COLLINS
SPANISH
COLLEGE
DICTIONARY

COLLINS
SPANISH
COLLEGE
DICTIONARY

SPANISH ▶ENGLISH ENGLISH ▶SPANISH

HarperCollins*Publishers*

second edition/segunda edición 1995

© **HarperCollins Publishers 1995**
© **William Collins Sons & Co. Ltd. 1989**

HarperCollins Publishers
P.O. Box, Glasgow G4 0NB, Great Britain
ISBN 0 00 470208 5 (Paperback)
ISBN 0 00 470730 3 (College)

Grijalbo Mondadori S.A.
Aragón 385, Barcelona 08013
ISBN 84 253 2792

Jeremy Butterfield • Mike Gonzalez • Gerry Breslin

contributors to second edition/colaboradores en la segunda edición
Teresa Alvarez García • Brian Steel
Ana Cristina Llompart • José Miguel Galván Déniz

editorial staff/redacción
Megan Thomson
Val McNulty • Irene Lakhani • Sharon Hunter
Tracy Lomas • Claire Evans • Jane Horwood

series editor/colección dirigida por
Lorna Sinclair Knight
editorial management/dirección editorial
Vivian Marr

Typeset by Morton Word Processing Ltd, Scarborough

Printed in Great Britain by
HarperCollins Manufacturing, Glasgow

ÍNDICE DE MATERIAS

CONTENTS

INTRODUCCIÓN

Si quieres aprender inglés o profundizar en los conocimientos ya adquiridos, si quieres leer o estudiar textos ingleses o conversar con personas de habla inglesa, acabas de escoger el compañero de trabajo ideal para poder hacerlo, ya estés en el instituto o en la universidad, seas turista, administrativo u hombre/mujer de negocios. Este diccionario, totalmente práctico y al día, abarca una gran parte del vocabulario cotidiano, del relacionado con el mundo de los negocios, de la actualidad, de la administración burocrática y del turismo. Como en todos nuestros diccionarios, hemos hecho hincapié en la lengua contemporánea y en las expresiones idiomáticas.

CÓMO USAR EL DICCIONARIO

Más abajo tienes las explicaciones necesarias para entender cómo está presentada la información en tu diccionario. Nuestro objetivo es darte la mayor información posible sin sacrificar por ello la claridad.

Las entradas

Éstos son los elementos que pueden componer una entrada cualquiera del diccionario:

Transcripción fonética

Ésta aparece inmediatamente después del lema (así denominamos a la palabra cabeza del artículo) y entre corchetes [ ]. Al igual que la mayor parte de los diccionarios actuales, hemos optado por el sistema denominado "alfabeto fonético internacional". En la página xiv encontrarás una lista completa de los caracteres utilizados en este sistema.

Información gramatical

Todas las voces incluidas en el diccionario pertenecen a una determinada categoría gramatical: sustantivo, verbo, adjetivo, pronombre, artículo, conjunción, abreviatura. Los sustantivos pueden ir en singular o en plural y, en español, pueden ser masculinos o femeninos. Los verbos pueden ser transitivos, intransitivos y en español también pronominales (o reflexivos). La categoría gramatical de cada voz aparece en *cursiva*, inmediatamente después de la transcripción fonética.

A menudo una misma palabra puede funcionar con distintas categorías gramaticales. Por ejemplo **deber** puede ser verbo o sustantivo, el término inglés **public** puede ser sustantivo o adjetivo. Incluso un mismo verbo como **importar** o como el inglés **to work** a veces será transitivo y a veces intransitivo, dependiendo de su significado. Para que te resulte más fácil encontrar la categoría gramatical que buscas, en el caso de que haya varias dentro de una misma entrada, y para que la presentación sea más clara, aquéllas aparecen separadas por rombos negros ♦.

Acepciones

La mayor parte de las palabras tienen más de un sentido. Así por ejemplo

crucero puede ser, entre otros, un tipo de barco o un tipo de viaje turístico, y según la acepción que busquemos la traducción varía: "cruise ship" en el primer caso y "cruise" en el segundo. Otras palabras se traducen de forma distinta según el contexto: **bajo** puede traducirse por "low", pero también por "small, short" si se trata de una persona, "ground" si de un piso etc. Para que puedas escoger la traducción más indicada para cada acepción o contexto hemos incorporado indicaciones de uso o significado, que aparecen entre paréntesis y en *cursiva*. Así figuran los anteriores ejemplos en el diccionario:

> **crucero** *nm* (*NAUT: barco*) cruise ship; (: *viaje*) cruise

> **bajo** *adj* (...) low; (*piso*) ground; (*de estatura*) small, short ...

De la misma forma, muchas voces tienen un sentido distinto según el contexto en el que se usen. Así por ejemplo, **giro** puede ser un movimiento, pero tiene un significado específico en gramática y finanzas. Con la incorporación de indicaciones de campo semántico (tales como *LINGÜÍSTICA* y *COMERCIO* en este caso), resulta más fácil saber cuál es la acepción que necesitamos. La mayoría de dichas acepciones aparecen abreviadas para ganar espacio:

> **giro** *nm* (*movimiento*) turn, revolution; (*LING*) expression; (*COM*) draft

Puede verse la lista completa de las abreviaturas que hemos utilizado en la página xii.

Traducciones

La mayor parte de las palabras españolas tienen su traducción al inglés y viceversa, como en los ejemplos que acabamos de ver. Sin embargo hay ocasiones en las que no hay un equivalente exacto en la lengua término, fundamentalmente por razones socio-culturales. En este caso hemos dado una traducción aproximada (que suele ser en realidad un equivalente cultural) y lo indicamos con el signo ≈. Este es el caso de **A road**, cuyo equivalente en español peninsular es "carretera nacional", o de **dual carriageway**, que equivale a "autovía": no se trata de traducciones propiamente dichas, puesto que ambos sistemas de carreteras son diferentes.

> **A road** *n* (*BRIT AUT*) ≈ carretera nacional

> **dual carriageway** *n* (*BRIT*) ≈ autovía

A veces es imposible encontrar incluso un equivalente aproximado, como en el caso de los platos o tradiciones regionales, por lo que se hace necesario dar una explicación en lugar de la traducción. Así ocurre, por ejemplo, con:

> **ceilidh** *n baile con música y danzas tradicionales escocesas o irlandesas*

Como puede verse, la explicación o glosa aparece en *cursiva*, para mayor claridad.

Así mismo, a menudo no se puede traducir palabra por palabra. Aunque **machine** se traduce normalmente por "máquina", **washing machine** es en realidad "lavadora". De la misma forma, la traducción al inglés de

hormiguero es "ant's nest", pero en la expresión **aquello era un hormiguero** la traducción será "it was swarming with people". Es en este tipo de situaciones en las que tu diccionario te será más útil, pues es muy completo en compuestos nominales, frases y expresiones idiomáticas.

Niveles lingüísticos

En español, sabemos instintivamente cuándo usar **eso son tonterías** y cuándo **eso son chorradas**. Sin embargo, a la hora de intentar comprender a alguien que está hablando en inglés o bien de expresarnos nosotros mismos en esa lengua, adquiere una importancia especial saber si una palabra es coloquial o no. Así pues, hemos marcado las palabras o expresiones inglesas que no suelen utilizarse más que en una situación familiar con la indicación (*col*) y aquéllas con las que hay que tener especial cuidado (pues pueden sonar muy vulgares a los oídos de mucha gente) con el signo de admiración (*col!*). No hemos añadido la indicación (*fam*) a la traducción inglesa cuando ésta tiene el mismo nivel que la palabra que se traduce pero a las traducciones que pueden resultar vulgares siempre las sigue el signo de admiración entre paréntesis (*!*).

Palabras clave

Algunas voces especialmente importantes o complejas en ambas lenguas requieren un tratamiento especial dentro del diccionario: verbos como **hacer** o **estar** en español, o **to have** o **to do** en inglés. Por ello, aparecen en un cuadro y bajo la denominación de "palabra clave", y como comprobarás, se ha hecho un análisis más profundo de ellas, pues son elementos básicos de la lengua.

Información de tipo cultural

Los artículos que aparecen separados del texto principal por dos líneas, una abajo y otra arriba, explican diversos aspectos de la cultura en países de habla española e inglesa, como la política, la educación, medios de comunicación y fiestas nacionales.

Nuevo orden alfabético en español

Tras la decisión tomada por la Real Academia Española en conjunción con las Academias hispanoamericanas, CH y LL ya no aparecen como letras independientes en este diccionario. Así por ejemplo **chapa** o **lluvia** se encuentran bajo la C y la L respectivamente. Conviene recordar que palabras como **cacha** y **callar** también han cambiado de lugar y ahora aparecen tras **cacerola** y **calizo**.

INTRODUCTION

You may be starting Spanish for the first time, or you may wish to extend your knowledge of the language. Perhaps you want to read and study Spanish books, newspapers and magazines, or perhaps simply have a conversation with Spanish speakers. Whatever the reason, whether you're a student, a tourist or want to use Spanish for business, this is the ideal book to help you understand and communicate. This modern, user-friendly dictionary gives priority to everyday vocabulary and the language of current affairs, business, computing and tourism, and, as in all Collins dictionaries, the emphasis is firmly placed on contemporary language and expressions.

HOW TO USE THE DICTIONARY

Below you will find an outline of how information is presented in your dictionary. Our aim is to give you the maximum amount of detail in the clearest and most helpful way.

Entries

A typical entry in your dictionary will be made up of the following elements:

Phonetic transcription

Phonetics appear in square brackets immediately after the headword. They are shown using the International Phonetic Alphabet (IPA), and a complete list of the symbols used in this system can be found on page xiv. The pronunciation given is for Castilian Spanish except where a word is solely used in Latin America, when we give the Latin American pronunciation. A further guide to the differences in types of Spanish pronunciation is given on page xiv.

Grammatical information

All words belong to one of the following parts of speech: noun, verb, adjective, adverb, pronoun, article, conjunction, preposition, abbreviation. Nouns can be singular or plural and, in Spanish, masculine or feminine. Verbs can be transitive, intransitive, reflexive or impersonal. Parts of speech appear in *italics* immediately after the phonetic spelling of the headword. The gender of the translation also appears in *italics* immediately following the key element of the translation, except where this is a regular masculine singular noun ending in "o", or a regular feminine singular noun ending in "a".

Often a word can have more than one part of speech. Just as the English word **chemical** can be an adjective or a noun, the Spanish word **conocido** can be an adjective ("(well-)known") or a noun ("acquaintance"). In the same way the verb **to walk** is sometimes transitive, ie it takes an object ("to walk the dog") and sometimes intransitive, ie it doesn't take an object ("to walk to school"). To help you find the meaning you are looking for quickly and for clarity of presentation, the different part of speech categories are separated by a black lozenge ♦.

Meaning divisions

Most words have more than one meaning. Take, for example, **punch** which can be, amongst other things, a blow with the fist or an object used for making holes. Other words are translated differently depending on the context in which they are used. The transitive verb **to put on**, for example, can be translated by "ponerse", "encender" etc depending on *what* it is you are putting on. To help you select the most appropriate translation in every context, entries are divided according to meaning. Each different meaning is introduced by an "indicator" in *italics* and in brackets. Thus, the examples given above will be shown as follows:

> **punch** n (*blow*) golpe m, puñetazo; (*tool*) punzón m

> **put on** vt (*clothes, lipstick etc*) ponerse; (*light etc*) encender

Likewise, some words can have a different meaning when used to talk about a specific subject area or field. For example **bishop**, which in a religious context means a high-ranking clergyman, is also the name of a chess piece. To show English speakers which translation to use, we have added "subject field labels" in capitals and in brackets, in this case (*CHESS*):

> **bishop** n obispo; (*CHESS*) alfil m

Field labels are often shortened to save space. You will find a complete list of abbreviations used in the dictionary on page xii.

Translations

Most English words have a direct translation in Spanish and vice versa, as shown in the examples given above. Sometimes, however, no exact equivalent exists in the target language. In such cases we have given an approximate equivalent, indicated by the sign ≈. An example is **British Rail**, the Spanish equivalent of which is "RENFE". There is no exact equivalent since the bodies in the two countries are quite different:

> **British Rail (BR)** n ≈ RENFE f (*SP*)

On occasion it is impossible to find even an approximate equivalent. This may be the case, for example, with the names of types of food:

> **fabada** nf bean and sausage stew

Here the translation (which doesn't exist) is replaced by an explanation. For increased clarity the explanation, or "gloss", is shown in *italics*.

It is often the case that a word, or a particular meaning of a word, cannot be translated in isolation. The translation of **Dutch**, for example, is "holandés/esa". However, the phrase **to go Dutch** is rendered by "pagar cada uno lo suyo". Even an expression as simple as **washing powder** needs a separate translation since it translates as "detergente (en polvo)", not "polvo para lavar". This is where your dictionary will prove to be particularly informative and useful since it contains an abundance of compounds, phrases and idiomatic expressions.

Levels of formality and familiarity

In English you instinctively know when to say **I'm broke** or **I'm a bit short of cash** and when to say **I don't have any money**. When you are trying to understand someone who is speaking Spanish, however, or when you yourself try to speak Spanish, it is important to know what is polite and what is less so, and what you can say in a relaxed situation but not in a formal context. To help you with this, on the Spanish-English side we have added the label (*fam*) to show that a Spanish meaning or expression is colloquial, while those meanings or expressions which are vulgar are given an exclamation mark (*fam!*), warning you they can cause serious offence. Note also that on the English-Spanish side, translations which are vulgar are followed by an exclamation mark in brackets.

Keywords

Words labelled in the text as *KEYWORD*s, such as **have** and **do** or their Spanish equivalents **tener** and **hacer**, have been given special treatment because they form the basic elements of the language. This extra help will ensure that you know how to use these complex words with confidence.

Cultural information

Entries which appear separated from the main text by a line above and below them explain aspects of culture in Spanish and English-speaking countries. Subject areas covered include politics, education, media and national festivals.

Spanish alphabetical order

In 1994 the **Real Academia Española** and the Spanish American language academies jointly decided to stop treating CH and LL as separate letters in Spanish, thereby bringing it into line with European spelling norms. This means that **chapa** and **lluvia** will be filed in letters C and L respectively. Of course, it should also be remembered that words like **cancha** and **callar**, with **ch** and **ll** in the middle of the words, will also have changed places alphabetically, now being found after **cáncer** and **cáliz** respectively. Spanish however still has one more letter than English with Ñ treated separately, between N and O.

ABREVIATURAS

ABBREVIATIONS

abreviatura	*ab(b)r*	abbreviation
adjetivo, locución adjetiva	*adj*	adjective, adjectival phrase
administración, lengua administrativa	*ADMIN*	administration
adverbio, locución adverbial	*adv*	adverb, adverbial phrase
agricultura	*AGR*	agriculture
alguien	*algn*	
América Latina	*AM*	Latin America
anatomía	*ANAT*	anatomy
arquitectura	*ARQ, ARCH*	architecture
astrología, astronomía	*ASTRO*	astrology, astronomy
el automóvil	*AUT(O)*	the motor car and motoring
aviación, viajes aéreos	*AVIAT*	flying, air travel
biología	*BIO(L)*	biology
botánica, flores	*BOT*	botany
inglés británico	*BRIT*	British English
química	*CHEM*	chemistry
	CINE	cinema
lengua familiar (! vulgar)	*col (!)*	colloquial usage (! particularly offensive)
comercio, finanzas, banca	*COM(M)*	commerce, finance, banking
informática	*COMPUT*	computing
conjunción	*conj*	conjunction
construcción	*CONSTR*	building
compuesto	*cpd*	compound element
cocina	*CULIN*	cookery
economía	*ECON*	economics
electricidad, electrónica	*ELEC*	electricity, electronics
enseñanza, sistema escolar	*ESCOL*	schooling, schools
España	*ESP*	Spain
especialmente	*esp*	especially
exclamación, interjección	*excl*	exclamation, interjection
femenino	*f*	feminine
lengua familiar (! vulgar)	*fam (!)*	colloquial usage (! particularly offensive)
ferrocarril	*FERRO*	railways
uso figurado	*fig*	figurative use
fotografía	*FOTO*	photography
(verbo inglés) del cual la partícula es inseparable	*fus*	(phrasal verb) where the particle is inseparable
generalmente	*gen*	generally
geografía, geología	*GEO*	geography, geology
geometría	*GEOM*	geometry
informática	*INFORM*	computing
invariable	*inv*	invariable
irregular	*irreg*	irregular
lo jurídico	*JUR*	law
América Latina	*LAM*	Latin America
gramática, lingüística	*LING*	grammar, linguistics
literatura	*LIT*	literature
masculino	*m*	masculine
matemáticas	*MAT(H)*	mathematics
medicina	*MED*	medical term, medicine
masculino/femenino	*m/f*	masculine/feminine

ABREVIATURAS

ABBREVIATIONS

lo militar, ejército	*MIL*	military matters
música	*MUS*	music
sustantivo, nombre	*n*	noun
navegación, náutica	*NAUT*	sailing, navigation
sustantivo no empleado en el plural	*no pl*	collective (uncountable) noun, not used in plural
sustantivo numérico	*num*	numeral noun
complemento	*obj*	(grammatical) object
	o.s.	oneself
peyorativo	*pey, pej*	derogatory, pejorative
fotografía	*PHOT*	photography
fisiología	*PHYSIOL*	physiology
plural	*pl*	plural
política	*POL*	politics
participio de pasado	*pp*	past participle
prefijo	*pref*	prefix
preposición	*prep*	preposition
pronombre	*pron*	pronoun
psicología, psiquiatría	*PSICO, PSYCH*	psychology, psychiatry
tiempo pasado	*pt*	past tense
ferrocarril	*RAIL*	railways
religión, lo eclesiástico	*REL*	religion, church service
	sb	somebody
enseñanza, sistema escolar	*SCOL*	schooling, schools
singular	*sg*	singular
España	*SP*	Spain
	sth	something
subjuntivo	*subjun*	subjunctive
sujeto	*su(b)j*	(grammatical) subject
sufijo	*suff*	suffix
tauromaquia	*TAUR*	bullfighting
también	*tb*	also
teatro	*TEAT*	
técnica, tecnología	*TEC(H)*	technical term, technology
telecomunicaciones	*TELEC, TEL*	telecommunications
	THEAT	theatre
imprenta, tipografía	*TIP, TYP*	typography, printing
televisión	*TV*	television
sistema universitario	*UNIV*	universities
inglés norteamericano	*US*	American English
verbo	*vb*	verb
verbo intransitivo	*vi*	intransitive verb
verbo pronominal	*vr*	reflexive verb
verbo transitivo	*vt*	transitive verb
zoología, animales	*ZOOL*	zoology
marca registrada	®	registered trademark
indica un equivalente cultural	≈	introduces a cultural equivalent

SPANISH PRONUNCIATION

Consonants

b	[b]	<u>b</u>om<u>b</u>a	see notes on *v* below
	[ß]	la<u>b</u>or	
c	[k]	<u>c</u>aja	*c* before *a*, *o* or *u* is pronounced as in *c*at
ce, ci	[θe, θi]	<u>ce</u>ro <u>ci</u>elo	*c* before *e* or *i* is pronounced as in *th*in and as *s* in *s*in in Latin America and parts
	[se, si][1]	vo<u>ce</u>ro noti<u>ci</u>ero	of Spain
ch	[tʃ]	<u>ch</u>iste	*ch* is pronounced as *ch* in *ch*air
d	[d]	<u>d</u>anés	at the beginning of a word or after *l* or *n*,
	[ð]	ciu<u>d</u>a<u>d</u>	*d* is pronounced as in English. In any other position it is like *th* in *the*
g	[g]	<u>g</u>afas <u>g</u>uerra	*g* before *a*, *o* or *u* is pronounced as in *g*ap, if at the beginning of a word or after *n*. In
	[ɣ]	pa<u>g</u>a	other positions the sound is softened
ge, gi	[xe, xi]	<u>ge</u>nte <u>gi</u>rar	*g* before *e* or *i* is pronounced similar to *ch* in Scottish lo*ch*
h		<u>h</u>aber	*h* is always silent in Spanish
j	[x]	<u>j</u>ugar	*j* is pronounced like *ch* in Scottish lo*ch*
ll	[ʎ]	ta<u>ll</u>e	*ll* is pronounced like the *lli* in mi*lli*on
ñ	[ɲ]	ni<u>ñ</u>o	*ñ* is pronounced like the *ni* in o*ni*on
q	[k]	<u>q</u>ue	*q* is pronounced as *k* in *k*ing
r, rr	[r]	quita<u>r</u>	*r* is always pronounced in Spanish, unlike
	[rr]	ga<u>rr</u>a	the silent *r* in dance*r*. *rr* and *r* at the beginning of a word are trilled, like a Scottish *r*
s	[s]	quizá<u>s</u> i<u>s</u>la	*s* is usually pronounced as in pa*ss*, but before *b*, *d*, *g*, *l*, *m* or *n* it is pronounced as in ro*s*e
v	[b]	<u>v</u>ía	*v* is pronounced something like *b*. At the
	[ß]	di<u>v</u>idir	beginning of a word or after *m* or *n* it is pronounced as *b* in *b*oy. In any other position it is pronounce with the lips in position to pronounce *b* of *b*oy, but not meeting
w	[b]	<u>w</u>áter	pronounced either like Spanish *b*, or like
	[w]	<u>w</u>hiskey	English *w*
z	[θ]	tena<u>z</u>	*z* is pronounced as *th*in *th*in and as *s* in
	[s][1]	i<u>z</u>ada	*s*in in Latin America and parts of Spain
	[ks]	tó<u>x</u>ico	*x* is pronounced as in to*x*in except in
	[s]	<u>x</u>enofobia	informal Spanish or at the beginning of a word

f, k, l, m, n, p and t are pronounced as in English.

[1]Only shown in Latin American entries.

Vowels

a	[a]	p<u>a</u>ta	not as long as *a* in f*a*r. When followed by a consonant in the same syllable (i.e. in a closed syllable), as in am*a*nte, the *a* is short, as in b*a*t
e	[e]	m<u>e</u>	like *e* in th*ey*. In a closed syllable, as in g*e*nte, the *e* is short as in p*e*t
i	[i]	p<u>i</u>no	as in m*ea*n or mach*i*ne
o	[o]	l<u>o</u>	as in l*o*cal. In a closed syllable, as in c*o*ntrol, the *o* is short as in c*o*t
u	[u]	l<u>u</u>nes	as in r*u*le. It is silent after *q*, and in *gue*, *gui*, unless marked *güe*, *güi* e.g. antig<u>ü</u>edad, when it is pronounced like *w* in *w*olf

Semivowels

i, y	[j]	b<u>i</u>en h<u>i</u>elo <u>y</u>unta	pronounced like *y* in *y*es
u	[w]	h<u>u</u>evo f<u>u</u>ente antig<u>ü</u>edad	unstressed *u* between consonant and vowel is pronounced like *w* in *w*ell. See also notes on *u* above

Dipthongs

ai, ay	[ai]	b<u>ai</u>le	as *i* in r*i*de
au	[au]	<u>au</u>to	as *ou* in sh*ou*t
ei, ey	[ei]	bu<u>ey</u>	as *ey* in gr*ey*
eu	[eu]	d<u>eu</u>da	both elements pronounced independently [e] + [u]
oi, oy	[oi]	h<u>oy</u>	as *oy* in t*oy*

Stress

The rules of stress in Spanish are as follows:

(a) when a word ends in a vowel or in *n* or *s*, the second last syllable is stressed: pat*a*ta, pat*a*tas, c*o*me, c*o*men

(b) when a word ends in a consonant other than *n* or *s*, the stress falls on the last syllable: par*e*d, habl*a*r

(c) when the rules set out in a and b are not applied, an acute accent appears over the stressed vowel: com*ú*n, geograf*í*a, ingl*é*s

In the phonetic transcription, the symbol ['] precedes the syllable on which the stress falls.

In general, we give the pronunciation of each entry in square brackets after the word in question.

PRONUNCIACIÓN INGLESA

Vocales y diptongos

	Ejemplo inglés	*Ejemplo español/explicación*
[ɑ:]	f<u>a</u>ther	Entre *a* de p<u>a</u>dre y *o* de n<u>o</u>che
[ʌ]	b<u>u</u>t, c<u>o</u>me	*a* muy breve
[æ]	m<u>a</u>n, c<u>a</u>t	Con los labios en la posición de *e* en p<u>e</u>na y luego se pronuncia el sonido *a* parecido *a* la a de c<u>a</u>rro
[ə]	fath<u>er</u>, <u>a</u>go	Vocal neutra parecida a una *e* u *o* casi muda
[ə:]	b<u>ir</u>d, h<u>ear</u>d	Entre *e* abierta, y *o* cerrada, sonido alargado
[ɛ]	g<u>e</u>t, b<u>e</u>d	Como en p<u>e</u>rro
[ɪ]	<u>i</u>t, b<u>i</u>g	Más breve que en s<u>i</u>
[i:]	t<u>ea</u>, s<u>ee</u>	Como en f<u>i</u>no
[ɔ]	h<u>o</u>t, w<u>a</u>sh	Como en t<u>o</u>rre
[ɔ:]	s<u>aw</u>, <u>a</u>ll	Como en p<u>o</u>r
[u]	p<u>u</u>t, b<u>oo</u>k	Sonido breve, más cerrado que en b<u>u</u>rro
[u:]	t<u>oo</u>, y<u>ou</u>	Sonido largo, como en <u>u</u>no
[aɪ]	fl<u>y</u>, h<u>igh</u>	Como en fr<u>ai</u>le
[au]	h<u>ow</u>, h<u>ou</u>se	Como en p<u>au</u>sa
[ɛə]	th<u>ere</u>, b<u>ear</u>	Casi como en v<u>ea</u>, pero el sonido *a* se mezcla con el indistinto [ə]
[eɪ]	d<u>ay</u>, ob<u>ey</u>	*e* cerrada seguida por una *i* débil
[ɪə]	h<u>ere</u>, h<u>ear</u>	Como en man<u>ía</u>, mezclándose el sonido *a* con el indistinto [ə]
[əu]	g<u>o</u>, n<u>o</u>te	[ə] seguido por una breve *u*
[ɔɪ]	b<u>oy</u>, <u>oi</u>l	Como en v<u>oy</u>
[uə]	p<u>oor</u>, s<u>ure</u>	*u* bastante larga más el sonido indistinto [ə]

Consonantes

	Ejemplo inglés	Ejemplo español/explicación
[b]	big, lobby	Como en tumban
[d]	mended	Como en conde, andar
[g]	go, get, big	Como en grande, gol
[dʒ]	gin, judge	Como en la ll andaluza y en Generalitat (catalán)
[ŋ]	sing	Como en vínculo
[h]	house, he	Como la jota hispanoamericana
[j]	young, yes	Como en ya
[k]	come, mock	Como en caña, Escocia
[r]	red, tread	Se pronuncia con la punta de la lengua hacia atrás y sin hacerla vibrar
[s]	sand, yes	Como en casa, sesión
[z]	rose, zebra	Como en desde, mismo
[ʃ]	she, machine	Como en chambre (francés), roxo (portugués)
[tʃ]	chin, rich	Como en chocolate
[v]	valley	Como en f, pero se retiran los dientes superiores vibrándolos contra el labio inferior
[w]	water, which	Como en la u de huevo, puede
[ʒ]	vision	Como en journal (francés)
[θ]	think, myth	Como en receta, zapato
[ð]	this, the	Como en la d de hablado, verdad

p, f, m, n, l, t iguales que en español

El signo * indica que la r final escrita apenas se pronuncia en inglés británico cuando la palabra siguiente empieza con vocal. El signo ['] indica la sílaba acentuada.

Por regla general, la pronunciación viene dada entre corchetes después de cada entrada léxica. Sin embargo, allí donde la entrada es un compuesto de dos o más palabras separadas, cada una de las cuales es objeto de entrada en alguna otra parte del diccionario, la pronunciación de cada palabra se encontrará en su correspondiente posición alfabética.

SPANISH VERB FORMS

1 Gerund *2* Imperative *3* Present *4* Preterite *5* Future *6* Present subjunctive *7* Imperfect subjunctive *8* Past participle *9* Imperfect

acertar *2* acierta *3* acierto, aciertas, acierta, aciertan *6* acierte, aciertes, acierte, acierten

acordar *2* acuerda *3* acuerdo, acuerdas, acuerda, acuerdan *6* acuerde, acuerdes, acuerde, acuerden

advertir *1* advirtiendo *2* advierte *3* advierto, adviertes, advierte, advierten *4* advirtió, advirtieron *6* advierta, adviertas, advierta, advirtamos, advirtáis, adviertan *7* advirtiera *etc*

agradecer *3* agradezco *6* agradezca *etc*

aparecer *3* aparezco *6* aparezca *etc*

aprobar *2* aprueba *3* apruebo, apruebas, aprueba, aprueban *6* apruebe, apruebes, apruebe, aprueben

atravesar *2* atraviesa *3* atravieso, atraviesas, atraviesa, atraviesan *6* atraviese, atravieses, atraviese, atraviesen

caber *3* quepo *4* cupe, cupiste, cupo, cupimos, cupisteis, cupieron *5* cabré *etc* *6* quepa *etc* *7* cupiera *etc*

caer *1* cayendo *3* caigo *4* cayó, cayeron *6* caiga *etc* *7* cayera *etc*

calentar *2* calienta *3* caliento, calientas, calienta, calientan *6* caliente, calientes, caliente, calienten

cerrar *2* cierra *3* cierro, cierras, cierra, cierran *6* cierre, cierres, cierre, cierren

COMER *1* comiendo *2* come, comed *3* como, comes, come, comemos, coméis, comen *4* comí, comiste, comió, comimos, comisteis, comieron *5* comeré, comerás, comerá, comeremos, comeréis, comerán *6* coma, comas, coma, comamos, comáis, coman *7* comiera, comieras, comiera, comiéramos, comierais, comieran *8* comido *9* comía, comías, comía, comíamos, comíais, comían

conocer *3* conozco *6* conozca *etc*

contar *2* cuenta *3* cuento, cuentas, cuenta, cuentan *6* cuente, cuentes, cuente, cuenten

costar *2* cuesta *3* cuesto, cuestas, cuesta, cuestan *6* cueste, cuestes, cueste, cuesten

dar *3* doy *4* di, diste, dio, dimos, disteis, dieron *7* diera *etc*

decir *2* di *3* digo *4* dije, dijiste, dijo, dijimos, dijisteis, dijeron *5* diré *etc* *6* diga *etc* *7* dijera *etc* *8* dicho

despertar *2* despierta *3* despierto, despiertas, despierta, despiertan *6* despierte, despiertes, despierte, despierten

divertir *1* divirtiendo *2* divierte *3* divierto, diviertes, divierte, divierten *4* divirtió, divirtieron *6* divierta, diviertas, divierta, divirtamos, divirtáis, diviertan *7* divirtiera *etc*

dormir *1* durmiendo *2* duerme *3* duermo, duermes, duerme, duermen *4* durmió, durmieron *6* duerma, duermas, duerma, durmamos, durmáis, duerman *7* durmiera *etc*

empezar *2* empieza *3* empiezo, empiezas, empieza, empiezan *4* empecé *6* empiece, empieces, empiece, empecemos, empecéis, empiecen

entender *2* entiende *3* entiendo, entiendes, entiende, entienden *6* entienda, entiendas, entienda, entiendan

ESTAR *2* está *3* estoy, estás, está, están *4* estuve, estuviste, estuvo, estuvimos, estuvisteis, estuvieron *6* esté, estés, esté, estén *7* estuviera *etc*

HABER *3* he, has, ha, hemos, han *4* hube, hubiste, hubo, hubimos, hubisteis, hubieron *5* habré *etc* *6* haya *etc* *7* hubiera *etc*

HABLAR *1* hablando *2* habla, hablad *3* hablo, hablas, habla, hablamos, habláis, hablan *4* hablé, hablaste, habló, hablamos, hablasteis, hablaron *5* hablaré, hablarás, hablará, hablaremos, hablaréis, hablarán *6* hable, hables, hable, hablemos, habléis, hablen *7* hablara, hablaras, hablara, habláramos, hablarais, hablaran *8* hablado *9* hablaba, hablabas, hablaba, hablábamos, hablabais, hablaban

hacer *2* haz *3* hago *4* hice, hiciste, hizo, hicimos, hicisteis, hicieron *5* haré *etc* *6* haga *etc* *7* hiciera *etc* *8* hecho

instruir *1* instruyendo *2* instruye *3* instruyo, instruyes, instruye, instruyen *4* instruyó, instruyeron *6* instruya *etc* *7* instruyera *etc*

ir *1* yendo *2* ve *3* voy, vas, va, vamos, vais, van *4* fui, fuiste, fue, fuimos, fuisteis, fueron *6* vaya, vayas, vaya, vayamos,

vayáis, vayan 7 fuera *etc* 8 iba, ibas, iba,
íbamos, ibais, iban
jugar 2 juega 3 juego, juegas, juega,
juegan 4 jugué 6 juegue *etc*
leer 1 leyendo 4 leyó, leyeron 7 leyera *etc*
morir 1 muriendo 2 muere 3 muero,
mueres, muere, mueren 4 murió,
murieron 6 muera, mueras, muera,
muramos, muráis, mueran 7 muriera *etc*
8 muerto
mostrar 2 muestra 3 muestro, muestras,
muestra, muestran 6 muestre, muestres,
muestre, muestren
mover 2 mueve 3 muevo, mueves, mueve,
mueven 6 mueva, muevas, mueva,
muevan
negar 2 niega 3 niego, niegas, niega,
niegan 4 negué 6 niegue, niegues,
niegue, neguemos, neguéis, nieguen
ofrecer 3 ofrezco 6 ofrezca *etc*
oír 1 oyendo 2 oye 3 oigo, oyes, oye, oyen
4 oyó, oyeron 6 oiga *etc* 7 oyera *etc*
oler 2 huele 3 huelo, hueles, huele, huelen
6 huela, huelas, huela, huelan
parecer 3 parezco 6 parezca *etc*
pedir 1 pidiendo 2 pide 3 pido, pides, pide,
piden 4 pidió, pidieron 6 pida *etc*
7 pidiera *etc*
pensar 2 piensa 3 pienso, piensas, piensa,
piensan 6 piense, pienses, piense,
piensen
perder 2 pierde 3 pierdo, pierdes, pierde,
pierden 6 pierda, pierdas, pierda,
pierdan
poder 1 pudiendo 2 puede 3 puedo,
puedes, puede, pueden 4 pude, pudiste,
pudo, pudimos, pudisteis, pudieron
5 podré *etc* 6 pueda, puedas, pueda,
puedan 7 pudiera *etc*
poner 2 pon 3 pongo 4 puse, pusiste, puso,
pusimos, pusisteis, pusieron 5 pondré
etc 6 ponga *etc* 7 pusiera *etc* 8 puesto
preferir 1 prefiriendo 2 prefiere 3 prefiero,
prefieres, prefiere, prefieren 4 prefirió,
prefirieron 6 prefiera, prefieras, prefiera,
prefiramos, prefiráis, prefieran
7 prefiriera *etc*
querer 2 quiere 3 quiero, quieres, quiere,
quieren 4 quise, quisiste, quiso,
quisimos, quisisteis, quisieron 5 querré
etc 6 quiera, quieras, quiera, quieran
7 quisiera *etc*
reír 2 ríe 3 río, ríes, ríe, ríen 4 rio, rieron
6 ría, rías, ría, riamos, riáis, rían 7 riera
etc
repetir 1 repitiendo 2 repite 3 repito,

repites, repite, repiten 4 repitió,
repitieron 6 repita *etc* 7 repitiera *etc*
rogar 2 ruega 3 ruego, ruegas, ruega,
ruegan 4 rogué 6 ruegue, ruegues,
ruegue, roguemos, roguéis, rueguen
saber 3 sé 4 supe, supiste, supo, supimos,
supisteis, supieron 5 sabré *etc* 6 sepa *etc*
7 supiera *etc*
salir 2 sal 3 salgo 5 saldré *etc* 6 salga *etc*
seguir 1 siguiendo 2 sigue 3 sigo, sigues,
sigue, siguen 4 siguió, siguieron 6 siga
etc 7 siguiera *etc*
sentar 2 sienta 3 siento, sientas, sienta,
sientan 6 siente, sientes, siente, sienten
sentir 1 sintiendo 2 siente 3 siento,
sientes, siente, sienten 4 sintió, sintieron
6 sienta, sientas, sienta, sintamos,
sintáis, sientan 7 sintiera *etc*
SER 2 sé 3 soy, eres, es, somos, sois, son
4 fui, fuiste, fue, fuimos, fuisteis, fueron
6 sea *etc* 7 fuera *etc* 9 era, eras, era,
éramos, erais, eran
servir 1 sirviendo 2 sirve 3 sirvo, sirves,
sirve, sirven 4 sirvió, sirvieron 6 sirva
etc 7 sirviera *etc*
soñar 2 sueña 3 sueño, sueñas, sueña,
sueñan 6 sueñe, sueñes, sueñe, sueñen
tener 2 ten 3 tengo, tienes, tiene, tienen
4 tuve, tuviste, tuvo, tuvimos, tuvisteis,
tuvieron 5 tendré *etc* 6 tenga *etc*
7 tuviera *etc*
traer 1 trayendo 3 traigo 4 traje, trajiste,
trajo, trajimos, trajisteis, trajeron
6 traiga *etc* 7 trajera *etc*
valer 2 val 3 valgo 5 valdré *etc* 6 valga *etc*
venir 2 ven 3 vengo, vienes, viene, vienen
4 vine, viniste, vino, vinimos, vinisteis,
vinieron 5 vendré *etc* 6 venga *etc*
7 viniera *etc*
ver 3 veo 6 vea *etc* 8 visto 9 veía *etc*
vestir 1 vistiendo 2 viste 3 visto, vistes,
viste, visten 4 vistió, vistieron 6 vista *etc*
7 vistiera *etc*
VIVIR 1 viviendo 2 vive, vivid 3 vivo,
vives, vive, vivimos, vivís, viven 4 viví,
viviste, vivió, vivimos, vivisteis,
vivieron 5 viviré, vivirás, vivirá,
viviremos, viviréis, vivirán 6 viva,
vivas, viva, vivamos, viváis, vivan
7 viviera, vivieras, viviera, viviéramos,
vivierais, vivieran 8 vivido 9 vivía,
vivías, vivía, vivíamos, vivíais, vivían
volver 2 vuelve 3 vuelvo, vuelves, vuelve,
vuelven 6 vuelva, vuelvas, vuelva,
vuelvan 8 vuelto

VERBOS IRREGULARES EN INGLÉS

present	pt	pp	present	pt	pp
arise	arose	arisen	eat	ate	eaten
awake	awoke	awoken	fall	fell	fallen
be (am, is, are; being)	was, were	been	feed	fed	fed
			feel	felt	felt
bear	bore	born(e)	fight	fought	fought
beat	beat	beaten	find	found	found
become	became	become	flee	fled	fled
befall	befell	befallen	fling	flung	flung
begin	began	begun	fly	flew	flown
behold	beheld	beheld	forbid	forbad(e)	forbidden
bend	bent	bent	forecast	forecast	forecast
beset	beset	beset	forget	forgot	forgotten
bet	bet, betted	bet, betted	forgive	forgave	forgiven
			forsake	forsook	forsaken
bid (at auction, cards)	bid	bid	freeze	froze	frozen
			get	got	got, (US) gotten
bid (say)	bade	bidden	give	gave	given
bind	bound	bound	go (goes)	went	gone
bite	bit	bitten	grind	ground	ground
bleed	bled	bled	grow	grew	grown
blow	blew	blown	hang	hung	hung
break	broke	broken	hang (execute)	hanged	hanged
breed	bred	bred			
bring	brought	brought	have	had	had
build	built	built	hear	heard	heard
burn	burnt, burned	burnt, burned	hide	hid	hidden
			hit	hit	hit
burst	burst	burst	hold	held	held
buy	bought	bought	hurt	hurt	hurt
can	could	(been able)	keep	kept	kept
cast	cast	cast	kneel	knelt, kneeled	knelt, kneeled
catch	caught	caught			
choose	chose	chosen	know	knew	known
cling	clung	clung	lay	laid	laid
come	came	come	lead	led	led
cost	cost	cost	lean	leant, leaned	leant, leaned
cost (work out price of)	costed	costed			
			leap	leapt, leaped	leapt, leaped
creep	crept	crept			
cut	cut	cut	learn	learnt, learned	learnt, learned
deal	dealt	dealt			
dig	dug	dug	leave	left	left
do (3rd person: he/she/it does)	did	done	lend	lent	lent
			let	let	let
			lie (lying)	lay	lain
			light	lit, lighted	lit, lighted
draw	drew	drawn	lose	lost	lost
dream	dreamed, dreamt	dreamed, dreamt	make	made	made
			may	might	—
drink	drank	drunk	mean	meant	meant
drive	drove	driven	meet	met	met
dwell	dwelt	dwelt	mistake	mistook	mistaken

present	pt	pp	present	pt	pp
mow	mowed	mown, mowed	spend	spent	spent
must	(had to)	(had to)	spill	spilt, spilled	spilt, spilled
pay	paid	paid			
put	put	put	spin	spun	spun
quit	quit, quitted	quit, quitted	spit	spat	spat
			spoil	spoiled, spoilt	spoiled, spoilt
read	read	read			
rid	rid	rid	spread	spread	spread
ride	rode	ridden	spring	sprang	sprung
ring	rang	rung	stand	stood	stood
rise	rose	risen	steal	stole	stolen
run	ran	run	stick	stuck	stuck
saw	sawed	sawed, sawn	sting	stung	stung
say	said	said	stink	stank	stunk
see	saw	seen	stride	strode	stridden
seek	sought	sought	strike	struck	struck
sell	sold	sold	strive	strove	striven
send	sent	sent	swear	swore	sworn
set	set	set	sweep	swept	swept
sew	sewed	sewn	swell	swelled	swollen, swelled
shake	shook	shaken			
shear	sheared	shorn, sheared	swim	swam	swum
shed	shed	shed	swing	swung	swung
shine	shone	shone	take	took	taken
shoot	shot	shot	teach	taught	taught
show	showed	shown	tear	tore	torn
shrink	shrank	shrunk	tell	told	told
shut	shut	shut	think	thought	thought
sing	sang	sung	throw	threw	thrown
sink	sank	sunk	thrust	thrust	thrust
sit	sat	sat	tread	trod	trodden
slay	slew	slain	wake	woke, waked	woken, waked
sleep	slept	slept			
slide	slid	slid	wear	wore	worn
sling	slung	slung	weave	wove	woven
slit	slit	slit	weave (wind)	weaved	weaved
smell	smelt, smelled	smelt, smelled	wed	wedded, wed	wedded, wed
sow	sowed	sown, sowed	weep	wept	wept
speak	spoke	spoken	win	won	won
speed	sped, speeded	sped, speeded	wind	wound	wound
			wring	wrung	wrung
spell	spelt, spelled	spelt, spelled	write	wrote	written

NÚMEROS

NUMBERS

uno (un, una)*	1	one
dos	2	two
tres	3	three
cuatro	4	four
cinco	5	five
seis	6	six
siete	7	seven
ocho	8	eight
nueve	9	nine
diez	10	ten
once	11	eleven
doce	12	twelve
trece	13	thirteen
catorce	14	fourteen
quince	15	fifteen
dieciséis	16	sixteen
diecisiete	17	seventeen
dieciocho	18	eighteen
diecinueve	19	nineteen
veinte	20	twenty
veintiuno(-un, -una)*	21	twenty-one
veintidós	22	twenty-two
treinta	30	thirty
treinta y uno(un, una)*	31	thirty-one
treinta y dos	32	thirty-two
cuarenta	40	forty
cincuenta	50	fifty
sesenta	60	sixty
setenta	70	seventy
ochenta	80	eighty
noventa	90	ninety
cien(ciento)**	100	a hundred, one hundred
ciento uno(un, una)*	101	a hundred and one
ciento dos	102	a hundred and two
ciento cincuenta y seis	156	a hundred and fifty-six
doscientos(as)	200	two hundred
trescientos(as)	300	three hundred
quinientos(as)	500	five hundred
mil	1,000	a thousand
mil tres	1,003	a thousand and three
dos mil	2,000	two thousand
un millón	1,000,000	a million

* 'uno' (+ 'veintiuno' etc) agrees in gender (but not number) with its noun: treinta y una personas; the masculine form is shortened to 'un' unless it stands alone: veintiún caballos, veintiuno.

** 'ciento' is used in compound numbers, except when it multiplies: ciento diez, but cien mil. 'Cien' is used before nouns: cien hombres, cien casas.

NÚMEROS

NUMBERS

primero(primer, primera), 1°, $1^{er}/1^a$, 1^{era}	first, 1st
segundo(a), $2^o/2^a$	second, 2nd
tercero(tercer, tercera), 3°, $3^{er}/3^a$, 3^{era}	third, 3rd
cuarto(a), $4^o/4^a$	fourth, 4th
quinto(a)	fifth, 5th
sexto(a)	sixth, 6th
séptimo(a)	seventh
octavo(a)	eighth
noveno(a); nono(a)	ninth
décimo(a)	tenth
undécimo(a)	eleventh
duodécimo(a)	twelfth
decimotercio(a)	thirteenth
decimocuarto(a)	fourteenth
decimoquinto(a)	fifteenth
decimosexto(a)	sixteenth
decimoséptimo(a)	seventeenth
decimoctavo(a)	eighteenth
decimonono(a)	nineteenth
vigésimo(a)	twentieth
vigésimo primero(a)	twenty-first
vigésimo segundo(a)	twenty-second
trigésimo(a)	thirtieth
trigésimo primero(a)	thirty-first
trigésimo segundo(a)	thirty-second
cuadragésimo(a)	fortieth
quincuagésimo(a)	fiftieth
sexagésimo(a)	sixtieth
septuagésimo(a)	seventieth
octogésimo(a)	eightieth
nonagésimo(a)	ninetieth
centésimo(a)	hundredth
centésimo primero(a)	hundred-and-first
milésimo(a)	thousandth

LA HORA

THE TIME

¿qué hora es?

what time is it?

es la una
son las cuatro
medianoche, las doce de la noche
la una (de la madrugada)

it's one o'clock
it's four o'clock
midnight
one o'clock (in the morning), one
  (a.m.)

la una y cinco
la una y diez
la una y cuarto *or* quince
la una y veinticinco

five past one
ten past one
a quarter past one, one fifteen
twenty-five past one, one twenty-
  five

la una y media *or* treinta
las dos menos veinticinco, la una
  treinta y cinco
las dos menos veinte, la una
  cuarenta
las dos menos cuarto, la una
  cuarenta y cinco
las dos menos diez, la una
  cincuenta
mediodía, las doce (de la mañana)
las dos (de la tarde)

las siete (de la tarde)

half-past one, one thirty
twenty-five to two, one thirty-five

twenty to two, one forty

a quarter to two, one forty-five

ten to two, one fifty

twelve o'clock, midday, noon
two o'clock (in the afternoon), two
  (p.m.)
seven o'clock (in the evening),
  seven (p.m.)

¿a qué hora?

at what time?

a medianoche
a las siete
a las una

at midnight
at seven o'clock
at one o'clock

en veinte minutos
hace diez minutos

in twenty minutes
ten minutes ago

LA FECHA

THE DATE

hoy
mañana
pasado mañana
ayer
antes de ayer, anteayer
la víspera
el día siguiente

today
tomorrow
the day after tomorrow
yesterday
the day before yesterday
the day before, the previous day
the next *or* following day

la mañana	morning
la tarde	evening
esta mañana	this morning
esta tarde	this evening
esta tarde	this afternoon
ayer por la mañana	yesterday morning
ayer por la tarde	yesterday evening
mañana por la mañana	tomorrow morning
mañana por la tarde	tomorrow evening
en la noche del sábado al domingo	during Saturday night, during the night of Saturday to Sunday
vendrá el sábado	he's coming on Saturday
los sábados	on Saturdays
todos los sábados	every Saturday
el sábado pasado	last Saturday
el sábado que viene, el próximo sábado	next Saturday
del sábado en ocho días	a week on Saturday
del sábado en quince días	a fortnight or two weeks on Saturday
de lunes a sábado	from Monday to Saturday
todos los días	every day
una vez a la semana	once a week
una vez ala mes	once a month
dos veces a la semana	twice a week
hace una semana o ocho días	a week ago
hace quince días	a fortnight or two weeks ago
el año pasado	last year
dentro de dos días	in two days
dentro de ocho días o una semana	in a week
dentro de quince días	in a fortnight or two weeks
el mes que viene, el próximo mes	next month
el año que viene, el próximo año	next year
¿a qué o a cuántos estamos?	*what day is it?*
el 1/24 octubre de 1996	the 1st/24th of October 1996, October 1st/24th 1996
en 1996	in 1996
mil novecientos noventa y cinco	nineteen ninety-five
44 a. de J.C.	44 BC
14 d. de J.C.	14 AD
en el (siglo) XIX	in the nineteenth century
en los años treinta	in the thirties
érase una vez ...	once upon a time ...

Español-Inglés
Spanish-English

A a

A, a [a] *nf* (*letra*) A, a; **A de Antonio** A for Andrew (*BRIT*) *o* Able (*US*).

================= *PALABRA CLAVE*

a [a] (*a+el = al*) *prep* **1** (*dirección*) to; **fueron ~ Madrid/Grecia** they went to Madrid/Greece; **me voy ~ casa** I'm going home
2 (*distancia*): **está ~ 15 km de aquí** it's 15 kms from here
3 (*posición*): **estar ~ la mesa** to be at table; **al lado de** next to, beside; **~ la derecha/izquierda** on the right/left; *V tb* **puerta**
4 (*tiempo*): **~ las 10/~ medianoche** at 10/midnight; **¿~ qué hora?** (at) what time?; **~ la mañana siguiente** the following morning; **~ los pocos días** after a few days; **estamos ~ 9 de julio** it's the 9th of July; **~ los 24 años** at the age of 24; **ocho horas al día** eight hours a day; **al año/~ la semana** (*AM*) a year/week later
5 (*manera*): **~ la francesa** the French way; **~ caballo** on horseback; **~ oscuras** in the dark; **~ rayas** striped; **le echaron ~ patadas** they kicked him out
6 (*medio, instrumento*): **~ lápiz** in pencil; **~ mano** by hand; **cocina ~ gas** gas stove
7 (*razón*): **~ 30 ptas el kilo** at 30 pesetas a kilo; **~ más de 50 kms por hora** at more than 50 kms per hour; **poco ~ poco** little by little
8 (*dativo*): **se lo di ~ él** I gave it to him; **se lo compré ~ él** I bought it from him
9 (*complemento directo*): **vi al policía** I saw the policeman
10 (*tras ciertos verbos*): **voy ~ verle** I'm going to see him; **empezó ~ trabajar** he started working *o* to work; **sabe ~ queso** it tastes of cheese
11 (*+infin*): **al verle, le reconocí inmediatamente** when I saw him I recognized him at once; **el camino ~ recorrer** the distance we (*etc*) have to travel; **¡~ callar!** keep quiet!; **¡~ comer!** let's eat!
12 (*a+que*): **¡~ que llueve!** I bet it's going to rain!; **¿~ qué viene eso?** what's the meaning of this?; **¿~ que sí va a venir?** he IS coming, isn't he?; **¿~ que no lo haces? – ¡~ que sí!** bet you don't do it! – yes, I WILL!

A. *abr* (*ESCOL:* = *aprobado*) pass.
AA *nfpl abr* = **Aerolíneas Argentinas**.
AA EE *abr* (= *Asuntos Exteriores*): **Min. de AA EE** ≈ FO (*BRIT*).
ab. *abr* (= *abril*) Apr.
abad, esa [a'βað, 'ðesa] *nm/f* abbot/abbess.
abadía [aβa'ðia] *nf* abbey.
abajo [a'βaxo] *adv* (*situación*) (down) below, underneath; (*en edificio*) downstairs; (*dirección*) down, downwards; **~ de** *prep* below, under; **el piso de ~** the downstairs flat; **la parte de ~** the lower part; **¡~ el gobierno!** down with the government!; **cuesta/río ~** downhill/downstream; **de arriba ~** from top to bottom; **el ~ firmante** the undersigned; **más ~** lower *o* further down.
abalance [aβa'lanθe] *etc vb V* **abalanzarse**.
abalanzarse [aβalan'θarse] *vr*: **~ sobre** *o* **contra** to throw o.s. at.
abalear [aβale'ar] *vt* (*AM fam*) to shoot.
abalorios [aβa'lorjos] *nmpl* (*chucherías*)

trinkets.

abanderado [aßande'raðo] *nm* standard bearer.

abandonado, a [aßando'naðo, a] *adj* derelict; (*desatendido*) abandoned; (*desierto*) deserted; (*descuidado*) neglected.

abandonar [aßando'nar] *vt* to leave; (*persona*) to abandon, desert; (*cosa*) to abandon, leave behind; (*descuidar*) to neglect; (*renunciar a*) to give up; (*INFORM*) to quit; ~**se** *vr*: ~**se a** to abandon o.s. to; ~**se al alcohol** to take to drink.

abandono [aßan'dono] *nm* (*acto*) desertion, abandonment; (*estado*) abandon, neglect; (*renuncia*) withdrawal, retirement; **ganar por** ~ to win by default.

abanicar [aßani'kar] *vt* to fan.

abanico [aßa'niko] *nm* fan; (*NAUT*) derrick; **en** ~ fan-shaped.

abanique [aßa'nike] *etc vb V* **abanicar**.

abaratar [aßara'tar] *vt* to lower the price of ♦ *vi,* ~**se** *vr* to go o come down in price.

abarcar [aßar'kar] *vt* to include, embrace; (*contener*) to comprise; (*AM*) to monopolize; **quien mucho abarca poco aprieta** don't bite off more than you can chew.

abarque [a'ßarke] *etc vb V* **abarcar**.

abarrotado, a [aßarro'taðo, a] *adj* packed; ~ **de** packed o bursting with.

abarrote [aßa'rrote] *nm* packing; ~**s** *nmpl* (*AM*) groceries, provisions.

abarrotería [aßarrote'ria] *nf* (*AM*) grocery store.

abarrotero, a [aßarro'tero, a] *nm/f* (*AM*) grocer.

abastecedor, a [aßasteθe'ðor, a] *adj* supplying ♦ *nm/f* supplier.

abastecer [aßaste'θer] *vt:* ~ **(de)** to supply (with).

abastecimiento [aßasteθi'mjento] *nm* supply.

abastezca [aßas'teθka] *etc vb V* **abastecer**.

abasto [a'ßasto] *nm* supply; (*abundancia*) abundance; **no dar** ~ **a algo** not to be able to cope with sth.

abatible [aßa'tißle] *adj:* **asiento** ~ tip-up seat.

abatido, a [aßa'tiðo, a] *adj* dejected, downcast; **estar muy** ~ to be very depressed.

abatimiento [aßati'mjento] *nm* (*depresión*) dejection, depression.

abatir [aßa'tir] *vt* (*muro*) to demolish; (*pájaro*) to shoot o bring down; (*fig*) to

depress; ~**se** *vr* to get depressed; ~**se sobre** to swoop o pounce on.

abdicación [aßðika'θjon] *nf* abdication.

abdicar [aßði'kar] *vi* to abdicate; ~ **en algn** to abdicate in favour of sb.

abdique [aß'ðike] *etc vb V* **abdicar**.

abdomen [aß'ðomen] *nm* abdomen.

abdominal [aßðomi'nal] *adj* abdominal ♦ *nm:* ~**es** (*DEPORTE*) abdominals; (*ANAT*) abdominals, stomach muscles.

abecedario [aßeθe'ðarjo] *nm* alphabet.

abedul [aße'ðul] *nm* birch.

abeja [a'ßexa] *nf* bee; (*fig: hormiguita*) hard worker.

abejorro [aße'xorro] *nm* bumblebee.

aberración [aßerra'θjon] *nf* aberration.

aberrante [aße'rrante] *adj* (*disparatado*) ridiculous.

abertura [aßer'tura] *nf* = **apertura**.

abertzale [aßer't ʃale] *adj, nm/f* Basque nationalist.

abeto [a'ßeto] *nm* fir.

abierto, a [a'ßjerto, a] *pp de* **abrir** ♦ *adj* open; (*fig: carácter*) frank.

abigarrado, a [aßiɣa'rraðo, a] *adj* multicoloured; (*fig*) motley.

abismal [aßis'mal] *adj* (*fig*) vast, enormous.

abismar [aßis'mar] *vt* to humble, cast down; ~**se** *vr* to sink; (*AM*) to be amazed; ~**se en** (*fig*) to be plunged into.

abismo [a'ßismo] *nm* abyss; **de sus ideas a las mías hay un** ~ our views are worlds apart.

abjurar [aßxu'rar] *vt* to abjure, forswear ♦ *vi:* ~ **de** to abjure, forswear.

ablandar [aßlan'dar] *vt* to soften up; (*conmover*) to touch; (*CULIN*) to tenderize ♦ *vi,* ~**se** *vr* to get softer.

abnegación [aßneɣa'θjon] *nf* self-denial.

abnegado, a [aßne'ɣaðo, a] *adj* self-sacrificing.

abobado, a [aßo'ßaðo, a] *adj* silly.

abobamiento [aßoßa'mjento] *nm* (*asombro*) bewilderment.

abocado, a [aßo'kaðo, a] *adj:* **verse** ~ **al desastre** to be heading for disaster.

abochornar [aßot ʃor'nar] *vt* to embarrass; ~**se** *vr* to get flustered; (*BOT*) to wilt; ~**se de** to get embarrassed about.

abofetear [aßofete'ar] *vt* to slap (in the face).

abogacía [aßoɣa'θia] *nf* legal profession; (*ejercicio*) practice of the law.

abogado, a [aßo'ɣaðo, a] *nm/f* lawyer; (*notario*) solicitor; (*asesor*) counsel; (*en tribunal*) barrister, advocate, attorney (*US*); ~ **defensor** defence lawyer o attorney (*US*); ~ **del diablo** devil's

advocate.
abogar [aβo'ɣar] *vi*: ~ **por** to plead for;
(*fig*) to advocate.
abogue [a'βoɣe] *etc vb V* **abogar**.
abolengo [aβo'lengo] *nm* ancestry,
lineage.
abolición [aβoli'θjon] *nf* abolition.
abolir [aβo'lir] *vt* to abolish; (*cancelar*) to
cancel.
abolladura [aβoʎa'ðura] *nf* dent.
abollar [aβo'ʎar] *vt* to dent.
abominable [aβomi'naβle] *adj* abominable.
abominación [aβomina'θjon] *nf*
abomination.
abonado, a [aβo'naðo, a] *adj* (*deuda*)
paid(-up) ♦ *nm/f* subscriber.
abonar [aβo'nar] *vt* to pay;(*deuda*) to
settle; (*terreno*) to fertilize; (*idea*) to
endorse; ~**se** *vr* to subscribe; ~ **dinero**
en una cuenta to pay money into an
account, credit money to an account.
abono [a'βono] *nm* payment; fertilizer;
subscription.
abordable [aβor'ðaβle] *adj* (*persona*)
approachable.
abordar [aβor'ðar] *vt* (*barco*) to board;
(*asunto*) to broach; (*individuo*) to
approach.
aborigen [aβo'rixen] *nm/f* aborigine.
aborrecer [aβorre'θer] *vt* to hate, loathe.
aborrezca [aβo'rreθka] *etc vb V* **aborrecer**.
abortar [aβor'tar] *vi* (*malparir*) to have a
miscarriage; (*deliberadamente*) to have
an abortion.
aborto [a'βorto] *nm* miscarriage; abortion.
abotagado, a [aβota'ɣaðo, a] *adj* swollen.
abotonar [aβoto'nar] *vt* to button (up), do
up.
abovedado, a [aβoβe'ðaðo, a] *adj* vaulted,
domed.
abr. *abr* (= *abril*) Apr.
abrace [a'βraθe] *etc vb V* **abrazar**.
abrasar [aβra'sar] *vt* to burn (up); (*AGR*) to
dry up, parch.
abrazadera [aβraθa'ðera] *nf* bracket.
abrazar [aβra'θar] *vt* to embrace, hug; ~**se**
vr to embrace, hug each other.
abrazo [a'βraθo] *nm* embrace, hug; **un** ~
(*en carta*) with best wishes.
abrebotellas [aβreβo'teʎas] *nm inv* bottle
opener.
abrecartas [aβre'kartas] *nm inv* letter
opener.
abrelatas [aβre'latas] *nm inv* tin (*BRIT*) *o* can
(*US*) opener.
abrevadero [aβreβa'ðero] *nm* watering
place.
abreviar [aβre'βjar] *vt* to abbreviate;

(*texto*) to abridge; (*plazo*) to reduce ♦ *vi*:
bueno, para ~ well, to cut a long story
short.
abreviatura [aβreβja'tura] *nf* abbreviation.
abridor [aβri'ðor] *nm* (*de botellas*) bottle
opener; (*de latas*) tin (*BRIT*) *o* can (*US*)
opener.
abrigar [aβri'ɣar] *vt* (*proteger*) to shelter;
(*suj: ropa*) to keep warm; (*fig*) to cherish;
~**se** *vr* to take shelter, protect o.s (*de*
from); (*con ropa*) to cover (o.s.) up;
¡**abrígate bien!** wrap up well!
abrigo [a'βriɣo] *nm* (*prenda*) coat, overcoat;
(*lugar protegido*) shelter; **al** ~ **de** in the
shelter of.
abrigue [a'βriɣe] *etc vb V* **abrigar**.
abril [a'βril] *nm* April.
abrillantar [aβriʎan'tar] *vt* (*pulir*) to polish;
(*fig*) to enhance.
abrir [a'βrir] *vt* to open (up); (*camino etc*) to
open up; (*apetito*) to whet; (*lista*) to head
♦ *vi* to open; ~**se** *vr* to open (up);
(*extenderse*) to open out; (*cielo*) to clear;
~ **un negocio** to start up a business; **en**
un ~ **y cerrar de ojos** in the twinkling of
an eye; ~**se paso** to find *o* force a way
through.
abrochar [aβro'tʃar] *vt* (*con botones*) to
button (up); (*zapato, con broche*) to do up;
~**se** *vr*: ~**se los zapatos** to tie one's
shoelaces.
abrogación [aβroɣa'θjon] *nf* repeal.
abrogar [aβro'ɣar] *vt* to repeal.
abrumador, a [aβruma'ðor, a] *adj* (*mayoría*)
overwhelming.
abrumar [aβru'mar] *vt* to overwhelm;
(*sobrecargar*) to weigh down.
abrupto, a [a'βrupto, a] *adj* abrupt;
(*empinado*) steep.
absceso [aβs'θeso] *nm* abscess.
absentismo [aβsen'tismo] *nm* (*de obreros*)
absenteeism.
absolución [aβsolu'θjon] *nf* (*REL*)
absolution; (*JUR*) acquittal.
absoluto, a [aβso'luto, a] *adj* absolute;
(*total*) utter, complete; **en** ~ *adv* not at
all.
absolver [aβsol'βer] *vt* to absolve; (*JUR*) to
pardon; (: *acusado*) to acquit.
absorbente [aβsor'βente] *adj* absorbent;
(*interesante*) absorbing, interesting;
(*exigente*) demanding.
absorber [aβsor'βer] *vt* to absorb;
(*embeber*) to soak up; ~**se** *vr* to become
absorbed.
absorción [aβsor'θjon] *nf* absorption;
(*COM*) takeover.
absorto, a [aβ'sorto, a] *pp de* **absorber** ♦ *adj*

absorbed, engrossed.
abstemio, a [aßs'temjo, a] *adj* teetotal.
abstención [aßsten'θjon] *nf* abstention.
abstendré [aßsten'dre] *etc vb V* **abstenerse**.
abstenerse [aßste'nerse] *vr*: ~ **(de)** to abstain *o* refrain (from).
abstenga [aßs'tenga] *etc vb V* **abstenerse**.
abstinencia [aßsti'nenθja] *nf* abstinence; (*ayuno*) fasting.
abstracción [aßstrak'θjon] *nf* abstraction.
abstracto, a [aß'strakto, a] *adj* abstract; **en** ~ in the abstract.
abstraer [aßstra'er] *vt* to abstract; ~**se** *vr* to be *o* become absorbed.
abstraído, a [aßstra'iðo, a] *adj* absent-minded.
abstraiga [aßs'traiva] *etc*, **abstraje** [aßs'traxe] *etc*, **abstrayendo** [aßstra'jendo] *etc vb V* **abstraer**.
abstuve [aßs'tuße] *etc vb V* **abstenerse**.
absuelto [aß'swelto] *pp de* **absolver**.
absurdo, a [aß'surðo, a] *adj* absurd; **lo** ~ **es que ...** the ridiculous thing is that ... ♦ *nm* absurdity.
abuchear [aßutʃe'ar] *vt* to boo.
abucheo [aßu'tʃeo] *nm* booing; **ganarse un** ~ (*TEAT*) to be booed.
abuela [a'ßwela] *nf* grandmother; **¡cuéntaselo a tu** ~**!** (*fam!*) do you think I was born yesterday? (*fam*); **no tener/ necesitar** ~ (*fam*) to be full of o.s./blow one's own trumpet.
abuelita [aßwe'lita] *nf* granny.
abuelo [a'ßwelo] *nm* grandfather; (*antepasado*) ancestor; ~**s** *nmpl* grandparents.
abulense [aßu'lense] *adj* of Ávila ♦ *nm/f* native *o* inhabitant of Ávila.
abulia [a'ßulja] *nf* lethargy.
abúlico, a [a'ßuliko, a] *adj* lethargic.
abultado, a [aßul'taðo, a] *adj* bulky.
abultar [aßul'tar] *vt* to enlarge; (*aumentar*) to increase; (*fig*) to exaggerate ♦ *vi* to be bulky.
abundancia [aßun'danθja] *nf*: **una** ~ **de** plenty of; **en** ~ in abundance.
abundante [aßun'dante] *adj* abundant, plentiful.
abundar [aßun'dar] *vi* to abound, be plentiful; ~ **en una opinión** to share an opinion.
aburguesarse [aßurxe'sarse] *vr* to become middle-class.
aburrido, a [aßu'rriðo, a] *adj* (*hastiado*) bored; (*que aburre*) boring.
aburrimiento [aßurri'mjento] *nm* boredom, tedium.
aburrir [aßu'rrir] *vt* to bore; ~**se** *vr* to be

bored, get bored; ~**se como una almeja** *u* **ostra** to be bored stiff.
abusar [aßu'sar] *vi* to go too far; ~ **de** to abuse.
abusivo, a [aßu'sißo, a] *adj* (*precio*) exorbitant.
abuso [a'ßuso] *nm* abuse; ~ **de confianza** betrayal of trust.
abyecto, a [aß'jekto, a] *adj* wretched, abject.
A.C. *abr* (= *Año de Cristo*) A.D.
a/c *abr* (= *al cuidado de*) c/o; (= *a cuenta*) on account.
acá [a'ka] *adv* (*lugar*) here; **pasearse de** ~ **para allá** to walk up and down; **¡vente para** ~**!** come over here!; **¿de cuándo** ~**?** since when?
acabado, a [aka'ßaðo, a] *adj* finished, complete; (*perfecto*) perfect; (*agotado*) worn out; (*fig*) masterly ♦ *nm* finish.
acabar [aka'ßar] *vt* (*llevar a su fin*) to finish, complete; (*consumir*) to use up; (*rematar*) to finish off ♦ *vi* to finish, end; (*morir*) to die; ~**se** *vr* to finish, stop; (*terminarse*) to be over; (*agotarse*) to run out; ~ **con** to put an end to; ~ **mal** to come to a sticky end; **esto acabará conmigo** this will be the end of me; ~ **de llegar** to have just arrived; **acababa de hacerlo** I had just done it; ~ **haciendo** *o* **por hacer algo** to end up (by) doing sth; **¡se acabó!** (*¡basta!*) that's enough!; (*se terminó*) it's all over!; **se me acabó el tabaco** I ran out of cigarettes.
acabóse [aka'ßose] *nm*: **esto es el** ~ this is the limit.
acacia [a'kaθja] *nf* acacia.
academia [aka'ðemja] *nf* academy; (*ESCOL*) private school; *V tb* **colegio**.
académico, a [aka'ðemiko, a] *adj* academic.
acaecer [akae'θer] *vi* to happen, occur.
acaezca [aka'eθka] *etc vb V* **acaecer**.
acallar [aka'ʎar] *vt* (*silenciar*) to silence; (*calmar*) to pacify.
acalorado, a [akalo'raðo, a] *adj* (*discusión*) heated.
acalorarse [akalo'rarse] *vr* (*fig*) to get heated.
acampada [akam'paða] *nf*: **ir de** ~ to go camping.
acampanado, a [akampa'naðo, a] *adj* flared.
acampar [akam'par] *vi* to camp.
acanalado, a [akana'laðo, a] *adj* (*hierro*) corrugated.
acanalar [akana'lar] *vt* to groove; (*ondular*) to corrugate.

acantilado [akanti'laðo] nm cliff.
acaparador, a [akapara'ðor, a] nm/f monopolizer.
acaparar [akapa'rar] vt to monopolize; (acumular) to hoard.
acápite [a'kapite] nm (AM) paragraph; **punto ~** full stop, new paragraph.
acaramelado, a [akarame'laðo, a] adj (CULIN) toffee-coated; (fig) sugary.
acariciar [akari'θjar] vt to caress; (esperanza) to cherish.
acarrear [akarre'ar] vt to transport; (fig) to cause, result in; **le acarreó muchos disgustos** it brought him lots of problems.
acaso [a'kaso] adv perhaps, maybe ♦ nm chance; **¿~ es mi culpa?** (AM fam) what makes you think it's my fault?; **(por) si ~** (just) in case.
acatamiento [akata'mjento] nm respect; (de la ley) observance.
acatar [aka'tar] vt to respect; (ley) to obey, observe.
acatarrarse [akata'rrarse] vr to catch a cold.
acaudalado, a [akauða'laðo, a] adj well-off.
acaudillar [akauði'ʎar] vt to lead, command.
acceder [akθe'ðer] vi to accede, agree; **~ a** (INFORM) to access.
accesible [akθe'siβle] adj accessible; **~ a** open to.
accésit, pl **accésits** [ak'θesit, ak'θesits] nm consolation prize.
acceso [ak'θeso] nm access, entry; (camino) access road; (MED) attack, fit; (de cólera) fit; (POL) accession; (INFORM) access; **~ aleatorio/directo/secuencial o en serie** (INFORM) random/direct/sequential o serial access; **de ~ múltiple** multi-access.
accesorio, a [akθe'sorjo, a] adj accessory ♦ nm accessory; **~s** nmpl (AUTO) accessories, extras; (TEAT) props.
accidentado, a [akθiðen'taðo, a] adj uneven; (montañoso) hilly; (azaroso) eventful ♦ nm/f accident victim.
accidental [akθiðen'tal] adj accidental; (empleo) temporary.
accidentarse [akθiðen'tarse] vr to have an accident.
accidente [akθi'ðente] nm accident; **por ~** by chance; **~s** nmpl unevenness sg, roughness sg.
acción [ak'θjon] nf action; (acto) action, act; (TEAT) plot; (COM) share; (JUR) action, lawsuit; **capital en acciones** share

capital; **~ liberada/ordinaria/preferente** fully-paid/ordinary/preference share.
accionamiento [akθjona'mjento] nm (de máquina) operation.
accionar [akθjo'nar] vt to work, operate; (INFORM) to drive.
accionista [akθjo'nista] nm/f shareholder.
acebo [a'θeβo] nm holly; (árbol) holly tree.
acechanza [aθe't∫anθa] nf = **acecho**.
acechar [aθe't∫ar] vt to spy on; (aguardar) to lie in wait for.
acecho [a'θet∫o] nm: **estar al ~ (de)** to lie in wait (for).
acedera [aθe'ðera] nf sorrel.
aceitar [aθei'tar] vt to oil, lubricate.
aceite [a'θeite] nm oil; (de oliva) olive oil; **~ de hígado de bacalao** cod-liver oil.
aceitera [aθei'tera] nf oilcan.
aceitoso, a [aθei'toso, a] adj oily.
aceituna [aθei'tuna] nf olive.
aceitunado, a [aθeitu'naðo, a] adj olive cpd; **de tez aceitunada** olive-skinned.
acelerador [aθelera'ðor] nm accelerator.
acelerar [aθele'rar] vt to accelerate; **~se** vr to hurry.
acelga [a'θelɣa] nf chard, beet.
acendrado, a [aθen'draðo, a] adj: **de ~ carácter español** typically Spanish.
acendrar [aθen'drar] vt to purify.
acento [a'θento] nm accent; (acentuación) stress; **~ cerrado** strong o thick accent.
acentuar [aθen'twar] vt to accent; to stress; (fig) to accentuate; (INFORM) to highlight.
acepción [aθep'θjon] nf meaning.
aceptación [aθepta'θjon] nf acceptance; (aprobación) approval.
aceptar [aθep'tar] vt to accept; to approve.
acequia [a'θekja] nf irrigation ditch.
acera [a'θera] nf pavement (BRIT), sidewalk (US).
acerado, a [aθe'raðo, a] adj steel; (afilado) sharp; (fig: duro) steely; (: mordaz) biting.
acerbo, a [a'θerβo, a] adj bitter; (fig) harsh.
acerca [a'θerka]: **~ de** adv about, concerning.
acercar [aθer'kar] vt to bring o move nearer; **~se** vr to approach, come near.
acerico [aθe'riko] nm pincushion.
acero [a'θero] nm steel; **~ inoxidable** stainless steel.
acerque [a'θerke] etc vb V **acercar**.
acérrimo, a [a'θerrimo, a] adj (partidario) staunch; (enemigo) bitter.
acertado, a [aθer'taðo, a] adj correct; (apropiado) apt; (sensato) sensible.
acertar [aθer'tar] vt (blanco) to hit; (solución) to get right; (adivinar) to guess

♦ *vi* to get it right, be right; ~ **a** to manage to; ~ **con** to happen *o* hit on.

acertijo [aθer'tixo] *nm* riddle, puzzle.

acervo [a'θerßo] *nm* heap; ~ **común** undivided estate.

achacar [atʃa'kar] *vt* to attribute.

achacoso, a [atʃa'koso, a] *adj* sickly.

achantar [atʃan'tar] *vt* (*fam*) to scare, frighten; ~**se** *vr* to back down.

achaque [a'tʃake] *etc vb V* **achacar** ♦ *nm* ailment.

achatar [atʃa'tar] *vt* to flatten.

achicar [atʃi'kar] *vt* to reduce; (*humillar*) to humiliate; (*NAUT*) to bale out; ~**se** (*ropa*) to shrink; (*fig*) to humble o.s.

achicharrar [atʃitʃa'rrar] *vt* to scorch, burn.

achicoria [atʃi'korja] *nf* chicory.

achinado, a [atʃi'naðo, a] *adj* (*ojos*) slanting; (*AM*) half-caste.

achique [a'tʃike] *etc vb V* **achicar**.

acholado, a [atʃo'laðo, a] *adj* (*AM*) half-caste.

achuchar [atʃu'tʃar] *vt* to crush.

achuchón [atʃu'tʃon] *nm* shove; **tener un** ~ (*MED*) to be poorly.

achuras [a'tʃuras] *nf* (*AM CULIN*) offal.

aciago, a [a'θjaɣo, a] *adj* ill-fated, fateful.

acicalar [aθika'lar] *vt* to polish; (*adornar*) to bedeck; ~**se** *vr* to get dressed up.

acicate [aθi'kate] *nm* spur; (*fig*) incentive.

acidez [aθi'ðeθ] *nf* acidity.

ácido, a ['aθiðo, a] *adj* sour, acid ♦ *nm* acid; (*fam: droga*) LSD.

acierto [a'θjerto] *etc vb V* **acertar** ♦ *nm* success; (*buen paso*) wise move; (*solución*) solution; (*habilidad*) skill, ability; (*al adivinar*) good guess; **fue un ~ suyo** it was a sensible choice on his part.

aclamación [aklama'θjon] *nf* acclamation; (*aplausos*) applause.

aclamar [akla'mar] *vt* to acclaim; to applaud.

aclaración [aklara'θjon] *nf* clarification, explanation.

aclarar [akla'rar] *vt* to clarify, explain; (*ropa*) to rinse ♦ *vi* to clear up; ~**se** *vr* (*suj: persona: explicarse*) to understand; (*fig: asunto*) to become clear; ~**se la garganta** to clear one's throat.

aclaratorio, a [aklara'torjo, a] *adj* explanatory.

aclimatación [aklimata'θjon] *nf* acclimatization.

aclimatar [aklima'tar] *vt* to acclimatize; ~**se** *vr* to become *o* get acclimatized; ~**se a algo** to get used to sth.

acné [ak'ne] *nm* acne.

acobardar [akoßar'ðar] *vt* to daunt, intimidate; ~**se** *vr* (*atemorizarse*) to be intimidated; (*echarse atrás*): ~**se (ante)** to shrink back (from).

acodarse [ako'ðarse] *vr*: ~ **en** to lean on.

acogedor, a [akoxe'ðor, a] *adj* welcoming; (*hospitalario*) hospitable.

acoger [ako'xer] *vt* to welcome; (*abrigar*) to shelter; ~**se** *vr* to take refuge; ~**se a** (*pretexto*) to take refuge in; (*ley*) to resort to.

acogida [ako'xiða] *nf* reception; refuge.

acoja [a'koxa] *etc vb V* **acoger**.

acojonante [akoxo'nante] *adj* (*ESP fam*) tremendous.

acolchar [akol'tʃar] *vt* to pad; (*fig*) to cushion.

acólito [a'kolito] *nm* (*REL*) acolyte; (*fig*) minion.

acometer [akome'ter] *vt* to attack; (*emprender*) to undertake.

acometida [akome'tiða] *nf* attack, assault.

acomodado, a [akomo'ðaðo, a] *adj* (*persona*) well-to-do.

acomodador, a [akomoða'ðor, a] *nm/f* usher(ette).

acomodar [akomo'ðar] *vt* to adjust; (*alojar*) to accommodate; ~**se** *vr* to conform; (*instalarse*) to install o.s.; (*adaptarse*) to adapt o.s.; **¡acomódese a su gusto!** make yourself comfortable!

acomodaticio, a [akomoða'tiθjo, a] *adj* (*pey*) accommodating, obliging; (*manejable*) pliable.

acompañamiento [akompaɲa'mjento] *nm* (*MUS*) accompaniment.

acompañante, a [akompa'ɲante, a] *nm/f* companion.

acompañar [akompa'ɲar] *vt* to accompany, go with; (*documentos*) to enclose; **¿quieres que te acompañe?** do you want me to come with you?; ~ **a algn a la puerta** to see sb to the door *o* out; **le acompaño en el sentimiento** please accept my condolences.

acompasar [akompa'sar] *vt* (*MUS*) to mark the rhythm of.

acomplejado, a [akomple'xaðo, a] *adj* neurotic.

acomplejar [akomple'xar] *vt* to give a complex to; ~**se** *vr*: ~**se (con)** to get a complex (about).

acondicionado, a [akondiθjo'naðo, a] *adj* (*TEC*) in good condition.

acondicionador [akondiθjona'ðor] *nm* conditioner.

acondicionar [akondiθjo'nar] *vt* to get

ready, prepare; (*pelo*) to condition.
acongojar [akongo'xar] *vt* to distress,
grieve.
aconsejable [akonse'xaßle] *adj* advisable.
aconsejar [akonse'xar] *vt* to advise,
counsel; ~**se** *vr*: ~**se con** *o* **de** to consult.
acontecer [akonte'θer] *vi* to happen,
occur.
acontecimiento [akonteθi'mjento] *nm*
event.
acontezca [akon'teθka] *etc vb* V **acontecer**.
acopiar [ako'pjar] *vt* (*recoger*) to gather;
(*COM*) to buy up.
acopio [a'kopjo] *nm* store, stock.
acoplador [akopla'ðor] *nm*: ~ **acústico**
(*INFORM*) acoustic coupler.
acoplamiento [akopla'mjento] *nm*
coupling, joint.
acoplar [ako'plar] *vt* to fit; (*ELEC*) to
connect; (*vagones*) to couple.
acoquinar [akoki'nar] *vt* to scare; ~**se** *vr* to
get scared.
acorazado, a [akora'θaðo, a] *adj* armour-
plated, armoured ♦ *nm* battleship.
acordar [akor'ðar] *vt* (*resolver*) to agree,
resolve; (*recordar*) to remind; ~**se** *vr* to
agree; ~**se (de algo)** to remember (sth).
acorde [a'korðe] *adj* (*MUS*) harmonious; ~
con (*medidas etc*) in keeping with ♦ *nm*
chord.
acordeón [akorðe'on] *nm* accordion.
acordonado, a [akorðo'naðo, a] *adj* (*calle*)
cordoned-off.
acorralar [akorra'lar] *vt* to round up,
corral; (*fig*) to intimidate.
acortar [akor'tar] *vt* to shorten; (*duración*)
to cut short; (*cantidad*) to reduce; ~**se** *vr*
to become shorter.
acosar [ako'sar] *vt* to pursue relentlessly;
(*fig*) to hound, pester; ~ **a algn a**
preguntas to pester sb with questions.
acoso [a'koso] *nm* relentless pursuit; (*fig*)
hounding; ~ **sexual** sexual harassment.
acostar [akos'tar] *vt* (*en cama*) to put to
bed; (*en suelo*) to lay down; (*barco*) to
bring alongside; ~**se** *vr* to go to bed; to
lie down.
acostumbrado, a [akostum'braðo, a] *adj*
(*habitual*) usual; **estar** ~ **a (hacer) algo** to
be used to (doing) sth.
acostumbrar [akostum'brar] *vt*: ~ **a algn a**
algo to get sb used to sth ♦ *vi*: ~ **(a hacer**
algo) to be in the habit (of doing sth);
~**se** *vr*: ~**se a** to get used to.
acotación [akota'θjon] *nf* (*apunte*)
marginal note; (*GEO*) elevation mark; (*de*
límite) boundary mark; (*TEAT*) stage
direction.

acotar [ako'tar] *vt* (*terreno*) to mark out;
(*fig*) to limit; (*caza*) to protect.
acotejar [akote'xar] *vt* (*AM*) to put in
order, arrange.
ácrata ['akrata] *adj, nm/f* anarchist.
acre ['akre] *adj* (*sabor*) sharp, bitter; (*olor*)
acrid; (*fig*) biting ♦ *nm* acre.
acrecentar [akreθen'tar] *vt* to increase,
augment.
acreciente [akre'θjente] *etc vb* V
acrecentar.
acreditado, a [akreði'taðo, a] *adj* (*POL*)
accredited; (*COM*): **una casa acreditada** a
reputable firm.
acreditar [akreði'tar] *vt* (*garantizar*) to
vouch for, guarantee; (*autorizar*) to
authorize; (*dar prueba de*) to prove; (*COM*:
abonar) to credit; (*embajador*) to
accredit; ~**se** *vr* to become famous;
(*demostrar valía*) to prove one's worth;
~**se de** to get a reputation for.
acreedor, a [akree'ðor, a] *adj*: ~ **a** worthy
of ♦ *nm/f* creditor; ~ **común/diferido/con**
garantía (*COM*) unsecured/deferred/
secured creditor.
acribillar [akrißi'ʎar] *vt*: ~ **a balazos** to
riddle with bullets.
acrimonia [akri'monja], **acritud** [akri'tuð]
nf acrimony.
acrobacia [akro'ßaθja] *nf* acrobatics; ~
aérea aerobatics.
acróbata [a'kroßata] *nm/f* acrobat.
acta ['akta] *nf* certificate; (*de comisión*)
minutes *pl*, record; ~ **de nacimiento/de**
matrimonio birth/marriage certificate;
~ **notarial** affidavit; **levantar** ~ (*JUR*) to
make a formal statement *o* deposition.
actitud [akti'tuð] *nf* attitude; (*postura*)
posture; **adoptar una** ~ **firme** to take a
firm stand.
activar [akti'ßar] *vt* to activate; (*acelerar*) to
speed up.
actividad [aktißi'ðað] *nf* activity; **estar en**
plena ~ to be in full swing.
activo, a [ak'tißo, a] *adj* active; (*vivo*)
lively ♦ *nm* (*COM*) assets *pl*; ~ **y pasivo**
assets and liabilities; ~ **circulante/fijo/**
inmaterial/invisible (*COM*) current/fixed/
intangible/invisible assets; ~ **realizable**
liquid assets; ~**s congelados** *o*
bloqueados frozen assets; **estar en** ~
(*MIL*) to be on active service.
acto ['akto] *nm* act, action; (*ceremonia*)
ceremony; (*TEAT*) act; **en el** ~
immediately; **hacer** ~ **de presencia**
(*asistir*) to attend (formally).
actor [ak'tor] *nm* actor; (*JUR*) plaintiff.
actora [ak'tora] *adj*: **parte** ~ prosecution;

(*demandante*) plaintiff.
actriz [ak'triθ] *nf* actress.
actuación [aktwa'θjon] *nf* action;
(*comportamiento*) conduct, behaviour;
(*JUR*) proceedings *pl*; (*desempeño*)
performance.
actual [ak'twal] *adj* present(-day), current;
el 6 del ~ the 6th of this month.
actualice [aktwa'liθe] *etc vb V* **actualizar.**
actualidad [aktwali'ðað] *nf* present; ~**es**
nfpl news *sg*; **en la** ~ nowadays, at
present; **ser de gran** ~ to be current.
actualización [aktwaliθa'θjon] *nf* updating,
modernization.
actualizar [aktwali'θar] *vt* to update,
modernize.
actualmente [aktwal'mente] *adv* at
present; (*hoy día*) nowadays.
actuar [ak'twar] *vi* (*obrar*) to work,
operate; (*actor*) to act, perform ♦ *vt* to
work, operate; ~ **de** to act as.
actuario, a [ak'twarjo] *nm/f* clerk; (*COM*)
actuary.
acuarela [akwa'rela] *nf* watercolour.
acuario [a'kwarjo] *nm* aquarium; **A~**
(*ASTRO*) Aquarius.
acuartelar [akwarte'lar] *vt* (*MIL*: *alojar*) to
quarter.
acuático, a [a'kwatiko, a] *adj* aquatic.
acuchillar [akutʃi'ʎar] *vt* (*TEC*) to plane
(down), smooth.
acuciar [aku'θjar] *vt* to urge on.
acuclillarse [akukli'ʎarse] *vr* to crouch
down.
ACUDE [a'kuðe] *nf abr* = *Asociación de
Consumidores y Usuarios de España.*
acudir [aku'ðir] *vi* to attend, turn up; ~ **a**
to turn to; ~ **en ayuda de** to go to the aid
of; ~ **a una cita** to keep an appointment;
~ **a una llamada** to answer a call; **no
tener a quién** ~ to have nobody to turn
to.
acuerdo [a'kwerðo] *etc vb V* **acordar** ♦ *nm*
agreement; (*POL*) resolution; ~ **de pago
respectivo** (*COM*) knock-for-knock
agreement; **A~ general sobre aranceles
aduaneros y comercio** (*COM*) General
Agreement on Tariffs and Trade; **tomar
un** ~ to pass a resolution; **¡de** ~**!**
agreed!; **de** ~ **con** (*persona*) in
agreement with; (*acción, documento*) in
accordance with; **de común** ~ by
common consent; **estar de** ~ (*persona*) to
agree; **llegar a un** ~ to come to an
understanding.
acueste [a'kweste] *etc vb V* **acostar.**
acullá [aku'ʎa] *adv* over there.
acumular [akumu'lar] *vt* to accumulate,

collect.
acunar [aku'nar] *vt* to rock (to sleep).
acuñar [aku'ɲar] *vt* (*moneda*) to mint;
(*frase*) to coin.
acuoso, a [a'kwoso, a] *adj* watery.
acupuntura [akupun'tura] *nf* acupuncture.
acurrucarse [akurru'karse] *vr* to crouch;
(*ovillarse*) to curl up.
acurruque [aku'rruke] *etc vb V*
acurrucarse.
acusación [akusa'θjon] *nf* accusation.
acusado, a [aku'saðo, a] *adj* (*JUR*) accused;
(*marcado*) marked; (*acento*) strong.
acusar [aku'sar] *vt* to accuse; (*revelar*) to
reveal; (*denunciar*) to denounce;
(*emoción*) to show; ~ **recibo** to
acknowledge receipt; **su rostro acusó
extrañeza** his face registered surprise;
~**se** *vr*: ~**se (de)** to confess (to).
acuse [a'kuse] *nm*: ~ **de recibo** acknowledgement of receipt.
acústico, a [a'kustiko, a] *adj* acoustic ♦ *nf*
(*de una sala etc*) acoustics *pl*; (*ciencia*)
acoustics *sg*.
ADA ['aða] *nf abr* (*ESP*. = *Ayuda del
Automovilista*) ≈ AA, RAC (*BRIT*), AAA
(*US*).
adagio [a'ðaxjo] *nm* adage; (*MUS*) adagio.
adalid [aða'lið] *nm* leader, champion.
adaptación [aðapta'θjon] *nf* adaptation.
adaptador [aðapta'ðor] *nm* (*ELEC*) adapter.
adaptar [aðap'tar] *vt* to adapt; (*acomodar*)
to fit; (*convertir*): ~ **(para)** to convert (to).
adecentar [aðeθen'tar] *vt* to tidy up.
adecuado, a [aðe'kwaðo, a] *adj* (*apto*)
suitable; (*oportuno*) appropriate; **el
hombre** ~ **para el puesto** the right man
for the job.
adecuar [aðe'kwar] *vt* (*adaptar*) to adapt;
(*hacer apto*) to make suitable.
adefesio [aðe'fesjo] *nm* (*fam*): **estaba
hecha un** ~ she looked a sight.
a. de J.C. *abr* (= *antes de Jesucristo*) B.C.
adelantado, a [aðelan'taðo, a] *adj*
advanced; (*reloj*) fast; **pagar por** ~ to pay
in advance.
adelantamiento [aðelanta'mjento] *nm*
advance, advancement; (*AUTO*)
overtaking.
adelantar [aðelan'tar] *vt* to move forward;
(*avanzar*) to advance; (*acelerar*) to speed
up; (*AUTO*) to overtake ♦ *vi* (*ir delante*) to
go ahead; (*progresar*) to improve; (*tb*:
~**se**) *vr*: *tomar la delantera*) to go forward,
advance; ~**se a algn** to get ahead of sb;
~**se a los deseos de algn** to anticipate
sb's wishes.
adelante [aðe'lante] *adv* forward(s),

onward(s), ahead ♦ *excl* come in!; **de hoy en ~** from now on; **más ~** later on; (*más allá*) further on.

adelanto [aðeˈlanto] *nm* advance; (*mejora*) improvement; (*progreso*) progress; (*dinero*) advance; **los ~s de la ciencia** the advances of science.

adelgace [aðelˈɣaθe] *etc vb V* **adelgazar.**

adelgazar [aðelɣaˈθar] *vt* to thin (down); (*afilar*) to taper ♦ *vi* to get thin; (*con régimen*) to slim down, lose weight.

ademán [aðeˈman] *nm* gesture; **ademanes** *nmpl* manners; **en ~ de** as if to.

además [aðeˈmas] *adv* besides; (*por otra parte*) moreover; (*también*) also; **~ de** besides, in addition to.

ADENA [aˈðena] *nf abr* (*ESP:* = *Asociación para la Defensa de la Naturaleza*) *organization for nature conservation.*

adentrarse [aðenˈtrarse] *vr*: **~ en** to go into, get inside; (*penetrar*) to penetrate (into).

adentro [aˈðentro] *adv* inside, in; **mar ~** out at sea; **tierra ~** inland ♦ *nm*: **dijo para sus ~s** he said to himself.

adepto, a [aˈðepto, a] *nm/f* supporter.

aderece [aðeˈreθe] *etc vb V* **aderezar.**

aderezar [aðereˈθar] *vt* (*ensalada*) to dress; (*comida*) to season.

aderezo [aðeˈreθo] *nm* dressing; seasoning.

adeudar [aðeuˈðar] *vt* to owe; **~se** *vr* to run into debt; **~ una suma en una cuenta** to debit an account with a sum.

a.D.g. *abr* (= *a Dios gracias*) D.G. (= *Deo gratias: thanks be to God*).

adherirse [aðeˈrirse] *vr*: **~ a** to adhere to; (*fig*) to follow.

adhesión [aðeˈsjon] *nf* adhesion; (*fig*) adherence.

adhesivo, a [aðeˈsiβo, a] *adj* adhesive ♦ *nm* sticker.

adhiera [aˈðjera] *etc*, **adhiriendo** [aðiˈrjendo] *etc vb V* **adherirse.**

adicción [aðikˈθjon] *nf* addiction.

adición [aðiˈθjon] *nf* addition.

adicional [aðiθjoˈnal] *adj* additional; (*INFORM*) add-on.

adicionar [aðiθjoˈnar] *vt* to add.

adicto, a [aˈðikto, a] *adj*: **~ a** (*droga etc*) addicted to; (*dedicado*) devoted to ♦ *nm/f* supporter, follower; (*toxicómano etc*) addict.

adiestrar [aðjesˈtrar] *vt* to train, teach; (*conducir*) to guide, lead; **~se** *vr* to practise; (*enseñarse*) to train o.s.

adinerado, a [aðineˈraðo, a] *adj* wealthy.

adiós [aˈðjos] *excl* (*para despedirse*) goodbye!, cheerio!; (*al pasar*) hello!

aditivo [aðiˈtiβo] *nm* additive.

adivinanza [aðiβiˈnanθa] *nf* riddle.

adivinar [aðiβiˈnar] *vt* (*profetizar*) to prophesy; (*conjeturar*) to guess.

adivino, a [aðiˈβino, a] *nm/f* fortune-teller.

adj *abr* (= *adjunto*) encl.

adjetivo [aðxeˈtiβo] *nm* adjective.

adjudicación [aðxuðikaˈθjon] *nf* award; (*COM*) adjudication.

adjudicar [aðxuðiˈkar] *vt* to award; **~se algo** *vr*: **~se algo** to appropriate sth.

adjudique [aðxuˈðike] *etc vb V* **adjudicar.**

adjuntar [aðxunˈtar] *vt* to attach, enclose.

adjunto, a [aðˈxunto, a] *adj* attached, enclosed ♦ *nm/f* assistant.

adminículo [aðmiˈnikulo] *nm* gadget.

administración [aðministraˈθjon] *nf* administration; (*dirección*) management; **~ pública** civil service; **A~ de Correos** General Post Office.

administrador, a [aðministraˈðor, a] *nm/f* administrator; manager(ess).

administrar [aðminisˈtrar] *vt* to administer.

administrativo, a [aðministraˈtiβo, a] *adj* administrative.

admirable [aðmiˈraβle] *adj* admirable.

admiración [aðmiraˈθjon] *nf* admiration; (*asombro*) wonder; (*LING*) exclamation mark.

admirar [aðmiˈrar] *vt* to admire; (*extrañar*) to surprise; **~se** *vr* to be surprised; **se admiró de saberlo** he was amazed to hear it; **no es de ~ que ...** it's not surprising that ...

admisible [aðmiˈsiβle] *adj* admissible.

admisión [aðmiˈsjon] *nf* admission; (*reconocimiento*) acceptance.

admitir [aðmiˈtir] *vt* to admit; (*aceptar*) to accept; (*dudas*) to leave room for; **esto no admite demora** this must be dealt with immediately.

admón. *abr* (= *administración*) admin.

admonición [aðmoniˈθjon] *nf* warning.

ADN *nm abr* (= *acido desoxirribonucleico*) DNA.

adobar [aðoˈβar] *vt* (*preparar*) to prepare; (*cocinar*) to season.

adobe [aˈðoβe] *nm* adobe, sun-dried brick.

adocenado, a [aðoθeˈnaðo, a] *adj* (*fam*) mediocre.

adoctrinar [aðoktriˈnar] *vt* to indoctrinate.

adolecer [aðoleˈθer] *vi*: **~ de** to suffer from.

adolescente [aðolesˈθente] *nm/f* adolescent, teenager ♦ *adj* adolescent, teenage.

adolezca [aðoˈleθka] etc vb V **adolecer**.
adonde [aˈðonde] adv (to) where.
adónde [aˈðonde] adv = **dónde**.
adondequiera [aðondeˈkjera] adv wherever.
adopción [aðopˈθjon] nf adoption.
adoptar [aðopˈtar] vt to adopt.
adoptivo, a [aðopˈtiβo, a] adj (padres) adoptive; (hijo) adopted.
adoquín [aðoˈkin] nm paving stone.
adorar [aðoˈrar] vt to adore.
adormecer [aðormeˈθer] vt to put to sleep; ~**se** vr to become sleepy; (dormirse) to fall asleep.
adormezca [aðorˈmeθka] etc vb V **adormecer**.
adormilarse [aðormiˈlarse] vr to doze.
adornar [aðorˈnar] vt to adorn.
adorno [aˈðorno] nm adornment; (decoración) decoration.
adosado, a [aðoˈsaðo, a] adj (casa) semidetached.
adquiera [aðˈkjera] etc vb V **adquirir**.
adquirir [aðkiˈrir] vt to acquire, obtain.
adquisición [aðkisiˈθjon] nf acquisition; (compra) purchase.
adrede [aˈðreðe] adv on purpose.
Adriático [aðˈrjatiko] nm: **el (Mar)** ~ the Adriatic (Sea).
adscribir [aðskriˈβir] vt to appoint; **estuvo adscrito al servicio de ...** he was attached to ...
adscrito [aðˈskrito] pp de **adscribir**.
aduana [aˈðwana] nf customs pl; (impuesto) (customs) duty.
aduanero, a [aðwaˈnero, a] adj customs cpd ♦ nm/f customs officer.
aducir [aðuˈθir] vt to adduce; (dar como prueba) to offer as proof.
adueñarse [aðweˈɲarse] vr: ~ **de** to take possession of.
adulación [aðulaˈθjon] nf flattery.
adular [aðuˈlar] vt to flatter.
adulterar [aðulteˈrar] vt to adulterate ♦ vi to commit adultery.
adulterio [aðulˈterjo] nm adultery.
adúltero, a [aˈðultero, a] adj adulterous ♦ nm/f adulterer/adulteress.
adulto, a [aˈðulto, a] adj, nm/f adult.
adusto, a [aˈðusto, a] adj stern; (austero) austere.
aduzca [aˈðuθka] etc vb V **aducir**.
advenedizo, a [aðβeneˈðiðo, a] nm/f upstart.
advenimiento [aðβeniˈmjento] nm arrival; (al trono) accession.
adverbio [aðˈβerβjo] nm adverb.
adversario, a [aðβerˈsarjo, a] nm/f adversary.
adversidad [aðβersiˈðað] nf adversity; (contratiempo) setback.
adverso, a [aðˈβerso, a] adj adverse; (suerte) bad.
advertencia [aðβerˈtenθja] nf warning; (prefacio) preface, foreword.
advertir [aðβerˈtir] vt (observar) to notice; (avisar): ~ **a algn de** to warn sb about o of.
Adviento [aðˈβjento] nm Advent.
advierta [aðˈβjerta] etc, **advirtiendo** [aðβirˈtjendo] etc vb V **advertir**.
adyacente [aðjaˈθente] adj adjacent.
aéreo, a [aˈereo, a] adj aerial; (tráfico) air cpd.
aerobic [aeˈroβik] nm aerobics sg.
aerodeslizador [aeroðesliθaˈðor] nm hovercraft.
aerodinámico, a [aeroði'namiko, a] adj aerodynamic.
aeródromo [aeˈroðromo] nm aerodrome.
aerograma [aeroˈɣrama] nm airmail letter.
aeromodelismo [aeromoðeˈlismo] nm model aircraft making, aeromodelling.
aeromozo, a [aeroˈmoso, a] nm/f (AM) flight attendant, air steward(ess).
aeronáutico, a [aeroˈnautiko, a] adj aeronautical.
aeronave [aeroˈnaβe] nm spaceship.
aeroplano [aeroˈplano] nm aeroplane.
aeropuerto [aeroˈpwerto] nm airport.
aerosol [aeroˈsol] nm aerosol, spray.
a/f abr (= a favor) in favour.
afabilidad [afaβiliˈðað] nf affability, pleasantness.
afable [aˈfaβle] adj affable, pleasant.
afamado, a [afaˈmaðo, a] adj famous.
afán [aˈfan] nm hard work; (deseo) desire; **con** ~ keenly.
afanar [afaˈnar] vt to harass; (fam) to pinch; ~**se** vr: ~**se por** to strive to.
afanoso, a [afaˈnoso, a] adj (trabajo) hard; (trabajador) industrious.
AFE [ˈafe] nf abr (= Asociación de Futbolistas Españoles) ≈ F.A.
afear [afeˈar] vt to disfigure.
afección [afekˈθjon] nf affection; (MED) disease.
afectación [afektaˈθjon] nf affectation.
afectado, a [afekˈtaðo, a] adj affected.
afectar [afekˈtar] vt to affect, have an effect on; (AM: dañar) to hurt; **por lo que afecta a esto** as far as this is concerned.
afectísimo , a [afekˈtisimo, a] adj affectionate; ~ **suyo** yours truly.
afectivo, a [afekˈtiβo, a] adj affective.
afecto, a [aˈfekto, a] adj: ~ **a** fond of; (JUR)

subject to ♦ *nm* affection; **tenerle** ~ **a algn** to be fond of sb.

afectuoso, a [afek'twoso, a] *adj* affectionate.

afeitar [afei'tar] *vt* to shave; ~**se** *vr* to shave.

afeminado, a [afemi'naðo, a] *adj* effeminate.

aferrar [afe'rrar] *vt* to moor; (*fig*) to grasp ♦ *vi* to moor; ~**se** *vr* (*agarrarse*) to cling on; ~**se a un principio** to stick to a principle; ~**se a una esperanza** to cling to a hope.

affmo., a. *abr* (= *afectísimo, a*) Yours.

Afganistán [afɣanis'tan] *nm* Afghanistan.

afgano, a [af'ɣano, a] *adj, nm/f* Afghan.

afiance [a'fjanθe] *etc vb V* **afianzar.**

afianzamiento [afjanθa'mjento] *nm* strengthening; security.

afianzar [afjan'θar] *vt* to strengthen, secure; ~**se** *vr* to steady o.s.; (*establecerse*) to become established.

afiche [a'fitʃe] *nm* (*AM*) poster.

afición [afi'θjon] *nf*: ~ **a** fondness *o* liking for; **la** ~ the fans *pl*; **pinto por** ~ I paint as a hobby.

aficionado, a [afiθjo'naðo, a] *adj* keen, enthusiastic; (*no profesional*) amateur ♦ *nm/f* enthusiast, fan; amateur.

aficionar [afiθjo'nar] *vt*: ~ **a algn a algo** to make sb like sth; ~**se** *vr*: ~**se a algo** to grow fond of sth.

afilado, a [afi'laðo, a] *adj* sharp.

afilador [afila'ðor] *nm* (*persona*) knife grinder.

afilalápices [afila'lapiθes] *nm inv* pencil sharpener.

afilar [afi'lar] *vt* to sharpen; ~**se** *vr* (*cara*) to grow thin.

afiliación [afilja'θjon] *nf* (*de sindicatos*) membership.

afiliado, a [afi'ljaðo, a] *adj* subsidiary ♦ *nm/f* affiliate.

afiliarse [afi'ljarse] *vr* to affiliate.

afín [a'fin] *adj* (*parecido*) similar; (*conexo*) related.

afinar [afi'nar] *vt* (*TEC*) to refine; (*MUS*) to tune ♦ *vi* to play/sing in tune.

afincarse [afin'karse] *vr* to settle.

afinidad [afini'ðað] *nf* affinity; (*parentesco*) relationship; **por** ~ by marriage.

afirmación [afirma'θjon] *nf* affirmation.

afirmar [afir'mar] *vt* to affirm, state; (*sostener*) to strengthen; ~**se** *vr* (*recuperar el equilibrio*) to steady o.s.; ~**se en lo dicho** to stand by what one has said.

afirmativo, a [afirma'tiβo, a] *adj* affirmative.

aflicción [aflik'θjon] *nf* affliction; (*dolor*) grief.

afligir [afli'xir] *vt* to afflict; (*apenar*) to distress; ~**se** *vr*: ~**se (por** *o* **con** *o* **de)** to grieve (about *o* at); **no te aflijas tanto** you must not let it affect you like this.

aflija [a'flixa] *etc vb V* **afligir.**

aflojar [aflo'xar] *vt* to slacken; (*desatar*) to loosen, undo; (*relajar*) to relax ♦ *vi* (*amainar*) to drop; (*bajar*) to go down; ~**se** *vr* to relax.

aflorar [aflo'rar] *vi* (*GEO, fig*) to come to the surface, emerge.

afluencia [aflu'enθja] *nf* flow.

afluente [aflu'ente] *adj* flowing ♦ *nm* (*GEO*) tributary.

afluir [aflu'ir] *vi* to flow.

afluya [a'fluja] *etc*, **afluyendo** [aflu'jendo] *etc vb V* **afluir.**

afmo., a. *abr* (= *afectísimo, a suyo, a*) Yours.

afónico, a [a'foniko, a] *adj*: **estar** ~ to have a sore throat; to have lost one's voice.

aforar [afo'rar] *vt* (*TEC*) to gauge; (*fig*) to value.

aforo [a'foro] *nm* (*TEC*) gauging; (*de teatro etc*) capacity; **el teatro tiene un** ~ **de 2,000** the theatre can seat 2,000.

afortunado, a [afortu'naðo, a] *adj* fortunate, lucky.

afrancesado, a [afranθe'saðo, a] *adj* francophile; (*pey*) Frenchified.

afrenta [a'frenta] *nf* affront, insult; (*deshonra*) dishonour (*BRIT*), dishonor (*US*), shame.

afrentoso, a [afren'toso, a] *adj* insulting; shameful.

África ['afrika] *nf* Africa; ~ **del Sur** South Africa.

africano, a [afri'kano, a] *adj, nm/f* African.

afrontar [afron'tar] *vt* to confront; (*poner cara a cara*) to bring face to face.

afuera [a'fwera] *adv* out, outside; **por** ~ on the outside; ~**s** *nfpl* outskirts.

ag. *abr* (= *agosto*) Aug.

agachar [aɣa'tʃar] *vt* to bend, bow; ~**se** *vr* to stoop, bend.

agalla [a'ɣaʎa] *nf* (*ZOOL*) gill; ~**s** *nfpl* (*MED*) tonsillitis *sg*; (*ANAT*) tonsils; **tener** ~**s** (*fam*) to have guts.

agarradera [aɣarra'ðera] *nf* (*AM*), **agarradero** [aɣarra'ðero] *nm* handle; ~**s** *npl* pull *sg*, influence *sg*.

agarrado, a [aɣa'rraðo, a] *adj* mean, stingy.

agarrar [aɣa'rrar] *vt* to grasp, grab; (*AM*) to take, catch ♦ *vi* (*planta*) to take root; ~**se** *vr* to hold on (tightly); (*meterse uno con otro*) to grapple (with each other);

agarrársela con algn (*AM*) to pick on sb; **agarró y se fue** (*esp AM fam*) he upped and went.

agarrotar [aɣarro'tar] *vt* (*lío*) to tie tightly; (*persona*) to squeeze tightly; (*reo*) to garrotte; **~se** *vr* (*motor*) to seize up; (*MED*) to stiffen.

agasajar [aɣasa'xar] *vt* to treat well, fête.

agave [a'ɣaβe] *nf* agave.

agazapar [aɣaθa'par] *vt* (*coger*) to grab hold of; **~se** *vr* (*agacharse*) to crouch down.

agencia [a'xenθja] *nf* agency; **~ de créditos/publicidad/viajes** credit/advertising/travel agency; **~ inmobiliaria** estate agent's (office) (*BRIT*), real estate office (*US*); **~ de matrimonios** marriage bureau.

agenciar [axen'θjar] *vt* to bring about; **~se** *vr* to look after o.s.; **~se algo** to get hold of sth.

agenda [a'xenda] *nf* diary; **~ telefónica** telephone directory.

agente [a'xente] *nm* agent; (*de policía*) policeman; **~ femenino** policewoman; **~ acreditado** (*COM*) accredited agent; **~ de bolsa** stockbroker; **~ inmobiliario** estate agent (*BRIT*), realtor (*US*); **~ de negocios** (*COM*) business agent; **~ de seguros** insurance broker; **~ de viajes** travel agent; **~s sociales** social partners.

ágil ['axil] *adj* agile, nimble.

agilidad [axili'ðað] *nf* agility, nimbleness.

agilizar [axili'θar] *vt* to speed up.

agitación [axita'θjon] *nf* (*de mano etc*) shaking, waving; (*de líquido etc*) stirring; agitation.

agitar [axi'tar] *vt* to wave, shake; (*líquido*) to stir; (*fig*) to stir up, excite; **~se** *vr* to get excited; (*inquietarse*) to get worried o upset.

aglomeración [aɣlomera'θjon] *nf:* **~ de tráfico/gente** traffic jam/mass of people.

aglomerar [aɣlome'rar] *vt*, **~se** *vr* to crowd together.

agnóstico, a [aɣ'nostiko, a] *adj, nm/f* agnostic.

ag.º *abr* = **ag.**

agobiante [aɣo'βjante] *adj* (*calor*) oppressive.

agobiar [aɣo'βjar] *vt* to weigh down; (*oprimir*) to oppress; (*cargar*) to burden; **sentirse agobiado por** to be overwhelmed by.

agobio [a'ɣoβjo] *nm* (*peso*) burden; (*fig*) oppressiveness.

agolpamiento [aɣolpa'mjento] *nm* crush.

agolparse [aɣol'parse] *vr* to crowd together.

agonía [aɣo'nia] *nf* death throes *pl*; (*fig*) agony, anguish.

agonice [aɣo'niθe] *etc vb* V **agonizar**.

agonizante [aɣoni'θante] *adj* dying.

agonizar [aɣoni'θar] *vi* (*tb:* **estar agonizando**) to be dying.

agorero, a [aɣo'rero, a] *adj* ominous ♦ *nm/f* soothsayer; **ave agorera** bird of ill omen.

agostar [aɣo'star] *vt* (*quemar*) to parch; (*fig*) to wither.

agosto [a'ɣosto] *nm* August; (*fig*) harvest; **hacer su ~** to make one's pile.

agotado, a [aɣo'taðo, a] *adj* (*persona*) exhausted; (*acabado*) finished; (*COM*) sold out; (: *libros*) out of print; (*pila*) flat.

agotador, a [aɣota'ðor, a] *adj* exhausting.

agotamiento [aɣota'mjento] *nm* exhaustion.

agotar [aɣo'tar] *vt* to exhaust; (*consumir*) to drain; (*recursos*) to use up, deplete; **~se** *vr* to be exhausted; (*acabarse*) to run out; (*libro*) to go out of print.

agraciado, a [aɣra'θjaðo, a] *adj* (*atractivo*) attractive; (*en sorteo etc*) lucky.

agraciar [aɣra'θjar] *vt* (*JUR*) to pardon; (*con premio*) to reward; (*hacer más atractivo*) to make more attractive.

agradable [aɣra'ðaβle] *adj* pleasant, nice.

agradar [aɣra'ðar] *vt, vi* to please; **~se** *vr* to like each other.

agradecer [aɣraðe'θer] *vt* to thank; (*favor etc*) to be grateful for; **le agradecería me enviara ...** I would be grateful if you would send me ...; **~se** *vr:* **¡se agradece!** much obliged!

agradecido, a [aɣraðe'θiðo, a] *adj* grateful; **¡muy ~!** thanks a lot!

agradecimiento [aɣraðeθi'mjento] *nm* thanks *pl*; gratitude.

agradezca [aɣra'ðeθka] *etc vb* V **agradecer**.

agrado [a'ɣraðo] *nm:* **ser de tu** *etc* **~** to be to your *etc* liking.

agrandar [aɣran'dar] *vt* to enlarge; (*fig*) to exaggerate; **~se** *vr* to get bigger.

agrario, a [a'ɣrarjo, a] *adj* agrarian, land *cpd*; (*política*) agricultural, farming *cpd*.

agravante [aɣra'βante] *adj* aggravating ♦ *nf* complication; **con la ~ de que ...** with the further difficulty that ...

agravar [aɣra'βar] *vt* (*pesar sobre*) to make heavier; (*irritar*) to aggravate; **~se** *vr* to worsen, get worse.

agraviar [aɣra'βjar] *vt* to offend; (*ser injusto con*) to wrong; **~se** *vr* to take offence.

agravio [a'ɣraβjo] *nm* offence; wrong;

(*JUR*) grievance.

agraz [a'ɣraθ] *nm* (*uva*) sour grape; **en ~** (*fig*) immature.

agredir [aɣre'ðir] *vt* to attack.

agregado [aɣre'ɣaðo] *nm* aggregate; (*persona*) attaché; (*profesor*) assistant professor.

agregar [aɣre'ɣar] *vt* to gather; (*añadir*) to add; (*persona*) to appoint.

agregue [a'ɣreɣe] *etc vb* V **agregar**.

agresión [aɣre'sjon] *nf* aggression; (*ataque*) attack.

agresivo, a [aɣre'siβo, a] *adj* aggressive.

agreste [a'ɣreste] *adj* (*rural*) rural; (*fig*) rough.

agriar [a'ɣrjar] *vt* (*fig*) to (turn) sour; **~se** *vr* to turn sour.

agrícola [a'ɣrikola] *adj* farming *cpd*, agricultural.

agricultor, a [aɣrikul'tor, a] *nm/f* farmer.

agricultura [aɣrikul'tura] *nf* agriculture, farming.

agridulce [aɣri'ðulθe] *adj* bittersweet; (*CULIN*) sweet and sour.

agrietarse [aɣrje'tarse] *vr* to crack; (*la piel*) to chap.

agrimensor, a [aɣrimen'sor, a] *nm/f* surveyor.

agringado, a [aɣrin'gaðo, a] *adj* gringolike.

agrio, a ['aɣrjo, a] *adj* bitter.

agronomía [aɣrono'mia] *nf* agronomy, agriculture.

agrónomo, a [a'ɣronomo, a] *nm/f* agronomist, agricultural expert.

agropecuario, a [aɣrope'kwarjo, a] *adj* farming *cpd*, agricultural.

agrupación [aɣrupa'θjon] *nf* group; (*acto*) grouping.

agrupar [aɣru'par] *vt* to group; (*INFORM*) to block; **~se** *vr* (*POL*) to form a group; (*juntarse*) to gather.

agua ['aɣwa] *nf* water; (*NAUT*) wake; (*ARQ*) slope of a roof; **~s** *nfpl* (*de joya*) water *sg*, sparkle *sg*; (*MED*) water *sg*, urine *sg*; (*NAUT*) waters; **~s abajo/arriba** downstream/upstream; **~ bendita/ destilada/potable** holy/distilled/drinking water; **~ caliente** hot water; **~ corriente** running water; **~ de colonia** eau de cologne; **~ mineral (con/sin gas)** (fizzy/ non-fizzy) mineral water; **~s jurisdiccionales** territorial waters; **~s mayores** excrement *sg*; **~ pasada no mueve molino** it's no use crying over spilt milk; **estar con el ~ al cuello** to be up to one's neck; **venir como ~ de mayo** to be a godsend.

aguacate [aɣwa'kate] *nm* avocado (pear).

aguacero [aɣwa'θero] *nm* (heavy) shower, downpour.

aguachirle [aɣwa'tʃirle] *nm* (*bebida*) slops *pl*.

aguado, a [a'ɣwaðo, a] *adj* watery, watered down ♦ *nf* (*AGR*) watering place; (*NAUT*) water supply; (*ARTE*) watercolour.

aguafiestas [aɣwa'fjestas] *nm/f inv* spoilsport.

aguafuerte [aɣwa'fwerte] *nf* etching.

aguaitar [aɣwai'tar] *vt* (*AM*) to watch.

aguanieve [aɣwa'njeβe] *nf* sleet.

aguantable [aɣwan'taβle] *adj* bearable, tolerable.

aguantar [aɣwan'tar] *vt* to bear, put up with; (*sostener*) to hold up ♦ *vi* to last; **~se** *vr* to restrain o.s.; **no sé cómo aguanta** I don't know how he can take it.

aguante [a'ɣwante] *nm* (*paciencia*) patience; (*resistencia*) endurance; (*DEPORTE*) stamina.

aguar [a'ɣwar] *vt* to water down; (*fig*): **~ la fiesta a algn** to spoil sb's fun.

aguardar [aɣwar'ðar] *vt* to wait for.

aguardentoso, a [aɣwarðen'toso, a] *adj* (*pey: voz*) husky, gruff.

aguardiente [aɣwar'ðjente] *nm* brandy, liquor.

aguarrás [aɣwa'rras] *nm* turpentine.

aguce [a'ɣuθe] *etc vb* V **aguzar**.

agudeza [aɣu'ðeθa] *nf* sharpness; (*ingenio*) wit.

agudice [aɣu'ðiθe] *etc vb* V **agudizar**.

agudizar [aɣuði'θar] *vt* to sharpen; (*crisis*) to make worse; **~se** *vr* to worsen, deteriorate.

agudo, a [a'ɣuðo, a] *adj* sharp; (*voz*) high-pitched, piercing; (*dolor, enfermedad*) acute.

agüe ['aɣwe] *etc vb* V **aguar**.

agüero [a'ɣwero] *nm*: **buen/mal ~** good/ bad omen; **ser de buen ~** to augur well; **pájaro de mal ~** bird of ill omen.

aguerrido, a [aɣe'rriðo, a] hardened; (*fig*) experienced.

aguijar [aɣi'xar] *vt* to goad; (*incitar*) to urge on ♦ *vi* to hurry along.

aguijón [aɣi'xon] *nm* sting; (*fig*) spur.

aguijonear [aɣixone'ar] *vt* = **aguijar**.

águila ['aɣila] *nf* eagle; (*fig*) genius.

aguileño, a [aɣi'leɲo, a] *adj* (*nariz*) aquiline; (*rostro*) sharp-featured.

aguinaldo [aɣi'naldo] *nm* Christmas box.

aguja [a'ɣuxa] *nf* needle; (*de reloj*) hand; (*ARQ*) spire; (*TEC*) firing-pin; **~s** *nfpl* (*ZOOL*) ribs; (*FERRO*) points.

agujerear [aɣuxere'ar] *vt* to make holes in; (*penetrar*) to pierce.

agujero [aɣu'xero] *nm* hole; (*COM*) deficit.

agujetas [aɣu'xetas] *nfpl* stitch *sg*; (*rigidez*) stiffness *sg*.

aguzar [aɣu'θar] *vt* to sharpen; (*fig*) to incite; ~ **el oído** to prick up one's ears.

aherrumbrarse [aerrum'brarse] *vr* to get rusty.

ahí [a'i] *adv* there; (*allá*) over there; **de ~ que** so that, with the result that; **~ llega** here he comes; **por ~** (*dirección*) that way; **¡hasta ~ hemos llegado!** so it has come to this!; **¡~ va!** (*objeto*) here it comes!; (*individuo*) there he goes!; **~ donde le ve** as sure as he's standing there.

ahijado, a [ai'xaðo, a] *nm/f* godson/daughter.

ahijar [ai'xar] *vt*: **~ algo a algn** (*fig*) to attribute sth to sb.

ahínco [a'inko] *nm* earnestness; **con ~** eagerly.

ahíto, a [a'ito, a] *adj*: **estoy ~** I'm full up.

ahogado, a [ao'ɣaðo, a] *adj* (*en agua*) drowned; (*emoción*) pent-up; (*grito*) muffled.

ahogar [ao'ɣar] *vt* (*en agua*) to drown; (*asfixiar*) to suffocate, smother; (*fuego*) to put out; **~se** *vr* (*en agua*) to drown; (*por asfixia*) to suffocate.

ahogo [a'oɣo] *nm* (*MED*) breathlessness; (*fig*) distress; (*problema económico*) financial difficulty.

ahogue [a'oɣe] *etc vb* V **ahogar**.

ahondar [aon'dar] *vt* to deepen, make deeper; (*fig*) to go deeply into ♦ *vi*: **~ en** to go deeply into.

ahora [a'ora] *adv* now; (*hace poco*) a moment ago, just now; (*dentro de poco*) in a moment; **~ voy** I'm coming; **~ mismo** right now; **~ bien** now then; **por ~** for the present.

ahorcado, a [aor'kaðo, a] *nm/f* hanged person.

ahorcar [aor'kar] *vt* to hang; **~se** *vr* to hang o.s.

ahorita [ao'rita], **ahoritita** [aori'tita] *adv* (*esp AM*: *fam*) right now.

ahorque [a'orke] *etc vb* V **ahorcar**.

ahorrar [ao'rrar] *vt* (*dinero*) to save; (*esfuerzos*) to save, avoid; **~se** *vr*: **~se molestias** to save o.s. trouble.

ahorrativo, a [aorra'tiβo, a] *adj* thrifty.

ahorro [a'orro] *nm* (*acto*) saving; (*frugalidad*) thrift; **~s** *nmpl* savings.

ahuecar [awe'kar] *vt* to hollow (out); (*voz*) to deepen ♦ *vi*: **¡ahueca!** (*fam*) beat it!

(*fam*); **~se** *vr* to give o.s. airs.

ahueque [a'weke] *etc vb* V **ahuecar**.

ahumar [au'mar] *vt* to smoke, cure; (*llenar de humo*) to fill with smoke ♦ *vi* to smoke; **~se** *vr* to fill with smoke.

ahuyentar [aujen'tar] *vt* to drive off, frighten off; (*fig*) to dispel.

AI *nf abr* (= *Amnistía Internacional*) AI.

aimara [ai'mara], **aimará** [aima'ra] *adj, nm/f* Aymara.

aindiado, a [aindi'aðo, a] *adj* (*AM*) Indian-like.

airado, a [ai'raðo, a] *adj* angry.

airar [ai'rar] *vt* to anger; **~se** *vr* to get angry.

aire ['aire] *nm* air; (*viento*) wind; (*corriente*) draught; (*MUS*) tune; **~s** *nmpl*: **darse ~s** to give o.s. airs; **al ~ libre** in the open air; **~ acondicionado** air conditioning; **tener ~ a** to look like; **estar de buen/mal ~** to be in a good/bad mood; **estar en el ~** (*RADIO*) to be on the air; (*fig*) to be up in the air.

airear [aire'ar] *vt* to ventilate; (*fig*: *asunto*) to air; **~se** *vr* to take the air.

airoso, a [ai'roso, a] *adj* windy; draughty; (*fig*) graceful.

aislado, a [ais'laðo, a] *adj* (*remoto*) isolated; (*incomunicado*) cut off; (*ELEC*) insulated.

aislante [ais'lante] *nm* (*ELEC*) insulator.

aislar [ais'lar] *vt* to isolate; (*ELEC*) to insulate; **~se** *vr* to cut o.s. off.

ajar [a'xar] *vt* to spoil; (*fig*) to abuse; **~se** *vr* to get crumpled; (*fig*: *piel*) to get wrinkled.

ajardinado, a [axarði'naðo, a] *adj* landscaped.

ajedrez [axe'ðreθ] *nm* chess.

ajenjo [a'xenxo] *nm* (*bebida*) absinth(e).

ajeno, a [a'xeno, a] *adj* (*que pertenece a otro*) somebody else's; **~ a** foreign to; **~ de** free from, devoid of; **por razones ajenas a nuestra voluntad** for reasons beyond our control.

ajetreado, a [axetre'aðo, a] *adj* busy.

ajetrearse [axetre'arse] *vr* (*atarearse*) to bustle about; (*fatigarse*) to tire o.s. out.

ajetreo [axe'treo] *nm* bustle.

ají [a'xi] *nm* chil(l)i, red pepper; (*salsa*) chil(l)i sauce.

ajiaco [axi'ako] *nm* (*AM*) potato and chil(l)i stew.

ajilimoje [axili'moxe] *nm* sauce of garlic and pepper; **~s** *nmpl* (*fam*) odds and ends.

ajo ['axo] *nm* garlic; **~ porro** *o* **puerro** leek; **(tieso) como un ~** (*fam*) snobbish; **estar**

en el ~ to be mixed up in it.
ajorca [a'xorka] *nf* bracelet.
ajuar [a'xwar] *nm* household furnishings
pl; (*de novia*) trousseau; (*de niño*) layette.
ajustado, a [axus'taðo, a] *adj* (*tornillo*)
tight; (*cálculo*) right; (*ropa*) tight(-
fitting); (*DEPORTE: resultado*) close.
ajustar [axus'tar] *vt* (*adaptar*) to adjust;
(*encajar*) to fit; (*TEC*) to engage; (*TIP*) to
make up; (*apretar*) to tighten; (*concertar*)
to agree (on); (*reconciliar*) to reconcile;
(*cuenta*) to settle ♦ *vi* to fit.
ajuste [a'xuste] *nm* adjustment; (*COSTURA*)
fitting; (*acuerdo*) compromise; (*de
cuenta*) settlement; (*INFORM*) patch.
al [al] = **a + el**; *V* **a**.
ala ['ala] *nf* wing; (*de sombrero*) brim;
(*futbolista*) winger; ~ **delta** hang-glider;
andar con el ~ **caída** to be downcast;
cortar las ~**s a algn** to clip sb's wings;
dar ~ **a algn** to encourage sb.
alabanza [ala'ßanθa] *nf* praise.
alabar [ala'ßar] *vt* to praise.
alacena [ala'θena] *nf* cupboard (*BRIT*),
closet (*US*).
alacrán [ala'kran] *nm* scorpion.
ALADI [a'laði] *nf abr* = *Asociación
Latinoamericana de Integración.*
alado, a [a'laðo, a] *adj* winged.
ALALC [a'lalk] *nf abr* (= *Asociación
Latinoamericana de Libre Comercio*)
LAFTA.
alambicado, a [alambi'kaðo, a] *adj*
distilled; (*fig*) affected.
alambicar [alambi'kar] *vt* to distil.
alambique [alam'bike] *etc vb V* **alambicar**
♦ *nm* still.
alambrada [alam'braða] *nf*, **alambrado**
[alam'braðo] *nm* wire fence; (*red*) wire
netting.
alambre [a'lambre] *nm* wire; ~ **de púas**
barbed wire.
alambrista [alam'brista] *nm/f* tightrope
walker.
alameda [ala'meða] *nf* (*plantío*) poplar
grove; (*lugar de paseo*) avenue,
boulevard.
álamo ['alamo] *nm* poplar; ~ **temblón**
aspen.
alano [a'lano] *nm* mastiff.
alarde [a'larðe] *nm* show, display; **hacer** ~
de to boast of.
alardear [alarðe'ar] *vi* to boast.
alargador [alarɣa'ðor] *nm* extension cable
o lead.
alargar [alar'ɣar] *vt* to lengthen, extend;
(*paso*) to hasten; (*brazo*) to stretch out;
(*cuerda*) to pay out; (*conversación*) to spin

out; ~**se** *vr* to get longer.
alargue [a'larɣe] *etc vb V* **alargar**.
alarido [ala'riðo] *nm* shriek.
alarma [a'larma] *nf* alarm; **voz de** ~
warning note; **dar la** ~ to raise the
alarm.
alarmante [alar'mante] *adj* alarming.
alarmar [alar'mar] *vt* to alarm; ~**se** *vr* to
get alarmed.
alavés, esa [ala'ßes, esa] *adj* of Álava
♦ *nm/f* native *o* inhabitant of Álava.
alazán [ala'θan] *nm* sorrel.
alba ['alßa] *nf* dawn.
albacea [alßa'θea] *nm/f* executor/executrix.
albaceteño, a [alßaθe'teɲo, a] *adj* of
Albacete ♦ *nm/f* native *o* inhabitant of
Albacete.
albahaca [al'ßaka] *nf* (*BOT*) basil.
Albania [al'ßanja] *nf* Albania.
albañal [alßa'ɲal] *nm* drain, sewer.
albañil [alßa'ɲil] *nm* bricklayer; (*cantero*)
mason.
albarán [alßa'ran] *nm* (*COM*) invoice.
albarda [al'ßarða] *nf* packsaddle.
albaricoque [alßari'koke] *nm* apricot.
albedrío [alße'ðrio] *nm*: **libre** ~ free will.
alberca [al'ßerka] *nf* reservoir; (*AM*)
swimming pool.
albergar [alßer'ɣar] *vt* to shelter;
(*esperanza*) to cherish; ~**se** *vr* (*refugiarse*)
to shelter; (*alojarse*) to lodge.
albergue [al'ßerɣe] *etc vb V* **albergar** ♦ *nm*
shelter, refuge; ~ **de juventud** youth
hostel.
albis ['alßis] *adv*: **quedarse en** ~ not to
have a clue.
albóndiga [al'ßondiɣa] *nf* meatball.
albor [al'ßor] *nm* whiteness; (*amanecer*)
dawn.
alborada [alßo'raða] *nf* dawn; (*diana*)
reveille.
alborear [alßore'ar] *vi* to dawn.
albornoz [alßor'noθ] *nm* (*de los árabes*)
burnous; (*para el baño*) bathrobe.
alboroce [alßo'roθe] *etc vb V* **alborozar**.
alborotar [alßoro'tar] *vi* to make a row ♦ *vt*
to agitate, stir up; ~**se** *vr* to get excited;
(*mar*) to get rough.
alboroto [alßo'roto] *nm* row, uproar.
alborozar [alßoro'θar] *vt* to gladden; ~**se** *vr*
to rejoice, be overjoyed.
alborozo [alßo'roθo] *nm* joy.
albricias [al'ßriθjas] *nfpl*: ¡~! good news!
álbum, *pl* **álbums** *o* **álbumes** ['alßum] *nm*
album.
albumen [al'ßumen] *nm* egg white,
albumen.
alcabala [alka'ßala] *nf* (*AM*) roadblock.

alcachofa [alka'tʃofa] *nf* (globe) artichoke; (*TIP*) golf ball; (*de ducha*) shower head.
alcahueta [alka'weta] *nf* procuress.
alcahuete [alka'wete] *nm* pimp.
alcalde, esa [al'kalde, alkal'desa] *nm/f* mayor(ess).
alcaldía [alkal'dia] *nf* mayoralty; (*lugar*) mayor's office.
álcali ['alkali] *nm* (*QUÍMICA*) alkali.
alcance [al'kanθe] *etc vb V* **alcanzar** ♦ *nm* (*MIL, RADIO*) range; (*fig*) scope; (*COM*) adverse balance, deficit; **estar al/fuera del ~ de algn** to be within/beyond one's reach; (*fig*) to be within one's powers/over one's head; **de gran ~** (*MIL*) long-range; (*fig*) far-reaching.
alcancía [alkan'θia] *nf* money box.
alcanfor [alkan'for] *nm* camphor.
alcantarilla [alkanta'riʎa] *nf* (*de aguas cloacales*) sewer; (*en la calle*) gutter.
alcanzar [alkan'θar] *vt* (*algo: con la mano, el pie*) to reach; (*alguien: en el camino etc*) to catch up (with); (*autobús*) to catch; (*suj: bala*) to hit, strike ♦ *vi* (*ser suficiente*) to be enough; **~ algo a algn** to hand sth to sb; **alcánzame la sal, por favor** pass the salt please; **~ a hacer** to manage to do.
alcaparra [alka'parra] *nf* (*BOT*) caper.
alcatraz [alka'traθ] *nm* gannet.
alcayata [alka'jata] *nf* hook.
alcázar [al'kaθar] *nm* fortress; (*NAUT*) quarter-deck.
alce ['alθe] *etc vb V* **alzar**.
alcista [al'θista] *adj* (*COM, ECON*): **mercado ~** bull market; **la tendencia ~** the upward trend ♦ *nm* speculator.
alcoba [al'koβa] *nf* bedroom.
alcohol [al'kol] *nm* alcohol; **no bebe ~** he doesn't drink (alcohol).
alcoholemia [alkoo'lemia] *nf* blood alcohol level; **prueba de la ~** breath test.
alcoholice [alko'liθe] *etc vb V* **alcoholizarse**.
alcohólico, a [al'koliko, a] *adj, nm/f* alcoholic.
alcoholímetro [alko'limetro] *nm* Breathalyser ®, drunkometer (*US*).
alcoholismo [alko'lismo] *nm* alcoholism.
alcoholizarse [alkoli'θarse] *vr* to become an alcoholic.
alcornoque [alkor'noke] *nm* cork tree; (*fam*) idiot.
alcotana [alko'tana] *nf* pickaxe; (*DEPORTE*) ice-axe.
alcurnia [al'kurnja] *nf* lineage.
alcuza [al'kusa] *nf* (*AM*) cruet.
aldaba [al'daβa] *nf* (door) knocker.
aldea [al'dea] *nf* village.

aldeano, a [alde'ano, a] *adj* village *cpd* ♦ *nm/f* villager.
ale ['ale] *excl* come on!, let's go!
aleación [alea'θjon] *nf* alloy.
aleatorio, a [alea'torjo, a] *adj* random, contingent; **acceso ~** (*INFORM*) random access.
aleccionador, a [alekθjona'ðor, a] *adj* instructive.
aleccionar [alekθjo'nar] *vt* to instruct; (*adiestrar*) to train.
aledaño, a [ale'ðaɲo, a] *adj*: **~ a** bordering on ♦ *nmpl* outskirts.
alegación [aleɣa'θjon] *nf* allegation.
alegar [ale'ɣar] *vt* (*dificultad etc*) to plead; (*JUR*) to allege ♦ *vi* (*AM*) to argue; **~ que** ... to give as an excuse that ...
alegato [ale'ɣato] *nm* (*JUR*) allegation; (*escrito*) indictment; (*declaración*) statement; (*AM*) argument.
alegoría [aleɣo'ria] *nf* allegory.
alegrar [ale'ɣrar] *vt* (*causar alegría*) to cheer (up); (*fuego*) to poke; (*fiesta*) to liven up; **~se** *vr* (*fam*) to get merry *o* tight; **~se de** to be glad about.
alegre [a'leɣre] *adj* happy, cheerful; (*fam*) merry, tight; (*licencioso*) risqué, blue.
alegría [ale'ɣria] *nf* happiness; merriment; **~ vital** joie de vivre.
alegrón [ale'ɣron] *nm* (*fig*) sudden joy.
alegue [a'leɣe] *etc vb V* **alegar**.
alejamiento [alexa'mjento] *nm* removal; (*distancia*) remoteness.
alejar [ale'xar] *vt* to move away, remove; (*fig*) to estrange; **~se** *vr* to move away.
alelado, a [ale'laðo, a] *adj* (*bobo*) foolish.
alelar [ale'lar] *vt* to bewilder.
aleluya [ale'luja] *nm* (*canto*) hallelujah.
alemán, ana [ale'man, ana] *adj, nm/f* German ♦ *nm* (*lengua*) German.
Alemania [ale'manja] *nf* Germany; **~ Occidental/Oriental** West/East Germany.
alentador, a [alenta'ðor, a] *adj* encouraging.
alentar [alen'tar] *vt* to encourage.
alergia [a'lerxja] *nf* allergy.
alero [a'lero] *nm* (*de tejado*) eaves *pl*; (*de foca, DEPORTE*) flipper; (*AUTO*) mudguard.
alerta [a'lerta] *adj inv, nm* alert.
aleta [a'leta] *nf* (*de pez*) fin; (*de ave*) wing; (*de coche*) mudguard.
aletargar [aletar'ɣar] *vt* to make drowsy; (*entumecer*) to make numb; **~se** *vr* to grow drowsy; to become numb.
aletargue [ale'tarɣe] *etc vb V* **aletargar**.
aletear [alete'ar] *vi* to flutter; (*ave*) to flap its wings; (*individuo*) to wave one's arms.

alevín [ale'ßin] *nm* fry, young fish.
alevosía [aleßo'sia] *nf* treachery.
alfabetización [alfaßetiθa'θjon] *nf*:
campaña de ~ literacy campaign.
alfabeto [alfa'ßeto] *nm* alphabet.
alfajor [alfa'xor] *nm* (*ESP: polvorón*) *cake eaten at Christmas time.*
alfalfa [al'falfa] *nf* alfalfa, lucerne.
alfaque [al'fake] *nm* (*NAUT*) bar, sandbank.
alfar [al'far] *nm* (*taller*) potter's workshop;
(*arcilla*) clay.
alfarería [alfare'ria] *nf* pottery; (*tienda*) pottery shop.
alfarero [alfa'rero] *nm* potter.
alféizar [al'feiθar] *nm* window-sill.
alférez [al'fereθ] *nm* (*MIL*) second lieutenant; (*NAUT*) ensign.
alfil [al'fil] *nm* (*AJEDREZ*) bishop.
alfiler [alfi'ler] *nm* pin; (*broche*) clip; (*pinza*) clothes peg (*BRIT*) o pin (*US*); ~ **de gancho** (*AM*) safety pin; **prendido con** ~**es** shaky.
alfiletero [alfile'tero] *nm* needle case.
alfombra [al'fombra] *nf* carpet; (*más pequeña*) rug.
alfombrar [alfom'brar] *vt* to carpet.
alfombrilla [alfom'briʎa] *nf* rug, mat.
alforja [al'forxa] *nf* saddlebag.
alforza [al'forθa] *nf* pleat.
algarabía [alɣara'ßia] *nf* (*fam*) gibberish;
(*griterío*) hullabaloo.
algarada [alɣa'raða] *nf* outcry; **hacer** o **levantar una** ~ to kick up a tremendous fuss.
Algarbe [al'ɣarße] *nm*: **el** ~ the Algarve.
algarroba [alɣa'rroßa] *nf* carob.
algarrobo [alɣa'rroßo] *nm* carob tree.
algas ['alɣas] *nfpl* seaweed *sg*.
algazara [alɣa'θara] *nf* din, uproar.
álgebra ['alxeßra] *nf* algebra.
álgido, a ['alxiðo, a] *adj* icy; (*momento etc*) crucial, decisive.
algo ['alɣo] *pron* something; (*en frases interrogativas*) anything ♦ *adv* somewhat, rather; **por** ~ **será** there must be some reason for it; **es** ~ **difícil** it's a bit awkward.
algodón [alɣo'ðon] *nm* cotton; (*planta*) cotton plant; ~ **de azúcar** candy floss (*BRIT*), cotton candy (*US*); ~ **hidrófilo** cotton wool (*BRIT*), absorbent cotton (*US*).
algodonero, a [alɣoðo'nero, a] *adj* cotton *cpd* ♦ *nm/f* cotton grower ♦ *nm* cotton plant.
algoritmo [alɣo'ritmo] *nm* algorithm.
alguacil [alɣwa'θil] *nm* bailiff; (*TAUR*) mounted official.

alguien ['alɣjen] *pron* someone, somebody;
(*en frases interrogativas*) anybody.
alguno, a [al'ɣuno, a] *adj* (*delante de nm*: **algún**) some; (*después de n*): **no tiene talento alguno** he has no talent, he hasn't any talent ♦ *pron* (*alguien*) someone, somebody; **algún que otro libro** some book or other; **algún día iré** I'll go one o some day; **sin interés alguno** without the slightest interest; **alguno que otro** an occasional one; **algunos piensan** some (people) think; **alguno de ellos** one of them.
alhaja [a'laxa] *nf* jewel; (*tesoro*) precious object, treasure.
alhelí [ale'li] *nm* wallflower, stock.
aliado, a [a'ljaðo, a] *adj* allied.
alianza [a'ljanθa] *nf* (*POL etc*) alliance;
(*anillo*) wedding ring.
aliar [a'ljar] *vt* to ally; ~**se** *vr* to form an alliance.
alias ['aljas] *adv* alias.
alicaído, a [alika'iðo, a] *adj* (*MED*) weak;
(*fig*) depressed.
alicantino, a [alikan'tino, a] *adj* of Alicante ♦ *nm/f* native o inhabitant of Alicante.
alicatar [alika'tar] *vt* to tile.
alicate(s) [ali'kate(s)] *nm(pl)* pliers *pl*; ~ **de uñas** nail clippers.
aliciente [ali'θjente] *nm* incentive;
(*atracción*) attraction.
alienación [aljena'θjon] *nf* alienation.
aliento [a'ljento] *etc vb V* **alentar** ♦ *nm* breath; (*respiración*) breathing; **sin** ~ breathless; **de un** ~ in one breath; (*fig*) in one go.
aligerar [alixe'rar] *vt* to lighten; (*reducir*) to shorten; (*aliviar*) to alleviate; (*mitigar*) to ease.
alijo [a'lixo] *nm* (*NAUT*) unloading;
(*contrabando*) smuggled goods.
alimaña [ali'maɲa] *nf* pest.
alimentación [alimenta'θjon] *nf* (*comida*) food; (*acción*) feeding; (*tienda*) grocer's (shop); ~ **continua** (*en fotocopiador etc*) stream feed.
alimentador [alimenta'ðor] *nm*: ~ **de papel** sheet-feeder.
alimentar [alimen'tar] *vt* to feed; (*nutrir*) to nourish; ~**se** *vr*: ~**se (de)** to feed (on).
alimenticio, a [alimen'tiθjo, a] *adj* food *cpd*;
(*nutritivo*) nourishing, nutritious.
alimento [ali'mento] *nm* food; (*nutrición*) nourishment; ~**s** *nmpl* (*JUR*) alimony *sg*.
alimón [ali'mon]: **al** ~ *adv* jointly, together.
alineación [alinea'θjon] *nf* alignment;
(*DEPORTE*) line-up.

alineado, a [aline'aðo, a] *adj* (*TIP*): **(no)** ~ **(un)justified;** ~ **a la izquierda/derecha** ranged left/right.

alinear [aline'ar] *vt* to align; (*TIP*) to justify; ~**se** *vr* to line up; ~**se en** to fall in with.

aliñar [ali'ɲar] *vt* (*CULIN*) to dress.

aliño [a'liɲo] *nm* (*CULIN*) dressing.

alisar [ali'sar] *vt* to smooth.

aliso [a'liso] *nm* alder.

alistamiento [alista'mjento] *nm* recruitment.

alistar [alis'tar] *vt* to recruit; ~**se** *vr* to enlist; (*inscribirse*) to enrol; (*AM: prepararse*) to get ready.

aliviar [ali'βjar] *vt* (*carga*) to lighten; (*persona*) to relieve; (*dolor*) to relieve, alleviate.

alivio [a'liβjo] *nm* alleviation, relief; ~ **de luto** half-mourning.

aljibe [al'xiβe] *nm* cistern.

allá [a'ʎa] *adv* (*lugar*) there; (*por ahí*) over there; (*tiempo*) then; ~ **abajo** down there; **más** ~ further on; **más** ~ **de** beyond; ¡~ **tú!** that's your problem!

allanamiento [aʎana'mjento] *nm* (*AM POLICÍA*) raid, search; ~ **de morada** housebreaking.

allanar [aʎa'nar] *vt* to flatten, level (out); (*igualar*) to smooth (out); (*fig*) to subdue; (*JUR*) to burgle, break into; (*AM POLICÍA*) to raid, search; ~**se** *vr* to fall down; ~**se a** to submit to, accept.

allegado, a [aʎe'ɣaðo, a] *adj* near, close ♦ *nm/f* relation.

allende [a'ʎende] *adv* on the other side ♦ *prep:* ~ **los mares** beyond the seas.

allí [a'ʎi] *adv* there; ~ **mismo** right there; **por** ~ over there; (*por ese camino*) that way.

alma ['alma] *nf* soul; (*persona*) person; (*TEC*) core; **se le cayó el** ~ **a los pies** he became very disheartened; **entregar el** ~ to pass away; **estar con el** ~ **en la boca** to be scared to death; **lo siento en el** ~ I am truly sorry; **tener el** ~ **en un hilo** to have one's heart in one's mouth; **estar como** ~ **en pena** to suffer; **ir como** ~ **que lleva el diablo** to go at breakneck speed.

almacén [alma'θen] *nm* (*depósito*) warehouse, store; (*MIL*) magazine; (*AM*) grocer's shop, foodstore, grocery store (*US*); **(grandes) almacenes** *nmpl* department store *sg*; ~ **depositario** (*COM*) depository.

almacenaje [almaθe'naxe] *nm* storage; ~ **secundario** (*INFORM*) backing storage.

almacenamiento [almaθena'mjento] *nm*

(*INFORM*) storage; ~ **temporal en disco** disk spooling.

almacenar [almaθe'nar] *vt* to store, put in storage; (*INFORM*) to store; (*proveerse*) to stock up with.

almacenero [almaθe'nero] *nm* warehouseman; (*AM*) grocer, shopkeeper.

almanaque [alma'nake] *nm* almanac.

almeja [al'mexa] *nf* clam.

almenas [al'menas] *nfpl* battlements.

almendra [al'mendra] *nf* almond.

almendro [al'mendro] *nm* almond tree.

almeriense [alme'rjense] *adj* of Almería ♦ *nm/f* native *o* inhabitant of Almería.

almiar [al'mjar] *nm* haystack.

almíbar [al'miβar] *nm* syrup.

almidón [almi'ðon] *nm* starch.

almidonado, a [almiðo'naðo, a] *adj* starched.

almidonar [almiðo'nar] *vt* to starch.

almirantazgo [almiran'taɣo] *nm* admiralty.

almirante [almi'rante] *nm* admiral.

almirez [almi'reθ] *nm* mortar.

almizcle [al'miθkle] *nm* musk.

almizclero [almiθ'klero] *nm* musk deer.

almohada [almo'aða] *nf* pillow; (*funda*) pillowcase.

almohadilla [almoa'ðiʎa] *nf* cushion; (*TEC*) pad; (*AM*) pincushion.

almohadillado, a [almoaði'ʎaðo, a] *adj* (*acolchado*) padded.

almohadón [almoa'ðon] *nm* large pillow.

almorcé [almor'θe], **almorcemos** [almor'θemos] *etc vb V* **almorzar.**

almorranas [almo'rranas] *nfpl* piles, haemorrhoids (*BRIT*), hemorrhoids (*US*).

almorzar [almor'θar] *vt:* ~ **una tortilla** to have an omelette for lunch ♦ *vi* to (have) lunch.

almuerce [al'mwerθe] *etc vb V* **almorzar.**

almuerzo [al'mwerθo] *etc vb V* **almorzar** ♦ *nm* lunch.

aló [a'lo] *excl* (*esp AM TELEC*) hello!

alocado, a [alo'kaðo, a] *adj* crazy.

alojamiento [aloxa'mjento] *nf* lodging(s) (*pl*); (*viviendas*) housing.

alojar [alo'xar] *vt* to lodge; ~**se** *vr:* ~**se en** to stay at; (*bala*) to lodge in.

alondra [a'londra] *nf* lark, skylark.

alpaca [al'paka] *nf* alpaca.

alpargata [alpar'ɣata] *nf* espadrille.

Alpes ['alpes] *nmpl:* **los** ~ the Alps.

alpinismo [alpi'nismo] *nm* mountaineering, climbing.

alpinista [alpi'nista] *nm/f* mountaineer, climber.

alpino, a [al'pino, a] *adj* alpine.
alpiste [al'piste] *nm* (*semillas*) birdseed; (*AM fam*: *dinero*) dough; (*fam*: *alcohol*) booze.
alquería [alke'ria] *nf* farmhouse.
alquilar [alki'lar] *vt* (*suj*: *propietario*: *inmuebles*) to let, rent (out); (: *coche*) to hire out; (: *TV*) to rent (out); (*suj*: *alquilador*. *inmuebles*, *TV*) to rent; (: *coche*) to hire; **"se alquila casa"** "house to let (*BRIT*) o to rent (*US*)" .
alquiler [alki'ler] *nm* renting, letting; hiring; (*arriendo*) rent; hire charge; **de** ~ for hire; ~ **de automóviles** car hire.
alquimia [al'kimja] *nf* alchemy.
alquitrán [alki'tran] *nm* tar.
alrededor [alreðe'ðor] *adv* around, about; ~**es** *nmpl* surroundings; ~ **de** *prep* around, about; **mirar a su** ~ to look (round) about one.
Alsacia [al'saθja] *nf* Alsace.
alta ['alta] *nf* (certificate of) discharge; **dar a algn de** ~ to discharge sb; **darse de** ~ (*MIL*) to join, enrol; (*DEPORTE*) to declare o.s. fit.
altanería [altane'ria] *nf* haughtiness, arrogance.
altanero, a [alta'nero, a] *adj* haughty, arrogant.
altar [al'tar] *nm* altar.
altavoz [alta'ßoθ] *nm* loudspeaker; (*amplificador*) amplifier.
alteración [altera'θjon] *nf* alteration; (*alboroto*) disturbance; ~ **del orden público** breach of the peace.
alterar [alte'rar] *vt* to alter; to disturb; ~**se** *vr* (*persona*) to get upset.
altercado [alter'kaðo] *nm* argument.
alternar [alter'nar] *vt* to alternate ♦ *vi*, ~**se** *vr* to alternate; (*turnar*) to take turns; ~ **con** to mix with.
alternativo, a [alterna'tißo, a] *adj* alternative; (*alterno*) alternating ♦ *nf* alternative; (*elección*) choice; **alternativas** *nfpl* ups and downs; **tomar la alternativa** (*TAUR*) to become a fully-qualified bullfighter.
alterno, a [al'terno, a] *adj* (*BOT*, *MAT*) alternate; (*ELEC*) alternating.
alteza [al'teθa] *nf* (*tratamiento*) highness.
altibajos [alti'ßaxos] *nmpl* ups and downs.
altillo [al'tiʎo] *nm* (*GEO*) small hill; (*AM*) attic.
altiplanicie [altipla'niθje] *nf*, **altiplano** [alti'plano] *nm* high plateau.
altisonante [altiso'nante] *adj* high-flown, high-sounding.
altitud [alti'tuð] *nf* altitude, height; **a una**

~ **de** at a height of.
altivez [alti'ßeθ] *nf* haughtiness, arrogance.
altivo, a [al'tißo, a] *adj* haughty, arrogant.
alto, a ['alto, a] *adj* high; (*persona*) tall; (*sonido*) high, sharp; (*noble*) high, lofty; (*GEO, clase*) upper ♦ *nm* halt; (*MUS*) alto; (*GEO*) hill; (*AM*) pile ♦ *adv* (*estar*) high; (*hablar*) loud, loudly ♦ *excl* halt!; **la pared tiene 2 metros de** ~ the wall is 2 metres high; **en alta mar** on the high seas; **en voz alta** in a loud voice; **las altas horas de la noche** the small (*BRIT*) o wee (*US*) hours; **en lo** ~ **de** at the top of; **pasar por** ~ to overlook; ~**s y bajos** ups and downs; **poner la radio más** ~ to turn the radio up; **¡más** ~, **por favor!** louder, please!
altoparlante [altopar'lante] *nm* (*AM*) loudspeaker.
altramuz [altra'muθ] *nm* lupin.
altruismo [al'truismo] *nm* altruism.
altura [al'tura] *nf* height; (*NAUT*) depth; (*GEO*) latitude; **la pared tiene 1.80 de** ~ the wall is 1 metre 80 (cm) high; **a esta** ~ **del año** at this time of the year; **estar a la** ~ **de las circunstancias** to rise to the occasion; **ha sido un partido de gran** ~ it has been a terrific match.
alubia [a'lußja] *nf* French bean, kidney bean.
alucinación [aluθina'θjon] *nf* hallucination.
alucinante [aluθi'nante] *adj* (*fam*: *estupendo*) great, super.
alucinar [aluθi'nar] *vi* to hallucinate ♦ *vt* to deceive; (*fascinar*) to fascinate.
alud [a'luð] *nm* avalanche; (*fig*) flood.
aludir [alu'ðir] *vi*: ~ **a** to allude to; **darse por aludido** to take the hint; **no te des por aludido** don't take it personally.
alumbrado [alum'braðo] *nm* lighting.
alumbramiento [alumbra'mjento] *nm* lighting; (*MED*) childbirth, delivery.
alumbrar [alum'brar] *vt* to light (up) ♦ *vi* (*iluminar*) to give light; (*MED*) to give birth.
aluminio [alu'minjo] *nm* aluminium (*BRIT*), aluminum (*US*).
alumnado [alum'naðo] *nm* (*UNIV*) student body; (*ESCOL*) pupils *pl*.
alumno, a [a'lumno, a] *nm/f* pupil, student.
alunice [alu'niθe] *etc vb V* **alunizar**.
alunizar [aluni'θar] *vi* to land on the moon.
alusión [alu'sjon] *nf* allusion.
alusivo, a [alu'sißo, a] *adj* allusive.
aluvión [alu'ßjon] *nm* (*GEO*) alluvium; (*fig*) flood; ~ **de improperios** torrent of abuse.
alvéolo [al'ßeolo] *nm* (*ANAT*) alveolus; (*fig*)

network.

alza ['alθa] *nf* rise; (*MIL*) sight; ~s fijas/graduables fixed/adjustable sights; al *o* en ~ (*precio*) rising; jugar al ~ to speculate on a rising *o* bull market; cotizarse *o* estar en ~ to be rising.

alzado, a [al'θaðo, a] *adj* (*gen*) raised; (*COM: precio*) fixed; (: *quiebra*) fradulent; por un tanto ~ for a lump sum ♦ *nf* (*de caballos*) height; (*JUR*) appeal.

alzamiento [alθa'mjento] *nm* (*aumento*) rise, increase; (*acción*) lifting, raising; (*mejor postura*) higher bid; (*rebelión*) rising; (*COM*) fraudulent bankruptcy.

alzar [al'θar] *vt* to lift (up); (*precio, muro*) to raise; (*cuello de abrigo*) to turn up; (*AGR*) to gather in; (*TIP*) to gather; ~se *vr* to get up, rise; (*rebelarse*) to revolt; (*COM*) to go fraudulently bankrupt; (*JUR*) to appeal; ~se con el premio to carry off the prize.

a.m. *abr* (*AM*: = *ante meridiem*) a.m.

ama ['ama] *nf* lady of the house; (*dueña*) owner; (*institutriz*) governess; (*madre adoptiva*) foster mother; ~ de casa housewife; ~ de cría *o* de leche wet-nurse; ~ de llaves housekeeper.

amabilidad [amaßili'ðað] *nf* kindness; (*simpatía*) niceness.

amabilísimo, a [amaßi'lisimo, a] *adj* *superlativo de* **amable.**

amable [a'maßle] *adj* kind; nice.

amaestrado, a [amaes'traðo, a] *adj* (*animal*) trained; (: *en circo etc*) performing.

amaestrar [amaes'trar] *vt* to train.

amagar [ama'ɣar] *vt, vi* to threaten.

amago [a'maɣo] *nm* threat; (*gesto*) threatening gesture; (*MED*) symptom.

amague [a'maɣe] *etc vb V* **amagar.**

amainar [amai'nar] *vt* (*NAUT*) to lower, take in; (*fig*) to calm ♦ *vi*, ~se *vr* to drop, die down; el viento amaina the wind is dropping.

amanerado, a [amane'raðo, a] *adj* affected.

amanezca [ama'neθka] *etc vb V* **amanecer.**

amansar [aman'sar] *vt* to tame; (*persona*) to subdue; ~se *vr* (*persona*) to calm down.

amante [a'mante] *adj*: ~ de fond of ♦ *nm/f* lover.

amanuense [ama'nwense] *nm* (*escribiente*) scribe; (*copista*) copyist; (*POL*) secretary.

amañar [ama'nar] *vt* (*gen*) to do skilfully; (*pey: resultado*) to alter.

amaño [a'mano] *nm* (*habilidad*) skill; ~s *nmpl* (*TEC*) tools; (*fig*) tricks.

amapola [ama'pola] *nf* poppy.

amar [a'mar] *vt* to love.

amargado, a [amar'ɣaðo, a] *adj* bitter; embittered.

amargar [amar'ɣar] *vt* to make bitter; (*fig*) to embitter; ~se *vr* to become embittered.

amargo, a [a'marɣo, a] *adj* bitter.

amargor [amar'ɣor] *nm* (*sabor*) bitterness; (*fig*) grief.

amargue [a'marɣe] *etc vb V* **amargar.**

amargura [amar'ɣura] *nf* = **amargor.**

amarillento, a [amari'ʎento, a] *adj* yellowish; (*tez*) sallow.

amarillismo [amari'ʎismo] *nm* (*de prensa*) sensationalist journalism.

amarillo, a [ama'riʎo, a] *adj*, *nm* yellow.

amarra [a'marra] *nf* (*NAUT*) mooring line; ~s *nfpl* (*fig*) protection *sg*; tener buenas ~s to have good connections; soltar ~s to set off.

amarrar [ama'rrar] *vt* to moor; (*sujetar*) to tie up.

amartillar [amarti'ʎar] *vt* (*fusil*) to cock.

amasar [ama'sar] *vt* to knead; (*mezclar*) to mix, prepare; (*confeccionar*) to concoct.

amasijo [ama'sixo] *nm* kneading; mixing; (*fig*) hotchpotch.

amateur ['amatur] *nm/f* amateur.

amatista [ama'tista] *nf* amethyst.

amazacotado, a [amaθako'taðo, a] *adj* (*terreno, arroz etc*) lumpy.

amazona [ama'θona] *nf* horsewoman.

Amazonas [ama'θonas] *nm*: el (Río) ~ the Amazon.

ambages [am'baxes] *nmpl*: sin ~ in plain language.

ámbar ['ambar] *nm* amber.

Amberes [am'beres] *nm* Antwerp.

ambición [ambi'θjon] *nf* ambition.

ambicionar [ambiθjo'nar] *vt* to aspire to.

ambicioso, a [ambi'θjoso, a] *adj* ambitious.

ambidextro, a [ambi'ðekstro, a] *adj* ambidextrous.

ambientación [ambjenta'θjon] *nf* (*CINE, LIT etc*) setting; (*RADIO etc*) sound effects *pl*.

amalgama [amal'ɣama] *nf* amalgam.

amalgamar [amalɣa'mar] *vt* to amalgamate; (*combinar*) to combine, mix.

amamantar [amaman'tar] *vt* to suckle, nurse.

amancebarse [amanθe'ßarse] *vr* (*pareja*) to live together.

amanecer [amane'θer] *vi* to dawn; (*fig*) to appear, begin to show ♦ *nm* dawn; el niño amaneció afiebrado the child woke up with a fever.

ambientador [ambjenta'ðor] *nm* air freshener.

ambientar [ambjen'tar] *vt* (*gen*) to give an atmosphere to; (*LIT etc*) to set.

ambiente [am'bjente] *nm* (*tb fig*) atmosphere; (*medio*) environment; (*AM*) room.

ambigüedad [ambixwe'ðað] *nf* ambiguity.

ambiguo, a [am'bixwo, a] *adj* ambiguous.

ámbito ['ambito] *nm* (*campo*) field; (*fig*) scope.

ambos, as ['ambos, as] *adj pl, pron pl* both.

ambulancia [ambu'lanθja] *nf* ambulance.

ambulante [ambu'lante] *adj* travelling, itinerant; (*biblioteca*) mobile.

ambulatorio [ambula'torjo] *nm* state health-service clinic.

ameba [a'meßa] *nf* amoeba.

amedrentar [ameðren'tar] *vt* to scare.

amén [a'men] *excl* amen; ~ **de** *prep* besides, in addition to; **en un decir** ~ in the twinkling of an eye; **decir** ~ **a todo** to have no mind of one's own.

amenace [ame'naθe] *etc vb V* **amenazar**.

amenaza [ame'naθa] *nf* threat.

amenazar [amena'θar] *vt* to threaten ♦ *vi*: ~ **con hacer** to threaten to do.

amenidad [ameni'ðað] *nf* pleasantness.

ameno, a [a'meno, a] *adj* pleasant.

América [a'merika] *nf* (*continente*) America, the Americas; (*EEUU*) America; (*Hispanoa~*) Latin *o* South America; ~ **del Norte/del Sur** North/South America; ~ **Central/Latina** Central/Latin America.

americanismo [amerika'nismo] *nm* Americanism.

americano, a [ameri'kano, a] *adj, nm/f* (*V América*) American; Latin *o* South American ♦ *nf* coat, jacket.

americe [ame'riθe] *etc vb V* **amerizar**.

amerindio, a [ame'rindjo, a] *adj, nm/f* Amerindian, American Indian.

amerizaje [ameri'θaxe] *nm* (*AVIAT*) landing (on the sea).

amerizar [ameri'θar] *vi* (*AVIAT*) to land (on the sea).

ametralladora [ametraʎa'ðora] *nf* machine gun.

amianto [a'mjanto] *nm* asbestos.

amigable [ami'xaßle] *adj* friendly.

amígdala [a'mixðala] *nf* tonsil.

amigdalitis [amixða'litis] *nf* tonsillitis.

amigo, a [a'mixo, a] *adj* friendly ♦ *nm/f* friend; (*amante*) lover; ~ **de lo ajeno** thief; ~ **corresponsal** penfriend; **hacerse** ~**s** to become friends; **ser** ~ **de** to like, be fond of; **ser muy** ~**s** to be close friends.

amigote [ami'xote] *nm* mate (*BRIT*), buddy.

amilanar [amila'nar] *vt* to scare; ~**se** *vr* to get scared.

aminorar [amino'rar] *vt* to diminish; (*reducir*) to reduce; ~ **la marcha** to slow down.

amistad [amis'tað] *nf* friendship; ~**es** *nfpl* friends.

amistoso, a [amis'toso, a] *adj* friendly.

amnesia [am'nesja] *nf* amnesia.

amnistía [amnis'tia] *nf* amnesty.

amnistiar [amnis'tjar] *vt* to amnesty, grant an amnesty to.

amo ['amo] *nm* owner; (*jefe*) boss.

amodorrarse [amoðo'rrarse] *vr* to get sleepy.

amolar [amo'lar] *vt* to annoy.

amoldar [amol'dar] *vt* to mould; (*adaptar*) to adapt.

amonestación [amonesta'θjon] *nf* warning; **amonestaciones** *nfpl* marriage banns.

amonestar [amone'star] *vt* to warn; to publish the banns of.

amoniaco [amo'njako] *nm* ammonia.

amontonar [amonto'nar] *vt* to collect, pile up; ~**se** *vr* (*gente*) to crowd together; (*acumularse*) to pile up; (*datos*) to accumulate; (*desastres*) to come one on top of another.

amor [a'mor] *nm* love; (*amante*) lover; **hacer el** ~ to make love; ~ **interesado** cupboard love; ~ **propio** self-respect; **por (el)** ~ **de Dios** for God's sake; **estar al** ~ **de la lumbre** to be close to the fire.

amoratado, a [amora'taðo, a] *adj* purple, blue with cold; (*con cardenales*) bruised.

amordace [amor'ðaθe] *etc vb V* **amordazar**.

amordazar [amorða'θar] *vt* to muzzle; (*fig*) to gag.

amorfo, a [a'morfo, a] *adj* amorphous, shapeless.

amorío [amo'rio] *nm* (*fam*) love affair.

amoroso, a [amo'roso, a] *adj* affectionate, loving.

amortajar [amorta'xar] *vt* (*fig*) to shroud.

amortice [amor'tiθe] *etc vb V* **amortizar**.

amortiguador [amortixwa'ðor] *nm* shock absorber; (*parachoques*) bumper; (*silenciador*) silencer; ~**es** *nmpl* (*AUTO*) suspension *sg*.

amortiguar [amorti'xwar] *vt* to deaden; (*ruido*) to muffle; (*color*) to soften.

amortigüe [amor'tixwe] *etc vb V* **amortiguar**.

amortización [amortiθa'θjon] *nf* redemption; repayment; (*COM*) capital allowance.

amortizar [amorti'θar] *vt* (*ECON: bono*) to redeem; (: *capital*) to write off; (: *préstamo*) to pay off.

amoscarse [amos'karse] *vr* to get cross.

amosque [a'moske] *etc vb* V **amoscarse.**

amotinar [amoti'nar] *vt* to stir up, incite (to riot); ~**se** *vr* to mutiny.

amparar [ampa'rar] *vt* to protect; ~**se** *vr* to seek protection; (*de la lluvia etc*) to shelter.

amparo [am'paro] *nm* help, protection; **al** ~ **de** under the protection of.

amperímetro [ampe'rimetro] *nm* ammeter.

amperio [am'perjo] *nm* ampère, amp.

ampliable [am'pljaβle] *adj* (*INFORM*) expandable.

ampliación [amplja'θjon] *nf* enlargement; (*extensión*) extension.

ampliar [am'pljar] *vt* to enlarge; to extend.

amplificación [amplifika'θjon] *nf* enlargement.

amplificador [amplifika'ðor] *nm* amplifier.

amplificar [amplifi'kar] *vt* to amplify.

amplifique [ampli'fike] *etc vb* V **amplificar.**

amplio, a ['ampljo, a] *adj* spacious; (*falda etc*) full; (*extenso*) extensive; (*ancho*) wide.

amplitud [ampli'tuð] *nf* spaciousness; extent; (*fig*) amplitude; ~ **de miras** broadmindedness; **de gran** ~ far-reaching.

ampolla [am'poʎa] *nf* blister; (*MED*) ampoule.

ampolleta [ampo'ʎeta] *nf* (*AM*) (light) bulb.

ampuloso, a [ampu'loso, a] *adj* bombastic, pompous.

amputar [ampu'tar] *vt* to cut off, amputate.

amueblar [amwe'βlar] *vt* to furnish.

amuleto [amu'leto] *nm* (lucky) charm.

amurallar [amura'ʎar] *vt* to wall up *o* in.

anacarado, a [anaka'raðo, a] *adj* mother-of-pearl *cpd.*

anacardo [ana'karðo] *nm* cashew (nut).

anaconda [ana'konda] *nf* anaconda.

anacronismo [anakro'nismo] *nm* anachronism.

ánade ['anaðe] *nm* duck.

anagrama [ana'ɣrama] *nm* anagram.

anales [a'nales] *nmpl* annals.

analfabetismo [analfaβe'tismo] *nm* illiteracy.

analfabeto, a [analfa'βeto, a] *adj, nm/f* illiterate.

analgésico [anal'xesiko] *nm* painkiller, analgesic.

analice [ana'liθe] *etc vb* V **analizar.**

análisis [a'nalisis] *nm inv* analysis; ~ **de costos-beneficios** cost-benefit analysis; ~ **de mercados** market research; ~ **de sangre** blood test.

analista [ana'lista] *nm/f* (*gen*) analyst; (*POL, HISTORIA*) chronicler; ~ **de sistemas** (*INFORM*) systems analyst.

analizar [anali'θar] *vt* to analyse.

analogía [analo'xia] *nf* analogy; **por** ~ **con** on the analogy of.

analógico, a [ana'loxico, a] *adj* analogue.

análogo, a [a'naloɣo, a] *adj* analogous, similar.

ananá(s) [ana'na(s)] *nm* pineapple.

anaquel [ana'kel] *nm* shelf.

anaranjado, a [anaran'xaðo, a] *adj* orange (-coloured).

anarquía [anar'kia] *nf* anarchy.

anarquismo [anar'kismo] *nm* anarchism.

anarquista [anar'kista] *nm/f* anarchist.

anatematizar [anatemati'θar] *vt* (*REL*) to anathematize; (*fig*) to curse.

anatemice [anate'miθe] *etc vb* V **anatemizar.**

anatomía [anato'mia] *nf* anatomy.

anca ['anka] *nf* rump, haunch; ~**s** *nfpl* (*fam*) behind *sg*; **llevar a algn en** ~**s** to carry sb behind one.

ancestral [anθes'tral] *adj* (*costumbre*) age-old.

ancho, a ['antʃo, a] *adj* wide; (*falda*) full; (*fig*) liberal ♦ *nm* width; (*FERRO*) gauge; **le viene muy** ~ **el cargo** (*fig*) the job is too much for him; **ponerse** ~ to get conceited; **quedarse tan** ~ to go on as if nothing had happened; **estar a sus anchas** to be at one's ease.

anchoa [an'tʃoa] *nf* anchovy.

anchura [an'tʃura] *nf* width; (*extensión*) wideness.

anchuroso, a [antʃu'roso, a] *adj* wide.

anciano, a [an'θjano, a] *adj* old, aged ♦ *nm/f* old man/woman ♦ *nm* elder.

ancla ['ankla] *nf* anchor; **levar** ~**s** to weigh anchor.

ancladero [ankla'ðero] *nm* anchorage.

anclar [an'klar] *vi* to (drop) anchor.

andadas [an'daðas] *nfpl* (*aventuras*) adventures; **volver a las** ~ to backslide.

andaderas [anda'ðeras] *nfpl* baby-walker *sg.*

andadura [anda'ðura] *nf* gait; (*de caballo*) pace.

Andalucía [andalu'θia] *nf* Andalusia.

andaluz, a [anda'luθ, a] *adj, nm/f* Andalusian.

andamio [an'damjo] *nm*, **andamiaje** [anda'mjaxe] *nm* scaffold(ing).

andanada [anda'naða] *nf (fig)* reprimand; **soltarle a algn una** ~ to give sb a rocket.

andante [an'dante] *adj*: **caballero** ~ knight errant.

andar [an'dar] *vt* to go, cover, travel ♦ *vi* to go, walk, travel; *(funcionar)* to go, work; *(estar)* to be ♦ *nm* walk, gait, pace; ~**se** *vr (irse)* to go away *o* off; ~ **a pie/a caballo/en bicicleta** to go on foot/on horseback/by bicycle; **¡anda!** *(sorpresa)* go on!; **anda en** *o* **por los 40** he's about 40; **¿en qué andas?** what are you up to?; **andamos mal de dinero/tiempo** we're badly off for money/we're short of time; ~**se por las ramas** to beat about the bush; **no** ~**se con rodeos** to call a spade a spade *(fam)*; **todo se andará** all in good time; **anda por aquí** it's round here somewhere; ~ **haciendo algo** to be doing sth.

andariego, a [anda'rjeɣo, a] *adj* fond of travelling.

andas ['andas] *nfpl* stretcher *sg*.

andén [an'den] *nm (FERRO)* platform; *(NAUT)* quayside; *(AM: acera)* pavement *(BRIT)*, sidewalk *(US)*.

Andes ['andes] *nmpl*: **los** ~ the Andes.

andinismo [andin'ismo] *nm (AM)* mountaineering, climbing.

andino, a [an'dino, a] *adj* Andean, of the Andes.

Andorra [an'dorra] *nf* Andorra.

andrajo [an'draxo] *nm* rag.

andrajoso, a [andra'xoso, a] *adj* ragged.

andurriales [andu'rrjales] *nmpl* out-of-the-way place *sg*, the sticks; **en esos** ~ in that godforsaken spot.

anduve [an'duβe], **anduviera** [andu'βjera] *etc vb V* **andar**.

anécdota [a'nekðota] *nf* anecdote, story.

anegar [ane'ɣar] *vt* to flood; *(ahogar)* to drown; ~**se** *vr* to drown; *(hundirse)* to sink.

anegue [a'neɣe] *etc vb V* **anegar**.

anejo, a [a'nexo, a] *adj* attached ♦ *nm (ARQ)* annexe.

anemia [a'nemja] *nf* anaemia.

anestesia [anes'tesja] *nf* anaesthetic; ~ **general/local** general/local anaesthetic.

anestesiar [aneste'sjar] *vt* to anaesthetize *(BRIT)* anesthetize *(US)*.

anestésico [anes'tesiko] *nm* anaesthetic.

anexar [anek'sar] *vt* to annex; *(documento)* to attach; *(INFORM)* to append.

anexión [anek'sjon] *nf*, **anexionamiento** [aneksjona'mjento] *nm* annexation.

anexionar [aneksjo'nar] *vt* to annex; ~**se** *vr*: ~ **un país** to annex a country.

anexo, a [a'nekso, a] *adj* attached ♦ *nm* annexe.

anfetamina [anfeta'mina] *nf* amphetamine.

anfibio, a [an'fiβjo, a] *adj* amphibious ♦ *nm* amphibian.

anfiteatro [anfite'atro] *nm* amphitheatre; *(TEAT)* dress circle.

anfitrión, ona [anfi'trjon, ona] *nm/f* host(ess).

ángel ['anxel] *nm* angel; ~ **de la guarda** guardian angel; **tener** ~ to have charm.

Ángeles ['anxeles] *nmpl*: **los** ~ Los Angeles.

angélico, a [an'xeliko, a], **angelical** [anxeli'kal] *adj* angelic(al).

angina [an'xina] *nf (MED)*: ~ **de pecho** angina; **tener** ~**s** to have a sore throat *o* throat infection.

anglicano, a [angli'kano, a] *adj*, *nm/f* Anglican.

anglicismo [angli'θismo] *nm* anglicism.

anglosajón, ona [anglosa'xon, 'xona] *adj*, *nm/f* Anglo-Saxon.

Angola [an'gola] *nf* Angola.

angoleño, a [ango'leɲo, a] *adj*, *nm/f* Angolan.

angosto, a [an'gosto, a] *adj* narrow.

anguila [an'gila] *nf* eel; ~**s** *nfpl* slipway *sg*.

angula [an'gula] *nf* elver, baby eel.

ángulo ['angulo] *nm* angle; *(esquina)* corner; *(curva)* bend.

angustia [an'gustja] *nf* anguish.

angustiar [angus'tjar] *vt* to distress, grieve; ~**se** *vr* to be distressed *(por* at, on account of*)*.

anhelante [ane'lante] *adj* eager; *(deseoso)* longing.

anhelar [ane'lar] *vt* to be eager for; to long for, desire ♦ *vi* to pant, gasp.

anhelo [a'nelo] *nm* eagerness; desire.

anhídrido [a'niðriðo] *nm*: ~ **carbónico** carbon dioxide.

anidar [ani'ðar] *vt (acoger)* to take in, shelter ♦ *vi* to nest; *(fig)* to make one's home.

anilina [ani'lina] *nf* aniline.

anilla [a'niʎa] *nf* ring; **(las)** ~**s** *(DEPORTE)* the rings.

anillo [a'niʎo] *nm* ring; ~ **de boda** wedding ring; ~ **de compromiso** engagement ring; **venir como** ~ **al dedo** to suit to a tee.

ánima ['anima] *nf* soul; **las** ~**s** the Angelus (bell) *sg*.

animación [anima'θjon] *nf* liveliness; *(vitalidad)* life; *(actividad)* bustle.

animado, a [ani'maðo, a] *adj (vivo)* lively;

(*vivaz*) animated; (*concurrido*) bustling; (*alegre*) in high spirits; **dibujos** ~**s** cartoon *sg.*

animador, a [anima'ðor, a] *nm/f* (*TV*) host(ess) ♦ *nf* (*DEPORTE*) cheerleader.

animadversión [animaðßer'sjon] *nf* ill-will, antagonism.

animal [ani'mal] *adj* animal; (*fig*) stupid ♦ *nm* animal; (*fig*) fool; (*bestia*) brute.

animalada [anima'laða] *nf* (*gen*) silly thing (to do *o* say); (*ultraje*) disgrace.

animar [ani'mar] *vt* (*BIO*) to animate, give life to; (*fig*) to liven up, brighten up, cheer up; (*estimular*) to stimulate; ~**se** *vr* to cheer up, feel encouraged; (*decidirse*) to make up one's mind.

ánimo ['animo] *nm* soul, mind; (*valentía*) courage ♦ *excl* cheer up!; **cobrar** ~ to take heart; **dar** ~**(s) a** to encourage.

animoso, a [ani'moso, a] *adj* brave; (*vivo*) lively.

aniñado, a [ani'ɲaðo, a] *adj* (*facción*) childlike; (*carácter*) childish.

aniquilar [aniki'lar] *vt* to annihilate, destroy.

anís [a'nis] *nm* (*grano*) aniseed; (*licor*) anisette.

aniversario [anißer'sarjo] *nm* anniversary.

Ankara [an'kara] *nf* Ankara.

ano ['ano] *nm* anus.

anoche [a'notʃe] *adv* last night; **antes de** ~ the night before last.

anochecer [anotʃe'θer] *vi* to get dark ♦ *nm* nightfall, dark; **al** ~ at nightfall.

anochezca [ano'tʃeθka] *etc vb* V **anochecer**.

anodino, a [ano'ðino, a] *adj* dull, anodyne.

anomalía [anoma'lia] *nf* anomaly.

anonadado, a [anona'ðaðo, a] *adj* stunned.

anonimato [anoni'mato] *nm* anonymity.

anónimo, a [a'nonimo, a] *adj* anonymous; (*COM*) limited ♦ *nm* (*carta*) anonymous letter; (: *maliciosa*) poison-pen letter.

anorak [ano'rak], *pl* **anoraks** *nm* anorak.

anorexia [ano'reksja] *nf* anorexia.

anormal [anor'mal] *adj* abnormal.

anotación [anota'θjon] *nf* note; annotation.

anotar [ano'tar] *vt* to note down; (*comentar*) to annotate.

anquilosado, a [ankilo'saðo, a] *adj* (*fig*) stale, out of date.

anquilosamiento [ankilosa'mjento] *nm* (*fig*) paralysis, stagnation.

ansia ['ansja] *nf* anxiety; (*añoranza*) yearning.

ansiar [an'sjar] *vt* to long for.

ansiedad [ansje'ðað] *nf* anxiety.

ansioso, a [an'sjoso, a] *adj* anxious;

(*anhelante*) eager; ~ **de** *o* **por algo** greedy for sth.

antagónico, a [anta'ɣoniko, a] *adj* antagonistic; (*opuesto*) contrasting.

antagonista [antaɣo'nista] *nm/f* antagonist.

antaño [an'taɲo] *adv* long ago.

Antártico [an'tartiko] *nm*: **el (océano)** ~ the Antarctic (Ocean).

Antártida [an'tartiða] *nf* Antarctica.

ante ['ante] *prep* before, in the presence of; (*encarado con*) faced with ♦ *nm* suede; ~ **todo** above all.

anteanoche [antea'notʃe] *adv* the night before last.

anteayer [antea'jer] *adv* the day before yesterday.

antebrazo [ante'ßraθo] *nm* forearm.

antecámara [ante'kamara] *nf* (*ARQ*) anteroom; (*antesala*) waiting room; (*POL*) lobby.

antecedente [anteθe'ðente] *adj* previous ♦ *nm*: ~**s** *nmpl* (*profesionales*) background *sg*; ~**s penales** criminal record; **no tener** ~**s** to have a clean record; **estar en** ~**s** to be well-informed; **poner a algn en** ~**s** to put sb in the picture.

anteceder [anteθe'ðer] *vt* to precede, go before.

antecesor, a [anteθe'sor, a] *nm/f* predecessor.

antedicho, a [ante'ðitʃo, a] *adj* aforementioned.

antelación [antela'θjon] *nf*: **con** ~ in advance.

antemano [ante'mano] *: **de** ~ *adv* beforehand, in advance.

antena [an'tena] *nf* antenna; (*de televisión etc*) aerial.

anteojeras [anteo'xeras] *nfpl* blinkers (*BRIT*), blinders (*US*).

anteojo [ante'oxo] *nm* eyeglass; ~**s** *nmpl* (*esp AM*) glasses, spectacles.

antepasados [antepa'saðos] *nmpl* ancestors.

antepecho [ante'petʃo] *nm* guardrail, parapet; (*repisa*) ledge, sill.

antepondré [antepon'dre] *etc vb* V **anteponer**.

anteponer [antepo'ner] *vt* to place in front; (*fig*) to prefer.

anteponga [ante'ponɣa] *etc vb* V **anteponer**.

anteproyecto [antepro'jekto] *nm* preliminary sketch; (*fig*) blueprint; (*POL*): ~ **de ley** draft bill.

antepuesto, a [ante'pwesto, a] *pp de* **anteponer**.

antepuse [ante'puse] *etc vb* V **anteponer**.

anterior [ante'rjor] *adj* preceding, previous.

anterioridad [anterjori'ðað] *nf*: **con ~ a** prior to, before.

anteriormente [anterjor'mente] *adv* previously, before.

antes ['antes] *adv* sooner; (*primero*) first; (*con prioridad*) before; (*hace tiempo*) previously, once; (*más bien*) rather ♦ *prep*: ~ **de** before ♦ *conj*: ~ **(de) que** before; ~ **bien** (but) rather; **dos días** ~ two days before *o* previously; **mucho/poco** ~ long/shortly before; ~ **muerto que esclavo** better dead than enslaved; **tomo el avión** ~ **que el barco** I take the plane rather than the boat; **cuanto** ~, **lo** ~ **posible** as soon as possible; **cuanto** ~ **mejor** the sooner the better.

antesala [ante'sala] *nf* anteroom.

antiadherente [antiaðe'rente] *adj* non-stick.

antiaéreo, a [antia'ereo, a] *adj* anti-aircraft.

antialcohólico, a [antial'koliko, a] *adj*: **centro** ~ (*MED*) detoxification unit.

antibalas [anti'ßalas] *adj inv*: **chaleco** ~ bulletproof jacket.

antibiótico [anti'ßjotiko] *nm* antibiotic.

anticiclón [antiθi'klon] *nm* (*METEOROLOGÍA*) anti-cyclone.

anticipación [antiθipa'θjon] *nf* anticipation; **con 10 minutos de** ~ 10 minutes early.

anticipado, a [antiθi'paðo, a] *adj* (in) advance; **por** ~ in advance.

anticipar [antiθi'par] *vt* to anticipate; (*adelantar*) to bring forward; (*COM*) to advance; ~**se** *vr*: ~**se a su época** to be ahead of one's time.

anticipo [anti'θipo] *nm* (*COM*) advance; *V tb* **anticipación**.

anticonceptivo, a [antikonθep'tißo, a] *adj*, *nm* contraceptive; **métodos** ~**s** contraceptive devices.

anticongelante [antikonxe'lante] *nm* antifreeze.

anticonstitucional [antikonstituθjo'nal] *adj* unconstitutional.

anticuado, a [anti'kwaðo, a] *adj* out-of-date, old-fashioned; (*desusado*) obsolete.

anticuario [anti'kwarjo] *nm* antique dealer.

anticuerpo [anti'kwerpo] *nm* (*MED*) antibody.

antidemocrático, a [antiðemo'kratiko, a] *adj* undemocratic.

antideportivo, a [antiðepor'tißo, a] *adj* unsporting.

antideslumbrante [antiðeslum'brante] *adj* (*INFORM*) anti-dazzle.

antidoping [anti'ðopin] *adj inv* anti-drug.

antídoto [an'tiðoto] *nm* antidote.

antidroga [anti'ðroɤa] *adj inv* anti-drug; **brigada** ~ drug squad.

antiestético, a [anties'tetiko, a] *adj* unsightly.

antifaz [anti'faθ] *nm* mask; (*velo*) veil.

antigás [anti'gas] *adj inv*: **careta** ~ gasmask.

antigualla [anti'ɤwaʎa] *nf* antique; (*reliquia*) relic; ~**s** *nfpl* old things.

antiguamente [antiɤwa'mente] *adv* formerly; (*hace mucho tiempo*) long ago.

antigüedad [antiɤwe'ðað] *nf* antiquity; (*artículo*) antique; (*rango*) seniority.

antiguo, a [an'tiɤwo, a] *adj* old, ancient; (*que fue*) former; **a la antigua** in the old-fashioned way.

antihigiénico, a [anti'xjeniko, a] *adj* unhygienic.

antihistamínico, a [antista'miniko, a] *adj*, *nm* antihistamine.

antiinflacionista [antinflaθjo'nista] *adj* anti-inflationary, counter-inflationary.

antillano, a [anti'ʎano, a] *adj*, *nm/f* West Indian.

Antillas [an'tiʎas] *nfpl*: **las** ~ the West Indies, the Antilles; **el mar de las** ~ the Caribbean Sea.

antílope [an'tilope] *nm* antelope.

antimonopolios [antimono'poljos] *adj inv*: **ley** ~ anti-trust law.

antinatural [antinatu'ral] *adj* unnatural.

antiparras [anti'parras] *nfpl* (*fam*) specs.

antipatía [antipa'tia] *nf* antipathy, dislike.

antipático, a [anti'patiko, a] *adj* disagreeable, unpleasant.

Antípodas [an'tipoðas] *nfpl*: **las** ~ the Antipodes.

antiquísimo, a [anti'kisimo, a] *adj* ancient.

antirreglamentario, a [antirreɤlamen 'tarjo, a] *adj* (*gen*) unlawful; (*POL etc*) unconstitutional.

antirrobo [anti'rroßo] *adj inv*: **(dispositivo)** ~ (*para casas etc*) burglar alarm; (*para coches*) car alarm.

antisemita [antise'mita] *adj* anti-Semitic ♦ *nm/f* anti-Semite.

antiséptico, a [anti'septiko, a] *adj*, *nm* antiseptic.

antiterrorista [antiterro'rista] *adj* antiterrorist; **la lucha** ~ the fight against terrorism.

antítesis [an'titesis] *nf inv* antithesis.

antojadizo, a [antoxa'ðiθo, a] *adj*

capricious.
antojarse [anto'xarse] *vr* (*desear*): **se me antoja comprarlo** I have a mind to buy it; (*pensar*): **se me antoja que** I have a feeling that.
antojo [an'toxo] *nm* caprice, whim; (*rosa*) birthmark; (*lunar*) mole; **hacer a su ~ to** do as one pleases.
antología [antolo'xia] *nf* anthology.
antonomasia [antono'masja] *nf*: **por ~ par** excellence.
antorcha [an'tortʃa] *nf* torch.
antro ['antro] *nm* cavern; **~ de corrupción** (*fig*) den of iniquity.
antropófago, a [antro'pofaxo, a] *adj, nm/f* cannibal.
antropología [antropolo'xia] *nf* anthropology.
antropólogo, a [antro'poloxo, a] *nm/f* anthropologist.
anual [a'nwal] *adj* annual.
anualidad [anwali'ðað] *nf* annuity, annual payment; **~ vitalicia** life annuity.
anuario [a'nwarjo] *nm* yearbook.
anudar [anu'ðar] *vt* to knot, tie; (*unir*) to join; **~se** *vr* to get tied up; **se me anudó la voz** I got a lump in my throat.
anulación [anula'θjon] *nf* annulment; cancellation; repeal.
anular [anu'lar] *vt* to annul, cancel; (*suscripción*) to cancel; (*ley*) to repeal
♦ *nm* ring finger.
anunciación [anunθja'θjon] *nf* announcement; **A~** (*REL*) Annunciation.
anunciante [anun'θjante] *nm/f* (*COM*) advertiser.
anunciar [anun'θjar] *vt* to announce; (*proclamar*) to proclaim; (*COM*) to advertise.
anuncio [a'nunθjo] *nm* announcement; (*señal*) sign; (*COM*) advertisement; (*cartel*) poster; (*TEAT*) bill; **~s por palabras** classified ads.
anverso [am'berso] *nm* obverse.
anzuelo [an'θwelo] *nm* hook; (*para pescar*) fish hook; **tragar el ~ to** swallow the bait.
añadido [aɲa'ðiðo] *nm* addition.
añadidura [aɲaði'ðura] *nf* addition, extra; **por ~ besides,** in addition.
añadir [aɲa'ðir] *vt* to add.
añejo, a [a'ɲexo, a] *adj* old; (*vino*) vintage; (*jamón*) well-cured.
añicos [a'ɲikos] *nmpl*: **hacer ~ to** smash, shatter; **hacerse ~ to** smash, shatter.
añil [a'ɲil] *nm* (*BOT, color*) indigo.
año ['aɲo] *nm* year; **¡Feliz A~ Nuevo!** Happy New Year!; **tener 15 ~s** to be 15

(years old); **los ~s 80** the eighties; **~ bisiesto/escolar** leap/school year; **~ fiscal** fiscal *o* tax year; **estar de buen ~** to be in good shape; **en el ~ de la nana** in the year dot; **el ~ que viene** next year.
añoranza [aɲo'ranθa] *nf* nostalgia; (*anhelo*) longing.
añorar [aɲo'rar] *vt* to long for.
añoso, a [a'ɲoso, a] *adj* ancient, old.
aovado, a [ao'ßaðo, a] *adj* oval.
aovar [ao'ßar] *vi* to lay eggs.
apabullar [apaßu'ʎar] *vt* (*lit, fig*) to crush.
apacentar [apaθen'tar] *vt* to pasture, graze.
apacible [apa'θißle] *adj* gentle, mild.
apaciente [apa'θjente] *etc vb V* **apacentar.**
apaciguar [apaθi'ɣwar] *vt* to pacify, calm (down).
apacigüe [apa'θiɣwe] *etc vb V* **apaciguar.**
apadrinar [apaðri'nar] *vt* to sponsor, support; (*REL*) to act as godfather to.
apagado, a [apa'ɣaðo, a] *adj* (*volcán*) extinct; (*color*) dull; (*voz*) quiet; (*sonido*) muted, muffled; (*persona*: *apático*) listless; **estar ~** (*fuego, luz*) to be out; (*radio, TV etc*) to be off.
apagar [apa'ɣar] *vt* to put out; (*color*) to tone down; (*sonido*) to silence, muffle; (*sed*) to quench; (*INFORM*) to toggle off; **~se** *vr* (*luz, fuego*) to go out; (*sonido*) to die away; (*pasión*) to wither; **~ el sistema** (*INFORM*) to close *o* shut down.
apagón [apa'ɣon] *nm* blackout, power cut.
apague [a'paɣe] *etc vb V* **apagar.**
apaisado, a [apai'saðo, a] *adj* (*papel*) landscape *cpd*.
apalabrar [apala'ßrar] *vt* to agree to; (*obrero*) to engage.
Apalaches [apa'latʃes] *nmpl*: **(Montes) ~** Appalachians.
apalear [apale'ar] *vt* to beat, thrash; (*AGR*) to winnow.
apañado, a [apa'ɲaðo, a] *adj* (*mañoso*) resourceful; (*arreglado*) tidy; (*útil*) handy.
apañar [apa'ɲar] *vt* to pick up; (*asir*) to take hold of, grasp; (*reparar*) to mend, patch up; **~se** *vr* to manage, get along; **apañárselas por su cuenta** to look after number one (*fam*).
apaño [a'paɲo] *nm* (*COSTURA*) patch; (*maña*) skill; **esto no tiene ~** there's no answer to this one.
aparador [apara'ðor] *nm* sideboard; (*escaparate*) shop window.
aparato [apa'rato] *nm* apparatus; (*máquina*) machine; (*doméstico*) appliance; (*boato*) ostentation; (*INFORM*)

device; ~ **de facsímil** facsimile (machine), fax; ~ **respiratorio** respiratory system; ~**s de mando** (*AVIAT etc*) controls.

aparatoso, a [apara'toso, a] *adj* showy, ostentatious.

aparcamiento [aparka'mjento] *nm* car park (*BRIT*), parking lot (*US*).

aparcar [apar'kar] *vt, vi* to park.

aparear [apare'ar] *vt* (*objetos*) to pair, match; (*animales*) to mate; ~**se** *vr* to form a pair; to mate.

aparecer [apare'θer] *vi*, ~**se** *vr* to appear; **apareció borracho** he turned up drunk.

aparejado, a [apare'xaðo, a] *adj* fit, suitable; **ir** ~ **con** to go hand in hand with; **llevar** *o* **traer** ~ to involve.

aparejador, a [aparexa'ðor, a] *nm/f* (*ARQ*) quantity surveyor.

aparejar [apare'xar] *vt* to prepare; (*caballo*) to saddle, harness; (*NAUT*) to fit out, rig out.

aparejo [apa'rexo] *nm* preparation; (*de caballo*) harness; (*NAUT*) rigging; (*de poleas*) block and tackle.

aparentar [aparen'tar] *vt* (*edad*) to look; (*fingir*): ~ **tristeza** to pretend to be sad.

aparente [apa'rente] *adj* apparent; (*adecuado*) suitable.

aparezca [apa'reθka] *etc vb V* **aparecer**.

aparición [apari'θjon] *nf* appearance; (*de libro*) publication; (*fantasma*) spectre.

apariencia [apa'rjenθja] *nf* (*outward*) appearance; **en** ~ outwardly, seemingly.

aparque [a'parke] *etc vb V* **aparcar**.

apartado, a [apar'taðo, a] *adj* separate; (*lejano*) remote ♦ *nm* (*tipográfico*) paragraph; ~ **(de correos)** post office box.

apartamento [aparta'mento] *nm* apartment, flat (*BRIT*).

apartamiento [aparta'mjento] *nm* separation; (*aislamiento*) remoteness; (*AM*) apartment, flat (*BRIT*).

apartar [apar'tar] *vt* to separate; (*quitar*) to remove; (*MINERALOGÍA*) to extract; ~**se** *vr* (*separarse*) to separate, part; (*irse*) to move away; (*mantenerse aparte*) to keep away.

aparte [a'parte] *adv* (*separadamente*) separately; (*además*) besides ♦ *prep*: ~ **de** apart from ♦ *nm* (*TEAT*) aside; (*tipográfico*) new paragraph; **"punto y** ~**"** "new paragraph".

apasionado, a [apasjo'naðo, a] *adj* passionate; (*pey*) biassed, prejudiced ♦ *nm/f* admirer.

apasionante [apasjo'nante] *adj* exciting.

apasionar [apasjo'nar] *vt* to arouse passion in; ~**se** *vr* to get excited; **le apasiona el fútbol** she's crazy about football.

apatía [apa'tia] *nf* apathy.

apático, a [a'patiko, a] *adj* apathetic.

apátrida [a'patriða] *adj* stateless.

Apdo. *nm abr* (= *Apartado (de Correos)*) P.O. Box.

apeadero [apea'ðero] *nm* halt, stopping place.

apearse [ape'arse] *vr* (*jinete*) to dismount; (*bajarse*) to get down *o* out; (*de coche*) to get out, alight; **no** ~ **del burro** to refuse to climb down.

apechugar [apetʃu'ɣar] *vi*: ~ **con algo** to face up to sth.

apechugue [ape'tʃuɣe] *etc vb V* **apechugar**.

apedrear [apeðre'ar] *vt* to stone.

apegarse [ape'ɣarse] *vr*: ~ **a** to become attached to.

apego [a'peɣo] *nm* attachment, devotion.

apegue [a'peɣe] *etc vb V* **apegarse**.

apelación [apela'θjon] *nf* appeal.

apelar [ape'lar] *vi* to appeal; ~ **a** (*fig*) to resort to.

apelativo [apela'tiβo] *nm* (*LING*) appellative; (*AM*) surname.

apellidar [apeʎi'ðar] *vt* to call, name; ~**se** *vr*: **se apellida Pérez** her (sur)name's Pérez.

apellido [ape'ʎiðo] *nm* surname.

In the Spanish-speaking world most people use two **apellidos**, *the first being their father's first surname, and the second their mother's first surname: eg the children of Juan García López, married to Carmen Pérez Rodríguez would have as their surname García Pérez. Married women retain their own surname(s) and sometimes add their husband's first surname on to theirs: eg Carmen Pérez de García. She could also be referred to as (la) Señora de García. In Latin America it is usual for the second surname to be shortened to an initial in correspondence eg: Juan García L.*

---

apelmazado, a [apelma'θaðo, a] *adj* compact, solid.

apelotonar [apeloto'nar] *vt* to roll into a ball; ~**se** *vr* (*gente*) to crowd together.

apenar [ape'nar] *vt* to grieve, trouble; (*AM: avergonzar*) to embarrass; ~**se** *vr* to grieve; (*AM*) to be embarrassed.

apenas [a'penas] *adv* scarcely, hardly ♦ *conj* as soon as, no sooner.

apéndice [a'pendiθe] nm appendix.
apendicitis [apendi'θitis] nf appendicitis.
Apeninos [ape'ninos] nmpl Apennines.
apercibimiento [aperθißi'mjento] nm (aviso) warning.
apercibir [aperθi'ßir] vt to prepare; (avisar) to warn; (JUR) to summon; (AM) to notice, see; ~se vr to get ready; ~se de to notice.
aperitivo [aperi'tißo] nm (bebida) aperitif; (comida) appetizer.
apero [a'pero] nm (AGR) implement; ~s nmpl farm equipment sg.
apertura [aper'tura] nf (gen) opening; (POL) openness, liberalization; (TEAT etc) beginning; ~ de un juicio hipotecario (COM) foreclosure.
aperturismo [apertu'rismo] nm (POL) (policy of) liberalization.
apesadumbrar [apesaðum'brar] vt to grieve, sadden; ~se vr to distress o.s.
apestar [apes'tar] vt to infect ♦ vi: ~ (a) to stink (of).
apestoso, a [apes'toso, a] adj (hediondo) stinking; (asqueroso) sickening.
apetecer [apete'θer] vt: ¿te apetece una tortilla? do you fancy an omelette?
apetecible [apete'θißle] adj desirable; (comida) tempting.
apetezca [ape'teθka] etc vb V apetecer.
apetito [ape'tito] nm appetite.
apetitoso, a [apeti'toso, a] adj (gustoso) appetizing; (fig) tempting.
apiadarse [apja'ðarse] vr: ~ de to take pity on.
ápice ['apiθe] nm apex; (fig) whit, iota; ni un ~ not a whit; no ceder un ~ not to budge an inch.
apicultor, a [apikul'tor, a] nm/f beekeeper, apiarist.
apicultura [apikul'tura] nf beekeeping.
apiladora [apila'ðora] nf (para máquina impresora) stacker.
apilar [api'lar] vt to pile o heap up; ~se vr to pile up.
apiñado, a [api'ɲaðo, a] adj (apretado) packed.
apiñar [api'ɲar] vt to crowd; ~se vr to crowd o press together.
apio ['apjo] nm celery.
apisonadora [apisona'ðora] nf (máquina) steamroller.
aplacar [apla'kar] vt to placate; ~se vr to calm down.
aplace [a'plaθe] etc vb V aplazar.
aplanamiento [aplana'mjento] nm smoothing, levelling.
aplanar [apla'nar] vt to smooth, level;

(allanar) to roll flat, flatten; ~se vr (edificio) to collapse; (persona) to get discouraged.
aplaque [a'plake] etc vb V aplacar.
aplastar [aplas'tar] vt to squash (flat); (fig) to crush.
aplatanarse [aplata'narse] vr to get lethargic.
aplaudir [aplau'ðir] vt to applaud.
aplauso [a'plauso] nm applause; (fig) approval, acclaim.
aplazamiento [aplaθa'mjento] nm postponement.
aplazar [apla'θar] vt to postpone, defer.
aplicación [aplika'θjon] nf application; (esfuerzo) effort; aplicaciones de gestión business applications.
aplicado, a [apli'kaðo, a] adj diligent, hard-working.
aplicar [apli'kar] vt (gen) to apply; (poner en vigor) to put into effect; (esfuerzos) to devote; ~se vr to apply o.s.
aplique [a'plike] etc vb V aplicar ♦ nm wall light o lamp.
aplomo [a'plomo] nm aplomb, self-assurance.
apocado, a [apo'kaðo, a] adj timid.
apocamiento [apoka'mjento] nm timidity; (depresión) depression.
apocarse [apo'karse] vr to feel small o humiliated.
apocopar [apoko'par] vt (LING) to shorten.
apócope [a'pokope] nf apocopation; gran es ~ de grande "gran" is the shortened form of "grande".
apócrifo, a [a'pokrifo, a] adj apocryphal.
apodar [apo'ðar] vt to nickname.
apoderado [apoðe'raðo] nm agent, representative.
apoderar [apoðe'rar] vt to authorize, empower; (JUR) to grant (a) power of attorney to; ~se vr: ~se de to take possession of.
apodo [a'poðo] nm nickname.
apogeo [apo'xeo] nm peak, summit.
apolillado, a [apoli'ʎaðo, a] adj moth-eaten.
apolillarse [apoli'ʎarse] vr to get moth-eaten.
apología [apolo'xia] nf eulogy; (defensa) defence.
apoltronarse [apoltro'narse] vr to get lazy.
apoplejía [apople'xia] nf apoplexy, stroke.
apoque [a'poke] etc vb V apocar.
apoquinar [apoki'nar] vt (fam) to cough up, fork out.
aporrear [aporre'ar] vt to beat (up).
aportación [aporta'θjon] nf contribution.

aportar [apor'tar] *vt* to contribute ♦ *vi* to reach port.

aposentar [aposen'tar] *vt* to lodge, put up.

aposento [apo'sento] *nm* lodging; (*habitación*) room.

apósito [a'posito] *nm* (*MED*) dressing.

apostar [apos'tar] *vt* to bet, stake; (*tropas etc*) to station, post ♦ *vi* to bet.

aposta(s) [a'posta(s)] *adv* on purpose.

apostatar [aposta'tar] *vi* (*REL*) to apostatize; (*fig*) to change sides.

a posteriori [aposte'rjori] *adv* at a later date *o* stage; (*LÓGICA*) a posteriori.

apostilla [apos'tiʎa] *nf* note, comment.

apóstol [a'postol] *nm* apostle.

apóstrofo [a'postrofo] *nm* apostrophe.

apostura [apos'tura] *nf* neatness, elegance.

apoteósico, a [apote'osiko, a] *adj* tremendous.

apoyar [apo'jar] *vt* to lean, rest; (*fig*) to support, back; ~**se** *vr*: ~**se en** to lean on.

apoyo [a'pojo] *nm* support, backing.

apreciable [apre'θjaßle] *adj* considerable; (*fig*) esteemed.

apreciación [apreθja'θjon] *nf* appreciation; (*COM*) valuation.

apreciar [apre'θjar] *vt* to evaluate, assess; (*COM*) to appreciate, value ♦ *vi* (*ECON*) to appreciate.

aprecio [a'preθjo] *nm* valuation, estimate; (*fig*) appreciation.

aprehender [apreen'der] *vt* to apprehend, detain; (*ver*) to see, observe.

aprehensión [apreen'sjon] *nf* detention, capture.

apremiante [apre'mjante] *adj* urgent, pressing.

apremiar [apre'mjar] *vt* to compel, force ♦ *vi* to be urgent, press.

apremio [a'premjo] *nm* urgency; ~ **de pago** demand note.

aprender [apren'der] *vt, vi* to learn; ~ **a conducir** to learn to drive; ~**se** *vr*: ~**se algo** to learn sth (off) by heart.

aprendiz, a [apren'diθ, a] *nmf* apprentice; (*principiante*) learner, trainee; ~ **de comercio** business trainee.

aprendizaje [aprendi'θaxe] *nm* apprenticeship.

aprensión [apren'sjon] *nm* apprehension, fear.

aprensivo, a [apren'sißo, a] *adj* apprehensive.

apresar [apre'sar] *vt* to seize; (*capturar*) to capture.

aprestar [apres'tar] *vt* to prepare, get ready; (*TEC*) to prime, size; ~**se** *vr* to get ready.

apresto [a'presto] *nm* (*gen*) preparation; (*sustancia*) size.

apresurado, a [apresu'raðo, a] *adj* hurried, hasty.

apresuramiento [apresura'mjento] *nm* hurry, haste.

apresurar [apresu'rar] *vt* to hurry, accelerate; ~**se** *vr* to hurry, make haste; **me apresuré a sugerir que ...** I hastily suggested that ...

apretado, a [apre'taðo, a] *adj* tight; (*escritura*) cramped.

apretar [apre'tar] *vt* to squeeze, press; (*mano*) to clasp; (*dientes*) to grit; (*TEC*) to tighten; (*presionar*) to press together, pack ♦ *vi* to be too tight; ~**se** *vr* to crowd together; ~ **la mano a algn** to shake sb's hand; ~ **el paso** to quicken one's step.

apretón [apre'ton] *nm* squeeze; ~ **de manos** handshake.

aprieto [a'prjeto] *etc vb V* **apretar** ♦ *nm* squeeze; (*dificultad*) difficulty, jam; **estar en un** ~ to be in a jam; **ayudar a algn a salir de un** ~ to help sb out of trouble.

a priori [apri'ori] *adv* beforehand; (*LÓGICA*) a priori.

aprisa [a'prisa] *adv* quickly, hurriedly.

aprisionar [aprisjo'nar] *vt* to imprison.

aprobación [aproßa'θjon] *nf* approval.

aprobado [apro'ßaðo] *nm* (*nota*) pass mark.

aprobar [apro'ßar] *vt* to approve (of); (*examen, materia*) to pass ♦ *vi* to pass.

apropiación [apropja'θjon] *nf* appropriation.

apropiado, a [apro'pjaðo, a] *adj* appropriate.

apropiarse [apro'pjarse] *vr*: ~ **de** to appropriate.

aprovechado, a [aproße'tʃaðo, a] *adj* industrious, hardworking; (*económico*) thrifty; (*pey*) unscrupulous.

aprovechamiento [aproßetʃa'mjento] *nm* use, exploitation.

aprovechar [aproße'tʃar] *vt* to use; (*explotar*) to exploit; (*experiencia*) to profit from; (*oferta, oportunidad*) to take advantage of ♦ *vi* to progress, improve; ~**se** *vr*: ~**se de** to make use of; (*pey*) to take advantage of; **¡que aproveche!** enjoy your meal!

aprovisionar [aproßisjo'nar] *vt* to supply.

aproximación [aproksima'θjon] *nf* approximation; (*de lotería*) consolation prize.

aproximadamente [aproksimaða'mente] *adv* approximately.

aproximado, a [aproksi'maðo, a] _adj_ approximate.

aproximar [aproksi'mar] _vt_ to bring nearer; ~**se** _vr_ to come near, approach.

apruebe [a'prweße] _etc vb_ V **aprobar**.

aptitud [apti'tuð] _nf_ aptitude; (_capacidad_) ability; ~ **para los negocios** business sense.

apto, a ['apto, a] _adj_ (_apropiado_) fit, suitable (_para_ for, to); (_hábil_) capable; ~**/no ~ para menores** (_CINE_) suitable/ unsuitable for children.

apuesto, a [a'pwesto, a] _etc vb_ V **apostar** ♦ _adj_ neat, elegant ♦ _nf_ bet, wager.

apuntador [apunta'ðor] _nm_ prompter.

apuntalar [apunta'lar] _vt_ to prop up.

apuntar [apun'tar] _vt_ (_con arma_) to aim at; (_con dedo_) to point at _o_ to; (_anotar_) to note (down); (_datos_) to record; (_TEAT_) to prompt; ~**se** _vr_ (_DEPORTE: tanto, victoria_) to score; (_ESCOL_) to enrol; ~ **una cantidad en la cuenta de algn** to charge a sum to sb's account; ~**se en un curso** to enrol on a course; **¡yo me apunto!** count me in!

apunte [a'punte] _nm_ note; (_TEAT: voz_) prompt; (: _texto_) prompt book.

apuñalar [apuɲa'lar] _vt_ to stab.

apurado, a [apu'raðo, a] _adj_ needy; (_difícil_) difficult; (_peligroso_) dangerous; (_AM_) hurried, rushed; **estar en una situación apurada** to be in a tight spot; **estar ~ to** be in a hurry.

apurar [apu'rar] _vt_ (_agotar_) to drain; (_recursos_) to use up; (_molestar_) to annoy; ~**se** _vr_ (_preocuparse_) to worry; (_esp AM: darse prisa_) to hurry.

apuro [a'puro] _nm_ (_aprieto_) fix, jam; (_escasez_) want, hardship; (_vergüenza_) embarrassment; (_AM_) haste, urgency.

aquejado, a [ake'xaðo, a] _adj:_ ~ **de** (_MED_) afflicted by.

aquejar [ake'xar] _vt_ (_afligir_) to distress; **le aqueja una grave enfermedad** he suffers from a serious disease.

aquel, aquella, aquellos, as [a'kel, a'keʎa, a'keʎos, as] _adj_ that; (_pl_) those.

aquél, aquélla, aquéllos, as [a'kel, a'keʎa, a'keʎos, as] _pron_ that (one); (_pl_) those (ones).

aquello [a'keʎo] _pron_ that, that business.

aquí [a'ki] _adv_ (_lugar_) here; (_tiempo_) now; ~ **arriba** up here; ~ **mismo** right here; ~ **yace** here lies; **de ~ a siete días** a week from now.

aquietar [akje'tar] _vt_ to quieten (down), calm (down).

Aquisgrán [akis'ɣran] _nm_ Aachen, Aix-la-Chapelle.

A.R. _abr_ (= _Alteza Real_) R.H.

ara ['ara] _nf_ (_altar_) altar; **en ~s de** for the sake of.

árabe ['araße] _adj_ Arab, Arabian, Arabic ♦ _nm/f_ Arab ♦ _nm_ (_LING_) Arabic.

Arabia [a'raßja] _nf_ Arabia; ~ **Saudí** _o_ **Saudita** Saudi Arabia.

arábigo, a [a'raßiɣo, a] _adj_ Arab, Arabian, Arabic.

arácnido [a'rakniðo] _nm_ arachnid.

arado [a'raðo] _nm_ plough.

aragonés, esa [araɣo'nes, esa] _adj, nm/f_ Aragonese ♦ _nm_ (_LING_) Aragonese

arancel [aran'θel] _nm_ tariff, duty; ~ **de aduanas** (customs) duty.

arandela [aran'dela] _nf_ (_TEC_) washer; (_chorrera_) frill.

araña [a'raɲa] _nf_ (_ZOOL_) spider; (_lámpara_) chandelier.

arañar [ara'ɲar] _vt_ to scratch.

arañazo [ara'ɲaθo] _nm_ scratch.

arar [a'rar] _vt_ to plough, till.

araucano, a [arau'kano, a] _adj, nm/f_ Araucanian.

arbitraje [arßi'traxe] _nm_ arbitration.

arbitrar [arßi'trar] _vt_ to arbitrate in; (_recursos_) to bring together; (_DEPORTE_) to referee ♦ _vi_ to arbitrate.

arbitrariedad [arßitrarje'ðað] _nf_ arbitrariness; (_acto_) arbitrary act.

arbitrario, a [arßi'trarjo] _adj_ arbitrary.

arbitrio [ar'ßitrjo] _nm_ free will; (_JUR_) adjudication, decision; **dejar al ~ de algn** to leave to sb's discretion.

árbitro ['arßitro] _nm_ arbitrator; (_DEPORTE_) referee; (_TENIS_) umpire.

árbol ['arßol] _nm_ (_BOT_) tree; (_NAUT_) mast; (_TEC_) axle, shaft.

arbolado, a [arßo'laðo, a] _adj_ wooded; (_camino_) tree-lined ♦ _nm_ woodland.

arboladura [arßola'ðura] _nf_ rigging.

arbolar [arßo'lar] _vt_ to hoist, raise.

arboleda [arßo'leða] _nf_ grove, plantation.

arbusto [ar'ßusto] _nm_ bush, shrub.

arca ['arka] _nf_ chest, box; **A~ de la Alianza** Ark of the Covenant; **A~ de Noé** Noah's Ark.

arcada [ar'kaða] _nf_ arcade; (_de puente_) arch, span; ~**s** _nfpl_ retching _sg_.

arcaico, a [ar'kaiko, a] _adj_ archaic.

arce ['arθe] _nm_ maple tree.

arcén [ar'θen] _nm_ (_de autopista_) hard shoulder; (_de carretera_) verge.

archiconocido, a [artʃikono'θiðo, a] _adj_ extremely well-known.

archipiélago [artʃi'pjelaɣo] _nm_

archipelago.

archisabido, a [artʃisa'βiðo, a] *adj*
extremely well-known.

archivador [artʃiβa'ðor] *nm* filing cabinet;
~ **colgante** suspension file.

archivar [artʃi'βar] *vt* to file (away);
(*INFORM*) to archive.

archivo [ar'tʃiβo] *nm* archive(s) (*pl*);
(*INFORM*) file, archive; **A~ Nacional**
Public Record Office; **~s policíacos**
police files; **nombre de ~** (*INFORM*)
filename; **~ maestro** (*INFORM*) master
file; **~ de transacciones** (*INFORM*)
transactions file.

arcilla [ar'θiʎa] *nf* clay.

arco ['arko] *nm* arch; (*MAT*) arc; (*MIL, MUS*)
bow; (*AM DEPORTE*) goal; ~ **iris** rainbow.

arcón [ar'kon] *nm* large chest.

arder [ar'ðer] *vt* to burn; ~ **sin llama** to
smoulder; **estar que arde** (*persona*) to
fume.

ardid [ar'ðið] *nm* ruse.

ardiente [ar'ðjente] *adj* ardent.

ardilla [ar'ðiʎa] *nf* squirrel.

ardor [ar'ðor] *nm* (*calor*) heat, warmth; (*fig*)
ardour; ~ **de estómago** heartburn.

ardoroso, a [arðo'roso, a] *adj* passionate.

arduo, a ['arðwo, a] *adj* arduous.

área ['area] *nf* area; (*DEPORTE*) penalty
area; ~ **de excedentes** (*INFORM*) overflow
area.

ARENA [a'rena] *nf abr* (*El Salvador: POL*)
= *Alianza Republicana Nacionalista*.

arena [a'rena] *nf* sand; (*de una lucha*) arena.

arenal [are'nal] *nm* (*arena movediza*)
quicksand.

arenga [a'renga] *nf* (*fam*) sermon.

arengar [aren'gar] *vt* to harangue.

arengue [a'renge] *etc vb V* **arengar**.

arenillas [are'niʎas] *nfpl* (*MED*) stones.

arenisca [are'niska] *nf* sandstone; (*cascajo*)
grit.

arenoso, a [are'noso, a] *adj* sandy.

arenque [a'renke] *nm* herring.

arepa [a'repa] *nf* (*AM*) corn pancake.

arete [a'rete] *nm* earring.

argamasa [arɣa'masa] *nf* mortar, plaster.

Argel [ar'xel] *n* Algiers.

Argelia [ar'xelja] *nf* Algeria.

argelino, a [arxe'lino, a] *adj, nm/f* Algerian.

Argentina [arxen'tina] *nf*: (**la**) ~ the
Argentine, Argentina.

argentino, a [arxen'tino, a] *adj*
Argentinian; (*de plata*) silvery ♦ *nm/f*
Argentinian.

argolla [ar'ɣoʎa] *nf* (*large*) ring; (*AM: de
matrimonio*) wedding ring.

argot [ar'ɣo] *nm, pl* **argots** [ar'ɣo, ar'ɣos]

slang.

argucia [ar'ɣuθja] *nf* subtlety, sophistry.

argüir [ar'ɣwir] *vt* to deduce; (*discutir*) to
argue; (*indicar*) to indicate, imply;
(*censurar*) to reproach ♦ *vi* to argue.

argumentación [arɣumenta'θjon] *nf* (line
of) argument.

argumentar [arɣumen'tar] *vt, vi* to argue.

argumento [arɣu'mento] *nm* argument;
(*razonamiento*) reasoning; (*de novela etc*)
plot; (*CINE, TV*) storyline.

arguyendo [arɣu'jendo] *etc vb V* **argüir**.

aria ['arja] *nf* aria.

aridez [ari'ðeθ] *nf* aridity, dryness.

árido, a ['ariðo, a] *adj* arid, dry; **~s** *nmpl*
dry goods.

Aries ['arjes] *nm* Aries.

ariete [a'rjete] *nm* battering ram.

ario, a ['arjo, a] *adj* Aryan.

arisco, a [a'risko, a] *adj* surly; (*insociable*)
unsociable.

aristocracia [aristo'kraθja] *nf* aristocracy.

aristócrata [aris'tokrata] *nm/f* aristocrat.

aristocrático, a [aristo'kratiko, a] *adj*
aristocratic.

aritmética [arit'metika] *nf* arithmetic.

aritmético, a [arit'metiko, a] *adj*
arithmetic(al) ♦ *nm/f* arithmetician.

arma ['arma] *nf* arm; **~s** *nfpl* arms; ~
blanca blade, knife; (*espada*) sword; ~
de fuego firearm; **~s cortas** small arms;
rendir las ~s to lay down one's arms; **ser
de ~s tomar** to be somebody to be
reckoned with.

armada [ar'maða] *nf* armada; (*flota*) fleet; *V
tb* **armado**.

armadillo [arma'ðiʎo] *nm* armadillo.

armado, a [ar'maðo, a] *adj* armed; (*TEC*)
reinforced.

armador [arma'ðor] *nm* (*NAUT*) shipowner.

armadura [arma'ðura] *nf* (*MIL*) armour;
(*TEC*) framework; (*ZOOL*) skeleton;
(*FÍSICA*) armature.

armamentista [armamen'tista],
armamentístico, a [armamen'tistiko, a]
adj arms *cpd*.

armamento [arma'mento] *nm* armament;
(*NAUT*) fitting-out.

armar [ar'mar] *vt* (*soldado*) to arm;
(*máquina*) to assemble; (*navío*) to fit out;
~la, ~ un lío to start a row; **~se** *vr*: **~se
de valor** to summon up one's courage.

armario [ar'marjo] *nm* wardrobe.

armatoste [arma'toste] *nm* (*mueble*)
monstrosity; (*máquina*) contraption.

armazón [arma'θon] *nf o m* body, chassis;
(*de mueble etc*) frame; (*ARQ*) skeleton.

Armenia [ar'menja] *nf* Armenia.

armería [arme'ria] nf (museo) military museum; (tienda) gunsmith's.

armiño [ar'miɲo] nm stoat; (piel) ermine.

armisticio [armis'tiθjo] nm armistice.

armonía [armo'nia] nf harmony.

armónica [ar'monika] nf harmonica; V tb **armónico**.

armonice [armo'niθe] etc vb V **armonizar**.

armónico, a [ar'moniko, a] adj harmonic.

armonioso, a [armo'njoso, a] adj harmonious.

armonizar [armoni'θar] vt to harmonize; (diferencias) to reconcile ♦ vi to harmonize; ~ **con** (fig) to be in keeping with; (colores) to tone in with.

arnés [ar'nes] nm armour; **arneses** nmpl harness sg.

aro ['aro] nm ring; (tejo) quoit; (AM: pendiente) earring; **entrar por el ~** to give in.

aroma [a'roma] nm aroma.

aromático, a [aro'matiko, a] adj aromatic.

arpa ['arpa] nf harp.

arpegio [ar'pexjo] nm (MUS) arpeggio.

arpía [ar'pia] nf (fig) shrew.

arpillera [arpi'ʎera] nf sacking, sackcloth.

arpón [ar'pon] nm harpoon.

arquear [arke'ar] vt to arch, bend; ~**se** vr to arch, bend.

arqueo [ar'keo] nm (gen) arching; (NAUT) tonnage.

arqueología [arkeolo'xia] nf archaeology.

arqueológico, a [arkeo'loxiko, a] adj archaeological.

arqueólogo, a [arke'oloɣo, a] nm/f archaeologist.

arquero [ar'kero] nm archer, bowman; (AM DEPORTE) goalkeeper.

arquetipo [arke'tipo] nm archetype.

arquitecto, a [arki'tekto, a] nm/f architect; ~ **paisajista** o **de jardines** landscape gardener.

arquitectónico, a [arkitek'toniko, a] adj architectural.

arquitectura [arkitek'tura] nf architecture.

arrabal [arra'βal] nm suburb; ~**es** nmpl outskirts.

arrabalero, a [arraβa'lero, a] adj (fig) common, coarse.

arracimarse [arraθi'marse] vr to cluster together.

arraigado, a [arrai'ɣaðo, a] adj deep-rooted; (fig) established.

arraigar [arrai'ɣar] vt to establish ♦ vi, ~**se** vr to take root; (persona) to settle.

arraigo [a'rraiɣo] nm (raíces) roots pl; (bienes) property; (influencia) hold; **hombre de ~** man of property.

arraigue [a'rraiɣe] etc vb V **arraigar**.

arrancada [arran'kaða] nf (arranque) sudden start.

arrancar [arran'kar] vt (sacar) to extract, pull out; (arrebatar) to snatch (away); (pedazo) to tear off; (página) to rip out; (suspiro) to heave; (AUTO) to start; (INFORM) to boot; (fig) to extract ♦ vi (AUTO, máquina) to start; (ponerse en marcha) to get going; ~ **información a algn** to extract information from sb; ~ **de** to stem from.

arranque [a'rranke] etc vb V **arrancar** ♦ nm sudden start; (AUTO) start; (fig) fit, outburst.

arras ['arras] nfpl pledge sg, security sg.

arrasar [arra'sar] vt (aplanar) to level, flatten; (destruir) to demolish.

arrastrado, a [arras'traðo, a] adj poor, wretched.

arrastrador [arrastra'ðor] nm (en máquina impresora) tractor.

arrastrar [arras'trar] vt to drag (along); (fig) to drag down, degrade; (suj: agua, viento) to carry away ♦ vi to drag, trail on the ground; ~**se** vr to crawl; (fig) to grovel; **llevar algo arrastrado** to drag sth along.

arrastre [a'rrastre] nm drag, dragging; (DEPORTE) crawl; **estar para el ~** (fig) to have had it; ~ **de papel por fricción/por tracción** (en máquina impresora) friction/tractor feed.

array [a'rrai] nm (INFORM) array; ~ **empaquetado** (INFORM) packed array.

arrayán [arra'jan] nm myrtle.

arre ['arre] excl gee up!

arrear [arre'ar] vt to drive on, urge on ♦ vi to hurry along.

arrebañar [arreβa'ɲar] vt (juntar) to scrape together.

arrebatado, a [arreβa'taðo, a] adj rash, impetuous; (repentino) sudden, hasty.

arrebatar [arreβa'tar] vt to snatch (away), seize; (fig) to captivate; ~**se** vr to get carried away, get excited.

arrebato [arre'βato] nm fit of rage, fury; (éxtasis) rapture; **en un ~ de cólera** in an outburst of anger.

arrebolar [arreβo'lar] vt to redden; ~**se** vr (enrojecer) to blush.

arrebujar [arreβu'xar] vt (objetos) to jumble together; ~**se** vr to wrap o.s. up.

arrechar [arre'tʃar] (AM) vt to arouse, excite; ~**se** vr to become aroused.

arrechucho [arre'tʃutʃo] nm (MED) turn.

arreciar [arre'θjar] vi to get worse; (viento) to get stronger.

arrecife [arre'θife] *nm* reef.

arredrar [arre'ðrar] *vt* (*hacer retirarse*) to drive back; **~se** *vr* (*apartarse*) to draw back; **~se ante algo** to shrink away from sth.

arreglado, a [arre'ɣlaðo, a] *adj* (*ordenado*) neat, orderly; (*moderado*) moderate, reasonable.

arreglar [arre'ɣlar] *vt* (*poner orden*) to tidy up; (*algo roto*) to fix, repair; (*problema*) to solve; **~se** *vr* to reach an understanding; **arreglárselas** (*fam*) to get by, manage.

arreglo [a'rreɣlo] *nm* settlement; (*orden*) order; (*acuerdo*) agreement; (*MUS*) arrangement, setting; (*INFORM*) array; **con ~ a** in accordance with; **llegar a un ~** to reach a compromise.

arrellanarse [arreʎa'narse] *vr* to sprawl; **~ en el asiento** to lie back in one's chair.

arremangar [arreman'gar] *vt* to roll up, turn up; **~se** *vr* to roll up one's sleeves.

arremangue [arre'mange] *etc vb V* **arremangar**.

arremeter [arreme'ter] *vt* to attack, assault; **~ contra algn** to attack sb.

arremetida [arreme'tiða] *nf* assault.

arremolinarse [arremoli'narse] *vr* to crowd around, mill around; (*corriente*) to swirl, eddy.

arrendador, a [arrenda'ðor, a] *nm/f* landlord/lady.

arrendamiento [arrenda'mjento] *nm* letting; (*el alquilar*) hiring; (*contrato*) lease; (*alquiler*) rent.

arrendar [arren'dar] *vt* to let; to hire; to lease; to rent.

arrendatario, a [arrenda'tarjo, a] *nm/f* tenant.

arreos [a'rreos] *nmpl* harness *sg*, trappings.

arrepentido, a [arrepen'tiðo, a] *nm/f* (*POL*) reformed terrorist.

arrepentimiento [arrepenti'mjento] *nm* regret, repentance.

arrepentirse [arrepen'tirse] *vr* to repent; **~ de (haber hecho) algo** to regret (doing) sth.

arrepienta [arre'pjenta] *etc*, **arrepintiendo** [arrepin'tjendo] *etc vb V* **arrepentirse**.

arrestar [arres'tar] *vt* to arrest; (*encarcelar*) to imprison.

arresto [a'rresto] *nm* arrest; (*MIL*) detention; (*audacia*) boldness, daring; **~ domiciliario** house arrest.

arriar [a'rrjar] *vt* (*velas*) to haul down; (*bandera*) to lower, strike; (*un cable*) to pay out.

arriate [a'rrjate] *nm* (*BOT*) bed; (*camino*) road.

════════ *PALABRA CLAVE*

arriba [a'rriβa] *adv* **1** (*posición*) above; **desde ~** from above; **~ del todo** at the very top, right on top; **Juan está ~** Juan is upstairs; **lo ~ mencionado** the aforementioned; **aquí/allí ~** up here/ there; **está hasta ~ de trabajo** (*fam*) he's up to his eyes in work (*fam*)
2 (*dirección*) up, upwards; **más ~** higher *o* further up; **calle ~** up the street
3: **de ~ abajo** from top to bottom; **mirar a algn de ~ abajo** to look sb up and down
4: **para ~: de 5000 pesetas para ~** from 5,000 pesetas up(wards); **de la cintura (para) ~** from the waist up
♦ *adj*: **de ~: el piso de ~** the upstairs flat (*BRIT*) *o* apartment; **la parte de ~** the top *o* upper part
♦ *prep*: **~ de** (*AM*) above; **~ de 200 dólares** more than 200 dollars
♦ *excl*: **¡~!** up!; **¡manos ~!** hands up!; **¡~ España!** long live Spain!

arribar [arri'βar] *vi* to put into port; (*esp AM*: *llegar*) to arrive.

arribista [arri'βista] *nm/f* parvenu(e), upstart.

arribo [a'rriβo] *nm* (*esp AM*) arrival.

arriendo [a'rrjendo] *etc vb V* **arrendar** ♦ *nm* = **arrendamiento**.

arriero [a'rrjero] *nm* muleteer.

arriesgado, a [arrjes'ɣaðo, a] *adj* (*peligroso*) risky; (*audaz*) bold, daring.

arriesgar [arrjes'ɣar] *vt* to risk; (*poner en peligro*) to endanger; **~se** *vr* to take a risk.

arriesgue [a'rrjesɣe] *etc vb V* **arriesgar**.

arrimar [arri'mar] *vt* (*acercar*) to bring close; (*poner de lado*) to set aside; **~se** *vr* to come close *o* closer; **~se a** to lean on; (*fig*) to keep company with; (*buscar ayuda*) to seek the protection of; **arrímate a mí** cuddle up to me.

arrinconado, a [arrinko'naðo, a] *adj* forgotten, neglected.

arrinconar [arrinko'nar] *vt* to put in a corner; (*fig*) to put on one side; (*abandonar*) to push aside.

arriscado, a [arris'kaðo, a] *adj* (*GEO*) craggy; (*fig*) bold, resolute.

arroba [a'rroβa] *nf* (*peso*) 25 pounds; **tiene talento por ~s** he has loads *o* bags of talent.

arrobado, a [arro'βaðo, a] *adj* entranced, enchanted.

arrobamiento [arroßa'mjento] *nm* ecstasy.
arrobar [arro'ßar] *vt* to enchant; ~**se** *vr* to be enraptured; (*místico*) to go into a trance.
arrodillarse [arroði'ʎarse] *vr* to kneel (down).
arrogancia [arro'ɣanθja] *nf* arrogance.
arrogante [arro'ɣante] *adj* arrogant.
arrojar [arro'xar] *vt* to throw, hurl; (*humo*) to emit, give out; (*COM*) to yield, produce; ~**se** *vr* to throw o hurl o.s.
arrojo [a'rroxo] *nm* daring.
arrollador, a [arroʎa'ðor, a] *adj* crushing, overwhelming.
arrollar [arro'ʎar] *vt* (*enrollar*) to roll up; (*suj: inundación*) to wash away; (*AUTO*) to run over; (*DEPORTE*) to crush.
arropar [arro'par] *vt* to cover (up), wrap up; ~**se** *vr* to wrap o.s. up.
arrostrar [arros'trar] *vt* to face (up to); ~**se** *vr*: ~**se con algn** to face up to sb.
arroyo [a'rrojo] *nm* stream; (*de la calle*) gutter; **poner a algn en el** ~ to turn sb onto the streets.
arroz [a'rroθ] *nm* rice; ~ **con leche** rice pudding.
arrozal [arro'θal] *nm* paddy field.
arruga [a'rruɣa] *nf* fold; (*de cara*) wrinkle; (*de vestido*) crease.
arrugar [arru'ɣar] *vt* to fold; to wrinkle; to crease; ~**se** *vr* to get wrinkled; to get creased.
arrugue [a'rruɣe] *etc vb V* **arrugar**.
arruinar [arrwi'nar] *vt* to ruin, wreck; ~**se** *vr* to be ruined.
arrullar [arru'ʎar] *vi* to coo ♦ *vt* to lull to sleep.
arrumaco [arru'mako] *nm* (*caricia*) caress; (*halago*) piece of flattery.
arrumbar [arrum'bar] *vt* (*objeto*) to discard; (*individuo*) to silence.
arrurruz [arrur'ruθ] *nm* arrowroot.
arsenal [arse'nal] *nm* naval dockyard; (*MIL*) arsenal.
arsénico [ar'seniko] *nm* arsenic.
arte ['arte] *nm* (*gen m en sg y siempre f en pl*) art; (*maña*) skill, guile; **por** ~ **de magia** (as if) by magic; **no tener** ~ **ni parte en algo** to have nothing whatsoever to do with sth; ~**s** *nfpl* arts; **Bellas A~s** Fine Art *sg*; ~**s y oficios** arts and crafts.
artefacto [arte'fakto] *nm* appliance; (*ARQUEOLOGÍA*) artefact.
arteria [ar'terja] *nf* artery.
arterial [arte'rjal] *adj* arterial; (*presión*) blood *cpd*.
arterio(e)sclerosis [arterjo(e)skle'rosis] *nf inv* hardening of the arteries,

arteriosclerosis.
artesa [ar'tesa] *nf* trough.
artesanía [artesa'nia] *nf* craftsmanship; (*artículos*) handicrafts *pl*.
artesano, a [arte'sano, a] *nm/f* artisan, craftsman/woman.
ártico, a ['artiko, a] *adj* Arctic ♦ *nm*: **el (océano) Á~** the Arctic (Ocean).
articulación [artikula'θjon] *nf* articulation; (*MED, TEC*) joint.
articulado, a [artiku'laðo, a] *adj* articulated; jointed.
articular [artiku'lar] *vt* to articulate; to join together.
articulista [artiku'lista] *nm/f* columnist, contributor (to a newspaper).
artículo [ar'tikulo] *nm* article; (*cosa*) thing, article; (*TV*) feature, report; ~ **de fondo** leader, editorial; ~**s** *nmpl* goods; ~**s de marca** (*COM*) proprietary goods.
artífice [ar'tifiθe] *nm* artist, craftsman; (*fig*) architect.
artificial [artifi'θjal] *adj* artificial.
artificio [arti'fiθjo] *nm* art, skill; (*artesanía*) craftsmanship; (*astucia*) cunning.
artillería [artiʎe'ria] *nf* artillery.
artillero [arti'ʎero] *nm* artilleryman, gunner.
artilugio [arti'luxjo] *nm* gadget.
artimaña [arti'maɲa] *nf* trap, snare; (*astucia*) cunning.
artista [ar'tista] *nm/f* (*pintor*) artist, painter; (*TEAT*) artist, artiste.
artístico, a [ar'tistiko, a] *adj* artistic.
artritis [ar'tritis] *nf* arthritis.
arveja [ar'ßexa] *nf* (*AM*) pea.
Arz. *abr* (= *Arzobispo*) Abp.
arzobispo [arθo'ßispo] *nm* archbishop.
as [as] *nm* ace; ~ **del fútbol** star player.
asa ['asa] *nf* handle; (*fig*) lever.
asado [a'saðo] *nm* roast (meat); (*AM: barbacoa*) barbecue.
asador [asa'ðor] *nm* (*varilla*) spit; (*aparato*) spit roaster.
asadura(s) [asa'ðura(s)] *nf(pl)* entrails *pl*, offal *sg*; (*CULIN*) chitterlings *pl*.
asaetar [asae'tar] *vt* (*fig*) to bother.
asalariado, a [asala'rjaðo, a] *adj* paid, wage-earning, salaried ♦ *nm/f* wage earner.
asaltador, a [asalta'ðor, a], **asaltante** [asal'tante] *nm/f* assailant.
asaltar [asal'tar] *vt* to attack, assault; (*fig*) to assail.
asalto [a'salto] *nm* attack, assault; (*DEPORTE*) round.
asamblea [asam'blea] *nf* assembly; (*reunión*) meeting.

asar [a'sar] *vt* to roast; ~ **al horno/a la parrilla** to bake/grill; **~se** *vr* (*fig*): **me aso de calor** I'm roasting; **aquí se asa uno vivo** it's boiling hot here.

asbesto [as'ßesto] *nm* asbestos.

ascendencia [asθen'denθja] *nf* ancestry; **de ~ francesa** of French origin.

ascender [asθen'der] *vi* (*subir*) to ascend, rise; (*ser promovido*) to gain promotion ♦ *vt* to promote; ~ **a** to amount to.

ascendiente [asθen'djente] *nm* influence ♦ *nm/f* ancestor.

ascensión [asθen'sjon] *nf* ascent; **la A~** the Ascension.

ascenso [as'θenso] *nm* ascent; (*promoción*) promotion.

ascensor [asθen'sor] *nm* lift (*BRIT*), elevator (*US*).

ascético, a [as'θetiko, a] *adj* ascetic.

ascienda [as'θjenda] *etc vb V* **ascender**.

asco ['asko] *nm*: **el ajo me da ~** I hate *o* loathe garlic; **hacer ~s de algo** to turn up one's nose at sth; **estar hecho un ~** to be filthy; **poner a algn de ~** to call sb all sorts of names *o* every name under the sun; **¡qué ~!** how revolting *o* disgusting!

ascua ['askwa] *nf* ember; **arrimar el ~ a su sardina** to look after number one; **estar en ~s** to be on tenterhooks.

aseado, a [ase'aðo, a] *adj* clean; (*arreglado*) tidy; (*pulcro*) smart.

asear [ase'ar] *vt* (*lavar*) to wash; (*ordenar*) to tidy (up).

asechanza [ase't∫anθa] *nf* trap, snare.

asediar [ase'ðjar] *vt* (*MIL*) to besiege, lay siege to; (*fig*) to chase, pester.

asedio [a'seðjo] *nm* siege; (*COM*) run.

asegurado, a [aseɣu'raðo, a] *adj* insured.

asegurador, a [aseɣura'ðor, a] *nm/f* insurer.

asegurar [aseɣu'rar] *vt* (*consolidar*) to secure, fasten; (*dar garantía de*) to guarantee; (*preservar*) to safeguard; (*afirmar, dar por cierto*) to assure, affirm; (*tranquilizar*) to reassure; (*tomar un seguro*) to insure; **~se** *vr* to assure o.s., make sure.

asemejarse [aseme'xarse] *vr* to be alike; ~ **a** to be like, resemble.

asentado, a [asen'taðo, a] *adj* established, settled.

asentar [asen'tar] *vt* (*sentar*) to seat, sit down; (*poner*) to place, establish; (*alisar*) to level, smooth down *o* out; (*anotar*) to note down ♦ *vi* to be suitable, suit.

asentimiento [asenti'mjento] *nm* assent, agreement.

asentir [asen'tir] *vi* to assent, agree.

aseo [a'seo] *nm* cleanliness; **~s** *nmpl* toilet *sg* (*BRIT*), restroom *sg* (*US*), cloakroom *sg*.

aséptico, a [a'septiko, a] *adj* germ-free, free from infection.

asequible [ase'kißle] *adj* (*precio*) reasonable; (*meta*) attainable; (*persona*) approachable.

aserradero [aserra'ðero] *nm* sawmill.

aserrar [ase'rrar] *vt* to saw.

asesinar [asesi'nar] *vt* to murder; (*POL*) to assassinate.

asesinato [asesi'nato] *nm* murder; assassination.

asesino, a [ase'sino, a] *nm/f* murderer, killer; (*POL*) assassin.

asesor, a [ase'sor, a] *nm/f* adviser, consultant; (*COM*) assessor, consultant; ~ **administrativo** management consultant.

asesorar [aseso'rar] *vt* (*JUR*) to advise, give legal advice to; (*COM*) to act as consultant to; **~se** *vr*: **~se con o de** to take advice from, consult.

asesoría [aseso'ria] *nf* (*cargo*) consultancy; (*oficina*) consultant's office.

asestar [ases'tar] *vt* (*golpe*) to deal; (*arma*) to aim; (*tiro*) to fire.

aseverar [aseße'rar] *vt* to assert.

asfaltado, a [asfal'taðo, a] *adj* asphalted ♦ *nm* (*pavimiento*) asphalt.

asfalto [as'falto] *nm* asphalt.

asfixia [as'fiksja] *nf* asphyxia, suffocation.

asfixiar [asfik'sjar] *vt* to asphyxiate, suffocate.

asga ['asɣa] *etc vb V* **asir**.

así [a'si] *adv* (*de esta manera*) in this way, like this, thus; (*aunque*) although; (*tan pronto como*) as soon as; ~ **que** so; ~ **como** as well as; ~ **y todo** even so; **¿no es ~?** isn't it?, didn't you? *etc*; ~ **de grande** this big; **¡~ sea!** so be it!; ~ **es la vida** such is life, that's life.

Asia ['asja] *nf* Asia.

asiático, a [a'sjatiko, a] *adj, nm/f* Asian, Asiatic.

asidero [asi'ðero] *nm* handle.

asiduidad [asiðwi'ðað] *nf* assiduousness.

asiduo, a [a'siðwo, a] *adj* assiduous; (*frecuente*) frequent ♦ *nm/f* regular (customer).

asiento [a'sjento] *etc vb V* **asentar, asentir** ♦ *nm* (*mueble*) seat, chair; (*de coche, en tribunal etc*) seat; (*localidad*) seat, place; (*fundamento*) site; ~ **delantero/trasero** front/back seat.

asierre [a'sjerre] *etc vb V* **aserrar**.

asignación [asiɣna'θjon] *nf* (*atribución*)

assignment; (*reparto*) allocation; (*COM*) allowance; ~ **(semanal)** pocket money; ~ **de presupuesto** budget appropriation.

asignar [asiɣ'nar] *vt* to assign, allocate.

asignatura [asiɣna'tura] *nf* subject; (*curso*) course; ~ **pendiente** (*fig*) matter pending.

asilado, a [asi'laðo, a] *nm/f* refugee.

asilo [a'silo] *nm* (*refugio*) asylum, refuge; (*establecimiento*) home, institution; ~ **político** political asylum.

asimilación [asimila'θjon] *nf* assimilation.

asimilar [asimi'lar] *vt* to assimilate.

asimismo [asi'mismo] *adv* in the same way, likewise.

asintiendo [asin't jendo] *etc vb V* **asentir**.

asir [a'sir] *vt* to seize, grasp; ~**se** *vr* to take hold; ~**se a** *o* **de** to seize.

asistencia [asis'tenθja] *nf* presence; (*TEAT*) audience; (*MED*) attendance; (*ayuda*) assistance; ~ **social** social *o* welfare work.

asistente, a [asis'tente, a] *nm/f* assistant ♦ *nm* (*MIL*) orderly ♦ *nf* daily help; **los** ~**s** those present; ~ **social** social worker.

asistido, a [asis'tiðo, a] *adj* (*AUTO*: *dirección*) power-assisted; ~ **por ordenador** computer-assisted.

asistir [asis'tir] *vt* to assist, help ♦ *vi*: ~ **a** to attend, be present at.

asma ['asma] *nf* asthma.

asno ['asno] *nm* donkey; (*fig*) ass.

asociación [asoθja'θjon] *nf* association; (*COM*) partnership.

asociado, a [aso'θjaðo, a] *adj* associate ♦ *nm/f* associate; (*COM*) partner.

asociar [aso'θjar] *vt* to associate; ~**se** *vr* to become partners.

asolar [aso'lar] *vt* to destroy.

asolear [asole'ar] *vt* to put in the sun; ~**se** *vr* to sunbathe.

asomar [aso'mar] *vt* to show, stick out ♦ *vi* to appear; ~**se** *vr* to appear, show up; ~ **la cabeza por la ventana** to put one's head out of the window.

asombrar [asom'brar] *vt* to amaze, astonish; ~**se** *vr*: ~**se (de)** (*sorprenderse*) to be amazed (at); (*asustarse*) to be frightened (at).

asombro [a'sombro] *nm* amazement, astonishment.

asombroso, a [asom'broso, a] *adj* amazing, astonishing.

asomo [a'somo] *nm* hint, sign; **ni por** ~ by no means.

asonancia [aso'nanθja] *nf* (*LIT*) assonance; (*fig*) connection; **no tener** ~ **con** to bear no relation to.

asorocharse [asoro't ʃarse] *vr* (*AM*) to get mountain sickness.

aspa ['aspa] *nf* (*cruz*) cross; (*de molino*) sail; **en** ~ X-shaped.

aspaviento [aspa'ßjento] *nm* exaggerated display of feeling; (*fam*) fuss.

aspecto [as'pekto] *nm* (*apariencia*) look, appearance; (*fig*) aspect; **bajo ese** ~ from that point of view.

aspereza [aspe'reθa] *nf* roughness; (*de fruta*) sharpness; (*de carácter*) surliness.

áspero, a ['aspero, a] *adj* rough; sharp; harsh.

aspersión [asper'sjon] *nf* sprinkling; (*AGR*) spraying.

aspersor [asper'sor] *nm* sprinkler.

aspiración [aspira'θjon] *nf* breath, inhalation; (*MUS*) short pause; **aspiraciones** *nfpl* aspirations.

aspiradora [aspira'ðora] *nf* vacuum cleaner, Hoover ®.

aspirante [aspi'rante] *nm/f* (*candidato*) candidate; (*DEPORTE*) contender.

aspirar [aspi'rar] *vt* to breathe in ♦ *vi*: ~ **a** to aspire to.

aspirina [aspi'rina] *nf* aspirin.

asquear [aske'ar] *vt* to sicken ♦ *vi* to be sickening; ~**se** *vr* to feel disgusted.

asquerosidad [askerosi'ðað] *nf* (*suciedad*) filth; (*dicho*) obscenity; (*truco*) dirty trick.

asqueroso, a [aske'roso, a] *adj* disgusting, sickening.

asta ['asta] *nf* lance; (*arpón*) spear; (*mango*) shaft, handle; (*ZOOL*) horn; **a media** ~ at half mast.

astado, a [as'taðo, a] *adj* horned ♦ *nm* bull.

asterisco [aste'risko] *nm* asterisk.

asteroide [aste'roiðe] *nm* asteroid.

astigmatismo [astiɣma'tismo] *nm* astigmatism.

astilla [as'tiʎa] *nf* splinter; (*pedacito*) chip; ~**s** *nfpl* firewood *sg*.

astillarse [asti'ʎarse] *vr* to splinter; (*fig*) to shatter.

astillero [asti'ʎero] *nm* shipyard.

astringente [astrin'xente] *adj, nm* astringent.

astro ['astro] *nm* star.

astrología [astrolo'xia] *nf* astrology.

astrólogo, a [as'troloɣo, a] *nm/f* astrologer.

astronauta [astro'nauta] *nm/f* astronaut.

astronave [astro'naße] *nm* spaceship.

astronomía [astrono'mia] *nf* astronomy.

astronómico, a [astro'nomiko, a] *adj* (*tb fig*) astronomical.

astrónomo, a [as'tronomo, a] *nm/f*

astronomer.

astroso, a [as'troso, a] *adj* (*desaliñado*) untidy; (*vil*) contemptible.

astucia [as'tuθja] *nf* astuteness; (*destreza*) clever trick.

asturiano, a [astu'rjano, a] *adj, nm/f* Asturian.

Asturias [as'turjas] *nfpl* Asturias; **Príncipe de** ~ crown prince.

astuto, a [as'tuto, a] *adj* astute; (*taimado*) cunning.

asueto [a'sweto] *nm* holiday; (*tiempo libre*) time off; **día de** ~ day off; **tarde de** ~ (*trabajo*) afternoon off; (*ESCOL*) half-holiday.

asumir [asu'mir] *vt* to assume.

asunción [asun'θjon] *nf* assumption.

asunto [a'sunto] *nm* (*tema*) matter, subject; (*negocio*) business; ¡**eso es** ~ **mio!** that's my business!; ~**s exteriores** foreign affairs; ~**s a tratar** agenda *sg*.

asustadizo, a [asusta'ðiθo, a] *adj* easily frightened.

asustar [asus'tar] *vt* to frighten; ~**se** *vr* to be/become frightened.

atacante [ata'kante] *nm/f* attacker.

atacar [ata'kar] *vt* to attack.

atadura [ata'ðura] *nf* bond, tie.

atajar [ata'xar] *vt* (*gen*) to stop; (*ruta de fuga*) to cut off; (*discurso*) to interrupt ♦ *vi* to take a short cut.

atajo [a'taxo] *nm* short cut; (*DEPORTE*) tackle.

atalaya [ata'laja] *nf* watchtower.

atañer [ata'ɲer] *vi*: ~ **a** to concern; **en lo que atañe a eso** with regard to this.

ataque [a'take] *etc vb V* **atacar** ♦ *nm* attack; ~ **cardíaco** heart attack.

atar [a'tar] *vt* to tie, tie up; ~ **la lengua a algn** (*fig*) to silence sb.

atardecer [atarðe'θer] *vi* to get dark ♦ *nm* evening; (*crepúsculo*) dusk.

atardezca [atar'ðeθka] *etc vb V* **atardecer.**

atareado, a [atare'aðo, a] *adj* busy.

atascar [atas'kar] *vt* to clog up; (*obstruir*) to jam; (*fig*) to hinder; ~**se** *vr* to stall; (*cañería*) to get blocked up; (*fig*) to get bogged down; (*en discurso*) to dry up.

atasco [a'tasko] *nm* obstruction; (*AUTO*) traffic jam.

atasque [a'taske] *etc vb V* **atascar.**

ataúd [ata'uð] *nm* coffin.

ataviar [ata'ßjar] *vt* to deck, array; ~**se** *vr* to dress up.

atavío [ata'ßio] *nm* attire, dress; ~**s** *nmpl* finery *sg*.

ateísmo [ate'ismo] *nm* atheism.

atemorice [atemo'riθe] *etc vb V* **atemorizar.**

atemorizar [atemori'θar] *vt* to frighten, scare; ~**se** *vr* to get frightened *o* scared.

Atenas [a'tenas] *nf* Athens.

atención [aten'θjon] *nf* attention; (*bondad*) kindness ♦ *excl* (be) careful!, look out!; **en** ~ **a esto** in view of this.

atender [aten'der] *vt* to attend to, look after; (*TEC*) to service; (*enfermo*) to care for; (*ruego*) to comply with ♦ *vi* to pay attention; ~ **a** to attend to; (*detalles*) to take care of.

atendré [aten'dre] *etc vb V* **atenerse.**

atenerse [ate'nerse] *vr*: ~ **a** to abide by, adhere to.

atenga [a'tenga] *etc vb V* **atenerse.**

ateniense [ate'njense] *adj, nm/f* Athenian.

atentado [aten'taðo] *nm* crime, illegal act; (*asalto*) assault; (*terrorista*) attack; ~ **contra la vida de algn** attempt on sb's life; ~ **golpista** (*POL*) attempted coup.

atentamente [atenta'mente] *adv*: **le saluda** ~ Yours faithfully.

atentar [aten'tar] *vi*: ~ **a** *o* **contra** to commit an outrage against.

atento, a [a'tento, a] *adj* attentive, observant; (*cortés*) polite, thoughtful; **su atenta (carta)** (*COM*) your letter.

atenuante [ate'nwante] *adj*: **circunstancias** ~**s** extenuating *o* mitigating circumstances ♦ *nmpl*: ~**s** extenuating *o* mitigating circumstances.

atenuar [ate'nwar] *vt* to attenuate; (*disminuir*) to lessen, minimize.

ateo, a [a'teo, a] *adj* atheistic ♦ *nm/f* atheist.

aterciopelado, a [aterθjope'laðo, a] *adj* velvety.

aterido, a [ate'riðo, a] *adj*: ~ **de frío** frozen stiff.

aterrador, a [aterra'ðor, a] *adj* frightening.

aterrar [ate'rrar] *vt* to frighten; (*aterrorizar*) to terrify; ~**se** *vr* to be frightened; to be terrified.

aterrice [ate'rriθe] *etc vb V* **aterrizar.**

aterrizaje [aterri'θaxe] *nm* landing; ~ **forzoso** forced landing.

aterrizar [aterri'θar] *vi* to land.

aterrorice [aterro'riθe] *etc vb V* **aterrorizar.**

aterrorizar [aterrori'θar] *vt* to terrify.

atesorar [ateso'rar] *vt* to hoard, store up.

atestado, a [ates'taðo, a] *adj* packed ♦ *nm* (*JUR*) affidavit.

atestar [ates'tar] *vt* to pack, stuff; (*JUR*) to attest, testify to.

atestiguar [atesti'ɣwar] *vt* to testify to, bear witness to.

atestigüe [ates'tiɣwe] *etc vb V* **atestiguar.**

atiborrar [atiβo'rrar] *vt* to fill, stuff; ~**se** *vr* to stuff o.s.

atice [a'tiθe] *etc vb V* **atizar.**

ático ['atiko] *nm* attic; ~ **de lujo** penthouse flat.

atienda [a'tjenda] *etc vb V* **atender.**

atildar [atil'dar] *vt* to criticize; (*TIP*) to put a tilde over; ~**se** *vr* to spruce o.s. up.

atinado, a [ati'naðo, a] *adj* correct; (*sensato*) sensible.

atinar [ati'nar] *vi* (*acertar*) to be right; ~ **con** *o* **en** (*solución*) to hit upon; ~ **a hacer** to manage to do.

atípico, a [a'tipiko, a] *adj* atypical.

atiplado, a [ati'plaðo, a] *adj* (*voz*) high-pitched.

atisbar [atis'βar] *vt* to spy on; (*echar ojeada*) to peep at.

atizar [ati'θar] *vt* to poke; (*horno etc*) to stoke; (*fig*) to stir up, rouse.

atlántico, a [at'lantiko, a] *adj* Atlantic ♦ *nm*: **el (océano) A~** the Atlantic (Ocean).

atlas ['atlas] *nm* atlas.

atleta [at'leta] *nm/f* athlete.

atlético, a [at'letiko, a] *adj* athletic.

atletismo [atle'tismo] *nm* athletics *sg.*

atmósfera [at'mosfera] *nf* atmosphere.

atmosférico, a [atmos'feriko, a] *adj* atmospheric.

atol(e) [a'tol(e)] *nm* (*AM*) cornflour drink.

atolladero [atoʎa'ðero] *nm*: **estar en un ~** to be in a jam.

atollarse [ato'ʎarse] *vr* to get stuck; (*fig*) to get into a jam.

atolondrado, a [atolon'draðo, a] *adj* scatterbrained.

atolondramiento [atolondra'mjento] *nm* bewilderment; (*insensatez*) silliness.

atómico, a [a'tomiko, a] *adj* atomic.

atomizador [atomiθa'ðor] *nm* atomizer.

átomo ['atomo] *nm* atom.

atónito, a [a'tonito, a] *adj* astonished, amazed.

atontado, a [aton'taðo, a] *adj* stunned; (*bobo*) silly, daft.

atontar [aton'tar] *vt* to stun; ~**se** *vr* to become confused.

atorar [ato'rar] *vt* to obstruct; ~**se** *vr* (*atragantarse*) to choke.

atormentar [atormen'tar] *vt* to torture; (*molestar*) to torment; (*acosar*) to plague, harass.

atornillar [atorni'ʎar] *vt* to screw on *o* down.

atorón [ato'ron] *nm* (*AM*) traffic jam.

atosigar [atosi'ɣar] *vt* to harass.

atosigue [ato'siɣe] *etc vb V* **atosigar.**

atrabiliario, a [atraβi'ljarjo, a] *adj* bad-tempered.

atracadero [atraka'ðero] *nm* pier.

atracador, a [atraka'ðor, a] *nm/f* robber.

atracar [atra'kar] *vt* (*NAUT*) to moor; (*robar*) to hold up, rob ♦ *vi* to moor; ~**se** *vr* (*hartarse*) to stuff o.s.

atracción [atrak'θjon] *nf* attraction.

atraco [a'trako] *nm* holdup, robbery.

atracón [atra'kon] *nm*: **darse** *o* **pegarse un ~ (de)** (*fam*) to pig out (on).

atractivo, a [atrak'tiβo, a] *adj* attractive ♦ *nm* attraction; (*belleza*) attractiveness.

atraer [atra'er] *vt* to attract; **dejarse ~ por** to be tempted by.

atragantarse [atraɣan'tarse] *vr*: ~ **(con algo)** to choke (on sth); **se me ha atragantado el chico ese/el inglés** I don't take to that boy/English.

atraiga [a'traiɣa] *etc*, **atraje** [a'traxe] *etc vb V* **atraer.**

atrancar [atran'kar] *vt* (*con tranca, barra*) to bar, bolt.

atranque [a'tranke] *etc vb V* **atrancar.**

atrapar [atra'par] *vt* to trap; (*resfriado etc*) to catch.

atraque [a'trake] *etc vb V* **atracar.**

atrás [a'tras] *adv* (*movimiento*) back(wards); (*lugar*) behind; (*tiempo*) previously; **ir hacia ~** to go back(wards); to go to the rear; **estar ~** to be behind *o* at the back.

atrasado, a [atra'saðo, a] *adj* slow; (*pago*) overdue, late; (*país*) backward.

atrasar [atra'sar] *vi* to be slow; ~**se** *vr* to remain behind; (*llegar tarde*) to arrive late.

atraso [a'traso] *nm* slowness; lateness, delay; (*de país*) backwardness; ~**s** *nmpl* arrears.

atravesado, a [atraβe'saðo, a] *adj*: **un tronco ~ en la carretera** a tree trunk lying across the road.

atravesar [atraβe'sar] *vt* (*cruzar*) to cross (over); (*traspasar*) to pierce; (*período*) to go through; (*poner al través*) to lay *o* put across; ~**se** *vr* to come in between; (*intervenir*) to interfere.

atraviese [atra'βjese] *etc vb V* **atravesar.**

atrayendo [atra'jendo] *vb V* **atraer.**

atrayente [atra'jente] *adj* attractive.

atreverse [atre'βerse] *vr* to dare; (*insolentarse*) to be insolent.

atrevido, a [atre'βiðo, a] *adj* daring; insolent.

atrevimiento [atreβi'mjento] *nm* daring; insolence.

atribución [atriβu'θjon] *nf* (*LIT*) attribution; **atribuciones** *nfpl* (*POL*) functions; (*ADMIN*)

responsibilities.
atribuir [atriβu'ir] *vt* to attribute;
(*funciones*) to confer.
atribular [atriβu'lar] *vt* to afflict, distress.
atributo [atri'βuto] *nm* attribute.
atribuya [atri'βuja] *etc*, **atribuyendo**
[atriβu'jendo] *etc vb V* **atribuir**.
atril [a'tril] *nm* lectern; (*MUS*) music stand.
atrincherarse [atrintʃe'rarse] *vr* (*MIL*) to
dig (o.s.) in; ~ **en** (*fig*) to hide behind.
atrio ['atrjo] *nm* (*REL*) porch.
atrocidad [atroθi'ðað] *nf* atrocity, outrage.
atrofiado, a [atro'fjaðo, a] *adj* (*extremidad*)
withered.
atrofiarse [atro'fjarse] *vr* (*tb fig*) to
atrophy.
atronador, a [atrona'ðor, a] *adj* deafening.
atropellar [atrope'ʎar] *vt* (*derribar*) to
knock over *o* down; (*empujar*) to push
(aside); (*AUTO*) to run over *o* down;
(*agraviar*) to insult; ~**se** *vr* to act hastily.
atropello [atro'peʎo] *nm* (*AUTO*) accident;
(*empujón*) push; (*agravio*) wrong;
(*atrocidad*) outrage.
atroz [a'troθ] *adj* atrocious, awful.
A.T.S. *nm/f abr* (= *Ayudante Técnico
Sanitario*) nurse.
atto., a. *abr* (= *atento, a*) Yours faithfully.
attrezzo [a'treθo] *nm* props *pl*.
atuendo [a'twendo] *nm* attire.
atufar [atu'far] *vt* (*suj: olor*) to overcome;
(*molestar*) to irritate; ~**se** *vr* (*fig*) to get
cross.
atún [a'tun] *nm* tuna, tunny.
aturdir [atur'ðir] *vt* to stun; (*suj: ruido*) to
deafen; (*fig*) to dumbfound, bewilder.
atur(r)ullar [atur(r)u'ʎar] *vt* to bewilder.
atusar [atu'sar] *vt* (*cortar*) to trim; (*alisar*)
to smooth (down).
atuve [a'tuβe] *etc vb V* **atenerse**.
audacia [au'ðaθja] *nf* boldness, audacity.
audaz [au'ðaθ] *adj* bold, audacious.
audible [au'ðiβle] *adj* audible.
audición [auði'θjon] *nf* hearing; (*TEAT*)
audition; ~ **radiofónica** radio concert.
audiencia [au'ðjenθja] *nf* audience; (*JUR*)
high court; (*POL*): ~ **pública** public
inquiry.
audífono [au'ðifono] *nm* hearing aid.
audiovisual [auðjoβi'swal] *adj* audiovisual.
auditivo, a [auði'tiβo, a] *adj* hearing *cpd*;
(*conducto, nervio*) auditory.
auditor [auði'tor] *nm* (*JUR*) judge-
advocate; (*COM*) auditor.
auditoría [auðito'ria] *nf* audit; (*profesión*)
auditing.
auditorio [auði'torjo] *nm* audience; (*sala*)
auditorium.
auge ['auxe] *nm* boom; (*clímax*) climax;
(*ECON*) expansion; **estar en** ~ to thrive.
augurar [auɣu'rar] *vt* to predict; (*presagiar*)
to portend.
augurio [au'ɣurjo] *nm* omen.
aula ['aula] *nf* classroom.
aullar [au'ʎar] *vi* to howl, yell.
aullido [au'ʎiðo] *nm* howl, yell.
aumentar [aumen'tar] *vt* to increase;
(*precios*) to put up; (*producción*) to step
up; (*con microscopio, anteojos*) to magnify
♦ *vi*, ~**se** *vr* to increase, be on the
increase.
aumento [au'mento] *nm* increase; rise.
aún [a'un] *adv* still, yet.
aun [a'un] *adv* even.
aunque [a'unke] *conj* though, although,
even though.
aúpa [a'upa] *excl* up!, come on!; (*fam*): **una
función de** ~ a slap-up do; **una paliza de**
~ a good hiding.
aupar [au'par] *vt* (*levantar*) to help up; (*fig*)
to praise.
aura ['aura] *nf* (*atmósfera*) aura.
aureola [aure'ola] *nf* halo.
auricular [auriku'lar] *nm* earpiece,
receiver; ~**es** *nmpl* headphones.
aurora [au'rora] *nf* dawn; ~ **boreal(is)**
northern lights *pl*.
auscultar [auskul'tar] *vt* (*MED: pecho*) to
listen to, sound.
ausencia [au'senθja] *nf* absence.
ausentarse [ausen'tarse] *vr* to go away;
(*por poco tiempo*) to go out.
ausente [au'sente] *adj* absent ♦ *nm/f*
(*ESCOL*) absentee; (*JUR*) missing person.
auspiciar [auspi'sjar] *vt* (*AM*) to back,
sponsor.
auspicios [aus'piθjos] *nmpl* auspices;
(*protección*) protection *sg*.
austeridad [austeri'ðað] *nf* austerity.
austero, a [aus'tero, a] *adj* austere.
austral [aus'tral] *adj* southern ♦ *nm*
monetary unit of Argentina (*1985-1991*).
Australia [aus'tralja] *nf* Australia.
australiano, a [austra'ljano, a] *adj, nm/f*
Australian.
Austria ['austrja] *nf* Austria.
austriaco, a [aus'trjako, a], **austríaco, a**
[aus'triako, a] *adj, nm/f* Austrian.
autenticar [autenti'kar] *vt* to authenticate.
auténtico, a [au'tentiko, a] *adj* authentic.
autentificar [autentifi'kar] *vt* to
authenticate.
autentique [auten'tike] *etc vb V* **autenticar**.
auto ['auto] *nm* (*coche*) car; (*JUR*) edict,
decree; (*: orden*) writ; ~**s** *nmpl* (*JUR*)

proceedings; (: *acta*) court record *sg*; ~ **de comparecencia** summons, subpoena; ~ **de ejecución** writ of execution.

autoadhesivo, a [autoaðe'sißo, a] *adj* self-adhesive; (*sobre*) self-sealing.

autoalimentación [autoalimenta'θjon] *nf* (*INFORM*): ~ **de hojas** automatic paper feed.

autobiografía [autoßjoɣra'fia] *nf* autobiography.

autobús [auto'ßus] *nm* bus (*BRIT*), (passenger) bus (*US*).

autocar [auto'kar] *nm* coach; ~ **de línea** intercity coach.

autocomprobación [autokomproßa'θjon] *nf* (*INFORM*) self-test.

autóctono, a [au'toktono, a] *adj* native, indigenous.

autodefensa [autoðe'fensa] *nf* self-defence.

autodeterminación [autoðetermina'θjon] *nf* self-determination.

autodidacta [autoði'ðakta] *adj* self-taught ♦ *nm/f*: **ser un(a)** ~ to be self-taught.

autoescuela [autoes'kwela] *nf* driving school.

autofinanciado, a [autofinan'θjaðo, a] *adj* self-financing.

autogestión [autoxes'tjon] *nf* self-management.

autógrafo [au'toɣrafo] *nm* autograph.

automación [automa'θjon] *nf* = **automatización.**

autómata [au'tomata] *nm* automaton.

automáticamente [auto'matikamente] *adv* automatically.

automatice [automa'tiθe] *etc vb V* **automatizar.**

automático, a [auto'matiko, a] *adj* automatic ♦ *nm* press stud.

automatización [automatiθa'θjon] *nf*: ~ **de fábricas** factory automation; ~ **de oficinas** office automation.

automatizar [automati'θar] *vt* to automate.

automotor, triz [automo'tor, 'triz] *adj* self-propelled ♦ *nm* diesel train.

automóvil [auto'moßil] *nm* (motor) car (*BRIT*), automobile (*US*).

automovilismo [automoßi'lismo] *nm* (*DEPORTE*) (sports) car racing.

automovilista [automoßi'lista] *nm/f* motorist, driver.

automovilístico, a [automoßi'listiko, a] *adj* (*industria*) car *cpd*.

autonomía [autono'mia] *nf* autonomy; (*ESP POL*) autonomy, self-government; (: *comunidad*) autonomous region.

autonómico, a [auto'nomiko, a] *adj* (*ESP*

POL) relating to autonomy, autonomous; **gobierno** ~ autonomous government.

autónomo, a [au'tonomo, a] *adj* autonomous; (*INFORM*) stand-alone, offline.

autopista [auto'pista] *nf* motorway (*BRIT*), freeway (*US*).

autopsia [au'topsja] *nf* autopsy.

autor, a [au'tor, a] *nm/f* author; **los ~es del atentado** those responsible for the attack.

autorice [auto'riθe] *etc vb V* **autorizar.**

autoridad [autori'ðað] *nf* authority; ~ **local** local authority.

autoritario, a [autori'tarjo, a] *adj* authoritarian.

autorización [autoriθa'θjon] *nf* authorization.

autorizado, a [autori'θaðo, a] *adj* authorized; (*aprobado*) approved.

autorizar [autori'θar] *vt* to authorize; to approve.

autorretrato [autorre'trato] *nm* self-portrait.

autoservicio [autoser'ßiθjo] *nm* self-service shop *o* store; (*restaurante*) self-service restaurant.

autostop [auto'stop] *nm* hitch-hiking; **hacer** ~ to hitch-hike.

autostopista [autosto'pista] *nm/f* hitch-hiker.

autosuficiencia [autosufi'θjenθja] *nf* self-sufficiency.

autosuficiente [autosufi'θjente] *adj* self-sufficient; (*pey*) smug.

autosugestión [autosuxes'tjon] *nf* autosuggestion.

autovía [auto'ßia] *nf* ≈ dual carriageway (*BRIT*), separated highway (*US*).

auxiliar [auksi'ljar] *vt* to help ♦ *nm/f* assistant.

auxilio [auk'siljo] *nm* assistance, help; **primeros ~s** first aid *sg*.

Av *abr* (= *Avenida*) Av(e).

a/v *abr* (*COM*: = *a vista*) at sight.

aval [a'ßal] *nm* guarantee; (*persona*) guarantor.

avalancha [aßa'lantʃa] *nf* avalanche.

avalar [aßa'lar] *vt* (*COM etc*) to underwrite; (*fig*) to endorse.

avalista [aßa'lista] *nm* (*COM*) endorser.

avance [a'ßanθe] *etc vb V* **avanzar** ♦ *nm* advance; (*pago*) advance payment; (*CINE*) trailer.

avanzado, a [aßan'θaðo, a] *adj* advanced; **de edad avanzada,** ~ **de edad** elderly.

avanzar [aßan'θar] *vt, vi* to advance.

avaricia [aßa'riθja] *nf* avarice, greed.

avaricioso, a [aβari'θjoso, a] *adj* avaricious, greedy.

avaro, a [a'βaro, a] *adj* miserly, mean ♦ *nm/f* miser.

avasallar [aβasa'ʎar] *vt* to subdue, subjugate.

avatar [aβa'tar] *nm* change; ~**es** ups and downs.

Avda *abr* (= *Avenida*) Av(e).

AVE ['aβe] *nm abr* (= *Alta Velocidad Española*) ≈ Bullet train.

ave ['aβe] *nf* bird; ~ **de rapiña** bird of prey.

avecinarse [aβeθi'narse] *vr* (*tormenta, fig*) to approach, be on the way.

avejentar [aβexen'tar] *vt, vi,* ~**se** *vr* to age.

avellana [aβe'ʎana] *nf* hazelnut.

avellano [aβe'ʎano] *nm* hazel tree.

avemaría [aβema'ria] *nm* Hail Mary, Ave Maria.

avena [a'βena] *nf* oats *pl.*

avendré [aβen'dre] *etc,* **avenga** [a'βenga] *etc vb V* **avenir.**

avenida [aβe'niða] *nf* (*calle*) avenue.

avenir [aβe'nir] *vt* to reconcile; ~**se** *vr* to come to an agreement, reach a compromise.

aventado, a [aβen'taðo, a] *adj* (*AM*) daring.

aventajado, a [aβenta'xaðo, a] *adj* outstanding.

aventajar [aβenta'xar] *vt* (*sobrepasar*) to surpass, outstrip.

aventar [aβen'tar] *vt* to fan, blow; (*grano*) to winnow; (*AM fam: echar*) to chuck out.

aventón [aβen'ton] *nm* (*AM*) push; **pedir** ~ to hitch a lift.

aventura [aβen'tura] *nf* adventure; ~ **sentimental** love affair.

aventurado, a [aβentu'raðo, a] *adj* risky.

aventurar [aβentu'rar] *vt* to risk; ~**se** *vr* to dare; ~**se a hacer algo** to venture to do sth.

aventurero, a [aβentu'rero, a] *adj* adventurous.

avergoncé [aβerɣon'θe], **avergoncemos** [aβerɣon'θemos] *etc vb V* **avergonzar.**

avergonzar [aβerɣon'θar] *vt* to shame; (*desconcertar*) to embarrass; ~**se** *vr* to be ashamed; to be embarrassed.

avergüence [aβer'ɣwenθe] *etc vb V* **avergonzar.**

avería [aβe'ria] *nf* (*TEC*) breakdown, fault.

averiado, a [aβe'rjaðo, a] *adj* broken-down.

averiar [aβe'rjar] *vt* to break; ~**se** *vr* to break down.

averiguación [aβeriɣwa'θjon] *nf* investigation; (*determinación*) ascertainment.

averiguar [aβeri'ɣwar] *vt* to investigate; (*descubrir*) to find out, ascertain.

averigüe [aβe'riɣwe] *etc vb V* **averiguar.**

aversión [aβer'sjon] *nf* aversion, dislike; **cobrar** ~ **a** to take a strong dislike to.

avestruz [aβes'truθ] *nm* ostrich.

aviación [aβja'θjon] *nf* aviation; (*fuerzas aéreas*) air force.

aviado, a [a'βjaðo, a] *adj*: **estar** ~ to be in a mess.

aviador, a [aβja'ðor, a] *nm/f* aviator, airman/woman.

aviar [a'βjar] *vt* to prepare, get ready.

avícola [a'βikola] *adj* poultry *cpd.*

avicultura [aβikul'tura] *nf* poultry farming.

avidez [aβi'ðeθ] *nf* avidity, eagerness.

ávido, a ['aβiðo, a] *adj* avid, eager.

aviente [a'βjente] *etc vb V* **aventar.**

avieso, a [a'βjeso, a] *adj* (*torcido*) distorted; (*perverso*) wicked.

avinagrado, a [aβina'ɣraðo, a] *adj* sour, acid.

avinagrarse [aβina'ɣrarse] *vr* to go *o* turn sour.

avine [a'βine] *etc vb V* **avenir.**

Aviñón [aβi'ɲon] *nm* Avignon.

avío [a'βio] *nm* preparation; ~**s** *nmpl* gear *sg*, kit *sg.*

avión [a'βjon] *nm* aeroplane; (*ave*) martin; ~ **de reacción** jet (plane); **por** ~ (*CORREOS*) by air mail.

avioneta [aβjo'neta] *nf* light aircraft.

avisar [aβi'sar] *vt* (*advertir*) to warn, notify; (*informar*) to tell; (*aconsejar*) to advise, counsel.

aviso [a'βiso] *nm* warning; (*noticia*) notice; (*COM*) demand note; (*INFORM*) prompt; ~ **escrito** notice in writing; **sin previo** ~ without warning; **estar sobre** ~ to be on the look-out.

avispa [a'βispa] *nf* wasp.

avispado, a [aβis'paðo, a] *adj* sharp, clever.

avispero [aβis'pero] *nm* wasp's nest.

avispón [aβis'pon] *nm* hornet.

avistar [aβis'tar] *vt* to sight, spot.

avitaminosis [aβitami'nosis] *nf inv* vitamin deficiency.

avituallar [aβitwa'ʎar] *vt* to supply with food.

avivar [aβi'βar] *vt* to strengthen, intensify; ~**se** *vr* to revive, acquire new life.

avizor [aβi'θor] *adj*: **estar ojo** ~ to be on the alert.

avizorar [aβiθo'rar] *vt* to spy on.

axila [ak'sila] *nf* armpit.

axioma [ak'sjoma] *nm* axiom.

ay [ai] *excl* (*dolor*) ow!, ouch!; (*aflicción*)

oh!, oh dear!; ¡~ **de mí!** poor me!

aya ['aja] *nf* governess; (*niñera*) nanny.

ayer [a'jer] *adv, nm* yesterday; **antes de ~** the day before yesterday; **~ por la tarde** yesterday afternoon/evening.

aymara, aymará [ai'mara, aima'ra] *adj, nm/f* Aymara.

ayo ['ajo] *nm* tutor.

ayote [a'jote] *nm* (*AM*) pumpkin.

Ayto. *abr* = **Ayuntamiento.**

ayuda [a'juða] *nf* help, assistance; (*MED*) enema ◆ *nm* page; **~ humanitaria** humanitarian aid.

ayudante, a [aju'ðante, a] *nm/f* assistant, helper; (*ESCOL*) assistant; (*MIL*) adjutant.

ayudar [aju'ðar] *vt* to help, assist.

ayunar [aju'nar] *vi* to fast.

ayunas [a'junas] *nfpl*: **estar en ~** (*no haber comido*) to be fasting; (*ignorar*) to be in the dark.

ayuno [a'juno] *nm* fasting.

ayuntamiento [ajunta'mjento] *nm* (*consejo*) town/city council; (*edificio*) town/city hall; (*cópula*) sexual intercourse.

azabache [aθa'βatʃe] *nm* jet.

azada [a'θaða] *nf* hoe.

azafata [aθa'fata] *nf* air hostess (*BRIT*) *o* stewardess.

azafate [asa'fate] *nm* (*AM*) tray.

azafrán [aθa'fran] *nm* saffron.

azahar [aθa'ar] *nm* orange/lemon blossom.

azalea [aθa'lea] *nf* azalea.

azar [a'θar] *nm* (*casualidad*) chance, fate; (*desgracia*) misfortune, accident; **por ~** by chance; **al ~** at random.

azaroso, a [aθa'roso, a] *adj* (*arriesgado*) risky; (*vida*) eventful.

Azerbaiyán [aθerba'jan] *nm* Azerbaijan.

azerbaiyano, a [aθerba'jano, a], **azerí** [aθe'ri] *adj, nm/f* Azerbaijani, Azeri.

azogue [a'θoɣe] *nm* mercury.

azor [a'θor] *nm* goshawk.

azoramiento [aθora'mjento] *nm* alarm; (*confusión*) confusion.

azorar [aθo'rar] *vt* to alarm; **~se** *vr* to get alarmed.

Azores [a'θores] *nfpl*: **las (Islas) ~** the Azores.

azotaina [aθo'taina] *nf* beating.

azotar [aθo'tar] *vt* to whip, beat; (*pegar*) to spank.

azote [a'θote] *nm* (*látigo*) whip; (*latigazo*) lash, stroke; (*en las nalgas*) spank; (*calamidad*) calamity.

azotea [aθo'tea] *nf* (flat) roof.

azteca [aθ'teka] *adj, nm/f* Aztec.

azúcar [a'θukar] *nm* sugar.

azucarado, a [aθuka'raðo, a] *adj* sugary, sweet.

azucarero, a [aθuka'rero, a] *adj* sugar *cpd* ◆ *nm* sugar bowl.

azuce [a'θuθe] *etc vb V* **azuzar.**

azucena [aθu'θena] *nf* white lily.

azufre [a'θufre] *nm* sulphur.

azul [a'θul] *adj, nm* blue; **~ celeste/marino** sky/navy blue.

azulejo [aθu'lexo] *nm* tile.

azulgrana [aθul'ɣrana] *adj inv* of Barcelona Football Club ◆ *nm*: **los A~** the Barcelona F.C. players *o* team.

azuzar [aθu'θar] *vt* to incite, egg on.

B b

B, b [(*ESP*) be, (*AM*) be'larɣa] *nf* (*letra*) B, b; **B de Barcelona** B for Benjamin (*BRIT*) *o* Baker (*US*).

baba ['baβa] *nf* spittle, saliva; **se le caía la ~** (*fig*) he was thrilled to bits.

babear [baβe'ar] *vi* (*echar saliva*) to slobber; (*niño*) to dribble; (*fig*) to drool, slaver.

babel [ba'βel] *nm o f* bedlam.

babero [ba'βero] *nm* bib.

Babia ['baβja] *nf*: **estar en ~** to be daydreaming.

bable ['baβle] *nm* Asturian (dialect).

babor [ba'βor] *nm* port (side); **a ~** to port.

babosada [baβo'saða] *nf*: **decir ~s** (*AM fam*) to talk rubbish.

baboso, a [ba'βoso, a] *adj* slobbering; (*ZOOL*) slimy; (*AM*) silly ◆ *nm/f* (*AM*) fool.

babucha [ba'βutʃa] *nf* slipper.

baca ['baka] *nf* (*AUTO*) luggage *o* roof rack.

bacalao [baka'lao] *nm* cod(fish).

bacanal [baka'nal] *nf* orgy.

bache ['batʃe] *nm* pothole, rut; (*fig*) bad patch.

bachillerato [batʃiʎe'rato] *nm* 2 year *secondary school course*; *V tb* **sistema educativo.**

bacilo [ba'θilo] *nm* bacillus, germ.

bacinica [baθi'nika] *nf*, **bacinilla** [baθi'niʎa] *nf* chamber pot.

bacteria [bak'terja] *nf* bacterium, germ.

bacteriológico, a [bakterjo'loxico, a] *adj* bacteriological; **guerra ~a** germ warfare.

báculo ['bakulo] *nm* stick, staff; (*fig*) support.
badajo [ba'ðaxo] *nm* clapper (*of a bell*).
bádminton ['baðminton] *nm* badminton.
baf(f)le ['baf(f)le] *nm* (*ELEC*) speaker.
bagaje [ba'ɣaxe] *nm* baggage; (*fig*) background.
bagatela [baɣa'tela] *nf* trinket, trifle.
Bahama [ba'ama]: **las (Islas) ~, las ~s** *nfpl* the Bahamas.
bahía [ba'ia] *nf* bay.
bailar [bai'lar] *vt, vi* to dance.
bailarín, ina [baila'rin, ina] *nm/f* dancer; (*de ballet*) ballet dancer.
baile ['baile] *nm* dance; (*formal*) ball.
baja ['baxa] *nf* drop, fall; (*ECON*) slump; (*MIL*) casualty; (*paro*) redundancy; **dar de ~** (*soldado*) to discharge; (*empleado*) to dismiss, sack; **darse de ~** (*retirarse*) to drop out; (*MED*) to go sick; (*dimitir*) to resign; **estar de ~** (*enfermo*) to be off sick; (*BOLSA*) to be dropping *o* falling; **jugar a la ~** (*ECON*) to speculate on a fall in prices; *V tb* **bajo**.
bajada [ba'xaða] *nf* descent; (*camino*) slope; (*de aguas*) ebb.
bajamar [baxa'mar] *nf* low tide.
bajar [ba'xar] *vi* to go *o* come down; (*temperatura, precios*) to drop, fall ♦ *vt* (*cabeza*) to bow; (*escalera*) to go *o* come down; (*radio etc*) to turn down; (*precio, voz*) to lower; (*llevar abajo*) to take down; **~se** *vr* (*de vehículo*) to get out; (*de autobús*) to get off; **~ de** (*coche*) to get out of; (*autobús*) to get off; **~le los humos a algn** (*fig*) to cut sb down to size.
bajeza [ba'xeθa] *nf* baseness; (*una ~*) vile deed.
bajío [ba'xio] *nm* shoal, sandbank; (*AM*) lowlands *pl*.
bajista [ba'xista] *nm/f* (*MUS*) bassist ♦ *adj* (*BOLSA*) bear *cpd*.
bajo, a ['baxo, a] *adj* (*terreno*) low(-lying); (*mueble, número, precio*) low; (*piso*) ground *cpd*; (*de estatura*) small, short; (*color*) pale; (*sonido*) faint, soft, low; (*voz, tono*) deep; (*metal*) base ♦ *adv* (*hablar*) softly, quietly; (*volar*) low ♦ *prep* under, below, underneath ♦ *nm* (*MUS*) bass; **hablar en voz baja** to whisper; **~ la lluvia** in the rain.
bajón [ba'xon] *nm* fall, drop.
bajura [ba'xura] *nf*: **pesca de ~** coastal fishing.
bakalao [baka'lao] *nm* (*MUS*) rave music.
bala ['bala] *nf* bullet; **~ de goma** plastic bullet.
balacera [bala'sera] *nf* (*AM*) shoot-out.

balada [ba'laða] *nf* ballad.
baladí [bala'ði] *adj* trivial.
baladronada [balaðro'naða] *nf* (*dicho*) boast, brag; (*hecho*) piece of bravado.
balance [ba'lanθe] *nm* (*COM*) balance; (: *libro*) balance sheet; (: *cuenta general*) stocktaking; **~ de comprobación** trial balance; **~ consolidado** consolidated balance sheet; **hacer ~** to take stock.
balancear [balanθe'ar] *vt* to balance ♦ *vi*, **~se** *vr* to swing (to and fro); (*vacilar*) to hesitate.
balanceo [balan'θeo] *nm* swinging.
balandro [ba'landro] *nm* yacht.
balanza [ba'lanθa] *nf* scales *pl*, balance; **~ comercial** balance of trade; **~ de pagos/ de poder(es)** balance of payments/of power; (*ASTRO*): **B~** Libra.
balar [ba'lar] *vi* to bleat.
balaustrada [balaus'traða] *nf* balustrade; (*pasamanos*) banister.
balazo [ba'laθo] *nm* (*tiro*) shot; (*herida*) bullet wound.
balboa [bal'ßoa] *nf* Panamanian currency unit.
balbucear [balßuθe'ar] *vi, vt* to stammer, stutter.
balbuceo [balßu'θeo] *nm* stammering, stuttering.
balbucir [balßu'θir] *vi, vt* to stammer, stutter.
balbuzca [bal'ßuθka] *etc vb V* **balbucir**.
Balcanes [bal'kanes] *nmpl*: **los (Montes) ~** the Balkans, the Balkan Mountains; **la Península de los ~** the Balkan Peninsula.
balcánico, a [bal'kaniko, a] *adj* Balkan.
balcón [bal'kon] *nm* balcony.
balda ['balda] *nf* (*estante*) shelf.
baldar [bal'dar] *vt* to cripple; (*agotar*) to exhaust.
balde ['balde] *nm* (*esp AM*) bucket, pail; **de ~** *adv* (for) free, for nothing; **en ~** *adv* in vain.
baldío, a [bal'dio, a] *adj* uncultivated; (*terreno*) waste; (*inútil*) vain ♦ *nm* wasteland.
baldosa [bal'dosa] *nf* (*azulejo*) floor tile; (*grande*) flagstone.
baldosín [baldo'sin] *nm* wall tile.
balear [bale'ar] *adj* Balearic, of the Balearic Islands ♦ *nm/f* native *o* inhabitant of the Balearic Islands ♦ *vt* (*AM*) to shoot (at).
Baleares [bale'ares] *nfpl*: **las (Islas) ~** the Balearics, the Balearic Islands.
balido [ba'liðo] *nm* bleat, bleating.
balín [ba'lin] *nm* pellet; **balines** *nmpl*

buckshot *sg.*

balística [ba'listika] *nf* ballistics *pl.*

baliza [ba'liθa] *nf (AVIAT)* beacon; *(NAUT)* buoy.

ballena [ba'ʎena] *nf* whale.

ballenero, a [baʎe'nero, a] *adj:* **industria ballenera** whaling industry ♦ *nm (pescador)* whaler; *(barco)* whaling ship.

ballesta [ba'ʎesta] *nf* crossbow; *(AUTO)* spring.

ballet, *pl* **ballets** [ba'le, ba'les] *nm* ballet.

balneario, a [balne'arjo, a] *adj:* **estación balnearia** (bathing) resort ♦ *nm* spa, health resort.

balompié [balom'pje] *nm* football.

balón [ba'lon] *nm* ball.

baloncesto [balon'θesto] *nm* basketball.

balonmano [balon'mano] *nm* handball.

balonvolea [balombo'lea] *nm* volleyball.

balsa ['balsa] *nf* raft; *(BOT)* balsa wood.

bálsamo ['balsamo] *nm* balsam, balm.

balsón [bal'son] *nm (AM)* swamp, bog.

báltico, a ['baltiko, a] *adj* Baltic; **el (Mar) B~** the Baltic (Sea).

baluarte [ba'lwarte] *nm* bastion, bulwark.

bambolearse [bambole'arse] *vr* to swing, sway; *(silla)* to wobble.

bamboleo [bambo'leo] *nm* swinging, swaying; wobbling.

bambú [bam'bu] *nm* bamboo.

banal [ba'nal] *adj* banal, trivial.

banana [ba'nana] *nf (AM)* banana.

bananal [bana'nal] *nm (AM)* banana plantation.

banano [ba'nano] *nm (AM)* banana tree.

banasta [ba'nasta] *nf* large basket, hamper.

banca ['banka] *nf (asiento)* bench; *(COM)* banking.

bancario, a [ban'karjo, a] *adj* banking *cpd,* bank *cpd;* **giro ~** bank draft.

bancarrota [banka'rrota] *nf* bankruptcy; **declararse en** *o* **hacer ~** to go bankrupt.

banco ['banko] *nm* bench; *(ESCOL)* desk; *(COM)* bank; *(GEO)* stratum; **~ comercial** *o* **mercantil** commercial bank; **~ por acciones** joint-stock bank; **~ de crédito/ de ahorros** credit/savings bank; **~ de arena** sandbank; **~ de datos** *(INFORM)* data bank; **~ de hielo** iceberg.

banda ['banda] *nf* band; *(cinta)* ribbon; *(pandilla)* gang; *(MUS)* brass band; *(NAUT)* side, edge; **la B~ Oriental** Uruguay; **~ sonora** soundtrack; **~ transportadora** conveyor belt.

bandada [ban'daða] *nf (de pájaros)* flock;

(de peces) shoal.

bandazo [ban'daθo] *nm:* **dar ~s** *(coche)* to veer from side to side.

bandeja [ban'dexa] *nf* tray; **~ de entrada/ salida** in-tray/out-tray.

bandera [ban'dera] *nf (de tela)* flag; *(estandarte)* banner; *(INFORM)* marker, flag; **izar la ~** to hoist the flag.

banderilla [bande'riʎa] *nf* banderilla; *(tapa)* savoury appetizer *(served on a cocktail stick).*

banderín [bande'rin] *nm* pennant, small flag.

banderola [bande'rola] *nf (MIL)* pennant.

bandido [ban'diðo] *nm* bandit.

bando ['bando] *nm (edicto)* edict, proclamation; *(facción)* faction; **pasar al otro ~** to change sides; **los ~s** *(REL)* the banns.

bandolera [bando'lera] *nf:* **bolsa de ~** shoulder bag.

bandolero [bando'lero] *nm* bandit, brigand.

bandoneón [bandone'on] *nm (AM)* large accordion.

BANESTO [ba'nesto] *nm abr* = *Banco Español de Crédito.*

banquero [ban'kero] *nm* banker.

banqueta [ban'keta] *nf* stool; *(AM: acera)* pavement *(BRIT),* sidewalk *(US).*

banquete [ban'kete] *nm* banquet; *(para convidados)* formal dinner; **~ de boda** wedding breakfast.

banquillo [ban'kiʎo] *nm (JUR)* dock, prisoner's bench; *(banco)* bench; *(para los pies)* footstool.

bañadera [baɲa'ðera] *nf (AM)* bath(tub).

bañado [ba'ɲaðo] *nm (AM)* swamp.

bañador [baɲa'ðor] *nm* swimming costume *(BRIT),* bathing suit *(US).*

bañar [ba'ɲar] *vt (niño)* to bath, bathe; *(objeto)* to dip; *(de barniz)* to coat; **~se** *vr (en el mar)* to bathe, swim; *(en la bañera)* to have a bath.

bañero, a [ba'ɲero, a] *nm* lifeguard ♦ *nf* bath(tub).

bañista [ba'ɲista] *nm/f* bather.

baño ['baɲo] *nm (en bañera)* bath; *(en río, mar)* dip, swim; *(cuarto)* bathroom; *(bañera)* bath(tub); *(capa)* coating; **ir a tomar los ~s** to take the waters.

baptista [bap'tista] *nm/f* Baptist.

baqueano, a, baquiano, a [bake'ano, a, baki'ano, a] *nm/f (AM)* guide.

baqueta [ba'keta] *nf (MUS)* drumstick.

bar [bar] *nm* bar.

barahúnda [bara'unda] *nf* uproar, hubbub.

baraja [ba'raxa] *nf* pack (of cards).

The **baraja española** is the traditional Spanish deck of cards and differs from a standard poker deck. The four **palos** (suits) are **oros** (golden coins), **copas** (goblets), **espadas** (swords), and **bastos** ("clubs", but not like the clubs in a poker pack). Every suit has 9 numbered cards, although for certain games only 7 are used, and 3 face cards: **sota** (Jack), **caballo** (≈ queen) and **rey** (king).

barajar [bara'xar] vt (naipes) to shuffle; (fig) to jumble up.

baranda [ba'randa], **barandilla** [baran'diʎa] nf rail, railing.

baratija [bara'tixa] nf trinket; (fig) trifle; ~s nfpl (COM) cheap goods.

baratillo [bara'tiʎo] nm (tienda) junkshop; (subasta) bargain sale; (conjunto de cosas) second-hand goods pl.

barato, a [ba'rato, a] adj cheap ♦ adv cheap, cheaply.

baratura [bara'tura] nf cheapness.

baraúnda [bara'unda] nf = **barahúnda**.

barba ['barβa] nf (mentón) chin; (pelo) beard; **tener** ~ to be unshaven; **hacer algo en las** ~**s de algn** to do sth under sb's very nose; **reírse en las** ~**s de algn** to laugh in sb's face.

barbacoa [barβa'koa] nf (parrilla) barbecue; (carne) barbecued meat.

barbaridad [barβari'ðað] nf barbarity; (acto) barbarism; (atrocidad) outrage; **una** ~ **de** (fam) loads of; **¡qué** ~! (fam) how awful!; **cuesta una** ~ (fam) it costs a fortune.

barbarie [bar'βarje] nf, **barbarismo** [barβa'rismo] nm barbarism; (crueldad) barbarity.

bárbaro, a ['barβaro, a] adj barbarous, cruel; (grosero) rough, uncouth ♦ nmlf barbarian ♦ adv: **lo pasamos** ~ (fam) we had a great time; **¡qué** ~! (fam) how marvellous!; **un éxito** ~ (fam) a terrific success; **es un tipo** ~ (fam) he's a great bloke.

barbecho [bar'βetʃo] nm fallow land.

barbero [bar'βero] nm barber, hairdresser.

barbilampiño [barβilam'piɲo] adj smooth-faced; (fig) inexperienced.

barbilla [bar'βiʎa] nf chin, tip of the chin.

barbitúrico [barβi'turiko] nm barbiturate.

barbo ['barβo] nm: ~ **de mar** red mullet.

barbotar [barβo'tar], **barbotear** [barβote'ar] vt, vi to mutter, mumble.

barbudo, a [bar'βuðo, a] adj bearded.

barbullar [barβu'ʎar] vi to jabber away.

barca ['barka] nf (small) boat; ~ **pesquera** fishing boat; ~ **de pasaje** ferry.

barcaza [bar'kaθa] nf barge; ~ **de desembarco** landing craft.

Barcelona [barθe'lona] nf Barcelona.

barcelonés, esa [barθelo'nes, esa] adj of o from Barcelona ♦ nmlf native o inhabitant of Barcelona.

barco ['barko] nm boat; (buque) ship; (COM etc) vessel; ~ **de carga** cargo boat; ~ **de guerra** warship; ~ **de vela** sailing ship; **ir en** ~ to go by boat.

baremo [ba'remo] nm scale; (tabla de cuentas) ready reckoner.

barítono [ba'ritono] nm baritone.

barman ['barman] nm barman.

Barna. abr = **Barcelona**.

barnice [bar'niθe] etc vb V **barnizar**.

barniz [bar'niθ] nm varnish; (en la loza) glaze; (fig) veneer.

barnizar [barni'θar] vt to varnish; (loza) to glaze.

barómetro [ba'rometro] nm barometer.

barón [ba'ron] nm baron.

baronesa [baro'nesa] nf baroness.

barquero [bar'kero] nm boatman.

barquilla [bar'kiʎa] nf (NAUT) log.

barquillo [bar'kiʎo] nm cone, cornet.

barra ['barra] nf bar, rod; (JUR) rail; (: banquillo) dock; (de un bar, café) bar; (de pan) French loaf; (palanca) lever; ~ **de carmín** o **de labios** lipstick; ~ **de espaciado** (INFORM) space bar; ~ **inversa** backslash; ~ **libre** free bar; **no pararse en** ~s to stick o stop at nothing.

barrabasada [barraβa'saða] nf (piece of) mischief.

barraca [ba'rraka] nf hut, cabin; (en Valencia) thatched farmhouse; (en feria) booth.

barracón [barra'kon] nm (caseta) big hut.

barragana [barra'ɣana] nf concubine.

barranca [ba'rranka] nf ravine, gully.

barranco [ba'rranko] nm ravine; (fig) difficulty.

barrena [ba'rrena] nf drill.

barrenar [barre'nar] vt to drill (through), bore.

barrendero, a [barren'dero, a] nmlf street-sweeper.

barreno [ba'rreno] nm large drill.

barreño [ba'rreɲo] nm washing-up bowl.

barrer [ba'rrer] vt to sweep; (quitar) to sweep away; (MIL, NAUT) to sweep, rake (with gunfire) ♦ vi to sweep up.

barrera [ba'rrera] nf barrier; (MIL) barricade; (FERRO) crossing gate; **poner** ~s **a** to hinder; ~ **arancelaria** (COM) tariff barrier; ~ **comercial** (*COM*) trade barrier.

barriada [ba'rrjaða] *nf* quarter, district.

barricada [barri'kaða] *nf* barricade.

barrida [ba'rriða] *nf*, **barrido** [ba'rriðo] *nm* sweep, sweeping.

barriga [ba'rriɣa] *nf* belly; (*panza*) paunch; (*vientre*) guts *pl*; **echar** ~ to get middle-age spread.

barrigón, ona [barri'ɣon, ona], **barrigudo, a** [barri'ɣuðo, a] *adj* potbellied.

barril [ba'rril] *nm* barrel, cask; **cerveza de** ~ draught beer.

barrio ['barrjo] *nm* (*vecindad*) area, neighborhood (*US*); (*en las afueras*) suburb; ~**s bajos** poor quarter *sg*; ~ **chino** red-light district.

barriobajero, a [barrjobßa'xero, a] *adj* (*vulgar*) common.

barro ['barro] *nm* (*lodo*) mud; (*objetos*) earthenware; (*MED*) pimple.

barroco, a [ba'rroko, a] *adj* Baroque; (*fig*) elaborate ♦ *nm* Baroque.

barrote [ba'rrote] *nm* (*de ventana etc*) bar.

barruntar [barrun'tar] *vt* (*conjeturar*) to guess; (*presentir*) to suspect.

barrunto [ba'rrunto] *nm* guess; suspicion.

bartola [bar'tola]: **a la** ~ *adv*: **tirarse a la** ~ to take it easy, be lazy.

bártulos ['bartulos] *nmpl* things, belongings.

barullo [ba'ruʎo] *nm* row, uproar.

basa ['basa] *nf* (*ARQ*) base.

basamento [basa'mento] *nm* base, plinth.

basar [ba'sar] *vt* to base; ~**se** *vr*: ~**se en** to be based on.

basca ['baska] *nf* nausea.

báscula ['baskula] *nf* (*platform*) scales *pl*; ~ **biestable** (*INFORM*) flip-flop, toggle.

bascular [basku'lar] *vt* (*INFORM*) to toggle.

base ['base] *nf* base; **a** ~ **de** on the basis of, based on; (*mediante*) by means of; **a** ~ **de bien** in abundance; ~ **de conocimiento** knowledge base; ~ **de datos** database.

básico, a ['basiko, a] *adj* basic.

Basilea [basi'lea] *nf* Basle.

basílica [ba'silika] *nf* basilica.

basilisco [basi'lisco] *nm* (*AM*) iguana; **estar hecho un** ~ to be hopping mad.

basket, básquet ['basket] *nm* basketball.

======== *PALABRA CLAVE* ========

bastante [bas'tante] *adj* **1** (*suficiente*) enough; ~ **dinero** enough *o* sufficient money; ~**s libros** enough books
2 (*valor intensivo*): ~ **gente** quite a lot of people; **tener** ~ **calor** to be rather hot;

hace ~ **tiempo que ocurrió** it happened quite *o* rather a long time ago
♦ *adv*: ~ **bueno/malo** quite good/rather bad; ~ **rico** pretty rich; **(lo)** ~ **inteligente (como) para hacer algo** clever enough *o* sufficiently clever to do sth; **voy a tardar** ~ I'm going to be a while *o* quite some time.

bastar [bas'tar] *vi* to be enough *o* sufficient; ~**se** *vr* to be self-sufficient; ~ **para** to be enough to; **¡basta!** (that's) enough!

bastardilla [bastar'ðiʎa] *nf* italics *pl*.

bastardo, a [bas'tarðo, a] *adj*, *nm/f* bastard.

bastidor [basti'ðor] *nm* frame; (*de coche*) chassis; (*ARTE*) stretcher; (*TEAT*) wing; **entre** ~**es** behind the scenes.

basto, a ['basto, a] *adj* coarse, rough
♦ *nmpl*: ~**s** (*NAIPES*) *one of the suits in the Spanish card deck*; *V tb* **Baraja Española**.

bastón [bas'ton] *nm* stick, staff; (*para pasear*) walking stick; ~ **de mando** baton.

bastonazo [basto'naθo] *nm* blow with a stick.

bastoncillo [baston'θiʎo] *nm* (*tb*: ~ **de algodón**) cotton bud.

basura [ba'sura] *nf* rubbish, refuse (*BRIT*), garbage (*US*).

basurero [basu'rero] *nm* (*hombre*) dustman (*BRIT*), garbage collector *o* man (*US*); (*lugar*) rubbish dump; (*cubo*) (rubbish) bin (*BRIT*), trash can (*US*).

bata ['bata] *nf* (*gen*) dressing gown; (*cubretodo*) smock, overall; (*MED, TEC etc*) lab(oratory) coat.

batacazo [bata'kaθo] *nm* bump.

batalla [ba'taʎa] *nf* battle; **de** ~ for everyday use.

batallar [bata'ʎar] *vi* to fight.

batallón [bata'ʎon] *nm* battalion.

batata [ba'tata] *nf* (*AM: CULIN*) sweet potato.

bate ['bate] *nm* (*DEPORTE*) bat.

batea [ba'tea] *nf* (*AM*) washing trough.

bateador [batea'ðor] *nm* (*DEPORTE*) batter, batsman.

batería [bate'ria] *nf* battery; (*MUS*) drums *pl*; (*TEAT*) footlights *pl*; ~ **de cocina** kitchen utensils *pl*.

batiburrillo [batißu'rriʎo] *nm* hotchpotch.

batido, a [ba'tiðo, a] *adj* (*camino*) beaten, well-trodden ♦ *nm* (*CULIN*) batter; ~ **(de leche)** milk shake ♦ *nf* (*AM*) (police) raid.

batidora [bati'ðora] *nf* beater, mixer; ~ **eléctrica** food mixer, blender.

batir [ba'tir] *vt* to beat, strike; (*vencer*) to beat, defeat; (*revolver*) to beat, mix; (*pelo*) to back-comb; ~**se** *vr* to fight; ~ **palmas** to clap, applaud.

baturro, a [ba'turro, a] *nm/f* Aragonese peasant.

batuta [ba'tuta] *nf* baton; **llevar la** ~ (*fig*) to be the boss.

baudio ['bauðjo] *nm* (*INFORM*) baud.

baúl [ba'ul] *nm* trunk; (*AM AUTO*) boot (*BRIT*), trunk (*US*).

bautice [bau'tiθe] *etc vb V* **bautizar**.

bautismo [bau'tismo] *nm* baptism, christening.

bautista [bau'tista] *adj, nm/f* Baptist.

bautizar [bauti'θar] *vt* to baptize, christen; (*fam: diluir*) to water down; (*dar apodo*) to dub.

bautizo [bau'tiθo] *nm* baptism, christening.

bávaro, a ['baβaro, a] *adj, nm/f* Bavarian.

Baviera [ba'βjera] *nf* Bavaria.

baya ['baja] *nf* berry; *V tb* **bayo**.

bayeta [ba'jeta] *nf* (*trapo*) floorcloth; (*AM: pañal*) nappy (*BRIT*), diaper (*US*).

bayo, a ['bajo, a] *adj* bay.

bayoneta [bajo'neta] *nf* bayonet.

baza ['baθa] *nf* trick; **meter** ~ to butt in.

bazar [ba'θar] *nm* bazaar.

bazo ['baθo] *nm* spleen.

bazofia [ba'θofja] *nf* pigswill (*BRIT*), hogwash (*US*); (*libro etc*) trash.

beatificar [beatifi'kar] *vt* to beatify.

beato, a [be'ato, a] *adj* blessed; (*piadoso*) pious.

bebe (*AM*), *pl* **bebes, bebé,** *pl* **bebés** ['beβe, 'beβes, be'βe, be'βes] *nm* baby.

bebedero, a [beβe'ðero, a] *nm* (*para animales*) drinking trough.

bebedizo, a [beβe'ðiθo, a] *adj* drinkable ♦ *nm* potion.

bebedor, a [beβe'ðor, a] *adj* hard-drinking.

bebé-probeta [be'βe-pro'βeta], *pl* **bebés-probeta** *nm/f* test-tube baby.

beber [be'βer] *vt, vi* to drink; ~ **a sorbos/ tragos** to sip/gulp; **se lo bebió todo** he drank it all up.

bebido, a [be'βiðo, a] *adj* drunk ♦ *nf* drink.

beca ['beka] *nf* grant, scholarship.

becado, a [be'kaðo, a] *nm/f*, **becario, a** [be'karjo, a] *nm/f* scholarship holder.

becerro [be'θerro] *nm* yearling calf.

bechamel [betʃa'mel] *nf* = **besamel**.

becuadro [be'kwaðro] *nm* (*MUS*) natural sign.

bedel [be'ðel] *nm* porter, janitor.

beduino, a [be'ðwino, a] *adj, nm/f* Bedouin.

befarse [be'farse] *vr*: ~ **de algo** to scoff at sth.

beige ['beix], **beis** ['beis] *adj, nm* beige.

béisbol ['beisβol] *nm* baseball.

bejuco [be'xuko] *nm* (*AM*) reed, liana.

beldad [bel'dað] *nf* beauty.

Belén [be'len] *nm* Bethlehem; **b~** (*de Navidad*) nativity scene, crib.

belga ['belɣa] *adj, nm/f* Belgian.

Bélgica ['belxika] *nf* Belgium.

Belgrado [bel'xraðo] *nm* Belgrade.

Belice [be'liθe] *nm* Belize.

bélico, a ['beliko, a] *adj* (*actitud*) warlike.

belicoso, a [beli'koso, a] *adj* (*guerrero*) warlike; (*agresivo*) aggressive, bellicose.

beligerante [belixe'rante] *adj* belligerent.

bellaco, a [be'ʎako, a] *adj* sly, cunning ♦ *nm* villain, rogue.

belladona [beʎa'ðona] *nf* deadly nightshade.

bellaquería [beʎake'ria] *nf* (*acción*) dirty trick; (*calidad*) wickedness.

belleza [be'ʎeθa] *nf* beauty.

bello, a ['beʎo, a] *adj* beautiful, lovely; **Bellas Artes** Fine Art *sg*.

bellota [be'ʎota] *nf* acorn.

bemol [be'mol] *nm* (*MUS*) flat; **esto tiene ~es** (*fam*) this is a tough one.

bencina [ben'sina] *nf* (*AM*) petrol (*BRIT*), gas (*US*).

bendecir [bende'θir] *vt* to bless; ~ **la mesa** to say grace.

bendición [bendi'θjon] *nf* blessing.

bendiga [ben'diɣa] *etc*, **bendije** [ben'dixe] *etc vb V* **bendecir**.

bendito, a [ben'dito, a] *pp de* **bendecir** ♦ *adj* (*santo*) blessed; (*agua*) holy; (*afortunado*) lucky; (*feliz*) happy; (*sencillo*) simple ♦ *nm/f* simple soul; ¡~ **sea Dios!** thank goodness!; **es un** ~ he's sweet; **dormir como un** ~ to sleep like a log.

benedictino, a [beneðik'tino, a] *adj, nm* Benedictine.

benefactor, a [benefak'tor, a] *nm/f* benefactor/benefactress.

beneficencia [benefi'θenθja] *nf* charity.

beneficiar [benefi'θjar] *vt* to benefit, be of benefit to; ~**se** *vr* to benefit, profit.

beneficiario, a [benefi'θjarjo, a] *nm/f* beneficiary; (*de cheque*) payee.

beneficio [bene'fiθjo] *nm* (*bien*) benefit, advantage; (*COM*) profit, gain; **a** ~ **de** for the benefit of; **en** ~ **propio** to one's own advantage; ~ **bruto/neto** gross/net profit; ~ **por acción** earnings *pl* per share.

beneficioso, a [benefi'θjoso, a] *adj* beneficial.

benéfico, a [be'nefiko, a] *adj* charitable;

sociedad ~a charity (organization).
benemérito, a [bene'merito, a] *adj*
meritorious ♦ *nf*: **la Benemérita** (*ESP*) the
Civil Guard; *V tb* **Guardia Civil.**
beneplácito [bene'plaθito] *nm* approval,
consent.
benevolencia [beneßo'lenθja] *nf*
benevolence, kindness.
benévolo, a [be'neßolo, a] *adj* benevolent,
kind.
Bengala [ben'gala] *nf* Bengal; **el Golfo de**
~ the Bay of Bengal.
bengala [ben'gala] *nf* (*MIL*) flare; (*fuego*)
Bengal light; (*materia*) rattan.
bengalí [benga'li] *adj, nm/f* Bengali.
benignidad [beniɣni'ðað] *nf* (*afabilidad*)
kindness; (*suavidad*) mildness.
benigno, a [be'niɣno, a] *adj* kind; (*suave*)
mild; (*MED: tumor*) benign, non-
malignant.
benjamín [benxa'min] *nm* youngest child.
beodo, a [be'oðo, a] *adj* drunk ♦ *nm/f*
drunkard.
berberecho [berße'retʃo] *nm* cockle.
berenjena [beren'xena] *nf* aubergine
(*BRIT*), eggplant (*US*).
berenjenal [berenxe'nal] *nm* (*AGR*)
aubergine bed; (*fig*) mess; **en buen** ~
nos hemos metido we've got ourselves
into a fine mess.
bergantín [berɣan'tin] *nm* brig(antine).
Berlín [ber'lin] *nm* Berlin.
berlinés, esa [berli'nes, esa] *adj* of o from
Berlin ♦ *nm/f* Berliner.
bermejo, a [ber'mexo, a] *adj* red.
bermellón [berme'ʎon] *nm* vermilion.
bermudas [ber'muðas] *nfpl* Bermuda
shorts.
berrear [berre'ar] *vi* to bellow, low.
berrido [be'rriðo] *nm* bellow(ing).
berrinche [be'rrintʃe] *nm* (*fam*) temper,
tantrum.
berro ['berro] *nm* watercress.
berza ['berθa] *nf* cabbage; ~ **lombarda** red
cabbage.
besamel [besa'mel], **besamela**
[besa'mela] *nf* (*CULIN*) white sauce,
bechamel sauce.
besar [be'sar] *vt* to kiss; (*fig: tocar*) to
graze; ~**se** *vr* to kiss (one another).
beso ['beso] *nm* kiss.
bestia ['bestja] *nf* beast, animal; (*fig*) idiot;
~ **de carga** beast of burden; ¡~! you
idiot!; **¡no seas** ~**!** (*bruto*) don't be such a
brute!; (*idiota*) don't be such an idiot!
bestial [bes'tjal] *adj* bestial; (*fam*) terrific.
bestialidad [bestjali'ðað] *nf* bestiality;
(*fam*) stupidity.

besugo [be'suɣo] *nm* sea bream; (*fam*)
idiot.
besuguera [besu'ɣera] *nf* (*CULIN*) fish pan.
besuquear [besuke'ar] *vt* to cover with
kisses; ~**se** *vr* to kiss and cuddle.
bético, a ['betiko, a] *adj* Andalusian.
betún [be'tun] *nm* shoe polish; (*QUÍMICA*)
bitumen, asphalt.
Bib. *abr* = **Biblioteca.**
biberón [biße'ron] *nm* feeding bottle.
Biblia ['bißlja] *nf* Bible.
bíblico, a ['bißliko, a] *adj* biblical.
bibliografía [bißljoɣra'fia] *nf* bibliography.
biblioteca [bißljo'teka] *nf* library;
(*estantes*) bookcase, bookshelves *pl*; ~ **de**
consulta reference library.
bibliotecario, a [bißljote'karjo, a] *nm/f*
librarian.
B.I.C. [bik] *nf abr* (= *Brigada de Investigación*
Criminal) ≈ CID (*BRIT*), FBI (*US*).
bicarbonato [bikarßo'nato] *nm*
bicarbonate.
bíceps ['biθeps] *nm inv* biceps.
bicho ['bitʃo] *nm* (*animal*) small animal;
(*sabandija*) bug, insect; (*TAUR*) bull; ~
raro (*fam*) queer fish.
bici ['biθi] *nf* (*fam*) bike.
bicicleta [biθi'kleta] *nf* bicycle, cycle; ~
estática/de montaña exercise/mountain
bike.
bicoca [bi'koka] *nf* (*ESP fam*) cushy job.
BID *n abr* (= *Banco Interamericano de*
Desarrollo) IDB.
bidé [bi'ðe] *nm* bidet.
bidireccional [biðirekθjo'nal] *adj*
bidirectional.
bidón [bi'ðon] *nm* (*grande*) drum;
(*pequeño*) can.
Bielorrusia [bjelo'rrusja] *nf* Belarus,
Byelorussia.
bielorruso, a [bjelo'rruso, a] *adj, nm/f*
Belaruso, Belorussian ♦ *nm* (*LING*)
Belarussian, Belorussian.

================== *PALABRA CLAVE*

bien [bjen] *nm* **1** (*bienestar*) good; **te lo digo**
por tu ~ I'm telling you for your own
good; **el** ~ **y el mal** good and evil
2 (*posesión*): ~**es** goods; ~**es de**
consumo/equipo consumer/capital
goods; ~**es inmuebles** o **raíces**/~**es**
muebles real estate *sg*/personal
property *sg*
♦ *adv* **1** (*de manera satisfactoria, correcta*
etc) well; **trabaja/come** ~ she works/eats
well; **contestó** ~ he answered correctly;
oler ~ to smell nice o good; **me siento** ~
I feel fine; **no me siento** ~ I don't feel

very well; **se está ~ aquí** it's nice here
2 (*frases*): **hiciste ~ en llamarme** you
were right to call me
3 (*valor intensivo*) very; **un cuarto ~
caliente** a nice warm room; **~ de veces**
lots of times; **~ se ve que** ... it's quite
clear that ...
4: estar ~: estoy muy ~ aquí I feel very
happy here; **¿te encuentras ~?** are you
all right?; **te está ~ la falda** (*ser la talla*)
the skirt fits you; (*sentar*) the skirt suits
you; **el libro está muy ~** the book is
really good; **está ~ que vengan** it's all
right for them to come; **¡está ~!** lo haré
oh all right, I'll do it; **ya está ~ de quejas**
that's quite enough complaining
5 (*de buena gana*): **yo ~ que iría pero** ...
I'd gladly go but ...
♦ *excl*: **¡~!** (*aprobación*) O.K!; **¡muy ~!**
well done!; **¡qué ~!** great!; **~, gracias, ¿y
usted?** fine thanks, and you?
♦ *adj inv*: **niño ~** rich kid; **gente ~** posh
people
♦ *conj* **1: ~** ... **~: ~ en coche ~ en tren**
either by car or by train
2: no ~ (*esp AM*): **no ~ llegue te llamaré**
as soon as I arrive I'll call you
3: si ~ even though; **V tb más.**

bienal [bje'nal] *adj* biennial.
bienaventurado, a [bjenaßentu'raðo, a]
adj (*feliz*) happy; (*afortunado*) fortunate;
(*REL*) blessed.
bienestar [bjenes'tar] *nm* well-being;
estado de ~ welfare state.
bienhechor, a [bjene'tʃor, a] *adj*
beneficent ♦ *nm/f* benefactor/
benefactress.
bienio ['bjenjo] *nm* two-year period.
bienvenido, a [bjembe'niðo, a] *adj*
welcome ♦ *excl* welcome! ♦ *nf* welcome;
dar la bienvenida a algn to welcome sb.
bies ['bjes] *nm*: **falda al ~** bias-cut skirt;
cortar al ~ to cut on the bias.
bifásico, a [bi'fasiko, a] *adj* (*ELEC*) two-
phase.
bife ['bife] *nm* (*AM*) steak.
bifocal [bifo'kal] *adj* bifocal.
bifurcación [bifurka'θjon] *nf* (*FERRO,
INFORM*) branch.
bifurcarse [bifur'karse] *vr* to fork.
bigamia [bi'ɣamja] *nf* bigamy.
bígamo, a [bi'ɣamo, a] *adj* bigamous ♦ *nm/f*
bigamist.
bígaro [bi'ɣaro] *nm* winkle.
bigote [bi'ɣote] *nm* (*tb*: **~s**) moustache.
bigotudo, a [biɣo'tuðo, a] *adj* with a big
moustache.

bigudí [biɣu'ði] *nm* (hair-)curler.
bikini [bi'kini] *nm* bikini; (*CULIN*) toasted
cheese and ham sandwich.
bilateral [bilate'ral] *adj* bilateral.
bilbaíno, a [bilßa'ino, a] *adj* of o from
Bilbao ♦ *nm/f* native o inhabitant of
Bilbao.
bilingüe [bi'lingwe] *adj* bilingual.
bilis ['bilis] *nf inv* bile.
billar [bi'ʎar] *nm* billiards *sg*; (*lugar*)
billiard hall; (*galería de atracciones*)
amusement arcade; **~ americano** pool.
billete [bi'ʎete] *nm* ticket; (*de banco*)
banknote (*BRIT*), bill (*US*); (*carta*) note; **~
sencillo, ~ de ida solamente/~ de ida y
vuelta** single (*BRIT*) o one-way (*US*)
ticket/return (*BRIT*) o round-trip (*US*)
ticket; **sacar (un) ~** to get a ticket; **un ~
de 5 libras** a five-pound note.
billetera [biʎe'tera] *nf*, **billetero** [biʎe'tero]
nm wallet.
billón [bi'ʎon] *nm* billion.
bimensual [bimen'swal] *adj* twice
monthly.
bimestral [bimes'tral] *adj* bimonthly.
bimestre [bi'mestre] *nm* two-month
period.
bimotor [bimo'tor] *adj* twin-engined ♦ *nm*
twin-engined plane.
binario, a [bi'narjo, a] *adj* (*INFORM*) binary.
bingo ['bingo] *nm* (*juego*) bingo; (*sala*)
bingo hall.
binóculo [bi'nokulo] *nm* pince-nez.
binomio [bi'nomjo] *nm* (*MAT*) binomial.
biodegradable [bioðeɣra'ðaßle] *adj*
biodegradable.
biodiversidad [bioðißersi'ðað] *nf*
biodiversity.
biografía [bioɣra'fia] *nf* biography.
biográfico, a [bio'ɣrafiko, a] *adj*
biographical.
biógrafo, a [bi'oɣrafo, a] *nm/f* biographer.
biología [biolo'xia] *nf* biology.
biológico, a [bio'loxiko, a] *adj* biological;
guerra biológica biological warfare.
biólogo, a [bi'oloɣo, a] *nm/f* biologist.
biombo ['bjombo] *nm* (folding) screen.
biopsia [bi'opsja] *nf* biopsy.
bioquímico, a [bio'kimiko, a] *adj*
biochemical ♦ *nm/f* biochemist ♦ *nf*
biochemistry.
biosfera [bios'fera] *nf* biosphere.
bióxido [bi'oksiðo] *nm* dioxide.
bipartidismo [biparti'ðismo] *nm* (*POL*)
two-party system.
biquini [bi'kini] *nm* = **bikini.**
birlar [bir'lar] *vt* (*fam*) to pinch.
birlibirloque [birlißir'loke] *nm*: **por arte de**

~ (as if) by magic.
Birmania [bir'manja] *nf* Burma.
birmano, a [bir'mano, a] *adj nm/f* Burmese.
birrete [bi'rrete] *nm (JUR)* judge's cap.
birria ['birrja] *nf (fam)*: **ser una** ~ to be rubbish; **ir hecho una** ~ to be o look a sight.
bis [bis] *excl* encore! ♦ *nm* encore ♦ *adv (dos veces)* twice; **viven en el 27** ~ they live at 27a.
bisabuelo, a [bisa'ßwelo, a] *nm/f* great-grandfather/mother; ~s *nmpl* great-grandparents.
bisagra [bi'saɣra] *nf* hinge.
bisbisar [bisßi'sar], **bisbisear** [bisßise'ar] *vt* to mutter, mumble.
bisbiseo [bisßi'seo] *nm* muttering.
biselar [bise'lar] *vt* to bevel.
bisexual [bisek'swal] *adj, nm/f* bisexual.
bisiesto [bi'sjesto] *adj*: **año** ~ leap year.
bisnieto, a [bis'njeto, a] *nm/f* great-grandson/daughter; ~s *nmpl* great-grandchildren.
bisonte [bi'sonte] *nm* bison.
bisoñé [biso'ɲe] *nm* toupée.
bisoño, a [bi'soɲo, a] *adj* green, inexperienced.
bistec [bis'tek], **bisté** [bis'te] *nm* steak.
bisturí [bistu'ri] *nm* scalpel.
bisutería [bisute'ria] *nf* imitation o costume jewellery.
bit [bit] *nm (INFORM)* bit; ~ **de parada** stop bit; ~ **de paridad** parity bit.
bitácora [bi'takora] *nf*: **cuaderno de** ~ logbook, ship's log.
bitio ['bitjo] *nm (INFORM)* bit.
bizantino, a [biθan'tino, a] *adj* Byzantine; *(fig)* pointless.
bizarría [biθa'rria] *nf (valor)* bravery; *(generosidad)* generosity.
bizarro, a [bi'θarro, a] *adj* brave; generous.
bizco, a ['biθko, a] *adj* cross-eyed.
bizcocho [biθ'kotʃo] *nm (CULIN)* sponge cake.
biznieto, a [biθ'njeto, a] *nm/f* = **bisnieto**.
bizquear [biθke'ar] *vi* to squint.
blanco, a ['blanko, a] *adj* white ♦ *nm/f* white man/woman, white ♦ *nm (color)* white; *(en texto)* blank; *(MIL, fig)* target ♦ *nf (MUS)* minim; **en** ~ blank; **cheque en** ~ blank cheque; **votar en** ~ to spoil one's vote; **quedarse en** ~ to be disappointed; **noche en** ~ sleepless night; **estar sin** ~ to be broke; **ser el** ~ **de las burlas** to be the butt of jokes.
blancura [blan'kura] *nf* whiteness.
blandengue [blan'denge] *adj (fam)* soft, weak.

blandir [blan'dir] *vt* to brandish.
blando, a ['blando, a] *adj* soft; *(tierno)* tender, gentle; *(carácter)* mild; *(fam)* cowardly ♦ *nm/f (POL etc)* soft-liner.
blandura [blan'dura] *nf* softness; tenderness; mildness.
blanquear [blanke'ar] *vt* to whiten; *(fachada)* to whitewash; *(paño)* to bleach; *(dinero)* to launder ♦ *vi* to turn white.
blanquecino, a [blanke'θino, a] *adj* whitish.
blanqueo [blan'keo] *nm (de pared)* whitewashing; *(de dinero)* laundering.
blasfemar [blasfe'mar] *vi* to blaspheme; *(fig)* to curse.
blasfemia [blas'femja] *nf* blasphemy.
blasfemo, a [blas'femo, a] *adj* blasphemous ♦ *nm/f* blasphemer.
blasón [bla'son] *nm* coat of arms; *(fig)* honour.
blasonar [blaso'nar] *vt* to emblazon ♦ *vi* to boast, brag.
bledo ['bleðo] *nm*: **(no) me importa un** ~ I couldn't care less.
blindado, a [blin'daðo, a] *adj (MIL)* armour-plated; *(antibalas)* bulletproof; **coche** o *(AM)* **carro** ~ armoured car; **puertas blindadas** security doors.
blindaje [blin'daxe] *nm* armour, armour-plating.
bloc, *pl* **blocs** [blok, blos] *nm* writing pad; *(ESCOL)* jotter; ~ **de dibujos** sketch pad.
bloque ['bloke] *nm (tb INFORM)* block; *(POL)* bloc; ~ **de cilindros** cylinder block.
bloquear [bloke'ar] *vt (NAUT etc)* to blockade; *(aislar)* to cut off; *(COM, ECON)* to freeze; **fondos bloqueados** frozen assets.
bloqueo [blo'keo] *nm* blockade; *(COM)* freezing, blocking.
bluejean [blu'jin] *nm (AM)* jeans *pl*, denims *pl*.
blusa ['blusa] *nf* blouse.
B.º *abr (FINANZAS*: = *banco)* bank; *(COM*: = *beneficiario)* beneficiary.
boa ['boa] *nf* boa.
boato [bo'ato] *nm* show, ostentation.
bobada [bo'ßaða] *nf* foolish action (o statement); **decir** ~s to talk nonsense.
bobalicón, ona [boßali'kon, ona] *adj* utterly stupid.
bobería [boße'ria] *nf* = **bobada**.
bobina [bo'ßina] *nf (TEC)* bobbin; *(FOTO)* spool; *(ELEC)* coil, winding.
bobo, a ['boßo, a] *adj (tonto)* daft, silly; *(cándido)* naïve ♦ *nm/f* fool, idiot ♦ *nm (TEAT)* clown, funny man.
boca ['boka] *nf* mouth; *(de crustáceo)*

pincer; (*de cañón*) muzzle; (*entrada*) mouth, entrance; (*INFORM*) slot; ~**s** *nfpl* (*de río*) mouth *sg*; ~ **abajo/arriba** face down/up; **a** ~ **jarro** point-blank; **se me hace la** ~ **agua** my mouth is watering; **todo salió a pedir de** ~ it all turned out perfectly; **en** ~ **de** (*esp AM*) according to; **la cosa anda de** ~ **en** ~ the story is going the rounds; **¡cállate la** ~**!** (*fam*) shut up!; **quedarse con la** ~ **abierta** to be dumbfounded; **no abrir la** ~ to keep quiet; ~ **del estómago** pit of the stomach; ~ **de metro** tube (*BRIT*) *o* subway (*US*) entrance.

bocacalle [boka'kaʎe] *nf* (entrance to a) street; **la primera** ~ the first turning *o* street.

bocadillo [boka'ðiʎo] *nm* sandwich.

bocado [bo'kaðo] *nm* mouthful, bite; (*de caballo*) bridle; ~ **de Adán** Adam's apple.

bocajarro [boka'xarro]: **a** ~ *adv* (*MIL*) at point-blank range; **decir algo a** ~ to say sth bluntly.

bocanada [boka'naða] *nf* (*de vino*) mouthful, swallow; (*de aire*) gust, puff.

bocata [bo'kata] *nm* (*fam*) sandwich.

bocazas [bo'kaθas] *nm/f inv* (*fam*) bigmouth.

boceto [bo'θeto] *nm* sketch, outline.

bocha ['botʃa] *nf* bowl; ~**s** *nfpl* bowls *sg*.

bochinche [bo'tʃintʃe] *nm* (*fam*) uproar.

bochorno [bo'tʃorno] *nm* (*vergüenza*) embarrassment; (*calor*): **hace** ~ it's very muggy.

bochornoso, a [botʃor'noso, a] *adj* muggy; embarrassing.

bocina [bo'θina] *nf* (*MUS*) trumpet; (*AUTO*) horn; (*para hablar*) megaphone; **tocar la** ~ (*AUTO*) to sound *o* blow one's horn.

bocinazo [boθi'naθo] *nm* (*AUTO*) toot, blast (of the horn).

bocio ['boθjo] *nm* (*MED*) goitre.

boda ['boða] *nf* (*tb*: ~**s**) wedding, marriage; (*fiesta*) wedding reception; ~**s de plata/de oro** silver/golden wedding *sg*.

bodega [bo'ðeɣa] *nf* (*de vino*) (wine) cellar; (*bar*) bar; (*restaurante*) restaurant; (*depósito*) storeroom; (*de barco*) hold.

bodegón [boðe'ɣon] *nm* (*ARTE*) still life.

bodrio [bo'ðrio] *nm*: **el libro es un** ~ the book is awful *o* rubbish.

B.O.E. ['boe] *nm abr* = **Boletín Oficial del Estado.**

bofe ['bofe] *nm* (*tb*: ~**s**: *de res*) lights *pl*; **echar los** ~**s** to slave (away).

bofetada [bofe'taða] *nf* slap (in the face); **dar de** ~**s a algn** to punch sb.

bofetón [bofe'ton] *nm* = **bofetada.**

boga ['boɣa] *nf*: **en** ~ in vogue.

bogar [bo'ɣar] *vi* (*remar*) to row; (*navegar*) to sail.

bogavante [boɣa'ßante] *nm* (*NAUT*) stroke, first rower; (*ZOOL*) lobster.

Bogotá [boɣo'ta] *n* Bogota.

bogotano, a [boɣo'tano, a] *adj* of *o* from Bogota ♦ *nm/f* native *o* inhabitant of Bogota.

bogue ['boɣe] *etc vb V* **bogar.**

bohemio, a [bo'emjo, a] *adj, nm/f* Bohemian.

boicot, *pl* **boicots** [boi'ko(t)] *nm* boycott.

boicotear [boikote'ar] *vt* to boycott.

boicoteo [boiko'teo] *nm* boycott.

boina ['boina] *nf* beret.

bola ['bola] *nf* ball; (*canica*) marble; (*NAIPES*) (grand) slam; (*betún*) shoe polish; (*mentira*) tale, story; ~**s** *nfpl* (*AM*) bolas; ~ **de billar** billiard ball; ~ **de nieve** snowball.

bolado [bo'laðo] *nm* (*AM*) deal.

bolchevique [boltʃe'ßike] *adj, nm/f* Bolshevik.

boleadoras [bolea'ðoras] *nfpl* (*AM*) bolas *sg*.

bolera [bo'lera] *nf* skittle *o* bowling alley.

bolero [bo'lero] *nm* bolero.

boleta [bo'leta] *nf* (*AM*: *permiso*) pass, permit; (: *para votar*) ballot.

boletería [bolete'ria] *nf* (*AM*) ticket office.

boletero, a [bole'tero, a] *nm/f* (*AM*) ticket seller.

boletín [bole'tin] *nm* bulletin; (*periódico*) journal, review; ~ **escolar** (*ESP*) school report; ~ **de noticias** news bulletin; ~ **de pedido** application form; ~ **de precios** price list; ~ **de prensa** press release.

The **Boletín Oficial del Estado**, *abbreviated to* **BOE**, *is the official government record of all laws and resolutions passed by* **las Cortes** (*Spanish Parliament*). *It is widely consulted, mainly because it also publishes the announcements for the* **oposiciones** (*public competitive examinations*).

boleto [bo'leto] *nm* (*esp AM*) ticket; ~ **de apuestas** betting slip.

boli ['boli] *nm* Biro ®.

boliche [bo'litʃe] *nm* (*bola*) jack; (*juego*) bowls *sg*; (*lugar*) bowling alley; (*AM*: *tienda*) small grocery store.

bólido ['boliðo] *nm* meteorite; (*AUTO*) racing car.

bolígrafo [bo'liɣrafo] *nm* ball-point pen, biro ®.

bolillo [bo'liʎo] *nm* (*COSTURA*) bobbin (for lacemaking).

bolívar [boˈliβar] *nm monetary unit of Venezuela.*

Bolivia [boˈliβja] *nf* Bolivia.

boliviano, a [boliˈβjano, a] *adj, nm/f* Bolivian.

bollo [ˈboʎo] *nm* (*pan*) roll; (*dulce*) scone; (*bulto*) bump, lump; (*abolladura*) dent; **~s** *nmpl* (*AM*) troubles.

bolo [ˈbolo] *nm* skittle; (*píldora*) (large) pill; **(juego de) ~s** skittles *sg*.

Bolonia [boˈlonja] *nf* Bologna.

bolsa [ˈbolsa] *nf* (*cartera*) purse; (*saco*) bag; (*AM*) pocket; (*ANAT*) cavity, sac; (*COM*) stock exchange; (*MINERÍA*) pocket; **~ de agua caliente** hot water bottle; **~ de aire** air pocket; **~ de (la) basura** bin-liner; **~ de dormir** (*AM*) sleeping bag; **~ de papel** paper bag; **~ de plástico** plastic (*o* carrier) bag; **"B~ de la propiedad"** "Property Mart"; **~ de trabajo** employment bureau; **jugar a la ~** to play the market.

bolsillo [bolˈsiʎo] *nm* pocket; (*cartera*) purse; **de ~** pocket *cpd*; **meterse a algn en el ~** to get sb eating out of one's hand.

bolsista [bolˈsista] *nm/f* stockbroker.

bolso [ˈbolso] *nm* (*bolsa*) bag; (*de mujer*) handbag.

boludo, a [boˈluðo, a] (*AM fam!*) *adj* stupid ♦ *nm/f* prat (!)

bomba [ˈbomba] *nf* (*MIL*) bomb; (*TEC*) pump; (*AM: borrachera*) drunkenness ♦ *adj* (*fam*): **noticia ~** bombshell ♦ *adv* (*fam*): **pasarlo ~** to have a great time; **~ atómica/de humo/de retardo** atomic/ smoke/time bomb; **~ de gasolina** petrol pump; **~ de incendios** fire engine.

bombacho, a [bomˈbatʃo, a] *adj* baggy.

bombardear [bombarðeˈar] *vt* to bombard; (*MIL*) to bomb.

bombardeo [bombarˈðeo] *nm* bombardment; bombing.

bombardero [bombarˈðero] *nm* bomber.

bombear [bombeˈar] *vt* (*agua*) to pump (out *o* up); (*MIL*) to bomb; (*FÚTBOL*) to lob; **~se** *vr* to warp.

bombero [bomˈbero] *nm* fireman; **(cuerpo de) ~s** fire brigade.

bombilla [bomˈbiʎa] *nf* (*ESP*), **bombillo** [bomˈbiʎo] *nm* (*AM*) (light) bulb.

bombín [bomˈbin] *nm* bowler hat.

bombo [ˈbombo] *nm* (*MUS*) bass drum; (*TEC*) drum; (*fam*) exaggerated praise; **hacer algo a ~ y platillo** to make a great song and dance about sth; **tengo la cabeza hecha un ~** I've got a splitting headache.

bombón [bomˈbon] *nm* chocolate; (*belleza*) gem.

bombona [bomˈbona] *nf*: **~ de butano** gas cylinder.

bombonería [bomboneˈria] *nf* sweetshop.

bonachón, ona [bonaˈtʃon, ona] *adj* good-natured.

bonaerense [bonaeˈrense] *adj* of *o* from Buenos Aires ♦ *nm/f* native *o* inhabitant of Buenos Aires.

bonancible [bonanˈθiβle] *adj* (*tiempo*) fair, calm.

bonanza [boˈnanθa] *nf* (*NAUT*) fair weather; (*fig*) bonanza; (*MINERÍA*) rich pocket *o* vein.

bondad [bonˈdað] *nf* goodness, kindness; **tenga la ~ de** (please) be good enough to.

bondadoso, a [bondaˈðoso, a] *adj* good, kind.

bongo [ˈboŋɣo] *nm* large canoe.

boniato [boˈnjato] *nm* sweet potato, yam.

bonificación [bonifikaˈθjon] *nf* (*COM*) allowance, discount; (*pago*) bonus; (*DEPORTE*) extra points *pl*.

bonito, a [boˈnito, a] *adj* (*lindo*) pretty; (*agradable*) nice ♦ *adv* (*AM fam*) well ♦ *nm* (*atún*) tuna (fish).

bono [ˈbono] *nm* voucher; (*FIN*) bond; **~ de billetes de metro** booklet of metro tickets; **~ del Tesoro** treasury bill.

bonobús [bonoˈβus] *nm* (*ESP*) bus pass.

Bono Loto, bonoloto [bonoˈloto] *nm o f* (*ESP*) *state-run weekly lottery*; *V tb* **lotería.**

boom, *pl* **booms** [ˈbum, ˈbums] *nm* boom.

boquear [bokeˈar] *vi* to gasp.

boquerón [bokeˈron] *nm* (*pez*) (kind of) anchovy; (*agujero*) large hole.

boquete [boˈkete] *nm* gap, hole.

boquiabierto, a [bokjaˈβjerto, a] *adj* open-mouthed (in astonishment); **quedar ~** to be left aghast.

boquilla [boˈkiʎa] *nf* (*para riego*) nozzle; (*para cigarro*) cigarette holder; (*MUS*) mouthpiece.

borbollar [borβoˈʎar], **borbollear** [borβoʎeˈar] *vi* to bubble.

borbollón [borβoˈʎon] *nm* bubbling; **hablar a borbollones** to gabble; **salir a borbollones** (*agua*) to gush out.

borbotar [borβoˈtar] *vi* = **borbollar.**

borbotón [borβoˈton] *nm*: **salir a borbotones** to gush out.

borda [ˈborða] *nf* (*NAUT*) gunwale; **echar** *o* **tirar algo por la ~** to throw sth overboard.

bordado [borˈðaðo] *nm* embroidery.

bordar [bor'ðar] *vt* to embroider.

borde ['borðe] *nm* edge, border; (*de camino etc*) side; (*en la costura*) hem; **al ~ de** (*fig*) on the verge o brink of; **ser ~** (*ESP fam*) to be a pain in the neck.

bordear [borðe'ar] *vt* to border.

bordillo [bor'ðiʎo] *nm* kerb (*BRIT*), curb (*US*).

bordo ['borðo] *nm* (*NAUT*) side; **a ~** on board.

Borgoña [bor'ɣoɲa] *nf* Burgundy.

borgoña [bor'ɣoɲa] *nm* burgundy.

boricua [bo'rikwa], **borinqueño, a** [borin'keɲo, a] *adj, nm/f* Puerto Rican.

borla ['borla] *nf* (*gen*) tassel; (*de gorro*) pompon.

borra ['borra] *nf* (*pelusa*) fluff; (*sedimento*) sediment.

borrachera [borra't ʃera] *nf* (*ebriedad*) drunkenness; (*orgía*) spree, binge.

borracho, a [bo'rratʃo, a] *adj* drunk ♦ *nm/f* (*que bebe mucho*) drunkard, drunk; (*temporalmente*) drunk, drunk man/woman ♦ *nm* (*CULIN*) cake soaked in liqueur or spirit.

borrador [borra'ðor] *nm* (*escritura*) first draft, rough sketch; (*cuaderno*) scribbling pad; (*goma*) rubber (*BRIT*), eraser; (*COM*) daybook; (*para pizarra*) duster; **hacer un nuevo ~ de** (*COM*) to redraft.

borrar [bo'rrar] *vt* to erase, rub out; (*tachar*) to delete; (*cinta*) to wipe out; (*INFORM: archivo*) to delete, erase; (*POL etc: eliminar*) to deal with.

borrasca [bo'rraska] *nf* (*METEOROLOGÍA*) storm.

borrascoso, a [borras'koso, a] *adj* stormy.

borrego, a [bo'rreɣo, a] *nm/f* lamb; (*oveja*) sheep; (*fig*) simpleton.

borricada [borri'kaða] *nf* foolish action/ statement.

borrico, a [bo'rriko, a] *nm* donkey; (*fig*) stupid man ♦ *nf* she-donkey; (*fig*) stupid woman.

borrón [bo'rron] *nm* (*mancha*) stain; **~ y cuenta nueva** let bygones be bygones.

borroso, a [bo'rroso, a] *adj* vague, unclear; (*escritura*) illegible; (*escrito*) smudgy; (*FOTO*) blurred.

Bósforo ['bosforo] *nm*: **el (Estrecho del) ~** the Bosp(h)orus.

Bosnia ['bosnja] *nf* Bosnia.

bosnio, a ['bosnjo, a] *adj, nm/f* Bosnian.

bosque ['boske] *nm* wood; (*grande*) forest.

bosquejar [boske'xar] *vt* to sketch.

bosquejo [bos'kexo] *nm* sketch.

bosta ['bosta] *nf* dung, manure.

bostece [bos'teθe] *etc vb* V **bostezar**.

bostezar [boste'θar] *vi* to yawn.

bostezo [bos'teθo] *nm* yawn.

bota ['bota] *nf* (*calzado*) boot; (*saco*) leather wine bottle; **ponerse las ~s** (*fam*) to strike it rich.

botadura [bota'ðura] *nf* launching.

botanas [bo'tanas] *nfpl* (*AM*) hors d'œuvres.

botánico, a [bo'taniko, a] *adj* botanical ♦ *nm/f* botanist ♦ *nf* botany.

botar [bo'tar] *vt* to throw, hurl; (*NAUT*) to launch; (*esp AM fam*) to throw out ♦ *vi* to bounce.

botarate [bota'rate] *nm* (*imbécil*) idiot.

bote ['bote] *nm* (*salto*) bounce; (*golpe*) thrust; (*vasija*) tin, can; (*embarcación*) boat; **de ~ en ~** packed, jammed full; **~ salvavidas** lifeboat; **dar un ~** to jump; **dar ~s** (*AUTO etc*) to bump; **~ de la basura** (*AM*) dustbin (*BRIT*), trashcan (*US*).

botella [bo'teʎa] *nf* bottle; **~ de vino** (*contenido*) bottle of wine; (*recipiente*) wine bottle.

botellero [bote'ʎero] *nm* wine rack.

botellín [bote'ʎin] *nm* small bottle.

botica [bo'tika] *nf* chemist's (shop) (*BRIT*), pharmacy.

boticario, a [boti'karjo, a] *nm/f* chemist (*BRIT*), pharmacist.

botijo [bo'tixo] *nm* (earthenware) jug; (*tren*) excursion train.

botín [bo'tin] *nm* (*calzado*) half boot; (*polaina*) spat; (*MIL*) booty; (*de ladrón*) loot.

botiquín [boti'kin] *nm* (*armario*) medicine chest; (*portátil*) first-aid kit.

botón [bo'ton] *nm* button; (*BOT*) bud; (*de florete*) tip; **~ de arranque** (*AUTO etc*) starter; **~ de oro** buttercup; **pulsar el ~** to press the button.

botones [bo'tones] *nm inv* bellboy, bellhop (*US*).

botulismo [botu'lismo] *nm* botulism, food poisoning.

bóveda ['boβeða] *nf* (*ARQ*) vault.

bovino, a [bo'ßino, a] *adj* bovine; (*AGR*): **ganado ~** cattle.

box ['boks] *nm* (*AM*) boxing.

boxeador [boksea'ðor] *nm* boxer.

boxear [bokse'ar] *vi* to box.

boxeo [bok'seo] *nm* boxing.

boya ['boja] *nf* (*NAUT*) buoy; (*flotador*) float.

boyante [bo'jante] *adj* (*NAUT*) buoyant; (*feliz*) buoyant; (*próspero*) prosperous.

bozal [bo'θal] *nm* (*de caballo*) halter; (*de perro*) muzzle.

bozo ['boθo] *nm* (*pelusa*) fuzz; (*boca*) mouth.

bracear [braθe'ar] *vi* (*agitar los brazos*) to wave one's arms.

bracero [bra'θero] *nm* labourer; (*en el campo*) farmhand.

braga ['braɣa] *nf* (*cuerda*) sling, rope; (*de bebé*) nappy, diaper (*US*); ~**s** *nfpl* (*de mujer*) panties.

braguero [bra'ɣero] *nm* (*MED*) truss.

bragueta [bra'ɣeta] *nf* fly (*BRIT*), flies *pl* (*BRIT*), zipper (*US*).

braguetazo [braɣe'taθo] *nm* marriage of convenience.

braille [breil] *nm* braille.

bramante [bra'mante] *nm* twine, string.

bramar [bra'mar] *vi* to bellow, roar.

bramido [bra'miðo] *nm* bellow, roar.

branquias ['brankjas] *nfpl* gills.

brasa ['brasa] *nf* live *o* hot coal; **carne a la** ~ grilled meat.

brasero [bra'sero] *nm* brazier; (*AM: chimenea*) fireplace.

Brasil [bra'sil] *nm*: (**el**) ~ Brazil.

brasileño, a [brasi'leɲo, a] *adj, nm/f* Brazilian.

bravata [bra'ßata] *nf* boast.

braveza [bra'ßeθa] *nf* (*valor*) bravery; (*ferocidad*) ferocity.

bravío, a [bra'ßio, a] *adj* wild; (*feroz*) fierce.

bravo, a ['braßo, a] *adj* (*valiente*) brave; (*bueno*) fine, splendid; (*feroz*) ferocious; (*salvaje*) wild; (*mar etc*) rough, stormy; (*CULIN*) hot, spicy ♦ *excl* bravo!

bravucón, ona [braßu'kon, ona] *adj* swaggering ♦ *nm/f* braggart.

bravura [bra'ßura] *nf* bravery; ferocity; (*pey*) boast.

braza ['braθa] *nf* fathom; **nadar a la** ~ to swim (the) breast-stroke.

brazada [bra'θaða] *nf* stroke.

brazalete [braθa'lete] *nm* (*pulsera*) bracelet; (*banda*) armband.

brazo ['braθo] *nm* arm; (*ZOOL*) foreleg; (*BOT*) limb, branch; ~**s** *nmpl* (*braceros*) hands, workers; ~ **derecho** (*fig*) right-hand man; **a** ~ **partido** hand-to-hand; **cogidos** *etc* **del** ~ arm in arm; **no dar su** ~ **a torcer** not to give way easily; **huelga de** ~**s caídos** sit-down strike.

brea ['brea] *nf* pitch, tar.

brebaje [bre'ßaxe] *nm* potion.

brecha ['bretʃa] *nf* breach; (*hoyo vacío*) gap, opening.

brécol ['brekol] *nm* broccoli.

brega ['breɣa] *nf* (*lucha*) struggle; (*trabajo*) hard work.

bregar [bre'ɣar] *vi* (*luchar*) to struggle; (*trabajar mucho*) to slog away.

bregue ['breɣe] *etc vb* V **bregar**.

breña ['breɲa] *nf* rough ground.

Bretaña [bre'taɲa] *nf* Brittany.

brete ['brete] *nm* (*cepo*) shackles *pl*; (*fig*) predicament; **estar en un** ~ to be in a jam.

breteles [bre'teles] *nmpl* (*AM*) straps.

bretón, ona [bre'ton, ona] *adj, nm/f* Breton.

breva ['breßa] *nf* (*BOT*) early fig; (*puro*) flat cigar; ¡**no caerá esa** ~! no such luck!

breve ['breße] *adj* short, brief; **en** ~ (*pronto*) shortly; (*en pocas palabras*) in short ♦ *nf* (*MUS*) breve.

brevedad [breße'ðað] *nf* brevity, shortness; **con** *o* **a la major** ~ as soon as possible.

breviario [bre'ßjarjo] *nm* (*REL*) breviary.

brezal [bre'θal] *nm* moor(land), heath.

brezo [bre'θo] *nm* heather.

bribón, ona [bri'ßon, ona] *adj* idle, lazy ♦ *nm/f* (*vagabundo*) vagabond; (*pícaro*) rascal, rogue.

bricolaje [briko'laxe] *nm* do-it-yourself, DIY.

brida ['briða] *nf* bridle, rein; (*TEC*) clamp; **a toda** ~ at top speed.

bridge [britʃ] *nm* (*NAIPES*) bridge.

brigada [bri'ɣaða] *nf* (*unidad*) brigade; (*trabajadores*) squad, gang ♦ *nm* warrant officer.

brigadier [briɣa'ðjer] *nm* brigadier (-general).

brillante [bri'ʎante] *adj* brilliant; (*color*) bright; (*joya*) sparkling ♦ *nm* diamond.

brillantez [briʎan'teθ] *nf* (*color etc*) brightness; (*fig*) brilliance.

brillar [bri'ʎar] *vi* (*tb fig*) to shine; (*joyas*) to sparkle; ~ **por su ausencia** to be conspicuous by one's absence.

brillo ['briʎo] *nm* shine; (*brillantez*) brilliance; (*fig*) splendour; **sacar** ~ **a** to polish.

brilloso, a [bri'ʎoso, a] *adj* (*AM*) = **brillante**.

brincar [brin'kar] *vi* to skip about, hop about, jump about; **está que brinca** he's hopping mad.

brinco ['brinko] *nm* jump, leap; **a** ~**s** by fits and starts; **de un** ~ at one bound.

brindar [brin'dar] *vi*: ~ **a** *o* **por** to drink (a toast) to ♦ *vt* to offer, present; **le brinda la ocasión de** it offers *o* affords him the opportunity to; ~**se** *vr*: ~**se a hacer algo** to offer to do sth.

brindis ['brindis] *nm inv* toast; (*TAUR*) (ceremony of) dedication.

brinque ['brinke] *etc vb* V **brincar**.

brío ['brio] *nm* spirit, dash.

brioso, a [bri'oso, a] *adj* spirited, dashing.
brisa ['brisa] *nf* breeze.
británico, a [bri'taniko, a] *adj* British ♦ *nm/f* Briton, British person; **los ~s** the British.
brizna ['briθna] *nf* (*hebra*) strand, thread; (*de hierba*) blade; (*trozo*) piece.
broca ['broka] *nf* (*COSTURA*) bobbin; (*TEC*) drill bit; (*clavo*) tack.
brocado [bro'kaðo] *nm* brocade.
brocal [bro'kal] *nm* rim.
brocha ['brotʃa] *nf* (large) paintbrush; **~ de afeitar** shaving brush; **pintor de ~ gorda** painter and decorator; (*fig*) poor painter.
brochazo [bro'tʃaθo] *nm* brush-stroke; **a grandes ~s** (*fig*) in general terms.
broche ['brotʃe] *nm* brooch.
broma ['broma] *nf* joke; (*inocentada*) practical joke; **en ~** in fun, as a joke; **gastar una ~ a algn** to play a joke on sb; **tomar algo a ~** to take sth as a joke.
bromear [brome'ar] *vi* to joke.
bromista [bro'mista] *adj* fond of joking ♦ *nm/f* joker, wag.
bromuro [bro'muro] *nm* bromide.
bronca ['bronka] *nf* row; (*regañada*) ticking-off; **armar una ~** to kick up a fuss; **echar una ~ a algn** to tell sb off.
bronce ['bronθe] *nm* bronze; (*latón*) brass.
bronceado, a [bronθe'aðo, a] *adj* bronze *cpd*; (*por el sol*) tanned ♦ *nm* (sun)tan; (*TEC*) bronzing.
bronceador [bronθea'ðor] *nm* suntan lotion.
broncearse [bronθe'arse] *vr* to get a suntan.
bronco, a ['bronko, a] *adj* (*manera*) rude, surly; (*voz*) harsh.
bronquios ['bronkjos] *nmpl* bronchial tubes.
bronquitis [bron'kitis] *nf inv* bronchitis.
brotar [bro'tar] *vt* (*tierra*) to produce ♦ *vi* (*BOT*) to sprout; (*aguas*) to gush (forth); (*lágrimas*) to well up; (*MED*) to break out.
brote ['brote] *nm* (*BOT*) shoot; (*MED, fig*) outbreak.
broza ['broθa] *nf* (*BOT*) dead leaves *pl*; (*fig*) rubbish.
bruces ['bruθes]: **de ~** *adv*: **caer** *o* **dar de ~** to fall headlong, fall flat.
bruja ['bruxa] *nf* witch.
Brujas ['bruxas] *nf* Bruges.
brujería [bruxe'ria] *nf* witchcraft.
brujo ['bruxo] *nm* wizard, magician.
brújula ['bruxula] *nf* compass.
bruma ['bruma] *nf* mist.
brumoso, a [bru'moso, a] *adj* misty.

bruñendo [bru'ɲenðo] *etc vb* V **bruñir**.
bruñido [bru'ɲiðo] *nm* polish.
bruñir [bru'ɲir] *vt* to polish.
brusco, a ['brusko, a] *adj* (*súbito*) sudden; (*áspero*) brusque.
Bruselas [bru'selas] *nf* Brussels.
brusquedad [bruske'ðað] *nf* suddenness; brusqueness.
brutal [bru'tal] *adj* brutal.
brutalidad [brutali'ðað] *nf* brutality.
bruto, a ['bruto, a] *adj* (*idiota*) stupid; (*bestial*) brutish; (*peso*) gross ♦ *nm* brute; **a la bruta, a lo ~** roughly; **en ~** raw, unworked.
Bs. *abr* = **bolívares**.
Bs.As. *abr* = **Buenos Aires**.
bucal [bu'kal] *adj* oral; **por vía ~** orally.
bucanero [buka'nero] *nm* buccaneer.
bucear [buθe'ar] *vi* to dive ♦ *vt* to explore.
buceo [bu'θeo] *nm* diving; (*fig*) investigation.
buche ['butʃe] *nm* (*de ave*) crop; (*ZOOL*) maw; (*fam*) belly.
bucle ['bukle] *nm* curl; (*INFORM*) loop.
budín [bu'ðin] *nm* pudding.
budismo [bu'ðismo] *nm* Buddhism.
budista [bu'ðista] *adj, nm/f* Buddhist.
buen [bwen] *adj* V **bueno**.
buenamente [bwena'mente] *adv* (*fácilmente*) easily; (*voluntariamente*) willingly.
buenaventura [bwenaβen'tura] *nf* (*suerte*) good luck; (*adivinación*) fortune; **decir** *o* **echar la ~ a algn** to tell sb's fortune.

═══════════════════ *PALABRA CLAVE*

bueno, a ['bweno, a] (*antes de nmsg*: **buen**) *adj* **1** (*excelente etc*) good; (*MED*) well; **es un libro ~, es un buen libro** it's a good book; **hace ~, hace buen tiempo** the weather is fine, it is fine; **es ~a persona** he's a good sort; **el ~ de Paco** good old Paco; **fue muy ~ conmigo** he was very nice *o* kind to me; **ya está ~** he's fine now
2 (*apropiado*): **ser ~ para** to be good for; **creo que vamos por buen camino** I think we're on the right track
3 (*irónico*): **le di un buen rapapolvo** I gave him a good *o* real ticking off; **¡buen conductor estás hecho!** some driver *o* a fine driver you are!; **¡estaría ~ que ...!** a fine thing it would be if ...!
4 (*atractivo, sabroso*): **está ~ este bizcocho** this sponge is delicious; **Julio está muy ~** (*fam*) Julio is a bit of alright
5 (*grande*) good, big; **un buen número de ...** a good number of ...; **un buen trozo**

de ... a nice big piece of ...
6 (*saludos*): **¡buen día!** (*AM*), **¡~s días!**
(good) morning!; **¡buenas (tardes)!** good
afternoon!; (*más tarde*) good evening!;
¡buenas noches! good night!
7 (*otras locuciones*): **estar de buenas** to
be in a good mood; **por las buenas o por
las malas** by hook or by crook; **de
buenas a primeras** all of a sudden
♦ *excl:* **¡~!** all right!; **~, ¿y qué?** well, so
what?; **~, lo que pasa es que** ... well, the
thing is ...; **pero ¡~!** well, I like that!; **~,
pues** ... right, (then) ...

Buenos Aires [bweno'saires] *nm* Buenos
Aires.
buey [bwei] *nm* ox.
búfalo ['bufalo] *nm* buffalo.
bufanda [bu'fanda] *nf* scarf.
bufar [bu'far] *vi* to snort.
bufete [bu'fete] *nm* (*despacho de abogado*)
lawyer's office; **establecer su ~** to set up
in legal practice.
buffer ['bufer] *nm* (*INFORM*) buffer.
bufón [bu'fon] *nm* clown.
bufonada [bufo'naða] *nf* (*dicho*) jest;
(*hecho*) piece of buffoonery; (*TEAT*)
farce.
buhardilla [buar'ðiʎa] *nf* attic.
búho ['buo] *nm* owl; (*fig*) hermit, recluse.
buhonero [buo'nero] *nm* pedlar.
buitre ['bwitre] *nm* vulture.
bujía [bu'xia] *nf* (*vela*) candle; (*ELEC*)
candle (power); (*AUTO*) spark plug.
bula ['bula] *nf* (*papal*) bull.
bulbo ['bulßo] *nm* (*BOT*) bulb.
bulevar [bule'ßar] *nm* boulevard.
Bulgaria [bul'xarja] *nf* Bulgaria.
búlgaro, a ['bulxaro, a] *adj, nm/f* Bulgarian.
bulimia [bu'limja] *nf* bulimia.
bulla ['buʎa] *nf* (*ruido*) uproar; (*de gente*)
crowd; **armar o meter ~** to kick up a
row.
bullendo [bu'ʎendo] *etc vb V* **bullir**.
bullicio [bu'ʎiθjo] *nm* (*ruido*) uproar;
(*movimiento*) bustle.
bullicioso, a [buʎi'θjoso, a] *adj* (*ruidoso*)
noisy, (*calle etc*) busy; (*situación*)
turbulent.
bullir [bu'ʎir] *vi* (*hervir*) to boil; (*burbujear*)
to bubble; (*mover*) to move, stir;
(*insectos*) to swarm; **~ de** (*fig*) to teem o
seethe with.
bulo ['bulo] *nm* false rumour.
bulto ['bulto] *nm* (*paquete*) package; (*fardo*)
bundle; (*tamaño*) size, bulkiness; (*MED*)
swelling, lump; (*silueta*) vague shape;
(*estatua*) bust, statue; **hacer ~** to take up

space; **escurrir el ~** to make o.s. scarce;
(*fig*) to dodge the issue.
buñuelo [bu'ɲwelo] *nm* ≈ doughnut, donut
(*US*).
BUP [bup] *nm abr* (*ESP ESCOL*:= *Bachillerato
Unificado y Polivalente*) *secondary
education for 14-17 age group;* V *tb*
sistema educativo.
buque ['buke] *nm* ship, vessel; **~ de guerra**
warship; **~ mercante** merchant ship; **~
de vela** sailing ship.
burbuja [bur'ßuxa] *nf* bubble; **hacer ~s** to
bubble; (*gaseosa*) to fizz.
burbujear [burßuxe'ar] *vi* to bubble.
burdel [bur'ðel] *nm* brothel.
Burdeos [bur'ðeos] *nm* Bordeaux.
burdo, a ['burðo, a] *adj* coarse, rough.
burgalés, esa [burxa'les, esa] *adj* of o from
Burgos ♦ *nm/f* native o inhabitant of
Burgos.
burgués, esa [bur'xes, esa] *adj* middle-
class, bourgeois; **pequeño ~** lower
middle-class; (*POL, pey*) petty bourgeois.
burguesía [burxe'sia] *nf* middle class,
bourgeoisie.
burla ['burla] *nf* (*mofa*) gibe; (*broma*) joke;
(*engaño*) trick; **hacer ~ de** to make fun
of.
burladero [burla'ðero] *nm* (bullfighter's)
refuge.
burlador, a [burla'ðor, a] *adj* mocking
♦ *nm/f* mocker; (*bromista*) joker ♦ *nm*
(*libertino*) seducer.
burlar [bur'lar] *vt* (*engañar*) to deceive;
(*seducir*) to seduce ♦ *vi*, **~se** *vr* to joke;
~se de to make fun of.
burlesco, a [bur'lesko, a] *adj* burlesque.
burlón, ona [bur'lon, ona] *adj* mocking.
buró [bu'ro] *nm* bureau.
burocracia [buro'kraθja] *nf* bureaucracy.
burócrata [bu'rokrata] *nm/f* bureaucrat.
buromática [buro'matika] *nf* office
automation.
burrada [bu'rraða] *nf* stupid act; **decir ~s**
to talk nonsense.
burro, a ['burro, a] *nm/f* (*ZOOL*) donkey;
(*fig*) ass, idiot ♦ *adj* stupid; **caerse del ~**
to realise one's mistake; **no ver tres en
un ~** to be as blind as a bat.
bursátil [bur'satil] *adj* stock-exchange *cpd*.
bus [bus] *nm* bus.
busca ['buska] *nf* search, hunt ♦ *nm*
bleeper, pager; **en ~ de** in search of.
buscador, a [buska'ðor, a] *adj, nm/f* searcher.
buscapiés [buska'pjes] *nm inv* jumping
jack (*BRIT*), firecracker (*US*).
buscapleitos [buska'pleitos] *nm/f inv*
troublemaker.

buscar [bus'kar] *vt* to look for; (*objeto perdido*) to have a look for; (*beneficio*) to seek; (*enemigo*) to seek out; (*traer*) to bring, fetch; (*provocar*) to provoke; (*INFORM*) to search ♦ *vi* to look, search, seek; **ven a ~me a la oficina** come and pick me up at the office; **~le 3 o 4 pies al gato** to split hairs; **"~ y reemplazar"** (*INFORM*) "search and replace"; **se busca secretaria** secretary wanted; **se la buscó** he asked for it.

buscavidas [buska'ßiðas] *nm/f inv* snooper; (*persona ambiciosa*) go-getter.

buscona [bus'kona] *nf* whore.

busilis [bu'silis] *nm inv* (*fam*) snag.

busque ['buske] *etc vb V* **buscar.**

búsqueda ['buskeða] *nf* = **busca.**

busto ['busto] *nm* (*ANAT, ARTE*) bust.

butaca [bu'taka] *nf* armchair; (*de cine, teatro*) stall, seat.

butano [bu'tano] *nm* butane (gas); **bombona de ~** gas cylinder.

butifarra [buti'farra] *nf* Catalan sausage.

buzo ['buθo] *nm* diver; (*AM: chandal*) tracksuit.

buzón [bu'θon] *nm* (*gen*) letter box; (*en la calle*) pillar box (*BRIT*); (*TELEC*) mailbox; **echar al ~** to post.

buzonear [buθone'ar] *vt* to leaflet.

byte [bait] *nm* (*INFORM*) byte.

Cc

C, c [θe, se (*esp AM*)] *nf* (*letra*) C, c; **C de Carmen** C for Charlie.

C. *abr* (= *centígrado*) C.; (= *compañía*) Co.

c. *abr* (= *capítulo*) ch.

C/ *abr* (= *calle*) St, Rd.

c/ *abr* (*COM*: = *cuenta*) a/c.

ca [ka] *excl* not a bit of it!

c.a. *abr* (= *corriente alterna*) A.C.

cabal [ka'ßal] *adj* (*exacto*) exact; (*correcto*) right, proper; (*acabado*) finished, complete; **~es** *nmpl*: **estar en sus ~es** to be in one's right mind.

cábala ['kaßala] *nf* (*REL*) cab(b)ala; (*fig*) cabal, intrigue; **~s** *nfpl* guess *sg*, supposition *sg*.

cabalgadura [kaßalɣa'ðura] *nf* mount, horse.

cabalgar [kaßal'ɣar] *vt, vi* to ride.

cabalgata [kaßal'ɣata] *nf* procession; *V tb* **Reyes Magos.**

cabalgue [ka'ßalɣe] *etc vb V* **cabalgar.**

cabalístico, a [kaßa'listiko, a] *adj* (*fig*) mysterious.

caballa [ka'ßaʎa] *nf* mackerel.

caballeresco, a [kaßaʎe'resko, a] *adj* noble, chivalrous.

caballería [kaßaʎe'ria] *nf* mount; (*MIL*) cavalry.

caballeriza [kaßaʎe'riθa] *nf* stable.

caballerizo [kaßaʎe'riθo] *nm* groom, stableman.

caballero [kaßa'ʎero] *nm* gentleman; (*de la orden de caballería*) knight; (*trato directo*) sir; **"C~s"** "Gents".

caballerosidad [kaßaʎerosi'ðað] *nf* chivalry.

caballete [kaßa'ʎete] *nm* (*AGR*) ridge; (*ARTE*) easel.

caballito [kaßa'ʎito] *nm* (*caballo pequeño*) small horse, pony; (*juguete*) rocking horse; **~s** *nmpl* merry-go-round *sg*; **~ de mar** seahorse; **~ del diablo** dragonfly.

caballo [ka'ßaʎo] *nm* horse; (*AJEDREZ*) knight; (*NAIPES*) ≈ queen; **~ de vapor** *o* **de fuerza** horsepower; **es su ~ de batalla** it's his hobby-horse; **~ blanco** (*COM*) backer; *V tb* **Baraja Española.**

cabaña [ka'ßaɲa] *nf* (*casita*) hut, cabin.

cabaré, cabaret, *pl* **cabarets** [kaßa're, kaßa'res] *nm* cabaret.

cabecear [kaßeθe'ar] *vi* to nod.

cabecera [kaße'θera] *nf* (*gen*) head; (*de distrito*) chief town; (*de cama*) headboard; (*IMPRENTA*) headline.

cabecilla [kaße'θiʎa] *nm* ringleader.

cabellera [kaße'ʎera] *nf* (head of) hair; (*de cometa*) tail.

cabello [ka'ßeʎo] *nm* (*tb*: **~s**) hair *sg*.

cabelludo [kaße'ʎuðo] *adj V* **cuero.**

caber [ka'ßer] *vi* (*entrar*) to fit, go; **caben 3 más** there's room for 3 more; **cabe preguntar si...** one might ask whether...; **cabe que venga más tarde** he may come later.

cabestrillo [kaßes'triʎo] *nm* sling.

cabestro [ka'ßestro] *nm* halter.

cabeza [ka'ßeθa] *nf* head; (*POL*) chief, leader ♦ *nm/f*: **~ rapada** skinhead; **caer de ~** to fall head first; **sentar la ~** to settle down; **~ de lectura/escritura** read/write head; **~ impresora** *o* **de impresión** printhead.

cabezada [kaße'θaða] *nf* (*golpe*) butt; **dar una ~** to nod off.

cabezal [kaße'θal] *nm*: **~ impresor** print head.

cabezazo [kaβe'θaθo] nm (golpe) headbutt; (FÚTBOL) header.

cabezón, ona [kaβe'θon, ona] adj with a big head; (vino) heady; (obstinado) obstinate, stubborn.

cabezota [kaβe'θota] adj inv obstinate, stubborn.

cabezudo, a [kaβe'θuðo, a] adj with a big head; (obstinado) obstinate, stubborn.

cabida [ka'βiða] nf space; **dar ~ a** to make room for; **tener ~ para** to have room for.

cabildo [ka'βildo] nm (de iglesia) chapter; (POL) town council.

cabina [ka'βina] nf (de camión) cabin; ~ **telefónica** (tele)phone box (BRIT) o booth.

cabizbajo, a [kaβiθ'βaxo, a] adj crestfallen, dejected.

cable ['kaβle] nm cable; (de aparato) lead; ~ **aéreo** (ELEC) overhead cable; **conectar con ~** (INFORM) to hardwire.

cabo ['kaβo] nm (de objeto) end, extremity; (MIL) corporal; (NAUT) rope, cable; (GEO) cape; (TEC) thread; **al ~ de 3 días** after 3 days; **de ~ a rabo** o **~** from beginning to end; (libro: leer) from cover to cover; **llevar a ~** to carry out; **atar ~s** to tie up the loose ends; **C~ de Buena Esperanza** Cape of Good Hope; **C~ de Hornos** Cape Horn; **las Islas de C~ Verde** the Cape Verde Islands.

cabra ['kaβra] nf goat; **estar como una ~** (fam) to be nuts.

cabré [ka'βre] etc vb V **caber**.

cabrear [kaβre'ar] vt to annoy; **~se** vr to fly off the handle.

cabrío, a [ka'βrio, a] adj goatish; **macho ~** (he-)goat, billy goat.

cabriola [ka'βrjola] nf caper.

cabritilla [kaβri'tiʎa] nf kid, kidskin.

cabrito [ka'βrito] nm kid.

cabrón [ka'βron] nm (fig: fam!) bastard (!).

cabronada [kaβro'naða] nf (fam!): **hacer una ~ a algn** to be a bastard to sb.

caca ['kaka] nf (palabra de niños) pooh ♦ excl: **no toques, ¡~!** don't touch, it's dirty!

cacahuete [kaka'wete] nm (ESP) peanut.

cacao [ka'kao] nm cocoa; (BOT) cacao.

cacarear [kakare'ar] vi (persona) to boast; (gallina) to cackle.

cacatúa [kaka'tua] nf cockatoo.

cacereño, a [kaθe'reɲo, a] adj of o from Cáceres ♦ nm/f native o inhabitant of Cáceres.

cacería [kaθe'ria] nf hunt.

cacerola [kaθe'rola] nf pan, saucepan.

cacha ['katʃa] nf (mango) handle; (nalga) buttock.

cachalote [katʃa'lote] nm sperm whale.

cacharro [ka'tʃarro] nm (vasija) (earthenware) pot; (cerámica) piece of pottery; (fam) useless object; **~s** nmpl pots and pans.

cachear [katʃe'ar] vt to search, frisk.

cachemir [katʃe'mir] nm cashmere.

cacheo [ka'tʃeo] nm searching, frisking.

cachete [ka'tʃete] nm (ANAT) cheek; (bofetada) slap (in the face).

cachimba [ka'tʃimba] nf, **cachimbo** [ka'tʃimbo] nm (AM) pipe.

cachiporra [katʃi'porra] nf truncheon.

cachivache [katʃi'βatʃe] nm piece of junk; **~s** nmpl trash sg, junk sg.

cacho, a ['katʃo, a] nm (small) bit; (AM: cuerno) horn.

cachondearse [katʃonde'arse] vr: **~ de algn** to tease sb.

cachondeo [katʃon'deo] nm (fam) farce, joke; (guasa) lark.

cachondo, a [ka'tʃondo, a] adj (ZOOL) on heat; (persona) randy, sexy; (gracioso) funny.

cachorro, a [ka'tʃorro, a] nm/f (perro) pup, puppy; (león) cub.

cacique [ka'θike] nm chief, local ruler; (POL) local party boss; (fig) despot.

caco ['kako] nm pickpocket.

cacofonía [kakofo'nia] nf cacophony.

cacto ['kakto] nm, **cactus** ['kaktus] nm inv cactus.

cada ['kaða] adj inv each; (antes de número) every; **~ día** each day, every day; **~ dos días** every other day; **~ uno/a** each one, every one; **~ vez más/menos** more and more/less and less; **uno de ~ diez** one out of every ten; **¿~ cuánto?** how often?

cadalso [ka'ðalso] nm scaffold.

cadáver [ka'ðaβer] nm (dead) body, corpse.

cadavérico, a [kaða'βeriko, a] adj cadaverous; (pálido) deathly pale.

cadena [ka'ðena] nf chain; (TV) channel; **reacción en ~** chain reaction; **trabajo en ~** assembly line work; **~ midi/mini** (MUS) midi/mini system; **~ perpetua** (JUR) life imprisonment; **~ de caracteres** (INFORM) character string.

cadencia [ka'ðenθja] nf cadence, rhythm.

cadera [ka'ðera] nf hip.

cadete [ka'ðete] nm cadet.

Cádiz ['kaðiθ] nm Cadiz.

caducar [kaðu'kar] vi to expire.

caducidad [kaðuθi'ðað] nf: **fecha de ~** expiry date; (de comida) sell-by date.

caduco, a [ka'ðuko, a] adj (idea etc) outdated, outmoded; **de hoja caduca**

·

deciduous.

caduque [ka'ðuke] *etc vb V* **caducar.**

C.A.E. *abr* (= *cóbrese al entregar*) COD.

caer [ka'er] *vi* to fall; (*premio*) to go; (*sitio*) to be, lie; (*pago*) to fall due; **~se** *vr* to fall (down); **dejar ~** to drop; **estar al ~** to be due to happen; (*persona*) to be about to arrive; **me cae bien/mal** I like/don't like him; **~ en la cuenta** to catch on; **su cumpleaños cae en viernes** her birthday falls on a Friday; **se me ha caído el guante** I've dropped my glove.

café, *pl* **cafés** [ka'fe, ka'fes] *nm* (*bebida, planta*) coffee; (*lugar*) café ♦ *adj* (*color*) brown; **~ con leche** white coffee; **~ solo, ~ negro** (*AM*) (small) black coffee.

cafeína [kafe'ina] *nf* caffein(e).

cafetal [kafe'tal] *nm* coffee plantation.

cafetera [kafe'tera] *nf V* **cafetero.**

cafetería [kafete'ria] *nf* cafe.

cafetero, a [kafe'tero, a] *adj* coffee *cpd* ♦ *nf* coffee pot; **ser muy ~** to be a coffee addict.

cafre ['kafre] *nm/f*: **como ~s** (*fig*) like savages.

cagalera [kaɣa'lera] *nf* (*fam!*): **tener ~** to have the runs.

cagar [ka'ɣar] (*fam!*) *vt* to shit (*!*); (*fig*) to bungle, mess up ♦ *vi* to have a shit (*!*); **~se** *vr*: **¡me cago en diez** (*etc*)! Christ! (*!*).

cague ['kaɣe] *etc vb V* **cagar.**

caído, a [ka'iðo, a] *adj* fallen; (*INFORM*) down ♦ *nf* fall; (*declive*) slope; (*disminución*) fall, drop; **~ del cielo** out of the blue; **a la caída del sol** at sunset; **sufrir una caída** to have a fall.

caiga ['kaiɣa] *etc vb V* **caer.**

caimán [kai'man] *nm* alligator.

Cairo ['kairo] *nm*: **el ~** Cairo.

caja ['kaxa] *nf* box; (*ataúd*) coffin, casket (*US*); (*para reloj*) case; (*de ascensor*) shaft; (*COM*) cashbox; (*ECON*) fund; (*donde se hacen los pagos*) cashdesk; (*en supermercado*) checkout, till; (*TIP*) case; **~ de ahorros** savings bank; **~ de cambios** gearbox; **~ fuerte, ~ de caudales** safe, strongbox; **ingresar en ~** to be paid in.

cajero, a [ka'xero, a] *nm/f* cashier; (*en banco*) (bank) teller ♦ *nm*: **~ automático** cash dispenser, automatic telling machine, A.T.M.

cajetilla [kaxe'tiʎa] *nf* (*de cigarrillos*) packet.

cajista [ka'xista] *nm/f* typesetter.

cajón [ka'xon] *nm* big box; (*de mueble*) drawer.

cal [kal] *nf* lime; **cerrar algo a ~ y canto** to

shut sth firmly.

cala ['kala] *nf* (*GEO*) cove, inlet; (*de barco*) hold.

calabacín [kalaßa'θin] *nm* (*BOT*) baby marrow, courgette, zucchini (*US*).

calabaza [kala'ßaθa] *nf* (*BOT*) pumpkin; **dar ~s a** (*candidato*) to fail.

calabozo [kala'ßoθo] *nm* (*cárcel*) prison; (*celda*) cell.

calado, a [ka'laðo, a] *adj* (*prenda*) lace *cpd* ♦ *nm* (*TEC*) fretwork; (*NAUT*) draught ♦ *nf* (*de cigarrillo*) puff; **estar ~** (**hasta los huesos**) to be soaked (to the skin).

calamar [kala'mar] *nm* squid.

calambre [ka'lambre] *nm* (*tb*: **~s**) cramp.

calamidad [kalami'ðað] *nf* calamity, disaster; (*persona*): **es una ~** he's a dead loss.

calamina [kala'mina] *nf* calamine.

cálamo ['kalamo] *nm* (*BOT*) stem; (*MUS*) reed.

calaña [ka'laɲa] *nf* model, pattern; (*fig*) nature, stamp.

calar [ka'lar] *vt* to soak, drench; (*penetrar*) to pierce, penetrate; (*comprender*) to see through; (*vela, red*) to lower; **~se** *vr* (*AUTO*) to stall; **~se las gafas** to stick one's glasses on.

calavera [kala'ßera] *nf* skull.

calcañal [kalka'ɲal], **calcañar** [kalka'ɲar] *nm* heel.

calcar [kal'kar] *vt* (*reproducir*) to trace; (*imitar*) to copy.

calce ['kalθe] *etc vb V* **calzar.**

calceta [kal'θeta] *nf* (knee-length) stocking; **hacer ~** to knit.

calcetín [kalθe'tin] *nm* sock.

calcinar [kalθi'nar] *vt* to burn, blacken.

calcio ['kalθjo] *nm* calcium.

calco ['kalko] *nm* tracing.

calcomanía [kalkoma'nia] *nf* transfer.

calculador, a [kalkula'ðor, a] *adj* calculating ♦ *nf* calculator.

calcular [kalku'lar] *vt* (*MAT*) to calculate, compute; **~ que ...** to reckon that ....

cálculo ['kalkulo] *nm* calculation; (*MED*) (gall)stone; (*MAT*) calculus; **~ de costo** costing; **~ diferencial** differential calculus; **obrar con mucho ~** to act cautiously.

caldear [kalde'ar] *vt* to warm (up), heat (up); (*metales*) to weld.

caldera [kal'dera] *nf* boiler.

calderero [kalde'rero] *nm* boilermaker.

calderilla [kalde'riʎa] *nf* (*moneda*) small change.

caldero [kal'dero] *nm* small boiler.

caldo ['kaldo] *nm* stock; (*consomé*)

consommé; ~ **de cultivo** (*BIO*) culture medium; **poner a ~ a algn** to tear sb off a strip; **los ~s jerezanos** sherries.

caldoso, a [kalˈdoso, a] *adj* (*guisado*) juicy; (*sopa*) thin.

calé [kaˈle] *adj* gipsy *cpd*.

calefacción [kalefakˈθjon] *nf* heating; ~ **central** central heating.

caleidoscopio [kaleiðosˈkopjo] *nm* kaleidoscope.

calendario [kalenˈdarjo] *nm* calendar.

calentador [kalentaˈðor] *nm* heater.

calentamiento [kalentaˈmjento] *nm* (*DEPORTE*) warm-up.

calentar [kalenˈtar] *vt* to heat (up); (*fam: excitar*) to turn on; (*AM: enfurecer*) to anger; **~se** *vr* to heat up, warm up; (*fig: discusión etc*) to get heated.

calentura [kalenˈtura] *nf* (*MED*) fever, (high) temperature; (*de boca*) mouth sore.

calenturiento, a [kalentuˈrjento, a] *adj* (*mente*) overactive.

calibrar [kaliˈβrar] *vt* to gauge, measure.

calibre [kaˈliβre] *nm* (*de cañón*) calibre, bore; (*diámetro*) diameter; (*fig*) calibre.

calidad [kaliˈðað] *nf* quality; **de ~** quality *cpd*; ~ **de borrador** (*INFORM*) draft quality; ~ **de carta** *o* **de correspondencia** (*INFORM*) letter quality; ~ **texto** (*INFORM*) text quality; ~ **de vida** quality of life; **en ~ de** in the capacity of.

cálido, a [ˈkaliðo, a] *adj* hot; (*fig*) warm.

caliente [kaˈljente] *etc vb V* **calentar** ♦ *adj* hot; (*fig*) fiery; (*disputa*) heated; (*fam: cachondo*) randy.

califa [kaˈlifa] *nm* caliph.

calificación [kalifikaˈθjon] *nf* qualification; (*de alumno*) grade, mark; ~ **de sobresaliente** first-class mark.

calificar [kalifiˈkar] *vt* to qualify; (*alumno*) to grade, mark; ~ **de** to describe as.

calificativo, a [kalifikaˈtiβo, a] *adj* qualifying ♦ *nm* qualifier, epithet.

califique [kaliˈfike] *etc vb V* **calificar**.

californiano, a [kaliforˈnjano, a] *adj, nm/f* Californian.

caligrafía [kaliɣraˈfia] *nf* calligraphy.

calima [kaˈlima] *nf* mist.

calina [kaˈlina] *nf* haze.

cáliz [ˈkaliθ] *nm* (*BOT*) calyx; (*REL*) chalice.

caliza [kaˈliθa] *nf* limestone.

callado, a [kaˈʎaðo, a] *adj* quiet, silent.

callar [kaˈʎar] *vt* (*asunto delicado*) to keep quiet about; (*say nothing about*; (*omitir*) to pass over in silence; (*persona, oposición*) to silence ♦ *vi*, **~se** *vr* to keep quiet, be silent; (*dejar de hablar*) to stop

talking; ¡**calla**!, be quiet!; ¡**cállate**!, ¡**cállese**! shut up!; ¡**cállate la boca**! shut your mouth!

calle [ˈkaʎe] *nf* street; (*DEPORTE*) lane; ~ **arriba/abajo** up/down the street; ~ **de sentido único** one-way street; **poner a algn (de patitas) en la ~** to kick sb out.

calleja [kaˈʎexa] *nf* alley, narrow street.

callejear [kaʎexeˈar] *vi* to wander (about) the streets.

callejero, a [kaʎeˈxero, a] *adj* street *cpd* ♦ *nm* street map.

callejón [kaʎeˈxon] *nm* alley, passage; (*GEO*) narrow pass; ~ **sin salida** cul-de-sac; (*fig*) blind alley.

callejuela [kaʎeˈxwela] *nf* side-street, alley.

callista [kaˈʎista] *nm/f* chiropodist.

callo [ˈkaʎo] *nm* callus; (*en el pie*) corn; **~s** *nmpl* (*CULIN*) tripe *sg*.

callosidad [kaʎosiˈðað] *nf* (*de pie*) corn; (*de mano*) callus.

calloso, a [kaˈʎoso, a] *adj* horny, rough.

calma [ˈkalma] *nf* calm; (*pachorra*) slowness; (*COM, ECON*) calm, lull; ~ **chicha** dead calm; ¡~!, ¡**con ~**! take it easy!

calmante [kalˈmante] *adj* soothing ♦ *nm* sedative, tranquillizer.

calmar [kalˈmar] *vt* to calm, calm down; (*dolor*) to relieve ♦ *vi*, **~se** *vr* (*tempestad*) to abate; (*mente etc*) to become calm.

calmoso, a [kalˈmoso, a] *adj* calm, quiet.

caló [kaˈlo] *nm* (*de gitanos*) gipsy language, Romany; (*argot*) slang.

calor [kaˈlor] *nm* heat; (~ *agradable*) warmth; **entrar en ~** to get warm; **tener ~** to be *o* feel hot.

caloría [kaloˈria] *nf* calorie.

calorífero, a [kaloˈrifero, a] *adj* heat-producing, heat-giving ♦ *nm* heating system.

calque [ˈkalke] *etc vb V* **calcar**.

calumnia [kaˈlumnja] *nf* slander; (*por escrito*) libel.

calumniar [kalumˈnjar] *vt* to slander; to libel.

calumnioso, a [kalumˈnjoso, a] *a* slanderous; libellous.

caluroso, a [kaluˈroso, a] *adj* hot; (*sin exceso*) warm; (*fig*) enthusiastic.

calva [ˈkalβa] *nf* bald patch; (*en bosque*) clearing.

calvario [kalˈβarjo] *nm* stations *pl* of the cross; (*fig*) cross, heavy burden.

calvicie [kalˈβiθje] *nf* baldness.

calvo, a [ˈkalβo, a] *adj* bald; (*terreno*) bare, barren; (*tejido*) threadbare ♦ *nm* bald man.

calza ['kalθa] *nf* wedge, chock.

calzado, a [kal'θaðo, a] *adj* shod ♦ *nm* footwear ♦ *nf* roadway, highway.

calzador [kalθa'ðor] *nm* shoehorn.

calzar [kal'θar] *vt* (*zapatos etc*) to wear; (*un mueble*) to put a wedge under; (*TEC: rueda etc*) to scotch; **~se** *vr*: **~se los zapatos** to put on one's shoes; **¿qué (número) calza?** what size do you take?

calzón [kal'θon] *nm* (*tb*: **calzones**) shorts *pl*; (*AM: de hombre*) pants *pl*; (: *de mujer*) panties *pl*.

calzonazos [kalθo'naθos] *nm inv* henpecked husband.

calzoncillos [kalθon'θiʎos] *nmpl* underpants.

cama ['kama] *nf* bed; (*GEO*) stratum; **~ individual/de matrimonio** single/double bed; **guardar ~** to be ill in bed.

camada [ka'maða] *nf* litter; (*de personas*) gang, band.

camafeo [kama'feo] *nm* cameo.

camaleón [kamale'on] *nm* chameleon.

cámara ['kamara] *nf* (*POL etc*) chamber; (*habitación*) room; (*sala*) hall; (*CINE*) cine camera; (*fotográfica*) camera; **~ de aire** inner tube; **~ alta/baja** upper/lower house; **~ de comercio** chamber of commerce; **~ de gas** gas chamber; **~ de video** video camera; **a ~ lenta** in slow motion.

camarada [kama'raða] *nm* comrade, companion.

camaradería [kamaraðe'ria] *nf* comradeship.

camarero, a [kama'rero, a] *nm* waiter ♦ *nf* (*en restaurante*) waitress; (*en casa, hotel*) maid.

camarilla [kama'riʎa] *nf* (*clan*) clique; (*POL*) lobby.

camarín [kama'rin] *nm* (*TEAT*) dressing room.

camarón [kama'ron] *nm* shrimp.

camarote [kama'rote] *nm* (*NAUT*) cabin.

cambiable [kam'bjaβle] *adj* (*variable*) changeable, variable; (*intercambiable*) interchangeable.

cambiante [kam'bjante] *adj* variable.

cambiar [kam'bjar] *vt* to change; (*trocar*) to exchange ♦ *vi* to change; **~se** *vr* (*mudarse*) to move; (*de ropa*) to change; **~(se) de ...** to change one's ...; **~ de idea/de ropa** to change one's mind/ clothes.

cambiazo [kam'bjaθo] *nm*: **dar el ~ a algn** to swindle sb.

cambio ['kambjo] *nm* change; (*trueque*) exchange; (*COM*) rate of exchange; (*oficina*) bureau de change; (*dinero menudo*) small change; **en ~** on the other hand; (*en lugar de eso*) instead; **~ de divisas** (*COM*) foreign exchange; **~ de línea** (*INFORM*) line feed; **~ de página** (*INFORM*) form feed; **~ a término** (*COM*) forward exchange; **~ de velocidades** gear lever; **~ de vía** points *pl*.

cambista [kam'bista] *nm* (*COM*) exchange broker.

Camboya [kam'boja] *nf* Cambodia, Kampuchea.

camboyano, a [kambo'jano, a] *a, nm/f* Cambodian, Kampuchean.

camelar [kame'lar] *vt* (*con mujer*) to flirt with; (*persuadir*) to cajole.

camelia [ka'melia] *nf* camellia.

camello [ka'meʎo] *nm* camel; (*fam: traficante*) pusher.

camelo [ka'melo] *nm*: **me huele a ~** it smells fishy.

camerino [kame'rino] *nm* (*TEAT*) dressing room.

camilla [ka'miʎa] *nf* (*MED*) stretcher.

caminante [kami'nante] *nm/f* traveller.

caminar [kami'nar] *vi* (*marchar*) to walk, go; (*viajar*) to travel, journey ♦ *vt* (*recorrer*) to cover, travel.

caminata [kami'nata] *nf* long walk.

camino [ka'mino] *nm* way, road; (*sendero*) track; **a medio ~** halfway (there); **en el ~** on the way, en route; **~ de** on the way to; **~ particular** private road; **~ vecinal** country road; **C~s, Canales y Puertos** (*UNIV*) Civil Engineering; **ir por buen ~** (*fig*) to be on the right track.

---

*The **Camino de Santiago** is a medieval pilgrim route stretching from the Pyrenees to Santiago de Compostela in north-west Spain, where tradition has it the body of the Apostle James is buried. Nowadays it is a popular tourist route as well as a religious one. The **concha** (cockleshell) is a symbol of the **Camino de Santiago**, because it is said that when St James' body was found it was covered in shells.*

---

camión [ka'mjon] *nm* lorry, truck (*US*); (*AM: autobús*) bus; **~ de bomberos** fire engine.

camionero [kamjo'nero] *nm* lorry *o* truck (*US*) driver, trucker (*esp US*).

camioneta [kamjo'neta] *nf* van, transit ®, light truck.

camisa [ka'misa] *nf* shirt; (*BOT*) skin; **~ de dormir** nightdress; **~ de fuerza**

straitjacket.
camisería [kamise'ria] *nf* outfitter's (shop).
camiseta [kami'seta] *nf* tee-shirt; (*ropa interior*) vest; (*de deportista*) top.
camisón [kami'son] *nm* nightdress, nightgown.
camomila [kamo'mila] *nf* camomile.
camorra [ka'morra] *nf*: **armar** ~ to kick up a row; **buscar** ~ to look for trouble.
camorrista [kamo'rrista] *nm/f* thug.
camote [ka'mote] *nm* (*AM*) sweet potato.
campal [kam'pal] *adj*: **batalla** ~ pitched battle.
campamento [kampa'mento] *nm* camp.
campana [kam'pana] *nf* bell.
campanada [kampa'naða] *nf* peal.
campanario [kampa'narjo] *nm* belfry.
campanilla [kampa'niʎa] *nf* (*campana*) small bell.
campante [kam'pante] *adj*: **siguió tan** ~ he went on as if nothing had happened.
campaña [kam'paɲa] *nf* (*MIL, POL*) campaign; **hacer** ~ (**en pro de/contra**) to campaign (for/against); ~ **de venta** sales campaign.
campechano, a [kampe't ʃano, a] *adj* open.
campeón, ona [kampe'on, ona] *nm/f* champion.
campeonato [kampeo'nato] *nm* championship.
campesino, a [kampe'sino, a] *adj* country *cpd*, rural; (*gente*) peasant *cpd* ♦ *nm/f* countryman/woman; (*agricultor*) farmer.
campestre [kam'pestre] *adj* country *cpd*, rural.
camping ['kampin] *nm* camping; (*lugar*) campsite; **ir de** *o* **hacer** ~ to go camping.
campiña [kam'piɲa] *nf* countryside.
campista [kam'pista] *nm/f* camper.
campo ['kampo] *nm* (*fuera de la ciudad*) country, countryside; (*AGR, ELEC, INFORM*) field; (*de fútbol*) pitch; (*de golf*) course; (*MIL*) camp; ~ **de batalla** battlefield; ~ **de minas** minefield; ~ **petrolífero** oilfield; ~ **visual** field of vision; ~ **de concentración/de internación/de trabajo** concentration/internment/labour camp.
camposanto [kampo'santo] *nm* cemetery.
CAMPSA ['kampsa] *nf abr* (*ESP COM*) = Compañía Arrendataria del Monopolio de Petróleos, S.A.
campus ['kampus] *nm inv* (*UNIV*) campus.
camuflaje [kamu'flaxe] *nm* camouflage.
camuflar [kamu'flar] *vt* to camouflage.
can [kan] *nm* dog, mutt (*fam*).
cana ['kana] *nf* V **cano**.
Canadá [kana'ða] *nm* Canada.

canadiense [kana'ðjense] *adj, nm/f* Canadian ♦ *nf* fur-lined jacket.
canal [ka'nal] *nm* canal; (*GEO*) channel, strait; (*de televisión*) channel; (*de tejado*) gutter; **C~ de la Mancha** English Channel; **C~ de Panamá** Panama Canal.
canalice [kana'liθe] *etc vb* V **canalizar**.
canalizar [kanali'θar] *vt* to channel.
canalla [ka'naʎa] *nf* rabble, mob ♦ *nm* swine.
canallada [kana'ʎaða] *nf* (*hecho*) dirty trick.
canalón [kana'lon] *nm* (*conducto vertical*) drainpipe; (*del tejado*) gutter; **canalones** *nmpl* (*CULIN*) cannelloni.
canapé, *pl* **canapés** [kana'pe, kana'pes] *nm* sofa, settee; (*CULIN*) canapé.
Canarias [ka'narjas] *nfpl*: **las (Islas)** ~ the Canaries, the Canary Isles.
canario, a [ka'narjo, a] *adj* of *o* from the Canary Isles ♦ *nm/f* native *o* inhabitant of the Canary Isles ♦ *nm* (*ZOOL*) canary.
canasta [ka'nasta] *nf* (round) basket.
canastilla [kanas'tiʎa] *nf* small basket; (*de niño*) layette.
canasto [ka'nasto] *nm* large basket.
cancela [kan'θela] *nf* (wrought-iron) gate.
cancelación [kanθela'θjon] *nf* cancellation.
cancelar [kanθe'lar] *vt* to cancel; (*una deuda*) to write off.
cáncer ['kanθer] *nm* (*MED*) cancer; **C~** (*ASTRO*) Cancer.
cancerígeno, a [kanθe'rixeno, a] *adj* carcinogenic.
cancha ['kant ʃa] *nf* (*de baloncesto, tenis etc*) court; (*AM: de fútbol etc*) pitch.
canciller [kanθi'ʎer] *nm* chancellor; **C~** (*AM*) Foreign Minister, ≈ Foreign Secretary (*BRIT*).
Cancillería [kansiʎe'ria] *nf* (*AM*) Foreign Ministry, ≈ Foreign Office (*BRIT*).
canción [kan'θjon] *nf* song; ~ **de cuna** lullaby.
cancionero [kanθjo'nero] *nm* song book.
candado [kan'daðo] *nm* padlock.
candela [kan'dela] *nf* candle.
candelabro [kande'laßro] *nm* candelabra.
candelero [kande'lero] *nm* (*para vela*) candlestick; (*de aceite*) oil lamp.
candente [kan'dente] *adj* red-hot; (*tema*) burning.
candidato, a [kandi'ðato, a] *nm/f* candidate; (*para puesto*) applicant.
candidatura [kandiða'tura] *nf* candidature.
candidez [kandi'ðeθ] *nf* (*sencillez*) simplicity; (*simpleza*) naiveté.
cándido, a ['kandiðo, a] *adj* simple; naive.
candil [kan'dil] *nm* oil lamp.

candilejas [kandi'lexas] *nfpl* (*TEAT*) footlights.

candor [kan'dor] *nm* (*sinceridad*) frankness; (*inocencia*) innocence.

canela [ka'nela] *nf* cinnamon.

canelo [ka'nelo] *nm*: **hacer el ~** to act the fool.

canelones [kane'lones] *nmpl* cannelloni.

cangrejo [kan'grexo] *nm* crab.

canguro [kan'guro] *nm* (*ZOOL*) kangaroo; (*de niños*) baby-sitter; **hacer de ~** to baby-sit.

caníbal [ka'niβal] *adj, nm/f* cannibal.

canica [ka'nika] *nf* marble.

caniche [ka'nitʃe] *nm* poodle.

canícula [ka'nikula] *nf* midsummer heat.

canijo, a [ka'nixo, a] *adj* frail, sickly.

canilla [ka'niʎa] *nf* (*TEC*) bobbin.

canino, a [ka'nino, a] *adj* canine ♦ *nm* canine (tooth).

canje [kan'xe] *nm* exchange; (*trueque*) swap.

canjear [kanxe'ar] *vt* to exchange; (*trocar*) to swap.

cano, a ['kano, a] *adj* grey-haired, white-haired ♦ *nf* (*tb*: **canas**) white *o* grey hair; **tener canas** to be going grey.

canoa [ka'noa] *nf* canoe.

canon ['kanon] *nm* canon; (*pensión*) rent; (*COM*) tax.

canonice [kano'niθe] *etc vb V* **canonizar**.

canónico, a [ka'noniko, a] *adj*: **derecho ~** canon law.

canónigo [ka'nonixo] *nm* canon.

canonizar [kanoni'θar] *vt* to canonize.

canoro, a [ka'noro, a] *adj* melodious.

canoso, a [ka'noso, a] *adj* (*pelo*) grey (*BRIT*), gray (*US*); (*persona*) grey-haired.

cansado, a [kan'saðo, a] *adj* tired, weary; (*tedioso*) tedious, boring; **estoy ~ de hacerlo** I'm sick of doing it.

cansancio [kan'sanθjo] *nm* tiredness, fatigue.

cansar [kan'sar] *vt* (*fatigar*) to tire, tire out; (*aburrir*) to bore; (*fastidiar*) to bother; **~se** *vr* to tire, get tired; (*aburrirse*) to get bored.

cantábrico, a [kan'taβriko, a] *adj* Cantabrian; **Mar C~** Bay of Biscay; **(Montes) C~s, Cordillera Cantábrica** Cantabrian Mountains.

cántabro, a ['kantaβro, a] *adj, nm/f* Cantabrian.

cantante [kan'tante] *adj* singing ♦ *nm/f* singer.

cantaor, a [kanta'or, a] *nm/f* Flamenco singer.

cantar [kan'tar] *vt* to sing ♦ *vi* to sing; (*insecto*) to chirp; (*rechinar*) to squeak; (*fam*: *criminal*) to squeal ♦ *nm* (*acción*) singing; (*canción*) song; (*poema*) poem; **~ a algn las cuarenta** to tell sb a few home truths; **~ a dos voces** to sing a duet.

cántara ['kantara] *nf* large pitcher.

cántaro ['kantaro] *nm* pitcher, jug.

cantautor, a [kantau'tor, a] *nm/f* singer-songwriter.

cante ['kante] *nm*: **~ jondo** flamenco singing.

cantera [kan'tera] *nf* quarry.

cántico ['kantiko] *nm* (*REL*) canticle; (*fig*) song.

cantidad [kanti'ðað] *nf* quantity, amount; (*ECON*) sum ♦ *adv* (*fam*) a lot; **~ alzada** lump sum; **~ de** lots of.

cantilena [kanti'lena] *nf* = **cantinela**.

cantimplora [kantim'plora] *nf* (*frasco*) water bottle, canteen.

cantina [kan'tina] *nf* canteen; (*de estación*) buffet; (*esp AM*) bar.

cantinela [kanti'nela] *nf* ballad, song.

canto ['kanto] *nm* singing; (*canción*) song; (*borde*) edge, rim; (*de un cuchillo*) back; **~ rodado** boulder.

cantón [kan'ton] *nm* canton.

cantor, a [kan'tor, a] *nm/f* singer.

canturrear [kanturre'ar] *vi* to sing softly.

canutas [ka'nutas] *nfpl*: **pasarlas ~** (*fam*) to have a rough time (of it).

canuto [ka'nuto] *nm* (*tubo*) small tube; (*fam*: *droga*) joint.

caña ['kaɲa] *nf* (*BOT*: *tallo*) stem, stalk; (*carrizo*) reed; (*vaso*) tumbler; (*de cerveza*) glass of beer; (*ANAT*) shinbone; (*AM*: *aguardiente*) cane liquor; **~ de azúcar** sugar cane; **~ de pescar** fishing rod.

cañada [ka'ɲaða] *nf* (*entre dos montañas*) gully, ravine; (*camino*) cattle track.

cáñamo ['kaɲamo] *nm* (*BOT*) hemp.

cañaveral [kaɲaβe'ral] *nm* (*BOT*) reedbed; (*AGR*) sugar-cane field.

cañería [kaɲe'ria] *nf* piping; (*tubo*) pipe.

caño ['kaɲo] *nm* (*tubo*) tube, pipe; (*de aguas servidas*) sewer; (*MUS*) pipe; (*NAUT*) navigation channel; (*de fuente*) jet.

cañón [ka'ɲon] *nm* (*MIL*) cannon; (*de fusil*) barrel; (*GEO*) canyon, gorge.

cañonazo [kaɲo'naθo] *nm* (*MIL*) gunshot.

cañonera [kaɲo'nera] *nf* (*tb*: **lancha ~**) gunboat.

caoba [ka'oβa] *nf* mahogany.

caos ['kaos] *nm* chaos.

caótico, a [ka'otiko, a] *adj* chaotic.

C.A.P. *nm abr* (= *Certificado de Aptitud*

Pedagógica) teaching certificate.
cap. *abr* (= *capítulo*) ch.
capa ['kapa] *nf* cloak, cape; (*CULIN*) coating; (*GEO*) layer, stratum; (*de pintura*) coat; **de ~ y espada** cloak-and-dagger; **so ~ de** under the pretext of; **~ de ozono** ozone layer; **~s sociales** social groups.
capacho [ka'patʃo] *nm* wicker basket.
capacidad [kapaθi'ðað] *nf* (*medida*) capacity; (*aptitud*) capacity, ability; **una sala con ~ para 900** a hall seating 900; **~ adquisitiva** purchasing power.
capacitación [kapaθita'θjon] *nf* training.
capacitar [kapaθi'tar] *vt*: **~ a algn para algo** to qualify sb for sth; (*TEC*) to train sb for sth.
capar [ka'par] *vt* to castrate, geld.
caparazón [kapara'θon] *nm* (*ZOOL*) shell.
capataz [kapa'taθ] *nm* foreman, chargehand.
capaz [ka'paθ] *adj* able, capable; (*amplio*) capacious, roomy; **es ~ que venga mañana** (*AM*) he'll probably come tomorrow.
capcioso, a [kap'θjoso, a] *adj* wily, deceitful; **pregunta capciosa** trick question.
capea [ka'pea] *nf* (*TAUR*) bullfight with young bulls.
capear [kape'ar] *vt* (*dificultades*) to dodge; **~ el temporal** to weather the storm.
capellán [kape'ʎan] *nm* chaplain; (*sacerdote*) priest.
caperuza [kape'ruθa] *nf* hood; (*de bolígrafo*) cap.
capi ['kapi] *nf* (*esp AM fam*) capital (city).
capicúa [kapi'kua] *nf* reversible number, *e.g.* 1441.
capilar [kapi'lar] *adj* hair *cpd.*
capilla [ka'piʎa] *nf* chapel.
capital [kapi'tal] *adj* capital ♦ *nm* (*COM*) capital ♦ *nf* (*de nación*) capital (city); (*tb*: **~ de provincia**) provincial capital, ≈ county town; **~ activo/en acciones** working/share *o* equity capital; **~ arriesgado** venture capital; **~ autorizado** *o* **social** authorised capital; **~ emitido** issued capital; **~ improductivo** idle money; **~ invertido** *o* **utilizado** capital employed; **~ pagado** paid-up capital; **~ de riesgo** risk capital; **~ social** equity *o* share capital; **inversión de ~es** capital investment; *V tb* **provincia**.
capitalice [kapita'liθe] *etc vb V* **capitalizar**.
capitalino, a [kapita'lino, a] *adj* (*AM*) of *o* from the capital ♦ *nm/f* native *o* inhabitant of the capital.

capitalismo [kapita'lismo] *nm* capitalism.
capitalista [kapita'lista] *adj*, *nm/f* capitalist.
capitalizar [kapitali'θar] *vt* to capitalize.
capitán [kapi'tan] *nm* captain; (*fig*) leader.
capitana [kapi'tana] *nf* flagship.
capitanear [kapitane'ar] *vt* to captain.
capitanía [kapita'nia] *nf* captaincy.
capitel [kapi'tel] *nm* (*ARQ*) capital.
capitolio [kapi'toljo] *nm* capitol.
capitulación [kapitula'θjon] *nf* (*rendición*) capitulation, surrender; (*acuerdo*) agreement, pact; **capitulaciones matrimoniales** marriage contract *sg.*
capitular [kapitu'lar] *vi* to come to terms, make an agreement; (*MIL*) to surrender.
capítulo [ka'pitulo] *nm* chapter.
capo [ka'po] *nm* drugs baron.
capó [ka'po] *nm* (*AUTO*) bonnet (*BRIT*), hood (*US*).
capón [ka'pon] *nm* capon.
caporal [kapo'ral] *nm* chief, leader.
capota [ka'pota] *nf* (*de mujer*) bonnet; (*AUTO*) hood (*BRIT*), top (*US*).
capote [ka'pote] *nm* (*abrigo: de militar*) greatcoat; (*de torero*) cloak.
capricho [ka'pritʃo] *nm* whim, caprice.
caprichoso, a [kapri'tʃoso, a] *adj* capricious.
Capricornio [kapri'kornjo] *nm* Capricorn.
cápsula ['kapsula] *nf* capsule; **~ espacial** space capsule.
captar [kap'tar] *vt* (*comprender*) to understand; (*RADIO*) to pick up; (*atención, apoyo*) to attract.
captura [kap'tura] *nf* capture; (*JUR*) arrest.
capturar [kaptu'rar] *vt* to capture; (*JUR*) to arrest; (*datos*) to input.
capucha [ka'putʃa] *nf* hood, cowl.
capullo [ka'puʎo] *nm* (*ZOOL*) cocoon; (*BOT*) bud; (*fam!*) berk (*BRIT*), jerk (*US*).
caqui ['kaki] *nm* khaki.
cara ['kara] *nf* (*ANAT, de moneda*) face; (*aspecto*) appearance; (*de disco*) side; (*fig*) boldness; (*descara*) cheek, nerve ♦ *prep*: **~ a** facing; **de ~ a** opposite, facing; **dar la ~** to face the consequences; **echar algo en ~ a algn** to reproach sb for sth; **¿~ o cruz?** heads or tails?; **¡ qué ~ más dura!** what a nerve!; **de una ~** (*disquete*) single-sided.
carabina [kara'βina] *nf* carbine, rifle; (*persona*) chaperone.
carabinero [karaβi'nero] *nm* (*de aduana*) customs officer; (*AM*) gendarme.
Caracas [ka'rakas] *nm* Caracas.
caracol [kara'kol] *nm* (*ZOOL*) snail; (*concha*) (sea)shell; **escalera de ~** spiral staircase.

caracolear [karakole'ar] *vi* (*caballo*) to prance about.

carácter, *pl* **caracteres** [ka'rakter, karak'teres] *nm* character; ~ **de cambio de página** (*INFORM*) form feed character; **caracteres de imprenta** (*TIP*) type(face) *sg*; ~ **libre** (*INFORM*) wildcard character; **tener buen/mal** ~ to be good-natured/bad tempered.

caracterice [karakte'riθe] *etc vb V* **caracterizar**.

característico, a [karakte'ristiko, a] *adj* characteristic ♦ *nf* characteristic.

caracterizar [karakteri'θar] *vt* (*distinguir*) to characterize, typify; (*honrar*) to confer (a) distinction on.

caradura [kara'ðura] *nm/f* cheeky person; **es un** ~ he's got a nerve.

carajillo [kara'xiʎo] *nm black coffee with brandy.*

carajo [ka'raxo] *nm* (*esp AM fam!*): ¡~! shit!(*!*); ¡**qué** ~! what the hell!; **me importa un** ~ I don't give a damn.

caramba [ka'ramba] *excl* well!, good gracious!

carámbano [ka'rambano] *nm* icicle.

carambola [karam'bola] *nf*: **por** ~ by a fluke.

caramelo [kara'melo] *nm* (*dulce*) sweet; (*azúcar fundido*) caramel.

carantoñas [karan'toɲas] *nfpl*: **hacer** ~ **a algn** to (try to) butter sb up.

caraqueño, a [kara'keɲo, a] *adj* of *o* from Caracas ♦ *nm/f* native *o* inhabitant of Caracas.

carátula [ka'ratula] *nf* (*máscara*) mask; (*TEAT*): **la** ~ the stage.

caravana [kara'ßana] *nf* caravan; (*fig*) group; (*de autos*) tailback.

carbón [kar'ßon] *nm* coal; ~ **de leña** charcoal; **papel** ~ carbon paper.

carbonatado, a [karßono'taðo, a] *adj* carbonated.

carbonato [karßo'nato] *nm* carbonate; ~ **sódico** sodium carbonate.

carboncillo [karßon'θiʎo] *nm* (*ARTE*) charcoal.

carbonice [karßo'niθe] *etc vb V* **carbonizar**.

carbonilla [karßo'niʎa] *nf* coal dust.

carbonizar [karßoni'θar] *vt* to carbonize; (*quemar*) to char; **quedar carbonizado** (*ELEC*) to be electrocuted.

carbono [kar'ßono] *nm* carbon.

carburador [karßura'ðor] *nm* carburettor.

carburante [karßu'rante] *nm* fuel.

carca [ˈkarka] *adj, nm/f inv* reactionary.

carcajada [karka'xaða] *nf* (loud) laugh, guffaw.

carcajearse [karkaxe'arse] *vr* to roar with laughter.

cárcel [ˈkarθel] *nf* prison, jail; (*TEC*) clamp.

carcelero, a [karθe'lero, a] *adj* prison *cpd* ♦ *nm/f* warder.

carcoma [kar'koma] *nf* woodworm.

carcomer [karko'mer] *vt* to bore into, eat into; (*fig*) to undermine; ~**se** *vr* to become worm-eaten; (*fig*) to decay.

carcomido, a [karko'miðo, a] *adj* worm-eaten; (*fig*) rotten.

cardar [kar'ðar] *vt* (*TEC*) to card, comb.

cardenal [karðe'nal] *nm* (*REL*) cardinal; (*MED*) bruise.

cárdeno, a [ˈkarðeno, a] *adj* purple; (*lívido*) livid.

cardiaco, a [kar'ðjako, a], **cardíaco, a** [kar'ðiako, a] *adj* cardiac; (*ataque*) heart *cpd*.

cardinal [karði'nal] *adj* cardinal.

cardiólogo, a [karðj'oloɣo, a] *nm/f* cardiologist.

cardo [ˈkarðo] *nm* thistle.

carear [kare'ar] *vt* to bring face to face; (*comparar*) to compare; ~**se** *vr* to come face to face, meet.

carecer [kare'θer] *vi*: ~ **de** to lack, be in need of.

carencia [ka'renθja] *nf* lack; (*escasez*) shortage; (*MED*) deficiency.

carente [ka'rente] *adj*: ~ **de** lacking in, devoid of.

carestía [kares'tia] *nf* (*escasez*) scarcity, shortage; (*COM*) high cost; **época de** ~ period of shortage.

careta [ka'reta] *nf* mask.

carey [ka'rei] *nm* (*tortuga*) turtle; (*concha*) tortoiseshell.

carezca [ka'reθka] *etc vb V* **carecer**.

carga [ˈkarɣa] *nf* (*peso, ELEC*) load; (*de barco*) cargo, freight; (*FINANZAS*) tax, duty; (*MIL*) charge; (*INFORM*) loading; (*obligación, responsabilidad*) duty, obligation; ~ **aérea** (*COM*) air cargo; ~ **útil** (*COM*) payload; **la** ~ **fiscal** the tax burden.

cargadero [karɣa'ðero] *nm* goods platform, loading bay.

cargado, a [kar'ɣaðo, a] *adj* loaded; (*ELEC*) live; (*café, té*) strong; (*cielo*) overcast.

cargador, a [karɣa'ðor, a] *nm/f* loader; (*NAUT*) docker ♦ *nm* (*INFORM*): ~ **de discos** disk pack.

cargamento [karɣa'mento] *nm* (*acción*) loading; (*mercancías*) load, cargo.

cargante [kar'ɣante] *adj* (*persona*) trying.

cargar [kar'ɣar] *vt* (*barco, arma*) to load; (*ELEC*) to charge; (*impuesto*) to impose;

(*COM: algo en cuenta*) to charge, debit; (*MIL: enemigo*) to charge ♦ *vi* (*AUTO*) to load (up); (*inclinarse*) to lean; (*INFORM*) to load, feed in; ~ **con** to pick up, carry away; ~**se** *vr* (*fam: estropear*) to break; (: *matar*) to bump off; (*ELEC*) to become charged.

cargo ['karɣo] *nm* (*COM etc*) charge, debit; (*puesto*) post, office; (*responsabilidad*) duty, obligation; (*fig*) weight, burden; (*JUR*) charge; **altos** ~**s** high-ranking officials; **una cantidad en** ~ **a algn** a sum chargeable to sb; **hacerse** ~ **de** to take charge of *o* responsibility for.

cargue ['karɣe] *etc vb* V **cargar**.

carguero [kar'ɣero] *nm* freighter, cargo boat; (*avión*) freight plane.

Caribe [ka'riße] *nm*: **el** ~ the Caribbean.

caribeño, a [kari'ßeɲo, a] *adj* Caribbean.

caricatura [karika'tura] *nf* caricature.

caricia [ka'riθja] *nf* caress; (*a animal*) pat, stroke.

caridad [kari'ðað] *nf* charity.

caries ['karjes] *nf inv* (*MED*) tooth decay.

carilla [ka'riʎa] *nf* (*TIP*) page.

cariño [ka'riɲo] *nm* affection, love; (*caricia*) caress; (*en carta*) love ....

cariñoso, a [kari'ɲoso, a] *adj* affectionate.

carioca [ka'rjoka] *adj* (*AM*) of *o* from Rio de Janeiro ♦ *nm/f* native *o* inhabitant of Rio de Janeiro.

carisma [ka'risma] *nm* charisma.

carismático, a [karis'matiko, a] *adj* charismatic.

caritativo, a [karita'tißo, a] *adj* charitable.

cariz [ka'riθ] *nm*: **tener** *o* **tomar buen/mal** ~ to look good/bad.

carmesí [karme'si] *adj, nm* crimson.

carmín [kar'min] *nm* (*color*) carmine; ~ **(de labios)** lipstick.

carnal [kar'nal] *adj* carnal; **primo** ~ first cousin.

carnaval [karna'ßal] *nm* carnival.

The 3 days before **miércoles de ceniza** (*Ash Wednesday*), *when fasting traditionally starts, are the time for* **carnaval,** *an exuberant celebration which dates back to pre-Christian times. Although in decline during the Franco years, the carnaval has grown in popularity recently in Spain, Cádiz and Tenerife being particularly well-known for their celebrations.* **El martes de carnaval** (*Shrove Tuesday*) *is the biggest day, with colourful street parades, fancy dress, fireworks and a general party atmosphere.*

---

carne ['karne] *nf* flesh; (*CULIN*) meat; ~ **de cañón** cannon fodder; ~ **de cerdo/de cordero/de ternera/de vaca** pork/lamb/veal/beef; ~ **picada** mince; ~ **de gallina** (*fig*) gooseflesh.

carné [kar'ne] *nm* = **carnet**.

carnero [kar'nero] *nm* sheep, ram; (*carne*) mutton.

carnet, *pl* **carnets** [kar'ne, kar'nes] *nm*: ~ **de conducir** driving licence; ~ **de identidad** identity card; V tb **Documento Nacional de Identidad**.

carnicería [karniθe'ria] *nf* butcher's (shop); (*fig: matanza*) carnage, slaughter.

carnicero, a [karni'θero, a] *adj* carnivorous ♦ *nm/f* (*tb fig*) butcher ♦ *nm* carnivore.

carnívoro, a [kar'nißoro, a] *adj* carnivorous ♦ *nm* carnivore.

carnoso, a [kar'noso, a] *adj* beefy, fat.

caro, a ['karo, a] *adj* dear; (*COM*) dear, expensive ♦ *adv* dear, dearly; **vender** ~ to sell at a high price.

carpa ['karpa] *nf* (*pez*) carp; (*de circo*) big top; (*AM: de camping*) tent.

carpeta [kar'peta] *nf* folder, file.

carpetazo [karpe'taθo] *nm*: **dar** ~ **a** to shelve.

carpintería [karpinte'ria] *nf* carpentry.

carpintero [karpin'tero] *nm* carpenter; **pájaro** ~ woodpecker.

carraca [ka'rraka] *nf* (*DEPORTE*) rattle.

carraspear [karraspe'ar] *vi* (*aclararse*) to clear one's throat.

carraspera [karras'pera] *nf* hoarseness.

carrera [ka'rrera] *nf* (*acción*) run(ning); (*espacio recorrido*) run; (*certamen*) race; (*trayecto*) course; (*profesión*) career; (*ESCOL, UNIV*) course; (*de taxi*) ride; (*en medias*) ladder; **a la** ~ at (full) speed; **caballo de** ~**(s)** racehorse; ~ **de armamentos** arms race.

carrerilla [karre'riʎa] *nf*: **decir algo de** ~ to reel sth off; **tomar** ~ to get up speed.

carreta [ka'rreta] *nf* wagon, cart.

carrete [ka'rrete] *nm* reel, spool; (*TEC*) coil.

carretera [karre'tera] *nf* (*main*) road, highway; ~ **nacional** ≈ A road (*BRIT*), state highway (*US*); ~ **de circunvalación** ring road.

carretilla [karre'tiʎa] *nf* trolley; (*AGR*) (wheel)barrow.

carril [ka'rril] *nm* furrow; (*de autopista*) lane; (*FERRO*) rail.

carrillo [ka'rriʎo] *nm* (*ANAT*) cheek; (*TEC*) pulley.

carro ['karro] *nm* cart, wagon; (*MIL*) tank; (*AM: coche*) car; (*TIP*) carriage; ~ **blindado** armoured car.

carrocería [karroθe'ria] *nf* body, bodywork *no pl* (*BRIT*).

carroña [ka'rroɲa] *nf* carrion *no pl*.

carroza [ka'rroθa] *nf* (*vehículo*) coach ♦ *nm/f* (*fam*) old fogey.

carruaje [ka'rrwaxe] *nm* carriage.

carrusel [karru'sel] *nm* merry-go-round, roundabout (*BRIT*).

carta ['karta] *nf* letter; (*CULIN*) menu; (*naipe*) card; (*mapa*) map; (*JUR*) document; ~ **de crédito** credit card; ~ **de crédito documentaria** (*COM*) documentary letter of credit; ~ **de crédito irrevocable** (*COM*) irrevocable letter of credit; ~ **certificada/urgente** registered/special delivery letter; ~ **marítima** chart; ~ **de pedido** (*COM*) order; ~ **verde** (*AUTO*) green card; ~ **de vinos** wine list; **echar una** ~ **al correo** to post a letter; **echar las** ~**s a algn** to tell sb's fortune.

cartabón [karta'ßon] *nm* set square.

cartearse [karte'arse] *vr* to correspond.

cartel [kar'tel] *nm* (*anuncio*) poster, placard; (*ESCOL*) wall chart; (*COM*) cartel.

cartelera [karte'lera] *nf* hoarding, billboard; (*en periódico etc*) listings *pl*, entertainments guide; **"en** ~**"** "showing".

cartera [kar'tera] *nf* (*de bolsillo*) wallet; (*de colegial, cobrador*) satchel; (*AM: de señora*) handbag (*BRIT*), purse (*US*); (*para documentos*) briefcase; **ministro sin** ~ (*POL*) minister without portfolio; **ocupa la** ~ **de Agricultura** he is Minister of Agriculture; ~ **de pedidos** (*COM*) order book; **efectos en** ~ (*ECON*) holdings.

carterista [karte'rista] *nm/f* pickpocket.

cartero [kar'tero] *nm* postman.

cartílago [kar'tilaɣo] *nm* cartilage.

cartilla [kar'tiʎa] *nf* (*ESCOL*) primer, first reading book; ~ **de ahorros** bank book.

cartografía [kartoɣra'fia] *nf* cartography.

cartón [kar'ton] *nm* cardboard.

cartucho [kar'tutʃo] *nm* (*MIL*) cartridge; (*bolsita*) paper cone; ~ **de datos** (*INFORM*) data cartridge.

cartulina [kartu'lina] *nf* fine cardboard, card.

CASA ['kasa] *nf abr* (*ESP AVIAT*) = *Construcciones Aeronáuticas S.A.*

casa ['kasa] *nf* house; (*hogar*) home; (*edificio*) building; (*COM*) firm, company; ~ **consistorial** town hall; ~ **de huéspedes** ≈ guest house; ~ **de socorro** first aid post; ~ **de citas** (*fam*) brothel; **ir a** ~ to go home; **salir de** ~ to go out; (*para*

siempre) to leave home; **echar la** ~ **por la ventana** (*gastar*) to spare no expense; *v tb* **hotel**.

casadero, a [kasa'ðero, a] *adj* marriageable.

casado, a [ka'saðo, a] *a* married ♦ *nm/f* married man/woman.

casamiento [kasa'mjento] *nm* marriage, wedding.

casar [ka'sar] *vt* to marry; (*JUR*) to quash, annul; ~**se** *vr* to marry, get married; ~**se por lo civil** to have a civil wedding, get married in a registry office (*BRIT*).

cascabel [kaska'ßel] *nm* (small) bell; (*ZOOL*) rattlesnake.

cascada [kas'kaða] *nf* waterfall.

cascajo [kas'kaxo] *nm* gravel, stone chippings *pl*.

cascanueces [kaska'nweθes] *nm inv*: **un** ~ a pair of nutcrackers.

cascar [kas'kar] *vt* to split; (*nuez*) to crack ♦ *vi* to chatter; ~**se** *vr* to crack, split, break (open).

cáscara ['kaskara] *nf* (*de huevo, fruta seca*) shell; (*de fruta*) skin; (*de limón*) peel.

cascarón [kaska'ron] *nm* (broken) eggshell.

cascarrabias [kaska'rraßjas] *nm/f inv* (*fam*) hothead.

casco ['kasko] *nm* (*de bombero, soldado*) helmet; (*cráneo*) skull; (*NAUT: de barco*) hull; (*ZOOL: de caballo*) hoof; (*botella*) empty bottle; (*de ciudad*): **el** ~ **antiguo** the old part; **el** ~ **urbano** the town centre; **los** ~**s azules** the UN peace-keeping force, the blue berets.

cascote [kas'kote] *nm* piece of rubble; ~**s** *nmpl* rubble *sg*.

caserío [kase'rio] *nm* hamlet, group of houses; (*casa*) country house.

casero, a [ka'sero, a] *adj*: **ser muy** ~ (*persona*) to be homeloving; **"comida casera"** "home cooking" ♦ *nm/f* (*propietario*) landlord/lady; (*COM*) house agent.

caserón [kase'ron] *nm* large (ramshackle) house.

caseta [ka'seta] *nf* hut; (*para bañista*) cubicle; (*de feria*) stall.

casete [ka'sete] *nm o f* cassette: ~ **digital** digital audio tape, DAT.

casi ['kasi] *adv* almost; ~ **nunca** hardly ever, almost never; ~ **nada** next to nothing; ~ **te caes** you almost *o* nearly fell.

casilla [ka'siʎa] *nf* (*casita*) hut, cabin; (*TEAT*) box office; (*para cartas*) pigeonhole; (*AJEDREZ*) square; **C**~ **postal**

o **de Correo(s)** (*AM*) P.O. Box; **sacar a algn de sus** ~ **s** to drive sb round the bend (*fam*), make sb lose his temper.
casillero [kasi'ʎero] *nm* (set of) pigeonholes.
casino [ka'sino] *nm* club; (*de juego*) casino.
caso ['kaso] *nm* case; (*suceso*) event; **en** ~ **de ... in case of ...; el** ~ **es que** the fact is that; **en el mejor de los** ~**s** at best; **en ese** ~ in that case; **en todo** ~ in any case; **en último** ~ as a last resort; **hacer** ~ **a** to pay attention to; **hacer** ~ **omiso de** to fail to mention, pass over; **hacer** *o* **venir al** ~ to be relevant.
caspa ['kaspa] *nf* dandruff.
Caspio ['kaspjo] *adj:* **Mar** ~ Caspian Sea.
casque ['kaske] *etc vb V* **cascar**.
casquillo [kas'kiʎo] *nm* (*de bombilla*) fitting; (*de bala*) cartridge case.
cassette [ka'set] *nf o m* = **casete**.
casta ['kasta] *nf* caste; (*raza*) breed; (*linaje*) lineage.
castaña [kas'taɲa] *nf V* **castaño**.
castañetear [kastaɲete'ar] *vi* (*dientes*) to chatter.
castaño, a [kas'taɲo, a] *adj* chestnut (-coloured), brown ♦ *nm* chestnut tree ♦ *nf* chestnut; (*fam: golpe*) punch; ~ **de Indias** horse chestnut tree.
castañuelas [kasta'ɲwelas] *nfpl* castanets.
castellano, a [kaste'ʎano, a] *adj* Castilian; (*fam*) Spanish ♦ *nm/f* Castilian; (*fam*) Spaniard ♦ *nm* (*LING*) Castilian, Spanish.

The term **castellano** *is now the most widely used term in Spain and Spanish America to refer to the Spanish language, since* **español** *is too closely associated with Spain as a nation. Of course some people maintain that* **castellano** *should only refer to the type of Spanish spoken in* **Castilla**.

castellonense [kasteʎo'nense] *adj* of *o* from Castellón de la Plana ♦ *nm/f* native *o* inhabitant of Castellón de la Plana.
castidad [kasti'ðað] *nf* chastity, purity.
castigar [kasti'ɣar] *vt* to punish; (*DEPORTE*) to penalize; (*afligir*) to afflict.
castigo [kas'tiɣo] *nm* punishment; (*DEPORTE*) penalty.
castigue [kas'tiɣe] *etc vb V* **castigar**.
Castilla [kas'tiʎa] *nf* Castile.
castillo [kas'tiʎo] *nm* castle.
castizo, a [kas'tiθo, a] *adj* (*LING*) pure; (*de buena casta*) purebred, pedigree; (*auténtico*) genuine.
casto, a ['kasto, a] *adj* chaste, pure.
castor [kas'tor] *nm* beaver.

castrar [kas'trar] *vt* to castrate; (*gato*) to doctor; (*BOT*) to prune.
castrense [kas'trense] *adj* army *cpd*, military.
casual [ka'swal] *adj* chance, accidental.
casualidad [kaswali'ðað] *nf* chance, accident; (*combinación de circunstancias*) coincidence; **¡qué** ~**!** what a coincidence!
casualmente [kaswal'mente] *adv* by chance.
cataclismo [kata'klismo] *nm* cataclysm.
catador [kata'ðor] *nm* taster.
catadura [kata'ðura] *nf* (*aspecto*) looks *pl*.
catalán, ana [kata'lan, ana] *adj, nm/f* Catalan ♦ *nm* (*LING*) Catalan; *V tb* **lenguas cooficiales**.
catalejo [kata'lexo] *nm* telescope.
catalizador [kataliθa'ðor] *nm* catalyst; (*AUTO*) catalytic converter.
catalogar [katalo'ɣar] *vt* to catalogue; ~ **(de)** (*fig*) to classify (as).
catálogo [ka'taloɣo] *nm* catalogue.
catalogue [kata'loɣe] *etc vb V* **catalogar**.
Cataluña [kata'luɲa] *nf* Catalonia.
cataplasma [kata'plasma] *nf* (*MED*) poultice.
catapulta [kata'pulta] *nf* catapult.
catar [ka'tar] *vt* to taste, sample.
catarata [kata'rata] *nf* (*GEO*) (water)fall; (*MED*) cataract.
catarro [ka'tarro] *nm* catarrh; (*constipado*) cold.
catarsis [ka'tarsis] *nf* catharsis.
catastro [ka'tastro] *nm* property register.
catástrofe [ka'tastrofe] *nf* catastrophe.
catear [kate'ar] *vt* (*fam*) to flunk.
catecismo [kate'θismo] *nm* catechism.
cátedra ['kateðra] *nf* (*UNIV*) chair, professorship; (*ESCOL*) principal teacher's post; **sentar** ~ **sobre un argumento** to take one's stand on an argument.
catedral [kate'ðral] *nf* cathedral.
catedrático, a [kate'ðratiko, a] *nm/f* professor; (*ESCOL*) principal teacher.
categoría [kateɣo'ria] *nf* category; (*rango*) rank, standing; (*calidad*) quality; **de** ~ (*hotel*) top-class; **de baja** ~ (*oficial*) low-ranking; **de segunda** ~ second-rate; **no tiene** ~ he has no standing.
categórico, a [kate'ɣoriko, a] *adj* categorical.
catequesis [kate'kesis] *nf* catechism lessons.
caterva [ka'terßa] *nf* throng, crowd.
cateto, a [ka'teto, a] *nm/f* yokel.
cátodo ['katoðo] *nm* cathode.

catolicismo [katoli'θismo] *nm* Catholicism.
católico, a [ka'toliko, a] *adj, nm/f* Catholic.
catorce [ka'torθe] *num* fourteen.
catre ['katre] *nm* camp bed (*BRIT*), cot (*US*); (*fam*) pit.
Cáucaso ['kaukaso] *nm* Caucasus.
cauce ['kauθe] *nm* (*de río*) riverbed; (*fig*) channel.
caucho ['kautʃo] *nm* rubber; (*AM: llanta*) tyre.
caución [kau'θjon] *nf* bail.
caucionar [kauθjo'nar] *vt* (*JUR*) to bail (out), go bail for.
caudal [kau'ðal] *nm* (*de río*) volume, flow; (*fortuna*) wealth; (*abundancia*) abundance.
caudaloso, a [kauða'loso, a] *adj* (*río*) large; (*persona*) wealthy, rich.
caudillaje [kauði'ʎaxe] *nm* leadership.
caudillo [kau'ðiʎo] *nm* leader, chief.
causa ['kausa] *nf* cause; (*razón*) reason; (*JUR*) lawsuit, case; **a** *o* **por ~ de** because of, on account of.
causar [kau'sar] *vt* to cause.
cáustico, a ['kaustiko, a] *adj* caustic.
cautela [kau'tela] *nf* caution, cautiousness.
cauteloso, a [kaute'loso, a] *adj* cautious, wary.
cautivar [kauti'ßar] *vt* to capture; (*fig*) to captivate.
cautiverio [kauti'ßerjo] *nm*, **cautividad** [kautißi'ðað] *nf* captivity.
cautivo, a [kau'tißo, a] *adj, nm/f* captive.
cauto, a ['kauto, a] *adj* cautious, careful.
cava ['kaßa] *nf* (*bodega*) (wine) cellar ♦ *nm* (*vino*) *champagne-type wine*.
cavar [ka'ßar] *vt* to dig; (*AGR*) to dig over.
caverna [ka'ßerna] *nf* cave, cavern.
cavernoso, a [kaßer'noso, a] *adj* cavernous; (*voz*) resounding.
caviar [ka'ßjar] *nm* caviar(e).
cavidad [kaßi'ðað] *nf* cavity.
cavilación [kaßila'θjon] *nf* deep thought.
cavilar [kaßi'lar] *vt* to ponder.
cayado [ka'jaðo] *nm* (*de pastor*) crook; (*de obispo*) crozier.
cayendo [ka'jendo] *etc vb V* **caer.**
caza ['kaθa] *nf* (*acción: gen*) hunting; (: *con fusil*) shooting; (*una ~*) hunt, chase; (*animales*) game; **coto de ~** hunting estate ♦ *nm* (*AVIAT*) fighter.
cazabe [ka'saße] *nm* (*AM*) cassava bread *o* flour.
cazador, a [kaθa'ðor, a] *nm/f* hunter/huntress ♦ *nf* jacket.
cazaejecutivos [kaθaexeku'tißos] *nm inv* (*COM*) headhunter.
cazar [ka'θar] *vt* to hunt; (*perseguir*) to

chase; (*prender*) to catch; **~las al vuelo** to be pretty sharp.
cazasubmarinos [kaθasußma'rinos] *nm inv* (*NAUT*) destroyer; (*AVIAT*) anti-submarine craft.
cazo ['kaθo] *nm* saucepan.
cazuela [ka'θwela] *nf* (*vasija*) pan; (*guisado*) casserole.
cazurro, a [ka'θurro, a] *adj* surly.
CC *nm abr* (*POL*: = *Comité Central*) Central Committee.
c/c. *abr* (*COM*: = *cuenta corriente*) current account.
CC.AA. *abr* (*ESP*) = **Comunidades Autónomas.**
CCI *nf abr* (*COM*: = *Cámara de Comercio Internacional*) ICC.
CC.OO. *nfpl abr* = **Comisiones Obreras.**
CD *nm abr* (= *compact disc*) CD ♦ *abr* (*POL*: = *Cuerpo Diplomático*) CD.
c/d *abr* (= *en casa de*) c/o; (= *con descuento*) with discount.
CDN *nm abr* (= *Centro Dramático Nacional*) ≈ RADA (*BRIT*).
CDS *nm abr* (= *Centro Democrático y Social*) *political party*.
CE *nm abr* (= *Consejo de Europa*) Council of Europe ♦ *nf abr* (= *Comunidad Europea*) EC.
cebada [θe'ßaða] *nf* barley.
cebar [θe'ßar] *vt* (*animal*) to fatten (up); (*anzuelo*) to bait; (*MIL, TEC*) to prime; **~se** *vr*: **~se en** to vent one's fury on, take it out on.
cebo ['θeßo] *nm* (*para animales*) feed, food; (*para peces, fig*) bait; (*de arma*) charge.
cebolla [θe'ßoʎa] *nf* onion.
cebolleta [θeßo'ʎeta] *nf* spring onion.
cebollino [θeßo'ʎino] *nm* spring onion.
cebón, ona [θe'ßon, ona] *adj* fat, fattened.
cebra ['θeßra] *nf* zebra; **paso de ~** zebra crossing.
CECA ['θeka] *nf abr* (= *Comunidad Europea del Carbón y del Acero*) ECSC.
ceca ['θeka] *nf*: **andar** *o* **ir de la ~ a la Meca** to chase about all over the place.
cecear [θeθe'ar] *vi* to lisp.
ceceo [θe'θeo] *nm* lisp.
cecina [θe'θina] *nf* cured *o* smoked meat.
cedazo [θe'ðaðo] *nm* sieve.
ceder [θe'ðer] *vt* (*entregar*) to hand over; (*renunciar a*) to give up, part with ♦ *vi* (*renunciar*) to give in, yield; (*disminuir*) to diminish, decline; (*romperse*) to give way; (*viento*) to drop; (*fiebre etc*) to abate; **"ceda el paso"** (*AUTO*) "give way".
cedro ['θeðro] *nm* cedar.
cédula ['θeðula] *nf* certificate, document;

~ **de identidad** (*AM*) identity card; ~ **en blanco** blank cheque; *V tb* **Documento Nacional de Identidad**.

CEE *nf abr* (= *Comunidad Económica Europea*) EEC.

cegar [θe'ɣar] *vt* to blind; (*tubería etc*) to block up, stop up ♦ *vi* to go blind; ~**se** *vr* to be blinded (*de* by).

cegué [θe'ɣe] *etc vb V* **cegar**.

ceguemos [θe'ɣemos] *etc vb V* **cegar**.

ceguera [θe'ɣera] *nf* blindness.

CEI *nf abr* (= *Comunidad de Estados Independientes*) CIS.

Ceilán [θei'lan] *nm* Ceylon, Sri Lanka.

ceja ['θexa] *nf* eyebrow; ~**s pobladas** bushy eyebrows; **arquear las** ~**s** to raise one's eyebrows; **fruncir las** ~**s** to frown.

cejar [θe'xar] *vi* (*fig*) to back down; **no** ~ to keep it up, stick at it.

cejijunto, a [θexi'xunto, a] *adj* with bushy eyebrows; (*fig*) scowling.

celada [θe'laða] *nf* ambush, trap.

celador, a [θela'ðor, a] *nm/f* (*de edificio*) watchman; (*de museo etc*) attendant; (*de cárcel*) warder.

celda ['θelda] *nf* cell.

celebérrimo, a [θele'βerrimo, a] *adj* *superlativo de* **célebre**.

celebración [θeleβra'θjon] *nf* celebration.

celebrar [θele'βrar] *vt* to celebrate; (*alabar*) to praise ♦ *vi* to be glad; ~**se** *vr* to occur, take place.

célebre ['θeleβre] *adj* celebrated, renowned.

celebridad [θeleβri'ðað] *nf* fame; (*persona*) celebrity.

celeridad [θeleri'ðað] *nf*: **con** ~ promptly.

celeste [θe'leste] *adj* sky-blue; (*cuerpo etc*) heavenly ♦ *nm* sky blue.

celestial [θeles'tjal] *adj* celestial, heavenly.

celibato [θeli'βato] *nm* celibacy.

célibe ['θeliβe] *adj, nm/f* celibate.

celo ['θelo] *nm* zeal; (*REL*) fervour; (*pey*) envy; ~**s** *nmpl* jealousy *sg*; **dar** ~**s a algn** to make sb jealous; **tener** ~**s de algn** to be jealous of sb; **en** ~ (*animales*) on heat.

celofán [θelo'fan] *nm* Cellophane ®.

celosía [θelo'sia] *nf* lattice (window).

celoso, a [θe'loso, a] *adj* (*envidioso*) jealous; (*trabajador*) zealous; (*desconfiado*) suspicious.

celta ['θelta] *adj* Celtic ♦ *nm/f* Celt.

célula ['θelula] *nf* cell.

celular [θelu'lar] *adj*: **tejido** ~ cell tissue.

celulitis [θelu'litis] *nf* (*enfermedad*) cellulitis; (*grasa*) cellulite.

celuloide [θelu'loiðe] *nm* celluloid.

celulosa [θelu'losa] *nf* cellulose.

cementerio [θemen'terjo] *nm* cemetery, graveyard; ~ **de coches** scrapyard.

cemento [θe'mento] *nm* cement; (*hormigón*) concrete; (*AM*: *cola*) glue.

CEN *nm abr* (*ESP*) = *Consejo de Economía Nacional*.

cena ['θena] *nf* evening meal, dinner.

cenagal [θena'ɣal] *nm* bog, quagmire.

cenar [θe'nar] *vt* to have for dinner, dine on ♦ *vi* to have dinner, dine.

cencerro [θen'θerro] *nm* cowbell; **estar como un** ~ (*fam*) to be round the bend.

cenicero [θeni'θero] *nm* ashtray.

ceniciento, a [θeni'θjento, a] *adj* ash-coloured, ashen.

cenit [θe'nit] *nm* zenith.

ceniza [θe'niθa] *nf* ash, ashes *pl*.

censar [θen'sar] *vt* to take a census of.

censo ['θenso] *nm* census; ~ **electoral** electoral roll.

censor [θen'sor] *nm* censor; ~ **de cuentas** (*COM*) auditor; ~ **jurado de cuentas** chartered (*BRIT*) *ou* certified public (*US*) accountant.

censura [θen'sura] *nf* (*POL*) censorship; (*moral*) censure, criticism.

censurable [θensu'raβle] *adj* reprehensible.

censurar [θensu'rar] *vt* (*idea*) to censure; (*cortar*: *película*) to censor.

centavo [θen'taβo] *nm* hundredth (part); (*AM*) cent.

centella [θen'teʎa] *nf* spark.

centellear [θenteʎe'ar] *vi* (*metal*) to gleam; (*estrella*) to twinkle; (*fig*) to sparkle.

centelleo [θente'ʎeo] *nm* gleam(ing); twinkling; sparkling.

centena [θen'tena] *nf* hundred.

centenar [θente'nar] *nm* hundred.

centenario, a [θente'narjo, a] *adj* one hundred years old ♦ *nm* centenary.

centeno [θen'teno] *nm* rye.

centésimo, a [θen'tesimo, a] *adj, nm* hundredth.

centígrado [θen'tiɣraðo] *adj* centigrade.

centigramo [θenti'ɣramo] *nm* centigramme.

centilitro [θenti'litro] *nm* centilitre (*BRIT*), centiliter (*US*).

centímetro [θen'timetro] *nm* centimetre (*BRIT*), centimeter (*US*).

céntimo, a ['θentimo, a] *adj* hundredth ♦ *nm* cent.

centinela [θenti'nela] *nm* sentry, guard.

centollo, a [θen'toʎo, a] *nm/f* large (*o* spider) crab.

central [θen'tral] *adj* central ♦ *nf* head

office; (*TEC*) plant; (*TELEC*) exchange; ~ **nuclear** nuclear power station.
centralice [θentra'liθe] *etc vb V* **centralizar**.
centralita [θentra'lita] *nf* (*TELEC*) switchboard.
centralización [θentraliθa'θjon] *nf* centralization.
centralizar [θentrali'θar] *vt* to centralize.
centrar [θen'trar] *vt* to centre.
céntrico, a ['θentriko, a] *adj* central.
centrifugar [θentrifu'ɣar] *vt* (*ropa*) to spin-dry.
centrífugo, a [θent'rifuɣo, a] *adj* centrifugal.
centrifugue [θentri'fuɣe] *etc vb V* **centrifugar**.
centrista [θen'trista] *adj* centre *cpd*.
centro ['θentro] *nm* centre; **ser del ~** (*POL*) to be a moderate; **~ de acogida (para niños)** children's home; **~ de beneficios** (*COM*) profit centre; **~ cívico** community centre; **~ comercial** shopping centre; **~ de computatión** computer centre; **~ (de determinación) de costos** (*COM*) cost centre; **~ delantero** (*DEPORTE*) centre forward; **~ docente** teaching institution; **~ juvenil** youth club; **~ social** community centre.
centroafricano, a [θentroafri'kano, a] *adj*: **la República Centroafricana** the Central African Republic.
centroamericano, a [θentroameri'kano, a] *adj*, *nm/f* Central American.
centrocampista [θentrokam'pista] *nm/f* (*DEPORTE*) midfielder.
ceñido, a [θe'ɲido, a] *adj* tight.
ceñir [θe'ɲir] *vt* (*rodear*) to encircle, surround; (*ajustar*) to fit (tightly); (*apretar*) to tighten; **~se** *vr*: **~se algo** to put sth on; **~se al asunto** to stick to the matter in hand.
ceño ['θeɲo] *nm* frown, scowl; **fruncir el ~** to frown, knit one's brow.
CEOE *nf abr* (= *Confederación Española de Organizaciones Empresariales*) ≈ CBI (*BRIT*).
cepa ['θepa] *nf* (*de vid, fig*) stock; (*BIO*) strain.
CEPAL [θe'pal] *nf abr* (= *Comisión Económica de las Naciones Unidas para la América Latina*) ECLA.
cepillar [θepi'ʎar] *vt* to brush; (*madera*) to plane (down).
cepillo [θe'piʎo] *nm* brush; (*para madera*) plane; (*REL*) poorbox, alms box.
cepo ['θepo] *nm* (*caza*) trap.
CEPSA ['θepsa] *nf abr* (*COM*) = *Compañía Española de Petróleos, S.A.*

CEPYME *nf abr* = *Confederación Española de la Pequeña y Mediana Empresa.*
cera ['θera] *nf* wax; **~ de abejas** beeswax.
cerámica [θe'ramika] *nf* pottery; (*arte*) ceramics *sg*.
ceramista [θera'mista] *nm/f* potter.
cerbatana [θerßa'tana] *nf* blowpipe.
cerca ['θerka] *nf* fence ♦ *adv* near, nearby, close; **por aquí ~** nearby ♦ *prep*: **~ de** (*cantidad*) nearly, about; (*distancia*) near, close to ♦ *nmpl*: **~s** foreground *sg*.
cercado [θer'kaðo] *nm* enclosure.
cercanía [θerka'nia] *nf* nearness, closeness; **~s** *nfpl* outskirts, suburbs; **tren de ~s** commuter *o* local train.
cercano, a [θer'kano, a] *adj* close, near; (*pueblo etc*) nearby; **C~ Oriente** Near East.
cercar [θer'kar] *vt* to fence in; (*rodear*) to surround.
cerciorar [θerθjo'rar] *vt* (*asegurar*) to assure; **~se** *vr* (*descubrir*) to find out (*de* about); (*asegurarse*) to make sure (*de* of).
cerco ['θerko] *nm* (*AGR*) enclosure; (*AM*) fence; (*MIL*) siege.
cerda ['θerða] *nf* (*de cepillo*) bristle; (*ZOOL*) sow.
cerdada [θer'ðaða] *nf* (*fam*): **hacer una ~ a algn** to play a dirty trick on sb.
Cerdeña [θer'ðeɲa] *nf* Sardinia.
cerdo ['θerðo] *nm* pig; **carne de ~** pork.
cereal [θere'al] *nm* cereal; **~es** *nmpl* cereals, grain *sg*.
cerebral [θere'ßral] *adj* (*tb fig*) cerebral; (*tumor*) brain *cpd*.
cerebro [θe'reßro] *nm* brain; (*fig*) brains *pl*; **ser un ~** (*fig*) to be brilliant.
ceremonia [θere'monja] *nf* ceremony; **reunión de ~** formal meeting; **hablar sin ~** to speak plainly.
ceremonial [θeremo'njal] *adj*, *nm* ceremonial.
ceremonioso, a [θeremo'njoso, a] *adj* ceremonious; (*cumplido*) formal.
cereza [θe'reθa] *nf* cherry.
cerezo [θe'reθo] *nm* cherry tree.
cerilla [θe'riʎa] *nf*, **cerillo** [se'riʎo] *nm* (*AM*) match.
cerner [θer'ner] *vt* to sift, sieve; **~se** *vr* to hover.
cero ['θero] *nm* nothing, zero; (*DEPORTE*) nil; **8 grados bajo ~** 8 degrees below zero; **a partir de ~** from scratch.
cerque ['θerke] *etc vb V* **cercar**.
cerrado, a [θe'rraðo, a] *adj* closed, shut; (*con llave*) locked; (*tiempo*) cloudy, overcast; (*curva*) sharp; (*acento*) thick, broad; **a puerta cerrada** (*JUR*) in camera.

cerradura [θerra'ðura] nf (acción) closing; (mecanismo) lock.

cerrajería [θerraxe'ria] nf locksmith's craft; (tienda) locksmith's (shop).

cerrajero, a [θerra'xero, a] nm/f locksmith.

cerrar [θe'rrar] vt to close, shut; (paso, carretera) to close; (grifo) to turn off; (trato, cuenta, negocio) to close ♦ vi to close, shut; (la noche) to come down; ~ con llave to lock; ~ el sistema (INFORM) to close o shut down the system; ~ un trato to strike a bargain; ~se vr to close, shut; (herida) to heal.

cerro ['θerro] nm hill; **andar por las ~s de Úbeda** to wander from the point, digress.

cerrojo [θe'rroxo] nm (herramienta) bolt; (de puerta) latch.

certamen [θer'tamen] nm competition, contest.

certero, a [θer'tero, a] adj (gen) accurate.

certeza [θer'teθa], **certidumbre** [θerti'ðumbre] nf certainty.

certificación [θertifika'θjon] nf certification; (JUR) affidavit.

certificado, a [θertifi'kaðo, a] adj certified; (CORREOS) registered ♦ nm certificate.

certificar [θertifi'kar] vt (asegurar, atestar) to certify.

certifique [θerti'fike] etc vb V **certificar.**

cervatillo [θerßa'tiʎo] nm fawn.

cervecería [θerßeθe'ria] nf (fábrica) brewery; (taberna) public house.

cerveza [θer'ßeθa] nf beer; ~ **de barril** draught beer.

cervical [θerßi'kal] adj cervical.

cerviz [θer'ßiθ] nf nape of the neck.

cesación [θesa'θjon] nf cessation, suspension.

cesante [θe'sante] adj redundant; (AM) unemployed; (ministro) outgoing; (diplomático) recalled ♦ nm/f redundant worker.

cesar [θe'sar] vi to cease, stop; (de un trabajo) to leave ♦ vt (en el trabajo) to dismiss; (alto cargo) to remove from office.

cesárea [θe'sarea] nf Caesarean (section).

cese ['θese] nm (de trabajo) dismissal; (de pago) suspension.

Cesid [θe'sið] nm abr (ESP: = Centro Superior de Investigación de la Defensa Nacional) military intelligence service.

cesión [θe'sjon] nf: ~ **de bienes** surrender of property.

césped ['θespeð] nm grass, lawn.

cesta ['θesta] nf basket.

cesto ['θesto] nm (large) basket, hamper.

cetrería [θetre'ria] nf falconry.

cetrino, a [θe'trino, a] adj (tez) sallow.

cetro ['θetro] nm sceptre.

Ceuta [θe'uta] nf Ceuta.

ceutí [θeu'ti] adj of o from Ceuta ♦ nm/f native o inhabitant of Ceuta.

C.F. nm abr (= Club de Fútbol) F.C.

CFC nm abr (= clorofluorocarbono) CFC.

cfr . abr (= confróntese, compárese) cf.

cg. abr (= centígramo) cg.

CGPJ nm abr (= Consejo General del Poder Judicial) governing body of Spanish legal system.

CGS nf abr (Guatemala, El Salvador) = Confederación General de Sindicatos.

CGT nf abr (Colombia, México, Nicaragua, ESP) = Confederación General de Trabajadores; (Argentina) = Confederación General del Trabajo.

Ch, ch [tʃe] nf former letter in the Spanish alphabet.

chabacano, a [tʃaßa'kano, a] adj vulgar, coarse.

chabola [tʃa'ßola] nf shack; ~**s** nfpl shanty town sg.

chabolismo [tʃaßo'lismo] nm: **el problema del** ~ the problem of substandard housing, the shanty town problem.

chacal [tʃa'kal] nm jackal.

chacarero [tʃaka'rero] nm (AM) small farmer.

chacha ['tʃatʃa] nf (fam) maid.

cháchara ['tʃatʃara] nf chatter; **estar de** ~ to chatter away.

chacra ['tʃakra] nf (AM) smallholding.

chafar [tʃa'far] vt (aplastar) to crush, flatten; (arruinar) to ruin.

chaflán [tʃa'flan] nm (TEC) bevel.

chal [tʃal] nm shawl.

chalado, a [tʃa'laðo, a] adj (fam) crazy.

chalé, pl **chalés** [tʃa'le, tʃa'les] nm = **chalet.**

chaleco [tʃa'leko] nm waistcoat, vest (US); ~ **antibala** bulletproof vest; ~ **salvavidas** life jacket.

chalet, pl **chalets** [tʃa'le, tʃa'les] nm villa, ≈ detached house; ~ **adosado** semi-detached house.

chalupa [tʃa'lupa] nf launch, boat.

chamaco, a [tʃa'mako, a] nm/f (AM) boy/girl.

chamarra [tʃa'marra] nf sheepskin jacket; (AM: poncho) blanket.

champán [tʃam'pan] nm, **champaña** [tʃam'paɲa] nm champagne.

champiñón [tʃampi'ɲon] nm mushroom.

champú [tʃam'pu] (pl **champúes,**

champús) *nm* shampoo.

chamuscar [tʃamus'kar] *vt* to scorch, sear, singe.

chamusque [tʃa'muske] *etc vb V* **chamuscar**.

chamusquina [tʃamus'kina] *nf* singeing.

chance ['tʃanθe] *nm* (*a veces nf*) (*AM*) chance, opportunity.

chanchada [tʃan'tʃaða] *nf* (*AM fam*) dirty trick.

chancho, a ['tʃantʃo, a] *nm/f* (*AM*) pig.

chanchullo [tʃan'tʃuʎo] *nm* (*fam*) fiddle, wangle.

chancla ['tʃankla] *nf*, **chancleta** [tʃan'kleta] *nf* flip-flop; (*zapato viejo*) old shoe.

chandal [tʃan'dal] *nm* tracksuit; ~ **(de tactel)** shellsuit.

chantaje [tʃan'taxe] *nm* blackmail; **hacer ~ a uno** to blackmail sb.

chanza ['tʃanθa] *nf* joke.

chao [tʃao] *excl* (*fam*) cheerio.

chapa ['tʃapa] *nf* (*de metal*) plate, sheet; (*de madera*) board, panel; (*de botella*) bottle top; (*insignia*) (lapel) badge; (*AM: AUTO*: ~ **de matrícula**) number (*BRIT*) *o* license (*US*) plate; (*AM cerradura*) lock; **de 3 ~s** (*madera*) 3-ply.

chapado, a [tʃa'paðo, a] *adj* (*metal*) plated; (*muebles etc*) finished.

chaparro, a [tʃa'parro, a] *adj* squat; (*AM: bajito*) short.

chaparrón [tʃapa'rron] *nm* downpour, cloudburst.

chapotear [tʃapote'ar] *vt* to sponge down ♦ *vi* (*fam*) to splash about.

chapucero, a [tʃapu'θero, a] *adj* rough, crude ♦ *nm/f* bungler.

chapurr(e)ar [tʃapurr(e)'ar] *vt* (*idioma*) to speak badly.

chapuza [tʃa'puθa] *nf* botched job.

chapuzón [tʃapu'θon] *nm*: **darse un ~** to go for a dip.

chaqué [tʃa'ke] *nm* morning coat.

chaqueta [tʃa'keta] *nf* jacket; **cambiar la ~** (*fig*) to change sides.

chaquetón [tʃake'ton] *nm* three-quarter-length coat.

charca ['tʃarka] *nf* pond, pool.

charco ['tʃarko] *nm* pool, puddle.

charcutería [tʃarkute'ria] *nf* (*tienda*) shop selling chiefly pork meat products; (*productos*) cooked pork meats *pl*.

charla ['tʃarla] *nf* talk, chat; (*conferencia*) lecture.

charlar [tʃar'lar] *vi* to talk, chat.

charlatán, ana [tʃarla'tan, ana] *nm/f* chatterbox; (*estafador*) trickster.

charol¹ [tʃa'rol] *nm* varnish; (*cuero*) patent leather.

charol² [tʃa'rol] *nm* (*AM*), **charola** [tʃa'rola] *nf* (*AM*) tray.

charqui ['tʃarki] *nm* (*AM*) dried beef, jerky (*US*).

charro, a ['tʃarro, a] *adj* Salamancan; (*AM*) Mexican; (*ropa*) loud, gaudy; (*AM: costumbres*) traditional ♦ *nm/f* Salamancan; Mexican.

chárter ['tʃarter] *adj inv*: **vuelo ~** charter flight.

chascarrillo [tʃaska'rriʎo] *nm* (*fam*) funny story.

chasco ['tʃasko] *nm* (*broma*) trick, joke; (*desengaño*) disappointment.

chasis ['tʃasis] *nm inv* (*AUTO*) chassis; (*FOTO*) plateholder.

chasquear [tʃaske'ar] *vt* (*látigo*) to crack; (*lengua*) to click.

chasquido [tʃas'kiðo] *nm* (*de lengua*) click; (*de látigo*) crack.

chatarra [tʃa'tarra] *nf* scrap (metal).

chato, a ['tʃato, a] *adj* flat; (*nariz*) snub ♦ *nm* wine tumbler; **beber unos ~s** to have a few drinks.

chau [tʃau], **chaucito** [tʃau'sito] *excl* (*fam*) cheerio.

chauvinismo [tʃoßi'nismo] *nm* chauvinism.

chauvinista [tʃoßi'nista] *adj*, *nm/f* chauvinist.

chaval, a [tʃa'ßal, a] *nm/f* kid (*fam*), lad/lass.

chavo ['tʃaßo] *nm* (*AM: fam*) bloke (*BRIT*), guy.

checo, a ['tʃeko, a] *adj*, *nm/f* Czech ♦ *nm* (*LING*) Czech.

checo(e)slovaco, a [tʃeko(e)slo'ßako, a] *adj*, *nm/f* Czech, Czechoslovak.

Checo(e)slovaquia [tʃeko(e)slo'ßakja] *nf* Czechoslovakia.

chepa ['tʃepa] *nf* hump.

cheque ['tʃeke] *nm* cheque (*BRIT*), check (*US*); ~ **abierto/en blanco/cruzado** open/blank/crossed cheque; ~ **al portador** cheque payable to bearer; ~ **caducado** stale cheque; ~ **de viajero** traveller's cheque.

chequeo [tʃe'keo] *nm* (*MED*) check-up; (*AUTO*) service.

chequera [tʃe'kera] *nf* (*AM*) chequebook (*BRIT*), checkbook (*US*).

chévere ['tʃeßere] *adj* (*AM*) great, fabulous (*fam*).

chicano, a [tʃi'kano, a] *adj*, *nm/f* chicano, Mexican-American.

chicha ['tʃitʃa] *nf* (*AM*) maize liquor.

chícharo ['tʃitʃaro] nm (AM) pea.
chicharra [tʃi'tʃarra] nf harvest bug, cicada.
chicharrón [tʃitʃa'rron] nm (pork) crackling.
chichón [tʃi'tʃon] nm bump, lump.
chicle ['tʃikle] nm chewing gum.
chico, a ['tʃiko, a] adj small, little ♦ nm/f child; (muchacho) boy; (muchacha) girl.
chicote [tʃi'kote] nm (AM) whip.
chiflado, a [tʃi'flaðo, a] adj (fam) crazy, round the bend ♦ nm/f nutcase.
chiflar [tʃi'flar] vt to hiss, boo ♦ vi (esp AM) to whistle.
Chile ['tʃile] nm Chile.
chile ['tʃile] nm chilli, pepper.
chileno, a [tʃi'leno, a] adj, nm/f Chilean.
chillar [tʃi'ʎar] vi (persona) to yell, scream; (animal salvaje) to howl; (cerdo) to squeal; (puerta) to creak.
chillido [tʃi'ʎiðo] nm (de persona) yell, scream; (de animal) howl; (de frenos) screech(ing).
chillón, ona [tʃi'ʎon, ona] adj (niño) noisy; (color) loud, gaudy.
chimenea [tʃime'nea] nf chimney; (hogar) fireplace.
chimpancé, pl **chimpancés** [tʃimpan'θe, tʃimpan'θes] nm chimpanzee.
China ['tʃina] nf: (la) ~ China.
china ['tʃina] nf pebble.
chinchar [tʃin'tʃar] (fam) vt to pester, annoy; ~**se** vr to get cross; ¡**chínchate!** tough!
chinche ['tʃintʃe] nf bug; (TEC) drawing pin (BRIT), thumbtack (US) ♦ nm/f nuisance, pest.
chincheta [tʃin'tʃeta] nf drawing pin (BRIT), thumbtack (US).
chinchorro [tʃin'tʃorro] nm (AM) hammock.
chingado, a [tʃin'gaðo, a] adj (esp AM fam!) lousy, bloody (!); **hijo de la ~a** bastard (!), son of a bitch (US!).
chingar [tʃin'gar] vt (AM: fam!) to fuck (up) (!), screw (up) (!); ~**se** vr (AM: emborracharse) to get pissed (BRIT), get plastered (!: fracasar) to fail.
chingue ['tʃinge] etc vb V chingar.
chino, a ['tʃino, a] adj, nm/f Chinese ♦ nm (LING) Chinese; (CULIN) chinois, conical strainer.
chip [tʃip] nm (INFORM) chip.
chipirón [tʃipi'ron] nm squid.
Chipre ['tʃipre] nf Cyprus.
chipriota [tʃi'prjota], **chipriote** [tʃi'prjote] adj Cypriot, Cyprian ♦ nm/f Cypriot.
chiquillada [tʃiki'ʎada] nf childish prank;

(AM: chiquillos) kids pl.
chiquillo, a [tʃi'kiʎo, a] nm/f kid (fam), youngster, child.
chiquito, a [tʃi'kito, a] adj very small, tiny ♦ nm/f kid (fam).
chirigota [tʃiri'ɣota] nf joke.
chirimbolo [tʃirim'bolo] nm thingummyjig (fam).
chirimoya [tʃiri'moja] nf custard apple.
chiringuito [tʃirin'gito] nm refreshment stall o stand.
chiripa [tʃi'ripa] nf fluke; **por** ~ by chance.
chirona [tʃi'rona], (AM) **chirola** [tʃi'rola] nf (fam) clink, jail.
chirriar [tʃi'rrjar] vi (goznes) to creak, squeak; (pájaros) to chirp, sing.
chirrido [tʃi'rriðo] nm creak(ing), squeak(ing); (de pájaro) chirp(ing).
chis [tʃis] excl sh!
chisme ['tʃisme] nm (habladurías) piece of gossip; (fam: objeto) thingummyjig.
chismoso, a [tʃis'moso, a] adj gossiping ♦ nm/f gossip.
chispa ['tʃispa] nf spark; (fig) sparkle; (ingenio) wit; (fam) drunkenness.
chispeante [tʃispe'ante] adj (tb fig) sparkling.
chispear [tʃispe'ar] vi to spark; (lloviznar) to drizzle.
chisporrotear [tʃisporrote'ar] vi (fuego) to throw out sparks; (leña) to crackle; (aceite) to hiss, splutter.
chistar [tʃistar] vi: **no** ~ not to say a word.
chiste ['tʃiste] nm joke, funny story; ~ **verde** blue joke.
chistera [tʃis'tera] nf top hat.
chistoso, a [tʃis'toso, a] adj (gracioso) funny, amusing; (bromista) witty.
chistu ['tʃistu] nm = **txistu**.
chivarse [tʃi'βarse] vr (fam) to grass.
chivatazo [tʃiβa'taθo] nm (fam) tip-off; **dar** ~ to inform.
chivo, a ['tʃiβo, a] nm/f (billy/nanny-)goat; ~ **expiatorio** scapegoat.
chocante [tʃo'kante] adj startling; (extraño) odd; (ofensivo) shocking.
chocar [tʃo'kar] vi (coches etc) to collide, crash; (MIL, fig) to clash ♦ vt to shock; (sorprender) to startle; ~ **con** to collide with; (fig) to run into, run up against; ¡**chócala!** (fam) put it there!
chochear [tʃotʃe'ar] vi to dodder, be senile.
chocho, a ['tʃotʃo, a] adj doddering, senile; (fig) soft, doting.
chocolate [tʃoko'late] adj chocolate ♦ nm chocolate; (fam) dope, marijuana.
chocolatería [tʃokolate'ria] nf chocolate

factory (o shop).

chófer ['tʃofer], **chofer** [tʃo'fer] (esp AM) nm driver.

chollo ['tʃoʎo] nm (fam) bargain, snip.

chomba ['tʃomba], **chompa** ['tʃompa] nf (AM) jumper, sweater.

chopo ['tʃopo] nm black poplar.

choque ['tʃoke] etc vb V **chocar** ♦ nm (impacto) impact; (golpe) jolt; (AUTO) crash; (fig) conflict.

chorizo [tʃo'riθo] nm hard pork sausage, (type of) salami; (ladrón) crook.

chorra ['tʃorra] nf luck.

chorrada [tʃo'rraða] nf (fam): ¡es una ~! that's crap! (!); **decir ~s** to talk crap (!).

chorrear [tʃorre'ar] vt to pour ♦ vi to gush (out), spout (out); (gotear) to drip, trickle.

chorreras [tʃo'rreras] nfpl (COSTURA) frill sg.

chorro ['tʃorro] nm jet; (caudalito) dribble, trickle; (fig) stream; **salir a ~s** to gush forth; **con propulsión a ~** jet-propelled.

chotearse [tʃote'arse] vr to joke.

choteo [tʃo'teo] nm kidding.

choto ['tʃoto] nm (cabrito) kid.

chovinismo [tʃoßi'nismo] nm = **chauvinismo**.

chovinista [tʃoßi'nista] adj, nmf = **chauvinista**.

choza ['tʃoθa] nf hut, shack.

chubasco [tʃu'ßasko] nm squall.

chubasquero [tʃußas'kero] nm oilskins pl.

chuchería [tʃutʃe'ria] nf trinket.

chucho ['tʃutʃo] nm (ZOOL) mongrel.

chufa ['tʃufa] nf chufa, earth almond, tiger nut; **horchata de ~s** drink made from chufas.

chuleta [tʃu'leta] nf chop, cutlet; (ESCOL etc: fam) crib.

chulo, a ['tʃulo, a] adj (encantador) charming; (aire) proud; (pey) fresh; (fam: estupendo) great, fantastic ♦ nm (pícaro) rascal; (madrileño) working-class Madrilenian; (rufián: tb: ~ **de putas**) pimp.

chumbera [tʃum'bera] nf prickly pear.

chungo, a ['tʃungo, a] (fam) adj lousy ♦ nf: **estar de chunga** to be in a merry mood.

chupa ['tʃupa] nf (fam) jacket.

chupado, a [tʃu'paðo, a] adj (delgado) skinny, gaunt; **está ~** (fam) it's simple, it's dead easy.

chupar [tʃu'par] vt to suck; (absorber) to absorb; **~se** vr to grow thin; **para ~se los dedos** mouthwatering.

chupatintas [tʃupa'tintas] nm inv penpusher.

chupe ['tʃupe] nm (AM) stew.

chupete [tʃu'pete] nm dummy (BRIT), pacifier (US).

chupetón [tʃupe'ton] nm suck.

churrasco [tʃu'rrasko] nm (AM) barbecue, barbecued meat.

churrería [tʃurre'ria] nf stall or shop which sells "churros".

churrete [tʃu'rrete] nm grease spot.

churretón [tʃurre'ton] nm stain.

churrigueresco, a [tʃurrige'resko, a] adj (ARQ) baroque; (fig) excessively ornate.

churro, a ['tʃurro, a] adj coarse ♦ nm (CULIN) (type of) fritter; (chapuza) botch, mess.

Churros, long fritters made with flour and water, are very popular in much of Spain and are often eaten with thick hot chocolate, either for breakfast or as a snack. In Madrid, they eat a thicker variety of **churro** called **porra**.

---

churruscar [tʃurrus'kar] vt to fry crisp.

churrusque [tʃu'rruske] etc vb V **churruscar**.

churumbel [tʃurum'bel] nm (fam) kid.

chus [tʃus] excl: **no decir ni ~ ni mus** not to say a word.

chusco, a ['tʃusko, a] adj funny.

chusma ['tʃusma] nf rabble, mob.

chutar [tʃu'tar] vi (DEPORTE) to shoot (at goal); **esto va que chuta** it's going fine.

chuzo ['tʃuθo] nm: **llueve a ~s, llueven ~s de punta** it's raining cats and dogs.

C.I. nm abr = **coeficiente intelectual** o **de inteligencia**.

Cía abr (= compañía) Co.

cianuro [θja'nuro] nm cyanide.

ciática ['θjatika] nf sciatica.

cibernética [θißer'netika] nf cybernetics sg.

cicatrice [θika'triθe] etc vb V **cicatrizar**.

cicatriz [θika'triθ] nf scar.

cicatrizar [θikatri'θar] vt to heal; **~se** vr to heal (up), form a scar.

cíclico, a ['θikliko, a] adj cyclical.

ciclismo [θi'klismo] nm cycling.

ciclista [θi'klista] nmf cyclist.

ciclo ['θiklo] nm cycle.

ciclomotor [θiklomo'tor] nm moped.

ciclón [θi'klon] nm cyclone.

cicloturismo [θiklotu'rismo] nm touring by bicycle.

cicuta [θi'kuta] nf hemlock.

ciego, a ['θjeɣo, a] etc vb V **cegar** ♦ adj blind ♦ nm/f blind man/woman; **a ciegas** blindly; **me puse ~a mariscos** (fam) I stuffed myself with seafood.

ciegue ['θjeɣe] *etc vb V* **cegar**.

cielo ['θjelo] *nm* sky; (*REL*) heaven; (*ARQ*: *tb*: ~ **raso**) ceiling; ¡~**s!** good heavens!; **ver el** ~ **abierto** to see one's chance.

ciempiés [θjem'pjes] *nm inv* centipede.

cien [θjen] *num V* **ciento**.

ciénaga ['θjenaɣa] *nf* marsh, swamp.

ciencia ['θjenθja] *nf* science; ~**s** *nfpl* science *sg*; **saber algo a** ~ **cierta** to know sth for certain.

ciencia-ficción ['θjenθjafik'θjon] *nf* science fiction.

cieno ['θjeno] *nm* mud, mire.

científico, a [θjen'tifiko, a] *adj* scientific ♦ *nm/f* scientist.

ciento ['θjento], **cien** *num* hundred; **pagar al 10 por ciento** to pay at 10 per cent.

cierne ['θjerne] *etc vb V* **cerner** ♦ *nm*: **en** ~ in blossom; **en** ~**(s)** (*fig*) in its infancy.

cierre ['θjerre] *etc vb V* **cerrar** ♦ *nm* closing, shutting; (*con llave*) locking; (*RADIO, TV*) close-down; ~ **de cremallera** zip (fastener); **precios de** ~ (*BOLSA*) closing prices; ~ **del sistema** (*INFORM*) system shutdown.

cierto, a ['θjerto, a] *adj* sure, certain; (*un tal*) a certain; (*correcto*) right, correct; ~ **hombre** a certain man; **ciertas personas** certain *o* some people; **sí, es** ~ yes, that's correct; **por** ~ by the way; **lo** ~ **es que ...** the fact is that ...; **estar en lo** ~ to be right.

ciervo ['θjerβo] *nm* (*ZOOL*) deer; (: *macho*) stag.

cierzo ['θjerθo] *nm* north wind.

CIES *nm abr* = *Consejo Interamericano Económico y Social*.

cifra ['θifra] *nf* number, figure; (*cantidad*) number, quantity; (*secreta*) code; ~ **global** lump sum; ~ **de negocios** (*COM*) turnover; **en** ~**s redondas** in round figures; ~ **de referencia** (*COM*) bench mark; ~ **de ventas** (*COM*) sales figures.

cifrado, a [θi'fraðo, a] *adj* in code.

cifrar [θi'frar] *vt* to code, write in code; (*resumir*) to abridge; (*calcular*) to reckon.

cigala [θi'ɣala] *nf* Norway lobster.

cigarra [θi'ɣarra] *nf* cicada.

cigarrera [θiɣa'rrera] *nf* cigar case.

cigarrillo [θiɣa'rriʎo] *nm* cigarette.

cigarro [θi'ɣarro] *nm* cigarette; (*puro*) cigar.

cigüeña [θi'ɣweɲa] *nf* stork.

cilíndrico, a [θi'lindriko, a] *adj* cylindrical.

cilindro [θi'lindro] *nm* cylinder.

cima ['θima] *nf* (*de montaña*) top, peak; (*de árbol*) top; (*fig*) height.

címbalo ['θimbalo] *nm* cymbal.

cimbrear [θimbre'ar] *vt* to brandish; ~**se** *vr* to sway.

cimentar [θimen'tar] *vt* to lay the foundations of; (*fig: reforzar*) to strengthen; (: *fundar*) to found.

cimiento [θi'mjento] *etc vb V* **cimentar** ♦ *nm* foundation.

cinc [θink] *nm* zinc.

cincel [θin'θel] *nm* chisel.

cincelar [θinθe'lar] *vt* to chisel.

cincha ['θintʃa] *nf* girth, saddle strap.

cincho ['θintʃo] *nm* sash, belt.

cinco ['θinko] *num* five; (*fecha*) fifth; **las** ~ five o'clock; **no estar en sus** ~ (*fam*) to be off one's rocker.

cincuenta [θin'kwenta] *num* fifty.

cincuentón, ona [θinkwen'ton, ona] *adj*, *nm/f* fifty-year-old.

cine ['θine] *nm* cinema; **el** ~ **mudo** silent films *pl*; **hacer** ~ to make films.

cineasta [θine'asta] *nm/f* (*director de cine*) film-maker *o* director.

cine-club ['θine'klub] *nm* film club.

cinéfilo, a [θi'nefilo, a] *nm/f* film buff.

cinematográfico, a [θinemato'ɣrafiko, a] *adj* cine-, film *cpd*.

cínico, a ['θiniko, a] *adj* cynical; (*descarado*) shameless ♦ *nm/f* cynic.

cinismo [θi'nismo] *nm* cynicism.

cinta ['θinta] *nf* band, strip; (*de tela*) ribbon; (*película*) reel; (*de máquina de escribir*) ribbon; (*métrica*) tape measure; (*magnetofónica*) tape; ~ **adhesiva** sticky tape; ~ **aislante** insulating tape; ~ **de carbón** carbon ribbon; ~ **magnética** (*INFORM*) magnetic tape; ~ **métrica** tape measure; ~ **de múltiples impactos** (*en impresora*) multistrike ribbon; ~ **de tela** (*para máquina de escribir*) fabric ribbon; ~ **transportadora** conveyor belt.

cinto ['θinto] *nm* belt, girdle.

cintura [θin'tura] *nf* waist; (*medida*) waistline.

cinturón [θintu'ron] *nm* belt; (*fig*) belt, zone; ~ **salvavidas** lifebelt; ~ **de seguridad** safety belt.

ciña ['θiɲa] *etc*, **ciñendo** [θi'ɲendo] *etc vb V* **ceñir**.

CIP [θip] *nm abr* = *Club Internacional de Prensa* (*Madrid*).

ciprés [θi'pres] *nm* cypress (tree).

circo ['θirko] *nm* circus.

circuito [θir'kwito] *nm* circuit; (*DEPORTE*) lap; **TV por** ~ **cerrado** closed-circuit TV; ~ **experimental** (*INFORM*) breadboard; ~ **impreso** printed circuit; ~ **lógico** (*INFORM*) logical circuit.

circulación [θirkula'θjon] *nf* circulation;

(*AUTO*) traffic; **"cerrado a la ~ rodada"** "closed to vehicles".

circular [θirku'lar] *adj*, *nf* circular ♦ *vt* to circulate ♦ *vi* to circulate; (*dinero*) to be in circulation; (*AUTO*) to drive; (*autobús*) to run.

círculo ['θirkulo] *nm* circle; (*centro*) clubhouse; (*POL*) political group.

circuncidar [θirkunθi'dar] *vt* to circumcise.

circunciso, a [θirkun'θiso, a] *pp de* **circuncidar**.

circundante [θirkun'dante] *adj* surrounding.

circundar [θirkun'dar] *vt* to surround.

circunferencia [θirkunfe'renθja] *nf* circumference.

circunloquio [θirkun'lokjo] *nm* circumlocution.

circunscribir [θirkunskri'ßir] *vt* to circumscribe; **~se** *vr* to be limited.

circunscripción [θirkunskrip'θjon] *nf* division; (*POL*) constituency.

circunscrito [θirkuns'krito] *pp de* **circunscribir**.

circunspección [θirkunspek'θjon] *nf* circumspection, caution.

circunspecto, a [θirkuns'pekto, a] *adj* circumspect, cautious.

circunstancia [θirkuns'tanθja] *nf* circumstance; **~s agravantes/ extenuantes** aggravating/extenuating circumstances; **estar a la altura de las ~s** to rise to the occasion.

circunvalación [θirkumbala'θjon] *nf*: **carretera de ~** ring road.

cirio ['θirjo] *nm* (wax) candle.

cirrosis [θi'rrosis] *nf* cirrhosis (of the liver).

ciruela [θi'rwela] *nf* plum; **~ pasa** prune.

ciruelo [θi'rwelo] *nm* plum tree.

cirugía [θiru'xia] *nf* surgery; **~ estética** *o* **plástica** plastic surgery.

cirujano [θiru'xano] *nm* surgeon.

cisco ['θisko] *nm*: **armar un ~** to kick up a row; **estar hecho ~** to be a wreck.

cisma ['θisma] *nm* schism; (*POL etc*) split.

cisne ['θisne] *nm* swan; **canto de ~** swan song.

cisterna [θis'terna] *nf* cistern, tank.

cistitis [θis'titis] *nf* cystitis.

cita ['θita] *nf* appointment, meeting; (*de novios*) date; (*referencia*) quotation; **acudir/faltar a una ~** to turn up for/miss an appointment

citación [θita'θjon] *nf* (*JUR*) summons *sg*.

citadino, a [sita'ðino, a] (*AM*) *adj* urban ♦ *nm/f* urban *o* city dweller.

citar [θi'tar] *vt* to make an appointment

with, arrange to meet; (*JUR*) to summons; (*un autor, texto*) to quote; **~se** *vr*: **~se con algn** to arrange to meet sb; **se citaron en el cine** they arranged to meet at the cinema.

cítara ['θitara] *nf* zither.

citología [θitolo'xia] *nf* smear test.

cítrico, a ['θitriko, a] *adj* citric ♦ *nm*: **~s** citrus fruits.

CiU *nm abr* (*POL*) = **Convergència i Unió**.

ciudad [θju'ðað] *nf* town; (*capital de país etc*) city; **~ universitaria** university campus; **C~ del Cabo** Cape Town; **la C~ Condal** Barcelona.

ciudadanía [θjuðaða'nia] *nf* citizenship.

ciudadano, a [θjuða'ðano, a] *adj* civic ♦ *nm/f* citizen.

ciudadrealeño, a [θjuðaðrea'leɲo, a] *adj* of *o* from Ciudad Real ♦ *nm/f* native *o* inhabitant of Ciudad Real.

cívico, a ['θißiko, a] *adj* civic; (*fig*) public-spirited.

civil [θi'ßil] *adj* civil ♦ *nm* (*guardia*) policeman.

civilice [θißi'liθe] *etc vb V* **civilizar**.

civilización [θißiliθa'θjon] *nf* civilization.

civilizar [θißili'θar] *vt* to civilize.

civismo [θi'ßismo] *nm* public spirit.

cizaña [θi'θaɲa] *nf* (*fig*) discord; **sembrar ~** to sow discord.

cl. *abr* (= *centilitro*) cl.

clamar [kla'mar] *vt* to clamour for, cry out for ♦ *vi* to cry out, clamour.

clamor [kla'mor] *nm* (*grito*) cry, shout; (*fig*) clamour, protest.

clamoroso, a [klamo'roso, a] *adj* (*éxito etc*) resounding.

clan ['klan] *nm* clan; (*de gángsters*) gang.

clandestinidad [klandestini'ðað] *nf* secrecy.

clandestino, a [klandes'tino, a] *adj* clandestine; (*POL*) underground.

clara ['klara] *nf* (*de huevo*) eggwhite.

claraboya [klara'ßoja] *nf* skylight.

clarear [klare'ar] *vi* (*el día*) to dawn; (*el cielo*) to clear up, brighten up; **~se** *vr* to be transparent.

clarete [kla'rete] *nm* rosé (wine).

claridad [klari'ðað] *nf* (*del día*) brightness; (*de estilo*) clarity.

clarificar [klarifi'kar] *vt* to clarify.

clarifique [klari'fike] *etc vb V* **clarificar**.

clarín [kla'rin] *nm* bugle.

clarinete [klari'nete] *nm* clarinet.

clarividencia [klarißi'ðenθja] *nf* clairvoyance; (*fig*) far-sightedness.

claro, a ['klaro, a] *adj* clear; (*luminoso*) bright; (*color*) light; (*evidente*) clear, evident; (*poco espeso*) thin ♦ *nm* (*en bosque*) clearing ♦ *adv* clearly ♦ *excl* of course!; **hablar** ~ (*fig*) to speak plainly; **a las claras** openly; **no sacamos nada en** ~ we couldn't get anything definite.

clase ['klase] *nf* class; (*tipo*) kind, sort; (*ESCOL etc*) class; (: *aula*) classroom; ~ **alta/media/obrera** upper/middle/ working class; **dar** ~**s** to teach.

clásico, a ['klasiko, a] *adj* classical; (*fig*) classic.

clasificable [klasifi'kaβle] *adj* classifiable.

clasificación [klasifika'θjon] *nf* classification; (*DEPORTE*) league (table); (*COM*) ratings *pl*.

clasificador [klasifika'ðor] *nm* filing cabinet.

clasificar [klasifi'kar] *vt* to classify; (*INFORM*) to sort; ~**se** *vr* (*DEPORTE: torneo*) to qualify.

clasifique [klasi'fike] *etc vb V* **clasificar**.

clasista [kla'sista] *adj* (*fam: actitud*) snobbish.

claudia ['klauðja] *nf* greengage.

claudicar [klauði'kar] *vi* (*fig*) to back down.

claudique [klau'ðike] *etc vb V* **claudicar**.

claustro ['klaustro] *nm* cloister; (*UNIV*) staff; (*junta*) senate.

claustrofobia [klaustro'foβja] *nf* claustrophobia.

cláusula ['klausula] *nf* clause; ~ **de exclusión** (*COM*) exclusion clause.

clausura [klau'sura] *nf* closing, closure.

clausurar [klausu'rar] *vt* (*congreso etc*) to close, bring to a close; (*POL etc*) to adjourn; (*cerrar*) to close (down).

clavado, a [kla'βaðo, a] *adj* nailed ♦ *excl* exactly!, precisely!

clavar [kla'βar] *vt* (*tablas etc*) to nail (together); (*con alfiler*) to pin; (*clavo*) to hammer in; (*cuchillo*) to stick, thrust; (*mirada*) to fix; (*fam: estafar*) to cheat.

clave ['klaβe] *nf* key; (*MUS*) clef ♦ *adj inv* key *cpd*; ~ **de búsqueda** (*INFORM*) search key; ~ **de clasificación** (*INFORM*) sort key.

clavel [kla'βel] *nm* carnation.

clavicémbalo [klaβi'θembalo] *nm* harpsichord.

clavicordio [klaβikor'ðjo] *nm* clavicord.

clavícula [kla'βikula] *nf* collar bone.

clavija [kla'βixa] *nf* peg, pin; (*MUS*) peg; (*ELEC*) plug.

clavo ['klaβo] *nm* (*de metal*) nail; (*BOT*) clove; **dar en el** ~ (*fig*) to hit the nail on the head.

claxon ['klakson], *pl* **claxons** *nm* horn; **tocar el** ~ to sound one's horn.

clemencia [kle'menθja] *nf* mercy, clemency.

clemente [kle'mente] *adj* merciful, clement.

cleptómano, a [klep'tomano, a] *nm/f* kleptomaniac.

clerical [kleri'kal] *adj* clerical.

clérigo ['kleriɣo] *nm* priest, clergyman.

clero ['klero] *nm* clergy.

cliché [kli'tʃe] *nm* cliché; (*TIP*) stencil; (*FOTO*) negative.

cliente, a ['kljente, a] *nm/f* client, customer.

clientela [kljen'tela] *nf* clientele, customers *pl*; (*COM*) goodwill; (*MED*) patients *pl*.

clima ['klima] *nm* climate.

climatizado, a [klimati'θaðo, a] *adj* air-conditioned.

clímax ['klimaks] *nm inv* climax.

clínico, a ['kliniko, a] *adj* clinical ♦ *nf* clinic; (*particular*) private hospital.

clip, *pl* **clips** [klip, klis] *nm* paper clip.

clítoris ['klitoris] *nm inv* clitoris.

cloaca [klo'aka] *nf* sewer, drain.

clonación [klona'θjon] *nf* cloning.

clorhídrico, a [klo'riðriko, a] *adj* hydrochloric.

cloro ['kloro] *nm* chlorine.

clorofila [kloro'fila] *nf* chlorophyl(l).

cloroformo [kloro'formo] *nm* chloroform.

cloruro [klo'ruro] *nm* chloride; ~ **sódico** sodium chloride.

club, *pl* **clubs** *o* **clubes** [klub, klus, 'kluβes] *nm* club; ~ **de jóvenes** youth club.

cm *abr* (= *centímetro*) cm.

C.N.T. *nf abr* (*ESP: Confederación Nacional de Trabajo*) *Anarchist Union Confederation*; (*AM*) = *Confederación Nacional de Trabajadores*.

coacción [koak'θjon] *nf* coercion, compulsion.

coaccionar [koakθjo'nar] *vt* to coerce, compel.

coagular [koaɣu'lar] *vt*, ~**se** *vr* (*sangre*) to clot; (*leche*) to curdle.

coágulo [ko'aɣulo] *nm* clot.

coalición [koali'θjon] *nf* coalition.

coartada [koar'taða] *nf* alibi.

coartar [koar'tar] *vt* to limit, restrict.

coba ['koβa] *nf*: **dar** ~ **a algn** to soft-soap sb.

cobarde [ko'βarðe] *adj* cowardly ♦ *nm/f* coward.

cobardía [koβar'ðia] *nf* cowardice.

cobaya [ko'βaja] *nf* guinea pig.

cobertizo [koβer'tiθo] *nm* shelter.

cobertor [koβer'tor] *nm* bedspread.

cobertura [koβer'tura] *nf* cover; (*COM*)

coverage; ~ **de dividendo** (*COM*)
dividend cover.
cobija [ko'ßixa] *nf* (*AM*) blanket.
cobijar [koßi'xar] *vt* (*cubrir*) to cover;
(*abrigar*) to shelter; ~**se** *vr* to take
shelter.
cobijo [ko'ßixo] *nm* shelter.
cobra ['koßra] *nf* cobra.
cobrador, a [koßra'ðor, a] *nm/f* (*de autobús*)
conductor/conductress; (*de impuestos,
gas*) collector.
cobrar [ko'ßrar] *vt* (*cheque*) to cash;
(*sueldo*) to collect, draw; (*objeto*) to
recover; (*precio*) to charge; (*deuda*) to
collect ♦ *vi* to draw one's pay; ~**se** *vr* to
recover, get on well; **cóbrese al entregar**
cash on delivery (COD) (*US*), collect on
delivery (COD) (*US*); **a** ~ (*COM*)
receivable; **cantidades por** ~ sums due.
cobre ['koßre] *nm* copper; (*AM fam*) cent;
~**s** *nmpl* brass instruments.
cobrizo, a [ko'ßriθo, a] *adj* coppery.
cobro ['koßro] *nm* (*de cheque*) cashing;
(*pago*) payment; **presentar al** ~ to cash;
V *tb* **llamada**.
coca ['koka] *nf* coca; (*droga*) coke.
Coca-Cola ® ['koka'kola] *nf* Coca-Cola ®.
cocaína [koka'ina] *nf* cocaine.
cocainómano, a [kokai'nomano, a] *nm/f*
cocaine addict.
cocción [kok'θjon] *nf* (*CULIN*) cooking; (*el
hervir*) boiling.
cocear [koθe'ar] *vi* to kick.
cocer [ko'θer] *vt, vi* to cook; (*en agua*) to
boil; (*en horno*) to bake.
coche ['kotʃe] *nm* (*AUTO*) car, automobile
(*US*); (*de tren, de caballos*) coach, carriage; (*para niños*) pram (*BRIT*), baby
carriage (*US*); ~ **de bomberos** fire
engine; ~ **celular** Black Maria, prison
van; ~ (**comedor**) (*FERRO*) (dining) car; ~
fúnebre hearse.
coche-bomba ['kotʃe'ßomba], *pl* **coches-
bomba** *nm* car bomb.
coche-cama ['kotʃe'kama], *pl* **coches-
cama** *nm* (*FERRO*) sleeping car, sleeper.
cochera [ko'tʃera] *nf* garage; (*de autobuses,
trenes*) depot.
coche-restaurante, *pl* **coches-
restaurante** ['kotʃeɾestau'rante] *nm*
(*FERRO*) dining-car, diner.
cochinada [kotʃi'naða] *nf* dirty trick.
cochinillo [kotʃi'niʎo] *nm* piglet, suckling
pig.
cochino, a [ko'tʃino, a] *adj* filthy, dirty
♦ *nm/f* pig.
cocido, a [ko'θiðo, a] *adj* boiled; (*fam*)
plastered ♦ *nm* stew.

cociente [ko'θjente] *nm* quotient.
cocina [ko'θina] *nf* kitchen; (*aparato*)
cooker, stove; (*acto*) cookery; ~ **casera**
home cooking; ~ **eléctrica** electric
cooker; ~ **francesa** French cuisine; ~ **de
gas** gas cooker.
cocinar [koθi'nar] *vt, vi* to cook.
cocinero, a [koθi'nero, a] *nm/f* cook.
coco ['koko] *nm* coconut; (*fantasma*)
bogeyman; (*fam: cabeza*) nut; **comer el** ~
a algn (*fam*) to brainwash sb.
cocodrilo [koko'ðrilo] *nm* crocodile.
cocotero [koko'tero] *nm* coconut palm.
cóctel ['koktel] *nm* (*bebida*) cocktail;
(*reunión*) cocktail party; ~ **Molotov**
Molotov cocktail, petrol bomb.
coctelera [kokte'lera] *nf* cocktail shaker.
cod. *abr* (= *código*) code.
codazo [ko'ðaθo] *nm*: **dar un** ~ **a algn** to
nudge sb.
codear [koðe'ar] *vi* to elbow, jostle; ~**se** *vr*:
~**se con** to rub shoulders with.
códice ['koðiθe] *nm* manuscript, codex.
codicia [ko'ðiθja] *nf* greed; (*fig*) lust.
codiciar [koði'θjar] *vt* to covet.
codicioso, a [koði'θjoso, a] *adj* covetous.
codificador [koðifika'ðor] *nm* (*INFORM*)
encoder; ~ **digital** digitizer.
codificar [koðifi'kar] *vt* (*mensaje*) to
(en)code; (*leyes*) to codify.
código ['koðixo] *nm* code; ~ **de barras**
(*COM*) bar code; ~ **binario** binary code;
~ **de caracteres** (*INFORM*) character
code; ~ **de (la) circulación** highway code;
~ **civil** common law; ~ **de control**
(*INFORM*) control code; ~ **máquina**
(*INFORM*) machine code; ~ **militar**
military law; ~ **de operación** (*INFORM*)
operational *o* machine code; ~ **penal**
penal code; ~ **de práctica** code of
practice.
codillo [ko'ðiʎo] *nm* (*ZOOL*) knee; (*TEC*)
elbow (joint).
codo ['koðo] *nm* (*ANAT, de tubo*) elbow;
(*ZOOL*) knee; **hablar por los** ~**s** to talk
nineteen to the dozen.
codorniz [koðor'niθ] *nf* quail.
coeficiente [koefi'θjente] *nm* (*MAT*)
coefficient; (*ECON etc*) rate; ~ **intelectual**
o **de inteligencia** I.Q.
coerción [koer'θjon] *nf* coercion.
coercitivo, a [koerθi'tißo, a] *adj* coercive.
coetáneo, a [koe'taneo, a] *nm/f*: ~**s**
contemporaries.
coexistencia [koeksis'tenθja] *nf*
coexistence.
coexistir [koeksis'tir] *vi* to coexist.
cofia ['kofja] *nf* (*de enfermera*) (white) cap.

cofradía [kofra'ðia] nf brotherhood, fraternity; V tb **Semana Santa**.

cofre ['kofre] nm (baúl) trunk; (de joyas) box; (AM AUTO) bonnet (BRIT), hood (US).

cogedor [koxe'ðor] nm dustpan.

coger [ko'xer] vt (ESP) to take (hold of); (objeto caído) to pick up; (frutas) to pick, harvest; (resfriado, ladrón, pelota) to catch; (AM fam!) to lay (!) ♦ vi: ~ **por el buen camino** to take the right road; ~**se** vr (el dedo) to catch; ~ **a algn desprevenido** to take sb unawares; ~**se a algo** to get hold of sth.

cogida [ko'xiða] nf gathering, harvesting; (de peces) catch; (TAUR) goring.

cogollo [ko'ɣoʎo] nm (de lechuga) heart; (fig) core, nucleus.

cogorza [ko'ɣorθa] nf (fam): **agarrar una** ~ to get smashed.

cogote [ko'ɣote] nm back o nape of the neck.

cohabitar [koaβi'tar] vi to live together, cohabit.

cohecho [ko'etʃo] nm (acción) bribery; (soborno) bribe.

coherencia [koe'renθja] nf coherence.

coherente [koe'rente] adj coherent.

cohesión [koe'sjon] nm cohesion.

cohete [ko'ete] nm rocket.

cohibido, a [koi'βiðo, a] adj (PSICO) inhibited; (tímido) shy; **sentirse** ~ to feel embarrassed.

cohibir [koi'βir] vt to restrain, restrict; ~**se** vr to feel inhibited.

COI nm abr (= Comité Olímpico Internacional) IOC.

coima ['koima] nf (AM fam) bribe.

coincidencia [koinθi'ðenθja] nf coincidence.

coincidir [koinθi'ðir] vi (en idea) to coincide, agree; (en lugar) to coincide.

coito ['koito] nm intercourse, coitus.

cojear [koxe'ar] vi (persona) to limp, hobble; (mueble) to wobble, rock.

cojera [ko'xera] nf lameness; (andar cojo) limp.

cojín [ko'xin] nm cushion.

cojinete [koxi'nete] nm small cushion, pad; (TEC) (ball) bearing.

cojo, a ['koxo, a] etc vb V **coger** ♦ adj (que no puede andar) lame, crippled; (mueble) wobbly ♦ nm/f lame person, cripple.

cojón [ko'xon] nm (fam!) ball (!), testicle; **¡cojones!** shit! (!).

cojonudo, a [koxo'nuðo, a] adj (ESP fam) great, fantastic.

col [kol] nf cabbage; ~**es de Bruselas** Brussels sprouts.

col., col.ª abr (= columna) col.

cola ['kola] nf tail; (de gente) queue; (lugar) end, last place; (para pegar) glue, gum; (de vestido) train; **hacer** ~ to queue (up).

colaboración [kolaβora'θjon] nf (gen) collaboration; (en periódico) contribution.

colaborador, a [kolaβora'ðor, a] nm/f collaborator; contributor.

colaborar [kolaβo'rar] vi to collaborate.

colación [kola'θjon] nf: **sacar a** ~ to bring up.

colado, a [ko'laðo, a] adj (metal) cast ♦ nf: **hacer la colada** to do the washing.

colador [kola'ðor] nm (de té) strainer; (para verduras etc) colander.

colapsar [kolap'sar] vt (tráfico etc) to bring to a standstill.

colapso [ko'lapso] nm collapse; ~ **nervioso** nervous breakdown.

colar [ko'lar] vt (líquido) to strain off; (metal) to cast ♦ vi to ooze, seep (through); ~**se** vr to jump the queue; (en mitin) to sneak in; (equivocarse) to slip up; ~**se en** to get into without paying; (en una fiesta) to gatecrash.

colateral [kolate'ral] nm collateral.

colcha ['koltʃa] nf bedspread.

colchón [kol'tʃon] nm mattress; ~ **inflable** inflatable mattress.

colchoneta [koltʃo'neta] nf (en gimnasio) mattress; ~ **hinchable** airbed.

colear [kole'ar] vi (perro) to wag its tail.

colección [kolek'θjon] nf collection.

coleccionar [kolekθjo'nar] vt to collect.

coleccionista [kolekθjo'nista] nm/f collector.

colecta [ko'lekta] nf collection.

colectivo, a [kolek'tiβo, a] adj collective, joint ♦ nm (AM: autobús) (small) bus; (: taxi) collective taxi.

colector [kolek'tor] nm collector; (sumidero) sewer.

colega [ko'leɣa] nm/f colleague.

colegiado, a [kole'xjaðo, a] adj (profesional) registered ♦ nm/f referee.

colegial, a [kole'xjal, a] adj (ESCOL etc) school cpd, college cpd ♦ nm/f schoolboy/girl.

colegio [ko'lexjo] nm college; (escuela) school; (de abogados etc) association; ~ **de internos** boarding school; **ir al** ~ to go to school.

A **colegio** is normally a private primary or secondary school. In the state system it means a primary school although these are also called **escuela**. State secondary

schools are called **institutos**.
*Extracurricular subjects, such as
computing or foreign languages, are offered
in private schools called* **academias**.

colegir [kole'xir] *vt (juntar)* to collect,
gather; *(deducir)* to infer, conclude.
cólera ['kolera] *nf (ira)* anger; **montar en** ~
to get angry ♦ *nm (MED)* cholera.
colérico, a [ko'leriko, a] *adj* angry, furious.
colesterol [koleste'rol] *nm* cholesterol.
coleta [ko'leta] *nf* pigtail.
coletazo [kole'taθo] *nm*: **dar un** ~ *(animal)*
to flap its tail; **los últimos** ~**s** death
throes.
coletilla [kole'tiʎa] *nf (en carta)* postscript;
(en conversación) filler phrase.
colgado, a [kol'xaðo, a] *pp de* **colgar** ♦ *adj*
hanging; *(ahorcado)* hanged; **dejar** ~ **a
algn** to let sb down.
colgajo [kol'xaxo] *nm* tatter.
colgante [kol'xante] *adj* hanging; *V* **puente**
♦ *nm (joya)* pendant.
colgar [kol'xar] *vt* to hang (up); *(tender:
ropa)* to hang out ♦ *vi* to hang; *(teléfono)*
to hang up.
colgué [kol'xe], **colguemos** [kol'xemos]
etc vb V **colgar**.
colibrí [koli'βri] *nm* hummingbird.
cólico ['koliko] *nm* colic.
coliflor [koli'flor] *nf* cauliflower.
coligiendo [koli'xjenðo] *etc vb V* **colegir**.
colija [ko'lixa] *etc vb V* **colegir**.
colilla [ko'liʎa] *nf* cigarette end, butt.
colina [ko'lina] *nf* hill.
colindante [kolin'dante] *adj* adjacent,
neighbouring.
colindar [kolin'dar] *vi* to adjoin, be
adjacent.
colisión [koli'sjon] *nf* collision; ~ **de frente**
head-on crash.
colitis [ko'litis] *nf inv*: **tener** ~ to have
diarrhoea.
collar [ko'ʎar] *nm* necklace; *(de perro)*
collar.
colmado, a [kol'maðo, a] *adj* full ♦ *nm*
grocer's (shop) *(BRIT)*, grocery store
(US).
colmar [kol'mar] *vt* to fill to the brim; *(fig)*
to fulfil, realize.
colmena [kol'mena] *nf* beehive.
colmillo [kol'miʎo] *nm (diente)* eye tooth;
(de elefante) tusk; *(de perro)* fang.
colmo ['kolmo] *nm* height, summit; **para** ~
de desgracias to cap it all; **¡eso es ya el**
~**!** that's beyond a joke!
colocación [koloka'θjon] *nf (acto)* placing;
(empleo) job, position; *(situación)* place,

position; *(COM)* placement.
colocar [kolo'kar] *vt* to place, put, position;
(poner en empleo) to find a job for; ~
dinero to invest money; ~**se** *vr* to place
o.s.; *(conseguir trabajo)* to find a job.
colofón [kolo'fon] *nm*: **como** ~ **de las
conversaciones** as a sequel to o
following the talks.
Colombia [ko'lombja] *nf* Colombia.
colombiano, a [kolom'bjano, a] *adj, nm/f*
Colombian.
colon ['kolon] *nm* colon.
colón [ko'lon] *nm (AM)* monetary unit of
Costa Rica and El Salvador.
Colonia [ko'lonja] *nf* Cologne.
colonia [ko'lonja] *nf* colony; *(de casas)*
housing estate; *(agua de* ~*)* cologne; ~
escolar summer camp (for
schoolchildren).
colonice [kolo'niθe] *etc vb V* **colonizar**.
colonización [koloniθa'θjon] *nf*
colonization.
colonizador, a [koloniθa'ðor, a] *adj*
colonizing ♦ *nm/f* colonist, settler.
colonizar [koloni'θar] *vt* to colonize.
colono [ko'lono] *nm (POL)* colonist, settler;
(AGR) tenant farmer.
coloque [ko'loke] *etc vb V* **colocar**.
coloquial [kolo'kjal] *adj* colloquial.
coloquio [ko'lokjo] *nm* conversation;
(congreso) conference; *(INFORM)*
handshake.
color [ko'lor] *nm* colour; **a todo** ~ in full
colour; **verlo todo** ~ **de rosa** to see
everything through rose-coloured
spectacles; **le salieron los** ~**es** she
blushed.
colorado, a [kolo'raðo, a] *adj (rojo)* red;
(AM: chiste) rude, blue; **ponerse** ~ to
blush.
colorante [kolo'rante] *nm* colouring
(matter).
colorar [kolo'rar] *vt* to colour; *(teñir)* to
dye.
colorear [kolore'ar] *vt* to colour.
colorete [kolo'rete] *nm* blusher.
colorido [kolo'riðo] *nm* colour(ing).
coloso [ko'loso] *nm* colossus.
columbrar [kolum'brar] *vt* to glimpse, spy.
columna [ko'lumna] *nf* column; *(pilar)*
pillar; *(apoyo)* support; ~ **blindada** *(MIL)*
armoured column; ~ **vertebral** spine,
spinal column.
columpiar [kolum'pjar] *vt*, ~**se** *vr* to swing.
columpio [ko'lumpjo] *nm* swing.
colza ['kolθa] *nf* rape; **aceite de** ~ rapeseed
oil.
coma ['koma] *nf* comma ♦ *nm (MED)* coma.

comadre [ko'maðre] *nf* (*madrina*)
godmother; (*vecina*) neighbour;
(*chismosa*) gossip.
comadrear [komaðre'ar] *vi* (*esp AM*) to
gossip.
comadreja [koma'ðrexa] *nf* weasel.
comadrona [koma'ðrona] *nf* midwife.
comandancia [koman'danθja] *nf*
command.
comandante [koman'dante] *nm*
commandant; (*grado*) major.
comandar [koman'dar] *vt* to command.
comando [ko'mando] *nm* (*MIL*: *mando*)
command; (: *grupo*) commando unit;
(*INFORM*) command; ~ **de búsqueda**
search command.
comarca [ko'marka] *nf* region; *V tb*
provincia.
comarcal [komar'kal] *adj* local.
comba ['komba] *nf* (*curva*) curve; (*en viga*)
warp; (*cuerda*) skipping rope; **saltar a la**
~ to skip.
combar [kom'bar] *vt* to bend, curve.
combate [kom'bate] *nm* fight; (*fig*) battle;
fuera de ~ out of action.
combatiente [komba'tjente] *nm*
combatant.
combatir [komba'tir] *vt* to fight, combat.
combatividad [kombatiβi'ðað] *nf* (*actitud*)
fighting spirit; (*agresividad*)
aggressiveness.
combativo, a [komba'tiβo, a] *adj* full of
fight.
combi ['kombi] *nm* fridge-freezer.
combinación [kombina'θjon] *nf*
combination; (*QUÍMICA*) compound;
(*bebida*) cocktail; (*plan*) scheme, setup;
(*prenda*) slip.
combinado, a [kombi'naðo, a] *adj*: **plato** ~
main course served with vegetables.
combinar [kombi'nar] *vt* to combine;
(*colores*) to match.
combustible [kombus'tiβle] *nm* fuel.
combustión [kombus'tjon] *nf* combustion.
comedia [ko'meðja] *nf* comedy; (*TEAT*)
play, drama; (*fig*) farce.
comediante [kome'ðjante] *nm/f* (*comic*)
actor/actress.
comedido, a [kome'ðiðo, a] *adj* moderate.
comedirse [kome'ðirse] *vr* to behave
moderately; (*ser cortés*) to be courteous.
comedor, a [kome'ðor, a] *nm/f* (*persona*)
glutton ♦ *nm* (*habitación*) dining room;
(*restaurante*) restaurant; (*cantina*)
canteen.
comencé [komen'θe], **comencemos**
[komen'θemos] *etc vb V* **comenzar**.
comensal [komen'sal] *nm/f* fellow guest/

diner.
comentar [komen'tar] *vt* to comment on;
(*fam*) to discuss; **comentó que...** he made
the comment that....
comentario [komen'tarjo] *nm* comment,
remark; (*LIT*) commentary; ~**s** *nmpl*
gossip *sg*; **dar lugar a** ~**s** to cause gossip.
comentarista [komenta'rista] *nm/f*
commentator.
comenzar [komen'θar] *vt, vi* to begin, start,
commence; ~ **a hacer algo** to begin *o*
start doing *o* to do sth.
comer [ko'mer] *vt* to eat; (*DAMAS, AJEDREZ*)
to take, capture; (*párrafo etc*) to skip ♦ *vi*
to eat; (*almorzar*) to have lunch; ~**se** *vr* to
eat up; ~ **el coco a** (*fam*) to brainwash; **¡a**
~! food's ready!
comercial [komer'θjal] *adj* commercial;
(*relativo al negocio*) business *cpd*.
comerciante [komer'θjante] *nm/f* trader,
merchant; (*tendero*) shopkeeper; ~
exclusivo (*COM*) sole trader.
comerciar [komer'θjar] *vi* to trade, do
business.
comercio [ko'merθjo] *nm* commerce,
trade; (*negocio*) business; (*grandes
empresas*) big business; (*fig*) dealings *pl*;
~ **autorizado** (*COM*) licensed trade; ~
exterior foreign trade.
comestible [komes'tiβle] *adj* eatable,
edible ♦ *nm*: ~**s** food *sg*, foodstuffs;
(*COM*) groceries.
cometa [ko'meta] *nm* comet ♦ *nf* kite.
cometer [kome'ter] *vt* to commit.
cometido [kome'tiðo] *nm* (*misión*) task,
assignment; (*deber*) commitment.
comezón [kome'θon] *nf* itch, itching.
cómic, pl cómics ['komik, 'komiks] *nm*
comic.
comicios [ko'miθjos] *nmpl* elections; (*voto*)
voting *sg*.
cómico, a ['komiko, a] *adj* comic(al) ♦ *nm/f*
comedian; (*de teatro*) (comic) actor/
actress.
comida [ko'miða] *etc vb V* **comedirse** ♦ *nf*
(*alimento*) food; (*almuerzo, cena*) meal;
(*de mediodía*) lunch; (*AM*) dinner.
comidilla [komi'ðiʎa] *nf*: **ser la** ~ **de la
ciudad** to be the talk of the town.
comience [ko'mjenθe] *etc vb V* **comenzar**.
comienzo [ko'mjenθo] *etc vb V* **comenzar**
♦ *nm* beginning, start; **dar** ~ **a un acto** to
begin a ceremony; ~ **del archivo**
(*INFORM*) top-of-file.
comillas [ko'miʎas] *nfpl* quotation marks.
comilón, ona [komi'lon, ona] *adj* greedy
♦ *nf* (*fam*) blow-out.
comino [ko'mino] *nm* cumin (seed); **no me**

importa un ~ I don't give a damn.
comisaría [komisa'ria] *nf* police station,
precinct (*US*); (*MIL*) commissariat.
comisario [komi'sarjo] *nm* (*MIL etc*)
commissary; (*POL*) commissar.
comisión [komi'sjon] *nf* (*COM*: *pago*)
commission, rake-off (*fam*); (: *junta*)
board; (*encargo*) assignment; ~ **mixta/**
permanente joint/standing committee;
Comisiones Obreras (*ESP*) *formerly*
Communist Union Confederation.
comisura [komi'sura] *nf*: ~ **de los labios**
corner of the mouth.
comité, *pl* **comités** *nm* [komi'te, komi'tes]
committee; ~ **de empresa** works
council.
comitiva [komi'tiβa] *nf* suite, retinue.
como ['komo] *adv* as; (*tal* ~) like;
(*aproximadamente*) about, approximately
♦ *conj* (*ya que, puesto que*) as, since; (*en*
seguida que) as soon as; (*si*: +*subjun*) if;
¡~ **no!** of course!; ~ **no lo haga hoy**
unless he does it today; ~ **si** as if; **es tan**
alto ~ **ancho** it is as high as it is wide.
cómo ['komo] *adv* how?, why? ♦ *excl* what?,
I beg your pardon? ♦ *nm*: **el** ~ **y el porqué**
the whys and wherefores; ¿~ **está Ud?**
how are you?; ¿~ **no?** why not?; ¡~ **no!**
(*esp AM*) of course!; ¿~ **son?** what are
they like?
cómoda ['komoδa] *nf* chest of drawers.
comodidad [komoδi'δaδ] *nf* comfort;
venga a su ~ come at your convenience.
comodín [komo'δin] *nm* joker; (*INFORM*)
wild card; **símbolo** ~ wild-card
character.
cómodo, a ['komoδo, a] *adj* comfortable;
(*práctico, de fácil uso*) convenient.
comodón, ona [komo'δon, ona] *adj*
comfort-loving ♦ *nm/f*: **ser un(a)** ~ to like
one's home comforts.
comoquiera [komo'kjera] *conj*: ~ **que**
(+ *subjun*) in whatever way; ~ **que sea**
eso however that may be.
comp. *abr* (= *compárese*) cp.
compacto, a [kom'pakto, a] *adj* compact.
compadecer [kompaδe'θer] *vt* to pity, be
sorry for; ~**se** *vr*: ~**se de** to pity, be
sorry for.
compadezca [kompa'δeθka] *etc vb V*
compadecer.
compadre [kom'paδre] *nm* (*padrino*)
godfather; (*esp AM*: *amigo*) friend, pal.
compaginar [kompaxi'nar] *vt*: ~ **A con B** to
bring A into line with B; ~**se** *vr*: ~**se con**
to tally with, square with.
compañerismo [kompaɲe'rismo] *nm*
comradeship.

compañero, a [kompa'ɲero, a] *nm/f*
companion; (*novio*) boyfriend/girlfriend;
~ **de clase** classmate.
compañía [kompa'ɲia] *nf* company; ~
afiliada associated company; ~
concesionadora franchiser; ~ **(no)**
cotizable (un)listed company; ~
inversionista investment trust; **hacer** ~ **a**
algn to keep sb company.
comparación [kompara'θjon] *nf*
comparison; **en** ~ **con** in comparison
with.
comparar [kompa'rar] *vt* to compare.
comparativo, a [kompara'tiβo, a] *adj*
comparative.
comparecencia [kompare'θenθja] *nf* (*JUR*)
appearance (in court); **orden de** ~
summons *sg.*
comparecer [kompare'θer] *vi* to appear (in
court).
comparezca [kompa'reθka] *etc vb V*
comparecer.
comparsa [kom'parsa] *nm/f* extra.
compartimento [komparti'mento],
compartimiento [komparti'mjento] *nm*
(*FERRO*) compartment; (*de mueble, cajón*)
section; ~ **estanco** (*fig*) watertight
compartment.
compartir [kompar'tir] *vt* to divide (up),
share (out).
compás [kom'pas] *nm* (*MUS*) beat, rhythm;
(*MAT*) compasses *pl*; (*NAUT etc*) compass;
al ~ in time.
compasión [kompa'sjon] *nf* compassion,
pity.
compasivo, a [kompa'siβo, a] *adj*
compassionate.
compatibilidad [kompatiβili'δaδ] *nf* (*tb*
INFORM) compatibility.
compatible [kompa'tiβle] *adj* compatible.
compatriota [kompa'trjota] *nm/f*
compatriot, fellow countryman/woman.
compendiar [kompen'djar] *vt* to
summarize; (*libro*) to abridge.
compendio [kom'pendjo] *nm* summary;
abridgement.
compenetración [kompenetra'θjon] *nf* (*fig*)
mutual understanding.
compenetrarse [kompene'trarse] *vr* (*fig*):
~ **(muy) bien** to get on (very) well
together.
compensación [kompensa'θjon] *nf*
compensation; (*JUR*) damages *pl*; (*COM*)
clearing.
compensar [kompen'sar] *vt* to
compensate; (*pérdida*) to make up for.
competencia [kompe'tenθja] *nf*
(*incumbencia*) domain, field; (*COM*)

receipt; (_JUR, habilidad_) competence; (_rivalidad_) competition.

competente [kompe'tente] _adj_ (_JUR, persona_) competent; (_conveniente_) suitable.

competer [kompe'ter] _vi_: ~ **a** to be the responsibility of, fall to.

competición [kompeti'θjon] _nf_ competition.

competidor, a [kompeti'ðor, a] _nm/f_ competitor.

competir [kompe'tir] _vi_ to compete.

competitivo, a [kompeti'tiβo, a] _adj_ competitive.

compilación [kompila'θjon] _nf_ compilation; **tiempo de ~** (_INFORM_) compile time.

compilador [kompila'ðor] _nm_ compiler.

compilar [kompi'lar] _vt_ to compile.

compinche [kom'pintʃe] _nm/f_ (_fam_) crony.

compita [kom'pita] _etc vb V_ **competir**.

complacencia [kompla'θenθja] _nf_ (_placer_) pleasure; (_satisfacción_) satisfaction; (_buena voluntad_) willingness.

complacer [kompla'θer] _vt_ to please; **~se** _vr_ to be pleased.

complaciente [kompla'θjente] _adj_ kind, obliging, helpful.

complazca [kom'plaθka] _etc vb V_ **complacer**.

complejo, a [kom'plexo, a] _adj, nm_ complex.

complementario, a [komplemen'tarjo, a] _adj_ complementary.

complemento [komple'mento] _nm_ (_de moda, diseño_) accessory; (_LING_) complement.

completar [komple'tar] _vt_ to complete.

completo, a [kom'pleto, a] _adj_ complete; (_perfecto_) perfect; (_lleno_) full ♦ _nm_ full complement.

complexión [komple'ksjon] _nf_ constitution.

complicación [komplika'θjon] _nf_ complication.

complicado, a [kompli'kaðo, a] _adj_ complicated; **estar ~ en** to be involved in.

complicar [kompli'kar] _vt_ to complicate.

cómplice ['kompliθe] _nm/f_ accomplice.

complique [kom'plike] _etc vb V_ **complicar**.

complot, _pl_ **complots** [kom'plo(t), kom'plos] _nm_ plot; (_conspiración_) conspiracy.

compondré [kompon'dre] _etc vb V_ **componer**.

componenda [kompo'nenda] _nf_ compromise; (_pey_) shady deal.

componente [kompo'nente] _adj, nm_ component.

componer [kompo'ner] _vt_ to make up, put together; (_MUS, LIT, IMPRENTA_) to compose; (_algo roto_) to mend, repair; (_adornar_) to adorn; (_arreglar_) to arrange; (_reconciliar_) to reconcile; **~se** _vr_: **~se de** to consist of; **componérselas para hacer algo** to manage to do sth.

componga [kom'ponga] _etc vb V_ **componer**.

comportamiento [komporta'mjento] _nm_ behaviour, conduct.

comportarse [kompor'tarse] _vr_ to behave.

composición [komposi'θjon] _nf_ composition.

compositor, a [komposi'tor, a] _nm/f_ composer.

compostelano, a [komposte'lano, a] _adj_ of _o_ from Santiago de Compostela ♦ _nm/f_ native _o_ inhabitant of Santiago de Compostela.

compostura [kompos'tura] _nf_ (_reparación_) mending, repair; (_composición_) composition; (_acuerdo_) agreement; (_actitud_) composure.

compota [kom'pota] _nf_ compote, preserve.

compra ['kompra] _nf_ purchase; **~s** _nfpl_ purchases, shopping _sg_; **hacer la ~/ir de ~s** to do the/go shopping; **~ a granel** (_COM_) bulk buying; **~ proteccionista** (_COM_) support buying.

comprador, a [kompra'ðor, a] _nm/f_ buyer, purchaser.

comprar [kom'prar] _vt_ to buy, purchase; **~ deudas** (_COM_) to factor.

compraventa [kompra'βenta] _nf_ (_JUR_) contract of sale.

comprender [kompren'der] _vt_ to understand; (_incluir_) to comprise, include.

comprensible [kompren'siβle] _adj_ understandable.

comprensión [kompren'sjon] _nf_ understanding; (_totalidad_) comprehensiveness.

comprensivo, a [kompren'siβo, a] _adj_ comprehensive; (_actitud_) understanding.

compresa [kom'presa] _nf_ compress; **~ higiénica** sanitary towel (_BRIT_) _o_ napkin (_US_).

compresión [kompre'sjon] _nf_ compression.

comprimido, a [kompri'miðo] _adj_ compressed ♦ _nm_ (_MED_) pill, tablet; **en caracteres ~s** (_TIP_) condensed.

comprimir [kompri'mir] _vt_ to compress;

(fig) to control; *(INFORM)* to pack.
comprobación [komproßa'θjon] *nf:* ~
general de cuentas *(COM)* general audit.
comprobante [kompro'ßante] *nm* proof;
(COM) voucher; ~ **(de pago)** receipt.
comprobar [kompro'ßar] *vt* to check;
(probar) to prove; *(TEC)* to check, test.
comprometedor, a [kompromete'ðor, a]
adj compromising.
comprometer [komprome'ter] *vt* to
compromise; *(exponer)* to endanger; ~**se**
vr to compromise o.s.; *(involucrarse)* to
get involved.
comprometido, a [komprome'tiðo, a] *a*
(situación) awkward; *(escritor etc)*
committed.
compromiso [kompro'miso] *nm*
(obligación) obligation; *(cita)*
engagement, date; *(cometido)*
commitment; *(convenio)* agreement;
(dificultad) awkward situation; **libre de** ~
(COM) without obligation.
comprueba [kom'prweßa] *etc vb V*
comprobar.
compuerta [kom'pwerta] *nf (en canal)*
sluice, floodgate; *(INFORM)* gate.
compuesto, a [kom'pwesto, a] *pp de*
componer ♦ *adj:* ~ **de** composed of, made
up of ♦ *nm* compound; *(MED)*
preparation.
compulsar [kompul'sar] *vt (cotejar)* to
collate, compare; *(JUR)* to make an
attested copy of.
compulsivo, a [kompul'sißo, a] *adj*
compulsive.
compungido, a [kompun'xiðo, a] *adj*
remorseful.
compuse [com'puse] *etc vb V* **componer.**
computador [komputa'ðor] *nm,*
computadora [komputa'ðora] *nf*
computer; ~ **central** mainframe
computer; ~ **especializado** dedicated
computer; ~ **personal** personal
computer.
computar [kompu'tar] *vt* to calculate,
compute.
cómputo ['komputo] *nm* calculation,
computation.
comulgar [komul'ɣar] *vi* to receive
communion.
comulgue [ko'mulɣe] *etc vb V* **comulgar.**
común [ko'mun] *adj (gen)* common;
(corriente) ordinary; **por lo** ~ generally
♦ *nm:* **el** ~ the community.
comuna [ko'muna] *nf* commune; *(AM)*
district.
comunicación [komunika'θjon] *nf*
communication; *(informe)* report.

comunicado [komuni'kaðo] *nm*
announcement; ~ **de prensa** press
release.
comunicar [komuni'kar] *vt* to
communicate; *(ARQ)* to connect ♦ *vi* to
communicate; to send a report; ~**se** *vr* to
communicate; **está comunicando** *(TELEC)*
the line's engaged *(BRIT)* o busy *(US)*.
comunicativo, a [komunika'tißo, a] *adj*
communicative.
comunidad [komuni'ðað] *nf* community; ~
autónoma autonomous region; ~ **de**
vecinos residents' association; **C**~
Económica Europea (CEE) European
Economic Community (EEC).

The 1978 Constitution provides for a degree
of self-government for the 19 regions, called
comunidades autónomas *or* **autonomías.**
Some, such as Catalonia and the Basque
Country, with their own language, history
and culture, have long felt separate from
the rest of Spain. This explains why some
of the **autonomías** *have more devolved*
powers than others, in all matters except
foreign affairs and national defence. The
regions are: **Andalucía, Aragón, Asturias,**
Islas Baleares, Canarias, Cantabria, Castilla y
León, Castilla-La Mancha, Cataluña,
Extremadura, Galicia, Madrid, Murcia,
Navarra, País Vasco, La Rioja, Comunidad
Valenciana, Ceuta, Melilla.

---

comunión [komu'njon] *nf* communion.
comunique [komu'nike] *etc vb V*
comunicar.
comunismo [komu'nismo] *nm*
communism.
comunista [komu'nista] *adj, nm/f*
communist.
comunitario, a [komuni'tarjo, a] *adj (de la*
CE) Community *cpd,* EC *cpd.*

=================== *PALABRA CLAVE*

con [kon] *prep* **1** *(medio, compañía, modo)*
with; **comer** ~ **cuchara** to eat with a
spoon; **café** ~ **leche** white coffee; **estoy**
~ **un catarro** I've got a cold; **pasear** ~
algn to go for a walk with sb; ~
habilidad skilfully
2 *(a pesar de):* ~ **todo, merece nuestros**
respetos all the same o even so, he
deserves our respect
3 *(para* ~*):* **es muy bueno para** ~ **los**
niños he's very good with (the) children
4 *(+infin):* ~ **llegar tan tarde se quedó**
sin comer by arriving o because he
arrived so late he missed out on eating;

~ **estudiar un poco apruebas** with a bit
of studying you should pass
5 (*queja*): ¡~ **las ganas que tenía de ir!**
and I really wanted to go (too)!
♦ *conj*: ~ **que: será suficiente ~ que le**
escribas it will be enough if you write to
her.

conato [ko'nato] *nm* attempt; ~ **de robo**
attempted robbery.
cóncavo, a ['konkaβo, a] *adj* concave.
concebir [konθe'βir] *vt* to conceive;
(*imaginar*) to imagine ♦ *vi* to conceive.
conceder [konθe'ðer] *vt* to concede.
concejal, a [konθe'xal, a] *nm/f* town
councillor.
concejo [kon'θexo] *nm* council.
concentración [konθentra'θjon] *nf*
concentration.
concentrar [konθen'trar] *vt*, ~**se** *vr* to
concentrate.
concéntrico, a [kon'θentriko, a] *adj*
concentric.
concepción [konθaβ'θjon] *nf* conception.
concepto [kon'θepto] *nm* concept; **por ~**
de as, by way of; **tener buen ~ de algn** to
think highly of sb; **bajo ningún ~** under
no circumstances.
conceptuar [konθep'twar] *vt* to judge.
concernir [konθer'nir] *vi*: **en lo que**
concierne a concerning.
concertar [konθer'tar] *vt* (*MUS*) to
harmonize; (*acordar: precio*) to agree;
(: *tratado*) to conclude; (*trato*) to arrange,
fix up; (*combinar: esfuerzos*) to
coordinate; (*reconciliar: personas*) to
reconcile ♦ *vi* to harmonize, be in tune.
concesión [konθe'sjon] *nf* concession;
(*COM: fabricación*) licence.
concesionario, a [konθesjo'narjo, a] *nm/f*
(*COM*) (licensed) dealer, agent,
concessionaire; (: *de venta*) franchisee;
(: *de transportes etc*) contractor.
concha ['kontʃa] *nf* shell; (*AM fam!*) cunt
(!)
conchabarse [kontʃa'βarse] *vr*: ~ **contra** to
gang up on.
conciencia [kon'θjenθja] *nf* (*moral*)
conscience; (*conocimiento*) awareness;
libertad de ~ freedom of worship;
tener/tomar ~ de to be/become aware
of; **tener la ~ limpia** *o* **tranquila** to have a
clear conscience; **tener plena ~ de** to be
fully aware of.
concienciar [konθjen'θjar] *vt* to make
aware; ~**se** *vr* to become aware.
concienzudo, a [konθjen'θuðo, a] *adj*
conscientious.

concierne [kon'θjerne] *etc vb V* **concernir**.
concierto [kon'θjerto] *etc vb V* **concertar**
♦ *nm* concert; (*obra*) concerto.
conciliación [konθilja'θjon] *nf* conciliation.
conciliar [konθi'ljar] *vt* to reconcile ♦ *adj*
(*REL*) of a council; ~ **el sueño** to get to
sleep.
concilio [kon'θiljo] *nm* council.
concisión [konθi'sjon] *nf* conciseness.
conciso, a [kon'θiso, a] *adj* concise.
conciudadano, a [konθjuða'ðano, a] *nm/f*
fellow citizen.
concluir [konklu'ir] *vt* (*acabar*) to conclude;
(*inferir*) to infer, deduce ♦ *vi*, ~**se** *vr* to
conclude; **todo ha concluido** it's all over.
conclusión [konklu'sjon] *nf* conclusion;
llegar a la ~ de que ... to come to the
conclusion that ....
concluya [kon'kluja] *etc vb V* **concluir**.
concluyente [konklu'jente] *adj* (*prueba*,
información) conclusive.
concordancia [konkor'ðanθja] *nf*
agreement.
concordar [konkor'ðar] *vt* to reconcile ♦ *vi*
to agree, tally.
concordia [kon'korðja] *nf* harmony.
concretamente [konkreta'mente] *adv*
specifically, to be exact.
concretar [konkre'tar] *vt* to make
concrete, make more specific;
(*problema*) to pinpoint; ~**se** *vr* to become
more definite.
concreto, a [kon'kreto, a] *adj, nm* (*AM*)
concrete; **en ~** (*en resumen*) to sum up;
(*específicamente*) specifically; **no hay**
nada en ~ there's nothing definite.
concubina [konku'βina] *nf* concubine.
concuerde [kon'kwerðe] *etc vb V*
concordar.
concupiscencia [konkupis'θenθja] *nf*
(*avancia*) greed; (*lujuria*) lustfulness.
concurrencia [konku'rrenθja] *nf* turnout.
concurrido, a [konku'rriðo, a] *a* (*calle*)
busy; (*local, reunión*) crowded.
concurrir [konku'rrir] *vi* (*juntarse: ríos*) to
meet, come together; (: *personas*) to
gather, meet.
concursante [konkur'sante] *nm*
competitor.
concursar [konkur'sar] *vi* to compete.
concurso [kon'kurso] *nm* (*de público*)
crowd; (*ESCOL, DEPORTE, competencia*)
competition; (*COM*) invitation to tender;
(*examen*) open competition; (*TV etc*) quiz;
(*ayuda*) help, cooperation.
condado [kon'daðo] *nm* county.
condal [kon'dal] *adj*: **la ciudad ~**
Barcelona.

conde ['konde] *nm* count.

condecoración [kondekora'θjon] *nf* (*MIL*) medal, decoration.

condecorar [kondeko'rar] *vt* to decorate.

condena [kon'dena] *nf* sentence; **cumplir una ~** to serve a sentence.

condenación [kondena'θjon] *nf* condemnation; (*REL*) damnation.

condenado, a [konde'naðo, a] *adj* (*JUR*) condemned; (*fam: maldito*) damned ♦ *nm/f* (*JUR*) convicted person.

condenar [konde'nar] *vt* to condemn; (*JUR*) to convict; **~se** *vr* (*JUR*) to confess (one's guilt); (*REL*) to be damned.

condensar [konden'sar] *vt* to condense.

condesa [kon'desa] *nf* countess.

condescendencia [kondesθen'denθja] *nf* condescension; **aceptar algo por ~** to accept sth so as not to hurt feelings.

condescender [kondesθen'der] *vi* to acquiesce, comply.

condescienda [kondes'θjenda] *etc vb V* **condescender**.

condición [kondi'θjon] *nf* (*gen*) condition; (*rango*) social class; **condiciones** *nfpl* (*cualidades*) qualities; (*estado*) condition; **a ~ de que ...** on condition that ...; **las condiciones del contrato** the terms of the contract; **condiciones de trabajo** working conditions; **condiciones de venta** conditions of sale.

condicional [kondiθjo'nal] *adj* conditional.

condicionamiento [kondiθjona'mjento] *nm* conditioning.

condicionar [kondiθjo'nar] *vt* (*acondicionar*) to condition; **~ algo a algo** to make sth conditional *o* dependent on sth.

condimento [kondi'mento] *nm* seasoning.

condiscípulo, a [kondis'θipulo, a] *nm/f* fellow student.

condolerse [kondo'lerse] *vr* to sympathize.

condominio [kondo'minjo] *nm* (*COM*) joint ownership; (*AM*) condominium, apartment.

condón [kon'don] *nm* condom.

condonar [kondo'nar] *vt* (*JUR: reo*) to reprieve; (*COM: deuda*) to cancel.

cóndor ['kondor] *nm* condor.

conducente [kondu'θente] *adj*: **~ a** conducive to, leading to.

conducir [kondu'θir] *vt* to take, convey; (*ELEC etc*) to carry; (*AUTO*) to drive; (*negocio*) to manage ♦ *vi* to drive; (*fig*) to lead; **~se** *vr* to behave.

conducta [kon'dukta] *nf* conduct, behaviour.

conducto [kon'dukto] *nm* pipe, tube; (*fig*) channel; (*ELEC*) lead; **por ~ de** through.

conductor, a [konduk'tor, a] *adj* leading, guiding ♦ *nm* (*FÍSICA*) conductor; (*de vehículo*) driver.

conduela [kon'dwela] *etc vb V* **condolerse**.

conduje [kon'duxe] *etc vb V* **conducir**.

conduzca [kon'duθka] *etc vb V* **conducir**.

conectado, a [konek'taðo, a] *a* (*ELEC*) connected, plugged in; (*INFORM*) on-line.

conectar [konek'tar] *vt* to connect (up), plug in; (*INFORM*) to toggle on; **~se** *vr* (*INFORM*) to log in (on).

conejillo [kone'xiʎo] *nm*: **~ de Indias** guinea pig.

conejo [ko'nexo] *nm* rabbit.

conexión [konek'sjon] *nf* connection; (*INFORM*) logging in (on).

confabularse [konfaβu'larse] *vr*: **~ (para hacer algo)** to plot, conspire (to do sth).

confección [konfek'θjon] *nf* (*preparación*) preparation, making-up; (*industria*) clothing industry; (*producto*) article; **de ~** (*ropa*) off-the-peg.

confeccionar [konfe(k)θjo'nar] *vt* to make (up).

confederación [konfeðera'θjon] *nf* confederation.

conferencia [konfe'renθja] *nf* conference; (*lección*) lecture; (*TELEC*) call; **~ de cobro revertido** (*TELEC*) reversed-charge (*BRIT*) *o* collect (*US*) call; **~ cumbre** summit (conference).

conferenciante [konferen'θjante] *nm/f* lecturer.

conferir [konfe'rir] *vt* to award.

confesar [konfe'sar] *vt* (*admitir*) to confess, admit; (*error*) to acknowledge; (*crimen*) to own up to.

confesión [konfe'sjon] *nf* confession.

confesionario [konfesjo'narjo] *nm* confessional.

confeso, a [kon'feso, a] *adj* (*JUR etc*) self-confessed.

confeti [kon'feti] *nm* confetti.

confiado, a [kon'fjaðo, a] *adj* (*crédulo*) trusting; (*seguro*) confident; (*presumido*) conceited, vain.

confianza [kon'fjanθa] *nf* trust; (*aliento, confidencia*) confidence; (*familiaridad*) intimacy, familiarity; (*pey*) vanity, conceit; **margen de ~** credibility gap; **tener ~ con algn** to be on close terms with sb.

confiar [kon'fjar] *vt* to entrust ♦ *vi* (*fiarse*) to trust; (*contar con*) to rely; **~se** *vr* to put one's trust.

confidencia [konfi'ðenθja] *nf* confidence.

confidencial [konfiðen'θjal] *adj*

confidential.
confidente [konfi'ðente] *nm/f* confidant/e;
(*policial*) informer.
confiera [kon'fjera] *etc vb V* **conferir**.
confiese [kon'fjese] *etc vb V* **confesar**.
configuración [konfiɣura'θjon] *nf* (*tb
INFORM*) configuration; **la ~ del terreno**
the lie of the land; **~ de bits** (*INFORM*) bit
pattern.
configurar [konfiɣu'rar] *vt* to shape, form.
confín [kon'fin] *nm* limit; **confines** *nmpl*
confines, limits.
confinar [konfi'nar] *vi* to confine;
(*desterrar*) to banish.
confiriendo [konfi'rjendo] *etc vb V*
conferir.
confirmación [konfirma'θjon] *nf*
confirmation; (*REL*) Confirmation.
confirmar [konfir'mar] *vt* to confirm; (*JUR
etc*) to corroborate; **la excepción
confirma la regla** the exception proves
the rule.
confiscar [konfis'kar] *vt* to confiscate.
confisque [kon'fiske] *etc vb V* **confiscar**.
confitado, a [konfi'taðo, a] *adj*: **fruta
confitada** crystallized fruit.
confite [kon'fite] *nm* sweet (*BRIT*), candy
(*US*).
confitería [konfite'ria] *nf* confectionery;
(*tienda*) confectioner's (shop).
confitura [konfi'tura] *nf* jam.
conflagración [konflaɣra'θjon] *nf*
conflagration.
conflictivo, a [konflik'tiβo, a] *adj* (*asunto,
propuesta*) controversial; (*país, situación*)
troubled.
conflicto [kon'flikto] *nm* conflict; (*fig*)
clash; (: *dificultad*): **estar en un ~** to be in
a jam; **~ laboral** labour dispute.
confluir [konflu'ir] *vi* (*ríos etc*) to meet;
(*gente*) to gather.
confluya [kon'fluja] *etc vb V* **confluir**.
conformar [konfor'mar] *vt* to shape,
fashion ♦ *vi* to agree; **~se** *vr* to conform;
(*resignarse*) to resign o.s.
conforme [kon'forme] *adj* alike, similar;
(*de acuerdo*) agreed, in agreement;
(*satisfecho*) satisfied ♦ *adv* as ♦ *excl*
agreed! ♦ *nm* agreement ♦ *prep*: **~ a** in
accordance with.
conformidad [konformi'ðað] *nf* (*semejanza*)
similarity; (*acuerdo*) agreement;
(*resignación*) resignation; **de/en ~ con** in
accordance with; **dar su ~** to consent.
conformismo [konfor'mismo] *nm*
conformism.
conformista [konfor'mista] *nm/f*
conformist.

confort, *pl* **conforts** [kon'for, kon'for(t)s]
nm comfort.
confortable [konfor'taβle] *adj*
comfortable.
confortar [konfor'tar] *vt* to comfort.
confraternidad [konfraterni'ðað] *nf*
brotherhood; **espíritu de ~** feeling of
unity.
confraternizar [konfraterni'θar] *vi* to
fraternize.
confrontación [konfronta'θjon] *nf*
confrontation.
confrontar [konfron'tar] *vt* to confront;
(*dos personas*) to bring face to face;
(*cotejar*) to compare ♦ *vi* to border.
confundir [konfun'dir] *vt* (*borrar*) to blur;
(*equivocar*) to mistake, confuse; (*mezclar*)
to mix; (*turbar*) to confuse; **~se** *vr*
(*hacerse borroso*) to become blurred;
(*turbarse*) to get confused; (*equivocarse*)
to make a mistake; (*mezclarse*) to mix.
confusión [konfu'sjon] *nf* confusion.
confusionismo [konfusjo'nismo] *nm*
confusion, uncertainty.
confuso, a [kon'fuso, a] *adj* (*gen*)
confused; (*recuerdo*) hazy; (*estilo*)
obscure.
congelación [konxela'θjon] *nf* freezing; **~
de créditos** credit freeze.
congelado, a [konxe'laðo, a] *adj* frozen
♦ *nmpl*: **~s** frozen food *sg o* foods.
congelador [konxela'ðor] *nm* freezer, deep
freeze.
congelar [konxe'lar] *vt* to freeze; **~se** *vr*
(*sangre, grasa*) to congeal.
congénere [kon'xenere] *nm/f*: **sus ~s** his
peers.
congeniar [konxe'njar] *vi* to get on (*BRIT*) *o*
along (*US*) (well).
congénito, a [kon'xenito, a] *adj*
congenital.
congestión [konxes'tjon] *nf* congestion.
congestionado, a [konxestjo'naðo, a] *adj*
congested.
congestionar [konxestjo'nar] *vt* to
congest; **~se** *vr* to become congested; **se
le congestionó la cara** his face became
flushed.
conglomerado [konglome'raðo] *nm*
conglomerate.
Congo ['kongo] *nm*: **el ~** the Congo.
congoja [kon'goxa] *nf* distress, grief.
congraciarse [kongra'θjarse] *vr* to
ingratiate o.s.
congratular [kongratu'lar] *vt* to
congratulate.
congregación [kongreɣa'θjon] *nf*
congregation.

congregar [kongre'ɣar] vt, ~**se** vr to gather together.

congregue [kon'greɣe] etc vb V **congregar**.

congresista [kongre'sista] nm/f delegate, congressman/woman.

congreso [kon'greso] nm congress; **C~ de los Diputados** (ESP POL) ≈ House of Commons (BRIT), House of Representatives (US); V tb **Las Cortes (españolas)**.

congrio ['kongrjo] nm conger (eel).

congruente [kon'grwente] adj congruent, congruous.

conífera [ko'nifera] nf conifer.

conjetura [konxe'tura] nf guess; (COM) guesstimate.

conjeturar [konxetu'rar] vt to guess.

conjugación [konxuɣa'θjon] nf conjugation.

conjugar [konxu'ɣar] vt to combine, fit together; (LING) to conjugate.

conjugue [kon'xuɣe] etc vb V **conjugar**.

conjunción [konxun'θjon] nf conjunction.

conjunctivitis [konxunti'βitis] nf conjunctivitis.

conjunto, a [kon'xunto, a] adj joint, united ♦ nm whole; (MUS) band; (vestido) ensemble; (INFORM) set; **en ~** as a whole; **~ integrado de programas** (INFORM) integrated software suite.

conjura [kon'xura] nf plot, conspiracy.

conjurar [konxu'rar] vt (REL) to exorcise; (peligro) to ward off ♦ vi to plot.

conjuro [kon'xuro] nm spell.

conllevar [konʎe'βar] vt to bear; (implicar) to imply, involve.

conmemoración [konmemora'θjon] nf commemoration.

conmemorar [konmemo'rar] vt to commemorate.

conmigo [kon'miɣo] pron with me.

conminar [konmi'nar] vt to threaten.

conmiseración [konmisera'θjon] nf pity, commiseration.

conmoción [konmo'θjon] nf shock; (POL) disturbance; (fig) upheaval; **~ cerebral** (MED) concussion.

conmovedor, a [konmoβe'ðor, a] adj touching, moving; (emocionante) exciting.

conmover [konmo'βer] vt to shake, disturb; (fig) to move; ~**se** vr (fig) to be moved.

conmueva [kon'mweβa] etc vb V **conmover**.

conmutación [konmuta'θjon] nf (INFORM) switching; **~ de mensajes** message switching; **~ por paquetes** packet switching.

conmutador [konmuta'ðor] nm switch; (AM TELEC) switchboard.

conmutar [konmu'tar] vt (JUR) to commute.

connivencia [konni'βenθja] nf: **estar en ~ con** to be in collusion with.

connotación [konnota'θjon] nf connotation.

cono ['kono] nm cone; **C~ Sur** Southern Cone.

conocedor, a [konoθe'ðor, a] adj expert, knowledgeable ♦ nm/f expert, connoisseur.

conocer [kono'θer] vt to know; (por primera vez) to meet, get to know; (entender) to know about; (reconocer) to recognize; ~**se** vr (una persona) to know o.s.; (dos personas) to (get to) know each other; **darse a ~** (presentarse) to make o.s. known; **se conoce que ...** (parece) apparently ....

conocido, a [kono'θiðo, a] adj (well-) known ♦ nm/f acquaintance.

conocimiento [konoθi'mjento] nm knowledge; (MED) consciousness; (NAUT: tb: **~ de embarque**) bill of lading; ~**s** nmpl (personas) acquaintances; (saber) knowledge sg; **hablar con ~ de causa** to speak from experience; ~ **(de embarque) aéreo** (COM) air waybill.

conozca [ko'noθka] etc vb V **conocer**.

conque ['konke] conj and so, so then.

conquense [kon'kense] adj of o from Cuenca ♦ nm/f native o inhabitant of Cuenca.

conquista [kon'kista] nf conquest.

conquistador, a [konkista'ðor, a] adj conquering ♦ nm conqueror.

conquistar [konkis'tar] vt (MIL) to conquer; (puesto, simpatía) to win; (enamorar) to win the heart of.

consabido, a [konsa'βiðo, a] adj (frase etc) old; (pey): **las consabidas excusas** the same old excuses.

consagrado, a [konsa'ɣraðo, a] adj (REL) consecrated; (actor) established.

consagrar [konsa'ɣrar] vt (REL) to consecrate; (fig) to devote.

consciente [kons'θjente] adj conscious; **ser o estar ~ de** to be aware of.

consecución [konseku'θjon] nf acquisition; (de fin) attainment.

consecuencia [konse'kwenθja] nf consequence, outcome; (firmeza) consistency; **de ~** of importance.

consecuente [konse'kwente] adj consistent.

consecutivo, a [konseku'tiβo, a] *adj* consecutive.

conseguir [konse'ɣir] *vt* to get, obtain; (*sus fines*) to attain.

consejería [konsexe'ria] *nf* (*POL*) ministry (*in a regional government*).

consejero, a [konse'xero, a] *nm/f* adviser, consultant; (*POL*) minister (*in a regional government*); (*COM*) director; (*en comisión*) member.

consejo [kon'sexo] *nm* advice; (*POL*) council; (*COM*) board; **un ~** a piece of advice; **~ de administración** board of directors; **~ de guerra** court-martial; **C~ de Europa** Council of Europe.

consenso [kon'senso] *nm* consensus.

consentido, a [konsen'tiðo, a] *adj* (*mimado*) spoiled.

consentimiento [konsenti'mjento] *nm* consent.

consentir [konsen'tir] *vt* (*permitir, tolerar*) to consent to; (*mimar*) to pamper, spoil ♦ *vi* to agree, consent; **~ que algn haga algo** to allow sb to do sth.

conserje [kon'serxe] *nm* caretaker; (*portero*) porter.

conserva [kon'serβa] *nf*: **en ~** (*alimentos*) tinned (*BRIT*), canned; **~s** tinned *o* canned foods.

conservación [konserβa'θjon] *nf* conservation; (*de alimentos, vida*) preservation.

conservador, a [konserβa'ðor, a] *adj* (*POL*) conservative ♦ *nm/f* conservative.

conservadurismo [konserβaðu'rismo] *nm* (*POL etc*) conservatism.

conservante [konser'βante] *nm* preservative.

conservar [konser'βar] *vt* (*gen*) to preserve; (*recursos*) to conserve, keep; (*alimentos, vida*) to preserve; **~se** *vr* to survive.

conservas [kon'serβas] *nfpl*: **~ (alimenticias)** tinned (*BRIT*) *o* canned goods.

conservatorio [konserβa'torjo] *nm* (*MUS*) conservatoire; (*AM*) greenhouse.

considerable [konsiðe'raβle] *adj* considerable.

consideración [konsiðera'θjon] *nf* consideration; (*estimación*) respect; **de ~** important; **De mi** *o* **nuestra (mayor) ~** (*AM*) Dear Sir(s) *o* Madam; **tomar en ~** to take into account.

considerado, a [konsiðe'raðo, a] *adj* (*atento*) considerate; (*respetado*) respected.

considerar [konsiðe'rar] *vt* (*gen*) to

consider; (*meditar*) to think about; (*tener en cuenta*) to take into account.

consienta [kon'sjenta] *etc vb V* **consentir**.

consigna [kon'siɣna] *nf* (*orden*) order, instruction; (*para equipajes*) left-luggage office (*BRIT*), checkroom (*US*).

consignación [konsiɣna'θjon] *nf* consignment; **~ de créditos** allocation of credits.

consignador [konsiɣna'ðor] *nm* (*COM*) consignor.

consignar [konsiɣ'nar] *vt* (*COM*) to send; (*créditos*) to allocate.

consignatario, a [konsiɣna'tarjo, a] *nm/f* (*COM*) consignee.

consigo [kon'siɣo] *etc vb V* **conseguir** ♦ *pron* (*m*) with him; (*f*) with her; (*usted*) with you; (*reflexivo*) with o.s.

consiguiendo [konsi'ɣjendo] *etc vb V* **conseguir**.

consiguiente [konsi'ɣjente] *adj* consequent; **por ~** and so, therefore, consequently.

consintiendo [konsin'tjendo] *etc vb V* **consentir**.

consistente [konsis'tente] *adj* consistent; (*sólido*) solid, firm; (*válido*) sound; **~ en** consisting of.

consistir [konsis'tir] *vi*: **~ en** (*componerse de*) to consist of; (*ser resultado de*) to be due to.

consola [kon'sola] *nf* console, control panel; (*mueble*) console table; **~ de juegos** games console; **~ de mando** (*INFORM*) control console; **~ de visualización** visual display console.

consolación [konsola'θjon] *nf* consolation.

consolar [konso'lar] *vt* to console.

consolidar [konsoli'ðar] *vt* to consolidate.

consomé, *pl* **consomés** [konso'me, konso'mes] *nm* consommé, clear soup.

consonancia [konso'nanθja] *nf* harmony; **en ~ con** in accordance with.

consonante [konso'nante] *adj* consonant, harmonious ♦ *nf* consonant.

consorcio [kon'sorθjo] *nm* (*COM*) consortium, syndicate.

consorte [kon'sorte] *nm/f* consort.

conspicuo, a [kons'pikwo, a] *adj* conspicuous.

conspiración [konspira'θjon] *nf* conspiracy.

conspirador, a [konspira'ðor, a] *nm/f* conspirator.

conspirar [konspi'rar] *vi* to conspire.

constancia [kons'tanθja] *nf* (*gen*) constancy; (*certeza*) certainly; **dejar ~ de algo** to put sth on record.

constante [kons'tante] *adj, nf* constant.

constar [kons'tar] *vi* (*evidenciarse*) to be clear *o* evident; ~ **(en)** to appear (in); ~ **de** to consist of; **hacer** ~ to put on record; **me consta que ...** I have evidence that ...; **que conste que lo hice por ti** believe me, I did it for your own good.

constatar [konsta'tar] *vt* (*controlar*) to check; (*observar*) to note.

constelación [konstela'θjon] *nf* constellation.

consternación [konsterna'θjon] *nf* consternation.

constipado, a [konsti'paðo, a] *adj*: **estar** ~ to have a cold ♦ *nm* cold.

constiparse [konsti'parse] *vr* to catch a cold.

constitución [konstitu'θjon] *nf* constitution; **Día de la C~** (*ESP*) Constitution Day (*6th December*).

constitucional [konstituθjo'nal] *adj* constitutional.

constituir [konstitu'ir] *vt* (*formar, componer*) to constitute, make up; (*fundar, erigir, ordenar*) to constitute, establish; (*ser*) to be; ~**se** *vr* (*POL etc: cuerpo*) to be composed of; (: *fundarse*) to be established.

constitutivo, a [konstitu'tiβo, a] *adj* constitutive, constituent.

constituya [konsti'tuja] *etc vb V* **constituir**.

constituyente [konstitu'jente] *adj* constituent.

constreñir [konstre'ɲir] *vt* (*obligar*) to compel, oblige; (*restringir*) to restrict.

constriño [kons'triɲo] *etc*, **constriñendo** [konstri'ɲendo] *etc vb V* **constreñir**.

construcción [konstruk'θjon] *nf* construction, building.

constructivo, a [konstruk'tiβo, a] *adj* constructive.

constructor, a [konstruk'tor, a] *nm/f* builder.

construir [konstru'ir] *vt* to build, construct.

construyendo [konstru'jendo] *etc vb V* **construir**.

consuelo [kon'swelo] *etc vb V* **consolar** ♦ *nm* consolation, solace.

consuetudinario, a [konswetuði'narjo, a] *adj* customary; **derecho** ~ common law.

cónsul ['konsul] *nm* consul.

consulado [konsu'laðo] *nm* (*sede*) consulate; (*cargo*) consulship.

consulta [kon'sulta] *nf* consultation; (*MED: consultorio*) consulting room; (*INFORM*) enquiry; **horas de** ~ surgery hours; **obra de** ~ reference book.

consultar [konsul'tar] *vt* to consult; ~ **un archivo** (*INFORM*) to interrogate a file.

consultor, a [konsul'tor, a] *nm*: ~ **en dirección de empresas** management consultant.

consultorio [konsul'torjo] *nm* (*MED*) surgery.

consumado, a [konsu'maðo, a] *adj* perfect; (*bribón*) out-and-out.

consumar [konsu'mar] *vt* to complete, carry out; (*crimen*) to commit; (*sentencia*) to carry out.

consumición [konsumi'θjon] *nf* consumption; (*bebida*) drink; (*comida*) food; ~ **mínima** cover charge.

consumido, a [konsu'miðo, a] *adj* (*flaco*) skinny.

consumidor, a [konsumi'ðor, a] *nm/f* consumer.

consumir [konsu'mir] *vt* to consume; ~**se** *vr* to be consumed; (*persona*) to waste away.

consumismo [konsu'mismo] *nm* (*COM*) consumerism.

consumo [kon'sumo] *nm* consumption; **bienes de** ~ consumer goods.

contabilice [kontaβi'liθe] *etc vb V* **contabilizar**.

contabilidad [kontaβili'ðað] *nf* accounting, book-keeping; (*profesión*) accountancy; (*COM*): ~ **analítica** variable costing; ~ **de costos** cost accounting; ~ **de doble partida** double-entry book-keeping; ~ **de gestión** management accounting; ~ **por partida simple** single-entry book-keeping.

contabilizar [kontaβi'liθar] *vt* to enter in the accounts.

contable [kon'taβle] *nm/f* bookkeeper; (*licenciado*) accountant; ~ **de costos** (*COM*) cost accountant.

contactar [kontak'tar] *vi*: ~ **con algn** to contact sb.

contacto [kon'takto] *nm* contact; **lentes de** ~ contact lenses; **estar en** ~ **con** to be in touch with.

contado, a [kon'taðo, a] *adj*: ~**s** (*escasos*) numbered, scarce, few ♦ *nm*: **al** ~ for cash; **pagar al** ~ to pay (in) cash; **precio al** ~ cash price.

contador [konta'ðor] *nm* (*aparato*) meter; (*AM: contable*) accountant.

contaduría [kontaðu'ria] *nf* accountant's office.

contagiar [konta'xjar] *vt* (*enfermedad*) to pass on, transmit; (*persona*) to infect; ~**se** *vr* to become infected.

contagio [kon'taxjo] *nm* infection.
contagioso, a [konta'xjoso, a] *adj*
infectious; (*fig*) catching.
contaminación [kontamina'θjon] *nf* (*gen*)
contamination; (*del ambiente etc*)
pollution.
contaminar [kontami'nar] *vt* (*gen*) to
contaminate; (*aire, agua*) to pollute; (*fig*)
to taint.
contante [kon'tante] *adj*: **dinero ~ (y
sonante)** hard cash.
contar [kon'tar] *vt* (*páginas, dinero*) to
count; (*anécdota etc*) to tell ♦ *vi* to count;
~se *vr* to be counted, figure; **~ con** to
rely on, count on; **sin ~** not to mention;
le cuento entre mis amigos I reckon him
among my friends.
contemplación [kontempla'θjon] *nf*
contemplation; **no andarse con
contemplaciones** not to stand on
ceremony.
contemplar [kontem'plar] *vt* to
contemplate; (*mirar*) to look at.
contemporáneo, a [kontempo'raneo, a]
adj, nm/f contemporary.
contemporizar [kontempori'θar] *vi*: **~ con**
to keep in with.
contención [konten'θjon] *nf* (*JUR*) suit;
muro de ~ retaining wall.
contencioso, a [konten'θjoso, a] *adj* (*JUR
etc*) contentious ♦ *nm* (*POL*) conflict,
dispute.
contender [konten'der] *vi* to contend; (*en
un concurso*) to compete.
contendiente [konten'djente] *nm/f*
contestant.
contendrá [konten'dra] *etc vb* V **contener**.
contenedor [kontene'ðor] *nm* container;
(*de escombros*) skip; **~ de (la) basura**
wheelie-bin (*BRIT*); **~ de vidrio** bottle
bank.
contener [konte'ner] *vt* to contain, hold;
(*risa etc*) to hold back, contain; **~se** *vr* to
control o restrain o.s.
contenga [kon'tenga] *etc vb* V **contener**.
contenido, a [konte'niðo, a] *adj*
(*moderado*) restrained; (*risa etc*)
suppressed ♦ *nm* contents *pl*, content.
contentar [konten'tar] *vt* (*satisfacer*) to
satisfy; (*complacer*) to please; (*COM*) to
endorse; **~se** *vr* to be satisfied.
contento, a [kon'tento, a] *adj* contented,
content; (*alegre*) pleased; (*feliz*) happy.
contestación [kontesta'θjon] *nf* answer,
reply; **~ a la demanda** (*JUR*) defence
plea.
contestador [kontesta'ðor] *nm*: **~
automático** answering machine.

contestar [kontes'tar] *vt* to answer (back),
reply; (*JUR*) to corroborate, confirm.
contestario, a [kontes'tarjo, a] *adj* anti-
establishment, nonconformist.
contexto [kon'teksto] *nm* context.
contienda [kon'tjenda] *nf* contest,
struggle.
contiene [kon'tjene] *etc vb* V **contener**.
contigo [kon'tixo] *pron* with you.
contiguo, a [kon'tixwo, a] *adj* (*de al lado*)
next; (*vecino*) adjacent, adjoining.
continental [kontinen'tal] *adj* continental.
continente [konti'nente] *adj, nm* continent.
contingencia [kontin'xenθja] *nf*
contingency; (*riesgo*) risk; (*posibilidad*)
eventuality.
contingente [kontin'xente] *adj* contingent
♦ *nm* contingent; (*COM*) quota.
continuación [kontinwa'θjon] *nf*
continuation; **a ~** then, next.
continuamente [kon'tinwamente] *adv* (*sin
interrupción*) continuously; (*a todas horas*)
constantly.
continuar [konti'nwar] *vt* to continue, go
on with; (*reanudar*) to resume ♦ *vi* to
continue, go on; **~ hablando** to continue
talking o to talk.
continuidad [kontinwi'ðað] *nf* continuity.
continuo, a [kon'tinwo, a] *adj* (*sin
interrupción*) continuous; (*acción
perseverante*) continual.
contonearse [kontone'arse] *vr* (*hombre*) to
swagger; (*mujer*) to swing her hips.
contorno [kon'torno] *nm* outline; (*GEO*)
contour; **~s** *nmpl* neighbourhood *sg*,
surrounding area *sg*.
contorsión [kontor'sjon] *nf* contortion.
contra ['kontra] *prep* against; (*COM: giro*)
on ♦ *adv* against ♦ *adj, nm/f* (*POL fam*)
counter-revolutionary ♦ *nm* con ♦ *nf*: **la
C~** (*nicaragüense*) the Contras *pl*.
contraalmirante [kontraalmi'rante] *nm*
rear admiral.
contraataque [kontraa'take] *nm*
counterattack.
contrabajo [kontra'βaxo] *nm* double bass.
contrabandista [kontraβan'dista] *nm/f*
smuggler.
contrabando [kontra'βando] *nm* (*acción*)
smuggling; (*mercancías*) contraband; **~
de armas** gun-running.
contracción [kontrak'θjon] *nf* contraction.
contrachapado [kontratʃa'paðo] *nm*
plywood.
contracorriente [kontrako'rrjente] *nf*
cross-current.
contradecir [kontraðe'θir] *vt* to contradict.
contradicción [kontraðik'θjon] *nf*

contradiction; **espíritu de** ~
contrariness.

contradicho [kontra'ðitʃo] *pp de*
contradecir.

contradiciendo [kontraði'θjendo] *etc vb* V
contradecir.

contradictorio, a [kontraðik'torjo, a] *adj*
contradictory.

contradiga [kontra'ðiɣa] *etc,* **contradije**
[kontra'ðixe], **contradirá** [kontraði'ra] *etc*
vb V **contradecir.**

contraer [kontra'er] *vt* to contract; (*hábito*)
to acquire; (*limitar*) to restrict; ~**se** *vr* to
contract; (*limitarse*) to limit o.s.

contraespionage [kontraespjo'naxe] *nm*
counter-espionage.

contrafuerte [kontra'fwerte] *nm* (*ARQ*)
buttress.

contragolpe [kontra'ɣolpe] *nm* backlash.

contrahaga [kontra'aɣa] *etc,* **contraharé**
[kontraa're] *etc vb* V **contrahacer.**

contrahecho, a [kontra'etʃo, a] *pp de*
contrahacer ♦ *adj* fake; (*ANAT*)
hunchbacked.

contrahice [kontra'iθe] *etc vb* V
contrahacer.

contraiga [kon'traiɣa] *etc vb* V **contraer.**

contraindicaciones [kontraindika'θjones]
nfpl (*MED*) contraindications.

contraje [kon'traxe] *etc vb* V **contraer.**

contralor [kontra'lor] *nm* (*AM*) government
accounting inspector.

contraluz [kontra'luθ] *nf* (*FOTO etc*) back
lighting; **a** ~ against the light.

contramaestre [kontrama'estre] *nm*
foreman.

contraofensiva [kontraofen'siβa] *nf*
counteroffensive.

contraorden [kontra'orðen] *nf* counter-
order, countermand.

contrapartida [kontrapar'tiða] *nf* (*COM*)
balancing entry; **como** ~ (**de**) in return
(for), as *o* in compensation (for).

contrapelo [kontra'pelo]: **a** ~ *adv* the
wrong way.

contrapesar [kontrape'sar] *vt* to
counterbalance; (*fig*) to offset.

contrapeso [kontra'peso] *nm*
counterweight; (*fig*) counterbalance;
(*COM*) makeweight.

contrapondré [kontrapon'dre] *etc vb* V
contraponer.

contraponer [kontrapo'ner] *vt* (*cotejar*) to
compare; (*oponer*) to oppose.

contraponga [kontra'ponga] *etc vb* V
contraponer.

contraportada [kontrapor'taða] *nf* (*de
revista*) back page.

contraproducente [kontraproðu'θente] *adj*
counterproductive.

contrapuesto [kontra'pwesto] *pp de*
contraponer.

contrapunto [kontra'punto] *nm*
counterpoint.

contrapuse [kontra'puse] *etc vb* V
contraponer.

contrariar [kontra'rjar] *vt* (*oponerse*) to
oppose; (*poner obstáculo*) to impede;
(*enfadar*) to vex.

contrariedad [kontrarje'ðað] *nf* (*oposición*)
opposition; (*obstáculo*) obstacle, setback;
(*disgusto*) vexation, annoyance.

contrario, a [kon'trarjo, a] *adj* contrary;
(*persona*) opposed; (*sentido, lado*)
opposite ♦ *nm/f* enemy, adversary;
(*DEPORTE*) opponent; **al** ~, **por el** ~ on the
contrary; **de lo** ~ otherwise.

Contrarreforma [kontrarre'forma] *nf*
Counter-Reformation.

contrarreloj [kontrarre'lo(x)] *nf* (*tb:* **prueba**
~) time trial.

contrarrestar [kontrarres'tar] *vt* to
counteract.

contrarrevolución [kontrarreβolu'θjon] *nf*
counter-revolution.

contrasentido [kontrasen'tiðo] *nm*
contradiction; **es un** ~ **que él** ... it
doesn't make sense for him to ... .

contraseña [kontra'seɲa] *nf* countersign;
(*frase*) password.

contrastar [kontras'tar] *vt* to resist ♦ *vi* to
contrast.

contraste [kon'traste] *nm* contrast.

contrata [kon'trata] *nf* (*JUR*) written
contract; (*empleo*) hiring.

contratar [kontra'tar] *vt* (*firmar un acuerdo
para*) to contract for; (*empleados,
obreros*) to hire, engage; (*DEPORTE*) to
sign up; ~**se** *vr* to sign on.

contratiempo [kontra'tjempo] *nm* (*revés*)
setback; (*accidente*) mishap; **a** ~ (*MUS*)
off-beat.

contratista [kontra'tista] *nm/f* contractor.

contrato [kon'trato] *nm* contract; ~ **de
compraventa** contract of sale; ~ **a precio
fijo** fixed-price contract; ~ **a término**
forward contract; ~ **de trabajo** contract
of employment *o* service.

contravalor [kontraβa'lor] *nm* exchange
value.

contravención [kontraβen'θjon] *nf*
contravention, violation.

contravendré [kontraβen'dre] *etc,*
contravenga [kontra'βenga] *etc vb* V
contravenir.

contravenir [kontraβe'nir] *vi:* ~ **a** to

contravene, violate.
contraventana [kontraßen'tana] *nf* shutter.
contraviene [kontra'ßjene] *etc*, **contraviniendo** [kontraßi'njendo] *etc vb* V **contravenir**.
contrayendo [kontra'jendo] *vb* V **contraer**.
contribución [kontrißu'θjon] *nf* (*municipal etc*) tax; (*ayuda*) contribution; **exento de contribuciones** tax-free.
contribuir [kontrißu'ir] *vt, vi* to contribute; (*COM*) to pay (in taxes).
contribuyendo [kontrißu'jendo] *etc vb* V **contribuir**.
contribuyente [kontrißu'jente] *nm/f* (*COM*) taxpayer; (*que ayuda*) contributor.
contrincante [kontrin'kante] *nm* opponent, rival.
control [kon'trol] *nm* control; (*inspección*) inspection, check; (*COM*): ~ **de calidad** quality control; ~ **de cambios** exchange control; ~ **de costos** cost control; ~ **de créditos** credit control; ~ **de existencias** stock control; ~ **de precios** price control.
controlador, a [kontrola'ðor, a] *nm/f* controller; ~ **aéreo** air-traffic controller.
controlar [kontro'lar] *vt* to control; to inspect, check; (*COM*) to audit.
controversia [kontro'ßersja] *nf* controversy.
contubernio [kontu'ßernjo] *nm* ring, conspiracy.
contumaz [kontu'maθ] *adj* obstinate, stubbornly disobedient.
contundente [kontun'dente] *adj* (*prueba*) conclusive; (*fig: argumento*) convincing; **instrumento** ~ blunt instrument.
contusión [kontu'sjon] *nf* bruise.
contuve [kon'tuße] *etc vb* V **contener**.
convalecencia [kombale'θenθja] *nf* convalescence.
convalecer [kombale'θer] *vi* to convalesce, get better.
convaleciente [kombale'θjente] *adj, nm/f* convalescent.
convalezca [komba'leθka] *etc vb* V **convalecer**.
convalidar [kombali'ðar] *vt* (*título*) to recognize.
convencer [komben'θer] *vt* to convince; (*persuadir*) to persuade.
convencimiento [kombenθi'mjento] *nm* (*acción*) convincing; (*persuasión*) persuasion; (*certidumbre*) conviction; **tener el** ~ **de que** ... to be convinced that ... .

convención [komben'θjon] *nf* convention.
convencional [kombenθjo'nal] *adj* conventional.
convendré [komben'dre] *etc*, **convenga** [kom'benga] *etc vb* V **convenir**.
conveniencia [kombe'njenθja] *nf* suitability; (*conformidad*) agreement; (*utilidad, provecho*) usefulness; ~**s** *nfpl* conventions; (*COM*) property *sg*; **ser de la** ~ **de algn** to suit sb.
conveniente [kombe'njente] *adj* suitable; (*útil*) useful; (*correcto*) fit, proper; (*aconsejable*) advisable.
convenio [kom'benjo] *nm* agreement, treaty; ~ **de nivel crítico** threshold agreement.
convenir [kombe'nir] *vi* (*estar de acuerdo*) to agree; (*ser conveniente*) to suit, be suitable; "**sueldo a** ~" "salary to be agreed"; **conviene recordar que** ... it should be remembered that ....
convento [kom'bento] *nm* monastery; (*de monjas*) convent.
convenza [kom'benθa] *etc vb* V **convencer**.
convergencia [komber'xenθja] *nf* convergence.
converger [komber'xer], **convergir** [komber'xir] *vi* to converge; **sus esfuerzos convergen a un fin común** their efforts are directed towards the same objective.
converja [kom'berxa] *etc vb* V **converger**, **convergir**.
conversación [kombersa'θjon] *nf* conversation.
conversar [komber'sar] *vi* to talk, converse.
conversión [komber'sjon] *nf* conversion.
converso, a [kom'berso, a] *nm/f* convert.
convertir [komber'tir] *vt* to convert; (*transformar*) to transform, turn; (*COM*) to (ex)change; ~**se** *vr* (*REL*) to convert.
convexo, a [kom'bekso, a] *adj* convex.
convicción [kombik'θjon] *nf* conviction.
convicto, a [kom'bikto, a] *adj* convicted; (*condenado*) condemned.
convidado, a [kombi'ðaðo, a] *nm/f* guest.
convidar [kombi'ðar] *vt* to invite.
conviene [kom'bjene] *etc vb* V **convenir**.
convierta [kom'bjerta] *etc vb* V **convertir**.
convincente [kombin'θente] *adj* convincing.
conviniendo [kombi'njendo] *etc vb* V **convenir**.
convirtiendo [kombir'tjendo] *etc vb* V **convertir**.
convite [kom'bite] *nm* invitation; (*banquete*) banquet.

convivencia [kombi'ßenθja] *nf* coexistence, living together.

convivir [kombi'ßir] *vi* to live together; (*POL*) to coexist.

convocar [kombo'kar] *vt* to summon, call (together).

convocatoria [komboka'torja] *nf* summons *sg*; (*anuncio*) notice of meeting; (*ESCOL*) examination session.

convoque [kom'boke] *etc vb V* **convocar.**

convoy [kom'boj] *nm* (*FERRO*) train.

convulsión [kombul'sjon] *nf* convulsion; (*POL etc*) upheaval.

conyugal [konju'yal] *adj* conjugal; **vida ~** married life.

cónyuge ['konyuxe] *nm/f* spouse, partner.

coña ['koɲa] *nf*: **tomar algo a ~** (*fam!*) to take sth as a joke.

coñac, *pl* **coñacs** ['koɲa(k), 'koɲas] *nm* cognac, brandy.

coñazo [ko'ɲaθo] *nm* (*fam*) pain; **dar el ~** to be a real pain.

coño ['koɲo] (*fam!*) *nm* cunt (*!*); (*AM pey*) Spaniard ♦ *excl* (*enfado*) shit (*!*); (*sorpresa*) bloody hell (*!*); **¡qué ~!** what a pain in the arse (*!*).

cooperación [koopera'θjon] *nf* cooperation.

cooperar [koope'rar] *vi* to cooperate.

cooperativo, a [koopera'tißo, a] *adj* cooperative ♦ *nf* cooperative.

coordenada [koorðe'naða] *nf* (*MAT*) coordinate; (*fig*): **~s** *nfpl* guidelines, framework *sg*.

coordinación [koorðina'θjon] *nf* coordination.

coordinador, a [koorðina'ðor, a] *nm/f* coordinator ♦ *nf* coordinating committee.

coordinar [koorði'nar] *vt* to coordinate.

copa ['kopa] *nf* (*tb DEPORTE*) cup; (*vaso*) glass; (*de árbol*) top; (*de sombrero*) crown; **~s** *nfpl* (*NAIPES*) one of the suits in the Spanish card deck; (**tomar una**) **~** (to have a) drink; **ir de ~s** to go out for a drink; *V tb* **Baraja Española.**

copar [ko'par] *vt* (*puestos*) to monopolize.

coparticipación [kopartiθipa'θjon] *nf* (*COM*) co-ownership.

COPE *nf abr* (= *Cadena de Ondas Populares Españolas*) Spanish radio network.

Copenhague [kope'naxe] Copenhagen.

copete [ko'pete] *nm* tuft (of hair); **de alto ~** aristocratic, upper-crust (*fam*).

copia ['kopja] *nf* copy; (*ARTE*) replica; (*COM etc*) duplicate; (*INFORM*): **~ impresa** hard copy; **~ de respaldo** *o* **de seguridad** backup copy; **hacer ~ de seguridad** to

back up; **~ de trabajo** working copy; **~ vaciada** dump.

copiadora [kopja'ðora] *nf* photocopier; **~ al alcohol** spirit duplicator.

copiar [ko'pjar] *vt* to copy; **~ al pie de la letra** to copy word for word.

copiloto [kopi'loto] *nm* (*AVIAT*) co-pilot; (*AUTO*) co-driver.

copioso, a [ko'pjoso, a] *adj* copious, plentiful.

copita [ko'pita] *nf* (small) glass; (*GOLF*) tee.

copla ['kopla] *nf* verse; (*canción*) (popular) song.

copo ['kopo] *nm*: **~s de maíz** cornflakes; **~ de nieve** snowflake.

coprocesador [koproθesa'ðor] *nm* (*INFORM*) co-processor.

coproducción [koproðuk'θjon] *nf* (*CINE etc*) joint production.

copropietarios [kopropje'tarjos] *nmpl* (*COM*) joint owners.

cópula ['kopula] *nf* copulation.

copular [kopu'lar] *vi* to copulate.

coqueta [ko'keta] *adj* flirtatious, coquettish ♦ *nf* (*mujer*) flirt.

coquetear [kokete'ar] *vi* to flirt.

coraje [ko'raxe] *nm* courage; (*ánimo*) spirit; (*ira*) anger.

coral [ko'ral] *adj* choral ♦ *nf* choir ♦ *nm* (*ZOOL*) coral.

Corán [ko'ran] *nm*: **el ~** the Koran.

coraza [ko'raθa] *nf* (*armadura*) armour; (*blindaje*) armour-plating.

corazón [kora'θon] *nm* heart; (*BOT*) core; **corazones** *nmpl* (*NAIPES*) hearts; **de buen ~** kind-hearted; **de todo ~** wholeheartedly; **estar mal del ~** to have heart trouble.

corazonada [koraθo'naða] *nf* impulse; (*presentimiento*) presentiment, hunch.

corbata [kor'ßata] *nf* tie.

corbeta [kor'ßeta] *nf* corvette.

Córcega ['korθexa] *nf* Corsica.

corcel [kor'θel] *nm* steed.

corchea [kor't ʃea] *nf* quaver.

corchete [kor't ʃete] *nm* catch, clasp; **~s** *nmpl* (*TIP*) square brackets.

corcho ['kort ʃo] *nm* cork; (*PESCA*) float.

corcovado, a [korko'ßaðo, a] *adj* hunchbacked ♦ *nm/f* hunchback.

cordel [kor'ðel] *nm* cord, line.

cordero [kor'ðero] *nm* lamb; (*piel*) lambskin.

cordial [kor'ðjal] *adj* cordial ♦ *nm* cordial, tonic.

cordialidad [korðjali'ðað] *nf* warmth, cordiality.

cordillera [korði'ʎera] *nf* range (of mountains).

Córdoba ['korðoßa] *nf* Cordova.

cordobés, esa [korðo'ßes, esa] *adj, nm/f* Cordovan.

cordón [kor'ðon] *nm* (*cuerda*) cord, string; (*de zapatos*) lace; (*ELEC*) flex, wire (*US*); (*MIL etc*) cordon.

cordura [kor'ðura] *nf* (*MED*) sanity; (*fig*) good sense.

Corea [ko'rea] *nf* Korea; ~ **del Norte/Sur** North/South Korea.

coreano, a [kore'ano, a] *adj, nm/f* Korean.

corear [kore'ar] *vt* to chorus.

coreografía [koreoɣra'fia] *nf* choreography.

corista [ko'rista] *nf* (*TEAT etc*) chorus girl.

cornada [kor'naða] *nf* (*TAUR etc*) butt, goring.

córner, *pl* **córners** ['korner, 'korners] *nm* corner (kick).

corneta [kor'neta] *nf* bugle.

cornisa [kor'nisa] *nf* cornice.

Cornualles [kor'nwaʎes] *nm* Cornwall.

cornudo, a [kor'nuðo, a] *adj* (*ZOOL*) horned; (*marido*) cuckolded.

coro ['koro] *nm* chorus; (*conjunto de cantores*) choir.

corolario [koro'larjo] *nm* corollary.

corona [ko'rona] *nf* crown; (*de flores*) garland.

coronación [korona'θjon] *nf* coronation.

coronar [koro'nar] *vt* to crown.

coronel [koro'nel] *nm* colonel.

coronilla [koro'niʎa] *nf* (*ANAT*) crown (of the head); **estar hasta la ~ (de)** to be utterly fed up (with).

corpiño [korpiɲo] *nm* bodice; (*AM: sostén*) bra.

corporación [korpora'θjon] *nf* corporation.

corporal [korpo'ral] *adj* corporal, bodily.

corporativo, a [korpora'tißo, a] *adj* corporate.

corpulento, a [korpu'lento, a] *adj* (*persona*) well-built.

corral [ko'rral] *nm* (*patio*) farmyard; (*AGR: de aves*) poultry yard; (*redil*) pen.

correa [ko'rrea] *nf* strap; (*cinturón*) belt; (*de perro*) lead, leash; ~ **transportadora** conveyor belt.

correaje [korre'axe] *nm* (*AGR*) harness.

corrección [korrek'θjon] *nf* correction; (*represión*) rebuke; (*cortesía*) good manners; (*INFORM*): ~ **por líneas** line editing; ~ **en pantalla** screen editing; ~ **(de pruebas)** (*TIP*) proofreading.

correccional [korrekθjo'nal] *nm* reformatory.

correcto, a [ko'rrekto, a] *adj* correct; (*persona*) well-mannered.

corrector, a [korrek'tor, a] *nm/f*: ~ **de pruebas** proofreader.

corredera [korre'ðera] *nf*: **puerta de ~** sliding door.

corredizo, a [korre'ðiθo, a] *adj* (*puerta etc*) sliding; (*nudo*) running.

corredor, a [korre'ðor, a] *adj* running; (*rápido*) fast ♦ *nm/f* (*DEPORTE*) runner ♦ *nm* (*pasillo*) corridor; (*balcón corrido*) gallery; (*COM*) agent, broker; (*pasillo*) corridor, passage; ~ **de bienes raíces** real-estate broker; ~ **de bolsa** stockbroker; ~ **de seguros** insurance broker.

corregir [korre'xir] *vt* (*error*) to correct; (*amonestar, reprender*) to rebuke, reprimand; ~**se** *vr* to reform.

correo [ko'rreo] *nm* post, mail; (*persona*) courier; **C~s** *nmpl* Post Office *sg*; ~ **aéreo** airmail; ~ **certificado** registered mail; ~ **electrónico** E-mail, electronic mail; ~ **urgente** special delivery; **a vuelta de ~** by return (of post).

correr [ko'rrer] *vt* to run; (*viajar*) to cover, travel; (*riesgo*) to run; (*aventura*) to have; (*cortinas*) to draw; (*cerrojo*) to shoot ♦ *vi* to run; (*líquido*) to run, flow; (*rumor*) to go round; ~**se** *vr* to slide, move; (*colores*) to run; (*fam: tener orgasmo*) to come; **echar a ~** to break into a run; ~ **con los gastos** to pay the expenses; **eso corre de mi cuenta** I'll take care of that.

correspondencia [korrespon'denθja] *nf* correspondence; (*FERRO*) connection; (*reciprocidad*) return; ~ **directa** (*COM*) direct mail.

corresponder [korrespon'der] *vi* to correspond; (*convenir*) to be suitable; (*pertenecer*) to belong; (*tocar*) to concern; (*favor*) to repay; ~**se** *vr* (*por escrito*) to correspond; (*amarse*) to love one another; **"a quien corresponda"** "to whom it may concern".

correspondiente [korrespon'djente] *adj* corresponding; (*respectivo*) respective.

corresponsal [korrespon'sal] *nm/f* (newspaper) correspondent; (*COM*) agent.

corretaje [korre'taxe] *nm* (*COM*) brokerage.

corretear [korrete'ar] *vi* to loiter.

corrido, a [ko'rriðo, a] *adj* (*avergonzado*) abashed; (*fluido*) fluent ♦ *nf* run, dash; (*de toros*) bullfight; **de ~** fluently; **3 noches corridas** 3 nights running; **un kilo ~ a** good kilo.

corriente [ko'rrjente] *adj* (*agua*) running;

(*fig*) flowing; (*dinero, cuenta etc*) current; (*común*) ordinary, normal ♦ *nf* current; (*fig: tendencia*) course ♦ *nm* current month; ~ *f* **de aire** draught; ~ **eléctrica** electric current; **las ~s modernas del arte** modern trends in art; **estar al ~ de** to be informed about.

corrigiendo [korri'xjendo] *etc vb V* **corregir.**

corrija [ko'rrixa] *etc vb V* **corregir.**

corrillo [ko'rriʎo] *nm* ring, circle (of people); (*fig*) clique.

corro ['korro] *nm* ring, circle (of people); (*baile*) ring-a-ring-a-roses; **la gente hizo** ~ the people formed a ring.

corroborar [korroβo'rar] *vt* to corroborate.

corroer [korro'er] *vt* (*tb fig*) to corrode, eat away; (*GEO*) to erode.

corromper [korrom'per] *vt* (*madera*) to rot; (*fig*) to corrupt.

corrompido, a [korrom'piðo, a] *adj* corrupt.

corrosivo, a [korro'siβo, a] *adj* corrosive.

corroyendo [korro'jendo] *etc vb V* **corroer.**

corrupción [korrup'θjon] *nf* rot, decay; (*fig*) corruption.

corrupto, a [ko'rrupto, a] *adj* corrupt.

corsario [kor'sarjo] *nm* privateer, corsair.

corsé [kor'se] *nm* corset.

corso, a ['korso, a] *adj, nm/f* Corsican.

cortacésped [korta'θespeð] *nm* lawn mower.

cortado, a [kor'taðo, a] *adj* (*con cuchillo*) cut; (*leche*) sour; (*confuso*) confused; (*desconcertado*) embarrassed; (*tímido*) shy ♦ *nm* white coffee (with a little milk).

cortadora [korta'ðora] *nf* cutter, slicer.

cortadura [korta'ðura] *nf* cut.

cortante [kor'tante] *adj* (*viento*) biting; (*frío*) bitter.

cortapisa [korta'pisa] *nf* (*restricción*) restriction; (*traba*) snag.

cortar [kor'tar] *vt* to cut; (*suministro*) to cut off; (*un pasaje*) to cut out; (*comunicación, teléfono*) to cut off ♦ *vi* to cut; (*AM TELEC*) to hang up; ~**se** *vr* (*turbarse*) to become embarrassed; (*leche*) to turn, curdle; ~ **por lo sano** to settle things once and for all; ~**se el pelo** to have one's hair cut; **se cortó la línea** *o* **el teléfono** I got cut off.

cortauñas [korta'uɲas] *nm inv* nail clippers *pl*.

corte ['korte] *nm* cut, cutting; (*filo*) edge; (*de tela*) piece, length; (*COSTURA*) tailoring ♦ *nf* (*real*) (royal) court; ~ **y confección** dressmaking; ~ **de corriente** *o* **luz** power cut; **me da** ~ **pedírselo** I'm

embarrassed to ask him for it; **¡qué ~ le di!** I left him with no comeback!; **C~ Internacional de Justicia** International Court of Justice; **las C~s** the Spanish Parliament *sg*; **hacer la ~ a** to woo, court.

> *The Spanish Parliament,* **Las Cortes (Españolas),** *has a Lower and an Upper Chamber, the* **Congreso de los Diputados** *and the* **Senado** *respectively. Members of Parliament are called* **diputados** *and are elected in national elections by proportional representation. Some Senate members,* **senadores,** *are chosen by being voted in during national elections and others are appointed by the regional parliaments.*

cortedad [korte'ðað] *nf* shortness; (*fig*) bashfulness, timidity.

cortejar [korte'xar] *vt* to court.

cortejo [kor'texo] *nm* entourage; ~ **fúnebre** funeral procession, cortège.

cortés [kor'tes] *adj* courteous, polite.

cortesano, a [korte'sano, a] *adj* courtly.

cortesía [korte'sia] *nf* courtesy.

corteza [kor'teθa] *nf* (*de árbol*) bark; (*de pan*) crust; (*de fruta*) peel, skin; (*de queso*) rind.

cortijo [kor'tixo] *nm* farmhouse.

cortina [kor'tina] *nf* curtain; ~ **de humo** smoke screen.

corto, a ['korto, a] *adj* (*breve*) short; (*tímido*) bashful; ~ **de luces** not very bright; ~ **de oído** hard of hearing; ~ **de vista** short-sighted; **estar** ~ **de fondos** to be short of funds.

cortocircuito [kortoθir'kwito] *nm* short-circuit.

cortometraje [kortome'traxe] *nm* (*CINE*) short.

Coruña [ko'ruɲa] *nf*: **La** ~ Corunna.

coruñés, esa [koru'ɲes, esa] *adj* of *o* from Corunna ♦ *nm/f* native *o* inhabitant of Corunna.

corvo, a ['korβo, a] *adj* curved; (*nariz*) hooked ♦ *nf* back of knee.

cosa ['kosa] *nf* thing; (*asunto*) affair; ~ **de** about; **eso es** ~ **mía** that's my business; **es poca** ~ it's not important; **¡qué ~ más rara!** how strange; **en** ~ **de 10 minutos** in about 10 minutes.

cosaco, a [ko'sako, a] *adj, nm/f* Cossack.

coscorrón [kosko'rron] *nm* bump on the head.

cosecha [ko'setʃa] *nf* (*AGR*) harvest; (*acto*) harvesting; (*de vino*) vintage; (*producción*) yield.

cosechadora [kosetʃa'ðora] *nf* combine harvester.

cosechar [kose't ʃar] *vt* to harvest, gather (in).

coser [ko'ser] *vt* to sew; (*MED*) to stitch (up).

cosido [ko'siðo] *nm* sewing.

cosmético, a [kos'metiko, a] *adj, nm* cosmetic ♦ *nf* cosmetics *pl.*

cosmopolita [kosmopo'lita] *adj* cosmopolitan.

cosmos ['kosmos] *nm* cosmos.

coso ['koso] *nm* bullring.

cosquillas [kos'kiʎas] *nfpl*: **hacer** ~ to tickle; **tener** ~ to be ticklish.

cosquilleo [koski'ʎeo] *nm* tickling (sensation).

costa ['kosta] *nf* (*GEO*) coast; **C~ Brava** Costa Brava; **C~ Cantábrica** Cantabrian Coast; **C~ de Marfil** Ivory Coast; **C~ del Sol** Costa del Sol; **a ~** (*COM*) at cost; **a ~ de** at the expense of; **a toda ~** at any price.

costado [kos'taðo] *nm* side; **de ~** (*dormir*) on one's side; **español por los 4 ~s** Spanish through and through.

costal [kos'tal] *nm* sack.

costalada [kosta'laða] *nf* bad fall.

costanera [kosta'nera] *nf* (*AM*) (seaside) promenade.

costar [kos'tar] *vt* (*valer*) to cost; **me cuesta hablarle** I find it hard to talk to him; **¿cuánto cuesta?** how much does it cost?

Costa Rica [kosta'rika] *nf* Costa Rica.

costarricense [kostarri'θense],
costarriqueño, a [kostarri'keɲo, a] *adj, nm/f* Costa Rican.

coste ['koste] *nm* (*COM*): ~ **promedio** average cost; ~**s fijos** fixed costs; *V tb* **costo.**

costear [koste'ar] *vt* to pay for; (*COM etc*) to finance; (*NAUT*) to sail along the coast of; ~**se** *vr* (*negocio*) to pay for itself, cover its costs.

costeño, a [kos'teɲo, a] *adj* coastal.

costero, a [kos'tero, a] *adj* coastal, coast *cpd.*

costilla [kos'tiʎa] *nf* rib; (*CULIN*) cutlet.

costo ['kosto] *nm* cost, price; ~ **directo** direct cost; ~ **de expedición** shipping charges; ~ **de sustitución** replacement cost; ~ **unitario** unit cost; ~ **de la vida** cost of living.

costoso, a [kos'toso, a] *adj* costly, expensive.

costra ['kostra] *nf* (*corteza*) crust; (*MED*) scab.

costumbre [kos'tumbre] *nf* custom, habit;

como de ~ as usual.

costura [kos'tura] *nf* sewing, needlework; (*confección*) dressmaking; (*zurcido*) seam.

costurera [kostu'rera] *nf* dressmaker.

costurero [kostu'rero] *nm* sewing box *o* case.

cota ['kota] *nf* (*GEO*) height above sea level; (*fig*) height.

cotarro [ko'tarro] *nm*: **dirigir el ~** (*fam*) to rule the roost.

cotejar [kote'xar] *vt* to compare.

cotejo [ko'texo] *nm* comparison.

cotice [ko'tiθe] *etc vb V* **cotizar.**

cotidiano, a [koti'ðjano, a] *adj* daily, day to day.

cotilla [ko'tiʎa] *nf* busybody, gossip.

cotillear [kotiʎe'ar] *vi* to gossip.

cotilleo [koti'ʎeo] *nm* gossip(ing).

cotización [kotiθa'θjon] *nf* (*COM*) quotation, price; (*de club*) dues *pl.*

cotizado, a [koti'θaðo, a] *adj* (*fig*) highly-prized.

cotizar [koti'θar] *vt* (*COM*) to quote, price; ~**se** *vr* (*fig*) to be highly prized; ~**se a** to sell at, fetch; (*BOLSA*) to stand at, be quoted at.

coto ['koto] *nm* (*terreno cercado*) enclosure; (*de caza*) reserve; (*COM*) price-fixing agreement; **poner ~ a** to put a stop to.

cotorra [ko'torra] *nf* (*ZOOL: loro*) parrot; (*fam: persona*) windbag.

COU [kou] *nm abr* (*ESP*: = *Curso de Orientación Universitario*) *one year course leading to final school leaving certificate and university entrance examinations; V tb* **sistema educativo.**

coyote [ko'jote] *nm* coyote, prairie wolf.

coyuntura [kojun'tura] *nf* (*ANAT*) joint; (*fig*) juncture, occasion; **esperar una ~ favorable** to await a favourable moment.

coz [koθ] *nf* kick.

CP *nm abr* (= *computador personal*) PC.

C.P. *abr* (*ESP*) = **Caja Postal.**

C.P.A. *nf abr* (= *Caja Postal de Ahorros*) Post Office Savings Bank.

CP/M *nm abr* (= *Programa de control para microprocesadores*) CP/M.

CPN *nm abr* (*ESP*) = **Cuerpo de la Policía Nacional.**

cps *abr* (= *caracteres por segundo*) c.p.s.

crac [krak] *nm* (*ECON*) crash.

cráneo ['kraneo] *nm* skull, cranium.

crápula ['krapula] *nf* drunkenness.

cráter ['krater] *nm* crater.

creación [krea'θjon] *nf* creation.

creador, a [krea'ðor, a] *adj* creative ♦ *nm/f* creator.

crear [kre'ar] *vt* to create, make; (*originar*) to originate; (*INFORM: archivo*) to create; ~**se** *vr* (*comité etc*) to be set up.

creativo, a [krea'tiβo, a] *adj* creative.

crecer [kre'θer] *vi* to grow; (*precio*) to rise; ~**se** *vr* (*engreírse*) to get cocky.

creces ['kreθes]: **con** ~ *adv* amply, fully.

crecido, a [kre'θiðo, a] *adj* (*persona, planta*) full-grown; (*cantidad*) large ♦ *nf* (*de río*) spate, flood.

creciente [kre'θjente] *adj* growing; (*cantidad*) increasing; (*luna*) crescent ♦ *nm* crescent.

crecimiento [kreθi'mjento] *nm* growth; (*aumento*) increase; (*COM*) rise.

credenciales [kreðen'θjales] *nfpl* credentials.

crédito ['kreðito] *nm* credit; **a** ~ on credit; **dar** ~ **a** to believe (in); ~ **al consumidor** consumer credit; ~ **rotativo** *o* **renovable** revolving credit.

credo ['kreðo] *nm* creed.

crédulo, a ['kreðulo, a] *adj* credulous.

creencia [kre'enθja] *nf* belief.

creer [kre'er] *vt, vi* to think, believe; (*considerar*) to think, consider; ~**se** *vr* to believe o.s. (to be); ~ **en** to believe in; **¡ya lo creo!** I should think so!

creíble [kre'iβle] *adj* credible, believable.

creído, a [kre'iðo, a] *adj* (*engreído*) conceited.

crema ['krema] *adj inv* cream (coloured) ♦ *nf* cream; (*natillas*) custard; **la** ~ **de la sociedad** the cream of society.

cremallera [krema'ʎera] *nf* zip (fastener) (*BRIT*), zipper (*US*).

crematorio [krema'torjo] *nm* crematorium (*BRIT*), crematory (*US*).

cremoso, a [kre'moso, a] *adj* creamy.

crepitar [krepi'tar] *vi* (*fuego*) to crackle.

crepúsculo [kre'puskulo] *nm* twilight, dusk.

crespo, a ['krespo, a] *adj* (*pelo*) curly.

crespón [kres'pon] *nm* crêpe.

cresta ['kresta] *nf* (*GEO, ZOOL*) crest.

Creta ['kreta] *nf* Crete.

cretino, a [kre'tino, a] *adj* cretinous ♦ *nm/f* cretin.

creyendo [kre'jendo] *etc vb V* **creer**.

creyente [kre'jente] *nm/f* believer.

crezca ['kreθka] *etc vb V* **crecer**.

cría ['kria] *etc vb V* **criar** ♦ *nf V* **crío, a**.

criada [kri'aða] *nf V* **criado, a**.

criadero [kria'ðero] *nm* nursery; (*ZOOL*) breeding place.

criadillas [kria'ðiʎas] *nfpl* (*CULIN*) bull's (*o* sheep's) testicles.

criado, a [kri'aðo, a] *nm* servant ♦ *nf* servant, maid.

criador [kria'ðor] *nm* breeder.

crianza [kri'anθa] *nf* rearing, breeding; (*fig*) breeding; (*MED*) lactation.

criar [kri'ar] *vt* (*amamantar*) to suckle, feed; (*educar*) to bring up; (*producir*) to grow, produce; (*animales*) to breed; ~**se** *vr* to grow (up); ~ **cuervos** to nourish a viper in one's bosom; **Dios los cría y ellos se juntan** birds of a feather flock together.

criatura [kria'tura] *nf* creature; (*niño*) baby, (small) child.

criba ['kriβa] *nf* sieve.

cribar [kri'βar] *vt* to sieve.

crimen ['krimen] *nm* crime; ~ **pasional** crime of passion.

criminal [krimi'nal] *adj, nm/f* criminal.

crin [krin] *nf* (*tb:* ~**es**) mane.

crío, a ['krio, a] *nm/f* (*fam: chico*) kid ♦ *nf* (*de animales*) rearing, breeding; (*animal*) young.

criollo, a [kri'oʎo, a] *adj* (*gen*) Creole; (*AM*) native (to America), national ♦ *nm/f* (*gen*) Creole; (*AM*) native American.

cripta ['kripta] *nf* crypt.

crisis ['krisis] *nf inv* crisis; ~ **nerviosa** nervous breakdown.

crisma ['krisma] *nf*: **romperle la** ~ **a algn** (*fam*) to knock sb's block off.

crisol [kri'sol] *nm* (*TEC*) crucible; (*fig*) melting pot.

crispación [krispa'θjon] *nf* tension.

crispar [kris'par] *vt* (*músculo*) to cause to contract; (*nervios*) to set on edge.

cristal [kris'tal] *nm* crystal; (*de ventana*) glass, pane; (*lente*) lens; **de** ~ glass *cpd*; ~ **ahumado/tallado** smoked/cut glass.

cristalería [kristale'ria] *nf* (*tienda*) glassware shop; (*objetos*) glassware.

cristalice [krista'liθe] *etc vb V* **cristalizar**.

cristalino, a [krista'lino, a] *adj* crystalline; (*fig*) clear ♦ *nm* lens of the eye.

cristalizar [kristali'θar] *vt, vi* to crystallize.

cristiandad [kristjan'dað] *nf*, **cristianismo** [kristja'nismo] *nm* Christianity.

cristiano, a [kris'tjano, a] *adj, nm/f* Christian; **hablar en** ~ to speak proper Spanish; (*fig*) to speak clearly.

Cristo ['kristo] *nm* (*dios*) Christ; (*crucifijo*) crucifix.

Cristóbal [kris'toβal] *nm*: ~ **Colón** Christopher Columbus.

criterio [kri'terjo] *nm* criterion; (*juicio*) judgement; (*enfoque*) attitude, approach; (*punto de vista*) view, opinion; ~ **de clasificación** (*INFORM*) sort criterion.

criticar [kriti'kar] *vt* to criticize.

crítico, a ['kritiko, a] *adj* critical ♦ *nm* critic ♦ *nf* criticism; (*TEAT etc*) review, notice; **la crítica** the critics *pl.*

critique [kri'tike] *etc vb V* **criticar.**

Croacia [kro'aθja] *nf* Croatia.

croar [kro'ar] *vi* to croak.

croata [kro'ata] *adj, nm/f* Croat(ian) ♦ *nm* (*LING*) Croat(ian).

croissan(t) [krwa'san] *nm* croissant.

crol ['krol] *nm* crawl.

cromado [kro'maðo] *nm* chromium plating, chrome.

cromo ['kromo] *nm* chrome; (*TIP*) coloured print.

cromosoma [kromo'soma] *nm* chromosome.

crónico, a ['kroniko, a] *adj* chronic ♦ *nf* chronicle, account; (*de periódico*) feature, article.

cronología [kronolo'xia] *nf* chronology.

cronológico, a [krono'loxiko, a] *adj* chronological.

cronometraje [kronome'traxe] *nm* timing.

cronometrar [kronome'trar] *vt* to time.

cronómetro [kro'nometro] *nm* (*DEPORTE*) stopwatch; (*TEC etc*) chronometer.

croqueta [kro'keta] *nf* croquette, rissole.

croquis ['krokis] *nm inv* sketch.

cruce ['kruθe] *etc vb V* **cruzar** ♦ *nm* crossing; (*de carreteras*) crossroads; (*AUTO etc*) junction, intersection; (*BIO: proceso*) crossbreeding; **luces de** ~ dipped headlights.

crucero [kru'θero] *nm* (*NAUT: barco*) cruise ship; (: *viaje*) cruise.

crucial [kru'θjal] *adj* crucial.

crucificar [kruθifi'kar] *vt* to crucify; (*fig*) to torment.

crucifijo [kruθi'fixo] *nm* crucifix.

crucifique [kruθi'fike] *etc vb V* **crucificar.**

crucigrama [kruθi'ɣrama] *nm* crossword (puzzle).

crudeza [kru'ðeθa] *nf* (*rigor*) harshness; (*aspereza*) crudeness.

crudo, a ['kruðo, a] *adj* raw; (*no maduro*) unripe; (*petróleo*) crude; (*rudo, cruel*) cruel; (*agua*) hard; (*clima etc*) harsh ♦ *nm* crude (oil).

cruel [krwel] *adj* cruel.

crueldad [krwel'ðað] *nf* cruelty.

cruento, a ['krwento, a] *adj* bloody.

crujido [kru'xiðo] *nm* (*de madera etc*) creak.

crujiente [kru'xjente] *adj* (*galleta etc*) crunchy.

crujir [kru'xir] *vi* (*madera etc*) to creak; (*dedos*) to crack; (*dientes*) to grind; (*nieve, arena*) to crunch.

cruz [kruθ] *nf* cross; (*de moneda*) tails *sg*; (*fig*) burden; ~ **gamada** swastika; **C~ Roja** Red Cross.

cruzado, a [kru'θaðo, a] *adj* crossed ♦ *nm* crusader ♦ *nf* crusade.

cruzar [kru'θar] *vt* to cross; (*palabras*) to exchange; ~**se** *vr* (*líneas etc*) to cross, intersect; (*personas*) to pass each other; ~**se de brazos** to fold one's arms; (*fig*) not to lift a finger to help; ~**se con algn en la calle** to pass sb in the street.

c.s.f. *abr* (= *costo, seguro y flete*) c.i.f.

CSIC [θe'sik] *nm abr* (*ESP ESCOL*) = *Consejo Superior de Investigaciones Científicas.*

cta, c.ta *nf abr* (= *cuenta*) a/c.

cta. cto. *abr* (= *carta de crédito*) L.C.

cte. *abr* (= *corriente, de los corrientes*) inst.

CTNE *nf abr* (*TELEC*) = *Compañía Telefónica Nacional de España.*

c/u *abr* (= *cada uno*) ea.

cuaco ['kwako] *nm* (*AM*) nag.

cuaderno [kwa'ðerno] *nm* notebook; (*de escuela*) exercise book; (*NAUT*) logbook.

cuadra ['kwaðra] *nf* (*caballeriza*) stable; (*AM*) (city) block.

cuadrado, a [kwa'ðraðo, a] *adj* square ♦ *nm* (*MAT*) square.

cuadragésimo, a [kwaðra'xesimo, a] *num* fortieth.

cuadrángulo [kwa'ðrangulo, a] *nm* quadrangle.

cuadrante [kwa'ðrante] *nm* quadrant.

cuadrar [kwa'ðrar] *vt* to square; (*TIP*) to justify ♦ *vi*: ~ **con** (*cuenta*) to square with, tally with; ~**se** *vr* (*soldado*) to stand to attention; ~ **por la derecha/izquierda** to right-/left-justify.

cuadrícula [kwa'ðrikula] *nf* (*TIP etc*) grid, ruled squares.

cuadriculado, a [kwaðriku'laðo, a] *adj*: **papel** ~ squared *o* graph paper.

cuadrilátero [kwaðri'latero] *nm* (*DEPORTE*) boxing ring; (*GEOM*) quadrilateral.

cuadrilla [kwa'ðriʎa] *nf* (*amigos*) party, group; (*pandilla*) gang; (*obreros*) team.

cuadro ['kwaðro] *nm* square; (*PINTURA*) painting; (*TEAT*) scene; (*diagrama: tb:* ~ **sinóptico**) chart, table, diagram; (*DEPORTE, MED*) team; (*POL*) executive; ~ **de mandos** control panel; **a** ~**s** check *cpd.*

cuadruplicarse [kwaðrupli'karse] *vr* to quadruple.

cuádruplo, a ['kwaðruplo, a], **cuádruple** ['kwaðruple] *adj* quadruple.

cuajado, a [kwa'xaðo, a] *adj*: ~ **de** (*fig*) full of ♦ *nf* (*de leche*) curd.

cuajar [kwa'xar] *vt* to thicken; (*leche*) to curdle; (*sangre*) to congeal; (*adornar*) to

adorn; (*CULIN*) to set ♦ *vi* (*nieve*) to lie;
(*fig*) to become set, become established;
(*idea*) to be received, be acceptable; **~se**
vr to curdle; to congeal; (*llenarse*) to fill
up.
cuajo ['kwaxo] *nm*: **arrancar algo de** ~ to
tear sth out by its roots.
cual [kwal] *adv* like, as ♦ *pron*: **el** ~ *etc*
which; (*persona: sujeto*) who; (: *objeto*)
whom; **lo** ~ (*relativo*) which; **allá cada** ~
every man to his own taste; **son a** ~ **más
gandul** each is as idle as the other; **cada**
~ each one ♦ *adj* such as; **tal** ~ just as it
is.
cuál [kwal] *pron interrogativo* which (one),
what.
cualesquier(a) [kwales'kjer(a)] *pl de*
cualquier(a).
cualidad [kwali'ðað] *nf* quality.
cualificado, a [kwalifi'kaðo, a] *adj* (*obrero*)
skilled, qualified.
cualquiera [kwal'kjera], **cualquier**
[kwal'kjer], *pl* **cualesquier(a)** *adj* any
♦ *pron* anybody, anyone; (*quienquiera*)
whoever; **en cualquier momento** any
time; **en cualquier parte** anywhere;
cualquiera que sea whichever it is;
(*persona*) whoever it is.
cuán [kwan] *adv* how.
cuando ['kwando] *adv* when; (*aún si*) if,
even if ♦ *conj* (*puesto que*) since ♦ *prep*:
yo, ~ **niño** ... when I was a child *o* as a
child I ...; ~ **no sea así** even if it is not
so; ~ **más** at (the) most; ~ **menos** at
least; ~ **no** if not, otherwise; **de** ~ **en** ~
from time to time; **ven** ~ **quieras** come
when(ever) you like.
cuándo ['kwando] *adv* when; **¿desde ~?,
¿de** ~ **acá?** since when?
cuantía [kwan'tia] *nf* (*alcance*) extent;
(*importancia*) importance.
cuantioso, a [kwan't joso, a] *adj*
substantial.

=========== *PALABRA CLAVE* ===========

cuanto, a ['kwanto, a] *adj* **1** (*todo*): **tiene
todo** ~ **desea** he's got everything he
wants; **le daremos ~s ejemplares
necesite** we'll give him as many copies
as *o* all the copies he needs; **~s hombres
la ven** all the men who see her
2: **unos ~s**: **había unos ~s periodistas**
there were (quite) a few journalists
3 (+*más*): ~ **más vino bebas peor te
sentirás** the more wine you drink the
worse you'll feel; **~s más, mejor** the
more the merrier
♦ *pron*: **tiene** ~ **desea** he has everything

he wants; **tome ~/~s quiera** take as
much/many as you want
♦ *adv*: **en** ~: **en** ~ **profesor** as a teacher;
en ~ **a mí** as for me; *V tb* **antes**
♦ *conj* **1**: ~ **más gana menos gasta** the
more he earns the less he spends; ~
más joven se es más se es confiado the
younger you are the more trusting you
are
2: **en** ~: **en** ~ **llegue/llegué** as soon as I
arrive/arrived.

cuánto, a ['kwanto, a] *adj* (*exclamación*)
what a lot of; (*interrogativo: sg*) how
much?; (: *pl*) how many? ♦ *pron, adv* how;
(*interrogativo: sg*) how much?; (: *pl*) how
many? ♦ *excl*: **¡~ me alegro!** I'm so glad!;
¡cuánta gente! what a lot of people!; **¿~
tiempo?** how long?; **¿~ cuesta?** how
much does it cost?; **¿a ~s estamos?**
what's the date?; **¿~ hay de aquí a
Bilbao?** how far is it from here to
Bilbao?; **Señor no sé ~s** Mr. So-and-So.
cuarenta [kwa'renta] *num* forty.
cuarentena [kwaren'tena] *nf* (*MED etc*)
quarantine; (*conjunto*) forty(-odd).
cuarentón, ona [kwaren'ton, ona] *adj*
forty-year-old, fortyish ♦ *nm/f* person of
about forty.
cuaresma [kwa'resma] *nf* Lent.
cuarta ['kwarta] *nf V* **cuarto**.
cuartear [kwarte'ar] *vt* to quarter; (*dividir*)
to divide up; **~se** *vr* to crack, split.
cuartel [kwar'tel] *nm* (*de ciudad*) quarter,
district; (*MIL*) barracks *pl*; ~ **general**
headquarters *pl*.
cuartelazo [kwarte'laθo] *nm* coup, military
uprising.
cuarteto [kwar'teto] *nm* quartet.
cuartilla [kwar'tiʎa] *nf* (*hoja*) sheet (of
paper); **~s** *nfpl* (*TIP*) copy *sg*.
cuarto, a ['kwarto, a] *adj* fourth ♦ *nm* (*MAT*)
quarter, fourth; (*habitación*) room ♦ *nf*
(*MAT*) quarter, fourth; (*palmo*) span; ~
de baño bathroom; ~ **de estar** living
room; ~ **de hora** quarter (of an) hour; ~
de kilo quarter kilo; **no tener un** ~ to be
broke (*fam*).
cuarzo ['kwarθo] *nm* quartz.
cuatrero [kwa'trero] *nm* (*AM*) rustler,
stock thief.
cuatrimestre [kwatri'mestre] *nm* four-
month period.
cuatro ['kwatro] *num* four; **las** ~ four
o'clock; **el** ~ **de octubre** (on) the fourth
of October; *V tb* **seis**.
cuatrocientos, as [kwatro'θjentos, as] *num*
four hundred; *V tb* **seiscientos**.

Cuba ['kußa] *nf* Cuba.
cuba ['kußa] *nf* cask, barrel; **estar como una ~** (*fam*) to be sloshed.
cubalibre [kußa'lißre] *nm* (white) rum and coke ®.
cubano, a [ku'ßano, a] *adj, nm/f* Cuban.
cubata [ku'ßata] *nm* = **cubalibre**.
cubertería [kußerte'ria] *nf* cutlery.
cúbico, a ['kußiko, a] *adj* cubic.
cubierto, a [ku'ßjerto, a] *pp de* **cubrir** ♦ *adj* covered; (*cielo*) overcast ♦ *nm* cover; (*en la mesa*) place ♦ *nf* cover, covering; (*neumático*) tyre; (*NAUT*) deck; **~s** *nmpl* cutlery *sg*; **a ~ de** covered with *o* in; **precio del ~** cover charge.
cubil [ku'ßil] *nm* den.
cubilete [kußi'lete] *nm* (*en juegos*) cup.
cubito [ku'ßito] *nm*: **~ de (la) basura** dustbin; **~ de hielo** ice cube.
cubo ['kußo] *nm* cube; (*balde*) bucket, tub; (*TEC*) drum.
cucaracha [kuka'ratʃa] *nf* cockroach.
cuchara [ku'tʃara] *nf* spoon; (*TEC*) scoop.
cucharada [kutʃa'raða] *nf* spoonful; **~ colmada** heaped spoonful.
cucharadita [kutʃara'ðita] *nf* teaspoonful.
cucharilla [kutʃa'riʎa] *nf* teaspoon.
cucharita [kutʃa'rita] *nf* teaspoon.
cucharón [kutʃa'ron] *nm* ladle.
cuchichear [kutʃitʃe'ar] *vi* to whisper.
cuchicheo [kutʃi'tʃeo] *nm* whispering.
cuchilla [ku'tʃiʎa] *nf* (large) knife; (*de arma blanca*) blade; **~ de afeitar** razor blade; **pasar a ~** to put to the sword.
cuchillada [kutʃi'ʎaða] *nf* (*golpe*) stab; (*herida*) knife *o* stab wound.
cuchillo [ku'tʃiʎo] *nm* knife.
cuchitril [kutʃi'tril] *nm* hovel; (*habitación etc*) pigsty.
cuclillas [ku'kliʎas] *nfpl*: **en ~** squatting.
cuco, a ['kuko, a] *adj* pretty; (*astuto*) sharp ♦ *nm* cuckoo.
cucurucho [kuku'rutʃo] *nm* paper cone, cornet.
cuece ['kweθe] *etc vb V* **cocer**.
cuele ['kwele] *etc vb V* **colar**.
cuelgue ['kwelɣe] *etc vb V* **colgar**.
cuello ['kweʎo] *nm* (*ANAT*) neck; (*de vestido, camisa*) collar.

cuenca ['kwenka] *nf* (*ANAT*) eye socket; (*GEO: valle*) bowl, deep valley; (: *fluvial*) basin.
cuenco ['kwenko] *nm* (earthenware) bowl.
cuenta ['kwenta] *etc vb V* **contar** ♦ *nf* (*cálculo*) count, counting; (*en café, restaurante*) bill; (*COM*) account; (*de collar*) bead; (*fig*) account; **a fin de ~s** in the end; **en resumidas ~s** in short; **caer en la ~** to catch on; **dar ~ a algn de sus actos** to account to sb for one's actions; **darse ~ de** to realize; **tener en ~** to bear in mind; **echar ~s** to take stock; **~ de atrás** countdown; **~ corriente/de ahorros/a plazo (fijo)** current/savings/deposit account; **~ de asignación** appropriation account; **~ de caja** cash account; **~ de capital** capital account; **~ por cobrar** account receivable; **~ de crédito** credit *o* loan account; **~ de gastos e ingresos** income and expenditure account; **~ por pagar** account payable; **abonar una cantidad en ~ a algn** to credit a sum to sb's account; **ajustar** *o* **liquidar una ~** to settle an account; **pasar la ~** to send the bill.
cuentagotas [kwenta'ɣotas] *nm inv* (*MED*) dropper; **a** *o* **con ~** (*fam, fig*) drop by drop, bit by bit.
cuentakilómetros [kwentaki'lometros] *nm inv* (*de distancias*) ≈ milometer, clock; (*velocímetro*) speedometer.
cuentista [kwen'tista] *nm/f* gossip; (*LIT*) short-story writer.
cuento ['kwento] *etc vb V* **contar** ♦ *nm* story; (*LIT*) short story; **~ de hadas** fairy story; **es el ~ de nunca acabar** it's an endless business; **eso no viene a ~** that's irrelevant.
cuerda ['kwerða] *nf* rope; (*hilo*) string; (*de reloj*) spring; (*MUS: de violín etc*) string; (*MAT*) chord; (*ANAT*) cord; **~ floja** tightrope; **~s vocales** vocal cords; **dar ~ a un reloj** to wind up a clock.
cuerdo, a ['kwerðo, a] *adj* sane; (*prudente*) wise, sensible.
cuerear [kwere'ar] *vt* (*AM*) to skin.
cuerno ['kwerno] *nm* (*ZOOL: gen*) horn; (: *de ciervo*) antler; **poner los ~s a** (*fam*) to cuckold; **saber a ~ quemado** to leave a nasty taste.
cuero ['kwero] *nm* (*ZOOL*) skin, hide; (*TEC*) leather; **en ~s** stark naked; **~ cabelludo** scalp.
cuerpo ['kwerpo] *nm* body; (*cadáver*) corpse; (*fig*) main part; **~ de bomberos** fire brigade; **~ diplomático** diplomatic

corps; **luchar** ~ **a** ~ to fight hand-to-hand; **tomar** ~ (*plan etc*) to take shape.

cuervo ['kwerβo] *nm* (*ZOOL*) raven, crow; *V* **criar**.

cuesta ['kwesta] *etc vb V* **costar** ♦ *nf* slope; (*en camino etc*) hill; ~ **arriba/abajo** uphill/downhill; **a** ~**s** on one's back.

cuestión [kwes'tjon] *nf* matter, question, issue; (*riña*) quarrel, dispute; **eso es otra** ~ that's another matter.

cuestionar [kwestjo'nar] *vt* to question.

cuestionario [kwestjo'narjo] *nm* questionnaire.

cueva ['kweβa] *nf* cave.

cueza ['kweθa] *etc vb V* **cocer**.

cuidado [kwi'ðaðo] *nm* care, carefulness; (*preocupación*) care, worry ♦ *excl* careful!, look out!; **eso me tiene sin** ~ I'm not worried about that.

cuidadoso, a [kwiða'ðoso, a] *adj* careful; (*preocupado*) anxious.

cuidar [kwi'ðar] *vt* (*MED*) to care for; (*ocuparse de*) to take care of, look after; (*detalles*) to pay attention to ♦ *vi*: ~ **de** to take care of, look after; ~**se** *vr* to look after o.s.; ~**se de hacer algo** to take care to do something.

cuita ['kwita] *nf* (*preocupación*) worry, trouble; (*pena*) grief.

culata [ku'lata] *nf* (*de fusil*) butt.

culatazo [kula'taθo] *nm* kick, recoil.

culebra [ku'leβra] *nf* snake; ~ **de cascabel** rattlesnake.

culebrear [kuleβre'ar] *vi* to wriggle along; (*río*) to meander.

culebrón [kule'βron] *nm* (*fam*) soap (opera).

culinario, a [kuli'narjo, a] *adj* culinary, cooking *cpd*.

culminación [kulmina'θjon] *nf* culmination.

culminante [kulmi'nante] *adj*: **momento** ~ climax, highlight, highspot.

culminar [kulmi'nar] *vi* to culminate.

culo ['kulo] *nm* (*fam: asentaderas*) bottom, backside, bum (*BRIT*); (: *ano*) arse(hole) (*BRIT!*), ass(hole) (*US!*); (*de vaso*) bottom.

culpa ['kulpa] *nf* fault; (*JUR*) guilt; ~**s** *nfpl* sins; **por** ~ **de** through, because of; **tener la** ~ (**de**) to be to blame (for).

culpabilidad [kulpaβili'ðað] *nf* guilt.

culpable [kul'paβle] *adj* guilty ♦ *nm/f* culprit; **confesarse** ~ to plead guilty; **declarar** ~ **a algn** to find sb guilty.

culpar [kul'par] *vt* to blame; (*acusar*) to accuse.

cultivadora [kultiβa'ðora] *nf* cultivator.

cultivar [kulti'βar] *vt* to cultivate; (*cosecha*)

to raise; (*talento*) to develop.

cultivo [kul'tiβo] *nm* (*acto*) cultivation; (*plantas*) crop; (*BIO*) culture.

culto, a ['kulto, a] *adj* (*cultivado*) cultivated; (*que tiene cultura*) cultured, educated ♦ *nm* (*homenaje*) worship; (*religión*) cult; (*POL etc*) cult.

cultura [kul'tura] *nf* culture.

cultural [kultu'ral] *adj* cultural.

culturismo [kultu'rismo] *nm* body-building.

cumbre ['kumbre] *nf* summit, top; (*fig*) top, height; **conferencia (en la)** ~ summit (conference).

cumpleaños [kumple'aɲos] *nm inv* birthday.

cumplido, a [kum'pliðo, a] *adj* complete, perfect; (*abundante*) plentiful; (*cortés*) courteous ♦ *nm* compliment; **visita de** ~ courtesy call.

cumplidor, a [kumpli'ðor, a] *adj* reliable.

cumplimentar [kumplimen'tar] *vt* to congratulate; (*órdenes*) to carry out.

cumplimiento [kumpli'mjento] *nm* (*de un deber*) fulfilment, execution, performance; (*acabamiento*) completion; (*COM*) expiry, end.

cumplir [kum'plir] *vt* (*orden*) to carry out, obey; (*promesa*) to carry out, fulfil; (*condena*) to serve; (*años*) to reach, attain ♦ *vi* (*pago*) to fall due; (*plazo*) to expire; ~**se** *vr* (*plazo*) to expire; (*plan etc*) to be fulfilled; (*vaticinio*) to come true; **hoy cumple dieciocho años** he is eighteen today; ~ **con** (*deberes*) to carry out, fulfil.

cúmulo ['kumulo] *nm* (*montón*) heap; (*nube*) cumulus.

cuna ['kuna] *nf* cradle, cot; **canción de** ~ lullaby.

cundir [kun'dir] *vi* (*noticia, rumor, pánico*) to spread; (*rendir*) to go a long way.

cuneta [ku'neta] *nf* ditch.

cuña ['kuɲa] *nf* (*TEC*) wedge; (*COM*) advertising spot; (*MED*) bedpan; **tener** ~**s** to have influence.

cuñado, a [ku'ɲaðo, a] *nm/f* brother/sister-in-law.

cuño ['kuɲo] *nm* (*TEC*) die-stamp; (*fig*) stamp.

cuota ['kwota] *nf* (*parte proporcional*) share; (*cotización*) fee, dues *pl*; ~ **inicial** (*COM*) down payment.

cupo ['kupo] *etc vb V* **caber** ♦ *nm* quota, share; (*COM*): ~ **de importación** import quota; ~ **de ventas** sales quota.

cupón [ku'pon] *nm* coupon; ~ **de la ONCE** o **de los ciegos** ONCE lottery ticket; *V tb* lotería.

cúpula ['kupula] *nf* (*ARQ*) dome.

cura ['kura] *nf* (*curación*) cure; (*método curativo*) treatment ♦ *nm* priest; ~ **de emergencia** emergency treatment.

curación [kura'θjon] *nf* cure; (*acción*) curing.

curado, a [ku'raðo, a] *adj* (*CULIN*) cured; (*pieles*) tanned.

curandero, a [kuran'dero, a] *nm/f* healer.

curar [ku'rar] *vt* (*MED*: *herida*) to treat, dress; (: *enfermo*) to cure; (*CULIN*) to cure, salt; (*cuero*) to tan ♦ *vi*, ~**se** *vr* to get well, recover.

curda ['kurða] (*fam*) *nm* drunk ♦ *nf*: **agarrar una/estar** ~ to get/be sloshed.

curiosear [kurjose'ar] *vt* to glance at, look over ♦ *vi* to look round, wander round; (*explorar*) to poke about.

curiosidad [kurjosi'ðað] *nf* curiosity.

curioso, a [ku'rjoso, a] *adj* curious; (*aseado*) neat ♦ *nm/f* bystander, onlooker; ¡**qué** ~! how odd!

curita [ku'rita] *nf* (*AM*) sticking plaster.

currante [ku'rrante] *nm/f* (*fam*) worker.

currar [ku'rrar] *vi* (*fam*), **currelar** [kurre'lar] *vi* (*fam*) to work.

currículo [ku'rrikulo] *nm*, **currículum** [ku'rrikulum] *nm* curriculum vitae.

curro ['kurro] *nm* (*fam*) work, job.

cursar [kur'sar] *vt* (*ESCOL*) to study.

cursi ['kursi] *adj* (*fam*) pretentious; (: *amanerado*) affected.

cursilada [kursi'laða] *nf*: ¡**qué** ~! how tacky!

cursilería [kursile'ria] *nf* (*vulgaridad*) bad taste; (*amaneramiento*) affectation.

cursillo [kur'siλo] *nm* short course.

cursiva [kur'siβa] *nf* italics *pl*.

curso ['kurso] *nm* (*dirección*) course; (*fig*) progress; (*ESCOL*) school year; (*UNIV*) academic year; **en** ~ (*año*) current; (*proceso*) going on, under way; **moneda de** ~ **legal** legal tender.

cursor [kur'sor] *nm* (*INFORM*) cursor; (*TEC*) slide.

curtido, a [kur'tiðo, a] *adj* (*cara etc*) weather-beaten; (*fig*: *persona*) experienced.

curtir [kur'tir] *vt* (*piel*) to tan; (*fig*) to harden.

curvo, a ['kurßo, a] *adj* (*gen*) curved; (*torcido*) bent ♦ *nf* (*gen*) curve, bend; **curva de rentabilidad** (*COM*) break-even chart.

cúspide ['kuspiðe] *nf* (*GEO*) summit, peak; (*fig*) top, pinnacle.

custodia [kus'toðja] *nf* (*cuidado*) safekeeping; (*JUR*) custody.

custodiar [kusto'ðjar] *vt* (*conservar*) to keep, take care of; (*vigilar*) to guard.

custodio [kus'toðjo] *nm* guardian, keeper.

cutáneo, a [ku'taneo, a] *adj* skin *cpd*.

cutícula [ku'tikula] *nf* cuticle.

cutis ['kutis] *nm inv* skin, complexion.

cutre ['kutre] *adj* (*fam*: *lugar*) grotty; (: *persona*) naff.

cuyo, a ['kujo, a] *pron* (*de quien*) whose; (*de que*) whose, of which; **la señora en cuya casa me hospedé** the lady in whose house I stayed; **el asunto cuyos detalles conoces** the affair the details of which you know; **por** ~ **motivo** for which reason.

C.V. *abr* (= *caballos de vapor*) H.P.

C y F *abr* (= *costo y flete*) C & F.

Dd

D, d [de] *nf* (*letre*) D, d; **D de Dolores** D for David (*BRIT*), D for Dog (*US*).

D. *abr* = **Don.**

D.ª *abr* = **Doña.**

dactilar [dakti'lar] *adj*: **huellas** ~**es** fingerprints.

dactilógrafo, a [dakti'loɣrafo, a] *nm/f* typist.

dádiva ['daðiβa] *nf* (*donación*) donation; (*regalo*) gift.

dadivoso, a [daði'ßoso, a] *adj* generous.

dado, a ['daðo, a] *pp de* **dar** ♦ *nm* die; ~**s** *nmpl* dice ♦ *adj*: **en un momento** ~ at a certain point; **ser** ~ **a** (**hacer algo**) to be very fond of (doing sth); ~ **que** *conj* given that.

daga ['daɣa] *nf* dagger.

daltónico, a [dal'toniko, a] *adj* colour-blind.

daltonismo [dalto'nismo] *nm* colour blindness.

dama ['dama] *nf* (*gen*) lady; (*AJEDREZ*) queen; ~**s** *nfpl* draughts; **primera** ~ (*TEAT*) leading lady; (*POL*) president's wife, first lady (*US*); ~ **de honor** (*de reina*) lady-in-waiting; (*de novia*) bridesmaid.

damasco [da'masko] *nm* (*tela*) damask; (*AM*: *árbol*) apricot tree; (: *fruta*) apricot.

damnificado, a [damnifi'kaðo, a] *nm/f*: **los**

~s the victims.

damnificar [damnifi'kar] *vt* to harm;
(*persona*) to injure.

damnifique [damni'fike] *etc vb V*
damnificar.

dance ['danθe] *etc vb V* **danzar**.

danés, esa [da'nes, esa] *adj* Danish ♦ *nm/f*
Dane ♦ *nm* (*LING*) Danish.

Danubio [da'nuβjo] *nm* Danube.

danza ['danθa] *nf* (*gen*) dancing; (*una ~*)
dance.

danzar [dan'θar] *vt, vi* to dance.

danzarín, ina [danθa'rin, ina] *nm/f* dancer.

dañar [da'nar] *vt* (*objeto*) to damage;
(*persona*) to hurt; (*estropear*) to spoil;
~**se** *vr* (*objeto*) to get damaged.

dañino, a [da'nino, a] *adj* harmful.

daño ['dano] *nm* (*a un objeto*) damage; (*a
una persona*) harm, injury; ~**s y
perjuicios** (*JUR*) damages; **hacer** ~ **a** to
damage; (*persona*) to hurt, injure;
hacerse ~ to hurt o.s.

DAO *abr* (=*Diseño Asistido por Ordenador*)
CAD.

══════════════ *PALABRA CLAVE*

dar [dar] *vt* **1** (*gen*) to give; (*obra de teatro*)
to put on; (*film*) to show; (*fiesta*) to have;
~ **algo a algn** to give sb sth *o* sth to sb;
~ **una patada a algn/algo** to kick sb/sth,
give sb/sth a kick; ~ **un susto a algn** to
give sb a fright; ~ **de beber a algn** to
give sb a drink

2 (*producir: intereses*) to yield; (*fruta*) to
produce

3 (*locuciones +n*): **da gusto escucharle**
it's a pleasure to listen to him; **me da
pena/asco** it frightens/sickens me; *V tb*
paseo *y otros sustantivos*

4 (*considerar*): ~ **algo por descontado/
entendido** to take sth for granted/as
read; ~ **algo por concluido** to consider
sth finished; **le dieron por desaparecido**
they gave him up as lost

5 (*hora*): **el reloj dio las 6** the clock
struck 6 (o'clock)

6: **me da lo mismo** it's all the same to
me; *V tb* **igual, más**

7: **¡y dale!** (*¡otra vez!*) not again!; **estar/
seguir dale que dale** *o* **te pego** *o*
(*AM*) **dale y dale** to go/keep on and on

♦ *vi* **1**: ~ **a** (*habitación*) to overlook, look
on to; (*accionar: botón etc*) to press, hit

2: ~ **con: dimos con él dos horas más
tarde** we came across him two hours
later; **al final di con la solución** I
eventually came up with the answer

3: ~ **en** (*blanco, suelo*) to hit; **el sol me da**

en la cara the sun is shining (right) in
my face

4: ~ **de sí** (*zapatos etc*) to stretch, give

5: ~ **para** to be enough for; **nuestro
presupuesto no da para más** our
budget's really tight

6: ~ **por: le ha dado por estudiar música**
now he's into studying music

7: ~ **que hablar** to set people talking;
una película que da que pensar a
thought-provoking film

♦ ~**se** *vr* **1**: ~**se un baño** to have a bath;
~**se un golpe** to hit o.s.

2: ~**se por vencido** to give up; **con eso
me doy por satisfecho** I'd settle for that

3 (*ocurrir*): **se han dado muchos casos**
there have been a lot of cases

4: ~**se a: se ha dado a la bebida** he's
taken to drinking

5: **se me dan bien/mal las ciencias** I'm
good/bad at science

6: **dárselas de: se las da de experto** he
fancies himself *o* poses as an expert.

dardo ['darðo] *nm* dart.

dársena ['darsena] *nf* (*NAUT*) dock.

datar [da'tar] *vi*: ~ **de** to date from.

dátil ['datil] *nm* date.

dativo [da'tiβo] *nm* (*LING*) dative.

dato ['dato] *nm* fact, piece of information;
(*MAT*) datum; ~**s** *nmpl* (*INFORM*) data; ~**s
de entrada/salida** input/output data; ~**s
personales** personal particulars.

dcha. *abr* (= *derecha*) r.h.

d. de J. C. *abr* (= *después de Jesucristo*)
A.D.

══════════════ *PALABRA CLAVE*

de [de] *prep* (*de+el = del*) **1** (*posesión,
pertenencia*) of; **la casa** ~ **Isabel/mis
padres** Isabel's/my parents' house; **es** ~
ellos/ella it's theirs/hers; **un libro** ~
Unamuno a book by Unamuno

2 (*origen, distancia, con números*) from;
soy ~ **Gijón** I'm from Gijón; ~ **8 a 20**
from 8 to 20; **5 metros** ~ **largo** 5 metres
long; **salir del cine** to go out of *o* leave
the cinema; ~ ... **en** ... from ... to ...; ~ **2
en 2** 2 by 2, 2 at a time; **9** ~ **cada 10** 9 out
of every 10

3 (*valor descriptivo*): **una copa** ~ **vino** a
glass of wine; **una silla** ~ **madera** a
wooden chair; **la mesa** ~ **la cocina** the
kitchen table; **un viaje** ~ **dos días** a two-
day journey; **un billete** ~ **1000 pesetas** a
1000 peseta note; **un niño** ~ **tres años** a
three-year-old (child); **una máquina** ~
coser a sewing machine; **la ciudad** ~

Madrid the city of Madrid; **el tonto** ~
Juan that idiot Juan; **ir vestido** ~ **gris** to
be dressed in grey; **la niña del vestido
azul** the girl in the blue dress; **la chica
del pelo largo** the girl with long hair;
trabaja ~ **profesora** she works as a
teacher; ~ **lado** sideways; ~ **atrás/
delante** rear/front
4 (*hora, tiempo*): **a las 8** ~ **la mañana** at 8
o'clock in the morning; ~ **día/noche** by
day/night; ~ **hoy en ocho días** a week
from now; ~ **niño era gordo** as a child
he was fat
5 (*comparaciones*): **más/menos** ~ **cien
personas** more/less than a hundred
people; **el más caro** ~ **la tienda** the most
expensive in the shop; **menos/más** ~ **lo
pensado** less/more than expected
6 (*causa*): **del calor** from the heat; ~
puro tonto out of sheer stupidity
7 (*tema*) about; **clases** ~ **inglés** English
classes; **¿sabes algo** ~ **él?** do you know
anything about him?; **un libro** ~ **física** a
physics book
8 (*adj + de + infin*): **fácil** ~ **entender** easy
to understand
9 (*oraciones pasivas*): **fue respetado** ~
todos he was loved by all
10 (*condicional + infin*) if; ~ **ser posible** if
possible; ~ **no terminarlo hoy** if I *etc*
don't finish it today.

dé [de] *vb V* **dar.**
deambular [deambu'lar] *vi* to stroll,
wander.
debajo [de'βaxo] *adv* underneath; ~ **de**
below, under; **por** ~ **de** beneath.
debate [de'βate] *nm* debate.
debatir [deβa'tir] *vt* to debate; ~**se** *vr* to
struggle.
debe ['deβe] *nm* (*en cuenta*) debit side; ~ **y
haber** debit and credit.
deber [de'βer] *nm* duty ♦ *vt* to owe ♦ *vi*:
debe (de) it must, it should; ~**se** *vr*: ~**se a**
to be owing *o* due to; ~**es** *nmpl* (*ESCOL*)
homework *sg*; **debo hacerlo** I must do it;
debe de ir he should go; **¿qué** *o* **cuánto le
debo?** how much is it?
debidamente [deβiða'mente] *adv* properly;
(*rellenar: documento, solicitud*) duly.
debido, a [de'βiðo, a] *adj* proper, due; ~ **a**
due to, because of; **en debida forma**
duly.
débil ['deβil] *adj* weak; (*persona:
físicamente*) feeble; (*salud*) poor; (*voz,
ruido*) faint; (*luz*) dim.
debilidad [deβili'ðað] *nf* weakness;
feebleness; dimness; **tener** ~ **por algn** to

have a soft spot for sb.
debilitar [deβili'tar] *vt* to weaken; ~**se** *vr* to
grow weak.
débito ['deβito] *nm* debit; (*deuda*) debt.
debutante [deβu'tante] *nm/f* beginner.
debutar [deβu'tar] *vi* to make one's debut.
década ['dekaða] *nf* decade.
decadencia [deka'ðenθja] *nf* (*estado*)
decadence; (*proceso*) decline, decay.
decadente [deca'ðente] *adj* decadent.
decaer [deka'er] *vi* (*declinar*) to decline;
(*debilitarse*) to weaken; (*salud*) to fail;
(*negocio*) to fall off.
decaído, a [deka'iðo, a] *adj*: **estar** ~
(*persona*) to be down.
decaiga [de'kaiɣa] *etc vb V* **decaer.**
decaimiento [dekai'mjento] *nm*
(*declinación*) decline; (*desaliento*)
discouragement; (*MED: depresión*)
depression.
decanato [deka'nato] *nm* (*cargo*) deanship;
(*despacho*) dean's office.
decano, a [de'kano, a] *nm/f* (*UNIV etc*) dean;
(*de grupo*) senior member.
decantar [dekan'tar] *vt* (*vino*) to decant.
decapitar [dekapi'tar] *vt* to behead.
decayendo [deka'jendo] *etc vb V* **decaer.**
decena [de'θena] *nf*: **una** ~ ten (or so).
decencia [de'θenθja] *nf* (*modestia*)
modesty; (*honestidad*) respectability.
decenio [de'θenjo] *nm* decade.
decente [de'θente] *adj* (*correcto*) proper;
(*honesto*) respectable.
decepción [deθep'θjon] *nf* disappointment.
decepcionante [deθepθjo'nante] *adj*
disappointing.
decepcionar [deθepθjo'nar] *vt* to
disappoint.
decibelio [deθi'βeljo] *nm* decibel.
decidido, a [deθi'ðiðo, a] *a* decided;
(*resuelto*) resolute.
decidir [deθi'ðir] *vt* (*persuadir*) to convince,
persuade; (*resolver*) to decide ♦ *vi* to
decide; ~**se** *vr*: ~**se a** to make up one's
mind to; ~**se por** to decide *o* settle on,
choose.
decimal [deθi'mal] *adj, nm* decimal.
décimo, a ['deθimo, a] *num* tenth ♦ *nf* (*MAT*)
tenth; **tiene unas** ~**as de fiebre** he has a
slight temperature.
decimoctavo, a [deθimok'taβo, a] *num*
eighteenth; *V tb* **sexto.**
decimocuarto, a [deθimo'kwarto, a] *num*
fourteenth; *V tb* **sexto.**
decimonoveno, a [deθimono'βeno, a] *num*
nineteenth; *V tb* **sexto.**
decimoquinto, a [deθimo'kinto, a] *num*
fifteenth; *V tb* **sexto.**

decimoséptimo, a [deθimo'septimo, a] *num* seventeenth; *V tb* **sexto**.

decimosexto, a [deθimo'seksto, a] *num* sixteenth; *V tb* **sexto**.

decimotercero, a [deθimoter'θero, a] *num* thirteenth; *V tb* **sexto**.

decir [de'θir] *vt* (*expresar*) to say; (*contar*) to tell; (*hablar*) to speak; (*indicar*) to show; (*revelar*) to reveal; (*fam*: *nombrar*) to call ♦ *nm* saying; ~**se** *vr*: **se dice** it is said, they say; (*se cuenta*) the story goes; **¿cómo se dice en inglés "cursi"?** what's the English for "cursi"?; ~ **para** *o* **entre sí** to say to o.s.; ~ **por** ~ to talk for talking's sake; **dar que** ~ **(a la gente)** to make people talk; **querer** ~ to mean; **es** ~ that is to say, namely; **ni que** ~ **tiene que ...** it goes without saying that ...; **como quien dice** so to speak; **¡quién lo diría!** would you believe it!; **el qué dirán** gossip; **¡diga!**, **¡dígame!** (*en tienda etc*) can I help you?; (*TELEC*) hello?; **le dije que fuera más tarde** I told her to go later; **es un** ~ it's just a phrase.

decisión [deθi'sjon] *nf* decision; (*firmeza*) decisiveness; (*voluntad*) determination.

decisivo, a [deθi'siβo, a] *adj* decisive.

declamar [dekla'mar] *vt, vi* to declaim; (*versos etc*) to recite.

declaración [deklara'θjon] *nf* (*manifestación*) statement; (*explicación*) explanation; (*JUR*: *testimonio*) evidence; ~ **de derechos** (*POL*) bill of rights; ~ **de impuestos** (*COM*) tax return; ~ **de ingresos** *o* **de la renta** income tax return; ~ **jurada** affidavit; **falsa** ~ (*JUR*) misrepresentation.

declarar [dekla'rar] *vt* to declare ♦ *vi* to declare; (*JUR*) to testify; ~**se** *vr* (*opinión*) to make one's opinion known; (*a una chica*) to propose; (*guerra, incendio*) to break out; ~ **culpable/inocente a algn** to find sb guilty/not guilty; ~**se culpable/inocente** to plead guilty/not guilty.

declinación [deklina'θjon] *nf* (*decaimiento*) decline; (*LING*) declension.

declinar [dekli'nar] *vt* (*gen, LING*) to decline; (*JUR*) to reject ♦ *vi* (*el día*) to draw to a close.

declive [de'kliβe] *nm* (*cuesta*) slope; (*inclinación*) incline; (*fig*) decline; (*COM*: *tb*: ~ **económico**) slump.

decodificador [dekoðifika'ðor] *nm* (*INFORM*) decoder.

decolorarse [dekolo'rarse] *vr* to become discoloured.

decomisar [dekomi'sar] *vt* to seize, confiscate.

decomiso [deko'miso] *nm* seizure.

decoración [dekora'θjon] *nf* decoration; (*TEAT*) scenery, set; ~ **de escaparates** window dressing.

decorado [deko'raðo] *nm* (*CINE, TEAT*) scenery, set.

decorador, a [dekora'ðor, a] *nm/f* (*de interiores*) (interior) decorator; (*TEAT*) stage *o* set designer.

decorar [deko'rar] *vt* to decorate.

decorativo, a [dekora'tiβo, a] *adj* ornamental, decorative.

decoro [de'koro] *nm* (*respeto*) respect; (*dignidad*) decency; (*recato*) propriety.

decoroso, a [deko'roso, a] *adj* (*decente*) decent; (*modesto*) modest; (*digno*) proper.

decrecer [dekre'θer] *vi* to decrease, diminish; (*nivel de agua*) to go down; (*días*) to draw in.

decrépito, a [de'krepito, a] *adj* decrepit.

decretar [dekre'tar] *vt* to decree.

decreto [de'kreto] *nm* decree; (*POL*) act.

decreto-ley [dekreto'lei], *pl* **decretos-leyes** *nm* decree.

decrezca [de'kreθka] *etc vb V* **decrecer**.

decúbito [de'kuβito] *nm* (*MED*): ~ **prono/supino** prone/supine position.

dedal [de'ðal] *nm* thimble.

dedalera [deða'lera] *nf* foxglove.

dédalo ['deðalo] *nm* (*laberinto*) labyrinth; (*fig*) tangle, mess.

dedicación [deðika'θjon] *nf* dedication; **con** ~ **exclusiva** *o* **plena** full-time.

dedicar [deði'kar] *vt* (*libro*) to dedicate; (*tiempo, dinero*) to devote; ~**se** *vr*: ~**se a** to devote o.s. to (*hacer algo* doing sth); (*carrera, estudio*) to go in for, take up; **¿a qué se dedica usted?** what do you do (for a living)?

dedicatoria [deðika'torja] *nf* (*de libro*) dedication.

dedillo [de'ðiʎo] *nm*: **saber algo al** ~ to have sth at one's fingertips.

dedique [de'ðike] *etc vb V* **dedicar**.

dedo ['deðo] *nm* finger; (*de vino etc*) drop; ~ **(del pie)** toe; ~ **pulgar** thumb; ~ **índice** index finger; ~ **mayor** *o* **cordial** middle finger; ~ **anular** ring finger; ~ **meñique** little finger; **contar con los** ~**s** to count on one's fingers; **comerse los** ~**s** to get very impatient; **entrar a** ~ to get a job by pulling strings; **hacer** ~ (*fam*) to hitch (a lift); **poner el** ~ **en la llaga** to put one's finger on it; **no tiene dos** ~**s de frente** he's pretty dim.

deducción [deðuk'θjon] *nf* deduction.

deducir [deðu'θir] *vt* (*concluir*) to deduce,

infer; (*COM*) to deduct.
deduje [de'ðuxe] *etc*, **dedujera**
[deðu'xera] *etc*, **deduzca** [de'ðuθka] *etc*
vb V **deducir**.
defección [defek'θjon] *nf* defection,
desertion.
defecto [de'fekto] *nm* defect, flaw; (*de
cara*) imperfection; ~ **de pronunciación**
speech defect; **por** ~ (*INFORM*) default; ~
latente (*COM*) latent defect.
defectuoso, a [defek'twoso, a] *adj*
defective, faulty.
defender [defen'der] *vt* to defend; (*ideas*)
to uphold; (*causa*) to champion; (*amigos*)
to stand up for; ~**se** *vr* to defend o.s.;
~ **bien** to give a good account of o.s.;
me defiendo en inglés (*fig*) I can get by
in English.
defendible [defen'diβle] *adj* defensible.
defensa [de'fensa] *nf* defence; (*NAUT*)
fender ♦ *nm* (*DEPORTE*) back; **en** ~ **propia**
in self-defence.
defensivo, a [defen'siβo, a] *adj* defensive
♦ *nf*: **a la defensiva** on the defensive.
defensor, a [defen'sor, a] *adj* defending
♦ *nm/f* (*abogado* ~) defending counsel;
(*protector*) protector; ~ **del pueblo** (*ESP*)
≈ ombudsman.
deferente [defe'rente] *adj* deferential.
deferir [defe'rir] *vt* (*JUR*) to refer, delegate
♦ *vi*: ~ **a** to defer to.
deficiencia [defi'θjenθja] *nf* deficiency.
deficiente [defi'θjente] *adj* (*defectuoso*)
defective; ~ **en** lacking *o* deficient in
♦ *nm/f*: **ser un** ~ **mental** to be mentally
handicapped.
déficit, ~**s** ['defiθit] *nm* (*COM*) deficit; (*fig*)
lack, shortage; ~ **presupuestario** budget
deficit.
deficitario, a [defiθi'tarjo, a] *adj* (*COM*) in
deficit; (*empresa*) loss-making.
defienda [de'fjenda] *etc vb V* **defender**.
defiera [de'fjera] *etc vb V* **deferir**.
definición [defini'θjon] *nf* definition;
(*INFORM: de pantalla*) resolution.
definido, a [defi'niðo, a] *adj* (*tb LING*)
definite; **bien** ~ well *o* clearly defined; ~
por el usuario (*INFORM*) user-defined.
definir [defi'nir] *vt* (*determinar*) to
determine, establish; (*decidir*, *INFORM*) to
define; (*aclarar*) to clarify.
definitivo, a [defini'tiβo, a] *adj* (*edición*,
texto) definitive; (*fecha*) definite; **en
definitiva** definitively; (*en conclusión*)
finally; (*en resumen*) in short.
defiriendo [defi'rjendo] *etc vb V* **deferir**.
deflacionario, a [deflaθjo'narjo, a],
deflacionista [deflaθjo'nista] *adj*

deflationary.
deflector [deflek'tor] *nm* (*TEC*) baffle.
deforestación [deforesta'θjon] *nf*
deforestation.
deformación [deforma'θjon] *nf* (*alteración*)
deformation; (*RADIO etc*) distortion.
deformar [defor'mar] *vt* (*gen*) to deform;
~**se** *vr* to become deformed.
deforme [de'forme] *adj* (*informe*)
deformed; (*feo*) ugly; (*mal hecho*)
misshapen.
deformidad [deformi'ðað] *nf* (*forma
anormal*) deformity; (*fig: defecto*) (*moral*)
shortcoming.
defraudar [defrau'ðar] *vt* (*decepcionar*) to
disappoint; (*estafar*) to cheat; to defraud;
~ **impuestos** to evade tax.
defunción [defun'θjon] *nf* decease,
demise.
degeneración [dexenera'θjon] *nf* (*de las
células*) degeneration; (*moral*)
degeneracy.
degenerar [dexene'rar] *vi* to degenerate;
(*empeorar*) to get worse.
deglutir [deɣlu'tir] *vt*, *vi* to swallow.
degolladero [deɣoʎa'ðero] *nm* (*ANAT*)
throat; (*cadalso*) scaffold; (*matadero*)
slaughterhouse.
degollar [deɣo'ʎar] *vt* to slaughter.
degradar [deɣra'ðar] *vt* to debase,
degrade; (*INFORM: datos*) to corrupt; ~**se**
vr to demean o.s.
degüelle [de'ɣweʎe] *etc vb V* **degollar**.
degustación [deɣusta'θjon] *nf* sampling,
tasting.
deificar [deifi'kar] *vt* (*persona*) to deify.
deifique [dei'fike] *etc vb V* **deificar**.
dejadez [dexa'ðeθ] *nf* (*negligencia*) neglect;
(*descuido*) untidiness, carelessness.
dejado, a [de'xaðo, a] *adj* (*desaliñado*)
slovenly; (*negligente*) careless;
(*indolente*) lazy.
dejar [de'xar] *vt* (*gen*) to leave; (*permitir*) to
allow, let; (*abandonar*) to abandon,
forsake; (*actividad*, *empleo*) to give up;
(*beneficios*) to produce, yield ♦ *vi*: ~ **de**
(*parar*) to stop; ~**se** *vr* (*abandonarse*) to let
o.s. go; **no puedo** ~ **de fumar** I can't give
up smoking; **no dejes de visitarles** don't
fail to visit them; **no dejes de comprar
un billete** make sure you buy a ticket; ~
a un lado to leave *o* set aside; ~ **caer** to
drop; ~ **entrar/salir** to let in/out; ~ **pasar**
to let through; **¡déjalo!** (*no te preocupes*)
don't worry about it; **te dejo en tu casa**
I'll drop you off at your place; **deja
mucho que desear** it leaves a lot to be
desired; ~**se persuadir** to allow o.s. to *o*

let o.s. be persuaded; **¡déjate de tonterías!** stop messing about!

deje ['dexe] *nm* (trace of) accent.

dejo ['dexo] *nm* (*LING*) accent.

del [del] = **de** + **el**; *V* **de.**

del. *abr* (*ADMIN*: = *Delegación*) district office.

delantal [delan'tal] *nm* apron.

delante [de'lante] *adv* in front; (*enfrente*) opposite; (*adelante*) ahead ♦ *prep*: ~ **de** in front of, before; **la parte de** ~ the front part; **estando otros** ~ with others present.

delantero, a [delan'tero, a] *adj* front; (*patas de animal*) fore ♦ *nm* (*DEPORTE*) forward ♦ *nf* (*de vestido, casa etc*) front part; (*TEAT*) front row; (*DEPORTE*) forward line; **llevar la delantera (a algn)** to be ahead (of sb).

delatar [dela'tar] *vt* to inform on *o* against, betray; **los delató a la policía** he reported them to the police.

delator, a [dela'tor, a] *nm/f* informer.

delegación [deleɣa'θjon] *nf* (*acción, delegados*) delegation; (*COM: oficina*) district office, branch; ~ **de poderes** (*POL*) devolution; ~ **de policía** police station.

delegado, a [dele'ɣaðo, a] *nm/f* delegate; (*COM*) agent.

delegar [dele'ɣar] *vt* to delegate.

delegue [de'leɣe] *etc vb V* **delegar.**

deleitar [delei'tar] *vt* to delight; ~**se** *vr*: ~**se con** *o* **en** to delight in, take pleasure in.

deleite [de'leite] *nm* delight, pleasure.

deletrear [deletre'ar] *vt* (*tb fig*) to spell (out).

deletreo [dele'treo] *nm* spelling; (*fig*) interpretation, decipherment.

deleznable [deleθ'naßle] *adj* (*frágil*) fragile; (*fig: malo*) poor; (*excusa*) feeble.

delfín [del'fin] *nm* dolphin.

delgadez [delɣa'ðeθ] *nf* thinness, slimness.

delgado, a [del'ɣaðo, a] *adj* thin; (*persona*) slim, thin; (*tierra*) poor; (*tela etc*) light, delicate ♦ *adv*: **hilar (muy)** ~ (*fig*) to split hairs.

deliberación [delißera'θjon] *nf* deliberation.

deliberar [deliße'rar] *vt* to debate, discuss ♦ *vi* to deliberate.

delicadeza [delika'ðeθa] *nf* delicacy; (*refinamiento, sutileza*) refinement.

delicado, a [deli'kaðo, a] *adj* delicate; (*sensible*) sensitive; (*rasgos*) dainty; (*gusto*) refined; (*situación: difícil*) tricky; (: *violento*) embarrassing; (*punto, tema*) sore; (*persona: difícil de contentar*) hard to

please; (: *sensible*) touchy, hypersensitive; (: *atento*) considerate.

delicia [de'liθja] *nf* delight.

delicioso, a [deli'θjoso, a] *adj* (*gracioso*) delightful; (*exquisito*) delicious.

delictivo, a [delik'tißo, a] *adj* criminal *cpd.*

delimitar [delimi'tar] *vt* to delimit.

delincuencia [delin'kwenθja] *nf*: ~ **juvenil** juvenile delinquency; **cifras de la** ~ crime rate.

delincuente [delin'kwente] *nm/f* delinquent; (*criminal*) criminal; ~ **sin antecedentes** first offender; ~ **habitual** hardened criminal.

delineante [deline'ante] *nm/f* draughtsman.

delinear [deline'ar] *vt* to delineate; (*dibujo*) to draw; (*contornos, fig*) to outline; ~ **un proyecto** to outline a project.

delinquir [delin'kir] *vi* to commit an offence.

delirante [deli'rante] *adj* delirious.

delirar [deli'rar] *vi* to be delirious, rave; (*fig: desatinar*) to talk nonsense.

delirio [de'lirjo] *nm* (*MED*) delirium; (*palabras insensatas*) ravings *pl*; ~ **de grandeza** megalomania; ~ **de persecución** persecution mania; **con** ~ (*fam*) madly; **¡fue el** ~! (*fam*) it was great!

delito [de'lito] *nm* (*gen*) crime; (*infracción*) offence.

delta ['delta] *nm* delta.

demacrado, a [dema'kraðo, a] *adj* emaciated.

demagogia [dema'ɣoxja] *nf* demagogy, demagoguery.

demagogo [dema'ɣoɣo] *nm* demagogue.

demanda [de'manda] *nf* (*pedido, COM*) demand; (*petición*) request; (*pregunta*) inquiry; (*reivindicación*) claim; (*JUR*) action, lawsuit; (*TEAT*) call; (*ELEC*) load; ~ **de pago** demand for payment; **escribir en** ~ **de ayuda** to write asking for help; **entablar** ~ (*JUR*) to sue; **presentar** ~ **de divorcio** to sue for divorce; ~ **final** final demand; ~ **indirecta** derived demand; ~ **de mercado** market demand.

demandado, a [deman'daðo, a] *nm/f* defendant; (*en divorcio*) respondent.

demandante [deman'dante] *nm/f* claimant; (*JUR*) plaintiff.

demandar [deman'dar] *vt* (*gen*) to demand; (*JUR*) to sue, file a lawsuit against, start proceedings against; ~ **a algn por calumnia/daños y perjuicios** to sue sb for libel/damages.

demarcación [demarka'θjon] *nf* (*de terreno*) demarcation.

demás [de'mas] *adj*: **los ~ niños** the other children, the remaining children ♦ *pron*: **los/las ~** the others, the rest (of them); **lo ~** the rest (of it); **por ~** moreover; (*en vano*) in vain; **y ~** etcetera.

demasía [dema'sia] *nf* (*exceso*) excess, surplus; **comer en ~** to eat to excess.

demasiado, a [dema'sjaðo, a] *adj*: **~ vino** too much wine ♦ *adv* (*antes de adj, adv*) too; **~s libros** too many books; **¡es ~!** it's too much!; **es ~ pesado para levantar** it is too heavy to lift; **~ lo sé** I know it only too well; **hace ~ calor** it's too hot.

demencia [de'menθja] *nf* (*locura*) madness.

demencial [demen'θjal] *adj* crazy.

demente [de'mente] *adj* mad, insane ♦ *nm/f* lunatic.

democracia [demo'kraθja] *nf* democracy.

demócrata [de'mokrata] *nm/f* democrat.

democratacristiano, a [demokrata kris'tjano, a], **democristiano, a** [demokris'tjano, a] *adj, nm/f* Christian Democrat.

democrático, a [demo'kratiko, a] *adj* democratic.

demográfico, a [demo'ɣrafiko, a] *adj* demographic, population *cpd*; **la explosión demográfica** the population explosion.

demoledor, a [demole'ðor, a] *adj* (*fig*: *argumento*) overwhelming; (: *ataque*) shattering.

demoler [demo'ler] *vt* to demolish; (*edificio*) to pull down.

demolición [demoli'θjon] *nf* demolition.

demonio [de'monjo] *nm* devil, demon; **¡~s!** hell!; **¿cómo ~s?** how the hell?; **¿qué ~s será?** what the devil can it be?; **¿dónde ~ lo habré dejado?** where the devil can I have left it?; **tener el ~ en el cuerpo** (*no parar*) to be always on the go.

demora [de'mora] *nf* delay.

demorar [demo'rar] *vt* (*retardar*) to delay, hold back; (*dilatar*) to hold up ♦ *vi* to linger, stay on; **~se** *vr* to linger, stay on; (*retrasarse*) to take a long time; **~se en hacer algo** (*esp AM*) to take time doing sth.

demos ['demos] *vb* V **dar**.

demostración [demostra'θjon] *nf* (*gen, MAT*) demonstration; (*de cariño, fuerza*) show; (*de teorema*) proof; (*de amistad*) gesture; (*de cólera, gimnasia*) display; **~ comercial** commercial exhibition.

demostrar [demos'trar] *vt* (*probar*) to prove; (*mostrar*) to show; (*manifestar*) to demonstrate.

demostrativo, a [demostra'tiβo, a] *adj* demonstrative.

demudado, a [demu'ðaðo, a] *adj* (*rostro*) pale; (*fig*) upset; **tener el rostro ~** to look pale.

demudar [demu'ðar] *vt* to change, alter; **~se** *vr* (*expresión*) to alter; (*perder color*) to change colour.

demuela [de'mwela] *etc vb* V **demoler**.

demuestre [de'mwestre] *etc vb* V **demostrar**.

den [den] *vb* V **dar**.

denegación [deneɣa'θjon] *nf* refusal, denial.

denegar [dene'ɣar] *vt* (*rechazar*) to refuse; (*negar*) to deny; (*JUR*) to reject.

denegué [dene'ɣe], **deneguemos** [dene'ɣemos] *etc*, **deniego** [de'njeɣo] *etc*, **deniegue** [de'njeɣe] *etc vb* V **denegar**.

dengue ['denɣe] *nm* dengue *o* breakbone fever.

denigrante [deni'ɣrante] *adj* (*injurioso*) insulting; (*deshonroso*) degrading.

denigrar [deni'ɣrar] *vt* (*desacreditar*) to denigrate; (*injuriar*) to insult.

denodado, a [deno'ðaðo, a] *adj* bold, brave.

denominación [denomina'θjon] *nf* (*acto*) naming; (*clase*) denomination.

The **denominación de origen**, *often abbreviated to* **D.O.**, *is a prestigious product classification given to designated regions by the awarding body, the* **Consejo Regulador de la Denominación de Origen**, *when their produce meets the required quality and production standards. It is often associated with* **manchego** *cheeses and many of the wines from the* **Rioja** *and* **Ribera de Duero** *regions.*

---

denominador [denomina'ðor] *nm*: **~ común** common denominator.

denostar [denos'tar] *vt* to insult.

denotar [deno'tar] *vt* (*indicar*) to indicate, denote.

densidad [densi'ðað] *nf* (*FÍSICA*) density; (*fig*) thickness; **~ de caracteres** (*INFORM*) pitch.

denso, a ['denso, a] *adj* (*apretado*) solid; (*espeso, pastoso*) thick; (*fig*) heavy.

dentado, a [den'taðo, a] *adj* (*rueda*) cogged; (*filo*) jagged; (*sello*) perforated; (*BOT*) dentate.

dentadura [denta'ðura] *nf* (set of) teeth *pl*; **~ postiza** false teeth *pl*.

dental [den'tal] *adj* dental.

dentellada [dente'ʎaða] *nf* (*mordisco*) bite, nip; (*señal*) tooth mark; **partir algo a ~s**

to sever sth with one's teeth.

dentera [den'tera] *nf* (*sensación desagradable*) the shivers *pl*.

dentición [denti'θjon] *nf* (*acto*) teething; (*ANAT*) dentition; **estar con la** ~ to be teething.

dentífrico, a [den'tifriko, a] *adj* dental, tooth *cpd* ♦ *nm* toothpaste; **pasta dentífrica** toothpaste.

dentista [den'tista] *nm/f* dentist.

dentro ['dentro] *adv* inside ♦ *prep*: ~ **de** in, inside, within; **allí** ~ in there; **mirar por** ~ to look inside; ~ **de lo posible** as far as possible; ~ **de todo** all in all; ~ **de tres meses** within three months.

denuedo [de'nweðo] *nm* boldness, daring.

denuesto [de'nwesto] *nm* insult.

denuncia [de'nunθja] *nf* (*delación*) denunciation; (*acusación*) accusation; (*de accidente*) report; **hacer** *o* **poner una** ~ to report an incident to the police.

denunciable [denun'θjaßle] *adj* indictable, punishable.

denunciante [denun'θjante] *nm/f* accuser; (*delator*) informer.

denunciar [denun'θjar] *vt* to report; (*delatar*) to inform on *o* against.

Dep. *abr* (= *Departamento*) Dept.; (= *Depósito*) dep.

deparar [depa'rar] *vt* (*brindar*) to provide *o* furnish with; (*suj: futuro, destino*) to have in store for; **los placeres que el viaje nos deparó** the pleasures which the trip afforded us.

departamento [departa'mento] *nm* (*sección administrativa*) department, section; (*AM: piso*) flat (*BRIT*), apartment (*US*); (*distrito*) department, province; ~ **de envíos** (*COM*) dispatch department; ~ **de máquinas** (*NAUT*) engine room.

departir [depar'tir] *vi* to talk, converse.

dependencia [depen'denθja] *nf* dependence; (*POL*) dependency; (*COM*) office, section; (*sucursal*) branch office; (*ARQ: cuarto*) room; ~**s** *nfpl* outbuildings.

depender [depen'der] *vi*: ~ **de** to depend on; (*contar con*) to rely on; (*de autoridad*) to be under, be answerable to; **depende** it (all) depends; **no depende de mí** it's not up to me.

dependienta [depen'djenta] *nf* saleswoman, shop assistant.

dependiente [depen'djente] *adj* dependent ♦ *nm* salesman, shop assistant.

depilación [depila'θjon] *nf* hair removal.

depilar [depi'lar] *vt* (*con cera: piernas*) to wax; (*cejas*) to pluck.

depilatorio, a [depila'torjo, a] *adj*

depilatory ♦ *nm* hair remover.

deplorable [deplo'raßle] *adj* deplorable.

deplorar [deplo'rar] *vt* to deplore.

depondré [depon'dre] *etc vb* V **deponer**.

deponer [depo'ner] *vt* (*armas*) to lay down; (*rey*) to depose; (*gobernante*) to oust; (*ministro*) to remove from office ♦ *vi* (*JUR*) to give evidence; (*declarar*) to make a statement.

deponga [de'ponga] *etc vb* V **deponer**.

deportación [deporta'θjon] *nf* deportation.

deportar [depor'tar] *vt* to deport.

deporte [de'porte] *nm* sport.

deportista [depor'tista] *adj* sports *cpd* ♦ *nm/f* sportsman/woman.

deportivo, a [depor'tißo, a] *adj* (*club, periódico*) sports *cpd* ♦ *nm* sports car.

deposición [deposi'θjon] *nf* (*de funcionario etc*) removal from office; (*JUR: testimonio*) evidence.

depositante [deposi'tante] *nm/f* depositor.

depositar [deposi'tar] *vt* (*dinero*) to deposit; (*mercaderías*) to put away, store; ~**se** *vr* to settle; ~ **la confianza en algn** to place one's trust in sb.

depositario, a [deposi'tarjo, a] *nm/f* trustee; ~ **judicial** official receiver.

depósito [de'posito] *nm* (*gen*) deposit; (*de mercaderías*) warehouse, store; (*de animales, coches*) pound; (*de agua, gasolina etc*) tank; (*en retrete*) cistern; ~ **afianzado** bonded warehouse; ~ **bancario** bank deposit; ~ **de cadáveres** mortuary; ~ **de maderas** timber yard; ~ **de suministro** feeder bin.

depravar [depra'ßar] *vt* to deprave, corrupt; ~**se** *vr* to become depraved.

depreciación [depreθja'θjon] *nf* depreciation.

depreciar [depre'θjar] *vt* to depreciate, reduce the value of; ~**se** *vr* to depreciate, lose value.

depredador, a [depreða'ðor, a] (*ZOOL*) *adj* predatory ♦ *nm* predator.

depredar [depre'ðar] *vt* to pillage.

depresión [depre'sjon] *nf* (*gen, MED*) depression; (*hueco*) hollow; (*en horizonte, camino*) dip; (*merma*) drop; (*ECON*) slump, recession; ~ **nerviosa** nervous breakdown.

deprimente [depri'mente] *adj* depressing.

deprimido, a [depri'miðo, a] *adj* depressed.

deprimir [depri'mir] *vt* to depress; ~**se** *vr* (*persona*) to become depressed.

deprisa [de'prisa] *adv* V **prisa**.

depuesto [de'pwesto] *pp de* **deponer**.

depuración [depura'θjon] *nf* purification; (*POL*) purge; (*INFORM*) debugging.

depurador [depura'ðor] *nm* purifier.

depuradora [depura'ðora] *nf* (*de agua*) water-treatment plant; (*tb*: ~ **de aguas residuales**) sewage farm.

depurar [depu'rar] *vt* to purify; (*purgar*) to purge; (*INFORM*) to debug.

depuse [de'puse] *etc vb V* **deponer**.

der., der.° *abr* (= *derecho*) r.

derecha [de'retʃa] *nf V* **derecho, a**.

derechazo [dere'tʃaθo] *nm* (*BOXEO*) right; (*TENIS*) forehand drive; (*TAUR*) *a pass with the cape*.

derechista [dere'tʃista] (*POL*) *adj* right-wing ♦ *nm/f* right-winger.

derecho, a [de'retʃo, a] *adj* right, right-hand ♦ *nm* (*privilegio*) right; (*título*) claim, title; (*lado*) right(-hand) side; (*leyes*) law ♦ *nf* right(-hand) side ♦ *adv* straight, directly; ~**s** *nmpl* dues; (*profesionales*) fees; (*impuestos*) taxes; (*de autor*) royalties; **la(s) derecha(s)** (*pl*) (*POL*) the Right; ~**s civiles** civil rights; ~**s de muelle** (*COM*) dock dues; ~**s de patente** patent rights; ~**s portuarios** (*COM*) harbour dues; ~ **de propiedad literaria** copyright; ~ **de retención** (*COM*) lien; ~ **de timbre** (*COM*) stamp duty; ~ **de votar** right to vote; ~ **a voto** voting right; **Facultad de D**~ Faculty of Law; **a derechas** rightly, correctly; **de derechas** (*POL*) right-wing; **"reservados todos los** ~**s"** "all rights reserved"; **¡no hay** ~**!** it's not fair!; **tener** ~ **a** to have a right to; **a la derecha** on the right; (*dirección*) to the right.

deriva [de'riβa] *nf*: **ir** *o* **estar a la** ~ to drift, be adrift.

derivación [deriβa'θjon] *nf* derivation.

derivado, a [deri'βaðo, a] *adj* derived ♦ *nm* (*LING*) derivative; (*INDUSTRIA, QUÍMICA*) by-product.

derivar [deri'βar] *vt* to derive; (*desviar*) to direct ♦ *vi*, ~**se** *vr* to derive, be derived; ~(**se**) **de** (*consecuencia*) to spring from.

dermatólogo, a [derma'toloɣo, a] *nm/f* dermatologist.

dérmico, a ['dermiko, a] *adj* skin *cpd*.

dermoprotector, a [dermoprotek'tor, a] *adj* protective.

derogación [deroɣa'θjon] *nf* repeal.

derogar [dero'ɣar] *vt* (*ley*) to repeal; (*contrato*) to revoke.

derogue [de'roɣe] *etc vb V* **derogar**.

derramamiento [derrama'mjento] *nm* (*dispersión*) spilling; (*fig*) squandering; ~ **de sangre** bloodshed.

derramar [derra'mar] *vt* to spill; (*verter*) to pour out; (*esparcir*) to scatter; ~**se** *vr* to pour out; ~ **lágrimas** to weep.

derrame [de'rrame] *nm* (*de líquido*) spilling; (*de sangre*) shedding; (*de tubo etc*) overflow; (*perdida*) leakage; (*MED*) discharge; (*declive*) slope; ~ **cerebral** brain haemorrhage; ~ **sinovial** water on the knee.

derrapar [derra'par] *vi* to skid.

derredor [derre'ðor] *adv*: **al** *o* **en** ~ **de** around, about.

derrengado, a [derren'gaðo, a] *adj* (*torcido*) bent; (*cojo*) crippled; **estar** ~ (*fig*) to ache all over; **dejar** ~ **a algn** (*fig*) to wear sb out.

derretido, a [derre'tiðo, a] *adj* melted; (*metal*) molten; **estar** ~ **por algn** (*fig*) to be crazy about sb.

derretir [derre'tir] *vt* (*gen*) to melt; (*nieve*) to thaw; (*fig*) to squander; ~**se** *vr* to melt.

derribar [derri'βar] *vt* to knock down; (*construcción*) to demolish; (*persona, gobierno, político*) to bring down.

derribo [de'rriβo] *nm* (*de edificio*) demolition; (*LUCHA*) throw; (*AVIAT*) shooting down; (*POL*) overthrow; ~**s** *nmpl* rubble *sg*, debris *sg*.

derrita [de'rrita] *etc vb V* **derretir**.

derrocar [derro'kar] *vt* (*gobierno*) to bring down, overthrow; (*ministro*) to oust.

derrochador, a [derrotʃa'ðor, a] *adj, nm/f* spendthrift.

derrochar [derro'tʃar] *vt* (*dinero, recursos*) to squander; (*energía, salud*) to be bursting with *o* full of.

derroche [de'rrotʃe] *nm* (*despilfarro*) waste, squandering; (*exceso*) extravagance; **con un** ~ **de buen gusto** with a fine display of good taste.

derroque [de'rroke] *etc vb V* **derrocar**.

derrota [de'rrota] *nf* (*NAUT*) course; (*MIL*) defeat, rout; **sufrir una grave** ~ (*fig*) to suffer a grave setback.

derrotar [derro'tar] *vt* (*gen*) to defeat.

derrotero [derro'tero] *nm* (*rumbo*) course; **tomar otro** ~ (*fig*) to adopt a different course.

derrotista [derro'tista] *adj, nm/f* defeatist.

derruir [derru'ir] *vt* to demolish, tear down.

derrumbamiento [derrumba'mjento] *nm* (*caída*) plunge; (*demolición*) demolition; (*desplome*) collapse; ~ **de tierra** landslide.

derrumbar [derrum'bar] *vt* to throw down; (*despeñar*) to fling *o* hurl down; (*volcar*) to upset; ~**se** *vr* (*hundirse*) to collapse; (: *techo*) to fall in, cave in; (*fig: esperanzas*)

to collapse.
derrumbe [de'rrumbe] *nm*
= **derrumbamiento**.
derruyendo [derru'jendo] *etc vb V* **derruir**.
des [des] *vb V* **dar**.
desabastecido, a [desaβaste'θiðo, a] *adj*:
estar ~ **de algo** to be short of *o* out of
sth.
desabotonar [desaβoto'nar] *vt* to
unbutton, undo ♦ *vi* (*flores*) to blossom;
~**se** *vr* to come undone.
desabrido, a [desa'βriðo, a] *adj* (*comida*)
insipid, tasteless; (*persona*: *soso*) dull;
(: *antipático*) rude, surly; (*respuesta*)
sharp; (*tiempo*) unpleasant.
desabrigado, a [desaβri'ɣaðo, a] *adj* (*sin*
abrigo) not sufficiently protected; (*fig*)
exposed.
desabrigar [desaβri'ɣar] *vt* (*quitar ropa a*) to
remove the clothing of; (*descubrir*) to
uncover; (*fig*) to deprive of protection;
~**se** *vr*: **me desabrigué en la cama** the
bedclothes came off.
desabrigue [desa'βriɣe] *etc vb V*
desabrigar.
desabrochar [desaβro't∫ar] *vt* (*botones,*
broches) to undo, unfasten; ~**se** *vr* (*ropa*
etc) to come undone.
desacatar [desaka'tar] *vt* (*ley*) to disobey.
desacato [desa'kato] *nm* (*falta de respeto*)
disrespect; (*JUR*) contempt.
desacertado, a [desaθer'taðo, a] *adj*
(*equivocado*) mistaken; (*inoportuno*)
unwise.
desacierto [desa'θjerto] *nm* (*error*)
mistake, error; (*dicho*) unfortunate
remark.
desaconsejable [desakonse'xaβle] *adj*
inadvisable.
desaconsejado, a [desakonse'xaðo, a] *adj*
ill-advised.
desaconsejar [desakonse'xar] *vt*: ~ **algo a**
algn to advise sb against sth.
desacoplar [desako'plar] *vt* (*ELEC*) to
disconnect; (*TEC*) to take apart.
desacorde [desa'korðe] *adj* (*MUS*)
discordant; (*fig*: *opiniones*) conflicting;
estar ~ **con algo** to disagree with sth.
desacreditar [desakreði'tar] *vt*
(*desprestigiar*) to discredit, bring into
disrepute; (*denigrar*) to run down.
desactivar [desakti'βar] *vt* to deactivate;
(*bomba*) to defuse.
desacuerdo [desa'kwerðo] *nm* (*conflicto*)
disagreement, discord; (*error*) error,
blunder; **en** ~ out of keeping.
desafiante [desa'fjante] *adj* (*insolente*)
defiant; (*retador*) challenging ♦ *nm/f*

challenger.
desafiar [desa'fjar] *vt* (*retar*) to challenge;
(*enfrentarse a*) to defy.
desafilado, a [desafi'laðo, a] *adj* blunt.
desafinado, a [desafi'naðo, a] *adj*: **estar** ~
to be out of tune.
desafinar [desafi'nar] *vi* to be out of tune;
~**se** *vr* to go out of tune.
desafío [desa'fio] *nm* (*reto*) challenge;
(*combate*) duel; (*resistencia*) defiance.
desaforadamente [desaforaða'mente] *adv*:
gritar ~ to shout one's head off.
desaforado, a [desafo'raðo, a] *adj* (*grito*)
ear-splitting; (*comportamiento*)
outrageous.
desafortunadamente [desafortunaða
'mente] *adv* unfortunately.
desafortunado, a [desafortu'naðo, a] *adj*
(*desgraciado*) unfortunate, unlucky.
desagradable [desaɣra'ðaβle] *adj*
(*fastidioso, enojoso*) unpleasant; (*irritante*)
disagreeable; **ser** ~ **con algn** to be rude
to sb.
desagradar [desaɣra'ðar] *vi* (*disgustar*) to
displease; (*molestar*) to bother.
desagradecido, a [desaɣraðe'θiðo, a] *adj*
ungrateful.
desagrado [desa'ɣraðo] *nm* (*disgusto*)
displeasure; (*contrariedad*)
dissatisfaction; **con** ~ unwillingly.
desagraviar [desaɣra'βjar] *vt* to make
amends to.
desagravio [desa'βraβjo] *nm* (*satisfacción*)
amends; (*compensación*) compensation.
desaguadero [desaɣwa'ðero] *nm* drain.
desagüe [de'saɣwe] *nm* (*de un líquido*)
drainage; (*cañería*: *tb*: **tubo de** ~)
drainpipe; (*salida*) outlet, drain.
desaguisado, a [desaɣi'saðo, a] *adj* illegal
♦ *nm* outrage.
desahogado, a [desao'ɣaðo, a] *adj*
(*holgado*) comfortable; (*espacioso*)
roomy.
desahogar [desao'ɣar] *vt* (*aliviar*) to ease,
relieve; (*ira*) to vent; ~**se** *vr* (*distenderse*)
to relax; (*desfogarse*) to let off steam
(*fam*); (*confesarse*) to confess, get sth off
one's chest (*fam*).
desahogo [desa'oɣo] *nm* (*alivio*) relief;
(*comodidad*) comfort, ease; **vivir con** ~ to
be comfortably off.
desahogue [desa'oɣe] *etc vb V* **desahogar**.
desahuciado, a [desau'θjaðo, a] *adj*
hopeless.
desahuciar [desau'θjar] *vt* (*enfermo*) to
give up hope for; (*inquilino*) to evict.
desahucio [de'sauθjo] *nm* eviction.
desairado, a [desai'raðo, a] *adj*

(*menospreciado*) disregarded; (*desgarbado*) shabby; (*sin éxito*) unsuccessful; **quedar** ~ to come off badly.

desairar [desai'rar] *vt* (*menospreciar*) to slight, snub; (*cosa*) to disregard; (*COM*) to default on.

desaire [des'aire] *nm* (*menosprecio*) slight; (*falta de garbo*) unattractiveness; **dar** *o* **hacer un** ~ **a algn** to offend sb; **¿me va usted a hacer ese** ~**?** I won't take no for an answer!

desajustar [desaxus'tar] *vt* (*desarreglar*) to disarrange; (*desconcertar*) to throw off balance; (*fig: planes*) to upset; ~**se** *vr* to get out of order; (*aflojarse*) to loosen.

desajuste [desa'xuste] *nm* (*de máquina*) disorder; (*avería*) breakdown; (*situación*) imbalance; (*desacuerdo*) disagreement.

desalentador, a [desalenta'ðor, a] *adj* discouraging.

desalentar [desalen'tar] *vt* (*desanimar*) to discourage; ~**se** *vr* to get discouraged.

desaliento [desa'ljento] *etc vb V* **desalentar** ♦ *nm* discouragement; (*abatimiento*) depression.

desaliñado, a [desali'ɲaðo, a] *adj* (*descuidado*) slovenly; (*raído*) shabby; (*desordenado*) untidy; (*negligente*) careless.

desaliño [desa'liɲo] *nm* (*descuido*) slovenliness; (*negligencia*) carelessness.

desalmado, a [desal'maðo, a] *adj* (*cruel*) cruel, heartless.

desalojar [desalo'xar] *vt* (*gen*) to remove, expel; (*expulsar, echar*) to eject; (*abandonar*) to move out of ♦ *vi* to move out; **la policía desalojó el local** the police cleared people out of the place.

desalquilar [desalki'lar] *vt* to vacate, move out; ~**se** *vr* to become vacant.

desamarrar [desama'rrar] *vt* to untie; (*NAUT*) to cast off.

desamor [desa'mor] *nm* (*frialdad*) indifference; (*odio*) dislike.

desamparado, a [desampa'raðo, a] *adj* (*persona*) helpless; (*lugar: expuesto*) exposed; (: *desierto*) deserted.

desamparar [desampa'rar] *vt* (*abandonar*) to desert, abandon; (*JUR*) to leave defenceless; (*barco*) to abandon.

desamparo [desam'paro] *nm* (*acto*) desertion; (*estado*) helplessness.

desamueblado, a [desamwe'ßlaðo, a] *adj* unfurnished.

desandar [desan'dar] *vt:* ~ **lo andado** *o* **el camino** to retrace one's steps.

desanduve [desan'duße] *etc,*

desanduviera [desandu'ßjera] *etc vb V* **desandar**.

desangelado, a [desanxe'laðo, a] *adj* (*habitación, edificio*) lifeless.

desangrar [desan'grar] *vt* to bleed; (*fig: persona*) to bleed dry; (*lago*) to drain; ~**se** *vr* to lose a lot of blood; (*morir*) to bleed to death.

desanimado, a [desani'maðo, a] *adj* (*persona*) downhearted; (*espectáculo, fiesta*) dull.

desanimar [desani'mar] *vt* (*desalentar*) to discourage; (*deprimir*) to depress; ~**se** *vr* to lose heart.

desánimo [de'sanimo] *nm* despondency; (*abatimiento*) dejection; (*falta de animación*) dullness.

desanudar [desanu'ðar] *vt* to untie; (*fig*) to clear up.

desapacible [desapa'θißle] *adj* unpleasant.

desaparecer [desapare'θer] *vi* to disappear; (*el sol, la luz*) to vanish; (~ *de vista*) to drop out of sight; (*efectos, señales*) to wear off ♦ *vt* (*esp AM POL*) to cause to disappear; (: *eufemismo*) to murder.

desaparecido, a [desapare'θiðo, a] *adj* missing; (*especie*) extinct ♦ *nm/f* (*AM POL*) kidnapped *o* missing person.

desaparezca [desapa'reθka] *etc vb V* **desaparecer**.

desaparición [desapari'θjon] *nf* disappearance; (*de especie etc*) extinction.

desapasionado, a [desapasjo'naðo, a] *adj* dispassionate, impartial.

desapego [desa'peɣo] *nm* (*frialdad*) coolness; (*distancia*) detachment.

desapercibido, a [desaperθi'ßiðo, a] *adj* unnoticed; (*desprevenido*) unprepared; **pasar** ~ to go unnoticed.

desaplicado, a [desapli'kaðo, a] *adj* slack, lazy.

desaprensivo, a [desapren'sißo, a] *adj* unscrupulous.

desaprobar [desapro'ßar] *vt* (*reprobar*) to disapprove of; (*condenar*) to condemn; (*no consentir*) to reject.

desaprovechado, a [desaproße't faðo, a] *adj* (*oportunidad, tiempo*) wasted; (*estudiante*) slack.

desaprovechar [desaproße't far] *vt* to waste; (*talento*) not to use to the full ♦ *vi* (*perder terreno*) to lose ground.

desapruebe [desa'prweße] *etc vb V* **desaprobar**.

desarmar [desar'mar] *vt* (*MIL, fig*) to disarm; (*TEC*) to take apart, dismantle.

desarme [de'sarme] *nm* disarmament.
desarraigado, a [desarrai'ɣaðo, a] *adj*
(*persona*) without roots, rootless.
desarraigar [desarrai'ɣar] *vt* to uproot; (*fig:
costumbre*) to root out; (: *persona*) to
banish.
desarraigo [desa'rraiɣo] *nm* uprooting.
desarraigue [desa'rraiɣe] *etc vb V*
desarraigar.
desarreglado, a [desarre'ɣlaðo, a] *adj*
(*desordenado*) disorderly, untidy;
(*hábitos*) irregular.
desarreglar [desarre'ɣlar] *vt* to mess up;
(*desordenar*) to disarrange; (*trastocar*) to
upset, disturb.
desarreglo [desa'rreɣlo] *nm* (*de casa,
persona*) untidiness; (*desorden*)
disorder; (*TEC*) trouble; (*MED*) upset;
viven en el mayor ~ they live in
complete chaos.
desarrollado, a [desarro'ʎaðo, a] *adj*
developed.
desarrollar [desarro'ʎar] *vt* (*gen*) to
develop; (*extender*) to unfold; (*teoría*) to
explain; ~**se** *vr* to develop; (*extenderse*)
to open (out); (*film*) to develop; (*fig*) to
grow; (*tener lugar*) to take place; **aquí
desarrollan un trabajo muy importante**
they carry on *o* out very important
work here; **la acción se desarrolla en
Roma** (*CINE etc*) the scene is set in Rome.
desarrollo [desa'rroʎo] *nm* development;
(*de acontecimientos*) unfolding; (*de
industria, mercado*) expansion, growth;
país en vías de ~ developing country; **la
industria está en pleno** ~ industry is
expanding steadily.
desarrugar [desarru'ɣar] *vt* (*alisar*) to
smooth (out); (*ropa*) to remove the
creases from.
desarrugue [desa'rruɣe] *etc vb V*
desarrugar.
desarticulado, a [desartiku'laðo, a] *adj*
disjointed.
desarticular [desartiku'lar] *vt* (*huesos*) to
dislocate, put out of joint; (*objeto*) to
take apart; (*grupo terrorista etc*) to break
up.
desaseado, a [desase'aðo, a] *adj* (*sucio*)
dirty; (*desaliñado*) untidy.
desaseo [desa'seo] *nm* (*suciedad*) dirtiness;
(*desarreglo*) untidiness.
desasga [de'sasɣa] *etc vb V* **desasir**.
desasir [desa'sir] *vt* to loosen; ~**se** *vr* to
extricate o.s.; ~**se de** to let go, give up.
desasosegar [desasose'ɣar] *vt* (*inquietar*)
to disturb, make uneasy; ~**se** *vr* to
become uneasy.

desasosegué [desasose'ɣe],
desasoseguemos [desasose'ɣemos] *etc*
vb V **desasosegar**.
desasosiego [desaso'sjeɣo] *etc vb V*
desasosegar ♦ *nm* (*intranquilidad*)
uneasiness, restlessness; (*ansiedad*)
anxiety; (*POL etc*) unrest.
desasosiegue [desaso'sjeɣue] *etc vb V*
desasosegar.
desastrado, a [desas'traðo, a] *adj*
(*desaliñado*) shabby; (*sucio*) dirty.
desastre [de'sastre] *nm* disaster; ¡un ~!
how awful!; **la función fue un** ~ the show
was a shambles.
desastroso, a [desas'troso, a] *adj*
disastrous.
desatado, a [desa'taðo, a] *adj* (*desligado*)
untied; (*violento*) violent, wild.
desatar [desa'tar] *vt* (*nudo*) to untie;
(*paquete*) to undo; (*perro, odio*) to
unleash; (*misterio*) to solve; (*separar*) to
detach; ~**se** *vr* (*zapatos*) to come untied;
(*tormenta*) to break; (*perder control de sí*)
to lose self-control; ~**se en injurias** to
pour out a stream of insults.
desatascar [desatas'kar] *vt* (*cañería*) to
unblock, clear; (*carro*) to pull out of the
mud; ~ **a algn** (*fig*) to get sb out of a
jam.
desatasque [desa'taske] *etc vb V*
desatascar.
desatención [desaten'θjon] *nf* (*descuido*)
inattention; (*distracción*) absent-
mindedness.
desatender [desaten'der] *vt* (*no prestar
atención a*) to disregard; (*abandonar*) to
neglect.
desatento, a [desa'tento, a] *adj* (*distraído*)
inattentive; (*descortés*) discourteous.
desatienda [desa'tjenda] *etc vb V*
desatender.
desatinado, a [desati'naðo, a] *adj* foolish,
silly.
desatino [desa'tino] *nm* (*idiotez*)
foolishness, folly; (*error*) blunder; ~**s**
nmpl nonsense *sg*; ¡qué ~! how silly!,
what rubbish!
desatornillar [desatorni'ʎar] *vt* to
unscrew.
desatrancar [desatran'kar] *vt* (*puerta*) to
unbolt; (*cañería*) to unblock.
desatranque [desa'tranke] *etc vb V*
desatrancar.
desautorice [desauto'riθe] *etc vb V*
desautorizar.
desautorizado, a [desautori'θaðo, a] *adj*
unauthorized.
desautorizar [desautori'θar] *vt* (*oficial*) to

deprive of authority; (*informe*) to deny.
desavendré [desaßen'dre] *etc vb V*
desavenir.
desavenencia [desaße'nenθja] *nf*
(*desacuerdo*) disagreement;
(*discrepancia*) quarrel.
desavenga [desa'ßenga] *etc vb V*
desavenir.
desavenido, a [desaße'niðo, a] *adj*
(*opuesto*) contrary; (*reñidos*) in
disagreement; **ellos están** ~**s** they
are at odds.
desavenir [desaße'nir] *vt* (*enemistar*) to
make trouble between; ~**se** *vr* to fall out.
desaventajado, a [desaßenta'xaðo, a] *adj*
(*inferior*) inferior; (*poco ventajoso*)
disadvantageous.
desaviene [desa'ßjene] *etc,*
desaviniendo [desaßi'njendo] *etc vb V*
desavenir.
desayunar [desaju'nar] *vi,* ~**se** *vr* to have
breakfast ♦ *vt* to have for breakfast; ~
con café to have coffee for breakfast; ~
con algo (*fig*) to get the first news of sth.
desayuno [desa'juno] *nm* breakfast.
desazón [desa'θon] *nf* (*angustia*) anxiety;
(*MED*) discomfort; (*fig*) annoyance.
desazonar [desaθo'nar] *vt* (*fig*) to annoy,
upset; ~**se** *vr* (*enojarse*) to be annoyed;
(*preocuparse*) to worry, be anxious.
desbancar [desßan'kar] *vt* (*quitar el puesto
a*) to oust; (*suplantar*) to supplant (in sb's
affections).
desbandada [desßan'daða] *nf* rush; ~
general mass exodus; **a la** ~ in disorder.
desbandarse [desßan'darse] *vr* (*MIL*) to
disband; (*fig*) to flee in disorder.
desbanque [des'ßanke] *etc vb V* **desbancar.**
desbarajuste [desßara'xuste] *nm*
confusion, disorder; ¡**qué** ~! what a
mess!
desbaratar [desßara'tar] *vt* (*gen*) to mess
up; (*plan*) to spoil; (*deshacer, destruir*) to
ruin ♦ *vi* to talk nonsense; ~**se** *vr*
(*máquina*) to break down; (*persona:
irritarse*) to fly off the handle (*fam*).
desbarrar [desßa'rrar] *vi* to talk nonsense.
desbloquear [desßloke'ar] *vt*
(*negociaciones, tráfico*) to get going
again; (*COM: cuenta*) to unfreeze.
desbocado, a [desßo'kaðo, a] *adj* (*caballo*)
runaway; (*herramienta*) worn.
desbocar [desßo'kar] *vt* (*vasija*) to break
the rim of; ~**se** *vr* (*caballo*) to bolt;
(*persona: soltar injurias*) to let out a
stream of insults.
desboque [des'ßoke] *etc vb V* **desbocar.**
desbordamiento [desßorða'mjento] *nm*

(*de río*) overflowing; (*INFORM*) overflow;
(*de cólera*) outburst; (*de entusiasmo*)
upsurge.
desbordar [desßor'ðar] *vt* (*sobrepasar*) to
go beyond; (*exceder*) to exceed ♦ *vi,* ~**se**
vr (*líquido, río*) to overflow; (*entusiasmo*)
to erupt; (*persona: exaltarse*) to get
carried away.
desbravar [desßra'ßar] *vt* (*caballo*) to break
in; (*animal*) to tame.
descabalgar [deskaßal'ɣar] *vi* to dismount.
descabalgue [deska'ßalɣe] *etc vb V*
descabalgar.
descabellado, a [deskaße'ʎaðo, a] *adj*
(*disparatado*) wild, crazy; (*insensato*)
preposterous.
descabellar [deskaße'ʎar] *vt* to ruffle;
(*TAUR: toro*) to give the coup de grace to.
descabezado, a [deskaße'θaðo, a] *adj* (*sin
cabeza*) headless; (*insensato*) wild.
descafeinado, a [deskafei'naðo, a] *adj*
decaffeinated ♦ *nm* decaffeinated
coffee, de-caff.
descalabrar [deskala'ßrar] *vt* to smash;
(*persona*) to hit; (*: en la cabeza*) to hit on
the head; (*NAUT*) to cripple; (*dañar*) to
harm, damage; ~**se** *vr* to hurt one's
head.
descalabro [deska'laßro] *nm* blow;
(*desgracia*) misfortune.
descalce [des'kalθe] *etc vb V* **descalzar.**
descalificación [deskalifika'θjon] *nf*
disqualification; **descalificaciones** *nfpl*
discrediting *sg.*
descalificar [deskalifi'kar] *vt* to disqualify;
(*desacreditar*) to discredit.
descalifique [deskali'fike] *etc vb V*
descalificar.
descalzar [deskal'θar] *vt* (*zapato*) to take
off.
descalzo, a [des'kalθo, a] *adj* barefoot(ed);
(*fig*) destitute; **estar (con los pies)** ~(**s**) to
be barefooted.
descambiar [deskam'bjar] *vt* to exchange.
descaminado, a [deskami'naðo, a] *adj*
(*equivocado*) on the wrong road; (*fig*)
misguided; **en eso no anda usted muy** ~
you're not far wrong there.
descamisado, a [deskami'saðo, a] *adj*
bare-chested.
descampado [deskam'paðo] *nm* open
space, piece of empty ground; **comer al**
~ to eat in the open air.
descansado, a [deskan'saðo, a] *adj* (*gen*)
rested; (*que tranquiliza*) restful.
descansar [deskan'sar] *vt* (*gen*) to rest;
(*apoyar*): ~ (**sobre**) to lean (on) ♦ *vi* to
rest, have a rest; (*echarse*) to lie down;

(*cadáver, restos*) to lie; ¡**que usted
descanse!** sleep well!; ~ **en** (*argumento*)
to be based on.
descansillo [deskan'siʎo] *nm* (*de escalera*)
landing.
descanso [des'kanso] *nm* (*reposo*) rest;
(*alivio*) relief; (*pausa*) break; (*DEPORTE*)
interval, half time; **día de** ~ day off; ~
de enfermedad/maternidad sick/
maternity leave; **tomarse unos días de** ~
to take a few days' leave *o* rest.
descapitalizado, a [deskapitali'θaðo, a] *adj*
undercapitalized.
descapotable [deskapo'taßle] *nm* (*tb:
coche* ~) convertible.
descarado, a [deska'raðo, a] *adj* (*sin
vergüenza*) shameless; (*insolente*) cheeky.
descarga [des'karɣa] *nf* (*ARQ, ELEC, MIL*)
discharge; (*NAUT*) unloading.
descargador [deskarɣa'ðor] *nm* (*de barcos*)
docker.
descargar [deskar'ɣar] *vt* to unload; (*golpe*)
to let fly; (*arma*) to fire; (*ELEC*) to
discharge; (*pila*) to run down;
(*conciencia*) to relieve; (*COM*) to take up;
(*persona: de una obligación*) to release;
(: *de una deuda*) to free; (*JUR*) to clear
♦ *vi* (*río*): ~ (**en**) to flow (into); ~**se** *vr* to
unburden o.s.; ~**se de algo** to get rid of
sth.
descargo [des'karɣo] *nm* (*de obligación*)
release; (*COM: recibo*) receipt; (: *de
deuda*) discharge; (*JUR*) evidence; ~ **de
una acusación** acquittal on a charge.
descargue [des'karɣe] *etc vb V* **descargar.**
descarnado, a [deskar'naðo, a] *adj*
scrawny; (*fig*) bare; (*estilo*)
straightforward.
descaro [des'karo] *nm* nerve.
descarriar [deska'rrjar] *vt* (*descaminar*) to
misdirect; (*fig*) to lead astray; ~**se** *vr*
(*perderse*) to lose one's way; (*separarse*)
to stray; (*pervertirse*) to err, go astray.
descarrilamiento [deskarrila'mjento] *nm*
(*de tren*) derailment.
descarrilar [deskarri'lar] *vi* to be derailed.
descartable [deskar'taßle] *adj* (*INFORM*)
temporary.
descartar [deskar'tar] *vt* (*rechazar*) to
reject; (*eliminar*) to rule out; ~**se** *vr*
(*NAIPES*) to discard; ~**se de** to shirk.
descascarar [deskaska'rar] *vt* (*naranja,
limón*) to peel; (*nueces, huevo duro*) to
shell; ~**se** *vr* to peel (off).
descascarillado, a [deskaskari'ʎaðo, a] *adj*
(*paredes*) peeling.
descendencia [desθen'denθja] *nf* (*origen*)
origin, descent; (*hijos*) offspring; **morir**

sin dejar ~ to die without issue.
descendente [desθen'dente] *adj* (*cantidad*)
diminishing; (*INFORM*) top-down.
descender [desθen'der] *vt* (*bajar: escalera*)
to go down ♦ *vi* to descend; (*temperatura,
nivel*) to fall, drop; (*líquido*) to run;
(*cortina etc*) to hang; (*fuerzas, persona*) to
fail, get weak; ~ **de** to be descended
from.
descendiente [desθen'djente] *nm/f*
descendant.
descenso [des'θenso] *nm* descent; (*de
temperatura*) drop; (*de producción*)
downturn; (*de calidad*) decline; (*MINERÍA*)
collapse; (*bajada*) slope; (*fig: decadencia*)
decline; (*de empleado etc*) demotion.
descentrado, a [desθen'traðo, a] *adj* (*pieza
de una máquina*) off-centre; (*rueda*) out of
true; (*persona*) bewildered;
(*desequilibrado*) unbalanced; (*problema*)
out of focus; **todavía está algo** ~ he is
still somewhat out of touch.
descentralice [desθentra'liθe] *etc vb V*
descentralizar.
descentralizar [desθentrali'θar] *vt* to
decentralize.
descerrajar [desθerra'xar] *vt* (*puerta*) to
break open.
descienda [des'θjenda] *etc vb V* **descender.**
descifrable [desθi'fraßle] *adj* (*gen*)
decipherable; (*letra*) legible.
descifrar [desθi'frar] *vt* (*escritura*) to
decipher; (*mensaje*) to decode;
(*problema*) to puzzle out; (*misterio*) to
solve.
descocado, a [desko'kaðo, a] *adj*
(*descarado*) cheeky; (*desvergonzado*)
brazen.
descoco [des'koko] *nm* (*descaro*) cheek;
(*atrevimiento*) brazenness.
descodificador [deskoðifika'ðor] *nm*
decoder.
descodificar [deskoðifi'kar] *vt* to decode.
descolgar [deskol'ɣar] *vt* (*bajar*) to take
down; (*desde una posición alta*) to lower;
(*de una pared etc*) to unhook; (*teléfono*) to
pick up; ~**se** *vr* to let o.s. down; ~**se por**
(*bajar escurriéndose*) to slip down; (*pared*)
to climb down; **dejó el teléfono
descolgado** he left the phone off the
hook.
descolgué [deskol'ɣe], **descolguemos**
[deskol'ɣemos] *etc vb V* **descolgar.**
descollar [desko'ʎar] *vi* (*sobresalir*) to
stand out; (*montaña etc*) to rise; **la obra
que más descuella de las suyas** his most
outstanding work.
descolocado, a [deskolo'kaðo, a] *adj:* **estar**

~ (*cosa*) to be out of place; (*criada*) to be unemployed.

descolorido, a [deskolo'riðo, a] *adj* (*color, tela*) faded; (*pálido*) pale; (*fig: estilo*) colourless.

descompaginar [deskompaxi'nar] *vt* (*desordenar*) to disarrange, mess up.

descompasado, a [deskompa'saðo, a] *adj* (*sin proporción*) out of all proportion; (*excesivo*) excessive; (*hora*) unearthly.

descompensar [deskompen'sar] *vt* to unbalance.

descompondré [deskompon'dre] *etc vb V* **descomponer**.

descomponer [deskompo'ner] *vt* (*gen, LING, MAT*) to break down; (*desordenar*) to disarrange, disturb; (*materia orgánica*) to rot, decompose; (*TEC*) to put out of order; (*facciones*) to distort; (*estómago etc*) to upset; (*planes*) to mess up; (*persona: molestar*) to upset; (: *irritar*) to annoy; ~**se** *vr* (*corromperse*) to rot, decompose; (*estómago*) to get upset; (*el tiempo*) to change (for the worse); (*TEC*) to break down.

descomponga [deskom'ponga] *etc vb V* **descomponer**.

descomposición [deskomposi'θjon] *nf* (*gen*) breakdown; (*de fruta etc*) decomposition; (*putrefacción*) rotting; (*de cara*) distortion; ~ **de vientre** (*MED*) stomach upset, diarrhoea.

descompostura [deskompos'tura] *nf* (*TEC*) breakdown; (*desorganización*) disorganization; (*desorden*) untidiness.

descompuesto, a [deskom'pwesto, a] *pp de* **descomponer** ♦ *adj* (*corrompido*) decomposed; (*roto*) broken (down).

descompuse [deskom'puse] *etc vb V* **descomponer**.

descomunal [deskomu'nal] *adj* (*enorme*) huge; (*fam: excelente*) fantastic.

desconcertado, a [deskonθer'taðo, a] *adj* disconcerted, bewildered.

desconcertar [deskonθer'tar] *vt* (*confundir*) to baffle; (*incomodar*) to upset, put out; (*orden*) to disturb; ~**se** *vr* (*turbarse*) to be upset; (*confundirse*) to be bewildered.

desconchado, a [deskon'tʃaðo, a] *adj* (*pintura*) peeling.

desconchar [deskon'tʃar] *vt* (*pared*) to strip off; (*loza*) to chip off.

desconcierto [deskon'θjerto] *etc vb V* **desconcertar** ♦ *nm* (*gen*) disorder; (*desorientación*) uncertainty; (*inquietud*) uneasiness; (*confusión*) bewilderment.

desconectado, a [deskonek'taðo, a] *adj* (*ELEC*) disconnected, switched off;

(*INFORM*) offline; **estar** ~ **de** (*fig*) to have no contact with.

desconectar [deskonek'tar] *vt* to disconnect; (*desenchufar*) to unplug; (*radio, televisión*) to switch off; (*INFORM*) to toggle off.

desconfiado, a [deskon'fjaðo, a] *adj* suspicious.

desconfianza [deskon'fjanθa] *nf* distrust.

desconfiar [deskon'fjar] *vi* to be distrustful; ~ **de** (*sospechar*) to mistrust, suspect; (*no tener confianza en*) to have no faith *o* confidence in; **desconfío de ello** I doubt it; **desconfíe de las imitaciones** (*COM*) beware of imitations.

desconforme [deskon'forme] *adj* = **disconforme**.

descongelar [deskonxe'lar] *vt* (*nevera*) to defrost; (*comida*) to thaw; (*AUTO*) to de-ice; (*COM, POL*) to unfreeze.

descongestionar [desconxestjo'nar] *vt* (*cabeza, tráfico*) to clear; (*calle, ciudad*) to relieve congestion in; (*fig: despejar*) to clear.

desconocer [deskono'θer] *vt* (*ignorar*) not to know, be ignorant of; (*no aceptar*) to deny; (*repudiar*) to disown.

desconocido, a [deskono'θiðo, a] *adj* unknown; (*que no se conoce*) unfamiliar; (*no reconocido*) unrecognized ♦ *nm/f* stranger; (*recién llegado*) newcomer; **está** ~ he is hardly recognizable.

desconocimiento [deskonoθi'mjento] *nm* (*falta de conocimientos*) ignorance; (*repudio*) disregard.

desconozca [desko'noθka] *etc vb V* **desconocer**.

desconsiderado, a [deskonsiðe'raðo, a] *adj* inconsiderate; (*insensible*) thoughtless.

desconsolado, a [deskonso'laðo, a] *adj* (*afligido*) disconsolate; (*cara*) sad; (*desanimado*) dejected.

desconsolar [deskonso'lar] *vt* to distress; ~**se** *vr* to despair.

desconsuelo [deskon'swelo] *etc vb V* **desconsolar** ♦ *nm* (*tristeza*) distress; (*desesperación*) despair.

descontado, a [deskon'taðo, a] *adj*: **por** ~ of course; **dar por** ~ (**que**) to take it for granted (that).

descontar [deskon'tar] *vt* (*deducir*) to take away, deduct; (*rebajar*) to discount.

descontento, a [deskon'tento, a] *adj* dissatisfied ♦ *nm* dissatisfaction, discontent.

descontrol [deskon'trol] *nm* (*fam*) lack of control.

descontrolado, a [deskontro'laðo, a] *adj* uncontrolled.

descontrolarse [deskontro'larse] *vr* (*persona*) to lose control.

desconvenir [deskombe'nir] *vi* (*personas*) to disagree; (*no corresponder*) not to fit; (*no convenir*) to be inconvenient.

desconvocar [deskombo'kar] *vt* to call off.

descorazonar [deskoraθo'nar] *vt* to discourage, dishearten; ~**se** *vr* to get discouraged, lose heart.

descorchador [deskortʃa'ðor] *nm* corkscrew.

descorchar [deskor'tʃar] *vt* to uncork, open.

descorrer [desko'rrer] *vt* (*cortina, cerrojo*) to draw back; (*velo*) to remove.

descortés [deskor'tes] *adj* (*mal educado*) discourteous; (*grosero*) rude.

descortesía [deskorte'sia] *nf* discourtesy; (*grosería*) rudeness.

descoser [desko'ser] *vt* to unstitch; ~**se** *vr* to come apart (at the seams); (*fam*: *descubrir un secreto*) to blurt out a secret; ~**se de risa** to split one's sides laughing.

descosido, a [desko'siðo, a] *adj* (*costura*) unstitched; (*desordenado*) disjointed ♦ *nm*: **como un** ~ (*obrar*) wildly; (*beber, comer*) to excess; (*estudiar*) like mad.

descoyuntar [deskojun'tar] *vt* (ANAT) to dislocate; (*hechos*) to twist; ~**se** *vr*: ~**se un hueso** (ANAT) to put a bone out of joint; ~**se de risa** (*fam*) to split one's sides laughing; **estar descoyuntado** (*persona*) to be double-jointed.

descrédito [des'kreðito] *nm* discredit; **caer en** ~ to fall into disrepute; **ir en** ~ **de** to be to the discredit of.

descreído, a [deskre'iðo, a] *adj* (*incrédulo*) incredulous; (*falto de fe*) unbelieving.

descremado, a [deskre'maðo, a] *adj* skimmed.

descremar [deskre'mar] *vt* (*leche*) to skim.

describir [deskri'ßir] *vt* to describe.

descripción [deskrip'θjon] *nf* description.

descrito [des'krito] *pp de* **describir**.

descuajar [deskwa'xar] *vt* (*disolver*) to melt; (*planta*) to pull out by the roots; (*extirpar*) to eradicate, wipe out; (*desanimar*) to dishearten.

descuajaringarse [deskwaxarin'garse] *vr* to fall to bits.

descuajaringue [deskwaxa'ringe] *etc vb V* **descuajaringarse**.

descuartice [deskwar'tiθe] *etc vb V* **descuartizar**.

descuartizar [deskwarti'θar] *vt* (*animal*) to carve up, cut up; (*fig*: *hacer pedazos*) to tear apart.

descubierto, a [desku'ßjerto, a] *pp de* **descubrir** ♦ *adj* uncovered, bare; (*persona*) bare-headed; (*cielo*) clear; (*coche*) open; (*campo*) treeless ♦ *nm* (*lugar*) open space; (COM: *en el presupuesto*) shortage; (: *bancario*) overdraft; **al** ~ in the open; **poner al** ~ to lay bare; **quedar al** ~ to be exposed; **estar en** ~ to be overdrawn.

descubridor, a [desku'ßri'ðor, a] *nm/f* discoverer.

descubrimiento [deskußri'mjento] *nm* (*hallazgo*) discovery; (*de criminal, fraude*) detection; (*revelación*) revelation; (*de secreto etc*) disclosure; (*de estatua etc*) unveiling.

descubrir [desku'ßrir] *vt* to discover, find; (*petróleo*) to strike; (*inaugurar*) to unveil; (*vislumbrar*) to detect; (*sacar a luz*: *crimen*) to bring to light; (*revelar*) to reveal, show; (*poner al descubierto*) to expose to view; (*naipes*) to lay down; (*quitar la tapa de*) to uncover; (*cacerola*) to take the lid off; (*enterarse de*: *causa, solución*) to find out; (*divisar*) to see, make out; (*delatar*) to give away, betray; ~**se** *vr* to reveal o.s.; (*quitarse sombrero*) to take off one's hat; (*confesar*) to confess; (*fig*: *salir a luz*) to come out *o* to light.

descuelga [des'kwelɣa] *etc*, **descuelgue** [des'kwelɣe] *etc vb V* **descolgar**.

descuelle [des'kweʎe] *etc vb V* **descollar**.

descuento [des'kwento] *etc vb V* **descontar** ♦ *nm* discount; ~ **del 3%** 3% off; **con** ~ at a discount; ~ **por pago al contado** (COM) cash discount; ~ **por volumen de compras** (COM) volume discount.

descuidado, a [deskwi'ðaðo, a] *adj* (*sin cuidado*) careless; (*desordenado*) untidy; (*olvidadizo*) forgetful; (*dejado*) neglected; (*desprevenido*) unprepared.

descuidar [deskwi'ðar] *vt* (*dejar*) to neglect; (*olvidar*) to overlook ♦ *vi*, ~**se** *vr* (*distraerse*) to be careless; (*estar desaliñado*) to let o.s. go; (*desprevenirse*) to drop one's guard; **¡descuida!** don't worry!

descuido [des'kwiðo] *nm* (*dejadez*) carelessness; (*olvido*) negligence; (*un* ~) oversight; **al** ~ casually; (*sin cuidado*) carelessly; **al menor** ~ if my *etc* attention wanders for a minute; **con** ~ thoughtlessly; **por** ~ by an oversight.

=========== *PALABRA CLAVE*

desde ['desðe] *prep* **1** (*lugar*) from; ~ **Burgos hasta mi casa hay 30 km** it's 30 kms from Burgos to my house; ~ **lejos** from a distance
2 (*posición*): **hablaba** ~ **el balcón** she was speaking from the balcony
3 (*tiempo*: +*adv*, *n*): ~ **ahora** from now on; ~ **entonces/la boda** since then/the wedding; ~ **niño** since I *etc* was a child; ~ **3 años atrás** since 3 years ago
4 (*tiempo*: +*vb*) since; for; **nos conocemos** ~ **1978/**~ **hace 20 años** we've known each other since 1978/for 20 years; **no le veo** ~ **1983/**~ **hace 5 años** I haven't seen him since 1983/for 5 years; **¿**~ **cuándo vives aquí?** how long have you lived here?
5 (*gama*): ~ **los más lujosos hasta los más económicos** from the most luxurious to the most reasonably priced
6: ~ **luego (que no)** of course (not)
♦ *conj*: ~ **que**: ~ **que recuerdo** for as long as I can remember; ~ **que llegó no ha salido** he hasn't been out since he arrived.

desdecir [desðe'θir] *vi*: ~ **de** (*no merecer*) to be unworthy of; (*no corresponder*) to clash with; ~**se** *vr*: ~**se de** to go back on.
desdén [des'ðen] *nm* scorn.
desdentado, a [desðen'taðo, a] *adj* toothless.
desdeñable [desðe'ɲaβle] *adj* contemptible; **nada** ~ far from negligible, considerable.
desdeñar [desðe'ɲar] *vt* (*despreciar*) to scorn.
desdeñoso, a [desðe'ɲoso, a] *adj* scornful.
desdibujar [desðiβu'xar] *vt* to blur (the outlines of); ~**se** *vr* to get blurred, fade (away); **el recuerdo se ha desdibujado** the memory has become blurred.
desdichado, a [desði'tʃaðo, a] *adj* (*sin suerte*) unlucky; (*infeliz*) unhappy; (*día*) ill-fated ♦ *nm/f* (*pobre desgraciado*) poor devil.
desdicho, a [des'ðitʃo, a] *pp de* **desdecir** ♦ *nf* (*desgracia*) misfortune; (*infelicidad*) unhappiness.
desdiciendo [desði'θjendo] *etc vb V* **desdecir**.
desdiga [des'ðiɣa] *etc*, **desdije** [des'dixe] *etc vb V* **desdecir**.
desdoblado, a [desðo'βlaðo, a] *adj* (*personalidad*) split.
desdoblar [desðo'βlar] *vt* (*extender*) to

spread out; (*desplegar*) to unfold.
deseable [dese'aβle] *adj* desirable.
desear [dese'ar] *vt* to want, desire, wish for; **¿qué desea la señora?** (*tienda etc*) what can I do for you, madam?; **estoy deseando que esto termine** I'm longing for this to finish.
desecar [dese'kar] *vt*, **desecarse** *vr* to dry up.
desechable [dese'tʃaβle] *adj* (*envase etc*) disposable.
desechar [dese'tʃar] *vt* (*basura*) to throw out *o* away; (*ideas*) to reject, discard; (*miedo*) to cast aside; (*plan*) to drop.
desecho [de'setʃo] *nm* (*desprecio*) contempt; (*lo peor*) dregs *pl*; ~**s** *nmpl* rubbish *sg*, waste *sg*; **de** ~ (*hierro*) scrap; (*producto*) waste; (*ropa*) cast-off.
desembalar [desemba'lar] *vt* to unpack.
desembarace [desemba'raθe] *etc vb V* **desembarazar**.
desembarazado, a [desembara'θaðo, a] *adj* (*libre*) clear, free; (*desenvuelto*) free and easy.
desembarazar [desembara'θar] *vt* (*desocupar*) to clear; (*desenredar*) to free; ~**se** *vr*: ~**se de** to free o.s. of, get rid of.
desembarazo [desemba'raθo] *nm* (*acto*) clearing; (*AM: parto*) birth; (*desenfado*) ease.
desembarcadero [desembarka'ðero] *nm* quay.
desembarcar [desembar'kar] *vt* (*personas*) to land; (*mercancías etc*) to unload ♦ *vi*, ~**se** *vr* (*de barco, avión*) to disembark.
desembarco [desem'barko] *nm* landing.
desembargar [desembar'xar] *vt* (*gen*) to free; (*JUR*) to remove the embargo on.
desembargue [desem'βarxe] *etc vb V* **desembargar**.
desembarque [desem'barke] *etc vb V* **desembarcar** ♦ *nm* disembarkation; (*de pasajeros*) landing; (*de mercancías*) unloading.
desembocadura [desemboka'ðura] *nf* (*de río*) mouth; (*de calle*) opening.
desembocar [desembo'kar] *vi*: ~ **en** to flow into; (*fig*) to result in.
desemboce [desem'boθe] *etc vb V* **desembozar**.
desembolsar [desembol'sar] *vt* (*pagar*) to pay out; (*gastar*) to lay out.
desembolso [desem'bolso] *nm* payment.
desemboque [desem'boke] *etc vb V* **desembocar**.
desembozar [desembo'θar] *vt* to unmask.
desembragar [desembra'xar] *vt* (*TEC*) to disengage; (*embrague*) to release ♦ *vi*

(*AUTO*) to declutch.
desembrague [desem'ßraɣe] *etc vb* V
desembragar.
desembrollar [desembro'ʎar] *vt* (*madeja*)
to unravel; (*asunto, malentendido*) to sort
out.
desembuchar [desembu'tʃar] *vt* to
disgorge; (*fig*) to come out with ♦ *vi*
(*confesar*) to spill the beans (*fam*);
¡**desembucha!** out with it!
desemejante [deseme'xante] *adj*
dissimilar; ~ **de** different from, unlike.
desemejanza [deseme'xanθa] *nf*
dissimilarity.
desempacar [desempa'kar] *vt* (*esp AM*) to
unpack.
desempañar [desempa'ɲar] *vt* (*cristal*) to
clean, demist.
desempaque [desem'pake] *etc vb* V
desempacar.
desempaquetar [desempake'tar] *vt* to
unpack, unwrap.
desempatar [desempa'tar] *vi* to break a
tie; **volvieron a jugar para** ~ they held a
play-off.
desempate [desem'pate] *nm* (*FÚTBOL*)
play-off; (*TENIS*) tie-break(er).
desempeñar [desempe'ɲar] *vt* (*cargo*) to
hold; (*papel*) to play; (*deber, función*) to
perform, carry out; (*lo empeñado*) to
redeem; ~**se** *vr* to get out of debt; ~ **un**
papel (*fig*) to play (a role).
desempeño [desem'peɲo] *nm* occupation;
(*de lo empeñado*) redeeming; **de mucho**
~ very capable.
desempleado, a [desemple'aðo, a] *adj*
unemployed, out of work ♦ *nm/f*
unemployed person.
desempleo [desem'pleo] *nm*
unemployment.
desempolvar [desempol'ßar] *vt* (*muebles*
etc) to dust; (*lo olvidado*) to revive.
desencadenar [desenkaðe'nar] *vt* to
unchain; (*ira*) to unleash; (*provocar*) to
cause, set off; ~**se** *vr* to break loose;
(*tormenta*) to burst; (*guerra*) to break out;
se desencadenó una lucha violenta a
violent struggle ensued.
desencajar [desenka'xar] *vt* (*hueso*) to put
out of joint; (*mandíbula*) to dislocate;
(*mecanismo, pieza*) to disconnect,
disengage.
desencantar [desenkan'tar] *vt* to
disillusion, disenchant.
desencanto [desen'kanto] *nm*
disillusionment, disenchantment.
desenchufar [desentʃu'far] *vt* to unplug,
disconnect.

desenfadado, a [desenfa'ðaðo, a] *adj*
(*desenvuelto*) uninhibited; (*descarado*)
forward; (*en el vestir*) casual.
desenfado [desen'faðo] *nm* (*libertad*)
freedom; (*comportamiento*) free and easy
manner; (*descaro*) forwardness;
(*desenvoltura*) self-confidence.
desenfocado, a [desenfo'kaðo, a] *adj*
(*FOTO*) out of focus.
desenfrenado, a [desenfre'naðo, a] *adj*
(*descontrolado*) uncontrolled;
(*inmoderado*) unbridled.
desenfrenarse [desenfre'narse] *vr*
(*persona: desmandarse*) to lose all self-
control; (*multitud*) to run riot;
(*tempestad*) to burst; (*viento*) to rage.
desenfreno [desen'freno] *nm* (*vicio*)
wildness; (*falta de control*) lack of self-
control; (*de pasiones*) unleashing.
desenganchar [desengan'tʃar] *vt* (*gen*) to
unhook; (*FERRO*) to uncouple; (*TEC*) to
disengage.
desengañar [desenga'ɲar] *vt* to disillusion;
(*abrir los ojos a*) to open the eyes of; ~**se**
vr to become disillusioned;
¡**desengáñate!** don't you believe it!
desengaño [desen'gaɲo] *nm*
disillusionment; (*decepción*)
disappointment; **sufrir un** ~ **amoroso** to
be disappointed in love.
desengrasar [desengra'sar] *vt* to degrease.
desenlace [desen'laθe] *etc vb* V **desenlazar**
♦ *nm* outcome; (*LIT*) ending.
desenlazar [desenla'θar] *vt* (*desatar*) to
untie; (*problema*) to solve; (*aclarar:*
asunto) to unravel; ~**se** *vr* (*desatarse*) to
come undone; (*LIT*) to end.
desenmarañar [desenmara'ɲar] *vt* (*fig*) to
unravel.
desenmascarar [desenmaska'rar] *vt* to
unmask, expose.
desenredar [desenre'ðar] *vt* to resolve.
desenrollar [desenro'ʎar] *vt* to unroll,
unwind.
desenroscar [desenros'kar] *vt* (*tornillo etc*)
to unscrew.
desenrosque [desen'roske] *etc vb* V
desenroscar.
desentenderse [desenten'derse] *vr*: ~ **de**
to pretend not to know about; (*apartarse*)
to have nothing to do with.
desentendido, a [desenten'diðo, a] *adj*:
hacerse el ~ to pretend not to notice; **se**
hizo el ~ he didn't take the hint.
desenterrar [desente'rrar] *vt* to exhume;
(*tesoro, fig*) to unearth, dig up.
desentierre [desen'tjerre] *etc vb* V
desenterrar.

desentonar [desento'nar] *vi* (*MUS*) to sing (*o* play) out of tune; (*no encajar*) to be out of place; (*color*) to clash.

desentorpecer [desentorpe'θer] *vt* (*miembro*) to stretch; (*fam: persona*) to polish up.

desentorpezca [desentor'peθka] *etc vb V* **desentorpecer.**

desentrañar [desentra'ɲar] *vt* (*misterio*) to unravel.

desentrenado, a [desentre'naðo, a] *adj* out of training.

desentumecer [desentume'θer] *vt* (*pierna etc*) to stretch; (*DEPORTE*) to loosen up.

desentumezca [desentu'meθka] *etc vb V* **desentumecer.**

desenvainar [desembai'nar] *vt* (*espada*) to draw, unsheathe.

desenvoltura [desembol'tura] *nf* (*libertad, gracia*) ease; (*descaro*) free and easy manner; (*al hablar*) fluency.

desenvolver [desembol'ßer] *vt* (*paquete*) to unwrap; (*fig*) to develop; ~**se** *vr* (*desarrollarse*) to unfold, develop; (*suceder*) to go off; (*prosperar*) to prosper; (*arreglárselas*) to cope.

desenvolvimiento [desembolßi'mjento] *nm* (*desarrollo*) development; (*de idea*) exposition.

desenvuelto, a [desem'bwelto, a] *pp de* **desenvolver** ♦ *adj* (*suelto*) easy; (*desenfadado*) confident; (*al hablar*) fluent; (*pey*) forward.

desenvuelva [desem'buelßa] *etc vb V* **desenvolver.**

deseo [de'seo] *nm* desire, wish; ~ **de saber** thirst for knowledge; **buen** ~ good intentions *pl*; **arder en** ~**s de algo** to yearn for sth.

deseoso, a [dese'oso, a] *adj:* **estar** ~ **de hacer** to be anxious to do.

deseque [de'seke] *etc vb V* **desecar.**

desequilibrado, a [desekili'ßraðo, a] *adj* unbalanced ♦ *nm/f* unbalanced person; ~ **mental** mentally disturbed person.

desequilibrar [desekili'ßrar] *vt* (*mente*) to unbalance; (*objeto*) to throw out of balance; (*persona*) to throw off balance.

desequilibrio [deseki'lißrio] *nm* (*de mente*) unbalance; (*entre cantidades*) imbalance; (*MED*) unbalanced mental condition.

desertar [deser'tar] *vt* (*JUR: derecho de apelación*) to forfeit ♦ *vi* to desert; ~ **de sus deberes** to neglect one's duties.

desértico, a [de'sertiko, a] *adj* desert *cpd*; (*vacío*) deserted.

desertor, a [deser'tor, a] *nm/f* deserter.

desesperación [desespera'θjon] *nf* desperation, despair; (*irritación*) fury; **es una** ~ it's maddening; **es una** ~ **tener que ...** it's infuriating to have to ....

desesperado, a [desespe'raðo, a] *adj* (*persona: sin esperanza*) desperate; (*caso, situación*) hopeless; (*esfuerzo*) furious ♦ *nm:* **como un** ~ like mad ♦ *nf:* **hacer algo a la desesperada** to do sth as a last resort *o* in desperation.

desesperance [desespe'ranθe] *etc vb V* **desesperanzar.**

desesperante [desespe'rante] *adj* (*exasperante*) infuriating; (*persona*) hopeless.

desesperanzar [desesperan'θar] *vt* to drive to despair; ~**se** *vr* to lose hope, despair.

desesperar [desespe'rar] *vt* to drive to despair; (*exasperar*) to drive to distraction ♦ *vi:* ~ **de** to despair of; ~**se** *vr* to despair, lose hope.

desespero [deses'pero] *nm* (*AM*) despair.

desestabilice [desestaßi'liθe] *etc vb V* **desestabilizar.**

desestabilizar [desestaßili'θar] *vt* to destabilize.

desestimar [desesti'mar] *vt* (*menospreciar*) to have a low opinion of; (*rechazar*) to reject.

desfachatez [desfatʃa'teθ] *nf* (*insolencia*) impudence; (*descaro*) rudeness.

desfalco [des'falko] *nm* embezzlement.

desfallecer [desfaʎe'θer] *vi* (*perder las fuerzas*) to become weak; (*desvanecerse*) to faint.

desfallecido, a [desfaʎe'θiðo, a] *adj* (*débil*) weak.

desfallezca [desfa'ʎeθka] *etc vb V* **desfallecer.**

desfasado, a [desfa'saðo, a] *adj* (*anticuado*) old-fashioned; (*TEC*) out of phase.

desfasar [desfa'sar] *vt* to phase out.

desfase [des'fase] *nm* (*diferencia*) gap.

desfavorable [desfaßo'raßle] *adj* unfavourable.

desfavorecer [desfaßore'θer] *vt* (*sentar mal*) not to suit.

desfavorezca [desfaßo're θka] *etc vb V* **desfavorecer.**

desfiguración [desfixura'θjon] *nf*, **desfiguramiento** [desfixura'mjento] *nm* (*de persona*) disfigurement; (*de monumento*) defacement; (*FOTO*) blurring.

desfigurar [desfixu'rar] *vt* (*cara*) to disfigure; (*cuerpo*) to deform; (*cuadro, monumento*) to deface; (*FOTO*) to blur; (*sentido*) to twist; (*suceso*) to misrepresent.

desfiladero [desfila'ðero] *nm* gorge, defile.

desfilar [desfi'lar] *vi* to parade; **desfilaron ante el general** they marched past the general.

desfile [des'file] *nm* procession; (*MIL*) parade; ~ **de modelos** fashion show.

desflorar [desflo'rar] *vt* (*mujer*) to deflower; (*arruinar*) to tarnish; (*asunto*) to touch on.

desfogar [desfo'ɣar] *vt* (*fig*) to vent ♦ *vi* (*NAUT: tormenta*) to burst; ~**se** *vr* (*fig*) to let off steam.

desfogue [des'foɣe] *etc vb V* **desfogar**.

desgajar [desɣa'xar] *vt* (*arrancar*) to tear off; (*romper*) to break off; (*naranja*) to split into segments; ~**se** *vr* to come off.

desgana [des'ɣana] *nf* (*falta de apetito*) loss of appetite; (*renuencia*) unwillingness; **hacer algo a** ~ to do sth unwillingly.

desganado, a [desɣa'naðo, a] *adj:* **estar** ~ (*sin apetito*) to have no appetite; (*sin entusiasmo*) to have lost interest.

desgañitarse [desɣaɲi'tarse] *vr* to shout o.s. hoarse.

desgarbado, a [desɣar'βaðo, a] *adj* (*sin gracia*) clumsy, ungainly.

desgarrador, a [desɣarra'ðor, a] *adj* heartrending.

desgarrar [desɣa'rrar] *vt* to tear (up); (*fig*) to shatter.

desgarro [des'ɣarro] *nm* (*en tela*) tear; (*aflicción*) grief; (*descaro*) impudence.

desgastar [desɣas'tar] *vt* (*deteriorar*) to wear away o down; (*estropear*) to spoil; ~**se** *vr* to get worn out.

desgaste [des'ɣaste] *nm* wear (and tear); (*de roca*) erosion; (*de cuerda*) fraying; (*de metal*) corrosion; ~ **económico** drain on one's resources.

desglosar [desɣlo'sar] *vt* to detach.

desgobierno [desɣo'ßjerno] *etc vb V* **desgobernar** ♦ *nm* (*POL*) misgovernment, misrule.

desgracia [des'ɣraθja] *nf* misfortune; (*accidente*) accident; (*vergüenza*) disgrace; (*contratiempo*) setback; **por** ~ unfortunately; **en el accidente no hay que lamentar** ~**s personales** there were no casualties in the accident; **caer en** ~ to fall from grace; **tener la** ~ **de** to be unlucky enough to.

desgraciadamente [desɣraθjaða'mente] *adv* unfortunately.

desgraciado, a [desɣra'θjaðo, a] *adj* (*sin suerte*) unlucky, unfortunate; (*miserable*) wretched; (*infeliz*) miserable ♦ *nm/f* (*malo*) swine; (*infeliz*) poor creature; **¡esa radio desgraciada!** (*esp AM*) that lousy radio!

desgraciar [desɣra'θjar] *vt* (*estropear*) to spoil; (*ofender*) to displease.

desgranar [desɣra'nar] *vt* (*trigo*) to thresh; (*guisantes*) to shell; ~ **un racimo** to pick the grapes from a bunch; ~ **mentiras** to come out with a string of lies.

desgravación [desɣraßa'θjon] *nf* (*COM*): ~ **de impuestos** tax relief; ~ **personal** personal allowance.

desgravar [desɣra'ßar] *vt* (*producto*) to reduce the tax o duty on.

desgreñado, a [desɣre'ɲaðo, a] *adj* dishevelled.

desguace [des'ɣwaθe] *nm* (*de coches*) scrapping; (*lugar*) scrapyard.

desguazar [desɣwa'θar] *vt* (*coche*) to scrap.

deshabitado, a [desaßi'taðo, a] *adj* uninhabited.

deshabitar [desaßi'tar] *vt* (*casa*) to leave empty; (*despoblar*) to depopulate.

deshacer [desa'θer] *vt* (*lo hecho*) to undo, unmake; (*proyectos: arruinar*) to spoil; (*casa*) to break up; (*TEC*) to take apart; (*enemigo*) to defeat; (*diluir*) to melt; (*contrato*) to break; (*intriga*) to solve; (*cama*) to strip; (*maleta*) to unpack; (*paquete*) to unwrap; (*nudo*) to untie; (*costura*) to unpick; ~**se** *vr* (*desatarse*) to come undone; (*estropearse*) to be spoiled; (*descomponerse*) to fall to pieces; (*disolverse*) to melt; (*despedazarse*) to come apart o undone; ~**se de** to get rid of; (*COM*) to dump, unload; ~**se en** (*cumplidos, elogios*) to be lavish with; ~**se en lágrimas** to burst into tears; ~**se por algo** to be crazy about sth.

deshaga [de'saɣa] *etc*, **desharé** [desa're] *etc vb V* **deshacer**.

des(h)arrapado, a [desarra'paðo, a] *adj* ragged; (**de aspecto**) ~ shabby.

deshecho, a [de'setʃo, a] *pp de* **deshacer** ♦ *adj* (*lazo, nudo*) undone; (*roto*) smashed; (*despedazado*) in pieces; (*cama*) unmade; (*MED: persona*) weak, emaciated; (*: salud*) broken; **estoy** ~ I'm shattered.

deshelar [dese'lar] *vt* (*cañería*) to thaw; (*heladera*) to defrost.

desheredar [desere'ðar] *vt* to disinherit.

deshice [de'siθe] *etc vb V* **deshacer**.

deshidratación [desiðrata'θjon] *nf* dehydration.

deshidratar [desiðra'tar] *vt* to dehydrate.

deshielo [des'jelo] *etc vb V* **deshelar** ♦ *nm* thaw.

deshilachar [desila'tʃar] *vt*, **deshilacharse** *vr* to fray.

deshilar [desi'lar] *vt* (*tela*) to unravel.

deshilvanado, a [desilßa'naðo, a] *adj* (*fig*) disjointed, incoherent.

deshinchar [desin't∫ar] *vt* (*neumático*) to let down; (*herida etc*) to reduce (the swelling of); ~**se** *vr* (*neumático*) to go flat; (*hinchazón*) to go down.

deshojar [deso'xar] *vt* (*árbol*) to strip the leaves off; (*flor*) to pull the petals off; ~**se** *vr* to lose its leaves *etc*.

deshollinar [desoʎi'nar] *vt* (*chimenea*) to sweep.

deshonesto, a [deso'nesto, a] *adj* (*no honrado*) dishonest; (*indecente*) indecent.

deshonor [deso'nor] *nm* dishonour, disgrace; (*un* ~) insult, affront.

deshonra [de'sonra] *nf* (*deshonor*) dishonour; (*vergüenza*) shame.

deshonrar [deson'rar] *vt* to dishonour.

deshonroso, a [deson'roso, a] *adj* dishonourable, disgraceful.

deshora [de'sora]: **a** ~ *adv* at the wrong time; (*llegar*) unexpectedly; (*acostarse*) at some unearthly hour.

deshuesar [deswe'sar] *vt* (*carne*) to bone; (*fruta*) to stone.

desidia [de'siðja] *nf* (*pereza*) idleness.

desierto, a [de'sjerto, a] *adj* (*casa, calle, negocio*) deserted; (*paisaje*) bleak ♦ *nm* desert.

designación [desiɣna'θjon] *nf* (*para un cargo*) appointment; (*nombre*) designation.

designar [desiɣ'nar] *vt* (*nombrar*) to designate; (*indicar*) to fix.

designio [de'siɣnjo] *nm* plan; **con el** ~ **de** with the intention of.

desigual [desi'ɣwal] *adj* (*lucha*) unequal; (*diferente*) different; (*terreno*) uneven; (*tratamiento*) unfair; (*cambiadizo: tiempo*) changeable; (: *carácter*) unpredictable.

desigualdad [desiɣwal'ðað] *nf* (*ECON, POL*) inequality; (*de carácter, tiempo*) unpredictability; (*de escritura*) unevenness; (*de terreno*) roughness.

desilusión [desilu'sjon] *nf* disillusionment; (*decepción*) disappointment.

desilusionar [desilusjo'nar] *vt* to disillusion; (*decepcionar*) to disappoint; ~**se** *vr* to become disillusioned.

desinencia [desi'nenθja] *nf* (*LING*) ending.

desinfectar [desinfek'tar] *vt* to disinfect.

desinfestar [desinfes'tar] *vt* to decontaminate.

desinflación [desinfla'θjon] *nf* (*COM*) disinflation.

desinflar [desin'flar] *vt* to deflate; ~**se** *vr* (*neumático*) to go down *o* flat.

desintegración [desinteɣra'θjon] *nf* disintegration; ~ **nuclear** nuclear fission.

desintegrar [desinte'ɣrar] *vt* (*gen*) to disintegrate; (*átomo*) to split; (*grupo*) to break up; ~**se** *vr* to disintegrate; to split; to break up.

desinterés [desinte'res] *nm* (*objetividad*) disinterestedness; (*altruismo*) unselfishness.

desinteresado, a [desintere'saðo, a] *adj* (*imparcial*) disinterested; (*altruista*) unselfish.

desintoxicar [desintoksi'kar] *vt* to detoxify; ~**se** *vr* (*drogadicto*) to undergo treatment for drug addiction; ~**se de** (*rutina, trabajo*) to get away from.

desintoxique [desintok'sike] *etc vb V* **desintoxicar**.

desistir [desis'tir] *vi* (*renunciar*) to stop, desist; ~ **de** (*empresa*) to give up; (*derecho*) to waive.

deslavazado, a [deslaßa'θaðo, a] *adj* (*lacio*) limp; (*desteñido*) faded; (*insípido*) colourless; (*incoherente*) disjointed.

desleal [desle'al] *adj* (*infiel*) disloyal; (*COM: competencia*) unfair.

deslealtad [desleal'tað] *nf* disloyalty.

desleído, a [desle'iðo, a] *adj* weak, woolly.

desleír [desle'ir] *vt* (*líquido*) to dilute; (*sólido*) to dissolve.

deslenguado, a [deslen'gwaðo, a] *adj* (*grosero*) foul-mouthed.

deslía [des'lia] *etc vb V* **desleír**.

desliar [des'ljar] *vt* (*desatar*) to untie; (*paquete*) to open; ~**se** *vr* to come undone.

deslice [des'liθe] *etc vb V* **deslizar**.

desliendo [desli'endo] *etc vb V* **desleír**.

desligar [desli'ɣar] *vt* (*desatar*) to untie, undo; (*separar*) to separate; ~**se** *vr* (*de un compromiso*) to extricate o.s.

desligue [des'liɣe] *etc vb V* **desligar**.

deslindar [deslin'dar] *vt* (*señalar las lindes de*) to mark out, fix the boundaries of; (*fig*) to define.

desliz [des'liθ] *nm* (*fig*) lapse; ~ **de lengua** slip of the tongue; **cometer un** ~ to slip up.

deslizar [desli'θar] *vt* to slip, slide; ~**se** *vr* (*escurrirse: persona*) to slip, slide; (: *coche*) to skid; (*aguas mansas*) to flow gently; (*error*) to creep in; (*tiempo*) to pass; (*persona: irse*) to slip away; ~**se en un cuarto** to slip into a room.

deslomar [deslo'mar] *vt* (*romper el lomo de*) to break the back of; (*fig*) to wear out; ~**se** *vr* (*fig fam*) to work one's guts out.

deslucido, a [deslu'θiðo, a] *adj* dull; (*torpe*)

awkward, graceless; (*deslustrado*) tarnished; (*fracasado*) unsuccessful; **quedar** ~ to make a poor impression.

deslucir [deslu'θir] *vt* (*deslustrar*) to tarnish; (*estropear*) to spoil, ruin; (*persona*) to discredit; **la lluvia deslució el acto** the rain ruined the ceremony.

deslumbrar [deslum'brar] *vt* (*con la luz*) to dazzle; (*cegar*) to blind; (*impresionar*) to dazzle; (*dejar perplejo a*) to puzzle, confuse.

deslustrar [deslus'trar] *vt* (*vidrio*) to frost; (*quitar lustre a*) to dull; (*reputación*) to sully.

desluzca [des'luθka] *etc vb V* **deslucir.**

desmadrarse [desma'ðrarse] *vr* (*fam*) to run wild.

desmadre [des'maðre] *nm* (*fam: desorganización*) chaos; (: *jaleo*) commotion.

desmán [des'man] *nm* (*exceso*) outrage; (*abuso de poder*) abuse.

desmandarse [desman'darse] *vr* (*portarse mal*) to behave badly; (*excederse*) to get out of hand; (*caballo*) to bolt.

desmano [des'mano]: **a** ~ *adv*: **me coge** *o* **pilla a** ~ it's out of my way.

desmantelar [desmante'lar] *vt* (*deshacer*) to dismantle; (*casa*) to strip; (*organización*) to disband; (*MIL*) to raze; (*andamio*) to take down; (*NAUT*) to unrig.

desmaquillador [desmakiʎa'ðor] *nm* make-up remover.

desmaquillarse [desmaki'ʎarse] *vr* to take off one's make up.

desmarcarse [desmar'karse] *vr*: ~ **de** (*DEPORTE*) to get clear of; (*fig*) to distance o.s. from.

desmayado, a [desma'jaðo, a] *adj* (*sin sentido*) unconscious; (*carácter*) dull; (*débil*) faint, weak; (*color*) pale.

desmayar [desma'jar] *vi* to lose heart; ~**se** *vr* (*MED*) to faint.

desmayo [des'majo] *nm* (*MED: acto*) faint; (*estado*) unconsciousness; (*depresión*) dejection; (*de voz*) faltering; **sufrir un** ~ to have a fainting fit.

desmedido, a [desme'ðiðo, a] *adj* excessive; (*ambición*) boundless.

desmejorado, a [desmexo'raðo, a] *adj*: **está muy desmejorada** (*MED*) she's not looking too well.

desmejorar [desmexo'rar] *vt* (*dañar*) to impair, spoil; (*MED*) to weaken.

desmembración [desmembra'θjon] *nf* dismemberment; (*fig*) break-up.

desmembrar [desmem'brar] *vt* (*MED*) to dismember; (*fig*) to separate.

desmemoriado, a [desmemo'rjaðo, a] *adj* forgetful, absent-minded.

desmentir [desmen'tir] *vt* (*contradecir*) to contradict; (*refutar*) to deny; (*rumor*) to scotch ♦ *vi*: ~ **de** to refute; ~**se** *vr* to contradict o.s.

desmenuce [desme'nuθe] *etc vb V* **desmenuzar.**

desmenuzar [desmenu'θar] *vt* (*deshacer*) to crumble; (*carne*) to chop; (*examinar*) to examine closely.

desmerecer [desmere'θer] *vt* to be unworthy of ♦ *vi* (*deteriorarse*) to deteriorate.

desmerezca [desme'reθka] *etc vb V* **desmerecer.**

desmesurado, a [desmesu'raðo, a] *adj* (*desmedido*) disproportionate; (*enorme*) enormous; (*ambición*) boundless; (*descarado*) insolent.

desmiembre [des'mjembre] *etc vb V* **desmembrar.**

desmienta [des'mjenta] *etc vb V* **desmentir.**

desmigajar [desmixa'xar], **desmigar** [desmi'ɣar] *vt* to crumble.

desmigue [des'miɣe] *etc vb V* **desmigar.**

desmilitarice [desmilita'riθe] *etc vb V* **desmilitarizar.**

desmilitarizar [desmilitari'θar] *vt* to demilitarize.

desmintiendo [desmin'tjendo] *etc vb V* **desmentir.**

desmochar [desmo'tʃar] *vt* (*árbol*) to lop; (*texto*) to cut, hack about.

desmontable [desmon'taβle] *adj* (*que se quita*) detachable; (*en compartimientos*) sectional; (*que se puede plegar etc*) collapsible.

desmontar [desmon'tar] *vt* (*deshacer*) to dismantle; (*motor*) to strip down; (*máquina*) to take apart; (*escopeta*) to uncock; (*tienda de campaña*) to take down; (*tierra*) to level; (*quitar los árboles a*) to clear; (*jinete*) to throw ♦ *vi* to dismount.

desmonte [des'monte] *nm* (*de tierra*) levelling; (*de árboles*) clearing; (*terreno*) levelled ground; (*FERRO*) cutting.

desmoralice [desmora'liθe] *etc vb V* **desmoralizar.**

desmoralizador, a [desmoraliθa'ðor, a] *adj* demoralizing.

desmoralizar [desmorali'θar] *vt* to demoralize.

desmoronado, a [desmoro'naðo, a] *adj* (*casa, edificio*) dilapidated.

desmoronamiento [desmorona'mjento]

nm (*tb fig*) crumbling.

desmoronar [desmoro'nar] *vt* to wear away, erode; **~se** *vr* (*edificio, dique*) to fall into disrepair; (*economía*) to decline.

desmovilice [desmoßi'liθe] *etc vb V* **desmovilizar**.

desmovilizar [desmoßili'θar] *vt* to demobilize.

desnacionalización [desnaθjonaliθa'θjon] *nf* denationalization.

desnacionalizado, a [desnaθjonali'θaðo, a] *adj* (*industria*) denationalized; (*persona*) stateless.

desnatado, a [desna'taðo, a] *adj* skimmed; (*yogur*) low fat.

desnatar [desna'tar] *vt* (*leche*) to skim; **leche sin** ~ whole milk.

desnaturalice [desnatura'liθe] *etc vb V* **desnaturalizar**.

desnaturalizado, a [desnaturali'θaðo, a] *adj* (*persona*) unnatural; **alcohol** ~ methylated spirits.

desnaturalizar [desnaturali'θar] *vt* (QUÍMICA) to denature; (*corromper*) to pervert; (*sentido de algo*) to distort; **~se** *vr* (*perder la nacionalidad*) to give up one's nationality.

desnivel [desni'ßel] *nm* (*de terreno*) unevenness; (POL) inequality; (*diferencia*) difference.

desnivelar [desniße'lar] *vt* (*terreno*) to make uneven; (*fig: desequilibrar*) to unbalance; (*balanza*) to tip.

desnuclearizado, a [desnukleari'θaðo, a] *adj*: **región desnuclearizada** nuclear-free zone.

desnudar [desnu'ðar] *vt* (*desvestir*) to undress; (*despojar*) to strip; **~se** *vr* (*desvestirse*) to get undressed.

desnudez [desnu'ðeθ] *nf* (*de persona*) nudity; (*fig*) bareness.

desnudo, a [des'nuðo, a] *adj* (*cuerpo*) naked; (*árbol, brazo*) bare; (*paisaje*) flat; (*estilo*) unadorned; (*verdad*) plain ♦ *nm/f* nude; ~ **de** devoid *o* bereft of; **la retrató al** ~ he painted her in the nude; **poner al** ~ to lay bare.

desnutrición [desnutri'θjon] *nf* malnutrition.

desnutrido, a [desnu'triðo, a] *adj* undernourished.

desobedecer [desoßeðe'θer] *vt, vi* to disobey.

desobedezca [desoße'ðeθka] *etc vb V* **desobedecer**.

desobediencia [desoße'ðjenθja] *nf* disobedience.

desocupación [desokupa'θjon] *nf* (AM) unemployment.

desocupado, a [desoku'paðo, a] *adj* at leisure; (*desempleado*) unemployed; (*deshabitado*) empty, vacant.

desocupar [desoku'par] *vt* to vacate; **~se** *vr* (*quedar libre*) to be free; **se ha desocupado aquella mesa** that table's free now.

desodorante [desoðo'rante] *nm* deodorant.

desoiga [de'soiɣa] *etc vb V* **desoír**.

desoír [deso'ir] *vt* to ignore, disregard.

desolación [desola'θjon] *nf* (*de lugar*) desolation; (*fig*) grief.

desolar [deso'lar] *vt* to ruin, lay waste.

desollar [deso'ʎar] *vt* (*quitar la piel a*) to skin; (*criticar*): ~ **vivo a** to criticize unmercifully.

desorbitado, a [desorßi'taðo, a] *adj* (*excesivo*) excessive; (*precio*) exorbitant; **con los ojos** ~**s** pop-eyed.

desorbitar [desorßi'tar] *vt* (*exagerar*) to exaggerate; (*interpretar mal*) to misinterpret; **~se** *vr* (*persona*) to lose one's sense of proportion; (*asunto*) to get out of hand.

desorden [de'sorðen] *nm* confusion; (*de casa, cuarto*) mess; (*político*) disorder; **desórdenes** *nmpl* (*alborotos*) disturbances; (*excesos*) excesses; **en** ~ (*gente*) in confusion.

desordenado, a [desorðe'naðo, a] *adj* (*habitación, persona*) untidy; (*objetos: revueltos*) in a mess, jumbled; (*conducta*) disorderly.

desordenar [desorðe'nar] *vt* (*gen*) to disarrange; (*pelo*) to mess up; (*cuarto*) to make a mess in; (*causar confusión a*) to throw into confusion.

desorganice [desorɣa'niθe] *etc vb V* **desorganizar**.

desorganizar [desorɣani'θar] *vt* to disorganize.

desorientar [desorjen'tar] *vt* (*extraviar*) to mislead; (*confundir, desconcertar*) to confuse; **~se** *vr* (*perderse*) to lose one's way.

desovar [deso'ßar] *vi* (*peces*) to spawn; (*insectos*) to lay eggs.

desoyendo [deso'jendo] *etc vb V* **desoír**.

despabilado, a [despaßi'laðo, a] *adj* (*despierto*) wide-awake; (*fig*) alert, sharp.

despabilar [despaßi'lar] *vt* (*despertar*) to wake up; (*fig: persona*) to liven up; (*trabajo*) to get through quickly ♦ *vi*, **~se** *vr* to wake up; (*fig*) to get a move on.

despachar [despa'tʃar] *vt* (*negocio*) to do, complete; (*resolver: problema*) to settle; (*correspondencia*) to deal with; (*fam:*

comida) to polish off; (: *bebida*) to knock back; (*enviar*) to send, dispatch; (*vender*) to sell, deal in; (*COM: cliente*) to attend to; (*billete*) to issue; (*mandar ir*) to send away ♦ *vi* (*decidirse*) to get things settled; (*apresurarse*) to hurry up; ~**se** *vr* to finish off; (*apresurarse*) to hurry up; ~**se de algo** to get rid of sth; ~**se a su gusto con algn** to give sb a piece of one's mind; **¿quién despacha?** is anybody serving?

despacho [des'patʃo] *nm* (*oficina*) office; (: *en una casa*) study; (*de paquetes*) dispatch; (*COM: venta*) sale (of goods); (*comunicación*) message; ~ **de billetes** *o* **boletos** (*AM*) booking office; ~ **de localidades** box office; **géneros sin** ~ unsaleable goods; **tener buen** ~ to find a ready sale.

despachurrar [despatʃu'rrar] *vt* (*aplastar*) to crush; (*persona*) to flatten.

despacio [des'paθjo] *adv* (*lentamente*) slowly; (*esp AM: en voz baja*) softly; ¡~! take it easy!

despacito [despa'θito] *adv* (*fam*) slowly; (*suavemente*) softly.

despampanante [despampa'nante] *adj* (*fam: chica*) stunning.

desparejado, a [despare'xaðo, a] *adj* odd.

desparpajo [despar'paxo] *nm* (*desenvoltura*) self-confidence; (*pey*) nerve.

desparramar [desparra'mar] *vt* (*esparcir*) to scatter; (*líquido*) to spill.

despatarrarse [despata'rrarse] *vr* (*abrir las piernas*) to open one's legs wide; (*caerse*) to tumble; (*fig*) to be flabbergasted.

despavorido, a [despaβo'riðo, a] *adj* terrified.

despecho [des'petʃo] *nm* spite; **a** ~ **de** in spite of; **por** ~ out of (sheer) spite.

despectivo, a [despek'tiβo, a] *adj* (*despreciativo*) derogatory; (*LING*) pejorative.

despedace [despe'ðaθe] *etc vb V* **despedazar**.

despedazar [despeða'θar] *vt* to tear to pieces.

despedida [despe'ðiða] *nf* (*adiós*) goodbye, farewell; (*antes de viaje*) send-off; (*en carta*) closing formula; (*de obrero*) sacking; (*INFORM*) logout; **cena/función de** ~ farewell dinner/performance; **regalo de** ~ parting gift; ~ **de soltero/ soltera** stag/hen party.

despedir [despe'ðir] *vt* (*visita*) to see off, show out; (*empleado*) to dismiss; (*inquilino*) to evict; (*objeto*) to hurl; (*olor etc*) to give out *o* off; ~**se** *vr* (*dejar un*

empleo) to give up one's job; (*INFORM*) to log out *o* off; ~**se de** to say goodbye to; **se despidieron** they said goodbye to each other.

despegado, a [despe'ɣaðo, a] *adj* (*separado*) detached; (*persona: poco afectuoso*) cold, indifferent ♦ *nm/f*: **es un** ~ he has cut himself off from his family.

despegar [despe'ɣar] *vt* to unstick; (*sobre*) to open ♦ *vi* (*avión*) to take off; (*cohete*) to blast off; ~**se** *vr* to come loose, come unstuck; **sin** ~ **los labios** without uttering a word.

despego [des'peɣo] *nm* detachment.

despegue [des'peɣe] *etc vb V* **despegar** ♦ *nm* takeoff; (*de cohete*) blastoff.

despeinado, a [despei'naðo, a] *adj* dishevelled, unkempt.

despeinar [despei'nar] *vt* (*pelo*) to ruffle; **¡me has despeinado todo!** you've completely ruined my hairdo!

despejado, a [despe'xaðo, a] *adj* (*lugar*) clear, free; (*cielo*) clear; (*persona*) wide-awake, bright.

despejar [despe'xar] *vt* (*gen*) to clear; (*misterio*) to clarify, clear up; (*MAT: incógnita*) to find ♦ *vi* (*el tiempo*) to clear; ~**se** *vr* (*tiempo, cielo*) to clear (up); (*misterio*) to become clearer; (*cabeza*) to clear; **¡despejen!** (*moverse*) move along!; (*salirse*) everybody out!

despeje [des'pexe] *nm* (*DEPORTE*) clearance.

despellejar [despeʎe'xar] *vt* (*animal*) to skin; (*criticar*) to criticize unmercifully; (*fam: arruinar*) to fleece.

despelotarse [despelo'tarse] *vr* (*fam*) to strip off; (*fig*) to let one's hair down.

despelote [despe'lote] (*fam*) *nm* (*AM: lío*) mess; **¡qué** *o* **vaya** ~! what a riot *o* laugh!

despenalizar [despenali'θar] *vt* to decriminalize.

despensa [des'pensa] *nf* (*armario*) larder; (*NAUT*) storeroom; (*provisión de comestibles*) stock of food.

despeñadero [despeɲa'ðero] *nm* (*GEO*) cliff, precipice.

despeñar [despe'ɲar] *vt* (*arrojar*) to fling down; ~**se** *vr* to fling o.s. down; (*caer*) to fall headlong.

desperdiciar [desperði'θjar] *vt* (*comida, tiempo*) to waste; (*oportunidad*) to throw away.

desperdicio [desper'ðiθjo] *nm* (*despilfarro*) squandering; (*residuo*) waste; ~**s** *nmpl* (*basura*) rubbish *sg*, refuse *sg*, garbage *sg*

(*US*); (*residuos*) waste *sg*; ~**s de cocina** kitchen scraps; **el libro no tiene** ~ the book is excellent from beginning to end.
desperdigar [desperði'ɣar] *vt* (*esparcir*) to scatter; (*energía*) to dissipate; ~**se** *vr* to scatter.
desperdigue [desper'ðiɣe] *etc vb V* **desperdigar.**
desperece [despe're0e] *etc vb V* **desperezarse.**
desperezarse [despere'0arse] *vr* to stretch.
desperfecto [desper'fekto] *nm* (*deterioro*) slight damage; (*defecto*) flaw, imperfection.
despertador [desperta'ðor] *nm* alarm clock; ~ **de viaje** travelling clock.
despertar [desper'tar] *vt* (*persona*) to wake up; (*recuerdos*) to revive; (*esperanzas*) to raise; (*sentimiento*) to arouse ♦ *vi*, ~**se** *vr* to awaken, wake up ♦ *nm* awakening; ~**se a la realidad** to wake up to reality.
despiadado a [despja'ðaðo, a] *adj* (*ataque*) merciless; (*persona*) heartless.
despido [des'piðo] *etc vb V* **despedir** ♦ *nm* dismissal, sacking; ~ **improcedente** *o* **injustificado** wrongful dismissal; ~ **injusto** unfair dismissal; ~ **libre** right to hire and fire; ~ **voluntario** voluntary redundancy.
despierto, a [des'pjerto, a] *etc vb V* **despertar** ♦ *adj* awake; (*fig*) sharp, alert.
despilfarrar [despilfa'rrar] *vt* (*gen*) to waste; (*dinero*) to squander.
despilfarro [despil'farro] *nm* (*derroche*) squandering; (*lujo desmedido*) extravagance.
despintar [despin'tar] *vt* (*quitar pintura a*) to take the paint off; (*hechos*) to distort ♦ *vi*: **A no despinta a B** A is in no way inferior to B; ~**se** *vr* (*desteñir*) to fade.
despiojar [despjo'xar] *vt* to delouse.
despistado, a [despis'taðo, a] *adj* (*distraído*) vague, absent-minded; (*poco práctico*) unpractical; (*confuso*) confused; (*desorientado*) off the track ♦ *nm/f* (*tipo: distraído*) scatterbrain, absent-minded person.
despistar [despis'tar] *vt* to throw off the track *o* scent; (*fig*) to mislead, confuse; ~**se** *vr* to take the wrong road; (*fig*) to become confused.
despiste [des'piste] *nm* (*AUTO etc*) swerve; (*error*) slip; (*distracción*) absent-mindedness; **tiene un terrible** ~ he's terribly absent-minded.
desplace [des'pla0e] *etc vb V* **desplazar.**
desplante [des'plante] *nm*: **hacer un** ~ a **algn** to be rude to sb.

desplazado, a [despla'0aðo, a] *adj* (*pieza*) wrongly placed ♦ *nm/f* (*inadaptado*) misfit; **sentirse un poco** ~ to feel rather out of place.
desplazamiento [despla0a'mjento] *nm* displacement; (*viaje*) journey; (*de opinión, votos*) shift, swing; (*INFORM*) scrolling; ~ **hacia arriba/abajo** (*INFORM*) scroll up/down.
desplazar [despla'0ar] *vt* (*gen*) to move; (*FÍSICA, NAUT, TEC*) to displace; (*tropas*) to transfer; (*suplantar*) to take the place of; (*INFORM*) to scroll; ~**se** *vr* (*persona, vehículo*) to travel, go; (*objeto*) to move, shift; (*votos, opinión*) to shift, swing.
desplegar [desple'ɣar] *vt* (*tela, papel*) to unfold, open out; (*bandera*) to unfurl; (*alas*) to spread; (*MIL*) to deploy; (*manifestar*) to display.
desplegué [desple'ɣe], **despleguemos** [desple'ɣemos] *etc vb V* **desplegar.**
despliegue [des'pljeɣe] *etc vb V* **desplegar** ♦ *nm* unfolding, opening; deployment, display.
desplomarse [desplo'marse] *vr* (*edificio, gobierno, persona*) to collapse; (*derrumbarse*) to topple over; (*precios*) to slump; **se ha desplomado el techo** the ceiling has fallen in.
desplumar [desplu'mar] *vt* (*ave*) to pluck; (*fam: estafar*) to fleece.
despoblado, a [despo'ßlaðo, a] *adj* (*sin habitantes*) uninhabited; (*con pocos habitantes*) depopulated; (*con insuficientes habitantes*) underpopulated ♦ *nm* deserted spot.
despojar [despo'xar] *vt* (*alguien: de sus bienes*) to divest of, deprive of; (*casa*) to strip, leave bare; (*de su cargo*) to strip of; ~**se** *vr* (*desnudarse*) to undress; ~**se de** (*ropa, hojas*) to shed; (*poderes*) to relinquish.
despojo [des'poxo] *nm* (*acto*) plundering; (*objetos*) plunder, loot; ~**s** *nmpl* (*de ave, res*) offal *sg*.
desposado, a [despo'saðo, a] *adj, nm/f* newly-wed.
desposar [despo'sar] *vt* (*suj: sacerdote: pareja*) to marry; ~**se** *vr* (*casarse*) to marry, get married.
desposeer [despose'er] *vt* (*despojar*) to dispossess; ~ **a algn de su autoridad** to strip sb of his authority.
desposeído, a [despose'iðo, a] *nm/f*: **los** ~**s** the have-nots.
desposeyendo [despose'jendo] *etc vb V* **desposeer.**
desposorios [despo'sorjos] *nmpl*

(*esponsales*) betrothal *sg*; (*boda*) marriage ceremony *sg*.

déspota ['despota] *nm/f* despot.

despotismo [despo'tismo] *nm* despotism.

despotricar [despotri'kar] *vi*: ~ **contra** to moan *o* complain about.

despotrique [despo'trike] *etc vb V* **despotricar**.

despreciable [despre'θjaßle] *adj* (*moralmente*) despicable; (*objeto*) worthless; (*cantidad*) negligible.

despreciar [despre'θjar] *vt* (*desdeñar*) to despise, scorn; (*afrentar*) to slight.

despreciativo, a [despreθja'tißo, a] *adj* (*observación, tono*) scornful, contemptuous; (*comentario*) derogatory.

desprecio [des'preθjo] *nm* scorn, contempt; slight.

desprender [despren'der] *vt* (*soltar*) to loosen; (*separar*) to separate; (*desatar*) to unfasten; (*olor*) to give off; ~**se** *vr* (*botón: caerse*) to fall off; (: *abrirse*) to unfasten; (*olor, perfume*) to be given off; ~**se de** to follow from; ~**se de algo** (*ceder*) to give sth up; (*desembarazarse*) to get rid of sth; **se desprende que** it transpires that.

desprendido, a [despren'dido, a] *adj* (*pieza*) loose; (*sin abrochar*) unfastened; (*desinteresado*) disinterested; (*generoso*) generous.

desprendimiento [desprendi'mjento] *nm* (*gen*) loosening; (*generosidad*) disinterestedness; (*indiferencia*) detachment; (*de gas*) leak; (*de tierra, rocas*) landslide.

despreocupado, a [despreoku'paðo, a] *adj* (*sin preocupación*) unworried, unconcerned; (*tranquilo*) nonchalant; (*en el vestir*) casual; (*negligente*) careless.

despreocuparse [despreoku'parse] *vr* to be carefree; (*dejar de inquietarse*) to stop worrying; (*ser indiferente*) to be unconcerned; ~ **de** to have no interest in.

desprestigiar [despresti'xjar] *vt* (*criticar*) to run down, disparage; (*desacreditar*) to discredit.

desprestigio [despres'tixjo] *nm* (*denigración*) disparagement; (*impopularidad*) unpopularity.

desprevenido, a [despreße'niðo, a] *adj* (*no preparado*) unprepared, unready; **coger** (*ESP*) *o* **agarrar** (*AM*) **a algn** ~ to catch sb unawares.

desproporción [despropor'θjon] *nf* disproportion, lack of proportion.

desproporcionado, a [desproporθjo'naðo, a] *adj* disproportionate, out of proportion.

despropósito [despro'posito] *nm* (*salida de tono*) irrelevant remark; (*disparate*) piece of nonsense.

desprovisto, a [despro'ßisto, a] *adj*: ~ **de** devoid of; **estar** ~ **de** to lack.

después [des'pwes] *adv* afterwards, later; (*desde entonces*) since (then); (*próximo paso*) next; **poco** ~ soon after; **un año** ~ a year later; ~ **se debatió el tema** next the matter was discussed ♦ *prep*: ~ **de** (*tiempo*) after, since; (*orden*) next (to); ~ **de comer** after lunch; ~ **de corregido el texto** after the text had been corrected; ~ **de esa fecha** (*pasado*) since that date; (*futuro*) from *o* after that date; ~ **de todo** after all; ~ **de verlo** after seeing it, after I *etc* saw it; **mi nombre está** ~ **del tuyo** my name comes next to yours ♦ *conj*: ~ **(de) que** after; ~ **(de) que lo escribí** after *o* since I wrote it, after writing it.

despuntar [despun'tar] *vt* (*lápiz*) to blunt ♦ *vi* (*BOT: plantas*) to sprout; (: *flores*) to bud; (*alba*) to break; (*día*) to dawn; (*persona: descollar*) to stand out.

desquiciar [deski'θjar] *vt* (*puerta*) to take off its hinges; (*descomponer*) to upset; (*persona: turbar*) to disturb; (: *volver loco a*) to unhinge.

desquitarse [deski'tarse] *vr* to obtain satisfaction; (*COM*) to recover a debt; (*fig: vengarse de*) to get one's own back; ~ **de una pérdida** to make up for a loss.

desquite [des'kite] *nm* (*satisfacción*) satisfaction; (*venganza*) revenge.

Dest. *abr* = **destinatario**.

destacado, a [desta'kaðo, a] *adj* outstanding.

destacamento [destaka'mento] *nm* (*MIL*) detachment.

destacar [desta'kar] *vt* (*ARTE: hacer resaltar*) to make stand out; (*subrayar*) to emphasize, point up; (*MIL*) to detach, detail; (*INFORM*) to highlight ♦ *vi*, ~**se** *vr* (*resaltarse*) to stand out; (*persona*) to be outstanding *o* exceptional; **quiero** ~ **que...** I wish to emphasize that...; ~**(se) contra** *o* **en** *o* **sobre** to stand out *o* be outlined against.

destajo [des'taxo] *nm*: **a** ~ (*por pieza*) by the job; (*con afán*) eagerly; **trabajar a** ~ to do piecework; (*fig*) to work one's fingers to the bone.

destapar [desta'par] *vt* (*botella*) to open; (*cacerola*) to take the lid off; (*descubrir*) to uncover; ~**se** *vr* (*descubrirse*) to get uncovered; (*revelarse*) to reveal one's true character.

destape [des'tape] *nm* nudity; (*fig*) permissiveness; **el ~ español** *the process of liberalization in Spain after Franco's death.*

destaque [des'take] *etc vb V* **destacar.**

destartalado, a [destarta'laðo, a] *adj* (*desordenado*) untidy; (*casa etc*: *grande*) rambling; (: *ruinoso*) tumbledown.

destellar [deste'ʎar] *vi* (*diamante*) to sparkle; (*metal*) to glint; (*estrella*) to twinkle.

destello [des'teʎo] *nm* (*de diamante*) sparkle; (*de metal*) glint; (*de estrella*) twinkle; (*de faro*) signal light; **no tiene un ~ de verdad** there's not a grain of truth in it.

destemplado, a [destem'plaðo, a] *adj* (*MUS*) out of tune; (*voz*) harsh; (*MED*) out of sorts; (*METEOROLOGÍA*) unpleasant, nasty.

destemplar [destem'plar] *vt* (*MUS*) to put out of tune; (*alterar*) to upset; **~se** *vr* (*MUS*) to lose its pitch; (*descomponerse*) to get out of order; (*persona: irritarse*) to get upset; (*MED*) to get out of sorts.

desteñir [deste'ɲir] *vt* to fade ♦ *vi*, **~se** *vr* to fade; **esta tela no destiñe** this fabric will not run.

desternillarse [desterni'ʎarse] *vr*: **~ de risa** to split one's sides laughing.

desterrado, a [deste'rraðo, a] *nm/f* (*exiliado*) exile.

desterrar [deste'rrar] *vt* (*exilar*) to exile; (*fig*) to banish, dismiss.

destetar [deste'tar] *vt* to wean.

destiempo [des'tjempo]: **a ~** *adv* at the wrong time.

destierro [des'tjerro] *etc vb V* **desterrar** ♦ *nm* exile; **vivir en el ~** to live in exile.

destilar [desti'lar] *vt* to distil; (*pus, sangre*) to ooze; (*fig: rebosar*) to exude; (: *revelar*) to reveal ♦ *vi* (*gotear*) to drip.

destilería [destile'ria] *nf* distillery; **~ de petróleo** oil refinery.

destinar [desti'nar] *vt* (*funcionario*) to appoint, assign; (*fondos*) to set aside; **es un libro destinado a los niños** it is a book (intended *o* meant) for children; **una carta que viene destinada a usted** a letter for you, a letter addressed to you.

destinatario, a [destina'tarjo, a] *nm/f* addressee; (*COM*) payee.

destino [des'tino] *nm* (*suerte*) destiny; (*de viajero*) destination; (*función*) use; (*puesto*) post, placement; **~ público** public appointment; **salir con ~ a** to leave for; **con ~ a Londres** (*avión, barco*) (bound) for London; (*carta*) to London.

destiña [des'tiɲa] *etc*, **destiñendo** [desti'ɲendo] *etc vb V* **desteñir.**

destitución [destitu'θjon] *nf* dismissal, removal.

destituir [destitu'ir] *vt* (*despedir*) to dismiss; (: *ministro, funcionario*) to remove from office.

destituyendo [destitu'jendo] *etc vb V* **destituir.**

destornillador [destorniʎa'ðor] *nm* screwdriver.

destornillar [destorni'ʎar] *vt*, **~se** *vr* (*tornillo*) to unscrew.

destreza [des'treθa] *nf* (*habilidad*) skill; (*maña*) dexterity.

destripar [destri'par] *vt* (*animal*) to gut; (*reventar*) to mangle.

destroce [de'stroθe] *etc vb V* **destrozar.**

destronar [destro'nar] *vt* (*rey*) to dethrone; (*fig*) to overthrow.

destroncar [destron'kar] *vt* (*árbol*) to chop off, lop; (*proyectos*) to ruin; (*discurso*) to interrupt.

destronque [des'tronke] *etc vb V* **destroncar.**

destrozar [destro'θar] *vt* (*romper*) to smash, break (up); (*estropear*) to ruin; (*nervios*) to shatter; **~ a algn en una discusión** to crush sb in an argument.

destrozo [des'troθo] *nm* (*acción*) destruction; (*desastre*) smashing; **~s** *nmpl* (*pedazos*) pieces; (*daños*) havoc *sg*.

destrucción [destruk'θjon] *nf* destruction.

destructor, a [destruk'tor, a] *adj* destructive ♦ *nm* (*NAUT*) destroyer.

destruir [destru'ir] *vt* to destroy; (*casa*) to demolish; (*equilibrio*) to upset; (*proyecto*) to spoil; (*esperanzas*) to dash; (*argumento*) to demolish.

destruyendo [destru'jendo] *etc vb V* **destruir.**

desuelle [de'sweʎe] *etc vb V* **desollar.**

desueve [de'sweβe] *etc vb V* **desovar.**

desunión [desu'njon] *nf* (*separación*) separation; (*discordia*) disunity.

desunir [desu'nir] *vt* to separate; (*TEC*) to disconnect; (*fig*) to cause a quarrel *o* rift between.

desuso [de'suso] *nm* disuse; **caer en ~** to fall into disuse, become obsolete; **una expresión caída en ~** an obsolete expression.

desvaído, a [desβa'iðo, a] *adj* (*color*) pale; (*contorno*) blurred.

desvalido, a [desβa'liðo, a] *adj* (*desprotegido*) destitute; (*sin fuerzas*) helpless; **niños ~s** waifs and strays.

desvalijar [desβali'xar] *vt* (*persona*) to rob;

(*casa, tienda*) to burgle; (*coche*) to break into.

desvalorice [desßalo'riθe] *etc vb V* **desvalorizar**.

desvalorizar [desßalori'θar] *vt* to devalue.

desván [des'ßan] *nm* attic.

desvanecer [desßane'θer] *vt* (*disipar*) to dispel; (*recuerdo, temor*) to banish; (*borrar*) to blur; ~**se** *vr* (*humo etc*) to vanish, disappear; (*duda*) to be dispelled; (*color*) to fade; (*recuerdo, sonido*) to fade away; (*MED*) to pass out.

desvanecido, a [desßane'θiðo, a] *adj* (*MED*) faint; **caer** ~ to fall in a faint.

desvanecimiento [desßaneθi'mjento] *nm* (*desaparición*) disappearance; (*de dudas*) dispelling; (*de colores*) fading; (*evaporación*) evaporation; (*MED*) fainting fit.

desvanezca [desßa'neθka] *etc vb V* **desvanecer**.

desvariar [desßa'rjar] *vi* (*enfermo*) to be delirious; (*delirar*) to talk nonsense.

desvarío [desßa'rio] *nm* delirium; (*desatino*) absurdity; ~**s** *nmpl* ravings.

desvelar [desße'lar] *vt* to keep awake; ~**se** *vr* (*no poder dormir*) to stay awake; (*vigilar*) to be vigilant *o* watchful; ~**se por algo** (*inquietarse*) to be anxious about sth; (*poner gran cuidado*) to take great care over sth.

desvelo [des'ßelo] *nm* lack of sleep; (*insomnio*) sleeplessness; (*fig*) vigilance; ~**s** *nmpl* (*preocupación*) anxiety *sg*, effort *sg*.

desvencijado, a [desßenθi'xaðo, a] *adj* (*silla*) rickety; (*máquina*) broken-down.

desvencijar [desßenθi'xar] *vt* (*romper*) to break; (*soltar*) to loosen; (*persona: agotar*) to exhaust; ~**se** *vr* to come apart.

desventaja [desßen'taxa] *nf* disadvantage; (*inconveniente*) drawback.

desventajoso, a [desßenta'xoso, a] *adj* disadvantageous, unfavourable.

desventura [desßen'tura] *nf* misfortune.

desventurado, a [desßentu'raðo, a] *adj* (*desgraciado*) unfortunate; (*de poca suerte*) ill-fated.

desvergonzado, a [desßerɣon'θaðo, a] *adj* (*sin vergüenza*) shameless; (*descarado*) insolent ♦ *nm/f* shameless person.

desvergüenza [desßer'ɣwenθa] *nf* (*descaro*) shamelessness; (*insolencia*) impudence; (*mala conducta*) effrontery; **esto es una** ~ this is disgraceful; **¡qué** ~! what a nerve!

desvestir [desßes'tir] *vt*, **desvestirse** *vr* to undress.

desviación [desßja'θjon] *nf* deviation; (*AUTO: rodeo*) diversion, detour; (: *carretera de circunvalación*) ring road (*BRIT*), circular route (*US*); ~ **de la circulación** traffic diversion; **es una** ~ **de sus principios** it is a departure from his usual principles.

desviar [des'ßjar] *vt* to turn aside; (*balón, flecha, golpe*) to deflect; (*pregunta*) to parry; (*ojos*) to avert, turn away; (*río*) to alter the course of; (*navío*) to divert, re-route; (*conversación*) to sidetrack; ~**se** *vr* (*apartarse del camino*) to turn aside; (: *barco*) to go off course; (*AUTO: dar un rodeo*) to make a detour; ~**se de un tema** to get away from the point.

desvincular [desßinku'lar] *vt* to free, release; ~**se** *vr* (*aislarse*) to be cut off; (*alejarse*) to cut o.s. off.

desvío [des'ßio] *etc vb V* **desviar** ♦ *nm* (*desviación*) detour, diversion; (*fig*) indifference.

desvirgar [desßir'ɣar] *vt* to deflower.

desvirtuar [desßir'twar] *vt* (*estropear*) to spoil; (*argumento, razonamiento*) to detract from; (*efecto*) to counteract; (*sentido*) to distort; ~**se** *vr* to spoil.

desvistiendo [desßis'tjendo] *etc vb V* **desvestir**.

desvitalizar [desßitali'θar] *vt* (*nervio*) to numb.

desvivirse [desßi'ßirse] *vr*: ~ **por** to long for, crave for; ~ **por los amigos** to do anything for one's friends.

detalladamente [detaʎaða'mente] *adv* (*con detalles*) in detail; (*extensamente*) at great length.

detallar [deta'ʎar] *vt* to detail; (*asunto por asunto*) to itemize.

detalle [de'taʎe] *nm* detail; (*fig*) gesture, token; **al** ~ in detail; (*COM*) retail *cpd*; **comercio al** ~ retail trade; **vender al** ~ to sell retail; **no pierde** ~ he doesn't miss a trick; **me observaba sin perder** ~ he watched my every move; **tiene muchos** ~**s** she is very considerate.

detallista [deta'ʎista] *nm/f* retailer ♦ *adj* (*meticuloso*) meticulous; **comercio** ~ retail trade.

detectar [detek'tar] *vt* to detect.

detective [detek'tiße] *nm/f* detective; ~ **privado** private detective.

detector [detek'tor] *nm* (*NAUT, TEC etc*) detector; ~ **de mentiras/de minas** lie/mine detector.

detención [deten'θjon] *nf* (*acción*) stopping; (*estancamiento*) stoppage; (*retraso*) holdup, delay; (*JUR: arresto*)

arrest; (*cuidado*) care; ~ **de juego**
(*DEPORTE*) stoppage of play; ~ **ilegal**
unlawful detention.
detendré [deten'dre] *etc vb V* **detener**.
detener [dete'ner] *vt* (*gen*) to stop; (*JUR*:
arrestar) to arrest; (: *encarcelar*) to detain;
(*objeto*) to keep; (*retrasar*) to hold up,
delay; (*aliento*) to hold; ~**se** *vr* to stop;
~**se en** (*demorarse*) to delay over, linger
over.
detenga [de'tenga] *etc vb V* **detener**.
detenidamente [deteniða'mente] *adv*
(*minuciosamente*) carefully;
(*extensamente*) at great length.
detenido, a [dete'niðo, a] *adj* (*arrestado*)
under arrest; (*minucioso*) detailed;
(*examen*) thorough; (*tímido*) timid ♦ *nm/f*
person under arrest, prisoner.
detenimiento [deteni'mjento] *nm* care;
con ~ thoroughly.
detentar [deten'tar] *vt* to hold; (*sin derecho*:
título) to hold unlawfully; (: *puesto*) to
occupy unlawfully.
detergente [deter'xente] *adj, nm*
detergent.
deteriorado, a [deterjo'raðo, a] *adj*
(*estropeado*) damaged; (*desgastado*)
worn.
deteriorar [deterjo'rar] *vt* to spoil,
damage; ~**se** *vr* to deteriorate.
deterioro [dete'rjoro] *nm* deterioration.
determinación [determina'θjon] *nf*
(*empeño*) determination; (*decisión*)
decision; (*de fecha, precio*) settling,
fixing.
determinado, a [determi'naðo, a] *adj*
(*preciso*) fixed, set; (*LING*: *artículo*)
definite; (*persona*: *resuelto*) determined;
un día ~ on a certain day; **no hay ningún
tema** ~ there is no particular theme.
determinar [determi'nar] *vt* (*plazo*) to fix;
(*precio*) to settle; (*daños, impuestos*) to
assess; (*pleito*) to decide; (*causar*) to
cause; ~**se** *vr* to decide; **el reglamento
determina que** ... the rule lays it down *o*
states that ...; **aquello determinó la caída
del gobierno** that brought about the fall
of the government; **esto le determinó**
this decided him.
detestable [detes'taßle] *adj* (*persona*)
hateful; (*acto*) detestable.
detestar [detes'tar] *vt* to detest.
detonación [detona'θjon] *nf* detonation;
(*sonido*) explosion.
detonante [deto'nante] *nm* (*fig*) trigger.
detonar [deto'nar] *vi* to detonate.
detractor, a [detrak'tor, a] *adj* disparaging
♦ *nm/f* detractor.

detrás [de'tras] *adv* behind; (*atrás*) at the
back ♦ *prep*: ~ **de** behind; **por** ~ **de algn**
(*fig*) behind sb's back; **salir de** ~ to come
out from behind; **por** ~ behind.
detrasito [detra'sito] *adv* (*AM fam*)
behind.
detrimento [detri'mento] *nm*: **en** ~ **de** to
the detriment of.
detuve [de'tuße] *etc vb V* **detener**.
deuda [de'uða] *nf* (*condición*) indebtedness,
debt; (*cantidad*) debt; ~ **a largo plazo**
long-term debt; ~ **exterior/pública**
foreign/national debt; ~ **incobrable** *o*
morosa bad debt; ~**s activas/pasivas**
assets/liabilities; **contraer** ~**s** to get
into debt.
deudor, a [deu'ðor, a] *nm/f* debtor; ~
hipotecario mortgager; ~ **moroso** slow
payer.
devaluación [deßalwa'θjon] *nf*
devaluation.
devaluar [deßalu'ar] *vt* to devalue.
devanar [deßa'nar] *vt* (*hilo*) to wind; ~**se** *vr*:
~**se los sesos** to rack one's brains.
devaneo [deßa'neo] *nm* (*MED*) delirium;
(*desatino*) nonsense; (*fruslería*) idle
pursuit; (*amorío*) flirtation.
devastar [deßas'tar] *vt* (*destruir*) to
devastate.
devendré [deßen'dre] *etc*, **devenga**
[de'ßenga] *etc vb V* **devenir**.
devengar [deßen'gar] *vt* (*salario*: *ganar*) to
earn; (: *tener que cobrar*) to be due;
(*intereses*) to bring in, accrue, earn.
devengue [de'ßenge] *etc vb V* **devengar**.
devenir [deße'nir] *vi*: ~ **en** to become, turn
into ♦ *nm* (*movimiento progresivo*) process
of development; (*transformación*)
transformation.
deviene [de'ßjene] *etc*, **deviniendo**
[deßi'njendo] *etc vb V* **devenir**.
devoción [deßo'θjon] *nf* devotion; (*afición*)
strong attachment.
devolución [deßolu'θjon] *nf* (*reenvío*)
return, sending back; (*reembolso*)
repayment; (*JUR*) devolution.
devolver [deßol'ßer] *vt* (*lo extraviado,
prestado*) to give back; (*a su sitio*) to put
back; (*carta al correo*) to send back;
(*COM*) to repay, refund; (*visita, la palabra*)
to return; (*salud, vista*) to restore; (*fam*:
vomitar) to throw up ♦ *vi* (*fam*) to be sick;
~**se** *vr* (*AM*) to return; ~ **mal por bien** to
return ill for good; ~ **la pelota a algn** to
give sb tit for tat.
devorar [deßo'rar] *vt* to devour; (*comer
ávidamente*) to gobble up; (*fig: fortuna*) to
run through; **todo lo devoró el fuego** the

fire consumed everything; **le devoran los celos** he is consumed with jealousy.
devoto, a [de'ßoto, a] *adj* (*REL: persona*) devout; (: *obra*) devotional; (*amigo*): ~ **(de algn)** devoted (to sb) ♦ *nm/f* admirer; **los ~s** (*REL*) the faithful; **su muy** ~ your devoted servant.
devuelto [de'ßwelto], **devuelva** [de'ßwelßa] *etc vb V* **devolver.**
D.F. *abr* (*México*) = *Distrito Federal.*
dg. *abr* (= *decigramo*) dg.
D.G. *abr* = *Dirección General*; (= *Director General*) D.G.
DGT *nf abr* = *Dirección General de Tráfico*; = *Dirección General de Turismo.*
di [di] *vb V* **dar; decir.**
día [dia] *nm* day; ~ **de asueto** day off; ~ **feriado** (*AM*) o **festivo** (public) holiday; ~ **hábil/inhábil** working/non-working day; ~ **domingo,** ~ **lunes** (*AM*) Sunday, Monday; ~ **lectivo** teaching day; ~ **libre** day off; **D~ de Reyes** Epiphany (*6 January*); **¿qué** ~ **es?** what's the date?; **estar/poner al** ~ to be/keep up to date; **el** ~ **de hoy/de mañana** today/tomorrow; **el** ~ **menos pensado** when you least expect it; **al** ~ **siguiente** on the following day; **todos los ~s** every day; **un** ~ **sí y otro no** every other day; **vivir al** ~ to live from hand to mouth; **de** ~ during the day, by day; **es de** ~ it's daylight; **del** ~ (*estilos*) fashionable; (*menú*) today's; **de un** ~ **para otro** any day now; **en pleno** ~ in full daylight; **en su** ~ in due time; **¡hasta otro ~!** so long!
diabetes [dia'betes] *nf* diabetes *sg.*
diabético, a [dia'betiko, a] *adj, nm/f* diabetic.
diablo ['djaßlo] *nm* (*tb fig*) devil; **pobre** ~ poor devil; **hace un frío de todos los ~s** it's hellishly cold.
diablura [dia'ßlura] *nf* prank; (*travesura*) mischief.
diabólico, a [dia'ßoliko, a] *adj* diabolical.
diadema [dia'ðema] *nf* (*para el pelo*) Alice band, headband; (*joya*) tiara.
diáfano, a ['djafano, a] *adj* (*tela*) diaphanous; (*agua*) crystal-clear.
diafragma [dia'fraɣma] *nm* diaphragm.
diagnosis [djaɣ'nosis] *nf inv*, **diagnóstico** [diaɣ'nostiko] *nm* diagnosis.
diagnosticar [djaɣnosti'kar] *vt* to diagnose.
diagonal [djaɣo'nal] *adj* diagonal ♦ *nf* (*GEOM*) diagonal; **en** ~ diagonally.
diagrama [dia'ɣrama] *nm* diagram; ~ **de barras** (*COM*) bar chart; ~ **de dispersión** (*COM*) scatter diagram; ~ **de flujo**

(*INFORM*) flowchart.
dial [di'al] *nm* dial.
dialecto [dja'lekto] *nm* dialect.
dialogar [djalo'ɣar] *vt* to write in dialogue form ♦ *vi* (*conversar*) to have a conversation; ~ **con** (*POL*) to hold talks with.
diálogo ['djaloɣo] *nm* dialogue.
dialogue [dja'loɣe] *etc vb V* **dialogar.**
diamante [dja'mante] *nm* diamond.
diametralmente [djametral'mente] *adv* diametrically; ~ **opuesto a** diametrically opposed to.
diámetro [di'ametro] *nm* diameter; ~ **de giro** (*AUTO*) turning circle; **faros de gran** ~ wide-angle headlights.
diana ['djana] *nf* (*MIL*) reveille; (*de blanco*) centre, bull's-eye.
diantre ['djantre] *nm*: **¡~!** (*fam*) oh hell!
diapasón [djapa'son] *nm* (*instrumento*) tuning fork; (*de violín etc*) fingerboard; (*de voz*) tone.
diapositiva [djaposi'tißa] *nf* (*FOTO*) slide, transparency.
diario, a ['djarjo, a] *adj* daily ♦ *nm* newspaper; (*libro diario*) diary; (: *COM*) daybook; (*COM: gastos*) daily expenses; ~ **de navegación** (*NAUT*) logbook; ~ **hablado** (*RADIO*) news (bulletin); ~ **de sesiones** parliamentary report; **a** ~ daily; **de** o **para** ~ everyday.
diarrea [dja'rrea] *nf* diarrhoea.
diatriba [dja'trißa] *nf* diatribe, tirade.
dibujante [dißu'xante] *nm/f* (*de bosquejos*) sketcher; (*de dibujos animados*) cartoonist; (*de moda*) designer; ~ **de publicidad** commercial artist.
dibujar [dißu'xar] *vt* to draw, sketch; ~**se** *vr* (*emoción*) to show; ~**se contra** to be outlined against.
dibujo [di'ßuxo] *nm* drawing; (*TEC*) design; (*en papel, tela*) pattern; (*en periódico*) cartoon; (*fig*) description; ~**s animados** cartoons; ~ **del natural** drawing from life.
dic., dic.e *abr* (= *diciembre*) Dec.
diccionario [dikθjo'narjo] *nm* dictionary.
dicharachero, a [ditʃara'tʃero, a] *adj* talkative ♦ *nm/f* (*ingenioso*) wit; (*parlanchín*) chatterbox.
dicho, a ['ditʃo, a] *pp de* **decir** ♦ *adj* (*susodicho*) aforementioned ♦ *nm* saying; (*proverbio*) proverb; (*ocurrencia*) bright remark ♦ *nf* (*buena suerte*) good luck; **mejor** ~ rather; ~ **y hecho** no sooner said than done.
dichoso, a [di'tʃoso, a] *adj* (*feliz*) happy; (*afortunado*) lucky; **¡aquel** ~ **coche!** (*fam*)

that blessed car!
diciembre [di'θjembre] *nm* December.
diciendo [di'θjendo] *etc vb V* **decir.**
dictado [dik'taðo] *nm* dictation; **escribir al
~** to take dictation; **los ~s de la
conciencia** (*fig*) the dictates of
conscience.
dictador [dikta'ðor] *nm* dictator.
dictadura [dikta'ðura] *nf* dictatorship.
dictáfono ® [dik'tafono] *nm* Dictaphone ®.
dictamen [dik'tamen] *nm* (*opinión*) opinion;
(*informe*) report; **~ contable** auditor's
report; **~ facultativo** (*MED*) medical
report.
dictar [dik'tar] *vt* (*carta*) to dictate; (*JUR:
sentencia*) to pass; (*decreto*) to issue; (*AM:
clase*) to give; (: *conferencia*) to deliver.
didáctico, a [di'ðaktiko, a] *adj* didactic;
(*material*) teaching *cpd*; (*juguete*)
educational.
diecinueve [djeθinu'eβe] *num* nineteen;
(*fecha*) nineteenth; *V tb* **seis.**
dieciochesco, a [djeθio'tʃesko, a] *adj*
eighteenth-century.
dieciocho [djeθi'otʃo] *num* eighteen;
(*fecha*) eighteenth; *V tb* **seis.**
dieciséis [djeθi'seis] *num* sixteen; (*fecha*)
sixteenth; *V tb* **seis.**
diecisiete [djeθi'sjete] *num* seventeen;
(*fecha*) seventeenth; *V tb* **seis.**
diente ['djente] *nm* (*ANAT, TEC*) tooth;
(*ZOOL*) fang; (: *de elefante*) tusk; (*de ajo*)
clove; **~ de león** dandelion; **~s postizos**
false teeth; **enseñar los ~s** (*fig*) to show
one's claws; **hablar entre ~s** to mutter,
mumble; **hincar el ~ en** (*comida*) to bite
into.
diera ['djera] *etc vb V* **dar.**
diéresis [di'eresis] *nf* diaeresis.
dieron ['djeron] *vb V* **dar.**
diesel ['disel] *adj:* **motor ~** diesel engine.
diestro, a ['djestro, a] *adj* (*derecho*) right;
(*hábil*) skilful; (: *con las manos*) handy
♦ *nm* (*TAUR*) matador ♦ *nf* right hand; **a ~
y siniestro** (*sin método*) wildly.
dieta ['djeta] *nf* diet; **~s** *nfpl* expenses;
estar a ~ to be on a diet.
dietético, a [dje'tetiko, a] *adj* dietetic
♦ *nm/f* dietician ♦ *nf* dietetics *sg*.
dietista [dje'tista] *nm/f* dietician.
diez [djeθ] *num* ten; (*fecha*) tenth; **hacer las
~ de últimas** (*NAIPES*) to sweep the
board; *V tb* **seis.**
diezmar [djeθ'mar] *vt* to decimate.
difamación [difama'θjon] *nf* slander; libel.
difamar [difa'mar] *vt* (*JUR: hablando*) to
slander; (: *por escrito*) to libel.
difamatorio, a [difama'torjo, a] *adj*

slanderous; libellous.
diferencia [dife'renθja] *nf* difference; **a ~
de** unlike; **hacer ~ entre** to make a
distinction between; **~ salarial** (*COM*)
wage differential.
diferencial [diferen'θjal] *nm* (*AUTO*)
differential.
diferenciar [diferen'θjar] *vt* to
differentiate between ♦ *vi* to differ; **~se**
vr to differ, be different; (*distinguirse*) to
distinguish o.s.
diferente [dife'rente] *adj* different.
diferido [dife'riðo] *nm:* **en ~** (*TV etc*)
recorded.
diferir [dife'rir] *vt* to defer.
difícil [di'fiθil] *adj* difficult; (*tiempos, vida*)
hard; (*situación*) delicate; **es un hombre
~** he's a difficult man to get on with.
difícilmente [di'fiθilmente] *adv* (*con
dificultad*) with difficulty; (*apenas*)
hardly.
dificultad [difikul'tað] *nf* difficulty;
(*problema*) trouble; (*objeción*) objection.
dificultar [difikul'tar] *vt* (*complicar*) to
complicate, make difficult; (*estorbar*) to
obstruct; **las restricciones dificultan el
comercio** the restrictions hinder trade.
dificultoso, a [difikul'toso, a] *adj* (*difícil*)
difficult, hard; (*fam: cara*) odd, ugly;
(*persona: exigente*) fussy.
difiera [di'fjera] *etc,* **difiriendo**
[difi'rjendo] *etc vb V* **diferir.**
difuminar [difumi'nar] *vt* to blur.
difundir [difun'dir] *vt* (*calor, luz*) to diffuse;
(*RADIO*) to broadcast; **~se** *vr* to spread
(out); **~ una noticia** to spread a piece of
news.
difunto, a [di'funto, a] *adj* dead, deceased
♦ *nm/f:* **el ~** the deceased.
difusión [difu'sjon] *nf* (*de calor, luz*)
diffusion; (*de noticia, teoría*)
dissemination; (*de programa*)
broadcasting; (*programa*) broadcast.
difuso, a [di'fuso, a] *adj* (*luz*) diffused;
(*conocimientos*) widespread; (*estilo,
explicación*) wordy.
diga ['diʝa] *etc vb V* **decir.**
digerir [dixe'rir] *vt* to digest; (*fig*) to
absorb; (*reflexionar sobre*) to think over.
digestión [dixes'tjon] *nf* digestion; **corte
de ~** indigestion.
digestivo, a [dixes'tiβo, a] *adj* digestive
♦ *nm* (*bebida*) liqueur, digestif.
digiera [di'xjera] *etc,* **digiriendo**
[dixi'rjendo] *etc vb V* **digerir.**
digital [dixi'tal] *adj* (*INFORM*) digital;
(*dactilar*) finger *cpd* ♦ *nf* (*BOT*) foxglove;
(*droga*) digitalis.

digitalizador [dixitaliθa'ðor] nm (INFORM) digitizer.

dignarse [diɣ'narse] vr to deign to.

dignidad [diɣni'ðað] nf dignity; (honra) honour; (rango) rank; (persona) dignitary; **herir la ~ de algn** to hurt sb's pride.

dignificar [diɣnifi'kar] vt to dignify.

dignifique [diɣni'fike] etc vb V **dignificar**.

digno, a ['diɣno, a] adj worthy; (persona: honesto) honourable; **~ de elogio** praiseworthy; **~ de mención** worth mentioning; **es ~ de verse** it is worth seeing; **poco ~** unworthy.

digresión [diɣre'sjon] nf digression.

dije ['dixe] etc, **dijera** [di'xera] etc vb V **decir**.

dilación [dila'θjon] nf delay; **sin ~** without delay, immediately.

dilapidar [dilapi'ðar] vt to squander, waste.

dilatación [dilata'θjon] nf (expansión) dilation.

dilatado, a [dila'taðo, a] adj dilated; (período) long drawn-out; (extenso) extensive.

dilatar [dila'tar] vt (gen) to dilate; (prolongar) to prolong; (aplazar) to delay; **~se** vr (pupila etc) to dilate; (agua) to expand.

dilema [di'lema] nm dilemma.

diligencia [dili'xenθja] nf diligence; (rapidez) speed; (ocupación) errand, job; (carruaje) stagecoach; **~s** nfpl (JUR) formalities; **~s judiciales** judicial proceedings; **~s previas** inquest sg.

diligente [dili'xente] adj diligent; **poco ~** slack.

dilucidar [diluθi'ðar] vt (aclarar) to elucidate, clarify; (misterio) to clear up.

diluir [dilu'ir] vt to dilute; (aguar, fig) to water down.

diluviar [dilu'βjar] vi to pour with rain.

diluvio [di'luβjo] nm deluge, flood; **un ~ de cartas** (fig) a flood of letters.

diluyendo [dilu'jendo] etc vb V **diluir**.

dimanar [dima'nar] vi: **~ de** to arise o spring from.

dimensión [dimen'sjon] nf dimension; **dimensiones** nfpl size sg; **tomar las dimensiones de** to take the measurements of.

dimes ['dimes] nmpl: **andar en ~ y diretes con algn** to bicker o squabble with sb.

diminutivo [diminu'tiβo] nm diminutive.

diminuto, a [dimi'nuto, a] adj tiny, diminutive.

dimisión [dimi'sjon] nf resignation.

dimitir [dimi'tir] vt (cargo) to give up; (despedir) to sack ♦ vi to resign.

dimos ['dimos] vb V **dar**.

Dinamarca [dina'marka] nf Denmark.

dinamarqués, esa [dinamar'kes, esa] adj Danish ♦ nm/f Dane ♦ nm (LING) Danish.

dinámico, a [di'namiko, a] adj dynamic ♦ nf dynamics sg.

dinamita [dina'mita] nf dynamite.

dinamitar [dinami'tar] vt to dynamite.

dinamo [di'namo], **dínamo** ['dinamo] nf (nm en AM) dynamo.

dinastía [dinas'tia] nf dynasty.

dineral [dine'ral] nm fortune.

dinero [di'nero] nm money; **~ en circulación** currency; **~ caro** (COM) dear money; **~ contante (y sonante)** hard cash; **~ de curso legal** legal tender; **~ efectivo** cash, ready cash; **es hombre de ~** he is a man of means; **andar mal de ~** to be short of money; **ganar ~ a espuertas** to make money hand over fist.

dinosaurio [dino'saurjo] nm dinosaur.

dintel [din'tel] nm lintel; (umbral) threshold.

diñar [di'nar] vt (fam) to give; **~la** to kick the bucket.

dio [djo] vb V **dar**.

diócesis ['djoθesis] nf inv diocese.

Dios [djos] nm God; **~ mediante** God willing; **a ~ gracias** thank heaven; **a la buena de ~** any old how; **una de ~ es Cristo** an almighty row; **~ los cría y ellos se juntan** birds of a feather flock together; **como ~ manda** as is proper; **¡~ mío!** (oh,) my God!; **¡por ~!** for God's sake!; **¡válgame ~!** bless my soul!

dios [djos] nm god.

diosa ['djosa] nf goddess.

Dip. abr (= Diputación) ≈ CC.

diploma [di'ploma] nm diploma.

diplomacia [diplo'maθja] nf diplomacy; (fig) tact.

diplomado, a [diplo'maðo, a] adj qualified ♦ nm/f holder of a diploma; (UNIV) graduate; V tb **licenciado**.

diplomático, a [diplo'matiko, a] adj (cuerpo) diplomatic; (que tiene tacto) tactful ♦ nm/f diplomat.

diptongo [dip'tongo] nm diphthong.

diputación [diputa'θjon] nf deputation; **~ permanente** (POL) standing committee; **~ provincial** ≈ county council.

diputado, a [dipu'taðo, a] nm/f delegate; (POL) ≈ member of parliament (BRIT), ≈ representative (US); V tb **Las Cortes (españolas)**.

dique ['dike] nm dyke; (rompeolas)

breakwater; ~ **de contención** dam.

Dir. *abr* = **dirección**; (= *director*) dir.

diré [di're] *etc vb V* **decir.**

dirección [direk'θjon] *nf* direction; (*fig*: *tendencia*) trend; (*señas, tb INFORM*) address; (*AUTO*) steering; (*gerencia*) management; (*de periódico*) editorship; (*en escuela*) headship; (*POL*) leadership; (*junta*) board of directors; (*despacho*) director's/manager's/headmaster's/editor's office; ~ **absoluta** (*INFORM*) absolute address; ~ **administrativa** office management; ~ **asistida** power-assisted steering; **D~ General de Seguridad/Turismo** State Security/Tourist Office; ~ **relativa** (*INFORM*) relative address; ~ **única o prohibida** one-way; **tomar la ~ de una empresa** to take over the running of a company.

direccionamiento [direkθjona'mjento] *nm* (*INFORM*) addressing.

directivo, a [direk'tiβo, a] *adj* (*junta*) managing; (*función*) administrative ♦ *nm/f* (*COM*) manager ♦ *nf* (*norma*) directive; (*tb*: **junta directiva**) board of directors.

directo, a [di'rekto, a] *adj* direct; (*línea*) straight; (*inmediato*) immediate; (*tren*) through; (*TV*) live; **en ~** (*INFORM*) on line; **transmitir en ~** to broadcast live.

director, a [direk'tor, a] *adj* leading ♦ *nm/f* director; (*ESCOL*) head (teacher) (*BRIT*), principal (*US*); (*gerente*) manager(ess); (*de compañía*) president; (*jefe*) head; (*PRENSA*) editor; (*de prisión*) governor; (*MUS*) conductor; ~ **adjunto** assistant manager; ~ **de cine** film director; ~ **comercial** marketing manager; ~ **ejecutivo** executive director; ~ **de empresa** company director; ~ **general** general manager; ~ **gerente** managing director; ~ **de sucursal** branch manager.

directorio [direk'torjo] *nm* (*INFORM*) directory.

directrices [direk'triθes] *nfpl* guidelines.

dirigente [diri'xente] *adj* leading ♦ *nm/f* (*POL*) leader; **los ~s del partido** the party leaders.

dirigible [diri'xiβle] *adj* (*AVIAT, NAUT*) steerable ♦ *nm* airship.

dirigir [diri'xir] *vt* to direct; (*acusación*) to level; (*carta*) to address; (*obra de teatro, film*) to produce, direct; (*MUS*) to conduct; (*comercio*) to manage; (*expedición*) to lead; (*sublevación*) to head; (*periódico*) to edit; (*guiar*) to guide; ~**se** *vr*: ~**se a** to go towards, make one's

way towards; (*hablar con*) to speak to; ~**se a algn solicitando algo** to apply to sb for sth; **"diríjase a ..."** "apply to ...".

dirigismo [diri'xismo] *nm* management, control; ~ **estatal** state control.

dirija [di'rixa] *etc vb V* **dirigir.**

dirimir [diri'mir] *vt* (*contrato, matrimonio*) to dissolve.

discado [dis'kaðo] *nm*: ~ **automático** autodial.

discernir [disθer'nir] *vt* to discern ♦ *vi* to distinguish.

discierna [dis'θjerna] *etc vb V* **discernir.**

disciplina [disθi'plina] *nf* discipline.

disciplinar [disθipli'nar] *vt* to discipline; (*enseñar*) to school; (*MIL*) to drill; (*azotar*) to whip.

discípulo, a [dis'θipulo, a] *nm/f* disciple; (*seguidor*) follower; (*ESCOL*) pupil.

disco ['disko] *nm* disc (*BRIT*), disk (*US*); (*DEPORTE*) discus; (*TELEC*) dial; (*AUTO*: *semáforo*) light; (*MUS*) record; (*INFORM*) disk; ~ **de arranque** boot disk; ~ **compacto** compact disc; ~ **de densidad sencilla/doble** single/double density disk; ~ **de larga duración** long-playing record (LP); ~ **flexible** *o* **floppy** floppy disk; ~ **de freno** brake disc; ~ **maestro** master disk; ~ **de reserva** backup disk; ~ **rígido** hard disk; ~ **de una cara/dos caras** single-/double-sided disk; ~ **virtual** ramdisk.

discóbolo [dis'koβolo] *nm* discus thrower.

discográfico, a [disko'γrafiko, a] *adj* record *cpd*; **casa discográfica** record company; **sello** ~ label.

díscolo, a ['diskolo, a] *adj* (*rebelde*) unruly.

disconforme [diskon'forme] *adj* differing; **estar ~ (con)** to be in disagreement (with).

discontinuo, a [diskon'tinwo, a] *adj* discontinuous; (*AUTO*: *línea*) broken.

discordar [diskor'ðar] *vi* (*MUS*) to be out of tune; (*estar en desacuerdo*) to disagree; (*colores, opiniones*) to clash.

discorde [dis'korðe] *adj* (*sonido*) discordant; (*opiniones*) clashing.

discordia [dis'korðja] *nf* discord.

discoteca [disko'teka] *nf* disco(theque).

discreción [diskre'θjon] *nf* discretion; (*reserva*) prudence; **¡a ~!** (*MIL*) stand easy!; **añadir azúcar a ~** (*CULIN*) add sugar to taste; **comer a ~** to eat as much as one wishes.

discrecional [diskreθjo'nal] *adj* (*facultativo*) discretionary; **parada ~** request stop.

discrepancia [diskre'panθja] *nf* (*diferencia*) discrepancy; (*desacuerdo*) disagreement.

discrepante [diskre'pante] adj divergent; **hubo varias voces ~s** there were some dissenting voices.

discrepar [diskre'par] vi to disagree.

discreto, a [dis'kreto, a] adj (diplomático) discreet; (sensato) sensible; (reservado) quiet; (sobrio) sober; (mediano) fair, fairly good; **le daremos un plazo ~** we'll allow him a reasonable time.

discriminación [diskrimina'θjon] nf discrimination.

discriminar [diskrimi'nar] vt to discriminate against; (diferenciar) to discriminate between.

discuerde [dis'kwerðe] etc vb V **discordar**.

disculpa [dis'kulpa] nf excuse; (pedir perdón) apology; **pedir ~s a/por** to apologize to/for.

disculpar [diskul'par] vt to excuse, pardon; **~se** vr to excuse o.s.; to apologize.

discurrir [disku'rrir] vt to contrive, think up ♦ vi (pensar, reflexionar) to think, meditate; (recorrer) to roam, wander; (río) to flow; (el tiempo) to pass, flow by.

discurso [dis'kurso] nm speech; **~ de clausura** closing speech; **pronunciar un ~** to make a speech; **en el ~ del tiempo** with the passage of time.

discusión [disku'sjon] nf (diálogo) discussion; (riña) argument; **tener una ~** to have an argument.

discutible [disku'tiβle] adj debatable; **de mérito ~** of dubious worth.

discutido, a [disku'tiðo, a] adj controversial.

discutir [disku'tir] vt (debatir) to discuss; (pelear) to argue about; (contradecir) to argue against ♦ vi to discuss; (disputar) to argue; **~ de política** to argue about politics; **¡no discutas!** don't argue!

disecar [dise'kar] vt (para conservar: animal) to stuff; (: planta) to dry.

diseminar [disemi'nar] vt to disseminate, spread.

disentir [disen'tir] vi to dissent, disagree.

diseñador, a [diseɲa'dor, a] nm/f designer.

diseñar [dise'ɲar] vt to design.

diseño [di'seɲo] nm (TEC) design; (ARTE) drawing; (COSTURA) pattern; **de ~ italiano** Italian-designed; **~ asistido por ordenador** computer-assisted design, CAD.

diseque [di'seke] etc vb V **disecar**.

disertar [diser'tar] vi to speak.

disfrace [dis'fraθe] etc vb V **disfrazar**.

disfraz [dis'fraθ] nm (máscara) disguise; (traje) fancy dress; (excusa) pretext; **bajo el ~ de** under the cloak of.

disfrazado, a [disfra'θaðo, a] adj disguised; **ir ~ de** to masquerade as.

disfrazar [disfra'θar] vt to disguise; **~se** vr to dress (o.s.) up; **~se de** to disguise o.s. as.

disfrutar [disfru'tar] vt to enjoy ♦ vi to enjoy o.s.; **¡que disfrutes!** have a good time; **~ de** to enjoy, possess; **~ de buena salud** to enjoy good health.

disfrute [dis'frute] nm (goce) enjoyment; (aprovechamiento) use.

disgregar [disɣre'ɣar] vt (desintegrar) to disintegrate; (manifestantes) to disperse; **~se** vr to disintegrate, break up.

disgregue [dis'ɣreɣe] etc vb V **disgregar**.

disgustar [disɣus'tar] vt (no gustar) to displease; (contrariar, enojar) to annoy; to upset; **~se** vr to be annoyed; (dos personas) to fall out; **estaba muy disgustado con el asunto** he was very upset about the affair.

disgusto [dis'ɣusto] nm (repugnancia) disgust; (contrariedad) annoyance; (desagrado) displeasure; (tristeza) grief; (riña) quarrel; (avería) misfortune; **hacer algo a ~** to do sth unwillingly; **matar a algn a ~s** to drive sb to distraction.

disidente [disi'ðente] nm dissident.

disienta [di'sjenta] etc vb V **disentir**.

disimulado, a [disimu'laðo, a] adj (solapado) furtive, underhand; (oculto) covert; **hacerse el ~** to pretend not to notice.

disimular [disimu'lar] vt (ocultar) to hide, conceal ♦ vi to dissemble.

disimulo [disi'mulo] nm (fingimiento) dissimulation; **con ~** cunningly.

disipar [disi'par] vt (duda, temor) to dispel; (esperanza) to destroy; (fortuna) to squander; **~se** vr (nubes) to vanish; (dudas) to be dispelled; (indisciplinarse) to dissipate.

diskette [dis'ket] nm (INFORM) diskette, floppy disk.

dislate [dis'late] nm (absurdo) absurdity; **~s** nmpl nonsense sg.

dislexia [dis'leksja] nf dyslexia.

dislocar [dislo'kar] vt (gen) to dislocate; (tobillo) to sprain.

disloque [dis'loke] etc vb V **dislocar** ♦ nm: **es el ~** (fam) it's the last straw.

disminución [disminu'θjon] nf diminution.

disminuido, a [disminu'iðo, a] nm/f: **~ mental/físico** mentally/physically-handicapped person.

disminuir [disminu'ir] vt to decrease, diminish; (estrechar) to lessen; (temperatura) to lower; (gastos, raciones) to cut down; (*dolor*) to relieve; (*autoridad, prestigio*) to weaken; (*entusiasmo*) to damp ♦ *vi* (*días*) to grow shorter; (*precios, temperatura*) to drop, fall; (*velocidad*) to slacken; (*población*) to decrease; (*beneficios, número*) to fall off; (*memoria, vista*) to fail.

disminuyendo [dismiɲuˈjendo] *etc vb V* **disminuir**.

disociar [disoˈθjar] *vt* to disassociate; ~**se** *vr* to disassociate o.s.

disoluble [disoˈluβle] *adj* soluble.

disolución [disoluˈθjon] *nf* (*acto*) dissolution; (*QUÍMICA*) solution; (*COM*) liquidation; (*moral*) dissoluteness.

disoluto, a [disoˈluto, a] *adj* dissolute.

disolvente [disolˈβente] *nm* (*solvent*) thinner.

disolver [disolˈβer] *vt* (*gen*) to dissolve; (*manifestación*) to break up; ~**se** *vr* to dissolve; (*COM*) to go into liquidation.

dispar [disˈpar] *adj* (*distinto*) different; (*irregular*) uneven.

disparado, a [dispaˈraðo, a] *adj*: **entrar** ~ to shoot in; **salir** ~ to shoot out; **ir** ~ to go like mad.

disparador [dispaˈraðor] *nm* (*de arma*) trigger; (*FOTO, TEC*) release; ~ **atómico** aerosol; ~ **de bombas** bomb release.

disparar [dispaˈrar] *vt, vi* to shoot, fire; ~**se** *vr* (*arma de fuego*) to go off; (*persona: marcharse*) to rush off; (*caballo*) to bolt; (*enojarse*) to lose control.

disparatado, a [disparaˈtaðo, a] *adj* crazy.

disparate [dispaˈrate] *nm* (*tontería*) foolish remark; (*error*) blunder; **decir** ~**s** to talk nonsense; **¡qué** ~**!** how absurd!; **costar un** ~ to cost a hell of a lot.

disparo [disˈparo] *nm* shot; (*acto*) firing; ~**s** *nmpl* shooting *sg*, (exchange of) shots (*sg*); ~ **inicial** (*de cohete*) blastoff.

dispendio [disˈpendjo] *nm* waste.

dispensar [dispenˈsar] *vt* to dispense; (*ayuda*) to give; (*honores*) to grant; (*disculpar*) to excuse; **¡usted dispense!** I beg your pardon!; ~ **a algn de hacer algo** to excuse sb from doing sth.

dispensario [dispenˈsarjo] *nm* (*clínica*) community clinic; (*de hospital*) outpatients' department.

dispersar [disperˈsar] *vt* to disperse; (*manifestación*) to break up; ~**se** *vr* to scatter.

disperso, a [disˈperso, a] *adj* scattered.

displicencia [displiˈθenθja] *nf* (*mal humor*) peevishness; (*desgana*) lack of enthusiasm.

displicente [displiˈθente] *adj*

(*malhumorado*) peevish; (*poco entusiasta*) unenthusiastic.

dispondré [disponˈdre] *etc vb V* **disponer**.

disponer [dispoˈner] *vt* (*arreglar*) to arrange; (*ordenar*) to put in order; (*preparar*) to prepare, get ready ♦ *vi*: ~ **de** to have, own; ~**se para** to prepare to, prepare for; **la ley dispone que ...** the law provides that ...; **no puede** ~ **de esos bienes** she cannot dispose of those properties.

disponga [disˈponga] *etc vb V* **disponer**.

disponibilidad [disponiβiliˈðað] *nf* availability; ~**es** *nfpl* (*COM*) resources, financial assets.

disponible [dispoˈniβle] *adj* available; (*tiempo*) spare; (*dinero*) on hand.

disposición [disposiˈθjon] *nf* arrangement, disposition; (*de casa, INFORM*) layout; (*ley*) order; (*cláusula*) provision; (*aptitud*) aptitude; ~ **de ánimo** attitude of mind; **última** ~ last will and testament; **a la** ~ **de** at the disposal of; **a su** ~ at your service.

dispositivo [disposiˈtiβo] *nm* device, mechanism; ~ **de alimentación** hopper; ~ **de almacenaje** storage device; ~ **periférico** peripheral (device); ~ **de seguridad** safety catch; (*fig*) security measure.

dispuesto, a [disˈpwesto, a] *pp de* **disponer** ♦ *adj* (*arreglado*) arranged; (*preparado*) disposed; (*persona: dinámico*) bright; **estar** ~**/poco** ~ **a hacer algo** to be inclined/reluctant to do sth.

dispuse [disˈpuse] *etc vb V* **disponer**.

disputa [disˈputa] *nf* (*discusión*) dispute, argument; (*controversia*) controversy.

disputar [dispuˈtar] *vt* (*discutir*) to dispute, question; (*contender*) to contend for ♦ *vi* to argue.

disquete [disˈkete] *nm* (*INFORM*) diskette, floppy disk.

disquetera [diskeˈtera] *nf* disk drive.

Dist. *abr* (= *distancia, Distrito*) dist.

distancia [disˈtanθja] *nf* distance; (*de tiempo*) interval; ~ **de parada** braking distance; ~ **del suelo** (*AUTO etc*) height off the ground; **a gran** o **a larga** ~ long-distance; **mantenerse a** ~ to keep one's distance; (*fig*) to remain aloof; **guardar las** ~**s** to keep one's distance.

distanciado, a [distanˈθjaðo, a] *adj* (*remoto*) remote; (*fig: alejado*) far apart; **estamos** ~**s en ideas** our ideas are poles apart.

distanciamiento [distanθjaˈmjento] *nm* (*acto*) spacing out; (*estado*) remoteness;

(*fig*) distance.
distanciar [distan'θjar] *vt* to space out;
  ~se *vr* to become estranged.
distante [dis'tante] *adj* distant.
distar [dis'tar] *vi*: **dista 5 kms de aquí** it is 5
  kms from here; **¿dista mucho?** is it far?;
  dista mucho de la verdad it's very far
  from the truth.
diste ['diste], **disteis** ['disteis] *vb V* **dar**.
distensión [disten'sjon] *nf* distension;
  (*POL*) détente; **~ muscular** (*MED*)
  muscular strain.
distinción [distin'θjon] *nf* distinction;
  (*elegancia*) elegance; (*honor*) honour; **a ~
  de** unlike; **sin ~** indiscriminately; **sin ~
  de edades** irrespective of age.
distinga [dis'tinga] *etc vb V* **distinguir**.
distinguido, a [distin'giðo, a] *adj*
  distinguished; (*famoso*) prominent,
  well-known; (*elegante*) elegant.
distinguir [distin'gir] *vt* to distinguish;
  (*divisar*) to make out; (*escoger*) to single
  out; (*caracterizar*) to mark out; **~se** *vr* to
  be distinguished; (*destacarse*) to
  distinguish o.s.; **a lo lejos no se distingue**
  it's not visible from a distance.
distintivo, a [distin'tiβo, a] *adj* distinctive;
  (*signo*) distinguishing ♦ *nm* (*de policía etc*)
  badge; (*fig*) characteristic.
distinto, a [dis'tinto, a] *adj* different;
  (*claro*) clear; **~s** several, various.
distorsión [distor'sjon] *nf* (*ANAT*) twisting;
  (*RADIO etc*) distortion.
distorsionar [distorsjo'nar] *vt*, *vi* to distort.
distracción [distrak'θjon] *nf* distraction;
  (*pasatiempo*) hobby, pastime; (*olvido*)
  absent-mindedness, distraction.
distraer [distra'er] *vt* (*atención*) to distract;
  (*divertir*) to amuse; (*fondos*) to embezzle
  ♦ *vi* to be relaxing; **~se** *vr* (*entretenerse*)
  to amuse o.s.; (*perder la concentración*) to
  allow one's attention to wander; **~ a
  algn de su pensamiento** to divert sb
  from his train of thought; **el pescar
  distrae** fishing is a relaxation.
distraído, a [distra'iðo, a] *adj* (*gen*)
  absent-minded; (*desatento*) inattentive;
  (*entretenido*) amusing ♦ *nm*: **hacerse el ~**
  to pretend not to notice; **con aire ~** idly;
  me miró distraída she gave me a casual
  glance.
distraiga [dis'traixa] *etc*, **distraje**
  [dis'traxe] *etc*, **distrajera** [distra'xera]
  etc, **distrayendo** [distra'jendo] *vb V*
  distraer.
distribución [distriβu'θjon] *nf* distribution;
  (*entrega*) delivery; (*en estadística*)
  distribution, incidence; (*ARQ*) layout; ~

de premios prize giving; **la ~ de los
  impuestos** the incidence of taxes.
distribuidor, a [distriβui'ðor, a] *nm/f*
  (*persona: gen*) distributor; (: *CORREOS*)
  sorter; (: *COM*) dealer; **su ~ habitual**
  your regular dealer.
distribuir [distriβu'ir] *vt* to distribute;
  (*prospectos*) to hand out; (*cartas*) to
  deliver; (*trabajo*) to allocate; (*premios*) to
  award; (*dividendos*) to pay; (*peso*) to
  distribute; (*ARQ*) to plan.
distribuyendo [distriβu'jendo] *etc vb V*
  distribuir.
distrito [dis'trito] *nm* (*sector, territorio*)
  region; (*barrio*) district; **~ electoral**
  constituency; **~ postal** postal district.
disturbio [dis'turβjo] *nm* disturbance;
  (*desorden*) riot; **los ~s** the troubles.
disuadir [diswa'ðir] *vt* to dissuade.
disuasión [diswa'sjon] *nf* dissuasion; (*MIL*)
  deterrent; **~ nuclear** nuclear deterrent.
disuasivo, a [diswa'siβo, a] *adj* dissuasive;
  arma disuasiva deterrent.
disuasorio, a [diswa'sorjo, a] *adj*
  = **disuasivo.**
disuelto [di'swelto] *pp de* **disolver.**
disuelva [di'swelβa] *etc vb V* **disolver.**
disuene [di'swene] *etc vb V* **disonar.**
disyuntiva [disjun'tiβa] *nf* (*dilema*)
  dilemma.
DIU ['diu] *nm abr* (= *dispositivo intrauterino*)
  I.U.D.
diurno, a ['djurno, a] *adj* day *cpd*, diurnal.
diva ['diβa] *nf* prima donna.
divagar [diβa'xar] *vi* (*desviarse*) to digress.
divague [di'βaxe] *etc vb V* **divagar.**
diván [di'βan] *nm* divan.
divergencia [diβer'xenθja] *nf* divergence.
divergir [diβer'xir] *vi* (*líneas*) to diverge;
  (*opiniones*) to differ; (*personas*) to
  disagree.
diverja [di'βerxa] *etc vb V* **divergir.**
diversidad [diβersi'ðað] *nf* diversity,
  variety.
diversificación [diβersifika'θjon] *nf* (*COM*)
  diversification.
diversificar [diβersifi'kar] *vt* to diversify.
diversifique [diβersi'fike] *etc vb V*
  diversificar.
diversión [diβer'sjon] *nf* (*gen*)
  entertainment; (*actividad*) hobby,
  pastime.
diverso, a [di'βerso, a] *adj* diverse;
  (*diferente*) different ♦ *nm*: **~s** (*COM*)
  sundries; **~s libros** several books.
divertido, a [diβer'tiðo, a] *adj* (*chiste*)
  amusing, funny; (*fiesta etc*) enjoyable;
  (*película, libro*) entertaining; **está ~**

(*irónico*) this is going to be fun.

divertir [diβer'tir] *vt* (*entretener, recrear*) to amuse, entertain; ~**se** *vr* (*pasarlo bien*) to have a good time; (*distraerse*) to amuse o.s.

dividendo [diβi'ðendo] *nm* (*COM*): ~**s** *nmpl* dividends; ~**s por acción** earnings per share; ~ **definitivo** final dividend.

dividir [diβi'ðir] *vt* (*gen*) to divide; (*separar*) to separate; (*distribuir*) to distribute, share out.

divierta [di'βjerta] *etc vb V* **divertir**.

divinidad [diβini'ðað] *nf* (*esencia divina*) divinity; **la D**~ God.

divino, a [di'βino, a] *adj* divine; (*fig*) lovely.

divirtiendo [diβir'tjendo] *etc vb V* **divertir**.

divisa [di'βisa] *nf* (*emblema, moneda*) emblem, badge; ~**s** *nfpl* currency *sg*; (*COM*) foreign exchange *sg*; **control de** ~**s** exchange control; ~ **de reserva** reserve currency.

divisar [diβi'sar] *vt* to make out, distinguish.

división [diβi'sjon] *nf* division; (*de partido*) split; (*de país*) partition.

divisorio, a [diβi'sorjo, a] *adj* (*línea*) dividing; **línea divisoria de las aguas** watershed.

divorciado, a [diβor'θjaðo, a] *adj* divorced; (*opinion*) split ♦ *nm/f* divorcé(e).

divorciar [diβor'θjar] *vt* to divorce; ~**se** *vr* to get divorced.

divorcio [di'βorθjo] *nm* divorce; (*fig*) split.

divulgación [diβulɣa'θjon] *nf* (*difusión*) spreading; (*popularización*) popularization.

divulgar [diβul'ɣar] *vt* (*desparramar*) to spread; (*popularizar*) to popularize; (*hacer circular*) to divulge, circulate; ~**se** *vr* (*secreto*) to leak out; (*rumor*) to get about.

divulgue [di'βulɣe] *etc vb V* **divulgar**.

dizque ['diske] *adv* (*AM fam*) apparently.

Dls., dls *abr* (*AM*) = **dólares**.

DM *abr* = **decimal**.

dm. *abr* (= *decímetro*) dm.

DNI *nm abr* (*ESP*) = **Documento Nacional de Identidad**.

Dña. *abr* = **Doña**.

do [do] *nm* (*MUS*) C.

D.O. *abr* = **Denominación de Origen**.

dobladillo [doβla'ðiʎo] *nm* (*de vestido*) hem; (*de pantalón: vuelta*) turn-up (*BRIT*), cuff (*US*).

doblaje [do'βlaxe] *nm* (*CINE*) dubbing.

doblar [do'βlar] *vt* to double; (*papel*) to fold; (*caño*) to bend; (*la esquina*) to turn,

go round; (*film*) to dub ♦ *vi* to turn; (*campana*) to toll; ~**se** *vr* (*plegarse*) to fold (up), crease; (*encorvarse*) to bend.

doble ['doβle] *adj* (*gen*) double; (*de dos aspectos*) dual; (*cuerda*) thick; (*fig*) two-faced ♦ *nm* double ♦ *nm/f* (*TEAT*) double, stand-in; ~**s** *nmpl* (*DEPORTE*) doubles *sg*; ~ **o nada** double or quits; ~ **página** double-page spread; **con** ~ **sentido** with a double meaning; **el** ~ twice the quantity *o* as much; **su sueldo es el** ~ **del mío** his salary is twice (as much as) mine; (*INFORM*): ~ **cara** double-sided; ~ **densidad** double density; ~ **espacio** double spacing.

doblegar [doβle'ɣar] *vt* to fold, crease; ~**se** *vr* to yield.

doblegue [do'βleɣe] *etc vb V* **doblegar**.

doblez [do'βleθ] *nm* (*pliegue*) fold, hem ♦ *nf* (*falsedad*) duplicity.

doc. *abr* (= *docena*) doz.; (= *documento*) doc.

doce ['doθe] *num* twelve; (*fecha*) twelfth; **las** ~ twelve o'clock; *V tb* **seis**.

docena [do'θena] *nf* dozen; **por** ~**s** by the dozen.

docente [do'θente] *adj*: **centro/personal** ~ teaching institution/staff.

dócil ['doθil] *adj* (*pasivo*) docile; (*manso*) gentle; (*obediente*) obedient.

docto, a ['dokto, a] *adj* learned, erudite ♦ *nm/f* scholar.

doctor, a [dok'tor, a] *nm/f* doctor; ~ **en filosofía** Doctor of Philosophy.

doctorado [dokto'raðo] *nm* doctorate.

doctorarse [dokto'rarse] *vr* to get a doctorate.

doctrina [dok'trina] *nf* doctrine, teaching.

documentación [dokumenta'θjon] *nf* documentation; (*de identidad etc*) papers *pl*.

documental [dokumen'tal] *adj, nm* documentary.

documentar [dokumen'tar] *vt* to document; ~**se** *vr* to gather information.

documento [doku'mento] *nm* (*certificado*) document; (*JUR*) exhibit; ~**s** *nmpl* papers; ~ **justificativo** voucher; **D**~ **Nacional de Identidad** national identity card.

A laminated plastic ID card with the holder's personal details and photograph, the Documento Nacional de Identidad is renewed every 10 years. People are required to carry it at all times and to produce it on request for the police. In Spain it is commonly known as the DNI or carnet de identidad. In Spanish America a similar card is called the **cédula (de identidad).**

dogma ['doɣma] *nm* dogma.
dogmático, a [doɣ'matiko, a] *adj* dogmatic.
dogo ['doɣo] *nm* bulldog.
dólar ['dolar] *nm* dollar.
dolencia [do'lenθja] *nf (achaque)* ailment; *(dolor)* ache.
doler [do'ler] *vt, vi* to hurt; *(fig)* to grieve; ~**se** *vr (de su situación)* to grieve, feel sorry; *(de las desgracias ajenas)* to sympathize; *(quejarse)* to complain; **me duele el brazo** my arm hurts; **no me duele el dinero** I don't mind about the money; **¡ahí le duele!** you've put your finger on it!
doliente [do'ljente] *adj (enfermo)* sick; *(dolorido)* aching; *(triste)* sorrowful; **la familia** ~ the bereaved family.
dolor [do'lor] *nm* pain; *(fig)* grief, sorrow; ~ **de cabeza** headache; ~ **de estómago** stomach ache; ~ **de oídos** earache; ~ **sordo** dull ache.
dolorido, a [dolo'riðo, a] *adj (MED)* sore; **la parte dolorida** the part which hurts.
doloroso, a [dolo'roso, a] *adj (MED)* painful; *(fig)* distressing.
domar [do'mar] *vt* to tame.
domesticado, a [domesti'kaðo, a] *adj (amansado)* tame.
domesticar [domesti'kar] *vt* to tame.
doméstico, a [do'mestiko, a] *adj* domestic ♦ *nm/f* servant; **economía doméstica** home economy; **gastos** ~**s** household expenses.
domestique [domes'tike] *etc vb* V **domesticar.**
domiciliación [domiθilja'θjon] *nf*: ~ **de pagos** *(COM)* standing order, direct debit.
domiciliar [domiθi'ljar] *vt* to domicile; ~**se** *vr* to take up (one's) residence.
domiciliario, a [domiθi'ljarjo, a] *adj*: **arresto** ~ house arrest.
domicilio [domi'θiljo] *nm* home; ~ **particular** private residence; ~ **social** *(COM)* head office, registered office; **servicio a** ~ delivery service; **sin** ~ **fijo** of no fixed abode.
dominante [domi'nante] *adj* dominant; *(person)* domineering.
dominar [domi'nar] *vt (gen)* to dominate; *(países)* to rule over; *(adversario)* to overpower; *(caballo, nervios, emoción)* to control; *(incendio, epidemia)* to bring under control; *(idiomas)* to be fluent in

♦ *vi* to dominate, prevail; ~**se** *vr* to control o.s.
domingo [do'mingo] *nm* Sunday; **D~ de Ramos** Palm Sunday; **D~ de Resurrección** Easter Sunday; *V tb* **sábado**; **Semana Santa.**
dominguero, a [domin'gero, a] *adj* Sunday *cpd*.
dominical [domini'kal] *adj* Sunday *cpd*; **periódico** ~ Sunday newspaper.
dominicano, a [domini'kano, a] *adj, nm/f* Dominican.
dominio [do'minjo] *nm (tierras)* domain; *(POL)* dominion; *(autoridad)* power, authority; *(supremacía)* supremacy; *(de las pasiones)* grip, hold; *(de idioma)* command; **ser del** ~ **público** to be widely known.
dominó [domi'no] *nm (pieza)* domino; *(juego)* dominoes.
dom.º *abr (= domingo)* Sun.
don [don] *nm (talento)* gift; **D~ Juan Gómez** Mr Juan Gomez, Juan Gomez Esq.; **tener** ~ **de gentes** to known how to handle people; ~ **de lenguas** gift for languages; ~ **de mando** (qualities of) leadership; ~ **de palabra** gift of the gab.

Don *or* **doña** *is a term used before someone's first name – eg Don Diego, Doña Inés – when showing respect or being polite to someone of a superior social standing or to an older person. It is becoming somewhat rare, but it does however continue to be used with names and surnames in official documents and in correspondence: eg Sr. D. Pedro Rodríguez Hernández, Sra. Dña Inés Rodríguez Hernández.*

---

donación [dona'θjon] *nf* donation.
donaire [do'naire] *nm* charm.
donante [do'nante] *nm/f* donor; ~ **de sangre** blood donor.
donar [do'nar] *vt* to donate.
donativo [dona'tiβo] *nm* donation.
doncella [don'θeʎa] *nf (criada)* maid.
donde ['donde] *adv* where ♦ *prep*: **el coche está allí** ~ **el farol** the car is over there by the lamppost *o* where the lamppost is; **por** ~ through which; **a** ~ to where, to which; **en** ~ where, in which; **es a** ~ **vamos nosotros** that's where we're going.
dónde ['donde] *adv interrogativo* where?; **¿a** ~ **vas?** where are you going (to)?; **¿de** ~ **vienes?** where have you come from?; **¿en** ~**?** where?; **¿por** ~**?** where?,

whereabouts?; ¿por ~ **se va al estadio?**
how do you get to the stadium?

dondequiera [donde'kjera] *adv* anywhere
♦ *conj:* ~ **que** wherever; **por** ~
everywhere, all over the place.

donostiarra [donos'tjarra] *adj* of *o* from
San Sebastián ♦ *nm/f* native *o* inhabitant
of San Sebastián.

doña ['doɲa] *nf:* **D~ Carmen Gómez** Mrs
Carmen Gómez; *V tb* **don.**

dopar [do'par] *vt* to dope, drug.

doping ['dopin] *nm* doping, drugging.

doquier [do'kjer] *adv:* **por** ~ all over,
everywhere.

dorado, a [do'raðo, a] *adj (color)* golden;
(TEC) gilt.

dorar [do'rar] *vt (TEC)* to gild; *(CULIN)* to
brown, cook lightly; ~ **la píldora** to
sweeten the pill.

dormilón, ona [dormi'lon, ona] *adj* fond of
sleeping ♦ *nm/f* sleepyhead.

dormir [dor'mir] *vt:* ~ **la siesta por la tarde**
to have an afternoon nap ♦ *vi* to sleep;
~**se** *vr (persona, brazo, pierna)* to fall
asleep; ~**la** *(fam)* to sleep it off; ~ **la**
mona *(fam)* to sleep off a hangover; ~
como un lirón *o* **tronco** to sleep like a
log; ~ **a pierna suelta** to sleep soundly.

dormitar [dormi'tar] *vi* to doze.

dormitorio [dormi'torjo] *nm* bedroom; ~
común dormitory.

dorsal [dor'sal] *adj* dorsal ♦ *nm (DEPORTE)*
number.

dorso ['dorso] *nm* back; **escribir algo al** ~
to write sth on the back; **"vease al ~"**
"see other side", "please turn over".

DOS *nm abr (= sistema operativo de disco)*
DOS.

dos [dos] *num* two; *(fecha)* second; **los** ~
the two of them, both of them; **cada** ~
por tres every five minutes; **de** ~ **en** ~
in twos; **estamos a** ~ *(TENIS)* the score is
deuce; *V tb* **seis.**

doscientos, as [dos'θjentos, as] *num* two
hundred.

dosel [do'sel] *nm* canopy.

dosificar [dosifi'kar] *vt (CULIN, MED,*
QUÍMICA) to measure out; *(no derrochar)*
to be sparing with.

dosifique [dosi'fike] *etc vb V* **dosificar.**

dosis ['dosis] *nf inv* dose, dosage.

dossier [do'sjer] *nm* dossier, file.

dotación [dota'θjon] *nf (acto, dinero)*
endowment; *(plantilla)* staff; *(NAUT)*
crew; **la** ~ **es insuficiente** we are under
staffed.

dotado, a [do'taðo, a] *adj* gifted; ~ **de**
(persona) endowed with; *(máquina)*

equipped with.

dotar [do'tar] *vt* to endow; *(TEC)* to fit;
(barco) to man; *(oficina)* to staff.

dote ['dote] *nf (de novia)* dowry; ~**s** *nfpl*
(talentos) gifts.

doy [doj] *vb V* **dar.**

Dpto. *abr (= Departamento)* dept.

Dr(a). *abr (= Doctor, Doctora)* Dr.

draga ['draxa] *nf* dredge.

dragado [dra'xaðo] *nm* dredging.

dragar [dra'xar] *vt* to dredge; *(minas)* to
sweep.

dragón [dra'xon] *nm* dragon.

drague ['draxe] *etc vb V* **dragar.**

drama ['drama] *nm* drama; *(obra)* play.

dramático, a [dra'matiko, a] *adj* dramatic
♦ *nm/f* dramatist; *(actor)* actor; **obra**
dramática play.

dramaturgo, a [drama'turxo, a] *nm/f*
dramatist, playwright.

dramón [dra'mon] *nm (TEAT)* melodrama;
¡qué ~! what a scene!

drástico, a ['drastiko, a] *adj* drastic.

drenaje [dre'naxe] *nm* drainage.

drenar [dre'nar] *vt* to drain.

droga ['droxa] *nf* drug; *(DEPORTE)* dope; **el**
problema de la ~ the drug problem.

drogadicto, a [droxa'ðikto, a] *nm/f* drug
addict.

drogar [dro'xar] *vt* to drug; *(DEPORTE)* to
dope; ~**se** *vr* to take drugs.

drogodependencia [droxoðepen'denθja]
nf drug addiction.

drogue ['droxe] *etc vb V* **drogar.**

droguería [droxe'ria] *nf* ≈ hardware shop
(BRIT) o store *(US)*.

dromedario [drome'ðarjo] *nm* dromedary.

Dto., D.to *abr* = **descuento.**

Dtor(a). *abr (= Director, Directora)* Dir.

ducado [du'kaðo] *nm* duchy, dukedom.

ducha ['dutʃa] *nf (baño)* shower; *(MED)*
douche.

ducharse [du'tʃarse] *vr* to take a shower.

ducho, a ['dutʃo, a] *adj:* ~ **en**
(experimentado) experienced in; *(hábil)*
skilled at.

dúctil ['duktil] *adj (metal)* ductile; *(persona)*
easily influenced.

duda ['duða] *nf* doubt; **sin** ~ no doubt,
doubtless; ¡sin ~! of course!; **no cabe** ~
there is no doubt about it; **no le quepa** ~
make no mistake about it; **no quiero**
poner en ~ **su conducta** I don't want to
call his behaviour into question; **sacar a**
algn de la ~ to settle sb's doubts; **tengo**
una ~ I have a query.

dudar [du'ðar] *vt* to doubt ♦ *vi* to doubt,
have doubts; ~ **acerca de algo** to be

uncertain about sth; **dudó en comprarlo** he hesitated to buy it; **dudan que sea verdad** they doubt whether o if it's true.

dudoso, a [du'ðoso, a] adj (incierto) hesitant; (sospechoso) doubtful; (conducta) dubious.

duelo ['dwelo] etc vb V **doler** ♦ nm (combate) duel; (luto) mourning; **batirse en** ~ to fight a duel.

duende ['dwende] nm imp, goblin; **tiene** ~ he's got real soul.

dueño, a ['dweno, a] nm/f (propietario) owner; (de pensión, taberna) landlord/ lady; (de casa, perro) master/mistress; (empresario) employer; **ser** ~ **de sí mismo** to have self-control; (libre) to be one's own boss; **eres** ~ **de hacer como te parezca** you're free to do as you think fit; **hacerse** ~ **de una situación** to take command of a situation.

duerma ['dwerma] etc vb V **dormir**.

duermevela [dwerme'ßela] nf (fam) nap, snooze.

Duero ['dwero] nm Douro.

dulce ['dulθe] adj sweet; (carácter, clima) gentle, mild ♦ adv gently, softly ♦ nm sweet.

dulcificar [dulθifi'kar] vt (fig) to soften.

dulcifique [dulθi'fike] etc vb V **dulcificar**.

dulzón, ona [dul'θon, ona] adj (alimento) sickly-sweet, too sweet; (canción etc) gooey.

dulzura [dul'θura] nf sweetness; (ternura) gentleness.

duna ['duna] nf dune.

Dunquerque [dun'kerke] nm Dunkirk.

dúo ['duo] nm duet, duo.

duodécimo, a [duo'deθimo, a] adj twelfth; V tb **sexto, a**.

dup., dup.do abr (= duplicado) duplicated.

dúplex ['dupleks] nm inv (piso) flat on two floors; (TELEC) link-up; (INFORM): ~ **integral** full duplex.

duplicar [dupli'kar] vt (hacer el doble de) to duplicate; (cantidad) to double; ~**se** vr to double.

duplique [du'plike] etc vb V **duplicar**.

duque ['duke] nm duke.

duquesa [du'kesa] nf duchess.

duración [dura'θjon] nf duration, length; (de máquina) life; ~ **media de la vida** average life expectancy; **de larga** ~ (enfermedad) lengthy; (pila) long-life; (disco) long-playing; **de poca** ~ short.

duradero, a [dura'ðero, a] adj (tela) hard-wearing; (fe, paz) lasting.

durante [du'rante] adv during; ~ **toda la noche** all night long; **habló** ~ **una hora**

he spoke for an hour.

durar [du'rar] vi (permanecer) to last; (recuerdo) to remain; (ropa) to wear (well).

durazno [du'rasno] nm (AM: fruta) peach; (: árbol) peach tree.

durex ['dureks] nm (AM: tira adhesiva) Sellotape ® (BRIT), Scotch tape ® (US).

dureza [du'reθa] nf (cualidad) hardness; (de carácter) toughness.

durmiendo [dur'mjendo] etc vb V **dormir**.

durmiente [dur'mjente] adj sleeping ♦ nm/f sleeper.

duro, a ['duro, a] adj hard; (carácter) tough; (pan) stale; (cuello, puerta) stiff; (clima, luz) harsh ♦ adv hard ♦ nm (moneda) five peseta coin; **el sector** ~ **del partido** the hardliners pl in the party; **ser** ~ **con algn** to be tough with o hard on sb; ~ **de mollera** (torpe) dense; ~ **de oído** hard of hearing; **trabajar** ~ to work hard; **estar sin un** ~ to be broke.

E e

E, e [e] nf (letra) E, e; **E de Enrique** E for Edward (BRIT) o Easy (US).

E abr (= este) E.

e [e] conj (delante de i- e hi-, pero no hie-) and; V tb **y**.

e/ abr (COM: = envío) shpt.

ebanista [eßa'nista] nm/f cabinetmaker.

ébano ['eßano] nm ebony.

ebrio, a ['eßrjo, a] adj drunk.

Ebro ['eßro] nm Ebro.

ebullición [eßuλi'θjon] nf boiling; **punto de** ~ boiling point.

eccema [ek'θema] nm (MED) eczema.

echar [e'tʃar] vt to throw; (agua, vino) to pour (out); (CULIN) to put in, add; (dientes) to cut; (discurso) to give; (empleado: despedir) to fire, sack; (hojas) to sprout; (cartas) to post; (humo) to emit, give out; (reprimenda) to deal out; (cuenta) to make up; (freno) to put on ♦ vi: ~ **a correr/llorar** to break into a run/burst into tears; ~ **a reír** to burst out laughing; ~**se** vr to lie down; ~ **abajo** (gobierno) to overthrow; (edificio) to demolish; ~ **la buenaventura a algn** to tell sb's fortune; ~ **la culpa a** to lay the blame on; ~ **de menos** to miss; ~**se atrás** to throw o.s. back(wards); (fig) to go back on what one has said; ~**se una novia** to get o.s. a girlfriend; ~**se una siestecita** to have a nap.

echarpe [e'tʃarpe] nm (woman's) stole.

eclesiástico, a [ekle'sjastiko, a] adj ecclesiastical; (autoridades etc) church cpd ♦ nm clergyman.

eclipsar [eklip'sar] vt to eclipse; (fig) to outshine, overshadow.

eclipse [e'klipse] nm eclipse.

eco ['eko] nm echo; **encontrar un ~ en** to produce a response from; **hacerse ~ de una opinión** to echo an opinion; **tener ~** to catch on.

ecografía [ekoɣra'fia] nf ultrasound.

ecología [ekolo'xia] nf ecology.

ecológico, a [eko'loxiko, a] adj ecological; (producto, método) environmentally-friendly; (agricultura) organic.

ecologista [ekolo'xista] adj environmental, conservation cpd ♦ nm/f environmentalist.

economato [ekono'mato] nm cooperative store.

economía [ekono'mia] nf (sistema) economy; (cualidad) thrift; ~ **dirigida** planned economy; ~ **doméstica** housekeeping; ~ **de mercado** market economy; ~ **mixta** mixed economy; ~ **sumergida** black economy; **hacer ~s** to economize; ~**s de escala** economies of scale.

economice [ekono'miθe] etc vb V economizar.

económico, a [eko'nomiko, a] adj (barato) cheap, economical; (persona) thrifty; (COM: año etc) financial; (: situación) economic.

economista [ekono'mista] nm/f economist.

economizar [ekonomi'θar] vt to economize on ♦ vi (ahorrar) to save up; (pey) to be miserly.

ecosistema [ekosis'tema] nm ecosystem.

ecu ['eku] nm ecu.

ecuación [ekwa'θjon] nf equation.

ecuador [ekwa'ðor] nm equator; **(el) E~** Ecuador.

ecuánime [e'kwanime] adj (carácter) level-headed; (estado) calm.

ecuatorial [ekwato'rjal] adj equatorial.

ecuatoriano, a [ekwato'rjano, a] adj, nm/f Ecuador(i)an.

ecuestre [e'kwestre] adj equestrian.

eczema [ek'θema] nm = **eccema**.

ed. abr (= edición) ed.

edad [e'ðað] nf age; **¿qué ~ tienes?** how

old are you?; **tiene ocho años de ~** he is eight (years old); **de ~ corta** young; **ser de ~ mediana/avanzada** to be middle-aged/getting on; **ser mayor de ~** to be of age; **llegar a mayor ~** to come of age; **ser menor de ~** to be under age; **la E~ Media** the Middle Ages; **la E~ de Oro** the Golden Age.

Edén [e'ðen] nm Eden.

edición [eði'θjon] nf (acto) publication; (ejemplar) edition; **"al cerrar la ~"** (TIP) "stop press".

edicto [e'ðikto] nm edict, proclamation.

edificante [eðifi'kante] adj edifying.

edificar [eðifi'kar] vt (ARQ) to build.

edificio [eði'fiθjo] nm building; (fig) edifice, structure.

edifique [eði'fike] etc vb V edificar.

Edimburgo [eðim'burɣo] nm Edinburgh.

editar [eði'tar] vt (publicar) to publish; (preparar textos, tb INFORM) to edit.

editor, a [eði'tor, a] nm/f (que publica) publisher; (redactor) editor ♦ adj: **casa ~a** publishing company.

editorial [eðito'rjal] adj editorial ♦ nm leading article, editorial ♦ nf (tb: **casa ~**) publishers.

editorialista [eðitorja'lista] nm/f leader-writer.

Edo. abr (AM) = **Estado**.

edredón [eðre'ðon] nm eiderdown, quilt; ~ **nórdico** continental quilt, duvet.

educación [eðuka'θjon] nf education; (crianza) upbringing; (modales) (good) manners pl; (formación) training; **sin ~** ill-mannered; **¡qué falta de ~!** how rude!

educado, a [eðu'kaðo, a] adj well-mannered; **mal ~** ill-mannered.

educar [eðu'kar] vt to educate; (criar) to bring up; (voz) to train.

educativo, a [eðuka'tiβo, a] adj educational; (política) education cpd.

eduque [e'ðuke] etc vb V educar.

EE.UU. nmpl abr (= Estados Unidos) USA.

efectista [efek'tista] adj sensationalist.

efectivamente [efektiβa'mente] adv (como respuesta) exactly, precisely; (verdadera-mente) really; (de hecho) in fact.

efectivo, a [efek'tiβo, a] adj effective; (real) actual, real ♦ nm: **pagar en ~** to pay (in) cash; **hacer ~ un cheque** to cash a cheque.

efecto [e'fekto] nm effect, result; (objetivo) purpose, end; ~**s** nmpl (personales) effects; (bienes) goods; (COM) assets; (ECON) bills, securities; ~ **invernadero** greenhouse effect; ~**s de consumo** consumer goods; ~**s a cobrar** bills

receivable; ~s **especiales** special
effects; ~s **personales** personal effects;
~ **secundarios** (COM) spin-off effects; ~s
sonoros sound effects; **hacer** o **surtir** ~
to have the desired effect; **hacer** ~
(impresionar) to make an impression;
llevar algo a ~ to carry sth out; **en** ~ in
fact; (respuesta) exactly, indeed.

efectuar [efek'twar] vt to carry out; (viaje)
to make.

efervescente [eferßes'θente] adj (bebida)
fizzy, bubbly.

eficacia [efi'kaθja] nf (de persona)
efficiency; (de medicamento etc)
effectiveness.

eficaz [efi'kaθ] adj (persona) efficient;
(acción) effective.

eficiencia [efi'θjenθja] nf efficiency.

eficiente [efi'θjente] adj efficient.

efigie [e'fixje] nf effigy.

efímero, a [e'fimero, a] adj ephemeral.

efusión [efu'sjon] nf outpouring; (en el
trato) warmth; **con** ~ effusively.

efusivo, a [efu'sißo, a] adj effusive; **mis
más efusivas gracias** my warmest
thanks.

EGB nf abr (ESP ESCOL: = Educación General
Básica) primary education for 6-14 year
olds; V tb **sistema educativo**.

Egeo [e'xeo] nm: **(Mar)** ~ Aegean (Sea).

egipcio, a [e'xipθjo, a] adj, nm/f Egyptian.

Egipto [e'xipto] nm Egypt.

egocéntrico, a [eɣo'θentriko, a] adj self-
centred.

egoísmo [eɣo'ismo] nm egoism.

egoísta [eɣo'ista] adj egoistical, selfish
♦ nm/f egoist.

ególatra [e'ɣolatra] adj big-headed.

egregio, a [e'ɣrexjo, a] adj eminent,
distinguished.

egresado, a [eɣre'saðo, a] nm/f (AM)
graduate.

egresar [eɣre'sar] vi (AM) to graduate.

eh [e] excl hey!, hi!

Eire ['eire] nm Eire.

ej. abr (= ejemplo) ex.

eje ['exe] nm (GEO, MAT) axis; (POL, fig)
axis, main line; (de rueda) axle; (de
máquina) shaft, spindle.

ejecución [exeku'θjon] nf execution;
(cumplimiento) fulfilment; (actuación)
performance; (JUR: embargo de deudor)
attachment.

ejecutar [exeku'tar] vt to execute, carry
out; (matar) to execute; (cumplir) to fulfil;
(MUS) to perform; (JUR: embargar) to
attach, distrain; (deseos) to fulfil;
(INFORM) to run.

ejecutivo, a [exeku'tißo, a] adj, nm/f executive; **el (poder)** ~ the Executive (Power).

ejecutor [exeku'tor] nm (tb: ~
testamentario) executor.

ejecutoria [exeku'torja] nf (JUR) final
judgment.

ejemplar [exem'plar] adj exemplary ♦ nm
example; (ZOOL) specimen; (de libro)
copy; (de periódico) number, issue; ~ **de
regalo** complimentary copy; **sin** ~
unprecedented.

ejemplificar [exemplifi'kar] vt to
exemplify, illustrate.

ejemplifique [exempli'fike] etc vb V
ejemplificar.

ejemplo [e'xemplo] nm example; (caso)
instance; **por** ~ for example; **dar** ~ to
set an example.

ejercer [exer'θer] vt to exercise; (funciones)
to perform; (negocio) to manage;
(influencia) to exert; (un oficio) to
practise; (poder) to wield ♦ vi: ~ **de** to
practise as.

ejercicio [exer'θiθjo] nm exercise; (MIL)
drill; (COM) fiscal o financial year;
(período) tenure; ~ **acrobático** (AVIAT)
stunt; ~ **comercial** business year; ~s
espirituales (REL) retreat sg; **hacer** ~ to
take exercise.

ejercitar [exerθi'tar] vt to exercise; (MIL) to
drill.

ejército [e'xerθito] nm army; **E~ del Aire/
de Tierra** Air Force/Army; ~ **de
ocupación** army of occupation; ~
permanente standing army; **entrar en el**
~ to join the army, join up.

ejerza [e'xerθa] etc vb V **ejercer**.

ejote [e'xote] nm (AM) green bean.

═══════════════ *PALABRA CLAVE*

el [el] (f **la**, pl **los, las**, neutro **lo**) art def **1** the;
**el libro/la mesa/los estudiantes/las
flores** the book/table/students/flowers;
me gusta el fútbol I like football; **está en
la cama** she's in bed
2 (con n abstracto o propio: no se traduce):
el amor/la juventud love/youth; ~ **Conde
Drácula** Count Dracula
3 (posesión: se traduce a menudo por adj
posesivo): **romperse el brazo** to break
one's arm; **levantó la mano** he put his
hand up; **se puso el sombrero** she put
her hat on
4 (valor descriptivo): **tener la boca
grande/los ojos azules** to have a big
mouth/blue eyes
5 (con días) on; **me iré el viernes** I'll
leave on Friday; **los domingos suelo ir a**

nadar on Sundays I generally go swimming
6 (*lo +adj*): **lo difícil/caro** what is difficult/expensive; (= *cuán*): **no se da cuenta de lo pesado que es** he doesn't realise how boring he is
♦ *pron demos* **1**: **mi libro y el de usted** my book and yours; **las de Pepe son mejores** Pepe's are better; **no la(s) blanca(s) sino la(s) gris(es)** not the white one(s) but the grey one(s)
2: **lo de**: **lo de ayer** what happened yesterday; **lo de las facturas** that business about the invoices
♦ *pron relativo*: **el que** *etc* **1** (*indef*): **el (los) que quiera(n) que se vaya(n)** anyone who wants to can leave; **llévese el/la que más le guste** take the one you like best
2 (*def*): **el que compré ayer** the one I bought yesterday; **los que se van** those who leave
3: **lo que**: **lo que pienso yo/más me gusta** what I think/like most
♦ *conj*: **el que**: **el que lo diga** the fact that he says so; **el que sea tan vago me molesta** his being so lazy bothers me
♦ *excl*: **¡el susto que me diste!** what a fright you gave me!
♦ *pron personal* **1** (*persona*: *m*) him; (: *f*) her; (: *pl*) them; **lo/las veo** I can see him/them
2 (*animal, cosa*: *sg*) it; (: *pl*) them; **lo** (*o* **la**) **veo** I can see it; **los** (*o* **las**) **veo** I can see them
3: **lo** (*como sustituto de frase*): **no lo sabía** I didn't know; **ya lo entiendo** I understand now.

él [el] *pron* (*persona*) he; (*cosa*) it; (*después de prep*: *persona*) him; (: *cosa*) it; **mis libros y los de** ~ my books and his.
elaboración [elaβora'θjon] *nf* (*producción*) manufacture; ~ **de presupuestos** (*COM*) budgeting.
elaborar [elaβo'rar] *vt* (*producto*) to make, manufacture; (*preparar*) to prepare; (*madera, metal etc*) to work; (*proyecto etc*) to work on *o* out.
elasticidad [elasti θi'ðað] *nf* elasticity.
elástico, a [e'lastiko, a] *adj* elastic; (*flexible*) flexible ♦ *nm* elastic; (*gomita*) elastic band.
elección [elek'θjon] *nf* election; (*selección*) choice, selection; **elecciones parciales** by-election *sg*; **elecciones generales** general election *sg*.
electo, a [e'lekto, a] *adj* elect; **el presidente** ~ the president-elect.
electorado [elekto'raðo] *nm* electorate,

voters *pl*.
electoral [elekto'ral] *adj* electoral.
electrice [elek'triθe] *etc vb V* **electrizar**.
electricidad [elektriθi'ðað] *nf* electricity.
electricista [elektri'θista] *nm/f* electrician.
eléctrico, a [e'lektriko, a] *adj* electric.
electrificar [elektrifi'kar] *vt* to electrify.
electrizar [elektri'θar] *vt* (*FERRO, fig*) to electrify.
electro... [elektro] *pref* electro....
electrocardiograma [elektrokarðjo'ɣrama] *nm* electrocardiogram.
electrocución [elektroku'θjon] *nf* electrocution.
electrocutar [elektroku'tar] *vt* to electrocute.
electrodo [elek'troðo] *nm* electrode.
electrodomésticos [elektroðo'mestikos] *nmpl* (*electrical*) household appliances; (*COM*) white goods.
electroimán [elektroi'man] *nm* electromagnet.
electromagnético, a [elektromaɣ'netiko, a] *adj* electromagnetic.
electrón [elek'tron] *nm* electron.
electrónico, a [elek'troniko, a] *adj* electronic ♦ *nf* electronics *sg*; **proceso** ~ **de datos** (*INFORM*) electronic data processing.
electrotecnia [elektro'teknja] *nf* electrical engineering.
electrotécnico, a [elektro'tekniko, a] *nm/f* electrical engineer.
elefante [ele'fante] *nm* elephant.
elegancia [ele'ɣanθja] *nf* elegance, grace; (*estilo*) stylishness.
elegante [ele'ɣante] *adj* elegant, graceful; (*traje etc*) smart, fashionable; (*decoración*) tasteful.
elegía [ele'xia] *nf* elegy.
elegir [ele'xir] *vt* (*escoger*) to choose, select; (*optar*) to opt for; (*presidente*) to elect.
elemental [elemen'tal] *adj* (*claro, obvio*) elementary; (*fundamental*) elemental, fundamental.
elemento [ele'mento] *nm* element; (*fig*) ingredient; (*AM*) person, individual; (*tipo raro*) odd person; (*de pila*) cell; ~**s** *nmpl* elements, rudiments; **estar en su** ~ to be in one's element; **vino a verle un** ~ someone came to see you.
elenco [e'lenko] *nm* catalogue, list; (*TEAT*) cast; (*AM: equipo*) team.
elepé [ele'pe] *nm* LP.
elevación [eleßa'θjon] *nf* elevation; (*acto*) raising, lifting; (*de precios*) rise; (*GEO*

etc) height, altitude.
elevador [eleßa'ðor] *nm* (*AM*) lift (*BRIT*), elevator (*US*).
elevar [ele'ßar] *vt* to raise, lift (up); (*precio*) to put up; (*producción*) to step up; (*informe etc*) to present; ~se *vr* (*edificio*) to rise; (*precios*) to go up; (*transportarse, enajenarse*) to get carried away; **la cantidad se eleva a ...** the total amounts to ... .
eligiendo [eli'xjenðo] *etc*, **elija** [e'lixa] *etc vb V* **elegir**.
eliminar [elimi'nar] *vt* to eliminate, remove; (*olor, persona*) to get rid of; (*DEPORTE*) to eliminate, knock out.
eliminatoria [elimina'torja] *nf* heat, preliminary (round).
elite [e'lite], **élite** ['elite] *nf* elite, élite.
elitista [eli'tista] *adj* elitist.
elixir [elik'sir] *nm* elixir; (*tb:* ~ **bucal**) mouthwash.
ella ['eʎa] *pron* (*persona*) she; (*cosa*) it; (*después de prep: persona*) her; (*: cosa*) it; **de** ~ hers.
ellas ['eʎas] *pron V* **ellos**.
ello ['eʎo] *pron neutro* it; **es por** ~ **que ...** that's why ....
ellos, as ['eʎos, as] *pron personal pl* they; (*después de prep*) them; **de** ~ theirs.
elocuencia [elo'kwenθja] *nf* eloquence.
elocuente [elo'kwente] *adj* eloquent; (*fig*) significant; **un dato** ~ a fact which speaks for itself.
elogiar [elo'xjar] *vt* to praise, eulogize.
elogio [e'loxjo] *nm* praise; **queda por encima de todo** ~ it's beyond praise; **hacer** ~ **de** to sing the praises of.
elote [e'lote] *nm* (*AM*) corn on the cob.
El Salvador *nm* El Salvador.
eludir [elu'ðir] *vt* (*evitar*) to avoid, evade; (*escapar*) to escape, elude.
E.M. *abr* (*MIL: = Estado Mayor*) G.S.
Em.ª *abr* = **Eminencia**.
emanar [ema'nar] *vi:* ~ **de** to emanate from, come from; (*derivar de*) to originate in.
emancipar [emanθi'par] *vt* to emancipate; ~se *vr* to become emancipated, free o.s.
embadurnar [embaður'nar] *vt* to smear.
embajada [emba'xaða] *nf* embassy.
embajador, a [embaxa'ðor, a] *nm/f* ambassador/ambassadress.
embaladura [embala'ðura] *nf* (*AM*), **embalaje** [emba'laxe] *nm* packing.
embalar [emba'lar] *vt* (*envolver*) to parcel, wrap (up); (*envasar*) to package ♦ *vi* to sprint.
embalsamar [embalsa'mar] *vt* to embalm.

embalsar [embal'sar] *vt* (*río*) to dam (up); (*agua*) to retain.
embalse [em'balse] *nm* (*presa*) dam; (*lago*) reservoir.
embarace [emba'raθe] *etc vb V* **embarazar**.
embarazada [embara'θaða] *adj f* pregnant ♦ *nf* pregnant woman.
embarazar [embara'θar] *vt* to obstruct, hamper; ~se *vr* (*aturdirse*) to become embarrassed; (*confundirse*) to get into a mess.
embarazo [emba'raθo] *nm* (*de mujer*) pregnancy; (*impedimento*) obstacle, obstruction; (*timidez*) embarrassment.
embarazoso, a [embara'θoso, a] *adj* (*molesto*) awkward; (*violento*) embarrassing.
embarcación [embarka'θjon] *nf* (*barco*) boat, craft; (*acto*) embarkation; ~ **de arrastre** trawler; ~ **de cabotaje** coasting vessel.
embarcadero [embarka'ðero] *nm* pier, landing stage.
embarcar [embar'kar] *vt* (*cargamento*) to ship, stow; (*persona*) to embark, put on board; (*fig*): ~ **a algn en una empresa** to involve sb in an undertaking; ~se *vr* to embark, go on board; (*marinero*) to sign on; (*AM: en tren etc*) to get on, get in.
embargar [embar'ɣar] *vt* (*frenar*) to restrain; (*sentidos*) to overpower; (*JUR*) to seize, impound.
embargo [em'barɣo] *nm* (*JUR*) seizure; (*COM etc*) embargo; **sin** ~ still, however, nonetheless.
embargue [em'barɣe] *etc vb V* **embargar**.
embarque [em'barke] *etc vb V* **embarcar**. ♦ *nm* shipment, loading.
embarrancar [embarran'kar] *vt, vi* (*NAUT*) to run aground; (*AUTO etc*) to run into a ditch.
embarranque [emba'rranke] *etc vb V* **embarrancar**.
embarullar [embaru'ʎar] *vt* to make a mess of.
embate [em'bate] *nm* (*de mar, viento*) beating, violence.
embaucador, a [embauka'ðor, a] *nm/f* (*estafador*) trickster; (*impostor*) impostor.
embaucar [embau'kar] *vt* to trick, fool.
embauque [em'bauke] *etc vb V* **embaucar**.
embeber [embe'ßer] *vt* (*absorber*) to absorb, soak up; (*empapar*) to saturate ♦ *vi* to shrink; ~se *vr:* ~se **en un libro** to be engrossed *o* absorbed in a book.
embelesado, a [embele'saðo, a] *adj* spellbound.

embelesar [embele'sar] *vt* to enchant; ~**se** *vr*: ~**se (con)** to be enchanted (by).

embellecer [embeʎe'θer] *vt* to embellish, beautify.

embellezca [embe'ʎeθka] *etc vb* V **embellecer.**

embestida [embes'tiða] *nf* attack, onslaught; (*carga*) charge.

embestir [embes'tir] *vt* to attack, assault; to charge, attack ♦ *vi* to attack.

embistiendo [embis'tjendo] *etc vb* V **embestir.**

emblanquecer [emblanke'θer] *vt* to whiten, bleach; ~**se** *vr* to turn white.

emblanquezca [emblan'keθka] *etc vb* V **emblanquecer.**

emblema [em'blema] *nm* emblem.

embobado, a [embo'ßaðo, a] *adj* (*atontado*) stunned, bewildered.

embobar [embo'ßar] *vt* (*asombrar*) to amaze; (*fascinar*) to fascinate; ~**se** *vr*: ~**se con** *o* **de** *o* **en** to be amazed at; to be fascinated by.

embocadura [emboka'ðura] *nf* narrow entrance; (*de río*) mouth; (*MUS*) mouthpiece.

embolado [embo'laðo] *nm* (*TEAT*) bit part, minor role; (*fam*) trick.

embolia [em'bolja] *nf* (*MED*) embolism; ~ **cerebral** clot on the brain.

émbolo ['embolo] *nm* (*AUTO*) piston.

embolsar [embol'sar] *vt* to pocket, put in one's pocket.

emboquillado, a [emboki'ʎaðo, a] *adj* (*cigarrillo*) tipped, filter *cpd.*

emborrachar [emborra'tʃar] *vt* to make drunk; ~**se** *vr* to get drunk.

emboscada [embos'kaða] *nf* (*celada*) ambush.

embotar [embo'tar] *vt* to blunt, dull; ~**se** *vr* (*adormecerse*) to go numb.

embotellamiento [emboteʎa'mjento] *nm* (*AUTO*) traffic jam.

embotellar [embote'ʎar] *vt* to bottle; ~**se** *vr* (*circulación*) to get into a jam.

embozo [em'boθo] *nm* muffler, mask; (*de sábana*) turn over.

embragar [embra'ɣar] *vt* (*AUTO, TEC*) to engage; (*partes*) to connect ♦ *vi* to let in the clutch.

embrague [em'braɣe] *etc vb* V **embragar** ♦ *nm* (*tb*: **pedal de ~**) clutch.

embravecer [embraβe'θer] *vt* to enrage, infuriate; ~**se** *vr* to become furious; (*mar*) to get rough; (*tormenta*) to rage.

embravecido, a [embraβe'θiðo, a] *adj* (*mar*) rough; (*persona*) furious.

embriagador, a [embrjaɣa'ðor, a] *adj* intoxicating.

embriagar [embrja'ɣar] *vt* (*emborrachar*) to make drunk; (*alegrar*) to delight; ~**se** *vr* (*emborracharse*) to get drunk.

embriague [em'brjaɣe] *etc vb* V **embriagar.**

embriaguez [embrja'ɣeθ] *nf* (*borrachera*) drunkenness.

embrión [em'brjon] *nm* embryo.

embrionario, a [embrjo'narjo, a] *adj* embryonic.

embrollar [embro'ʎar] *vt* (*asunto*) to confuse, complicate; (*persona*) to involve, embroil; ~**se** *vr* (*confundirse*) to get into a muddle *o* mess.

embrollo [em'broʎo] *nm* (*enredo*) muddle, confusion; (*aprieto*) fix, jam.

embromado, a [embro'maðo, a] *adj* (*AM fam*) tricky, difficult.

embromar [embro'mar] *vt* (*burlarse de*) to tease, make fun of; (*AM fam*: *molestar*) to annoy.

embrujado, a [embru'xaðo, a] *adj* (*persona*) bewitched; **casa embrujada** haunted house.

embrujo [em'bruxo] *nm* (*de mirada etc*) charm, magic.

embrutecer [embrute'θer] *vt* (*atontar*) to stupefy; ~**se** *vr* to be stupefied.

embrutezca [embru'teθka] *etc vb* V **embrutecer.**

embudo [em'buðo] *nm* funnel.

embuste [em'buste] *nm* trick; (*mentira*) lie; (*hum*) fib.

embustero, a [embus'tero, a] *adj* lying, deceitful ♦ *nm/f* (*tramposo*) cheat; (*mentiroso*) liar; (*hum*) fibber.

embutido [embu'tiðo] *nm* (*CULIN*) sausage; (*TEC*) inlay.

embutir [embu'tir] *vt* to insert; (*TEC*) to inlay; (*llenar*) to pack tight, cram.

emergencia [emer'xenθja] *nf* emergency; (*surgimiento*) emergence.

emergente [emer'xente] *adj* resultant, consequent; (*nación*) emergent.

emerger [emer'xer] *vi* to emerge, appear.

emeritense [emeri'tense] *adj* of *o* from Mérida ♦ *nm/f* native *o* inhabitant of Mérida.

emerja [e'merxa] *etc vb* V **emerger.**

emigración [emiɣra'θjon] *nf* emigration; (*de pájaros*) migration.

emigrado, a [emi'ɣraðo, a] *nm/f* emigrant; (*POL etc*) émigré(e).

emigrante [emi'ɣrante] *adj, nm/f* emigrant.

emigrar [emi'ɣrar] *vi* (*personas*) to emigrate; (*pájaros*) to migrate.

eminencia [emi'nenθja] *nf* eminence; (*en títulos*): **Su E~** His Eminence; **Vuestra**

E~ Your Eminence.

eminente [emi'nente] *adj* eminent, distinguished; (*elevado*) high.

emisario [emi'sarjo] *nm* emissary.

emisión [emi'sjon] *nf* (*acto*) emission; (*COM etc*) issue; (*RADIO, TV: acto*) broadcasting; (: *programa*) broadcast, programme, program (*US*); ~ **de acciones** (*COM*) share issue; ~ **gratuita de acciones** (*COM*) rights issue; ~ **de valores** (*COM*) flotation.

emisor, a [emi'sor, a] *nm* transmitter ♦ *nf* radio *o* broadcasting station.

emitir [emi'tir] *vt* (*olor etc*) to emit, give off; (*moneda etc*) to issue; (*opinión*) to express; (*voto*) to cast; (*señal*) to send out; (*RADIO*) to broadcast; ~ **una señal sonora** to beep.

emoción [emo'θjon] *nf* emotion; (*excitación*) excitement; (*sentimiento*) feeling; ¡**qué** ~! how exciting!; (*irónico*) what a thrill!

emocionado, a [emoθjo'naðo, a] *adj* deeply moved, stirred.

emocionante [emoθjo'nante] *adj* (*excitante*) exciting, thrilling.

emocionar [emoθjo'nar] *vt* (*excitar*) to excite, thrill; (*conmover*) to move, touch; (*impresionar*) to impress; ~**se** *vr* to get excited.

emotivo, a [emo'tiβo, a] *adj* emotional.

empacar [empa'kar] *vt* (*gen*) to pack; (*en caja*) to bale, crate.

empacharse [empa't∫arse] *vr* (*MED*) to get indigestion.

empacho [em'pat∫o] *nm* (*MED*) indigestion; (*fig*) embarrassment.

empadronamiento [empaðrona'mjento] *nm* census; (*de electores*) electoral register.

empadronarse [empaðro'narse] *vr* (*POL: como elector*) to register.

empalagar [empala'ɣar] *vt* (*suj: comida*) to cloy; (*hartar*) to pall on ♦ *vi* to pall.

empalagoso, a [empala'ɣoso, a] *adj* cloying; (*fig*) tiresome.

empalague [empa'laɣe] *etc vb V* **empalagar**.

empalizada [empali'θaða] *nf* fence; (*MIL*) palisade.

empalmar [empal'mar] *vt* to join, connect ♦ *vi* (*dos caminos*) to meet, join.

empalme [em'palme] *nm* joint, connection; (*de vías*) junction; (*de trenes*) connection.

empanada [empa'naða] *nf* pie, pasty.

empanar [empa'nar] *vt* (*CULIN*) to cook *o* roll in breadcrumbs *o* pastry.

empantanarse [empanta'narse] *vr* to get

swamped; (*fig*) to get bogged down.

empañarse [empa'ɲarse] *vr* (*nublarse*) to get misty, steam up.

empapar [empa'par] *vt* (*mojar*) to soak, saturate; (*absorber*) to soak up, absorb; ~**se** *vr*: ~**se de** to soak up.

empapelar [empape'lar] *vt* (*paredes*) to paper.

empaque [em'pake] *etc vb V* **empacar**.

empaquetar [empake'tar] *vt* to pack, parcel up; (*COM*) to package.

emparedado [empare'ðaðo] *nm* sandwich.

emparejar [empare'xar] *vt* to pair ♦ *vi* to catch up.

emparentar [emparen'tar] *vi*: ~ **con** to marry into.

empariente [empa'rjente] *etc vb V* **emparentar**.

empastar [empas'tar] *vt* (*embadurnar*) to paste; (*diente*) to fill.

empaste [em'paste] *nm* (*de diente*) filling.

empatar [empa'tar] *vi* to draw, tie.

empate [em'pate] *nm* draw, tie; **un** ~ **a cero** a no-score draw.

empecé [empe'θe], **empecemos** [empe'θemos] *etc vb V* **empezar**.

empecinado, a [empeθi'naðo, a] *adj* stubborn.

empedernido, a [empeðer'niðo, a] *adj* hard, heartless; (*fijado*) hardened, inveterate; **un fumador** ~ a heavy smoker.

empedrado, a [empe'ðraðo, a] *adj* paved ♦ *nm* paving.

empedrar [empe'ðrar] *vt* to pave.

empeine [em'peine] *nm* (*de pie, zapato*) instep.

empellón [empe'ʎon] *nm* push, shove; **abrirse paso a empellones** to push *o* shove one's way past *o* through.

empeñado, a [empe'ɲaðo, a] *adj* (*persona*) determined; (*objeto*) pawned.

empeñar [empe'ɲar] *vt* (*objeto*) to pawn, pledge; (*persona*) to compel; ~**se** *vr* (*obligarse*) to bind o.s., pledge o.s.; (*endeudarse*) to get into debt; ~**se en hacer** to be set on doing, be determined to do.

empeño [em'peɲo] *nm* (*determinación*) determination; (*cosa prendada*) pledge; **casa de** ~**s** pawnshop; **con** ~ insistently; (*con celo*) eagerly; **tener** ~ **en hacer algo** to be bent on doing sth.

empeoramiento [empeora'mjento] *nm* worsening.

empeorar [empeo'rar] *vt* to make worse, worsen ♦ *vi* to get worse, deteriorate.

empequeñecer [empekeɲe'θer] *vt* to

dwarf; (fig) to belittle.
empequeñezca [empeke'ɲeθka] etc vb V
empequeñecer.
emperador [empera'ðor] nm emperor.
emperatriz [empera'triθ] nf empress.
emperrarse [empe'rrarse] vr to get
stubborn; ~ **en algo** to persist in sth.
empezar [empe'θar] vt, vi to begin, start;
empezó a llover it started to rain; **bueno,
para** ~ well, to start with.
empiece [em'pjeθe] etc vb V **empezar.**
empiedre [em'pjeðre] etc vb V **empedrar.**
empiezo [em'pjeθo] etc vb V **empezar.**
empinado, a [empi'naðo, a] adj steep.
empinar [empi'nar] vt to raise; (botella) to
tip up; ~**se** vr (persona) to stand on
tiptoe; (animal) to rear up; (camino) to
climb steeply; ~ **el codo** to booze (fam).
empingorotado, a [empingoro'taðo, a] adj
(fam) stuck-up.
empírico, a [em'piriko, a] adj empirical.
emplace [em'plaθe] etc vb V **emplazar.**
emplaste [em'plaste], **emplasto**
[em'plasto] nm (MED) plaster.
emplazamiento [emplaθa'mjento] nm site,
location; (JUR) summons sg.
emplazar [empla'θar] vt (ubicar) to site,
place, locate; (JUR) to summons;
(convocar) to summon.
empleado, a [emple'aðo, a] nm/f (gen)
employee; (de banco etc) clerk; ~ **público**
civil servant.
emplear [emple'ar] vt (usar) to use,
employ; (dar trabajo a) to employ; ~**se** vr
(conseguir trabajo) to be employed;
(ocuparse) to occupy o.s.; ~ **mal el
tiempo** to waste time; **¡te está bien
empleado!** it serves you right!
empleo [em'pleo] nm (puesto) job; (puestos:
colectivamente) employment; (uso) use,
employment; **"modo de ~"**
"instructions for use".
emplumar [emplu'mar] vt (estafar) to
swindle.
empobrecer [empoβre'θer] vt to
impoverish; ~**se** vr to become poor o
impoverished.
empobrecimiento [empoβreθi'mjento] nm
impoverishment.
empobrezca [empo'βreθka] etc vb V
empobrecer.
empollar [empo'ʎar] vt to incubate; (ESCOL
fam) to swot (up) ♦ vi (gallina) to brood;
(ESCOL fam) to swot.
empollón, ona [empo'ʎon, ona] nm/f
(ESCOL fam) swot.
empolvar [empol'βar] vt (cara) to powder;
~**se** vr to powder one's face; (superficie)

to get dusty.
emponzoñar [emponθo'ɲar] vt (esp fig) to
poison.
emporio [em'porjo] nm emporium, trading
centre; (AM: gran almacén) department
store.
empotrado, a [empo'traðo, a] adj (armario
etc) built-in.
empotrar [empo'trar] vt to embed;
(armario etc) to build in.
emprendedor, a [emprende'ðor, a] adj
enterprising.
emprender [empren'der] vt to undertake;
(empezar) to begin, embark on;
(acometer) to tackle, take on; ~ **marcha a**
to set out for.
empresa [em'presa] nf enterprise; (COM:
sociedad) firm, company; (: negocio)
business; (esp TEAT) management; ~
filial (COM) affiliated company; ~ **matriz**
(COM) parent company.
empresario, a [empre'sarjo, a] nm/f (COM)
businessman/woman, entrepreneur;
(TEC) manager; (MUS: de ópera etc)
impresario; ~ **de pompas fúnebres**
undertaker (BRIT), mortician (US).
empréstito [em'prestito] nm (public) loan;
(COM) loan capital.
empujar [empu'xar] vt to push, shove.
empuje [em'puxe] nm thrust; (presión)
pressure; (fig) vigour, drive.
empujón [empu'xon] nm push, shove;
abrirse paso a empujones to shove one's
way through.
empuñadura [empuɲa'ðura] nf (de espada)
hilt; (de herramienta etc) handle.
empuñar [empu'ɲar] vt (asir) to grasp,
take (firm) hold of; ~ **las armas** (fig) to
take up arms.
emulación [emula'θjon] nf emulation.
emular [emu'lar] vt to emulate; (rivalizar) to
rival.
émulo, a ['emulo, a] nm/f rival,
competitor.
emulsión [emul'sjon] nf emulsion.

=========================== PALABRA CLAVE

en [en] prep **1** (posición) in; (: sobre) on; **está**
~ **el cajón** it's in the drawer; ~
Argentina/La Paz in Argentina/La Paz; ~
el colegio/la oficina at school/the office;
~ **casa** at home; **está** ~ **el suelo/quinto
piso** it's on the floor/the fifth floor; ~ **el
periódico** in the paper
2 (dirección) into; **entró** ~ **el aula** she
went into the classroom; **meter algo** ~ **el
bolso** to put sth into one's bag; **ir de
puerta** ~ **puerta** to go from door to door

3 (*tiempo*) in; on; ~ **1605/3 semanas/ invierno** in 1605/3 weeks/winter; ~ **(el mes de) enero** in (the month of) January; ~ **aquella ocasión/época** on that occasion/at that time
4 (*precio*) for; **lo vendió ~ 20 dólares** he sold it for 20 dollars
5 (*diferencia*) by; **reducir/aumentar ~ una tercera parte/un 20 por ciento** to reduce/increase by a third/20 per cent
6 (*manera, forma*): ~ **avión/autobús** by plane/bus; **escrito ~ inglés** written in English; ~ **serio** seriously; ~ **espiral/ círculo** in a spiral/circle
7 (*después de vb que indica gastar etc*) on; **han cobrado demasiado ~ dietas** they've charged too much to expenses; **se le va la mitad del sueldo ~ comida** half his salary goes on food
8 (*tema, ocupación*): **experto ~ la materia** expert on the subject; **trabaja ~ la construcción** he works in the building industry
9 (*adj* + ~ + *infin*): **lento ~ reaccionar** slow to react.

enagua(s) [ena‍ɣwa(s)] *nf(pl)* (*esp AM*) petticoat.
enajenación [enaxena'θjon] *nf*, **enajenamiento** [enaxena'mjento] *nm* alienation; (*fig: distracción*) absent-mindedness; (:: *embelesamiento*) rapture, trance; ~ **mental** mental derangement.
enajenar [enaxe'nar] *vt* to alienate; (*fig*) to carry away.
enamorado, a [enamo'raðo, a] *adj* in love ♦ *nm/f* lover; **estar ~ (de)** to be in love (with).
enamorar [enamo'rar] *vt* to win the love of; ~**se** *vr*: ~**se (de)** to fall in love (with).
enano, a [e'nano, a] *adj* tiny, dwarf ♦ *nm/f* dwarf; (*pey*) runt.
enarbolar [enarßo'lar] *vt* (*bandera etc*) to hoist; (*espada etc*) to brandish.
enardecer [enarðe'θer] *vt* (*pasiones*) to fire, inflame; (*persona*) to fill with enthusiasm; ~**se** *vr* to get excited; ~**se por** to get enthusiastic about.
enardezca [enar'deθka] *etc vb V* **enardecer**.
encabece [enka'ßeθe] *etc vb V* **encabezar**.
encabezado [enkaße'θaðo] *nm* (*COM*) header.
encabezamiento [enkaßeθa'mjento] *nm* (*de carta*) heading; (*COM*) billhead, letterhead; (*de periódico*) headline; (*preámbulo*) foreword, preface; ~ **normal** (*TIP etc*) running head.
encabezar [enkaße'θar] *vt* (*movimiento,*

revolución) to lead, head; (*lista*) to head; (*carta*) to put a heading to; (*libro*) to entitle.
encadenar [enkaðe'nar] *vt* to chain (together); (*poner grilletes a*) to shackle.
encajar [enka'xar] *vt* (*ajustar*): ~ **en** to fit (into); (*meter a la fuerza*) to push in; (*máquina etc*) to house; (*partes*) to join; (*fam: golpe*) to give, deal; (*entrometer*) to insert ♦ *vi* to fit (well); (*fig: corresponder a*) to match; ~**se** *vr*: ~**se en un sillón** to squeeze into a chair.
encaje [en'kaxe] *nm* (*labor*) lace.
encajonar [enkaxo'nar] *vt* to box (up), put in a box.
encalar [enka'lar] *vt* (*pared*) to whitewash.
encallar [enka'ʎar] *vi* (*NAUT*) to run aground.
encaminado, a [enkami'naðo, a] *adj*: **medidas encaminadas a ...** measures designed to *o* aimed at ....
encaminar [enkami'nar] *vt* to direct, send; ~**se** *vr*: ~**se a** to set out for; ~ **por** (*expedición etc*) to route via.
encandilar [enkandi'lar] *vt* to dazzle; (*persona*) to daze, bewilder.
encanecer [enkane'θer] *vi*, **encanecerse** *vr* (*pelo*) to go grey.
encanezca [enka'neθka] *etc vb V* **encanecer**.
encantado, a [enkan'taðo, a] *adj* delighted; ¡~! how do you do!, pleased to meet you.
encantador, a [enkanta'ðor, a] *adj* charming, lovely ♦ *nm/f* magician, enchanter/enchantress.
encantar [enkan'tar] *vt* to charm, delight; (*cautivar*) to fascinate; (*hechizar*) to bewitch, cast a spell on.
encanto [en'kanto] *nm* (*magia*) spell, charm; (*fig*) charm, delight; (*expresión de ternura*) sweetheart; **como por ~** as if by magic.
encapotado, a [enkapo'taðo, a] *adj* (*cielo*) overcast.
encapricharse [enkapri'tʃarse] *vr*: **se ha encaprichado con ir** he's taken it into his head to go; **se ha encaprichado** he's digging his heels in.
encaramar [enkara'mar] *vt* (*subir*) to raise, lift up; ~**se** *vr* (*subir*) to perch; ~**se a** (*árbol etc*) to climb.
encararse [enka'rarse] *vr*: ~ **a** *o* **con** to confront, come face to face with.
encarcelar [enkarθe'lar] *vt* to imprison, jail.
encarecer [enkare'θer] *vt* to put up the price of ♦ *vi*, ~**se** *vr* to get dearer.

encarecidamente [enkareθiða'mente] *adv* earnestly.

encarecimiento [enkareθi'mjento] *nm* price increase.

encarezca [enka'reθka] *etc vb V* **encarecer.**

encargado, a [enkar'ɣaðo, a] *adj* in charge ♦ *nm/f* agent, representative; (*responsable*) person in charge.

encargar [enkar'ɣar] *vt* to entrust; (*COM*) to order; (*recomendar*) to urge, recommend; ~**se** *vr*: ~**se de** to look after, take charge of; ~ **algo a algn** to put sb in charge of sth.

encargo [en'karɣo] *nm* (*pedido*) assignment, job; (*responsabilidad*) responsibility; (*recomendación*) recommendation; (*COM*) order.

encargue [en'karɣe] *etc vb V* **encargar.**

encariñarse [enkari'ɲarse] *vr*: ~ **con** to grow fond of, get attached to.

encarnación [enkarna'θjon] *nf* incarnation, embodiment.

encarnado, a [enkar'naðo, a] *adj* (*color*) red; **ponerse** ~ to blush.

encarnar [enkar'nar] *vt* to personify; (*TEAT: papel*) to play ♦ *vi* (*REL etc*) to become incarnate.

encarnizado, a [enkarni'θaðo, a] *adj* (*lucha*) bloody, fierce.

encarrilar [enkarri'lar] *vt* (*tren*) to put back on the rails; (*fig*) to correct, put on the right track.

encasillar [enkasi'ʎar] *vt* (*TEAT*) to typecast; (*clasificar. pey*) to pigeonhole.

encasquetar [enkaske'tar] *vt* (*sombrero*) to pull down *o* on; ~**se** *vr*: ~**se el sombrero** to pull one's hat down *o* on; ~ **algo a algn** to offload sth onto sb.

encauce [en'kauθe] *etc vb V* **encauzar.**

encausar [enkau'sar] *vt* to prosecute, sue.

encauzar [enkau'θar] *vt* to channel; (*fig*) to direct.

encendedor [enθende'ðor] *nm* lighter.

encender [enθen'der] *vt* (*con fuego*) to light; (*incendiar*) to set fire to; (*luz, radio*) to put on, switch on; (*INFORM*) to toggle on, switch on; (*avivar: pasiones etc*) to inflame; (*despertar: entusiasmo*) to arouse; (*odio*) to awaken; ~**se** *vr* to catch fire; (*excitarse*) to get excited; (*de cólera*) to flare up; (*el rostro*) to blush.

encendidamente [enθendiða'mente] *adv* passionately.

encendido, a [enθen'diðo, a] *adj* alight; (*aparato*) (switched) on; (*mejillas*) glowing; (*cara: por el vino etc*) flushed; (*mirada*) passionate ♦ *nm* (*AUTO*) ignition; (*de faroles*) lighting.

encerado, a [enθe'raðo, a] *adj* (*suelo*) waxed, polished ♦ *nm* (*ESCOL*) blackboard; (*hule*) oilcloth.

encerar [enθe'rar] *vt* (*suelo*) to wax, polish.

encerrar [enθe'rrar] *vt* (*confinar*) to shut in *o* up; (*con llave*) to lock in *o* up; (*comprender, incluir*) to include, contain; ~**se** *vr* to shut *o* lock o.s. up *o* in.

encerrona [enθe'rrona] *nf* trap.

encestar [enθes'tar] *vi* to score a basket.

encharcar [entʃar'kar] *vt* to swamp, flood; ~**se** *vr* to become flooded.

encharque [en'tʃarke] *etc vb V* **encharcar.**

enchufar [entʃu'far] *vt* (*ELEC*) to plug in; (*TEC*) to connect, fit together; (*COM*) to merge.

enchufe [en'tʃufe] *nm* (*ELEC: clavija*) plug; (: *toma*) socket; (*de dos tubos*) joint, connection; (*fam: influencia*) contact, connection; (: *puesto*) cushy job; ~ **de clavija** jack plug; **tiene un** ~ **en el ministerio** he can pull strings at the ministry.

encía [en'θia] *nf* (*ANAT*) gum.

enciclopedia [enθiklo'peðja] *nf* encyclopaedia.

encienda [en'θjenda] *etc vb V* **encender.**

encierro [en'θjerro] *etc vb V* **encerrar** ♦ *nm* shutting in *o* up; (*calabozo*) prison; (*AGR*) pen; (*TAUR*) penning.

encima [en'θima] *adv* (*sobre*) above, over; (*además*) besides; ~ **de** (*en*) on, on top of; (*sobre*) above, over; (*además de*) besides, on top of; **por** ~ **de** over; ¿**llevas dinero** ~? have you (got) any money on you?; **se me vino** ~ it took me by surprise.

encina [en'θina] *nf* (holm) oak.

encinta [en'θinta] *adj f* pregnant.

enclave [en'klaβe] *nm* enclave.

enclenque [en'klenke] *adj* weak, sickly.

encoger [enko'xer] *vt* (*gen*) to shrink, contract; (*fig: asustar*) to scare; (: *desanimar*) to discourage; ~**se** *vr* to shrink, contract; (*fig*) to cringe; ~**se de hombros** to shrug one's shoulders.

encoja [en'koxa] *etc vb V* **encoger.**

encolar [enko'lar] *vt* (*engomar*) to glue, paste; (*pegar*) to stick down.

encolerice [enkole'riθe] *etc vb V* **encolerizar.**

encolerizar [enkoleri'θar] *vt* to anger, provoke; ~**se** *vr* to get angry.

encomendar [enkomen'dar] *vt* to entrust, commend; ~**se** *vr*: ~**se a** to put one's trust in.

encomiar [enko'mjar] *vt* to praise, pay tribute to.

encomienda [enko'mjenda] *etc vb V*

encomendar ♦ *nf* (*encargo*) charge, commission; (*elogio*) tribute; (*AM*) parcel, package; ~ **postal** (*AM*) parcel post.

encomio [en'komjo] *nm* praise, tribute.

encono [en'kono] *nm* (*rencor*) rancour, spite.

encontrado, a [enkon'traðo, a] *adj* (*contrario*) contrary, conflicting; (*hostil*) hostile.

encontrar [enkon'trar] *vt* (*hallar*) to find; (*inesperadamente*) to meet, run into; ~**se** *vr* to meet (each other); (*situarse*) to be (situated); (*persona*) to find o.s., be; (*entrar en conflicto*) to crash, collide; ~**se con** to meet; ~**se bien (de salud)** to feel well; **no se encuentra aquí en este momento** he's not in at the moment.

encontronazo [enkontro'naθo] *nm* collision, crash.

encorvar [enkor'ßar] *vt* to curve; (*inclinar*) to bend (down); ~**se** *vr* to bend down, bend over.

encrespado, a [enkres'paðo, a] *adj* (*pelo*) curly; (*mar*) rough.

encrespar [enkres'par] *vt* (*cabellos*) to curl; (*fig*) to anger, irritate; ~**se** *vr* (*el mar*) to get rough; (*fig*) to get cross o irritated.

encrucijada [enkruθi'xaða] *nf* crossroads *sg*; (*empalme*) junction.

encuadernación [enkwaðerna'θjon] *nf* binding; (*taller*) binder's.

encuadernador, a [enkwaðerna'ðor, a] *nm/f* bookbinder.

encuadrar [enkwa'ðrar] *vt* (*retrato*) to frame; (*ajustar*) to fit, insert; (*encerrar*) to contain.

encubierto [enku'ßjerto] *pp de* **encubrir**.

encubrir [enku'ßrir] *vt* (*ocultar*) to hide, conceal; (*criminal*) to harbour, shelter; (*ayudar*) to be an accomplice in.

encuentro [en'kwentro] *etc vb V* **encontrar** ♦ *nm* (*de personas*) meeting; (*AUTO etc*) collision, crash; (*DEPORTE*) match, game; (*MIL*) encounter.

encuesta [en'kwesta] *nf* inquiry, investigation; (*sondeo*) public opinion poll; ~ **judicial** post mortem.

encumbrado, a [enkum'braðo, a] *adj* eminent, distinguished.

encumbrar [enkum'brar] *vt* (*persona*) to exalt; ~**se** *vr* (*fig*) to become conceited.

endeble [en'deßle] *adj* (*argumento, excusa, persona*) weak.

endémico, a [en'demiko, a] *adj* endemic.

endemoniado, a [endemo'njaðo, a] *adj* possessed (of the devil); (*travieso*) devilish.

enderece [ende're θe] *etc vb V* **enderezar**.

enderezar [endere'θar] *vt* (*poner derecho*) to straighten (out); (: *verticalmente*) to set upright; (*fig*) to straighten o sort out; (*dirigir*) to direct; ~**se** *vr* (*persona sentada*) to sit up straight.

endeudarse [endeu'ðarse] *vr* to get into debt.

endiablado, a [endja'ßlaðo, a] *adj* devilish, diabolical; (*hum*) mischievous.

endibia [en'dißja] *nf* endive.

endilgar [endil'ɣar] *vt* (*fam*): ~ **algo a algn** to lumber sb with sth; ~ **un sermón a algn** to give sb a lecture.

endilgue [en'dilɣe] *etc vb V* **endilgar**.

endiñar [endi'ɲar] *vt*: ~ **algo a algn** to land sth on sb.

endomingarse [endomin'garse] *vr* to dress up, put on one's best clothes.

endomingue [endo'minge] *etc vb V* **endomingarse**.

endosar [endo'sar] *vt* (*cheque etc*) to endorse.

endulce [en'dulθe] *etc vb V* **endulzar**.

endulzar [endul'θar] *vt* to sweeten; (*suavizar*) to soften.

endurecer [endure'θer] *vt* to harden; ~**se** *vr* to harden, grow hard.

endurecido, a [endure'θiðo, a] *adj* (*duro*) hard; (*fig*) hardy, tough; **estar ~ a algo** to be hardened o used to sth.

endurezca [endu'reθka] *etc vb V* **endurecer**.

ene. *abr* (= *enero*) Jan.

enemigo, a [ene'miɣo, a] *adj* enemy, hostile ♦ *nm/f* enemy ♦ *nf* enmity, hostility; **ser ~ de** (*persona*) to dislike; (*suj: tendencia*) to be inimical to.

enemistad [enemis'tað] *nf* enmity.

enemistar [enemis'tar] *vt* to make enemies of, cause a rift between; ~**se** *vr* to become enemies; (*amigos*) to fall out.

energético, a [ener'xetiko, a] *adj*: **política energética** energy policy.

energía [ener'xia] *nf* (*vigor*) energy, drive; (*TEC, ELEC*) energy, power; ~ **atómica/eléctrica/eólica** atomic/electric/wind power.

enérgico, a [e'nerxiko, a] *adj* (*gen*) energetic; (*ataque*) vigorous; (*ejercicio*) strenuous; (*medida*) bold; (*voz, modales*) forceful.

energúmeno, a [ener'xumeno, a] *nm/f* madman/woman; **ponerse como un ~ con algn** to get furious with sb.

enero [e'nero] *nm* January.

enervar [ener'ßar] *vt* (*poner nervioso a*) to get on sb's nerves.

enésimo, a [e'nesimo, a] *adj* (*MAT*) nth; **por enésima vez** (*fig*) for the umpteenth time.

enfadado, a [enfa'ðaðo, a] *adj* angry, annoyed.

enfadar [enfa'ðar] *vt* to anger, annoy; **~se** *vr* to get angry *o* annoyed.

enfado [en'faðo] *nm* (*enojo*) anger, annoyance; (*disgusto*) trouble, bother.

énfasis ['enfasis] *nm* emphasis, stress; **poner ~ en** to stress.

enfático, a [en'fatiko, a] *adj* emphatic.

enfatizado, a [enfati'θaðo, a] *adj*: **en caracteres ~s** (*INFORM*) emphasized.

enfermar [enfer'mar] *vt* to make ill ♦ *vi* to fall ill, be taken ill; **su actitud me enferma** his attitude makes me sick; **~ del corazón** to develop heart trouble.

enfermedad [enferme'ðað] *nf* illness; **~ venérea** venereal disease.

enfermera [enfer'mera] *nf* V **enfermero**.

enfermería [enferme'ria] *nf* infirmary; (*de colegio etc*) sick bay.

enfermero, a [enfer'mero, a] *nm* (male) nurse ♦ *nf* nurse; **enfermera jefa** matron.

enfermizo, a [enfer'miθo, a] *adj* (*persona*) sickly, unhealthy; (*fig*) unhealthy.

enfermo, a [en'fermo, a] *adj* ill, sick ♦ *nm/f* invalid, sick person; (*en hospital*) patient.

enfilar [enfi'lar] *vt* (*aguja*) to thread; (*calle*) to go down.

enflaquecer [enflake'θer] *vt* (*adelgazar*) to make thin; (*debilitar*) to weaken.

enflaquezca [enfla'keθka] *etc vb* V **enflaquecer**.

enfocar [enfo'kar] *vt* (*foto etc*) to focus; (*problema etc*) to consider, look at.

enfoque [en'foke] *etc vb* V **enfocar** ♦ *nm* focus; (*acto*) focusing; (*óptica*) approach.

enfrascado, a [enfras'kaðo, a] *adj*: **estar ~ en algo** (*fig*) to be wrapped up in sth.

enfrascarse [enfras'karse] *vr*: **~ en un libro** to bury o.s. in a book.

enfrasque [en'fraske] *etc vb* V **enfrascar**.

enfrentamiento [enfrenta'mjento] *nm* confrontation.

enfrentar [enfren'tar] *vt* (*peligro*) to face (up to), confront; (*oponer*) to bring face to face; **~se** *vr* (*dos personas*) to face *o* confront each other; (*DEPORTE: dos equipos*) to meet; **~se a** *o* **con** to face up to, confront.

enfrente [en'frente] *adv* opposite; **~ de** *prep* opposite, facing; **la casa de ~** the house opposite, the house across the street.

enfriamiento [enfria'mjento] *nm* chilling, refrigeration; (*MED*) cold, chill.

enfriar [enfri'ar] *vt* (*alimentos*) to cool, chill; (*algo caliente*) to cool down;

(*habitación*) to air, freshen; (*entusiasmo*) to dampen; **~se** *vr* to cool down; (*MED*) to catch a chill; (*amistad*) to cool.

enfurecer [enfure'θer] *vt* to enrage, madden; **~se** *vr* to become furious, fly into a rage; (*mar*) to get rough.

enfurezca [enfu'reθka] *etc vb* V **enfurecer**.

engalanar [engala'nar] *vt* (*adornar*) to adorn; (*ciudad*) to decorate; **~se** *vr* to get dressed up.

enganchar [engan'tʃar] *vt* to hook; (*ropa*) to hang up; (*dos vagones*) to hitch up; (*TEC*) to couple, connect; (*MIL*) to recruit; (*fam: atraer: persona*) to rope into; **~se** *vr* (*MIL*) to enlist, join up; **~se (a)** (*drogas*) to get hooked (on).

enganche [en'gantʃe] *nm* hook; (*TEC*) coupling, connection; (*acto*) hooking (up); (*MIL*) recruitment, enlistment; (*AM: depósito*) deposit.

engañar [enga'ɲar] *vt* to deceive; (*estafar*) to cheat, swindle ♦ *vi*: **las apariencias engañan** appearances are deceptive; **~se** *vr* (*equivocarse*) to be wrong; (*asimismo*) to deceive *o* kid o.s.; **engaña a su mujer** he's unfaithful to *o* cheats on his wife.

engaño [en'gaɲo] *nm* deceit; (*estafa*) trick, swindle; (*error*) mistake, misunderstanding; (*ilusión*) delusion.

engañoso, a [enga'ɲoso, a] *adj* (*tramposo*) crooked; (*mentiroso*) dishonest, deceitful; (*aspecto*) deceptive; (*consejo*) misleading.

engarce [en'garθe] *etc vb* V **engarzar**.

engarzar [engar'θar] *vt* (*joya*) to set, mount; (*fig*) to link, connect.

engatusar [engatu'sar] *vt* (*fam*) to coax.

engendrar [enxen'drar] *vt* to breed; (*procrear*) to beget; (*fig*) to cause, produce.

engendro [en'xendro] *nm* (*BIO*) foetus; (*fig*) monstrosity; (*idea*) brainchild.

englobar [englo'βar] *vt* (*comprender*) to include, comprise; (*incluir*) to lump together.

engomar [engo'mar] *vt* to glue, stick.

engordar [engor'ðar] *vt* to fatten ♦ *vi* to get fat, put on weight.

engorro [en'gorro] *nm* bother, nuisance.

engorroso, a [engo'rroso, a] *adj* bothersome, trying.

engranaje [engra'naxe] *nm* (*AUTO*) gear; (*juego*) gears *pl*.

engrandecer [engrande'θer] *vt* to enlarge, magnify; (*alabar*) to praise, speak highly of; (*exagerar*) to exaggerate.

engrandezca [engran'deθka] *etc vb* V

engrandecer.

engrasar [engra'sar] *vt* (*TEC*: *poner grasa*) to grease; (: *lubricar*) to lubricate, oil; (*manchar*) to make greasy.

engrase [en'grase] *nm* greasing, lubrication.

engreído, a [engre'iðo, a] *adj* vain, conceited.

engrosar [engro'sar] *vt* (*ensanchar*) to enlarge; (*aumentar*) to increase; (*hinchar*) to swell.

engrudo [en'gruðo] *nm* paste.

engruese [en'grwese] *etc vb V* **engrosar.**

engullir [engu'ʎir] *vt* to gobble, gulp (down).

enhebrar [ene'ßrar] *vt* to thread.

enhiesto, a [e'njesto, a] *adj* (*derecho*) erect; (*bandera*) raised; (*edificio*) lofty.

enhorabuena [enora'ßwena] *excl* congratulations.

enigma [e'niɣma] *nm* enigma; (*problema*) puzzle; (*misterio*) mystery.

enigmático, a [eniɣ'matiko, a] *adj* enigmatic.

enjabonar [enxaßo'nar] *vt* to soap; (*barba*) to lather; (*fam*: *adular*) to soft-soap; (: *regañar*) to tick off.

enjalbegar [enxalße'ɣar] *vt* (*pared*) to whitewash.

enjalbegue [enxal'ßeɣe] *etc vb V* **enjalbegar.**

enjambre [en'xamßre] *nm* swarm.

enjaular [enxau'lar] *vt* to (put in a) cage; (*fam*) to jail, lock up.

enjuagar [enxwa'ɣar] *vt* (*ropa*) to rinse (out).

enjuague [en'xwaɣe] *etc vb V* **enjuagar** ♦ *nm* (*MED*) mouthwash; (*de ropa*) rinse, rinsing.

enjugar [enxu'ɣar] *vt* to wipe (off); (*lágrimas*) to dry; (*déficit*) to wipe out.

enjugue [en'xuɣe] *etc vb V* **enjugar.**

enjuiciar [enxwi'θjar] *vt* (*JUR*: *procesar*) to prosecute, try; (*fig*) to judge.

enjuto, a [en'xuto, a] *adj* dry, dried up; (*fig*) lean, skinny.

enlace [en'laθe] *etc vb V* **enlazar** ♦ *nm* link, connection; (*relación*) relationship; (*tb*: ~ **matrimonial**) marriage; (*de trenes*) connection; ~ **de datos** data link; ~ **sindical** shop steward; ~ **telefónico** telephone link-up.

enlazar [enla'θar] *vt* (*unir con lazos*) to bind together; (*atar*) to tie; (*conectar*) to link, connect; (*AM*) to lasso.

enlodar [enlo'ðar] *vt* to cover in mud; (*fig*: *manchar*) to stain; (: *rebajar*) to debase.

enloquecer [enloke'θer] *vt* to drive mad ♦ *vi*, ~**se** *vr* to go mad.

enloquezca [enlo'keθka] *etc vb V* **enloquecer.**

enlutado, a [enlu'taðo, a] *adj* (*persona*) in mourning.

enlutar [enlu'tar] *vt* to dress in mourning; ~**se** *vr* to go into mourning.

enmarañar [enmara'ɲar] *vt* (*enredar*) to tangle up, entangle; (*complicar*) to complicate; (*confundir*) to confuse; ~**se** *vr* (*enredarse*) to become entangled; (*confundirse*) to get confused.

enmarcar [enmar'kar] *vt* (*cuadro*) to frame; (*fig*) to provide a setting for.

enmarque [en'marke] *etc vb V* **enmarcar.**

enmascarar [enmaska'rar] *vt* to mask; (*intenciones*) to disguise; ~**se** *vr* to put on a mask.

enmendar [enmen'dar] *vt* to emend, correct; (*constitución etc*) to amend; (*comportamiento*) to reform; ~**se** *vr* to reform, mend one's ways.

enmienda [en'mjenda] *etc vb V* **enmendar** ♦ *nf* correction; amendment; reform.

enmohecerse [enmoe'θerse] *vr* (*metal*) to rust, go rusty; (*muro, plantas*) to go mouldy.

enmohezca [enmo'eθka] *etc vb V* **enmohecerse.**

enmudecer [enmuðe'θer] *vt* to silence ♦ *vi*, ~**se** *vr* (*perder el habla*) to fall silent; (*guardar silencio*) to remain silent; (*por miedo*) to be struck dumb.

enmudezca [enmu'ðeθka] *etc vb V* **enmudecer.**

ennegrecer [enneɣre'θer] *vt* (*poner negro*) to blacken; (*oscurecer*) to darken; ~**se** *vr* to turn black; (*oscurecerse*) to get dark, darken.

ennegrezca [enne'ɣreθka] *etc vb V* **ennegrecer.**

ennoblecer [ennoße'θer] *vt* to ennoble.

ennoblezca [enno'ßleθka] *etc vb V* **ennoblecer.**

en.º *abr* (= *enero*) Jan.

enojadizo, a [enoxa'ðiθo, a] *adj* irritable, short-tempered.

enojar [eno'xar] (*esp AM*) *vt* (*encolerizar*) to anger; (*disgustar*) to annoy, upset; ~**se** *vr* to get angry; to get annoyed.

enojo [e'noxo] (*esp AM*) *nm* (*cólera*) anger; (*irritación*) annoyance; ~**s** *nmpl* trials, problems.

enojoso, a [eno'xoso, a] *adj* annoying.

enorgullecerse [enorɣuʎe'θerse] *vr* to be proud of; ~ **de** to pride o.s. on, be proud of.

enorgullezca [enorɣu'ʎeθka] *etc vb V* **enorgullecerse.**

enorme [e'norme] *adj* enormous, huge; (*fig*) monstrous.

enormidad [enormi'ðað] *nf* hugeness, immensity.

enraice [en'raiθe] *etc vb V* **enraizar**.

enraizar [enrai'θar] *vi* to take root.

enrarecido, a [enrare'θiðo, a] *adj* rarefied.

enredadera [enreða'ðera] *nf* (*BOT*) creeper, climbing plant.

enredar [enre'ðar] *vt* (*cables, hilos etc*) to tangle (up), entangle; (*situación*) to complicate, confuse; (*meter cizaña*) to sow discord among o between; (*implicar*) to embroil, implicate; ~**se** *vr* to get entangled, get tangled (up); (*situación*) to get complicated; (*persona*) to get embroiled.

enredo [en'reðo] *nm* (*maraña*) tangle; (*confusión*) mix-up, confusion; (*intriga*) intrigue; (*apuro*) jam; (*amorío*) love affair.

enrejado [enre'xaðo] *nm* grating; (*de ventana*) lattice; (*en jardín*) trellis.

enrevesado, a [enreße'saðo, a] *adj* (*asunto*) complicated, involved.

enriquecer [enrike'θer] *vt* to make rich; (*fig*) to enrich; ~**se** *vr* to get rich.

enriquezca [enri'keθka] *etc vb V* **enriquecer**.

enrojecer [enroxe'θer] *vt* to redden ♦ *vi*, ~**se** *vr* (*persona*) to blush.

enrojezca [enro'xeθka] *etc vb V* **enrojecer**.

enrolar [enro'lar] *vt* (*MIL*) to enlist; (*reclutar*) to recruit; ~**se** *vr* (*MIL*) to join up; (*afiliarse*) to enrol, sign on.

enrollar [enro'ʎar] *vt* to roll (up), wind (up); ~**se** *vr*: ~**se con algn** to get involved with sb.

enroque [en'roke] *nm* (*AJEDREZ*) castling.

enroscar [enros'kar] *vt* (*torcer, doblar*) to twist; (*arrollar*) to coil (round), wind; (*tornillo, rosca*) to screw in; ~**se** *vr* to coil, wind.

enrosque [en'roske] *etc vb V* **enroscar**.

ensalada [ensa'laða] *nf* salad; (*lío*) mix-up.

ensaladilla [ensala'ðiʎa] *nf* (*tb:* ~ **rusa**) ≈ Russian salad.

ensalce [en'salθe] *etc vb V* **ensalzar**.

ensalzar [ensal'θar] *vt* (*alabar*) to praise, extol; (*exaltar*) to exalt.

ensamblador [ensambla'ðor] *nm* (*INFORM*) assembler.

ensambladura [ensambla'ðura] *nf*, **ensamblaje** [ensam'blaxe] *nm* assembly; (*TEC*) joint.

ensamblar [ensam'blar] *vt* (*montar*) to assemble; (*madera etc*) to join.

ensanchar [ensan'tʃar] *vt* (*hacer más ancho*) to widen; (*agrandar*) to enlarge, expand; (*COSTURA*) to let out; ~**se** *vr* to get wider, expand; (*pey*) to give o.s. airs.

ensanche [en'santʃe] *nm* (*de calle*) widening; (*de negocio*) expansion.

ensangrentado, a [ensangren'taðo, a] *adj* bloodstained, covered with blood.

ensangrentar [ensangren'tar] *vt* to stain with blood.

ensangriente [ensan'grjente] *etc vb V* **ensangrentar**.

ensañarse [ensa'ɲarse] *vr*: ~ **con** to treat brutally.

ensartar [ensar'tar] *vt* (*gen*) to string (together); (*carne*) to spit, skewer.

ensayar [ensa'jar] *vt* to test, try (out); (*TEAT*) to rehearse.

ensayista [ensa'jista] *nmlf* essayist.

ensayo [en'sajo] *nm* test, trial; (*QUÍMICA*) experiment; (*TEAT*) rehearsal; (*DEPORTE*) try; (*ESCOL, LITERATURA*) essay; **pedido de** ~ (*COM*) trial order; ~ **general** (*TEAT*) dress rehearsal; (*MUS*) full rehearsal.

enseguida [ense'ɣuiða] *adv* at once, right away; ~ **termino** I've nearly finished, I shan't be long now.

ensenada [ense'naða] *nf* inlet, cove.

enseña [en'seɲa] *nf* ensign, standard.

enseñante [ense'ɲante] *nmlf* teacher.

enseñanza [ense'ɲanθa] *nf* (*educación*) education; (*acción*) teaching; (*doctrina*) teaching, doctrine; ~ **primaria/ secundaria/superior** primary/ secondary/higher education.

enseñar [ense'ɲar] *vt* (*educar*) to teach; (*instruir*) to teach, instruct; (*mostrar, señalar*) to show.

enseres [en'seres] *nmpl* belongings.

ENSIDESA [ensi'ðesa] *abr* (*ESP COM*) = *Empresa Nacional Siderúrgica, S. A.*

ensillar [ensi'ʎar] *vt* to saddle (up).

ensimismarse [ensimis'marse] *vr* (*abstraerse*) to become lost in thought; (*estar absorto*) to be lost in thought; (*AM*) to become conceited.

ensopar [enso'par] *vt* (*AM*) to soak.

ensordecer [ensorðe'θer] *vt* to deafen ♦ *vi* to go deaf.

ensordezca [ensor'ðeθka] *etc vb V* **ensordecer**.

ensortijado, a [ensorti'xaðo, a] *adj* (*pelo*) curly.

ensuciar [ensu'θjar] *vt* (*manchar*) to dirty, soil; (*fig*) to defile; ~**se** *vr* (*mancharse*) to get dirty; (*niño*) to dirty (o wet) o.s.

ensueño [en'sweɲo] *nm* (*sueño*) dream, fantasy; (*ilusión*) illusion; (*soñando despierto*) daydream; **de** ~ dream-like.

entablado [enta'ßlaðo] *nm* (*piso*) floorboards *pl*; (*armazón*) boarding.

entablar [enta'ßlar] *vt* (*recubrir*) to board (up); (*AJEDREZ, DAMAS*) to set up; (*conversación*) to strike up; (*JUR*) to file ♦ *vi* to draw.

entablillar [entaßli'ʎar] *vt* (*MED*) to (put in a) splint.

entallado, a [enta'ʎaðo, a] *adj* waisted.

entallar [enta'ʎar] *vt* (*traje*) to tailor ♦ *vi*: **el traje entalla bien** the suit fits well.

ente ['ente] *nm* (*organización*) body, organization; (*compañía*) company; (*fam*: *persona*) odd character; (*ser*) being; ~ **público** (*ESP*) state(-owned) body.

entender [enten'der] *vt* (*comprender*) to understand; (*darse cuenta*) to realize; (*querer decir*) to mean ♦ *vi* to understand; (*creer*) to think, believe ♦ *nm*: **a mi** ~ in my opinion; ~ **de** to know all about; ~ **algo de** to know a little about; ~ **en** to deal with, have to do with; **~se** *vr* (*comprenderse*) to be understood; (*2 personas*) to get on together; (*ponerse de acuerdo*) to agree, reach an agreement; **dar a** ~ **que ...** to lead to believe that ...; **~se mal** to get on badly; **¿entiendes?** (do you) understand?

entendido, a [enten'diðo, a] *adj* (*comprendido*) understood; (*hábil*) skilled; (*inteligente*) knowledgeable ♦ *nm/f* (*experto*) expert ♦ *excl* agreed!

entendimiento [entendi'mjento] *nm* (*comprensión*) understanding; (*inteligencia*) mind, intellect; (*juicio*) judgement.

enterado, a [ente'raðo, a] *adj* well-informed; **estar** ~ **de** to know about, be aware of; **no darse por** ~ to pretend not to understand.

enteramente [entera'mente] *adv* entirely, completely.

enterarse [ente'rarse] *vr*: ~ **(de)** to find out (about); **para que te enteres ...** (*fam*) for your information ...

entereza [ente'reθa] *nf* (*totalidad*) entirety; (*fig*: *carácter*) strength of mind; (*honradez*) integrity.

enternecedor, a [enterneθe'ðor, a] *adj* touching.

enternecer [enterne'θer] *vt* (*ablandar*) to soften; (*apiadar*) to touch, move; **~se** *vr* to be touched, be moved.

enternezca [enter'neθka] *etc vb V* **enternecer.**

entero, a [en'tero, a] *adj* (*total*) whole, entire; (*fig*: *recto*) honest; (: *firme*) firm, resolute ♦ *nm* (*MAT*) integer; (*COM*: *punto*) point; (*AM*: *pago*) payment; **las acciones han subido dos ~s** the shares have gone up two points.

enterrador [enterra'ðor] *nm* gravedigger.

enterrar [ente'rrar] *vt* to bury; (*fig*) to forget.

entibiar [enti'ßjar] *vt* (*enfriar*) to cool; (*calentar*) to warm; **~se** *vr* (*fig*) to cool.

entidad [enti'ðað] *nf* (*empresa*) firm, company; (*organismo*) body; (*sociedad*) society; (*FILOSOFÍA*) entity.

entienda [en'tjenda] *etc vb V* **entender.**

entierro [en'tjerro] *etc vb V* **enterrar** ♦ *nm* (*acción*) burial; (*funeral*) funeral.

entomología [entomolo'xia] *nf* entomology.

entomólogo, a [ento'moloɣo, a] *nm/f* entomologist.

entonación [entona'θjon] *nf* (*LING*) intonation; (*fig*) conceit.

entonar [ento'nar] *vt* (*canción*) to intone; (*colores*) to tone; (*MED*) to tone up ♦ *vi* to be in tune; **~se** *vr* (*engreírse*) to give o.s. airs.

entonces [en'tonθes] *adv* then, at that time; **desde** ~ since then; **en aquel** ~ at that time; **(pues)** ~ and so; **el** ~ **embajador de España** the then Spanish ambassador.

entornar [entor'nar] *vt* (*puerta, ventana*) to half close, leave ajar; (*los ojos*) to screw up.

entorno [en'torno] *nm* setting, environment; ~ **de redes** (*INFORM*) network environment.

entorpecer [entorpe'θer] *vt* (*entendimiento*) to dull; (*impedir*) to obstruct, hinder; (: *tránsito*) to slow down, delay.

entorpezca [entor'peθka] *etc vb V* **entorpecer.**

entrado, a [en'traðo, a] *adj*: ~ **en años** elderly; **(una vez)** ~ **el verano** in the summer(time), when summer comes ♦ *nf* (*acción*) entry, access; (*sitio*) entrance, way in; (*principio*) beginning; (*COM*) receipts *pl*, takings *pl*; (*CULIN*) entrée; (*DEPORTE*) innings *sg*; (*TEAT*) house, audience; (*para el cine etc*) ticket; (*INFORM*) input; (*ECON*): **entradas** *nfpl* income *sg*; **entradas brutas** gross receipts; **entradas y salidas** (*COM*) income and expenditure; **entrada de aire** (*TEC*) air intake *o* inlet; **de entrada** right away; "**entrada gratis**" "admission free"; **entrada de datos vocal** (*INFORM*) voice input; **tiene entradas** he's losing his hair.

entrante [en'trante] *adj* next, coming; (*POL*) incoming ♦ *nm* inlet; (*CULIN*) starter; **mes/año** ~ next month/year.

entraña [en'traɲa] *nf* (*fig: centro*) heart, core; (*raíz*) root; ~**s** *nfpl* (*ANAT*) entrails; (*fig*) heart *sg*.

entrañable [entra'ɲaβle] *adj* (*persona, lugar*) dear; (*relación*) close; (*acto*) intimate.

entrañar [entra'ɲar] *vt* to entail.

entrar [en'trar] *vt* (*introducir*) to bring in; (*persona*) to show in; (*INFORM*) to input ♦ *vi* (*meterse*) to go *o* come in, enter; (*comenzar*): ~ **diciendo** to begin by saying; **entré en** *o* **a** (*AM*) **la casa** I went into the house; **le entraron ganas de reír** he felt a sudden urge to laugh; **no me entra** I can't get the hang of it.

entre ['entre] *prep* (*dos*) between; (*en medio de*) among(st); (*por*): **se abrieron paso ~ la multitud** they forced their way through the crowd; ~ **una cosa y otra** what with one thing and another; ~ **más estudia más aprende** (*AM*) the more he studies the more he learns.

entreabierto [entrea'βjerto] *pp de* **entreabrir.**

entreabrir [entrea'βrir] *vt* to half-open, open halfway.

entreacto [entre'akto] *nm* interval.

entrecano, a [entre'kano, a] *a* greying; **ser** ~ (*persona*) to be going grey.

entrecejo [entre'θexo] *nm*: **fruncir el** ~ to frown.

entrechocar [entretʃo'kar] *vi* (*dientes*) to chatter.

entrechoque [entre'tʃoke] *etc vb V* **entrechocar.**

entrecomillado, a [entrekomi'ʎaðo, a] *adj* in inverted commas.

entrecortado, a [entrekor'taðo, a] *adj* (*respiración*) laboured, difficult; (*habla*) faltering.

entrecot [entre'ko(t)] *nm* (*CULIN*) sirloin steak.

entrecruce [entre'kruθe] *etc vb V* **entrecruzarse.**

entrecruzarse [entrekru'θarse] *vr* (*BIO*) to interbreed.

entredicho [entre'ðitʃo] *nm* (*JUR*) injunction; **poner en** ~ to cast doubt on; **estar en** ~ to be in doubt.

entrega [en'treɣa] *nf* (*de mercancías*) delivery; (*de premios*) presentation; (*de novela etc*) instalment; "~ **a domicilio**" "door-to-door delivery service".

entregar [entre'ɣar] *vt* (*dar*) to hand (over), deliver; (*ejercicios*) to hand in;

~**se** *vr* (*rendirse*) to surrender, give in, submit; ~**se a** (*dedicarse*) to devote o.s. to; **a** ~ (*COM*) to be supplied.

entregue [en'treɣe] *etc vb V* **entregar.**

entrelace [entre'laθe] *etc vb V* **entrelazar.**

entrelazar [entrela'θar] *vt* to entwine.

entremedias [entre'meðjas] *adv* (*en medio*) in between, halfway.

entremeses [entre'meses] *nmpl* hors d'œuvres.

entremeter [entreme'ter] *vt* to insert, put in; ~**se** *vr* to meddle, interfere.

entremetido, a [entreme'tiðo, a] *adj* meddling, interfering.

entremezclar [entremeθ'klar] *vt*, ~**se** *vr* to intermingle.

entrenador, a [entrena'ðor, a] *nm/f* trainer, coach.

entrenamiento [entrena'mjento] *nm* training.

entrenar [entre'nar] *vt* (*DEPORTE*) to train; (*caballo*) to exercise ♦ *vi*, ~**se** *vr* to train.

entrepierna [entre'pjerna] *nf* (*tb*: ~**s**) crotch, crutch.

entresacar [entresa'kar] *vt* to pick out, select.

entresaque [entre'sake] *etc vb V* **entresacar.**

entresuelo [entre'swelo] *nm* mezzanine, entresol; (*TEAT*) dress *o* first circle.

entretanto [entre'tanto] *adv* meanwhile, meantime.

entretejer [entrete'xer] *vt* to interweave.

entretela [entre'tela] *nf* (*de ropa*) interlining; ~**s** *nfpl* heart-strings.

entretención [entreten'sjon] *nf* (*AM*) entertainment.

entretendré [entreten'dre] *etc vb V* **entretener.**

entretener [entrete'ner] *vt* (*divertir*) to entertain, amuse; (*detener*) to hold up, delay; (*mantener*) to maintain; ~**se** *vr* (*divertirse*) to amuse o.s.; (*retrasarse*) to delay, linger; **no le entretengo más** I won't keep you any longer.

entretenga [entre'tenga] *etc vb V* **entretener.**

entretenido, a [entrete'niðo, a] *adj* entertaining, amusing.

entretenimiento [entreteni'mjento] *nm* entertainment, amusement; (*mantenimiento*) upkeep, maintenance.

entretiempo [entre'tjempo] *nm*: **ropa de** ~ clothes *for spring and autumn.*

entretiene [entre'tjene] *etc*, **entretuve** [entre'tuβe] *etc vb V* **entretener.**

entreveía [entreβe'ia] *etc vb V* **entrever.**

entrever [entre'βer] *vt* to glimpse, catch a

glimpse of.

entrevista [entre'ßista] *nf* interview.

entrevistar [entreßis'tar] *vt* to interview; ~**se con** to have an interview with, see; **el ministro se entrevistó con el Rey ayer** the minister had an audience with the King yesterday.

entrevisto [entre'ßisto] *pp de* **entrever.**

entristecer [entriste'θer] *vt* to sadden, grieve; ~**se** *vr* to grow sad.

entristezca [entris'teθka] *etc vb V* **entristecer.**

entrometerse [entrome'terse] *vr:* ~ **(en)** to interfere (in *o* with).

entrometido, a [entrome'tiðo, a] *adj* interfering, meddlesome.

entroncar [entron'kar] *vi* to be connected *o* related.

entronque [en'tronke] *etc vb V* **entroncar.**

entuerto [en'twerto] *nm* wrong, injustice; ~**s** *nmpl* (*MED*) afterpains.

entumecer [entume'θer] *vt* to numb, benumb; ~**se** *vr* (*por el frío*) to go *o* become numb.

entumecido, a [entume'θiðo, a] *adj* numb, stiff.

entumezca [entu'meθka] *etc vb V* **entumecer.**

enturbiar [entur'ßjar] *vt* (*el agua*) to make cloudy; (*fig*) to confuse; ~**se** *vr* (*oscurecerse*) to become cloudy; (*fig*) to get confused, become obscure.

entusiasmar [entusjas'mar] *vt* to excite, fill with enthusiasm; (*gustar mucho*) to delight; ~**se** *vr:* ~**se con** *o* **por** to get enthusiastic *o* excited about.

entusiasmo [entu'sjasmo] *nm* enthusiasm; (*excitación*) excitement.

entusiasta [entu'sjasta] *adj* enthusiastic ♦ *nm/f* enthusiast.

enumerar [enume'rar] *vt* to enumerate.

enunciación [enunθja'θjon] *nf,* **enunciado** [enun'θjaðo] *nm* enunciation; (*declaración*) declaration, statement.

enunciar [enun'θjar] *vt* to enunciate; to declare, state.

envainar [embai'nar] *vt* to sheathe.

envalentonar [embalento'nar] *vt* to give courage to; ~**se** *vr* (*pey: jactarse*) to boast, brag.

envanecer [embane'θer] *vt* to make conceited; ~**se** *vr* to grow conceited.

envanezca [emba'neθka] *etc vb V* **envanecer.**

envasar [emba'sar] *vt* (*empaquetar*) to pack, wrap; (*enfrascar*) to bottle; (*enlatar*) to can; (*embolsar*) to pocket.

envase [em'base] *nm* packing, wrapping; bottling; canning; pocketing; (*recipiente*) container; (*paquete*) package; (*botella*) bottle; (*lata*) tin (*BRIT*), can.

envejecer [embexe'θer] *vt* to make old, age ♦ *vi,* ~**se** *vr* (*volverse viejo*) to grow old; (*parecer viejo*) to age.

envejecido, a [embexe'θiðo, a] *adj* old, aged; (*de aspecto*) old-looking.

envejezca [embe'xeθka] *etc vb V* **envejecer.**

envenenar [embene'nar] *vt* to poison; (*fig*) to embitter.

envergadura [emberɣa'ðura] *nf* (*expansión*) expanse; (*NAUT*) breadth; (*fig*) scope; **un programa de gran** ~ a wide-ranging programme.

envés [em'bes] *nm* (*de tela*) back, wrong side.

enviado, a [em'bjaðo, a] *nm/f* (*POL*) envoy; ~ **especial** (*de periódico, TV*) special correspondent.

enviar [em'bjar] *vt* to send.

enviciar [embi'θjar] *vt* to corrupt ♦ *vi* (*trabajo etc*) to be addictive; ~**se** *vr:* ~**se (con** *o* **en)** to get addicted (to).

envidia [em'biðja] *nf* envy; **tener** ~ **a** to envy, be jealous of.

envidiar [embi'ðjar] *vt* (*desear*) to envy; (*tener celos de*) to be jealous of.

envidioso, a [embi'ðjoso, a] *adj* envious, jealous.

envío [em'bio] *nm* (*acción*) sending; (*de mercancías*) consignment; (*de dinero*) remittance; (*en barco*) shipment; **gastos de** ~ postage and packing; ~ **contra reembolso** COD shipment.

enviudar [embju'ðar] *vi* to be widowed.

envoltura [embol'tura] *nf* (*cobertura*) cover; (*embalaje*) wrapper, wrapping.

envolver [embol'ßer] *vt* to wrap (up); (*cubrir*) to cover; (*enemigo*) to surround; (*implicar*) to involve, implicate.

envuelto [em'bwelto], **envuelva** [em'bwelßa] *etc vb V* **envolver.**

enyesar [enje'sar] *vt* (*pared*) to plaster; (*MED*) to put in plaster.

enzarzarse [enθar'θarse] *vr:* ~ **en algo** to get mixed up in sth.

epa ['epa], **épale** ['epale] (*AM*) *excl* hey!, wow!

E.P.D. *abr* (= *en paz descanse*) R.I.P.

epicentro [epi'θentro] *nm* epicentre.

épico, a ['epiko, a] *adj* epic ♦ *nf* epic (poetry).

epidemia [epi'ðemja] *nf* epidemic.

epidémico, a [epi'ðemiko, a] *adj* epidemic.

epidermis [epi'ðermis] *nf* epidermis.

epifanía [epifa'nia] *nf* Epiphany.

epilepsia [epi'lepsja] *nf* epilepsy.

epiléptico, a [epi'leptiko, a] *adj, nm/f*
epileptic.

epílogo [e'piloɣo] *nm* epilogue.

episcopado [episko'paðo] *nm* (*cargo*)
bishopric; (*obispos*) bishops *pl*
(*collectively*).

episodio [epi'soðjo] *nm* episode; (*suceso*)
incident.

epístola [e'pistola] *nf* epistle.

epitafio [epi'tafjo] *nm* epitaph.

epíteto [e'piteto] *nm* epithet.

época ['epoka] *nf* period, time; (*temporada*)
season; (*HISTORIA*) age, epoch; **hacer** ~ **to**
be epoch-making.

equidad [eki'ðað] *nf* equity, fairness.

equilibrar [ekili'ßrar] *vt* to balance.

equilibrio [eki'lißrjo] *nm* balance,
equilibrium; ~ **político** balance of
power.

equilibrista [ekili'ßrista] *nm/f* (*funámbulo*)
tightrope walker; (*acróbata*) acrobat.

equinoccio [eki'nokθjo] *nm* equinox.

equipaje [eki'paxe] *nm* luggage (*BRIT*),
baggage (*US*); (*avíos*) equipment, kit; ~
de mano hand luggage; **hacer el** ~ **to**
pack.

equipar [eki'par] *vt* (*proveer*) to equip.

equiparar [ekipa'rar] *vt* (*igualar*) to put on
the same level; (*comparar*) to compare
(*con* with); ~**se** *vr*: ~**se con** to be on a
level with.

equipo [e'kipo] *nm* (*conjunto de cosas*)
equipment; (*DEPORTE, grupo*) team; (*de
obreros*) shift; (*de máquinas*) plant;
(*turbinas etc*) set; ~ **de caza** hunting gear;
~ **físico** (*INFORM*) hardware; ~ **médico**
medical team; ~ **de música** music
centre.

equis ['ekis] *nf* (the letter) X.

equitación [ekita'θjon] *nf* (*acto*) riding;
(*arte*) horsemanship.

equitativo, a [ekita'tißo, a] *adj* equitable,
fair.

equivaldré [ekißal'dre] *etc vb V* **equivaler.**

equivalencia [ekißa'lenθja] *nf* equivalence.

equivalente [ekißa'lente] *adj, nm*
equivalent.

equivaler [ekißa'ler] *vi*: ~ **a** to be
equivalent *o* equal to; (*en rango*) to rank
as.

equivalga [eki'ßalɣa] *etc vb V* **equivaler.**

equivocación [ekißoka'θjon] *nf* mistake,
error; (*malentendido*) misunderstanding.

equivocado, a [ekißo'kaðo, a] *adj* wrong,
mistaken.

equivocarse [ekißo'karse] *vr* to be wrong,
make a mistake; ~ **de camino** to take
the wrong road.

equívoco, a [e'kißoko, a] *adj* (*dudoso*)
suspect; (*ambiguo*) ambiguous ♦ *nm*
ambiguity; (*malentendido*)
misunderstanding.

equivoque [eki'ßoke] *etc vb V* **equivocar.**

era ['era] *vb V* **ser** ♦ *nf* era, age; (*AGR*)
threshing floor.

erais ['erais], **éramos** ['eramos], **eran**
['eran] *vb V* **ser.**

erario [e'rarjo] *nm* exchequer, treasury.

eras ['eras], **eres** ['eres] *vb V* **ser.**

erección [erek'θjon] *nf* erection.

ergonomía [erɣono'mia] *nf* ergonomics *sg*,
human engineering.

erguir [er'ɣir] *vt* to raise, lift; (*poner
derecho*) to straighten; ~**se** *vr* to
straighten up.

erice [e'riθe] *etc vb V* **erizarse.**

erigir [eri'xir] *vt* to erect, build; ~**se** *vr*: ~**se
en** to set o.s. up as.

erija [e'rixa] *etc vb V* **erigir.**

erizado, a [eri'θaðo, a] *adj* bristly.

erizarse [eri'θarse] *vr* (*pelo: de perro*) to
bristle; (: *de persona*) to stand on end.

erizo [e'riθo] *nm* hedgehog; ~ **de mar** sea
urchin.

ermita [er'mita] *nf* hermitage.

ermitaño, a [ermi'taɲo, a] *nm/f* hermit.

erosión [ero'sjon] *nf* erosion.

erosionar [erosjo'nar] *vt* to erode.

erótico, a [e'rotiko, a] *adj* erotic.

erotismo [ero'tismo] *nm* eroticism.

erradicar [erraði'kar] *vt* to eradicate.

erradique [erra'ðike] *etc vb V* **erradicar.**

errado, a [e'rraðo, a] *adj* mistaken, wrong.

errante [e'rrante] *adj* wandering, errant.

errar [e'rrar] *vi* (*vagar*) to wander, roam;
(*equivocarse*) to be mistaken ♦ *vt*: ~ **el
camino** to take the wrong road; ~ **el tiro**
to miss.

errata [e'rrata] *nf* misprint.

erre ['erre] *nf* (the letter) R; ~ **que** ~
stubbornly.

erróneo, a [e'rroneo, a] *adj* (*equivocado*)
wrong, mistaken; (*falso*) false, untrue.

error [e'rror] *nm* error, mistake; (*INFORM*)
bug; ~ **de imprenta** misprint; ~ **de
lectura/escritura** (*INFORM*) read/write
error; ~ **sintáctico** syntax error; ~
judicial miscarriage of justice.

Ertzaintza [er'tʃantʃa] *nf* Basque police; *V
tb* **policía.**

eructar [eruk'tar] *vt* to belch, burp.

eructo [e'rukto] *nm* belch.

erudición [eruði'θjon] *nf* erudition,
learning.

erudito, a [eru'ðito, a] *adj* erudite, learned
♦ *nm/f* scholar; **los** ~**s en esta materia** the

experts in this field.

erupción [erup'θjon] *nf* eruption; (*MED*) rash; (*de violencia*) outbreak; (*de ira*) outburst.

es [es] *vb V* **ser.**

E/S *abr* (*INFORM*: *entrada/salida*) I/O.

esa ['esa], **esas** ['esas] *adj demostrativo V* **ese.**

ésa ['esa], **ésas** ['esas] *pron V* **ése.**

esbelto, a [es'βelto, a] *adj* slim, slender.

esbirro [es'βirro] *nm* henchman.

esbozar [esβo'θar] *vt* to sketch, outline.

esbozo [es'βoθo] *nm* sketch, outline.

escabeche [eska'βetʃe] *nm* brine; (*de aceitunas etc*) pickle; **en ~** pickled.

escabechina [eskaβe'tʃina] *nf* (*batalla*) massacre; **hacer una ~** (*ESCOL*) to fail a lot of students.

escabroso, a [eska'βroso, a] *adj* (*accidentado*) rough, uneven; (*fig*) tough, difficult; (: *atrevido*) risqué.

escabullirse [eskaβu'ʎirse] *vr* to slip away; (*largarse*) to clear out.

escacharrar [eskatʃa'rrar] *vt* (*fam*) to break; **~se** *vr* to get broken.

escafandra [eska'fandra] *nf* (*buzo*) diving suit; (**~ espacial**) spacesuit.

escala [es'kala] *nf* (*proporción, MUS*) scale; (*de mano*) ladder; (*AVIAT*) stopover; (*de colores etc*) range; **~ de tiempo** time scale; **~ de sueldos** salary scale; **una investigación a ~ nacional** a nationwide inquiry; **reproducir según ~** to reproduce to scale; **hacer ~ en** to stop off *o* over at.

escalada [eska'laða] *nf* (*de montaña*) climb; (*de pared*) scaling.

escalafón [eskala'fon] *nm* (*escala de salarios*) salary scale, wage scale.

escalar [eska'lar] *vt* to climb, scale ♦ *vi* (*MIL, POL*) to escalate.

escaldar [eskal'dar] *vt* (*quemar*) to scald; (*escarmentar*) to teach a lesson.

escalera [eska'lera] *nf* stairs *pl*, staircase; (*escala*) ladder; (*NAIPES*) run; (*de camión*) tailboard; **~ mecánica** escalator; **~ de caracol** spiral staircase; **~ de incendios** fire escape.

escalerilla [eskale'riʎa] *nf* (*de avión*) steps *pl*.

escalfar [eskal'far] *vt* (*huevos*) to poach.

escalinata [eskali'nata] *nf* staircase.

escalofriante [eskalo'frjante] *adj* chilling.

escalofrío [eskalo'frio] *nm* (*MED*) chill; **~s** *nmpl* (*fig*) shivers.

escalón [eska'lon] *nm* step, stair; (*de escalera*) rung; (*fig: paso*) step; (*al éxito*) ladder.

escalonar [eskalo'nar] *vt* to spread out;

(*tierra*) to terrace; (*horas de trabajo*) to stagger.

escalope [eska'lope] *nm* (*CULIN*) escalope.

escama [es'kama] *nf* (*de pez, serpiente*) scale; (*de jabón*) flake; (*fig*) resentment.

escamar [eska'mar] *vt* (*pez*) to scale; (*producir recelo*) to make wary.

escamotear [eskamote'ar] *vt* (*fam: robar*) to lift, swipe; (*hacer desaparecer*) to make disappear.

escampar [eskam'par] *vb impersonal* to stop raining.

escanciar [eskan'θjar] *vt* (*vino*) to pour (out).

escandalice [eskanda'liθe] *etc vb V* **escandalizar.**

escandalizar [eskandali'θar] *vt* to scandalize, shock; **~se** *vr* to be shocked; (*ofenderse*) to be offended.

escándalo [es'kandalo] *nm* scandal; (*alboroto, tumulto*) row, uproar; **armar un ~** to make a scene; **¡es un ~!** it's outrageous!

escandaloso, a [eskanda'loso, a] *adj* scandalous, shocking; (*risa*) hearty; (*niño*) noisy.

Escandinavia [eskandi'naβja] *nf* Scandinavia.

escandinavo, a [eskandi'naβo, a] *adj, nm/f* Scandinavian.

escáner [es'kaner] *nm* scanner.

escaño [es'kaɲo] *nm* bench; (*POL*) seat.

escapada [eska'paða] *nf* (*huida*) escape, flight; (*deportes*) breakaway; (*viaje*) quick trip.

escapar [eska'par] *vi* (*gen*) to escape, run away; (*DEPORTE*) to break away; **~se** *vr* to escape, get away; (*agua, gas, noticias*) to leak (out); **se me escapa su nombre** his name escapes me.

escaparate [eskapa'rate] *nm* shop window; (*COM*) showcase.

escapatoria [eskapa'torja] *nf*: **no tener ~** (*fig*) to have no way out.

escape [es'kape] *nm* (*huida*) escape; (*de agua, gas*) leak; (*de motor*) exhaust; **salir a ~** to rush out.

escapismo [eska'pismo] *nm* escapism.

escaquearse [eskake'arse] *vr* (*fam*) to duck out.

escarabajo [eskara'βaxo] *nm* beetle.

escaramuza [eskara'muθa] *nf* skirmish; (*fig*) brush.

escarbar [eskar'βar] *vt* (*gallina*) to scratch; (*fig*) to inquire into, investigate.

escarceos [eskar'θeos] *nmpl*: **en sus ~ con la política** in his occasional forays into politics; **~ amorosos** flirtations.

escarcha [es'kartʃa] *nf* frost.

escarlata [eskar'lata] *adj inv* scarlet.
escarlatina [eskarla'tina] *nf* scarlet fever.
escarmentar [eskarmen'tar] *vt* to punish severely ♦ *vi* to learn one's lesson; ¡**para que escarmientes!** that'll teach you!
escarmiento [eskar'mjento] *etc vb V* **escarmentar** ♦ *nm* (*ejemplo*) lesson; (*castigo*) punishment.
escarnio [es'karnjo] *nm* mockery; (*injuria*) insult.
escarola [eska'rola] *nf* (*BOT*) endive.
escarpado, a [eskar'paðo, a] *adj* (*pendiente*) sheer, steep; (*rocas*) craggy.
escasamente [eskasa'mente] *adv* (*insuficientemente*) scantily; (*apenas*) scarcely.
escasear [eskase'ar] *vi* to be scarce.
escasez [eska'seθ] *nf* (*falta*) shortage, scarcity; (*pobreza*) poverty; **vivir con ~** to live on the breadline.
escaso, a [es'kaso, a] *adj* (*poco*) scarce; (*raro*) rare; (*ralo*) thin, sparse; (*limitado*) limited; (*recursos*) scanty; (*público*) sparse; (*posibilidad*) slim; (*visibilidad*) poor.
escatimar [eskati'mar] *vt* (*limitar*) to skimp (on), be sparing with; **no ~ esfuerzos (para)** to spare no effort (to).
escayola [eska'jola] *nf* plaster.
escayolar [eskajo'lar] *vt* to put in plaster.
escena [es'θena] *nf* scene; (*decorado*) scenery; (*escenario*) stage; **poner en ~** to put on.
escenario [esθe'narjo] *nm* (*TEAT*) stage; (*CINE*) set; (*fig*) scene; **el ~ del crimen** the scene of the crime; **el ~ político** the political scene.
escenografía [esθenoɣra'fia] *nf* set *o* stage design.
escepticismo [esθepti'θismo] *nm* scepticism.
escéptico, a [es'θeptiko, a] *adj* sceptical ♦ *nm/f* sceptic.
escindir [esθin'dir] *vt* to split; **~se** *vr* (*facción*) to split off; **~se en** to split into.
escisión [esθi'sjon] *nf* (*MED*) excision; (*fig, POL*) split; **~ nuclear** nuclear fission.
esclarecer [esklare'θer] *vt* (*iluminar*) to light up, illuminate; (*misterio, problema*) to shed light on.
esclarezca [eskla'reθka] *etc vb V* **esclarecer.**
esclavice [eskla'ßiθe] *etc vb V* **esclavizar.**
esclavitud [esklaßi'tuð] *nf* slavery.
esclavizar [esklaßi'θar] *vt* to enslave.
esclavo, a [es'klaßo, a] *nm/f* slave.
esclusa [es'klusa] *nf* (*de canal*) lock; (*compuerta*) floodgate.

escoba [es'koßa] *nf* broom; **pasar la ~** to sweep up.
escobazo [esko'ßaθo] *nm* (*golpe*) blow with a broom; **echar a algn a ~s** to kick sb out.
escobilla [esko'ßiʎa] *nf* brush.
escocer [esko'θer] *vi* to burn, sting; **~se** *vr* to chafe, get chafed.
escocés, esa [esko'θes, esa] *adj* Scottish; (*whisky*) Scotch ♦ *nm/f* Scotsman/woman, Scot ♦ *nm* (*LING*) Scots *sg*; **tela escocesa** tartan.
Escocia [es'koθja] *nf* Scotland.
escoger [esko'xer] *vt* to choose, pick, select.
escogido, a [esko'xiðo, a] *adj* chosen, selected; (*calidad*) choice, select; (*persona*): **ser muy ~** to be very fussy.
escoja [es'koxa] *etc vb V* **escoger.**
escolar [esko'lar] *adj* school *cpd* ♦ *nm/f* schoolboy/girl, pupil.
escolaridad [eskolari'ðað] *nf* schooling; **libro de ~** school record.
escolarización [eskolariθa'θjon] *nf*: **~ obligatoria** compulsory education.
escolarizado, a [eskolari'θaðo, a] *adj, nm/f*: **los ~s** those in *o* attending school.
escollo [es'koʎo] *nm* (*arrecife*) reef, rock; (*fig*) pitfall.
escolta [es'kolta] *nf* escort.
escoltar [eskol'tar] *vt* to escort; (*proteger*) to guard.
escombros [es'kombros] *nmpl* (*basura*) rubbish *sg*; (*restos*) debris *sg*.
esconder [eskon'der] *vt* to hide, conceal; **~se** *vr* to hide.
escondidas [eskon'diðas] *nfpl* (*AM*) hide-and-seek *sg*; **a ~** secretly; **hacer algo a ~ de algn** to do sth behind sb's back.
escondite [eskon'dite] *nm* hiding place; (*juego*) hide-and-seek.
escondrijo [eskon'drixo] *nm* hiding place, hideout.
escopeta [esko'peta] *nf* shotgun; **~ de aire comprimido** air gun.
escoria [es'korja] *nf* (*desecho mineral*) slag; (*fig*) scum, dregs *pl*.
Escorpio [es'korpjo] *nm* (*ASTRO*) Scorpio.
escorpión [eskor'pjon] *nm* scorpion.
escotado, a [esko'taðo, a] *adj* low-cut.
escotar [esko'tar] *vt* (*vestido: ajustar*) to cut to fit; (*cuello*) to cut low.
escote [es'kote] *nm* (*de vestido*) low neck; **pagar a ~** to share the expenses.
escotilla [esko'tiʎa] *nf* (*NAUT*) hatchway.
escotillón [eskoti'ʎon] *nm* trapdoor.
escozor [esko'θor] *nm* (*dolor*) sting(ing).
escribano, a [eskri'ßano, a], **escribiente**

[eskri'βjente] *nm/f* clerk; (*secretario judicial*) court o lawyer's clerk.

escribir [eskri'βir] *vt, vi* to write; ~ **a máquina** to type; **¿cómo se escribe?** how do you spell it?

escrito, a [es'krito, a] *pp de* **escribir** ♦ *adj* written, in writing; (*examen*) written ♦ *nm* (*documento*) document; (*manuscrito*) text, manuscript; **por** ~ in writing.

escritor, a [eskri'tor, a] *nm/f* writer.

escritorio [eskri'torjo] *nm* desk; (*oficina*) office.

escritura [eskri'tura] *nf* (*acción*) writing; (*caligrafía*) (hand)writing; (*JUR: documento*) deed; (*COM*) indenture; ~ **de propiedad** title deed; **Sagrada E~** (Holy) Scripture; ~ **social** articles *pl* of association.

escroto [es'kroto] *nm* scrotum.

escrúpulo [es'krupulo] *nm* scruple; (*minuciosidad*) scrupulousness.

escrupuloso, a [eskrupu'loso, a] *adj* scrupulous.

escrutar [eskru'tar] *vt* to scrutinize, examine; (*votos*) to count.

escrutinio [eskru'tinjo] *nm* (*examen atento*) scrutiny; (*POL: recuento de votos*) count(ing).

escuadra [es'kwaðra] *nf* (*TEC*) square; (*MIL etc*) squad; (*NAUT*) squadron; (*de coches etc*) fleet.

escuadrilla [eskwa'ðriʎa] *nf* (*de aviones*) squadron.

escuadrón [eskwa'ðron] *nm* squadron.

escuálido, a [es'kwaliðo, a] *adj* skinny, scraggy; (*sucio*) squalid.

escucha [es'kutʃa] *nf* (*acción*) listening ♦ *nm* (*TELEC: sistema*) monitor; (*oyente*) listener; **estar a la** ~ to listen in; **estar de** ~ to spy; ~**s telefónicas** (phone) tapping *sg*.

escuchar [esku'tʃar] *vt* to listen to; (*consejo*) to heed; (*esp AM: oír*) to hear ♦ *vi* to listen; ~**se** *vr*: **se escucha muy mal** (*TELEC*) it's a very bad line.

escudarse [esku'ðarse] *vr*: ~ **en** (*fig*) to hide behind.

escudería [eskuðe'ria] *nf*: **la** ~ **Ferrari** the Ferrari team.

escudero [esku'ðero] *nm* squire.

escudilla [esku'ðiʎa] *nf* bowl, basin.

escudo [es'kuðo] *nm* shield; ~ **de armas** coat of arms.

escudriñar [eskuðri'ɲar] *vt* (*examinar*) to investigate, scrutinize; (*mirar de lejos*) to scan.

escuece [es'kweθe] *etc vb V* **escocer**.

escuela [es'kwela] *nf* (*tb fig*) school; ~ **normal** teacher training college; ~

técnica superior *university offering 5-year courses in engineering and technical subjects*; ~ **universitaria** *university offering 3-year diploma courses*; ~ **de párvulos** kindergarten; *V tb* **colegio**.

escueto, a [es'kweto, a] *adj* plain; (*estilo*) simple; (*explicación*) concise.

escueza [es'kweθa] *etc vb V* **escocer**.

escuincle [es'kwinkle] *nm* (*AM fam*) kid.

esculpir [eskul'pir] *vt* to sculpt; (*grabar*) to engrave; (*tallar*) to carve.

escultor, a [eskul'tor, a] *nm/f* sculptor.

escultura [eskul'tura] *nf* sculpture.

escupidera [eskupi'ðera] *nf* spittoon.

escupir [esku'pir] *vt* to spit (out) ♦ *vi* to spit.

escupitajo [eskupi'taxo] *nm* (*fam*) gob of spit.

escurreplatos [eskurre'platos] *nm inv* plate rack.

escurridizo, a [eskurri'ðiθo, a] *adj* slippery.

escurrir [esku'rrir] *vt* (*ropa*) to wring out; (*verduras, platos*) to drain ♦ *vi* (*los líquidos*) to drip; ~**se** *vr* (*secarse*) to drain; (*resbalarse*) to slip, slide; (*escaparse*) to slip away.

ese[1] ['ese] *nf* (the letter) S; **hacer** ~**s** (*carretera*) to zigzag; (*borracho*) to reel about.

ese[2] ['ese], **esa** ['esa], **esos** ['esos], **esas** ['esas] *adj demostrativo* (*sg*) that; (*pl*) those.

ése ['ese], **ésa** ['esa], **ésos** ['esos], **ésas** ['esas] *pron* (*sg*) that (one); (*pl*) those (ones); **ése ... éste** ... the former ... the latter ...; **¡no me vengas con ésas!** don't give me any more of that nonsense!

esencia [e'senθja] *nf* essence.

esencial [esen'θjal] *adj* essential; (*principal*) chief; **lo** ~ the main thing.

esfera [es'fera] *nf* sphere; (*de reloj*) face; ~ **de acción** scope; ~ **terrestre** globe.

esférico, a [es'feriko, a] *adj* spherical.

esfinge [es'finxe] *nf* sphinx.

esforcé [esfor'θe], **esforcemos** [esfor'θemos] *etc vb V* **esforzar**.

esforzado, a [esfor'θaðo, a] *adj* (*enérgico*) energetic, vigorous.

esforzarse [esfor'θarse] *vr* to exert o.s., make an effort.

esfuerce [es'fwerθe] *etc vb V* **esforzar**.

esfuerzo [es'fwerθo] *etc vb V* **esforzar** ♦ *nm* effort; **sin** ~ effortlessly.

esfumarse [esfu'marse] *vr* (*apoyo, esperanzas*) to fade away; (*persona*) to vanish.

esgrima [es'ɣrima] *nf* fencing.

esgrimidor [esɣrimi'ðor] *nm* fencer.
esgrimir [esɣri'mir] *vt* (*arma*) to brandish; (*argumento*) to use ♦ *vi* to fence.
esguince [es'ɣinθe] *nm* (*MED*) sprain.
eslabón [esla'ßon] *nm* link; ~ **perdido** (*BIO, fig*) missing link.
eslabonar [eslaßo'nar] *vt* to link, connect.
eslálom [es'lalom] *nm* slalom.
eslavo, a [es'laßo, a] *adj* Slav, Slavonic ♦ *nm/f* Slav ♦ *nm* (*LING*) Slavonic.
eslogan [es'loɣan] *nm, pl* **eslogans** = **slogan.**
eslora [es'lora] *nf* (*NAUT*) length.
eslovaco, a [eslo'ßako, a] *adj, nm/f* Slovak, Slovakian ♦ *nm* (*LING*) Slovak, Slovakian.
Eslovaquia [eslo'ßakja] *nf* Slovakia.
Eslovenia [eslo'ßenja] *nf* Slovenia.
esloveno, a [eslo'ßeno, a] *adj, nm/f* Slovene, Slovenian ♦ *nm* (*LING*) Slovene, Slovenian.
esmaltar [esmal'tar] *vt* to enamel.
esmalte [es'malte] *nm* enamel; ~ **de uñas** nail varnish *o* polish.
esmerado, a [esme'raðo, a] *adj* careful, neat.
esmeralda [esme'ralda] *nf* emerald.
esmerarse [esme'rarse] *vr* (*aplicarse*) to take great pains, exercise great care; (*afanarse*) to work hard; (*hacer lo mejor*) to do one's best.
esmero [es'mero] *nm* (great) care.
esmirriado, a [esmi'rrjaðo, a] *adj* puny.
esmoquin [es'mokin] *nm* dinner jacket (*BRIT*), tuxedo (*US*).
esnob [es'nob] *adj inv* (*persona*) snobbish; (*coche etc*) posh ♦ *nm/f* snob.
esnobismo [esno'ßismo] *nm* snobbery.
eso ['eso] *pron* that, that thing *o* matter; ~ **de su coche** that business about his car; ~ **de ir al cine** all that about going to the cinema; **a** ~ **de las cinco** at about five o'clock; **en** ~ thereupon, at that point; **por** ~ therefore; ~ **es** that's it; **nada de** ~ far from it; ¡~ **sí que es vida!** now this is really living!; **por** ~ **te lo dije** that's why I told you; **y** ~ **que llovía** in spite of the fact it was raining.
esófago [e'sofaɣo] *nm* (*ANAT*) oesophagus.
esos ['esos] *adj demostrativo V* **ese.**
ésos ['esos] *pron V* **ése.**
esotérico, a [eso'teriko, a] *adj* esoteric.
esp. *abr* (= *español*) Sp., Span.
espabilado, a [espaßi'laðo, a] *adj* quick-witted.
espabilar [espaßi'lar] *vt*, **espabilarse** *vr* = **despabilar(se).**
espachurrar [espatʃu'rrar] *vt* to squash; ~**se** *vr* to get squashed.

espaciado [espa'θjaðo] *nm* (*INFORM*) spacing.
espacial [espa'θjal] *adj* (*del espacio*) space *cpd.*
espaciar [espa'θjar] *vt* to space (out).
espacio [es'paθjo] *nm* space; (*MUS*) interval; (*RADIO, TV*) programme, program (*US*); **el** ~ space; **ocupar mucho** ~ to take up a lot of room; **a dos** ~**s, a doble** ~ (*TIP*) double-spaced; **por** ~ **de** during, for.
espacioso, a [espa'θjoso, a] *adj* spacious, roomy.
espada [es'paða] *nf* sword ♦ *nm* swordsman; (*TAUR*) matador; ~**s** *nfpl* (*NAIPES*) one of the suits in the Spanish card deck; **estar entre la** ~ **y la pared** to be between the devil and the deep blue sea; *V tb* **baraja española.**
espadachín [espaða'tʃin] *nm* (*esgrimidor*) skilled swordsman.
espaguetis [espa'ɣetis] *nmpl* spaghetti *sg.*
espalda [es'palda] *nf* (*gen*) back; (*NATACIÓN*) backstroke; ~**s** *nfpl* (*hombros*) shoulders; **a** ~**s de algn** behind sb's back; **estar de** ~**s** to have one's back turned; **tenderse de** ~**s** to lie (down) on one's back; **volver la** ~ **a algn** to cold-shoulder sb.
espaldarazo [espalda'raθo] *nm* (*tb fig*) slap on the back.
espaldilla [espal'ðiʎa] *nf* shoulder blade.
espantadizo, a [espanta'ðiθo, a] *adj* timid, easily frightened.
espantajo [espan'taxo] *nm*,
espantapájaros [espanta'paxaros] *nm inv* scarecrow.
espantar [espan'tar] *vt* (*asustar*) to frighten, scare; (*ahuyentar*) to frighten off; (*asombrar*) to horrify, appal; ~**se** *vr* to get frightened *o* scared; to be appalled.
espanto [es'panto] *nm* (*susto*) fright; (*terror*) terror; (*asombro*) astonishment; ¡**qué** ~! how awful!
espantoso, a [espan'toso, a] *adj* frightening, terrifying; (*ruido*) dreadful.
España [es'paɲa] *nf* Spain; **la** ~ **de pandereta** touristy Spain.
español, a [espa'ɲol, a] *adj* Spanish ♦ *nm/f* Spaniard ♦ *nm* (*LING*) Spanish; *V tb* **castellano.**
españolice [espaɲo'liθe] *etc vb V* **españolizar.**
españolizar [espaɲoli'θar] *vt* to make Spanish, Hispanicize; ~**se** *vr* to adopt Spanish ways.
esparadrapo [espara'ðrapo] *nm* (sticking)

plaster, Band-Aid ® (*US*).

esparcido, a [espar'θiðo, a] *adj* scattered.

esparcimiento [esparθi'mjento] *nm*
(*dispersión*) spreading; (*derramamiento*)
scattering; (*fig*) cheerfulness.

esparcir [espar'θir] *vt* to spread; (*derramar*)
to scatter; ~**se** *vr* to spread (out); to
scatter; (*divertirse*) to enjoy o.s.

espárrago [es'parraɣo] *nm* (*tb*: ~**s**)
asparagus; **estar hecho un** ~ to be as
thin as a rake; **¡vete a freír** ~**s!** (*fam*) go
to hell!

esparto [es'parto] *nm* esparto (grass).

esparza [es'parθa] *etc vb V* **esparcir**.

espasmo [es'pasmo] *nm* spasm.

espátula [es'patula] *nf* (*MED*) spatula;
(*ARTE*) palette knife; (*CULIN*) fish slice.

especia [es'peθja] *nf* spice.

especial [espe'θjal] *adj* special.

especialidad [espeθjali'ðað] *nf* speciality,
specialty (*US*); (*ESCOL*: *ramo*) specialism.

especialista [espeθja'lista] *nm/f* specialist;
(*CINE*) stuntman/woman.

especializado, a [espeθjali'θaðo, a] *adj*
specialized; (*obrero*) skilled.

especialmente [espeθjal'mente] *adv*
particularly, especially.

especie [es'peθje] *nf* (*BIO*) species; (*clase*)
kind, sort; **pagar en** ~ to pay in kind.

especificar [espeθifi'kar] *vt* to specify.

específico, a [espe'θifiko, a] *adj* specific.

especifique [espeθi'fike] *etc vb V*
especificar.

espécimen [es'peθimen], *pl* **especímenes**
nm specimen.

espectáculo [espek'takulo] *nm* (*gen*)
spectacle; (*TEAT etc*) show; (*función*)
performance; **dar un** ~ to make a scene.

espectador, a [espekta'ðor, a] *nm/f*
spectator; (*de incidente*) onlooker; **los**
~**es** (*TEAT*) the audience *sg*.

espectro [es'pektro] *nm* ghost; (*fig*)
spectre.

especulación [espekula'θjon] *nf*
speculation; ~ **bursátil** speculation on
the Stock Market.

especular [espeku'lar] *vt*, *vi* to speculate.

especulativo, a [espekula'tiβo, a] *adj*
speculative.

espejismo [espe'xismo] *nm* mirage.

espejo [es'pexo] *nm* mirror; (*fig*) model; ~
retrovisor rear-view mirror; **mirarse al**
~ to look (at o.s.) in the mirror.

espeleología [espeleolo'xia] *nf* potholing.

espeluznante [espeluθ'nante] *adj*
horrifying, hair-raising.

espera [es'pera] *nf* (*pausa, intervalo*) wait;
(*JUR*: *plazo*) respite; **en** ~ **de** waiting for;

(*con expectativa*) expecting; **en** ~ **de su
contestación** awaiting your reply.

esperance [espe'ranθe] *etc vb V*
esperanzar.

esperanza [espe'ranθa] *nf* (*confianza*) hope;
(*expectativa*) expectation; **hay pocas** ~**s
de que venga** there is little prospect of
his coming.

esperanzador, a [esperanθa'ðor, a] *adj*
hopeful, encouraging.

esperanzar [esperan'θar] *vt* to give hope
to.

esperar [espe'rar] *vt* (*aguardar*) to wait for;
(*tener expectativa de*) to expect; (*desear*)
to hope for ♦ *vi* to wait; to expect; to
hope; ~**se** *vr*: **como podía** ~**se** as was to
be expected; **hacer** ~ **a uno** to keep sb
waiting; **ir a** ~ **a uno** to go and meet sb;
~ **un bebé** to be expecting (a baby).

esperma [es'perma] *nf* sperm.

espermatozoide [espermato'θoiðe] *nm*
spermatozoid.

esperpento [esper'pento] *nm* (*persona*)
sight (*fam*); (*disparate*) (piece of)
nonsense.

espesar [espe'sar] *vt* to thicken; ~**se** *vr* to
thicken, get thicker.

espeso, a [es'peso, a] *adj* thick; (*bosque*)
dense; (*nieve*) deep; (*sucio*) dirty.

espesor [espe'sor] *nm* thickness; (*de nieve*)
depth.

espesura [espe'sura] *nf* (*bosque*) thicket.

espetar [espe'tar] *vt* (*reto, sermón*) to give.

espía [es'pia] *nm/f* spy.

espiar [espi'ar] *vt* (*observar*) to spy on ♦ *vi*:
~ **para** to spy for.

espiga [es'piɣa] *nf* (*BOT*: *de trigo etc*) ear;
(: *de flores*) spike.

espigado, a [espi'ɣaðo, a] *adj* (*BOT*) ripe;
(*fig*) tall, slender.

espigón [espi'ɣon] *nm* (*BOT*) ear; (*NAUT*)
breakwater.

espina [es'pina] *nf* thorn; (*de pez*) bone; ~
dorsal (*ANAT*) spine; **me da mala** ~ I
don't like the look of it.

espinaca [espi'naka] *nf* (*tb*: ~**s**) spinach.

espinar [espi'nar] *nm* (*matorral*) thicket.

espinazo [espi'naθo] *nm* spine, backbone.

espinilla [espi'niʎa] *nf* (*ANAT*: *tibia*)
shin(bone); (: *en la piel*) blackhead.

espino [es'pino] *nm* hawthorn.

espinoso, a [espi'noso, a] *adj* (*planta*)
thorny, prickly; (*fig*) bony; (*problema*)
knotty.

espionaje [espjo'naxe] *nm* spying,
espionage.

espiral [espi'ral] *adj, nf* spiral; **la** ~
inflacionista the inflationary spiral.

espirar [espi'rar] *vt, vi* to breathe out, exhale.

espiritista [espiri'tista] *adj, nm/f* spiritualist.

espíritu [es'piritu] *nm* spirit; (*mente*) mind; (*inteligencia*) intelligence; (*REL*) spirit, soul; **E~ Santo** Holy Ghost; **con ~ amplio** with an open mind.

espiritual [espiri'twal] *adj* spiritual.

espita [es'pita] *nf* tap (*BRIT*), faucet (*US*).

esplendidez [esplendi'ðeθ] *nf* (*abundancia*) lavishness; (*magnificencia*) splendour.

espléndido, a [es'plendiðo, a] *adj* (*magnífico*) magnificent, splendid; (*generoso*) generous, lavish.

esplendor [esplen'dor] *nm* splendour.

espliego [es'pljeɣo] *nm* lavender.

espolear [espole'ar] *vt* to spur on.

espoleta [espo'leta] *nf* (*de bomba*) fuse.

espolvorear [espolßore'ar] *vt* to dust, sprinkle.

esponja [es'ponxa] *nf* sponge; (*fig*) sponger.

esponjoso, a [espon'xoso, a] *adj* spongy.

esponsales [espon'sales] *nmpl* betrothal *sg*.

espontaneidad [espontanei'ðað] *nf* spontaneity.

espontáneo, a [espon'taneo, a] *adj* spontaneous; (*improvisado*) impromptu; (*persona*) natural.

espora [es'pora] *nf* spore.

esporádico, a [espo'raðiko, a] *adj* sporadic.

esposa [es'posa] *nf* V **esposo.**

esposar [espo'sar] *vt* to handcuff.

esposo, a [es'poso, a] *nm* husband ♦ *nf* wife; **esposas** *nfpl* handcuffs.

espuela [es'pwela] *nf* spur; (*fam: trago*) one for the road.

espuerta [es'pwerta] *nf* basket, pannier.

espuma [es'puma] *nf* foam; (*de cerveza*) froth, head; (*de jabón*) lather; (*de olas*) surf.

espumadera [espuma'ðera] *nf* skimmer.

espumarajo [espuma'raxo] *nm* froth, foam; **echar ~s (de rabia)** to splutter with rage.

espumoso, a [espu'moso, a] *adj* frothy, foamy; (*vino*) sparkling.

esputo [es'puto] *nm* (*saliva*) spit; (*MED*) sputum.

esqueje [es'kexe] *nm* (*BOT*) cutting.

esquela [es'kela] *nf*: **~ mortuoria** announcement of death.

esquelético, a [eske'letiko, a] *adj* (*fam*) skinny.

esqueleto [eske'leto] *nm* skeleton; (*lo esencial*) bare bones (of a matter); **en ~**

unfinished.

esquema [es'kema] *nm* (*diagrama*) diagram; (*dibujo*) plan; (*plan*) scheme; (*FILOSOFÍA*) schema.

esquemático, a [eske'matiko, a] *adj* schematic; **un resumen ~** a brief outline.

esquí [es'ki], *pl* **esquís** *nm* (*objeto*) ski; (*deporte*) skiing; **~ acuático** water-skiing; **hacer ~** to go skiing.

esquiador, a [eskja'ðor, a] *nm/f* skier.

esquiar [es'kjar] *vi* to ski.

esquila [es'kila] *nf* (*campanilla*) small bell; (*encerro*) cowbell.

esquilar [eski'lar] *vt* to shear.

esquimal [eski'mal] *adj, nm/f* Eskimo.

esquina [es'kina] *nf* corner; **doblar la ~** to turn the corner.

esquinazo [eski'naθo] *nm*: **dar ~ a algn** to give sb the slip.

esquirla [es'kirla] *nf* splinter.

esquirol [eski'rol] *nm* blackleg.

esquivar [eski'ßar] *vt* to avoid; (*evadir*) to dodge, elude.

esquivo, a [es'kiβo, a] *adj* (*altanero*) aloof; (*desdeñoso*) scornful, disdainful.

esquizofrenia [eskiθo'frenja] *nf* schizophrenia.

esta ['esta] *adj demostrativo* V **este.**

ésta ['esta] *pron* V **éste.**

está [es'ta] *vb* V **estar.**

estabilice [estaßi'liθe] *etc vb* V **estabilizar.**

estabilidad [estaßili'ðað] *nf* stability.

estabilización [estaßiliθa'θjon] *nf* (*COM*) stabilization.

estabilizar [estaßili'θar] *vt* to stabilize; (*fijar*) to make steady; (*precios*) to peg; **~se** *vr* to become stable.

estable [es'taßle] *adj* stable.

establecer [estaßle'θer] *vt* to establish; (*fundar*) to set up; (*colonos*) to settle; (*récord*) to set (up); **~se** *vr* to establish o.s.; (*echar raíces*) to settle (down); (*COM*) to start up.

establecimiento [estaßleθi'mjento] *nm* establishment; (*fundación*) institution; (*de negocio*) start-up; (*de colonias*) settlement; (*local*) establishment; **~ comercial** business house.

establezca [esta'ßleθka] *etc vb* V **establecer.**

establo [es'taßlo] *nm* (*AGR*) stall; (: *esp AM*) barn.

estaca [es'taka] *nf* stake, post; (*de tienda de campaña*) peg.

estacada [esta'kaða] *nf* (*cerca*) fence, fencing; (*palenque*) stockade; **dejar a algn en la ~** to leave sb in the lurch.

estación [esta'θjon] *nf* station; (*del año*) season; ~ **de autobuses/ferrocarril** bus/railway station; ~ **balnearia (de turistas)** seaside resort; ~ **de servicio** service station; ~ **terminal** terminus; ~ **de trabajo** (*COM*) work station; ~ **transmisora** transmitter; ~ **de visualización** display unit.

estacionamiento [estaθjona'mjento] *nm* (*AUTO*) parking; (*MIL*) stationing.

estacionar [estaθjo'nar] *vt* (*AUTO*) to park; (*MIL*) to station.

estacionario, a [estaθjo'narjo, a] *adj* stationary; (*COM: mercado*) slack.

estada [es'taða], **estadía** [esta'ðia] *nf* (*AM*) stay.

estadio [es'taðjo] *nm* (*fase*) stage, phase; (*DEPORTE*) stadium.

estadista [esta'ðista] *nm* (*POL*) statesman; (*ESTADÍSTICA*) statistician.

estadística [esta'ðistika] *nf* (*una* ~) figure, statistic; (*ciencia*) statistics *sg*.

estado [es'taðo] *nm* (*POL: condición*) state; ~ **civil** marital status; ~ **de cuenta(s)** bank statement, statement of accounts; ~ **de excepción** (*POL*) state of emergency; ~ **financiero** (*COM*) financial statement; ~ **mayor** (*MIL*) staff; ~ **de pérdidas y ganancias** (*COM*) profit and loss statement, operating statement; **E~s Unidos (EE.UU.)** United States (of America) (USA); **estar en** ~ (**de buena esperanza**) to be pregnant.

estadounidense [estaðouni'ðense] *adj* United States *cpd*, American ♦ *nm/f* United States citizen, American.

estafa [es'tafa] *nf* swindle, trick; (*COM etc*) racket.

estafar [esta'far] *vt* to swindle, defraud.

estafeta [esta'feta] *nf* (*oficina de correos*) post office; ~ **diplomática** diplomatic bag.

estalactita [estalak'tita] *nf* stalactite.

estalagmita [estalaɣ'mita] *nf* stalagmite.

estallar [esta'ʎar] *vi* to burst; (*bomba*) to explode, go off; (*volcán*) to erupt; (*vidrio*) to shatter; (*látigo*) to crack; (*epidemia, guerra, rebelión*) to break out; ~ **en llanto** to burst into tears.

estallido [esta'ʎiðo] *nm* explosion; (*de látigo, trueno*) crack; (*fig*) outbreak.

estambre [es'tambre] *nm* (*tela*) worsted; (*BOT*) stamen.

Estambul [estam'bul] *nm* Istanbul.

estamento [esta'mento] *nm* (social) class.

estampa [es'tampa] *nf* (*impresión, imprenta*) print, engraving; (*imagen, figura: de persona*) appearance.

estampado, a [estam'paðo, a] *adj* printed ♦ *nm* (*impresión: acción*) printing; (: *efecto*) print; (*marca*) stamping.

estampar [estam'par] *vt* (*imprimir*) to print; (*marcar*) to stamp; (*metal*) to engrave; (*poner sello en*) to stamp; (*fig*) to stamp, imprint.

estampida [estam'piða] *nf* stampede.

estampido [estam'piðo] *nm* bang, report.

estampilla [estam'piʎa] *nf* (*sello de goma*) (rubber) stamp; (*AM*) (postage) stamp.

están [es'tan] *vb V* **estar**.

estancado, a [estan'kaðo, a] *adj* (*agua*) stagnant.

estancamiento [estanka'mjento] *nm* stagnation.

estancar [estan'kar] *vt* (*aguas*) to hold up, hold back; (*COM*) to monopolize; (*fig*) to block, hold up; ~**se** *vr* to stagnate.

estancia [es'tanθja] *nf* (*permanencia*) stay; (*sala*) room; (*AM*) farm, ranch.

estanciero [estan'sjero] *nm* (*AM*) farmer, rancher.

estanco, a [es'tanko, a] *adj* watertight ♦ *nm* tobacconist's (shop).

Cigarettes, tobacco, postage stamps and official forms are all sold under state monopoly and usually through a shop called an **estanco**. *Tobacco products are also sold in* **quioscos** *and bars but are generally more expensive. The number of* **estanco** *licences is regulated by the state.*

---

estándar [es'tandar] *adj, nm* standard.

estandarice [estanda'riθe] *etc vb V* **estandarizar**.

estandarizar [estandari'θar] *vt* to standardize.

estandarte [estan'darte] *nm* banner, standard.

estanque [es'tanke] *etc vb V* **estancar** ♦ *nm* (*lago*) pool, pond; (*AGR*) reservoir.

estanquero, a [estan'kero, a] *nm/f* tobacconist.

estante [es'tante] *nm* (*armario*) rack, stand; (*biblioteca*) bookcase; (*anaquel*) shelf; (*AM*) prop.

estantería [estante'ria] *nf* shelving, shelves *pl*.

estaño [es'taɲo] *nm* tin.

====================== *PALABRA CLAVE*

estar [es'tar] *vi* **1** (*posición*) to be; **está en la plaza** it's in the square; **¿está Juan?** is Juan in?; **estamos a 30 km de Junín** we're 30 kms from Junín
2 (+*adj o adv: estado*) to be; ~ **enfermo**

to be ill; **está muy elegante** he's looking very smart; ~ **lejos** to be far (away); **¿cómo estás?** how are you keeping?

3 (+*gerundio*) to be; **estoy leyendo** I'm reading

4 (*uso pasivo*): **está condenado a muerte** he's been condemned to death; **está envasado en ...** it's packed in ...

5: ~ **a:** **¿a cuántos estamos?** what's the date today?; **estamos a 5 de mayo** it's the 5th of May; **las manzanas están a 200 ptas** apples are (selling at) 200 pesetas; **estamos a 25 grados** it's 25 degrees today

6 (*locuciones*): **¿estamos?** (*¿de acuerdo?*) okay?; (*¿listo?*) ready?; **¡ya está bien!** that's enough!; **¿está la comida?** is dinner ready?; **¡ya está!**, (*AM*) **¡ya estuvo!** that's it!

7: ~ **con:** **está con gripe** he's got (the) flu

8: ~ **de:** ~ **de vacaciones/viaje** to be on holiday/away *o* on a trip; **está de camarero** he's working as a waiter

9: ~ **para:** **está para salir** he's about to leave; **no estoy para bromas** I'm not in the mood for jokes

10: ~ **por** (*propuesta etc*) to be in favour of; (*persona etc*) to support, side with; **está por limpiar** it still has to be cleaned; **¡estoy por dejarlo!** I think I'm going to leave this!

11 (+*que*): **está que rabia** (*fam*) he's hopping mad (*fam*); **estoy que me caigo de sueño** I'm terribly sleepy, I can't keep my eyes open

12: ~ **sin:** ~ **sin dinero** to have no money; **está sin terminar** it isn't finished yet

♦ ~**se** *vr*: **se estuvo en la cama toda la tarde** he stayed in bed all afternoon; **¡estáte quieto!** stop fidgeting!

estárter [es'tarter] *nm* (*AUTO*) choke.
estas ['estas] *adj demostrativo* V **este**.
éstas ['estas] *pron* V **éste**.
estás [es'tas] *vb* V **estar**.
estatal [esta'tal] *adj* state *cpd*.
estático, a [es'tatiko, a] *adj* static.
estatua [es'tatwa] *nf* statue.
estatura [esta'tura] *nf* stature, height.
estatus [es'tatus] *nm inv* status.
estatutario, a [estatu'tarjo, a] *adj* statutory.
estatuto [esta'tuto] *nm* (*JUR*) statute; (*de ciudad*) bye-law; (*de comité*) rule; ~**s sociales** (*COM*) articles of association.
este[1] ['este] *adj* (*lado*) east; (*dirección*) easterly ♦ *nm* east; **en la parte del** ~ in

the eastern part.
este[2] ['este], **esta** ['esta], **estos** ['estos], **estas** ['estas] *adj demostrativo* (*sg*) this; (*pl*) these; (*AM: como muletilla*) er, um.
éste ['este], **ésta** ['esta], **éstos** ['estos], **éstas** ['estas] *pron* (*sg*) this (one); (*pl*) these (ones); **ése ... éste ...** the former ... the latter ....
esté [es'te] *vb* V **estar**.
estela [es'tela] *nf* wake, wash; (*fig*) trail.
estelar [este'lar] *adj* (*ASTRO*) stellar; (*TEAT*) star *cpd*.
estén [es'ten] *vb* V **estar**.
estenografía [estenoɣra'fia] *nf* shorthand.
estentóreo, a [esten'toreo, a] *adj* (*sonido*) strident; (*voz*) booming.
estepa [es'tepa] *nf* (*GEO*) steppe.
estera [es'tera] *nf* (*alfombra*) mat; (*tejido*) matting.
estercolero [esterko'lero] *nm* manure heap, dunghill.
estéreo [es'tereo] *adj inv*, *nm* stereo.
estereofónico, a [estereo'foniko, a] *adj* stereophonic.
estereotipar [estereoti'par] *vt* to stereotype.
estereotipo [estereo'tipo] *nm* stereotype.
estéril [es'teril] *adj* sterile, barren; (*fig*) vain, futile.
esterilice [esteri'liθe] *etc vb* V **esterilizar**.
esterilizar [esterili'θar] *vt* to sterilize.
esterilla [este'riʎa] *nf* (*alfombrilla*) small mat.
esterlina [ester'lina] *adj*: **libra** ~ pound sterling.
esternón [ester'non] *nm* breastbone.
estero [es'tero] *nm* (*AM*) swamp.
estertor [ester'tor] *nm* death rattle.
estés [es'tes] *vb* V **estar**.
esteta [es'teta] *nm/f* aesthete.
esteticienne [esteti'θjen] *nf* beautician.
estético, a [es'tetiko, a] *adj* aesthetic ♦ *nf* aesthetics *sg*.
estetoscopio [estetos'kopjo] *nm* stethoscope.
estibador [estiβa'ðor] *nm* stevedore.
estibar [esti'βar] *vt* (*NAUT*) to stow.
estiércol [es'tjerkol] *nm* dung, manure.
estigma [es'tiɣma] *nm* stigma.
estigmatice [estiɣma'tiθe] *etc vb* V **estigmatizar**.
estigmatizar [estiɣmati'θar] *vt* to stigmatize.
estilarse [esti'larse] *vr* (*estar de moda*) to be in fashion; (*usarse*) to be used.
estilice [esti'liθe] *etc vb* V **estilizar**.
estilizar [estili'θar] *vt* to stylize; (*TEC*) to design.

estilo [es'tilo] *nm* style; (*TEC*) stylus; (*NATACIÓN*) stroke; ~ **de vida** lifestyle; **al** ~ **de** in the style of; **algo por el** ~ something along those lines.

estilográfica [estilo'ɣrafika] *nf* fountain pen.

estima [es'tima] *nf* esteem, respect.

estimación [estima'θjon] *nf* (*evaluación*) estimation; (*aprecio, afecto*) esteem, regard.

estimado, a [esti'maðo, a] *adj* esteemed; "E~ **Señor**" "Dear Sir".

estimar [esti'mar] *vt* (*evaluar*) to estimate; (*valorar*) to value; (*apreciar*) to esteem, respect; (*pensar, considerar*) to think, reckon.

estimulante [estimu'lante] *adj* stimulating ♦ *nm* stimulant.

estimular [estimu'lar] *vt* to stimulate; (*excitar*) to excite; (*animar*) to encourage.

estímulo [es'timulo] *nm* stimulus; (*ánimo*) encouragement; (*INFORM*) prompt.

estío [es'tio] *nm* summer.

estipendio [esti'pendjo] *nm* salary; (*COM*) stipend.

estipulación [estipula'θjon] *nf* stipulation, condition.

estipular [estipu'lar] *vt* to stipulate.

estirado, a [esti'raðo, a] *adj* (*tenso*) (stretched *o* drawn) tight; (*fig: persona*) stiff, pompous; (*engreído*) stuck-up.

estirar [esti'rar] *vt* to stretch; (*dinero, suma etc*) to stretch out; (*cuello*) to crane; (*dinero*) to eke out; (*discurso*) to spin out; ~ **la pata** (*fam*) to kick the bucket; ~**se** *vr* to stretch.

estirón [esti'ron] *nm* pull, tug; (*crecimiento*) spurt, sudden growth; **dar un** ~ (*niño*) to shoot up.

estirpe [es'tirpe] *nf* stock, lineage.

estival [esti'ßal] *adj* summer *cpd*.

esto ['esto] *pron* this, this thing *o* matter; (*como muletilla*) er, um; ~ **de la boda** this business about the wedding; **en** ~ at this *o* that point; **por** ~ for this reason.

estocada [esto'kaða] *nf* (*acción*) stab; (*TAUR*) death blow.

Estocolmo [esto'kolmo] *nm* Stockholm.

estofa [es'tofa] *nf*: **de baja** ~ poor-quality.

estofado [esto'faðo] *nm* stew.

estofar [esto'far] *vt* (*bordar*) to quilt; (*CULIN*) to stew.

estoico, a [es'toiko, a] *adj* (*FILOSOFÍA*) stoic(al); (*fig*) cold, indifferent.

estomacal [estoma'kal] *adj* stomach *cpd*; **trastorno** ~ stomach upset.

estómago [es'tomaɣo] *nm* stomach; **tener** ~ to be thick-skinned.

Estonia [es'tonja] *nf* Estonia.

estonio, a [es'tonjo, a] *adj, nm/f* Estonian ♦ *nm* (*LING*) Estonian.

estoque [es'toke] *nm* rapier, sword.

estorbar [estor'ßar] *vt* to hinder, obstruct; (*fig*) to bother, disturb ♦ *vi* to be in the way.

estorbo [es'torßo] *nm* (*molestia*) bother, nuisance; (*obstáculo*) hindrance, obstacle.

estornino [estor'nino] *nm* starling.

estornudar [estornu'ðar] *vi* to sneeze.

estornudo [estor'nuðo] *nm* sneeze.

estos ['estos] *adj demostrativo* V **este**.

éstos ['estos] *pron* V **éste**.

estoy [es'toi] *vb* V **estar**.

estrabismo [estra'ßismo] *nm* squint.

estrado [es'traðo] *nm* (*tarima*) platform; (*MUS*) bandstand; ~**s** *nmpl* law courts.

estrafalario, a [estrafa'larjo, a] *adj* odd, eccentric; (*desarreglado*) slovenly, sloppy.

estrago [es'traɣo] *nm* ruin, destruction; **hacer** ~**s en** to wreak havoc among.

estragón [estra'ɣon] *nm* (*CULIN*) tarragon.

estrambótico, a [estram'botiko, a] *adj* odd, eccentric.

estrangulación [estrangula'θjon] *nf* strangulation.

estrangulador, a [estrangula'ðor, a] *nm/f* strangler ♦ *nm* (*TEC*) throttle; (*AUTO*) choke.

estrangulamiento [estrangula'mjento] *nm* (*AUTO*) bottleneck.

estrangular [estrangu'lar] *vt* (*persona*) to strangle; (*MED*) to strangulate.

estraperlista [estraper'lista] *nm/f* black marketeer.

estraperlo [estra'perlo] *nm* black market.

estratagema [estrata'xema] *nf* (*MIL*) stratagem; (*astucia*) cunning.

estratega [estra'teɣa] *nm/f* strategist.

estrategia [estra'texja] *nf* strategy.

estratégico, a [estra'texiko, a] *adj* strategic.

estratificar [estratifi'kar] *vt* to stratify.

estratifique [estrati'fike] *etc vb* V **estratificar**.

estrato [es'trato] *nm* stratum, layer.

estratosfera [estratos'fera] *nf* stratosphere.

estrechar [estre'tʃar] *vt* (*reducir*) to narrow; (*vestido*) to take in; (*persona*) to hug, embrace; ~**se** *vr* (*reducirse*) to narrow, grow narrow; (*2 personas*) to embrace; ~ **la mano** to shake hands.

estrechez [estre'tʃeθ] *nf* narrowness; (*de ropa*) tightness; (*intimidad*) intimacy;

(*COM*) want *o* shortage of money; **estrecheces** *nfpl* financial difficulties.

estrecho, a [es'tretʃo, a] *adj* narrow; (*apretado*) tight; (*íntimo*) close, intimate; (*miserable*) mean ♦ *nm* strait; ~ **de miras** narrow-minded; **E~ de Gibraltar** Straits of Gibraltar.

estrella [es'treʎa] *nf* star; ~ **fugaz** shooting star; ~ **de mar** starfish; **tener (buena)/ mala** ~ to be lucky/unlucky.

estrellado, a [estre'ʎaðo, a] *adj* (*forma*) star-shaped; (*cielo*) starry; (*huevos*) fried.

estrellar [estre'ʎar] *vt* (*hacer añicos*) to smash (to pieces); (*huevos*) to fry; ~**se** *vr* to smash; (*chocarse*) to crash; (*fracasar*) to fail.

estrellato [estre'ʎato] *nm* stardom.

estremecer [estreme'θer] *vt* to shake; ~**se** *vr* to shake, tremble; ~ **de** (*horror*) to shudder with; (*frío*) to shiver with.

estremecimiento [estremeθi'mjento] *nm* (*temblor*) trembling, shaking.

estremezca [estre'meθka] *etc vb V* **estremecer**.

estrenar [estre'nar] *vt* (*vestido*) to wear for the first time; (*casa*) to move into; (*película, obra de teatro*) to present for the first time; ~**se** *vr* (*persona*) to make one's début; (*película*) to have its premiere; (*TEAT*) to open.

estreno [es'treno] *nm* (*primer uso*) first use; (*CINE etc*) premiere.

estreñido, a [estre'ɲiðo, a] *adj* constipated.

estreñimiento [estreɲi'mjento] *nm* constipation.

estreñir [estre'ɲir] *vt* to constipate.

estrépito [es'trepito] *nm* noise, racket; (*fig*) fuss.

estrepitoso, a [estrepi'toso, a] *adj* noisy; (*fiesta*) rowdy.

estrés [es'tres] *nm* stress.

estresante [estre'sante] *adj* stressful.

estría [es'tria] *nf* groove; ~**s (en el cutis)** stretchmarks.

estribación [estriβa'θjon] *nf* (*GEO*) spur; **estribaciones** *nfpl* foothills.

estribar [estri'βar] *vi*: ~ **en** to rest on, be supported by; **la dificultad estriba en el texto** the difficulty lies in the text.

estribillo [estri'βiʎo] *nm* (*LITERATURA*) refrain; (*MUS*) chorus.

estribo [es'triβo] *nm* (*de jinete*) stirrup; (*de coche, tren*) step; (*de puente*) support; (*GEO*) spur; **perder los ~s** to fly off the handle.

estribor [estri'βor] *nm* (*NAUT*) starboard.

estricnina [estrik'nina] *nf* strychnine.

estricto, a [es'trikto, a] *adj* (*riguroso*) strict; (*severo*) severe.

estridente [estri'ðente] *adj* (*color*) loud; (*voz*) raucous.

estro ['estro] *nm* inspiration.

estrofa [es'trofa] *nf* verse.

estropajo [estro'paxo] *nm* scourer.

estropeado, a [estrope'aðo, a] *adj*: **está ~** it's not working.

estropear [estrope'ar] *vt* (*arruinar*) to spoil; (*dañar*) to damage; (: *máquina*) to break; ~**se** *vr* (*objeto*) to get damaged; (*coche*) to break down; (*la piel etc*) to be ruined.

estropicio [estro'piθjo] *nm* (*rotura*) breakage; (*efectos*) harmful effects *pl*.

estructura [estruk'tura] *nf* structure.

estruendo [es'trwendo] *nm* (*ruido*) racket, din; (*fig*: *alboroto*) uproar, turmoil.

estrujar [estru'xar] *vt* (*apretar*) to squeeze; (*aplastar*) to crush; (*fig*) to drain, bleed.

estuario [es'twarjo] *nm* estuary.

estuche [es'tutʃe] *nm* box, case.

estudiante [estu'ðjante] *nmlf* student.

estudiantil [estuðjan'til] *adj inv* student *cpd*.

estudiantina [estuðjan'tina] *nf* student music group.

estudiar [estu'ðjar] *vt* to study; (*propuesta*) to think about *o* over; ~ **para abogado** to study to become a lawyer.

estudio [es'tuðjo] *nm* study; (*encuesta*) research; (*proyecto*) plan; (*piso*) studio flat; (*CINE, ARTE, RADIO*) studio; ~**s** *nmpl* studies; (*erudición*) learning *sg*; **cursar** *o* **hacer** ~**s** to study; ~ **de casos prácticos** case study; ~ **de desplazamientos y tiempos** (*COM*) time and motion study; ~**s de motivación** motivational research *sg*; ~ **del trabajo** (*COM*) work study; ~ **de viabilidad** (*COM*) feasibility study.

estudioso, a [estu'ðjoso, a] *adj* studious.

estufa [es'tufa] *nf* heater, fire.

estulticia [estul'tiθja] *nf* foolishness.

estupefaciente [estupefa'θjente] *adj, nm* narcotic.

estupefacto, a [estupe'fakto, a] *adj* speechless, thunderstruck.

estupendamente [estupenda'mente] *adv* (*fam*): **estoy ~** I feel great; **le salió ~** he did it very well.

estupendo, a [estu'pendo, a] *adj* wonderful, terrific; (*fam*) great; ¡~! that's great!, fantastic!

estupidez [estupi'ðeθ] *nf* (*torpeza*) stupidity; (*acto*) stupid thing (to do); **fue una ~ mía** that was a silly thing for me to do *o* say.

estúpido, a [es'tupiðo, a] *adj* stupid, silly.

estupor [estu'por] *nm* stupor; (*fig*) astonishment, amazement.

estupro [es'tupro] *nm* rape.

estuve [es'tuße] *etc*, **estuviera** [estu'ßjera] *etc vb V* **estar**.

esvástica [es'ßastika] *nf* swastika.

ET *abr* = *Ejército de Tierra*.

ETA ['eta] *nf abr* (*POL*: = *Euskadi Ta Askatasuna*) ETA.

etapa [e'tapa] *nf* (*de viaje*) stage; (*DEPORTE*) leg; (*parada*) stopping place; (*fig*) stage, phase; **por ~s** gradually *o* in stages.

etarra [e'tarra] *adj* ETA *cpd* ♦ *nm/f* member of ETA.

etc. *abr* (= *etcétera*) etc.

etcétera [et'θetera] *adv* etcetera.

etéreo, a [e'tereo, a] *adj* ethereal.

eternice [eter'niθe] *etc vb V* **eternizar**.

eternidad [eterni'ðað] *nf* eternity.

eternizarse [eterni'θarse] *vr*: ~ **en hacer algo** to take ages to do sth.

eterno, a [e'terno, a] *adj* eternal, everlasting; (*despectivo*) never-ending.

ético, a ['etiko, a] *adj* ethical ♦ *nf* ethics.

etimología [etimolo'xia] *nf* etymology.

etiqueta [eti'keta] *nf* (*modales*) etiquette; (*rótulo*) label, tag; **de ~** formal.

etnia ['etnja] *nf* ethnic group.

étnico, a ['etniko, a] *adj* ethnic.

EU(A) *abr* (*esp AM*) = **Estados Unidos (de América)**.

eucalipto [euka'lipto] *nm* eucalyptus.

Eucaristía [eukaris'tia] *nf* Eucharist.

eufemismo [eufe'mismo] *nm* euphemism.

euforia [eu'forja] *nf* euphoria.

eufórico, a [eu'foriko, a] *adj* euphoric.

eunuco [eu'nuko] *nm* eunuch.

eurodiputado, a [euroðipu'taðo, a] *nm/f* Euro MP, MEP.

Europa [eu'ropa] *nf* Europe.

europeice [euro'peiθe] *etc vb V* **europeizar**.

europeizar [europei'θar] *vt* to Europeanize; **~se** *vr* to become Europeanized.

europeo, a [euro'peo, a] *adj, nm/f* European.

Euskadi [eus'kaði] *nm* the Basque Provinces *pl*.

euskera, eusquera [eus'kera] *nm* (*LING*) Basque; *V tb* **lenguas cooficiales**.

eutanasia [euta'nasja] *nf* euthanasia.

evacuación [eßakwa'θjon] *nf* evacuation.

evacuar [eßa'kwar] *vt* to evacuate.

evadir [eßa'ðir] *vt* to evade, avoid; **~se** *vr* to escape.

evaluación [eßalwa'θjon] *nf* evaluation, assessment.

evaluar [eßa'lwar] *vt* to evaluate, assess.

evangélico, a [eßan'xeliko, a] *adj* evangelical.

evangelio [eßan'xeljo] *nm* gospel.

evaporación [eßapora'θjon] *nf* evaporation.

evaporar [eßapo'rar] *vt* to evaporate; **~se** *vr* to vanish.

evasión [eßa'sjon] *nf* escape, flight; (*fig*) evasion; **~ fiscal** *o* **tributaria** tax evasion.

evasivo, a [eßa'sißo, a] *adj* evasive, non-committal ♦ *nf* (*pretexto*) excuse; **contestar con evasivas** to avoid giving a straight answer.

evento [e'ßento] *nm* event; (*eventualidad*) eventuality.

eventual [eßen'twal] *adj* possible, conditional (upon circumstances); (*trabajador*) casual, temporary.

Everest [eße'rest] *nm*: **el (Monte) ~** (Mount) Everest.

evidencia [eßi'ðenθja] *nf* evidence, proof; **poner en ~** to make clear; **ponerse en ~** (*persona*) to show o.s. up.

evidenciar [eßiðen'θjar] *vt* (*hacer patente*) to make evident; (*probar*) to prove, show; **~se** *vr* to be evident.

evidente [eßi'ðente] *adj* obvious, clear, evident.

evitar [eßi'tar] *vt* (*evadir*) to avoid; (*impedir*) to prevent; (*peligro*) to escape; (*molestia*) to save; (*tentación*) to shun; **si puedo ~lo** if I can help it.

evocador, a [eßoka'ðor, a] *adj* (*sugestivo*) evocative.

evocar [eßo'kar] *vt* to evoke, call forth.

evolución [eßolu'θjon] *nf* (*desarrollo*) evolution, development; (*cambio*) change; (*MIL*) manoeuvre.

evolucionar [eßoluθjo'nar] *vi* to evolve; (*MIL, AVIAT*) to manoeuvre.

evoque [e'ßoke] *etc vb V* **evocar**.

ex [eks] *adj* ex-; **el ~ ministro** the former minister, the ex-minister.

exabrupto [eksa'ßrupto] *nm* interjection.

exacción [eksak'θjon] *nf* (*acto*) exaction; (*de impuestos*) demand.

exacerbar [eksaθer'ßar] *vt* to irritate, annoy.

exactamente [eksakta'mente] *adv* exactly.

exactitud [eksakti'tuð] *nf* exactness; (*precisión*) accuracy; (*puntualidad*) punctuality.

exacto, a [ek'sakto, a] *adj* exact; accurate; punctual; **¡~!** exactly!; **eso no es del todo ~** that's not quite right; **para ser ~** to be precise.

exageración [eksaxera'θjon] *nf* exaggeration.

exagerado, a [eksaxe'raðo, a] *adj* (*relato*) exaggerated; (*precio*) excessive; (*persona*) over-demonstrative; (*gesto*) theatrical.

exagerar [eksaxe'rar] *vt* to exaggerate; (*exceder*) to overdo.

exaltado, a [eksal'taðo, a] *adj* (*apasionado*) over-excited, worked up; (*exagerado*) extreme; (*fanático*) hot-headed; (*discurso*) impassioned ♦ *nm/f* (*fanático*) hothead; (*POL*) extremist.

exaltar [eksal'tar] *vt* to exalt, glorify; ~**se** *vr* (*excitarse*) to get excited o worked up.

examen [ek'samen] *nm* examination; (*de problema*) consideration; ~ **de** (*encuesta*) inquiry into; ~ **de ingreso** entrance examination; ~ **de conducir** driving test; ~ **eliminatorio** qualifying examination.

examinar [eksami'nar] *vt* to examine; (*poner a prueba*) to test; (*inspeccionar*) to inspect; ~**se** *vr* to be examined, take an examination.

exánime [ek'sanime] *adj* lifeless; (*fig*) exhausted.

exasperar [eksaspe'rar] *vt* to exasperate; ~**se** *vr* to get exasperated, lose patience.

Exc.ª *abr* = **Excelencia**.

excarcelar [ekskarθe'lar] *vt* to release (from prison).

excavador, a [ekskaßa'ðor, a] *nm/f* (*persona*) excavator ♦ *nf* (*TEC*) digger.

excavar [ekska'ßar] *vt* to excavate, dig (out).

excedencia [eksθe'ðenθja] *nf* (*MIL*) leave; (*ESCOL*) sabbatical.

excedente [eksθe'ðente] *adj, nm* excess, surplus.

exceder [eksθe'ðer] *vt* to exceed, surpass; ~**se** *vr* (*extralimitarse*) to go too far; (*sobrepasarse*) to excel o.s.

excelencia [eksθe'lenθja] *nf* excellence; **E**~ Excellency; **por** ~ par excellence.

excelente [eksθe'lente] *adj* excellent.

excelso, a [eks'θelso, a] *adj* lofty, sublime.

excentricidad [eksθentriθi'ðað] *nf* eccentricity.

excéntrico, a [eks'θentriko, a] *adj, nm/f* eccentric.

excepción [eksθep'θjon] *nf* exception; **la** ~ **confirma la regla** the exception proves the rule.

excepcional [eksθepθjo'nal] *adj* exceptional.

excepto [eks'θepto] *adv* excepting, except (for).

exceptuar [eksθep'twar] *vt* to except, exclude.

excesivo, a [eksθe'sißo, a] *adj* excessive.

exceso [eks'θeso] *nm* excess; (*COM*) surplus; ~ **de equipaje/peso** excess luggage/weight; ~ **de velocidad** speeding; **en** o **por** ~ excessively.

excitación [eksθita'θjon] *nf* (*sensación*) excitement; (*acción*) excitation.

excitado, a [eksθi'taðo, a] *adj* excited; (*emociones*) aroused.

excitante [eksθi'tante] *adj* exciting; (*MED*) stimulating ♦ *nm* stimulant.

excitar [eksθi'tar] *vt* to excite; (*incitar*) to urge; (*emoción*) to stir up; (*esperanzas*) to raise; (*pasión*) to arouse; ~**se** *vr* to get excited.

exclamación [eksklama'θjon] *nf* exclamation.

exclamar [ekskla'mar] *vi* to exclaim; ~**se** *vr*: ~**se** (**contra**) to complain (about).

excluir [eksklu'ir] *vt* to exclude; (*dejar fuera*) to shut out; (*solución*) to reject; (*posibilidad*) to rule out.

exclusión [eksklu'sjon] *nf* exclusion.

exclusiva [eksklu'sißa] *nf* V **exclusivo**.

exclusive [eksklu'siße] *prep* exclusive of, not counting.

exclusivo, a [eksklu'sißo, a] *adj* exclusive ♦ *nf* (*PRENSA*) exclusive, scoop; (*COM*) sole right o agency; **derecho** ~ sole o exclusive right.

excluyendo [eksklu'jendo] *etc vb* V **excluir**.

Excma., Excmo. *abr* (= *Excelentísima, Excelentísimo*) *courtesy title*.

excombatiente [ekskomba'tjente] *nm* ex-serviceman, war veteran (*US*).

excomulgar [ekskomul'var] *vt* (*REL*) to excommunicate.

excomulgue [eksko'mulɣe] *etc vb* V **excomulgar**.

excomunión [ekskomu'njon] *nf* excommunication.

excoriar [eksko'rjar] *vt* to flay, skin.

excremento [ekskre'mento] *nm* excrement.

exculpar [ekskul'par] *vt* to exonerate; (*JUR*) to acquit; ~**se** *vr* to exonerate o.s.

excursión [ekskur'sjon] *nf* excursion, outing; **ir de** ~ to go (off) on a trip.

excursionista [ekskursjo'nista] *nm/f* (*turista*) sightseer.

excusa [eks'kusa] *nf* excuse; (*disculpa*) apology; **presentar sus** ~**s** to excuse o.s.

excusado, a [eksku'saðo, a] *adj* unnecessary; (*disculpado*) excused, forgiven.

excusar [eksku'sar] *vt* to excuse; (*evitar*) to avoid, prevent; ~**se** *vr* (*disculparse*) to apologize.

execrable [ekse'kraßle] *adj* appalling.

exención [eksen'θjon] *nf* exemption.

exento, a [ek'sento, a] *pp de* **eximir** ♦ *adj* exempt.

exequias [ek'sekjas] *nfpl* funeral rites.

exfoliar [eksfo'ljar] *vt* to exfoliate.

exhalación [eksala'θjon] *nf* (*del aire*) exhalation; (*vapor*) fumes *pl*, vapour; (*rayo*) shooting star; **salir como una** ~ to shoot out.

exhalar [eksa'lar] *vt* to exhale, breathe out; (*olor etc*) to give off; (*suspiro*) to breathe, heave.

exhaustivo, a [eksaus'tiβo, a] *adj* exhaustive.

exhausto, a [ek'sausto, a] *adj* exhausted, worn-out.

exhibición [eksiβi'θjon] *nf* exhibition; (*demostración*) display, show; (*de película*) showing; (*de equipo*) performance.

exhibicionista [eksiβiθjo'nista] *adj, nm/f* exhibitionist.

exhibir [eksi'βir] *vt* to exhibit; to display, show; (*cuadros*) to exhibit; (*artículos*) to display, show; (*pasaporte*) to show; (*película*) to screen; (*mostrar con orgullo*) to show off; ~**se** *vr* (*mostrarse en público*) to show o.s. off; (*fam: indecentemente*) to expose o.s.

exhortación [eksorta'θjon] *nf* exhortation.

exhortar [eksor'tar] *vt*: ~ **a** to exhort to.

exhumar [eksu'mar] *vt* to exhume.

exigencia [eksi'xenθja] *nf* demand, requirement.

exigente [eksi'xente] *adj* demanding; (*profesor*) strict; **ser** ~ **con algn** to be hard on sb.

exigir [eksi'xir] *vt* (*gen*) to demand, require; (*impuestos*) to exact, levy; ~ **el pago** to demand payment.

exiguo, a [ek'siɣwo, a] *adj* (*cantidad*) meagre; (*objeto*) tiny.

exija [e'ksixa] *etc vb V* **exigir**.

exiliado, a [eksi'ljaðo, a] *adj* exiled, in exile ♦ *nm/f* exile.

exiliar [eksi'ljar] *vt* to exile; ~**se** *vr* to go into exile.

exilio [ek'siljo] *nm* exile.

eximio, a [ek'simjo, a] *adj* (*eminente*) distinguished, eminent.

eximir [eksi'mir] *vt* to exempt.

existencia [eksis'tenθja] *nf* existence; ~**s** *nfpl* stock *sg*; ~ **de mercancías** (*COM*) stock-in-trade; **tener en** ~ to have in stock; **amargar la** ~ **a algn** to make sb's life a misery.

existir [eksis'tir] *vi* to exist, be.

éxito ['eksito] *nm* (*resultado*) result, outcome; (*triunfo*) success; (*MUS, TEAT*) hit; ~ **editorial** bestseller; ~ **rotundo** smash hit; **tener** ~ to be successful.

exitoso, a [eksi'toso, a] *adj* (*esp AM*) successful.

éxodo ['eksoðo] *nm* exodus; **el** ~ **rural** the drift from the land.

ex oficio [ekso'fiθjo] *adj, adv* ex officio.

exonerar [eksone'rar] *vt* to exonerate; ~ **de una obligación** to free from an obligation.

exorcice [eksor'θiθe] *etc vb V* **exorcizar**.

exorcismo [eksor'θismo] *nm* exorcism.

exorcizar [eksorθi'θar] *vt* to exorcize.

exótico, a [ek'sotiko, a] *adj* exotic.

expandido, a [ekspan'diðo, a] *adj*: **en caracteres** ~**s** (*INFORM*) double width.

expandir [ekspan'dir] *vt* to expand; (*COM*) to expand, enlarge; ~**se** *vr* to expand, spread.

expansión [ekspan'sjon] *nf* expansion; (*recreo*) relaxation; **la** ~ **económica** economic growth; **economía en** ~ expanding economy.

expansionarse [ekspansjo'narse] *vr* (*dilatarse*) to expand; (*recrearse*) to relax.

expansivo, a [ekspan'siβo, a] *adj* expansive; (*efusivo*) communicative.

expatriado, a [ekspa'trjaðo, a] *nm/f* (*emigrado*) expatriate; (*exiliado*) exile.

expatriarse [ekspa'trjarse] *vr* to emigrate; (*POL*) to go into exile.

expectación [ekspekta'θjon] *nf* (*esperanza*) expectation; (*ilusión*) excitement.

expectativa [ekspekta'tiβa] *nf* (*espera*) expectation; (*perspectiva*) prospect; ~ **de vida** life expectancy; **estar a la** ~ to wait and see (what will happen).

expedición [ekspeði'θjon] *nf* (*excursión*) expedition; **gastos de** ~ shipping charges.

expedientar [ekspeðjen'tar] *vt* to open a file on; (*funcionario*) to discipline, start disciplinary proceedings against.

expediente [ekspe'ðjente] *nm* expedient; (*JUR: procedimento*) action, proceedings *pl*; (: *papeles*) dossier, file, record; ~ **judicial** court proceedings *pl*; ~ **académico** (student's) record.

expedir [ekspe'ðir] *vt* (*despachar*) to send, forward; (*pasaporte*) to issue; (*cheque*) to make out.

expedito, a [ekspe'ðito, a] *adj* (*libre*) clear, free.

expeler [ekspe'ler] *vt* to expel, eject.

expendedor, a [ekspende'ðor, a] *nm/f* (*vendedor*) dealer; (*TEAT*) ticket agent ♦ *nm* (*aparato*) (vending) machine; ~ **de cigarrillos** cigarette machine.

expendeduría [ekspendedu'ria] *nf* (*estanco*)

tobacconist's (shop) (*BRIT*), cigar store (*US*).

expendio [eks'pendjo] *nm* (*AM*) small shop (*BRIT*) *o* store (*US*).

expensas [eks'pensas] *nfpl* (*JUR*) costs; **a ~ de** at the expense of.

experiencia [ekspe'rjenθja] *nf* experience.

experimentado, a [eksperimen'taðo, a] *adj* experienced.

experimentar [eksperimen'tar] *vt* (*en laboratorio*) to experiment with; (*probar*) to test, try out; (*notar, observar*) to experience; (*deterioro, pérdida*) to suffer; (*aumento*) to show; (*sensación*) to feel.

experimento [eksperi'mento] *nm* experiment.

experto, a [eks'perto, a] *adj* expert ♦ *nm/f* expert.

expiar [ekspi'ar] *vt* to atone for.

expida [eks'piða] *etc vb V* **expedir**.

expirar [ekspi'rar] *vi* to expire.

explanada [ekspla'naða] *nf* (*paseo*) esplanade; (*a orillas del mar*) promenade.

explayarse [ekspla'jarse] *vr* (*en discurso*) to speak at length; **~ con algn** to confide in sb.

explicación [eksplika'θjon] *nf* explanation.

explicar [ekspli'kar] *vt* to explain; (*teoría*) to expound; (*UNIV*) to lecture in; **~se** *vr* to explain (o.s.); **no me lo explico** I can't understand it.

explícito, a [eks'pliθito, a] *adj* explicit.

explique [eks'plike] *etc vb V* **explicar**.

exploración [eksplora'θjon] *nf* exploration; (*MIL*) reconnaissance.

explorador, a [eksplora'ðor, a] *nm/f* (*pionero*) explorer; (*MIL*) scout ♦ *nm* (*MED*) probe; (*radar*) (radar) scanner.

explorar [eksplo'rar] *vt* to explore; (*MED*) to probe; (*radar*) to scan.

explosión [eksplo'sjon] *nf* explosion.

explosivo, a [eksplo'sißo, a] *adj* explosive.

explotación [eksplota'θjon] *nf* exploitation; (*de planta etc*) running; (*de mina*) working; (*de recurso*) development; **~ minera** mine; **gastos de ~** operating costs.

explotar [eksplo'tar] *vt* to exploit; (*planta*) to run, operate; (*mina*) to work ♦ *vi* (*bomba etc*) to explode, go off.

expondré [ekspon'dre] *etc vb V* **exponer**.

exponer [ekspo'ner] *vt* to expose; (*cuadro*) to display; (*vida*) to risk; (*idea*) to explain; (*teoría*) to expound; (*hechos*) to set out; **~se** *vr*: **~se a (hacer) algo** to run the risk of (doing) sth.

exponga [eks'ponga] *etc vb V* **exponer**.

exportación [eksporta'θjon] *nf* (*acción*) export; (*mercancías*) exports *pl*.

exportador, a [eksporta'ðor, a] *adj* (*país*) exporting ♦ *nm/f* exporter.

exportar [ekspor'tar] *vt* to export.

exposición [eksposi'θjon] *nf* (*gen*) exposure; (*de arte*) show, exhibition; (*COM*) display; (*feria*) show, fair; (*explicación*) explanation; (*de teoría*) exposition; (*narración*) account, statement.

exprés [eks'pres] *adj inv* (*café*) espresso ♦ *nm* (*FERRO*) express (train).

expresamente [ekspresa'mente] *adv* (*concretamente*) expressly; (*a propósito*) on purpose.

expresar [ekspre'sar] *vt* to express; (*redactar*) to phrase, put; (*emoción*) to show; **~se** *vr* to express o.s.; (*dato*) to be stated; **como abajo se expresa** as stated below.

expresión [ekspre'sjon] *nf* expression; **~ familiar** colloquialism.

expresivo, a [ekspre'sißo, a] *adj* expressive; (*cariñoso*) affectionate.

expreso, a [eks'preso, a] *adj* (*explícito*) express; (*claro*) specific, clear; (*tren*) fast ♦ *nm* (*FERRO*) fast train ♦ *adv*: **mandar ~** to send by express (delivery).

exprimidor [eksprimi'ðor] *nm* (lemon) squeezer.

exprimir [ekspri'mir] *vt* (*fruta*) to squeeze; (*zumo*) to squeeze out.

ex profeso [ekspro'feso] *adv* expressly.

expropiar [ekspro'pjar] *vt* to expropriate.

expuesto, a [eks'pwesto, a] *pp de* **exponer** ♦ *adj* exposed; (*cuadro etc*) on show, on display; **según lo ~ arriba** according to what has been stated above.

expulsar [ekspul'sar] *vt* (*echar*) to eject, throw out; (*alumno*) to expel; (*despedir*) to sack, fire; (*DEPORTE*) to send off.

expulsión [ekspul'sjon] *nf* expulsion; sending-off.

expurgar [ekspur'xar] *vt* to expurgate.

expuse [eks'puse] *etc vb V* **exponer**.

exquisito, a [ekski'sito, a] *adj* exquisite; (*comida*) delicious; (*afectado*) affected.

Ext. *abr* (= *Exterior*) ext.; (= *Extensión*) ext.

éxtasis ['ekstasis] *nm* (*tb droga*) ecstasy.

extemporáneo, a [ekstempo'raneo, a] *adj* unseasonal.

extender [eksten'der] *vt* to extend; (*los brazos*) to stretch out, hold out; (*mapa, tela*) to spread (out), open (out); (*mantequilla*) to spread; (*certificado*) to issue; (*cheque, recibo*) to make out; (*documento*) to draw up; **~se** *vr* to extend; (*terreno*) to stretch *o* spread (out); (*persona: en el suelo*) to stretch out; (*en el tiempo*) to extend, last; (*costumbre, epidemia*) to spread; (*guerra*) to escalate; ~**se sobre un tema** to enlarge on a subject.

extendido, a [eksten'diðo, a] *adj* (*abierto*) spread out, open; (*brazos*) outstretched; (*costumbre etc*) widespread.

extensible [eksten'siβle] *adj* extending.

extensión [eksten'sjon] *nf* (*de terreno, mar*) expanse, stretch; (*MUS*) range; (*de conocimientos*) extent; (*de programa*) scope; (*de tiempo*) length, duration; (*TELEC*) extension; ~ **de plazo** (*COM*) extension; **en toda la** ~ **de la palabra** in every sense of the word; **de** ~ (*INFORM*) add-on.

extenso, a [eks'tenso, a] *adj* extensive.

extenuar [ekste'nwar] *vt* (*debilitar*) to weaken.

exterior [ekste'rjor] *adj* (*de fuera*) external; (*afuera*) outside, exterior; (*apariencia*) outward; (*deuda, relaciones*) foreign ♦ *nm* exterior, outside; (*aspecto*) outward appearance; (*DEPORTE*) wing(er); (*países extranjeros*) abroad; **asuntos** ~**es** foreign affairs; **al** ~ outwardly, on the outside; **en el** ~ abroad; **noticias del** ~ foreign o overseas news.

exteriorice [eksterjo'riθe] *etc vb V* **exteriorizar**.

exteriorizar [eksterjori'θar] *vt* (*emociones*) to show, reveal.

exteriormente [eksterjor'mente] *adv* outwardly.

exterminar [ekstermi'nar] *vt* to exterminate.

exterminio [ekster'minjo] *nm* extermination.

externo, a [eks'terno, a] *adj* (*exterior*) external, outside; (*superficial*) outward ♦ *nm/f* day pupil.

extienda [eks'tjenda] *etc vb V* **extender**.

extinción [ekstin'θjon] *nf* extinction.

extinga [eks'tinga] *etc vb V* **extinguir**.

extinguido, a [ekstin'giðo, a] *adj* (*animal, volcán*) extinct; (*fuego*) out, extinguished.

extinguir [ekstin'gir] *vt* (*fuego*) to extinguish, put out; (*raza, población*) to wipe out; ~**se** *vr* (*fuego*) to go out; (*BIO*) to die out, become extinct.

extinto, a [eks'tinto, a] *adj* extinct.

extintor [ekstin'tor] *nm* (fire) extinguisher.

extirpar [ekstir'par] *vt* (*vicios*) to eradicate, stamp out; (*MED*) to remove (surgically).

extorsión [ekstor'sjon] *nf* blackmail.

extra ['ekstra] *adj inv* (*tiempo*) extra; (*vino*)

vintage; (*chocolate*) good-quality; (*gasolina*) high-octane ♦ *nm/f* extra ♦ *nm* (*bono*) bonus; (*periódico*) special edition.

extracción [ekstrak'θjon] *nf* extraction; (*en lotería*) draw; (*de carbón*) mining.

extracto [eks'trakto] *nm* extract.

extractor [ekstrak'tor] *nm* (*tb:* ~ **de humos**) extractor fan.

extradición [ekstraði'θjon] *nf* extradition.

extraditar [ekstraði'tar] *vt* to extradite.

extraer [ekstra'er] *vt* to extract, take out.

extrafino, a [ekstra'fino, a] *adj* extra-fine; **azúcar** ~ caster sugar.

extraiga [eks'traixa] *etc*, **extraje** [eks'traxe] *etc*, **extrajera** [ekstra'xera] *etc vb V* **extraer**.

extralimitarse [ekstralimi'tarse] *vr* to go too far.

extranjerismo [ekstranxe'rismo] *nm* foreign word o phrase *etc*.

extranjero, a [ekstran'xero, a] *adj* foreign ♦ *nm/f* foreigner ♦ *nm* foreign lands *pl*; **en el** ~ abroad.

extrañamiento [ekstraɲa'mjento] *nm* estrangement.

extrañar [ekstra'ɲar] *vt* (*sorprender*) to find strange o odd; (*echar de menos*) to miss; ~**se** *vr* (*sorprenderse*) to be amazed, be surprised; (*distanciarse*) to become estranged, grow apart; **me extraña** I'm surprised.

extrañeza [ekstra'ɲeθa] *nf* (*rareza*) strangeness, oddness; (*asombro*) amazement, surprise.

extraño, a [eks'traɲo, a] *adj* (*extranjero*) foreign; (*raro, sorprendente*) strange, odd.

extraoficial [ekstraofi'θjal] *adj* unofficial, informal.

extraordinario, a [ekstraorði'narjo, a] *adj* extraordinary; (*edición, número*) special ♦ *nm* (*de periódico*) special edition; **horas extraordinarias** overtime *sg*.

extrarradio [ekstra'rraðjo] *nm* suburbs *pl*.

extrasensorial [ekstrasenso'rjal] *adj*: **percepción** ~ extrasensory perception.

extraterrestre [ekstrate'rrestre] *adj* of o from outer space ♦ *nm/f* creature from outer space.

extravagancia [ekstraβa'xanθja] *nf* oddness; outlandishness; (*rareza*) peculiarity; ~**s** *nfpl* (*tonterías*) nonsense *sg*.

extravagante [ekstraβa'xante] *adj* (*excéntrico*) eccentric; (*estrafalario*) outlandish.

extraviado, a [ekstra'βjaðo, a] *adj* lost, missing.

extraviar [ekstra'ßjar] *vt* to mislead, misdirect; (*perder*) to lose, misplace; **~se** *vr* to lose one's way, get lost; (*objeto*) to go missing, be mislaid.

extravío [ekstra'ßio] *nm* loss; (*fig*) misconduct.

extrayendo [ekstra'jendo] *vb* V **extraer**.

extremado, a [ekstre'maðo, a] *adj* extreme, excessive.

Extremadura [ekstrema'ðura] *nf* Estremadura.

extremar [ekstre'mar] *vt* to carry to extremes; **~se** *vr* to do one's utmost, make every effort.

extremaunción [ekstremaun'θjon] *nf* extreme unction, last rites *pl*.

extremidad [ekstremi'ðað] *nf* (*punta*) extremity; (*fila*) edge; **~es** *nfpl* (*ANAT*) extremities.

extremista [ekstre'mista] *adj, nm/f* extremist.

extremo, a [eks'tremo, a] *adj* extreme; (*más alejado*) furthest; (*último*) last ♦ *nm* end; (*situación*) extreme; **E~ Oriente** Far East; **en último ~** as a last resort; **pasar de un ~ a otro** (*fig*) to go from one extreme to the other; **con ~** in the extreme; **la extrema derecha** (*POL*) the far right; **~ derecho/izquierdo** (*DEPORTE*) outside right/left.

extrínseco, a [eks'trinseko, a] *adj* extrinsic.

extrovertido, a [ekstroßer'tiðo, a] *adj* extrovert, outgoing ♦ *nm/f* extrovert.

exuberancia [eksuße'ranθja] *nf* exuberance.

exuberante [eksuße'rante] *adj* exuberant; (*fig*) luxuriant, lush.

exudar [eksu'ðar] *vt, vi* to exude.

exultar [eksul'tar] *vi:* **~ (en)** to exult (in); (*pey*) to gloat (over).

exvoto [eks'ßoto] *nm* votive offering.

eyaculación [ejakula'θjon] *nf* ejaculation.

eyacular [ejaku'lar] *vt, vi* to ejaculate.

Ff

F, f ['efe] *nf* (*letra*) F, f; **F de Francia** F for Frederick (*BRIT*), F for Fox (*US*).

fa [fa] *nm* (*MUS*) F.

f.ª *abr* (*COM*: = *factura*) Inv.

f.a.b. *abr* (= *franco a bordo*) f.o.b.

fabada [fa'ßaða] *nf bean and sausage stew.*

fábrica ['faßrika] *nf* factory; **~ de moneda** mint; **marca de ~** trademark; **precio de ~** factory price.

fabricación [faßrika'θjon] *nf* (*manufactura*) manufacture; (*producción*) production; **de ~ casera** home-made; **de ~ nacional** home produced; **~ en serie** mass production.

fabricante [faßri'kante] *nm/f* manufacturer.

fabricar [faßri'kar] *vt* (*manufacturar*) to manufacture, make; (*construir*) to build; (*cuento*) to fabricate, devise; **~ en serie** to mass-produce.

fabril [fa'ßril] *adj:* **industria ~** manufacturing industry.

fabrique [fa'ßrike] *etc vb* V **fabricar**.

fábula ['faßula] *nf* (*cuento*) fable; (*chisme*) rumour; (*mentira*) fib.

fabuloso, a [faßu'loso, a] *adj* fabulous, fantastic.

FACA ['faka] *nm abr* (*ESP AVIAT*) = *Futuro Avión de Combate y Ataque.*

facción [fak'θjon] *nf* (*POL*) faction; **facciones** *nfpl* (*del rostro*) features.

faceta [fa'θeta] *nf* facet.

facha ['fatʃa] (*fam*) *nm/f* fascist, right-wing extremist ♦ *nf* (*aspecto*) look; (*cara*) face; **¡qué ~ tienes!** you look a sight!

fachada [fa'tʃaða] *nf* (*ARQ*) façade, front; (*TIP*) title page; (*fig*) façade, outward show.

facial [fa'θjal] *adj* facial.

fácil ['faθil] *adj* (*simple*) easy; (*sencillo*) simple, straightforward; (*probable*) likely; (*respuesta*) facile; **~ de usar** (*INFORM*) user-friendly.

facilidad [faθili'ðað] *nf* (*capacidad*) ease; (*sencillez*) simplicity; (*de palabra*) fluency; **~es** *nfpl* facilities; **"~es de pago"** (*COM*) "credit facilities", "payment terms".

facilitar [faθili'tar] *vt* (*hacer fácil*) to make easy; (*proporcionar*) to provide; (*documento*) to issue; **le agradecería me facilitara** ... I would be grateful if you could let me have ....

fácilmente ['faθilmente] *adv* easily.

facsímil [fak'simil] *nm* (*documento*) facsimile; **enviar por** ~ to fax.

factible [fak'tiβle] *adj* feasible.

factor [fak'tor] *nm* factor; (*COM*) agent; (*FERRO*) freight clerk.

factoría [fakto'ria] *nf* (*COM: agencia*) agency; (: *fábrica*) factory.

factura [fak'tura] *nf* (*cuenta*) bill; (*nota de pago*) invoice; (*hechura*) manufacture; **presentar** ~ **a** to invoice.

facturación [faktura'θjon] *nf* (*COM*) invoicing; (: *ventas*) turnover; ~ **de equipajes** luggage check-in.

facturar [faktu'rar] *vt* (*COM*) to invoice, charge for; (*AVIAT*) to check in; (*equipaje*) to register, check (*US*).

facultad [fakul'taθ] *nf* (*aptitud, ESCOL etc*) faculty; (*poder*) power.

facultativo, a [fakulta'tiβo, a] *adj* optional; (*de un oficio*) professional; **prescripción facultativa** medical prescription.

FAD *nm abr* (*ESP*) = *Fondo de Ayuda y Desarrollo.*

faena [fa'ena] *nf* (*trabajo*) work; (*quehacer*) task, job; ~**s domésticas** housework *sg.*

faenar [fae'nar] *vi* to fish.

fagot [fa'ɣot] *nm* (*MUS*) bassoon.

faisán [fai'san] *nm* pheasant.

faja ['faxa] *nf* (*para la cintura*) sash; (*de mujer*) corset; (*de tierra*) strip.

fajo ['faxo] *nm* (*de papeles*) bundle; (*de billetes*) role, wad.

falange [fa'lanxe] *nf*: **la F**~ (*POL*) the Falange.

falda ['falda] *nf* (*prenda de vestir*) skirt; (*GEO*) foothill; ~ **escocesa** kilt.

fálico, a ['faliko, a] *adj* phallic.

falla ['faʎa] *nf* (*defecto*) fault, flaw.

fallar [fa'ʎar] *vt* (*JUR*) to pronounce sentence on; (*NAIPES*) to trump ♦ *vi* (*memoria*) to fail; (*plan*) to go wrong; (*motor*) to miss; ~ **a algn** to let sb down.

---

*In the week of the 19th of March (the feast of St Joseph, **San José**), Valencia honours its patron saint with a spectacular fiesta called **las Fallas**. The **Fallas** are huge sculptures, made of wood, cardboard, paper and cloth, depicting famous politicians and other targets for ridicule, which are set alight and burned by the*

---

falleros, members of the competing local groups who have just spent months preparing them.

---

fallecer [faʎe'θer] *vi* to pass away, die.

fallecido, a [faʎe'θiðo, a] *adj* late ♦ *nm/f* deceased.

fallecimiento [faʎeθi'mjento] *nm* decease, demise.

fallero, a [fa'ʎero, a] *nm/f* maker of "Fallas".

fallezca [fa'ʎeθka] *etc vb V* **fallecer.**

fallido, a [fa'ʎiðo, a] *adj* vain; (*intento*) frustrated, unsuccessful; (*esperanza*) disappointed.

fallo ['faʎo] *nm* (*JUR*) verdict, ruling; (*decisión*) decision; (*de jurado*) findings; (*fracaso*) failure; (*DEPORTE*) miss; (*INFORM*) bug.

falo ['falo] *nm* phallus.

falsear [false'ar] *vt* to falsify; (*firma etc*) to forge ♦ *vi* (*MUS*) to be out of tune.

falsedad [false'ðað] *nf* falseness; (*hipocresía*) hypocrisy; (*mentira*) falsehood.

falsificación [falsifika'θjon] *nf* (*acto*) falsification; (*objeto*) forgery.

falsificar [falsifi'kar] *vt* (*firma etc*) to forge; (*voto etc*) to rig; (*moneda*) to counterfeit.

falsifique [falsi'fike] *etc vb V* **falsificar.**

falso, a ['falso, a] *adj* false; (*erróneo*) wrong, mistaken; (*firma, documento*) forged; (*documento, moneda etc*) fake; **en** ~ falsely; **dar un paso en** ~ to trip; (*fig*) to take a false step.

falta ['falta] *nf* (*defecto*) fault, flaw; (*privación*) lack, want; (*ausencia*) absence; (*carencia*) shortage; (*equivocación*) mistake; (*JUR*) default; (*DEPORTE*) foul; (*TENIS*) fault; ~ **de ortografía** spelling mistake; ~ **de respeto** disrespect; **echar en** ~ to miss; **hacer** ~ **hacer algo** to be necessary to do sth; **me hace** ~ **una pluma** I need a pen; **sin** ~ without fail; **por** ~ **de** through *o* for lack of.

faltar [fal'tar] *vi* (*escasear*) to be lacking, be wanting; (*ausentarse*) to be absent, be missing; **¿falta algo?** is anything missing?; **falta mucho todavía** there's plenty of time yet; **¿falta mucho?** is there long to go?; **faltan 2 horas para llegar** there are 2 hours to go till arrival; ~ **(al respeto) a algn** to be disrespectful to sb; ~ **a una cita** to miss an appointment; ~ **a la verdad** to lie; **¡no faltaba más!** that's the last straw!

falto, a ['falto, a] *adj* (*desposeído*) deficient,

lacking; (*necesitado*) poor, wretched; **estar ~ de** to be short of.

fama ['fama] *nf* (*renombre*) fame; (*reputación*) reputation.

famélico, a [fa'meliko, a] *adj* starving.

familia [fa'milja] *nf* family; **~ política** in-laws *pl*.

familiar [fami'ljar] *adj* (*relativo a la familia*) family *cpd*; (*conocido, informal*) familiar; (*estilo*) informal; (*LING*) colloquial ♦ *nm/f* relative, relation.

familiarice [familja'riθe] *etc vb* V **familiarizarse**.

familiaridad [familjari'ðað] *nf* familiarity; (*informalidad*) homeliness.

familiarizarse [familjari'θarse] *vr*: **~ con** to familiarize o.s. with.

famoso, a [fa'moso, a] *adj* (*renombrado*) famous.

fan, *pl* **fans** [fan, fans] *nm* fan.

fanático, a [fa'natiko, a] *adj* fanatical ♦ *nm/f* fanatic; (*CINE, DEPORTE etc*) fan.

fanatismo [fana'tismo] *nm* fanaticism.

fanfarrón, ona [fanfa'rron, ona] *adj* boastful; (*pey*) showy.

fanfarronear [fanfarrone'ar] *vi* to boast.

fango ['fango] *nm* mud.

fangoso, a [fan'goso, a] *adj* muddy.

fantasear [fantase'ar] *vi* to fantasize; **~ con una idea** to toy with an idea.

fantasía [fanta'sia] *nf* fantasy, imagination; (*MUS*) fantasia; (*capricho*) whim; **joyas de ~** imitation jewellery *sg*.

fantasma [fan'tasma] *nm* (*espectro*) ghost, apparition; (*presumido*) show-off.

fantástico, a [fan'tastiko, a] *adj* (*irreal, fam*) fantastic.

fanzine [fan'θine] *nm* fanzine.

FAO ['fao] *nf abr* (= *Organización de las Naciones Unidas para la Agricultura y la Alimentación*) FAO.

faquir [fa'kir] *nm* fakir.

faraón [fara'on] *nm* Pharaoh.

faraónico, a [fara'oniko, a] *adj* Pharaonic; (*fig*) grandiose.

fardar [far'ðar] *vi* to show off; **~ de** to boast about.

fardo ['farðo] *nm* bundle; (*fig*) burden.

faringe [fa'rinxe] *nf* pharynx.

faringitis [farin'xitis] *nf* pharyngitis.

farmacéutico, a [farma'θeutiko, a] *adj* pharmaceutical ♦ *nm/f* chemist (*BRIT*), pharmacist.

farmacia [far'maθja] *nf* (*ciencia*) pharmacy; (*tienda*) chemist's (shop) (*BRIT*), pharmacy, drugstore (*US*); **~ de turno** duty chemist.

fármaco ['farmako] *nm* medicine, drug.

faro ['faro] *nm* (*NAUT: torre*) lighthouse; (*señal*) beacon; (*AUTO*) headlamp; **~s antiniebla** fog lamps; **~s delanteros/traseros** headlights/rear lights.

farol [fa'rol] *nm* (*luz*) lantern, lamp; (*FERRO*) headlamp; (*poste*) lamppost; **echarse un ~** (*fam*) to show off.

farola [fa'rola] *nf* street lamp (*BRIT*) o light (*US*), lamppost.

farruco, a [fa'rruko, a] *adj* (*fam*): **estar** o **ponerse ~** to get aggressive.

farsa ['farsa] *nf* (*gen*) farce.

farsante [far'sante] *nm/f* fraud, fake.

FASA ['fasa] *nf abr* (*ESP AUTO*) = *Fábrica de Automóviles, S.A.*

fascículo [fas'θikulo] *nm* (*gen*) part, instalment (*BRIT*), installment (*US*).

fascinante [fasθi'nante] *adj* fascinating.

fascinar [fasθi'nar] *vt* to fascinate; (*encantar*) to captivate.

fascismo [fas'θismo] *nm* fascism.

fascista [fas'θista] *adj, nm/f* fascist.

fase ['fase] *nf* phase.

fastidiar [fasti'ðjar] *vt* (*disgustar*) to annoy, bother; (*estropear*) to spoil; **~se** *vr* (*disgustarse*) to get annoyed o cross; ¡**no fastidies!** you're joking!; ¡**que se fastidie!** (*fam*) he'll just have to put up with it!

fastidio [fas'tiðjo] *nm* (*disgusto*) annoyance.

fastidioso, a [fasti'ðjoso, a] *adj* (*molesto*) annoying.

fastuoso, a [fas'twoso, a] *adj* (*espléndido*) magnificent; (*banquete etc*) lavish.

fatal [fa'tal] *adj* (*gen*) fatal; (*desgraciado*) ill-fated; (*fam: malo, pésimo*) awful ♦ *adv* terribly; **lo pasó ~** he had a terrible time (of it).

fatalidad [fatali'ðað] *nf* (*destino*) fate; (*mala suerte*) misfortune.

fatídico, a [fa'tiðiko, a] *adj* fateful.

fatiga [fa'tiɣa] *nf* (*cansancio*) fatigue, weariness; **~s** *nfpl* hardships.

fatigar [fati'ɣar] *vt* to tire, weary; **~se** *vr* to get tired.

fatigoso, a [fati'ɣoso, a] *adj* (*cansador*) tiring.

fatigue [fa'tiɣe] *etc vb* V **fatigar**.

fatuo, a ['fatwo, a] *adj* (*vano*) fatuous; (*presuntuoso*) conceited.

fauces ['fauθes] *nfpl* (*ANAT*) gullet *sg*; (*fam*) jaws.

fauna ['fauna] *nf* fauna.

favor [fa'ßor] *nm* favour (*BRIT*), favor (*US*); **haga el ~ de ...** would you be so good as to ..., kindly ...; **por ~** please; **a ~** in favo(u)r; **a ~ de** to be in favo(u)r of;

(*COM*) to the order of.

favorable [faßo'raßle] *adj* favourable (*BRIT*), favorable (*US*); (*condiciones etc*) advantageous.

favorecer [faßore'θer] *vt* to favour (*BRIT*), favor (*US*); (*amparar*) to help; (*vestido etc*) to become, flatter; **este peinado le favorece** this hairstyle suits him.

favorezca [faßo're θka] *etc vb V* **favorecer**.

favorito, a [faßo'rito, a] *adj, nm/f* favourite (*BRIT*), favorite (*US*).

fax [faks] *nm inv* fax; **mandar por** ~ to fax.

faz [faθ] *nf* face; **la** ~ **de la tierra** the face of the earth.

F.C., f.c. *abr* = **ferrocarril**.

FE *nf abr* = *Falange Española*.

fe [fe] *nf* (*REL*) faith; (*confianza*) belief; (*documento*) certificate; **de buena** ~ (*JUR*) bona fide; **prestar** ~ **a** to believe, credit; **actuar con buena/mala** ~ to act in good/bad faith; **dar** ~ **de** to bear witness to; ~ **de erratas** errata.

fealdad [feal'daθ] *nf* ugliness.

feb., feb.º *abr* (= *febrero*) Feb.

febrero [fe'ßrero] *nm* February.

febril [fe'ßril] *adj* feverish; (*movido*) hectic.

fecha ['fetʃa] *nf* date; ~ **límite** *o* **tope** closing *o* last date; ~ **límite de venta** (*de alimentos*) sell-by date; ~ **de caducidad** (*de alimentos*) sell-by date; (*de contrato*) expiry date; **en** ~ **próxima** soon; **hasta la** ~ to date, so far; ~ **de vencimiento** (*COM*) due date; ~ **de vigencia** (*COM*) effective date.

fechar [fe'tʃar] *vt* to date.

fechoría [fetʃo'ria] *nf* misdeed.

fécula ['fekula] *nf* starch.

fecundación [fekunda'θjon] *nf* fertilization; ~ **in vitro** in vitro fertilization, I.V.F.

fecundar [fekun'dar] *vt* (*generar*) to fertilize, make fertile.

fecundidad [fekundi'ðaθ] *nf* fertility; (*fig*) productiveness.

fecundo, a [fe'kundo, a] *adj* (*fértil*) fertile; (*fig*) prolific; (*productivo*) productive.

FED *nm abr* (= *Fondo Europeo de Desarrollo*) EDF.

FEDER *nm abr* (= *Fondo Europeo de Desarrollo Regional*) ERDF.

federación [feðera'θjon] *nf* federation.

federal [feðe'ral] *adj* federal.

federalismo [feðera'lismo] *nm* federalism.

FEF [fef] *nf abr* = *Federación Española de Fútbol*.

felicidad [feliθi'ðaθ] *nf* (*satisfacción, contento*) happiness; ~**es** *nfpl* best wishes, congratulations.

felicitación [feliθita'θjon] *nf* (*tarjeta*) greetings card; **felicitaciones** *nfpl* (*enhorabuena*) congratulations; ~ **navideña** *o* **de Navidad** Christmas Greetings.

felicitar [feliθi'tar] *vt* to congratulate.

feligrés, esa [feli'ɣres, esa] *nm/f* parishioner.

felino, a [fe'lino, a] *adj* cat-like; (*ZOOL*) feline ♦ *nm* feline.

feliz [fe'liθ] *adj* (*contento*) happy; (*afortunado*) lucky.

felonía [felo'nia] *nf* felony, crime.

felpa ['felpa] *nf* (*terciopelo*) plush; (*toalla*) towelling.

felpudo [fel'puðo] *nm* doormat.

femenino, a [feme'nino, a] *adj* feminine; (*ZOOL etc*) female ♦ *nm* (*LING*) feminine.

feminismo [femi'nismo] *nm* feminism.

feminista [femi'nista] *adj, nm/f* feminist.

fenomenal [fenome'nal] *adj* phenomenal; (*fam*) great, terrific.

fenómeno [fe'nomeno] *nm* phenomenon; (*fig*) freak, accident ♦ *adv*: **lo pasamos** ~ we had a great time ♦ *excl* great!, marvellous!

feo, a ['feo, a] *adj* (*gen*) ugly; (*desagradable*) bad, nasty ♦ *nm* insult; **hacer un** ~ **a algn** to offend sb; **más** ~ **que Picio** as ugly as sin.

féretro ['feretro] *nm* (*ataúd*) coffin; (*sarcófago*) bier.

feria ['ferja] *nf* (*gen*) fair; (*AM: mercado*) market; (*descanso*) holiday, rest day; (*AM: cambio*) small change; ~ **comercial** trade fair; ~ **de muestras** trade show.

feriado, a [fe'rjaðo, a] (*AM*) *adj*: **día** ~ (public) holiday ♦ *nm* (public) holiday.

fermentar [fermen'tar] *vi* to ferment.

fermento [fer'mento] *nm* leaven, leavening.

ferocidad [feroθi'ðaθ] *nf* fierceness, ferocity.

ferocísimo, a [fero'θisimo, a] *adj superlativo de* **feroz**.

feroz [fe'roθ] *adj* (*cruel*) cruel; (*salvaje*) fierce.

férreo, a ['ferreo, a] *adj* iron *cpd*; (*TEC*) ferrous; (*fig*) (of) iron.

ferretería [ferrete'ria] *nf* (*tienda*) ironmonger's (shop) (*BRIT*), hardware store.

ferrocarril [ferroka'rril] *nm* railway, railroad (*US*); ~ **de vía estrecha/única** narrow-gauge/single-track railway *o* line.

ferroviario, a [ferrovja'rjo, a] *adj* rail *cpd*, railway *cpd* (*BRIT*), railroad *cpd* (*US*) ♦ *nm*:

~**s** railway (*BRIT*) *o* railroad (*US*) workers.

fértil ['fertil] *adj* (*productivo*) fertile; (*rico*) rich.

fertilice [ferti'liθe] *etc vb* V **fertilizar.**

fertilidad [fertili'ðað] *nf* (*gen*) fertility; (*productividad*) fruitfulness.

fertilizante [fertili'θante] *nm* fertilizer.

fertilizar [fertili'θar] *vt* to fertilize.

ferviente [fer'βjente] *adj* fervent.

fervor [fer'ßor] *nm* fervour (*BRIT*), fervor (*US*).

fervoroso, a [ferßo'roso, a] *adj* fervent.

festejar [feste'xar] *vt* (*agasajar*) to wine and dine, fête; (*galantear*) to court; (*celebrar*) to celebrate.

festejo [fes'texo] *nm* (*diversión*) entertainment; (*galanteo*) courtship; (*fiesta*) celebration.

festín [fes'tin] *nm* feast, banquet.

festival [festi'ßal] *nm* festival.

festividad [festißi'ðað] *nf* festivity.

festivo, a [fes'tißo, a] *adj* (*de fiesta*) festive; (*fig*) witty; (*CINE, LIT*) humorous; **día** ~ holiday.

fetiche [fe'titʃe] *nm* fetish.

fetichista [feti'tʃista] *adj* fetishistic ♦ *nm/f* fetishist.

fétido, a ['fetiðo, a] *adj* (*hediondo*) foul-smelling.

feto ['feto] *nm* foetus; (*fam*) monster.

F.E.V.E. *nf abr* (= *Ferrocarriles Españoles de Vía Estrecha*) *Spanish narrow-gauge railways.*

FF.AA. *nfpl abr* (*MIL*) = **Fuerzas Armadas.**

FF.CC. *nmpl abr* = **Ferrocarriles.**

fiable [fi'aßle] *adj* (*persona*) trustworthy; (*máquina*) reliable.

fiado [fi'aðo] *nm:* **comprar al** ~ to buy on credit; **en** ~ on bail.

fiador, a [fia'ðor, a] *nm/f* (*JUR*) surety, guarantor; (*COM*) backer; **salir** ~ **por algn** to stand bail for sb.

fiambre ['fjambre] *adj* (*CULIN*) (served) cold ♦ *nm* (*CULIN*) cold meat (*BRIT*), cold cut (*US*); (*fam*) corpse, stiff.

fiambrera [fjam'brera] *nf* ≈ lunch box, dinner pail (*US*).

fianza ['fjanθa] *nf* surety; (*JUR*): **libertad bajo** ~ release on bail.

fiar [fi'ar] *vt* (*salir garante de*) to guarantee; (*JUR*) to stand bail *o* bond (*US*) for; (*vender a crédito*) to sell on credit; (*secreto*) to confide ♦ *vi:* ~ (**de**) to trust (in); **ser de** ~ to be trustworthy; ~**se** *vr:* ~ **de** to trust (in), rely on.

fiasco ['fjasko] *nm* fiasco.

fibra ['fißra] *nf* fibre (*BRIT*), fiber (*US*); (*fig*)

vigour (*BRIT*), vigor (*US*); ~ **óptica** (*INFORM*) optical fibre (*BRIT*) *o* fiber (*US*).

ficción [fik'θjon] *nf* fiction.

ficha ['fitʃa] *nf* (*TELEC*) token; (*en juegos*) counter, marker; (*en casino*) chip; (*COM, ECON*) tally, check (*US*); (*INFORM*) file; (*tarjeta*) (index) card; (*ELEC*) plug; (*en hotel*) registration form; ~ **policíaca** police dossier.

fichaje [fi'tʃaxe] *nm* signing(-up).

fichar [fi'tʃar] *vt* (*archivar*) to file, index; (*DEPORTE*) to sign (up) ♦ *vi* (*deportista*) to sign (up); (*obrero*) to clock in *o* on; **estar fichado** to have a record.

fichero [fi'tʃero] *nm* card index; (*archivo*) filing cabinet; (*COM*) box file; (*INFORM*) file, archive; (*de policía*) criminal records; ~ **activo** (*INFORM*) active file; ~ **archivado** (*INFORM*) archived file; ~ **indexado** (*INFORM*) index file; ~ **de reserva** (*INFORM*) backup file; ~ **de tarjetas** card index; **nombre de** ~ filename.

ficticio, a [fik'tiθjo, a] *adj* (*imaginario*) fictitious; (*falso*) fabricated.

ficus ['fikus] *nm inv* (*BOT*) rubber plant.

fidedigno, a [fiðe'ðiɣno, a] *adj* reliable.

fideicomiso [fiðeiko'miso] *nm* (*COM*) trust.

fidelidad [fiðeli'ðað] *nf* (*lealtad*) fidelity, loyalty; (*exactitud: de dato etc*) accuracy; **alta** ~ high fidelity, hi-fi.

fidelísimo, a [fiðe'lisimo, a] *adj superlativo de* **fiel.**

fideos [fi'ðeos] *nmpl* noodles.

fiduciario, a [fiðu'θjarjo, a] *nm/f* fiduciary.

fiebre ['fjeßre] *nf* (*MED*) fever; (*fig*) excitement; ~ **amarilla/del heno** yellow/hay fever; ~ **palúdica** malaria; **tener** ~ to have a temperature.

fiel [fjel] *adj* (*leal*) faithful, loyal; (*fiable*) reliable; (*exacto*) accurate ♦ *nm* (*aguja*) needle, pointer; **los** ~**es** the faithful.

fieltro ['fjeltro] *nm* felt.

fiera ['fjera] *nf* V **fiero.**

fiereza [fje're θa] *nf* (*ZOOL*) wildness; (*bravura*) fierceness.

fiero, a ['fjero, a] *adj* (*cruel*) cruel; (*feroz*) fierce; (*duro*) harsh ♦ *nm/f* (*fig*) fiend ♦ *nf* (*animal feroz*) wild animal *o* beast; (*fig*) dragon.

fierro ['fjerro] *nm* (*AM*) iron.

fiesta ['fjesta] *nf* party; (*de pueblo*) festival; **la** ~ **nacional** bullfighting; (**día de**) ~ (public) holiday; **mañana es** ~ it's a holiday tomorrow; ~ **de guardar** (*REL*) day of obligation.

Fiestas *can be official public holidays (such as the* **Día de la Constitución**)*, or special holidays for each* **comunidad autónoma***, many of which are religious feast days. All over Spain there are also special local* **fiestas** *for a patron saint or the Virgin Mary. These often last several days and can include religious processions, carnival parades, bullfights, dancing and feasts of typical local produce.*

FIFA *nf abr* (= *Federación Internacional de Fútbol Asociación*) FIFA.

figura [fiˈɣura] *nf* (*gen*) figure; (*forma, imagen*) shape, form; (*NAIPES*) face card.

figurado, a [fiɣuˈraðo, a] *adj* figurative.

figurante [fiɣuˈrante] *nm/f* (*TEAT*) walk-on part; (*CINE*) extra.

figurar [fiɣuˈrar] *vt* (*representar*) to represent; (*fingir*) to feign ♦ *vi* to figure; ~**se** *vr* (*imaginarse*) to imagine; (*suponer*) to suppose; **ya me lo figuraba** I thought as much.

fijador [fixaˈðor] *nm* (*FOTO etc*) fixative; (*de pelo*) gel.

fijar [fiˈxar] *vt* (*gen*) to fix; (*cartel*) to post, put up; (*estampilla*) to affix, stick (on); (*pelo*) to set; (*fig*) to settle (on), decide; ~**se** *vr*: ~**se en** to notice; ¡**fíjate!** just imagine!; ¿**te fijas?** see what I mean?

fijo, a [ˈfixo, a] *adj* (*gen*) fixed; (*firme*) firm; (*permanente*) permanent; (*trabajo*) steady; (*color*) fast ♦ *adv*: **mirar** ~ to stare.

fila [ˈfila] *nf* row; (*MIL*) rank; (*cadena*) line; (*MIL*) rank; (*en marcha*) file; ~ **india** single file; **ponerse en** ~ to line up, get into line; **primera** ~ front row.

filántropo, a [fiˈlantropo, a] *nm/f* philanthropist.

filarmónico, a [filarˈmoniko, a] *adj, nf* philharmonic.

filatelia [filaˈtelja] *nf* philately, stamp collecting.

filatelista [filateˈlista] *nm/f* philatelist, stamp collector.

filete [fiˈlete] *nm* (*carne*) fillet steak; (*de cerdo*) tenderloin; (*pescado*) fillet; (*MEC: rosca*) thread.

filiación [filjaˈθjon] *nf* (*POL etc*) affiliation; (*señas*) particulars *pl*; (*MIL, POLICÍA*) records *pl*.

filial [fiˈljal] *adj* filial ♦ *nf* subsidiary; (*sucursal*) branch.

filibustero [filiβusˈtero] *nm* pirate.

Filipinas [filiˈpinas] *nfpl*: **las (Islas)** ~ the Philippines.

filipino, a [filiˈpino, a] *adj, nm/f* Philippine.

film [film], *pl* **films** *nm* = **filme**.

filmación [filmaˈθjon] *nf* filming, shooting.

filmar [filˈmar] *vt* to film, shoot.

filme [ˈfilme] *nm* film, movie (*US*).

filmoteca [filmoˈteka] *nf* film library.

filo [ˈfilo] *nm* (*gen*) edge; **sacar** ~ **a** to sharpen; **al** ~ **del medio día** at about midday; **de doble** ~ double-edged.

filología [filoloˈxia] *nf* philology.

filólogo, a [fiˈloloɣo, a] *nm/f* philologist.

filón [fiˈlon] *nm* (*MINERÍA*) vein, lode; (*fig*) gold mine.

filoso, a [fiˈloso, a] *adj* (*AM*) sharp.

filosofía [filosoˈfia] *nf* philosophy.

filosófico, a [filoˈsofiko, a] *adj* philosophic(al).

filósofo, a [fiˈlosofo, a] *nm/f* philosopher.

filtración [filtraˈθjon] *nf* (*TEC*) filtration; (*INFORM*) sorting; (*fig: de fondos*) misappropriation; (*de datos*) leak.

filtrar [filˈtrar] *vt, vi* to filter, strain; (*información*) to leak; ~**se** *vr* to filter; (*fig: dinero*) to dwindle.

filtro [ˈfiltro] *nm* (*TEC, utensilio*) filter.

filudo, a [fiˈluðo, a] *adj* (*AM*) sharp.

fin [fin] *nm* end; (*objetivo*) aim, purpose; **a** ~ **de cuentas** at the end of the day; **al** ~ **y al cabo** when all's said and done; **a** ~ **de** in order to; **por** ~ finally; **en** ~ (*resumiendo*) in short; ¡**en** ~! (*resignación*) oh, well!; ~ **de archivo** (*INFORM*) end-of-file; ~ **de semana** weekend; **sin** ~ endless(ly).

final [fiˈnal] *adj* final ♦ *nm* end, conclusion ♦ *nf* (*DEPORTE*) final.

finalice [finaˈliθe] *etc vb V* **finalizar**.

finalidad [finaliˈðað] *nf* finality; (*propósito*) purpose, aim.

finalista [finaˈlista] *nm/f* finalist.

finalizar [finaliˈθar] *vt* to end, finish ♦ *vi* to end, come to an end; ~ **la sesión** (*INFORM*) to log out *o* off.

financiación [finanθjaˈθjon] *nf* financing.

financiar [finanˈθjar] *vt* to finance.

financiero, a [finanˈθjero, a] *adj* financial ♦ *nm/f* financier.

financista [finanˈsista] *nm/f* (*AM*) financier.

finanzas [fiˈnanθas] *nfpl* finances.

finca [ˈfinka] *nf* country estate.

fineza [fiˈneθa] *nf* (*cualidad*) fineness; (*modales*) refinement.

fingir [finˈxir] *vt* (*simular*) to simulate, feign; (*pretextar*) to sham, fake ♦ *vi* (*aparentar*) to pretend; ~**se** *vr*: ~**se dormido** to pretend to be asleep.

finiquitar [finikiˈtar] *vt* (*ECON: cuenta*) to settle and close.

Finisterre [finisˈterre] *nm*: **el cabo de** ~

Cape Finisterre.
finja ['finxa] *etc vb V* **fingir**.
finlandés, esa [finlan'des, esa] *adj* Finnish
♦ *nm/f* Finn ♦ *nm* (*LING*) Finnish.
Finlandia [fin'landja] *nf* Finland.
fino, a ['fino, a] *adj* fine; (*delgado*) slender;
(*de buenas maneras*) polite, refined;
(*inteligente*) shrewd; (*punta*) sharp;
(*gusto*) discriminating; (*oído*) sharp;
(*jerez*) fino, dry ♦ *nm* (*jerez*) dry sherry.
finura [fi'nura] *nf* (*calidad*) fineness;
(*cortesía*) politeness; (*elegancia*)
elegance; (*agudeza*) shrewdness.
FIP [fip] *nf abr* (*ESP*) = *Formación Intensiva
Profesional*.
firma ['firma] *nf* signature; (*COM*) firm,
company.
firmamento [firma'mento] *nm* firmament.
firmante [fir'mante] *adj, nm/f* signatory; **los
abajo ~s** the undersigned.
firmar [fir'mar] *vt* to sign; **~ un contrato**
(*COM: colocarse*) to sign on; **firmado y
sellado** signed and sealed.
firme ['firme] *adj* firm; (*estable*) stable;
(*sólido*) solid; (*constante*) steady;
(*decidido*) resolute; (*duro*) hard; **¡~s!**
(*MIL*) attention!; **oferta en ~** (*COM*) firm
offer ♦ *nm* road (surface).
firmemente [firme'mente] *adv* firmly.
firmeza [fir'meθa] *nf* firmness; (*constancia*)
steadiness; (*solidez*) solidity.
fiscal [fis'kal] *adj* fiscal ♦ *nm* (*JUR*) ≈ Crown
Prosecutor, Procurator Fiscal (*Escocia*),
district attorney (*US*).
fiscalice [fiska'liθe] *etc vb V* **fiscalizar**.
fiscalizar [fiskali'θar] *vt* (*controlar*) to
control; (*registrar*) to inspect (officially);
(*fig*) to criticize.
fisco ['fisko] *nm* (*hacienda*) treasury,
exchequer; **declarar algo al ~** to declare
sth for tax purposes.
fisgar [fis'ɣar] *vt* to pry into.
fisgón, ona [fis'ɣon, ona] *adj* nosey.
fisgue ['fisɣe] *etc vb V* **fisgar**.
físico, a ['fisiko, a] *adj* physical ♦ *nm*
physique; (*aspecto*) appearance, looks
♦ *nm/f* physicist ♦ *nf* physics *sg*.
fisioterapeuta [fisjotera'peuta] *nm/f*
physiotherapist.
fisioterapia [fisjote'rapja] *nf*
physiotherapy.
fisioterapista [fisjotera'pista] *nm/f* (*AM*)
physiotherapist.
fisonomía [fisono'mia] *nf* physiognomy,
features *pl*.
fisonomista [fisono'mista] *nm/f*: **ser buen
~** to have a good memory for faces.
flac(c)idez [fla(k)θi'ðeθ] *nf* softness,

flabbiness.
flác(c)ido, a ['fla(k)θiðo, a] *adj* flabby.
flaco, a ['flako, a] *adj* (*muy delgado*)
skinny, thin; (*débil*) weak, feeble.
flagrante [fla'ɣrante] *adj* flagrant.
flamante [fla'mante] *adj* (*fam*) brilliant;
(: *nuevo*) brand-new.
flamear [flame'ar] *vt* (*CULIN*) to flambé.
flamenco, a [fla'menko, a] *adj* (*de Flandes*)
Flemish; (*baile, música*) gipsy ♦ *nm/f*
Fleming; **los ~s** the Flemish ♦ *nm* (*LING*)
Flemish; (*baile, música*) flamenco; (*ZOOL*)
flamingo.
flan [flan] *nm* creme caramel.
flanco ['flanko] *nm* side; (*MIL*) flank.
Flandes ['flandes] *nm* Flanders.
flanquear [flanke'ar] *vt* to flank; (*MIL*) to
outflank.
flaquear [flake'ar] *vi* (*debilitarse*) to
weaken; (*persona*) to slack.
flaqueza [fla'keθa] *nf* (*delgadez*) thinness,
leanness; (*fig*) weakness.
flaquísimo, a [fla'kisimo, a] *adj superlativo
de* **flaco**.
flash [flas], *pl* **flashes** [flas] *nm* (*FOTO*)
flash.
flato ['flato] *nm*: **el** (*o* **un**) **~** the (*o* a) stitch.
flauta ['flauta] (*MUS*) *nf* flute ♦ *nm/f* flautist,
flute player; **¡la gran ~!** (*AM*) my God!;
hijo de la gran ~ (*AM fam!*) bastard (!),
son of a bitch (*US!*).
flecha ['fletʃa] *nf* arrow.
flechazo [fle't ʃaθo] *nm* (*acción*) bowshot;
(*fam*): **fue un ~** it was love at first sight.
fleco ['fleko] *nm* fringe.
flema ['flema] *nm* phlegm.
flemático, a [fle'matiko, a] *adj* phlegmatic;
(*tono etc*) matter-of-fact.
flemón [fle'mon] *nm* (*MED*) gumboil.
flequillo [fle'kiʎo] *nm* (*pelo*) fringe.
fletar [fle'tar] *vt* (*COM*) to charter;
(*embarcar*) to load; (*AUTO*) to lease
(-purchase).
flete ['flete] *nm* (*carga*) freight; (*alquiler*)
charter; (*precio*) freightage; **~ debido**
(*COM*) freight forward; **~ sobre compras**
(*COM*) freight inward.
flexible [flek'sißle] *adj* flexible; (*individuo*)
compliant.
flexión [flek'sjon] *nf* (*DEPORTE*) bend; (: *en
el suelo*) press-up.
flexo ['flekso] *nm* adjustable table lamp.
flipper ['fliper] *nm* pinball machine.
flirtear [flirte'ar] *vi* to flirt.
FLN *nm abr* (*POL: ESP, Perú, Venezuela*)
= *Frente de Liberación Nacional*.
flojear [floxe'ar] *vi* (*piernas: al andar*) to
give way; (*alumno*) to do badly; (*cosecha*,

mercado) to be poor.
flojera [flo'xera] *nf* (*AM*) laziness; **me da** ~
I can't be bothered.
flojo, a ['floxo, a] *adj* (*gen*) loose; (*sin
fuerzas*) limp; (*débil*) weak; (*viento*) light;
(*bebida*) weak; (*trabajo*) poor; (*actitud*)
slack; (*precio*) low; (*COM: mercado*) dull,
slack; (*AM*) lazy.
flor [flor] *nf* flower; (*piropo*) compliment; **la
~ y nata de la sociedad** (*fig*) the cream
of society; **en la ~ de la vida** in the
prime of life; **a ~ de** on the surface of.
flora ['flora] *nf* flora.
florecer [flore'θer] *vi* (*BOT*) to flower,
bloom; (*fig*) to flourish.
floreciente [flore'θjente] *adj* (*BOT*) in
flower, flowering; (*fig*) thriving.
Florencia [flo'renθja] *nf* Florence.
florero [flo'rero] *nm* vase.
florezca [flo'reθka] *etc vb* V **florecer**.
florista [flo'rista] *nm/f* florist.
floristería [floriste'ria] *nf* florist's (shop).
flota ['flota] *nf* fleet.
flotación [flota'θjon] *nf* (*COM*) flotation.
flotador [flota'ðor] *nm* (*gen*) float; (*para
nadar*) rubber ring; (*de cisterna*) ballcock.
flotante [flo'tante] *adj* floating; (*INFORM*):
de coma ~ floating-point.
flotar [flo'tar] *vi* to float.
flote ['flote] *nm*: **a ~** afloat; **ponerse a ~**
(*fig*) to get back on one's feet.
FLS *nm abr* (*POL: Nicaragua*) = Frente de
Liberación Sandinista.
fluctuación [fluktwa'θjon] *nf* fluctuation.
fluctuante [fluk'twante] *adj* fluctuating.
fluctuar [fluk'twar] *vi* (*oscilar*) to fluctuate.
fluidez [flui'ðeθ] *nf* fluidity; (*fig*) fluency.
fluido, a ['flwiðo, a] *adj* fluid; (*lenguaje*)
fluent; (*estilo*) smooth ♦ *nm* (*líquido*) fluid.
fluir [flu'ir] *vi* to flow.
flujo ['fluxo] *nm* flow; (*POL*) swing; (*NAUT*)
rising tide; **~ y reflujo** ebb and flow; **~
de sangre** (*MED*) haemorrhage (*BRIT*),
hemorrhage (*US*); **~ positivo/negativo
de efectivo** (*COM*) positive/negative cash
flow.
flúor ['fluor] *nm* fluorine; (*en dentífrico*)
fluoride.
fluorescente [flwores'θente] *adj*
fluorescent ♦ *nm* (*tb*: **tubo ~**) fluorescent
tube.
fluoruro [flwo'ruro] *nm* fluoride.
fluvial [flußi'al] *adj* fluvial, river *cpd*.
fluyendo [flu'jendo] *etc vb* V **fluir**.
F.M. *nf abr* (= Frecuencia Modulada) F.M.
FMI *nm abr* (= Fondo Monetario
Internacional) I.M.F.
F.N. *nf abr* (*ESP POL*) = Fuerza Nueva ♦ *nm*

= Frente Nacional.
FNPT *nm abr* (*ESP*) = Fondo Nacional de
Protección del Trabajo.
f.° *abr* (= folio) fo., fol.
foca ['foka] *nf* seal.
foco ['foko] *nm* focus; (*centro*) focal point;
(*fuente*) source; (*de incendio*) seat; (*ELEC*)
floodlight; (*TEAT*) spotlight; (*AM*) (*light*)
bulb, light.
fofo, a ['fofo, a] *adj* (*esponjoso*) soft,
spongy; (*músculo*) flabby.
fogata [fo'xata] *nf* (*hoguera*) bonfire.
fogón [fo'xon] *nm* (*de cocina*) ring, burner.
fogoso, a [fo'xoso, a] *adj* spirited.
foja ['foxa] *nf* (*AM*) sheet (of paper); **~ de
servicios** record (file).
fol. *abr* (= folio) fo., fol.
folder, fólder ['folder] *nm* (*AM*) folder.
folio ['foljo] *nm* folio; (*hoja*) leaf.
folklore [fol'klore] *nm* folklore.
folklórico, a [fol'kloriko, a] *adj* traditional.
follaje [fo'ʎaxe] *nm* foliage.
follar [fo'ʎar] *vt, vi* (*fam!*) to fuck (*!*).
folletinesco, a [foʎetin'esko, a] *adj*
melodramatic.
folleto [fo'ʎeto] *nm* pamphlet; (*COM*)
brochure; (*prospecto*) leaflet; (*ESCOL etc*)
handout.
follón [fo'ʎon] *nm* (*fam: lío*) mess;
(: *conmoción*) fuss, rumpus, shindy;
armar un ~ to kick up a fuss; **se armó un
~** there was a hell of a row.
fomentar [fomen'tar] *vt* (*MED*) to foment;
(*fig: promover*) to promote, foster; (*odio
etc*) to stir up.
fomento [fo'mento] *nm* (*fig: ayuda*)
fostering; (*promoción*) promotion.
fonda ['fonda] *nf* ≈ guest house; V *tb* **hotel**.
fondear [fonde'ar] *vt* (*NAUT: sondear*) to
sound; (*barco*) to search.
fondo ['fondo] *nm* (*de caja etc*) bottom;
(*medida*) depth; (*de coche, sala*) back;
(*ARTE etc*) background; (*reserva*) fund;
(*fig: carácter*) nature; **~s** *nmpl* (*COM*)
funds, resources; **~ de amortización**
(*COM*) sinking fund; **F~ Monetario
Internacional** International Monetary
Fund; **~ del mar** sea bed *o* floor; **una
investigación a ~** a thorough
investigation; **en el ~** at bottom, deep
down; **tener buen ~** to be good natured.
fonética [fo'netika] *nf* phonetics *sg*.
fono ['fono] *nm* (*AM*) telephone (number).
fonógrafo [fo'noxrafo] *nm* (*esp AM*)
gramophone, phonograph (*US*).
fonología [fonolo'xia] *nf* phonology.
fontanería [fontane'ria] *nf* plumbing.
fontanero [fonta'nero] *nm* plumber.

footing ['futin] *nm* jogging; **hacer** ~ to jog.
F.O.P. [fop] *nfpl abr (ESP)* = **Fuerzas del Orden Público**.
forajido [fora'xiðo] *nm* outlaw.
foráneo, a [fo'raneo, a] *adj* foreign ♦ *nm/f* outsider.
forastero, a [foras'tero, a] *nm/f* stranger.
forcé [for'θe] *vb V* **forzar**.
forcejear [forθexe'ar] *vi (luchar)* to struggle.
forcemos [for'θemos] *etc vb V* **forzar**.
fórceps ['forθeps] *nm inv* forceps.
forense [fo'rense] *adj* forensic ♦ *nm/f* pathologist.
forestal [fores'tal] *adj* forest *cpd*.
forjar [for'xar] *vt* to forge; *(formar)* to form.
forma ['forma] *nf (figura)* form, shape; *(molde)* mould, pattern; *(MED)* fitness; *(método)* way, means; **estar en** ~ to be fit; ~ **de pago** *(COM)* method of payment; **las** ~**s** the conventions; **de** ~ **que** ... so that ...; **de todas** ~**s** in any case.
formación [forma'θjon] *nf (gen)* formation; *(enseñanza)* training; ~ **profesional** vocational training; ~ **fuera del trabajo** off-the-job training; ~ **en el trabajo** *o* **sobre la práctica** on-the-job training.
formal [for'mal] *adj (gen)* formal; *(fig: persona)* serious; *(: de fiar)* reliable; *(conducta)* steady.
formalice [forma'liθe] *etc vb V* **formalizar**.
formalidad [formali'ðað] *nf* formality; seriousness; reliability; steadiness.
formalizar [formali'θar] *vt (JUR)* to formalize; *(plan)* to draw up; *(situación)* to put in order, regularize; ~**se** *vr (situación)* to be put in order, be regularized.
formar [for'mar] *vt (componer)* to form, shape; *(constituir)* to make up, constitute; *(ESCOL)* to train, educate ♦ *vi (MIL)* to fall in; *(DEPORTE)* to line up; ~**se** *vr (ESCOL)* to be trained *(o educated)*; *(cobrar forma)* to form, take form; *(desarrollarse)* to develop.
formatear [formate'ar] *vt (INFORM)* to format.
formateo [forma'teo] *nm (INFORM)* formatting.
formato [for'mato] *nm (INFORM)*: **sin** ~ *(disco, texto)* unformatted; ~ **de registro** record format.
formica ® [for'mika] *nf* Formica ®.
formidable [formi'ðaβle] *adj (temible)* formidable; *(asombroso)* tremendous.
fórmula ['formula] *nf* formula.
formular [formu'lar] *vt (queja)* to lodge; *(petición)* to draw up; *(pregunta)* to pose,

formulate; *(idea)* to formulate.
formulario [formu'larjo] *nm* form; ~ **de solicitud/de pedido** *(COM)* application/ order form; **llenar un** ~ to fill in a form; ~ **contínuo desplegable** *(INFORM)* fanfold paper.
fornicar [forni'kar] *vi* to fornicate.
fornido, a [for'niðo, a] *adj* well-built.
fornique [for'nike] *etc vb V* **fornicar**.
foro ['foro] *nm (gen)* forum; *(JUR)* court.
forofo, a [fo'rofo, a] *nm/f* fan.
FORPPA ['forpa] *nm abr (ESP)* = *Fondo de Ordenación y Regulación de Productos y Precios Agrarios.*
FORPRONU [for'pronu] *nf abr (= Fuerza de Protección de las Naciones Unidas)* UNPROFOR.
forrado, a [fo'rraðo, a] *adj (ropa)* lined; *(fam)* well-heeled.
forrar [fo'rrar] *vt (abrigo)* to line; *(libro)* to cover; *(coche)* to upholster; ~**se** *vr (fam)* to line one's pockets.
forro ['forro] *nm (de cuaderno)* cover; *(costura)* lining; *(de sillón)* upholstery.
fortalecer [fortale'θer] *vt* to strengthen; ~**se** *vr* to fortify o.s.; *(opinión etc)* to become stronger.
fortaleza [forta'leθa] *nf (MIL)* fortress, stronghold; *(fuerza)* strength; *(determinación)* resolution.
fortalezca [forta'leθka] *etc vb V* **fortalecer**.
fortificar [fortifi'kar] *vt* to fortify; *(fig)* to strengthen.
fortifique [forti'fike] *etc vb V* **fortificar**.
fortísimo, a [for'tisimo, a] *adj superlativo de* **fuerte**.
fortuito, a [for'twito, a] *adj* accidental, chance *cpd*.
fortuna [for'tuna] *nf (suerte)* fortune, (good) luck; *(riqueza)* fortune, wealth.
forzar [for'θar] *vt (puerta)* to force (open); *(compeler)* to compel; *(violar)* to rape; *(ojos etc)* to strain.
forzoso, a [for'θoso, a] *adj* necessary; *(inevitable)* inescapable; *(obligatorio)* compulsory.
forzudo, a [for'θuðo, a] *adj* burly.
fosa ['fosa] *nf (sepultura)* grave; *(en tierra)* pit; *(MED)* cavity; ~**s nasales** nostrils.
fosfato [fos'fato] *nm* phosphate.
fosforescente [fosfores'θente] *adj* phosphorescent.
fósforo ['fosforo] *nm (QUÍMICA)* phosphorus; *(esp AM: cerilla)* match.
fósil ['fosil] *adj* fossil, fossilized ♦ *nm* fossil.
foso ['foso] *nm* ditch; *(TEAT)* pit; *(AUTO)*: ~ **de reconocimiento** inspection pit.

foto ['foto] nf photo, snap(shot); **sacar una** ~ to take a photo o picture.

fotocopia [foto'kopja] nf photocopy.

fotocopiadora [fotokopja'ðora] nf photocopier.

fotocopiar [fotoko'pjar] vt to photocopy.

fotogénico, a [foto'xeniko, a] adj photogenic.

fotografía [fotoɣra'fia] nf (arte) photography; (una ~) photograph.

fotografiar [fotoɣra'fjar] vt to photograph.

fotógrafo, a [fo'toɣrafo, a] nm/f photographer.

fotomatón [fotoma'ton] nm (cabina) photo booth.

fotómetro [fo'tometro] nm (FOTO) light meter.

fotonovela [fotono'ßela] nf photo-story.

foulard [fu'lar] nm (head)scarf.

FP nf abr (ESP: ESCOL, COM) = Formación Profesional ♦ nm abr (POL) = Frente Popular.

FPLP nm abr (POL: = Frente Popular para la Liberación de Palestina) PFLP.

Fr. abr (= Fray, franco) Fr.

frac [frak], pl **fracs** o **fraques** ['frakes] nm dress coat, tails.

fracasar [fraka'sar] vi (gen) to fail; (plan etc) to fall through.

fracaso [fra'kaso] nm (desgracia, revés) failure; (de negociaciones etc) collapse, breakdown.

fracción [frak'θjon] nf fraction; (POL) faction, splinter group.

fraccionamiento [fraksjona'mjento] nm (AM) housing estate.

fractura [frak'tura] nf fracture, break.

fragancia [fra'ɣanθja] nf (olor) fragrance, perfume.

fragante [fra'ɣante] adj fragrant, scented.

fraganti [fra'ɣanti]: **in** ~ adv: **coger a algn in** ~ to catch sb red-handed.

fragata [fra'ɣata] nf frigate.

frágil ['fraxil] adj (débil) fragile; (COM) breakable; (fig) frail, delicate.

fragilidad [fraxili'ðað] nf fragility; (de persona) frailty.

fragmento [fraɣ'mento] nm fragment; (pedazo) piece; (de discurso) excerpt; (de canción) snatch.

fragor [fra'ɣor] nm (ruido intenso) din.

fragua ['fraɣwa] nf forge.

fraguar [fra'ɣwar] vt to forge; (fig) to concoct ♦ vi to harden.

fragüe ['fraɣwe] etc vb V **fraguar.**

fraile ['fraile] nm (REL) friar; (: monje) monk.

frambuesa [fram'bwesa] nf raspberry.

francés, esa [fran'θes, esa] adj French

♦ nm/f Frenchman/woman ♦ nm (LING) French.

Francia ['franθja] nf France.

franco, a ['franko, a] adj (cándido) frank, open; (COM: exento) free ♦ nm (moneda) franc; ~ **de derechos** duty-free; ~ **al costado del buque** (COM) free alongside ship; ~ **puesto sobre vagón** (COM) free on rail; ~ **a bordo** free on board.

francotirador, a [frankotira'ðor, a] nm/f sniper.

franela [fra'nela] nf flannel.

franja ['franxa] nf fringe; (de uniforme) stripe; (de tierra etc) strip.

franquear [franke'ar] vt (camino) to clear; (carta, paquete postal) to frank, stamp; (obstáculo) to overcome; (COM etc) to free, exempt.

franqueo [fran'keo] nm postage.

franqueza [fran'keθa] nf (candor) frankness.

franquicia [fran'kiθja] nf exemption; ~ **aduanera** exemption from customs duties.

franquismo [fran'kismo] nm: **el** ~ (sistema) the Franco system; (período) the Franco years.

The political reign and style of government of Francisco Franco (from the end of the Spanish Civil War in 1939 until his death in 1975) are commonly called **franquismo**. *He was a powerful, authoritarian, right-wing dictator, who promoted a traditional, Catholic and self-sufficient country. From the 1960s Spain gradually opened its doors to the international community, coinciding with a rise in economic growth and internal political opposition. On his death Spain became a democratic constitutional monarchy.*

---

franquista [fran'kista] adj pro-Franco ♦ nm/f supporter of Franco.

frasco ['frasko] nm bottle, flask; ~ **al vacío** (vacuum) flask.

frase ['frase] nf sentence; (locución) phrase, expression; ~ **hecha** set phrase; (despectivo) cliché.

fraternal [frater'nal] adj brotherly, fraternal.

fraude ['frauðe] nm (cualidad) dishonesty; (acto) fraud, swindle.

fraudulento, a [frauðu'lento, a] adj fraudulent.

frazada [fra'saða] nf (AM) blanket.

frecuencia [fre'kwenθja] nf frequency; **con** ~ frequently, often; ~ **de red** (INFORM) mains frequency; ~ **del reloj** (*INFORM*) clock speed; ~ **telefónica** voice frequency.

frecuentar [frekwen'tar] *vt* (*lugar*) to frequent; (*persona*) to see frequently *o* often; ~ **la buena sociedad** to mix in high society.

frecuente [fre'kwente] *adj* frequent; (*costumbre*) common; (*vicio*) rife.

fregadero [freɣa'ðero] *nm* (kitchen) sink.

fregado, a [fre'gaðo, a] *adj* (*AM fam!*) damn, bloody (*!*).

fregar [fre'ɣar] *vt* (*frotar*) to scrub; (*platos*) to wash (up); (*AM*) to annoy.

fregón, ona [fre'ɣon, ona] *adj* = **fregado** ♦ *nf* (*utensilio*) mop; (*pey: sirvienta*) skivvy.

fregué [fre'ɣe], **freguemos** [fre'ɣemos] *etc vb V* **fregar**.

freidora [frei'ðora] *nf* deep-fat fryer.

freír [fre'ir] *vt* to fry.

fréjol ['frexol] *nm* = **fríjol**.

frenar [fre'nar] *vt* to brake; (*fig*) to check.

frenazo [fre'naθo] *nm*: **dar un** ~ to brake sharply.

frenesí [frene'si] *nm* frenzy.

frenético, a [fre'netiko, a] *adj* frantic; **ponerse** ~ to lose one's head.

freno ['freno] *nm* (*TEC, AUTO*) brake; (*de cabalgadura*) bit; (*fig*) check.

frente ['frente] *nm* (*ARQ, MIL, POL*) front; (*de objeto*) front part ♦ *nf* forehead, brow; ~ **de batalla** battle front; **hacer** ~ **común con algn** to make common cause with sb; ~ **a** in front of; (*en situación opuesta*) opposite; **chocar de** ~ to crash head-on; **hacer** ~ **a** to face up to.

fresa ['fresa] *nf* (*ESP: fruta*) strawberry; (*de dentista*) drill.

fresco, a ['fresko, a] *adj* (*nuevo*) fresh; (*huevo*) newly-laid; (*frío*) cool; (*descarado*) cheeky, bad-mannered ♦ *nm* (*aire*) fresh air; (*ARTE*) fresco; (*AM: bebida*) fruit juice *o* drink ♦ *nm/f* (*fam*) shameless person; (*persona insolente*) impudent person; **tomar el** ~ to get some fresh air; **¡qué** ~! what a cheek!

frescor [fres'kor] *nm* freshness.

frescura [fres'kura] *nf* freshness; (*descaro*) cheek, nerve; (*calma*) calmness.

fresno ['fresno] *nm* ash (tree).

fresón [fre'son] *nm* strawberry.

frialdad [frjal'dað] *nf* (*gen*) coldness; (*indiferencia*) indifference.

fricción [frik'θjon] *nf* (*gen*) friction; (*acto*) rub(bing); (*MED*) massage; (*POL, fig etc*) friction, trouble.

friega ['frjeɣa] *etc*, **friegue** ['frjeɣe] *etc vb V* **fregar**.

friendo [fri'endo] *etc vb V* **freír**.

frigidez [frixi'ðeθ] *nf* frigidity.

frígido, a ['frixiðo, a] *adj* frigid.

frigorífico, a [friɣo'rifiko, a] *adj* refrigerating ♦ *nm* refrigerator; (*camión*) freezer lorry *o* truck (*US*); **instalación frigorífica** cold-storage plant.

frijol [fri'xol], **fríjol** ['frixol] *nm* kidney bean.

frió [fri'o] *vb V* **freír**.

frío, a ['frio, a] *etc vb V* **freír** ♦ *adj* cold; (*fig: indiferente*) unmoved, indifferent; (*poco entusiasta*) chilly ♦ *nm* cold(ness); indifference; **¡que** ~! how cold it is!

friolento, a [frjo'lento, a] (*AM*), **friolero, a** [frjo'lero, a] *adj* sensitive to cold.

frito, a ['frito, a] *pp de* **freír** ♦ *adj* fried ♦ *nm* fry; **me trae** ~ **ese hombre** I'm sick and tired of that man; ~**s variados** mixed grill.

frívolo, a ['friβolo, a] *adj* frivolous.

frondoso, a [fron'doso, a] *adj* leafy.

frontal [fron'tal] *nm*: **choque** ~ head-on collision.

frontera [fron'tera] *nf* frontier; (*línea divisoria*) border; (*zona*) frontier area.

fronterizo, a [fronte'riθo, a] *adj* frontier *cpd*; (*contiguo*) bordering.

frontón [fron'ton] *nm* (*DEPORTE: cancha*) pelota court; (: *juego*) pelota.

frotar [fro'tar] *vt* to rub; (*fósforo*) to strike; ~**se** *vr*: ~**se las manos** to rub one's hands.

frs. *abr* (= *francos*) fr.

fructífero, a [fruk'tifero, a] *adj* productive, fruitful.

frugal [fru'ɣal] *adj* frugal.

fruncir [frun'θir] *vt* (*COSTURA*) to gather; (*ceño*) to frown; (*labios*) to purse.

frunza ['frunθa] *etc vb V* **fruncir**.

frustración [frustra'θjon] *nf* frustration.

frustrar [frus'trar] *vt* to frustrate; ~**se** *vr* to be frustrated; (*plan etc*) to fail.

fruta ['fruta] *nf* fruit.

frutal [fru'tal] *adj* fruit-bearing, fruit *cpd* ♦ *nm*: (**árbol**) ~ fruit tree.

frutería [frute'ria] *nf* fruit shop.

frutero, a [fru'tero, a] *adj* fruit *cpd* ♦ *nm/f* fruiterer ♦ *nm* fruit dish *o* bowl.

frutilla [fru'tiʎa] *nf* (*AM*) strawberry.

fruto ['fruto] *nm* (*BOT*) fruit; (*fig: resultado*) result, outcome; ~**s secos** ≈ nuts and raisins.

FSLN *nm abr* (*POL: Nicaragua*) = *Frente Sandinista de Liberación Nacional*.

fue [fwe] *vb V* **ser, ir**.

fuego ['fweɣo] nm (gen) fire; (CULIN: gas) burner, ring; (fig: pasión) fire, passion; ~s **artificiales** o **de artificio** fireworks; **prender** ~ **a** to set fire to; **a** ~ **lento** on a low flame o gas; ¡**alto el** ~! cease fire!; **estar entre dos** ~s to be in the crossfire; ¿**tienes** ~? have you (got) a light?

fuelle ['fweʎe] nm bellows pl.

fuel-oil [fuel'oil] nm paraffin (BRIT), kerosene (US).

fuente ['fwente] nf fountain; (manantial, fig) spring; (origen) source; (plato) large dish; ~ **de alimentación** (INFORM) power supply; **de** ~ **desconocida/fidedigna** from an unknown/reliable source.

fuera ['fwera] etc vb ser, ir ♦ adv out(side); (en otra parte) away; (excepto, salvo) except, save ♦ prep: ~ **de** outside; (fig) besides; ~ **de alcance** out of reach; ~ **de combate** out of action; (boxeo) knocked out; ~ **de sí** beside o.s.; **por** ~ (on the) outside; **los de** ~ strangers, newcomers; **estar** ~ (en el extranjero) to be abroad.

fuera-borda [fwera'βorða] nm inv outboard engine o motor.

fuerce ['fwerθe] etc vb V forzar.

fuereño, a [fwe'reɲo, a] nm/f (AM) outsider.

fuero ['fwero] nm (carta municipal) municipal charter; (leyes locales) local o regional law code; (privilegio) privilege; (autoridad) jurisdiction; (fig): **en mi** etc ~ **interno** in my etc heart of hearts ..., deep down ....

fuerte ['fwerte] adj strong; (golpe) hard; (ruido) loud; (comida) rich; (lluvia) heavy; (dolor) intense ♦ adv strongly; hard; loud(ly) ♦ nm (MIL) fort, strongpoint; (fig): **el canto no es mi** ~ singing is not my strong point.

fuerza ['fwerθa] etc vb V forzar ♦ nf (fortaleza) strength; (TEC, ELEC) power; (coacción) force; (violencia) violence; (MIL: tb: ~s) forces pl; ~ **de arrastre** (TEC) pulling power; ~ **de brazos** manpower; ~ **mayor** force majeure; ~ **bruta** brute force; ~s **armadas** (FF.AA.) armed forces; ~ **de Orden Público (F.O.P.)** police (forces); ~ **vital** vitality; **a** ~ **de** by (dint of); **cobrar** ~s to recover one's strength; **tener** ~s **para** to have the strength to; **hacer algo a la** ~ to be forced to do sth; **con** ~ **legal** (COM) legally binding; **a la** ~, **por** ~ of necessity; ~ **de voluntad** willpower.

fuete ['fwete] nm (AM) whip.

fuga ['fuɣa] nf (huida) flight, escape; (de enamorados) elopement; (de gas etc) leak; ~ **de cerebros** (fig) brain drain.

fugarse [fu'ɣarse] vr to flee, escape.

fugaz [fu'ɣaθ] adj fleeting.

fugitivo, a [fuxi'tiβo, a] adj fugitive, fleeing ♦ nm/f fugitive.

fugue ['fuɣe] etc vb V **fugarse**.

fui [fwi] etc vb V **ser, ir**.

fulano, a [fu'lano, a] nm/f so-and-so, what's-his-name.

fulgor [ful'ɣor] nm brilliance.

fulminante [fulmi'nante] adj (pólvora) fulminating; (fig: mirada) withering; (MED) fulminant; (fam) terrific, tremendous.

fulminar [fulmi'nar] vt: **caer fulminado por un rayo** to be struck down by lightning; ~ **a algn con la mirada** to look daggers at sb.

fumador, a [fuma'ðor, a] nm/f smoker; **no** ~ non-smoker.

fumar [fu'mar] vt, vi to smoke; ~**se** vr (disipar) to squander; ~ **en pipa** to smoke a pipe.

fumigar [fumi'ɣar] vt to fumigate.

funámbulo, a [fu'nambulo, a], **funambulista** [funambu'lista] nm/f tightrope walker.

función [fun'θjon] nf function; (de puesto) duties pl; (TEAT etc) show; **entrar en funciones** to take up one's duties; ~ **de tarde/de noche** matinée/evening performance.

funcional [funθjo'nal] adj functional.

funcionamiento [funθjona'mjento] nm functioning; (TEC) working; **en** ~ (COM) on stream; **entrar en** ~ to come into operation.

funcionar [funθjo'nar] vi (gen) to function; (máquina) to work; "**no funciona**" "out of order".

funcionario, a [funθjo'narjo, a] nm/f official; (público) civil servant.

funda ['funda] nf (gen) cover; (de almohada) pillowcase; ~ **protectora del disco** (INFORM) disk-jacket.

fundación [funda'θjon] nf foundation.

fundado, a [fun'daðo, a] adj (justificado) well-founded.

fundamental [fundamen'tal] adj fundamental, basic.

fundamentalismo [fundamenta'lismo] nm fundamentalism.

fundamentalista [fundamenta'lista] adj, nm/f fundamentalist.

fundamentar [fundamen'tar] vt (poner base) to lay the foundations of; (establecer) to found; (fig) to base.

fundamento [funda'mento] *nm* (*base*) foundation; (*razón*) grounds; **eso carece de** ~ that is groundless.

fundar [fun'dar] *vt* to found; (*crear*) to set up; (*fig: basar*): ~ **(en)** to base *o* found (on); ~**se** *vr:* ~**se en** to be founded on.

fundición [fundi'θjon] *nf* (*acción*) smelting; (*fábrica*) foundry; (*TIP*) fount (*BRIT*), font.

fundir [fun'dir] *vt* (*gen*) to fuse; (*metal*) to smelt, melt down; (*COM*) to merge; (*estatua*) to cast; ~**se** *vr* (*colores etc*) to merge, blend; (*unirse*) to fuse together; (*ELEC: fusible, lámpara etc*) to blow; (*nieve etc*) to melt.

fúnebre ['funeßre] *adj* funeral *cpd*, funereal.

funeral [fune'ral] *nm* funeral.

funeraria [fune'rarja] *nf* undertaker's (*BRIT*), mortician's (*US*).

funesto, a [fu'nesto, a] *adj* ill-fated; (*desastroso*) fatal.

fungir [fun'xir] *vi:* ~ **de** (*AM*) to act as.

furgón [fur'ɣon] *nm* wagon.

furgoneta [furɣo'neta] *nf* (*AUTO, COM*) (transit) van (*BRIT*), pickup (truck) (*US*).

furia ['furja] *nf* (*ira*) fury; (*violencia*) violence.

furibundo, a [furi'ßundo, a] *adj* furious.

furioso, a [fu'rjoso, a] *adj* (*iracundo*) furious; (*violento*) violent.

furor [fu'ror] *nm* (*cólera*) rage; (*pasión*) frenzy, passion; **hacer** ~ to be a sensation.

furtivo, a [fur'tißo, a] *adj* furtive ♦ *nm* poacher.

furúnculo [fu'runkulo] *nm* (*MED*) boil.

fuselaje [fuse'laxe] *nm* fuselage.

fusible [fu'sißle] *nm* fuse.

fusil [fu'sil] *nm* rifle.

fusilamiento [fusila'mjento] *nm* (*JUR*) execution by firing squad.

fusilar [fusi'lar] *vt* to shoot.

fusión [fu'sjon] *nf* (*gen*) melting; (*unión*) fusion; (*COM*) merger, amalgamation.

fusionar [fusjo'nar] *vt* to fuse (together); (*COM*) to merge; ~**se** *vr* (*COM*) to merge, amalgamate.

fusta ['fusta] *nf* (*látigo*) riding crop.

fútbol ['futßol] *nm* football.

futbolín [futßo'lin] *nm* table football.

futbolista [futßo'lista] *nm/f* footballer.

fútil ['futil] *adj* trifling.

futilidad [futili'ðað], **futileza** [futi'leθa] *nf* triviality.

futón [fu'ton] *nm* futon.

futuro, a [fu'turo, a] *adj* future ♦ *nm* future; (*LING*) future tense; ~**s** *nmpl* (*COM*) futures.

G g

G, g [xe] *nf* (*letra*) G, g; **G de Gerona** G for George.

g/ *abr* = **giro.**

gabacho, a [ga'ßatʃo, a] *adj* Pyrenean; (*fam*) Frenchified ♦ *nm/f* Pyrenean villager; (*fam*) Frenchy.

gabán [ga'ßan] *nm* overcoat.

gabardina [gaßar'ðina] *nf* (*tela*) gabardine; (*prenda*) raincoat.

gabinete [gaßi'nete] *nm* (*POL*) cabinet; (*estudio*) study; (*de abogados etc*) office; ~ **de consulta/de lectura** consulting/ reading room.

gacela [ga'θela] *nf* gazelle.

gaceta [ga'θeta] *nf* gazette.

gacetilla [gaθe'tiʎa] *nf* (*en periódico*) news in brief; (*de personalidades*) gossip column.

gachas ['gatʃas] *nfpl* porridge *sg.*

gacho, a ['gatʃo, a] *adj* (*encorvado*) bent down; (*orejas*) drooping.

gaditano, a [gaði'tano, a] *adj* of *o* from Cadiz ♦ *nm/f* native *o* inhabitant of Cadiz.

GAE *nm abr* (*ESP MIL*) = *Grupo Aéreo Embarcado.*

gaélico, a [ga'eliko, a] *adj* Gaelic ♦ *nm/f* Gael ♦ *nm* (*LING*) Gaelic.

gafar [ga'far] *vt* (*fam: traer mala suerte*) to put a jinx on.

gafas ['gafas] *nfpl* glasses; ~ **oscuras** dark glasses; ~ **de sol** sunglasses.

gafe ['gafe] *adj:* **ser** ~ to be jinxed ♦ *nm* (*fam*) jinx.

gaita ['gaita] *nf* flute; (~ *gallega*) bagpipes *pl*; (*dificultad*) bother; (*cosa engorrosa*) tough job.

gajes ['gaxes] *nmpl* (*salario*) pay *sg*; **los** ~ **del oficio** occupational hazards; ~ **y emolumentos** perquisites.

gajo ['gaxo] *nm* (*gen*) bunch; (*de árbol*) bough; (*de naranja*) segment.

gala ['gala] *nf* full dress; (*fig: lo mejor*) cream, flower; ~**s** *nfpl* finery *sg*; **estar de** ~ to be in one's best clothes; **hacer** ~ **de** to display, show off; **tener algo a** ~ to be proud of sth.

galaico, a [ga'laiko, a] *adj* Galician.

galán [ga'lan] *nm* lover, gallant; (*hombre*

atractivo) ladies' man; (*TEAT*): **primer ~** leading man.

galante [ga'lante] *adj* gallant; (*atento*) charming; (*cortés*) polite.

galantear [galante'ar] *vt* (*hacer la corte a*) to court, woo.

galanteo [galan'teo] *nm* (*coqueteo*) flirting; (*de pretendiente*) wooing.

galantería [galante'ria] *nf* (*caballerosidad*) gallantry; (*cumplido*) politeness; (*piropo*) compliment.

galápago [ga'lapaɣo] *nm* (*ZOOL*) freshwater tortoise.

galardón [galar'ðon] *nm* award, prize.

galardonar [galarðo'nar] *vt* (*premiar*) to reward; (*una obra*) to award a prize for.

galaxia [ga'laksja] *nf* galaxy.

galbana [gal'ßana] *nf* (*pereza*) sloth, laziness.

galeote [gale'ote] *nm* galley slave.

galera [ga'lera] *nf* (*nave*) galley; (*carro*) wagon; (*MED*) hospital ward; (*TIP*) galley.

galería [gale'ria] *nf* (*gen*) gallery; (*balcón*) veranda(h); (*de casa*) corridor; (*fam: público*) audience; **~ secreta** secret passage.

Gales ['gales] *nm*: **(el País de) ~** Wales.

galés, esa [ga'les, esa] *adj* Welsh ♦ *nm/f* Welshman/woman ♦ *nm* (*LING*) Welsh.

galgo, a ['galɣo, a] *nm/f* greyhound.

Galia ['galja] *nf* Gaul.

Galicia [ga'liθja] *nf* Galicia.

galicismo [gali'θismo] *nm* gallicism.

Galilea [gali'lea] *nf* Galilee.

galimatías [galima'tias] *nm inv* (*asunto*) rigmarole; (*lenguaje*) gibberish, nonsense.

gallardía [gaʎar'ðia] *nf* (*galantería*) dash; (*gracia*) gracefulness; (*valor*) bravery; (*elegancia*) elegance; (*nobleza*) nobleness.

gallego, a [ga'ʎeɣo, a] *adj* Galician; (*AM pey*) Spanish ♦ *nm/f* Galician; (*AM pey*) Spaniard ♦ *nm* (*LING*) Galician; *V tb* **lenguas cooficiales.**

galleta [ga'ʎeta] *nf* biscuit; (*fam: bofetada*) whack, slap.

gallina [ga'ʎina] *nf* hen ♦ *nm* (*fam*) coward; **~ ciega** blind man's buff; **~ llueca** broody hen.

gallinazo [gaʎi'naso] *nm* (*AM*) turkey buzzard.

gallinero [gaʎi'nero] *nm* (*criadero*) henhouse; (*TEAT*) gods *sg*, top gallery; (*voces*) hubbub.

gallo ['gaʎo] *nm* cock, rooster; (*MUS*) false *o* wrong note; (*cambio de voz*) break in the voice; **en menos que canta un ~** in an instant.

galo, a ['galo, a] *adj* Gallic; (= *francés*) French ♦ *nm/f* Gaul.

galón [ga'lon] *nm* (*COSTURA*) braid; (*MIL*) stripe; (*medida*) gallon.

galopante [galo'pante] *adj* galloping.

galopar [galo'par] *vi* to gallop.

galope [ga'lope] *nm* gallop; **al ~** (*fig*) in great haste; **a ~ tendido** at full gallop.

galvanice [galßa'niθe] *etc vb V* **galvanizar.**

galvanizar [galßani'θar] *vt* to galvanize.

gama ['gama] *nf* (*MUS*) scale; (*fig*) range; (*ZOOL*) doe.

gamba ['gamba] *nf* prawn.

gamberrada [gambe'rraða] *nf* act of hooliganism.

gamberro, a [gam'berro, a] *nm/f* hooligan, lout.

gamo ['gamo] *nm* (*ZOOL*) buck.

gamuza [ga'muθa] *nf* chamois; (*bayeta*) duster; (*AM: piel*) suede.

gana ['gana] *nf* (*deseo*) desire, wish; (*apetito*) appetite; (*voluntad*) will; (*añoranza*) longing; **de buena ~** willingly; **de mala ~** reluctantly; **me dan ~s de** I feel like, I want to; **tener ~s de** to feel like; **no me da la (real) ~** I don't (damned well) want to; **son ~s de molestar** they're just trying to be awkward.

ganadería [ganaðe'ria] *nf* (*ganado*) livestock; (*ganado vacuno*) cattle *pl*; (*cría, comercio*) cattle raising.

ganadero, a [gana'ðero, a] *adj* stock *cpd* ♦ *nm* stockman.

ganado [ga'naðo] *nm* livestock; **~ caballar/cabrío** horses *pl*/goats *pl*; **~ lanar** *u* **ovejuno** sheep *pl*; **~ porcino/vacuno** pigs *pl*/cattle *pl*.

ganador, a [gana'ðor, a] *adj* winning ♦ *nm/f* winner; (*ECON*) earner.

ganancia [ga'nanθja] *nf* (*lo ganado*) gain; (*aumento*) increase; (*beneficio*) profit; **~s** *nfpl* (*ingresos*) earnings; (*beneficios*) profit *sg*, winnings; **~s y pérdidas** profit and loss; **~ bruta/líquida** gross/net profit; **~s de capital** capital gains; **sacar ~ de** to draw profit from.

ganapán [gana'pan] *nm* (*obrero casual*) odd-job man; (*individuo tosco*) lout.

ganar [ga'nar] *vt* (*obtener*) to get, obtain; (*sacar ventaja*) to gain; (*COM*) to earn; (*DEPORTE, premio*) to win; (*derrotar*) to beat; (*alcanzar*) to reach; (*MIL: objetivo*) to take; (*apoyo*) to gain, win ♦ *vi* (*DEPORTE*) to win; **~se** *vr*: **~se la vida** to earn one's living; **se lo ha ganado** he deserves it; **~ tiempo** to gain time.

ganchillo [gan'tʃiʎo] *nm* (*para croché*)

crochet hook; (*arte*) crochet work.

gancho ['gantʃo] *nm* (*gen*) hook; (*colgador*) hanger; (*pey: revendedor*) tout; (*fam: atractivo*) sex appeal; (*BOXEO: golpe*) hook.

gandul, a [gan'dul, a] *adj, nmlf* good-for-nothing.

ganga ['ganga] *nf* (*cosa*) bargain; (*buena situación*) cushy job.

Ganges ['ganxes] *nm*: **el (Río)** ~ the Ganges.

ganglio ['gangljo] *nm* (*ANAT*) ganglion; (*MED*) swelling.

gangrena [gan'grena] *nf* gangrene.

gansada [gan'saða] *nf* (*fam*) stupid thing (to do).

ganso, a ['ganso, a] *nmlf* (*ZOOL*) gander/goose; (*fam*) idiot.

Gante ['gante] *nm* Ghent.

ganzúa [gan'θua] *nf* skeleton key ♦ *nmlf* burglar.

gañán [ga'ɲan] *nm* farmhand, farm labourer.

garabatear [garaßate'ar] *vt* to scribble, scrawl.

garabato [gara'ßato] *nm* (*gancho*) hook; (*garfio*) grappling iron; (*escritura*) scrawl, scribble; (*fam*) sex appeal.

garaje [ga'raxe] *nm* garage.

garante [ga'rante] *adj* responsible ♦ *nmlf* guarantor.

garantía [garan'tia] *nf* guarantee; (*seguridad*) pledge; (*compromiso*) undertaking; (*JUR: caución*) warranty; **de máxima** ~ absolutely guaranteed; ~ **de trabajo** job security.

garantice [garan'tiθe] *etc vb V* **garantizar**.

garantizar [garanti'θar] *vt* (*hacerse responsable de*) to vouch for; (*asegurar*) to guarantee.

garbanzo [gar'ßanθo] *nm* chickpea.

garbeo [gar'ßeo] *nm*: **darse un** ~ to go for a walk.

garbo ['garßo] *nm* grace, elegance; (*aire*) jauntiness; (*de mujer*) glamour; **andar con** ~ to walk gracefully.

garboso, a [gar'ßoso, a] *adj* graceful, elegant.

garete [ga'rete] *nm*: **irse al** ~ to go to the dogs.

garfio ['garfjo] *nm* grappling iron; (*gancho*) hook; (*ALPINISMO*) climbing iron.

gargajo [gar'xaxo] *nm* phlegm, sputum.

garganta [gar'xanta] *nf* (*interna*) throat; (*externa, de botella*) neck; (*GEO: barranco*) ravine; (*desfiladero*) narrow pass.

gargantilla [garxan'tiʎa] *nf* necklace.

gárgara ['garxara] *nf* gargle, gargling;

hacer ~**s** to gargle; **¡vete a hacer** ~**s!** (*fam*) go to blazes!

gárgola ['garxola] *nf* gargoyle.

garita [ga'rita] *nf* cabin, hut; (*MIL*) sentry box; (*puesto de vigilancia*) lookout post.

garito [ga'rito] *nm* (*lugar*) gaming house *o* den.

garra ['garra] *nf* (*de gato, TEC*) claw; (*de ave*) talon; (*fam*) hand, paw; (*fig: de canción etc*) bite; **caer en las** ~**s de algn** to fall into sb's clutches.

garrafa [ga'rrafa] *nf* carafe, decanter.

garrafal [garra'fal] *adj* enormous, terrific; (*error*) terrible.

garrapata [garra'pata] *nf* (*ZOOL*) tick.

garrotazo [garro'taθo] *nm* blow with a stick *o* club.

garrote [ga'rrote] *nm* (*palo*) stick; (*porra*) club, cudgel; (*suplicio*) garrotte.

garza ['garθa] *nf* heron.

gas [gas] *nm* gas; (*vapores*) fumes *pl*; ~**es de escape** exhaust (fumes).

gasa ['gasa] *nf* gauze; (*de pañal*) nappy liner.

gaseoso, a [gase'oso, a] *adj* gassy, fizzy ♦ *nf* lemonade, pop (*fam*).

gasoducto [gaso'ðukto] *nm* gas pipeline.

gasoil [ga'soil], **gasóleo** [ga'soleo] *nm* diesel (oil).

gasolina [gaso'lina] *nf* petrol, gas(oline) (*US*); ~ **sin plomo** unleaded petrol.

gasolinera [gasoli'nera] *nf* petrol (*BRIT*) *o* gas (*US*) station.

gastado, a [gas'taðo, a] *adj* (*ropa*) worn out; (*usado: frase etc*) trite.

gastar [gas'tar] *vt* (*dinero, tiempo*) to spend; (*consumir*) to use (up), consume; (*desperdiciar*) to waste; (*llevar*) to wear; ~**se** *vr* to wear out; (*terminarse*) to run out; (*estropearse*) to waste; ~ **bromas** to crack jokes; **¿qué número gastas?** what size (shoe) do you take?

gasto ['gasto] *nm* (*desembolso*) expenditure, spending; (*cantidad gastada*) outlay, expense; (*consumo, uso*) use; (*desgaste*) waste; ~**s** *nmpl* (*desembolsos*) expenses; (*cargos*) charges, costs; ~ **corriente** (*COM*) revenue expenditure; ~ **fijo** (*COM*) fixed charge; ~**s bancarios** bank charges; ~**s corrientes** running expenses; ~**s de distribución** (*COM*) distribution costs; ~**s generales** overheads; ~**s de mantenimiento** maintenance expenses; ~**s operacionales** operating costs; ~**s de tramitación** (*COM*) handling charge *sg*; ~**s vencidos** (*COM*) accrued charges; **cubrir** ~**s** to cover expenses; **meterse en**

~s to incur expense.

gastronomía [gastrono'mia] *nf* gastronomy.

gata ['gata] *nf* (*ZOOL*) she-cat; **andar a ~s** to go on all fours.

gatear [gate'ar] *vi* to go on all fours.

gatillo [ga'tiʎo] *nm* (*de arma de fuego*) trigger; (*de dentista*) forceps.

gato ['gato] *nm* (*ZOOL*) cat; (*TEC*) jack; **~ de Angora** Angora cat; **~ montés** wildcat; **dar a algn ~ por liebre** to take sb in; **aquí hay ~ encerrado** there's something fishy here.

gatuno, a [ga'tuno, a] *adj* feline.

gaucho, a ['gautʃo, a] *adj, nm/f* gaucho.

gaveta [ga'ßeta] *nf* drawer.

gavilán [gaßi'lan] *nm* sparrowhawk.

gavilla [ga'ßiʎa] *nf* sheaf.

gaviota [ga'ßjota] *nf* seagull.

gay [ge] *adj, nm* gay, homosexual.

gazapo [ga'θapo] *nm* young rabbit.

gaznate [gaθ'nate] *nm* (*pescuezo*) gullet; (*garganta*) windpipe.

gazpacho [gaθ'patʃo] *nm* gazpacho.

gel [xel] *nm* gel.

gelatina [xela'tina] *nf* jelly; (*polvos etc*) gelatine.

gema ['xema] *nf* gem.

gemelo, a [xe'melo, a] *adj, nm/f* twin; **~s** *nmpl* (*de camisa*) cufflinks; **~s de campo** field glasses, binoculars; **~s de teatro** opera glasses.

gemido [xe'miðo] *nm* (*quejido*) moan, groan; (*lamento*) wail, howl.

Géminis ['xeminis] *nm* (*ASTRO*) Gemini.

gemir [xe'mir] *vi* (*quejarse*) to moan, groan; (*animal*) to whine; (*viento*) to howl.

gen [xen] *nm* gene.

gen. *abr* (*LING*) = **género; genitivo.**

gendarme [xen'darme] *nm* (*AM*) policeman.

genealogía [xenealo'xia] *nf* genealogy.

generación [xenera'θjon] *nf* generation; **primera/segunda/tercera/cuarta ~** (*INFORM*) first/second/third/fourth generation.

generado, a [xene'raðo, a] *adj* (*INFORM*): **~ por ordenador** computer generated.

generador [xenera'ðor] *nm* generator; **~ de programas** (*INFORM*) program generator.

general [xene'ral] *adj* general; (*común*) common; (*pey: corriente*) rife; (*frecuente*) usual ♦ *nm* general; **~ de brigada/de división** brigadier-/major-general; **por lo o en ~** in general.

generalice [xenera'liθe] *etc vb V* **generalizar.**

generalidad [xenerali'ðað] *nf* generality.

Generalitat [jenerali'tat] *nf regional government of Catalonia;* **~ Valenciana** *regional government of Valencia.*

generalización [xeneraliθa'θjon] *nf* generalization.

generalizar [xenerali'θar] *vt* to generalize; **~se** *vr* to become generalized, spread; (*difundirse*) to become widely known.

generalmente [xeneral'mente] *adv* generally.

generar [xene'rar] *vt* to generate.

genérico, a [xe'neriko, a] *adj* generic.

género ['xenero] *nm* (*clase*) kind, sort; (*tipo*) type; (*BIO*) genus; (*LING*) gender; (*COM*) material; **~s** *nmpl* (*productos*) goods; **~ humano** human race; **~ chico** (*zarzuela*) Spanish operetta; **~s de punto** knitwear *sg*.

generosidad [xenerosi'ðað] *nf* generosity.

generoso, a [xene'roso, a] *adj* generous.

genético, a [xe'netiko, a] *adj* genetic ♦ *nf* genetics *sg*.

genial [xe'njal] *adj* inspired; (*idea*) brilliant; (*afable*) genial.

genialidad [xenjali'ðað] *nf* (*singularidad*) genius; (*acto genial*) stroke of genius; **es una ~ suya** it's one of his brilliant ideas.

genio ['xenjo] *nm* (*carácter*) nature, disposition; (*humor*) temper; (*facultad creadora*) genius; **mal ~** bad temper; **~ vivo** quick *o* hot temper; **de mal ~** bad-tempered.

genital [xeni'tal] *adj* genital ♦ *nm:* **~es** genitals, genital organs.

genocidio [xeno'θiðjo] *nm* genocide.

Génova ['xenoßa] *nf* Genoa.

genovés, esa [xeno'ßes, esa] *adj, nm/f* Genoese.

gente ['xente] *nf* (*personas*) people *pl*; (*raza*) race; (*nación*) nation; (*parientes*) relatives *pl*; **~ bien/baja** posh/lower-class people *pl*; **~ menuda** (*niños*) children *pl*; **es buena ~** (*fam: esp AM*) he's a good sort; **una ~ como Vd** (*AM*) a person like you.

gentil [xen'til] *adj* (*elegante*) graceful; (*encantador*) charming; (*REL*) gentile.

gentileza [xenti'leθa] *nf* grace; charm; (*cortesía*) courtesy; **por ~ de** by courtesy of.

gentilicio, a [xenti'liθjo, a] *adj* (*familiar*) family *cpd*.

gentío [xen'tio] *nm* crowd, throng.

gentuza [xen'tuθa] *nf* (*pey: plebe*) rabble; (: *chusma*) riffraff.

genuflexión [xenuflek'sjon] *nf* genuflexion.

genuino, a [xe'nwino, a] *adj* genuine.

GEO ['xeo] *nmpl abr* (*ESP.* = *Grupos Especiales de Operaciones*) *Special Police Units used in anti-terrorist operations etc.*

geografía [xeoɣra'fia] *nf* geography.

geográfico, a [xeo'ɣrafiko, a] *adj* geographic(al).

geología [xeolo'xia] *nf* geology.

geólogo, a [xe'oloɣo, a] *nm/f* geologist.

geometría [xeome'tria] *nf* geometry.

geométrico, a [xeo'metriko, a] *adj* geometric(al).

Georgia [xe'orxja] *nf* Georgia.

georgiano, a [xeor'xjano, a] *adj, nm/f* Georgian ♦ *nm* (*LING*) Georgian.

geranio [xe'ranjo] *nm* (*BOT*) geranium.

gerencia [xe'renθja] *nf* management; (*cargo*) post of manager; (*oficina*) manager's office.

gerente [xe'rente] *nm/f* (*supervisor*) manager; (*jefe*) director.

geriatría [xerja'tria] *nf* (*MED*) geriatrics *sg.*

geriátrico, a [xer'jatriko, a] *adj* geriatric.

germano, a [xer'mano, a] *adj* German, Germanic ♦ *nm/f* German.

germen ['xermen] *nm* germ.

germinar [xermi'nar] *vi* to germinate; (*brotar*) to sprout.

gerundense [xerun'dense] *adj* of *o* from Gerona ♦ *nm/f* native *o* inhabitant of Gerona.

gerundio [xe'rundjo] *nm* (*LING*) gerund.

gestación [xesta'θjon] *nf* gestation.

gesticulación [xestikula'θjon] *nf* (*ademán*) gesticulation; (*mueca*) grimace.

gesticular [xestiku'lar] *vi* (*con ademanes*) to gesture; (*con muecas*) to make faces.

gestión [xes'tjon] *nf* management; (*diligencia, acción*) negotiation; **hacer las gestiones preliminares** to do the groundwork; **~ de cartera** (*COM*) portfolio management; **~ financiera** (*COM*) financial management; **~ interna** (*INFORM*) housekeeping; **~ de personal** personnel management; **~ de riesgos** (*COM*) risk management.

gestionar [xestjo'nar] *vt* (*lograr*) to try to arrange; (*llevar*) to manage.

gesto ['xesto] *nm* (*mueca*) grimace; (*ademán*) gesture; **hacer ~s** to make faces.

gestor, a [xes'tor, a] *adj* managing ♦ *nm/f* manager; (*promotor*) promoter; (*agente*) business agent.

gestoría [xesto'ria] *nf agency undertaking business with government departments, insurance companies etc.*

Gibraltar [xißral'tar] *nm* Gibraltar.

gibraltareño, a [xißralta'reɲo, a] *adj* of *o* from Gibraltar ♦ *nm/f* native *o* inhabitant of Gibraltar.

gigante [xi'ɣante] *adj, nm/f* giant.

gijonés [xixo'nes, esa] *adj* of *o* from Gijón ♦ *nm/f* native *o* inhabitant of Gijón.

gilipollas [xili'poʎas] (*fam*) *adj inv* daft ♦ *nm/f* berk.

gilipollez [xilipo'ʎez] *nf* (*fam*): **es una ~** that's a load of crap (*!*); **decir gilipolleces** to talk crap (*!*).

gima ['xima] *etc vb* V **gemir.**

gimnasia [xim'nasja] *nf* gymnastics *pl*; **confundir la ~ con la magnesia** to get things mixed up.

gimnasio [xim'nasjo] *nm* gym(nasium).

gimnasta [xim'nasta] *nm/f* gymnast.

gimotear [ximote'ar] *vi* to whine, whimper; (*lloriquear*) to snivel.

Ginebra [xi'neßra] *n* Geneva.

ginebra [xi'neßra] *nf* gin.

ginecología [xinekolo'xia] *nf* gyn(a)ecology.

ginecológico, a [xineko'loxiko, a] *adj* gyn(a)ecological.

ginecólogo, a [xine'koloɣo, a] *nm/f* gyn(a)ecologist.

gira ['xira] *nf* tour, trip.

girar [xi'rar] *vt* (*dar la vuelta*) to turn (around); (: *rápidamente*) to spin; (*COM: giro postal*) to draw; (*comerciar: letra de cambio*) to issue ♦ *vi* to turn (round); (*dar vueltas*) to rotate; (*rápido*) to spin; **la conversación giraba en torno a las elecciones** the conversation centred on the election; **~ en descubierto** to overdraw.

giratorio, a [xira'torjo, a] *adj* (*gen*) revolving; (*puente*) swing *cpd*; (*silla*) swivel *cpd.*

giro ['xiro] *nm* (*movimiento*) turn, revolution; (*LING*) expression; (*COM*) draft; (*de sucesos*) trend, course; **~ bancario** money order, bank giro; **~ de existencias** (*COM*) stock turnover; **~ postal** postal order; **~ a la vista** (*COM*) sight draft.

gis [xis] *nm* (*AM*) chalk.

gitano, a [xi'tano, a] *adj, nm/f* gypsy.

glacial [gla'θjal] *adj* icy, freezing.

glaciar [gla'θjar] *nm* glacier.

glándula ['glandula] *nf* (*ANAT, BOT*) gland.

glicerina [gliθe'rina] *nf* (*TEC*) glycerin(e).

global [glo'ßal] *adj* (*en conjunto*) global; (*completo*) total; (*investigación*) full; (*suma*) lump *cpd.*

globo ['gloßo] *nm* (*esfera*) globe, sphere;

(*aeróstato, juguete*) balloon.

glóbulo ['gloβulo] *nm* globule; (*ANAT*) corpuscle; ~ **blanco/rojo** white/red corpuscle.

gloria ['glorja] *nf* glory; (*fig*) delight; (*delicia*) bliss.

glorieta [glo'rjeta] *nf* (*de jardín*) bower, arbour, (*US*) arbor; (*AUTO*) roundabout (*BRIT*), traffic circle (*US*); (*plaza redonda*) circus; (*cruce*) junction.

glorificar [glorifi'kar] *vt* (*enaltecer*) to glorify, praise.

glorifique [glori'fike] *etc vb* V **glorificar.**

glorioso, a [glo'rjoso, a] *adj* glorious.

glosa ['glosa] *nf* comment; (*explicación*) gloss.

glosar [glo'sar] *vt* (*comentar*) to comment on.

glosario [glo'sarjo] *nm* glossary.

glotón, ona [glo'ton, ona] *adj* gluttonous, greedy ♦ *nm/f* glutton.

glotonería [glotone'ria] *nf* gluttony, greed.

glúteo ['gluteo] *nm* (*fam: nalga*) buttock.

gnomo ['nomo] *nm* gnome.

gobernación [goβerna'θjon] *nf* government, governing; (*POL*) Provincial Governor's office; **Ministro de la G**~ Minister of the Interior, Home Secretary (*BRIT*).

gobernador, a [goβerna'ðor, a] *adj* governing ♦ *nm/f* governor.

gobernanta [goβer'nanta] *nf* (*esp AM: niñera*) governess.

gobernante [goβer'nante] *adj* governing ♦ *nm* ruler, governor ♦ *nf* (*en hotel etc*) housekeeper.

gobernar [goβer'nar] *vt* (*dirigir*) to guide, direct; (*POL*) to rule, govern ♦ *vi* to govern; (*NAUT*) to steer; ~ **mal** to misgovern.

gobierno [go'βjerno] *etc vb* V **gobernar** ♦ *nm* (*POL*) government; (*gestión*) management; (*dirección*) guidance, direction; (*NAUT*) steering; (*puesto*) governorship.

goce ['goθe] *etc vb* V **gozar** ♦ *nm* enjoyment.

godo, a ['goðo, a] *nm/f* Goth; (*AM pey*) Spaniard.

gol [gol] *nm* goal.

golear [gole'ar] *vt* (*marcar*) to score a goal against.

golf [golf] *nm* golf.

golfo, a ['golfo, a] *nm/f* (*pilluelo*) street urchin; (*vago*) tramp; (*gorrón*) loafer; (*gamberro*) lout ♦ *nm* (*GEO*) gulf ♦ *nf* (*fam: prostituta*) slut, whore, hooker (*US*).

golondrina [golon'drina] *nf* swallow.

golosina [golo'sina] *nf* titbit; (*dulce*) sweet.

goloso, a [go'loso, a] *adj* sweet-toothed; (*fam: glotón*) greedy.

golpe ['golpe] *nm* blow; (*de puño*) punch; (*de mano*) smack; (*de remo*) stroke; (*FÚTBOL*) kick; (*TENIS etc*) hit, shot; (*mala suerte*) misfortune; (*fam: atraco*) job, heist (*US*); (*fig: choque*) clash; **no dar** ~ to be bone idle; **de un** ~ with one blow; **de** ~ suddenly; ~ **(de estado)** coup (d'état); ~ **de gracia** coup de grâce (*tb fig*); ~ **de fortuna/maestro** stroke of luck/genius; **cerrar una puerta de** ~ to slam a door.

golpear [golpe'ar] *vt, vi* to strike, knock; (*asestar*) to beat; (*de puño*) to punch; (*golpetear*) to tap; (*mesa*) to bang.

golpista [gol'pista] *adj*: **intentona** ~ coup attempt ♦ *nm/f* participant in a coup (d'état).

golpiza [gol'pisa] *nf*: **dar una** ~ **a algn** (*AM*) to beat sb up.

goma ['goma] *nf* (*caucho*) rubber; (*elástico*) elastic; (*tira*) rubber *o* elastic (*BRIT*) band; (*fam: preservativo*) condom; (*droga*) hashish; (*explosivo*) plastic explosive; ~ **(de borrar)** eraser, rubber (*BRIT*); ~ **de mascar** chewing gum; ~ **de pegar** gum, glue.

goma-espuma [gomaes'puma] *nf* foam rubber.

gomina [go'mina] *nf* hair gel.

gomita [go'mita] *nf* rubber *o* elastic (*BRIT*) band.

góndola ['gondola] *nf* (*barco*) gondola; (*de tren*) goods wagon.

gordo, a ['gorðo, a] *adj* (*gen*) fat; (*persona*) plump; (*agua*) hard; (*fam*) enormous ♦ *nm/f* fat man *o* woman; **el (premio)** ~ (*en lotería*) first prize; ¡~! (*fam*) fatty!

gordura [gor'ðura] *nf* fat; (*corpulencia*) fatness, stoutness.

gorgojo [gor'xoxo] *nm* (*insecto*) grub.

gorgorito [gorɣ'rito] *nm* (*gorjeo*) trill, warble.

gorila [go'rila] *nm* gorilla; (*fam*) tough, thug; (*guardaespaldas*) bodyguard.

gorjear [gorxe'ar] *vi* to twitter, chirp.

gorjeo [gor'xeo] *nm* twittering, chirping.

gorra ['gorra] *nf* (*gen*) cap; (*de niño*) bonnet; (*militar*) bearskin; ~ **de montar/ de paño/de punto/de visera** riding/ cloth/knitted/peaked cap; **andar** *o* **ir** *o* **vivir de** ~ to sponge, scrounge; **entrar de** ~ (*fam*) to gatecrash.

gorrión [go'rrjon] *nm* sparrow.

gorro ['gorro] *nm* cap; (*de niño, mujer*) bonnet; **estoy hasta el** ~ I am fed up.

gorrón, ona [go'rron, ona] *nm* pebble;

(*TEC*) pivot ♦ *nm/f* scrounger.

gorronear [gorrone'ar] *vi* (*fam*) to sponge, scrounge.

gota ['gota] *nf* (*gen*) drop; (*de pintura*) blob; (*de sudor*) bead; (*MED*) gout; ~ **a** ~ drop by drop; **caer a** ~**s** to drip.

gotear [gote'ar] *vi* to drip; (*escurrir*) to trickle; (*salirse*) to leak; (*cirio*) to gutter; (*lloviznar*) to drizzle.

gotera [go'tera] *nf* leak.

gótico, a ['gotiko, a] *adj* Gothic.

gozar [go'θar] *vi* to enjoy o.s.; ~ **de** (*disfrutar*) to enjoy; (*poseer*) to possess; ~ **de buena salud** to enjoy good health.

gozne ['goθne] *nm* hinge.

gozo ['goθo] *nm* (*alegría*) joy; (*placer*) pleasure; **¡mi** ~ **en el pozo!** that's torn it!, just my luck!

g.p. *nm abr* (= *giro postal*) m.o.

gr. *abr* (= *gramo(s)*) g.

grabación [graβa'θjon] *nf* recording.

grabado, a [gra'βaðo, a] *adj* (*MUS*) recorded; (*en cinta*) taped, on tape ♦ *nm* print, engraving; ~ **al agua fuerte** etching; ~ **al aguatinta** aquatint; ~ **en cobre** copperplate; ~ **en madera** woodcut; ~ **rupestre** rock carving.

grabador, a [graβa'ðor, a] *nm/f* engraver ♦ *nf* tape-recorder; ~**a de cassettes** cassette recorder.

grabar [gra'βar] *vt* to engrave; (*discos, cintas*) to record; (*impresionar*) to impress.

gracejo [gra'θexo] *nm* (*humor*) wit, humour; (*elegancia*) grace.

gracia ['graθja] *nf* (*encanto*) grace, gracefulness; (*REL*) grace; (*chiste*) joke; (*humor*) humour, wit; **¡muchas** ~**s!** thanks very much!; ~**s a** thanks to; **tener** ~ (*chiste etc*) to be funny; **¡qué** ~**!** how funny!; (*irónico*) what a nerve!; **no me hace** ~ (*broma*) it's not funny; (*plan*) I am not too keen; **con** ~**s anticipadas/ repetidas** thanking you in advance/ again; **dar las** ~**s a algn por algo** to thank sb for sth.

grácil ['graθil] *adj* (*sutil*) graceful; (*delgado*) slender; (*delicado*) delicate.

gracioso, a [gra'θjoso, a] *adj* (*garboso*) graceful; (*chistoso*) funny; (*cómico*) comical; (*agudo*) witty; (*título*) gracious ♦ *nm/f* (*TEAT*) comic character, fool; **su graciosa Majestad** His/Her Gracious Majesty.

grada ['graða] *nf* (*de escalera*) step; (*de anfiteatro*) tier, row; ~**s** *nfpl* (*de estadio*) terraces.

gradación [graða'θjon] *nf* gradation; (*serie*) graded series.

gradería [graðe'ria] *nf* (*gradas*) (flight of) steps *pl*; (*de anfiteatro*) tiers *pl*, rows *pl*; ~ **cubierta** covered stand.

grado ['graðo] *nm* degree; (*etapa*) stage, step; (*nivel*) rate; (*de parentesco*) order of lineage; (*de aceite, vino*) grade; (*grada*) step; (*ESCOL*) class, year, grade (*US*); (*UNIV*) degree; (*LING*) degree of comparison; (*MIL*) rank; **de buen** ~ willingly; **en sumo** ~, **en** ~ **superlativo** in the highest degree.

graduación [graðwa'θjon] *nf* (*acto*) gradation; (*clasificación*) rating; (*del alcohol*) proof, strength; (*ESCOL*) graduation; (*MIL*) rank; **de alta** ~ high-ranking.

gradual [gra'ðwal] *adj* gradual.

graduar [gra'ðwar] *vt* (*gen*) to graduate; (*medir*) to gauge; (*TEC*) to calibrate; (*UNIV*) to confer a degree on; (*MIL*) to commission; ~**se** *vr* to graduate; ~**se la vista** to have one's eyes tested.

grafía [gra'fia] *nf* (*escritura*) writing; (*ortografía*) spelling.

gráfico, a ['grafiko, a] *adj* graphic; (*fig: vívido*) vivid, lively ♦ *nm* diagram ♦ *nf* graph; ~ **de barras** (*COM*) bar chart; ~ **de sectores** *o* **de tarta** (*COM*) pie chart; ~**s** *nmpl* (*tb INFORM*) graphics; ~**s empresariales** (*COM*) business graphics.

grafito [gra'fito] *nm* (*TEC*) graphite, black lead.

grafología [grafolo'xia] *nf* graphology.

gragea [gra'xea] *nf* (*MED*) pill; (*caramelo*) dragée.

grajo ['graxo] *nm* rook.

Gral. *abr* (*MIL*: = *General*) Gen.

gramático, a [gra'matiko, a] *nm/f* (*persona*) grammarian ♦ *nf* grammar.

gramo ['gramo] *nm* gramme (*BRIT*), gram (*US*).

gran [gran] *adj V* **grande**.

grana ['grana] *nf* (*BOT*) seedling; (*color*) scarlet; **ponerse como la** ~ to go as red as a beetroot.

granada [gra'naða] *nf* pomegranate; (*MIL*) grenade; ~ **de mano** hand grenade; ~ **de metralla** shrapnel shell.

granadilla [grana'ðiʎa] *nf* (*AM*) passion fruit.

granadino, a [grana'ðino, a] *adj* of *o* from Granada ♦ *nm/f* native *o* inhabitant of Granada ♦ *nf* grenadine.

granar [gra'nar] *vi* to seed.

granate [gra'nate] *adj inv* maroon ♦ *nm* garnet; (*color*) maroon.

Gran Bretaña [grambre'taɲa] *nf* Great

Britain.
Gran Canaria [granka'narja] *nf* Grand
Canary.
grancanario, a [granka'narjo, a] *adj* of *o*
from Grand Canary ♦ *nm/f* native *o*
inhabitant of Grand Canary.
grande ['grande], **gran** *adj* (*de tamaño*) big,
large; (*alto*) tall; (*distinguido*) great;
(*impresionante*) grand ♦ *nm* grandee;
¿cómo es de ~? how big is it?, what size
is it?; **pasarlo en ~** to have a
tremendous time.
grandeza [gran'deθa] *nf* greatness;
(*tamaño*) bigness; (*esplendidez*)
grandness; (*nobleza*) nobility.
grandioso, a [gran'djoso, a] *adj*
magnificent, grand.
grandullón, ona [granðu'ʎon, ona] *adj*
oversized.
granel [gra'nel] *nm* (*montón*) heap; **a ~**
(*COM*) in bulk.
granero [gra'nero] *nm* granary, barn.
granice [gra'niθe] *etc vb V* **granizar.**
granito [gra'nito] *nm* (*AGR*) small grain;
(*roca*) granite.
granizada [grani'θaða] *nf* hailstorm; (*fig*)
hail; **una ~ de balas** a hail of bullets.
granizado [grani'θaðo] *nm* iced drink; **~
de café** iced coffee.
granizar [grani'θar] *vi* to hail.
granizo [gra'niθo] *nm* hail.
granja ['granxa] *nf* (*gen*) farm; **~ avícola**
chicken *o* poultry farm.
granjear [granxe'ar] *vt* (*cobrar*) to earn;
(*ganar*) to win; (*avanzar*) to gain; **~se** *vr*
(*amistad etc*) to gain for o.s.
granjero, a [gran'xero, a] *nm/f* farmer.
grano ['grano] *nm* grain; (*semilla*) seed;
(*baya*) berry; (*MED*) pimple, spot;
(*partícula*) particle; (*punto*) speck; **~s**
nmpl cereals; **~ de café** coffee bean; **ir al
~** to get to the point.
granuja [gra'nuxa] *nm* rogue; (*golfillo*)
urchin.
grapa ['grapa] *nf* staple; (*TEC*) clamp;
(*sujetador*) clip, fastener; (*ARQ*) cramp.
grapadora [grapa'ðora] *nf* stapler.
GRAPO ['grapo] *nm abr* (*ESP POL*) = Grupo
de Resistencia Antifascista Primero de
Octubre.
grasa ['grasa] *nf V* **graso.**
grasiento, a [gra'sjento, a] *adj* greasy; (*de
aceite*) oily; (*mugriento*) filthy.
graso, a ['graso, a] *adj* fatty; (*aceitoso*)
greasy, oily ♦ *nf* (*gen*) grease; (*de cocina*)
fat, lard; (*sebo*) suet; (*mugre*) filth;
(*AUTO*) oil; (*lubricante*) grease; **~ de
ballena** blubber; **~ de pescado** fish oil.

grasoso, a [gra'soso, a] *adj* (*AM*) greasy,
sticky.
gratificación [gratifika'θjon] *nf* (*propina*)
tip; (*aguinaldo*) gratuity; (*bono*) bonus;
(*recompensa*) reward.
gratificar [gratifi'kar] *vt* (*dar propina*) to
tip; (*premiar*) to reward; **"se gratificará"**
"a reward is offered".
gratifique [grati'fike] *etc vb V* **gratificar.**
gratinar [grati'nar] *vt* to cook au gratin.
gratis ['gratis] *adv* free, for nothing.
gratitud [grati'tuð] *nf* gratitude.
grato, a ['grato, a] *adj* (*agradable*) pleasant,
agreeable; (*bienvenido*) welcome; **nos es
~ informarle que ...** we are pleased to
inform you that ....
gratuito, a [gra'twito, a] *adj* (*gratis*) free;
(*sin razón*) gratuitous; (*acusación*)
unfounded.
grava ['graßa] *nf* (*guijos*) gravel; (*piedra
molida*) crushed stone; (*en carreteras*)
road metal.
gravamen [gra'ßamen] *nm* (*carga*) burden;
(*impuesto*) tax; **libre de ~** (*ECON*) free
from encumbrances.
gravar [gra'ßar] *vt* to burden; (*COM*) to tax;
(*ECON*) to assess for tax; **~ con
impuestos** to burden with taxes.
grave ['graße] *adj* heavy; (*fig, MED*) grave,
serious; (*importante*) important; (*herida*)
severe; (*MUS*) low, deep; (*LING: acento*)
grave; **estar ~** to be seriously ill.
gravedad [graße'ðað] *nf* gravity; (*fig*)
seriousness; (*grandeza*) importance;
(*dignidad*) dignity; (*MUS*) depth.
grávido, a ['graßiðo, a] *adj* (*preñada*)
pregnant.
gravilla [gra'ßiʎa] *nf* gravel.
gravitación [graßita'θjon] *nf* gravitation.
gravitar [graßi'tar] *vi* to gravitate; **~ sobre**
to rest on.
gravoso, a [gra'ßoso, a] *adj* (*pesado*)
burdensome; (*costoso*) costly.
graznar [graθ'nar] *vi* (*cuervo*) to squawk;
(*pato*) to quack; (*hablar ronco*) to croak.
graznido [graθ'niðo] *nm* squawk; croak.
Grecia ['greθja] *nf* Greece.
gregario, a [gre'ɣarjo, a] *adj* gregarious;
instinto ~ herd instinct.
gremio ['gremjo] *nm* (*asociación*)
professional association, guild.
greña ['greɲa] *nf* (*cabellos*) shock of hair;
(*maraña*) tangle; **andar a la ~** to bicker,
squabble.
greñudo, a [gre'ɲuðo, a] *adj* (*persona*)
dishevelled; (*hair*) tangled.
gresca ['greska] *nf* uproar; (*trifulca*) row.
griego, a ['grjeɣo, a] *adj* Greek, Grecian

♦ *nm/f* Greek ♦ *nm* (*LING*) Greek.

grieta ['grjeta] *nf* crack; (*hendidura*) chink; (*quiebra*) crevice; (*MED*) chap; (*POL*) rift.

grifa ['grifa] *nf* (*fam: droga*) marijuana.

grifo ['grifo] *nm* tap (*BRIT*), faucet (*US*); (*AM*) petrol (*BRIT*) o gas (*US*) station.

grilletes [gri'ʎetes] *nmpl* fetters, shackles.

grillo ['griʎo] *nm* (*ZOOL*) cricket; (*BOT*) shoot; ~**s** *nmpl* shackles, irons.

grima ['grima] *nf* (*horror*) loathing; (*desagrado*) reluctance; (*desazón*) uneasiness; **me da** ~ it makes me sick.

gringo, a ['gringo, a] (*AM*) *adj* (*pey: extranjero*) foreign; (: *norteamericano*) Yankee; (*idioma*) foreign ♦ *nm/f* foreigner; Yank.

gripa ['gripa] *nf* (*AM*) flu, influenza.

gripe ['gripe] *nf* flu, influenza.

gris [gris] *adj* grey.

grisáceo, a [gri'saθeo, a] *adj* greyish.

grisoso, a [gri'soso, a] *adj* (*AM*) greyish, grayish (*esp US*).

gritar [gri'tar] *vt, vi* to shout, yell; ¡**no grites!** stop shouting!

grito ['grito] *nm* shout, yell; (*de horror*) scream; **a** ~ **pelado** at the top of one's voice; **poner el** ~ **en el cielo** to scream blue murder; **es el último** ~ (*de moda*) it's all the rage.

groenlandés, esa [groenlan'des, esa] *adj* Greenland *cpd* ♦ *nm/f* Greenlander.

Groenlandia [groen'landja] *nf* Greenland.

grosella [gro'seʎa] *nf* (red)currant; ~ **negra** blackcurrant.

grosería [grose'ria] *nf* (*actitud*) rudeness; (*comentario*) vulgar comment; (*palabrota*) swearword.

grosero, a [gro'sero, a] *adj* (*poco cortés*) rude, bad-mannered; (*ordinario*) vulgar, crude.

grosor [gro'sor] *nm* thickness.

grotesco, a [gro'tesko, a] *adj* grotesque; (*absurdo*) bizarre.

grúa ['grua] *nf* (*TEC*) crane; (*de petróleo*) derrick; ~ **corrediza o móvil/de pescante/puente/de torre** travelling/jib/overhead/tower crane.

grueso, a ['grweso, a] *adj* thick; (*persona*) stout; (*calidad*) coarse ♦ *nm* bulk; (*espesor*) thickness; (*densidad*) density; (*de gente*) main body, mass; **el** ~ **de** the bulk of.

grulla ['gruʎa] *nf* (*ZOOL*) crane.

grumete [gru'mete] *nm* (*NAUT*) cabin o ship's boy.

grumo ['grumo] *nm* (*coágulo*) clot, lump; (*masa*) dollop.

gruñido [gru'ɲiðo] *nm* grunt, growl; (*fig*) grumble.

gruñir [gru'ɲir] *vi* (*animal*) to grunt, growl; (*fam*) to grumble.

gruñón, ona [gru'ɲon, ona] *adj* grumpy ♦ *nm/f* grumbler.

grupa ['grupa] *nf* (*ZOOL*) rump.

grupo ['grupo] *nm* group; (*TEC*) unit, set; (*de árboles*) cluster; ~ **sanguíneo** blood group.

gruta ['gruta] *nf* grotto.

Gta. *abr* (*AUTO*) = **Glorieta**.

guaca ['gwaka] *nf* Indian tomb.

guacamole [gwaka'mole] *nm* (*AM*) avocado salad.

guachimán [gwatʃi'man] *nm* (*AM*) night watchman.

guadalajareño, a [gwaðalaxa'reɲo, a] *adj* of o from Guadalajara ♦ *nm/f* native o inhabitant of Guadalajara.

Guadalquivir [gwaðalki'ßir] *nm*: **el (Río)** ~ the Guadalquivir.

guadaña [gwa'ðaɲa] *nf* scythe.

guadañar [gwaða'ɲar] *vt* to scythe, mow.

Guadiana [gwa'ðjana] *nm*: **el (Río)** ~ the Guadiana.

guagua ['gwaɣwa] *nf* (*AM, Canarias*) bus; (*AM: criatura*) baby.

guajolote [gwajo'lote] *nm* (*AM*) turkey.

guano ['gwano] *nm* guano.

guantada [gwan'taða] *nf*, **guantazo** [gwan'taθo] *nm* slap.

guante ['gwante] *nm* glove; **se ajusta como un** ~ it fits like a glove; **echar el** ~ **a algn** to catch hold of sb; (*fig: policía*) to catch sb.

guapo, a ['gwapo, a] *adj* good-looking; (*mujer*) pretty, attractive; (*hombre*) handsome; (*elegante*) smart ♦ *nm* lover, gallant; (*AM fam*) tough guy, bully.

guaraní [gwara'ni] *adj, nm/f* Guarani ♦ *nm* (*moneda*) monetary unit of Paraguay.

guarapo [gwa'rapo] *nm* (*AM*) fermented cane juice.

guarda ['gwarða] *nm/f* (*persona*) warden, keeper ♦ *nf* (*acto*) guarding; (*custodia*) custody; (*TIP*) flyleaf, endpaper; ~ **forestal** game warden.

guarda(a)gujas [gwarða'ɣuxas] *nm inv* (*FERRO*) switchman.

guardabarros [gwarða'ßarros] *nm inv* mudguard (*BRIT*), fender (*US*).

guardabosques [gwarða'ßoskes] *nm inv* gamekeeper.

guardacoches [gwarða'kotʃes] *nm/f inv* (*celador*) parking attendant.

guardacostas [gwarða'kostas] *nm inv* coastguard vessel.

guardador, a [gwarða'ðor, a] *adj* protective; (*tacaño*) mean, stingy ♦ *nm/f* guardian, protector.

guardaespaldas [gwardaes'paldas] *nm/f inv* bodyguard.

guardameta [gwarða'meta] *nm* goalkeeper.

guardapolvo [gwarda'polβo] *nm* dust cover; (*prenda de vestir*) overalls *pl*.

guardar [gwar'ðar] *vt* (*gen*) to keep; (*vigilar*) to guard, watch over; (*conservar*) to put away; (*dinero: ahorrar*) to save; (*promesa etc*) to keep; (*ley*) to observe; (*rencor*) to bear, harbour; (*INFORM: archivo*) to save; ~**se** *vr* (*preservarse*) to protect o.s.; ~**se de algo** (*evitar*) to avoid sth; (*abstenerse*) to refrain from sth; ~**se de hacer algo** to be careful not to do sth; **guardársela a algn** to have it in for sb.

guardarropa [gwarða'rropa] *nm* (*armario*) wardrobe; (*en establecimiento público*) cloakroom.

guardería [gwarðe'ria] *nf* nursery.

guardia ['gwarðja] *nf* (*MIL*) guard; (*cuidado*) care, custody ♦ *nm/f* guard; (*policía*) policeman/woman; **estar de** ~ to be on guard; **montar** ~ to mount guard; **la G**~ **Civil** the Civil Guard; ~ **municipal** *o* **urbana** municipal police; **un** ~ **civil** a Civil Guard(sman); **un(a)** ~ **nacional** a policeman/woman; ~ **urbano** traffic policeman.

The **Guardia Civil** is a branch of the **Ejército de Tierra** (*Army*) run along military lines, which fulfils a policing role outside large urban communities and is under the joint control of the Spanish Ministry of Defence and the Ministry of the Interior. It is also known as **La Benemérita**.

---

guardián, ana [gwar'ðjan, ana] *nm/f* (*gen*) guardian, keeper.

guarecer [gware'θer] *vt* (*proteger*) to protect; (*abrigar*) to shelter; ~**se** *vr* to take refuge.

guarezca [gwa're θka] *etc vb V* **guarecer**.

guarida [gwa'riða] *nf* (*de animal*) den, lair; (*de persona*) haunt, hideout; (*refugio*) refuge.

guarnecer [gwarne'θer] *vt* (*equipar*) to provide; (*adornar*) to adorn; (*TEC*) to reinforce.

guarnezca [gwar'neθka] *etc vb V* **guarnecer**.

guarnición [gwarni'θjon] *nf* (*de vestimenta*) trimming; (*de piedra*) mount; (*CULIN*) garnish; (*arneses*) harness; (*MIL*) garrison.

guarrada [gwa'rraða] *nf* (*fam*) (*cosa sucia*) dirty mess; (*acto o dicho obsceno*) obscenity; **hacer una** ~ **a algn** to do the dirty on sb.

guarrería [gwarre'ria] *nf* = **guarrada**.

guarro, a ['gwarro, a] *nm/f* (*fam*) pig; (*fig*) dirty *o* slovenly person.

guasa ['gwasa] *nf* joke; **con** *o* **de** ~ jokingly, in fun.

guasón, ona [gwa'son, ona] *adj* witty; (*bromista*) joking ♦ *nm/f* wit; joker.

Guatemala [gwate'mala] *nf* Guatemala.

guatemalteco, a [gwatemal'teko, a] *adj*, *nm/f* Guatemalan.

guateque [gwa'teke] *nm* (*fiesta*) party, binge.

guay [gwai] *adj* (*fam*) super, great.

guayaba [gwa'jaβa] *nf* (*BOT*) guava.

Guayana [gwa'jana] *nf* Guyana, Guiana.

gubernamental [guβernamen'tal], **gubernativo, a** [guβerna'tiβo, a] *adj* governmental.

guedeja [ge'ðexa] *nf* long hair.

guerra ['gerra] *nf* war; (*arte*) warfare; (*pelea*) struggle; ~ **atómica/bacteriológica/nuclear/de guerrillas** atomic/germ/nuclear/guerrilla warfare; **Primera/Segunda G**~ **Mundial** First/Second World War; ~ **de precios** (*COM*) price war; ~ **civil/fría** civil/cold war; ~ **a muerte** fight to the death; **de** ~ military, war *cpd*; **estar en** ~ to be at war; **dar** ~ to be annoying.

guerrear [gerre'ar] *vi* to wage war.

guerrero, a [ge'rrero, a] *adj* fighting; (*carácter*) warlike ♦ *nm/f* warrior.

guerrilla [ge'rriʎa] *nf* guerrilla warfare; (*tropas*) guerrilla band *o* group.

guerrillero, a [gerri'ʎero, a] *nm/f* guerrilla (fighter); (*contra invasor*) partisan.

gueto ['geto] *nm* ghetto.

guía ['gia] *etc vb V* **guiar** ♦ *nm/f* (*persona*) guide ♦ *nf* (*libro*) guidebook; (*manual*) handbook; (*INFORM*) prompt; ~ **de ferrocarriles** railway timetable; ~ **telefónica** telephone directory; ~ **del turista/del viajero** tourist/traveller's guide.

guiar [gi'ar] *vt* to guide, direct; (*dirigir*) to lead; (*orientar*) to advise; (*AUTO*) to steer; ~**se** *vr*: ~**se por** to be guided by.

guijarro [gi'xarro] *nm* pebble.

guillotina [giʎo'tina] *nf* guillotine.

guinda ['ginda] *nf* morello cherry; (*licor*) cherry liqueur.

guindar [gin'dar] *vt* to hoist; (*fam: robar*) to nick.

guindilla [gin'diʎa] *nf* chil(l)i pepper.

Guinea [gi'nea] *nf* Guinea.

guineo, a [gi'neo, a] *adj* Guinea *cpd*,
Guinean ♦ *nm/f* Guinean.
guiñapo [gi'ɲapo] *nm* (*harapo*) rag;
(*persona*) rogue.
guiñar [gi'ɲar] *vi* to wink.
guiño ['giɲo] *nm* (*parpadeo*) wink; (*muecas*)
grimace; **hacer ~s a** (*enamorados*) to
make eyes at.
guiñol [gi'ɲol] *nm* (*TEAT*) puppet theatre.
guión [gi'on] *nm* (*LING*) hyphen, dash;
(*esquema*) summary, outline; (*CINE*)
script.
guionista [gjo'nista] *nm/f* scriptwriter.
guipuzcoano, a [gipuθko'ano, a] *adj* of *o*
from Guipúzcoa ♦ *nm/f* native *o*
inhabitant of Guipúzcoa.
guiri ['giri] *nm/f* (*fam, pey*) foreigner.
guirigay [giri'gai] *nm* (*griterío*) uproar;
(*confusión*) chaos.
guirnalda [gir'nalda] *nf* garland.
guisa ['gisa] *nf*: **a ~ de** as, like.
guisado [gi'saðo] *nm* stew.
guisante [gi'sante] *nm* pea.
guisar [gi'sar] *vt, vi* to cook; (*fig*) to
arrange.
guiso ['giso] *nm* cooked dish.
guita ['gita] *nf* twine; (*fam: dinero*) dough.
guitarra [gi'tarra] *nf* guitar.
guitarrista [gita'rrista] *nm/f* guitarist.
gula ['gula] *nf* gluttony, greed.
gusano [gu'sano] *nm* maggot, worm; (*de
mariposa, polilla*) caterpillar; (*fig*) worm;
(*ser despreciable*) creep; **~ de seda** silk-
worm.
gustar [gus'tar] *vt* to taste, sample ♦ *vi* to
please, be pleasing; **~ de algo** to like *o*
enjoy sth; **me gustan las uvas** I like
grapes; **le gusta nadar** she likes *o* enjoys
swimming; **¿gusta Ud?** would you like
some?; **como Ud guste** as you wish.
gusto ['gusto] *nm* (*sentido, sabor*) taste;
(*agrado*) liking; (*placer*) pleasure; **tiene
un ~ amargo** it has a bitter taste; **tener
buen ~** to have good taste; **sobre ~s no
hay nada escrito** there's no accounting
for tastes; **de buen/mal ~** in good/bad
taste; **sentirse a ~** to feel at ease;
¡mucho o tanto ~ (en conocerle)! how do
you do?, pleased to meet you; **el ~ es
mío** the pleasure is mine; **tomar ~ a** to
take a liking to; **con ~** willingly, gladly.
gustoso, a [gus'toso, a] *adj* (*sabroso*) tasty;
(*agradable*) pleasant; (*con voluntad*)
willing, glad; **lo hizo ~** he did it gladly.
gutural [gutu'ral] *adj* guttural.
guyanés, esa [gwaja'nes, esa] *adj, nm/f*
Guyanese.

H h

H, h ['atʃe] *nf* (*letra*) H, h; **H de Historia** H
for Harry (*BRIT*) *o* How (*US*).
H. *abr* (*QUÍMICA*: = *Hidrógeno*) H;
(= *Hectárea(s)*) ha.; (*COM*: = *Haber*) cr.
h. *abr* (= *hora(s)*) h., hr(s).; (= *hacia*) c.
♦ *nmpl abr* (= *habitantes*) pop.
ha [a] *vb* V **haber**.
Ha. *abr* (= *Hectárea(s)*) ha.
haba ['aßa] *nf* bean; **son ~s contadas** it
goes without saying; **en todas partes
cuecen ~s** it's the same (story) the
whole world over.
Habana [a'ßana] *nf*: **la ~** Havana.
habanero, a [aßa'nero, a] *adj* of *o* from
Havana ♦ *nm/f* native *o* inhabitant of
Havana ♦ *nf* (*MUS*) habanera.
habano [a'ßano] *nm* Havana cigar.
habeas corpus [a'ßeas'korpus] *nm* (*LAW*)
habeas corpus.

━━━━━━━ *PALABRA CLAVE*

haber [a'ßer] *vb aux* **1** (*tiempos compuestos*)
to have; **había comido** I have/had eaten;
antes/después de ~lo visto before
seeing/after seeing *o* having seen it; **si
lo hubiera sabido habría ido** if I had
known I would have gone
2: **¡~lo dicho antes!** you should have
said so before!; **¿habráse visto (cosa
igual)?** have you ever seen anything like
it?
3: **~ de: he de hacerlo** I must do it; **ha de
llegar mañana** it should arrive
tomorrow
♦ *vb impers* **1** (*existencia: sg*) there is; (*: pl*)
there are; **hay un hermano/dos
hermanos** there is one brother/there are
two brothers; **¿cuánto hay de aquí a
Sucre?** how far is it from here to
Sucre?; **habrá unos 4 grados** it must be
about 4 degrees; **no hay quien te
entienda** there's no understanding you
2 (*obligación*): **hay que hacer algo**
something must be done; **hay que
apuntarlo para acordarse** you have to
write it down to remember
3: **¡hay que ver!** well I never!
4: **¡no hay de o por (AM) qué!** don't

mention it!, not at all!
5: ¿qué hay? (*¿qué pasa?*) what's up?,
what's the matter?; (*¿qué tal?*) how's it
going?
♦ **~se** *vr*: **habérselas con algn** to have it
out with sb
♦ *vt*: **he aquí unas sugerencias** here are
some suggestions; **todos los inventos
habidos y por ~** all inventions present
and future; **en el encuentro habido ayer**
in yesterday's game
♦ *nm* (*en cuenta*) credit side; **~es** *nmpl*
assets; **¿cuánto tengo en el ~?** how
much do I have in my account?; **tiene
varias novelas en su ~** he has several
novels to his credit.

habichuela [aβi'tʃwela] *nf* kidney bean.
hábil ['aβil] *adj* (*listo*) clever, smart; (*capaz*)
fit, capable; (*experto*) expert; **día ~**
working day.
habilidad [aβili'ðað] *nf* (*gen*) skill, ability;
(*inteligencia*) cleverness; (*destreza*)
expertness, expertise; (*JUR*)
competence; **~ (para)** fitness (for); **tener
~ manual** to be clever with one's hands.
habilitación [aβilita'θjon] *nf* qualification;
(*colocación de muebles*) fitting out;
(*financiamiento*) financing; (*oficina*)
paymaster's office.
habilitado [aβili'taðo] *nm* paymaster.
habilitar [aβili'tar] *vt* to qualify; (*autorizar*)
to authorize; (*capacitar*) to enable; (*dar
instrumentos*) to equip; (*financiar*) to
finance.
hábilmente [aβil'mente] *adv* skilfully,
expertly.
habitable [aβi'taβle] *adj* inhabitable.
habitación [aβita'θjon] *nf* (*cuarto*) room;
(*casa*) dwelling, abode; (*BIO: morada*)
habitat; **~ sencilla** *o* **individual** single
room; **~ doble** *o* **de matrimonio** double
room.
habitante [aβi'tante] *nm/f* inhabitant.
habitar [aβi'tar] *vt* (*residir en*) to inhabit;
(*ocupar*) to occupy ♦ *vi* to live.
hábitat, *pl* **hábitats** ['aβitat, 'aβitats] *nm*
habitat.
hábito ['aβito] *nm* habit; **tener el ~ de
hacer algo** to be in the habit of doing
sth.
habitual [aβi'twal] *adj* habitual.
habituar [aβi'twar] *vt* to accustom; **~se** *vr*:
~se a to get used to.
habla ['aβla] *nf* (*capacidad de hablar*)
speech; (*idioma*) language; (*dialecto*)
dialect; **perder el ~** to become
speechless; **de ~ francesa** French-

speaking; **estar al ~** to be in contact;
(*TELEC*) to be on the line; **¡González al ~!**
(*TELEC*) Gonzalez speaking!
hablador, a [aβla'ðor, a] *adj* talkative
♦ *nm/f* chatterbox.
habladuría [aβlaðu'ria] *nf* rumour; **~s** *nfpl*
gossip *sg*.
hablante [a'βlante] *adj* speaking ♦ *nm/f*
speaker.
hablar [a'βlar] *vt* to speak, talk ♦ *vi* to
speak; **~se** *vr* to speak to each other; **~
con** to speak to; **¡hable!**, **¡puede ~!**
(*TELEC*) you're through!; **de eso ni ~** no
way, that's not on; **~ alto/bajo/claro** to
speak loudly/quietly/plainly *o* bluntly; **~
de** to speak of *o* about; **"se habla inglés"**
"English spoken here"; **no se hablan**
they are not on speaking terms.
habré [a'βre] *etc* *vb* V **haber.**
hacedor, a [aθe'ðor, a] *nm/f* maker.
hacendado, a [aθen'daðo, a] *adj* property-
owning ♦ *nm* (*terrateniente*) large
landowner.
hacendoso, a [aθen'doso, a] *adj*
industrious, hard-working.

═══════════════════ *PALABRA CLAVE*

hacer [a'θer] *vt* **1** (*fabricar, producir,
conseguir*) to make; (*construir*) to build; **~
una película/un ruido** to make a film/
noise; **el guisado lo hice yo** I made *o*
cooked the stew; **~ amigos** to make
friends
2 (*ejecutar: trabajo etc*) to do; **~ la colada**
to do the washing; **~ la comida** to do the
cooking; **¿qué haces?** what are you
doing?; **¡eso está hecho!** you've got it!;
~ el tonto/indio to act the fool/clown; **~
el malo** *o* **el papel del malo** (*TEAT*) to play
the villain
3 (*estudios, algunos deportes*) to do; **~
español/económicas** to do *o* study
Spanish/economics; **~ yoga/gimnasia** to
do yoga/go to gym
4 (*transformar, incidir en*): **esto lo hará
más difícil** this will make it more
difficult; **salir te hará sentir mejor** going
out will make you feel better; **te hace
más joven** it makes you look younger
5 (*cálculo*): **2 y 2 hacen 4** 2 and 2 make 4;
éste hace 100 this one makes 100
6 (+*sub*): **esto hará que ganemos** this
will make us win; **harás que no quiera
venir** you'll stop him wanting to come
7 (*como sustituto de vb*) to do; **él bebió y
yo hice lo mismo** he drank and I did
likewise
8: no hace más que criticar all he does is

criticize

◆ *vb semi-aux*: ~ +*infin* **1** (*directo*): **les hice
venir** I made *o* had them come; ~
trabajar a los demás to get others to
work

2 (*por intermedio de otros*): ~ **reparar
algo** to get sth repaired

◆ *vi* **1**: **haz como que no lo sabes** act as if
you don't know; **hiciste bien en
decírmelo** you were right to tell me

2 (*ser apropiado*): **si os hace** if it's alright
with you

3: ~ **de**: ~ **de madre para uno** to be like a
mother to sb; (*TEAT*): ~ **de Otelo** to play
Othello; **la tabla hace de mesa** the board
does as a table

◆ *vb impers* **1**: **hace calor/frío** it's hot/cold;
V tb **bueno; sol; tiempo**

2 (*tiempo*): **hace 3 años** 3 years ago;
hace un mes que voy/no voy I've been
going/I haven't been for a month; **no le
veo desde hace mucho** I haven't seen
him for a long time

3: **¿cómo has hecho para llegar tan
rápido?** how did you manage to get here
so quickly?

◆ ~**se** *vr* **1** (*volverse*) to become; **se
hicieron amigos** they became friends;
~**se viejo** to get *o* grow old; **se hace
tarde** it's getting late

2: ~**se algo: me hice un traje** I got a suit
made

3 (*acostumbrarse*): ~**se a** to get used to;
~**se a la idea** to get used to the idea

4: **se hace con huevos y leche** it's made
out of eggs and milk; **eso no se hace**
that's not done

5 (*obtener*): ~**se de** *o* **con algo** to get
hold of sth

6 (*fingirse*): ~**se el sordo/sueco** to turn a
deaf ear/pretend to not to notice.

hacha ['atʃa] *nf* axe; (*antorcha*) torch.
hachazo [a'tʃaθo] *nm* axe blow.
hache ['atʃe] *nf* (the letter) H; **llámele
usted** ~ call it what you will.
hachís [a'tʃis] *nm* hashish.
hacia ['aθja] *prep* (*en dirección de, actitud*)
towards; (*cerca de*) near; ~ **arriba/abajo**
up(wards)/down(wards); ~ **mediodía**
about noon.
hacienda [a'θjenda] *nf* (*propiedad*)
property; (*finca*) farm; (*AM*) ranch; ~
pública public finance; **(Ministerio de)
H**~ Exchequer (*BRIT*), Treasury
Department (*US*).
hacinar [aθi'nar] *vt* to pile (up); (*AGR*) to
stack; (*fig*) to overcrowd.

hada ['aða] *nf* fairy; ~ **madrina** fairy
godmother.
hado ['aðo] *nm* fate, destiny.
haga ['aɣa] *etc vb V* **hacer.**
Haití [ai'ti] *nm* Haiti.
haitiano, a [ai'tjano, a] *adj, nm/f* Haitian.
hala ['ala] *excl* (*vamos*) come on!; (*anda*)
get on with it!
halagar [ala'ɣar] *vt* (*lisonjear*) to flatter.
halago [a'laɣo] *nm* (*adulación*) flattery.
halague [a'laɣe] *etc vb V* **halagar.**
halagüeño, a [ala'ɣweɲo, a] *adj* flattering.
halcón [al'kon] *nm* falcon, hawk.
hálito ['alito] *nm* breath.
halitosis [ali'tosis] *nf* halitosis, bad breath.
hallar [a'ʎar] *vt* (*gen*) to find; (*descubrir*) to
discover; (*toparse con*) to run into; ~**se** *vr*
to be (situated); (*encontrarse*) to find o.s.;
se halla fuera he is away; **no se halla** he
feels out of place.
hallazgo [a'ʎaθɣo] *nm* discovery; (*cosa*)
find.
halo ['alo] *nm* halo.
halógeno, a [a'loxeno, a] *adj*: **faro** ~
halogen lamp.
halterofilia [altero'filja] *nf* weightlifting.
hamaca [a'maka] *nf* hammock.
hambre ['ambre] *nf* hunger; (*carencia*)
famine; (*inanición*) starvation; (*fig*)
longing; **tener** ~ to be hungry.
hambriento, a [am'brjento, a] *adj* hungry,
starving ◆ *nm/f* starving person; **los** ~**s**
the hungry; ~ **de** hungry *o* longing for.
hambruna [am'bruna] *nf* famine.
Hamburgo [am'burxo] *nm* Hamburg.
hamburguesa [ambur'ɣesa] *nf*
hamburger, burger.
hampa ['ampa] *nf* underworld.
hampón [am'pon] *nm* thug.
han [an] *vb V* **haber.**
haragán, ana [ara'ɣan, ana] *adj, nm/f* good-
for-nothing.
haraganear [araɣane'ar] *vi* to idle, loaf
about.
harapiento, a [ara'pjento, a] *adj* tattered,
in rags.
harapo [a'rapo] *nm* rag.
hardware ['xardwer] *nm* (*INFORM*)
hardware.
haré [a're] *etc vb V* **hacer.**
harén [a'ren] *nm* harem.
harina [a'rina] *nf* flour; **eso es** ~ **de otro
costal** that's another kettle of fish.
harinero, a [ari'nero, a] *nm/f* flour
merchant.
harinoso, a [ari'noso, a] *adj* floury.
hartar [ar'tar] *vt* to satiate, glut; (*fig*) to
tire, sicken; ~**se** *vr* (*de comida*) to fill o.s.,

gorge o.s.; (*cansarse*) to get fed up (*de* with).

hartazgo [ar'taθɣo] *nm* surfeit, glut.

harto, a ['arto, a] *adj* (*lleno*) full; (*cansado*) fed up ♦ *adv* (*bastante*) enough; (*muy*) very; **estar** ~ **de** to be fed up with; **¡estoy** ~ **de decírtelo!** I'm sick and tired of telling you (so)!

hartura [ar'tura] *nf* (*exceso*) surfeit; (*abundancia*) abundance; (*satisfacción*) satisfaction.

has [as] *vb* V **haber.**

Has. *abr* (= *Hectáreas*) ha.

hasta ['asta] *adv* even ♦ *prep* (*alcanzando a*) as far as, up/down to; (*de tiempo: a tal hora*) till, until; (: *antes de*) before ♦ *conj:* ~ **que** until; ~ **luego** *o* **ahora** (*fam*)/**el sábado** see you soon/on Saturday; ~ **la fecha** (up) to date; ~ **nueva orden** until further notice; ~ **en Valencia hiela a veces** even in Valencia it freezes sometimes.

hastiar [as'tjar] *vt* (*gen*) to weary; (*aburrir*) to bore; ~**se** *vr:* ~**se de** to get fed up with.

hastío [as'tio] *nm* weariness; boredom.

hatajo [a'taxo] *nm:* **un** ~ **de gamberros** a bunch of hooligans.

hatillo [a'tiʎo] *nm* belongings *pl*, kit; (*montón*) bundle, heap.

Hawai [a'wai] *nm* (*tb:* **las Islas** ~) Hawaii.

hawaianas [awa'janas] *nfpl* (*esp AM*) flip-flops (*BRIT*), thongs.

hawaiano, a [awa'jano, a] *adj, nm/f* Hawaiian.

hay [ai] *vb* V **haber.**

Haya ['aja] *nf:* **la** ~ The Hague.

haya ['aja] *etc vb* V **haber** ♦ *nf* beech tree.

hayal [a'jal] *nm* beech grove.

haz [aθ] *vb* V **hacer** ♦ *nm* bundle, bunch; (*rayo: de luz*) beam ♦ *nf:* ~ **de la tierra** face of the earth.

hazaña [a'θaɲa] *nf* feat, exploit; **sería una** ~ it would be a great achievement.

hazmerreír [aθmerre'ir] *nm inv* laughing stock.

HB *abr* (= *Herri Batasuna*) *Basque political party.*

he [e] *vb* V **haber** ♦ *adv:* ~ **aquí** here is, here are; ~ **aquí por qué** ... that is why ....

hebilla [e'βiʎa] *nf* buckle, clasp.

hebra ['eβra] *nf* thread; (*BOT: fibra*) fibre, grain.

hebreo, a [e'βreo, a] *adj, nm/f* Hebrew ♦ *nm* (*LING*) Hebrew.

Hébridas ['eβriðas] *nfpl:* **las** ~ the Hebrides.

hechice [e'tʃiθe] *etc vb* V **hechizar.**

hechicero, a [etʃi'θero, a] *nm/f* sorcerer/sorceress.

hechizar [etʃi'θar] *vt* to cast a spell on, bewitch.

hechizo [e'tʃiθo] *nm* witchcraft, magic; (*acto de magia*) spell, charm.

hecho, a ['etʃo, a] *pp de* **hacer** ♦ *adj* complete; (*maduro*) mature; (*COSTURA*) ready-to-wear ♦ *nm* deed, act; (*dato*) fact; (*cuestión*) matter; (*suceso*) event ♦ *excl* agreed!, done!; **¡bien** ~! well done!; **de** ~ in fact, as a matter of fact; (*POL etc: adj, adv*) de facto; **de** ~ **y de derecho** de facto and de jure; ~ **a la medida** made-to-measure; **a lo** ~, **pecho** it's no use crying over spilt milk.

hechura [e'tʃura] *nf* making, creation; (*producto*) product; (*forma*) form, shape; (*de persona*) build; (*TEC*) craftsmanship.

hectárea [ek'tarea] *nf* hectare.

heder [e'ðer] *vi* to stink, smell; (*fig*) to be unbearable.

hediondez [eðjon'deθ] *nf* stench, stink; (*cosa*) stinking thing.

hediondo, a [e'ðjondo, a] *adj* stinking.

hedor [e'ðor] *nm* stench.

hegemonía [exemo'nia] *nf* hegemony.

helada [e'laða] *nf* frost.

heladera [ela'ðera] *nf* (*AM: refrigerador*) refrigerator.

heladería [elaðe'ria] *nf* ice-cream stall (*o* parlour).

helado, a [e'laðo, a] *adj* frozen; (*glacial*) icy; (*fig*) chilly, cold ♦ *nm* ice-cream; **dejar** ~ **a algn** to dumbfound sb.

helador, a [ela'ðor, a] *adj* (*viento etc*) icy, freezing.

helar [e'lar] *vt* to freeze, ice (up); (*dejar atónito*) to amaze; (*desalentar*) to discourage ♦ *vi*, ~**se** *vr* to freeze; (*AVIAT, FERRO etc*) to ice (up), freeze up; (*líquido*) to set.

helecho [e'letʃo] *nm* bracken, fern.

helénico, a [e'leniko, a] *adj* Hellenic, Greek.

heleno, a [e'leno, a] *nm/f* Hellene, Greek.

hélice ['eliθe] *nf* spiral; (*TEC*) propeller; (*MAT*) helix.

helicóptero [eli'koptero] *nm* helicopter.

helio ['eljo] *nm* helium.

helmántico, a [el'mantiko, a] *adj* of *o* from Salamanca.

helvético, a [el'βetiko, a] *adj, nm/f* Swiss.

hematoma [ema'toma] *nm* bruise.

hembra ['embra] *nf* (*BOT, ZOOL*) female; (*mujer*) woman; (*TEC*) nut; **un elefante** ~ a she-elephant.

hemeroteca [emero'teka] *nf* newspaper

library.
hemiciclo [emi'θiklo] *nm*: **el ~** (*POL*) the floor.
hemisferio [emis'ferjo] *nm* hemisphere.
hemofilia [emo'filja] *nf* haemophilia (*BRIT*), hemophilia (*US*).
hemorragia [emo'rraxja] *nf* haemorrhage (*BRIT*), hemorrhage (*US*).
hemorroides [emo'rroiðes] *nfpl* haemorrhoids (*BRIT*), hemorrhoids (*US*).
hemos ['emos] *vb V* **haber**.
henar [e'nar] *nm* meadow, hayfield.
henchir [en'tʃir] *vt* to fill, stuff; **~se** *vr* (*llenarse de comida*) to stuff o.s. (with food); (*inflarse*) to swell (up).
Hendaya [en'daja] *nf* Hendaye.
hender [en'der] *vt* to cleave, split.
hendidura [endi'ðura] *nf* crack, split; (*GEO*) fissure.
henequén [ene'ken] *nm* (*AM*) henequen.
heno ['eno] *nm* hay.
hepatitis [epa'titis] *nf inv* hepatitis.
herbario, a [er'ßarjo, a] *adj* herbal ♦ *nm* (*colección*) herbarium; (*especialista*) herbalist; (*botánico*) botanist.
herbicida [erßi'θiða] *nm* weedkiller.
herbívoro, a [er'ßißoro, a] *adj* herbivorous.
herboristería [erßoriste'ria] *nf* herbalist's shop.
heredad [ere'ðað] *nf* landed property; (*granja*) farm.
heredar [ere'ðar] *vt* to inherit.
heredero, a [ere'ðero, a] *nm/f* heir(ess); **~ del trono** heir to the throne.
hereditario, a [ereði'tarjo, a] *adj* hereditary.
hereje [e'rexe] *nm/f* heretic.
herejía [ere'xia] *nf* heresy.
herencia [e'renθja] *nf* inheritance; (*fig*) heritage; (*BIO*) heredity.
herético, a [e'retiko, a] *adj* heretical.
herido, a [e'riðo, a] *adj* injured, wounded; (*fig*) offended ♦ *nm/f* casualty ♦ *nf* wound, injury.
herir [e'rir] *vt* to wound, injure; (*fig*) to offend; (*conmover*) to touch, move.
hermana [er'mana] *nf V* **hermano**.
hermanar [erma'nar] *vt* to match; (*unir*) to join; (*ciudades*) to twin.
hermanastro, a [erma'nastro, a] *nm/f* stepbrother/sister.
hermandad [erman'dað] *nf* brotherhood; (*de mujeres*) sisterhood; (*sindicato etc*) association.
hermano, a [er'mano, a] *adj* similar ♦ *nm* brother ♦ *nf* sister; **~ gemelo** twin brother; **~ político** brother-in-law; **~ primo** first cousin; **mis ~s** my brothers,

my brothers and sisters; **hermana política** sister-in-law.
hermético, a [er'metiko, a] *adj* hermetic; (*fig*) watertight.
hermoso, a [er'moso, a] *adj* beautiful, lovely; (*estupendo*) splendid; (*guapo*) handsome.
hermosura [ermo'sura] *nf* beauty; (*de hombre*) handsomeness.
hernia ['ernja] *nf* hernia, rupture; **~ discal** slipped disc.
herniarse [er'njarse] *vr* to rupture o.s.; (*fig*) to break one's back.
héroe ['eroe] *nm* hero.
heroicidad [eroiθi'ðað] *nf* heroism; (*una ~*) heroic deed.
heroico, a [e'roiko, a] *adj* heroic.
heroína [ero'ina] *nf* (*mujer*) heroine; (*droga*) heroin.
heroinómano, a [eroi'nomano, a] *nm/f* heroin addict.
heroísmo [ero'ismo] *nm* heroism.
herpes ['erpes] *nmpl o nfpl* (*MED: gen*) herpes *sg*; (: *de la piel*) shingles *sg*.
herradura [erra'ðura] *nf* horseshoe.
herraje [e'rraxe] *nm* (*trabajos*) ironwork.
herramienta [erra'mjenta] *nf* tool.
herrería [erre'ria] *nf* smithy; (*TEC*) forge.
herrero [e'rrero] *nm* blacksmith.
herrumbre [e'rrumbre] *nf* rust.
herrumbroso, a [errum'broso, a] *adj* rusty.
hervidero [erßi'ðero] *nm* (*fig*) swarm; (*POL etc*) hotbed.
hervir [er'ßir] *vi* to boil; (*burbujear*) to bubble; (*fig*): **~ de** to teem with; **~ a fuego lento** to simmer.
hervor [er'ßor] *nm* boiling; (*fig*) ardour, fervour.
heterogéneo, a [etero'xeneo, a] *adj* heterogeneous.
heterosexual [eterosek'swal] *adj, nm/f* heterosexual.
hez [eθ] *nf* (*tb*: **heces** *pl*) dregs.
hibernar [ißer'nar] *vi* to hibernate.
híbrido, a ['ißriðo, a] *adj* hybrid.
hice ['iθe] *etc vb V* **hacer**.
hidalgo, a [i'ðalɣo, a] *adj* noble; (*honrado*) honourable (*BRIT*), honorable (*US*) ♦ *nm/f* noble(man/woman).
hidratante [iðra'tante] *adj*: **crema ~** moisturizing cream, moisturizer.
hidratar [iðra'tar] *vt* to moisturize.
hidrato [i'ðrato] *nm* hydrate; **~ de carbono** carbohydrate.
hidráulico, a [i'ðrauliko, a] *adj* hydraulic ♦ *nf* hydraulics *sg*.
hidro... [iðro] *pref* hydro..., water-....
hidroavión [iðroa'ßjon] *nm* seaplane.

hidroeléctrico, a [iðroe'lektriko, a] *adj* hydroelectric.

hidrófilo, a [i'ðrofilo, a] *adj* absorbent; **algodón ~** cotton wool (*BRIT*), absorbent cotton (*US*).

hidrofobia [iðro'foβja] *nf* hydrophobia, rabies.

hidrófugo, a [i'ðrofuɣo, a] *adj* damp-proof.

hidrógeno [i'ðroxeno] *nm* hydrogen.

hieda ['jeða] *etc vb* **V heder.**

hiedra ['jeðra] *nf* ivy.

hiel [jel] *nf* gall, bile; (*fig*) bitterness.

hielo ['jelo] *etc vb* **V helar ♦** *nm* (*gen*) ice; (*escarcha*) frost; (*fig*) coldness, reserve; **romper el ~** (*fig*) to break the ice.

hiena ['jena] *nf* (*ZOOL*) hyena.

hiera ['jera] *etc vb* **V herir.**

hierba ['jerβa] *nf* (*pasto*) grass; (*CULIN, MED*: *planta*) herb; **mala ~** weed; (*fig*) evil influence.

hierbabuena [jerβa'βwena] *nf* mint.

hierro ['jerro] *nm* (*metal*) iron; (*objeto*) iron object; **~ acanalado** corrugated iron; **~ colado** *o* **fundido** cast iron; **de ~** iron *cpd*.

hierva ['jerβa] *etc vb* **V hervir.**

hígado ['iɣaðo] *nm* liver; **~s** *nmpl* (*fig*) guts; **echar los ~s** to wear o.s. out.

higiene [i'xjene] *nf* hygiene.

higiénico, a [i'xjeniko, a] *adj* hygienic.

higo ['iɣo] *nm* fig; **~ seco** dried fig; **~ chumbo** prickly pear; **de ~s a brevas** once in a blue moon.

higuera [i'ɣera] *nf* fig tree.

hijastro, a [i'xastro, a] *nm/f* stepson/daughter.

hijo, a ['ixo, a] *nm/f* son/daughter, child; (*uso vocativo*) dear; **~s** *nmpl* children, sons and daughters; **sin ~s** childless; **~/hija político/a** son-/daughter-in-law; **~ pródigo** prodigal son; **~ de papá/mamá** daddy's/mummy's boy; **~ de puta** (*fam!*) bastard (*!*), son of a bitch (*!*); **cada ~ de vecino** any Tom, Dick or Harry.

hilacha [i'latʃa] *nf* ravelled thread; **~ de acero** steel wool.

hilado, a [i'laðo, a] *adj* spun.

hilandero, a [ilan'dero, a] *nm/f* spinner.

hilar [i'lar] *vt* to spin; (*fig*) to reason, infer; **~ delgado** to split hairs.

hilera [i'lera] *nf* row, file.

hilo ['ilo] *nm* thread; (*BOT*) fibre; (*tela*) linen; (*metal*) wire; (*de agua*) trickle, thin stream; (*de luz*) beam, ray; (*de conversación*) thread, theme; (*de pensamientos*) train; **~ dental** dental floss; **colgar de un ~** (*fig*) to hang by a thread; **traje de ~** linen suit.

hilvanar [ilβa'nar] *vt* (*COSTURA*) to tack

(*BRIT*), baste (*US*); (*fig*) to do hurriedly.

Himalaya [ima'laja] *nm*: **el ~, los Montes ~** the Himalayas.

himno ['imno] *nm* hymn; **~ nacional** national anthem.

hincapié [inka'pje] *nm*: **hacer ~ en** to emphasize, stress.

hincar [in'kar] *vt* to drive (in), thrust (in); (*diente*) to sink; **~se** *vr*: **~se de rodillas** (*esp AM*) to kneel down.

hincha ['intʃa] *nm/f* (*fam*: *DEPORTE*) fan.

hinchado, a [in'tʃaðo, a] *adj* (*gen*) swollen; (*persona*) pompous ♦ *nf* (group of) supporters *o* fans.

hinchar [in'tʃar] *vt* (*gen*) to swell; (*inflar*) to blow up, inflate; (*fig*) to exaggerate; **~se** *vr* (*inflarse*) to swell up; (*fam*: *llenarse*) to stuff o.s.; (*fig*) to get conceited; **~se de reír** to have a good laugh.

hinchazón [intʃa'θon] *nf* (*MED*) swelling; (*protuberancia*) bump, lump; (*altivez*) arrogance.

hindú [in'du] *adj, nm/f* Hindu.

hinojo [i'noxo] *nm* fennel.

hinque ['inke] *etc vb* **V hincar.**

hipar [i'par] *vi* to hiccup.

hiper... [iper] *pref* hyper....

hiperactivo, a [iperak'tiβo, a] *adj* hyperactive.

hipermercado [ipermer'kaðo] *nm* hypermarket, superstore.

hipersensible [ipersen'siβle] *adj* hypersensitive.

hipertensión [iperten'sjon] *nf* high blood pressure, hypertension.

hípico, a ['ipiko, a] *adj* horse *cpd*, equine; **club ~** riding club.

hipnosis [ip'nosis] *nf inv* hypnosis.

hipnotice [ipno'tiθe] *etc vb* **V hipnotizar.**

hipnotismo [ipno'tismo] *nm* hypnotism.

hipnotizar [ipnoti'θar] *vt* to hypnotize.

hipo ['ipo] *nm* hiccups *pl*; **quitar el ~ a algn** to cure sb's hiccups.

hipocondría [ipokon'dria] *nf* hypochondria.

hipocondríaco, a [ipokon'driako, a] *adj, nm/f* hypochondriac.

hipocresía [ipokre'sia] *nf* hypocrisy.

hipócrita [i'pokrita] *adj* hypocritical ♦ *nm/f* hypocrite.

hipodérmico, a [ipo'ðermiko, a] *adj*: **aguja hipodérmica** hypodermic needle.

hipódromo [i'poðromo] *nm* racetrack.

hipopótamo [ipo'potamo] *nm* hippopotamus.

hipoteca [ipo'teka] *nf* mortgage; **redimir una ~** to pay off a mortgage.

hipotecar [ipote'kar] *vt* to mortgage; (*fig*)

to jeopardize.
hipotecario, a [ipote'karjo, a] *adj*
mortgage *cpd.*
hipótesis [i'potesis] *nf inv* hypothesis; **es
una ~ (nada más)** that's just a theory.
hipotético, a [ipo'tetiko, a] *adj*
hypothetic(al).
hiriendo [i'rjendo] *etc vb V* herir.
hiriente [i'rjente] *adj* offensive, wounding.
hirsuto, a [ir'suto, a] *adj* hairy.
hirviendo [ir'ßjendo] *etc vb V* hervir.
hisopo [i'sopo] *nm (REL)* sprinkler; *(BOT)*
hyssop; *(de algodón)* swab.
hispánico, a [is'paniko, a] *adj* Hispanic,
Spanish.
hispanidad [ispani'ðað] *nf (cualidad)*
Spanishness; *(POL)* Spanish o Hispanic
world.
hispanista [ispa'nista] *nm/f (UNIV etc)*
Hispan(ic)ist.
hispano, a [is'pano, a] *adj* Hispanic,
Spanish, Hispano- ♦ *nm/f* Spaniard.
Hispanoamérica [ispanoa'merika] *nf*
Spanish o Latin America.
hispanoamericano, a [ispanoameri'kano,
a] *adj, nm/f* Spanish o Latin American.
hispanohablante [ispanoa'ßlante],
hispanoparlante [ispanopar'lante] *adj*
Spanish-speaking.
histeria [is'terja] *nf* hysteria.
histérico, a [is'teriko, a] *adj* hysterical.
histerismo [iste'rismo] *nm (MED)* hysteria;
(fig) hysterics.
histograma [isto'xrama] *nm* histogram.
historia [is'torja] *nf* history; *(cuento)* story,
tale; **~s** *nfpl (chismes)* gossip *sg;* **dejarse
de ~s** to come to the point; **pasar a la ~**
to go down in history.
historiador, a [istorja'ðor, a] *nm/f*
historian.
historial [isto'rjal] *nm* record; *(profesional)*
curriculum vitae, c.v., résumé *(US);*
(MED) case history.
histórico, a [is'toriko, a] *adj* historical;
(fig) historic.
historieta [isto'rjeta] *nf* tale, anecdote;
(dibujos) comic strip.
histrionismo [istrjo'nismo] *nm (TEAT)*
acting; *(fig)* histrionics *pl.*
hito ['ito] *nm (fig)* landmark; *(objetivo)*
goal, target; *(fig)* milestone.
hizo ['iθo] *vb V* hacer.
Hna(s). *abr (= Hermana(s))* Sr(s).
Hno(s). *abr (= Hermano(s))* Bro(s).
hocico [o'θiko] *nm* snout; *(fig)* grimace.
hockey ['xoki] *nm* hockey; **~ sobre hielo**
ice hockey.
hogar [o'xar] *nm* fireplace, hearth; *(casa)*

home; *(vida familiar)* home life.
hogareño, a [oxa'reɲo, a] *adj* home *cpd;*
(persona) home-loving.
hogaza [o'xaθa] *nf (pan)* large loaf.
hoguera [o'xera] *nf (gen)* bonfire; *(para
herejes)* stake.
hoja ['oxa] *nf (gen)* leaf; *(de flor)* petal; *(de
hierba)* blade; *(de papel)* sheet; *(página)*
page; *(formulario)* form; *(de puerta)* leaf;
~ de afeitar razor blade; **~ de cálculo
electrónico** spreadsheet; **~ de trabajo**
(INFORM) worksheet; **de ~ ancha** broad-
leaved; **de ~ caduca/perenne**
deciduous/evergreen.
hojalata [oxa'lata] *nf* tin(plate).
hojaldre [o'xaldre] *nm (CULIN)* puff pastry.
hojarasca [oxa'raska] *nf (hojas)* dead o
fallen leaves *pl; (fig)* rubbish.
hojear [oxe'ar] *vt* to leaf through, turn the
pages of.
hola ['ola] *excl* hello!
Holanda [o'landa] *nf* Holland.
holandés, esa [olan'des, esa] *adj* Dutch
♦ *nm/f* Dutchman/woman; **los holandeses**
the Dutch ♦ *nm (LING)* Dutch.
holgado, a [ol'xaðo, a] *adj* loose, baggy;
(rico) well-to-do.
holgar [ol'xar] *vi (descansar)* to rest;
(sobrar) to be superfluous; **huelga decir
que** it goes without saying that.
holgazán, ana [olxa'θan, ana] *adj* idle, lazy
♦ *nm/f* loafer.
holgazanear [olxaθane'ar] *vi* to laze o loaf
around.
holgura [ol'xura] *nf* looseness, bagginess;
(TEC) play, free movement; *(vida)*
comfortable living, luxury.
hollar [o'ʎar] *vt* to tread (on), trample.
hollín [o'ʎin] *nm* soot.
hombre ['ombre] *nm* man; *(raza humana):* **el
~** man(kind) ♦ *excl:* **¡sí ~!** *(claro)* of
course!; *(para énfasis)* man, old chap; **~
de negocios** businessman; **~-rana**
frogman; **~ de bien** o **pro** honest man; **~
de confianza** right-hand man; **~ de
estado** statesman; **el ~ medio** the
average man.
hombrera [om'brera] *nf* shoulder strap.
hombro ['ombro] *nm* shoulder; **arrimar el
~** to lend a hand; **encogerse de ~s** to
shrug one's shoulders.
hombruno, a [om'bruno, a] *adj* mannish.
homenaje [ome'naxe] *nm (gen)* homage;
(tributo) tribute; **un partido ~** a benefit
match.
homeopatía [omeopa'tia] *nf*
hom(o)eopathy.
homeopático, a [omeo'patiko, a] *adj*

hom(o)eopathic.

homicida [omi'θiða] *adj* homicidal ♦ *nm/f* murderer.

homicidio [omi'θiðjo] *nm* murder, homicide; (*involuntario*) manslaughter.

homologación [omoloɣa'θjon] *nf* (*de sueldo, condiciones*) parity.

homologar [omolo'ɣar] *vt* (COM) to standardize; (ESCOL) to officially approve; (DEPORTE) to officially recognize; (*sueldos*) to equalize.

homólogo, a [o'moloɣo, a] *nm/f* counterpart, opposite number.

homónimo [o'monimo] *nm* (*tocayo*) namesake.

homosexual [omosek'swal] *adj, nm/f* homosexual.

hondo, a ['ondo, a] *adj* deep; **lo** ~ the depth(s) (*pl*), the bottom; **con ~ pesar** with deep regret.

hondonada [ondo'naða] *nf* hollow, depression; (*cañón*) ravine; (GEO) lowland.

hondura [on'dura] *nf* depth, profundity.

Honduras [on'duras] *nf* Honduras.

hondureño, a [ondu'reɲo, a] *adj, nm/f* Honduran.

honestidad [onesti'ðað] *nf* purity, chastity; (*decencia*) decency.

honesto, a [o'nesto, a] *adj* chaste; decent, honest; (*justo*) just.

hongo ['oŋgo] *nm* (BOT: gen) fungus; (: *comestible*) mushroom; (: *venenoso*) toadstool; (*sombrero*) bowler (hat) (BRIT), derby (US); **~s del pie** footrot *sg*, athlete's foot *sg*.

honor [o'nor] *nm* (gen) honour (BRIT), honor (US); (*gloria*) glory; **~ profesional** professional etiquette; **en ~ a la verdad** to be fair.

honorable [ono'raßle] *adj* honourable (BRIT), honorable (US).

honorario, a [ono'rarjo, a] *adj* honorary ♦ *nm*: **~s** fees.

honorífico, a [ono'rifiko, a] *adj* honourable (BRIT), honorable (US); **mención honorífica** hono(u)rable mention.

honra ['onra] *nf* (gen) honour; (*renombre*) good name; **~s fúnebres** funeral rites; **tener algo a mucha ~** to be proud of sth.

honradez [onra'ðeθ] *nf* honesty; (*de persona*) integrity.

honrado, a [on'raðo, a] *adj* honest, upright.

honrar [on'rar] *vt* to honour; **~se** *vr*: **~se con algo/de hacer algo** to be honoured by sth/to do sth.

honroso, a [on'roso, a] *adj* (*honrado*)

honourable; (*respetado*) respectable.

hora ['ora] *nf* hour; (*tiempo*) time; **¿qué ~ es?** what time is it?; **¿a qué ~?** at what time?; **media ~** half an hour; **a la ~ de comer/de recreo** at lunchtime/at playtime; **a primera ~** first thing (in the morning); **a última ~** at the last moment; **"última ~"** "stop press"; **noticias de última ~** last-minute news; **a altas ~s** in the small hours; **a la ~ en punto** on the dot; **¡a buena ~!** about time, too!; **en mala ~** unluckily; **dar la ~** to strike the hour; **poner el reloj en ~** to set one's watch; **~s de oficina/de trabajo** office/working hours; **~s de visita** visiting times; **~s extras** *o* **extraordinarias** overtime *sg*; **~s punta** rush hours; **no ver la ~ de** to look forward to; **¡ya era ~!** and about time too!

horadar [ora'ðar] *vt* to drill, bore.

horario, a [o'rarjo, a] *adj* hourly, hour *cpd* ♦ *nm* timetable; **~ comercial** business hours.

horca ['orka] *nf* gallows *sg*; (AGR) pitchfork.

horcajadas [orka'xaðas]: **a ~** *adv* astride.

horchata [or'tʃata] *nf* cold drink made from tiger nuts and water, tiger nut milk.

horda ['orða] *nf* horde.

horizontal [oriθon'tal] *adj* horizontal.

horizonte [ori'θonte] *nm* horizon.

horma ['orma] *nf* mould; **~ (de calzado)** last; **~ de sombrero** hat block.

hormiga [or'miɣa] *nf* ant; **~s** *nfpl* (MED) pins and needles.

hormigón [ormi'ɣon] *nm* concrete; **~ armado/pretensado** reinforced/prestressed concrete.

hormigueo [ormi'ɣeo] *nm* (*comezón*) itch; (*fig*) uneasiness.

hormiguero [ormi'ɣero] *nm* (ZOOL) ant's nest; **era un ~** it was swarming with people.

hormona [or'mona] *nf* hormone.

hornada [or'naða] *nf* batch of loaves (*etc*).

hornillo [or'niʎo] *nm* (*cocina*) portable stove.

horno ['orno] *nm* (CULIN) oven; (TEC) furnace; (*para cerámica*) kiln; **~ microondas** microwave (oven); **alto ~** blast furnace; **~ crematorio** crematorium.

horóscopo [o'roskopo] *nm* horoscope.

horquilla [or'kiʎa] *nf* hairpin; (AGR) pitchfork.

horrendo, a [o'rrendo, a] *adj* horrendous,

frightful.
horrible [o'rriβle] *adj* horrible, dreadful.
horripilante [orripi'lante] *adj* hair-raising, horrifying.
horripilar [orripi'lar] *vt*: ~ **a algn** to horrify sb; ~**se** *vr* to be horrified.
horror [o'rror] *nm* horror, dread; (*atrocidad*) atrocity; ¡**qué** ~! (*fam*) how awful!; **estudia horrores** he studies a hell of a lot.
horrorice [orro'riθe] *etc vb V* **horrorizar**.
horrorizar [orrori'θar] *vt* to horrify, frighten; ~**se** *vr* to be horrified.
horroroso, a [orro'roso, a] *adj* horrifying, ghastly.
hortaliza [orta'liθa] *nf* vegetable.
hortelano, a [orte'lano, a] *nm/f* (market) gardener.
hortera [or'tera] *adj* (*fam*) vulgar, naff.
horterada [orte'raða] *nf* (*fam*): **es una** ~ it's really naff.
hortícola [or'tikola] *adj* horticultural.
horticultura [ortikul'tura] *nf* horticulture.
hortofrutícola [ortofru'tikola] *adj* fruit and vegetable *cpd*.
hosco, a ['osko, a] *adj* dark; (*persona*) sullen, gloomy.
hospedaje [ospe'ðaxe] *nm* (cost of) board and lodging.
hospedar [ospe'ðar] *vt* to put up; ~**se** *vr*: ~**se (con/en)** to stay *o* lodge (with/at).
hospedería [ospeðe'ria] *nf* (*edificio*) inn; (*habitación*) guest room.
hospicio [os'piθjo] *nm* (*para niños*) orphanage.
hospital [ospi'tal] *nm* hospital.
hospitalario, a [ospita'larjo, a] *adj* (*acogedor*) hospitable.
hospitalice [ospita'liθe] *etc vb V* **hospitalizar**.
hospitalidad [ospitali'ðað] *nf* hospitality.
hospitalizar [ospitali'θar] *vt* to send *o* take to hospital, hospitalize.
hosquedad [oske'ðað] *nf* sullenness.
hostal [os'tal] *nm* small hotel; *V tb* **hotel**.
hostelería [ostele'ria] *nf* hotel business *o* trade.
hostia ['ostja] *nf* (*REL*) host, consecrated wafer; (*fam: golpe*) whack, punch ♦ *excl*: ¡~**(s)**! (*fam!*) damn!
hostigar [osti'ɣar] *vt* to whip; (*fig*) to harass, pester.
hostigue [os'tiɣe] *etc vb V* **hostigar**.
hostil [os'til] *adj* hostile.
hostilidad [ostili'ðað] *nf* hostility.
hotel [o'tel] *nm* hotel.

In Spain you can choose from the following categories of accommodation, in descending order of quality and price: **hotel** (*from 5 stars to 1*), **hostal, pensión, casa de huéspedes, fonda**. Quality can vary widely even within these categories. The State also runs luxury hotels called **paradores**, which are usually sited in places of particular historical interest and are often historic buildings themselves.

hotelero, a [ote'lero, a] *adj* hotel *cpd* ♦ *nm/f* hotelier.
hoy [oi] *adv* (*este día*) today; (*en la actualidad*) now(adays) ♦ *nm* present time; ~ (**en**) **día** now(adays); **el día de** ~, ~ **día** (*AM*) this very day; ~ **por** ~ right now; **de** ~ **en ocho días** a week today; **de** ~ **en adelante** from now on.
hoya ['oja] *nf* pit; (*sepulcro*) grave; (*GEO*) valley.
hoyo ['ojo] *nm* hole, pit; (*tumba*) grave; (*GOLF*) hole; (*MED*) pockmark.
hoyuelo [oj'welo] *nm* dimple.
hoz [oθ] *nf* sickle.
hube ['uβe] *etc vb V* **haber**.
hucha ['utʃa] *nf* money box.
hueco, a ['weko, a] *adj* (*vacío*) hollow, empty; (*resonante*) booming; (*sonido*) resonant; (*persona*) conceited; (*estilo*) pompous ♦ *nm* hollow, cavity; (*agujero*) hole; (*de escalera*) well; (*de ascensor*) shaft; (*vacante*) vacancy; ~ **de la mano** hollow of the hand.
huela ['wela] *etc vb V* **oler**.
huelga ['welɣa] *etc vb V* **holgar** ♦ *nf* strike; **declararse en** ~ to go on strike, come out on strike; ~ **general** general strike; ~ **de hambre** hunger strike; ~ **oficial** official strike.
huelgue ['welɣe] *etc vb V* **holgar**.
huelguista [wel'ɣista] *nm/f* striker.
huella ['weʎa] *nf* (*acto de pisar, pisada*) tread(ing); (*marca del paso*) footprint, footstep; (: *de animal, máquina*) track; ~ **digital** fingerprint; **sin dejar** ~ without leaving a trace.
huérfano, a ['werfano, a] *adj* orphan(ed); (*fig*) unprotected ♦ *nm/f* orphan.
huerta ['werta] *nf* market garden (*BRIT*), truck farm (*US*); (*Murcia, Valencia*) irrigated region.
huerto ['werto] *nm* kitchen garden; (*de árboles frutales*) orchard.
hueso ['weso] *nm* (*ANAT*) bone; (*de fruta*) stone, pit (*US*); **sin** ~ (*carne*) boned; **estar en los** ~**s** to be nothing but skin and

bone; **ser un** ~ (*profesor*) to be terribly strict; **un** ~ **duro de roer** a hard nut to crack.

huesoso, a [we'soso, a] *adj* (*esp AM*) bony.

huésped, a ['wespeð, a] *nm/f* (*invitado*) guest; (*habitante*) resident; (*anfitrión*) host(ess).

huesudo, a [we'suðo, a] *adj* bony, big-boned.

huevas ['weßas] *nfpl* eggs, roe *sg*; (*AM: fam!*) balls (*!*).

huevera [we'ßera] *nf* eggcup.

huevo ['weßo] *nm* egg; (*fam!*) ball (*!*), testicle; ~ **duro/escalfado/estrellado** *o* **frito/pasado por agua** hard-boiled/poached/fried/soft-boiled egg; ~**s revueltos** scrambled eggs; **me costó un** ~ (*fam!*) it was hard work; **tener** ~**s** (*fam!*) to have guts.

huevón, ona [we'ßon, ona] *nm/f* (*AM fam!*) stupid bastard (*!*), stupid idiot.

huida [u'iða] *nf* escape, flight; ~ **de capitales** (*COM*) flight of capital.

huidizo, a [ui'ðiθo, a] *adj* (*tímido*) shy; (*pasajero*) fleeting.

huir [u'ir] *vt* (*escapar*) to flee, escape; (*evadir*) to avoid ♦ *vi* to flee, run away; ~**se** *vr* (*escaparse*) to escape.

hule ['ule] *nm* (*encerado*) oilskin; (*esp AM*) rubber.

hulla ['uʎa] *nf* bituminous coal.

humanice [uma'niθe] *etc vb* V **humanizar.**

humanidad [umani'ðað] *nf* (*género humano*) man(kind); (*cualidad*) humanity; (*fam: gordura*) corpulence.

humanitario, a [umani'tarjo, a] *adj* humanitarian; (*benévolo*) humane.

humanizar [umani'θar] *vt* to humanize; ~**se** *vr* to become more human.

humano, a [u'mano, a] *adj* (*gen*) human; (*humanitario*) humane ♦ *nm* human; **ser** ~ human being.

humareda [uma'reða] *nf* cloud of smoke.

humeante [ume'ante] *adj* smoking, smoky.

humedad [ume'ðað] *nf* (*del clima*) humidity; (*de pared etc*) dampness; **a prueba de** ~ damp-proof.

humedecer [umeðe'θer] *vt* to moisten, wet; ~**se** *vr* to get wet.

humedezca [ume'ðeθka] *etc vb* V **humedecer.**

húmedo, a ['umeðo, a] *adj* (*mojado*) damp, wet; (*tiempo etc*) humid.

humildad [umil'dað] *nf* humility, humbleness.

humilde [u'milde] *adj* humble, modest; (*clase etc*) low, modest.

humillación [umiʎa'θjon] *nf* humiliation.

humillante [umi'ʎante] *adj* humiliating.

humillar [umi'ʎar] *vt* to humiliate; ~**se** *vr* to humble o.s., grovel.

humo ['umo] *nm* (*de fuego*) smoke; (*gas nocivo*) fumes *pl*; (*vapor*) steam, vapour; ~**s** *nmpl* (*fig*) conceit *sg*; **irse todo en** ~ (*fig*) to vanish without trace; **bajar los** ~**s a algn** to take sb down a peg or two.

humor [u'mor] *nm* (*disposición*) mood, temper; (*lo que divierte*) humour; **de buen/mal** ~ in a good/bad mood.

humorismo [umo'rismo] *nm* humour.

humorista [umo'rista] *nm/f* comic.

humorístico, a [umo'ristiko, a] *adj* funny, humorous.

hundimiento [undi'mjento] *nm* (*gen*) sinking; (*colapso*) collapse.

hundir [un'dir] *vt* to sink; (*edificio, plan*) to ruin, destroy; ~**se** *vr* to sink, collapse; (*fig: arruinarse*) to be ruined; (*desaparecer*) to disappear; **se hundió la economía** the economy collapsed; **se hundieron los precios** prices slumped.

húngaro, a ['ungaro, a] *adj, nm/f* Hungarian ♦ *nm* (*LING*) Hungarian, Magyar.

Hungría [un'gria] *nf* Hungary.

huracán [ura'kan] *nm* hurricane.

huraño, a [u'raɲo, a] *adj* shy; (*antisocial*) unsociable.

hurgar [ur'ɣar] *vt* to poke, jab; (*remover*) to stir (up); ~**se** *vr*: ~**se (las narices)** to pick one's nose.

hurgonear [urɣone'ar] *vt* to poke.

hurgue ['urɣe] *etc vb* V **hurgar.**

hurón [u'ron] *nm* (*ZOOL*) ferret.

hurra ['urra] *excl* hurray!, hurrah!

hurtadillas [urta'ðiʎas]: **a** ~ *adv* stealthily, on the sly.

hurtar [ur'tar] *vt* to steal; ~**se** *vr* to hide, keep out of the way.

hurto ['urto] *nm* theft, stealing; (*lo robado*) (piece of) stolen property, loot.

husmear [usme'ar] *vt* (*oler*) to sniff out, scent; (*fam*) to pry into ♦ *vi* to smell bad.

huso ['uso] *nm* (*TEC*) spindle; (*de torno*) drum.

huy ['ui] *excl* (*dolor*) ow!, ouch!; (*sorpresa*) well!; (*alivio*) phew!; ¡~, **perdona!** oops, sorry!

huyendo [u'jendo] *etc vb* V **huir.**

I i

I, i [i] nf (letra) I, i; **I de Inés** I for Isaac (BRIT) o Item (US).
I.A. abr = **inteligencia artificial.**
iba ['iβa] etc vb V **ir.**
Iberia [i'βerja] nf Iberia.
ibérico, a [i'βeriko, a] adj Iberian; **la Península ibérica** the Iberian Peninsula.
ibero, a [i'βero, a], **íbero, a** ['iβero, a] adj, nm/f Iberian.
iberoamericano, a [iβeroameri'kano, a] adj, nm/f Latin American.
íbice ['iβiθe] nm ibex.
ibicenco, a [iβi'θenko, a] adj of o from Ibiza ♦ nm/f native o inhabitant of Ibiza.
Ibiza [i'βiθa] nf Ibiza.
ice ['iθe] etc vb V **izar.**
iceberg [iθe'ber] nm iceberg.
ICONA [i'kona] nm abr (ESP) = Instituto Nacional para la Conservación de la Naturaleza.
icono [i'kono] nm (tb INFORM) icon.
iconoclasta [ikono'klasta] adj iconoclastic ♦ nm/f iconoclast.
ictericia [ikte'riθja] nf jaundice.
íd. abr = **ídem.**
I+D abr (= Investigación y Desarrollo) R&D.
ida ['iða] nf going, departure; ~ **y vuelta** round trip, return; ~**s y venidas** comings and goings.
IDE [iðe] nf abr (= Iniciativa de Defensa Estratégica) SDI.
idea [i'ðea] nf idea; (impresión) opinion; (propósito) intention; ~ **genial** brilliant idea; **a mala** ~ out of spite; **no tengo la menor** ~ I haven't a clue.
ideal [iðe'al] adj, nm ideal.
idealice [iðea'liθe] etc vb V **idealizar.**
idealista [iðea'lista] adj idealistic ♦ nm/f idealist.
idealizar [iðeali'θar] vt to idealize.
idear [iðe'ar] vt to think up; (aparato) to invent; (viaje) to plan.
ídem ['iðem] pron ditto.
idéntico, a [i'ðentiko, a] adj identical.
identidad [iðenti'ðað] nf identity; ~ **corporativa** corporate identity o image.
identificación [iðentifika'θjon] nf identification.

identificar [iðentifi'kar] vt to identify; ~**se** vr: ~**se con** to identify with.
identifique [iðenti'fike] etc vb V **identificar.**
ideología [iðeolo'xia] nf ideology.
ideológico, a [iðeo'loxiko, a] adj ideological.
idílico, a [i'ðiliko, a] adj idyllic.
idilio [i'ðiljo] nm love affair.
idioma [i'ðjoma] nm language.
idiomático, a [iðjo'matiko, a] adj idiomatic.
idiota [i'ðjota] adj idiotic ♦ nm/f idiot.
idiotez [iðjo'teθ] nf idiocy.
idolatrar [iðola'trar] vt (fig) to idolize.
ídolo ['iðolo] nm (tb fig) idol.
idoneidad [iðonei'ðað] nf suitability; (capacidad) aptitude.
idóneo, a [i'ðoneo, a] adj suitable.
iglesia [i'ɣlesja] nf church; ~ **parroquial** parish church; ¡**con la** ~ **hemos topado!** now we're really up against it!
iglú [i'ɣlu] nm igloo; (contenedor) bottle bank.
ignición [iɣni'θjon] nf ignition.
ignominia [iɣno'minja] nf ignominy.
ignominioso, a [iɣnomi'njoso, a] adj ignominious.
ignorado, a [iɣno'raðo, a] adj unknown; (dato) obscure.
ignorancia [iɣno'ranθja] nf ignorance; **por** ~ through ignorance.
ignorante [iɣno'rante] adj ignorant, uninformed ♦ nm/f ignoramus.
ignorar [iɣno'rar] vt not to know, be ignorant of; (no hacer caso a) to ignore; **ignoramos su paradero** we don't know his whereabouts.
ignoto, a [iɣ'noto, a] adj unknown.
igual [i'ɣwal] adj equal; (similar) like, similar; (mismo) (the) same; (constante) constant; (temperatura) even ♦ nm/f equal; **al** ~ **que** prep, conj like, just like; ~ **que** the same as; **sin** ~ peerless; **me da** o **es** ~ I don't care, it makes no difference; **no tener** ~ to be unrivalled; **son** ~**es** they're the same.
iguala [i'ɣwala] nf equalization; (COM) agreement.
igualada [iɣwa'laða] nf equalizer.
igualar [iɣwa'lar] vt (gen) to equalize, make equal; (terreno) to make even; (COM) to agree upon; ~**se** vr (platos de balanza) to balance out; ~**se (a)** (equivaler) to be equal (to).
igualdad [iɣwal'dað] nf equality; (similaridad) sameness; (uniformidad) uniformity; **en** ~ **de condiciones** on an equal basis.

igualmente [iɣwal'mente] *adv* equally; (*también*) also, likewise ♦ *excl* the same to you!

iguana [i'ɣwana] *nf* iguana.

ikurriña [iku'rriɲa] *nf* Basque flag.

ilegal [ile'ɣal] *adj* illegal.

ilegitimidad [ilexitimi'ðað] *nf* illegitimacy.

ilegítimo, a [ile'xitimo, a] *adj* illegitimate.

ileso, a [i'leso, a] *adj* unhurt, unharmed.

ilícito, a [i'liθito, a] *adj* illicit.

ilimitado, a [ilimi'taðo, a] *adj* unlimited.

Ilma., Ilmo. *abr* (= *Ilustrísima, Ilustrísimo*) courtesy title.

ilógico, a [i'loxiko, a] *adj* illogical.

iluminación [ilumina'θjon] *nf* illumination; (*alumbrado*) lighting; (*fig*) enlightenment.

iluminar [ilumi'nar] *vt* to illuminate, light (up); (*fig*) to enlighten.

ilusión [ilu'sjon] *nf* illusion; (*quimera*) delusion; (*esperanza*) hope; (*emoción*) excitement, thrill; **hacerse ilusiones** to build up one's hopes; **no te hagas ilusiones** don't build up your hopes *o* get too excited.

ilusionado, a [ilusjo'naðo, a] *adj* excited.

ilusionar [ilusjo'nar] *vt*: ~ **a algn** (*falsamente*) to build up sb's hopes; ~**se** *vr* (*falsamente*) to build up one's hopes; (*entusiasmarse*) to get excited; **me ilusiona mucho el viaje** I'm really excited about the trip.

ilusionista [ilusjo'nista] *nm/f* conjurer.

iluso, a [i'luso, a] *adj* gullible, easily deceived ♦ *nm/f* dreamer, visionary.

ilusorio, a [ilu'sorjo, a] *adj* (*de ilusión*) illusory, deceptive; (*esperanza*) vain.

ilustración [ilustra'θjon] *nf* illustration; (*saber*) learning, erudition; **la I~** the Enlightenment.

ilustrado, a [ilus'traðo, a] *adj* illustrated; learned.

ilustrar [ilus'trar] *vt* to illustrate; (*instruir*) to instruct; (*explicar*) to explain, make clear; ~**se** *vr* to acquire knowledge.

ilustre [i'lustre] *adj* famous, illustrious.

imagen [i'maxen] *nf* (*gen*) image; (*dibujo, TV*) picture; (*REL*) statue; **ser la viva ~ de** to be the spitting *o* living image of; **a su ~** in one's own image.

imaginación [imaxina'θjon] *nf* imagination; (*fig*) fancy; **ni por ~** on no account; **no se me pasó por la ~ que ...** it never even occurred to me that ....

imaginar [imaxi'nar] *vt* (*gen*) to imagine; (*idear*) to think up; (*suponer*) to suppose; ~**se** *vr* to imagine; **¡imagínate!** just imagine!, just fancy!; **imagínese que ...**

suppose that ...; **me imagino que sí** I should think so.

imaginario, a [imaxi'narjo, a] *adj* imaginary.

imaginativo, a [imaxina'tiβo, a] *adj* imaginative ♦ *nf* imagination.

imán [i'man] *nm* magnet.

iman(t)ar [ima'n(t)ar] *vt* to magnetize.

imbécil [im'beθil] *nm/f* imbecile, idiot.

imbecilidad [imbeθili'ðað] *nf* imbecility, stupidity.

imberbe [im'berße] *adj* beardless.

imborrable [imbo'rraßle] *adj* indelible; (*inolvidable*) unforgettable.

imbuir [imbu'ir] *vi* to imbue.

imbuyendo [imbu'jendo] *etc vb V* **imbuir**.

imitación [imita'θjon] *nf* imitation; (*parodia*) mimicry; **a ~ de** in imitation of; **desconfíe de las imitaciones** (*COM*) beware of copies *o* imitations.

imitador, a [imita'ðor, a] *adj* imitative ♦ *nm/f* imitator; (*TEAT*) mimic.

imitar [imi'tar] *vt* to imitate; (*parodiar, remedar*) to mimic, ape; (*copiar*) to follow.

impaciencia [impa'θjenθja] *nf* impatience.

impacientar [impaθjen'tar] *vt* to make impatient; (*enfadar*) to irritate; ~**se** *vr* to get impatient; (*inquietarse*) to fret.

impaciente [impa'θjente] *adj* impatient; (*nervioso*) anxious.

impacto [im'pakto] *nm* impact; (*esp AM: fig*) shock.

impagado, a [impa'ɣaðo, a] *adj* unpaid, still to be paid.

impar [im'par] *adj* odd ♦ *nm* odd number.

imparable [impa'raßle] *adj* unstoppable.

imparcial [impar'θjal] *adj* impartial, fair.

imparcialidad [imparθjali'ðað] *nf* impartiality, fairness.

impartir [impar'tir] *vt* to impart, give.

impasible [impa'sißle] *adj* impassive.

impávido, a [im'paβiðo, a] *adj* fearless, intrepid.

IMPE ['impe] *nm abr* (*ESP COM*) = *Instituto de la Mediana y Pequeña Empresa.*

impecable [impe'kaßle] *adj* impeccable.

impedido, a [impe'ðiðo, a] *adj*: **estar ~ to** be an invalid ♦ *nm/f*: **ser un ~ físico** to be an invalid.

impedimento [impeði'mento] *nm* impediment, obstacle.

impedir [impe'ðir] *vt* (*obstruir*) to impede, obstruct; (*estorbar*) to prevent; ~ **el tráfico** to block the traffic.

impeler [impe'ler] *vt* to drive, propel; (*fig*) to impel.

impenetrabilidad [impenetraßili'ðað] *nf*

impenetrability.
impenetrable [impene'traßle] *adj*
impenetrable; (*fig*) incomprehensible.
impensable [impen'saßle] *adj* unthinkable.
impepinable [impepi'naßle] *adj* (*fam*)
certain, inevitable.
imperante [impe'rante] *adj* prevailing.
imperar [impe'rar] *vi* (*reinar*) to rule, reign;
(*fig*) to prevail, reign; (*precio*) to be
current.
imperativo, a [impera'tiβo, a] *adj* (*persona*)
imperious; (*urgente, LING*) imperative.
imperceptible [imperθep'tiβle] *adj*
imperceptible.
imperdible [imper'ðiβle] *nm* safety pin.
imperdonable [imperðo'naβle] *adj*
unforgivable, inexcusable.
imperecedero, a [impereθe'ðero, a] *adj*
undying.
imperfección [imperfek'θjon] *nf*
imperfection; (*falla*) flaw, fault.
imperfecto, a [imper'fekto, a] *adj* faulty,
imperfect ♦ *nm* (*LING*) imperfect tense.
imperial [impe'rjal] *adj* imperial.
imperialismo [imperja'lismo] *nm*
imperialism.
imperialista [imperja'lista] *adj*
imperialist(ic) ♦ *nmf* imperialist.
impericia [impe'riθja] *nf* (*torpeza*)
unskilfulness; (*inexperiencia*)
inexperience.
imperio [im'perjo] *nm* empire; (*autoridad*)
rule, authority; (*fig*) pride, haughtiness;
vale un ~ (*fig*) it's worth a fortune.
imperioso, a [impe'rjoso, a] *adj* imperious;
(*urgente*) urgent; (*imperativo*)
imperative.
impermeable [imperme'aβle] *adj* (*a prueba
de agua*) waterproof ♦ *nm* raincoat, mac
(*BRIT*).
impersonal [imperso'nal] *adj* impersonal.
impertérrito, a [imper'territo, a] *adj*
undaunted.
impertinencia [imperti'nenθja] *nf*
impertinence.
impertinente [imperti'nente] *adj*
impertinent.
imperturbable [impertur'βaβle] *adj*
imperturbable; (*sereno*) unruffled;
(*impasible*) impassive.
ímpetu ['impetu] *nm* (*impulso*) impetus,
impulse; (*impetuosidad*) impetuosity;
(*violencia*) violence.
impetuosidad [impetwosi'ðað] *nf*
impetuousness; (*violencia*) violence.
impetuoso, a [impe'twoso, a] *adj*
impetuous; (*río*) rushing; (*acto*) hasty.
impida [im'piða] *etc vb V* **impedir**.

impío, a [im'pio, a] *adj* impious, ungodly;
(*cruel*) cruel, pitiless.
implacable [impla'kaβle] *adj* implacable,
relentless.
implantación [implanta'θjon] *nf*
introduction; (*BIO*) implantation.
implantar [implan'tar] *vt* (*costumbre*) to
introduce; (*BIO*) to implant; ~**se** *vr* to be
introduced.
implicar [impli'kar] *vt* to involve; (*entrañar*)
to imply; **esto no implica que** ... this does
not mean that ....
implícito, a [im'pliθito, a] *adj* (*tácito*)
implicit; (*sobreentendido*) implied.
implique [im'plike] *etc vb V* **implicar**.
implorar [implo'rar] *vt* to beg,
implore.
impondré [impon'dre] *etc vb V* **imponer**.
imponente [impo'nente] *adj*
(*impresionante*) impressive, imposing;
(*solemne*) grand ♦ *nmf* (*COM*) depositor.
imponer [impo'ner] *vt* (*gen*) to impose;
(*tarea*) to set; (*exigir*) to exact; (*miedo*) to
inspire; (*COM*) to deposit; ~**se** *vr* to
assert o.s.; (*prevalecer*) to prevail;
(*costumbre*) to grow up; ~**se un deber** to
assume a duty.
imponga [im'ponga] *etc vb V* **imponer**.
imponible [impo'niβle] *adj* (*COM*) taxable,
subject to tax; (*importación*) dutiable,
subject to duty; **no** ~ tax-free, tax-
exempt (*US*).
impopular [impopu'lar] *adj* unpopular.
importación [importa'θjon] *nf* (*acto*)
importing; (*mercancías*) imports *pl*.
importancia [impor'tanθja] *nf* importance;
(*valor*) value, significance; (*extensión*)
size, magnitude; **no dar** ~ **a** to consider
unimportant; (*fig*) to make light of; **no
tiene** ~ it's nothing.
importante [impor'tante] *adj* important;
valuable, significant.
importar [impor'tar] *vt* (*del extranjero*) to
import; (*costar*) to amount to; (*implicar*)
to involve ♦ *vi* to be important, matter;
me importa un bledo I don't give a
damn; **¿le importa que fume?** do you
mind if I smoke?; **¿te importa
prestármelo?** would you mind lending it
to me?; **¿qué importa?** what difference
does it make?; **no importa** it doesn't
matter; **no le importa** he doesn't care, it
doesn't bother him; **"no importa precio"**
"cost no object".
importe [im'porte] *nm* (*total*) amount;
(*valor*) value.
importunar [importu'nar] *vt* to bother,
pester.

importuno, a [impor'tuno, a] *adj*
(*inoportuno, molesto*) inopportune;
(*indiscreto*) troublesome.

imposibilidad [imposiβili'ðað] *nf*
impossibility; **mi ~ para hacerlo** my
inability to do it.

imposibilitado, a [imposiβili'taðo, a] *adj:*
verse ~ para hacer algo to be unable to
do sth.

imposibilitar [imposiβili'tar] *vt* to make
impossible, prevent.

imposible [impo'siβle] *adj* impossible;
(*insoportable*) unbearable, intolerable; **es
~ it's** out of the question; **es ~ de
predecir** it's impossible to forecast *o*
predict.

imposición [imposi'θjon] *nf* imposition;
(*COM*) tax; (*inversión*) deposit; **efectuar
una ~** to make a deposit.

impostor, a [impos'tor, a] *nm/f* impostor.

impostura [impos'tura] *nf* fraud,
imposture.

impotencia [impo'tenθja] *nf* impotence.

impotente [impo'tente] *adj* impotent.

impracticable [imprakti'kaβle] *adj*
(*irrealizable*) impracticable; (*intransitable*)
impassable.

imprecar [impre'kar] *vi* to curse.

imprecisión [impreθi'sjon] *nf* lack of
precision, vagueness.

impreciso, a [impre'θiso, a] *adj* imprecise,
vague.

impredecible [impreðe'θiβle],
impredictible [impreðik'tiβle] *adj*
unpredictable.

impregnar [impreɣ'nar] *vt* to impregnate;
(*fig*) to pervade; **~se** *vr* to become
impregnated.

imprenta [im'prenta] *nf* (*acto*) printing;
(*aparato*) press; (*casa*) printer's; (*letra*)
print.

impreque [im'preke] *etc vb V*
imprecar.

imprescindible [impresθin'diβle] *adj*
essential, vital.

impresión [impre'sjon] *nf* impression;
(*IMPRENTA*) printing; (*edición*) edition;
(*FOTO*) print; (*marca*) imprint; **~ digital**
fingerprint.

impresionable [impresjo'naβle] *adj*
(*sensible*) impressionable.

impresionado, a [impresjo'naðo, a] *adj*
impressed; (*FOTO*) exposed.

impresionante [impresjo'nante] *adj*
impressive; (*tremendo*) tremendous;
(*maravilloso*) great, marvellous.

impresionar [impresjo'nar] *vt* (*conmover*)
to move; (*afectar*) to impress, strike;

(*película fotográfica*) to expose; **~se** *vr* to
be impressed; (*conmoverse*) to be
moved.

impresionista [impresjo'nista] *adj*
impressionist(ic); (*ARTE*) impressionist
♦ *nm/f* impressionist.

impreso, a [im'preso, a] *pp de* **imprimir**
♦ *adj* printed ♦ *nm* printed paper/book
etc; **~s** *nmpl* printed matter *sg*; **~ de
solicitud** application form.

impresora [impre'sora] *nf* (*INFORM*)
printer; **~ de chorro de tinta** ink-jet
printer; **~ (por) láser** laser printer; **~ de
línea** line printer; **~ de matriz (de
agujas)** dot-matrix printer; **~ de rueda** *o*
de margarita daisy-wheel printer.

imprevisible [impreβi'siβle] *adj*
unforeseeable; (*individuo*) unpredictable.

imprevisión [impreβi'sjon] *nf* short-
sightedness; (*irreflexión*)
thoughtlessness.

imprevisto, a [impre'βisto, a] *adj*
unforeseen; (*inesperado*) unexpected
♦ *nm:* **~s** (*dinero*) incidentals, unforeseen
expenses.

imprimir [impri'mir] *vt* to stamp; (*textos*) to
print; (*INFORM*) to output, print out.

improbabilidad [improβaβili'ðað] *nf*
improbability, unlikelihood.

improbable [impro'βaβle] *adj* improbable;
(*inverosímil*) unlikely.

improcedente [improθe'ðente] *adj*
inappropriate; (*JUR*) inadmissible.

improductivo, a [improðuk'tiβo, a] *adj*
unproductive.

impronunciable [impronun'θjaβle] *adj*
unpronounceable.

improperio [impro'perjo] *nm* insult; **~s**
nmpl abuse *sg*.

impropiedad [impropje'ðað] *nf*
impropriety (of language).

impropio, a [im'propjo, a] *adj* improper;
(*inadecuado*) inappropriate.

improvisación [improβisa'θjon] *nf*
improvization.

improvisado, a [improβi'saðo, a] *adj*
improvised, impromptu.

improvisar [improβi'sar] *vt* to improvise;
(*comida*) to rustle up ♦ *vi* to improvise;
(*MUS*) to extemporize; (*TEAT etc*) to ad-
lib.

improviso [impro'βiso] *adv* **de ~**
unexpectedly, suddenly; (*MUS etc*)
impromptu.

imprudencia [impru'ðenθja] *nf*
imprudence; (*indiscreción*) indiscretion;
(*descuido*) carelessness.

imprudente [impru'ðente] *adj* imprudent;

indiscreet.

Impte. *abr* (= *Importe*) amt.

impúdico, a [im'puðiko, a] *adj* shameless; (*lujurioso*) lecherous.

impudor [impu'ðor] *nm* shamelessness; (*lujuria*) lechery.

impuesto, a [im'pwesto, a] *pp de* **imponer** ♦ *adj* imposed ♦ *nm* tax; (*derecho*) duty; **anterior al** ~ pre-tax; **sujeto a** ~ taxable; ~ **de lujo** luxury tax; ~ **de plusvalía** capital gains tax; ~ **sobre la propiedad** property tax; ~ **sobre la renta** income tax; ~ **sobre la renta de las personas físicas (IRPF)** personal income tax; ~ **sobre la riqueza** wealth tax; ~ **de transferencia de capital** capital transfer tax; ~ **de venta** sales tax; ~ **sobre el valor añadido (IVA)** value added tax (VAT).

impugnar [impuɣ'nar] *vt* to oppose, contest; (*refutar*) to refute, impugn.

impulsar [impul'sar] *vt* = **impeler**.

impulsivo, a [impul'siβo, a] *adj* impulsive.

impulso [im'pulso] *nm* impulse; (*fuerza, empuje*) thrust, drive; (*fig: sentimiento*) urge, impulse; **a** ~**s del miedo** driven on by fear.

impune [im'pune] *adj* unpunished.

impunemente [impune'mente] *adv* with impunity.

impureza [impu'reθa] *nf* impurity; (*fig*) lewdness.

impuro, a [im'puro, a] *adj* impure; lewd.

impuse [im'puse] *etc vb V* **imponer**.

imputación [imputa'θjon] *nf* imputation.

imputar [impu'tar] *vt*: ~ **a** to attribute to, to impute to.

inabordable [inaβor'ðaβle] *adj* unapproachable.

inacabable [inaka'βaβle] *adj* (*infinito*) endless; (*interminable*) interminable.

inaccesible [inakθe'siβle] *adj* inaccessible; (*fig: precio*) beyond one's reach, prohibitive; (*individuo*) aloof.

inacción [inak'θjon] *nf* inactivity.

inaceptable [inaθep'taβle] *adj* unacceptable.

inactividad [inaktiβi'ðað] *nf* inactivity; (*COM*) dullness.

inactivo, a [inak'tiβo, a] *adj* inactive; (*COM*) dull; (*población*) non-working.

inadaptación [inaðapta'θjon] *nf* maladjustment.

inadaptado, a [inaðap'taðo, a] *adj* maladjusted ♦ *nm/f* misfit.

inadecuado, a [inaðe'kwaðo, a] *adj* (*insuficiente*) inadequate; (*inapto*) unsuitable.

inadmisible [inaðmi'siβle] *adj* inadmissible.

inadvertido, a [inaðßer'tiðo, a] *adj* (*no visto*) unnoticed.

inagotable [inaɣo'taβle] *adj* inexhaustible.

inaguantable [inaɣwan'taβle] *adj* unbearable.

inalámbrico, a [ina'lambriko, a] *adj* cordless.

inalcanzable [inalkan'θaβle] *adj* unattainable.

inalterable [inalte'raβle] *adj* immutable, unchangeable.

inamovible [inamo'βiβle] *adj* fixed, immovable; (*TEC*) undetachable.

inanición [inani'θjon] *nf* starvation.

inanimado, a [inani'maðo, a] *adj* inanimate.

inapelable [inape'laβle] *adj* (*JUR*) unappealable; (*fig*) irremediable.

inapetencia [inape'tenθja] *nf* lack of appetite.

inaplicable [inapli'kaβle] *adj* not applicable.

inapreciable [inapre'θjaβle] *adj* invaluable.

inarrugable [inarru'ɣaβle] *adj* crease-resistant.

inasequible [inase'kiβle] *adj* unattainable.

inaudito, a [inau'ðito, a] *adj* unheard-of.

inauguración [inauɣura'θjon] *nf* inauguration; (*de exposición*) opening.

inaugurar [inauɣu'rar] *vt* to inaugurate; to open.

I.N.B. *abr* (= *Instituto Nacional de Bachillerato*) ≈ comprehensive school (*BRIT*), high school (*US*).

I.N.B.A. *abr* (*AM*) = *Instituto Nacional de Bellas Artes.*

inca ['inka] *nm/f* Inca.

INCAE [in'kae] *nm abr* = *Instituto Centroamericano de Administración de Empresas.*

incaico, a [in'kaiko, a] *adj* Inca.

incalculable [inkalku'laβle] *adj* incalculable.

incandescente [inkandes'θente] *adj* incandescent.

incansable [inkan'saβle] *adj* tireless, untiring.

incapacidad [inkapaθi'ðað] *nf* incapacity; (*incompetencia*) incompetence; ~ **física/mental** physical/mental disability.

incapacitar [inkapaθi'tar] *vt* (*inhabilitar*) to incapacitate, handicap; (*descalificar*) to disqualify.

incapaz [inka'paθ] *adj* incapable; ~ **de hacer algo** unable to do sth.

incautación [inkauta'θjon] *nf* seizure,

confiscation.

incautarse [inkau'tarse] *vr*: ~ **de** to seize,
confiscate.

incauto, a [in'kauto, a] *adj* (*imprudente*)
incautious, unwary.

incendiar [inθen'djar] *vt* to set fire to; (*fig*)
to inflame; **~se** *vr* to catch fire.

incendiario, a [inθen'djarjo, a] *adj*
incendiary ♦ *nm/f* fire-raiser, arsonist.

incendio [in'θendjo] *nm* fire; ~
intencionado arson.

incentivo [inθen'tiβo] *nm* incentive.

incertidumbre [inθerti'ðumbre] *nf*
(*inseguridad*) uncertainty; (*duda*) doubt.

incesante [inθe'sante] *adj* incessant.

incesto [in'θesto] *nm* incest.

incidencia [inθi'ðenθja] *nf* (*MAT*) incidence;
(*fig*) effect.

incidente [inθi'ðente] *nm* incident.

incidir [inθi'ðir] *vi*: ~ **en** (*influir*) to
influence; (*afectar*) to affect; ~ **en un
error** to be mistaken.

incienso [in'θjenso] *nm* incense.

incierto, a [in'θjerto, a] *adj* uncertain.

incineración [inθinera'θjon] *nf*
incineration; (*de cadáveres*) cremation.

incinerar [inθine'rar] *vt* to burn; to
cremate.

incipiente [inθi'pjente] *adj* incipient.

incisión [inθi'sjon] *nf* incision.

incisivo, a [inθi'siβo, a] *adj* sharp, cutting;
(*fig*) incisive.

inciso [in'θiso] *nm* (*LING*) clause, sentence;
(*coma*) comma; (*JUR*) subsection.

incitante [inθi'tante] *adj* (*estimulante*)
exciting; (*provocativo*) provocative.

incitar [inθi'tar] *vt* to incite, rouse.

incivil [inθi'βil] *adj* rude, uncivil.

inclemencia [inkle'menθja] *nf* (*severidad*)
harshness, severity; (*del tiempo*)
inclemency.

inclemente [inkle'mente] *adj* harsh,
severe; inclement.

inclinación [inklina'θjon] *nf* (*gen*)
inclination; (*de tierras*) slope, incline; (*de
cabeza*) nod, bow; (*fig*) leaning, bent.

inclinado, a [inkli'naðo, a] *adj* (*objeto*)
leaning; (*superficie*) sloping.

inclinar [inkli'nar] *vt* to incline; (*cabeza*) to
nod, bow; **~se** *vr* to lean, slope; (*en
reverencia*) to bow; (*encorvarse*) to stoop;
~se a (*parecerse*) to take after,
resemble; **~se ante** to bow down to; **me
inclino a pensar que ...** I'm inclined to
think that ....

incluir [inklu'ir] *vt* to include; (*incorporar*)
to incorporate; (*meter*) to enclose; **todo
incluido** (*COM*) inclusive, all-in.

inclusive [inklu'siβe] *adv* inclusive ♦ *prep*
including.

incluso, a [in'kluso, a] *adj* included ♦ *adv*
inclusively; (*hasta*) even.

incluyendo [inklu'jendo] *etc vb V* **incluir**.

incobrable [inko'βraβle] *adj* irrecoverable;
(*deuda*) bad.

incógnita [in'koɣnita] *nf* (*fig*) mystery.

incógnito [in'koɣnito]: **de** ~ *adv* incognito.

incoherencia [inkoe'renθja] *nf*
incoherence; (*falta de conexión*)
disconnectedness.

incoherente [inkoe'rente] *adj* incoherent.

incoloro, a [inko'loro, a] *adj* colourless.

incólume [in'kolume] *adj* safe; (*indemne*)
unhurt, unharmed.

incombustible [inkombus'tiβle] *adj* (*gen*)
fire-resistant; (*telas*) fireproof.

incomodar [inkomo'ðar] *vt* to
inconvenience; (*molestar*) to bother,
trouble; (*fastidiar*) to annoy; **~se** *vr* to put
o.s. out; (*fastidiarse*) to get annoyed; **no
se incomode** don't bother.

incomodidad [inkomoði'ðað] *nf*
inconvenience; (*fastidio, enojo*)
annoyance; (*de vivienda*) discomfort.

incómodo, a [in'komoðo, a] *adj*
(*inconfortable*) uncomfortable; (*molesto*)
annoying; (*inconveniente*) inconvenient;
sentirse ~ to feel ill at ease.

incomparable [inkompa'raβle] *adj*
incomparable.

incomparecencia [inkompare'θenθja] *nf*
(*JUR etc*) failure to appear.

incompatible [inkompa'tiβle] *adj*
incompatible.

incompetencia [inkompe'tenθja] *nf*
incompetence.

incompetente [inkompe'tente] *adj*
incompetent.

incompleto, a [inkom'pleto, a] *adj*
incomplete, unfinished.

incomprendido, a [inkompren'diðo, a] *adj*
misunderstood.

incomprensible [inkompren'siβle] *adj*
incomprehensible.

incomunicado, a [inkomuni'kaðo, a] *adj*
(*aislado*) cut off, isolated; (*confinado*) in
solitary confinement.

incomunicar [inkomuni'kar] *vt* (*gen*) to cut
off; (*preso*) to put into solitary
confinement; **~se** *vr* (*fam*) to go into
one's shell.

incomunique [inkomu'nike] *etc vb V*
incomunicar.

inconcebible [inkonθe'βiβle] *adj*
inconceivable.

inconcluso, a [inkon'kluso, a] *adj*

(*inacabado*) unfinished.
incondicional [inkondiθjo'nal] *adj*
unconditional; (*apoyo*) wholehearted;
(*partidario*) staunch.
inconexo, a [inko'nekso, a] *adj*
unconnected; (*desunido*) disconnected;
(*incoherente*) incoherent.
inconfeso, a [inkon'feso, a] *adj*
unconfessed; **un homosexual** ~ a closet
homosexual.
inconformista [inkonfor'mista] *adj, nm/f*
nonconformist.
inconfundible [inkonfun'diβle] *adj*
unmistakable.
incongruente [inkon'grwente] *adj*
incongruous.
inconmensurable [inkonmensu'raβle] *adj*
immeasurable, vast.
inconsciencia [inkons'θjenθja] *nf*
unconsciousness; (*fig*) thoughtlessness.
inconsciente [inkons'θjente] *adj*
unconscious; thoughtless; (*ignorante*)
unaware; (*involuntario*) unwitting.
inconsecuencia [inkonse'kwenθja] *nf*
inconsistency.
inconsecuente [inkonse'kwente] *adj*
inconsistent.
inconsiderado, a [inkonsiðe'raðo, a] *adj*
inconsiderate.
inconsistente [inkonsis'tente] *adj*
inconsistent; (*CULIN*) lumpy; (*endeble*)
weak; (*tela*) flimsy.
inconstancia [inkons'tanθja] *nf*
inconstancy; (*de tiempo*) changeability;
(*capricho*) fickleness.
inconstante [inkons'tante] *adj* inconstant;
changeable; fickle.
incontable [inkon'taβle] *adj* countless,
innumerable.
incontestable [inkontes'taβle] *adj*
unanswerable; (*innegable*) undeniable.
incontinencia [inkonti'nenθja] *nf*
incontinence.
incontrolado, a [inkontro'laðo, a] *adj*
uncontrolled.
incontrovertible [inkontroβer'tiβle] *adj*
undeniable, incontrovertible.
inconveniencia [inkombe'njenθja] *nf*
unsuitability, inappropriateness;
(*descortesía*) impoliteness.
inconveniente [inkombe'njente] *adj*
unsuitable; impolite ♦ *nm* obstacle;
(*desventaja*) disadvantage; **el** ~ **es que** ...
the trouble is that ...; **no hay** ~ **en** *o* **para
hacer eso** there is no objection to doing
that; **no tengo** ~ I don't mind.
incordiar [inkor'ðjar] *vt* (*fam*) to hassle.
incorporación [inkorpora'θjon] *nf*

incorporation; (*fig*) inclusion.
incorporado, a [inkorpo'raðo, a] *adj* (*TEC*)
built-in.
incorporar [inkorpo'rar] *vt* to incorporate;
(*abarcar*) to embody; (*CULIN*) to mix; ~**se**
vr to sit up; ~**se a** to join.
incorrección [inkorrek'θjon] *nf*
incorrectness, inaccuracy; (*descortesía*)
bad-mannered behaviour.
incorrecto, a [inko'rrekto, a] *adj* incorrect,
wrong; (*comportamiento*) bad-mannered.
incorregible [inkorre'xiβle] *adj*
incorrigible.
incorruptible [inkorrup'tiβle] *adj*
incorruptible.
incorrupto, a [inko'rrupto, a] *adj*
uncorrupted; (*fig*) pure.
incredulidad [inkreðuli'ðað] *nf* incredulity;
(*escepticismo*) scepticism.
incrédulo, a [in'kreðulo, a] *adj*
incredulous, unbelieving; sceptical.
increíble [inkre'iβle] *adj* incredible.
incrementar [inkremen'tar] *vt* (*aumentar*)
to increase; (*alzar*) to raise; ~**se** *vr* to
increase.
incremento [inkre'mento] *nm* increment;
(*aumento*) rise, increase; ~ **de precio**
rise in price.
increpar [inkre'par] *vt* to reprimand.
incriminar [inkrimi'nar] *vt* (*JUR*) to
incriminate.
incruento, a [in'krwento, a] *adj* bloodless.
incrustar [inkrus'tar] *vt* to incrust; (*piedras:
en joya*) to inlay; (*fig*) to graft; (*TEC*) to
set.
incubar [inku'βar] *vt* to incubate; (*fig*) to
hatch.
incuestionable [inkwestjo'naβle] *adj*
unchallengeable.
inculcar [inkul'kar] *vt* to inculcate.
inculpar [inkul'par] *vt*: ~ **de** (*acusar*) to
accuse of; (*achacar, atribuir*) to charge
with, blame for.
inculque [in'kulke] *etc vb V* **inculcar**.
inculto, a [in'kulto, a] *adj* (*persona*)
uneducated, uncultured; (*fig: grosero*)
uncouth ♦ *nm/f* ignoramus.
incumbencia [inkum'benθja] *nf* obligation;
no es de mi ~ it is not my field.
incumbir [inkum'bir] *vi*: ~ **a** to be
incumbent upon; **no me incumbe a mí** it
is no concern of mine.
incumplimiento [inkumpli'mjento] *nm*
non-fulfilment; (*COM*) repudiation; ~ **de
contrato** breach of contract; **por** ~ by
default.
incurable [inku'raβle] *adj* (*enfermedad*)
incurable; (*paciente*) incurably ill.

incurrir [inku'rrir] *vi*: ~ **en** to incur; (*crimen*) to commit; ~ **en un error** to make a mistake.

indagación [indaɣa'θjon] *nf* investigation; (*búsqueda*) search; (*JUR*) inquest.

indagar [inda'ɣar] *vt* to investigate; to search; (*averiguar*) to ascertain.

indague [in'daɣe] *etc vb V* **indagar**.

indebido, a [inde'ßiðo, a] *adj* undue; (*dicho*) improper.

indecencia [inde'θenθja] *nf* indecency; (*dicho*) obscenity.

indecente [inde'θente] *adj* indecent, improper; (*lascivo*) obscene.

indecible [inde'θißle] *adj* unspeakable; (*indescriptible*) indescribable.

indeciso, a [inde'θiso, a] *adj* (*por decidir*) undecided; (*vacilante*) hesitant.

indefenso, a [inde'fenso, a] *adj* defenceless.

indefinido, a [indefi'niðo, a] *adj* indefinite; (*vago*) vague, undefined.

indeleble [inde'leßle] *adj* indelible.

indemne [in'demne] *adj* (*objeto*) undamaged; (*persona*) unharmed, unhurt.

indemnice [indem'niθe] *etc vb V* **indemnizar**.

indemnización [indemniθa'θjon] *nf* (*acto*) indemnification; (*suma*) indemnity; ~ **de cese** redundancy payment; ~ **de despido** severance pay; **doble** ~ double indemnity.

indemnizar [indemni'θar] *vt* to indemnify; (*compensar*) to compensate.

independencia [indepen'denθja] *nf* independence.

independice [indepen'diθe] *etc vb V* **independizar**.

independiente [indepen'djente] *adj* (*libre*) independent; (*autónomo*) self-sufficient; (*INFORM*) stand-alone.

independizar [independi'θar] *vt* to make independent; ~**se** *vr* to become independent.

indescifrable [indesθi'fraßle] *adj* (*MIL*: *código*) indecipherable; (*fig*: *misterio*) impenetrable.

indeseable [indese'aßle] *adj*, *nm/f* undesirable.

indeterminado, a [indetermi'naðo, a] *adj* (*tb LING*) indefinite; (*desconocido*) indeterminate.

India ['indja] *nf*: **la** ~ India.

indiano, a [in'djano, a] *adj* (Spanish-) American ♦ *nm* Spaniard who has made good in America.

indicación [indika'θjon] *nf* indication;

(*dato*) piece of information; (*señal*) sign; (*sugerencia*) suggestion, hint; **indicaciones** *nfpl* (*COM*) instructions.

indicado, a [indi'kaðo, a] *adj* (*apto*) right, appropriate.

indicador [indika'ðor] *nm* indicator; (*TEC*) gauge, meter; (*aguja*) hand, pointer; (*de carretera*) roadsign; ~ **de encendido** (*INFORM*) power-on indicator.

indicar [indi'kar] *vt* (*mostrar*) to indicate, show; (*suj*: *termómetro etc*) to read, register; (*señalar*) to point to.

indicativo, a [indika'tißo, a] *adj* indicative ♦ *nm* (*RADIO*) call sign; ~ **de nacionalidad** (*AUTO*) national identification plate.

índice ['indiθe] *nm* index; (*catálogo*) catalogue; (*ANAT*) index finger, forefinger; ~ **del coste de (la) vida** cost-of-living index; ~ **de crédito** credit rating; ~ **de materias** table of contents; ~ **de natalidad** birth rate; ~ **de precios al por menor (IPM)** (*COM*) retail price index (RPI).

indicio [in'diθjo] *nm* indication, sign; (*en pesquisa etc*) clue; (*INFORM*) marker, mark.

indiferencia [indife'renθja] *nf* indifference; (*apatía*) apathy.

indiferente [indife'rente] *adj* indifferent; **me es** ~ it makes no difference to me.

indígena [in'dixena] *adj* indigenous, native ♦ *nm/f* native.

indigencia [indi'xenθja] *nf* poverty, need.

indigenista [indixe'nista] (*AM*) *adj* pro-Indian ♦ *nm/f* (*estudiante*) student of Indian cultures; (*POL etc*) promoter of Indian cultures.

indigestar [indixes'tar] *vt* to cause indigestion to; ~**se** *vr* to get indigestion.

indigestión [indixes'tjon] *nf* indigestion.

indigesto, a [indi'xesto, a] *adj* undigested; (*indigestible*) indigestible; (*fig*) turgid.

indignación [indixna'θjon] *nf* indignation.

indignante [indiɣ'nante] *adj* outrageous, infuriating.

indignar [indiɣ'nar] *vt* to anger, make indignant; ~**se** *vr*: ~**se por** to get indignant about.

indigno, a [in'diɣno, a] *adj* (*despreciable*) low, contemptible; (*inmerecido*) unworthy.

indio, a ['indjo, a] *adj*, *nm/f* Indian.

indique [in'dike] *etc vb V* **indicar**.

indirecto, a [indi'rekto, a] *adj* indirect ♦ *nf* insinuation, innuendo; (*sugerencia*) hint.

indisciplina [indisθi'plina] *nf* (*gen*) lack of discipline; (*MIL*) insubordination.

indiscreción [indiskre'θjon] *nf*

(*imprudencia*) indiscretion; (*irreflexión*) tactlessness; (*acto*) gaffe, faux pas; ..., **si no es** ~ ..., if I may say so.

indiscreto, a [indis'kreto, a] *adj* indiscreet.

indiscriminado, a [indiskrimi'naðo, a] *adj* indiscriminate.

indiscutible [indisku'tiβle] *adj* indisputable, unquestionable.

indispensable [indispen'saβle] *adj* indispensable.

indispondré [indispon'dre] *etc vb V* **indisponer**.

indisponer [indispo'ner] *vt* to spoil, upset; (*salud*) to make ill; ~**se** *vr* to fall ill; ~**se con algn** to fall out with sb.

indisponga [indis'poŋga] *etc vb V* **indisponer**.

indisposición [indisposi'θjon] *nf* indisposition; (*desgana*) unwillingness.

indispuesto, a [indis'pwesto, a] *pp de* **indisponer** ♦ *adj* indisposed; **sentirse** ~ to feel unwell *o* indisposed.

indispuse [indis'puse] *etc vb V* **indisponer**.

indistinto, a [indis'tinto, a] *adj* indistinct; (*vago*) vague.

individual [indiβi'ðwal] *adj* individual; (*habitación*) single ♦ *nm* (*DEPORTE*) singles *sg*.

individuo, a [indi'βiðwo, a] *adj* individual ♦ *nm* individual.

Indochina [indo'tʃina] *nf* Indochina.

indocumentado, a [indokumen'taðo, a] *adj* without identity papers.

indoeuropeo, a [indoeuro'peo, a] *adj, nm/f* Indo-European.

índole ['indole] *nf* (*naturaleza*) nature; (*clase*) sort, kind.

indolencia [indo'lenθja] *nf* indolence, laziness.

indoloro, a [in'doloro, a] *adj* painless.

indomable [indo'maβle] *adj* (*animal*) untameable; (*espíritu*) indomitable.

indómito, a [in'domito, a] *adj* indomitable.

Indonesia [indo'nesja] *nf* Indonesia.

indonesio, a [indo'nesjo, a] *adj, nm/f* Indonesian.

inducción [induk'θjon] *nf* (*FILOSOFÍA, ELEC*) induction; **por** ~ by induction.

inducir [indu'θir] *vt* to induce; (*inferir*) to infer; (*persuadir*) to persuade; ~ **a algn en el error** to mislead sb.

indudable [indu'ðaβle] *adj* undoubted; (*incuestionable*) unquestionable; **es** ~ **que** ... there is no doubt that ....

indulgencia [indul'xenθja] *nf* indulgence; (*JUR etc*) leniency; **proceder sin** ~ **contra** to proceed ruthlessly against.

indultar [indul'tar] *vt* (*perdonar*) to pardon,

reprieve; (*librar de pago*) to exempt.

indulto [in'dulto] *nm* pardon; exemption.

indumentaria [indumen'tarja] *nf* (*ropa*) clothing, dress.

industria [in'dustrja] *nf* industry; (*habilidad*) skill; ~ **agropecuaria** farming and fishing; ~ **pesada** heavy industry; ~ **petrolífera** oil industry.

industrial [indus'trjal] *adj* industrial ♦ *nm* industrialist.

industrializar [industrjali'θar] *vt* to industrialize; ~**se** *vr* to become industrialized.

INE ['ine] *nm abr* (*ESP*) = *Instituto Nacional de Estadística*.

inédito, a [i'neðito, a] *adj* (*libro*) unpublished; (*nuevo*) unheard-of.

inefable [ine'faβle] *adj* ineffable, indescribable.

ineficacia [inefi'kaθja] *nf* (*de medida*) ineffectiveness; (*de proceso*) inefficiency.

ineficaz [inefi'kaθ] *adj* (*inútil*) ineffective; (*ineficiente*) inefficient.

ineludible [inelu'ðiβle] *adj* inescapable, unavoidable.

INEM, Inem [i'nem] *nm abr* (*ESP*: = *Instituto Nacional de Empleo*) ≈ Department of Employment (*BRIT*).

INEN ['inen] *nm abr* (*México*) = *Instituto Nacional de Energía Nuclear*.

inenarrable [inena'rraβle] *adj* inexpressible.

ineptitud [inepti'tuð] *nf* ineptitude, incompetence.

inepto, a [i'nepto, a] *adj* inept, incompetent.

inequívoco, a [ine'kiβoko, a] *adj* unequivocal; (*inconfundible*) unmistakable.

inercia [i'nerθja] *nf* inertia; (*pasividad*) passivity.

inerme [i'nerme] *adj* (*sin armas*) unarmed; (*indefenso*) defenceless.

inerte [i'nerte] *adj* inert; (*inmóvil*) motionless.

inescrutable [ineskru'taβle] *adj* inscrutable.

inesperado, a [inespe'raðo, a] *adj* unexpected, unforeseen.

inestable [ines'taβle] *adj* unstable.

inestimable [inesti'maβle] *adj* inestimable; **de valor** ~ invaluable.

inevitable [ineβi'taβle] *adj* inevitable.

inexactitud [ineksakti'tuð] *nf* inaccuracy.

inexacto, a [inek'sakto, a] *adj* inaccurate; (*falso*) untrue.

inexistente [ineksis'tente] *adj* non-

existent.
inexorable [inekso'raßle] *adj* inexorable.
inexperiencia [inekspe'rjenθja] *nf*
inexperience, lack of experience.
inexperto, a [ineks'perto, a] *adj* (*novato*)
inexperienced.
inexplicable [inekspli'kaßle] *adj*
inexplicable.
inexpresable [inekspre'saßle] *adj*
inexpressible.
inexpresivo, a [inekspre'sißo, a] *adj*
inexpressive; (*ojos*) dull; (*cara*) wooden.
inexpugnable [inekspuɣ'naßle] *adj* (*MIL*)
impregnable; (*fig*) firm.
infalible [infa'lißle] *adj* infallible;
(*indefectible*) certain, sure; (*plan*)
foolproof.
infame [in'fame] *adj* infamous.
infamia [in'famja] *nf* infamy; (*deshonra*)
disgrace.
infancia [in'fanθja] *nf* infancy, childhood;
jardín de la ~ nursery school.
infanta [in'fanta] *nf* (*hija del rey*) infanta,
princess.
infante [in'fante] *nm* (*hijo del rey*) infante,
prince.
infantería [infante'ria] *nf* infantry.
infantil [infan'til] *adj* child's, children's;
(*pueril, aniñado*) infantile; (*cándido*)
childlike.
infarto [in'farto] *nm* (*tb*: ~ **de miocardio**)
heart attack.
infatigable [infati'ɣaßle] *adj* tireless,
untiring.
infección [infek'θjon] *nf* infection.
infeccioso, a [infek'θjoso, a] *adj*
infectious.
infectar [infek'tar] *vt* to infect; ~**se** *vr*: ~**se**
(**de**) (*tb fig*) to become infected (with).
infecundidad [infekundi'ðað] *nf* (*de tierra*)
infertility, barrenness; (*de mujer*)
sterility.
infecundo, a [infe'kundo, a] *adj* infertile,
barren; sterile.
infeliz [infe'liθ] *adj* (*desgraciado*) unhappy,
wretched; (*inocente*) gullible ♦ *nmlf*
(*desgraciado*) wretch; (*inocentón*)
simpleton.
inferior [infe'rjor] *adj* inferior; (*situación,
MAT*) lower ♦ *nmlf* inferior, subordinate;
cualquier número ~ **a 9** any number less
than *o* under *o* below 9; **una cantidad** ~ a
lesser quantity.
inferioridad [inferjori'ðað] *nf* inferiority;
estar en ~ **de condiciones** to be at a
disadvantage.
inferir [infe'rir] *vt* (*deducir*) to infer,
deduce; (*causar*) to cause.

infernal [infer'nal] *adj* infernal.
infértil [in'fertil] *adj* infertile.
infestar [infes'tar] *vt* to infest.
infidelidad [infiðeli'ðað] *nf* (*gen*) infidelity,
unfaithfulness.
infiel [in'fjel] *adj* unfaithful, disloyal;
(*falso*) inaccurate ♦ *nmlf* infidel,
unbeliever.
infiera [in'fjera] *etc vb V* **inferir**.
infierno [in'fjerno] *nm* hell; **¡vete al** ~! go
to hell; **está en el quinto** ~ it's at the
back of beyond.
infiltrar [infil'trar] *vt* to infiltrate; ~**se** *vr* to
infiltrate, filter; (*líquidos*) to percolate.
ínfimo, a ['infimo, a] *adj* (*vil*) vile, mean;
(*más bajo*) lowest; (*peor*) worst;
(*miserable*) wretched.
infinidad [infini'ðað] *nf* infinity;
(*abundancia*) great quantity; ~ **de** vast
numbers of; ~ **de veces** countless times.
infinitivo [infini'tißo] *nm* infinitive.
infinito, a [infi'nito, a] *adj* infinite; (*fig*)
boundless ♦ *adv* infinitely ♦ *nm* infinite;
(*MAT*) infinity; **hasta lo** ~ ad infinitum.
infiriendo [infi'rjendo] *etc vb V* **inferir**.
inflación [infla'θjon] *nf* (*hinchazón*)
swelling; (*monetaria*) inflation; (*fig*)
conceit.
inflacionario, a [inflaθjo'narjo, a] *adj*
inflationary.
inflacionismo [inflaθjo'nismo] *nm* (*ECON*)
inflation.
inflacionista [inflaθjo'nista] *adj*
inflationary.
inflamar [infla'mar] *vt* to set on fire; (*MED,
fig*) to inflame; ~**se** *vr* to catch fire; to
become inflamed.
inflar [in'flar] *vt* (*hinchar*) to inflate, blow
up; (*fig*) to exaggerate; ~**se** *vr* to swell
(up); (*fig*) to get conceited.
inflexible [inflek'sißle] *adj* inflexible; (*fig*)
unbending.
infligir [infli'xir] *vt* to inflict.
inflija [in'flixa] *etc vb V* **infligir**.
influencia [in'flwenθja] *nf* influence.
influenciar [inflwen'θjar] *vt* to influence.
influir [influ'ir] *vt* to influence ♦ *vi* to have
influence, carry weight; ~ **en** *o* **sobre** to
influence, affect; (*contribuir a*) to have a
hand in.
influjo [in'fluxo] *nm* influence; ~ **de
capitales** (*ECON etc*) capital influx.
influyendo [influ'jendo] *etc vb V* **influir**.
influyente [influ'jente] *adj* influential.
información [informa'θjon] *nf*
information; (*noticias*) news *sg*; (*informe*)
report; (*INFORM: datos*) data; (*JUR*)
inquiry; **I**~ (*oficina*) Information; (*TELEC*)

Directory Enquiries (*BRIT*), Directory Assistance (*US*); (*mostrador*) Information Desk; **una ~** a piece of information; **abrir una ~** (*JUR*) to begin proceedings; **~ deportiva** (*en periódico*) sports section.

informal [infor'mal] *adj* (*gen*) informal.

informante [infor'mante] *nm/f* informant.

informar [infor'mar] *vt* (*gen*) to inform; (*revelar*) to reveal, make known ♦ *vi* (*JUR*) to plead; (*denunciar*) to inform; (*dar cuenta de*) to report on; **~se** *vr* to find out; **~se de** to inquire into.

informática [infor'matika] *nf* V **informático**.

informatice [informa'tiθe] *etc vb* V **informatizar**.

informático, a [infor'matiko, a] *adj* computer *cpd* ♦ *nf* (*TEC*) information technology; computing; (*ESCOL*) computer science *o* studies; **~ de gestión** commercial computing.

informativo, a [informa'tiβo, a] *adj* (*libro*) informative; (*folleto*) information *cpd*; (*RADIO, TV*) news *cpd* ♦ *nm* (*RADIO, TV*) news programme.

informatización [informatiθa'θjon] *nf* computerization.

informatizar [informati'θar] *vt* to computerize.

informe [in'forme] *adj* shapeless ♦ *nm* report; (*dictamen*) statement; (*MIL*) briefing; (*JUR*) plea; **~s** *nmpl* information *sg*; (*datos*) data; **~ anual** annual report; **~ del juez** summing-up.

infortunio [infor'tunjo] *nm* misfortune.

infracción [infrak'θjon] *nf* infraction, infringement; (*AUTO*) offence.

infraestructura [infraestruk'tura] *nf* infrastructure.

in fraganti [infra'ɣanti] *adv*: **pillar a algn ~** to catch sb red-handed.

infranqueable [infranke'aβle] *adj* impassable; (*fig*) insurmountable.

infrarrojo, a [infra'rroxo, a] *adj* infrared.

infravalorar [infraβalo'rar] *vt* to undervalue; (*FIN*) to underestimate.

infringir [infrin'xir] *vt* to infringe, contravene.

infrinja [in'frinxa] *etc vb* V **infringir**.

infructuoso, a [infruk'twoso, a] *adj* fruitless, unsuccessful.

infundado, a [infun'daðo, a] *adj* groundless, unfounded.

infundir [infun'dir] *vt* to infuse, instil; **~ ánimo a algn** to encourage sb; **~ miedo a algn** to intimidate sb.

infusión [infu'sjon] *nf* infusion; **~ de manzanilla** camomile tea.

Ing. *abr* = **Ingeniero**.

ingeniar [inxe'njar] *vt* to think up, devise; **~se** *vr* to manage; **~se para** to manage to.

ingeniería [inxenje'ria] *nf* engineering; **~ genética** genetic engineering; **~ de sistemas** (*INFORM*) systems engineering.

ingeniero, a [inxe'njero, a] *nm/f* engineer; **~ de sonido** sound engineer; **~ de caminos** civil engineer.

ingenio [in'xenjo] *nm* (*talento*) talent; (*agudeza*) wit; (*habilidad*) ingenuity, inventiveness; (*TEC*): **~ azucarero** sugar refinery.

ingenioso, a [inxe'njoso, a] *adj* ingenious, clever; (*divertido*) witty.

ingente [in'xente] *adj* huge, enormous.

ingenuidad [inxenwi'ðað] *nf* ingenuousness; (*sencillez*) simplicity.

ingenuo, a [in'xenwo, a] *adj* ingenuous.

ingerir [inxe'rir] *vt* to ingest; (*tragar*) to swallow; (*consumir*) to consume.

ingiera [in'xjera] *etc*, **ingiriendo** [inxi'rjenðo] *etc vb* V **ingerir**.

Inglaterra [ingla'terra] *nf* England.

ingle ['ingle] *nf* groin.

inglés, esa [in'gles, esa] *adj* English ♦ *nm/f* Englishman/woman ♦ *nm* (*LING*) English; **los ingleses** the English.

ingratitud [ingrati'tuð] *nf* ingratitude.

ingrato, a [in'grato, a] *adj* ungrateful; (*tarea*) thankless.

ingravidez [ingraβi'ðeθ] *nf* weightlessness.

ingrediente [ingre'ðjente] *nm* ingredient; **~s** *nmpl* (*AM: tapas*) titbits.

ingresar [ingre'sar] *vt* (*dinero*) to deposit ♦ *vi* to come *o* go in; **~ a** (*esp AM*) to enter; **~ en** (*club*) to join; (*MIL, ESCOL*) to enrol in; **~ en el hospital** to go into hospital.

ingreso [in'greso] *nm* (*entrada*) entry; (: *en hospital etc*) admission; (*MIL, ESCOL*) enrolment; **~s** *nmpl* (*dinero*) income *sg*; (: *COM*) takings *pl*; **~ gravable** taxable income *sg*; **~s accesorios** fringe benefits; **~s brutos** gross receipts; **~s devengados** earned income *sg*; **~s exentos de impuestos** non-taxable income *sg*; **~s personales disponibles** disposable personal income *sg*.

íngrimo, a ['ingrimo, a] *adj* (*AM: tb* **~ y solo**) all alone.

inhábil [i'naβil] *adj* unskilful, clumsy.

inhabilitar [inaβili'tar] *vt* (*POL, MED*): **~ a algn (para hacer algo)** to disqualify sb (from doing sth).

inhabitable [inaβi'taβle] *adj* uninhabitable.

inhabituado, a [inaβi'twaðo, a] *adj* unaccustomed.

inhalador [inala'ðor] *nm* (*MED*) inhaler.
inhalar [ina'lar] *vt* to inhale.
inherente [ine'rente] *adj* inherent.
inhibición [iniβi'θjon] *nf* inhibition.
inhibir [ini'βir] *vt* to inhibit; (*REL*) to restrain; **~se** *vr* to keep out.
inhospitalario, a [inospita'larjo, a], **inhóspito, a** [i'nospito, a] *adj* inhospitable.
inhumación [inuma'θjon] *nf* burial, interment.
inhumano, a [inu'mano, a] *adj* inhuman.
INI ['ini] *nm abr* = **Instituto Nacional de Industria**.
inicial [ini'θjal] *adj, nf* initial.
inicialice [iniθja'liθe] *etc vb* V **inicializar**.
inicializar [iniθjali'θar] *vt* (*INFORM*) to initialize.
iniciar [ini'θjar] *vt* (*persona*) to initiate; (*empezar*) to begin, commence; (*conversación*) to start up; **~ a algn en un secreto** to let sb into a secret; **~ la sesión** (*INFORM*) to log in *o* on.
iniciativa [iniθja'tiβa] *nf* initiative; (*liderazgo*) leadership; **la ~ privada** private enterprise.
inicio [i'niθjo] *nm* start, beginning.
inicuo, a [i'nikwo, a] *adj* iniquitous.
inigualado, a [inixwa'laðo, a] *adj* unequalled.
ininteligible [ininteli'xiβle] *adj* unintelligible.
ininterrumpido, a [ininterrum'piðo, a] *adj* uninterrupted; (*proceso*) continuous; (*progreso*) steady.
injerencia [inxe'renθja] *nf* interference.
injertar [inxer'tar] *vt* to graft.
injerto [in'xerto] *nm* graft; **~ de piel** skin graft.
injuria [in'xurja] *nf* (*agravio, ofensa*) offence; (*insulto*) insult; **~s** *nfpl* abuse *sg*.
injuriar [inxu'rjar] *vt* to insult.
injurioso, a [inxu'rjoso, a] *adj* offensive; insulting.
injusticia [inxus'tiθja] *nf* injustice, unfairness; **con ~** unjustly.
injusto, a [in'xusto, a] *adj* unjust, unfair.
inmaculado, a [inmaku'laðo, a] *adj* immaculate, spotless.
inmadurez [inmaðu're θ] *nf* immaturity.
inmaduro, a [inma'ðuro, a] *adj* immature; (*fruta*) unripe.
inmediaciones [inmeðja'θjones] *nfpl* neighbourhood *sg*, environs.
inmediatez [inmeðja'teθ] *nf* immediacy.
inmediato, a [inme'ðjato, a] *adj* immediate; (*contiguo*) adjoining; (*rápido*) prompt; (*próximo*) neighbouring, next;

de ~ (*esp AM*) immediately.
inmejorable [inmexo'raβle] *adj* unsurpassable; (*precio*) unbeatable.
inmemorable [inmemo'raβle], **inmemorial** [inmemo'rjal] *adj* immemorial.
inmenso, a [in'menso, a] *adj* immense, huge.
inmerecido, a [inmere'θiðo, a] *adj* undeserved.
inmersión [inmer'sjon] *nf* immersion; (*buzo*) dive.
inmigración [inmiɣra'θjon] *nf* immigration.
inmigrante [inmi'ɣrante] *adj, nm/f* immigrant.
inminente [inmi'nente] *adj* imminent, impending.
inmiscuirse [inmisku'irse] *vr* to interfere, meddle.
inmiscuyendo [inmisku'jendo] *etc vb* V **inmiscuirse**.
inmobiliario, a [inmoβi'ljarjo, a] *adj* real-estate *cpd*, property *cpd* ♦ *nf* estate agency.
inmolar [inmo'lar] *vt* to immolate, sacrifice.
inmoral [inmo'ral] *adj* immoral.
inmortal [inmor'tal] *adj* immortal.
inmortalice [inmorta'liθe] *etc vb* V **inmortalizar**.
inmortalizar [inmortali'θar] *vt* to immortalize.
inmotivado, a [inmoti'βaðo, a] *adj* motiveless; (*sospecha*) groundless.
inmóvil [in'moβil] *adj* immobile.
inmovilizar [inmoβili'θar] *vt* to immobilize; (*paralizar*) to paralyse; **~se** *vr*: **se le ha inmovilizado la pierna** her leg was paralysed.
inmueble [in'mweβle] *adj*: **bienes ~s** real estate *sg*, landed property *sg* ♦ *nm* property.
inmundicia [inmun'diθja] *nf* filth.
inmundo, a [in'mundo, a] *adj* filthy.
inmune [in'mune] *adj* (*MED*) immune.
inmunidad [inmuni'ðað] *nf* immunity; (*fisco*) exemption; **~ diplomática/ parlamentaria** diplomatic/parliamentary immunity.
inmunitario, a [inmuni'tarjo, a] *adj*: **sistema ~** immune system.
inmunización [inmuniθa'θjon] *nf* immunization.
inmunizar [inmuni'θar] *vt* to immunize.
inmutable [inmu'taβle] *adj* immutable; **permaneció ~** he didn't flinch.
inmutarse [inmu'tarse] *vr*: **siguió sin ~** he

carried on unperturbed.
innato, a [in'nato, a] *adj* innate.
innecesario, a [inneθe'sarjo, a] *adj* unnecessary.
innegable [inne'ɣaßle] *adj* undeniable.
innoble [in'noßle] *adj* ignoble.
innovación [innoßa'θjon] *nf* innovation.
innovador, a [innoßa'ðor, a] *adj* innovatory, innovative ♦ *nm/f* innovator.
innovar [inno'ßar] *vt* to introduce.
innumerable [innume'raßle] *adj* countless.
inocencia [ino'θenθja] *nf* innocence.
inocentada [inoθen'taða] *nf* practical joke.
inocente [ino'θente] *adj* (*ingenuo*) naive, innocent; (*inculpable*) innocent; (*sin malicia*) harmless ♦ *nm/f* simpleton; **día de los (Santos) l~s** ≈ April Fool's Day.

---

*The 28th December, **el día de los (Santos) Inocentes**, is when the Church commemorates the story of Herod's slaughter of the innocent children of Judea in the time of Christ. On this day Spaniards play **inocentadas** (practical jokes) on each other, much like our April Fools' Day pranks, eg typically sticking a **monigote** (cut-out paper figure) on someone's back, or broadcasting unlikely news stories.*

---

inocuidad [inokwi'ðað] *nf* harmlessness.
inocular [inoku'lar] *vt* to inoculate.
inocuo, a [i'nokwo, a] *adj* (*sustancia*) harmless.
inodoro, a [ino'ðoro, a] *adj* odourless ♦ *nm* toilet (*BRIT*), lavatory (*BRIT*), washroom (*US*).
inofensivo, a [inofen'sißo, a] *adj* inoffensive.
inolvidable [inolßi'ðaßle] *adj* unforgettable.
inoperante [inope'rante] *adj* ineffective.
inopinado, a [inopi'naðo, a] *adj* ineffective.
inoportuno, a [inopor'tuno, a] *adj* untimely; (*molesto*) inconvenient; (*inapropiado*) inappropriate.
inoxidable [inoksi'ðaßle] *adj* stainless; **acero** ~ stainless steel.
inquebrantable [inkeßran'taßle] *adj* unbreakable; (*fig*) unshakeable.
inquiera [in'kjera] *etc vb V* **inquirir**.
inquietante [inkje'tante] *adj* worrying.
inquietar [inkje'tar] *vt* to worry, trouble; ~**se** *vr* to worry, get upset.
inquieto, a [in'kjeto, a] *adj* anxious, worried; **estar** ~ **por** to be worried about.
inquietud [inkje'tuð] *nf* anxiety, worry.

inquilino, a [inki'lino, a] *nm/f* tenant; (*COM*) lessee.
inquina [in'kina] *nf* (*aversión*) dislike; (*rencor*) ill will; **tener** ~ **a algn** to have a grudge against sb.
inquiriendo [inki'rjendo] *etc vb V* **inquirir**.
inquirir [inki'rir] *vt* to enquire into, investigate.
insaciable [insa'θjaßle] *adj* insatiable.
insalubre [insa'lußre] *adj* unhealthy; (*condiciones*) insanitary.
INSALUD [insa'luð] *nm abr* (*ESP*) = Instituto Nacional de la Salud.
insano, a [in'sano, a] *adj* (*loco*) insane; (*malsano*) unhealthy.
insatisfacción [insatisfak'θjon] *nf* dissatisfaction.
insatisfecho, a [insatis'fetʃo, a] *adj* (*condición*) unsatisfied; (*estado de ánimo*) dissatisfied.
inscribir [inskri'ßir] *vt* to inscribe; (*en lista*) to put; (*en censo*) to register; ~**se** *vr* to register; (*ESCOL etc*) to enrol.
inscripción [inskrip'θjon] *nf* inscription; (*ESCOL etc*) enrolment; (*en censo*) registration.
inscrito [ins'krito] *pp de* **inscribir**.
insecticida [insekti'θiða] *nm* insecticide.
insecto [in'sekto] *nm* insect.
inseguridad [inseɣuri'ðað] *nf* insecurity.
inseguro, a [inse'ɣuro, a] *adj* insecure; (*inconstante*) unsteady; (*incierto*) uncertain.
inseminación [insemina'θjon] *nf*: ~ **artificial** artificial insemination (A.I.).
inseminar [insemi'nar] *vt* to inseminate, fertilize.
insensato, a [insen'sato, a] *adj* foolish, stupid.
insensibilice [insensißi'liθe] *etc vb V* **insensibilizar**.
insensibilidad [insensißili'ðað] *nf* (*gen*) insensitivity; (*dureza de corazón*) callousness.
insensibilizar [insensißili'θar] *vt* to desensitize; (*MED*) to anaesthetize (*BRIT*), anesthetize (*US*); (*eufemismo*) to knock out o unconscious.
insensible [insen'sißle] *adj* (*gen*) insensitive; (*movimiento*) imperceptible; (*sin sentido*) numb.
inseparable [insepa'raßle] *adj* inseparable.
INSERSO [in'serso] *nm abr* (= Instituto Nacional de Servicios Sociales) branch of social services.
insertar [inser'tar] *vt* to insert.
inservible [inser'ßißle] *adj* useless.
insidioso, a [insi'ðjoso, a] *adj* insidious.

insigne [in'siɣne] *adj* distinguished; (*famoso*) notable.
insignia [in'siɣnja] *nf* (*señal distintivo*) badge; (*estandarte*) flag.
insignificante [insiɣnifi'kante] *adj* insignificant.
insinuar [insi'nwar] *vt* to insinuate, imply; ~se *vr*: ~se con algn to ingratiate o.s. with sb.
insípido, a [in'sipiðo, a] *adj* insipid.
insistencia [insis'tenθja] *nf* insistence.
insistir [insis'tir] *vi* to insist; ~ en algo to insist on sth; (*enfatizar*) to stress sth.
in situ [in'situ] *adv* on the spot, in situ.
insobornable [insoβor'naβle] *adj* incorruptible.
insociable [inso'θjaβle] *adj* unsociable.
insolación [insola'θjon] *nf* (*MED*) sunstroke.
insolencia [inso'lenθja] *nf* insolence.
insolente [inso'lente] *adj* insolent.
insólito, a [in'solito, a] *adj* unusual.
insoluble [inso'luβle] *adj* insoluble.
insolvencia [insol'βenθja] *nf* insolvency.
insomne [in'somne] *adj* sleepless ♦ *nm/f* insomniac.
insomnio [in'somnjo] *nm* insomnia.
insondable [inson'daβle] *adj* bottomless.
insonorización [insonoriθa'θjon] *nf* soundproofing.
insonorizado, a [insonori'θaðo, a] *adj* (*cuarto etc*) soundproof.
insoportable [insopor'taβle] *adj* unbearable.
insoslayable [insosla'jaβle] *adj* unavoidable.
insospechado, a [insospe'tʃaðo, a] *adj* (*inesperado*) unexpected.
insostenible [insoste'niβle] *adj* untenable.
inspección [inspek'θjon] *nf* inspection, check; I~ inspectorate; ~ técnica (de vehículos) ≈ MOT (test) (*BRIT*).
inspeccionar [inspekθjo'nar] *vt* (*examinar*) to inspect, examine; (*controlar*) to check; (*INFORM*) to peek.
inspector, a [inspek'tor, a] *nm/f* inspector.
inspectorado [inspekto'raðo] *nm* inspectorate.
inspiración [inspira'θjon] *nf* inspiration.
inspirador, a [inspira'ðor, a] *adj* inspiring.
inspirar [inspi'rar] *vt* to inspire; (*MED*) to inhale; ~se *vr*: ~se en to be inspired by.
instalación [instala'θjon] *nf* (*equipo*) fittings *pl*, equipment; ~ eléctrica wiring.
instalar [insta'lar] *vt* (*establecer*) to instal; (*erguir*) to set up, erect; ~se *vr* to establish o.s.; (*en una vivienda*) to move into.

instancia [ins'tanθja] *nf* (*solicitud*) application; (*ruego*) request; (*JUR*) petition; a ~ de at the request of; en última ~ in the last resort.
instantáneo, a [instan'taneo, a] *adj* instantaneous ♦ *nf* snap(shot); café ~ instant coffee.
instante [ins'tante] *nm* instant, moment; en un ~ in a flash.
instar [ins'tar] *vt* to press, urge.
instaurar [instau'rar] *vt* (*establecer*) to establish, set up.
instigador, a [instiɣa'ðor, a] *nm/f* instigator; ~ de un delito (*JUR*) accessory before the fact.
instigar [insti'ɣar] *vt* to instigate.
instigue [ins'tiɣe] *etc vb V* **instigar.**
instintivo, a [instin'tiβo, a] *adj* instinctive.
instinto [ins'tinto] *nm* instinct; por ~ instinctively.
institución [institu'θjon] *nf* institution, establishment; ~ benéfica charitable foundation.
instituir [institu'ir] *vt* to establish; (*fundar*) to found.
instituto [insti'tuto] *nm* (*gen*) institute; I~ Nacional de Enseñanza (*ESP*) ≈ comprehensive (*BRIT*) o high (*US*) school; I~ Nacional de Industria (INI) (*ESP COM*) ≈ National Enterprise Board (*BRIT*) .
institutriz [institu'triθ] *nf* governess.
instituyendo [institu'jendo] *etc vb V* **instituir.**
instrucción [instruk'θjon] *nf* instruction; (*enseñanza*) education, teaching; (*JUR*) proceedings *pl*; (*MIL*) training; (*DEPORTE*) coaching; (*conocimientos*) knowledge; (*INFORM*) statement; **instrucciones para el uso** directions for use; **instrucciones de funcionamiento** operating instructions.
instructivo, a [instruk'tiβo, a] *adj* instructive.
instruir [instru'ir] *vt* (*gen*) to instruct; (*enseñar*) to teach, educate; (*JUR: proceso*) to prepare, draw up; ~se *vr* to learn, teach o.s.
instrumento [instru'mento] *nm* (*gen*, MUS) instrument; (*herramienta*) tool, implement; (*COM*) indenture; (*JUR*) legal document; ~ de percusión/cuerda/viento percussion/string(ed)/wind instrument.
instruyendo [instru'jendo] *etc vb V* **instruir.**
insubordinarse [insuβorði'narse] *vr* to rebel.
insuficiencia [insufi'θjenθja] *nf* (*carencia*)

lack; (*inadecuación*) inadequacy; ~ **cardíaca/renal** heart/kidney failure.

insuficiente [insufi'θjente] *adj* (*gen*) insufficient; (*ESCOL: nota*) unsatisfactory.

insufrible [insu'friβle] *adj* insufferable.

insular [insu'lar] *adj* insular.

insulina [insu'lina] *nf* insulin.

insulso, a [in'sulso, a] *adj* insipid; (*fig*) dull.

insultar [insul'tar] *vt* to insult.

insulto [in'sulto] *nm* insult.

insumisión [insumi'sjon] *nf* refusal to do military service or community service.

insumiso, a [insu'miso, a] *adj* (*rebelde*) rebellious ♦ *nm/f* (*POL*) person who refuses to do military service or community service; *V tb* **mili**.

insuperable [insupe'raβle] *adj* (*excelente*) unsurpassable; (*problema etc*) insurmountable.

insurgente [insur'xente] *adj, nm/f* insurgent.

insurrección [insurrek'θjon] *nf* insurrection, rebellion.

insustituible [insusti'twiβle] *adj* irreplaceable.

intachable [inta'tʃaβle] *adj* irreproachable.

intacto, a [in'takto, a] *adj* (*sin tocar*) untouched; (*entero*) intact.

integrado, a [inte'ɣraðo, a] *adj* (*INFORM*): **circuito** ~ integrated circuit.

integral [inte'ɣral] *adj* integral; (*completo*) complete; (*TEC*) built-in; **pan** ~ wholemeal bread.

integrante [inte'ɣrante] *adj* integral ♦ *nm/f* member.

integrar [inte'ɣrar] *vt* to make up, compose; (*MAT, fig*) to integrate.

integridad [inteɣri'ðað] *nf* wholeness; (*carácter, tb INFORM*) integrity; **en su** ~ completely.

integrismo [inte'ɣrismo] *nm* fundamentalism.

integrista [inte'ɣrista] *adj, nm/f* fundamentalist.

íntegro, a ['inteɣro, a] *adj* whole, entire; (*texto*) uncut, unabridged; (*honrado*) honest.

intelectual [intelek'twal] *adj, nm/f* intellectual.

intelectualidad [intelektwali'ðað] *nf* intelligentsia, intellectuals *pl*.

inteligencia [inteli'xenθja] *nf* intelligence; (*ingenio*) ability; ~ **artificial** artificial intelligence.

inteligente [inteli'xente] *adj* intelligent.

inteligible [inteli'xiβle] *adj* intelligible.

intemperancia [intempe'ranθja] *nf* excess, intemperance.

intemperie [intem'perje] *nf*: **a la** ~ outdoors, in the open air.

intempestivo, a [intempes'tiβo, a] *adj* untimely.

intención [inten'θjon] *nf* (*gen*) intention, purpose; **con segundas intenciones** maliciously; **con** ~ deliberately.

intencionado, a [intenθjo'naðo, a] *adj* deliberate; **bien** ~ well-meaning; **mal** ~ ill-disposed, hostile.

intendencia [inten'denθja] *nf* management, administration; (*MIL: tb*: **cuerpo de** ~) ≈ service corps.

intensidad [intensi'ðað] *nf* (*gen*) intensity; (*ELEC, TEC*) strength; (*de recuerdo*) vividness; **llover con** ~ to rain hard.

intensificar [intensifi'kar] *vt*, **intensificarse** *vr* to intensify.

intensifique [intensi'fike] *etc vb V* **intensificar**.

intensivo, a [inten'siβo, a] *adj* intensive; **curso** ~ crash course.

intenso, a [in'tenso, a] *adj* intense; (*impresión*) vivid; (*sentimiento*) profound, deep.

intentar [inten'tar] *vt* (*tratar*) to try, attempt.

intento [in'tento] *nm* (*intención*) intention, purpose; (*tentativa*) attempt.

intentona [inten'tona] *nf* (*POL*) attempted coup.

interaccionar [interakθjo'nar] *vi* (*INFORM*) to interact.

interactivo, a [interak'tiβo, a] *adj* interactive; (*INFORM*): **computación interactiva** interactive computing.

intercalación [interkala'θjon] *nf* (*INFORM*) merging.

intercalar [interka'lar] *vt* to insert; (*INFORM: archivos, texto*) to merge.

intercambiable [interkam'bjaβle] *adj* interchangeable.

intercambio [inter'kambjo] *nm* (*canje*) exchange; (*trueque*) swap.

interceder [interθe'ðer] *vi* to intercede.

interceptar [interθep'tar] *vt* to intercept, cut off; (*AUTO*) to hold up.

interceptor [interθep'tor] *nm* interceptor; (*TEC*) trap.

intercesión [interθe'sjon] *nf* intercession.

interés [inte'res] *nm* (*gen, COM*) interest; (*importancia*) concern; (*parte*) share, part; (*pey*) self-interest; ~ **compuesto** compound interest; ~ **simple** simple interest; **con un** ~ **de 9 por ciento** at an interest of 9%; **dar a** ~ to lend at interest; **tener** ~ **en** (*COM*) to hold a share in; **intereses acumulados** accrued interest *sg*; **intereses por cobrar** interest receivable *sg*; **intereses creados** vested interests; **intereses por pagar** interest payable *sg*.

interesado, a [intere'saðo, a] *adj* interested; (*prejuiciado*) prejudiced; (*pey*) mercenary, self-seeking ♦ *nm/f* person concerned; (*firmante*) the undersigned.

interesante [intere'sante] *adj* interesting.

interesar [intere'sar] *vt* to interest, be of interest to ♦ *vi* to interest, be of interest; (*importar*) to be important; ~**se** *vr*: ~**se en** *o* **por** to take an interest in; **no me interesan los toros** bullfighting does not appeal to me.

interestatal [interesta'tal] *adj* inter-state.

interface [inter'faθe], **interfase** [inter'fase] *nm* (*INFORM*) interface; ~ **hombre/ máquina/por menús** man/machine/menu interface.

interfaz [inter'faθ] *nm* = **interface**.

interferencia [interfe'renθja] *nf* interference.

interferir [interfe'rir] *vt* to interfere with; (*TELEC*) to jam ♦ *vi* to interfere.

interfiera [inter'fjera] *etc*, **interfiriendo** [interfi'rjendo] *etc vb V* **interferir**.

interfono [inter'fono] *nm* intercom.

ínterin ['interin] *adv* meanwhile ♦ *nm* interim; **en el** ~ in the meantime.

interino, a [inte'rino, a] *adj* temporary; (*empleado etc*) provisional ♦ *nm/f* temporary holder of a post; (*MED*) locum; (*ESCOL*) supply teacher; (*TEAT*) stand-in.

interior [inte'rjor] *adj* inner, inside; (*COM*) domestic, internal ♦ *nm* interior, inside; (*fig*) soul, mind; (*DEPORTE*) inside forward; **Ministerio del I**~ ≈ Home Office (*BRIT*), Ministry of the Interior; **dije para mi** ~ I said to myself.

interjección [interxek'θjon] *nf* interjection.

interlínea [inter'linea] *nf* (*INFORM*) line feed.

interlocutor, a [interloku'tor, a] *nm/f* speaker; (*al teléfono*) person at the other end (of the line); **mi** ~ the person I was speaking to.

intermediario, a [interme'ðjarjo, a] *adj* (*mediador*) mediating ♦ *nm/f* intermediary, go-between; (*mediador*) mediator.

intermedio, a [inter'meðjo, a] *adj* intermediate; (*tiempo*) intervening ♦ *nm*

interval; (*POL*) recess.

interminable [intermi'naßle] *adj* endless, interminable.

intermitente [intermi'tente] *adj* intermittent ♦ *nm* (*AUTO*) indicator.

internacional [internaθjo'nal] *adj* international.

internado [inter'naðo] *nm* boarding school.

internamiento [interna'mjento] *nm* internment.

internar [inter'nar] *vt* to intern; (*en un manicomio*) to commit; ~**se** *vr* (*penetrar*) to penetrate; ~**se en** to go into *o* right inside; ~**se en un estudio** to study a subject in depth.

interno, a [in'terno, a] *adj* internal, interior; (*POL etc*) domestic ♦ *nm/f* (*alumno*) boarder.

interpelación [interpela'θjon] *nf* appeal, plea.

interpelar [interpe'lar] *vt* (*rogar*) to implore; (*hablar*) to speak to; (*POL*) to ask for explanations, question formally.

interpondré [interpon'dre] *etc vb V* **interponer**.

interponer [interpo'ner] *vt* to interpose, put in; ~**se** *vr* to intervene.

interponga [inter'ponga] *etc vb V* **interponer**.

interposición [interposi'θjon] *nf* insertion.

interpretación [interpreta'θjon] *nf* interpretation; (*MUS, TEAT*) performance; **mala** ~ misinterpretation.

interpretar [interpre'tar] *vt* to interpret.

intérprete [in'terprete] *nm/f* (*LING*) interpreter, translator; (*MUS, TEAT*) performer, artist(e).

interpuesto [inter'pwesto], **interpuse** [inter'puse] *etc vb V* **interponer**.

interrogación [interoxa'θjon] *nf* interrogation; (*LING: tb:* **signo de** ~) question mark; (*TELEC*) polling.

interrogante [interro'xante] *adj* questioning ♦ *nm* question mark; (*fig*) question mark, query.

interrogar [interro'xar] *vt* to interrogate, question.

interrogatorio [interoxa'torjo] *nm* interrogation; (*MIL*) debriefing; (*JUR*) examination.

interrogue [inte'rroxe] *etc vb V* **interrogar**.

interrumpir [interrum'pir] *vt* to interrupt; (*vacaciones*) to cut short; (*servicio*) to cut off; (*tráfico*) to block.

interrupción [interrup'θjon] *nf* interruption.

interruptor [interrup'tor] *nm* (*ELEC*) switch.
intersección [intersek'θjon] *nf* intersection; (*AUTO*) junction.
interurbano, a [interur'ßano, a] *adj* inter city; (*TELEC*) long-distance.
intervalo [inter'ßalo] *nm* interval; (*descanso*) break; **a ~s** at intervals, every now and then.
intervención [interßen'θjon] *nf* supervision; (*COM*) audit(ing); (*MED*) operation; (*TELEC*) tapping; (*participación*) intervention; **~ quirúrgica** surgical operation; **la política de no ~** the policy of non-intervention.
intervencionista [interßenθjo'nista] *adj*: **no ~** (*COM*) laissez-faire.
intervendré [interßen'dre] *etc*, **intervenga** [inter'ßenga] *etc vb V* **intervenir**.
intervenir [interße'nir] *vt* (*controlar*) to control, supervise; (*COM*) to audit; (*MED*) to operate on; (*TELEC*) to tap ♦ *vi* (*participar*) to take part, participate; (*mediar*) to intervene.
interventor, a [interßen'tor, a] *nm/f* inspector; (*COM*) auditor.
interviniendo [interßi'njendo] *etc vb V* **intervenir**.
interviú [inter'ßju] *nf* interview.
intestino [intes'tino] *nm* intestine.
inti ['inti] *nm monetary unit of Peru.*
intimar [inti'mar] *vt* to intimate, announce; (*mandar*) to order ♦ *vi*, **~se** *vr* to become friendly.
intimidad [intimi'ðað] *nf* intimacy; (*familiaridad*) familiarity; (*vida privada*) private life; (*JUR*) privacy.
intimidar [intimi'ðar] *vt* to intimidate, scare.
íntimo, a ['intimo, a] *adj* intimate; (*pensamientos*) innermost; (*vida*) personal, private; **una boda íntima** a quiet wedding.
intolerable [intole'raßle] *adj* intolerable, unbearable.
intolerancia [intole'ranθja] *nf* intolerance.
intoxicación [intoksika'θjon] *nf* poisoning; **~ alimenticia** food poisoning.
intraducible [intraðu'θißle] *adj* untranslatable.
intranquilice [intranki'liθe] *etc vb V* **intranquilizarse**.
intranquilizarse [intrankili'θarse] *vr* to get worried *o* anxious.
intranquilo, a [intran'kilo, a] *adj* worried.
intranscendente [intransθen'dente] *adj* unimportant.
intransferible [intransfe'rißle] *adj* not

transferable.
intransigente [intransi'xente] *adj* intransigent.
intransitable [intransi'taßle] *adj* impassable.
intransitivo, a [intransi'tißo, a] *adj* intransitive.
intratable [intra'taßle] *adj* (*problema*) intractable; (*dificultad*) awkward; (*individuo*) unsociable.
intrepidez [intrepi'ðeθ] *nf* courage, bravery.
intrépido, a [in'trepiðo, a] *adj* intrepid, fearless.
intriga [in'triɣa] *nf* intrigue; (*plan*) plot.
intrigar [intri'ɣar] *vt*, *vi* to intrigue.
intrigue [in'triɣe] *etc vb V* **intrigar**.
intrincado, a [intrin'kaðo, a] *adj* intricate.
intrínseco, a [in'trinseko, a] *adj* intrinsic.
introducción [introðuk'θjon] *nf* introduction; (*de libro*) foreword; (*INFORM*) input.
introducir [introðu'θir] *vt* (*gen*) to introduce; (*moneda*) to insert; (*INFORM*) to input, enter.
introduje [intro'ðuxe] *etc*, **introduzca** [intro'ðuθka] *etc vb V* **introducir**.
intromisión [intromi'sjon] *nf* interference, meddling.
introvertido, a [introßer'tiðo, a] *adj*, *nm/f* introvert.
intruso, a [in'truso, a] *adj* intrusive ♦ *nm/f* intruder.
intuición [intwi'θjon] *nf* intuition.
intuir [intu'ir] *vt* to know by intuition, intuit.
intuyendo [intu'jendo] *etc vb V* **intuir**.
inundación [inunda'θjon] *nf* flood(ing).
inundar [inun'dar] *vt* to flood; (*fig*) to swamp, inundate.
inusitado, a [inusi'taðo, a] *adj* unusual.
inútil [i'nutil] *adj* useless; (*esfuerzo*) vain, fruitless.
inutilice [inuti'liθe] *etc vb V* **inutilizar**.
inutilidad [inutili'ðað] *nf* uselessness.
inutilizar [inutili'θar] *vt* to make unusable, put out of action; (*incapacitar*) to disable; **~se** *vr* to become useless.
invadir [imba'ðir] *vt* to invade.
invalidar [imbali'ðar] *vt* to invalidate.
invalidez [imbali'ðeθ] *nf* (*MED*) disablement; (*JUR*) invalidity.
inválido, a [im'baliðo, a] *adj* invalid; (*JUR*) null and void ♦ *nm/f* invalid.
invariable [imba'rjable] *adj* invariable.
invasión [imba'sjon] *nf* invasion.
invasor, a [imba'sor, a] *adj* invading ♦ *nm/f* invader.

invencible [imben'θißle] *adj* invincible;
(*timidez, miedo*) unsurmountable.
invención [imben'θjon] *nf* invention.
inventar [imben'tar] *vt* to invent.
inventario [imben'tarjo] *nm* inventory;
(*COM*) stocktaking.
inventiva [imben'tißa] *nf* inventiveness.
invento [im'bento] *nm* invention; (*fig*)
brainchild; (*pey*) silly idea.
inventor, a [imben'tor, a] *nm/f* inventor.
invernadero [imberna'ðero] *nm*
greenhouse.
invernal [imber'nal] *adj* wintry, winter *cpd*.
invernar [imber'nar] *vi* (*ZOOL*) to hibernate.
inverosímil [imbero'simil] *adj* implausible.
inversión [imber'sjon] *nf* (*COM*)
investment; ~ **de capitales** capital
investment; **inversiones extranjeras**
foreign investment *sg*.
inverso, a [im'berso, a] *adj* inverse,
opposite; **en el orden** ~ in reverse order;
a la inversa inversely, the other way
round.
inversor, a [imber'sor, a] *nm/f* (*COM*)
investor.
invertebrado, a [imberte'ßraðo, a] *adj, nm*
invertebrate.
invertido, a [imber'tiðo, a] *adj* inverted; (*al
revés*) reversed; (*homosexual*)
homosexual ♦ *nm/f* homosexual.
invertir [imber'tir] *vt* (*COM*) to invest;
(*volcar*) to turn upside down; (*tiempo etc*)
to spend.
investigación [imbestiɣa'θjon] *nf*
investigation; (*indagación*) inquiry;
(*UNIV*) research; ~ **y desarrollo** (*COM*)
research and development (R & D); ~
de los medios de publicidad media
research; ~ **del mercado** market
research.
investigador, a [imbestiɣa'ðor, a] *nm/f*
investigator; (*UNIV*) research fellow.
investigar [imbesti'ɣar] *vt* to investigate;
(*estudiar*) to do research into.
investigue [imbes'tiɣe] *etc vb V* **investigar**.
investir [imbes'tir] *vt*: ~ **a algn con algo** to
confer sth on sb; **fue investido Doctor
Honoris Causa** he was awarded an
honorary doctorate.
invicto, a [im'bikto, a] *adj* unconquered.
invidente [imbi'ðente] *adj* sightless ♦ *nm/f*
blind person; **los** ~**s** the sightless.
invierno [im'bjerno] *nm* winter.
invierta [im'bjerta] *etc vb V* **invertir**.
inviolabilidad [imbjolaßili'ðað] *nf*
inviolability; ~ **parlamentaria**
parliamentary immunity.
invirtiendo [imbir'tjendo] *etc vb V* **invertir**.

invisible [imbi'sißle] *adj* invisible;
exportaciones/importaciones ~**s**
invisible exports/imports.
invitación [imbita'θjon] *nf* invitation.
invitado, a [imbi'taðo, a] *nm/f* guest.
invitar [imbi'tar] *vt* to invite; (*incitar*) to
entice; ~ **a algn a hacer algo** to invite sb
to do sth; ~ **a algo** to pay for sth; **nos
invitó a cenar fuera** she took us out for
dinner; **invito yo** it's on me.
in vitro [im'bitro] *adv* in vitro.
invocar [imbo'kar] *vt* to invoke, call on;
(*INFORM*) to call.
involucrar [imbolu'krar] *vt*: ~ **algo en un
discurso** to bring something irrelevant
into a discussion; ~ **a algn en algo** to
involve sb in sth; ~**se** *vr* (*interesarse*) to
get involved.
involuntario, a [imbolun'tarjo, a] *adj*
involuntary; (*ofensa etc*) unintentional.
invoque [im'boke] *etc vb V* **invocar**.
inyección [injek'θjon] *nf* injection.
inyectar [injek'tar] *vt* to inject.
ión [i'on] *nm* ion.
IPC *nm abr* (*ESP*: = *índice de precios al
consumo*) CPI.
IPM *nm abr* (= *índice de precios al por
menor*) RPI.

═══════════════ *PALABRA CLAVE*

ir [ir] *vi* **1** to go; (*a pie*) to walk; (*viajar*) to
travel; ~ **caminando** to walk; **fui en tren**
I went *o* travelled by train; **voy a la calle**
I'm going out; ~ **en coche/en bicicleta** to
drive/cycle; ~ **a pie** to walk, go on foot;
~ **de pesca** to go fishing; ¡(**ahora**) **voy!**
(I'm just) coming!
2: ~ (**a**) **por**: ~ (**a**) **por el médico** to fetch
the doctor
3 (*progresar: persona, cosa*) to go; **el
trabajo va muy bien** work is going very
well; **¿cómo te va?** how are things
going?; **me va muy bien** I'm getting on
very well; **le fue fatal** it went awfully
badly for him
4 (*funcionar*): **el coche no va muy bien**
the car isn't running very well
5 (*sentar*): **me va estupendamente** (*ropa,
color*) it suits me really well;
(*medicamento*) it works really well for
me; ~ **bien con algo** to go well with sth
6 (*aspecto*): **iba muy bien vestido** he was
very well dressed; ~ **con zapatos negros**
to wear black shoes
7 (*locuciones*): **¿vino?** – ¡**que va!** did he
come? – of course not!; **vamos, no llores**
come on, don't cry; ¡**vaya coche!**
(*admiración*) what a car!, that's some

car!; (*desprecio*) that's a terrible car!; **¡vaya!** (*regular*) so so; (*desagrado*) come on!; **¡vamos!** come on!; **¡que le vaya bien!** (*adiós*) take care!
8: no vaya a ser: tienes que correr, no vaya a ser que pierdas el tren you'll have to run so as not to miss the train
9: no me *etc* **va ni me viene** I *etc* don't care
♦ *vb aux* **1:** ~ **a: voy/iba a hacerlo hoy** I am/was going to do it today
2 (*+gerundio*): **iba anocheciendo** it was getting dark; **todo se me iba aclarando** everything was gradually becoming clearer to me
3 (*+pp = pasivo*): **van vendidos 300 ejemplares** 300 copies have been sold so far
♦ ~**se** *vr* **1:** **¿por dónde se va al zoológico?** which is the way to the zoo?
2 (*marcharse*) to leave; **ya se habrán ido** they must already have left *o* gone; **¡vámonos!**, (*AM*) **¡nos fuimos!** let's go!; **¡vete!** go away!; **¡vete a saber!** your guess is as good as mine!, who knows!

ira ['ira] *nf* anger, rage.
iracundo, a [ira'kundo, a] *adj* irascible.
Irak [i'rak] *nm* = **Iraq**.
Irán [i'ran] *nm* Iran.
iraní [ira'ni] *adj, nm/f* Iranian.
Iraq [i'rak] *nm* Iraq.
iraquí [ira'ki] *adj, nm/f* Iraqui.
irascible [iras'θiβle] *adj* irascible.
irguiendo [ir'ɣjendo] *etc vb V* **erguir**.
iris ['iris] *nm inv* (*arco* ~) rainbow; (*ANAT*) iris.
Irlanda [ir'landa] *nf* Ireland; ~ **del Norte** Northern Ireland, Ulster.
irlandés, esa [irlan'des, esa] *adj* Irish ♦ *nm/f* Irishman/woman ♦ *nm* (*LING*) Gaelic, Irish; **los irlandeses** *npl* the Irish.
ironía [iro'nia] *nf* irony.
irónico, a [i'roniko, a] *adj* ironic(al).
IRPF *nm abr* (*ESP*) = *impuesto sobre la renta de las personas físicas.*
irracional [irraθjo'nal] *adj* irrational.
irrazonable [irraθo'naβle] *adj* unreasonable.
irreal [irre'al] *adj* unreal.
irrealizable [irreali'θaβle] *adj* (*gen*) unrealizable; (*meta*) unrealistic.
irrebatible [irreβa'tiβle] *adj* irrefutable.
irreconocible [irrekono'θiβle] *adj* unrecognizable.
irrecuperable [irrekupe'raβle] *adj* irrecoverable, irretrievable.
irreembolsable [irreembol'saβle] *adj* (*COM*)

non-returnable.
irreflexión [irreflek'sjon] *nf* thoughtlessness; (*ímpetu*) rashness.
irregular [irreɣu'lar] *adj* irregular; (*situación*) abnormal, anomalous; **margen izquierdo/derecho** ~ (*texto*) ragged left/right (margin).
irregularidad [irreɣulari'ðað] *nf* irregularity.
irremediable [irreme'ðjaβle] *adj* irremediable; (*vicio*) incurable.
irreprochable [irrepro'tʃaβle] *adj* irreproachable.
irresistible [irresis'tiβle] *adj* irresistible.
irresoluto, a [irreso'luto, a] *adj* irresolute, hesitant; (*sin resolver*) unresolved.
irrespetuoso, a [irrespe'twoso, a] *adj* disrespectful.
irresponsable [irrespon'saβle] *adj* irresponsible.
irreverente [irreβe'rente] *adj* disrespectful.
irreversible [irreβer'siβle] *adj* irreversible.
irrevocable [irreβo'kaβle] *adj* irrevocable.
irrigar [irri'ɣar] *vt* to irrigate.
irrigue [i'rriɣe] *etc vb V* **irrigar**.
irrisorio, a [irri'sorjo, a] *adj* derisory, ridiculous; (*precio*) bargain *cpd*.
irritación [irrita'θjon] *nf* irritation.
irritar [irri'tar] *vt* to irritate, annoy; ~**se** *vr* to get angry, lose one's temper.
irrompible [irrom'piβle] *adj* unbreakable.
irrumpir [irrum'pir] *vi:* ~ **en** to burst *o* rush into.
irrupción [irrup'θjon] *nf* irruption; (*invasión*) invasion.
IRTP *nm abr* (*ESP:* = *impuesto sobre el rendimiento del trabajo personal*) ≈ PAYE.
isla ['isla] *nf* (*GEO*) island; **I~s Británicas** British Isles; **I~s Filipinas/Malvinas/Canarias** Philippines/Falklands/Canaries.
Islam [is'lam] *nm* Islam.
islámico, a [is'lamiko, a] *adj* Islamic.
islandés, esa [islan'des, esa] *adj* Icelandic ♦ *nm/f* Icelander ♦ *nm* (*LING*) Icelandic.
Islandia [is'landja] *nf* Iceland.
isleño, a [is'leɲo, a] *adj* island *cpd* ♦ *nm/f* islander.
islote [is'lote] *nm* small island.
isotónico, a [iso'toniko, a] *adj* isotonic.
isótopo [i'sotopo] *nm* isotope.
Israel [isra'el] *nm* Israel.
israelí [israe'li] *adj, nm/f* Israeli.
istmo ['istmo] *nm* isthmus; **el I~ de Panamá** the Isthmus of Panama.
Italia [i'talja] *nf* Italy.
italiano, a [ita'ljano, a] *adj, nm/f* Italian

♦ *nm* (*LING*) Italian.
itinerante [itine'rante] *adj* travelling; (*embajador*) roving.
itinerario [itine'rarjo] *nm* itinerary, route.
ITV *nf abr* (= *Inspección Técnica de Vehículos*) ≈ MOT (test) (*BRIT*).
IVA ['iβa] *nm abr* (*ESP COM*: = *Impuesto sobre el Valor Añadido*) VAT.
IVP *nm abr* = *Instituto Venezolano de Petroquímica*.
izada [i'saða] *nf* (*AM*) lifting, raising.
izar [i'θar] *vt* to hoist.
izda, izq.ª *abr* = **izquierda**.
izdo, izq, izq.º *abr* = **izquierdo**.
izquierda [iθ'kjerða] *nf V* **izquierdo**.
izquierdista [iθkjer'ðista] *adj* leftist, left-wing ♦ *nm/f* left-winger, leftist.
izquierdo, a [iθ'kjerðo, a] *adj* left ♦ *nf* left; (*POL*) left (wing); **a la ~** on the left; **es un cero a la ~** (*fam*) he is a nonentity; **conducción por la ~** left-hand drive.

J j

J, j ['xota] *nf* (*letra*) J, j; **J de José** J for Jack (*BRIT*) *o* Jig (*US*).
jabalí [xaβa'li] *nm* wild boar.
jabalina [xaβa'lina] *nf* javelin.
jabato, a [xa'βato, a] *adj* brave, bold ♦ *nm* young wild boar.
jabón [xa'βon] *nm* soap; (*fam: adulación*) flattery; **~ de afeitar** shaving soap; **~ de tocador** toilet soap; **dar ~ a algn** to soft-soap sb.
jabonar [xaβo'nar] *vt* to soap.
jaca ['xaka] *nf* pony.
jacinto [xa'θinto] *nm* hyacinth.
jactancia [xak'tanθja] *nf* boasting, boastfulness.
jactarse [xak'tarse] *vr*: **~ (de)** to boast *o* brag (about *o* of).
jadear [xaðe'ar] *vi* to pant, gasp for breath.
jadeo [xa'ðeo] *nm* panting, gasping.
jaguar [xa'ɣwar] *nm* jaguar.
jalar [xa'lar] *vt* (*AM*) to pull.
jalbegue [xal'βeɣe] *nm* (*pintura*) whitewash.
jalea [xa'lea] *nf* jelly.
jaleo [xa'leo] *nm* racket, uproar; **armar un ~** to kick up a racket.

jalón [xa'lon] *nm* (*AM*) tug.
jalonar [xalo'nar] *vt* to stake out; (*fig*) to mark.
Jamaica [xa'maika] *nf* Jamaica.
jamaicano, a [xamai'kano, a] *adj, nm/f* Jamaican.
jamás [xa'mas] *adv* never, not ... ever; (*interrogativo*) ever; **¿~ se vio tal cosa?** did you ever see such a thing?
jamón [xa'mon] *nm* ham; **~ dulce/serrano** boiled/cured ham.
Japón [xa'pon] *nm*: **el ~** Japan.
japonés, esa [xapo'nes, esa] *adj, nm/f* Japanese ♦ *nm* (*LING*) Japanese.
jaque ['xake] *nm*: **~ mate** checkmate.
jaqueca [xa'keka] *nf* (very bad) headache, migraine.
jarabe [xa'raβe] *nm* syrup; **~ para la tos** cough syrup *o* mixture.
jarana [xa'rana] *nf* (*juerga*) spree (*fam*); **andar/ir de ~** to be/go on a spree.
jarcia ['xarθja] *nf* (*NAUT*) ropes *pl*, rigging.
jardín [xar'ðin] *nm* garden; **~ botánico** botanical garden; **~ de (la) infancia** (*ESP*) *o* **de niños** (*AM*) *o* **infantil** (*AM*) kindergarten, nursery school.
jardinería [xarðine'ria] *nf* gardening.
jardinero, a [xarði'nero, a] *nm/f* gardener.
jarra ['xarra] *nf* jar; (*jarro*) jug; (*de leche*) churn; (*de cerveza*) mug; **de *o* en ~s** with arms akimbo.
jarro ['xarro] *nm* jug.
jarrón [xa'rron] *nm* vase; (*ARQUEOLOGÍA*) urn.
jaspeado, a [xaspe'ado, a] *adj* mottled, speckled.
jaula ['xaula] *nf* cage; (*embalaje*) crate.
jauría [xau'ria] *nf* pack of hounds.
jazmín [xaθ'min] *nm* jasmine.
J. C. *abr* = **Jesucristo**.
jeep, pl jeeps ® [jip, jips] *nm* jeep ®.
jefa ['xefa] *nf V* **jefe**.
jefatura [xefa'tura] *nf* (*liderato*) leadership; (*sede*) central office; **J~ de la aviación civil** ≈ Civil Aviation Authority; **~ de policía** police headquarters *sg*.
jefazo [xe'faθo] *nm* bigwig.
jefe, a ['xefe, a] *nm/f* (*gen*) chief, head; (*patrón*) boss; (*POL*) leader; (*COM*) manager(ess); **~ de camareros** head waiter; **~ de cocina** chef; **~ ejecutivo** (*COM*) chief executive; **~ de estación** stationmaster; **~ de estado** head of state; **~ de oficina** (*COM*) office manager; **~ de producción** (*COM*) production manager; **~ supremo** commander-in-chief; **ser el ~** (*fig*) to be the boss.
JEN [xen] *nf abr* (*ESP*) = *Junta de Energía*

Nuclear.

jengibre [xen'xiβre] *nm* ginger.

jeque ['xeke] *nm* sheik(h).

jerarquía [xerar'kia] *nf* (*orden*) hierarchy; (*rango*) rank.

jerárquico, a [xe'rarkiko, a] *adj* hierarchic(al).

jerez [xe'reθ] *nm* sherry; **J~ de la Frontera** Jerez.

jerezano, a [xere'θano, a] *adj* of *o* from Jerez ♦ *nm/f* native *o* inhabitant of Jerez.

jerga ['xerɣa] *nf* (*tela*) coarse cloth; (*lenguaje*) jargon; ~ **informática** computer jargon.

jerigonza [xeri'xonθa] *nf* (*jerga*) jargon, slang; (*galimatías*) nonsense, gibberish.

jeringa [xe'ringa] *nf* syringe; (*AM*) annoyance, bother; ~ **de engrase** grease gun.

jeringar [xerin'gar] *vt* to annoy, bother.

jeringue [xe'ringe] *etc vb V* **jeringar.**

jeringuilla [xerin'guiʎa] *nf* hypodermic (syringe).

jeroglífico [xero'ɣlifiko] *nm* hieroglyphic.

jersey [xer'sei], *pl* **jerseys** *nm* jersey, pullover, jumper.

Jerusalén [xerusa'len] *n* Jerusalem.

Jesucristo [xesu'kristo] *nm* Jesus Christ.

jesuita [xe'swita] *adj, nm* Jesuit.

Jesús [xe'sus] *nm* Jesus; ¡~! good heavens!; (*al estornudar*) bless you!

jet, *pl* **jets** [jet, jet] *nm* jet (plane) ♦ *nf*: **la ~ the jet set.**

jeta ['xeta] *nf* (*ZOOL*) snout; (*fam: cara*) mug; ¡**que ~ tienes!** (*fam: insolencia*) you've got a nerve!

jíbaro, a ['xiβaro, a] *adj, nm/f* Jibaro (Indian).

jícara ['xikara] *nf* small cup.

jiennense [xjen'nense] *adj* of *o* from Jaén ♦ *nm/f* native *o* inhabitant of Jaén.

jilguero [xil'ɣero] *nm* goldfinch.

jinete, a [xi'nete, a] *nm/f* horseman/woman.

jipijapa [xipi'xapa] *nm* (*AM*) straw hat.

jira ['xira] *nf* (*de tela*) strip; (*excursión*) picnic.

jirafa [xi'rafa] *nf* giraffe.

jirón [xi'ron] *nm* rag, shred.

JJ.OO. *nmpl abr* = **Juegos Olímpicos.**

jocosidad [xokosi'ðað] *nf* humour; (*chiste*) joke.

jocoso, a [xo'koso, a] *adj* humorous, jocular.

joder [xo'ðer] (*fam!*) *vt* to fuck (*!*), screw (*!*); (*fig: fastidiar*) to piss off (*!*), bug; ~**se** *vr* (*fracasar*) to fail; ¡~! damn it!; **se jodió todo** everything was ruined.

jodido, a [xo'ðiðo, a] *adj* (*fam!: difícil*)

awkward; **estoy ~** I'm knackered *o* buggered (*!*).

jofaina [xo'faina] *nf* washbasin.

jojoba [xo'xoβa] *nf* jojoba.

jolgorio [xol'ɣorjo] *nm* (*juerga*) fun, revelry.

jonrón [xon'ron] *nm* home run.

Jordania [xor'ðanja] *nf* Jordan.

jornada [xor'naða] *nf* (*viaje de un día*) day's journey; (*camino o viaje entero*) journey; (*día de trabajo*) working day; ~ **de 8 horas** 8-hour day; (**trabajar a**) ~ **partida** (to work a) split shift.

jornal [xor'nal] *nm* (day's) wage.

jornalero, a [xorna'lero, a] *nm/f* (day) labourer.

joroba [xo'roβa] *nf* hump.

jorobado, a [xoro'βaðo, a] *adj* hunchbacked ♦ *nm/f* hunchback.

jorobar [xoro'βar] *vt* to annoy, pester, bother; ~**se** *vr* to get cross; ¡**hay que ~se!** to hell with it!; **esto me joroba** I'm fed up with this!

jota ['xota] *nf* letter J; (*danza*) Aragonese dance; (*fam*) jot, iota; **no saber ~** to have no idea.

joven ['xoβen] *adj* young ♦ *nm* young man, youth ♦ *nf* young woman, girl.

jovencito, a [xoβen'θito, a] *nm/f* youngster.

jovial [xo'βjal] *adj* cheerful, jolly.

jovialidad [xoβjali'ðað] *nf* cheerfulness, jolliness.

joya ['xoja] *nf* jewel, gem; (*fig: persona*) gem; ~**s de fantasía** imitation jewellery *sg.*

joyería [xoje'ria] *nf* (*joyas*) jewellery; (*tienda*) jeweller's (shop).

joyero [xo'jero] *nm* (*persona*) jeweller; (*caja*) jewel case.

The **Noche de San Juan** (*evening of the Feast of Saint John*) *on the 24th June is a* **fiesta** *coinciding with the summer solstice, and which has taken the place of other ancient pagan festivals. Traditionally fire plays a major part in these festivities, which can last for days in certain areas. Celebrations and dancing take place around* **hogueras** (*bonfires*) *in towns and villages across the country.*

---

juanete [xwa'nete] *nm* (*del pie*) bunion.

jubilación [xuβila'θjon] *nf* (*retiro*) retirement.

jubilado, a [xuβi'laðo, a] *adj* retired ♦ *nm/f* retired person, pensioner (*BRIT*), senior citizen.

jubilar [xuβi'lar] *vt* to pension off, retire;

(*fam*) to discard; ~**se** *vr* to retire.
jubileo [xuβi'leo] *nm* jubilee.
júbilo ['xuβilo] *nm* joy, rejoicing.
jubiloso, a [xuβi'loso, a] *adj* jubilant.
judaísmo [xuða'ismo] *nm* Judaism.
judía [xu'ðia] *nf* V **judío**.
judicatura [xuðika'tura] *nf* (*cargo de juez*) office of judge; (*cuerpo de jueces*) judiciary.
judicial [xuði'θjal] *adj* judicial.
judío, a [xu'ðio, a] *adj* Jewish ♦ *nm* Jew ♦ *nf* Jewess, Jewish woman; (*CULIN*) bean; **judía blanca** haricot bean; **judía verde** French o string bean.
juego ['xweɣo] *etc vb* V **jugar** ♦ *nm* (*gen*) play; (*pasatiempo, partido*) game; (*en casino*) gambling; (*deporte*) sport; (*conjunto*) set; (*herramientas*) kit; ~ **de azar** game of chance; ~ **de café** coffee set; ~ **de caracteres** (*INFORM*) font; ~ **limpio/sucio** fair/foul o dirty play; **J~s Olímpicos** Olympic Games; ~ **de programas** (*INFORM*) suite of programs; **fuera de** ~ (*DEPORTE: persona*) offside; (: *pelota*) out of play; **por** ~ in fun, for fun.
juegue ['xweɣe] *etc vb* V **jugar.**
juerga ['xwerɣa] *nf* binge; (*fiesta*) party; **ir de** ~ to go out on a binge.
juerguista [xwer'ɣista] *nm/f* reveller.
jueves ['xweβes] *nm inv* Thursday.
juez [xweθ] *nm/f* (*f tb:* **jueza**) judge; (*TENIS*) umpire; ~ **de línea** linesman; ~ **de paz** justice of the peace; ~ **de salida** starter.
jugada [xu'ɣaða] *nf* play; **buena** ~ good move (o shot o stroke) *etc*.
jugador, a [xuɣa'ðor, a] *nm/f* player; (*en casino*) gambler.
jugar [xu'ɣar] *vt* to play; (*en casino*) to gamble; (*apostar*) to bet ♦ *vi* to play; to gamble; (*COM*) to speculate; ~**se** *vr* to gamble (away); ~**se el todo por el todo** to stake one's all, go for bust; **¿quién juega?** whose move is it?; **¡me la han jugado!** (*fam*) I've been had!
jugarreta [xuɣa'rreta] *nf* (*mala jugada*) bad move; (*trampa*) dirty trick; **hacer una** ~ **a algn** to play a dirty trick on sb.
juglar [xu'ɣlar] *nm* minstrel.
jugo ['xuɣo] *nm* (*BOT, de fruta*) juice; (*fig*) essence, substance; ~ **de naranja** (*esp AM*) orange juice.
jugoso, a [xu'ɣoso, a] *adj* juicy; (*fig*) substantial, important.
jugué [xu'ɣe], **juguemos** [xu'ɣemos] *etc vb* V **jugar.**
juguete [xu'ɣete] *nm* toy.
juguetear [xuɣete'ar] *vi* to play.
juguetería [xuɣete'ria] *nf* toyshop.

juguetón, ona [xuɣe'ton, ona] *adj* playful.
juicio ['xwiθjo] *nm* judgement; (*sana razón*) sanity, reason; (*opinión*) opinion; (*JUR: proceso*) trial; **estar fuera de** ~ to be out of one's mind; **a mi** ~ in my opinion.
juicioso, a [xwi'θjoso, a] *adj* wise, sensible.
JUJEM [xu'xem] *nf abr* (*ESP MIL*) = **Junta de Jefes del Estado Mayor.**
jul. *abr* (= *julio*) Jul.
julio ['xuljo] *nm* July.
jumento, a [xu'mento, a] *nm/f* donkey.
jun. *abr* (= *junio*) Jun.
junco ['xunko] *nm* rush, reed.
jungla ['xungla] *nf* jungle.
junio ['xunjo] *nm* June.
junta ['xunta] *nf* V **junto.**
juntar [xun'tar] *vt* to join, unite; (*maquinaria*) to assemble, put together; (*dinero*) to collect; ~**se** *vr* to join, meet; (*reunirse: personas*) to meet, assemble; (*arrimarse*) to approach, draw closer; ~**se con algn** to join sb.
junto, a ['xunto, a] *adj* joined; (*unido*) united; (*anexo*) near, close; (*contiguo, próximo*) next, adjacent ♦ *nf* (*asamblea*) meeting, assembly; (*comité, consejo*) board, council, committee; (*MIL, POL*) junta; (*articulación*) joint ♦ *adv*: **todo** ~ all at once ♦ *prep*: ~ **a** near (to), next to; ~**s** together; **junta constitutiva** (*COM*) statutory meeting; **junta directiva** (*COM*) board of management; **junta general extraordinaria** (*COM*) extraordinary general meeting.
juntura [xun'tura] *nf* (*punto de unión*) join, junction; (*articulación*) joint.
jura ['xura] *nf* oath, pledge; ~ **de bandera** (ceremony of taking the) oath of allegiance.
jurado [xu'raðo] *nm* (*JUR: individuo*) juror; (: *grupo*) jury; (*de concurso: grupo*) panel (of judges); (: *individuo*) member of a panel.
juramentar [xuramen'tar] *vt* to swear in, administer the oath to; ~**se** *vr* to be sworn in, take the oath.
juramento [xura'mento] *nm* oath; (*maldición*) oath, curse; **bajo** ~ on oath; **prestar** ~ to take the oath; **tomar** ~ **a** to swear in, administer the oath to.
jurar [xu'rar] *vt, vi* to swear; ~ **en falso** to commit perjury; **jurárselas a algn** to have it in for sb.
jurídico, a [xu'riðiko, a] *adj* legal, juridical.
jurisdicción [xurisðik'θjon] *nf* (*poder, autoridad*) jurisdiction; (*territorio*)

district.
jurisprudencia [xurispru'ðenθja] *nf* jurisprudence.
jurista [xu'rista] *nmf* jurist.
justamente [xusta'mente] *adv* justly, fairly; (*precisamente*) just, exactly.
justicia [xus'tiθja] *nf* justice; (*equidad*) fairness, justice; **de** ~ deservedly.
justiciero, a [xusti'θjero, a] *adj* just, righteous.
justificable [xustifi'kaßle] *adj* justifiable.
justificación [xustifika'θjon] *nf* justification; ~ **automática** (*INFORM*) automatic justification.
justificado, a [xustifi'kaðo, a] *adj* (*TIP*): **(no)** ~ (un)justified.
justificante [xustifi'kante] *nm* voucher; ~ **médico** sick note.
justificar [xustifi'kar] *vt* (*tb TIP*) to justify; (*probar*) to verify.
justifique [xusti'fike] *etc vb V* **justificar**.
justo, a ['xusto, a] *adj* (*equitativo*) just, fair, right; (*preciso*) exact, correct; (*ajustado*) tight ♦ *adv* (*precisamente*) exactly, precisely; (*apenas a tiempo*) just in time; ¡~! that's it!, correct!; **llegaste muy** ~ you just made it; **vivir muy** ~ to be hard up.
juvenil [xuße'nil] *adj* youthful.
juventud [xußen'tuð] *nf* (*adolescencia*) youth; (*jóvenes*) young people *pl.*
juzgado [xuθ'ɣaðo] *nm* tribunal; (*JUR*) court.
juzgar [xuθ'ɣar] *vt* to judge; **a** ~ **por** ... to judge by ..., judging by ...; ~ **mal** to misjudge; **júzguelo usted mismo** see for yourself.

Kenia ['kenja] *nf* Kenya.
keniata [ke'njata] *adj, nmf* Kenyan.
kepí, kepis [ke'pi, 'kepis] *nm* (*esp AM*) kepi, military hat.
kerosene [kero'sene] *nm* kerosene.
kg. *abr* (= *kilogramo(s)*) kg.
kilate [ki'late] *nm* = **quilate**.
kilo ['kilo] *nm* kilo.
kilobyte ['kiloßait] *nm* (*INFORM*) kilobyte.
kilogramo [kilo'ɣramo] *nm* kilogramme (*BRIT*), kilogram (*US*).
kilolitro [kilo'litro] *nm* kilolitre (*BRIT*), kiloliter (*US*).
kilometraje [kilome'traxe] *nm* distance in kilometres, ≈ mileage.
kilométrico, a [kilo'metriko, a] *adj* kilometric; (*fam*) very long; **(billete)** ~ (*FERRO*) mileage ticket.
kilómetro [ki'lometro] *nm* kilometre (*BRIT*), kilometer (*US*).
kiloocteto [kilook'teto] *nm* (*INFORM*) kilobyte.
kilovatio [kilo'ßatjo] *nm* kilowatt.
kiosco ['kjosko] *nm* = **quiosco**.
Kirguizistán [kirɣiθis'tan] *nm* Kirghizia.
kiwi ['kiwi] *nm* kiwi (fruit).
km *abr* (= *kilómetro(s)*) km.
km/h *abr* (= *kilómetros por hora*) km/h.
knock-out ['nokau], **K.O.** ['kao] *nm* knockout; (*golpe*) knockout blow; **dejar** *o* **poner a algn** ~ to knock sb out.
k.p.h. *abr* (= *kilómetros por hora*) km/h.
k.p.l. *abr* (= *kilómetros por litro*) ≈ m.p.g.
kurdo, a ['kurðo, a] *adj* Kurdish ♦ *nmf* Kurd ♦ *nm* (*LING*) Kurdish.
kuwaití [kußai'ti] *adj, nmf* Kuwaiti.
kv *abr* (= *kilovatio*) kw.
kv/h *abr* (= *kilovatios-hora*) kw-h.

Kk

K, k [ka] *nf* (*letra*) K, k; **K de Kilo** K for King.
K *abr* (= *1.000*) K; (*INFORM*: = *1.024*) K.
Kampuchea [kampu'tʃea] *nf* Kampuchea.
karaoke [kara'oke] *nm* karaoke.
karate [ka'rate] *nm* karate.
KAS *nf abr* (= *Koordinadora Abertzale Sozialista*) *Basque nationalist umbrella group.*
Kazajstán [kaθaxs'tan] *nm* Kazakhstan.
k/c. *abr* (= *kilociclos*) kc.

Ll

L, l ['ele] *nf* (*letra*) L, l; **L de Lorenzo** L for Lucy (*BRIT*) *o* Love (*US*).
l. *abr* (= *litro(s)*) l.; (*JUR*) = **ley**; (*LITERATURA*: = *libro*) bk.
L/ *abr* (*COM*) = **letra**.
la [la] *artículo definido fsg* the ♦ *pron* her; (*usted*) you; (*cosa*) it ♦ *nm* (*MUS*) A; **está en** ~ **cárcel** he's in jail; ~ **del sombrero rojo** the woman/girl/one in the red hat.

laberinto [laße'rinto] *nm* labyrinth.
labia ['laßja] *nf* fluency; (*pey*) glibness;
tener mucha ~ to have the gift of the
gab.
labial [la'ßjal] *adj* labial.
labio ['laßjo] *nm* lip; (*de vasija etc*) edge,
rim; ~ **inferior/superior** lower/upper lip.
labor [la'ßor] *nf* labour; (*AGR*) farm work;
(*tarea*) job, task; (*COSTURA*) needlework,
sewing; (*punto*) knitting; ~ **de equipo**
teamwork; ~ **de ganchillo** crochet.
laborable [laßo'raßle] *adj* (*AGR*) workable;
día ~ working day.
laboral [laßo'ral] *adj* (*accidente,
conflictividad*) industrial; (*jornada*)
working; (*derecho, relaciones*) labour *cpd.*
laboralista [laßora'lista] *adj*: **abogado** ~
labour lawyer.
laborar [laßo'rar] *vi* to work.
laboratorio [laßora'torjo] *nm* laboratory.
laborioso, a [laßo'rjoso, a] *a* (*persona*)
hard-working; (*trabajo*) tough.
laborista [laßo'rista] (*BRIT POL*) *adj*: **Partido
L**~ Labour Party ♦ *nm/f* Labour Party
member *o* supporter.
labrado, a [la'ßraðo, a] *adj* worked;
(*madera*) carved; (*metal*) wrought ♦ *nm*
(*AGR*) cultivated field.
Labrador [laßra'ðor] *nm* Labrador.
labrador, a [laßra'ðor, a] *nm/f* farmer.
labranza [la'ßranθa] *nf* (*AGR*) cultivation.
labrar [la'ßrar] *vt* (*gen*) to work; (*madera
etc*) to carve; (*fig*) to cause, bring about.
labriego, a [la'ßrjeɣo, a] *nm/f* peasant.
laca ['laka] *nf* lacquer; (*de pelo*) hairspray;
~ **de uñas** nail varnish.
lacayo [la'kajo] *nm* lackey.
lacerar [laθe'rar] *vt* to lacerate.
lacio, a ['laθjo, a] *adj* (*pelo*) lank, straight.
lacón [la'kon] *nm* shoulder of pork.
lacónico, a [la'koniko, a] *adj* laconic.
lacra ['lakra] *nf* (*defecto*) blemish; ~ **social**
social disgrace.
lacrar [la'krar] *vt* (*cerrar*) to seal (with
sealing wax).
lacre ['lakre] *nm* sealing wax.
lacrimógeno, a [lakri'moxeno, a] *adj* (*fig*)
sentimental; **gas** ~ tear gas.
lacrimoso, a [lakri'moso, a] *adj* tearful.
lactancia [lak'tanθja] *nf* breast-feeding.
lactar [lak'tar] *vt, vi* to suckle, breast-feed.
lácteo, a ['lakteo, a] *adj*: **productos** ~**s**
dairy products.
ladear [laðe'ar] *vt* to tip, tilt ♦ *vi* to tilt; ~**se**
vr to lean; (*DEPORTE*) to swerve; (*AVIAT*)
to bank, turn.
ladera [la'ðera] *nf* slope.
ladino, a [la'ðino, a] *adj* cunning.

lado ['laðo] *nm* (*gen*) side; (*fig*) protection;
(*MIL*) flank; ~ **izquierdo** left(-hand) side;
~ **a** ~ side by side; **al** ~ **de** next to,
beside; **hacerse a un** ~ to stand aside;
poner de ~ to put on its side; **poner a un**
~ to put aside; **me da de** ~ I don't care;
por un ~ ..., **por otro** ~ ... on the one
hand ..., on the other (hand), ...; **por
todos** ~**s** on all sides, all round (*BRIT*).
ladrar [la'ðrar] *vi* to bark.
ladrido [la'ðriðo] *nm* bark, barking.
ladrillo [la'ðriʎo] *nm* (*gen*) brick; (*azulejo*)
tile.
ladrón, ona [la'ðron, ona] *nm/f* thief.
lagar [la'ɣar] *nm* (wine/oil) press.
lagartija [laɣar'tixa] *nf* (small) lizard, wall
lizard.
lagarto [la'ɣarto] *nm* (*ZOOL*) lizard; (*AM*)
alligator.
lago ['laɣo] *nm* lake.
Lagos ['laɣos] *nm* Lagos.
lágrima ['laɣrima] *nf* tear.
lagrimal [laɣri'mal] *nm* (inner) corner of
the eye.
lagrimear [laɣrime'ar] *vi* to weep; (*ojos*)
to water.
laguna [la'ɣuna] *nf* (*lago*) lagoon; (*en
escrito, conocimientos*) gap.
laico, a ['laiko, a] *adj* lay ♦ *nm/f* layman/
woman.
laja ['laxa] *nf* rock.
lamber [lam'ber] *vt* (*AM*) to lick.
lambiscón, ona [lambis'kon, ona] *adj*
flattering ♦ *nm/f* flatterer.
lameculos [lame'kulos] *nm/f inv* (*fam*)
arselicker (*!*), crawler.
lamentable [lamen'taßle] *adj* lamentable,
regrettable; (*miserable*) pitiful.
lamentación [lamenta'θjon] *nf*
lamentation; **ahora no sirven
lamentaciones** it's no good crying over
spilt milk.
lamentar [lamen'tar] *vt* (*sentir*) to regret;
(*deplorar*) to lament; ~**se** *vr* to lament; **lo
lamento mucho** I'm very sorry.
lamento [la'mento] *nm* lament.
lamer [la'mer] *vt* to lick.
lámina ['lamina] *nf* (*plancha delgada*) sheet;
(*para estampar, estampa*) plate; (*grabado*)
engraving.
laminar [lami'nar] *vt* (*en libro*) to laminate;
(*TEC*) to roll.
lámpara ['lampara] *nf* lamp; ~ **de alcohol/
gas** spirit/gas lamp; ~ **de pie** standard
lamp.
lamparilla [lampa'riʎa] *nf* nightlight.
lamparón [lampa'ron] *nm* (*MED*) scrofula;
(*mancha*) (large) grease spot.

lampiño, a [lam'piɲo, a] *adj* (*sin pelo*) hairless.

lana ['lana] *nf* wool; (*tela*) woollen (*BRIT*) o woolen (*US*) cloth; (*AM fam: dinero*) dough; (**hecho**) **de** ~ wool *cpd*.

lance ['lanθe] *etc vb V* **lanzar** ♦ *nm* (*golpe*) stroke; (*suceso*) event, incident.

lanceta [lan'seta] *nf* (*AM*) sting.

lancha ['lantʃa] *nf* launch; ~ **motora** motorboat; ~ **de pesca** fishing boat; ~ **salvavidas/torpedera** lifeboat/torpedo boat; ~ **neumática** rubber dinghy.

lanero, a [la'nero, a] *adj* wool *cpd*.

langosta [lan'gosta] *nf* (*insecto*) locust; (*crustáceo*) lobster (: *de río*) crayfish.

langostino [langos'tino] *nm* prawn; (*de agua dulce*) crayfish.

languidecer [langiðe'θer] *vi* to languish.

languidez [langi'ðeθ] *nf* languor.

languidezca [langi'ðeθka] *etc vb V* **languidecer**.

lánguido, a ['langiðo, a] *adj* (*gen*) languid; (*sin energía*) listless.

lanilla [la'niʎa] *nf* nap; (*tela*) thin flannel cloth.

lanolina [lano'lina] *nf* lanolin(e).

lanudo, a [la'nuðo, a] *adj* woolly, fleecy.

lanza ['lanθa] *nf* (*arma*) lance, spear; **medir** ~**s** to cross swords.

lanzacohetes [lanθako'etes] *nm inv* rocket launcher.

lanzadera [lanθa'ðera] *nf* shuttle.

lanzado, a [lan'θaðo, a] *adj* (*atrevido*) forward; (*decidido*) determined; **ir** ~ (*rápido*) to fly along.

lanzallamas [lanθa'ʎamas] *nm inv* flamethrower.

lanzamiento [lanθa'mjento] *nm* (*gen*) throwing; (*NAUT, COM*) launch, launching; ~ **de pesos** putting the shot.

lanzar [lan'θar] *vt* (*gen*) to throw; (*con violencia*) to fling; (*DEPORTE: pelota*) to bowl; (: *US*) to pitch; (*NAUT, COM*) to launch; (*JUR*) to evict; (*grito*) to give, utter; ~**se** *vr* to throw o.s.; (*fig*) to take the plunge; ~**se a** (*fig*) to embark upon.

Lanzarote [lanθa'rote] *nm* Lanzarote.

lanzatorpedos [lanθator'peðos] *nm inv* torpedo tube.

lapa ['lapa] *nf* limpet.

La Paz *nf* La Paz.

lapicero [lapi'θero] *nm* pencil; (*AM*) propelling (*BRIT*) o mechanical (*US*) pencil; (: *bolígrafo*) Biro ®.

lápida ['lapiða] *nf* stone; ~ **conmemorativa** memorial stone; ~ **mortuoria** headstone.

lapidar [lapi'ðar] *vt* to stone; (*TEC*) to polish, lap.

lapidario, a [lapi'ðarjo, a] *adj, nm* lapidary.

lápiz ['lapiθ] *nm* pencil; ~ **de color** coloured pencil; ~ **de labios** lipstick; ~ **óptico** o **luminoso** light pen.

lapón, ona [la'pon, ona] *adj* Lapp ♦ *nm/f* Laplander, Lapp ♦ *nm* (*LING*) Lapp.

Laponia [la'ponja] *nf* Lapland.

lapso ['lapso] *nm* lapse; (*error*) error; ~ **de tiempo** interval of time.

lapsus ['lapsus] *nm inv* error, mistake.

LAR [lar] *nf abr* (*ESP JUR*) = *Ley de Arrendamientos Rústicos*.

largamente [larɣa'mente] *adv* for a long time; (*relatar*) at length.

largar [lar'ɣar] *vt* (*soltar*) to release; (*aflojar*) to loosen; (*lanzar*) to launch; (*fam*) to let fly; (*velas*) to unfurl; (*AM*) to throw; ~**se** *vr* (*fam*) to beat it; ~**se a** (*AM*) to start to.

largo, a ['larɣo, a] *adj* (*longitud*) long; (*tiempo*) lengthy; (*persona: alta*) tall; (: *fig*) generous ♦ *nm* length; (*MUS*) largo; **dos años** ~**s** two long years; **a** ~ **plazo** in the long term; **tiene 9 metros de** ~ it is 9 metres long; **a lo** ~ (*posición*) lengthways; **a lo** ~ **de** along; (*tiempo*) all through, throughout; **a la larga** in the long run; **me dio largas con una promesa** she put me off with a promise; ¡~ **de aquí!** (*fam*) clear off!

largometraje [larɣome'traxe] *nm* full-length o feature film.

largue ['larɣe] *etc vb V* **largar**.

larguero [lar'ɣero] *nm* (*ARQ*) main beam, chief support; (*de puerta*) jamb; (*DEPORTE*) crossbar; (*en cama*) bolster.

largueza [lar'ɣeθa] *nf* generosity.

larguirucho, a [larɣi'rutʃo, a] *adj* lanky, gangling.

larguísimo, a [lar'ɣisimo, a] *adj superlativo de* **largo**.

largura [lar'ɣura] *nf* length.

laringe [la'rinxe] *nf* larynx.

laringitis [larin'xitis] *nf* laryngitis.

larva ['larβa] *nf* larva.

las [las] *artículo definido fpl* the ♦ *pron* them; ~ **que cantan** the ones/women/girls who sing.

lasaña [la'saɲa] *nf* lasagne, lasagna.

lasca ['laska] *nf* chip of stone.

lascivia [las'θiβja] *nf* lewdness; (*lujuria*) lust; (*fig*) playfulness.

lascivo, a [las'θiβo, a] *adj* lewd.

láser ['laser] *nm* laser.

Las Palmas *nf* Las Palmas.

lástima ['lastima] *nf* (*pena*) pity; **dar** ~ to be pitiful; **es una** ~ **que** it's a pity that;

¡qué ~! what a pity!; **estar hecho una ~** to be a sorry sight.
lastimar [lasti'mar] *vt* (*herir*) to wound; (*ofender*) to offend; **~se** *vr* to hurt o.s.
lastimero, a [lasti'mero, a] *adj* pitiful, pathetic.
lastre ['lastre] *nm* (TEC, NAUT) ballast; (*fig*) dead weight.
lata ['lata] *nf* (*metal*) tin; (*envase*) tin, can; (*fam*) nuisance; **en ~** tinned; **dar (la) ~** to be a nuisance.
latente [la'tente] *adj* latent.
lateral [late'ral] *adj* side, lateral ♦ *nm* (TEAT) wings *pl*.
latido [la'tiðo] *nm* (*del corazón*) beat; (*de herida*) throb(bing).
latifundio [lati'fundjo] *nm* large estate.
latifundista [latifun'dista] *nm/f* owner of a large estate.
latigazo [lati'ɣaθo] *nm* (*golpe*) lash; (*sonido*) crack; (*fig: regaño*) dressing-down.
látigo ['latiɣo] *nm* whip.
latiguillo [lati'ɣiʎo] *nm* (TEAT) hamming.
latín [la'tin] *nm* Latin; **saber (mucho) ~** (*fam*) to be pretty sharp.
latinajo [lati'naxo] *nm* dog Latin; **echar ~s** to come out with Latin words.
latino, a [la'tino, a] *adj* Latin.
Latinoamérica [latinoa'merika] *nf* Latin America.
latinoamericano, a [latinoameri'kano, a] *adj, nm/f* Latin American.
latir [la'tir] *vi* (*corazón, pulso*) to beat.
latitud [lati'tuð] *nf* (GEO) latitude; (*fig*) breadth, extent.
lato, a ['lato, a] *adj* broad.
latón [la'ton] *nm* brass.
latoso, a [la'toso, a] *adj* (*molesto*) annoying; (*aburrido*) boring.
latrocinio [latro'θinjo] *nm* robbery.
LAU *nf abr* (ESP JUR) = Ley de Arrendamientos Urbanos.
laúd [la'uð] *nm* lute.
laudatorio, a [lauða'torjo, a] *adj* laudatory.
laudo ['lauðo] *nm* (JUR) decision, finding.
laurear [laure'ar] *vt* to honour, reward.
laurel [lau'rel] *nm* (BOT) laurel; (CULIN) bay.
Lausana [lau'sana] *nf* Lausanne.
lava ['laβa] *nf* lava.
lavable [la'βaβle] *adj* washable.
lavabo [la'βaβo] *nm* (*jofaina*) washbasin; (*retrete*) lavatory (BRIT), toilet (BRIT), washroom (US).
lavadero [laβa'ðero] *nm* laundry.
lavado [la'βaðo] *nm* washing; (*de ropa*) wash, laundry; (ARTE) wash; **~ de**

cerebro brainwashing.
lavadora [laβa'ðora] *nf* washing machine.
lavanda [la'βanda] *nf* lavender.
lavandería [laβande'ria] *nf* laundry; **~ automática** launderette.
lavaparabrisas [laβapara'βrisas] *nm inv* windscreen washer.
lavaplatos [laβa'platos] *nm inv* dishwasher.
lavar [la'βar] *vt* to wash; (*borrar*) to wipe away; **~se** *vr* to wash o.s.; **~se las manos** to wash one's hands; (*fig*) to wash one's hands of it; **~ y marcar** (*pelo*) to shampoo and set; **~ en seco** to dry-clean.
lavativa [laβa'tiβa] *nf* (MED) enema.
lavavajillas [laβaβa'xiʎas] *nm inv* dishwasher.
laxante [lak'sante] *nm* laxative.
laxitud [laksi'tuð] *nf* laxity, slackness.
lazada [la'θaða] *nf* bow.
lazarillo [laθa'riʎo] *nm*: **perro de ~** guide dog.
lazo ['laθo] *nm* knot; (*lazada*) bow; (*para animales*) lasso; (*trampa*) snare; (*vínculo*) tie; **~ corredizo** slipknot.
LBE *nf abr* (ESP JUR) = Ley Básica de Empleo.
lb(s) *abr* = **libra(s)**.
L/C *abr* (= Letra de Crédito) B/E.
Lda., Ldo. *abr* = **Licenciado, a**.
le [le] *pron* (*directo*) him (*o* her); (: *usted*) you; (*indirecto*) to him (*o* her *o* it); (: *usted*) to you.
leal [le'al] *adj* loyal.
lealtad [leal'tað] *nf* loyalty.
lebrel [le'βrel] *nm* greyhound.
lección [lek'θjon] *nf* lesson; **~ práctica** object lesson; **dar lecciones** to teach, give lessons; **dar una ~ a algn** (*fig*) to teach sb a lesson.
leche ['letʃe] *nf* milk; (*fam!*) semen, spunk (*!*); **dar una ~ a algn** (*fam*) to belt sb; **estar de mala ~** (*fam*) to be in a foul mood; **tener mala ~** (*fam*) to be a nasty piece of work; **~ condensada/en polvo** condensed/powdered milk; **~ desnatada** skimmed milk; **~ de magnesia** milk of magnesia; **¡~!** hell!
lechera [le'tʃera] *nf V* **lechero**.
lechería [letʃe'ria] *nf* dairy.
lechero, a [le'tʃero, a] *adj* milk *cpd* ♦ *nm* milkman ♦ *nf* (*vendedora*) milkmaid; (*recipiente*) milk pan; (*para servir*) milk churn.
lecho ['letʃo] *nm* (*cama, de río*) bed; (GEO) layer; **~ mortuorio** deathbed.
lechón [le'tʃon] *nm* sucking (BRIT) *o* suckling (US) pig.
lechoso, a [le'tʃoso, a] *adj* milky.

lechuga [le'tʃuɣa] *nf* lettuce.
lechuza [le'tʃuθa] *nf* (barn) owl.
lectivo, a [lek'tiβo, a] *adj* (*horas*) teaching *cpd*; **año** *o* **curso** ~ (*ESCOL*) school year; (*UNIV*) academic year.
lector, a [lek'tor, a] *nm/f* reader; (*ESCOL, UNIV*) (conversation) assistant ♦ *nm*: ~ **óptico de caracteres** (*INFORM*) optical character reader ♦ *nf*: ~**a de fichas** (*INFORM*) card reader.
lectura [lek'tura] *nf* reading; ~ **de marcas sensibles** (*INFORM*) mark sensing.
leer [le'er] *vt* to read; ~ **entre líneas** to read between the lines.
legación [leɣa'θjon] *nf* legation.
legado [le'ɣaðo] *nm* (*don*) bequest; (*herencia*) legacy; (*enviado*) legate.
legajo [le'ɣaxo] *nm* file, bundle (of papers).
legal [le'ɣal] *adj* legal, lawful; (*persona*) trustworthy.
legalice [leɣa'liθe] *etc vb V* **legalizar**.
legalidad [leɣali'ðað] *nf* legality.
legalizar [leɣali'θar] *vt* to legalize; (*documento*) to authenticate.
legaña [le'ɣaɲa] *nf* sleep (*in eyes*).
legar [le'ɣar] *vt* to bequeath, leave.
legatario, a [leɣa'tarjo, a] *nm/f* legatee.
legendario, a [lexen'darjo, a] *adj* legendary.
legible [le'xiβle] *adj* legible; ~ **por máquina** (*INFORM*) machine-readable.
legión [le'xjon] *nf* legion.
legionario, a [lexjo'narjo, a] *adj* legionary ♦ *nm* legionnaire.
legislación [lexisla'θjon] *nf* legislation; (*leyes*) laws *pl*; ~ **antimonopolio** (*COM*) anti-trust legislation.
legislar [lexis'lar] *vt* to legislate.
legislativo, a [lexisla'tiβo, a] *adj*: (**elecciones) legislativas** ≈ general election.
legislatura [lexisla'tura] *nf* (*POL*) period of office.
legitimar [lexiti'mar] *vt* to legitimize.
legítimo, a [le'xitimo, a] *adj* (*genuino*) authentic; (*legal*) legitimate, rightful.
lego, a ['leɣo, a] *adj* (*REL*) secular; (*ignorante*) ignorant ♦ *nm* layman.
legua ['leɣwa] *nf* league; **se ve** (*o* **nota**) **a la** ~ you can tell (it) a mile off.
legue ['leɣe] *etc vb V* **legar**.
leguleyo [leɣu'lejo] *nm* (*pey*) petty *o* shyster (*US*) lawyer.
legumbres [le'ɣumbres] *nfpl* pulses.
leído, a [le'iðo, a] *adj* well-read.
lejanía [lexa'nia] *nf* distance.
lejano, a [le'xano, a] *adj* far-off; (*en el tiempo*) distant; (*fig*) remote; **L~ Oriente** Far East.
lejía [le'xia] *nf* bleach.
lejísimos [le'xisimos] *adv* a long, long way.
lejos ['lexos] *adv* far, far away; **a lo** ~ in the distance; **de** *o* **desde** ~ from a distance; **está muy** ~ it's a long way (away); **¿está** ~? is it far?; ~ **de** *prep* far from.
lelo, a ['lelo, a] *adj* silly ♦ *nm/f* idiot.
lema ['lema] *nm* motto; (*POL*) slogan.
lencería [lenθe'ria] *nf* (*telas*) linen, drapery; (*ropa interior*) lingerie.
lendakari [lenda'kari] *nm head of the Basque Autonomous Government.*
lengua ['lengwa] *nf* tongue; ~ **materna** mother tongue; ~ **de tierra** (*GEO*) spit *o* tongue of land; **dar a la** ~ to chatter; **morderse la** ~ to hold one's tongue; **sacar la** ~ **a algn** (*fig*) to cock a snook at sb.

Under the Spanish constitution **lenguas cooficiales** *or* **oficiales** *enjoy the same status as* **castellano** *in those regions which have retained their own distinct language, ie in Galicia,* **gallego***; in the Basque Country,* **euskera***; in Catalonia and the Balearic Islands,* **catalán***. The regional governments actively promote their own language through the media and the education system. Of the three regions with their own language, Catalonia has the highest number of people who speak the* lengua cooficial.

lenguado [len'gwaðo] *nm* sole.
lenguaje [len'gwaxe] *nm* language; (*forma de hablar*) (mode of) speech; ~ **comercial** business language; ~ **ensamblador** *o* **de alto nivel** (*INFORM*) high-level language; ~ **máquina** (*INFORM*) machine language; ~ **original** source language; ~ **periodístico** journalese; ~ **de programación** (*INFORM*) programming language; **en** ~ **llano** ≈ in plain English.
lenguaraz [lengwa'raθ] *adj* talkative; (*pey*) foul-mouthed.
lengüeta [len'gweta] *nf* (*ANAT*) epiglottis; (*de zapatos, MUS*) tongue.
lenidad [leni'ðað] *nf* lenience.
Leningrado [lenin'graðo] *nm* Leningrad.
lente ['lente] *nm o nf* lens; (*lupa*) magnifying glass; ~**s** *pl* glasses; ~**s de contacto** contact lenses.
lenteja [len'texa] *nf* lentil.
lentejuela [lente'xwela] *nf* sequin.
lentilla [len'tiʎa] *nf* contact lens.
lentitud [lenti'tuð] *nf* slowness; **con** ~

slowly.
lento, a ['lento, a] *adj* slow.
leña ['leɲa] *nf* firewood; **dar ~ a** to thrash; **echar ~ al fuego** to add fuel to the flames.
leñador, a [leɲa'ðor, a] *nm/f* woodcutter.
leño ['leɲo] *nm* (*trozo de árbol*) log; (*madera*) timber; (*fig*) blockhead.
Leo ['leo] *nm* (*ASTRO*) Leo.
león [le'on] *nm* lion; **~ marino** sea lion.
leonera [leo'nera] *nf* (*jaula*) lion's cage; **parece una ~** it's shockingly dirty.
leonés, esa [leo'nes, esa] *adj, nm/f* Leonese ♦ *nm* (*LING*) Leonese.
leonino, a [leo'nino, a] *adj* leonine.
leopardo [leo'parðo] *nm* leopard.
leotardos [leo'tarðos] *nmpl* tights.
lepra ['lepra] *nf* leprosy.
leprosería [leprose'ria] *nf* leper colony.
leproso, a [le'proso, a] *nm/f* leper.
lerdo, a ['lerðo, a] *adj* (*lento*) slow; (*patoso*) clumsy.
leridano, a [leri'ðano, a] *adj* of *o* from Lérida ♦ *nm/f* native *o* inhabitant of Lérida.
les [les] *pron* (*directo*) them; (: *ustedes*) you; (*indirecto*) to them; (: *ustedes*) to you.
lesbiana [les'βjana] *nf* lesbian.
lesión [le'sjon] *nf* wound, lesion; (*DEPORTE*) injury.
lesionado, a [lesjo'naðo, a] *adj* injured ♦ *nm/f* injured person.
lesionar [lesjo'nar] *vt* (*dañar*) to hurt; (*herir*) to wound; **~se** *vr* to get hurt.
letal [le'tal] *adj* lethal.
letanía [leta'nia] *nf* litany; (*retahíla*) long list.
letárgico, a [le'tarxiko, a] *adj* lethargic.
letargo [le'tarɣo] *nm* lethargy.
letón, ona [le'ton, ona] *adj, nm/f* Latvian ♦ *nm* (*LING*) Latvian.
Letonia [le'tonja] *nf* Latvia.
letra ['letra] *nf* letter; (*escritura*) handwriting; (*COM*) letter, bill, draft; (*MUS*) lyrics *pl*; **~s** *nfpl* (*UNIV*) arts; **~ bastardilla/negrilla** italics *pl*/bold type; **~ de cambio** bill of exchange; **~ de imprenta** print; **~ inicial/capital/mayúscula/minúscula** initial/capital/small letter; **lo tomó al pie de la ~** he took it literally; **~ bancaria** (*COM*) bank draft; **~ de patente** (*COM*) letters patent *pl*; **escribir 4 ~s a algn** to drop a line to sb.
letrado, a [le'traðo, a] *adj* learned; (*fam*) pedantic ♦ *nm/f* lawyer.
letrero [le'trero] *nm* (*cartel*) sign; (*etiqueta*) label.
letrina [le'trina] *nf* latrine.

leucemia [leu'θemja] *nf* leukaemia.
leucocito [leuko'θito] *nm* white blood cell, leucocyte.
leva ['leβa] *nf* (*NAUT*) weighing anchor; (*MIL*) levy; (*TEC*) lever.
levadizo, a [leβa'ðiθo, a] *adj*: **puente ~** drawbridge.
levadura [leβa'ðura] *nf* yeast, leaven; **~ de cerveza** brewer's yeast.
levantamiento [leβanta'mjento] *nm* raising, lifting; (*rebelión*) revolt, rising; (*GEO*) survey; **~ de pesos** weightlifting.
levantar [leβan'tar] *vt* (*gen*) to raise; (*del suelo*) to pick up; (*hacia arriba*) to lift (up); (*plan*) to make, draw up; (*mesa*) to clear; (*campamento*) to strike; (*fig*) to cheer up, hearten; **~se** *vr* to get up; (*enderezarse*) to straighten up; (*rebelarse*) to rebel; (*sesión*) to be adjourned; (*niebla*) to lift; (*viento*) to rise; **~se (de la cama)** to get up, get out of bed; **~ el ánimo** to cheer up.
levante [le'βante] *nm* east; (*viento*) east wind; **el L~** region of Spain extending from Castellón to Murcia.
levantino, a [leβan'tino, a] *adj* of *o* from the *Levante* ♦ *nm/f*: **los ~s** the people of the *Levante*.
levar [le'βar] *vi* to weigh anchor.
leve ['leβe] *adj* light; (*fig*) trivial; (*mínimo*) slight.
levedad [leβe'ðað] *nf* lightness; (*fig*) levity.
levita [le'βita] *nf* frock coat.
léxico, a ['leksiko, a] *adj* lexical ♦ *nm* (*vocabulario*) vocabulary; (*LING*) lexicon.
ley [lei] *nf* (*gen*) law; (*metal*) standard; **decreto-~** decree law; **de buena ~** (*fig*) genuine; **según la ~** in accordance with the law, by law, in law.
leyenda [le'jenda] *nf* legend; (*TIP*) inscription.
leyendo [le'jendo] *etc vb V* leer.
liar [li'ar] *vt* to tie (up); (*unir*) to bind; (*envolver*) to wrap (up); (*enredar*) to confuse; (*cigarrillo*) to roll; **~se** *vr* (*fam*) to get involved; (*confundirse*) to get mixed up; **~se a palos** to get involved in a fight.
lib. *abr* (= *libro*) bk.
libanés, esa [liβa'nes, esa] *adj, nm/f* Lebanese.
Líbano ['liβano] *nm*: **el ~** the Lebanon.
libar [li'βar] *vt* to suck.
libelo [li'βelo] *nm* satire, lampoon; (*JUR*) petition.
libélula [li'βelula] *nf* dragonfly.
liberación [liβera'θjon] *nf* liberation; (*de la cárcel*) release.

liberado, a [liße'raðo, a] *adj* liberated; (*COM*) paid-up, paid-in (*US*).

liberal [liße'ral] *adj, nm/f* liberal.

liberalidad [lißerali'ðað] *nf* liberality, generosity.

liberar [liße'rar] *vt* to liberate.

libertad [lißer'tað] *nf* liberty, freedom; ~ **de asociación/de culto/de prensa/de comercio/de palabra** freedom of association/of worship/of the press/of trade/of speech; ~ **condicional** probation; ~ **bajo palabra** parole; ~ **bajo fianza** bail; **estar en** ~ to be free; **poner a algn en** ~ to set sb free.

libertador, a [lißerta'ðor, a] *adj* liberating ♦ *nm/f* liberator; **El L~** (*AM*) The Liberator.

libertar [lißer'tar] *vt* (*preso*) to set free; (*de una obligación*) to release; (*eximir*) to exempt.

libertinaje [lißerti'naxe] *nm* licentiousness.

libertino, a [lißer'tino, a] *adj* permissive ♦ *nm/f* permissive person.

Libia ['lißja] *nf* Libya.

libidinoso, a [lißiði'noso, a] *adj* lustful; (*viejo*) lecherous.

libido [li'ßiðo] *nf* libido.

libio, a ['lißjo, a] *adj, nm/f* Libyan.

libra ['lißra] *nf* pound; **L~** (*ASTRO*) Libra; ~ **esterlina** pound sterling.

librador, a [lißra'ðor, a] *nm/f* drawer.

libramiento [lißra'mjento] *nm* rescue; (*COM*) delivery.

libranza [li'ßranθa] *nf* (*COM*) draft; (*letra de cambio*) bill of exchange.

librar [li'ßrar] *vt* (*de peligro*) to save; (*batalla*) to wage, fight; (*de impuestos*) to exempt; (*cheque*) to make out; (*JUR*) to exempt; **~se** *vr*: **~se de** to escape from, free o.s. from; **de buena nos hemos librado** we're well out of that.

libre ['lißre] *adj* (*gen*) free; (*lugar*) unoccupied; (*tiempo*) spare; (*asiento*) vacant; (*COM*): ~ **a bordo** free on board; ~ **de franqueo** post-free; ~ **de impuestos** free of tax; **tiro** ~ free kick; **los 100 metros** ~ the 100 metres freestyle (*race*); **al aire** ~ in the open air; **¿estás ~?** are you free?

librecambio [lißre'kambjo] *nm* free trade.

librecambista [lißrekam'bista] *adj* free-trade *cpd* ♦ *nm* free-trader.

librería [lißre'ria] *nf* (*tienda*) bookshop; (*estante*) bookcase; ~ **de ocasión** secondhand bookshop.

librero, a [li'ßrero, a] *nm/f* bookseller.

libreta [li'ßreta] *nf* notebook; (*pan*) one-pound loaf; ~ **de ahorros** savings book.

libro ['lißro] *nm* book; ~ **de actas** minute book; ~ **de bolsillo** paperback; ~ **de cabecera** bedside book; ~ **de caja** (*COM*) cashbook; ~ **de caja auxiliar** (*COM*) petty cash book; ~ **de cocina** cookery book (*BRIT*), cookbook (*US*); ~ **de consulta** reference book; ~ **de cuentas** account book; ~ **de cuentos** storybook; ~ **de cheques** cheque (*BRIT*) o check (*US*) book; ~ **diario** journal; ~ **de entradas y salidas** (*COM*) daybook; ~ **de honor** visitors' book; ~ **mayor** (*COM*) general ledger; ~ **de reclamaciones** complaints book; ~ **de texto** textbook.

Lic. *abr* = **Licenciado, a**.

licencia [li'θenθja] *nf* (*gen*) licence; (*permiso*) permission; ~ **por enfermedad/con goce de sueldo** sick/paid leave; ~ **de armas/de caza** gun/game licence; ~ **de exportación** (*COM*) export licence; ~ **poética** poetic licence.

licenciado, a [liθen'θjaðo, a] *adj* licensed ♦ *nm/f* graduate; **L~ en Filosofía y Letras** ≈ Bachelor of Arts.

> *When students finish University after an average of five years they receive the degree of* **licenciado**. *If the course is only three years such as Nursing, or if they choose not to do the optional two-year specialization, they are awarded the degree of* **diplomado**. **Cursos de posgrado**, *postgraduate courses, are becoming increasingly popular, especially one-year specialist courses called* **masters**.

licenciar [liθen'θjar] *vt* (*empleado*) to dismiss; (*permitir*) to permit, allow; (*soldado*) to discharge; (*estudiante*) to confer a degree upon; **~se** *vr*: **~se en letras** to get an arts degree.

licenciatura [liθenθja'tura] *nf* (*título*) degree; (*estudios*) degree course.

licencioso, a [liθen'θjoso, a] *adj* licentious.

liceo [li'θeo] *nm* (*esp AM*) (high) school.

licitación [liθita'θjon] *nf* bidding; (*oferta*) tender, offer.

licitador [liθita'ðor] *nm* bidder.

licitar [liθi'tar] *vt* to bid for ♦ *vi* to bid.

lícito, a ['liθito, a] *adj* (*legal*) lawful; (*justo*) fair, just; (*permisible*) permissible.

licor [li'kor] *nm* spirits *pl* (*BRIT*), liquor (*US*); (*con hierbas etc*) liqueur.

licra ® ['likra] *nf* Lycra ®.

licuadora [likwa'ðora] *nf* blender.

licuar [li'kwar] *vt* to liquidize.

lid [lið] *nf* combat; (*fig*) controversy.

líder ['liðer] *nm/f* leader.

liderato [liðe'rato] *nm* = **liderazgo**.
liderazgo [liðe'raɣo] *nm* leadership.
lidia ['liðja] *nf* bullfighting; (*una ~*)
bullfight; **toros de ~** fighting bulls.
lidiar [li'ðjar] *vt*, *vi* to fight.
liebre ['ljeßre] *nf* hare; **dar gato por ~** to
con.
Lieja ['ljexa] *nf* Liège.
lienzo ['ljenθo] *nm* linen; (*ARTE*) canvas;
(*ARQ*) wall.
lifting ['liftin] *nm* facelift.
liga ['liɣa] *nf* (*de medias*) garter,
suspender; (*confederación*) league; (*AM*:
gomita) rubber band.
ligadura [liɣa'ðura] *nf* bond, tie; (*MED,
MUS*) ligature.
ligamento [liɣa'mento] *nm* (*ANAT*)
ligament; (*atadura*) tie; (*unión*) bond.
ligar [li'ɣar] *vt* (*atar*) to tie; (*unir*) to join;
(*MED*) to bind up; (*MUS*) to slur; (*fam*) to
get off with, pick up ♦ *vi* to mix, blend;
(*fam*) to get off with sb; (*2 personas*) to
get off with one another; **~se** *vr* (*fig*) to
commit o.s.; **~ con** (*fam*) to get off with,
pick up; **~se a algn** to get off with *o* pick
up sb.
ligereza [lixe'reθa] *nf* lightness; (*rapidez*)
swiftness; (*agilidad*) agility;
(*superficialidad*) flippancy.
ligero, a [li'xero, a] *adj* (*de peso*) light;
(*tela*) thin; (*rápido*) swift, quick; (*ágil*)
agile, nimble; (*de importancia*) slight; (*de
carácter*) flippant, superficial ♦ *adv*
quickly, swiftly; **a la ligera** superficially;
juzgar a la ligera to jump to conclusions.
light ['lait] *adj inv* (*cigarrillo*) low-tar;
(*comida*) diet *cpd*.
ligón [li'ɣon] *nm* (*fam*) Romeo.
ligue ['liɣe] *etc vb V* **ligar** ♦ *nm/f* boyfriend/
girlfriend ♦ *nm* (*persona*) pick-up.
liguero [li'ɣero] *nm* suspender (*BRIT*) *o*
garter (*US*) belt.
lija ['lixa] *nf* (*ZOOL*) dogfish; **(papel de) ~**
sandpaper.
lijar [li'xar] *vt* to sand.
lila ['lila] *adj inv*, *nf* lilac ♦ *nm* (*fam*) twit.
lima ['lima] *nf* file; (*BOT*) lime; **~ de uñas**
nail file; **comer como una ~** to eat like a
horse.
limar [li'mar] *vt* to file; (*alisar*) to smooth
over; (*fig*) to polish up.
limbo ['limbo] *nm* (*REL*) limbo; **estar en el
~** to be on another planet.
limitación [limita'θjon] *nf* limitation, limit;
~ de velocidad speed limit.
limitado, a [limi'taðo, a] *adj* limited;
sociedad limitada (*COM*) limited
company.

limitar [limi'tar] *vt* to limit; (*reducir*) to
reduce, cut down ♦ *vi*: **~ con** to border
on; **~se** *vr*: **~se a** to limit *o* confine o.s.
to.
límite ['limite] *nm* (*gen*) limit; (*fin*) end;
(*frontera*) border; **como ~** at (the) most;
(*fecha*) at the latest; **no tener ~s** to know
no bounds; **~ de crédito** (*COM*) credit
limit; **~ de página** (*INFORM*) page break;
~ de velocidad speed limit.
limítrofe [li'mitrofe] *adj* bordering,
neighbouring.
limón [li'mon] *nm* lemon ♦ *adj*: **amarillo ~**
lemon-yellow.
limonada [limo'naða] *nf* lemonade.
limonero [limo'nero] *nm* lemon tree.
limosna [li'mosna] *nf* alms *pl*; **pedir ~** to
beg; **vivir de ~** to live on charity.
limpiabotas [limpja'ßotas] *nm/f inv*
bootblack (*BRIT*), shoeshine boy/girl.
limpiacristales [limpjakris'tales] *nm inv*
(*detergente*) window cleaner.
limpiador, a [limpja'ðor, a] *adj* cleaning,
cleansing ♦ *nm/f* cleaner.
limpiaparabrisas [limpjapara'ßrisas] *nm inv*
windscreen (*BRIT*) *o* windshield (*US*)
wiper.
limpiar [lim'pjar] *vt* to clean; (*con trapo*) to
wipe; (*quitar*) to wipe away; (*zapatos*) to
shine, polish; (*casa*) to tidy up; (*fig*) to
clean up; (: *purificar*) to cleanse, purify;
(*MIL*) to mop up; **~ en seco** to dry-clean.
limpieza [lim'pjeθa] *nf* (*estado*)
cleanliness; (*acto*) cleaning; (: *de las
calles*) cleansing; (: *de zapatos*) polishing;
(*habilidad*) skill; (*fig*: *POLICÍA*) clean-up;
(*pureza*) purity; (*MIL*): **operación de ~**
mopping-up operation; **~ étnica** ethnic
cleansing; **~ en seco** dry cleaning.
limpio, a ['limpjo, a] *adj* clean;
(*moralmente*) pure; (*ordenado*) tidy;
(*despejado*) clear; (*COM*) clear, net; (*fam*)
honest ♦ *adv*: **jugar ~** to play fair; **pasar a
~** to make a fair copy; **sacar algo en ~**
to get benefit from sth; **~ de** free from.
linaje [li'naxe] *nm* lineage, family.
linaza [li'naθa] *nf* linseed; **aceite de ~**
linseed oil.
lince ['linθe] *nm* lynx; **ser un ~** (*fig*:
observador) to be very observant;
(: *astuto*) to be shrewd.
linchar [lin'tʃar] *vt* to lynch.
lindante [lin'dante] *adj* adjoining; **~ con**
bordering on.
lindar [lin'dar] *vi* to adjoin; **~ con** to
border on; (*ARQ*) to abut on.
linde ['linde] *nm o nf* boundary.
lindero, a [lin'dero, a] *adj* adjoining ♦ *nm*

boundary.

lindo, a ['lindo, a] *adj* pretty, lovely ♦ *adv* (*esp AM: fam*) nicely, very well; **canta muy ~** (*AM*) he sings beautifully; **se divertían de lo ~** they enjoyed themselves enormously.

línea ['linea] *nf* (*gen, moral, POL etc*) line; (*talle*) figure; (*INFORM*): **en ~** on line; **fuera de ~** off line; **~ de estado** status line; **~ de formato** format line; **~ aérea** airline; **~ de alto el fuego** ceasefire line; **~ de fuego** firing line; **~ de meta** goal line; (*de carrera*) finishing line; **~ de montaje** assembly line; **~ dura** (*POL*) hard line; **~ recta** straight line; **la ~ de 1995** (*moda*) the 1995 look.

lineal [line'al] *adj* linear; (*INFORM*) on-line.

lingote [lin'gote] *nm* ingot.

lingüista [lin'gwista] *nm/f* linguist.

lingüística [lin'gwistika] *nf* linguistics *sg.*

linimento [lini'mento] *nm* liniment.

lino ['lino] *nm* linen; (*BOT*) flax.

linóleo [li'noleo] *nm* lino, linoleum.

linterna [lin'terna] *nf* lantern, lamp; **~ eléctrica** *o* **a pilas** torch (*BRIT*), flashlight (*US*).

lío ['lio] *nm* bundle; (*desorden*) muddle, mess; (*fam: follón*) fuss; (: *relación amorosa*) affair; **armar un ~** to make a fuss; **meterse en un ~** to get into a jam; **tener un ~ con algn** to be having an affair with sb.

lipotimia [lipo'timja] *nf* blackout.

liquen ['liken] *nm* lichen.

liquidación [likiða'θjon] *nf* liquidation; (*cuenta*) settlement; **venta de ~** clearance sale.

liquidar [liki'ðar] *vt* (*QUÍMICA*) to liquefy; (*COM*) to liquidate; (*deudas*) to pay off; (*empresa*) to wind up; **~ a algn** to bump sb off, rub sb out (*fam*).

liquidez [liki'ðeθ] *nf* liquidity.

líquido, a ['likiðo, a] *adj* liquid; (*ganancia*) net ♦ *nm* liquid; (*COM: efectivo*) ready cash *o* money; (: *ganancia*) net amount *o* profit; **~ imponible** net taxable income.

lira ['lira] *nf* (*MUS*) lyre; (*moneda*) lira.

lírico, a ['liriko, a] *adj* lyrical.

lirio ['lirjo] *nm* (*BOT*) iris.

lirismo [li'rismo] *nm* lyricism; (*sentimentalismo*) sentimentality.

lirón [li'ron] *nm* (*ZOOL*) dormouse; (*fig*) sleepyhead.

Lisboa [lis'βoa] *nf* Lisbon.

lisboeta [lisβo'eta] *adj* of *o* from Lisbon ♦ *nm/f* native *o* inhabitant of Lisbon.

lisiado, a [li'sjaðo, a] *adj* injured ♦ *nm/f* cripple.

lisiar [li'sjar] *vt* to maim; **~se** *vr* to injure o.s.

liso, a ['liso, a] *adj* (*terreno*) flat; (*cabello*) straight; (*superficie*) even; (*tela*) plain; **lisa y llanamente** in plain language, plainly.

lisonja [li'sonxa] *nf* flattery.

lisonjear [lisonxe'ar] *vt* to flatter; (*fig*) to please.

lisonjero, a [lison'xero, a] *adj* flattering; (*agradable*) gratifying, pleasing ♦ *nm/f* flatterer.

lista ['lista] *nf* list; (*de alumnos*) school register; (*de libros*) catalogue; (*de correos*) poste restante; (*de platos*) menu; (*de precios*) price list; **pasar ~** to call the roll; (*ESCOL*) to call the register; **~ de correos** poste restante; **~ de direcciones** mailing list; **~ electoral** electoral roll; **~ de espera** waiting list; **tela a ~s** striped material.

listado, a [lis'taðo, a] *adj* striped ♦ *nm* (*COM, INFORM*) listing; **~ paginado** (*INFORM*) paged listing.

listar [lis'tar] *vt* (*INFORM*) to list.

listo, a ['listo, a] *adj* (*perspicaz*) smart, clever; (*preparado*) ready; **~ para usar** ready-to-use; **¿estás ~?** are you ready?; **pasarse de ~** to be too clever by half.

listón [lis'ton] *nm* (*tela*) ribbon; (*de madera, metal*) strip.

litera [li'tera] *nf* (*en barco, tren*) berth; (*en dormitorio*) bunk, bunk bed.

literal [lite'ral] *adj* literal.

literario, a [lite'rarjo, a] *adj* literary.

literato, a [lite'rato, a] *nm/f* writer.

literatura [litera'tura] *nf* literature.

litigante [liti'γante] *nm/f* litigant, claimant.

litigar [liti'γar] *vt* to fight ♦ *vi* (*JUR*) to go to law; (*fig*) to dispute, argue.

litigio [li'tixjo] *nm* (*JUR*) lawsuit; (*fig*): **en ~ con** in dispute with.

litigue [li'tiγe] *etc vb V* **litigar**.

litografía [litoγra'fia] *nf* lithography; (*una ~*) lithograph.

litoral [lito'ral] *adj* coastal ♦ *nm* coast, seaboard.

litro ['litro] *nm* litre, liter (*US*).

Lituania [li'twanja] *nf* Lithuania.

lituano, a [li'twano, a] *adj, nm/f* Lithuanian ♦ *nm* (*LING*) Lithuanian.

liturgia [li'turxja] *nf* liturgy.

liviano, a [li'βjano, a] *adj* (*persona*) fickle; (*cosa, objeto*) trivial; (*AM*) light.

lívido, a ['liβiðo, a] *adj* livid.

living ['liβin], *pl* **livings** *nm* (*esp AM*) sitting room.

Ll, ll ['eʎe] *nf former letter in the Spanish*

alphabet.

llaga ['ʎaɣa] nf wound.

llagar [ʎa'ɣar] vt to make sore; (herir) to wound.

llague ['ʎaɣe] etc vb V **llagar.**

llama ['ʎama] nf flame; (fig) passion; (ZOOL) llama; **en ~s** burning, ablaze.

llamada [ʎa'maða] nf call; (a la puerta) knock; (: timbre) ring; ~ **a cobro revertido** reverse-charge call; ~ **al orden** call to order; ~ **a pie de página** reference note; ~ **a procedimiento** (INFORM) procedure call; ~ **interurbana** trunk call.

llamado [ʎa'maðo] nm (AM) (telephone) call; (llamamiento) appeal, call.

llamamiento [ʎama'mjento] nm call; **hacer un ~ a algn para que haga algo** to appeal to sb to do sth.

llamar [ʎa'mar] vt to call; (convocar) to summon; (invocar) to invoke; (atraer con gesto) to beckon; (atención) to attract; (TELEC: tb: ~ **por teléfono**) to call, ring up, telephone; (MIL) to call up ♦ vi (por teléfono) to phone; (a la puerta) to knock (o ring); (por señas) to beckon; ~**se** vr to be called, be named; **¿cómo se llama usted?** what's your name?; **¿quién llama?** (TELEC) who's calling?, who's that?; **no me llama la atención** (fam) I don't fancy it.

llamarada [ʎama'raða] nf (llamas) blaze; (rubor) flush; (fig) flare-up.

llamativo, a [ʎama'tiβo, a] adj showy; (color) loud.

llamear [ʎame'ar] vi to blaze.

llanamente [ʎana'mente] adv (lisamente) smoothly; (sin ostentaciones) plainly; (sinceramente) frankly; V tb **liso.**

llaneza [ʎa'neθa] nf (gen) simplicity; (honestidad) straightforwardness, frankness.

llano, a ['ʎano, a] adj (superficie) flat; (persona) straightforward; (estilo) clear ♦ nm plain, flat ground.

llanta ['ʎanta] nf (wheel) rim; (AM: neumático) tyre; (: cámara) (inner) tube.

llanto ['ʎanto] nm weeping; (fig) lamentation; (canción) dirge, lament.

llanura [ʎa'nura] nf (lisura) flatness, smoothness; (GEO) plain.

llave ['ʎaβe] nf key; (de gas, agua) tap (BRIT), faucet (US); (MECÁNICA) spanner; (de la luz) switch; (MUS) key; ~ **inglesa** monkey wrench; ~ **maestra** master key; ~ **de contacto** (AUTO) ignition key; ~ **de paso** stopcock; **echar** ~ **a** to lock up.

llavero [ʎa'βero] nm keyring.

llavín [ʎa'βin] nm latchkey.

llegada [ʎe'ɣaða] nf arrival.

llegar [ʎe'ɣar] vt to bring up, bring over ♦ vi to arrive; (bastar) to be enough; ~**se** vr: ~**se a** to approach; ~ **a** (alcanzar) to reach; to manage to, succeed in; ~ **a saber** to find out; ~ **a ser famoso/el jefe** to become famous/the boss; ~ **a las manos** to come to blows; ~ **a las manos de** to come into the hands of; **no llegues tarde** don't be late; **esta cuerda no llega** this rope isn't long enough.

llegue ['ʎeɣe] etc vb V **llegar.**

llenar [ʎe'nar] vt to fill; (superficie) to cover; (espacio, tiempo) to fill, take up; (formulario) to fill in o out; (deber) to fulfil; (fig) to heap; ~**se** vr to fill (up); ~**se de** (fam) to stuff o.s. with.

lleno, a ['ʎeno, a] adj full, filled; (repleto) full up ♦ nm (abundancia) abundance; (TEAT) full house; **dar de ~ contra un muro** to hit a wall head-on.

llevadero, a [ʎeβa'ðero, a] adj bearable, tolerable.

llevar [ʎe'βar] vt to take; (ropa) to wear; (cargar) to carry; (quitar) to take away; (en coche) to drive; (transportar) to transport; (ruta) to follow, keep to; (traer: dinero) to carry; (suj: camino etc): ~ **a** to lead to; (MAT) to carry; (aguantar) to bear; (negocio) to conduct, direct; to manage; ~**se** vr to carry off, take away; **llevamos dos días aquí** we have been here for two days; **él me lleva 2 años** he's 2 years older than me; ~ **adelante** (fig) to carry forward; ~ **por delante a uno** (en coche etc) to run sb over; (fig) to ride roughshod over sb; ~ **la ventaja** to be winning o in the lead; ~ **los libros** (COM) to keep the books; **llevo las de perder** I'm likely to lose; **no las lleva todas consigo** he's not all there; **nos llevó a cenar fuera** she took us out for a meal; ~**se a uno por delante** (atropellar) to run sb over; ~**se bien** to get on well (together).

llorar [ʎo'rar] vt to cry, weep ♦ vi to cry, weep; (ojos) to water; ~ **a moco tendido** to sob one's heart out; ~ **de risa** to cry with laughter.

lloriquear [ʎorike'ar] vi to snivel, whimper.

lloro ['ʎoro] nm crying, weeping.

llorón, ona [ʎo'ron, ona] adj tearful ♦ nmlf cry-baby.

lloroso, a [ʎo'roso, a] adj (gen) weeping, tearful; (triste) sad, sorrowful.

llover [ʎo'ßer] *vi* to rain; ~ **a cántaros** o **a cubos** o **a mares** to rain cats and dogs, pour (down); **ser una cosa llovida del cielo** to be a godsend; **llueve sobre mojado** it never rains but it pours.
llovizna [ʎo'ßiθna] *nf* drizzle.
lloviznar [ʎoßiθ'nar] *vi* to drizzle.
llueve ['ʎweße] *etc vb V* **llover**.
lluvia ['ʎußja] *nf* rain; (*cantidad*) rainfall; (*fig: balas etc*) hail, shower; ~ **radioactiva** radioactive fallout; **día de** ~ rainy day; **una** ~ **de regalos a** shower of gifts.
lluvioso, a [ʎu'ßjoso, a] *adj* rainy.
lo [lo] *artículo definido neutro*: ~ **bueno** the good ♦ *pron* (*persona*) him; (*cosa*) it; ~ **mío** what is mine; ~ **difícil es que ...** the difficult thing about it is that ...; **no saben** ~ **aburrido que es** they don't know how boring it is; **viste a** ~ **americano** he dresses in the American style; ~ **de** that matter of; ~ **que** what, that which; **toma** ~ **que quieras** take what(ever) you want; ~ **que sea** whatever; **¡toma** ~ **que he dicho!** I stand by what I said!
loa ['loa] *nf* praise.
loable [lo'aßle] *adj* praiseworthy.
LOAPA [lo'apa] *nf abr* (*ESP JUR*) = *Ley Orgánica de Armonización del Proceso Autónomo*.
loar [lo'ar] *vt* to praise.
lobato [lo'ßato] *nm* (*ZOOL*) wolf cub.
lobo ['loßo] *nm* wolf; ~ **de mar** (*fig*) sea dog; ~ **marino** seal.
lóbrego, a ['loßreɣo, a] *adj* dark; (*fig*) gloomy.
lóbulo ['loßulo] *nm* lobe.
LOC *nm abr* (= *lector óptico de caracteres*) OCR.
local [lo'kal] *adj* local ♦ *nm* place, site; (*oficinas*) premises *pl*.
localice [loka'liθe] *etc vb V* **localizar**.
localidad [lokali'ðað] *nf* (*barrio*) locality; (*lugar*) location; (*TEAT*) seat, ticket.
localizar [lokali'θar] *vt* (*ubicar*) to locate, find; (*encontrar*) to find, track down; (*restringir*) to localize; (*situar*) to place.
loción [lo'θjon] *nf* lotion, wash.
loco, a ['loko, a] *adj* mad; (*fig*) wild, mad ♦ *nm/f* lunatic, madman/woman; ~ **de atar**, ~ **de remate**, ~ **rematado** raving mad; **a lo** ~ without rhyme or reason; **ando** ~ **con el examen** the exam is driving me crazy; **estar** ~ **de alegría** to be overjoyed o over the moon.
locomoción [lokomo'θjon] *nf* locomotion.
locomotora [lokomo'tora] *nf* engine, locomotive.
locuaz [lo'kwaθ] *adj* loquacious, talkative.

locución [loku'θjon] *nf* expression.
locura [lo'kura] *nf* madness; (*acto*) crazy act.
locutor, a [loku'tor, a] *nm/f* (*RADIO*) announcer; (*comentarista*) commentator; (*TV*) newscaster, newsreader.
locutorio [loku'torjo] *nm* (*TELEC*) telephone box o booth.
lodo ['lodo] *nm* mud.
logia ['loxja] *nf* (*MIL, de masones*) lodge; (*ARQ*) loggia.
lógico, a ['loxiko, a] *adj* logical; (*correcto*) natural; (*razonable*) reasonable ♦ *nm* logician ♦ *nf* logic; **es** ~ **que ...** it stands to reason that ...; **ser de una lógica aplastante** to be as clear as day.
logístico, a [lo'xistiko, a] *adj* logistical ♦ *nf* logistics *pl*.
logotipo [loɣo'tipo] *nm* logo.
logrado, a [lo'ɣrado, a] *adj* accomplished.
lograr [lo'ɣrar] *vt* (*obtener*) to get, obtain; (*conseguir*) to achieve, attain; ~ **hacer** to manage to do; ~ **que algn venga** to manage to get sb to come; ~ **acceso a** (*INFORM*) to access.
logro [lo'ɣro] *nm* achievement, success; (*COM*) profit.
logroñés, esa [loɣro'ɲes, esa] *adj* of o from Logroño ♦ *nm/f* native o inhabitant of Logroño.
LOGSE *nf abr* (= *Ley Orgánica de Ordenación General del Sistema Educativo*) educational reform act.
Loira ['loira] *nm* Loire.
loma ['loma] *nf* hillock, low ridge.
Lombardía [lombar'ðia] *nf* Lombardy.
lombriz [lom'briθ] *nf* (*earth*)worm.
lomo ['lomo] *nm* (*de animal*) back; (*CULIN: de cerdo*) pork loin; (: *de vaca*) rib steak; (*de libro*) spine.
lona ['lona] *nf* canvas.
loncha ['lontʃa] *nf* = **lonja**.
lonche ['lontʃe] *nm* (*AM*) lunch.
lonchería [lontʃe'ria] *nf* (*AM*) snack bar, diner o (*US*).
londinense [londi'nense] *adj* London *cpd*, of o from London ♦ *nm/f* Londoner.
Londres ['londres] *nm* London.
longaniza [longa'niθa] *nf* pork sausage.
longevidad [lonxeßi'ðað] *nf* longevity.
longitud [lonxi'tuð] *nf* length; (*GEO*) longitude; **tener 3 metros de** ~ to be 3 metres long; ~ **de onda** wavelength; **salto de** ~ long jump.
longitudinal [lonxituði'nal] *adj* longitudinal.
lonja ['lonxa] *nf* slice; (*de tocino*) rasher; (*COM*) market, exchange; ~ **de pescado**

fish market.
lontananza [lonta'nanθa] *nf* background;
  en ~ far away, in the distance.
loor [lo'or] *nm* praise.
Lorena [lo'rena] *nf* Lorraine.
loro ['loro] *nm* parrot.
los [los] *artículo definido mpl* the ♦ *pron* them;
  (*ustedes*) you; **mis libros y** ~ **de usted** my
  books and yours.
losa ['losa] *nf* stone; ~ **sepulcral**
  gravestone.
lote ['lote] *nm* portion, share; (*COM*) lot;
  (*INFORM*) batch.
lotería [lote'ria] *nf* lottery; (*juego*) lotto; **le
  tocó la** ~ he won a big prize in the
  lottery; (*fig*) he struck lucky; ~ **nacional**
  national lottery; ~ **primitiva** (*ESP*) *type
  of state-run lottery.*

Millions of pounds are spent every year on
loterías, *lotteries. There is the weekly*
Lotería Nacional *which is very popular
especially at Christmas. Other weekly
lotteries are the* **Bono Loto** *and the* (**Lotería**)
Primitiva. *One of the most famous lotteries
is run by the wealthy and influential
society for the blind,* **la ONCE**, *and the form
is called* **el cupón de la ONCE** *or* **el cupón de
los ciegos**.

---

lotero, a [lo'tero, a] *nm/f* seller of lottery
  tickets.
Lovaina [lo'βaina] *nf* Louvain.
loza ['loθa] *nf* crockery; ~ **fina** china.
lozanía [loθa'nia] *nf* (*lujo*) luxuriance.
lozano, a [lo'θano, a] *adj* luxuriant;
  (*animado*) lively.
lubina [lu'βina] *nf* (*ZOOL*) sea bass.
lubricante [luβri'kante] *adj, nm* lubricant.
lubricar [luβri'kar], **lubrificar** [luβrifi'kar]
  vt to lubricate.
lubrifique [luβri'fike] *etc vb V* **lubrificar**.
lubrique [lu'βrike] *etc vb V* **lubricar**.
lucense [lu'θense] *adj* of *o* from Lugo ♦ *nm/f*
  native *o* inhabitant of Lugo.
Lucerna [lu'θerna] *nf* Lucerne.
lucero [lu'θero] *nm* (*ASTRO*) bright star;
  (*fig*) brilliance; ~ **del alba/de la tarde**
  morning/evening star.
luces ['luθes] *nfpl de* **luz**.
lucha ['lutʃa] *nf* fight, struggle; ~ **de clases**
  class struggle; ~ **libre** wrestling.
luchar [lu'tʃar] *vi* to fight.
lucidez [luθi'ðeθ] *nf* lucidity.
lucido, a [lu'θiðo, a] *adj* (*espléndido*)
  splendid, brilliant; (*elegante*) elegant;
  (*exitoso*) successful.
lúcido, a ['luθiðo, a] *adj* lucid.

luciérnaga [lu'θjernaɣa] *nf* glow-worm.
lucimiento [luθi'mjento] *nm* (*brillo*)
  brilliance; (*éxito*) success.
lucio ['luθjo] *nm* (*ZOOL*) pike.
lucir [lu'θir] *vt* to illuminate, light (up);
  (*ostentar*) to show off ♦ *vi* (*brillar*) to
  shine; (*AM: parecer*) to look, seem; ~**se** *vr*
  (*irónico*) to make a fool of o.s.;
  (*ostentarse*) to show off; **la casa luce
  limpia** the house looks clean.
lucrativo, a [lukra'tiβo, a] *adj* lucrative,
  profitable; **institución no lucrativa** non
  profit-making institution.
lucro ['lukro] *nm* profit, gain; ~**s y daños**
  (*COM*) profit and loss *sg.*
luctuoso, a [luk'twoso, a] *adj* mournful.
lúdico, a ['luðiko, a] *adj* playful; (*actividad*)
  recreational.
ludopatía [luðopa'tia] *nf* addiction to
  gambling (*o* videogames).
luego ['lweɣo] *adv* (*después*) next; (*más
  tarde*) later, afterwards; (*AM fam: en
  seguida*) at once, immediately; **desde** ~
  of course; **¡hasta** ~! see you later!, so
  long!; **¿y** ~**?** what next?
lugar [lu'ɣar] *nm* place; (*sitio*) spot; (*pueblo*)
  village, town; **en** ~ **de** instead of; **en
  primer** ~ in the first place, firstly; **dar** ~
  a to give rise to; **hacer** ~ to make room;
  fuera de ~ out of place; **tener** ~ to take
  place; ~ **común** commonplace; **yo en su**
  ~ if I were him; **no hay** ~ **para
  preocupaciones** there is no cause for
  concern.
lugareño, a [luɣa'reɲo, a] *adj* village *cpd*
  ♦ *nm/f* villager.
lugarteniente [luɣarte'njente] *nm* deputy.
lúgubre ['luɣuβre] *adj* mournful.
lujo ['luxo] *nm* luxury; (*fig*) profusion,
  abundance; **de** ~ luxury *cpd*, de luxe.
lujoso, a [lu'xoso, a] *adj* luxurious.
lujuria [lu'xurja] *nf* lust.
lumbago [lum'baɣo] *nm* lumbago.
lumbre ['lumbre] *nf* (*luz*) light; (*fuego*) fire;
  cerca de la ~ near the fire, at the
  fireside; **¿tienes** ~**?** (*para cigarro*) have
  you got a light?
lumbrera [lum'brera] *nf* luminary; (*fig*)
  leading light.
luminoso, a [lumi'noso, a] *adj* luminous,
  shining; (*idea*) bright, brilliant.
luna ['luna] *nf* moon; (*vidrio: escaparate*)
  plate glass; (: *de un espejo*) glass; (: *de
  gafas*) lens; (*fig*) crescent; ~ **creciente/
  llena/menguante/nueva** crescent/full/
  waning/new moon; ~ **de miel**
  honeymoon; **estar en la** ~ to have one's
  head in the clouds.

lunar [lu'nar] *adj* lunar ♦ *nm (ANAT)* mole; **tela a ~es** spotted material.
lunes ['lunes] *nm inv* Monday.
luneta [lu'neta] *nf* lens.
lupa ['lupa] *nf* magnifying glass.
lusitano, a [lusi'tano, a], **luso, a** ['luso, a] *adj, nm/f* Portuguese.
lustrador [lustra'ðor] *nm (AM)* bootblack.
lustrar [lus'trar] *vt (esp AM) (mueble)* to polish; *(zapatos)* to shine.
lustre ['lustre] *nm* polish; *(fig)* lustre; **dar ~ a** to polish.
lustro ['lustro] *nm* period of five years.
lustroso, a [lus'troso, a] *adj* shining.
luterano, a [lute'rano, a] *adj* Lutheran.
luto ['luto] *nm* mourning; *(congoja)* grief, sorrow; **llevar el o vestirse de ~** to be in mourning.
luxación [luksa'θjon] *nf (MED)* dislocation; **tener una ~ de tobillo** to have a dislocated ankle.
Luxemburgo [luksem'burɣo] *nm* Luxembourg.
luz [luθ], *pl* **luces** *nf (tb fig)* light; *(fam)* electricity; **dar a ~ un niño** to give birth to a child; **sacar a la ~** to bring to light; **dar la ~** to switch on the light; **encender** *(ESP)* **o prender** *(AM)***/apagar la ~** to switch the light on/off; **les cortaron la ~** their (electricity) supply was cut off; **a la ~ de** in the light of; **a todas luces** by any reckoning; **hacer la ~ sobre** to shed light on; **tener pocas luces** to be dim *o* stupid; **~ de la luna/del sol** *o* **solar** moonlight/sunlight; **~ eléctrica** electric light; **~ roja/verde** red/green light; **~ de cruce** *(AUTO)* dipped headlight; **~ de freno** brake light; **~ intermitente/trasera** flashing/rear light; **luces de tráfico** traffic lights; **el Siglo de las Luces** the Age of Enlightenment; **traje de luces** bullfighter's costume.

M m

M, m ['eme] *nf (letra)* M, m; **M de Madrid** M for Mike.
M. *abr (FERRO)* = **Metro**.
m. *abr* (= *metro(s)*) m; (= *minuto(s)*) min., m; (= *masculino*) m., masc.
M.ª *abr* = **María**.
macabro, [ma'kaβro, a] *adj* macabre.
macaco [ma'kako] *nm (ZOOL)* rhesus monkey; *(fam)* runt, squirt.
macana [ma'kana] *nf (AM: porra)* club; (: *mentira*) lie, fib; (: *tontería*) piece of nonsense.
macanudo, a [maka'nuðo, a] *adj (AM fam)* great.
macarra [ma'karra] *nm (fam)* thug.
macarrones [maka'rrones] *nmpl* macaroni *sg*.
Macedonia [maθe'ðonja] *nf* Macedonia.
macedonia [maθe'ðonja] *nf:* **~ de frutas** fruit salad.
macedonio [maθe'ðonjo] *adj, nm/f* Macedonian ♦ *nm (LING)* Macedonian.
macerar [maθe'rar] *vt (CULIN)* to soak, macerate; **~se** *vr* to soak, soften.
maceta [ma'θeta] *nf (de flores)* pot of flowers; *(para plantas)* flowerpot.
macetero [maθe'tero] *nm* flowerpot stand *o* holder.
machacar [matʃa'kar] *vt* to crush, pound; *(moler)* to grind (up); *(aplastar)* to mash ♦ *vi (insistir)* to go on, keep on.
machacón, ona [matʃa'kon, ona] *adj (pesado)* tiresome; *(insistente)* insistent; *(monótono)* monotonous.
machamartillo [matʃamar'tiλo]: **a ~** *adv:* **creer a ~** *(firmemente)* to believe firmly.
machaque [ma'tʃake] *etc vb V* **machacar**.
machete [ma'tʃete] *nm* machete, (large) knife.
machismo [ma'tʃismo] *nm* sexism; male chauvinism.
machista [ma'tʃista] *adj, nm* sexist; male chauvinist.
macho ['matʃo] *adj* male; *(fig)* virile ♦ *nm* male; *(fig)* he-man, tough guy (*US*); *(TEC: perno)* pin, peg; *(ELEC)* pin, plug; *(COSTURA)* hook.

macilento, a [maθi'lento, a] *adj* (*pálido*) pale; (*ojeroso*) haggard.

macizo, a [ma'θiθo, a] *adj* (*grande*) massive; (*fuerte, sólido*) solid ♦ *nm* mass, chunk; (*GEO*) massif.

macramé [makra'me] *nm* macramé.

macrobiótico, a [makro'ßjotiko, a] *adj* macrobiotic.

macro-comando [makroko'mando] *nm* (*INFORM*) macro (command).

macroeconomía [makroekono'mia] *nf* (*COM*) macroeconomics *sg.*

mácula ['makula] *nf* stain, blemish.

macuto [ma'kuto] *nm* (*MIL*) knapsack.

Madagascar [maðaɤas'kar] *nm* Madagascar.

madeja [ma'ðexa] *nf* (*de lana*) skein, hank.

madera [ma'ðera] *nf* wood; (*fig*) nature, character; (: *aptitud*) aptitude; **una ~ a** piece of wood; **~ contrachapada o laminada** plywood; **tiene buena ~** he's made of solid stuff; **tiene ~ de futbolista** he's got the makings of a footballer.

maderaje [maðe'raxe], **maderamen** [maðe'ramen] *nm* timber; (*trabajo*) woodwork, timbering.

maderero [maðe'rero] *nm* timber merchant.

madero [ma'ðero] *nm* beam; (*fig*) ship.

madrastra [ma'ðrastra] *nf* stepmother.

madre ['maðre] *adj* mother *cpd*; (*AM*) tremendous ♦ *nf* mother; (*de vino etc*) dregs *pl*; **~ adoptiva/política/soltera** foster mother/mother-in-law/unmarried mother; **la M~ Patria** the Mother Country; **sin ~** motherless; **¡~ mía!** oh dear!; **¡tu ~!** (*fam!*) fuck off! (*!*); **salirse de ~** (*río*) to burst its banks; (*persona*) to lose all self-control.

madreperla [maðre'perla] *nf* mother-of-pearl.

madreselva [maðre'selßa] *nf* honeysuckle.

Madrid [ma'ðrið] *n* Madrid.

madriguera [maðri'ɤera] *nf* burrow.

madrileño, a [maðri'leɲo, a] *adj* of *o* from Madrid ♦ *nm/f* native *o* inhabitant of Madrid.

Madriles [ma'ðriles] *nmpl*: **Los ~** (*fam*) Madrid *sg.*

madrina [ma'ðrina] *nf* godmother; (*ARQ*) prop, shore; (*TEC*) brace; **~ de boda** bridesmaid.

madroño [ma'ðroɲo] *nm* (*BOT*) strawberry tree, arbutus.

madrugada [maðru'ɤaða] *nf* early morning, small hours; (*alba*) dawn, daybreak; **a las 4 de la ~** at 4 o'clock in the morning.

madrugador, a [maðruɤa'ðor, a] *adj* early-rising.

madrugar [maðru'ɤar] *vi* to get up early; (*fig*) to get a head start.

madrugue [ma'ðruɤe] *etc vb V* **madrugar.**

madurar [maðu'rar] *vt, vi* (*fruta*) to ripen; (*fig*) to mature.

madurez [maðu'reθ] *nf* ripeness; (*fig*) maturity.

maduro, a [ma'ðuro, a] *adj* ripe; (*fig*) mature; **poco ~** unripe.

MAE *nm abr* (*ESP POL*) = *Ministerio de Asuntos Exteriores.*

maestra [ma'estra] *nf V* **maestro.**

maestría [maes'tria] *nf* mastery; (*habilidad*) skill, expertise; (*AM*) Master's Degree.

maestro, a [ma'estro, a] *adj* masterly; (*perito*) skilled, expert; (*principal*) main; (*educado*) trained ♦ *nm/f* master/mistress; (*profesor*) teacher ♦ *nm* (*autoridad*) authority; (*MUS*) maestro; (*obrero*) skilled workman; **~ albañil** master mason; **~ de obras** foreman.

mafia ['mafja] *nf* mafia; **la M~** the Mafia.

mafioso [ma'fjoso] *nm* gangster.

Magallanes [maɤa'ʎanes] *nm*: **Estrecho de ~** Strait of Magellan.

magia ['maxja] *nf* magic.

mágico, a ['maxiko, a] *adj* magic(al) ♦ *nm/f* magician.

magisterio [maxis'terjo] *nm* (*enseñanza*) teaching; (*profesión*) teaching profession; (*maestros*) teachers *pl.*

magistrado [maxis'traðo] *nm* magistrate; **Primer M~** (*AM*) President, Prime Minister.

magistral [maxis'tral] *adj* magisterial; (*fig*) masterly.

magistratura [maxistra'tura] *nf* magistracy; **M~ del Trabajo** (*ESP*) ≈ Industrial Tribunal.

magnánimo, a [maɤ'nanimo, a] *adj* magnanimous.

magnate [maɤ'nate] *nm* magnate, tycoon; **~ de la prensa** press baron.

magnesio [maɤ'nesjo] *nm* (*QUÍMICA*) magnesium.

magnetice [maɤne'tiθe] *etc vb V* **magnetizar.**

magnético, a [maɤ'netiko, a] *adj* magnetic.

magnetismo [maɤne'tismo] *nm* magnetism.

magnetizar [maɤneti'θar] *vt* to magnetize.

magnetofón [maɤneto'fon], **magnetófono** [maɤne'tofono] *nm* tape recorder.

magnetofónico, a [maɤneto'foniko, a] *adj*:

cinta **magnetofónica** recording tape.

magnicidio [maɣni'θiðjo] *nm* assassination (*of an important person*).

magnífico, a [maɣ'nifiko, a] *adj* splendid, magnificent.

magnitud [maɣni'tuð] *nf* magnitude.

mago, a ['maɣo, a] *nm/f* magician, wizard; **los Reyes M~s** the Magi, the Three Wise Men; *V tb* **Reyes Magos.**

magrear [maɣre'ar] *vt* (*fam*) to touch up.

magro, a ['maɣro, a] *adj* (*persona*) thin, lean; (*carne*) lean.

maguey [ma'ɣei] *nm* (*BOT*) agave.

magulladura [maɣuʎa'ðura] *nf* bruise.

magullar [maɣu'ʎar] *vt* (*amoratar*) to bruise; (*dañar*) to damage; (*fam: golpear*) to bash, beat.

Maguncia [ma'ɣunθja] *nf* Mainz.

mahometano, a [maome'tano, a] *adj* Mohammedan.

mahonesa [mao'nesa] *nf* = **mayonesa.**

maicena [mai'θena] *nf* cornflour, corn starch (*US*).

maillot [ma'jot] *nm* swimming costume; (*DEPORTE*) vest.

maître ['metre] *nm* head waiter.

maíz [ma'iθ] *nm* maize (*BRIT*), corn (*US*); sweet corn.

maizal [mai'θal] *nm* maize field, cornfield.

majadero, a [maxa'ðero, a] *adj* silly, stupid.

majar [ma'xar] *vt* to crush, grind.

majareta [maxa'reta] *adj* (*fam*) cracked, potty.

majestad [maxes'tað] *nf* majesty; **Su M~** His/Her Majesty; **(Vuestra) M~** Your Majesty.

majestuoso, a [maxes'twoso, a] *adj* majestic.

majo, a ['maxo, a] *adj* nice; (*guapo*) attractive, good-looking; (*elegante*) smart.

mal [mal] *adv* badly; (*equivocadamente*) wrongly; (*con dificultad*) with difficulty ♦ *adj* = **malo, a** ♦ *nm* evil; (*desgracia*) misfortune; (*daño*) harm, damage; (*MED*) illness ♦ *conj*: ~ **que le pese** whether he likes it or not; **me entendió** ~ he misunderstood me; **hablar** ~ **de algn** to speak ill of sb; **huele** ~ it smells bad; **ir de** ~ **en peor** to go from bad to worse; **oigo/veo** ~ I can't hear/see very well; **si** ~ **no recuerdo** if my memory serves me right; **¡menos ~!** just as well!; ~ **que bien** rightly or wrongly; **no hay** ~ **que por bien no venga** every cloud has a silver lining; ~ **de ojo** evil eye.

malabarismo [malaβa'rismo] *nm* juggling.

malabarista [malaβa'rista] *nm/f* juggler.

malaconsejado, a [malakonse'xaðo, a] *adj* ill-advised.

malacostumbrado, a [malakostum'braðo, a] *adj* (*consentido*) spoiled.

malacostumbrar [malakostum'brar] *vt*: ~ **a algn** to get sb into bad habits.

malagueño, a [mala'ɣeɲo, a] *adj* of *o* from Málaga ♦ native *o* inhabitant of Málaga.

Malaisia [ma'laisja] *nf* Malaysia.

malaria [ma'larja] *nf* malaria.

Malasia [ma'lasja] *nf* Malaysia.

malavenido, a [malaβe'niðo, a] *adj* incompatible.

malayo, a [ma'lajo, a] *adj* Malay(an) ♦ *nm/f* Malay ♦ *nm* (*LING*) Malay.

Malaysia [ma'laisia] *nf* Malaysia.

malcarado, a [malka'raðo, a] *adj* ugly, grim-faced.

malcriado, a [mal'krjaðo, a] *adj* (*consentido*) spoiled.

malcriar [mal'krjar] *vt* to spoil, pamper.

maldad [mal'dað] *nf* evil, wickedness.

maldecir [malde'θir] *vt* to curse ♦ *vi*: ~ **de** to speak ill of.

maldiciendo [maldi'θjendo] *etc vb V* **maldecir.**

maldición [maldi'θjon] *nf* curse; **¡~!** curse it!, damn!

maldiga [mal'diɣa] *etc*, **maldije** [mal'dixe] *etc vb V* **maldecir.**

maldito, a [mal'dito, a] *adj* (*condenado*) damned; (*perverso*) wicked ♦ *nm*: **el** ~ the devil; **¡~ sea!** damn it!; **no le hace** ~ **(el) caso** he doesn't take a blind bit of notice.

maleable [male'aβle] *adj* malleable.

maleante [male'ante] *adj* wicked ♦ *nm/f* criminal, crook.

malecón [male'kon] *nm* pier, jetty.

maledicencia [maleði'θenθja] *nf* slander, scandal.

maleducado, a [maleðu'kaðo, a] *adj* bad-mannered, rude.

maleficio [male'fiθjo] *nm* curse, spell.

malentendido [malenten'diðo] *nm* misunderstanding.

malestar [males'tar] *nm* (*gen*) discomfort; (*enfermedad*) indisposition; (*fig: inquietud*) uneasiness; (*POL*) unrest; **siento un** ~ **en el estómago** my stomach is upset.

maleta [ma'leta] *nf* case, suitcase; (*AUTO*) boot (*BRIT*), trunk (*US*); **hacer la** ~ to pack.

maletera [male'tera] *nf* (*AM AUTO*) boot (*BRIT*), trunk (*US*).

maletero [male'tero] *nm* (*AUTO*) boot

(BRIT), trunk (US); (persona) porter.

maletín [male'tin] nm small case, bag; (portafolio) briefcase.

malevolencia [maleßo'lenθja] nf malice, spite.

malévolo, a [ma'leßolo, a] adj malicious, spiteful.

maleza [ma'leθa] nf (hierbas malas) weeds pl; (arbustos) thicket.

malgache [mal'ɣatʃe] adj of o from Madagascar ♦ nm/f native o inhabitant of Madagascar.

malgastar [malɣas'tar] vt (tiempo, dinero) to waste; (recursos) to squander; (salud) to ruin.

malhaya [ma'laja] excl (esp AM: fam!) damn (it)! (!); ¡~ **sea/sean!** damn it/them! (!).

malhechor, a [male'tʃor, a] nm/f delinquent; (criminal) criminal.

malherido, a [male'riðo, a] adj badly injured.

malhumorado, a [malumo'raðo, a] adj bad-tempered.

malicia [ma'liθja] nf (maldad) wickedness; (astucia) slyness, guile; (mala intención) malice, spite; (carácter travieso) mischievousness.

malicioso, a [mali'θjoso, a] adj wicked, evil; sly, crafty; malicious, spiteful; mischievous.

malignidad [maliɣni'ðað] nf (MED) malignancy; (malicia) malice.

maligno, a [ma'liɣno, a] adj evil; (dañino) pernicious, harmful; (malévolo) malicious; (MED) malignant ♦ nm: **el** ~ the devil.

malintencionado, a [malintenθjo'naðo, a] adj (comentario) hostile; (persona) malicious.

malla ['maʎa] nf (de una red) mesh; (red) network; (AM: de baño) swimsuit; (de ballet, gimnasia) leotard; ~**s** nfpl tights; ~ **de alambre** wire mesh.

Mallorca [ma'ʎorka] nf Majorca.

mallorquín, ina [maʎor'kin, ina] adj, nm/f Majorcan ♦ nm (LING) Majorcan.

malnutrido, a [malnu'triðo, a] adj undernourished.

malo, a ['malo, a] adj (mal before nmsg) bad; (calidad) poor; (falso) false; (espantoso) dreadful; (niño) naughty ♦ nm/f villain ♦ nm (CINE fam) bad guy ♦ nf spell of bad luck; **estar** ~ to be ill; **andar a malas con algn** to be on bad terms with sb; **estar de malas** (mal humor) to be in a bad mood; **lo** ~ **es que** ... the trouble is that ....

malograr [malo'ɣrar] vt to spoil; (plan) to

upset; (ocasión) to waste; ~**se** vr (plan etc) to fail, come to grief; (persona) to die before one's time.

maloliente [malo'ljente] adj stinking, smelly.

malparado, a [malpa'raðo, a] adj: **salir** ~ to come off badly.

malpensado, a [malpen'saðo, a] adj evil-minded.

malquerencia [malke'renθja] nf dislike.

malquistar [malkis'tar] vt: ~ **a dos personas** to cause a rift between two people; ~**se** vr to fall out.

malsano, a [mal'sano, a] adj unhealthy.

malsonante [malso'nante] adj (palabra) nasty, rude.

Malta ['malta] nf Malta.

malta ['malta] nf malt.

malteada [malte'aða] nf (AM) milk shake.

maltés, esa [mal'tes, esa] adj, nm/f Maltese.

maltraer [maltra'er] vt (abusar) to insult, abuse; (maltratar) to ill-treat.

maltratar [maltra'tar] vt to ill-treat, mistreat.

maltrecho, a [mal'tretʃo, a] adj battered, damaged.

malva ['malßa] nf mallow; ~ **loca** hollyhock; (de color de) ~ mauve.

malvado, a [mal'ßaðo, a] adj evil, villainous.

malvavisco [malßa'ßisko] nm marshmallow.

malvender [malßen'der] vt to sell off cheap o at a loss.

malversación [malßersa'θjon] nf embezzlement, misappropriation.

malversar [malßer'sar] vt to embezzle, misappropriate.

Malvinas [mal'ßinas] nfpl: **Islas** ~ Falkland Islands.

mama ['mama], pl **mamás** nf (de animal) teat; (de mujer) breast.

mamá [ma'ma] nf (fam) mum, mummy.

mamacita [mama'sita] nf (AM fam) mum, mummy.

mamadera [mama'dera] nf (AM) baby's bottle.

mamagrande [mama'grande] nf (AM) grandmother.

mamar [ma'mar] vt (pecho) to suck; (fig) to absorb, assimilate ♦ vi to suck; **dar de** ~ to (breast-)feed; (animal) to suckle.

mamarracho [mama'rratʃo] nm sight, mess.

mambo ['mambo] nf (MUS) mambo.

mamífero, a [ma'mifero, a] adj mammalian, mammal cpd ♦ nm mammal.

mamón, ona [ma'mon, ona] adj small,

baby *cpd* ♦ *nm/f* small baby; (*fam!*)
wanker (*!*).

mamotreto [mamo'treto] *nm* hefty
volume; (*fam*) whacking great thing.

mampara [mam'para] *nf* (*entre
habitaciones*) partition; (*biombo*) screen.

mamporro [mam'porro] *nm* (*fam*): **dar un ~
a** to clout.

mampostería [mamposte'ria] *nf* masonry.

mamut [ma'mut] *nm* mammoth.

maná [ma'na] *nm* manna.

manada [ma'naða] *nf* (*ZOOL*) herd; (: *de
leones*) pride; (: *de lobos*) pack; **llegaron
en ~s** (*fam*) they came in droves.

Managua [ma'naɣwa] *n* Managua.

manantial [manan'tjal] *nm* spring; (*fuente*)
fountain; (*fig*) source.

manar [ma'nar] *vt* to run with, flow with
♦ *vi* to run, flow; (*abundar*) to abound.

manaza [ma'naθa] *nf* big hand ♦ *adj, nm/f inv*:
~s: ser un ~s to be clumsy.

mancebo [man'θeβo] *nm* (*joven*) young
man.

mancha ['mantʃa] *nf* stain, mark; (*de tinta*)
blot; (*de vegetación*) patch; (*imperfección*)
stain, blemish, blot; (*boceto*) sketch,
outline; **la M~** La Mancha.

manchado, a [man'tʃaðo, a] *adj* (*sucio*)
dirty; (*animal*) spotted; (*ave*) speckled;
(*tinta*) smudged.

manchar [man'tʃar] *vt* to stain, mark;
(*ZOOL*) to patch; (*ensuciar*) to soil, dirty;
~se *vr* to get dirty; (*fig*) to dirty one's
hands.

manchego, a [man'tʃeɣo, a] *adj* of *o* from
La Mancha ♦ *nm/f* native *o* inhabitant of
La Mancha.

mancilla [man'θiʎa] *nf* stain, blemish.

mancillar [manθi'ʎar] *vt* to stain, sully.

manco, a ['manko, a] *adj* one-armed; one-
handed; (*fig*) defective, faulty; **no ser ~**
to be useful *o* active.

mancomunar [mankomu'nar] *vt* to unite,
bring together; (*recursos*) to pool; (*JUR*)
to make jointly responsible.

mancomunidad [mankomuni'ðað] *nf*
union, association; (*comunidad*)
community; (*JUR*) joint responsibility.

mandado [man'daðo] *nm* (*orden*) order;
(*recado*) commission, errand.

mandamás [manda'mas] *adj, nm/f inv* boss;
ser un ~ to be very bossy.

mandamiento [manda'mjento] *nm* (*orden*)
order, command; (*REL*) commandment;
~ judicial warrant.

mandar [man'dar] *vt* (*ordenar*) to order;
(*dirigir*) to lead, command; (*país*) to rule
over; (*enviar*) to send; (*pedir*) to order,

ask for ♦ *vi* to be in charge; (*pey*) to be
bossy; **~se** *vr*: **~se mudar** (*AM fam*) to go
away, clear off; **¿mande?** pardon?,
excuse me? (*US*); **¿manda usted algo
más?** is there anything else?; **~ a algn a
paseo** *o* **a la porra** to tell sb to go to hell;
se lo mandaremos por correo we'll post
it to you; **~ hacer un traje** to have a suit
made.

mandarín [manda'rin] *nm* petty
bureaucrat.

mandarina [manda'rina] *nf* (*fruta*)
tangerine, mandarin (orange).

mandatario, a [manda'tarjo, a] *nm/f*
(*representante*) agent; **primer ~** (*esp AM*)
head of state.

mandato [man'dato] *nm* (*orden*) order;
(*POL: período*) term of office; (: *territorio*)
mandate; (*INFORM*) command; **~ judicial**
(*search*) warrant.

mandíbula [man'diβula] *nf* jaw.

mandil [man'dil] *nm* (*delantal*) apron.

Mandinga [man'dinɣa] *nm* (*AM*) Devil.

mandioca [man'djoka] *nf* cassava.

mando ['mando] *nm* (*MIL*) command; (*de
país*) rule; (*el primer lugar*) lead; (*POL*)
term of office; (*TEC*) control; **~ a la
izquierda** left-hand drive; **los altos ~s**
the high command *sg*; **~ por botón**
push-button control; **al ~ de** in charge
of; **tomar el ~** to take the lead.

mandolina [mando'lina] *nf* mandolin(e).

mandón, ona [man'don, ona] *adj* bossy,
domineering.

manecilla [mane'θiʎa] *nf* (*TEC*) pointer; (*de
reloj*) hand.

manejable [mane'xaβle] *adj* manageable;
(*fácil de usar*) handy.

manejar [mane'xar] *vt* to manage;
(*máquina*) to work, operate; (*caballo etc*)
to handle; (*casa*) to run, manage; (*AM
AUTO*) to drive ♦ *vi* (*AM AUTO*) to drive;
~se *vr* (*comportarse*) to act, behave;
(*arreglárselas*) to manage; "**~ con
cuidado**" "handle with care".

manejo [ma'nexo] *nm* management;
handling; running; driving; (*facilidad de
trato*) ease, confidence; (*de idioma*)
command; **~s** *nmpl* intrigues; **tengo ~
del francés** I have a good command of
French.

manera [ma'nera] *nf* way, manner,
fashion; (*ARTE, LITERATURA etc: estilo*)
manner, style; **~s** *nfpl* (*modales*)
manners; **su ~ de ser** the way he is;
(*aire*) his manner; **de mala ~** (*fam*) badly,
unwillingly; **de ninguna ~** no way, by no
means; **de otra ~** otherwise; **de todas ~s**

at any rate; **en gran** ~ to a large extent; **sobre** ~ exceedingly; **a mi** ~ **de ver** in my view; **no hay** ~ **de persuadirle** there's no way of convincing him.

manga ['manga] *nf (de camisa)* sleeve; *(de riego)* hose; **de** ~ **corta/larga** short-/long-sleeved; **andar** ~ **por hombro** *(desorden)* to be topsy-turvy; **tener** ~ **ancha** to be easy-going.

mangante [man'gante] *adj (descarado)* brazen ♦ *nm (mendigo)* beggar.

mangar [man'gar] *vt (unir)* to plug in; *(fam: birlar)* to pinch, nick, swipe; *(mendigar)* to beg.

mango ['mango] *nm* handle; *(BOT)* mango; ~ **de escoba** broomstick.

mangonear [mangone'ar] *vt* to boss about ♦ *vi* to be bossy.

mangue ['mange] *etc vb V* **mangar.**

manguera [man'gera] *nf (de riego)* hose; *(tubo)* pipe; ~ **de incendios** fire hose.

manía [ma'nia] *nf (MED)* mania; *(fig: moda)* rage, craze; *(disgusto)* dislike; *(malicia)* spite; **tiene** ~**s** she's a bit fussy; **tener** ~ **a algn** to dislike sb.

maníaco, a [ma'niako, a] *adj* maniac(al) ♦ *nm/f* maniac.

maniatar [manja'tar] *vt* to tie the hands of.

maniático, a [ma'njatiko, a] *adj* maniac(al); *(loco)* crazy; *(tiquismiquis)* fussy ♦ *nm/f* maniac.

manicomio [mani'komjo] *nm* mental hospital *(BRIT)*, insane asylum *(US)*.

manicuro, a [mani'kuro, a] *nm/f* manicurist ♦ *nf* manicure.

manido, a [ma'niðo, a] *adj (tema etc)* trite, stale.

manifestación [manifesta'θjon] *nf (declaración)* statement, declaration; *(demostración)* show, display; *(POL)* demonstration.

manifestante [manifes'tante] *nm/f* demonstrator.

manifestar [manifes'tar] *vt* to show, manifest; *(declarar)* to state, declare; ~**se** *vr* to show, become apparent; *(POL: desfilar)* to demonstrate; *(: reunirse)* to hold a mass meeting.

manifiesto, a [mani'fjesto, a] *etc vb V* **manifestar** ♦ *adj* clear, manifest ♦ *nm* manifesto; *(ANAT, NAUT)* manifest; **poner algo de** ~ *(aclarar)* to make sth clear; *(revelar)* to reveal sth; **quedar** ~ to be plain *o* clear.

manija [ma'nixa] *nf* handle.

manilla [ma'niʎa] *nf (de reloj)* hand; *(AM)* handle, lever; ~**s (de hierro)** *nfpl* handcuffs.

manillar [mani'ʎar] *nm* handlebars *pl.*

maniobra [ma'njoßra] *nf* manœuvring; *(maneja)* handling; *(fig: movimiento)* manœuvre, move; *(: estratagema)* trick, stratagem; ~**s** *nfpl* manœuvres.

maniobrar [manio'ßrar] *vt* to manœuvre; *(manejar)* to handle ♦ *vi* to manœuvre.

manipulación [manipula'θjon] *nf* manipulation; *(COM)* handling.

manipular [manipu'lar] *vt* to manipulate; *(manejar)* to handle.

maniquí [mani'ki] *nm/f* model ♦ *nm* dummy.

manirroto, a [mani'rroto, a] *adj* lavish, extravagant ♦ *nm/f* spendthrift.

maní(s) [ma'ni] *nm, pl* **maníes** *o* **manises** *(AM: cacahuete)* peanut; *(: planta)* groundnut plant.

manita [ma'nita] *nf* little hand; ~**s de plata** artistic hands.

manitas [ma'nitas] *adj inv* good with one's hands ♦ *nm/f inv:* **ser un** ~ to be very good with one's hands.

manito [ma'nito] *nm (AM: en conversación)* mate *(fam)*, chum.

manivela [mani'ßela] *nf* crank.

manjar [man'xar] *nm (tasty)* dish.

mano¹ ['mano] *nf* hand; *(ZOOL)* foot, paw; *(de pintura)* coat; *(serie)* lot, series; **a** ~ by hand; **a** ~ **derecha/izquierda** on *(o* to) the right(-hand side)/left(-hand side); **hecho a** ~ handmade; **a** ~**s llenas** lavishly, generously; **de primera** ~ (at) first hand; **de segunda** ~ (at) second hand; **robo a** ~ **armada** armed robbery; **Pedro es mi** ~ **derecha** Pedro is my right-hand man; ~ **de obra** labour, manpower; ~ **de santo** sure remedy; **darse la(s)** ~**(s)** to shake hands; **echar una** ~ to lend a hand; **echar una** ~ **a** to lay hands on; **echar** ~ **de** to make use of; **estrechar la** ~ **a algn** to shake sb's hand; **traer** *o* **llevar algo entre** ~**s** to deal *o* be busy with sth; **está en tus** ~**s** it's up to you; **se le fue la** ~ his hand slipped; *(fig)* he went too far; **¡**~**s a la obra!** to work!

mano² ['mano] *nm (AM fam)* friend, mate.

manojo [ma'noxo] *nm* handful, bunch; ~ **de llaves** bunch of keys.

manómetro [ma'nometro] *nm (pressure)* gauge.

manopla [ma'nopla] *nf (paño)* flannel; ~**s** *nfpl* mittens.

manoseado, a [manose'aðo, a] *adj* well-worn.

manosear [manose'ar] *vt (tocar)* to handle, touch; *(desordenar)* to mess up, rumple; *(insistir en)* to overwork; *(acariciar)* to caress, fondle; *(pey: persona)* to feel *o* touch up.

manotazo [mano'taθo] *nm* slap, smack.

mansalva [man'salßa]: **a ~** *adv* indiscriminately.

mansedumbre [manse'ðumbre] *nf* gentleness, meekness; (*de animal*) tameness.

mansión [man'sjon] *nf* mansion.

manso, a ['manso, a] *adj* gentle, mild; (*animal*) tame.

manta ['manta] *nf* blanket; (*AM*) poncho.

manteca [man'teka] *nf* fat; (*AM*) butter; **~ de cacahuete/cacao** peanut/cocoa butter; **~ de cerdo** lard.

mantecado [mante'kaðo] *nm* ice cream.

mantecoso, a [mante'koso, a] *adj* fat, greasy; **queso ~** soft cheese.

mantel [man'tel] *nm* tablecloth.

mantelería [mantele'ria] *nf* table linen.

mantendré [manten'dre] *etc vb* V **mantener.**

mantener [mante'ner] *vt* to support, maintain; (*alimentar*) to sustain; (*conservar*) to keep; (*TEC*) to maintain, service; **~se** *vr* (*seguir de pie*) to be still standing; (*no ceder*) to hold one's ground; (*subsistir*) to sustain o.s., keep going; **~ algo en equilibrio** to keep sth balanced; **~se a distancia** to keep one's distance; **~se firme** to hold one's ground.

mantenga [man'tenga] *etc vb* V **mantener.**

mantenimiento [manteni'mjento] *nm* maintenance; sustenance; (*sustento*) support.

mantequería [manteke'ria] *nf* (*ultramarinos*) grocer's (shop).

mantequilla [mante'kiʎa] *nf* butter.

mantilla [man'tiʎa] *nf* mantilla; **~s** *nfpl* baby clothes; **estar en ~s** (*persona*) to be terribly innocent; (*proyecto*) to be in its infancy.

manto ['manto] *nm* (*capa*) cloak; (*de ceremonia*) robe, gown.

mantón [man'ton] *nm* shawl.

mantuve [man'tuße] *etc vb* V **mantener.**

manual [ma'nwal] *adj* manual ♦ *nm* manual, handbook; **habilidad ~** manual skill.

manubrio [ma'nußrio] *nm* (*AM AUTO*) steering wheel.

manufactura [manufak'tura] *nf* manufacture; (*fábrica*) factory.

manufacturado, a [manufaktu'raðo, a] *adj* manufactured.

manuscrito, a [manus'krito, a] *adj* handwritten ♦ *nm* manuscript.

manutención [manuten'θjon] *nf*

maintenance; (*sustento*) support.

manzana [man'θana] *nf* apple; (*ARQ*) block; **~ de la discordia** (*fig*) bone of contention.

manzanal [manθa'nal] *nm* apple orchard.

manzanilla [manθa'niʎa] *nf* (*planta*) camomile; (*infusión*) camomile tea; (*vino*) manzanilla.

manzano [man'θano] *nm* apple tree.

maña ['maɲa] *nf* (*gen*) skill, dexterity; (*pey*) guile; (*costumbre*) habit; (*una ~*) trick, knack; **con ~** craftily.

mañana [ma'ɲana] *adv* tomorrow ♦ *nm* future ♦ *nf* morning; **de** *o* **por la ~** in the morning; **¡hasta ~!** see you tomorrow!; **pasado ~** the day after tomorrow; **~ por la ~** tomorrow morning.

mañanero, a [maɲa'nero, a] *adj* early-rising.

maño, a ['maɲo, a] *adj* Aragonese ♦ *nm/f* native *o* inhabitant of Aragon.

mañoso, a [ma'ɲoso, a] *adj* (*hábil*) skilful; (*astuto*) smart, clever.

mapa ['mapa] *nm* map.

mapuche, a [ma'putʃhe, a] *adj, nm/f* Mapuche, Araucanian.

maqueta [ma'keta] *nf* (*scale*) model.

maquiavélico, a [makja'ßeliko, a] *adj* Machiavellian.

maquillador, a [makiʎa'ðor, a] *nm/f* (*TEAT etc*) make-up artist.

maquillaje [maki'ʎaxe] *nm* make-up; (*acto*) making up.

maquillar [maki'ʎar] *vt* to make up; **~se** *vr* to put on (some) make-up.

máquina ['makina] *nf* machine; (*de tren*) locomotive, engine; (*FOTO*) camera; (*AM: coche*) car; (*fig*) machinery; (: *proyecto*) plan, project; **a toda ~** at full speed; **escrito a ~** typewritten; **~ de escribir** typewriter; **~ de coser/lavar** sewing/washing machine; **~ de facsímil** facsimile (machine), fax; **~ de franqueo** franking machine; **~ tragaperras** fruit machine; (*COM*) slot machine.

maquinación [makina'θjon] *nf* machination, plot.

maquinal [maki'nal] *adj* (*fig*) mechanical, automatic.

maquinar [maki'nar] *vt, vi* to plot.

maquinaria [maki'narja] *nf* (*máquinas*) machinery; (*mecanismo*) mechanism, works *pl.*

maquinilla [maki'niʎa] *nf* small machine; (*torno*) winch; **~ de afeitar** razor; **~ eléctrica** electric razor.

maquinista [maki'nista] *nm* (*FERRO*) engine driver (*BRIT*), engineer (*US*); (*TEC*) operator; (*NAUT*) engineer.

mar [mar] *nm* sea; ~ **de fondo**
groundswell; ~ **llena** high tide; ~
adentro *o* **afuera** out at sea; **en alta** ~ on
the high seas; **por** ~ by sea *o* boat;
hacerse a la ~ to put to sea; **a** ~**es** in
abundance; **un** ~ **de** lots of; **es la** ~ **de**
guapa she is ever so pretty; **el M**~
Negro/Báltico the Black/Baltic Sea; **el**
M~ **Muerto/Rojo** the Dead/Red Sea; **el**
M~ **del Norte** the North Sea.

mar. *abr* (= *marzo*) Mar.

maraca [ma'raka] *nf* maraca.

maraña [ma'raɲa] *nf* (*maleza*) thicket;
(*confusión*) tangle.

maravilla [mara'ßiʎa] *nf* marvel, wonder;
(*BOT*) marigold; **hacer** ~**s** to work
wonders; **a** (**las mil**) ~**s** wonderfully
well.

maravillar [maraßi'ʎar] *vt* to astonish,
amaze; ~**se** *vr* to be astonished, be
amazed.

maravilloso, a [maraßi'ʎoso, a] *adj*
wonderful, marvellous.

marbellí [marße'ʎi] *adj* of *o* from Marbella.
♦ *nm/f* native *o* inhabitant of Marbella.

marca ['marka] *nf* mark; (*sello*) stamp;
(*COM*) make, brand; (*de ganado*) brand;
(: *acto*) branding; (*NAUT*) seamark;
(: *boya*) marker; (*DEPORTE*) record; **de** ~
excellent, outstanding; ~ **de fábrica**
trademark; ~ **propia** own brand; ~
registrada registered trademark.

marcación [marka'θjon] *nf* (*TELEC*): ~
automática autodial.

marcado, a [mar'kaðo, a] *adj* marked,
strong.

marcador [marka'ðor] *nm* marker;
(*rotulador*) marker (pen); (*de libro*)
bookmark; (*DEPORTE*) scoreboard;
(: *persona*) scorer.

marcapasos [marka'pasos] *nm inv*
pacemaker.

marcar [mar'kar] *vt* to mark; (*número de*
teléfono) to dial; (*gol*) to score; (*números*)
to record, keep a tally of; (*el pelo*) to set;
(*ganado*) to brand; (*suj: termómetro*) to
read, register; (: *reloj*) to show; (*tarea*) to
assign; (*COM*) to put a price on ♦ *vi*
(*DEPORTE*) to score; (*TELEC*) to dial; **mi**
reloj marca las 2 it's 2 o'clock by my
watch; ~ **el compás** (*MUS*) to keep time;
~ **el paso** (*MIL*) to mark time.

marcha ['martʃa] *nf* march; (*DEPORTE*)
walk; (*TEC*) running, working; (*AUTO*)
gear; (*velocidad*) speed; (*fig*) progress;
(*dirección*) course; **dar** ~ **atrás** to
reverse, put into reverse; **estar en** ~ to

be under way, be in motion; **hacer algo**
sobre la ~ to do sth as you *etc* go along;
poner en ~ to put into gear; **ponerse en**
~ to start, get going; **a** ~**s forzadas** (*fig*)
with all speed; **¡en** ~**!** (*MIL*) forward
march!; (*fig*) let's go!; "~ **moderada**"
(*AUTO*) "drive slowly"; **que tiene** *o* **de**
mucha ~ (*fam*) very lively.

marchante, a [mar'tʃante, a] *nm/f* dealer,
merchant.

marchar [mar'tʃar] *vi* (*ir*) to go; (*funcionar*)
to work, go; (*fig*) to go, proceed; ~**se** *vr*
to go (away), leave; **todo marcha bien**
everything is going well.

marchitar [martʃi'tar] *vt* to wither, dry up;
~**se** *vr* (*BOT*) to wither; (*fig*) to fade away.

marchito, a [mar'tʃito, a] *adj* withered,
faded; (*fig*) in decline.

marchoso, a [mar'tʃoso, a] *adj* (*fam:*
animado) lively; (: *moderno*) modern.

marcial [mar'θjal] *adj* martial, military.

marciano, a [mar'θjano, a] *adj* Martian, of
o from Mars.

marco ['marko] *nm* frame; (*DEPORTE*)
goalposts *pl*; (*moneda*) mark; (*fig*)
setting; (*contexto*) framework; ~ **de**
chimenea mantelpiece.

marea [ma'rea] *nf* tide; (*llovizna*) drizzle; ~
alta/baja high/low tide; ~ **negra** oil slick.

mareado, a [mare'aðo, a] *adj*: **estar** ~ (*con*
náuseas) to feel sick; (*aturdido*) to feel
dizzy.

marear [mare'ar] *vt* (*fig: irritar*) to annoy,
upset; (*MED*): ~ **a algn** to make sb feel
sick; ~**se** *vr* (*tener náuseas*) to feel sick;
(*desvanecerse*) to feel faint; (*aturdirse*) to
feel dizzy; (*fam: emborracharse*) to get
tipsy.

marejada [mare'xaða] *nf* (*NAUT*) swell,
heavy sea.

maremágnum [mare'maxnum] *nm* (*fig*)
ocean, abundance.

maremoto [mare'moto] *nm* tidal wave.

mareo [ma'reo] *nm* (*náusea*) sick feeling;
(*aturdimiento*) dizziness; (*fam: lata*)
nuisance.

marfil [mar'fil] *nm* ivory.

margarina [marxa'rina] *nf* margarine.

margarita [marxa'rita] *nf* (*BOT*) daisy;
(*rueda*) ~ (*en máquina impresora*) daisy
wheel.

margen ['marxen] *nm* (*borde*) edge,
border; (*fig*) margin, space ♦ *nf* (*de río*
etc) bank; ~ **de beneficio** *o* **de ganancia**
profit margin; ~ **comercial** mark-up; ~
de confianza credibility gap; **dar** ~ **para**
to give an opportunity for; **dejar a algn**
al ~ to leave sb out (in the cold);

mantenerse al ~ to keep out (of things); **al** ~ **de lo que digas** despite what you say.

marginado, a [marxi'naðo, a] *nm/f* outcast.

marginal [marxi'nal] *adj (tema, error)* minor; *(grupo)* fringe *cpd*; *(anotación)* marginal.

marginar [marxi'nar] *vt* to exclude.

maría [ma'ria] *nf (fam: mujer)* housewife.

mariachi [ma'rjatʃi] *nm (música)* mariachi music; *(grupo)* mariachi band; *(persona)* mariachi player.

marica [ma'rika] *nm (fam)* sissy; *(homosexual)* queer.

Maricastaña [marikas'taɲa] *nf*: **en los días** *o* **en tiempos de** ~ way back, in the good old days.

maricón [mari'kon] *nm (fam)* queer.

marido [ma'riðo] *nm* husband.

marihuana [mari'wənə] *nf* marijuana, cannabis.

marimacho [mari'matʃo] *nf (fam)* mannish woman.

marimorena [marimo'rena] *nf* fuss, row; **armar una** ~ to kick up a row.

marina [ma'rina] *nf* navy; ~ **mercante** merchant navy.

marinero, a [mari'nero, a] *adj* sea *cpd*; *(barco)* seaworthy ♦ *nm* sailor, seaman.

marino, a [ma'rino, a] *adj* sea *cpd*, marine ♦ *nm* sailor; ~ **de agua dulce/de cubierta/de primera** landlubber/ deckhand/able seaman.

marioneta [marjo'neta] *nf* puppet.

mariposa [mari'posa] *nf* butterfly.

mariposear [maripose'ar] *vi (revolotear)* to flutter about; *(ser inconstante)* to be fickle; *(coquetear)* to flirt.

mariquita [mari'kita] *nm (fam)* sissy; *(homosexual)* queer ♦ *nf (ZOOL)* ladybird *(BRIT)*, ladybug *(US)*.

marisco [ma'risko] *nm (tb: ~s)* shellfish, seafood.

marisma [ma'risma] *nf* marsh, swamp.

marisquería [mariske'ria] *nf* shellfish bar, seafood restaurant.

marítimo, a [ma'ritimo, a] *adj* sea *cpd*, maritime.

marmita [mar'mita] *nf* pot.

mármol ['marmol] *nm* marble.

marmóreo, a [mar'moreo, a] *adj* marble.

marmota [mar'mota] *nf (ZOOL)* marmot; *(fig)* sleepyhead.

maroma [ma'roma] *nf* rope.

marque ['marke] *etc vb V* **marcar**.

marqués, esa [mar'kes, esa] *nm/f* marquis/marchioness.

marquesina [marke'sina] *nf (de parada)* bus-shelter.

marquetería [markete'ria] *nf* marquetry, inlaid work.

marranada [marra'naða] *nf (fam)*: **es una** ~ that's disgusting; **hacer una** ~ **a algn** to do the dirty on sb.

marrano, a [ma'rrano, a] *adj* filthy, dirty ♦ *nm (ZOOL)* pig; *(malo)* swine; *(sucio)* dirty pig.

marras ['marras]: **de** ~ *adv*: **es el problema de** ~ it's the same old problem.

marrón [ma'rron] *adj* brown.

marroquí [marro'ki] *adj, nm/f* Moroccan ♦ *nm* Morocco (leather).

Marruecos [ma'rrwekos] *nm* Morocco.

marta ['marta] *nf (animal)* (pine) marten; *(piel)* sable.

Marte ['marte] *nm* Mars.

martes ['martes] *nm inv* Tuesday; ~ **de carnaval** Shrove Tuesday; *V tb* **Carnaval**.

martillar [marti'ʎar], **martillear** [martiʎe'ar] *vt* to hammer.

martilleo [marti'ʎeo] *nm* hammering.

martillo [mar'tiʎo] *nm* hammer; *(de presidente de asamblea, comité)* gavel; ~ **neumático** pneumatic drill *(BRIT)*, jackhammer *(US)*.

Martinica [marti'nika] *nf* Martinique.

mártir ['martir] *nm/f* martyr.

martirice [marti'riðe] *etc vb V* **martirizar**.

martirio [mar'tirjo] *nm* martyrdom; *(fig)* torture, torment.

martirizar [martiri'θar] *vt (REL)* to martyr; *(fig)* to torture, torment.

maruja [ma'ruxa] *nf (fam)* = **maría**.

marxismo [mark'sismo] *nm* Marxism.

marxista [mark'sista] *adj, nm/f* Marxist.

marzo ['marθo] *nm* March.

mas [mas] *conj* but.

═══════════════ *PALABRA CLAVE*

más [mas] *adj, adv* **1**: ~ **(que, de)** *(compar)* more (than), ...+er (than); ~ **grande/ inteligente** bigger/more intelligent; **trabaja** ~ **(que yo)** he works more (than me); ~ **de 6** more than 6; **es** ~ **de medianoche** it's after midnight; **durar** ~ to last longer; *V tb* **cada**

2 *(superl)*: **el** ~ **the most, ...+est; el** ~ **grande/inteligente (de)** the biggest/most intelligent (in)

3 *(negativo)*: **no tengo** ~ **dinero** I haven't got any more money; **no viene** ~ **por aquí** he doesn't come round here any more; **no sé** ~ I don't know any more, that's all I know

4 *(adicional)*: **un kilómetro** ~ one more kilometre; **no le veo** ~ **solución que ...** I

see no other solution than to ...; ¿**algo** ~**?**
anything else?; (*en tienda*) will that be
all?; ¿**quién** ~**?** anybody else?
5 (+*adj*: *valor intensivo*): ¡**qué perro** ~
sucio! what a filthy dog!; ¡**es** ~ **tonto!**
he's so stupid!
6 (*locuciones*): ~ **o menos** more or less;
los ~ most people; **es** ~ in fact,
furthermore; ~ **bien** rather; ¡**qué** ~ **da!**
what does it matter!; *V tb* **no**
7: por ~: **por** ~ **que lo intento** no matter
how much *o* hard I try; **por** ~ **que**
quisiera ayudar
much as I should like to help
8: de ~: **veo que aquí estoy de** ~ I can
see I'm not needed here; **tenemos uno**
de ~ we've got one extra
9: (*AM*): **no** ~ only, just; **ayer no** ~ just
yesterday
♦ *prep*: **2** ~ **2 son 4** 2 and *o* plus 2 are 4
♦ *nm inv*: **este trabajo tiene sus** ~ **y sus**
menos this job's got its good points and
its bad points.

masa ['masa] *nf* (*mezcla*) dough; (*volumen*)
volume, mass; (*FÍSICA*) mass; **en** ~ **en**
masse; las ~**s** (*POL*) the masses.
masacrar [masa'krar] *vt* to massacre.
masacre [ma'sakre] *nf* massacre.
masaje [ma'saxe] *nm* massage; **dar** ~ **a** to
massage.
masajista [masa'xista] *nm/f* masseur/
masseuse.
mascar [mas'kar] *vt, vi* to chew; (*fig*) to
mumble, mutter.
máscara ['maskara] *nf* (*tb INFORM*) mask ♦
nm/f masked person; ~ **antigás** gas mask.
mascarada [maska'raða] *nf* masquerade.
mascarilla [maska'riʎa] *nf* mask; (*vaciado*)
deathmask; (*maquillaje*) face pack.
mascarón [maska'ron] *nm* large mask; ~
de proa figurehead.
mascota [mas'kota] *nf* mascot.
masculino, a [masku'lino, a] *adj*
masculine; (*BIO*) male ♦ *nm* (*LING*)
masculine.
mascullar [masku'ʎar] *vt* to mumble,
mutter.
masificación [masifika'θjon] *nf*
overcrowding.
masilla [ma'siʎa] *nf* putty.
masivo, a [ma'sißo, a] *adj* (*en masa*) mass.
masón [ma'son] *nm* (free)mason.
masonería [masone'ria] *nf* (free)masonry.
masoquista [maso'kista] *adj* masochistic
♦ *nm/f* masochist.
masque ['maske] *etc vb V* **mascar**.
mastectomía [mastekto'mia] *nf*

mastectomy.
máster, *pl* **masters** ['master, 'masters] *nm*
postgraduate degree; *V tb* **licenciado**.
masticar [masti'kar] *vt* to chew; (*fig*) to
ponder over.
mástil ['mastil] *nm* (*de navío*) mast; (*de*
guitarra) neck.
mastín [mas'tin] *nm* mastiff.
mastique [mas'tike] *etc vb V* **masticar**.
masturbación [masturßa'θjon] *nf*
masturbation.
masturbarse [mastur'ßarse] *vr* to
masturbate.
Mat. *abr* = **Matemáticas**.
mata ['mata] *nf* (*arbusto*) bush, shrub; (*de*
hierbas) tuft; (*campo*) field; (*manojo*) tuft,
blade; ~**s** *nfpl* scrub *sg*; ~ **de pelo** mop of
hair; **a salto de** ~ (*día a día*) from day to
day; (*al azar*) haphazardly.
matadero [mata'ðero] *nm* slaughterhouse,
abattoir.
matador, a [mata'ðor, a] *adj* killing ♦ *nm/f*
killer ♦ *nm* (*TAUR*) matador, bullfighter.
matamoscas [mata'moskas] *nm inv* (*palo*)
fly swat.
matanza [ma'tanθa] *nf* slaughter.
matar [ma'tar] *vt* to kill; (*tiempo, pelota*) to
kill ♦ *vi* to kill; ~**se** *vr* (*suicidarse*) to kill
o.s., commit suicide; (*morir*) to be *o* get
killed; (*gastarse*) to wear o.s. out; ~ **el**
hambre to stave off hunger; ~ **a algn a**
disgustos make sb's life a misery; ~**las**
callando to go about things slyly; ~**se**
trabajando to kill o.s. with work; ~**se**
por hacer algo to struggle to do sth.
matarife [mata'rife] *nm* slaughterman.
matasanos [mata'sanos] *nm inv* quack.
matasellos [mata'seʎos] *nm inv* postmark.
mate ['mate] *adj* (*sin brillo*: *color*) dull, matt
♦ *nm* (*en ajedrez*) (check)mate; (*AM*:
hierba) maté; (: *vasija*) gourd.
matemático, a [mate'matiko, a] *adj*
mathematical ♦ *nm/f* mathematician
♦ **matemáticas** *nfpl* mathematics *sg*.
materia [ma'terja] *nf* (*gen*) matter; (*TEC*)
material; (*ESCOL*) subject; **en** ~ **de** on
the subject of; (*en cuanto a*) as regards;
~ **prima** raw material; **entrar en** ~ to get
down to business.
material [mate'rjal] *adj* material; (*dolor*)
physical; (*real*) real; (*literal*) literal ♦ *nm*
material; (*TEC*) equipment; ~ **de**
construcción building material; ~**es de**
derribo rubble *sg*.
materialismo [materja'lismo] *nm*
materialism.
materialista [materja'lista] *adj*
materialist(ic).

materialmente [materjal'mente] _adv_ materially; (_fig_) absolutely.

maternal [mater'nal] _adj_ motherly, maternal.

maternidad [materni'ðað] _nf_ motherhood, maternity.

materno, a [ma'terno, a] _adj_ maternal; (_lengua_) mother _cpd_.

matice [ma'tiθe] _etc vb V_ **matizar**.

matinal [mati'nal] _adj_ morning _cpd_.

matiz [ma'tiθ] _nm_ shade; (_de sentido_) shade, nuance; (_ironía etc_) touch.

matizar [mati'θar] _vt_ (_variar_) to vary; (_ARTE_) to blend; ~ **de** to tinge with.

matón [ma'ton] _nm_ bully.

matorral [mato'rral] _nm_ thicket.

matraca [ma'traka] _nf_ rattle; (_fam_) nuisance.

matraz [ma'traθ] _nm_ (_QUÍMICA_) flask.

matriarcado [matrjar'kaðo] _nm_ matriarchy.

matrícula [ma'trikula] _nf_ (_registro_) register; (_ESCOL: inscripción_) registration; (_AUTO_) registration number; (: _placa_) number plate.

matricular [matriku'lar] _vt_ to register, enrol.

matrimonial [matrimo'njal] _adj_ matrimonial.

matrimonio [matri'monjo] _nm_ (_pareja_) (married) couple; (_acto_) marriage; ~ **civil/clandestino** civil/secret marriage; **contraer** ~ (**con**) to marry.

matriz [ma'triθ] _nf_ (_ANAT_) womb; (_TEC_) mould; (_MAT_) matrix; **casa** ~ (_COM_) head office.

matrona [ma'trona] _nf_ (_persona de edad_) matron.

matutino, a [matu'tino, a] _adj_ morning _cpd_.

maula ['maula] _adj_ (_persona_) good-for-nothing ♦ _nm/f_ (_vago_) idler, slacker ♦ _nf_ (_persona_) dead loss (_fam_).

maullar [mau'ʎar] _vi_ to mew, miaow.

maullido [mau'ʎiðo] _nm_ mew(ing), miaow(ing).

Mauricio [mau'riθjo] _nm_ Mauritius.

Mauritania [mauri'tanja] _nf_ Mauritania.

mausoleo [mauso'leo] _nm_ mausoleum.

maxilar [maksi'lar] _nm_ jaw(bone).

máxima ['maksima] _nf V_ **máximo**.

máxime ['maksime] _adv_ especially.

máximo, a ['maksimo, a] _adj_ maximum; (_más alto_) highest; (_más grande_) greatest ♦ _nm_ maximum ♦ _nf_ maxim; ~ **jefe** _o_ **líder** (_AM_) President, leader; **como** ~ at most; **al** ~ to the utmost.

maxisingle [maksi'singel] _nm_ twelve-inch (single).

maya ['maja] _adj_ Mayan ♦ _nm/f_ Maya(n).

mayo ['majo] _nm_ May.

mayonesa [majo'nesa] _nf_ mayonnaise.

mayor [ma'jor] _adj_ main, chief; (_adulto_) grown-up, adult; (_JUR_) of age; (_de edad avanzada_) elderly; (_MUS_) major; (_comparativo: de tamaño_) bigger; (: _de edad_) older; (_superlativo: de tamaño_) biggest; (_tb: fig_) greatest; (: _de edad_) oldest ♦ _nm_ chief, boss; (_adulto_) adult; **al por** ~ wholesale; ~ **de edad** adult; _V tb_ **mayores**.

mayoral [majo'ral] _nm_ foreman.

mayordomo [major'ðomo] _nm_ butler.

mayoreo [majo'reo] _nm_ (_AM_) wholesale (trade).

mayores [ma'jores] _nmpl_ grown-ups; **llegar a** ~**es** to get out of hand.

mayoría [majo'ria] _nf_ majority, greater part; **en la** ~ **de los casos** in most cases; **en su** ~ on the whole.

mayorista [majo'rista] _nm/f_ wholesaler.

mayoritario, a [majori'tarjo, a] _adj_ majority _cpd_; **gobierno** ~ majority government.

mayúsculo, a [ma'juskulo, a] _adj_ (_fig_) big, tremendous ♦ _nf_ capital (letter); **mayúsculas** _nfpl_ capitals; (_TIP_) upper case _sg_.

maza ['maθa] _nf_ (_arma_) mace; (_DEPORTE_) bat; (_POLO_) stick.

mazacote [maθa'kote] _nm_ hard mass; (_CULIN_) dry doughy food; (_ARTE, LITERATURA etc_) mess, hotchpotch.

mazapán [maθa'pan] _nm_ marzipan.

mazmorra [maθ'morra] _nf_ dungeon.

mazo ['maθo] _nm_ (_martillo_) mallet; (_de mortero_) pestle; (_de flores_) bunch; (_DEPORTE_) bat.

mazorca [ma'θorka] _nf_ (_BOT_) spike; (_de maíz_) cob, ear.

MCAC _nm abr_ = _Mercado Común de la América Central_.

MCI _nm abr_ = _Mercado Común Iberoamericano_.

me [me] _pron_ (_directo_) me; (_indirecto_) (to) me; (_reflexivo_) (to) myself; **¡dámelo!** give it to me!; ~ **lo compró** (_de mí_) he bought it from me; (_para mí_) he bought it for me.

meandro [me'andro] _nm_ meander.

mear [me'ar] (_fam_) _vt_ to piss on (!) ♦ _vi_ to pee, piss (!), have a piss (!); ~**se** _vr_ to wet o.s.

Meca ['meka] _nf_: **La** ~ Mecca.

mecánica [me'kanika] _nf V_ **mecánico**.

mecanice [meka'niθe] _etc vb V_ **mecanizar**.

mecánico, a [me'kaniko, a] _adj_

mechanical; (*repetitivo*) repetitive ♦ *nm/f*
mechanic ♦ *nf* (*estudio*) mechanics *sg*;
(*mecanismo*) mechanism.

mecanismo [meka'nismo] *nm* mechanism;
(*engranaje*) gear.

mecanizar [mekani'θar] *vt* to mechanize.

mecanografía [mekanoɣra'fia] *nf*
typewriting.

mecanografiado, a [mekanoɣra'fjaðo, a]
adj typewritten ♦ *nm* typescript.

mecanógrafo, a [meka'noɣrafo, a] *nm/f*
(*copy*) typist.

mecate [me'kate] *nm* (*AM*) rope.

mecedor [mese'ðor] *nm* (*AM*), **mecedora**
[meθe'ðora] *nf* rocking chair.

mecenas [me'θenas] *nm inv* patron.

mecenazgo [meθe'naɣo] *nm* patronage.

mecer [me'θer] *vt* (*cuna*) to rock; ~**se** *vr* to
rock; (*rama*) to sway.

mecha ['metʃa] *nf* (*de vela*) wick; (*de
bomba*) fuse; **a toda** ~ at full speed;
ponerse ~**s** to streak one's hair.

mechero [me'tʃero] *nm* (*cigarette*) lighter.

mechón [me'tʃon] *nm* (*gen*) tuft; (*manojo*)
bundle; (*de pelo*) lock.

medalla [me'ðaʎa] *nf* medal.

media ['meðja] *nf V* medio.

mediación [meða'θjon] *nf* mediation; **por**
~ **de** through.

mediado, a [me'ðjaðo, a] *adj* half-full;
(*trabajo*) half-completed; **a** ~**s de** in the
middle of, halfway through.

medianamente [meðjana'mente] *adv*
(*moderadamente*) moderately, fairly;
(*regularmente*) moderately well.

mediano, a [me'ðjano, a] *adj* (*regular*)
medium, average; (*mediocre*) mediocre
♦ *nf* (*AUT*) central reservation, median
(*US*); (**de tamaño**) ~ medium-sized.

medianoche [meðja'notʃe] *nf* midnight.

mediante [me'ðjante] *adv* by (means of),
through.

mediar [me'ðjar] *vi* (*tiempo*) to elapse;
(*interceder*) to mediate, intervene;
(*existir*) to exist; **media el hecho de que**
... there is the fact that ....

medicación [meðika'θjon] *nf* medication,
treatment.

medicamento [meðika'mento] *nm*
medicine, drug.

medicina [meði'θina] *nf* medicine.

medicinal [meði'θi'nal] *adj* medicinal.

medición [meði'θjon] *nf* measurement.

médico, a ['meðiko, a] *adj* medical ♦ *nm/f*
doctor; ~ **de cabecera** family doctor; ~
pediatra paediatrician; ~ **residente**
house physician, intern (*US*).

medida [me'ðiða] *nf* measure; (*medición*)

measurement; (*de camisa, zapato etc*)
size, fitting; (*prudencia*) moderation,
prudence; **en cierta/gran** ~ up to a
point/to a great extent; **un traje a la** ~
made-to-measure suit; ~ **de cuello** collar
size; **a** ~ **de** in proportion to; (*de acuerdo
con*) in keeping with; **con** ~ with
restraint; **sin** ~ immoderately; **a** ~ **que**
... (at the same time) as ...; **tomar** ~**s** to
take steps.

medieval [meðje'ßal] *adj* medieval.

medio, a ['meðjo, a] *adj* half (a); (*punto*)
mid, middle; (*promedio*) average ♦ *adv*
half-; (*esp AM*: *un tanto*) rather, quite
♦ *nm* (*centro*) middle, centre; (*promedio*)
average; (*método*) means, way;
(*ambiente*) environment ♦ *nf* (*prenda de
vestir*) stocking, (*AM*) sock; (*promedio*)
average; ~**s** *nfpl* tights; **media hora** half
an hour; ~ **litro** half a litre; **las tres y
media** half past three; **M~ Oriente**
Middle East; **a** ~ **camino** halfway
(there); ~ **dormido** half asleep; ~
enojado (*esp AM*) rather annoyed; **lo dejó
a** ~**s** he left it half-done; **ir a** ~**s** to go
fifty-fifty; **a** ~ **terminar** half finished; **en**
~ in the middle; (*entre*) in between; **por**
~ **de** by (means of), through; **en los** ~**s
financieros** in financial circles;
encontrarse en su ~ to be in one's
element; ~ **circulante** (*COM*) money
supply; *V tb* **medios**.

medioambiental [meðjoambjen'tal] *adj*
environmental.

mediocre [me'ðjokre] *adj* middling,
average; (*pey*) mediocre.

mediocridad [meðjokri'ðað] *nf* middling
quality; (*pey*) mediocrity.

mediodía [meðjo'ðia] *nm* midday, noon.

mediopensionista [meðjopensjo'nista]
nm/f day boy/girl.

medios ['meðjos] *nmpl* means, resources;
los ~ **de comunicación** the media.

medir [me'ðir] *vt* (*gen*) to measure ♦ *vi* to
measure; ~**se** *vr* (*moderarse*) to be
moderate, act with restraint; **¿cuánto
mides?** — **mido 1.50 m** how tall are you?
— I am 1.50 m tall.

meditabundo, a [meðita'ßundo, a] *adj*
pensive.

meditar [meði'tar] *vt* to ponder, think
over, meditate on; (*planear*) to think out
♦ *vi* to ponder, think, meditate.

mediterráneo, a [meðite'rraneo, a] *adj*
Mediterranean ♦ *nm*: **el (mar) M~** the
Mediterranean (Sea).

medrar [me'ðrar] *vi* to increase, grow;
(*mejorar*) to improve; (*prosperar*) to

prosper, thrive; (*animal, planta etc*) to grow.

medroso, a [me'ðroso, a] *adj* fearful, timid.

médula ['meðula] *nf* (*ANAT*) marrow; (*BOT*) pith; ~ **espinal** spinal cord; **hasta la ~** (*fig*) to the core.

medusa [me'ðusa] *nf* (*ESP*) jellyfish.

megabyte ['meɣaßait] *nm* (*INFORM*) megabyte.

megafonía [meɣafo'nia] *nf* PA *o* public address system.

megáfono [me'ɣafono] *nm* public address system.

megalomanía [meɣaloma'nia] *nf* megalomania.

megalómano, a [meɣa'lomano, a] *nm/f* megalomaniac.

megaocteto [meɣaok'teto] *nm* (*INFORM*) megabyte.

mejicano, a [mexi'kano, a] *adj, nm/f* Mexican.

Méjico ['mexiko] *nm* Mexico.

mejilla [me'xiʎa] *nf* cheek.

mejillón [mexi'ʎon] *nm* mussel.

mejor [me'xor] *adj, adv* (*comparativo*) better; (*superlativo*) best; **lo ~** the best thing; **lo ~ de la vida** the prime of life; **a lo ~** probably; (*quizá*) maybe; ~ **dicho** rather; **tanto ~** so much the better; **es el ~ de todos** he's the best of all.

mejora [me'xora] *nf*, **mejoramiento** [mexora'mjento] *nm* improvement.

mejorar [mexo'rar] *vt* to improve, make better ♦ *vi*, ~**se** *vr* to improve, get better; (*COM*) to do well, prosper; ~ **a** to be better than; **los negocios mejoran** business is picking up.

mejoría [mexo'ria] *nf* improvement; (*restablecimiento*) recovery.

mejunje [me'xunxe] *nm* (*pey*) concoction.

melancolía [melanko'lia] *nf* melancholy.

melancólico, a [melan'koliko, a] *adj* (*triste*) sad, melancholy; (*soñador*) dreamy.

melena [me'lena] *nf* (*de persona*) long hair; (*ZOOL*) mane.

melillense [meli'ʎense] *adj* of *o* from Melilla ♦ *nm/f* native *o* inhabitant of Melilla.

mella ['meʎa] *nf* (*rotura*) notch, nick; **hacer ~** (*fig*) to make an impression.

mellizo, a [me'ʎiθo, a] *adj, nm/f* twin.

melocotón [meloko'ton] *nm* (*ESP*) peach.

melodía [melo'ðia] *nf* melody; (*aire*) tune.

melodrama [melo'ðrama] *nm* melodrama.

melodramático, a [meloðra'matiko, a] *adj* melodramatic.

melón [me'lon] *nm* melon.

melopea [melo'pea] *nf* (*fam*): **tener una ~** to be sloshed.

meloso, a [me'loso, a] *adj* honeyed, sweet; (*empalagoso*) sickly, cloying; (*voz*) sweet; (*zalamero*) smooth.

membrana [mem'brana] *nf* membrane.

membrete [mem'brete] *nm* letterhead; **papel con ~** headed notepaper.

membrillo [mem'briʎo] *nm* quince; **carne de ~** quince jelly.

memo, a ['memo, a] *adj* silly, stupid ♦ *nm/f* idiot.

memorable [memo'raßle] *adj* memorable.

memorándum [memo'randum] *nm* (*libro*) notebook; (*comunicación*) memorandum.

memoria [me'morja] *nf* (*gen*) memory; (*artículo*) (learned) paper; ~**s** *nfpl* (*de autor*) memoirs; ~ **anual** annual report; **aprender algo de ~** to learn sth by heart; **si tengo buena ~** if my memory serves me right; **venir a la ~** to come to mind; (*INFORM*): ~ **de acceso aleatorio** random access memory, RAM; ~ **auxiliar** backing storage; ~ **fija** read-only memory, ROM; ~ **fija programable** programmable memory; ~ **del teclado** keyboard memory.

memorice [memo'riθe] *etc vb* V **memorizar**.

memorizar [memori'θar] *vt* to memorize.

menaje [me'naxe] *nm* (*muebles*) furniture; (*utensilios domésticos*) household equipment; ~ **de cocina** kitchenware.

mención [men'θjon] *nf* mention; **digno de ~** noteworthy; **hacer ~ de** to mention.

mencionar [menθjo'nar] *vt* to mention; (*nombrar*) to name; **sin ~ ...** let alone ....

mendicidad [mendiθi'ðað] *nf* begging.

mendigar [mendi'ɣar] *vt* to beg (for).

mendigo, a [men'diɣo, a] *nm/f* beggar.

mendigue [men'diɣe] *etc vb* V **mendigar**.

mendrugo [men'druɣo] *nm* crust.

menear [mene'ar] *vt* to move; (*cola*) to wag; (*cadera*) to swing; (*fig*) to handle; ~**se** *vr* to shake; (*balancearse*) to sway; (*moverse*) to move; (*fig*) to get a move on.

menester [menes'ter] *nm* (*necesidad*) necessity; ~**es** *nmpl* (*deberes*) duties; **es ~ hacer algo** it is necessary to do sth, sth must be done.

menestra [me'nestra] *nf*: ~ **de verduras** vegetable stew.

mengano, a [men'gano, a] *nm/f* Mr (*o* Mrs *o* Miss) So-and-so.

mengua ['mengwa] *nf* (*disminución*) decrease; (*falta*) lack; (*pobreza*) poverty; (*fig*) discredit; **en ~ de** to the detriment of.

menguante [men'gwante] adj decreasing, diminishing; (luna) waning; (marea) ebb cpd.

menguar [men'gwar] vt to lessen, diminish; (fig) to discredit ♦ vi to diminish, decrease; (fig) to decline.

mengüe ['mengwe] etc vb V **menguar.**

menopausia [meno'pausja] nf menopause.

menor [me'nor] adj (más pequeño: comparativo) smaller; (número) less, lesser; (: superlativo) smallest; (número) least; (más joven: comparativo) younger; (: superlativo) youngest; (MUS) minor ♦ nm/f (joven) young person, juvenile; **Juanito es ~ que Pepe** Juanito is younger than Pepe; **ella es la ~ de todas** she is the youngest of all; **no tengo la ~ idea** I haven't the faintest idea; **al por ~** retail; **~ de edad** under age.

Menorca [me'norka] nf Minorca.

menorquín, ina [menor'kin, ina] adj, nm/f Minorcan.

======================= *PALABRA CLAVE*

menos [menos] adj **1**: **~ (que, de)** (compar: cantidad) less (than); (: número) fewer (than); **con ~ entusiasmo** with less enthusiasm; **~ gente** fewer people; V tb **cada**
2 (superl): **es el que ~ culpa tiene** he is the least to blame; **donde ~ problemas hay** where there are fewest problems
♦ adv **1** (compar): **~ (que, de)** less (than); **me gusta ~ que el otro** I like it less than the other one; **~ de 5** less than 5; **~ de lo que piensas** less than you think
2 (superl): **es el ~ listo (de su clase)** he's the least bright (in his class); **de todas ellas es la que ~ me agrada** out of all of them she's the one I like least; **(por) lo ~** at (the very) least; **es lo ~ que puedo hacer** it's the least I can do; **lo ~ posible** as little as possible
3 (locuciones): **no quiero verle y ~ visitarle** I don't want to see him let alone visit him; **tenemos 7 (de) ~** we're 7 short; **eso es lo de ~** that's the least of it; **¡todo ~ eso!** anything but that!; **al/ por lo ~** at (the very) least; **si al ~** if only
♦ prep except; (cifras) minus; **todos ~ él** everyone except (for) him; **5 ~ 2** 5 minus 2; **las 7 ~ 20** (hora) 20 to 7
♦ conj: **a ~ que: a ~ que venga mañana** unless he comes tomorrow.

menoscabar [menoska'βar] vt (estropear) to damage, harm; (fig) to discredit.

menospreciar [menospre'θjar] vt to underrate, undervalue; (despreciar) to scorn, despise.

menosprecio [menos'preθjo] nm underrating, undervaluation; scorn, contempt.

mensaje [men'saxe] nm message; **~ de error** (INFORM) error message.

mensajero, a [mensa'xero, a] nm/f messenger.

menstruación [menstrwa'θjon] nf menstruation.

menstruar [mens'trwar] vi to menstruate.

mensual [men'swal] adj monthly; **100 ptas ~es** 100 ptas. a month.

mensualidad [menswali'ðað] nf (salario) monthly salary; (COM) monthly payment o instalment.

menta ['menta] nf mint.

mentado, a [men'taðo, a] adj (mencionado) aforementioned; (famoso) well-known ♦ nf: **hacerle una mentada a algn** (AM fam) to (seriously) insult sb.

mental [men'tal] adj mental.

mentalidad [mentali'ðað] nf mentality, way of thinking.

mentalizar [mentali'θar] vt (sensibilizar) to make aware; (convencer) to convince; (preparar mentalmente) to psych up; **~se** vr (concienciarse) to become aware; (prepararse mentalmente) to get psyched up; **~se de que ...** (convencerse) to get it into one's head that ...

mentar [men'tar] vt to mention, name; **~ la madre a algn** to swear at sb.

mente ['mente] nf mind; (inteligencia) intelligence; **no tengo en ~ hacer eso** it is not my intention to do that.

mentecato, a [mente'kato, a] adj silly, stupid ♦ nm/f fool, idiot.

mentir [men'tir] vi to lie; **¡miento!** sorry, I'm wrong!

mentira [men'tira] nf (una ~) lie; (acto) lying; (invención) fiction; **~ piadosa** white lie; **una ~ como una casa** a whopping great lie (fam); **parece ~ que ...** it seems incredible that ..., I can't believe that ....

mentiroso, a [menti'roso, a] adj lying; (falso) deceptive ♦ nm/f liar.

mentís [men'tis] nm inv denial; **dar el ~ a** to deny.

mentón [men'ton] nm chin.

menú [me'nu] nm (tb INFORM) menu; (en restaurante) set meal; **guiado por ~** (INFORM) menu-driven.

menudear [menuðe'ar] vt (repetir) to repeat frequently ♦ vi (ser frecuente) to

menudencia – mesurar

be frequent; (*detallar*) to go into great detail.

menudencia [menu'ðenθja] *nf* (*bagatela*) trifle; ~s *nfpl* odds and ends.

menudeo [menu'ðeo] *nm* retail sales *pl*.

menudillos [menu'ðiʎos] *nmpl* giblets.

menudo, a [me'nuðo, a] *adj* (*pequeño*) small, tiny; (*sin importancia*) petty, insignificant; ¡~ negocio! (*fam*) some deal!; a ~ often, frequently.

meñique [me'ɲike] *nm* little finger.

meollo [me'oʎo] *nm* (*fig*) essence, core.

mequetrefe [meke'trefe] *nm* good-for-nothing, whippersnapper.

mercader [merka'ðer] *nm* merchant.

mercadería [merkaðe'ria] *nf* commodity; ~s *nfpl* goods, merchandise *sg*.

mercado [mer'kaðo] *nm* market; ~ en baja falling market; M~ Común Common Market; ~ de demanda/de oferta seller's/buyer's market; ~ laboral labour market; ~ objetivo target market; ~ de productos básicos commodity market; ~ de valores stock market; ~ exterior/interior o nacional/libre overseas/home/free market.

mercancía [merkan'θia] *nf* commodity; ~s *nfpl* goods, merchandise *sg*; ~s en depósito bonded goods; ~s perecederas perishable goods.

mercancías [merkan'θias] *nm inv* goods train, freight train (*US*).

mercantil [merkan'til] *adj* mercantile, commercial.

mercenario, a [merθe'narjo, a] *adj, nm* mercenary.

mercería [merθe'ria] *nf* (*artículos*) haberdashery (*BRIT*), notions *pl* (*US*); (*tienda*) haberdasher's shop (*BRIT*), drapery (*BRIT*), notions store (*US*).

Mercosur [merko'sur] *nm abr* = Mercado Común del Sur.

mercurio [mer'kurjo] *nm* mercury.

merecedor, a [mereθe'ðor, a] *adj* deserving; ~ de confianza trustworthy.

merecer [mere'θer] *vt* to deserve, merit ♦ *vi* to be deserving, be worthy; merece la pena it's worthwhile.

merecido, a [mere'θiðo, a] *adj* (well) deserved; llevarse su ~ to get one's deserts.

merendar [meren'dar] *vt* to have for tea ♦ *vi* to have tea; (*en el campo*) to have a picnic.

merendero [meren'dero] *nm* (*café*) tearoom; (*en el campo*) picnic spot.

merengue [me'renge] *nm* meringue.

merezca [me'reθka] *etc vb V* merecer.

meridiano [meri'ðjano] *nm* (*ASTRO, GEO*) meridian; la explicación es de una claridad meridiana the explanation is as clear as day.

meridional [meriðjo'nal] *adj* Southern ♦ *nm/f* Southerner.

merienda [me'rjenda] *etc vb V* merendar ♦ *nf* (light) tea, afternoon snack; (*de campo*) picnic; ~ de negros free-for-all.

mérito ['merito] *nm* merit; (*valor*) worth, value; hacer ~s to make a good impression; restar ~ a to detract from.

meritorio, a [meri'torjo, a] *adj* deserving.

merluza [mer'luθa] *nf* hake; coger una ~ (*fam*) to get sozzled.

merma ['merma] *nf* decrease; (*pérdida*) wastage.

mermar [mer'mar] *vt* to reduce, lessen ♦ *vi* to decrease, dwindle.

mermelada [merme'laða] *nf* jam; ~ de naranja marmalade.

mero, a ['mero, a] *adj* mere, simple; (*AM fam*) real ♦ *adv* (*AM*) just, right ♦ *nm* (*ZOOL*) grouper; el ~ ~ (*AM fam*) the boss.

merodear [meroðe'ar] *vi* (*MIL*) to maraud; (*de noche*) to prowl (about); (*curiosear*) to snoop around.

mes [mes] *nm* month; (*salario*) month's pay; el ~ corriente this o the current month.

mesa ['mesa] *nf* table; (*de trabajo*) desk; (*COM*) counter; (*en mitin*) platform; (*GEO*) plateau; (*ARQ*) landing; ~ de noche/de tijera/de operaciones u operatoria bedside/folding/operating table; ~ redonda (*reunión*) round table; ~ digitalizadora (*INFORM*) graph pad; ~ directiva board; ~ y cama bed and board; poner/quitar la ~ to lay/clear the table.

mesarse [me'sarse] *vr*: ~ el pelo o los cabellos to tear one's hair.

mesera [me'sera] *nf* (*AM*) waitress.

mesero [me'sero] *nm* (*AM*) waiter.

meseta [me'seta] *nf* (*GEO*) meseta, tableland; (*ARQ*) landing.

mesilla [me'siʎa], **mesita** [me'sita] *nf*: ~ de noche bedside table.

mesón [me'son] *nm* inn.

mestizo, a [mes'tiθo, a] *adj* half-caste, of mixed race; (*ZOOL*) crossbred ♦ *nm/f* half-caste.

mesura [me'sura] *nf* (*calma*) calm; (*moderación*) moderation, restraint; (*cortesía*) courtesy.

mesurar [mesu'rar] *vt* (*contener*) to restrain; ~se *vr* to restrain o.s.

meta ['meta] *nf* goal; (*de carrera*) finish; (*fig*) goal, aim, objective.
metabolismo [metaßo'lismo] *nm* metabolism.
metafísico, a [meta'fisiko, a] *adj* metaphysical ♦ *nf* metaphysics *sg.*
metáfora [me'tafora] *nf* metaphor.
metafórico, a [meta'foriko, a] *adj* metaphorical.
metal [me'tal] *nm* (*materia*) metal; (*MUS*) brass.
metálico, a [me'taliko, a] *adj* metallic; (*de metal*) metal ♦ *nm* (*dinero contante*) cash.
metalurgia [meta'lurxja] *nf* metallurgy.
metalúrgico, a [meta'lurxiko, a] *adj* metallurgic(al); **industria ~a** engineering industry.
metamorfosear [metamorfose'ar] *vt*: ~ **(en)** to metamorphose *o* transform (into).
metamorfosis [metamor'fosis] *nf inv* metamorphosis, transformation.
metedura [mete'ðura] *nf*: ~ **de pata** (*fam*) blunder.
meteorito [meteo'rito] *nm* meteorite.
meteoro [mete'oro] *nm* meteor.
meteorología [meteorolo'xia] *nf* meteorology.
meteorólogo, a [meteo'roloyo, a] *nm/f* meteorologist; (*RADIO, TV*) weather reporter.
meter [me'ter] *vt* (*colocar*) to put, place; (*introducir*) to put in, insert; (*involucrar*) to involve; (*causar*) to make, cause; **~se** *vr*: **~se en** to go into, enter; (*fig*) to interfere in, meddle in; **~se a** to start; **~se a escritor** to become a writer; **~se con algn** to provoke sb, pick a quarrel with sb; ~ **prisa a algn** to hurry sb up.
meticuloso, a [metiku'loso, a] *adj* meticulous, thorough.
metido, a [me'tiðo, a] *adj*: **estar muy ~ en un asunto** to be deeply involved in a matter; ~ **en años** elderly; ~ **en carne** plump.
metódico, a [me'toðiko, a] *adj* methodical.
metodismo [meto'ðismo] *nm* Methodism.
método ['metoðo] *nm* method.
metodología [metoðolo'xia] *nf* methodology.
metomentodo [metomen'toðo] *nm inv* meddler, busybody.
metraje [me'traxe] *nm* (*CINE*) length; **cinta de largo/corto** ~ full-length film/short.
metralla [me'traʎa] *nf* shrapnel.
metralleta [metra'ʎeta] *nf* sub-machine-gun.
métrico, a ['metriko, a] *adj* metric ♦ *nf*

metrics *pl*; **cinta métrica** tape measure.
metro ['metro] *nm* metre; (*tren*: *tb*: **metropolitano**) underground (*BRIT*), subway (*US*); (*instrumento*) rule; ~ **cuadrado/cúbico** square/cubic metre.
metrópoli [me'tropoli], **metrópolis** [me'tropolis] *nf* (*ciudad*) metropolis; (*colonial*) mother country.
mexicano, a [mexi'kano, a] *adj, nm/f* (*AM*) Mexican.
México ['mexiko] *nm* (*AM*) Mexico; **Ciudad de** ~ Mexico City.
mezcla ['meθkla] *nf* mixture; (*fig*) blend.
mezclar [meθ'klar] *vt* to mix (up); (*armonizar*) to blend; (*combinar*) to merge; **~se** *vr* to mix, mingle; ~ **en** to get mixed up in, get involved in.
mezcolanza [meθko'lanθa] *nf* hotchpotch, jumble.
mezquindad [meθkin'daδ] *nf* (*cicatería*) meanness; (*miras estrechas*) pettiness; (*acto*) mean action.
mezquino, a [meθ'kino, a] *adj* (*cicatero*) mean ♦ *nm/f* (*avaro*) mean person; (*miserable*) petty individual.
mezquita [meθ'kita] *nf* mosque.
MF *abr* (= *Modulación de Frecuencia*) FM.
mg. *abr* (= *miligramo(s)*) mg.
mi [mi] *adj posesivo* my ♦ *nm* (*MUS*) E.
mí [mi] *pron* me, myself; **¿y a** ~ **qué?** so what?
miaja ['mjaxa] *nf* crumb; **ni una** ~ (*fig*) not the least little bit.
miau [mjau] *nm* miaow.
michelín [mitʃe'lin] *nm* (*fam*) spare tyre.
mico ['miko] *nm* monkey.
micro ['mikro] *nm* (*RADIO*) mike, microphone; (*AM*: *pequeño*) minibus; (: *grande*) coach, bus.
microbio [mi'kroßjo] *nm* microbe.
microbús [mikro'ßus] *nm* minibus.
microchip [mikro'tʃip] *nm* microchip.
microcomputador [mikrokomputa'ðor] *nm*, **microcomputadora** [mikrokomputa'ðora] *nf* micro(computer).
microeconomía [mikroekono'mia] *nf* microeconomics *sg.*
microficha [mikro'fitʃa] *nf* microfiche.
microfilm [mikro'film], *pl* **microfilms** [mikro'films] *nm* microfilm.
micrófono [mi'krofono] *nm* microphone.
microinformática [mikroinfor'matika] *nf* microcomputing.
micrómetro [mi'krometro] *nm* micrometer.
microonda [mikro'onda] *nf* microwave; **(horno)** ~**s** microwave (oven).
microordenador [mikroordena'ðor] *nm*

microcomputer.
micropastilla [mikropas'tiʎa],
microplaqueta [mikropla'keta] *nf*
(*INFORM*) chip, wafer.
microplaquita [mikropla'kita] *nf*: ~ **de**
silicio silicon chip.
microprocesador [mikroprocesa'ðor] *nm*
microprocessor.
microprograma [mikropro'ɣrama] *nm*
(*INFORM*) firmware.
microscópico, a [mikros'kopiko, a] *adj*
microscopic.
microscopio [mikros'kopjo] *nm*
microscope.
midiendo [mi'ðjendo] *etc vb V* **medir**.
miedo ['mjeðo] *nm* fear; (*nerviosismo*)
apprehension, nervousness; **meter** ~ **a**
to scare, frighten; **tener** ~ to be afraid;
de ~ wonderful, marvellous; **¡qué** ~**!**
(*fam*) how awful!; **me da** ~ it scares me;
hace un frío de ~ (*fam*) it's terribly cold.
miedoso, a [mje'ðoso, a] *adj* fearful,
timid.
miel [mjel] *nf* honey; **no hay** ~ **sin hiel**
there's no rose without a thorn.
miembro ['mjembro] *nm* limb; (*socio*)
member; (*de institución*) fellow; ~ **viril**
penis.
mientes ['mjentes] *etc vb V* **mentar**; **mentir**
♦ *nfpl*: **no parar** ~ **en** to pay no attention
to; **traer a las** ~ to recall.
mientras ['mjentras] *conj* while; (*duración*)
as long as ♦ *adv* meanwhile; ~ **(que)**
whereas; ~ **tanto** meanwhile; ~ **más**
tiene, más quiere the more he has, the
more he wants.
miérc. *abr* (= *miércoles*) Wed.
miércoles ['mjerkoles] *nm inv* Wednesday;
~ **de ceniza** Ash Wednesday; *V tb*
Carnaval.
mierda ['mjerða] *nf* (*fam!*) shit (*!*), crap (*!*);
(*fig*) filth, dirt; **¡vete a la** ~! go to hell!
mies [mjes] *nf* (*ripe*) corn, wheat, grain.
miga ['miɣa] *nf* crumb; (*fig: meollo*)
essence; **hacer buenas** ~**s** (*fam*) to get on
well; **esto tiene su** ~ there's more to this
than meets the eye.
migaja [mi'ɣaxa] *nf*: **una** ~ **de** (*un poquito*)
a little; ~**s** *nfpl* crumbs; (*pey*) left-overs.
migración [miɣra'θjon] *nf* migration.
migratorio, a [miɣra'torjo, a] *adj*
migratory.
mil [mil] *num* thousand; **dos** ~ **libras** two
thousand pounds.
milagro [mi'laɣro] *nm* miracle; **hacer** ~**s**
(*fig*) to work wonders.
milagroso, a [mila'ɣroso, a] *adj*
miraculous.

Milán [mi'lan] *nm* Milan.
milenario, a [mile'narjo, a] *adj* millennial;
(*fig*) very ancient.
milenio [mi'lenjo] *nm* millennium.
milésimo, a [mi'lesimo, a] *num* thousandth.
mili ['mili] *nf*: **hacer la** ~ (*fam*) to do one's
military service.

La **mili**, *military service, is compulsory in
Spain although the number of months'
service has been reduced and recruits are
now posted close to their home town. There
continues to be strong opposition from*
objetores de conciencia, *conscientious
objectors, who are obliged to do* **Prestación
Social Sustitutoria** *in place of military
service; this usually involves doing
community service and lasts longer. Those
who refuse to do either of these,* **los
insumisos**, *can be sent to prison.*

milicia [mi'liθja] *nf* (*MIL*) militia; (*servicio
militar*) military service.
miligramo [mili'ɣramo] *nm* milligram.
milímetro [mi'limetro] *nm* millimetre
(*BRIT*), millimeter (*US*).
militante [mili'tante] *adj* militant.
militar [mili'tar] *adj* military ♦ *nm/f* soldier
♦ *vi* to serve in the army; (*fig*) to
militate, fight.
militarismo [milita'rismo] *nm* militarism.
milla ['miʎa] *nf* mile; ~ **marina** nautical
mile.
millar [mi'ʎar] *num* thousand; **a** ~**es** in
thousands.
millón [mi'ʎon] *num* million.
millonario, a [miʎo'narjo, a] *nm/f*
millionaire.
millonésimo, a [miʎo'nesimo, a] *num*
millionth.
mimado, a [mi'maðo, a] *adj* spoiled.
mimar [mi'mar] *vt* to spoil, pamper.
mimbre ['mimbre] *nm* wicker; **de** ~ wicker
cpd, wickerwork.
mimetismo [mime'tismo] *nm* mimicry.
mímica ['mimika] *nf* (*para comunicarse*)
sign language; (*imitación*) mimicry.
mimo ['mimo] *nm* (*caricia*) caress; (*de niño*)
spoiling; (*TEAT*) mime; (: *actor*) mime
artist.
mina ['mina] *nf* mine; (*pozo*) shaft; (*de
lápiz*) lead refill; **hullera** *o* ~ **de carbón**
coalmine.
minar [mi'nar] *vt* to mine; (*fig*) to
undermine.
mineral [mine'ral] *adj* mineral ♦ *nm* (*GEO*)
mineral; (*mena*) ore.
minería [mine'ria] *nf* mining.

minero, a [mi'nero, a] *adj* mining *cpd* ♦ *nm/f* miner.

miniatura [minja'tura] *adj inv*, *nf* miniature.

minicadena [minika'ðena] *nf* (*MUS*) mini hi-fi.

minicomputador [minikomputa'ðor] *nm* minicomputer.

minidisco [mini'ðisko] *nm* diskette.

minifalda [mini'falda] *nf* miniskirt.

minifundio [mini'fundjo] *nm* smallholding, small farm.

minimizar [minimi'θar] *vt* to minimize.

mínimo, a ['minimo, a] *adj* minimum; (*insignificante*) minimal ♦ *nm* minimum; **precio/salario** ~ minimum price/wage; **lo** ~ **que pueden hacer** the least they can do.

minino, a [mi'nino, a] *nm/f* (*fam*) puss, pussy.

ministerio [minis'terjo] *nm* ministry (*BRIT*), department (*US*); **M~ de Asuntos Exteriores** Foreign Office (*BRIT*), State Department (*US*); **M~ del Comercio e Industria** Department of Trade and Industry; **M~ de (la) Gobernación** *o* **del Interior** ≈ Home Office (*BRIT*), Ministry of the Interior; **M~ de Hacienda** Treasury (*BRIT*), Treasury Department (*US*).

ministro, a [mi'nistro, a] *nm/f* minister, secretary (*esp US*); **M~ de Hacienda** Chancellor of the Exchequer, Secretary of the Treasury (*US*); **M~ de (la) Gobernación** *o* **del Interior** ≈ Home Secretary (*BRIT*), Secretary of the Interior (*US*).

minoría [mino'ria] *nf* minority.

minorista [mino'rista] *nm* retailer.

mintiendo [min'tjendo] *etc vb V* **mentir**.

minucia [mi'nuθja] *nf* (*detalle insignificante*) trifle; (*bagatela*) mere nothing.

minuciosidad [minuθjosi'ðað] *nf* (*meticulosidad*) thoroughness, meticulousness.

minucioso, a [minu'θjoso, a] *adj* thorough, meticulous; (*prolijo*) very detailed.

minúsculo, a [mi'nuskulo, a] *adj* tiny, minute ♦ *nf* small letter; **minúsculas** *nfpl* (*TIP*) lower case *sg*.

minusvalía [minusßa'lia] *nf* physical handicap; (*COM*) depreciation, capital loss.

minusválido, a [minus'ßaliðo, a] *adj* (physically) handicapped *o* disabled ♦ *nm/f* disabled person.

minuta [mi'nuta] *nf* (*de comida*) menu; (*de abogado etc*) fee.

minutero [minu'tero] *nm* minute hand.

minuto [mi'nuto] *nm* minute.

Miño ['miɲo] *nm*: **el (río)** ~ the Miño.

mío, a ['mio, a] *adj, pron*: **el** ~ mine; **un amigo** ~ a friend of mine; **lo** ~ what is mine; **los** ~**s** my people, my relations.

miope ['mjope] *adj* short-sighted.

miopía [mjo'pia] *nf* near- *o* short-sightedness.

MIR [mir] *nm abr* (*POL*) = *Movimiento de Izquierda Revolucionaria*; (*ESP MED*) = *Médico Interno y Residente*.

mira ['mira] *nf* (*de arma*) sight(s) (*pl*); (*fig*) aim, intention; **de amplias/estrechas** ~**s** broad-/narrow-minded.

mirada [mi'raða] *nf* look, glance; (*expresión*) look, expression; ~ **de soslayo** sidelong glance; ~ **fija** stare, gaze; ~ **perdida** distant look; **echar una** ~ **a** to glance at; **levantar/bajar la** ~ to look up/down; **resistir la** ~ **de algn** to stare sb out.

mirado, a [mi'raðo, a] *adj* (*sensato*) sensible; (*considerado*) considerate; **bien/mal** ~ well/not well thought of.

mirador [mira'ðor] *nm* viewpoint, vantage point.

miramiento [mira'mjento] *nm* (*consideración*) considerateness; **tratar sin** ~**s a algn** to ride roughshod over sb.

mirar [mi'rar] *vt* to look at; (*observar*) to watch; (*considerar*) to consider, think over; (*vigilar, cuidar*) to watch, look after ♦ *vi* to look; (*ARQ*) to face; ~**se** *vr* (*dos personas*) to look at each other; ~ **algo/a algn de reojo** *o* **de través** to look askance at sth/sb; ~ **algo/a algn por encima del hombro** to look down on sth/sb; ~ **bien/mal** to think highly of/have a poor opinion of; ~ **fijamente** to stare *o* gaze at; ~ **por** (*fig*) to look after; ~ **por la ventana** to look out of the window; ~**se al espejo** to look at o.s. in the mirror; ~**se a los ojos** to look into each other's eyes.

mirilla [mi'riʎa] *nf* (*agujero*) spyhole, peephole.

mirlo ['mirlo] *nm* blackbird.

misa ['misa] *nf* mass; ~ **del gallo** midnight mass (*on Christmas Eve*); ~ **de difuntos** requiem mass; **como en** ~ in dead silence; **estos datos van a** ~ (*fig*) these facts are utterly trustworthy.

misántropo [mi'santropo] *nm* misanthrope, misanthropist.

miscelánea [misθe'lanea] *nf* miscellany.

miserable [mise'raßle] *adj* (*avaro*) mean, stingy; (*nimio*) miserable, paltry; (*lugar*) squalid; (*fam*) vile, despicable ♦ *nm/f* (*malvado*) rogue.

miseria [mi'serja] *nf* misery; (*pobreza*) poverty; (*tacañería*) meanness, stinginess; (*condiciones*) squalor; **una ~** a pittance.

misericordia [miseri'korðja] *nf* (*compasión*) compassion, pity; (*perdón*) forgiveness, mercy.

misil [mi'sil] *nm* missile.

misión [mi'sjon] *nf* mission; (*tarea*) job, duty; (*POL*) assignment; **misiones** *nfpl* (*REL*) overseas missions.

misionero, a [misjo'nero, a] *nm/f* missionary.

mismamente [misma'mente] *adv* (*fam: sólo*) only, just.

mismísimo, a [mis'misimo, a] *adj superlativo* selfsame, very (same).

mismo, a ['mismo, a] *adj* (*semejante*) same; (*después de pronombre*) -self; (*para énfasis*) very ♦ *adv*: **aquí/ayer/hoy ~** right here/only yesterday/this very day; **ahora ~** right now ♦ *conj*: **lo ~ que** just like, just as; **por lo ~** for the same reason; **el ~ traje** the same suit; **en ese ~ momento** at that very moment; **vino el ~ Ministro** the Minister himself came; **yo ~ lo vi** I saw it myself; **lo hizo por sí ~** he did it by himself; **lo ~ the** same (thing); **da lo ~** it's all the same; **quedamos en las mismas** we're no further forward.

misógino [mi'soxino] *nm* misogynist.

miss [mis] *nf* beauty queen.

misterio [mis'terjo] *nm* mystery; (*lo secreto*) secrecy.

misterioso, a [miste'rjoso, a] *adj* mysterious; (*inexplicable*) puzzling.

misticismo [misti'θismo] *nm* mysticism.

místico, a ['mistiko, a] *adj* mystic(al) ♦ *nm/f* mystic ♦ *nf* mysticism.

mitad [mi'tað] *nf* (*medio*) half; (*centro*) middle; **~ (y) ~** half-and-half; (*fig*) yes and no; **a ~ de precio** (at) half-price; **en o a ~ del camino** halfway along the road; **cortar por la ~** to cut through the middle.

mítico, a ['mitiko, a] *adj* mythical.

mitigar [miti'ɣar] *vt* to mitigate; (*dolor*) to relieve; (*sed*) to quench; (*ira*) to appease; (*preocupación*) to allay; (*soledad*) to alleviate.

mitigue [mi'tiɣe] *etc vb V* **mitigar**.

mitin ['mitin] *nm* (*esp POL*) meeting.

mito ['mito] *nm* myth.

mitología [mitolo'xia] *nf* mythology.

mitológico, a [mito'loxiko, a] *adj* mythological.

mixto, a ['miksto, a] *adj* mixed; (*comité*) joint.

ml. *abr* (= *mililitro*) ml.

mm. *abr* (= *milímetro*) mm.

m/n *abr* (*ECON*) = **moneda nacional.**

M.º *abr* (*POL*: = *Ministerio*) Min.

m/o *abr* (*COM*) = **mi orden.**

mobiliario [moβi'ljarjo] *nm* furniture.

MOC *nm abr* = **Movimiento de Objeción de Conciencia.**

mocasín [moka'sin] *nm* moccasin.

mocedad [moθe'ðað] *nf* youth.

mochila [mo'tʃila] *nf* rucksack (*BRIT*), backpack.

moción [mo'θjon] *nf* motion; **~ compuesta** (*POL*) composite motion.

moco ['moko] *nm* mucus; **limpiarse los ~s** to blow one's nose; **no es ~ de pavo** it's no trifle.

mocoso, a [mo'koso, a] *adj* snivelling; (*fig*) ill-bred ♦ *nm/f* (*fam*) brat.

moda ['moða] *nf* fashion; (*estilo*) style; **de o a la ~** in fashion, fashionable; **pasado de ~** out of fashion; **vestido a la última ~** trendily dressed.

modal [mo'ðal] *adj* modal ♦ *nm*: **~es** *nmpl* manners.

modalidad [moðali'ðað] *nf* (*clase*) kind, variety; (*manera*) way; (*INFORM*) mode; **~ de texto** (*INFORM*) text mode.

modelar [moðe'lar] *vt* to model.

modelo [mo'ðelo] *adj inv* model ♦ *nm/f* model ♦ *nm* (*patrón*) pattern; (*norma*) standard.

módem ['moðem] *nm* (*INFORM*) modem.

moderado, a [moðe'raðo, a] *adj* moderate.

moderar [moðe'rar] *vt* to moderate; (*violencia*) to restrain, control; (*velocidad*) to reduce; **~se** *vr* to restrain o.s., control o.s.

modernice [moðer'niθe] *etc vb V* **modernizar**.

modernizar [moðerni'θar] *vt* to modernize; (*INFORM*) to upgrade.

moderno, a [mo'ðerno, a] *adj* modern; (*actual*) present-day; (*equipo etc*) up-to-date.

modestia [mo'ðestja] *nf* modesty.

modesto, a [mo'ðesto, a] *adj* modest.

módico, a ['moðiko, a] *adj* moderate, reasonable.

modificar [moðifi'kar] *vt* to modify.

modifique [moði'fike] *etc vb V* **modificar**.

modismo [mo'ðismo] *nm* idiom.

modisto, a [mo'ðisto, a] *nm/f* dressmaker.

modo ['moðo] *nm* (*manera, forma*) way, manner; (*INFORM, MUS*) mode; (*LING*) mood; **~s** *nmpl* manners; **"~ de empleo"** "instructions for use"; **~ de gobierno**

form of government; **a ~ de** like; **de este ~** in this way; **de ningún ~** in no way; **de todos ~s** at any rate; **de un ~ u otro** (in) one way or another.

modorra [mo'ðorra] *nf* drowsiness.

modoso, a [mo'ðoso, a] *adj* (*educado*) quiet, well-mannered.

modulación [moðula'θjon] *nf* modulation; **~ de frecuencia** (*RADIO*) frequency modulation, FM.

módulo ['moðulo] *nm* module; (*de mueble*) unit.

mofarse [mo'farse] *vr*: **~ de** to mock, scoff at.

moflete [mo'flete] *nm* fat cheek, chubby cheek.

mogollón [moɣo'ʎon] (*fam*) *nm*: **~ de discos** *etc* loads of records *etc* ♦ *adv*: **un ~** a hell of a lot.

mohín [mo'in] *nm* (*mueca*) (wry) face; (*pucheros*) pout.

mohino, a [mo'ino, a] *adj* (*triste*) gloomy, depressed; (*enojado*) sulky.

moho ['moo] *nm* (*BOT*) mould, mildew; (*en metal*) rust.

mohoso, a [mo'oso, a] *adj* mouldy; rusty.

mojado, a [mo'xaðo, a] *adj* wet; (*húmedo*) damp; (*empapado*) drenched.

mojar [mo'xar] *vt* to wet; (*humedecer*) to damp(en), moisten; (*calar*) to soak; **~se** *vr* to get wet; **~ el pan en el café** to dip *o* dunk one's bread in one's coffee.

mojigato, a [moxi'ɣato, a] *adj* (*hipócrita*) hypocritical; (*santurrón*) sanctimonious; (*gazmoño*) prudish ♦ *nm/f* hypocrite; sanctimonious person; prude.

mojón [mo'xon] *nm* (*hito*) landmark; (*en un camino*) signpost; (*~ kilométrico*) milestone.

mol. *abr* (= *molécula*) mol.

molar [mo'lar] *nm* molar ♦ *vt* (*fam*): **lo que más me mola es** ... what I'm really into is ...; **¿te mola un pitillo?** do you fancy a smoke?

Moldavia [mol'ðaßja], **Moldova** [mol'ðoßa] *nf* Moldavia, Moldova.

moldavo, a [mol'ðaßo, a] *adj, nm/f* Moldavian, Moldovan.

molde ['molde] *nm* mould; (*vaciado*) cast; (*de costura*) pattern; (*fig*) model.

moldear [molde'ar] *vt* to mould; (*en yeso etc*) to cast.

mole ['mole] *nf* mass, bulk; (*edificio*) pile.

molécula [mo'lekula] *nf* molecule.

moler [mo'ler] *vt* to grind, crush; (*pulverizar*) to pound; (*trigo etc*) to mill; (*cansar*) to tire out, exhaust; **~ a algn a palos** to give sb a beating.

molestar [moles'tar] *vt* to bother; (*fastidiar*) to annoy; (*incomodar*) to inconvenience, put out; (*perturbar*) to trouble, upset ♦ *vi* to be a nuisance; **~se** *vr* to bother; (*incomodarse*) to go to a lot of trouble; (*ofenderse*) to take offence; **¿le molesta el ruido?** do you mind the noise?; **siento ~le** I'm sorry to trouble you.

molestia [mo'lestja] *nf* bother, trouble; (*incomodidad*) inconvenience; (*MED*) discomfort; **no es ninguna ~** it's no trouble at all.

molesto, a [mo'lesto, a] *adj* (*que fastidia*) annoying; (*incómodo*) inconvenient; (*inquieto*) uncomfortable, ill at ease; (*enfadado*) annoyed; **estar ~** (*MED*) to be in some discomfort; **estar ~ con algn** (*fig*) to be cross with sb; **me sentí ~** I felt embarrassed.

molido, a [mo'liðo, a] *adj* (*machacado*) ground; (*pulverizado*) powdered; **estar ~** (*fig*) to be exhausted *o* dead beat.

molinero [moli'nero] *nm* miller.

molinillo [moli'niʎo] *nm* hand mill; **~ de carne/café** mincer/coffee grinder.

molino [mo'lino] *nm* (*edificio*) mill; (*máquina*) grinder.

mollera [mo'ʎera] *nf* (*ANAT*) crown of the head; (*fam: seso*) brains *pl*; **duro de ~** (*estúpido*) thick.

Molucas [mo'lukas] *nfpl*: **las (Islas) ~** the Moluccas, the Molucca Islands.

molusco [mo'lusko] *nm* mollusc.

momentáneo, a [momen'taneo, a] *adj* momentary.

momento [mo'mento] *nm* (*gen*) moment; (*TEC*) momentum; **de ~** at the moment, for the moment; **en ese ~** at that moment, just then; **por el ~** for the time being.

momia ['momja] *nf* mummy.

mona ['mona] *nf V* **mono**.

Mónaco ['monako] *nm* Monaco.

monada [mo'naða] *nf* (*de niño*) charming habit; (*cosa primorosa*) lovely thing; (*chica*) pretty girl; **¡qué ~!** isn't it cute?

monaguillo [mona'ɣiʎo] *nm* altar boy.

monarca [mo'narka] *nm/f* monarch, ruler.

monarquía [monar'kia] *nf* monarchy.

monárquico, a [mo'narkiko, a] *nm/f* royalist, monarchist.

monasterio [monas'terjo] *nm* monastery.

Moncloa [mon'kloa] *nf*: **la ~** *official residence of the Spanish Prime Minister.*

monda ['monda] *nf* (*poda*) pruning; (: *de árbol*) lopping; (: *de fruta*) peeling; (*cáscara*) skin; **¡es la ~!** (*fam: fantástico*)

it's great!; (: *el colmo*) it's the limit!;
(: *persona*: *gracioso*) he's a knockout!
mondadientes [monda'ðjentes] *nm inv*
toothpick.
mondar [mon'dar] *vt* (*limpiar*) to clean;
(*pelar*) to peel; ~**se** *vr*: ~**se de risa** (*fam*)
to split one's sides laughing.
moneda [mo'neða] *nf* (*tipo de dinero*)
currency, money; (*pieza*) coin; **una** ~ **de
5 pesetas** a 5 peseta coin; ~ **de curso
legal** tender; ~ **extranjera** foreign
exchange; ~ **única** single currency; **es** ~
corriente (*fig*) it's common knowledge.
monedero [mone'ðero] *nm* purse.
monegasco, a [mone'ɣasko, a] *adj* of *o*
from Monaco, Monegasque ♦ *nm/f*
Monegasque.
monetario, a [mone'tarjo, a] *adj*
monetary, financial.
monetarista [moneta'rista] *adj, nm/f*
monetarist.
mongólico, a [mon'goliko, a] *adj, nm/f*
Mongol.
monigote [moni'ɣote] *nm* (*dibujo*) doodle;
(*de papel*) cut-out figure; (*pey*) wimp; *V tb*
Día de los (Santos) Inocentes.
monitor [moni'tor] *nm* (*INFORM*) monitor;
~ **en color** colour monitor; ~ **fósfor
verde** green screen.
monja ['monxa] *nf* nun.
monje ['monxe] *nm* monk.
mono, a ['mono, a] *adj* (*bonito*) lovely,
pretty; (*gracioso*) nice, charming ♦ *nm/f*
monkey, ape ♦ *nm* dungarees *pl*; (*overo-
les*) overalls *pl*; (*fam*: *de drogas*) cold
turkey; **una chica muy mona** a very
pretty girl; **dormir la** ~ to sleep it off.
monóculo [mo'nokulo] *nm* monocle.
monografía [monoɣra'fia] *nf* monograph.
monolingüe [mono'lingwe] *adj*
monolingual.
monólogo [mo'noloɣo] *nm* monologue.
monomando [mono'mando] *nm* (*tb*: **grifo**
~) mixer tap.
monoparental [monoparen'tal] *adj*: **familia**
~ single-parent family.
monopatín [monopa'tin] *nm* skateboard.
monopolice [monopo'liθe] *etc vb V*
monopolizar.
monopolio [mono'poljo] *nm* monopoly; ~
total absolute monopoly.
monopolista [monopo'lista] *adj, nm/f*
monopolist.
monopolizar [monopoli'θar] *vt* to
monopolize.
monosílabo, a [mono'silaβo, a] *adj*
monosyllabic ♦ *nm* monosyllable.
monotonía [monoto'nia] *nf* (*sonido*)

monotone; (*fig*) monotony.
monótono, a [mo'notono, a] *adj*
monotonous.
mono-usuario, a [monou'swarjo, a] *adj*
(*INFORM*) single-user.
monóxido [mo'noksiðo] *nm* monoxide; ~
de carbono carbon monoxide.
Mons. *abr* (*REL*) = **Monseñor**.
monseñor [monse'ɲor] *nm* monsignor.
monserga [mon'serɣa] *nf* (*lenguaje
confuso*) gibberish; (*tonterías*) drivel.
monstruo ['monstrwo] *nm* monster ♦ *adj
inv* fantastic.
monstruoso, a [mons'trwoso, a] *adj*
monstrous.
monta ['monta] *nf* total, sum; **de poca** ~
unimportant, of little account.
montacargas [monta'karɣas] *nm inv*
service lift (*BRIT*), freight elevator (*US*).
montador [monta'ðor] *nm* (*para montar*)
mounting block; (*profesión*) fitter; (*CINE*)
film editor.
montaje [mon'taxe] *nm* assembly;
(*organización*) fitting up; (*TEAT*) décor;
(*CINE*) montage.
montante [mon'tante] *nm* (*poste*) upright;
(*soporte*) stanchion; (*ARQ*: *de puerta*)
transom; (: *de ventana*) mullion; (*suma*)
amount, total.
montaña [mon'taɲa] *nf* (*monte*) mountain;
(*sierra*) mountains *pl*, mountainous area;
(*AM*: *selva*) forest; ~ **rusa** roller coaster.
montañero, a [monta'ɲero, a] *adj*
mountain *cpd* ♦ *nm/f* mountaineer,
climber.
montañés, esa [monta'ɲes, esa] *adj*
mountain *cpd*; (*de Santander*) of *o* from
the Santander region ♦ *nm/f* highlander;
native *o* inhabitant of the Santander
region.
montañismo [monta'ɲismo] *nm*
mountaineering, climbing.
montañoso, a [monta'ɲoso, a] *adj*
mountainous.
montar [mon'tar] *vt* (*subir a*) to mount, get
on; (*caballo etc*) to ride; (*TEC*) to
assemble, put together; (*negocio*) to set
up; (*colocar*) to lift on to; (*CINE*: *película*)
to edit; (*TEAT*: *obra*) to stage, put on;
(*CULIN*: *batir*) to whip, beat
♦ *vi* to mount, get on; (*sobresalir*) to
overlap; ~ **en cólera** to get angry; ~ **un
número** *o* **numerito** to make a scene;
tanto monta it makes no odds.
montaraz [monta'raθ] *adj* mountain *cpd*,
highland *cpd*; (*pey*) uncivilized.
monte ['monte] *nm* (*montaña*) mountain;
(*bosque*) woodland; (*área sin cultivar*) wild

area, wild country; ~ **de piedad**
pawnshop; ~ **alto** forest; ~ **bajo**
scrub(land).

montera [mon'tera] *nf* (*sombrero*) cloth
cap; (*de torero*) bullfighter's hat.

monto ['monto] *nm* total, amount.

montón [mon'ton] *nm* heap, pile; **un ~ de**
(*fig*) heaps of, lots of; **a montones** by the
score, galore.

montura [mon'tura] *nf* (*cabalgadura*)
mount; (*silla*) saddle; (*arreos*) harness;
(*de joya*) mounting; (*de gafas*) frame.

monumental [monumen'tal] *adj* (*tb fig*)
monumental; **zona ~** area of historical
interest.

monumento [monu'mento] *nm* monument;
(*de conmemoración*) memorial.

monzón [mon'θon] *nm* monsoon.

moña ['moɲa] *nf* hair ribbon.

moño ['moɲo] *nm* (*de pelo*) bun; **estar
hasta el ~** (*fam*) to be fed up to the back
teeth.

MOPTMA *nm abr* = **Ministerio de Obras
Públicas, Transporte y Medio Ambiente.**

moqueta [mo'keta] *nf* fitted carpet.

moquillo [mo'kiʎo] *nm* (*enfermedad*)
distemper.

mora ['mora] *nf* (*BOT*) mulberry;
(: *zarzamora*) blackberry; (*COM*): **en ~** in
arrears.

morado, a [mo'raðo, a] *adj* purple, violet
♦ *nm* bruise ♦ *nf* (*casa*) dwelling, abode;
pasarlas moradas to have a tough time
of it.

moral [mo'ral] *adj* moral ♦ *nf* (*ética*) ethics
pl; (*moralidad*) morals *pl*, morality;
(*ánimo*) morale; **tener baja la ~** to be in
low spirits.

moraleja [mora'lexa] *nf* moral.

moralice [mora'liθe] *etc vb* V **moralizar.**

moralidad [morali'ðað] *nf* morals *pl*,
morality.

moralizar [morali'θar] *vt* to moralize.

morar [mo'rar] *vi* to live, dwell.

moratón [mora'ton] *nm* bruise.

moratoria [mora'torja] *nf* moratorium.

morbo ['morβo] *nm* (*fam*) morbid pleasure.

morbosidad [morβosi'ðað] *nf* morbidity.

morboso, a [mor'βoso, a] *adj* morbid.

morcilla [mor'θiʎa] *nf* blood sausage,
≈ black pudding (*BRIT*).

mordaz [mor'ðaθ] *adj* (*crítica*) biting,
scathing.

mordaza [mor'ðaθa] *nf* (*para la boca*) gag;
(*TEC*) clamp.

morder [mor'ðer] *vt* to bite; (*mordisquear*)
to nibble; (*fig: consumir*) to eat away, eat
into ♦ *vi*, **~se** *vr* to bite; **está que muerde**

he's hopping mad; **~se la lengua** to hold
one's tongue.

mordida [mor'ðiða] *nf* (*AM fam*) bribe.

mordisco [mor'ðisko] *nm* bite.

mordisquear [morðiske'ar] *vt* to nibble at.

moreno, a [mo'reno, a] *adj* (*color*) (dark)
brown; (*de tez*) dark; (*de pelo ~*) dark-
haired; (*negro*) black ♦ *nm/f* (*de tez*) dark-
skinned man/woman; (*de pelo*) dark-
haired man/woman.

morfina [mor'fina] *nf* morphine.

morfinómano, a [morfi'nomano, a] *adj*
addicted to hard drugs ♦ *nm/f* drug
addict.

morgue ['morgue] *nf* (*AM*) mortuary (*BRIT*),
morgue (*US*).

moribundo, a [mori'βundo, a] *adj* dying
♦ *nm/f* dying person.

morir [mo'rir] *vi* to die; (*fuego*) to die
down; (*luz*) to go out; **~se** *vr* to die; (*fig*)
to be dying; (*FERRO etc: vías*) to end;
(*calle*) to come out; **fue muerto a tiros/en
un accidente** he was shot (dead)/was
killed in an accident; **~ de frío/hambre**
to die of cold/starve to death; **¡me
muero de hambre!** (*fig*) I'm starving!;
~se por algo to be dying for sth; **~se
por algn** to be crazy about sb.

mormón, ona [mor'mon, ona] *nm/f*
Mormon.

moro, a ['moro, a] *adj* Moorish ♦ *nm/f*
Moor; **¡hay ~s en la costa!** watch out!

moroso, a [mo'roso, a] *adj* (*lento*) slow
♦ *nm* (*COM*) bad debtor, defaulter;
deudor ~ (*COM*) slow payer.

morral [mo'rral] *nm* haversack.

morriña [mo'rriɲa] *nf* homesickness; **tener
~** to be homesick.

morro ['morro] *nm* (*ZOOL*) snout, nose;
(*AUTO, AVIAT*) nose; (*fam: labio*) (thick)
lip; **beber a ~** to drink from the bottle;
caer de ~ to nosedive; **estar de ~s (con
algn)** to be in a bad mood (with sb);
tener ~ to have a nerve.

morrocotudo, a [morroko'tuðo, a] *adj*
(*fam*) (*fantástico*) smashing; (*riña, golpe*)
tremendous; (*fuerte*) strong; (*pesado*)
heavy; (*difícil*) awkward.

morsa ['morsa] *nf* walrus.

morse ['morse] *nm* Morse (code).

mortadela [morta'ðela] *nf* mortadella,
bologna sausage.

mortaja [mor'taxa] *nf* shroud; (*TEC*)
mortise; (*AM*) cigarette paper.

mortal [mor'tal] *adj* mortal; (*golpe*) deadly.

mortalidad [mortali'ðað], **mortandad**
[mortan'dað] *nf* mortality.

mortecino, a [morte'θino, a] *adj* (*débil*)

weak; (*luz*) dim; (*color*) dull.
mortero [mor'tero] *nm* mortar.
mortífero, a [mor'tifero, a] *adj* deadly,
lethal.
mortificar [mortifi'kar] *vt* to mortify;
(*atormentar*) to torment.
mortifique [morti'fike] *etc vb V*
mortificar.
mortuorio, a [mor'tworjo, a] *adj*
mortuary, death *cpd.*
Mosa ['mosa] *nm*: **el (Río)** ~ the Meuse.
mosaico [mo'saiko] *nm* mosaic.
mosca ['moska] *nf* fly; **por si las** ~**s** just in
case; **estar** ~ (*desconfiar*) to smell a rat;
tener la ~ **en** *o* **detrás de la oreja** to be
wary.
moscovita [mosko'ßita] *adj* Muscovite,
Moscow *cpd* ♦ *nm/f* Muscovite.
Moscú [mos'ku] *nm* Moscow.
mosquear [moske'ar] (*fam*) *vt* (*hacer
sospechar*) to make suspicious; (*fastidiar*)
to annoy; ~**se** *vr* (*enfadarse*) to get
annoyed; (*ofenderse*) to take offence.
mosquita [mos'kita] *nf*: **parece una** ~
muerta he looks as though butter
wouldn't melt in his mouth.
mosquitero [moski'tero] *nm* mosquito
net.
mosquito [mos'kito] *nm* mosquito.
Mossos ['mosos] *nmpl*: ~ **d'Esquadra**
Catalan police; *V tb* **policía.**
mostaza [mos'taθa] *nf* mustard.
mosto ['mosto] *nm* unfermented grape
juice.
mostrador [mostra'ðor] *nm* (*de tienda*)
counter; (*de café*) bar.
mostrar [mos'trar] *vt* to show; (*exhibir*) to
display, exhibit; (*explicar*) to explain;
~**se** *vr*: ~**se amable** to be kind; to prove
to be kind; **no se muestra muy
inteligente** he doesn't seem (to be) very
intelligent; ~ **en pantalla** (*INFORM*) to
display.
mota ['mota] *nf* speck, tiny piece; (*en
diseño*) dot.
mote ['mote] *nm* (*apodo*) nickname.
motín [mo'tin] *nm* (*del pueblo*) revolt,
rising; (*del ejército*) mutiny.
motivación [motißa'θjon] *nf* motivation.
motivar [moti'ßar] *vt* (*causar*) to cause,
motivate; (*explicar*) to explain, justify.
motivo [mo'tißo] *nm* motive, reason;
(*ARTE, MUS*) motif; **con** ~ **de** (*debido a*)
because of; (*en ocasión de*) on the
occasion of; (*con el fin de*) in order to; **sin**
~ for no reason at all.
moto ['moto] *nf*, **motocicleta**
[motoθi'kleta] *nf* motorbike (*BRIT*),

motorcycle.
motoneta [moto'neta] *nf* (*AM*) Vespa ®.
motor, a [mo'tor, a] *adj* (*TEC*) motive;
(*ANAT*) motor ♦ *nm* motor, engine; ~ **a
chorro** *o* **de reacción/de explosión** jet
engine/internal combustion engine ♦ *nf*
motorboat.
motorismo [moto'rismo] *nm*
motorcycling.
motorista [moto'rista] *nm/f* (*esp AM*:
automovilista) motorist; (: *motociclista*)
motorcyclist.
motorizado, a [motori'θaðo, a] *adj*
motorized.
motosierra [moto'sjerra] *nf* mechanical
saw.
motriz [mo'triz] *adj*: **fuerza** ~ motive
power; (*fig*) driving force.
movedizo, a [moße'ðiθo, a] *adj* (*inseguro*)
unsteady; (*fig*) unsettled, changeable;
(*persona*) fickle.
mover [mo'ßer] *vt* to move; (*cambiar de
lugar*) to shift; (*cabeza: para negar*) to
shake; (: *para asentir*) to nod; (*accionar*) to
drive; (*fig*) to cause, provoke; ~**se** *vr* to
move; (*mar*) to get rough; (*viento*) to rise;
(*fig: apurarse*) to get a move on;
(: *transformarse*) to be on the move.
movible [mo'ßißle] *adj* (*no fijo*) movable;
(*móvil*) mobile; (*cambiadizo*)
changeable.
movido, a [mo'ßiðo, a] *adj* (*FOTO*) blurred;
(*persona: activo*) active; (*mar*) rough; (*día*)
hectic ♦ *nf* move; **la movida madrileña**
the Madrid scene.
móvil ['moßil] *adj* mobile; (*pieza de
máquina*) moving; (*mueble*) movable ♦ *nm*
motive.
movilice [moßi'liθe] *etc vb V* **movilizar.**
movilidad [moßili'ðað] *nf* mobility.
movilizar [moßili'θar] *vt* to mobilize.
movimiento [moßi'mjento] *nm* (*gen*,
LITERATURA, POL) movement; (*TEC*)
motion; (*actividad*) activity; (*MUS*)
tempo; **el M~** the Falangist Movement;
~ **de bloques** (*INFORM*) block move; ~ **de
mercancías** (*COM*) turnover, volume of
business; ~ **obrero/sindical** workers'/
trade union movement; ~ **sísmico** earth
tremor.
Mozambique [moθam'bike] *nm*
Mozambique.
mozambiqueño, a [moθambi'keɲo, a] *adj*,
nm/f Mozambican.
mozo, a ['moθo, a] *adj* (*joven*) young;
(*soltero*) single, unmarried ♦ *nm/f* (*joven*)
youth, young man/girl; (*camarero*)
waiter; (*camarera*) waitress; ~ **de**

estación porter.

MPAIAC [emepa'jak] *nm abr* (*ESP POL*) = *Movimiento para la Autodeterminación y la Independencia del Archipiélago Canario*.

mucama [mu'kama] *nf* (*AM*) maid.

muchacho, a [mu'tʃatʃo, a] *nm/f* (*niño*) boy/girl; (*criado*) servant/servant *o* maid.

muchedumbre [mutʃe'ðumbre] *nf* crowd.

muchísimo, a [mu'tʃisimo, a] *adj* (*superlativo de* mucho) lots and lots of, ever so much ♦ *adv* ever so much.

═══════════ *PALABRA CLAVE*

mucho, a ['mutʃo, a] *adj* **1** (*cantidad*) a lot of, much; (*número*) lots of, a lot of, many; ~ **dinero** a lot of money; **hace** ~ **calor** it's very hot; **muchas amigas** lots *o* a lot of *o* many friends

2 (*sg: fam*): **ésta es mucha casa para él** this house is much too big for him; **había** ~ **borracho** there were a lot *o* lots of drunks

♦ *pron*: **tengo** ~ **que hacer** I've got a lot to do; ~**s dicen que** ... a lot of people say that ...; *V tb* **tener**

♦ *adv* **1**: **me gusta** ~ I like it a lot *o* very much; **lo siento** ~ I'm very sorry; **come** ~ he eats a lot; **trabaja** ~ he works hard; **¿te vas a quedar** ~? are you going to be staying long?; ~ **más/menos** much *o* a lot more/less

2 (*respuesta*) very; **¿estás cansado? – ¡**~**!** are you tired? – very!

3 (*locuciones*): **como** ~ at (the) most; **el mejor con** ~ by far the best; **¡ni** ~ **menos!** far from it!; **no es rico ni** ~ **menos** he's far from being rich

4: **por** ~ **que: por** ~ **que le creas** however much *o* no matter how much you believe him.

────────────────────────

muda ['muða] *nf* (*de ropa*) change of clothing; (*ZOOL*) moult; (*de serpiente*) slough.

mudanza [mu'ðanθa] *nf* (*cambio*) change; (*de casa*) move; **estar de** ~ to be moving.

mudar [mu'ðar] *vt* to change; (*ZOOL*) to shed ♦ *vi* to change; ~**se** *vr* (*la ropa*) to change; ~**se de casa** to move house.

mudo, a ['muðo, a] *adj* dumb; (*callado, película*) silent; (*LING: letra*) mute; (: *consonante*) voiceless; **quedarse** ~ (**de**) (*fig*) to be dumb with; **quedarse** ~ **de asombro** to be speechless.

mueble ['mweβle] *nm* piece of furniture; ~**s** *nmpl* furniture *sg*.

mueble-bar [mweβle'βar] *nm* cocktail cabinet.

mueca ['mweka] *nf* face, grimace; **hacer** ~**s a** to make faces at.

muela ['mwela] *etc vb V* **moler** ♦ *nf* (*diente*) tooth; (: *de atrás*) molar; (*de molino*) millstone; (*de afilar*) grindstone; ~ **del juicio** wisdom tooth.

muelle ['mweʎe] *adj* (*blando*) soft; (*fig*) soft, easy ♦ *nm* spring; (*NAUT*) wharf; (*malecón*) jetty.

muera ['mwera] *etc vb V* **morir**.

muerda ['mwerða] *etc vb V* **morder**.

muermo ['mwermo] *nm* (*fam*) wimp.

muerte ['mwerte] *nf* death; (*homicidio*) murder; **dar** ~ **a** to kill; **de mala** ~ (*fam*) lousy, rotten; **es la** ~ (*fam*) it's deadly boring.

muerto, a ['mwerto, a] *pp de* **morir** ♦ *adj* dead; (*color*) dull ♦ *nm/f* dead man/ woman; (*difunto*) deceased; (*cadáver*) corpse; **cargar con el** ~ (*fam*) to carry the can; **echar el** ~ **a algn** to pass the buck; **hacer el** ~ (*nadando*) to float; **estar** ~ **de cansancio** to be dead tired.

muesca ['mweska] *nf* nick.

muestra ['mwestra] *etc vb V* **mostrar** ♦ *nf* (*señal*) indication, sign; (*demostración*) demonstration; (*prueba*) proof; (*estadística*) sample; (*modelo*) model, pattern; (*testimonio*) token; **dar** ~**s de** to show signs of; ~ **al azar** (*COM*) random sample.

muestrario [mwes'trarjo] *nm* collection of samples; (*exposición*) showcase.

muestreo [mwes'treo] *nm* sample, sampling.

mueva [mweβa] *etc vb V* **mover**.

mugir [mu'xir] *vi* (*vaca*) to moo.

mugre ['muɣre] *nf* dirt, filth, muck.

mugriento, a [mu'ɣrjento, a] *adj* dirty, filthy mucky.

mugroso, a [muɣ'roso, a] *adj* (*AM*) filthy, grubby.

muja ['muxa] *etc vb V* **mugir**.

mujer [mu'xer] *nf* woman; (*esposa*) wife.

mujeriego [muxe'rjeɣo] *nm* womaniser.

mula ['mula] *nf* mule.

muladar [mula'ðar] *nm* dungheap, dunghill.

mulato, a [mu'lato, a] *adj*, *nm/f* mulatto.

muleta [mu'leta] *nf* (*para andar*) crutch; (*TAUR*) stick with red cape attached.

muletilla [mule'tiʎa] *nf* (*palabra*) pet word, tag; (*de cómico*) catch phrase.

mullido, a [mu'ʎiðo, a] *adj* (*cama*) soft; (*hierba*) soft, springy.

multa ['multa] *nf* fine; **echar** *o* **poner una** ~

a to fine.

multar [mul'tar] *vt* to fine; (*DEPORTE*) to penalize.

multiacceso [multjak'θeso] *adj* (*INFORM*) multi-access.

multicine [multi'θine] *nm* multiscreen cinema.

multicolor [multiko'lor] *adj* multicoloured.

multicopista [multiko'pista] *nm* duplicator.

multimillonario, a [multimiʎo'narjo, a] *adj* (*contrato*) multimillion pound *o* dollar *cpd* ♦ *nm/f* multimillionaire/-millionairess.

multinacional [multinaθjo'nal] *adj, nf* multinational.

múltiple ['multiple] *adj* multiple; (*pl*) many, numerous; **de tarea** ~ (*INFORM*) multi-tasking; **de usuario** ~ (*INFORM*) multi-user.

multiplicar [multipli'kar] *vt* (*MAT*) to multiply; (*fig*) to increase; ~**se** *vr* (*BIO*) to multiply; (*fig*) to be everywhere at once.

multiplique [multi'plike] *etc vb V* **multiplicar**.

múltiplo ['multiplo] *adj, nm* multiple.

multitud [multi'tuð] *nf* (*muchedumbre*) crowd; ~ **de** lots of.

multitudinario, a [multituði'narjo, a] *adj* (*numeroso*) multitudinous; (*de masa*) mass *cpd*.

mundanal [munda'nal] *adj* worldly; **lejos del** ~ **ruido** far from the madding crowd.

mundano, a [mun'dano, a] *adj* worldly; (*de moda*) fashionable.

mundial [mun'djal] *adj* world-wide, universal; (*guerra, récord*) world *cpd*.

mundialmente [mundjal'mente] *adv* worldwide; ~ **famoso** world-famous.

mundo ['mundo] *nm* world; (*ámbito*) world, circle; **el otro** ~ the next world; **el** ~ **del espectáculo** show business; **todo el** ~ everybody; **tener** ~ to be experienced, know one's way around; **el** ~ **es un pañuelo** it's a small world; **no es nada del otro** ~ it's nothing special; **se le cayó el** ~ **(encima)** his world fell apart.

Munich ['munitʃ] *nm* Munich.

munición [muni'θjon] *nf* (*MIL: provisiones*) stores *pl*, supplies *pl*; (*: de armas*) ammunition.

municipal [muniθi'pal] *adj* (*elección*) municipal; (*concejo*) town *cpd*, local; (*piscina etc*) public ♦ *nm* (*guardia*) policeman.

municipio [muni'θipjo] *nm* (*ayuntamiento*) town council, corporation; (*territorio administrativo*) town, municipality.

muñeca [mu'ɲeka] *nf* (*ANAT*) wrist; (*juguete*) doll.

muñeco [mu'ɲeko] *nm* (*figura*) figure; (*marioneta*) puppet; (*fig*) puppet, pawn; (*niño*) pretty little boy; ~ **de nieve** snowman.

muñequera [muɲe'kera] *nf* wristband.

muñón [mu'ɲon] *nm* (*ANAT*) stump.

mural [mu'ral] *adj* mural, wall *cpd* ♦ *nm* mural.

muralla [mu'raʎa] *nf* (*city*) wall(s) (*pl*).

murciano, a [mur'θjano, a] *adj* of *o* from Murcia ♦ *nm/f* native *o* inhabitant of Murcia.

murciélago [mur'θjelaɣo] *nm* bat.

murga ['murɣa] *nf* (*banda*) band of street musicians; **dar la** ~ to be a nuisance.

murmullo [mur'muʎo] *nm* murmur(ing); (*cuchicheo*) whispering; (*de arroyo*) murmur, rippling; (*de hojas, viento*) rustle, rustling; (*ruido confuso*) hum(ming).

murmuración [murmura'θjon] *nf* gossip; (*críticas*) backbiting.

murmurador, a [murmura'ðor, a] *adj* gossiping; (*criticón*) backbiting ♦ *nm/f* gossip; backbiter.

murmurar [murmu'rar] *vi* to murmur, whisper; (*criticar*) to criticize; (*cotillear*) to gossip.

muro ['muro] *nm* wall; ~ **de contención** retaining wall.

mus [mus] *nm* card game.

musaraña [musa'raɲa] *nf* (*ZOOL*) shrew; (*insecto*) creepy-crawly; **pensar en las** ~**s** to daydream.

muscular [musku'lar] *adj* muscular.

músculo ['muskulo] *nm* muscle.

musculoso, a [musku'loso, a] *adj* muscular.

museo [mu'seo] *nm* museum; ~ **de arte** *o* **de pintura** art gallery; ~ **de cera** waxworks.

musgo ['musɣo] *nm* moss.

musical [musi'kal] *adj, nm* musical.

músico, a ['musiko, a] *adj* musical ♦ *nm/f* musician ♦ *nf* music; **irse con la música a otra parte** to clear off.

musitar [musi'tar] *vt, vi* to mutter, mumble.

muslo ['muslo] *nm* thigh; (*de pollo*) leg, drumstick.

mustio, a ['mustjo, a] *adj* (*persona*) depressed, gloomy; (*planta*) faded, withered.

musulmán, ana [musul'man, ana] *nm/f* Moslem, Muslim.

mutación [muta'θjon] *nf* (*BIO*) mutation;

(: *cambio*) (sudden) change.
mutilar [muti'lar] *vt* to mutilate; (*a una persona*) to maim.
mutis ['mutis] *nm inv* (*TEAT*) exit; **hacer ~** (*TEAT*: *retirarse*) to exit, go off; (*fig*) to say nothing.
mutismo [mu'tismo] *nm* silence.
mutualidad [mutwali'ðað] *nf* (*reciprocidad*) mutual character; (*asociación*) friendly o benefit (*US*) society.
mutuamente [mutwa'mente] *adv* mutually.
mutuo, a ['mutwo, a] *adj* mutual.
muy [mwi] *adv* very; (*demasiado*) too; **M~ Señor mío** Dear Sir; **~ bien** (*de acuerdo*) all right; **~ de noche** very late at night; **eso es ~ de él** that's just like him; **eso es ~ español** that's typically Spanish.

N n

N, n ['ene] *nf* (*letra*) N, n; **N de Navarra** N for Nellie (*BRIT*) o Nan (*US*).
N *abr* (= *norte*) N.
N. *abr* (= *noviembre*) Nov; (*AM*: = *moneda nacional*) local currency; **le entregaron sólo N.$2.000** they only gave him $2000 pesos.
N.º *abr* (= *número*) No.
n. *abr* (*LING*: = *nombre*) n; (= *nacido*) b.
n/ *abr* = *nuestro, a*.
nabo ['naβo] *nm* turnip.
nácar ['nakar] *nm* mother-of-pearl.
nacer [na'θer] *vi* to be born; (*huevo*) to hatch; (*vegetal*) to sprout; (*río*) to rise; (*fig*) to begin, originate, have its origins; **nació para poeta** he was born to be a poet; **nadie nace enseñado** we all have to learn; **nació una sospecha en su mente** a suspicion formed in her mind.
nacido, a [na'θiðo, a] *adj* born; **recién ~** newborn.
naciente [na'θjente] *adj* new, emerging; (*sol*) rising.
nacimiento [naθi'mjento] *nm* birth; (*fig*) birth, origin; (*de Navidad*) Nativity; (*linaje*) descent, family; (*de río*) source; **ciego de ~** blind from birth.
nación [na'θjon] *nf* nation; (*pueblo*) people; **Naciones Unidas** United Nations.
nacional [naθjo'nal] *adj* national; (*COM,*

ECON) domestic, home *cpd*.
nacionalice [naθjona'liθe] *etc vb V* nacionalizar.
nacionalidad [naθjonali'ðað] *nf* nationality; (*ESP POL*) autonomous region.
nacionalismo [naθjona'lismo] *nm* nationalism.
nacionalista [naθjona'lista] *adj, nm/f* nationalist.
nacionalizar [naθjonali'θar] *vt* to nationalize; **~se** *vr* (*persona*) to become naturalized.
nada ['naða] *pron* nothing ♦ *adv* not at all, in no way ♦ *nf* nothingness; **no decir ~** (*más*) to say nothing (else), not to say anything (else); **¡~ más!** that's all; **de ~** don't mention it; **~ de eso** nothing of the kind; **antes de ~** right away; **como si ~** as if it didn't matter; **no ha sido ~** it's nothing; **la ~** the void.
nadador, a [naða'ðor, a] *nm/f* swimmer.
nadar [na'ðar] *vi* to swim; **~ en la abundancia** (*fig*) to be rolling in money.
nadie ['naðje] *pron* nobody, no-one; **~ habló** nobody spoke; **no había ~** there was nobody there, there wasn't anybody there; **es un don ~** he's a nobody o nonentity.
nadita [na'ðita] (*esp AM: fam*) = **nada**.
nado ['naðo]: **a ~** *adv*: **pasar a ~** to swim across.
nafta ['nafta] *nf* (*AM*) petrol (*BRIT*), gas(oline) (*US*).
naftalina [nafta'lina] *nf*: **bolas de ~** mothballs.
náhuatl ['nawatl] *adj, nm* Nahuatl.
naipe ['naipe] *nm* (playing) card; **~s** *nmpl* cards.
nal. *abr* (= *nacional*) nat.
nalgas ['nalɣas] *nfpl* buttocks.
Namibia [na'miβja] *nf* Namibia.
nana ['nana] *nf* lullaby.
napias ['napjas] *nfpl* (*fam*) conk *sg*.
Nápoles ['napoles] *nf* Naples.
napolitano, a [napoli'tano, a] *adj* of o from Naples, Neapolitan ♦ *nm/f* Neapolitan.
naranja [na'ranxa] *adj inv, nf* orange; **media ~** (*fam*) better half; **¡~s de la China!** nonsense!
naranjada [naran'xaða] *nf* orangeade.
naranjo [na'ranxo] *nm* orange tree.
Narbona [nar'βona] *nf* Narbonne.
narcisista [narθi'sista] *adj* narcissistic.
narciso [nar'θiso] *nm* narcissus.
narcotice [narko'tiθe] *etc vb V* **narcotizar**.
narcótico, a [nar'kotiko, a] *adj, nm* narcotic.

narcotizar [narkoti'θar] *vt* to drug.
narcotraficante [narkotrafi'kante] *nm/f* narcotics *o* drug trafficker.
narcotráfico [narko'trafiko] *nm* narcotics *o* drug trafficking.
nardo ['narðo] *nm* lily.
narices [na'riθes] *nfpl V* **nariz.**
narigón, ona [nari'ɣon, ona], **narigudo, a** [nari'ɣuðo, a] *adj* big-nosed.
nariz [na'riθ] *nf* nose; **narices** *nfpl* nostrils; **¡narices!** (*fam*) rubbish!; **delante de las narices de algn** under one's (very) nose; **estar hasta las narices** to be completely fed up; **meter las narices en algo** to poke one's nose into sth.
narración [narra'θjon] *nf* narration.
narrador, a [narra'ðor, a] *nm/f* narrator.
narrar [na'rrar] *vt* to narrate, recount.
narrativo, a [narra'tiβo, a] *adj* narrative
♦ *nf* narrative, story.
nasal [na'sal] *adj* nasal.
N.ª S.ra *abr* = **Nuestra Señora.**
nata ['nata] *nf* cream (*tb fig*); (*en leche cocida etc*) skin; ~ **batida** whipped cream.
natación [nata'θjon] *nf* swimming.
natal [na'tal] *adj* natal; (*país*) native; **ciudad** ~ home town.
natalicio [nata'liθjo] *nm* birthday.
natalidad [natali'ðað] *nf* birth rate.
natillas [na'tiʎas] *nfpl* (egg) custard *sg.*
natividad [natiβi'ðað] *nf* nativity.
nativo, a [na'tiβo, a] *adj, nm/f* native.
nato, a ['nato, a] *adj* born; **un músico** ~ a born musician.
natural [natu'ral] *adj* natural; (*fruta etc*) fresh ♦ *nm/f* native ♦ *nm* disposition, temperament; **buen** ~ good nature; **fruta al** ~ fruit in its own juice.
naturaleza [natura'leθa] *nf* nature; (*género*) nature, kind; ~ **muerta** still life.
naturalice [natura'liθe] *etc vb V* **naturalizarse.**
naturalidad [naturali'ðað] *nf* naturalness.
naturalización [naturaliθa'θjon] *nf* naturalization.
naturalizarse [naturali'θarse] *vr* to become naturalized; (*aclimatarse*) to become acclimatized.
naturalmente [natural'mente] *adv* naturally; **¡~!** of course!
naturista [natu'rista] *adj* (*MED*) naturopathic ♦ *nm/f* naturopath.
naufragar [naufra'ɣar] *vi* (*barco*) to sink; (*gente*) to be shipwrecked; (*fig*) to fail.
naufragio [nau'fraxjo] *nm* shipwreck.
náufrago, a ['naufraɣo, a] *nm/f* castaway, shipwrecked person.

naufrague [nau'fraɣe] *etc vb V* **naufragar.**
náusea ['nausea] *nf* nausea; **me da** ~**s** it makes me feel sick.
nauseabundo, a [nausea'ßundo, a] *adj* nauseating, sickening.
náutico, a ['nautiko, a] *adj* nautical; **club** ~ sailing *o* yacht club ♦ *nf* navigation, seamanship.
navaja [na'βaxa] *nf* (*cortaplumas*) clasp knife (*BRIT*), penknife; ~ **(de afeitar)** razor.
navajazo [naβa'xaθo] *nm* (*herida*) gash; (*golpe*) slash.
naval [na'ßal] *adj* (*MIL*) naval; **construcción** ~ shipbuilding; **sector** ~ shipbuilding industry.
Navarra [na'ßarra] *nf* Navarre.
navarro, a [na'ßarro, a] *adj* of *o* from Navarre, Navarrese ♦ *nm/f* Navarrese ♦ *nm* (*LING*) Navarrese.
nave ['naße] *nf* (*barco*) ship, vessel; (*ARQ*) nave; ~ **espacial** spaceship; **quemar las** ~**s** to burn one's boats.
navegación [naßeɣa'θjon] *nf* navigation; (*viaje*) sea journey; ~ **aérea** air traffic; ~ **costera** coastal shipping; ~ **fluvial** river navigation.
navegante [naße'ɣante] *nm/f* navigator.
navegar [naße'ɣar] *vi* (*barco*) to sail; (*avión*) to fly ♦ *vt* to sail; to fly; (*dirigir el rumbo de*) to navigate.
navegue [na'ßeɣe] *etc vb V* **navegar.**
navidad [naßi'ðað] *nf* Christmas; ~**es** *nfpl* Christmas time *sg*; **día de** ~ Christmas Day; **por** ~**es** at Christmas (time); **¡felices** ~**es!** Merry Christmas.
navideño, a [naßi'ðeɲo, a] *adj* Christmas *cpd.*
navío [na'ßio] *nm* ship.
nazi ['naθi] *adj, nm/f* Nazi.
nazismo [na'θismo] *nm* Nazism.
n/cta *abr* (*COM*) = **nuestra cuenta.**
N. de la R. *abr* (= *nota de la redacción*) editor's note.
N. de la T./del T. *abr* (= *nota de la traductora/del traductor*) translator's note.
NE *abr* (= *nor(d)este*) NE.
neblina [ne'ßlina] *nf* mist.
nebuloso, a [neßu'loso, a] *adj* foggy; (*calinoso*) misty; (*indefinido*) nebulous, vague ♦ *nf* nebula.
necedad [neθe'ðað] *nf* foolishness; (*una* ~) foolish act.
necesario, a [neθe'sarjo, a] *adj* necessary; **si fuera** *o* **fuese** ~ if need(s) be.
neceser [neθe'ser] *nm* vanity case; (*bolsa grande*) holdall.
necesidad [neθesi'ðað] *nf* need; (*lo*

inevitable) necessity; (*miseria*) poverty, need; **en caso de** ~ in case of need *o* emergency; **hacer sus** ~**es** to relieve o.s.

necesitado, a [neθesi'taðo, a] *adj* needy, poor; ~ **de** in need of.

necesitar [neθesi'tar] *vt* to need, require ♦ *vi*: ~ **de** to have need of; ~**se** *vr* to be needed; (*anuncios*) **"necesítase coche"** "car wanted".

necio, a ['neθjo, a] *adj* foolish ♦ *nm/f* fool.

necrología [nekrolo'xia] *nf* obituary.

necrópolis [ne'kropolis] *nf inv* cemetery.

néctar ['nektar] *nm* nectar.

nectarina [nekta'rina] *nf* nectarine.

neerlandés, esa [neerlan'des, esa] *adj* Dutch ♦ *nm/f* Dutchman/woman ♦ *nm* (*LING*) Dutch; **los neerlandeses** the Dutch.

nefando, a [ne'fando, a] *adj* unspeakable.

nefasto, a [ne'fasto, a] *adj* ill-fated, unlucky.

negación [neɣa'θjon] *nf* negation; (*LING*) negative; (*rechazo*) refusal, denial.

negado, a [ne'ɣaðo, a] *adj*: ~ **para** inept at, unfitted for.

negar [ne'ɣar] *vt* (*renegar, rechazar*) to refuse; (*prohibir*) to refuse, deny; (*desmentir*) to deny; ~**se** *vr*: ~**se a hacer algo** to refuse to do sth.

negativo, a [neɣa'tiβo, a] *adj* negative ♦ *nm* (*FOTO*) negative; (*MAT*) minus ♦ *nf* (*gen*) negative; (*rechazo*) refusal, denial; **negativa rotunda** flat refusal.

negligencia [neɣli'xenθja] *nf* negligence.

negligente [neɣli'xente] *adj* negligent.

negociable [neɣo'θjaβle] *adj* (*COM*) negotiable.

negociación [neɣoθja'θjon] *nf* negotiation.

negociado [neɣo'θjaðo] *nm* department, section.

negociante [neɣo'θjante] *nm/f* businessman/woman.

negociar [neɣo'θjar] *vt, vi* to negotiate; ~ **en** to deal in, trade in.

negocio [ne'ɣoθjo] *nm* (*COM*) business; (*asunto*) affair, business; (*operación comercial*) deal, transaction; (*AM*) shop, store; (*lugar*) place of business; **los** ~**s** business *sg*; **hacer** ~ to do business; **el** ~ **del libro** the book trade; ~ **autorizado** licensed trade; **hombre de** ~**s** businessman; ~ **sucio** shady deal; **hacer un buen** ~ to pull off a profitable deal; **¡mal** ~**!** it looks bad!

negra ['neɣra] *nf V* **negro** ♦ *nf* (*MUS*) crotchet.

negrita [ne'ɣrita] *nf* (*TIP*) bold face; **en** ~ in bold (type).

negro, a ['neɣro, a] *adj* black; (*suerte*) awful, atrocious; (*humor etc*) sad; (*lúgubre*) gloomy ♦ *nm* (*color*) black ♦ *nm/f* Negro/Negress, black ♦ *nf* (*MUS*) crotchet; ~ **como la boca del lobo** pitch-black; **estoy** ~ **con esto** I'm getting desperate about it; **ponerse** ~ (*fam*) to get cross.

negrura [ne'ɣrura] *nf* blackness.

negué [ne'ɣe], **neguemos** [ne'ɣemos] *etc vb V* **negar.**

nene, a ['nene, a] *nm/f* baby, small child.

nenúfar [ne'nufar] *nm* water lily.

neologismo [neolo'xismo] *nm* neologism.

neón [ne'on] *nm* neon.

neoyorquino, a [neojor'kino, a] *adj* New York *cpd* ♦ *nm/f* New Yorker.

neozelandés, esa [neoθelan'des, esa] *adj* New Zealand *cpd* ♦ *nm/f* New Zealander.

nepotismo [nepo'tismo] *nm* nepotism.

nervio ['nerβjo] *nm* (*ANAT*) nerve; (: *tendón*) tendon; (*fig*) vigour; (*TEC*) rib; **crispar los** ~**s a algn, poner los** ~**s de punta a algn** to get on sb's nerves.

nerviosismo [nerβjo'sismo] *nm* nervousness, nerves *pl*.

nervioso, a [ner'βjoso, a] *adj* nervous; (*sensible*) nervy, highly-strung; (*impaciente*) restless; **¡no te pongas** ~**!** take it easy!

nervudo, a [ner'βuðo, a] *adj* tough; (*mano*) sinewy.

neto, a ['neto, a] *adj* clear; (*limpio*) clean; (*COM*) net.

neumático, a [neu'matiko, a] *adj* pneumatic ♦ *nm* (*ESP*) tyre (*BRIT*), tire (*US*); ~ **de recambio** spare tyre.

neumonía [neumo'nia] *nf* pneumonia.

neura ['neura] (*fam*) *nm/f* (*persona*) neurotic ♦ *nf* (*obsesión*) obsession.

neuralgia [neu'ralxja] *nf* neuralgia.

neurálgico, a [neu'ralxiko, a] *adj* neuralgic; (*fig: centro*) nerve *cpd*.

neurastenia [neuras'tenja] *nf* neurasthenia; (*fig*) excitability.

neurasténico, a [neuras'teniko, a] *adj* neurasthenic; excitable.

neurólogo, a [neu'roloɣo, a] *nm/f* neurologist.

neurona [neu'rona] *nf* neuron.

neurosis [neu'rosis] *nf inv* neurosis.

neurótico, a [neu'rotiko, a] *adj, nm/f* neurotic.

neutral [neu'tral] *adj* neutral.

neutralice [neutra'liθe] *etc vb V* **neutralizar.**

neutralizar [neutrali'θar] *vt* to neutralize; (*contrarrestar*) to counteract.

neutro, a ['neutro, a] *adj* (*BIO, LING*) neuter.

neutrón [neu'tron] *nm* neutron.
nevado, a [ne'ßaðo, a] *adj* snow-covered;
(*montaña*) snow-capped; (*fig*) snowy,
snow-white ♦ *nf* snowstorm; (*caída de
nieve*) snowfall.
nevar [ne'ßar] *vi* to snow ♦ *vt* (*fig*) to
whiten.
nevera [ne'ßera] *nf* (*ESP*) refrigerator
(*BRIT*), icebox (*US*).
nevisca [ne'ßiska] *nf* flurry of snow.
nexo ['nekso] *nm* link, connection.
n/f *abr* (*COM*) = *nuestro favor.*
ni [ni] *conj* nor, neither; (*tb*: ~ **siquiera**) not
even; ~ **que** not even if; ~ **blanco** ~
negro neither white nor black; ~ **el uno**
~ **el otro** neither one nor the other.
Nicaragua [nika'raɣwa] *nf* Nicaragua.
nicaragüense [nikara'ɣwense] *adj, nm/f*
Nicaraguan.
nicho ['nitʃo] *nm* niche.
nicotina [niko'tina] *nf* nicotine.
nido ['niðo] *nm* nest; (*fig*) hiding place; ~
de ladrones den of thieves.
niebla ['njeßla] *nf* fog; (*neblina*) mist; **hay** ~
it is foggy.
niego ['njeɣo] *etc*, **niegue** ['njeɣe] *etc vb V*
negar.
nieto, a ['njeto, a] *nm/f* grandson/daughter;
~**s** *nmpl* grandchildren.
nieve ['njeße] *etc vb V* **nevar** ♦ *nf* snow;
(*AM*) ice cream; **copo de** ~ snowflake.
N.I.F. *nm abr* (= *Número de Identificación
Fiscal*) *ID number used for tax purposes.*
Nigeria [ni'xerja] *nf* Nigeria.
nigeriano, a [nixe'rjano, a] *adj, nm/f*
Nigerian.
nigromancia [niɣro'manθja] *nf*
necromancy, black magic.
nihilista [nii'lista] *adj* nihilistic ♦ *nm*
nihilist.
Nilo ['nilo] *nm*: **el (Río)** ~ the Nile.
nimbo ['nimbo] *nm* (*aureola*) halo; (*nube*)
nimbus.
nimiedad [nimje'ðað] *nf* small-
mindedness; (*trivialidad*) triviality; (*una
~*) trifle, tiny detail.
nimio, a ['nimjo, a] *adj* trivial,
insignificant.
ninfa ['ninfa] *nf* nymph.
ninfómana [nin'fomana] *nf*
nymphomaniac.
ninguno, a [nin'guno, a] *adj* (**ningún** *delante
de nmsg*) no ♦ *pron* (*nadie*) nobody; (*ni uno*)
none, not one; (*ni uno ni otro*) neither; **de
ninguna manera** by no means, not at all;
no voy a ninguna parte I'm not going
anywhere.
niña ['nina] *nf V* **niño.**

niñera [ni'nera] *nf* nursemaid, nanny.
niñería [nine'ria] *nf* childish act.
niñez [ni'neθ] *nf* childhood; (*infancia*)
infancy.
niño, a ['nino, a] *adj* (*joven*) young;
(*inmaduro*) immature ♦ *nm* (*chico*) boy,
child ♦ *nf* girl, child; (*ANAT*) pupil; **los** ~**s**
the children; ~ **bien** rich kid; ~ **expósito**
foundling; ~ **de pecho** babe-in-arms; ~
prodigio child prodigy; **de** ~ as a child;
ser el ~ **mimado de algn** to be sb's pet;
ser la niña de los ojos de algn to be the
apple of sb's eye.
nipón, ona [ni'pon, ona] *adj, nm/f* Japanese;
los nipones the Japanese.
níquel ['nikel] *nm* nickel.
niquelar [nike'lar] *vt* (*TEC*) to nickel-plate.
níspero ['nispero] *nm* medlar.
nitidez [niti'ðeθ] *nf* (*claridad*) clarity; (: *de
atmósfera*) brightness; (: *de imagen*)
sharpness.
nítido, a ['nitiðo, a] *adj* bright; (*fig*) pure;
(*imagen*) clear, sharp.
nitrato [ni'trato] *nm* nitrate.
nitrógeno [ni'troxeno] *nm* nitrogen.
nitroglicerina [nitroxliθe'rina] *nf*
nitroglycerine.
nivel [ni'ßel] *nm* (*GEO*) level; (*norma*) level,
standard; (*altura*) height; ~ **de aceite** oil
level; ~ **de aire** spirit level; ~ **de vida**
standard of living; **al** ~ **de** on a level
with, at the same height as; (*fig*) on a
par with; **a 900m sobre el** ~ **del mar** at
900m above sea level.
nivelado, a [niße'laðo, a] *adj* level, flat;
(*TEC*) flush.
nivelar [niße'lar] *vt* to level out; (*fig*) to
even up; (*COM*) to balance.
Niza ['niθa] *nf* Nice.
n/l. *abr* (*COM*) = *nuestra letra.*
NNE *abr* (= *nornordeste*) NNE.
NNO *abr* (= *nornoroeste*) NNW.
NN. UU. *nfpl abr* (= *Naciones Unidas*) UN
sg.
NO *abr* (= *noroeste*) NW.
no [no] *adv* no; (*con verbo*) not ♦ *excl* no!; ~
tengo nada I don't have anything, I have
nothing; ~ **es el mío** it's not mine; **ahora**
~ not now; ¿~ **lo sabes?** don't you
know?; ~ **mucho** not much; ~ **bien
termine, lo entregaré** as soon as I finish
I'll hand it over; **¡a que** ~ **lo sabes!** I bet
you don't know!; **¡cómo** ~! of course!;
pacto de ~ **agresión** non-aggression
pact; **los países** ~ **alineados** the nonaligned countries; **el** ~ **va más** the
ultimate; **la** ~ **intervención** non-
intervention.

n/o *abr* (*COM*) = *nuestra orden.*

noble ['noßle] *adj, nmf* noble; **los ~s** the nobility *sg.*

nobleza [noß'leθa] *nf* nobility.

noche ['notʃe] *nf* night, night-time; (*la tarde*) evening; (*fig*) darkness; **de ~, por la ~** at night; **ayer por la ~** last night; **esta ~** tonight; **(en) toda la ~** all night; **hacer ~ en un sitio** to spend the night in a place; **se hace de ~** it's getting dark.

Nochebuena [notʃe'ßwena] *nf* Christmas Eve.

> On **Nochebuena** in Spanish homes there is normally a large supper when family members come from all over to be together. The more religiously inclined attend la **misa del gallo** at midnight. The tradition of receiving Christmas presents from Santa Claus that night is becoming more and more widespread and gradually replacing the tradition of **los Reyes Magos** (The Three Wise Men) on the 6th of January.

Nochevieja [notʃe'ßjexa] *nf* New Year's Eve; *V tb* **uvas.**

noción [no'θjon] *nf* notion; **nociones** *nfpl* elements, rudiments.

nocivo, a [no'θißo, a] *adj* harmful.

noctambulismo [noktambu'lismo] *nm* sleepwalking.

noctámbulo, a [nok'tambulo, a] *nmf* sleepwalker.

nocturno, a [nok'turno, a] *adj* (*de la noche*) nocturnal, night *cpd*; (*de la tarde*) evening *cpd* ♦ *nm* nocturne.

nodriza [no'ðriθa] *nf* wet nurse; **buque o nave ~** supply ship.

Noé [no'e] *nm* Noah.

nogal [no'ɣal] *nm* walnut tree; (*madera*) walnut.

nómada ['nomaða] *adj* nomadic ♦ *nmf* nomad.

nomás [no'mas] *adv*: (*AM*: *gen*) just; (: *tan sólo*) only; **así ~** (*AM fam*) just like that; **ayer ~** only yesterday ♦ *conj* (*AM*: *en cuanto*) ~ **se fue se acordó** no sooner had she left than she remembered.

nombramiento [nombra'mjento] *nm* naming; (*a un empleo*) appointment; (*POL etc*) nomination; (*MIL*) commission.

nombrar [nom'brar] *vt* (*gen*) to name; (*mencionar*) to mention; (*designar*) to appoint, nominate; (*MIL*) to commission.

nombre ['nombre] *nm* name; (*sustantivo*) noun; (*fama*) renown; **~ y apellidos** name in full; **~ común/propio** common/proper noun; **~ de pila/de soltera** Christian/

maiden name; **~ de fichero** (*INFORM*) file name; **en ~ de** in the name of, on behalf of; **sin ~** nameless; **su conducta no tiene ~** his behaviour is utterly despicable.

nomenclatura [nomenkla'tura] *nf* nomenclature.

nomeolvides [nomeol'ßiðes] *nm inv* forget-me-not.

nómina ['nomina] *nf* (*lista*) list; (*COM*: *tb*: **~s**) payroll.

nominal [nomi'nal] *adj* nominal; (*valor*) face *cpd*; (*LING*) noun *cpd*, substantival.

nominar [nomi'nar] *vt* to nominate.

nominativo, a [nomina'tißo, a] *adj* (*LING*) nominative; (*COM*): **un cheque ~ a X** a cheque made out to X.

non [non] *adj* odd, uneven ♦ *nm* odd number; **pares y ~es** odds and evens.

nonagésimo, a [nona'xesimo, a] *num* ninetieth.

nono, a ['nono, a] *num* ninth.

nordeste [nor'ðeste] *adj* north-east, north-eastern, north-easterly ♦ *nm* north-east; (*viento*) north-east wind, north-easterly.

nórdico, a ['norðiko, a] *adj* (*del norte*) northern, northerly; (*escandinavo*) Nordic, Norse ♦ *nmf* northerner; (*escandinavo*) Norseman/woman ♦ *nm* (*LING*) Norse.

noreste [no'reste] *adj, nm* = **nordeste.**

noria ['norja] *nf* (*AGR*) waterwheel; (*de carnaval*) big (*BRIT*) o Ferris (*US*) wheel.

norma ['norma] *nf* standard, norm, rule; (*patrón*) pattern; (*método*) method.

normal [nor'mal] *adj* (*corriente*) normal; (*habitual*) usual, natural; (*TEC*) standard; **Escuela N~** teacher training college; **(gasolina) ~** two-star petrol.

normalice [norma'liθe] *etc vb* V **normalizar.**

normalidad [normali'ðað] *nf* normality; **restablecer la ~** to restore order.

normalización [normaliθa'θjon] *nf* (*COM*) standardization.

normalizar [normali'θar] *vt* (*reglamentar*) to normalize; (*COM, TEC*) to standardize; **~se** *vr* to return to normal.

normalmente [normal'mente] *adv* (*con normalidad*) normally; (*habitualmente*) usually.

Normandía [norman'dia] *nf* Normandy.

normando, a [nor'mando, a] *adj, nmf* Norman.

normativo, a [norma'tißo, a] *adj*: **es ~ en todos los coches nuevos** it is standard in all new cars ♦ *nf* regulations *pl.*

noroeste [noro'este] *adj* north-west, north-western, north-westerly ♦ *nm*

north-west; (*viento*) north-west wind, north-westerly.
norte ['norte] *adj* north, northern, northerly ♦ *nm* north; (*fig*) guide.
Norteamérica [nortea'merika] *nf* North America.
norteamericano, a [norteameri'kano, a] *adj*, *nm/f* (North) American.
norteño, a [nor'teɲo, a] *adj* northern ♦ *nm/f* northerner.
Noruega [no'rweɣa] *nf* Norway.
noruego, a [no'rweɣo, a] *adj*, *nm/f* Norwegian ♦ *nm* (*LING*) Norwegian.
nos [nos] *pron* (*directo*) us; (*indirecto*) (to) us; (*reflexivo*) (to) ourselves; (*recíproco*) (to) each other; ~ **levantamos a las 7** we get up at 7.
nosocomio [noso'komio] *nm* (*AM*) hospital.
nosotros, as [no'sotros, as] *pron* (*sujeto*) we; (*después de prep*) us; ~ (**mismos**) ourselves.
nostalgia [nos'talxja] *nf* nostalgia, homesickness.
nostálgico, a [nos'talxiko, a] *adj* nostalgic, homesick.
nota ['nota] *nf* note; (*ESCOL*) mark; (*de fin de año*) report; (*UNIV etc*) footnote; (*COM*) account; ~ **de aviso** advice note; ~ **de crédito/débito** credit/debit note; ~ **de gastos** expenses claim; ~ **de sociedad** gossip column; **tomar** ~**s** to take notes.
notable [no'taßle] *adj* noteworthy, notable; (*ESCOL etc*) outstanding ♦ *nm/f* notable.
notar [no'tar] *vt* to notice, note; (*percibir*) to feel; (*ver*) to see; ~**se** *vr* to be obvious; **se nota que** ... one observes that ....
notaría [nota'ria] *nf* (*profesión*) profession of notary; (*despacho*) notary's office.
notarial [nota'rjal] *adj* (*estilo*) legal; **acta** ~ affidavit.
notario [no'tarjo] *nm* notary; (*abogado*) solicitor.
noticia [no'tiθja] *nf* (*información*) piece of news; (*TV etc*) news item; **las** ~**s** the news *sg*; **según nuestras** ~**s** according to our information; **tener** ~**s de algn** to hear from sb.
noticiario [noti'θjarjo] *nm* (*CINE*) newsreel; (*TV*) news bulletin.
noticiero [noti'θjero] *nm* newspaper, gazette; (*AM*: *tb*: ~ **telediario**) news bulletin.
notificación [notifika'θjon] *nf* notification.
notificar [notifi'kar] *vt* to notify, inform.
notifique [noti'fike] *etc vb V* **notificar**.
notoriedad [notorje'ðað] *nf* fame, renown.
notorio, a [no'torjo, a] *adj* (*público*) well-known; (*evidente*) obvious.
nov. *abr* (= *noviembre*) Nov.

novatada [noßa'taða] *nf* (*burla*) teasing, hazing (*US*); **pagar la** ~ to learn the hard way.
novato, a [no'ßato, a] *adj* inexperienced ♦ *nm/f* beginner, novice.
novecientos, as [noße'θjentos, as] *num* nine hundred.
novedad [noße'ðað] *nf* (*calidad de nuevo*) newness, novelty; (*noticia*) piece of news; (*cambio*) change, (new) development; (*sorpresa*) surprise; ~**es** *nfpl* (*noticia*) latest (news) *sg*.
novedoso, a [noße'ðoso, a] *adj* novel.
novel [no'ßel] *adj* new; (*inexperto*) inexperienced ♦ *nm/f* beginner.
novela [no'ßela] *nf* novel; ~ **policíaca** detective story.
novelero, a [noße'lero, a] *adj* highly imaginative.
novelesco, a [noße'lesko, a] *adj* fictional; (*romántico*) romantic; (*fantástico*) fantastic.
novelista [noße'lista] *nm/f* novelist.
novelística [noße'listika] *nf*: **la** ~ fiction, the novel.
noveno, a [no'ßeno, a] *num* ninth.
noventa [no'ßenta] *num* ninety.
novia ['noßja] *nf V* **novio**.
noviazgo [no'ßjaθvo] *nm* engagement.
novicio, a [no'ßiθjo, a] *nm/f* novice.
noviembre [no'ßjembre] *nm* November.
novilla [no'ßiʎa] *nf* heifer.
novillada [noßi'ʎaða] *nf* (*TAUR*) *bullfight with young bulls.*
novillero [noßi'ʎero] *nm* novice bullfighter.
novillo [no'ßiʎo] *nm* young bull, bullock; **hacer** ~**s** (*fam*) to play truant (*BRIT*) o hooky (*US*).
novio, a ['noßjo, a] *nm/f* boyfriend/ girlfriend; (*prometido*) fiancé/fiancée; (*recién casado*) bridegroom/bride; **los** ~**s** the newly-weds.
novísimo, a [no'ßisimo, a] *adj superlativo de* **nuevo, a**.
NPI *nm abr* (*INFORM*: = *número personal de identificación*) PIN.
N. S. *abr* = *Nuestro Señor*.
ntra., ntro. *abr* = **nuestra, nuestro**.
NU *nfpl abr* (= *Naciones Unidas*) UN *sg*.
nubarrón [nußa'rron] *nm* storm cloud.
nube ['nuße] *nf* cloud; (*MED*: *ocular*) cloud, film; (*fig*) mass; **una** ~ **de críticas** a storm of criticism; **los precios están por las** ~**s** prices are sky-high; **estar en las** ~**s** to be away with the fairies.
nublado, a [nu'ßlaðo, a] *adj* cloudy ♦ *nm* storm cloud.
nublar [nu'ßlar] *vt* (*oscurecer*) to darken;

(*confundir*) to cloud; ~**se** *vr* to cloud over.

nuca ['nuka] *nf* nape of the neck.

nuclear [nukle'ar] *adj* nuclear.

nuclearizado, a [nukleari'θaðo, a] *adj*: **países ~s** countries possessing nuclear weapons.

núcleo ['nukleo] *nm* (*centro*) core; (*FÍSICA*) nucleus.

nudillo [nu'ðiʎo] *nm* knuckle.

nudista [nu'dista] *adj, nm/f* nudist.

nudo ['nuðo] *nm* knot; (*unión*) bond; (*de problema*) crux; (*FERRO*) junction; (*fig*) lump; ~ **corredizo** slipknot; **con un ~ en la garganta** with a lump in one's throat.

nudoso, a [nu'ðoso, a] *adj* knotty; (*tronco*) gnarled; (*bastón*) knobbly.

nueces ['nweθes] *nfpl de* **nuez.**

nuera ['nwera] *nf* daughter-in-law.

nuestro, a ['nwestro, a] *adj posesivo* our ♦ *pron* ours; ~ **padre** our father; **un amigo ~** a friend of ours; **es el ~** it's ours; **los ~s** our people; (*DEPORTE*) our *o* the local team *o* side.

nueva ['nweßa] *nf* V **nuevo.**

Nueva Escocia *nf* Nova Scotia.

nuevamente [nweßa'mente] *adv* (*otra vez*) again; (*de nuevo*) anew.

Nueva York [-'jork] *nf* New York.

Nueva Zeland(i)a [-θe'land(j)a] *nf* New Zealand.

nueve ['nweße] *num* nine.

nuevo, a ['nweßo, a] *adj* (*gen*) new ♦ *nf* piece of news; **¿qué hay de ~?** (*fam*) what's new?; **de ~** again.

Nuevo Méjico *nm* New Mexico.

nuez [nweθ], *pl* **nueces** *nf* (*del nogal*) walnut; (*fruto*) nut; ~ **de Adán** Adam's apple; ~ **moscada** nutmeg.

nulidad [nuli'ðað] *nf* (*incapacidad*) incompetence; (*abolición*) nullity; (*individuo*) nonentity; **es una ~** he's a dead loss.

nulo, a ['nulo, a] *adj* (*inepto, torpe*) useless; (*inválido*) (null and) void; (*DEPORTE*) drawn, tied.

núm. *abr* (= *número*) no.

numen ['numen] *nm* inspiration.

numeración [numera'θjon] *nf* (*cifras*) numbers *pl*; (*arábiga, romana etc*) numerals *pl*; ~ **de línea** (*INFORM*) line numbering.

numerador [numera'ðor] *nm* (*MAT*) numerator.

numeral [nume'ral] *nm* numeral.

numerar [nume'rar] *vt* to number; ~**se** *vr* (*MIL etc*) to number off.

numerario, a [nume'rarjo, a] *adj* numerary; **profesor ~** permanent *o* tenured member of teaching staff ♦ *nm* hard cash.

numérico, a [nu'meriko, a] *adj* numerical.

número ['numero] *nm* (*gen*) number; (*tamaño: de zapato*) size; (*ejemplar: de diario*) number, issue; (*TEAT etc*) turn, act, number; **sin ~** numberless, unnumbered; ~ **binario** (*INFORM*) binary number; ~ **de matrícula/de teléfono** registration/telephone number; ~ **personal de identificación** (*INFORM etc*) personal identification number; ~ **de serie** (*COM*) serial number; ~ **atrasado** back number.

numeroso, a [nume'roso, a] *adj* numerous; **familia numerosa** large family.

numerus ['numerus] *nm*: ~ **clausus** (*UNIV*) restricted *o* selective entry.

nunca ['nunka] *adv* (*jamás*) never; (*con verbo negativo*) ever; ~ **lo pensé** I never thought it; **no viene** ~ he never comes; ~ **más** never again.

nuncio ['nunθjo] *nm* (*REL*) nuncio.

nupcial [nup'θjal] *adj* wedding *cpd*.

nupcias ['nupθjas] *nfpl* wedding *sg*, nuptials.

nutria ['nutrja] *nf* otter.

nutrición [nutri'θjon] *nf* nutrition.

nutrido, a [nu'triðo, a] *adj* (*alimentado*) nourished; (*fig: grande*) large; (*abundante*) abundant; **mal ~** undernourished; ~ **de** full of.

nutrir [nu'trir] *vt* to feed, nourish; (*fig*) to feed, strengthen.

nutritivo, a [nutri'tißo, a] *adj* nourishing, nutritious.

nylon [ni'lon] *nm* nylon.

Ñ ñ

Ñ, ñ ['eɲe] *nf* (*letra*) Ñ, ñ.

ñato, a ['ɲato, a] *adj* (*AM*) snub-nosed.

ñoñería [ɲoɲe'ria], **ñoñez** [ɲo'ɲeθ] *nf* insipidness.

ñoño, a ['ɲoɲo, a] *adj* (*soso*) insipid; (*persona: débil*) spineless.

ñoquis ['ɲokis] *nmpl* (*CULIN*) gnocchi.

O o

O, o [o] *nf* (*letra*) O, o; **O de Oviedo** O for Oliver (*BRIT*) *o* Oboe (*US*).

O *abr* (= *oeste*) W.

o [o] *conj* or; ~ ... ~ either ... or; ~ **sea** that is.

ó [o] *conj* (*en números para evitar confusión*) or; **5 ~ 6** 5 or 6.

o/ *nm* (*COM*: = *orden*) o.

OACI *nf abr* (= *Organización de la Aviación Civil Internacional*) ICAO.

oasis [o'asis] *nm inv* oasis.

obcecado, a [oßße'kaðo, a] *adj* blind; (*terco*) stubborn.

obcecarse [oßße'karse] *vr* to be obstinate; ~ **en hacer** to insist on doing.

obceque [oß'θeke] *etc vb V* **obcecarse**.

obedecer [oßeðe'θer] *vt* to obey; ~ **a** (*MED etc*) to yield to; (*fig*) ~ **a** ..., ~ **al hecho de que** ... to be due to ..., arise from ....

obedezca [oße'ðeθka] *etc vb V* **obedecer**.

obediencia [oße'ðjenθja] *nf* obedience.

obediente [oße'ðjente] *adj* obedient.

obertura [oßer'tura] *nf* overture.

obesidad [oßesi'ðað] *nf* obesity.

obeso, a [o'ßeso, a] *adj* obese.

óbice ['oßiθe] *nm* obstacle, impediment.

obispado [oßis'paðo] *nm* bishopric.

obispo [o'ßispo] *nm* bishop.

óbito ['oßito] *nm* demise.

objeción [oßxe'θjon] *nf* objection; **hacer una ~, poner objeciones** to raise objections, object.

objetar [oßxe'tar] *vt, vi* to object.

objetivo, a [oßxe'tißo, a] *adj* objective ♦ *nm* objective; (*fig*) aim; (*FOTO*) lens.

objeto [oß'xeto] *nm* (*cosa*) object; (*fin*) aim.

objetor, a [oßxe'tor, a] *nm/f* objector; ~ **de conciencia** conscientious objector; *V tb* **mili**.

oblea [o'ßlea] *nf* (*REL, fig*) wafer; (*INFORM*) chip, wafer.

oblicuo, a [o'ßlikwo, a] *adj* oblique; (*mirada*) sidelong.

obligación [oßliɣa'θjon] *nf* obligation; (*COM*) bond, debenture.

obligar [oßli'ɣar] *vt* to force; ~**se** *vr*: ~**se a** to commit o.s. to.

obligatorio, a [oßliɣa'torjo, a] *adj* compulsory, obligatory.

obligue [o'ßliɣe] *etc vb V* **obligar**.

oboe [o'ßoe] *nm* oboe; (*músico*) oboist.

Ob.po *abr* (= *Obispo*) Bp.

obra ['oßra] *nf* work; (*hechura*) piece of work; (*ARQ*) construction, building; (*libro*) book; (*MUS*) opus; (*TEAT*) play; ~ **de arte** work of art; ~ **maestra** masterpiece; ~ **de consulta** reference book; ~**s completas** complete works; ~ **benéfica** charity; "~**s**" (*en carretera*) "men at work"; ~**s públicas** public works; **por ~ de** thanks to (the efforts of); ~**s son amores y no buenas razones** actions speak louder than words.

obrar [o'ßrar] *vt* to work; (*tener efecto*) to have an effect on ♦ *vi* to act, behave; (*tener efecto*) to have an effect; **la carta obra en su poder** the letter is in his/her possession.

obr. cit. *abr* (= *obra citada*) op. cit.

obrero, a [o'ßrero, a] *adj* working; (*movimiento*) labour *cpd*; **clase obrera** working class ♦ *nm/f* (*gen*) worker; (*sin oficio*) labourer.

obscenidad [oßsθeni'ðað] *nf* obscenity.

obsceno, a [oßs'θeno, a] *adj* obscene.

obscu... = oscu...

obsequiar [oßse'kjar] *vt* (*ofrecer*) to present; (*agasajar*) to make a fuss of, lavish attention on.

obsequio [oß'sekjo] *nm* (*regalo*) gift; (*cortesía*) courtesy, attention.

obsequioso, a [oßse'kjoso, a] *adj* attentive.

observación [oßserßa'θjon] *nf* observation; (*reflexión*) remark; (*objeción*) objection.

observador, a [oßserßa'ðor, a] *adj* observant ♦ *nm/f* observer.

observancia [oßser'ßanθja] *nf* observance.

observar [oßser'ßar] *vt* to observe; (*notar*) to notice; (*leyes*) to observe, respect; (*reglas*) to abide by.

observatorio [oßserßa'torjo] *nm* observatory; ~ **del tiempo** weather station.

obsesión [oßse'sjon] *nf* obsession.

obsesionar [oßsesjo'nar] *vt* to obsess.

obseso, a [oß'seso, a] *nm/f* (*sexual*) sex maniac.

obsolescencia [oßsoles'θenθja] *nf*: ~ **incorporada** (*COM*) built-in obsolescence.

obsoleto, a [oßso'leto, a] *adj* obsolete.

obstaculice [oßstaku'liθe] *etc vb V* **obstaculizar**.

obstaculizar [oßstakuli'θar] *vt* (*dificultar*) to hinder, hamper.

obstáculo [oßs'takulo] *nm* (*gen*) obstacle;

(*impedimento*) hindrance, drawback.
obstante [oßs'tante]: **no** ~ *adv*
nevertheless; (*de todos modos*) all the
same ♦ *prep* in spite of.
obstetra [oßs'tetra] *nm/f* obstetrician.
obstetricia [oßste'triθja] *nf* obstetrics *sg*.
obstinado, a [oßsti'naðo, a] *adj* (*gen*)
obstinate; (*terco*) stubborn.
obstinarse [oßsti'narse] *vr* to dig one's
heels in; ~ **en** to persist in.
obstrucción [oßstruk'θjon] *nf* obstruction.
obstruir [oßstru'ir] *vt* to obstruct;
(*bloquear*) to block; (*estorbar*) to hinder.
obstruyendo [oßstru'jendo] *etc vb V*
obstruir.
obtención [oßten'θjon] *nf* (*COM*)
procurement.
obtendré [oßten'dre] *etc vb V* **obtener**.
obtener [oßte'ner] *vt* (*conseguir*) to obtain;
(*ganar*) to gain.
obtenga [oß'tenga] *etc vb V* **obtener**.
obturación [oßtura'θjon] *nf* plugging,
stopping; (*FOTO*): **velocidad de** ~ shutter
speed.
obturador [oßtura'ðor] *nm* (*FOTO*) shutter.
obtuso, a [oß'tuso, a] *adj* (*filo*) blunt; (*MAT,
fig*) obtuse.
obtuve [oß'tuße] *etc vb V* **obtener**.
obús [o'ßus] *nm* (*MIL*) shell.
obviar [oß'ßjar] *vt* to obviate, remove.
obvio, a ['oßßjo, a] *adj* obvious.
oca ['oka] *nf* goose; (*tb*: **juego de la** ~)
≈ snakes and ladders.
ocasión [oka'sjon] *nf* (*oportunidad*)
opportunity, chance; (*momento*)
occasion, time; (*causa*) cause; **de** ~
secondhand; **con** ~ **de** on the occasion
of; **en algunas ocasiones** sometimes;
aprovechar la ~ to seize one's
opportunity.
ocasionar [okasjo'nar] *vt* to cause.
ocaso [o'kaso] *nm* sunset; (*fig*) decline.
occidental [okθiðen'tal] *adj* western ♦ *nm/f*
westerner ♦ *nm* west.
occidente [okθi'ðente] *nm* west; **el O**~ the
West.
occiso, a [ok'θiso, a] *nm/f*: **el** ~ the
deceased; (*de asesinato*) the victim.
O.C.D.E. *nf abr* (= *Organización de
Cooperación y Desarrollo Económicos*)
OECD.
océano [o'θeano] *nm* ocean; **el** ~ **Índico** the
Indian Ocean.
ochenta [o't ʃenta] *num* eighty.
ocho ['ot ʃo] *num* eight; (*fecha*) eighth; ~
días a week.
ochocientos, as [ot ʃo'θjentos, as] *num*
eight hundred.

OCI ['oθi] *nf abr* (*POL: Venezuela, Perú*)
= *Oficina Central de Información.*
ocio ['oθjo] *nm* (*tiempo*) leisure; (*pey*)
idleness; **"guía del** ~" "what's on".
ociosidad [oθjosi'ðað] *nf* idleness.
ocioso, a [o'θjoso, a] *adj* (*inactivo*) idle;
(*inútil*) useless.
oct. *abr* (= *octubre*) Oct.
octanaje [okta'naxe] *nm*: **de alto** ~ high
octane.
octano [ok'tano] *nm* octane.
octavilla [okta'ßiʎa] *nm* leaflet, pamphlet.
octavo, a [ok'taßo, a] *num* eighth.
octeto [ok'teto] *nm* (*INFORM*) byte.
octogenario, a [oktoxe'narjo, a] *adj, nm/f*
octogenarian.
octubre [ok'tußre] *nm* October.
OCU ['oku] *nf abr* (*ESP.* = *Organización de
Consumidores y Usuarios*) ≈ Consumers'
Association.
ocular [oku'lar] *adj* ocular, eye *cpd*; **testigo**
~ eyewitness.
oculista [oku'lista] *nm/f* oculist.
ocultar [okul'tar] *vt* (*esconder*) to hide;
(*callar*) to conceal; (*disfrazar*) to screen;
~**se** *vr* to hide (o.s.); ~**se a la vista** to
keep out of sight.
oculto, a [o'kulto, a] *adj* hidden; (*fig*)
secret.
ocupación [okupa'θjon] *nf* occupation;
(*tenencia*) occupancy.
ocupado, a [oku'paðo, a] *adj* (*persona*)
busy; (*plaza*) occupied, taken; (*teléfono*)
engaged; **¿está ocupada la silla?** is that
seat taken?
ocupar [oku'par] *vt* (*gen*) to occupy;
(*puesto*) to hold, fill; (*individuo*) to
engage; (*obreros*) to employ; (*confiscar*)
to seize; ~**se** *vr*: ~**se de** *o* **en** to concern
o.s. with; (*cuidar*) to look after; ~**se de lo
suyo** to mind one's own business.
ocurrencia [oku'rrenθja] *nf* (*ocasión*)
occurrence; (*agudeza*) witticism.
ocurrir [oku'rrir] *vi* to happen; ~**se** *vr*: **se
me ocurrió que ...** it occurred to me that
...; **¿se te ocurre algo?** can you think of *o*
come up with anything? **¿qué ocurre?**
what's going on?
oda ['oða] *nf* ode.
ODECA [o'ðeka] *nf abr* = *Organización de
Estados Centroamericanos.*
odiar [o'ðjar] *vt* to hate.
odio ['oðjo] *nm* (*gen*) hate, hatred;
(*disgusto*) dislike.
odioso, a [o'ðjoso, a] *adj* (*gen*) hateful;
(*malo*) nasty.
odisea [oði'sea] *nf* odyssey.
odontología [oðontolo'xia] *nf* dentistry,

dental surgery.

odontólogo, a [oðon'toloɣo, a] *nm/f* dentist, dental surgeon.

odre ['oðre] *nm* wineskin.

O.E.A. *nf abr* (= *Organización de Estados Americanos*) O.A.S.

OECE *nf abr* (= *Organización Europea de Cooperación Económica*) OEEC.

OELA [o'ela] *nf abr* = *Organización de Estados Latinoamericanos.*

oeste [o'este] *nm* west; **una película del ~ a** western.

ofender [ofen'der] *vt* (*agraviar*) to offend; (*insultar*) to insult; **~se** *vr* to take offence.

ofensa [o'fensa] *nf* offence; (*insulto*) slight.

ofensivo, a [ofen'siβo, a] *adj* (*insultante*) insulting; (*MIL*) offensive ♦ *nf* offensive.

oferta [o'ferta] *nf* offer; (*propuesta*) proposal; (*para contrato*) bid, tender; **la ~ y la demanda** supply and demand; **artículos en ~** goods on offer; **~ excedentaria** (*COM*) excess supply; **~ monetaria** money supply; **~ pública de adquisición (OPA)** (*COM*) takeover bid; **~s de trabajo** (*en periódicos*) situations vacant column.

offset ['ofset] *nm* offset.

oficial [ofi'θjal] *adj* official ♦ *nm* official; (*MIL*) officer.

oficialista [ofisja'lista] *adj* (*AM*) (pro-) government; **el candidato ~** the governing party's candidate.

oficiar [ofi'θjar] *vt* to inform officially ♦ *vi* (*REL*) to officiate.

oficina [ofi'θina] *nf* office; **~ de colocación** employment agency; **~ de información** information bureau; **~ de objetos perdidos** lost property office (*BRIT*), lost-and-found department (*US*); **~ de turismo** tourist office.

oficinista [ofiθi'nista] *nm/f* clerk; **los ~s** white-collar workers.

oficio [o'fiθjo] *nm* (*profesión*) profession; (*puesto*) post; (*REL*) service; (*función*) function; (*comunicado*) official letter; **ser del ~** to be an old hand; **tener mucho ~** to have a lot of experience; **~ de difuntos** funeral service; **de ~** officially.

oficioso, a [ofi'θjoso, a] *adj* (*pey*) officious; (*no oficial*) unofficial, informal.

ofimática [ofi'matika] *nf* office automation.

ofrecer [ofre'θer] *vt* (*dar*) to offer; (*proponer*) to propose; **~se** *vr* (*persona*) to offer o.s., volunteer; (*situación*) to present itself; **¿qué se le ofrece?, ¿se le ofrece algo?** what can I do for you?, can I get you anything?

ofrecimiento [ofreθi'mjento] *nm* offer, offering.

ofrendar [ofren'dar] *vt* to offer, contribute.

ofrezca [o'freθka] *etc vb V* **ofrecer**.

oftalmología [oftalmolo'xia] *nf* ophthalmology.

oftalmólogo, a [oftal'mologo, a] *nm/f* ophthalmologist.

ofuscación [ofuska'θjon] *nf*, **ofuscamiento** [ofuska'mjento] *nm* (*fig*) bewilderment.

ofuscar [ofus'kar] *vt* (*confundir*) to bewilder; (*enceguecer*) to dazzle, blind.

ofusque [o'fuske] *etc vb V* **ofuscar**.

ogro ['oɣro] *nm* ogre.

OIC *nf abr* = *Organización Interamericana del Café*; (*COM*) = *Organización Internacional del Comercio*.

oída [o'iða] *nf*: **de ~s** by hearsay.

oído [o'iðo] *nm* (*ANAT, MUS*) ear; (*sentido*) hearing; **~ interno** inner ear; **de ~** by ear; **apenas pude dar crédito a mis ~** I could scarcely believe my ears; **hacer ~s sordos a** to turn a deaf ear to.

OIEA *nm abr* (= *Organismo International de Energía Atómica*) IAEA.

oiga ['oiɣa] *etc vb V* **oír**.

OIR [o'ir] *nf abr* (= *Organización Internacional para los Refugiados*) IRO.

oír [o'ir] *vt* (*gen*) to hear; (*esp AM: escuchar*) to listen to; **¡oye!** (*sorpresa*) I say!, say! (*US*); **¡oiga!** (*TELEC*) hullo?; **~ misa** to attend mass; **como quien oye llover** without paying (the slightest) attention.

O.I.T. *nf abr* (= *Organización Internacional del Trabajo*) ILO.

ojal [o'xal] *nm* buttonhole.

ojalá [oxa'la] *excl* if only (it were so)!, some hope! ♦ *conj* if only...!, would that...!; **~ que venga hoy** I hope he comes today; **¡~ pudiera!** I wish I could!

ojeada [oxe'aða] *nf* glance; **echar una ~ a** to take a quick look at.

ojera [o'xera] *nf*: **tener ~s** to have bags under one's eyes.

ojeriza [oxe'riθa] *nf* ill-will; **tener ~ a** to have a grudge against, have it in for.

ojeroso, a [oxe'roso, a] *adj* haggard.

ojete [o'xete] *nm* eye(let).

ojo ['oxo] *nm* eye; (*de puente*) span; (*de cerradura*) keyhole ♦ *excl* careful!; **tener ~ para** to have an eye for; **~s saltones** bulging *o* goggle eyes; **~ de buey** porthole; **~ por ~** an eye for an eye; **en un abrir y cerrar de ~s** in the twinkling of an eye; **a ~s vistas** openly; (*crecer etc*) before one's (very) eyes; **a** ~ **(de buen cubero)** roughly; ~**s que no ven, corazón que no siente** out of sight, out of mind; **ser el** ~ **derecho de algn** (*fig*) to be the apple of sb's eye.

okupa [o'kupa] *nmf* (*fam*) squatter.

ola ['ola] *nf* wave; ~ **de calor/frío** heatwave/cold spell; **la nueva** ~ the latest fashion; (*CINE, MUS*) (the) new wave.

OLADE [o'laðe] *nf abr* = *Organización Latinoamericana de Energía*.

olé [o'le] *excl* bravo!, olé!

oleada [ole'aða] *nf* big wave, swell; (*fig*) wave.

oleaje [ole'axe] *nm* swell.

óleo ['oleo] *nm* oil.

oleoducto [oleo'ðukto] *nm* (oil) pipeline.

oler [o'ler] *vt* (*gen*) to smell; (*inquirir*) to pry into; (*fig: sospechar*) to sniff out ♦ *vi* to smell; ~ **a** to smell of; **huele mal** it smells bad, it stinks.

olfatear [olfate'ar] *vt* to smell; (*fig: sospechar*) to sniff out; (*inquirir*) to pry into.

olfato [ol'fato] *nm* sense of smell.

oligarquía [olixar'kia] *nf* oligarchy.

olimpiada [olim'piaða] *nf*: **la** ~ *o* **las** ~**s** the Olympics.

olímpicamente [o'limpikamente] *adv*: **pasar** ~ **de algo** to totally ignore sth.

olímpico, a [o'limpiko, a] *adj* Olympian; (*deportes*) Olympic.

oliva [o'lißa] *nf* (*aceituna*) olive; **aceite de** ~ olive oil.

olivar [oli'ßar] *nm* olive grove *o* plantation.

olivo [o'lißo] *nm* olive tree.

olla ['oʎa] *nf* pan; (*para hervir agua*) kettle; (*comida*) stew; ~ **a presión** pressure cooker.

olmo ['olmo] *nm* elm (tree).

olor [o'lor] *nm* smell.

oloroso, a [olo'roso, a] *adj* scented.

OLP *nf abr* (= *Organización para la Liberación de Palestina*) PLO.

olvidadizo, a [olßiða'ðiθo, a] *adj* (*desmemoriado*) forgetful; (*distraído*) absent-minded.

olvidar [olßi'ðar] *vt* to forget; (*omitir*) to omit; (*abandonar*) to leave behind; ~**se** *vr* (*fig*) to forget o.s.; **se me olvidó** I forgot.

olvido [ol'ßiðo] *nm* oblivion; (*acto*) oversight; (*descuido*) slip; **caer en el** ~ to fall into oblivion.

O.M. *abr* (*POL*) = *Orden Ministerial*.

ombligo [om'blivo] *nm* navel.

OMI *nf abr* (= *Organización Marítima Internacional*) IMO.

ominoso, a [omi'noso, a] *adj* ominous.

omisión [omi'sjon] *nf* (*abstención*) omission; (*descuido*) neglect.

omiso, a [o'miso, a] *adj*: **hacer caso** ~ **de** to ignore, pass over.

omitir [omi'tir] *vt* to leave *o* miss out, omit.

ómnibus ['omnißus] *nm* (*AM*) bus.

omnipotente [omnipo'tente] *adj* omnipotent.

omnipresente [omnipre'sente] *adj* omnipresent.

omnívoro, a [om'nißoro, a] *adj* omnivorous.

omoplato [omo'plato], **omóplato** [o'moplato] *nm* shoulder-blade.

OMS *nf abr* (= *Organización Mundial de la Salud*) WHO.

ONCE ['onθe] *nf abr* (= *Organización Nacional de Ciegos Españoles*) *charity for the blind*.

once ['onθe] *num* eleven ♦ *nm* (*AM*): ~**s** *nmpl* tea break *sg*.

onda ['onda] *nf* wave; ~ **corta/larga/media** short/long/medium wave; ~**s acústicas/ hertzianas** acoustic/Hertzian waves; ~ **sonora** sound wave.

ondear [onde'ar] *vi* to wave; (*tener ondas*) to be wavy; (*agua*) to ripple; ~**se** *vr* to swing, sway.

ondulación [ondula'θjon] *nf* undulation.

ondulado, a [ondu'laðo, a] *adj* wavy ♦ *nm* wave.

ondulante [ondu'lante] *adj* undulating.

ondular [ondu'lar] *vt* (*el pelo*) to wave ♦ *vi*, ~**se** *vr* to undulate.

oneroso, a [one'roso, a] *adj* onerous.

ONG *nf abr* (= *organización no gubernamental*) NGO.

onomástica, a [ono'mastiko, a] *adj*: **fiesta onomástica** saint's day ♦ *nm* saint's day.

ONU ['onu] *nf abr* V **Organización de las Naciones Unidas**.

onubense [onu'ßense] *adj* of *o* from Huelva ♦ *nmf* native *o* inhabitant of Huelva.

ONUDI [o'nuði] *nf abr* (= *Organización de las Naciones Unidas para el Desarrollo Industrial*) UNIDO (*United Nations Industrial Development Organization*).

onza ['onθa] *nf* ounce.

O.P. *nfpl abr* = **obras públicas**; (*COM*) = *Oficina Principal*.

OPA *nf abr* (= *oferta público de adquisición*) takeover bid.

opaco, a [o'pako, a] *adj* opaque; (*fig*) dull.

ópalo ['opalo] *nm* opal.

opción [op'θjon] *nf* (*gen*) option; (*derecho*) right, option; **no hay** ~ there is no alternative.

opcional [opθjo'nal] *adj* optional.

O.P.E.P. [o'pep] *nf abr* (= *Organización de Países Exportadores de Petróleo*) OPEC.

ópera ['opera] *nf* opera; ~ **bufa** *o* **cómica** comic opera.

operación [opera'θjon] *nf (gen)* operation; (*COM*) transaction, deal; ~ **"llave en manos"** (*INFORM*) turnkey operation; ~ **a plazo** (*COM*) forward transaction; **operaciones accesorias** (*INFORM*) housekeeping; **operaciones a término** (*COM*) futures.

operador, a [opera'ðor, a] *nmf* operator; (*CINE: proyección*) projectionist; (: *rodaje*) cameraman.

operante [ope'rante] *adj* operating.

operar [ope'rar] *vt (producir)* to produce, bring about; (*MED*) to operate on ♦ *vi* (*COM*) to operate, deal; ~**se** *vr* to occur; (*MED*) to have an operation; **se han operado grandes cambios** great changes have been made *o* have taken place.

operario, a [ope'rarjo, a] *nmf* operative, worker.

opereta [ope'reta] *nf* operetta.

opinar [opi'nar] *vt (estimar)* to think ♦ *vi* (*enjuiciar*) to give one's opinion; ~ **bien de** to think well of, have a good opinion of.

opinión [opi'njon] *nf (creencia)* belief; (*criterio*) opinion; **la** ~ **pública** public opinion.

opio ['opjo] *nm* opium.

opíparo, a [o'piparo, a] *adj* sumptuous.

opondré [opon'dre] *etc vb V* **oponer**.

oponente [opo'nente] *nmf* opponent.

oponer [opo'ner] *vt (resistencia)* to put up, offer; (*negativa*) to raise; ~**se** *vr (objetar)* to object; (*estar frente a frente*) to be opposed; (*dos personas*) to oppose each other; ~ **A a B** to set A against B; **me opongo a pensar que** ... I refuse to believe *o* think that ....

oponga [o'ponga] *etc vb V* **oponer**.

Oporto [o'porto] *nm* Oporto.

oporto [o'porto] *nm* port.

oportunidad [oportuni'ðað] *nf (ocasión)* opportunity; (*posibilidad*) chance.

oportunismo [oportu'nismo] *nm* opportunism.

oportunista [oportu'nista] *nmf* opportunist; (*infección*) opportunistic.

oportuno, a [opor'tuno, a] *adj (en su tiempo)* opportune, timely; (*respuesta*) suitable; **en el momento** ~ at the right moment.

oposición [oposi'θjon] *nf* opposition;

oposiciones *nfpl* public examinations; **ganar un puesto por oposiciones** to win a post by public competitive examination; **hacer oposiciones a, presentarse a unas oposiciones a** to sit a competitive examination for.

> *The **oposiciones** are exams held every year for posts nationally and locally in the public sector, State education, the Judiciary etc. These posts are permanent and the number of candidates is high so the exams are tough. The candidates, **opositores**, have to study a great number of subjects relating to their field and also the Constitution. People can spend years studying and resitting exams.*

opositar [oposi'tar] *vi* to sit a public entrance examination.

opositor, a [oposi'tor, a] *nmf (ADMIN)* candidate to a public examination; (*adversario*) opponent.

opresión [opre'sjon] *nf* oppression.

opresivo, a [opre'siβo, a] *adj* oppressive.

opresor, a [opre'sor, a] *nmf* oppressor.

oprimir [opri'mir] *vt* to squeeze; (*asir*) to grasp; (*pulsar*) to press; (*fig*) to oppress.

oprobio [o'proβjo] *nm (infamia)* ignominy; (*descrédito*) shame.

optar [op'tar] *vi (elegir)* to choose; ~ **a** *o* **por** to opt for.

optativo, a [opta'tiβo, a] *adj* optional.

óptico, a ['optiko, a] *adj* optic(al) ♦ *nmf* optician ♦ *nf* optics *sg*; (*fig*) viewpoint.

optimismo [opti'mismo] *nm* optimism.

optimista [opti'mista] *nmf* optimist.

óptimo, a ['optimo, a] *adj (el mejor)* very best.

opuesto, a [o'pwesto, a] *pp de* **oponer** ♦ *adj* (*contrario*) opposite; (*antagónico*) opposing.

opulencia [opu'lenθja] *nf* opulence.

opulento, a [opu'lento, a] *adj* opulent.

opuse [o'puse] *etc vb V* **oponer**.

ORA ['ora] *nf abr (ESP.* = *Operación de Regulación de Aparcamientos) parking regulations.

ora ['ora] *adv*: ~ **tú** ~ **yo** now you, now me.

oración [ora'θjon] *nf (discurso)* speech; (*REL*) prayer; (*LING*) sentence.

oráculo [o'rakulo] *nm* oracle.

orador, a [ora'ðor, a] *nmf* orator; (*conferenciante*) speaker.

oral [o'ral] *adj* oral; **por vía** ~ (*MED*) orally.

orangután [orangu'tan] *nm* orang-utan.

orar [o'rar] *vi (REL)* to pray.

oratoria [ora'torja] *nf* oratory.

orbe ['orße] *nm* orb, sphere; (*fig*) world; **en todo el ~** all over the globe.

órbita ['orßita] *nf* orbit; (*ANAT: ocular*) (eye-)socket.

orden ['orðen] *nm* (*gen*) order; (*INFORM*) command; **~ público** public order, law and order; (*números*) **del ~ de** about; **de primer ~** first-rate; **en ~ de prioridad** in order of priority ♦ *nf* (*gen*) order; **~ bancaria** banker's order; **~ de compra** (*COM*) purchase order; **~ del día** agenda; **eso ahora está a la ~ del día** that is now the order of the day; **a la ~ de usted** at your service; **dar la ~ de hacer algo** to give the order to do sth.

ordenación [orðena'θjon] *nf* (*estado*) order; (*acto*) ordering; (*REL*) ordination.

ordenado, a [orðe'naðo, a] *adj* (*metódico*) methodical; (*arreglado*) orderly.

ordenador [orðena'ðor] *nm* computer; **~ central** mainframe computer; **~ de gestión** business computer; **~ portátil** laptop (computer); **~ de sobremesa** desktop computer.

ordenamiento [orðena'mjento] *nm* legislation.

ordenanza [orðe'nanθa] *nf* ordinance; **~s municipales** by-laws ♦ *nm* (*COM etc*) messenger; (*MIL*) orderly; (*bedel*) porter.

ordenar [orðe'nar] *vt* (*mandar*) to order; (*poner orden*) to put in order, arrange; **~se** *vr* (*REL*) to be ordained.

ordeñadora [orðeɲa'ðora] *nf* milking machine.

ordeñar [orðe'ɲar] *vt* to milk.

ordinariez [orðina'rjeθ] *nf* (*cualidad*) coarseness, vulgarity; (*una ~*) coarse remark *o* joke *etc*.

ordinario, a [orði'narjo, a] *adj* (*común*) ordinary, usual; (*vulgar*) vulgar, common.

ordinograma [orðino'ɣrama] *nm* flowchart.

orear [ore'ar] *vt* to air; **~se** *vr* (*ropa*) to air.

orégano [o'reɣano] *nm* oregano.

oreja [o'rexa] *nf* ear; (*MECÁNICA*) lug, flange.

orensano, a [oren'sano, a] *adj* of *o* from Orense ♦ *nm/f* native *o* inhabitant of Orense.

orfanato [orfa'nato] *nm*, **orfanatorio** [orfana'torjo] *nm* orphanage.

orfandad [orfan'dað] *nf* orphanhood.

orfebre [or'feßre] *nm* gold-/silversmith.

orfebrería [orfeßre'ria] *nf* gold/silver work.

orfelinato [orfeli'nato] *nm* orphanage.

orfeón [orfe'on] *nm* (*MUS*) choral society.

organice [orɣa'niθe] *etc vb* V **organizar**.

orgánico, a [or'ɣaniko, a] *adj* organic.

organigrama [orɣani'ɣrama] *nm* flow chart; (*de organización*) organization chart.

organillo [orɣa'niʎo] *nm* barrel organ.

organismo [orɣa'nismo] *nm* (*BIO*) organism; (*POL*) organization; **O~ Internacional de Energía Atómica** International Atomic Energy Agency.

organista [orɣa'nista] *nm/f* organist.

organización [orɣaniθa'θjon] *nf* organization; **O~ de las Naciones Unidas (ONU)** United Nations Organization **O~ del Tratado del Atlántico Norte (OTAN)** North Atlantic Treaty Organization (NATO).

organizador, a [orɣaniθa'ðor, a] *adj* organizing; **el comité ~** the organizing committee ♦ *nm/f* organizer.

organizar [orɣani'θar] *vt* to organize.

órgano ['orɣano] *nm* organ.

orgasmo [or'ɣasmo] *nm* orgasm.

orgía [or'xia] *nf* orgy.

orgullo [or'ɣuʎo] *nm* (*altanería*) pride; (*autorespeto*) self-respect.

orgulloso, a [orɣu'ʎoso, a] *adj* (*gen*) proud; (*altanero*) haughty.

orientación [orjenta'θjon] *nf* (*posición*) position; (*dirección*) direction; **~ profesional** occupational guidance.

oriental [orjen'tal] *adj* oriental; (*región etc*) eastern ♦ *nm/f* oriental.

orientar [orjen'tar] *vt* (*situar*) to orientate; (*señalar*) to point; (*dirigir*) to direct; (*guiar*) to guide; **~se** *vr* to get one's bearings; (*decidirse*) to decide on a course of action.

oriente [o'rjente] *nm* east; **el O~** the East, the Orient; **Cercano/Medio/Lejano O~** Near/ Middle/Far East.

orificio [ori'fiθjo] *nm* orifice.

origen [o'rixen] *nm* origin; (*nacimiento*) lineage, birth; **dar ~ a** to cause, give rise to.

original [orixi'nal] *adj* (*nuevo*) original; (*extraño*) odd, strange ♦ *nm* original; (*TIP*) manuscript; (*TEC*) master (copy).

originalidad [orixinali'ðað] *nf* originality.

originar [orixi'nar] *vt* to originate; **~se** *vr* to originate.

originario, a [orixi'narjo, a] *adj* (*nativo*) native; (*primordial*) original; **ser ~ de** to originate from; **país ~** country of origin.

orilla [o'riʎa] *nf* (*borde*) border; (*de río*) bank; (*de bosque, tela*) edge; (*de mar*) shore; **a ~s de** on the banks of.

orillar [ori'ʎar] *vt* (*bordear*) to skirt, go round; (*COSTURA*) to edge; (*resolver*) to wind up; (*tocar: asunto*) to touch briefly on; (*dificultad*) to avoid.

orín [o'rin] *nm* rust.

orina [o'rina] *nf* urine.

orinal [ori'nal] *nm* (chamber) pot.

orinar [ori'nar] *vi* to urinate; ~**se** *vr* to wet o.s.

orines [o'rines] *nmpl* urine *sg*.

oriundo, a [o'rjundo, a] *adj*: ~ **de** native of.

orla ['orla] *nf* edge, border; (*ESCOL*) graduation photograph.

ornamentar [ornamen'tar] *vt* (*adornar*, *ataviar*) to adorn; (*revestir*) to bedeck.

ornar [or'nar] *vt* to adorn.

ornitología [ornitolo'xia] *nf* ornithology, bird watching.

ornitólogo, a [orni'toloxo, a] *nmlf* ornithologist.

oro ['oro] *nm* gold; ~ **en barras** gold ingots; **de** ~ gold, golden; **no es** ~ **todo lo que reluce** all that glitters is not gold; **hacerse de** ~ to make a fortune; *V tb* **oros**.

orondo, a [o'rondo, a] *adj* (*vasija*) rounded; (*individuo*) smug, self-satisfied.

oropel [oro'pel] *nm* tinsel.

oros ['oros] *nmpl* (*NAIPES*) one of the suits in the Spanish card deck; *V tb* **Baraja Española**.

orquesta [or'kesta] *nf* orchestra; ~ **de cámara/sinfónica** chamber/symphony orchestra; ~ **de jazz** jazz band.

orquestar [orkes'tar] *vt* to orchestrate.

orquídea [or'kiðea] *nf* orchid.

ortiga [or'tixa] *nf* nettle.

ortodoncia [orto'ðonθja] *nf* orthodontics *sg*.

ortodoxo, a [orto'ðokso, a] *adj* orthodox.

ortografía [ortoxra'fia] *nf* spelling.

ortopedia [orto'peðja] *nf* orthop(a)edics *sg*.

ortopédico, a [orto'peðiko, a] *adj* orthop(a)edic.

oruga [o'ruxa] *nf* caterpillar.

orujo [o'ruxo] *nm* type of strong grape liqueur made from grape pressings.

orzuelo [or'θwelo] *nm* (*MED*) stye.

os [os] *pron* (*gen*) (to) you; (*a vosotros*) (to) you; (*reflexivo*) (to) yourselves; (*mutuo*) (to) each other; **vosotros** ~ **laváis** you wash yourselves; **¡callar~!** (*fam*) shut up!

osa ['osa] *nf* (she-)bear; **O~ Mayor/Menor** Great/Little Bear, Ursa Major/Minor.

osadía [osa'ðia] *nf* daring; (*descaro*) impudence.

osamenta [osa'menta] *nf* skeleton.

osar [o'sar] *vi* to dare.

oscense [os'θense] *adj* of o from Huesca. ♦ *nmlf* native o inhabitant of Huesca.

oscilación [osθila'θjon] *nf* (*movimiento*) oscillation; (*fluctuación*) fluctuation; (*vacilación*) hesitation; (*columpio*) swinging, movement to and fro.

oscilar [osθi'lar] *vi* to oscillate; to fluctuate; to hesitate.

ósculo ['oskulo] *nm* kiss.

oscurecer [oskure'θer] *vt* to darken ♦ *vi* to grow dark; ~**se** *vr* to grow o get dark.

oscurezca [osku're θka] *etc vb V* **oscurecer**.

oscuridad [oskuri'ðað] *nf* obscurity; (*tinieblas*) darkness.

oscuro, a [os'kuro, a] *adj* dark; (*fig*) obscure; (*indefinido*) confused; (*cielo*) overcast, cloudy; (*futuro etc*) uncertain; **a oscuras** in the dark.

óseo, a ['oseo, a] *adj* bony; (*MED etc*) bone *cpd*.

oso ['oso] *nm* bear; ~ **blanco/gris/pardo** polar/grizzly/brown bear; ~ **de peluche** teddy bear; ~ **hormiguero** anteater; **hacer el** ~ to play the fool.

Ostende [os'tende] *nm* Ostend.

ostensible [osten'siβle] *adj* obvious.

ostensiblemente [ostensiβle'mente] *adv* perceptibly, visibly.

ostentación [ostenta'θjon] *nf* (*gen*) ostentation; (*acto*) display.

ostentar [osten'tar] *vt* (*gen*) to show; (*pey*) to flaunt, show off; (*poseer*) to have, possess.

ostentoso, a [osten'toso, a] *adj* ostentatious, showy.

osteópata [oste'opata] *nmlf* osteopath.

ostra ['ostra] *nf* oyster ♦ *excl*: **¡~s!** (*fam*) sugar!

ostracismo [ostra'θismo] *nm* ostracism.

OTAN ['otan] *nf abr V* **Organización del Tratado del Atlántico Norte**.

OTASE [o'tase] *nf abr* (= *Organización del Tratado del Sudeste Asiático*) SEATO.

otear [ote'ar] *vt* to observe; (*fig*) to look into.

otero [o'tero] *nm* low hill, hillock.

otitis [o'titis] *nf* earache.

otoñal [oto'ɲal] *adj* autumnal.

otoño [o'toɲo] *nm* autumn, fall (*US*).

otorgamiento [otorxa'mjento] *nm* conferring, granting; (*JUR*) execution.

otorgar [otor'xar] *vt* (*conceder*) to concede; (*dar*) to grant; (*poderes*) to confer; (*premio*) to award.

otorgue [o'torxe] *etc vb V* **otorgar**.

otorrinolaringólogo, a [otorrinolarin'go loxo, a] *nmlf* (*MED*: *tb*: **otorrino**) ear, nose and throat specialist.

═══════════ PALABRA CLAVE

otro, a ['otro, a] *adj* **1** (*distinto: sg*) another;
(*: pl*) other; **otra cosa/persona**
something/someone else; **con ~s amigos**
with other *o* different friends; **a/en otra**
parte elsewhere, somewhere else
2 (*adicional*): **tráigame ~ café (más), por**
favor can I have another coffee please;
~s 10 días más another 10 days
♦ *pron* **1** (*sg*) another one; **el ~** the other
one; **(los) ~s** (the) others; **¡otra!** (*MUS*)
more!; **de ~** somebody *o* someone else's;
que lo haga ~ let somebody *o* someone
else do it; **ni uno ni ~** neither one nor
the other
2 (*recíproco*): **se odian (la) una a (la) otra**
they hate one another *o* each other
3: **~ tanto: comer ~ tanto** to eat the
same *o* as much again; **recibió una**
decena de telegramas y otras tantas
llamadas he got about ten telegrams and
as many calls.

otrora [o'trora] *adv* formerly; **el ~ señor**
del país the one-time ruler of the
country.
OUA *nf abr* (= *Organización de la Unidad*
Africana) OAU.
ovación [oβa'θjon] *nf* ovation.
ovacionar [oβaθjo'nar] *vt* to cheer.
oval [o'βal], **ovalado, a** [oβa'laðo, a] *adj*
oval.
óvalo ['oβalo] *nm* oval.
ovario [o'βarjo] *nm* ovary.
oveja [o'βexa] *nf* sheep; **~ negra** (*fig*) black
sheep (of the family).
overol [oβe'rol] *nm* (*AM*) overalls *pl*.
ovetense [oβe'tense] *adj* of *o* from Oviedo
♦ *nm/f* native *o* inhabitant of Oviedo.
ovillo [o'βiʎo] *nm* (*de lana*) ball; (*fig*) tangle;
hacerse un ~ to curl up (into a ball).
OVNI ['oβni] *nm abr* (= *objeto volante no*
identificado) UFO.
ovulación [oβula'θjon] *nf* ovulation.
óvulo ['oβulo] *nm* ovum.
oxidación [oksiða'θjon] *nf* rusting.
oxidar [oksi'ðar] *vt* to rust; **~se** *vr* to go
rusty; (*TEC*) to oxidize.
óxido ['oksiðo] *nm* oxide.
oxigenado, a [oksixe'naðo, a] *adj*
(*QUÍMICA*) oxygenated; (*pelo*) bleached.
oxigenar [oksixe'nar] *vt* to oxygenate; **~se**
vr to become oxygenated; (*fam*) to get
some fresh air.
oxígeno [ok'sixeno] *nm* oxygen.
oyendo [o'jendo] *etc vb V* **oír**.
oyente [o'jente] *nm/f* listener, hearer;

(*ESCOL*) unregistered *o* occasional
student.

═══════════ *P p*

P, p [pe] *nf* (*letra*) P, p; **P de París** P for
Peter.
P *abr* (*REL*: = *padre*) Fr.; = **papa**.
p. *abr* (= *página*) p.
p.a. *abr* = **por autorización**.
pabellón [paβe'ʎon] *nm* bell tent; (*ARQ*)
pavilion; (*de hospital etc*) block, section;
(*bandera*) flag; **~ de conveniencia** (*COM*)
flag of convenience; **~ de la oreja** outer
ear.
pábilo ['paβilo] *nm* wick.
pábulo ['paβulo] *nm* food; **dar ~ a** to feed,
encourage.
PAC *nf abr* (= *Política Agrícola Común*) CAP.
pacense [pa'θense] *adj* of *o* from Badajoz
♦ *nm/f* native *o* inhabitant of Badajoz.
paceño, a [pa'θeɲo, a] *adj* of *o* from La
Paz ♦ *nm/f* native *o* inhabitant of La Paz.
pacer [pa'θer] *vi* to graze ♦ *vt* to graze on.
pachá [pa'tʃa] *nm*: **vivir como un ~** to live
like a king.
pachanguero, a [patʃan'gero, a] *adj* (*pey*:
música) *noisy and catchy*.
pachorra [pa'tʃorra] *nf* (*indolencia*)
slowness; (*tranquilidad*) calmness.
pachucho, a [pa'tʃutʃo, a] *adj* (*fruta*)
overripe; (*persona*) off-colour, poorly.
paciencia [pa'θjenθja] *nf* patience; **¡~!** be
patient!; **¡~ y barajar!** don't give up!;
perder la ~ to lose one's temper.
paciente [pa'θjente] *adj, nm/f* patient.
pacificación [paθifika'θjon] *nf* pacification.
pacificar [paθifi'kar] *vt* to pacify;
(*tranquilizar*) to calm.
pacífico, a [pa'θifiko, a] *adj* peaceful;
(*persona*) peace-loving; (*existencia*)
pacific; **el (Océano) P~** the Pacific
(Ocean).
pacifique [paθi'fike] *etc vb V* **pacificar**.
pacifismo [paθi'fismo] *nm* pacifism.
pacifista [paθi'fista] *nm/f* pacifist.
pacotilla [pako'tiʎa] *nf* trash; **de ~** shoddy.
pactar [pak'tar] *vt* to agree to, agree on
♦ *vi* to come to an agreement.
pacto ['pakto] *nm* (*tratado*) pact; (*acuerdo*)
agreement.

padecer [paðe'θer] *vt* (*sufrir*) to suffer; (*soportar*) to endure, put up with; (*ser víctima de*) to be a victim of ♦ *vi*: ~ **de** to suffer from.

padecimiento [paðeθi'mjento] *nm* suffering.

padezca [pa'ðeθka] *etc vb V* **padecer**.

padrastro [pa'ðrastro] *nm* stepfather.

padre ['paðre] *nm* father ♦ *adj* (*fam*): **un éxito** ~ a tremendous success; ~**s** *nmpl* parents; ~ **espiritual** confessor; **P~ Nuestro** Lord's Prayer; ~ **político** father-in-law; **García** ~ García senior; **¡tu** ~**!** (*fam!*) up yours! (*!*).

padrino [pa'ðrino] *nm* godfather; (*fig*) sponsor, patron; ~**s** *nmpl* godparents; ~ **de boda** best man.

padrón [pa'ðron] *nm* (*censo*) census, roll; (*de socios*) register.

paella [pa'eʎa] *nf* paella, *dish of rice with meat, shellfish etc*.

paga ['paɣa] *nf* (*dinero pagado*) payment; (*sueldo*) pay, wages *pl*.

pagadero, a [paɣa'ðero, a] *adj* payable; ~ **a la entrega/a plazos** payable on delivery/in instalments.

pagano, a [pa'ɣano, a] *adj, nm/f* pagan, heathen.

pagar [pa'ɣar] *vt* (*gen*) to pay; (*las compras, crimen*) to pay for; (*deuda*) to pay (off); (*fig: favor*) to repay ♦ *vi* to pay; ~**se** *vr*: ~**se con algo** to be content with sth; **¡me las pagarás!** I'll get you for this!

pagaré [paɣa're] *nm* I.O.U.

página ['paxina] *nf* page; ~**s amarillas** Yellow Pages ®.

paginación [paxina'θjon] *nf* (*INFORM, TIP*) pagination.

paginar [paxi'nar] *vt* (*INFORM, TIP*) to paginate.

pago ['paɣo] *nm* (*dinero*) payment; (*fig*) return; ~ **anticipado/a cuenta/a la entrega/en especie/inicial** advance payment/payment on account/cash on delivery/payment in kind/down payment; ~ **a título gracioso** ex gratia payment; **en** ~ **de** in return for.

pág(s). *abr* (= *página(s)*) p(p).

pague ['paɣe] *etc vb V* **pagar**.

paila ['paila] *nf* (*AM*) frying pan.

país [pa'is] *nm* (*gen*) country; (*región*) land; **los Países Bajos** the Low Countries; **el P~ Vasco** the Basque Country.

paisaje [pai'saxe] *nm* countryside, landscape; (*vista*) scenery.

paisano, a [pai'sano, a] *adj* of the same country ♦ *nm/f* (*compatriota*) fellow countryman/woman; **vestir de** ~

(*soldado*) to be in civilian clothes; (*guardia*) to be in plain clothes.

paja ['paxa] *nf* straw; (*fig*) trash, rubbish; (*en libro, ensayo*) padding, waffle; **riñeron por un quítame allá esas** ~**s** they quarrelled over a trifle.

pajar [pa'xar] *nm* hay loft.

pajarita [paxa'rita] *nf* bow tie.

pájaro ['paxaro] *nm* bird; (*fam: astuto*) clever fellow; **tener la cabeza a** ~**s** to be featherbrained.

pajita [pa'xita] *nf* (drinking) straw.

pajizo, a [pa'xiθo, a] *adj* (*de paja*) straw *cpd*; (*techo*) thatched; (*color*) straw-coloured.

pakistaní [pakista'ni] *adj, nm/f* Pakistani.

pala ['pala] *nf* (*de mango largo*) spade; (*de mango corto*) shovel; (*raqueta etc*) bat; (*: de tenis*) racquet; (*CULIN*) slice; ~ **matamoscas** fly swat.

palabra [pa'laβra] *nf* (*gen, promesa*) word; (*facultad*) (power of) speech; (*derecho de hablar*) right to speak; **faltar a su** ~ to go back on one's word; **quedarse con la** ~ **en la boca** to stop short; (*en reunión, comité etc*) **tomar la** ~ to speak, take the floor; **pedir la** ~ to ask to be allowed to speak; **tener la** ~ to have the floor; **no encuentro** ~**s para expresarme** words fail me.

palabrería [palaβre'ria] *nf* hot air.

palabrota [pala'βrota] *nf* swearword.

palacio [pa'laθjo] *nm* palace; (*mansión*) mansion, large house; ~ **de justicia** courthouse; ~ **municipal** town/city hall.

palada [pa'laða] *nf* shovelful, spadeful; (*de remo*) stroke.

paladar [pala'ðar] *nm* palate.

paladear [palaðe'ar] *vt* to taste.

palanca [pa'lanka] *nf* lever; (*fig*) pull, influence; ~ **de cambio** (*AUTO*) gear lever, gearshift (*US*); ~ **de freno** (*AUTO*) brake lever; ~ **de gobierno** *o* **de control** (*INFORM*) joystick.

palangana [palan'gana] *nf* washbasin.

palco ['palko] *nm* box.

palenque [pa'lenke] *nm* (*cerca*) stockade, fence; (*área*) arena, enclosure; (*de gallos*) pit.

palentino, a [palen'tino, a] *adj* of *o* from Palencia ♦ *nm/f* native *o* inhabitant of Palencia.

paleolítico, a [paleo'litiko, a] *adj* paleolithic.

paleontología [paleontolo'xia] *nf* paleontology.

Palestina [pales'tina] *nf* Palestine.

palestino, a [pales'tino, a] *adj, nm/f* Palestinian.

palestra [pa'lestra] *nf*: **salir** *o* **saltar a la** ~ to come into the spotlight.

paleto, a [pa'leto, a] *nm/f* yokel, hick (US)
♦ *nf* (*pala*) small shovel; (*ARTE*) palette; (*ANAT*) shoulder blade; (*AM*) ice lolly.

paliar [pa'ljar] *vt* (*mitigar*) to mitigate; (*disfrazar*) to conceal.

paliativo [palja'tiβo] *nm* palliative.

palidecer [paliðe'θer] *vi* to turn pale.

palidez [pali'ðeθ] *nf* paleness.

palidezca [pali'ðeθka] *etc vb V* **palidecer**.

pálido, a ['paliðo, a] *adj* pale.

palillo [pa'liʎo] *nm* small stick; (*para dientes*) toothpick; ~**s (chinos)** chopsticks; **estar hecho un** ~ to be as thin as a rake.

palio ['paljo] *nm* canopy.

palique [pa'like] *nm*: **estar de** ~ (*fam*) to have a chat.

paliza [pa'liθa] *nf* beating, thrashing; **dar** *o* **propinar** (*fam*) **una** ~ **a algn** to give sb a thrashing.

palma ['palma] *nf* (*ANAT*) palm; (*árbol*) palm tree; **batir** *o* **dar** ~**s** to clap, applaud; **llevarse la** ~ to triumph, win.

palmada [pal'maða] *nf* slap; ~**s** *nfpl* clapping *sg*, applause *sg*.

Palma de Mallorca *nf* Palma.

palmar [pal'mar] *vi* (*tb*: ~**la**) to die, kick the bucket.

palmarés [palma'res] *nm* (*lista*) list of winners; (*historial*) track record.

palmear [palme'ar] *vi* to clap.

palmero, a [pal'mero, a] *adj* of the island of Palma ♦ *nm/f* native *o* inhabitant of the island of Palma ♦ *nm* (*AM*), *nf* palm tree.

palmo ['palmo] *nm* (*medida*) span; (*fig*) small amount; ~ **a** ~ inch by inch.

palmotear [palmote'ar] *vi* to clap, applaud.

palmoteo [palmo'teo] *nm* clapping, applause.

palo ['palo] *nm* stick; (*poste*) post, pole; (*mango*) handle, shaft; (*golpe*) blow, hit; (*de golf*) club; (*de béisbol*) bat; ~ (*NAUT*) mast; (*NAIPES*) suit; **vermut a** ~ **seco** straight vermouth; **de tal** ~ **tal astilla** like father like son.

paloma [pa'loma] *nf* dove, pigeon; ~ **mensajera** carrier *o* homing pigeon.

palomilla [palo'miʎa] *nf* moth; (*TEC: tuerca*) wing nut; (*soporte*) bracket.

palomitas [palo'mitas] *nfpl* popcorn *sg*.

palpable [pal'paβle] *adj* palpable; (*fig*) tangible.

palpar [pal'par] *vt* to touch, feel.

palpitación [palpita'θjon] *nf* palpitation.

palpitante [palpi'tante] *adj* palpitating; (*fig*) burning.

palpitar [palpi'tar] *vi* to palpitate; (*latir*) to beat.

palta ['palta] *nf* (*AM*) avocado.

palúdico, a [pa'luðiko, a] *adj* marshy.

paludismo [palu'ðismo] *nm* malaria.

palurdo, a [pa'lurðo, a] *adj* coarse, uncouth ♦ *nm/f* yokel, hick (US).

pamela [pa'mela] *nf* sun hat.

pampa ['pampa] *nf* (*AM*) pampa(s), prairie.

pamplinas [pam'plinas] *nfpl* nonsense *sg*.

pamplonés, esa [pamplo'nes, esa], **pamplonica** [pamplo'nika] *adj* of *o* from Pamplona ♦ *nm/f* native *o* inhabitant of Pamplona.

pan [pan] *nm* bread; (*una barra*) loaf; ~ **de molde** sliced loaf; ~ **integral** wholemeal bread; ~ **rallado** breadcrumbs *pl*; **eso es** ~ **comido** it's a cinch; **llamar al** ~ ~ **y al vino vino** to call a spade a spade.

pana ['pana] *nf* corduroy.

panadería [panaðe'ria] *nf* baker's (shop).

panadero, a [pana'ðero, a] *nm/f* baker.

panal [pa'nal] *nm* honeycomb.

Panamá [pana'ma] *nm* Panama.

panameño, a [pana'meɲo, a] *adj* Panamanian.

pancarta [pan'karta] *nf* placard, banner.

pancho, a ['pantʃo, a] *adj*: **estar tan** ~ to remain perfectly calm.

pancito [pan'sito] *nm* (*AM*) (bread) roll.

páncreas ['pankreas] *nm* pancreas.

panda ['panda] *nm* panda ♦ *nf* gang.

pandereta [pande'reta] *nf* tambourine.

pandilla [pan'diʎa] *nf* set, group; (*de criminales*) gang; (*pey*) clique.

pando, a ['pando, a] *adj* sagging.

panel [pa'nel] *nm* panel; ~ **acústico** acoustic screen.

panera [pa'nera] *nf* bread basket.

panfleto [pan'fleto] *nm* (*POL etc*) pamphlet; lampoon.

pánico ['paniko] *nm* panic.

panificadora [panifika'ðora] *nf* bakery.

panorama [pano'rama] *nm* panorama; (*vista*) view.

panqué [pan'ke] *nm* (*AM*) pancake.

pantaletas [panta'letas] *nfpl* (*AM*) panties.

pantalla [pan'taʎa] *nf* (*de cine*) screen; (*cubreluz*) lampshade; (*INFORM*) screen, display; **servir de** ~ **a** to be a blind for; ~ **de cristal líquido** liquid crystal display; ~ **táctil** touch-sensitive screen; ~ **de ayuda** help screen; ~ **plana** plane screen.

pantalón [panta'lon] *nm*, **pantalones** [panta'lones] *nmpl* trousers *pl*, pants *pl* (US); **pantalones vaqueros** jeans *pl*.

pantano [pan'tano] *nm* (*ciénaga*) marsh,

swamp; (*depósito: de agua*) reservoir; (*fig*) jam, fix, difficulty.

pantera [pan'tera] *nf* panther.

pantis ['pantis] *nmpl* tights.

pantomima [panto'mima] *nf* pantomime.

pantorrilla [panto'rriʎa] *nf* calf (of the leg).

pantufla [pan'tufla] *nf* slipper.

panty ['panti] *nm* = **pantis**.

panza ['panθa] *nf* belly, paunch.

panzón, ona [pan'θon, ona], **panzudo, a** [pan'θuðo, a] *adj* fat, potbellied.

pañal [pa'ɲal] *nm* nappy, diaper (*US*); **estar todavía en ~es** to be still wet behind the ears.

pañería [paɲe'ria] *nf* (*artículos*) drapery; (*tienda*) draper's (shop), dry-goods store (*US*).

paño ['paɲo] *nm* (*tela*) cloth; (*pedazo de tela*) (piece of) cloth; (*trapo*) duster, rag; **~ de cocina** dishcloth; **~ higiénico** sanitary towel; **~s menores** underclothes; **~s calientes** (*fig*) half-measures; **no andarse con ~s calientes** to pull no punches.

pañuelo [pa'ɲwelo] *nm* handkerchief, hanky (*fam*); (*para la cabeza*) (head)scarf.

papa ['papa] *nf* (*AM*) potato ♦ *nm*: **el P~** the Pope.

papá [pa'pa] *nm, pl* **papás** (*fam*) dad, daddy, pop (*US*); **~s** *nmpl* parents; **hijo de ~** Hooray Henry (*fam*).

papada [pa'paða] *nf* double chin.

papagayo [papa'ɣajo] *nm* parrot.

papanatas [papa'natas] *nm inv* (*fam*) sucker, simpleton.

paparrucha [papa'rrutʃa] *nf* (*tontería*) piece of nonsense.

papaya [pa'paja] *nf* papaya.

papear [pape'ar] *vt, vi* (*fam*) to eat.

papel [pa'pel] *nm* (*gen*) paper; (*hoja de papel*) sheet of paper; (*TEAT*) part, role; **~es** *nmpl* identification papers; **~ de calco/carbón/de cartas** tracing paper/carbon paper/stationery; **~ contínuo** (*INFORM*) continuous stationery; **~ de envolver/de empapelar** brown paper, wrapping paper/wallpaper; **~ de aluminio/higiénico** tinfoil/toilet paper; **~ del** *o* **de pagos al Estado** government bonds *pl*; **~ de lija** sandpaper; **~ moneda** paper money; **~ plegado (en abanico** *o* **en acordeón)** fanfold paper; **~ secante** blotting paper; **~ térmico** thermal paper.

papeleo [pape'leo] *nm* red tape.

papelera [pape'lera] *nf* (*cesto*) wastepaper basket; (*escritorio*) desk.

papelería [papele'ria] *nf* (*tienda*) stationer's (shop).

papeleta [pape'leta] *nf* (*pedazo de papel*) slip *o* bit of paper; (*POL*) ballot paper; (*ESCOL*) report; **¡vaya ~!** this is a tough one!

paperas [pa'peras] *nfpl* mumps *sg*.

papilla [pa'piʎa] *nf* (*de bebé*) baby food; (*pey*) mush; **estar hecho ~** to be dog-tired.

paquete [pa'kete] *nm* (*caja*) packet; (*bulto*) parcel; (*AM fam*) nuisance, bore; (*INFORM*) package (*of software*); (*vacaciones*) package tour; **~ de aplicaciones** (*INFORM*) applications package; **~ integrado** (*INFORM*) integrated package; **~ de gestión integrado** combined management suite; **~s postales** parcel post *sg*.

paquistaní [pakista'ni] = **pakistaní**.

par [par] *adj* (*igual*) like, equal; (*MAT*) even ♦ *nm* equal; (*de guantes*) pair; (*de veces*) couple; (*dignidad*) peer; (*GOLF, COM*) par ♦ *nf* par; **~es o nones** odds or evens; **abrir de ~ en ~** to open wide; **a la ~** par; **sobre/bajo la ~** above/below par.

para ['para] *prep* (*gen*) for; **no es ~ comer** it's not for eating; **decir ~ sí** to say to o.s.; **¿~ qué lo quieres?** what do you want it for?; **se casaron ~ separarse otra vez** they married only to separate again; **~ entonces** by then *o* that time; **lo tendré ~ mañana** I'll have it for tomorrow; **ir ~ casa** to go home, head for home; **~ profesor es muy estúpido** he's very stupid for a teacher; **¿quién es usted ~ gritar así?** who are you to shout like that?; **tengo bastante ~ vivir** I have enough to live on.

parabellum [paraße'lum] *nm* (automatic) pistol.

parabién [para'ßjen] *nm* congratulations *pl*.

parábola [pa'raßola] *nf* parable; (*MAT*) parabola.

parabólica [para'ßolika] *nf* (*tb*: **antena ~**) satellite dish.

parabrisas [para'ßrisas] *nm inv* windscreen, windshield (*US*).

paracaídas [paraka'iðas] *nm inv* parachute.

paracaidista [parakai'ðista] *nm/f* parachutist; (*MIL*) paratrooper.

parachoques [para'tʃokes] *nm inv* bumper, fender (*US*); shock absorber.

parada [pa'raða] *nf* V **parado**.

paradero [para'ðero] *nm* stopping-place; (*situación*) whereabouts.

parado, a [pa'raðo, a] *adj* (*persona*) motionless, standing still; (*fábrica*) closed, at a standstill; (*coche*) stopped; (*AM: de pie*) standing (up); (*sin empleo*) unemployed, idle; (*confuso*) confused ♦ *nf* (*gen*) stop; (*acto*) stopping; (*de industria*) shutdown, stoppage; (*lugar*) stopping-place; **salir bien** ~ to come off well; **parada de autobús** bus stop; **parada discrecional** request stop; **parada en seco** sudden stop; **parada de taxis** taxi rank.

paradoja [para'ðoxa] *nf* paradox.

paradójico, a [para'ðoxiko, a] *adj* paradoxical.

parador [para'ðor] *nm* (luxury) hotel.

parafrasear [parafrase'ar] *vt* to paraphrase.

paráfrasis [pa'rafrasis] *nf inv* paraphrase.

paraguas [pa'raɣwas] *nm inv* umbrella.

Paraguay [para'ɣwai] *nm*: **el** ~ Paraguay.

paraguayo, a [para'ɣwajo, a] *adj, nm/f* Paraguayan.

paraíso [para'iso] *nm* paradise, heaven; ~ **fiscal** (*COM*) tax haven.

paraje [pa'raxe] *nm* place, spot.

paralelo, a [para'lelo, a] *adj, nm* parallel; **en** ~ (*ELEC, INFORM*) (in) parallel.

paralice [para'liθe] *etc vb V* **paralizar**.

parálisis [pa'ralisis] *nf inv* paralysis; ~ **cerebral** cerebral palsy; ~ **progresiva** creeping paralysis.

paralítico, a [para'litiko, a] *adj, nm/f* paralytic.

paralizar [parali'θar] *vt* to paralyse; ~**se** *vr* to become paralysed; (*fig*) to come to a standstill.

parámetro [pa'rametro] *nm* parameter.

paramilitar [paramili'tar] *adj* paramilitary.

páramo ['paramo] *nm* bleak plateau.

parangón [paran'ɡon] *nm*: **sin** ~ incomparable.

paraninfo [para'ninfo] *nm* (*ESCOL*) assembly hall.

paranoia [para'noia] *nf* paranoia.

paranoico, a [para'noiko, a] *adj, nm/f* paranoid.

paranormal [paranor'mal] *adj* paranormal.

parapetarse [parape'tarse] *vr* to shelter.

parapléjico, a [para'plexiko, a] *adj, nm/f* paraplegic.

parar [pa'rar] *vt* to stop; (*progreso etc*) to check, halt; (*golpe*) to ward off ♦ *vi* to stop; (*hospedarse*) to stay, put up; ~**se** *vr* to stop; (*AM*) to stand up; **no** ~ **de hacer algo** to keep on doing sth; **ha parado de llover** it has stopped raining; **van a** ~ **en la comisaría** they're going to end up in the police station; **no sabemos en qué va a** ~ **todo esto** we don't know where all

this is going to end; ~**se a hacer algo** to stop to do sth; ~**se en** to pay attention to.

pararrayos [para'rrajos] *nm inv* lightning conductor.

parásito, a [pa'rasito, a] *nm/f* parasite.

parasol [para'sol] *nm* parasol, sunshade.

parcela [par'θela] *nf* plot, piece of ground, smallholding.

parche ['partʃe] *nm* patch.

parchís [par'tʃis] *nm* ludo.

parcial [par'θjal] *adj* (*pago*) part-; (*eclipse*) partial; (*juez*) prejudiced, biased.

parcialidad [parθjali'ðað] *nf* (*prejuicio*) prejudice, bias.

parco, a ['parko, a] *adj* (*frugal*) sparing; (*moderado*) moderate.

pardillo, a [par'ðiʎo, a] *adj* (*pey*) provincial ♦ *nm/f* (*pey*) country bumpkin ♦ *nm* (*ZOOL*) linnet.

pardo, a ['parðo, a] *adj* (*color*) brown; (*cielo*) overcast; (*voz*) flat, dull.

parear [pare'ar] *vt* (*juntar, hacer par*) to match, put together; (*calcetines*) to put into pairs; (*BIO*) to mate, pair.

parecer [pare'θer] *nm* (*opinión*) opinion, view; (*aspecto*) looks *pl* ♦ *vi* (*tener apariencia*) to seem, look; (*asemejarse*) to look like, seem like; (*aparecer, llegar*) to appear; ~**se** *vr* to look alike, resemble each other; ~**se a** to look like, resemble; **al** ~ apparently; **me parece que** I think (that), it seems to me that.

parecido, a [pare'θiðo, a] *adj* similar ♦ *nm* similarity, likeness, resemblance; ~ **a** like, similar to; **bien** ~ good-looking, nice-looking.

pared [pa'reð] *nf* wall; ~ **divisoria/ medianera** dividing/party wall; **subirse por las** ~**es** (*fam*) to go up the wall.

paredón [pare'ðon] *nm*: **llevar a algn al** ~ to put sb up against a wall, shoot sb.

parejo, a [pa'rexo, a] *adj* (*igual*) equal; (*liso*) smooth, even ♦ *nf* (*dos*) pair; (*: de personas*) couple; (*el otro: de un par*) other one (of a pair); (*: persona*) partner; (*Guardias*) Civil Guard patrol.

parentela [paren'tela] *nf* relations *pl*.

parentesco [paren'tesko] *nm* relationship.

paréntesis [pa'rentesis] *nm inv* parenthesis; (*digresión*) digression; (*en escrito*) bracket.

parezca [pa'reθka] *etc vb V* **parecer**.

parida [pa'riða] *nf*: ~ **mental** (*fam*) dumb idea.

paridad [pari'ðað] *nf* (*ECON*) parity.

pariente, a [pa'rjente, a] *nm/f* relative, relation.

parihuela [pari'wela] *nf* stretcher.
paripé [pari'pe] *nm*: **hacer el** ~ to put on an act.
parir [pa'rir] *vt* to give birth to ♦ *vi* (*mujer*) to give birth, have a baby; (*yegua*) to foal; (*vaca*) to calve.
París [pa'ris] *nm* Paris.
parisiense [pari'sjense] *adj, nmf* Parisian.
paritario, a [pari'tarjo, a] *adj* equal.
parking ['parkin] *nm* car park, parking lot (*US*).
parlamentar [parlamen'tar] *vi* (*negociar*) to parley.
parlamentario, a [parlamen'tarjo, a] *adj* parliamentary ♦ *nmf* member of parliament.
parlamento [parla'mento] *nm* (*POL*) parliament; (*JUR*) speech.
parlanchín, ina [parlan'tʃin, ina] *adj* loose-tongued, indiscreet ♦ *nmf* chatterbox.
parlante [par'lante] *nm* (*AM*) loudspeaker.
parlar [par'lar] *vi* to chatter (away).
parlotear [parlote'ar] *vi* to chatter, prattle.
parloteo [parlo'teo] *nm* chatter, prattle.
parné [par'ne] *nm* (*fam: dinero*) dough.
paro ['paro] *nm* (*huelga*) stoppage (of work), strike; (*desempleo*) unemployment; ~ **cardiaco** cardiac arrest; **subsidio de** ~ unemployment benefit; **hay** ~ **en la industria** work in the industry is at a standstill; ~ **del sistema** (*INFORM*) system shutdown.
parodia [pa'roðja] *nf* parody.
parodiar [paro'ðjar] *vt* to parody.
parpadear [parpaðe'ar] *vi* (*los ojos*) to blink; (*luz*) to flicker.
parpadeo [parpa'ðeo] *nm* (*de ojos*) blinking, winking; (*de luz*) flickering.
párpado ['parpaðo] *nm* eyelid.
parque ['parke] *nm* (*lugar verde*) park; ~ **de atracciones/de bomberos/zoológico** fairground/fire station/zoo.
parqué, parquet [par'ke] *nm* parquet.
parqueadero [parkea'ðero] *nm* (*AM*) car park, parking lot (*US*).
parquímetro [par'kimetro] *nm* parking meter.
parra ['parra] *nf* grapevine.
párrafo ['parrafo] *nm* paragraph; **echar un** ~ (*fam*) to have a chat.
parranda [pa'rranda] *nf* (*fam*) spree, binge.
parrilla [pa'rriʎa] *nf* (*CULIN*) grill; (*AM AUTO*) roof-rack; ~ (**de salida**) (*AUTO*) starting grid; **carne a la** ~ grilled meat.
parrillada [parri'ʎaða] *nf* barbecue.
párroco ['parroko] *nm* parish priest.
parroquia [pa'rrokja] *nf* parish; (*iglesia*) parish church; (*COM*) clientele,

customers *pl*.
parroquiano, a [parro'kjano, a] *nmf* parishioner; client, customer.
parsimonia [parsi'monja] *nf* (*frugalidad*) sparingness; (*calma*) deliberateness; **con** ~ calmly.
parte ['parte] *nm* message; (*informe*) report; ~ **meteorológico** weather forecast ♦ *nf* part; (*lado, cara*) side; (*de reparto*) share; (*JUR*) party; **en alguna** ~ **de Europa** somewhere in Europe; **en cualquier** ~ anywhere; **por ahí no se va a ninguna** ~ that leads nowhere; (*fig*) this is getting us nowhere; **en gran** ~ to a large extent; **la mayor** ~ **de los españoles** most Spaniards; **de algún tiempo a esta** ~ for some time past; **de** ~ **de algn** on sb's behalf; **¿de** ~ **de quién?** (*TELEC*) who is speaking?; **por** ~ **de** on the part of; **yo por mi** ~ I for my part; **por una** ~ ... **por otra** ~ on the one hand, ... on the other (hand); **dar** ~ **a algn** to report to sb; **tomar** ~ to take part.
partera [par'tera] *nf* midwife.
parterre [par'terre] *nm* (*de flores*) (flower)bed.
partición [parti'θjon] *nf* division, sharing-out; (*POL*) partition.
participación [partiθipa'θjon] *nf* (*acto*) participation, taking part; (*parte*) share; (*COM*) share, stock (*US*); (*de lotería*) shared prize; (*aviso*) notice, notification; ~ **en los beneficios** profit-sharing; ~ **minoritaria** minority interest.
participante [partiθi'pante] *nmf* participant.
participar [partiθi'par] *vt* to notify, inform ♦ *vi* to take part, participate; ~ **en una empresa** (*COM*) to invest in an enterprise; **le participo que** ... I have to tell you that ....
partícipe [par'tiθipe] *nmf* participant; **hacer** ~ **a algn de algo** to inform sb of sth.
participio [parti'θipjo] *nm* participle; ~ **de pasado/presente** past/present participle.
partícula [par'tikula] *nf* particle.
particular [partiku'lar] *adj* (*especial*) particular, special; (*individual, personal*) private, personal ♦ *nm* (*punto, asunto*) particular, point; (*individuo*) individual; **tiene coche** ~ he has a car of his own; **no dijo mucho sobre el** ~ he didn't say much about the matter.
particularice [partikula'riθe] *etc vb V* **particularizar**.

particularidad [partikulari'ðað] *nf*
peculiarity; **tiene la ~ de que** ... one of
its special features is (that) ....

particularizar [partikulari'θar] *vt* to
distinguish; (*especificar*) to specify;
(*detallar*) to give details about.

partida [par'tiða] *nf* (*salida*) departure;
(*COM*) entry, item; (*juego*) game; (*grupo,
bando*) band, group; **mala ~** dirty trick;
~ de nacimiento/matrimonio/defunción
birth/marriage/death certificate; **echar
una ~** to have a game.

partidario, a [parti'ðarjo, a] *adj* partisan
♦ *nm/f* (*DEPORTE*) supporter; (*POL*) partisan.

partidismo [parti'ðismo] *nm* (*JUR*)
partisanship, bias; (*POL*) party politics.

partido [par'tiðo] *nm* (*POL*) party;
(*encuentro*) game, match; (*apoyo*)
support; (*equipo*) team; **~ amistoso**
(*DEPORTE*) friendly game; **~ de fútbol**
football match; **sacar ~ de** to profit
from, benefit from; **tomar ~** to take
sides.

partir [par'tir] *vt* (*dividir*) to split, divide;
(*compartir, distribuir*) to share (out),
distribute; (*romper*) to break open, split
open; (*rebanada*) to cut (off) ♦ *vi* (*tomar
camino*) to set off, set out; (*comenzar*) to
start (off *o* out); **~se** *vr* to crack *o* split *o*
break (in two *etc*); **a ~ de** (starting)
from; **~se de risa** to split one's sides
(laughing).

partitura [parti'tura] *nf* score.

parto ['parto] *nm* birth, delivery; (*fig*)
product, creation; **estar de ~** to be in
labour.

parvulario [parβu'larjo] *nm* nursery
school, kindergarten.

párvulo, a ['parβulo, a] *nm/f* infant.

pasa ['pasa] *nf* V **paso**.

pasable [pa'saβle] *adj* passable.

pasada [pa'saða] *nf* V **pasado**.

pasadizo [pasa'ðiθo] *nm* (*pasillo*) passage,
corridor; (*callejuela*) alley.

pasado, a [pa'saðo, a] *adj* past; (*malo:
comida, fruta*) bad; (*muy cocido*)
overdone; (*anticuado*) out of date ♦ *nm*
past; (*LING*) past (tense) ♦ *nf* passing,
passage; (*acción de pulir*) rub, polish; **~
mañana** the day after tomorrow; **el mes
~** last month; **~s dos días** after two
days; **lo ~, ~** let bygones be bygones; **~
de moda** old-fashioned; **~ por agua**
(*huevo*) boiled; **de pasada** in passing,
incidentally; **una mala pasada** a dirty
trick.

pasador [pasa'ðor] *nm* (*gen*) bolt; (*de pelo*)
pin, grip, slide; **~es** *nmpl* (*AM: cordones*)

shoelaces.

pasaje [pa'saxe] *nm* (*gen*) passage; (*pago
de viaje*) fare; (*los pasajeros*) passengers
pl; (*pasillo*) passageway.

pasajero, a [pasa'xero, a] *adj* passing;
(*ave*) migratory ♦ *nm/f* passenger;
(*viajero*) traveller.

pasamanos [pasa'manos] *nm inv* rail,
handrail; (*de escalera*) banister.

pasamontañas [pasamon'taɲas] *nm inv*
balaclava (helmet).

pasaporte [pasa'porte] *nm* passport.

pasar [pa'sar] *vt* (*gen*) to pass; (*tiempo*) to
spend; (*durezas*) to suffer, endure;
(*noticia*) to give, pass on; (*película*) to
show; (*persona*) to take, conduct; (*río*) to
cross; (*barrera*) to pass through; (*falta*) to
overlook, tolerate; (*contrincante*) to
surpass, do better than; (*coche*) to
overtake; (*contrabando*) to smuggle (in/
out); (*enfermedad*) to give, infect with
♦ *vi* (*gen*) to pass, go; (*terminarse*) to be
over; (*ocurrir*) to happen; **~se** *vr* (*efectos*)
to pass, be over; (*flores*) to fade; (*comida*)
to go bad, go off; (*fig*) to overdo it, go
too far *o* over the top; **~ de** to go
beyond, exceed; **¡pase!** come in!; **nos
hicieron ~** they showed us in; **~ por** to
fetch; **~ por alto** to skip; **~ por una crisis**
to go through a crisis; **se hace ~ por
médico** he passes himself off as a
doctor; **~lo bien/bomba** *o* **de maravilla**
to have a good/great time; **~se al
enemigo** to go over to the enemy; **~se
de la raya** to go too far; **¡no te pases!**
don't try me!; **se me pasó** I forgot; **se
me pasó el turno** I missed my turn; **no
se le pasa nada** nothing escapes him, he
misses nothing; **ya se te pasará** you'll
get over it; **¿qué pasa?** what's
happening?, what's going on?, what's
up?; **¡cómo pasa el tiempo!** time just
flies!; **pase lo que pase** come what may;
el autobús pasa por nuestra casa the bus
goes past our house.

pasarela [pasa'rela] *nf* footbridge; (*en
barco*) gangway.

pasatiempo [pasa'tjempo] *nm* pastime,
hobby; (*distracción*) amusement.

Pascua, pascua ['paskwa] *nf*: **~ (de
Resurrección)** Easter; **~ de Navidad**
Christmas; **~s** *nfpl* Christmas time *sg*;
¡felices ~s! Merry Christmas; **de ~s a
Ramos** once in a blue moon; **hacer la ~ a**
(*fam*) to annoy, bug.

pase ['pase] *nm* pass; (*CINE*) performance,
showing; (*COM*) permit; (*JUR*) licence.

pasear [pase'ar] *vt* to take for a walk;

(*exhibir*) to parade, show off ♦ *vi*, ~**se** *vr*
to walk, go for a walk; ~ **en coche** to go
for a drive.

paseo [pa'seo] *nm* (*avenida*) avenue;
(*distancia corta*) short walk; ~ **marítimo**
promenade; **dar un** ~ to go for a walk;
mandar a algn a ~ to tell sb to go to
blazes; ¡**vete a** ~! get lost!

pasillo [pa'siʎo] *nm* passage, corridor.

pasión [pa'sjon] *nf* passion.

pasional [pasjo'nal] *adj* passionate; **crimen**
~ crime of passion.

pasivo, a [pa'siβo, a] *adj* passive; (*inactivo*)
inactive ♦ *nm* (*COM*) liabilities *pl*, debts *pl*;
(*de cuenta*) debit side; ~ **circulante**
current liabilities.

pasma ['pasma] *nm* (*fam*) cop.

pasmado, a [pas'maðo, a] *adj* (*asombrado*)
astonished; (*atontado*) bewildered.

pasmar [pas'mar] *vt* (*asombrar*) to amaze,
astonish; ~**se** *vr* to be amazed *o*
astonished.

pasmo ['pasmo] *nm* amazement,
astonishment; (*fig*) wonder, marvel.

pasmoso, a [pas'moso, a] *adj* amazing,
astonishing.

paso, a ['paso, a] *adj* dried ♦ *nm* (*gen, de
baile*) step; (*modo de andar*) walk; (*huella*)
footprint; (*rapidez*) speed, pace, rate;
(*camino accesible*) way through, passage;
(*cruce*) crossing; (*pasaje*) passing,
passage; (*REL*) religious float *or*
sculpture; (*GEO*) pass; (*estrecho*) strait;
(*fig*) step, measure; (*apuro*) difficulty ♦ *nf*
raisin; **pasa de Corinto/de Esmirna**
currant/sultana; ~ **a** ~ step by step; **a
ese** ~ (*fig*) at that rate; **salir al** ~ **de** *o* **a**
to waylay; **salir del** ~ to get out of
trouble; **dar un** ~ **en falso** to trip; (*fig*) to
take a false step; **estar de** ~ to be
passing through; ~ **atrás** step
backwards; (*fig*) backward step; ~
elevado/subterráneo flyover/subway,
underpass (*US*); **prohibido el** ~ no entry;
ceda el ~ give way; *V tb* **Semana Santa**.

pasota [pa'sota] *adj, nm/f* (*fam*) ≈ dropout;
ser un (tipo) ~ to be a bit of a dropout;
(*ser indiferente*) not to care about
anything.

pasotismo [paso'tismo] *nm* underground *o*
alternative culture.

pasta ['pasta] *nf* (*gen*) paste; (*CULIN: masa*)
dough; (: *de bizcochos etc*) pastry; (*fam*)
money, dough; (*encuadernación*)
hardback; ~**s** *nfpl* (*bizcochos*) pastries,
small cakes; (*fideos, espaguetis etc*)
noodles, spaghetti *sg etc*; ~ **de dientes** *o*
dentífrica toothpaste; ~ **de madera** wood

pulp.

pastar [pas'tar] *vt, vi* to graze.

pastel [pas'tel] *nm* (*dulce*) cake; (*de carne*)
pie; (*ARTE*) pastel; (*fig*) plot; ~**es** *nmpl*
pastry *sg*, confectionery *sg*.

pastelería [pastele'ria] *nf* cake shop,
pastry shop.

pasteurizado, a [pasteuri'θaðo, a] *adj*
pasteurized.

pastilla [pas'tiʎa] *nf* (*de jabón, chocolate*)
cake, bar; (*píldora*) tablet, pill.

pastizal [pasti'θal] *nm* pasture.

pasto ['pasto] *nm* (*hierba*) grass; (*lugar*)
pasture, field; (*fig*) food, nourishment.

pastor, a [pas'tor, a] *nm/f* shepherd(ess)
♦ *nm* clergyman, pastor; (*ZOOL*)
sheepdog; ~ **alemán** Alsatian.

pastoso, a [pas'toso, a] *adj* (*material*)
doughy, pasty; (*lengua*) furry; (*voz*)
mellow.

pat. *abr* (= *patente*) pat.

pata ['pata] *nf* (*pierna*) leg; (*pie*) foot; (*de
muebles*) leg; ~**s arriba** upside down; **a
cuatro** ~**s** on all fours; **meter la** ~ to put
one's foot in it; ~ **de cabra** (*TEC*)
crowbar; ~**s de gallo** crow's feet; **tener
buena/mala** ~ to be lucky/unlucky.

patada [pa'taða] *nf* stamp; (*puntapié*) kick;
a ~**s** in abundance; (*trato*) roughly; **echar
a algn a** ~**s** to kick sb out.

patagón, ona [pata'ɣon, ona] *adj, nm/f*
Patagonian.

Patagonia [pata'ɣonja] *nf*: **la** ~ Patagonia.

patalear [patale'ar] *vi* to stamp one's feet.

pataleo [pata'leo] *nm* stamping.

patán [pa'tan] *nm* rustic, yokel.

patata [pa'tata] *nf* potato; ~**s fritas** *o* **a la
española** chips, French fries; ~**s a la
inglesa** crisps; **ni** ~ (*fam*) nothing at all;
no entendió ni ~ he didn't understand a
single word.

paté [pa'te] *nm* pâté.

patear [pate'ar] *vt* (*pisar*) to stamp on,
trample (on); (*pegar con el pie*) to kick
♦ *vi* to stamp (with rage), stamp one's foot.

patentar [paten'tar] *vt* to patent.

patente [pa'tente] *adj* obvious, evident;
(*COM*) patent ♦ *nf* patent.

patera [pa'tera] *nf* boat.

paternal [pater'nal] *adj* fatherly, paternal.

paternalista [paterna'lista] *adj* (*tono,
actitud etc*) patronizing.

paternidad [paterni'ðað] *nf* fatherhood,
parenthood; (*JUR*) paternity.

paterno, a [pa'terno, a] *adj* paternal.

patético, a [pa'tetiko, a] *adj* pathetic,
moving.

patíbulo [pa'tiβulo] *nm* scaffold,

gallows sg.

patilla [pa'tiʎa] nf (de gafas) arm; (de pelo) sideburn.

patín [pa'tin] nm skate; (de tobogán) runner; ~ **de hielo** ice skate; ~ **de ruedas** roller skate.

patinaje [pati'naxe] nm skating.

patinar [pati'nar] vi to skate; (resbalarse) to skid, slip; (fam) to slip up, blunder.

patinazo [pati'naθo] nm (AUTO) skid; **dar un** ~ (fam) to blunder.

patio ['patjo] nm (de casa) patio, courtyard; ~ **de recreo** playground.

pato ['pato] nm duck; **pagar el** ~ (fam) to take the blame, carry the can.

patológico, a [pato'loxiko, a] adj pathological.

patoso, a [pa'toso, a] adj awkward, clumsy.

patraña [pa'traɲa] nf story, fib.

patria ['patrja] nf native land, mother country; ~ **chica** home town.

patrimonio [patri'monjo] nm inheritance; (fig) heritage; (COM) net worth.

patriota [pa'trjota] nmlf patriot.

patriotero, a [patrjo'tero, a] adj chauvinistic.

patriótico, a [pa'trjotiko, a] adj patriotic.

patriotismo [patrjo'tismo] nm patriotism.

patrocinador, a [patroθina'ðor, a] nmlf sponsor.

patrocinar [patroθi'nar] vt to sponsor; (apoyar) to back, support.

patrocinio [patro'θinjo] nm sponsorship; backing, support.

patrón, ona [pa'tron, ona] nmlf (jefe) boss, chief, master/mistress; (propietario) landlord/lady; (REL) patron saint ♦ nm (COSTURA) pattern; (TEC) standard; ~ **oro** gold standard.

patronal [patro'nal] adj: **la clase** ~ management; **cierre** ~ lockout.

patronato [patro'nato] nm sponsorship; (acto) patronage; (COM) employers' association; (fundación) trust; **el** ~ **de turismo** the tourist board.

patrulla [pa'truʎa] nf patrol.

patrullar [patru'ʎar] vi to patrol.

paulatino, a [paula'tino, a] adj gradual, slow.

paupérrimo, a [pau'perrimo, a] adj very poor, poverty-stricken.

pausa ['pausa] nf pause; (intervalo) break; (interrupción) interruption; (TEC: en videograbadora) hold; **con** ~ slowly.

pausado, a [pau'saðo, a] adj slow, deliberate.

pauta ['pauta] nf line, guide line.

pavimento [paßi'mento] nm (ARQ) flooring.

pavo ['paßo] nm turkey; (necio) silly thing, idiot; ~ **real** peacock; ¡no seas ~! don't be silly!

pavonearse [paßone'arse] vr to swagger, show off.

pavor [pa'ßor] nm dread, terror.

payasada [paja'saða] nf ridiculous thing (to do); ~**s** nfpl clowning sg.

payaso, a [pa'jaso, a] nmlf clown.

payo, a ['pajo, a] adj, nmlf non-gipsy.

paz [paθ] nf peace; (tranquilidad) peacefulness, tranquillity; **dejar a algn en** ~ to leave sb alone o in peace; **hacer las paces** to make peace; (fig) to make up; ¡haya ~! stop it!

pazca ['paθka] etc vb V **pacer.**

PC nm abr (POL: = Partido Comunista) CP.

P.C.E. nm abr = Partido Comunista Español.

PCL nf abr (= pantalla de cristal líquido) LCD.

PCUS [pe'kus] nm abr (= Partido Comunista de la Unión Soviética) Soviet Communist Party.

P.D. abr (= posdata) P.S.

pdo. abr (= pasado) ult.

peaje [pe'axe] nm toll; **autopista de** ~ toll motorway, turnpike (US).

peatón [pea'ton] nm pedestrian; **paso de peatones** pedestrian crossing, crosswalk (US).

peca ['peka] nf freckle.

pecado [pe'kaðo] nm sin.

pecador, a [peka'ðor, a] adj sinful ♦ nmlf sinner.

pecaminoso, a [pekami'noso, a] adj sinful.

pecar [pe'kar] vi (REL) to sin; (fig): ~ **de generoso** to be too generous.

pecera [pe'θera] nf goldfish bowl.

pecho ['petʃo] nm (ANAT) chest; (de mujer) breast(s) (pl), bosom; (corazón) heart, breast; (valor) courage, spirit; **dar el** ~ **a** to breast-feed; **tomar algo a** ~ to take sth to heart; **no le cabía en el** ~ he was bursting with happiness.

pechuga [pe'tʃuɣa] nf breast (of chicken etc).

pecoso, a [pe'koso, a] adj freckled.

peculiar [peku'ljar] adj special, peculiar; (característico) typical, characteristic.

peculiaridad [pekuljari'ðað] nf peculiarity; special feature, characteristic.

pedagogía [peðaɣo'xia] nf education.

pedagogo [peða'ɣoɣo] nm pedagogue, teacher.

pedal [pe'ðal] nm pedal; ~ **de embrague** clutch (pedal); ~ **de freno** footbrake.

pedalear [peðale'ar] vi to pedal.

pedante [pe'ðante] *adj* pedantic ♦ *nm/f*
pedant.

pedantería [peðante'ria] *nf* pedantry.

pedazo [pe'ðaθo] *nm* piece, bit; **hacerse ~s**
to fall to pieces; (*romperse*) to smash,
shatter; **un ~ de pan** a scrap of bread;
(*fig*) a terribly nice person.

pedernal [peðer'nal] *nm* flint.

pedestal [peðes'tal] *nm* base; **tener/poner
a algn en un ~** to put sb on a pedestal.

pedestre [pe'ðestre] *adj* pedestrian;
carrera ~ foot race.

pediatra [pe'ðjatra] *nm/f* paediatrician
(*BRIT*), pediatrician (*US*).

pediatría [peðja'tria] *nf* paediatrics *sg*
(*BRIT*), pediatrics *sg* (*US*).

pedicuro, a [peði'kuro, a] *nm/f* chiropodist
(*BRIT*), podiatrist (*US*).

pedido [pe'ðiðo] *nm* (*COM: mandado*) order;
(*petición*) request; **~s en cartera** (*COM*)
backlog *sg*.

pedigrí [peði'vri] *nm* pedigree.

pedir [pe'ðir] *vt* to ask for, request;
(*comida, COM: mandar*) to order; (*exigir:
precio*) to ask; (*necesitar*) to need,
demand, require ♦ *vi* to ask; **~ prestado**
to borrow; **~ disculpas** to apologize; **me
pidió que cerrara la puerta** he asked me
to shut the door; **¿cuánto piden por el
coche?** how much are they asking for
the car?

pedo ['peðo] (*fam*) *adj inv*: **estar ~** to be
pissed (*!*) ♦ *nm* fart (*!*).

pedrada [pe'ðraða] *nf* throw of a stone;
(*golpe*) blow from a stone; **herir a algn de
una ~** to hit sb with a stone.

pedrea [pe'ðrea] *nf* (*granizada*) hailstorm;
(*de lotería*) minor prizes.

pedrisco [pe'ðrisko] *nm* (*granizo*) hail;
(*granizada*) hailstorm.

Pedro ['peðro] *nm* Peter; **entrar como ~
por su casa** to come in as if one owned
the place.

pega ['peva] *nf* (*dificultad*) snag; **de ~** false,
dud; **poner ~s** to raise objections.

pegadizo, a [peva'ðiθo, a] *adj* (*canción etc*)
catchy.

pegajoso, a [peva'xoso, a] *adj* sticky,
adhesive.

pegamento [peva'mento] *nm* gum.

pegar [pe'var] *vt* (*papel, sellos*) to stick
(on); (*con cola*) to glue; (*cartel*) to post,
stick up; (*coser*) to sew (on); (*unir: partes*)
to join, fix together; (*MED*) to give, infect
with; (*dar: golpe*) to give, deal ♦ *vi*
(*adherirse*) to stick, adhere; (*ir juntos:
colores*) to match, go together; (*golpear*)
to hit; (*quemar: el sol*) to strike hot, burn

(*fig*); **~se** *vr* (*gen*) to stick; (*dos personas*)
to hit each other, fight; **~le a algo** to be a
great one for sth; **~ un grito** to let out a
yell; **~ un salto** to jump (with fright); **~
fuego** to catch fire; **~ en** to touch; **~se
un tiro** to shoot o.s.; **no pega** that doesn't
seem right; **ese sombrero no pega con el
abrigo** that hat doesn't go with the coat.

pegatina [peva'tina] *nf* (*POL etc*) sticker.

pego ['pevo] *nm*: **dar el ~** (*pasar por
verdadero*) to look like the real thing.

pegote [pe'vote] *nm* (*fig*) patch, ugly
mend; **tirarse ~s** (*fam*) to come on
strong.

pegue ['peve] *etc vb V* **pegar**.

peinado [pei'naðo] *nm* (*en peluquería*)
hairdo; (*estilo*) hair style.

peinar [pei'nar] *vt* to comb sb's hair; (*hacer
estilo*) to style; **~se** *vr* to comb one's hair.

peine ['peine] *nm* comb.

peineta [pei'neta] *nf* ornamental comb.

p.ej. *abr* (= *por ejemplo*) e.g.

Pekín [pe'kin] *n* Peking.

pela ['pela] *nf* (*ESP fam*) peseta; *V tb* **pelas**.

pelado, a [pe'laðo, a] *adj* (*cabeza*) shorn;
(*fruta*) peeled; (*campo, fig*) bare; (*fam: sin
dinero*) broke.

pelaje [pe'laxe] *nm* (*ZOOL*) fur, coat; (*fig*)
appearance.

pelambre [pe'lambre] *nm* long hair, mop.

pelar [pe'lar] *vt* (*fruta, patatas*) to peel;
(*cortar el pelo a*) to cut the hair of; (*quitar
la piel: animal*) to skin; (*ave*) to pluck;
(*habas etc*) to shell; **~se** *vr* (*la piel*) to peel
off; **corre que se las pela** (*fam*) he runs
like nobody's business.

pelas ['pelas] (*ESP fam*) *nfpl* dough.

peldaño [pel'daɲo] *nm* step; (*de escalera
portátil*) rung.

pelea [pe'lea] *nf* (*lucha*) fight; (*discusión*)
quarrel, row.

peleado, a [pele'aðo, a] *adj*: **estar ~** (**con
algn**) to have fallen out (with sb).

pelear [pele'ar] *vi* to fight; **~se** *vr* to fight;
(*reñirse*) to fall out, quarrel.

pelele [pe'lele] *nm* (*figura*) guy, dummy;
(*fig*) puppet.

peletería [pelete'ria] *nf* furrier's, fur shop.

peliagudo, a [pelja'vuðo, a] *adj* tricky.

pelícano [pe'likano] *nm* pelican.

película [pe'likula] *nf* (*CINE*) film, movie
(*US*); (*cobertura ligera*) film, thin
covering; (*FOTO: rollo*) roll *o* reel of film;
~ de dibujos (**animados**) cartoon film; **~
muda** silent film; **de ~** (*fam*) astonishing,
out of this world.

peligrar [peli'vrar] *vi* to be in danger.

peligro [pe'livro] *nm* danger; (*riesgo*) risk;

"~ de muerte" "danger"; **correr ~ de** to be in danger of; **con ~ de la vida** at the risk of one's life.

peligrosidad [peliɣrosi'ðað] *nf* danger, riskiness.

peligroso, a [peli'ɣroso, a] *adj* dangerous; risky.

pelirrojo, a [peli'rroxo, a] *adj* red-haired, red-headed.

pellejo [pe'ʎexo] *nm* (*de animal*) skin, hide; **salvar el ~** to save one's skin.

pellizcar [peʎiθ'kar] *vt* to pinch, nip.

pellizco [pe'ʎiθko] *nm* (*gen*) pinch.

pellizque [pe'ʎiθke] *etc vb* V **pellizcar**.

pelma ['pelma] *nm/f*, **pelmazo** [pel'maθo] *nm* (*fam*) pest.

pelo ['pelo] *nm* (*cabellos*) hair; (*de barba, bigote*) whisker; (*de animal: pellejo*) fur, coat; (*de perro etc*) hair, coat; (*de ave*) down; (*de tejido*) nap; (*TEC*) fibre; **a ~** bareheaded; (*desnudo*) naked; **al ~** just right; **venir al ~** to be exactly what one needs; **por los ~s** by the skin of one's teeth; **escaparse por un ~** to have a close shave; **se me pusieron los ~s de punta** my hair stood on end; **no tener ~s en la lengua** to be outspoken, not mince words; **tomar el ~ a algn** to pull sb's leg.

pelón, ona [pe'lon, ona] *adj* hairless, bald.

pelota [pe'lota] *nf* ball; (*fam: cabeza*) nut (*fam*); **en ~(s)** stark naked; **~ vasca** pelota; **devolver la ~ a algn** (*fig*) to turn the tables on sb; **hacer la ~ (a algn)** to creep (to sb).

pelotera [pelo'tera] *nf* (*fam*) barney.

pelotón [pelo'ton] *nm* (*MIL*) squad, detachment.

peluca [pe'luka] *nf* wig.

peluche [pe'lutʃe] *nm*: **muñeco de ~** soft toy.

peludo, a [pe'luðo, a] *adj* hairy, shaggy.

peluquería [peluke'ria] *nf* hairdresser's; (*para hombres*) barber's (shop).

peluquero, a [pelu'kero, a] *nm/f* hairdresser; barber.

peluquín [pelu'kin] *nm* toupée.

pelusa [pe'lusa] *nf* (*BOT*) down; (*COSTURA*) fluff.

pelvis ['pelβis] *nf* pelvis.

PEMEX [pe'meks] *nm abr* = *Petróleos Mejicanos*.

PEN [pen] *nm abr* (*ESP*) = *Plan Energético Nacional*.

pena ['pena] *nf* (*congoja*) grief, sadness; (*remordimiento*) regret; (*dificultad*) trouble; (*dolor*) pain; (*AM: vergüenza*) shame; (*JUR*) sentence; (*DEPORTE*) penalty; **~ capital** capital punishment; **~ de muerte** death penalty; **~ pecuniaria** fine; **merecer** *o* **valer la ~** to be worthwhile; **a duras ~s** with great difficulty; **so ~ de** on pain of; **me dan ~** I feel sorry for them; **¿no te da ~ hacerlo?** (*AM*) aren't you embarrassed doing that?; **¡qué ~!** what a shame *o* pity!

penal [pe'nal] *adj* penal ♦ *nm* (*cárcel*) prison.

penalidad [penali'ðað] *nf* (*problema, dificultad*) trouble, hardship; (*JUR*) penalty, punishment.

penalizar [penali'θar] *vt* to penalize.

penalti, penalty [pe'nalti] *nm* (*DEPORTE*) penalty.

penar [pe'nar] *vt* to penalize; (*castigar*) to punish ♦ *vi* to suffer.

pendejo, a [pen'dexo, a] *nm/f* (*AM fam!*) wanker (*BRIT!*), jerk (*US!*).

pender [pen'der] *vi* (*colgar*) to hang; (*JUR*) to be pending.

pendiente [pen'djente] *adj* pending, unsettled ♦ *nm* earring ♦ *nf* hill, slope; **tener una asignatura ~** to have to resit a subject.

pendón [pen'don] *nm* banner, standard.

péndulo ['pendulo] *nm* pendulum.

pene ['pene] *nm* penis.

penene [pe'nene] *nm/f* = **PNN**.

penetración [penetra'θjon] *nf* (*acto*) penetration; (*agudeza*) sharpness, insight.

penetrante [pene'trante] *adj* (*herida*) deep; (*persona, arma*) sharp; (*sonido*) penetrating, piercing; (*mirada*) searching; (*viento, ironía*) biting.

penetrar [pene'trar] *vt* to penetrate, pierce; (*entender*) to grasp ♦ *vi* to penetrate, go in; (*líquido*) to soak in; (*emoción*) to pierce.

penicilina [peniθi'lina] *nf* penicillin.

península [pe'ninsula] *nf* peninsula; **P~ Ibérica** Iberian Peninsula.

peninsular [peninsu'lar] *adj* peninsular.

penique [pe'nike] *nm* penny; **~s** *nmpl* pence.

penitencia [peni'tenθja] *nf* (*remordimiento*) penitence; (*castigo*) penance; **en ~** as a penance.

penitencial [peniten'θjal] *adj* penitential.

penitenciaría [penitenθja'ria] *nf* prison, penitentiary.

penitenciario, a [peniten'θjarjo, a] *adj* prison *cpd*.

penoso, a [pe'noso, a] *adj* laborious, difficult.

pensado, a [pen'saðo, a] *adj*: **bien/mal ~**

well intentioned/cynical; **en el momento menos** ~ when least expected.

pensador, a [pensa'ðor, a] *nm/f* thinker.

pensamiento [pensa'mjento] *nm* (*gen*) thought; (*mente*) mind; (*idea*) idea; (*BOT*) pansy; **no le pasó por el** ~ it never occurred to him.

pensar [pen'sar] *vt* to think; (*considerar*) to think over, think out; (*proponerse*) to intend, plan, propose; (*imaginarse*) to think up, invent ♦ *vi* to think; ~ **en** to think of *o* about; (*anhelar*) to aim at, aspire to; **dar que** ~ **a algn** to give sb food for thought.

pensativo, a [pensa'tißo, a] *adj* thoughtful, pensive.

pensión [pen'sjon] *nf* (*casa*) ≈ guest house; (*dinero*) pension; (*cama y comida*) board and lodging; ~ **de jubilación** retirement pension; ~ **escalada** graduated pension; ~ **completa** full board; **media** ~ half board.

pensionista [pensjo'nista] *nm/f* (*jubilado*) (old-age) pensioner; (*quien vive en pensión*) lodger; (*ESCOL*) boarder.

pentágono [pen'taɣono] *nm* pentagon: **el P~** (*US*) the Pentagon.

pentagrama [penta'ɣrama] *nm* (*MUS*) stave, staff.

penúltimo, a [pe'nultimo, a] *adj* penultimate, second last.

penumbra [pe'numbra] *nf* half-light, semi-darkness.

penuria [pe'nurja] *nf* shortage, want.

peña ['peɲa] *nf* (*roca*) rock; (*cuesta*) cliff, crag; (*grupo*) group, circle; (*DEPORTE*) supporters' club.

peñasco [pe'ɲasko] *nm* large rock, boulder.

peñón [pe'ɲon] *nm* crag; **el P~** the Rock (of Gibraltar).

peón [pe'on] *nm* labourer; (*AM*) farm labourer, farmhand; (*TEC*) spindle, shaft; (*AJEDREZ*) pawn.

peonza [pe'onθa] *nf* spinning top.

peor [pe'or] *adj* (*comparativo*) worse; (*superlativo*) worst ♦ *adv* worse; worst; **de mal en** ~ from bad to worse; **tanto** ~ so much the worse; **A es** ~ **que B** A is worse than B; **Z es el** ~ **de todos** Z is the worst of all.

pepenar [pepe'nar] *vi* (*AM*) to sift through rubbish *o* garbage.

pepinillo [pepi'niʎo] *nm* gherkin.

pepino [pe'pino] *nm* cucumber; **(no) me importa un** ~ I don't care two hoots.

pepita [pe'pita] *nf* (*BOT*) pip; (*MINERÍA*) nugget.

pepito [pe'pito] *nm* meat sandwich.

peque ['peke] *etc vb* V **pecar.**

pequeñez [peke'ɲeθ] *nf* smallness, littleness; (*trivialidad*) trifle, triviality.

pequeño, a [pe'keɲo, a] *adj* small, little; (*cifra*) small, low; (*bajo*) short; ~ **burgués** lower middle-class.

pequinés, esa [peki'nes, esa] *adj, nm/f* Pekinese.

pera ['pera] *adj inv* classy; **niño** ~ spoiled upper-class brat ♦ *nf* pear; **eso es pedir** ~**s al olmo** that's asking the impossible.

peral [pe'ral] *nm* pear tree.

percance [per'kanθe] *nm* setback, misfortune.

per cápita [per'kapita] *adj*: **renta** ~ per capita income.

percatarse [perka'tarse] *vr*: ~ **de** to notice, take note of.

percebe [per'θeße] *nm* (*ZOOL*) barnacle; (*fam*) idiot.

percepción [perθep'θjon] *nf* (*vista*) perception; (*idea*) notion, idea; (*COM*) collection.

perceptible [perθep'tißle] *adj* perceptible, noticeable; (*COM*) payable, receivable.

percha ['pertʃa] *nf* (*poste*) pole, support; (*gancho*) peg; (*de abrigos*) coat stand; (*colgador*) coat hanger; (*de ave*) perch.

perchero [per'tʃero] *nm* clothes rack.

percibir [perθi'ßir] *vt* to perceive, notice; (*ver*) to see; (*peligro etc*) to sense; (*COM*) to earn, receive, get.

percusión [perku'sjon] *nf* percussion.

percusor [perku'sor], **percutor** [perku'tor] *nm* (*TEC*) hammer; (*de arma*) firing pin.

perdedor, a [perðe'ðor, a] *adj* losing ♦ *nm/f* loser.

perder [per'ðer] *vt* to lose; (*tiempo, palabras*) to waste; (*oportunidad*) to lose, miss; (*tren*) to miss ♦ *vi* to lose; ~**se** *vr* (*extraviarse*) to get lost; (*desaparecer*) to disappear, be lost to view; (*arruinarse*) to be ruined; **echar a** ~ (*comida*) to spoil, ruin; (*oportunidad*) to waste; **tener buen** ~ to be a good loser; **¡no te lo pierdas!** don't miss it!; **he perdido la costumbre** I have got out of the habit.

perdición [perði'θjon] *nf* perdition; (*fig*) ruin.

pérdida ['perðiða] *nf* loss; (*de tiempo*) waste; (*COM*) net loss; ~**s** *nfpl* (*COM*) losses; **¡no tiene** ~**!** you can't go wrong!; ~ **contable** (*COM*) book loss.

perdido, a [per'ðiðo, a] *adj* lost; **estar** ~ **por** to be crazy about; **es un caso** ~ he is a hopeless case.

perdigón [perði'ɣon] *nm* pellet.

perdiz [per'ðiθ] *nf* partridge.
perdón [per'ðon] *nm* (*disculpa*) pardon, forgiveness; (*clemencia*) mercy; ¡~! sorry!, I beg your pardon!; **con** ~ if I may, if you don't mind.
perdonar [perðo'nar] *vt* to pardon, forgive; (*la vida*) to spare; (*excusar*) to exempt, excuse ♦ *vi* to pardon, forgive; ¡**perdone (usted)**! sorry!, I beg your pardon!; **perdone, pero me parece que ...** excuse me, but I think ...
perdurable [perðu'raßle] *adj* lasting; (*eterno*) everlasting.
perdurar [perðu'rar] *vi* (*resistir*) to last, endure; (*seguir existiendo*) to stand, still exist.
perecedero, a [pereθe'ðero, a] *adj* perishable.
perecer [pere'θer] *vi* to perish, die.
peregrinación [pereɣrina'θjon] *nf* (*REL*) pilgrimage.
peregrino, a [pere'ɣrino] *adj* (*extraño*) strange; (*singular*) rare ♦ *nm/f* pilgrim.
perejil [pere'xil] *nm* parsley.
perenne [pe'renne] *adj* everlasting, perennial.
perentorio, a [peren'torjo, a] *adj* (*urgente*) urgent; (*terminante*) peremptory; (*fijo*) set, fixed.
pereza [pe'reθa] *nf* (*flojera*) laziness; (*lentitud*) sloth, slowness.
perezca [pe'reθka] *etc vb V* **perecer**.
perezoso, a [pere'θoso, a] *adj* lazy; slow, sluggish.
perfección [perfek'θjon] *nf* perfection; **a la** ~ to perfection.
perfeccionar [perfekθjo'nar] *vt* to perfect; (*acabar*) to complete, finish.
perfecto, a [per'fekto, a] *adj* perfect ♦ *nm* (*LING*) perfect (tense).
perfidia [per'fiðja] *nf* perfidy, treachery.
pérfido, a ['perfiðo, a] *adj* perfidious, treacherous.
perfil [per'fil] *nm* (*parte lateral*) profile; (*silueta*) silhouette, outline; (*TEC*) (cross) section; ~**es** *nmpl* features; (*fig*) social graces; ~ **del cliente** (*COM*) customer profile; **en** ~ from the side, in profile.
perfilado, a [perfi'laðo, a] *adj* (*bien formado*) well-shaped; (*largo: cara*) long.
perfilar [perfi'lar] *vt* (*trazar*) to outline; (*dar carácter a*) to shape, give character to; ~**se** *vr* to be silhouetted (*en* against); **el proyecto se va perfilando** the project is taking shape.
perforación [perfora'θjon] *nf* perforation; (*con taladro*) drilling.
perforadora [perfora'ðora] *nf* drill; ~ **de**

fichas card-punch.
perforar [perfo'rar] *vt* to perforate; (*agujero*) to drill, bore; (*papel*) to punch a hole in ♦ *vi* to drill, bore.
perfumado, a [perfu'maðo, a] *adj* scented, perfumed.
perfumar [perfu'mar] *vt* to scent, perfume.
perfume [per'fume] *nm* perfume, scent.
pergamino [perɣa'mino] *nm* parchment.
pericia [pe'riθja] *nf* skill, expertise.
periferia [peri'ferja] *nf* periphery; (*de ciudad*) outskirts *pl*.
periférico, a [peri'feriko, a] *adj* peripheral ♦ *nm* (*INFORM*) peripheral; (*AM: AUTO*) ring road; **barrio** ~ outlying district.
perilla [pe'riʎa] *nf* goatee.
perímetro [pe'rimetro] *nm* perimeter.
periódico, a [pe'rjoðiko, a] *adj* periodic(al) ♦ *nm* (news)paper; ~ **dominical** Sunday (news)paper.
periodismo [perjo'ðismo] *nm* journalism.
periodista [perjo'ðista] *nm/f* journalist.
periodístico, a [perjo'ðistiko, a] *adj* journalistic.
periodo [pe'rjoðo], **período** [pe'rioðo] *nm* period; ~ **contable** (*COM*) accounting period.
peripecias [peri'peθjas] *nfpl* adventures.
peripuesto, a [peri'pwesto, a] *adj* dressed up; **tan** ~ all dressed up (to the nines).
perito, a [pe'rito, a] *adj* (*experto*) expert; (*diestro*) skilled, skilful ♦ *nm/f* expert; skilled worker; (*técnico*) technician.
perjudicar [perxuði'kar] *vt* (*gen*) to damage, harm; (*fig*) to prejudice.
perjudicial [perxuði'θjal] *adj* damaging, harmful; (*en detrimento*) detrimental.
perjudique [perxu'ðike] *etc vb V* **perjudicar**.
perjuicio [per'xwiθjo] *nm* damage, harm; **en/sin** ~ **de** to the detriment of/without prejudice to.
perjurar [perxu'rar] *vi* to commit perjury.
perla ['perla] *nf* pearl; **me viene de** ~**s** it suits me fine.
permanecer [permane'θer] *vi* (*quedarse*) to stay, remain; (*seguir*) to continue to be.
permanencia [perma'nenθja] *nf* (*duración*) permanence; (*estancia*) stay.
permanente [perma'nente] *adj* (*que queda*) permanent; (*constante*) constant; (*comisión etc*) standing ♦ *nf* perm; **hacerse una** ~ to have one's hair permed.
permanezca [perma'neθka] *etc vb V* **permanecer**.
permisible [permi'sißle] *adj* permissible, allowable.

permiso [per'miso] *nm* permission;
(*licencia*) permit, licence (*BRIT*), license
(*US*); **con** ~ excuse me; **estar de** ~ (*MIL*)
to be on leave; ~ **de conducir** *o*
conductor driving licence (*BRIT*),
driver's license (*US*); ~ **de exportación/
importación** export/import licence; ~
por asuntos familiares compassionate
leave.

permitir [permi'tir] *vt* to permit, allow;
~**se** *vr*: ~**se algo** to allow o.s. sth; **no me
puedo** ~ **ese lujo** I can't afford that; **¿me
permite?** may I?; **si lo permite el tiempo**
weather permitting.

permuta [per'muta] *nf* exchange.

permutar [permu'tar] *vt* to switch,
exchange; ~ **destinos con algn** to swap *o*
exchange jobs with sb.

pernicioso, a [perni'θjoso, a] *adj* (*maligno,
MED*) pernicious; (*persona*) wicked.

perno ['perno] *nm* bolt.

pernoctar [pernok'tar] *vi* to stay for the
night.

pero ['pero] *conj* but; (*aún*) yet ♦ *nm*
(*defecto*) flaw, defect; (*reparo*) objection;
¡no hay ~ **que valga!** there are no buts
about it.

perogrullada [peroɣru'ʎaða] *nf* platitude,
truism.

perol [pe'rol] *nm*, **perola** [pe'rola] *nf* pan.

peronista [pero'nista] *adj, nm/f* Peronist.

perorata [pero'rata] *nf* long-winded
speech.

perpendicular [perpendiku'lar] *adj*
perpendicular; **el camino es** ~ **al río** the
road is at right angles to the river.

perpetrar [perpe'trar] *vt* to perpetrate.

perpetuamente [perpetwa'mente] *adv*
perpetually.

perpetuar [perpe'twar] *vt* to perpetuate.

perpetuo, a [per'petwo, a] *adj* perpetual;
(*JUR etc: condena*) life *cpd*.

Perpiñán [perpi'ɲan] *nm* Perpignan.

perplejo, a [per'plexo, a] *adj* perplexed,
bewildered.

perra ['perra] *nf* bitch; (*fam: dinero*) money;
(: *manía*) mania, crazy idea; (: *rabieta*)
tantrum; **estar sin una** ~ to be flat broke.

perrera [pe'rrera] *nf* kennel.

perro ['perro] *nm* dog; ~ **caliente** hot dog;
"~ **peligroso**" "beware of the dog"; **ser**
~ **viejo** to be an old hand; **tiempo de** ~**s**
filthy weather; ~ **que ladra no muerde**
his bark is worse than his bite.

persa ['persa] *adj, nm/f* Persian ♦ *nm* (*LING*)
Persian.

persecución [perseku'θjon] *nf* pursuit,
hunt, chase; (*REL, POL*) persecution.

perseguir [perse'ɣir] *vt* to pursue, hunt;
(*cortejar*) to chase after; (*molestar*) to
pester, annoy; (*REL, POL*) to persecute;
(*JUR*) to prosecute.

perseverante [perseβe'rante] *adj*
persevering, persistent.

perseverar [perseve'rar] *vi* to persevere,
persist; ~ **en** to persevere in, persist
with.

persiana [per'sjana] *nf* (Venetian) blind.

persiga [per'siɣa] *etc vb V* **perseguir.**

persignarse [persiɣ'narse] *vr* to cross o.s.

persiguiendo [persi'ɣjenðo] *etc vb V*
perseguir.

persistente [persis'tente] *adj* persistant.

persistir [persis'tir] *vi* to persist.

persona [per'sona] *nf* person; **10** ~**s** 10
people; **tercera** ~ third party; (*LING*)
third person; **en** ~ in person *o* the flesh;
por ~ a head; **es buena** ~ he's a good
sort.

personaje [perso'naxe] *nm* important
person, celebrity; (*TEAT*) character.

personal [perso'nal] *adj* (*particular*)
personal; (*para una persona*) single, for
one person ♦ *nm* (*plantilla*) personnel,
staff; (*NAUT*) crew; (*fam: gente*) people.

personalidad [personali'ðað] *nf*
personality; (*JUR*) status.

personalizar [personali'θar] *vt* to
personalize ♦ *vi* (*al hablar*) to name
names.

personarse [perso'narse] *vr* to appear in
person; ~ **en** to present o.s. at, report to.

personero, a [perso'nero, a] *nm/f* (*AM*)
(government) official.

personificar [personifi'kar] *vt* to personify.

personifique [personi'fike] *etc vb V*
personificar.

perspectiva [perspek'tiβa] *nf* perspective;
(*vista, panorama*) view, panorama;
(*posibilidad futura*) outlook, prospect;
tener algo en ~ to have sth in view.

perspicacia [perspi'kaθja] *nf* discernment,
perspicacity.

perspicaz [perspi'kaθ] *adj* shrewd.

persuadir [perswa'ðir] *vt* (*gen*) to
persuade; (*convencer*) to convince; ~**se**
vr to become convinced.

persuasión [perswa'sjon] *nf* (*acto*)
persuasion; (*convicción*) conviction.

persuasivo, a [perwa'siβo, a] *adj*
persuasive; convincing.

pertenecer [pertene'θer] *vi*: ~ **a** to belong
to; (*fig*) to concern.

perteneciente [pertene'θjente] *adj*: ~ **a**
belonging to.

pertenencia [perte'nenθja] *nf* ownership;

~s *nfpl* possessions, property *sg*.

pertenezca [perte'neθka] *etc vb* V **pertenecer**.

pértiga ['pertiɣa] *nf* pole; **salto de** ~ pole vault.

pertinaz [perti'naθ] *adj* (*persistente*) persistent; (*terco*) obstinate.

pertinente [perti'nente] *adj* relevant, pertinent; (*apropiado*) appropriate; ~ **a** concerning, relevant to.

pertrechar [pertre'tʃar] *vt* (*gen*) to supply; (*MIL*) to supply with ammunition and stores; ~**se** *vr*: ~**se de algo** to provide o.s. with sth.

pertrechos [per'tretʃos] *nmpl* (*gen*) implements; (*MIL*) supplies and stores.

perturbación [perturßa'θjon] *nf* (*POL*) disturbance; (*MED*) upset, disturbance; ~ **del orden público** breach of the peace.

perturbador, a [perturßa'ðor, a] *adj* (*que perturba*) perturbing, disturbing; (*subversivo*) subversive.

perturbar [pertur'ßar] *vt* (*el orden*) to disturb; (*MED*) to upset, disturb; (*mentalmente*) to perturb.

Perú [pe'ru] *nm*: **el** ~ Peru.

peruano, a [pe'rwano, a] *adj, nm/f* Peruvian.

perversión [perßer'sjon] *nf* perversion.

perverso, a [perßerso, a] *adj* perverse; (*depravado*) depraved.

pervertido, a [perßer'tiðo, a] *adj* perverted ♦ *nm/f* pervert.

pervertir [perßer'tir] *vt* to pervert, corrupt.

pervierta [per'ßjerta] *etc*, **pervirtiendo** [perßir'tjendo] *etc vb* V **pervertir**.

pesa ['pesa] *nf* weight; (*DEPORTE*) shot.

pesadez [pesa'ðeθ] *nf* (*calidad de pesado*) heaviness; (*lentitud*) slowness; (*aburrimiento*) tediousness; **es una** ~ **tener que ...** it's a bind having to ....

pesadilla [pesa'ðiʎa] *nf* nightmare, bad dream; (*fig*) worry, obsession.

pesado, a [pe'saðo, a] *adj* (*gen*) heavy; (*lento*) slow; (*difícil, duro*) tough, hard; (*aburrido*) tedious, boring; (*bochornoso*) sultry ♦ *nm/f* bore; **tener el estómago** ~ to feel bloated; **¡no seas** ~! come off it!

pesadumbre [pesa'ðumbre] *nf* grief, sorrow.

pésame ['pesame] *nm* expression of condolence, message of sympathy; **dar el** ~ to express one's condolences.

pesar [pe'sar] *vt* to weigh; (*fig*) to weigh heavily on; (*afligir*) to grieve ♦ *vi* to weigh; (*ser pesado*) to weigh a lot, be heavy; (*fig: opinión*) to carry weight ♦ *nm* (*sentimiento*) regret; (*pena*) grief, sorrow; **a** ~ **de (que)** in spite of, despite; **no me pesa haberlo hecho** I'm not sorry I did it.

pesca ['peska] *nf* (*acto*) fishing; (*cantidad de pescado*) catch; ~ **de altura/en bajura** deep sea/coastal fishing; **ir de** ~ to go fishing.

pescadería [peskaðe'ria] *nf* fish shop, fishmonger's.

pescadilla [peska'ðiʎa] *nf* whiting.

pescado [pes'kaðo] *nm* fish.

pescador, a [peska'ðor, a] *nm/f* fisherman/woman.

pescar [pes'kar] *vt* (*coger*) to catch; (*tratar de coger*) to fish for; (*fam: lograr*) to get hold of, land; (*conseguir: trabajo*) to manage to get; (*sorprender*) to catch unawares ♦ *vi* to fish, go fishing.

pescuezo [pes'kweθo] *nm* neck.

pese ['pese] *prep*: ~ **a** despite, in spite of.

pesebre [pe'seßre] *nm* manger.

peseta [pe'seta] *nf* peseta.

pesetero, a [pese'tero, a] *adj* money-grubbing.

pesimismo [pesi'mismo] *nm* pessimism.

pesimista [pesi'mista] *adj* pessimistic ♦ *nm/f* pessimist.

pésimo, a ['pesimo, a] *adj* abominable, vile.

peso ['peso] *nm* weight; (*balanza*) scales *pl*; (*AM COM*) monetary unit; (*moneda*) peso; (*DEPORTE*) shot; ~ **bruto/neto** gross/net weight; ~ **mosca/pesado** fly-/heavyweight; **de poco** ~ light(weight); **levantamiento de** ~s weightlifting; **vender a** ~ to sell by weight; **argumento de** ~ weighty argument; **eso cae de su** ~ that goes without saying.

pesque ['peske] *etc vb* V **pescar**.

pesquero, a [pes'kero, a] *adj* fishing *cpd*.

pesquisa [pes'kisa] *nf* inquiry, investigation.

pestaña [pes'tana] *nf* (*ANAT*) eyelash; (*borde*) rim.

pestañear [pestane'ar] *vi* to blink.

peste ['peste] *nf* plague; (*fig*) nuisance; (*mal olor*) stink, stench; ~ **negra** Black Death; **echar** ~s to swear, fume.

pesticida [pesti'θiða] *nm* pesticide.

pestilencia [pesti'lenθja] *nf* (*mal olor*) stink, stench.

pestillo [pes'tiʎo] *nm* bolt, latch; (*cerrojo*) catch; (*picaporte*) (door) handle.

petaca [pe'taka] *nf* (*de cigarrillos*) cigarette case; (*de pipa*) tobacco pouch; (*AM: maleta*) suitcase.

pétalo ['petalo] *nm* petal.

petanca [pe'tanka] *nf* a game in which

metal bowls are thrown at a target bowl.

petardo [pe'tarðo] *nm* firework, firecracker.

petición [peti'θjon] *nf (pedido)* request, plea; *(memorial)* petition; *(JUR)* plea; **a ~ de** at the request of; **~ de aumento de salarios** wage demand o claim.

petirrojo [peti'rroxo] *nm* robin.

peto ['peto] *nm (corpiño)* bodice; *(TAUR)* horse's padding.

pétreo, a ['petreo, a] *adj* stony, rocky.

petrificar [petrifi'kar] *vt* to petrify.

petrifique [petri'fike] *etc vb V* **petrificar**.

petrodólar [petro'ðolar] *nm* petrodollar.

petróleo [pe'troleo] *nm* oil, petroleum.

petrolero, a [petro'lero, a] *adj* petroleum *cpd* ♦ *nm (COM)* oil man; *(buque)* (oil) tanker.

petulancia [petu'lanθja] *nf (insolencia)* vanity, opinionated nature.

peyorativo, a [pejora'tiβo, a] *adj* pejorative.

pez [peθ] *nm* fish; **~ de colores** goldfish; **~ espada** swordfish; **estar como el ~ en el agua** to feel completely at home.

pezón [pe'θon] *nm* teat, nipple.

pezuña [pe'θuɲa] *nf* hoof.

piadoso, a [pja'ðoso, a] *adj (devoto)* pious, devout; *(misericordioso)* kind, merciful.

Piamonte [pja'monte] *nm* Piedmont.

pianista [pja'nista] *nm/f* pianist.

piano ['pjano] *nm* piano; **~ de cola** grand piano.

piar [pjar] *vi* to cheep.

piara ['pjara] *nf (manada)* herd, drove.

PIB *nm abr (ESP COM: = Producto Interno Bruto)* GDP.

pibe, a ['piβe, a] *nm/f (AM)* boy/girl, kid, child.

pica ['pika] *nf (MIL)* pike; *(TAUR)* goad; **poner una ~ en Flandes** to bring off something difficult.

picadero [pika'ðero] *nm* riding school.

picadillo [pika'ðiʎo] *nm* mince, minced meat.

picado, a [pi'kaðo, a] *adj* pricked, punctured; *(mar)* choppy; *(diente)* bad; *(tabaco)* cut; *(enfadado)* cross.

picador [pika'ðor] *nm (TAUR)* picador; *(minero)* faceworker.

picadora [pika'ðora] *nf* mincer.

picadura [pika'ðura] *nf (pinchazo)* puncture; *(de abeja)* sting; *(de mosquito)* bite; *(tabaco picado)* cut tobacco.

picana [pi'kana] *(AM) nf (AGR)* cattle prod; *(POL: para tortura)* electric prod.

picante [pi'kante] *adj (comida, sabor)* hot;

(comentario) racy, spicy.

picaporte [pika'porte] *nm (tirador)* handle; *(pestillo)* latch.

picar [pi'kar] *vt (agujerear, perforar)* to prick, puncture; *(billete)* to punch, clip; *(abeja)* to sting; *(mosquito, serpiente)* to bite; *(persona)* to nibble (at); *(incitar)* to incite, goad; *(dañar, irritar)* to annoy, bother; *(quemar: lengua)* to burn, sting ♦ *vi (pez)* to bite, take the bait; *(el sol)* to burn, scorch; *(abeja, MED)* to sting; *(mosquito)* to bite; **~se** *vr (agriarse)* to turn sour, go off; *(mar)* to get choppy; *(ofenderse)* to take offence; **me pican los ojos** my eyes sting; **me pica el brazo** my arm itches.

picardía [pikar'ðia] *nf* villainy; *(astucia)* slyness, craftiness; *(una ~)* dirty trick; *(palabra)* rude/bad word o expression.

picaresco, a [pika'resko, a] *adj (travieso)* roguish, rascally; *(LIT)* picaresque.

pícaro, a ['pikaro, a] *adj (malicioso)* villainous; *(travieso)* mischievous ♦ *nm (astuto)* sly sort; *(sinvergüenza)* rascal, scoundrel.

picazón [pika'θon] *nf (comezón)* itch; *(ardor)* sting(ing feeling); *(remordimiento)* pang of conscience.

pichón, ona [pi'tʃon, ona] *nm/f (paloma)* young pigeon; *(apelativo)* darling, dearest.

pico ['piko] *nm (de ave)* beak; *(punto agudo)* peak, sharp point; *(TEC)* pick, pickaxe; *(GEO)* peak, summit; *(labia)* talkativeness; **no abrir el ~** to keep quiet; **~ parásito** *(ELEC)* spike; **y ~ and a bit**; **son las 3 y ~** it's just after 3; **tiene 50 libros y ~** he has 50-odd books; **me costó un ~** it cost me quite a bit.

picor [pi'kor] *nm* itch; *(ardor)* sting(ing feeling).

picota [pi'kota] *nf* pillory; **poner a algn en la ~** *(fig)* to ridicule sb.

picotada [piko'taða] *nf*, **picotazo** [piko'taθo] *nm (de pájaro)* peck; *(de insecto)* sting, bite.

picotear [pikote'ar] *vt* to peck ♦ *vi* to nibble, pick.

pictórico, a [pik'toriko, a] *adj* pictorial; **tiene dotes pictóricas** she has a talent for painting.

picudo, a [pi'kuðo, a] *adj* pointed, with a point.

pidiendo [pi'ðjendo] *etc vb V* **pedir**.

pie [pje] *(pl ~s) nm (gen, MAT)* foot; *(de cama, página, escalera)* foot, bottom; *(TEAT)* cue; *(fig: motivo)* motive, basis; *(: fundamento)* foothold; **~s planos** flat feet; **ir a ~** to go on foot, walk; **estar de ~** to be standing (up); **ponerse de ~** to stand up; **al ~ de la letra** (*citar*) literally, verbatim; (*copiar*) exactly, word for word; **de ~s a cabeza** from head to foot; **en ~ de guerra** on a war footing; **sin ~s ni cabeza** pointless, absurd; **dar ~ a** to give cause for; **no dar ~ con bola** to be no good at anything; **saber de qué ~ cojea algn** to know sb's weak spots.

piedad [pje'ðað] *nf* (*lástima*) pity, compassion; (*clemencia*) mercy; (*devoción*) piety, devotion; **tener ~ de** to take pity on.

piedra ['pjeðra] *nf* stone; (*roca*) rock; (*de mechero*) flint; (*METEOROLOGÍA*) hailstone; **primera ~** foundation stone; **~ de afilar** grindstone; **~ arenisca/caliza** sand-/limestone.

piel [pjel] *nf* (*ANAT*) skin; (*ZOOL*) skin, hide; (*de oso*) fur; (*cuero*) leather; (*BOT*) skin, peel ♦ *nm/f*: **~ roja** redskin.

pienso ['pjenso] *etc vb V* **pensar** ♦ *nm* (*AGR*) feed.

pierda ['pjerða] *etc vb V* **perder**.

pierna ['pjerna] *nf* leg; **en ~s** bare-legged.

pieza ['pjeθa] *nf* piece; (*esp AM: habitación*) room; (*MUS*) piece, composition; (*TEAT*) work, play; **~ de recambio** *o* **repuesto** spare (part), extra (*US*); **~ de ropa** article of clothing; **quedarse de una ~** to be dumbfounded.

pigmento [piɣ'mento] *nm* pigment.

pigmeo, a [piɣ'meo, a] *adj, nm/f* pigmy.

pijama [pi'xama] *nm* pyjamas *pl*.

pijo, a ['pixo, a] *nm/f* (*fam*) upper-class twit.

pijotada [pixo'taða] *nf* nuisance.

pila ['pila] *nf* (*ELEC*) battery; (*montón*) heap, pile; (*fuente*) sink; (*REL: tb*: **~ bautismal**) font; **nombre de ~** Christian *o* first name; **tengo una ~ de cosas que hacer** (*fam*) I have heaps *o* stacks of things to do; **~ de discos** (*INFORM*) disk pack.

pilar [pi'lar] *nm* pillar; (*de puente*) pier; (*fig*) prop, mainstay.

píldora ['pildora] *nf* pill; **la ~ (anticonceptiva)** the pill; **tragarse la ~** to be taken in.

pileta [pi'leta] *nf* basin, bowl; (*AM: de cocina*) sink; (: *piscina*) swimming pool.

pillaje [pi'ʎaxe] *nm* pillage, plunder.

pillar [pi'ʎar] *vt* (*fam: coger*) to catch; (: *agarrar*) to grasp, seize; (: *entender*) to grasp, catch on to; (*suj: coche etc*) to run over; **~ un resfriado** (*fam*) to catch a cold.

pillo, a ['piʎo, a] *adj* villainous; (*astuto*) sly,

crafty ♦ *nm/f* rascal, rogue, scoundrel.

pilón [pi'lon] *nm* pillar, post; (*ELEC*) pylon; (*bebedero*) drinking trough; (*de fuente*) basin.

pilotar [pilo'tar] *vt* (*avión*) to pilot; (*barco*) to steer.

piloto [pi'loto] *nm* pilot; (*AUTO*) rear light, tail light; (*conductor*) driver ♦ *adj inv*: **planta ~** pilot plant; **luz ~** side light.

piltrafa [pil'trafa] *nf* (*carne*) poor quality meat; (*fig*) worthless object; (: *individuo*) wretch.

pimentón [pimen'ton] *nm* (*polvo*) paprika.

pimienta [pi'mjenta] *nf* pepper.

pimiento [pi'mjento] *nm* pepper, pimiento.

pimpante [pim'pante] *adj* (*encantador*) charming; (*tb*: **tan ~**) smug, self-satisfied.

PIN *nm abr* (*ESP COM*: = *Producto Interior Neto*) net domestic product.

pin, *pl* pins [pin, pins] *nm* badge.

pinacoteca [pinako'teka] *nf* art gallery.

pinar [pi'nar] *nm* pinewood.

pincel [pin'θel] *nm* paintbrush.

pincelada [pinθe'laða] *nf* brushstroke; **última ~** (*fig*) finishing touch.

pinchadiscos [pintʃa'diskos] *nm/f inv* disc jockey, DJ.

pinchar [pin'tʃar] *vt* (*perforar*) to prick, pierce; (*neumático*) to puncture; (*incitar*) to prod ♦ *vi* (*MUS fam*) to be DJ; **~se** *vr* (*con droga*) to inject o.s.; (*neumático*) to burst, puncture; **no ~ ni cortar** (*fam*) to cut no ice; **tener un neumático pinchado** to have a puncture *o* a flat tyre.

pinchazo [pin'tʃaθo] *nm* (*perforación*) prick; (*de llanta*) puncture, flat (*US*).

pinche ['pintʃe] *nm* (*de cocina*) kitchen boy, scullion.

pinchito [pin'tʃito] *nm* shish kebab.

pincho ['pintʃo] *nm* point; (*aguijón*) spike; (*CULIN*) savoury (snack); **~ moruno** shish kebab; **~ de tortilla** small slice of omelette.

ping-pong ['pimpon] *nm* table tennis.

pingüe ['piŋgwe] *adj* (*grasoso*) greasy; (*cosecha*) bumper *cpd*; (*negocio*) lucrative.

pingüino [piŋ'gwino] *nm* penguin.

pinitos [pi'nitos] *nmpl*: **hacer sus primeros ~** to take one's first steps.

pino ['pino] *nm* pine (tree); **vivir en el quinto ~** to live at the back of beyond.

pinta ['pinta] *nf* spot; (*gota*) spot, drop; (*aspecto*) appearance, look(s) (*pl*); (*medida*) pint; **tener buena ~** to look good, look well; **por la ~** by the look of it.

pintado, a [pin'taðo, a] *adj* spotted; *(de muchos colores)* colourful ♦ *nf* piece of political graffiti; **~s** *nfpl* political graffiti *sg*; **me sienta que ni ~, viene que ni ~** it suits me a treat.

pintar [pin'tar] *vt* to paint ♦ *vi* to paint; *(fam)* to count, be important; **~se** *vr* to put on make-up; **pintárselas solo para hacer algo** to manage to do sth by o.s.; **no pinta nada** *(fam)* he has no say.

pintor, a [pin'tor, a] *nm/f* painter; **~ de brocha gorda** house painter; *(fig)* bad painter.

pintoresco, a [pinto'resko, a] *adj* picturesque.

pintura [pin'tura] *nf* painting; **~ a la acuarela** watercolour; **~ al óleo** oil painting; **~ rupestre** cave painting.

pinza ['pinθa] *nf* (*ZOOL*) claw; *(para colgar ropa)* clothes peg, clothespin (*US*); (*TEC*) pincers *pl*; **~s** *nfpl* (*para depilar*) tweezers.

piña ['piɲa] *nf* (*fruto del pino*) pine cone; *(fruta)* pineapple; *(fig)* group.

piñón [pi'ɲon] *nm* (*BOT*) pine nut; (*TEC*) pinion.

PÍO *nm abr* (*ESP*: = *Patronato de Igualdad de Oportunidades*) ≈ Equal Opportunities Board.

pío, a ['pio, a] *adj* (*devoto*) pious, devout; *(misericordioso)* merciful ♦ *nm*: **no decir ni ~** not to breathe a word.

piojo ['pjoxo] *nm* louse.

piojoso, a [pjo'xoso, a] *adj* lousy; *(sucio)* dirty.

piolet [pjo'le], *pl* **~s** [-s] *nm* ice axe.

pionero, a [pjo'nero, a] *adj* pioneering ♦ *nm/f* pioneer.

pipa ['pipa] *nf* pipe; (*BOT*) seed, pip.

pipí [pi'pi] *nm* (*fam*): **hacer ~** to have a wee(-wee).

pipiolo [pi'pjolo] *nm* youngster; *(novato)* novice, greenhorn.

pique ['pike] *etc vb V* **picar** ♦ *nm* *(resentimiento)* pique, resentment; *(rivalidad)* rivalry, competition; **irse a ~** to sink; *(familia)* to be ruined; **tener un ~ con algn** to have a grudge against sb.

piqueta [pi'keta] *nf* pick(axe).

piquete [pi'kete] *nm* (*agujerito*) small hole; (*MIL*) squad, party; *(de obreros)* picket; **~ secundario** secondary picket.

pirado, a [pi'raðo, a] *adj* (*fam*) round the bend.

piragua [pi'raɣwa] *nf* canoe.

piragüismo [pira'ɣwismo] *nm* (*DEPORTE*) canoeing.

pirámide [pi'ramiðe] *nf* pyramid.

piraña [pi'raɲa] *nf* piranha.

pirarse [pi'rarse] *vr*: **~(las)** *(largarse)* to beat it *(fam)*; (*ESCOL*) to cut class.

pirata [pi'rata] *adj*: **edición/disco ~** pirate edition/bootleg record ♦ *nm* pirate; (*tb*: **~ informático**) hacker.

pirenaico, a [pire'naiko, a] *adj* Pyrenean.

Pirineo(s) [piri'neo(s)] *nm(pl)* Pyrenees *pl*.

pirómano, a [pi'romano, a] *nm/f* (*PSICO*) pyromaniac; (*JUR*) arsonist.

piropo [pi'ropo] *nm* compliment, (piece of) flattery; **echar ~s a** to make flirtatious remarks to.

pirueta [pi'rweta] *nf* pirouette.

piruleta [piru'leta] *nf* lollipop.

pirulí [piru'li] *nm* lollipop.

pis [pis] *nm* (*fam*) pee; **hacer ~** to have a pee.

pisada [pi'saða] *nf* (*paso*) footstep; *(huella)* footprint.

pisar [pi'sar] *vt* (*caminar sobre*) to walk on, tread on; (*apretar con el pie*) to press; *(fig)* to trample on, walk all over ♦ *vi* to tread, step, walk; **~ el acelerador** to step on the accelerator; **~ fuerte** *(fig)* to act determinedly.

piscifactoría [pisθifakto'ria] *nf* fish farm.

piscina [pis'θina] *nf* swimming pool.

Piscis ['pisθis] *nm* (*ASTRO*) Pisces.

piso ['piso] *nm* (*suelo, de edificio*) floor; (*AM*) ground; *(apartamento)* flat, apartment; **primer ~** (*ESP*) first o second (*US*) floor; (*AM*) ground o first (*US*) floor.

pisotear [pisote'ar] *vt* to trample (on o underfoot); *(fig: humillar)* to trample on.

pisotón [piso'ton] *nm* (*con el pie*) stamp.

pista ['pista] *nf* track, trail; *(indicio)* clue; (*INFORM*) track; **~ de auditoría** (*COM*) audit trail; **~ de aterrizaje** runway; **~ de baile** dance floor; **~ de tenis** tennis court; **~ de hielo** ice rink; **estar sobre la ~ de algn** to be on sb's trail.

pisto ['pisto] *nm* (*CULIN*) ratatouille; **darse ~** *(fam)* to show off.

pistola [pis'tola] *nf* pistol; (*TEC*) spray-gun.

pistolero, a [pisto'lero, a] *nm/f* gunman, gangster ♦ *nf* holster.

pistón [pis'ton] *nm* (*TEC*) piston; (*MUS*) key.

pitar [pi'tar] *vt* (*hacer sonar*) to blow; *(partido)* to referee; *(rechiflar)* to whistle at, boo; *(actor, obra)* to hiss ♦ *vi* to whistle; (*AUTO*) to sound o toot one's horn; (*AM*) to smoke; **salir pitando** to beat it.

pitido [pi'tiðo] *nm* whistle; *(sonido agudo)* beep; *(sonido corto)* pip.

pitillera [piti'ʎera] *nf* cigarette case.

pitillo [pi'tiʎo] *nm* cigarette.

pito ['pito] *nm* whistle; *(de coche)* horn;

(*cigarrillo*) cigarette; (*fam: de marijuana*) joint; (*fam!*) prick (*!*); **me importa un** ~ I don't care two hoots.

pitón [pi'ton] *nm* (*ZOOL*) python.

pitonisa [pito'nisa] *nf* fortune-teller.

pitorrearse [pitorre'arse] *vr*: ~ **de** to scoff at, make fun of.

pitorreo [pito'rreo] *nm* joke, laugh; **estar de** ~ to be in a joking mood.

píxel ['piksel] *nm* (*INFORM*) pixel.

piyama [pi'jama] *nm* (*AM*) pyjamas *pl*, pajamas (*US*) *pl*.

pizarra [pi'θarra] *nf* (*piedra*) slate; (*encerado*) blackboard.

pizca ['piθka] *nf* pinch, spot; (*fig*) spot, speck, trace; **ni** ~ not a bit.

pizza ['pitsa] *nf* pizza.

placa ['plaka] *nf* plate; (*MED*) dental plate; (*distintivo*) badge; ~ **de matrícula** number plate; ~ **madre** (*INFORM*) mother board.

placaje [pla'kaxe] *nm* tackle.

placard [pla'kar] *nm* (*AM*) built-in cupboard, (clothes) closet (*US*).

placenta [pla'θenta] *nf* placenta; (*tras el parto*) afterbirth.

placentero, a [plaθen'tero, a] *adj* pleasant, agreeable.

placer [pla'θer] *nm* pleasure; **a** ~ at one's pleasure.

plácido, a ['plaθiðo, a] *adj* placid.

plafón [pla'fon] *nm* (*AM*) ceiling.

plaga ['playa] *nf* pest; (*MED*) plague; (*fig*) swarm.

plagar [pla'yar] *vt* to infest, plague; (*llenar*) to fill; **plagado de** riddled with; **han plagado la ciudad de carteles** they have plastered the town with posters.

plagiar [pla'gjar] *vt* to plagiarize; (*AM*) to kidnap.

plagiario, a [pla'gjario, a] *nm/f* plagiarist; (*AM*) kidnapper.

plagio ['plaxjo] *nm* plagiarism; (*AM*) kidnap.

plague ['playe] *etc vb* V **plagar**.

plan [plan] *nm* (*esquema, proyecto*) plan; (*idea, intento*) idea, intention; (*de curso*) programme; ~ **cotizable de jubilación** contributory pension scheme; ~ **de estudios** curriculum, syllabus; ~ **de incentivos** (*COM*) incentive scheme; **tener** ~ (*fam*) to have a date; **tener un** ~ (*fam*) to have an affair; **en** ~ **cachondeo** for a laugh; **en** ~ **económico** (*fam*) on the cheap; **vamos en** ~ **de turismo** we're going as tourists; **si te pones en ese** ~ ... if that's your attitude ...

plana ['plana] *nf* V **plano**.

plancha ['plantʃa] *nf* (*para planchar*) iron; (*rótulo*) plate, sheet; (*NAUT*) gangway; (*CULIN*) grill; **pescado a la** ~ grilled fish.

planchado, a [plan'tʃaðo, a] *adj* (*ropa*) ironed; (*traje*) pressed ♦ *nm* ironing.

planchar [plan'tʃar] *vt* to iron ♦ *vi* to do the ironing.

planeador [planea'ðor] *nm* glider.

planear [plane'ar] *vt* to plan ♦ *vi* to glide.

planeta [pla'neta] *nm* planet.

planetario, a [plane'tarjo, a] *adj* planetary ♦ *nm* planetarium.

planicie [pla'niθje] *nf* plain.

planificación [planifika'θjon] *nf* planning; ~ **corporativa** (*COM*) corporate planning; ~ **familiar** family planning; **diagrama de** ~ (*COM*) planner.

planilla [pla'niʎa] *nf* (*AM*) form.

plano, a ['plano, a] *adj* flat, level, even; (*liso*) smooth ♦ *nm* (*MAT, TEC, AVIAT*) plane; (*FOTO*) shot; (*ARQ*) plan; (*GEO*) map; (*de ciudad*) map, street plan ♦ *nf* sheet of paper, page; (*TEC*) trowel **primer** ~ close-up; **caer de** ~ to fall flat; **rechazar algo de** ~ to turn sth down flat; **le daba el sol de** ~ (*fig*) the sun shone directly on it; **en primera plana** on the front page; **plana mayor** staff.

planta ['planta] *nf* (*BOT, TEC*) plant; (*ANAT*) sole of the foot, foot; ~ **baja** ground floor.

plantación [planta'θjon] *nf* (*AGR*) plantation; (*acto*) planting.

plantar [plan'tar] *vt* (*BOT*) to plant; (*puesto*) to put in; (*levantar*) to erect, set up; ~**se** *vr* to stand firm; ~ **a algn en la calle** to chuck sb out; **dejar plantado a algn** (*fam*) to stand sb up; ~**se en** to reach, get to.

plantear [plante'ar] *vt* (*problema*) to pose; (*dificultad*) to raise; **se lo plantearé** I'll put it to him.

plantel [plan'tel] *nm* (*fig*) group, set.

plantilla [plan'tiʎa] *nf* (*de zapato*) insole; (*personal*) personnel; **ser de** ~ to be on the staff.

plantío [plan'tio] *nm* (*acto*) planting; (*lugar*) plot, bed, patch.

plantón [plan'ton] *nm* (*MIL*) guard, sentry; (*fam*) long wait; **dar (un)** ~ **a algn** to stand sb up.

plañir [pla'ɲir] *vi* to mourn.

plasma ['plasma] *nm* plasma.

plasmar [plas'mar] *vt* (*dar forma*) to mould, shape; (*representar*) to represent ♦ *vi*: ~ **en** to take the form of.

plasta ['plasta] *nf* soft mass, lump; (*desastre*) botch, mess.

plasticidad [plastiθiˈðað] *nf* (*fig*) expressiveness.

plástico, a [ˈplastiko, a] *adj* plastic ♦ *nf* (art of) sculpture, modelling ♦ *nm* plastic.

plastificar [plastifiˈkar] *vt* (*documento*) to laminate.

plastifique [plastiˈfike] *etc vb V* **plastificar.**

plastilina [plastiˈlina] *nf* Plasticine ®.

plata [ˈplata] *nf* (*metal*) silver; (*cosas hechas de plata*) silverware; (*AM*) cash, dough (*fam*); **hablar en ~** to speak bluntly *o* frankly.

plataforma [plataˈforma] *nf* platform; **~ de lanzamiento/perforación** launch(ing) pad/drilling rig.

plátano [ˈplatano] *nm* (*fruta*) banana; (*árbol*) plane tree.

platea [plaˈtea] *nf* (*TEAT*) pit.

plateado, a [plateˈaðo, a] *adj* silver; (*TEC*) silver-plated.

platense [plaˈtense] (*fam*) = **ríoplatense.**

plática [ˈplatika] *nf* (*AM*) talk, chat; (*REL*) sermon.

platicar [platiˈkar] *vi* (*AM*) to talk, chat.

platillo [plaˈtiʎo] *nm* saucer; (*de limosnas*) collecting bowl; **~s** *nmpl* cymbals; **~ volador** *o* **volante** flying saucer; **pasar el ~** to pass the hat round.

platina [plaˈtina] *nf* (*MUS*) tape deck.

platino [plaˈtino] *nm* platinum; **~s** *nmpl* (*AUTO*) (contact) points.

platique [plaˈtike] *etc vb V* **platicar.**

plato [ˈplato] *nm* plate, dish; (*parte de comida*) course; (*guiso*) dish; **~ frutero/ sopero** fruit/soup dish; **pagar los ~s rotos** (*fam*) to carry the can (*fam*).

plató [plaˈto] *nm* set.

platónico, a [plaˈtoniko, a] *adj* platonic.

playa [ˈplaja] *nf* beach; (*costa*) seaside; **~ de estacionamiento** (*AM*) car park.

playero, a [plaˈjero, a] *adj* beach *cpd* ♦ *nf* (*AM*: *camiseta*) T-shirt; **~s** *nfpl* canvas shoes; (*TENIS*) tennis shoes.

plaza [ˈplaθa] *nf* square; (*mercado*) market(place); (*sitio*) room, space; (*en vehículo*) seat, place; (*colocación*) post, job; **~ de abastos** food market; **~ mayor** main square; **~ de toros** bullring; **hacer la ~** to do the daily shopping; **reservar una ~** to reserve a seat; **el hotel tiene 100 ~s** the hotel has 100 beds.

plazca [ˈplaθka] *etc vb V* **placer.**

plazo [ˈplaθo] *nm* (*lapso de tiempo*) time, period, term; (*fecha de vencimiento*) expiry date; (*pago parcial*) instalment; **a corto/largo ~** short-/long-term; **comprar a ~s** to buy on hire purchase, pay for in instalments; **nos dan un ~ de 8 días** they allow us a week.

plazoleta [plaθoˈleta], **plazuela** [plaˈθwela] *nf* small square.

pleamar [pleaˈmar] *nf* high tide.

plebe [ˈpleβe] *nf*: **la ~** the common people *pl*, the masses *pl*; (*pey*) the plebs *pl*.

plebeyo, a [pleˈβejo, a] *adj* plebeian; (*pey*) coarse, common.

plebiscito [pleβisˈθito] *nm* plebiscite.

pleca [ˈpleka] *nf* (*INFORM*) backslash.

plegable [pleˈɣaβle] *adj* pliable; (*silla*) folding.

plegar [pleˈɣar] *vt* (*doblar*) to fold, bend; (*COSTURA*) to pleat; **~se** *vr* to yield, submit.

plegaria [pleˈɣarja] *nf* (*oración*) prayer.

plegué [pleˈɣe], **pleguemos** [pleˈɣemos] *etc vb V* **plegar.**

pleitear [pleiteˈar] *vi* (*JUR*) to plead, conduct a lawsuit; (*litigar*) to go to law.

pleito [ˈpleito] *nm* (*JUR*) lawsuit, case; (*fig*) dispute, feud; **~s** *nmpl* litigation *sg*; **entablar ~** to bring an action *o* a lawsuit; **poner ~** to sue.

plenario, a [pleˈnarjo, a] *adj* plenary, full.

plenilunio [pleniˈlunjo] *nm* full moon.

plenitud [pleniˈtuð] *nf* plenitude, fullness; (*abundancia*) abundance.

pleno, a [ˈpleno, a] *adj* full; (*completo*) complete ♦ *nm* plenum; **en ~** as a whole; (*por unanimidad*) unanimously; **en ~ día** in broad daylight; **en ~ verano** at the height of summer; **en plena cara** full in the face.

pletina *nf* (*MUS*) tape deck.

pleuresía [pleureˈsia] *nf* pleurisy.

plexiglás [pleksiˈɣlas] *nm* acrylic.

pliego [ˈpljeɣo] *etc vb V* **plegar** ♦ *nm* (*hoja*) sheet (of paper); (*carta*) sealed letter/ document; **~ de condiciones** details *pl*, specifications *pl*.

pliegue [ˈpljeɣe] *etc vb V* **plegar** ♦ *nm* fold, crease; (*de vestido*) pleat.

plisado [pliˈsaðo] *nm* pleating.

plomero [ploˈmero] *nm* (*AM*) plumber.

plomizo, a [ploˈmiθo, a] *adj* leaden, lead-coloured.

plomo [ˈplomo] *nm* (*metal*) lead; (*ELEC*) fuse; **caer a ~** to fall heavily *o* flat.

pluma [ˈpluma] *nf* (*ZOOL*) feather; **~ estilográfica, ~ fuente** (*AM*) fountain pen.

plumazo [pluˈmaθo] *nm* (*lit, fig*) stroke of the pen.

plumero [pluˈmero] *nm* (*quitapolvos*) feather duster; **ya te veo el ~** I know what you're up to.

plumón [pluˈmon] *nm* (*AM*) felt-tip pen.

plural [plu'ral] *adj* plural ♦ *nm*: **en ~** in the plural.

pluralidad [plurali'ðað] *nf* plurality; **una ~ de votos** a majority of votes.

pluriempleo [pluriem'pleo] *nm* moonlighting.

plus [plus] *nm* bonus.

plusmarquista [plusmar'kista] *nm/f* (*DEPORTE*) record holder.

plusvalía [plusßa'lia] *nf* (*mayor valor*) appreciation, added value; (*COM*) goodwill.

plutocracia [pluto'kraθja] *nf* plutocracy.

PM *nf abr* (*MIL*: = *Policía Militar*) MP.

p.m. *abr* (= *post meridiem*) p.m.; (= *por minuto*) per minute.

PMA *nm abr* (= *Programa Mundial de Alimentos*) World Food Programme.

pmo. *abr* (= *próximo*) prox.

PN *nf abr* (*MIL*: = *Policía Naval*) Naval Police.

PNB *nm abr* (*ESP COM*: = *producto nacional bruto*) GNP.

P.N.D. *nm abr* (*ESCOL*: = *personal no docente*) non-teaching staff.

PNN *nm/f abr* (= *profesor no numerario*) untenured teacher; (*ESP COM*: = *producto nacional neto*) net national product.

PNUD *nm abr* (= *Programa de las Naciones Unidas para el Desarrollo*) United Nations Development Programme.

PNV *nm abr* (*ESP POL*) = *Partido Nacional Vasco*.

P.º *abr* (= *Paseo*) Av(e).

p.o. *abr* = **por orden.**

p.º n.º *abr* (= *peso neto*) nt. wt.

población [poßla'θjon] *nf* population; (*pueblo, ciudad*) town, city; **~ activa** working population.

poblado, a [po'ßlaðo, a] *adj* inhabited; (*barba*) thick; (*cejas*) bushy ♦ *nm* (*aldea*) village; (*pueblo*) (small) town; **~ de** (*lleno*) filled with; **densamente ~** densely populated.

poblador, a [poßla'ðor, a] *nm/f* settler, colonist.

poblar [po'ßlar] *vt* (*colonizar*) to colonize; (*fundar*) to found; (*habitar*) to inhabit; **~se** *vr*: **~se de** to fill up with; (*irse cubriendo*) to become covered with.

pobre ['poßre] *adj* poor ♦ *nm/f* poor person; (*mendigo*) beggar; **los ~s** the poor; **¡~!** poor thing!; **~ diablo** (*fig*) poor wretch *o* devil.

pobreza [po'ßreθa] *nf* poverty.

pocho, a ['potʃo, a] *adj* (*flor, color*) faded, discoloured; (*persona*) pale; (*fruta*) overripe; (*deprimido*) depressed.

pocilga [po'θilɣa] *nf* pigsty.

pocillo [po'siʎo] *nm* (*AM*) coffee cup.

pócima ['poθima], **poción** [po'θjon] *nf* potion; (*brebaje*) concoction, nasty drink.

═══════════════════ **PALABRA CLAVE**

poco, a ['poko, a] *adj* **1** (*sg*) little, not much; **~ tiempo** little *o* not much time; **de ~ interés** of little interest, not very interesting; **poca cosa** not much
2 (*pl*) few, not many; **unos ~s** a few, some; **~s niños comen lo que les conviene** few children eat what they should
♦ *adv* **1** little, not much; **cuesta ~** it doesn't cost much; **~ más o menos** more or less
2 (+*adj*: = *negativo, antónimo*): **~ amable/inteligente** not very nice/intelligent
3: por ~ me caigo I almost fell
4 (*tiempo*): **~ después** soon after that; **dentro de ~** shortly; **hace ~** a short time ago, not long ago; **a ~ de haberse casado** shortly after getting married
5: ~ a ~ little by little
6 (*AM*): **¿a ~ no está divino?** isn't it just divine?; **de a ~** gradually
♦ *nm* a little, a bit; **un ~ triste/de dinero** a little sad/money.

poda ['poða] *nf* (*acto*) pruning; (*temporada*) pruning season.

podar [po'ðar] *vt* to prune.

podenco [po'ðenko] *nm* hound.

═══════════════════ **PALABRA CLAVE**

poder [po'ðer] *vi* **1** (*capacidad*) can, be able to; **no puedo hacerlo** I can't do it, I'm unable to do it
2 (*permiso*) can, may, be allowed to; **¿se puede?** may I (*o* we)?; **puedes irte ahora** you may go now; **no se puede fumar en este hospital** smoking is not allowed in this hospital
3 (*posibilidad*) may, might, could; **puede llegar mañana** he may *o* might arrive tomorrow; **pudiste haberte hecho daño** you might *o* could have hurt yourself; **¡podías habérmelo dicho antes!** you might have told me before!
4: puede (ser) perhaps; **puede que lo sepa Tomás** Tomás may *o* might know
5: ¡no puedo más! I've had enough!; **no pude menos que dejarlo** I couldn't help but leave it; **es tonto a más no ~** he's as stupid as they come
6: ~ con: ¿puedes con eso? can you manage that?; **no puedo con este crío**

this kid's too much for me
7: él me puede (*fam*) he's stronger than me
♦ *nm* power; **el ~** the Government; **~ adquisitivo** purchasing power; **detentar** *u* **ocupar** *o* **estar en el ~** to be in power *o* office; **estar** *u* **obrar en ~ de** to be in the hands *o* possession of; **por ~(es)** by proxy.

poderío [poðe'rio] *nm* power; (*autoridad*) authority.
poderoso, a [poðe'roso, a] *adj* powerful.
podio ['poðjo] *nm* podium.
podólogo, a [po'ðoloɣo, a] *nm/f* chiropodist (*BRIT*), podiatrist (*US*).
podré [po'ðre] *etc vb V* **poder**.
podrido, a [po'ðriðo, a] *adj* rotten, bad; (*fig*) rotten, corrupt.
podrir [po'ðrir] = **pudrir**.
poema [po'ema] *nm* poem.
poesía [poe'sia] *nf* poetry.
poeta [po'eta] *nm* poet.
poético, a [po'etiko, a] *adj* poetic(al).
poetisa [poe'tisa] *nf* (woman) poet.
póker ['poker] *nm* poker.
polaco, a [po'lako, a] *adj* Polish ♦ *nm/f* Pole ♦ *nm* (*LING*) Polish.
polar [po'lar] *adj* polar.
polarice [pola'riθe] *etc vb V* **polarizar**.
polaridad [polari'ðað] *nf* polarity.
polarizar [polari'θar] *vt* to polarize.
polea [po'lea] *nf* pulley.
polémica [po'lemika] *nf* polemics *sg*; (*una ~*) controversy.
polemice [pole'miθe] *etc vb V* **polemizar**.
polémico, a [po'lemiko, a] *adj* polemic(al).
polemizar [polemi'θar] *vi* to indulge in a polemic, argue.
polen ['polen] *nm* pollen.
poleo [po'leo] *nm* pennyroyal.
poli ['poli] *nm* (*fam*) cop (*fam*) ♦ *nf*: **la ~** the cops *pl* (*fam*).
policía [poli'θia] *nm/f* policeman/woman ♦ *nf* police.

There are two branches of the police, both armed: the **policía nacional**, *in charge of national security and public order in general, and the* **policía municipal**, *with duties of regulating traffic and policing the local community. Catalonia and the Basque Country have their own police forces, the* **Mossos d'Esquadra** *and the* **Ertzaintza** *respectively.*

policíaco, a [poli'θiako, a] *adj* police *cpd*; **novela policíaca** detective story.

polideportivo [poliðepor'tiβo] *nm* sports centre.
poliéster [poli'ester] *nm* polyester.
polietileno [polieti'leno] *nm* polythene (*BRIT*), polyethylene (*US*).
polifacético, a [polifa'θetiko, a] *adj* (*persona, talento*) many-sided, versatile.
poligamia [poli'ɣamja] *nf* polygamy.
polígamo, a [po'liɣamo, a] *adj* polygamous ♦ *nm* polygamist.
polígono [po'liɣono] *nm* (*MAT*) polygon; (*solar*) building lot; (*zona*) area; (*unidad vecina*) housing estate; **~ industrial** industrial estate.
polígrafo [po'liɣrafo] *nm* polygraph.
polilla [po'liʎa] *nf* moth.
Polinesia [poli'nesja] *nf* Polynesia.
polinesio, a [poli'nesjo, a] *adj, nm/f* Polynesian.
polio ['poljo] *nf* polio.
Polisario [poli'sarjo] *nm abr* (*POL: tb*: **Frente ~**) = *Frente Político de Liberación del Sáhara y Río de Oro.*
politécnico [poli'tekniko] *nm* polytechnic.
politicastro [politi'kastro] *nm* (*pey*) politician, politico.
político, a [po'litiko, a] *adj* political; (*discreto*) tactful; (*pariente*) in-law ♦ *nm/f* politician ♦ *nf* politics *sg*; (*económica, agraria*) policy; **padre ~** father-in-law; **política exterior/de ingresos y precios** foreign/prices and incomes policy.
póliza ['poliθa] *nf* certificate, voucher; (*impuesto*) tax *o* fiscal stamp; **~ de seguro(s)** insurance policy.
polizón [poli'θon] *nm* (*AVIAT, NAUT*) stowaway.
pollera [po'ʎera] *nf* (*criadero*) hencoop; (*AM*) skirt, overskirt.
pollería [poʎe'ria] *nf* poulterer's (shop).
pollo ['poʎo] *nm* chicken; (*joven*) young man; (*señorito*) playboy; **~ asado** roast chicken.
polo ['polo] *nm* (*GEO, ELEC*) pole; (*helado*) ice lolly; (*DEPORTE*) polo; (*suéter*) polo-neck; **P~ Norte/Sur** North/South Pole; **esto es el ~ opuesto de lo que dijo antes** this is the exact opposite of what he said before.
Polonia [po'lonja] *nf* Poland.
poltrona [pol'trona] *nf* reclining chair, easy chair.
polución [polu'θjon] *nf* pollution; **~ ambiental** environmental pollution.
polvera [pol'βera] *nf* powder compact.
polvo ['polβo] *nm* dust; (*QUÍMICA, CULIN, MED*) powder; (*fam!*) screw(!); **en ~** powdered; **~ de talco** talcum powder;

estar hecho ~ to be worn out o
exhausted; **hacer algo** ~ to smash sth;
hacer ~ **a algn** to shatter sb; *V tb* **polvos.**

pólvora ['polßora] *nf* gunpowder; (*fuegos
artificiales*) fireworks *pl*; **propagarse
como la** ~ (*noticia*) to spread like
wildfire.

polvoriento, a [polßo'rjento, a] *adj*
(*superficie*) dusty; (*sustancia*) powdery.

polvorín [polßo'rin] *nm* (*fig*) powder keg.

polvorosa [polßo'rosa] *adj* (*fam*): **poner
pies en** ~ to beat it.

polvos ['polßos] *nmpl* powder *sg*.

polvoso, a [pol'ßoso, a] *adj* (*AM*) dusty.

pomada [po'maða] *nf* pomade.

pomelo [po'melo] *nm* grapefruit.

pómez ['pomeθ] *nf*: **piedra** ~ pumice
stone.

pomo ['pomo] *nm* handle.

pompa ['pompa] *nf* (*burbuja*) bubble;
(*bomba*) pump; (*esplendor*) pomp,
splendour; ~**s funebres** funeral *sg*.

pomposo, a [pom'poso, a] *adj* splendid,
magnificent; (*pey*) pompous.

pómulo ['pomulo] *nm* cheekbone.

ponche ['pontʃe] *nm* punch.

poncho ['pontʃo] *nm* (*AM*) poncho, cape.

ponderar [ponde'rar] *vt* (*considerar*) to
weigh up, consider; (*elogiar*) to praise
highly, speak in praise of.

pondré [pon'dre] *etc vb V* **poner.**

ponencia [po'nenθja] *nf* (*exposición*)
(learned) paper, communication;
(*informe*) report.

==================== *PALABRA CLAVE*

poner [po'ner] *vt* **1** to put; (*colocar*) to
place, set; (*ropa*) to put on; (*problema, la
mesa*) to set; (*interés*) to show;
(*telegrama*) to send; (*obra de teatro*) to put
on; (*película*) to show; **ponlo más alto**
turn it up; **¿qué ponen en el Excelsior?**
what's on at the Excelsior?; ~ **algo a
secar** to put sth (out) to dry; **¡no pongas
esa cara!** don't look at me like that!

2 (*tienda*) to open; (*instalar: gas etc*) to
put in; (*radio, TV*) to switch o turn on

3 (*suponer*): **pongamos que ...** let's
suppose that ...

4 (*contribuir*): **el gobierno ha puesto otro
millón** the government has contributed
another million

5 (*TELEC*): **póngame con el Sr. López** can
you put me through to Mr. López?

6 (*estar escrito*) to say; **¿qué pone aquí?**
what does it say here?

7: ~ **de: le han puesto de director general**
they've appointed him general manager

8 (+*adj*) to make; **me estás poniendo
nerviosa** you're making me nervous

9 (*dar nombre*): **al hijo le pusieron Diego**
they called their son Diego

♦ *vi* (*gallina*) to lay

♦ ~**se** *vr* **1** (*colocarse*): **se puso a mi lado**
he came and stood beside me; **tú pónte
en esa silla** you go and sit on that chair

2 (*vestido, cosméticos*) to put on; **¿por
qué no te pones el vestido nuevo?** why
don't you put on o wear your new dress?

3 (*sol*) to set

4 (+*adj*) to get, become; to turn; ~**se
enfermo/gordo/triste** to get ill/fat/sad;
se puso muy serio he got very serious;
después de lavarla la tela se puso azul
after washing it the material turned
blue; **¡no te pongas así!** don't be like
that!; ~**se cómodo** to make o.s.
comfortable

5: ~**se a: se puso a llorar** he started to
cry; **tienes que** ~**te a estudiar** you must
get down to studying

6: ~**se a bien con algn** to make it up with
sb; ~**se a mal con algn** to get on the
wrong side of sb

7 (*AM*): **se me pone que ...** it seems to
me that ..., I think that ....

ponga ['ponga] *etc vb V* **poner.**

poniente [po'njente] *nm* west.

pontevedrés, esa [ponteße'ðres, esa] *adj*
of o from Pontevedra ♦ *nm/f* native o
inhabitant of Pontevedra.

pontificado [pontifi'kaðo] *nm* papacy,
pontificate.

pontífice [pon'tifiθe] *nm* pope, pontiff; **el
Sumo P**~ His Holiness the Pope.

pontón [pon'ton] *nm* pontoon.

ponzoña [pon'θoɲa] *nf* poison,
venom.

ponzoñoso, a [ponθo'ɲoso, a] *adj*
poisonous, venomous.

pop [pop] *adj inv, nm* (*MUS*) pop.

popa ['popa] *nf* stern; **a** ~ astern, abaft; **de**
~ **a proa** fore and aft.

popular [popu'lar] *adj* popular; (*del pueblo*)
of the people.

popularice [popula'riθe] *etc vb V*
popularizarse.

popularidad [populari'ðað] *nf* popularity.

popularizarse [populari'θarse] *vr* to
become popular.

poquísimo, a [po'kisimo, a] *adj* (*superlativo
de* **poco**) very little; (*pl*) very few; (*casi
nada*) hardly any.

poquito [po'kito] *nm*: **un** ~ a little bit ♦ *adv*
a little, a bit; **a** ~**s** bit by bit.

===================== PALABRA CLAVE

por [por] *prep* **1** (*objetivo*) for; **luchar ~ la patria** to fight for one's country; **hazlo ~ mí** do it for my sake
2 (+*infin*): **~ no llegar tarde** so as not to arrive late; **~ citar unos ejemplos** to give a few examples
3 (*causa*) out of, because of; **no es ~ eso** that's not the reason; **~ escasez de fondos** through *o* for lack of funds
4 (*tiempo*): **~ la mañana/noche** in the morning/at night; **se queda ~ una semana** she's staying (for) a week
5 (*lugar*): **pasar ~ Madrid** to pass through Madrid; **ir a Guayaquil ~ Quito** to go to Guayaquil via Quito; **caminar ~ la calle** to walk along the street; **~ allí** over there; **se va ~ ahí** we have to go that way; **¿~ dónde?** which way?; **está ~ el norte** it's somewhere in the north; **~ todo el país** throughout the country
6 (*cambio, precio*): **te doy uno nuevo ~ el que tienes** I'll give you a new one (in return) for the one you've got; **lo vendí ~ 15 dólares** I sold it for 15 dollars
7 (*valor distributivo*): **550 pesetas ~ hora/cabeza** 550 pesetas an *o* per hour/a *o* per head; **10 ~ ciento** 10 per cent; **80 (kms) ~ hora** 80 (km) an *o* per hour
8 (*modo, medio*) by; **~ correo/avión** by post/air; **día ~ día** day by day; **~ orden** in order; **entrar ~ la entrada principal** to go in through the main entrance
9 (*agente*) by; **hecho ~ él** done by him; "**dirigido ~**" "directed by"
10: **10 ~ 10 son 100** 10 by 10 is 100
11 (*en lugar de*): **vino él ~ su jefe** he came instead of his boss
12: **~ mí que revienten** as far as I'm concerned they can drop dead
13 (*evidencia*): **~ lo que dicen** judging by *o* from what they say
14: **estar/quedar ~ hacer** to be still *o* remain to be done
15: **~ (muy) difícil que sea** however hard it is *o* may be; **~ más que lo intente** no matter how *o* however hard I try
16: **~ qué** why; **¿~ qué?** why?; **¿~?** (*fam*) why (do you ask)?

porcelana [porθe'lana] *nf* porcelain; (*china*) china.
porcentaje [porθen'taxe] *nm* percentage; **~ de actividad** (*INFORM*) hit rate.
porche ['portʃe] *nm* (*de una plaza*) arcade; (*de casa*) porch.
porción [por'θjon] *nf* (*parte*) portion, share;

(*cantidad*) quantity, amount.
pordiosero, a [porðjo'sero, a] *nm/f* beggar.
porfía [por'fia] *nf* persistence; (*terquedad*) obstinacy.
porfiado, a [por'fjaðo, a] *adj* persistent; obstinate.
porfiar [por'fjar] *vi* to persist, insist; (*disputar*) to argue stubbornly.
pormenor [porme'nor] *nm* detail, particular.
pormenorice [pormeno'riθe] *etc vb V* **pormenorizar**.
pormenorizar [pormenori'θar] *vt* to (set out in) detail ♦ *vi* to go into detail.
porno ['porno] *adj inv* porno ♦ *nm* porn.
pornografía [pornoxra'fia] *nf* pornography.
poro ['poro] *nm* pore.
poroso, a [po'roso, a] *adj* porous.
poroto [po'roto] *nm* (*AM*) kidney bean.
porque ['porke] *conj* (*a causa de*) because; (*ya que*) since; **~ sí** because I feel like it.
porqué [por'ke] *nm* reason, cause.
porquería [porke'ria] *nf* (*suciedad*) filth, muck, dirt; (*acción*) dirty trick; (*objeto*) small thing, trifle; (*fig*) rubbish.
porqueriza [porke'riθa] *nf* pigsty.
porra ['porra] *nf* (*arma*) stick, club; (*cachiporra*) truncheon; **¡~s!** oh heck!; **¡vete a la ~!** go to heck!
porrazo [po'rraθo] *nm* (*golpe*) blow; (*caída*) bump; **de un ~** in one go.
porro ['porro] *nm* joint.
porrón [po'rron] *nm* glass wine jar with a long spout.
port [por(t)] *nm* (*INFORM*) port.
portaaviones [port(a)a'βjones] *nm inv* aircraft carrier.
portada [por'taða] *nf* (*TIP*) title page; (: *de revista*) cover.
portador, a [porta'ðor, a] *nm/f* carrier, bearer; (*COM*) bearer, payee; (*MED*) carrier; **ser ~ del virus del sida** to be HIV-positive.
portaequipajes [portaeki'paxes] *nm inv* boot (*BRIT*), trunk (*US*); (*baca*) luggage rack.
portafolio(s) [porta'foljo(s)] *nm* (*AM*) briefcase; **~ de inversiones** (*COM*) investment portfolio.
portal [por'tal] *nm* (*entrada*) vestibule, hall; (*pórtico*) porch, doorway; (*puerta de entrada*) main door; (*DEPORTE*) goal; **~es** *nmpl* arcade *sg*.
portaligas [porta'lixas] *nm inv* (*AM*) suspender belt.
portamaletas [portama'letas] *nm inv* roof rack.

portamonedas [portamo'neðas] *nm inv* purse.

portar [por'tar] *vt* to carry, bear; ~**se** *vr* to behave, conduct o.s.; ~**se mal** to misbehave; **se portó muy bien conmigo** he treated me very well.

portátil [por'tatil] *adj* portable.

portaviones [porta'βjones] *nm inv* aircraft carrier.

portavoz [porta'βoθ] *nm/f* spokesman/ woman.

portazo [por'taθo] *nm*: **dar un** ~ to slam the door.

porte ['porte] *nm* (*COM*) transport; (*precio*) transport charges *pl*; (*CORREOS*) postage; ~ **debido** (*COM*) carriage forward; ~ **pagado** (*COM*) carriage paid, post-paid.

portento [por'tento] *nm* marvel, wonder.

portentoso, a [porten'toso, a] *adj* marvellous, extraordinary.

porteño, a [por'teɲo, a] *adj* of o from Buenos Aires ♦ *nm/f* native o inhabitant of Buenos Aires.

portería [porte'ria] *nf* (*oficina*) porter's office; (*gol*) goal.

portero, a [por'tero, a] *nm/f* porter; (*conserje*) caretaker; (*DEPORTE*) goalkeeper.

pórtico ['portiko] *nm* (*porche*) portico, porch; (*fig*) gateway; (*arcada*) arcade.

portilla [por'tiʎa] *nf*, **portillo** [por'tiʎo] *nm* gate.

portón [pro'ton] *nm* proton.

portorriqueño, a [portorri'keɲo, a] *adj*, *nm/f* Puerto Rican.

portuario, a [por'twarjo, a] *adj* (*del puerto*) port *cpd*, harbour *cpd*; (*del muelle*) dock *cpd*; **trabajador** ~ docker.

Portugal [portu'ɣal] *nm* Portugal.

portugués, esa [portu'ɣes, esa] *adj*, *nm/f* Portuguese ♦ *nm* (*LING*) Portuguese.

porvenir [porβe'nir] *nm* future.

pos [pos]: **en** ~ **de**: *prep* after, in pursuit of.

posada [po'saða] *nf* (*refugio*) shelter, lodging; (*mesón*) guest house; **dar** ~ **a** to give shelter to, take in.

posaderas [posa'ðeras] *nfpl* backside *sg*, buttocks.

posar [po'sar] *vt* (*en el suelo*) to lay down, put down; (*la mano*) to place, put gently ♦ *vi* to sit, pose; ~**se** *vr* to settle; (*pájaro*) to perch; (*avión*) to land, come down.

posdata [pos'ðata] *nf* postscript.

pose ['pose] *nf* (*ARTE, afectación*) pose.

poseedor, a [posee'ðor, a] *nm/f* owner, possessor; (*de récord, puesto*) holder.

poseer [pose'er] *vt* to have, possess, own; (*ventaja*) to enjoy; (*récord, puesto*) to hold.

poseído, a [pose'iðo, a] *adj* possessed; **estar muy** ~ **de** to be very vain about.

posesión [pose'sjon] *nf* possession; **tomar** ~ **(de)** to take over.

posesionarse [posesjo'narse] *vr*: ~ **de** to take possession of, take over.

posesivo, a [pose'sißo, a] *adj* possessive.

poseyendo [pose'jendo] *etc vb* V **poseer**.

posgrado [pos'ɣraðo] *nm* = **postgrado**.

posgraduado, a [posɣra'ðwaðo, a] *adj*, *nm/f* = **postgraduado**.

posibilidad [posißili'ðað] *nf* possibility; (*oportunidad*) chance.

posibilitar [posißili'tar] *vt* to make possible, permit; (*hacer factible*) to make feasible.

posible [po'sißle] *adj* possible; (*factible*) feasible ♦ *nm*: ~**s** means; (*bienes*) funds, assets; **de ser** ~ if possible; **en o dentro de lo** ~ as far as possible; **lo antes** ~ as quickly as possible.

posición [posi'θjon] *nf* (*gen*) position; (*rango social*) status.

positivo, a [posi'tißo, a] *adj* positive ♦ *nf* (*FOTO*) print.

poso ['poso] *nm* sediment.

posoperatorio, a [posopera'torjo, a] *adj*, *nm* = **postoperatorio**.

posponer [pospo'ner] *vt* to put behind o below; (*aplazar*) to postpone.

posponga [pos'ponga] *etc*, **pospuesto** [pos'pwesto], **pospuse** [pos'puse] *etc vb* V **posponer**.

posta ['posta] *nf* (*de caballos*) relay, team; **a** ~ on purpose, deliberately.

postal [pos'tal] *adj* postal ♦ *nf* postcard.

poste ['poste] *nm* (*de telégrafos*) post, pole; (*columna*) pillar.

póster ['poster], *pl* **posters** ['posters] *nm* poster.

postergar [poster'ɣar] *vt* (*esp AM*) to put off, postpone, delay.

postergue [pos'terɣe] *etc vb* V **postergar**.

posteridad [posteri'ðað] *nf* posterity.

posterior [poste'rjor] *adj* back, rear; (*siguiente*) following, subsequent; (*más tarde*) later; **ser** ~ **a** to be later than.

posterioridad [posterjori'ðað] *nf*: **con** ~ later, subsequently.

postgrado [post'ɣraðo] *nm*: **curso de** ~ postgraduate course.

postgraduado, a [postɣra'ðwaðo, a] *adj*, *nm/f* postgraduate.

pos(t)guerra [pos(t)'ɣerra] *nf* postwar period; **en la** ~ after the war.

postigo [pos'tiɣo] *nm* (*portillo*) postern;

(*contraventana*) shutter.
postín [pos'tin] *nm* (*fam*) elegance; **de** ~
posh; **darse** ~ to show off.
postizo, a [pos'tiθo, a] *adj* false, artificial;
(*sonrisa*) false, phoney ♦ *nm* hairpiece.
postoperatorio, a [postopera'torjo, a] *adj*
postoperative ♦ *nm* postoperative
period.
postor, a [pos'tor, a] *nm/f* bidder; **mejor** ~
highest bidder.
postrado, a [pos'traðo, a] *adj* prostrate.
postrar [pos'trar] *vt* (*derribar*) to cast
down, overthrow; (*humillar*) to humble;
(*MED*) to weaken, exhaust; ~**se** *vr* to
prostrate o.s.
postre ['postre] *nm* sweet, dessert ♦ *nf*: **a la**
~ in the end, when all is said and done;
para ~ (*fam*) to crown it all; **llegar a los**
~**s** (*fig*) to come too late.
postrero, a [pos'trero, a] *adj* (*delante de
nmsg*: **postrer**: *último*) last; (*: que viene
detrás*) rear.
postrimerías [postrime'rias] *nfpl* final
stages.
postulado [postu'laðo] *nm* postulate.
postulante [postu'lante] *nm/f* petitioner;
(*REL*) postulant.
póstumo, a ['postumo, a] *adj* posthumous.
postura [pos'tura] *nf* (*del cuerpo*) posture,
position; (*fig*) attitude, position.
post-venta [pos'βenta] *adj* (*COM*) after-
sales.
potable [po'taβle] *adj* drinkable.
potaje [po'taxe] *nm* thick vegetable soup.
pote ['pote] *nm* pot, jar.
potencia [po'tenθja] *nf* power; (*capacidad*)
capacity; ~ **(en caballos)** horsepower; **en**
~ potential, in the making; **las grandes**
~**s** the great powers.
potencial [poten'θjal] *adj, nm* potential.
potenciar [poten'θjar] *vt* (*promover*) to
promote; (*fortalecer*) to boost.
potente [po'tente] *adj* powerful.
potestad [potes'tað] *nf* authority; **patria** ~
paternal authority.
potosí [poto'si] *nm* fortune; **cuesta un** ~ it
costs the earth.
potra ['potra] *nf* (*ZOOL*) filly; **tener** ~ to be
lucky.
potro ['potro] *nm* (*ZOOL*) colt; (*DEPORTE*)
vaulting horse.
pozo ['poθo] *nm* well; (*de río*) deep pool;
(*de mina*) shaft; ~ **negro** cesspool; **ser un**
~ **de ciencia** (*fig*) to be deeply learned.
PP *abr* (= *por poderes*) pp; (= *porte pagado*)
carriage paid.
p.p.m. *abr* (= *palabras por minuto*) wpm.
práctica ['praktika] *nf* V **práctico**.

practicable [prakti'kaβle] *adj* practicable;
(*camino*) passable, usable.
prácticamente ['praktikamente] *adv*
practically.
practicante [prakti'kante] *nm/f* (*MED*:
ayudante de doctor) medical assistant;
(*: enfermero*) nurse; (*quien practica algo*)
practitioner ♦ *adj* practising.
practicar [prakti'kar] *vt* to practise;
(*deporte*) to go in for, play; (*ejecutar*) to
carry out, perform.
práctico, a ['praktiko, a] *adj* (*gen*)
practical; (*conveniente*) handy; (*instruído*:
persona) skilled, expert ♦ *nf* practice;
(*método*) method; (*arte, capacidad*) skill;
en la práctica in practice.
practique [prak'tike] *etc vb* V **practicar**.
pradera [pra'ðera] *nf* meadow; (*de Canadá*)
prairie.
prado ['praðo] *nm* (*campo*) meadow, field;
(*pastizal*) pasture; (*AM*) lawn.
Praga ['praγa] *nf* Prague.
pragmático, a [praγ'matiko, a] *adj*
pragmatic.
preámbulo [pre'ambulo] *nm* preamble,
introduction; **decir algo sin** ~**s** to say sth
without beating about the bush.
precalentamiento [prekalenta'mjento] *nm*
(*DEPORTE*) warm-up.
precalentar [prekalen'tar] *vt* to preheat.
precaliente [preka'ljente] *etc vb* V
precalentar.
precario, a [pre'karjo, a] *adj* precarious.
precaución [prekau'θjon] *nf* (*medida
preventiva*) preventive measure,
precaution; (*prudencia*) caution,
wariness.
precaver [preka'βer] *vt* to guard against;
(*impedir*) to forestall; ~**se** *vr*: ~**se de** *o*
contra algo to (be on one's) guard
against sth.
precavido, a [preka'βiðo, a] *adj* cautious,
wary.
precedencia [preθe'ðenθja] *nf* precedence;
(*prioridad*) priority; (*superioridad*)
greater importance, superiority.
precedente [preθe'ðente] *adj* preceding;
(*anterior*) former ♦ *nm* precedent; **sin**
~**(s)** unprecedented; **establecer** *o* **sentar**
un ~ to establish *o* set a precedent.
preceder [preθe'ðer] *vt, vi* to precede, go/
come before.
precepto [pre'θepto] *nm* precept.
preceptor [preθep'tor] *nm* (*maestro*)
teacher; (*: particular*) tutor.
preciado, a [pre'θjaðo, a] *adj* (*estimado*)
esteemed, valuable.
preciar [pre'θjar] *vt* to esteem, value; ~**se**

vr to boast; ~**se de** to pride o.s. on.

precintar [preθin'tar] *vt* (*local*) to seal off; (*producto*) to seal.

precinto [pre'θinto] *nm* (*COM*: *tb*: ~ **de garantía**) seal.

precio ['preθjo] *nm* (*de mercado*) price; (*costo*) cost; (*valor*) value, worth; (*de viaje*) fare; ~ **de coste** *o* **de cobertura** cost price; ~ **al contado** cash price; ~ **al detalle** *o* **al por menor** retail price; ~ **al detallista** trade price; ~ **de entrega inmediata** spot price; ~ **de oferta** offer price; ~ **de oportunidad** bargain price; ~ **de salida** upset price; ~ **tope** top price; ~ **unitario** unit price; **no tener** ~ (*fig*) to be priceless; "**no importa** ~" "cost no object".

preciosidad [preθjosi'ðað] *nf* (*valor*) (high) value, (great) worth; (*encanto*) charm; (*cosa bonita*) beautiful thing; **es una** ~ it's lovely, it's really beautiful.

precioso, a [pre'θjoso, a] *adj* precious; (*de mucho valor*) valuable; (*fam*) lovely, beautiful.

precipicio [preθi'piθjo] *nm* cliff, precipice; (*fig*) abyss.

precipitación [preθipita'θjon] *nf* (*prisa*) haste; (*lluvia*) rainfall; (*QUÍMICA*) precipitation.

precipitado, a [preθipi'taðo, a] *adj* hasty, rash; (*salida*) hasty, sudden ♦ *nm* (*QUÍMICA*) precipitate.

precipitar [preθipi'tar] *vt* (*arrojar*) to hurl, throw; (*apresurar*) to hasten; (*acelerar*) to speed up, accelerate; (*QUÍMICA*) to precipitate; ~**se** *vr* to throw o.s.; (*apresurarse*) to rush; (*actuar sin pensar*) to act rashly; ~**se hacia** to rush towards.

precisado, a [preθi'saðo, a] *adj*: **verse** ~ **a hacer algo** to be obliged to do sth.

precisamente [preθisa'mente] *adv* precisely; (*justo*) precisely, exactly, just; ~ **por eso** for that very reason; ~ **fue él quien lo dijo** as a matter of fact he said it; **no es eso** ~ it's not really that.

precisar [preθi'sar] *vt* (*necesitar*) to need, require; (*fijar*) to determine exactly, fix; (*especificar*) to specify; (*señalar*) to pinpoint.

precisión [preθi'sjon] *nf* (*exactitud*) precision.

preciso, a [pre'θiso, a] *adj* (*exacto*) precise; (*necesario*) necessary, essential; (*estilo, lenguaje*) concise; **es** ~ **que lo hagas** you must do it.

precocidad [prekoθi'ðað] *nf* precociousness, precocity.

preconcebido, a [prekonθe'βiðo, a] *adj* preconceived.

preconice [preko'niθe] *etc vb V* **preconizar**.

preconizar [prekoni'θar] *vt* (*aconsejar*) to advise; (*prever*) to foresee.

precoz [pre'koθ] *adj* (*persona*) precocious; (*calvicie*) premature.

precursor, a [prekur'sor, a] *nm/f* precursor.

predecesor, a [preðeθe'sor, a] *nm/f* predecessor.

predecir [preðe'θir] *vt* to predict, foretell, forecast.

predestinado, a [preðesti'naðo, a] *adj* predestined.

predeterminar [preðetermi'nar] *vt* to predetermine.

predicado [preði'kaðo] *nm* predicate.

predicador, a [preðika'ðor, a] *nm/f* preacher.

predicar [preði'kar] *vt, vi* to preach.

predicción [preðik'θjon] *nf* prediction; (*pronóstico*) forecast; ~ **del tiempo** weather forecast(ing).

predicho [pre'ðitʃo], **prediga** [pre'ðiɣa] *etc*, **predije** [pre'ðixe] *etc vb V* **predecir**.

predilecto, a [preði'lekto, a] *adj* favourite.

predique [pre'ðike] *etc vb V* **predicar**.

prediré [preði're] *etc vb V* **predecir**.

predispondré [preðispon'dre] *etc vb V* **predisponer**.

predisponer [preðispo'ner] *vt* to predispose; (*pey*) to prejudice.

predisponga [preðis'ponga] *etc vb V* **predisponer**.

predisposición [preðisposi'θjon] *nf* predisposition, inclination; prejudice, bias; (*MED*) tendency.

predispuesto [preðis'pwesto], **predispuse** [preðis'puse] *etc vb V* **predisponer**.

predominante [preðomi'nante] *adj* predominant; (*preponderante*) prevailing; (*interés*) controlling.

predominar [preðomi'nar] *vt* to dominate ♦ *vi* to predominate; (*prevalecer*) to prevail.

predominio [preðo'minjo] *nm* predominance; prevalence.

preescolar [preesko'lar] *adj* preschool.

preestreno [prees'treno] *nm* preview, press view.

prefabricado, a [prefaβri'kaðo, a] *adj* prefabricated.

prefacio [pre'faθjo] *nm* preface.

preferencia [prefe'renθja] *nf* preference; **de** ~ preferably, for preference; **localidad de** ~ reserved seat.

preferible [prefe'riβle] *adj* preferable.

preferir [prefe'rir] *vt* to prefer.
prefiera [pre'fjera] *etc vb* V **preferir**.
prefijo [pre'fixo] *nm* prefix.
prefiriendo [prefi'rjendo] *etc vb* V **preferir**.
pregón [pre'ɣon] *nm* proclamation, announcement.
pregonar [preɣo'nar] *vt* to proclaim, announce; (*mercancía*) to hawk.
pregonero [preɣo'nero] *nm* town crier.
pregunta [pre'ɣunta] *nf* question; ~ **capciosa** catch question; **hacer una** ~ to ask a question.
preguntar [preɣun'tar] *vt* to ask; (*cuestionar*) to question ♦ *vi* to ask; ~**se** *vr* to wonder; ~ **por algn** to ask for sb; ~ **por la salud de algn** to ask after sb's health.
preguntón, ona [preɣun'ton, ona] *adj* inquisitive.
prehistórico, a [preis'toriko, a] *adj* prehistoric.
prejuicio [pre'xwiθjo] *nm* prejudgement; (*preconcepción*) preconception; (*pey*) prejudice, bias.
prejuzgar [prexuθ'ɣar] *vt* (*predisponer*) to prejudge.
prejuzgue [pre'xuθɣe] *etc vb* V **prejuzgar**.
preliminar [prelimi'nar] *adj, nm* preliminary.
preludio [pre'luðjo] *nm* (*MUS, fig*) prelude.
premamá [prema'ma] *adj*: **vestido** ~ maternity dress.
prematrimonial [prematrimo'njal] *adj*: **relaciones** ~**es** premarital sex.
prematuro, a [prema'turo, a] *adj* premature.
premeditación [premeðita'θjon] *nf* premeditation.
premeditado, a [premeði'taðo, a] *adj* premeditated, deliberate; (*intencionado*) wilful.
premeditar [premeði'tar] *vt* to premeditate.
premiar [pre'mjar] *vt* to reward; (*en un concurso*) to give a prize to.
premio ['premjo] *nm* reward; prize; (*COM*) premium; ~ **gordo** first prize.
premisa [pre'misa] *nf* premise.
premonición [premoni'θjon] *nf* premonition.
premura [pre'mura] *nf* (*prisa*) haste, urgency.
prenatal [prena'tal] *adj* antenatal, prenatal.
prenda ['prenda] *nf* (*ropa*) garment, article of clothing; (*garantía*) pledge; (*fam*) darling!; ~**s** *nfpl* talents, gifts; **dejar algo en** ~ to pawn sth; **no soltar** ~ to give

nothing away; (*fig*) not to say a word.
prendar [pren'dar] *vt* to captivate, enchant; ~**se de algo** to fall in love with sth.
prendedor [prende'ðor] *nm* brooch.
prender [pren'der] *vt* (*captar*) to catch, capture; (*detener*) to arrest; (*coser*) to pin, attach; (*sujetar*) to fasten; (*AM*) to switch on ♦ *vi* to catch; (*arraigar*) to take root; ~**se** *vr* (*encenderse*) to catch fire.
prendido, a [pren'diðo, a] *adj* (*AM: luz etc*) on.
prensa ['prensa] *nf* press; **la P~** the press; **tener mala** ~ to have o get a bad press; **la** ~ **nacional** the national press.
prensar [pren'sar] *vt* to press.
preñado, a [pre'naðo, a] *adj* (*mujer*) pregnant; ~ **de** pregnant with, full of.
preocupación [preokupa'θjon] *nf* worry, concern; (*ansiedad*) anxiety.
preocupado, a [preoku'paðo, a] *adj* worried, concerned; anxious.
preocupar [preoku'par] *vt* to worry; ~**se** *vr* to worry; ~**se de algo** (*hacerse cargo*) to take care of sth; ~**se por algo** to worry about sth.
preparación [prepara'θjon] *nf* (*acto*) preparation; (*estado*) preparedness, readiness; (*entrenamiento*) training.
preparado, a [prepa'raðo, a] *adj* (*dispuesto*) prepared; (*CULIN*) ready (to serve) ♦ *nm* (*MED*) preparation; ¡~**s, listos, ya!** ready, steady, go!
preparar [prepa'rar] *vt* (*disponer*) to prepare, get ready; (*TEC: tratar*) to prepare, process, treat; (*entrenar*) to teach, train; ~**se** *vr*: ~**se a** o **para hacer algo** to prepare o get ready to do sth.
preparativo, a [prepara'tiβo] *adj* preparatory, preliminary ♦ *nm*: ~**s** *nmpl* preparations.
preparatoria [prepara'torja] *nf* (*AM*) sixth form college (*BRIT*), senior high school (*US*).
preposición [preposi'θjon] *nf* preposition.
prepotencia [prepo'tenθja] *nf* abuse of power; (*POL*) high-handedness; (*soberbia*) arrogance.
prepotente [prepo'tente] *adj* (*POL*) high-handed; (*soberbio*) arrogant.
prerrogativa [prerroɣa'tiβa] *nf* prerogative, privilege.
presa ['presa] *nf* (*cosa apresada*) catch; (*víctima*) victim; (*de animal*) prey; (*de agua*) dam; **hacer** ~ **en** to clutch (on to), seize; **ser** ~ **de** (*fig*) to be a prey to.
presagiar [presa'xjar] *vt* to threaten.
presagio [pre'saxjo] *nm* omen.

presbítero [pres'ßitero] *nm* priest.

prescindir [presθin'dir] *vi*: ~ **de** (*privarse de*) to do without, go without; (*descartar*) to dispense with; **no podemos ~ de él** we can't manage without him.

prescribir [preskri'ßir] *vt* to prescribe.

prescripción [preskrip'θjon] *nf* prescription; ~ **facultativa** medical prescription.

prescrito [pres'krito] *pp de* **prescribir**.

preseleccionar [preselekθjo'nar] *vt* (*DEPORTE*) to seed.

presencia [pre'senθja] *nf* presence; **en ~ de** in the presence of.

presencial [presen'θjal] *adj*: **testigo ~** eyewitness.

presenciar [presen'θjar] *vt* to be present at; (*asistir a*) to attend; (*ver*) to see, witness.

presentación [presenta'θjon] *nf* presentation; (*introducción*) introduction.

presentador, a [presenta'ðor, a] *nm/f* compère.

presentar [presen'tar] *vt* to present; (*ofrecer*) to offer; (*mostrar*) to show, display; (*renuncia*) to tender; (*moción*) to propose; (*a una persona*) to introduce; **~se** *vr* (*llegar inesperadamente*) to appear, turn up; (*ofrecerse: como candidato*) to run, stand; (*aparecer*) to show, appear; (*solicitar empleo*) to apply; **~ al cobro** (*COM*) to present for payment; **~se a la policía** to report to the police.

presente [pre'sente] *adj* present ♦ *nm* present; (*LING*) present (tense); (*regalo*) gift; **los ~s** those present; **hacer ~** to state, declare; **tener ~** to remember, bear in mind; **la carta ~, la ~** this letter.

presentimiento [presenti'mjento] *nm* premonition, presentiment.

presentir [presen'tir] *vt* to have a premonition of.

preservación [preserßa'θjon] *nf* protection, preservation.

preservar [preser'ßar] *vt* to protect, preserve.

preservativo [preserßa'tißo] *nm* sheath, condom.

presidencia [presi'ðenθja] *nf* presidency; (*de comité*) chairmanship; **ocupar la ~** to preside, be in *o* take the chair.

presidente [presi'ðente] *nm/f* president; chairman/woman; (*en parlamento*) speaker; (*JUR*) presiding magistrate.

presidiario [presi'ðjarjo] *nm* convict.

presidio [pre'siðjo] *nm* prison, penitentiary.

presidir [presi'ðir] *vt* (*dirigir*) to preside at,

preside over; (: *comité*) to take the chair at; (*dominar*) to dominate, rule ♦ *vi* to preside; to take the chair.

presienta [pre'sjenta] *etc*, **presintiendo** [presin'tjendo] *etc vb V* **presentir**.

presión [pre'sjon] *nf* pressure; ~ **arterial** *o* **sanguínea** blood pressure; **a ~** under pressure.

presionar [presjo'nar] *vt* to press; (*botón*) to push, press; (*fig*) to press, put pressure on ♦ *vi*: ~ **para** *o* **por** to press for.

preso, a ['preso, a] *adj*: **estar ~ de terror** *o* **pánico** to be panic-stricken ♦ *nm/f* prisoner; **tomar** *o* **llevar ~ a algn** to arrest sb, take sb prisoner.

prestación [presta'θjon] *nf* (*aportación*) lending; (*INFORM*) capability; (*servicio*) service; (*subsidio*) benefit; **prestaciones** *nfpl* (*AUTO*) performance features; ~ **de juramento** oath-taking; ~ **personal** obligatory service; **P~ Social Sustitutoria** community service for conscientious objectors; *V tb* **mili**.

prestado, a [pres'taðo, a] *adj* on loan; **dar algo ~** to lend sth; **pedir ~** to borrow.

prestamista [presta'mista] *nm/f* moneylender.

préstamo ['prestamo] *nm* loan; ~ **con garantía** loan against collateral; ~ **hipotecario** mortgage.

prestar [pres'tar] *vt* to lend, loan; (*atención*) to pay; (*ayuda*) to give; (*servicio*) to do, render; (*juramento*) to take, swear; **~se** *vr* (*ofrecerse*) to offer *o* volunteer.

prestatario, a [presta'tarjo, a] *nm/f* borrower.

presteza [pres'teθa] *nf* speed, promptness.

prestidigitador [prestiðixita'ðor] *nm* conjurer.

prestigio [pres'tixjo] *nm* prestige; (*reputación*) face; (*renombre*) good name.

prestigioso, a [presti'xjoso, a] *adj* (*honorable*) prestigious; (*famoso, renombrado*) renowned, famous.

presto, a ['presto, a] *adj* (*rápido*) quick, prompt; (*dispuesto*) ready ♦ *adv* at once, right away.

presumido, a [presu'miðo, a] *adj* conceited.

presumir [presu'mir] *vt* to presume ♦ *vi* (*tener aires*) to be conceited; **según cabe ~** as may be presumed, presumably; ~ **de listo** to think o.s. very smart.

presunción [presun'θjon] *nf* presumption; (*sospecha*) suspicion; (*vanidad*) conceit.

presunto, a [pre'sunto, a] *adj* (*supuesto*)

supposed, presumed; (así llamado) so-called.

presuntuoso, a [presun'twoso, a] adj conceited, presumptuous.

presupondré [presupon'dre] etc vb V **presuponer**.

presuponer [presupo'ner] vt to presuppose.

presuponga [presu'ponga] etc vb V **presuponer**.

presupuestar [presupwes'tar] vi to budget ♦ vt: ~ **algo** to budget for sth.

presupuestario, a [presupwes'tarjo, a] adj (FINANZAS) budgetary, budget cpd.

presupuesto [presu'pwesto] pp de **presuponer** ♦ nm (FINANZAS) budget; (estimación: de costo) estimate; **asignación de** ~ (COM) budget appropriation.

presupuse [presu'puse] etc vb V **presuponer**.

presuroso, a [presu'roso, a] adj (rápido) quick, speedy; (que tiene prisa) hasty.

pretencioso, a [preten'θjoso, a] adj pretentious.

pretender [preten'der] vt (intentar) to try to, seek to; (reivindicar) to claim; (buscar) to seek, try for; (cortejar) to woo, court; ~ **que** to expect that; **¿qué pretende usted?** what are you after?

pretendiente [preten'djente] nmlf (candidato) candidate, applicant; (amante) suitor.

pretensión [preten'sjon] nf (aspiración) aspiration; (reivindicación) claim; (orgullo) pretension.

pretérito, a [pre'terito, a] adj (LING) past; (fig) past, former.

pretextar [preteks'tar] vt to plead, use as an excuse.

pretexto [pre'teksto] nm pretext; (excusa) excuse; **so** ~ **de** under pretext of.

pretil [pre'til] nm (valla) parapet; (baranda) handrail.

prevalecer [preβale'θer] vi to prevail.

prevaleciente [preβale'θjente] adj prevailing, prevalent.

prevalezca [preβa'leθka] etc vb V **prevalecer**.

prevención [preβen'θjon] nf (preparación) preparation; (estado) preparedness, readiness; (medida) prevention; (previsión) foresight, forethought; (precaución) precaution.

prevendré [preβen'dre] etc, **prevenga** [pre'βenga] etc vb V **prevenir**.

prevenido, a [preβe'niðo, a] adj prepared, ready; (cauteloso) cautious; **estar** ~

(preparado) to be ready; **ser** ~ (cuidadoso) to be cautious; **hombre** ~ **vale por dos** forewarned is forearmed.

prevenir [preβe'nir] vt (impedir) to prevent; (prever) to foresee, anticipate; (predisponer) to prejudice, bias; (avisar) to warn; (preparar) to prepare, get ready; ~**se** vr to get ready, prepare; ~**se contra** to take precautions against.

preventivo, a [preβen'tiβo, a] adj preventive, precautionary.

prever [pre'βer] vt to foresee; (anticipar) to anticipate.

previniendo [preβi'njendo] etc vb V **prevenir**.

previo, a [' preβjo, a] adj (anterior) previous, prior ♦ prep: ~ **acuerdo de los otros** subject to the agreement of the others; ~ **pago de los derechos** on payment of the fees.

previsible [preβi'siβle] adj foreseeable.

previsión [preβi'sjon] nf (perspicacia) foresight; (predicción) forecast; (prudencia) caution; ~ **de ventas** (COM) sales forecast.

previsor, a [preβi'sor, a] adj (precavido) far-sighted; (prudente) thoughtful.

previsto [pre'βisto] pp de **prever**.

P.R.I. nm abr (AM) = **Partido Revolucionario Institucional**.

prieto, a [' prjeto, a] adj (oscuro) dark; (AM) dark(-skinned); (fig) mean; (comprimido) tight, compressed.

prima [' prima] nf V **primo**.

primacía [prima'θia] nf primacy.

primar [pri'mar] vi (tener primacía) to occupy first place; ~ **sobre** to have priority over.

primario, a [pri'marjo, a] adj primary ♦ nf primary education; V tb **sistema educativo**.

primavera [prima'βera] nf (temporada) spring; (período) springtime.

primaveral [primaβe'ral] adj spring cpd, springlike.

primero, a [pri'mero, a] adj (delante de nmsg: **primer**) first; (fig) prime; (anterior) former; (básico) fundamental ♦ adv first; (más bien) sooner, rather ♦ nf (AUTO) first gear; (FERRO) first class; **de primera** (fam) first-class, first-rate; **de buenas a primeras** suddenly; **primera dama** (TEAT) leading lady.

primicia [pri'miθja] nf (PRENSA) scoop; ~**s** nfpl (tb fig) first fruits.

primitivo, a [primi'tiβo, a] adj primitive; (original) original; (COM: acción) ordinary ♦ nf: (**Lotería**) **Primitiva** weekly state-run lottery; V tb **lotería.**

primo, a ['primo, a] adj (MAT) prime ♦ nm/f cousin; (fam) fool, dupe ♦ nf (COM) bonus; (seguro) premium; (a la exportación) subsidy; ~ **hermano** first cousin; **materias primas** raw materials; **hacer el** ~ to be taken for a ride.

primogénito, a [primo'xenito] adj first-born.

primor [pri'mor] nm (cuidado) care; **es un** ~ it's lovely.

primordial [primor'ðjal] adj basic, fundamental.

primoroso, a [primo'roso] adj exquisite, fine.

princesa [prin'θesa] nf princess.

principado [prinθi'paðo] nm principality.

principal [prinθi'pal] adj principal, main; (más destacado) foremost; (piso) first, second (US); (INFORM) foreground ♦ nm (jefe) chief, principal.

príncipe ['prinθipe] nm prince; ~ **heredero** crown prince; **P~ de Asturias** King's son and heir to the Spanish throne; ~ **de gales** (tela) check.

principiante [prinθi'pjante] nm/f beginner; (novato) novice.

principio [prin'θipjo] nm (comienzo) beginning, start; (origen) origin; (base) rudiment, basic idea; (moral) principle; **a ~s de** at the beginning of; **desde el** ~ from the first; **en un** ~ at first.

pringar [prin'gar] vt (CULIN: pan) to dip; (ensuciar) to dirty; ~**se** vr to get splashed o soiled; ~ **a algn en un asunto** (fam) to involve sb in a matter.

pringoso, a [prin'goso] adj greasy; (pegajoso) sticky.

pringue ['pringe] etc vb V **pringar** ♦ nm (grasa) grease, fat, dripping.

prioridad [priori'ðað] nf priority; (AUTO) right of way.

prioritario, a [priori'tarjo] adj (INFORM) foreground.

prisa ['prisa] nf (apresuramiento) hurry, haste; (rapidez) speed; (urgencia) (sense of) urgency; **correr** ~ to be urgent; **darse** ~ to hurry up; **estar de o tener** ~ to be in a hurry.

prisión [pri'sjon] nf (cárcel) prison; (período de cárcel) imprisonment.

prisionero, a [prisjo'nero] nm/f prisoner.

prismáticos [pris'matikos] nmpl binoculars.

privación [priβa'θjon] nf deprivation; (falta) want, privation; **privaciones** nfpl hardships, privations.

privado, a [pri'βaðo] adj (particular) private; (POL: favorito) favourite (BRIT), favorite (US); **en** ~ privately, in private; "~ **y confidencial**" "private and confidential".

privar [pri'βar] vt to deprive; ~**se** vr: ~**se de** (abstenerse) to deprive o.s. of; (renunciar) to give up.

privativo, a [priβa'tiβo, a] adj exclusive.

privatizar [priβati'θar] vt to privatize.

privilegiado, a [priβile'xjaðo, a] adj privileged; (memoria) very good ♦ nm/f (afortunado) privileged person.

privilegiar [priβile'xjar] vt to grant a privilege to; (favorecer) to favour.

privilegio [priβi'lexjo] nm privilege; (concesión) concession.

pro [pro] nm o nf profit, advantage ♦ prep: **asociación** ~ **ciegos** association for the blind ♦ pref: ~ **soviético/americano** pro-Soviet/-American; **en** ~ **de** on behalf of, for; **los** ~**s y los contras** the pros and cons.

proa ['proa] nf (NAUT) bow, prow.

probabilidad [proβaβili'ðað] nf probability, likelihood; (oportunidad, posibilidad) chance, prospect.

probable [pro'βaβle] adj probable, likely; **es** ~ **que** + subjun it is probable o likely that; **es** ~ **que no venga** he probably won't come.

probador [proβa'ðor] nm (persona) taster (of wine etc); (en una tienda) fitting room.

probar [pro'βar] vt (demostrar) to prove; (someter a prueba) to test, try out; (ropa) to try on; (comida) to taste ♦ vi to try; ~**se** vr: ~**se un traje** to try on a suit.

probeta [pro'βeta] nf test tube.

problema [pro'βlema] nm problem.

procaz [pro'kaθ] adj insolent, impudent.

procedencia [proθe'ðenθja] nf (principio) source, origin; (lugar de salida) point of departure.

procedente [proθe'ðente] adj (razonable) reasonable; (conforme a derecho) proper, fitting; ~ **de** coming from, originating in.

proceder [proθe'ðer] vi (avanzar) to proceed; (actuar) to act; (ser correcto) to be right (and proper), be fitting ♦ nm (comportamiento) behaviour, conduct; **no procede obrar así** it is not right to act like that; ~ **de** to come from, originate in.

procedimiento [proθeði'mjento] nm procedure; (proceso) process; (método) means, method; (trámite) proceedings pl.

prócer ['proθer] nm (persona eminente) worthy; (líder) great man, leader; (esp

AM) national hero.
procesado, a [proθe'saðo, a] *nm/f* accused (person).
procesador [proθesa'ðor] *nm*: ~ **de textos** (*INFORM*) word processor.
procesamiento [proθesa'mjento] *nm* (*INFORM*) processing; ~ **de datos** data processing; ~ **por lotes** batch processing; ~ **solapado** multiprogramming; ~ **de textos** word processing.
procesar [proθe'sar] *vt* to try, put on trial; (*INFORM*) to process.
procesión [proθe'sjon] *nf* procession; **la ~ va por dentro** he keeps his troubles to himself.
proceso [pro'θeso] *nm* process; (*JUR*) trial; (*lapso*) course (of time); (*INFORM*): ~ **(automático) de datos** (automatic) data processing; ~ **no prioritario** background process; ~ **por pasadas** batch processing; ~ **en tiempo real** real-time programming.
proclama [pro'klama] *nf* (*acto*) proclamation; (*cartel*) poster.
proclamar [prokla'mar] *vt* to proclaim.
proclive [pro'kliβe] *adj*: ~ **(a)** inclined *o* prone (to).
procreación [prokrea'θjon] *nf* procreation.
procrear [prokre'ar] *vt, vi* to procreate.
procurador, a [prokura'ðor, a] *nm/f* attorney, solicitor.
procurar [proku'rar] *vt* (*intentar*) to try, endeavour; (*conseguir*) to get, obtain; (*asegurar*) to secure; (*producir*) to produce.
prodigar [proði'ɣar] *vt* to lavish; ~**se** *vr*: ~**se en** to be lavish with.
prodigio [pro'ðixjo] *nm* prodigy; (*milagro*) wonder, marvel; **niño** ~ child prodigy.
prodigioso, a [proði'xjoso, a] *adj* prodigious, marvellous.
pródigo, a ['proðiɣo, a] *adj* (*rico*) rich, productive; **hijo** ~ prodigal son.
producción [proðuk'θjon] *nf* production; (*suma de productos*) output; (*producto*) product; ~ **en serie** mass production.
producir [proðu'θir] *vt* to produce; (*generar*) to cause, bring about; (*impresión*) to give; (*COM: interés*) to bear; ~**se** *vr* (*gen*) to come about, happen; (*hacerse*) to be produced, be made; (*estallar*) to break out; (*accidente*) to take place.
productividad [proðuktiβi'ðað] *nf* productivity.
productivo, a [proðuk'tiβo, a] *adj* productive; (*provechoso*) profitable.
producto [pro'ðukto] *nm* (*resultado*)

product; *producción*) production; ~ **alimenticio** foodstuff; ~ **(nacional) bruto** gross (national) product; ~ **interno bruto** gross domestic product.
productor, a [proðuk'tor, a] *adj* productive, producing ♦ *nm/f* producer.
produje [pro'ðuxe], **produjera** [proðu'xera], **produzca** [pro'ðuθka] *etc vb V* **producir**.
proeza [pro'eθa] *nf* exploit, feat.
profanar [profa'nar] *vt* to desecrate, profane.
profano, a [pro'fano, a] *adj* profane ♦ *nm/f* (*inexperto*) layman/woman; **soy** ~ **en música** I don't know anything about music.
profecía [profe'θia] *nf* prophecy.
proferir [profe'rir] *vt* (*palabra, sonido*) to utter; (*injuria*) to hurl, let fly.
profesar [profe'sar] *vt* (*declarar*) to profess; (*practicar*) to practise.
profesión [profe'sjon] *nf* profession; (*confesión*) avowal; **abogado de** ~, **de** ~ **abogado** a lawyer by profession.
profesional [profesjo'nal] *adj* professional.
profesor, a [profe'sor, a] *nm/f* teacher; (*instructor*) instructor; (~ **de universidad**) lecturer; ~ **adjunto** assistant lecturer, associate professor (*US*).
profesorado [profeso'raðo] *nm* (*profesión*) teaching profession; (*cuerpo*) teaching staff, faculty (*US*); (*cargo*) professorship.
profeta [pro'feta] *nm/f* prophet.
profetice [profe'tiθe] *etc vb V* **profetizar**.
profetizar [profeti'θar] *vt, vi* to prophesy.
profiera [pro'fjera] *etc*, **profiriendo** [profi'rjendo] *etc vb V* **proferir**.
profilaxis [profi'laksis] *nf inv* prevention.
prófugo, a ['profuɣo, a] *nm/f* fugitive; (*desertor*) deserter.
profundice [profun'diθe] *etc vb V* **profundizar**.
profundidad [profundi'ðað] *nf* depth; **tener una** ~ **de 30 cm** to be 30 cm deep.
profundizar [profundi'θar] *vt* (*fig*) to go deeply into, study in depth.
profundo, a [pro'fundo, a] *adj* deep; (*misterio, pensador*) profound; **poco** ~ shallow.
profusión [profu'sjon] *nf* (*abundancia*) profusion; (*prodigalidad*) wealth.
progenie [pro'xenje] *nf* offspring.
progenitor [proxeni'tor] *nm* ancestor; ~**es** *nmpl* (*fam*) parents.
programa [pro'ɣrama] *nm* programme; (*INFORM*) program; ~ **de estudios** curriculum, syllabus; ~ **verificador de**

ortografía (*INFORM*) spelling checker.
programación [proɣrama'θjon] *nf*
(*INFORM*) programming; ~ **estructurada**
structured programming.
programador, a [proɣrama'ðor, a] *nm/f*
(computer) programmer; ~ **de**
aplicaciones applications programmer.
programar [proɣra'mar] *vt* (*INFORM*) to
programme.
programería [proɣrame'ria] *nf* (*INFORM*): ~
fija firmware.
progre ['proɣre] *adj* (*fam*) liberal.
progresar [proɣre'sar] *vi* to progress,
make progress.
progresión [proɣres'jon] *nf*: ~
geométrica/aritmética geometric/
arithmetic progression.
progresista [proɣre'sista] *adj*, *nm/f*
progressive.
progresivo, a [proɣre'siβo, a] *adj*
progressive; (*gradual*) gradual;
(*continuo*) continuous.
progreso [pro'ɣreso] *nm* (*tb*: ~**s**) progress;
hacer ~**s** to progress, advance.
prohibición [proiβi'θjon] *nf* prohibition,
ban; **levantar la** ~ **de** to remove the ban
on.
prohibir [proi'βir] *vt* to prohibit, ban,
forbid; **se prohíbe fumar** no smoking.
prohibitivo, a [proiβi'tiβo, a] *adj*
prohibitive.
prójimo, a ['proximo, a] *nm* fellow man
♦ *nm/f* (*vecino*) neighbour.
prole ['prole] *nf* (*descendencia*) offspring.
proletariado [proleta'rjaðo] *nm*
proletariat.
proletario, a [prole'tarjo, a] *adj*, *nm/f*
proletarian.
proliferación [prolifera'θjon] *nf*
proliferation; ~ **de armas nucleares**
spread of nuclear arms.
proliferar [prolife'rar] *vi* to proliferate.
prolífico, a [pro'lifiko, a] *adj* prolific.
prolijo, a [pro'lixo, a] *adj* long-winded,
tedious; (*AM*) neat.
prólogo ['proloɣo] *nm* prologue;
(*preámbulo*) preface, introduction.
prolongación [prolonga'θjon] *nf*
extension.
prolongado, a [prolon'gaðo, a] *adj* (*largo*)
long; (*alargado*) lengthy.
prolongar [prolon'gar] *vt* (*gen*) to extend;
(*en el tiempo*) to prolong; (*calle, tubo*) to
make longer, extend; ~**se** *vr* (*alargarse*)
to extend, go on.
prolongue [pro'longe] *etc vb V* **prolongar**.
prom. *abr* (= *promedio*) av.
promedio [pro'meðjo] *nm* average; (*de*

distancia) middle, mid-point.
promesa [pro'mesa] *nf* promise ♦ *adj*:
jugador ~ promising player; **faltar a una**
~ to break a promise.
prometer [prome'ter] *vt* to promise ♦ *vi* to
show promise; ~**se** *vr* (*dos personas*) to
get engaged.
prometido, a [prome'tiðo, a] *adj* promised;
engaged ♦ *nm/f* fiancé/fiancée.
prominente [promi'nente] *adj* prominent.
promiscuidad [promiskwi'ðað] *nf*
promiscuity.
promiscuo, a [pro'miskwo, a] *adj*
promiscuous.
promoción [promo'θjon] *nf* promotion;
(*año*) class, year; ~ **por correspondencia**
directa (*COM*) direct mailshot; ~ **de**
ventas sales promotion *o* drive.
promocionar [promoθjo'nar] *vt* (*COM*: *dar*
publicidad) to promote.
promontorio [promon'torjo] *nm*
promontory.
promotor [promo'tor] *nm* promoter;
(*instigador*) instigator.
promover [promo'βer] *vt* to promote;
(*causar*) to cause; (*juicio*) to bring;
(*motín*) to instigate, stir up.
promueva [pro'mweβa] *etc vb V* **promover**.
promulgar [promul'ɣar] *vt* to promulgate;
(*fig*) to proclaim.
promulgue [pro'mulɣe] *etc vb V*
promulgar.
pronombre [pro'nombre] *nm* pronoun.
pronosticar [pronosti'kar] *vt* to predict,
foretell, forecast.
pronóstico [pro'nostiko] *nm* prediction,
forecast; (*profecía*) omen; (*MED*:
diagnóstico) prognosis; **de** ~ **leve** slight,
not serious; ~ **del tiempo** weather
forecast.
pronostique [pronos'tike] *etc vb V*
pronosticar.
prontitud [pronti'tuð] *nf* speed, quickness.
pronto, a ['pronto, a] *adj* (*rápido*) prompt,
quick; (*preparado*) ready ♦ *adv* quickly,
promptly; (*en seguida*) at once, right
away; (*dentro de poco*) soon; (*temprano*)
early ♦ *nm* urge, sudden feeling; **tener**
~**s de enojo** to be quick-tempered; **al** ~
at first; **de** ~ suddenly; **¡hasta** ~**!** see
you soon!; **lo más** ~ **posible** as soon as
possible; **por lo** ~ meanwhile, for the
present; **tan** ~ **como** as soon as.
pronunciación [pronunθja'θjon] *nf*
pronunciation.
pronunciado, a [pronun'θjaðo, a] *adj*
(*marcado*) pronounced; (*curva etc*) sharp;
(*facciones*) marked.

pronunciamiento [pronunθja'mjento] *nm* (*rebelión*) insurrection.

pronunciar [pronun'θjar] *vt* to pronounce; (*discurso*) to make, deliver; (*JUR*: *sentencia*) to pass, pronounce; ~**se** *vr* to revolt, rise, rebel; (*declararse*) to declare o.s.; ~**se sobre** to pronounce on.

propagación [propaɣa'θjon] *nf* propagation; (*difusión*) spread(ing).

propaganda [propa'ɣanda] *nf* (*política*) propaganda; (*comercial*) advertising; **hacer ~ de** (*COM*) to advertise.

propagar [propa'ɣar] *vt* to propagate; (*difundir*) to spread, disseminate; ~**se** *vr* (*BIO*) to propagate; (*fig*) to spread.

propague [pro'paɣe] *etc vb V* **propagar**.

propalar [propa'lar] *vt* (*divulgar*) to divulge; (*publicar*) to publish an account of.

propano [pro'pano] *nm* propane.

propasarse [propa'sarse] *vr* (*excederse*) to go too far; (*sexualmente*) to take liberties.

propensión [propen'sjon] *nf* inclination, propensity.

propenso, a [pro'penso, a] *adj*: ~ **a** prone *o* inclined to; **ser ~ a hacer algo** to be inclined *o* have a tendency to do sth.

propiamente [propja'mente] *adv* properly; (*realmente*) really, exactly; ~ **dicho** real, true.

propicio, a [pro'piθjo, a] *adj* favourable, propitious.

propiedad [propje'ðað] *nf* property; (*posesión*) possession, ownership; (*conveniencia*) suitability; (*exactitud*) accuracy; ~ **particular** private property; ~ **pública** (*COM*) public ownership; **ceder algo a algn en ~** to transfer to sb the full rights over sth.

propietario, a [propje'tarjo, a] *nm/f* owner, proprietor.

propina [pro'pina] *nf* tip; **dar algo de ~** to give something extra.

propinar [propi'nar] *vt* (*golpe*) to strike; (*azotes*) to give.

propio, a ['propjo, a] *adj* own, of one's own; (*característico*) characteristic, typical; (*conveniente*) proper; (*mismo*) selfsame, very; **el ~ ministro** the minister himself; **¿tienes casa propia?** have you a house of your own?; **eso es muy ~ de él** that's just like him; **tiene un olor muy ~** it has a smell of its own.

propondré [propon'dre] *etc vb V* **proponer**.

proponente [propo'nente] *nm* proposer, mover.

proponer [propo'ner] *vt* to propose, put

forward; (*candidato*) to propose, nominate; (*problema*) to pose; ~**se** *vr* to propose, plan, intend.

proponga [pro'ponga] *etc vb V* **proponer**.

proporción [propor'θjon] *nf* proportion; (*MAT*) ratio; (*razón, porcentaje*) rate; **proporciones** *nfpl* dimensions; (*fig*) size *sg*; **en ~ con** in proportion to.

proporcionado, a [proporθjo'naðo, a] *adj* proportionate; (*regular*) medium, middling; (*justo*) just right; **bien ~** well-proportioned.

proporcional [proporθjo'nal] *adj* proportional; ~ **a** proportional to.

proporcionar [proporθjo'nar] *vt* (*dar*) to give, supply, provide; **esto le proporciona una renta anual de ...** this brings him a yearly income of ....

proposición [proposi'θjon] *nf* proposition; (*propuesta*) proposal.

propósito [pro'posito] *nm* (*intención*) purpose; (*intento*) aim, intention ♦ *adv*: **a ~** by the way, incidentally; **a ~ de** about, with regard to.

propuesto, a [pro'pwesto, a] *pp de* **proponer** ♦ *nf* proposal.

propugnar [propuɣ'nar] *vt* to uphold.

propulsar [propul'sar] *vt* to drive, propel; (*fig*) to promote, encourage.

propulsión [propul'sjon] *nf* propulsion; ~ **a chorro** *o* **por reacción** jet propulsion.

propuse [pro'puse] *etc vb V* **proponer**.

prorrata [pro'rrata] *nf* (*porción*) share, quota, prorate (*US*) ♦ *adv* (*COM*) pro rata.

prorratear [prorrate'ar] *vt* (*dividir*) to share out, prorate (*US*).

prórroga ['prorroɣa] *nf* (*gen*) extension; (*JUR*) stay; (*COM*) deferment.

prorrogable [prorro'ɣaβle] *adj* which can be extended.

prorrogar [prorro'ɣar] *vt* (*período*) to extend; (*decisión*) to defer, postpone.

prorrogue [pro'rroɣe] *etc vb V* **prorrogar**.

prorrumpir [prorrum'pir] *vi* to burst forth, break out; ~ **en gritos** to start shouting; ~ **en lágrimas** to burst into tears.

prosa ['prosa] *nf* prose.

prosaico, a [pro'saiko, a] *adj* prosaic, dull.

proscribir [proskri'βir] *vt* to prohibit, ban; (*desterrar*) to exile, banish; (*partido*) to proscribe.

proscripción [proskrip'θjon] *nf* prohibition, ban; banishment; proscription.

proscrito, a [pros'krito, a] *pp de* **proscribir** ♦ *adj* (*prohibido*) banned; (*desterrado*) outlawed ♦ *nm/f* (*exilado*) exile; (*bandido*) outlaw.

prosecución [proseku'θjon] *nf*
continuation; (*persecución*) pursuit.
proseguir [prose'yir] *vt* to continue, carry
on, proceed with; (*investigación, estudio*)
to pursue ♦ *vi* to continue, go on.
prosiga [pro'siya] *etc*, **prosiguiendo**
[prosi'xjenðo] *etc vb V* **proseguir**.
prosista [pro'sista] *nm/f* (*escritor*) prose
writer.
prospección [prospek'θjon] *nf* exploration;
(*del petróleo, del oro*) prospecting.
prospecto [pros'pekto] *nm* prospectus;
(*folleto*) leaflet, sheet of instructions.
prosperar [prospe'rar] *vi* to prosper,
thrive, flourish.
prosperidad [prosperi'ðað] *nf* prosperity;
(*éxito*) success.
próspero, a ['prospero, a] *adj* prosperous,
thriving, flourishing; (*que tiene éxito*)
successful.
prostíbulo [pros'tiβulo] *nm* brothel.
prostitución [prostitu'θjon] *nf*
prostitution.
prostituir [prosti'twir] *vt* to prostitute; ~**se**
vr to prostitute o.s., become a prostitute.
prostituta [prosti'tuta] *nf* prostitute.
prostituyendo [prostitu'jendo] *etc vb V*
prostituir.
protagonice [protayo'niθe] *etc vb V*
protagonizar.
protagonista [protayo'nista] *nm/f*
protagonist; (*LIT: personaje*) main
character, hero(ine).
protagonizar [protayoni'θar] *vt* to head,
take the chief role in.
protección [protek'θjon] *nf* protection.
proteccionismo [protekθjo'nismo] *nm*
(*COM*) protectionism.
protector, a [protek'tor, a] *adj* protective,
protecting; (*tono*) patronizing ♦ *nm/f*
protector; (*bienhechor*) patron; (*de la
tradición*) guardian.
proteger [prote'xer] *vt* to protect; ~ **contra
grabación** *o* **contra escritura** (*INFORM*) to
write-protect.
protegido, a [prote'xiðo, a] *nm/f* protégé/
protégée.
proteína [prote'ina] *nf* protein.
proteja [pro'texa] *etc vb V* **proteger**.
prótesis ['protesis] *nf* (*MED*) prosthesis.
protesta [pro'testa] *nf* protest;
(*declaración*) protestation.
protestante [protes'tante] *adj* Protestant.
protestar [protes'tar] *vt* to protest,
declare; (*fe*) to protest ♦ *vi* to protest;
(*objetar*) to object; **cheque protestado
por falta de fondos** cheque referred to
drawer.

protocolo [proto'kolo] *nm* protocol; **sin ~s**
(*formalismo*) informal(ly), without
formalities.
protón [pro'ton] *nm* proton.
prototipo [proto'tipo] *nm* prototype; (*ideal*)
model.
protuberancia [protuβe'ranθja] *nf*
protuberance.
prov. *abr* (= *provincia*) prov.
provecho [pro'βetʃo] *nm* advantage,
benefit; (*FINANZAS*) profit; ¡**buen ~!** bon
appétit!; **en ~ de** to the benefit of; **sacar
~ de** to benefit from, profit by.
provechoso, a [proβe'tʃoso, a] *adj*
(*ventajoso*) advantageous; (*beneficioso*)
beneficial, useful; (*FINANZAS: lucrativo*)
profitable.
proveedor, a [proβee'ðor, a] *nm/f*
(*abastecedor*) supplier; (*distribuidor*)
dealer.
proveer [proβe'er] *vt* to provide, supply;
(*preparar*) to provide, get ready;
(*vacante*) to fill; (*negocio*) to transact,
dispatch ♦ *vi*: ~ **a** to provide for; ~**se** *vr*:
~**se de** to provide o.s. with.
provendré [proβen'dre] *etc*, **provenga**
[pro'βenga] *etc vb V* **provenir**.
provenir [proβe'nir] *vi*: ~ **de** to come from,
stem from.
Provenza [pro'βenθa] *nf* Provence.
proverbial [proβer'βjal] *adj* proverbial;
(*fig*) notorious.
proverbio [pro'βerβjo] *nm* proverb.
proveyendo [proβe'jendo] *etc vb V*
proveer.
providencia [proβi'ðenθja] *nf* providence;
(*previsión*) foresight; ~**s** *nfpl* measures,
steps.
provincia [pro'βinθja] *nf* province; (*ESP:
ADMIN*) ≈ county, ≈ region (*Scot*); **un
pueblo de ~(s)** a country town.

---

*Spain is divided up into 55 administrative
provincias, including the islands, and
territories in North Africa. Each one has a
capital de provincia, which generally bears
the same name. **Provincias** are grouped by
geography, history and culture into
comunidades autónomas. It should be
noted that the term **comarca** normally has
a purely geographical function in Spanish,
but in Catalonia it designates
administrative boundaries.*

---

provinciano, a [proβin'θjano, a] *adj*
provincial; (*del campo*) country *cpd*.
proviniendo [proβi'njendo] *etc vb V*
provenir.

provisión [pro'βi'sjon] *nf* provision; (*abastecimiento*) provision, supply; (*medida*) measure, step.

provisional [proβisjo'nal] *adj* provisional.

provisorio, a [proβi'sorjo, a] *adj* (*esp AM*) provisional.

provisto, a [pro'βisto, a] *adj*: ~ **de** provided *o* supplied with; (*que tiene*) having, possessing.

provocación [proβoka'θjon] *nf* provocation.

provocador, a [proβoka'ðor, a] *adj* provocative, provoking.

provocar [proβo'kar] *vt* to provoke; (*alentar*) to tempt, invite; (*causar*) to bring about, lead to; (*promover*) to promote; (*estimular*) to rouse, stir, stimulate; (*protesta, explosión*) to cause, spark off; (*AM*): **¿te provoca un café?** would you like a coffee?

provocativo, a [proβoka'tiβo, a] *adj* provocative.

provoque [pro'βoke] *etc vb V* **provocar.**

proxeneta [prokse'neta] *nm/f* go-between; (*de prostitutas*) pimp/procuress.

próximamente [proksima'mente] *adv* shortly, soon.

proximidad [proksimi'ðað] *nf* closeness, proximity.

próximo, a ['proksimo, a] *adj* near, close; (*vecino*) neighbouring; (*el que viene*) next; **en fecha próxima** at an early date; **el mes** ~ next month.

proyección [projek'θjon] *nf* projection; (*CINE*) showing; (*diapositiva*) slide, transparency; (*influencia*) influence; **el tiempo de** ~ **es de 35 minutos** the film runs for 35 minutes.

proyectar [projek'tar] *vt* (*objeto*) to hurl, throw; (*luz*) to cast, shed; (*CINE*) to screen, show; (*planear*) to plan.

proyectil [projek'til] *nm* projectile, missile; ~ **(tele)dirigido** guided missile.

proyecto [pro'jekto] *nm* plan; (*idea*) project; (*estimación de costo*) detailed estimate; **tener algo en** ~ to be planning sth; ~ **de ley** (*POL*) bill.

proyector [projek'tor] *nm* (*CINE*) projector.

prudencia [pru'ðenθja] *nf* (*sabiduría*) wisdom, prudence; (*cautela*) care.

prudente [pru'ðente] *adj* sensible, wise, prudent; (*cauteloso*) careful.

prueba ['prweβa] *etc vb V* **probar ♦** *nf* proof; (*ensayo*) test, trial; (*cantidad*) taste, sample; (*saboreo*) testing, sampling; (*de ropa*) fitting; (*DEPORTE*) event; **a** ~ on trial; (*COM*) on approval; **a** ~ **de** proof against; **a** ~ **de agua/fuego** waterproof/

fireproof; ~ **de capacitación** (*COM*) proficiency test; ~ **de fuego** (*fig*) acid test; ~ **de vallas** hurdles; **someter a** ~ **to** put to the test; **¿tiene usted** ~ **de ello?** can you prove it?, do you have proof?

prurito [pru'rito] *nm* itch; (*de bebé*) nappy rash; (*anhelo*) urge.

psico... [siko] *pref* psycho...

psicoanálisis [sikoa'nalisis] *nm* psychoanalysis.

psicoanalista [sikoana'lista] *nm/f* psychoanalyst.

psicología [sikolo'xia] *nf* psychology.

psicológico, a [siko'loxiko, a] *adj* psychological.

psicólogo, a [si'koloɣo, a] *nm/f* psychologist.

psicópata [si'kopata] *nm/f* psychopath.

psicosis [si'kosis] *nf inv* psychosis.

psicosomático, a [sikoso'matiko, a] *adj* psychosomatic.

psicoterapia [sikote'rapja] *nf* psychotherapy.

psiquiatra [si'kjatra] *nm/f* psychiatrist.

psiquiátrico, a [si'kjatriko, a] *adj* psychiatric ♦ *nm* mental hospital.

psíquico, a ['sikiko, a] *adj* psychic(al).

PSOE [pe'soe] *nm abr* = *Partido Socialista Obrero Español.*

PSS *nf abr* (= *Prestación Social Sustitutoria*) *community service for conscientious objectors.*

Pta. *abr* (*GEO*: = *Punta*) Pt.

pta(s). *abr* = **peseta(s).**

ptmo. *abr* (*COM*) = **préstamo.**

pts. *abr* = **pesetas.**

púa ['pua] *nf* sharp point; (*para guitarra*) plectrum; **alambre de** ~s barbed wire.

pub [puβ/paβ/paf] *nm* bar.

púber, a ['puβer, a] *adj, nm/f* adolescent.

pubertad [puβer'tað] *nf* puberty.

publicación [puβlika'θjon] *nf* publication.

publicar [puβli'kar] *vt* (*editar*) to publish; (*hacer público*) to publicize; (*divulgar*) to make public, divulge.

publicidad [puβliθi'ðað] *nf* publicity; (*COM*) advertising; **dar** ~ **a** to publicize, give publicity to; ~ **gráfica** display advertising; ~ **en el punto de venta** point-of-sale advertising.

publicitar [puβliθi'tar] *vt* to publicize.

publicitario, a [puβliθi'tarjo, a] *adj* publicity *cpd*; advertising *cpd*.

público, a ['puβliko, a] *adj* public ♦ *nm* public; (*TEAT etc*) audience; (*DEPORTE*) spectators *pl*, crowd; (*restaurantes etc*) clients *pl*; **el gran** ~ the general public; **hacer** ~ to publish; (*difundir*) to disclose;

~ **objetivo** (*COM*) target audience.
publique [pu'ßlike] *etc vb V* **publicar.**
pucherazo [putʃe'raθo] *nm* (*fraude*)
electoral fiddle; **dar** ~ to rig an election.
puchero [pu'tʃero] *nm* (*CULIN: olla*) cooking
pot; (: *guiso*) stew; **hacer** ~**s** to pout.
pudibundo, a [puði'ßundo, a] *adj* bashful.
púdico, a ['puðiko, a] *adj* modest;
(*pudibundo*) bashful.
pudiendo [pu'ðjendo] *etc vb V* **poder.**
pudiente [pu'ðjente] *adj* (*opulento*)
wealthy; (*poderoso*) powerful.
pudín [pu'ðin] *nm* pudding.
pudor [pu'ðor] *nm* modesty; (*vergüenza*)
(sense of) shame.
pudoroso, a [puðo'roso, a] *adj* (*modesto*)
modest; (*casto*) chaste.
pudrir [pu'ðrir] *vt* to rot; (*fam*) to upset,
annoy; ~**se** *vr* to rot, decay; (*fig*) to rot,
languish.
pueblerino, a [pweßle'rino, a] *adj*
(*lugareño*) small-town *cpd*; (*persona*)
rustic, provincial ♦ *nm/f* (*aldeano*)
country person.
pueblo ['pweßlo] *etc vb V* **poblar** ♦ *nm*
people; (*nación*) nation; (*aldea*) village;
(*plebe*) common people; (*población
pequeña*) small town, country town.
pueda ['pweða] *etc vb V* **poder.**
puente ['pwente] *nm* (*gen*) bridge; (*NAUT:
tb*: ~ **de mando**) bridge; (: *cubierta*) deck;
~ **aéreo** airlift; ~ **colgante** suspension
bridge; ~ **levadizo** drawbridge; **hacer
(el)** ~ (*fam*) to take a long weekend.
puenting ['pwentin] *nm* bungee jumping.
puerco, a ['pwerko, a] *adj* (*sucio*) dirty,
filthy; (*obsceno*) disgusting ♦ *nm/f* pig/
sow.
pueril [pwe'ril] *adj* childish.
puerro ['pwerro] *nm* leek.
puerta ['pwerta] *nf* door; (*de jardín*) gate;
(*portal*) doorway; (*fig*) gateway; (*gol*)
goal; (*INFORM*) port; **a la** ~ at the door; **a
~ cerrada** behind closed doors; ~
corredera/giratoria sliding/swing *o*
revolving door; ~ **principal/trasera** *o* **de
servicio** front/back door; ~ **(de
transmisión en) paralelo/serie** (*INFORM*)
parallel/serial port; **tomar la** ~ (*fam*) to
leave.
puerto ['pwerto] *nm* (*tb INFORM*) port; (*de
mar*) seaport; (*paso*) pass; (*fig*) haven,
refuge; **llegar a un** ~ (*fig*) to get over a
difficulty.
Puerto Rico [pwerto'riko] *nm* Puerto Rico.
puertorriqueño, a [pwertorri'keɲo, a] *adj*,
nm/f Puerto Rican.
pues [pwes] *adv* (*entonces*) then;

(¡*entonces!*) well, well then; (*así que*) so
♦ *conj* (*porque*) since; ~ ... **no sé** well ... I
don't know.
puesto, a ['pwesto, a] *pp de* **poner** ♦ *adj*
dressed ♦ *nm* (*lugar, posición*) place;
(*trabajo*) post, job; (*MIL*) post; (*COM*) stall;
(*quiosco*) kiosk ♦ *nf* (*apuesta*) bet, stake; ~ **de mercado**
market stall; ~ **de policía** police station;
~ **de socorro** first aid post; **puesta en
escena** staging; **puesta en marcha**
starting; **puesta del sol** sunset; **puesta a
cero** (*INFORM*) reset.
pugna ['puɣna] *nf* battle, conflict.
pugnar [puɣ'nar] *vi* (*luchar*) to struggle,
fight; (*pelear*) to fight.
puja ['puxa] *nf* (*esfuerzo*) attempt; (*en una
subasta*) bid.
pujante [pu'xante] *adj* strong, vigorous.
pujar [pu'xar] *vt* (*precio*) to raise, push up
♦ *vi* (*en licitación*) to bid, bid up; (*fig:
esforzarse*) to struggle, strain.
pulcro, a ['pulkro, a] *adj* neat, tidy.
pulga ['pulɣa] *nf* flea; **tener malas** ~**s** to be
short-tempered.
pulgada [pul'ɣaða] *nf* inch.
pulgar [pul'ɣar] *nm* thumb.
pulgón [pul'ɣon] *nm* plant louse, greenfly.
pulir [pu'lir] *vt* to polish; (*alisar*) to smooth;
(*fig*) to polish up, touch up.
pulla ['puʎa] *nf* cutting remark.
pulmón [pul'mon] *nm* lung; **a pleno** ~
(*respirar*) deeply; (*gritar*) at the top of
one's voice; ~ **de acero** iron lung.
pulmonía [pulmo'nia] *nf* pneumonia.
pulpa ['pulpa] *nf* pulp; (*de fruta*) flesh, soft
part.
pulpería [pulpe'ria] *nf* (*AM*) small grocery
store.
púlpito ['pulpito] *nm* pulpit.
pulpo ['pulpo] *nm* octopus.
pulsación [pulsa'θjon] *nf* beat, pulsation;
(*ANAT*) throb(bing); (*en máquina de
escribir*) tap; (*de pianista, mecanógrafo*)
touch; ~ **(de una tecla)** (*INFORM*)
keystroke; ~ **doble** (*INFORM*) strikeover.
pulsador [pulsa'ðor] *nm* button, push
button.
pulsar [pul'sar] *vt* (*tecla*) to touch, tap;
(*MUS*) to play; (*botón*) to press, push ♦ *vi*
to pulsate; (*latir*) to beat, throb.
pulsera [pul'sera] *nf* bracelet; **reloj de** ~
wristwatch.
pulso ['pulso] *nm* (*MED*) pulse; **hacer algo a
~** to do sth unaided *o* by one's own
efforts.
pulular [pulu'lar] *vi* (*estar plagado*): ~ **(de)**
to swarm (with).

pulverice [pulße'riθe] _etc vb_ V **pulverizar.**
pulverizador [pulßeriθa'ðor] _nm_ spray, spray gun.
pulverizar [pulßeri'θar] _vt_ to pulverize; (_líquido_) to spray.
puna ['puna] _nf_ (_AM MED_) mountain sickness.
punce ['punθe] _etc vb_ V **punzar.**
punción [pun'θjon] _nf_ (_MED_) puncture.
pundonor [pundo'nor] _nm_ (_dignidad_) self-respect.
punición [puni'θjon] _nf_ punishment.
punitivo, a [puni'tißo, a] _adj_ punitive.
punki ['punki] _adj, nm/f_ punk.
punta ['punta] _nf_ point, tip; (_extremidad_) end; (_promontorio_) headland; (_COSTURA_) corner; (_TEC_) small nail; (_fig_) touch, trace; **horas ~s** peak hours, rush hours; **sacar ~ a** to sharpen; **de ~** on end; **de ~ a ~** from one end to the other; **estar de ~** to be edgy; **ir de ~ en blanco** to be all dressed up to the nines; **tener algo en la ~ de la lengua** to have sth on the tip of one's tongue; **se le pusieron los pelos de ~** her hair stood on end.
puntada [pun'taða] _nf_ (_COSTURA_) stitch.
puntal [pun'tal] _nm_ prop, support.
puntapié [punta'pje], _pl_ **puntapiés** _nm_ kick; **echar a algn a ~s** to kick sb out.
punteado, a [punte'aðo, a] _adj_ (_moteado_) dotted; (_diseño_) of dots ♦ _nm_ (_MUS_) twang.
puntear [punte'ar] _vt_ to tick, mark; (_MUS_) to pluck.
puntería [punte'ria] _nf_ (_de arma_) aim, aiming; (_destreza_) marksmanship.
puntero, a [pun'tero, a] _adj_ leading ♦ _nm_ (_señal, INFORM_) pointer; (_dirigente_) leader.
puntiagudo, a [puntja'ɣuðo, a] _adj_ sharp, pointed.
puntilla [pun'tiʎa] _nf_ (_TEC_) tack, braid; (_COSTURA_) lace edging; (**andar) de ~s** (to walk) on tiptoe.
puntilloso, a [punti'ʎoso, a] _adj_ (_pundonoroso_) punctilious; (_susceptible_) touchy.
punto ['punto] _nm_ (_gen_) point; (_señal diminuta_) spot, dot; (_lugar_) spot, place; (_momento_) point, moment; (_en un examen_) mark; (_tema_) item; (_COSTURA_) stitch; (_INFORM: impresora_) pitch; (: _pantalla_) pixel; **a ~** ready; **estar a ~ de** to be on the point of _o_ about to; **llegar a ~** to come just at the right moment; **al ~** at once; **en ~** on the dot; **estar en su ~** (_CULIN_) to be done to a turn; **hasta cierto ~** to some extent; **hacer ~** to knit; **poner**

un motor en ~ to tune an engine; **~ de partida/de congelación/de fusión** starting/freezing/melting point; **~ de vista** point of view, viewpoint; **~ muerto** dead centre; (_AUTO_) neutral (gear); **~s a tratar** matters to be discussed, agenda _sg_; **~ final** full stop; **dos ~s** colon; **~ y coma** semicolon; **~ acápite** (_AM_) full stop, new paragraph; **~ de interrogación** question mark; **~s suspensivos** suspension points; **~ de equilibrio/de pedido** (_COM_) breakeven/reorder point; **~ inicial** _o_ **de partida** (_INFORM_) home; **~ de referencia/de venta** (_COM_) benchmark point/point-of-sale.
puntuación [puntwa'θjon] _nf_ punctuation; (_puntos: en examen_) mark(s) (_pl_); (: _DEPORTE_) score.
puntual [pun'twal] _adj_ (_a tiempo_) punctual; (_cálculo_) exact, accurate; (_informe_) reliable.
puntualice [puntwa'liθe] _etc vb_ V **puntualizar.**
puntualidad [puntwali'ðað] _nf_ punctuality; exactness, accuracy; reliability.
puntualizar [puntwali'θar] _vt_ to fix, specify.
puntuar [pun'twar] _vt_ (_LING, TIP_) to punctuate; (_examen_) to mark ♦ _vi_ (_DEPORTE_) to score, count.
punzada [pun'θaða] _nf_ (_puntura_) prick; (_MED_) stitch; (_dolor_) twinge (of pain).
punzante [pun'θante] _adj_ (_dolor_) shooting, sharp; (_herramienta_) sharp; (_comentario_) biting.
punzar [pun'θar] _vt_ to prick, pierce ♦ _vi_ to shoot, stab.
punzón [pun'θon] _nm_ (_TEC_) punch.
puñado [pu'ɲaðo] _nm_ handful (_tb fig_); **a ~s** by handfuls.
puñal [pu'ɲal] _nm_ dagger.
puñalada [puɲa'laða] _nf_ stab.
puñeta [pu'ɲeta] _nf_: **¡~!, ¡qué ~(s)!** (_fam!_) hell!; **mandar a algn a hacer ~s** (_fam_) to tell sb to go to hell.
puñetazo [puɲe'taθo] _nm_ punch.
puño ['puɲo] _nm_ (_ANAT_) fist; (_cantidad_) fistful, handful; (_COSTURA_) cuff; (_de herramienta_) handle; **como un ~** (_verdad_) obvious; (_palpable_) tangible, visible; **de ~ y letra del poeta** in the poet's own handwriting.
pupila [pu'pila] _nf_ (_ANAT_) pupil.
pupitre [pu'pitre] _nm_ desk.
puré [pu're], _pl_ **purés** _nm_ puree; (_sopa_) (thick) soup; **~ de patatas** mashed potatoes; **estar hecho ~** (_fig_) to be knackered.

pureza [pu'reθa] *nf* purity.
purga ['purɣa] *nf* purge.
purgante [pur'ɣante] *adj, nm* purgative.
purgar [pur'ɣar] *vt* to purge; (*POL: depurar*)
to purge, liquidate; **~se** *vr* (*MED*) to take
a purge.
purgatorio [purɣa'torjo] *nm* purgatory.
purgue ['purɣe] *etc vb* V **purgar**.
purificar [purifi'kar] *vt* to purify; (*refinar*)
to refine.
purifique [puri'fike] *etc vb* V **purificar**.
puritano, a [puri'tano, a] *adj* (*actitud*)
puritanical; (*iglesia, tradición*) puritan
♦ *nm/f* puritan.
puro, a ['puro, a] *adj* pure; (*depurado*)
unadulterated; (*oro*) solid; (*cielo*) clear;
(*verdad*) simple, plain ♦ *adv*: **de ~
cansado** out of sheer tiredness ♦ *nm*
cigar; **por pura casualidad** by sheer
chance.
púrpura ['purpura] *nf* purple.
purpúreo, a [pur'pureo, a] *adj* purple.
pus [pus] *nm* pus.
puse ['puse] *etc vb* V **poner**.
pústula ['pustula] *nf* pimple, sore.
puta ['puta] *nf* whore, prostitute.
putada [pu'taða] *nf* (*fam!*): **hacer una ~ a
algn** to play a dirty trick on sb; **¡qué ~!**
what a pain in the arse!(*!*).
putería [pute'ria] *nf* (*prostitución*)
prostitution; (*prostíbulo*) brothel.
putrefacción [putrefak'θjon] *nf* rotting,
putrefaction.
pútrido, a ['putriðo, a] *adj* rotten.
puzzle ['puθle] *nm* puzzle.
PVP *abr* (*ESP. = Precio Venta al Público*)
≈ RRP.
PYME *nf abr* (*= Pequeña y Mediana
Empresa*) SME.

Q q

Q, q [ku] *nf* (*letra*) Q, q; **Q de Querido** Q for
Queen.
q.e.g.e. *abr* (*= que en gloria esté*) R.I.P.
q.e.p.d. *abr* (*= que en paz descanse*)
R.I.P.
q.e.s.m. *abr* (*= que estrecha su mano*)
courtesy formula.
qm. *abr* = **quintal(es) métrico(s)**.
qts. *abr* = **quilates**.

═══════════════ *PALABRA CLAVE*

que [ke] *conj* **1** (*con oración subordinada*:
muchas veces no se traduce) that; **dijo ~
vendría** he said (that) he would come;
espero ~ lo encuentres I hope (that) you
find it; **dile ~ me llame** ask him to call
me; *V tb* **el**
2 (*en oración independiente*): **¡~ entre!**
send him in; **¡que se mejore tu padre!** I
hope your father gets better; **¡~ lo haga
él!** he can do it!; (*orden*) get him to do it!
3 (*enfático*): **¿me quieres? – ¡~ sí!** do you
love me? – of course!; **te digo ~ sí** I'm
telling you
4 (*consecutivo: muchas veces no se
traduce*) that; **es tan grande ~ no lo
puedo levantar** it's so big (that) I can't
lift it
5 (*comparaciones*) than; **yo ~ tú/él** if I
were you/him; *V tb* **más; menos**
6 (*valor disyuntivo*): **~ le guste o no**
whether he likes it or not; **~ venga o ~
no venga** whether he comes or not
7 (*porque*): **no puedo, ~ tengo ~
quedarme en casa** I can't, I've got to
stay in
8: siguió toca ~ toca he kept on playing
♦ *pron* **1** (*cosa*) that, which; (*+prep*)
which; **el sombrero ~ te compraste** the
hat (that *o* which) you bought; **la cama
en ~ dormí** the bed (that *o* which) I
slept in; **el día (en) ~ ella nació** the day
(when) she was born
2 (*persona: suj*) that, who; (: *objeto*) that,
whom; **el amigo ~ me acompañó al
museo** the friend that *o* who went to the
museum with me: **la chica ~ invité** the
girl (that *o* whom) I invited.

qué [ke] *adj* what?, which? ♦ *pron* what?; **¡~
divertido/asco!** how funny/revolting!; **¡~
día más espléndido!** what a glorious
day!; **¿~ edad tienes?** how old are you?;
¿de ~ me hablas? what are you saying
to me?; **¿~ tal?** how are you?, how are
things?; **¿~ hay (de nuevo)?** what's
new?; **¿~ más?** anything else?
quebrada [ke'ßraða] *nf* V **quebrado**.
quebradero [keßra'ðero] *nm*: **~ de cabeza**
headache, worry.
quebradizo, a [keßra'ðiθo, a] *adj* fragile;
(*persona*) frail.
quebrado, a [ke'ßraðo, a] *adj* (*roto*)
broken; (*terreno*) rough, uneven ♦ *nm/f*
bankrupt ♦ *nm* (*MAT*) fraction ♦ *nf* ravine;
~ rehabilitado discharged bankrupt.
quebradura [keßra'ðura] *nf* (*fisura*) fissure;

(*MED*) rupture.

quebrantamiento [keβranta'mjento] *nm* (*acto*) breaking; (*de ley*) violation; (*estado*) exhaustion.

quebrantar [keβran'tar] *vt* (*infringir*) to violate, transgress; ~**se** *vr* (*persona*) to fail in health.

quebranto [ke'βranto] *nm* damage, harm; (*decaimiento*) exhaustion; (*dolor*) grief, pain.

quebrar [ke'βrar] *vt* to break, smash ♦ *vi* to go bankrupt; ~**se** *vr* to break, get broken; (*MED*) to be ruptured.

quechua ['ketʃua] *adj, nm/f* Quechua.

queda ['keða] *nf*: (**toque de**) ~ curfew.

quedar [ke'ðar] *vi* to stay, remain; (*encontrarse*) to be; (*restar*) to remain, be left; ~**se** *vr* to remain, stay (behind); ~ **en** (*acordar*) to agree on/to; (*acabar siendo*) to end up as; ~ **por hacer** to be still to be done; ~ **ciego/mudo** to be left blind/dumb; **no te queda bien ese vestido** that dress doesn't suit you; **quedamos a las seis** we agreed to meet at six; **eso queda muy lejos** that's a long way (away); **nos quedan 12 kms para llegar al pueblo** there are still 12 kms before we get to the village; **no queda otra** there's no alternative; ~**se (con) algo** to keep sth; ~**se con algn** (*fam*) to swindle sb; ~**se en nada** to come to nothing *o* nought; ~**se sin** to run out of.

quedo, a ['keðo, a] *adj* still ♦ *adv* softly, gently.

quehacer [kea'θer] *nm* task, job; ~**es** (**domésticos**) household chores.

queja ['kexa] *nf* complaint.

quejarse [ke'xarse] *vr* (*enfermo*) to moan, groan; (*protestar*) to complain; ~ **de que** ... to complain (about the fact) that ....

quejica [ke'xika] *adj* grumpy, complaining ♦ *nm/f* grumbler, whinger.

quejido [ke'xiðo] *nm* moan.

quejoso, a [ke'xoso, a] *adj* complaining.

quema ['kema] *nf* fire; (*combustión*) burning.

quemado, a [ke'maðo, a] *adj* burnt; (*irritado*) annoyed.

quemadura [kema'ðura] *nf* burn, scald; (*de sol*) sunburn; (*de fusible*) blow-out.

quemar [ke'mar] *vt* to burn; (*fig: malgastar*) to burn up, squander; (*COM: precios*) to slash, cut; (*fastidiar*) to annoy, bug ♦ *vi* to be burning hot; ~**se** *vr* (*consumirse*) to burn (up); (*del sol*) to get sunburnt.

quemarropa [kema'rropa]: **a** ~ *adv* point-blank.

quemazón [kema'θon] *nf* burn; (*calor*)

intense heat; (*sensación*) itch.

quena ['kena] *nf* (*AM*) Indian flute.

quepo ['kepo] *etc vb V* **caber**.

querella [ke'reʎa] *nf* (*JUR*) charge; (*disputa*) dispute.

querellarse [kere'ʎarse] *vr* to file a complaint.

querencia [ke'renθja] *nf* (*ZOOL*) homing instinct; (*fig*) homesickness.

═══════════ *PALABRA CLAVE*

querer [ke'rer] *vt* **1** (*desear*) to want; **quiero más dinero** I want more money; **quisiera** *o* **querría un té** I'd like a tea; **quiero ayudar/que vayas** I want to help/you to go; **como Vd quiera** as you wish, as you please; **ven cuando quieras** come when you like; **lo hizo sin** ~ he didn't mean to do it; **no quiero** I don't want to; **le pedí que me dejara ir pero no quiso** I asked him to let me go but he refused
2 (*preguntas: para pedir u ofrecer algo*): **¿quiere abrir la ventana?** could you open the window?; **¿quieres echarme una mano?** can you give me a hand?; **¿quiere un café?** would you like some coffee?
3 (*amar*) to love; (*tener cariño a*) to be fond of; **quiere mucho a sus hijos** he's very fond of his children
4 (*requerir*): **esta planta quiere más luz** this plant needs more light
5: ~ **decir** to mean; **¿qué quieres decir?** what do you mean?

querido, a [ke'riðo, a] *adj* dear ♦ *nm/f* darling; (*amante*) lover; **nuestra querida patria** our beloved country.

querosén [kero'sen], **querosene** [kero'sene] *nm* (*AM*) kerosene, paraffin.

querré [ke'rre] *etc vb V* **querer**.

quesería [kese'ria] *nf* dairy; (*fábrica*) cheese factory.

quesero, a [ke'sero, a] *adj*: **la industria quesera** the cheese industry ♦ *nm/f* cheesemaker ♦ *nf* cheese dish.

queso ['keso] *nm* cheese; ~ **rallado** grated cheese; ~ **crema** cream cheese; **dárselas con** ~ **a algn** (*fam*) to take sb in.

quetzal [ket'sal] *nm monetary unit of Guatemala*.

quicio ['kiθjo] *nm* hinge; **estar fuera de** ~ to be beside o.s.; **sacar a algn de** ~ to drive sb up the wall.

quid [kið] *nm* gist, crux; **dar en el** ~ to hit the nail on the head.

quiebra ['kjeβra] *nf* break, split; (*COM*) bankruptcy; (*ECON*) slump.

quiebro ['kjeβro] *etc vb V* **quebrar** ♦ *nm* (*del*

cuerpo) swerve.

quien [kjen] *pron relativo* (*suj*) who; (*complemento*) whom; (*indefinido*): ~ **dice eso es tonto** whoever says that is a fool; **hay ~ piensa que** there are those who think that; **no hay ~ lo haga** no-one will do it; ~ **más,** ~ **menos tiene sus problemas** everybody has problems.

quién [kjen] *pron interrogativo* who; (*complemento*) whom; *¿*~ **es?** who is it?, who's there?; (*TELEC*) who's calling?

quienquiera [kjen'kjera] (*pl* **quienesquiera**) *pron* whoever.

quiera ['kjera] *etc vb V* querer.

quieto, a ['kjeto, a] *adj* still; (*carácter*) placid; **¡estáte ~!** keep still!

quietud [kje'tuð] *nf* stillness.

quijada [ki'xaða] *nf* jaw, jawbone.

quijote [ki'xote] *nm* dreamer; **Don Q~** Don Quixote.

quil. *abr* = **quilates.**

quilate [ki'late] *nm* carat.

quilla ['kiʎa] *nf* keel.

quilo... ['kilo... = **kilo...**

quimera [ki'mera] *nf* (*sueño*) pipe dream.

quimérico, a [ki'meriko, a] *adj* fantastic.

químico, a ['kimiko, a] *adj* chemical ♦ *nm/f* chemist ♦ *nf* chemistry.

quimioterapia [kimiote'rapia] *nf* chemotherapy.

quina ['kina] *nf* quinine.

quincallería [kinkaʎe'ria] *nf* ironmonger's (shop), hardware store (*US*).

quince ['kinθe] *num* fifteen; ~ **días** a fortnight.

quinceañero, a [kinθea'ɲero, a] *adj* fifteen-year-old; (*adolescente*) teenage ♦ *nm/f* fifteen-year-old; (*adolescente*) teenager.

quincena [kin'θena] *nf* fortnight; (*pago*) fortnightly pay.

quincenal [kinθe'nal] *adj* fortnightly.

quincuagésimo, a [kinkwa'xesimo, a] *num* fiftieth.

quiniela [ki'njela] *nf* football pools *pl*; ~**s** *nfpl* pools coupon *sg*.

quinientos, as [ki'njentos, as] *num* five hundred.

quinina [ki'nina] *nf* quinine.

quinqué [kin'ke] *nm* oil lamp.

quinquenal [kinke'nal] *adj* five-year *cpd*.

quinqui ['kinki] *nm* delinquent.

quinta ['kinta] *nf V* quinto.

quintaesencia [kintae'senθja] *nf* quintessence.

quintal [kin'tal] *nm* (*Castilla: peso*) = *46kg*; ~ **métrico** = *100kg.*

quinteto [kin'teto] *nm* quintet.

quinto, a ['kinto, a] *adj* fifth ♦ *nm* (*MIL*) conscript, draftee ♦ *nf* country house; (*MIL*) call-up, draft.

quintuplo, a [kin'tuplo, a] *adj* quintuple, five-fold.

quiosco ['kjosko] *nm* (*de música*) bandstand; (*de periódicos*) news stand (*also selling sweets, cigarettes etc*).

quirófano [ki'rofano] *nm* operating theatre.

quiromancia [kiro'manθja] *nf* palmistry.

quirúrgico, a [ki'rurxiko, a] *adj* surgical.

quise ['kise] *etc vb V* querer.

quisque ['kiske] *pron* (*fam*): **cada** *o* **todo ~** (*absolutely*) everyone.

quisquilloso [kiski'ʎoso, a] *adj* (*susceptible*) touchy; (*meticuloso*) pernickety.

quiste ['kiste] *nm* cyst.

quitaesmalte [kitaes'malte] *nm* nail polish remover.

quitamanchas [kita'mantʃas] *nm inv* stain remover.

quitanieves [kita'njeβes] *nm inv* snowplough (*BRIT*), snowplow (*US*).

quitar [ki'tar] *vt* to remove, take away; (*ropa*) to take off; (*dolor*) to relieve; (*vida*) to take; (*de periódicos*) to reduce; (*hurtar*) to remove, steal ♦ *vi*: **¡quita de ahí!** get away!; ~**se** *vr* to withdraw; (*mancha*) to come off *o* out; (*ropa*) to take off; **me quita mucho tiempo** it takes up a lot of my time; **el café me quita el sueño** coffee stops me sleeping; ~ **de en medio a algn** to get rid of sb; ~**se algo de encima** to get rid of sth; ~**se del tabaco** to give up smoking; **se quitó el sombrero** he took off his hat.

quitasol [kita'sol] *nm* sunshade (*BRIT*), parasol.

quite ['kite] *nm* (*esgrima*) parry; (*evasión*) dodge; **estar al ~** to be ready to go to sb's aid.

Quito ['kito] *n* Quito.

quizá(s) [ki'θa(s)] *adv* perhaps, maybe.

quórum ['kworum] *pl* **quórums** ['kworum] *nm* quorum.

R r

R, r ['erre] *nf* (*letra*) R, r; **R de Ramón** R for Robert (*BRIT*) o Roger (*US*).

R. *abr* = **Remite, Remitente**.

rabadilla [raβa'ðiʎa] *nf* base of the spine.

rábano ['raβano] *nm* radish; **me importa un ~** I don't give a damn.

rabia ['raβja] *nf* (*MED*) rabies *sg*; (*fig*: *ira*) fury, rage; **¡qué ~!** isn't it infuriating!; **me da ~** it maddens me; **tener ~ a algn** to have a grudge against sb.

rabiar [ra'βjar] *vi* to have rabies; to rage, be furious; **~ por algo** to long for sth.

rabieta [ra'βjeta] *nf* tantrum, fit of temper.

rabino [ra'βino] *nm* rabbi.

rabioso, a [ra'βjoso, a] *adj* rabid; (*fig*) furious.

rabo ['raβo] *nm* tail.

racanear [rakane'ar] *vi* (*fam*) to skive.

rácano ['rakano] *nm* (*fam*) slacker, skiver.

RACE *nm abr* (= *Real Automóvil Club de España*) ≈ RAC.

racha ['ratʃa] *nf* gust of wind; (*serie*) string, series; **buena/mala ~** spell of good/bad luck.

racial [ra'θjal] *adj* racial, race *cpd*.

racimo [ra'θimo] *nm* bunch.

raciocinio [raθjo'θinjo] *nm* reason; (*razonamiento*) reasoning.

ración [ra'θjon] *nf* portion; **raciones** *nfpl* rations.

racional [raθjo'nal] *adj* (*razonable*) reasonable; (*lógico*) rational.

racionalice [raθjona'liθe] *etc vb V* **racionalizar**.

racionalizar [raθjonali'θar] *vt* to rationalize; (*COM*) to streamline.

racionamiento [raθjona'mjento] *nm* (*COM*) rationing.

racionar [raθjo'nar] *vt* to ration (out).

racismo [ra'θismo] *nm* racialism, racism.

racista [ra'θista] *adj, nm/f* racist.

radar [ra'ðar] *nm* radar.

radiación [raðja'θjon] *nf* radiation; (*TELEC*) broadcasting.

radiactividad [raðjaktiβi'ðað] *nf* radioactivity.

radiado, a [ra'ðjaðo, a] *adj* radio *cpd*, broadcast.

radiador [raðja'ðor] *nm* radiator.

radial [ra'ðjal] *adj* (*AM*) radio *cpd*.

radiante [ra'ðjante] *adj* radiant.

radiar [ra'ðjar] *vt* to radiate; (*TELEC*) to broadcast; (*MED*) to give radiotherapy to.

radical [raði'kal] *adj, nm/f* radical ♦ *nm* (*LING*) root; (*MAT*) square-root sign.

radicar [raði'kar] *vi* to take root; **~ en** to lie o consist in; **~se** *vr* to establish o.s., put down (one's) roots.

radio ['raðjo] *nf* radio; (*aparato*) radio (set) ♦ *nm* (*MAT*) radius; (*AM*) radio; (*QUÍMICA*) radium; **~ de acción** extent of one's authority, sphere of influence.

radioactivo, a [raðjoak'tiβo, a] *adj* radioactive.

radioaficionado, a [raðjoafiθjo'naðo, a] *nm/f* radio ham.

radiocasete [raðjoka'sete] *nm* radiocassette (player).

radiodifusión [raðjodifu'sjon] *nf* broadcasting.

radioemisora [raðjoemi'sora] *nf* transmitter, radio station.

radiofónico, a [raðjo'foniko, a] *adj* radio *cpd*.

radiografía [raðjoɣra'fia] *nf* X-ray.

radiólogo, a [ra'ðjoloɣo, a] *nm/f* radiologist.

radionovela [raðjono'βela] *nf* radio series.

radiotaxi [raðjo'taksi] *nm* radio taxi.

radioterapia [raðjote'rapja] *nf* radiotherapy.

radioyente [raðjo'jente] *nm/f* listener.

radique [ra'ðike] *etc vb V* **radicar**.

RAE *nf abr* = **Real Academia Española**.

ráfaga ['rafaɣa] *nf* gust; (*de luz*) flash; (*de tiros*) burst.

raído, a [ra'iðo, a] *adj* (*ropa*) threadbare; (*persona*) shabby.

raigambre [rai'ɣambre] *nf* (*BOT*) roots *pl*; (*fig*) tradition.

raíz [ra'iθ] (*pl* **raíces**) *nf* root; **~ cuadrada** square root; **a ~ de** as a result of; (*después de*) immediately after.

raja ['raxa] *nf* (*de melón etc*) slice; (*hendedura*) slit, split; (*grieta*) crack.

rajar [ra'xar] *vt* to split; (*fam*) to slash; **~se** *vr* to split, crack; **~se de** to back out of.

rajatabla [raxa'taβla]: **a ~** *adv* (*estrictamente*) strictly, to the letter.

ralea [ra'lea] *nf* (*pey*) kind, sort.

ralenti [ra'lenti] *nm* (*TV etc*) slow motion; (*AUTO*) neutral; **al ~** in slow motion; (*AUTO*) ticking over.

rallador [raʎa'ðor] *nm* grater.

rallar [ra'ʎar] *vt* to grate.

ralo, a ['ralo, a] *adj* thin, sparse.

RAM [ram] *nf abr* (= *random access memory*) RAM.

rama ['rama] *nf* bough, branch; **andarse por las ~s** (*fig, fam*) to beat about the bush.

ramaje [ra'maxe] *nm* branches *pl*, foliage.

ramal [ra'mal] *nm* (*de cuerda*) strand; (*FERRO*) branch line; (*AUTO*) branch (road).

rambla ['rambla] *nf* (*avenida*) avenue.

ramera [ra'mera] *nf* whore, hooker (*US*).

ramificación [ramifika'θjon] *nf* ramification.

ramificarse [ramifi'karse] *vr* to branch out.

ramifique [rami'fike] *etc vb* V **ramificarse**.

ramillete [rami'ʎete] *nm* bouquet; (*fig*) select group.

ramo ['ramo] *nm* branch, twig; (*sección*) department, section; (*sector*) field, sector.

rampa ['rampa] *nf* ramp.

ramplón, ona [ram'plon, ona] *adj* uncouth, coarse.

rana ['rana] *nf* frog; **salto de ~** leapfrog; **cuando las ~s críen pelos** when pigs fly.

ranchero [ran'tʃero] *nm* (*AM*) rancher; (*pequeño propietario*) smallholder.

rancho ['rantʃo] *nm* (*MIL*) food; (*AM: grande*) ranch; (: *pequeño*) small farm.

rancio, a ['ranθjo, a] *adj* (*comestibles*) stale, rancid; (*vino*) aged, mellow; (*fig*) ancient.

rango ['rango] *nm* rank; (*prestigio*) standing.

ranura [ra'nura] *nf* groove; (*de teléfono etc*) slot; **~ de expansión** (*INFORM*) expansion slot.

rap [rap] *nm* (*MUS*) rap.

rapacidad [rapaθi'ðað] *nf* rapacity.

rapapolvo [rapa'polßo] *nm*: **echar un ~ a algn** to give sb a ticking off.

rapar [ra'par] *vt* to shave; (*los cabellos*) to crop.

rapaz [ra'paθ] *adj* (*ZOOL*) predatory ♦ *nm/f* (*f*: **rapaza**) young boy/girl.

rape ['rape] *nm* quick shave; (*pez*) angler (fish); **al ~** cropped.

rapé [ra'pe] *nm* snuff.

rapidez [rapi'ðeθ] *nf* speed, rapidity.

rápido, a ['rapiðo, a] *adj* fast, quick ♦ *adv* quickly ♦ *nm* (*FERRO*) express; **~s** *nmpl* rapids.

rapiña [ra'piɲa] *nm* robbery; **ave de ~** bird of prey.

rap(p)el [ra'pel] *nm* (*DEPORTE*) abseiling.

raptar [rap'tar] *vt* to kidnap.

rapto ['rapto] *nm* kidnapping; (*impulso*) sudden impulse; (*éxtasis*) ecstasy, rapture.

raqueta [ra'keta] *nf* racquet.

raquítico, a [ra'kitiko, a] *adj* stunted; (*fig*) poor, inadequate.

raquitismo [raki'tismo] *nm* rickets *sg*.

rareza [ra'reθa] *nf* rarity; (*fig*) eccentricity.

raro, a ['raro, a] *adj* (*poco común*) rare; (*extraño*) odd, strange; (*excepcional*) remarkable; **¡qué ~!** how (very) odd!; **¡(qué) cosa más rara!** how strange!

ras [ras] *nm*: **a ~ de** level with; **a ~ de tierra** at ground level.

rasar [ra'sar] *vt* to level.

rascacielos [raska'θjelos] *nm inv* skyscraper.

rascar [ras'kar] *vt* (*con las uñas etc*) to scratch; (*raspar*) to scrape; **~se** *vr* to scratch (o.s.).

rasgar [ras'ɣar] *vt* to tear, rip (up).

rasgo ['rasɣo] *nm* (*con pluma*) stroke; **~s** *nmpl* features, characteristics; **a grandes ~s** in outline, broadly.

rasgue ['rasɣe] *etc vb* V **rasgar**.

rasguear [rasɣe'ar] *vt* (*MUS*) to strum.

rasguñar [rasɣu'ɲar] *vt* to scratch; (*bosquejar*) to sketch.

rasguño [ras'ɣuɲo] *nm* scratch.

raso, a ['raso, a] *adj* (*liso*) flat, level; (*a baja altura*) very low ♦ *nm* satin; (*campo llano*) flat country; **cielo ~** clear sky; **al ~** in the open.

raspado [ras'paðo] *nm* (*MED*) scrape.

raspador [raspa'ðor] *nm* scraper.

raspadura [raspa'ðura] *nf* (*acto*) scrape, scraping; (*marca*) scratch; **~s** *nfpl* scrapings.

raspar [ras'par] *vt* to scrape; (*arañar*) to scratch; (*limar*) to file ♦ *vi* (*manos*) to be rough; (*vino*) to be sharp, have a rough taste.

rasque ['raske] *etc vb* V **rascar**.

rastra ['rastra] *nf*: **a ~s** by dragging; (*fig*) unwillingly.

rastreador [rastrea'ðor] *nm* tracker; **~ de minas** minesweeper.

rastrear [rastre'ar] *vt* (*seguir*) to track; (*minas*) to sweep.

rastrero, a [ras'trero, a] *adj* (*BOT, ZOOL*) creeping; (*fig*) despicable, mean.

rastrillar [rastri'ʎar] *vt* to rake.

rastrillo [ras'triʎo] *nm* rake; (*AM*) safety razor.

rastro ['rastro] *nm* (*AGR*) rake; (*pista*) track, trail; (*vestigio*) trace; (*mercado*) fleamarket; **el R~** *the Madrid fleamarket*; **perder el ~** to lose the scent; **desaparecer sin ~** to vanish without

trace.
rastrojo [ras'troxo] _nm_ stubble.
rasurador [rasura'ðor] _nm_, (_AM_)
rasuradora [rasura'ðora] _nf_ electric
shaver _o_ razor.
rasurarse [rasu'rarse] _vr_ to shave.
rata ['rata] _nf_ rat.
ratear [rate'ar] _vt_ (_robar_) to steal.
ratero, a [ra'tero, a] _adj_ light-fingered
♦ _nm/f_ pickpocket; (_AM: de casas_) burglar.
ratificar [ratifi'kar] _vt_ to ratify.
ratifique [rati'fike] _etc vb V_ ratificar.
rato ['rato] _nm_ while, short time; **a ~s**
from time to time; **al poco ~** shortly
after, soon afterwards; **~s libres** _o_ **de
ocio** leisure _sg_, spare _o_ free time _sg_; **hay
para ~** there's still a long way to go;
pasar el ~ to kill time; **pasar un buen/
mal ~** to have a good/rough time.
ratón [ra'ton] _nm_ (_tb INFORM_) mouse.
ratonera [rato'nera] _nf_ mousetrap.
RAU _nf abr_ (= _República Árabe Unida_) UAR.
raudal [rau'ðal] _nm_ torrent; **a ~es** in
abundance; **entrar a ~es** to pour in.
raudo, a ['rauðo, a] _adj_ (_rápido_) swift;
(_precipitado_) rushing.
raya ['raja] _nf_ line; (_marca_) scratch; (_en
tela_) stripe; (_TIP_) hyphen; (_de pelo_)
parting; (_límite_) boundary; (_pez_) ray; **a
~s** striped; **pasarse de la ~** to overstep
the mark, go too far; **tener a ~** to keep
in check.
rayado, a [ra'jaðo, a] _adj_ (_papel_) ruled;
(_tela, diseño_) striped.
rayar [ra'jar] _vt_ to line; to scratch;
(_subrayar_) to underline ♦ _vi_: **~ en** _o_ **con** to
border on; **al ~ el alba** at first light.
rayo ['rajo] _nm_ (_del sol_) ray, beam; (_de luz_)
shaft; (_en una tormenta_) (flash of)
lightning; **~ solar** _o_ **de sol** sunbeam; **~s
infrarrojos** infrared rays; **~s X** X-rays;
como un ~ like a shot; **la noticia cayó
como un ~** the news was a bombshell;
pasar como un ~ to flash past.
raza ['raθa] _nf_ race; (_de animal_) breed; **~
humana** human race; **de pura ~** (_caballo_)
thoroughbred; (_perro etc_) pedigree.
razón [ra'θon] _nf_ reason; (_justicia_) right,
justice; (_razonamiento_) reasoning;
(_motivo_) reason, motive; (_proporción_)
rate; (_MAT_) ratio; **a ~ de 10 cada día** at
the rate of 10 a day; **"~: ..."** "inquiries
to ..."; **en ~ de** with regard to; **perder la
~** to go out of one's mind; **dar ~ a algn**
to agree that sb is right; **dar ~ de** to
give an account of, report on; **tener/no
tener ~** to be right/wrong; **~ directa/
inversa** direct/inverse proportion; **~ de**

ser raison d'être.
razonable [raθo'naßle] _adj_ reasonable;
(_justo, moderado_) fair.
razonado, a [raθo'naðo, a] _adj_ (_COM: cuenta
etc_) itemized.
razonamiento [raθona'mjento] _nm_ (_juicio_)
judgement; (_argumento_) reasoning.
razonar [raθo'nar] _vt, vi_ to reason, argue.
RDA _nf_ = **República Democrática Alemana**.
Rdo. _abr_ (_REL:_ = _Reverendo_) Rev.
re [re] _nm_ (_MUS_) D.
reabierto [rea'ßjerto] _pp de_ reabrir.
reabrir [rea'ßrir] _vt_, **~se** _vr_ to reopen.
reacción [reak'θjon] _nf_ reaction; **avión a ~**
jet plane; **~ en cadena** chain reaction.
reaccionar [reakθjo'nar] _vi_ to react.
reaccionario, a [reakθjo'narjo, a] _adj_
reactionary.
reacio, a [re'aθjo, a] _adj_ stubborn; **ser** _o_
estar ~ a to be opposed to.
reactivar [reakti'ßar] _vt_ to reactivate; **~se**
_vr_ (_economía_) to be on the upturn.
reactor [reak'tor] _nm_ reactor; (_avión_) jet
plane; **~ nuclear** nuclear reactor.
readaptación [reaðapta'θjon] _nf_: **~
profesional** industrial retraining.
readmitir [reaðmi'tir] _vt_ to readmit.
reafirmar [reafir'mar] _vt_ to reaffirm.
reagrupar [reaɣru'par] _vt_ to regroup.
reajustar [reaxus'tar] _vt_ (_INFORM_) to reset.
reajuste [rea'xuste] _nm_ readjustment; **~
salarial** wage increase; **~ de plantilla**
rationalization.
real [re'al] _adj_ real; (_del rey, fig_) royal;
(_espléndido_) grand ♦ _nm_ (_de feria_)
fairground.

_The **Real Academia Española (RAE)** is the
regulatory body for the Spanish language in
Spain and was founded in 1713. It produces
dictionaries and grammars bearing its own
name, and is considered the authority on
the language, although it has been critized
for being too conservative. In 1994, along
with the Spanish American academias, it
approved a change to the Spanish
alphabet, no longer treating "ch" and "ll"
as separate letters. "ñ" continues to be
treated separately._

---

realce [re'alθe] _etc vb V_ realzar ♦ _nm_ (_TEC_)
embossing; (_lustre, fig_) splendour (_BRIT_),
splendor (_US_); (_ARTE_) highlight; **poner de
~** to emphasize.
real-decreto [re'alde'kreto] (_pl_ **~es-~s**) _nm_
royal decree.
realeza [rea'leθa] _nf_ royalty.
realice [rea'liθe] _etc vb V_ realizar.

realidad [reali'ðað] nf reality; (verdad) truth; ~ **virtual** virtual reality; **en** ~ in fact.

realismo [rea'lismo] nm realism.

realista [rea'lista] nmlf realist.

realización [realiθa'θjon] nf fulfilment, realization; (COM) selling up (BRIT), conversion into money (US); ~ **de plusvalías** profit-taking.

realizador, a [realiθa'ðor, a] nmlf (TV etc) producer.

realizar [reali'θar] vt (objetivo) to achieve; (plan) to carry out; (viaje) to make, undertake; (COM) to realize; ~**se** vr to come about, come true; ~**se como persona** to fulfil one's aims in life.

realmente [real'mente] adv really.

realojar [realo'xar] vt to rehouse.

realquilar [realki'lar] vt (subarrendar) to sublet; (alquilar de nuevo) to relet.

realzar [real'θar] vt (TEC) to raise; (embellecer) to enhance; (acentuar) to highlight.

reanimar [reani'mar] vt to revive; (alentar) to encourage; ~**se** vr to revive.

reanudar [reanu'ðar] vt (renovar) to renew; (historia, viaje) to resume.

reaparición [reapari'θjon] nf reappearance; (vuelta) return.

reapertura [reaper'tura] nf reopening.

rearme [re'arme] nm rearmament.

reata [re'ata] nf (AM) lasso.

reavivar [reaβi'βar] vt (persona) to revive; (fig) to rekindle.

rebaja [re'βaxa] nf reduction, lowering; (COM) discount; **"grandes ~s"** "big reductions", "sale".

rebajar [reβa'xar] vt (bajar) to lower; (reducir) to reduce; (precio) to cut; (disminuir) to lessen; (humillar) to humble; ~**se** vr: ~**se a hacer algo** to stoop to doing sth.

rebanada [reβa'naða] nf slice.

rebañar [reβa'nar] vt to scrape clean.

rebaño [re'βano] nm herd; (de ovejas) flock.

rebasar [reβa'sar] vt (tb: ~ **de**) to exceed; (AUTO) to overtake.

rebatir [reβa'tir] vt to refute; (rebajar) to reduce; (ataque) to repel.

rebato [re'βato] nm alarm; (ataque) surprise attack; **llamar** o **tocar a** ~ (fig) to sound the alarm.

rebeca [re'βeka] nf cardigan.

rebelarse [reβe'larse] vr to rebel, revolt.

rebelde [re'βelde] adj rebellious; (niño) unruly ♦ nmlf rebel; **ser** ~ **a** to be in revolt against, rebel against.

rebeldía [reβel'dia] nf rebelliousness; (desobediencia) disobedience; (JUR) default.

rebelión [reβe'ljon] nf rebellion.

rebenque [re'βenke] nm (AM) whip.

reblandecer [reβlande'θer] vt to soften.

reblandezca [reβlan'deθka] etc vb V reblandecer.

rebobinar [reβoβi'nar] vt to rewind.

reboce [re'βoθe] etc vb V rebozar.

rebosante [reβo'sante] adj: ~ **de** (fig) brimming o overflowing with.

rebosar [reβo'sar] vi to overflow; (abundar) to abound, be plentiful; ~ **de salud** to be bursting o brimming with health.

rebotar [reβo'tar] vt to bounce; (rechazar) to repel.

rebote [re'βote] nm rebound; **de** ~ on the rebound.

rebozado, a [reβo'θaðo, a] adj (CULIN) fried in batter o breadcrumbs o flour.

rebozar [reβo'θar] vt to wrap up; (CULIN) to fry in batter etc.

rebozo [reβo'θo] nm: **sin** ~ openly.

rebuscado, a [reβus'kaðo, a] adj affected.

rebuscar [reβus'kar] vi (en bolsillo, cajón) to fish; (en habitación) to search high and low.

rebuznar [reβuθ'nar] vi to bray.

recabar [reka'βar] vt (obtener) to manage to get; ~ **fondos** to collect money.

recadero [reka'ðero] nm messenger.

recado [re'kaðo] nm message; **dejar/tomar un** ~ (TELEC) to leave/take a message.

recaer [reka'er] vi to relapse; ~ **en** to fall to o on; (criminal etc) to fall back into, relapse into; (premio) to go to.

recaída [reka'iða] nf relapse.

recaiga [re'kaiγa] etc vb V recaer.

recalcar [rekal'kar] vt (fig) to stress, emphasize.

recalcitrante [rekalθi'trante] adj recalcitrant.

recalentamiento [rekalenta'mjento] nm: ~ **global** global warming.

recalentar [rekalen'tar] vt (comida) to warm up, reheat; (demasiado) to overheat; ~**se** vr to overheat, get too hot.

recaliente [reka'ljente] etc vb V recalentar.

recalque [re'kalke] etc vb V recalcar.

recámara [re'kamara] nf side room; (AM) bedroom.

recamarera [rekama'rera] nf (AM) maid.

recambio [re'kambjo] nm spare; (de pluma) refill; **piezas de** ~ spares.

recapacitar [rekapaθi'tar] vi to reflect.

recapitular [rekapitu'lar] vt to recap.

recargable [rekar'γaβle] adj (batería, pila)

rechargeable; (*mechero, pluma*) refillable.

recargado, a [rekar'ɣaðo, a] *adj* overloaded; (*exagerado*) over-elaborate.

recargar [rekar'ɣar] *vt* to overload; (*batería*) to recharge; (*mechero, pluma*) to refill.

recargo [re'karɣo] *nm* surcharge; (*aumento*) increase.

recargue [re'karɣe] *etc vb V* **recargar**.

recatado, a [reka'taðo, a] *adj* (*modesto*) modest, demure; (*prudente*) cautious.

recato [re'kato] *nm* (*modestia*) modesty, demureness; (*cautela*) caution.

recauchutado, a [rekautʃu'taðo, a] *adj* remould *cpd*.

recaudación [rekauða'θjon] *nf* (*acción*) collection; (*cantidad*) takings *pl*; (*en deporte*) gate; (*oficina*) tax office.

recaudador, a [rekauða'ðor, a] *nm/f* tax collector.

recaudar [rekau'ðar] *vt* to collect.

recaudo [re'kauðo] *nm* (*impuestos*) collection; (*JUR*) surety; **estar a buen ~** to be in safekeeping; **poner algo a buen ~** to put sth in a safe place.

recayendo [reka'jendo] *etc vb V* **recaer**.

rece ['reθe] *etc vb V* **rezar**.

recelar [reθe'lar] *vt*: **~ que** (*sospechar*) to suspect that; (*temer*) to fear that ♦ *vi*: **~(se) de** to distrust.

recelo [re'θelo] *nm* distrust, suspicion.

receloso, a [reθe'loso, a] *adj* distrustful, suspicious.

recepción [reθep'θjon] *nf* reception; (*acto de recibir*) receipt.

recepcionista [reθepθjo'nista] *nm/f* receptionist.

receptáculo [reθep'takulo] *nm* receptacle.

receptivo, a [reθep'tiβo, a] *adj* receptive.

receptor, a [reθep'tor, a] *nm/f* recipient ♦ *nm* (*TELEC*) receiver; **descolgar el ~** to pick up the receiver.

recesión [reθe'sjon] *nf* (*COM*) recession.

receta [re'θeta] *nf* (*CULIN*) recipe; (*MED*) prescription.

recetar [reθe'tar] *vt* to prescribe.

rechace [re'tʃaθe] *etc vb V* **rechazar**.

rechazar [retʃa'θar] *vt* to repel, drive back; (*idea*) to reject; (*oferta*) to turn down.

rechazo [re'tʃaθo] *nm* (*de fusil*) recoil; (*rebote*) rebound; (*negación*) rebuff.

rechifla [re'tʃifla] *nf* hissing, booing; (*fig*) derision.

rechinar [retʃi'nar] *vi* to creak; (*dientes*) to grind; (*máquina*) to clank, clatter; (*metal seco*) to grate; (*motor*) to hum.

rechistar [retʃis'tar] *vi*: **sin ~** without complaint.

rechoncho, a [re'tʃontʃo, a] *adj* (*fam*) stocky, thickset (*BRIT*), heavy-set (*US*).

rechupete [retʃu'pete]: **de ~** *adj* (*comida*) delicious.

recibidor [reθiβi'ðor] *nm* entrance hall.

recibimiento [reθiβi'mjento] *nm* reception, welcome.

recibir [reθi'βir] *vt* to receive; (*dar la bienvenida*) to welcome; (*salir al encuentro de*) to go and meet ♦ *vi* to entertain; **~se** *vr*: **~se de** to qualify as.

recibo [re'θiβo] *nm* receipt; **acusar ~ de** to acknowledge receipt of.

reciclaje [reθi'klaxe] *nm* recycling; (*de trabajadores*) retraining; **cursos de ~** refresher courses.

reciclar [reθi'klar] *vt* to recycle; (*trabajador*) to retrain.

recién [re'θjen] *adv* recently, newly; (*AM*) just, recently; **~ casado** newly-wed; **el ~ llegado** the newcomer; **el ~ nacido** the newborn child; **~ a las seis** only at six o'clock.

reciente [re'θjente] *adj* recent; (*fresco*) fresh.

recientemente [reθjente'mente] *adv* recently.

recinto [re'θinto] *nm* enclosure; (*área*) area, place.

recio, a ['reθjo, a] *adj* strong, tough; (*voz*) loud ♦ *adv* hard; loud(ly).

recipiente [reθi'pjente] *nm* (*objeto*) container, receptacle; (*persona*) recipient.

reciprocidad [reθiproθi'ðað] *nf* reciprocity.

recíproco, a [re'θiproco, a] *adj* reciprocal.

recital [reθi'tal] *nm* (*MUS*) recital; (*LIT*) reading.

recitar [reθi'tar] *vt* to recite.

reclamación [reklama'θjon] *nf* claim, demand; (*queja*) complaint; **~ salarial** pay claim.

reclamar [rekla'mar] *vt* to claim, demand ♦ *vi*: **~ contra** to complain about; **~ a algn en justicia** to take sb to court.

reclamo [re'klamo] *nm* (*anuncio*) advertisement; (*tentación*) attraction.

reclinar [rekli'nar] *vt* to recline, lean; **~se** *vr* to lean back.

recluir [reklu'ir] *vt* to intern, confine.

reclusión [reklu'sjon] *nf* (*prisión*) prison; (*refugio*) seclusion; **~ perpetua** life imprisonment.

recluso, a [re'kluso, a] *adj* imprisoned; **población reclusa** prison population ♦ *nm/f* (*solitario*) recluse; (*JUR*) prisoner.

recluta [re'kluta] *nm/f* recruit ♦ *nf*

recruitment.

reclutamiento [rekluta'mjento] *nm*
recruitment.

recluyendo [reklu'jendo] *etc vb* V **recluir**.

recobrar [reko'ßrar] *vt* (*recuperar*) to
recover; (*rescatar*) to get back; (*ciudad*)
to recapture; (*tiempo*) to make up (for);
~**se** *vr* to recover.

recochineo [rekot ʃi'neo] *nm* (*fam*)
mickey-taking.

recodo [re'koðo] *nm* (*de río, camino*) bend.

recogedor, a [rekoxe'ðor, a] *nm/f* picker,
harvester.

recoger [reko'xer] *vt* to collect; (*AGR*) to
harvest; (*fruta*) to pick; (*levantar*) to pick
up; (*juntar*) to gather; (*pasar a buscar*) to
come for, get; (*dar asilo*) to give shelter
to; (*faldas*) to gather up; (*mangas*) to roll
up; (*pelo*) to put up; ~**se** *vr* (*retirarse*) to
retire; **me recogieron en la estación** they
picked me up at the station.

recogido, a [reko'xiðo, a] *adj* (*lugar*) quiet,
secluded; (*pequeño*) small ♦ *nf* (*CORREOS*)
collection; (*AGR*) harvest; **recogida de
datos** (*INFORM*) data capture.

recogimiento [rekoxi'mjento] *nm*
collection; (*AGR*) harvesting.

recoja [re'koxa] *etc vb* V **recoger**.

recolección [rekolek'θjon] *nf* (*AGR*)
harvesting; (*colecta*) collection.

recomencé [rekomen'θe],
recomencemos [rekomen'θemos] *etc vb*
V **recomenzar**.

recomendable [rekomen'daßle] *adj*
recommendable; **poco** ~ inadvisable.

recomendación [rekomenda'θjon] *nf*
(*sugerencia*) suggestion,
recommendation; (*referencia*) reference;
carta de ~ **para** letter of introduction to.

recomendar [rekomen'dar] *vt* to suggest,
recommend; (*confiar*) to entrust.

recomenzar [rekomen'θar] *vt, vi* to begin
again, recommence.

recomience [reko'mjenθe] *etc vb* V
recomenzar.

recomiende [reko'mjende] *etc vb* V
recomendar.

recomienzo [reko'mjenθo] *etc vb* V
recomenzar.

recompensa [rekom'pensa] *nf* reward,
recompense; (*compensación*): ~ (**de una
pérdida**) compensation (for a loss);
como *o* **en** ~ **por** in return for.

recompensar [rekompen'sar] *vt* to reward,
recompense.

recompondré [rekompon'dre] *etc vb* V
recomponer.

recomponer [rekompo'ner] *vt* to mend;

(*INFORM: texto*) to reformat.

recomponga [rekom'ponga] *etc,*
recompuesto [rekom'pwesto],
recompuse [rekom'puse] *etc vb* V
recomponer.

reconciliación [rekonθilja'θjon] *nf*
reconciliation.

reconciliar [rekonθi'ljar] *vt* to reconcile;
~**se** *vr* to become reconciled.

recóndito, a [re'kondito, a] *adj* (*lugar*)
hidden, secret.

reconfortar [rekonfor'tar] *vt* to comfort.

reconocer [rekono'θer] *vt* to recognize; ~
los hechos to face the facts.

reconocido, a [rekono'θiðo, a] *adj*
recognized; (*agradecido*) grateful.

reconocimiento [rekonoθi'mjento] *nm*
recognition; (*registro*) search;
(*inspección*) examination; (*gratitud*)
gratitude; (*confesión*) admission; ~
óptico de caracteres (*INFORM*) optical
character recognition; ~ **de la voz**
(*INFORM*) speech recognition.

reconozca [reko'noθka] *etc vb* V **reconocer**.

reconquista [rekon'kista] *nf* reconquest.

reconquistar [rekonkis'tar] *vt* (*MIL*) to
reconquer; (*fig*) to recover, win back.

reconstituyente [rekonstitu'jente] *nm*
tonic.

reconstruir [rekonstru'ir] *vt* to reconstruct.

reconstruyendo [rekonstru'jendo] *etc vb* V
reconstruir.

reconversión [recomber'sjon] *nf*
restructuring, reorganization; (*tb*: ~
industrial) rationalization.

recopilación [rekopila'θjon] *nf* (*resumen*)
summary; (*compilación*) compilation.

recopilar [rekopi'lar] *vt* to compile.

récord ['rekorð] *adj inv* record; **cifras** ~
record figures ♦ *nm, pl* **records, récords**
['rekorð] record; **batir el** ~ to break the
record.

recordar [rekor'ðar] *vt* (*acordarse de*) to
remember; (*traer a la memoria*) to recall;
(*acordar a otro*) to remind ♦ *vi* to
remember; **recuérdale que me debe 5
dólares** remind him that he owes me 5
dollars; **que yo recuerde** as far as I can
remember; **creo** ~, **si mal no recuerdo** if
my memory serves me right.

recordatorio [rekorða'torjo] *nm* (*de
fallecimiento*) in memoriam card; (*de
bautizo, comunión*) commemorative card.

recorrer [reko'rrer] *vt* (*país*) to cross,
travel through; (*distancia*) to cover;
(*registrar*) to search; (*repasar*) to look
over.

recorrido [reko'rriðo] *nm* run, journey;

tren de largo ~ main-line *o* inter-city (*BRIT*) train.

recortado, a [rekor'taðo, a] *adj* uneven, irregular.

recortar [rekor'tar] *vt* (*papel*) to cut out; (*el pelo*) to trim; (*dibujar*) to draw in outline; **~se** *vr* to stand out, be silhouetted.

recorte [re'korte] *nm* (*acción, de prensa*) cutting; (*de telas, chapas*) trimming; ~ **presupuestario** budget cut; ~ **salarial** wage cut.

recostado, a [rekos'taðo, a] *adj* leaning; **estar** ~ to be lying down.

recostar [rekos'tar] *vt* to lean; **~se** *vr* to lie down.

recoveco [reko'ßeko] *nm* (*de camino, río etc*) bend; (*en casa*) cubbyhole.

recreación [rekrea'θjon] *nf* recreation.

recrear [rekre'ar] *vt* (*entretener*) to entertain; (*volver a crear*) to recreate.

recreativo, a [rekrea'tißo, a] *adj* recreational.

recreo [re'kreo] *nm* recreation; (*ESCOL*) break, playtime.

recriminar [rekrimi'nar] *vt* to reproach ♦ *vi* to recriminate; **~se** *vr* to reproach each other.

recrudecer [rekruðe'θer] *vt, vi*, **recrudecerse** *vr* to worsen.

recrudecimiento [rekruðeθi'mjento] *nm* upsurge.

recrudezca [recru'ðeθka] *etc vb V* **recrudecer**.

recta ['rekta] *nf V* **recto**.

rectangular [rektangu'lar] *adj* rectangular.

rectángulo, a [rek'tangulo, a] *adj* rectangular ♦ *nm* rectangle.

rectificable [rektifi'kaßle] *adj* rectifiable; **fácilmente** ~ easily rectified.

rectificación [rektifika'θjon] *nf* correction.

rectificar [rektifi'kar] *vt* to rectify; (*volverse recto*) to straighten ♦ *vi* to correct o.s.

rectifique [rekti'fike] *etc vb V* **rectificar**.

rectitud [rekti'tuð] *nf* straightness; (*fig*) rectitude.

recto, a ['rekto, a] *adj* straight; (*persona*) honest, upright; (*estricto*) strict; (*juez*) fair; (*juicio*) sound ♦ *nm* rectum; (*ATLETISMO*) straight ♦ *nf* straight line; **en el sentido** ~ **de la palabra** in the proper sense of the word; **recta final** *o* **de llegada** home straight.

rector, a [rek'tor, a] *adj* governing ♦ *nm/f* head, chief; (*ESCOL*) rector, president (*US*).

rectorado [rekto'raðo] *nm* (*cargo*) rectorship, presidency (*US*); (*oficina*)

rector's office.

recuadro [re'kwaðro] *nm* box; (*TIP*) inset.

recubrir [reku'ßir] *vt* to cover.

recuento [re'kwento] *nm* inventory; **hacer el** ~ **de** to count *o* reckon up.

recuerdo [re'kwerðo] *etc vb V* **recordar** ♦ *nm* souvenir; **~s** *nmpl* memories; ¡**~s a tu madre!** give my regards to your mother!; "**R~ de Mallorca**" "a present from Majorca"; **contar los ~s** to reminisce.

recueste [re'kweste] *etc vb V* **recostar**.

recular [reku'lar] *vi* to back down.

recuperable [rekupe'raßle] *adj* recoverable.

recuperación [rekupera'θjon] *nf* recovery; ~ **de datos** (*INFORM*) data retrieval.

recuperar [rekupe'rar] *vt* to recover; (*tiempo*) to make up; (*INFORM*) to retrieve; **~se** *vr* to recuperate.

recurrir [reku'rrir] *vi* (*JUR*) to appeal; ~ **a** to resort to; (*persona*) to turn to.

recurso [re'kurso] *nm* resort; (*medio*) means *pl*, resource; (*JUR*) appeal; **como último** ~ as a last resort; **~s económicos** economic resources; **~s naturales** natural resources.

recusar [reku'sar] *vt* to reject, refuse.

red [reð] *nf* net, mesh; (*FERRO, INFORM*) network; (*ELEC, de agua*) mains, supply system; (*de tiendas*) chain; (*trampa*) trap; **estar conectado con la** ~ to be connected to the mains; ~ **local** (*INFORM*) local area network; ~ **de transmisión** (*INFORM*) data network.

redacción [reðak'θjon] *nf* (*acción*) writing; (*ESCOL*) essay, composition; (*limpieza de texto*) editing; (*personal*) editorial staff.

redactar [reðak'tar] *vt* to draw up, draft; (*periódico, INFORM*) to edit.

redactor, a [reðak'tor, a] *nm/f* writer; (*en periódico*) editor.

redada [re'ðaða] *nf* (*PESCA*) cast, throw; (*fig*) catch; ~ **policial** police raid, round-up.

redención [reðen'θjon] *nf* redemption.

redentor, a [reðen'tor, a] *adj* redeeming ♦ *nm/f* (*COM*) redeemer.

redescubierto [reðesku'ßjerto] *pp de* **redescubrir**.

redescubrir [reðesku'ßrir] *vt* to rediscover.

redesignar [reðesix'nar] *vt* (*INFORM*) to rename.

redicho, a [re'ðitʃo, a] *adj* affected.

redil [re'ðil] *nm* sheepfold.

redimir [reði'mir] *vt* to redeem; (*rehén*) to ransom.

redistribución [reðistrißu'θjon] *nf* (*COM*)

redeployment.
rédito ['reðito] *nm* interest, yield.
redoblar [reðo'βlar] *vt* to redouble ♦ *vi*
(*tambor*) to play a roll on the drums.
redoble [re'ðoßle] *nm* (*MUS*) drumroll,
drumbeat; (*de trueno*) roll.
redomado, a [reðo'maðo, a] *adj* (*astuto*)
sly, crafty; (*perfecto*) utter.
redonda [re'ðonda] *nf V* **redondo.**
redondear [reðonde'ar] *vt* to round, round
off; (*cifra*) to round up.
redondel [reðon'del] *nm* (*círculo*) circle;
(*TAUR*) bullring, arena; (*AUTO*)
roundabout.
redondo, a [re'ðondo, a] *adj* (*circular*)
round; (*completo*) complete ♦ *nf*: **a la**
redonda around, round about; **en**
muchas millas a la redonda for many
miles around; **rehusar en** ~ to give a flat
refusal.
reducción [reðuk'θjon] *nf* reduction; ~ **del**
activo (*COM*) divestment; ~ **de precios**
(*COM*) price-cutting.
reducido, a [reðu'θiðo, a] *adj* reduced;
(*limitado*) limited; (*pequeño*) small;
quedar ~ **a** to be reduced to.
reducir [reðu'θir] *vt* to reduce, limit;
(*someter*) to bring under control; ~**se** *vr*
to diminish; (*MAT*): ~ **(a)** to reduce (to),
convert (into); ~ **las millas a kilómetros**
to convert miles into kilometres; ~**se a**
(*fig*) to come *o* boil down to.
reducto [re'ðukto] *nm* redoubt.
reduje [re'ðuxe] *etc vb V* **reducir.**
redundancia [reðun'danθja] *nf*
redundancy.
reduzca [re'ðuθka] *etc vb V* **reducir.**
reedición [re(e)ði'θjon] *nf* reissue.
reeditar [re(e)ði'tar] *vt* to reissue.
reelección [re(e)lek'θjon] *nf* re-election.
reelegir [re(e)le'xir] *vt* to re-elect.
reembolsable [re(e)mbol'saßle] *adj* (*COM*)
redeemable, refundable.
reembolsar [re(e)mbol'sar] *vt* (*persona*) to
reimburse; (*dinero*) to repay, pay back;
(*depósito*) to refund.
reembolso [re(e)m'bolso] *nm*
reimbursement; refund; **enviar algo**
contra ~ to send sth cash on delivery;
contra ~ **del flete** freight forward; ~
fiscal tax rebate.
reemplace [re(e)m'plaθe] *etc vb V*
reemplazar.
reemplazar [re(e)mpla'θar] *vt* to replace.
reemplazo [re(e)m'plaθo] *nm* replacement;
de ~ (*MIL*) reserve.
reencuentro [re(e)n'kwentro] *nm* reunion.
reengancharse [re(e)ngan'tʃarse] *vr* (*MIL*)

to re-enlist.
reestreno [re(e)s'treno] *nm* rerun.
reestructurar [re(e)struktu'rar] *vt* to
restructure.
reexportación [re(e)ksporta'θjon] *nf* (*COM*)
re-export.
reexportar [re(e)kspor'tar] *vt* (*COM*) to re-
export.
REF *nm abr* (*ESP ECON*) = *Régimen*
Económico Fiscal.
Ref.ª *abr* (= *referencia*) ref.
refacción [refak'θjon] *nf* (*AM*) repair(s);
refacciones *nfpl* (*piezas de repuesto*) spare
parts.
referencia [refe'renθja] *nf* reference; **con**
~ **a** with reference to; **hacer** ~ **a** to refer
o allude to; ~ **comercial** (*COM*) trade
reference.
referéndum [refe'rendum], *pl*
referéndums *nm* referendum.
referente [refe'rente] *adj*: ~ **a** concerning,
relating to.
referir [refe'rir] *vt* (*contar*) to tell, recount;
(*relacionar*) to refer, relate; ~**se** *vr*: ~**se a**
to refer to; ~ **al lector a un apéndice** to
refer the reader to an appendix; ~ **a**
(*COM*) to convert into; **por lo que se**
refiere a eso as for that, as regards that.
refiera [re'fjera] *etc vb V* **referir.**
refilón [refi'lon]: **de** ~ *adv* obliquely; **mirar**
a algn de ~ to look out of the corner of
one's eye at sb.
refinado, a [refi'naðo, a] *adj* refined.
refinamiento [refina'mjento] *nm*
refinement; ~ **por pasos** (*INFORM*)
stepwise refinement.
refinar [refi'nar] *vt* to refine.
refinería [refine'ria] *nf* refinery.
refiriendo [refi'rjendo] *etc vb V* **referir.**
reflector [reflek'tor] *nm* reflector; (*ELEC*)
spotlight; (*AVIAT*, *MIL*) searchlight.
reflejar [refle'xar] *vt* to reflect; ~**se** *vr* to be
reflected.
reflejo, a [re'flexo, a] *adj* reflected;
(*movimiento*) reflex ♦ *nm* reflection;
(*ANAT*) reflex; (*en el pelo*): ~**s** *nmpl*
highlights; **tiene el pelo castaño con** ~**s**
rubios she has chestnut hair with blond
streaks.
reflexión [reflek'sjon] *nf* reflection.
reflexionar [refleksjo'nar] *vt* to reflect on
♦ *vi* to reflect; (*detenerse*) to pause (to
think); ¡**reflexione!** you think it over!
reflexivo, a [reflek'sißo, a] *adj* thoughtful;
(*LING*) reflexive.
refluir [reflu'ir] *vi* to flow back.
reflujo [re'fluxo] *nm* ebb.
refluyendo [reflu'jendo] *etc vb V* **refluir.**

reforcé [refor'θe], **reforcemos**
[refor'θemos] *etc vb V* **reforzar**.

reforma [re'forma] *nf* reform; (*ARQ etc*)
repair; ~ **agraria** agrarian reform.

reformar [refor'mar] *vt* to reform;
(*modificar*) to change, alter; (*texto*) to
revise; (*ARQ*) to repair; ~**se** *vr* to mend
one's ways.

reformatear [reformate'ar] *vt* (*INFORM*:
disco) to reformat.

reformatorio [reforma'torjo] *nm*
reformatory; ~ **de menores** remand
home.

reformista [refor'mista] *adj*, *nmf* reformist.

reforzamiento [reforθa'mjento] *nm*
reinforcement.

reforzar [refor'θar] *vt* to strengthen; (*ARQ*)
to reinforce; (*fig*) to encourage.

refractario, a [refrak'tarjo, a] *adj* (*TEC*)
heat-resistant; **ser ~ a una reforma** to
resist o be opposed to a reform.

refrán [re'fran] *nm* proverb, saying.

refregar [refre'ɣar] *vt* to scrub.

refrenar [refre'nar] *vt* to check, restrain.

refrendar [refren'dar] *vt* (*firma*) to endorse,
countersign; (*ley*) to approve.

refrescante [refres'kante] *adj* refreshing,
cooling.

refrescar [refres'kar] *vt* to refresh ♦ *vi* to
cool down; ~**se** *vr* to get cooler; (*tomar
aire fresco*) to go out for a breath of
fresh air; (*beber*) to have a drink.

refresco [re'fresko] *nm* soft drink, cool
drink; "~**s**" "refreshments".

refresque [re'freske] *etc vb V* **refrescar**.

refriega [re'frjeɣa] *etc vb V* **refregar** ♦ *nf*
scuffle, brawl.

refriegue [re'frjeɣe] *etc vb V* **refregar**.

refrigeración [refrixera'θjon] *nf*
refrigeration; (*de casa*) air-conditioning.

refrigerado, a [refrixe'raðo, a] *adj* cooled;
(*sala*) air-conditioned.

refrigerador [refrixera'ðor] *nm*, (*AM*)
refrigeradora [refrixera'ðora] *nf*
refrigerator, icebox (*US*).

refrigerar [refrixe'rar] *vt* to refrigerate;
(*sala*) to air-condition.

refrito [re'frito] *nm* (*CULIN*): **un ~ de
cebolla y tomate** sautéed onions and
tomatoes; **un ~** (*fig*) a rehash.

refuerce [re'fwerθe] *etc vb V* **reforzar**.

refuerzo [re'fwerθo] *etc vb V* **reforzar** ♦ *nm*
reinforcement; (*TEC*) support.

refugiado, a [refu'xjaðo, a] *nmf* refugee.

refugiarse [refu'xjarse] *vr* to take refuge,
shelter.

refugio [re'fuxjo] *nm* refuge; (*protección*)
shelter; (*AUTO*) street o traffic island; ~

alpino o **de montaña** mountain hut; ~
subterráneo (*MIL*) underground shelter.

refulgencia [reful'xenθja] *nf* brilliance.

refulgir [reful'xir] *vi* to shine, be dazzling.

refulja [re'fulxa] *etc vb V* **refulgir**.

refundir [refun'dir] *vt* to recast; (*escrito etc*)
to adapt, rewrite.

refunfuñar [refunfu'nar] *vi* to grunt,
growl; (*quejarse*) to grumble.

refunfuñón, ona [refunfu'non, ona] (*fam*)
adj grumpy ♦ *nm/f* grouch.

refutación [refuta'θjon] *nf* refutation.

refutar [refu'tar] *vt* to refute.

regadera [reɣa'ðera] *nf* watering can; (*AM*)
shower; **estar como una ~** (*fam*) to be as
mad as a hatter.

regadío [reɣa'ðio] *nm* irrigated land.

regalado, a [reɣa'laðo, a] *adj* comfortable,
luxurious; (*gratis*) free, for nothing; **lo
tuvo ~** it was handed to him on a plate.

regalar [reɣa'lar] *vt* (*dar*) to give (as a
present); (*entregar*) to give away;
(*mimar*) to pamper, make a fuss of; ~**se**
vr to treat o.s. to.

regalía [reɣa'lia] *nf* privilege, prerogative;
(*COM*) bonus; (*de autor*) royalty.

regaliz [reɣa'liθ] *nm* liquorice.

regalo [re'ɣalo] *nm* (*obsequio*) gift,
present; (*gusto*) pleasure; (*comodidad*)
comfort.

regañadientes [reɣana'ðjentes]: **a ~** *adv*
reluctantly.

regañar [reɣa'nar] *vt* to scold ♦ *vi* to
grumble; (*dos personas*) to fall out,
quarrel.

regañón, ona [reɣa'non, ona] *adj* nagging.

regar [re'ɣar] *vt* to water, irrigate; (*fig*) to
scatter, sprinkle.

regata [re'ɣata] *nf* (*NAUT*) race.

regatear [reɣate'ar] *vt* (*COM*) to bargain
over; (*escatimar*) to be mean with ♦ *vi* to
bargain, haggle; (*DEPORTE*) to dribble;
no ~ esfuerzo to spare no effort.

regateo [reɣa'teo] *nm* bargaining;
(*DEPORTE*) dribbling; (*del cuerpo*) swerve,
dodge.

regazo [re'ɣaθo] *nm* lap.

regencia [re'xenθja] *nf* regency.

regeneración [rexenera'θjon] *nf*
regeneration.

regenerar [rexene'rar] *vt* to regenerate.

regentar [rexen'tar] *vt* to direct, manage;
(*puesto*) to hold in an acting capacity;
(*negocio*) to be in charge of.

regente, a [re'xente, a] *adj* (*príncipe*)
regent; (*director*) managing ♦ *nm* (*COM*)
manager; (*POL*) regent.

régimen ['reximen], *pl* **regímenes**

[re'ximenes] *nm* regime; (*reinado*) rule; (*MED*) diet; (*reglas*) (set of) rules *pl*; (*manera de vivir*) lifestyle; **estar a** ~ to be on a diet.

regimiento [rexi'mjento] *nm* regiment.

regio, a ['rexjo, a] *adj* royal, regal; (*fig: suntuoso*) splendid; (*AM fam*) great, terrific.

región [re'xjon] *nf* region; (*área*) area.

regional [rexjo'nal] *adj* regional.

regir [re'xir] *vt* to govern, rule; (*dirigir*) to manage, run; (*ECON, JUR, LING*) to govern ♦ *vi* to apply, be in force.

registrador [rexistra'ðor] *nm* registrar, recorder.

registrar [rexis'trar] *vt* (*buscar*) to search; (*en cajón*) to look through; (*inspeccionar*) to inspect; (*anotar*) to register, record; (*INFORM, MUS*) to record; ~**se** *vr* to register; (*ocurrir*) to happen.

registro [re'xistro] *nm* (*acto*) registration; (*MUS, libro*) register; (*lista*) list, record; (*INFORM*) record; (*inspección*) inspection, search; ~ **civil** registry office; ~ **electoral** voting register; ~ **de la propiedad** land registry (office).

regla ['rexla] *nf* (*ley*) rule, regulation; (*de medir*) ruler, rule; (*MED: período*) period; (~ *científica*) law, principle; **no hay** ~ **sin excepción** every rule has its exception.

reglamentación [rexlamenta'θjon] *nf* (*acto*) regulation; (*lista*) rules *pl*.

reglamentar [rexlamen'tar] *vt* to regulate.

reglamentario, a [rexlamen'tarjo, a] *adj* statutory; **en la forma reglamentaria** in the properly established way.

reglamento [rexla'mento] *nm* rules *pl*, regulations *pl*; ~ **del tráfico** highway code.

reglar [re'xlar] *vt* (*acciones*) to regulate; ~**se** *vr*: ~**se por** to be guided by.

regocijarse [rexoθi'xarse] *vr*: ~ **de** o **por** to rejoice at, be glad about.

regocijo [rexo'θixo] *nm* joy, happiness.

regodearse [rexoðe'arse] *vr* to be glad, be delighted; (*pey*): ~ **con** o **en** to gloat over.

regodeo [rexo'ðeo] *nm* delight; (*pey*) perverse pleasure.

regresar [rexre'sar] *vi* to come/go back, return; ~**se** *vr* (*AM*) to return.

regresivo, a [rexre'siβo, a] *adj* backward; (*fig*) regressive.

regreso [re'xreso] *nm* return; **estar de** ~ to be back, be home.

regué [re'xe], **reguemos** [re'xemos] *etc vb* V **regar**.

reguero [re'xero] *nm* (*de sangre*) trickle;

(*de humo*) trail.

regulación [rexula'θjon] *nf* regulation; (*TEC*) adjustment; (*control*) control; ~ **de empleo** redundancies *pl*; ~ **del tráfico** traffic control.

regulador [rexula'ðor] *nm* (*TEC*) regulator; (*de radio etc*) knob, control.

regular [rexu'lar] *adj* regular; (*normal*) normal, usual; (*común*) ordinary; (*organizado*) regular, orderly; (*mediano*) average; (*fam*) not bad, so-so ♦ *adv*: **estar** ~ to be so-so o alright ♦ *vt* (*controlar*) to control, regulate; (*TEC*) to adjust; **por lo** ~ as a rule.

regularice [rexula'riθe] *etc vb* V **regularizar**.

regularidad [rexulari'ðað] *nf* regularity; **con** ~ regularly.

regularizar [rexulari'θar] *vt* to regularize.

regusto [re'xusto] *nm* aftertaste.

rehabilitación [reaβilita'θjon] *nf* rehabilitation; (*ARQ*) restoration.

rehabilitar [reaβili'tar] *vt* to rehabilitate; (*ARQ*) to restore; (*reintegrar*) to reinstate.

rehacer [rea'θer] *vt* (*reparar*) to mend, repair; (*volver a hacer*) to redo, repeat; ~**se** *vr* (*MED*) to recover.

rehaga [re'axa] *etc*, **reharé** [rea're] *etc*, **rehaz** [re'aθ], **rehecho** [re'etʃo] *vb* V **rehacer**.

rehén [re'en] *nm/f* hostage.

rehice [re'iθe] *etc*, **rehizo** [re'iθo] *vb* V **rehacer**.

rehogar [reo'xar] *vt* to sauté, toss in oil.

rehuir [reu'ir] *vt* to avoid, shun.

rehusar [reu'sar] *vt, vi* to refuse.

rehuyendo [reu'jendo] *etc vb* V **rehuir**.

reina ['reina] *nf* queen.

reinado [rei'naðo] *nm* reign.

reinante [rei'nante] *adj* (*fig*) prevailing.

reinar [rei'nar] *vi* to reign; (*fig: prevalecer*) to prevail, be general.

reincidir [reinθi'ðir] *vi* to relapse; (*criminal*) to repeat an offence.

reincorporarse [reinkorpo'rarse] *vr*: ~ **a** to rejoin.

reinicializar [reiniθjali'θar] *vt* (*INFORM*) to reset.

reino ['reino] *nm* kingdom; **el R**~ **Unido** the United Kingdom.

reinserción [reinser'θjon] *nf* rehabilitation.

reinsertar [reinser'tar] *vt* to rehabilitate.

reintegración [reintexra'θjon] *nf* (*COM*) reinstatement.

reintegrar [reinte'xrar] *vt* (*reconstituir*) to reconstruct; (*persona*) to reinstate; (*dinero*) to refund, pay back; ~**se** *vr*: ~**se a** to return to.

reintegro [rein'texro] *nm* refund,

reimbursement; (*en banco*) withdrawal.

reír [re'ir] *vi*, **reírse** *vr* to laugh; ~**se** de to laugh at.

reiterado, a [reite'raðo, a] *adj* repeated.

reiterar [reite'rar] *vt* to reiterate; (*repetir*) to repeat.

reivindicación [reißindika'θjon] *nf* (*demanda*) claim, demand; (*justificación*) vindication.

reivindicar [reißindi'kar] *vt* to claim.

reivindique [reißin'dike] *etc vb V* **reivindicar**.

reja ['rexa] *nf* (*de ventana*) grille, bars *pl*; (*en la calle*) grating.

rejamos [re'xamos] *etc vb V* **regir**.

rejilla [re'xiʎa] *nf* grating, grille; (*muebles*) wickerwork; (*de ventilación*) vent; (*de coche etc*) luggage rack.

rejuvenecer [rexußene'θer] *vt*, *vi* to rejuvenate.

rejuvenezca [rexuße'neθka] *etc vb V* **rejuvenecer**.

relación [rela'θjon] *nf* relation, relationship; (*MAT*) ratio; (*lista*) list; (*narración*) report; ~ **costo-efectivo** *o* **costo-rendimiento** (*COM*) cost-effectiveness; **relaciones** *nfpl* (*enchufes*) influential friends, connections; **relaciones carnales** sexual relations; **relaciones comerciales** business connections; **relaciones empresariales/ humanas** industrial/human relations; **relaciones laborales/públicas** labour/ public relations; **con ~ a, en ~ con** in relation to; **estar en** *o* **tener buenas relaciones con** to be on good terms with.

relacionar [relaθjo'nar] *vt* to relate, connect; ~**se** *vr* to be connected *o* linked.

relajación [relaxa'θjon] *nf* relaxation.

relajado, a [rela'xaðo, a] *adj* (*disoluto*) loose; (*cómodo*) relaxed; (*MED*) ruptured.

relajante [rela'xante] *adj* relaxing; (*MED*) sedative.

relajar [rela'xar] *vt*, **relajarse** *vr* to relax.

relamerse [rela'merse] *vr* to lick one's lips.

relamido, a [rela'miðo, a] *adj* (*pulcro*) overdressed; (*afectado*) affected.

relámpago [re'lampaɣo] *nm* flash of lightning ♦ *adj* lightning *cpd*; **como un ~** as quick as lightning, in a flash; **visita/ huelga ~** lightning visit/strike.

relampaguear [relampaɣe'ar] *vi* to flash.

relanzar [relan'θar] *vt* to relaunch.

relatar [rela'tar] *vt* to tell, relate.

relatividad [relatißi'ðað] *nf* relativity.

relativo, a [rela'tißo, a] *adj* relative; **en lo ~ a** concerning.

relato [re'lato] *nm* (*narración*) story, tale.

relax [re'las] *nm* rest; "**R~**" (*en anuncio*) "Personal services".

relegar [rele'ɣar] *vt* to relegate; ~ **algo al olvido** to banish sth from one's mind.

relegue [re'leɣe] *etc vb V* **relegar**.

relevante [rele'ßante] *adj* eminent, outstanding.

relevar [rele'ßar] *vt* (*sustituir*) to relieve; ~**se** *vr* to relay; ~ **a algn de un cargo** to relieve sb of his post.

relevo [re'leßo] *nm* relief; **carrera de ~s** relay race; ~ **con cinta** (*INFORM*) tape relay; **coger** *o* **tomar el ~** to take over, stand in.

relieve [re'ljeße] *nm* (*ARTE, TEC*) relief; (*fig*) prominence, importance; **bajo ~** bas-relief; **un personaje de ~** an important man; **dar ~ a** to highlight.

religión [reli'xjon] *nf* religion.

religioso, a [reli'xjoso, a] *adj* religious ♦ *nm/f* monk/nun.

relinchar [relin'tʃar] *vi* to neigh.

relincho [re'lintʃo] *nm* neigh; (*acto*) neighing.

reliquia [re'likja] *nf* relic; ~ **de familia** heirloom.

rellano [re'ʎano] *nm* (*ARQ*) landing.

rellenar [reʎe'nar] *vt* (*llenar*) to fill up; (*CULIN*) to stuff; (*COSTURA*) to pad; (*formulario etc*) to fill in *o* out.

relleno, a [re'ʎeno, a] *adj* full up; (*CULIN*) stuffed ♦ *nm* stuffing; (*de tapicería*) padding.

reloj [re'lo(x)] *nm* clock; ~ **de pie** grandfather clock; ~ (**de pulsera**) wristwatch; ~ **de sol** sundial; ~ **despertador** alarm (clock); **como un ~** like clockwork; **contra (el)** ~ against the clock.

relojería [reloxe'ria] *nf* (*tienda*) watchmaker's (shop); **aparato de ~** clockwork; **bomba de ~** time bomb.

relojero, a [relo'xero, a] *nm/f* clockmaker; watchmaker.

reluciente [relu'θjente] *adj* brilliant, shining.

relucir [relu'θir] *vi* to shine; (*fig*) to excel; **sacar algo a ~** to show sth off.

relumbrante [relum'brante] *adj* dazzling.

relumbrar [relum'brar] *vi* to dazzle, shine brilliantly.

reluzca [re'luθka] *etc vb V* **relucir**.

remachar [rema'tʃar] *vt* to rivet; (*fig*) to hammer home, drive home.

remache [re'matʃe] *nm* rivet.

remanente [rema'nente] *nm* remainder; (*COM*) balance; (*de producto*) surplus.

remangarse [reman'garse] *vr* to roll one's

sleeves up.

remanso [re'manso] *nm* pool.

remar [re'mar] *vi* to row.

rematado, a [rema'taðo, a] *adj* complete, utter; **es un loco** ~ he's a raving lunatic.

rematar [rema'tar] *vt* to finish off; (*animal*) to put out of its misery; (*COM*) to sell off cheap ♦ *vi* to end, finish off; (*DEPORTE*) to shoot.

remate [re'mate] *nm* end, finish; (*punta*) tip; (*DEPORTE*) shot; (*ARQ*) top; (*COM*) auction sale; **de o para** ~ to crown it all (*BRIT*), to top it off.

remediable [reme'ðjaßle] *adj*: **fácilmente** ~ easily remedied.

remediar [reme'ðjar] *vt* (*gen*) to remedy; (*subsanar*) to make good, repair; (*evitar*) to avoid; **sin poder** ~**lo** without being able to prevent it.

remedio [re'meðjo] *nm* remedy; (*JUR*) recourse, remedy; **poner** ~ **a** to correct, stop; **no tener más** ~ to have no alternative; **¡qué** ~**!** there's no other way; **como último** ~ as a last resort; **sin** ~ inevitable; (*MED*) hopeless.

remedo [re'meðo] *nm* imitation; (*pey*) parody.

remendar [remen'dar] *vt* to repair; (*con parche*) to patch; (*fig*) to correct.

remesa [re'mesa] *nf* remittance; (*COM*) shipment.

remiendo [re'mjendo] *etc vb V* **remendar** ♦ *nm* mend; (*con parche*) patch; (*cosido*) darn; (*fig*) correction.

remilgado, a [remil'ɣaðo, a] *adj* prim; (*afectado*) affected.

remilgo [re'milɣo] *nm* primness; (*afectación*) affectation.

reminiscencia [reminis'θenθja] *nf* reminiscence.

remirar [remi'rar] *vt* (*volver a mirar*) to look at again; (*examinar*) to look hard at.

remisión [remi'sjon] *nf* (*acto*) sending, shipment; (*REL*) forgiveness, remission; **sin** ~ hopelessly.

remiso, a [re'miso, a] *adj* remiss.

remite [re'mite] *nm* (*en sobre*) name and address of sender.

remitente [remi'tente] *nm/f* (*CORREOS*) sender.

remitir [remi'tir] *vt* to remit, send ♦ *vi* to slacken.

remo ['remo] *nm* (*de barco*) oar; (*DEPORTE*) rowing; **cruzar un río a** ~ to row across a river.

remoce [re'moθe] *etc vb V* **remozar**.

remodelación [remodela'θjon] *nf* (*POL*): ~ **del gobierno** cabinet reshuffle.

remojar [remo'xar] *vt* to steep, soak; (*galleta etc*) to dip, dunk; (*fam*) to celebrate with a drink.

remojo [re'moxo] *nm* steeping, soaking; (*por la lluvia*) drenching, soaking; **dejar la ropa en** ~ to leave clothes to soak.

remojón [remo'xon] *nm* soaking; **darse un** ~ (*fam*) to go (in) for a dip.

remolacha [remo'latʃa] *nf* beet, beetroot (*BRIT*).

remolcador [remolka'ðor] *nm* (*NAUT*) tug; (*AUTO*) breakdown lorry.

remolcar [remol'kar] *vt* to tow.

remolino [remo'lino] *nm* eddy; (*de agua*) whirlpool; (*de viento*) whirlwind; (*de gente*) crowd.

remolón, ona [remo'lon, ona] *adj* lazy ♦ *nm/f* slacker, shirker.

remolque [re'molke] *etc vb V* **remolcar** ♦ *nm* tow, towing; (*cuerda*) towrope; **llevar a** ~ to tow.

remontar [remon'tar] *vt* to mend; (*obstáculo*) to negotiate, get over; ~**se** *vr* to soar; ~**se a** (*COM*) to amount to; (*en tiempo*) to go back to, date from; ~ **el vuelo** to soar.

rémora ['remora] *nf* hindrance.

remorder [remor'ðer] *vt* to distress, disturb.

remordimiento [remorði'mjento] *nm* remorse.

remotamente [remota'mente] *adv* vaguely.

remoto, a [re'moto, a] *adj* remote.

remover [remo'ßer] *vt* to stir; (*tierra*) to turn over; (*objetos*) to move round.

remozar [remo'θar] *vt* (*ARQ*) to refurbish; (*fig*) to brighten *o* polish up.

remuerda [re'mwerða] *etc vb V* **remorder**.

remueva [re'mweßa] *etc vb V* **remover**.

remuneración [remunera'θjon] *nf* remuneration.

remunerado, a [remune'raðo, a] *adj*: **trabajo bien/mal** ~ well-/badly-paid job.

remunerar [remune'rar] *vt* to remunerate; (*premiar*) to reward.

renacer [rena'θer] *vi* to be reborn; (*fig*) to revive.

renacimiento [renaθi'mjento] *nm* rebirth; **el R**~ the Renaissance.

renacuajo [rena'kwaxo] *nm* (*ZOOL*) tadpole.

renal [re'nal] *adj* renal, kidney *cpd*.

Renania [re'nanja] *nf* Rhineland.

renazca [re'naθka] *etc vb V* **renacer**.

rencilla [ren'θiʎa] *nf* quarrel; ~**s** *nfpl* bickering *sg*.

rencor [ren'kor] *nm* rancour, bitterness; (*resentimiento*) ill feeling, resentment;

guardar ~ **a** to have a grudge against.
rencoroso, a [renko'roso, a] *adj* spiteful.
rendición [rendi'θjon] *nf* surrender.
rendido, a [ren'diðo, a] *adj* (*sumiso*)
submissive; (*agotado*) worn-out,
exhausted; (*enamorado*) devoted.
rendija [ren'dixa] *nf* (*hendedura*) crack;
(*abertura*) aperture; (*fig*) rift, split; (*JUR*)
loophole.
rendimiento [rendi'mjento] *nm*
(*producción*) output; (*COM*) yield,
profit(s) (*pl*); (*TEC, COM*) efficiency; ~ **de
capital** (*COM*) return on capital.
rendir [ren'dir] *vt* (*vencer*) to defeat;
(*producir*) to produce; (*dar beneficio*) to
yield; (*agotar*) to exhaust ♦ *vi* to pay;
(*COM*) to yield, produce; ~**se** *vr*
(*someterse*) to surrender; (*ceder*) to
yield; (*cansarse*) to wear o.s. out; ~
homenaje *o* **culto a** to pay homage to; **el
negocio no rinde** the business doesn't
pay.
renegado, a [rene'xaðo, a] *adj, nm/f*
renegade.
renegar [rene'xar] *vt* (*negar*) to deny
vigorously ♦ *vi* (*blasfemar*) to blaspheme;
~ **de** (*renunciar*) to renounce; (*quejarse*)
to complain about.
renegué [rene'xe], **reneguemos**
[rene'xemos] *etc vb V* **renegar**.
RENFE ['renfe] *nf abr ESP*. = *Red Nacional de
Ferrocarriles Españoles*.
renglón [ren'glon] *nm* (*línea*) line; (*COM*)
item, article; **a** ~ **seguido** immediately
after.
rengo, a ['rengo, a] *adj* (*AM*) lame.
reniego [re'njexo] *etc*, **reniegue**
[re'njexe] *etc vb V* **renegar**.
reno ['reno] *nm* reindeer.
renombrado, a [renom'braðo, a] *adj*
renowned.
renombre [re'nombre] *nm* renown.
renovable [reno'ßaßle] *adj* renewable.
renovación [renoßa'θjon] *nf* (*de contrato*)
renewal; (*ARQ*) renovation.
renovar [reno'ßar] *vt* to renew; (*ARQ*) to
renovate; (*sala*) to redecorate.
renquear [renke'ar] *vi* to limp; (*fam*) to get
along, scrape by.
renta ['renta] *nf* (*ingresos*) income;
(*beneficio*) profit; (*alquiler*) rent; ~
gravable *o* **imponible** taxable income; ~
nacional (bruta) (gross) national income;
~ **no salarial** unearned income; ~ **sobre
el terreno** (*COM*) ground rent; ~ **vitalicia**
annuity; **política de** ~**s** incomes policy;
vivir de sus ~**s** to live on one's private
income.

rentabilizar [rentaßili'θar] *vt* to make
profitable.
rentable [ren'taßle] *adj* profitable; **no** ~
unprofitable.
rentar [ren'tar] *vt* to produce, yield; (*AM*)
to rent.
rentista [ren'tista] *nm/f* (*accionista*)
shareholder (*BRIT*), stockholder (*US*).
renuencia [re'nwenθja] *nf* reluctance.
renuente [re'nwente] *adj* reluctant.
renueve [re'nweße] *etc vb V* **renovar**.
renuncia [re'nunθja] *nf* resignation.
renunciar [renun'θjar] *vt* to renounce, give
up ♦ *vi* to resign; ~ **a hacer algo** to give
up doing sth.
reñido, a [re'niðo, a] *adj* (*batalla*) bitter,
hard-fought; **estar** ~ **con algn** to be on
bad terms with sb; **está** ~ **con su familia**
he has fallen out with his family.
reñir [re'nir] *vt* (*regañar*) to scold ♦ *vi* (*estar
peleado*) to quarrel, fall out; (*combatir*) to
fight.
reo ['reo] *nm/f* culprit, offender; (*JUR*)
accused.
reojo [re'oxo]: **de** ~ *adv* out of the corner
of one's eye.
reorganice [reorxa'niθe] *etc vb V*
reorganizar.
reorganizar [reorxani'θar] *vt* to
reorganize.
Rep *abr* = **República**.
reparación [repara'θjon] *nf* (*acto*) mending,
repairing; (*TEC*) repair; (*fig*) amends,
reparation; "**reparaciones en el acto**"
"repairs while you wait".
reparar [repa'rar] *vt* to repair; (*fig*) to make
amends for; (*suerte*) to retrieve;
(*observar*) to observe ♦ *vi*: ~ **en** (*darse
cuenta de*) to notice; (*poner atención en*) to
pay attention to; **sin** ~ **en los gastos**
regardless of the cost.
reparo [re'paro] *nm* (*advertencia*)
observation; (*duda*) doubt; (*dificultad*)
difficulty; (*escrúpulo*) scruple, qualm;
poner ~**s (a)** to raise objections (to);
(*criticar*) to criticize; **no tuvo** ~ **en
hacerlo** he did not hesitate to do it.
repartición [reparti'θjon] *nf* distribution;
(*división*) division.
repartidor, a [reparti'ðor, a] *nm/f*
distributor; ~ **de leche** milkman.
repartir [repar'tir] *vt* to distribute, share
out; (*COM, CORREOS*) to deliver; (*MIL*) to
partition; (*libros*) to give out; (*comida*) to
serve out; (*NAIPES*) to deal.
reparto [re'parto] *nm* distribution; (*COM,
CORREOS*) delivery; (*TEAT, CINE*) cast;
(*AM: urbanización*) housing estate (*BRIT*),

real estate development (*US*); "~ **a domicilio**" "home delivery service".

repasar [repa'sar] *vt* (*ESCOL*) to revise; (*MECÁNICA*) to check, overhaul; (*COSTURA*) to mend.

repaso [re'paso] *nm* revision; (*MECÁNICA*) overhaul, checkup; (*COSTURA*) mending; ~ **general** servicing, general overhaul; **curso de** ~ refresher course.

repatriar [repa'trjar] *vt* to repatriate; ~**se** *vr* to return home.

repelente [repe'lente] *adj* repellent, repulsive.

repeler [repe'ler] *vt* to repel; (*idea, oferta*) to reject.

repensar [repen'sar] *vt* to reconsider.

repente [re'pente] *nm* sudden movement; (*fig*) impulse; **de** ~ suddenly; ~ **de ira** fit of anger.

repentice [repen'tiθe] *etc vb V* **repentizar**.

repentino, a [repen'tino, a] *adj* sudden; (*imprevisto*) unexpected.

repentizar [repenti'θar] *vi* (*MUS*) to sight-read.

repercusión [reperku'sjon] *nf* repercussion; **de amplia** *o* **ancha** ~ far-reaching.

repercutir [reperku'tir] *vi* (*objeto*) to rebound; (*sonido*) to echo; ~ **en** (*fig*) to have repercussions *o* effects on.

repertorio [reper'torjo] *nm* list; (*TEAT*) repertoire.

repesca [re'peska] *nf* (*ESCOL fam*) resit.

repetición [repeti'θjon] *nf* repetition.

repetido, a [repe'tiðo, a] *adj* repeated; **repetidas veces** repeatedly.

repetir [repe'tir] *vt* to repeat; (*plato*) to have a second helping of; (*TEAT*) to give as an encore, sing *etc* again ♦ *vi* to repeat; (*sabor*) to come back; ~**se** *vr* to repeat o.s.; (*suceso*) to recur.

repetitivo, a [repeti'tißo, a] *adj* repetitive, repetitious.

repicar [repi'kar] *vi* (*campanas*) to ring (out).

repiense [re'pjense] *etc vb V* **repensar**.

repipi [re'pipi] *adj* la-di-da ♦ *nf*: **es una** ~ she's a little madam.

repique [re'pike] *etc vb V* **repicar** ♦ *nm* pealing, ringing.

repiqueteo [repike'teo] *nm* pealing; (*de tambor*) drumming.

repisa [re'pisa] *nf* ledge, shelf; ~ **de chimenea** mantelpiece; ~ **de ventana** windowsill.

repitiendo [repi'tjendo] *etc vb V* **repetir**.

replantear [replante'ar] *vt* (*cuestión pública*) to readdress; (*problema personal*)

to reconsider; (*en reunión*) to raise again; ~**se** *vr*: ~**se algo** to reconsider sth.

replegarse [reple'ɣarse] *vr* to fall back, retreat.

replegué [reple'ɣe], **repleguemos** [reple'ɣemos] *etc vb V* **replegarse**.

repleto, a [re'pleto, a] *adj* replete, full up; ~ **de** filled *o* crammed with.

réplica ['replika] *nf* answer; (*ARTE*) replica; **derecho de** ~ right of *o* to reply.

replicar [repli'kar] *vi* to answer; (*objetar*) to argue, answer back.

repliego [re'pljeɣo] *etc vb V* **replegarse**.

repliegue [re'pljeɣe] *etc vb V* **replegarse** ♦ *nm* (*MIL*) withdrawal.

replique [re'plike] *etc vb V* **replicar**.

repoblación [repoßla'θjon] *nf* repopulation; (*de río*) restocking; ~ **forestal** reafforestation.

repoblar [repo'ßlar] *vt* to repopulate; to restock.

repollo [re'poʎo] *nm* cabbage.

repondré [repon'dre] *etc vb V* **reponer**.

reponer [repo'ner] *vt* to replace, put back; (*máquina*) to re-set; (*TEAT*) to revive; ~**se** *vr* to recover; ~ **que** to reply that.

reponga [re'ponga] *etc vb V* **reponer**.

reportaje [repor'taxe] *nm* report, article; ~ **gráfico** illustrated report.

reportar [repor'tar] *vt* (*traer*) to bring, carry; (*conseguir*) to obtain; (*fig*) to check; ~**se** *vr* (*contenerse*) to control o.s.; (*calmarse*) to calm down; **la cosa no le reportó sino disgustos** the affair brought him nothing but trouble.

reportero, a [repor'tero, a] *nm/f* reporter; ~ **gráfico/a** news photographer.

reposacabezas [reposaka'ßeθas] *nm inv* headrest.

reposado, a [repo'saðo, a] *adj* (*descansado*) restful; (*tranquilo*) calm.

reposar [repo'sar] *vi* to rest, repose; (*muerto*) to lie, rest.

reposición [reposi'θjon] *nf* replacement; (*CINE*) second showing; (*TEAT*) revival.

reposo [re'poso] *nm* rest.

repostar [repos'tar] *vt* to replenish; (*AUTO*) to fill up (with petrol *o* gasoline).

repostería [reposte'ria] *nf* (*arte*) confectionery, pastry-making; (*tienda*) confectioner's (shop).

repostero, a [repos'tero, a] *nm/f* confectioner.

reprender [repren'der] *vt* to reprimand; (*niño*) to scold.

reprensión [repren'sjon] *nf* rebuke, reprimand; (*de niño*) telling-off, scolding.

represa [re'presa] *nf* dam; (*lago artificial*) lake, pool.

represalia [repre'salja] *nf* reprisal; **tomar ~s** to take reprisals, retaliate.

representación [representa'θjon] *nf* representation; (*TEAT*) performance; **en ~ de** representing; **por ~** by proxy; **~ visual** (*INFORM*) display.

representante [represen'tante] *nm/f* (*POL, COM*) representative; (*TEAT*) performer.

representar [represen'tar] *vt* to represent; (*significar*) to mean; (*TEAT*) to perform; (*edad*) to look; **~se** *vr* to imagine; **tal acto representaría la guerra** such an act would mean war.

representativo, a [representa'tiβo, a] *adj* representative.

represión [repre'sjon] *nf* repression.

represivo, a [repre'siβo, a] *adj* repressive.

reprimenda [repri'menda] *nf* reprimand, rebuke.

reprimir [repri'mir] *vt* to repress; **~se** *vr*: **~se de hacer algo** to stop o.s. from doing sth.

reprobación [reproβa'θjon] *nf* reproval; (*culpa*) blame.

reprobar [repro'βar] *vt* to censure, reprove.

réprobo, a ['reproβo, a] *nm/f* reprobate.

reprochar [repro'tʃar] *vt* to reproach; (*censurar*) to condemn, censure.

reproche [re'protʃe] *nm* reproach.

reproducción [reproðuk'θjon] *nf* reproduction.

reproducir [reproðu'θir] *vt* to reproduce; **~se** *vr* to breed; (*situación*) to recur.

reproductor, a [reproðuk'tor, a] *adj* reproductive ♦ *nm*: **~ de discos compactos** CD player.

reproduje [repro'ðuxe], **reprodujera** [reproðu'xera] *etc*, **reproduzca** [repro'ðuθka] *etc vb V* **reproducir**.

repruebe [re'prweβe] *etc vb V* **reprobar**.

reptar [rep'tar] *vi* to creep, crawl.

reptil [rep'til] *nm* reptile.

república [re'puβlika] *nf* republic; **R~ Dominicana** Dominican Republic; **R~ Democrática Alemana (RDA)** German Democratic Republic; **R~ Federal Alemana (RFA)** Federal Republic of Germany; **R~ Árabe Unida** United Arab Republic.

republicano, a [repuβli'kano, a] *adj, nm/f* republican.

repudiar [repu'ðjar] *vt* to repudiate; (*fe*) to renounce.

repudio [re'puðjo] *nm* repudiation.

repueble [re'pweβle] *etc vb V* **repoblar**.

repuesto [re'pwesto] *pp de* **reponer** ♦ *nm* (*pieza de recambio*) spare (part); (*abastecimiento*) supply; **rueda de ~** spare wheel; **y llevamos otro de ~** and we have another as a spare *o* in reserve.

repugnancia [repuɣ'nanθja] *nf* repugnance.

repugnante [repuɣ'nante] *adj* repugnant, repulsive.

repugnar [repuɣ'nar] *vt* to disgust ♦ *vi*, **~se** *vr* (*contradecirse*) to contradict each other; (*dar asco*) to be disgusting.

repujar [repu'xar] *vt* to emboss.

repulsa [re'pulsa] *nf* rebuff.

repulsión [repul'sjon] *nf* repulsion, aversion.

repulsivo, a [repul'siβo, a] *adj* repulsive.

repuse [re'puse] *etc vb V* **reponer**.

reputación [reputa'θjon] *nf* reputation.

reputar [repu'tar] *vt* to consider, deem.

requemado, a [reke'maðo, a] *adj* (*quemado*) scorched; (*bronceado*) tanned.

requemar [reke'mar] *vt* (*quemar*) to scorch; (*secar*) to parch; (*CULIN*) to overdo, burn; (*la lengua*) to burn, sting.

requerimiento [rekeri'mjento] *nm* request; (*demanda*) demand; (*JUR*) summons.

requerir [reke'rir] *vt* (*pedir*) to ask, request; (*exigir*) to require; (*ordenar*) to call for; (*llamar*) to send for, summon.

requesón [reke'son] *nm* cottage cheese.

requete... [rekete] *pref* extremely.

requiebro [re'kjeβro] *nm* (*piropo*) compliment, flirtatious remark.

réquiem ['rekjem] *nm* requiem.

requiera [re'kjera] *etc*, **requiriendo** [reki'rjendo] *etc vb V* **requerir**.

requisa [re'kisa] *nf* (*inspección*) survey, inspection; (*MIL*) requisition.

requisar [reki'sar] *vt* (*MIL*) to requisition; (*confiscar*) to seize, confiscate.

requisito [reki'sito] *nm* requirement, requisite; **~ previo** prerequisite; **tener los ~s para un cargo** to have the essential qualifications for a post.

res [res] *nf* beast, animal.

resabio [re'saβjo] *nm* (*maña*) vice, bad habit; (*dejo*) (unpleasant) aftertaste.

resaca [re'saka] *nf* (*en el mar*) undertow, undercurrent; (*fig*) backlash; (*fam*) hangover.

resaltar [resal'tar] *vi* to project, stick out; (*fig*) to stand out.

resarcir [resar'θir] *vt* to compensate; (*pagar*) to repay; **~se** *vr* to make up for; **~ a algn de una pérdida** to compensate sb for a loss; **~ a algn de una cantidad** to repay sb a sum.

resarza [re'sarθa] *etc vb* V **resarcir**.

resbalada [resßa'laða] *nf* (*AM*) slip.

resbaladizo, a [resßala'ðiθo, a] *adj* slippery.

resbalar [resßa'lar] *vi*, **resbalarse** *vr* to slip, slide; (*fig*) to slip (up); **le resbalaban las lágrimas por las mejillas** tears were trickling down his cheeks.

resbalón [resßa'lon] *nm* (*acción*) slip; (*deslizamiento*) slide; (*fig*) slip.

rescatar [reska'tar] *vt* (*salvar*) to save, rescue; (*objeto*) to get back, recover; (*cautivos*) to ransom.

rescate [res'kate] *nm* rescue; (*objeto*) recovery; **pagar un** ~ to pay a ransom.

rescindir [resθin'dir] *vt* (*contrato*) to annul, rescind.

rescisión [resθi'sjon] *nf* cancellation.

rescoldo [res'koldo] *nm* embers *pl*.

resecar [rese'kar] *vt* to dry off, dry thoroughly; (*MED*) to cut out, remove; ~**se** *vr* to dry up.

reseco, a [re'seko, a] *adj* very dry; (*fig*) skinny.

resentido, a [resen'tiðo, a] *adj* resentful; **es un** ~ he's bitter.

resentimiento [resenti'mjento] *nm* resentment, bitterness.

resentirse [resen'tirse] *vr* (*debilitarse*: *persona*) to suffer; ~ **con** to resent; ~ **de** (*consecuencias*) to feel the effects of.

reseña [re'seɲa] *nf* (*cuenta*) account; (*informe*) report; (*LIT*) review.

reseñar [rese'ɲar] *vt* to describe; (*LIT*) to review.

reseque [re'seke] *etc vb* V **resecar**.

reserva [re'serßa] *nf* reserve; (*reservación*) reservation; **a** ~ **de que** ... unless ...; **con toda** ~ in strictest confidence; **de** ~ spare; **tener algo de** ~ to have sth in reserve; ~ **de indios** Indian reservation; (*COM*): ~ **para amortización** depreciation allowance; ~ **de caja** *o* **en efectivo** cash reserves; ~**s del Estado** government stock; ~**s en oro** gold reserves.

reservado, a [reser'ßaðo, a] *adj* reserved; (*retraído*) cold, distant ♦ *nm* private room; (*FERRO*) reserved compartment.

reservar [reser'ßar] *vt* (*guardar*) to keep; (*FERRO, TEAT etc*) to reserve, book; ~**se** *vr* to save o.s.; (*callar*) to keep to o.s.; ~ **con exceso** to overbook.

resfriado [res'friaðo] *nm* cold.

resfriarse [res'friarse] *vr* to cool off; (*MED*) to catch (a) cold.

resfrío [resf'rio] *nm* (*esp AM*) cold.

resguardar [resɣwar'ðar] *vt* to protect, shield; ~**se** *vr*: ~**se de** to guard against.

resguardo [res'ɣwarðo] *nm* defence; (*vale*) voucher; (*recibo*) receipt, slip.

residencia [resi'ðenθja] *nf* residence; (*UNIV*) hall of residence; ~ **para ancianos** *o* **jubilados** rest home.

residencial [resiðen'θjal] *adj* residential ♦ *nf* (*urbanización*) housing estate (*BRIT*), real estate development (*US*).

residente [resi'ðente] *adj, nm/f* resident.

residir [resi'ðir] *vi* to reside, live; ~ **en** to reside *o* lie in; (*consistir en*) to consist of.

residual [resi'ðwal] *adj* residual; **aguas** ~**es** sewage.

residuo [re'siðwo] *nm* residue; ~**s atmosféricos** *o* **radiactivos** fallout *sg*.

resienta [re'sjenta] *etc vb* V **resentir**.

resignación [resiɣna'θjon] *nf* resignation.

resignarse [resiɣ'narse] *vr*: ~ **a** *o* **con** to resign o.s. to, be resigned to.

resina [re'sina] *nf* resin.

resintiendo [resin'tjendo] *etc vb* V **resentir**.

resistencia [resis'tenθja] *nf* (*dureza*) endurance, strength; (*oposición, ELEC*) resistance; **la R**~ (*MIL*) the Resistance.

resistente [resis'tente] *adj* strong, hardy; (*TEC*) resistant; ~ **al calor** heat-resistant.

resistir [resis'tir] *vt* (*soportar*) to bear; (*oponerse a*) to resist, oppose; (*aguantar*) to put up with ♦ *vi* to resist; (*aguantar*) to last, endure; ~**se** *vr*: ~**se a** to refuse to, resist; **no puedo** ~ **este frío** I can't bear *o* stand this cold; **me resisto a creerlo** I refuse to believe it; **se le resiste la química** chemistry escapes her.

resol [re'sol] *nm* glare of the sun.

resollar [reso'ʎar] *vi* to breathe noisily, wheeze.

resolución [resolu'θjon] *nf* resolution; (*decisión*) decision; (*moción*) motion; ~ **judicial** legal ruling; **tomar una** ~ to take a decision.

resoluto, a [reso'luto, a] *adj* resolute.

resolver [resol'ßer] *vt* to resolve; (*solucionar*) to solve, resolve; (*decidir*) to decide, settle; ~**se** *vr* to make up one's mind.

resonancia [reso'nanθja] *nf* (*del sonido*) resonance; (*repercusión*) repercussion; (*fig*) wide effect, impact.

resonante [reso'nante] *adj* resonant, resounding; (*fig*) tremendous.

resonar [reso'nar] *vi* to ring, echo.

resoplar [reso'plar] *vi* to snort; (*por cansancio*) to puff.

resoplido [reso'pliðo] *nm* heavy breathing.

resorte [re'sorte] *nm* spring; (*fig*) lever.

respaldar [respal'dar] *vt* to back (up),

support; (*INFORM*) to back up; ~**se** *vr* to lean back; ~**se con** *o* **en** (*fig*) to take one's stand on.

respaldo [res'paldo] *nm* (*de sillón*) back; (*fig*) support, backing.

respectivo, a [respek'tiβo, a] *adj* respective; **en lo** ~ **a** with regard to.

respecto [res'pekto] *nm*: **al** ~ on this matter; **con** ~ **a,** ~ **de** with regard to, in relation to.

respetable [respe'taβle] *adj* respectable.

respetar [respe'tar] *vt* to respect.

respeto [res'peto] *nm* respect; (*acatamiento*) deference; ~**s** *nmpl* respects; **por** ~ **a** out of consideration for; **presentar sus** ~**s a** to pay one's respects to.

respetuoso, a [respe'twoso, a] *adj* respectful.

respingo [res'pingo] *nm* start, jump.

respiración [respira'θjon] *nf* breathing; (*MED*) respiration; (*ventilación*) ventilation.

respirar [respi'rar] *vt, vi* to breathe; **no dejar** ~ **a algn** to keep on at sb; **estuvo escuchándole sin** ~ he listened to him in complete silence.

respiratorio, a [respira'torjo, a] *adj* respiratory.

respiro [res'piro] *nm* breathing; (*fig: descanso*) respite, rest; (*COM*) period of grace.

resplandecer [resplande'θer] *vi* to shine.

resplandeciente [resplande'θjente] *adj* resplendent, shining.

resplandezca [resplan'deθka] *etc vb V* **resplandecer**.

resplandor [resplan'dor] *nm* brilliance, brightness; (*del fuego*) blaze.

responder [respon'der] *vt* to answer ♦ *vi* to answer; (*fig*) to respond; (*pey*) to answer back; (*corresponder*) to correspond; ~ **a** (*situación etc*) to respond to; ~ **a una pregunta** to answer a question; ~ **a una descripción** to fit a description; ~ **de** *o* **por** to answer for.

respondón, ona [respon'don, ona] *adj* cheeky.

responsabilice [responsaβi'liθe] *etc vb V* **responsabilizarse**.

responsabilidad [responsaβili'ðað] *nf* responsibility; **bajo mi** ~ on my authority; ~ **ilimitada** (*COM*) unlimited liability.

responsabilizarse [responsaβili'θarse] *vr* to make o.s. responsible, take charge.

responsable [respon'sable] *adj* responsible; **la persona** ~ the person in

charge; **hacerse** ~ **de algo** to assume responsibility for sth.

respuesta [res'pwesta] *nf* answer, reply; (*reacción*) response.

resquebrajar [reskeβra'xar] *vt*, **resquebrajarse** *vr* to crack, split.

resquemor [reske'mor] *nm* resentment.

resquicio [res'kiθjo] *nm* chink; (*hendedura*) crack.

resta ['resta] *nf* (*MAT*) remainder.

restablecer [restaβle'θer] *vt* to re-establish, restore; ~**se** *vr* to recover.

restablecimiento [restaβleθi'mjento] *nm* re-establishment; (*restauración*) restoration; (*MED*) recovery.

restablezca [resta'βleθka] *etc vb V* **restablecer**.

restallar [resta'ʎar] *vi* to crack.

restante [res'tante] *adj* remaining; **lo** ~ the remainder; **los** ~**s** the rest, those left (over).

restar [res'tar] *vt* (*MAT*) to subtract; (*descontar*) to deduct; (*fig*) to take away ♦ *vi* to remain, be left.

restauración [restaura'θjon] *nf* restoration.

restaurador, a [restaura'ðor, a] *nm/f* (*persona*) restorer.

restaurante [restau'rante] *nm* restaurant.

restaurar [restau'rar] *vt* to restore.

restitución [restitu'θjon] *nf* return, restitution.

restituir [restitu'ir] *vt* (*devolver*) to return, give back; (*rehabilitar*) to restore.

restituyendo [restitu'jendo] *etc vb V* **restituir**.

resto ['resto] *nm* (*residuo*) rest, remainder; (*apuesta*) stake; ~**s** *nmpl* remains; (*CULIN*) leftovers, scraps; ~**s mortales** mortal remains.

restregar [restre'xar] *vt* to scrub, rub.

restregué [restre'xe], **restreguemos** [restre'xemos] *etc vb V* **restregar**.

restricción [restrik'θjon] *nf* restriction; **sin** ~ **de** without restrictions on *o* as to; **hablar sin restricciones** to talk freely.

restrictivo, a [restrik'tiβo, a] *adj* restrictive.

restriego [res'trjexo] *etc*, **restriegue** [res'trjexe] *etc vb V* **restregar**.

restringir [restrin'xir] *vt* to restrict, limit.

restrinja [res'trinxa] *etc vb V* **restringir**.

resucitar [resuθi'tar] *vt, vi* to resuscitate, revive.

resuello [re'sweʎo] *etc vb V* **resollar** ♦ *nm* (*aliento*) breath.

resuelto, a [re'swelto, a] *pp de* **resolver** ♦ *adj* resolute, determined; **estar** ~ **a**

algo to be set on sth; **estar ~ a hacer algo** to be determined to do sth.
resuelva [re'swelßa] etc vb V **resolver.**
resuene [re'swene] etc vb V **resonar.**
resulta [re'sulta] nf result; **de ~s de** as a result of.
resultado [resul'taðo] nm result; (conclusión) outcome; **~s** nmpl (INFORM) output sg; **dar ~** to produce results.
resultante [resul'tante] adj resulting, resultant.
resultar [resul'tar] vi (ser) to be; (llegar a ser) to turn out to be; (salir bien) to turn out well; (seguir) to ensue; **~ a** (COM) to amount to; **~ de** to stem from; **~ en** to result in, produce; **resulta que ...** (por consecuencia) it follows that ...; (parece que) it seems that ...; **el conductor resultó muerto** the driver was killed; **no resultó** it didn't work o come off; **me resulta difícil hacerlo** it's difficult for me to do it.
resumen [re'sumen] nm summary, résumé; **en ~** in short.
resumir [resu'mir] vt to sum up; (condensar) to summarize; (cortar) to abridge, cut down; (condensar) to summarize; **~se** vr: **la situación se resume en pocas palabras** the situation can be summed up in a few words.
resurgir [resur'xir] vi (reaparecer) to reappear.
resurrección [resurrek'θjon] nf resurrection.
retablo [re'taßlo] nm altarpiece.
retaguardia [reta'ɣwarðja] nf rearguard.
retahíla [reta'ila] nf series, string; (de injurias) volley, stream.
retal [re'tal] nm remnant.
retar [re'tar] vt (gen) to challenge; (desafiar) to defy, dare.
retardar [retar'ðar] vt (demorar) to delay; (hacer más lento) to slow down; (retener) to hold back.
retardo [re'tarðo] nm delay.
retazo [re'taθo] nm snippet (BRIT), fragment.
RETD nf abr (ESP TELEC) = Red Especial de Transmisión de Datos.
rete... ['rete] pref very, extremely.
retén [re'ten] nm (AM) roadblock, checkpoint.
retención [reten'θjon] nf retention; (de pago) deduction; **~ de llamadas** (TELEC) hold facility.
retendré [reten'dre] etc vb V **retener.**
retener [rete'ner] vt (guardar) to retain, keep; (intereses) to withhold.

retenga [re'tenga] etc vb V **retener.**
reticencia [reti'θenθja] nf (sugerencia) insinuation, (malevolent) suggestion; (engaño) half-truth.
reticente [reti'θente] adj (insinuador) insinuating; (engañoso) deceptive.
retiene [re'tjene] etc vb V **retener.**
retina [re'tina] nf retina.
retintín [retin'tin] nm jangle, jingle; **decir algo con ~** to say sth sarcastically.
retirado, a [reti'raðo, a] adj (lugar) remote; (vida) quiet; (jubilado) retired ♦ nf (MIL) retreat; (de dinero) withdrawal; (de embajador) recall; (refugio) safe place; **batirse en retirada** to retreat.
retirar [reti'rar] vt to withdraw; (la mano) to draw back; (quitar) to remove; (dinero) to take out, withdraw; (jubilar) to retire, pension off; **~se** vr to retreat, withdraw; (jubilarse) to retire; (acostarse) to retire, go to bed.
retiro [re'tiro] nm retreat; (jubilación, tb DEPORTE) retirement; (pago) pension; (lugar) quiet place.
reto ['reto] nm dare, challenge.
retocar [reto'kar] vt to touch up, retouch.
retoce [re'toθe] etc vb V **retozar.**
retoño [re'toɲo] nm sprout, shoot; (fig) offspring, child.
retoque [re'toke] etc vb V **retocar** ♦ nm retouching.
retorcer [retor'θer] vt to twist; (argumento) to turn, twist; (manos, lavado) to wring; **~se** vr to become twisted; (persona) to writhe; **~se de dolor** to writhe in o squirm with pain.
retorcido, a [retor'θiðo, a] adj (tb fig) twisted.
retorcimiento [retorθi'mjento] nm twist, twisting; (fig) deviousness.
retórico, a [re'toriko, a] adj rhetorical; (pey) affected, windy ♦ nf rhetoric; (pey) affectedness.
retornable [retor'naßle] adj returnable.
retornar [retor'nar] vt to return, give back ♦ vi to return, go/come back.
retorno [re'torno] nm return; **~ del carro** (INFORM, TIP) carriage return; **~ del carro automático** (INFORM) wordwrap, word wraparound.
retortero [retor'tero] nm: **andar al ~** to bustle about, have heaps of things to do; **andar al ~ por algn** to be madly in love with sb.
retortijón [retorti'xon] nm twist, twisting; **~ de tripas** stomach cramp.
retorzamos [retor'θamos] etc vb V **retorcer.**

retozar [reto'θar] *vi* (*juguetear*) to frolic, romp; (*saltar*) to gambol.

retozón, ona [reto'θon, ona] *adj* playful.

retracción [retrak'θjon] *nf* retraction.

retractarse [retrak'tarse] *vr* to retract; **me retracto** I take that back.

retraerse [retra'erse] *vr* to retreat, withdraw.

retraído, a [retra'iðo, a] *adj* shy, retiring.

retraiga [re'traiɣa] *etc vb V* **retraerse**.

retraimiento [retrai'mjento] *nm* retirement; (*timidez*) shyness.

retraje [re'traxe] *etc*, **retrajera** [retra'xera] *etc vb V* **retraerse**.

retransmisión [retransmi'sjon] *nf* repeat (broadcast).

retransmitir [retransmi'tir] *vt* (*mensaje*) to relay; (*TV etc*) to repeat, retransmit; (: *en vivo*) to broadcast live.

retrasado, a [retra'saðo, a] *adj* late; (*MED*) mentally retarded; (*país etc*) backward, underdeveloped; **estar** ~ (*reloj*) to be slow; (*persona, industria*) to be o lag behind.

retrasar [retra'sar] *vt* (*demorar*) to postpone, put off; (*retardar*) to slow down ♦ *vi*, **~se** *vr* (*atrasarse*) to be late; (*reloj*) to be slow; (*producción*) to fall (away); (*quedarse atrás*) to lag behind.

retraso [re'traso] *nm* (*demora*) delay; (*lentitud*) slowness; (*tardanza*) lateness; (*atraso*) backwardness; **~s** *nmpl* (*COM*) arrears; (*deudas*) deficit *sg*, debts; **llegar con** ~ to arrive late; **llegar con 25 minutos de** ~ to be 25 minutes late; **llevo un** ~ **de 6 semanas** I'm 6 weeks behind (with my work *etc*); ~ **mental** mental deficiency.

retratar [retra'tar] *vt* (*ARTE*) to paint the portrait of; (*fotografiar*) to photograph; (*fig*) to depict, describe; **~se** *vr* to have one's portrait painted; to have one's photograph taken.

retratista [retra'tista] *nm/f* (*pintura*) (portrait) painter; (*FOTO*) photographer.

retrato [re'trato] *nm* portrait; (*FOTO*) photograph; (*descripción*) portrayal, depiction; (*fig*) likeness; **ser el vivo** ~ **de** to be the spitting image of.

retrato-robot [re'tratoro'ßo(t)], *pl* **retratos-robot** *nm* identikit picture.

retrayendo [retra'jendo] *etc vb V* **retraerse**.

retreta [re'treta] *nf* retreat.

retrete [re'trete] *nm* toilet.

retribución [retrißu'θjon] *nf* (*recompensa*) reward; (*pago*) pay, payment.

retribuir [retrißu'ir] *vt* (*recompensar*) to reward; (*pagar*) to pay.

retribuyendo [retrißu'jendo] *etc vb V* **retribuir**.

retro... [retro] *pref* retro....

retroactivo, a [retroak'tißo, a] *adj* retroactive, retrospective; **dar efecto** ~ **a un pago** to backdate a payment.

retroalimentación [retroalimenta'θjon] *nf* (*INFORM*) feedback.

retroceder [retroθe'ðer] *vi* (*echarse atrás*) to move back(wards); (*fig*) to back down; **no** ~ to stand firm; **la policía hizo** ~ **a la multitud** the police forced the crowd back.

retroceso [retro'θeso] *nm* backward movement; (*MED*) relapse; (*COM*) recession, depression; (*fig*) backing down.

retrógrado, a [re'troɣraðo, a] *adj* retrograde, retrogressive; (*POL*) reactionary.

retropropulsión [retropropul'sjon] *nf* jet propulsion.

retrospectivo, a [retrospek'tißo, a] *adj* retrospective; **mirada retrospectiva** backward glance.

retrovisor [retroßi'sor] *nm* rear-view mirror.

retuerce [re'twerθe] *etc*, **retuerza** [re'twerθa] *etc vb V* **retorcer**.

retumbante [retum'bante] *adj* resounding.

retumbar [retum'bar] *vi* to echo, resound; (*continuamente*) to reverberate.

retuve [re'tuße] *etc vb V* **retener**.

reuma ['reuma] *nm* rheumatism.

reumático, a [reu'matiko, a] *adj* rheumatic.

reumatismo [reuma'tismo] *nm* rheumatism.

reunificar [reunifi'kar] *vt* to reunify.

reunifique [reuni'fike] *etc vb V* **reunificar**.

reunión [reu'njon] *nf* (*asamblea*) meeting; (*fiesta*) party; ~ **en la cumbre** summit meeting; ~ **de ventas** (*COM*) sales meeting.

reunir [reu'nir] *vt* (*juntar*) to reunite, join (together); (*recoger*) to gather (together); (*personas*) to bring o get together; (*cualidades*) to combine; **~se** *vr* (*personas: en asamblea*) to meet, gather; **reunió a sus amigos para discutirlo** he got his friends together to talk it over.

reválida [re'ßaliða] *nf* (*ESCOL*) final examination.

revalidar [reßali'ðar] *vt* (*ratificar*) to confirm, ratify.

revalorar [reßalo'rar] *vt* to revalue, reassess.

revalor(iz)ación [reßalor(iθ)a'θjon] *nf*

revaluation; (*ECON*) reassessment.

revancha [re'ßantʃa] *nf* revenge; (*DEPORTE*) return match; (*BOXEO*) return fight.

revelación [reßela'θjon] *nf* revelation.

revelado [reße'laðo] *nm* developing.

revelador, a [reßela'ðor, a] *adj* revealing.

revelar [reße'lar] *vt* to reveal; (*secreto*) to disclose; (*mostrar*) to show; (*FOTO*) to develop.

revendedor, a [reßende'ðor, a] *nm/f* retailer; (*pey*) ticket tout.

revendré [reßen'dre] *etc*, **revenga** [re'ßenga] *etc vb V* **revenirse**.

revenirse [reße'nirse] *vr* to shrink; (*comida*) to go bad *o* off; (*vino*) to sour; (*CULIN*) to get tough.

reventa [re'ßenta] *nf* resale; (*especulación*) speculation; (*de entradas*) touting.

reventar [reßen'tar] *vt* to burst, explode; (*molestar*) to annoy, rile ♦ *vi*, ~**se** *vr* (*estallar*) to burst, explode; **me revienta tener que ponérmelo** I hate having to wear it; ~ **de** (*fig*) to be bursting with; ~ **por** to be bursting to.

reventón [reßen'ton] *nm* (*AUTO*) blow-out (*BRIT*), flat (*US*).

reverberación [reßerßera'θjon] *nf* reverberation.

reverberar [reßerße'rar] *vi* (*luz*) to play, be reflected; (*superficie*) to shimmer; (*nieve*) to glare; (*sonido*) to reverberate.

reverbero [reßer'ßero] *nm* play; shimmer, shine; glare; reverberation.

reverencia [reße'renθja] *nf* reverence; (*inclinación*) bow.

reverenciar [reßeren'θjar] *vt* to revere.

reverendo, a [reße'rendo, a] *adj* reverend; (*fam*) big, awful; **un** ~ **imbécil** an awful idiot.

reverente [reße'rente] *adj* reverent.

reversible [reßer'sißle] *adj* reversible.

reverso [re'ßerso] *nm* back, other side; (*de moneda*) reverse.

revertir [reßer'tir] *vi* to revert; ~ **en beneficio de** to be to the advantage of; ~ **en perjuicio de** to be to the detriment of.

revés [re'ßes] *nm* back, wrong side; (*fig*) reverse, setback; (*DEPORTE*) backhand; **al** ~ the wrong way round; (*de arriba abajo*) upside down; (*ropa*) inside out; **y al** ~ and vice versa; **volver algo al** ~ to turn sth round; (*ropa*) to turn sth inside out; **los reveses de la fortuna** the blows of fate.

revestir [reßes'tir] *vt* (*poner*) to put on; (*cubrir*) to cover, coat; (*cualidad*) to have, possess; ~**se** *vr* (*REL*) to put on one's vestments; (*ponerse*) to put on; ~ **con** *o*

de to arm o.s. with; **el acto revestía gran solemnidad** the ceremony had great dignity.

reviejo, a [re'ßjexo, a] *adj* very old, ancient.

reviene [re'ßjene] *etc vb V* **revenirse**.

reviente [re'ßjente] *etc vb V* **reventar**.

revierta [re'ßjerta] *etc vb V* **revertir**.

reviniendo [reßi'njendo] *etc vb V* **revenirse**.

revirtiendo [reßir'tjendo] *etc vb V* **revertir**.

revisar [reßi'sar] *vt* (*examinar*) to check; (*texto etc*) to revise; (*JUR*) to review.

revisión [reßi'sjon] *nf* revision; ~ **aduanera** customs inspection; ~ **de cuentas** audit.

revisor, a [reßi'sor, a] *nm/f* inspector; (*FERRO*) ticket collector; ~ **de cuentas** auditor.

revista [re'ßista] *etc vb V* **revestir** ♦ *nf* magazine, review; (*sección*) section, page; (*TEAT*) revue; (*inspección*) inspection; ~ **literaria** literary review; ~ **de libros** book reviews (page); **pasar** ~ **a** to review, inspect.

revivir [reßi'ßir] *vt* (*recordar*) to revive memories of ♦ *vi* to revive.

revocación [reßoka'θjon] *nf* repeal.

revocar [reßo'kar] *vt* (*decisión*) to revoke; (*ARQ*) to plaster.

revolcar [reßol'kar] *vt* to knock down, send flying; ~**se** *vr* to roll about.

revolcón [reßol'kon] *nm* tumble.

revolotear [reßolote'ar] *vi* to flutter.

revoloteo [reßolo'teo] *nm* fluttering.

revolqué [reßol'ke], **revolquemos** [reßol'kemos] *etc vb V* **revolcar**.

revoltijo [reßol'tixo] *nm* mess, jumble.

revoltoso, a [reßol'toso, a] *adj* (*travieso*) naughty, unruly.

revolución [reßolu'θjon] *nf* revolution.

revolucionar [reßoluθjo'nar] *vt* to revolutionize.

revolucionario, a [reßoluθjo'narjo, a] *adj, nm/f* revolutionary.

revolver [reßol'ßer] *vt* (*desordenar*) to disturb, mess up; (*agitar*) to shake; (*líquido*) to stir; (*mover*) to move about; (*POL*) to stir up ♦ *vi*: ~ **en** to go through, rummage (about) in; ~**se** *vr* (*en cama*) to toss and turn; (*METEOROLOGÍA*) to break, turn stormy; ~**se contra** to turn on *o* against; **han revuelto toda la casa** they've turned the whole house upside down.

revólver [re'ßolßer] *nm* revolver.

revoque [re'ßoke] *etc vb V* **revocar**.

revuelco [re'ßwelko] *etc vb V* **revolcar**.

revuelo [re'ßwelo] *nm* fluttering; (*fig*) commotion; **armar** *o* **levantar un gran** ~

to cause a great stir.
revuelque [re'ßwelke] *etc vb V* **revolcar.**
revuelto, a [re'ßwelto, a] *pp de* **revolver**
♦ *adj (mezclado)* mixed-up, in disorder;
(mar) rough; *(tiempo)* unsettled ♦ *nf*
(motín) revolt; *(agitación)* commotion;
todo estaba ~ everything was in
disorder *o* was topsy-turvy.
revuelva [re'ßwelßa] *etc vb V* **revolver.**
revulsivo [reßul'sißo] *nm*: **servir de** ~ to
have a salutary effect.
rey [rei] *nm* king; **los R~es** the King and
Queen; *V tb* **Baraja Española.**

---

*The night before the 6th of January (the
Epiphany), which is a holiday in Spain,
children go to bed expecting* **los Reyes
Magos,** *the Three Wise Men who visited the
baby Jesus, to bring them presents. Twelfth
night processions, known as* **cabalgatas,**
*take place that evening, when 3 people
dressed as* **los Reyes Magos** *arrive in the
town by land or sea to the delight of the
children.*

---

reyerta [re'jerta] *nf* quarrel, brawl.
rezagado, a [reθa'ɣaðo, a] *adj*: **quedar** ~ to
be left behind; *(estar retrasado)* to be
late, be behind ♦ *nm/f* straggler.
rezagar [reθa'ɣar] *vt (dejar atrás)* to leave
behind; *(retrasar)* to delay, postpone; **~se**
vr (atrasarse) to fall behind.
rezague [re'θaɣe] *etc vb V* **rezagar.**
rezar [re'θar] *vi* to pray; ~ **con** *(fam)* to
concern, have to do with.
rezo [ˈreθo] *nm* prayer.
rezongar [reθon'gar] *vi* to grumble;
(murmurar) to mutter; *(refunfuñar)* to
growl.
rezongue [re'θoŋge] *etc vb V* **rezongar.**
rezumar [reθu'mar] *vt* to ooze ♦ *vi* to leak;
~se *vr* to leak out.
RFA *nf abr* = **República Federal Alemana.**
ría [ˈria] *nf* estuary.
riachuelo [rja'tʃwelo] *nm* stream.
riada [riˈaða] *nf* flood.
ribera [ri'ßera] *nf (de río)* bank; (: *área)*
riverside.
ribete [ri'ßete] *nm (de vestido)* border; *(fig)*
addition.
ribetear [rißete'ar] *vt* to edge, border.
rice [ˈriθe] *etc vb V* **rizar.**
ricino [ri'θino] *nm*: **aceite de** ~ castor oil.
rico, a [ˈriko, a] *adj (adinerado)* rich,
wealthy; *(lujoso)* luxurious; *(comida)*
delicious; *(niño)* lovely, cute ♦ *nm/f* rich
person; **nuevo** ~ nouveau riche.
rictus [ˈriktus] *nm (mueca)* sneer, grin; ~

de amargura bitter smile.
ridiculez [riðiku'leθ] *nf* absurdity.
ridiculice [riðiku'liθe] *etc vb V* **ridiculizar.**
ridiculizar [riðikuli'θar] *vt* to ridicule.
ridículo, a [ri'ðikulo, a] *adj* ridiculous;
hacer el ~ to make a fool of o.s.; **poner a
algn en** ~ to make a fool of sb; **ponerse
en** ~ to make a fool *o* laughing-stock of
o.s.
riego [ˈrjeɣo] *etc vb V* **regar** ♦ *nm*
(aspersión) watering; *(irrigación)*
irrigation.
riegue [ˈrjeɣe] *etc vb V* **regar.**
riel [rjel] *nm* rail.
rienda [ˈrjenda] *nf* rein; *(fig)* restraint,
moderating influence; **dar** ~ **suelta a** to
give free rein to; **llevar las** ~**s** to be in
charge.
riendo [ˈrjendo] *vb V* **reír.**
riesgo [ˈrjesɣo] *nm* risk; **seguro a** *o* **contra
todo** ~ comprehensive insurance; ~
para la salud health hazard; **correr el** ~
de to run the risk of.
Rif [rif] *nm* Rif(f).
rifa [ˈrifa] *nf (lotería)* raffle.
rifar [ri'far] *vt* to raffle.
rifeño, a [ri'feɲo, a] *adj* of the Rif(f),
Rif(f)ian ♦ *nm/f* Rif(f)ian, Rif(f).
rifle [ˈrifle] *nm* rifle.
rigidez [rixi'ðeθ] *nf* rigidity, stiffness; *(fig)*
strictness.
rígido, a [ˈrixiðo, a] *adj* rigid, stiff;
(moralmente) strict, inflexible; *(cara)*
wooden, expressionless.
rigiendo [ri'xjendo] *etc vb V* **regir.**
rigor [ri'ɣor] *nm* strictness, rigour; *(dureza)*
toughness; *(inclemencia)* harshness;
(meticulosidad) accuracy; **el** ~ **del verano**
the hottest part of the summer; **con
todo** ~ **científico** with scientific
precision; **de** ~ de rigueur, essential;
después de los saludos de ~ after the
inevitable greetings.
riguroso, a [riɣu'roso, a] *adj* rigorous;
(METEOROLOGÍA) harsh; *(severo)* severe.
rija [ˈrixa] *etc vb V* **regir** ♦ *nf* quarrel.
rima [ˈrima] *nf* rhyme; ~**s** *nfpl* verse *sg*; ~
imperfecta assonance; ~ **rimando** *(fam)*
merrily.
rimar [ri'mar] *vi* to rhyme.
rimbombante [rimbom'bante] *adj (fig)*
pompous.
rímel, rímmel [ˈrimel] *nm* mascara.
rimero [ri'mero] *nm* stack, pile.
Rin [rin] *nm* Rhine.
rincón [rin'kon] *nm* corner *(inside)*.
rindiendo [rin'djendo] *etc vb V* **rendir.**
ring [riŋ] *nm (BOXEO)* ring.

rinoceronte [rinoθe'ronte] *nm* rhinoceros.
riña ['riɲa] *nf* (*disputa*) argument; (*pelea*) brawl.
riñendo [ri'ɲendo] *etc vb V* **reñir**.
riñón [ri'ɲon] *nm* kidney; **me costó un ~** (*fam*) it cost me an arm and a leg; **tener riñones** to have guts.
río ['rio] *etc vb V* **reír** ♦ *nm* river; (*fig*) torrent, stream; **~ abajo/arriba** downstream/upstream; **cuando el ~ suena, agua lleva** there's no smoke without fire.
rió [ri'o] *vb V* **reír**.
Río de Janeiro ['rioðexa'neiro] *nm* Rio de Janeiro.
Río de la Plata ['rioðela'plata] *nm* Rio de la Plata, River Plate.
Rioja [ri'oxa] *nf*: **La ~** La Rioja ♦ *nm*: **r~** rioja wine.
riojano, a [rjo'xano, a] *adj, nm/f* Riojan.
rioplatense [riopla'tense] *adj* of *o* from the River Plate region ♦ *nm/f* native *o* inhabitant of the River Plate region.
riqueza [ri'keθa] *nf* wealth, riches *pl*; (*cualidad*) richness.
risa ['risa] *nf* laughter; (*una* ~) laugh; **¡qué ~!** what a laugh!; **caerse** *o* **morirse de ~** to split one's sides laughing, die laughing; **tomar algo a ~** to laugh sth off.
risco ['risko] *nm* crag, cliff.
risible [ri'siβle] *adj* ludicrous, laughable.
risotada [riso'taða] *nf* guffaw, loud laugh.
ristra ['ristra] *nf* string.
ristre ['ristre] *nm*: **en ~** at the ready.
risueño, a [ri'sweɲo, a] *adj* (*sonriente*) smiling; (*contento*) cheerful.
ritmo ['ritmo] *nm* rhythm; **a ~ lento** slowly; **trabajar a ~ lento** to go slow.
rito ['rito] *nm* rite.
ritual [ri'twal] *adj, nm* ritual.
rival [ri'βal] *adj, nm/f* rival.
rivalice [riβa'liθe] *etc vb V* **rivalizar**.
rivalidad [riβali'ðað] *nf* rivalry, competition.
rivalizar [riβali'θar] *vi*: **~ con** to rival, compete with.
rizado, a [ri'θaðo, a] *adj* (*pelo*) curly; (*superficie*) ridged; (*terreno*) undulating; (*mar*) choppy ♦ *nm* curls *pl*.
rizar [ri'θar] *vt* to curl; **~se** *vr* (*el pelo*) to curl; (*agua*) to ripple; (*el mar*) to become choppy.
rizo ['riθo] *nm* curl; (*agua*) ripple.
Rma. *abr* (= *Reverendísima*) courtesy title.
Rmo. *abr* (= *Reverendísimo*) Rt. Rev.
RNE *nf abr* = *Radio Nacional de España*.
R. O. *abr* (= *Real Orden*) royal order.

robar [ro'βar] *vt* to rob; (*objeto*) to steal; (*casa etc*) to break into; (*NAIPES*) to draw; (*atención*) to steal, capture; (*paciencia*) to exhaust.
roble ['roβle] *nm* oak.
robledal [roβle'ðal], **robledo** [ro'βleðo] *nm* oakwood.
robo ['roβo] *nm* robbery, theft; (*objeto robado*) stolen article *o* goods *pl*; **¡esto es un ~!** this is daylight robbery!
robot [ro'βo(t)], *pl* **robots** *adj*, *nm* robot ♦ *nm* (*tb*: **~ de cocina**) food processor.
robótica [ro'βotika] *nf* robotics *sg*.
robustecer [roβuste'θer] *vt* to strengthen.
robustezca [roβus'teθka] *etc vb V* **robustecer**.
robusto, a [ro'βusto, a] *adj* robust, strong.
ROC *abr* (*INFORM*: = *reconocimiento óptico de caracteres*) OCR.
roca ['roka] *nf* rock; **la R~** the Rock (of Gibraltar).
roce ['roθe] *etc vb V* **rozar** ♦ *nm* rub, rubbing; (*caricia*) brush; (*TEC*) friction; (*en la piel*) graze; **tener ~ con** to have a brush with.
rociar [ro'θjar] *vt* to sprinkle, spray.
rocín [ro'θin] *nm* nag, hack.
rocío [ro'θio] *nm* dew.
rock [rok] *adj inv, nm* (*MUS*) rock (*cpd*).
rockero, a [ro'kero, a] *adj* rock *cpd* ♦ *nm/f* rocker.
rocoso, a [ro'koso, a] *adj* rocky.
rodado, a [ro'ðaðo, a] *adj* (*con ruedas*) wheeled ♦ *nf* rut.
rodaja [ro'ðaxa] *nf* (*raja*) slice.
rodaje [ro'ðaxe] *nm* (*CINE*) shooting, filming; (*AUTO*): **en ~** running in.
rodamiento [roða'mjento] *nm* (*AUTO*) tread.
Ródano ['roðano] *nm* Rhône.
rodar [ro'ðar] *vt* (*vehículo*) to wheel (along); (*escalera*) to roll down; (*viajar por*) to travel (over) ♦ *vi* to roll; (*coche*) to go, run; (*CINE*) to shoot, film; (*persona*) to move about (from place to place), drift; **echarlo todo a ~** (*fig*) to mess it all up.
Rodas ['roðas] *nf* Rhodes.
rodear [roðe'ar] *vt* to surround ♦ *vi* to go round; **~se** *vr*: **~se de amigos** to surround o.s. with friends.
rodeo [ro'ðeo] *nm* (*ruta indirecta*) long way round, roundabout way; (*desvío*) detour; (*evasión*) evasion; (*AM*) rodeo; **dejarse de ~s** to talk straight; **hablar sin ~s** to come to the point, speak plainly.
rodilla [ro'ðiʎa] *nf* knee; **de ~s** kneeling.
rodillo [ro'ðiʎo] *nm* roller; (*CULIN*) rolling-pin; (*en máquina de escribir, impresora*)

platen.
rododendro [roðo'ðendro] *nm*
rhododendron.
roedor, a [roe'ðor, a] *adj* gnawing ♦ *nm*
rodent.
roer [ro'er] *vt* (*masticar*) to gnaw; (*corroer,
fig*) to corrode.
rogar [ro'ɣar] *vt* (*pedir*) to beg, ask for ♦ *vi*
(*suplicar*) to beg, plead; **~se** *vr*: **se ruega
no fumar** please do not smoke; **~ que**
+ *subjun* to ask to ...; **ruegue a este señor
que nos deje en paz** please ask this
gentleman to leave us alone; **no se hace
de ~** he doesn't have to be asked twice.
rogué [ro'ɣe], **roguemos** [ro'ɣemos] *etc
vb V* **rogar**.
rojizo, a [ro'xiθo, a] *adj* reddish.
rojo, a ['roxo, a] *adj* red ♦ *nm* red (colour);
(*POL*) red; **ponerse ~** to turn red, blush;
al ~ vivo red-hot.
rol [rol] *nm* list, roll; (*esp AM: papel*) role.
rollizo, a [ro'ʎiθo, a] *adj* (*objeto*)
cylindrical; (*persona*) plump.
rollo, a ['roʎo, a] *adj* (*fam*) boring, tedious
♦ *nm* roll; (*de cuerda*) coil; (*madera*) log;
(*fam*) bore; (*discurso*) boring speech;
¡qué ~! what a carry-on!; **la conferencia
fue un ~** the lecture was a big drag.
ROM [rom] *nf abr* (= *memoria de sólo
lectura*) ROM.
Roma ['roma] *nf* Rome; **por todas partes se
va a ~** all roads lead to Rome.
romance [ro'manθe] *nm* (*LING*) Romance
language; (*LIT*) ballad; **hablar en ~** to
speak plainly.
románico, a [ro'maniko, a] *adj, nm*
Romanesque.
romano, a [ro'mano, a] *adj* Roman, of
Rome ♦ *nm/f* Roman.
romanticismo [romanti'θismo] *nm*
romanticism.
romántico, a [ro'mantiko, a] *adj* romantic.
rombo ['rombo] *nm* (*GEOM*) rhombus;
(*diseño*) diamond; (*TIP*) lozenge.
romería [rome'ria] *nf* (*REL*) pilgrimage;
(*excursión*) trip, outing.

*Originally a pilgrimage to a shrine or
church to express devotion to Our Lady or
a local Saint, the* **romería** *has also become
a rural fiesta which accompanies the
pilgrimage. People come from all over to
attend, bringing their own food and drink,
and spend the day in celebration.*

romero, a [ro'mero, a] *nm/f* pilgrim ♦ *nm*
rosemary.
romo, a ['romo, a] *adj* blunt; (*fig*) dull.

rompecabezas [rompeka'βeθas] *nm inv*
riddle, puzzle; (*juego*) jigsaw (puzzle).
rompehielos [rompe'jelos] *nm inv*
icebreaker.
rompeolas [rompe'olas] *nm inv*
breakwater.
romper [rom'per] *vt* to break; (*hacer
pedazos*) to smash; (*papel, tela etc*) to
tear, rip; (*relaciones*) to break off ♦ *vi*
(*olas*) to break; (*sol, diente*) to break
through; **~ un contrato** to break a
contract; **~ a** to start (suddenly) to; **~ a
llorar** to burst into tears; **~ con algn** to
fall out with sb; **ha roto con su novio** she
has broken up with her fiancé.
rompimiento [rompi'mjento] *nm* (*acto*)
breaking; (*fig*) break; (*quiebra*) crack; **~
de relaciones** breaking off of relations.
ron [ron] *nm* rum.
roncar [ron'kar] *vi* (*al dormir*) to snore;
(*animal*) to roar.
roncha ['rontʃa] *nf* (*cardenal*) bruise;
(*hinchazón*) swelling.
ronco, a ['ronko, a] *adj* (*afónico*) hoarse;
(*áspero*) raucous.
ronda ['ronda] *nf* (*de bebidas etc*) round;
(*patrulla*) patrol; (*de naipes*) hand, game;
ir de ~ to do one's round.
rondar [ron'dar] *vt* to patrol; (*a una
persona*) to hang round; (*molestar*) to
harass; (*a una chica*) to court ♦ *vi* to
patrol; (*fig*) to prowl round; (*MUS*) to go
serenading.
rondeño, a [ron'deɲo, a] *adj* of o from
Ronda ♦ *nm/f* native o inhabitant of
Ronda.
ronque ['ronke] *etc vb V* **roncar**.
ronquera [ron'kera] *nf* hoarseness.
ronquido [ron'kiðo] *nm* snore, snoring.
ronronear [ronrone'ar] *vi* to purr.
ronroneo [ronro'neo] *nm* purr.
roña ['roɲa] *nf* (*veterinaria*) mange; (*mugre*)
dirt, grime; (*óxido*) rust.
roñica [ro'ɲika] *nm/f* (*fam*) skinflint.
roñoso, a [ro'ɲoso, a] *adj* (*mugriento*)
filthy; (*tacaño*) mean.
ropa ['ropa] *nf* clothes *pl*, clothing; **~
blanca** linen; **~ de cama** bed linen; **~
interior** underwear; **~ lavada** o **para
lavar** washing; **~ planchada** ironing; **~
sucia** dirty clothes *pl*, washing; **~ usada**
secondhand clothes.
ropaje [ro'paxe] *nm* gown, robes *pl*.
ropero [ro'pero] *nm* linen cupboard;
(*guardarropa*) wardrobe.
roque ['roke] *nm* (*AJEDREZ*) rook, castle;
estar ~ to be fast asleep.
rosa ['rosa] *adj inv* pink ♦ *nf* rose; (*ANAT*)

red birthmark; ~ **de los vientos** the compass; **estar como una** ~ to feel as fresh as a daisy; **(color) de** ~ pink.

rosado, a [ro'saðo, a] *adj* pink ♦ *nm* rosé.

rosal [ro'sal] *nm* rosebush.

rosaleda [rosa'leða] *nf* rose bed *o* garden.

rosario [ro'sarjo] *nm* (REL) rosary; (*fig: serie*) string; **rezar el** ~ to say the rosary.

rosbif [ros'ßif] *nm* roast beef.

rosca ['roska] *nf* (*de tornillo*) thread; (*de humo*) coil, spiral; (*pan, postre*) ring-shaped roll/pastry; **hacer la** ~ **a algn** (*fam*) to suck up to sb; **pasarse de** ~ (*fig*) to go too far.

Rosellón [rose'ʎon] *nm* Roussillon.

rosetón [rose'ton] *nm* rosette; (ARQ) rose window.

rosquilla [ros'kiʎa] *nf* small ring-shaped cake; (*de humo*) ring.

rosticería [rostise'ria] *nf* (AM) roast chicken shop.

rostro ['rostro] *nm* (*cara*) face; (*fig*) cheek.

rotación [rota'θjon] *nf* rotation; ~ **de cultivos** crop rotation.

rotativo, a [rota'tiβo, a] *adj* rotary ♦ *nm* newspaper.

roto, a ['roto, a] *pp de* **romper** ♦ *adj* broken; (*en pedazos*) smashed; (*tela, papel*) torn; (*vida*) shattered ♦ *nm* (*en vestido*) hole, tear.

rótula ['rotula] *nf* kneecap; (TEC) ball-and-socket joint.

rotulador [rotula'ðor] *nm* felt-tip pen.

rotular [rotu'lar] *vt* (*carta, documento*) to head, entitle; (*objeto*) to label.

rótulo ['rotulo] *nm* (*título*) heading, title; (*etiqueta*) label; (*letrero*) sign.

rotundo, a [ro'tundo, a] *adj* round; (*enfático*) emphatic.

rotura [ro'tura] *nf* (*rompimiento*) breaking; (MED) fracture.

roturar [rotu'rar] *vt* to plough.

roulote [ru'lote] *nf* caravan (BRIT), trailer (US).

rozado, a [ro'θaðo, a] *adj* worn.

rozadura [roθa'ðura] *nf* abrasion, graze.

rozar [ro'θar] *vt* (*frotar*) to rub; (*ensuciar*) to dirty; (MED) to graze; (*tocar ligeramente*) to shave, skim; (*fig*) to touch *o* border on; ~**se** *vr* to rub (together); ~ **con** (*fam*) to rub shoulders with.

Rte. *abr* = **remite, remitente.**

RTVE *nf abr* (TV) = **Radiotelevisión Española.**

Ruán [ru'an] *nm* Rouen.

rubéola [ru'ßeola] *nf* German measles, rubella.

rubí [ru'ßi] *nm* ruby; (*de reloj*) jewel.

rubio, a ['rußjo, a] *adj* fair-haired, blond(e)

♦ *nm/f* blond/blonde; **tabaco** ~ Virginia tobacco; (*cerveza*) **rubia** lager.

rubor [ru'ßor] *nm* (*sonrojo*) blush; (*timidez*) bashfulness.

ruborice [rußo'riθe] *etc vb V* **ruborizarse.**

ruborizarse [rußori'θarse] *vr* to blush.

ruboroso, a [rußo'roso, a] *adj* blushing.

rúbrica ['rußrika] *nf* (*título*) title, heading; (*de la firma*) flourish; **bajo la** ~ **de** under the heading of.

rubricar [rußri'kar] *vt* (*firmar*) to sign with a flourish; (*concluir*) to sign and seal.

rubrique [ru'ßrike] *etc vb V* **rubricar.**

rudeza [ru'ðeθa] *nf* (*tosquedad*) coarseness; (*sencillez*) simplicity.

rudimentario, a [ruðimen'tarjo, a] *adj* rudimentary, basic.

rudo, a ['ruðo, a] *adj* (*sin pulir*) unpolished; (*grosero*) coarse; (*violento*) violent; (*sencillo*) simple.

rueda ['rweða] *nf* wheel; (*círculo*) ring, circle; (*rodaja*) slice, round; (*en impresora etc*) sprocket; ~ **delantera/trasera/de repuesto** front/back/spare wheel; ~ **impresora** (INFORM) print wheel; ~ **de prensa** press conference.

ruedo ['rweðo] *etc vb V* **rodar** ♦ *nm* (*contorno*) edge, border; (*de vestido*) hem; (*círculo*) circle; (TAUR) arena, bullring; (*esterilla*) (round) mat.

ruego ['rweɣo] *etc vb V* **rogar** ♦ *nm* request; **a** ~ **de** at the request of; **"~s y preguntas"** "question and answer session".

ruegue ['rweɣe] *etc vb V* **rogar.**

rufián [ru'fjan] *nm* scoundrel.

rugby ['ruɣßi] *nm* rugby.

rugido [ru'xiðo] *nm* roar.

rugir [ru'xir] *vi* to roar; (*toro*) to bellow; (*estómago*) to rumble.

rugoso, a [ru'ɣoso, a] *adj* (*arrugado*) wrinkled; (*áspero*) rough; (*desigual*) ridged.

ruibarbo [rwi'ßarßo] *nm* rhubarb.

ruido ['rwiðo] *nm* noise; (*sonido*) sound; (*alboroto*) racket, row; (*escándalo*) commotion, rumpus; ~ **de fondo** background noise; **hacer** *o* **meter** ~ to cause a stir.

ruidoso, a [rwi'ðoso, a] *adj* noisy, loud; (*fig*) sensational.

ruin [rwin] *adj* contemptible, mean.

ruina ['rwina] *nf* ruin; (*colapso*) collapse; (*de persona*) ruin, downfall; **estar hecho una** ~ to be a wreck; **la empresa le llevó a la** ~ the venture ruined him (financially).

ruindad [rwin'dað] *nf* lowness, meanness;

(_acto_) low o mean act.
ruinoso, a [rwi'noso, a] _adj_ ruinous;
(_destartalado_) dilapidated, tumbledown;
(_COM_) disastrous.
ruiseñor [rwise'nor] _nm_ nightingale.
ruja ['ruxa] _etc vb V_ **rugir.**
ruleta [ru'leta] _nf_ roulette.
rulo ['rulo] _nm_ (_para el pelo_) curler.
rulot(e) [ru'lot(e)] _nf_ caravan (_BRIT_), trailer
(_US_).
Rumania [ru'manja] _nf_ Rumania.
rumano, a [ru'mano, a] _adj, nm/f_ Rumanian.
rumba ['rumba] _nf_ rumba.
rumbo ['rumbo] _nm_ (_ruta_) route, direction;
(_ángulo de dirección_) course, bearing;
(_fig_) course of events; **con ~ a** in the
direction of; **ir con ~ a** to be heading
for; (_NAUT_) to be bound for.
rumboso, a [rum'boso, a] _adj_ (_generoso_)
generous.
rumiante [ru'mjante] _nm_ ruminant.
rumiar [ru'mjar] _vt_ to chew; (_fig_) to chew
over ♦ _vi_ to chew the cud.
rumor [ru'mor] _nm_ (_ruido sordo_) low sound;
(_murmuración_) murmur, buzz.
rumorearse [rumore'arse] _vr_: **se rumorea
que** it is rumoured that.
rumoroso, a [rumo'roso, a] _adj_ full of
sounds; (_arroyo_) murmuring.
runrún [run'run] _nm_ (_voces_) murmur,
sound of voices; (_fig_) rumour; (_de una
máquina_) whirr.
rupestre [ru'pestre] _adj_ rock _cpd_; **pintura ~**
cave painting.
ruptura [rup'tura] _nf_ (_gen_) rupture;
(_disputa_) split; (_de contrato_) breach; (_de
relaciones_) breaking-off.
rural [ru'ral] _adj_ rural.
Rusia ['rusja] _nf_ Russia.
ruso, a ['ruso, a] _adj, nm/f_ Russian ♦ _nm_
(_LING_) Russian.
rústico, a ['rustiko, a] _adj_ rustic; (_ordinario_)
coarse, uncouth ♦ _nm/f_ yokel ♦ _nf_: **libro en
rústica** paperback (book).
ruta ['ruta] _nf_ route.
rutina [ru'tina] _nf_ routine; **~ diaria** daily
routine; **por ~** as a matter of course.
rutinario, a [ruti'narjo, a] _adj_ routine.

S s

S, s ['ese] _nf_ S, s; **S de Sábado** S for Sugar.
S _abr_ (= _san, santo, a_) St.; (= _sur_) S.
s. _abr_ (= _siglo_) c.; (= _siguiente_) foll.
s/ _abr_ (_COM_) = **su(s).**
S.ª _abr_ (= _Sierra_) Mts.
S.A. _abr_ (= _Sociedad Anónima_) Ltd., Inc.
(_US_); (= _Su Alteza_) H.H.
sáb. _abr_ (= _sábado_) Sun.
sábado ['saβaðo] _nm_ Saturday; (_de los
judíos_) Sabbath; **del ~ en ocho días** a
week on Saturday; **un ~ sí y otro no,
cada dos ~s** every other Saturday; **S~
Santo** Holy Saturday; _V tb_ **Semana
Santa.**
sabana [sa'βana] _nf_ savannah.
sábana ['saβana] _nf_ sheet; **se le pegan las
~s** he can't get up in the morning.
sabandija [saβan'dixa] _nf_ (_bicho_) bug; (_fig_)
louse.
sabañón [saβa'non] _nm_ chilblain.
sabático, a [sa'βatiko, a] _adj_ (_REL, UNIV_)
sabbatical.
sabelotodo [saβelo'toðo] _nm/f inv_ know-all.
saber [sa'βer] _vt_ to know; (_llegar a conocer_)
to find out, learn; (_tener capacidad de_) to
know how to ♦ _vi_: **~ a** to taste of, taste
like ♦ _nm_ knowledge, learning; **~se** _vr_: **se
sabe que ...** it is known that ...; **no se
sabe** nobody knows; **a ~** namely; **¿sabes
conducir/nadar?** can you drive/swim?;
¿sabes francés? do you o can you speak
French?; **~ de memoria** to know by
heart; **lo sé** I know; **hacer ~** to inform,
let know; **que yo sepa** as far as I know;
vete o **anda a ~** your guess is as good as
mine, who knows!; **¿sabe?** (_fam_) you
know (what I mean)?; **le sabe mal que
otro la saque a bailar** it upsets him that
anybody else should ask her to dance.
sabido, a [sa'βiðo, a] _adj_ (_consabido_) well-
known; **como es ~** as we all know.
sabiduría [saβiðu'ria] _nf_ (_conocimientos_)
wisdom; (_instrucción_) learning; **~ popular**
folklore.
sabiendas [sa'βjendas]: **a ~** _adv_
knowingly; **a ~ de que ...** knowing full
well that ....
sabihondo, a [sa'βjondo, a] _adj, nm/f_

know-all, know-it-all (*US*).

sabio, a ['saβjo,a] *adj* (*docto*) learned; (*prudente*) wise, sensible.

sablazo [sa'βlaθo] *nm* (*herida*) sword wound; (*fam*) sponging; **dar un ~ a algn** to tap sb for money.

sable [sa'βle] *nm* sabre.

sabor [sa'βor] *nm* taste, flavour; (*fig*) flavour; **sin ~** flavourless.

saborear [saβore'ar] *vt* to taste, savour; (*fig*) to relish.

sabotaje [saβo'taxe] *nm* sabotage.

saboteador, a [saβotea'ðor, a] *nm/f* saboteur.

sabotear [saβote'ar] *vt* to sabotage.

Saboya [sa'βoja] *nf* Savoy.

sabré [sa'βre] *etc vb V* **saber.**

sabroso, a [sa'βroso, a] *adj* tasty; (*fig fam*) racy, salty.

saca ['saka] *nf* big sack; **~ de correo(s)** mailbag; (*COM*) withdrawal.

sacacorchos [saka'kortʃos] *nm inv* corkscrew.

sacapuntas [saka'puntas] *nm inv* pencil sharpener.

sacar [sa'kar] *vt* to take out; (*fig: extraer*) to get (out); (*quitar*) to remove, get out; (*hacer salir*) to bring out; (*fondos: de cuenta*) to draw out, withdraw; (*obtener: legado etc*) to get; (*demostrar*) to show; (*conclusión*) to draw; (*novela etc*) to publish, bring out; (*ropa*) to take off; (*obra*) to make; (*premio*) to receive; (*entradas*) to get; (*TENIS*) to serve; (*FÚTBOL*) to put into play; **~ adelante** (*niño*) to bring up; **~ a algn a bailar** to dance with sb; **~ a algn de sí** to infuriate sb; **~ una foto** to take a photo; **~ la lengua** to stick out one's tongue; **~ buenas/malas notas** to get good/bad marks.

sacarina [saka'rina] *nf* saccharin(e).

sacerdote [saθer'ðote] *nm* priest.

saciar [sa'θjar] *vt* (*hartar*) to satiate; (*fig*) to satisfy; **~se** *vr* (*fig*) to be satisfied.

saciedad [saθje'ðað] *nf* satiety; **hasta la ~** (*comer*) one's fill; (*repetir*) ad nauseam.

saco ['sako] *nm* bag; (*grande*) sack; (*su contenido*) bagful; (*AM: chaqueta*) jacket; **~ de dormir** sleeping bag.

sacramento [sakra'mento] *nm* sacrament.

sacrificar [sakrifi'kar] *vt* to sacrifice; (*animal*) to slaughter; (*perro etc*) to put to sleep; **~se** *vr* to sacrifice o.s.

sacrificio [sakri'fiθjo] *nm* sacrifice.

sacrifique [sakri'fike] *etc vb V* **sacrificar.**

sacrilegio [sakri'lexjo] *nm* sacrilege.

sacrílego, a [sa'krileɣo, a] *adj* sacrilegious.

sacristán [sakris'tan] *nm* verger.

sacristía [sakris'tia] *nf* sacristy.

sacro, a ['sakro, a] *adj* sacred.

sacudida [saku'ðiða] *nf* (*agitación*) shake, shaking; (*sacudimiento*) jolt, bump; (*fig*) violent change; (*POL etc*) upheaval; **~ eléctrica** electric shock.

sacudir [saku'ðir] *vt* to shake; (*golpear*) to hit; (*ala*) to flap; (*alfombra*) to beat; **~ a algn** (*fam*) to belt sb.

sádico, a ['saðiko, a] *adj* sadistic ♦ *nm/f* sadist.

sadismo [sa'ðismo] *nm* sadism.

sadomasoquismo [saðomaso'kismo] *nm* sadomasochism, S & M.

sadomasoquista [saðomaso'kista] *adj* sadomasochistic ♦ *nm/f* sadomasochist.

saeta [sa'eta] *nf* (*flecha*) arrow; (*MUS*) *sacred song in flamenco style.*

safari [sa'fari] *nm* safari.

sagacidad [saɣaθi'ðað] *nf* shrewdness, cleverness.

sagaz [sa'ɣaθ] *adj* shrewd, clever.

Sagitario [saxi'tarjo] *nm* (*ASTRO*) Sagittarius.

sagrado, a [sa'ɣraðo, a] *adj* sacred, holy.

Sáhara ['saara] *nm*: **el ~** the Sahara (desert).

saharaui [saxa'rawi] *adj* Saharan ♦ *nm/f* native *o* inhabitant of the Sahara.

sajón, ona [sa'xon, 'xona] *adj, nm/f* Saxon.

Sajonia [sa'xonja] *nf* Saxony.

sal [sal] *vb ver* **salir** ♦ *nf* salt; (*gracia*) wit; (*encanto*) charm; **~es de baño** bath salts; **~ gorda** *o* **de cocina** kitchen *o* cooking salt.

sala ['sala] *nf* (*cuarto grande*) large room; (**~ de estar**) living room; (*TEAT*) house, auditorium; (*de hospital*) ward; **~ de apelación** court; **~ de conferencias** lecture hall; **~ de espera** waiting room; **~ de embarque** departure lounge; **~ de estar** living room; **~ de fiestas** function room; **~ de juntas** (*COM*) boardroom.

salado, a [sa'laðo, a] *adj* salty; (*fig*) witty, amusing; **agua salada** salt water.

salar [sa'lar] *vt* to salt, add salt to.

salarial [sala'rjal] *adj* (*aumento, revisión*) wage *cpd*, salary *cpd*, pay *cpd*.

salario [sa'larjo] *nm* wage, pay.

salchicha [sal'tʃitʃa] *nf* (pork) sausage.

salchichón [saltʃi'tʃon] *nm* (salami-type) sausage.

saldar [sal'dar] *vt* to pay; (*vender*) to sell off; (*fig*) to settle, resolve.

saldo ['saldo] *nm* (*pago*) settlement; (*de una cuenta*) balance; (*lo restante*) remnant(s) (*pl*), remainder; (*liquidación*)

sale; (*COM*): ~ **anterior** balance brought forward; ~ **acreedor/deudor** *o* **pasivo** credit/debit balance; ~ **final** final balance.
saldré [sal'dre] *etc vb V* **salir**.
salero [sa'lero] *nm* salt cellar; (*ingenio*) wit; (*encanto*) charm.
salga ['salɣa] *etc vb V* **salir**.
salida [sa'liða] *nf* (*puerta etc*) exit, way out; (*acto*) leaving, going out; (*de tren*, *AVIAT*) departure; (*COM*, *TEC*) output, production; (*fig*) way out; (*resultado*) outcome; (*COM: oportunidad*) opening; (*GEO*, *válvula*) outlet; (*de gas*) escape; (*ocurrencia*) joke; **calle sin ~** cul-de-sac; **a la ~ del teatro** after the theatre; **dar la ~** (*DEPORTE*) to give the starting signal; ~ **de incendios** fire escape; ~ **impresa** (*INFORM*) hard copy; **no hay ~** there's no way out of it; **no tenemos otra ~** we have no option; **tener ~s** to be witty.
salido, a [sa'liðo, a] *adj* (*fam*) randy.
saliente [sa'ljente] *adj* (*ARQ*) projecting; (*sol*) rising; (*fig*) outstanding.
salina [sa'lina] *nf* salt mine; ~**s** *nfpl* saltworks *sg*.

===== *PALABRA CLAVE* =====

salir [sa'lir] *vi* **1** (*persona*) to come *o* go out; (*tren*, *avión*) to leave; **Juan ha salido** Juan has gone out; **salió de la cocina** he came out of the kitchen; **salimos de Madrid a las 8** we left Madrid at 8 (o'clock); **salió corriendo (del cuarto)** he ran out (of the room); ~ **de un apuro** to get out of a jam
2 (*pelo*) to grow; (*diente*) to come through; (*disco, libro*) to come out; (*planta, número de lotería*) to come up; ~ **a la superficie** to come to the surface; **anoche salió en la tele** she appeared *o* was on TV last night; **salió en todos los periódicos** it was in all the papers; **le salió un trabajo** he got a job
3 (*resultar*): **la muchacha nos salió muy trabajadora** the girl turned out to be a very hard worker; **la comida te ha salido exquisita** the food was delicious; **sale muy caro** it's very expensive; **la entrevista que hice me salió bien/mal** the interview I did turned out *o* went well/badly; **nos salió a 5.000 ptas cada uno** it worked out at 5,000 pesetas each; **no salen las cuentas** it doesn't work out *o* add up; ~ **ganando** to come out on top; ~ **perdiendo** to lose out
4 (*DEPORTE*) to start; (*NAIPES*) to lead
5: ~ **con algn** to go out with sb
6: ~ **adelante: no sé como haré para ~**

♦ ~**se** *vr* **1** (*líquido*) to spill; (*animal*) to escape
2 (*desviarse*): ~**se de la carretera** to leave *o* go off the road; ~**se de lo normal** to be unusual; ~**se del tema** to get off the point
3: ~**se con la suya** to get one's own way

saliva [sa'liβa] *nf* saliva.
salivadera [saliβa'ðera] *nf* (*AM*) spittoon.
salmantino, a [salman'tino, a] *adj* of *o* from Salamanca ♦ *nm/f* native *o* inhabitant of Salamanca.
salmo ['salmo] *nm* psalm.
salmón [sal'mon] *nm* salmon.
salmonete [salmo'nete] *nm* red mullet.
salmuera [sal'mwera] *nf* pickle, brine.
salón [sa'lon] *nm* (*de casa*) living-room, lounge; (*muebles*) lounge suite; ~ **de belleza** beauty parlour; ~ **de baile** dance hall; ~ **de sesiones** assembly hall.
salpicadero [salpika'ðero] *nm* (*AUTO*) dashboard.
salpicar [salpi'kar] *vt* (*de barro, pintura*) to splash; (*rociar*) to sprinkle, spatter; (*esparcir*) to scatter.
salpicón [salpi'kon] *nm* (*acto*) splashing; (*CULIN*) meat *o* fish salad.
salpimentar [salpimen'tar] *vt* (*CULIN*) to season.
salpique [sal'pike] *etc vb V* **salpicar**.
salsa ['salsa] *nf* sauce; (*con carne asada*) gravy; (*fig*) spice; ~ **mayonesa** mayonnaise; **estar en su ~** (*fam*) to be in one's element.
saltamontes [salta'montes] *nm inv* grasshopper.
saltar [sal'tar] *vt* to jump (over), leap (over); (*dejar de lado*) to skip, miss out ♦ *vi* to jump, leap; (*pelota*) to bounce; (*al aire*) to fly up; (*quebrarse*) to break; (*al agua*) to dive; (*fig*) to explode, blow up; (*botón*) to come off; (*corcho*) to pop out; ~**se** *vr* (*omitir*) to skip, miss; **salta a la vista** it's obvious; ~**se todas las reglas** to break all the rules.
salteado, a [salte'aðo, a] *adj* (*CULIN*) sauté(ed).
salteador [saltea'ðor] *nm* (*tb*: ~ **de caminos**) highwayman.
saltear [salte'ar] *vt* (*robar*) to rob (in a holdup); (*asaltar*) to assault, attack; (*CULIN*) to sauté.
saltimbanqui [saltim'banki] *nm/f* acrobat.
salto ['salto] *nm* jump, leap; (*al agua*) dive; **a ~s** by jumping; ~ **de agua** waterfall; ~ **de altura** high jump; ~ **de cama**

negligee; ~ **mortal** somersault;
(*INFORM*): ~ **de línea** line feed; ~ **de línea**
automático wordwrap; ~ **de página**
formfeed.

saltón, ona [sal'ton, ona] *adj* (*ojos*)
bulging, popping; (*dientes*) protruding.

salubre [sa'luβre] *adj* healthy, salubrious.

salud [sa'luð] *nf* health; **estar bien/mal de**
~ to be in good/poor health; **¡(a su) ~!**
cheers!, good health!; **beber a la ~ de** to
drink (to) the health of.

saludable [salu'ðaβle] *adj* (*de buena salud*)
healthy; (*provechoso*) good, beneficial.

saludar [salu'ðar] *vt* to greet; (*MIL*) to
salute; **ir a ~ a algn** to drop in to see sb;
salude de mi parte a X give my regards
to X; **le saluda atentamente** (*en carta*)
yours faithfully.

saludo [sa'luðo] *nm* greeting; ~**s** (*en carta*)
best wishes, regards; **un ~ afectuoso** o
cordial yours sincerely.

salva ['salβa] *nf* (*MIL*) salvo; **una ~ de**
aplausos thunderous applause.

salvación [salβa'θjon] *nf* salvation;
(*rescate*) rescue.

salvado [sal'βaðo] *nm* bran.

salvador [salβa'ðor] *nm* rescuer, saviour;
el S~ the Saviour; **El S~** El Salvador;
San S~ San Salvador.

salvadoreño, a [salβaðo'reɲo, a] *adj, nm/f*
Salvadoran, Salvadorian.

salvaguardar [salβaɣwar'ðar] *vt* to
safeguard; (*INFORM*) to back up, make a
backup copy of.

salvajada [salβa'xaða] *nf* savage deed,
atrocity.

salvaje [sal'βaxe] *adj* wild; (*tribu*) savage.

salvajismo [salβa'xismo] *nm* savagery.

salvamento [salβa'mento] *nm* (*acción*)
rescue; (*de naufragio*) salvage; ~ **y**
socorrismo life-saving.

salvar [sal'βar] *vt* (*rescatar*) to save, rescue;
(*resolver*) to overcome, resolve; (*cubrir*
distancias) to cover, travel; (*hacer*
excepción) to except, exclude; (*un barco*)
to salvage; ~**se** *vr* to save o.s., escape;
¡sálvese el que pueda! every man for
himself!

salvavidas [salβa'βiðas] *adj inv*: **bote/**
chaleco/cinturón ~ lifeboat/lifejacket/
lifebelt.

salvedad [salβe'ðað] *nf* reservation,
qualification; **con la ~ de que ...** with the
proviso that ....

salvia ['salβja] *nf* sage.

salvo, a ['salβo, a] *adj* safe ♦ *prep* except
(for), save; ~ **error u omisión** (*COM*)
errors and omissions excepted; **a ~ out**

of danger; ~ **que** unless.

salvoconducto [salβokon'dukto] *nm* safe-
conduct.

samba ['samba] *nf* samba.

san [san] *nm* (*apócope de* **santo**) saint; ~
Juan St. John; V tb **Juan**.

sanar [sa'nar] *vt* (*herida*) to heal; (*persona*)
to cure ♦ *vi* (*persona*) to get well,
recover; (*herida*) to heal.

sanatorio [sana'torjo] *nm* sanatorium.

sanción [san'θjon] *nf* sanction.

sancionar [sanθjo'nar] *vt* to sanction.

sancocho [san'kotʃo] *nm* (*AM*) stew.

sandalia [san'dalja] *nf* sandal.

sándalo ['sandalo] *nm* sandal(wood).

sandez [san'deθ] *nf* (*cualidad*) foolishness;
(*acción*) stupid thing; **decir sandeces** to
talk nonsense.

sandía [san'dia] *nf* watermelon.

sandinista [sanði'nista] *adj, nm/f*
Sandinist(a).

sandwich ['sandwitʃ], *pl* **sandwichs** o
sandwiches *nm* sandwich.

saneamiento [sanea'mjento] *nm*
sanitation.

sanear [sane'ar] *vt* to drain; (*indemnizar*) to
compensate; (*ECON*) to reorganize.

The **Sanfermines** *are a week of fiestas in
Pamplona, the capital of Navarre, made
famous by Ernest Hemingway. From the
7th of July, the feast of* **San Fermín**, *crowds
of mainly young people take to the streets
drinking, singing and dancing. Early in the
morning bulls are released along the
narrow streets leading to the bullring, and
people risk serious injury by running out in
front of them, a custom which is also
typical of many Spanish villages.*

---

sangrante [san'grante] *adj* (*herida*)
bleeding; (*fig*) flagrant.

sangrar [san'grar] *vt, vi* to bleed; (*texto*) to
indent.

sangre ['sangre] *nf* blood; ~ **fría** sangfroid;
a ~ fría in cold blood.

sangría [san'gria] *nf* (*MED*) bleeding;
(*CULIN*) sangria, *sweetened drink of red
wine with fruit,* ≈ fruit cup.

sangriento, a [san'grjento, a] *adj* bloody.

sanguijuela [sangi'xwela] *nf* (*ZOOL, fig*)
leech.

sanguinario, a [sangi'narjo, a] *adj*
bloodthirsty.

sanguíneo, a [san'gineo, a] *adj* blood *cpd*.

sanguinolento, a [sangino'lento, a] *adj*
(*que echa sangre*) bleeding; (*manchado*)
bloodstained; (*ojos*) bloodshot.

sanidad [sani'ðað] *nf* sanitation; (*calidad de sano*) health, healthiness; ~ **pública** public health (department).

sanitario, a [sani'tarjo, a] *adj* sanitary; (*de la salud*) health *cpd* ♦ *nm*: ~**s** *nmpl* toilets (*BRIT*), restroom *sg* (*US*).

San Marino [sanma'rino] *nm*: (**La República de**) ~ San Marino.

sano, a ['sano, a] *adj* healthy; (*sin daños*) sound; (*comida*) wholesome; (*entero*) whole, intact; ~ **y salvo** safe and sound.

santanderino, a [santande'rino, a] *adj* of o from Santander ♦ *nm/f* native o inhabitant of Santander.

Santiago [san'tjaɣo] *nm*: ~ (**de Chile**) Santiago.

santiamén [santja'men] *nm*: **en un** ~ in no time at all.

santidad [santi'ðað] *nf* holiness, sanctity.

santificar [santifi'kar] *vt* to sanctify, make holy.

santifique [santi'fike] *etc vb V* **santificar**.

santiguarse [santi'ɣwarse] *vr* to make the sign of the cross.

santigüe [san'tiɣwe] *etc vb V* **santiguarse**.

santo, a ['santo, a] *adj* holy; (*fig*) wonderful, miraculous ♦ *nm/f* saint ♦ *nm* saint's day; **hacer su santa voluntad** to do as one jolly well pleases; **¿a ~ de qué ...?** why on earth ...?; **se le fue el ~ al cielo** he forgot what he was about to say; ~ **y seña** password.

> As well as celebrating their birthday Spaniards have traditionally celebrated **el santo**, their Saint's day, when the Saint they were called after at birth, eg San **Pedro** or la Virgen de los **Dolores**, is honoured in the Christian calendar. This is a custom which is gradually dying out.

santuario [san'twarjo] *nm* sanctuary, shrine.

saña ['saɲa] *nf* rage, fury.

sapo ['sapo] *nm* toad.

saque ['sake] *etc vb V* **sacar** ♦ *nm* (*TENIS*) service, serve; (*FÚTBOL*) throw-in; ~ **inicial** kick-off; ~ **de esquina** corner (kick); **tener buen** ~ to eat heartily.

saquear [sake'ar] *vt* (*MIL*) to sack; (*robar*) to loot, plunder; (*fig*) to ransack.

saqueo [sa'keo] *nm* sacking; looting, plundering; ransacking.

S.A.R. *abr* (= *Su Alteza Real*) HRH.

sarampión [saram'pjon] *nm* measles *sg*.

sarape [sa'rape] *nm* (*AM*) blanket.

sarcasmo [sar'kasmo] *nm* sarcasm.

sarcástico, a [sar'kastiko, a] *adj* sarcastic.

sarcófago [sar'kofaɣo] *nm* sarcophagus.

sardina [sar'ðina] *nf* sardine.

sardo, a ['sarðo, a] *adj*, *nm/f* Sardinian.

sardónico, a [sar'ðoniko, a] *adj* sardonic; (*irónico*) ironical, sarcastic.

sargento [sar'xento] *nm* sergeant.

sarmiento [sar'mjento] *nm* vine shoot.

sarna ['sarna] *nf* itch; (*MED*) scabies.

sarpullido [sarpu'ʎiðo] *nm* (*MED*) rash.

sarro ['sarro] *nm* deposit; (*en dientes*) tartar.

sarta ['sarta] *nf* (*fig*): **una** ~ **de mentiras** a pack of lies.

sartén [sar'ten] *nf* frying pan; **tener la** ~ **por el mango** to rule the roost.

sastre ['sastre] *nm* tailor.

sastrería [sastre'ria] *nf* (*arte*) tailoring; (*tienda*) tailor's (shop).

Satanás [sata'nas] *nm* Satan.

satélite [sa'telite] *nm* satellite.

satinado, a [sati'naðo, a] *adj* glossy ♦ *nm* gloss, shine.

sátira ['satira] *nf* satire.

satírico, a [sa'tiriko, a] *adj* satiric(al).

sátiro [sa'tiro] *nm* (*MITOLOGÍA*) satyr; (*fig*) sex maniac.

satisfacción [satisfak'θjon] *nf* satisfaction.

satisfacer [satisfa'θer] *vt* to satisfy; (*gastos*) to meet; (*deuda*) to pay; (*COM: letra de cambio*) to honour (*BRIT*), honor (*US*); (*pérdida*) to make good; ~**se** *vr* to satisfy o.s., be satisfied; (*vengarse*) to take revenge.

satisfaga [satis'faɣa] *etc*, **satisfaré** [satisfa're] *etc vb V* **satisfacer**.

satisfecho, a [satis'fetʃo, a] *pp de* **satisfacer** ♦ *adj* satisfied; (*contento*) content(ed), happy; (*tb*: ~ **de sí mismo**) self-satisfied, smug.

satisfice [satis'fiθe] *etc vb V* **satisfacer**.

saturación [satura'θjon] *nf* saturation; **llegar a la** ~ to reach saturation point.

saturar [satu'rar] *vt* to saturate; ~**se** *vr* (*mercado, aeropuerto*) to reach saturation point; **¡estoy saturado de tanta televisión!** I can't take any more television!

sauce ['sauθe] *nm* willow; ~ **llorón** weeping willow.

saúco [sa'uko] *nm* (*BOT*) elder.

saudí [sau'ði] *adj*, *nm/f* Saudi.

sauna ['sauna] *nf* sauna.

savia ['saβja] *nf* sap.

saxo ['sakso] *nm* sax.

saxofón [sakso'fon] *nm* saxophone.

saya ['saja] *nf* (*falda*) skirt; (*enagua*) petticoat.

sayo ['sajo] *nm* smock.

sazón [sa'θon] *nf* (*de fruta*) ripeness; **a la ~ then**, at that time.
sazonado, a [saθo'naðo, a] *adj* (*fruta*) ripe; (*CULIN*) flavoured, seasoned.
sazonar [saθo'nar] *vt* to ripen; (*CULIN*) to flavour, season.
s/c *abr* (*COM*: = *su casa*) your firm; (: = *su cuenta*) your account.
Sdo. *abr* (*COM*: = *Saldo*) bal.
SE *abr* (= *sudeste*) SE.

═══════════════ *PALABRA CLAVE*

se [se] *pron* **1** (*reflexivo: sg: m*) himself; (: *f*) herself; (: *pl*) themselves; (: *cosa*) itself; (: *de Vd*) yourself; (: *de Vds*) yourselves; (*indefinido*) oneself; ~ **mira en el espejo** he looks at himself in the mirror; **¡siénte~!** sit down!; ~ **durmió** he fell asleep; ~ **está preparando** she's getting (herself) ready; *para usos léxicos del pron ver el vb en cuestión, p.ej.* **arrepentirse**
2 (*como complemento indirecto*) to him; to her; to them; to it; to you; ~ **lo dije ayer** (*a Vd*) I told you yesterday; ~ **compró un sombrero** he bought himself a hat; ~ **rompió la pierna** he broke his leg; **cortar~ el pelo** to get one's hair cut; (*uno mismo*) to cut one's hair; ~ **comió un pastel** he ate a cake
3 (*uso recíproco*) each other, one another; ~ **miraron (el uno al otro)** they looked at each other *o* one another
4 (*en oraciones pasivas*): **se han vendido muchos libros** a lot of books have been sold; **"~ vende coche"** "car for sale"
5 (*impers*): ~ **dice que** people say that, it is said that; **allí ~ come muy bien** the food there is very good, you can eat very well there.

sé [se] *vb V* **saber, ser**.
sea ['sea] *etc vb V* **ser**.
SEAT ['seat] *nf abr* = *Sociedad Española de Automóviles de Turismo*.
sebo ['seßo] *nm* fat, grease.
Sec. *abr* (= *Secretario*) Sec.
seca ['seka] *nf V* **seco**.
secado [se'kaðo] *nm* drying; ~ **a mano** blow-dry.
secador [seka'ðor] *nm*: ~ **para el pelo** hairdryer.
secadora [seka'ðora] *nf* tumble dryer; ~ **centrífuga** spin-dryer.
secano [se'kano] *nm* (*AGR*: *tb*: **tierra de ~**) dry land *o* region; **cultivo de ~** dry farming.
secante [se'kante] *adj* (*viento*) drying ♦ *nm* blotting paper.

secar [se'kar] *vt* to dry; (*superficie*) to wipe dry; (*frente, suelo*) to mop; (*líquido*) to mop up; (*tinta*) to blot; ~**se** *vr* to dry (off); (*río, planta*) to dry up.
sección [sek'θjon] *nf* section; (*COM*) department; ~ **deportiva** (*en periódico*) sports page(s).
seco, a ['seko, a] *adj* dry; (*fruta*) dried; (*persona: magro*) thin, skinny; (*carácter*) cold; (*antipático*) disagreeable; (*respuesta*) sharp, curt ♦ *nf* dry season; **habrá pan a secas** there will be just bread; **decir algo a secas** to say sth curtly; **parar en ~** to stop dead.
secreción [sekre'θjon] *nf* secretion.
secretaría [sekreta'ria] *nf* secretariat; (*oficina*) secretary's office.
secretariado [sekreta'rjaðo] *nm* (*oficina*) secretariat; (*cargo*) secretaryship; (*curso*) secretarial course.
secretario, a [sekre'tarjo, a] *nm/f* secretary; ~ **adjunto** (*COM*) assistant secretary.
secreto, a [se'kreto, a] *adj* secret; (*información*) confidential; (*persona*) secretive ♦ *nm* secret; (*calidad*) secrecy.
secta ['sekta] *nf* sect.
sectario, a [sek'tarjo, a] *adj* sectarian.
sector [sek'tor] *nm* sector (*tb INFORM*); (*de opinión*) section; (*fig: campo*) area, field; ~ **privado/público** (*COM, ECON*) private/public sector.
secuela [se'kwela] *nf* consequence.
secuencia [se'kwenθja] *nf* sequence.
secuestrar [sekwes'trar] *vt* to kidnap; (*avión*) to hijack; (*bienes*) to seize, confiscate.
secuestro [se'kwestro] *nm* kidnapping; hijack; seizure, confiscation.
secular [seku'lar] *adj* secular.
secundar [sekun'dar] *vt* to second, support.
secundario, a [sekun'darjo, a] *adj* secondary; (*carretera*) side *cpd*; (*INFORM*) background *cpd* ♦ *nf* secondary education; *V tb* **sistema educativo**.
sed [seð] *nf* thirst; (*fig*) thirst, craving; **tener ~** to be thirsty.
seda ['seða] *nf* silk; ~ **dental** dental floss.
sedal [se'ðal] *nm* fishing line.
sedante [se'ðante] *nm* sedative.
sede ['seðe] *nf* (*de gobierno*) seat; (*de compañía*) headquarters *pl*, head office; **Santa S~** Holy See.
sedentario, a [seðen'tarjo, a] *adj* sedentary.
SEDIC [se'ðik] *nf abr* = *Sociedad Española de*

Documentación e Información Científica.

sedición [seði'θjon] *nf* sedition.

sediento, a [se'ðjento, a] *adj* thirsty.

sedimentar [seðimen'tar] *vt* to deposit; ~**se** *vr* to settle.

sedimento [seði'mento] *nm* sediment.

sedoso, a [se'ðoso, a] *adj* silky, silken.

seducción [seðuk'θjon] *nf* seduction.

seducir [seðu'θir] *vt* to seduce; (*sobornar*) to bribe; (*cautivar*) to charm, fascinate; (*atraer*) to attract.

seductor, a [seðuk'tor, a] *adj* seductive; charming, fascinating; attractive; (*engañoso*) deceptive, misleading ♦ *nm/f* seducer.

seduje [se'ðuxe] *etc*, **seduzca** [se'ðuθka] *etc vb V* **seducir**.

sefardí [sefar'ði], **sefardita** [sefar'ðita] *adj* Sephardi(c) ♦ *nm/f* Sephardi.

segador, a [seɣa'ðor, a] *nm/f* (*persona*) harvester ♦ *nf* (*TEC*) mower, reaper.

segadora-trilladora [seɣa'ðoratriʎa'ðora] *nf* combine harvester.

segar [se'ɣar] *vt* (*mies*) to reap, cut; (*hierba*) to mow, cut; (*esperanzas*) to ruin.

seglar [se'ɣlar] *adj* secular, lay.

segoviano, a [seɣo'ßjano, a] *adj* of o from Segovia ♦ *nm/f* native o inhabitant of Segovia.

segregación [seɣreɣa'θjon] *nf* segregation; ~ **racial** racial segregation.

segregar [seɣre'ɣar] *vt* to segregate, separate.

segregue [se'ɣreɣe] *etc vb V* **segregar**.

segué [se'ɣe], **seguemos** [se'ɣemos] *etc vb V* **segar**.

seguidamente [seɣiða'mente] *adv* (*sin parar*) without a break; (*inmediatamente después*) immediately after.

seguido, a [se'ɣiðo, a] *adj* (*continuo*) continuous, unbroken; (*recto*) straight ♦ *adv* (*directo*) straight (on); (*después*) after; (*AM: a menudo*) often ♦ *nf*: **en seguida** at once, right away; **5 días ~s** 5 days running, 5 days in a row; **en seguida termino** I've nearly finished, I shan't be long now.

seguimiento [seɣi'mjento] *nm* chase, pursuit; (*continuación*) continuation.

seguir [se'ɣir] *vt* to follow; (*venir después*) to follow on, come after; (*proseguir*) to continue; (*perseguir*) to chase, pursue; (*indicio*) to follow up; (*mujer*) to court ♦ *vi* (*gen*) to follow; (*continuar*) to continue, carry o go on; ~**se** *vr* to follow; **a ~** to be continued; **sigo sin comprender** I still don't understand; **sigue lloviendo** it's

still raining; **sigue** (*en carta*) P.T.O.; (*en libro, TV*) continued; "**hágase ~**" "please forward"; **¡siga!** (*AM: pase*) come in!

según [se'ɣun] *prep* according to ♦ *adv*: ~ (**y conforme**) it all depends ♦ *conj* as; ~ **esté el tiempo** depending on the weather; ~ **me consta** as far as I know; **está ~ lo dejaste** it is just as you left it.

segundo, a [se'ɣundo, a] *adj* second; (*en discurso*) secondly ♦ *nm* (*gen, medida de tiempo*) second; (*piso*) second floor ♦ *nf* (*sentido*) second meaning; ~ (**de a bordo**) (*NAUT*) first mate; **segunda (clase)** (*FERRO*) second class; **segunda (marcha)** (*AUTO*) second (gear); **de segunda mano** second hand.

seguramente [seɣura'mente] *adv* surely; (*con certeza*) for sure, with certainty; (*probablemente*) probably; **¿lo va a comprar?** — ~ is he going to buy it? — I should think so.

seguridad [seɣuri'ðað] *nf* safety; (*del estado, de casa etc*) security; (*certidumbre*) certainty; (*confianza*) confidence; (*estabilidad*) stability; ~ **social** social security; ~ **contra incendios** fire precautions *pl*; ~ **en sí mismo** (self-) confidence.

seguro, a [se'ɣuro, a] *adj* (*cierto*) sure, certain; (*fiel*) trustworthy; (*libre de peligro*) safe; (*bien defendido, firme*) secure; (*datos etc*) reliable; (*fecha*) firm ♦ *adv* for sure, certainly ♦ *nm* (*dispositivo*) safety device; (*de cerradura*) tumbler; (*de arma*) safety catch; (*COM*) insurance; ~ **contra accidentes/incendios** fire/accident insurance; ~ **contra terceros/a todo riesgo** third party/comprehensive insurance; ~ **dotal con beneficios** with-profits endowment assurance; **S~ de Enfermedad** ≈ National Insurance; ~ **marítimo** marine insurance; ~ **mixto** endowment assurance; ~ **temporal** term insurance; ~ **de vida** life insurance.

seis [seis] *num* six; ~ **mil** six thousand; **tiene ~ años** she is six (years old); **unos** ~ about six; **hoy es el** ~ today is the sixth.

seiscientos, as [seis'θjentos, as] *num* six hundred.

seísmo [se'ismo] *nm* tremor, earthquake.

selección [selek'θjon] *nf* selection; ~ **múltiple** multiple choice; ~ **nacional** (*DEPORTE*) national team.

seleccionador, a [selekθjona'ðor, a] *nm/f* (*DEPORTE*) selector.

seleccionar [selekθjo'nar] *vt* to pick, choose, select.

selectividad [selektiβi'ðað] *nf* (*UNIV*) entrance examination.

School leavers wishing to go on to University sit the dreaded **selectividad** in June, with resits in September. When student numbers are too high for a particular course only the best students get their choice. Some of the others then wait a year to sit the exam again rather than do a course they don't want.

selecto, a [se'lekto, a] *adj* select, choice; (*escogido*) selected.

sellado, a [se'ʎaðo, a] *adj* (*documento oficial*) sealed; (*pasaporte*) stamped.

sellar [se'ʎar] *vt* (*documento oficial*) to seal; (*pasaporte, visado*) to stamp; (*marcar*) to brand; (*pacto, labios*) to seal.

sello ['seʎo] *nm* stamp; (*precinto*) seal; (*fig: tb:* ~ **distintivo**) hallmark; ~ **fiscal** revenue stamp; ~**s de prima** (*COM*) trading stamps.

selva ['selβa] *nf* (*bosque*) forest, woods *pl*; (*jungla*) jungle; **la S~ Negra** the Black Forest.

selvático, a [sel'βatiko, a] *adj* woodland *cpd*; (*BOT*) wild.

semáforo [se'maforo] *nm* (*AUTO*) traffic lights *pl*; (*FERRO*) signal.

semana [se'mana] *nf* week; ~ **inglesa** 5-day (working) week; ~ **laboral** working week; **S~ Santa** Holy Week; **entre** ~ during the week.

Semana Santa is a holiday in Spain; all regions take **Viernes Santo**, Good Friday, **Sábado Santo**, Holy Saturday, and **Domingo de Resurrección**, Easter Sunday. Other holidays at this time vary according to each region. There are spectacular **procesiones** all over the country, with members of **cofradías** (brotherhoods) dressing in hooded robes and parading their **pasos** (religious floats or sculptures) through the streets. Seville has the most renowned celebrations, on account of the religious fervour shown by the locals.

semanal [sema'nal] *adj* weekly.

semanario [sema'narjo] *nm* weekly (magazine).

semántica [se'mantika] *nf* semantics *sg*.

semblante [sem'blante] *nm* face; (*fig*) look.

semblanza [sem'blanθa] *nf* biographical sketch, profile.

sembrar [sem'brar] *vt* to sow; (*objetos*) to sprinkle, scatter about; (*noticias etc*) to spread.

semejante [seme'xante] *adj* (*parecido*) similar; (*tal*) such; ~**s** alike, similar ♦ *nm* fellow man, fellow creature; **son muy** ~**s** they are very much alike; **nunca hizo cosa** ~ he never did such a *o* any such thing.

semejanza [seme'xanθa] *nf* similarity, resemblance; **a** ~ **de** like, as.

semejar [seme'xar] *vi* to seem like, resemble; ~**se** *vr* to look alike, be similar.

semen ['semen] *nm* semen.

semental [semen'tal] *nm* (*macho*) stud.

sementera [semen'tera] *nf* (*acto*) sowing; (*temporada*) seedtime; (*tierra*) sown land.

semestral [semes'tral] *adj* half-yearly, bi-annual.

semestre [se'mestre] *nm* period of six months; (*US UNIV*) semester; (*COM*) half-yearly payment.

semicírculo [semi'θirkulo] *nm* semicircle.

semiconductor [semikonduk'tor] *nm* semiconductor.

semiconsciente [semikons'θjente] *adj* semiconscious.

semidesnatado, a [semiðesna'taðo, a] *adj* semi-skimmed.

semifinal [semifi'nal] *nf* semifinal.

semiinconsciente [semi(i)nkons'θjente] *adj* semiconscious.

semilla [se'miʎa] *nf* seed.

semillero [semi'ʎero] *nm* (*AGR etc*) seedbed; (*fig*) hotbed.

seminario [semi'narjo] *nm* (*REL*) seminary; (*ESCOL*) seminar.

semiseco [semi'seko] *nm* medium-dry.

semita [se'mita] *adj* Semitic ♦ *nm/f* Semite.

sémola ['semola] *nf* semolina.

sempiterno, a [sempi'terno, a] *adj* everlasting.

Sena ['sena] *nm*: **el** ~ the (river) Seine.

senado [se'naðo] *nm* senate; *V tb* **Las Cortes (españolas)**.

senador, a [sena'ðor, a] *nm/f* senator.

sencillez [senθi'ʎeθ] *nf* simplicity; (*de persona*) naturalness.

sencillo, a [sen'θiʎo, a] *adj* simple; (*carácter*) natural, unaffected; (*billete*) single ♦ *nm* (*disco*) single; (*AM*) small change.

senda ['senda] *nf*, **sendero** [sen'dero] *nm* path, track; **Sendero Luminoso** the Shining Path (guerrilla movement).

senderismo [sende'rismo] *nm* trekking.

sendos, as ['sendos, as] *adj pl*: **les dio** ~ **golpes** he hit both of them.

senil [se'nil] *adj* senile.

seno ['seno] *nm* (*ANAT*) bosom, bust; (*fig*)

bosom; ~s *nmpl* breasts; ~ **materno** womb.

sensación [sensa'θjon] *nf* sensation; (*sentido*) sense; (*sentimiento*) feeling; **causar** *o* **hacer** ~ to cause a sensation.

sensacional [sensaθjo'nal] *adj* sensational.

sensatez [sensa'teθ] *nf* common sense.

sensato, a [sen'sato, a] *adj* sensible.

sensibilidad [sensiβili'ðað] *nf* sensitivity; (*para el arte*) feel.

sensibilizar [sensiβili'θar] *vt*: ~ **a la población/opinión pública** to raise public awareness.

sensible [sen'sible] *adj* sensitive; (*apreciable*) perceptible, appreciable; (*pérdida*) considerable.

sensiblero, a [sensi'ßlero, a] *adj* sentimental, slushy.

sensitivo, a [sensi'tißo, a], **sensorial** [senso'rjal] *adj* sense *cpd*.

sensor [sen'sor] *nm*: ~ **de fin de papel** paper out sensor.

sensual [sen'swal] *adj* sensual.

sentado, a [sen'taðo, a] *adj* (*establecido*) settled; (*carácter*) sensible ♦ *nf* sitting; (*POL*) sit-in, sit-down protest; **dar por** ~ to take for granted, assume; **dejar algo** ~ to establish sth firmly; **estar** ~ to sit, be sitting (down); **de una sentada** at one sitting.

sentar [sen'tar] *vt* to sit, seat; (*fig*) to establish ♦ *vi* (*vestido*) to suit; (*alimento*): ~ **bien/mal a** to agree/disagree with; ~**se** *vr* (*persona*) to sit, sit down; (*el tiempo*) to settle (down); (*los depósitos*) to settle; **¡siéntese!** (do) sit down, take a seat.

sentencia [sen'tenθja] *nf* (*máxima*) maxim, saying; (*JUR*) sentence; (*INFORM*) statement; ~ **de muerte** death sentence.

sentenciar [senten'θjar] *vt* to sentence.

sentido, a [sen'tiðo, a] *adj* (*pérdida*) regrettable; (*carácter*) sensitive ♦ *nm* sense; (*sentimiento*) feeling; (*significado*) sense, meaning; (*dirección*) direction; **mi más** ~ **pésame** my deepest sympathy; ~ **del humor** sense of humour; ~ **común** common sense; **en el buen** ~ **de la palabra** in the best sense of the word; **sin** ~ meaningless; **tener** ~ to make sense; ~ **único** one-way (street).

sentimental [sentimen'tal] *adj* sentimental; **vida** ~ love life.

sentimiento [senti'mjento] *nm* (*emoción*) feeling, emotion; (*sentido*) sense; (*pesar*) regret, sorrow.

sentir [sen'tir] *vt* to feel; (*percibir*) to perceive, sense; (*esp AM*: *oír*) to hear;

(*lamentar*) to regret, be sorry for; (*música etc*) to have a feeling for ♦ *vi* to feel; (*lamentarse*) to feel sorry ♦ *nm* opinion, judgement; ~**se** *vr* to feel; **lo siento** I'm sorry; ~**se mejor/mal** to feel better/ill; ~**se como en su casa** to feel at home.

seña ['seɲa] *nf* sign; (*MIL*) password; ~**s** *nfpl* address *sg*; ~**s personales** personal description *sg*; **por más** ~**s** moreover; **dar** ~**s de** to show signs of.

señal [se'ɲal] *nf* sign; (*síntoma*) symptom; (*indicio*) indication; (*FERRO, TELEC*) signal; (*marca*) mark; (*COM*) deposit; (*INFORM*) marker, mark; **en** ~ **de** as a token of, as a sign of; **dar** ~**es de** to show signs of; ~ **de auxilio/de peligro** distress/danger signal; ~ **de llamada** ringing tone; ~ **para marcar** dialling tone.

señalado, a [seɲa'laðo, a] *adj* (*persona*) distinguished; (*pey*) notorious.

señalar [seɲa'lar] *vt* to mark; (*indicar*) to point out, indicate; (*significar*) to denote; (*referirse a*) to allude to; (*fijar*) to fix, settle; (*pey*) to criticize.

señalice [seɲa'liθe] *etc vb V* **señalizar**.

señalización [seɲaliθa'θjon] *nf* signposting; signals *pl*.

señalizar [seɲali'θar] *vt* (*AUTO*) to put up road signs on; (*FERRO*) to put signals on; (*AUTO*: *ruta*): **está bien señalizada** it's well signposted.

señas ['seɲas] *nfpl V* **seña**.

señor, a [se'ɲor, a] *adj* (*fam*) lordly ♦ *nm* (*hombre*) man; (*caballero*) gentleman; (*dueño*) owner, master; (*trato: antes de nombre propio*) Mr; (: *hablando directamente*) sir ♦ *nf* (*dama*) lady; (*trato: antes de nombre propio*) Mrs; (: *hablando directamente*) madam; (*esposa*) wife; **los** ~**es González** Mr and Mrs González; **S~ Don Jacinto Benavente** (*en sobre*) Mr J. Benavente, J. Benavente Esq.; **S~ Director ...** (*de periódico*) Dear Sir ...; ~ **juez** my lord, your worship (*US*); ~ **Presidente** Mr Chairman *o* President; **Muy** ~ **mío** Dear Sir; **Muy** ~**es nuestros** Dear Sirs; **Nuestro S~** (*REL*) Our Lord; **¿está la señora?** is the lady of the house in?; **la señora de Smith** Mrs Smith; **Nuestra Señora** (*REL*) Our Lady.

señoría [seɲo'ria] *nf* rule; **su** *o* **vuestra S~** your *o* his/her lordship/ladyship.

señorío [seɲo'rio] *nm* manor; (*fig*) rule.

señorita [seɲo'rita] *nf* (*gen*) Miss; (*mujer joven*) young lady; (*maestra*) schoolteacher.

señorito [seɲo'rito] *nm* young gentleman;

(*lenguaje de criados*) master; (*pey*) toff.
señuelo [se'ɲwelo] *nm* decoy.
Sep. *abr* (= *septiembre*) Sept.
sepa ['sepa] *etc vb* V **saber**.
separable [sepa'raßle] *adj* separable; (*TEC*)
   detachable.
separación [separa'θjon] *nf* separation;
   (*división*) division; (*distancia*) gap,
   distance; ~ **de bienes** division of
   property.
separado, a [sepa'raðo, a] *adj* separate;
   (*TEC*) detached; **vive** ~ **de su mujer** he is
   separated from his wife; **por** ~
   separately.
separador [separa'ðor] *nm* (*INFORM*)
   delimiter.
separadora [separa'ðora] *nf*: ~ **de hojas**
   burster.
separar [sepa'rar] *vt* to separate; (*silla de la
   mesa*) to move away; (*TEC: pieza*) to
   detach; (*persona: de un cargo*) to remove,
   dismiss; (*dividir*) to divide; ~**se** *vr* (*parte*)
   to come away; (*partes*) to come apart;
   (*persona*) to leave, go away; (*matrimonio*)
   to separate.
separata [sepa'rata] *nf* offprint.
separatismo [separa'tismo] *nm* (*POL*)
   separatism.
sepelio [se'peljo] *nm* burial, interment.
sepia ['sepja] *nf* cuttlefish.
Sept. *abr* (= *septiembre*) Sept.
septentrional [septentrjo'nal] *adj* north
   cpd, northern.
septiembre [sep'tjembre] *nm* September.
séptimo, a ['septimo, a] *adj, nm* seventh.
septuagésimo, a [septwa'xesimo, a] *adj*
   seventieth.
sepulcral [sepul'kral] *adj* sepulchral; (*fig*)
   gloomy, dismal.
sepulcro [se'pulkro] *nm* tomb, grave,
   sepulchre.
sepultar [sepul'tar] *vt* to bury; (*en
   accidente*) to trap; **quedaban sepultados
   en la caverna** they were trapped in the
   cave.
sepultura [sepul'tura] *nf* (*acto*) burial;
   (*tumba*) grave, tomb; **dar** ~ **a** to bury;
   recibir ~ to be buried.
sepulturero, a [sepultu'rero, a] *nm/f*
   gravedigger.
seque ['seke] *etc vb* V **secar**.
sequedad [seke'ðað] *nf* dryness; (*fig*)
   brusqueness, curtness.
sequía [se'kia] *nf* drought.
séquito ['sekito] *nm* (*de rey etc*) retinue;
   (*POL*) followers *pl*.
SER *nf abr* (= *Sociedad Española de
   Radiodifusión*) Spanish radio network.

ser [ser] *vi* **1** (*descripción, identidad*) to be;
   es médica/muy alta she's a doctor/very
   tall; **la familia es de Cuzco** his (*o* her *etc*)
   family is from Cuzco; ~ **de madera** to be
   made of wood; **soy Ana** it's Ana
   2 (*propiedad*): **es de Joaquín** it's
   Joaquín's, it belongs to Joaquín
   3 (*horas, fechas, números*): **es la una** it's
   one o'clock; **son las seis y media** it's
   half-past six; **es el 1 de junio** it's the
   first of June; **somos/son seis** there are
   six of us/them; **2 y 2 son 4** 2 and 2 are *o*
   make 4
   4 (*suceso*): **¿qué ha sido eso?** what was
   that?; **la fiesta es en mi casa** the party's
   at my house; **¿qué será de mí?** what will
   become of me?; **"érase una vez ..."**
   "once upon a time ..."
   5 (*en oraciones pasivas*): **ha sido
   descubierto ya** it's already been
   discovered
   6: **es de esperar que** ... it is to be hoped *o*
   I *etc* hope that ...
   7 (*locuciones con sub*): **o sea** that is to
   say; **sea él sea su hermana** either him or
   his sister; **tengo que irme, no sea que
   mis hijos estén esperándome** I have to
   go in case my children are waiting for
   me
   8: **a** *o* **de no** ~ **por él** ... but for him ...
   9: **a no** ~ **que**: **a no** ~ **que tenga uno ya**
   unless he's got one already
   ♦ *nm* being; ~ **humano** human being; ~
   vivo living creature.

Serbia ['serßja] *nf* Serbia.
serbio, a ['serßjo, a] *adj* Serbian ♦ *nm/f*
   Serb.
serenarse [sere'narse] *vr* to calm down;
   (*mar*) to grow calm; (*tiempo*) to clear up.
serenidad [sereni'ðað] *nf* calmness.
sereno, a [se'reno, a] *adj* (*persona*) calm,
   unruffled; (*el tiempo*) fine, settled; (*ambiente*) calm, peaceful ♦ *nm* night watchman.
serial [se'rjal] *nm* serial.
serie ['serje] *nf* series; (*cadena*) sequence,
   succession; (*TV etc*) serial; (*de
   inyecciones*) course; **fuera de** ~ out of
   order; (*fig*) special, out of the ordinary;
   fabricación en ~ mass production;
   (*INFORM*): **interface/impresora en** ~
   serial interface/printer.
seriedad [serje'ðað] *nf* seriousness;
   (*formalidad*) reliability; (*de crisis*)
   gravity, seriousness.

serigrafía [seriɣra'fia] *nf* silk screen printing.

serio, a ['serjo, a] *adj* serious; reliable, dependable; grave, serious; **poco** ~ (*actitud*) undignified; (*carácter*) unreliable; **en** ~ seriously.

sermón [ser'mon] *nm* (*REL*) sermon.

sermonear [sermone'ar] *vt* (*fam*) to lecture ♦ *vi* to sermonize.

seropositivo, a [seroposi'tiβo, a] *adj* HIV-positive.

serpentear [serpente'ar] *vi* to wriggle; (*camino, río*) to wind, snake.

serpentina [serpen'tina] *nf* streamer.

serpiente [ser'pjente] *nf* snake; ~ **boa** boa constrictor; ~ **de cascabel** rattlesnake.

serranía [serra'nia] *nf* mountainous area.

serrano, a [se'rrano, a] *adj* highland *cpd*, hill *cpd* ♦ *nm/f* highlander.

serrar [se'rrar] *vt* to saw.

serrín [se'rrin] *nm* sawdust.

serrucho [se'rrutʃo] *nm* handsaw.

Servia ['serβja] *nf* Serbia.

servicial [serβi'θjal] *adj* helpful, obliging.

servicio [ser'βiθjo] *nm* service; (*CULIN etc*) set; ~**s** *nmpl* toilet(s) (*pl*); **estar de** ~ to be on duty; ~ **aduanero** *o* **de aduana** customs service; ~ **a domicilio** home delivery service; ~ **incluido** (*en hotel etc*) service charge included; ~ **militar** military service; ~ **público** (*COM*) public utility.

servidor, a [serβi'ðor, a] *nm/f* servant ♦ *nm* (*INFORM*) server; **su seguro** ~ (**s.s.s.**) yours faithfully; **un** ~ (*el que habla o escribe*) your humble servant.

servidumbre [serβi'ðumbre] *nf* (*sujeción*) servitude; (*criados*) servants *pl*, staff.

servil [ser'βil] *adj* servile.

servilleta [serβi'ʎeta] *nf* serviette, napkin.

servilletero [serβiʎe'tero] *nm* napkin ring.

servir [ser'βir] *vt* to serve; (*comida*) to serve out *o* up; (*TENIS etc*) to serve ♦ *vi* to serve; (*camarero*) to serve, wait; (*tener utilidad*) to be of use, be useful; ~**se** *vr* to serve *o* help o.s.; **¿en qué puedo** ~**le?** how can I help you?; ~ **vino a algn** to pour out wine for sb; ~ **de guía** to act *o* serve as a guide; **no sirve para nada** it's no use at all; ~**se de algo** to make use of sth, use sth; **sírvase pasar** please come in.

sesantía [θesan'tia] *nf* (*AM*) unemployment.

sesenta [se'senta] *num* sixty.

sesentón, ona [sesen'ton, ona] *adj*, *nm/f* sixty-year-old.

sesgado, a [ses'ɣaðo, a] *adj* slanted, slanting.

sesgo ['sesɣo] *nm* slant; (*fig*) slant, twist.

sesión [se'sjon] *nf* (*POL*) session, sitting; (*CINE*) showing; (*TEAT*) performance; **abrir/levantar la** ~ to open/close *o* adjourn the meeting; **la segunda** ~ the second house.

seso ['seso] *nm* brain; (*fig*) intelligence; ~**s** *nmpl* (*CULIN*) brains; **devanarse los** ~**s** to rack one's brains.

sesudo, a [se'suðo, a] *adj* sensible, wise.

set, *pl* **sets** [set, sets] *nm* (*TENIS*) set.

Set. *abr* (= *setiembre*) Sept.

seta ['seta] *nf* mushroom; ~ **venenosa** toadstool.

setecientos, as [sete'θjentos, as] *num* seven hundred.

setenta [se'tenta] *num* seventy.

setiembre [se'tjembre] *nm* = **septiembre**.

seto ['seto] *nm* fence; ~ **vivo** hedge.

seudo... [seuðo] *pref* pseudo....

seudónimo [seu'ðonimo] *nm* pseudonym.

Seúl [se'ul] *nm* Seoul.

s.e.u.o. *abr* (= *salvo error u omisión*) E & O E.

severidad [seβeri'ðað] *nf* severity.

severo, a [se'βero, a] *adj* severe; (*disciplina*) strict; (*frío*) bitter.

Sevilla [se'βiʎa] *nf* Seville.

sevillano, a [seβi'ʎano, a] *adj* of *o* from Seville ♦ *nm/f* native *o* inhabitant of Seville.

sexagenario, a [seksaxe'narjo, a] *adj* sixty-year-old ♦ *nm/f* person in his/her sixties.

sexagésimo, a [seksa'xesimo, a] *num* sixtieth.

sexo ['sekso] *nm* sex; **el** ~ **femenino/masculino** the female/male sex.

sexto, a ['seksto, a] *num* sixth; **Juan S**~ John the Sixth.

sexual [sek'swal] *adj* sexual; **vida** ~ sex life.

sexualidad [sekswali'ðað] *nf* sexuality.

s.f. *abr* (= *sin fecha*) no date.

s/f *abr* (*COM*: = *su favor*) your favour.

sgte(s). *abr* (= *siguiente(s)*) foll.

si [si] *conj* if; (*en pregunta indirecta*) if, whether ♦ *nm* (*MUS*) B; ~ ... ~ ... whether ... or ...; **me pregunto** ~ ... I wonder if *o* whether ...; ~ **no** if not, otherwise; ¡~ **fuera verdad!** if only it were true!; **por** ~ **viene** in case he comes.

sí [si] *adv* yes ♦ *nm* consent ♦ *pron* (*uso impersonal*) oneself; (*sg: m*) himself; (: *f*) herself; (: *de cosa*) itself; (: *de usted*) yourself; (*pl*) themselves; (: *de ustedes*) yourselves; (: *recíproco*) each other; **él no**

quiere pero yo ~ he doesn't want to but I do; **ella** ~ **vendrá** she will certainly come, she is sure to come; **claro que** ~ of course; **creo que** ~ I think so; **porque** ~ because that's the way it is; (*porque lo digo yo*) because I say so; ¡~ **que lo es!** I'll say it is!; ¡**eso** ~ **que no!** never!; **se ríe de** ~ **misma** she laughs at herself; **cambiaron una mirada entre** ~ they gave each other a look; **de por** ~ in itself.

siamés, esa [sja'mes, esa] *adj, nm/f* Siamese.

sibarita [siβa'rita] *adj* sybaritic ♦ *nm/f* sybarite.

sicario [si'karjo] *nm* hired killer.

Sicilia [si'θilja] *nf* Sicily.

siciliano, a [siθi'ljano, a] *adj, nm/f* Sicilian ♦ *nm* (*LING*) Sicilian.

SIDA ['siða] *nm abr* (= *síndrome de inmunodeficiencia adquirida*) AIDS.

sida ['siða] *nm* AIDS.

siderurgia [siðe'rurxja] *nf* iron and steel industry.

siderúrgico, a [siðe'rurxico, a] *adj* iron and steel *cpd*.

sidra ['siðra] *nf* cider.

siega ['sjeɣa] *etc vb V* segar ♦ *nf* (*cosechar*) reaping; (*segar*) mowing; (*época*) harvest (time).

siegue ['sjeɣe] *etc vb V* segar.

siembra ['sjembra] *etc vb V* sembrar ♦ *nf* sowing.

siempre ['sjempre] *adv* always; (*todo el tiempo*) all the time; (*AM: así y todo*) still ♦ *conj*: ~ **que ...** (+ *indic*) whenever ...; (+ *subjun*) provided that ...; **es lo de** ~ it's the same old story; **como** ~ as usual; **para** ~ forever; ~ **me voy mañana** (*AM*) I'm still leaving tomorrow.

sien [sjen] *nf* (*ANAT*) temple.

siento ['sjento] *etc vb V* sentar, sentir.

sierra ['sjerra] *etc vb V* serrar ♦ *nf* (*TEC*) saw; (*GEO*) mountain range; **S~ Leona** Sierra Leone.

siervo, a ['sjerβo, a] *nm/f* slave.

siesta ['sjesta] *nf* siesta, nap; **dormir la** *o* **echarse una** *o* **tomar una** ~ to have an afternoon nap *o* a doze.

siete ['sjete] *num* seven ♦ *excl* (*AM fam*): ¡**la gran** ~! wow!, hell!; **hijo de la gran** ~ (*fam!*) bastard(*!*), son of a bitch (*US!*).

sífilis ['sifilis] *nf* syphilis.

sifón [si'fon] *nm* syphon; **whisky con** ~ whisky and soda.

siga ['siɣa] *etc vb V* seguir.

sigilo [si'xilo] *nm* secrecy; (*discreción*) discretion.

sigla ['siɣla] *nf* initial, abbreviation.

siglo ['siɣlo] *nm* century; (*fig*) age; **S~ de las Luces** Age of Enlightenment; **S~ de Oro** Golden Age.

significación [siɣnifika'θjon] *nf* significance.

significado [siɣnifi'kaðo] *nm* significance; (*de palabra etc*) meaning.

significar [siɣnifi'kar] *vt* to mean, signify; (*notificar*) to make known, express.

significativo, a [siɣnifika'tiβo, a] *adj* significant.

signifique [siɣni'fike] *etc vb V* significar.

signo ['siɣno] *nm* sign; ~ **de admiración** *o* **exclamación** exclamation mark; ~ **igual** equals sign; ~ **de interrogación** question mark; ~ **de más/de menos** plus/minus sign; ~**s de puntuación** punctuation marks.

siguiendo [si'ɣjendo] *etc vb V* seguir.

siguiente [si'ɣjente] *adj* following; (*próximo*) next.

silbar [sil'βar] *vt, vi* to whistle; (*silbato*) to blow; (*TEAT etc*) to hiss.

silbato [sil'βato] *nm* (*instrumento*) whistle.

silbido [sil'βiðo] *nm* whistle, whistling; (*abucheo*) hiss.

silenciador [silenθja'ðor] *nm* silencer.

silenciar [silen'θjar] *vt* (*persona*) to silence; (*escándalo*) to hush up.

silencio [si'lenθjo] *nm* silence, quiet; **en el** ~ **más absoluto** in dead silence; **guardar** ~ to keep silent.

silencioso, a [silen'θjoso, a] *adj* silent, quiet.

sílfide ['silfiðe] *nf* sylph.

silicio [si'liθjo] *nm* silicon.

silla ['siʎa] *nf* (*asiento*) chair; (*tb*: ~ **de montar**) saddle; ~ **de ruedas** wheelchair.

sillería [siʎe'ria] *nf* (*asientos*) chairs *pl*, set of chairs; (*REL*) choir stalls *pl*; (*taller*) chairmaker's workshop.

sillín [si'ʎin] *nm* saddle, seat.

sillón [si'ʎon] *nm* armchair, easy chair.

silueta [si'lweta] *nf* silhouette; (*de edificio*) outline; (*figura*) figure.

silvestre [sil'βestre] *adj* (*BOT*) wild; (*fig*) rustic, rural.

sima ['sima] *nf* abyss, chasm.

simbolice [simbo'liθe] *etc vb V* simbolizar.

simbólico, a [sim'boliko, a] *adj* symbolic(al).

simbolizar [simboli'θar] *vt* to symbolize.

símbolo ['simbolo] *nm* symbol; ~ **gráfico** (*INFORM*) icon.

simetría [sime'tria] *nf* symmetry.

simétrico, a [si'metriko, a] *adj* symmetrical.

simiente [si'mjente] *nf* seed.

similar [simi'lar] *adj* similar.
similitud [simili'tuð] *nf* similarity, resemblance.
simio ['simjo] *nm* ape.
simpatía [simpa'tia] *nf* liking; (*afecto*) affection; (*amabilidad*) kindness; (*de ambiente*) friendliness; (*de persona, lugar*) charm, attractiveness; (*solidaridad*) mutual support, solidarity; **tener ~ a** to like; **la famosa ~ andaluza** that well-known Andalusian charm.
simpatice [simpa'tiθe] *etc vb V* **simpatizar**.
simpático, a [sim'patiko, a] *adj* nice, pleasant; (*bondadoso*) kind; **no le hemos caído muy ~s** she didn't much take to us.
simpatiquísimo, a [simpati'kisimo, a] *adj* (*superl de* **simpático**) ever so nice; ever so kind.
simpatizante [simpati'θante] *nm/f* sympathizer.
simpatizar [simpati'θar] *vi*: **~ con** to get on well with.
simple ['simple] *adj* simple; (*elemental*) simple, easy; (*mero*) mere; (*puro*) pure, sheer ♦ *nm/f* simpleton; **un ~ soldado** an ordinary soldier.
simpleza [sim'pleθa] *nf* simpleness; (*necedad*) silly thing.
simplicidad [simpliθi'ðað] *nf* simplicity.
simplificar [simplifi'kar] *vt* to simplify.
simplifique [simpli'fike] *etc vb V* **simplificar**.
simplón, ona [sim'plon, ona] *adj* simple, gullible ♦ *nm/f* simple soul.
simposio [sim'posjo] *nm* symposium.
simulacro [simu'lakro] *nm* (*apariencia*) semblance; (*fingimiento*) sham.
simular [simu'lar] *vt* to simulate; (*fingir*) to feign, sham.
simultanear [simultane'ar] *vt*: **~ dos cosas** to do two things simultaneously.
simultáneo, a [simul'taneo, a] *adj* simultaneous.
sin [sin] *prep* without; (*a no ser por*) but for ♦ *conj*: **~ que** (+ *subjun*) without; **~ decir nada** without a word; **~ verlo yo** without my seeing it; **platos ~ lavar** unwashed *o* dirty dishes; **la ropa está ~ lavar** the clothes are unwashed; **~ que lo sepa él** without his knowing; **~ embargo** however.
sinagoga [sina'ɣoɣa] *nf* synagogue.
Sinaí [sina'i] *nm*: **El ~** Sinai, the Sinai Peninsula; **el Monte ~** Mount Sinai.
sinceridad [sinθeri'ðað] *nf* sincerity.
sincero, a [sin'θero, a] *adj* sincere; (*persona*) genuine; (*opinión*) frank;

(*felicitaciones*) heartfelt.
síncope ['sinkope] *nm* (*desmayo*) blackout; **~ cardíaco** (*MED*) heart failure.
sincronice [sinkro'niθe] *etc vb V* **sincronizar**.
sincronizar [sinkroni'θar] *vt* to synchronize.
sindical [sindi'kal] *adj* union *cpd*, trade-union *cpd*.
sindicalista [sindika'lista] *adj* trade-union *cpd* ♦ *nm/f* trade unionist.
sindicar [sindi'kar] *vt* (*obreros*) to organize, unionize; **~se** *vr* (*obrero*) to join a union.
sindicato [sindi'kato] *nm* (*de trabajadores*) trade(s) *o* labor (*US*) union; (*de negociantes*) syndicate.
sindique [sin'dike] *etc vb V* **sindicar**.
síndrome ['sindrome] *nm* syndrome; **~ de abstinencia** withdrawal symptoms.
sine qua non [sine'kwanon] *adj*: **condición ~** sine qua non.
sinfín [sin'fin] *nm*: **un ~ de** a great many, no end of.
sinfonía [sinfo'nia] *nf* symphony.
sinfónico, a [sin'foniko, a] *adj* (*música*) symphonic; **orquesta sinfónica** symphony orchestra.
Singapur [singa'pur] *nm* Singapore.
singular [singu'lar] *adj* singular; (*fig*) outstanding, exceptional; (*pey*) peculiar, odd ♦ *nm* (*LING*) singular; **en ~** in the singular.
singularice [singula'riθe] *etc vb V* **singularizar**.
singularidad [singulari'ðað] *nf* singularity, peculiarity.
singularizar [singulari'θar] *vt* to single out; **~se** *vr* to distinguish o.s., stand out.
siniestro, a [si'njestro, a] *adj* left; (*fig*) sinister ♦ *nm* (*accidente*) accident; (*desastre*) natural disaster.
sinnúmero [sin'numero] *nm* = **sinfín**.
sino ['sino] *nm* fate, destiny ♦ *conj* (*pero*) but; (*salvo*) except, save; **no son 8 ~ 9** there are not 8 but 9; **todos ~ él** all except him.
sinónimo, a [si'nonimo, a] *adj* synonymous ♦ *nm* synonym.
sinrazón [sinra'θon] *nf* wrong, injustice.
sinsabor [sinsa'ßor] *nm* (*molestia*) trouble; (*dolor*) sorrow; (*preocupación*) uneasiness.
sintaxis [sin'taksis] *nf* syntax.
síntesis ['sintesis] *nf inv* synthesis.
sintetice [sinte'tiθe] *etc vb V* **sintetizar**.
sintético, a [sin'tetiko, a] *adj* synthetic.
sintetizador [sintetiθa'ðor] *nm* synthesizer.

sintetizar [sinteti'θar] *vt* to synthesize.
sintiendo [sin'tjendo] *etc vb* V **sentir**.
síntoma ['sintoma] *nm* symptom.
sintomático, a [sinto'matiko, a] *adj* symptomatic.
sintonía [sinto'nia] *nf* (*RADIO*) tuning; (*melodía*) signature tune.
sintonice [sinto'niθe] *etc vb* V **sintonizar**.
sintonizador [sintoniθa'ðor] *nm* (*RADIO*) tuner.
sintonizar [sintoni'θar] *vt* (*RADIO*) to tune (in) to, pick up.
sinuoso, a [si'nwoso, a] *adj* (*camino*) winding; (*rumbo*) devious.
sinvergüenza [simber'ɣwenθa] *nm/f* rogue, scoundrel.
sionismo [sjo'nismo] *nm* Zionism.
siquiera [si'kjera] *conj* even if, even though ♦ *adv* (*esp AM*) at least; **ni** ~ not even; ~ **bebe algo** at least drink something.
sirena [si'rena] *nf* siren, mermaid; (*bocina*) siren, hooter.
Siria ['sirja] *nf* Syria.
sirio, a ['sirjo, a] *adj, nm/f* Syrian.
sirviendo [sir'ßjendo] *etc vb* V **servir**.
sirviente, a [sir'ßjente, a] *nm/f* servant.
sisa ['sisa] *nf* petty theft; (*COSTURA*) dart; (*sobaquera*) armhole.
sisar [si'sar] *vt* (*robar*) to thieve; (*COSTURA*) to take in.
sisear [sise'ar] *vt*, *vi* to hiss.
sísmico, a ['sismiko, a] *adj*: **movimiento** ~ earthquake.
sismógrafo [sis'moɣrafo] *nm* seismograph.
sistema [sis'tema] *nm* system; (*método*) method; ~ **impositivo** *o* **tributario** taxation, tax system; ~ **pedagógico** educational system; ~ **de alerta inmediata** early-warning system; ~ **binario** (*INFORM*) binary system; ~ **experto** expert system; ~ **de facturación** (*COM*) invoicing system; ~ **de fondo fijo** (*COM*) imprest system; ~ **de lógica compartida** (*INFORM*) shared logic system; ~ **métrico** metric system; ~ **operativo (en disco)** (*INFORM*) (disk-based) operating system.

The reform of the Spanish **sistema educativo** (*education system*) *begun in the early 90s has replaced the courses* **EGB, BUP** *and* **COU** *with the following:* **Primaria***: a compulsory 6 years;* **Secundaria** *a compulsory 4 years;* **Bachillerato** *an optional 2 year secondary school course, essential for those wishing to go on to higher education.*

---

sistemático, a [siste'matiko, a] *adj* systematic.
sitiar [si'tjar] *vt* to besiege, lay siege to.
sitio ['sitjo] *nm* (*lugar*) place; (*espacio*) room, space; (*MIL*) siege; **¿hay** ~**?** is there any room?; **hay** ~ **de sobra** there's plenty of room.
situación [sitwa'θjon] *nf* situation, position; (*estatus*) position, standing.
situado, a [si'twaðo, a] *adj* situated, placed; **estar** ~ (*COM*) to be financially secure.
situar [si'twar] *vt* to place, put; (*edificio*) to locate, situate.
S.L. *abr* (*COM*: = *Sociedad Limitada*) Ltd.
slip [es'lip], *pl* **slips** *nm* pants *pl*, briefs *pl*.
slot [es'lot], *pl* **slots** *nm*: ~ **de expansión** expansion slot.
S.M. *abr* (= *Su Majestad*) HM.
SME *nm abr* (= *Sistema Monetario Europeo*) EMS; **(mecanismo de cambios del)** ~ ERM.
smoking [(e)'smokin] (*pl* ~**s**) *nm* dinner jacket (*BRIT*), tuxedo (*US*).
s/n *abr* (= *sin número*) no number.
snob [es'nob] = **esnob**.
SO *abr* (= *suroeste*) SW.
so [so] *excl* whoa!; **¡**~ **burro!** you idiot! ♦ *prep* under.
s/o *abr* (*COM*: = *su orden*) your order.
sobaco [so'ßako] *nm* armpit.
sobado, a [so'ßaðo, a] *adj* (*ropa*) worn; (*arrugado*) crumpled; (*libro*) well-thumbed; (*CULIN*: *masa*) short.
sobar [so'ßar] *vt* (*tela*) to finger; (*ropa*) to rumple, mess up; (*músculos*) to rub, massage.
soberanía [soßera'nia] *nf* sovereignty.
soberano, a [soße'rano, a] *adj* sovereign; (*fig*) supreme ♦ *nm/f* sovereign; **los** ~**s** the king and queen.
soberbio, a [so'ßerßjo, a] *adj* (*orgulloso*) proud; (*altivo*) haughty, arrogant; (*fig*) magnificent, superb ♦ *nf* pride; haughtiness, arrogance; magnificence.
sobornar [soßor'nar] *vt* to bribe.
soborno [so'ßorno] *nm* (*un* ~) bribe; (*el* ~) bribery.
sobra ['soßra] *nf* excess, surplus; ~**s** *nfpl* left-overs, scraps; **de** ~ surplus, extra; **lo sé de** ~ I'm only too aware of it; **tengo de** ~ I've more than enough.
sobradamente [soßraða'mente] *adv* amply; (*saber*) only too well.
sobrado, a [so'ßraðo, a] *adj* (*más que suficiente*) more than enough; (*superfluo*) excessive ♦ *adv* too, exceedingly;

sobradas veces repeatedly.
sobrante [so'ßrante] *adj* remaining, extra
♦ *nm* surplus, remainder.
sobrar [so'ßrar] *vt* to exceed, surpass ♦ *vi*
(*tener de más*) to be more than enough;
(*quedar*) to remain, be left (over).
sobrasada [soßra'saða] *nf* ≈ sausage
spread.
sobre ['soßre] *prep* (*gen*) on; (*encima*) on
(top of); (*por encima de, arriba de*) over,
above; (*más que*) more than; (*además*) in
addition to, besides; (*alrededor de*) about;
(*porcentaje*) in, out of; (*tema*) about, on
♦ *nm* envelope; ~ **todo** above all; **3 ~ 100**
3 in a 100, 3 out of every 100; **un libro ~
Tirso** a book about Tirso; ~ **de ventanilla**
window envelope.
sobrecama [soßre'kama] *nf* bedspread.
sobrecapitalice [soßrekapita'liθe] *etc vb V*
sobrecapitalizar.
sobrecapitalizar [soßrekapitali'θar] *vi* to
overcapitalize.
sobrecargar [soßrekar'ɣar] *vt* (*camión*) to
overload; (*COM*) to surcharge.
sobrecargue [soßre'karɣe] *etc vb V*
sobrecargar.
sobrecoger [soßreko'xer] *vt* (*sobresaltar*) to
startle; (*asustar*) to scare; ~**se** *vr*
(*sobresaltarse*) to be startled; (*asustarse*)
to get scared; (*quedar impresionado*): ~**se
(de)** to be overawed (by).
sobrecoja [soßre'koxa] *etc vb V*
sobrecoger.
sobredosis [soßre'ðosis] *nf inv* overdose.
sobre(e)ntender [soßre(e)nten'der] *vt* to
understand; (*adivinar*) to deduce, infer;
~**se** *vr*: **se sobre(e)ntiende que ...** it is
implied that ....
sobreescribir [soßreeskri'ßir] *vt* (*INFORM*)
to overwrite.
sobre(e)stimar [soßre(e)sti'mar] *vt* to
overestimate.
sobregiro [soßre'xiro] *nm* (*COM*) overdraft.
sobrehumano, a [soßreu'mano, a] *adj*
superhuman.
sobreimprimir [soßreimpri'mir] *vt* (*COM*) to
merge.
sobrellevar [soßreʎe'ßar] *vt* (*fig*) to bear,
endure.
sobremesa [soßre'mesa] *nf* (*después de
comer*) sitting on after a meal; (*INFORM*)
desktop; **conversación de ~** table talk.
sobremodo [soßre'moðo] *adv* very much,
enormously.
sobrenatural [soßrenatu'ral] *adj*
supernatural.
sobrenombre [soßre'nombre] *nm*
nickname.

sobrepasar [soßrepa'sar] *vt* to exceed,
surpass.
sobrepondré [soßrepon'dre] *etc vb V*
sobreponer.
sobreponer [soßrepo'ner] *vt* (*poner encima*)
to put on top; (*añadir*) to add; ~**se** *vr*: ~**se
a** to overcome.
sobreponga [soßre'ponga] *etc vb V*
sobreponer.
sobreprima [soßre'prima] *nf* (*COM*)
loading.
sobreproducción [soßreproðuk'θjon] *nf*
overproduction.
sobrepuesto [soßre'pwesto], **sobrepuse**
[soßre'puse] *etc vb V* **sobreponer**.
sobresaldré [soßresal'dre] *etc*,
sobresalga [soßre'salɣa] *etc vb V*
sobresalir.
sobresaliente [soßresa'ljente] *adj*
projecting; (*fig*) outstanding, excellent;
(*UNIV etc*) first class ♦ *nm* (*UNIV etc*) first
class (mark), distinction.
sobresalir [soßresa'lir] *vi* to project, jut
out; (*fig*) to stand out, excel.
sobresaltar [soßresal'tar] *vt* (*asustar*) to
scare, frighten; (*sobrecoger*) to startle.
sobresalto [soßre'salto] *nm* (*movimiento*)
start; (*susto*) scare; (*turbación*) sudden
shock.
sobreseer [soßrese'er] *vt*: ~ **una causa**
(*JUR*) to stop a case.
sobrestadía [soßresta'ðia] *nf* (*COM*)
demurrage.
sobretensión [soßreten'sjon] *nf* (*ELEC*): ~
transitoria surge.
sobretiempo [soßre'tjempo] *nm* (*AM*)
overtime.
sobretodo [soßre'toðo] *nm* overcoat.
sobrevendré [soßreßen'dre] *etc*,
sobrevenga [soßre'ßenga] *etc vb V*
sobrevenir.
sobrevenir [soßreße'nir] *vi* (*ocurrir*) to
happen (unexpectedly); (*resultar*) to
follow, ensue.
sobreviene [soßre'ßjene] *etc*, **sobrevine**
[soßre'ßine] *etc vb V* **sobrevenir**.
sobreviviente [soßreßi'ßjente] *adj*
surviving ♦ *nm/f* survivor.
sobrevivir [soßreßi'ßir] *vi* to survive;
(*persona*) to outlive; (*objeto etc*) to
outlast.
sobrevolar [soßreßo'lar] *vt* to fly over.
sobrevuele [soßre'ßwele] *etc vb V*
sobrevolar.
sobriedad [soßrje'ðað] *nf* sobriety,
soberness; (*moderación*) moderation,
restraint.
sobrino, a [so'ßrino, a] *nm/f* nephew/niece.

sobrio, a ['soβrjo, a] *adj* (*moderado*)
moderate, restrained.

socarrón, ona [soka'rron, ona] *adj*
(*sarcástico*) sarcastic, ironic(al).

socavar [soka'βar] *vt* to undermine;
(*excavar*) to dig underneath o below.

socavón [soka'βon] *nm* (*en mina*) gallery;
(*hueco*) hollow; (*en la calle*) hole.

sociable [so'θjaβle] *adj* (*persona*) sociable,
friendly; (*animal*) social.

social [so'θjal] *adj* social; (*COM*) company
cpd.

socialdemócrata [soθjalde'mokrata] *adj*
social-democratic ♦ *nm/f* social
democrat.

socialice [soθja'liθe] *etc vb V* **socializar**.

socialista [soθja'lista] *adj, nm/f* socialist.

socializar [soθjali'θar] *vt* to socialize.

sociedad [soθje'ðað] *nf* society; (*COM*)
company; ~ **de ahorro y préstamo**
savings and loan society; ~ **anónima**
(S.A.) limited company (Ltd) (*BRIT*),
incorporated company (Inc) (*US*); ~ **de**
beneficiencia friendly society (*BRIT*),
benefit association (*US*); ~ **de cartera**
investment trust; ~ **comanditaria** (*COM*)
co-ownership; ~ **conjunta** (*COM*) joint
venture; ~ **inmobiliaria** building society
(*BRIT*), savings and loan (society) (*US*); ~
de responsabilidad limitada (*COM*)
private limited company.

socio, a ['soθjo, a] *nm/f* (*miembro*)
member; (*COM*) partner; ~ **activo** active
partner; ~ **capitalista** o **comanditario**
sleeping o silent (*US*) partner.

socioeconómico, a [soθjoeko'nomiko, a]
adj socio-economic.

sociología [soθjolo'xia] *nf* sociology.

sociólogo, a [so'θjoloɣo, a] *nm/f*
sociologist.

socorrer [soko'rrer] *vt* to help.

socorrido, a [soko'rriðo, a] *adj* (*tienda*)
well-stocked; (*útil*) handy; (*persona*)
helpful.

socorrismo [soko'rrismo] *nm* life-saving.

socorrista [soko'rrista] *nm/f* first aider; (*en*
piscina, playa) lifeguard.

socorro [so'korro] *nm* (*ayuda*) help, aid;
(*MIL*) relief; ¡~! help!

soda ['soða] *nf* (*sosa*) soda; (*bebida*) soda
(water).

sódico, a ['soðiko, a] *adj* sodium *cpd*.

soez [so'eθ] *adj* dirty, obscene.

sofá [so'fa] *nm* sofa, settee.

sofá-cama [so'fakama] *nm* studio couch,
sofa bed.

Sofia ['sofja] *nf* Sofia.

sofisticación [sofistika'θjon] *nf*
sophistication.

sofisticado, a [sofisti'kaðo, a] *adj*
sophisticated.

sofocado, a [sofo'kaðo, a] *adj*: **estar** ~ (*fig*)
to be out of breath; (*ahogarse*) to feel
stifled.

sofocar [sofo'kar] *vt* to suffocate; (*apagar*)
to smother, put out; ~**se** *vr* to suffocate;
(*fig*) to blush, feel embarrassed.

sofoco [so'foko] *nm* suffocation; (*azoro*)
embarrassment.

sofocón [sofo'kon] *nm*: **llevarse** o **pasar un**
~ to have a sudden shock.

sofreír [sofre'ir] *vt* to fry lightly.

sofría [so'fria] *etc*, **sofriendo** [so'frjendo]
etc, **sofrito** [so'frito] *vb V* **sofreír**.

soft(ware) ['sof(wer)] *nm* (*INFORM*)
software.

soga ['soɣa] *nf* rope.

sois [sois] *vb V* **ser**.

soja ['soxa] *nf* soya.

sojuzgar [soxuθ'ɣar] *vt* to subdue, rule
despotically.

sojuzgue [so'xuθɣe] *etc vb V* **sojuzgar**.

sol [sol] *nm* sun; (*luz*) sunshine, sunlight;
(*MUS*) G; ~ **naciente/poniente** rising/
setting sun; **tomar el** ~ to sunbathe;
hace ~ it is sunny.

solace [so'laθe] *etc vb V* **solazar**.

solamente [sola'mente] *adv* only, just.

solapa [so'lapa] *nf* (*de chaqueta*) lapel; (*de*
libro) jacket.

solapado, a [sola'paðo, a] *adj* sly,
underhand.

solar [so'lar] *adj* solar, sun *cpd* ♦ *nm*
(*terreno*) plot (of ground); (*local*)
undeveloped site.

solaz [so'laθ] *nm* recreation, relaxation.

solazar [sola'θar] *vt* (*divertir*) to amuse; ~**se**
vr to enjoy o.s., relax.

soldada [sol'daða] *nf* pay.

soldado [sol'daðo] *nm* soldier; ~ **raso**
private.

soldador [solda'ðor] *nm* soldering iron;
(*persona*) welder.

soldar [sol'dar] *vt* to solder, weld; (*unir*) to
join, unite.

soleado, a [sole'aðo, a] *adj* sunny.

soledad [sole'ðað] *nf* solitude; (*estado*
infeliz) loneliness.

solemne [so'lemne] *adj* solemn; (*tontería*)
utter; (*error*) complete.

solemnidad [solemni'ðað] *nf* solemnity.

soler [so'ler] *vi* to be in the habit of, be
accustomed to; **suele salir a las ocho** she
usually goes out at 8 o'clock; **solíamos ir**
todos los años we used to go every
year.

solera [so'lera] *nf* (*tradición*) tradition; **vino de** ~ vintage wine.

solfeo [sol'feo] *nm* singing of scales; **ir a clases de** ~ to take singing lessons.

solicitar [soliθi'tar] *vt* (*permiso*) to ask for, seek; (*puesto*) to apply for; (*votos*) to canvass for; (*atención*) to attract; (*persona*) to pursue, chase after.

solícito, a [so'liθito, a] *adj* (*diligente*) diligent; (*cuidadoso*) careful.

solicitud [soliθi'tuð] *nf* (*calidad*) great care; (*petición*) request; (*a un puesto*) application.

solidaridad [soliðari'ðað] *nf* solidarity; **por** ~ **con** (*POL etc*) out of *o* in solidarity with.

solidario, a [soli'ðarjo, a] *adj* (*participación*) joint, common; (*compromiso*) mutually binding; **hacerse** ~ **de** to declare one's solidarity with.

solidarizarse [soliðari'θarse] *vr*: ~ **con algn** to support sb, sympathize with sb.

solidez [soli'ðeθ] *nf* solidity.

sólido, a ['soliðo, a] *adj* solid; (*TEC*) solidly made; (*bien construido*) well built.

soliloquio [soli'lokjo] *nm* soliloquy.

solista [so'lista] *nm/f* soloist.

solitario, a [soli'tarjo, a] *adj* (*persona*) lonely, solitary; (*lugar*) lonely, desolate ♦ *nm/f* (*reclusa*) recluse; (*en la sociedad*) loner ♦ *nm* solitaire ♦ *nf* tapeworm.

soliviantar [solißjan'tar] *vt* to stir up, rouse (to revolt); (*enojar*) to anger; (*sacar de quicio*) to exasperate.

solloce [so'ʎoθe] *etc vb* V **sollozar**.

sollozar [soʎo'θar] *vi* to sob.

sollozo [so'ʎoθo] *nm* sob.

solo, a ['solo, a] *adj* (*único*) single, sole; (*sin compañía*) alone; (*MUS*) solo; (*solitario*) lonely; **hay una sola dificultad** there is just one difficulty; **a solas** alone, by o.s.

sólo ['solo] *adv* only, just; (*exclusivamente*) solely; **tan** ~ only just.

solomillo [solo'miʎo] *nm* sirloin.

solsticio [sols'tiθjo] *nm* solstice.

soltar [sol'tar] *vt* (*dejar ir*) to let go of; (*desprender*) to unfasten, loosen; (*librar*) to release, set free; (*amarras*) to cast off; (*AUTO: freno etc*) to release; (*suspiro*) to heave; (*risa etc*) to let out; ~**se** *vr* (*desanudarse*) to come undone; (*desprenderse*) to come off; (*adquirir destreza*) to become expert; (*en idioma*) to become fluent.

soltero, a [sol'tero, a] *adj* single, unmarried ♦ *nm* bachelor ♦ *nf* single woman, spinster.

solterón [solte'ron] *nm* confirmed bachelor.

solterona [solte'rona] *nf* spinster, maiden lady; (*pey*) old maid.

soltura [sol'tura] *nf* looseness, slackness; (*de los miembros*) agility, ease of movement; (*en el hablar*) fluency, ease.

soluble [so'lußle] *adj* (*QUÍMICA*) soluble; (*problema*) solvable; ~ **en agua** soluble in water.

solución [solu'θjon] *nf* solution; ~ **de continuidad** break in continuity.

solucionar [soluθjo'nar] *vt* (*problema*) to solve; (*asunto*) to settle, resolve.

solvencia [sol'ßenθja] *nf* (*COM: estado*) solvency; (: *acción*) settlement, payment.

solventar [solßen'tar] *vt* (*pagar*) to settle, pay; (*resolver*) to resolve.

solvente [sol'ßente] *adj* solvent, free of debt.

Somalia [so'malja] *nf* Somalia.

sombra ['sombra] *nf* shadow; (*como protección*) shade; ~**s** *nfpl* darkness *sg*, shadows; **sin** ~ **de duda** without a shadow of doubt; **tener buena/mala** ~ (*suerte*) to be lucky/unlucky; (*carácter*) to be likeable/disagreeable.

sombrero [som'brero] *nm* hat; ~ **hongo** bowler (hat), derby (*US*); ~ **de copa** *o* **de pelo** (*AM*) top hat.

sombrilla [som'briʎa] *nf* parasol, sunshade.

sombrío, a [som'brio, a] *adj* (*oscuro*) shady; (*fig*) sombre, sad; (*persona*) gloomy.

somero, a [so'mero, a] *adj* superficial.

someter [some'ter] *vt* (*país*) to conquer; (*persona*) to subject to one's will; (*informe*) to present, submit; ~**se** *vr* to give in, yield, submit; ~**se a** to submit to; ~**se a una operación** to undergo an operation.

sometimiento [someti'mjento] *nm* (*estado*) submission; (*acción*) presentation.

somier [so'mjer] *pl* **somiers** *nm* spring mattress.

somnífero [som'nifero] *nm* sleeping pill *o* tablet.

somnolencia [somno'lenθja] *nf* sleepiness, drowsiness.

somos ['somos] *vb* V **ser**.

son [son] *vb* V **ser** ♦ *nm* sound; **en** ~ **de broma** as a joke.

sonado, a [so'naðo, a] *adj* (*comentado*) talked-of; (*famoso*) famous; (*COM: pey*) hyped(-up).

sonajero [sona'xero] *nm* (baby's) rattle.

sonambulismo [sonambu'lismo] *nm*

sleepwalking.
sonámbulo, a [so'nambulo, a] *nm/f*
sleepwalker.
sonar [so'nar] *vt (campana)* to ring;
(trompeta, sirena) to blow ♦ *vi* to sound;
(hacer ruido) to make a noise; *(LING)* to be
sounded, be pronounced; *(ser conocido)*
to sound familiar; *(campana)* to ring;
(reloj) to strike, chime; **~se** *vr*: **~se (la
nariz)** to blow one's nose; **es un nombre
que suena** it's a name that's in the news;
me suena ese nombre that name rings a
bell.
sonda ['sonda] *nf (NAUT)* sounding; *(TEC)*
bore, drill; *(MED)* probe.
sondear [sonde'ar] *vt* to sound; to bore
(into), drill; to probe, sound; *(fig)* to
sound out.
sondeo [son'deo] *nm* sounding; boring,
drilling; *(encuesta)* poll, enquiry; **~ de la
opinión pública** public opinion poll.
sónico, a ['soniko, a] *adj* sonic, sound *cpd*.
sonido [so'niðo] *nm* sound.
sonoro, a [so'noro, a] *adj* sonorous;
(resonante) loud, resonant; *(LING)* voiced;
efectos ~s sound effects.
sonreír [sonre'ir] *vi*, **sonreírse** *vr* to smile.
sonría [son'ria] *etc*, **sonriendo**
[son'rjendo] *etc vb V* **sonreír**.
sonriente [son'rjente] *adj* smiling.
sonrisa [son'risa] *nf* smile.
sonrojar [sonro'xar] *vt*: **~ a algn** to make
sb blush; **~se** *vr*: **~se (de)** to blush (at).
sonrojo [son'roxo] *nm* blush.
sonsacar [sonsa'kar] *vt* to wheedle, coax;
~ a algn to pump sb for information.
sonsaque [son'sake] *etc vb V* **sonsacar**.
sonsonete [sonso'nete] *nm (golpecitos)*
tap(ping); *(voz monótona)* monotonous
delivery, singsong (voice).
soñador, a [soɲa'ðor, a] *nm/f* dreamer.
soñar [so'ɲar] *vt, vi* to dream; **~ con** to
dream about *o* of; **soñé contigo anoche** I
dreamed about you last night.
soñoliento, a [soɲo'ljento, a] *adj* sleepy,
drowsy.
sopa ['sopa] *nf* soup; **~ de fideos** noodle
soup.
sopero, a [so'pero, a] *adj (plato, cuchara)*
soup *cpd* ♦ *nm* soup plate ♦ *nf* soup tureen.
sopesar [sope'sar] *vt* to try the weight of;
(fig) to weigh up.
sopetón [sope'ton] *nm*: **de ~** suddenly,
unexpectedly.
soplar [so'plar] *vt (polvo)* to blow away,
blow off; *(inflar)* to blow up; *(vela)* to
blow out; *(ayudar a recordar)* to prompt;
(birlar) to nick; *(delatar)* to split on ♦ *vi* to

blow; *(delatar)* to squeal; *(beber)* to
booze, bend the elbow.
soplete [so'plete] *nm* blowlamp; **~
soldador** welding torch.
soplo ['soplo] *nm* blow, puff; *(de viento)*
puff, gust.
soplón, ona [so'plon, ona] *nm/f (fam:
chismoso)* telltale; (: *de policía)* informer,
grass.
soponcio [so'ponθjo] *nm* dizzy spell.
sopor [so'por] *nm* drowsiness.
soporífero, a [sopo'rifero, a] *adj* sleep-
inducing; *(fig)* soporific ♦ *nm* sleeping
pill.
soportable [sopor'taßle] *adj* bearable.
soportal [sopor'tal] *nm* porch; **~es** *nmpl*
arcade *sg*.
soportar [sopor'tar] *vt* to bear, carry; *(fig)*
to bear, put up with.
soporte [so'porte] *nm* support; *(fig)* pillar,
support; *(INFORM)* medium; **~ de
entrada/salida** input/output medium.
soprano [so'prano] *nf* soprano.
sor [sor] *nf*: **S~ María** Sister Mary.
sorber [sor'ßer] *vt (chupar)* to sip; *(inhalar)*
to sniff, inhale; *(absorber)* to soak up,
absorb.
sorbete [sor'ßete] *nm* sherbet.
sorbo ['sorßo] *nm (trago)* gulp, swallow;
(chupada) sip; **beber a ~s** to sip.
sordera [sor'ðera] *nf* deafness.
sórdido, a ['sorðiðo, a] *adj* dirty, squalid.
sordo, a ['sorðo, a] *adj (persona)* deaf;
(ruido) dull; *(LING)* voiceless ♦ *nm/f* deaf
person; **quedarse ~** to go deaf.
sordomudo, a [sorðo'muðo, a] *adj* deaf
and dumb ♦ *nm/f* deaf-mute.
soriano, a [so'rjano, a] *adj* of *o* from Soria
♦ *nm/f* native *o* inhabitant of Soria.
sorna ['sorna] *nf (malicia)* slyness; *(tono
burlón)* sarcastic tone.
soroche [so'rotʃe] *nm (AM MED)* mountain
sickness.
sorprendente [sorpren'dente] *adj*
surprising.
sorprender [sorpren'der] *vt* to surprise;
(asombrar) to amaze; *(sobresaltar)* to
startle; *(coger desprevenido)* to catch
unawares; **~se** *vr*: **~se (de)** to be
surprised *o* amazed (at).
sorpresa [sor'presa] *nf* surprise.
sorpresivo, a [sorpre'sißo, a] *adj (AM)*
surprising; *(imprevisto)* sudden.
sortear [sorte'ar] *vt* to draw lots for; *(rifar)*
to raffle; *(dificultad)* to dodge, avoid.
sorteo [sor'teo] *nm (en lotería)* draw; *(rifa)*
raffle.
sortija [sor'tixa] *nf* ring; *(rizo)* ringlet, curl.

sortilegio [sorti'lexjo] *nm (hechicería)*
sorcery; *(hechizo)* spell.
sosegado, a [sose'ɣaðo, a] *adj* quiet, calm.
sosegar [sose'ɣar] *vt* to quieten, calm; *(el
ánimo)* to reassure ♦ *vi* to rest.
sosegué [sose'ɣe], **soseguemos**
[sose'ɣemos] *etc vb V* **sosegar**.
sosiego [so'sjeɣo] *etc vb V* **sosegar** ♦ *nm*
quiet(ness), calm(ness).
sosiegue [so'sjeɣe] *etc vb V* **sosegar**.
soslayar [sosla'jar] *vt (preguntas)* to get
round.
soslayo [sos'lajo]: **de** ~ *adv* obliquely,
sideways; **mirar de** ~ to look out of the
corner of one's eye (at).
soso, a ['soso, a] *adj (CULIN)* tasteless; *(fig)*
dull, uninteresting.
sospecha [sos'petʃa] *nf* suspicion.
sospechar [sospe'tʃar] *vt* to suspect ♦ *vi:* ~
de to be suspicious of.
sospechoso, a [sospe'tʃoso, a] *adj*
suspicious; *(testimonio, opinión)* suspect
♦ *nm/f* suspect.
sostén [sos'ten] *nm (apoyo)* support;
(sujetador) bra; *(alimentación)*
sustenance, food.
sostendré [sosten'dre] *etc vb V* **sostener**.
sostener [soste'ner] *vt* to support;
(mantener) to keep up, maintain;
(alimentar) to sustain, keep going; ~**se** *vr*
to support o.s.; *(seguir)* to continue,
remain.
sostenga [sos'tenga] *etc vb V* **sostener**.
sostenido, adj [soste'niðo, a] *adj*
continuous, sustained; *(prolongado)*
prolonged; *(MUS)* sharp ♦ *nm (MUS)*
sharp.
sostuve [sos'tuβe] *etc vb V* **sostener**.
sota ['sota] *nf (NAIPES)* ≈ jack; *V tb* **baraja
española**.
sotana [so'tana] *nf (REL)* cassock.
sótano ['sotano] *nm* basement.
sotavento [sota'βento] *nm (NAUT)* lee,
leeward.
soterrar [sote'rrar] *vt* to bury; *(esconder)* to
hide away.
sotierre [so'tjerre] *etc vb V* **soterrar**.
soviético, a [so'βjetiko, a] *adj, nm/f* Soviet;
los ~**s** the Soviets, the Russians.
soy [soi] *vb V* **ser**.
soya ['soja] *nf (AM)* soya (bean).
SP *abr (AUTO)* = **servicio público**.
SPM *nm abr* (= *síndrome premenstrual*)
PMS.
spooling [es'pulin] *nm (INFORM)* spooling.
sport [es'por(t)] *nm* sport.
spot [es'pot], *pl* **spot** *nm (publicitario)* ad.
squash [es'kwas] *nm (DEPORTE)* squash.

Sr. *abr* (= *Señor*) Mr.
Sra. *abr* (= *Señora*) Mrs.
S.R.C. *abr* (= *se ruega contestación*)
R.S.V.P.
Sres., Srs. *abr* (= *Señores*) Messrs.
Sri Lanka [sri'lanka] *nm* Sri Lanka.
Srta. *abr* = **Señorita**.
SS *abr* (= *Santos, Santas*) SS.
ss. *abr* (= *siguientes*) foll.
S.S. *abr (REL:* = *Su Santidad)* H.H.
SS.MM. *abr* (= *Sus Majestades*) Their
Royal Highnesses.
Sta. *abr* (= *Santa*) St; (= *Señorita*) Miss.
stand, *pl* **stands** [es'tan, es'tan(s)] *nm*
(COM) stand.
stárter [es'tarter] *nm (AUTO)* self-starter,
starting motor.
status ['status, es'tatus] *nm inv* status.
statu(s) quo [es'tatu(s)'kuo] *nm* status
quo.
Sto. *abr* (= *Santo*) St.
stop, *pl* **stops** [es'top, es'top(s)] *nm (AUTO)*
stop sign.
su [su] *pron (de él)* his; *(de ella)* her; *(de una
cosa)* its; *(de ellos, ellas)* their; *(de usted,
ustedes)* your.
suave ['swaβe] *adj* gentle; *(superficie)*
smooth; *(trabajo)* easy; *(música, voz)* soft,
sweet; *(clima, sabor)* mild.
suavice [swa'βiθe] *etc vb V* **suavizar**.
suavidad [swaβi'ðað] *nf* gentleness; *(de
superficie)* smoothness; *(de música)*
softness, sweetness.
suavizante [swaβi'θante] *nm* conditioner.
suavizar [swaβi'θar] *vt* to soften; *(quitar la
aspereza)* to smooth (out); *(pendiente)* to
ease; *(colores)* to tone down; *(carácter)* to
mellow; *(dureza)* to temper.
subalimentado, a [suβalimen'taðo, a] *adj*
undernourished.
subalterno, a [suβal'terno, a] *adj*
(importancia) secondary; *(personal)*
minor, auxiliary ♦ *nm* subordinate.
subarrendar [suβarren'dar] *vt (COM)* to
lease back.
subarriendo [suβa'rrjendo] *nm (COM)*
leaseback.
subasta [su'βasta] *nf* auction; **poner en** *o*
sacar a pública ~ to put up for public
auction; ~ **a la rebaja** Dutch auction.
subastador, a [suβasta'ðor, a] *nm/f*
auctioneer.
subastar [suβas'tar] *vt* to auction (off).
subcampeón, ona [suβkampe'on, ona]
nm/f runner-up.
subconsciente [suβkons'θjente] *adj*
subconscious.
subcontratar [suβkontra'tar] *vt (COM)* to

subcontract.
subcontrato [sußkon'trato] *nm* (*COM*)
subcontract.
subdesarrollado, a [sußðesarro'ʎaðo, a]
adj underdeveloped.
subdesarrollo [sußðesa'rroʎo] *nm*
underdevelopment.
subdirector, a [sußðirek'tor, a] *nm/f*
assistant *o* deputy manager.
subdirectorio [sußðirek'torjo] *nm* (*INFORM*)
subdirectory.
súbdito, a ['sußðito, a] *nm/f* subject.
subdividir [sußðißi'ðir] *vt* to subdivide.
subempleo [sußem'pleo] *nm*
underemployment.
subestimar [sußesti'mar] *vt* to
underestimate, underrate.
subido, a [su'ßiðo, a] *adj* (*color*) bright,
strong; (*precio*) high ♦ *nf* (*de montaña etc*)
ascent, climb; (*de precio*) rise, increase;
(*pendiente*) slope, hill.
subíndice [su'ßindiθe] *nm* (*INFORM, TIP*)
subscript.
subir [su'ßir] *vt* (*objeto*) to raise, lift up;
(*cuesta, calle*) to go up; (*colina, montaña*)
to climb; (*precio*) to raise, put up;
(*empleado etc*) to promote ♦ *vi* to go/come
up; (*a un coche*) to get in; (*a un autobús,
tren*) to get on; (*precio*) to rise, go up; (*en
el empleo*) to be promoted; (*río, marea*) to
rise; ~**se** *vr* to get up, climb; ~**se a un
coche** to get in(to) a car.
súbito, a ['sußito, a] *adj* (*repentino*) sudden;
(*imprevisto*) unexpected.
subjetivo, a [sußxe'tißo, a] *adj* subjective.
subjuntivo [sußxun'tißo] *nm* subjunctive
(mood).
sublevación [sußleßa'θjon] *nf* revolt,
rising.
sublevar [sußle'ßar] *vt* to rouse to revolt;
~**se** *vr* to revolt, rise.
sublimar [sußli'mar] *vt* (*persona*) to exalt;
(*deseos etc*) to sublimate.
sublime [su'ßlime] *adj* sublime.
subliminal [sußlimi'nal] *adj* subliminal.
submarinista [sußmari'nista] *nm/f*
underwater explorer.
submarino, a [sußma'rino, a] *adj*
underwater ♦ *nm* submarine.
subnormal [sußnor'mal] *adj* subnormal
♦ *nm/f* subnormal person.
suboficial [sußofi'θjal] *nm* non-commissioned officer.
subordinado, a [sußorði'naðo, a] *adj, nm/f*
subordinate.
subproducto [sußpro'ðukto] *nm* by-
product.
subrayado [sußra'jaðo] *nm* underlining.

subrayar [sußra'jar] *vt* to underline;
(*recalcar*) to underline, emphasize.
subrepticio, a [sußrep'tiθjo, a] *adj*
surreptitious.
subrutina [sußru'tina] *nf* (*INFORM*) subroutine.
subsanar [sußsa'nar] *vt* (*reparar*) to make
good; (*perdonar*) to excuse; (*sobreponerse
a*) to overcome.
subscribir [sußskri'ßir] *vt* = **suscribir**.
subscrito [sußs'krito] *pp de* **subscribir**.
subsecretario, a [sußsekre'tarjo, a] *nm/f*
undersecretary, assistant secretary.
subsidiariedad [sußsiðjarie'ðað] *nf* (*POL*)
subsidiarity.
subsidiario, a [sußsi'ðjarjo, a] *adj*
subsidiary.
subsidio [suß'siðjo] *nm* (*ayuda*) aid,
financial help; (*subvención*) subsidy,
grant; (*de enfermedad, paro etc*) benefit,
allowance.
subsistencia [sußsis'tenθja] *nf*
subsistence.
subsistir [sußsis'tir] *vi* to subsist; (*vivir*) to
live; (*sobrevivir*) to survive, endure.
subsuelo [sußs'welo] *nm* subsoil.
subterfugio [sußter'fuxjo] *nm* subterfuge.
subterráneo, a [sußte'rraneo, a] *adj*
underground, subterranean ♦ *nm*
underpass, underground passage; (*AM*)
underground railway, subway (*US*).
subtítulo [sußs'titulo] *nm* subtitle,
subheading.
suburbano, a [sußur'ßano, a] *adj*
suburban.
suburbio [su'ßurßjo] *nm* (*barrio*) slum
quarter; (*afueras*) suburbs *pl*.
subvención [sußßen'θjon] *nf* subsidy,
subvention, grant; ~ **estatal** state
subsidy *o* support; ~ **para la inversión**
(*COM*) investment grant.
subvencionar [sußßenθjo'nar] *vt* to
subsidize.
subversión [sußßer'sjon] *nf* subversion.
subversivo, a [sußßer'sißo, a] *adj*
subversive.
subyacente [sußja'θente] *adj* underlying.
subyugar [sußju'ɣar] *vt* (*país*) to
subjugate, subdue; (*enemigo*) to
overpower; (*voluntad*) to dominate.
subyugue [sub'juxe] *etc vb V* **subyugar**.
succión [suk'θjon] *nf* suction.
succionar [sukθjo'nar] *vt* (*sorber*) to suck;
(*TEC*) to absorb, soak up.
sucedáneo, a [suθe'ðaneo, a] *adj*
substitute ♦ *nm* substitute (food).
suceder [suθe'ðer] *vi* to happen; ~ **a**
(*seguir*) to succeed, follow; **lo que sucede**

es que ... the fact is that ...; ~ **al trono** to succeed to the throne.

sucesión [suθe'sjon] *nf* succession; (*serie*) sequence, series; (*hijos*) issue, offspring.

sucesivamente [suθesiβa'mente] *adv*: **y así** ~ and so on.

sucesivo, a [suθe'siβo, a] *adj* successive, following; **en lo** ~ in future, from now on.

suceso [su'θeso] *nm* (*hecho*) event, happening; (*incidente*) incident.

sucesor, a [suθe'sor, a] *nm/f* successor; (*heredero*) heir/heiress.

suciedad [suθje'ðað] *nf* (*estado*) dirtiness; (*mugre*) dirt, filth.

sucinto, a [su'θinto, a] *adj* (*conciso*) succinct, concise.

sucio, a ['suθjo, a] *adj* dirty; (*mugriento*) grimy; (*manchado*) grubby; (*borroso*) smudged; (*conciencia*) bad; (*conducta*) vile; (*táctica*) dirty, unfair.

Sucre ['sukre] *n* Sucre.

sucre ['sukre] *nm* Ecuadorean monetary unit.

suculento, a [suku'lento, a] *adj* (*sabroso*) tasty; (*jugoso*) succulent.

sucumbir [sukum'bir] *vi* to succumb.

sucursal [sukur'sal] *nf* branch (office); (*filial*) subsidiary.

Sudáfrica [su'ðafrika] *nf* South Africa.

sudafricano, a [suðafri'kano, a] *adj*, *nm/f* South African.

Sudamérica [suða'merika] *nf* South America.

sudamericano, a [suðameri'kano, a] *adj*, *nm/f* South American.

sudanés, esa [suða'nes, esa] *adj*, *nm/f* Sudanese.

sudar [su'ðar] *vt*, *vi* to sweat; (*BOT*) to ooze, give out o off.

sudeste [su'ðeste] *adj* south-east(ern); (*rumbo, viento*) south-easterly ♦ *nm* south-east; (*viento*) south-east wind.

sudoeste [suðo'este] *adj* south-west(ern); (*rumbo, viento*) south-westerly ♦ *nm* south-west; (*viento*) south-west wind.

sudor [su'ðor] *nm* sweat.

sudoroso, a [suðo'roso, a] *adj* sweaty, sweating.

Suecia ['sweθja] *nf* Sweden.

sueco, a ['sweko, a] *adj* Swedish ♦ *nm/f* Swede ♦ *nm* (*LING*) Swedish; **hacerse el** ~ to pretend not to hear o understand.

suegro, a ['sweɣro, a] *nm/f* father-/mother-in-law; **los** ~**s** one's in-laws.

suela ['swela] *nf* (*de zapato, tb pescado*) sole.

sueldo ['sweldo] *etc vb V* **soldar** ♦ *nm* pay, wage(s) (*pl*).

suelo ['swelo] *etc vb V* **soler** ♦ *nm* (*tierra*) ground; (*de casa*) floor.

suelto, a ['swelto, a] *etc vb V* **soltar** ♦ *adj* loose; (*libre*) free; (*separado*) detached; (*ágil*) quick, agile; (*corriente*) fluent, flowing ♦ *nm* (loose) change, small change; **está muy** ~ **en inglés** he is very good at o fluent in English.

suene ['swene] *etc vb V* **sonar**.

sueño ['sweɲo] *etc vb V* **soñar** ♦ *nm* sleep; (*somnolencia*) sleepiness, drowsiness; (*lo soñado, fig*) dream; ~ **pesado** o **profundo** deep o heavy sleep; **tener** ~ to be sleepy.

suero ['swero] *nm* (*MED*) serum; (*de leche*) whey.

suerte ['swerte] *nf* (*fortuna*) luck; (*azar*) chance; (*destino*) fate, destiny; (*condición*) lot; (*género*) sort, kind; **lo echaron a** ~**s** they drew lots o tossed up for it; **tener** ~ to be lucky; **de otra** ~ otherwise, if not; **de** ~ **que** so that, in such a way that.

suéter ['sweter], *pl* **suéters** *nm* sweater.

suficiencia [sufi'θjenθja] *nf* (*cabida*) sufficiency; (*idoneidad*) suitability; (*aptitud*) adequacy.

suficiente [sufi'θjente] *adj* enough, sufficient.

sufijo [su'fixo] *nm* suffix.

sufragar [sufra'ɣar] *vt* (*ayudar*) to help; (*gastos*) to meet; (*proyecto*) to pay for.

sufragio [su'fraxjo] *nm* (*voto*) vote; (*derecho de voto*) suffrage.

sufrague [su'fraɣe] *etc vb V* **sufragar**.

sufrido, a [su'friðo, a] *adj* (*de carácter fuerte*) tough; (*paciente*) long-suffering; (*tela*) hard-wearing; (*color*) that does not show the dirt; (*marido*) complaisant.

sufrimiento [sufri'mjento] *nm* suffering.

sufrir [su'frir] *vt* (*padecer*) to suffer; (*soportar*) to bear, stand, put up with; (*apoyar*) to hold up, support ♦ *vi* to suffer.

sugerencia [suxe'renθja] *nf* suggestion.

sugerir [suxe'rir] *vt* to suggest; (*sutilmente*) to hint; (*idea: incitar*) to prompt.

sugestión [suxes'tjon] *nf* suggestion; (*sutil*) hint; (*poder*) hypnotic power.

sugestionar [suxestjo'nar] *vt* to influence.

sugestivo, a [suxes'tiβo, a] *adj* stimulating; (*atractivo*) attractive; (*fascinante*) fascinating.

sugiera [su'xjera] *etc*, **sugiriendo** [suxi'rjendo] *etc vb V* **sugerir**.

suicida [sui'θiða] *adj* suicidal ♦ *nm/f*

suicidal person; (*muerto*) suicide, person who has committed suicide.

suicidarse [sui̯θi'ðarse] *vr* to commit suicide, kill o.s.

suicidio [sui'θiðjo] *nm* suicide.

Suiza ['swiθa] *nf* Switzerland.

suizo, a ['swiθo, a] *adj, nm/f* Swiss ♦ *nm* sugared bun.

sujeción [suxe'θjon] *nf* subjection.

sujetador [suxeta'ðor] *nm* fastener, clip; (*prenda femenina*) bra, brassiere.

sujetapapeles [suxetapa'peles] *nm inv* paper clip.

sujetar [suxe'tar] *vt* (*fijar*) to fasten; (*detener*) to hold down; (*fig*) to subject, subjugate; (*pelo etc*) to keep o hold in place; (*papeles*) to fasten together; ~**se** *vr* to subject o.s.

sujeto, a [su'xeto, a] *adj* fastened, secure ♦ *nm* subject; (*individuo*) individual; (*fam: tipo*) fellow, character, type, guy (*US*); ~ **a** subject to.

sulfurar [sulfu'rar] *vt* (*TEC*) to sulphurate; (*sacar de quicio*) to annoy; ~**se** *vr* (*enojarse*) to get riled, see red, blow up.

sulfuro [sul'furo] *nm* sulphide.

suma ['suma] *nf* (*cantidad*) total, sum; (*de dinero*) sum; (*acto*) adding (up), addition; **en** ~ in short; ~ **y sigue** (*COM*) carry forward.

sumador [suma'ðor] *nm* (*INFORM*) adder.

sumamente [suma'mente] *adv* extremely, exceedingly.

sumar [su'mar] *vt* to add (up); (*reunir*) to collect, gather ♦ *vi* to add up.

sumario, a [su'marjo, a] *adj* brief, concise ♦ *nm* summary.

sumergir [sumer'xir] *vt* to submerge; (*hundir*) to sink; (*bañar*) to immerse, dip; ~**se** *vr* (*hundirse*) to sink beneath the surface.

sumerja [su'merxa] *etc vb V* **sumergir**.

sumidero [sumi'ðero] *nm* drain, sewer; (*TEC*) sump.

suministrador, a [suministra'ðor, a] *nm/f* supplier.

suministrar [suminis'trar] *vt* to supply, provide.

suministro [sumi'nistro] *nm* supply; (*acto*) supplying, providing.

sumir [su'mir] *vt* to sink, submerge; (*fig*) to plunge; ~**se** *vr* (*objeto*) to sink; ~**se en el estudio** to become absorbed in one's studies.

sumisión [sumi'sjon] *nf* (*acto*) submission; (*calidad*) submissiveness, docility.

sumiso, a [su'miso, a] *adj* submissive, docile.

súmmum ['sumum] *nm inv* (*fig*) height.

sumo, a ['sumo, a] *adj* great, extreme; (*mayor*) highest, supreme ♦ *nm* sumo (wrestling); **a lo** ~ at most.

suntuoso, a [sun'twoso, a] *adj* sumptuous, magnificent; (*lujoso*) lavish.

sup. *abr* (= *superior*) sup.

supe ['supe] *etc vb V* **saber**.

supeditar [supeði'tar] *vt* to subordinate; (*sojuzgar*) to subdue; (*oprimir*) to oppress; ~**se** *vr*: ~**se a** to subject o.s. to.

supensivo, a [suspen'siβo, a] *adj*: **puntos** ~**s** dots, suspension points.

super... [super] *pref* super..., over....

súper ['super] *adj* (*fam*) super, great.

superable [supe'raβle] *adj* (*dificultad*) surmountable; (*tarea*) that can be performed.

superación [supera'θjon] *nf* (*tb:* ~ **personal**) self-improvement.

superar [supe'rar] *vt* (*sobreponerse a*) to overcome; (*rebasar*) to surpass, do better than; (*pasar*) to go beyond; (*marca, récord*) to break; (*etapa: dejar atrás*) to get past; ~**se** *vr* to excel o.s.

superávit [supe'raβit], *pl* **superávits** *nm* surplus.

superchería [supertʃe'ria] *nf* fraud, trick, swindle.

superficial [superfi'θjal] *adj* superficial; (*medida*) surface *cpd*.

superficie [super'fiθje] *nf* surface; (*área*) area; **grandes** ~**s** (*COM*) superstores.

superfluo, a [su'perflwo, a] *adj* superfluous.

superíndice [supe'rindiθe] *nm* (*INFORM, TIP*) superscript.

superintendente [superinten'dente] *nm/f* supervisor, superintendent.

superior [supe'rjor] *adj* (*piso, clase*) upper; (*temperatura, número, nivel*) higher; (*mejor: calidad, producto*) superior, better ♦ *nm/f* superior.

superiora [supe'rjora] *nf* (*REL*) mother superior.

superioridad [superjori'ðað] *nf* superiority.

superlativo, a [superla'tiβo, a] *adj, nm* superlative.

supermercado [supermer'kaðo] *nm* supermarket.

superpoblación [superpoβla'θjon] *nf* overpopulation; (*congestionamiento*) overcrowding.

superponer [superpo'ner] *vt* (*INFORM*) to overstrike.

superposición [superposi'θjon] *nf* (*en impresora*) overstrike.

superpotencia [superpo'tenθja] *nf* superpower, great power.

superproducción [superproðuk'θjon] *nf* overproduction.

supersónico, a [super'soniko, a] *adj* supersonic.

superstición [supersti'θjon] *nf* superstition.

supersticioso, a [supersti'θjoso, a] *adj* superstitious.

supervisar [superßi'sar] *vt* to supervise; (*COM*) to superintend.

supervisor, a [superßi'sor, a] *nm/f* supervisor.

supervivencia [superßi'ßenθja] *nf* survival.

superviviente [superßi'ßjente] *adj* surviving ♦ *nm/f* survivor.

suplantar [suplan'tar] *vt* (*persona*) to supplant; (*hacerse pasar por otro*) to take the place of.

suplementario, a [suplemen'tarjo, a] *adj* supplementary.

suplemento [suple'mento] *nm* supplement.

suplencia [su'plenθja] *nf* substitution, replacement; (*etapa*) period during which one deputizes *etc*.

suplente [su'plente] *adj* substitute; (*disponible*) reserve ♦ *nm/f* substitute.

supletorio, a [suple'torjo, a] *adj* supplementary; (*adicional*) extra ♦ *nm* supplement; **mesa supletoria** spare table.

súplica ['suplika] *nf* request; (*REL*) supplication; (*JUR: instancia*) petition; **~s** *nfpl* entreaties.

suplicar [supli'kar] *vt* (*cosa*) to beg (for), plead for; (*persona*) to beg, plead with; (*JUR*) to appeal to, petition.

suplicio [su'pliθjo] *nm* torture; (*tormento*) torment; (*emoción*) anguish; (*experiencia penosa*) ordeal.

suplique [su'plike] *etc vb V* **suplicar**.

suplir [su'plir] *vt* (*compensar*) to make good, make up for; (*reemplazar*) to replace, substitute ♦ *vi*: **~ a** to take the place of, substitute for.

supo ['supo] *etc vb V* **saber**.

supondré [supon'dre] *etc vb V* **suponer**.

suponer [supo'ner] *vt* to suppose; (*significar*) to mean; (*acarrear*) to involve ♦ *vi* to count, have authority; **era de ~ que** ... it was to be expected that ....

suponga [su'ponga] *etc vb V* **suponer**.

suposición [suposi'θjon] *nf* supposition.

supositorio [suposi'torjo] *nm* suppository.

supremacía [suprema'θia] *nf* supremacy.

supremo, a [su'premo, a] *adj* supreme.

supresión [supre'sjon] *nf* suppression; (*de derecho*) abolition; (*de dificultad*) removal; (*de palabra etc*) deletion; (*de restricción*) cancellation, lifting.

suprimir [supri'mir] *vt* to suppress; (*derecho, costumbre*) to abolish; (*dificultad*) to remove; (*palabra etc, INFORM*) to delete; (*restricción*) to cancel, lift.

supuestamente [supwesta'mente] *adv* supposedly.

supuesto, a [su'pwesto, a] *pp de* **suponer** ♦ *adj* (*hipotético*) supposed; (*falso*) false ♦ *nm* assumption, hypothesis ♦ *conj*: **~ que** since; **dar por ~ algo** to take sth for granted; **por ~** of course.

supurar [supu'rar] *vi* to fester, suppurate.

supuse [su'puse] *etc vb V* **suponer**.

sur [sur] *adj* southern; (*rumbo*) southerly ♦ *nm* south; (*viento*) south wind.

Suráfrica [su'rafrika] *etc* = **Sudáfrica** *etc*.

Suramérica [sura'merika] *etc* = **Sudamérica** *etc*.

surcar [sur'kar] *vt* to plough; (*superficie*) to cut, score.

surco ['surko] *nm* (*en metal, disco*) groove; (*AGR*) furrow.

surcoreano, a [surkore'ano, a] *adj, nm/f* South Korean.

sureño, a [su'reɲo, a] *adj* southern ♦ *nm/f* southerner.

sureste [su'reste] = **sudeste**.

surf [surf] *nm* surfing.

surgir [sur'xir] *vi* to arise, emerge; (*dificultad*) to come up, crop up.

surja ['surxa] *etc vb V* **surgir**.

suroeste [suro'este] = **sudoeste**.

surque ['surke] *etc vb V* **surcar**.

surrealismo [surrea'lismo] *nm* surrealism.

surrealista [surrea'lista] *adj, nm/f* surrealist.

surtido, a [sur'tiðo, a] *adj* mixed, assorted ♦ *nm* (*selección*) selection, assortment; (*abastecimiento*) supply, stock.

surtidor [surti'ðor] *nm* (*chorro*) jet, spout; (*fuente*) fountain; **~ de gasolina** petrol (*BRIT*) o gas (*US*) pump.

surtir [sur'tir] *vt* to supply, provide; (*efecto*) to have, produce ♦ *vi* to spout, spurt; **~se** *vr*: **~se de** to provide o.s. with.

susceptible [susθep'tißle] *adj* susceptible; (*sensible*) sensitive; **~ de** capable of.

suscitar [susθi'tar] *vt* to cause, provoke; (*discusión*) to start; (*duda, problema*) to raise; (*interés, sospechas*) to arouse.

suscribir [suskri'ßir] *vt* (*firmar*) to sign; (*respaldar*) to subscribe to, endorse; (*COM: acciones*) to take out an option on;

~se *vr* to subscribe; ~ **a algn a una revista** to take out a subscription to a journal for sb.

suscripción [suskrip'θjon] *nf* subscription.

suscrito, a [sus'krito, a] *pp de* **suscribir** ♦ *adj*: ~ **en exceso** oversubscribed.

susodicho, a [suso'ditʃo, a] *adj* above-mentioned.

suspender [suspen'der] *vt* (*objeto*) to hang (up), suspend; (*trabajo*) to stop, suspend; (*ESCOL*) to fail.

suspense [sus'pense] *nm* suspense.

suspensión [suspen'sjon] *nf* suspension; (*fig*) stoppage, suspension; (*JUR*) stay; ~ **de fuego** *o* **de hostilidades** ceasefire, cessation of hostilities; ~ **de pagos** suspension of payments.

suspenso, a [sus'penso, a] *adj* hanging, suspended; (*ESCOL*) failed ♦ *nm* (*ESCOL*) fail(ure); **quedar** *o* **estar en** ~ to be pending.

suspicacia [suspi'kaθja] *nf* suspicion, mistrust.

suspicaz [suspi'kaθ] *adj* suspicious, distrustful.

suspirar [suspi'rar] *vi* to sigh.

suspiro [sus'piro] *nm* sigh.

sustancia [sus'tanθja] *nf* substance; ~ **gris** (*ANAT*) grey matter; **sin** ~ lacking in substance, shallow.

sustancial [sustan'θjal] *adj* substantial.

sustancioso, a [sustan'θjoso, a] *adj* substantial; (*discurso*) solid.

sustantivo, a [sustan'tiβo, a] *adj* substantive; (*LING*) substantival, noun *cpd* ♦ *nm* noun, substantive.

sustentar [susten'tar] *vt* (*alimentar*) to sustain, nourish; (*objeto*) to hold up, support; (*idea, teoría*) to maintain, uphold; (*fig*) to sustain, keep going.

sustento [sus'tento] *nm* support; (*alimento*) sustenance, food.

sustituir [sustitu'ir] *vt* to substitute, replace.

sustituto, a [susti'tuto, a] *nm/f* substitute, replacement.

sustituyendo [sustitu'jendo] *etc vb V* **sustituir**.

susto ['susto] *nm* fright, scare; **dar un** ~ **a algn** to give sb a fright; **darse** *o* **pegarse un** ~ (*fam*) to get a fright.

sustraer [sustra'er] *vt* to remove, take away; (*MAT*) to subtract.

sustraiga [sus'traiɣa] *etc*, **sustraje** [sus'traxe] *etc*, **sustrajera** [sustra'xera] *etc vb V* **sustraer**.

sustrato [sus'trato] *nm* substratum.

sustrayendo [sustra'jendo] *etc vb V* sustraer.

susurrar [susu'rrar] *vi* to whisper.

susurro [su'surro] *nm* whisper.

sutil [su'til] *adj* (*aroma*) subtle; (*tenue*) thin; (*hilo, hebra*) fine; (*olor*) delicate; (*brisa*) gentle; (*diferencia*) fine, subtle; (*inteligencia*) sharp, keen.

sutileza [suti'leθa] *nf* subtlety; (*delgadez*) thinness; (*delicadeza*) delicacy; (*agudeza*) keenness.

sutura [su'tura] *nf* suture.

suturar [sutu'rar] *vt* to suture; (*juntar con puntos*) to stitch.

suyo, a ['sujo, a] *adj* (*con artículo o después del verbo ser: de él*) his; (: *de ella*) hers; (: *de ellos, ellas*) theirs; (: *de usted, ustedes*) yours; (*después de un nombre: de él*) of his; (: *de ella*) of hers; (: *de ellos, ellas*) of theirs; (: *de usted, ustedes*) of yours; **lo** ~ (what is) his; (*su parte*) his share, what he deserves; **los** ~**s** (*familia*) one's family *o* relations; (*partidarios*) one's own people *o* supporters; ~ **afectísimo** (*en carta*) yours faithfully *o* sincerely; **de** ~ in itself; **eso es muy** ~ that's just like him; **hacer de las suyas** to get up to one's old tricks; **ir a la suya, ir a lo** ~ to go one's own way; **salirse con la suya** to get one's way.

T t

T, t [te] *nf* (*letra*) T, t; **T de Tarragona** T for Tommy.

t *abr* = **tonelada**.

T. *abr* (= *Telefón, Telégrafo*) tel.; (*COM*) = **Tarifa; Tasa**.

t. *abr* (= *tomo(s)*) vol(s).

Tabacalera [taβaka'lera] *nf* Spanish state tobacco monopoly.

tabaco [ta'βako] *nm* tobacco; (*fam*) cigarettes *pl*.

tábano ['taβano] *nm* horsefly.

tabaquería [tabake'ria] *nf* tobacconist's (*BRIT*), cigar store (*US*).

tabarra [ta'βarra] *nf* (*fam*) nuisance; **dar la** ~ to be a pain in the neck.

taberna [ta'βerna] *nf* bar.

tabernero, a [taβer'nero, a] *nm/f* (*encargado*) publican; (*camarero*) barman/barmaid.

tabique [ta'ßike] *nm* (*pared*) thin wall; (*para dividir*) partition.

tabla ['taßla] *nf* (*de madera*) plank; (*estante*) shelf; (*de anuncios*) board; (*lista, catálogo*) list; (*mostrador*) counter; (*de vestido*) pleat; (*ARTE*) panel; ~s *nfpl* (*TAUR, TEAT*) boards; **hacer ~s** to draw; ~ **de consulta** (*INFORM*) lookup table.

tablado [ta'ßlaðo] *nm* (*plataforma*) platform; (*suelo*) plank floor; (*TEAT*) stage.

tablao [ta'ßlao] *nm* (*tb:* ~ **flamenco**) flamenco show.

tablero [ta'ßlero] *nm* (*de madera*) plank, board; (*pizarra*) blackboard; (*de ajedrez, damas*) board; (*AUTO*) dashboard; ~ **de gráficos** (*INFORM*) graph pad.

tableta [ta'ßleta] *nf* (*MED*) tablet; (*de chocolate*) bar.

tablilla [ta'ßliʎa] *nf* small board; (*MED*) splint.

tablón [ta'ßlon] *nm* (*de suelo*) plank; (*de techo*) beam; (*de anuncios*) notice board.

tabú [ta'ßu] *nm* taboo.

tabulación [taßula'θjon] *nf* (*INFORM*) tab(bing).

tabulador [taßula'ðor] *nm* (*INFORM, TIP*) tab.

tabuladora [taßula'ðora] *nf:* ~ **eléctrica** electric accounting machine.

tabular [taßu'lar] *vt* to tabulate; (*INFORM*) to tab.

taburete [taßu'rete] *nm* stool.

tacaño, a [ta'kaɲo, a] *adj* (*avaro*) mean; (*astuto*) crafty.

tacha ['tatʃa] *nf* (*defecto*) flaw, defect; (*TEC*) stud; **poner ~ a** to find fault with; **sin ~** flawless.

tachar [ta'tʃar] *vt* (*borrar*) to cross out; (*corregir*) to correct; (*criticar*) to criticize; ~ **de** to accuse of.

tacho ['tatʃo] *nm* (*AM*) bucket, pail.

tachón [ta'tʃon] *nm* erasure; (*tachadura*) crossing-out; (*TEC*) ornamental stud; (*COSTURA*) trimming.

tachuela [ta'tʃwela] *nf* (*clavo*) tack.

tácito, a ['taθito, a] *adj* tacit; (*acuerdo*) unspoken; (*LING*) understood; (*ley*) unwritten.

taciturno, a [taθi'turno, a] *adj* (*callado*) silent; (*malhumorado*) sullen.

taco ['tako] *nm* (*BILLAR*) cue; (*libro de billetes*) book; (*manojo de billetes*) wad; (*AM*) heel; (*tarugo*) peg; (*fam: bocado*) snack; (: *palabrota*) swear word; (: *trago de vino*) swig; (*Méjico*) filled tortilla; **armarse o hacerse un** ~ to get into a mess.

tacógrafo [ta'koɣrafo] *nm* (*COM*) tachograph.

tacón [ta'kon] *nm* heel; **de** ~ **alto** high-heeled.

taconear [takone'ar] *vi* (*dar golpecitos*) to tap with one's heels; (*MIL etc*) to click one's heels.

taconeo [tako'neo] *nm* (heel) tapping *o* clicking.

táctico, a ['taktiko, a] *adj* tactical ♦ *nf* tactics *pl*.

tacto ['takto] *nm* touch; (*acción*) touching; (*fig*) tact.

TAE *nf abr* (= *tasa anual equivalente*) APR.

tafetán [tafe'tan] *nm* taffeta; **tafetanes** *nmpl* (*fam*) frills; ~ **adhesivo** *o* **inglés** sticking plaster.

tafilete [tafi'lete] *nm* morocco leather.

tahona [ta'ona] *nf* (*panadería*) bakery; (*molino*) flourmill.

tahur [ta'ur] *nm* gambler; (*pey*) cheat.

tailandés, esa [tailan'des, esa] *adj, nm/f* Thai ♦ *nm* (*LING*) Thai.

Tailandia [tai'landja] *nf* Thailand.

taimado, a [tai'maðo, a] *adj* (*astuto*) sly; (*resentido*) sullen.

taita ['taita] *nm* dad, daddy.

tajada [ta'xaða] *nf* slice; (*fam*) rake-off; **sacar** ~ to get one's share.

tajante [ta'xante] *adj* sharp; (*negativa*) emphatic; **es una persona** ~ he's an emphatic person.

tajar [ta'xar] *vt* to cut, slice.

Tajo ['taxo] *nm* Tagus.

tajo ['taxo] *nm* (*corte*) cut; (*filo*) cutting edge; (*GEO*) cleft.

tal [tal] *adj* such; **un** ~ **García** a man called García; ~ **vez** perhaps ♦ *pron* (*persona*) someone, such a one; (*cosa*) something, such a thing; ~ **como** such as; ~ **para cual** tit for tat; (*dos iguales*) two of a kind; **hablábamos de que si** ~ **si cual** we were talking about this, that and the other ♦ *adv:* ~ **como** (*igual*) just as; ~ **cual** (*como es*) just as it is; ~ **el padre, cual el hijo** like father, like son; **¿qué ~?** how are things?; **¿qué** ~ **te gusta?** how do you like it? ♦ *conj:* **con** ~ **(de) que** provided that.

tala ['tala] *nf* (*de árboles*) tree felling.

taladradora [talaðra'ðora] *nf* drill; ~ **neumática** pneumatic drill.

taladrar [tala'ðrar] *vt* to drill; (*fig: suj: ruido*) to pierce.

taladro [ta'laðro] *nm* (*gen*) drill; (*hoyo*) drill hole; ~ **neumático** pneumatic drill.

talante [ta'lante] *nm* (*humor*) mood; (*voluntad*) will, willingness.

talar [ta'lar] *vt* to fell, cut down; (*fig*) to devastate.

talco ['talko] *nm* (*polvos*) talcum powder; (*MINERALOGÍA*) talc.

talega [ta'leɣa] *nf* sack.

talego [ta'leɣo] *nm* sack; **tener ~** (*fam*) to have money.

talento [ta'lento] *nm* talent; (*capacidad*) ability; (*don*) gift.

Talgo ['talgo] *nm abr* (*FERRO = tren articulado ligero Goicoechea-Oriol*) high-speed train.

talidomida [taliðo'miða] *nm* thalidomide.

talismán [talis'man] *nm* talisman.

talla ['taʎa] *nf* (*estatura, fig, MED*) height, stature; (*de ropa*) size, fitting; (*palo*) measuring rod; (*ARTE: de madera*)) carving; (*de piedra*) sculpture.

tallado, a [ta'ʎaðo, a] *adj* carved ♦ *nm* (*de madera*) carving; (*de piedra*) sculpture.

tallar [ta'ʎar] *vt* (*trabajar*) to work, carve; (*grabar*) to engrave; (*medir*) to measure; (*repartir*) to deal ♦ *vi* to deal.

tallarín [taʎa'rin] *nm* noodle.

talle ['taʎe] *nm* (*ANAT*) waist; (*medida*) size; (*física*) build; (: *de mujer*) figure; (*fig*) appearance; **de ~ esbelto** with a slim figure.

taller [ta'ʎer] *nm* (*TEC*) workshop; (*fábrica*) factory; (*AUTO*) garage; (*de artista*) studio.

tallo ['taʎo] *nm* (*de planta*) stem; (*de hierba*) blade; (*brote*) shoot; (*col*) cabbage; (*CULIN*) candied peel.

talmente [tal'mente] *adv* (*de esta forma*) in such a way; (*hasta tal punto*) to such an extent; (*exactamente*) exactly.

talón [ta'lon] *nm* (*gen*) heel; (*COM*) counterfoil; (*TEC*) rim; **~ de Aquiles** Achilles heel.

talonario [talo'narjo] *nm* (*de cheques*) cheque book; (*de billetes*) book of tickets; (*de recibos*) receipt book.

tamaño, a [ta'maɲo, a] *adj* (*tan grande*) such a big; (*tan pequeño*) such a small ♦ *nm* size; **de ~ natural** full-size; **¿de qué ~ es?** what size is it?

tamarindo [tama'rindo] *nm* tamarind.

tambaleante [tambale'ante] *adj* (*persona*) staggering; (*mueble*) wobbly; (*vehículo*) swaying.

tambalearse [tambale'arse] *vr* (*persona*) to stagger; (*mueble*) to wobble; (*vehículo*) to sway.

también [tam'bjen] *adv* (*igualmente*) also, too, as well; (*además*) besides; **estoy cansado — yo ~** I'm tired — so am I *o* me too.

tambor [tam'bor] *nm* drum; (*ANAT*) eardrum; **~ del freno** brake drum; **~**

magnético (*INFORM*) magnetic drum.

tamboril [tambo'ril] *nm* small drum.

tamborilear [tamborile'ar] *vi* (*MUS*) to drum; (*con los dedos*) to drum with one's fingers.

tamborilero [tambori'lero] *nm* drummer.

Támesis ['tamesis] *nm* Thames.

tamice [ta'miθe] *etc vb V* **tamizar**.

tamiz [ta'miθ] *nm* sieve.

tamizar [tami'θar] *vt* to sieve.

tampoco [tam'poko] *adv* nor, neither; **yo ~ lo compré** I didn't buy it either.

tampón [tam'pon] *nm* plug; (*MED*) tampon.

tan [tan] *adv* so; **~ es así que** so much so that; **¡qué cosa ~ rara!** how strange!; **no es una idea ~ buena** it is not such a good idea.

tanatorio [tana'torjo] *nm* (*privado*) funeral home *o* parlour; (*público*) mortuary.

tanda ['tanda] *nf* (*gen*) series; (*de inyecciones*) course; (*juego*) set; (*turno*) shift; (*grupo*) gang.

tándem ['tandem] *nm* tandem; (*POL*) duo.

tanga ['tanga] *nm* (*bikini*) tanga; (*ropa interior*) tanga briefs.

tangente [tan'xente] *nf* tangent; **salirse por la ~** to go off at a tangent.

Tánger ['tanxer] *n* Tangier.

tangerino, a [tanxe'rino, a] *adj* of *o* from Tangier ♦ *nm/f* native *o* inhabitant of Tangier.

tangible [tan'xiβle] *adj* tangible.

tango ['tango] *nm* tango.

tanino [ta'nino] *nm* tannin.

tanque ['tanke] *nm* (*gen*) tank; (*AUTO, NAUT*) tanker.

tanqueta [tan'keta] *nf* (*MIL*) small tank, armoured vehicle.

tantear [tante'ar] *vt* (*calcular*) to reckon (up); (*medir*) to take the measure of; (*probar*) to test, try out; (*tomar la medida*: *persona*) to take the measurements of; (*considerar*) to weigh up ♦ *vi* (*DEPORTE*) to score.

tanteo [tan'teo] *nm* (*cálculo*) (rough) calculation; (*prueba*) test, trial; (*DEPORTE*) scoring; (*adivinanzas*) guesswork; **al ~** by trial and error.

tantísimo, a [tan'tisimo, a] *adj* so much; **~s** so many.

tanto, a ['tanto, a] *adj* (*cantidad*) so much, as much; **~s** so many, as many; **20 y ~s** 20-odd ♦ *adv* (*cantidad*) so much, as much; (*tiempo*) so long, as long; **~ tú como yo** both you and I; **~ como eso** it's not as bad as that; **~ más ... cuanto que** it's all the more ... because; **~ mejor/peor** so much the better/the worse; **~ si**

viene como si va whether he comes or whether he goes; ~ **es así que** so much so that; **por** ~, **por lo** ~ therefore; **me he vuelto ronco de** o **con** ~ **hablar** I have become hoarse with so much talking ♦ conj: **con** ~ **que** provided (that); **en** ~ **que** while; **hasta** ~ **(que)** until such time as ♦ nm (suma) certain amount; (proporción) so much; (punto) point; (gol) goal; ~ **alzado** agreed price; ~ **por ciento** percentage; **al** ~ up to date; **estar al** ~ **de los acontecimientos** to be fully abreast of events; **un** ~ **perezoso** somewhat lazy; **al** ~ **de que** because of the fact that ♦ pron: **cada uno paga** ~ each one pays so much; **uno de** ~s one of many; **a** ~s **de agosto** on such and such a day in August; **entre** ~ meanwhile.

tañer [ta'ɲer] vt (MUS) to play; (campana) to ring.

T/año abr = toneladas por año.

TAO nf abr (= traducción asistida por ordenador) MAT.

tapa ['tapa] nf (de caja, olla) lid; (de botella) top; (de libro) cover; (comida) snack.

tapacubos [tapa'kuβos] nm inv hub cap.

tapadera [tapa'ðera] nf lid, cover.

tapado [ta'paðo] nm (AM: abrigo) coat.

tapar [ta'par] vt (cubrir) to cover; (envolver) to wrap o cover up; (la vista) to obstruct; (persona, falta) to conceal; (AM) to fill; ~**se** vr to wrap o.s. up.

tapete [ta'pete] nm table cover; **estar sobre el** ~ (fig) to be under discussion.

tapia ['tapja] nf (garden) wall.

tapiar [ta'pjar] vt to wall in.

tapice [ta'piθe] etc vb V **tapizar**.

tapicería [tapiθe'ria] nf tapestry; (para muebles) upholstery; (tienda) upholsterer's (shop).

tapicero, a [tapi'θero, a] nm/f (de muebles) upholsterer.

tapiz [ta'piθ] nm (alfombra) carpet; (tela tejida) tapestry.

tapizar [tapi'θar] vt (pared) to wallpaper; (suelo) to carpet; (muebles) to upholster.

tapón [ta'pon] nm (corcho) stopper; (TEC) plug; (MED) tampon; ~ **de rosca** o **de tuerca** screw-top.

taponar [tapo'nar] vt (botella) to cork; (tubería) to block.

taponazo [tapo'naθo] nm (de tapón) pop.

tapujo [ta'puxo] nm (embozo) muffler; (engaño) deceit; **sin** ~s honestly.

taquigrafía [takiɣra'fia] nf shorthand.

taquígrafo, a [ta'kiɣrafo, a] nm/f shorthand writer.

taquilla [ta'kiʎa] nf (de estación etc) booking office; (de teatro) box office; (suma recogida) takings pl; (archivador) filing cabinet.

taquillero, a [taki'ʎero, a] adj: **función taquillera** box office success ♦ nm/f ticket clerk.

taquimecanografía [takimekanoɣra'fia] nf shorthand and typing.

taquímetro [ta'kimetro] nm speedometer; (de control) tachymeter.

tara ['tara] nf (defecto) defect; (COM) tare.

tarado, a [ta'raðo, a] adj (COM) defective, imperfect; (idiota) stupid; (loco) crazy, nuts ♦ nm/f idiot, cretin.

tarántula [ta'rantula] nf tarantula.

tararear [tarare'ar] vi to hum.

tardanza [tar'ðanθa] nf (demora) delay; (lentitud) slowness.

tardar [tar'ðar] vi (tomar tiempo) to take a long time; (llegar tarde) to be late; (demorar) to delay; **¿tarda mucho el tren?** does the train take long?; **a más** ~ at the (very) latest; ~ **en hacer algo** to be slow o take a long time to do sth; **no tardes en venir** come soon, come before long.

tarde ['tarðe] adv (hora) late; (fuera de tiempo) too late ♦ nf (de día) afternoon; (de noche) evening; ~ **o temprano** sooner or later; **de** ~ **en** ~ from time to time; **¡buenas** ~s! (de día) good afternoon!; (de noche) good evening!; **a** o **por la** ~ in the afternoon; in the evening.

tardío, a [tar'ðio, a] adj (retrasado) late; (lento) slow (to arrive).

tardo, a ['tarðo, a] adj (lento) slow; (torpe) dull; ~ **de oído** hard of hearing.

tarea [ta'rea] nf task; ~s nfpl (ESCOL) homework sg; ~ **de ocasión** chore.

tarifa [ta'rifa] nf (lista de precios) price list; (COM) tariff; ~ **básica** basic rate; ~ **completa** all-in cost; ~ **a destajo** piece rate; ~ **doble** double time.

tarima [ta'rima] nf (plataforma) platform; (taburete) stool; (litera) bunk.

tarjeta [tar'xeta] nf card; ~ **postal/de crédito/de Navidad** postcard/credit card/Christmas card; ~ **de circuitos** (INFORM) circuit board; ~ **comercial** (COM) calling card; ~ **dinero** cash card; ~ **gráficos** (INFORM) graphics card; ~ **de multifunción** (INFORM) multiplication card.

tarot [ta'rot] nm tarot.

tarraconense [tarrako'nense] adj of o from Tarragona ♦ nm/f native o inhabitant of Tarragona.

tarro ['tarro] *nm* jar, pot.
tarta ['tarta] *nf* (*pastel*) cake; (*torta*) tart.
tartajear [tartaxe'ar] *vi* to stammer.
tartamudear [tartamuðe'ar] *vi* to stutter, stammer.
tartamudo, a [tarta'muðo, a] *adj* stuttering, stammering ♦ *nm/f* stutterer, stammerer.
tartárico, a [tar'tariko, a] *adj*: **ácido ~** tartaric acid.
tártaro ['tartaro] *adj, nm* Tartar ♦ *nm* (*QUIMICA*) tartar.
tarugo, a [ta'ruɣo, a] *adj* stupid ♦ *nm* (*de madera*) lump.
tarumba [ta'rumba] *adj* (*confuso*) confused.
tasa ['tasa] *nf* (*precio*) (fixed) price, rate; (*valoración*) valuation; (*medida, norma*) measure, standard; ~ **básica** (*COM*) basic rate; ~ **de cambio** exchange rate; **de ~ cero** (*COM*) zero-rated; ~ **de crecimiento** growth rate; ~ **de interés/de nacimiento** rate of interest/birth rate; ~ **de rendimiento** (*COM*) rate of return; **~s universitarias** university fees.
tasación [tasa'θjon] *nf* assessment, valuation; (*fig*) appraisal.
tasador, a [tasa'ðor, a] *nm/f* valuer; (*COM*: *de impuestos*) assessor.
tasar [ta'sar] *vt* (*arreglar el precio*) to fix a price for; (*valorar*) to value, assess; (*limitar*) to limit.
tasca ['taska] *nf* (*fam*) pub.
tata ['tata] *nm* (*fam*) dad(dy) ♦ *nf* (*niñera*) nanny, maid.
tatarabuelo, a [tatara'ßwelo, a] *nm/f* great-great-grandfather/mother; **los ~s** one's great-great-grandparents.
tatuaje [ta'twaxe] *nm* (*dibujo*) tattoo; (*acto*) tattooing.
tatuar [ta'twar] *vt* to tattoo.
taumaturgo [tauma'turɣo] *nm* miracle-worker.
taurino, a [tau'rino, a] *adj* bullfighting *cpd*.
Tauro ['tauro] *nm* Taurus.
tauromaquia [tauro'makja] *nf* (art of) bullfighting.
tautología [tautolo'xia] *nf* tautology.
taxativo, a [taksa'tißo, a] *adj* (*restringido*) limited; (*sentido*) specific.
taxi ['taksi] *nm* taxi.
taxidermia [taksi'ðermja] *nf* taxidermy.
taxímetro [tak'simetro] *nm* taximeter.
taxista [tak'sista] *nm/f* taxi driver.
Tayikistán [tajikis'tan] *nm* Tajikistan.
taza ['taθa] *nf* cup; (*de retrete*) bowl; ~ **para café** coffee cup.
tazón [ta'θon] *nm* mug, large cup;

(*escudilla*) basin.
TCI *nf abr* (= *tarjeta de circuito impreso*) PCB.
te [te] *pron* (*complemento de objeto*) you; (*complemento indirecto*) (to) you; (*reflexivo*) (to) yourself; **¿~ duele mucho el brazo?** does your arm hurt a lot?; ~ **equivocas** you're wrong; **¡cálma~!** calm yourself!
té [te], *pl* **tés** *nm* tea; (*reunión*) tea party.
tea ['tea] *nf* (*antorcha*) torch.
teatral [tea'tral] *adj* theatre *cpd*; (*fig*) theatrical.
teatro [te'atro] *nm* theatre; (*LITERATURA*) plays *pl*, drama; **el ~** (*carrera*) the theatre, acting; ~ **de aficionados/de variedades** amateur/variety theatre, vaudeville theater (*US*); **hacer ~** (*fig*) to make a fuss.
tebeo [te'ßeo] *nm* children's comic.
techado [te'tʃaðo] *nm* (*techo*) roof; **bajo ~** under cover.
techo ['tetʃo] *nm* (*externo*) roof; (*interno*) ceiling.
techumbre [te'tʃumbre] *nf* roof.
tecla ['tekla] *nf* (*INFORM, MUS, TIP*) key; (*INFORM*): ~ **de anulación/de borrar** cancel/delete key; ~ **de control/de edición** control/edit key; ~ **con flecha** arrow key; ~ **programable** user-defined key; ~ **de retorno/de tabulación** return/tab key; ~ **del cursor** cursor key; **~s de control direccional del cursor** cursor control keys.
teclado [te'klaðo] *nm* keyboard (*tb INFORM*); ~ **numérico** (*INFORM*) numeric keypad.
teclear [tekle'ar] *vi* to strum; (*fam*) to drum ♦ *vt* (*INFORM*) to key (in), type in, keyboard.
tecleo [te'kleo] *nm* (*MUS*: *sonido*) strumming; (: *forma de tocar*) fingering; (*fam*) drumming.
tecnicismo [tekni'θismo] *nm* (*carácter técnico*) technical nature; (*LING*) technical term.
técnico, a ['tekniko, a] *adj* technical ♦ *nm* technician; (*experto*) expert ♦ *nf* (*procedimientos*) technique; (*arte, oficio*) craft.
tecnicolor [tekniko'lor] *nm* Technicolor ®.
tecnócrata [tek'nokrata] *nm/f* technocrat.
tecnología [teknolo'xia] *nf* technology; ~ **de estado sólido** (*INFORM*) solid-state technology; ~ **de la información** information technology.
tecnológico, a [tekno'loxiko, a] *adj* technological.

tecnólogo, a [tek'noloɣo, a] *nm/f*
technologist.
tedio ['teðjo] *nm* (*aburrimiento*) boredom;
(*apatía*) apathy; (*fastidio*) depression.
tedioso, a [te'ðjoso, a] *adj* boring;
(*cansado*) wearisome, tedious.
Teherán [tee'ran] *nm* Teheran.
teja ['texa] *nf* (*azulejo*) tile; (*BOT*) lime
(tree).
tejado [te'xaðo] *nm* (tiled) roof.
tejano, a [te'xano, a] *adj, nm/f* Texan ♦ *nmpl*:
~**s** (*vaqueros*) jeans.
Tejas ['texas] *nm* Texas.
tejemaneje [texema'nexe] *nm* (*actividad*)
bustle; (*lío*) fuss, to-do; (*intriga*) intrigue.
tejer [te'xer] *vt* to weave; (*tela de araña*) to
spin; (*AM*) to knit; (*fig*) to fabricate ♦ *vi*:
~ **y destejer** to chop and change.
tejido [te'xiðo] *nm* fabric; (*estofa, tela*)
(knitted) material; (*ANAT*) tissue;
(*textura*) texture.
tejo ['texo] *nm* (*BOT*) yew (tree).
tel. *abr* (= *teléfono*) tel.
tela ['tela] *nf* (*material*) material; (*de fruta,
en líquido*) skin; (*del ojo*) film; **hay** ~ **para
rato** there's lots to talk about; **poner en**
~ **de juicio** to (call in) question; ~ **de
araña** cobweb, spider's web.
telar [te'lar] *nm* (*máquina*) loom; (*de teatro*)
gridiron; ~**es** *nmpl* textile mill *sg*.
telaraña [tela'raɲa] *nf* cobweb, spider's
web.
tele... [tele] *pref* tele...
tele ['tele] *nf* (*fam*) TV.
telecargar [telekar'ɣar] *vt* (*INFORM*) to
download.
telecomunicación [telekomunika'θjon] *nf*
telecommunication.
telecontrol [telekon'trol] *nm* remote
control.
telecopiadora [telekopja'ðora] *nf*: ~
facsímil fax copier.
telediario [tele'ðjarjo] *nm* television news.
teledifusión [teleðifu'sjon] *nf* (television)
broadcast.
teledirigido, a [teleðiri'xiðo, a] *adj*
remote-controlled.
teléf. *abr* (= *teléfono*) tel.
teleférico [tele'feriko] *nm* (*tren*) cable-
railway; (*de esquí*) ski-lift.
telefilm [tele'film], **telefilme** [tele'filme]
nm TV film.
telefonazo [telefo'naθo] *nm* (*fam*)
telephone call; **te daré un** ~ I'll give you
a ring.
telefonear [telefone'ar] *vi* to telephone.
telefónicamente [tele'fonikamente] *adv* by
(tele)phone.

telefónico, a [tele'foniko, a] *adj* telephone
cpd ♦ *nf*: **Telefónica** (*ESP*) Spanish
national telephone company, ≈ British
Telecom.
telefonista [telefo'nista] *nm/f* telephonist.
teléfono [te'lefono] *nm* (tele)phone; ~
móvil mobile phone; **está hablando por**
~ he's on the phone.
telefoto [tele'foto] *nf* telephoto.
telegrafía [teleɣra'fia] *nf* telegraphy.
telégrafo [te'leɣrafo] *nm* telegraph; (*fam:
persona*) telegraph boy.
telegrama [tele'ɣrama] *nm* telegram.
teleimpresor [teleimpre'sor] *nm*
teleprinter.
telemática [tele'matika] *nf* telematics *sg*.
telémetro [te'lemetro] *nm* rangefinder.
telenovela [teleno'βela] *nf* soap (opera).
teleobjetivo [teleobxe'tiβo] *nm* telephoto
lens.
telepatía [telepa'tia] *nf* telepathy.
telepático, a [tele'patiko, a] *adj* telepathic.
teleproceso [telepro'θeso] *nm*
teleprocessing.
telescópico, a [tele'skopiko, a] *adj*
telescopic.
telescopio [tele'skopjo] *nm* telescope.
telesilla [tele'siʎa] *nm* chairlift.
telespectador, a [telespekta'ðor, a] *nm/f*
viewer.
telesquí [teles'ki] *nm* ski-lift.
teletex(to) [tele'teks(to)] *nm* teletext.
teletipista [teleti'pista] *nm/f* teletypist.
teletipo [tele'tipo] *nm* teletype(writer).
televentas [tele'βentas] *nfpl* telesales.
televidente [teleβi'ðente] *nm/f* viewer.
televisar [teleβi'sar] *vt* to televise.
televisión [teleβi'sjon] *nf* television; ~ **en
color/por satélite** colour/satellite
television.
televisivo, a [teleβi'siβo, a] *adj* television
cpd.
televisor [teleβi'sor] *nm* television set.
télex ['teleks] *nm* telex; **máquina** ~ telex
(machine); **enviar por** ~ to telex.
telón [te'lon] *nm* curtain; ~ **de boca/
seguridad** front/safety curtain; ~ **de
acero** (*POL*) iron curtain; ~ **de fondo**
backcloth, background.
telonero, a [telo'nero, a] *nm/f* support act;
los ~**s** (*MUS*) the support band.
tema ['tema] *nm* (*asunto*) subject, topic;
(*MUS*) theme; ~**s de actualidad** current
affairs ♦ *nf* (*obsesión*) obsession; (*manía*)
ill-will; **tener** ~ **a algn** to have a grudge
against sb.
temario [te'marjo] *nm* (*ESCOL*) set of top-
ics; (*de una conferencia*) agenda.

temático, a [te'matiko, a] *adj* thematic ♦ *nf* subject matter.

tembladera [tembla'ðera] *nf* shaking; (*AM*) quagmire.

temblar [tem'blar] *vi* to shake, tremble; (*de frío*) to shiver.

tembleque [tem'bleke] *adj* shaking ♦ *nm* shaking.

temblón, ona [tem'blon, ona] *adj* shaking.

temblor [tem'blor] *nm* trembling; (*AM: de tierra*) earthquake.

tembloroso, a [temblo'roso, a] *adj* trembling.

temer [te'mer] *vt* to fear ♦ *vi* to be afraid; **temo que Juan llegue tarde** I am afraid Juan may be late.

temerario, a [teme'rarjo, a] *adj* (*imprudente*) rash; (*descuidado*) reckless; (*arbitrario*) hasty.

temeridad [temeri'ðað] *nf* (*imprudencia*) rashness; (*audacia*) boldness.

temeroso, a [teme'roso, a] *adj* (*miedoso*) fearful; (*que inspira temor*) frightful.

temible [te'miβle] *adj* fearsome.

temor [te'mor] *nm* (*miedo*) fear; (*duda*) suspicion.

témpano ['tempano] *nm* (*MUS*) kettledrum; ~ **de hielo** ice floe.

temperamento [tempera'mento] *nm* temperament; **tener** ~ to be temperamental.

temperar [tempe'rar] *vt* to temper, moderate.

temperatura [tempera'tura] *nf* temperature.

tempestad [tempes'tað] *nf* storm; ~ **en un vaso de agua** (*fig*) storm in a teacup.

tempestuoso, a [tempes'twoso, a] *adj* stormy.

templado, a [tem'plaðo, a] *adj* (*moderado*) moderate; (: *en el comer*) frugal; (: *en el beber*) abstemious; (*agua*) lukewarm; (*clima*) mild; (*MUS*) in tune, well-tuned.

templanza [tem'planθa] *nf* moderation; (*en el beber*) abstemiousness; (*del clima*) mildness.

templar [tem'plar] *vt* (*moderar*) to moderate; (*furia*) to restrain; (*calor*) to reduce; (*solución*) to dilute; (*afinar*) to tune (up); (*acero*) to temper ♦ *vi* to moderate; ~**se** *vr* to be restrained.

temple ['temple] *nm* (*humor*) mood; (*coraje*) courage; (*ajuste*) tempering; (*afinación*) tuning; (*pintura*) tempera.

templo ['templo] *nm* (*iglesia*) church; (*pagano etc*) temple; ~ **metodista** Methodist chapel.

temporada [tempo'raða] *nf* time, period; (*estación, social, DEPORTE*) season; **en plena** ~ at the height of the season.

temporal [tempo'ral] *adj* (*no permanente*) temporary; (*REL*) temporal ♦ *nm* storm.

temporario, a [tempo'rarjo, a] *adj* (*AM*) temporary.

tempranero, a [tempra'nero, a] *adj* (*BOT*) early; (*persona*) early-rising.

temprano, a [tem'prano, a] *adj* early ♦ *adv* early; (*demasiado pronto*) too soon, too early; **lo más** ~ **posible** as soon as possible.

ten [ten] *vb* V **tener**.

tenacidad [tenaθi'ðað] *nf* (*gen*) tenacity; (*dureza*) toughness; (*terquedad*) stubbornness.

tenacillas [tena'θiλas] *nfpl* (*gen*) tongs; (*para el pelo*) curling tongs; (*MED*) forceps.

tenaz [te'naθ] *adj* (*material*) tough; (*persona*) tenacious; (*pegajoso*) sticky; (*terco*) stubborn.

tenaza(s) [te'naθa(s)] *nf(pl)* (*MED*) forceps; (*TEC*) pliers; (*ZOOL*) pincers.

tendal [ten'dal] *nm* awning.

tendedero [tende'ðero] *nm* (*para ropa*) drying-place; (*cuerda*) clothes line.

tendencia [ten'denθja] *nf* tendency; (*proceso*) trend; ~ **imperante** prevailing tendency; ~ **del mercado** run of the market; **tener** ~ **a** to tend *o* have a tendency to.

tendenciosidad [tendenθjosi'ðað] *nf* tendentiousness.

tendencioso, a [tenden'θjoso, a] *adj* tendentious.

tender [ten'der] *vt* (*extender*) to spread out; (*ropa*) to hang out; (*vía férrea, cable*) to lay; (*cuerda*) to stretch; (*trampa*) to set ♦ *vi* to tend; ~**se** *vr* to lie down; (*fig: dejarse llevar*) to let o.s. go; (: *dejar ir*) to let things go; ~ **la cama/la mesa** (*AM*) to make the bed/lay the table.

ténder ['tender] *nm* (*FERRO*) tender.

tenderete [tende'rete] *nm* (*puesto*) stall; (*carretilla*) barrow; (*exposición*) display of goods.

tendero, a [ten'dero, a] *nm/f* shopkeeper.

tendido, a [ten'diðo, a] *adj* (*acostado*) lying down, flat; (*colgado*) hanging ♦ *nm* (*ropa*) washing; (*TAUR*) front rows *pl* of seats; (*colocación*) laying; (*ARQ: enyesado*) coat of plaster; **a galope** ~ flat out.

tendón [ten'don] *nm* tendon.

tendré [ten'dre] *etc vb* V **tener**.

tenducho [ten'dutʃo] *nm* small dirty shop.

tenebroso, a [tene'ßroso, a] *adj* (*oscuro*) dark; (*fig*) gloomy; (*siniestro*) sinister.

tenedor [tene'ðor] *nm* (*CULIN*) fork; (*poseedor*) holder; ~ **de libros** book-keeper; ~ **de acciones** shareholder; ~ **de póliza** policyholder.

teneduría [teneðu'ria] *nf* keeping; ~ **de libros** book-keeping.

tenencia [te'nenθja] *nf* (*de casa*) tenancy; (*de oficio*) tenure; (*de propiedad*) possession; ~ **asegurada** security of tenure; ~ **ilícita de armas** illegal possession of weapons.

══════════════ *PALABRA CLAVE*

tener [te'ner] *vt* **1** (*poseer, gen*) to have; (*en la mano*) to hold; **¿tienes un boli?** have you got a pen?; **va a ~ un niño** she's going to have a baby; **tiene los ojos azules** he's got blue eyes; **¡ten** (*o* **tenga**)!, **¡aquí tienes** (*o* **tiene**)!** here you are!
2 (*edad, medidas*) to be; **tiene 7 años** she's 7 (years old); **tiene 15 cm de largo** it's 15 cm long
3 (*sentimientos, sensaciones*): ~ **sed/ hambre/frío/calor** to be thirsty/hungry/cold/hot; ~ **celos** to be jealous; ~ **cuidado** to be careful; ~ **razón** to be right; ~ **suerte** to be lucky
4 (*considerar*): **lo tengo por brillante** I consider him to be brilliant; ~ **en mucho a algn** to think very highly of sb
5 (+*pp*, +*adj*, +*gerundio*): **tengo terminada ya la mitad del trabajo** I've done half the work already; **tenía el sombrero puesto** he had his hat on; **tenía pensado llamarte** I had been thinking of phoning you; **nos tiene hartos** we're fed up with him; **me ha tenido tres horas esperando** he kept me waiting three hours
6: ~ **que hacer algo** to have to do sth; **tengo que acabar este trabajo hoy** I have to finish this job today
7: **¿qué tienes, estás enfermo?** what's the matter with you, are you ill?
8 (*locuciones*): **¿conque ésas tenemos?** so it's like that, then?; **no las tengo todas conmigo** I'm a bit unsure (about it); **lo tiene difícil** he'll have a hard job
♦ ~**se** *vr* **1**: ~**se en pie** to stand up
2: ~**se por** to think o.s.; **se tiene por un gran cantante** he thinks himself a great singer.

tenga ['tenga] *etc vb V* **tener**.
tenia ['tenja] *nf* tapeworm.
teniente [te'njente] *nm* lieutenant; ~ **coronel** lieutenant colonel.
tenis ['tenis] *nm* tennis; ~ **de mesa** table tennis.
tenista [te'nista] *nm/f* tennis player.
tenor [te'nor] *nm* (*tono*) tone; (*sentido*) meaning; (*MUS*) tenor; **a** ~ **de** on the lines of.
tenorio [te'norjo] *nm* (*fam*) ladykiller, Don Juan.
tensar [ten'sar] *vt* to tauten; (*arco*) to draw.
tensión [ten'sjon] *nf* tension; (*TEC*) stress; (*MED*): ~ **arterial** blood pressure; ~ **nerviosa** nervous strain; **tener la** ~ **alta** to have high blood pressure.
tenso, a ['tenso, a] *adj* tense; (*relaciones*) strained.
tentación [tenta'θjon] *nf* temptation.
tentáculo [ten'takulo] *nm* tentacle.
tentador, a [tenta'ðor, a] *adj* tempting ♦ *nm/f* tempter/temptress.
tentar [ten'tar] *vt* (*tocar*) to touch, feel; (*seducir*) to tempt; (*atraer*) to attract; (*probar*) to try (out); (*MED*) to probe; ~ **hacer algo** to try to do sth.
tentativa [tenta'tiβa] *nf* attempt; ~ **de asesinato** attempted murder.
tentempié [tentem'pje] *nm* (*fam*) snack.
tenue ['tenwe] *adj* (*delgado*) thin, slender; (*alambre*) fine; (*insustancial*) tenuous; (*sonido*) faint; (*neblina*) light; (*lazo, vínculo*) slight.
teñir [te'ɲir] *vt* to dye; (*fig*) to tinge; ~**se el pelo** to dye one's hair.
teología [teolo'xia] *nf* theology.
teólogo, a [te'oloɣo, a] *nm/f* theologist, theologian.
teorema [teo'rema] *nm* theorem.
teoría [teo'ria] *nf* theory; **en** ~ in theory.
teóricamente [te'orikamente] *adv* theoretically.
teorice [teo'riθe] *etc vb V* **teorizar**.
teórico, a [te'oriko, a] *adj* theoretic(al) ♦ *nm/f* theoretician, theorist.
teorizar [teori'θar] *vi* to theorize.
tequila [te'kila] *nm o f* tequila.
TER [ter] *nm abr* (*FERRO*) = **tren español rápido**.
terapeuta [tera'peuta] *nm/f* therapist.
terapéutico, a [tera'peutiko, a] *adj* therapeutic(al) ♦ *nf* therapeutics *sg*.
terapia [te'rapja] *nf* therapy; ~ **laboral** occupational therapy.
tercer [ter'θer] *adj V* **tercero**.
tercermundista [terθermun'dista] *adj* Third World *cpd*.
tercero, a [ter'θero, a] *adj* third (*delante de nmsg*: **tercer**) ♦ *nm* (*árbitro*) mediator; (*JUR*) third party.
terceto [ter'θeto] *nm* trio.
terciado, a [ter'θjaðo, a] *adj* slanting;

azúcar ~ brown sugar.

terciar [ter'θjar] vt (MAT) to divide into three; (inclinarse) to slope; (llevar) to wear across one's chest ♦ vi (participar) to take part; (hacer de árbitro) to mediate; ~**se** vr to arise.

terciario, a [ter'θjarjo, a] adj tertiary.

tercio ['terθjo] nm third.

terciopelo [terθjo'pelo] nm velvet.

terco, a ['terko, a] adj obstinate, stubborn; (material) tough.

tergal ® [ter'ɣal] nm Terylene ®.

tergiversación [terxiβersa'θjon] nf (deformación) distortion; (evasivas) prevarication.

tergiversar [terxiβer'sar] vt to distort ♦ vi to prevaricate.

termal [ter'mal] adj thermal.

termas ['termas] nfpl hot springs.

térmico, a ['termiko, a] adj thermic, thermal, heat cpd.

terminación [termina'θjon] nf (final) end; (conclusión) conclusion, ending.

terminal [termi'nal] adj terminal ♦ nm (ELEC, INFORM) terminal; ~ **conversacional** interactive terminal; ~ **de pantalla** visual display unit ♦ nf (AVIAT, FERRO) terminal.

terminante [termi'nante] adj (final) final, definitive; (tajante) categorical.

terminar [termi'nar] vt (completar) to complete, finish; (concluir) to end ♦ vi (llegar a su fin) to end; (parar) to stop; (acabar) to finish; ~**se** vr to come to an end; ~ **por hacer algo** to end up (by) doing sth.

término ['termino] nm end, conclusion; (parada) terminus; (límite) boundary; (en discusión) point; (LING, COM) term; ~ **medio** average; (fig) middle way; **en otros ~s** in other words; **en último ~** (a fin de cuentas) in the last analysis; (como último recurso) as a last resort; **en ~s de** in terms of; **según los ~s del contrato** according to the terms of the contract.

terminología [terminolo'xia] nf terminology.

termita [ter'mita] nf termite.

termo ['termo] nm Thermos ® (flask).

termodinámico, a [termoði'namiko, a] adj thermodynamic ♦ nf thermodynamics sg.

termoimpresora [termoimpre'sora] nf thermal printer.

termómetro [ter'mometro] nm thermometer.

termonuclear [termonukle'ar] adj thermonuclear.

termostato [termos'tato] nm thermostat.

ternero, a [ter'nero, a] nm/f (animal) calf ♦ nf (carne) veal.

terneza [ter'neθa] nf tenderness.

ternilla [ter'niʎa] nf gristle; (cartílago) cartilage.

terno ['terno] nm (traje) three-piece suit; (conjunto) set of three.

ternura [ter'nura] nf (trato) tenderness; (palabra) endearment; (cariño) fondness.

terquedad [terke'ðað] nf obstinacy; (dureza) harshness.

terrado [te'rraðo] nm terrace.

Terranova [terra'noβa] nf Newfoundland.

terraplén [terra'plen] nm (AGR) terrace; (FERRO) embankment; (MIL) rampart; (cuesta) slope.

terráqueo, a [te'rrakeo, a] adj: **globo** ~ globe.

terrateniente [terrate'njente] nm landowner.

terraza [te'rraθa] nf (balcón) balcony; (techo) flat roof; (AGR) terrace.

terremoto [terre'moto] nm earthquake.

terrenal [terre'nal] adj earthly.

terreno, a [te'rreno, a] adj (de la tierra) earthly, worldly ♦ nm (tierra) land; (parcela) plot; (suelo) soil; (fig) field; **un** ~ a piece of land; **sobre el** ~ on the spot; **ceder/perder** ~ to give/lose ground; **preparar el** ~ **(a)** (fig) to pave the way (for).

terrestre [te'rrestre] adj terrestrial; (ruta) land cpd.

terrible [te'rriβle] adj (espantoso) terrible; (aterrador) dreadful; (tremendo) awful.

territorial [territo'rjal] adj territorial.

territorio [terri'torjo] nm territory; ~ **bajo mandato** mandated territory.

terrón [te'rron] nm (de azúcar) lump; (de tierra) clod, lump; **terrones** nmpl land sg.

terror [te'rror] nm terror.

terrorífico, a [terro'rifiko, a] adj terrifying.

terrorismo [terro'rismo] nm terrorism.

terrorista [terro'rista] adj, nm/f terrorist.

terroso, a [te'rroso, a] adj earthy.

terruño [te'rruɲo] nm (pedazo) clod; (parcela) plot; (fig) native soil; **apego al** ~ attachment to one's native soil.

terso, a ['terso, a] adj (liso) smooth; (pulido) polished; (fig: estilo) flowing.

tersura [ter'sura] nf smoothness; (brillo) shine.

tertulia [ter'tulja] nf (reunión informal) social gathering; (grupo) group, circle; (sala) clubroom; ~ **literaria** literary circle.

tesina [te'sina] nf dissertation.

tesis ['tesis] nf inv thesis.

tesón [te'son] nm (firmeza) firmness; (tenacidad) tenacity.

tesorería [tesore'ria] nf treasurership.

tesorero, a [teso'rero, a] nm/f treasurer.

tesoro [te'soro] nm treasure; **T~ público** (POL) Exchequer.

test, pl **tests** [tes(t), tes(t)] nm test.

testaferro [testa'ferro] nm figurehead.

testamentaría [testamenta'ria] nf execution of a will.

testamentario, a [testamen'tarjo, a] adj testamentary ♦ nm/f executor/executrix.

testamento [testa'mento] nm will.

testar [tes'tar] vi to make a will.

testarada [testa'raða] nf, **testarazo** [testa'raθo] nm: **darse un(a) ~** (fam) to bump one's head.

testarudo, a [testa'ruðo, a] adj stubborn.

testículo [tes'tikulo] nm testicle.

testificar [testifi'kar] vt to testify; (fig) to attest ♦ vi to give evidence.

testifique [testi'fike] etc vb V **testificar**.

testigo [tes'tiɣo] nm/f witness; **~ de cargo/descargo** witness for the prosecution/defence; **~ ocular** eye witness; **poner a algn por ~** to cite sb as a witness.

testimonial [testimo'njal] adj (prueba) testimonial; (gesto) token.

testimoniar [testimo'njar] vt to testify to; (fig) to show.

testimonio [testi'monjo] nm testimony; **en ~ de** as a token o mark of; **falso ~** perjured evidence, false witness.

teta ['teta] nf (de biberón) teat; (ANAT) nipple; (fam) breast; (fam!) tit (!).

tétanos ['tetanos] nm tetanus.

tetera [te'tera] nf teapot; **~ eléctrica** (electric) kettle.

tetilla [te'tiʎa] nf (ANAT) nipple; (de biberón) teat.

tétrico, a ['tetriko, a] adj gloomy, dismal.

textil [teks'til] adj textile.

texto ['teksto] nm text.

textual [teks'twal] adj textual; **palabras ~es** exact words.

textura [teks'tura] nf (de tejido) texture; (de mineral) structure.

tez [teθ] nf (cutis) complexion; (color) colouring.

tfno. abr (= teléfono) tel.

ti [ti] pron you; (reflexivo) yourself.

tía ['tia] nf (pariente) aunt; (mujer cualquiera) girl, bird (col); (fam: pej: vieja) old bag; (: prostituta) whore.

Tibet [ti'ßet] nm: **El ~** Tibet.

tibetano, a [tiße'tano, a] adj, nm/f Tibetan ♦ nm (LING) Tibetan.

tibia ['tißja] nf tibia.

tibieza [ti'ßjeθa] nf (temperatura) tepidness; (fig) coolness.

tibio, a ['tißjo, a] adj lukewarm, tepid.

tiburón [tißu'ron] nm shark.

tic [tik] nm (ruido) click; (de reloj) tick; **~ nervioso** (MED) nervous tic.

tico, a ['tiko, a] adj, nm/f (AM fam) Costa Rican.

tictac [tik'tak] nm (de reloj) tick tock.

tiemble ['tjemble] etc vb V **temblar**.

tiempo ['tjempo] nm (gen) time; (época, período) age, period; (METEOROLOGÍA) weather; (LING) tense; (edad) age; (de juego) half; **a ~** in time; **a un o al mismo ~** at the same time; **al poco ~** very soon (after); **andando el ~** in due course; **cada cierto ~** every so often; **con ~** in time; **con el ~** eventually; **de ~ en ~** from time to time; **en mis ~s** in my time; **en los buenos ~s** in the good old days; **hace buen/mal ~** the weather is fine/bad; **estar a ~** to be in time; **hace ~** some time ago; **hacer ~** to while away the time; **¿qué ~ tiene?** how old is he?; **motor de 2 ~s** two-stroke engine; **~ compartido** (INFORM) time sharing; **~ de ejecución** (INFORM) run time; **~ inactivo** (COM) downtime; **~ libre** spare time; **~ de paro** (COM) idle time; **a ~ partido** (trabajar) part-time; **~ preferencial** (COM) prime time; **en ~ real** (INFORM) real time.

tienda ['tjenda] etc vb V **tender** ♦ nf shop; (más grande) store; (NAUT) awning; **~ de campaña** tent.

tiene ['tjene] etc vb V **tener**.

tienta ['tjenta] nf (MED) probe; (fig) tact; **andar a ~s** to grope one's way along.

tiento ['tjento] etc vb V **tentar** ♦ nm (tacto) touch; (precaución) wariness; (pulso) steady hand; (ZOOL) feeler, tentacle.

tierno, a ['tjerno, a] adj (blando, dulce) tender; (fresco) fresh.

tierra ['tjerra] nf earth; (suelo) soil; (mundo) world; (país) country, land; (ELEC) earth, ground (US); **~ adentro** inland; **~ natal** native land; **echar ~ a un asunto** to hush an affair up; **no es de estas ~s** he's not from these parts; **la T~ Santa** the Holy Land.

tieso, a ['tjeso, a] etc vb V **tesar** ♦ adj (rígido) rigid; (duro) stiff; (fig: testarudo) stubborn; (fam: orgulloso) conceited ♦ adv strongly.

tiesto ['tjesto] nm flowerpot; (pedazo)

piece of pottery.
tifoidea [tifoi'ðea] *nf* typhoid.
tifón [ti'fon] *nm* (*huracán*) typhoon; (*de mar*) tidal wave.
tifus ['tifus] *nm* typhus; ~ **icteroides** yellow fever.
tigre ['tiɣre] *nm* tiger; (*AM*) jaguar.
tijera [ti'xera] *nf* (*una* ~) (pair of) scissors *pl*; (*ZOOL*) claw; (*persona*) gossip; **de** ~ folding; ~**s** *nfpl* scissors; (*para plantas*) shears; **unas** ~**s** a pair of scissors.
tijeretear [tixerete'ar] *vt* to snip ♦ *vi* (*fig*) to meddle.
tila ['tila] *nf* (*BOT*) lime tree; (*CULIN*) lime flower tea.
tildar [til'dar] *vt*: ~ **de** to brand as.
tilde ['tilde] *nf* (*defecto*) defect; (*trivialidad*) triviality; (*TIP*) tilde.
tilín [ti'lin] *nm* tinkle.
tilo ['tilo] *nm* lime tree.
timador, a [tima'ðor, a] *nm/f* swindler.
timar [ti'mar] *vt* (*robar*) to steal; (*estafar*) to swindle; (*persona*) to con; ~**se** *vr* (*fam*) to make eyes (*con algn* at sb).
timbal [tim'bal] *nm* small drum.
timbrar [tim'brar] *vt* to stamp; (*sellar*) to seal; (*carta*) to postmark.
timbrazo [tim'braθo] *nm* ring; **dar un** ~ to ring the bell.
timbre ['timbre] *nm* (*sello*) stamp; (*campanilla*) bell; (*tono*) timbre; (*COM*) stamp duty.
timidez [timi'ðeθ] *nf* shyness.
tímido, a ['timiðo, a] *adj* shy, timid.
timo ['timo] *nm* swindle; **dar un** ~ **a algn** to swindle sb.
timón [ti'mon] *nm* helm, rudder; (*AM*) steering wheel; **coger el** ~ (*fig*) to take charge.
timonel [timo'nel] *nm* helmsman.
timorato, a [timo'rato, a] *adj* God-fearing; (*mojigato*) sanctimonious.
tímpano ['timpano] *nm* (*ANAT*) eardrum; (*MUS*) small drum.
tina ['tina] *nf* tub; (*AM: baño*) bath(tub).
tinaja [ti'naxa] *nf* large earthen jar.
tinerfeño, a [tiner'feɲo, a] *adj* of *o* from Tenerife ♦ *nm/f* native *o* inhabitant of Tenerife.
tinglado [tin'glaðo] *nm* (*cobertizo*) shed; (*fig: truco*) trick; (*intriga*) intrigue; **armar un** ~ to lay a plot.
tinieblas [ti'njeβlas] *nfpl* darkness *sg*; (*sombras*) shadows; **estamos en** ~ **sobre sus proyectos** (*fig*) we are in the dark about his plans.
tino ['tino] *nm* (*habilidad*) skill; (*MIL*) marksmanship; (*juicio*) insight;

(*moderación*) moderation; **sin** ~ immoderately; **coger el** ~ to get the feel *o* hang of it.
tinta ['tinta] *nf* ink; (*TEC*) dye; (*ARTE*) colour; ~ **china** Indian ink; ~**s** *nfpl* (*fig*) shades; **medias** ~**s** (*fig*) half measures; **saber algo de buena** ~ to have sth on good authority.
tinte ['tinte] *nm* (*acto*) dyeing; (*fig*) tinge; (*barniz*) veneer.
tintero [tin'tero] *nm* inkwell; **se le quedó en el** ~ he clean forgot about it.
tintinear [tintine'ar] *vt* to tinkle.
tinto, a ['tinto, a] *adj* (*teñido*) dyed; (*manchado*) stained ♦ *nm* red wine.
tintorera [tinto'rera] *nf* shark.
tintorería [tintore'ria] *nf* dry cleaner's.
tintorero [tinto'rero] *nm* dry cleaner('s).
tintura [tin'tura] *nf* (*acto*) dyeing; (*QUÍMICA*) dye; (*farmacéutico*) tincture.
tiña ['tiɲa] *etc vb V* **teñir** ♦ *nf* (*MED*) ringworm.
tío ['tio] *nm* (*pariente*) uncle; (*fam: viejo*) old fellow; (: *individuo*) bloke, chap, guy (*US*).
tiovivo [tio'βiβo] *nm* roundabout.
típico, a ['tipiko, a] *adj* typical; (*pintoresco*) picturesque.
tiple ['tiple] *nm* soprano (voice) ♦ *nf* soprano.
tipo ['tipo] *nm* (*clase*) type, kind; (*norma*) norm; (*patrón*) pattern; (*fam: hombre*) fellow, bloke, guy (*US*); (*ANAT*) build; (: *de mujer*) figure; (*IMPRENTA*) type; ~ **bancario/de descuento** bank/discount rate; ~ **de interés** interest rate; ~ **de interés vigente** (*COM*) standard rate; ~ **de cambio** exchange rate; ~ **base** (*COM*) base rate; ~ **a término** (*COM*) forward rate; **dos** ~**s sospechosos** two suspicious characters; ~ **de letra** (*INFORM, TIP*) typeface; ~ **de datos** (*INFORM*) data type.
tipografía [tipoɣra'fia] *nf* (*tipo*) printing; (*lugar*) printing press.
tipográfico, a [tipo'ɣrafiko, a] *adj* printing.
tipógrafo, a [ti'poɣrafo, a] *nm/f* printer.
tíque(t) ['tike], *pl* **tíque(t)s** ['tikes] *nm* ticket; (*en tienda*) cash slip.
tiquismiquis [tikis'mikis] *nm* fussy person ♦ *nmpl* (*querellas*) squabbling *sg*; (*escrúpulos*) silly scruples.
tira ['tira] *nf* strip; (*fig*) abundance ♦ *nm*: ~ **y afloja** give and take; (*cautela*) caution; **la** ~ **de ...** (*fam*) lots of ....
tirabuzón [tiraβu'θon] *nm* corkscrew; (*rizo*) curl.
tiradero [tira'ðero] *nm* (*AM*) rubbish dump.

tirado, a [ti'raðo, a] _adj_ (_barato_) dirt-cheap; (_fam: fácil_) very easy ♦ _nf_ (_acto_) cast, throw; (_distancia_) distance; (_serie_) series; (_TIP_) printing, edition; **de una tirada** at one go; **está ~** (_fam_) it's a cinch.

tirador, a [tira'ðor, a] _nm/f_ (_persona_) shooter ♦ _nm_ (_mango_) handle; (_ELEC_) flex; **~ certero** sniper.

tiralíneas [tira'lineas] _nm inv_ ruling-pen.

tiranía [tira'nia] _nf_ tyranny.

tiránico, a [ti'raniko, a] _adj_ tyrannical.

tiranizar [tirani'θar] _vt_ (_pueblo, empleado_) to tyrannize.

tirano, a [ti'rano, a] _adj_ tyrannical ♦ _nm/f_ tyrant.

tirante [ti'rante] _adj_ (_cuerda_) tight, taut; (_relaciones_) strained ♦ _nm_ (_ARQ_) brace; (_TEC_) stay; (_correa_) shoulder strap; **~s** _nmpl_ braces, suspenders (_US_).

tirantez [tiran'teθ] _nf_ tightness; (_fig_) tension.

tirar [ti'rar] _vt_ to throw; (_volcar_) to upset; (_derribar_) to knock down _o_ over; (_tiro_) to fire; (_cohete_) to launch; (_bomba_) to drop; (_edificio_) to pull down; (_desechar_) to throw out _o_ away; (_disipar_) to squander; (_imprimir_) to print; (_dar. golpe_) to deal ♦ _vi_ (_disparar_) to shoot; (_jalar_) to pull; (_fig_) to draw; (_interesar_) to appeal; (_fam: andar_) to go; (_tender a, buscar realizar_) to tend to; (_DEPORTE_) to shoot; **~se** _vr_ to throw o.s.; (_fig_) to demean o.s.; (_fam !_) to screw (_!_); **~ abajo** to bring down, destroy; **tira más a su padre** he takes more after his father; **~ de algo** to pull _o_ tug (on) sth; **ir tirando** to manage; **~ a la derecha** to turn _o_ go right; **a todo ~** at the most.

tirita [ti'rita] _nf_ (sticking) plaster, bandaid (_US_).

tiritar [tiri'tar] _vi_ to shiver.

tiritona [tiri'tona] _nf_ shivering (fit).

tiro ['tiro] _nm_ (_lanzamiento_) throw; (_disparo_) shot; (_tiroteo_) shooting; (_DEPORTE_) shot; (_TENIS, GOLF_) drive; (_alcance_) range; (_de escalera_) flight (of stairs); (_golpe_) blow; (_engaño_) hoax; **~ al blanco** target practice; **caballo de ~** cart-horse; **andar de ~s largos** to be all dressed up; **al ~** (_AM_) at once; **de a ~** (_AM fam_) completely; **se pegó un ~** he shot himself; **le salió el ~ por la culata** it backfired on him.

tiroides [ti'roiðes] _nm inv_ thyroid.

Tirol [ti'rol] _nm_: **El ~** the Tyrol.

tirolés, esa [tiro'les, esa] _adj, nm/f_ Tyrolean.

tirón [ti'ron] _nm_ (_sacudida_) pull, tug; **de un ~** in one go; **dar un ~ a** to pull at, tug at.

tirotear [tirote'ar] _vt_ to shoot at; **~se** _vr_ to exchange shots.

tiroteo [tiro'teo] _nm_ exchange of shots, shooting; (_escaramuza_) skirmish.

tirria ['tirrja] _nf_: **tener una ~ a algn** to have a grudge against sb.

tísico, a ['tisiko, a] _adj, nm/f_ consumptive.

tisis ['tisis] _nf_ consumption, tuberculosis.

tít. _abr_ = **título**.

titánico, a [ti'taniko, a] _adj_ titanic.

títere ['titere] _nm_ puppet; **no dejar ~ con cabeza** to turn everything upside-down.

titilar [titi'lar] _vi_ (_luz, estrella_) to twinkle; (_parpado_) to flutter.

titiritero, a [titiri'tero, a] _nm/f_ (_acróbata_) acrobat; (_malabarista_) juggler.

titubeante [tituße'ante] _adj_ (_inestable_) shaky, tottering; (_farfullante_) stammering; (_dudoso_) hesitant.

titubear [tituße'ar] _vi_ to stagger; (_tartamudear_) to stammer; (_vacilar_) to hesitate.

titubeo [titu'ßeo] _nm_ staggering; stammering; hesitation.

titulado, a [titu'laðo, a] _adj_ (_libro_) entitled; (_persona_) titled.

titular [titu'lar] _adj_ titular ♦ _nm/f_ (_de oficina_) occupant; (_de pasaporte_) holder ♦ _nm_ headline ♦ _vt_ to title; **~se** _vr_ to be entitled.

título ['titulo] _nm_ (_gen_) title; (_de diario_) headline; (_certificado_) professional qualification; (_universitario_) university degree; (_COM_) bond; (_fig_) right; **~s** _nmpl_ qualifications; **a ~ de** by way of; (_en calidad de_) in the capacity of; **a ~ de curiosidad** as a matter of interest; **~ de propiedad** title deed; **~s convertibles de interés fijo** (_COM_) convertible loan stock _sg_.

tiza ['tiθa] _nf_ chalk; **una ~** a piece of chalk.

tizna ['tiθna] _nf_ grime.

tiznar [tiθ'nar] _vt_ to blacken; (_manchar_) to smudge, stain; (_fig_) to tarnish.

tizón [ti'θon], **tizo** ['tiθo] _nm_ brand; (_fig_) stain.

TLC _nm abr_ (= _Tratado de Libre Comercio_) NAFTA.

Tm. _abr_ = **tonelada(s) métrica(s)**.

toalla [to'aʎa] _nf_ towel.

tobillo [to'ßiʎo] _nm_ ankle.

tobogán [toßo'ɣan] _nm_ toboggan; (_montaña rusa_) switchback; (_resbaladilla_) chute, slide.

toca ['toka] _nf_ headdress.

tocadiscos [toka'ðiskos] _nm inv_ record player.

tocado, a [to'kaðo, a] *adj* (*fruta etc*) rotten;
♦ *nm* headdress; **estar ~ de la cabeza**
(*fam*) to be weak in the head.

tocador [toka'ðor] *nm* (*mueble*) dressing
table; (*cuarto*) boudoir; (*neceser*) toilet
case; (*fam*) ladies' room.

tocante [to'kante]: **~ a** *prep* with regard
to; **en lo ~ a** as for, so far as concerns.

tocar [to'kar] *vt* to touch; (*sentir*) to feel;
(*con la mano*) to handle; (*MUS*) to play;
(*campana*) to ring; (*tambor*) to beat;
(*trompeta*) to blow; (*topar con*) to run
into, strike; (*referirse a*) to allude to; (*ser
emparentado con*) to be related to ♦ *vi* (*a
la puerta*) to knock (on *o* at the door); (*ser
de turno*) to fall to, be the turn of; (*ser
hora*) to be due; (*atañer*) to concern; **~se**
vr (*cubrirse la cabeza*) to cover one's head;
(*tener contacto*) to touch (each other);
~le a algn to fall to sb's lot; **~ en** (*NAUT*)
to call at; **por lo que a mí me toca** as far
as I am concerned; **esto toca en la locura**
this verges on madness.

tocateja [toka'texa] (*fam*): **a ~** *adv* in
readies.

tocayo, a [to'kajo, a] *nm/f* namesake.

tocino [to'θino] *nm* (bacon) fat; **~ de
panceta** bacon.

todavía [toða'βia] *adv* (*aun*) even; (*aún*)
still, yet; **~ más** yet *o* still more; **~ no**
not yet; **~ en 1970** as late as 1970; **está
lloviendo ~** it's still raining.

toditito, a [toði'tito, a], **todito, a** [to'ðito,
a] *adj* (*AM fam*) (absolutely) all.

══════════════ *PALABRA CLAVE*

todo, a ['toðo, a] *adj* **1** (*sg*) all; **toda la
carne** all the meat; **toda la noche** all
night, the whole night; **~ el libro** the
whole book; **toda una botella** a whole
bottle; **~ lo contrario** quite the opposite;
está toda sucia she's all dirty; **a toda
velocidad** at full speed; **por ~ el país**
throughout the whole country; **es ~ un
hombre** he's every inch a man; **soy ~
oídos** I'm all ears
2 (*pl*) all; every; **~s los libros** all the
books; **todas las noches** every night; **~s
los que quieran salir** all those who want
to leave; **~s vosotros** all of you
♦ *pron* **1** everything, all; **~s** everyone,
everybody; **lo sabemos ~** we know
everything; **~s querían más tiempo**
everybody *o* everyone wanted more
time; **nos marchamos ~s** all of us left;
corriendo y ~, no llegaron a tiempo even
though they ran, they still didn't arrive
in time

2 (*con preposición*): **a pesar de ~** even so,
in spite of everything; **con ~ él me sigue
gustando** even so I still like him; **le
llamaron de todo** they called him all the
names under the sun; **no me agrada del
~** I don't entirely like it
♦ *adv* all; **vaya ~ seguido** keep straight
on *o* ahead
♦ *nm*: **como un ~** as a whole; **arriba del ~**
at the very top.

todopoderoso, a [toðopoðe'roso, a] *adj* all
powerful; (*REL*) almighty.

todoterreno [toðote'rreno] *nm* (*tb:
vehículo ~*) four-by-four.

toga ['toɣa] *nf* toga; (*ESCOL*) gown.

Tokio ['tokjo] *n* Tokyo.

toldo ['toldo] *nm* (*para el sol*) sunshade;
(*tienda*) marquee; (*fig*) pride.

tole ['tole] *nm* (*fam*) commotion.

toledano, a [tole'ðano, a] *adj* of *o* from
Toledo ♦ *nm/f* native *o* inhabitant of
Toledo.

tolerable [tole'raβle] *adj* tolerable.

tolerancia [tole'ranθja] *nf* tolerance.

tolerante [tole'rante] *adj* tolerant; (*fig*)
open-minded.

tolerar [tole'rar] *vt* to tolerate; (*resistir*) to
endure.

Tolón [to'lon] *nm* Toulon.

toma ['toma] *nf* (*gen*) taking; (*MED*) dose;
(*ELEC*: *tb*: **~ de corriente**) socket; (*MEC*)
inlet; **~ de posesión** (*por presidente*)
taking up office; **~ de tierra** (*AVIAT*)
landing.

tomadura [toma'ðura] *nf*: **~ de pelo** hoax.

tomar [to'mar] *vt* (*gen, CINE, FOTO, TV*) to
take; (*actitud*) to adopt; (*aspecto*) to take
on; (*notas*) to take down; (*beber*) to drink
♦ *vi* to take; (*AM*) to drink; **~se** *vr* to take;
~se por to consider o.s. to be; **¡toma!**
here you are!; **~ asiento** to sit down; **~ a
algn por loco** to think sb mad; **~ a bien/a
mal** to take well/badly; **~ en serio** to
take seriously; **~ el pelo a algn** to pull
sb's leg; **~la con algn** to pick a quarrel
with sb; **~ por escrito** to write down;
toma y daca give and take.

tomate [to'mate] *nm* tomato.

tomatera [toma'tera] *nf* tomato plant.

tomavistas [toma'βistas] *nm inv* movie
camera.

tomillo [to'miʎo] *nm* thyme.

tomo ['tomo] *nm* (*libro*) volume; (*fig*)
importance.

ton [ton] *abr* = **tonelada** ♦ *nm*: **sin ~ ni son**
without rhyme or reason.

tonada [to'naða] *nf* tune.

tonalidad [tonali'ðað] *nf* tone.

tonel [to'nel] *nm* barrel.

tonelada [tone'laða] *nf* ton; ~ **métrica** metric ton.

tonelaje [tone'laxe] *nm* tonnage.

tonelero [tone'lero] *nm* cooper.

tongo ['toŋgo] *nm* (*DEPORTE*) fix.

tónico, a ['toniko, a] *adj* tonic ♦ *nm* (*MED*) tonic ♦ *nf* (*MUS*) tonic; (*fig*) keynote.

tonificador, a [tonifika'ðor, a], **tonificante** [tonifi'kante] *adj* invigorating, stimulating.

tonificar [tonifi'kar] *vt* to tone up.

tonifique [toni'fike] *etc vb V* **tonificar**.

tonillo [to'niʎo] *nm* monotonous voice.

tono ['tono] *nm* (*MUS*) tone; (*altura*) pitch; (*color*) shade; **fuera de** ~ inappropriate; ~ **de marcar** (*TELEC*) dialling tone; **darse** ~ to put on airs.

tontear [tonte'ar] *vi* (*fam*) to fool about; (*enamorados*) to flirt.

tontería [tonte'ria] *nf* (*estupidez*) foolishness; (*una* ~) silly thing; ~**s** *nfpl* rubbish *sg*, nonsense *sg*.

tonto, a ['tonto, a] *adj* stupid; (*ridículo*) silly ♦ *nm/f* fool; (*payaso*) clown; **a tontas y a locas** anyhow; **hacer(se) el** ~ to act the fool.

topacio [to'paθjo] *nm* topaz.

topar [to'par] *vt* (*tropezar*) to bump into; (*encontrar*) to find, come across; (*cabra etc*) to butt ♦ *vi*: ~ **contra** *o* **en** to run into; ~ **con** to run up against; **el problema topa en eso** that's where the problem lies.

tope ['tope] *adj* maximum ♦ *nm* (*fin*) end; (*límite*) limit; (*riña*) quarrel; (*FERRO*) buffer; (*AUTO*) bumper; **al** ~ end to end; **fecha** ~ closing date; **precio** ~ top price; **sueldo** ~ maximum salary; ~ **de tabulación** tab stop.

tópico, a ['topiko, a] *adj* topical; (*MED*) local ♦ *nm* platitude, cliché; **de uso** ~ for external application.

topo ['topo] *nm* (*ZOOL*) mole; (*fig*) blunderer.

topografía [topoɣra'fia] *nf* topography.

topógrafo, a [to'poɣrafo, a] *nm/f* topographer; (*agrimensor*) surveyor.

toponimia [topo'nimja] *nf* place names *pl*; (*estudio*) study of place names.

toque ['toke] *etc vb V* **tocar** ♦ *nm* touch; (*MUS*) beat; (*de campana*) ring, chime; (*MIL*) bugle call; (*fig*) crux; **dar un** ~ **a** to test; **dar el último** ~ **a** to put the final touch to; ~ **de queda** curfew.

toquetear [tokete'ar] *vt* to handle; (*fam!*) to touch up.

toquilla [to'kiʎa] *nf* (*chal*) shawl.

torax ['toraks] *nm inv* thorax.

torbellino [torbe'ʎino] *nm* whirlwind; (*fig*) whirl.

torcedura [torθe'ðura] *nf* twist; (*MED*) sprain.

torcer [tor'θer] *vt* to twist; (*la esquina*) to turn; (*MED*) to sprain; (*cuerda*) to plait; (*ropa, manos*) to wring; (*persona*) to corrupt; (*sentido*) to distort ♦ *vi* (*cambiar de dirección*) to turn; ~**se** *vr* to twist; (*doblar*) to bend; (*desviarse*) to go astray; (*fracasar*) to go wrong; ~ **el gesto** to scowl; ~**se un pie** to twist one's foot; **el coche torció a la derecha** the car turned right.

torcido, a [tor'θiðo, a] *adj* twisted; (*fig*) crooked ♦ *nm* curl.

tordo, a ['torðo, a] *adj* dappled ♦ *nm* thrush.

torear [tore'ar] *vt* (*fig: evadir*) to dodge; (*toro*) to fight ♦ *vi* to fight bulls.

toreo [to'reo] *nm* bullfighting.

torero, a [to'rero, a] *nm/f* bullfighter.

toril [to'ril] *nm* bullpen.

tormenta [tor'menta] *nf* storm; (*fig: confusión*) turmoil.

tormento [tor'mento] *nm* torture; (*fig*) anguish.

tormentoso, a [tormen'toso, a] *adj* stormy.

tornar [tor'nar] *vt* (*devolver*) to return, give back; (*transformar*) to transform ♦ *vi* to go back; ~**se** *vr* (*ponerse*) to become; (*volver*) to return.

tornasol [torna'sol] *nm* (*BOT*) sunflower; **papel de** ~ litmus paper.

tornasolado, a [tornaso'laðo, a] *adj* (*brillante*) iridescent; (*reluciente*) shimmering.

torneo [tor'neo] *nm* tournament.

tornero, a [tor'nero, a] *nm/f* machinist.

tornillo [tor'niʎo] *nm* screw; **apretar los** ~**s a algn** to apply pressure on sb; **le falta un** ~ (*fam*) he's got a screw loose.

torniquete [torni'kete] *nm* (*puerta*) turnstile; (*MED*) tourniquet.

torno ['torno] *nm* (*TEC: grúa*) winch; (: *de carpintero*) lathe; (*tambor*) drum; ~ **de banco** vice, vise (*US*); **en** ~ **(a)** round, about.

toro ['toro] *nm* bull; (*fam*) he-man; **los** ~**s** bullfighting *sg*.

toronja [to'ronxa] *nf* grapefruit.

torpe ['torpe] *adj* (*poco hábil*) clumsy, awkward; (*movimiento*) sluggish; (*necio*) dim; (*lento*) slow; (*indecente*) crude; (*no honrado*) dishonest.

torpedo [tor'peðo] *nm* torpedo.
torpemente [torpe'mente] *adv* (*sin destreza*) clumsily; (*lentamente*) slowly.
torpeza [tor'peθa] *nf* (*falta de agilidad*) clumsiness; (*lentitud*) slowness; (*rigidez*) stiffness; (*error*) mistake; (*crudeza*) obscenity.
torre ['torre] *nf* tower; (*de petróleo*) derrick; (*de electricidad*) pylon; (*AJEDREZ*) rook; (*AVIAT, MIL, NAUT*) turret.
torrefacto, a [torre'fakto, a] *adj*: **café ~** high roast coffee.
torrencial [torren'θjal] *adj* torrential.
torrente [to'rrente] *nm* torrent.
tórrido, a ['torriðo, a] *adj* torrid.
torrija [to'rrixa] *nf* fried bread; **~s** French toast *sg*.
torsión [tor'sjon] *nf* twisting.
torso ['torso] *nm* torso.
torta ['torta] *nf* cake; (*fam*) slap; **~ de huevos** (*AM*) omelette; **no entendió ni ~** he didn't understand a word of it.
tortazo [tor'taθo] *nm* (*bofetada*) slap; (*de coche*) crash.
tortícolis [tor'tikolis] *nm inv* stiff neck.
tortilla [tor'tiʎa] *nf* omelette; (*AM*) maize pancake; **~ francesa/española** plain/potato omelette; **cambiar o volver la ~ a algn** to turn the tables on sb.
tortillera [torti'ʎera] *nf* (*fam!*) lesbian.
tórtola ['tortola] *nf* turtledove.
tortuga [tor'tuɣa] *nf* tortoise; **~ marina** turtle.
tortuoso, a [tor'twoso, a] *adj* winding.
tortura [tor'tura] *nf* torture.
torturar [tortu'rar] *vt* to torture.
torvo, a ['torβo, a] *adj* grim, fierce.
torzamos [tor'θamos] *etc vb V* **torcer**.
tos [tos] *nf inv* cough; **~ ferina** whooping cough.
Toscana [tos'kana] *nf*: **La ~** Tuscany.
tosco, a ['tosko, a] *adj* coarse.
toser [to'ser] *vi* to cough; **no hay quien le tosa** he's in a class by himself.
tostado, a [tos'taðo, a] *adj* toasted; (*por el sol*) dark brown; (*piel*) tanned ♦ *nf* tan; (*pan*) piece of toast; **tostadas** *nfpl* toast *sg*.
tostador [tosta'ðor] *nm* toaster.
tostar [tos'tar] *vt* to toast; (*café*) to roast; (*al sol*) to tan; **~se** *vr* to get brown.
tostón [tos'ton] *nm*: **ser un ~** to be a drag.
total [to'tal] *adj* total ♦ *adv* in short; (*al fin y al cabo*) when all is said and done ♦ *nm* total; **en ~** in all; **~ que** to cut a long story short; **~ de comprobación** (*INFORM*) hash total; **~ debe/haber** (*COM*) debit/assets total.
totalidad [totali'ðað] *nf* whole.

totalitario, a [totali'tarjo, a] *adj* totalitarian.
totalmente [to'talmente] *adv* totally.
tóxico, a ['toksiko, a] *adj* toxic ♦ *nm* poison.
toxicómano, a [toksi'komano, a] *adj* addicted to drugs ♦ *nm/f* drug addict.
toxina [to'ksina] *nf* toxin.
tozudo, a [to'θuðo, a] *adj* obstinate.
traba ['traβa] *nf* bond, tie; (*cadena*) fetter; **poner ~s a** to restrain.
trabajador, a [traβaxa'ðor, a] *nm/f* worker ♦ *adj* hard-working.
trabajar [traβa'xar] *vt* to work; (*arar*) to till; (*empeñarse en*) to work at; (*empujar: persona*) to push; (*convencer*) to persuade ♦ *vi* to work; (*esforzarse*) to strive; **¡a ~!** let's get to work!; **~ por hacer algo** to strive to do sth.
trabajo [tra'βaxo] *nm* work; (*tarea*) task; (*POL*) labour; (*fig*) effort; **tomarse el ~ de** to take the trouble to; **~ por turno/a destajo** shift work/piecework; **~ en proceso** (*COM*) work-in-progress.
trabajoso, a [traβa'xoso, a] *adj* hard; (*MED*) pale.
trabalenguas [traβa'lengwas] *nm inv* tongue twister.
trabar [tra'βar] *vt* (*juntar*) to join, unite; (*atar*) to tie down, fetter; (*agarrar*) to seize; (*amistad*) to strike up; **~se** *vr* to become entangled; (*reñir*) to squabble; **se le traba la lengua** he gets tongue-tied.
trabazón [traβa'θon] *nf* (*TEC*) joining, assembly; (*fig*) bond, link.
trabucar [traβu'kar] *vt* (*confundir*) to confuse, mix up; (*palabras*) to misplace.
trabuque [tra'βuke] *etc vb V* **trabucar**.
tracción [trak'θjon] *nf* traction; **~ delantera/trasera** front-wheel/rear-wheel drive.
trace ['traθe] *etc vb V* **trazar**.
tractor [trak'tor] *nm* tractor.
trad. *abr* (= *traducido*) trans.
tradición [traði'θjon] *nf* tradition.
tradicional [traðiθjo'nal] *adj* traditional.
traducción [traðuk'θjon] *nf* translation; **~ asistida por ordenador** computer-assisted translation.
traducible [traðu'θiβle] *adj* translatable.
traducir [traðu'θir] *vt* to translate; **~se** *vr*: **~se en** (*fig*) to entail, result in.
traductor, a [traðuk'tor, a] *nm/f* translator.
traduzca [tra'ðuθka] *etc vb V* **traducir**.
traer [tra'er] *vt* to bring; (*llevar*) to carry; (*ropa*) to wear; (*incluir*) to carry; (*fig*) to cause; **~se** *vr*: **~se algo** to be up to sth; **~se bien/mal** to dress well/badly; **traérselas** to be annoying; **~ consigo** to involve, entail; **es un problema que se**

las trae it's a difficult problem.
traficante [trafi'kante] *nm/f* trader, dealer.
traficar [trafi'kar] *vi* to trade; ~ **con** (*pey*) to deal illegally in.
tráfico ['trafiko] *nm* (*COM*) trade; (*AUTO*) traffic.
trafique [tra'fike] *etc vb* V **traficar.**
tragaderas [traɣa'ðeras] *nfpl* (*garganta*) throat *sg*, gullet *sg*; (*credulidad*) gullibility *sg*.
tragaluz [traɣa'luθ] *nm* skylight.
tragamonedas [traɣamo'neðas] *nm inv*, **tragaperras** [traɣa'perras] *nm inv* slot machine.
tragar [tra'ɣar] *vt* to swallow; (*devorar*) to devour, bolt down; ~**se** *vr* to swallow; (*tierra*) to absorb, soak up; **no le puedo ~** (*persona*) I can't stand him.
tragedia [tra'xeðja] *nf* tragedy.
trágico, a ['traxiko, a] *adj* tragic.
trago ['traɣo] *nm* (*líquido*) drink; (*comido de golpe*) gulp; (*fam: de bebida*) swig; (*desgracia*) blow; ~ **amargo** (*fig*) hard time.
trague ['traɣe] *etc vb* V **tragar.**
traición [trai'θjon] *nf* treachery; (*JUR*) treason; (*una ~*) act of treachery.
traicionar [traiθjo'nar] *vt* to betray.
traicionero, a [traiθjo'nero, a] = **traidor, a.**
traída [tra'iða] *nf* carrying; ~ **de aguas** water supply.
traidor, a [trai'ðor, a] *adj* treacherous ♦ *nm/f* traitor.
traiga ['traiɣa] *etc vb* V **traer.**
trailer, *pl* **trailers** ['trailer, 'trailer(s)] *nm* trailer.
traje ['traxe] *etc vb* V **traer** ♦ *nm* (*gen*) dress; (*de hombre*) suit; (~ *típico*) costume; (*fig*) garb; ~ **de baño** swimsuit; ~ **de luces** bullfighter's costume; ~ **hecho a la medida** made-to-measure suit.
trajera [tra'xera] *etc vb* V **traer.**
trajín [tra'xin] *nm* haulage; (*fam: movimiento*) bustle; **trajines** *nmpl* goings-on.
trajinar [traxi'nar] *vt* (*llevar*) to carry, transport ♦ *vi* (*moverse*) to bustle about; (*viajar*) to travel around.
trama ['trama] *nf* (*fig*) link; (: *intriga*) plot; (*de tejido*) weft.
tramar [tra'mar] *vt* to plot; (*TEC*) to weave; ~**se** *vr* (*fig*): **algo se está tramando** there's something going on.
tramitar [trami'tar] *vt* (*asunto*) to transact; (*negociar*) to negotiate; (*manejar*) to handle.
trámite ['tramite] *nm* (*paso*) step; (*JUR*)

transaction; ~**s** *nmpl* (*burocracia*) paperwork *sg*, procedures; (*JUR*) proceedings.
tramo ['tramo] *nm* (*de tierra*) plot; (*de escalera*) flight; (*de vía*) section.
tramoya [tra'moja] *nf* (*TEAT*) piece of stage machinery; (*fig*) trick.
tramoyista [tramo'jista] *nm/f* scene shifter; (*fig*) trickster.
trampa ['trampa] *nf* trap; (*en el suelo*) trapdoor; (*prestidigitación*) conjuring trick; (*engaño*) trick; (*fam*) fiddle; (*de pantalón*) fly; **caer en la ~** to fall into the trap; **hacer ~s** (*hacer juegos de manos*) to juggle, conjure; (*trampear*) to cheat.
trampear [trampe'ar] *vt, vi* to cheat.
trampilla [tram'piʎa] *nf* trap, hatchway.
trampolín [trampo'lin] *nm* trampoline; (*de piscina etc*) diving board.
tramposo, a [tram'poso, a] *adj* crooked, cheating ♦ *nm/f* crook, cheat.
tranca ['tranka] *nf* (*palo*) stick; (*viga*) beam; (*de puerta, ventana*) bar; (*borrachera*) binge; **a ~s y barrancas** with great difficulty.
trancar [tran'kar] *vt* to bar ♦ *vi* to stride along.
trancazo [tran'kaθo] *nm* (*golpe*) blow.
trance ['tranθe] *nm* (*momento difícil*) difficult moment; (*situación crítica*) critical situation; (*estado hipnotizado*) trance; **estar en ~ de muerte** to be at death's door.
tranco ['tranko] *nm* stride.
tranque ['tranke] *etc vb* V **trancar.**
tranquilamente [tran'kilamente] *adv* (*sin preocupaciones: leer, trabajar*) peacefully; (*sin enfadarse: hablar, discutir*) calmly.
tranquilice [tranki'liθe] *etc vb* V **tranquilizar.**
tranquilidad [trankili'ðað] *nf* (*calma*) calmness, stillness; (*paz*) peacefulness.
tranquilizador, a [trankiliθa'ðor, a] *adj* (*música*) soothing; (*hecho*) reassuring.
tranquilizante [trankili'θante] *nm* tranquillizer.
tranquilizar [trankili'θar] *vt* (*calmar*) to calm (down); (*asegurar*) to reassure.
tranquilo, a [tran'kilo, a] *adj* (*calmado*) calm; (*apacible*) peaceful; (*mar*) calm; (*mente*) untroubled.
Trans. *abr* (*COM*) = **transferencia.**
transacción [transak'θjon] *nf* transaction.
transar [tran'sar] *vi* (*AM*) = **transigir.**
transatlántico, a [transat'lantiko, a] *adj* transatlantic ♦ *nm* (ocean) liner.
transbordador [transβorða'ðor] *nm* ferry.
transbordar [transβor'ðar] *vt* to transfer;

~**se** *vr* to change.

transbordo [trans'ßorðo] *nm* transfer; **hacer** ~ to change (trains).

transcender [transθen'der] *vt* = **trascender**.

transcribir [transkri'ßir] *vt* to transcribe.

transcurrir [transku'rrir] *vi* (*tiempo*) to pass; (*hecho*) to turn out.

transcurso [trans'kurso] *nm* passing, lapse; **en el** ~ **de 8 días** in the course of a week.

transeúnte [transe'unte] *adj* transient ♦ *nm/f* passer-by.

transexual [transe'kswal] *adj*, *nm/f* transsexual.

transferencia [transfe'renθja] *nf* transference; (*COM*) transfer; ~ **bancaria** banker's order; ~ **de crédito** (*COM*) credit transfer; ~ **electrónica de fondos** (*COM*) electronic funds transfer.

transferir [transfe'rir] *vt* to transfer; (*aplazar*) to postpone.

transfiera [trans'fjera] *etc vb V* **transferir**.

transfigurar [transfixu'rar] *vt* to transfigure.

transfiriendo [transfi'rjendo] *etc vb V* **transferir**.

transformación [transforma'θjon] *nf* transformation.

transformador [transforma'ðor] *nm* transformer.

transformar [transfor'mar] *vt* to transform; (*convertir*) to convert.

tránsfuga ['transfuɣa] *nm/f* (*MIL*) deserter; (*POL*) turncoat.

transfusión [transfu'sjon] *nf* (*tb*: ~ **de sangre**) (blood) transfusion.

transgredir [transɣre'dir] *vt* to transgress.

transgresión [transɣre'sjon] *nf* transgression.

transición [transi'θjon] *nf* transition; **período de** ~ transitional period.

transido, a [tran'siðo, a] *adj* overcome; ~ **de angustia** beset with anxiety; ~ **de dolor** racked with pain.

transigir [transi'xir] *vi* to compromise; (*ceder*) to make concessions.

transija [tran'sixa] *etc vb V* **transigir**.

Transilvania [transil'ßanja] *nf* Transylvania.

transistor [transis'tor] *nm* transistor.

transitable [transi'taßle] *adj* (*camino*) passable.

transitar [transi'tar] *vi* to go (from place to place).

transitivo, a [transi'tißo, a] *adj* transitive.

tránsito ['transito] *nm* transit; (*AUTO*) traffic; (*parada*) stop; **horas de máximo** ~

rush hours; **"se prohíbe el** ~**"** "no thoroughfare."

transitorio, a [transi'torjo, a] *adj* transitory.

transmisión [transmi'sjon] *nf* (*RADIO, TV*) transmission, broadcast(ing); (*transferencia*) transfer; ~ **en circuito** hookup; ~ **en directo/exterior** live/ outside broadcast; ~ **de datos** (**en paralelo/en serie**) (*INFORM*) (parallel/ serial) data transfer *o* transmission; **plena/media** ~ **bidireccional** (*INFORM*) full/half duplex.

transmitir [transmi'tir] *vt* to transmit; (*RADIO, TV*) to broadcast; (*enfermedad*) to give, pass on.

transparencia [transpa'renθja] *nf* transparency; (*claridad*) clearness, clarity; (*foto*) slide.

transparentar [transparen'tar] *vt* to reveal ♦ *vi* to be transparent.

transparente [transpa'rente] *adj* transparent; (*aire*) clear; (*ligero*) diaphanous ♦ *nm* curtain.

transpirar [transpi'rar] *vi* to perspire; (*fig*) to transpire.

transpondré [transpon'dre] *etc vb V* **transponer**.

transponer [transpo'ner] *vt* to transpose; (*cambiar de sitio*) to move about ♦ *vi* (*desaparecer*) to disappear; (*ir más allá*) to go beyond; ~**se** *vr* to change places; (*ocultarse*) to hide; (*sol*) to go down.

transponga [trans'ponga] *etc vb V* **transponer**.

transportador [transporta'ðor] *nm* (*MECÁNICA*): ~ **de correa** belt conveyor.

transportar [transpor'tar] *vt* to transport; (*llevar*) to carry.

transporte [trans'porte] *nm* transport; (*COM*) haulage; **Ministerio de T**~**s** Ministry of Transport.

transpuesto [trans'pwesto], **transpuse** [trans'puse] *etc vb V* **transponer**.

transversal [transßer'sal] *adj* transverse, cross ♦ *nf* (*tb*: **calle** ~) cross street.

transversalmente [transßersal'mente] *adv* obliquely.

tranvía [tram'bia] *nm* tram, streetcar (*US*).

trapecio [tra'peθjo] *nm* trapeze.

trapecista [trape'θista] *nm/f* trapeze artist.

trapero, a [tra'pero, a] *nm/f* ragman.

trapicheos [trapi't∫eos] *nmpl* (*fam*) schemes, fiddles.

trapisonda [trapi'sonda] *nf* (*jaleo*) row; (*estafa*) swindle.

trapo ['trapo] *nm* (*tela*) rag; (*de cocina*) cloth; ~**s** *nmpl* (*fam: de mujer*) clothes, dresses; **a todo** ~ under full sail; **soltar el** ~ (*llorar*) to burst into tears.

tráquea ['trakea] *nf* trachea, windpipe.

traqueteo [trake'teo] *nm* (*crujido*) crack; (*golpeteo*) rattling.

tras [tras] *prep* (*detrás*) behind; (*después*) after; ~ **de** besides; **día** ~ **día** day after day; **uno** ~ **otro** one after the other.

trascendencia [trasθen'denθja] *nf* (*importancia*) importance; (*filosofía*) transcendence.

trascendental [trasθenden'tal] *adj* important; transcendental.

trascender [trasθen'der] *vi* (*oler*) to smell; (*noticias*) to come out, leak out; (*eventos, sentimientos*) to spread, have a wide effect; ~ **a** (*afectar*) to reach, have an effect on; (*oler a*) to smack of; **en su novela todo trasciende a romanticismo** everything in his novel smacks of romanticism.

trascienda [tras'θjenda] *etc vb V* **trascender**.

trasegar [trase'ɣar] *vt* (*mover*) to move about; (*vino*) to decant.

trasegué [trase'ɣe], **traseguemos** [trase'ɣemos] *etc vb V* **trasegar**.

trasero, a [tra'sero, a] *adj* back, rear ♦ *nm* (*ANAT*) bottom; ~**s** *nmpl* ancestors.

trasfondo [tras'fondo] *nm* background.

trasgo ['trasɣo] *nm* (*duende*) goblin.

trasgredir [trasɣre'ðir] *vt* to contravene.

trashumante [trasu'mante] *adj* migrating.

trasiego [tra'sjeɣo] *etc vb V* **trasegar** ♦ *nm* (*cambiar de sitio*) move, switch; (*de vino*) decanting; (*trastorno*) upset.

trasiegue [tra'sjeɣe] *etc vb V* **trasegar**.

trasladar [trasla'ðar] *vt* to move; (*persona*) to transfer; (*postergar*) to postpone; (*copiar*) to copy; (*interpretar*) to interpret; ~**se** *vr* (*irse*) to go; (*mudarse*) to move; ~**se a otro puesto** to move to a new job.

traslado [tras'laðo] *nm* move; (*mudanza*) move, removal; (*de persona*) transfer; (*copia*) copy; ~ **de bloque** (*INFORM*) block move, cut-and-paste.

traslucir [traslu'θir] *vt* to show; ~**se** *vr* to be translucent; (*fig*) to be revealed.

trasluz [tras'luθ] *nm* reflected light; **al** ~ against *o* up to the light.

trasluzca [tras'luθka] *etc vb V* **traslucir**.

trasmano [tras'mano]: **a** ~ *adv* (*fuera de alcance*) out of reach; (*apartado*) out of the way.

trasnochado, a [trasno'tʃaðo, a] *adj* dated.

trasnochador, a [trasnotʃa'ðor, a] *adj* given to staying up late ♦ *nm/f* (*fig*) night bird.

trasnochar [trasno'tʃar] *vi* (*acostarse tarde*) to stay up late; (*no dormir*) to have a sleepless night; (*pasar la noche*) to stay the night.

traspasar [traspa'sar] *vt* (*bala*) to pierce, go through; (*propiedad*) to sell, transfer; (*calle*) to cross over; (*límites*) to go beyond; (*ley*) to break; **"traspaso negocio"** "business for sale".

traspaso [tras'paso] *nm* transfer; (*fig*) anguish.

traspié [tras'pje], *pl* **traspiés** *nm* (*caída*) stumble; (*tropezón*) trip; (*fig*) blunder.

trasplantar [trasplan'tar] *vt* to transplant.

trasplante [tras'plante] *nm* transplant.

traspuesto, a [tras'pwesto, a] *adj*: **quedarse** ~ to doze off.

trastada [tras'taða] *nf* (*fam*) prank.

trastazo [tras'taθo] *nm* (*fam*) bump; **darse un** ~ (*persona*) to bump o.s.; (*en coche*) to have a bump.

traste ['traste] *nm* (*MUS*) fret; **dar al** ~ **con algo** to ruin sth; **ir al** ~ to fall through.

trastero [tras'tero] *nm* lumber room.

trastienda [tras'tjenda] *nf* backshop; **obtener algo por la** ~ to get sth by underhand means.

trasto ['trasto] *nm* (*mueble*) piece of furniture; (*tarro viejo*) old pot; (*pey: cosa*) piece of junk; (: *persona*) dead loss; ~**s** *nmpl* (*TEAT*) scenery *sg*; **tirar los** ~**s a la cabeza** to have a blazing row.

trastocar [trasto'kar] *vt* (*papeles*) to mix up.

trastornado, a [trastor'naðo, a] *adj* (*loco*) mad; (*agitado*) crazy.

trastornar [trastor'nar] *vt* to overturn, upset; (*fig: ideas*) to confuse; (: *nervios*) to shatter; (: *persona*) to drive crazy; ~**se** *vr* (*plan*) to fall through.

trastorno [tras'torno] *nm* (*acto*) overturning; (*confusión*) confusion; (*POL*) disturbance, upheaval; (*MED*) upset; ~ **estomacal** stomach upset; ~ **mental** mental disorder, breakdown.

trasunto [tra'sunto] *nm* copy.

trasvase [tras'βase] *nm* (*de río*) diversion.

tratable [tra'taβle] *adj* friendly.

tratado [tra'taðo] *nm* (*POL*) treaty; (*COM*) agreement; (*LITERATURA*) treatise.

tratamiento [trata'mjento] *nm* treatment; (*TEC*) processing; (*de problema*) handling; ~ **de datas** (*INFORM*) data processing; ~ **de gráficos** (*INFORM*) graphics processing; ~ **de márgenes** margin settings; ~ **de textos** (*INFORM*) word processing; ~ **por lotes** (*INFORM*) batch processing; ~ **de tú** familiar address.

tratante [tra'tante] *nm/f* dealer, merchandizer.

tratar [tra'tar] *vt* (*ocuparse de*) to treat; (*manejar, TEC*) to handle; (*INFORM*) to process; (*MED*) to treat; (*dirigirse a*: *persona*) to address ♦ *vi*: ~ **de** (*hablar sobre*) to deal with, be about; (*intentar*) to try to; ~ **con** (*COM*) to trade in; (*negociar*) to negotiate with; (*tener contactos*) to have dealings with; ~**se** *vr* to treat each other; **se trata de la nueva piscina** it's about the new pool; **¿de qué se trata?** what's it about?

trato ['trato] *nm* dealings *pl*; (*relaciones*) relationship; (*comportamiento*) manner; (*COM, JUR*) agreement, contract; (*título*) (form of) address; **de** ~ **agradable** pleasant; **de fácil** ~ easy to get on with; ~ **equitativo** fair deal; **¡**~ **hecho!** it's a deal!; **malos** ~**s** ill-treatment *sg*.

trauma ['trauma] *nm* trauma.

traumático, a [trau'matiko, a] *adj* traumatic.

través [tra'ßes] *nm* (*contratiempo*) reverse; **al** ~ across, crossways; **a** ~ **de** across; (*sobre*) over; (*por*) through; **de** ~ across; (*de lado*) sideways.

travesaño [traße'saɲo] *nm* (*ARQ*) crossbeam; (*DEPORTE*) crossbar.

travesía [traße'sia] *nf* (*calle*) cross-street; (*NAUT*) crossing.

travesti [tra'ßesti] *nm/f* transvestite.

travesura [traße'sura] *nf* (*broma*) prank; (*ingenio*) wit.

travieso, a [tra'ßjeso, a] *adj* (*niño*) naughty; (*adulto*) restless; (*ingenioso*) witty ♦ *nf* crossing; (*ARQ*) crossbeam; (*FERRO*) sleeper.

trayecto [tra'jekto] *nm* (*ruta*) road, way; (*viaje*) journey; (*tramo*) stretch; (*curso*) course; **final del** ~ end of the line.

trayectoria [trajek'torja] *nf* trajectory; (*desarrollo*) development, path; **la** ~ **actual del partido** the party's present line.

trayendo [tra'jendo] *etc vb V* **traer**.

traza ['traθa] *nf* (*ARQ*) plan, design; (*aspecto*) looks *pl*; (*señal*) sign; (*engaño*) trick; (*habilidad*) skill; (*INFORM*) trace.

trazado, a [tra'θaðo, a] *adj*: **bien** ~ shapely, well-formed ♦ *nm* (*ARQ*) plan, design; (*fig*) outline; (*de carretera etc*) line, route.

trazador [traθa'ðor] *nm* plotter; ~ **plano** flatbed plotter.

trazar [tra'θar] *vt* (*ARQ*) to plan; (*ARTE*) to sketch; (*fig*) to trace; (*itinerario: hacer*) to plot; (*plan*) to follow.

trazo ['traθo] *nm* (*línea*) line; (*bosquejo*) sketch; ~**s** *nmpl* (*de cara*) lines, features.

TRB *abr* = **toneladas de registro bruto**.

trébol ['treßol] *nm* (*BOT*) clover; ~**es** *nmpl* (*NAIPES*) clubs.

trece ['treθe] *num* thirteen; **estar en sus** ~ to stand firm.

trecho ['tretʃo] *nm* (*distancia*) distance; (*de tiempo*) while; (*fam*) piece; **de** ~ **en** ~ at intervals.

tregua ['treɣwa] *nf* (*MIL*) truce; (*fig*) lull; **sin** ~ without respite.

treinta ['treinta] *num* thirty.

treintena [trein'tena] *nf* (about) thirty.

tremendo, a [tre'mendo, a] *adj* (*terrible*) terrible; (*imponente: cosa*) imposing; (*fam: fabuloso*) tremendous; (*divertido*) entertaining.

trémulo, a ['tremulo, a] *adj* quivering; (*luz*) flickering.

tren [tren] *nm* (*FERRO*) train; ~ **de aterrizaje** undercarriage; ~ **directo/expreso/(de) mercancías/de pasajeros/suplementario** through/fast/goods *o* freight/passenger/relief train; ~ **de vida** way of life.

trenca ['trenka] *nf* duffel coat.

trence ['trenθe] *etc vb V* **trenzar**.

trenza ['trenθa] *nf* (*de pelo*) plait.

trenzar [tren'θar] *vt* (*el pelo*) to plait ♦ *vi* (*en baile*) to weave in and out; ~**se** *vr* (*AM*) to become involved.

trepa ['trepa] *nf* (*subida*) climb; (*ardid*) trick.

trepador(a) [trepa'ðor(a)] *nm/f* (*fam*): **ser un(a)** ~ to be on the make ♦ *nf* (*BOT*) climber.

trepar [tre'par] *vt, vi* to climb; (*TEC*) to drill.

trepidación [trepiða'θjon] *nf* shaking, vibration.

trepidar [trepi'ðar] *vi* to shake, vibrate.

tres [tres] *num* three; (*fecha*) third; **las** ~ three o'clock.

trescientos, as [tres'θjentos, as] *num* three hundred.

tresillo [tre'siʎo] *nm* three-piece suite; (*MUS*) triplet.

treta ['treta] *nf* (*COM etc*) gimmick; (*fig*) trick.

tri... [tri] *pref* tri..., three-....

tríada ['triaða] *nf* triad.

triangular [trjangu'lar] *adj* triangular.

triángulo [tri'angulo] *nm* triangle.

tribal [tri'ßal] *adj* tribal.

tribu ['trißu] *nf* tribe.

tribuna [tri'ßuna] *nf* (*plataforma*) platform; (*DEPORTE*) stand; (*fig*) public speaking; ~ **de la prensa** press box; ~ **del acusado** (*JUR*) dock; ~ **del jurado** jury box.

tribunal [triˈβuˈnal] *nm* (*juicio*) court; (*comisión, fig*) tribunal; (*ESCOL: examinadores*) board of examiners; **T~ Supremo** High Court, (*US*) Supreme Court; **T~ de Justicia de las Comunidades Europeas** European Court of Justice.

tributar [triβuˈtar] *vt* to pay; (*las gracias*) to give; (*cariño*) to show.

tributario, a [triβuˈtarjo, a] *adj* (*GEO, POL*) tributary *cpd*; (*ECON*) tax *cpd*, taxation *cpd* ♦ *nm* (*GEO*) tributary ♦ *nm/f* (*COM*) taxpayer; **sistema ~** tax system.

tributo [triˈβuto] *nm* (*COM*) tax.

trice [ˈtriθe] *etc vb V* **trizar**.

triciclo [triˈθiklo] *nm* tricycle.

tricornio [triˈkornjo] *nm* three-cornered hat.

tricota [triˈkota] *nf* (*AM*) knitted sweater.

tricotar [trikoˈtar] *vi* to knit.

tridimensional [triðimensjoˈnal] *adj* three-dimensional.

trienal [trjeˈnal] *adj* three-year.

trifulca [triˈfulka] *nf* (*fam*) row, shindy.

trigal [triˈɣal] *nm* wheat field.

trigésimo, a [triˈxesimo, a] *num* thirtieth.

trigo [ˈtriɣo] *nm* wheat; **~s** *nmpl* wheat field(s) (*pl*).

trigueño, a [triˈɣeɲo, a] *adj* (*pelo*) corn-coloured; (*piel*) olive-skinned.

trillado, a [triˈʎaðo, a] *adj* threshed; (*fig*) trite, hackneyed.

trilladora [triʎaˈðora] *nf* threshing machine.

trillar [triˈʎar] *vt* (*AGR*) to thresh; (*fig*) to frequent.

trillizos, as [triˈʎiθos, as] *nmpl/nfpl* triplets.

trilogía [triloˈxia] *nf* triology.

trimestral [trimesˈtral] *adj* quarterly; (*ESCOL*) termly.

trimestre [triˈmestre] *nm* (*ESCOL*) term; (*COM*) quarter, financial period; (: *pago*) quarterly payment.

trinar [triˈnar] *vi* (*MUS*) to trill; (*ave*) to sing, warble; **está que trina** he's hopping mad.

trincar [trinˈkar] *vt* (*atar*) to tie up; (*NAUT*) to lash; (*agarrar*) to pinion.

trinchante [trinˈtʃante] *nm* (*para cortar carne*) carving knife; (*tenedor*) meat fork.

trinchar [trinˈtʃar] *vt* to carve.

trinchera [trinˈtʃera] *nf* (*fosa*) trench; (*para vía*) cutting; (*impermeable*) trench-coat.

trineo [triˈneo] *nm* sledge.

trinidad [triniˈðað] *nf* trio; (*REL*): **la T~** the Trinity.

trino [ˈtrino] *nm* trill.

trinque [ˈtrinke] *etc vb V* **trincar**.

trinquete [trinˈkete] *nm* (*TEC*) pawl; (*NAUT*) foremast.

trío [ˈtrio] *nm* trio.

tripa [ˈtripa] *nf* (*ANAT*) intestine; (*fig, fam*) belly; **~s** *nfpl* (*ANAT*) insides; (*CULIN*) tripe *sg*; **tener mucha ~** to be fat; **me duelen las ~s** I have a stomach ache.

tripartito, a [triparˈtito, a] *adj* tripartite.

triple [ˈtriple] *adj* triple; (*tres veces*) threefold.

triplicado, a [tripliˈkaðo, a] *adj*: **por ~** in triplicate.

triplicar [tripliˈkar] *vt* to treble.

triplo [ˈtriplo] *adj* = **triple**.

trípode [ˈtripoðe] *nm* tripod.

Trípoli [ˈtripoli] *nm* Tripoli.

tríptico [ˈtriptiko] *nm* (*ARTE*) triptych; (*documento*) three-part document.

tripulación [tripulaˈθjon] *nf* crew.

tripulante [tripuˈlante] *nm/f* crewman/woman.

tripular [tripuˈlar] *vt* (*barco*) to man; (*AUTO*) to drive.

triquiñuela [trikiˈɲwela] *nf* trick.

tris [tris] *nm* crack; **en un ~** in an instant; **estar en un ~ de hacer algo** to be within an inch of doing sth.

triste [ˈtriste] *adj* (*afligido*) sad; (*sombrío*) melancholy, gloomy; (*desolado*) desolate; (*lamentable*) sorry, miserable; (*viejo*) old; (*único*) single; **no queda sino un ~ penique** there's just one miserable penny left.

tristeza [trisˈteθa] *nf* (*aflicción*) sadness; (*melancolía*) melancholy; (*de lugar*) desolation; (*pena*) misery.

tristón, ona [trisˈton, ona] *adj* sad, downhearted.

trituradora [trituraˈðora] *nf* shredder.

triturar [trituˈrar] *vt* (*moler*) to grind; (*mascar*) to chew; (*documentos*) to shred.

triunfador, a [triunfaˈðor, a] *adj* triumphant; (*ganador*) winning ♦ *nm/f* winner.

triunfal [triunˈfal] *adj* triumphant; (*arco*) triumphal.

triunfante [triunˈfante] *adj* triumphant; (*ganador*) winning.

triunfar [triunˈfar] *vi* (*tener éxito*) to triumph; (*ganar*) to win; (*NAIPES*) to be trumps; **triunfan corazones** hearts are trumps; **~ en la vida** to succeed in life.

triunfo [triˈunfo] *nm* triumph; (*NAIPES*) trump.

trivial [triˈβjal] *adj* trivial.

trivialice [triβjaˈliθe] *etc vb V* **trivializar**.

trivializar [triβjaliˈθar] *vt* to minimize, play

down.

triza ['triθa] *nf* bit, piece; **hacer algo ~s** to smash sth to bits; (*papel*) to tear sth to shreds.

trocar [tro'kar] *vt* (*COM*) to exchange; (*dinero, de lugar*) to change; (*palabras*) to exchange; (*confundir*) to confuse; (*vomitar*) to vomit; **~se** *vr* (*confundirse*) to get mixed up; (*transformarse*): **~se (en)** to change (into).

trocear [troθe'ar] *vt* to cut up.

trocha ['trotʃa] *nf* (*sendero*) by-path; (*atajo*) short cut.

troche ['trotʃe]: **a ~ y moche** *adv* helter-skelter, pell-mell.

trofeo [tro'feo] *nm* (*premio*) trophy; (*éxito*) success.

trola ['trola] *nf* (*fam*) fib.

tromba ['tromba] *nf* whirlwind; **~ de agua** cloudburst.

trombón [trom'bon] *nm* trombone.

trombosis [trom'bosis] *nf inv* thrombosis.

trompa ['trompa] *nf* (*MUS*) horn; (*de elefante*) trunk; (*trompo*) humming top; (*hocico*) snout; (*ANAT*) tube, duct ♦ *nm* (*MUS*) horn player; **~ de Falopio** Fallopian tube; **cogerse una ~** (*fam*) to get tight.

trompada [trom'paða] *nf*, **trompazo** [trom'paθo] *nm* (*choque*) bump, bang; (*puñetazo*) punch.

trompeta [trom'peta] *nf* trumpet; (*clarín*) bugle ♦ *nm* trumpeter.

trompetilla [trompe'tiʎa] *nf* ear trumpet.

trompicón [trompi'kon]: **a trompicones** *adv* in fits and starts.

trompo ['trompo] *nm* spinning top.

trompón [trom'pon] *nm* bump.

tronado, a [tro'naðo, a] *adj* broken-down.

tronar [tro'nar] *vt* (*AM*) to shoot, execute ♦ *vi* to thunder; (*fig*) to rage; (*fam*) to go broke.

tronchar [tron'tʃar] *vt* (*árbol*) to chop down; (*fig: vida*) to cut short; (*esperanza*) to shatter; (*persona*) to tire out; **~se** *vr* to fall down; **~se de risa** to split one's sides with laughter.

tronco ['tronko] *nm* (*de árbol, ANAT*) trunk; (*de planta*) stem; **estar hecho un ~** to be sound asleep.

tronera [tro'nera] *nf* (*MIL*) loophole; (*ARQ*) small window.

trono ['trono] *nm* throne.

tropa ['tropa] *nf* (*MIL*) troop; (*soldados*) soldiers *pl*; (*soldados rasos*) ranks *pl*; (*gentío*) mob.

tropecé [trope'θe], **tropecemos** [trope'θemos] *etc vb V* **tropezar**.

tropel [tro'pel] *nm* (*muchedumbre*) crowd; (*prisa*) rush; (*montón*) throng; **acudir** *etc* **en ~** to come *etc* in a mad rush.

tropelía [trope'lia] *nm* outrage.

tropezar [trope'θar] *vi* to trip, stumble; (*fig*) to slip up; **~se** *vr* (*dos personas*) to run into each other; **~ con** (*encontrar*) to run into; (*topar con*) to bump into.

tropezón [trope'θon] *nm* trip; (*fig*) blunder; (*traspié*): **dar un ~** to trip.

tropical [tropi'kal] *adj* tropical.

trópico ['tropiko] *nm* tropic.

tropiece [tro'pjeθe] *etc vb V* **tropezar**.

tropiezo [tro'pjeθo] *etc vb V* **tropezar** ♦ *nm* (*error*) slip, blunder; (*desgracia*) misfortune; (*revés*) setback; (*obstáculo*) snag; (*discusión*) quarrel.

troqué [tro'ke], **troquemos** [tro'kemos] *etc vb V* **trocar**.

trotamundos [trota'mundos] *nm inv* globetrotter.

trotar [tro'tar] *vi* to trot; (*viajar*) to travel about.

trote ['trote] *nm* trot; (*fam*) travelling; **de mucho ~** hard-wearing.

Troya ['troja] *nf* Troy; **aquí fue ~** now there's nothing but ruins.

trozo ['troθo] *nm* bit, piece; (*LITERATURA, MUS*) passage; **a ~s** in bits.

trucha ['trutʃa] *nf* (*pez*) trout; (*TEC*) crane.

truco ['truko] *nm* (*habilidad*) knack; (*engaño*) trick; (*CINE*) trick effect *o* photography; **~s** *nmpl* billiards *sg*; **~ publicitario** advertising gimmick.

trueco ['trweko] *etc vb V* **trocar**.

trueno ['trweno] *etc vb V* **tronar** ♦ *nm* (*gen*) thunder; (*estampido*) boom; (*de arma*) bang.

trueque ['trweke] *etc vb V* **trocar** ♦ *nm* exchange; (*COM*) barter.

trufa ['trufa] *nf* (*BOT*) truffle; (*fig: fam*) fib.

truhán, ana [tru'an, ana] *nm/f* rogue.

truncado, a [trun'kaðo, a] *adj* truncated.

truncar [trun'kar] *vt* (*cortar*) to truncate; (*la vida etc*) to cut short; (*el desarrollo*) to stunt.

trunque ['trunke] *etc vb V* **truncar**.

tu [tu] *adj* your.

tú [tu] *pron* you.

tubérculo [tu'βerkulo] *nm* (*BOT*) tuber.

tuberculosis [tuβerku'losis] *nf inv* tuberculosis.

tubería [tuβe'ria] *nf* pipes *pl*, piping; (*conducto*) pipeline.

tubo ['tuβo] *nm* tube, pipe; **~ de desagüe** drainpipe; **~ de ensayo** test-tube; **~ de escape** exhaust (pipe); **~ digestivo** alimentary canal.

tuerca ['twerka] *nf (TEC)* nut.
tuerce ['twerθe] *etc vb V* torcer.
tuerto, a ['twerto, a] *adj (torcido)* twisted; *(ciego)* blind in one eye ♦ *nm/f* one-eyed person ♦ *nm (ofensa)* wrong; **a tuertas** upside-down.
tuerza ['twerθa] *etc vb V* torcer.
tueste ['tweste] *etc vb V* tostar.
tuétano ['twetano] *nm (ANAT: médula)* marrow; *(BOT)* pith; **hasta los ~s** through and through, utterly.
tufo ['tufo] *nm* vapour; *(fig: pey)* stench.
tugurio [tu'ɣurjo] *nm* slum.
tul [tul] *nm* tulle.
tulipán [tuli'pan] *nm* tulip.
tullido, a [tu'ʎiðo, a] *adj* crippled; *(cansado)* exhausted.
tumba ['tumba] *nf (sepultura)* tomb; *(sacudida)* shake; *(voltereta)* somersault; **ser (como) una ~** to keep one's mouth shut.
tumbar [tum'bar] *vt* to knock down; *(doblar)* to knock over; *(fam: suj: olor)* to overpower ♦ *vi* to fall down; **~se** *vr (echarse)* to lie down; *(extenderse)* to stretch out.
tumbo ['tumbo] *nm (caída)* fall; *(de vehículo)* jolt; *(momento crítico)* critical moment.
tumbona [tum'bona] *nf* lounger.
tumefacción [tumefak'θjon] *nf* swelling.
tumor [tu'mor] *nm* tumour.
tumulto [tu'multo] *nm* turmoil; *(POL: motín)* riot.
tuna ['tuna] *nf (MUS)* student music group *V tb* **tuno.**

A **tuna** *is made up of university students, or quite often former students, who dress up in costumes from the* **Edad de Oro,** *the Spanish Golden Age. These musical troupes go through the town playing their guitars, lutes and tambourines and serenade the young ladies in the halls of residence, or make impromptu appearances at weddings or parties singing traditional Spanish songs for a few* **pesetas.**

tunante [tu'nante] *adj* rascally ♦ *nm* rogue, villain; ¡~! you villain!
tunda ['tunda] *nf (de tela)* shearing; *(golpeo)* beating.
tundir [tun'dir] *vt (tela)* to shear; *(hierba)* to mow; *(fig)* to exhaust; *(fam: golpear)* to beat.
tunecino, a [tune'θino, a] *adj, nm/f* Tunisian.
túnel ['tunel] *nm* tunnel.

Túnez ['tuneθ] *nm* Tunis.
túnica ['tunika] *nf* tunic; *(vestido largo)* long dress; *(ANAT, BOT)* tunic.
Tunicia [tu'niθja] *nf* Tunisia.
tuno, a ['tuno, a] *nm/f (fam)* rogue ♦ *nm (MUS)* member of a "tuna".
tuntún [tun'tun]: **al ~** *adv* thoughtlessly.
tupamaro, a [tupa'maro, a] *adj, nm/f (AM)* urban guerrilla.
tupé [tu'pe] *nm* quiff.
tupí [tu'pi], **tupí-guaraní** [tupigwara'ni] *adj, nm/f* Tupi-Guarani.
tupido, a [tu'piðo, a] *adj (denso)* dense; *(fig: torpe)* dim; *(tela)* close-woven.
turba ['turßa] *nf (combustible)* turf; *(muchedumbre)* crowd.
turbación [turßa'θjon] *nf (molestia)* disturbance; *(preocupación)* worry.
turbado, a [tur'ßaðo, a] *adj (molesto)* disturbed; *(preocupado)* worried.
turbante [tur'ßante] *nm* turban.
turbar [tur'ßar] *vt (molestar)* to disturb; *(incomodar)* to upset; **~se** *vr* to be disturbed.
turbina [tur'ßina] *nf* turbine.
turbio, a ['turßjo, a] *adj (agua etc)* cloudy; *(vista)* dim, blurred; *(tema)* unclear, confused; *(negocio)* shady ♦ *adv* indistinctly.
turbión [tur'ßjon] *nf* downpour; *(fig)* shower, hail.
turbo ['turßo] *adj inv* turbo(-charged) ♦ *nm (tb coche)* turbo.
turbohélice [turßo'eliθe] *nm* turboprop.
turbulencia [turßu'lenθja] *nf* turbulence; *(fig)* restlessness.
turbulento, a [turßu'lento, a] *adj* turbulent; *(fig: intranquilo)* restless; *(: ruidoso)* noisy.
turco, a ['turko, a] *adj* Turkish ♦ *nm/f* Turk ♦ *nm (LING)* Turkish.
Turena [tu'rena] *nf* Touraine.
turgente [tur'xente], **túrgido, a** ['turxiðo, a] *adj (hinchado)* turgid, swollen.
Turín [tu'rin] *nm* Turin.
turismo [tu'rismo] *nm* tourism; *(coche)* saloon car; **hacer ~** to go travelling (abroad).
turista [tu'rista] *nm/f* tourist; *(vacacionista)* holidaymaker *(BRIT)*, vacationer *(US)*.
turístico, a [tu'ristiko, a] *adj* tourist *cpd.*
Turkmenistán [turkmeni'stan] *nm* Turkmenistan.
turnar [tur'nar] *vi*, **turnarse** *vr* to take (it in) turns.
turno ['turno] *nm (oportunidad, orden de prioridad)* opportunity; *(DEPORTE etc)* turn; **es su ~** it's his turn (next); **~ de**

día/de noche (*INDUSTRIA*) day/night shift.
turolense [turo'lense] *adj* of *o* from Teruel
♦ *nmf* native *o* inhabitant of Teruel.
turquesa [tur'kesa] *nf* turquoise.
Turquía [tur'kia] *nf* Turkey.
turrón [tu'rron] *nm* (*dulce*) nougat; (*fam*)
sinecure, cushy job *o* number.
tute ['tute] *nm* (*NAIPES*) *card game*; **darse
un** ~ to break one's back.
tutear [tute'ar] *vt* to address as familiar
"tú"; ~**se** *vr* to be on familiar terms.
tutela [tu'tela] *nf* (*legal*) guardianship;
(*instrucción*) guidance; **estar bajo la** ~ **de**
(*fig*) to be under the protection of.
tutelar [tute'lar] *adj* tutelary ♦ *vt* to
protect.
tutor, a [tu'tor, a] *nmf* (*legal*) guardian;
(*ESCOL*) tutor; ~ **de curso** form master/
mistress.
tuve ['tuße] *etc vb V* **tener**.
tuyo, a ['tujo, a] *adj* yours, of yours ♦ *pron*
yours; **los** ~**s** (*fam*) your relations, your
family.
TVE *nf abr* = *Televisión Española*.

U u

U, u [u] *nf* (*letra*) U, u; **viraje en U** U-turn; **U
de Ulises** U for Uncle.
u [u] *conj* or.
UAR [war] *nfpl abr* (*ESP*) = *Unidades
Antiterroristas Rurales*.
ubérrimo, a [u'ßerrimo, a] *adj* very rich,
fertile.
ubicación [ußika'θjon] *nf* (*esp AM*) place,
position, location.
ubicado, a [ußi'kaðo, a] *adj* (*esp AM*)
situated.
ubicar [ußi'kar] *vt* (*esp AM*) to place,
situate; (: *fig*) to install in a post;
(: *encontrar*) to find; ~**se** *vr* to be situated,
be located.
ubicuo, a [u'ßikwo, a] *adj* ubiquitous.
ubique [u'ßike] *etc vb V* **ubicar**.
ubre ['ußre] *nf* udder.
Ucrania [u'kranja] *nf* Ukraine.
ucraniano, a [ukra'njano, a] *adj*, *nmf*
Ukrainian ♦ *nm* (*LING*) Ukrainian.
ucranio [u'kranjo] *nm* (*LING*) Ukrainian.
Ud(s) *abr* = **usted(es)**.
UE *nf abr* (= *Unión Europea*) EU.

UEFA *nf abr* (= *Unión de Asociaciones de
Fútbol Europeo*) UEFA.
UEO *nf abr* (= *Unión Europea Occidental*)
WEU.
UEP *nf abr* = *Unión Europea de Pagos*.
uf [uf] *excl* (*cansancio*) phew!; (*repugnancia*)
ugh!
ufanarse [ufa'narse] *vr* to boast; ~ **de** to
pride o.s. on.
ufano, a [u'fano, a] *adj* (*arrogante*)
arrogant; (*presumido*) conceited.
UGT *nf abr V* **Unión General de
Trabajadores**.
ujier [u'xjer] *nm* usher; (*portero*)
doorkeeper.
úlcera ['ulθera] *nf* ulcer.
ulcerar [ulθe'rar] *vt* to make sore; ~**se** *vr* to
ulcerate.
ulterior [ulte'rjor] *adj* (*más allá*) farther,
further; (*subsecuente, siguiente*)
subsequent.
ulteriormente [ulterjor'mente] *adv* later,
subsequently.
últimamente ['ultimamente] *adv*
(*recientemente*) lately, recently;
(*finalmente*) finally; (*como último recurso*)
as a last resort.
ultimar [ulti'mar] *vt* to finish; (*finalizar*) to
finalize; (*AM: rematar*) to finish off,
murder.
ultimátum [ulti'matum] *nm*, *pl*
ultimátums ultimatum.
último, a ['ultimo, a] *adj* last; (*más reciente*)
latest, most recent; (*más bajo*) bottom;
(*más alto*) top; (*fig*) final, extreme; **en las
últimas** on one's last legs; **por** ~ finally.
ultra ['ultra] *adj* ultra ♦ *nmf* extreme
right-winger.
ultracongelar [ultrakonxe'lar] *vt* to deep-
freeze.
ultraderecha [ultraðe'retʃa] *nf* extreme
right (wing).
ultrajar [ultra'xar] *vt* (*escandalizar*) to
outrage; (*insultar*) to insult, abuse.
ultraje [ul'traxe] *nm* outrage; insult.
ultraligero [ultrali'xero] *nm* microlight
(*BRIT*), microlite (*US*).
ultramar [ultra'mar] *nm*: **de** *o* **en** ~ abroad,
overseas; **los países de** ~ the overseas
countries.
ultramarino, a [ultrama'rino, a] *adj*
overseas, foreign ♦ *nmpl*: ~**s** groceries;
tienda de ~**s** grocer's (shop).
ultranza [ul'tranθa]: **a** ~ *adv* to the death;
(*a todo trance*) at all costs; (*completo*)
outright; (*POL etc*) out-and-out, extreme;
un nacionalista a ~ a rabid nationalist.
ultrarrojo, a [ultra'rroxo, a] *adj*

= **infrarrojo, a.**

ultrasónico, a [ultra'soniko, a] *adj*
ultrasonic.

ultratumba [ultra'tumba] *nf*: **la vida de** ~
the next life; **una voz de** ~ a ghostly
voice.

ultravioleta [ultraβjo'leta] *adj inv*
ultraviolet.

ulular [ulu'lar] *vi* to howl; (*búho*) to hoot.

umbilical [umbili'kal] *adj*: **cordón** ~
umbilical cord.

umbral [um'bral] *nm* (*gen*) threshold; ~ **de
rentabilidad** (*COM*) break-even point.

umbrío, a [um'brio, a] *adj* shady.

===================== *PALABRA CLAVE*

un, una [un, 'una] *art indef* a; (*antes de vocal*)
an; **una mujer/naranja** a woman/an orange
♦ *adj* **1: unos** (*o* **unas**)**: hay unos regalos para
ti** there are some presents for you; **hay
unas cervezas en la nevera** there are some
beers in the fridge

2 (*enfático*): **¡hace un frío!** it's so cold!;
¡tiene una casa! he's got some house!

U.N.A.M. ['unam] *nf abr* = *Universidad
Nacional Autónoma de México.*

unánime [u'nanime] *adj* unanimous.

unanimidad [unanimi'ðað] *nf* unanimity;
por ~ unanimously.

unción [un'θjon] *nf* anointing.

uncir [un'θir] *vt* to yoke.

undécimo, a [un'deθimo, a] *adj, nm/f* eleventh.

UNED [u'ned] *nf abr* (*ESP UNIV*: =
*Universidad Nacional de Enseñanza a
Distancia*) ≈ Open University (*BRIT*).

ungir [un'xir] *vt* to rub with ointment;
(*REL*) to anoint.

ungüento [un'gwento] *nm* ointment; (*fig*)
salve, balm.

únicamente ['unikamente] *adv* solely;
(*solamente*) only.

unicidad [uniθi'ðað] *nf* uniqueness.

único, a ['uniko, a] *adj* only; (*solo*) sole,
single; (*sin par*) unique; **hijo** ~ only child.

unidad [uni'ðað] *nf* unity; (*TEC*) unit; ~
móvil (*TV*) mobile unit; (*INFORM*): ~
central system unit, central processing
unit; ~ **de control** control unit; ~ **de
disco** disk drive; ~ **de entrada/salida**
input/output device; ~ **de información**
data item; ~ **periférica** peripheral
device; ~ **de presentación visual** *o* **de
visualización** visual display unit; ~
procesadora central central processing
unit.

unido, a [u'niðo, a] *adj* joined, linked; (*fig*)

united.

unifamiliar [unifamil'jar] *adj*: **vivienda** ~
single-family home.

unificar [unifi'kar] *vt* to unite, unify.

unifique [uni'fike] *etc vb V* **unificar**.

uniformado, a [unifor'maðo, a] *adj*
uniformed, in uniform.

uniformar [unifor'mar] *vt* to make
uniform; (*TEC*) to standardize.

uniforme [uni'forme] *adj* uniform, equal;
(*superficie*) even ♦ *nm* uniform.

uniformidad [uniformi'ðað] *nf* uniformity;
(*llaneza*) levelness, evenness.

unilateral [unilate'ral] *adj* unilateral.

unión [u'njon] *nf* (*gen*) union; (*acto*)
uniting, joining; (*calidad*) unity; (*TEC*)
joint; (*fig*) closeness, togetherness; **en** ~
con (together) with, accompanied by; ~
aduanera customs union; **U~ General de
Trabajadores (UGT)** (*ESP*) *Socialist
Union Confederation*; **U~ Europea**
European Union; **la U~ Soviética** the
Soviet Union; **punto de** ~ (*TEC*) junction.

unir [u'nir] *vt* (*juntar*) to join, unite; (*atar*) to
tie, fasten; (*combinar*) to combine ♦ *vi*
(*ingredientes*) to mix well; ~**se** *vr* to join
together, unite; (*empresas*) to merge; **les
une una fuerte simpatía** they are bound
by (a) strong affection; ~**se en
matrimonio** to marry.

unisex [uni'seks] *adj inv* unisex.

unísono [u'nisono] *nm*: **al** ~ in unison.

unitario, a [uni'tarjo, a] *adj* unitary; (*REL*)
Unitarian ♦ *nm/f* (*REL*) Unitarian.

universal [uniβer'sal] *adj* universal;
(*mundial*) world *cpd*; **historia** ~ world
history.

universidad [uniβersi'ðað] *nf* university; ~
laboral polytechnic, poly.

universitario, a [uniβersi'tarjo, a] *adj*
university *cpd* ♦ *nm/f* (*profesor*) lecturer;
(*estudiante*) (university) student.

universo [uni'βerso] *nm* universe.

unja ['unxa] *etc vb V* **ungir**.

===================== *PALABRA CLAVE*

uno, a ['uno, a] *adj* one; **es todo** ~ it's all
one and the same; ~**s pocos** a few; ~**s
cien** about a hundred

♦ *pron* **1** one; **quiero** ~ **solo** I only want
one; ~ **de ellos** one of them; **una de dos**
either one or the other; **no doy una hoy** I
can't do anything right today

2 (*alguien*) somebody, someone;
conozco a ~ **que se te parece** I know
somebody *o* someone who looks like
you; ~**s querían quedarse** some (people)
wanted to stay

3 (*impersonal*) one; ~ **mismo** oneself; ~ **nunca sabe qué hacer** one never knows what to do
4: ~**s ... otros ...** some ... others; **una y otra son muy agradables** they're both very nice; **(los)** ~**(s) a (los) otro(s)** each other, one another ♦ *nf* one; **es la una** it's one o'clock ♦ *num* (number) one; **el día** ~ the first.

untar [un'tar] *vt* (*gen*) to rub; (*engrasar*) to grease, oil; (*MED*) to rub (with ointment); (*fig*) to bribe; ~**se** *vr* (*fig*) to be crooked; ~ **el pan con mantequilla** to spread butter on one's bread.
unto ['unto] *nm* animal fat; (*MED*) ointment.
unza ['unθa] *etc vb V* **uncir**.
uña ['uɲa] *nf* (*ANAT*) nail; (*del pie*) toenail; (*garra*) claw; (*casco*) hoof; (*arrancaclavos*) claw; **ser** ~ **y carne** to be as thick as thieves; **enseñar** *o* **mostrar** *o* **sacar las** ~**s** to show one's claws.
UOE *nf abr* (*ESP MIL*) = *Unidad de Operaciones Especiales*.
UPA *nf abr* = *Unión Panamericana*.
UPC *nf abr* (= *unidad procesadora central*) CPU.
uperizado, a [uperi'θaðo, a] *adj*: **leche uperizada** UHT milk.
Urales [u'rales] *nmpl* (*tb*: **Montes** ~) Urals.
uralita ® [ura'lita] *nf* corrugated asbestos cement.
uranio [u'ranjo] *nm* uranium.
urbanidad [urβani'ðað] *nf* courtesy, politeness.
urbanismo [urβa'nismo] *nm* town planning.
urbanista [urβa'nista] *nm/f* town planner.
urbanización [urβaniθa'θjon] *nf* (*colonia, barrio*) estate, housing scheme.
urbanizar [urβani'θar] *vt* to develop.
urbano, a [ur'βano, a] *adj* (*de ciudad*) urban, town *cpd*; (*cortés*) courteous, polite.
urbe ['urβe] *nf* large city, metropolis.
urdimbre [ur'ðimbre] *nf* (*de tejido*) warp; (*intriga*) intrigue.
urdir [ur'ðir] *vt* to warp; (*fig*) to plot, contrive.
urgencia [ur'xenθja] *nf* urgency; (*prisa*) haste, rush; **salida de** ~ emergency exit; **servicios de** ~ emergency services.
urgente [ur'xente] *adj* urgent; (*insistente*) insistent; **carta** ~ registered (*BRIT*) *o* special delivery (*US*) letter.
urgir [ur'xir] *vi* to be urgent; **me urge** I'm in a hurry for it; **me urge terminarlo** I

must finish it as soon as I can.
urinario, a [uri'narjo, a] *adj* urinary ♦ *nm* urinal, public lavatory, comfort station (*US*).
urja ['urxa] *etc vb V* **urgir**.
urna ['urna] *nf* urn; (*POL*) ballot box; **acudir a las** ~**s** (*fig*: *persona*) to (go and) vote; (: *gobierno*) to go to the country.
urología [urolo'xia] *nf* urology.
urólogo, a [u'roloɣo, a] *nm/f* urologist.
urraca [u'rraka] *nf* magpie.
URSS *nf abr* (= *Unión de Repúblicas Socialistas Soviéticas*) USSR.
Uruguay [uru'ɣwai] *nm*: **El** ~ Uruguay.
uruguayo, a [uru'ɣwajo, a] *adj, nm/f* Uruguayan.
usado, a [u'saðo, a] *adj* (*gen*) used; (*ropa etc*) worn; **muy** ~ worn out.
usanza [u'sanθa] *nf* custom, usage.
usar [u'sar] *vt* to use; (*ropa*) to wear; (*tener costumbre*) to be in the habit of ♦ *vi*: ~ **de** to make use of; ~**se** *vr* to be used; (*ropa*) to be worn *o* in fashion.
USO *nf abr* (*ESP*: = *Unión Sindical Obrera*) *workers' union*.
uso ['uso] *nm* use; (*MECÁNICA etc*) wear; (*costumbre*) usage, custom; (*moda*) fashion; **al** ~ in keeping with custom; **al** ~ **de** in the style of; **de** ~ **externo** (*MED*) for external application; **estar en el** ~ **de la palabra** to be speaking, have the floor; ~ **y desgaste** (*COM*) wear and tear.
usted [us'teð] *pron* (*sg*: *abr* **Ud** *o* **Vd**: *formal*) you *sg*; ~**es** (*pl*: *abr* **Uds** *o* **Vds**: *formal*) you *pl*; (*AM*: *formal y fam*) you *pl*.
usual [u'swal] *adj* usual.
usuario, a [usw'arjo, a] *nm/f* user; ~ **final** (*COM*) end user.
usufructo [usu'frukto] *nm* use; ~ **vitalicio (de)** life interest (in).
usura [u'sura] *nf* usury.
usurero, a [usu'rero, a] *nm/f* usurer.
usurpar [usur'par] *vt* to usurp.
utensilio [uten'siljo] *nm* tool; (*CULIN*) utensil.
útero ['utero] *nm* uterus, womb.
útil ['util] *adj* useful; (*servible*) usable, serviceable ♦ *nm* tool; **día** ~ working day, weekday; **es muy** ~ **tenerlo aquí cerca** it's very handy having it here close by.
utilice [uti'liθe] *etc vb V* **utilizar**.
utilidad [utili'ðað] *nf* usefulness, utility; (*COM*) profit; ~**es líquidas** net profit *sg*.
utilitario [utili'tarjo] *nm* (*INFORM*) utility.
utilizar [utili'θar] *vt* to use, utilize; (*explotar*) to harness.
utopía [uto'pia] *nf* Utopia.

utópico, a [u'topiko, a] *adj* Utopian.
uva ['ußa] *nf* grape; ~ **pasa** raisin; ~ **de Corinto** currant; **estar de mala** ~ to be in a bad mood.

In Spain **Las uvas** play a big part on New Years' Eve **(Nochevieja)**, when on the stroke of midnight people from every part of Spain, at home, in restaurants or in the **plaza mayor** eat a grape for each stroke of the clock of the **Puerta del Sol** in Madrid. It is said to bring luck for the following year.

---

uve ['uße] *nf* name of the letter *V*; **en forma de** ~ V-shaped; ~ **doble** name of the letter *W*.
UVI ['ußi] *nf abr* (*ESP MED*: = unidad de vigilancia intensiva) ICU.

V v

V, v [(*ESP*) 'uße, (*AM*) be'lkorta, betʃika] *nf* (*letra*) V, v; **V de Valencia** V for Victor.
V. *abr* (= *visto*) approved, passed.
v. *abr* (= *voltio*) v.; (= *véase*) v.; (= *verso*) v.
va [ba] *vb V* **ir**.
V.A. *abr* = *Vuestra Alteza*.
vaca ['baka] *nf* (*animal*) cow; (*carne*) beef; (*cuero*) cowhide; ~**s flacas/gordas** (*fig*) bad/good times.
vacaciones [baka'θjones] *nfpl* holiday(s); **estar/irse** *o* **marcharse de** ~ to be/go (away) on holiday.
vacante [ba'kante] *adj* vacant, empty ♦ *nf* vacancy.
vaciado, a [ba'θjaðo, a] *adj* (*hecho en molde*) cast in a mould; (*hueco*) hollow ♦ *nm* cast, mould(ing).
vaciar [ba'θjar] *vt* to empty (out); (*ahuecar*) to hollow out; (*moldear*) to cast; (*INFORM*) to dump ♦ *vi* (*río*) to flow (*en* into); ~**se** *vr* to empty; (*fig*) to blab, spill the beans.
vaciedad [baθje'ðað] *nf* emptiness.
vacilación [baθila'θjon] *nf* hesitation.
vacilante [baθi'lante] *adj* unsteady; (*habla*) faltering; (*luz*) flickering; (*fig*) hesitant.
vacilar [baθi'lar] *vi* to be unsteady; to falter; to flicker; to hesitate, waver; (*persona*) to stagger, stumble; (*memoria*) to fail; (*esp AM*: *divertirse*) to have a great time.

vacilón [baθi'lon] *nm* (*esp AM*): **estar** *o* **ir de** ~ to have a great time.
vacío, a [ba'θio, a] *adj* empty; (*puesto*) vacant; (*desocupado*) idle; (*vano*) vain; (*charla etc*) light, superficial ♦ *nm* emptiness; (*FÍSICA*) vacuum; (*un* ~) (empty) space; **hacer el** ~ **a algn** to send sb to Coventry.
vacuna [ba'kuna] *nf* vaccine.
vacunar [baku'nar] *vt* to vaccinate; ~**se** *vr* to get vaccinated.
vacuno, a [ba'kuno, a] *adj* bovine.
vacuo, a ['bakwo, a] *adj* empty.
vadear [baðe'ar] *vt* (*río*) to ford; (*problema*) to overcome; (*persona*) to sound out.
vado ['baðo] *nm* ford; (*solución*) solution; (*descanso*) respite.
vagabundear [baɣabunde'ar] *vi* (*andar sin rumbo*) to wander, roam; (*ser vago*) to be a tramp *o* bum (*US*).
vagabundo, a [baɣa'ßundo, a] *adj* wandering; (*pey*) vagrant ♦ *nm/f* (*errante*) wanderer; (*vago*) tramp, bum (*US*).
vagamente [baɣa'mente] *adv* vaguely.
vagancia [ba'ɣanθja] *nf* vagrancy.
vagar [ba'ɣar] *vi* to wander; (*pasear*) to saunter up and down; (*no hacer nada*) to idle ♦ *nm* leisure.
vagido [ba'xiðo] *nm* wail.
vagina [ba'xina] *nf* vagina.
vago, a ['baɣo, a] *adj* vague; (*perezoso*) lazy; (*ambulante*) wandering ♦ *nm/f* (*vagabundo*) tramp, bum (*US*); (*flojo*) lazybones *sg*, idler.
vagón [ba'ɣon] *nm* (*de pasajeros*) carriage; (*de mercancías*) wagon; ~ **cama/restaurante** sleeping/dining car.
vague ['baɣe] *etc vb V* **vagar**.
vaguear [baɣe'ar] *vi* to laze around.
vaguedad [baɣe'ðað] *nf* vagueness.
vahído [ba'iðo] *nm* dizzy spell.
vaho ['bao] *nm* (*vapor*) vapour, steam; (*olor*) smell; (*respiración*) breath; ~**s** *nmpl* (*MED*) inhalation *sg*.
vaina ['baina] *nf* sheath ♦ *nm* (*AM*) nuisance.
vainilla [bai'niʎa] *nf* vanilla.
vainita [bai'nita] *nf* (*AM*) green *o* French bean.
vais [bais] *vb V* **ir**.
vaivén [bai'ßen] *nm* to-and-fro movement; (*de tránsito*) coming and going; **vaivenes** *nmpl* (*fig*) ups and downs.
vajilla [ba'xiʎa] *nf* crockery, dishes *pl*; (*una* ~) service; ~ **de porcelana** chinaware.
val [bal], **valdré** [bal'dre] *etc vb V* **valer**.
vale ['bale] *nm* voucher; (*recibo*) receipt; (*pagaré*) I.O.U.; ~ **de regalo** gift voucher

o token.

valedero, a [bale'ðero, a] *adj* valid.

valenciano, a [balen'θjano, a] *adj, nm/f* Valencian ♦ *nm (LING)* Valencian.

valentía [balen'tia] *nf* courage, bravery; *(pey)* boastfulness; *(acción)* heroic deed.

valentísimo, a [balen'tisimo, a] *adj (superl de* **valiente)** very brave, courageous.

valentón, ona [balen'ton, ona] *adj* blustering.

valer [ba'ler] *vt* to be worth; *(MAT)* to equal; *(costar)* to cost; *(amparar)* to aid, protect ♦ *vi (ser útil)* to be useful; *(ser válido)* to be valid; **~se** *vr* to defend o.s. ♦ *nm* worth, value; **~ la pena** to be worthwhile; **¿vale?** O.K.?; **¡vale!** *(¡basta!)* that'll do!; **¡eso no vale!** that doesn't count!; **no vale nada** it's no good; *(mercancía)* it's worthless; *(argumento)* it's no use; **no vale para nada** he's no good at all; **más vale tarde que nunca** better late than never; **más vale que nos vayamos** we'd better go; **~se de** to make use of, take advantage of; **~se por sí mismo** to help *o* manage by o.s.

valga ['balɣa] *etc vb V* **valer.**

valía [ba'lia] *nf* worth; **de gran ~** *(objeto)* very valuable.

validar [bali'ðar] *vt* to validate; *(POL)* to ratify.

validez [bali'ðeθ] *nf* validity; **dar ~ a** to validate.

válido, a ['baliðo, a] *adj* valid.

valiente [ba'ljente] *adj* brave, valiant; *(audaz)* bold; *(pey)* boastful; *(con ironía)* fine, wonderful ♦ *nm/f* brave man/ woman.

valija [ba'lixa] *nf* case; *(AM)* suitcase; *(mochila)* satchel; *(CORREOS)* mailbag; **~ diplomática** diplomatic bag.

valioso, a [ba'ljoso, a] *adj* valuable; *(rico)* wealthy.

valla ['baʎa] *nf* fence; *(DEPORTE)* hurdle; *(fig)* barrier; **~ publicitaria** billboard.

vallar [ba'ʎar] *vt* to fence in.

valle ['baʎe] *nm* valley, vale.

vallisoletano, a [baʎisole'tano, a] *adj* of *o* from Valladolid ♦ *nm/f* native *o* inhabitant of Valladolid.

valor [ba'lor] *nm* value, worth; *(precio)* price; *(valentía)* valour, courage; *(importancia)* importance; *(cara)* nerve, cheek *(fam)*; **sin ~** worthless; **~ adquisitivo** *o* **de compra** purchasing power; **dar ~ a** to attach importance to; **quitar ~ a** to minimize the importance of; *(COM)*: **~ según balance** book value; **~ comercial** *o* **de mercado** market value;

~ contable/desglosado asset/break-up value; **~ de escasez** scarcity value; **~ intrínseco** intrinsic value; **~ a la par** par value; **~ neto** net worth; **~ de rescate/de sustitución** surrender/replacement value; *V tb* **valores.**

valoración [balora'θjon] *nf* valuation.

valorar [balo'rar] *vt* to value; *(tasar)* to price; *(fig)* to assess.

valores [ba'lores] *nmpl (COM)* securities; **~ en cartera** *o* **habidos** investments.

vals [bals] *nm* waltz.

válvula ['balβula] *nf* valve.

vamos ['bamos] *vb V* **ir.**

vampiro, iresa [bam'piro, i'resa] *nm/f* vampire ♦ *nf (CINE)* vamp, femme fatale.

van [ban] *vb V* **ir.**

vanagloriarse [banaɣlo'rjarse] *vr* to boast.

vandalismo [banda'lismo] *nm* vandalism.

vándalo, a ['bandalo, a] *nm/f* vandal.

vanguardia [ban'gwardja] *nf* vanguard; **de ~** *(ARTE)* avant-garde; **estar en** *o* **ir a la ~ de** *(fig)* to be in the forefront of.

vanguardista [bangwar'ðista] *adj* avant-garde.

vanidad [bani'ðað] *nf* vanity; *(inutilidad)* futility; *(irrealidad)* unreality.

vanidoso, a [bani'ðoso, a] *adj* vain, conceited.

vano, a ['bano, a] *adj (irreal)* unreal; *(irracional)* unreasonable; *(inútil)* vain, useless; *(persona)* vain, conceited; *(frívolo)* frivolous.

vapor [ba'por] *nm* vapour; *(vaho)* steam; *(de gas)* fumes *pl*; *(neblina)* mist; **~es** *nmpl (MED)* hysterics; **al ~** *(CULIN)* steamed.

vaporice [bapo'riθe] *etc vb V* **vaporizar.**

vaporizador [baporiθa'ðor] *nm (perfume etc)* spray.

vaporizar [bapori'θar] *vt* to vaporize; *(perfume)* to spray.

vaporoso, a [bapo'roso, a] *adj* vaporous; *(vahoso)* steamy; *(tela)* light, airy.

vapulear [bapule'ar] *vt* to thrash; *(fig)* to slate.

vaque ['bake] *etc vb V* **vacar.**

vaquería [bake'ria] *nf* dairy.

vaquero, a [ba'kero, a] *adj* cattle *cpd* ♦ *nm* cowboy; **~s** *nmpl* jeans.

vaquilla [ba'kiʎa] *nf* heifer.

vara ['bara] *nf* stick, pole; *(TEC)* rod; **~ mágica** magic wand.

varado, a [ba'raðo, a] *adj (NAUT)* stranded; **estar ~** to be aground.

varar [ba'rar] *vt* to beach ♦ *vi*, **~se** *vr* to be beached.

varear [bare'ar] *vt* to hit, beat; *(frutas)* to

knock down (with poles).
variable [ba'rjaßle] *adj, nf* variable (*tb INFORM*).
variación [barja'θjon] *nf* variation; **sin ~** unchanged.
variado, a [ba'rjaðo, a] *adj* varied; (*dulces, galletas*) assorted; **entremeses ~s** a selection of starters.
variante [ba'rjante] *adj* variant ♦ *nf* (*alternativa*) alternative; (*AUTO*) bypass.
variar [ba'rjar] *vt* (*cambiar*) to change; (*poner variedad*) to vary; (*modificar*) to modify; (*cambiar de posición*) to switch around ♦ *vi* to vary; **~ de** to differ from; **~ de opinión** to change one's mind; **para ~** just for a change.
varicela [bari'θela] *nf* chicken pox.
varices [ba'riθes] *nfpl* varicose veins.
variedad [barje'ðað] *nf* variety.
varilla [ba'riʎa] *nf* stick; (*BOT*) twig; (*TEC*) rod; (*de rueda*) spoke; **~ mágica** magic wand.
vario, a ['barjo, a] *adj* (*variado*) varied; (*multicolor*) motley; (*cambiable*) changeable; **~s** various, several.
variopinto, a [barjo'pinto, a] *adj* diverse; **un público ~** a mixed audience.
varita [ba'rita] *nf*: **~ mágica** magic wand.
varón [ba'ron] *nm* male, man.
varonil [baro'nil] *adj* manly.
Varsovia [bar'soßja] *nf* Warsaw.
vas [bas] *vb V* **ir**.
vasco, a ['basko, a], **vascongado, a** [baskon'gaðo, a] *adj, nm/f* Basque ♦ *nm* (*LING*) Basque ♦ *nfpl*: **las Vascongadas** the Basque Country *sg o* Provinces.
vascuence [bas'kwenθe] *nm* (*LING*) Basque.
vasectomía [basekto'mia] *nf* vasectomy.
vaselina [base'lina] *nf* Vaseline ®.
vasija [ba'sixa] *nf* (earthenware) vessel.
vaso ['baso] *nm* glass, tumbler; (*ANAT*) vessel; (*cantidad*) glass(ful); **~ de vino** glass of wine; **~ para vino** wineglass.
vástago ['bastayo] *nm* (*BOT*) shoot; (*TEC*) rod; (*fig*) offspring.
vasto, a ['basto, a] *adj* vast, huge.
váter ['bater] *nm* lavatory, W.C.
Vaticano [bati'kano] *nm*: **el ~** the Vatican; **la Ciudad del ~** the Vatican City.
vaticinar [batiθi'nar] *vt* to prophesy, predict.
vaticinio [bati'θinjo] *nm* prophecy.
vatio ['batjo] *nm* (*ELEC*) watt.
vaya ['baja] *etc vb V* **ir**.
Vda. *abr* = **viuda**.
Vd(s) *abr* = **usted(es)**.
ve [be] *vb V* **ir, ver**.
vea ['bea] *etc vb V* **ver**.

vecinal [beθi'nal] *adj* (*camino, impuesto etc*) local.
vecindad [beθin'dað] *nf*, **vecindario** [beθin'darjo] *nm* neighbourhood; (*habitantes*) residents *pl*.
vecino, a [be'θino, a] *adj* neighbouring ♦ *nm/f* neighbour; (*residente*) resident; **somos ~s** we live next door to one another.
vector [bek'tor] *nm* vector.
veda ['beða] *nf* prohibition; (*temporada*) close season.
vedado [be'ðaðo] *nm* preserve.
vedar [be'ðar] *vt* (*prohibir*) to ban, prohibit; (*idea, plan*) to veto; (*impedir*) to stop, prevent.
vedette [be'ðet] *nf* (*TEAT, CINE*) star(let).
vega ['bexa] *nf* fertile plain *o* valley.
vegetación [bexeta'θjon] *nf* vegetation.
vegetal [bexe'tal] *adj, nm* vegetable.
vegetar [bexe'tar] *vi* to vegetate.
vegetariano, a [bexeta'rjano, a] *adj, nm/f* vegetarian.
vegetativo, a [bexeta'tißo, a] *adj* vegetative.
vehemencia [bee'menθja] *nf* (*insistencia*) vehemence; (*pasión*) passion; (*fervor*) fervour; (*violencia*) violence.
vehemente [bee'mente] *adj* vehement; passionate; fervent; violent.
vehículo [be'ikulo] *nm* vehicle; (*MED*) carrier; **~ de servicio público** public service vehicle; **~ espacial** spacecraft.
veinte ['beinte] *num* twenty; (*orden, fecha*) twentieth; **el siglo ~** the twentieth century.
veintena [bein'tena] *nf*: **una ~** (about) twenty, a score.
vejación [bexa'θjon] *nf* vexation; (*humillación*) humiliation.
vejamen [be'xamen] *nm* satire.
vejar [be'xar] *vt* (*irritar*) to annoy, vex; (*humillar*) to humiliate.
vejatorio, a [bexa'torjo, a] *adj* humiliating, degrading.
vejez [be'xeθ] *nf* old age.
vejiga [be'xixa] *nf* (*ANAT*) bladder.
vela ['bela] *nf* (*de cera*) candle; (*NAUT*) sail; (*insomnio*) sleeplessness; (*vigilia*) vigil; (*MIL*) sentry duty; (*fam*) snot; **a toda ~** (*NAUT*) under full sail; **estar a dos ~s** (*fam*) to be skint; **pasar la noche en ~** to have a sleepless night.
velado, a [be'laðo, a] *adj* veiled; (*sonido*) muffled; (*FOTO*) blurred ♦ *nf* soirée.
velador [bela'ðor] *nm* watchman; (*candelero*) candlestick; (*AM*) bedside table.

velar [be'lar] *vt* (*vigilar*) to keep watch over; (*cubrir*) to veil ♦ *vi* to stay awake; ~ **por** to watch over, look after.

velatorio [bela'torjo] *nm* (*funeral*) wake.

veleidad [belei'ðað] *nf* (*ligereza*) fickleness; (*capricho*) whim.

velero [be'lero] *nm* (*NAUT*) sailing ship; (*AVIAT*) glider.

veleta [be'leta] *nmf* fickle person ♦ *nf* weather vane.

veliz [be'lis] *nm* (*AM*) suitcase.

vello ['beʎo] *nm* down, fuzz.

vellón [be'ʎon] *nm* fleece.

velloso, a [be'ʎoso, a] *adj* fuzzy.

velludo, a [be'ʎuðo, a] *adj* shaggy ♦ *nm* plush, velvet.

velo ['belo] *nm* veil; ~ **de paladar** (*ANAT*) soft palate.

velocidad [beloθi'ðað] *nf* speed; (*TEC*) rate, pace, velocity; (*MECÁNICA, AUTO*) gear; **¿a qué ~?** how fast?; **de alta ~** high-speed; **cobrar ~** to pick up *o* gather speed; **meter la segunda ~** to change into second gear; ~ **máxima de impresión** (*INFORM*) maximum print speed.

velocímetro [belo'θimetro] *nm* speedometer.

velódromo [be'loðromo] *nm* cycle track.

veloz [be'loθ] *adj* fast, swift.

ven [ben] *vb V* venir.

vena ['bena] *nf* vein; (*fig*) vein, disposition; (*GEO*) seam, vein.

venablo [be'naβlo] *nm* javelin.

venado [be'naðo] *nm* deer; (*CULIN*) venison.

venal [be'nal] *adj* (*ANAT*) venous; (*pey*) venal.

venalidad [benali'ðað] *nf* venality.

vencedor, a [benθe'ðor, a] *adj* victorious ♦ *nmf* victor, winner.

vencer [ben'θer] *vt* (*dominar*) to defeat, beat; (*derrotar*) to vanquish; (*superar, controlar*) to overcome, master ♦ *vi* (*triunfar*) to win (through), triumph; (*pago*) to fall due; (*plazo*) to expire; **dejarse ~** to yield, give in.

vencido, a [ben'θiðo, a] *adj* (*derrotado*) defeated, beaten; (*COM*) payable, due ♦ *adv*: **pagar ~** to pay in arrears; **le pagan por meses ~s** he is paid at the end of the month; **darse por ~** to give up.

vencimiento [benθi'mjento] *nm* collapse; (*COM: plazo*) expiration; **a su ~** when it falls due.

venda ['benda] *nf* bandage.

vendaje [ben'daxe] *nm* bandage, dressing.

vendar [ben'dar] *vt* to bandage; ~ **los ojos** to blindfold.

vendaval [benda'βal] *nm* (*viento*) gale; (*huracán*) hurricane.

vendedor, a [bende'ðor, a] *nmf* seller; ~ **ambulante** hawker, pedlar (*BRIT*), peddler (*US*).

vender [ben'der] *vt* to sell; (*comerciar*) to market; (*traicionar*) to sell out, betray; ~**se** *vr* to be sold; ~ **al contado/al por mayor/al por menor/a plazos** to sell for cash/wholesale/retail/on credit; **"se vende"** "for sale"; **"véndese coche"** "car for sale"; ~ **al descubierto** to sell short.

vendimia [ben'dimja] *nf* grape harvest; **la ~ de 1973** the 1973 vintage.

vendimiar [bendi'mjar] *vi* to pick grapes.

vendré [ben'dre] *etc vb V* **venir**.

Venecia [be'neθja] *nf* Venice.

veneciano, a [bene'θjano, a] *adj, nmf* Venetian.

veneno [be'neno] *nm* poison, venom.

venenoso, a [bene'noso, a] *adj* poisonous.

venerable [bene'raβle] *adj* venerable.

veneración [benera'θjon] *nf* veneration.

venerar [bene'rar] *vt* (*reconocer*) to venerate; (*adorar*) to worship.

venéreo, a [be'nereo, a] *adj* venereal.

venezolano, a [beneθo'lano, a] *adj, nmf* Venezuelan.

Venezuela [bene'θwela] *nf* Venezuela.

venga ['benga] *etc vb V* **venir**.

vengador, a [benga'ðor, a] *adj* avenging ♦ *nmf* avenger.

venganza [ben'ganθa] *nf* vengeance, revenge.

vengar [ben'gar] *vt* to avenge; ~**se** *vr* to take revenge.

vengativo, a [benga'tiβo, a] *adj* (*persona*) vindictive.

vengue ['benge] *etc vb V* **vengar**.

venia ['benja] *nf* (*perdón*) pardon; (*permiso*) consent; **con su ~** by your leave.

venial [be'njal] *adj* venial.

venida [be'niða] *nf* (*llegada*) arrival; (*regreso*) return; (*fig*) rashness.

venidero, a [beni'ðero, a] *adj* coming, future; **en lo ~** in (the) future.

venir [be'nir] *vi* to come; (*llegar*) to arrive; (*ocurrir*) to happen; ~**se abajo** to collapse; ~ **a menos** (*persona*) to lose status; (*empresa*) to go downhill; ~ **bien** to be suitable, come just right; (*ropa, gusto*) to suit; ~ **mal** to be unsuitable *o* inconvenient, come awkwardly; **el año que viene** next year; **¡ven acá!** come (over) here!; **¡venga!** (*fam*) come on!

venta ['benta] *nf* (*COM*) sale; (*posada*) inn; ~ **a plazos** hire purchase; ~ **al contado/**

al por mayor/al por menor *o* **al detalle** cash sale/wholesale/retail; ~ **a domicilio** door-to-door selling; ~ **y arrendamiento al vendedor** sale and lease back; ~ **de liquidación** clearance sale; **estar de** *o* **en** ~ to be (up) for sale *o* on the market; ~**s brutas** gross sales; ~**s a término** forward sales.

ventaja [ben'taxa] *nf* advantage; **llevar la** ~ (*en carrera*) to be leading *o* ahead.

ventajoso, a [benta'xoso, a] *adj* advantageous.

ventana [ben'tana] *nf* window; ~ **de guillotina/galería** sash/bay window; ~ **de la nariz** nostril.

ventanilla [venta'niʎa] *nf* (*de taquilla, tb INFORM*) window.

ventearse [bente'arse] *vr* (*romperse*) to crack; (*ANAT*) to break wind.

ventilación [bentila'θjon] *nf* ventilation; (*corriente*) draught; (*fig*) airing.

ventilador [bentila'ðor] *nm* ventilator; (*eléctrico*) fan.

ventilar [benti'lar] *vt* to ventilate; (*a secar*) to put out to dry; (*fig*) to air, discuss.

ventisca [ben'tiska] *nf* blizzard.

ventisquero [bentis'kero] *nm* snowdrift.

ventolera [bento'lera] *nf* (*ráfaga*) gust of wind; (*idea*) whim, wild idea; **le dio la** ~ **de comprarlo** he had a sudden notion to buy it.

ventosear [bentose'ar] *vi* to break wind.

ventosidad [bentosi'ðað] *nf* flatulence.

ventoso, a [ben'toso, a] *adj* windy ♦ *nf* (*ZOOL*) sucker; (*instrumento*) suction pad.

ventrículo [ben'trikulo] *nm* ventricle.

ventrílocuo, a [ben'trilokwo, a] *nm/f* ventriloquist.

ventriloquia [bentri'lokja] *nf* ventriloquism.

ventura [ben'tura] *nf* (*felicidad*) happiness; (*buena suerte*) luck; (*destino*) fortune; **a la (buena)** ~ at random.

venturoso, a [bentu'roso, a] *adj* happy; (*afortunado*) lucky, fortunate.

venza ['benθa] *etc vb V* **vencer.**

ver [ber] *vt, vi* to see; (*mirar*) to look at, watch; (*investigar*) to look into; (*entender*) to see, understand; ~**se** *vr* (*encontrarse*) to meet; (*dejarse* ~) to be seen; (*hallarse: en un apuro*) to find o.s., be ♦ *nm* looks *pl*, appearance; **a** ~ let's see; **a** ~ **si** ... I wonder if ...; **por lo que veo** apparently; **dejarse** ~ to become apparent; **no tener nada que** ~ **con** to have nothing to do with; **a mi modo de** ~ as I see it; **merece** ~**se** it's worth seeing; **no lo veo** I can't see it; **¡nos vemos!** see you (later)!;

¡habráse visto! did you ever! (*fam*); **¡viera(n)** *o* **hubiera(n) visto qué casa!** (*AM fam*) if only you'd seen the house!, what a house!; **ya se ve que** ... it is obvious that ...; **si te vi no me acuerdo** they *etc* just don't want to know.

vera ['bera] *nf* edge, verge; (*de río*) bank; **a la** ~ **de** near, next to.

veracidad [beraθi'ðað] *nf* truthfulness.

veraneante [berane'ante] *nm/f* holidaymaker, (summer) vacationer (*US*).

veranear [berane'ar] *vi* to spend the summer.

veraneo [bera'neo] *nm*: **estar de** ~ to be away on (one's summer) holiday; **lugar de** ~ holiday resort.

veraniego, a [bera'njeɣo, a] *adj* summer *cpd*.

verano [be'rano] *nm* summer.

veras ['beras] *nfpl* truth *sg*; **de** ~ really, truly; **esto va de** ~ this is serious.

veraz [be'raθ] *adj* truthful.

verbal [ber'ßal] *adj* verbal; (*mensaje etc*) oral.

verbena [ber'ßena] *nf* street party.

verbigracia [berßi'xraθja] *adv* for example.

verbo ['berßo] *nm* verb.

verborrea [berßo'rrea] *nf* verbosity, verbal diarrhoea.

verboso, a [ber'ßoso, a] *adj* verbose.

verdad [ber'ðað] *nf* (*lo verídico*) truth; (*fiabilidad*) reliability ♦ *adv* really; **¿~?, ¿no es** ~**?** isn't it?, aren't you?, don't you? *etc*; **de** ~ *adj* real, proper; **a decir** ~, **no quiero** to tell (you) the truth, I don't want to; **la pura** ~ the plain truth.

verdaderamente [berðaðera'mente] *adv* really, indeed, truly.

verdadero, a [berða'ðero, a] *adj* (*veraz*) true, truthful; (*fiable*) reliable; (*fig*) real.

verde ['berðe] *adj* green; (*fruta etc*) green, unripe; (*chiste etc*) blue, smutty, dirty ♦ *nm* green; **viejo** ~ dirty old man; **poner** ~ **a algn** to give sb a dressing-down.

verdear [berðe'ar], **verdecer** [berðe'θer] *vi* to turn green.

verdezca [ber'ðeθka] *etc vb V* **verdecer.**

verdor [ber'ðor] *nm* (*lo verde*) greenness; (*BOT*) verdure; (*fig*) youthful vigour.

verdugo [ber'ðuɣo] *nm* executioner; (*BOT*) shoot; (*cardenal*) weal.

verdulero, a [berðu'lero, a] *nm/f* greengrocer.

verdura [ber'ðura] *nf* greenness; ~**s** *nfpl* (*CULIN*) greens.

vereda [be'reða] *nf* path; (*AM*) pavement, sidewalk (*US*); **meter a algn en** ~ to bring sb into line.

veredicto [bere'ðikto] nm verdict.

vergel [ber'xel] nm lush garden.

vergonzoso, a [berɣon'θoso, a] adj shameful; (tímido) timid, bashful.

vergüenza [ber'ɣwenθa] nf shame, sense of shame; (timidez) bashfulness; (pudor) modesty; **tener ~ to be ashamed; me da ~ decírselo** I feel too shy o it embarrasses me to tell him; **¡qué ~!** (de situación) what a disgrace!; (a persona) shame on you!

vericueto [beri'kweto] nm rough track.

verídico, a [be'riðiko, a] adj true, truthful.

verificar [berifi'kar] vt to check; (corroborar) to verify (tb INFORM); (testamento) to prove; (llevar a cabo) to carry out; **~se** vr to occur, happen; (mitin etc) to be held; (profecía etc) to come o prove true.

verifique [beri'fike] etc vb V **verificar.**

verja ['berxa] nf iron gate; (cerca) railing(s) (pl); (rejado) grating.

vermut [ber'mu], pl **vermuts** nm vermouth ♦ nf (esp AM) matinée.

verosímil [bero'simil] adj likely, probable; (relato) credible.

verosimilitud [berosimili'tuð] nf likeliness, probability.

verruga [be'rruɣa] nf wart.

versado, a [ber'saðo, a] adj: **~ en** versed in.

Versalles [ber'saʎes] nm Versailles.

versar [ber'sar] vi to go round, turn; **~ sobre** to deal with, be about.

versátil [ber'satil] adj versatile.

versículo [ber'sikulo] nm (REL) verse.

versión [ber'sjon] nf version; (traducción) translation.

verso ['berso] nm (gen) verse; **un ~ a** line of poetry; **~ libre/suelto** free/blank verse.

vértebra ['berteßra] nf vertebra.

vertebrado, a [berte'ßraðo, a] adj, nm/f vertebrate.

vertebral [berte'ßral] adj vertebral; **columna ~** spine.

vertedero [berte'ðero] nm rubbish dump, tip.

verter [ber'ter] vt (vaciar) to empty, pour (out); (tirar) to dump ♦ vi to flow.

vertical [berti'kal] adj vertical; (postura, piano etc) upright ♦ nf vertical.

vértice ['bertiθe] nm vertex, apex.

vertiente [ber'tjente] nf slope.

vertiginoso, a [bertixi'noso, a] adj giddy, dizzy.

vértigo ['bertiɣo] nm vertigo; (mareo) dizziness; (actividad) intense activity; **de**

~ (fam: velocidad) giddy; (: ruido) tremendous; (: talento) fantastic.

vesícula [be'sikula] nf blister; **~ biliar** gall bladder.

vespa ® ['bespa] nf (motor) scooter.

vespertino, a [besper'tino, a] adj evening cpd.

vespino ® [bes'pino] nm o f ≈ moped.

vestíbulo [bes'tißulo] nm hall; (de teatro) foyer.

vestido [bes'tiðo] nm (ropa) clothes pl, clothing; (de mujer) dress, frock.

vestigio [bes'tixjo] nm (trazo) trace; (señal) sign; **~s** nmpl remains.

vestimenta [besti'menta] nf clothing.

vestir [bes'tir] vt (poner: ropa) to put on; (llevar: ropa) to wear; (cubrir) to clothe, cover; (pagar: la ropa) to clothe, pay for the clothing of; (sastre) to make clothes for ♦ vi (ponerse: ropa) to dress; (verse bien) to look good; **~se** vr to get dressed, dress o.s.; **traje de ~** (formal) formal suit; **estar vestido de** to be dressed o clad in; (como disfraz) to be dressed as.

vestuario [bes'twarjo] nm clothes pl, wardrobe; (TEAT: para actores) dressing room; (: para público) cloakroom; (DEPORTE) changing room.

Vesubio [be'sußjo] nm Vesuvius.

veta ['beta] nf (vena) vein, seam; (raya) streak; (de madera) grain.

vetar [be'tar] vt to veto.

veterano, a [bete'rano, a] adj, nm/f veteran.

veterinario, a [beteri'narjo, a] nm/f vet(erinary surgeon) ♦ nf veterinary science.

veto ['beto] nm veto.

vetusto, a [be'tusto, a] adj ancient.

vez [beθ] nf time; (turno) turn; **a la ~ que** at the same time as; **a su ~** in its turn; **cada ~ más/menos** more and more/less and less; **una ~** once; **dos veces** twice; **de una ~** in one go; **de una ~ para siempre** once and for all; **en ~ de** instead of; **a veces** sometimes; **otra ~** again; **una y otra ~** repeatedly; **pocas veces** seldom; **de ~ en cuando** from time to time; **7 veces 9** 7 times 9; **hacer las veces de** to stand in for; **tal ~** perhaps; **¿lo viste alguna ~?** did you ever see it?; **¿cuántas veces?** how often?; **érase una ~** once upon a time (there was).

v. g., v. gr. abr (= verbigracia) viz.

vía ['bia] nf (calle) road; (ruta) track, route; (FERRO) line; (fig) way; (ANAT) passage, tube ♦ prep via, by way of; **por ~ bucal** orally; **por ~ judicial** by legal means; **por**

~ **oficial** through official channels; **por ~ de** by way of; **en ~s de** in the process of; **un país en ~s de desarrollo** a developing country; ~ **aérea** airway; **V~ Láctea** Milky Way; ~ **pública** public highway *o* thoroughfare; ~ **única** one-way street; **el tren está en la** ~ **8** the train is (standing) at platform 8.

viable ['bjaßle] *adj (COM)* viable; *(plan etc)* feasible.

viaducto [bja'ðukto] *nm* viaduct.

viajante [bja'xante] *nm* commercial traveller, traveling salesman (*US*).

viajar [bja'xar] *vi* to travel, journey.

viaje ['bjaxe] *nm* journey; *(gira)* tour; *(NAUT)* voyage; *(COM: carga)* load; **los ~s** travel *sg*; **estar de** ~ to be on a journey; ~ **de ida y vuelta** round trip; ~ **de novios** honeymoon.

viajero, a [bja'xero, a] *adj* travelling (*BRIT*), traveling (*US*); *(ZOOL)* migratory ♦ *nm/f* *(quien viaja)* traveller; *(pasajero)* passenger.

vial [bjal] *adj* road *cpd*, traffic *cpd.*

vianda ['bjanda] *nf (tb:* ~**s)** food.

viáticos ['bjatikos] *nmpl (COM)* travelling (*BRIT*) *o* traveling (*US*) expenses.

víbora ['bißora] *nf* viper.

vibración [bißra'θjon] *nf* vibration.

vibrador [bißra'ðor] *nm* vibrator.

vibrante [bi'ßrante] *adj* vibrant, vibrating.

vibrar [bi'ßrar] *vt* to vibrate ♦ *vi* to vibrate; *(pulsar)* to throb, beat, pulsate.

vicario [bi'karjo] *nm* curate.

vicecónsul [biθe'konsul] *nm* vice-consul.

vicegerente [biθexe'rente] *nm/f* assistant manager.

vicepresidente [biθepresi'ðente] *nm/f* vice president; *(de comité etc)* vice-chairman.

viceversa [biθe'ßersa] *adv* vice versa.

viciado, a [bi'θjaðo, a] *adj (corrompido)* corrupt; *(contaminado)* foul, contaminated.

viciar [bi'θjar] *vt (pervertir)* to pervert; *(adulterar)* to adulterate; *(falsificar)* to falsify; *(JUR)* to nullify; *(estropear)* to spoil; *(sentido)* to twist; ~**se** *vr* to become corrupted; *(aire, agua)* to be(come) polluted.

vicio ['biθjo] *nm (libertinaje)* vice; *(mala costumbre)* bad habit; *(mimo)* spoiling; *(alabeo)* warp, warping; **de** *o* **por** ~ out of sheer habit.

vicioso, a [bi'θjoso, a] *adj (muy malo)* vicious; *(corrompido)* depraved; *(mimado)* spoiled ♦ *nm/f* depraved person; *(adicto)* addict.

vicisitud [biθisi'tuð] *nf* vicissitude.

víctima ['biktima] *nf* victim; *(de accidente etc)* casualty.

victimario [bikti'marjo] *nm (AM)* killer, murderer.

victoria [bik'torja] *nf* victory.

victorioso, a [bikto'rjoso, a] *adj* victorious.

vicuña [bi'kuɲa] *nf* vicuna.

vid [bið] *nf* vine.

vida ['biða] *nf* life; *(duración)* lifetime; *(modo de vivir)* way of life; **¡~!, ¡~ mía!** *(saludo cariñoso)* my love!; **de por** ~ for life; **de** ~ **airada** *o* **libre** loose-living; **en la/mi** ~ never; **estar con** ~ to be still alive; **ganarse la** ~ to earn one's living; **¡esto es ~!** this is the life!; **le va la** ~ **en esto** his life depends on it.

vidente [bi'ðente] *nm/f (adivino)* clairvoyant; *(no ciego)* sighted person.

vídeo ['biðeo] *nm* video *(recorder)*; **cinta de** ~ videotape; **película de** ~ videofilm; **grabar en** ~ to record, (video)tape; ~ **compuesto/ inverso** (*INFORM*) composite/reverse video.

videocámara [biðeo'kamara] *nf* video camera; *(pequeña)* camcorder.

videocassette [biðeoka'set] *nm* video cassette.

videoclip [biðeo'klip] *nm* (music) video.

videoclub [biðeo'klub] *nm* video club; *(tienda)* video shop.

videodatos [biðeo'ðatos] *nmpl (COM)* viewdata.

videojuego [biðeo'xweɣo] *nm* video game.

videotex(o) [biðeo'teks(o)] *nm* Videotex ®.

vidriero, a [bi'ðrjero, a] *nm/f* glazier ♦ *nf (ventana)* stained-glass window; *(AM: de tienda)* shop window; *(puerta)* glass door.

vidrio ['biðrjo] *nm* glass; *(AM)* window; ~ **cilindrado/inastillable** plate/splinter-proof glass.

vidrioso, a [bi'ðrjoso, a] *adj* glassy; *(frágil)* fragile, brittle; *(resbaladizo)* slippery.

viejo, a ['bjexo, a] *adj* old ♦ *nm/f* old man/ woman; **mi ~/vieja** *(fam)* my old man/ woman; **hacerse** *o* **ponerse** ~ to grow *o* get old.

Viena ['bjena] *nf* Vienna.

viene ['bjene] *etc vb V* venir.

vienés, esa [bje'nes, esa] *adj, nm/f* Viennese.

viento ['bjento] *nm* wind; *(olfato)* scent; **contra** ~ **y marea** at all costs; **ir** ~ **en popa** to go splendidly; *(negocio)* to prosper.

vientre ['bjentre] *nm* belly; *(matriz)* womb; ~**s** *nmpl* bowels; **hacer de** ~ to have a movement of the bowels.

vier. *abr* (= *viernes*) Fri.

viernes ['bjernes] *nm inv* Friday; **V~ Santo** Good Friday; *V tb* **Semana Santa**.

vierta ['bjerta] *etc vb V* **verter.**

Vietnam [bjet'nam] *nm*: **el ~** Vietnam.

vietnamita [bjetna'mita] *adj, nm/f* Vietnamese.

viga ['biɣa] *nf* beam, rafter; (*de metal*) girder.

vigencia [bi'xenθja] *nf* validity; (*de contrato etc*) term, life; **estar/entrar en ~** to be in/come into effect *o* force.

vigente [bi'xente] *adj* valid, in force; (*imperante*) prevailing.

vigésimo, a [bi'xesimo, a] *num* twentieth.

vigía [bi'xia] *nm* look-out ♦ *nf* (*atalaya*) watchtower; (*acción*) watching.

vigilancia [bixi'lanθja] *nf* vigilance.

vigilante [bixi'lante] *adj* vigilant ♦ *nm* caretaker; (*en cárcel*) warder; (*en almacén*) shopwalker (*BRIT*), floor-walker (*US*); **~ jurado** security guard (*licensed to carry a gun*); **~ nocturno** night watchman.

vigilar [bixi'lar] *vt* to watch over; (*cuidar*) to look after, keep an eye on ♦ *vi* to be vigilant; (*hacer guardia*) to keep watch.

vigilia [vi'xilja] *nf* wakefulness; (*REL*) fast; **comer de ~** to fast.

vigor [bi'ɣor] *nm* vigour, vitality; **en ~** in force; **entrar/poner en ~** to take/put into effect.

vigoroso, a [biɣo'roso, a] *adj* vigorous.

VIH *nm abr* (= *virus de inmunodeficiencia humana*) HIV.

vil [bil] *adj* vile, low.

vileza [bi'leθa] *nf* vileness; (*acto*) base deed.

vilipendiar [bilipen'djar] *vt* to vilify, revile.

villa ['biʎa] *nf* (*pueblo*) small town; (*municipalidad*) municipality; **la V~** (*ESP*) Madrid; **~ miseria** shanty town.

villancico [biʎan'θiko] *nm* (Christmas) carol.

villorrio [bi'ʎorrjo] *nm* one-horse town, dump; (*AM*: *barrio pobre*) shanty town.

vilo ['bilo]: **en ~** *adv* in the air, suspended; (*fig*) on tenterhooks, in suspense; **estar** *o* **quedar en ~** to be left in suspense.

vinagre [bi'naɣre] *nm* vinegar.

vinagrera [bina'ɣrera] *nf* vinegar bottle; **~s** *nfpl* cruet stand *sg*.

vinagreta [bina'ɣreta] *nf* French dressing.

vinatería [binate'ria] *nf* wine shop.

vinatero, a [bina'tero, a] *adj* wine *cpd* ♦ *nm* wine merchant.

vinculación [binkula'θjon] *nf* (*lazo*) link, bond; (*acción*) linking.

vincular [binku'lar] *vt* to link, bind.

vínculo ['binkulo] *nm* link, bond.

vindicar [bindi'kar] *vt* to vindicate; (*vengar*) to avenge; (*JUR*) to claim.

vinícola [bi'nikola] *adj* (*industria*) wine *cpd*; (*región*) wine-growing *cpd*.

vinicultura [binikul'tura] *nf* wine growing.

vino ['bino] *etc vb V* **venir** ♦ *nm* wine; **~ de solera/seco/tinto** vintage/dry/red wine; **~ de Jerez** sherry; **~ de Oporto** port (wine).

viña ['biɲa] *nf*, **viñedo** [bi'ɲeðo] *nm* vineyard.

viñeta [bi'ɲeta] *nf* (*en historieta*) cartoon.

viola ['bjola] *nf* viola.

violación [bjola'θjon] *nf* violation; (*JUR*) offence, infringement; (*estupro*): **~ (sexual)** rape; **~ de contrato** (*COM*) breach of contract.

violar [bjo'lar] *vt* to violate; (*JUR*) to infringe; (*cometer estupro*) to rape.

violencia [bjo'lenθja] *nf* (*fuerza*) violence, force; (*embarazo*) embarrassment; (*acto injusto*) unjust act.

violentar [bjolen'tar] *vt* to force; (*casa*) to break into; (*agredir*) to assault; (*violar*) to violate.

violento, a [bjo'lento, a] *adj* violent; (*furioso*) furious; (*situación*) embarrassing; (*acto*) forced, unnatural; (*difícil*) awkward; **me es muy ~** it goes against the grain with me.

violeta [bjo'leta] *nf* violet.

violín [bjo'lin] *nm* violin.

violón [bjo'lon] *nm* double bass.

violoncelo [bjolon'θelo] *nm* cello.

virador [bira'ðor] *nm* (*para fotocopiadora*) toner.

viraje [bi'raxe] *nm* turn; (*de vehículo*) swerve; (*de carretera*) bend; (*fig*) change of direction.

virar [bi'rar] *vi* to turn; to swerve; to change direction.

virgen ['birxen] *adj* virgin; (*cinta*) blank ♦ *nm/f* virgin; **la Santísima V~** (*REL*) the Blessed Virgin.

virginidad [birxini'ðað] *nf* virginity.

Virgo ['birɣo] *nm* Virgo.

viril [bi'ril] *adj* virile.

virilidad [birili'ðað] *nf* virility.

virrey [bi'rrei] *nm* viceroy.

virtual [bir'twal] *adj* (*real*) virtual; (*en potencia*) potential.

virtud [bir'tuð] *nf* virtue; **en ~ de** by virtue of.

virtuoso, a [bir'twoso, a] *adj* virtuous

♦ *nm/f* virtuoso.
viruela [bi'rwela] *nf* smallpox; ~s *nfpl* pockmarks; ~s **locas** chickenpox *sg*.
virulento, a [biru'lento, a] *adj* virulent.
virus ['birus] *nm inv* virus.
viruta [bi'ruta] *nf* wood *o* metal shaving.
vis [bis] *nf*: ~ **cómica** sense of humour.
visa ['bisa] *nf* (*AM*), **visado** [bi'saðo] *nm* visa; ~ **de permanencia** residence permit.
visar [bi'sar] *vt* (*pasaporte*) to visa; (*documento*) to endorse.
víscera ['bisθera] *nf* internal organ; ~s *nfpl* entrails.
visceral [bisθe'ral] *adj* (*odio*) deep-rooted; **reacción** ~ gut reaction.
viscoso, a [bis'koso, a] *adj* viscous.
visera [bi'sera] *nf* visor.
visibilidad [bisiβili'ðað] *nf* visibility.
visible [bi'siβle] *adj* visible; (*fig*) obvious; **exportaciones/importaciones** ~s (*COM*) visible exports/imports.
visillo [bi'siʎo] *nm* lace curtain.
visión [bi'sjon] *nf* (*ANAT*) vision, (eye)sight; (*fantasía*) vision, fantasy; (*panorama*) view; **ver visiones** to see *o* be seeing things.
visionario, a [bisjo'narjo, a] *adj* (*que prevé*) visionary; (*alucinado*) deluded ♦ *nm/f* visionary; (*chalado*) lunatic.
visita [bi'sita] *nf* call, visit; (*persona*) visitor; **horas/tarjeta de** ~ visiting hours/card; ~ **de cortesía/de cumplido/de despedida** courtesy/formal/farewell visit; **hacer una** ~ to pay a visit; **ir de** ~ to go visiting.
visitar [bisi'tar] *vt* to visit, call on; (*inspeccionar*) to inspect.
vislumbrar [bislum'brar] *vt* to glimpse, catch a glimpse of.
vislumbre [bis'lumbre] *nf* glimpse; (*centelleo*) gleam; (*idea vaga*) glimmer.
viso ['biso] *nm* (*de metal*) glint, gleam; (*de tela*) sheen; (*aspecto*) appearance; **hay un** ~ **de verdad en esto** there is an element of truth in this.
visón [bi'son] *nm* mink.
visor [bi'sor] *nm* (*FOTO*) viewfinder.
víspera ['bispera] *nf* eve, day before; **la** ~ *o* **en** ~s **de** on the eve of.
vista ['bista] *nf* sight, vision; (*capacidad de ver*) (eye)sight; (*mirada*) look(s) (*pl*); (*FOTO etc*) view; (*JUR*) hearing ♦ *nm* customs officer; **a primera** ~ at first glance; ~ **general** overview; **fijar** *o* **clavar la** ~ **en** to stare at; **hacer la** ~ **gorda** to turn a blind eye; **volver la** ~ to look back; **está a la** ~ **que** it's obvious that; **a**

la ~ (*COM*) at sight; **en** ~ **de** in view of; **en** ~ **de que** in view of the fact that; **¡hasta la** ~!** so long!, see you!; **con** ~s **a** with a view to; **V** *tb* **visto, a.**
vistazo [bis'taθo] *nm* glance; **dar** *o* **echar un** ~ **a** to glance at.
visto, a ['bisto, a] *etc vb* **V vestir** ♦ *pp de* **ver** ♦ *adj* seen; (*considerado*) considered ♦ *nm*: ~ **bueno** approval; "~ **bueno**" "approved"; **por lo** ~ evidently; **dar el** ~ **bueno a algo** to give sth the go-ahead; **está** ~ **que** it's clear that; **está bien/mal** ~ it's acceptable/unacceptable; **está muy** ~ it is very common; **estaba** ~ it had to be; ~ **que** *conj* since, considering that.
vistoso, a [bis'toso, a] *adj* colourful; (*alegre*) gay; (*pey*) gaudy.
visual [bi'swal] *adj* visual.
visualice [biswa'liθe] *etc vb* **V visualizar.**
visualizador [biswaliθa'ðor] *nm* (*INFORM*) display screen, VDU.
visualizar [biswali'θar] *vt* (*imaginarse*) to visualize; (*INFORM*) to display.
vital [bi'tal] *adj* life *cpd*, living *cpd*; (*fig*) vital; (*persona*) lively, vivacious.
vitalicio, a [bita'liθjo, a] *adj* for life.
vitalidad [bitali'ðað] *nf* vitality.
vitamina [bita'mina] *nf* vitamin.
vitaminado, a [bitami'naðo, a] *adj* with added vitamins.
vitamínico, a [bita'miniko, a] *adj* vitamin *cpd*; **complejos** ~s vitamin compounds.
viticultor, a [bitikul'tor, a] *nm/f* vine grower.
viticultura [bitikul'tura] *nf* vine growing.
vitorear [bitore'ar] *vt* to cheer, acclaim.
vítores ['bitores] *nmpl* cheers.
vitoriano, a [bito'rjano, a] *adj* of *o* from Vitoria ♦ *nm/f* native *o* inhabitant of Vitoria.
vítreo, a ['bitreo, a] *adj* vitreous.
vitrina [bi'trina] *nf* glass case; (*en casa*) display cabinet; (*AM*) shop window.
vituperar [bitupe'rar] *vt* to condemn.
vituperio [bitu'perjo] *nm* (*condena*) condemnation; (*censura*) censure; (*insulto*) insult.
viudez [bju'ðeθ] *nf* widowhood.
viudo, a [bi'bjuðo, a] *adj* widowed ♦ *nm* widower ♦ *nf* widow.
viva ['biβa] *excl* hurrah! ♦ *nm* cheer; **¡**~ **el rey!** long live the King!
vivacidad [biβaθi'ðað] *nf* (*vigor*) vigour; (*vida*) vivacity.
vivamente [biβa'mente] *adv* in lively fashion; (*descripción etc*) vividly; (*protesta*) sharply; (*emoción*) acutely.

vivaracho, a [biβa'ratʃo, a] *adj* jaunty, lively; (*ojos*) bright, twinkling.

vivaz [bi'βaθ] *adj* (*que dura*) enduring; (*vigoroso*) vigorous; (*vivo*) lively.

vivencia [bi'βenθja] *nf* experience.

víveres ['biβeres] *nmpl* provisions.

vivero [bi'βero] *nm* (*HORTICULTURA*) nursery; (*para peces*) fishpond; (: *COM*) fish farm.

viveza [bi'βeθa] *nf* liveliness; (*agudeza*) sharpness.

vividor, a [biβi'ðor, a] *adj* (*pey*) opportunistic ♦ *nm* (*aprovechado*) hustler.

vivienda [bi'βjenda] *nf* (*alojamiento*) housing; (*morada*) dwelling; ~**s protegidas** *o* **sociales** council housing *sg* (*BRIT*), public housing *sg* (*US*).

viviente [bi'βjente] *adj* living.

vivificar [biβifi'kar] *vt* to give life to.

vivifique [biβi'fike] *etc vb V* **vivificar**.

vivir [bi'βir] *vt* (*experimentar*) to live *o* go through ♦ *vi* (*gen, COM*): ~ (**de**) to live (by, off, on) ♦ *nm* life, living; ¡**viva!** hurray!; ¡**viva el rey!** long live the king!

vivo, a ['biβo, a] *adj* living, live, alive; (*fig*) vivid; (*movimiento*) quick; (*color*) bright; (*protesta etc*) strong; (*astuto*) smart, clever; **en** ~ (*TV etc*) live; **llegar a lo** ~ to cut to the quick.

vizcaíno, a [biθka'ino, a] *adj, nm/f* Biscayan.

Vizcaya [biθ'kaja] *nf* Biscay; **el Golfo de** ~ the Bay of Biscay.

V.M. *abr* = **Vuestra Majestad**.

V.O. *abr* = *versión original*.

V.ºB.º *abr* = *visto bueno*.

vocablo [bo'kaβlo] *nm* (*palabra*) word; (*término*) term.

vocabulario [bokaβu'larjo] *nm* vocabulary, word list.

vocación [boka'θjon] *nf* vocation.

vocacional [bokasjo'nal] *nf* (*AM*) ≈ technical college.

vocal [bo'kal] *adj* vocal ♦ *nm/f* member (of a committee *etc*) ♦ *nm* non-executive director ♦ *nf* vowel.

vocalice [boka'liθe] *etc vb V* **vocalizar**.

vocalizar [bokali'θar] *vt* to vocalize.

voceador [bosea'ðor] *nm* (*AM*): ~ **de periódicos** newspaper vendor *o* seller.

vocear [boθe'ar] *vt* (*para vender*) to cry; (*aclamar*) to acclaim; (*fig*) to proclaim ♦ *vi* to yell.

vocerío [boθe'rio] *nm* shouting; (*escándalo*) hullabaloo.

vocero, a [bo'sero, a] *nm/f* (*AM*) spokesman/woman.

vociferar [boθife'rar] *vt* to shout; (*jactarse*)

to proclaim boastfully ♦ *vi* to yell.

vocinglero, a [boθin'glero, a] *adj* vociferous; (*gárrulo*) garrulous; (*fig*) blatant.

vodevil [boðe'βil] *nm* music hall, variety, (*US*) vaudeville.

vodka ['boðka] *nm* vodka.

vodú [bo'ðu] *nm* voodoo.

vol *abr* = **volumen**.

volado, a [bo'laðo, a] *adj*: **estar** ~ (*fam: inquieto*) to be worried; (: *loco*) to be crazy.

volador, a [bola'ðor, a] *adj* flying.

voladura [bola'ðura] *nf* blowing up, demolition; (*MINERÍA*) blasting.

volandas [bo'landas]: **en** ~ *adv* in *o* through the air; (*fig*) swiftly.

volante [bo'lante] *adj* flying ♦ *nm* (*de máquina, coche*) steering wheel; (*de reloj*) balance; (*nota*) note; **ir al** ~ to be at the wheel, be driving.

volar [bo'lar] *vt* (*demolir*) to blow up, demolish ♦ *vi* to fly; (*fig: correr*) to rush, hurry; (*fam: desaparecer*) to disappear; **voy volando** I must dash; ¡**cómo vuela el tiempo!** how time flies!

volátil [bo'latil] *adj* volatile; (*fig*) changeable.

volcán [bol'kan] *nm* volcano.

volcánico, a [bol'kaniko, a] *adj* volcanic.

volcar [bol'kar] *vt* to upset, overturn; (*tumbar, derribar*) to knock over; (*vaciar*) to empty out ♦ *vi* to overturn; ~**se** *vr* to tip over; (*barco*) to capsize.

voleibol [bolei'βol] *nm* volleyball.

voleo [bo'leo] *nm* volley; **a(l)** ~ haphazardly; **de un** ~ quickly.

Volga ['bolɣa] *nm* Volga.

volición [boli'θjon] *nf* volition.

volqué [bol'ke], **volquemos** [bol'kemos] *etc vb V* **volcar**.

volquete [bol'kete] *nm* dumper, dump truck (*US*).

voltaje [bol'taxe] *nm* voltage.

voltear [bolte'ar] *vt* to turn over; (*volcar*) to knock over; (*doblar*) to peal ♦ *vi* to roll over; ~**se** *vr* (*AM*) to turn round; ~ **a hacer algo** (*AM*) to do sth again.

voltereta [bolte'reta] *nf* somersault; ~ **sobre las manos** handspring; ~ **lateral** cartwheel.

voltio ['boltjo] *nm* volt.

voluble [bo'luβle] *adj* fickle.

volumen [bo'lumen] *nm* volume; ~ **monetario** money supply; ~ **de negocios** turnover; **bajar el** ~ to turn down the volume; **poner la radio a todo** ~ to turn the radio up full.

voluminoso, a [bolumi'noso, a] *adj* voluminous; (*enorme*) massive.

voluntad [bolun'tað] *nf* will, willpower; (*deseo*) desire, wish; (*afecto*) fondness; **a ~ at** will; (*cantidad*) as much as one likes; **buena ~** goodwill; **mala ~** ill will, malice; **por causas ajenas a mi ~** for reasons beyond my control.

voluntario, a [bolun'tarjo, a] *adj* voluntary ♦ *nm/f* volunteer.

voluntarioso, a [bolunta'rjoso, a] *adj* headstrong.

voluptuoso, a [bolup'twoso, a] *adj* voluptuous.

volver [bol'ßer] *vt* to turn; (*boca abajo*) to turn (over); (*voltear*) to turn round, turn upside down; (*poner al revés*) to turn inside out; (*devolver*) to return; (*transformar*) to change, transform; (*manga*) to roll up ♦ *vi* to return, go/come back; **~se** *vr* to turn round; (*llegar a ser*) to become; **~ la espalda** to turn one's back; **~ bien por mal** to return good for evil; **~ a hacer** to do again; **~ en sí** to come to o round, regain consciousness; **~ la vista atrás** to look back; **~ loco a algn** to drive sb mad; **~se loco** to go mad.

vomitar [bomi'tar] *vt, vi* to vomit.

vómito ['bomito] *nm* (*acto*) vomiting; (*resultado*) vomit.

voracidad [boraθi'ðað] *nf* voracity.

vorágine [bo'raxine] *nf* whirlpool; (*fig*) maelstrom.

voraz [bo'raθ] *adj* voracious; (*fig*) fierce.

vórtice ['bortiθe] *nm* whirlpool; (*de aire*) whirlwind.

vos [bos] *pron* (*AM*) you.

voseo [bo'seo] *nm* (*AM*) addressing a person as "vos", *familiar usage.*

Vosgos ['bosɣos] *nmpl* Vosges.

vosotros, as [bo'sotros, as] *pron* you *pl*; (*reflexivo*) yourselves; **entre ~** among yourselves.

votación [bota'θjon] *nf* (*acto*) voting; (*voto*) vote; **~ a mano alzada** show of hands; **someter algo a ~** to put sth to the vote.

votar [bo'tar] *vt* (*POL: partido etc*) to vote for; (*proyecto: aprobar*) to pass; (*REL*) to vow ♦ *vi* to vote.

voto ['boto] *nm* vote; (*promesa*) vow; (*maldición*) oath, curse; **~s** *nmpl* (good) wishes; **~ de bloque/de grupo** block/card vote; **~ de censura/de (des)confianza/de gracias** vote of censure/(no) confidence/thanks; **dar su ~** to cast one's vote.

voy [boi] *vb V* **ir.**

voz [boθ] *nf* voice; (*grito*) shout; (*chisme*) rumour; (*LING: palabra*) word; (: *forma*) voice; **dar voces** to shout, yell; **llamar a algn a voces** to shout to sb; **llevar la ~ cantante** (*fig*) to be the boss; **tener la ~ tomada** to be hoarse; **tener ~ y voto** to have the right to speak; **a media ~** in a low voice; **a ~ en cuello** o **en grito** at the top of one's voice; **de viva ~** verbally; **en ~ alta** aloud; **~ de mando** command.

vozarrón [boθa'rron] *nm* booming voice.

vra., vro. *abr* = **vuestra, vuestro.**

Vto. *abr* (*COM*) = **vencimiento.**

vudú [bu'ðu] *nm* voodoo.

vuelco ['bwelko] *etc vb V* **volcar** ♦ *nm* spill, overturning; (*fig*) collapse; **mi corazón dio un ~** my heart missed a beat.

vuelo ['bwelo] *etc vb V* **volar** ♦ *nm* flight; (*encaje*) lace, frill; (*de falda etc*) loose part; (*fig*) importance; **de altos ~s** (*fig: plan*) grandiose; (: *persona*) ambitious; **alzar el ~** to take flight; (*fig*) to dash off; **coger al ~** to catch in flight; **~ en picado** dive; **~ libre** hang-gliding; **~ regular** scheduled flight; **falda de mucho ~** full o wide skirt.

vuelque ['bwelke] *etc vb V* **volcar.**

vuelta ['bwelta] *nf* turn; (*curva*) bend, curve; (*regreso*) return; (*revolución*) revolution; (*paseo*) stroll; (*circuito*) lap; (*de papel, tela*) reverse; (*de pantalón*) turn-up (*BRIT*), cuff (*US*); (*dinero*) change; **~ a empezar** back to square one; **~ al mundo** world trip; **V~ a Francia** Tour de France; **~ cerrada** hairpin bend; **a la ~** (*ESP*) on one's return; **a la ~ de la esquina, a la ~** (*AM*) round the corner; **a ~ de correo** by return of post; **dar ~s** to turn, revolve; **dar ~s a una idea** to turn over an idea (in one's mind); **dar una ~** to go for a walk; **dar media ~** (*AUTO*) to do a U-turn; (*fam*) to beat it; **estar de ~** (*fam*) to be back; **poner a algn de ~ y media** to heap abuse on sb; **no tiene ~ de hoja** there's no alternative.

vueltita [bwel'tita] *nf* (*esp AM fam*) (little) walk; (: *en coche*) (little) drive.

vuelto ['bwelto] *pp de* **volver** ♦ *nm* (*AM: moneda*) change.

vuelva ['bwelßa] *etc vb V* **volver.**

vuestro, a ['bwestro, a] *adj* your; (*después de n*) of yours ♦ *pron*: **el ~/la vuestra/los ~s/las vuestras** yours; **lo ~** (what is) yours; **un amigo ~** a friend of yours; **una idea vuestra** an idea of yours.

vulgar [bul'ɣar] *adj* (*ordinario*) vulgar; (*común*) common.

vulgarice [bulɣa'riθe] *etc vb V* **vulgarizar.**

vulgaridad [bulɣari'ðað] *nf* commonness; (*acto*) vulgarity; (*expresión*) coarse expression; ~**es** *nfpl* banalities.
vulgarismo [bulɣa'rismo] *nm* popular form of a word.
vulgarizar [bulɣari'θar] *vt* to popularize.
vulgo ['bulɣo] *nm* common people.
vulnerable [bulne'raβle] *adj* vulnerable.
vulnerar [bulne'rar] *vt* to harm, damage; (*derechos*) to interfere with; (*JUR, COM*) to violate.
vulva ['bulβa] *nf* vulva.

W w

W, w ['uβe'doβle, (*AM*) 'doβleβe] *nf* (*letra*) W, w; **W de Washington** W for William.
walkie-talkie [walki'talki] *nm* walkie-talkie.
walkman ® ['wal(k)man] *nm* Walkman ®.
wáter ['bater] *nm* lavatory.
waterpolo [water'polo] *nm* waterpolo.
wátman ['watman] *adj inv* (*fam*) cool.
whisky ['wiski] *nm* whisky.
Winchester ['wintʃester] *nm* (*INFORM*): **disco** ~ Winchester disk.
windsurf ['winsurf] *nm* windsurfing.

X x

X, x ['ekis] *nf* (*letra*) X, x; **X de Xiquena** X for Xmas.
xenofobia [seno'foβja] *nf* xenophobia.
xenófobo, a [se'nofoβo, a] *adj* xenophobic ♦ *nm/f* xenophobe.
xerografía [seroɣra'fia] *nf* xerography.
xilófono [si'lofono] *nm* xylophone.
Xunta ['ʃunta] *nf* (*tb* ~ **de Galicia**) *regional government of Galicia*.

Y y

Y, y [i'ɣrjeɣa] *nf* (*letra*) Y, y; **Y de Yegua** Y for Yellow (*BRIT*) *o* Yoke (*US*).
y [i] *conj* and; (*AM fam: pues*) well; ¿~ **eso?** why?, how so?; ¡~ **los demás?** what about the others?; ~ **bueno, ...** (*AM*) well ...
ya [ja] *adv* (*gen*) already; (*ahora*) now; (*en seguida*) at once; (*pronto*) soon ♦ *excl* all right!; (*por supuesto*) of course! ♦ *conj* (*ahora que*) now that; ~ **no** not any more, no longer; ~ **lo sé** I know; ~ **dice que sí,** ~ **dice que no** first he says yes, then he says no; ¡~, ~! yes, yes!; (*con impaciencia*) all right!, O.K.!; ¡~ **voy!** (*enfático: no se suele traducir*) coming!; ~ **que** since.
yacer [ja'θer] *vi* to lie.
yacimiento [jaθi'mjento] *nm* bed, deposit; ~ **petrolífero** oilfield.
Yakarta [ja'karta] *nf* Jakarta.
yanqui ['janki] *adj* Yankee ♦ *nm/f* Yank, Yankee.
yate ['jate] *nm* yacht.
yazca ['jaθka] *etc vb V* **yacer**.
yedra ['jeðra] *nf* ivy.
yegua ['jeɣwa] *nf* mare.
yema ['jema] *nf* (*del huevo*) yoke; (*BOT*) leaf bud; (*fig*) best part; ~ **del dedo** fingertip.
Yemen ['jemen] *nm*: **el** ~ **del Norte** Yemen; **el** ~ **del Sur** Southern Yemen.
yemení [jeme'ni] *adj, nm/f* Yemeni.
yendo ['jendo] *vb V* **ir**.
yerba ['jerβa] *nf* = **hierba**.
yerbatero, a [jerβa'tero, a] *adj* (*AM*) maté ♦ *nm/f* (*AM*) herbal healer.
yerga ['jerɣa] *etc*, **yergue** ['jerɣe] *etc vb V* **erguir**.
yermo, a ['jermo, a] *adj* barren; (*de gente*) uninhabited ♦ *nm* waste land.
yerno ['jerno] *nm* son-in-law.
yerre ['jerre] *etc vb V* **errar**.
yerto, a ['jerto, a] *adj* stiff.
yesca ['jeska] *nf* tinder.
yeso ['jeso] *nm* (*GEO*) gypsum; (*ARQ*) plaster.
yo ['jo] *pron personal* I; **soy** ~ it's me, it is I; ~ **que tú/usted** if I were you.

yodo ['joðo] nm iodine.
yoga ['joɣa] nm yoga.
yogur(t) [jo'ɣur(t)] nm yogurt.
yogurtera [joɣur'tera] nf yogurt maker.
yuca ['juka] nf yucca.
yudo ['juðo] nm judo.
yugo ['juɣo] nm yoke.
Yugoslavia [juɣos'laβja] nf Yugoslavia.
yugoslavo, a [juɣos'laβo, a] adj
Yugoslavian ♦ nm/f Yugoslav.
yugular [juɣu'lar] adj jugular.
yunque ['junke] nm anvil.
yunta ['junta] nf yoke.
yuntero [jun'tero] nm ploughman.
yute ['jute] nm jute.
yuxtapondré [jukstapond're] etc vb V
yuxtaponer.
yuxtaponer [jukstapo'ner] vt to juxtapose.
yuxtaponga [juksta'ponga] etc vb V
yuxtaponer.
yuxtaposición [jukstaposi'θjon] nf
juxtaposition.
yuxtapuesto [juksta'pwesto], **yuxtapuse**
[juksta'puse] etc vb V **yuxtaponer**.

Z z

Z, z ['θeta, (esp AM) 'seta] nf (letra) Z, z; **Z de
Zaragoza** Z for Zebra.
zafar [θa'far] vt (soltar) to untie; (superficie)
to clear; ~**se** vr (escaparse) to escape;
(ocultarse) to hide o.s. away; (TEC) to slip
off; ~**se de** (persona) to get away from.
zafio, a ['θafjo, a] adj coarse.
zafiro [θa'firo] nm sapphire.
zaga ['θaɣa] nf rear; **a la** ~ behind, in the
rear.
zagal [θa'ɣal] nm boy, lad.
zagala [θa'ɣala] nf girl, lass.
zaguán [θa'ɣwan] nm hallway.
zaherir [θae'rir] vt (criticar) to criticize; (fig:
herir) to wound.
zahiera etc, **zahiriendo** [θa'jera,
θai'rjendo] etc vb V **zaherir**.
zahorí [θao'ri] nm clairvoyant.
zaino, a ['θaino, a] adj (color de caballo)
chestnut; (pérfido) treacherous; (animal)
vicious.
zalamería [θalame'ria] nf flattery.
zalamero, a [θala'mero, a] adj flattering;
(relamido) suave.

zamarra [θa'marra] nf (piel) sheepskin;
(saco) sheepskin jacket.
Zambeze [θam'beθe] nm Zambezi.
zambo, a ['θambo, a] adj knock-kneed
♦ nm/f (AM) half-breed (of Negro and
Indian parentage); (mulato) mulatto ♦ nf
samba.
zambullida [θambu'ʎiða] nf dive, plunge.
zambullirse [θambu'ʎirse] vr to dive;
(ocultarse) to hide o.s.
zamorano, a [θamo'rano, a] adj of o from
Zamora ♦ nm/f native o inhabitant of
Zamora.
zampar [θam'par] vt (esconder) to hide o
put away (hurriedly); (comer) to gobble;
(arrojar) to hurl ♦ vi to eat voraciously;
~**se** vr (chocar) to bump; (fig) to
gatecrash.
zanahoria [θana'orja] nf carrot.
zancada [θan'kaða] nf stride.
zancadilla [θanka'ðiʎa] nf trip; (fig)
stratagem; **echar la** ~ **a algn** to trip sb up.
zancajo [θan'kaxo] nm (ANAT) heel; (fig)
dwarf.
zanco ['θanko] nm stilt.
zancudo, a [θan'kuðo, a] adj long-legged
♦ nm (AM) mosquito.
zángano ['θangano] nm drone; (holgazán)
idler, slacker.
zanja ['θanxa] nf (fosa) ditch; (tumba)
grave.
zanjar [θan'xar] vt (fosa) to ditch, trench;
(problema) to surmount; (conflicto) to
resolve.
zapapico [θapa'piko] nm pick, pickaxe.
zapata [θa'pata] nf half-boot; (MECÁNICA)
shoe.
zapateado [θapate'aðo] nm (flamenco) tap
dance.
zapatear [θapate'ar] vt (tocar) to tap with
one's foot; (patear) to kick; (fam) to ill-
treat ♦ vi to tap with one's feet.
zapatería [θapate'ria] nf (oficio)
shoemaking; (tienda) shoe-shop; (fábrica)
shoe factory.
zapatero, a [θapa'tero, a] nm/f shoemaker;
~ **remendón** cobbler.
zapatilla [θapa'tiʎa] nf slipper; (TEC)
washer; (para deporte) training shoe.
zapato [θa'pato] nm shoe.
zapear [θape'ar] vi to flick through the
channels.
zapping ['θapin] nm channel-hopping;
hacer ~ to channel-hop.
zar [θar] nm tsar, czar.
zarabanda [θara'ßanda] nf saraband; (fig)
whirl.
Zaragoza [θara'ɣoθa] nf Saragossa.

zaragozano, a [θaraˠo'θano, a] *adj* of *o* from Saragossa ♦ *nm/f* native *o* inhabitant of Saragossa.

zaranda [θa'randa] *nf* sieve.

zarandear [θarande'ar] *vt* to sieve; (*fam*) to shake vigorously.

zarpa ['θarpa] *nf* (*garra*) claw, paw; **echar la** ~ **a** to claw at; (*fam*) to grab.

zarpar [θar'par] *vi* to weigh anchor.

zarpazo [θar'paθo] *nm*: **dar un** ~ to claw.

zarza ['θarθa] *nf* (*BOT*) bramble.

zarzal [θar'θal] *nm* (*matorral*) bramble patch.

zarzamora [θarθa'mora] *nf* blackberry.

zarzuela [θar'θwela] *nf* Spanish light opera; **la Z**~ *home of the Spanish Royal Family.*

zigzag [θiˠ'θaˠ] *adj* zigzag.

zigzaguear [θiˠθaˠe'ar] *vi* to zigzag.

zinc [θink] *nm* zinc.

zíper ['siper] *nm* (*AM*) zip, zipper (*US*).

zócalo ['θokalo] *nm* (*ARQ*) plinth, base; (*de pared*) skirting board.

zoco ['θoko] *nm* (Arab) market, souk.

zodíaco [θo'ðiako] *nm* zodiac; **signo del** ~ star sign.

zona ['θona] *nf* zone; ~ **fronteriza** border area; ~ **del dólar** (*COM*) dollar area; ~ **de fomento** *o* **de desarrollo** development area.

zonzo, a ['sonso, a] *adj* (*AM*) silly.

zoología [θoolo'xia] *nf* zoology.

zoológico, a [θoo'loxiko, a] *adj* zoological ♦ *nm* (*tb*: **parque** ~) zoo.

zoólogo, a [θo'oloˠo, a] *nm/f* zoologist.

zoom [θum] *nm* zoom lens.

zopenco, a [θo'penko, a] (*fam*) *adj* dull, stupid ♦ *nm/f* clot, nitwit.

zopilote [sopi'lote] *nm* (*AM*) buzzard.

zoquete [θo'kete] *nm* (*madera*) block; (*pan*) crust; (*fam*) blockhead.

zorro, a ['θorro, a] *adj* crafty ♦ *nm/f* fox/ vixen ♦ *nf* (*fam*) whore, tart, hooker (*US*).

zote ['θote] (*fam*) *adj* dim, stupid ♦ *nm/f* dimwit.

zozobra [θo'θoßra] *nf* (*fig*) anxiety.

zozobrar [θoθo'ßrar] *vi* (*hundirse*) to capsize; (*fig*) to fail.

zueco ['θweko] *nm* clog.

zulo ['θulo] *nm* (*de armas*) cache.

zumbar [θum'bar] *vt* (*burlar*) to tease; (*golpear*) to hit ♦ *vi* to buzz; (*fam*) to be very close; ~**se** *vr*: ~**se de** to tease; **me zumban los oídos** I have a buzzing *o* ringing in my ears.

zumbido [θum'biðo] *nm* buzzing; (*fam*) punch; ~ **de oídos** buzzing *o* ringing in the ears.

zumo ['θumo] *nm* juice; (*ganancia*) profit; ~ **de naranja** (fresh) orange juice.

zurcir [θur'θir] *vt* (*coser*) to darn; (*fig*) to put together; **¡que las zurzan!** to blazes with them!

zurdo, a ['θurðo, a] *adj* (*mano*) left; (*persona*) left-handed.

zurrar [θu'rrar] *vt* (*TEC*) to dress; (*fam*: *pegar duro*) to wallop; (: *aplastar*) to flatten; (: *criticar*) to criticize harshly.

zurriagazo [θurrja'ˠaθo] *nm* lash, stroke; (*desgracia*) stroke of bad luck.

zurrón [θu'rron] *nm* pouch.

zurza ['θurθa] *etc vb* V **zurcir**.

zutano, a [θu'tano, a] *nm/f* so-and-so.

English-Spanish
Inglés-Español

Aa

A, a [eɪ] *n* (*letter*) A, a; (*SCOL: mark*) ≈
sobresaliente; (*MUS*): **A** la *m*; **A for
Andrew,** (*US*) **A for Able** A de Antonio; **A
road** *n* (*BRIT AUT*) ≈ carretera nacional; **A
shares** *npl* (*BRIT STOCK EXCHANGE*)
acciones *fpl* de clase A.

══════════ *KEYWORD*

a [ə] *indef art* (*before vowel or silent h*: **an**) **1**
un(a); ~ **book** un libro; **an apple** una
manzana; **she's** ~ **nurse** (ella) es
enfermera; **I haven't got** ~ **car** no tengo
coche
2 (*instead of the number "one"*) un(a); ~
year ago hace un año; ~ **hundred/
thousand pounds** cien/mil libras
3 (*in expressing ratios, prices etc*): **3** ~
day/week 3 al día/a la semana; **10 km an
hour** 10 km por hora; **£5** ~ **person** £5 por
persona; **30p** ~ **kilo** 30p el kilo; **3 times** ~
month 3 veces al mes.

a. *abbr* = **acre.**
AA *n abbr* (*BRIT*: = *Automobile Association*)
≈ RACE *m* (*SP*); = *Alcoholics Anonymous*;
(*US*: = *Associate in/of Arts*) título
universitario; (= *anti-aircraft*) A.A.
AAA *n abbr* (= *American Automobile
Association*) ≈ RACE *m* (*SP*); ['θriː'eɪz]
(*BRIT*: = *Amateur Athletics Association*)
asociación de atletismo amateur.
A & R *n abbr* (*MUS*) (= *artists and repertoire*)
nuevos artistas y canciones; ~ **man**
descubridor de jóvenes talentos.
AAUP *n abbr* (= *American Association of
University Professors*) asociación de
profesores universitarios.
AB *abbr* (*BRIT*) = **able-bodied seaman;**

(*Canada*) = *Alberta.*
aback [ə'bæk] *adv*: **to be taken** ~ quedar(se)
desconcertado.
abandon [ə'bændən] *vt* abandonar;
(*renounce*) renunciar a ♦ *n* abandono;
(*wild behaviour*): **with** ~ con desenfreno;
to ~ **ship** abandonar el barco.
abandoned [ə'bændənd] *adj* (*child, house
etc*) abandonado; (*unrestrained*: *manner*)
desinhibido.
abase [ə'beɪs] *vt*: **to** ~ **o.s.** (**so far as to do
...**) rebajarse (hasta el punto de hacer ...).
abashed [ə'bæʃt] *adj* avergonzado.
abate [ə'beɪt] *vi* moderarse; (*lessen*)
disminuir; (*calm down*) calmarse.
abatement [ə'beɪtmənt] *n* (*of pollution,
noise*) disminución *f*.
abattoir ['æbətwɑː*] *n* (*BRIT*) matadero.
abbey ['æbɪ] *n* abadía.
abbot ['æbət] *n* abad *m*.
abbreviate [ə'briːvɪeɪt] *vt* abreviar.
abbreviation [əbriːvɪ'eɪʃən] *n* (*short form*)
abreviatura; (*act*) abreviación *f*.
ABC *n abbr* (= *American Broadcasting
Company*) cadena de televisión.
abdicate ['æbdɪkeɪt] *vt, vi* abdicar.
abdication [æbdɪ'keɪʃən] *n* abdicación *f*.
abdomen ['æbdəmən] *n* abdomen *m*.
abdominal [æb'dɒmɪnl] *adj* abdominal.
abduct [æb'dʌkt] *vt* raptar, secuestrar.
abductor [æb'dʌktə*] *n* raptor(a) *m/f*,
secuestrador(a) *m/f*.
abduction [æb'dʌkʃən] *n* rapto, secuestro.
Aberdonian [æbə'dəʊnɪən] *adj* de Aberdeen
♦ *n* nativo/a *or* habitante *m/f* de Aberdeen.
aberration [æbə'reɪʃən] *n* aberración *f*; **in a
moment of mental** ~ en un momento de
enajenación mental.

abet [ə'bɛt] *vt see* **aid**.

abeyance [ə'beɪəns] *n*: **in ~** (*law*) en desuso; (*matter*) en suspenso.

abhor [əb'hɔː*] *vt* aborrecer, abominar (de).

abhorrent [əb'hɔrənt] *adj* aborrecible, detestable.

abide [ə'baɪd] *vt*: **I can't ~ it/him** no lo/le puedo ver *or* aguantar; **to ~ by** *vt fus* atenerse a.

abiding [ə'baɪdɪŋ] *adj* (*memory etc*) perdurable.

ability [ə'bɪlɪtɪ] *n* habilidad *f*, capacidad *f*; (*talent*) talento; **to the best of my ~** lo mejor que pueda *etc*.

abject ['æbdʒɛkt] *adj* (*poverty*) sórdido; (*apology*) rastrero; (*coward*) vil.

ablaze [ə'bleɪz] *adj* en llamas, ardiendo.

able ['eɪbl] *adj* capaz; (*skilled*) hábil; **to be ~ to do sth** poder hacer algo.

able-bodied ['eɪbl'bɔdɪd] *adj* sano; **~ seaman** marinero de primera.

ably ['eɪblɪ] *adv* hábilmente.

ABM *n abbr* = **anti-ballistic missile**.

abnormal [æb'nɔːml] *adj* anormal.

abnormality [æbnɔː'mælɪtɪ] *n* (*condition*) anormalidad *f*; (*instance*) anomalía.

aboard [ə'bɔːd] *adv* a bordo ♦ *prep* a bordo de; **~ the train** en el tren.

abode [ə'bəud] *n* (*old*) morada; (*LAW*) domicilio; **of no fixed ~** sin domicilio fijo.

abolish [ə'bɔlɪʃ] *vt* suprimir, abolir.

abolition [æbəu'lɪʃən] *n* supresión *f*, abolición *f*.

abominable [ə'bɔmɪnəbl] *adj* abominable.

aborigine [æbə'rɪdʒɪnɪ] *n* aborigen *m/f*.

abort [ə'bɔːt] *vt* abortar; (*COMPUT*) interrumpir ♦ *vi* (*COMPUT*) interrumpir el programa.

abortion [ə'bɔːʃən] *n* aborto (provocado); **to have an ~** abortar.

abortionist [ə'bɔːʃənɪst] *n* persona que practica abortos.

abortive [ə'bɔːtɪv] *adj* fracasado.

abound [ə'baund] *vi*: **to ~ (in** *or* **with)** abundar (de *or* en).

===================================== *KEYWORD*

about [ə'baut] *adv* **1** (*approximately*) más o menos, aproximadamente; **~ a hundred/ thousand** *etc* unos(unas) *or* como cien/ mil *etc*; **it takes ~ 10 hours** se tarda unas *or* más o menos 10 horas; **at ~ 2 o'clock** sobre las dos; **I've just ~ finished** casi he terminado

2 (*referring to place*) por todas partes; **to leave things lying ~** dejar las cosas (tiradas) por ahí; **to run ~** correr por todas partes; **to walk ~** pasearse, ir y venir; **is Paul ~?** ¿está por aquí Paul?; **it's the other way ~** es al revés

3: **to be ~ to do sth** estar a punto de hacer algo; **I'm not ~ to do all that for nothing** no pienso hacer todo eso para nada

♦ *prep* **1** (*relating to*) de, sobre, acerca de; **a book ~ London** un libro sobre *or* acerca de Londres; **what is it ~?** (*book, film*) ¿de qué se trata?; **we talked ~ it** hablamos de eso *or* ello; **what** *or* **how ~ doing this?** ¿qué tal si hacemos esto?

2 (*referring to place*) por; **to walk ~ the town** caminar por la ciudad.

───────────────────────────────

about face, about turn *n* (*MIL*) media vuelta; (*fig*) cambio radical.

above [ə'bʌv] *adv* encima, por encima, arriba ♦ *prep* encima de; **mentioned ~** susodicho; **~ all** sobre todo; **he's not ~ a bit of blackmail** es capaz hasta de hacer chantaje.

above board *adj* legítimo.

above-mentioned [əbʌv'mɛnʃnd] *adj* susodicho.

abrasion [ə'breɪʒən] *n* (*on skin*) abrasión *f*.

abrasive [ə'breɪzɪv] *adj* abrasivo.

abreast [ə'brɛst] *adv* uno al lado de otro; **to keep ~ of** mantenerse al corriente de.

abridge [ə'brɪdʒ] *vt* abreviar.

abroad [ə'brɔːd] *adv* (*to be*) en el extranjero; (*to go*) al extranjero; **there is a rumour ~ that ...** corre el rumor de que ...

abrupt [ə'brʌpt] *adj* (*sudden: departure*) repentino; (*manner*) brusco.

abruptly [ə'brʌptlɪ] *adv* (*leave*) repentinamente; (*speak*) bruscamente.

abscess ['æbsɪs] *n* absceso.

abscond [əb'skɔnd] *vi* fugarse.

absence ['æbsəns] *n* ausencia; **in the ~ of** (*person*) en ausencia de; (*thing*) a falta de.

absent ['æbsənt] *adj* ausente; **~ without leave (AWOL)** ausente sin permiso.

absentee [æbsən'tiː] *n* ausente *m/f*.

absenteeism [æbsən'tiːɪzəm] *n* absentismo.

absent-minded [æbsənt'maɪndɪd] *adj* distraído.

absolute ['æbsəluːt] *adj* absoluto; **~ monopoly** monopolio total.

absolutely [æbsə'luːtlɪ] *adv* totalmente; **oh yes, ~!** ¡claro *or* por supuesto que sí!

absolution [æbsə'luːʃən] *n* (*REL*) absolución *f*.

absolve [əb'zɔlv] *vt*: **to ~ sb (from)** absolver a alguien (de).

absorb [əb'zɔːb] *vt* absorber; **to be ~ed in a**

book estar enfrascado en un libro.
absorbent [əb'zɔːbənt] *adj* absorbente.
absorbent cotton *n* (*US*) algodón *m* hidrófilo.
absorbing [əb'zɔːbɪŋ] *adj* absorbente; (*book etc*) interesantísimo.
absorption [əb'zɔːpʃən] *n* absorción *f.*
abstain [əb'steɪn] *vi*: **to ~ (from)** abstenerse (de).
abstemious [əb'stiːmɪəs] *adj* abstemio.
abstention [əb'stɛnʃən] *n* abstención *f.*
abstinence ['æbstɪnəns] *n* abstinencia.
abstract ['æbstrækt] *adj* abstracto.
abstruse [æb'struːs] *adj* abstruso, oscuro.
absurd [əb'sɔːd] *adj* absurdo.
absurdity [əb'sɔːdɪtɪ] *n* absurdo.
ABTA ['æbtə] *n abbr* = *Association of British Travel Agents.*
abundance [ə'bʌndəns] *n* abundancia.
abundant [ə'bʌndənt] *adj* abundante.
abuse [ə'bjuːs] *n* (*insults*) insultos *mpl*, improperios *mpl*; (*misuse*) abuso ♦ *vt* [ə'bjuːz] (*ill-treat*) maltratar; (*take advantage of*) abusar de; **open to ~** sujeto al abuso.
abusive [ə'bjuːsɪv] *adj* ofensivo.
abysmal [ə'bɪzməl] *adj* pésimo; (*ignorance*) supino.
abyss [ə'bɪs] *n* abismo.
AC *abbr* (= *alternating current*) corriente *f* alterna ♦ *n abbr* (*US*) = *athletic club.*
a/c *abbr* (*BANKING etc*) = *account, account current.*
academic [ækə'dɛmɪk] *adj* académico, universitario; (*pej: issue*) puramente teórico ♦ *n* estudioso/a; (*lecturer*) profesor(a) *m/f* universitario/a; **~ year** (*UNIV*) año académico.
academy [ə'kædəmɪ] *n* (*learned body*) academia; (*school*) instituto, colegio; **~ of music** conservatorio.
ACAS ['eɪkæs] *n abbr* (*BRIT*: = *Advisory, Conciliation and Arbitration Service*) ≈ Instituto de Mediación, Arbitraje y Conciliación.
accede [æk'siːd] *vi*: **to ~ to** acceder a.
accelerate [æk'sɛləreɪt] *vt* acelerar ♦ *vi* acelerarse.
acceleration [æksɛlə'reɪʃən] *n* aceleración *f.*
accelerator [æk'sɛləreɪtə*] *n* (*BRIT*) acelerador *m.*
accent ['æksɛnt] *n* acento.
accentuate [æk'sɛntjueɪt] *vt* (*syllable*) acentuar; (*need, difference etc*) recalcar, subrayar.
accept [ək'sɛpt] *vt* aceptar; (*approve*) aprobar; (*concede*) admitir.
acceptable [ək'sɛptəbl] *adj* aceptable;

admisible.
acceptance [ək'sɛptəns] *n* aceptación *f*; aprobación *f*; **to meet with general ~** recibir la aprobación general.
access ['æksɛs] *n* acceso ♦ *vt* (*COMPUT*) acceder a; **the burglars gained ~ through a window** los ladrones lograron entrar por una ventana; **to have ~ to** tener acceso a.
accessible [æk'sɛsəbl] *adj* accesible.
accession [æk'sɛʃən] *n* (*of monarch*) subida, ascenso; (*addition*) adquisición *f.*
accessory [æk'sɛsərɪ] *n* accesorio; **toilet accessories** artículos *mpl* de tocador.
access road *n* carretera de acceso; (*to motorway*) carril *m* de acceso.
access time *n* (*COMPUT*) tiempo de acceso.
accident ['æksɪdənt] *n* accidente *m*; (*chance*) casualidad *f*; **by ~** (*unintentionally*) sin querer; (*by coincidence*) por casualidad; **~s at work** accidentes *mpl* de trabajo; **to meet with** *or* **to have an ~** tener *or* sufrir un accidente.
accidental [æksɪ'dɛntl] *adj* accidental, fortuito.
accidentally [æksɪ'dɛntəlɪ] *adv* sin querer; por casualidad.
accident insurance *n* seguro contra accidentes.
accident-prone ['æksɪdənt'prəun] *adj* propenso a los accidentes.
acclaim [ə'kleɪm] *vt* aclamar, aplaudir ♦ *n* aclamación *f*, aplausos *mpl.*
acclamation [æklə'meɪʃən] *n* (*approval*) aclamación *f*; (*applause*) aplausos *mpl*; **by ~** por aclamación.
acclimatize [ə'klaɪmətaɪz], (*US*) **acclimate** [ə'klaɪmət] *vt*: **to become ~d** aclimatarse.
accolade ['ækəuleɪd] *n* (*prize*) premio; (*praise*) alabanzas *fpl*, homenaje *m.*
accommodate [ə'kɔmədeɪt] *vt* alojar, hospedar; (*oblige, help*) complacer; **this car ~s 4 people comfortably** en este coche caben 4 personas cómodamente.
accommodating [ə'kɔmədeɪtɪŋ] *adj* servicial, complaciente.
accommodation *n*, (*US*) **accommodations** *npl* [əkɔmə'deɪʃən(z)] alojamiento; "**~ to let**" "se alquilan habitaciones"; **seating ~** asientos *mpl.*
accompaniment [ə'kʌmpənɪmənt] *n* acompañamiento.
accompanist [ə'kʌmpənɪst] *n* (*MUS*) acompañante *m/f.*
accompany [ə'kʌmpənɪ] *vt* acompañar.
accomplice [ə'kʌmplɪs] *n* cómplice *m/f.*
accomplish [ə'kʌmplɪʃ] *vt* (*finish*) acabar;

(*aim*) realizar; (*task*) llevar a cabo.

accomplished [əˈkʌmplɪʃt] *adj* experto, hábil.

accomplishment [əˈkʌmplɪʃmənt] *n* (*ending*) conclusión *f*; (*bringing about*) realización *f*; (*skill*) talento.

accord [əˈkɔːd] *n* acuerdo ♦ *vt* conceder; **of his own** ~ espontáneamente; **with one** ~ de *or* por común acuerdo.

accordance [əˈkɔːdəns] *n*: **in** ~ **with** de acuerdo con.

according [əˈkɔːdɪŋ]: ~ **to** *prep* según; (*in accordance with*) conforme a; **it went** ~ **to plan** salió según lo previsto.

accordingly [əˈkɔːdɪŋlɪ] *adv* (*thus*) por consiguiente.

accordion [əˈkɔːdɪən] *n* acordeón *m*.

accordionist [əˈkɔːdɪənɪst] *n* acordeonista *m/f*.

accost [əˈkɒst] *vt* abordar, dirigirse a.

account [əˈkaunt] *n* (*COMM*) cuenta, factura; (*report*) informe *m*; ~**s** *npl* (*COMM*) cuentas *fpl*; **"** ~ **payee only"** "únicamente en cuenta del beneficiario"; **your** ~ **is still outstanding** su cuenta está todavía pendiente; **of little** ~ de poca importancia; **on** ~ a crédito; **to buy sth on** ~ comprar algo a crédito; **on no** ~ bajo ningún concepto; **on** ~ **of** a causa de, por motivo de; **to take into** ~, **take** ~ **of** tener en cuenta; **to keep an** ~ **of** llevar la cuenta de; **to bring sb to** ~ **for sth/for having done sth** pedirle cuentas a algn por algo/por haber hecho algo.

▶**account for** *vt fus* (*explain*) explicar; **all the children were** ~**ed for** no faltaba ningún niño.

accountability [əkauntəˈbɪlɪtɪ] *n* responsabilidad *f*.

accountable [əˈkauntəbl] *adj*: ~ **(for)** responsable (de).

accountancy [əˈkauntənsɪ] *n* contabilidad *f*.

accountant [əˈkauntənt] *n* contable *m/f*, contador(a) *m/f* (*LAM*).

accounting [əˈkauntɪŋ] *n* contabilidad *f*.

accounting period *n* período contable, ejercicio financiero.

account number *n* (*at bank etc*) número de cuenta.

account payable *n* cuenta por pagar.

account receivable *n* cuenta por cobrar.

accoutrements [əˈkuːtrəmənts] *npl* equipo, pertrechos *mpl*.

accredited [əˈkredɪtɪd] *adj* (*agent etc*) autorizado, acreditado.

accretion [əˈkriːʃən] *n* acumulación *f*.

accrue [əˈkruː] *vi* (*mount up*) aumentar, incrementarse; (*interest*) acumularse; **to**

~ **to** corresponder a; ~**d charges** gastos *mpl* vencidos; ~**d interest** interés *m* acumulado.

accumulate [əˈkjuːmjuleɪt] *vt* acumular ♦ *vi* acumularse.

accumulation [əkjuːmjuˈleɪʃən] *n* acumulación *f*.

accuracy [ˈækjurəsɪ] *n* exactitud *f*, precisión *f*.

accurate [ˈækjurɪt] *adj* (*number*) exacto; (*answer*) acertado; (*shot*) certero.

accurately [ˈækjurɪtlɪ] *adv* (*count, shoot, answer*) con precisión.

accursed [əˈkəst] *adj* maldito.

accusation [ækjuˈzeɪʃən] *n* acusación *f*.

accusative [əˈkjuːzətɪv] *n* acusativo.

accuse [əˈkjuːz] *vt* acusar; (*blame*) echar la culpa a.

accused [əˈkjuːzd] *n* acusado/a.

accuser [əˈkjuːzə*] *n* acusador(a) *m/f*.

accustom [əˈkʌstəm] *vt* acostumbrar; **to** ~ **o.s. to sth** acostumbrarse a algo.

accustomed [əˈkʌstəmd] *adj*: ~ **to** acostumbrado a.

AC/DC *abbr* = *alternating current/direct current*.

ACE [eɪs] *n abbr* = *American Council on Education*.

ace [eɪs] *n* as *m*.

acerbic [əˈsəːbɪk] *adj* acerbo; (*fig*) mordaz.

acetate [ˈæsɪteɪt] *n* acetato.

ache [eɪk] *n* dolor *m* ♦ *vi* doler; (*yearn*): **to** ~ **to do sth** ansiar hacer algo; **I've got stomach** ~ *or* (*US*) **a stomach** ~ tengo dolor de estómago, me duele el estómago; **my head** ~**s** me duele la cabeza.

achieve [əˈtʃiːv] *vt* (*reach*) alcanzar; (*realize*) realizar; (*victory, success*) lograr, conseguir.

achievement [əˈtʃiːvmənt] *n* (*completion*) realización *f*; (*success*) éxito.

Achilles heel [əˈkɪliːz-] *n* talón *m* de Aquiles.

acid [ˈæsɪd] *adj* ácido; (*bitter*) agrio ♦ *n* ácido.

acidity [əˈsɪdɪtɪ] *n* acidez *f*; (*MED*) acedía.

acid rain *n* lluvia ácida.

acid test *n* (*fig*) prueba de fuego.

acknowledge [əkˈnɒlɪdʒ] *vt* (*letter: also*: ~ **receipt of**) acusar recibo de; (*fact*) reconocer.

acknowledgement [əkˈnɒlɪdʒmənt] *n* acuse *m* de recibo; reconocimiento; ~**s** (*in book*) agradecimientos *mpl*.

ACLU *n abbr* (= *American Civil Liberties Union*) unión americana por libertades civiles.

acme ['ækmɪ] n súmmum m.

acne ['æknɪ] n acné m.

acorn ['eɪkɔːn] n bellota.

acoustic [ə'kuːstɪk] adj acústico.

acoustic coupler [-'kʌplə*] n (COMPUT) acoplador m acústico.

acoustics [ə'kuːstɪks] n, npl acústica sg.

acquaint [ə'kweɪnt] vt: to ~ sb with sth (inform) poner a algn al corriente de algo; to be ~ed with (person) conocer; (fact) estar al corriente de.

acquaintance [ə'kweɪntəns] n conocimiento; (person) conocido/a; to make sb's ~ conocer a algn.

acquiesce [ækwɪ'ɛs] vi (agree): to ~ (in) consentir (en), conformarse (con).

acquire [ə'kwaɪə*] vt adquirir.

acquired [ə'kwaɪəd] adj adquirido; it's an ~ taste es algo a lo que uno se aficiona poco a poco.

acquisition [ækwɪ'zɪʃən] n adquisición f.

acquisitive [ə'kwɪzɪtɪv] adj codicioso.

acquit [ə'kwɪt] vt absolver, exculpar; to ~ o.s. well defenderse bien.

acquittal [ə'kwɪtl] n absolución f, exculpación f.

acre ['eɪkə*] n acre m.

acreage ['eɪkərɪdʒ] n extensión f.

acrid ['ækrɪd] adj (smell) acre; (fig) mordaz, sarcástico.

acrimonious [ækrɪ'məʊnɪəs] adj (remark) mordaz; (argument) reñido.

acrobat ['ækrəbæt] n acróbata m/f.

acrobatic [ækrə'bætɪk] adj acrobático.

acrobatics [ækrə'bætɪks] npl acrobacias fpl.

acronym ['ækrənɪm] n siglas fpl.

across [ə'krɒs] prep (on the other side of) al otro lado de; (crosswise) a través de ♦ adv de un lado a otro, de una parte a otra; a través, al través; to run/swim ~ atravesar corriendo/nadando; ~ from enfrente de; the lake is 12 km ~ el lago tiene 12 km de ancho; to get sth ~ to sb (fig) hacer comprender algo a algn.

acrylic [ə'krɪlɪk] adj acrílico.

act [ækt] n acto, acción f; (THEAT) acto; (in music-hall etc) número; (LAW) decreto, ley f ♦ vi (behave) comportarse; (THEAT) actuar; (pretend) fingir; (take action) tomar medidas ♦ vt (part) hacer, representar; ~ of God fuerza mayor; it's only an ~ es cuento; to catch sb in the ~ coger a algn in fraganti or con las manos en la masa; to ~ Hamlet hacer el papel de Hamlet; to ~ as actuar or hacer de; ~ing in my capacity as chairman, I ... en mi calidad de presidente, yo ...; it ~s as a deterrent sirve para disuadir; he's only ~ing está

fingiendo nada más.

▶**act on** vt: to ~ on sth actuar or obrar sobre algo.

▶**act out** vt (event) representar; (fantasies) realizar.

acting ['æktɪŋ] adj suplente ♦ n: to do some ~ hacer algo de teatro; he is the ~ manager es el gerente en funciones.

action ['ækʃən] n acción f, acto; (MIL) acción f; (LAW) proceso, demanda; to put a plan into ~ poner un plan en acción or en marcha; killed in ~ (MIL) muerto en acto de servicio or en combate; out of ~ (person) fuera de combate; (thing) averiado, descompuesto; to take ~ tomar medidas; to bring an ~ against sb entablar or presentar demanda contra algn.

action replay n (TV) repetición f.

activate ['æktɪveɪt] vt activar.

active ['æktɪv] adj activo, enérgico; (volcano) en actividad; to play an ~ part in colaborar activamente en; ~ file (COMPUT) fichero activo.

active duty (AD) n (US MIL) servicio activo.

actively ['æktɪvlɪ] adv (participate) activamente; (discourage, dislike) enérgicamente.

active partner n (COMM) socio activo.

activist ['æktɪvɪst] n activista m/f.

activity [æk'tɪvɪtɪ] n actividad f.

actor ['æktə*] n actor m.

actress ['aektrɪs] n actriz f.

ACTT n abbr (BRIT: = Association of Cinematographic, Television and Allied Technicians) sindicato de técnicos de cine y televisión.

actual ['æktjuəl] adj verdadero, real.

actually ['æktjuəlɪ] adv realmente, en realidad.

actuary ['æktjuərɪ] n (COMM) actuario/a (de seguros).

actuate ['æktjueɪt] vt mover, impulsar.

acumen ['ækjumən] n perspicacia; business ~ talento para los negocios.

acupuncture ['ækjupʌŋktʃə*] n acupuntura.

acute [ə'kjuːt] adj agudo.

acutely [ə'kjuːtlɪ] adv profundamente, extremadamente.

AD adv abbr (= Anno Domini) A.C. ♦ n abbr (US MIL) see active duty.

ad [æd] n abbr = advertisement.

adage ['ædɪdʒ] n refrán m, adagio.

Adam ['ædəm] n Adán m; ~'s apple n nuez f (de la garganta).

adamant ['ædəmənt] adj firme, inflexible.

adapt [ə'dæpt] *vt* adaptar; (*reconcile*) acomodar ♦ *vi*: **to ~ (to)** adaptarse (a), ajustarse (a).

adaptability [ədæptə'bılıtı] *n* (*of person, device etc*) adaptabilidad *f*.

adaptable [ə'dæptəbl] *adj* (*device*) adaptable; (*person*) acomodadizo, que se adapta.

adaptation [ædæp'teıʃən] *n* adaptación *f*.

adapter, adaptor [ə'dæptə*] *n* (*ELEC*) adaptador *m*.

ADC *n abbr* (*MIL*) = *aide-de-camp*; (*US*: = *Aid to Dependent Children*) *ayuda para niños dependientes*.

add [æd] *vt* añadir, agregar (*esp LAM*); (*figures: also*: ~ **up**) sumar ♦ *vi*: **to ~ to** (*increase*) aumentar, acrecentar.

▶**add on** *vt* añadir.

▶**add up** *vt* (*figures*) sumar ♦ *vi* (*fig*): **it doesn't ~ up** no tiene sentido; **it doesn't ~ up to much** es poca cosa, no tiene gran *or* mucha importancia.

addendum [ə'dɛndəm] *n* ad(d)enda *m or f*.

adder ['ædə*] *n* víbora.

addict ['ædıkt] *n* (*to drugs etc*) adicto/a; (*enthusiast*) aficionado/a, entusiasta *m/f*; **heroin ~** heroinómano/a.

addicted [ə'dıktıd] *adj*: **to be ~ to** ser adicto a; ser aficionado a.

addiction [ə'dıkʃən] *n* (*dependence*) hábito morboso; (*enthusiasm*) afición *f*.

addictive [ə'dıktıv] *adj* que causa adicción.

adding machine ['ædıŋ-] *n* calculadora.

Addis Ababa ['ædıs'æbəbə] *n* Addis Abeba *m*.

addition [ə'dıʃən] *n* (*adding up*) adición *f*; (*thing added*) añadidura, añadido; **in ~** además, por añadidura; **in ~ to** además de.

additional [ə'dıʃənl] *adj* adicional.

additive ['ædıtıv] *n* aditivo.

addled ['ædld] *adj* (*BRIT*: *rotten*) podrido; (: *fig*) confuso.

address [ə'drɛs] *n* dirección *f*, señas *fpl*; (*speech*) discurso; (*COMPUT*) dirección *f* ♦ *vt* (*letter*) dirigir; (*speak to*) dirigirse a, dirigir la palabra a; **form of ~** tratamiento; **absolute/relative ~** (*COMPUT*) dirección *f* absoluta/relativa; **to ~ o.s. to sth** (*issue, problem*) abordar.

address book *n* agenda (de direcciones).

addressee [ædrɛ'si:] *n* destinatario/a.

Aden ['eıdn] *n* Adén *m*.

adenoids ['ædınɔıdz] *npl* vegetaciones *fpl* (adenoideas).

adept ['ædɛpt] *adj*: **~ at** experto *or* ducho en.

adequacy ['ædıkwəsı] *n* idoneidad *f*.

adequate ['ædıkwıt] *adj* (*satisfactory*) adecuado; (*enough*) suficiente; **to feel ~ to a task** sentirse con fuerzas para una tarea.

adequately ['ædıkwıtlı] *adv* adecuadamente.

adhere [əd'hıə*] *vi*: **to ~ to** adherirse a; (*fig*: *abide by*) observar.

adherent [əd'hıərənt] *n* partidario/a.

adhesion [əd'hi:ʒən] *n* adherencia.

adhesive [əd'hi:zıv] *adj*, *n* adhesivo.

adhesive tape *n* (*BRIT*) cinta adhesiva; (*US*: *MED*) esparadrapo.

ad hoc [æd'hɔk] *adj* (*decision*) ad hoc; (*committee*) formado con fines específicos ♦ *adv* ad hoc.

adieu [ə'dju:] *excl* ¡vaya con Dios!

ad inf ['æd'ınf] *adv* hasta el infinito.

adjacent [ə'dʒeısənt] *adj*: **~ to** contiguo a, inmediato a.

adjective ['ædʒɛktıv] *n* adjetivo.

adjoin [ə'dʒɔın] *vt* estar contiguo a; (*land*) lindar con.

adjoining [ə'dʒɔınıŋ] *adj* contiguo, vecino.

adjourn [ə'dʒə:n] *vt* aplazar; (*session*) suspender, levantar; (*US*: *end*) terminar ♦ *vi* suspenderse; **the meeting has been ~ed till next week** se ha levantado la sesión hasta la semana que viene; **they ~ed to the pub** (*col*) se trasladaron al bar.

adjournment [ə'dʒə:nmənt] *n* (*period*) suspensión *f*; (*postponement*) aplazamiento.

Adjt. *abbr* = **adjutant**.

adjudicate [ə'dʒu:dıkeıt] *vi* sentenciar; (*contest*) hacer de árbitro en, juzgar; (*claim*) decidir.

adjudication [ədʒu:dı'keıʃən] *n* fallo.

adjudicator [ə'dʒu:dıkeıtə*] *n* juez *m*, árbitro.

adjust [ə'dʒʌst] *vt* (*change*) modificar; (*arrange*) arreglar; (*machine*) ajustar ♦ *vi*: **to ~ (to)** adaptarse (a).

adjustable [ə'dʒʌstəbl] *adj* ajustable.

adjuster [ə'dʒʌstə*] *n see* **loss adjuster**.

adjustment [ə'dʒʌstmənt] *n* modificación *f*; arreglo; (*of prices, wages*) ajuste *m*.

adjutant ['ædʒətənt] *n* ayudante *m*.

ad-lib [æd'lıb] *vt*, *vi* improvisar ♦ *adv*: **ad lib** a voluntad, a discreción.

adman ['ædmæn] *n* (*col*) publicista *m*.

admin ['ædmın] *n abbr* (*col*) = **administration**.

administer [əd'mınıstə*] *vt* proporcionar; (*justice*) administrar.

administration [ædmını'streıʃən] *n* administración *f*; (*government*) gobierno;

the A~ (*US*) la Administración.
administrative [əd'mɪnɪstrətɪv] *adj* administrativo.
administrator [əd'mɪnɪstreɪtə*] *n* administrador(a) *m/f*.
admirable ['ædmərəbl] *adj* admirable.
admiral ['ædmərəl] *n* almirante *m*.
Admiralty ['ædmərəltɪ] *n* (*BRIT*) Ministerio de Marina, Almirantazgo.
admiration [ædmə'reɪʃən] *n* admiración *f*.
admire [əd'maɪə*] *vt* admirar.
admirer [əd'maɪərə*] *n* admirador(a) *m/f*; (*suitor*) pretendiente *m*.
admiring [əd'maɪərɪŋ] *adj* (*expression*) de admiración.
admissible [əd'mɪsəbl] *adj* admisible.
admission [əd'mɪʃən] *n* (*exhibition, nightclub*) entrada; (*enrolment*) ingreso; (*confession*) confesión *f*; "~ *free*" "entrada gratis *or* libre"; **by his own** ~ él mismo reconoce que.
admit [əd'mɪt] *vt* dejar entrar, dar entrada a; (*permit*) admitir; (*acknowledge*) reconocer; "**this ticket ~s two**" "entrada para 2 personas"; **children not ~ted** se prohíbe la entrada a (los) menores de edad; **I must ~ that** ... debo reconocer que ...
▶**admit of** *vt fus* admitir, permitir.
▶**admit to** *vt fus* confesarse culpable de.
admittance [əd'mɪtəns] *n* entrada; "**no ~**" "se prohíbe la entrada", "prohibida la entrada".
admittedly [əd'mɪtədlɪ] *adv* de acuerdo que.
admonish [əd'mɒnɪʃ] *vt* amonestar; (*advise*) aconsejar.
ad nauseam [æd'nɔːsɪæm] *adv* hasta la saciedad.
ado [ə'duː] *n*: **without (any) more ~** sin más (ni más).
adolescence [ædəu'lɛsns] *n* adolescencia.
adolescent [ædəu'lɛsnt] *adj, n* adolescente *m/f*.
adopt [ə'dɒpt] *vt* adoptar.
adopted [ə'dɒptɪd] *adj* adoptivo.
adoption [ə'dɒpʃən] *n* adopción *f*.
adoptive [ə'dɒptɪv] *adj* adoptivo.
adorable [ə'dɔːrəbl] *adj* adorable.
adoration [ædə'reɪʃən] *n* adoración *f*.
adore [ə'dɔː*] *vt* adorar.
adoring [ə'dɔːrɪŋ] *adj*: **to his ~ public** a un público que le adora *or* le adoraba *etc*.
adorn [ə'dɔːn] *vt* adornar.
adornment [ə'dɔːnmənt] *n* adorno.
ADP *n abbr see* **automatic data processing**.
adrenalin [ə'drɛnəlɪn] *n* adrenalina.
Adriatic [eɪdrɪ'ætɪk] *n*: **the ~ (Sea)** el (Mar)

Adriático.
adrift [ə'drɪft] *adv* a la deriva; **to come ~** (*boat*) ir a la deriva, soltarse; (*wire, rope etc*) soltarse.
adroit [ə'drɔɪt] *adj* diestro, hábil.
ADT *abbr* (*US*: = *Atlantic Daylight Time*) *hora de verano de Nueva York*.
adulation [ædju'leɪʃən] *n* adulación *f*.
adult ['ædʌlt] *n* adulto/a ♦ *adj*: ~ **education** educación *f* para adultos.
adulterate [ə'dʌltəreɪt] *vt* adulterar.
adulterer [ə'dʌltərə*] *n* adúltero.
adulteress [ə'dʌltrɪs] *n* adúltera.
adultery [ə'dʌltərɪ] *n* adulterio.
adulthood ['ædʌlthud] *n* edad *f* adulta.
advance [əd'vɑːns] *n* adelanto, progreso; (*money*) anticipo; (*MIL*) avance *m* ♦ *vt* avanzar, adelantar; (*money*) anticipar ♦ *vi* avanzar, adelantarse; **in ~** por adelantado; (*book*) con antelación; **to make ~s to sb** (*gen*) ponerse en contacto con algn; (*amorously*) insinuarse a algn.
advanced *adj* avanzado; (*SCOL: studies*) adelantado; ~ **in years** entrado en años.
advancement [əd'vɑːnsmənt] *n* progreso; (*in rank*) ascenso.
advance notice *n* previo aviso.
advance payment *n* (*part sum*) anticipo.
advantage [əd'vɑːntɪdʒ] *n* (*also TENNIS*) ventaja; **to take ~ of** aprovecharse de; **it's to our ~** es ventajoso para nosotros.
advantageous [ædvən'teɪdʒəs] *adj* ventajoso, provechoso.
advent ['ædvənt] *n* advenimiento; **A~** Adviento.
adventure [əd'vɛntʃə*] *n* aventura.
adventure playground *n* parque *m* infantil.
adventurous [əd'vɛntʃərəs] *adj* aventurero; (*bold*) arriesgado.
adverb ['ædvəːb] *n* adverbio.
adversary ['ædvəsərɪ] *n* adversario, contrario.
adverse ['ædvəːs] *adj* adverso, contrario; ~ **to** adverso a.
adversity [əd'vəːsɪtɪ] *n* infortunio.
advert ['ædvəːt] *n abbr* (*BRIT*) = **advertisement**.
advertise ['ædvətaɪz] *vi* hacer propaganda; (*in newspaper etc*) poner un anuncio, anunciarse; **to ~ for** (*staff*) buscar por medio de anuncios ♦ *vt* anunciar.
advertisement [əd'vəːtɪsmənt] *n* (*COMM*) anuncio.
advertiser ['ædvətaɪzə*] *n* anunciante *m/f*.
advertising ['ædvətaɪzɪŋ] *n* publicidad *f*, propaganda; anuncios *mpl*.
advertising agency *n* agencia de

publicidad.

advertising campaign *n* campaña de publicidad.

advice [əd'vaɪs] *n* consejo, consejos *mpl*; (*notification*) aviso; **a piece of** ~ un consejo; **to take legal** ~ consultar a un abogado; **to ask (sb) for** ~ pedir consejo (a algn).

advice note *n* (*BRIT*) nota de aviso.

advisable [əd'vaɪzəbl] *adj* aconsejable, conveniente.

advise [əd'vaɪz] *vt* aconsejar; **to** ~ **sb of sth** (*inform*) informar a algn de algo; **to** ~ **sb against sth/doing sth** desaconsejar algo a algn/aconsejar a algn que no haga algo; **you will be well/ill** ~**d to go** deberías/no deberías ir.

advisedly [əd'vaɪzɪdlɪ] *adv* (*deliberately*) deliberadamente.

adviser [əd'vaɪzə*] *n* consejero/a; (*business adviser*) asesor(a) *m/f*.

advisory [əd'vaɪzərɪ] *adj* consultivo; **in an** ~ **capacity** como asesor.

advocate ['ædvəkeɪt] *vt* (*argue for*) abogar por; (*give support to*) ser partidario de ♦ *n* ['ædvəkɪt] abogado/a.

advt. *abbr* = **advertisement.**

AEA *n abbr* (*BRIT*: = *Atomic Energy Authority*) consejo de energía nuclear.

AEC *n abbr* (*US*: = *Atomic Energy Commission*) AEC *f*.

AEEU *n abbr* (*BRIT*: = *Amalgamated Engineering and Electrical Union*) sindicato mixto de ingenieros y electricistas.

Aegean [iː'dʒiːən] *n*: **the** ~ (**Sea**) el (Mar) Egeo.

aegis ['iːdʒɪs] *n*: **under the** ~ **of** bajo la tutela de.

aeon ['iːən] *n* eón *m*.

aerial ['ɛərɪəl] *n* antena ♦ *adj* aéreo.

aerie ['ɛərɪ] *n* (*US*) aguilera.

aero- ['ɛərəu] *pref* aero-.

aerobatics [ɛərəu'bætɪks] *npl* acrobacia aérea.

aerobics [ɛə'rəubɪks] *nsg* aerobic *m*, aerobismo (*LAM*).

aerodrome ['ɛərədrəum] *n* (*BRIT*) aeródromo.

aerodynamic [ɛərəudaɪ'næmɪk] *adj* aerodinámico.

aeronautics [ɛərəu'nɔːtɪks] *nsg* aeronáutica.

aeroplane ['ɛərəpleɪn] *n* (*BRIT*) avión *m*.

aerosol ['ɛərəsɔl] *n* aerosol *m*.

aerospace industry ['ɛərəuspeɪs-] *n* industria aeroespacial.

aesthetic [iːs'θɛtɪk] *adj* estético.

aesthetics [iːs'θɛtɪks] *npl* estética.

a.f. *abbr* = **audiofrequency.**

afar [ə'fɑː*] *adv* lejos; **from** ~ desde lejos.

AFB *n abbr* (*US*) = *Air Force Base.*

AFDC *n abbr* (*US*: = *Aid to Families with Dependent Children*) ayuda a familias con hijos menores.

affable ['æfəbl] *adj* afable.

affair [ə'fɛə*] *n* asunto; (*also*: **love** ~) aventura *f* amorosa; ~**s** (*business*) asuntos *mpl*; **the Watergate** ~ el asunto (de) Watergate.

affect [ə'fɛkt] *vt* afectar, influir en; (*move*) conmover.

affectation [æfɛk'teɪʃən] *n* afectación *f*.

affected [ə'fɛktɪd] *adj* afectado.

affection [ə'fɛkʃən] *n* afecto, cariño.

affectionate [ə'fɛkʃənɪt] *adj* afectuoso, cariñoso.

affectionately [ə'fɛkʃənɪtlɪ] *adv* afectuosamente.

affidavit [æfɪ'deɪvɪt] *n* (*LAW*) declaración *f* jurada.

affiliated [ə'fɪlɪeɪtɪd] *adj* afiliado; ~ **company** empresa *or* compañía filial *or* subsidiaria.

affinity [ə'fɪnɪtɪ] *n* afinidad *f*.

affirm [ə'fəːm] *vt* afirmar.

affirmation [æfə'meɪʃən] *n* afirmación *f*.

affirmative [ə'fəːmətɪv] *adj* afirmativo.

affix [ə'fɪks] *vt* (*signature*) estampar; (*stamp*) pegar.

afflict [ə'flɪkt] *vt* afligir.

affliction [ə'flɪkʃən] *n* enfermedad *f*, aflicción *f*.

affluence ['æfluəns] *n* opulencia, riqueza.

affluent ['æfluənt] *adj* adinerado, acaudalado; **the** ~ **society** la sociedad opulenta.

afford [ə'fɔːd] *vt* poder permitirse; (*provide*) proporcionar; **can we** ~ **a car?** ¿podemos permitirnos el gasto de comprar un coche?

affordable [ə'fɔːdəbl] *adj* asequible.

affray [ə'freɪ] *n* refriega, reyerta.

affront [ə'frʌnt] *n* afrenta, ofensa.

affronted [ə'frʌntɪd] *adj* ofendido.

Afghan ['æfgæn] *adj*, *n* afgano/a *m/f*.

Afghanistan [æf'gænɪstæn] *n* Afganistán *m*.

afield [ə'fiːld] *adv*: **far** ~ muy lejos.

AFL-CIO *n abbr* (*US*: = *American Federation of Labor and Congress of Industrial Organizations*) confederación sindicalista.

afloat [ə'fləut] *adv* (*floating*) a flote; (*at sea*) en el mar.

afoot [ə'fut] *adv*: **there is something** ~ algo se está tramando.

aforesaid [ə'fɔːsɛd] *adj* susodicho; (*COMM*) mencionado anteriormente.

afraid [ə'freɪd] *adj*: **to be ~ of** (*person*) tener miedo a; (*thing*) tener miedo de; **to be ~ to** tener miedo de, temer; **I am ~ that** me temo que; **I'm ~ so** ¡me temo que sí!, ¡lo siento, pero es así!; **I'm ~ not** me temo que no.

afresh [ə'frɛʃ] *adv* de nuevo, otra vez.

Africa ['æfrɪkə] *n* África.

African ['æfrɪkən] *adj*, *n* africano/a *m/f*.

Afrikaans [æfrɪ'kɑːns] *n* africaans *m*.

Afrikaner [æfrɪ'kɑːnə*] *n* africánder *m/f*.

Afro-American ['æfrəʊə'merɪkən] *adj*, *n* afroamericano/a *m/f*.

AFT *n abbr* (= *American Federation of Teachers*) sindicato de profesores.

aft [ɑːft] *adv* (*to be*) en popa; (*to go*) a popa.

after ['ɑːftə*] *prep* (*time*) después de; (*place, order*) detrás de, tras ♦ *adv* después ♦ *conj* después (de) que; **what/who are you ~?** ¿qué/a quién buscas?; **the police are ~ him** la policía le está buscando; **~ having done/he left** después de haber hecho/ después de que se marchó; **~ dinner** después de cenar *or* comer; **the day ~ tomorrow** pasado mañana; **to ask ~ sb** preguntar por algn; **~ all** después de todo, al fin y al cabo; **~ you!** ¡Vd primero!; **quarter ~ two** (*US*) las 2 y cuarto.

afterbirth ['ɑːftəbɜːθ] *n* placenta.

aftercare ['ɑːftəkeə*] *n* (*MED*) asistencia postoperatoria.

after-effects ['ɑːftərɪfɛkts] *npl* secuelas *fpl*, efectos *mpl*.

afterlife ['ɑːftəlaɪf] *n* vida después de la muerte.

aftermath ['ɑːftəmɑːθ] *n* consecuencias *fpl*, resultados *mpl*.

afternoon [ɑːftə'nuːn] *n* tarde *f*; **good ~!** ¡buenas tardes!

afters ['ɑːftəz] *n* (*col: dessert*) postre *m*.

after-sales service [ɑːftə'seɪlz-] *n* (*BRIT COMM: for car, washing machine etc*) servicio de asistencia pos-venta.

after-shave (lotion) ['ɑːftəʃeɪv-] *n* loción *f* para después del afeitado, aftershave *m*.

aftershock ['ɑːftəʃɒk] *n* (*of earthquake*) pequeño temblor *m* posterior.

aftertaste ['ɑːftəteɪst] *n* regusto.

afterthought ['ɑːftəθɔːt] *n* ocurrencia (tardía).

afterwards ['ɑːftəwədz] *adv* después, más tarde.

again [ə'gɛn] *adv* otra vez, de nuevo; **to do sth ~** volver a hacer algo; **~ and ~** una y otra vez; **now and ~** de vez en cuando.

against [ə'gɛnst] *prep* (*opposed*) en contra de; (*close to*) contra, junto a; **I was leaning**

~ the desk estaba apoyado en el escritorio; **(as)** ~ frente a.

age [eɪdʒ] *n* edad *f*; (*old ~*) vejez *f*; (*period*) época ♦ *vi* envejecer(se) ♦ *vt* envejecer; **what ~ is he?** ¿qué edad *or* cuántos años tiene?; **he is 20 years of ~** tiene 20 años; **under ~** menor de edad; **to come of ~** llegar a la mayoría de edad; **it's been ~s since I saw you** hace siglos que no te veo.

aged [eɪdʒd] *adj*: ~ **10** de 10 años de edad ♦ *npl* ['eɪdʒɪd]: **the ~** los ancianos.

age group *n*: **to be in the same ~** tener la misma edad; **the 40 to 50 ~** las personas de 40 a 50 años.

ageing ['eɪdʒɪŋ] *adj* que envejece; (*pej*) en declive ♦ *n* envejecimiento.

ageless ['eɪdʒlɪs] *adj* (*eternal*) eterno; (*ever young*) siempre joven.

age limit *n* límite *m* de edad, edad *f* tope.

agency ['eɪdʒənsɪ] *n* agencia; **through** *or* **by the ~ of** por medio de.

agenda [ə'dʒɛndə] *n* orden *m* del día; **on the ~** (*COMM*) en el orden del día.

agent ['eɪdʒənt] *n* (*gen*) agente *m/f*; (*representative*) representante *m/f*, delegado/a.

aggravate ['ægrəveɪt] *vt* agravar; (*annoy*) irritar, exasperar.

aggravating ['ægrəveɪtɪŋ] *adj* irritante, molesto.

aggravation [ægrə'veɪʃən] *n* agravamiento.

aggregate ['ægrɪgeɪt] *n* conjunto.

aggression [ə'grɛʃən] *n* agresión *f*.

aggressive [ə'grɛsɪv] *adj* agresivo; (*vigorous*) enérgico.

aggressiveness [ə'grɛsɪvnɪs] *n* agresividad *f*.

aggressor [ə'grɛsə*] *n* agresor(a) *m/f*.

aggrieved [ə'griːvd] *adj* ofendido, agraviado.

aggro ['ægrəʊ] *n* (*col*) (*physical violence*) bronca; (*bad feeling*) mal rollo; (*hassle*) rollo, movida.

aghast [ə'gɑːst] *adj* horrorizado.

agile ['ædʒaɪl] *adj* ágil.

agility [ə'dʒɪlɪtɪ] *n* agilidad *f*.

agitate ['ædʒɪteɪt] *vt* (*shake*) agitar; (*trouble*) inquietar; **to ~ for** hacer campaña en pro de *or* en favor de.

agitated ['ædʒɪteɪtɪd] *adj* agitado.

agitator ['ædʒɪteɪtə*] *n* agitador(a) *m/f*.

AGM *n abbr see* **annual general meeting**.

agnostic [æg'nɒstɪk] *adj*, *n* agnóstico/a *m/f*.

ago [ə'gəʊ] *adv*: **2 days ~** hace 2 días; **not long ~** hace poco; **how long ~?** ¿hace cuánto tiempo?; **as long ~ as 1960** ya en 1960.

agog [ə'gɒg] *adj* (*anxious*) ansioso; (*excited*):

(all) ~ (for) (todo) emocionado (por).
agonize ['ægənaɪz] *vi*: **to ~ (over)** atormentarse (por).
agonized ['ægənaɪzd] *adj* angustioso.
agonizing ['ægənaɪzɪŋ] *adj (pain)* atroz; *(suspense)* angustioso.
agony ['ægənɪ] *n (pain)* dolor *m* atroz; *(distress)* angustia; **to be in ~** retorcerse de dolor.
agony aunt *n (BRIT col)* consejera sentimental.
agony column *n* consultorio sentimental.
agree [ə'griː] *vt (price)* acordar, quedar en ♦ *vi (statements etc)* coincidir, concordar; **to ~ (with)** *(person)* estar de acuerdo (con), ponerse de acuerdo (con); **to ~ to do** aceptar hacer; **to ~ to sth** consentir en algo; **to ~ that** *(admit)* estar de acuerdo en que; **it was ~d that ...** se acordó que ...; **garlic doesn't ~ with me** el ajo no me sienta bien.
agreeable [ə'griːəbl] *adj* agradable; *(person)* simpático; *(willing)* de acuerdo, conforme.
agreeably [ə'griːəblɪ] *adv* agradablemente.
agreed [ə'griːd] *adj (time, place)* convenido.
agreement [ə'griːmənt] *n* acuerdo; *(COMM)* contrato; **in ~** de acuerdo, conforme; **by mutual ~** de común acuerdo.
agricultural [ægrɪ'kʌltʃərəl] *adj* agrícola.
agriculture ['ægrɪkʌltʃə*] *n* agricultura.
aground [ə'graund] *adv*: **to run ~** encallar, embarrancar.
ahead [ə'hed] *adv* delante; **~ of** delante de; *(fig: schedule etc)* antes de; **~ of time** antes de la hora; **to be ~ of sb** *(fig)* llevar ventaja *or* la delantera a algn; **go right** *or* **straight ~** siga adelante; **they were (right) ~ of us** iban (justo) delante de nosotros.
ahoy [ə'hɔɪ] *excl* ¡oiga!
AI *n abbr* = *Amnesty International*; *(COMPUT)* = *artificial intelligence*.
AIB *n abbr (BRIT: = Accident Investigation Bureau)* oficina de investigación de accidentes.
AID *n abbr (= artificial insemination by donor)* inseminación artificial por donante; *(US: = Agency for International Development)* Agencia Internacional para el Desarrollo.
aid [eɪd] *n* ayuda, auxilio ♦ *vt* ayudar, auxiliar; **in ~ of** a beneficio de; **with the ~ of** con la ayuda de; **to ~ and abet** *(LAW)* ser cómplice.
aide [eɪd] *n (POL)* ayudante *m/f*.
AIDS [eɪdz] *n abbr (= acquired immune (or immuno-)deficiency syndrome)* SIDA *m*, sida *m*.

AIH *abbr (= artificial insemination by husband)* inseminación artificial por esposo.
ailing ['eɪlɪŋ] *adj (person, economy)* enfermizo.
ailment ['eɪlmənt] *n* enfermedad *f*, achaque *m*.
aim [eɪm] *vt (gun)* apuntar; *(missile, remark)* dirigir; *(blow)* asestar ♦ *vi (also*: **take ~)** apuntar ♦ *n* puntería; *(objective)* propósito, meta; **to ~ at** *(objective)* aspirar a, pretender; **to ~ to do** tener como objetivo hacer, aspirar a hacer.
aimless ['eɪmlɪs] *adj* sin propósito, sin objeto.
aimlessly ['eɪmlɪslɪ] *adv* sin rumbo fijo.
ain't [eɪnt] *(col)* = **am not; aren't; isn't**.
air [ɛə*] *n* aire *m*; *(appearance)* aspecto ♦ *vt (room)* ventilar; *(clothes, bed, grievances, ideas)* airear; *(views)* hacer público ♦ *cpd* aéreo; **to throw sth into the ~** *(ball etc)* lanzar algo al aire; **by ~** *(travel)* en avión; **to be on the ~** *(RADIO, TV: programme)* estarse emitiendo; *(: station)* estar emitiendo.
airbag ['ɛəbæg] *n* airbag *m inv*.
air base *n (MIL)* base *f* aérea.
air bed *n (BRIT)* colcheta inflable *or* neumática.
airborne ['ɛəbɔːn] *adj (in the air)* en el aire; *(MIL)* aerotransportado; **as soon as the plane was ~** tan pronto como el avión estuvo en el aire.
air cargo *n* carga aérea.
air-conditioned ['ɛəkən'dɪʃənd] *adj* climatizado.
air conditioning [-kən'dɪʃənɪŋ] *n* aire *m* acondicionado.
air-cooled ['ɛəkuːld] *adj* refrigerado por aire.
aircraft ['ɛəkrɑːft] *n*, *pl inv* avión *m*.
aircraft carrier *n* porta(a)viones *m inv*.
air cushion *n* cojín *m* de aire; *(AVIAT)* colchón *m* de aire.
airdrome ['ɛədrəum] *n (US)* aeródromo.
airfield ['ɛəfiːld] *n* campo de aviación.
Air Force *n* fuerzas aéreas *fpl*, aviación *f*.
air freight *n* flete *m* por avión.
air freshener *n* ambientador *m*.
air gun *n* escopeta de aire comprimido.
air hostess *(BRIT) n* azafata, aeromoza *(LAM)*.
airily ['ɛərɪlɪ] *adv* muy a la ligera.
airing ['ɛərɪŋ] *n*: **to give an ~ to** *(linen)* airear; *(room)* ventilar; *(fig: ideas etc)* airear, someter a discusión.
air letter *n (BRIT)* carta aérea.
airlift ['ɛəlɪft] *n* puente *m* aéreo.

airline ['ɛəlaɪn] n línea aérea.
airliner ['ɛəlaɪnə*] n avión m de pasajeros.
airlock ['ɛəlɔk] n (in pipe) esclusa de aire.
airmail ['ɛəmeɪl] n: **by** ~ por avión.
air mattress n colchón m inflable or
  neumático.
airplane ['ɛəpleɪn] n (US) avión m.
air pocket n bolsa de aire.
airport ['ɛəpɔːt] n aeropuerto.
air raid n ataque m aéreo.
air rifle n escopeta de aire comprimido.
airsick ['ɛəsɪk] adj: **to be** ~ marearse (en
  avión).
airspeed ['ɛəspiːd] n velocidad f de vuelo.
airstrip ['ɛəstrɪp] n pista de aterrizaje.
air terminal n terminal f.
airtight ['ɛətaɪt] adj hermético.
air time n (RADIO, TV) tiempo en antena.
air traffic control n control m de tráfico
  aéreo.
air traffic controller n controlador(a) m/f
  aéreo/a.
airway ['ɛəweɪ] n (AVIAT) vía aérea; (ANAT)
  vía respiratoria.
airy ['ɛərɪ] adj (room) bien ventilado;
  (manners) despreocupado.
aisle [aɪl] n (of church) nave f lateral; (of
  theatre, plane) pasillo.
ajar [ə'dʒɑː*] adj entreabierto.
AK abbr (US) = Alaska.
aka abbr (= also known as) alias.
akin [ə'kɪn] adj: ~ **to** semejante a.
AL abbr (US) = Alabama.
ALA n abbr = American Library Association.
Ala. abbr (US) = Alabama.
alabaster ['æləbɑːstə*] n alabastro.
à la carte [ælæ'kɑːt] adv a la carta.
alacrity [ə'lækrɪtɪ] n: **with** ~ con la mayor
  prontitud.
alarm [ə'lɑːm] n alarma; (anxiety) inquietud
  f ♦ vt asustar, alarmar.
alarm clock n despertador m.
alarmed [ə'lɑːmd] adj (person) alarmado,
  asustado; (house, car etc) con alarma.
alarming [ə'lɑːmɪŋ] adj alarmante.
alarmingly [ə'lɑːmɪŋlɪ] adv de forma
  alarmante; ~ **quickly** a una velocidad
  alarmante.
alarmist [ə'lɑːmɪst] n alarmista m/f.
alas [ə'læs] adv desgraciadamente ♦ excl
  ¡ay!
Alas. abbr (US) = Alaska.
Alaska [ə'læskə] n Alaska.
Albania [æl'beɪnɪə] n Albania.
Albanian [æl'beɪnɪən] adj albanés/esa ♦ n
  albanés/esa m/f; (LING) albanés m.
albatross ['ælbətrɔs] n albatros m.
albeit [ɔːl'biːɪt] conj (although) aunque.

album ['ælbəm] n álbum m; (L.P.) elepé m.
albumen ['ælbjumɪn] n albúmina f.
alchemy ['ælkɪmɪ] n alquimia.
alcohol ['ælkəhɔl] n alcohol m.
alcohol-free adj sin alcohol.
alcoholic [ælkə'hɔlɪk] adj, n alcohólico/a m/f.
alcoholism ['ælkəhɔlɪzəm] n alcoholismo.
alcove ['ælkəuv] n nicho, hueco.
Ald. abbr = alderman.
alderman ['ɔːldəmən] n concejal m.
ale [eɪl] n cerveza.
alert [ə'lɔːt] adj alerta inv; (sharp) despierto,
  despabilado ♦ n alerta m, alarma ♦ vt
  poner sobre aviso; **to** ~ **sb (to sth)** poner
  sobre aviso or alertar a algn (de algo); **to**
  ~ **sb to the dangers of sth** poner sobre
  aviso or alertar a algn de los peligros de
  algo; **to be on the** ~ estar alerta or sobre
  aviso.
alertness [ə'lɔːtnɪs] n vigilancia.
Aleutian Islands [ə'luːʃən-] npl Islas fpl
  Aleutianas.
Alexandria [ælɪg'zɑːndrɪə] n Alejandría.
alfresco [æl'frɛskəu] adj, adv al aire libre.
algebra ['ældʒɪbrə] n álgebra.
Algeria [æl'dʒɪərɪə] n Argelia.
Algerian [æl'dʒɪərɪən] adj, n argelino/a m/f.
Algiers [æl'dʒɪəz] n Argel m.
algorithm ['ælgərɪðəm] n algoritmo.
alias ['eɪlɪəs] adv alias, conocido por ♦ n
  alias m.
alibi ['ælɪbaɪ] n coartada.
alien ['eɪlɪən] n (foreigner) extranjero/a
  ♦ adj: ~ **to** ajeno a.
alienate ['eɪlɪəneɪt] vt enajenar, alejar.
alienation [eɪlɪə'neɪʃən] n alejamiento m.
alight [ə'laɪt] adj ardiendo ♦ vi apearse,
  bajar.
align [ə'laɪn] vt alinear.
alignment [ə'laɪnmənt] n alineación f; **the
  desks are out of** ~ los pupitres no están
  bien alineados.
alike [ə'laɪk] adj semejantes, iguales ♦ adv
  igualmente, del mismo modo; **to look** ~
  parecerse.
alimony ['ælɪmənɪ] n (LAW) pensión f
  alimenticia.
alive [ə'laɪv] adj (gen) vivo; (lively) activo.
alkali ['ælkəlaɪ] n álcali m.

━━━━━━━━━━━━━━━━━━━━━━━━━━━━ KEYWORD

all [ɔːl] adj (sg) todo/a; (pl) todos/as; ~ **day**
  todo el día; ~ **night** toda la noche; ~ **men**
  todos los hombres; ~ **five came** vinieron
  los cinco; ~ **the books** todos los libros; ~
  the time/his life todo el tiempo/toda su
  vida; **for** ~ **their efforts** a pesar de todos
  sus esfuerzos

♦ *pron* **1** todo; **I ate it** ~, **I ate** ~ **of it** me lo comí todo; ~ **of them** todos (ellos); ~ **of us went** fuimos todos; ~ **the boys went** fueron todos los chicos; **is that** ~? ¿eso es todo?, ¿algo más?; (*in shop*) ¿algo más?, ¿alguna cosa más?

2 (*in phrases*): **above** ~ sobre todo; por encima de todo; **after** ~ después de todo; **at** ~: **anything at** ~ lo que sea; **not at** ~ (*in answer to question*) en absoluto; (*in answer to thanks*) ¡de nada!, ¡no hay de qué!; **I'm not at** ~ **tired** no estoy nada cansado/a; **anything at** ~ **will do** cualquier cosa viene bien; ~ **in** ~ a fin de cuentas

♦ *adv*: ~ **alone** completamente solo/a; **to be/feel** ~ **in** estar rendido; **it's not as hard as** ~ **that** no es tan difícil como lo pintas; ~ **the more/the better** tanto más/mejor; ~ **but** casi; **the score is 2** ~ están empatados a 2.

all-around ['ɔːlə'raund] *adj* (*US*) = **all-round**.
allay [ə'leɪ] *vt* (*fears*) aquietar; (*pain*) aliviar.
all clear *n* (*after attack etc*) fin *m* de la alerta; (*fig*) luz *f* verde.
allegation [ælɪ'ɡeɪʃən] *n* alegato.
allege [ə'lɛdʒ] *vt* pretender; **he is** ~**d to have said** ... se afirma que él dijo ....
alleged [ə'lɛdʒd] *adj* supuesto, presunto.
allegedly [ə'lɛdʒɪdlɪ] *adv* supuestamente, según se afirma.
allegiance [ə'liːdʒəns] *n* lealtad *f*.
allegory ['ælɪɡərɪ] *n* alegoría.
all-embracing ['ɔːləm'breɪsɪŋ] *adj* universal.
allergic [ə'lɜːdʒɪk] *adj*: ~ **to** alérgico a.
allergy ['ælədʒɪ] *n* alergia.
alleviate [ə'liːvɪeɪt] *vt* aliviar.
alleviation [əliːvɪ'eɪʃən] *n* alivio.
alley ['ælɪ] *n* (*street*) callejuela; (*in garden*) paseo.
alleyway ['ælɪweɪ] *n* callejón *m*.
alliance [ə'laɪəns] *n* alianza.
allied ['ælaɪd] *adj* aliado; (*related*) relacionado.
alligator ['ælɪɡeɪtə*] *n* caimán *m*.
all-important ['ɔːlɪm'pɔːtənt] *adj* de suma importancia.
all-in ['ɔːlɪn] *adj* (*BRIT*) (*also adv: charge*) todo incluido.
all-in wrestling *n* lucha libre.
alliteration [əlɪtə'reɪʃən] *n* aliteración *f*.
all-night ['ɔːl'naɪt] *adj* (*café*) abierto toda la noche; (*party*) que dura toda la noche.
allocate ['æləkeɪt] *vt* (*share out*) repartir; (*devote*) asignar.
allocation [ælə'keɪʃən] *n* (*of money*) ración

f, cuota; (*distribution*) reparto.
allot [ə'lɒt] *vt* asignar; **in the** ~**ted time** en el tiempo asignado.
allotment [ə'lɒtmənt] *n* porción *f*; (*garden*) parcela.
all-out ['ɔːlaut] *adj* (*effort etc*) supremo ♦ *adv*: **all out** con todas las fuerzas, a fondo.
allow [ə'lau] *vt* (*permit*) permitir, dejar; (*a claim*) admitir; (*sum to spend, time estimated*) dar, conceder; (*concede*): **to** ~ **that** reconocer que; **to** ~ **sb to do** permitir a alguien hacer; **smoking is not** ~**ed** prohibido *or* se prohíbe fumar; **he is** ~**ed to** ... se le permite ...; **we must** ~ **3 days for the journey** debemos dejar 3 días para el viaje.
► **allow for** *vt fus* tener en cuenta.
allowance [ə'lauəns] *n* concesión *f*; (*payment*) subvención *f*, pensión *f*; (*discount*) descuento, rebaja; **to make** ~**s for** (*person*) disculpar a; (*thing: take into account*) tener en cuenta.
alloy ['ælɔɪ] *n* aleación *f*.
all right *adv* (*feel, work*) bien; (*as answer*) ¡de acuerdo!, ¡está bien!
all-round ['ɔːl'raund] *adj* completo; (*view*) amplio.
all-rounder ['ɔːl'raundə*] *n*: **to be a good** ~ ser una persona que hace de todo.
allspice ['ɔːlspaɪs] *n* pimienta inglesa *or* de Jamaica.
all-time ['ɔːl'taɪm] *adj* (*record*) de todos los tiempos.
allude [ə'luːd] *vi*: **to** ~ **to** aludir a.
alluring [ə'ljuərɪŋ] *adj* seductor(a), atractivo.
allusion [ə'luːʒən] *n* referencia, alusión *f*.
ally *n* ['ælaɪ] aliado/a ♦ *vt* [ə'laɪ]: **to** ~ **o.s. with** aliarse con.
almanac ['ɔːlmənæk] *n* almanaque *m*.
almighty [ɔːl'maɪtɪ] *adj* todopoderoso.
almond ['ɑːmənd] *n* (*fruit*) almendra; (*tree*) almendro.
almost ['ɔːlməust] *adv* casi; **he** ~ **fell** casi *or* por poco se cae.
alms [ɑːmz] *npl* limosna *sg*.
aloft [ə'lɒft] *adv* arriba.
alone [ə'ləun] *adj* solo ♦ *adv* sólo, solamente; **to leave sb** ~ dejar a algn en paz; **to leave sth** ~ no tocar algo; **let** ~ ... y mucho menos, y no digamos ...
along [ə'lɒŋ] *prep* a lo largo de, por ♦ *adv*: **is he coming** ~ **with us?** ¿viene con nosotros?; **he was limping** ~ iba cojeando; ~ **with** junto con; **all** ~ (*all the time*) desde el principio.
alongside [ə'lɒŋ'saɪd] *prep* al lado de ♦ *adv* (*NAUT*) de costado; **we brought our boat**

~ atracamos nuestro barco.
aloof [ə'luːf] *adj* distante ♦ *adv*: **to stand** ~ mantenerse a distancia.
aloud [ə'laud] *adv* en voz alta.
alphabet ['ælfəbet] *n* alfabeto.
alphabetical [ælfə'betɪkəl] *adj* alfabético; **in** ~ **order** por orden alfabético.
alphanumeric [ælfənjuː'merɪk] *adj* alfanumérico.
alpine ['ælpaɪn] *adj* alpino, alpestre.
Alps [ælps] *npl*: **the** ~ los Alpes.
already [ɔːl'redɪ] *adv* ya.
alright ['ɔːl'raɪt] *adv* (*BRIT*) = **all right**.
Alsatian [æl'seɪʃən] *n* (*dog*) pastor *m* alemán.
also ['ɔːlsəu] *adv* también, además.
Alta. *abbr* (*Canada*) = *Alberta*.
altar ['ɔltə*] *n* altar *m*.
alter ['ɔltə*] *vt* cambiar, modificar ♦ *vi* cambiarse, modificarse.
alteration [ɔltə'reɪʃən] *n* cambio, modificación *f*; ~**s** *npl* (*ARCH*) reformas *fpl*; (*SEWING*) arreglos *mpl*; **timetable subject to** ~ el horario puede cambiar.
altercation [ɔltə'keɪʃən] *n* altercado.
alternate [ɔl'tɜːnɪt] *adj* alterno ♦ *vi* ['ɔltəneɪt]: **to** ~ (**with**) alternar (con); **on** ~ **days** en días alternos.
alternately [ɔl'tɜːnɪtlɪ] *adv* alternativamente, por turno.
alternating ['ɔltəneɪtɪŋ] *adj* (*current*) alterno.
alternative [ɔl'tɜːnətɪv] *adj* alternativo ♦ *n* alternativa.
alternatively [ɔl'tɜːnətɪvlɪ] *adv*: ~ **one could** ... por otra parte se podría....
alternative medicine *n* medicina alternativa.
alternator ['ɔltəneɪtə*] *n* (*AUT*) alternador *m*.
although [ɔːl'ðəu] *conj* aunque, si bien.
altitude ['æltɪtjuːd] *n* altitud *f*, altura.
altitude sickness *n* mal *m* de altura, soroche *m* (*LAM*).
alto ['æltəu] *n* (*female*) contralto *f*; (*male*) alto.
altogether [ɔːltə'geðə*] *adv* completamente, del todo; (*on the whole, in all*) en total, en conjunto; **how much is that** ~? ¿cuánto es todo *or* en total?
altruism ['æltruɪzəm] *n* altruismo.
altruistic [æltru'ɪstɪk] *adj* altruista.
aluminium [ælju'mɪnɪəm], (*US*) **aluminum** [ə'luːmɪnəm] *n* aluminio.
always ['ɔːlweɪz] *adv* siempre.
Alzheimer's ['æltshaɪməz] (*also*: ~ **disease**) enfermedad *f* de Alzheimer.
AM *abbr* = *amplitude modulation*.

am [æm] *vb see* **be**.
a.m. *adv abbr* (= *ante meridiem*) de la mañana.
AMA *n abbr* = *American Medical Association*.
amalgam [ə'mælgəm] *n* amalgama.
amalgamate [ə'mælgəmeɪt] *vi* amalgamarse ♦ *vt* amalgamar.
amalgamation [əmælgə'meɪʃən] *n* (*COMM*) fusión *f*.
amass [ə'mæs] *vt* amontonar, acumular.
amateur ['æmətə*] *n* aficionado/a, amateur *m/f*; ~ **dramatics** dramas *mpl* presentados por aficionados, representación *f* de aficionados.
amateurish ['æmətərɪʃ] *adj* (*pej*) torpe, inexperto.
amaze [ə'meɪz] *vt* asombrar, pasmar; **to be** ~**d (at)** asombrarse (de).
amazement [ə'meɪzmənt] *n* asombro, sorpresa; **to my** ~ para mi sorpresa.
amazing [ə'meɪzɪŋ] *adj* extraordinario, asombroso; (*bargain, offer*) increíble.
amazingly [ə'meɪzɪŋlɪ] *adv* extraordinariamente.
Amazon ['æməzən] *n* (*GEO*) Amazonas *m*; (*MYTHOLOGY*) amazona ♦ *cpd*: **the** ~ **basin/jungle** la cuenca/selva del Amazonas.
Amazonian [æmə'zəunɪən] *adj* amazónico.
ambassador [æm'bæsədə*] *n* embajador(a) *m/f*.
amber ['æmbə*] *n* ámbar *m*; **at** ~ (*BRIT AUT*) en amarillo.
ambidextrous [æmbɪ'dekstrəs] *adj* ambidextro.
ambience ['æmbɪəns] *n* ambiente *m*.
ambiguity [æmbɪ'gjuːɪtɪ] *n* ambigüedad *f*; (*of meaning*) doble sentido.
ambiguous [æm'bɪgjuəs] *adj* ambiguo.
ambition [æm'bɪʃən] *n* ambición *f*; **to achieve one's** ~ realizar su ambición.
ambitious [æm'bɪʃəs] *adj* ambicioso; (*plan*) grandioso.
ambivalent [æm'bɪvələnt] *adj* ambivalente; (*pej*) equívoco.
amble ['æmbl] *vi* (*gen*: ~ **along**) deambular, andar sin prisa.
ambulance ['æmbjuləns] *n* ambulancia.
ambulanceman/woman ['æmbjulənsmən/wumən] *n* ambulanciero/a.
ambush ['æmbuʃ] *n* emboscada ♦ *vt* tender una emboscada a; (*fig*) coger (*SP*) *or* agarrar (*LAM*) por sorpresa.
ameba [ə'miːbə] *n* (*US*) = **amoeba**.
ameliorate [ə'miːlɪəreɪt] *vt* mejorar.
amelioration [əmiːlɪə'reɪʃən] *n* mejora.
amen [ɑː'men] *excl* amén.
amenable [ə'miːnəbl] *adj*: ~ **to** (*advice etc*)

sensible a.
amend [ə'mɛnd] *vt (law, text)* enmendar; **to make ~s** *(apologize)* enmendarlo, dar cumplida satisfacción.
amendment [ə'mɛndmənt] *n* enmienda.
amenities [ə'miːnɪtɪz] *npl* comodidades *fpl.*
amenity [ə'miːnɪtɪ] *n* servicio.
America [ə'mɛrɪkə] *n* América (del Norte).
American [ə'mɛrɪkən] *adj, n* (norte)americano/a *m/f,* estadounidense *m/f.*
Americanism [ə'mɛrɪkənɪzəm] *n* americanismo.
americanize [ə'mɛrɪkənaɪz] *vt* americanizar.
Amerindian [æmər'ɪndɪən] *adj, n* amerindio/a.
amethyst ['æmɪθɪst] *n* amatista.
Amex ['æmɛks] *n abbr = American Stock Exchange.*
amiable ['eɪmɪəbl] *adj (kind)* amable, simpático.
amicable ['æmɪkəbl] *adj* amistoso, amigable.
amicably ['æmɪkəblɪ] *adv* amigablemente, amistosamente; **to part ~** separarse amistosamente.
amid(st) [ə'mɪd(st)] *prep* entre, en medio de.
amiss [ə'mɪs] *adv:* **to take sth ~** tomar algo a mal; **there's something ~** pasa algo.
ammo ['æməu] *n abbr (col)* = **ammunition.**
ammonia [ə'məunɪə] *n* amoníaco.
ammunition [æmju'nɪʃən] *n* municiones *fpl;* *(fig)* argumentos *mpl.*
ammunition dump *n* depósito de municiones.
amnesia [æm'niːzɪə] *n* amnesia.
amnesty ['æmnɪstɪ] *n* amnistía; **to grant an ~** amnistiar (a); **A~ International** Amnistía Internacional.
amoeba, *(US)* **ameba** [ə'miːbə] *n* amiba.
amok [ə'mɔk] *adv:* **to run ~** enloquecerse, desbocarse.
among(st) [ə'mʌŋ(st)] *prep* entre, en medio de.
amoral [æ'mɔrəl] *adj* amoral.
amorous ['æmərəs] *adj* cariñoso.
amorphous [ə'mɔːfəs] *adj* amorfo.
amortization [əmɔːtaɪ'zeɪʃən] *n* amortización *f.*
amount [ə'maunt] *n (gen)* cantidad *f;* *(of bill etc)* suma, importe *m* ♦ *vi:* **to ~ to** *(total)* sumar; *(be same as)* equivaler a, significar; **this ~s to a refusal** esto equivale a una negativa; **the total ~** *(of money)* la suma total.
amp(ère) ['æmp(ɛə*)] *n* amperio; **a 13 amp**

plug un enchufe de 13 amperios.
ampersand ['æmpəsænd] *n* signo &, "y" comercial.
amphetamine [æm'fɛtəmiːn] *n* anfetamina.
amphibian [æm'fɪbɪən] *n* anfibio.
amphibious [æm'fɪbɪəs] *adj* anfibio.
amphitheatre, *(US)* **amphitheater** ['æmfɪθɪətə*] *n* anfiteatro.
ample ['æmpl] *adj (spacious)* amplio; *(abundant)* abundante; **to have ~ time** tener tiempo de sobra.
amplifier ['æmplɪfaɪə*] *n* amplificador *m.*
amplify ['æmplɪfaɪ] *vt* amplificar, aumentar; *(explain)* explicar.
amply ['æmplɪ] *adv* ampliamente.
ampoule, *(US)* **ampule** ['æmpuːl] *n (MED)* ampolla.
amputate ['æmpjuteɪt] *vt* amputar.
amputee [æmpju'tiː] *n* persona que ha sufrido una amputación.
Amsterdam ['æmstədæm] *n* Amsterdam *m.*
amt *abbr* = **amount.**
amuck [ə'mʌk] *adv* = **amok.**
amuse [ə'mjuːz] *vt* divertir; *(distract)* distraer, entretener; **to ~ o.s. with sth/ by doing sth** distraerse con algo/ haciendo algo; **he was ~d at the joke** le divirtió el chiste.
amusement [ə'mjuːzmənt] *n* diversión *f;* *(pastime)* pasatiempo; *(laughter)* risa; **much to my ~** con gran regocijo mío.
amusement arcade *n* salón *m* de juegos.
amusement park *n* parque *m* de atracciones.
amusing [ə'mjuːzɪŋ] *adj* divertido.
an [æn, ən, n] *indef art see* **a.**
ANA *n abbr = American Newspaper Association; American Nurses Association.*
anachronism [ə'nækrənɪzəm] *n* anacronismo.
anaemia [ə'niːmɪə] *n* anemia.
anaemic [ə'niːmɪk] *adj* anémico; *(fig)* flojo.
anaesthetic [ænɪs'θɛtɪk] *n* anestesia; **local/ general ~** anestesia local/general.
anaesthetist [æ'niːsθɪtɪst] *n* anestesista *m/f.*
anagram ['ænəgræm] *n* anagrama *m.*
anal ['eɪnl] *adj* anal.
analgesic [ænæl'dʒiːsɪk] *adj, n* analgésico.
analogous [ə'næləgəs] *adj:* **~ to** *or* **with** análogo a.
analog(ue) ['ænəlɔg] *adj (computer, watch)* analógico.
analogy [ə'nælədʒɪ] *n* analogía; **to draw an ~ between** señalar la analogía entre.
analyse ['ænəlaɪz] *vt (BRIT)* analizar.
analysis, *pl* **analyses** [ə'næləsɪs, -siːz] *n* análisis *m inv.*
analyst ['ænəlɪst] *n (political ~)* analista *m/f,*

(*psycho~*) psicoanalista *m/f*.
analytic(al) [ænəˈlɪtɪk(əl)] *adj* analítico.
analyze [ˈænəlaɪz] *vt* (*US*) = **analyse**.
anarchic [æˈnɑːkɪk] *adj* anárquico.
anarchist [ˈænəkɪst] *adj, n* anarquista *m/f*.
anarchy [ˈænəkɪ] *n* anarquía, desorden *m*.
anathema [əˈnæθɪmə] *n*: **that is ~ to him** eso es pecado para él.
anatomical [ænəˈtɒmɪkəl] *adj* anatómico.
anatomy [əˈnætəmɪ] *n* anatomía.
ANC *n abbr* = *African National Congress*.
ancestor [ˈænsɪstə*] *n* antepasado.
ancestral [ænˈsɛstrəl] *adj* ancestral.
ancestry [ˈænsɪstrɪ] *n* ascendencia, abolengo.
anchor [ˈæŋkə*] *n* ancla, áncora ♦ *vi* (*also*: **to drop ~**) anclar, echar el ancla ♦ *vt* (*fig*) sujetar, afianzar; **to weigh ~** levar anclas.
anchorage [ˈæŋkərɪdʒ] *n* ancladero.
anchor man, anchor woman *n* (*RADIO, TV*) presentador(a) *m/f*.
anchovy [ˈæntʃəvɪ] *n* anchoa.
ancient [ˈeɪnʃənt] *adj* antiguo; **~ monument** monumento histórico.
ancillary [ænˈsɪlərɪ] *adj* (*worker, staff*) auxiliar.
and [ænd] *conj* y; (*before i, hi*) e; **~ so on** etcétera; **try ~ come** procure *or* intente venir; **better ~ better** cada vez mejor.
Andalusia [ændəˈluːzɪə] *n* Andalucía.
Andean [ˈændɪən] *adj* andino/a; **~ high plateau** altiplanicie *f*, altiplano (*LAM*).
Andes [ˈændiːz] *npl*: **the ~** los Andes.
anecdote [ˈænɪkdəʊt] *n* anécdota.
anemia [əˈniːmɪə] *n* (*US*) = **anaemia**.
anemic [əˈniːmɪk] *adj* (*US*) = **anaemic**.
anemone [əˈnɛmənɪ] *n* (*BOT*) anémone *f*; **sea ~** anémona.
anesthetic [ænɪsˈθɛtɪk] *adj, n* (*US*) = **anaesthetic**.
anesthetist [æˈniːsθɪtɪst] *n* (*US*) = **anaesthetist**.
anew [əˈnjuː] *adv* de nuevo, otra vez.
angel [ˈeɪndʒəl] *n* ángel *m*.
angel dust *n* polvo de ángel.
angelic [ænˈdʒɛlɪk] *adj* angélico.
anger [ˈæŋɡə*] *n* ira, cólera, enojo (*LAM*) ♦ *vt* enojar, enfurecer.
angina [ænˈdʒaɪnə] *n* angina (del pecho).
angle [ˈæŋɡl] *n* ángulo; **from their ~** desde su punto de vista.
angler [ˈæŋɡlə*] *n* pescador(a) *m/f* (de caña).
Anglican [ˈæŋɡlɪkən] *adj, n* anglicano/a.
anglicize [ˈæŋɡlɪsaɪz] *vt* anglicanizar.
angling [ˈæŋɡlɪŋ] *n* pesca con caña.
Anglo- [ˈæŋɡləʊ] *pref* anglo… .

Angola [æŋˈɡəʊlə] *n* Angola.
Angolan [æŋˈɡəʊlən] *adj, n* angoleño/a *m/f*.
angrily [ˈæŋɡrɪlɪ] *adv* enojado, enfadado.
angry [ˈæŋɡrɪ] *adj* enfadado, enojado (*esp LAM*); **to be ~ with sb/at sth** estar enfadado con algn/por algo; **to get ~** enfadarse, enojarse (*esp LAM*).
anguish [ˈæŋɡwɪʃ] *n* (*physical*) tormentos *mpl*; (*mental*) angustia.
anguished [ˈæŋɡwɪʃt] *adj* angustioso.
angular [ˈæŋɡjulə*] *adj* (*shape*) angular; (*features*) anguloso.
animal [ˈænɪməl] *adj, n* animal *m*.
animal rights [-raɪts] *npl* derechos *mpl* de los animales.
animate [ˈænɪmeɪt] *vt* (*enliven*) animar; (*encourage*) estimular, alentar ♦ [ˈænɪmɪt] *adj* vivo, animado.
animated [ˈænɪmeɪtɪd] *adj* vivo, animado.
animation [ænɪˈmeɪʃən] *n* animación *f*.
animosity [ænɪˈmɒsɪtɪ] *n* animosidad *f*, rencor *m*.
aniseed [ˈænɪsiːd] *n* anís *m*.
Ankara [ˈæŋkərə] *n* Ankara.
ankle [ˈæŋkl] *n* tobillo *m*.
ankle sock *n* calcetín *m*.
annex [ˈænɛks] *n* (*also*: *Brit*: **annexe**) (*building*) edificio anexo ♦ *vt* [æˈnɛks] (*territory*) anexar.
annihilate [əˈnaɪəleɪt] *vt* aniquilar.
annihilation [ənaɪəˈleɪʃən] *n* aniquilación *f*.
anniversary [ænɪˈvɜːsərɪ] *n* aniversario.
annotate [ˈænəuteɪt] *vt* anotar.
announce [əˈnaʊns] *vt* (*gen*) anunciar; (*inform*) comunicar; **he ~d that he wasn't going** declaró que no iba.
announcement [əˈnaʊnsmənt] *n* (*gen*) anuncio; (*declaration*) declaración *f*; **I'd like to make an ~** quisiera anunciar algo.
announcer [əˈnaʊnsə*] *n* (*RADIO, TV*) locutor(a) *m/f*.
annoy [əˈnɔɪ] *vt* molestar, fastidiar, fregar (*LAM*), embromar (*LAM*); **to be ~ed (at sth/with sb)** estar enfadado *or* molesto (por algo/con algn); **don't get ~ed!** ¡no se enfade!
annoyance [əˈnɔɪəns] *n* enojo; (*thing*) molestia.
annoying [əˈnɔɪɪŋ] *adj* molesto, fastidioso, fregado (*LAM*), embromado (*LAM*); (*person*) pesado.
annual [ˈænjuəl] *adj* anual ♦ *n* (*BOT*) anual *m*; (*book*) anuario.
annual general meeting (AGM) *n* junta general anual.
annually [ˈænjuəlɪ] *adv* anualmente, cada año.
annual report *n* informe *m or* memoria

anual.

annuity [əˈnjuːɪtɪ] *n* renta *or* pensión *f* vitalicia.

annul [əˈnʌl] *vt* anular; (*law*) revocar.

annulment [əˈnʌlmənt] *n* anulación *f*.

annum [ˈænəm] *n see* per annum.

Annunciation [ənʌnsɪˈeɪʃən] *n* Anunciación *f*.

anode [ˈænəud] *n* ánodo.

anoint [əˈnɔɪnt] *vt* untar.

anomalous [əˈnɔmələs] *adj* anómalo.

anomaly [əˈnɔmɔlɪ] *n* anomalía.

anon. [əˈnɔn] *abbr* = anonymous.

anonymity [ænəˈnɪmɪtɪ] *n* anonimato.

anonymous [əˈnɔnɪməs] *adj* anónimo; **to remain** ~ quedar en el anonimato.

anorak [ˈænəræk] *n* anorak *m*.

anorexia [ænəˈrɛksɪə] *n* (*MED*) anorexia.

anorexic [ænəˈrɛksɪk] *adj*, *n* anoréxico/a *m/f*.

another [əˈnʌðə*] *adj*: ~ **book** otro libro; ~ **beer?** ¿(quieres) otra cerveza?; **in ~ 5 years** en cinco años más ♦ *pron* otro; *see also* one.

ANSI *n abbr* (= *American National Standards Institution*) oficina de normalización de EEUU.

answer [ˈɑːnsə*] *n* respuesta, contestación *f*; (*to problem*) solución *f* ♦ *vi* contestar, responder ♦ *vt* (*reply to*) contestar a, responder a; (*problem*) resolver; **to ~ the phone** contestar el teléfono; **in ~ to your letter** contestando *or* en contestación a su carta; **to ~ the bell** *or* **the door** abrir la puerta.

▶**answer back** *vi* replicar, ser respondón/ona.

▶**answer for** *vt fus* responder de *or* por.

▶**answer to** *vt fus* (*description*) corresponder a.

answerable [ˈɑːnsərəbl] *adj*: ~ **to sb for sth** responsable ante algn de algo.

answering machine [ˈɑːnsərɪŋ-] *n* contestador *m* automático.

ant [ænt] *n* hormiga.

ANTA *n abbr* = American National Theater and Academy.

antagonism [ænˈtægənɪzəm] *n* antagonismo *m*.

antagonist [ænˈtægənɪst] *n* antagonista *m/f*, adversario/a.

antagonistic [æntægəˈnɪstɪk] *adj* antagónico; (*opposed*) contrario, opuesto.

antagonize [ænˈtægənaɪz] *vt* provocar la enemistad de.

Antarctic [æntˈɑːktɪk] *adj* antártico ♦ *n*: **the ~** el Antártico.

Antarctica [ænˈtɑːktɪkə] *n* Antártida.

Antarctic Circle *n* Círculo Polar Antártico.

Antarctic Ocean *n* Océano Antártico.

ante [ˈæntɪ] *n*: **to up the ~** subir la apuesta.

ante... [ˈæntɪ] *pref* ante....

anteater [ˈæntiːtə*] *n* oso hormiguero.

antecedent [æntɪˈsiːdənt] *n* antecedente *m*.

antechamber [ˈæntɪtʃeɪmbə*] *n* antecámara.

antelope [ˈæntɪləup] *n* antílope *m*.

antenatal [æntɪˈneɪtl] *adj* prenatal.

antenatal clinic *n* clínica prenatal.

antenna [ænˈtɛnə], *pl* ~**e** [-niː] *n* antena.

anteroom [ˈæntɪrum] *n* antesala.

anthem [ˈænθəm] *n*: **national ~** himno nacional.

anthology [ænˈθɔlədʒɪ] *n* antología.

anthropologist [ænθrəˈpɔlədʒɪst] *n* antropólogo/a.

anthropology [ænθrəˈpɔlədʒɪ] *n* antropología.

anti... [æntɪ] *pref* anti....

anti-aircraft [ˈæntɪˈɛəkrɑːft] *adj* antiaéreo.

antiballistic [æntɪbəˈlɪstɪk] *adj* antibalístico.

antibiotic [æntɪbaɪˈɔtɪk] *adj*, *n* antibiótico.

antibody [ˈæntɪbɔdɪ] *n* anticuerpo.

anticipate [ænˈtɪsɪpeɪt] *vt* (*foresee*) prever; (*expect*) esperar, contar con; (*forestall*) anticiparse a, adelantarse a; **this is worse than I ~d** esto es peor de lo que esperaba; **as ~d** según se esperaba.

anticipation [æntɪsɪˈpeɪʃən] *n* previsión *f*; esperanza; anticipación *f*.

anticlimax [æntɪˈklaɪmæks] *n* decepción *f*.

anticlockwise [æntɪˈklɔkwaɪz] *adv* en dirección contraria a la de las agujas del reloj.

antics [ˈæntɪks] *npl* payasadas *fpl*.

anticyclone [æntɪˈsaɪkləun] *n* anticiclón *m*.

antidote [ˈæntɪdəut] *n* antídoto.

antifreeze [ˈæntɪfriːz] *n* anticongelante *m*.

antihistamine [æntɪˈhɪstəmiːn] *n* antihistamínico.

Antilles [ænˈtɪliːz] *npl*: **the ~** las Antillas.

antipathy [ænˈtɪpəθɪ] *n* (*between people*) antipatía; (*to person, thing*) aversión *f*.

antiperspirant [ˈæntɪpəːspɪrənt] *n* antitranspirante *m*.

Antipodean [æntɪpəˈdiːən] *adj* antípoda.

Antipodes [ænˈtɪpədiːz] *npl*: **the ~** las Antípodas.

antiquarian [æntɪˈkwɛərɪən] *n* anticuario/a.

antiquated [ˈæntɪkweɪtɪd] *adj* anticuado.

antique [ænˈtiːk] *n* antigüedad *f* ♦ *adj* antiguo.

antique dealer *n* anticuario/a.

antique shop *n* tienda de antigüedades.

antiquity [ænˈtɪkwɪtɪ] *n* antigüedad *f*.

anti-Semitic [ˈæntɪsɪˈmɪtɪk] *adj* antisemita.

anti-Semitism [æntɪ'sɛmɪtɪzəm] *n* antisemitismo.
antiseptic [æntɪ'sɛptɪk] *adj, n* antiséptico.
antisocial [æntɪ'səuʃəl] *adj* antisocial.
antitank [æntɪ'tæŋk] *adj* antitanque.
antithesis, *pl* **antitheses** [æn'tɪθɪsɪs, -siːz] *n* antítesis *f inv*.
antitrust [æntɪ'trʌst] *adj*: ~ **legislation** legislación *f* antimonopolio.
antlers ['æntləz] *npl* cornamenta.
anus ['eɪnəs] *n* ano.
anvil ['ænvɪl] *n* yunque *m*.
anxiety [æŋ'zaɪətɪ] *n* (*worry*) inquietud *f*; (*eagerness*) ansia, anhelo.
anxious ['æŋkʃəs] *adj* (*worried*) inquieto; (*keen*) deseoso; **I'm very ~ about you** me tienes muy preocupado.
anxiously ['æŋkʃəslɪ] *adv* con inquietud, de manera angustiada.

=========================== *KEYWORD*

any ['ɛnɪ] *adj* **1** (*in questions etc*) algún/alguna; **have you ~ butter/children?** ¿tienes mantequilla/hijos?; **if there are ~ tickets left** si quedan billetes, si queda algún billete
2 (*with negative*): **I haven't ~ money/books** no tengo dinero/libros
3 (*no matter which*) cualquier; **~ excuse will do** valdrá *or* servirá cualquier excusa; **choose ~ book you like** escoge el libro que quieras; **~ teacher you ask will tell you** cualquier profesor al que preguntes te lo dirá
4 (*in phrases*): **in ~ case** de todas formas, en cualquier caso; **~ day now** cualquier día (de estos); **at ~ moment** en cualquier momento, de un momento a otro; **at ~ rate** en todo caso; **~ time: come (at) ~ time** ven cuando quieras; **he might come (at) ~ time** podría llegar de un momento a otro
♦ *pron* **1** (*in questions etc*): **have you got ~?** ¿tienes alguno/a?; **can ~ of you sing?** ¿sabe cantar alguno de vosotros/ustedes?
2 (*with negative*): **I haven't ~ (of them)** no tengo ninguno
3 (*no matter which one(s)*): **take ~ of those books (you like)** toma el libro que quieras de ésos
♦ *adv* **1** (*in questions etc*): **do you want ~ more soup/sandwiches?** ¿quieres más sopa/bocadillos?; **are you feeling ~ better?** ¿te sientes algo mejor?
2 (*with negative*): **I can't hear him ~ more** ya no le oigo; **don't wait ~ longer** no esperes más.

anybody ['ɛnɪbɔdɪ] *pron* cualquiera, cualquier persona; (*in interrogative sentences*) alguien; (*in negative sentences*): **I don't see ~** no veo a nadie.
anyhow ['ɛnɪhau] *adv* de todos modos, de todas maneras; (*carelessly*) de cualquier manera; (*haphazardly*) de cualquier modo; **I shall go ~** iré de todas maneras.
anyone ['ɛnɪwʌn] = **anybody**.
anyplace ['ɛnɪpleɪs] *adv* (*US*) = **anywhere**.
anything ['ɛnɪθɪŋ] *pron* (*see* **anybody**) cualquier cosa; (*in interrogative sentences*) algo; (*in negative sentences*) nada; (*everything*) todo; **~ else?** ¿algo más?; **it can cost ~ between £15 and £20** puede costar entre 15 y 20 libras.
anytime ['ɛnɪtaɪm] *adv* (*at any moment*) en cualquier momento, de un momento a otro; (*whenever*) no importa cuándo, cuando quiera.
anyway ['ɛnɪweɪ] *adv* de todas maneras; de cualquier modo.
anywhere ['ɛnɪwɛə*] *adv* (*see* **anybody**) dondequiera; (*interrogative*) en algún sitio; (*negative sense*) en ningún sitio; (*everywhere*) en *or* por todas partes; **I don't see him ~** no le veo en ningún sitio; **~ in the world** en cualquier parte del mundo.
Anzac ['ænzæk] *n abbr* (= *Australia-New Zealand Army Corps*).
apace [ə'peɪs] *adv* aprisa.
apart [ə'pɑːt] *adv* aparte, separadamente; **10 miles ~** separados por 10 millas; **to take ~** desmontar; **~ from** *prep* aparte de.
apartheid [ə'pɑːteɪt] *n* apartheid *m*.
apartment [ə'pɑːtmənt] *n* (*US*) piso, departamento (*LAM*), apartamento; (*room*) cuarto.
apartment block *or* **building** (*US*) bloque *m* de pisos.
apathetic [æpə'θɛtɪk] *adj* apático, indiferente.
apathy ['æpəθɪ] *n* apatía, indiferencia.
APB *n abbr* (*US*: = *all points bulletin*) expresión usada por la policía que significa "descubrir y aprehender al sospechoso".
ape [eɪp] *n* mono ♦ *vt* imitar, remedar.
Apennines ['æpənaɪnz] *npl*: **the ~** los Apeninos *mpl*.
aperitif [ə'pɛrɪtiːf] *n* aperitivo.
aperture ['æpətʃuə*] *n* rendija, resquicio; (*PHOT*) abertura.
APEX ['eɪpɛks] *n abbr* (*AVIAT* = *advance purchase excursion*) APEX *m*.
apex ['eɪpɛks] *n* ápice *m*; (*fig*) cumbre *f*.
aphid ['eɪfɪd] *n* pulgón *m*.

aphorism ['æfərɪzəm] n aforismo.
aphrodisiac [æfrəu'dɪzɪæk] adj, n afrodisíaco.
API n abbr = American Press Institute.
apiece [ə'piːs] adv cada uno.
aplomb [ə'plɔm] n aplomo, confianza.
APO n abbr (US: = Army Post Office) servicio postal del ejército.
Apocalypse [ə'pɔkəlɪps] n Apocalipsis m.
apocryphal [ə'pɔkrɪfəl] adj apócrifo.
apolitical [eɪpə'lɪtɪkl] adj apolítico.
apologetic [əpɔlə'dʒɛtɪk] adj (look, remark) de disculpa.
apologetically [əpɔlə'dʒɛtɪkəlɪ] adv con aire de disculpa, excusándose, disculpándose.
apologize [ə'pɔlədʒaɪz] vi: to ~ (for sth to sb) disculparse (con algn por algo).
apology [ə'pɔlədʒɪ] n disculpa, excusa; please accept my apologies le ruego me disculpe.
apoplectic [æpə'plɛktɪk] adj (MED) apoplético; (col): ~ with rage furioso.
apoplexy ['æpəplɛksɪ] n apoplegía.
apostle [ə'pɔsl] n apóstol m/f.
apostrophe [ə'pɔstrəfɪ] n apóstrofo m.
appal [ə'pɔːl] vt horrorizar, espantar.
Appalachian Mountains [æpə'leɪʃən-] npl: the ~ los (Montes) Apalaches.
appalling [ə'pɔːlɪŋ] adj espantoso; (awful) pésimo; she's an ~ cook es una cocinera malísima.
apparatus [æpə'reɪtəs] n aparato; (in gymnasium) aparatos mpl.
apparel [ə'pærl] n (US) indumentaria.
apparent [ə'pærənt] adj aparente; (obvious) manifiesto, evidente; it is ~ that está claro que.
apparently [ə'pærəntlɪ] adv por lo visto, al parecer, dizque (LAM).
apparition [æpə'rɪʃən] n aparición f.
appeal [ə'piːl] vi (LAW) apelar ♦ n (LAW) apelación f; (request) llamamiento, llamado (LAM); (plea) súplica; (charm) atractivo, encanto; to ~ for solicitar; to ~ to (subj: person) rogar a, suplicar a; (: thing) atraer, interesar; to ~ to sb for mercy rogarle misericordia a alguien; it doesn't ~ to me no me atrae, no me llama la atención; right of ~ derecho de apelación.
appealing [ə'piːlɪŋ] adj (nice) atractivo; (touching) conmovedor(a), emocionante.
appear [ə'pɪə*] vi aparecer, presentarse; (LAW) comparecer; (publication) salir (a luz), publicarse; (seem) parecer; it would ~ that parecería que.
appearance [ə'pɪərəns] n aparición f; (look, aspect) apariencia, aspecto; to keep up

~s salvar las apariencias; to all ~s al parecer.
appease [ə'piːz] vt (pacify) apaciguar; (satisfy) satisfacer.
appeasement [ə'piːzmənt] n (POL) apaciguamiento.
append [ə'pɛnd] vt (COMPUT) añadir (al final).
appendage [ə'pɛndɪdʒ] n añadidura.
appendicitis [əpɛndɪ'saɪtɪs] n apendicitis f.
appendix, pl **appendices** [ə'pɛndɪks, -dɪsiːz] n apéndice m; to have one's ~ out operarse de apendicitis.
appetite ['æpɪtaɪt] n apetito; (fig) deseo, anhelo; that walk has given me an ~ ese paseo me ha abierto el apetito.
appetizer ['æpɪtaɪzə*] n (drink) aperitivo; (food) tapas fpl (SP).
appetizing ['æpɪtaɪzɪŋ] adj apetitoso.
applaud [ə'plɔːd] vt, vi aplaudir.
applause [ə'plɔːz] n aplausos mpl.
apple ['æpl] n manzana.
apple tree n manzano.
appliance [ə'plaɪəns] n aparato; electrical ~s electrodomésticos mpl.
applicable [ə'plɪkəbl] adj aplicable, pertinente; the law is ~ from January la ley es aplicable or se pone en vigor a partir de enero; to be ~ to referirse a.
applicant ['æplɪkənt] n candidato/a; solicitante m/f.
application [æplɪ'keɪʃən] n aplicación f; (for a job, a grant etc) solicitud f.
application form n solicitud f.
applications package n (COMPUT) paquete m de programas de aplicación.
applied [ə'plaɪd] adj (science, art) aplicado.
apply [ə'plaɪ] vt: to ~ (to) aplicar (a); (fig) emplear (para) ♦ vi: to ~ to (ask) dirigirse a; (be suitable for) ser aplicable a; (be relevant to) tener que ver con; to ~ for (permit, grant, job) solicitar; to ~ the brakes echar el freno; to ~ o.s. to aplicarse a, dedicarse a.
appoint [ə'pɔɪnt] vt (to post) nombrar; (date, place) fijar, señalar.
appointee [əpɔɪn'tiː] n persona nombrada.
appointment [ə'pɔɪntmənt] n (engagement) cita; (date) compromiso; (act) nombramiento; (post) puesto; to make an ~ (with) (doctor) pedir hora (con); (friend) citarse (con); "~s (vacant)" "ofertas de trabajo"; by ~ mediante cita.
apportion [ə'pɔːʃən] vt repartir.
appraisal [ə'preɪzl] n evaluación f.
appraise [ə'preɪz] vt (value) tasar, valorar; (situation etc) evaluar.
appreciable [ə'priːʃəbl] adj sensible.

appreciably [ə'priːʃəblɪ] *adv* sensiblemente, de manera apreciable.

appreciate [ə'priːʃɪeɪt] *vt* (*like*) apreciar, tener en mucho; (*be grateful for*) agradecer; (*be aware of*) comprender ♦ *vi* (*COMM*) aumentar en valor; **1 ~d your help** agradecí tu ayuda.

appreciation [əpriːʃɪ'eɪʃən] *n* aprecio; reconocimiento, agradecimiento; aumento en valor.

appreciative [ə'priːʃɪətɪv] *adj* agradecido.

apprehend [æprɪ'hɛnd] *vt* percibir; (*arrest*) detener.

apprehension [æprɪ'hɛnʃən] *n* (*fear*) aprensión *f*.

apprehensive [æprɪ'hɛnsɪv] *adj* aprensivo.

apprentice [ə'prɛntɪs] *n* aprendiz(a) *m/f* ♦ *vt*: **to be ~d to** estar de aprendiz con.

apprenticeship [ə'prɛntɪsʃɪp] *n* aprendizaje *m*; **to serve one's ~** hacer el aprendizaje.

appro. ['æprəu] *abbr* (*BRIT COMM: col*) = **approval**.

approach [ə'prəutʃ] *vi* acercarse ♦ *vt* acercarse a; (*be approximate*) aproximarse a; (*ask, apply to*) dirigirse a; (*problem*) abordar ♦ *n* acercamiento; aproximación *f*; (*access*) acceso; (*proposal*) proposición *f*; (*to problem etc*) enfoque *m*; **to ~ sb about sth** hablar con algn sobre algo.

approachable [ə'prəutʃəbl] *adj* (*person*) abordable; (*place*) accesible.

approach road *n* vía de acceso.

approbation [æprə'beɪʃən] *n* aprobación *f*.

appropriate [ə'prəuprɪɪt] *adj* apropiado, conveniente ♦ *vt* [-rɪeɪt] (*take*) apropiarse de; (*allot*): **to ~ sth for** destinar algo a; **~ for or to** apropiado para; **it would not be ~ for me to comment** no estaría bien *or* sería pertinente que yo diera mi opinión.

appropriation [əprəuprɪ'eɪʃən] *n* asignación *f*.

approval [ə'pruːvəl] *n* aprobación *f*, visto bueno; **on ~** (*COMM*) a prueba; **to meet with sb's ~** obtener la aprobación de algn.

approve [ə'pruːv] *vt* aprobar.

▶**approve of** *vt fus* aprobar.

approved school *n* (*BRIT*) correccional *m*.

approx. *abbr* (= *approximately*) aprox.

approximate [ə'prɔksɪmɪt] *adj* aproximado.

approximately [ə'prɔksɪmɪtlɪ] *adv* aproximadamente, más o menos.

approximation [əprɔksɪ'meɪʃən] *n* aproximación *f*.

Apr. *abbr* (= *April*) abr.

apr *n abbr* (= *annual percentage rate*) tasa de interés anual.

apricot ['eɪprɪkɔt] *n* albaricoque *m* (*SP*), damasco (*LAM*).

April ['eɪprəl] *n* abril *m*; **~ Fools' Day** *n* ≈ día *m* de los (Santos) Inocentes.

> El 1 de abril es **April Fools' Day** en la tradición anglosajona. Tal día se les gastan bromas a los más desprevenidos, quienes reciben la denominación de **April Fool** (≈ inocente), y tanto la prensa escrita como la televisión difunden alguna historia falsa con la que sumarse al espíritu del día.

apron ['eɪprən] *n* delantal *m*; (*AVIAT*) pista.

apse [æps] *n* (*ARCH*) ábside *m*.

APT *n abbr* (*BRIT*) = advanced passenger train.

Apt. *abbr* = **apartment**.

apt [æpt] *adj* (*to the point*) acertado, oportuno; (*appropriate*) apropiado; **~ to do** (*likely*) propenso a hacer.

aptitude ['æptɪtjuːd] *n* aptitud *f*, capacidad *f*.

aptitude test *n* prueba de aptitud.

aptly ['æptlɪ] *adj* acertadamente.

aqualung ['ækwəlʌŋ] *n* escafandra autónoma.

aquarium [ə'kwɛərɪəm] *n* acuario.

Aquarius [ə'kwɛərɪəs] *n* Acuario.

aquatic [ə'kwætɪk] *adj* acuático.

aqueduct ['ækwɪdʌkt] *n* acueducto.

AR *abbr* (*US*) = Arkansas.

ARA *n abbr* (*BRIT*) = Associate of the Royal Academy.

Arab ['ærəb] *adj, n* árabe *m/f*.

Arabia [ə'reɪbɪə] *n* Arabia.

Arabian [ə'reɪbɪən] *adj* árabe, arábigo.

Arabian Desert *n* Desierto de Arabia.

Arabian Sea *n* Mar *m* de Omán.

Arabic ['ærəbɪk] *adj* (*language, manuscripts*) árabe, arábigo ♦ *n* árabe *m*; **~ numerals** numeración *f* arábiga.

arable ['ærəbl] *adj* cultivable.

Aragon ['ærəgən] *n* Aragón *m*.

ARAM *n abbr* (*BRIT*) = Associate of the Royal Academy of Music.

arbiter ['ɑːbɪtə*] *n* árbitro.

arbitrary ['ɑːbɪtrərɪ] *adj* arbitrario.

arbitrate ['ɑːbɪtreɪt] *vi* arbitrar.

arbitration [ɑːbɪ'treɪʃən] *n* arbitraje *m*; **the dispute went to ~** el conflicto laboral fue sometido al arbitraje.

arbitrator ['ɑːbɪtreɪtə*] *n* árbitro.

ARC *n abbr* = American Red Cross.

arc [ɑːk] *n* arco.

arcade [ɑː'keɪd] *n* (*ARCH*) arcada; (*round a square*) soportales *mpl*; (*shopping ~*) galería comercial.

arch [ɑːtʃ] n arco; (*vault*) bóveda; (*of foot*) empeine m ♦ vt arquear.

archaeological [ɑːkɪəˈlɒdʒɪkl] adj arqueológico.

archaeologist [ɑːkɪˈɔlədʒɪst] n arqueólogo/a.

archaeology [ɑːkɪˈɔlədʒɪ] n arqueología.

archaic [ɑːˈkeɪɪk] adj arcaico.

archangel [ˈɑːkeɪndʒəl] n arcángel m.

archbishop [ɑːtʃˈbɪʃəp] n arzobispo.

arched [ɑːtʃt] adj abovedado.

archenemy [ɑːtʃˈɛnəmɪ] n enemigo jurado.

archeology [ɑːkɪˈɔlədʒɪ] etc (*US*) = **archaeology** etc.

archer [ˈɑːtʃə*] n arquero/a.

archery [ˈɑːtʃərɪ] n tiro al arco.

archetypal [ˈɑːkɪtaɪpəl] adj arquetípico.

archetype [ˈɑːkɪtaɪp] n arquetipo.

archipelago [ɑːkɪˈpɛlɪgəu] n archipiélago.

architect [ˈɑːkɪtɛkt] n arquitecto/a.

architectural [ɑːkɪˈtɛktʃərəl] adj arquitectónico.

architecture [ˈɑːkɪtɛktʃə*] n arquitectura.

archive [ˈɑːkaɪv] n (*often pl: also* COMPUT) archivo.

archive file n (COMPUT) fichero archivado.

archives [ˈɑːkaɪvz] npl archivo sg.

archivist [ˈɑːkɪvɪst] n archivero/a.

archway [ˈɑːtʃweɪ] n arco, arcada.

ARCM n abbr (BRIT) = Associate of the Royal College of Music.

Arctic [ˈɑːktɪk] adj ártico ♦ n: the ~ el Ártico.

Arctic Circle n Círculo Polar Ártico.

Arctic Ocean n Océano (Glacial) Ártico.

ARD n abbr (US MED) = acute respiratory disease.

ardent [ˈɑːdənt] adj (*desire*) ardiente; (*supporter, lover*) apasionado.

ardour, (*US*) **ardor** [ˈɑːdə*] n ardor m, pasión f.

arduous [ˈɑːdjuəs] adj (*gen*) arduo; (*journey*) penoso.

are [ɑː*] vb see **be**.

area [ˈɛərɪə] n área; (MATH etc) superficie f, extensión f; (*zone*) región f, zona; **the London** ~ la zona de Londres.

area code n (US TEL) prefijo.

arena [əˈriːnə] n arena; (*of circus*) pista; (*for bullfight*) plaza, ruedo.

aren't [ɑːnt] = **are not**.

Argentina [ɑːdʒənˈtiːnə] n Argentina.

Argentinian [ɑːdʒənˈtɪnɪən] adj, n argentino/a m/f.

arguable [ˈɑːgjuəbl] adj: **it is ~ whether ...** es dudoso que + subjun.

arguably [ˈɑːgjuəblɪ] adv: **it is ~ ...** es discutiblemente ....

argue [ˈɑːgjuː] vt (*debate: case, matter*) mantener, argüir ♦ vi (*quarrel*) discutir; (*reason*) razonar, argumentar; **to ~ that** sostener que; **to ~ about sth (with sb)** pelearse (con algn) por algo.

argument [ˈɑːgjumənt] n (*reasons*) argumento; (*quarrel*) discusión f; (*debate*) debate m; ~ **for/against** argumento en pro/contra de.

argumentative [ɑːgjuˈmɛntətɪv] adj discutidor(a).

aria [ˈɑːrɪə] n (MUS) aria.

ARIBA n abbr (BRIT) = Associate of the Royal Institute of British Architects.

arid [ˈærɪd] adj árido.

aridity [əˈrɪdɪtɪ] n aridez f.

Aries [ˈɛərɪz] n Aries m.

arise [əˈraɪz], pt **arose**, pp **arisen** [əˈrɪzn] vi (*rise up*) levantarse, alzarse; (*emerge*) surgir, presentarse; **to ~ from** derivar de; **should the need ~** si fuera necesario.

aristocracy [ærɪsˈtɔkrəsɪ] n aristocracia.

aristocrat [ˈærɪstəkræt] n aristócrata m/f.

aristocratic [ərɪstəˈkrætɪk] adj aristocrático.

arithmetic [əˈrɪθmətɪk] n aritmética.

arithmetical [ærɪθˈmɛtɪkl] adj aritmético.

Ariz. abbr (US) = Arizona.

Ark [ɑːk] n: **Noah's ~** el Arca f de Noé.

Ark. abbr (US) = Arkansas.

arm [ɑːm] n (ANAT) brazo ♦ vt armar; ~ **in ~** cogidos del brazo; see also **arms**.

armaments [ˈɑːməmənts] npl (*weapons*) armamentos mpl.

armchair [ˈɑːmtʃɛə*] n sillón m, butaca.

armed [ɑːmd] adj armado; **the ~ forces** las fuerzas armadas.

armed robbery n robo a mano armada.

Armenia [ɑːˈmiːnɪə] n Armenia.

Armenian [ɑːˈmiːnɪən] adj armenio ♦ n armenio/a; (LING) armenio.

armful [ˈɑːmful] n brazada.

armistice [ˈɑːmɪstɪs] n armisticio.

armour, (*US*) **armor** [ˈɑːmə*] n armadura.

armo(u)red car n coche m or carro (LAM) blindado.

armo(u)ry [ˈɑːmərɪ] n arsenal m.

armpit [ˈɑːmpɪt] n sobaco, axila.

armrest [ˈɑːmrɛst] n reposabrazos m inv, brazo.

arms [ɑːmz] npl (*weapons*) armas fpl; (HERALDRY) escudo sg.

arms control n control m de armamentos.

arms race n carrera de armamentos.

army [ˈɑːmɪ] n ejército.

aroma [əˈrəumə] n aroma m, fragancia.

aromatherapy [ərəuməˈθɛrəpɪ] n aromaterapia.

aromatic [ærə'mætɪk] *adj* aromático, fragante.
arose [ə'rəuz] *pt of* **arise**.
around [ə'raund] *adv* alrededor; (*in the area*) a la redonda ♦ *prep* alrededor de.
arousal [ə'rauzəl] *n* (*sexual*) excitación *f*; (*of feelings, interest*) despertar *m*.
arouse [ə'rauz] *vt* despertar.
arrange [ə'reɪndʒ] *vt* arreglar, ordenar; (*programme*) organizar ♦ *vi*: **we have ~d for a taxi to pick you up** hemos organizado todo para que le recoja un taxi; **to ~ to do sth** quedar en hacer algo; **it was ~d that ...** se quedó en que ....
arrangement [ə'reɪndʒmənt] *n* arreglo; (*agreement*) acuerdo; **~s** *npl* (*plans*) planes *mpl*, medidas *fpl*; (*preparations*) preparativos *mpl*; **to come to an ~ (with sb)** llegar a un acuerdo (con algn); **by ~** a convenir; **I'll make ~s for you to be met** haré los preparativos para que le estén esperando.
arrant ['ærənt] *adj*: **~ nonsense** una verdadera tontería.
array [ə'reɪ] *n* (*COMPUT*) matriz *f*; **~ of** (*things*) serie *f* or colección *f* de; (*people*) conjunto de.
arrears [ə'rɪəz] *npl* atrasos *mpl*; **in ~** (*COMM*) en mora; **to be in ~ with one's rent** estar retrasado en el pago del alquiler.
arrest [ə'rɛst] *vt* detener; (*sb's attention*) llamar ♦ *n* detención *f*; **under ~** detenido.
arresting [ə'rɛstɪŋ] *adj* (*fig*) llamativo.
arrival [ə'raɪvəl] *n* llegada, arribo (*LAM*); **new ~** recién llegado/a.
arrive [ə'raɪv] *vi* llegar, arribar (*LAM*).
arrogance ['ærəgəns] *n* arrogancia, prepotencia (*LAM*).
arrogant ['ærəgənt] *adj* arrogante, prepotente (*LAM*).
arrow ['ærəu] *n* flecha.
arse [ɑːs] *n* (*BRIT col!*) culo, trasero.
arsenal ['ɑːsɪnl] *n* arsenal *m*.
arsenic ['ɑːsnɪk] *n* arsénico.
arson ['ɑːsn] *n* incendio provocado.
art [ɑːt] *n* arte *m*; (*skill*) destreza; (*technique*) técnica; **A~s** *npl* (*SCOL*) Letras *fpl*; **work of ~** obra de arte.
artefact ['ɑːtɪfækt] *n* artefacto.
arterial [ɑː'tɪərɪəl] *adj* (*ANAT*) arterial; (*road etc*) principal.
artery ['ɑːtərɪ] *n* (*MED, road etc*) arteria.
artful ['ɑːtful] *adj* (*cunning: person, trick*) mañoso.
art gallery *n* pinacoteca, museo de pintura; (*COMM*) galería de arte.
arthritis [ɑː'θraɪtɪs] *n* artritis *f*.

artichoke ['ɑːtɪtʃəuk] *n* alcachofa; **Jerusalem ~** aguaturma.
article ['ɑːtɪkl] *n* artículo, objeto, cosa; (*in newspaper*) artículo; (*BRIT LAW: training*): **~s** *npl* contrato *sg* de aprendizaje; **~s of clothing** prendas *fpl* de vestir.
articles of association *npl* (*COMM*) estatutos *mpl* sociales, escritura social.
articulate *adj* [ɑː'tɪkjulɪt] (*speech*) claro; (*person*) que se expresa bien ♦ *vi* [ɑː'tɪkjuleɪt] articular.
articulated lorry *n* (*BRIT*) trailer *m*.
artifice ['ɑːtɪfɪs] *n* artificio, truco.
artificial [ɑːtɪ'fɪʃəl] *adj* artificial; (*teeth etc*) postizo.
artificial insemination *n* inseminación *f* artificial.
artificial intelligence (A.I.) *n* inteligencia artificial (I.A.).
artificial respiration *n* respiración *f* artificial.
artillery [ɑː'tɪlərɪ] *n* artillería.
artisan ['ɑːtɪzæn] *n* artesano/a.
artist ['ɑːtɪst] *n* artista *m/f*; (*MUS*) intérprete *m/f*.
artistic [ɑː'tɪstɪk] *adj* artístico.
artistry ['ɑːtɪstrɪ] *n* arte *m*, habilidad *f* (artística).
artless ['ɑːtlɪs] *adj* (*innocent*) natural, sencillo; (*clumsy*) torpe.
art school *n* escuela de bellas artes.
artwork ['ɑːtwɔːk] *n* material *m* gráfico.
arty ['ɑːtɪ] *adj* artistoide.
ARV *n abbr* (= *American Revised Version*) *traducción americana de la Biblia.*
AS *n abbr* (*US UNIV*: = *Associate in/of Science*) *título universitario* ♦ *abbr* (*US*) = *American Samoa.*

━━━━━━━━━━━━━━ *KEYWORD*

as [æz] *conj* **1** (*referring to time: while*) mientras; (: *when*) cuando; **she wept ~ she told her story** lloraba mientras contaba lo que le ocurrió; **~ the years go by** a medida que pasan los años, con el paso de los años; **he came in ~ I was leaving** entró cuando me marchaba; **~ from tomorrow** a partir de *or* desde mañana
2 (*in comparisons*): **~ big ~** tan grande como; **twice ~ big ~** el doble de grande que; **~ much money/many books ~** tanto dinero/tantos libros como; **~ soon ~** en cuanto, no bien (*LAM*)
3 (*since, because*) como, ya que; **~ I don't**

speak German I can't understand him
como no hablo alemán no le entiendo, no
le entiendo ya que no hablo alemán
4 (*although*): **much ~ I like them,** ...
aunque me gustan, ...
5 (*referring to manner, way*): **do ~ you
wish** haz lo que quieras; **~ she said** como
dijo; **he gave it to me ~ a present** me lo
dio de regalo; **it's on the left ~ you go in**
según se entra, a la izquierda
6 (*concerning*): **~ for** *or* **to that** por *or* en
lo que respecta a eso
7: **~ if** *or* **though** como si; **he looked ~ if
he was ill** parecía como si estuviera
enfermo, tenía aspecto de enfermo; *see
also* **long; such; well**
♦ *prep* (*in the capacity of*): **he works ~ a
barman** trabaja de barman; **~ chairman
of the company, he** ... como presidente de
la compañía, ...

ASA *n abbr* (= *American Standards
Association*) *instituto de normalización*;
(*BRIT*: = *Advertising Standards Authority*)
*departamento de control de la
publicidad*; (: = *Amateur Swimming
Association*) *federación amateur de
natación.*
a.s.a.p. *abbr* (= *as soon as possible*) cuanto
antes, lo más pronto posible.
asbestos [æz'bɛstəs] *n* asbesto, amianto.
ascend [ə'sɛnd] *vt* subir, ascender.
ascendancy [ə'sɛndənsɪ] *n* ascendiente *m*,
dominio.
ascendant [ə'sɛndənt] *n*: **to be in the ~**
estar en auge, ir ganando predominio.
Ascension [ə'sɛnʃən] *n*: **the ~** la Ascensión.
Ascension Island *n* Isla Ascensión.
ascent [ə'sɛnt] *n* subida; (*slope*) cuesta,
pendiente *f*; (*of plane*) ascenso.
ascertain [æsə'teɪn] *vt* averiguar.
ascetic [ə'sɛtɪk] *adj* ascético.
asceticism [ə'sɛtɪsɪzəm] *n* ascetismo.
ASCII ['æskiː] *n abbr* (= *American Standard
Code for Information Interchange*) ASCII.
ascribe [ə'skraɪb] *vt*: **to ~ sth to** atribuir
algo a.
ASCU *n abbr* (*US*) = *Association of State
Colleges and Universities.*
ASE *n abbr* = *American Stock Exchange.*
ASH [æʃ] *n abbr* (*BRIT*: = *Action on Smoking
and Health*) *organización anti-tabaco.*
ash [æʃ] *n* ceniza; (*tree*) fresno.
ashamed [ə'ʃeɪmd] *adj* avergonzado; **to be
~ of** avergonzarse de.
ashcan ['æʃkæn] *n* (*US*) cubo *or* bote *m*
(*LAM*) de la basura.
ashen ['æʃn] *adj* pálido.

ashore [ə'ʃɔː*] *adv* en tierra.
ashtray ['æʃtreɪ] *n* cenicero.
Ash Wednesday *n* miércoles *m* de ceniza.
Asia ['eɪʃə] *n* Asia.
Asian ['eɪʃən], **Asiatic** [eɪsɪ'ætɪk] *adj, n*
asiático/a *m/f.*
aside [ə'saɪd] *adv* a un lado ♦ *n* aparte *m*; **~
from** *prep* (*as well as*) aparte or además de.
ask [ɑːsk] *vt* (*question*) preguntar; (*demand*)
pedir; (*invite*) invitar ♦ *vi*: **to ~ about sth**
preguntar acerca de algo; **to ~ sb sth/to
do sth** preguntar algo a algn/pedir a algn
que haga algo; **to ~ sb about sth**
preguntar algo a algn; **to ~ (sb) a
question** hacer una pregunta (a algn); **to
~ sb the time** preguntar la hora a algn;
to ~ sb out to dinner invitar a cenar a
algn.
▸**ask after** *vt fus* preguntar por.
▸**ask for** *vt fus* pedir; **it's just ~ing for
trouble** *or* **for it** es buscarse problemas.
askance [ə'skɑːns] *adv*: **to look ~ at sb**
mirar con recelo a algn.
askew [ə'skjuː] *adv* sesgado, ladeado.
asking price *n* (*COMM*) precio inicial.
asleep [ə'sliːp] *adj* dormido; **to fall ~**
dormirse, quedarse dormido.
ASLEF ['æzlɛf] *n abbr* (*BRIT*: = *Associated
Society of Locomotive Engineers and
Firemen*) *sindicato de ferroviarios.*
asp [æsp] *n* áspid *m.*
asparagus [əs'pærəgəs] *n* espárragos *mpl.*
ASPCA *n abbr* = *American Society for the
Prevention of Cruelty to Animals.*
aspect ['æspɛkt] *n* aspecto, apariencia;
(*direction in which a building etc faces*)
orientación *f.*
aspersions [əs'pəːʃənz] *npl*: **to cast ~ on**
difamar a, calumniar a.
asphalt ['æsfælt] *n* asfalto.
asphyxiate [æs'fɪksɪeɪt] *vt* asfixiar.
asphyxiation [aesfɪksɪ'eɪʃən] *n* asfixia.
aspirate ['æspəreɪt] *vt* aspirar ♦ *adj*
['æspərɪt] aspirado.
aspirations [æspə'reɪʃənz] *npl* aspiraciones
fpl; (*ambition*) ambición *f.*
aspire [əs'paɪə*] *vi*: **to ~ to** aspirar a,
ambicionar.
aspirin ['æsprɪn] *n* aspirina.
aspiring [əs'paɪərɪŋ] *adj*: **an ~ actor** un
aspirante a actor.
ass [æs] *n* asno, burro; (*col*) imbécil *m/f*; (*US
col!*) culo, trasero.
assailant [ə'seɪlənt] *n* agresor(a) *m/f.*
assassin [ə'sæsɪn] *n* asesino/a.
assassinate [ə'sæsɪneɪt] *vt* asesinar.
assassination [əsæsɪ'neɪʃən] *n* asesinato.
assault [ə'sɔːlt] *n* (*gen*: *attack*) asalto,

agresión f ♦ vt asaltar, agredir; (*sexually*) violar.
assemble [ə'sɛmbl] vt reunir, juntar; (*TECH*) montar ♦ vi reunirse, juntarse.
assembler [ə'sɛmblə*] n (*COMPUT*) ensamblador m.
assembly [ə'sɛmblɪ] n (*meeting*) reunión f, asamblea; (*construction*) montaje m.
assembly language n (*COMPUT*) lenguaje m ensamblador.
assembly line n cadena de montaje.
assent [ə'sɛnt] n asentimiento, aprobación f ♦ vi consentir, asentir; **to ~ (to sth)** consentir (en algo).
assert [ə'səːt] vt afirmar; (*insist on*) hacer valer; **to ~ o.s.** imponerse.
assertion [ə'səːʃən] n afirmación f.
assertive [ə'səːtɪv] adj enérgico, agresivo, perentorio.
assess [ə'sɛs] vt valorar, calcular; (*tax, damages*) fijar; (*property etc: for tax*) gravar.
assessment [ə'sɛsmənt] n valoración f; gravamen m; (*judgment*): **~ (of)** juicio (sobre).
assessor [ə'sɛsə*] n asesor(a) m/f; (*of tax*) tasador(a) m/f.
asset ['æsɛt] n posesión f; (*quality*) ventaja; **~s** npl (*funds*) activo sg, fondos mpl.
asset-stripping ['æsɛt'strɪpɪŋ] n (*COMM*) acaparamiento de activos.
assiduous [ə'sɪdjuəs] adj asiduo.
assign [ə'saɪn] vt (*date*) fijar; (*task*) asignar; (*resources*) destinar; (*property*) traspasar.
assignment [ə'saɪnmənt] n asignación f; (*task*) tarea.
assimilate [ə'sɪmɪleɪt] vt asimilar.
assimilation [əsɪmɪ'leɪʃən] n asimilación f.
assist [ə'sɪst] vt ayudar.
assistance [ə'sɪstəns] n ayuda, auxilio.
assistant [ə'sɪstənt] n ayudante m/f; (*BRIT: also: shop ~*) dependiente/a m/f.
assistant manager n subdirector(a) m/f.
assizes [ə'saɪzɪz] npl sesión f de un tribunal.
associate [ə'səuʃɪɪt] adj asociado ♦ n socio/a, colega m/f; (*in crime*) cómplice m/f; (*member*) miembro/a ♦ vb [ə'səuʃɪeɪt] vt asociar; (*ideas*) relacionar ♦ vi: **to ~ with sb** tratar con alguien; **~ director** subdirector/a m/f; **~d company** compañía afiliada.
association [əsəusɪ'eɪʃən] n asociación f; (*COMM*) sociedad f; **in ~ with** en asociación con.
association football n (*BRIT*) fútbol m.
assorted [ə'sɔːtɪd] adj surtido, variado; **in ~ sizes** en distintos tamaños.
assortment [ə'sɔːtmənt] n surtido.

Asst. abbr = **Assistant**.
assuage [ə'sweɪdʒ] vt mitigar.
assume [ə'sjuːm] vt (*suppose*) suponer; (*responsibilities etc*) asumir; (*attitude, name*) adoptar, tomar.
assumed name n nombre m falso.
assumption [ə'sʌmpʃən] n (*supposition*) suposición f, presunción f; (*act*) asunción f; **on the ~ that** suponiendo que.
assurance [ə'ʃuərəns] n garantía, promesa; (*confidence*) confianza, aplomo; (*BRIT: insurance*) seguro; **I can give you no ~s** no puedo hacerle ninguna promesa.
assure [ə'ʃuə*] vt asegurar.
assured [ə'ʃuəd] adj seguro.
assuredly [ə'ʃuərɪdlɪ] adv indudablemente.
AST n abbr (= *Atlantic Standard Time*) hora oficial del este del Canadá.
asterisk ['æstərɪsk] n asterisco.
astern [ə'stəːn] adv a popa.
asteroid ['æstərɔɪd] n asteroide m.
asthma ['æsmə] n asma.
asthmatic [æs'mætɪk] adj, n asmático/a m/f.
astigmatism [ə'stɪgmətɪzəm] n astigmatismo.
astir [ə'stəː*] adv en acción.
astonish [ə'stɔnɪʃ] vt asombrar, pasmar.
astonishing [ə'stɔnɪʃɪŋ] adj asombroso, pasmoso; **I find it ~ that ...** me asombra or pasma que ....
astonishingly [ə'stɔnɪʃɪŋlɪ] adv increíblemente, asombrosamente.
astonishment [ə'stɔnɪʃmənt] n asombro, sorpresa; **to my ~** con gran sorpresa mía.
astound [ə'staund] vt asombrar, pasmar.
astounding [ə'staundɪŋ] adj asombroso.
astray [ə'streɪ] adv: **to go ~** extraviarse; **to lead ~** llevar por mal camino; **to go ~ in one's calculations** equivocarse en sus cálculos.
astride [ə'straɪd] prep a caballo or horcajadas sobre.
astringent [əs'trɪndʒənt] adj, n astringente m.
astrologer [əs'trɔlədʒə*] n astrólogo/a.
astrology [əs'trɔlədʒɪ] n astrología.
astronaut ['æstrənɔːt] n astronauta m/f.
astronomer [əs'trɔnəmə*] n astrónomo/a.
astronomical [æstrə'nɔmɪkəl] adj astronómico.
astronomy [aes'trɔnəmɪ] n astronomía.
astrophysics ['æstrəu'fɪzɪks] n astrofísica.
astute [əs'tjuːt] adj astuto.
asunder [ə'sʌndə*] adv: **to tear ~** hacer pedazos.
ASV n abbr (= *American Standard Version*) traducción americana de la Biblia.

asylum [ə'saɪləm] *n* (*refuge*) asilo; (*hospital*) manicomio; **to seek political** ~ pedir asilo político.
asymmetric(al) [eɪsɪ'mɛtrɪk(l)] *adj* asimétrico.

━━━━━━━━━━━━━━ *KEYWORD*

at [æt] *prep* **1** (*referring to position*) en; (*direction*) a; ~ **the top** en lo alto; ~ **home/school** en casa/la escuela; **to look** ~ **sth/sb** mirar algo/a algn
2 (*referring to time*): ~ **4 o'clock** a las 4; ~ **night** por la noche; ~ **Christmas** en Navidad; ~ **times** a veces
3 (*referring to rates, speed etc*): ~ **£1 a kilo** a una libra el kilo; **two** ~ **a time** de dos en dos; ~ **50 km/h** a 50 km/h
4 (*referring to manner*): ~ **a stroke** de un golpe; ~ **peace** en paz
5 (*referring to activity*): **to be** ~ **work** estar trabajando; (*in the office etc*) estar en el trabajo; **to play** ~ **cowboys** jugar a los vaqueros; **to be good** ~ **sth** ser bueno en algo
6 (*referring to cause*): **shocked/surprised/annoyed** ~ **sth** asombrado/sorprendido/fastidiado por algo; **I went** ~ **his suggestion** fui a instancias suyas.

━━━━━━━━━━━━━━

ate [ɛt, eɪt] *pt of* eat.
atheism ['eɪθɪɪzəm] *n* ateísmo.
atheist ['eɪθɪɪst] *n* ateo/a.
Athenian [ə'θiːnɪən] *adj, n* ateniense *m/f*.
Athens ['æθɪnz] *n* Atenas *f*.
athlete ['æθliːt] *n* atleta *m/f*.
athletic [æθ'lɛtɪk] *adj* atlético.
athletics [æθ'lɛtɪks] *n* atletismo.
Atlantic [ət'læntɪk] *adj* atlántico ♦ *n*: **the** ~ **(Ocean)** el (Océano) Atlántico.
atlas ['ætləs] *n* atlas *m*.
Atlas Mountains *npl*: **the** ~ el Atlas.
A.T.M. *n abbr* (= *Automated Telling Machine*) cajero automático.
atmosphere ['ætməsfɪə*] *n* (*air*) atmósfera; (*fig*) ambiente *m*.
atom ['ætəm] *n* átomo.
atomic [ə'tɒmɪk] *adj* atómico.
atom(ic) bomb *n* bomba atómica.
atomic power *n* energía atómica.
atomizer ['ætəmaɪzə*] *n* atomizador *m*.
atone [ə'təun] *vi*: **to** ~ **for** expiar.
atonement [ə'təunmənt] *n* expiación *f*.
A to Z ® *n* guía alfabética; (*map*) callejero.
ATP *n abbr* (= *Association of Tennis Professionals*) sindicato de jugadores de tenis profesionales.
atrocious [ə'trəuʃəs] *adj* atroz; (*fig*) horrible, infame.

atrocity [ə'trɒsɪtɪ] *n* atrocidad *f*.
atrophy ['ætrəfɪ] *n* atrofia ♦ *vi* atrofiarse.
attach [ə'tætʃ] *vt* sujetar; (*stick*) pegar; (*document, letter*) adjuntar; **to be** ~**ed to sb/sth** (*to like*) tener cariño a algn/algo; **the** ~**ed letter** la carta adjunta.
attaché [ə'tæʃeɪ] *n* agregado/a.
attaché case *n* (*BRIT*) maletín *m*.
attachment [ə'tætʃmənt] *n* (*tool*) accesorio; (*love*): ~ **(to)** apego (a), cariño (a).
attack [ə'tæk] *vt* (*MIL*) atacar; (*criminal*) agredir, asaltar; (*task etc*) emprender ♦ *n* ataque *m*, asalto; (*on sb's life*) atentado; **heart** ~ infarto (de miocardio).
attacker [ə'tækə*] *n* agresor(a) *m/f*, asaltante *m/f*.
attain [ə'teɪn] *vt* (*also*: ~ **to**) alcanzar; (*achieve*) lograr, conseguir.
attainments [ə'teɪnmənts] *npl* (*skill*) talento *sg*.
attempt [ə'tɛmpt] *n* tentativa, intento; (*attack*) atentado ♦ *vt* intentar, tratar de; **he made no** ~ **to help** ni siquiera intentó ayudar.
attempted [ə'tɛmptɪd] *adj*: ~ **murder/burglary/suicide** tentativa *or* intento de asesinato/robo/suicidio.
attend [ə'tɛnd] *vt* asistir a; (*patient*) atender.
▶**attend to** *vt fus* (*needs, affairs etc*) ocuparse de; (*speech etc*) prestar atención a; (*customer*) atender a.
attendance [ə'tɛndəns] *n* asistencia, presencia; (*people present*) concurrencia.
attendant [ə'tɛndənt] *n* sirviente/a *m/f*, mozo/a; (*THEAT*) acomodador(a) *m/f* ♦ *adj* concomitante.
attention [ə'tɛnʃən] *n* atención *f* ♦ *excl* (*MIL*) ¡firme(s)!; **for the** ~ **of...** (*ADMIN*) a la atención de...; **it has come to my** ~ **that ...** me he enterado de que ....
attentive [ə'tɛntɪv] *adj* atento; (*polite*) cortés.
attenuate [ə'tɛnjueɪt] *vt* atenuar.
attest [ə'tɛst] *vi*: **to** ~ **to** dar fe de.
attic ['ætɪk] *n* desván *m*, altillo (*LAM*), entretecho (*LAM*).
attitude ['ætɪtjuːd] *n* (*gen*) actitud *f*; (*disposition*) disposición *f*.
attorney [ə'təːnɪ] *n* (*US: lawyer*) abogado/a; (*having proxy*) apoderado.
Attorney General *n* (*BRIT*) ≈ Presidente *m* del Consejo del Poder Judicial (*SP*); (*US*) ≈ ministro de justicia.
attract [ə'trækt] *vt* atraer; (*attention*) llamar.
attraction [ə'trækʃən] *n* (*gen*) encanto, atractivo; (*PHYSICS, towards sth*)

atracción f.

attractive [ə'træktɪv] adj atractivo.

attribute ['ætrɪbjuːt] n atributo ♦ vt [ə'trɪbjuːt]: **to ~ sth to** atribuir algo a; (accuse) achacar algo a.

attrition [ə'trɪʃən] n: **war of ~** guerra de agotamiento or desgaste.

Atty. Gen. abbr = **Attorney General.**

ATV n abbr (= all terrain vehicle) vehículo todo terreno.

atypical [eɪ'tɪpɪkl] adj atípico.

aubergine ['əʊbəʒiːn] n (BRIT) berenjena.

auburn ['ɔːbən] adj color castaño rojizo.

auction ['ɔːkʃən] n (also: **sale by ~**) subasta ♦ vt subastar.

auctioneer [ɔːkʃə'nɪə*] n subastador(a) m/f.

auction room n sala de subastas.

audacious [ɔː'deɪʃəs] adj (bold) audaz, osado; (impudent) atrevido, descarado.

audacity [ɔː'dæsɪtɪ] n audacia, atrevimiento; (pej) descaro.

audible ['ɔːdɪbl] adj audible, que se puede oír.

audience ['ɔːdɪəns] n auditorio; (gathering) público; (interview) audiencia.

audio-typist ['ɔːdɪəʊ'taɪpɪst] n mecanógrafo/a de dictáfono.

audiovisual [ɔːdɪəʊ'vɪzjʊəl] adj audiovisual.

audiovisual aid n ayuda or medio audiovisual.

audit ['ɔːdɪt] vt revisar, intervenir.

audition [ɔː'dɪʃən] n audición f ♦ vi: **to ~ for the part of** hacer una audición para el papel de.

auditor ['ɔːdɪtə*] n interventor(a) m/f, censor(a) m/f de cuentas.

auditorium [ɔːdɪ'tɔːrɪəm] n auditorio.

Aug. abbr (= August) ag.

augment [ɔːg'mɛnt] vt, vi aumentar.

augur ['ɔːgə*] vi: **it ~s well** es de buen agüero.

August ['ɔːgəst] n agosto.

august [ɔː'gʌst] adj augusto.

aunt [ɑːnt] n tía.

auntie, aunty ['ɑːntɪ] n diminutive of **aunt.**

au pair ['əʊ'pɛə*] n (also: **~ girl**) au pair f.

aura ['ɔːrə] n aura; (atmosphere) ambiente m.

auspices ['ɔːspɪsɪz] npl: **under the ~ of** bajo los auspicios de.

auspicious [ɔːs'pɪʃəs] adj propicio, de buen augurio.

austere [ɔs'tɪə*] adj austero; (manner) adusto.

austerity [ɔ'stɛrɪtɪ] n austeridad f.

Australasia [ɔːstrə'leɪzɪə] n Australasia.

Australia [ɔs'treɪlɪə] n Australia.

Australian [ɔs'treɪlɪən] adj, n australiano/a

m/f.

Austria ['ɔstrɪə] n Austria.

Austrian ['ɔstrɪən] adj, n austríaco/a m/f.

AUT n abbr (BRIT: = Association of University Teachers) sindicato de profesores de universidad.

authentic [ɔː'θɛntɪk] adj auténtico.

authenticate [ɔː'θɛntɪkeɪt] vt autentificar.

authenticity [ɔːθɛn'tɪsɪtɪ] n autenticidad f.

author ['ɔːθə*] n autor(a) m/f.

authoritarian [ɔːθɔrɪ'tɛərɪən] adj autoritario.

authoritative [ɔː'θɔrɪtətɪv] adj autorizado; (manner) autoritario.

authority [ɔː'θɔrɪtɪ] n autoridad f; **the authorities** npl las autoridades; **to have ~ to do sth** tener autoridad para hacer algo.

authorization [ɔːθəraɪ'zeɪʃən] n autorización f.

authorize ['ɔːθəraɪz] vt autorizar.

authorized capital n (COMM) capital m autorizado or social.

autistic [ɔː'tɪstɪk] adj autista.

auto ['ɔːtəʊ] n (US) coche m, carro (LAM), auto (LAM), automóvil m.

autobiographical [ɔːtəbaɪə'græfɪkəl] adj autobiográfico.

autobiography [ɔːtəbaɪ'ɔgrəfɪ] n autobiografía.

autocratic [ɔːtə'krætɪk] adj autocrático.

Autocue ® ['ɔːtəʊkjuː] n autocue m, teleapuntador m.

autograph ['ɔːtəgrɑːf] n autógrafo ♦ vt firmar; (photo etc) dedicar.

autoimmune [ɔːtəʊɪ'mjuːn] adj autoinmune.

automat ['ɔːtəmæt] n (US) restaurante m de autoservicio.

automate ['ɔːtəmeɪt] vt automatizar.

automated ['ɔːtəmeɪtɪd] adj automatizado.

automatic [ɔːtə'mætɪk] adj automático ♦ n (gun) pistola automática; (washing machine) lavadora.

automatically [ɔːtə'mætɪklɪ] adv automáticamente.

automatic data processing (ADP) n proceso automático de datos.

automation [ɔːtə'meɪʃən] n automatización f.

automaton, pl **automata** [ɔː'tɔmətən, -tə] n autómata.

automobile ['ɔːtəməbiːl] n (US) coche m, carro (LAM), automóvil m.

autonomous [ɔː'tɔnəməs] adj autónomo.

autonomy [ɔː'tɔnəmɪ] n autonomía.

autopsy ['ɔːtɔpsɪ] n autopsia.

autumn ['ɔːtəm] n otoño.

auxiliary [ɔːg'zɪlɪərɪ] adj auxiliar.

AV *n abbr* (= *Authorized Version*) traducción inglesa de la Biblia ♦ *abbr* = **audiovisual**.

Av. *abbr* (= *avenue*) Av., Avda.

avail [ə'veɪl] *vt*: **to ~ o.s. of** aprovechar(se) de, valerse de ♦ *n*: **to no ~** en vano, sin resultado.

availability [əveɪlə'bɪlɪtɪ] *n* disponibilidad *f*.

available [ə'veɪləbl] *adj* disponible; (*obtainable*) asequible; **to make sth ~ to sb** poner algo a la disposición de algn; **is the manager ~?** ¿está libre el gerente?

avalanche ['ævəlɑːnʃ] *n* alud *m*, avalancha.

avant-garde ['ævɑ̃ŋ'gɑːd] *adj* de vanguardia.

avarice ['ævərɪs] *n* avaricia.

avaricious [ævə'rɪʃəs] *adj* avaricioso.

avdp. *abbr* = *avoirdupois*.

Ave. *abbr* (= *avenue*) Av., Avda.

avenge [ə'vɛndʒ] *vt* vengar.

avenue ['ævənjuː] *n* avenida; (*fig*) camino, vía.

average ['ævərɪdʒ] *n* promedio, media ♦ *adj* (*mean*) medio; (*ordinary*) regular, corriente ♦ *vt* calcular el promedio de; **on ~** por término medio.

▶**average out** *vi*: **to ~ out at** salir a un promedio de.

averse [ə'vɜːs] *adj*: **to be ~ to sth/doing** sentir aversión *or* antipatía por algo/por hacer.

aversion [ə'vɜːʃən] *n* aversión *f*, repugnancia.

avert [ə'vɜːt] *vt* prevenir; (*blow*) desviar; (*one's eyes*) apartar.

aviary ['eɪvɪərɪ] *n* pajarera.

aviation [eɪvɪ'eɪʃən] *n* aviación *f*.

aviator ['eɪvɪeɪtə*] *n* aviador(a) *m/f*.

avid ['ævɪd] *adj* ávido, ansioso.

avidly ['ævɪdlɪ] *adv* ávidamente, con avidez.

avocado [ævə'kɑːdəu] *n* (*also*: *Brit*: **~ pear**) aguacate *m*, palta (*LAM*).

avoid [ə'vɔɪd] *vt* evitar, eludir.

avoidable [ə'vɔɪdəbl] *adj* evitable, eludible.

avoidance [ə'vɔɪdəns] *n* evasión *f*.

avow [ə'vau] *vt* prometer.

avowal [ə'vauəl] *n* promesa, voto.

avowed [ə'vaud] *adj* declarado.

AVP *n abbr* (*US*) = *assistant vice-president*.

avuncular [ə'vʌŋkjulə*] *adj* paternal.

AWACS ['eɪwæks] *n abbr* (= *airborne warning and control system*) AWACS *m*.

await [ə'weɪt] *vt* esperar, aguardar; **long ~ed** largamente esperado.

awake [ə'weɪk] *adj* despierto ♦ (*vb*: *pt* **awoke**, *pp* **awoken** *or* **awaked**) *vt* despertar ♦ *vi* despertarse; **to be ~** estar despierto.

awakening [ə'weɪknɪŋ] *n* despertar *m*.

award [ə'wɔːd] *n* (*prize*) premio; (*medal*) condecoración *f*; (*LAW*) fallo, sentencia; (*act*) concesión *f* ♦ *vt* (*prize*) otorgar, conceder; (*LAW*: *damages*) adjudicar.

aware [ə'wɛə*] *adj* consciente; (*awake*) despierto; (*informed*) enterado; **to become ~ of** darse cuenta de, enterarse de; **I am fully ~ that** sé muy bien que.

awareness [ə'wɛənɪs] *n* conciencia, conocimiento.

awash [ə'wɔʃ] *adj* inundado.

away [ə'weɪ] *adv* (*gen*) fuera; (*far ~*) lejos; **two kilometres ~** a dos kilómetros (de distancia); **two hours ~ by car** a dos horas en coche; **the holiday was two weeks ~** faltaban dos semanas para las vacaciones; **~ from** lejos de, fuera de; **he's ~ for a week** estará ausente una semana; **he's ~ in Barcelona** está en Barcelona; **to take ~** llevar(se); **to work/pedal ~** seguir trabajando/pedaleando; **to fade ~** desvanecerse; (*sound*) apagarse.

away game *n* (*SPORT*) partido de fuera.

awe [ɔː] *n* respeto, temor *m* reverencial.

awe-inspiring ['ɔːɪnspaɪərɪŋ], **awesome** ['ɔːsəm] *adj* imponente, pasmoso.

awestruck ['ɔːstrʌk] *adj* pasmado.

awful ['ɔːfʊl] *adj* terrible; **an ~ lot of** (*people, cars, dogs*) la mar de, muchísimos.

awfully ['ɔːfəlɪ] *adv* (*very*) terriblemente.

awhile [ə'waɪl] *adv* (durante) un rato, algún tiempo.

awkward ['ɔːkwəd] *adj* (*clumsy*) desmañado, torpe; (*shape, situation*) incómodo; (*difficult*: *question*) difícil; (*problem*) complicado.

awkwardness ['ɔːkwədnɪs] *n* (*clumsiness*) torpeza; (*of situation*) incomodidad *f*.

awl [ɔːl] *n* lezna, subilla.

awning ['ɔːnɪŋ] *n* (*of shop*) toldo; (*of window etc*) marquesina.

awoke [ə'wəuk], **awoken** [ə'wəukən] *pt*, *pp of* **awake**.

AWOL ['eɪwɔl] *abbr* (*MIL*) *see* **absent without leave**.

awry [ə'raɪ] *adv*: **to be ~** estar descolocado *or* atravesado; **to go ~** salir mal, fracasar.

axe, (*US*) **ax** [æks] *n* hacha ♦ *vt* (*employee*) despedir; (*project etc*) cortar; (*jobs*) reducir; **to have an ~ to grind** (*fig*) tener un interés creado *or* algún fin interesado.

axes ['æksiːz] *npl of* **axis**.

axiom ['æksɪəm] *n* axioma *m*.

axiomatic [æksɪə'mætɪk] *adj* axiomático.

axis, *pl* **axes** ['æksɪs, -siːz] *n* eje *m*.

axle ['æksl] n eje m, árbol m.
ay(e) [aɪ] excl (yes) sí; **the ayes** npl los que votan a favor.
AYH n abbr = American Youth Hostels.
AZ abbr (US) = Arizona.
azalea [ə'zeɪlɪə] n azalea.
Azerbaijan [æzəbaɪ'dʒɑːn] n Azerbaiyán m.
Azerbaijani [æzəbaɪ'dʒɑːni], **Azeri** [ə'zɛəri] adj, n azerbaiyano/a, azerí m/f.
Azores [ə'zɔːz] npl: **the ~** las (Islas) Azores.
AZT n abbr (= azidothymidine) AZT m.
Aztec ['æztɛk] adj, n azteca m/f.
azure ['eɪʒə*] adj celeste.

B b

B, b [biː] n (letter) B, b f; (SCOL: mark) N; (MUS) si m; **B for Benjamin**, (US) **B for Baker** B de Barcelona; **B road** (BRIT AUT) ≈ carretera secundaria.
b. abbr = born.
BA n abbr = British Academy; (SCOL) = Bachelor of Arts; see also **Bachelor's Degree**.
babble ['bæbl] vi farfullar.
babe [beɪb] n criatura.
baboon [bə'buːn] n mandril m.
baby ['beɪbɪ] n bebé m/f.
baby carriage n (US) cochecito.
babyish ['beɪbɪɪʃ] adj infantil.
baby-minder ['beɪbɪ'maɪndə*] n niñera f (cualificada).
baby-sit ['beɪbɪsɪt] vi hacer de canguro.
baby-sitter ['beɪbɪsɪtə*] n canguro m/f.
bachelor ['bætʃələ*] n soltero; **B~ of Arts/ Science (BA/BSc)** licenciado/a en Filosofía y Letras/Ciencias.

Se denomina **Bachelor's Degree** a la titulación que se recibe al finalizar el primer ciclo universitario, normalmente después de un período de estudio de tres o cuatro años. Las titulaciones más frecuentes son las de Letras, **BA (Bachelor of Arts)**, Ciencias, **BSc (Bachelor of Science)**, Educación, **BEd (Bachelor of Education)** y Derecho, **LLB (Bachelor of Laws)**.

back [bæk] n (of person) espalda; (of animal) lomo; (of hand, page) dorso; (as opposed to front) parte f de atrás; (of room) fondo; (of chair) respaldo; (FOOTBALL) defensa m; **to have one's ~ to the wall** (fig) estar entre la espada y la pared; **to break the ~ of a job** hacer lo más difícil de un trabajo; **~ to front** al revés; **at the ~ of my mind was the thought that ...** en el fondo tenía la idea de que ... ♦ vt (candidate: also: ~ **up**) respaldar, apoyar; (horse: at races) apostar a; (car) dar marcha atrás a or con ♦ vi (car etc) dar marcha atrás ♦ adj (in compounds) de atrás; **~ seats/wheels** (AUT) asientos mpl/ruedas fpl traseros/as; **~ garden/room** jardín m/habitación f de atrás; **~ payments** pagos mpl con efecto retroactivo; **~ rent** renta atrasada; **to take a ~ seat** (fig) pasar a segundo plano ♦ adv (not forward) (hacia) atrás; **he's ~** (returned) ha vuelto; **he ran ~** volvió corriendo; **throw the ball ~** (restitution) devuelve la pelota; **can I have it ~?** ¿me lo devuelve?; **he called ~** (again) volvió a llamar; **~ and forth** de acá para allá; **as far ~ as the 13th century** ya en el siglo XIII; **when will you be ~?** ¿cuándo volverá?
▸**back down** vi echarse atrás.
▸**back on to** vt fus: **the house ~s on to the golf course** por atrás la casa da al campo de golf.
▸**back out** vi (of promise) volverse atrás.
▸**back up** vt (support: person) apoyar, respaldar; (: theory) defender; (car) dar marcha atrás a; (COMPUT) hacer una copia de reserva de.
backache ['bækeɪk] n dolor m de espalda.
backbencher ['bæk'bɛntʃə*] n (BRIT) see **backbenches**.

Reciben el nombre genérico de **the backbenches** los escaños más alejados del pasillo central en la Cámara de los Comunes del Parlamento británico, que son ocupados por los **backbenchers**, los miembros de la cámara que no tienen cargo en el gobierno o en la oposición.

backbiting ['bækbaɪtɪŋ] n murmuración f.
backbone ['bækbəun] n columna vertebral; **the ~ of the organization** el pilar de la organización.
backchat ['bæktʃæt] n réplicas fpl.
backcloth ['bækklɔθ] n telón m de fondo.
backcomb ['bækkəum] vt cardar.
backdate [bæk'deɪt] vt (letter) poner fecha atrasada a; **~d pay rise** aumento de sueldo con efecto retroactivo.
backdrop ['bækdrɔp] n = **backcloth**.
backer ['bækə*] n partidario/a; (COMM)

promotor(a) *m/f*.
backfire [bæk'faɪə*] *vi* (*AUT*) petardear;
(*plans*) fallar, salir mal.
backgammon ['bækgæmən] *n*
backgammon *m*.
background ['bækgraund] *n* fondo; (*of
events*) antecedentes *mpl*; (*basic
knowledge*) bases *fpl*; (*experience*)
conocimientos *mpl*, educación *f* ♦ *cpd*
(*noise, music*) de fondo; (*COMPUT*)
secundario; ~ **reading** lectura de
preparación; **family ~** origen *m*,
antecedentes *mpl* familiares.
backhand ['bækhænd] *n* (*TENNIS: also*: ~
stroke) revés *m*.
backhanded ['bæk'hændɪd] *adj* (*fig*)
ambiguo, equívoco.
backhander ['bæk'hændə*] *n* (*BRIT: bribe*)
soborno.
backing ['bækɪŋ] *n* (*fig*) apoyo, respaldo;
(*COMM*) respaldo financiero; (*MUS*)
acompañamiento.
backlash ['bæklæʃ] *n* reacción *f* (en contra).
backlog ['bæklɔg] *n*: ~ **of work** trabajo
atrasado.
back number *n* (*of magazine etc*) número
atrasado.
backpack ['bækpæk] *n* mochila.
backpacker ['bækpækə*] *n* mochilero/a.
back pay *n* atrasos *mpl*.
backpedal ['bækpɛdl] *vi* (*fig*) volverse/
echarse atrás.
backseat driver ['bæksiːt-] *n* pasajero que
se empeña en aconsejar al conductor.
backside ['bæksaɪd] *n* (*col*) trasero.
backslash ['bækslæʃ] *n* pleca, barra
inversa.
backslide ['bækslaɪd] *vi* reincidir, recaer.
backspace ['bækspeɪs] *vi* (*in typing*)
retroceder.
backstage [bæk'steɪdʒ] *adv* entre
bastidores.
back-street ['bækstriːt] *adj* de barrio; ~
abortionist persona que practica abortos
clandestinos.
backstroke ['bækstrəuk] *n* espalda.
backtrack ['bæktræk] *vi* (*fig*) = **backpedal**.
backup ['bækʌp] *adj* (*train, plane*)
suplementario; (*COMPUT: disk, file*) de
reserva ♦ *n* (*support*) apoyo; (*also*: ~ **file**)
copia de reserva; (*US: congestion*)
embotellamiento, retención *f*.
back-up lights *npl* (*US*) luces *fpl* de marcha
atrás.
backward ['bækwəd] *adj* (*movement*) hacia
atrás; (*person, country*) atrasado; (*shy*)
tímido.
backwardness ['bækwədnɪs] *n* atraso.

backwards ['bækwədz] *adv* (*move, go*)
hacia atrás; (*read a list*) al revés; (*fall*) de
espaldas; **to know sth ~ or** (*US*) ~ **and
forwards** (*col*) saberse algo al dedillo.
backwater ['bækwɔːtə*] *n* (*fig*) lugar *m*
atrasado *or* apartado.
backyard [bæk'jɑːd] *n* patio trasero.
bacon ['beɪkən] *n* tocino, bacon *m*, beicon
m.
bacteria [bæk'tɪərɪə] *npl* bacterias *fpl*.
bacteriology [bæktɪərɪ'ɔlədʒɪ] *n*
bacteriología.
bad [bæd] *adj* malo; (*serious*) grave; (*meat,
food*) podrido, pasado; **to go ~** pasarse;
to have a ~ time of it pasarlo mal; **I feel ~
about it** (*guilty*) me siento culpable; ~
debt (*COMM*) cuenta incobrable; **in ~ faith**
de mala fe.
baddie, baddy ['bædɪ] *n* (*col: CINE etc*)
malo/a.
bade [bæd, beɪd] *pt of* **bid**.
badge [bædʒ] *n* insignia; (*metal* ~) chapa;
(*of policeman*) placa; (*stick-on*) pegatina.
badger ['bædʒə*] *n* tejón *m*.
badly ['bædlɪ] *adv* (*work, dress etc*) mal; ~
wounded gravemente herido; **he needs it
~** le hace mucha falta; **to be ~ off (for
money)** andar mal de dinero; **things are
going ~** las cosas van muy mal.
bad-mannered ['bæd'mænəd] *adj* mal
educado.
badminton ['bædmɪntən] *n* bádminton *m*.
bad-tempered ['bæd'tɛmpəd] *adj* de mal
genio *or* carácter; (*temporary*) de mal
humor.
baffle ['bæfl] *vt* desconcertar, confundir.
baffling ['bæflɪŋ] *adj* incomprensible.
bag [bæg] *n* bolsa; (*handbag*) bolso; (*satchel*)
mochila; (*case*) maleta; (*of hunter*) caza
♦ *vt* (*col: take*) coger (*SP*), agarrar (*LAM*),
pescar; **~s of** (*col: lots of*) un montón de;
to pack one's ~s hacer las maletas.
bagful ['bægful] *n* saco (lleno).
baggage ['bægɪdʒ] *n* equipaje *m*.
baggage claim *n* recogida de equipajes.
baggy ['bægɪ] *adj* (*trousers*) ancho, holgado.
Baghdad [bæg'dæd] *n* Bagdad *m*.
bag lady *n* (*col*) *mujer sin hogar cargada
de bolsas*.
bagpipes ['bægpaɪps] *npl* gaita *sg*.
bag-snatcher ['bægsnætʃə*] *n* (*BRIT*)
ladrón/ona *m/f* de bolsos.
bag-snatching ['bægsnætʃɪŋ] *n* (*BRIT*) tirón
m (de bolsos).
Bahamas [bə'hɑːməz] *npl*: **the ~** las (Islas)
Bahama.
Bahrain [bɑː'reɪn] *n* Bahrein *m*.
bail [beɪl] *n* fianza ♦ *vt* (*prisoner: also*: **grant**

~ **to)** poner en libertad bajo fianza; (*boat:
also*: ~ **out)** achicar; **on** ~ (*prisoner*) bajo
fianza; **to be released on** ~ ser puesto en
libertad bajo fianza; **to** ~ **sb out** pagar la
fianza de algn; *see also* **bale**.

bailiff ['beɪlɪf] *n* alguacil *m*.

bait [beɪt] *n* cebo ♦ *vt* poner el cebo en.

bake [beɪk] *vt* cocer (al horno) ♦ *vi* (*cook*)
cocerse; (*be hot*) hacer un calor terrible.

baked beans *npl* judías *fpl* en salsa de
tomate.

baker ['beɪkə*] *n* panadero/a.

baker's dozen *n* docena del fraile.

bakery ['beɪkərɪ] *n* (*for bread*) panadería;
(*for cakes*) pastelería.

baking ['beɪkɪŋ] *n* (*act*) cocción *f*; (*batch*)
hornada.

baking powder *n* levadura (en polvo).

baking tin *n* molde *m* (para horno).

balaclava [bælə'klɑːvə] *n* (*also*: ~ **helmet**)
pasamontañas *m inv*.

balance ['bæləns] *n* equilibrio; (*COMM: sum*)
balance *m*; (*remainder*) resto; (*scales*)
balanza ♦ *vt* equilibrar; (*budget*) nivelar;
(*account*) saldar; (*compensate*)
compensar; ~ **of trade/payments** balanza
de comercio/pagos; ~ **carried forward**
balance *m* pasado a cuenta nueva; ~
brought forward saldo de hoja anterior;
to ~ **the books** hacer el balance.

balanced ['bælənst] *adj* (*personality, diet*)
equilibrado.

balance sheet *n* balance *m*.

balcony ['bælkənɪ] *n* (*open*) balcón *m*;
(*closed*) galería.

bald [bɔːld] *adj* calvo; (*tyre*) liso.

baldness ['bɔːldnɪs] *n* calvicie *f*.

bale [beɪl] *n* (*AGR*) paca, fardo.

▶**bale out** *vi* (*of a plane*) lanzarse en
paracaídas ♦ *vt* (*NAUT*) achicar; **to** ~ **sb
out of a difficulty** sacar a algn de un
apuro.

Balearic Islands [bælɪ'ærɪk-] *npl*: **the** ~ las
(Islas) Baleares.

baleful ['beɪlful] *adj* (*look*) triste; (*sinister*)
funesto, siniestro.

balk [bɔːk] *vi*: **to** ~ **(at)** resistirse (a);
(*horse*) plantarse (ante).

Balkan ['bɔːlkən] *adj* balcánico ♦ *n*: **the** ~**s**
los Balcanes.

ball [bɔːl] *n* (*sphere*) bola; (*football*) balón *m*;
(*for tennis, golf etc*) pelota; (*dance*) baile *m*;
to be on the ~ (*fig: competent*) ser un
enterado; (: *alert*) estar al tanto; **to play** ~
(with sb) jugar a la pelota (con algn); (*fig*)
cooperar; **to start the** ~ **rolling** (*fig*)
empezar; **the** ~ **is in your court** (*fig*) le
toca a usted.

ballad ['bæləd] *n* balada, romance *m*.

ballast ['bæləst] *n* lastre *m*.

ball bearing *n* cojinete *m* de bolas.

ballcock ['bɔːlkɔk] *n* llave *f* de bola *or* de
flotador.

ballerina [bælə'riːnə] *n* bailarina.

ballet ['bæleɪ] *n* ballet *m*.

ballet dancer *n* bailarín/ina *m/f* (de ballet).

ballistic [bə'lɪstɪk] *adj* balístico;
intercontinental ~ **missile** misil *m*
balístico intercontinental.

ballistics [bə'lɪstɪks] *n* balística.

balloon [bə'luːn] *n* globo; (*in comic strip*)
bocadillo ♦ *vi* dispararse.

balloonist [bə'luːnɪst] *n* aeróstata *m/f*.

ballot ['bælət] *n* votación *f*.

ballot box *n* urna (electoral).

ballot paper *n* papeleta.

ballpark ['bɔːlpɑːk] *n* (*US*) estadio de
béisbol.

ball-point pen ['bɔːlpɔɪnt-] *n* bolígrafo.

ballroom ['bɔːlrum] *n* salón *m* de baile.

balm [bɑːm] *n* (*also fig*) bálsamo.

balmy ['bɑːmɪ] *adj* (*breeze, air*) suave; (*col*)
= **barmy**.

BALPA ['bælpə] *n abbr* (= *British Airline
Pilots' Association*) *sindicato de pilotos de
líneas aéreas*.

balsa (wood) ['bɔːlsə-] *n* (madera de)
balsa.

Baltic ['bɔːltɪk] *adj* báltico ♦ *n*: **the** ~ **(Sea)** el
(Mar) Báltico.

balustrade ['bæləstreɪd] *n* barandilla.

bamboo [bæm'buː] *n* bambú *m*.

bamboozle [bæm'buːzl] *vt* (*col*) embaucar,
engatusar.

ban [bæn] *n* prohibición *f* ♦ *vt* prohibir;
(*exclude*) excluir; **he was** ~**ned from
driving** le retiraron el carnet de
conducir.

banal [bə'nɑːl] *adj* banal, vulgar.

banana [bə'nɑːnə] *n* plátano, banana (*LAM*).

band [bænd] *n* (*group*) banda; (*gang*)
pandilla; (*strip*) faja, tira; (*at a dance*)
orquesta; (*MIL*) banda; (*rock* ~) grupo.

▶**band together** *vi* juntarse, asociarse.

bandage ['bændɪdʒ] *n* venda, vendaje *m* ♦ *vt*
vendar.

Band-Aid ® ['bændeɪd] *n* (*US*) tirita, curita
(*LAM*).

bandit ['bændɪt] *n* bandido; **one-armed** ~
máquina tragaperras.

bandstand ['bændstænd] *n* quiosco de
música.

bandwagon ['bændwægən] *n*: **to jump on
the** ~ (*fig*) subirse al carro.

bandy ['bændɪ] *vt* (*jokes, insults*)
intercambiar.

bandy-legged ['bændɪ'lɛgd] *adj* patizambo.
bane [beɪn] *n*: **it** (*or* **he** *etc*) **is the ~ of my life** me amarga la vida.
bang [bæŋ] *n* estallido; (*of door*) portazo; (*blow*) golpe *m* ♦ *vt* golpear ♦ *vi* estallar ♦ *adv*: **to be ~ on time** (*col*) llegar en punto; **to ~ the door** dar un portazo; **to ~ into sth** chocar con algo, golpearse contra algo; *see also* **bangs**.
banger ['bæŋə*] *n* (*BRIT*: *car*: *also*: **old ~**) armatoste *m*, cacharro; (*BRIT col*: *sausage*) salchicha; (*firework*) petardo.
Bangkok [bæŋ'kɔk] *n* Bangkok *m*.
Bangladesh [bæŋglə'dɛʃ] *n* Bangladesh *f*.
bangle ['bæŋgl] *n* brazalete *m*, ajorca.
bangs [bæŋz] *npl* (*US*) flequillo *sg*.
banish ['bænɪʃ] *vt* desterrar.
banister(s) ['bænɪstə(z)] *n*(*pl*) barandilla *f*, pasamanos *m inv*.
banjo, *pl* ~**es** *or* ~**s** ['bændʒəu] *n* banjo.
bank [bæŋk] *n* (*COMM*) banco; (*of river, lake*) ribera, orilla; (*of earth*) terraplén *m* ♦ *vi* (*AVIAT*) ladearse; (*COMM*): **to ~ with** tener la cuenta en.
▶**bank on** *vt fus* contar con.
bank account *n* cuenta bancaria.
bank balance *n* saldo.
bank card *n* = **banker's card**.
bank charges *npl* comisión *fsg*.
bank draft *n* letra de cambio.
banker ['bæŋkə*] *n* banquero; ~**'s card** (*BRIT*) tarjeta bancaria; ~**'s order** orden *f* bancaria.
bank giro *n* giro bancario.
bank holiday *n* (*BRIT*) día *m* festivo *or* de fiesta.

El término **bank holiday** *se aplica en el Reino Unido a todo día festivo oficial en el que cierran bancos y comercios. Los más destacados coinciden con Navidad, Semana Santa, finales de mayo y finales de agosto. Al contrario que en los países de tradición católica, no se celebran las festividades dedicadas a los santos.*

---

banking ['bæŋkɪŋ] *n* banca.
bank loan *n* préstamo bancario.
bank manager *n* director(a) *m/f* (de sucursal) de banco.
banknote ['bæŋknəut] *n* billete *m* de banco.
bank rate *n* tipo de interés bancario.
bankrupt ['bæŋkrʌpt] *n* quebrado/a ♦ *adj* quebrado, insolvente; **to go ~** quebrar, hacer bancarrota; **to be ~** estar en quiebra.
bankruptcy ['bæŋkrʌptsɪ] *n* quiebra, bancarrota.

bank statement *n* extracto de cuenta.
banner ['bænə*] *n* bandera; (*in demonstration*) pancarta.
banns [bænz] *npl* amonestaciones *fpl*.
banquet ['bæŋkwɪt] *n* banquete *m*.
banter ['bæntə*] *n* guasa, bromas *fpl*.
BAOR *n abbr* (= *British Army of the Rhine*) fuerzas británicas en Alemania.
baptism ['bæptɪzəm] *n* bautismo; (*act*) bautizo.
baptize [bæp'taɪz] *vt* bautizar.
bar [bɑ:*] *n* barra; (*on door*) tranca; (*of window, cage*) reja; (*of soap*) pastilla; (*fig: hindrance*) obstáculo; (*prohibition*) prohibición *f*; (*pub*) bar *m*, cantina (*esp LAM*); (*counter: in pub*) barra, mostrador *m*; (*MUS*) barra ♦ *vt* (*road*) obstruir; (*window, door*) atrancar; (*person*) excluir; (*activity*) prohibir; **behind ~s** entre rejas; **the B~** (*LAW: profession*) la abogacía; (: *people*) el cuerpo de abogados; ~ **none** sin excepción.
Barbados [bɑ:'beɪdɔs] *n* Barbados *m*.
barbarian [bɑ:'bɛərɪən] *n* bárbaro/a.
barbaric [bɑ:'bærɪk] *adj* bárbaro.
barbarity [bɑ:'bærɪtɪ] *n* barbaridad *f*.
barbarous ['bɑ:bərəs] *adj* bárbaro.
barbecue ['bɑ:bɪkju:] *n* barbacoa, asado (*LAM*).
barbed wire ['bɑ:bd-] *n* alambre *m* de espino.
barber ['bɑ:bə*] *n* peluquero, barbero.
barbiturate [bɑ:'bɪtjurɪt] *n* barbitúrico.
Barcelona [bɑ:sɪ'ləunə] *n* Barcelona.
bar chart *n* gráfico de barras.
bar code *n* código de barras.
bare [bɛə*] *adj* desnudo; (*head*) descubierto ♦ *vt* desnudar; **to ~ one's teeth** enseñar los dientes.
bareback ['bɛəbæk] *adv* a pelo.
barefaced ['bɛəfeɪst] *adj* descarado.
barefoot ['bɛəfut] *adj*, *adv* descalzo.
bareheaded [bɛə'hɛdɪd] *adj* descubierto, sin sombrero.
barely ['bɛəlɪ] *adv* apenas.
bareness ['bɛənɪs] *n* desnudez *f*.
Barents Sea ['bærənts-] *n*: **the ~** el Mar de Barents.
bargain ['bɑ:gɪn] *n* pacto; (*transaction*) negocio; (*good buy*) ganga ♦ *vi* negociar; (*haggle*) regatear; **into the ~** además, por añadidura.
▶**bargain for** *vt fus* (*col*): **he got more than he ~ed for** le resultó peor de lo que esperaba.
bargaining ['bɑ:gənɪŋ] *n* negociación *f*; regateo; ~ **table** mesa de negociaciones.
bargaining position *n*: **to be in a strong/**

weak ~ estar/no estar en una posición de fuerza para negociar.

barge [bɑːdʒ] *n* barcaza.

►**barge in** *vi* irrumpir; (*conversation*) entrometerse.

►**barge into** *vt fus* dar contra.

baritone ['bærɪtəun] *n* barítono.

barium meal ['bɛərɪəm-] *n* (*MED*) sulfato de bario.

bark [bɑːk] *n* (*of tree*) corteza; (*of dog*) ladrido ♦ *vi* ladrar.

barley ['bɑːlɪ] *n* cebada.

barley sugar *n* azúcar *m* cande.

barmaid ['bɑːmeɪd] *n* camarera.

barman ['bɑːmən] *n* camarero, barman *m*.

barmy ['bɑːmɪ] *adj* (*col*) chiflado, chalado.

barn [bɑːn] *n* granero; (*for animals*) cuadra.

barnacle ['bɑːnəkl] *n* percebe *m*.

barn owl *n* lechuza.

barometer [bə'rɔmɪtə*] *n* barómetro.

baron ['bærən] *n* barón *m*; (*fig*) magnate *m*; **the press** ~**s** los magnates de la prensa.

baroness ['bærənɪs] *n* baronesa.

baroque [bə'rɔk] *adj* barroco.

barrack ['bærək] *vt* (*BRIT*) abuchear.

barracking ['bærəkɪŋ] *n*: **to give sb a** ~ (*BRIT*) abuchear a algn.

barracks ['bærəks] *npl* cuartel *msg*.

barrage ['bærɑːʒ] *n* (*MIL*) cortina de fuego; (*dam*) presa; (*fig: of criticism etc*) lluvia, aluvión *m*; **a** ~ **of questions** una lluvia de preguntas.

barrel ['bærəl] *n* barril *m*; (*of wine*) tonel *m*, cuba; (*of gun*) cañón *m*.

barren ['bærən] *adj* estéril.

barricade [bærɪ'keɪd] *n* barricada ♦ *vt* cerrar con barricadas.

barrier ['bærɪə*] *n* barrera; (*crash* ~) barrera.

barrier cream *n* crema protectora.

barring ['bɑːrɪŋ] *prep* excepto, salvo.

barrister ['bærɪstə*] *n* (*BRIT*) abogado/a.

En el sistema legal inglés **barrister** es el abogado que se ocupa de defender los casos de sus clientes en los tribunales superiores. El equivalente escocés es **advocate**. Normalmente actúan según instrucciones de un **solicitor**, abogado de despacho que no toma parte activa en los juicios de dichos tribunales. El título de **barrister** lo otorga el órgano colegiado correspondiente, **the Inns of Court**.

barrow ['bærəu] *n* (*cart*) carretilla.

barstool ['bɑːstuːl] *n* taburete *m* (de bar).

Bart. *abbr* (*BRIT*) = baronet.

bartender ['bɑːtɛndə*] *n* (*US*) camarero, barman *m*.

barter ['bɑːtə*] *vt*: **to** ~ **sth for sth** trocar algo por algo.

base [beɪs] *n* base *f* ♦ *vt*: **to** ~ **sth on** basar or fundar algo en ♦ *adj* bajo, infame; **to** ~ **at** (*troops*) estacionar en; **I'm** ~**d in London** (*work*) trabajo en Londres.

baseball ['beɪsbɔːl] *n* béisbol *m*.

base camp *n* campamento base.

Basel ['bɑːzəl] *n* Basilea.

baseless ['beɪslɪs] *adj* infundado.

baseline ['beɪslaɪn] *n* (*TENNIS*) línea de fondo.

basement ['beɪsmənt] *n* sótano.

base rate *n* tipo base.

bases ['beɪsiːz] *npl of* **basis**; ['beɪsɪz] *npl of* **base**.

bash [bæʃ] *n*: **I'll have a** ~ (**at it**) lo intentaré ♦ *vt* (*col*) golpear.

►**bash up** *vt* (*col: car*) destrozar; (: *person*) aporrear, vapulear.

bashful ['bæʃful] *adj* tímido, vergonzoso.

bashing ['bæʃɪŋ] *n* (*col*) paliza; **to go Paki-/queer-**~ ir a dar una paliza a los paquistaníes/a los maricas.

BASIC ['beɪsɪk] *n* BASIC *m*.

basic ['beɪsɪk] *adj* (*salary etc*) básico; (*elementary: principles*) fundamental.

basically ['beɪsɪklɪ] *adv* fundamentalmente, en el fondo.

basic rate *n* (*of tax*) base *f* mínima imponible.

basil ['bæzl] *n* albahaca.

basin ['beɪsn] *n* (*vessel*) cuenco, tazón *m*; (*GEO*) cuenca; (*also:* **wash**~) palangana, jofaina; (*in bathroom*) lavabo.

basis ['beɪsɪs], *pl* **-ses** [-siːz] *n* base *f*; **on the** ~ **of what you've said** en base a lo que has dicho.

bask [bɑːsk] *vi*: **to** ~ **in the sun** tomar el sol.

basket ['bɑːskɪt] *n* cesta, cesto.

basketball ['bɑːskɪtbɔːl] *n* baloncesto.

basketball player *n* jugador(a) *m/f* de baloncesto.

basketwork ['bɑːskɪtwəːk] *n* cestería.

Basle [bɑːl] *n* Basilea.

basmati rice [bəz'mætɪ-] *n* arroz *m* basmati.

Basque [bæsk] *adj*, *n* vasco/a *m/f*.

Basque Country *n* Euskadi *m*, País *m* Vasco.

bass [beɪs] *n* (*MUS*) bajo.

bass clef *n* clave *f* de fa.

bassoon [bə'suːn] *n* fagot *m*.

bastard ['bɑːstəd] *n* bastardo/a; (*col!*) cabrón *m*, hijo de puta (*!*).

baste [beɪst] *vt* (*CULIN*) rociar (con su salsa).

bastion ['bæstɪən] *n* bastión *m*, baluarte *m*.

bat [bæt] *n* (*ZOOL*) murciélago; (*for ball games*) palo; (*for cricket, baseball*) bate *m*; (*BRIT: for table tennis*) pala; **he didn't ~ an eyelid** ni pestañeó, ni se inmutó.

batch [bætʃ] *n* lote *m*, remesa; (*of bread*) hornada.

batch processing *n* (*COMPUT*) proceso por lotes.

bated ['beɪtɪd] *adj*: **with ~ breath** sin respirar.

bath [bɑːθ, *pl* bɑːðz] *n* (*action*) baño; (*~tub*) bañera, tina (*esp LAM*) ♦ *vt* bañar; **to have a ~** bañarse, darse un baño; *see also* **baths**.

bathchair ['bɑːθtʃeə*] *n* silla de ruedas.

bathe [beɪð] *vi* bañarse; (*US*) darse un baño, bañarse ♦ *vt* (*wound etc*) lavar; (*US*) bañar, dar un baño a.

bather ['beɪðə*] *n* bañista *m/f*.

bathing ['beɪðɪŋ] *n* baño.

bathing cap *n* gorro de baño.

bathing costume, (*US*) **bathing suit** *n* bañador *m*, traje *m* de baño.

bathing trunks *npl* bañador *msg*.

bathmat ['bɑːθmæt] *n* alfombrilla de baño.

bathrobe ['bɑːθrəub] *n* albornoz *m*.

bathroom ['bɑːθrum] *n* (cuarto de) baño.

baths [bɑːðz] *npl* piscina *sg*.

bath towel *n* toalla de baño.

bathtub ['bɑːθtʌb] *n* bañera.

batman ['bætmən] *n* (*BRIT*) ordenanza *m*.

baton ['bætən] *n* (*MUS*) batuta.

battalion [bə'tælɪən] *n* batallón *m*.

batten ['bætn] *n* (*CARPENTRY*) listón *m*; (*NAUT*) junquillo, sable *m*.

▶**batten down** *vt* (*NAUT*): **to ~ down the hatches** atrancar las escotillas.

batter ['bætə*] *vt* maltratar, apalear; (*subj: wind, rain*) azotar ♦ *n* batido.

battered ['bætəd] *adj* (*hat, pan*) estropeado.

battery ['bætərɪ] *n* batería; (*of torch*) pila.

battery charger *n* cargador *m* de baterías.

battery farming *n* cría intensiva.

battle ['bætl] *n* batalla; (*fig*) lucha ♦ *vi* luchar; **that's half the ~** (*col*) ya hay medio camino andado; **to fight a losing ~** (*fig*) luchar por una causa perdida.

battlefield ['bætlfiːld] *n* campo *m* de batalla.

battlements ['bætlmənts] *npl* almenas *fpl*.

battleship ['bætlʃɪp] *n* acorazado.

batty ['bætɪ] *adj* (*col: person*) chiflado; (: *idea*) de chiflado.

bauble ['bɔːbl] *n* chuchería.

baud [bɔːd] *n* (*COMPUT*) baudio.

baud rate *n* (*COMPUT*) velocidad *f* (de transmisión) en baudios.

bauxite ['bɔːksaɪt] *n* bauxita.

Bavaria [bə'veərɪə] *n* Baviera.

Bavarian [bə'veərɪən] *adj*, *n* bávaro/a *m/f*.

bawdy ['bɔːdɪ] *adj* indecente; (*joke*) verde.

bawl [bɔːl] *vi* chillar, gritar.

bay [beɪ] *n* (*GEO*) bahía; (*for parking*) parking *m*, estacionamiento; (*loading ~*) patio de carga; (*BOT*) laurel *m* ♦ *vi* aullar; **to hold sb at ~** mantener a alguien a raya.

bay leaf *n* (hoja de) laurel *m*.

bayonet ['beɪənɪt] *n* bayoneta.

bay window *n* ventana saledizа.

bazaar [bə'zɑː*] *n* bazar *m*.

bazooka [bə'zuːkə] *n* bazuca.

BB *n abbr* (*BRIT*: = *Boys' Brigade*) organización juvenil para chicos.

B. & B. *n abbr* = **bed and breakfast**.

BBB *n abbr* (*US*: = *Better Business Bureau*) *organismo para la defensa del consumidor.*

BBC *n abbr* (= *British Broadcasting Corporation*) BBC *f*.

---

*La **BBC** es el organismo público británico de radio y televisión, autónomo en cuanto a su política de programas pero regulado por un estatuto (**BBC charter**) que ha de aprobar el Parlamento. Tiene dos cadenas nacionales de televisión (**BBC1** y **BBC2**) y un servicio mundial (**World Service TV**), así como cinco cadenas de radio nacional, numerosas de radio local y una mundial (**World Service**), en varios idiomas. A no tener publicidad, se financia a través de operaciones comerciales paralelas y del cobro de una licencia anual obligatoria (**TV licence**) para los que tienen aparato de televisión.*

BC *ad abbr* (= *before Christ*) a. de J.C. ♦ *abbr* (*Canada*) = *British Columbia*.

BCG *n abbr* (= *Bacillus Calmette-Guérin*) *vacuna de la tuberculosis.*

BD *n abbr* (= *Bachelor of Divinity*) *Licenciado/a en Teología.*

B/D *abbr* = **bank draft**.

BDS *n abbr* (= *Bachelor of Dental Surgery*) *título universitario.*

=============================== *KEYWORD*

be [biː] (*pt* **was, were**, *pp* **been**) *aux vb* **1** (*with present participle: forming continuous tenses*): **what are you doing?** ¿qué estás haciendo?, ¿qué haces?; **they're coming tomorrow** vienen mañana; **I've been waiting for you for hours** llevo horas esperándote

2 (*with pp: forming passives*) ser (*but often*

replaced by active or reflexive constructions); **to ~ murdered** ser asesinado; **the box had been opened** habían abierto la caja; **the thief was nowhere to ~ seen** no se veía al ladrón por ninguna parte **3** (*in tag questions*): **it was fun, wasn't it?** fue divertido, ¿no? *or* ¿verdad?; **he's good-looking, isn't he?** es guapo, ¿no te parece?; **she's back again, is she?** entonces, ¿ha vuelto? **4** (*+to +infin*): **the house is to ~ sold** (*necessity*) hay que vender la casa; (*future*) van a vender la casa; **he's not to open it** no tiene que abrirlo; **he was to have come yesterday** debía de haber venido ayer; **am I to understand that ...?** ¿debo entender que ...?

♦ *vb +complement* **1** (*with n or num complement*) ser; **he's a doctor** es médico; **2 and 2 are 4** 2 y 2 son 4 **2** (*with adj complement*: *expressing permanent or inherent quality*) ser; (: *expressing state seen as temporary or reversible*) estar; **I'm English** soy inglés/esa; **she's tall/pretty** es alta/bonita; **he's young** es joven; **~ careful/good/quiet** ten cuidado/pórtate bien/cállate; **I'm tired** estoy cansado/a; **I'm warm** tengo calor; **it's dirty** está sucio/a **3** (*of health*) estar; **how are you?** ¿cómo estás?; **he's very ill** está muy enfermo; **I'm better now** ya estoy mejor **4** (*of age*) tener; **how old are you?** ¿cuántos años tienes?; **I'm sixteen (years old)** tengo dieciséis años **5** (*cost*) costar; **how much was the meal?** ¿cuánto fue *or* costó la comida?; **that'll ~ £5.75, please** son £5.75, por favor; **this shirt is £17** esta camisa cuesta £17

♦ *vi* **1** (*exist, occur etc*) existir, haber; **the best singer that ever was** el mejor cantante que existió jamás; **is there a God?** ¿hay un Dios?, ¿existe Dios?; **~ that as it may** sea como sea; **so ~ it** así sea **2** (*referring to place*) estar; **I won't ~ here tomorrow** no estaré aquí mañana **3** (*referring to movement*): **where have you been?** ¿dónde has estado?

♦ *impers vb* **1** (*referring to time*): **it's 5 o'clock** son las 5; **it's the 28th of April** estamos a 28 de abril **2** (*referring to distance*): **it's 10 km to the village** el pueblo está a 10 km **3** (*referring to the weather*): **it's too hot/cold** hace demasiado calor/frío; **it's windy today** hace viento hoy

4 (*emphatic*): **it's me** soy yo; **it was Maria who paid the bill** fue María la que pagó la cuenta.

B/E *abbr* = **bill of exchange.**
beach [biːtʃ] *n* playa ♦ *vt* varar.
beach buggy [-bʌgɪ] *n* buggy *m*.
beachcomber ['biːtʃkəumə*] *n* raquero/a.
beachwear ['biːtʃwɛə*] *n* ropa de playa.
beacon ['biːkən] *n* (*lighthouse*) faro; (*marker*) guía; (*radio ~*) radiofaro.
bead [biːd] *n* cuenta, abalorio; (*of dew, sweat*) gota; **~s** *npl* (*necklace*) collar *m*.
beady ['biːdɪ] *adj* (*eyes*) pequeño y brillante.
beagle ['biːgl] *n* sabueso pequeño, beagle *m*.
beak [biːk] *n* pico.
beaker ['biːkə*] *n* vaso.
beam [biːm] *n* (*ARCH*) viga; (*of light*) rayo, haz *m* de luz; (*RADIO*) rayo ♦ *vi* brillar; (*smile*) sonreír; **to drive on full** *or* **main ~** conducir con las luces largas.
beaming ['biːmɪŋ] *adj* (*sun, smile*) radiante.
bean [biːn] *n* judía, fríjol/frijol *m* (*esp LAM*); **runner/broad ~** habichuela/haba; **coffee ~** grano de café.
beanpole ['biːnpəul] *n* (*col*) espárrago.
beansprouts ['biːnsprauts] *npl* brotes *mpl* de soja.
bear [bɛə*] *n* oso; (*STOCK EXCHANGE*) bajista *m* ♦ (*vb: pt* **bore**, *pp* **borne**) *vt* (*weight etc*) llevar; (*cost*) pagar; (*responsibility*) tener; (*traces, signs*) mostrar; (*produce: fruit*) dar; (*COMM: interest*) devengar; (*endure*) soportar, aguantar; (*stand up to*) resistir a; (*children*) tener, dar a luz ♦ *vi*: **to ~ right/left** torcer a la derecha/izquierda; **I can't ~ him** no le puedo ver, no lo soporto; **to bring pressure to ~ on sb** ejercer presión sobre algn.
▶**bear on** *vt fus* tener que ver con, referirse a.
▶**bear out** *vt fus* (*suspicions*) corroborar, confirmar; (*person*) confirmar lo dicho por.
▶**bear up** *vi* (*cheer up*) animarse; **he bore up well under the strain** resistió bien la presión.
▶**bear with** *vt fus* (*sb's moods, temper*) tener paciencia con.
bearable ['bɛərəbl] *adj* soportable, aguantable.
beard [bɪəd] *n* barba.
bearded ['bɪədɪd] *adj* con barba.
bearer ['bɛərə*] *n* (*of news, cheque*) portador(a) *m/f*; (*of passport*) titular *m/f*.
bearing ['bɛərɪŋ] *n* porte *m*; (*connection*)

relación *f*; **(ball)** ~s *npl* cojinetes *mpl* a bolas; **to take a** ~ marcarse; **to find one's** ~**s** orientarse.

bearskin ['bɛəskɪn] *n* (*MIL*) gorro militar (*de piel de oso*).

beast [biːst] *n* bestia; (*col*) bruto, salvaje *m*.

beastly ['biːstlɪ] *adj* bestial; (*awful*) horrible.

beat [biːt] *n* (*of heart*) latido; (*MUS*) ritmo, compás *m*; (*of policeman*) ronda ♦ (*vb: pt* **beat**, *pp* **beaten**) *vt* (*hit*) golpear; (*eggs*) batir; (*defeat*) vencer, derrotar; (*better*) sobrepasar; (*drum*) tocar; (*rhythm*) marcar ♦ *vi* (*heart*) latir; **off the** ~**en track** aislado; **to** ~ **about the bush** andarse con rodeos; **to** ~ **it** largarse; **that** ~**s everything!** (*col*) ¡eso es el colmo!; **to** ~ **on a door** dar golpes en una puerta.

▶**beat down** *vt* (*door*) derribar a golpes; (*price*) conseguir rebajar, regatear; (*seller*) hacer rebajar el precio ♦ *vi* (*rain*) llover a cántaros; (*sun*) caer de plomo.

▶**beat off** *vt* rechazar.

▶**beat up** *vt* (*col*: *person*) dar una paliza a.

beater ['biːtə*] *n* (*for eggs, cream*) batidora.

beating ['biːtɪŋ] *n* paliza, golpiza (*LAM*); **to take a** ~ recibir una paliza.

beat-up ['biːt'ʌp] *adj* (*col*) destartalado.

beautiful ['bjuːtɪful] *adj* hermoso, bello, lindo (*esp LAM*).

beautifully ['bjuːtɪfəlɪ] *adv* de maravilla.

beautify ['bjuːtɪfaɪ] *vt* embellecer.

beauty ['bjuːtɪ] *n* belleza, hermosura; (*concept, person*) belleza; **the** ~ **of it is that ...** lo mejor de esto es que ....

beauty contest *n* concurso de belleza.

beauty queen *n* reina de la belleza.

beauty salon *n* salón *m* de belleza.

beauty sleep *n*: **to get one's** ~ *no perder horas de sueño.*

beauty spot *n* lunar *m* postizo; (*BRIT: TOURISM*) lugar *m* pintoresco.

beaver ['biːvə*] *n* castor *m*.

becalmed [bɪ'kɑːmd] *adj* encalmado.

became [bɪ'keɪm] *pt of* **become**.

because [bɪ'kɔz] *conj* porque; ~ **of** *prep* debido a, a causa de.

beck [bɛk] *n*: **to be at the** ~ **and call of** estar a disposición de.

beckon ['bɛkən] *vt* (*also:* ~ **to**) llamar con señas.

become [bɪ'kʌm] (*irreg: like* **come**) *vi* (+ *noun*) hacerse, llegar a ser; (+ *adj*) ponerse, volverse ♦ *vt* (*suit*) favorecer, sentar bien a; **to** ~ **fat** engordar; **to** ~ **angry** enfadarse; **it became known that ...** se descubrió que ....

becoming [bɪ'kʌmɪŋ] *adj* (*behaviour*)

decoroso; (*clothes*) favorecedor(a).

becquerel [bɛkə'rɛl] *n* becquerelio.

BECTU *n abbr* (*BRIT*) = *Broadcasting Entertainment Cinematographic and Theatre Union*.

BEd *n abbr* (= *Bachelor of Education*) título universitario; *see also* **Bachelor's Degree**.

bed [bɛd] *n* cama; (*of flowers*) macizo; (*of sea, lake*) fondo; (*of coal, clay*) capa; **to go to** ~ acostarse.

▶**bed down** *vi* acostarse.

bed and breakfast (B & B) *n* ≈ pensión *f*.

Se llama **Bed and Breakfast** *a la casa de hospedaje particular, o granja si es en el campo, que ofrece cama y desayuno a tarifas inferiores a las de un hotel. El servicio se suele anunciar con carteles colocados en las ventanas del establecimiento, en el jardín o en la carretera y en ellos aparece a menudo únicamente el símbolo* **B & B**.

---

bedbug ['bɛdbʌg] *n* chinche *f*.

bedclothes ['bɛdkləuðz] *npl* ropa de cama.

bedding ['bɛdɪŋ] *n* ropa de cama.

bedeck [bɪ'dɛk] *vt* engalanar, adornar.

bedevil [bɪ'dɛvl] *vt* (*dog*) acosar; (*trouble*) fastidiar.

bedfellow ['bɛdfɛləu] *n*: **they are strange** ~**s** (*fig*) hacen una pareja rara.

bedlam ['bɛdləm] *n* confusión *f*.

bedpan ['bɛdpæn] *n* cuña.

bedraggled [bɪ'drægld] *adj* desastrado.

bedridden ['bɛdrɪdn] *adj* postrado (en cama).

bedrock ['bɛdrɔk] *n* (*GEO*) roca firme; (*fig*) pilar *m*.

bedroom ['bɛdrum] *n* dormitorio, alcoba.

Beds *abbr* (*BRIT*) = *Bedfordshire*.

bed settee *n* sofá-cama *m*.

bedside ['bɛdsaɪd] *n*: **at sb's** ~ a la cabecera de alguien.

bedside lamp *n* lámpara de noche.

bedsit(ter) ['bɛdsɪt(ə*)] *n* (*BRIT*) estudio.

bedspread ['bɛdsprɛd] *n* cubrecama *m*, colcha.

bedtime ['bɛdtaɪm] *n* hora de acostarse; **it's** ~ es hora de acostarse *or* de irse a la cama.

bee [biː] *n* abeja; **to have a** ~ **in one's bonnet (about sth)** tener una idea fija (de algo).

beech [biːtʃ] *n* haya.

beef [biːf] *n* carne *f* de vaca; **roast** ~ rosbif *m*.

▶**beef up** *vt* (*col*) reforzar.

beefburger ['biːfbəːgə*] *n* hamburguesa.

beefeater ['biːfiːtə*] n alabardero de la Torre de Londres.

beehive ['biːhaɪv] n colmena.

bee-keeping ['biːkiːpɪŋ] n apicultura.

beeline ['biːlaɪn] n: **to make a ~ for** ir derecho a.

been [biːn] pp of **be**.

beep [biːp] n pitido ♦ vi pitar.

beeper ['biːpə*] n (of doctor etc) busca m inv.

beer [bɪə*] n cerveza.

beer belly n (col) barriga (de bebedor de cerveza).

beer can n bote m or lata de cerveza.

beet [biːt] n (US) remolacha.

beetle ['biːtl] n escarabajo.

beetroot ['biːtruːt] n (BRIT) remolacha.

befall [bɪ'fɔːl] vi (vt) (irreg: like **fall**) acontecer (a).

befit [bɪ'fɪt] vt convenir a, corresponder a.

before [bɪ'fɔː*] prep (of time) antes de; (of space) delante de ♦ conj antes (de) que ♦ adv (time) antes; (space) delante, adelante; **~ going** antes de marcharse; **~ she goes** antes de que se vaya; **the week ~** la semana anterior; **I've never seen it ~** no lo he visto nunca.

beforehand [bɪ'fɔːhænd] adv de antemano, con anticipación.

befriend [bɪ'frɛnd] vt ofrecer amistad a.

befuddled [bɪ'fʌdld] adj aturdido, atontado.

beg [bɛg] vi pedir limosna, mendigar ♦ vt pedir, rogar; (entreat) suplicar; **I ~ your pardon** (apologising) perdóneme; (not hearing) ¿perdón?

began [bɪ'gæn] pt of **begin**.

beggar ['bɛgə*] n mendigo/a.

begin, pt **began**, pp **begun** [bɪ'gɪn, -gæn, -gʌn] vt, vi empezar, comenzar; **to ~ doing** or **to do sth** empezar a hacer algo; **I can't ~ to thank you** no encuentro palabras para agradecerle; **to ~ with, I'd like to know ...** en primer lugar, quisiera saber ...; **~ning from Monday** a partir del lunes.

beginner [bɪ'gɪnə*] n principiante m/f.

beginning [bɪ'gɪnɪŋ] n principio, comienzo; **right from the ~** desde el principio.

begrudge [bɪ'grʌdʒ] vt: **to ~ sb sth** tenerle envidia a alguien por algo.

beguile [bɪ'gaɪl] vt (enchant) seducir.

beguiling [bɪ'gaɪlɪŋ] adj seductor(a), atractivo.

begun [bɪ'gʌn] pp of **begin**.

behalf [bɪ'hɑːf] n: **on ~ of**, (US) **in ~ of** en nombre de; (for benefit of) por.

behave [bɪ'heɪv] vi (person) portarse, comportarse; (thing) funcionar; (well: also: ~ **o.s.**) portarse bien.

behaviour, (US) **behavior** [bɪ'heɪvjə*] n comportamiento, conducta.

behead [bɪ'hɛd] vt decapitar.

beheld [bɪ'hɛld] pt, pp of **behold**.

behind [bɪ'haɪnd] prep detrás de ♦ adv detrás, por detrás, atrás ♦ n trasero; **to be ~ (schedule)** ir retrasado; **~ the scenes** (fig) entre bastidores; **we're ~ them in technology** (fig) nos dejan atrás en tecnología; **to leave sth ~** olvidar or dejarse algo; **to be ~ with sth** estar atrasado en algo; **to be ~ with payments (on sth)** estar atrasado en el pago (de algo).

behold [bɪ'həʊld] (irreg: like **hold**) vt contemplar.

beige [beɪʒ] adj (color) beige.

being ['biːɪŋ] n ser m; **to come into ~** nacer, aparecer.

Beirut [beɪ'ruːt] n Beirut m.

Belarus [bɛlə'rus] n Bielorrusia.

Belarussian [bɛlə'rʌʃən] adj, n bielorruso/a ♦ n (LING) bielorruso.

belated [bɪ'leɪtɪd] adj atrasado, tardío.

belch [bɛltʃ] vi eructar ♦ vt (also: ~ **out**: smoke etc) vomitar, arrojar.

beleaguered [bɪ'liːgəd] adj asediado.

Belfast ['bɛlfɑːst] n Belfast m.

belfry ['bɛlfrɪ] n campanario.

Belgian ['bɛldʒən] adj, n belga m/f.

Belgium ['bɛldʒəm] n Bélgica.

Belgrade [bɛl'greɪd] n Belgrado.

belie [bɪ'laɪ] vt (give false impression of) desmentir, contradecir.

belief [bɪ'liːf] n (opinion) opinión f; (trust, faith) fe f; (acceptance as true) creencia; **it's beyond ~** es increíble; **in the ~ that** creyendo que.

believable [bɪ'liːvəbl] adj creíble.

believe [bɪ'liːv] vt, vi creer; **to ~ (that)** creer (que); **to ~ in** (God, ghosts) creer en; (method) ser partidario de; **he is ~d to be abroad** se cree que está en el extranjero; **I don't ~ in corporal punishment** no soy partidario del castigo corporal.

believer [bɪ'liːvə*] n (in idea, activity) partidario/a; (REL) creyente m/f, fiel m/f.

belittle [bɪ'lɪtl] vt despreciar.

Belize [bɛ'liːz] n Belice f.

bell [bɛl] n campana; (small) campanilla; (on door) timbre m; (animal's) cencerro; (on toy etc) cascabel m; **that rings a ~** (fig) eso me suena.

bellboy ['bɛlbɔɪ] n, (US) **bellhop** ['bɛlhɒp] n botones m inv.

belligerent [bɪ'lɪdʒərənt] adj (at war) beligerante; (fig) agresivo.

bellow ['bɛləu] *vi* bramar; (*person*) rugir
♦ *vt* (*orders*) gritar.
bellows ['bɛləuz] *npl* fuelle *msg*.
bell push *n* pulsador *m* de timbre.
belly ['bɛlɪ] *n* barriga, panza.
bellyache ['bɛlɪeɪk] *n* dolor *m* de barriga *or*
de tripa ♦ *vi* (*col*) gruñir.
bellyful ['bɛlɪful] *n*: **to have had a ~ of ...**
(*col*) estar más que harto de ....
belong [bɪ'lɔŋ] *vi*: **to ~ to** pertenecer a;
(*club etc*) ser socio de; **this book ~s here**
este libro va aquí.
belongings [bɪ'lɔŋɪŋz] *npl*: **personal ~**
pertenencias *fpl*.
Belorussia [bɛləu'rʌʃə] *n* Bielorrusia.
Belorussian [bɛləu'rʌʃən] *adj, n* =
Belarussian.
beloved [bɪ'lʌvɪd] *adj, n* querido/a *m/f*,
amado/a *m/f*.
below [bɪ'ləu] *prep* bajo, debajo de ♦ *adv*
abajo, (por) debajo; **see ~** véase más
abajo.
belt [bɛlt] *n* cinturón *m*; (*TECH*) correa,
cinta ♦ *vt* (*thrash*) golpear con correa;
industrial ~ cinturón industrial.
►**belt out** *vt* (*song*) cantar a voz en grito *or*
a grito pelado.
►**belt up** *vi* (*AUT*) ponerse el cinturón de
seguridad; (*fig, col*) cerrar el pico.
beltway ['bɛltweɪ] *n* (*US AUT*) carretera de
circunvalación.
bemoan [bɪ'məun] *vt* lamentar.
bemused [bɪ'mju:zd] *adj* perplejo.
bench [bɛntʃ] *n* banco; **the B~** (*LAW*) el
tribunal; (*people*) la judicatura.
bench mark *n* punto de referencia.
bend [bɛnd] *vb* (*pt, pp* **bent** [bɛnt]) *vt* doblar;
(*body, head*) inclinar ♦ *vi* inclinarse; (*road*)
curvarse ♦ *n* (*BRIT: in road, river*) recodo;
(*in pipe*) codo; *see also* **bends.**
►**bend down** *vi* inclinarse, doblarse.
►**bend over** *vi* inclinarse.
bends [bɛndz] *npl* (*MED*) *apoplejía por*
cambios bruscos de presión.
beneath [bɪ'ni:θ] *prep* bajo, debajo de;
(*unworthy of*) indigno de ♦ *adv* abajo, (por)
debajo.
benefactor ['bɛnɪfæktə*] *n* bienhechor *m*.
benefactress ['bɛnɪfæktrɪs] *n* bienhechora.
beneficial [bɛnɪ'fɪʃəl] *adj*: **~ to** beneficioso
para.
beneficiary [bɛnɪ'fɪʃərɪ] *n* (*LAW*)
beneficiario/a.
benefit ['bɛnɪfɪt] *n* beneficio, provecho;
(*allowance of money*) subsidio ♦ *vt*
beneficiar ♦ *vi*: **he'll ~ from it** le sacará
provecho; **unemployment ~** subsidio de
desempleo.

Benelux ['bɛnɪlʌks] *n* Benelux *m*.
benevolence [bɪ'nɛvələns] *n* benevolencia.
benevolent [bɪ'nɛvələnt] *adj* benévolo.
BEng *n abbr* (= *Bachelor of Engineering*)
título universitario.
benign [bɪ'naɪn] *adj* (*person, MED*) benigno;
(*smile*) afable.
bent [bɛnt] *pt, pp of* **bend** ♦ *n* inclinación *f*
♦ *adj* (*wire, pipe*) doblado, torcido; **to be**
~ on estar empeñado en.
bequeath [bɪ'kwi:ð] *vt* legar.
bequest [bɪ'kwɛst] *n* legado.
bereaved [bɪ'ri:vd] *adj* afligido ♦ *n*: **the ~**
los afligidos *mpl*.
bereavement [bɪ'ri:vmənt] *n* aflicción *f*.
beret ['bɛreɪ] *n* boina.
Bering Sea ['bɛərɪŋ-] *n*: **the ~** el Mar de
Bering.
berk [bə:k] *n* (*BRIT col*) capullo/a (*!*).
Berks *abbr* (*BRIT*) = **Berkshire.**
Berlin [bə:'lɪn] *n* Berlín *m*; **East/West ~**
Berlín del Este/Oeste.
berm [bə:m] *n* (*US AUT*) arcén *m*.
Bermuda [bə:'mju:də] *n* las (Islas)
Bermudas.
Bermuda shorts *npl* bermudas *mpl or fpl*.
Bern [bə:n] *n* Berna.
berry ['bɛrɪ] *n* baya.
berserk [bə'sə:k] *adj*: **to go ~** perder los
estribos.
berth [bə:θ] *n* (*bed*) litera; (*cabin*) camarote
m; (*for ship*) amarradero ♦ *vi* atracar,
amarrar; **to give sb a wide ~** (*fig*) evitar
encontrarse con algn.
beseech *pt, pp* **besought** [bɪ'si:tʃ, -'sɔ:t] *vt*
suplicar.
beset *pt, pp* **beset** [bɪ'sɛt] *vt* (*person*) acosar
♦ *adj*: **a policy ~ with dangers** una política
rodeada de peligros.
besetting [bɪ'sɛtɪŋ] *adj*: **his ~ sin** su
principal falta.
beside [bɪ'saɪd] *prep* junto a, al lado de;
(*compared with*) comparado con; **to be ~**
o.s. with anger estar fuera de sí; **that's ~**
the point eso no tiene nada que ver con
el asunto.
besides [bɪ'saɪdz] *adv* además ♦ *prep* (*as well*
as) además de; (*except*) excepto.
besiege [bɪ'si:dʒ] *vt* (*town*) sitiar; (*fig*)
asediar.
besmirch [bɪ'smə:tʃ] *vt* (*fig*) manchar,
mancillar.
besotted [bɪ'sɔtɪd] *adj*: **~ with** chiflado por.
bespoke [bɪ'spəuk] *adj* (*garment*) hecho a la
medida; **~ tailor** sastre *m* que
confecciona a la medida.
best [bɛst] *adj* (el/la) mejor ♦ *adv* (lo) mejor;
the ~ part of (*quantity*) la mayor parte de;

at ~ en el mejor de los casos; **to make the ~ of sth** sacar el mejor partido de algo; **to do one's ~** hacer todo lo posible; **to the ~ of my knowledge** que yo sepa; **to the ~ of my ability** como mejor puedo; **the ~ thing to do is ...** lo mejor (que se puede hacer) es ...; **he's not exactly patient at the ~ of times** no es que tenga mucha paciencia precisamente.

bestial ['bɛstɪəl] *adj* bestial.

best man *n* padrino de boda.

bestow [bɪ'stəu] *vt* otorgar; (*honour, praise*) dispensar; **to ~ sth on sb** conceder *or* dar algo a algn.

bestseller ['bɛst'sɛlə*] *n* éxito de ventas, best-seller *m*.

bet [bɛt] *n* apuesta ♦ *vt*, *vi* (*pt, pp* **bet** *or* **betted**) apostar (*on* a); **it's a safe ~** (*fig*) es cosa segura.

Bethlehem ['bɛθlɪhɛm] *n* Belén *m*.

betray [bɪ'treɪ] *vt* traicionar; (*inform on*) delatar.

betrayal [bɪ'treɪəl] *n* traición *f*.

better ['bɛtə*] *adj* mejor ♦ *adv* mejor ♦ *vt* mejorar; (*record etc*) superar ♦ *n*: **to get the ~ of sb** quedar por encima de algn; **you had ~ do it** más vale que lo hagas; **he thought ~ of it** cambió de parecer; **to get ~** mejorar(se); (*MED*) reponerse; **that's ~!** ¡eso es!; **I had ~ go** tengo que irme; **a change for the ~** una mejora; **~ off** *adj* más acomodado.

betting ['bɛtɪŋ] *n* juego, apuestas *fpl*.

betting shop *n* (*BRIT*) casa de apuestas.

between [bɪ'twiːn] *prep* entre ♦ *adv* (*also* **in ~**: *time*) mientras tanto; (: *place*) en medio; **the road ~ here and London** la carretera de aquí a Londres; **we only had 5 ~ us** teníamos sólo 5 entre todos.

bevel ['bɛvəl] *n* (*also*: **~ edge**) bisel *m*, chaflán *m*.

beverage ['bɛvərɪdʒ] *n* bebida.

bevy ['bɛvɪ] *n*: **a ~ of** una bandada de.

bewail [bɪ'weɪl] *vt* lamentar.

beware [bɪ'wɛə*] *vi*: **to ~ (of)** tener cuidado (con) ♦ *excl* ¡cuidado!

bewildered [bɪ'wɪldəd] *adj* aturdido, perplejo.

bewildering [bɪ'wɪldərɪŋ] *adj* desconcertante.

bewitching [bɪ'wɪtʃɪŋ] *adj* hechicero, encantador(a).

beyond [bɪ'jɔnd] *prep* más allá de; (*exceeding*) además de, fuera de; (*above*) superior a ♦ *adv* más allá, más lejos; **~ doubt** fuera de toda duda; **~ repair** irreparable.

b/f *abbr* (= *brought forward*) saldo previo.

BFPO *n abbr* (= *British Forces Post Office*) servicio postal del ejército.

bhp *n abbr* (= *brake horsepower*) potencia al freno.

bi ... [baɪ] *pref* bi ....

biannual [baɪ'ænjuəl] *adj* semestral.

bias ['baɪəs] *n* (*prejudice*) prejuicio; (*preference*) predisposición *f*.

bias(s)ed ['baɪəst] *adj* parcial; **to be ~ against** tener perjuicios contra.

biathlon [baɪ'æθlən] *n* biatlón *m*.

bib [bɪb] *n* babero.

Bible ['baɪbl] *n* Biblia.

biblical ['bɪblɪkəl] *adj* bíblico.

bibliography [bɪblɪ'ɔgrəfɪ] *n* bibliografía.

bicarbonate of soda [baɪ'kɑːbənɪt-] *n* bicarbonato de soda.

bicentenary [baɪsɛn'tiːnərɪ], (*US*) **bicentennial** [baɪsɛn'tɛnɪəl] *n* bicentenario.

biceps ['baɪsɛps] *n* bíceps *m*.

bicker ['bɪkə*] *vi* reñir.

bickering ['bɪkərɪŋ] *n* riñas *fpl*, altercados *mpl*.

bicycle ['baɪsɪkl] *n* bicicleta.

bicycle path *n* camino para ciclistas.

bicycle pump *n* bomba de bicicleta.

bid [bɪd] *n* (*at auction*) oferta, puja, postura; (*attempt*) tentativa, conato ♦ *vi* (*pt, pp* **bid**) hacer una oferta ♦ *vt* (*pt* **bade** [bæd], *pp* **bidden** ['bɪdn]) mandar, ordenar; **to ~ sb good day** dar a algn los buenos días.

bidder ['bɪdə*] *n*: **the highest ~** el mejor postor.

bidding ['bɪdɪŋ] *n* (*at auction*) ofertas *fpl*, puja; (*order*) orden *f*, mandato.

bide [baɪd] *vt*: **to ~ one's time** esperar el momento adecuado.

bidet ['biːdeɪ] *n* bidet *m*.

bidirectional ['baɪdɪ'rɛkʃənl] *adj* bidireccional.

biennial [baɪ'ɛnɪəl] *adj*, *n* bienal *f*.

bier [bɪə*] *n* féretro.

bifocals [baɪ'fəuklz] *npl* gafas *fpl or* anteojos *mpl* (*LAM*) bifocales.

big [bɪg] *adj* grande; **~ business** gran negocio; **to do things in a ~ way** hacer las cosas en grande.

bigamy ['bɪgəmɪ] *n* bigamia.

big dipper [-'dɪpə*] *n* montaña rusa.

big end *n* (*AUT*) cabeza de biela.

biggish ['bɪgɪʃ] *adj* más bien grande; (*man*) más bien alto.

bigheaded ['bɪg'hɛdɪd] *adj* engreído.

bigot ['bɪgət] *n* fanático/a, intolerante *m/f*.

bigoted ['bɪgətɪd] *adj* fanático, intolerante.

bigotry ['bɪgətrɪ] *n* fanatismo, intolerancia.

big toe *n* dedo gordo (del pie).

big top *n* (*circus*) circo; (*main tent*) carpa principal.
big wheel *n* (*at fair*) noria.
bigwig ['bɪgwɪg] *n* (*col*) pez *m* gordo.
bike [baɪk] *n* bici *f*.
bikini [bɪ'kiːnɪ] *n* bikini *m*.
bilateral [baɪ'lætərl] *adj* (*agreement*) bilateral.
bile [baɪl] *n* bilis *f*.
bilge [bɪldʒ] *n* (*water*) agua de sentina.
bilingual [baɪ'lɪŋgwəl] *adj* bilingüe.
bilious ['bɪlɪəs] *adj* bilioso (*also fig*).
bill [bɪl] *n* (*gen*) cuenta; (*invoice*) factura; (*POL*) proyecto de ley; (*US*: *banknote*) billete *m*; (*of bird*) pico; (*notice*) cartel *m*; (*THEAT*) programa *m* ♦ *vt* extender *or* pasar la factura a; **may I have the ~ please?** ¿puede traerme la cuenta, por favor?; **~ of exchange** letra de cambio; **~ of lading** conocimiento de embarque; **~ of sale** escritura de venta; **"post no ~s"** "prohibido fijar carteles".
billboard ['bɪlbɔːd] *n* (*US*) valla publicitaria.
billet ['bɪlɪt] *n* alojamiento ♦ *vt*: **to ~ sb (on sb)** alojar a algn (con algn).
billfold ['bɪlfəʊld] *n* (*US*) cartera.
billiards ['bɪljədz] *n* billar *m*.
billion ['bɪljən] *n* (*BRIT*) billón *m*; (*US*) mil millones *mpl*.
billow ['bɪləʊ] *n* (*of smoke*) nube *f*; (*of sail*) ondulación *f* ♦ *vi* (*smoke*) salir en nubes; (*sail*) ondear, ondular.
billowy ['bɪləʊɪ] *adj* ondulante.
billy ['bɪlɪ] *n* (*US*) porra.
billy goat *n* macho cabrío.
bimbo ['bɪmbəʊ] *n* (*col*) tía buena sin seso.
bin [bɪn] *n* (*gen*) cubo *or* bote *m* (*LAM*) de la basura; **litter~** *n* (*BRIT*) papelera.
binary ['baɪnərɪ] *adj* (*MATH*) binario; **~ code** código binario; **~ system** sistema *m* binario.
bind, *pt*, *pp* **bound** [baɪnd, baʊnd] *vt* atar, liar; (*wound*) vendar; (*book*) encuadernar; (*oblige*) obligar.
▶**bind over** *vt* (*LAW*) obligar por vía legal.
▶**bind up** *vt* (*wound*) vendar; **to be bound up in** (*work, research etc*) estar absorto en; **to be bound up with** (*person*) estar estrechamente ligado a.
binder ['baɪndə*] *n* (*file*) archivador *m*.
binding ['baɪndɪŋ] *adj* (*contract*) vinculante.
binge [bɪndʒ] *n* borrachera, juerga; **to go on a ~** ir de juerga.
bingo ['bɪŋgəʊ] *n* bingo *m*.
bin-liner ['bɪnlaɪnə*] *n* bolsa de la basura.
binoculars [bɪ'nɒkjʊləz] *npl* prismáticos *mpl*, gemelos *mpl*.

biochemistry [baɪə'kɛmɪstrɪ] *n* bioquímica.
biodegradable ['baɪəʊdɪ'greɪdəbl] *adj* biodegradable.
biodiversity ['baɪəʊdaɪ'vɜːsɪtɪ] *n* biodiversidad *f*.
biofuel ['baɪəʊfjʊəl] *n* biocarburante *m*.
biographer [baɪ'ɒgrəfə*] *n* biógrafo/a.
biographical [baɪə'græfɪkəl] *adj* biográfico.
biography [baɪ'ɒgrəfɪ] *n* biografía.
biological [baɪə'lɒdʒɪkəl] *adj* biológico.
biological clock *n* reloj *m* biológico.
biologist [baɪ'ɒlədʒɪst] *n* biólogo/a.
biology [baɪ'ɒlədʒɪ] *n* biología.
biophysics ['baɪəʊ'fɪzɪks] *nsg* biofísica.
biopic ['baɪəʊpɪk] *n* filme *m* biográfico.
biopsy ['baɪɒpsɪ] *n* biopsia.
biosphere ['baɪəsfɪə*] *n* biosfera.
biotechnology ['baɪəʊtɛk'nɒlədʒɪ] *n* biotecnología.
biped ['baɪpɛd] *n* bípedo.
birch [bɜːtʃ] *n* abedul *m*; (*cane*) vara.
bird [bɜːd] *n* ave *f*, pájaro; (*BRIT col*: *girl*) chica.
birdcage ['bɜːdkeɪdʒ] *n* jaula.
bird of prey *n* ave *f* de presa.
bird's-eye view ['bɜːdzaɪ-] *n* vista de pájaro.
bird watcher *n* ornitólogo/a.
Biro ® ['baɪrəʊ] *n* bolígrafo.
birth [bɜːθ] *n* nacimiento; (*MED*) parto; **to give ~ to** parir, dar a luz a; (*fig*) dar origen a.
birth certificate *n* partida de nacimiento.
birth control *n* control *m* de natalidad; (*methods*) métodos *mpl* anticonceptivos.
birthday ['bɜːθdeɪ] *n* cumpleaños *m inv*.
birthplace ['bɜːθpleɪs] *n* lugar *m* de nacimiento.
birth rate *n* (tasa de) natalidad *f*.
Biscay ['bɪskeɪ] *n*: **the Bay of ~** el Mar Cantábrico, el golfo de Vizcaya.
biscuit ['bɪskɪt] *n* (*BRIT*) galleta.
bisect [baɪ'sɛkt] *vt* (*also MATH*) bisecar.
bisexual ['baɪ'sɛksjuəl] *adj*, *n* bisexual *m/f*.
bishop ['bɪʃəp] *n* obispo; (*CHESS*) alfil *m*.
bistro ['biːstrəʊ] *n* café-bar *m*.
bit [bɪt] *pt of* **bite** ♦ *n* trozo, pedazo, pedacito; (*COMPUT*) bit *m*; (*for horse*) freno, bocado; **a ~ of** un poco de; **a ~ mad** algo loco; **~ by ~** poco a poco; **to come to ~s** (*break*) hacerse pedazos; **to do one's ~** aportar su granito de arena; **bring all your ~s and pieces** trae todas tus cosas.
bitch [bɪtʃ] *n* (*dog*) perra; (*col!*) zorra (!).
bite [baɪt] *vt*, *vi* (*pt* **bit** [bɪt], *pp* **bitten** ['bɪtn]) morder; (*insect etc*) picar ♦ *n* (*wound*: *of dog, snake etc*) mordedura; (*of insect*)

picadura; (*mouthful*) bocado; **to ~ one's nails** morderse las uñas; **let's have a ~ (to eat)** comamos algo.

biting ['baɪtɪŋ] *adj* (*wind*) que traspasa los huesos; (*criticism*) mordaz.

bit part *n* (*THEAT*) papel *m* sin importancia, papelito.

bitten ['bɪtn] *pp of* bite.

bitter ['bɪtə*] *adj* amargo; (*wind, criticism*) cortante, penetrante; (*icy: weather*) glacial; (*battle*) encarnizado ♦ *n* (*BRIT: beer*) *cerveza típica británica a base de lúpulos.*

bitterly ['bɪtəlɪ] *adv* (*disappoint, complain, weep*) desconsoladamente; (*oppose, criticise*) implacablemente; (*jealous*) agriamente; **it's ~ cold** hace un frío glacial.

bitterness ['bɪtənɪs] *n* amargura; (*anger*) rencor *m*.

bitty ['bɪtɪ] *adj* deshilvanado.

bitumen ['bɪtjumɪn] *n* betún *m*.

bivouac ['bɪvuæk] *n* vivac *m*, vivaque *m*.

bizarre [bɪ'zɑ:*] *adj* raro, estrafalario.

bk *abbr* = bank, book.

BL *n abbr* (= *Bachelor of Law(s), Bachelor of Letters*) título universitario; (*US*: = *Bachelor of Literature*) título universitario.

bl *abbr* = bill of lading.

blab [blæb] *vi* cantar ♦ *vt* (*also*: ~ out) soltar, contar.

black [blæk] *adj* (*colour*) negro; (*dark*) oscuro ♦ *n* (*colour*) color *m* negro; (*person*): **B~** negro/a ♦ *vt* (*shoes*) lustrar; (*BRIT: INDUSTRY*) boicotear; **to give sb a ~ eye** ponerle a algn el ojo morado; **~ coffee** café *m* solo; **there it is in ~ and white** (*fig*) ahí está bien claro; **to be in the ~** (*in credit*) tener saldo positivo; **~ and blue** *adj* amoratado.
►**black out** *vi* (*faint*) desmayarse.

black belt *n* (*SPORT*) cinturón *m* negro; (*US*: *area*) zona negra.

blackberry ['blækbərɪ] *n* zarzamora.

blackbird ['blækbə:d] *n* mirlo.

blackboard ['blækbɔ:d] *n* pizarra.

black box *n* (*AVIAT*) caja negra.

Black Country *n* (*BRIT*): **the ~** *región industrial del centro de Inglaterra.*

blackcurrant ['blæk'kʌrənt] *n* grosella negra.

black economy *n* economía sumergida.

blacken ['blækən] *vt* ennegrecer; (*fig*) denigrar.

Black Forest *n*: **the ~** la Selva Negra.

blackguard ['blægɑ:d] *n* canalla *m*, pillo.

black hole *n* (*ASTRO*) agujero negro.

black ice *n* hielo invisible en la carretera.

blackjack ['blækdʒæk] *n* (*US*) veintiuna.

blackleg ['blækleg] *n* (*BRIT*) esquirol *m/f*.

blacklist ['blæklɪst] *n* lista negra ♦ *vt* poner en la lista negra.

blackmail ['blækmeɪl] *n* chantaje *m* ♦ *vt* chantajear.

blackmailer ['blækmeɪlə*] *n* chantajista *m/f*.

black market *n* mercado negro, estraperlo.

blackness ['blæknɪs] *n* negrura.

blackout ['blækaut] *n* (*TV, ELEC*) apagón *m*; (*fainting*) desmayo, pérdida de conocimiento.

black pepper *n* pimienta negra.

Black Sea *n*: **the ~** el Mar Negro.

black sheep *n* oveja negra.

blacksmith ['blæksmɪθ] *n* herrero.

black spot *n* (*AUT*) punto negro.

bladder ['blædə*] *n* vejiga.

blade [bleɪd] *n* hoja; (*cutting edge*) filo; **a ~ of grass** una brizna de hierba.

blame [bleɪm] *n* culpa ♦ *vt*: **to ~ sb for sth** echar a algn la culpa de algo; **to be to ~ (for)** tener la culpa (de); **I'm not to ~** yo no tengo la culpa; **and I don't ~ him** y lo comprendo perfectamente.

blameless ['bleɪmlɪs] *adj* (*person*) inocente.

blanch [blɑ:ntʃ] *vi* (*person*) palidecer; (*CULIN*) escaldar.

bland [blænd] *adj* suave; (*taste*) soso.

blank [blæŋk] *adj* en blanco; (*shot*) de fogueo; (*look*) sin expresión ♦ *n* blanco, espacio en blanco; cartucho de fogueo; **to draw a ~** (*fig*) no conseguir nada.

blank cheque, (*US*) **blank check** *n* cheque *m* en blanco.

blanket ['blæŋkɪt] *n* manta, frazada (*LAM*), cobija (*LAM*) ♦ *adj* (*statement, agreement*) comprensivo, general; **to give ~ cover** (*subj: insurance policy*) dar póliza a todo riesgo.

blankly ['blæŋklɪ] *adv*: **she looked at me ~** me miró sin comprender.

blare [blɛə*] *vi* (*brass band, horns, radio*) resonar.

blasé ['blɑ:zeɪ] *adj* de vuelta de todo.

blaspheme [blæs'fi:m] *vi* blasfemar.

blasphemous ['blæsfɪməs] *adj* blasfemo.

blasphemy ['blæsfɪmɪ] *n* blasfemia.

blast [blɑ:st] *n* (*of wind*) ráfaga, soplo; (*of whistle*) toque *m*; (*of explosive*) carga explosiva; (*force*) choque *m* ♦ *vt* (*blow up*) volar; (*blow open*) abrir con carga explosiva ♦ *excl* (*BRIT col*) ¡maldito sea!; **(at) full ~** (*also fig*) a toda marcha.
►**blast off** *vi* (*spacecraft etc*) despegar.

blast furnace *n* alto horno.

blast-off ['blɑ:stɔf] *n* (*SPACE*) lanzamiento.

blatant ['bleɪtənt] *adj* descarado.
blatantly ['bleɪtəntlɪ] *adv*: **it's ~ obvious** está clarísimo.
blather ['blæðə*] *vi* decir tonterías.
blaze [bleɪz] *n* (*fire*) fuego; (*flames*) llamarada; (*glow: of fire, sun etc*) resplandor *m*; (*fig*) arranque *m* ♦ *vi* (*fire*) arder con llamaradas; (*fig*) brillar ♦ *vt*: **to ~ a trail** (*fig*) abrir (un) camino; **in a ~ of publicity** bajo los focos de la publicidad.
blazer ['bleɪzə*] *n* chaqueta de uniforme de colegial o de socio de club.
bleach [bliːtʃ] *n* (*also*: **household ~**) lejía ♦ *vt* (*linen*) blanquear.
bleached [bliːtʃt] *adj* (*hair*) de colorado; (*clothes*) blanqueado.
bleachers ['bliːtʃəz] *npl* (*US SPORT*) gradas *fpl*.
bleak [bliːk] *adj* (*countryside*) desierto; (*landscape*) desolado, desierto; (*weather*) desapacible; (*smile*) triste; (*prospect, future*) poco prometedor(a).
bleary-eyed ['blɪərɪ'aɪd] *adj*: **to be ~** tener ojos de cansado.
bleat [bliːt] *vi* balar.
bleed, *pt, pp* **bled** [bliːd, blɛd] *vt* sangrar; (*brakes, radiator*) desaguar ♦ *vi* sangrar.
bleeding ['bliːdɪŋ] *adj* sangrante.
bleep [bliːp] *n* pitido ♦ *vi* pitar ♦ *vt* llamar por el busca.
bleeper ['bliːpə*] *n* (*of doctor etc*) busca *m*.
blemish ['blɛmɪʃ] *n* mancha, tacha.
blench [blɛntʃ] *vi* (*shrink back*) acobardarse; (*grow pale*) palidecer.
blend [blɛnd] *n* mezcla ♦ *vt* mezclar ♦ *vi* (*colours etc*) combinarse, mezclarse.
blender ['blɛndə*] *n* (*CULIN*) batidora.
bless, *pt, pp* **blessed** *or* **blest** [blɛs, blɛst] *vt* bendecir.
blessed ['blɛsɪd] *adj* (*REL: holy*) santo, bendito; (: *happy*) dichoso; **every ~ day** cada santo día.
blessing ['blɛsɪŋ] *n* bendición *f*; (*advantage*) beneficio, ventaja; **to count one's ~s** agradecer lo que se tiene; **it was a ~ in disguise** no hay mal que por bien no venga.
blew [bluː] *pt of* **blow**.
blight [blaɪt] *vt* (*hopes etc*) frustrar, arruinar.
blimey ['blaɪmɪ] *excl* (*BRIT col*) ¡caray!
blind [blaɪnd] *adj* ciego ♦ *n* (*for window*) persiana ♦ *vt* cegar; (*dazzle*) deslumbrar.
blind alley *n* callejón *m* sin salida.
blind corner *n* (*BRIT*) esquina *or* curva sin visibilidad.
blind date *n* cita a ciegas.
blinders ['blaɪndəz] *npl* (*US*) anteojeras *fpl*.

blindfold ['blaɪndfəuld] *n* venda ♦ *adj, adv* con los ojos vendados ♦ *vt* vendar los ojos a.
blinding ['blaɪndɪŋ] *adj* (*flash, light*) cegador; (*pain*) intenso.
blindingly ['blaɪndɪŋlɪ] *adv*: **it's ~ obvious** salta a la vista.
blindly ['blaɪndlɪ] *adv* a ciegas, ciegamente.
blindness ['blaɪndnɪs] *n* ceguera.
blind spot *n* (*AUT*) ángulo muerto; **to have a ~ about sth** estar ciego para algo.
blink [blɪŋk] *vi* parpadear, pestañear; (*light*) oscilar; **to be on the ~** (*col*) estar estropeado.
blinkers ['blɪŋkəz] *npl* (*esp Brit*) anteojeras *fpl*.
blinking ['blɪŋkɪŋ] *adj* (*col*): **this ~...** este condenado....
blip [blɪp] *n* señal *f* luminosa; (*on graph*) pequeña desviación *f*; (*fig*) pequeña anomalía.
bliss [blɪs] *n* felicidad *f*.
blissful ['blɪsful] *adj* dichoso; **in ~ ignorance** feliz en tu ignorancia.
blissfully ['blɪsfulɪ] *adv* (*sigh, smile*) con felicidad; **~ happy** sumamente feliz.
blister ['blɪstə*] *n* (*on skin, paint*) ampolla ♦ *vi* ampollarse.
blistering ['blɪstərɪŋ] *adj* (*heat*) abrasador(a).
blithely ['blaɪðlɪ] *adv* alegremente, despreocupadamente.
blithering ['blɪðərɪŋ] *adj* (*col*): **this ~ idiot** este tonto perdido.
BLit(t) *n abbr* (= *Bachelor of Literature*) título universitario.
blitz [blɪts] *n* bombardeo aéreo; **to have a ~ on sth** (*fig*) emprenderla con algo.
blizzard ['blɪzəd] *n* ventisca.
BLM *n abbr* (*US*) = *Bureau of Land Management*.
bloated ['bləutɪd] *adj* hinchado.
blob [blɔb] *n* (*drop*) gota; (*stain, spot*) mancha.
bloc [blɔk] *n* (*POL*) bloque *m*.
block [blɔk] *n* bloque *m* (*also COMPUT*); (*in pipes*) obstáculo; (*of buildings*) manzana ♦ *vt* (*gen*) obstruir, cerrar; (*progress*) estorbar; (*COMPUT*) agrupar; **~ of flats** (*BRIT*) bloque *m* de pisos; **mental ~** amnesia temporal; **~ and tackle** (*TECH*) aparejo de polea; **3 ~s from here** a 3 manzanas *or* cuadras (*LAM*) de aquí.
►**block up** *vt* tapar, obstruir; (*pipe*) atascar.
blockade [blɔ'keɪd] *n* bloqueo ♦ *vt* bloquear.
blockage ['blɔkɪdʒ] *n* estorbo, obstrucción *f*.

block booking *n* reserva en grupo.
blockbuster ['blɔkbʌstə*] *n* (*book*) best-seller *m*; (*film*) éxito de público.
block capitals *npl* mayúsculas *fpl*.
block letters *npl* letras *fpl* de molde.
block release *n* (*BRIT*) exención *f* por estudios.
block vote *n* (*BRIT*) voto por delegación.
bloke [bləuk] *n* (*BRIT col*) tipo, tío.
blond(e) [blɔnd] *adj, n* rubio/a *m/f*.
blood [blʌd] *n* sangre *f*; **new ~** (*fig*) gente *f* nueva.
blood bank *n* banco de sangre.
blood count *n* recuento de glóbulos rojos y blancos.
blood donor *n* donante *m/f* de sangre.
blood group *n* grupo sanguíneo.
bloodhound ['blʌdhaund] *n* sabueso.
bloodless ['blʌdlɪs] *adj* (*pale*) exangüe; (*revolt etc*) sin derramamiento de sangre, incruento.
bloodletting ['blʌdletɪŋ] *n* (*MED*) sangría; (*fig*) sangría, carnicería.
blood poisoning *n* septicemia de la sangre.
blood pressure *n* tensión *f* sanguínea; **to have high/low ~** tener la tensión alta/baja.
bloodshed ['blʌdʃed] *n* baño de sangre.
bloodshot ['blʌdʃɔt] *adj* inyectado en sangre.
bloodstained ['blʌdsteɪnd] *adj* manchado de sangre.
bloodstream ['blʌdstri:m] *n* corriente *f* sanguínea.
blood test *n* análisis *m* de sangre.
bloodthirsty ['blʌdθə:stɪ] *adj* sanguinario.
blood transfusion *n* transfusión *f* de sangre.
blood type *n* grupo sanguíneo.
blood vessel *n* vaso sanguíneo.
bloody ['blʌdɪ] *adj* sangriento; (*BRIT col!*): **this ~...** este condenado *or* puñetero *or* fregado (*LAM*) ... (!) ♦ *adv* (*BRIT col!*): **~ strong/good** terriblemente fuerte/bueno.
bloody-minded ['blʌdɪ'maɪndɪd] *adj* (*BRIT col*) con malas pulgas.
bloom [blu:m] *n* floración *f*; **in ~** en flor ♦ *vi* florecer.
blooming ['blu:mɪŋ] *adj* (*col*): **this ~...** este condenado....
blossom ['blɔsəm] *n* flor *f* ♦ *vi* florecer; (*fig*) desarrollarse; **to ~ into** (*fig*) convertirse en.
blot [blɔt] *n* borrón *m* ♦ *vt* (*dry*) secar; (*stain*) manchar; **to ~ out** *vt* (*view*) tapar; (*memories*) borrar; **to be a ~ on the landscape** estropear el paisaje; **to ~**

one's copy book (*fig*) manchar su reputación.
blotchy ['blɔtʃɪ] *adj* (*complexion*) lleno de manchas.
blotter ['blɔtə*] *n* secante *m*.
blotting paper ['blɔtɪŋ-] *n* papel *m* secante.
blotto ['blɔtəu] *adj* (*col*) mamado.
blouse [blauz] *n* blusa.
blow [bləu] *n* golpe *m* ♦ *vb* (*pt* **blew**, *pp* **blown** [blu:, bləun]) *vi* soplar; (*fuse*) fundirse ♦ *vt* (*glass*) soplar; (*fuse*) quemar; (*instrument*) tocar; **to come to ~s** llegar a golpes; **to ~ one's nose** sonarse.
►**blow away** *vt* llevarse, arrancar.
►**blow down** *vt* derribar.
►**blow off** *vt* arrebatar.
►**blow out** *vt* apagar ♦ *vi* apagarse; (*tyre*) reventar.
►**blow over** *vi* amainar.
►**blow up** *vi* estallar ♦ *vt* volar; (*tyre*) inflar; (*PHOT*) ampliar.
blow-dry ['bləudraɪ] *n* secado con secador de mano ♦ *vt* secar con secador de mano.
blowlamp ['bləulæmp] *n* (*BRIT*) soplete *m*, lámpara de soldar.
blow-out ['bləuaut] *n* (*of tyre*) pinchazo; (*col: big meal*) banquete *m*, festín *m*.
blowtorch ['bləutɔ:tʃ] *n* = **blowlamp**.
blow-up ['bləuʌp] *n* (*PHOT*) ampliación *f*.
blowzy ['blauzɪ] *adj* (*BRIT*) dejado, desaliñado.
BLS *n abbr* (*US*) = *Bureau of Labor Statistics*.
blubber ['blʌbə*] *n* grasa de ballena ♦ *vi* (*pej*) lloriquear.
bludgeon ['blʌdʒən] *vt*: **to ~ sb into doing sth** coaccionar a algn a hacer algo.
blue [blu:] *adj* azul; **~ film** película porno; **~ joke** chiste verde; **once in a ~ moon** de higos a brevas; **to come out of the ~** (*fig*) ser completamente inesperado; *see also* **blues**.
blue baby *n* niño azul *or* cianótico.
bluebell ['blu:bel] *n* campanilla, campánula azul.
blue-blooded [blu:'blʌdɪd] *adj* de sangre azul.
bluebottle ['blu:bɔtl] *n* moscarda, mosca azul.
blue cheese *n* queso azul.
blue-chip ['blu:tʃɪp] *n*: **~ investment** inversión *f* asegurada.
blue-collar worker ['blu:kɔlə*-] *n* obrero/a.
blue jeans *npl* tejanos *mpl*, vaqueros *mpl*.
blueprint ['blu:prɪnt] *n* proyecto; **~ (for)** (*fig*) anteproyecto (de).
blues [blu:z] *npl*: **the ~** (*MUS*) el blues; **to have the ~** estar triste.
bluff [blʌf] *vi* tirarse un farol, farolear ♦ *n*

bluff *m*, farol *m*; (*GEO*) precipicio, despeñadero; **to call sb's** ~ coger a algn en un renuncio.

bluish ['bluːɪʃ] *adj* azulado.

blunder ['blʌndə*] *n* patinazo, metedura de pata ♦ *vi* cometer un error, meter la pata; **to** ~ **into sb/sth** tropezar con algn/algo.

blunt [blʌnt] *adj* (*knife*) desafilado; (*person*) franco, directo ♦ *vt* embotar, desafilar; **this pencil is** ~ este lápiz está despuntado; ~ **instrument** (*LAW*) instrumento contundente.

bluntly ['blʌntlɪ] *adv* (*speak*) francamente, de modo terminante.

bluntness ['blʌntnɪs] *n* (*of person*) franqueza, brusquedad *f*.

blur [blə:*] *n* aspecto borroso ♦ *vt* (*vision*) enturbiar; (*memory*) empañar.

blurb [blə:b] *n* propaganda.

blurred [blə:d] *adj* borroso.

blurt [blə:t]: **to** ~ **out** *vt* (*say*) descolgarse con, dejar escapar.

blush [blʌʃ] *vi* ruborizarse, ponerse colorado ♦ *n* rubor *m*.

blusher ['blʌʃə*] *n* colorete *m*.

bluster ['blʌstə*] *n* fanfarronada, bravata ♦ *vi* fanfarronear, echar bravatas.

blustering ['blʌstərɪŋ] *adj* (*person*) fanfarrón/ona.

blustery ['blʌstərɪ] *adj* (*weather*) tempestuoso, tormentoso.

Blvd *abbr* = boulevard.

BM *n abbr* = *British Museum*; (*UNIV*: = *Bachelor of Medicine*) título universitario.

BMA *n abbr* = *British Medical Association*.

BMJ *n abbr* = *British Medical Journal*.

BMus *n abbr* (= *Bachelor of Music*) título universitario.

BMX *n abbr* (= *bicycle motocross*) BMX *f*; ~ **bike** bici(cleta) *f* BMX.

BO *n abbr* (*col*: = *body odour*) olor *m* a sudor; (*US*) = **box office**.

boa ['bəuə] *n* boa.

boar [bɔ:*] *n* verraco, cerdo.

board [bɔ:d] *n* tabla, tablero; (*on wall*) tablón *m*; (*for chess etc*) tablero; (*committee*) junta, consejo; (*in firm*) mesa *or* junta directiva; (*NAUT*, *AVIAT*): **on** ~ a bordo ♦ *vt* (*ship*) embarcarse en; (*train*) subir a; **full** ~ (*BRIT*) pensión *f* completa; **half** ~ (*BRIT*) media pensión; ~ **and lodging** alojamiento y comida; **to go by the** ~ (*fig*) irse por la borda; **above** ~ (*fig*) sin tapujos; **across the** ~ (*fig*: *adv*) en todos los niveles; (*: adj*) general.

▶**board up** *vt* (*door*) tapar, cegar.

boarder ['bɔ:də*] *n* huésped(a) *m/f*; (*SCOL*) interno/a.

board game *n* juego de tablero.

boarding card ['bɔ:dɪŋ-] *n* (*BRIT*: *AVIAT*, *NAUT*) tarjeta de embarque.

boarding house ['bɔ:dɪŋ-] *n* casa de huéspedes.

boarding party ['bɔ:dɪŋ-] *n* brigada de inspección.

boarding pass ['bɔ:dɪŋ-] *n* (*US*) = **boarding card**.

boarding school ['bɔ:dɪŋ-] *n* internado.

board meeting *n* reunión *f* de la junta directiva.

board room *n* sala de juntas.

boardwalk ['bɔ:dwɔ:k] *n* (*US*) paseo entablado.

boast [bəust] *vi*: **to** ~ **(about** *or* **of)** alardear (de) ♦ *vt* ostentar ♦ *n* alarde *m*, baladronada.

boastful ['bəustfəl] *adj* presumido, jactancioso.

boastfulness ['bəustfulnɪs] *n* fanfarronería, jactancia.

boat [bəut] *n* barco, buque *m*; (*small*) barca, bote *m*; **to go by** ~ ir en barco.

boater ['bəutə*] *n* (*hat*) canotié *m*.

boating ['bəutɪŋ] *n* canotaje *m*.

boatman ['bəutmən] *n* barquero.

boat people *npl* refugiados que huyen en barca.

boatswain ['bəusn] *n* contramaestre *m*.

bob [bɔb] *vi* (*boat, cork on water: also:* ~ **up and down**) menearse, balancearse ♦ *n* (*BRIT col*) = **shilling**.

▶**bob up** *vi* (re)aparecer de repente.

bobbin ['bɔbɪn] *n* (*of sewing machine*) carrete *m*, bobina.

bobby ['bɔbɪ] *n* (*BRIT col*) poli *m/f*.

bobsleigh ['bɔbsleɪ] *n* bob *m*, trineo de competición *f*.

bode [bəud] *vi*: **to** ~ **well/ill (for)** ser de buen/mal agüero (para).

bodice ['bɔdɪs] *n* corpiño.

-bodied ['bɔdɪd] *adj suff* de cuerpo ....

bodily ['bɔdɪlɪ] *adj* (*comfort, needs*) corporal; (*pain*) corpóreo ♦ *adv* (*in person*) en persona; (*carry*) corporalmente; (*lift*) en peso.

body ['bɔdɪ] *n* cuerpo; (*corpse*) cadáver *m*; (*of car*) caja, carrocería; (*also:* **stocking**) body *m*; (*fig: organization*) organización *f*; (*: public* ~) organismo; (*: quantity*) masa; (*: of speech, document*) parte *f* principal; **ruling** ~ directiva; **in a** ~ todos juntos, en masa.

body blow *n* (*fig*) palo.

body-building ['bɔdɪˈbɪldɪŋ] *n* culturismo.

bodyguard ['bɔdɪgɑ:d] *n* guardaespaldas *m inv*.

body language n lenguaje m gestual.
body search n cacheo; **to carry out a** ~ **on sb** registrar a algn; **to submit to** or **undergo a** ~ ser registrado.
bodywork ['bɒdɪwɜːk] n carrocería.
boffin ['bɒfɪn] n (BRIT) científico/a.
bog [bɒg] n pantano, ciénaga ♦ vt: **to get** ~**ged down** (fig) empantanarse, atascarse.
boggle ['bɒgl] vi: **the mind** ~**s!** ¡no puedo creerlo!
Bogotá [bəʊgə'tɑː] n Bogotá.
bogus ['bəʊgəs] adj falso, fraudulento; (person) fingido.
Bohemia [bə'hiːmɪə] n Bohemia.
Bohemian [bə'hiːmɪən] adj, n bohemio/a m/f.
boil [bɔɪl] vt cocer; (eggs) pasar por agua ♦ vi hervir ♦ n (MED) furúnculo, divieso; **to bring to the** ~ calentar hasta que hierva; **to come to the** (BRIT) or **a** (US) ~ comenzar a hervir; ~**ed egg** huevo pasado por agua; ~**ed potatoes** patatas fpl or papas fpl (LAM) cocidas.
►**boil down** vi (fig): **to** ~ **down to** reducirse a.
►**boil over** vi (liquid) rebosar; (anger, resentment) llegar al colmo.
boiler ['bɔɪlə*] n caldera.
boiler suit n (BRIT) mono, overol m (LAM).
boiling ['bɔɪlɪŋ] adj: **I'm** ~ (**hot**) (col) estoy asado.
boiling point n punto de ebullición f.
boil-in-the-bag [bɔɪlɪnðə'bæg] adj: ~ **meals** platos que se cuecen en su misma bolsa.
boisterous ['bɔɪstərəs] adj (noisy) bullicioso; (excitable) exuberante; (crowd) tumultuoso.
bold [bəʊld] adj (brave) valiente, audaz; (pej) descarado; (outline) grueso; (colour) vivo; ~ **type** (TYP) negrita.
boldly ['bəʊldlɪ] adv audazmente.
boldness ['bəʊldnɪs] n valor m, audacia; (cheek) descaro.
Bolivia [bə'lɪvɪə] n Bolivia.
Bolivian [bə'lɪvɪən] adj, n boliviano/a m/f.
bollard ['bɒləd] n (BRIT AUT) poste m.
bolshy ['bɒlʃɪ] adj (BRIT col) protestón/ona; **to be in a** ~ **mood** tener el día protestón.
bolster ['bəʊlstə*] n travesero, cabezal m.
►**bolster up** vt reforzar; (fig) alentar.
bolt [bəʊlt] n (lock) cerrojo; (with nut) perno, tornillo ♦ adv: ~ **upright** rígido, erguido ♦ vt (door) echar el cerrojo a; (food) engullir ♦ vi fugarse; (horse) desbocarse.
bomb [bɒm] n bomba ♦ vt bombardear.
bombard [bɒm'bɑːd] vt bombardear; (fig) asediar.

bombardment [bɒm'bɑːdmənt] n bombardeo.
bombastic [bɒm'bæstɪk] adj rimbombante; (person) pomposo.
bomb disposal n desactivación f de explosivos.
bomb disposal expert n artificiero/a.
bomber ['bɒmə*] n (AVIAT) bombardero; (terrorist) persona que pone bombas.
bombing ['bɒmɪŋ] n bombardeo.
bomb scare n amenaza de bomba.
bombshell ['bɒmʃɛl] n obús m, granada; (fig) bomba.
bomb site n lugar m donde estalló una bomba.
bona fide ['bəʊnə'faɪdɪ] adj genuino, auténtico.
bonanza [bə'nænzə] n bonanza.
bond [bɒnd] n (binding promise) fianza; (FINANCE) bono; (link) vínculo, lazo; **in** ~ (COMM) en depósito bajo fianza.
bondage ['bɒndɪdʒ] n esclavitud f.
bonded goods ['bɒndɪd-] npl mercancías fpl en depósito de aduanas.
bonded warehouse ['bɒndɪd-] n depósito de aduanas.
bone [bəʊn] n hueso; (of fish) espina ♦ vt deshuesar; quitar las espinas a; ~ **of contention** manzana de la discordia.
bone china n porcelana fina.
bone-dry ['bəʊn'draɪ] adj completamente seco.
bone idle adj gandul.
bone marrow n médula; ~ **transplant** transplante m de médula.
boner ['bəʊnə*] n (US col) plancha, patochada.
bonfire ['bɒnfaɪə*] n hoguera, fogata.
bonk [bɒŋk] vt, vi (hum, col) chingar (!).
bonkers ['bɒŋkəz] adj (BRIT col) majareta.
Bonn [bɒn] n Bonn m.
bonnet ['bɒnɪt] n gorra; (BRIT: of car) capó m.
bonny ['bɒnɪ] adj (esp Scottish) bonito, hermoso, lindo.
bonus ['bəʊnəs] n (at Christmas etc) paga extraordinaria; (merit award) sobrepaga, prima.
bony ['bəʊnɪ] adj (arm, face, MED: tissue) huesudo; (meat) lleno de huesos; (fish) lleno de espinas; (thin: person) flaco, delgado.
boo [buː] vt abuchear.
boob [buːb] n (col: mistake) disparate m, sandez f; (: breast) teta.
booby prize ['buːbɪ-] n premio de consolación (al último).
booby trap ['buːbɪ-] n (MIL etc) trampa

explosiva.

book [buk] *n* libro; (*notebook*) libreta; (*of
stamps etc*) librillo; **~s** (*COMM*) cuentas
fpl, contabilidad *f* ♦ *vt* (*ticket, seat, room*)
reservar; (*driver*) fichar; (*FOOTBALL*)
amonestar; **to keep the ~s** llevar las
cuentas *or* los libros; **by the ~** según las
reglas; **to throw the ~ at sb** echar un
rapapolvo a algn.
►**book in** *vi* (*at hotel*) registrarse.
►**book up** *vt*: **all seats are ~ed up** todas las
plazas están reservadas; **the hotel is ~ed
up** el hotel está lleno.

bookable ['bukəbl] *adj*: **seats are ~** los
asientos se pueden reservar (de
antemano).

bookcase ['bukkeɪs] *n* librería, estante *m*
para libros.

booking office ['bukɪŋ-] *n* (*BRIT: RAIL*)
despacho de billetes *or* boletos (*LAM*);
(: *THEAT*) taquilla, boletería (*LAM*).

book-keeping ['buk'ki:pɪŋ] *n* contabilidad
f.

booklet ['buklɪt] *n* folleto.

bookmaker ['bukmeɪkə*] *n* corredor *m* de
apuestas.

bookseller ['buksɛlə*] *n* librero/a.

bookshelf ['bukʃɛlf] *n* estante *m*.

bookshop ['bukʃɔp] *n* librería.

bookstall ['bukstɔːl] *n* quiosco de libros.

book store *n* = **bookshop**.

book token *n* vale *m* para libros.

book value *n* (*COMM*) valor *m* contable.

bookworm ['bukwɜːm] *n* (*fig*) ratón *m* de
biblioteca.

boom [bu:m] *n* (*noise*) trueno, estampido;
(*in prices etc*) alza rápida; (*ECON*) boom *m*,
auge *m* ♦ *vi* (*cannon*) hacer gran
estruendo, retumbar; (*ECON*) estar en
alza.

boomerang ['bu:məræŋ] *n* bumerang *m*
(*also fig*) ♦ *vi*: **to ~ on sb** (*fig*) ser
contraproducente para algn.

boom town *n* ciudad *f* de crecimiento
rápido.

boon [bu:n] *n* favor *m*, beneficio.

boorish ['buərɪʃ] *adj* grosero.

boost [bu:st] *n* estímulo, empuje *m* ♦ *vt*
estimular, empujar; (*increase: sales,
production*) aumentar; **to give a ~ to**
(*morale*) levantar; **it gave a ~ to his
confidence** le dio confianza en sí mismo.

booster ['bu:stə*] *n* (*MED*) reinyección *f*;
(*TV*) repetidor *m*; (*ELEC*) elevador *m* de
tensión; (*also*: **~ rocket**) cohete *m*.

boot [bu:t] *n* bota; (*ankle ~*) botín *m*,
borceguí *m*; (*BRIT: of car*) maleta,
maletero, baúl *m* (*LAM*) ♦ *vt* dar un

puntapié a; (*COMPUT*) arrancar; **to ~** (*in
addition*) además, por añadidura; **to give
sb the ~** (*col*) despedir a algn, poner a
algn en la calle.

booth [bu:ð] *n* (*at fair*) barraca; (*telephone
~, voting ~*) cabina.

bootleg ['bu:tlɛg] *adj* de contrabando; **~
record** disco pirata.

booty ['bu:tɪ] *n* botín *m*.

booze [bu:z] (*col*) *n* bebida ♦ *vi*
emborracharse.

boozer ['bu:zə*] *n* (*col: person*) bebedor(a)
m/f; (: *BRIT: pub*) bar *m*.

border ['bɔːdə*] *n* borde *m*, margen *m*; (*of a
country*) frontera ♦ *adj* fronterizo; **the B~s**
*región fronteriza entre Escocia e
Inglaterra*.
►**border on** *vt fus* lindar con; (*fig*) rayar en.

borderline ['bɔːdəlaɪn] *n* (*fig*) frontera.

bore [bɔː*] *pt of* **bear** ♦ *vt* (*hole*) taladrar;
(*person*) aburrir ♦ *n* (*person*) pelmazo,
pesado; (*of gun*) calibre *m*.

bored [bɔːd] *adj* aburrido; **he's ~ to tears** *or*
to death *or* **stiff** está aburrido como una
ostra, está muerto de aburrimiento.

boredom ['bɔːdəm] *n* aburrimiento.

boring ['bɔːrɪŋ] *adj* aburrido, pesado.

born [bɔːn] *adj*: **to be ~** nacer; **I was ~ in
1960** nací en 1960.

born-again [bɔːnə'gɛn] *adj*: **~ Christian**
evangelista *m/f*.

borne [bɔːn] *pp of* **bear**.

Borneo ['bɔːnɪəu] *n* Borneo.

borough ['bʌrə] *n* municipio.

borrow ['bɔrəu] *vt*: **to ~ sth (from sb)** tomar
algo prestado (a alguien); **may I ~ your
car?** ¿me prestas tu coche?

borrower ['bɔrəuə*] *n* prestatario/a.

borrowing ['bɔrəuɪŋ] *n* préstamos *mpl*.

borstal ['bɔːstl] *n* (*BRIT*) reformatorio (de
menores).

Bosnia ['bɔznɪə] *n* Bosnia.

**Bosnia-Herzegovina, Bosnia-
Hercegovina** ['bɔːsnɪəhɛrzə'gəuvi:nə] *n*
Bosnia-Herzegovina.

Bosnian ['bɔznɪən] *adj, n* bosnio/a.

bosom ['buzəm] *n* pecho; (*fig*) seno; **~
friend** *n* amigo/a íntimo/a *or* del alma.

boss [bɔs] *n* jefe/a *m/f*; (*employer*) patrón/
ona *m/f*; (*political etc*) cacique *m* ♦ *vt* (*also*:
~ about *or* **around**) mangonear; **stop
~ing everyone about!** ¡deja de dar
órdenes *or* de mangonear a todos!

bossy ['bɔsɪ] *adj* mandón/ona.

bosun ['bəusn] *n* contramaestre *m*.

botanical [bə'tænɪkl] *adj* botánico.

botanist ['bɔtənɪst] *n* botanista *m/f*.

botany ['bɔtənɪ] *n* botánica.

botch [bɔtʃ] vt (also: ~ **up**) arruinar, estropear.
both [bəʊθ] adj, pron ambos/as, los/las dos; ~ **of us went, we ~ went** fuimos los dos, ambos fuimos ♦ adv: ~ **A and B** tanto A como B.
bother ['bɔðə*] vt (worry) preocupar; (disturb) molestar, fastidiar, fregar (LAM), embromar (LAM) ♦ vi (gen: ~ **o.s.**) molestarse ♦ n: **what a ~!** ¡qué lata! ♦ excl ¡maldita sea!, ¡caramba!; **I'm sorry to ~ you** perdona que te moleste; **to ~ doing** tomarse la molestia de hacer; **please don't ~** no te molestes.
Botswana [bɔt'swɑːnə] n Botswana.
bottle ['bɔtl] n botella; (small) frasco; (baby's) biberón m ♦ vt embotellar; ~ **of wine/milk** botella de vino/de leche; **wine/milk ~** botella de vino/de leche.
►**bottle up** vt (fig) contener, reprimir.
bottle bank n contenedor m de vidrio, iglú m.
bottleneck ['bɔtlnɛk] n embotellamiento.
bottle-opener ['bɔtləʊpnə*] n abrebotellas m inv.
bottom ['bɔtəm] n (of box, sea) fondo; (buttocks) trasero, culo; (of page, mountain, tree) pie m; (of list) final m ♦ adj (lowest) más bajo; (last) último; **to get to the ~ of sth** (fig) llegar al fondo de algo.
bottomless ['bɔtəmlɪs] adj sin fondo, insondable.
bottom line n: **the ~** lo fundamental; **the ~ is he has to go** el caso es que tenemos que despedirle.
botulism ['bɔtjulɪzəm] n botulismo.
bough [baʊ] n rama.
bought [bɔːt] pt, pp of **buy**.
bouillon cube ['buːjɔn-] n (US) cubito de caldo.
boulder ['bəʊldə*] n canto rodado.
bounce [baʊns] vi (ball) (re)botar; (cheque) ser rechazado ♦ vt hacer (re)botar ♦ n (rebound) (re)bote m; **he's got plenty of ~** (fig) tiene mucha energía.
bouncer ['baʊnsə*] n (col) forzudo, gorila m.
bouncy castle ® ['baʊnsɪ-] n castillo inflable.
bound [baʊnd] pt, pp of **bind** ♦ n (leap) salto; (gen pl: limit) límite m ♦ vi (leap) saltar ♦ adj: ~ **by** rodeado de; **to be ~ to do sth** (obliged) tener el deber de hacer algo; **he's ~ to come** es seguro que vendrá; "**out of ~s to the public**" "prohibido el paso"; ~ **for** con destino a.
boundary ['baʊndrɪ] n límite m, lindero.
boundless ['baʊndlɪs] adj ilimitado.

bountiful ['baʊntɪful] adj (person) liberal, generoso; (God) bondadoso; (supply) abundante.
bounty ['baʊntɪ] n (generosity) generosidad f; (reward) prima.
bounty hunter n cazarrecompensas m inv.
bouquet ['bukeɪ] n (of flowers) ramo, ramillete m; (of wine) aroma m.
bourbon ['buəbən] n (US: also: ~ **whiskey**) whisky m americano, bourbon m.
bourgeois ['buəʒwɑː] adj, n burgués/esa m/f.
bout [baʊt] n (of malaria etc) ataque m; (BOXING etc) combate m, encuentro.
boutique [buːˈtiːk] n boutique f, tienda de ropa.
bow [bəʊ] n (knot) lazo; (weapon, MUS) arco; [baʊ] (of the head) reverencia; (NAUT: also: ~**s**) proa ♦ vi [baʊ] inclinarse, hacer una reverencia; (yield): **to ~ to** or **before** ceder ante, someterse a; **to ~ to the inevitable** resignarse a lo inevitable.
bowels ['baʊəlz] npl intestinos mpl, vientre m.
bowl [bəʊl] n tazón m, cuenco; (for washing) palangana, jofaina; (ball) bola; (US: stadium) estadio ♦ vi (CRICKET) arrojar la pelota; see also **bowls**.
bow-legged ['bəʊˈlɛgɪd] adj estevado.
bowler ['bəʊlə*] n (CRICKET) lanzador m (de la pelota); (BRIT: also: ~ **hat**) hongo, bombín m.
bowling ['bəʊlɪŋ] n (game) bolos mpl, bochas fpl.
bowling alley n bolera.
bowling green n pista para bochas.
bowls [bəʊlz] n juego de los bolos, bochas fpl.
bow tie ['bəʊ-] n corbata de lazo, pajarita.
box [bɔks] n (also: **cardboard ~**) caja, cajón m; (for jewels) estuche m; (for money) cofre m; (crate) cofre m, arca; (THEAT) palco ♦ vt encajonar ♦ vi (SPORT) boxear.
boxer ['bɔksə*] n (person) boxeador m; (dog) bóxer m.
box file n fichero.
boxing ['bɔksɪŋ] n (SPORT) boxeo, box m (LAM).

El día después de Navidad es **Boxing Day**, *fiesta en todo el Reino Unido, aunque si el 26 de diciembre cae en domingo el día de descanso se traslada al lunes. En dicho día solía ser tradición entregar* **Christmas boxes** *(aguinaldos) a empleados, proveedores a domicilio, carteros etc.*

---

boxing gloves npl guantes mpl de boxeo.
boxing ring n ring m, cuadrilátero.

box number n (*for advertisements*) apartado.
box office n taquilla, boletería (*LAM*).
boxroom ['bɒksrum] n trastero.
boy [bɔɪ] n (*young*) niño; (*older*) muchacho.
boycott ['bɔɪkɔt] n boicot m ♦ vt boicotear.
boyfriend ['bɔɪfrɛnd] n novio.
boyish ['bɔɪɪʃ] adj de muchacho, inmaduro.
boy scout n boy scout m.
Bp abbr = **bishop.**
BPOE n abbr (*US:* = *Benevolent and Protective Order of Elks*) organización benéfica.
BR abbr see **British Rail.**
bra [brɑː] n sostén m, sujetador m, corpiño (*LAM*).
brace [breɪs] n refuerzo, abrazadera; (*BRIT: on teeth*) corrector m; (*tool*) berbiquí m ♦ vt asegurar, reforzar; **to ~ o.s. (for)** (*fig*) prepararse (para); see also **braces.**
bracelet ['breɪslɪt] n pulsera, brazalete m, pulso (*LAM*).
braces ['breɪsɪz] npl (*BRIT*) tirantes mpl, suspensores mpl (*LAM*); (*US: on teeth*) corrector m.
bracing ['breɪsɪŋ] adj vigorizante, tónico.
bracken ['brækən] n helecho.
bracket ['brækɪt] n (*TECH*) soporte m, puntal m; (*group*) clase f, categoría; (*also:* **brace ~**) soporte m, abrazadera; (*also:* **round ~**) paréntesis m inv; (*gen:* **square ~**) corchete m ♦ vt (*fig: also:* **~ together**) agrupar; **income ~** nivel m económico; **in ~s** entre paréntesis.
brackish ['brækɪʃ] adj (*water*) salobre.
brag [bræg] vi jactarse.
braid [breɪd] n (*trimming*) galón m; (*of hair*) trenza.
Braille [breɪl] n Braille m.
brain [breɪn] n cerebro; **~s** npl sesos mpl; **she's got ~s** es muy lista.
brainchild ['breɪntʃaɪld] n invención f.
braindead ['breɪndɛd] adj (*MED*) clínicamente muerto; (*col*) subnormal, tarado.
brainless ['breɪnlɪs] adj estúpido, insensato.
brainstorm ['breɪnstɔːm] n (*fig*) ataque m de locura, frenesí m; (*US: brainwave*) idea luminosa or genial, inspiración f.
brainstorming ['breɪnstɔːmɪŋ] n discusión intensa para solucionar problemas.
brainwash ['breɪnwɒʃ] vt lavar el cerebro a.
brainwave ['breɪnweɪv] n idea luminosa or genial, inspiración f.
brainy ['breɪnɪ] adj muy listo or inteligente.
braise [breɪz] vt cocer a fuego lento.
brake [breɪk] n (*on vehicle*) freno ♦ vt, vi frenar.

brake drum n tambor m de freno.
brake fluid n líquido de frenos.
brake light n luz f de frenado.
brake pedal n pedal m de freno.
bramble ['bræmbl] n (*fruit*) zarza.
bran [bræn] n salvado.
branch [brɑːntʃ] n rama; (*fig*) ramo; (*COMM*) sucursal f ♦ vi ramificarse; (*fig*) extenderse.
►**branch out** vi ramificarse.
branch line n (*RAIL*) ramal m, línea secundaria.
branch manager n director(a) m/f de sucursal.
brand [brænd] n marca; (*iron*) hierro de marcar ♦ vt (*cattle*) marcar con hierro candente.
brandish ['brændɪʃ] vt blandir.
brand name n marca.
brand-new ['brænd'njuː] adj flamante, completamente nuevo.
brandy ['brændɪ] n coñac m, brandy m.
brash [bræʃ] adj (*rough*) tosco; (*cheeky*) descarado.
Brasilia [brə'zɪlɪə] n Brasilia.
brass [brɑːs] n latón m; **the ~** (*MUS*) los cobres.
brass band n banda de metal.
brassière ['bræsɪə*] n sostén m, sujetador m.
brass tacks npl: **to get down to ~** ir al grano.
brat [bræt] n (*pej*) mocoso/a.
bravado [brə'vɑːdəu] n fanfarronería.
brave [breɪv] adj valiente, valeroso ♦ n guerrero indio ♦ vt (*challenge*) desafiar; (*resist*) aguantar.
bravely ['breɪvlɪ] adv valientemente, con valor.
bravery ['breɪvərɪ] n valor m, valentía.
bravo [brɑː'vəu] excl ¡bravo!, ¡olé!
brawl [brɔːl] n pendencia, reyerta ♦ vi pelearse.
brawn [brɔːn] n fuerza muscular; (*meat*) carne f en gelatina.
brawny ['brɔːnɪ] adj fornido, musculoso.
bray [breɪ] n rebuzno ♦ vi rebuznar.
brazen ['breɪzn] adj descarado, cínico ♦ vt: **to ~ it out** echarle cara al asunto.
brazier ['breɪzɪə*] n brasero.
Brazil [brə'zɪl] n (el) Brasil.
Brazilian [brə'zɪlɪən] adj, n brasileño/a m/f.
breach [briːtʃ] vt abrir brecha en ♦ n (*gap*) brecha; (*estrangement*) ruptura; (*breaking*): **~ of confidence** abuso de confianza; **~ of contract** infracción f de contrato; **~ of the peace** perturbación f del órden público; **in ~ of** por

incumplimiento or infracción de.

bread [brɛd] n pan m; (col: money) pasta, lana (LAM); ~ **and butter** n pan con mantequilla; (fig) pan (de cada día) ♦ adj común y corriente; **to earn one's daily** ~ ganarse el pan; **to know which side one's** ~ **is buttered (on)** saber dónde aprieta el zapato.

breadbin ['brɛdbɪn] n panera.

breadboard ['brɛdbɔːd] n (COMPUT) circuito experimental.

breadbox ['brɛdbɔks] n (US) panera.

breadcrumbs ['brɛdkrʌmz] npl migajas fpl; (CULIN) pan msg rallado.

breadline ['brɛdlaɪn] n: **on the** ~ en la miseria.

breadth [brɛtθ] n anchura; (fig) amplitud f.

breadwinner ['brɛdwɪnə*] n sostén m de la familia.

break [breɪk] vb (pt **broke** [brəuk], pp **broken** ['brəukən]) vt (gen) romper; (promise) no cumplir; (fall) amortiguar; (journey) interrumpir; (law) violar, infringir; (record) batir; (news) comunicar ♦ vi romperse, quebrarse; (storm) estallar; (weather) cambiar ♦ n (gap) abertura; (crack) grieta; (fracture) fractura; (in relations) ruptura; (rest) descanso; (time) intervalo; (: at school) (período de) recreo; (holiday) vacaciones fpl; (chance) oportunidad f; (escape) evasión f, fuga; **to** ~ **with sb** (fig) romper con algn; **to** ~ **even** vi cubrir los gastos; **to** ~ **free or loose** vi escaparse; **lucky** ~ (col) chiripa, racha de buena suerte; **to have or take a** ~ (few minutes) descansar; **without a** ~ sin descanso or descansar.

▶**break down** vt (door etc) echar abajo, derribar; (resistance) vencer, acabar con; (figures, data) analizar, descomponer; (undermine) acabar con ♦ vi estropearse; (MED) sufrir un colapso; (AUT) averiarse, descomponerse (LAM); (person) romper a llorar.

▶**break in** vt (horse etc) domar ♦ vi (burglar) forzar una entrada.

▶**break into** vt fus (house) forzar.

▶**break off** vi (speaker) pararse, detenerse; (branch) partir ♦ vt (talks) suspender; (engagement) romper.

▶**break open** vt (door etc) abrir por la fuerza, forzar.

▶**break out** vi estallar; **to** ~ **out in spots** salir a algn granos.

▶**break through** vi: **the sun broke through** asomó el sol ♦ vt fus (defences, barrier) abrirse paso por; (crowd) abrirse paso por.

▶**break up** vi (partnership) disolverse; (friends) romper ♦ vt (rocks, ice etc) partir; (crowd) disolver.

breakable ['breɪkəbl] adj quebradizo ♦ n: ~**s** cosas fpl frágiles.

breakage ['breɪkɪdʒ] n rotura; **to pay for** ~**s** pagar por los objetos rotos.

breakaway ['breɪkəweɪ] adj (group etc) disidente.

break-dancing ['breɪkdɑːnsɪŋ] n break m.

breakdown ['breɪkdaun] n (AUT) avería; (in communications) interrupción f; (MED: also: **nervous** ~) colapso, crisis f nerviosa; (of figures) desglose m.

breakdown van n (BRIT) (camión m) grúa.

breaker ['breɪkə*] n rompiente m, ola grande.

breakeven ['breɪk'iːvn] cpd: ~ **chart** gráfico del punto de equilibrio; ~ **point** punto de break-even or de equilibrio.

breakfast ['brɛkfəst] n desayuno.

breakfast cereal n cereales mpl para el desayuno.

break-in ['breɪkɪn] n robo con allanamiento de morada.

breaking and entering ['breɪkɪŋənd 'ɛntərɪŋ] n (LAW) violación f de domicilio, allanamiento de morada.

breaking point ['breɪkɪŋ-] n punto de ruptura.

breakthrough ['breɪkθruː] n ruptura; (fig) avance m, adelanto.

break-up ['breɪkʌp] n (of partnership, marriage) disolución f.

break-up value n (COMM) valor m de liquidación.

breakwater ['breɪkwɔːtə*] n rompeolas m inv.

breast [brɛst] n (of woman) pecho, seno; (chest) pecho; (of bird) pechuga.

breast-feed ['brɛstfiːd] vt, vi (irreg: like **feed**) amamantar, dar el pecho.

breaststroke ['brɛststrəuk] n braza de pecho.

breath [brɛθ] n aliento, respiración f; **out of** ~ sin aliento, sofocado; **to go out for a** ~ **of air** salir a tomar el fresco.

Breathalyser ® ['brɛθəlaɪzə*] n (BRIT) alcoholímetro m; ~ **test** n prueba de alcoholemia.

breathe [briːð] vt, vi respirar; (noisily) resollar; **I won't** ~ **a word about it** no diré ni una palabra de ello.

▶**breathe in** vt, vi aspirar.

▶**breathe out** vt, vi espirar.

breather ['briːðə*] n respiro, descanso.

breathing ['briːðɪŋ] n respiración f.

breathing space n (fig) respiro, pausa.

breathless ['brεθlɪs] *adj* sin aliento, jadeante; (*with excitement*) pasmado.
breathtaking ['brεθteɪkɪŋ] *adj* imponente, pasmoso.
breath test *n* prueba de la alcoholemia.
-bred [brεd] *suff*: **to be well/ill~** estar bien/mal criado.
breed [briːd] *vb* (*pt, pp* **bred** [brεd]) *vt* criar; (*fig: hate, suspicion*) crear, engendrar ♦ *vi* reproducirse, procrear ♦ *n* raza, casta.
breeder ['briːdə*] *n* (*person*) criador(a) *m/f*; (*PHYSICS: also:* ~ **reactor**) reactor *m*.
breeding ['briːdɪŋ] *n* (*of person*) educación *f*.
breeze [briːz] *n* brisa.
breezeblock ['briːzblɔk] *n* (*BRIT*) bovedilla.
breezy ['briːzɪ] *adj* de mucho viento, ventoso; (*person*) despreocupado.
Breton ['brεtən] *adj* bretón/ona ♦ *n* bretón/ona *m/f*; (*LING*) bretón *m*.
brevity ['brεvɪtɪ] *n* brevedad *f*.
brew [bruː] *vt* (*tea*) hacer; (*beer*) elaborar; (*plot*) tramar ♦ *vi* hacerse; elaborarse; tramarse; (*storm*) amenazar.
brewer ['bruːə*] *n* cervecero, fabricante *m* de cerveza.
brewery ['bruːərɪ] *n* fábrica de cerveza.
briar ['braɪə*] *n* (*thorny bush*) zarza; (*wild rose*) escaramujo, rosa silvestre.
bribe [braɪb] *n* soborno ♦ *vt* sobornar, cohechar; **to ~ sb to do sth** sobornar a algn para que haga algo.
bribery ['braɪbərɪ] *n* soborno, cohecho.
bric-a-brac ['brɪkəbræk] *n inv* baratijas *fpl*.
brick [brɪk] *n* ladrillo.
bricklayer ['brɪkleɪə*] *n* albañil *m*.
brickwork ['brɪkwəːk] *n* enladrillado.
brickworks ['brɪkwəːks] *n* ladrillar *m*.
bridal ['braɪdl] *adj* nupcial.
bride [braɪd] *n* novia.
bridegroom ['braɪdgruːm] *n* novio.
bridesmaid ['braɪdzmeɪd] *n* dama de honor.
bridge [brɪdʒ] *n* puente *m*; (*NAUT*) puente *m* de mando; (*of nose*) caballete *m*; (*CARDS*) bridge *m* ♦ *vt* (*river*) tender un puente sobre.
bridgehead ['brɪdʒhεd] *n* cabeza de puente.
bridging loan ['brɪdʒɪŋ-] *n* crédito provisional.
bridle ['braɪdl] *n* brida, freno ♦ *vt* poner la brida a; (*fig*) reprimir, refrenar ♦ *vi* (*in anger etc*) picarse.
bridle path *n* camino de herradura.
brief [briːf] *adj* breve, corto ♦ *n* (*LAW*) escrito ♦ *vt* (*inform*) informar; (*instruct*) dar instrucciones a; **in ~** ... en resumen ...; **to ~ sb (about sth)** informar a algn (sobre algo).

briefcase ['briːfkeɪs] *n* cartera, portafolio(s) *m inv* (*LAM*).
briefing ['briːfɪŋ] *n* (*PRESS*) informe *m*.
briefly *adv* (*smile, glance*) brevemente; (*explain, say*) brevemente, en pocas palabras.
briefs [briːfs] *npl* (*for men*) calzoncillos *mpl*; (*for women*) bragas *fpl*.
Brig. *abbr* = **brigadier.**
brigade [brɪ'geɪd] *n* (*MIL*) brigada.
brigadier [brɪgə'dɪə*] *n* general *m* de brigada.
bright [braɪt] *adj* claro; (*room*) luminoso; (*day*) de sol; (*person: clever*) listo, inteligente; (*: lively*) alegre, animado; (*colour*) vivo; **to look on the ~ side** mirar el lado bueno.
brighten ['braɪtn] (*also:* ~ **up**) *vt* (*room*) hacer más alegre ♦ *vi* (*weather*) despejarse; (*person*) animarse, alegrarse.
brill [brɪl] *adj* (*BRIT col*) guay.
brilliance ['brɪljəns] *n* brillo, brillantez *f*; (*fig: of person*) inteligencia.
brilliant ['brɪljənt] *adj* (*light, idea, person, success*) brillante; (*clever*) genial.
brilliantly ['brɪljəntlɪ] *adv* brillantemente.
brim [brɪm] *n* borde *m*; (*of hat*) ala.
brimful ['brɪm'ful] *adj* lleno hasta el borde; (*fig*) rebosante.
brine [braɪn] *n* (*CULIN*) salmuera.
bring, *pt, pp* **brought** [brɪŋ, brɔːt] *vt* (*thing*) traer; (*person*) conducir; **to ~ to an end** terminar con algo; **I can't ~ myself to sack him** no soy capaz de echarle.
►**bring about** *vt* ocasionar, producir.
►**bring back** *vt* volver a traer; (*return*) devolver.
►**bring down** *vt* bajar; (*price*) rebajar.
►**bring forward** *vt* adelantar; (*BOOKKEEPING*) sumar y seguir.
►**bring in** *vt* (*harvest*) recoger; (*person*) hacer entrar *or* pasar; (*object*) traer; (*POL: bill, law*) presentar; (*LAW: verdict*) pronunciar; (*produce: income*) producir, rendir.
►**bring off** *vt* (*task, plan*) lograr, conseguir; (*deal*) cerrar.
►**bring out** *vt* (*object*) sacar; (*new product*) sacar; (*book*) publicar.
►**bring round** *vt* (*unconscious person*) hacer volver en sí; (*convince*) convencer.
►**bring up** *vt* (*person*) educar, criar; (*carry up*) subir; (*question*) sacar a colación; (*food: vomit*) devolver, vomitar.
brink [brɪŋk] *n* borde *m*; **on the ~ of doing sth** a punto de hacer algo; **she was on the ~ of tears** estaba al borde de las lágrimas.

brisk [brɪsk] *adj* (*walk*) enérgico, vigoroso; (*speedy*) rápido; (*wind*) fresco; (*trade*) activo, animado; (*abrupt*) brusco; **business is ~** el negocio va bien *or* a paso activo.

brisket ['brɪskɪt] *n* falda de vaca.

bristle ['brɪsl] *n* cerda ♦ *vi* erizarse.

bristly ['brɪslɪ] *adj* (*beard, hair*) erizado; **to have a ~ chin** tener la barba crecida.

Brit [brɪt] *n abbr* (*col*: = *British person*) británico/a.

Britain ['brɪtən] *n* (*also*: **Great ~**) Gran Bretaña.

British ['brɪtɪʃ] *adj* británico; **the ~** *npl* los británicos; **the ~ Isles** *npl* las Islas Británicas.

British Rail (BR) *n* ≈ RENFE *f* (*SP*).

British Summer Time *n* hora de verano británica.

Briton ['brɪtən] *n* británico/a.

brittle ['brɪtl] *adj* quebradizo, frágil.

Br(o). *abbr* (*REL*) = **brother.**

broach [brəutʃ] *vt* (*subject*) abordar.

broad [brɔːd] *adj* ancho, amplio; (*accent*) cerrado ♦ *n* (*US col*) tía; **in ~ daylight** en pleno día; **the ~ outlines** las líneas generales.

broad bean *n* haba.

broadcast ['brɔːdkɑːst] *n* emisión *f* ♦ *vb* (*pt, pp* **broadcast**) *vt* (*RADIO*) emitir; (*TV*) transmitir ♦ *vi* emitir; transmitir.

broadcaster ['brɔːdkɑːstə*] *n* locutor(a) *m/f*.

broadcasting ['brɔːdkɑːstɪŋ] *n* radiodifusión *f*, difusión *f*.

broadcasting station *n* emisora.

broaden ['brɔːdn] *vt* ensanchar ♦ *vi* ensancharse.

broadly ['brɔːdlɪ] *adv* en general.

broad-minded ['brɔːd'maɪndɪd] *adj* tolerante, liberal.

broadsheet ['brɔːdʃiːt] *n* (*BRIT*) periódico de gran formato (*no sensacionalista*); *see also* **quality press.**

brocade [brə'keɪd] *n* brocado.

broccoli ['brɔkəlɪ] *n* brécol *m*, bróculi *m*.

brochure ['brəuʃjuə*] *n* folleto.

brogue [brəug] *n* (*accent*) acento regional; (*shoe*) (*tipo de*) zapato de cuero grueso.

broil [brɔɪl] *vt* (*US*) asar a la parrilla.

broiler ['brɔɪlə*] *n* (*fowl*) pollo (para asar).

broke [brəuk] *pt of* **break** ♦ *adj* (*col*) pelado, sin una perra; **to go ~** quebrar.

broken ['brəukən] *pp of* **break** ♦ *adj* (*stick*) roto; (*fig*: *marriage*) deshecho; (: *promise, vow*) violado; **~ leg** pierna rota; **in ~ English** en un inglés chapurreado.

broken-down ['brəukn'daun] *adj* (*car*) averiado; (*machine*) estropeado; (*house*) destartalado.

broken-hearted ['brəukn'hɑːtɪd] *adj* con el corazón destrozado.

broker ['brəukə*] *n* corredor(a) *m/f* de bolsa.

brokerage ['brəukərɪdʒ] *n* corretaje *m*.

brolly ['brɔlɪ] *n* (*BRIT col*) paraguas *m inv*.

bronchitis [brɔŋ'kaɪtɪs] *n* bronquitis *f*.

bronze [brɔnz] *n* bronce *m*.

bronzed [brɔnzd] *adj* bronceado.

brooch [brəutʃ] *n* broche *m*.

brood [bruːd] *n* camada, cría; (*children*) progenie *f* ♦ *vi* (*hen*) empollar; **to ~ over** dar vueltas a, rumiar.

broody ['bruːdɪ] *adj* (*fig*) triste, melancólico.

brook [bruk] *n* arroyo.

broom [brum] *n* escoba; (*BOT*) retama.

broomstick ['brumstɪk] *n* palo de escoba.

Bros. *abbr* (*COMM*: = *Brothers*) Hnos.

broth [brɔθ] *n* caldo.

brothel ['brɔθl] *n* burdel *m*.

brother ['brʌðə*] *n* hermano.

brotherhood ['brʌðəhud] *n* hermandad *f*.

brother-in-law ['brʌðərɪn'lɔː] *n* cuñado.

brotherly ['brʌðəlɪ] *adj* fraternal.

brought [brɔːt] *pt, pp of* **bring.**

brow [brau] *n* (*forehead*) frente *f*; (*of hill*) cumbre *f*.

browbeat ['braubiːt] *vt* (*irreg*: *like* **beat**) intimidar.

brown [braun] *adj* marrón; (*hair*) castaño; (*tanned*) moreno ♦ *n* (*colour*) marrón *m* ♦ *vt* (*tan*) poner moreno; (*CULIN*) dorar; **to go ~** (*person*) ponerse moreno; (*leaves*) dorarse.

brown bread *n* pan *m* moreno.

brownie ['braunɪ] *n* niña exploradora.

brown paper *n* papel *m* de estraza.

brown rice *n* arroz *m* integral.

brown sugar *n* azúcar *m* moreno.

browse [brauz] *vi* (*animal*) pacer; (*among books*) hojear libros; **to ~ through a book** hojear un libro.

bruise [bruːz] *n* (*on person*) cardenal *m*, hematoma *m* ♦ *vt* (*leg etc*) magullar; (*fig*: *feelings*) herir.

Brum [brʌm] *n abbr*, **Brummagem** ['brʌmədʒəm] *n* (*col*) = **Birmingham.**

Brummie ['brʌmɪ] *n* (*col*) habitante *m/f* de Birmingham.

brunch [brʌntʃ] *n* desayuno-almuerzo.

brunette [bruː'nɛt] *n* morena, morocha (*LAM*).

brunt [brʌnt] *n*: **to bear the ~ of** llevar el peso de.

brush [brʌʃ] *n* cepillo, escobilla (*LAM*); (*large*) escoba; (*for painting, shaving etc*)

brocha; (*artist's*) pincel *m*; (*BOT*) maleza ♦ *vt* cepillar; (*gen*: ~ **past**, ~ **against**) rozar al pasar; **to have a** ~ **with the police** tener un roce con la policía.
► **brush aside** *vt* rechazar, no hacer caso a.
► **brush up** *vt* (*knowledge*) repasar, refrescar.
brushed [brʌʃt] *adj* (*nylon, denim etc*) afelpado; (*TECH: steel, chrome etc*) cepillado.
brushwood ['brʌʃwud] *n* (*bushes*) maleza; (*sticks*) leña.
brusque [bruːsk] *adj* (*person, manner*) brusco; (*tone*) áspero.
Brussels ['brʌslz] *n* Bruselas.
Brussels sprout *n* col *f* de Bruselas.
brutal ['bruːtl] *adj* brutal.
brutality [bruːˈtælɪtɪ] *n* brutalidad *f*.
brutalize ['bruːtəlaɪz] *vt* (*harden*) embrutecer; (*ill-treat*) tratar brutalmente a.
brute [bruːt] *n* bruto; (*person*) bestia ♦ *adj*: **by** ~ **force** por la fuerza bruta.
brutish ['bruːtɪʃ] *adj* brutal.
BS *n abbr* (*US*: = *Bachelor of Science*) título universitario.
bs *abbr* = **bill of sale**.
BSA *n abbr* = *Boy Scouts of America*.
BSc *abbr* = **Bachelor of Science**; *see also* **Bachelor's Degree**.
BSE *n abbr* (= *bovine spongiform encephalopathy*) encefalopatía espongiforme bovina.
BSI *n abbr* (= *British Standards Institution*) *institución británica de normalización.*
BST *n abbr* (= *British Summer Time*) *hora de verano británica.*
Bt. *abbr* (*BRIT*) = *baronet*.
btu *n abbr* (= *British thermal unit*) ≈ *1054.2 julios.*
bubble ['bʌbl] *n* burbuja; (*in paint*) ampolla ♦ *vi* burbujear, borbotar.
bubble bath *n* espuma para el baño.
bubble gum *n* chicle *m*.
bubblejet printer ['bʌbldʒet-] *n* impresora de inyección por burbujas.
bubbly ['bʌblɪ] *adj* (*person*) vivaracho; (*liquid*) con burbujas ♦ *n* (*col*) champán *m*.
Bucharest [buːkəˈrest] *n* Bucarest *m*.
buck [bʌk] *n* macho; (*US col*) dólar *m* ♦ *vi* corcovear; **to pass the** ~ **(to sb)** echar (a algn) el muerto.
► **buck up** *vi* (*cheer up*) animarse, cobrar ánimo ♦ *vt*: **to** ~ **one's ideas up** poner más empeño.
bucket ['bʌkɪt] *n* cubo, balde *m* (*esp LAM*) ♦ *vi*: **the rain is** ~**ing (down)** (*col*) está

lloviendo a cántaros.

Buckingham Palace *es la residencia oficial del monarca británico en Londres. Data de 1703 y fue en principio el palacio del Duque de Buckingham, para pasar a manos de Jorge III en 1762. Fue reconstruido el siglo pasado y reformado después a principios de este siglo. Hoy en día parte del palacio está abierto al público.*

buckle ['bʌkl] *n* hebilla ♦ *vt* abrochar con hebilla ♦ *vi* torcerse, combarse.
► **buckle down** *vi* poner empeño.
Bucks [bʌks] *abbr* (*BRIT*) = Buckinghamshire.
bud [bʌd] *n* brote *m*, yema; (*of flower*) capullo ♦ *vi* brotar, echar brotes.
Budapest [bjuːdəˈpest] *n* Budapest *m*.
Buddhism ['budɪzm] *n* Budismo.
Buddhist ['budɪst] *adj, n* budista *m/f*.
budding ['bʌdɪŋ] *adj* en ciernes, en embrión.
buddy ['bʌdɪ] *n* (*US*) compañero, compinche *m*.
budge [bʌdʒ] *vt* mover; (*fig*) hacer ceder ♦ *vi* moverse.
budgerigar ['bʌdʒərɪgaː*] *n* periquito.
budget ['bʌdʒɪt] *n* presupuesto ♦ *vi*: **to** ~ **for sth** presupuestar algo; **I'm on a tight** ~ no puedo gastar mucho; **she works out her** ~ **every month** planea su presupuesto todos los meses.
budgie ['bʌdʒɪ] *n* = **budgerigar**.
Buenos Aires ['bweɪnɔsˈaɪrɪz] *n* Buenos Aires *m* ♦ *adj* bonaerense, porteño (*LAM*).
buff [bʌf] *adj* (*colour*) color *m* de ante ♦ *n* (*enthusiast*) entusiasta *m/f*.
buffalo ['bʌfələu], *pl* ~ *or* **buffaloes** *n* (*BRIT*) búfalo; (*US: bison*) bisonte *m*.
buffer ['bʌfə*] *n* amortiguador *m*; (*COMPUT*) memoria intermedia, buffer *m*.
buffering ['bʌfərɪŋ] *n* (*COMPUT*) almacenamiento en memoria intermedia.
buffer zone *n* zona (que sirve de) colchón.
buffet ['bufeɪ] *n* (*BRIT: bar*) bar *m*, cafetería; (*food*) buffet *m* ♦ *vt* ['bʌfɪt] (*strike*) abofetear; (*wind etc*) golpear.
buffet car *n* (*BRIT RAIL*) coche-restaurante *m*.
buffet lunch *n* buffet *m* (almuerzo).
buffoon [bəˈfuːn] *n* bufón *m*.
bug [bʌg] *n* (*insect*) chinche *m*; (: *gen*) bicho, sabandija; (*germ*) microbio, bacilo; (*spy device*) micrófono oculto; (*COMPUT*) fallo, error *m* ♦ *vt* (*annoy*) fastidiar; (*room*) poner un micrófono oculto en; (*phone*) pinchar; **I've got the travel** ~ (*fig*) me encanta viajar; **it really** ~**s me** me

fastidia *or* molesta mucho.
bugbear ['bʌgbɛə*] *n* pesadilla.
bugle ['bjuːgl] *n* corneta, clarín *m*.
build [bɪld] *n* (*of person*) talle *m*, tipo ♦ *vt* (*pt, pp* **built** [bɪlt]) construir, edificar.
▶**build on** *vt fus* (*fig*) basar en.
▶**build up** *vt* (*MED*) fortalecer; (*stocks*) acumular; (*establish: business*) fomentar, desarrollar; (: *reputation*) crear(se); (*increase: production*) aumentar; **don't ~ your hopes up too soon** no te hagas demasiadas ilusiones.
builder ['bɪldə*] *n* constructor(a) *m/f*; (*contractor*) contratista *m/f*.
building ['bɪldɪŋ] *n* (*act of*) construcción *f*; (*habitation, offices*) edificio.
building contractor *n* contratista *m/f* de obras.
building industry *n* construcción *f*.
building site *n* solar *m* (*SP*), obra (*LAM*).
building society *n* (*BRIT*) sociedad *f* de préstamo inmobiliario.

En el Reino Unido existe un tipo de entidad financiera llamada **building society** *de la que sus clientes son también propietarios y cuyos servicios son similares a los de los bancos, aunque se centran fundamentalmente en créditos hipotecarios y cuentas de ahorro. Son la entidad más utilizada por el público en general a la hora de pedir créditos para la compra de la vivienda.*

---

building trade *n* = **building industry**.
build-up ['bɪldʌp] *n* (*publicity*): **to give sb/ sth a good ~** hacer mucha propaganda de algn/algo.
built [bɪlt] *pt, pp of* **build**.
built-in ['bɪlt'ɪn] *adj* (*cupboard*) empotrado; (*device*) interior, incorporado; **~ obsolescence** caducidad *f* programada.
built-up ['bɪltʌp] *adj* (*area*) urbanizado.
bulb [bʌlb] *n* (*BOT*) bulbo; (*ELEC*) bombilla, bombillo (*LAM*), foco (*LAM*).
bulbous ['bʌlbəs] *adj* bulboso.
Bulgaria [bʌl'gɛərɪə] *n* Bulgaria.
Bulgarian [bʌl'gɛərɪən] *adj* búlgaro ♦ *n* búlgaro/a; (*LING*) búlgaro.
bulge [bʌldʒ] *n* bombeo, pandeo; (*in birth rate, sales*) alza, aumento ♦ *vi* bombearse, pandearse; (*pocket etc*) hacer bulto.
bulimia [bə'lɪmɪə] *n* bulimia.
bulk [bʌlk] *n* (*mass*) bulto, volumen *m*; (*major part*) grueso; **in ~** (*COMM*) a granel; **the ~ of** la mayor parte de; **to buy in ~** comprar en grandes cantidades.
bulk buying *n* compra a granel.

bulk carrier *n* (buque *m*) granelero.
bulkhead ['bʌlkhɛd] *n* mamparo.
bulky ['bʌlkɪ] *adj* voluminoso, abultado.
bull [bul] *n* toro; (*STOCK EXCHANGE*) alcista *m/f* de bolsa; (*REL*) bula.
bulldog ['buldɔg] *n* dogo.
bulldoze ['buldəuz] *vt* mover con excavadora; **I was ~d into doing it** (*fig col*) me obligaron a hacerlo.
bulldozer ['buldəuzə*] *n* buldozer *m*, excavadora.
bullet ['bulɪt] *n* bala; **~ wound** balazo.
bulletin ['bulɪtɪn] *n* comunicado, parte *m*; (*journal*) boletín *m*.
bulletin board *n* (*US*) tablón *m* de anuncios; (*COMPUT*) tablero de noticias.
bulletproof ['bulɪtpruːf] *adj* a prueba de balas; **~ vest** chaleco anti-balas.
bullfight ['bulfaɪt] *n* corrida de toros.
bullfighter ['bulfaɪtə*] *n* torero.
bullfighting ['bulfaɪtɪŋ] *n* los toros *mpl*, el toreo; (*art of* ~) tauromaquia.
bullion ['buljən] *n* oro *or* plata en barras.
bullock ['bulək] *n* novillo.
bullring ['bulrɪŋ] *n* plaza de toros.
bull's-eye ['bulzaɪ] *n* blanco, diana.
bullshit ['bulʃɪt] (*col!*) *excl* chorradas ♦ *n* chorradas *fpl* ♦ *vi* decir chorradas ♦ *vt*: **to ~ sb** quedarse con algn.
bully ['bulɪ] *n* valentón *m*, matón *m* ♦ *vt* intimidar, tiranizar.
bum [bʌm] *n* (*BRIT: col: backside*) culo; (: *tramp*) vagabundo; (*col: esp US: idler*) holgazán/ana *m/f*, flojo/a.
bumble ['bʌmbl] *vi* (*walk unsteadily*) andar de forma vacilante; (*fig*) farfullar, trastabillar.
bumblebee ['bʌmblbiː] *n* abejorro.
bumbling ['bʌmblɪŋ] *n* divagación *f*.
bumf [bʌmf] *n* (*col: forms etc*) papeleo.
bump [bʌmp] *n* (*blow*) tope *m*, choque *m*; (*jolt*) sacudida; (*noise*) choque *m*, topetón *m*; (*on road etc*) bache *m*; (*on head*) chichón *m* ♦ *vt* (*strike*) chocar contra, topetar ♦ *vi* dar sacudidas.
▶**bump into** *vt fus* chocar contra, tropezar con; (*person*) topar con; (*col: meet*) tropezar con, toparse con.
bumper ['bʌmpə*] *n* (*BRIT*) parachoques *m inv* ♦ *adj*: **~ crop/harvest** cosecha abundante.
bumper cars *npl* (*US*) autos *or* coches *mpl* de choque.
bumph [bʌmf] *n* = **bumf**.
bumptious ['bʌmpʃəs] *adj* engreído, presuntuoso.
bumpy ['bʌmpɪ] *adj* (*road*) lleno de baches; (*journey, flight*) agitado.

bun [bʌn] n (*BRIT*: *cake*) pastel m; (*US*: *bread*) bollo; (*of hair*) moño.

bunch [bʌntʃ] n (*of flowers*) ramo; (*of keys*) manojo; (*of bananas*) piña; (*of people*) grupo; (*pej*) pandilla.

bundle ['bʌndl] n (*gen*) bulto, fardo; (*of sticks*) haz m; (*of papers*) legajo ♦ vt (*also*: ~ **up**) atar, envolver; **to** ~ **sth/sb into** meter algo/a algn precipitadamente en.

bun fight n (*BRIT col*: *tea party*) merienda; (: *function*) fiesta oficial.

bung [bʌŋ] n tapón m, bitoque m ♦ vt (*throw*: *also*: ~ **into**) arrojar; (*also*: ~ **up**: *pipe*, *hole*) tapar; **my nose is** ~**ed up** (*col*) tengo la nariz atascada *or* taponada.

bungalow ['bʌŋɡələu] n bungalow m, chalé m.

bungee jumping ['bʌndʒiː'dʒʌmpɪŋ] n puenting m, banyi m.

bungle ['bʌŋɡl] vt chapucear.

bunion ['bʌnjən] n juanete m.

bunk [bʌŋk] n litera; ~ **beds** npl literas fpl.

bunker ['bʌŋkə*] n (*coal store*) carbonera; (*MIL*) refugio; (*GOLF*) bunker m.

bunk off vi: **to** ~ **school** (*BRIT col*) pirarse las clases; **I'll** ~ **at 3 this afternoon** me voy a pirar a las 3 esta tarde.

bunny ['bʌnɪ] n (*also*: ~ **rabbit**) conejito.

Bunsen burner ['bʌnsn-] n mechero Bunsen.

bunting ['bʌntɪŋ] n empavesada, banderas fpl.

buoy [bɔɪ] n boya.

▶**buoy up** vt mantener a flote; (*fig*) animar.

buoyancy ['bɔɪənsɪ] n (*of ship*) flotabilidad f.

buoyant ['bɔɪənt] adj (*carefree*) boyante, optimista; (*COMM*: *market*, *prices etc*) sostenido.

BUPA ['buːpə] n abbr (= *British United Provident Association*) seguro médico privado.

burden ['bəːdn] n carga ♦ vt cargar; **to be a** ~ **to sb** ser una carga para algn.

bureau, pl ~**x** ['bjuərəu, -z] n (*BRIT*: *writing desk*) escritorio, buró m; (*US*: *chest of drawers*) cómoda; (*office*) oficina, agencia.

bureaucracy [bjuə'rɔkrəsɪ] n burocracia.

bureaucrat ['bjuərəkræt] n burócrata m/f.

bureaucratic [bjuərə'krætɪk] adj burocrático.

burgeon ['bəːdʒən] vi (*develop rapidly*) crecer, incrementarse; (*trade etc*) florecer.

burger ['bəːɡə*] n hamburguesa.

burglar ['bəːɡlə*] n ladrón/ona m/f.

burglar alarm n alarma f contra robo.

burglarize ['bəːɡləraɪz] vt (*US*) robar (con

allanamiento).

burglary ['bəːɡlərɪ] n robo con allanamiento *or* fractura, robo de una casa.

burgle ['bəːɡl] vt robar (con allanamiento).

Burgundy ['bəːɡəndɪ] n Borgoña.

burial ['bɛrɪəl] n entierro.

burial ground n cementerio.

burlap ['bəːlæp] n arpillera.

burlesque [bəː'lɛsk] n parodia.

burly ['bəːlɪ] adj fornido, membrudo.

Burma ['bəːmə] n Birmania; *see also* **Myanmar**.

Burmese [bəː'miːz] adj birmano ♦ n (*pl inv*) birmano/a; (*LING*) birmano.

burn [bəːn] vb (pt, pp **burned** or **burnt** [bəːnt]) vt quemar; (*house*) incendiar ♦ vi quemarse, arder; incendiarse; (*sting*) escocer ♦ n (*MED*) quemadura; **the cigarette** ~**t a hole in her dress** se ha quemado el vestido con el cigarrillo; **I've** ~**t myself!** ¡me he quemado!

▶**burn down** vt incendiar.

▶**burn out** vt (*subj*: *writer etc*): **to** ~ **o.s. out** agotarse.

burner ['bəːnə*] n (*gas*) quemador m.

burning ['bəːnɪŋ] adj ardiente; (*building*, *forest*) en llamas.

Cada veinticinco de enero los escoceses celebran la llamada **Burns' Night** *(noche de Burns), en honor al poeta escocés Robert Burns (1759-1796). Es tradición hacer una cena en la que, al son de la música de la gaita escocesa, se sirve* **haggis**, *plato tradicional de asadura de cordero cocida en el estómago del animal, acompañado de nabos y puré de patatas. Durante la misma se recitan poemas del autor y varios discursos conmemorativos de carácter festivo.*

---

burp [bəːp] (*col*) n eructo ♦ vi eructar.

burrow ['bʌrəu] n madriguera ♦ vt hacer una madriguera.

bursar ['bəːsə*] n tesorero; (*BRIT*: *student*) becario/a.

bursary ['bəːsərɪ] n (*BRIT*) beca.

burst [bəːst] vb (pt, pp **burst**) vt (*balloon*, *pipe*) reventar; (*banks etc*) romper ♦ vi reventarse; romperse; (*tyre*) pincharse; (*bomb*) estallar ♦ n (*explosion*) estallido; (*also*: ~ **pipe**) reventón m; **the river has** ~ **its banks** el río se ha desbordado; **to** ~ **into flames** estallar en llamas; **to** ~ **out laughing** soltar la carcajada; **to** ~ **into tears** deshacerse en lágrimas; **to be** ~**ing with** reventar de; **a** ~ **of energy** una

bury – button

explosión de energía; **a ~ of applause** una salva de aplausos; **a ~ of speed** una escapada; **to ~ open** *vi* abrirse de golpe.
▶**burst into** *vt fus* (*room etc*) irrumpir en.
bury ['berɪ] *vt* enterrar; (*body*) enterrar, sepultar; **to ~ the hatchet** enterrar el hacha (de guerra), echar pelillos a la mar.
bus [bʌs] *n* autobús *m*, camión *m* (*LAM*).
bus boy *n* (*US*) ayudante *m/f* de camarero.
bush [buʃ] *n* arbusto; (*scrub land*) monte *m* bajo; **to beat about the ~** andar(se) con rodeos.
bushed [buʃt] *adj* (*col*) molido.
bushel ['buʃl] *n* (*measure: Brit*) = 36,36 *litros*; (: *US*) = 35,24 *litros*.
bush fire *n* incendio en el monte.
bushy ['buʃɪ] *adj* (*beard, eyebrows*) poblado; (*hair*) espeso; (*fur*) tupido.
busily ['bɪzɪlɪ] *adv* afanosamente.
business ['bɪznɪs] *n* (*matter, affair*) asunto; (*trading*) comercio, negocios *mpl*; (*firm*) empresa, casa; (*occupation*) oficio; **to be away on ~** estar en viaje de negocios; **it's my ~ to...** me toca *or* corresponde...; **it's none of my ~** no es asunto mío; **he means ~** habla en serio; **he's in the insurance ~** se dedica a los seguros; **I'm here on ~** estoy aquí por mi trabajo; **to do ~ with sb** hacer negocios con algn.
business address *n* dirección *f* comercial.
business card *n* tarjeta de visita.
businesslike ['bɪznɪslaɪk] *adj* (*company*) serio; (*person*) eficiente.
businessman ['bɪznɪsmən] *n* hombre *m* de negocios.
business trip *n* viaje *m* de negocios.
businesswoman ['bɪznɪswumən] *n* mujer *f* de negocios.
busker ['bʌskə*] *n* (*BRIT*) músico/a ambulante.
bus route *n* recorrido del autobús.
bus station *n* estación *f or* terminal *f* de autobuses.
bus-stop ['bʌsstɔp] *n* parada de autobús, paradero (*LAM*).
bust [bʌst] *n* (*ANAT*) pecho ♦ *adj* (*col: broken*) roto, estropeado ♦ *vt* (*col: POLICE: arrest*) detener; **to go ~** quebrar.
bustle ['bʌsl] *n* bullicio, movimiento ♦ *vi* menearse, apresurarse.
bustling ['bʌslɪŋ] *adj* (*town*) animado, bullicioso.
bust-up ['bʌstʌp] *n* (*col*) riña.
busty ['bʌstɪ] *adj* (*col*) pechugona, con buena delantera.
busy ['bɪzɪ] *adj* ocupado, atareado; (*shop, street*) concurrido, animado ♦ *vt*: **to ~ o.s.**

with ocuparse en; **he's a ~ man** (*normally*) es un hombre muy ocupado; (*temporarily*) está muy ocupado; **the line's ~** (*esp US*) está comunicando.
busybody ['bɪzɪbɔdɪ] *n* entrometido/a.
busy signal *n* (*US TEL*) señal *f* de comunicando.

══════════════ *KEYWORD*

but [bʌt] *conj* **1** pero; **he's not very bright, ~ he's hard-working** no es muy inteligente, pero es trabajador
2 (*in direct contradiction*) sino; **he's not English ~ French** no es inglés sino francés; **he didn't sing ~ he shouted** no cantó sino que gritó
3 (*showing disagreement, surprise etc*): **~ that's far too expensive!** ¡pero eso es carísimo!; **~ it does work!** ¡(pero) sí que funciona!
♦ *prep* (*apart from, except*) menos, salvo; **we've had nothing ~ trouble** no hemos tenido más que problemas; **no-one ~ him can do it** nadie más que él puede hacerlo; **the last ~ one** el penúltimo; **who ~ a lunatic would do such a thing?** ¡sólo un loco haría una cosa así!; **~ for you/your help** si no fuera por ti/tu ayuda; **anything ~ that** cualquier cosa menos eso
♦ *adv* (*just, only*): **she's ~ a child** no es más que una niña; **had I ~ known** si lo hubiera sabido; **I can ~ try** al menos lo puedo intentar; **it's all ~ finished** está casi acabado.

butane ['bjuːteɪn] *n* (*also: ~ gas*) (gas *m*) butano.
butch [butʃ] *adj* (*pej: woman*) machirula, marimacho; (*col: man*) muy macho.
butcher ['butʃə*] *n* carnicero/a ♦ *vt* hacer una carnicería con; (*cattle etc for meat*) matar; **~'s (shop)** carnicería.
butler ['bʌtlə*] *n* mayordomo.
butt [bʌt] *n* (*cask*) tonel *m*; (*for rain*) tina; (*thick end*) cabo, extremo; (*of gun*) culata; (*of cigarette*) colilla; (*BRIT fig: target*) blanco ♦ *vt* dar cabezadas contra, topetar.
▶**butt in** *vi* (*interrupt*) interrumpir.
butter ['bʌtə*] *n* mantequilla, manteca (*LAM*) ♦ *vt* untar con mantequilla.
butter bean *n* judía blanca.
buttercup ['bʌtəkʌp] *n* ranúnculo.
butterfingers ['bʌtəfɪŋgəz] *n* (*col*) torpe *m/f*.
butterfly ['bʌtəflaɪ] *n* mariposa; (*SWIMMING: also: ~ stroke*) (braza de) mariposa.
buttocks ['bʌtəks] *npl* nalgas *fpl*.
button ['bʌtn] *n* botón *m* ♦ *vt* (*also: ~ up*)

abotonar, abrochar ♦ *vi* abrocharse.
buttonhole ['bʌtnhəʊl] *n* ojal *m*; (*flower*)
flor *f* que se lleva en el ojal ♦ *vt* obligar a
escuchar.
buttress ['bʌtrɪs] *n* contrafuerte *m*; (*fig*)
apoyo, sostén *m*.
buxom ['bʌksəm] *adj* (*woman*) frescachona,
rolliza.
buy [baɪ] *vb* (*pt, pp* **bought** [bɔ:t]) *vt* comprar
♦ *n* compra; **to ~ sb sth/sth from sb**
comprarle algo a algn; **to ~ sb a drink**
invitar a algn a una copa; **a good/bad ~**
una buena/mala compra.
►**buy back** *vt* volver a comprar.
►**buy in** *vt* proveerse *or* abastecerse de.
►**buy into** *vt fus* comprar acciones en.
►**buy off** *vt* (*col*: *bribe*) sobornar.
►**buy out** *vt* (*partner*) comprar la parte de.
buyer ['baɪə*] *n* comprador(a) *m/f*; **~'s**
market mercado favorable al comprador.
buy-out ['baɪaʊt] *n* (*COMM*) adquisición *f* de
(la totalidad de) las acciones.
buzz [bʌz] *n* zumbido; (*col*: *phone call*)
llamada (telefónica) ♦ *vt* (*call on intercom*)
llamar; (*with buzzer*) hacer sonar; (*AVIAT*:
plane, building) pasar rozando ♦ *vi*
zumbar; **my head is ~ing** me zumba la
cabeza.
►**buzz off** *vi* (*BRIT col*) largarse.
buzzard ['bʌzəd] *n* (*BRIT*) águila ratonera;
(*US*) buitre *m*, gallinazo (*LAM*).
buzzer ['bʌzə*] *n* timbre *m*.
buzz word *n* palabra que está de moda.

============================== *KEYWORD*

by [baɪ] *prep* **1** (*referring to cause, agent*) por;
de; **abandoned ~ his mother** abandonado
por su madre; **surrounded ~ enemies**
rodeado de enemigos; **a painting ~**
Picasso un cuadro de Picasso
2 (*referring to method, manner, means*): **~**
bus/car/train en autobús/coche/tren; **to**
pay ~ cheque pagar con cheque(s); **~**
moonlight/candlelight a la luz de la luna/
una vela; **~ saving hard, he ...**
ahorrando, ...
3 (*via, through*) por; **we came ~ Dover**
vinimos por Dover
4 (*close to, past*): **the house ~ the river** la
casa junto al río; **she rushed ~ me** pasó a
mi lado como una exhalación; **I go ~ the**
post office every day paso por delante de
Correos todos los días
5 (*time: not later than*) para; (: *during*): **~**
daylight de día; **~ 4 o'clock** para las
cuatro; **~ this time tomorrow** mañana a
estas horas; **~ the time I got here it was**
too late cuando llegué ya era demasiado

tarde
6 (*amount*): **~ the metre/kilo** por metro/
kilo; **paid ~ the hour** pagado por hora
7 (*MATH, measure*): **to divide/multiply ~ 3**
dividir/multiplicar por 3; **a room 3**
metres ~ 4 una habitación de 3 metros
por 4; **it's broader ~ a metre** es un metro
más ancho; **the bus missed me ~ inches**
no me pilló el autobús por un pelo
8 (*according to*) según, de acuerdo con;
it's 3 o'clock ~ my watch según mi reloj,
son las tres; **it's all right ~ me** por mí,
está bien
9: (**all**) **~ oneself** *etc* todo solo; **he did it**
(**all**) **~ himself** lo hizo él solo; **he was**
standing (**all**) **~ himself in a corner** estaba
de pie solo en un rincón
10: **~ the way** a propósito, por cierto; **this**
wasn't my idea, ~ the way pues, no fue
idea mía
♦ *adv* **1** *see* **go; pass** *etc*
2: **~ and ~** finalmente; **they'll come back**
~ and ~ acabarán volviendo; **~ and large**
en líneas generales, en general.

bye(-bye) ['baɪ('baɪ)] *excl* adiós, hasta
luego, chao (*esp LAM*).
by(e)-law ['baɪlɔ:] *n* ordenanza municipal.
by-election ['baɪɪlekʃən] *n* (*BRIT*) elección *f*
parcial.

Se celebra una **by-election** *en el Reino*
Unido y otros países de la **Commonwealth**
cuando es necesario reemplazar a un
parlamentario (**Member of Parliament**)
cesado o fallecido durante una legislatura.
Dichas elecciones tienen lugar únicamente
en el área electoral representada por el
citado parlamentario, su **constituency**.

bygone ['baɪgɒn] *adj* pasado, del pasado
♦ *n*: **let ~s be ~s** lo pasado, pasado está.
Byelorussia [bjɛləʊ'rʌʃə] *n* Bielorrusia.
Byelorussian [bjɛləʊ'rʌʃən] *adj, n* =
Belorussian.
bypass ['baɪpɑ:s] *n* carretera de
circunvalación; (*MED*) (operación *f* de)
by-pass *m* ♦ *vt* evitar.
by-product ['baɪprɒdʌkt] *n* subproducto,
derivado.
bystander ['baɪstændə*] *n* espectador(a) *m/*
f.
byte [baɪt] *n* (*COMPUT*) byte *m*, octeto.
byway ['baɪweɪ] *n* camino poco
frecuentado.
byword ['baɪwə:d] *n*: **to be a ~ for** ser
sinónimo de.
by-your-leave ['baɪjɔ:'li:v] *n*: **without so**

much as a ~ sin decir nada, sin dar ningún tipo de explicación.

C c

C, c [siː] n (*letter*) C, c f; (*MUS*): **C do** m; **C for Charlie** C de Carmen.

C *abbr* (= *Celsius, centigrade*) C.

c *abbr* (= *century*) S.; (= *circa*) hacia; (*US etc*) = **cent(s)**.

CA n abbr = **Central America**; (*BRIT*) = **chartered accountant**; (*US*) = **California**.

ca. *abbr* (= *circa*) c.

c/a *abbr* = **capital account, credit account, current account**.

CAA n abbr (*BRIT*: = *Civil Aviation Authority*) organismo de control y desarrollo de la aviación civil.

CAB n abbr (*BRIT*: = *Citizens' Advice Bureau*) ≈ Servicio de Información Ciudadana.

cab [kæb] n taxi m; (*of truck*) cabina.

cabaret ['kæbəreɪ] n cabaret m.

cabbage ['kæbɪdʒ] n col f, berza.

cabbie, cabby ['kæbɪ] n (*col*) taxista m/f.

cab driver n taxista m/f.

cabin ['kæbɪn] n cabaña; (*on ship*) camarote m.

cabin cruiser n yate m de motor.

cabinet ['kæbɪnɪt] n (*POL*) consejo de ministros; (*furniture*) armario; (*also*: **display ~**) vitrina.

cabinet-maker ['kæbɪnɪt'meɪkə*] n ebanista m.

cabinet minister n ministro/a (del gabinete).

cable ['keɪbl] n cable m ♦ vt cablegrafiar.

cable-car ['keɪblkɑː*] n teleférico.

cablegram ['keɪblɡræm] n cablegrama m.

cable television n televisión f por cable.

cache [kæʃ] n (*drugs*) alijo; (*arms*) zulo.

cackle ['kækl] vi cacarear.

cactus, pl **cacti** ['kæktəs, -taɪ] n cacto.

CAD n abbr (= *computer-aided design*) DAO m.

caddie, caddy ['kædɪ] n (*GOLF*) cadi m.

cadence ['keɪdəns] n ritmo; (*MUS*) cadencia.

cadet [kə'dɛt] n (*MIL*) cadete m; **police ~** cadete m de policía.

cadge [kædʒ] vt gorronear.

cadger ['kædʒə*] n gorrón/ona m/f.

cadre ['kædrɪ] n cuadro.

Caesarean, (*US*) **Cesarean** [siː'zɛərɪən] adj: **~ (section)** cesárea.

CAF abbr (*BRIT*: = *cost and freight*) C y F.

café ['kæfeɪ] n café m.

cafeteria [kæfɪ'tɪərɪə] n cafetería (*con autoservicio para comer*).

caffein(e) ['kæfiːn] n cafeína.

cage [keɪdʒ] n jaula ♦ vt enjaular.

cagey ['keɪdʒɪ] adj (*col*) cauteloso, reservado.

cagoule [kə'ɡuːl] n canguro.

cahoots [kə'huːts] n: **to be in ~ (with sb)** estar conchabado (con algn).

CAI n abbr (= *computer-aided instruction*) enseñanza asistida por ordenador.

Cairo ['kaɪərəu] n El Cairo.

cajole [kə'dʒəul] vt engatusar.

cake [keɪk] n pastel m; (*of soap*) pastilla; **he wants to have his ~ and eat it** (*fig*) quiere estar en misa y repicando; **it's a piece of ~** (*col*) es pan comido.

caked [keɪkt] adj: **~ with** cubierto de.

cake shop n pastelería.

Cal. abbr (*US*) = *California*.

calamine ['kæləmaɪn] n calamina.

calamitous [kə'læmɪtəs] adj calamitoso.

calamity [kə'læmɪtɪ] n calamidad f.

calcium ['kælsɪəm] n calcio.

calculate ['kælkjuleɪt] vt (*estimate: chances, effect*) calcular.

▶**calculate on** *vt fus*: **to ~ on sth/on doing sth** contar con algo/con hacer algo.

calculated ['kælkjuleɪtɪd] adj: **we took a ~ risk** calculamos el riesgo.

calculating ['kælkjuleɪtɪŋ] adj (*scheming*) calculador(a).

calculation [kælkju'leɪʃən] n cálculo, cómputo.

calculator ['kælkjuleɪtə*] n calculadora.

calculus ['kælkjuləs] n cálculo.

calendar ['kæləndə*] n calendario; **~ month/year** n mes m/año civil.

calf, pl **calves** [kɑːf, kɑːvz] n (*of cow*) ternero, becerro; (*of other animals*) cría; (*also*: **~skin**) piel f de becerro; (*ANAT*) pantorrilla, canilla (*LAM*).

caliber ['kælɪbə*] n (*US*) = **calibre**.

calibrate ['kælɪbreɪt] vt (*gun etc*) calibrar; (*scale of measuring instrument*) graduar.

calibre, (*US*) **caliber** ['kælɪbə*] n calibre m.

calico ['kælɪkəu] n calicó m.

Calif. abbr (*US*) = *California*.

California [kælɪ'fɔːnɪə] n California.

calipers ['kælɪpəz] npl (*US*) = **callipers**.

call [kɔːl] vt (*gen, also TEL*) llamar; (*announce: flight*) anunciar; (*meeting, strike*) convocar ♦ vi (*shout*) llamar;

(*telephone*) llamar (por teléfono), telefonear; (*visit: also*: ~ **in**, ~ **round**) hacer una visita ♦ *n* (*shout, TEL*) llamada, llamado (*LAM*); (*of bird*) canto; (*appeal*) llamamiento, llamado (*LAM*); (*summons: for flight etc*) llamada; (*fig: lure*) llamada; **to be** ~**ed** (*person, object*) llamarse; **to** ~ **sb names** poner verde a algn; **let's** ~ **it a day** (*col*) ¡dejémoslo!, ¡ya está bien!; **who is** ~**ing?** ¿de parte de quién?; **London** ~**ing** (*RADIO*) aquí Londres; **on** ~ (*nurse, doctor etc*) de guardia; **please give me a** ~ **at 7** despiérteme *or* llámeme a las 7, por favor; **long-distance** ~ conferencia (interurbana); **to make a** ~ llamar por teléfono; **port of** ~ puerto de escala; **to pay a** ~ **on sb** pasarse a ver a algn; **there's not much** ~ **for these items** estos artículos no tienen mucha demanda.

► **call at** *vt fus* (*ship*) hacer escala en, tocar en; (*train*) parar en.

► **call back** *vi* (*return*) volver; (*TEL*) volver a llamar.

► **call for** *vt fus* (*demand*) pedir, exigir; (*fetch*) venir por.

► **call in** *vt* (*doctor, expert, police*) llamar.

► **call off** *vt* suspender; **the strike was** ~**ed off** se desconvocó la huelga.

► **call on** *vt fus* (*visit*) ir a ver; (*turn to*) acudir a.

► **call out** *vi* gritar, dar voces ♦ *vt* (*doctor*) llamar; (*police, troops*) hacer intervenir.

► **call up** *vt* (*MIL*) llamar a filas.

Callanetics ® [kælə'nɛtɪks] *nsg* gimnasia de repetición de pequeños ejercicios musculares.

callbox ['kɔːlbɔks] *n* (*BRIT*) cabina telefónica.

caller ['kɔːlə*] *n* visita *f*; (*TEL*) usuario/a; **hold the line,** ~**!** ¡no cuelgue!

call girl *n* prostituta.

call-in ['kɔːlɪn] *n* (*US*) programa de línea abierta al público.

calling ['kɔːlɪŋ] *n* vocación *f*; (*profession*) profesión *f*.

calling card *n* tarjeta de visita.

callipers, (*US*) **calipers** ['kælɪpəz] *npl* (*MED*) aparato ortopédico; (*MATH*) calibrador *m*.

callous ['kæləs] *adj* insensible, cruel.

callousness ['kæləsnɪs] *n* insensibilidad, crueldad *f*.

callow ['kæləu] *adj* inexperto, novato.

calm [kɑːm] *adj* tranquilo; (*sea*) tranquilo, en calma ♦ *n* calma, tranquilidad *f* ♦ *vt* calmar, tranquilizar.

► **calm down** *vi* calmarse, tranquilizarse ♦ *vt* calmar, tranquilizar.

calmly ['kɑːmlɪ] *adv* tranquilamente, con calma.

calmness ['kɑːmnɪs] *n* calma.

Calor gas ® ['kælə*-] *n* butano.

calorie ['kælərɪ] *n* caloría; **low-**~ **product** producto bajo en calorías.

calve [kɑːv] *vi* parir.

calves [kɑːvz] *npl of* **calf**.

CAM *n abbr* (= *computer-aided manufacturing*) producción *f* asistida por ordenador.

camber ['kæmbə*] *n* (*of road*) combadura.

Cambodia [kæm'bəudjə] *n* Camboya.

Cambodian [kæm'bəudjən] *adj, n* camboyano/a *m/f*.

Cambs *abbr* (*BRIT*) = **Cambridgeshire**.

camcorder ['kæmkɔːdə*] *n* videocámara.

came [keɪm] *pt of* **come**.

camel ['kæməl] *n* camello.

cameo ['kæmɪəu] *n* camafeo.

camera ['kæmərə] *n* cámara *or* máquina fotográfica; (*CINE, TV*) cámara; (*movie* ~) cámara, tomavistas *m inv*; **in** ~ a puerta cerrada.

cameraman ['kæmərəmən] *n* cámara *m*.

Cameroon, Cameroun [kæme'ruːn] *n* Camerún *m*.

camomile tea ['kæməmaɪl-] *n* manzanilla.

camouflage ['kæməflɑːʒ] *n* camuflaje *m* ♦ *vt* camuflar.

camp [kæmp] *n* campo, campamento ♦ *vi* acampar ♦ *adj* afectado, afeminado; **to go** ~**ing** ir *or* hacer camping.

campaign [kæm'peɪn] *n* (*MIL, POL etc*) campaña ♦ *vi*: **to** ~ **(for/against)** hacer campaña (a favor de/en contra de).

campaigner [kæm'peɪnə*] *n*: ~ **for** defensor(a) *m/f* de; ~ **against** persona que hace campaña contra.

campbed ['kæmpbɛd] *n* (*BRIT*) cama plegable.

camper ['kæmpə*] *n* campista *m/f*; (*vehicle*) caravana.

camping ['kæmpɪŋ] *n* camping *m*.

campsite ['kæmpsaɪt] *n* camping *m*.

campus ['kæmpəs] *n* campus *m*.

camshaft ['kæmʃɑːft] *n* árbol *m* de levas.

can [kæn] *aux vb see next headword* ♦ *n* (*of oil, water*) bidón *m*; (*tin*) lata, bote *m* ♦ *vt* enlatar; (*preserve*) conservar en lata; **a** ~ **of beer** una lata *or* un bote de cerveza; **to carry the** ~ (*col*) pagar el pato.

═══════════════════ *KEYWORD*

can (*negative* **cannot, can't**; *conditional and pt* **could**) *aux vb* **1** (*be able to*) poder; **you** ~ **do it if you try** puedes hacerlo si lo intentas; **I** ~**'t see you** no te veo; ~ **you hear me?**

(*not translated*) ¿me oyes?
2 (*know how to*) saber; **I ~ swim/play tennis/drive** sé nadar/jugar al tenis/conducir; **~ you speak French?** ¿hablas *or* sabes hablar francés?
3 (*may*) poder; **~ I use your phone?** ¿me dejas *or* puedo usar tu teléfono?; **could I have a word with you?** ¿podría hablar contigo un momento?
4 (*expressing disbelief, puzzlement etc*): **it ~'t be true!** ¡no puede ser (verdad)!; **what** *CAN* **he want?** ¿qué querrá?
5 (*expressing possibility, suggestion etc*): **he could be in the library** podría estar en la biblioteca; **she could have been delayed** puede que se haya retrasado.

Canada ['kænədə] *n* Canadá *m*.
Canadian [kə'neɪdɪən] *adj*, *n* canadiense *m/f*.
canal [kə'næl] *n* canal *m*.
canary [kə'nɛərɪ] *n* canario.
Canary Islands, Canaries [kə'nɛərɪz] *npl* las (Islas) Canarias.
Canberra ['kænbərə] *n* Canberra.
cancel ['kænsəl] *vt* cancelar; (*train*) suprimir; (*appointment, cheque*) anular; (*cross out*) tachar.
▶**cancel out** *vt* (*MATH*) anular; (*fig*) contrarrestar; **they ~ each other out** se anulan mutuamente.
cancellation [kænsə'leɪʃən] *n* cancelación *f*; supresión *f*.
cancer ['kænsə*] *n* cáncer *m*; **C~** (*ASTRO*) Cáncer *m*.
cancerous ['kænsərəs] *adj* canceroso.
cancer patient *n* enfermo/a *m/f* de cáncer.
cancer research *n* investigación *f* del cáncer.
C and F *abbr* (= *cost and freight*) C y F.
candid ['kændɪd] *adj* franco, abierto.
candidacy ['kændɪdəsɪ] *n* candidatura.
candidate ['kændɪdeɪt] *n* candidato/a.
candidature ['kændɪdətʃə*] *n* (*BRIT*) = **candidacy**.
candidly ['kændɪdlɪ] *adv* francamente, con franqueza.
candle ['kændl] *n* vela; (*in church*) cirio.
candle holder *n see* **candlestick**.
candlelight ['kændllaɪt] *n*: **by ~** a la luz de una vela.
candlestick ['kændlstɪk] *n* (*also:* **candle holder**: *single*) candelero; (: *low*) palmatoria; (*bigger, ornate*) candelabro.
candour, (*US*) **candor** ['kændə*] *n* franqueza.
candy ['kændɪ] *n* azúcar *m* cande; (*US*) caramelo ♦ *vt* (*fruit*) escarchar.
candy-floss ['kændɪflɔs] *n* (*BRIT*) algodón *m*

(azucarado).
cane [keɪn] *n* (*BOT*) caña; (*for baskets, chairs etc*) mimbre *m*; (*stick*) vara, palmeta; (: *for walking*) bastón *m* ♦ *vt* (*BRIT SCOL*) castigar (con palmeta); **~ liquor** caña.
canine ['kænaɪn] *adj* canino.
canister ['kænɪstə*] *n* bote *m*.
cannabis ['kænəbɪs] *n* canabis *m*.
canned [kænd] *adj* en lata, de lata; (*col: music*) grabado; (: *drunk*) mamado.
cannibal ['kænɪbəl] *n* caníbal *m/f*, antropófago/a.
cannibalism ['kænɪbəlɪzəm] *n* canibalismo.
cannon, *pl* **~** *or* **~s** ['kænən] *n* cañón *m*.
cannonball ['kænənbɔːl] *n* bala (de cañón).
cannon fodder *n* carne *f* de cañón.
cannot ['kænɔt] = **can not**.
canny ['kænɪ] *adj* avispado.
canoe [kə'nuː] *n* canoa; (*SPORT*) piragua.
canoeing [kə'nuːɪŋ] *n* (*SPORT*) piragüismo.
canoeist [kə'nuːɪst] *n* piragüista *m/f*.
canon ['kænən] *n* (*clergyman*) canónigo; (*standard*) canon *m*.
canonize ['kænənaɪz] *vt* canonizar.
can opener *n* abrelatas *m inv*.
canopy ['kænəpɪ] *n* dosel *m*, toldo.
can't [kænt] = **can not**.
Cantab. *abbr* (*BRIT:* = *cantabrigiensis*) = *of Cambridge*.
cantankerous [kæn'tæŋkərəs] *adj* arisco, malhumorado.
canteen [kæn'tiːn] *n* (*eating place*) comedor *m*; (*BRIT: of cutlery*) juego.
canter ['kæntə*] *n* medio galope ♦ *vi* ir a medio galope.
cantilever ['kæntɪliːvə*] *n* viga voladiza.
canvas ['kænvəs] *n* (*material*) lona; (*painting*) lienzo; (*NAUT*) velamen *m*; **under ~** (*camping*) en tienda de campaña.
canvass ['kænvəs] *vt* (*POL: district*) hacer campaña (puerta a puerta) en; (: *person*) hacer campaña (puerta a puerta) a favor de; (*COMM: district*) sondear el mercado en; (: *citizens, opinions*) sondear.
canvasser ['kænvəsə*] *n* (*POL*) representante *m/f* electoral; (*COMM*) corredor(a) *m/f*.
canyon ['kænjən] *n* cañón *m*.
CAP *n abbr* (= *Common Agricultural Policy*) PAC *f*.
cap [kæp] *n* (*hat*) gorra; (*for swimming*) gorro; (*of pen*) capuchón *m*; (*of bottle*) tapón *m*; (: *metal*) chapa; (*contraceptive*) diafragma *m* ♦ *vt* (*outdo*) superar; (*BRIT SPORT*) seleccionar (para el equipo nacional); **and to ~ it all, he ...** y para colmo, él ....
capability [keɪpə'bɪlɪtɪ] *n* capacidad *f*.

capable ['keɪpəbl] *adj* capaz.
capacious [kə'peɪʃəs] *adj* amplio.
capacity [kə'pæsɪtɪ] *n* capacidad *f*; (*position*) calidad *f*; **filled to** ~ lleno a reventar; **this work is beyond my** ~ este trabajo es superior a mí; **in an advisory** ~ como asesor.
cape [keɪp] *n* capa; (*GEO*) cabo.
Cape of Good Hope *n* Cabo de Buena Esperanza.
caper ['keɪpə*] *n* (*CULIN: also:* ~**s**) alcaparra; (*prank*) travesura.
Cape Town *n* Ciudad *f* del Cabo.
capital ['kæpɪtl] *n* (*also:* ~ **city**) capital *f*; (*money*) capital *m*; (*also:* ~ **letter**) mayúscula.
capital account *n* cuenta de capital.
capital allowance *n* desgravación *f* sobre bienes del capital.
capital assets *n* activo fijo.
capital expenditure *n* inversión *f* de capital.
capital gains tax *n* impuesto sobre la plusvalía.
capital goods *npl* bienes *mpl* de capital.
capital-intensive [kæpɪtlɪn'tɛnsɪv] *adj* de utilización intensiva de capital.
capital investment *n* inversión *f* de capital.
capitalism ['kæpɪtəlɪzəm] *n* capitalismo.
capitalist ['kæpɪtəlɪst] *adj*, *n* capitalista *m/f*.
capitalize ['kæpɪtəlaɪz] *vt* (*COMM: provide with capital*) capitalizar.
▶**capitalize on** *vt fus* (*fig*) sacar provecho de, aprovechar.
capital punishment *n* pena de muerte.
capital transfer tax *n* impuesto sobre plusvalía de cesión.
Capitol ['kæpɪtl] *n*: **the** ~ el Capitolio.

> *El Capitolio* (**Capitol**) *es el edificio en el que se reúne el Congreso de los Estados Unidos* (**Congress**), *situado en la ciudad de Washington. Por extensión, también se suele llamar así al edificio en el que tienen lugar las sesiones parlamentarias de la cámara de representantes de muchos de los estados.*

capitulate [kə'pɪtjuleɪt] *vi* capitular, rendirse.
capitulation [kəpɪtju'leɪʃən] *n* capitulación *f*, rendición *f*.
capricious [kə'prɪʃəs] *adj* caprichoso.
Capricorn ['kæprɪkɔːn] *n* Capricornio.
caps [kæps] *abbr* (= *capital letters*) may.
capsize [kæp'saɪz] *vt* volcar, hacer zozobrar ♦ *vi* volcarse, zozobrar.

capstan ['kæpstən] *n* cabrestante *m*.
capsule ['kæpsjuːl] *n* cápsula.
Capt. *abbr* = **Captain**.
captain ['kæptɪn] *n* capitán *m* ♦ *vt* capitanear, ser el capitán de.
caption ['kæpʃən] *n* (*heading*) título; (*to picture*) leyenda, pie *m*.
captivate ['kæptɪveɪt] *vt* cautivar, encantar.
captive ['kæptɪv] *adj*, *n* cautivo/a *m/f*.
captivity [kæp'tɪvɪtɪ] *n* cautiverio.
captor ['kæptə*] *n* captor(a) *m/f*.
capture ['kæptʃə*] *vt* capturar; (*place*) tomar; (*attention*) captar, llamar ♦ *n* captura; toma; (*data* ~) formulación *f* de datos.
car [kɑː*] *n* coche *m*, carro (*LAM*), automóvil *m*, auto (*LAM*); (*US RAIL*) vagón *m*; **by** ~ en coche.
Caracas [kə'rækəs] *n* Caracas *m*.
carafe [kə'ræf] *n* garrafa.
caramel ['kærəməl] *n* caramelo.
carat ['kærət] *n* quilate *m*; **18-**~ **gold** oro de 18 quilates.
caravan ['kærəvæn] *n* (*BRIT*) caravana, remolque *m*; (*of camels*) caravana.
caravan site *n* (*BRIT*) camping *m* para caravanas.
caraway ['kærəweɪ] *n*: ~ **seed** carvi *m*.
carbohydrates [kɑːbəu'haɪdreɪts] *npl* (*foods*) hidratos *mpl* de carbono.
carbolic [kɑː'bɔlɪk] *adj*: ~ **acid** ácido carbólico, fenol *m*.
car bomb *n* coche-bomba *m*.
carbon ['kɑːbən] *n* carbono.
carbonated ['kɑːbəneɪtɪd] *adj* (*drink*) con gas.
carbon copy *n* copia al carbón.
carbon dioxide *n* dióxido de carbono, anhídrido carbónico.
carbon monoxide *n* monóxido de carbono.
carbon paper *n* papel *m* carbón.
carbon ribbon *n* cinta de carbón.
car boot sale *n* mercadillo (*de objetos usados expuestos en el maletero del coche*).
carburettor, (*US*) **carburetor** [kɑːbju'rɛtə*] *n* carburador *m*.
carcass ['kɑːkəs] *n* (*animal*) res *f* muerta; (*dead body*) cadáver *m*.
carcinogenic [kɑːsɪnə'dʒɛnɪk] *adj* cancerígeno.
card [kɑːd] *n* (*thin cardboard*) cartulina; (*playing* ~) carta, naipe *m*; (*visiting* ~, *greetings* ~ *etc*) tarjeta; (*index* ~) ficha; **membership** ~ carnet *m*; **to play** ~**s** jugar a las cartas *or* los naipes.
cardamom ['kɑːdəməm] *n* cardamomo.

cardboard ['kɑːdbɔːd] n cartón m, cartulina.

cardboard box n caja de cartón.

cardboard city n zona de marginados sin hogar (*que se refugian entre cartones*).

card-carrying member ['kɑːdkærɪŋ-] n miembro con carnet.

card game n juego de naipes or cartas.

cardiac ['kɑːdɪæk] adj cardíaco.

cardigan ['kɑːdɪgən] n chaqueta (de punto), rebeca.

cardinal ['kɑːdɪnl] adj cardinal ♦ n cardenal m.

cardinal number n número cardinal.

card index n fichero.

cardphone ['kɑːdfəun] n *cabina que funciona con tarjetas telefónicas*.

cardsharp ['kɑːdʃɑːp] n fullero/a.

card vote n voto por delegación.

CARE [kɛə*] n abbr (= *Cooperative for American Relief Everywhere*) *sociedad benéfica*.

care [kɛə*] n cuidado; (*worry*) preocupación f; (*charge*) cargo, custodia ♦ vi: **to ~ about** preocuparse por; **~ of (c/o)** en casa de, al cuidado de; (: *on letter*) para (entregar a); **in sb's ~** a cargo de algn; **the child has been taken into ~** pusieron al niño bajo custodia del gobierno; **"with ~"** **"¡frágil!"**; **to take ~ to** cuidarse de, tener cuidado de; **to take ~ of** vt cuidar; (*details, arrangements*) encargarse de; **I don't ~** no me importa; **I couldn't ~ less** me trae sin cuidado.

▶**care for** vt fus cuidar; (*like*) querer.

careen [kə'riːn] vi (*ship*) inclinarse, escorar ♦ vt carenar.

career [kə'rɪə*] n carrera (profesional); (*occupation*) profesión f ♦ vi (*also*: **~ along**) correr a toda velocidad.

career girl n mujer f dedicada a su profesión.

careers officer n consejero/a de orientación profesional.

carefree ['kɛəfriː] adj despreocupado.

careful ['kɛəful] adj cuidadoso; (*cautious*) cauteloso; **(be) ~!** ¡ten cuidado!; **he's very ~ with his money** mira mucho el dinero; (*pej*) es muy tacaño.

carefully ['kɛəfəlɪ] adv con cuidado, cuidadosamente.

careless ['kɛəlɪs] adj descuidado; (*heedless*) poco atento.

carelessly ['kɛəlɪslɪ] adv sin cuidado, a la ligera.

carelessness ['kɛəlɪsnɪs] n descuido, falta de atención.

carer ['kɛərə*] n *persona que cuida de*

enfermos, ancianos o disminuidos.

caress [kə'rɛs] n caricia ♦ vt acariciar.

caretaker ['kɛəteɪkə*] n portero/a, conserje m/f.

caretaker government n gobierno provisional.

car-ferry ['kɑːfɛrɪ] n transbordador m para coches.

cargo, pl ~es ['kɑːgəu] n cargamento, carga.

cargo boat n buque m de carga, carguero.

cargo plane n avión m de carga.

car hire n alquiler m de coches.

Caribbean [kærɪ'biːən] adj caribe, caribeño; **the ~ (Sea)** el (Mar) Caribe.

caricature ['kærɪkətjuə*] n caricatura.

caring ['kɛərɪŋ] adj humanitario.

carnage ['kɑːnɪdʒ] n matanza, carnicería.

carnal ['kɑːnl] adj carnal.

carnation [kɑː'neɪʃən] n clavel m.

carnival ['kɑːnɪvəl] n carnaval m; (*US*) parque m de atracciones.

carnivore ['kɑːnɪvɔː*] n carnívoro/a.

carnivorous [kɑː'nɪvrəs] adj carnívoro.

carol ['kærəl] n: **(Christmas) ~** villancico.

carouse [kə'rauz] vi estar de juerga.

carousel [kærə'sɛl] n (*US*) tiovivo, caballitos mpl.

carp [kɑːp] n (*fish*) carpa.

▶**carp at** or **about** vt fus sacar faltas de.

car park n (*BRIT*) aparcamiento, parking m, playa de estacionamiento (*LAM*).

carpenter ['kɑːpɪntə*] n carpintero.

carpentry ['kɑːpɪntrɪ] n carpintería.

carpet ['kɑːpɪt] n alfombra ♦ vt alfombrar; **fitted ~** moqueta.

carpet bombing n bombardeo de arrasamiento.

carpet slippers npl zapatillas fpl.

carpet sweeper [-'swiːpə*] n cepillo mecánico.

car phone n teléfono de coche.

carping ['kɑːpɪŋ] adj (*critical*) criticón/ona.

carriage ['kærɪdʒ] n coche m; (*BRIT RAIL*) vagón m; (*for goods*) transporte m; (*of typewriter*) carro; (*bearing*) porte m; **~ forward** porte m debido; **~ free** franco de porte; **~ paid** porte pagado; **~ inwards/ outwards** gastos mpl de transporte a cargo del comprador/vendedor.

carriage return n (*on typewriter etc*) tecla de regreso.

carriageway ['kærɪdʒweɪ] n (*BRIT: part of road*) calzada; **dual ~** autovía.

carrier ['kærɪə*] n transportista m/f; (*company*) empresa de transportes; (*MED*) portador(a) m/f.

carrier bag n (*BRIT*) bolsa de papel or

plástico.
carrier pigeon *n* paloma mensajera.
carrion ['kærɪən] *n* carroña.
carrot ['kærət] *n* zanahoria.
carry ['kærɪ] *vt* (*subj: person*) llevar; (*transport*) transportar; (*a motion, bill*) aprobar; (*involve: responsibilities etc*) entrañar, conllevar; (*COMM: stock*) tener en existencia; (: *interest*) llevar; (*MATH: figure*) llevarse ♦ *vi* (*sound*) oírse; **to get carried away** (*fig*) entusiasmarse; **this loan carries 10% interest** este empréstito devenga un interés del 10 por ciento.
► **carry forward** *vt* (*MATH, COMM*) pasar a la página/columna siguiente.
► **carry on** *vi* (*continue*) seguir (adelante), continuar; (*fam: complain*) montar el número ♦ *vt* seguir, continuar.
► **carry out** *vt* (*orders*) cumplir; (*investigation*) llevar a cabo, realizar.
carrycot ['kærɪkɔt] *n* (*BRIT*) cuna portátil, capazo.
carry-on ['kærɪ'ɔn] *n* (*col*) follón *m*.
cart [kɑːt] *n* carro, carreta ♦ *vt* cargar con.
carte blanche ['kɑːt'blɒnʃ] *n*: **to give sb ~** dar carta blanca a algn.
cartel [kɑː'tɛl] *n* (*COMM*) cartel *m*.
cartilage ['kɑːtɪlɪdʒ] *n* cartílago.
cartographer [kɑː'tɔgrəfə*] *n* cartógrafo/a.
carton ['kɑːtən] *n* caja (de cartón); (*of cigarettes*) cartón *m*.
cartoon [kɑː'tuːn] *n* (*PRESS*) chiste *m*; (*comic strip*) historieta, tira cómica; (*film*) dibujos *mpl* animados.
cartoonist [kɑː'tuːnɪst] *n* humorista *m/f* gráfico.
cartridge ['kɑːtrɪdʒ] *n* cartucho.
cartwheel ['kɑːtwiːl] *n*: **to turn a ~** dar una voltereta lateral.
carve [kɑːv] *vt* (*meat*) trinchar; (*wood*) tallar; (*stone*) cincelar, esculpir; (*on tree*) grabar.
► **carve up** *vt* dividir, repartir; (*meat*) trinchar.
carving ['kɑːvɪŋ] *n* (*in wood etc*) escultura, talla.
carving knife *n* trinchante *m*.
car wash *n* túnel *m* de lavado.
Casablanca [kæsə'blæŋkə] *n* Casablanca.
cascade [kæs'keɪd] *n* salto de agua, cascada; (*fig*) chorro ♦ *vi* caer a chorros.
case [keɪs] *n* (*container*) caja; (*MED*) caso; (*for jewels etc*) estuche *m*; (*LAW*) causa, proceso; (*BRIT: also*: **suit~**) maleta; **lower/upper ~** (*TYP*) caja baja/alta; **in ~ of** en caso de; **in any ~** en todo caso; **just in ~** por si acaso; **to have a good ~** tener buenas razones; **there's a strong ~ for**

reform hay razones sólidas para exigir una reforma.
case history *n* (*MED*) historial *m* médico, historia clínica.
case study *n* estudio de casos prácticos.
cash [kæʃ] *n* (dinero) efectivo; (*col: money*) dinero ♦ *vt* cobrar, hacer efectivo; **to pay (in) ~** pagar al contado; **~ on delivery (COD)** entrega contra reembolso; **~ with order** paga al hacer el pedido; **to be short of ~** estar pelado, estar sin blanca.
► **cash in** *vt* (*insurance policy etc*) cobrar ♦ *vi*: **to ~ in on sth** sacar partido *or* aprovecharse de algo.
cash account *n* cuenta de caja.
cash and carry *n* cash and carry *m*, autoservicio mayorista.
cashbook ['kæʃbuk] *n* libro de caja.
cash box *n* hucha.
cash card *n* tarjeta *f* de(l) cajero (automático).
cash desk *n* (*BRIT*) caja.
cash discount *n* descuento por pago al contado.
cash dispenser *n* cajero automático.
cashew [kæ'ʃuː] *n* (*also*: **~ nut**) anacardo.
cash flow *n* flujo de fondos, cash-flow *m*, movimiento de efectivo.
cashier [kæ'ʃɪə*] *n* cajero/a ♦ *vt* (*MIL*) destituir, expulsar.
cashmere ['kæʃmɪə*] *n* cachemir *m*, cachemira.
cash payment *n* pago al contado.
cash price *n* precio al contado.
cash register *n* caja.
cash reserves *npl* reserva en efectivo.
cash sale *n* venta al contado.
casing ['keɪsɪŋ] *n* revestimiento.
casino [kə'siːnəu] *n* casino.
cask [kɑːsk] *n* tonel *m*, barril *m*.
casket ['kɑːskɪt] *n* cofre *m*, estuche *m*; (*US: coffin*) ataúd *m*.
Caspian Sea ['kæspɪən-] *n*: **the ~** el Mar Caspio.
cassava [kə'sɑːvə] *n* mandioca.
casserole ['kæsərəul] *n* (*food, pot*) cazuela.
cassette [kæ'sɛt] *n* cas(s)et(t)e *m or f*.
cassette deck *n* platina.
cassette player, cassette recorder *n* cas(s)et(t)e *m*.
cassock ['kæsək] *n* sotana.
cast [kɑːst] *vb* (*pt, pp* **cast**) *vt* (*throw*) echar, arrojar, lanzar; (*skin*) mudar, perder; (*metal*) fundir; (*THEAT*): **to ~ sb as Othello** dar a algn el papel de Otelo ♦ *n* (*THEAT*) reparto; (*mould*) forma, molde *m*; (*also*: **plaster ~**) vaciado; **to ~ loose** soltar; **to ~ one's vote** votar.

►**cast aside** *vt* (*reject*) descartar, desechar.
►**cast away** *vt* desechar.
►**cast down** *vt* derribar.
►**cast off** *vi* (*NAUT*) soltar amarras; (*KNITTING*) cerrar los puntos ◊ *vt* (*KNITTING*) cerrar; **to ~ sb off** abandonar a algn, desentenderse de algn.
►**cast on** *vt* (*KNITTING*) montar.
castanets [kæstə'nɛts] *npl* castañuelas *fpl*.
castaway ['kɑːstəwəɪ] *n* náufrago/a.
caste [kɑːst] *n* casta.
caster sugar ['kɑːstə*-] *n* (*BRIT*) azúcar *m* en polvo.
Castile [kæs'tiːl] *n* Castilla.
Castilian [kæs'tɪlɪən] *adj, n* castellano/a ◊ *n* (*LING*) castellano.
casting vote ['kɑːstɪŋ-] *n* (*BRIT*) voto decisivo.
cast iron *n* hierro fundido *or* colado ◊ *adj* (*fig: alibi*) irrebatible; (*will*) férreo.
castle ['kɑːsl] *n* castillo; (*CHESS*) torre *f*.
castor ['kɑːstə*] *n* (*wheel*) ruedecilla.
castor oil *n* aceite *m* de ricino.
castrate [kæs'treɪt] *vt* castrar.
casual ['kæʒjul] *adj* (*by chance*) fortuito; (*irregular: work etc*) eventual, temporero; (*unconcerned*) despreocupado; (*informal: clothes*) de sport.
casually ['kæʒjuli] *adv* por casualidad; de manera despreocupada.
casualty ['kæʒjultɪ] *n* víctima, herido; (*dead*) muerto; (*MIL*) baja; **heavy casualties** numerosas bajas *fpl*.
casualty ward *n* urgencias *fpl*.
cat [kæt] *n* gato.
catacombs ['kætəkuːmz] *npl* catacumbas *fpl*.
Catalan ['kætəlæn] *adj, n* catalán/ana *m/f*.
catalogue, (*US*) catalog ['kætəlɒg] *n* catálogo ◊ *vt* catalogar.
Catalonia [kætə'ləʊnɪə] *n* Cataluña.
catalyst ['kætəlɪst] *n* catalizador *m*.
catalytic converter [kætə'lɪtɪkkən'vəːtə*] *n* catalizador *m*.
catapult ['kætəpʌlt] *n* tirachinas *m inv*.
cataract ['kætərækt] *n* (*MED*) cataratas *fpl*.
catarrh [kə'tɑː*] *n* catarro.
catastrophe [kə'tæstrəfɪ] *n* catástrofe *f*.
catastrophic [kætə'strɒfɪk] *adj* catastrófico.
catcall ['kætkɔːl] *n* (*at meeting etc*) rechifla, silbido.
catch [kætʃ] *vb* (*pt, pp* **caught** [kɔːt]) *vt* coger (*SP*), agarrar (*LAM*); (*arrest*) atrapar, coger (*SP*); (*grasp*) asir; (*breath*) recobrar; (*person: by surprise*) pillar; (*attract: attention*) captar; (*MED*) pillar, coger; (*also: ~ up*) alcanzar ◊ *vi* (*fire*)

encenderse; (*in branches etc*) engancharse ◊ *n* (*fish etc*) captura; (*act of catching*) cogida; (*trick*) trampa; (*of lock*) pestillo, cerradura; **to ~ fire** prenderse; (*house*) incendiarse; **to ~ sight of** divisar.
►**catch on** *vi* (*understand*) caer en la cuenta; (*grow popular*) tener éxito, cuajar.
►**catch out** *vt* (*fig: with trick question*) hundir.
►**catch up** *vi* (*fig*) ponerse al día.
catching ['kætʃɪŋ] *adj* (*MED*) contagioso.
catchment area ['kætʃmənt-] *n* (*BRIT*) zona de captación.
catch phrase *n* frase *f* de moda.
catch-22 ['kætʃtwɛntɪ'tuː] *n*: **it's a ~ situation** es un callejón sin salida, es un círculo vicioso.
catchy ['kætʃɪ] *adj* (*tune*) pegadizo.
catechism ['kætɪkɪzəm] *n* (*REL*) catecismo.
categoric(al) [kætɪ'gɒrɪk(əl)] *adj* categórico, terminante.
categorically [kætɪ'gɒrɪkəlɪ] *adv* categóricamente, terminantemente.
categorize ['kætɪgəraɪz] *vt* clasificar.
category ['kætɪgərɪ] *n* categoría.
cater ['keɪtə*] *vi*: **to ~ for** (*BRIT*) abastecer a; (*needs*) atender a; (*consumers*) proveer a.
caterer ['keɪtərə*] *n* abastecedor(a) *m/f*, proveedor(a) *m/f*.
catering ['keɪtərɪŋ] *n* (*trade*) hostelería.
caterpillar ['kætəpɪlə*] *n* oruga.
caterpillar track *n* rodado de oruga.
cat flap *n* gatera.
cathedral [kə'θiːdrəl] *n* catedral *f*.
cathode-ray tube ['kæθəʊdreɪ'tjuːb] *n* tubo de rayos catódicos.
catholic ['kæθəlɪk] *adj* católico; **C~** *adj, n* (*REL*) católico/a *m/f*.
CAT scanner [kæt-] (*MED*) *n abbr* (= *computerized axial tomography scanner*) escáner *m* TAC.
cat's-eye ['kætsaɪ] *n* (*BRIT AUT*) catafaro.
catsup ['kætsəp] *n* (*US*) ketchup, catsup *m*.
cattle ['kætl] *npl* ganado *sg*.
catty ['kætɪ] *adj* malicioso.
catwalk ['kætwɔːk] *n* pasarela.
Caucasian [kɔː'keɪzɪən] *adj, n* caucásico/a *m/f*.
Caucasus ['kɔːkəsəs] *n* Cáucaso.
caucus ['kɔːkəs] *n* (*POL: local committee*) comité *m* local; (: *US: to elect candidates*) comité *m* electoral; (: *group*) camarilla política.
caught [kɔːt] *pt, pp of* **catch**.
cauliflower ['kɒlɪflaʊə*] *n* coliflor *f*.
cause [kɔːz] *n* causa; (*reason*) motivo,

razón *f* ♦ *vt* causar; (*provoke*) provocar; **to ~ sb to do sth** hacer que algn haga algo.
causeway ['kɔːzweɪ] *n* (*road*) carretera elevada; (*embankment*) terraplén *m*.
caustic ['kɔːstɪk] *adj* cáustico; (*fig*) mordaz.
cauterize ['kɔːtəraɪz] *vt* cauterizar.
caution ['kɔːʃən] *n* cautela, prudencia; (*warning*) advertencia, amonestación *f* ♦ *vt* amonestar.
cautious ['kɔːʃəs] *adj* cauteloso, prudente, precavido.
cautiously ['kɔːʃəslɪ] *adv* con cautela.
cautiousness ['kɔːʃəsnɪs] *n* cautela.
cavalcade [kævəl'keɪd] *n* cabalgata.
cavalier [kævə'lɪə*] *n* (*knight*) caballero ♦ *adj* (*pej: offhand: person, attitude*) arrogante, desdeñoso.
cavalry ['kævəlrɪ] *n* caballería.
cave [keɪv] *n* cueva, caverna ♦ *vi*: **to go caving** ir en una expedición espeleológica.
►**cave in** *vi* (*roof etc*) derrumbarse, hundirse.
caveman ['keɪvmæn] *n* cavernícola *m*.
cavern ['kævən] *n* caverna.
cavernous ['kævənəs] *adj* (*cheeks, eyes*) hundido.
caviar(e) ['kævɪɑː*] *n* caviar *m*.
cavity ['kævɪtɪ] *n* hueco, cavidad *f*.
cavity wall insulation *n* aislamiento térmico.
cavort [kə'vɔːt] *vi* hacer cabrioladas.
cayenne [keɪ'ɛn] *n*: **~ pepper** pimentón *m* picante.
CB *n abbr* (= *Citizens' Band (Radio)*) frecuencias de radio usadas para la comunicación privada; (*BRIT*: = *Companion of (the Order of) the Bath*) título de nobleza.
CBC *n abbr* (= *Canadian Broadcasting Corporation*) cadena de radio y televisión.
CBE *n abbr* (= *Companion of (the Order of) the British Empire*) título de nobleza.
CBI *n abbr* (= *Confederation of British Industry*) ≈ C.E.O.E. *f* (*SP*).
CBS *n abbr* (*US*: = *Columbia Broadcasting System*) cadena de radio y televisión.
CC *abbr* (*BRIT*) = *County Council*.
cc *abbr* (= *cubic centimetres*) cc, cm³; (*on letter etc*) = *carbon copy*.
CCA *n abbr* (*US*: = *Circuit Court of Appeals*) tribunal de apelación itinerante.
CCU *n abbr* (*US*: = *coronary care unit*) unidad *f* de cuidados cardiológicos.
CD *n abbr* (= *compact disc*) CD *m*; **~ player** reproductor *m* de compact disc; (*MIL*) = *Civil Defence (Corps)* (*BRIT*), *Civil Defense* (*US*) ♦ *abbr* (*BRIT*: = *Corps Diplomatique*)

CD.
CDC *n abbr* (*US*) = *center for disease control*.
CD-I ® *n* (= *Compact Disc Interactive*) CD-I *m*, disco *m* compacto interactivo.
Cdr. *abbr* = **Commander**.
CD-ROM *n abbr* (= *compact disc read-only memory*) CD-ROM *m*.
CDT *n abbr* (*US*: = *Central Daylight Time*) hora de verano del centro.
cease [siːs] *vt* cesar.
ceasefire ['siːsfaɪə*] *n* alto *m* el fuego.
ceaseless ['siːslɪs] *adj* incesante.
ceaselessly ['siːslɪslɪ] *adv* sin cesar.
CED *n abbr* (*US*) = *Committee for Economic Development*.
cedar ['siːdə*] *n* cedro.
cede [siːd] *vt* ceder.
CEEB *n abbr* (*US*: = *College Entrance Examination Board*) tribunal para las pruebas de acceso a la universidad.
ceilidh ['keɪlɪ] *n* baile con música y danzas tradicionales escocesas o irlandesas.
ceiling ['siːlɪŋ] *n* techo; (*fig: upper limit*) límite *m*, tope *m*.
celebrate ['sɛlɪbreɪt] *vt* celebrar; (*have a party*) festejar ♦ *vi*: **let's ~!** ¡vamos a celebrarlo!
celebrated ['sɛlɪbreɪtɪd] *adj* célebre.
celebration [sɛlɪ'breɪʃən] *n* celebración *f*, festejo.
celebrity [sɪ'lɛbrɪtɪ] *n* celebridad *f*.
celeriac [sə'lɛrɪæk] *n* apio-nabo.
celery ['sɛlərɪ] *n* apio.
celestial [sɪ'lɛstɪəl] *adj* (*of sky*) celeste; (*divine*) celestial.
celibacy ['sɛlɪbəsɪ] *n* celibato.
cell [sɛl] *n* celda; (*BIOL*) célula; (*ELEC*) elemento.
cellar ['sɛlə*] *n* sótano; (*for wine*) bodega.
cellist ['tʃɛlɪst] *n* violoncelista *m/f*.
cello ['tʃɛləʊ] *n* violoncelo.
cellophane ['sɛləfeɪn] *n* celofán *m*.
cellphone ['sɛlfəʊn] *n* teléfono celular.
cellular ['sɛljʊlə*] *adj* celular.
celluloid ['sɛljʊlɔɪd] *n* celuloide *m*.
cellulose ['sɛljʊləʊs] *n* celulosa.
Celsius ['sɛlsɪəs] *adj* centígrado.
Celt [kɛlt, sɛlt] *n* celta *m/f*.
Celtic ['kɛltɪk, 'sɛltɪk] *adj* celta, céltico ♦ *n* (*LING*) celta.
cement [sə'mɛnt] *n* cemento ♦ *vt* cementar; (*fig*) cimentar.
cement mixer *n* hormigonera.
cemetery ['sɛmɪtrɪ] *n* cementerio.
cenotaph ['sɛnətɑːf] *n* cenotafio.
censor ['sɛnsə*] *n* censor(a) *m/f* ♦ *vt* (*cut*) censurar.
censorship ['sɛnsəʃɪp] *n* censura.

censure ['sɛnʃə*] vt censurar.
census ['sɛnsəs] n censo.
cent [sɛnt] n (US: coin) centavo; see also **per**.
centenary [sɛn'tiːnərɪ], (US) **centennial** [sɛn'tɛnɪəl] n centenario.
center ['sɛntə*] n (US) = **centre**.
centigrade ['sɛntɪɡreɪd] adj centígrado.
centilitre, (US) **centiliter** ['sɛntɪliːtə*] n centilitro.
centimetre, (US) **centimeter** ['sɛntɪmiːtə*] n centímetro.
centipede ['sɛntɪpiːd] n ciempiés m inv.
central ['sɛntrəl] adj central; (of house etc) céntrico.
Central African Republic n República Centroafricana.
Central America n Centroamérica.
Central American adj, n centroamericano/a m/f.
central heating n calefacción f central.
centralize ['sɛntrəlaɪz] vt centralizar.
central processing unit (CPU) n (COMPUT) unidad f procesadora central, unidad f central de proceso.
central reservation n (BRIT AUT) mediana.
centre, (US) **center** ['sɛntə*] n centro ♦ vt centrar; **to ~ (on)** (concentrate) concentrar (en).
centrefold, (US) **centerfold** ['sɛntəfəuld] n página central plegable.
centre-forward ['sɛntə'fɔːwəd] n (SPORT) delantero centro.
centre-half ['sɛntə'hɑːf] n (SPORT) medio centro.
centrepiece, (US) **centerpiece** ['sɛntəpiːs] n punto central.
centre spread n (BRIT) páginas fpl centrales.
centre-stage n: **to take ~** pasar a primer plano.
centrifuge ['sɛntrɪfjuːdʒ] n centrifugadora.
century ['sɛntjurɪ] n siglo; **20th ~** siglo veinte; **in the twentieth ~** en el siglo veinte.
CEO n abbr (US) = **chief executive officer**.
ceramic [sɪ'ræmɪk] adj de cerámica.
ceramics [sɪ'ræmɪks] n cerámica.
cereal ['siːrɪəl] n cereal m.
cerebral ['sɛrɪbrəl] adj cerebral.
ceremonial [sɛrɪ'məunɪəl] n ceremonial.
ceremony ['sɛrɪmənɪ] n ceremonia; **to stand on ~** hacer ceremonias, andarse con cumplidos.
cert [səːt] n (BRIT col): **it's a dead ~** ¡es cosa segura!
certain ['səːtən] adj seguro; (correct) cierto; (particular) cierto; **for ~** a ciencia cierta.
certainly ['səːtənlɪ] adv desde luego, por

supuesto.
certainty ['səːtəntɪ] n certeza, certidumbre f, seguridad f.
certificate [sə'tɪfɪkɪt] n certificado.
certified ['səːtɪfaɪd] adj: **~ mail** (US) correo certificado.
certified public accountant (CPA) n (US) contable m/f diplomado/a.
certify ['səːtɪfaɪ] vt certificar.
cervical ['səːvɪkl] adj: **~ cancer** cáncer m cervical; **~ smear** citología.
cervix ['səːvɪks] n cerviz f, cuello del útero.
Cesarean [sɪ'zɛərɪən] adj, n (US) = **Caesarean**.
cessation [sə'seɪʃən] n cese m, suspensión f.
cesspit ['sɛspɪt] n pozo negro.
CET n abbr (= Central European Time) hora de Europa central.
Ceylon [sɪ'lɔn] n Ceilán m.
cf. abbr (= compare) cfr.
CFC n abbr (= chlorofluorocarbon) CFC m.
c/f abbr (COMM) = carried forward.
CG n abbr (US) = **coastguard**.
cg abbr (= centigram) cg.
CH n abbr (BRIT: = Companion of Honour) título de nobleza.
ch abbr (BRIT: = central heating) cal. cen.
ch. abbr (= chapter) cap.
Chad [tʃæd] n Chad m.
chafe [tʃeɪf] vt (rub) rozar; (irritate) irritar; **to ~ (against)** (fig) irritarse or enojarse (con).
chaffinch ['tʃæfɪntʃ] n pinzón m (vulgar).
chagrin ['ʃæɡrɪn] n (annoyance) disgusto; (disappointment) desazón f.
chain [tʃeɪn] n cadena ♦ vt (also: **~ up**) encadenar.
chain reaction n reacción f en cadena.
chain-smoke ['tʃeɪnsməuk] vi fumar un cigarrillo tras otro.
chain store n tienda de una cadena, ≈ grandes almacenes mpl.
chair [tʃɛə*] n silla; (armchair) sillón m; (of university) cátedra ♦ vt (meeting) presidir; **the ~** (US: electric ~) la silla eléctrica; **please take a ~** siéntese or tome asiento, por favor.
chairlift ['tʃɛəlɪft] n telesilla m.
chairman ['tʃɛəmən] n presidente m.
chairperson ['tʃɛəpəːsn] n presidente/a m/f.
chairwoman ['tʃɛəwumən] n presidenta.
chalet ['ʃæleɪ] n chalet m (de madera).
chalice ['tʃælɪs] n cáliz m.
chalk [tʃɔːk] n (GEO) creta; (for writing) tiza, gis m (LAM).
▶**chalk up** vt apuntar; (fig: success, victory) apuntarse.
challenge ['tʃælɪndʒ] n desafío, reto ♦ vt

desafiar, retar; (*statement, right*) poner en
duda; **to ~ sb to do sth** retar a algn a que
haga algo.
challenger ['tʃælɪndʒə*] *n* (*SPORT*)
contrincante *m/f*.
challenging ['tʃælɪndʒɪŋ] *adj* que supone un
reto; (*tone*) de desafío.
chamber ['tʃeɪmbə*] *n* cámara, sala; **~ of
commerce** cámara de comercio.
chambermaid ['tʃeɪmbəmeɪd] *n* camarera.
chamber music *n* música de cámara.
chamberpot ['tʃeɪmbəpɔt] *n* orinal *m*.
chameleon [kə'miːlɪən] *n* camaleón *m*.
chamois ['ʃæmwɑː] *n* gamuza.
champagne [ʃæm'peɪn] *n* champaña *m*,
champán *m*.
champers ['ʃæmpəz] *nsg* (*col*) champán *m*.
champion ['tʃæmpɪən] *n* campeón/ona *m/f*;
(*of cause*) defensor(a) *m/f*, paladín *m/f* ♦ *vt*
defender, apoyar.
championship ['tʃæmpɪənʃɪp] *n*
campeonato.
chance [tʃɑːns] *n* (*coincidence*) casualidad *f*;
(*luck*) suerte *f*; (*fate*) azar *m*; (*opportunity*)
ocasión *f*, oportunidad *f*, chance *m or f*
(*LAM*); (*likelihood*) posibilidad *f*; (*risk*)
riesgo ♦ *vt* arriesgar, probar ♦ *adj*
fortuito, casual; **to ~ it** arriesgarse,
intentarlo; **to take a ~** arriesgarse; **by ~**
por casualidad; **it's the ~ of a lifetime** es
la oportunidad de su vida; **the ~s are that**
... lo más probable es que ...; **to ~ to do
sth** (*happen*) hacer algo por casualidad.
▶**chance (up)on** *vt fus* tropezar(se) con.
chancel ['tʃɑːnsəl] *n* coro y presbiterio.
chancellor ['tʃɑːnsələ*] *n* canciller *m*; **C~ of
the Exchequer** (*BRIT*) Ministro de
Economía y Hacienda; *see also* **Downing
Street**.
chancy ['tʃɑːnsɪ] *adj* (*col*) arriesgado.
chandelier [ʃændə'lɪə*] *n* araña (de luces).
change [tʃeɪndʒ] *vt* cambiar; (*clothes,
house*) cambiarse de, mudarse de;
(*transform*) transformar ♦ *vi* cambiar(se);
(*trains*) hacer transbordo; (*be
transformed*): **to ~ into** transformarse en
♦ *n* cambio; (*alteration*) modificación *f*,
transformación *f*; (*coins*) suelto; (*money
returned*) vuelta, vuelto (*LAM*); **to ~
mind** cambiar de opinión *or* idea; **to ~
gear** (*AUT*) cambiar de marcha; **she ~d
into an old skirt** se puso una falda vieja;
for a ~ para variar; **can you give me ~
for £1?** ¿tiene cambio de una libra?; **keep
the ~** quédese con la vuelta.
changeable ['tʃeɪndʒəbl] *adj* (*weather*)
cambiable; (*person*) variable.
changeless ['tʃeɪndʒlɪs] *adj* inmutable.

change machine *n* máquina de cambio.
changeover ['tʃeɪndʒəuvə*] *n* (*to new
system*) cambio.
changing ['tʃeɪndʒɪŋ] *adj* cambiante.
changing room *n* (*BRIT*) vestuario.
channel ['tʃænl] *n* (*TV*) canal *m*; (*of river*)
cauce *m*; (*of sea*) estrecho; (*groove, fig:
medium*) conducto, medio ♦ *vt* (*river etc*)
encauzar; **to ~ into** (*fig: interest, energies*)
encauzar a, dirigir a; **the (English) C~** el
Canal (de la Mancha); **the C~ Islands** las
Islas Anglonormandas; **~s of
communication** canales *mpl* de
comunicación; **green/red ~** (*CUSTOMS*)
pasillo verde/rojo.
Channel Tunnel *n*: **the ~** el túnel del
Canal de la Mancha, el Eurotúnel.
chant [tʃɑːnt] *n* canto; (*of crowd*) gritos *mpl*
♦ *vt* cantar; **the demonstrators ~ed their
disapproval** los manifestantes corearon
su desaprobación.
chaos ['keɪɔs] *n* caos *m*.
chaos theory *n* teoría del caos.
chaotic [keɪ'ɔtɪk] *adj* caótico.
chap [tʃæp] *n* (*BRIT col: man*) tío, tipo; **old ~**
amigo (mío).
chapel ['tʃæpəl] *n* capilla.
chaperone ['ʃæpərəun] *n* carabina.
chaplain ['tʃæplɪn] *n* capellán *m*.
chapped [tʃæpt] *adj* agrietado.
chapter ['tʃæptə*] *n* capítulo.
char [tʃɑː*] *vt* (*burn*) carbonizar,
chamuscar ♦ *n* (*BRIT*) = **charlady**.
character ['kærɪktə*] *n* carácter *m*,
naturaleza, índole *f*; (*in novel, film*)
personaje *m*; (*role*) papel *m*; (*individuality,
COMPUT*) carácter *m*; **a person of good ~**
una persona de buena reputación.
character code *n* código de caracteres.
characteristic [kærɪktə'rɪstɪk] *adj*
característico ♦ *n* característica.
characterize ['kærɪktəraɪz] *vt* caracterizar.
charade [ʃə'rɑːd] *n* farsa, comedia; **~s**
(*game*) charadas *fpl*.
charcoal ['tʃɑːkəul] *n* carbón *m* vegetal;
(*ART*) carboncillo.
charge [tʃɑːdʒ] *n* carga; (*LAW*) cargo,
acusación *f*; (*cost*) precio, coste *m*;
(*responsibility*) cargo; (*task*) encargo ♦ *vt*
(*LAW*) acusar (*with de*); (*gun, battery, MIL:
enemy*) cargar; (*price*) pedir; (*customer*)
cobrar; (*sb with task*) encargar ♦ *vi*
precipitarse; (*make pay*) cobrar; **~s** *npl*:
bank ~s comisiones *fpl* bancarias; **extra ~**
recargo, suplemento; **free of ~** gratis; **to
reverse the ~s** (*BRIT TEL*) llamar a cobro
revertido; **to take ~ of** hacerse cargo de,
encargarse de; **to be in ~ of** estar

encargado de; **how much do you ~?**
¿cuánto cobra usted?; **to ~ an expense
(up) to sb's account** cargar algo a cuenta
de algn; **~ it to my account** póngalo *or*
cárguelo a mi cuenta.
charge account *n* (*US*) cuenta abierta *or* a
crédito.
charge card *n* tarjeta de cuenta.
chargé d'affaires ['ʃɑːʒeɪdæ'fɛəʳ] *n*
encargado de negocios.
chargehand ['tʃɑːdʒhænd] *n* capataz *m*.
charger ['tʃɑːdʒəʳ] *n* (*also*: **battery ~**)
cargador *m* (de baterías); (*old*: *warhorse*)
caballo de batalla.
chariot ['tʃærɪət] *n* carro.
charisma [kæ'rɪzmə] *n* carisma *m*.
charitable ['tʃærɪtəbl] *adj* caritativo.
charity ['tʃærɪtɪ] *n* (*gen*) caridad *f*;
(*organization*) organización *f* benéfica.
charlady ['tʃɑːleɪdɪ] *n* (*BRIT*) mujer *f* de la
limpieza.
charlatan ['ʃɑːlətən] *n* charlatán *m*.
charm [tʃɑːm] *n* encanto, atractivo; (*spell*)
hechizo; (*object*) amuleto ♦ *vt* encantar;
hechizar.
charm bracelet *n* pulsera amuleto.
charming ['tʃɑːmɪŋ] *adj* encantador(a);
(*person*) simpático.
chart [tʃɑːt] *n* (*table*) cuadro; (*graph*)
gráfica; (*map*) carta de navegación;
(*weather ~*) mapa *m* meteorológico ♦ *vt*
(*course*) trazar; (*sales, progress*) hacer una
gráfica de; **to be in the ~s** (*record, pop
group*) estar en la lista de éxitos.
charter ['tʃɑːtəʳ] *vt* (*bus*) alquilar; (*plane,
ship*) fletar ♦ *n* (*document*) estatuto, carta;
on ~ en alquiler, alquilado.
chartered accountant (CA) *n* (*BRIT*)
contable *m/f* diplomado/a.
charter flight *n* vuelo chárter.
charwoman ['tʃɑːwumən] *n* = **charlady**.
chase [tʃeɪs] *vt* (*pursue*) perseguir; (*hunt*)
cazar ♦ *n* persecución *f*; caza; **to ~ after**
correr tras.
►**chase up** *vt* (*information*) tratar de
conseguir; **to ~ sb up about sth** recordar
algo a algn.
chasm ['kæzəm] *n* abismo.
chassis ['ʃæsɪ] *n* chasis *m*.
chaste [tʃeɪst] *adj* casto.
chastened ['tʃeɪsənd] *adj* escarmentado.
chastening ['tʃeɪsnɪŋ] *adj* aleccionador(a).
chastity ['tʃæstɪtɪ] *n* castidad *f*.
chat [tʃæt] *vi* (*also*: **have a ~**) charlar ♦ *n*
charla.
►**chat up** *vt* (*col*: *girl*) ligar con, enrollarse
con.
chatline ['tʃætlaɪn] *n* línea (telefónica)

múltiple, party line *f*.
chat show *n* (*BRIT*) programa *m* de
entrevistas.
chattel ['tʃætl] *n* bien *m* mueble.
chatter ['tʃætəʳ] *vi* (*person*) charlar; (*teeth*)
castañetear ♦ *n* (*of birds*) parloteo; (*of
people*) charla, cháchara.
chatterbox ['tʃætəbɔks] *n* parlanchín/ina
m/f.
chattering classes ['tʃætərɪŋ'klɑːsɪz] *npl*:
the ~ (*col*: *pej*) los intelectualillos.
chatty ['tʃætɪ] *adj* (*style*) informal; (*person*)
hablador(a).
chauffeur ['ʃəufəʳ] *n* chófer *m*.
chauvinist ['ʃəuvɪnɪst] *n* (*male ~*) machista
m; (*nationalist*) chovinista *m/f*, patriotero/a
m/f.
ChE *abbr* = *chemical engineer*.
cheap [tʃiːp] *adj* barato; (*joke*) de mal
gusto, chabacano; (*poor quality*) malo;
(*reduced*: *ticket*) económico, (:*fare*) barato
♦ *adv* barato.
cheapen ['tʃiːpn] *vt* rebajar el precio de,
abaratar.
cheaply ['tʃiːplɪ] *adv* barato, a bajo precio.
cheat [tʃiːt] *vi* hacer trampa; (*in exam*)
copiar ♦ *vt* estafar, timar ♦ *n* trampa;
estafa; (*person*) tramposo/a; **he's been
~ing on his wife** ha estado engañando a
su esposa.
cheating ['tʃiːtɪŋ] *n* trampa.
check [tʃɛk] *vt* comprobar; (*count*) contar;
(*halt*) frenar; (*restrain*) refrenar,
restringir ♦ *vi*: **to ~ with sb** consultar con
algn; (*official etc*) informarse por ♦ *n*
(*inspection*) control *m*, inspección *f*; (*curb*)
freno; (*bill*) nota, cuenta; (*US*) = **cheque**;
(*pattern*: *gen pl*) cuadro ♦ *adj* (*also*: **~ed**:
pattern, cloth) a cuadros; **to keep a ~ on
sth/sb** controlar algo/a algn.
►**check in** *vi* (*in hotel*) registrarse; (*at
airport*) facturar ♦ *vt* (*luggage*) facturar.
►**check out** *vi* (*of hotel*) desocupar la
habitación ♦ *vt* (*investigate*: *story*)
comprobar; (:*person*) informarse sobre.
►**check up** *vi*: **to ~ up on sth** comprobar
algo; **to ~ up on sb** investigar a algn.
checkbook ['tʃɛkbuk] *n* (*US*) =
chequebook.
checkered ['tʃɛkəd] *adj* (*US*) = **chequered**.
checkers ['tʃɛkəz] *n* (*US*) damas *fpl*.
check-in ['tʃɛkɪn] *n* (*also*: **~ desk**: *at airport*)
mostrador *m* de facturación.
checking account ['tʃɛkɪŋ-] *n* (*US*) cuenta
corriente.
checklist ['tʃɛklɪst] *n* lista.
checkmate ['tʃɛkmeɪt] *n* jaque *m* mate.
checkout ['tʃɛkaut] *n* (*in supermarket*) caja.

checkpoint ['tʃɛkpɔɪnt] n (punto de) control m, retén m (LAM).
checkroom ['tʃɛkrum] n (US) consigna.
checkup ['tʃɛkʌp] n (MED) reconocimiento general; (of machine) revisión f.
cheek [tʃiːk] n mejilla; (impudence) descaro.
cheekbone ['tʃiːkbəun] n pómulo.
cheeky ['tʃiːkɪ] adj fresco, descarado.
cheep [tʃiːp] n (of bird) pío ♦ vi piar.
cheer [tʃɪə*] vt vitorear, ovacionar; (gladden) alegrar, animar ♦ vi dar vivas ♦ n viva m; ~s npl vítores mpl; ~s! ¡salud!
►**cheer on** vt (person etc) animar con aplausos or gritos.
►**cheer up** vi animarse ♦ vt alegrar, animar.
cheerful ['tʃɪəful] adj alegre.
cheerfulness ['tʃɪəfulnɪs] n alegría.
cheering ['tʃɪərɪŋ] n ovaciones fpl, vítores mpl.
cheerio [tʃɪərɪ'əu] excl (BRIT) ¡hasta luego!
cheerleader ['tʃɪəliːdə*] n animador(a) m/f.
cheerless ['tʃɪəlɪs] adj triste, sombrío.
cheese [tʃiːz] n queso.
cheeseboard ['tʃiːzbɔːd] n tabla de quesos.
cheeseburger ['tʃiːzbəːgə*] n hamburguesa con queso.
cheesecake ['tʃiːzkeɪk] n pastel m de queso.
cheetah ['tʃiːtə] n guepardo.
chef [ʃɛf] n jefe/a m/f de cocina.
chemical ['kɛmɪkəl] adj químico ♦ n producto químico.
chemist ['kɛmɪst] n (BRIT: pharmacist) farmacéutico/a; (scientist) químico/a; ~'s (shop) n (BRIT) farmacia.
chemistry ['kɛmɪstrɪ] n química.
chemotherapy [kiːməu'θɛrəpɪ] n quimioterapia.
cheque, (US) **check** [tʃɛk] n (BRIT) cheque m; **to pay by** ~ pagar con cheque.
chequebook, (US) **checkbook** ['tʃɛkbuk] n talonario (de cheques), chequera (LAM).
cheque card n (BRIT) tarjeta de identificación bancaria.
chequered, (US) **checkered** ['tʃɛkəd] adj (fig) accidentado; (pattern) de cuadros.
cherish ['tʃɛrɪʃ] vt (love) querer, apreciar; (protect) cuidar; (hope etc) abrigar.
cheroot [ʃə'ruːt] n puro (cortado en los dos extremos).
cherry ['tʃɛrɪ] n cereza.
Ches abbr (BRIT) = Cheshire.
chess [tʃɛs] n ajedrez m.
chessboard ['tʃɛsbɔːd] n tablero (de ajedrez).
chessman ['tʃɛsmən] n pieza (de ajedrez).

chest [tʃɛst] n (ANAT) pecho; (box) cofre m; **to get sth off one's** ~ (col) desahogarse; ~ **of drawers** n cómoda.
chest measurement n talla (de chaqueta etc).
chestnut ['tʃɛsnʌt] n castaña; (also: ~ **tree**) castaño; (colour) castaño ♦ adj (color) castaño inv.
chesty ['tʃɛstɪ] adj (cough) de bronquios, de pecho.
chew [tʃuː] vt mascar, masticar.
chewing gum ['tʃuːɪŋ-] n chicle m.
chic [ʃiːk] adj elegante.
chicanery [ʃɪ'keɪnərɪ] n embustes mpl, sofismas mpl.
Chicano [tʃɪ'kɑːnəu] adj, n chicano/a.
chick [tʃɪk] n pollito, polluelo; (US col) chica.
chicken ['tʃɪkɪn] n gallina, pollo; (food) pollo; (col: coward) gallina m/f.
►**chicken out** vi (col) rajarse; **to** ~ **out of doing sth** rajarse y no hacer algo.
chickenpox ['tʃɪkɪnpɔks] n varicela.
chickpea ['tʃɪkpiː] n garbanzo.
chicory ['tʃɪkərɪ] n (for coffee) achicoria; (salad) escarola.
chide [tʃaɪd] vt: **to** ~ **sb for sth** reprender a algn por algo.
chief [tʃiːf] n jefe/a m/f ♦ adj principal, máximo (esp LAM); **C~ of Staff** (MIL) Jefe m del Estado mayor.
chief executive, (US) **chief executive officer** n director m general.
chiefly ['tʃiːflɪ] adv principalmente.
chieftain ['tʃiːftən] n jefe m, cacique m.
chiffon ['ʃɪfɔn] n gasa.
chilblain ['tʃɪlbleɪn] n sabañón m.
child, pl ~**ren** [tʃaɪld, 'tʃɪldrən] n niño/a; (offspring) hijo/a.
child benefit n (BRIT) subsidio por cada hijo pequeño.
childbirth ['tʃaɪldbəːθ] n parto.
childhood ['tʃaɪldhud] n niñez f, infancia.
childish ['tʃaɪldɪʃ] adj pueril, infantil.
childless ['tʃaɪldlɪs] adj sin hijos.
childlike ['tʃaɪldlaɪk] adj de niño, infantil.
child minder n (BRIT) niñera, madre f de día.
child prodigy n niño/a prodigio inv.
children's home n centro de acogida para niños.
child's play n (fig): **this is** ~ esto es coser y cantar.
Chile ['tʃɪlɪ] n Chile m.
Chilean ['tʃɪlɪən] adj, n chileno/a m/f.
chill [tʃɪl] n frío; (MED) resfriado ♦ adj frío ♦ vt enfriar; (CULIN) refrigerar.
►**chill out** vi (esp US col) tranquilizarse.

chil(l)i ['tʃɪlɪ] n (BRIT) chile m, ají m (LAM).
chilling ['tʃɪlɪŋ] adj escalofriante.
chilly ['tʃɪlɪ] adj frío.
chime [tʃaɪm] n repique m, campanada ♦ vi repicar, sonar.
chimney ['tʃɪmnɪ] n chimenea.
chimney sweep n deshollinador m.
chimpanzee [tʃɪmpæn'zi:] n chimpancé m.
chin [tʃɪn] n mentón m, barbilla.
China ['tʃaɪnə] n China.
china ['tʃaɪnə] n porcelana; (crockery) loza.
Chinese [tʃaɪ'ni:z] adj chino ♦ n (pl inv) chino/a; (LING) chino.
chink [tʃɪŋk] n (opening) rendija, hendedura; (noise) tintineo.
chintz [tʃɪnts] n cretona.
chinwag ['tʃɪnwæg] n (BRIT col): **to have a ~** echar una parrafada.
chip [tʃɪp] n (gen pl: CULIN: BRIT) patata or papa (LAM) frita; (: US: also: **potato ~**) patata or papa (LAM) frita; (of wood) astilla; (stone) lasca; (in gambling) ficha; (COMPUT) chip m ♦ vt (cup, plate) desconchar; **when the ~s are down** (fig) a la hora de la verdad.
►**chip in** vi (col: interrupt) interrumpir, meterse; (: contribute) contribuir.
chipboard ['tʃɪpbɔːd] n madera aglomerada.
chipmunk ['tʃɪpmʌŋk] n ardilla listada.

> *Se denomina* **chip shop** *o* **fish-and-chip shop** *a un tipo de tienda popular de comida rápida en la que se despachan platos tradicionales británicos, principalmente filetes de pescado rebozado frito y patatas fritas.*

chiropodist [kɪ'rɔpədɪst] n (BRIT) podólogo/a.
chiropody [kɪ'rɔpədɪ] n podología.
chirp [tʃəːp] vi gorjear; (cricket) cantar ♦ n (of cricket) canto.
chirpy ['tʃəːpɪ] adj alegre, animado.
chisel ['tʃɪzl] n (for wood) escoplo; (for stone) cincel m.
chit [tʃɪt] n nota.
chitchat ['tʃɪtʃæt] n chismes mpl, habladurías fpl.
chivalrous ['ʃɪvəlrəs] adj caballeroso.
chivalry ['ʃɪvəlrɪ] n caballerosidad f.
chives [tʃaɪvz] npl cebollinos mpl.
chloride ['klɔːraɪd] n cloruro.
chlorinate ['klɔːrɪneɪt] vt clorar.
chlorine ['klɔːriːn] n cloro.
chock-a-block ['tʃɔkə'blɔk], **chock-full** [tʃɔk'ful] adj atestado.
chocolate ['tʃɔklɪt] n chocolate m.

choice [tʃɔɪs] n elección f; (preference) preferencia ♦ adj escogido; **I did it by** or **from ~** lo hice de buena gana; **a wide ~** un gran surtido, una gran variedad.
choir ['kwaɪə*] n coro.
choirboy ['kwaɪəbɔɪ] n niño de coro.
choke [tʃəuk] vi ahogarse; (on food) atragantarse ♦ vt ahogar; (block) atascar ♦ n (AUT) estárter m.
choker ['tʃəukə*] n (necklace) gargantilla.
cholera ['kɔlərə] n cólera m.
cholesterol [kɔ'lestərəl] n colesterol m.
choose, pt **chose,** pp **chosen** [tʃuːz, tʃəuz, 'tʃəuzn] vt escoger, elegir; (team) seleccionar; **to ~ between** elegir or escoger entre; **to ~ from** escoger entre.
choosy ['tʃuːzɪ] adj remilgado.
chop [tʃɔp] vt (wood) cortar, talar; (CULIN: also: **~ up**) picar ♦ n tajo, golpe m cortante; (CULIN) chuleta; **~s** npl (jaws) boca sg; **to get the ~** (col: project) ser suprimido; (: person: be sacked) ser despedido.
chopper ['tʃɔpə*] n (helicopter) helicóptero.
choppy ['tʃɔpɪ] adj (sea) picado, agitado.
chopsticks ['tʃɔpstɪks] npl palillos mpl.
choral ['kɔːrəl] adj coral.
chord [kɔːd] n (MUS) acorde m.
chore [tʃɔː*] n faena, tarea; (routine task) trabajo rutinario.
choreographer [kɔrɪ'ɔgrəfə*] n coreógrafo/a.
choreography [kɔrɪ'ɔgrəfɪ] n coreografía.
chorister ['kɔrɪstə*] n corista m/f; (US) director(a) m/f de un coro.
chortle ['tʃɔːtl] vi reírse satisfecho.
chorus ['kɔːrəs] n coro; (repeated part of song) estribillo.
chose [tʃəuz] pt of **choose**.
chosen ['tʃəuzn] pp of **choose**.
chow [tʃau] n (dog) perro chino.
chowder ['tʃaudə*] n (esp US) sopa de pescado.
Christ [kraɪst] n Cristo.
christen ['krɪsn] vt bautizar.
christening ['krɪsnɪŋ] n bautizo.
Christian ['krɪstɪən] adj, n cristiano/a m/f.
Christianity [krɪstɪ'ænɪtɪ] n cristianismo.
Christian name n nombre m de pila.
Christmas ['krɪsməs] n Navidad f; **Merry ~!** ¡Felices Navidades!, ¡Felices Pascuas!
Christmas card n crismas m inv, tarjeta de Navidad.
Christmas Day n día m de Navidad.
Christmas Eve n Nochebuena.
Christmas Island n Isla Christmas.
Christmas tree n árbol m de Navidad.
chrome [krəum] n = **chromium plating**.

chromium ['krəumɪəm] n cromo; (also: ~ **plating**) cromado.
chromosome ['krəuməsəum] n cromosoma m.
chronic ['krɔnɪk] adj crónico; (fig: liar, smoker) empedernido.
chronicle ['krɔnɪkl] n crónica.
chronological [krɔnə'lɔdʒɪkəl] adj cronológico.
chrysalis ['krɪsəlɪs] n (BIO) crisálida.
chrysanthemum [krɪ'sænθəməm] n crisantemo.
chubby ['tʃʌbɪ] adj rechoncho.
chuck [tʃʌk] vt tirar; **to ~ (up or in)** vt (BRIT) dejar, mandar a paseo.
chuckle ['tʃʌkl] vi reírse entre dientes.
chuffed [tʃʌft] adj (col): **to be ~ (about sth)** estar encantado (con algo).
chug [tʃʌg] vi (also: ~ **along**: train) ir despacio; (: fig) ir tirando.
chum [tʃʌm] n amiguete/a m/f, coleguilla m/f.
chump [tʃʌmp] n (col) tonto/a, estúpido/a.
chunk [tʃʌŋk] n pedazo, trozo.
chunky ['tʃʌŋkɪ] adj (furniture etc) achaparrado; (person) fornido; (knitwear) de lana gorda, grueso.
Chunnel [tʃʌnl] n = **Channel Tunnel**.
church [tʃəːtʃ] n iglesia; **the C~ of England** la Iglesia Anglicana.
churchyard ['tʃəːtʃjɑːd] n cementerio, camposanto.
churlish ['tʃəːlɪʃ] adj grosero; (mean) arisco.
churn [tʃəːn] n (for butter) mantequera; (for milk) lechera.
▶**churn out** vt producir en serie.
chute [ʃuːt] n (also: **rubbish ~**) vertedero; (BRIT: children's slide) tobogán m.
chutney ['tʃʌtnɪ] n salsa picante de frutas y especias.
CIA n abbr (US: = Central Intelligence Agency) CIA f, Agencia Central de Inteligencia.
cicada [sɪ'kɑːdə] n cigarra.
CID n abbr (BRIT: = Criminal Investigation Department) ≈ B.I.C. f (SP).
cider ['saɪdə*] n sidra.
C.I.F. abbr (= cost, insurance and freight) c.s.f.
cigar [sɪ'gɑː*] n puro.
cigarette [sɪgə'rɛt] n cigarrillo, pitillo.
cigarette case n pitillera.
cigarette end n colilla.
cigarette holder n boquilla.
C-in-C abbr = **commander-in-chief**.
cinch [sɪntʃ] n: **it's a ~** está tirado.
Cinderella [sɪndə'rɛlə] n Cenicienta.
cinders ['sɪndəz] npl cenizas fpl.

cine-camera ['sɪnɪ'kæmərə] n (BRIT) cámara cinematográfica.
cine-film ['sɪnɪfɪlm] n (BRIT) película de cine.
cinema ['sɪnəmə] n cine m.
cinnamon ['sɪnəmən] n canela.
cipher ['saɪfə*] n clave f; (fig) cero; **in ~** en clave.
circle ['səːkl] n círculo; (in theatre) anfiteatro ♦ vi dar vueltas ♦ vt (surround) rodear, cercar; (move round) dar la vuelta a.
circuit ['səːkɪt] n circuito; (track) pista; (lap) vuelta.
circuit board n tarjeta de circuitos.
circuitous [səː'kjuɪtəs] adj indirecto.
circular ['səːkjulə*] adj circular ♦ n circular f; (as advertisement) panfleto.
circulate ['səːkjuleɪt] vi circular; (person: socially) alternar, circular ♦ vt poner en circulación.
circulation [səːkju'leɪʃən] n circulación f; (of newspaper etc) tirada.
circumcise ['səːkəmsaɪz] vt circuncidar.
circumference [sə'kʌmfərəns] n circunferencia.
circumscribe ['səːkəmskraɪb] vt circunscribir.
circumspect ['səːkəmspɛkt] adj circunspecto, prudente.
circumstances ['səːkəmstənsɪz] npl circunstancias fpl; (financial condition) situación f económica; **in the ~** en or dadas las circunstancias; **under no ~** de ninguna manera, bajo ningún concepto.
circumstantial [səːkəm'stænʃəl] adj detallado; **~ evidence** prueba indiciaria.
circumvent ['səːkəmvɛnt] vt (rule etc) burlar.
circus ['səːkəs] n circo; (also: **C~**: in place names) Plaza.
cirrhosis [sɪ'rəusɪs] n (also: ~ **of the liver**) cirrosis f inv.
CIS n abbr (= Commonwealth of Independent States) CEI f.
cissy ['sɪsɪ] n = **sissy**.
cistern ['sɪstən] n tanque m, depósito; (in toilet) cisterna.
citation [saɪ'teɪʃən] n cita; (LAW) citación f; (MIL) mención f.
cite [saɪt] vt citar.
citizen ['sɪtɪzn] n (POL) ciudadano/a; (of city) habitante m/f.
Citizens' Advice Bureau n (BRIT) organización voluntaria británica que aconseja especialmente en temas legales o financieros.
citizenship ['sɪtɪznʃɪp] n ciudadanía.

citric ['sɪtrɪk] *adj*: ~ **acid** ácido cítrico.
citrus fruits ['sɪtrəs-] *npl* cítricos *mpl*.
city ['sɪtɪ] *n* ciudad *f*; **the C**~ centro financiero de Londres.
city centre *n* centro de la ciudad.
City Hall *n* (*US*) ayuntamiento.
City Technology College *n* (*BRIT*) ≈ Centro de formación profesional.
civic ['sɪvɪk] *adj* cívico; (*authorities*) municipal.
civic centre *n* (*BRIT*) centro de administración municipal.
civil ['sɪvɪl] *adj* civil; (*polite*) atento, cortés; (*well-bred*) educado.
civil defence *n* protección *f* civil.
civil engineer *n* ingeniero/a de caminos.
civil engineering *n* ingeniería de caminos.
civilian [sɪ'vɪlɪən] *adj* civil; (*clothes*) de paisano ♦ *n* civil *m/f*.
civilization [sɪvɪlaɪ'zeɪʃən] *n* civilización *f*.
civilized ['sɪvɪlaɪzd] *adj* civilizado.
civil law *n* derecho civil.
civil liberties *npl* libertades *fpl* civiles.
civil rights *npl* derechos *mpl* civiles.
civil servant *n* funcionario/a (del Estado).
Civil Service *n* administración *f* pública.
civil war *n* guerra civil.
civvies ['sɪvɪz] *npl*: **in** ~ (*col*) de paisano.
cl *abbr* (= *centilitre*) cl.
clad [klæd] *adj*: ~ **(in)** vestido (de).
claim [kleɪm] *vt* exigir, reclamar; (*rights etc*) reivindicar; (*assert*) pretender ♦ *vi* (*for insurance*) reclamar ♦ *n* (*for expenses*) reclamación *f*; (*LAW*) demanda; (*pretension*) pretensión *f*; **to put in a** ~ **for sth** presentar una demanda por algo.
claimant ['kleɪmənt] *n* (*ADMIN, LAW*) demandante *m/f*.
claim form *n* solicitud *f*.
clairvoyant [klɛə'vɔɪənt] *n* clarividente *m/f*.
clam [klæm] *n* almeja.
▶**clam up** *vi* (*col*) cerrar el pico.
clamber ['klæmbə*] *vi* trepar.
clammy ['klæmɪ] *adj* (*cold*) frío y húmedo; (*sticky*) pegajoso.
clamour, (*US*) **clamor** ['klæmə*] *n* (*noise*) clamor *m*; (*protest*) protesta ♦ *vi*: **to** ~ **for sth** clamar por algo, pedir algo a voces.
clamp [klæmp] *n* abrazadera; (*laboratory* ~) grapa; (*wheel* ~) cepo ♦ *vt* afianzar (con abrazadera).
▶**clamp down on** *vt fus* (*subj: government, police*) poner coto a.
clampdown ['klæmpdaun] *n* restricción *f*; **there has been a** ~ **on terrorism** se ha puesto coto al terrorismo.
clan [klæn] *n* clan *m*.

clandestine [klæn'dɛstɪn] *adj* clandestino.
clang [klæŋ] *n* estruendo ♦ *vi* sonar con estruendo.
clanger [klæŋə*] *n*: **to drop a** ~ (*BRIT col*) meter la pata.
clansman ['klænzmən] *n* miembro del clan.
clap [klæp] *vi* aplaudir ♦ *vt* (*hands*) batir ♦ *n* (*of hands*) palmada; **to** ~ **one's hands** dar palmadas, batir las palmas; **a** ~ **of thunder** un trueno.
clapping ['klæpɪŋ] *n* aplausos *mpl*.
claptrap ['klæptræp] *n* (*col*) gilipolleces *fpl*.
claret ['klærət] *n* burdeos *m inv*.
clarification [klærɪfɪ'keɪʃən] *n* aclaración *f*.
clarify ['klærɪfaɪ] *vt* aclarar.
clarinet [klærɪ'nɛt] *n* clarinete *m*.
clarity ['klærɪtɪ] *n* claridad *f*.
clash [klæʃ] *n* estruendo; (*fig*) choque *m* ♦ *vi* enfrentarse; (*personalities, interests*) oponerse, chocar; (*colours*) desentonar; (*dates, events*) coincidir.
clasp [klɑːsp] *n* broche *m*; (*on jewels*) cierre *m* ♦ *vt* abrochar; (*hand*) apretar; (*embrace*) abrazar.
class [klɑːs] *n* (*gen*) clase *f*; (*group, category*) clase *f*, categoría ♦ *cpd* de clase ♦ *vt* clasificar.
class-conscious ['klɑːs'kɔnʃəs] *adj* clasista, con conciencia de clase.
classic ['klæsɪk] *adj* clásico ♦ *n* (*work*) obra clásica, clásico; ~**s** *npl* (*UNIV*) clásicas *fpl*.
classical ['klæsɪkəl] *adj* clásico; ~ **music** música clásica.
classification [klæsɪfɪ'keɪʃən] *n* clasificación *f*.
classified ['klæsɪfaɪd] *adj* (*information*) reservado.
classified advertisement *n* anuncio por palabras.
classify ['klæsɪfaɪ] *vt* clasificar.
classless ['klɑːslɪs] *adj*: ~ **society** sociedad *f* sin clases.
classmate ['klɑːsmeɪt] *n* compañero/a de clase.
classroom ['klɑːsrum] *n* aula.
classy ['klɑːsɪ] *adj* (*col*) elegante, con estilo.
clatter ['klætə*] *n* ruido, estruendo; (*of hooves*) trápala ♦ *vi* hacer ruido *or* estruendo.
clause [klɔːz] *n* cláusula; (*LING*) oración *f*.
claustrophobia [klɔːstrə'fəubɪə] *n* claustrofobia.
claustrophobic [klɔːstrə'fəubɪk] *adj* claustrofóbico; **I feel** ~ me entra claustrofobia.
claw [klɔː] *n* (*of cat*) uña; (*of bird of prey*) garra; (*of lobster*) pinza; (*TECH*) garfio ♦ *vi*: **to** ~ **at** arañar; (*tear*) desgarrar.

clay [kleɪ] n arcilla.
clean [kliːn] adj limpio; (copy) en limpio; (lines) bien definido ♦ vt limpiar ♦ adv: he ~ forgot lo olvidó por completo; to come ~ (col: admit guilt) confesarlo todo; to have a ~ driving licence tener el carnet de conducir sin sanciones; to ~ one's teeth lavarse los dientes.
►**clean off** vt limpiar.
►**clean out** vt limpiar (a fondo).
►**clean up** vt limpiar, asear ♦ vi (fig: make profit): to ~ up on sacar provecho de.
clean-cut ['kliːn'kʌt] adj bien definido; (outline) nítido; (person) de buen parecer.
cleaner ['kliːnə*] n encargado/a m/f de la limpieza; (also: dry ~) tintorero/a.
cleaning ['kliːnɪŋ] n limpieza.
cleaning lady n señora de la limpieza, asistenta.
cleanliness ['klɛnlɪnɪs] n limpieza.
cleanse [klɛnz] vt limpiar.
cleanser ['klɛnzə*] n detergente m; (cosmetic) loción f or crema limpiadora.
clean-shaven ['kliːn'ʃeɪvn] adj bien afeitado.
cleansing department ['klɛnzɪŋ-] n (BRIT) servicio municipal de limpieza.
clean sweep n: to make a ~ (SPORT) arrasar, barrer.
clear [klɪə*] adj claro; (road, way) libre; (profit) neto; (majority) absoluto ♦ vt (space) despejar, limpiar; (LAW: suspect) absolver; (obstacle) salvar, saltar por encima de; (debt) liquidar; (cheque) aceptar; (site, woodland) desmontar ♦ vi (fog etc) despejarse ♦ n: to be in the ~ (out of debt) estar libre de deudas; (out of suspicion) estar fuera de toda sospecha; (out of danger) estar fuera de peligro ♦ adv: ~ of a distancia de; to make o.s. ~ explicarse claramente; to make it ~ to sb that ... hacer entender a algn que ...; I have a ~ day tomorrow mañana tengo el día libre; to keep ~ of sth/sb evitar algo/a algn; to ~ a profit of ... sacar una ganancia de ...; to ~ the table recoger or quitar la mesa.
►**clear off** vi (col: leave) marcharse, mandarse mudar (LAM).
►**clear up** vt limpiar; (mystery) aclarar, resolver.
clearance ['klɪərəns] n (removal) despeje m; (permission) acreditación f.
clear-cut ['klɪə'kʌt] adj bien definido, claro.
clearing ['klɪərɪŋ] n (in wood) claro.
clearing bank n (BRIT) banco central.
clearing house n (COMM) cámara de compensación.

clearly ['klɪəlɪ] adv claramente.
clearway ['klɪəweɪ] n (BRIT) carretera en la que no se puede estacionar.
cleaver ['kliːvə] n cuchilla (de carnicero).
clef [klɛf] n (MUS) clave f.
cleft [klɛft] n (in rock) grieta, hendedura.
clemency ['klɛmənsɪ] n clemencia.
clement ['klɛmənt] adj (weather) clemente, benigno.
clench [klɛntʃ] vt apretar, cerrar.
clergy ['kləːdʒɪ] n clero.
clergyman ['kləːdʒɪmən] n clérigo.
clerical ['klɛrɪkəl] adj de oficina; (REL) clerical; (error) de copia.
clerk [klɑːk, (US) kləːrk] n oficinista m/f; (US) dependiente/a m/f, vendedor(a) m/f; C~ of the Court secretario/a de juzgado.
clever ['klɛvə*] adj (mentally) inteligente, listo; (skilful) hábil; (device, arrangement) ingenioso.
cleverly ['klɛvəlɪ] adv ingeniosamente.
clew [kluː] n (US) = clue.
cliché ['kliːʃeɪ] n cliché m, frase f hecha.
click [klɪk] vt (tongue) chasquear; to ~ one's heels taconear.
client ['klaɪənt] n cliente m/f.
clientele [kliːɑːn'tɛl] n clientela.
cliff [klɪf] n acantilado.
cliffhanger ['klɪfhæŋə*] n: it was a ~ estuvimos etc en ascuas hasta el final.
climactic [klaɪ'mæktɪk] adj culminante.
climate ['klaɪmɪt] n clima m; (fig) clima m, ambiente m.
climax ['klaɪmæks] n punto culminante; (of play etc) clímax m; (sexual ~) orgasmo.
climb [klaɪm] vi subir, trepar; (plane) elevarse, remontar el vuelo ♦ vt (stairs) subir; (tree) trepar a; (mountain) escalar ♦ n subida, ascenso; to ~ over a wall saltar una tapia.
►**climb down** vi (fig) volverse atrás.
climbdown ['klaɪmdaun] n vuelta atrás.
climber ['klaɪmə*] n escalador(a) m/f.
climbing ['klaɪmɪŋ] n escalada.
clinch [klɪntʃ] vt (deal) cerrar; (argument) rematar.
clincher ['klɪntʃə*] n (col): that was the ~ for me eso me hizo decidir.
cling [klɪŋ], pt, pp **clung** [klɪŋ, klʌŋ] vi: to ~ (to) agarrarse (a); (clothes) pegarse (a).
clingfilm ['klɪŋfɪlm] n plástico adherente.
clinic ['klɪnɪk] n clínica.
clinical ['klɪnɪkl] adj clínico; (fig) frío, impasible.
clink [klɪŋk] vi tintinear.
clip [klɪp] n (for hair) horquilla; (also: paper ~) sujetapapeles m inv, clip m; (clamp) grapa ♦ vt (cut) cortar; (hedge) podar;

(also: ~ **together**) unir.
clippers ['klɪpəz] npl (for gardening) tijeras fpl de podar; (for hair) maquinilla sg; (for nails) cortauñas m inv.
clipping ['klɪpɪŋ] n (from newspaper) recorte m.
clique [kliːk] n camarilla.
cloak [kləuk] n capa, manto ♦ vt (fig) encubrir, disimular.
cloakroom ['kləukrum] n guardarropa m; (BRIT: WC) lavabo, aseos mpl, baño (esp LAM).
clobber ['klɔbə*] n (col) bártulos mpl, trastos mpl ♦ vt dar una paliza a.
clock [klɔk] n reloj m; (in taxi) taxímetro; **to work against the** ~ trabajar contra reloj; **around the** ~ las veinticuatro horas; **to sleep round the** ~ dormir un día entero; **30,000 on the** ~ (AUT) treinta mil millas en el cuentakilómetros.
►**clock in, clock on** vi fichar, picar.
►**clock off, clock out** vi fichar or picar la salida.
►**clock up** vt hacer.
clockwise ['klɔkwaɪz] adv en el sentido de las agujas del reloj.
clockwork ['klɔkwəːk] n aparato de relojería ♦ adj (toy, train) de cuerda.
clog [klɔg] n zueco, chanclo ♦ vt atascar ♦ vi atascarse.
cloister ['klɔɪstə*] n claustro.
clone [kləun] n clon m.
close adj, adv and derivatives [kləus] adj cercano, próximo; (near): ~ **(to)** cerca (de); (print, weave) tupido, compacto; (friend) íntimo; (connection) estrecho; (examination) detallado, minucioso; (weather) bochornoso; (atmosphere) sofocante; (room) mal ventilado ♦ adv cerca; ~ **by,** ~ **at hand** adj, adv muy cerca; ~ **to** prep cerca de; **to have a** ~ **shave** (fig) escaparse por un pelo; **how** ~ **is Edinburgh to Glasgow?** ¿qué distancia hay de Edimburgo a Glasgow?; **at** ~ **quarters** de cerca ♦ vb and derivatives [kləuz] vt cerrar; (end) concluir, terminar ♦ vi (shop etc) cerrar; (end) concluir(se), terminar(se) ♦ n (end) fin m, final m, conclusión f; **to bring sth to a** ~ terminar algo.
►**close down** vi cerrar definitivamente.
►**close in** vi (hunters) acercarse rodeando, rodear; (evening, night) caer; (fog) cerrarse; **to** ~ **in on sb** rodear or cercar a algn; **the days are closing in** los días son cada vez más cortos.
►**close off** vt (area) cerrar al tráfico or al público.

closed [kləuzd] adj (shop etc) cerrado.
closed-circuit ['kləuzd'səːkɪt] adj: ~ **television** televisión f por circuito cerrado.
closed shop n empresa en la que todo el personal está afiliado a un sindicato.
close-knit ['kləus'nɪt] adj (fig) muy unido.
closely ['kləuslɪ] adv (study) con detalle; (listen) con atención; (watch: person, events) de cerca; **we are** ~ **related** somos parientes cercanos; **a** ~ **guarded secret** un secreto rigurosamente guardado.
close season [kləuz-] n (FOOTBALL) temporada de descanso; (HUNTING) veda.
closet ['klɔzɪt] n (cupboard) armario, placar(d) m (LAM).
close-up ['kləusʌp] n primer plano.
closing ['kləuzɪŋ] adj (stages, remarks) último, final; ~ **price** (STOCK EXCHANGE) cotización f de cierre.
closing time n hora de cierre.
closure ['kləuʒə*] n cierre m.
clot [klɔt] n (gen: blood ~) embolia; (col: idiot) imbécil m/f ♦ vi (blood) coagularse.
cloth [klɔθ] n (material) tela, paño; (table ~) mantel m; (rag) trapo.
clothe [kləuð] vt vestir; (fig) revestir.
clothes [kləuðz] npl ropa sg; **to put one's** ~ **on** vestirse, ponerse la ropa; **to take one's** ~ **off** desvestirse, desnudarse.
clothes brush n cepillo (para la ropa).
clothes line n cuerda (para tender la ropa).
clothes peg, (US) clothes pin n pinza.
clothing ['kləuðɪŋ] n = **clothes.**
clotted cream ['klɔtɪd-] n nata muy espesa.
cloud [klaud] n nube f; (storm ~) nubarrón m ♦ vt (liquid) enturbiar; **every** ~ **has a silver lining** no hay mal que por bien no venga; **to** ~ **the issue** empañar el problema.
►**cloud over** vi (also fig) nublarse.
cloudburst ['klaudbəːst] n chaparrón m.
cloud-cuckoo-land ['klaud'kuku:'lænd] n Babia.
cloudy ['klaudɪ] adj nublado; (liquid) turbio.
clout [klaut] n (fig) influencia, peso ♦ vt dar un tortazo a.
clove [kləuv] n clavo; ~ **of garlic** diente m de ajo.
clover ['kləuvə*] n trébol m.
clown [klaun] n payaso ♦ vi (also: ~ **about,** ~ **around**) hacer el payaso.
cloying ['klɔɪɪŋ] adj (taste) empalagoso.
club [klʌb] n (society) club m; (weapon) porra, cachiporra; (also: golf ~) palo ♦ vt aporrear ♦ vi: **to** ~ **together** (join forces)

unir fuerzas; ~s *npl* (*CARDS*) tréboles *mpl*.
club car *n* (*US RAIL*) coche *m* salón.
club class *n* (*AVIAT*) clase *f* preferente.
clubhouse ['klʌbhaus] *n local social, sobre todo en clubs deportivos.*
club soda *n* (*US*) soda.
cluck [klʌk] *vi* cloquear.
clue [kluː] *n* pista; (*in crosswords*) indicación *f*; **I haven't a** ~ no tengo ni idea.
clued up, (*US*) **clued in** [kluːd-] *adj* (*col*) al tanto, al corriente.
clueless ['kluːlis] *adj* (*col*) desorientado.
clump [klʌmp] *n* (*of trees*) grupo.
clumsy ['klʌmzi] *adj* (*person*) torpe; (*tool*) difícil de manejar.
clung [klʌŋ] *pt, pp of* **cling**.
cluster ['klʌstə*] *n* grupo; (*BOT*) racimo ♦ *vi* agruparse, apiñarse.
clutch [klʌtʃ] *n* (*AUT*) embrague *m*; (*pedal*) (pedal *m* de) embrague *m*; **to fall into sb's ~es** caer en las garras de algn ♦ *vt* agarrar.
clutter ['klʌtə*] *vt* (*also*: ~ **up**) atestar, llenar desordenadamente ♦ *n* desorden *m*, confusión *f*.
CM *abbr* (*US*) = North Mariana Islands.
cm *abbr* (= centimetre) cm.
CNAA *n abbr* (*BRIT*: = Council for National Academic Awards*) organismo no universitario que otorga diplomas.
CND *n abbr* (= Campaign for Nuclear Disarmament*) plataforma pro desarme nuclear.
CO *n abbr* = **commanding officer**; (*BRIT*) = Commonwealth Office ♦ *abbr* (*US*) = Colorado.
Co. *abbr* = **county**; = **company**.
c/o *abbr* (= care of*) c/a, a/c.
coach [kəutʃ] *n* (*bus*) autocar *m* (*SP*), autobús *m*; (*horse-drawn*) coche *m*; (*ceremonial*) carroza; (*of train*) vagón *m*, coche *m*; (*SPORT*) entrenador(a) *m/f*, instructor(a) *m/f* ♦ *vt* (*SPORT*) entrenar; (*student*) preparar, enseñar.
coach trip *n* excursión *f* en autocar.
coagulate [kəu'ægjuleit] *vi* coagularse.
coal [kəul] *n* carbón *m*.
coal face *n* frente *m* de carbón.
coalfield ['kəulfiːld] *n* yacimiento de carbón.
coalition [kəuə'liʃən] *n* coalición *f*.
coal man *n* carbonero.
coalmine ['kəulmaın] *n* mina de carbón.
coalminer ['kəulmaınə*] *n* minero (de carbón).
coalmining ['keulmaınıŋ] *n* minería (de carbón).

coarse [kɔːs] *adj* basto, burdo; (*vulgar*) grosero, ordinario.
coast [kəust] *n* costa, litoral *m* ♦ *vi* (*AUT*) ir en punto muerto.
coastal ['kəustl] *adj* costero.
coaster ['kəustə*] *n* buque *m* costero, barco de cabotaje.
coastguard ['kəustgɑːd] *n* guardacostas *m inv*.
coastline ['kəustlaın] *n* litoral *m*.
coat [kəut] *n* (*jacket*) chaqueta, saco *m* (*LAM*); (*overcoat*) abrigo; (*of animal*) pelo, lana; (*of paint*) mano *f*, capa ♦ *vt* cubrir, revestir.
coat hanger *n* percha, gancha (*LAM*).
coating ['kəutıŋ] *n* capa, baño.
coat of arms *n* escudo de armas.
co-author ['kəu'ɔːθə*] *n* coautor(a) *m/f*.
coax [kəuks] *vt* engatusar.
cob [kɔb] *n see* **corn**.
cobbler ['kɔblə*] *n* zapatero (remendón).
cobbles ['kɔblz], **cobblestones** ['kɔblstəunz] *npl* adoquines *mpl*.
COBOL ['kəubɔl] *n* COBOL *m*.
cobra ['kəubrə] *n* cobra.
cobweb ['kɔbwεb] *n* telaraña.
cocaine [kə'keın] *n* cocaína.
cock [kɔk] *n* (*rooster*) gallo; (*male bird*) macho ♦ *vt* (*gun*) amartillar.
cock-a-hoop [kɔkə'huːp] *adj*: **to be** ~ estar más contento que unas pascuas.
cockatoo [kɔkə'tuː] *n* cacatúa.
cockerel ['kɔkərl] *n* gallito, gallo joven.
cock-eyed ['kɔkaıd] *adj* bizco; (*fig: crooked*) torcido; (: *idea*) disparatado.
cockle ['kɔkl] *n* berberecho.
cockney ['kɔknı] *n habitante de ciertos barrios de Londres.*
cockpit ['kɔkpıt] *n* (*in aircraft*) cabina.
cockroach ['kɔkrəutʃ] *n* cucaracha.
cocktail ['kɔkteıl] *n* combinado, cóctel *m*; **prawn** ~ cóctel *m* de gambas.
cocktail cabinet *n* mueble-bar *m*.
cocktail party *n* cóctel *m*.
cocktail shaker [-ʃeıkə*] *n* coctelera.
cocky ['kɔkı] *adj* farruco, flamenco.
cocoa ['kəukəu] *n* cacao; (*drink*) chocolate *m*.
coconut ['kəukənʌt] *n* coco.
cocoon [kə'kuːn] *n* capullo.
cod [kɔd] *n* bacalao.
COD *abbr see* **cash on delivery, collect on delivery** (*US*).
code [kəud] *n* código; (*cipher*) clave *f*; (*TEL*) prefijo; ~ **of behaviour** código de conducta; ~ **of practice** código profesional.
codeine ['kəudiːn] *n* codeína.

codger [ˈkɔdʒə*] n (BRIT col): **an old ~** un abuelo.
codicil [ˈkɔdɪsɪl] n codicilo.
codify [ˈkəudɪfaɪ] vt codificar.
cod-liver oil [ˈkɔdlɪvə*-] n aceite m de hígado de bacalao.
co-driver [ˈkəuˈdraɪvə*] n (in race) copiloto m/f; (of lorry) segundo conductor m.
co-ed [ˈkəuɛd] adj abbr = **coeducational** ♦ n abbr (US: = female student) alumna de una universidad mixta; (BRIT: school) colegio mixto.
coeducational [kəuɛdjuˈkeɪʃənl] adj mixto.
coerce [kəuˈəːs] vt forzar, coaccionar.
coercion [kəuˈəːʃən] n coacción f.
coexistence [ˈkəuɪgˈzɪstəns] n coexistencia.
C. of C. n abbr = **chamber of commerce.**
C of E abbr = **Church of England.**
coffee [ˈkɔfɪ] n café m; **white ~, (US) ~ with cream** café con leche.
coffee bar n (BRIT) cafetería.
coffee bean n grano de café.
coffee break n descanso (para tomar café).
coffee cup n taza de café, pocillo (LAM).
coffeepot [ˈkɔfɪpɔt] n cafetera.
coffee table n mesita baja.
coffin [ˈkɔfɪn] n ataúd m.
C of I abbr = **Church of Ireland.**
C of S abbr = **Church of Scotland.**
cog [kɔg] n diente m.
cogent [ˈkəudʒənt] adj lógico, convincente.
cognac [ˈkɔnjæk] n coñac m.
cogwheel [ˈkɔgwiːl] n rueda dentada.
cohabit [kəuˈhæbɪt] vi (formal): **to ~ (with sb)** cohabitar (con algn).
coherent [kəuˈhɪərənt] adj coherente.
cohesion [kəuˈhiːʒən] n cohesión f.
cohesive [kəuˈhiːsɪv] adj (fig) cohesivo, unido.
COI n abbr (BRIT: = Central Office of Information) servicio de información gubernamental.
coil [kɔɪl] n rollo; (of rope) vuelta; (of smoke) espiral f; (AUT, ELEC) bobina, carrete m; (contraceptive) DIU m ♦ vt enrollar.
coin [kɔɪn] n moneda ♦ vt acuñar; (word) inventar, acuñar.
coinage [ˈkɔɪnɪdʒ] n moneda.
coin-box [ˈkɔɪnbɔks] n (BRIT) caja recaudadora.
coincide [kəuɪnˈsaɪd] vi coincidir.
coincidence [kəuˈɪnsɪdəns] n casualidad f, coincidencia.
coin-operated [ˈkɔɪnˈɔpəreɪtɪd] adj (machine) que funciona con monedas.
Coke ® [kəuk] n Coca Cola ® f.
coke [kəuk] n (coal) coque m.

Col. abbr (= colonel) col; (US) = Colorado.
COLA n abbr (US: = cost-of-living adjustment) reajuste salarial de acuerdo con el coste de la vida.
colander [ˈkɔləndə*] n escurridor m.
cold [kəuld] adj frío ♦ n frío; (MED) resfriado; **it's ~** hace frío; **to be ~** tener frío; **to catch a ~** coger un catarro, resfriarse, acatarrarse; **in ~ blood** a sangre fría; **the room's getting ~** está empezando a hacer frío en la habitación; **to give sb the ~ shoulder** tratar a algn con frialdad.
cold-blooded [ˈkəuldˈblʌdɪd] adj (ZOOL) de sangre fría.
cold cream n crema.
coldly [ˈkəuldlɪ] adj fríamente.
cold sore n calentura, herpes m labial.
cold sweat n: **to be in a ~ (about sth)** tener sudores fríos (por algo).
cold turkey n (col) mono.
Cold War n: **the ~** la guerra fría.
coleslaw [ˈkəulslɔ:] n ensalada de col con zanahoria.
colic [ˈkɔlɪk] n cólico.
colicky [ˈkɔlɪkɪ] adj: **to be ~** tener un cólico.
collaborate [kəˈlæbəreɪt] vi colaborar.
collaboration [kəlæbəˈreɪʃən] n colaboración f; (POL) colaboracionismo.
collaborator [kəˈlæbəreɪtə*] n colaborador(a) m/f; (POL) colaboracionista m/f.
collage [kɔˈlɑːʒ] n collage m.
collagen [ˈkɔlədʒən] n colágeno.
collapse [kəˈlæps] vi (gen) hundirse, derrumbarse; (MED) sufrir un colapso ♦ n (gen) hundimiento; (MED) colapso; (of government) caída; (of plans, scheme) fracaso; (of business) ruina.
collapsible [kəˈlæpsəbl] adj plegable.
collar [ˈkɔlə*] n (of coat, shirt) cuello; (for dog, TECH) collar m ♦ vt (col: person) agarrar; (: object) birlar.
collarbone [ˈkɔləbəun] n clavícula.
collate [kɔˈleɪt] vt cotejar.
collateral [kɔˈlætərəl] n (COMM) garantía subsidiaria.
collation [kəˈleɪʃən] n colación f.
colleague [ˈkɔliːg] n colega m/f.
collect [kəˈlɛkt] vt reunir; (as a hobby) coleccionar; (BRIT: call and pick up) recoger; (wages) cobrar; (debts) recaudar; (donations, subscriptions) colectar ♦ vi (crowd) reunirse ♦ adv: **to call ~ (US TEL)** llamar a cobro revertido; **to ~ one's thoughts** reponerse, recobrar el dominio de sí mismo; **~ on delivery (COD)** (US) entrega contra reembolso.

collection [kə'lɛkʃən] *n* colección *f*; (*of fares, wages*) cobro; (*of post*) recogida.
collective [kə'lɛktɪv] *adj* colectivo.
collective bargaining *n* negociación *f* del convenio colectivo.
collector [kə'lɛktə*] *n* coleccionista *m/f*; (*of taxes etc*) recaudador(a) *m/f*; ~'s item *or* piece pieza de coleccionista.
college ['kɒlɪdʒ] *n* colegio; (*of technology, agriculture etc*) escuela.
collide [kə'laɪd] *vi* chocar.
collie ['kɒlɪ] *n* (*dog*) collie *m*, perro pastor escocés.
colliery ['kɒlɪərɪ] *n* (*BRIT*) mina de carbón.
collision [kə'lɪʒən] *n* choque *m*, colisión *f*; to be on a ~ course (*also fig*) ir rumbo al desastre.
colloquial [kə'ləʊkwɪəl] *adj* coloquial.
collusion [kə'luːʒən] *n* confabulación *f*, connivencia; in ~ with en connivencia con.
Colo. *abbr* (*US*) = *Colorado*.
cologne [kə'ləʊn] *n* (*also:* eau de ~) (agua de) colonia.
Colombia [kə'lɒmbɪə] *n* Colombia.
Colombian [kə'lɒmbɪən] *adj, n* colombiano/a *m/f*.
colon ['kəʊlən] *n* (*sign*) dos puntos; (*MED*) colon *m*.
colonel ['kɜːnl] *n* coronel *m*.
colonial [kə'ləʊnɪəl] *adj* colonial.
colonize ['kɒlənaɪz] *vt* colonizar.
colonnade [kɒlə'neɪd] *n* columnata *f*.
colony ['kɒlənɪ] *n* colonia.
color ['kʌlə*] *etc* (*US*) = colour.
Colorado beetle [kɒlə'rɑːdəʊ-] *n* escarabajo de la patata.
colossal [kə'lɒsl] *adj* colosal.
colour, (*US*) **color** ['kʌlə*] *n* color *m* ♦ *vt* colorear, pintar; (*dye*) teñir ♦ *vi* (*blush*) sonrojarse; ~s *npl* (*of party, club*) colores *mpl*.
colo(u)r bar *n* segregación *f* racial.
colo(u)r-blind ['kʌləblaɪnd] *adj* daltónico.
colo(u)red ['kʌləd] *adj* de color; (*photo*) en color; (*of race*) de color.
colo(u)r film *n* película en color.
colo(u)rful ['kʌləful] *adj* lleno de color; (*person*) pintoresco.
colo(u)ring ['kʌlərɪŋ] *n* colorido, color; (*substance*) colorante *m*.
colo(u)rless ['kʌləlɪs] *adj* incoloro, sin color.
colo(u)r scheme *n* combinación *f* de colores.
colour supplement *n* (*BRIT PRESS*) suplemento semanal *or* dominical.
colo(u)r television *n* televisión *f* en color.

colt [kəʊlt] *n* potro.
column ['kɒləm] *n* columna; (*fashion* ~, *sports* ~ *etc*) sección *f*, columna; the editorial ~ el editorial.
columnist ['kɒləmnɪst] *n* columnista *m/f*.
coma ['kəʊmə] *n* coma *m*.
comb [kəʊm] *n* peine *m*; (*ornamental*) peineta ♦ *vt* (*hair*) peinar; (*area*) registrar a fondo, peinar.
combat ['kɒmbæt] *n* combate *m* ♦ *vt* combatir.
combination [kɒmbɪ'neɪʃən] *n* (*gen*) combinación *f*.
combination lock *n* cerradura de combinación.
combine [kəm'baɪn] *vt* combinar; (*qualities*) reunir ♦ *vi* combinarse ♦ *n* ['kɒmbaɪn] (*ECON*) cartel *m*; a ~d effort un esfuerzo conjunto.
combine (harvester) *n* cosechadora.
combo ['kɒmbəʊ] *n* (*JAZZ etc*) conjunto.
combustion [kəm'bʌstʃən] *n* combustión *f*.

======================================= *KEYWORD*

come [kʌm] (*pt* came, *pp* come) *vi* 1 (*movement towards*) venir; to ~ running venir corriendo; ~ with me ven conmigo
2 (*arrive*) llegar; he's ~ here to work ha venido aquí para trabajar; to ~ home volver a casa; we've just ~ from Seville acabamos de llegar de Sevilla; coming! ¡voy!
3 (*reach*): to ~ to llegar a; the bill came to £40 la cuenta ascendía a cuarenta libras
4 (*occur*): an idea came to me se me ocurrió una idea; if it ~s to it llegado el caso
5 (*be, become*): to ~ loose/undone *etc* aflojarse/desabrocharse, desatarse *etc*; I've ~ to like him por fin ha llegado a gustarme
►**come about** *vi* suceder, ocurrir
►**come across** *vt fus* (*person*) encontrarse con; (*thing*) encontrar ♦ *vi*: to ~ across well/badly causar buena/mala impresión
►**come away** *vi* (*leave*) marcharse; (*become detached*) desprenderse
►**come back** *vi* (*return*) volver; (*reply*): can I ~ back to you on that one? volvamos sobre ese punto
►**come by** *vt fus* (*acquire*) conseguir
►**come down** *vi* (*price*) bajar; (*building*) derrumbarse; (*: be demolished*) ser derribado
►**come forward** *vi* presentarse
►**come from** *vt fus* (*place, source*) ser de
►**come in** *vi* (*visitor*) entrar; (*train, report*)

llegar; (*fashion*) ponerse de moda; (*on deal etc*) entrar
►**come in for** *vt fus* (*criticism etc*) recibir
►**come into** *vt fus* (*money*) heredar; (*be involved*) tener que ver con; **to ~ into fashion** ponerse de moda
►**come off** *vi* (*button*) soltarse, desprenderse; (*attempt*) salir bien
►**come on** *vi* (*pupil, work, project*) marchar; (*lights*) encenderse; (*electricity*) volver; **~ on!** ¡vamos!
►**come out** *vi* (*fact*) salir a la luz; (*book, sun*) salir; (*stain*) quitarse; **to ~ out (on strike)** declararse en huelga; **to ~ out for/against** declararse a favor/en contra de
►**come over** *vt fus*: **I don't know what's ~ over him!** ¡no sé lo que le pasa!
►**come round** *vi* (*after faint, operation*) volver en sí
►**come through** *vi* (*survive*) sobrevivir; (*telephone call*): **the call came through** recibimos la llamada
►**come to** *vi* (*wake*) volver en sí; (*total*) sumar; **how much does it ~ to?** ¿cuánto es en total?, ¿a cuánto asciende?
►**come under** *vt fus* (*heading*) entrar dentro de; (*influence*) estar bajo
►**come up** *vi* (*sun*) salir; (*problem*) surgir; (*event*) aproximarse; (*in conversation*) mencionarse
►**come up against** *vt fus* (*resistance etc*) tropezar con
►**come up to** *vt fus* llegar hasta; **the film didn't ~ up to our expectations** la película no fue tan buena como esperábamos
►**come up with** *vt fus* (*idea*) sugerir; (*money*) conseguir
►**come upon** *vt fus* (*find*) dar con.

comeback ['kʌmbæk] *n* (*reaction*) reacción *f*; (*response*) réplica; **to make a ~** (*THEAT*) volver a las tablas.
Comecon ['kɔmɪkɔn] *n abbr* (= *Council for Mutual Economic Aid*) COMECON *m*.
comedian [kə'miːdɪən] *n* humorista *m*.
comedienne [kəmiːdɪ'ɛn] *n* humorista.
comedown ['kʌmdaun] *n* revés *m*.
comedy ['kɔmɪdɪ] *n* comedia.
comet ['kɔmɪt] *n* cometa *m*.
comeuppance [kʌm'ʌpəns] *n*: **to get one's ~** llevar su merecido.
comfort ['kʌmfət] *n* comodidad *f*, confort *m*; (*well-being*) bienestar *m*; (*solace*) consuelo; (*relief*) alivio ♦ *vt* consolar; *see also* **comforts**.
comfortable ['kʌmfətəbl] *adj* cómodo;

(*income*) adecuado; (*majority*) suficiente; **I don't feel very ~ about it** la cosa me tiene algo preocupado.
comfortably ['kʌmfətəblɪ] *adv* (*sit*) cómodamente; (*live*) holgadamente.
comforter ['kʌmfətə*] *n* (*US: pacifier*) chupete *m*; (: *bed cover*) colcha.
comforts ['kʌmfəts] *npl* comodidades *fpl*.
comfort station *n* (*US*) servicios *mpl*.
comic ['kɔmɪk] *adj* (*also*: ~**al**) cómico, gracioso ♦ *n* (*magazine*) tebeo; (*for adults*) cómic *m*.
comic strip *n* tira cómica.
coming ['kʌmɪŋ] *n* venida, llegada ♦ *adj* que viene; (*next*) próximo; (*future*) venidero; ~**(s) and going(s)** *n(pl)* ir y venir *m*, ajetreo; **in the ~ weeks** en las próximas semanas.
Comintern ['kɔmɪntəːn] *n* Comintern *m*.
comma ['kɔmə] *n* coma.
command [kə'mɑːnd] *n* orden *f*, mandato; (*MIL: authority*) mando; (*mastery*) dominio; (*COMPUT*) orden *f*, comando ♦ *vt* (*troops*) mandar; (*give orders to*) mandar, ordenar; (*be able to get*) disponer de; (*deserve*) merecer; **to have at one's ~** (*money, resources etc*) disponer de; **to have/take ~ of** estar al/asumir el mando de.
command economy *n* economía dirigida.
commandeer [kɔmən'dɪə*] *vt* requisar.
commander [kə'mɑːndə*] *n* (*MIL*) comandante *m/f*, jefe/a *m/f*.
commanding [kə'mɑːndɪŋ] *adj* (*appearance*) imponente; (*voice, tone*) imperativo; (*lead*) abrumador(a); (*position*) dominante.
commanding officer *n* comandante *m*.
commandment [kə'mɑːndmənt] *n* (*REL*) mandamiento.
command module *n* módulo de mando.
commando [kə'mɑːndəu] *n* comando.
commemorate [kə'mɛməreɪt] *vt* conmemorar.
commemoration [kəmɛmə'reɪʃən] *n* conmemoración *f*.
commemorative [kə'mɛmərətɪv] *adj* conmemorativo.
commence [kə'mɛns] *vt, vi* comenzar.
commend [kə'mɛnd] *vt* (*praise*) elogiar, alabar; (*recommend*) recomendar; (*entrust*) encomendar.
commendable [kə'mɛndəbl] *adj* encomiable.
commendation [kɔmɛn'deɪʃən] *n* (*for bravery etc*) elogio, encomio.
commensurate [kə'mɛnʃərɪt] *adj*: **~ with** en proporción a.
comment ['kɔmɛnt] *n* comentario ♦ *vt*: **to ~**

that comentar *or* observar que ♦ *vi*: **to ~ (on)** comentar, hacer comentarios (sobre); **"no ~"** "no tengo nada que decir", "sin comentarios".
commentary ['kɔməntərɪ] *n* comentario.
commentator ['kɔmənteɪtə*] *n* comentarista *m/f*.
commerce ['kɔmɜːs] *n* comercio.
commercial [kə'mɜːʃəl] *adj* comercial ♦ *n* (*TV*) anuncio.
commercial bank *n* banco comercial.
commercial break *n* intermedio para publicidad.
commercialism [kə'mɜːʃəlɪzəm] *n* comercialismo.
commercial television *n* televisión *f* comercial.
commercial vehicle *n* vehículo comercial.
commiserate [kə'mɪzəreɪt] *vi*: **to ~ with** compadecerse de, condolerse de.
commission [kə'mɪʃən] *n* (*committee, fee, order for work of art etc*) comisión *f*; (*act*) perpetración *f* ♦ *vt* (*MIL*) nombrar; (*work of art*) encargar; **out of ~** (*machine*) fuera de servicio; **~ of inquiry** comisión *f* investigadora; **I get 10% ~** me dan el diez por ciento de comisión; **to ~ sb to do sth** encargar a algn que haga algo; **to ~ sth from sb** (*painting etc*) encargar algo a algn.
commissionaire [kəmɪʃə'nɛə*] *n* (*BRIT*) portero, conserje *m*.
commissioner [kə'mɪʃənə*] *n* comisario; (*POLICE*) comisario *m* de policía.
commit [kə'mɪt] *vt* (*act*) cometer; (*to sb's care*) entregar; **to ~ o.s. (to do)** comprometerse (a hacer); **to ~ suicide** suicidarse; **to ~ sb for trial** remitir a algn al tribunal.
commitment [kə'mɪtmənt] *n* compromiso.
committed [kə'mɪtɪd] *adj* (*writer, politician etc*) comprometido.
committee [kə'mɪtɪ] *n* comité *m*; **to be on a ~** ser miembro/a de un comité.
committee meeting *n* reunión *f* del comité.
commodious [kə'məʊdɪəs] *adj* grande, espacioso.
commodity [kə'mɔdɪtɪ] *n* mercancía.
commodity exchange *n* bolsa de productos *or* de mercancías.
commodity market *n* mercado de productos básicos.
commodore ['kɔmədɔː*] *n* comodoro.
common ['kɔmən] *adj* (*gen*) común; (*pej*) ordinario ♦ *n* campo común; **in ~** en común; **in ~ use** de uso corriente.

common cold *n*: **the ~** el resfriado.
common denominator *n* común denominador *m*.
commoner ['kɔmənə*] *n* plebeyo/a.
common land *n* campo comunal, ejido.
common law *n* ley *f* consuetudinaria.
common-law ['kɔmənlɔː] *adj*: **~ wife** esposa de hecho.
commonly ['kɔmənlɪ] *adv* comúnmente.
Common Market *n* Mercado Común.
commonplace ['kɔmənpleɪs] *adj* corriente.
commonroom ['kɔmənrum] *n* sala de reunión.
Commons ['kɔmənz] *npl* (*BRIT POL*): **the ~** (la Cámara de) los Comunes.
common sense *n* sentido común.
Commonwealth ['kɔmənwɛlθ] *n*: **the ~** la Comunidad (Británica) de Naciones, la Commonwealth.

> La **Commonwealth** es la asociación de estados soberanos independientes y territorios asociados que formaban parte del antiguo Imperio Británico. Éste pasó a llamarse así después de la Segunda Guerra Mundial, aunque ya desde 1931 se le conocía como **British Commonwealth of Nations**. Todos los estados miembros reconocen al monarca británico como **Head of the Commonwealth**.

commotion [kə'məʊʃən] *n* tumulto, confusión *f*.
communal ['kɔmjuːnl] *adj* comunal; (*kitchen*) común.
commune ['kɔmjuːn] *n* (*group*) comuna ♦ *vi* [kə'mjuːn]: **to ~ with** comunicarse con.
communicate [kə'mjuːnɪkeɪt] *vt* comunicar ♦ *vi*: **to ~ (with)** comunicarse (con).
communication [kəmjuːnɪ'keɪʃən] *n* comunicación *f*.
communication cord *n* (*BRIT*) timbre *m* de alarma.
communications network *n* red *f* de comunicaciones.
communications satellite *n* satélite *m* de comunicaciones.
communicative [kə'mjuːnɪkətɪv] *adj* comunicativo.
communion [kə'mjuːnɪən] *n* (*also*: **Holy C~**) comunión *f*.
communiqué [kə'mjuːnɪkeɪ] *n* comunicado, parte *m*.
communism ['kɔmjunɪzəm] *n* comunismo.
communist ['kɔmjunɪst] *adj, n* comunista *m/f*.
community [kə'mjuːnɪtɪ] *n* comunidad *f*; (*large group*) colectividad *f*; (*local*)

vecindario.

community centre *n* centro social.

community chest *n* (*US*) fondo social.

community health centre *n* centro médico, casa de salud.

community spirit *n* civismo.

commutation ticket [kɔmju'teɪʃən-] *n* (*US*) billete *m* de abono.

commute [kə'mjuːt] *vi* viajar a diario de casa al trabajo ♦ *vt* conmutar.

commuter [kə'mjuːtə*] *n persona que viaja a diario de casa al trabajo.*

compact [kəm'pækt] *adj* compacto; (*style*) conciso; (*packed*) apretado ♦ *n* ['kɔmpækt] (*pact*) pacto; (*also:* **powder ~**) polvera.

compact disc *n* compact disc *m*, disco compacto.

compact disc player *n* lector *m or* reproductor *m* de discos compactos.

companion [kəm'pænɪən] *n* compañero/a.

companionship [kəm'pænjənʃɪp] *n* compañerismo.

companionway [kəm'pænjənweɪ] *n* (*NAUT*) escalerilla.

company ['kʌmpənɪ] *n* (*gen*) compañía; (*COMM*) empresa, compañía; **to keep sb ~** acompañar a algn; **Smith and C~** Smith y Compañía.

company car *n* coche *m* de la empresa.

company director *n* director(a) *m/f* de empresa.

company secretary *n* (*BRIT*) administrador(a) *m/f* de empresa.

comparable ['kɔmpərəbl] *adj* comparable.

comparative [kəm'pærətɪv] *adj* (*freedom, luxury, cost*) relativo; (*study, linguistics*) comparado.

comparatively [kəm'pærətɪvlɪ] *adv* (*relatively*) relativamente.

compare [kəm'pɛə*] *vt* comparar ♦ *vi:* **to ~ (with)** poder compararse (con); **~d with** *or* **to** comparado con *or* a; **how do the prices ~?** ¿cómo son los precios en comparación?

comparison [kəm'pærɪsn] *n* comparación *f*; **in ~ (with)** en comparación (con).

compartment [kəm'pɑːtmənt] *n* compartim(i)ento; (*RAIL*) departamento, compartimento.

compass ['kʌmpəs] *n* brújula; **~es** *npl* compás *m*; **within the ~ of** al alcance de.

compassion [kəm'pæʃən] *n* compasión *f*.

compassionate [kəm'pæʃənɪt] *adj* compasivo; **on ~ grounds** por compasión.

compassionate leave *n* permiso por asuntos familiares.

compatibility [kəmpætɪ'bɪlɪtɪ] *n* compatibilidad *f*.

compatible [kəm'pætɪbl] *adj* compatible.

compel [kəm'pɛl] *vt* obligar.

compelling [kəm'pɛlɪŋ] *adj* (*fig: argument*) convincente.

compendium [kəm'pɛndɪəm] *n* compendio.

compensate ['kɔmpənseɪt] *vt* compensar ♦ *vi:* **to ~ for** compensar.

compensation [kɔmpən'seɪʃən] *n* (*for loss*) indemnización *f*.

compère ['kɔmpɛə*] *n* presentador(a) *m/f*.

compete [kəm'piːt] *vi* (*take part*) competir; (*vie with*) competir, hacer la competencia.

competence ['kɔmpɪtəns] *n* capacidad *f*, aptitud *f*.

competent ['kɔmpɪtənt] *adj* competente, capaz.

competing [kəm'piːtɪŋ] *adj* (*rival*) competidor(a); (*ideas*) contrapuesto.

competition [kɔmpɪ'tɪʃən] *n* (*contest*) concurso; (*SPORT*) competición *f*; (*ECON, rivalry*) competencia; **in ~ with** en competencia con.

competitive [kəm'pɛtɪtɪv] *adj* (*ECON, SPORT*) competitivo; (*spirit*) competidor(a), de competencia; (*selection*) por concurso.

competitor [kəm'pɛtɪtə*] *n* (*rival*) competidor(a) *m/f*; (*participant*) concursante *m/f*.

compile [kəm'paɪl] *vt* recopilar.

complacency [kəm'pleɪsnsɪ] *n* autosatisfacción *f*.

complacent [kəm'pleɪsənt] *adj* autocomplaciente.

complain [kəm'pleɪn] *vi* (*gen*) quejarse; (*COMM*) reclamar.

complaint [kəm'pleɪnt] *n* (*gen*) queja; (*COMM*) reclamación *f*; (*LAW*) demanda, querella; (*MED*) enfermedad *f*.

complement ['kɔmplɪmənt] *n* complemento; (*esp ship's crew*) dotación *f* ♦ *vt* ['kɔmplɪment] (*enhance*) complementar.

complementary [kɔmplɪ'mɛntərɪ] *adj* complementario.

complete [kəm'pliːt] *adj* (*full*) completo; (*finished*) acabado ♦ *vt* (*fulfil*) completar; (*finish*) acabar; (*a form*) rellenar; **it's a ~ disaster** es un desastre total.

completely [kəm'pliːtlɪ] *adv* completamente.

completion [kəm'pliːʃən] *n* (*gen*) conclusión *f*, terminación *f*; **to be nearing ~** estar a punto de terminarse; **on ~ of contract** cuando se realice el contrato.

complex ['kɔmplɛks] *adj* complejo ♦ *n* (*gen*) complejo.

complexion [kəm'plɛkʃən] *n* (*of face*) tez *f*,

cutis *m*; (*fig*) aspecto.
complexity [kəm'plɛksɪtɪ] *n* complejidad *f*.
compliance [kəm'plaɪəns] *n* (*submission*)
sumisión *f*; (*agreement*) conformidad *f*; **in**
~ **with** de acuerdo con.
compliant [kəm'plaɪənt] *adj* sumiso;
conforme.
complicate ['kɔmplɪkeɪt] *vt* complicar.
complicated ['kɔmplɪkeɪtɪd] *adj*
complicado.
complication [kɔmplɪ'keɪʃən] *n*
complicación *f*.
complicity [kəm'plɪsɪtɪ] *n* complicidad *f*.
compliment ['kɔmplɪmənt] *n* (*formal*)
cumplido; (*flirtation*) piropo ♦ *vt* felicitar;
~**s** *npl* saludos *mpl*; **to pay sb a** ~ (*formal*)
hacer cumplidos a algn; (*flirt*) piropear,
echar piropos a algn; **to** ~ **sb (on sth/on
doing sth)** felicitar a algn (por algo/por
haber hecho algo).
complimentary [kɔmplɪ'mɛntərɪ] *adj*
elogioso; (*copy*) de regalo; ~ **ticket**
invitación *f*.
compliments slip *n* saluda *m*.
comply [kəm'plaɪ] *vi*: **to** ~ **with** acatar.
component [kəm'pəunənt] *adj* componente
♦ *n* (*TECH*) pieza, componente *m*.
compose [kəm'pəuz] *vt* componer; **to be
~d of** componerse de, constar de; **to** ~
o.s. tranquilizarse.
composed [kəm'pəuzd] *adj* sosegado.
composer [kəm'pəuzə*] *n* (*MUS*)
compositor(a) *m/f*.
composite ['kɔmpəzɪt] *adj* compuesto; ~
motion (*COMM*) moción *f* compuesta.
composition [kɔmpə'zɪʃən] *n* composición *f*.
compositor [kəm'pɔzɪtə*] *n* (*TYP*) cajista
m/f.
compos mentis ['kɔmpəs'mɛntɪs] *adj*: **to be**
~ estar en su sano juicio.
compost ['kɔmpɔst] *n* abono.
compost heap *n* montón de basura
orgánica para abono.
composure [kəm'pəuʒə*] *n* serenidad *f*,
calma.
compound ['kɔmpaund] *n* (*CHEM*)
compuesto; (*LING*) término compuesto;
(*enclosure*) recinto ♦ *adj* (*gen*) compuesto;
(*fracture*) complicado ♦ *vt* [kəm'paund] (*fig*:
problem, difficulty) agravar.
comprehend [kɔmprɪ'hɛnd] *vt* comprender.
comprehension [kɔmprɪ'hɛnʃən] *n*
comprensión *f*.
comprehensive [kɔmprɪ'hɛnsɪv] *adj* (*broad*)
extenso; (*general*) de conjunto; ~ (**school**)
n centro estatal de enseñanza
secundaria, ≈ Instituto Nacional de
Bachillerato (*SP*).

En los años 60 se creó un nuevo tipo de
centro educativo de enseñanza secundaria
(aproximadamente de los once años en
adelante) denominado **comprehensive
school**, abierto a todos los alumnos
independientemente de sus capacidades,
con el que se intentó poner fin a la división
tradicional entre centros de enseñanzas
teóricas para acceder a la educación
superior (**grammar schools**) y otros de
enseñanzas básicamente profesionales
(**secondary modern schools**).

comprehensive insurance policy *n*
seguro a todo riesgo.
compress [kəm'prɛs] *vt* comprimir ♦ *n*
['kɔmprɛs] (*MED*) compresa.
compression [kəm'prɛʃən] *n* compresión *f*.
comprise [kəm'praɪz] *vt* (*also*: **be ~d of**)
comprender, constar de.
compromise ['kɔmprəmaɪz] *n* solución *f*
intermedia; (*agreement*) arreglo ♦ *vt*
comprometer ♦ *vi* transigir, transar
(*LAM*) ♦ *cpd* (*decision, solution*) de término
medio.
compulsion [kəm'pʌlʃən] *n* obligación *f*;
under ~ a la fuerza, por obligación.
compulsive [kəm'pʌlsɪv] *adj* compulsivo.
compulsory [kəm'pʌlsərɪ] *adj* obligatorio.
compulsory purchase *n* expropiación *f*.
compunction [kəm'pʌŋkʃən] *n* escrúpulo;
to have no ~ **about doing sth** no tener
escrúpulos en hacer algo.
computer [kəm'pjuːtə*] *n* ordenador *m*,
computador *m*, computadora.
computer game *n* juego de ordenador.
computerize [kəm'pjuːtəraɪz] *vt* (*data*)
computerizar; (*system*) informatizar.
computer language *n* lenguaje *m* de
ordenador *or* computadora.
computer literate *adj*: **to be** ~ tener
conocimientos de informática a nivel de
usuario.
computer peripheral *n* periférico.
computer program *n* programa *m*
informático *or* de ordenador.
computer programmer *n*
programador(a) *m/f*.
computer programming *n* programación
f.
computer science *n* informática.
computing [kəm'pjuːtɪŋ] *n* (*activity*)
informática.
comrade ['kɔmrɪd] *n* compañero/a.
comradeship ['kɔmrɪdʃɪp] *n* camaradería,
compañerismo.
comsat ® ['kɔmsæt] *n abbr*

= **communications satellite.**

con [kɔn] vt timar, estafar ♦ n timo, estafa; **to ~ sb into doing sth** (col) engañar a algn para que haga algo.

concave ['kɔn'keɪv] adj cóncavo.

conceal [kən'siːl] vt ocultar; (thoughts etc) disimular.

concede [kən'siːd] vt reconocer; (game) darse por vencido en; (territory) ceder ♦ vi darse por vencido.

conceit [kən'siːt] n orgullo, presunción f.

conceited [kən'siːtɪd] adj orgulloso.

conceivable [kən'siːvəbl] adj concebible; **it is ~ that** ... es posible que ....

conceivably [kən'siːvəblɪ] adv: **he may ~ be right** es posible que tenga razón.

conceive [kən'siːv] vt, vi concebir; **to ~ of sth/of doing sth** imaginar algo/imaginarse haciendo algo.

concentrate ['kɔnsəntreɪt] vi concentrarse ♦ vt concentrar.

concentration [kɔnsən'treɪʃən] n concentración f.

concentration camp n campo de concentración.

concentric [kən'sɛntrɪk] adj concéntrico.

concept ['kɔnsɛpt] n concepto.

conception [kən'sɛpʃən] n (idea) concepto, idea; (BIOL) concepción f.

concern [kən'səːn] n (matter) asunto; (COMM) empresa; (anxiety) preocupación f ♦ vt tener que ver con; (affect) atañer, concernir; **to be ~ed (about)** interesarse (por), preocuparse (por); **to be ~ed with** tratar de; **"to whom it may ~"** "a quien corresponda"; **the department ~ed** (under discussion) el departamento en cuestión; (relevant) el departamento competente; **as far as I am ~ed** en cuanto a mí, por lo que a mí se refiere.

concerning [kən'səːnɪŋ] prep sobre, acerca de.

concert ['kɔnsət] n concierto.

concerted [kən'səːtəd] adj (efforts etc) concertado.

concert hall n sala de conciertos.

concertina [kɔnsə'tiːnə] n concertina.

concerto [kən'tʃəːtəu] n concierto.

concession [kən'sɛʃən] n concesión f; (price ~) descuento; **tax ~** privilegio fiscal.

concessionaire [kənsɛʃə'nɛə*] n concesionario/a.

concessionary [kən'sɛʃənərɪ] adj (ticket, fare) con descuento, a precio reducido.

conciliation [kənsɪlɪ'eɪʃən] n conciliación f.

conciliatory [kən'sɪlɪətrɪ] adj conciliador(a).

concise [kən'saɪs] adj conciso.

conclave ['kɔnkleɪv] n cónclave m.

conclude [kən'kluːd] vt (finish) concluir; (treaty etc) firmar; (agreement) llegar a; (decide): **to ~ that** ... llegar a la conclusión de que ... ♦ vi (events) concluir, terminar.

concluding [kən'kluːdɪŋ] adj (remarks etc) final.

conclusion [kən'kluːʒən] n conclusión f; **to come to the ~ that** llegar a la conclusión de que.

conclusive [kən'kluːsɪv] adj decisivo, concluyente.

conclusively [kən'kluːsɪvlɪ] adv concluyentemente.

concoct [kən'kɔkt] vt (food, drink) preparar; (story) inventar; (plot) tramar.

concoction [kən'kɔkʃən] n (food) mezcla; (drink) brebaje m.

concord ['kɔŋkɔːd] n (harmony) concordia; (treaty) acuerdo.

concourse ['kɔŋkɔːs] n (hall) vestíbulo.

concrete ['kɔnkriːt] n hormigón m ♦ adj concreto.

concrete mixer n hormigonera.

concur [kən'kəː*] vi estar de acuerdo.

concurrently [kən'kʌrntlɪ] adv al mismo tiempo.

concussion [kən'kʌʃən] n conmoción f cerebral.

condemn [kən'dɛm] vt condenar.

condemnation [kɔndɛm'neɪʃən] n (gen) condena; (blame) censura.

condensation [kɔndɛn'seɪʃən] n condensación f.

condense [kən'dɛns] vi condensarse ♦ vt condensar; (text) abreviar.

condensed milk n leche f condensada.

condescend [kɔndɪ'sɛnd] vi condescender; **to ~ to sb** tratar a algn con condescendencia; **to ~ to do sth** dignarse hacer algo.

condescending [kɔndɪ'sɛndɪŋ] adj superior.

condition [kən'dɪʃən] n condición f; (of health) estado; (disease) enfermedad f ♦ vt condicionar; **on ~ that** a condición (de) que; **weather ~s** condiciones atmosféricas; **in good/poor ~** en buenas/malas condiciones, en buen/mal estado; **~s of sale** condiciones de venta.

conditional [kən'dɪʃənl] adj condicional.

conditioned reflex [kən'dɪʃənd-] n reflejo condicionado.

conditioner [kən'dɪʃənə*] n (for hair) suavizante m, acondicionador m.

condo ['kɔndəu] n (US col) = **condominium.**

condolences [kən'dəulənsız] *npl* pésame *msg*.

condom ['kɔndəm] *n* condón *m*.

condominium [kɔndə'mınıəm] *n* (*US: building*) bloque *m* de pisos *or* apartamentos (*propiedad de quienes lo habitan*), condominio (*LAM*); (: *apartment*) piso *or* apartamento (en propiedad), condominio (*LAM*).

condone [kən'dəun] *vt* condonar.

conducive [kən'dju:sıv] *adj*: ~ **to** conducente a.

conduct ['kɔndʌkt] *n* conducta, comportamiento ♦ *vt* [kən'dʌkt] (*lead*) conducir; (*manage*) llevar, dirigir; (*MUS*) dirigir ♦ *vi* (*MUS*) llevar la batuta; **to** ~ **o.s.** comportarse.

conducted tour *n* (*BRIT*) visita con guía.

conductor [kən'dʌktə*] *n* (*of orchestra*) director(a) *m/f*; (*US: on train*) revisor(a) *m/f*; (*on bus*) cobrador *m*; (*ELEC*) conductor *m*.

conductress [kən'dʌktrıs] *n* (*on bus*) cobradora.

cone [kəun] *n* cono; (*pine* ~) piña; (*for ice cream*) cucurucho.

confectioner [kən'fɛkʃənə*] *n* (*of cakes*) pastelero/a; (*of sweets*) confitero/a; ~**'s (shop)** *n* pastelería; confitería.

confectionery [kən'fɛkʃənrı] *n* pasteles *mpl*; dulces *mpl*.

confederate [kən'fɛdrıt] *adj* confederado ♦ *n* (*pej*) cómplice *m/f*; (*US: HISTORY*) confederado/a.

confederation [kənfɛdə'reıʃən] *n* confederación *f*.

confer [kən'fəː*] *vt* otorgar (*on a*) ♦ *vi* conferenciar; **to** ~ **(with sb about sth)** consultar (*con algn sobre algo*).

conference ['kɔnfərns] *n* (*meeting*) reunión *f*; (*convention*) congreso; **to be in** ~ estar en una reunión.

conference room *n* sala de conferencias.

confess [kən'fɛs] *vt* confesar ♦ *vi* confesar; (*REL*) confesarse.

confession [kən'fɛʃən] *n* confesión *f*.

confessional [kən'fɛʃənl] *n* confesionario.

confessor [kən'fɛsə*] *n* confesor *m*.

confetti [kən'fɛtı] *n* confeti *m*.

confide [kən'faıd] *vi*: **to** ~ **in** confiar en.

confidence ['kɔnfıdns] *n* (*gen, also: self-*~) confianza; (*secret*) confidencia; **in** ~ (*speak, write*) en confianza; **to have (every)** ~ **that** estar seguro *or* confiado de que; **motion of no** ~ moción *f* de censura; **to tell sb sth in strict** ~ decir algo a algn de manera confidencial.

confidence trick *n* timo.

confident ['kɔnfıdənt] *adj* seguro de sí mismo.

confidential [kɔnfı'dɛnʃəl] *adj* confidencial; (*secretary*) de confianza.

confidentiality [kɔnfıdɛnʃı'ælıtı] *n* confidencialidad *f*.

configuration [kənfıgju'reıʃən] *n* (*also COMPUT*) configuración *f*.

confine [kən'faın] *vt* (*limit*) limitar; (*shut up*) encerrar; **to** ~ **o.s. to doing sth** limitarse a hacer algo.

confined [kən'faınd] *adj* (*space*) reducido.

confinement [kən'faınmənt] *n* (*prison*) reclusión *f*; (*MED*) parto; **in solitary** ~ incomunicado.

confines ['kɔnfaınz] *npl* confines *mpl*.

confirm [kən'fəːm] *vt* confirmar.

confirmation [kɔnfə'meıʃən] *n* confirmación *f*.

confirmed [kən'fəːmd] *adj* empedernido.

confiscate ['kɔnfıskeıt] *vt* confiscar.

confiscation [kɔnfıs'keıʃən] *n* incautación *f*.

conflagration [kɔnflə'greıʃən] *n* conflagración *f*.

conflict ['kɔnflıkt] *n* conflicto ♦ *vi* [kən'flıkt] (*opinions*) estar reñido; (*reports, evidence*) contradecirse.

conflicting [kən'flıktıŋ] *adj* (*reports, evidence, opinions*) contradictorio.

conform [kən'fɔːm] *vi*: **to** ~ **to** (*laws*) someterse a; (*usages, mores*) amoldarse a; (*standards*) ajustarse a.

conformist [kən'fɔːmıst] *n* conformista *m/f*.

confound [kən'faund] *vt* confundir; (*amaze*) pasmar.

confounded [kən'faundıd] *adj* condenado.

confront [kən'frʌnt] *vt* (*problems*) hacer frente a; (*enemy, danger*) enfrentarse con.

confrontation [kɔnfrən'teıʃən] *n* enfrentamiento, confrontación *f*.

confrontational [kɔnfrən'teıʃənəl] *adj* conflictivo.

confuse [kən'fjuːz] *vt* (*perplex*) desconcertar; (*mix up*) confundir.

confused [kən'fjuːzd] *adj* confuso; (*person*) desconcertado; **to get** ~ desconcertarse; (*muddled up*) hacerse un lío.

confusing [kən'fjuːzıŋ] *adj* confuso.

confusion [kən'fjuːʒən] *n* confusión *f*.

congeal [kən'dʒiːl] *vi* coagularse.

congenial [kən'dʒiːnıəl] *adj* agradable.

congenital [kən'dʒɛnıtl] *adj* congénito.

congested [kən'dʒɛstıd] *adj* (*gen*) atestado; (*telephone lines*) saturado.

congestion [kən'dʒɛstʃən] *n* congestión *f*.

conglomerate [kən'glɔmərət] *n* (*COMM, GEO*) conglomerado.

conglomeration [kənglɔmə'reɪʃən] n conglomeración f.

Congo ['kɔŋgəʊ] n (state) Congo.

congratulate [kən'grætjuleɪt] vt felicitar.

congratulations [kəngrætju'leɪʃənz] npl: ~ (on) felicitaciones fpl (por); ~! ¡enhorabuena!, ¡felicidades!

congregate ['kɔŋgrɪgeɪt] vi congregarse.

congregation [kɔŋgrɪ'geɪʃən] n (in church) fieles mpl.

congress ['kɔŋgrɛs] n congreso; (US POL): C~ el Congreso (de los Estados Unidos).

---

*En el Congreso de los Estados Unidos (**Congress**) se elaboran y aprueban las leyes federales. Consta de dos cámaras: la Cámara de Representantes (**House of Representatives**), cuyos 435 miembros son elegidos cada dos años por voto popular directo y en número proporcional a los habitantes de cada estado, y el Senado (**Senate**), con 100 senadores (**senators**), 2 por estado, de los que un tercio se elige cada dos años y el resto cada seis.*

---

congressman ['kɔŋgrɛsmən] n (US) diputado, miembro del Congreso.

congresswoman ['kɔŋgrɛswumən] n (US) diputada, miembro f del Congreso.

conical ['kɔnɪkl] adj cónico.

conifer ['kɔnɪfə*] n conífera.

coniferous [kə'nɪfərəs] adj (forest) conífero.

conjecture [kən'dʒɛktʃə*] n conjetura.

conjugal ['kɔndʒugl] adj conyugal.

conjugate ['kɔndʒugeɪt] vt conjugar.

conjunction [kən'dʒʌŋkʃən] n conjunción f; **in ~ with** junto con.

conjunctivitis [kəndʒʌŋktɪ'vaɪtɪs] n conjuntivitis f.

conjure ['kʌndʒə*] vi hacer juegos de manos.

▶**conjure up** vt (ghost, spirit) hacer aparecer; (memories) evocar.

conjurer ['kʌndʒərə*] n ilusionista m/f.

conjuring trick ['kʌndʒərɪŋ-] n juego de manos.

conker ['kɔŋkə*] n (BRIT) castaño de Indias.

conk out [kɔŋk-] vi (col) estropearse, fastidiarse, descomponerse (LAM).

con man n timador m.

Conn. abbr (US) = Connecticut.

connect [kə'nɛkt] vt juntar, unir; (ELEC) conectar; (pipes) empalmar; (fig) relacionar, asociar ♦ vi: **to ~ with** (train) enlazar con; **to be ~ed with** (associated) estar relacionado con; (related) estar emparentado con; **I am trying to ~ you** (TEL) estoy intentando ponerle al habla.

connection [kə'nɛkʃən] n juntura, unión f; (ELEC) conexión f; (TECH) empalme m; (RAIL) enlace m; (TEL) comunicación f; (fig) relación f; **what is the ~ between them?** ¿qué relación hay entre ellos?; **in ~ with** con respecto a, en relación a; **she has many business ~s** tiene muchos contactos profesionales; **to miss/make a ~** perder/coger el enlace.

connive [kə'naɪv] vi: **to ~ at** hacer la vista gorda a.

connoisseur [kɔnɪ'sə:*] n experto/a, entendido/a.

connotation [kɔnə'teɪʃən] n connotación f.

conquer ['kɔŋkə*] vt (territory) conquistar; (enemy, feelings) vencer.

conqueror ['kɔŋkərə*] n conquistador(a) m/f.

conquest ['kɔŋkwɛst] n conquista.

cons [kɔnz] npl see **convenience, pro.**

conscience ['kɔnʃəns] n conciencia; **in all ~** en conciencia.

conscientious [kɔnʃɪ'ɛnʃəs] adj concienzudo; (objection) de conciencia.

conscientious objector n objetor m de conciencia.

conscious ['kɔnʃəs] adj consciente; (deliberate: insult, error) premeditado, intencionado; **to become ~ of sth/that** darse cuenta de algo/de que.

consciousness ['kɔnʃəsnɪs] n conciencia; (MED) conocimiento.

conscript ['kɔnskrɪpt] n recluta m/f.

conscription [kən'skrɪpʃən] n servicio militar (obligatorio).

consecrate ['kɔnsɪkreɪt] vt consagrar.

consecutive [kən'sɛkjutɪv] adj consecutivo; **on 3 ~ occasions** en 3 ocasiones consecutivas.

consensus [kən'sɛnsəs] n consenso; **the ~ of opinion** el consenso general.

consent [kən'sɛnt] n consentimiento ♦ vi: **to ~ to** consentir en; **by common ~** de común acuerdo.

consenting adults [kən'sɛntɪŋ-] npl adultos con capacidad de consentir.

consequence ['kɔnsɪkwəns] n consecuencia; **in ~** por consiguiente.

consequently ['kɔnsɪkwəntlɪ] adv por consiguiente.

conservation [kɔnsə'veɪʃən] n conservación f; (of nature) conservación, protección f.

conservationist [kɔnsə'veɪʃnɪst] n conservacionista m/f.

conservative [kən'sə:vətɪv] adj conservador(a); (cautious) moderado; C~ adj, n (BRIT POL) conservador(a) m/f; **the**

C~ Party el partido conservador (británico).
conservatory [kən'sɔːvətrɪ] *n (greenhouse)* invernadero.
conserve [kən'sɔːv] *vt* conservar ♦ *n* conserva.
consider [kən'sɪdə*] *vt* considerar; *(take into account)* tomar en cuenta; *(study)* estudiar, examinar; **to ~ doing sth** pensar en (la posibilidad de) hacer algo; **all things ~ed** pensándolo bien; **~ yourself lucky** ¡date por satisfecho!
considerable [kən'sɪdərəbl] *adj* considerable.
considerably [kən'sɪdərəblɪ] *adv* bastante, considerablemente.
considerate [kən'sɪdərɪt] *adj* considerado.
consideration [kənsɪdə'reɪʃən] *n* consideración *f*; *(reward)* retribución *f*; **to be under ~** estar estudiándose; **my first ~ is my family** mi primera consideración es mi familia.
considered [kən'sɪdəd] *adj*: **it's my ~ opinion that** ... depués de haber reflexionado mucho, pienso que ....
considering [kən'sɪdərɪŋ] *prep*: **~ (that)** teniendo en cuenta (que).
consign [kən'saɪn] *vt* consignar.
consignee [kɔnsaɪ'niː] *n* consignatario/a.
consignment [kɔn'saɪnmənt] *n* envío.
consignment note *n (COMM)* talón *m* de expedición.
consignor [kən'saɪnə*] *n* remitente *m/f*.
consist [kən'sɪst] *vi*: **to ~ of** consistir en.
consistency [kən'sɪstənsɪ] *n (of person etc)* consecuencia, coherencia; *(thickness)* consistencia.
consistent [kən'sɪstənt] *adj (person, argument)* consecuente, coherente; *(results)* constante.
consolation [kɔnsə'leɪʃən] *n* consuelo.
console [kən'səul] *vt* consolar ♦ *n* ['kɔnsəul] *(control panel)* consola.
consolidate [kən'sɔlɪdeɪt] *vt* consolidar.
consols ['kɔnsɔlz] *npl (BRIT STOCK EXCHANGE)* valores *mpl* consolidados.
consommé [kən'sɔmeɪ] *n* consomé *m*, caldo.
consonant ['kɔnsənənt] *n* consonante *f*.
consort ['kɔnsɔːt] *n* consorte *m/f* ♦ *vi* [kən'sɔːt]: **to ~ with sb** *(often pej)* asociarse con algn; **prince ~** príncipe *m* consorte.
consortium [kən'sɔːtɪəm] *n* consorcio.
conspicuous [kən'spɪkjuəs] *adj (visible)* visible; *(garish etc)* llamativo; *(outstanding)* notable; **to make o.s. ~** llamar la atención.

conspiracy [kən'spɪrəsɪ] *n* conjura, complot *m*.
conspiratorial [kənspɪrə'tɔːrɪəl] *adj* de conspirador.
conspire [kən'spaɪə*] *vi* conspirar.
constable ['kʌnstəbl] *n (BRIT)* agente *m/f* (de policía); **chief ~ ≈** jefe *m/f* de policía.
constabulary [kən'stæbjulərɪ] *n ≈* policía.
constancy ['kɔnstənsɪ] *n* constancia; fidelidad *f*.
constant ['kɔnstənt] *adj (gen)* constante; *(loyal)* leal, fiel.
constantly ['kɔnstəntlɪ] *adv* constantemente.
constellation [kɔnstə'leɪʃən] *n* constelación *f*.
consternation [kɔnstə'neɪʃən] *n* consternación *f*.
constipated ['kɔnstɪpeɪtəd] *adj* estreñido.
constipation [kɔnstɪ'peɪʃən] *n* estreñimiento.
constituency [kən'stɪtjuənsɪ] *n (POL)* distrito electoral; *(people)* electorado.

Constituency *es la denominación que recibe un distrito o circunscripción electoral y el grupo de electores registrados en ella en el sistema electoral británico. Cada circunscripción elige a un diputado* (**Member of Parliament**), *el cual se halla disponible semanalmente para las consultas y peticiones de sus electores durante ciertas horas a la semana, tiempo al que se llama* **surgery**.

---

constituency party *n* partido local.
constituent [kən'stɪtjuənt] *n (POL)* elector(a) *m/f*; *(part)* componente *m*.
constitute ['kɔnstɪtjuːt] *vt* constituir.
constitution [kɔnstɪ'tjuːʃən] *n* constitución *f*.
constitutional [kɔnstɪ'tjuːʃənl] *adj* constitucional; **~ monarchy** monarquía constitucional.
constrain [kən'streɪn] *vt* obligar.
constrained [kən'streɪnd] *adj*: **to feel ~ to ...** sentirse obligado a ....
constraint [kən'streɪnt] *n (force)* fuerza; *(limit)* restricción *f*; *(restraint)* reserva; *(embarrassment)* cohibición *f*.
constrict [kən'strɪkt] *vt* oprimir.
constriction [kən'strɪkʃən] *n* constricción *f*, opresión *f*.
construct [kən'strʌkt] *vt* construir.
construction [kən'strʌkʃən] *n* construcción *f*; *(fig: interpretation)* interpretación *f*; **under ~** en construcción.
construction industry *n* industria de la

construcción.
constructive [kən'strʌktɪv] *adj* constructivo.
construe [kən'struː] *vt* interpretar.
consul ['kɔnsl] *n* cónsul *m/f*.
consulate ['kɔnsjulɪt] *n* consulado.
consult [kən'sʌlt] *vt, vi* consultar; **to ~ sb (about sth)** consultar a algn (sobre algo).
consultancy [kən'sʌltənsɪ] *n* (*COMM*) consultoría; (*MED*) puesto de especialista.
consultant [kən'sʌltənt] *n* (*BRIT MED*) especialista *m/f*; (*other specialist*) asesor(a) *m/f*, consultor(a) *m/f*.
consultation [kɔnsəl'teɪʃən] *n* consulta; **in ~ with** en consulta con.
consultative [kən'sʌltətɪv] *adj* consultivo.
consulting room *n* (*BRIT*) consulta, consultorio.
consume [kən'sjuːm] *vt* (*eat*) comerse; (*drink*) beberse; (*fire etc, COMM*) consumir.
consumer [kən'sjuːmə*] *n* (*of electricity, gas etc*) consumidor(a) *m/f*.
consumer association *n* asociación *f* de consumidores.
consumer credit *n* crédito al consumidor.
consumer durables *npl* bienes *mpl* de consumo duraderos.
consumer goods *npl* bienes *mpl* de consumo.
consumerism [kən'sjuːmərɪzəm] *n* consumismo.
consumer society *n* sociedad *f* de consumo.
consumer watchdog *n* organización *f* protectora del consumidor.
consummate ['kɔnsʌmeɪt] *vt* consumar.
consumption [kən'sʌmpʃən] *n* consumo; (*MED*) tisis *f*; **not fit for human ~** no apto para el consumo humano.
cont. *abbr* (= *continued*) sigue.
contact ['kɔntækt] *n* contacto; (*person: pej*) enchufe *m* ♦ *vt* ponerse en contacto con; **~ lenses** *npl* lentes *fpl* de contacto; **to be in ~ with sb/sth** estar en contacto con algn/algo; **business ~s** relaciones *fpl* comerciales.
contagious [kən'teɪdʒəs] *adj* contagioso.
contain [kən'teɪn] *vt* contener; **to ~ o.s.** contenerse.
container [kən'teɪnə*] *n* recipiente *m*; (*for shipping etc*) contenedor *m*.
containerize [kən'teɪnəraɪz] *vt* transportar en contenedores.
container ship *n* buque *m* contenedor, portacontenedores *m inv*.
contaminate [kən'tæmɪneɪt] *vt* contaminar.
contamination [kəntæmɪ'neɪʃən] *n* contaminación *f*.

cont'd *abbr* (= *continued*) sigue.
contemplate ['kɔntəmpleɪt] *vt* (*gen*) contemplar; (*reflect upon*) considerar; (*intend*) pensar.
contemplation [kɔntəm'pleɪʃən] *n* contemplación *f*.
contemporary [kən'tempərərɪ] *adj, n* (*of the same age*) contemporáneo/a *m/f*.
contempt [kən'tempt] *n* desprecio; **~ of court** (*LAW*) desacato (a los tribunales *or* a la justicia).
contemptible [kən'temptɪbl] *adj* despreciable, desdeñable.
contemptuous [kən'temptjuəs] *adj* desdeñoso.
contend [kən'tend] *vt* (*argue*) afirmar ♦ *vi* (*struggle*) luchar; **he has a lot to ~ with** tiene que hacer frente a muchos problemas.
contender [kən'tendə*] *n* (*SPORT*) contendiente *m/f*.
content [kən'tent] *adj* (*happy*) contento; (*satisfied*) satisfecho ♦ *vt* contentar; satisfacer ♦ *n* ['kɔntent] contenido; **~s** *npl* contenido *msg*; (*table of*) **~s** índice *m* de materias; (*in magazine*) sumario; **to be ~ with** conformarse con; **to ~ o.s. with sth/with doing sth** conformarse con algo/con hacer algo.
contented [kən'tentɪd] *adj* contento; satisfecho.
contentedly [kən'tentɪdlɪ] *adv* con aire satisfecho.
contention [kən'tenʃən] *n* discusión *f*; (*belief*) argumento; **bone of ~** manzana de la discordia.
contentious [kən'tenʃəs] *adj* discutible.
contentment [kən'tentmənt] *n* satisfacción *f*.
contest ['kɔntest] *n* contienda; (*competition*) concurso ♦ *vt* [kən'test] (*dispute*) impugnar; (*LAW*) disputar, litigar; (*POL: election, seat*) presentarse como candidato/a a.
contestant [kən'testənt] *n* concursante *m/f*; (*in fight*) contendiente *m/f*.
context ['kɔntekst] *n* contexto; **in/out of ~** en/fuera de contexto.
continent ['kɔntɪnənt] *n* continente *m*; **the C~** (*BRIT*) el continente europeo, Europa; **on the C~** en el continente europeo, en Europa.
continental [kɔntɪ'nentl] *adj* continental; (*BRIT: European*) europeo.
continental breakfast *n* desayuno estilo europeo.
continental quilt *n* (*BRIT*) edredón *m*.
contingency [kən'tɪndʒənsɪ]

contingencia.
contingent [kənˈtɪndʒənt] n (*group*)
representación f.
continual [kənˈtɪnjuəl] adj continuo.
continually [kənˈtɪnjuəlɪ] adv
continuamente.
continuation [kəntɪnjuˈeɪʃən] n
prolongación f; (*after interruption*)
reanudación f; (*story, episode*)
continuación f.
continue [kənˈtɪnjuː] vi, vt seguir,
continuar; ~d on page 10 sigue en la
página 10.
continuing education [kənˈtɪnjuɪŋ] n
educación f continua de adultos.
continuity [kɒntɪˈnjuɪtɪ] n (*also CINE*)
continuidad f.
continuity girl n (*CINE*) secretaria de
continuidad.
continuous [kənˈtɪnjuəs] adj continuo; ~
performance (*CINE*) sesión f continua; ~
stationery papel m continuo.
continuously [kənˈtɪnjuəslɪ] adv
continuamente.
contort [kənˈtɔːt] vt retorcer.
contortion [kənˈtɔːʃən] n (*movement*)
contorsión f.
contortionist [kənˈtɔːʃənɪst] n
contorsionista m/f.
contour [ˈkɒntuə*] n contorno; (*also*: ~ **line**)
curva de nivel.
contraband [ˈkɒntrəbænd] n contrabando
♦ adj de contrabando.
contraception [kɒntrəˈsɛpʃən] n
contracepción f.
contraceptive [kɒntrəˈsɛptɪv] adj, n
anticonceptivo.
contract [ˈkɒntrækt] n contrato ♦ cpd
[ˈkɒntrækt] (*price, date*) contratado, de
contrato; (*work*) bajo contrato ♦ vb
[kənˈtrækt] vi (*COMM*): **to ~ to do sth**
comprometerse por contrato a hacer
algo; (*become smaller*) contraerse,
encogerse ♦ vt contraer; **to be under ~ to
do sth** estar bajo contrato para hacer
algo; ~ **of employment** or **of service**
contrato de trabajo.
▶**contract in** vi tomar parte.
▶**contract out** vi: **to ~ out (of)** optar por
no tomar part (en); **to ~ out of a pension
scheme** dejar de cotizar en un plan de
jubilación.
contraction [kənˈtrækʃən] n contracción f.
contractor [kənˈtræktə*] n contratista m/f.
contractual [kənˈtræktjuəl] adj contractual.
contradict [kɒntrəˈdɪkt] vt (*declare to be
wrong*) desmentir; (*be contrary to*)
contradecir.

contradiction [kɒntrəˈdɪkʃən] n
contradicción f; **to be in ~ with**
contradecir.
contradictory [kɒntrəˈdɪktərɪ] adj
(*statements*) contradictorio; **to be ~ to**
contradecir.
contralto [kənˈtræltəu] n contralto f.
contraption [kənˈtræpʃən] n (*pej*) artilugio
m.
contrary [ˈkɒntrərɪ] adj (*opposite, different*)
contrario; [kənˈtrɛərɪ] (*perverse*) terco ♦ n:
on the ~ al contrario; **unless you hear to
the ~** a no ser que le digan lo contrario;
~ **to what we thought** al contrario de lo
que pensábamos.
contrast [ˈkɒntrɑːst] n contraste m ♦ vt
[kənˈtrɑːst] contrastar; **in ~ to** or **with** a
diferencia de.
contrasting [kənˈtrɑːstɪŋ] adj (*opinion*)
opuesto; (*colour*) que hace contraste.
contravene [kɒntrəˈviːn] vt contravenir.
contravention [kɒntrəˈvɛnʃən] n: ~ **(of)**
contravención f (de).
contribute [kənˈtrɪbjuːt] vi contribuir ♦ vt:
to ~ to (*gen*) contribuir a; (*newspaper*)
colaborar en; (*discussion*) intervenir en.
contribution [kɒntrɪˈbjuːʃən] n (*money*)
contribución f; (*to debate*) intervención f;
(*to journal*) colaboración f.
contributor [kənˈtrɪbjutə*] n (*to newspaper*)
colaborador(a) m/f.
contributory [kənˈtrɪbjutərɪ] adj (*cause*)
contribuyente; **it was a ~ factor in ...** fue
un factor que contribuyó en ....
contributory pension scheme n plan m
cotizable de jubilación.
contrivance [kənˈtraɪvəns] n (*machine,
device*) aparato, dispositivo.
contrive [kənˈtraɪv] vt (*invent*) idear ♦ vi: **to
~ to do** lograr hacer; (*try*) procurar
hacer.
control [kənˈtrəul] vt controlar; (*traffic etc*)
dirigir; (*machinery*) manejar; (*temper*)
dominar; (*disease, fire*) dominar,
controlar ♦ n (*command*) control m; (*of
car*) conducción f; (*check*) freno; ~**s** npl
mandos mpl; **to ~ o.s.** controlarse,
dominarse; **everything is under ~** todo
está bajo control; **to be in ~ of** estar al
mando de; **the car went out of ~** el coche
se descontroló.
control group n (*MED, PSYCH etc*) grupo de
control.
control key n (*COMPUT*) tecla de control.
controlled economy n economía dirigida.
controller [kənˈtrəulə*] n controlador(a)
m/f.
controlling interest [kənˈtrəulɪŋ-] n

participación *f* mayoritaria.
control panel *n* (*on aircraft, ship, TV etc*)
tablero de instrumentos.
control point *n* (puesto de) control *m*.
control room *n* (*NAUT, MIL*) sala de
mandos; (*RADIO, TV*) sala de control.
control tower *n* (*AVIAT*) torre *f* de control.
control unit *n* (*COMPUT*) unidad *f* de
control.
controversial [kɔntrə'vəːʃl] *adj* polémico.
controversy ['kɔntrəvəːsɪ] *n* polémica.
conurbation [kɔnəː'beɪʃən] *n* conurbación *f*.
convalesce [kɔnvə'lɛs] *vi* convalecer.
convalescence [kɔnvə'lɛsns] *n*
convalecencia.
convalescent [kɔnvə'lɛsnt] *adj, n*
convaleciente *m/f*.
convector [kən'vɛktə*] *n* calentador *m* de
convección.
convene [kən'viːn] *vt* (*meeting*) convocar
♦ *vi* reunirse.
convenience [kən'viːnɪəns] *n* (*comfort*)
comodidad *f*; (*advantage*) ventaja; **at your
earliest** ~ (*COMM*) tan pronto como le sea
posible; **all modern ~s**, (*BRIT*) **all mod
cons** todo confort.
convenience foods *npl* platos *mpl*
preparados.
convenient [kən'viːnɪənt] *adj* (*useful*) útil;
(*place*) conveniente; (*time*) oportuno; **if it
is** ~ **for you** si le viene bien.
conveniently [kən'viːnɪəntlɪ] *adv* (*happen*)
oportunamente; (*situated*)
convenientemente.
convent ['kɔnvənt] *n* convento.
convent school *n* colegio de monjas.
convention [kən'venʃən] *n* convención *f*;
(*meeting*) asamblea.
conventional [kən'venʃənl] *adj*
convencional.
converge [kən'vəːdʒ] *vi* converger.
conversant [kən'vəːsnt] *adj*: **to be** ~ **with**
estar familiarizado con.
conversation [kɔnvə'seɪʃən] *n*
conversación *f*.
conversational [kɔnvə'seɪʃənl] *adj* (*familiar*)
familiar; (*talkative*) locuaz; ~ **mode**
(*COMPUT*) modo de conversación.
converse ['kɔnvəːs] *n* inversa ♦ *vi* [kən'vəːs]
conversar; **to** ~ (**with sb about sth**)
conversar *or* platicar (*LAM*) (con algn de
algo).
conversely [kɔn'vəːslɪ] *adv* a la inversa.
conversion [kən'vəːʃən] *n* conversión *f*;
(*house* ~) reforma, remodelación *f*.
conversion table *n* tabla de
equivalencias.
convert [kən'vəːt] *vt* (*REL, COMM*) convertir;

(*alter*) transformar ♦ *n* ['kɔnvəːt]
converso/a.
convertible [kən'vəːtəbl] *adj* convertible
♦ *n* descapotable *m*; ~ **loan stock**
obligaciones *fpl* convertibles.
convex ['kɔn'vɛks] *adj* convexo.
convey [kən'veɪ] *vt* transportar; (*thanks*)
comunicar; (*idea*) expresar.
conveyance [kən'veɪəns] *n* (*of goods*)
transporte *m*; (*vehicle*) vehículo, medio de
transporte.
conveyancing [kən'veɪənsɪŋ] *n* (*LAW*)
preparación *f* de escrituras de traspaso.
conveyor belt [kən'veɪə*-] *n* cinta
transportadora.
convict [kən'vɪkt] *vt* (*gen*) condenar; (*find
guilty*) declarar culpable a ♦ *n* ['kɔnvɪkt]
presidiario/a.
conviction [kən'vɪkʃən] *n* condena; (*belief*)
creencia, convicción *f*.
convince [kən'vɪns] *vt* convencer; **to** ~ **sb
(of sth/that)** convencer a algn (de algo/de
que).
convinced [kən'vɪnst] *adj*: ~ **of/that**
convencido de/de que.
convincing [kən'vɪnsɪŋ] *adj* convincente.
convincingly [kən'vɪnsɪŋlɪ] *adv* de modo
convincente, convincentemente.
convivial [kən'vɪvɪəl] *adj* (*person*) sociable;
(*atmosphere*) alegre.
convoluted ['kɔnvəluːtɪd] *adj* (*argument etc*)
enrevesado; (*shape*) enrollado,
enroscado.
convoy ['kɔnvɔɪ] *n* convoy *m*.
convulse [kən'vʌls] *vt* convulsionar; **to be
~d with laughter** dislocarse de risa.
convulsion [kən'vʌlʃən] *n* convulsión *f*.
coo [kuː] *vi* arrullar.
cook [kuk] *vt* cocinar; (*stew etc*) guisar;
(*meal*) preparar ♦ *vi* hacerse; (*person*)
cocinar ♦ *n* cocinero/a.
►**cook up** *vt* (*col: excuse, story*) inventar.
cookbook ['kukbuk] *n* libro de cocina.
cooker ['kukə*] *n* cocina.
cookery ['kukərɪ] *n* cocina.
cookery book *n* (*BRIT*) = **cookbook**.
cookie ['kukɪ] *n* (*US*) galleta.
cooking ['kukɪŋ] *n* cocina ♦ *cpd* (*apples*)
para cocinar; (*utensils, salt, foil*) de cocina.
cooking chocolate *n* chocolate *m* fondant
or de hacer.
cookout ['kukaut] *n* (*US*) comida al aire
libre.
cool [kuːl] *adj* fresco; (*not hot*) tibio; (*not
afraid*) tranquilo; (*unfriendly*) frío ♦ *vt*
enfriar ♦ *vi* enfriarse; **it is** ~ (*weather*)
hace fresco; **to keep sth** ~ *or* **in a** ~ **place**
conservar algo fresco *or* en un sitio

fresco.

▶**cool down** vi enfriarse; (fig: person, situation) calmarse.

coolant ['ku:lənt] n refrigerante m.

cool box, (US) **cooler** ['ku:lə*] n nevera portátil.

cooling ['ku:lɪŋ] adj refrescante.

cooling-off period [ku:lɪŋ'ɔf-] n (INDUSTRY) plazo de negociaciones.

cooling tower n torre f de refrigeración.

coolly ['ku:lɪ] adv (calmly) con tranquilidad; (audaciously) descaradamente; (unenthusiastically) fríamente, con frialdad.

coolness ['ku:lnɪs] n frescura; tranquilidad f; (hostility) frialdad f; (indifference) falta de entusiasmo.

coop [ku:p] n gallinero ♦ vt: **to ~ up** (fig) encerrar.

co-op ['kəuɔp] n abbr (= Cooperative (Society)) cooperativa.

cooperate [kəu'ɔpəreɪt] vi cooperar, colaborar; **will he ~?** ¿querrá cooperar?

cooperation [kəuɔpə'reɪʃən] n cooperación f, colaboración f.

cooperative [kəu'ɔpərətɪv] adj cooperativo; (person) dispuesto a colaborar ♦ n cooperativa.

co-opt [kəu'ɔpt] vt: **to ~ sb into sth** nombrar a algn para algo.

coordinate [kəu'ɔːdɪneɪt] vt coordinar ♦ n [kəu'ɔːdɪnət] (MATH) coordenada; **~s** npl (clothes) coordinados mpl.

coordination [kəuɔːdɪ'neɪʃən] n coordinación f.

coot [ku:t] n focha f (común).

co-ownership [kəu'əunəʃɪp] n co-propiedad f.

cop [kɔp] n (col) poli m.

cope [kəup] vi: **to ~ with** poder con; (problem) hacer frente a.

Copenhagen [kəupən'heɪgən] n Copenhague m.

copier ['kɔpɪə*] n (photo~) (foto)copiadora.

co-pilot ['kəu'paɪlət] n copiloto m/f.

copious ['kəupɪəs] adj copioso, abundante.

copper ['kɔpə*] n (metal) cobre m; (col: policeman) poli m; **~s** npl perras fpl; (small change) calderilla.

coppice ['kɔpɪs], **copse** [kɔps] n bosquecillo.

copulate ['kɔpjuleɪt] vi copular.

copulation [kɔpju'leɪʃən] n cópula.

copy ['kɔpɪ] n copia, (of book) ejemplar m; (of magazine) número; (material: for printing) original m ♦ vt copiar (also COMPUT); (imitate) copiar, imitar; **to make good ~** (fig) ser una noticia de interés;

rough **~** borrador m; **fair ~** copia en limpio.

▶**copy out** vt copiar.

copycat ['kɔpɪkæt] n (pej) imitador(a) m/f.

copyright ['kɔpɪraɪt] n derechos mpl de autor.

copy typist n mecanógrafo/a.

coral ['kɔrəl] n coral m.

coral reef n arrecife m (de coral).

Coral Sea n: **the ~** el Mar del Coral.

cord [kɔːd] n cuerda; (ELEC) cable m; (fabric) pana; **~s** npl (trousers) pantalones mpl de pana.

cordial ['kɔːdɪəl] adj cordial ♦ n cordial m.

cordless ['kɔːdlɪs] adj sin hilos.

cordon ['kɔːdn] n cordón m.

▶**cordon off** vt acordonar.

Cordova ['kɔːdəvə] n Córdoba.

corduroy ['kɔːdərɔɪ] n pana.

CORE [kɔː*] n abbr (US) = Congress of Racial Equality.

core [kɔː*] n (of earth, nuclear reactor) centro, núcleo; (of fruit) corazón m; (of problem etc) esencia, meollo ♦ vt quitar el corazón de.

Corfu [kɔː'fu] n Corfú m.

coriander [kɔrɪ'ændə*] n culantro, cilantro.

cork [kɔːk] n corcho; (tree) alcornoque m.

corkage ['kɔːkɪdʒ] n precio que se cobra en un restaurante por una botella de vino traída de fuera.

corked [kɔːkt] adj (wine) con sabor a corcho.

corkscrew ['kɔːkskru:] n sacacorchos m inv.

cormorant ['kɔːmərnt] n cormorán m.

Corn abbr (BRIT) = Cornwall.

corn [kɔːn] n (BRIT: wheat) trigo; (US: maize) maíz m, choclo (LAM); (on foot) callo; **~ on the cob** (CULIN) maíz en la mazorca.

cornea ['kɔːnɪə] n córnea.

corned beef ['kɔːnd-] n carne f de vaca acecinada.

corner ['kɔːnə*] n (outside) esquina; (inside) rincón m; (in road) curva; (FOOTBALL) córner m, saque m de esquina ♦ vt (trap) arrinconar; (COMM) acaparar ♦ vi (in car) tomar las curvas; **to cut ~s** atajar.

corner flag n (FOOTBALL) banderola de esquina.

corner kick n (FOOTBALL) córner m, saque m de esquina.

cornerstone ['kɔːnəstəun] n piedra angular.

cornet ['kɔːnɪt] n (MUS) corneta; (BRIT: of ice cream) cucurucho.

cornflakes ['kɔːnfleɪks] npl copos mpl de maíz, cornflakes mpl.

cornflour ['kɔːnflauə*] n (BRIT) harina de

maíz.
cornice ['kɔːnɪs] n cornisa.
Cornish ['kɔːnɪʃ] adj de Cornualles.
corn oil n aceite m de maíz.
cornstarch ['kɔːnstɑːtʃ] n (US) = **cornflour**.
cornucopia [kɔːnjuˈkəupɪə] n cornucopia.
Cornwall ['kɔːnwəl] n Cornualles m.
corny ['kɔːnɪ] adj (col) gastado.
corollary [kəˈrɔlərɪ] n corolario.
coronary ['kɔrənərɪ] n: ~ **(thrombosis)**
infarto.
coronation [kɔrəˈneɪʃən] n coronación f.
coroner ['kɔrənə*] n juez m/f de instrucción.
coronet ['kɔrənɪt] n corona.
Corp. abbr = **corporation**.
corporal ['kɔːpərl] n cabo ♦ adj: ~
punishment castigo corporal.
corporate ['kɔːpərɪt] adj corporativo.
corporate hospitality n obsequios a los
clientes por cortesía de la empresa.
corporate identity, corporate image n
(of organization) identidad f corporativa.
corporation [kɔːpəˈreɪʃən] n (of town)
ayuntamiento; (COMM) corporación f.
corps [kɔː*], pl **corps** [kɔːz] n cuerpo; **press**
~ gabinete m de prensa.
corpse [kɔːps] n cadáver m.
corpulent ['kɔːpjulənt] adj corpulento/a.
Corpus Christi ['kɔːpəsˈkrɪstɪ] n Corpus m
(Christi).
corpuscle ['kɔːpʌsl] n corpúsculo.
corral [kəˈrɑːl] n corral m.
correct [kəˈrɛkt] adj correcto, (accurate)
exacto ♦ vt corregir; **you are** ~ tiene
razón.
correction [kəˈrɛkʃən] n rectificación f,
(erasure) tachadura.
correlate ['kɔrɪleɪt] vi: **to** ~ **with** tener
correlación con.
correlation [kɔrɪˈleɪʃən] n correlación f.
correspond [kɔrɪsˈpɔnd] vi (write)
escribirse; (be equal to) corresponder.
correspondence [kɔrɪsˈpɔndəns] n
correspondencia.
correspondence course n curso por
correspondencia.
correspondent [kɔrɪsˈpɔndənt] n
corresponsal m/f.
corresponding [kɔrɪsˈpɔndɪŋ] adj
correspondiente.
corridor ['kɔrɪdɔː*] n pasillo.
corroborate [kəˈrɔbəreɪt] vt corroborar.
corroboration [kərɔbəˈreɪʃən] n
corroboración f, confirmación f.
corrode [kəˈrəud] vt corroer ♦ vi corroerse.
corrosion [kəˈrəuʒən] n corrosión f.
corrosive [kəˈrəusɪv] adj corrosivo.
corrugated ['kɔrəgeɪtɪd] adj ondulado.

corrugated cardboard n cartón m
ondulado.
corrugated iron n chapa ondulada.
corrupt [kəˈrʌpt] adj corrompido; (person)
corrupto ♦ vt corromper; (bribe)
sobornar; (data) degradar; ~ **practices**
(dishonesty, bribery) corrupción f.
corruption [kəˈrʌpʃən] n corrupción f; (of
data) alteración f.
corset ['kɔːsɪt] n faja; (old-style) corsé m.
Corsica ['kɔːsɪkə] n Córcega.
Corsican ['kɔːsɪkən] adj, n corso/a m/f.
cortège [kɔːˈteɪʒ] n cortejo, comitiva.
cortisone ['kɔːtɪzəun] n cortisona.
c.o.s. abbr (= cash on shipment) pago al
embarcar.
cosh [kɔʃ] n (BRIT) cachiporra.
cosignatory ['kəuˈsɪgnətərɪ] n
cosignatario/a.
cosine ['kəusaɪn] n coseno.
cosiness ['kəuzɪnɪs] n comodidad f;
(atmosphere) lo acogedor.
cos lettuce [kɔs-] n lechuga romana.
cosmetic [kɔzˈmɛtɪk] n cosmético ♦ adj
(also fig) cosmético; (surgery) estético.
cosmic ['kɔzmɪk] adj cósmico.
cosmonaut ['kɔzmənɔːt] n cosmonauta m/f.
cosmopolitan [kɔzməˈpɔlɪtn] adj
cosmopolita.
cosmos ['kɔzmɔs] n cosmos m.
cosset ['kɔsɪt] vt mimar.
cost [kɔst] n (gen) coste m, costo; (price)
precio; ~**s** npl (LAW) costas fpl ♦ vb (pt, pp
cost) vi costar, valer ♦ vt preparar el
presupuesto de; **how much does it** ~?
¿cuánto cuesta?, ¿cuánto vale?; **what will
it** ~ **to have it repaired?** ¿cuánto costará
repararlo?; **the** ~ **of living** el coste or
costo de la vida; **at all** ~**s** cueste lo que
cueste.
cost accountant n contable m de costos.
co-star ['kəustɑː*] n coprotagonista m/f.
Costa Rica ['kɔstəˈriːkə] n Costa Rica.
Costa Rican ['kɔstəˈriːkən] adj, n
costarriqueño/a m/f, costarricense m/f.
cost centre n centro (de determinación)
de coste.
cost control n control m de costes.
cost-effective [kɔstɪˈfɛktɪv] adj (COMM)
rentable.
cost-effectiveness ['kɔstɪˈfɛktɪvnɪs] n
relación f coste-rendimiento.
costing ['kɔstɪŋ] n cálculo del coste.
costly ['kɔstlɪ] adj (expensive) costoso.
cost-of-living [kɔstəvˈlɪvɪŋ] adj: ~
allowance n plus m de carestía de vida; ~
index n índice m del coste de vida.
cost price n (BRIT) precio de coste.

costume ['kɔstjuːm] *n* traje *m*; (*BRIT: also:* **swimming ~**) traje de baño.
costume jewellery *n* bisutería.
cosy, (*US*) **cozy** ['kəʊzɪ] *adj* cómodo, a gusto; (*room, atmosphere*) acogedor(a).
cot [kɔt] *n* (*BRIT: child's*) cuna; (*US: folding bed*) cama plegable.
cot death *n* muerte *f* en la cuna.
Cotswolds ['kɔtswəʊldz] *npl* región de colinas del suroeste inglés.
cottage ['kɔtɪdʒ] *n* casita de campo.
cottage cheese *n* requesón *m*.
cottage industry *n* industria artesanal.
cottage pie *n* pastel de carne cubierta de puré de patatas.
cotton ['kɔtn] *n* algodón *m*; (*thread*) hilo.
▶**cotton on** *vi* (*col*): **to ~ on (to sth)** caer en la cuenta (de algo).
cotton candy *n* (*US*) algodón *m* (azucarado).
cotton wool *n* (*BRIT*) algodón *m* (hidrófilo).
couch [kautʃ] *n* sofá *m*; (*in doctor's surgery*) camilla.
couchette [kuːʃɛt] *n* litera.
couch potato *n* (*col*) persona comodona que no se mueve en todo el día.
cough [kɔf] *vi* toser ♦ *n* tos *f*.
▶**cough up** *vt* escupir.
cough drop *n* pastilla para la tos.
cough mixture *n* jarabe *m* para la tos.
could [kud] *pt of* **can**.
couldn't ['kudnt] = **could not**.
council ['kaunsl] *n* consejo; **city** *or* **town ~** ayuntamiento; **C~ of Europe** Consejo de Europa.
council estate *n* (*BRIT*) barriada de viviendas sociales de alquiler.
council house *n* (*BRIT*) vivienda social de alquiler.
councillor ['kaunslə*] *n* concejal *m/f*.
council tax *n* (*BRIT*) contribución *f* municipal (*dependiente del valor de la vivienda*).
counsel ['kaunsl] *n* (*advice*) consejo; (*lawyer*) abogado/a ♦ *vt* aconsejar; **~ for the defence/the prosecution** abogado/a defensor(a)/fiscal; **to ~ sth/sb to do sth** aconsejar algo/a algn que haga algo.
counsellor, (*US*) **counselor** ['kaunslə*] *n* consejero/a; (*US LAW*) abogado/a.
count [kaunt] *vt* (*gen*) contar; (*include*) incluir ♦ *vi* contar ♦ *n* cuenta; (*of votes*) escrutinio; (*nobleman*) conde *m*; (*sum*) total *m*, suma; **to ~ the cost of** calcular el coste de; **not ~ing the children** niños aparte; **10 ~ing him** diez incluyéndolo a él, diez con él; **~ yourself lucky** date por satisfecho; **that doesn't ~!** ¡eso no vale!;

to ~ (up) to 10 contar hasta diez; **it ~s for very little** cuenta poco; **to keep ~ of sth** llevar la cuenta de algo.
▶**count on** *vt fus* contar con; **to ~ on doing sth** contar con hacer algo.
▶**count up** *vt* contar.
countdown ['kauntdaun] *n* cuenta atrás.
countenance ['kauntɪnəns] *n* semblante *m*, rostro ♦ *vt* (*tolerate*) aprobar, consentir.
counter ['kauntə*] *n* (*in shop*) mostrador *m*; (*position: in post office, bank*) ventanilla; (*in games*) ficha; (*TECH*) contador *m* ♦ *vt* contrarrestar; (*blow*) parar; (*attack*) contestar a ♦ *adv*: **~ to** contrario a; **to buy under the ~** (*fig*) comprar de estraperlo *or* bajo mano; **to ~ sth with sth/by doing sth** contestar algo con algo/haciendo algo.
counteract ['kauntər'ækt] *vt* contrarrestar.
counterattack ['kauntərə'tæk] *n* contraataque *m* ♦ *vi* contraatacar.
counterbalance ['kauntə'bæləns] *n* contrapeso.
counter-clockwise ['kauntə'klɔkwaɪz] *adv* en sentido contrario al de las agujas del reloj.
counter-espionage ['kauntər'ɛspɪɑːʒ] *n* contraespionaje *m*.
counterfeit ['kauntəfɪt] *n* falsificación *f* ♦ *vt* falsificar ♦ *adj* falso, falsificado.
counterfoil ['kauntəfɔɪl] *n* (*BRIT*) matriz *f*, talón *m*.
counterintelligence ['kauntərɪn'tɛlɪdʒəns] *n* contraespionaje *m*.
countermand ['kauntəmɑːnd] *vt* revocar.
counter-measure ['kauntəmɛʒə*] *n* contramedida.
counteroffensive ['kauntərə'fɛnsɪv] *n* contraofensiva.
counterpane ['kauntəpeɪn] *n* colcha.
counterpart ['kauntəpɑːt] *n* (*of person*) homólogo/a.
counter-productive [kauntəprə'dʌktɪv] *adj* contraproducente.
counterproposal ['kauntəprə'pəuzl] *n* contrapropuesta.
countersign ['kauntəsaɪn] *vt* ratificar, refrendar.
countess ['kauntɪs] *n* condesa.
countless ['kauntlɪs] *adj* innumerable.
countrified ['kʌntrɪfaɪd] *adj* rústico.
country ['kʌntrɪ] *n* país *m*; (*native land*) patria; (*as opposed to town*) campo; (*region*) región *f*, tierra; **in the ~** en el campo; **mountainous ~** región *f* montañosa.
country and western (music) *n* música country.

country dancing n (BRIT) baile m regional.
country house n casa de campo.
countryman ['kʌntrɪmən] n (national) compatriota m; (rural) hombre m del campo.
countryside ['kʌntrɪsaɪd] n campo.
countrywide ['kʌntrɪ'waɪd] adj nacional ♦ adv por todo el país.
county ['kaʊntɪ] n condado; see also **district council**.
county council n (BRIT) ≈ diputación f provincial.
county town n cabeza de partido.
coup, ~s [kuː, -z] n golpe m; (triumph) éxito; (also: ~ d'état) golpe de estado.
coupé ['kuːpeɪ] n cupé m.
couple ['kʌpl] n (of things) par m; (of people) pareja; (married ~) matrimonio ♦ vt (ideas, names) unir, juntar; (machinery) acoplar; **a ~ of** un par de.
couplet ['kʌplɪt] n pareado.
coupling ['kʌplɪŋ] n (RAIL) enganche m.
coupon ['kuːpɔn] n cupón m; (pools ~) boleto (de quiniela).
courage ['kʌrɪdʒ] n valor m, valentía.
courageous [kə'reɪdʒəs] adj valiente.
courgette [kuə'ʒet] n (BRIT) calabacín m.
courier ['kʊrɪə*] n mensajero/a; (diplomatic) correo; (for tourists) guía m/f (de turismo).
course [kɔːs] n (direction) dirección f; (of river, SCOL) curso; (of ship) rumbo; (fig) proceder m; (GOLF) campo; (part of meal) plato; **of ~** adv desde luego, naturalmente; **of ~!** ¡claro!, ¡cómo no! (LAM): **(no) of ~ not!** ¡claro que no!, ¡por supuesto que no!; **in due ~** a su debido tiempo; **in the ~ of the next few days** durante los próximos días; **we have no other ~ but to** ... no tenemos más remedio que ...; **there are 2 ~s open to us** se nos ofrecen dos posibilidades; **the best ~ would be to** ... lo mejor sería ...; **~ of treatment** (MED) tratamiento.
court [kɔːt] n (royal) corte f; (LAW) tribunal m, juzgado; (TENNIS) pista, cancha (LAM) ♦ vt (woman) cortejar; (fig: favour, popularity) solicitar, buscar; (: death, disaster, danger etc) buscar; **to take to ~** demandar; **~ of appeal** tribunal m de apelación.
courteous ['kɔːtɪəs] adj cortés.
courtesan [kɔːtɪ'zæn] n cortesana.
courtesy ['kɔːtəsɪ] n cortesía; **by ~ of** (por) cortesía de.
courtesy light n (AUT) luz f interior.
court-house ['kɔːthaʊs] n (US) palacio de justicia.
courtier ['kɔːtɪə*] n cortesano.

court martial, pl **courts martial** ['kɔːt'mɑːʃəl] n consejo de guerra ♦ vt someter a consejo de guerra.
courtroom ['kɔːtrum] n sala de justicia.
court shoe n zapato de mujer de estilo clásico.
courtyard ['kɔːtjɑːd] n patio.
cousin ['kʌzn] n primo/a; **first ~** primo/a carnal.
cove [kəʊv] n cala, ensenada.
covenant ['kʌvənənt] n convenio ♦ vt: **to ~ £20 per year to a charity** concertar el pago de veinte libras anuales a una sociedad benéfica.
Coventry ['kɔvəntrɪ] n: **to send sb to ~** (fig) hacer el vacío a algn.
cover ['kʌvə*] vt cubrir; (with lid) tapar; (chairs etc) revestir; (distance) cubrir, recorrer; (include) abarcar; (protect) abrigar; (journalist) investigar; (issues) tratar ♦ n cubierta; (lid) tapa; (for chair etc) funda; (for bed) cobertor m; (envelope) sobre m; (of magazine) portada; (shelter) abrigo; (insurance) cobertura; **to take ~** (shelter) protegerse, resguardarse; **under ~** (indoors) bajo techo; **under ~ of darkness** al amparo de la oscuridad; **under separate ~** (COMM) por separado; **£10 will ~ everything** con diez libras cubriremos todos los gastos.
►**cover up** vt (child, object) cubrir completamente, tapar; (fig: hide: truth, facts) ocultar; **to ~ up for sb** (fig) encubrir a algn.
coverage ['kʌvərɪdʒ] n alcance m; (in media) reportaje m; (INSURANCE) cobertura.
coveralls ['kʌvərɔːlz] npl (US) mono sg.
cover charge n precio del cubierto.
covering ['kʌvərɪŋ] n cubierta, envoltura.
covering letter, (US) **cover letter** n carta de explicación.
cover note n (INSURANCE) póliza provisional.
cover price n precio de cubierta.
covert ['kəʊvət] adj (secret) secreto, encubierto; (dissembled) furtivo.
cover-up ['kʌvərʌp] n encubrimiento.
covet ['kʌvɪt] vt codiciar.
covetous ['kʌvɪtəs] adj codicioso.
cow [kaʊ] n vaca ♦ vt intimidar.
coward ['kaʊəd] n cobarde m/f.
cowardice ['kaʊədɪs] n cobardía.
cowardly ['kaʊədlɪ] adj cobarde.
cowboy ['kaʊbɔɪ] n vaquero.
cower ['kaʊə*] vi encogerse (de miedo).
co-worker ['kəʊwɜːkə*] n colaborador(a) m/f.

cowshed ['kauʃɛd] n establo.
cowslip ['kauslɪp] n (BOT) primavera, prímula.
coxswain ['kɔksn] n (abbr: **cox**) timonel m.
coy [kɔɪ] adj tímido.
coyote [kɔɪ'əutɪ] n coyote m.
cozy ['kəuzɪ] adj (US) = **cosy**.
CP n abbr (= Communist Party) PC m.
cp. abbr (= compare) cfr.
c/p abbr (BRIT) = **carriage paid**.
CPA n abbr (US) = **certified public accountant**.
CPI n abbr (= Consumer Price Index) IPC m.
Cpl. abbr (MIL) = **corporal**.
CP/M n abbr (= Central Program for Microprocessors) CP/M m.
c.p.s. abbr (= characters per second) c.p.s.
CPSA n abbr (BRIT: = Civil and Public Services Association) sindicato de funcionarios.
CPU n abbr = **central processing unit**.
cr. abbr = **credit, creditor**.
crab [kræb] n cangrejo.
crab apple n manzana silvestre.
crack [kræk] n grieta; (noise) crujido; (: of whip) chasquido; (joke) chiste m; (col: drug) crack m; (attempt): **to have a ~ at sth** intentar algo ♦ vt agrietar, romper; (nut) cascar; (safe) forzar; (whip etc) chasquear; (knuckles) crujir; (joke) contar; (case: solve) resolver; (code) descifrar ♦ adj (athlete) de primera clase; **to ~ jokes** (col) bromear.
▶**crack down on** vt fus reprimir fuertemente, adoptar medidas severas contra.
▶**crack up** vi sufrir una crisis nerviosa.
crackdown ['krækdaun] n: ~ **(on)** (on crime) campaña (contra); (on spending) reducción f (en).
cracker ['krækə*] n (biscuit) galleta salada, cráquer m; (Christmas ~) sorpresa (navideña).
crackle ['krækl] vi crepitar.
crackling ['kræklɪŋ] n (on radio, telephone) interferencia; (of fire) chisporroteo, crepitación f; (of leaves etc) crujido; (of pork) chicharrón m.
crackpot ['krækpɔt] (col) n pirado/a ♦ adj de pirado.
cradle ['kreɪdl] n cuna ♦ vt (child) mecer, acunar; (object) abrazar.
craft [krɑːft] n (skill) arte m; (trade) oficio; (cunning) astucia; (boat) embarcación f.
craftsman ['krɑːftsmən] n artesano.
craftsmanship ['krɑːftsmənʃɪp] n artesanía.
crafty ['krɑːftɪ] adj astuto.
crag [kræg] n peñasco.

craggy ['krægɪ] adj escarpado.
cram [kræm] vt (fill): **to ~ sth with** llenar algo (a reventar) de; (put): **to ~ sth into** meter algo a la fuerza en ♦ vi (for exams) empollar.
crammed [kræmd] adj atestado.
cramp [kræmp] n (MED) calambre m; (TECH) grapa ♦ vt (limit) poner trabas a.
cramped [kræmpt] adj apretado; (room) minúsculo.
crampon ['kræmpən] n crampón m.
cranberry ['krænbərɪ] n arándano.
crane [kreɪn] n (TECH) grúa; (bird) grulla ♦ vt, vi: **to ~ forward, to ~ one's neck** estirar el cuello.
cranium ['kreɪnɪəm] n cráneo.
crank [kræŋk] n manivela; (person) chiflado/a.
crankshaft ['kræŋkʃɑːft] n cigüeñal m.
cranky ['kræŋkɪ] adj (eccentric) maniático; (bad-tempered) de mal genio.
cranny ['krænɪ] n see **nook**.
crap [kræp] n (col!) mierda (!).
crappy ['kræpɪ] adj (col) chungo.
craps [kræps] n (US) dados mpl.
crash [kræʃ] n (noise) estrépito; (of cars, plane) accidente m; (of business) quiebra; (STOCK EXCHANGE) crac m ♦ vt (plane) estrellar ♦ vi (plane) estrellarse; (two cars) chocar; (fall noisily) caer con estrépito; **he ~ed the car into a wall** estrelló el coche contra una pared or tapia.
crash barrier n (AUT) barrera de protección.
crash course n curso acelerado.
crash helmet n casco (protector).
crash landing n aterrizaje m forzoso.
crass [kræs] adj grosero, maleducado.
crate [kreɪt] n caja, cajón m de embalaje; (col) armatoste m.
crater ['kreɪtə*] n cráter m.
cravat(e) [krə'væt] n pañuelo.
crave [kreɪv] vt, vi: **to ~ (for)** ansiar, anhelar.
craving ['kreɪvɪŋ] n (for food, cigarettes, etc) ansias fpl; (during pregnancy) antojo.
crawl [krɔːl] vi (drag o.s.) arrastrarse; (child) andar a gatas, gatear; (vehicle) avanzar (lentamente); (col): **to ~ to sb** dar coba a algn, hacerle la pelota a algn ♦ n (SWIMMING) crol m.
crawler lane [krɔːlə-] n (BRIT AUT) carril m para tráfico lento.
crayfish ['kreɪfɪʃ] n, pl inv (freshwater) cangrejo (de río); (saltwater) cigala.
crayon ['kreɪən] n lápiz m de color.
craze [kreɪz] n manía; (fashion) moda.
crazed [kreɪzd] adj (look, person) loco,

demente; (*pottery, glaze*) agrietado, cuarteado.

crazy ['kreɪzɪ] *adj* (*person*) loco; (*idea*) disparatado; **to go** ~ volverse loco; **to be** ~ **about sb/sth** (*col*) estar loco por algn/algo.

crazy paving *n pavimento de baldosas irregulares.*

creak [kriːk] *vi* crujir; (*hinge etc*) chirriar, rechinar.

cream [kriːm] *n* (*of milk*) nata, crema; (*lotion*) crema; (*fig*) flor *f* y nata ♦ *adj* (*colour*) color *m* crema; **whipped** ~ nata batida.

►**cream off** *vt* (*fig*) (*best talents, part of profits*) separar lo mejor de.

cream cake *n* pastel *m* de nata.

cream cheese *n* queso fresco cremoso.

creamery ['kriːmərɪ] *n* (*shop*) quesería; (*factory*) central *f* lechera.

creamy ['kriːmɪ] *adj* cremoso.

crease [kriːs] *n* (*fold*) pliegue *m*; (*in trousers*) raya; (*wrinkle*) arruga ♦ *vt* (*fold*) doblar, plegar; (*wrinkle*) arrugar ♦ *vi* (*wrinkle up*) arrugarse.

crease-resistant ['kriːsrɪzɪstənt] *adj* inarrugable.

create [kriː'eɪt] *vt* (*also COMPUT*) crear; (*impression*) dar; (*fuss, noise*) hacer.

creation [kriː'eɪʃən] *n* creación *f.*

creative [kriː'eɪtɪv] *adj* creativo.

creativity [kriːeɪ'tɪvɪtɪ] *n* creatividad *f.*

creator [kriː'eɪtə*] *n* creador(a) *m/f.*

creature ['kriːtʃə*] *n* (*living thing*) criatura; (*animal*) animal *m*; (*insect*) bicho.

creature comforts *npl* comodidades *fpl* materiales.

crèche, creche [krɛʃ] *n* (*BRIT*) guardería (infantil).

credence ['kriːdəns] *n*: **to lend** *or* **give** ~ **to** creer en, dar crédito a.

credentials [krɪ'dɛnʃlz] *npl* credenciales *fpl*; (*letters of reference*) referencias *fpl.*

credibility [krɛdɪ'bɪlɪtɪ] *n* credibilidad *f.*

credible ['krɛdɪbl] *adj* creíble; (*witness, source*) fidedigno.

credit ['krɛdɪt] *n* (*gen*) crédito; (*merit*) honor *m*, mérito ♦ *vt* (*COMM*) abonar; (*believe*) creer, dar crédito a ♦ *adj* crediticio; **to be in** ~ (*person, bank account*) tener saldo a favor; **on** ~ a crédito; (*col*) al fiado; **he's a** ~ **to his family** hace honor a su familia; **to** ~ **sb with** (*fig*) reconocer a algn el mérito de; *see also* **credits.**

creditable ['krɛdɪtəbl] *adj* estimable, digno de elogio.

credit account *n* cuenta de crédito.

credit agency *n* agencia de informes comerciales.

credit balance *n* saldo acreedor.

credit card *n* tarjeta de crédito.

credit control *n* control *m* de créditos.

credit facilities *npl* facilidades *fpl* de crédito.

credit limit *n* límite *m* de crédito.

credit note *n* nota de crédito.

creditor ['krɛdɪtə*] *n* acreedor(a) *m/f.*

credits ['krɛdɪts] *npl* (*CINE*) títulos *mpl or* rótulos *mpl* de crédito, créditos *mpl.*

credit transfer *n* transferencia de crédito.

creditworthy ['krɛdɪtwəːðɪ] *adj* solvente.

credulity [krɪ'djuːlɪtɪ] *n* credulidad *f.*

creed [kriːd] *n* credo.

creek [kriːk] *n* cala, ensenada; (*US*) riachuelo.

creel [kriːl] *n* nasa.

creep, *pt*, *pp* **crept** [kriːp, krɛpt] *vi* (*animal*) deslizarse; (*plant*) trepar; **to** ~ **up on sb** acercarse sigilosamente a algn; (*fig: old age etc*) acercarse ♦ *n* (*col*): **he's a** ~ ¡qué lameculos es!; **it gives me the** ~**s** me da escalofríos.

creeper ['kriːpə*] *n* enredadera.

creepers ['kriːpəz] *npl* (*US: for baby*) pelele *msg.*

creepy ['kriːpɪ] *adj* (*frightening*) horripilante.

creepy-crawly ['kriːpɪ'krɔːlɪ] *n* (*col*) bicho.

cremate [krɪ'meɪt] *vt* incinerar.

cremation [krɪ'meɪʃən] *n* incineración *f,* cremación *f.*

crematorium, *pl* **crematoria** [krɛmə'tɔːrɪəm, -'tɔːrɪə] *n* crematorio.

creosote ['krɪəsəut] *n* creosota.

crêpe [kreɪp] *n* (*fabric*) crespón *m*; (*also:* ~ **rubber**) crep(é) *m.*

crêpe bandage *n* (*BRIT*) venda elástica.

crêpe paper *n* papel *m* crep(é).

crêpe sole *n* (*on shoes*) suela de crep(é).

crept [krɛpt] *pt, pp of* **creep.**

crescent ['krɛsnt] *n* media luna; (*street*) calle *f* (*en forma de semicírculo*).

cress [krɛs] *n* berro.

crest [krɛst] *n* (*of bird*) cresta; (*of hill*) cima, cumbre *f*; (*of helmet*) cimera; (*of coat of arms*) blasón *m.*

crestfallen ['krɛstfɔːlən] *adj* alicaído.

Crete [kriːt] *n* Creta.

cretin ['krɛtɪn] *n* cretino/a.

crevasse [krɪ'væs] *n* grieta.

crevice ['krɛvɪs] *n* grieta, hendedura.

crew [kruː] *n* (*of ship etc*) tripulación *f*; (*CINE etc*) equipo; (*gang*) pandilla, banda; (*MIL*) dotación *f.*

crew-cut ['kruːkʌt] *n* corte *m* al rape.

crew-neck ['kruːnɛk] n cuello de caja.
crib [krɪb] n pesebre m ♦ vt (col) plagiar; (SCOL) copiar.
crick [krɪk] n: ~ **in the neck** tortícolis f inv.
cricket ['krɪkɪt] n (insect) grillo; (game) críquet m.
cricketer ['krɪkɪtə*] n jugador(a) m/f de críquet.
crime [kraɪm] n crimen m; (less serious) delito.
crime wave n ola de crímenes or delitos.
criminal ['krɪmɪnl] n criminal m/f, delincuente m/f ♦ adj criminal; (law) penal.
Criminal Investigation Department (CID) n ≈ Brigada de Investigación Criminal (B.I.C. f) (SP).
crimp [krɪmp] vt (hair) rizar.
crimson ['krɪmzn] adj carmesí.
cringe [krɪndʒ] vi encogerse.
crinkle ['krɪŋkl] vt arrugar.
crinkly ['krɪŋklɪ] adj (hair) rizado, crespo.
cripple ['krɪpl] n lisiado/a, cojo/a ♦ vt lisiar, mutilar; (ship, plane) inutilizar; (production, exports) paralizar; ~d with arthritis paralizado por la artritis.
crippling ['krɪplɪŋ] adj (injury etc) debilitador(a); (prices, taxes) devastador(a).
crisis, pl **crises** ['kraɪsɪs, -siːz] n crisis f.
crisp [krɪsp] adj fresco; (toast, snow) crujiente; (manner) seco.
crisps [krɪsps] npl (BRIT) patatas fpl fritas.
crisscross ['krɪskrɔs] adj entrelazado, entrecruzado ♦ vt entrecruzar(se).
criterion, pl **criteria** [kraɪ'tɪərɪən, -'tɪərɪə] n criterio.
critic ['krɪtɪk] n crítico/a.
critical ['krɪtɪkl] adj (gen) crítico; (illness) grave; **to be ~ of sb/sth** criticar a algn/algo.
critically ['krɪtɪklɪ] adv (speak etc) en tono crítico; (ill) gravemente.
criticism ['krɪtɪsɪzm] n crítica.
criticize ['krɪtɪsaɪz] vt criticar.
critique [krɪ'tiːk] n crítica.
croak [krəʊk] vi (frog) croar; (raven) graznar ♦ n (of raven) graznido.
Croat ['krəʊæt] adj, n = **Croatian.**
Croatia [krəʊ'eɪʃə] n Croacia.
Croatian [krəʊ'eɪʃən] adj, n croata m/f ♦ n (LING) croata m.
crochet ['krəʊʃeɪ] n ganchillo.
crock [krɔk] n cántaro; (col: person: also: old ~) carcamal m/f, vejestorio; (: car etc) cacharro.
crockery ['krɔkərɪ] n (plates, cups etc) loza, vajilla.
crocodile ['krɔkədaɪl] n cocodrilo.

crocus ['krəʊkəs] n azafrán m.
croft [krɔft] n granja pequeña.
crofter ['krɔftə*] n pequeño granjero.
croissant ['krwasã] n croissant m, medialuna (esp LAM).
crone [krəʊn] n arpía, bruja.
crony ['krəʊnɪ] n compinche m/f.
crook [kruk] n (fam) ladrón/ona m/f; (of shepherd) cayado; (of arm) pliegue m.
crooked ['krukɪd] adj torcido; (path) tortuoso; (fam) sucio.
crop [krɔp] n (produce) cultivo; (amount produced) cosecha; (riding ~) látigo de montar; (of bird) buche m ♦ vt cortar, recortar; (subj: animals: grass) pacer.
▶**crop up** vi surgir, presentarse.
crop spraying [-'spreɪɪŋ] n fumigación f de los cultivos.
croquet ['krəʊkeɪ] n croquet m.
croquette [krə'kɛt] n croqueta (de patata).
cross [krɔs] n cruz f ♦ vt (street etc) cruzar, atravesar; (thwart: person) contrariar, ir contra ♦ vi: **the boat ~es from Santander to Plymouth** el barco hace la travesía de Santander a Plymouth ♦ adj de mal humor, enojado; **it's a ~ between geography and sociology** es una mezcla de geografía y sociología; **to ~ o.s.** santiguarse; **they've got their lines ~ed** (fig) hay un malentendido entre ellos; **to be/get ~ with sb (about sth)** estar enfadado/enfadarse con algn (por algo).
▶**cross out** vt tachar.
▶**cross over** vi cruzar.
crossbar ['krɔsbɑː*] n travesaño; (of bicycle) barra.
crossbow ['krɔsbəʊ] n ballesta.
cross-Channel ferry ['krɔs'tʃænl-] n transbordador m que cruza el Canal de la Mancha.
cross-check ['krɔstʃɛk] n verificación f ♦ vt verificar.
cross-country (race) ['krɔs'kʌntrɪ-] n carrera a campo traviesa, cross m.
cross-dressing [krɔs'drɛsɪŋ] n travestismo.
cross-examination ['krɔsɪgzæmɪ'neɪʃən] n interrogatorio.
cross-examine ['krɔsɪg'zæmɪn] vt interrogar.
cross-eyed ['krɔsaɪd] adj bizco.
crossfire ['krɔsfaɪə*] n fuego cruzado.
crossing ['krɔsɪŋ] n (road) cruce m; (rail) paso a nivel; (sea passage) travesía; (also: pedestrian ~) paso de peatones.
crossing guard n (US) persona encargada de ayudar a los niños a cruzar la calle.
crossing point n paso; (at border) paso fronterizo.

cross purposes *npl*: **to be at ~ with sb** tener un malentendido con algn.
cross-question ['krɔs'kwɛstʃən] *vt* interrogar.
cross-reference ['krɔs'rɛfrəns] *n* remisión *f*.
crossroads ['krɔsrəudz] *nsg* cruce *m*; (*fig*) encrucijada.
cross section *n* corte *m* transversal; (*of population*) muestra (representativa).
crosswalk ['krɔswɔːk] *n* (*US*) paso de peatones.
crosswind ['krɔswɪnd] *n* viento de costado.
crossword ['krɔswəːd] *n* crucigrama *m*.
crotch [krɔtʃ] *n* (*of garment*) entrepierna.
crotchet ['krɔtʃɪt] *n* (*BRIT MUS*) negra.
crotchety ['krɔtʃɪtɪ] *adj* (*person*) arisco.
crouch [krautʃ] *vi* agacharse.
croup [kruːp] *n* (*MED*) crup *m*.
croupier ['kruːpɪə] *n* crupier *m/f*.
crouton ['kruːtɔn] *n* cubito de pan frito.
crow [krəu] *n* (*bird*) cuervo; (*of cock*) canto, cacareo ♦ *vi* (*cock*) cantar; (*fig*) jactarse.
crowbar ['krəubaː*] *n* palanca.
crowd [kraud] *n* muchedumbre *f*; (*SPORT*) público; (*common herd*) vulgo ♦ *vt* (*gather*) amontonar; (*fill*) llenar ♦ *vi* (*gather*) reunirse; (*pile up*) amontonarse; **~s of people** gran cantidad de gente.
crowded ['kraudɪd] *adj* (*full*) atestado; (*well-attended*) concurrido.
crowd scene *n* (*CINE, THEAT*) escena con muchos comparsas.
crown [kraun] *n* corona; (*of head*) coronilla; (*of hat*) copa; (*of hill*) cumbre *f* ♦ *vt* (*also tooth*) coronar; **and to ~ it all ...** (*fig*) y para colmo *or* remate ....
crown court *n* (*LAW*) tribunal *m* superior.

> En el sistema legal inglés los delitos graves como asesinato, violación o atraco son juzgados por un jurado en un tribunal superior llamado **crown court** con sede en noventa ciudades. Los jueces de paz (**Justice of the Peace**) juzgan delitos menores e infracciones de la ley en juzgados llamados **Magistrates' Courts**. Es el juez de paz quien decide remitir los casos pertinentes a la **crown court**, que en caso de recursos se remite al tribunal de apelación, **Court of Appeal**.

crowning ['kraunɪŋ] *a* (*achievement, glory*) máximo.
crown jewels *npl* joyas *fpl* reales.
crown prince *n* príncipe *m* heredero.
crow's feet ['krəuzfiːt] *npl* patas *fpl* de gallo.
crucial ['kruːʃl] *adj* crucial, decisivo; **his approval is ~ to the success of the project** su aprobación es crucial para el éxito del proyecto.
crucifix ['kruːsɪfɪks] *n* crucifijo.
crucifixion [kruːsɪ'fɪkʃən] *n* crucifixión *f*.
crucify ['kruːsɪfaɪ] *vt* crucificar; (*fig*) martirizar.
crude [kruːd] *adj* (*materials*) bruto; (*fig*: *basic*) tosco; (: *vulgar*) ordinario.
crude (oil) *n* (petróleo) crudo.
cruel ['kruəl] *adj* cruel.
cruelty ['kruəltɪ] *n* crueldad *f*.
cruet ['kruːɪt] *n* vinagreras *fpl*.
cruise [kruːz] *n* crucero ♦ *vi* (*ship*) navegar; (*holidaymakers*) hacer un crucero; (*car*) ir a velocidad constante.
cruise missile *n* misil *m* de crucero.
cruiser ['kruːzə*] *n* crucero.
cruising speed ['kruːzɪŋ-] *n* velocidad *f* de crucero.
crumb [krʌm] *n* miga, migaja.
crumble ['krʌmbl] *vt* desmenuzar ♦ *vi* (*gen*) desmenuzarse; (*building*) desmoronarse.
crumbly ['krʌmblɪ] *adj* desmenuzable.
crummy ['krʌmɪ] *adj* (*col: poor quality*) pésimo, cutre (*SP*); (: *unwell*) fatal.
crumpet ['krʌmpɪt] *n* ≈ bollo para tostar.
crumple ['krʌmpl] *vt* (*paper*) estrujar; (*material*) arrugar.
crunch [krʌntʃ] *vt* (*with teeth*) ronzar; (*underfoot*) hacer crujir ♦ *n* (*fig*) hora de la verdad.
crunchy ['krʌntʃɪ] *adj* crujiente.
crusade [kruː'seɪd] *n* cruzada ♦ *vi*: **to ~ for/against** (*fig*) hacer una campaña en pro de/en contra de.
crusader [kruː'seɪdə*] *n* (*fig*) paladín *m/f*.
crush [krʌʃ] *n* (*crowd*) aglomeración *f* ♦ *vt* (*gen*) aplastar; (*paper*) estrujar; (*cloth*) arrugar; (*grind, break up: garlic, ice*) picar; (*fruit*) exprimir; (*grapes*) exprimir, prensar; **to have a ~ on sb** estar enamorado de algn.
crush barrier *n* barrera de seguridad.
crushing ['krʌʃɪŋ] *adj* aplastante; (*burden*) agobiante.
crust [krʌst] *n* corteza.
crustacean [krʌs'teɪʃən] *n* crustáceo.
crusty ['krʌstɪ] *adj* (*bread*) crujiente; (*person*) de mal carácter; (*remark*) brusco.
crutch [krʌtʃ] *n* (*MED*) muleta; (*support*) apoyo.
crux [krʌks] *n*: **the ~** lo esencial, el quid.
cry [kraɪ] *vi* llorar; (*shout: also: ~ out*) gritar ♦ *n* grito; (*of animal*) aullido; (*weep*): **she had a good ~** lloró a lágrima viva; **what are you ~ing about?** ¿por qué lloras?; **to ~ for help** pedir socorro a voces; **it's a far**

~ **from** ... (*fig*) dista mucho de ....
▶**cry off** *vi* retirarse.
crypt [krɪpt] *n* cripta.
cryptic ['krɪptɪk] *adj* enigmático.
crystal ['krɪstl] *n* cristal *m*.
crystal-clear ['krɪstl'klɪə*] *adj* claro como el agua; (*fig*) cristalino.
crystallize ['krɪstəlaɪz] *vt* (*fig*) cristalizar ♦ *vi* cristalizarse; ~**d fruits** frutas *fpl* escarchadas.
CSA *n abbr* = *Confederate States of America*; (= *Child Support Agency*) organismo que supervisa el pago de la pensión a hijos de padres separados.
CSC *n abbr* (= *Civil Service Commission*) comisión para la contratación de funcionarios.
CSE *n abbr* (*BRIT*: = *Certificate of Secondary Education*) ≈ título de BUP.
CS gas *n* (*BRIT*) gas *m* lacrimógeno.
CST *n abbr* (*US*: = *Central Standard Time*) huso horario.
CT, Ct. *abbr* (*US*) = *Connecticut*.
ct *abbr* = **carat.**
CTC *n abbr* (*BRIT*: *city technology college*) ≈ centro de formación profesional.
cu. *abbr* = **cubic.**
cub [kʌb] *n* cachorro; (*also*: ~ **scout**) niño explorador.
Cuba ['kjuːbə] *n* Cuba.
Cuban ['kjuːbən] *adj*, *n* cubano/a *m/f*.
cubbyhole ['kʌbɪhəul] *n* cuchitril *m*.
cube [kjuːb] *n* cubo; (*of sugar*) terrón *m* ♦ *vt* (*MATH*) elevar al cubo.
cube root *n* raíz *f* cúbica.
cubic ['kjuːbɪk] *adj* cúbico; ~ **capacity** (*AUT*) capacidad *f* cúbica.
cubicle ['kjuːbɪkl] *n* (*at pool*) caseta; (*for bed*) cubículo.
cubism ['kjuːbɪzəm] *n* cubismo.
cuckoo ['kuːkuː] *n* cuco.
cuckoo clock *n* reloj *m* de cuco.
cucumber ['kjuːkʌmbə*] *n* pepino.
cuddle ['kʌdl] *vt* abrazar ♦ *vi* abrazarse.
cuddly ['kʌdlɪ] *adj* mimoso; (*toy*) de peluche.
cudgel ['kʌdʒəl] *vt*: **to** ~ **one's brains** devanarse los sesos.
cue [kjuː] *n* (*snooker* ~) taco; (*THEAT etc*) entrada.
cuff [kʌf] *n* (*BRIT*: *of shirt, coat etc*) puño; (*US*: *of trousers*) vuelta; (*blow*) bofetada ♦ *vt* bofetear; **off the** ~ *adv* improvisado.
cufflinks ['kʌflɪŋks] *npl* gemelos *mpl*.
cu. in. *abbr* = **cubic inches.**
cuisine [kwɪ'ziːn] *n* cocina.
cul-de-sac ['kʌldəsæk] *n* callejón *m* sin salida.

culinary ['kʌlɪnərɪ] *adj* culinario.
cull [kʌl] *vt* (*select*) entresacar; (*kill selectively*: *animals*) matar selectivamente ♦ *n* matanza selectiva; **seal** ~ matanza selectiva de focas.
culminate ['kʌlmɪneɪt] *vi*: **to** ~ **in** culminar en.
culmination [kʌlmɪ'neɪʃən] *n* culminación *f*, colmo.
culottes [kuː'lɒts] *npl* falda *f* pantalón.
culpable ['kʌlpəbl] *adj* culpable.
culprit ['kʌlprɪt] *n* culpable *m/f*.
cult [kʌlt] *n* culto; **a** ~ **figure** un ídolo.
cultivate ['kʌltɪveɪt] *vt* (*also fig*) cultivar.
cultivated ['kʌltɪveɪtɪd] *adj* culto.
cultivation [kʌltɪ'veɪʃən] *n* cultivo; (*fig*) cultura.
cultural ['kʌltʃərəl] *adj* cultural.
culture ['kʌltʃə*] *n* (*also fig*) cultura.
cultured ['kʌltʃəd] *adj* culto.
cumbersome ['kʌmbəsəm] *adj* voluminoso.
cumin ['kʌmɪn] *n* (*spice*) comino.
cummerbund ['kʌməbʌnd] *n* faja, fajín *m*.
cumulative ['kjuːmjulətɪv] *adj* cumulativo.
cunning ['kʌnɪŋ] *n* astucia ♦ *adj* astuto; (*clever*: *device, idea*) ingenioso.
cunt [kʌnt] *n* (*col!*) *n* coño (!); (*insult*) mamonazo/a (!).
cup [kʌp] *n* taza; (*prize, event*) copa; **a** ~ **of tea** una taza de té.
cupboard ['kʌbəd] *n* armario, placar(d) *m* (*LAM*).
cup final *n* (*FOOTBALL*) final *f* de copa.
cupful ['kʌpful] *n* taza.
Cupid ['kjuːpɪd] *n* Cupido.
cupola ['kjuːpələ] *n* cúpula.
cuppa ['kʌpə] *n* (*BRIT col*) (taza de) té *m*.
cup-tie ['kʌptaɪ] *n* (*BRIT*) partido de copa.
cur [kəː*] *n* perro de mala raza; (*person*) canalla *m*.
curable ['kjuərəbl] *adj* curable.
curate ['kjuərɪt] *n* coadjutor *m*.
curator [kjuə'reɪtə*] *n* director(a) *m/f*.
curb [kəːb] *vt* refrenar; (*powers, spending*) limitar ♦ *n* freno; (*US*: *kerb*) bordillo.
curd cheese [kəːd-] *n* requesón *m*.
curdle ['kəːdl] *vi* cuajarse.
curds [kəːdz] *npl* requesón *msg*.
cure [kjuə*] *vt* curar ♦ *n* cura, curación *f*; **to be** ~**d of sth** curarse de algo; **to take a** ~ tomar un remedio.
cure-all ['kjuərɔːl] *n* (*also fig*) panacea.
curfew ['kəːfjuː] *n* toque *m* de queda.
curio ['kjuərɪəu] *n* curiosidad *f*.
curiosity [kjuərɪ'ɒsɪtɪ] *n* curiosidad *f*.
curious ['kjuərɪəs] *adj* curioso; **I'm** ~ **about him** me intriga.
curiously ['kjuərɪəslɪ] *adv* curiosamente; ~

enough, ... aunque parezca extraño ....

curl [kə:l] *n* rizo; (*of smoke etc*) espiral *f*, voluta ♦ *vt* (*hair*) rizar; (*paper*) arrollar; (*lip*) fruncir ♦ *vi* rizarse; arrollarse.
►**curl up** *vi* arrollarse; (*person*) hacerse un ovillo; (*fam*) morirse de risa.

curler ['kə:lə*] *n* bigudí *m*.

curlew ['kə:lu:] *n* zarapito.

curling tongs, (*US*) **curling irons** ['kə:lɪŋ-] *npl* tenacillas *fpl*.

curly ['kə:lɪ] *adj* rizado.

currant ['kʌrnt] *n* pasa; (*black, red*) grosella.

currency ['kʌrnsɪ] *n* moneda; **to gain** ~ (*fig*) difundirse.

current ['kʌrnt] *n* corriente *f* ♦ *adj* actual; **direct/alternating** ~ corriente directa/alterna; **the** ~ **issue of a magazine** el último número de una revista; **in** ~ **use** de uso corriente.

current account *n* (*BRIT*) cuenta corriente.

current affairs *npl* (noticias *fpl* de) actualidad *f*.

current assets *npl* (*COMM*) activo disponible.

current liabilities *npl* (*COMM*) pasivo circulante.

currently ['kʌrntlɪ] *adv* actualmente.

curriculum, *pl* ~**s** *or* **curricula** [kə'rɪkjuləm, -lə] *n* plan *m* de estudios.

curriculum vitae (CV) [-'vi:taɪ] *n* currículum *m* (vitae).

curry ['kʌrɪ] *n* curry *m* ♦ *vt:* **to** ~ **favour with** buscar el favor de.

curry powder *n* curry *m* en polvo.

curse [kə:s] *vi* echar pestes ♦ *vt* maldecir ♦ *n* maldición *f*; (*swearword*) palabrota.

cursor ['kə:sə*] *n* (*COMPUT*) cursor *m*.

cursory ['kə:sərɪ] *adj* rápido, superficial.

curt [kə:t] *adj* seco.

curtail [kə:'teɪl] *vt* (*cut short*) acortar; (*restrict*) restringir.

curtain ['kə:tn] *n* cortina; (*THEAT*) telón *m*; **to draw the** ~**s** (*together*) cerrar las cortinas; (*apart*) abrir las cortinas.

curtain call *n* (*THEAT*) llamada a escena.

curtain ring *n* anilla.

curts(e)y ['kə:tsɪ] *n* reverencia ♦ *vi* hacer una reverencia.

curvature ['kə:vətʃə*] *n* curvatura.

curve [kə:v] *n* curva ♦ *vt, vi* torcer.

curved [kə:vd] *adj* curvo.

cushion ['kuʃən] *n* cojín *m*; (*SNOOKER*) banda ♦ *vt* (*seat*) acolchar; (*shock*) amortiguar.

cushy ['kuʃɪ] *adj* (*col*): **a** ~ **job** un chollo; **to have a** ~ **time** tener la vida arreglada.

custard ['kʌstəd] *n* (*for pouring*) natillas *fpl*.

custard powder *n* polvos *mpl* para natillas.

custodial sentence [kʌs'təudɪəl-] *n* pena de prisión.

custodian [kʌs'təudɪən] *n* guardián/ana *m/f*; (*of museum etc*) conservador(a) *m/f*.

custody ['kʌstədɪ] *n* custodia; **to take sb into** ~ detener a algn; **in the** ~ **of** al cuidado *or* cargo de.

custom ['kʌstəm] *n* costumbre *f*; (*COMM*) clientela; *see also* **customs**.

customary ['kʌstəmərɪ] *adj* acostumbrado; **it is** ~ **to do** ... es la costumbre hacer ....

custom-built ['kʌstəm'bɪlt] *adj* = **custom-made**.

customer ['kʌstəmə*] *n* cliente *m/f*; **he's an awkward** ~ (*col*) es un tipo difícil.

customer profile *n* perfil *m* del cliente.

customized ['kʌstəmaɪzd] *adj* (*car etc*) hecho a encargo.

custom-made ['kʌstəm'meɪd] *adj* hecho a la medida.

customs ['kʌstəmz] *npl* aduana *sg*; **to go through (the)** ~ pasar la aduana.

Customs and Excise *n* (*BRIT*) Aduanas *fpl* y Arbitrios.

customs officer *n* aduanero/a, funcionario/a de aduanas.

cut [kʌt] *vb* (*pt, pp* **cut**) *vt* cortar; (*price*) rebajar; (*record*) grabar; (*reduce*) reducir; (*col: avoid: class, lecture*) fumarse, faltar a ♦ *vi* cortar; (*intersect*) cruzarse ♦ *n* corte *m*; (*in skin*) corte, cortadura; (*with sword*) tajo; (*of knife*) cuchillada; (*in salary etc*) recorte *m*; (*slice of meat*) tajada; **to** ~ **one's finger** cortarse un dedo; **to get one's hair** ~ cortarse el pelo; **to** ~ **sb dead** negarle el saludo *or* cortarle (*LAM*) a algn; **it** ~**s both ways** (*fig*) tiene doble filo; **to** ~ **a tooth** echar un diente; **power** ~ (*BRIT*) apagón *m*.
►**cut back** *vt* (*plants*) podar; (*production, expenditure*) reducir.
►**cut down** *vt* (*tree*) cortar, derribar; (*consumption, expenses*) reducir; **to** ~ **sb down to size** (*fig*) bajarle los humos a algn.
►**cut in** *vi:* **to** ~ **in (on)** (*interrupt: conversation*) interrumpir, intervenir (en); (*AUT*) cerrar el paso (a).
►**cut off** *vt* cortar; (*fig*) aislar; (*troops*) cercar; **we've been** ~ **off** (*TEL*) nos han cortado la comunicación.
►**cut out** *vt* (*shape*) recortar; (*delete*) suprimir.
►**cut up** *vt* cortar (en pedazos); (*chop: food*) trinchar, cortar.

cut-and-dried ['kʌtən'draɪd] *adj* (*also:* **cut-and-dry**) arreglado de antemano, seguro.

cutback ['kʌtbæk] *n* reducción *f.*
cute [kjuːt] *adj* lindo, mono; *(shrewd)* listo.
cuticle ['kjuːtɪkl] *n* cutícula.
cutlery ['kʌtlərɪ] *n* cubiertos *mpl.*
cutlet ['kʌtlɪt] *n* chuleta.
cutoff ['kʌtɔf] *n* (*also:* ~ **point**) límite *m.*
cutout ['kʌtaut] *n* (*cardboard* ~) recortable *m.*
cut-price ['kʌt'praɪs], (*US*) **cut-rate** ['kʌt'reɪt] *adj* a precio reducido.
cutthroat ['kʌtθrəut] *n* asesino/a ♦ *adj* feroz; ~ **competition** competencia encarnizada *or* despiadada.
cutting ['kʌtɪŋ] *adj* (*gen*) cortante; (*remark*) mordaz ♦ *n* (*BRIT: from newspaper*) recorte *m;* (: *RAIL*) desmonte *m;* (*CINE*) montaje *m.*
cutting edge *n* (*of knife*) filo; (*fig*) vanguardia; **a country on** *or* **at the** ~ **of space technology** un país puntero en tecnología del espacio.
CV *n abbr see* **curriculum vitae.**
C & W *n abbr* = **country and western** (**music**).
cwo *abbr* (*COMM*) = **cash with order.**
cwt. *abbr* = **hundredweight(s).**
cyanide ['saɪənaɪd] *n* cianuro.
cybernetics [saɪbə'nɛtɪks] *nsg* cibernética.
cyclamen ['sɪkləmən] *n* ciclamen *m.*
cycle ['saɪkl] *n* ciclo; (*bicycle*) bicicleta ♦ *vi* ir en bicicleta.
cycle race *n* carrera ciclista.
cycle rack *n* soporte *m* para bicicletas.
cycling ['saɪklɪŋ] *n* ciclismo.
cycling holiday *n* vacaciones *fpl* en bicicleta.
cyclist ['saɪklɪst] *n* ciclista *m/f.*
cyclone ['saɪkləun] *n* ciclón *m.*
cygnet ['sɪgnɪt] *n* pollo de cisne.
cylinder ['sɪlɪndə*] *n* cilindro.
cylinder block *n* bloque *m* de cilindros.
cylinder capacity *n* cilindrada.
cylinder head *n* culata de cilindro.
cylinder-head gasket *n* junta de culata.
cymbals ['sɪmblz] *npl* platillos *mpl,* címbalos *mpl.*
cynic ['sɪnɪk] *n* cínico/a.
cynical ['sɪnɪkl] *adj* cínico.
cynicism ['sɪnɪsɪzəm] *n* cinismo.
CYO *n abbr* (*US*) = **Catholic Youth Organization.**
cypress ['saɪprɪs] *n* ciprés *m.*
Cypriot ['sɪprɪət] *adj, n* chipriota *m/f.*
Cyprus ['saɪprəs] *n* Chipre *f.*
cyst [sɪst] *n* quiste *m.*
cystitis [sɪs'taɪtɪs] *n* cistitis *f.*
CZ *n abbr* (*US:* = *Central Zone*) zona del Canal de Panamá.
czar [zɑː*] *n* zar *m.*

czarina [zɑː'riːnə] *n* zarina.
Czech [tʃɛk] *adj* checo ♦ *n* checo/a; (*LING*) checo; **the** ~ **Republic** la República Checa.
Czechoslovak [tʃɛkə'sləuvæk] *adj, n* = **Czechoslovakian.**
Czechoslovakia [tʃɛkəslə'vækɪə] *n* Checoslovaquia.
Czechoslovakian [tʃɛkəslə'vækɪən] *adj, n* checoslovaco/a *m/f.*

Dd

D, d [diː] *n* (*letter*) D, d; (*MUS*): **D** re *m;* **D for David,** (*US*) **D for Dog** D de Dolores.
D *abbr* (*US POL*) = **democrat(ic).**
d *abbr* (*BRIT: old*) = **penny.**
d. *abbr* = **died.**
DA *n abbr* (*US*) = **district attorney.**
dab [dæb] *v:* **to** ~ **ointment onto a wound** aplicar pomada sobre una herida; **to** ~ **with paint** dar unos toques de pintura ♦ *n* (*light stroke*) toque *m;* (*small amount*) pizca.
dabble ['dæbl] *vi:* **to** ~ **in** hacer por afición.
Dacca ['dækə] *n* Dacca.
dachshund ['dækshund] *n* perro tejonero.
Dacron ® ['deɪkrɔn] *n* (*US*) terylene *m.*
dad [dæd], **daddy** ['dædɪ] *n* papá *m.*
daddy-long-legs [dædɪ'lɔŋlɛgz] *n* típula.
daffodil ['dæfədɪl] *n* narciso.
daft [dɑːft] *adj* chiflado.
dagger ['dægə*] *n* puñal *m,* daga; **to look** ~**s at sb** fulminar a algn con la mirada.
dahlia ['deɪljə] *n* dalia.
daily ['deɪlɪ] *adj* diario, cotidiano ♦ *n* (*paper*) diario; (*domestic help*) asistenta ♦ *adv* todos los días, cada día; **twice** ~ dos veces al día.
dainty ['deɪntɪ] *adj* delicado; (*tasteful*) elegante.
dairy ['dɛərɪ] *n* (*shop*) lechería; (*on farm*) vaquería ♦ *adj* (*cow etc*) lechero.
dairy cow *n* vaca lechera.
dairy farm *n* vaquería.
dairy produce *n* productos *mpl* lácteos.
dais ['deɪɪs] *n* estrado.
daisy ['deɪzɪ] *n* margarita.
daisy wheel *n* (*on printer*) (rueda) margarita.
daisy-wheel printer *n* impresora de

margarita.

Dakar ['dækə*] n Dakar m.

dale [deɪl] n valle m.

dally ['dælɪ] vi entretenerse.

dalmatian [dæl'meɪʃən] n (dog) (perro) dálmata m.

dam [dæm] n presa; (reservoir) embalse ♦ vt embalsar.

damage ['dæmɪdʒ] n daño; (fig) perjuicio; (to machine) avería ♦ vt dañar; perjudicar; averiar; ~ **to property** daños materiales.

damages ['dæmɪdʒɪz] npl (LAW) daños y perjuicios; **to pay £5000 in** ~ pagar £5000 por daños y perjuicios.

damaging ['dæmɪdʒɪŋ] adj: ~ **(to)** perjudicial (a).

Damascus [də'mɑːskəs] n Damasco.

dame [deɪm] n (title) dama; (US col) tía; (THEAT) vieja; see also **pantomime**.

damn [dæm] vt condenar; (curse) maldecir ♦ n (col): **I don't give a** ~ me importa un pito ♦ adj (col: also: ~**ed**) maldito, fregado (LAM); ~ **(it)!** ¡maldito sea!

damnable ['dæmnəbl] adj (col: behaviour) detestable; (: weather) horrible.

damnation [dæm'neɪʃən] n (REL) condenación f ♦ excl (col) ¡maldición!, ¡maldito sea!

damning ['dæmɪŋ] adj (evidence) irrecusable.

damp [dæmp] adj húmedo, mojado ♦ n humedad f ♦ vt (also: ~**en**) (cloth, rag) mojar; (enthusiasm) enfriar.

dampcourse ['dæmpkɔːs] n aislante m hidrófugo.

damper ['dæmpə*] n (MUS) sordina; (of fire) regulador m de tiro; **to put a** ~ **on things** ser un jarro de agua fría.

dampness ['dæmpnɪs] n humedad f.

damson ['dæmzən] n ciruela damascena.

dance [dɑːns] n baile m ♦ vi bailar; **to** ~ **about** saltar.

dance hall n salón m de baile.

dancer ['dɑːnsə*] n bailador(a) m/f; (professional) bailarín/ina m/f.

dancing ['dɑːnsɪŋ] n baile m.

D and C n abbr (MED: = dilation and curettage) raspado.

dandelion ['dændɪlaɪən] n diente m de león.

dandruff ['dændrəf] n caspa.

dandy ['dændɪ] n dandi m ♦ adj (US col) estupendo.

Dane [deɪn] n danés/esa m/f.

danger ['deɪndʒə*] n peligro; (risk) riesgo; ~**!** (on sign) ¡peligro!; **to be in** ~ **of** correr riesgo de; **out of** ~ fuera de peligro.

danger list n (MED): **to be on the** ~ estar grave.

dangerous ['deɪndʒərəs] adj peligroso.

dangerously ['deɪndʒərəslɪ] adv peligrosamente; ~ **ill** gravemente enfermo.

danger zone n área or zona de peligro.

dangle ['dæŋgl] vt colgar ♦ vi pender, estar colgado.

Danish ['deɪnɪʃ] adj danés/esa ♦ n (LING) danés m.

Danish pastry n pastel m de almendra.

dank [dæŋk] adj húmedo y malsano.

Danube ['dænjuːb] n Danubio.

dapper ['dæpə*] adj pulcro, apuesto.

Dardanelles [dɑːdə'nɛlz] npl Dardanelos mpl.

dare [dɛə*] vt: **to** ~ **sb to do** desafiar a algn a hacer ♦ vi: **to** ~ **(to) do sth** atreverse a hacer algo; **I** ~ **say** (I suppose) puede ser, a lo mejor; **I** ~ **say he'll turn up** puede ser que or quizás venga; **I** ~**n't tell him** no me atrevo a decírselo.

daredevil ['dɛədɛvl] n temerario/a, atrevido/a.

Dar-es-Salaam ['dɑːrɛssə'lɑːm] n Dar es Salaam m.

daring ['dɛərɪŋ] adj (person) osado; (plan, escape) atrevido ♦ n atrevimiento, osadía.

dark [dɑːk] adj oscuro; (hair, complexion) moreno; (fig: cheerless) triste, sombrío ♦ n (gen) oscuridad f; (night) tinieblas fpl; ~ **chocolate** chocolate m amargo; **it is/is getting** ~ es de noche/está oscureciendo; **in the** ~ **about** (fig) ignorante de; **after** ~ después del anochecer.

darken ['dɑːkn] vt oscurecer; (colour) hacer más oscuro ♦ vi oscurecerse; (cloud over) nublarse.

dark glasses npl gafas fpl oscuras.

dark horse n (fig) incógnita.

darkly ['dɑːklɪ] adv (gloomily) tristemente; (sinisterly) siniestramente.

darkness ['dɑːknɪs] n (in room) oscuridad f; (night) tinieblas fpl.

darkroom ['dɑːkrum] n cuarto oscuro.

darling ['dɑːlɪŋ] adj, n querido/a m/f.

darn [dɑːn] vt zurcir.

dart [dɑːt] n dardo; (in sewing) pinza ♦ vi precipitarse; **to** ~ **away/along** vi salir/ marchar disparado.

dartboard ['dɑːtbɔːd] n diana.

darts [dɑːts] n dardos mpl.

dash [dæʃ] n (small quantity: of liquid) gota, chorrito; (: of solid) pizca; (sign) guión m; (: long) raya ♦ vt (break) romper, estrellar; (hopes) defraudar ♦ vi precipitarse, ir de prisa; **a** ~ **of soda** un poco or chorrito de sifón or soda.

► **dash away, dash off** vi marcharse

apresuradamente.
dashboard ['dæʃbɔːd] n (AUT) salpicadero.
dashing ['dæʃɪŋ] adj gallardo.
dastardly ['dæstədlɪ] adj ruin, vil.
DAT n abbr (= digital audio tape) cas(s)et(t)e m or f digital.
data ['deɪtə] npl datos mpl.
database ['deɪtəbeɪs] n base f de datos.
data capture n recogida de datos.
data link n enlace m de datos.
data processing n proceso or procesamiento de datos.
data transmission n transmisión f de datos.
date [deɪt] n (day) fecha; (with friend) cita; (fruit) dátil m ♦ vt fechar; (col: girl etc) salir con; **what's the ~ today?** ¿qué fecha es hoy?; **~ of birth** fecha de nacimiento; **closing ~** fecha tope; **to ~** adv hasta la fecha; **out of ~** pasado de moda; **up to ~** moderno; puesto al día; **to bring up to ~** (correspondence, information) poner al día; (method) actualizar; **to bring sb up to ~** poner a algn al corriente; **letter ~d 5th July** or (US) **July 5th** carta fechada el 5 de julio.
dated ['deɪtɪd] adj anticuado.
date rape n violación ocurrida durante una cita con un conocido.
date stamp n matasellos m inv; (on fresh foods) sello de fecha.
dative ['deɪtɪv] n dativo.
daub [dɔːb] vt embadurnar.
daughter ['dɔːtə] n hija.
daughter-in-law ['dɔːtərɪnlɔː] n nuera, hija política.
daunting ['dɔːntɪŋ] adj desalentador(a).
davenport ['dævnpɔːt] n escritorio; (US: sofa) sofá m.
dawdle ['dɔːdl] vi (waste time) perder el tiempo; (go slowly) andar muy despacio; **to ~ over one's work** trabajar muy despacio.
dawn [dɔːn] n alba, amanecer m ♦ vi amanecer; (fig): **it ~ed on him that ...** cayó en la cuenta de que ...; **at ~** al amanecer; **from ~ to dusk** de sol a sol.
dawn chorus n canto de los pájaros al amanecer.
day [deɪ] n día m; (working ~) jornada; **the ~ before** el día anterior; **the ~ after tomorrow** pasado mañana; **the ~ before yesterday** anteayer, antes de ayer; **the ~ after, the following ~** el día siguiente; **by ~ de día; ~ by ~** día a día; **(on) the ~ that ...** el día que ...; **to work an 8-hour ~** trabajar 8 horas diarias or al día; **he works 8 hours a ~** trabaja 8 horas al día;

paid by the ~ pagado por día; **these ~s, in the present ~** hoy en día.
daybook ['deɪbuk] n (BRIT) diario or libro de entradas y salidas.
daybreak ['deɪbreɪk] n amanecer m.
day-care centre ['deɪkeə-] n centro de día; (for children) guardería infantil.
daydream ['deɪdriːm] n ensueño ♦ vi soñar despierto.
daylight ['deɪlaɪt] n luz f (del día).
daylight robbery n: **it's ~!** (fig, col) ¡es un robo descarado!
Daylight Saving Time n (US) hora de verano.
day-release course [deɪrɪˈliːs-] n curso de formación de un día a la semana.
day return (ticket) n (BRIT) billete m de ida y vuelta (en un día).
day shift n turno de día.
daytime ['deɪtaɪm] n día m.
day-to-day ['deɪtəˈdeɪ] adj cotidiano, diario; (expenses) diario; **on a ~ basis** día por día.
day trip n excursión f (de un día).
day tripper n excursionista m/f.
daze [deɪz] vt (stun) aturdir ♦ n: **in a ~** aturdido.
dazed [deɪzd] adj aturdido.
dazzle ['dæzl] vt deslumbrar.
dazzling ['dæzlɪŋ] adj (light, smile) deslumbrante; (colour) fuerte.
DBS n abbr (= direct broadcasting by satellite) transmisión vía satélite.
DC abbr (ELEC) = **direct current**; (US) = District of Columbia.
DCC ® n abbr (= digital compact cassette) cas(s)et(t)e m digital compacto.
DD n abbr (= Doctor of Divinity) título universitario.
dd. abbr (COMM) = delivered.
D/D abbr = direct debit.
D-day ['diːdeɪ] n (fig) día m clave.
DDS n abbr (US: = Doctor of Dental Science; Doctor of Dental Surgery) títulos universitarios.
DDT n abbr (= dichlorodiphenyltri-chloroethane) DDT m.
DE abbr (US) = Delaware.
DEA n abbr (US: = Drug Enforcement Administration) brigada especial dedicada a la lucha contra el tráfico de estupefacientes.
deacon ['diːkən] n diácono.
dead [dɛd] adj muerto; (limb) dormido; (battery) agotado ♦ adv totalmente; (exactly) justo; **he was ~ on arrival** ingresó cadáver; **to shoot sb ~** matar a algn a tiros; **~ tired** muerto (de

cansancio); **to stop** ~ parar en seco; **the line has gone** ~ (TEL) se ha cortado la línea; **the** ~ npl los muertos.
dead beat adj: **to be** ~ (col) estar hecho polvo.
deaden ['dɛdn] vt (blow, sound) amortiguar; (pain) calmar, aliviar.
dead end n callejón m sin salida.
dead-end ['dɛdɛnd] adj: **a** ~ **job** un trabajo sin porvenir.
dead heat n (SPORT) empate m.
deadline ['dɛdlaɪn] n fecha tope; **to work to a** ~ trabajar con una fecha tope.
deadlock ['dɛdlɔk] n punto muerto.
dead loss n (col): **to be a** ~ (person) ser un inútil; (thing) ser una birria.
deadly ['dɛdlɪ] adj mortal, fatal; ~ **dull** aburridísimo.
deadly nightshade [-'naɪtʃeɪd] n belladona.
deadpan ['dɛdpæn] adj sin expresión.
Dead Sea n: **the** ~ el Mar Muerto.
dead season n (TOURISM) temporada baja.
deaf [dɛf] adj sordo; **to turn a** ~ **ear to sth** hacer oídos sordos a algo.
deaf-aid ['dɛfeɪd] n audífono.
deaf-and-dumb ['dɛfən'dʌm] adj (person) sordomudo; (alphabet) para sordomudos.
deafen ['dɛfn] vt ensordecer.
deafening ['dɛfnɪŋ] adj ensordecedor(a).
deaf-mute ['dɛfmjuːt] n sordomudo/a.
deafness ['dɛfnɪs] n sordera.
deal [diːl] n (agreement) pacto, convenio; (business) negocio, transacción f; (CARDS) reparto ♦ vt (pt, pp dealt) (gen) dar; **a great** ~ **(of)** bastante, mucho; **it's a** ~! (col) ¡trato hecho!, ¡de acuerdo!; **to do a** ~ **with sb** hacer un trato con algn; **he got a bad/fair** ~ **from them** le trataron mal/bien.
▶**deal in** vt fus tratar en, comerciar en.
▶**deal with** vt fus (people) tratar con; (problem) ocuparse de; (subject) tratar de.
dealer ['diːlə*] n comerciante m/f; (CARDS) mano f.
dealership ['diːləʃɪp] n concesionario.
dealings ['diːlɪŋz] npl (COMM) transacciones fpl; (relations) relaciones fpl.
dealt [dɛlt] pt, pp of **deal**.
dean [diːn] n (REL) deán m; (SCOL) decano/a.
dear [dɪə*] adj querido; (expensive) caro ♦ n: **my** ~ querido/a; ~ **me!** ¡Dios mío!; **D**~ **Sir/Madam** (in letter) Muy señor mío, Estimado señor/Estimada señora, De mi/nuestra (mayor) consideración (esp LAM); **D**~ **Mr/Mrs X** Estimado/a señor(a) X.
dearly ['dɪəlɪ] adv (love) mucho; (pay) caro.

dearth [dəːθ] n (of food, resources, money) escasez f.
death [dɛθ] n muerte f.
deathbed ['dɛθbɛd] n lecho de muerte.
death certificate n partida de defunción.
death duties npl (BRIT) derechos mpl de sucesión.
deathly ['dɛθlɪ] adj mortal; (silence) profundo.
death penalty n pena de muerte.
death rate n tasa de mortalidad.
death row n: **to be on** ~ (US) estar condenado a muerte.
death sentence n condena a muerte.
death squad n escuadrón m de la muerte.
deathtrap ['dɛθtræp] n lugar m (or vehículo etc) muy peligroso.
deb [dɛb] n abbr (col) = **debutante**.
debacle [deɪ'bɑːkl] n desastre m, catástrofe f.
debar [dɪ'bɑː*] vt: **to** ~ **sb from doing** prohibir a algn hacer.
debase [dɪ'beɪs] vt degradar.
debatable [dɪ'beɪtəbl] adj discutible; **it is** ~ **whether ...** es discutible si ....
debate [dɪ'beɪt] n debate m ♦ vt discutir.
debauched [dɪ'bɔːtʃt] adj vicioso.
debauchery [dɪ'bɔːtʃərɪ] n libertinaje m.
debenture [dɪ'bɛntʃə*] n (COMM) bono, obligación f.
debenture capital n capital m hipotecario.
debilitate [dɪ'bɪlɪteɪt] vt debilitar.
debilitating [dɪ'bɪlɪteɪtɪŋ] adj (illness etc) debilitante.
debit ['dɛbɪt] n debe m ♦ vt: **to** ~ **a sum to sb** or **to sb's account** cargar una suma en cuenta a algn.
debit balance n saldo deudor or pasivo.
debit note n nota de débito or cargo.
debonair [dɛbə'nɛə*] adj jovial, cortés/esa.
debrief [diː'briːf] vt hacer dar parte.
debriefing [diː'briːfɪŋ] n relación f (de un informe).
debris ['dɛbriː] n escombros mpl.
debt [dɛt] n deuda; **to be in** ~ tener deudas; ~**s of £5000** deudas de cinco mil libras; **bad** ~ deuda incobrable.
debt collector n cobrador(a) m/f de deudas.
debtor ['dɛtə*] n deudor(a) m/f.
debug ['diː'bʌg] vt (COMPUT) depurar.
debunk [diː'bʌŋk] vt (col: theory) desprestigiar, desacreditar; (: claim) desacreditar; (: person, institution) desenmascarar.
début ['deɪbjuː] n presentación f.
debutante ['dɛbjutænt] n debutante f.
Dec. abbr (= December) dic.

decade ['dɛkeɪd] n década, decenio.
decadence ['dɛkədəns] n decadencia.
decadent ['dɛkədənt] adj decadente.
de-caff ['diːkæf] n (col) descafeinado.
decaffeinated [dɪ'kæfɪneɪtɪd] adj
descafeinado.
decamp [dɪ'kæmp] vi (col) escaparse,
largarse, rajarse (LAM).
decant [dɪ'kænt] vt decantar.
decanter [dɪ'kæntə*] n jarra, decantador m.
decathlon [dɪ'kæθlən] n decatlón m.
decay [dɪ'keɪ] n (fig) decadencia; (of
building) desmoronamiento; (of tooth)
caries f inv ♦ vi (rot) pudrirse; (fig) decaer.
decease [dɪ'siːs] n fallecimiento ♦ vi
fallecer.
deceased [dɪ'siːst] adj difunto.
deceit [dɪ'siːt] n engaño.
deceitful [dɪ'siːtful] adj engañoso.
deceive [dɪ'siːv] vt engañar.
decelerate [diː'sɛləreɪt] vt moderar la
marcha de ♦ vi decelerar.
December [dɪ'sɛmbə*] n diciembre m.
decency ['diːsənsɪ] n decencia.
decent ['diːsənt] adj (proper) decente;
(person) amable, bueno.
decently ['diːsəntlɪ] adv (respectably)
decentemente; (kindly) amablemente.
decentralization [diːsɛntrəlaɪ'zeɪʃən] n
descentralización f.
decentralize [diː'sɛntrəlaɪz] vt
descentralizar.
deception [dɪ'sɛpʃən] n engaño.
deceptive [dɪ'sɛptɪv] adj engañoso.
decibel ['dɛsɪbɛl] n decibel(io) m.
decide [dɪ'saɪd] vt (person) decidir;
(question, argument) resolver ♦ vi: to ~ to
do/that decidir hacer/que; to ~ on sth
tomar una decisión sobre algo; to ~
against doing sth decidir en contra de
hacer algo.
decided [dɪ'saɪdɪd] adj (resolute) decidido;
(clear, definite) indudable.
decidedly [dɪ'saɪdɪdlɪ] adv decididamente.
deciding [dɪ'saɪdɪŋ] adj decisivo.
deciduous [dɪ'sɪdjuəs] adj de hoja caduca.
decimal ['dɛsɪməl] adj decimal ♦ n decimal
f; to 3 ~ places con 3 cifras decimales.
decimalize ['dɛsɪməlaɪz] vt convertir al
sistema decimal.
decimal point n coma decimal.
decimal system n sistema m métrico
decimal.
decimate ['dɛsɪmeɪt] vt diezmar.
decipher [dɪ'saɪfə*] vt descifrar.
decision [dɪ'sɪʒən] n decisión f; to make a ~
tomar una decisión.
decisive [dɪ'saɪsɪv] adj (influence) decisivo;

(manner, person) decidido; (reply) tajante.
deck [dɛk] n (NAUT) cubierta; (of bus) piso;
(of cards) baraja; **cassette** ~ platina; **to go
up on** ~ subir a (la) cubierta; **below** ~ en
la bodega.
deckchair ['dɛktʃɛə*] n tumbona.
deckhand ['dɛkhænd] n marinero de
cubierta.
declaration [dɛklə'reɪʃən] n declaración f.
declare [dɪ'klɛə*] vt (gen) declarar.
declassify [diː'klæsɪfaɪ] vt permitir que
salga a la luz.
decline [dɪ'klaɪn] n decaimiento,
decadencia; (lessening) disminución f ♦ vt
rehusar ♦ vi decaer; disminuir; ~ **in living
standards** disminución f del nivel de vida;
to ~ **to do sth** rehusar hacer algo.
declutch ['diː'klʌtʃ] vi desembragar.
decode [diː'kəud] vt descifrar.
decoder [diː'kəudə*] n (COMPUT, TV)
de(s)codificador m.
decompose [diːkəm'pəuz] vi
descomponerse.
decomposition [diːkɔmpə'zɪʃən] n
descomposición f.
decompression [diːkəm'prɛʃən] n
descompresión f.
decompression chamber n cámara de
descompresión.
decongestant [diːkən'dʒɛstənt] n
descongestionante.
decontaminate [diːkən'tæmɪneɪt] vt
descontaminar.
decontrol [diːkən'trəul] vt (trade) quitar
controles a; (prices) descongelar.
décor ['deɪkɔ:*] n decoración f; (THEAT)
decorado.
decorate ['dɛkəreɪt] vt (paint) pintar;
(paper) empapelar; (adorn): to ~ (with)
adornar (de), decorar (de).
decoration [dɛkə'reɪʃən] n adorno; (act)
decoración f; (medal) condecoración f.
decorative ['dɛkərətɪv] adj decorativo.
decorator ['dɛkəreɪtə*] n (workman) pintor
m decorador.
decorum [dɪ'kɔ:rəm] n decoro.
decoy ['diːkɔɪ] n señuelo; **police** ~ trampa
or señuelo policial.
decrease ['diːkriːs] n disminución f ♦ (vb:
[dɪ'kriːs]) vt disminuir, reducir ♦ vi
reducirse; **to be on the** ~ ir
disminuyendo.
decreasing [dɪ'kriːsɪŋ] adj decreciente.
decree [dɪ'kriː] n decreto ♦ vt: to ~ (that)
decretar (que); ~ **absolute/nisi** sentencia
absoluta/provisional de divorcio.
decrepit [dɪ'krɛpɪt] adj (person) decrépito;
(building) ruinoso.

decry [dɪ'kraɪ] vt criticar, censurar.
dedicate ['dedɪkeɪt] vt dedicar.
dedicated ['dedɪkeɪtɪd] adj dedicado; (COMPUT) especializado; ~ **word processor** procesador m de textos especializado or dedicado.
dedication [dedɪ'keɪʃən] n (devotion) dedicación f; (in book) dedicatoria.
deduce [dɪ'djuːs] vt deducir.
deduct [dɪ'dʌkt] vt restar; (from wage etc) descontar, deducir.
deduction [dɪ'dʌkʃən] n (amount deducted) descuento; (conclusion) deducción f, conclusión f.
deed [diːd] n hecho, acto; (feat) hazaña; (LAW) escritura; ~ **of covenant** escritura de contrato.
deem [diːm] vt (formal) juzgar, considerar; **to ~ it wise to do** considerar prudente hacer.
deep [diːp] adj profundo; (voice) bajo; (breath) profundo, a pleno pulmón ♦ adv: **the spectators stood 20 ~** los espectadores se formaron de 20 en fondo; **to be 4 metres ~** tener 4 metros de profundidad.
deepen ['diːpn] vt ahondar, profundizar ♦ vi (darkness) intensificarse.
deep-freeze ['diːp'friːz] n arcón m congelador.
deep-fry ['diːp'fraɪ] vt freír en aceite abundante.
deeply ['diːplɪ] adv (breathe) profundamente, a pleno pulmón; (interested, moved, grateful) profundamente, hondamente; **to regret sth ~** sentir algo profundamente.
deep-rooted ['diːp'ruːtɪd] adj (prejudice, habit) profundamente arraigado; (affection) profundo.
deep-sea ['diːp'siː] adj: ~ **diver** buzo; ~ **diving** buceo de altura.
deep-seated ['diːp'siːtɪd] adj (beliefs) (profundamente) arraigado.
deep-set ['diːpset] adj (eyes) hundido.
deer [dɪə*] n, pl inv ciervo.
deerstalker ['dɪəstɔːkə*] n (hat) gorro de cazador.
deface [dɪ'feɪs] vt desfigurar, mutilar.
defamation [defə'meɪʃən] n difamación f.
defamatory [dɪ'fæmətrɪ] adj difamatorio.
default [dɪ'fɔːlt] vi faltar al pago; (SPORT) no presentarse, no comparecer ♦ n (COMPUT) defecto; **by ~** (LAW) en rebeldía; (SPORT) por incomparecencia; **to ~ on a debt** dejar de pagar una deuda.
defaulter [dɪ'fɔːltə*] n (in debt) moroso/a.
default option n (COMPUT) opción f por

defecto.
defeat [dɪ'fiːt] n derrota ♦ vt derrotar, vencer; (fig: efforts) frustrar.
defeatism [dɪ'fiːtɪzəm] n derrotismo.
defeatist [dɪ'fiːtɪst] adj, n derrotista m/f.
defecate ['defəkeɪt] vi defecar.
defect ['diːfɛkt] n defecto ♦ vi [dɪ'fɛkt]: **to ~ to the enemy** pasarse al enemigo; **physical ~** defecto físico; **mental ~** deficiencia mental.
defective [dɪ'fɛktɪv] adj (gen) defectuoso; (person) anormal.
defector [dɪ'fɛktə*] n tránsfuga m/f.
defence, (US) **defense** [dɪ'fɛns] n defensa; **the Ministry of D~** el Ministerio de Defensa; **witness for the ~** testigo de descargo.
defenceless [dɪ'fɛnslɪs] adj indefenso.
defence spending n gasto militar.
defend [dɪ'fɛnd] vt defender; (decision, action) defender; (opinion) mantener.
defendant [dɪ'fɛndənt] n acusado/a; (in civil case) demandado/a.
defender [dɪ'fɛndə*] n defensor(a) m/f.
defending champion [dɪ'fɛndɪŋ-] n (SPORT) defensor(a) m/f del título.
defending counsel n (LAW) abogado defensor.
defense [dɪ'fɛns] n (US) = **defence.**
defensive [dɪ'fɛnsɪv] adj defensivo ♦ n defensiva; **on the ~** a la defensiva.
defer [dɪ'fɜː*] vt (postpone) aplazar; **to ~ to** diferir a; (submit): **to ~ to sb/sb's opinion** someterse a algn/a la opinión de algn.
deference ['defərəns] n deferencia, respeto; **out of** or **in ~ to** por respeto a.
deferential [defə'renʃəl] adj respetuoso.
deferred [dɪ'fɜːd] adj: ~ **creditor** acreedor m diferido.
defiance [dɪ'faɪəns] n desafío; **in ~ of** en contra de.
defiant [dɪ'faɪənt] adj (insolent) insolente; (challenging) retador(a).
defiantly [dɪ'faɪəntlɪ] adv con aire de desafío.
deficiency [dɪ'fɪʃənsɪ] n (lack) falta; (COMM) déficit m; (defect) defecto.
deficient [dɪ'fɪʃənt] adj (lacking) insuficiente; (incomplete) incompleto; (defective) defectuoso; (mentally) anormal; ~ **in** deficiente en.
deficit ['defɪsɪt] n déficit m.
defile [dɪ'faɪl] vt manchar; (violate) violar.
define [dɪ'faɪn] vt (also COMPUT) definir.
definite ['defɪnɪt] adj (fixed) determinado; (clear, obvious) claro; **he was ~ about it** no dejó lugar a dudas (sobre ello).
definitely ['defɪnɪtlɪ] adv: **he's ~ mad** no

cabe duda de que está loco.
definition [dɛfɪ'nɪʃən] *n* definición *f.*
definitive [dɪ'fɪnɪtɪv] *adj* definitivo.
deflate [diː'fleɪt] *vt* (*gen*) desinflar;
(*pompous person*) quitar *or* rebajar los
humos a; (*ECON*) deflacionar.
deflation [diː'fleɪʃən] *n* (*ECON*) deflación *f.*
deflationary [diː'fleɪʃənrɪ] *adj* (*ECON*)
deflacionario.
deflect [dɪ'flɛkt] *vt* desviar.
defog [diː'fɔg] *vt* desempañar.
defogger [diː'fɔgə*] *n* (*US AUT*) dispositivo
antivaho.
deform [dɪ'fɔːm] *vt* deformar.
deformed [dɪ'fɔːmd] *adj* deformado.
deformity [dɪ'fɔːmɪtɪ] *n* deformación *f.*
defraud [dɪ'frɔːd] *vt* estafar; **to ~ sb of sth**
estafar algo a algn.
defray [dɪ'freɪ] *vt*: **to ~ sb's expenses**
reembolsar a algn los gastos.
defrost [diː'frɔst] *vt* (*frozen food*, *fridge*)
descongelar.
defroster [diː'frɔstə*] *n* (*US*) eliminador *m*
de vaho.
deft [dɛft] *adj* diestro, hábil.
defunct [dɪ'fʌŋkt] *adj* difunto; (*organization*
etc) ya desaparecido.
defuse [diː'fjuːz] *vt* desarmar; (*situation*)
calmar, apaciguar.
defy [dɪ'faɪ] *vt* (*resist*) oponerse a;
(*challenge*) desafiar; (*order*) contravenir.
degenerate [dɪ'dʒɛnəreɪt] *vi* degenerar
♦ *adj* [dɪ'dʒɛnərɪt] degenerado.
degradation [dɛgrə'deɪʃən] *n* degradación
f.
degrade [dɪ'greɪd] *vt* degradar.
degrading [dɪ'greɪdɪŋ] *adj* degradante.
degree [dɪ'griː] *n* grado; (*SCOL*) título; **10
~s below freezing** 10 grados bajo cero; **to
have a ~ in maths** ser licenciado/a en
matemáticas; **by ~s** (*gradually*) poco a
poco, por etapas; **to some ~, to a certain
~** hasta cierto punto; **a considerable ~ of
risk** un gran índice de riesgo.
dehydrated [diː'haɪ'dreɪtɪd] *adj*
deshidratado; (*milk*) en polvo.
dehydration [diːhaɪ'dreɪʃən] *n*
deshidratación *f.*
de-ice [diː'aɪs] *vt* (*windscreen*) deshelar.
de-icer [diː'aɪsə*] *n* descongelador *m.*
deign [deɪn] *vi*: **to ~ to do** dignarse hacer.
deity [ˈdiːɪtɪ] *n* deidad *f*, divinidad *f.*
déjà vu [deɪʒɑː'vuː] *n*: **I had a sense of ~**
sentía como si ya lo hubiera vivido.
dejected [dɪ'dʒɛktɪd] *adj* abatido,
desanimado.
dejection [dɪ'dʒɛkʃən] *n* abatimiento.
Del. *abbr* (*US*) = *Delaware.*

del. *abbr* = *delete.*
delay [dɪ'leɪ] *vt* demorar, aplazar; (*person*)
entretener; (*train*) retrasar; (*payment*)
aplazar ♦ *vi* tardar ♦ *n* demora, retraso;
without ~ en seguida, sin tardar.
delayed-action [dɪleɪd'ækʃən] *adj* (*bomb
etc*) de acción retardada.
delectable [dɪ'lɛktəbl] *adj* (*person*)
encantador(a); (*food*) delicioso.
delegate [ˈdɛlɪgɪt] *n* delegado/a ♦ *vt*
[ˈdɛlɪgeɪt] delegar; **to ~ sth to sb/sb to do
sth** delegar algo en algn/en algn para
hacer algo.
delegation [dɛlɪ'geɪʃən] *n* (*of work etc*)
delegación *f.*
delete [dɪ'liːt] *vt* suprimir, tachar;
(*COMPUT*) suprimir, borrar.
Delhi [ˈdɛlɪ] *n* Delhi *m.*
deli [ˈdɛlɪ] *n* = **delicatessen.**
deliberate [dɪ'lɪbərɪt] *adj* (*intentional*)
intencionado; (*slow*) pausado, lento ♦ *vi*
[dɪ'lɪbəreɪt] deliberar.
deliberately [dɪ'lɪbərɪtlɪ] *adv* (*on purpose*) a
propósito; (*slowly*) pausadamente.
deliberation [dɪlɪbə'reɪʃən] *n* (*consideration*)
reflexión *f*; (*discussion*) deliberación *f*,
discusión *f.*
delicacy [ˈdɛlɪkəsɪ] *n* delicadeza; (*choice
food*) manjar *m.*
delicate [ˈdɛlɪkɪt] *adj* (*gen*) delicado;
(*fragile*) frágil.
delicately [ˈdɛlɪkɪtlɪ] *adv* con delicadeza,
delicadamente; (*act, express*) con
discreción.
delicatessen [dɛlɪkə'tɛsn] *n tienda
especializada en comida exótica.*
delicious [dɪ'lɪʃəs] *adj* delicioso, rico.
delight [dɪ'laɪt] *n* (*feeling*) placer *m*, deleite
m; (*object*) encanto, delicia ♦ *vt* encantar,
deleitar; **to take ~ in** deleitarse en.
delighted [dɪ'laɪtɪd] *adj*: **~ (at or with/to
do)** encantado (con/de hacer); **to be ~
that** estar encantado de que; **I'd be ~** con
mucho *or* todo gusto.
delightful [dɪ'laɪtful] *adj* encantador(a),
delicioso.
delimit [diː'lɪmɪt] *vt* delimitar.
delineate [dɪ'lɪnɪeɪt] *vt* delinear.
delinquency [dɪ'lɪŋkwənsɪ] *n* delincuencia.
delinquent [dɪ'lɪŋkwənt] *adj, n* delincuente
m/f.
delirious [dɪ'lɪrɪəs] *adj* (*MED, fig*) delirante;
to be ~ delirar, desvariar.
delirium [dɪ'lɪrɪəm] *n* delirio.
deliver [dɪ'lɪvə*] *vt* (*distribute*) repartir;
(*hand over*) entregar; (*message*)
comunicar; (*speech*) pronunciar; (*blow*)
lanzar, dar; (*MED*) asistir al parto de.

deliverance [dɪ'lɪvrəns] n liberación f.
delivery [dɪ'lɪvərɪ] n reparto; entrega; (of speaker) modo de expresarse; (MED) parto, alumbramiento; **to take ~ of** recibir.
delivery note n nota de entrega.
delivery van n furgoneta de reparto.
delta ['dɛltə] n delta m.
delude [dɪ'luːd] vt engañar.
deluge ['dɛljuːdʒ] n diluvio ♦ vt (fig): **to ~ (with)** inundar (de).
delusion [dɪ'luːʒən] n ilusión f, engaño.
de luxe [də'lʌks] adj de lujo.
delve [dɛlv] vi: **to ~ into** hurgar en.
Dem. abbr (US POL) = **democrat(ic).**
demand [dɪ'mɑːnd] vt (gen) exigir; (rights) reclamar; (need) requerir ♦ n (gen) exigencia; (claim) reclamación f; (ECON) demanda; **to ~ sth (from or of sb)** exigir algo (a algn); **to be in ~** ser muy solicitado; **on ~** a solicitud.
demanding [dɪ'mɑːndɪŋ] adj (boss) exigente; (work) absorbente.
demarcation [diːmɑː'keɪʃən] n demarcación f.
demarcation dispute n conflicto de definición or demarcación del trabajo.
demean [dɪ'miːn] vt: **to ~ o.s.** rebajarse.
demeanour, (US) **demeanor** [dɪ'miːnə*] n porte m, conducta, comportamiento.
demented [dɪ'mɛntɪd] adj demente.
demi- ['dɛmɪ] pref semi..., medio....
demilitarize [diː'mɪlɪtəraɪz] vt desmilitarizar; **~d zone** zona desmilitarizada.
demise [dɪ'maɪz] n (death) fallecimiento.
demist [diː'mɪst] vt (AUT) eliminar el vaho de.
demister [diː'mɪstə*] n (AUT) eliminador m de vaho.
demo ['dɛməʊ] n abbr (col: = demonstration) manifestación f.
demobilization [diː'məʊbɪlaɪ'zeɪʃən] n desmovilización f.
democracy [dɪ'mɔkrəsɪ] n democracia.
democrat ['dɛməkræt] n demócrata m/f.
democratic [dɛmə'krætɪk] adj democrático; **the D~ Party** el partido demócrata (estadounidense).
demography [dɪ'mɔɡrəfɪ] n demografía.
demolish [dɪ'mɔlɪʃ] vt derribar, demoler.
demolition [dɛmə'lɪʃən] n derribo, demolición f.
demon ['diːmən] n (evil spirit) demonio ♦ cpd temible.
demonstrate ['dɛmənstreɪt] vt demostrar ♦ vi manifestarse; **to ~ (for/against)** manifestarse (a favor de/en contra de).

demonstration [dɛmən'streɪʃən] n (POL) manifestación f; (proof) prueba, demostración f; **to hold a ~** (POL) hacer una manifestación.
demonstrative [dɪ'mɔnstrətɪv] adj (person) expresivo; (LING) demostrativo.
demonstrator ['dɛmənstreɪtə*] n (POL) manifestante m/f.
demoralize [dɪ'mɔrəlaɪz] vt desmoralizar.
demote [dɪ'məʊt] vt degradar.
demotion [dɪ'məʊʃən] n degradación f; (COMM) descenso.
demur [dɪ'məː*] vi: **to ~ (at)** hacer objeciones (a), vacilar (ante) ♦ n: **without ~** sin objeción.
demure [dɪ'mjʊə*] adj recatado.
demurrage [dɪ'mʌrɪdʒ] n sobrestadía.
den [dɛn] n (of animal) guarida; (study) estudio.
denationalization [diːnæʃnəlaɪ'zeɪʃən] n desnacionalización f.
denationalize [diː'næʃnəlaɪz] vt desnacionalizar.
denatured alcohol [diː'neɪtʃəd-] n (US) alcohol m desnaturalizado.
denial [dɪ'naɪəl] n (refusal) negativa; (of report etc) denegación f.
denier ['dɛnɪə*] n denier m.
denim ['dɛnɪm] n tela vaquera; see also **denims.**
denim jacket n chaqueta vaquera, saco vaquero (LAM).
denims ['dɛnɪms] npl vaqueros mpl.
denizen ['dɛnɪzn] n (inhabitant) habitante m/f; (foreigner) residente m/f extranjero/a.
Denmark ['dɛnmɑːk] n Dinamarca.
denomination [dɪnɔmɪ'neɪʃən] n valor m; (REL) confesión f.
denominator [dɪ'nɔmɪneɪtə*] n denominador m.
denote [dɪ'nəʊt] vt indicar, significar.
denounce [dɪ'naʊns] vt denunciar.
dense [dɛns] adj (thick) espeso; (: foliage etc) tupido; (stupid) torpe.
densely [dɛnslɪ] adv: **~ populated** con una alta densidad de población.
density ['dɛnsɪtɪ] n densidad f; **single/double-~ disk** n disco de densidad sencilla/de doble densidad.
dent [dɛnt] n abolladura ♦ vt (also: **make a ~ in**) abollar.
dental ['dɛntl] adj dental.
dental floss [-flɔs] n seda dental.
dental surgeon n odontólogo/a.
dentifrice ['dɛntɪfrɪs] n dentífrico.
dentist ['dɛntɪst] n dentista m/f; **~'s surgery** (BRIT) consultorio dental.
dentistry ['dɛntɪstrɪ] n odontología.

dentures ['dɛntʃəz] *npl* dentadura *sg* (postiza).

denude [dɪ'njuːd] *vt:* **to ~ of** despojar de.

denunciation [dɪnʌnsɪ'eɪʃən] *n* denuncia, denunciación *f.*

deny [dɪ'naɪ] *vt* negar; (*charge*) rechazar; (*report*) desmentir; **to ~ o.s.** privarse (de); **he denies having said it** niega haberlo dicho.

deodorant [diː'əudərənt] *n* desodorante *m.*

depart [dɪ'paːt] *vi* irse, marcharse; (*train*) salir; **to ~ from** (*fig: differ from*) apartarse de.

departed [dɪ'paːtɪd] *adj* (*bygone: days, glory*) pasado; (*dead*) difunto ♦ *n:* **the (dear) ~** el/la/los/las difunto/a/os/as.

department [dɪ'paːtmənt] *n* (*COMM*) sección *f*; (*SCOL*) departamento; (*POL*) ministerio; **that's not my ~** (*fig*) no tiene que ver conmigo; **D~ of State** (*US*) Ministerio de Asuntos Exteriores.

departmental [diːpaːt'mɛntl] *adj* (*dispute*) departamental; (*meeting*) departamental, de departamento; **~ manager** jefe/a *m/f* de sección *or* de departamento *or* de servicio.

department store *n* gran almacén *m.*

departure [dɪ'paːtʃə*] *n* partida, ida; (*of train*) salida; **a new ~** un nuevo rumbo.

departure lounge *n* (*at airport*) sala de embarque.

depend [dɪ'pɛnd] *vi:* **to ~ (up)on** (*be dependent upon*) depender de; (*rely on*) contar con; **it ~s** depende, según; **~ing on the result** según el resultado.

dependable [dɪ'pɛndəbl] *adj* (*person*) formal, serio.

dependant [dɪ'pɛndənt] *n* dependiente *m/f.*

dependence [dɪ'pɛndəns] *n* dependencia.

dependent [dɪ'pɛndənt] *adj:* **to be ~ (on)** depender (de) ♦ *n* = **dependant.**

depict [dɪ'pɪkt] *vt* (*in picture*) pintar; (*describe*) representar.

depilatory [dɪ'pɪlətrɪ] *n* (*also:* **~ cream**) depilatorio.

depleted [dɪ'pliːtɪd] *adj* reducido.

deplorable [dɪ'plɔːrəbl] *adj* deplorable.

deplore [dɪ'plɔː*] *vt* deplorar.

deploy [dɪ'plɔɪ] *vt* desplegar.

depopulate [diː'pɔpjuleɪt] *vt* despoblar.

depopulation ['diːpɔpjuˈleɪʃən] *n* despoblación *f.*

deport [dɪ'pɔːt] *vt* deportar.

deportation [diːpɔːˈteɪʃən] *n* deportación *f.*

deportation order *n* orden *f* de expulsión *or* deportación.

deportee [diːpɔːˈtiː] *n* deportado/a.

deportment [dɪ'pɔːtmənt] *n* comportamiento.

depose [dɪ'pəuz] *vt* deponer.

deposit [dɪ'pɔzɪt] *n* depósito; (*CHEM*) sedimento; (*of ore, oil*) yacimiento ♦ *vt* (*gen*) depositar; **to put down a ~ of £50** dejar un depósito de 50 libras.

deposit account *n* (*BRIT*) cuenta de ahorros.

depositor [dɪ'pɔzɪtə*] *n* depositante *m/f*, cuentacorrentista *m/f.*

depository [dɪ'pɔzɪtərɪ] *n* almacén *m* depositario.

depot ['dɛpəu] *n* (*storehouse*) depósito; (*for vehicles*) parque *m.*

deprave [dɪ'preɪv] *vt* depravar.

depraved [dɪ'preɪvd] *adj* depravado, vicioso.

depravity [dɪ'prævɪtɪ] *n* depravación *f*, vicio.

deprecate ['dɛprɪkeɪt] *vt* desaprobar, lamentar.

deprecating ['dɛprɪkeɪtɪŋ] *adj* (*disapproving*) de desaprobación; (*apologetic*): **a ~ smile** una sonrisa de disculpa.

depreciate [dɪ'priːʃɪeɪt] *vi* depreciarse, perder valor.

depreciation [dɪpriːʃɪ'eɪʃən] *n* depreciación *f.*

depress [dɪ'prɛs] *vt* deprimir; (*press down*) apretar.

depressant [dɪ'prɛsnt] *n* (*MED*) calmante *m*, sedante *m.*

depressed [dɪ'prɛst] *adj* deprimido; (*COMM: market, economy*) deprimido; (*area*) deprimido (económicamente); **to get ~** deprimirse.

depressing [dɪ'prɛsɪŋ] *adj* deprimente.

depression [dɪ'prɛʃən] *n* depresión *f*; **the economy is in a state of ~** la economía está deprimida.

deprivation [dɛprɪ'veɪʃən] *n* privación *f*; (*loss*) pérdida.

deprive [dɪ'praɪv] *vt:* **to ~ sb of** privar a algn de.

deprived [dɪ'praɪvd] *adj* necesitado.

dept. *abbr* (= *department*) dto.

depth [dɛpθ] *n* profundidad *f*; **at a ~ of 3 metres** a 3 metros de profundidad; **to be out of one's ~** (*swimmer*) perder pie; (*fig*) estar perdido; **to study sth in ~** estudiar algo a fondo; **in the ~s of** en lo más hondo de.

depth charge *n* carga de profundidad.

deputation [dɛpjuˈteɪʃən] *n* delegación *f.*

deputize ['dɛpjutaɪz] *vi:* **to ~ for sb** sustituir a algn.

deputy ['dɛpjutɪ] *adj:* **~ head**

subdirector(a) *m/f* ♦ *n* sustituto/a, suplente *m/f*; (*POL*) diputado/a; (*agent*) representante *m/f*.

deputy leader *n* (*POL*) vicepresidente/a *m/f*.

derail [dɪ'reɪl] *vt*: **to be ~ed** descarrilarse.

derailment [dɪ'reɪlmənt] *n* descarrilamiento.

deranged [dɪ'reɪndʒd] *adj* trastornado.

derby ['dəːbɪ] *n* (*US*) hongo.

Derbys *abbr* (*BRIT*) = **Derbyshire**.

deregulate [diː'rɛgjuleɪt] *vt* desreglamentar.

deregulation [diːrɛgjʊ'leɪʃən] *n* desreglamentación *f*.

derelict ['dɛrɪlɪkt] *adj* abandonado.

deride [dɪ'raɪd] *vt* ridiculizar, mofarse de.

derision [dɪ'rɪʒən] *n* irrisión *f*, mofas *fpl*.

derisive [dɪ'raɪsɪv] *adj* burlón/ona.

derisory [dɪ'raɪzərɪ] *adj* (*sum*) irrisorio; (*laughter, person*) burlón/ona, irónico.

derivation [dɛrɪ'veɪʃən] *n* derivación *f*.

derivative [dɪ'rɪvətɪv] *n* derivado ♦ *adj* (*work*) poco original.

derive [dɪ'raɪv] *vt* derivar ♦ *vi*: **to ~ from** derivarse de.

derived [dɪ'raɪvd] *adj* derivado.

dermatitis [dəːmə'taɪtɪs] *n* dermatitis *f*.

dermatology [dəːmə'tɔlədʒɪ] *n* dermatología.

derogatory [dɪ'rɔgətərɪ] *adj* despectivo.

derrick ['dɛrɪk] *n* torre *f* de perforación.

derv [dəːv] *n* (*BRIT*) gasoil *m*.

DES *n abbr* (*BRIT*: = *Department of Education and Science*) *ministerio de educación y ciencia*.

descend [dɪ'sɛnd] *vt*, *vi* descender, bajar; **to ~ from** descender de; **in ~ing order of importance** de mayor a menor importancia.

▶**descend on** *vt fus* (*subj: enemy, angry person*) caer sobre; (: *misfortune*) sobrevenir; (*fig: gloom, silence*) invadir; **visitors ~ed (up)on us** las visitas nos invadieron.

descendant [dɪ'sɛndənt] *n* descendiente *m/f*.

descent [dɪ'sɛnt] *n* descenso; (*GEO*) pendiente *f*, declive *m*; (*origin*) descendencia.

describe [dɪs'kraɪb] *vt* describir.

description [dɪs'krɪpʃən] *n* descripción *f*; (*sort*) clase *f*, género; **of every ~** de toda clase.

descriptive [dɪs'krɪptɪv] *adj* descriptivo.

desecrate ['dɛsɪkreɪt] *vt* profanar.

desegregation [diːsɛgrɪ'geɪʃən] *n* desegregación *f*.

desert ['dɛzət] *n* desierto ♦ *vb* [dɪ'zəːt] *vt* abandonar, desamparar ♦ *vi* (*MIL*) desertar; *see also* **deserts**.

deserter [dɪ'zəːtə*] *n* desertor(a) *m/f*.

desertion [dɪ'zəːʃən] *n* deserción *f*.

desert island *n* isla desierta.

deserts [dɪ'zəːts] *npl*: **to get one's just ~** llevarse su merecido.

deserve [dɪ'zəːv] *vt* merecer, ser digno de, ameritar (*LAM*).

deservedly [dɪ'zəːvɪdlɪ] *adv* con razón.

deserving [dɪ'zəːvɪŋ] *adj* (*person*) digno; (*action, cause*) meritorio.

desiccated ['dɛsɪkeɪtɪd] *adj* desecado.

design [dɪ'zaɪn] *n* (*sketch*) bosquejo; (*of dress, car*) diseño; (*pattern*) dibujo ♦ *vt* (*gen*) diseñar; **industrial ~** diseño industrial; **to have ~s on sb** tener la(s) mira(s) puesta(s) en algn; **to be ~ed for sb/sth** estar hecho para algn/algo.

designate ['dɛzɪgneɪt] *vt* (*appoint*) nombrar; (*destine*) designar ♦ *adj* ['dɛzɪgnɪt] designado.

designation [dɛzɪg'neɪʃən] *n* (*appointment*) nombramiento; (*name*) denominación *f*.

designer [dɪ'zaɪnə*] *n* diseñador(a) *m/f*; (*fashion ~*) modisto/a.

desirability [dɪzaɪərə'bɪlɪtɪ] *n* ventaja, atractivo.

desirable [dɪ'zaɪərəbl] *adj* (*proper*) deseable; (*attractive*) atractivo; **it is ~ that** es conveniente que.

desire [dɪ'zaɪə*] *n* deseo ♦ *vt* desear; **to ~ sth/to do sth/that** desear algo/hacer algo/que.

desirous [dɪ'zaɪərəs] *adj* deseoso.

desist [dɪ'zɪst] *vi*: **to ~ (from)** desistir (de).

desk [dɛsk] *n* (*in office*) escritorio; (*for pupil*) pupitre *m*; (*in hotel, at airport*) recepción *f*; (*BRIT: in shop, restaurant*) caja.

desktop computer ['dɛsktɔp-] *n* ordenador *m* de sobremesa.

desktop publishing ['dɛsktɔp-] *n* autoedición *f*.

desolate ['dɛsəlɪt] *adj* (*place*) desierto; (*person*) afligido.

desolation [dɛsə'leɪʃən] *n* (*of place*) desolación *f*; (*of person*) aflicción *f*.

despair [dɪs'pɛə*] *n* desesperación *f* ♦ *vi*: **to ~ of** desesperar de; **in ~** desesperado.

despatch [dɪs'pætʃ] *n*, *vt* = **dispatch**.

desperate ['dɛspərɪt] *adj* desesperado; (*fugitive*) peligroso; (*measures*) extremo; **we are getting ~** estamos al borde de desesperación.

desperately ['dɛspərɪtlɪ] *adv* desesperadamente; (*very*) terriblemente, gravemente; **~ ill** gravemente enfermo.

desperation [dɛspə'reɪʃən] *n* desesperación *f*; **in ~** desesperado.

despicable [dɪs'pɪkəbl] *adj* vil, despreciable.

despise [dɪs'paɪz] *vt* despreciar.

despite [dɪs'paɪt] *prep* a pesar de, pese a.

despondent [dɪs'pɒndənt] *adj* deprimido, abatido.

despot ['dɛspɒt] *n* déspota *m/f*.

dessert [dɪ'zɜːt] *n* postre *m*.

dessertspoon [dɪ'zɜːtspuːn] *n* cuchara (de postre).

destabilize [diː'steɪbɪlaɪz] *vt* desestabilizar.

destination [dɛstɪ'neɪʃən] *n* destino.

destine ['dɛstɪn] *vt* destinar.

destined ['dɛstɪnd] *adj*: **~ for London** con destino a Londres.

destiny ['dɛstɪnɪ] *n* destino.

destitute ['dɛstɪtjuːt] *adj* desamparado, indigente.

destitution [dɛstɪ'tjuːʃən] *n* indigencia, miseria.

destroy [dɪs'trɔɪ] *vt* destruir; (*finish*) acabar con.

destroyer [dɪs'trɔɪə*] *n* (*NAUT*) destructor *m*.

destruction [dɪs'trʌkʃən] *n* destrucción *f*; (*fig*) ruina.

destructive [dɪs'trʌktɪv] *adj* destructivo, destructor(a).

desultory ['dɛsəltərɪ] *adj* (*reading*) poco metódico; (*conversation*) inconexo; (*contact*) intermitente.

detach [dɪ'tætʃ] *vt* separar; (*unstick*) despegar.

detachable [dɪ'tætʃəbl] *adj* separable; (*TECH*) desmontable.

detached [dɪ'tætʃt] *adj* (*attitude*) objetivo, imparcial.

detached house *n* chalé *m*, chalet *m*.

detachment [dɪ'tætʃmənt] *n* separación *f*; (*MIL*) destacamento; (*fig*) objetividad *f*, imparcialidad *f*.

detail ['diːteɪl] *n* detalle *m*; (*MIL*) destacamento ♦ *vt* detallar; (*MIL*) destacar; **in ~** detalladamente; **to go into ~(s)** entrar en detalles.

detailed ['diːteɪld] *adj* detallado.

detain [dɪ'teɪn] *vt* retener; (*in captivity*) detener.

detainee [diːteɪ'niː] *n* detenido/a.

detect [dɪ'tɛkt] *vt* (*discover*) descubrir; (*MED, POLICE*) identificar; (*MIL, RADAR, TECH*) detectar; (*notice*) percibir.

detection [dɪ'tɛkʃən] *n* descubrimiento; identificación *f*; **crime ~** investigación *f*; **to escape ~** (*criminal*) escaparse sin ser descubierto; (*mistake*) pasar inadvertido.

detective [dɪ'tɛktɪv] *n* detective *m*.

detective story *n* novela policíaca.

detector [dɪ'tɛktə*] *n* detector *m*.

détente [deɪ'tɑːnt] *n* distensión *f*, detente *f*.

detention [dɪ'tɛnʃən] *n* detención *f*, arresto.

deter [dɪ'tɜː*] *vt* (*dissuade*) disuadir; (*prevent*) impedir; **to ~ sb from doing sth** disuadir a algn de que haga algo.

detergent [dɪ'tɜːdʒənt] *n* detergente *m*.

deteriorate [dɪ'tɪərɪəreɪt] *vi* deteriorarse.

deterioration [dɪtɪərɪə'reɪʃən] *n* deterioro.

determination [dɪtɜːmɪ'neɪʃən] *n* resolución *f*.

determine [dɪ'tɜːmɪn] *vt* determinar; **to ~ to do sth** decidir hacer algo.

determined [dɪ'tɜːmɪnd] *adj*: **to be ~ to do sth** estar decidido *or* resuelto a hacer algo; **a ~ effort** un esfuerzo enérgico.

deterrence [dɪ'tɜːns] *n* disuasión *f*.

deterrent [dɪ'tɛrənt] *n* fuerza de disuasión; **to act as a ~** servir para prevenir.

detest [dɪ'tɛst] *vt* aborrecer.

detestable [dɪ'tɛstəbl] *adj* aborrecible.

dethrone [diː'θrəun] *vt* destronar.

detonate ['dɛtəneɪt] *vi* estallar ♦ *vt* hacer detonar.

detonator ['dɛtəneɪtə*] *n* detonador *m*, fulminante *m*.

detour ['diːtuə*] *n* (*gen, US AUT: diversion*) desvío ♦ *vt* (*US: traffic*) desviar; **to make a ~** dar un rodeo.

detract [dɪ'trækt] *vt*: **to ~ from** quitar mérito a, restar valor a.

detractor [dɪ'træktə*] *n* detractor(a) *m/f*.

detriment ['dɛtrɪmənt] *n*: **to the ~ of** en perjuicio de; **without ~ to** sin detrimento de, sin perjuicio para.

detrimental [dɛtrɪ'mɛntl] *adj* perjudicial.

deuce [djuːs] *n* (*TENNIS*) cuarenta iguales.

devaluation [dɪvælju'eɪʃən] *n* devaluación *f*.

devalue [dɪ'vælju:] *vt* devaluar.

devastate ['dɛvəsteɪt] *vt* devastar; **he was ~d by the news** las noticias le dejaron desolado.

devastating ['dɛvəsteɪtɪŋ] *adj* devastador(a); (*fig*) arrollador(a).

devastation [dɛvəs'teɪʃən] *n* devastación *f*, ruina.

develop [dɪ'vɛləp] *vt* desarrollar; (*PHOT*) revelar; (*disease*) contraer; (*habit*) adquirir ♦ *vi* desarrollarse; (*advance*) progresar; **this land is to be ~ed** se va a construir en este terreno; **to ~ a taste for sth** tomar gusto a algo; **to ~ into** transformarse *or* convertirse en.

developer [dɪ'vɛləpə*] *n* (*property ~*)

promotor(a) m/f.

developing country n país m en (vías de) desarrollo.

development [dɪ'vɛləpmənt] n desarrollo; (advance) progreso; (of affair, case) desenvolvimiento; (of land) urbanización f.

development area n zona de fomento or desarrollo.

deviant ['diːvɪənt] adj anómalo, pervertido.

deviate ['diːvɪeɪt] vi: **to ~ (from)** desviarse (de).

deviation [diːvɪ'eɪʃən] n desviación f.

device [dɪ'vaɪs] n (scheme) estratagema, recurso; (apparatus) aparato, mecanismo; (explosive ~) artefacto explosivo.

devil ['dɛvl] n diablo, demonio.

devilish ['dɛvlɪʃ] adj diabólico.

devil-may-care ['dɛvlmeɪ'kɛə*] adj despreocupado.

devil's advocate n: **to play (the) ~** hacer de abogado del diablo.

devious ['diːvɪəs] adj intricado, enrevesado; (person) taimado.

devise [dɪ'vaɪz] vt idear, inventar.

devoid [dɪ'vɔɪd] adj: **~ of** desprovisto de.

devolution [diːvə'luːʃən] n (POL) descentralización f.

devolve [dɪ'vɔlv] vi: **to ~ (up)on** recaer sobre.

devote [dɪ'vəʊt] vt: **to ~ sth to** dedicar algo a.

devoted [dɪ'vəʊtɪd] adj (loyal) leal, fiel; **the book is ~ to politics** el libro trata de política.

devotee [dɛvəʊ'tiː] n devoto/a.

devotion [dɪ'vəʊʃən] n dedicación f; (REL) devoción f.

devour [dɪ'vaʊə*] vt devorar.

devout [dɪ'vaʊt] adj devoto.

dew [djuː] n rocío.

dexterity [dɛks'tɛrɪtɪ] n destreza.

dext(e)rous ['dɛkstrəs] adj (skilful) diestro, hábil; (movement) ágil.

dg abbr (= decigram) dg.

diabetes [daɪə'biːtiːz] n diabetes f.

diabetic [daɪə'bɛtɪk] n diabético/a ♦ adj diabético; (chocolate, jam) para diabéticos.

diabolical [daɪə'bɔlɪkəl] adj diabólico; (col: dreadful) horrendo, horroroso.

diagnose ['daɪəgnəʊz] vt diagnosticar.

diagnosis, pl **diagnoses** [daɪəg'nəʊsɪs, -siːz] n diagnóstico.

diagonal [daɪ'ægənl] adj diagonal ♦ n diagonal f.

diagram ['daɪəgræm] n diagrama m, esquema m.

dial ['daɪəl] n esfera; (of radio) dial m; (: tuner) sintonizador m; (of phone) disco ♦ vt (number) marcar, discar (LAM); **to ~ a wrong number** equivocarse de número; **can I ~ London direct?** ¿puedo marcar un número de Londres directamente?

dial. abbr = **dialect.**

dial code n (US) prefijo.

dialect ['daɪəlɛkt] n dialecto.

dialling code ['daɪəlɪŋ-] n (BRIT) prefijo.

dialling tone n (BRIT) señal f or tono de marcar.

dialogue, (US) **dialog** ['daɪəlɔg] n diálogo.

dial tone n (US) señal f or tono de marcar.

dialysis [daɪ'ælɪsɪs] n diálisis f.

diameter [daɪ'æmɪtə*] n diámetro.

diametrically [daɪə'mɛtrɪklɪ] adv: **~ opposed (to)** diametralmente opuesto (a).

diamond ['daɪəmənd] n diamante m; **~s** npl (CARDS) diamantes mpl.

diamond ring n anillo or sortija de diamantes.

diaper ['daɪəpə*] n (US) pañal m.

diaphragm ['daɪəfræm] n diafragma m.

diarrhoea, (US) **diarrhea** [daɪə'riːə] n diarrea.

diary ['daɪərɪ] n (daily account) diario; (book) agenda; **to keep a ~** escribir un diario.

diatribe ['daɪətraɪb] n: **~ (against)** diatriba (contra).

dice [daɪs] n, pl inv dados mpl ♦ vt (CULIN) cortar en cuadritos.

dicey ['daɪsɪ] adj (col): **it's a bit ~** (risky) es un poco arriesgado; (doubtful) es un poco dudoso.

dichotomy [daɪ'kɔtəmɪ] n dicotomía.

dickhead ['dɪkhɛd] n (BRIT col!) gilipollas m inv.

Dictaphone ® ['dɪktəfəʊn] n dictáfono ®.

dictate [dɪk'teɪt] vt dictar ♦ n ['dɪkteɪt] dictado.

▶**dictate to** vt fus (person) dar órdenes a; **I won't be ~d to** no recibo órdenes de nadie.

dictation [dɪk'teɪʃən] n (to secretary etc) dictado; **at ~ speed** para tomar al dictado.

dictator [dɪk'teɪtə*] n dictador m.

dictatorship [dɪk'teɪtəʃɪp] n dictadura.

diction ['dɪkʃən] n dicción f.

dictionary ['dɪkʃənrɪ] n diccionario.

did [dɪd] pt of **do.**

didactic [daɪ'dæktɪk] adj didáctico.

diddle ['dɪdl] vt estafar, timar.

didn't ['dɪdənt] = **did not.**

die [daɪ] vi morir; **to ~ (of or from)** morirse (de); **to be dying** morirse, estar muriéndose; **to be dying for sth/to do sth**

morirse por algo/de ganas de hacer algo.
▶**die away** *vi* (*sound, light*) desvanecerse.
▶**die down** *vi* (*gen*) apagarse; (*wind*)
amainar.
▶**die out** *vi* desaparecer, extinguirse.
diehard ['daɪhɑːd] *n* intransigente *m/f*.
diesel ['diːzl] *n* diesel *m*.
diesel engine *n* motor *m* diesel.
diesel fuel, diesel oil *n* gas-oil *m*.
diet ['daɪət] *n* dieta; (*restricted food*)
régimen *m* ♦ *vi* (*also:* **be on a ~**) estar a
dieta, hacer régimen; **to live on a ~ of**
alimentarse de.
dietician [daɪə'tɪʃən] *n* dietista *m/f*.
differ ['dɪfə*] *vi* (*be different*) ser distinto,
diferenciarse; (*disagree*) discrepar.
difference ['dɪfrəns] *n* diferencia; (*quarrel*)
desacuerdo; **it makes no ~ to me** me da
igual *or* lo mismo; **to settle one's ~s**
arreglarse.
different ['dɪfrənt] *adj* diferente, distinto.
differential [dɪfə'rɛnʃəl] *n* diferencial *f*.
differentiate [dɪfə'rɛnʃɪeɪt] *vt* distinguir
♦ *vi* diferenciarse; **to ~ between**
distinguir entre.
differently ['dɪfrəntlɪ] *adv* de otro modo, en
forma distinta.
difficult ['dɪfɪkəlt] *adj* difícil; **~ to
understand** difícil de entender.
difficulty ['dɪfɪkəltɪ] *n* dificultad *f*; **to have
difficulties with** (*police, landlord etc*) tener
problemas con; **to be in ~** estar en
apuros.
diffidence ['dɪfɪdəns] *n* timidez *f*, falta de
confianza en sí mismo.
diffident ['dɪfɪdənt] *adj* tímido.
diffuse [dɪ'fjuːs] *adj* difuso ♦ *vt* [dɪ'fjuːz]
difundir.
dig [dɪg] *vt* (*pt, pp* **dug** [dʌg]) (*hole*) cavar;
(*ground*) remover; (*coal*) extraer; (*nails
etc*) hincar ♦ *n* (*prod*) empujón *m*;
(*archaeological*) excavación *f*; (*remark*)
indirecta; **to ~ into** (*savings*) consumir; **to
~ into one's pockets for sth** hurgar en el
bolsillo buscando algo; **to ~ one's nails
into** clavar las uñas en; *see also* **digs**.
▶**dig in** *vi* (*also:* **~ o.s. in:** *MIL*)
atrincherarse; (*col: eat*) hincar los
dientes ♦ *vt* (*compost*) añadir al suelo;
(*knife, claw*) clavar; **to ~ in one's heels**
(*fig*) mantenerse en sus trece.
▶**dig out** *vt* (*hole*) excavar; (*survivors, car
from snow*) sacar.
▶**dig up** *vt* desenterrar; (*plant*)
desarraigar.
digest [daɪ'dʒɛst] *vt* (*food*) digerir; (*facts*)
asimilar ♦ *n* ['daɪdʒɛst] resumen *m*.
digestible [daɪ'dʒɛstəbl] *adj* digerible.

digestion [dɪ'dʒɛstʃən] *n* digestión *f*.
digestive [daɪ'dʒɛstɪv] *adj* (*juices, system*)
digestivo.
digit ['dɪdʒɪt] *n* (*number*) dígito; (*finger*)
dedo.
digital ['dɪdʒɪtl] *adj* digital.
digital compact cassette *n* cas(s)et(t)e *m*
or f digital compacto.
digital computer *n* ordenador *m* digital.
dignified ['dɪgnɪfaɪd] *adj* grave, solemne;
(*action*) decoroso.
dignify ['dɪgnɪfaɪ] *vt* dignificar.
dignitary ['dɪgnɪtərɪ] *n* dignatario/a.
dignity ['dɪgnɪtɪ] *n* dignidad *f*.
digress [daɪ'grɛs] *vi:* **to ~ from** apartarse
de.
digression [daɪ'grɛʃən] *n* digresión *f*.
digs [dɪgz] *npl* (*BRIT: col*) pensión *f*,
alojamiento.
dike [daɪk] *n* = **dyke**.
dilapidated [dɪ'læpɪdeɪtɪd] *adj*
desmoronado, ruinoso.
dilate [daɪ'leɪt] *vt* dilatar ♦ *vi* dilatarse.
dilatory ['dɪlətərɪ] *adj* (*person*) lento; (*action*)
dilatorio.
dilemma [daɪ'lɛmə] *n* dilema *m*; **to be in a ~**
estar en un dilema.
dilettante [dɪlɪ'tæntɪ] *n* diletante *m/f*.
diligence ['dɪlɪdʒəns] *n* diligencia.
diligent ['dɪlɪdʒənt] *adj* diligente.
dill [dɪl] *n* eneldo.
dilly-dally ['dɪlɪ'dælɪ] *vi* (*hesitate*) vacilar;
(*dawdle*) entretenerse.
dilute [daɪ'luːt] *vt* diluir.
dim [dɪm] *adj* (*light*) débil; (*sight*) turbio;
(*outline*) borroso; (*stupid*) lerdo; (*room*)
oscuro ♦ *vt* (*light*) bajar; **to take a ~ view
of sth** tener una pobre opinión de algo.
dime [daɪm] *n* (*US*) *moneda de diez
centavos*.
dimension [dɪ'mɛnʃən] *n* dimensión *f*.
-dimensional [dɪ'mɛnʃənl] *adj suff*: **two~** de
dos dimensiones.
dimensions [dɪ'mɛnʃənz] *npl* dimensiones
fpl.
diminish [dɪ'mɪnɪʃ] *vt, vi* disminuir.
diminished [dɪ'mɪnɪʃt] *adj:* **~ responsibility**
(*LAW*) responsabilidad *f* disminuida.
diminutive [dɪ'mɪnjutɪv] *adj* diminuto ♦ *n*
(*LING*) diminutivo.
dimly ['dɪmlɪ] *adv* débilmente; (*not clearly*)
vagamente.
dimmer ['dɪmə*] *n* (*also:* **~ switch**)
regulador *m* (de intensidad); (*US AUT*)
interruptor *m*.
dimple ['dɪmpl] *n* hoyuelo.
dimwitted ['dɪm'wɪtɪd] *adj* (*col*) lerdo, de
pocas luces.

din [dɪn] *n* estruendo, estrépito ♦ *vt*: **to ~ sth into sb** (*col*) meter algo en la cabeza a algn.

dine [daɪn] *vi* cenar.

diner ['daɪnə*] *n* (*person: in restaurant*) comensal *m/f*; (*BRIT RAIL*) = **dining car**; (*US*) restaurante económico.

dinghy ['dɪŋgɪ] *n* bote *m*; (*also*: **rubber ~**) lancha (neumática).

dingy ['dɪndʒɪ] *adj* (*room*) sombrío; (*dirty*) sucio; (*dull*) deslucido.

dining car ['daɪnɪŋ-] *n* (*BRIT*) coche-restaurante *m*.

dining room ['daɪnɪŋ-] *n* comedor *m*.

dinner ['dɪnə*] *n* (*evening meal*) cena, comida (*LAM*); (*lunch*) comida; (*public*) cena, banquete *m*; **~'s ready!** ¡la cena está servida!

dinner jacket *n* smoking *m*.

dinner party *n* cena.

dinner time *n* hora de cenar *or* comer.

dinosaur ['daɪnəsɔ:*] *n* dinosaurio.

dint [dɪnt] *n*: **by ~ of (doing) sth** a fuerza de (hacer) algo.

diocese ['daɪəsɪs] *n* diócesis *f*.

dioxide [daɪ'ɔksaɪd] *n* bióxido; **carbon ~** bióxido de carbono.

Dip. *abbr* (*BRIT*) = **diploma**.

dip [dɪp] *n* (*slope*) pendiente *f*; (*in sea*) chapuzón *m* ♦ *vt* (*in water*) mojar; (*ladle etc*) meter; (*BRIT AUT*): **to ~ one's lights** poner la luz de cruce ♦ *vi* inclinarse hacia abajo.

diphtheria [dɪf'θɪərɪə] *n* difteria.

diphthong ['dɪfθɔŋ] *n* diptongo.

diploma [dɪ'pləumə] *n* diploma *m*.

diplomacy [dɪ'pləuməsɪ] *n* diplomacia.

diplomat ['dɪpləmæt] *n* diplomático/a *m/f*.

diplomatic [dɪplə'mætɪk] *adj* diplomático; **to break off ~ relations** romper las relaciones diplomáticas.

diplomatic corps *n* cuerpo diplomático.

diplomatic immunity *n* inmunidad *f* diplomática.

dipstick ['dɪpstɪk] *n* (*AUT*) varilla de nivel (del aceite).

dipswitch ['dɪpswɪtʃ] *n* (*BRIT AUT*) interruptor *m*.

dire [daɪə*] *adj* calamitoso.

direct [daɪ'rɛkt] *adj* (*gen*) directo; (*manner, person*) franco ♦ *vt* dirigir; **can you ~ me to...?** ¿puede indicarme dónde está...?; **to ~ sb to do sth** mandar a algn hacer algo.

direct access *n* (*COMPUT*) acceso directo.

direct cost *n* costo directo.

direct current *n* corriente *f* continua.

direct debit *n* domiciliación *f* bancaria de recibos; **to pay by ~** domiciliar el pago.

direct dialling *n* servicio automático de llamadas.

direction [dɪ'rɛkʃən] *n* dirección *f*; **sense of ~** sentido de la orientación; **~s** *npl* (*advice*) órdenes *fpl*, instrucciones *fpl*; (*to a place*) señas *fpl*; **in the ~ of** hacia, en dirección a; **~s for use** modo de empleo; **to ask for ~s** preguntar el camino.

directional [dɪ'rɛkʃənl] *adj* direccional.

directive [daɪ'rɛktɪv] *n* orden *f*, instrucción *f*; **a government ~** una orden del gobierno.

direct labour *n* mano *f* de obra directa.

directly [dɪ'rɛktlɪ] *adv* (*in straight line*) directamente; (*at once*) en seguida.

direct mail *n* correspondencia personalizada.

direct mailshot *n* (*BRIT*) promoción *f* por correspondencia personalizada.

directness [dɪ'rɛktnɪs] *n* (*of person, speech*) franqueza.

director [dɪ'rɛktə*] *n* director(a) *m/f*; **managing ~** director(a) *m/f* gerente.

Director of Public Prosecutions *n* ≈ fiscal *m/f* general del Estado.

directory [dɪ'rɛktərɪ] *n* (*TEL*) guía (telefónica); (*street ~*) callejero; (*trade ~*) directorio de comercio; (*COMPUT*) directorio.

directory enquiries, (*US*) **directory assistance** *n* (*service*) (servicio de) información *f*.

dirt [də:t] *n* suciedad *f*.

dirt-cheap ['də:t'tʃi:p] *adj* baratísimo.

dirt road *n* (*US*) camino sin firme.

dirty ['də:tɪ] *adj* sucio; (*joke*) verde, colorado (*LAM*) ♦ *vt* ensuciar; (*stain*) manchar.

dirty trick *n* mala jugada, truco sucio.

disability [dɪsə'bɪlɪtɪ] *n* incapacidad *f*.

disability allowance *n* pensión *f* de invalidez.

disable [dɪs'eɪbl] *vt* (*subj: illness, accident*) dejar incapacitado *or* inválido; (*tank, gun*) inutilizar; (*LAW: disqualify*) incapacitar.

disabled [dɪs'eɪbld] *adj* minusválido.

disabuse [dɪsə'bju:z] *vt* desengañar.

disadvantage [dɪsəd'vɑ:ntɪdʒ] *n* desventaja, inconveniente *m*.

disadvantaged [dɪsəd'vɑ:ntɪdʒd] *adj* (*person*) desventajado.

disadvantageous [dɪsædvən'teɪdʒəs] *adj* desventajoso.

disaffected [dɪsə'fɛktɪd] *adj* descontento; **to be ~ (to *or* towards)** estar descontento (de).

disaffection [dɪsə'fɛkʃən] *n* desafecto, descontento.

disagree [dɪsə'griː] *vi* (*differ*) discrepar; **to ~ (with)** no estar de acuerdo (con); **I ~ with you** no estoy de acuerdo contigo.

disagreeable [dɪsə'grɪəbl] *adj* desagradable.

disagreement [dɪsə'griːmənt] *n* (*gen*) desacuerdo; (*quarrel*) riña; **to have a ~ with sb** estar en desacuerdo con algn.

disallow ['dɪsə'lau] *vt* (*goal*) anular; (*claim*) rechazar.

disappear [dɪsə'pɪə*] *vi* desaparecer.

disappearance [dɪsə'pɪərəns] *n* desaparición *f*.

disappoint [dɪsə'pɔɪnt] *vt* decepcionar; (*hopes*) defraudar.

disappointed [dɪsə'pɔɪntɪd] *adj* decepcionado.

disappointing [dɪsə'pɔɪntɪŋ] *adj* decepcionante.

disappointment [dɪsə'pɔɪntmənt] *n* decepción *f*.

disapproval [dɪsə'pruːvəl] *n* desaprobación *f*.

disapprove [dɪsə'pruːv] *vi*: **to ~ of** desaprobar.

disapproving [dɪsə'pruːvɪŋ] *adj* de desaprobación, desaprobador(a).

disarm [dɪs'ɑːm] *vt* desarmar.

disarmament [dɪs'ɑːməmənt] *n* desarme *m*.

disarmament talks *npl* conversaciones *fpl* de *or* sobre desarme.

disarming [dɪs'ɑːmɪŋ] *adj* (*smile*) que desarma, encantador(a).

disarray [dɪsə'reɪ] *n*: **in ~** (*troops*) desorganizado; (*thoughts*) confuso; (*hair, clothes*) desarreglado; **to throw into ~** provocar el caos.

disaster [dɪ'zɑːstə*] *n* desastre *m*.

disaster area *n* zona catastrófica.

disastrous [dɪ'zɑːstrəs] *adj* desastroso.

disband [dɪs'bænd] *vt* disolver ♦ *vi* desbandarse.

disbelief [dɪsbə'liːf] *n* incredulidad *f*; **in ~** con incredulidad.

disbelieve ['dɪsbə'liːv] *vt* (*person, story*) poner en duda, no creer.

disc [dɪsk] *n* disco; (*COMPUT*) = **disk**.

disc. *abbr* (*COMM*) = **discount**.

discard [dɪs'kɑːd] *vt* (*old things*) tirar; (*fig*) descartar.

discern [dɪ'səːn] *vt* percibir, discernir; (*understand*) comprender.

discernible [dɪ'səːnəbl] *adj* perceptible.

discerning [dɪ'səːnɪŋ] *adj* perspicaz.

discharge [dɪs'tʃɑːdʒ] *vt* (*task, duty*) cumplir; (*ship etc*) descargar; (*patient*) dar de alta; (*employee*) despedir; (*soldier*) licenciar; (*defendant*) poner en libertad;

(*settle: debt*) saldar ♦ *n* ['dɪstʃɑːdʒ] (*ELEC*) descarga; (*vaginal ~*) emisión *f* vaginal; (*dismissal*) despedida; (*of duty*) desempeño; (*of debt*) pago, descargo; (*of gas, chemicals*) escape *m*; **~d bankrupt** quebrado/a rehabilitado/a.

disciple [dɪ'saɪpl] *n* discípulo/a.

disciplinary ['dɪsɪplɪnərɪ] *adj*: **to take ~ action against sb** disciplinar a algn.

discipline ['dɪsɪplɪn] *n* disciplina ♦ *vt* disciplinar; **to ~ o.s. to do sth** obligarse a hacer algo.

disc jockey (DJ) *n* pinchadiscos *m/f inv*.

disclaim [dɪs'kleɪm] *vt* negar tener.

disclaimer [dɪs'kleɪmə*] *n* rectificación *f*; **to issue a ~** hacer una rectificación.

disclose [dɪs'kləuz] *vt* revelar.

disclosure [dɪs'kləuʒə*] *n* revelación *f*.

disco ['dɪskəu] *n abbr* = **discothèque**.

discolouration, (*US*) **discoloration** [dɪskʌlə'reɪʃən] *n* descoloramiento, decoloración *f*.

discolo(u)red [dɪs'kʌləd] *adj* descolorido.

discomfort [dɪs'kʌmfət] *n* incomodidad *f*; (*unease*) inquietud *f*; (*physical*) malestar *m*.

disconcert [dɪskən'səːt] *vt* desconcertar.

disconnect [dɪskə'nɛkt] *vt* (*gen*) separar; (*ELEC etc*) desconectar; (*supply*) cortar (el suministro) a.

disconsolate [dɪs'kɔnsəlɪt] *adj* desconsolado.

discontent [dɪskən'tɛnt] *n* descontento.

discontented [dɪskən'tɛntɪd] *adj* descontento.

discontinue [dɪskən'tɪnjuː] *vt* interrumpir; (*payments*) suspender.

discord ['dɪskɔːd] *n* discordia; (*MUS*) disonancia.

discordant [dɪs'kɔːdənt] *adj* disonante.

discothèque ['dɪskəutɛk] *n* discoteca.

discount ['dɪskaunt] *n* descuento ♦ *vt* [dɪs'kaunt] descontar; (*report etc*) descartar; **at a ~** con descuento; **~ for cash** descuento por pago en efectivo; **to give sb a ~ on sth** hacer un descuento a algn en algo.

discount house *n* (*FINANCE*) banco de descuento; (*COMM: also*: **discount store**) ≈ tienda de saldos.

discount rate *n* (*COMM*) tipo de descuento.

discount store *n* ≈ tienda de saldos.

discourage [dɪs'kʌrɪdʒ] *vt* desalentar; (*oppose*) oponerse a; (*dissuade, deter*) desanimar, disuadir.

discouragement [dɪs'kʌrɪdʒmənt] *n* (*dissuasion*) disuasión *f*; (*depression*) desánimo, desaliento; **to act as a ~ to**

servir para disuadir.

discouraging [dɪs'kʌrɪdʒɪŋ] *adj* desalentador(a).

discourteous [dɪs'kɜ:tɪəs] *adj* descortés.

discover [dɪs'kʌvə*] *vt* descubrir.

discovery [dɪs'kʌvərɪ] *n* descubrimiento.

discredit [dɪs'kredɪt] *vt* desacreditar.

discreet [dɪ'skri:t] *adj* (*tactful*) discreto; (*careful*) circunspecto, prudente.

discreetly [dɪ'skri:tlɪ] *adv* discretamente.

discrepancy [dɪ'skrepənsɪ] *n* (*difference*) diferencia; (*disagreement*) discrepancia.

discretion [dɪ'skreʃən] *n* (*tact*) discreción *f*; (*care*) prudencia, circunspección *f*; **use your own** ~ haz lo que creas oportuno.

discretionary [dɪ'skreʃənrɪ] *adj* (*powers*) discrecional.

discriminate [dɪ'skrɪmɪneɪt] *vi:* **to** ~ **between** distinguir entre; **to** ~ **against** discriminar contra.

discriminating [dɪ'skrɪmɪneɪtɪŋ] *adj* entendido.

discrimination [dɪskrɪmɪ'neɪʃən] *n* (*discernment*) perspicacia; (*bias*) discriminación *f*; **racial/sexual** ~ discriminación racial/sexual.

discus ['dɪskəs] *n* disco.

discuss [dɪ'skʌs] *vt* (*gen*) discutir; (*a theme*) tratar.

discussion [dɪ'skʌʃən] *n* discusión *f*; **under** ~ en discusión.

disdain [dɪs'deɪn] *n* desdén *m* ♦ *vt* desdeñar.

disease [dɪ'zi:z] *n* enfermedad *f*.

diseased [dɪ'zi:zd] *adj* enfermo.

disembark [dɪsɪm'bɑ:k] *vt, vi* desembarcar.

disembarkation [dɪsembɑ:'keɪʃən] *n* desembarque *m*.

disenchanted [dɪsɪn'tʃɑːntɪd] *adj:* ~ **(with)** desilusionado (con).

disenfranchise ['dɪsɪn'fræntʃaɪz] *vt* privar del derecho al voto; (*COMM*) privar de franquicias.

disengage [dɪsɪn'geɪdʒ] *vt* soltar; **to** ~ **the clutch** (*AUT*) desembragar.

disentangle [dɪsɪn'tæŋgl] *vt* desenredar.

disfavour, (*US*) **disfavor** [dɪs'feɪvə*] *n* desaprobación *f*.

disfigure [dɪs'fɪgə*] *vt* desfigurar.

disgorge [dɪs'gɔːdʒ] *vt* verter.

disgrace [dɪs'greɪs] *n* ignominia; (*downfall*) caída; (*shame*) vergüenza, escándalo ♦ *vt* deshonrar.

disgraceful [dɪs'greɪsful] *adj* vergonzoso; (*behaviour*) escandaloso.

disgruntled [dɪs'grʌntld] *adj* disgustado, descontento.

disguise [dɪs'gaɪz] *n* disfraz *m* ♦ *vt* disfrazar; (*voice*) disimular; (*feelings etc*)

ocultar; **in** ~ disfrazado; **to** ~ **o.s. as** disfrazarse de; **there's no disguising the fact that** ... no puede ocultarse el hecho de que ....

disgust [dɪs'gʌst] *n* repugnancia ♦ *vt* repugnar, dar asco a.

disgusting [dɪs'gʌstɪŋ] *adj* repugnante, asqueroso.

dish [dɪʃ] *n* (*gen*) plato; **to do** *or* **wash the** ~**es** fregar los platos.

▶**dish out** *vt* (*money, exam papers*) repartir; (*food*) servir; (*advice*) dar.

▶**dish up** *vt* servir.

dishcloth ['dɪʃklɔθ] *n* paño de cocina, bayeta.

dishearten [dɪs'hɑːtn] *vt* desalentar.

dishevelled, (*US*) **disheveled** [dɪ'ʃevəld] *adj* (*hair*) despeinado; (*clothes, appearance*) desarreglado.

dishonest [dɪs'ɔnɪst] *adj* (*person*) poco honrado, tramposo; (*means*) fraudulento.

dishonesty [dɪs'ɔnɪstɪ] *n* falta de honradez.

dishonour, (*US*) **dishonor** [dɪs'ɔnə*] *n* deshonra.

dishono(u)rable [dɪs'ɔnərəbl] *adj* deshonroso.

dish soap *n* (*US*) lavavajillas *m inv*.

dishtowel ['dɪʃtauəl] *n* (*US*) trapo de fregar.

dishwasher ['dɪʃwɔʃə*] *n* lavaplatos *m inv*; (*person*) friegaplatos *m/f inv*.

dishy ['dɪʃɪ] *adj* (*BRIT col*) buenón/ona.

disillusion [dɪsɪ'lu:ʒən] *vt* desilusionar; **to become** ~**ed (with)** quedar desilusionado (con).

disillusionment [dɪsɪ'lu:ʒənmənt] *n* desilusión *f*.

disincentive [dɪsɪn'sentɪv] *n* freno; **to act as a** ~ **(to)** actuar de freno (a); **to be a** ~ **to** ser un freno a.

disinclined ['dɪsɪn'klaɪnd] *adj:* **to be** ~ **to do sth** estar poco dispuesto a hacer algo.

disinfect [dɪsɪn'fekt] *vt* desinfectar.

disinfectant [dɪsɪn'fektənt] *n* desinfectante *m*.

disinflation [dɪsɪn'fleɪʃən] *n* desinflación *f*.

disinformation [dɪsɪnfə'meɪʃən] *n* desinformación *f*.

disingenuous [dɪsɪn'dʒenjuəs] *adj* poco sincero, falso.

disinherit [dɪsɪn'herɪt] *vt* desheredar.

disintegrate [dɪs'ɪntɪgreɪt] *vi* disgregarse, desintegrarse.

disinterested [dɪs'ɪntrəstɪd] *adj* desinteresado.

disjointed [dɪs'dʒɔɪntɪd] *adj* inconexo.

disk [dɪsk] *n* (*COMPUT*) disco, disquete *m*; **single-/double-sided** ~ disco de una

cara/dos caras.
disk drive *n* disc drive *m*.
diskette [dɪs'ket] *n* diskette *m*, disquete *m*, disco flexible.
disk operating system (DOS) *n* sistema *m* operativo de discos (DOS).
dislike [dɪs'laɪk] *n* antipatía, aversión *f* ♦ *vt* tener antipatía a; **to take a ~ to sb/sth** cogerle *or* agarrarle (*LAM*) antipatía a algn/algo; **I ~ the idea** no me gusta la idea.
dislocate ['dɪsləkeɪt] *vt* dislocar; **he ~d his shoulder** se dislocó el hombro.
dislodge [dɪs'lɒdʒ] *vt* sacar; (*enemy*) desalojar.
disloyal [dɪs'lɔɪəl] *adj* desleal.
dismal ['dɪzml] *adj* (*dark*) sombrío; (*depressing*) triste; (*very bad*) fatal.
dismantle [dɪs'mæntl] *vt* desmontar, desarmar.
dismay [dɪs'meɪ] *n* consternación *f* ♦ *vt* consternar; **much to my ~** para gran consternación mía.
dismiss [dɪs'mɪs] *vt* (*worker*) despedir; (*official*) destituir; (*idea, LAW*) rechazar; (*possibility*) descartar ♦ *vi* (*MIL*) romper filas.
dismissal [dɪs'mɪsl] *n* despedida; destitución *f*.
dismount [dɪs'maʊnt] *vi* apearse; (*rider*) desmontar.
disobedience [dɪsə'biːdɪəns] *n* desobediencia.
disobedient [dɪsə'biːdɪənt] *adj* desobediente.
disobey [dɪsə'beɪ] *vt* desobedecer; (*rule*) infringir.
disorder [dɪs'ɔːdə*] *n* desorden *m*; (*rioting*) disturbio; (*MED*) trastorno; (*disease*) enfermedad *f*; **civil ~** desorden *m* civil.
disorderly [dɪs'ɔːdəlɪ] *adj* (*untidy*) desordenado; (*meeting*) alborotado; **~ conduct** (*LAW*) conducta escandalosa.
disorganized [dɪs'ɔːgənaɪzd] *adj* desorganizado.
disorientated [dɪs'ɔːrɪenteɪtəd] *adj* desorientado.
disown [dɪs'əʊn] *vt* renegar de.
disparaging [dɪs'pærɪdʒɪŋ] *adj* despreciativo; **to be ~ about sth/sb** menospreciar algo/a algn.
disparate ['dɪspərɪt] *adj* dispar.
disparity [dɪs'pærɪtɪ] *n* disparidad *f*.
dispassionate [dɪs'pæʃənɪt] *adj* (*unbiased*) imparcial; (*unemotional*) desapasionado.
dispatch [dɪs'pætʃ] *vt* enviar; (*kill*) despachar; (*deal with: business*) despachar ♦ *n* (*sending*) envío; (*speed*)

prontitud *f*; (*PRESS*) informe *m*; (*MIL*) parte *m*.
dispatch department *n* (*COMM*) departamento de envíos.
dispatch rider *n* (*MIL*) correo.
dispel [dɪs'pel] *vt* disipar, dispersar.
dispensary [dɪs'pensərɪ] *n* dispensario.
dispensation [dɪspen'seɪʃən] *n* (*REL*) dispensa.
dispense [dɪs'pens] *vt* dispensar, repartir; (*medicine*) preparar.
▶**dispense with** *vt fus* (*make unnecessary*) prescindir de.
dispenser [dɪs'pensə*] *n* (*container*) distribuidor *m* automático.
dispensing chemist [dɪs'pensɪŋ-] *n* (*BRIT*) farmacia.
dispersal [dɪs'pɜːsl] *n* dispersión *f*.
disperse [dɪs'pɜːs] *vt* dispersar ♦ *vi* dispersarse.
dispirited [dɪ'spɪrɪtɪd] *adj* desanimado, desalentado.
displace [dɪs'pleɪs] *vt* (*person*) desplazar; (*replace*) reemplazar.
displaced person *n* (*POL*) desplazado/a.
displacement [dɪs'pleɪsmənt] *n* cambio de sitio.
display [dɪs'pleɪ] *n* (*exhibition*) exposición *f*; (*COMPUT*) visualización *f*; (*MIL*) desfile *m*; (*of feeling*) manifestación *f*; (*pej*) aparato, pompa ♦ *vt* exponer; manifestar; (*ostentatiously*) lucir; **on ~** (*exhibits*) expuesto, exhibido; (*goods*) en el escaparate.
display advertising *n* publicidad *f* gráfica.
displease [dɪs'pliːz] *vt* (*offend*) ofender; (*annoy*) fastidiar; **~d with** disgustado con.
displeasure [dɪs'pleʒə*] *n* disgusto.
disposable [dɪs'pəʊzəbl] *adj* (*not reusable*) desechable; **~ personal income** ingresos *mpl* personales disponibles.
disposable nappy *n* pañal *m* desechable.
disposal [dɪs'pəʊzl] *n* (*sale*) venta; (*of house*) traspaso; (*by giving away*) donación *f*; (*arrangement*) colocación *f*; (*of rubbish*) destrucción *f*; **at one's ~** a la disposición de algn; **to put sth at sb's ~** poner algo a disposición de algn.
disposed [dɪs'pəʊzd] *adj*: **~ to do** dispuesto a hacer.
dispose of [dɪs'pəʊz] *vt fus* (*time, money*) disponer de; (*unwanted goods*) deshacerse de; (*COMM: sell*) traspasar, vender; (*throw away*) tirar.
disposition [dɪspə'zɪʃən] *n* disposición *f*; (*temperament*) carácter *m*.
dispossess ['dɪspə'zes] *vt*: **to ~ sb (of)**

desposeer a algn (de).
disproportion [dɪsprə'pɔːʃən] *n* desproporción *f*.
disproportionate [dɪsprə'pɔːʃənət] *adj* desproporcionado.
disprove [dɪs'pruːv] *vt* refutar.
dispute [dɪs'pjuːt] *n* disputa; (*verbal*) discusión *f*; (*also*: **industrial** ~) conflicto (laboral) ♦ *vt* (*argue*) disputar; (*question*) cuestionar; **to be in** *or* **under** ~ (*matter*) discutirse; (*territory*) estar en disputa; (*JUR*) estar en litigio.
disqualification [dɪskwɔlɪfɪ'keɪʃən] *n* inhabilitación *f*; (*SPORT, from driving*) descalificación *f*.
disqualify [dɪs'kwɔlɪfaɪ] *vt* (*SPORT*) desclasificar; **to** ~ **sb for sth/from doing sth** incapacitar a algn para algo/hacer algo.
disquiet [dɪs'kwaɪət] *n* preocupación *f*, inquietud *f*.
disquieting [dɪs'kwaɪətɪŋ] *adj* inquietante.
disregard [dɪsrɪ'gɑːd] *vt* desatender; (*ignore*) no hacer caso de ♦ *n* (*indifference*: *to feelings, danger, money*): ~ **(for)** indiferencia (a); ~ **(of)** (*non-observance*: *of law, rules*) violación *f* (de).
disrepair [dɪsrɪ'pɛə*] *n*: **to fall into** ~ (*building*) desmoronarse; (*street*) deteriorarse.
disreputable [dɪs'rɛpjutəbl] *adj* (*person, area*) de mala fama; (*behaviour*) vergonzoso.
disrepute ['dɪsrɪ'pjuːt] *n* descrédito, ignominia; **to bring into** ~ desacreditar.
disrespectful [dɪsrɪ'spɛktful] *adj* irrespetuoso.
disrupt [dɪs'rʌpt] *vt* (*meeting, public transport, conversation*) interrumpir; (*plans*) desbaratar, alternar, trastornar.
disruption [dɪs'rʌpʃən] *n* trastorno; desbaratamiento; interrupción *f*.
disruptive [dɪs'rʌptɪv] *adj* (*influence*) disruptivo; (*strike action*) perjudicial.
dissatisfaction [dɪssætɪs'fækʃən] *n* disgusto, descontento.
dissatisfied [dɪs'sætɪsfaɪd] *adj* insatisfecho.
dissect [dɪ'sɛkt] *vt* (*also fig*) disecar.
disseminate [dɪ'sɛmɪneɪt] *vt* divulgar, difundir.
dissent [dɪ'sɛnt] *n* disensión *f*.
dissenter [dɪ'sɛntə*] *n* (*REL, POL etc*) disidente *m/f*.
dissertation [dɪsə'teɪʃən] *n* (*UNIV*) tesina; *see also* **master's degree**.
disservice [dɪs'sɜːvɪs] *n*: **to do sb a** ~ perjudicar a alguien.
dissident ['dɪsɪdnt] *adj, n* disidente *m/f*.

dissimilar [dɪ'sɪmɪlə*] *adj* distinto.
dissipate ['dɪsɪpeɪt] *vt* disipar; (*waste*) desperdiciar.
dissipated ['dɪsɪpeɪtɪd] *adj* disoluto.
dissipation [dɪsɪ'peɪʃən] *n* disipación *f*; (*moral*) libertinaje *m*, vicio; (*waste*) derroche *m*.
dissociate [dɪ'səuʃɪeɪt] *vt* disociar; **to** ~ **o.s. from** disociarse de.
dissolute ['dɪsəluːt] *adj* disoluto.
dissolution [dɪsə'luːʃən] *n* (*of organization, marriage, POL*) disolución *f*.
dissolve [dɪ'zɔlv] *vt* (*gen, COMM*) disolver ♦ *vi* disolverse.
dissuade [dɪ'sweɪd] *vt*: **to** ~ **sb (from)** disuadir a algn (de).
distaff ['dɪstæf] *n*: ~ **side** rama femenina.
distance ['dɪstns] *n* distancia; **in the** ~ a lo lejos; **what** ~ **is it to London?** ¿qué distancia hay de aquí a Londres?; **it's within walking** ~ se puede ir andando.
distant ['dɪstnt] *adj* lejano; (*manner*) reservado, frío.
distaste [dɪs'teɪst] *n* repugnancia.
distasteful [dɪs'teɪstful] *adj* repugnante, desagradable.
Dist. Atty. *abbr* (*US*) = **district attorney**.
distemper [dɪs'tɛmpə*] *n* (*of dogs*) moquillo.
distend [dɪ'stɛnd] *vt* dilatar, hinchar ♦ *vi* dilatarse, hincharse.
distended [dɪ'stɛndɪd] *adj* (*stomach*) hinchado.
distil, (*US*) **distill** [dɪs'tɪl] *vt* destilar.
distillery [dɪs'tɪlərɪ] *n* destilería.
distinct [dɪs'tɪŋkt] *adj* (*different*) distinto; (*clear*) claro; (*unmistakeable*) inequívoco; **as** ~ **from** a diferencia de.
distinction [dɪs'tɪŋkʃən] *n* distinción *f*; (*in exam*) sobresaliente *m*; **a writer of** ~ un escritor destacado; **to draw a** ~ **between** hacer una distinción entre.
distinctive [dɪs'tɪŋktɪv] *adj* distintivo.
distinctly [dɪs'tɪŋktlɪ] *adv* claramente.
distinguish [dɪs'tɪŋgwɪʃ] *vt* distinguir ♦ *vi*: **to** ~ **(between)** distinguir (entre).
distinguished [dɪs'tɪŋgwɪʃt] *adj* (*eminent*) distinguido; (*career*) eminente; (*refined*) distinguido, de categoría.
distinguishing [dɪs'tɪŋgwɪʃɪŋ] *adj* (*feature*) distintivo.
distort [dɪs'tɔːt] *vt* torcer, retorcer; (*account, news*) desvirtuar, deformar.
distortion [dɪs'tɔːʃən] *n* deformación *f*; (*of sound*) distorsión *f*; (*of truth etc*) tergiversación *f*; (*of facts*) falseamiento.
distract [dɪs'trækt] *vt* distraer.
distracted [dɪs'træktɪd] *adj* distraído.

distracting [dɪs'træktɪŋ] *adj* que distrae la atención, molesto.

distraction [dɪs'trækʃən] *n* distracción *f*; (*confusion*) aturdimiento; (*amusement*) diversión *f*; **to drive sb to** ~ (*distress, anxiety*) volver loco a algn.

distraught [dɪs'trɔːt] *adj* turbado, enloquecido.

distress [dɪs'trɛs] *n* (*anguish*) angustia; (*want*) miseria; (*pain*) dolor *m*; (*danger*) peligro ♦ *vt* afligir; (*pain*) doler; **in** ~ (*ship etc*) en peligro.

distressing [dɪs'trɛsɪŋ] *adj* angustioso; doloroso.

distress signal *n* señal *f* de socorro.

distribute [dɪs'trɪbjuːt] *vt* (*gen*) distribuir; (*share out*) repartir.

distribution [dɪstrɪ'bjuːʃən] *n* distribución *f*.

distribution cost *n* gastos *mpl* de distribución.

distributor [dɪs'trɪbjutə*] *n* (*AUT*) distribuidor *m*; (*COMM*) distribuidora.

district ['dɪstrɪkt] *n* (*of country*) zona, región *f*; (*of town*) barrio; (*ADMIN*) distrito.

district attorney *n* (*US*) fiscal *m/f*.

district council *n* ≈ municipio.

> *En Inglaterra y Gales, con la excepción de Londres, la administración local corre a cargo del* **district council**, *responsable de los servicios municipales como vivienda, urbanismo, recolección de basuras, salud medioambiental etc. La mayoría de sus miembros son elegidos a nivel local cada cuatro años. Hay un total de 369* **districts** *(distritos), repartidos en 53* **counties** *(condados), que se financian a través de los impuestos municipales y partidas presupuestarias del Estado. Éste controla sus gastos a través de una comisión independiente.*

district manager *n* representante *m/f* regional.

district nurse *n* (*BRIT*) enfermera que atiende a pacientes a domicilio.

distrust [dɪs'trʌst] *n* desconfianza ♦ *vt* desconfiar de.

distrustful [dɪs'trʌstful] *adj* desconfiado.

disturb [dɪs'təːb] *vt* (*person: bother, interrupt*) molestar; (*meeting*) interrumpir; (*disorganize*) desordenar; **sorry to** ~ **you** perdone la molestia.

disturbance [dɪs'təːbəns] *n* (*political etc*) disturbio; (*violence*) alboroto; (*of mind*) trastorno; **to cause a** ~ causar alboroto; ~ **of the peace** alteración *f* del orden

público.

disturbed [dɪs'təːbd] *adj* (*worried, upset*) preocupado, angustiado; **to be emotionally/mentally** ~ tener problemas emocionales/ser un trastornado mental.

disturbing [dɪs'təːbɪŋ] *adj* inquietante, perturbador(a).

disuse [dɪs'juːs] *n*: **to fall into** ~ caer en desuso.

disused [dɪs'juːzd] *adj* abandonado.

ditch [dɪtʃ] *n* zanja; (*irrigation* ~) acequia ♦ *vt* (*col*) deshacerse de.

dither ['dɪðə*] *vi* vacilar.

ditto ['dɪtəu] *adv* ídem, lo mismo.

divan [dɪ'væn] *n* diván *m*.

divan bed *n* cama turca.

dive [daɪv] *n* (*from board*) salto; (*underwater*) buceo; (*of submarine*) inmersión *f*; (*AVIAT*) picada ♦ *vi* saltar; bucear; sumergirse; picar.

diver ['daɪvə*] *n* (*SPORT*) saltador(a) *m/f*; (*underwater*) buzo.

diverge [daɪ'vəːdʒ] *vi* divergir.

divergent [daɪ'vəːdʒənt] *adj* divergente.

diverse [daɪ'vəːs] *adj* diversos/as, varios/as.

diversification [daɪvəːsɪfɪ'keɪʃən] *n* diversificación *f*.

diversify [daɪ'vəːsɪfaɪ] *vt* diversificar.

diversion [daɪ'vəːʃən] *n* (*BRIT AUT*) desviación *f*; (*distraction, MIL*) diversión *f*.

diversionary tactics [daɪ'vəːʃənrɪ-] *npl* tácticas *fpl* de diversión.

diversity [daɪ'vəːsɪtɪ] *n* diversidad *f*.

divert [daɪ'vəːt] *vt* (*BRIT: train, plane, traffic*) desviar; (*amuse*) divertir.

divest [daɪ'vɛst] *vt*: **to** ~ **sb of sth** despojar a alguien de algo.

divide [dɪ'vaɪd] *vt* dividir; (*separate*) separar ♦ *vi* dividirse; (*road*) bifurcarse; **to** ~ **(between, among)** repartir *or* dividir (entre); **40** ~**d by 5** 40 dividido por 5.

▶**divide out** *vt*: **to** ~ **out (between, among)** (*sweets, tasks etc*) repartir (entre).

divided [dɪ'vaɪdɪd] *adj* (*country, couple*) dividido, separado; (*opinions*) en desacuerdo.

divided highway *n* (*US*) carretera de doble calzada.

dividend ['dɪvɪdɛnd] *n* dividendo; (*fig*) beneficio.

dividend cover *n* cobertura de dividendo.

dividers [dɪ'vaɪdəz] *npl* compás *m* de puntas.

divine [dɪ'vaɪn] *adj* divino ♦ *vt* (*future*) vaticinar; (*truth*) alumbrar; (*water, metal*) descubrir, detectar.

diving ['daɪvɪŋ] *n* (*SPORT*) salto; (*underwater*) buceo.

diving board – do

diving board *n* trampolín *m*.
diving suit *n* escafandra.
divinity [dɪ'vɪnɪtɪ] *n* divinidad *f*; (*SCOL*) teología.
divisible [dɪ'vɪzɪbl] *adj* divisible.
division [dɪ'vɪʒən] *n* (*also BRIT FOOTBALL*) división *f*; (*sharing out*) repartimiento; (*BRIT POL*) votación *f*; ~ **of labour** división *f* del trabajo.
divisive [dɪ'vaɪsɪv] *adj* divisivo.
divorce [dɪ'vɔ:s] *n* divorcio ♦ *vt* divorciarse de.
divorced [dɪ'vɔ:st] *adj* divorciado.
divorcee [dɪvɔ:'si:] *n* divorciado/a.
divot ['dɪvət] *n* (*GOLF*) chuleta.
divulge [daɪ'vʌldʒ] *vt* divulgar, revelar.
D.I.Y. *adj, n abbr* (*BRIT*) = **do-it-yourself**.
dizziness ['dɪzɪnɪs] *n* vértigo.
dizzy ['dɪzɪ] *adj* (*person*) mareado; (*height*) vertiginoso; **to feel** ~ marearse; **I feel** ~ estoy mareado.
DJ *n abbr see* **disc jockey.**
d.j. *n abbr* = **dinner jacket.**
Djakarta [dʒə'kɑːtə] *n* Yakarta.
DJIA *n abbr* (*US STOCK EXCHANGE*) = *Dow Jones Industrial Average.*
dl *abbr* (= *decilitre(s)*) dl.
DLit(t) *abbr* (= *Doctor of Literature, Doctor of Letters*) título universitario.
DLO *n abbr* (= *dead-letter office*) oficina de Correos que se encarga de las cartas que no llegan a su destino.
dm *abbr* (= *decimetre(s)*) dm.
DMus *abbr* (= *Doctor of Music*) título universitario.
DMZ *n abbr* (= *demilitarized zone*) zona desmilitarizada.
DNA *n abbr* = (*deoxyribonucleic acid*) ADN *m*.

================== *KEYWORD*

do [du:] (*pt* **did**, *pp* **done**) *n* **1** (*inf: party etc*): **we're having a little** ~ **on Saturday** damos una fiestecita el sábado; **it was rather a grand** ~ fue un acontecimiento a lo grande
2: the ~**s and don'ts** lo que se debe y no se debe hacer
♦ *aux vb* **1** (*in negative constructions: not translated*) **I don't understand** no entiendo
2 (*to form questions: not translated*) ~ **you speak English?** ¿habla (usted) inglés?; **didn't you know?** ¿no lo sabías?; **what** ~ **you think?** ¿qué opinas?
3 (*for emphasis, in polite expressions*): **people** ~ **make mistakes sometimes** a veces sí se cometen errores; **she does seem rather late** a mí también me parece que se ha retrasado; ~ **sit down/help**

yourself siéntate/sírvete por favor; ~ **take care!** ¡ten cuidado! ¿eh?; **I** *DO* **wish I could ...** ojalá (que) pudiera ...; **but I** *DO* **like it** pero, sí (que) me gusta
4 (*used to avoid repeating vb*): **she sings better than I** ~ canta mejor que yo; ~ **you agree?** — **yes, I** ~**/no, I don't** ¿estás de acuerdo? — sí (lo estoy)/no (lo estoy); **she lives in Glasgow** — **so** ~ **I** vive en Glasgow — yo también; **he didn't like it and neither did we** no le gustó a nosotros tampoco; **who made this mess?** — **I did** ¿quién hizo esta chapuza? — yo; **he asked me to help him and I did** me pidió que le ayudara y lo hice
5 (*in question tags*): **you like him, don't you?** te gusta, ¿verdad? *or* ¿no?; **I don't know him,** ~ **I?** creo que no le conozco; **he laughed, didn't he?** se rió ¿no?
♦ *vt* **1** (*gen, carry out, perform etc*): **what are you** ~**ing tonight?** ¿qué haces esta noche?; **what can I** ~ **for you?** (*in shop*) ¿en qué puedo servirle?; **what does he** ~ **for a living?** ¿a qué se dedica?; **I'll** ~ **all I can** haré todo lo que pueda; **what have you done with my slippers?** ¿qué has hecho con mis zapatillas?; **to** ~ **the washing-up/cooking** fregar los platos/cocinar; **to** ~ **one's teeth/hair/nails** lavarse los dientes/arreglarse el pelo/arreglarse las uñas
2 (*AUT etc*): **the car was** ~**ing 100** el coche iba a 100; **we've done 200 km already** ya hemos hecho 200 km; **he can** ~ **100 in that car** puede ir a 100 en ese coche
3 (*visit: city, museum*) visitar, recorrer
4 (*cook*): **a steak – well done please** un filete bien hecho, por favor
♦ *vi* **1** (*act, behave*) hacer; ~ **as I** ~ haz como yo
2 (*get on, fare*): **he's** ~**ing well/badly at school** va bien/mal en la escuela; **the firm is** ~**ing well** la empresa anda *or* va bien; **how** ~ **you** ~**?** mucho gusto; (*less formal*) ¿qué tal?
3 (*suit*): **will it** ~**?** ¿sirve?, ¿está *or* va bien?; **it doesn't** ~ **to upset her** cuidado en ofenderla
4 (*be sufficient*) bastar; **will £10** ~**?** ¿será bastante con £10?; **that'll** ~ así está bien; **that'll** ~**!** (*in annoyance*) ¡ya está bien!, ¡basta ya!; **to make** ~ (**with**) arreglárselas (con)
▶**do away with** *vt fus* (*kill, disease*) eliminar; (*abolish: law etc*) abolir; (*withdraw*) retirar
▶**do out of** *vt fus*: **to** ~ **sb out of sth** pisar

algo a algn
▶**do up** *vt* (*laces*) atar; (*zip, dress, shirt*) abrochar; (*renovate: room, house*) renovar
▶**do with** *vt fus* (*need*): **I could ~ with a drink/some help** no me vendría mal un trago/un poco de ayuda; (*be connected*) tener que ver con; **what has it got to ~ with you?** ¿qué tiene que ver contigo?
▶**do without** *vi*: **if you're late for dinner then you'll ~ without** si llegas tarde tendrás que quedarte sin cenar ♦ *vt fus* pasar sin; **I can ~ without a car** puedo pasar sin coche.

do. *abbr* = **ditto.**
DOA *abbr* = *dead on arrival.*
d.o.b. *abbr* = *date of birth.*
doc [dɔk] *n* (*col*) médico/a.
docile ['dəʊsaɪl] *adj* dócil.
dock [dɔk] *n* (*NAUT: wharf*) dársena, muelle *m*; (*LAW*) banquillo (de los acusados); **~s** *npl* muelles *mpl*, puerto *sg* ♦ *vi* (*enter ~*) atracar (en el muelle) ♦ *vt* (*pay etc*) descontar.
dock dues *npl* derechos *mpl* de muelle.
docker ['dɔkə*] *n* trabajador *m* portuario, estibador *m*.
docket ['dɔkɪt] *n* (*on parcel etc*) etiqueta.
dockyard ['dɔkjaːd] *n* astillero.
doctor ['dɔktə*] *n* médico; (*Ph.D. etc*) doctor(a) *m/f* ♦ *vt* (*fig*) arreglar, falsificar; (*drink etc*) adulterar.
doctorate ['dɔktərɪt] *n* doctorado.

*El grado más alto que conceden las universidades es el doctorado (**doctorate**), tras un período de estudio e investigación original no inferior a tres años que culmina con la presentación de una tesis (**thesis**) en la que se exponen los resultados. El título más frecuente es el de **PhD** (**Doctor of Philosophy**), que se obtiene en Letras, Ciencias e Ingeniería, aunque también existen otros doctorados específicos en Música, Derecho etc.*

Doctor of Philosophy (Ph.D.) *n* Doctor *m* (en Filosofía y Letras).
doctrinaire [dɔktrɪ'nɛə*] *adj* doctrinario.
doctrine ['dɔktrɪn] *n* doctrina.
docudrama [dɔkju'draːmə] *n* (*TV*) docudrama *m*.
document ['dɔkjumənt] *n* documento ♦ *vt* documentar.
documentary [dɔkju'mɛntərɪ] *adj* documental ♦ *n* documental *m*.
documentation [dɔkjumen'teɪʃən] *n* documentación *f*.

DOD *n abbr* (*US*: = *Department of Defense*) Ministerio de Defensa.
doddering ['dɔdərɪŋ] *adj*, **doddery** ['dɔdərɪ] *adj* vacilante.
doddle ['dɔdl] *n*: **it's a ~** (*BRIT col*) es pan comido.
Dodecanese (Islands) [dəʊdɪkə'niːz-] *n*(*pl*) Dodecaneso *sg*.
dodge [dɔdʒ] *n* (*of body*) regate *m*; (*fig*) truco ♦ *vt* (*gen*) evadir; (*blow*) esquivar ♦ *vi* escabullirse; (*SPORT*) hacer una finta; **to ~ out of the way** echarse a un lado; **to ~through the traffic** esquivar el tráfico.
dodgems ['dɔdʒəmz] *npl* (*BRIT*) autos *or* coches *mpl* de choque.
dodgy ['dɔdʒɪ] (*col*) *adj* (*uncertain*) dudoso; (*shady*) sospechoso; (*risky*) arriesgado.
DOE *n abbr* (*BRIT*) = **Department of the Environment**; (*US*) = *Department of Energy.*
doe [dəʊ] *n* (*deer*) cierva, gama; (*rabbit*) coneja.
does [dʌz] *vb see* **do.**
doesn't ['dʌznt] = **does not.**
dog [dɔg] *n* perro ♦ *vt* seguir (de cerca); (*fig: memory etc*) perseguir; **to go to the ~s** (*person*) echarse a perder; (*nation etc*) ir a la ruina.
dog biscuit *n* galleta de perro.
dog collar *n* collar *m* de perro; (*fig*) alzacuello(s) *msg*.
dog-eared ['dɔgɪəd] *adj* sobado; (*page*) con la esquina doblada.
dogfish ['dɔgfɪʃ] *n* cazón *m*, perro marino.
dog food *n* comida para perros.
dogged ['dɔgɪd] *adj* tenaz, obstinado.
doggy ['dɔgɪ] *n* (*col*) perrito.
doggy bag *n* bolsa para llevarse las sobras de la comida.
dogma ['dɔgmə] *n* dogma *m*.
dogmatic [dɔg'mætɪk] *adj* dogmático.
do-gooder [duː'gudə*] *n* (*col pej*): **to be a ~** ser una persona bien intencionada *or* un filantropista.
dogsbody ['dɔgzbɔdɪ] *n* (*BRIT*) burro de carga.
doily ['dɔɪlɪ] *n* pañito de adorno.
doing ['duːɪŋ] *n*: **this is your ~** esto es obra tuya.
doings ['duːɪŋz] *npl* (*events*) sucesos *mpl*; (*acts*) hechos *mpl*.
do-it-yourself [duːɪtjɔː'sɛlf] *n* bricolaje *m*.
doldrums ['dɔldrəmz] *npl*: **to be in the ~** (*person*) estar abatido; (*business*) estar estancado.
dole [dəʊl] *n* (*BRIT: payment*) subsidio de paro; **on the ~** parado.
▶**dole out** *vt* repartir.
doleful ['dəʊlful] *adj* triste, lúgubre.

doll [dɔl] n muñeca.
▶**doll up** vt: **to ~ o.s. up** ataviarse.
dollar ['dɔlə*] n dólar m.
dollop ['dɔləp] n buena cucharada.
dolly ['dɔlɪ] n muñeca.
dolphin ['dɔlfɪn] n delfín m.
domain [də'meɪn] n (fig) campo,
competencia; (land) dominios mpl.
dome [dəum] n (ARCH) cúpula; (shape)
bóveda.
domestic [də'mestɪk] adj (animal, duty)
doméstico; (flight, news, policy) nacional.
domesticated [də'mestɪkeɪtɪd] adj
domesticado; (person: home-loving)
casero, hogareño.
domesticity [dəumes'tɪsɪtɪ] n vida casera.
domestic servant n sirviente/a m/f.
domicile ['dɔmɪsaɪl] n domicilio.
dominant ['dɔmɪnənt] adj dominante.
dominate ['dɔmɪneɪt] vt dominar.
domination [dɔmɪ'neɪʃən] n dominación f.
domineering [dɔmɪ'nɪərɪŋ] adj dominante.
Dominican Republic [də'mɪnɪkən-] n
República Dominicana.
dominion [də'mɪnɪən] n dominio.
domino, pl **~es** ['dɔmɪnəu] n ficha de
dominó.
dominoes ['dɔmɪnəuz] n (game) dominó.
don [dɔn] n (BRIT) profesor(a) m/f de
universidad.
donate [də'neɪt] vt donar.
donation [də'neɪʃən] n donativo.
done [dʌn] pp of **do.**
donkey ['dɔŋkɪ] n burro.
donkey-work ['dɔŋkɪwɔːk] n (BRIT col)
trabajo pesado.
donor ['dəunə*] n donante m/f.
donor card n carnet m de donante de
órganos.
don't [dəunt] = **do not.**
donut ['dəunʌt] n (US) = **doughnut.**
doodle ['duːdl] n garabato ♦ vi pintar
dibujitos or garabatos.
doom [duːm] n (fate) suerte f; (death)
muerte f ♦ vt: **to be ~ed to failure** estar
condenado al fracaso.
doomsday ['duːmzdeɪ] n día m del juicio
final.
door [dɔː*] n puerta; (of car) portezuela;
(entry) entrada; **from ~ to ~** de puerta en
puerta.
doorbell ['dɔːbel] n timbre m.
door handle n tirador m; (of car) manija.
door knocker n aldaba.
doorman ['dɔːmən] n (in hotel) portero.
doormat ['dɔːmæt] n felpudo, estera.
doorstep ['dɔːstep] n peldaño; **on your ~**
en la puerta de casa; (fig) al lado de casa.

door-to-door ['dɔːtə'dɔː*] adj: **~ selling**
venta a domicilio.
doorway ['dɔːweɪ] n entrada, puerta; **in the
~** en la puerta.
dope [dəup] n (col: person) imbécil m/f;
(: information) información f, informes mpl
♦ vt (horse etc) drogar.
dopey ['dəupɪ] adj atontado.
dormant ['dɔːmənt] adj inactivo; (latent)
latente.
dormer ['dɔːmə*] n (also: **~ window**)
buhardilla.
dormitory ['dɔːmɪtrɪ] n (BRIT) dormitorio;
(US: hall of residence) residencia, colegio
mayor.
dormouse, pl **dormice** ['dɔːmaus, -maɪs] n
lirón m.
Dors abbr (BRIT) = **Dorset.**
DOS n abbr see **disk operating system.**
dosage ['dəusɪdʒ] n (on medicine bottle)
dosis f inv, dosificación f.
dose [dəus] n (of medicine) dosis f inv; **a ~ of
flu** un ataque de gripe ♦ vt: **to ~ o.s. with**
automedicarse con.
dosser ['dɔsə*] n (BRIT col) mendigo/a; (lazy
person) vago/a.
doss house ['dɔs-] n (BRIT) pensión f de
mala muerte.
dossier ['dɔsɪeɪ] n: **~ (on)** expediente m
(sobre).
DOT n abbr (US: = Department of
Transportation) ministerio de transporte.
dot [dɔt] n punto; **~ted with** salpicado de;
on the ~ en punto.
dot command n (COMPUT) instrucción f
(precedida) de punto.
dote [dəut]: **to ~ on** vt fus adorar, idolatrar.
dot-matrix printer [dɔt'meɪtrɪks-] n
impresora matricial or de matriz.
dotted line ['dɔtɪd-] n línea de puntos; **to
sign on the ~** firmar.
dotty ['dɔtɪ] adj (col) disparatado, chiflado.
double ['dʌbl] adj doble ♦ adv (twice): **to
cost ~** costar el doble ♦ n (gen) doble m
♦ vt doblar; (efforts) redoblar ♦ vi
doblarse; (have two uses etc): **to ~ as**
hacer las veces de; **~ five two six (5526)**
(TELEC) cinco cinco dos seis; **spelt with a
~ "s"** escrito con dos "eses"; **on the ~,**
(BRIT) **at the ~** corriendo.
▶**double back** vi (person) volver sobre sus
pasos.
▶**double up** vi (bend over) doblarse; (share
bedroom) compartir.
double bass n contrabajo.
double bed n cama matrimonial.
double-breasted ['dʌbl'brestɪd] adj
cruzado.

double-check ['dʌbltʃɛk] vt volver a revisar ♦ vi: **I'll ~** voy a revisarlo otra vez.

double cream n nata enriquecida.

doublecross ['dʌbl'krɔs] vt (*trick*) engañar; (*betray*) traicionar.

doubledecker ['dʌbl'dɛkə*] n autobús m de dos pisos.

double glazing n (*BRIT*) doble acristalamiento.

double indemnity n doble indemnización f.

double-page ['dʌblpeɪdʒ] adj: **~ spread** doble página.

double room n cuarto para dos.

doubles ['dʌblz] n (*TENNIS*) juego de dobles.

double time n tarifa doble.

double whammy [-'wæmɪ] n (*col*) palo doble.

doubly ['dʌblɪ] adv doblemente.

doubt [daut] n duda ♦ vt dudar; (*suspect*) dudar de; **to ~ that** dudar que; **there is no ~ that** no cabe duda de que; **without (a) ~** sin duda (alguna); **beyond ~** fuera de duda; **I ~ it very much** lo dudo mucho.

doubtful ['dautful] adj dudoso; (*person*) sospechoso; **to be ~ about sth** tener dudas sobre algo; **I'm a bit ~** no estoy convencido.

doubtless ['dautlɪs] adv sin duda.

dough [dəu] n masa, pasta; (*col*: *money*) pasta, lana (*LAM*).

doughnut ['dəunʌt] n buñuelo.

douse [daus] vt (*drench*: *with water*) mojar; (*extinguish*: *flames*) apagar.

dove [dʌv] n paloma.

Dover ['dəuvə*] n Dover.

dovetail ['dʌvteɪl] vi (*fig*) encajar.

dowager ['dauɪdʒə*] n: **~ duchess** duquesa viuda.

dowdy ['daudɪ] adj desaliñado; (*inelegant*) poco elegante.

Dow-Jones average ['daudʒəunz-] n (*US*) índice m Dow-Jones.

Dow-Jones Index n (*US*) índice m Dow-Jones.

down [daun] n (*fluff*) pelusa; (*feathers*) plumón m, flojel m; (*hill*) loma ♦ adv (*~wards*) abajo, hacia abajo; (*on the ground*) por/en tierra ♦ prep abajo ♦ vt (*col*: *drink*) beberse, tragar(se); **~ with X!** ¡abajo X!; **~ there** allí abajo; **~ here** aquí abajo; **I'll be ~ in a minute** ahora bajo; **England is two goals ~** Inglaterra está perdiendo por dos tantos; **I've been ~ with flu** he estado con gripe; **the price of meat is ~** ha bajado el precio de la carne;

I've got it ~ in my diary lo he apuntado en mi agenda; **to pay £2 ~** dejar £2 de depósito; **he went ~ the hill** fue cuesta abajo; **~ under** (*in Australia etc*) en Australia/Nueva Zelanda; **to ~ tools** (*fig*) declararse en huelga.

down-and-out ['daunəndaut] n (*tramp*) vagabundo/a.

down-at-heel ['daunət'hi:l] adj venido a menos; (*appearance*) desaliñado.

downbeat ['daunbi:t] n (*MUS*) compás m ♦ adj (*gloomy*) pesimista.

downcast ['daunkɑ:st] adj abatido.

downer ['daunə*] n (*col*: *drug*) tranquilizante; **to be on a ~** estar pasando un mal bache.

downfall ['daunfɔ:l] n caída, ruina.

downgrade [daun'greɪd] vt (*job*) degradar; (*hotel*) bajar de categoría a.

downhearted [daun'hɑ:tɪd] adj desanimado.

downhill [daun'hɪl] adv: **to go ~** ir cuesta abajo; (*business*) estar en declive.

Downing Street *es la calle de Londres en la que tienen su residencia oficial tanto el Primer Ministro (***Prime Minister***) como el Ministro de Economía (***Chancellor of the Exchequer***). El primero vive en el nº10 y el segundo en el nº11. Es una calle cerrada al público que se encuentra en el barrio de Westminster, en el centro de Londres.*
*****Downing Street** se usa también en lenguaje periodístico para referirse al jefe del gobierno británico.*

download ['daunləud] vt (*COMPUT*) transferir, telecargar.

down-market ['daun'mɑ:kɪt] adj de escasa calidad.

down payment n entrada, pago al contado.

downplay ['daunpleɪ] vt (*US*) quitar importancia a.

downpour ['daunpɔ:*] n aguacero.

downright ['daunraɪt] adj (*nonsense*, *lie*) manifiesto; (*refusal*) terminante.

downsize [daun'saɪz] vt reducir la plantilla de.

Down's syndrome [daunz-] n síndrome m de Down.

downstairs [daun'stɛəz] adv (*below*) (en el piso de) abajo; (*motion*) escaleras abajo; **to come** (*or* **go**) **~** bajar la escalera.

downstream [daun'stri:m] adv aguas *or* río abajo.

downtime ['dauntaɪm] n (*COMM*) tiempo inactivo.

down-to-earth [dauntu'ə:θ] *adj* práctico.
downtown [daun'taun] *adv* en el centro de la ciudad.
downtrodden ['dauntrɔdn] *adj* oprimido.
downward ['daunwəd] *adv* hacia abajo
♦ *adj*: **a ~ trend** una tendencia descendente.
downward(s) ['daunwəd(z)] *adv* hacia abajo; **face ~s** (*person*) boca abajo; (*object*) cara abajo.
dowry ['dauri] *n* dote *f*.
doz. *abbr* = **dozen.**
doze [dəuz] *vi* dormitar.
▶**doze off** *vi* echar una cabezada.
dozen ['dʌzn] *n* docena; **a ~ books** una docena de libros; **~s of** cantidad de; **~s of times** cantidad de veces; **80p a ~** 80 peniques la docena.
DPh., D. Phil. *n abbr* (= *Doctor of Philosophy*) título universitario.
DPP *n abbr* (*BRIT*) = **Director of Public Prosecutions.**
DPT *n abbr* (= *diphtheria, pertussis, tetanus*) vacuna trivalente.
DPW *n abbr* (*US*: = *Department of Public Works*) ministerio de obras públicas.
Dr, Dr. *abbr* (= *doctor*) Dr.
Dr. *abbr* (*in street names*) = **Drive.**
dr *abbr* (*COMM*) = **debtor.**
drab [dræb] *adj* gris, monótono.
draft [drɑːft] *n* (*first copy: of document, report*) borrador *m*; (*COMM*) giro; (*US: call-up*) quinta ♦ *vt* (*write roughly*) hacer un borrador de; *see also* **draught.**
draftsman ['drɑːftsmən] *etc* (*US*) = **draughtsman** *etc.*
drag [dræg] *vt* arrastrar; (*river*) dragar, rastrear ♦ *vi* arrastrarse por el suelo ♦ *n* (*AVIAT: resistance*) resistencia aerodinámica; (*col*) lata; (*women's clothing*): **in ~** travestido.
▶**drag away** *vt*: **to ~ away (from)** separar a rastras (de).
▶**drag on** *vi* ser interminable.
dragnet ['drægnet] *n* (*NAUT*) rastra; (*fig*) emboscada.
dragon ['drægən] *n* dragón *m*.
dragonfly ['drægənflaɪ] *n* libélula.
dragoon [drə'guːn] *n* (*cavalryman*) dragón *m* ♦ *vt*: **to ~ sb into doing sth** forzar a algn a hacer algo.
drain [dreɪn] *n* desaguadero; (*in street*) sumidero; (*~ cover*) rejilla del sumidero ♦ *vt* (*land, marshes*) desecar; (*MED*) drenar; (*reservoir*) desecar; (*fig*) agotar ♦ *vi* escurrirse; **to be a ~ on** consumir, agotar; **to feel ~ed (of energy)** (*fig*) sentirse agotado.
drainage ['dreɪnɪdʒ] *n* (*act*) desagüe *m*;

(*MED, AGR*) drenaje *m*; (*sewage*) alcantarillado.
draining board ['dreɪnɪŋ-], (*US*) **drainboard** ['dreɪnbɔːd] *n* escurridero, escurridor *m*.
drainpipe ['dreɪnpaɪp] *n* tubo de desagüe.
drake [dreɪk] *n* pato (macho).
dram [dræm] *n* (*drink*) traguito, copita.
drama ['drɑːmə] *n* (*art*) teatro; (*play*) drama *m*.
dramatic [drə'mætɪk] *adj* dramático.
dramatist ['dræmətɪst] *n* dramaturgo/a.
dramatize ['dræmətaɪz] *vt* (*events etc*) dramatizar; (*adapt: novel: for TV, cinema*) adaptar.
drank [dræŋk] *pt of* **drink.**
drape [dreɪp] *vt* cubrir.
draper ['dreɪpə*] *n* (*BRIT*) pañero, mercero.
drapes [dreɪps] *npl* (*US*) cortinas *fpl*.
drastic ['dræstɪk] *adj* (*measure, reduction*) severo; (*change*) radical.
draught, (*US*) **draft** [drɑːft] *n* (*of air*) corriente *f* de aire; (*drink*) trago; (*NAUT*) calado; **on ~** (*beer*) de barril.
draught beer *n* cerveza de barril.
draughtboard ['drɑːftbɔːd] (*BRIT*) *n* tablero de damas.
draughts [drɑːfts] *n* (*BRIT*) juego de damas.
draughtsman, (*US*) **draftsman** ['drɑːftsmən] *n* proyectista *m*, delineante *m*.
draughtsmanship, (*US*) **draftsmanship** ['drɑːftsmənʃɪp] *n* (*drawing*) dibujo lineal; (*skill*) habilidad *f* para el dibujo.
draw [drɔː] *vb* (*pt* **drew**, *pp* **drawn** [druː, drɔːn]) *vt* (*pull*) tirar; (*take out*) sacar; (*attract*) atraer; (*picture*) dibujar; (*money*) retirar; (*formulate: conclusion*): **to ~ (from)** sacar (de); (*comparison, distinction*): **to ~ (between)** hacer (entre) ♦ *vi* (*SPORT*) empatar ♦ *n* (*SPORT*) empate *m*; (*lottery*) sorteo; (*attraction*) atracción *f*; **to ~ near** *vi* acercarse.
▶**draw back** *vi*: **to ~ back (from)** echarse atrás (de).
▶**draw in** *vi* (*car*) aparcar; (*train*) entrar en la estación.
▶**draw on** *vt* (*resources*) utilizar, servirse de; (*imagination, person*) recurrir a.
▶**draw out** *vi* (*lengthen*) alargarse.
▶**draw up** *vi* (*stop*) pararse ♦ *vt* (*document*) redactar; (*plans*) trazar.
drawback ['drɔːbæk] *n* inconveniente *m*, desventaja.
drawbridge ['drɔːbrɪdʒ] *n* puente *m* levadizo.
drawee [drɔː'iː] *n* girado, librado.
drawer [drɔː*] *n* cajón *m*; (*of cheque*)

librador(a) *m/f*.
drawing ['drɔːɪŋ] *n* dibujo.
drawing board *n* tablero (de dibujante).
drawing pin *n* (*BRIT*) chincheta *m*.
drawing room *n* salón *m*.
drawl [drɔːl] *n* habla lenta y cansina.
drawn [drɔːn] *pp of* **draw** ♦ *adj* (*haggard*: *with
tiredness*) ojeroso; (: *with pain*) macilento.
drawstring ['drɔːstrɪŋ] *n* cordón *m*.
dread [drɛd] *n* pavor *m*, terror *m* ♦ *vt* temer,
tener miedo *or* pavor a.
dreadful ['drɛdful] *adj* espantoso; **I feel ~!**
(*ill*) ¡me siento fatal *or* malísimo!;
(*ashamed*) ¡qué vergüenza!
dream [driːm] *n* sueño ♦ *vt, vi* (*pt, pp*
dreamed *or* **dreamt** [drɛmt]) soñar; **to
have a ~ about sb/sth** soñar con algn/
algo; **sweet ~s!** ¡que sueñes con los
angelitos!
▶**dream up** *vt* (*reason, excuse*) inventar;
(*plan, idea*) idear.
dreamer ['driːmə*] *n* soñador(a) *m/f*.
dream world *n* mundo imaginario *or* de
ensueño.
dreamy ['driːmɪ] *adj* (*person*) soñador(a),
distraído; (*music*) de sueño.
dreary ['drɪərɪ] *adj* monótono, aburrido.
dredge [drɛdʒ] *vt* dragar.
▶**dredge up** *vt* sacar con draga; (*fig*:
unpleasant facts) pescar, sacar a luz.
dredger ['drɛdʒə*] *n* (*ship, machine*) draga;
(: *CULIN*) tamiz *m*.
dregs [drɛgz] *npl* heces *fpl*.
drench [drɛntʃ] *vt* empapar; **~ed to the
skin** calado hasta los huesos.
dress [drɛs] *n* vestido; (*clothing*) ropa ♦ *vt*
vestir; (*wound*) vendar; (*CULIN*) aliñar;
(*shop window*) decorar, arreglar ♦ *vi*
vestirse; **to ~ o.s., get ~ed** vestirse; **she
~es very well** se viste muy bien.
▶**dress up** *vi* vestirse de etiqueta; (*in fancy
dress*) disfrazarse.
dress circle *n* (*BRIT*) principal *m*.
dress designer *n* modisto/a.
dresser ['drɛsə*] *n* (*furniture*) aparador *m*;
(: *US*) tocador *m*; (*THEAT*) camarero/a.
dressing ['drɛsɪŋ] *n* (*MED*) vendaje *m*;
(*CULIN*) aliño.
dressing gown *n* (*BRIT*) bata.
dressing room *n* (*THEAT*) camarín *m*;
(*SPORT*) vestidor *m*.
dressing table *n* tocador *m*.
dressmaker ['drɛsmeɪkə*] *n* modista,
costurera.
dressmaking ['drɛsmeɪkɪŋ] *n* costura.
dress rehearsal *n* ensayo general.
dress shirt *n* camisa de frac.
dressy ['drɛsɪ] *adj* (*col*) elegante.

drew [druː] *pt of* **draw**.
dribble ['drɪbl] *vi* gotear, caer gota a gota;
(*baby*) babear ♦ *vt* (*ball*) driblar, regatear.
dried [draɪd] *adj* (*gen*) seco; (*fruit*) paso;
(*milk*) en polvo.
drier ['draɪə*] *n* = **dryer**.
drift [drɪft] *n* (*of current etc*) velocidad *f*; (*of
sand*) montón *m*; (*of snow*) ventisquero;
(*meaning*) significado ♦ *vi* (*boat*) ir a la
deriva; (*sand, snow*) amontonarse; **to
catch sb's ~** cogerle el hilo a algn; **to let
things ~** dejar las cosas como están; **to ~
apart** (*friends*) seguir su camino; (*lovers*)
disgustarse, romper.
drifter ['drɪftə*] *n* vagabundo/a.
driftwood ['drɪftwud] *n* madera flotante.
drill [drɪl] *n* taladro; (*bit*) broca; (*of dentist*)
fresa; (*for mining etc*) perforadora,
barrena; (*MIL*) instrucción *f* ♦ *vt* perforar,
taladrar; (*soldiers*) ejercitar; (*pupils*: *in
grammar*) hacer ejercicios con ♦ *vi* (*for oil*)
perforar.
drilling ['drɪlɪŋ] *n* (*for oil*) perforación *f*.
drilling rig *n* (*on land*) torre *f* de
perforación; (*at sea*) plataforma de
perforación.
drily ['draɪlɪ] *adv* secamente.
drink [drɪŋk] *n* bebida ♦ *vt, vi* (*pt* **drank**, *pp*
drunk) beber, tomar (*LAM*); **to have a ~**
tomar algo; tomar una copa *or* un trago;
a ~ of water un trago de agua; **to invite
sb for ~s** invitar a algn a tomar unas
copas; **there's food and ~ in the kitchen**
hay de comer y de beber en la cocina;
would you like something to ~? ¿quieres
beber *or* tomar algo?
▶**drink in** *vt* (*subj*: *person*: *fresh air*)
respirar; (*story, sight*) beberse.
drinkable ['drɪŋkəbl] *adj* (*not poisonous*)
potable; (*palatable*) aguantable.
drink-driving [drɪŋk'draɪvɪŋ] *n*: **to be
charged with ~** ser acusado de conducir
borracho *or* en estado de embriaguez.
drinker ['drɪŋkə*] *n* bebedor(a) *m/f*.
drinking ['drɪŋkɪŋ] *n* (*drunkenness*) beber *m*.
drinking fountain *n* fuente *f* de agua
potable.
drinking water *n* agua potable.
drip [drɪp] *n* (*act*) goteo; (*one ~*) gota; (*MED*)
gota a gota *m*; (*sound*: *of water etc*) goteo;
(*col*: *spineless person*) soso/a ♦ *vi* gotear,
caer gota a gota.
drip-dry ['drɪp'draɪ] *adj* (*shirt*) de lava y pon.
dripping ['drɪpɪŋ] *n* (*animal fat*) pringue *m*
♦ *adj*: **~ wet** calado.
drive [draɪv] *n* paseo (en coche); (*journey*)
viaje *m* (en coche); (*also*: **~way**) entrada;
(*street*) calle; (*energy*) energía, vigor *m*;

(PSYCH) impulso; (SPORT) ataque m; (COMPUT: also: **disk** ~) disc drive m ♦ vb (pt **drove,** pp **driven** [drəuv, 'drɪvn]) vt (car) conducir, manejar (LAM); (nail) clavar; (push) empujar; (TECH: motor) impulsar ♦ vi (AUT: at controls) conducir; (: travel) pasearse en coche; **to go for a** ~ dar una vuelta en coche; **it's 3 hours'** ~ **from London** es un viaje de 3 horas en coche desde Londres; **left-/right-hand** ~ conducción f a la izquierda/derecha; **front-/rear-wheel** ~ tracción f delantera/trasera; **sales** ~ promoción f de ventas; **to** ~ **sb mad** volverle loco a algn; **to** ~ **sb to (do) sth** empujar a algn a (hacer) algo; **he** ~**s a taxi** es taxista; **he** ~**s a Mercedes** tiene un Mercedes; **can you** ~? ¿sabes conducir or (LAM) manejar?; **to** ~ **at 50 km an hour** ir a 50km por hora.

▶**drive at** vt fus (fig: intend, mean) querer decir, insinuar.

▶**drive on** vi no parar, seguir adelante ♦ vt (incite, encourage) empujar.

drive-by ['draɪvbaɪ] n: ~ **shooting** tiroteo desde el coche.

drive-in ['draɪvɪn] adj (esp US): ~ **cinema** autocine m.

drivel ['drɪvl] n (col) tonterías fpl.

driven ['drɪvn] pp of **drive**.

driver ['draɪvə*] n conductor(a) m/f, chofer m (LAM); (of taxi) taxista m/f.

driver's license n (US) carnet m or permiso de conducir.

driveway ['draɪvweɪ] n camino de entrada.

driving ['draɪvɪŋ] n conducir m, manejar m (LAM) ♦ adj (force) impulsor(a).

driving instructor n instructor(a) m/f de autoescuela.

driving lesson n clase f de conducir.

driving licence n (BRIT) carnet m or permiso de conducir.

driving school n autoescuela.

driving test n examen m de conducir.

drizzle ['drɪzl] n llovizna, garúa (LAM) ♦ vi lloviznar.

droll [drəul] adj gracioso.

dromedary ['drɔmɪdərɪ] n dromedario.

drone [drəun] vi (bee, aircraft, engine) zumbar; (also: ~ **on**) murmurar sin interrupción ♦ n zumbido; (male bee) zángano.

drool [dru:l] vi babear; **to** ~ **over sb/sth** caérsele la baba por algn/algo.

droop [dru:p] vi (fig) decaer, desanimarse.

drop [drɔp] n (of water) gota; (fall: in price) bajada; (: in salary) disminución f ♦ vt (allow to fall) dejar caer; (voice, eyes, price) bajar; (set down from car) dejar ♦ vi (price,

temperature) bajar; (wind) calmarse, amainar; (numbers, attendance) disminuir; ~**s** npl (MED) gotas fpl; **cough** ~**s** pastillas fpl para la tos; **a** ~ **of 10%** una bajada del 10 por ciento; **to** ~ **anchor** echar el ancla; **to** ~ **sb a line** mandar unas líneas a algn.

▶**drop in** vi (col: visit): **to** ~ **in (on)** pasar por casa (de).

▶**drop off** vi (sleep) dormirse ♦ vt (passenger) bajar, dejar.

▶**drop out** vi (withdraw) retirarse.

droplet ['drɔplɪt] n gotita.

dropout ['drɔpaut] n (from society) marginado/a; (from university) estudiante m/f que ha abandonado los estudios.

dropper ['drɔpə*] n (MED) cuentagotas m inv.

droppings ['drɔpɪŋz] npl excremento sg.

dross [drɔs] n (coal, fig) escoria.

drought [draut] n sequía.

drove [drəuv] pt of **drive**.

drown [draun] vt (also: ~ **out**: sound) ahogar ♦ vi ahogarse.

drowse [drauz] vi estar medio dormido.

drowsy ['drauzɪ] adj soñoliento; **to be** ~ tener sueño.

drudge [drʌdʒ] n esclavo del trabajo.

drudgery ['drʌdʒərɪ] n trabajo pesado or monótono.

drug [drʌg] n (MED) medicamento, droga; (narcotic) droga ♦ vt drogar; **to be on** ~**s** drogarse; **he's on** ~**s** se droga.

drug addict n drogadicto/a.

druggist ['drʌgɪst] n (US) farmacéutico/a.

drug peddler n traficante m/f de drogas.

drugstore ['drʌgstɔ:*] n (US) tienda (de comestibles, periódicos y medicamentos).

drug trafficker n narcotraficante m/f.

drum [drʌm] n tambor m; (large) bombo; (for oil, petrol) bidón m ♦ vi tocar el tambor; (with fingers) tamborilear ♦ vt: **to** ~ **one's fingers on the table** tamborilear con los dedos sobre la mesa; ~**s** npl batería sg.

▶**drum up** vt (enthusiasm, support) movilizar, fomentar.

drummer ['drʌmə*] n (in military band) tambor m/f; (in jazz/pop group) batería m/f.

drumstick ['drʌmstɪk] n (MUS) palillo, baqueta; (chicken leg) muslo (de pollo).

drunk [drʌŋk] pp of **drink** ♦ adj borracho ♦ n (also: ~**ard**) borracho/a; **to get** ~ emborracharse.

drunken ['drʌŋkən] adj borracho.

drunkenness ['drʌŋkənnɪs] n embriaguez f.

dry [draɪ] adj seco; (day) sin lluvia; (climate) árido, seco; (humour) agudo; (uninteresting: lecture) aburrido, pesado

♦ *vt* secar; (*tears*) enjugarse ♦ *vi* secarse; on ~ land en tierra firme; to ~ one's hands/hair/eyes secarse las manos/el pelo/las lágrimas.

▶**dry up** *vi* (*supply, imagination etc*) agotarse; (*in speech*) atascarse.

dry-clean ['draɪˈkliːn] *vt* limpiar *or* lavar en seco; "~ only" (*on label*) "limpieza *or* lavado en seco".

dry-cleaner's ['draɪˈkliːnəz] *n* tintorería.

dry-cleaning ['draɪˈkliːnɪŋ] *n* lavado en seco.

dry dock *n* (*NAUT*) dique *m* seco.

dryer ['draɪə*] *n* (*for hair*) secador *m*; (*for clothes*) secadora.

dry goods *npl* (*COMM*) mercería *sg*.

dry goods store *n* (*US*) mercería.

dry ice *n* nieve *f* carbónica, hielo seco.

dryness ['draɪnɪs] *n* sequedad *f*.

dry rot *n* putrefacción *f*.

dry run *n* (*fig*) ensayo.

dry ski slope *n* pista artificial de esquí.

DSc *n abbr* (= *Doctor of Science*) título universitario.

DST *n abbr* (*US*: = *Daylight Saving Time*) hora de verano.

DT *n abbr* (*COMPUT*) = **data transmission**.

DTI *n abbr* (*BRIT*) = *Department of Trade and Industry*.

DTP *n abbr* = **desktop publishing**.

DT's *n abbr* (*col*: = *delirium tremens*) delirium *m* tremens.

dual ['djuəl] *adj* doble.

dual carriageway *n* (*BRIT*) ≈ autovía.

dual-control ['djuəlkən'trəul] *adj* de doble mando.

dual nationality *n* doble nacionalidad *f*.

dual-purpose ['djuəl'pɜ:pəs] *adj* de doble uso.

dubbed [dʌbd] *adj* (*CINE*) doblado.

dubious ['djuːbɪəs] *adj* indeciso; (*reputation, company*) dudoso; (*character*) sospechoso; I'm very ~ about it tengo mis dudas sobre ello.

Dublin ['dʌblɪn] *n* Dublín.

Dubliner ['dʌblɪnə*] *n* dublinés/esa *m/f*.

duchess ['dʌtʃɪs] *n* duquesa.

duck [dʌk] *n* pato ♦ *vi* agacharse ♦ *vt* (*plunge in water*) zambullir.

duckling ['dʌklɪŋ] *n* patito.

duct [dʌkt] *n* conducto, canal *m*.

dud [dʌd] *n* (*shell*) obús *m* que no estalla; (*object, tool*): it's a ~ es una filfa ♦ *adj*: ~ cheque (*BRIT*) cheque *m* sin fondos.

due [djuː] *adj* (*proper*) debido; (*fitting*) conveniente, oportuno ♦ *adv*: ~ north derecho al norte; ~s *npl* (*for club, union*) cuota *sg*; (*in harbour*) derechos *mpl*; in ~ course a su debido tiempo; ~ to debido a; to be ~ to deberse a; the train is ~ to arrive at 8.00 el tren tiene (prevista) la llegada a las ocho; the rent's ~ on the 30th hay que pagar el alquiler el día 30; I am ~ 6 days' leave me deben 6 días de vacaciones; she is ~ back tomorrow ella debe volver mañana.

due date *n* fecha de vencimiento.

duel ['djuəl] *n* duelo.

duet [djuːˈɛt] *n* dúo.

duff [dʌf] *adj* sin valor.

duffel bag ['dʌfl-] *n* macuto.

duffel coat ['dʌfl-] *n* trenca.

dug [dʌg] *pt, pp of* **dig**.

dugout ['dʌgaut] *n* (*canoe*) piragua (*hecha de un solo tronco*); (*SPORT*) banquillo; (*MIL*) refugio subterráneo.

duke [djuːk] *n* duque *m*.

dull [dʌl] *adj* (*light*) apagado; (*stupid*) torpe; (*boring*) pesado; (*sound, pain*) sordo; (*weather, day*) gris ♦ *vt* (*pain, grief*) aliviar; (*mind, senses*) entorpecer.

duly ['djuːlɪ] *adv* debidamente; (*on time*) a su debido tiempo.

dumb [dʌm] *adj* mudo; (*stupid*) estúpido; to be struck ~ (*fig*) quedar boquiabierto.

dumbbell ['dʌmbɛl] *n* (*SPORT*) pesa.

dumbfounded [dʌmˈfaundɪd] *adj* pasmado.

dummy ['dʌmɪ] *n* (*tailor's model*) maniquí *m*; (*BRIT*: *for baby*) chupete *m* ♦ *adj* falso, postizo; ~ run ensayo.

dump [dʌmp] *n* (*heap*) montón *m* de basura; (*place*) basurero, vertedero; (*col*) tugurio; (*MIL*) depósito; (*COMPUT*) copia vaciada ♦ *vt* (*put down*) dejar; (*get rid of*) deshacerse de; (*COMPUT*) vaciar; (*COMM*: *goods*) inundar el mercado de; to be (down) in the ~s (*col*) tener murria, estar deprimido.

dumping ['dʌmpɪŋ] *n* (*ECON*) dumping *m*; (*of rubbish*): "no ~" "prohibido verter basura".

dumpling ['dʌmplɪŋ] *n bola de masa hervida*.

dumpy ['dʌmpɪ] *adj* regordete/a.

dunce [dʌns] *n* zopenco.

dune [djuːn] *n* duna.

dung [dʌŋ] *n* estiércol *m*.

dungarees [dʌŋgəˈriːz] *npl* mono *sg*, overol *msg* (*LAM*).

dungeon ['dʌndʒən] *n* calabozo.

dunk [dʌŋk] *vt* mojar.

duo ['djuːəu] *n* (*gen, MUS*) dúo.

duodenal [djuːəˈdiːnl] *adj* (*ulcer*) de duodeno.

duodenum [djuːəˈdiːnəm] *n* duodeno.

dupe [djuːp] *n* (*victim*) víctima ♦ *vt* engañar.

duplex ['dju:plɛks] *n* (*US: also:* ~ **apartment**) dúplex *m*.
duplicate ['dju:plɪkət] *n* duplicado; (*copy of letter etc*) copia ♦ *adj* (*copy*) duplicado ♦ *vt* ['dju:plɪkeɪt] duplicar; (*on machine*) multicopiar; **in** ~ por duplicado.
duplicate key *n* duplicado de una llave.
duplicating machine ['dju:plɪkeɪtɪŋ-], **duplicator** ['dju:plɪkeɪtə*] *n* multicopista *m*.
duplicity [dju:'plɪsɪtɪ] *n* doblez *f*, duplicidad *f*.
Dur *abbr* (*BRIT*) = Durham.
durability [djuərə'bɪlɪtɪ] *n* durabilidad *f*.
durable ['djuərəbl] *adj* duradero.
duration [djuə'reɪʃən] *n* duración *f*.
duress [djuə'rɛs] *n*: **under** ~ por coacción.
Durex ® ['djuərɛks] *n* (*BRIT*) preservativo.
during ['djuərɪŋ] *prep* durante.
dusk [dʌsk] *n* crepúsculo, anochecer *m*.
dusky ['dʌskɪ] *adj* oscuro; (*complexion*) moreno.
dust [dʌst] *n* polvo ♦ *vt* (*furniture*) desempolvar; (*cake etc*): **to** ~ **with** espolvorear de.
▶**dust off** *vt* (*also fig*) desempolvar, quitar el polvo de.
dustbin ['dʌstbɪn] *n* (*BRIT*) cubo de la basura, balde *m* (*LAM*).
dustbin liner *n* bolsa de basura.
duster ['dʌstə*] *n* paño, trapo; (*feather* ~) plumero.
dust jacket *n* sobrecubierta.
dustman ['dʌstmən] *n* (*BRIT*) basurero.
dustpan ['dʌstpæn] *n* cogedor *m*.
dust storm *n* vendaval *m* de polvo.
dusty ['dʌstɪ] *adj* polvoriento.
Dutch [dʌtʃ] *adj* holandés/esa ♦ *n* (*LING*) holandés *m* ♦ *adv*: **to go** ~ pagar a escote; **the** ~ *npl* los holandeses.
Dutch auction *n* subasta a la rebaja.
Dutchman ['dʌtʃmən], **Dutchwoman** ['dʌtʃwumən] *n* holandés/esa *m/f*.
dutiful ['dju:tɪful] *adj* (*child*) obediente; (*husband*) sumiso; (*employee*) cumplido.
duty ['dju:tɪ] *n* deber *m*; (*tax*) derechos *mpl* de aduana; (*MED: in hospital*) servicio, guardia; **on** ~ de servicio; (*at night etc*) de guardia; **off** ~ libre (de servicio); **to make it one's** ~ **to do sth** encargarse de hacer algo sin falta; **to pay** ~ **on sth** pagar los derechos sobre algo.
duty-free [dju:tɪ'fri:] *adj* libre de derechos de aduana; ~ **shop** tienda libre de impuestos.
duty officer *n* (*MIL etc*) oficial *m/f* de guardia.
duvet ['du:veɪ] *n* (*BRIT*) edredón *m*

(nórdico).
DV *abbr* (= *Deo volente*) Dios mediante.
DVLA *n abbr* (*BRIT*: = *Driver and Vehicle Licensing Agency*) organismo encargado de la expedición de permisos de conducir y matriculación de vehículos.
DVM *n abbr* (*US*: = *Doctor of Veterinary Medicine*) título universitario.
dwarf [dwɔ:f], *pl* **dwarves** [dwɔ:vz] *n* enano ♦ *vt* empequeñecer.
dwell [dwɛl], *pt, pp* **dwelt** [dwɛlt] *vi* morar.
▶**dwell on** *vt fus* explayarse en.
dweller ['dwɛlə*] *n* habitante *m*; **city** ~ habitante *m* de la ciudad.
dwelling ['dwɛlɪŋ] *n* vivienda.
dwelt [dwɛlt] *pt, pp of* **dwell**.
dwindle ['dwɪndl] *vi* menguar, disminuir.
dwindling ['dwɪndlɪŋ] *adj* (*strength, interest*) menguante; (*resources, supplies*) en disminución.
dye [daɪ] *n* tinte *m* ♦ *vt* teñir; **hair** ~ tinte *m* para el pelo.
dying ['daɪɪŋ] *adj* moribundo, agonizante; (*moments*) final; (*words*) último.
dyke [daɪk] *n* (*BRIT*) dique *m*; (*channel*) arroyo, acequia; (*causeway*) calzada.
dynamic [daɪ'næmɪk] *adj* dinámico.
dynamics [daɪ'næmɪks] *n or npl* dinámica *sg*.
dynamite ['daɪnəmaɪt] *n* dinamita ♦ *vt* dinamitar.
dynamo ['daɪnəməu] *n* dinamo *f or m* (*LAM*).
dynasty ['dɪnəstɪ] *n* dinastía.
dysentery ['dɪsɪntrɪ] *n* disentería.
dyslexia [dɪs'lɛksɪə] *n* dislexia.
dyslexic [dɪs'lɛksɪk] *adj, n* disléxico/a *m/f*.
dyspepsia [dɪs'pɛpsɪə] *n* dispepsia.
dystrophy ['dɪstrəfɪ] *n* distrofia; **muscular** ~ distrofia muscular.

E e

E, e [i:] *n* (*letter*) E, e *f*; (*MUS*) mi *m*; **E for Edward**, (*US*) **E for Easy** E de Enrique.
E *abbr* (= *east*) E ♦ *n abbr* (= *Ecstasy*) éxtasis *m*.
E111 *n abbr* (*also:* **form** ~) impreso E111.
ea. *abbr* = **each**.
E.A. *abbr* (*US*: = *educational age*) nivel escolar.
each [i:tʃ] *adj* cada *inv* ♦ *pron* cada uno; ~ **other** el uno al otro; **they hate** ~ **other** se

odian (entre ellos *or* mutuamente); ~ **day** cada día; **they have 2 books** ~ tienen 2 libros cada uno; **they cost £5** ~ cuestan cinco libras cada uno; ~ **of us** cada uno de nosotros.

eager ['iːɡəʳ] *adj* (*gen*) impaciente; (*hopeful*) ilusionado; (*keen*) entusiasmado; (: *pupil*) apasionado; **to be** ~ **to do sth** estar deseoso de hacer algo; **to be** ~ **for** ansiar, anhelar.

eagerly ['iːɡəlɪ] *adv* con impaciencia; con ilusión; con entusiasmo.

eagerness ['iːɡənɪs] *n* impaciencia; ilusión *f*; entusiasmo.

eagle ['iːɡl] *n* águila.

E and OE *abbr* = **errors and omissions excepted.**

ear [ɪəʳ] *n* oreja; (*sense of hearing*) oído; (*of corn*) espiga; **up to the** ~**s in debt** abrumado de deudas.

earache ['ɪəreɪk] *n* dolor *m* de oídos.

eardrum ['ɪədrʌm] *n* tímpano.

earful ['ɪəful] *n*: **to give sb an** ~ (*col*) echar una bronca a algn.

earl [əːl] *n* conde *m*.

early ['əːlɪ] *adv* (*gen*) temprano; (*ahead of time*) con tiempo, con anticipación ♦ *adj* (*gen*) temprano; (*reply*) pronto; (*man*) primitivo; (*first: Christians, settlers*) primero; **to have an** ~ **night** acostarse temprano; **in the** ~ *or* ~ **in the spring/ 19th century** a principios de primavera/ del siglo diecinueve; **you're** ~! ¡has llegado temprano *or* pronto!; ~ **in the morning/afternoon** a primeras horas de la mañana/tarde; **she's in her** ~ **forties** tiene poco más de cuarenta años; **at your earliest convenience** (*COMM*) con la mayor brevedad posible; **I can't come any earlier** no puedo llegar antes.

early retirement *n* jubilación *f* anticipada.

early warning system *n* sistema *m* de alerta inmediata.

earmark ['ɪəmaːk] *vt*: **to** ~ **for** reservar para, destinar a.

earn [əːn] *vt* (*gen*) ganar; (*interest*) devengar; (*praise*) ganarse; **to** ~ **one's living** ganarse la vida.

earned income *n* renta del trabajo.

earnest ['əːnɪst] *adj* serio, formal ♦ *n* (*also*: ~ **money**) anticipo, señal *f*; **in** ~ *adv* en serio.

earnings ['əːnɪŋz] *npl* (*personal*) ingresos *mpl*; (*of company etc*) ganancias *fpl*.

earphones ['ɪəfəunz] *npl* auriculares *mpl*.

earplugs ['ɪəplʌɡz] *npl* tapones *mpl* para los oídos.

earring ['ɪərɪŋ] *n* pendiente *m*, arete *m* (*esp*

LAM).

earshot ['ɪəʃɔt] *n*: **out of/within** ~ fuera del/al alcance del oído.

earth [əːθ] *n* (*gen*) tierra; (*BRIT: ELEC*) toma de tierra ♦ *vt* (*BRIT: ELEC*) conectar a tierra.

earthenware ['əːθnwɛəʳ] *n* loza (de barro).

earthly ['əːθlɪ] *adj* terrenal, mundano; ~ **paradise** paraíso terrenal; **there is no** ~ **reason to think** ... no existe razón para pensar ....

earthquake ['əːθkweɪk] *n* terremoto.

earth-shattering ['əːθʃætərɪŋ] *adj* trascendental.

earthworm ['əːθwəːm] *n* lombriz *f*.

earthy ['əːθɪ] *adj* (*fig: uncomplicated*) sencillo; (: *coarse*) grosero.

earwig ['ɪəwɪɡ] *n* tijereta.

ease [iːz] *n* facilidad *f*; (*comfort*) comodidad *f* ♦ *vt* (*task*) facilitar; (*pain*) aliviar; (*loosen*) soltar; (*relieve: pressure, tension*) aflojar; (*weight*) aligerar; (*help pass*): **to** ~ **sth in/ out** meter/sacar algo con cuidado ♦ *vi* (*situation*) relajarse; **with** ~ con facilidad; **to feel at** ~/**ill at** ~ sentirse a gusto/a disgusto; **at** ~! (*MIL*) ¡descansen!

►**ease off, ease up** *vi* (*work, business*) aflojar; (*person*) relajarse.

easel ['iːzl] *n* caballete *m*.

easily ['iːzɪlɪ] *adv* fácilmente.

easiness ['iːzɪnɪs] *n* facilidad *f*; (*of manners*) soltura.

east [iːst] *n* este *m*, oriente *m* ♦ *adj* del este, oriental ♦ *adv* al este, hacia el este; **the E~** el Oriente; (*POL*) el Este.

Easter ['iːstəʳ] *n* Pascua (de Resurrección).

Easter egg *n* huevo de Pascua.

Easter holidays *npl* Semana Santa *sg*.

Easter Island *n* Isla de Pascua.

easterly ['iːstəlɪ] *adj* (*to the east*) al este; (*from the east*) del este.

Easter Monday *n* lunes *m* de Pascua.

eastern ['iːstən] *adj* del este, oriental; **E~ Europe** Europa del Este; **the E~ bloc** (*POL*) los países del Este.

Easter Sunday *n* Domingo de Resurrección.

East Germany *n* (*formerly*) Alemania Oriental *or* del Este.

eastward(s) ['iːstwəd(z)] *adv* hacia el este.

easy ['iːzɪ] *adj* fácil; (*life*) holgado, cómodo; (*relaxed*) natural ♦ *adv*: **to take it** *or* **things** ~ (*not worry*) no preocuparse; (*go slowly*) tomarlo con calma; (*rest*) descansar; **payment on** ~ **terms** (*COMM*) facilidades de pago; **I'm** ~ (*col*) me da igual, no me importa; **easier said than done** del dicho al hecho hay buen trecho.

easy chair *n* butaca.
easy-going ['iːzɪ'gəʊɪŋ] *adj* acomodadizo.
easy touch [iːzɪ'tʌtʃ] *n*: **he's an ~** (*col*) es fácil de convencer.
eat, *pt* **ate,** *pp* **eaten** [iːt, eɪt, 'iːtn] *vt* comer.
▶**eat away** *vt* (*subj: sea*) desgastar; (: *acid*) corroer.
▶**eat into, eat away at** *vt fus* corroer.
▶**eat out** *vi* comer fuera.
▶**eat up** *vt* (*meal etc*) comerse; **it ~s up electricity** devora la electricidad.
eatable ['iːtəbl] *adj* comestible.
eau de Cologne [əʊdəkə'ləʊn] *n* (agua de) colonia.
eaves [iːvz] *npl* alero *sg*.
eavesdrop ['iːvzdrɒp] *vi*: **to ~ (on sb)** escuchar a escondidas *or* con disimulo (a algn).
ebb [ɛb] *n* reflujo ♦ *vi* bajar; (*fig: also:* **~ away**) decaer; **~ and flow** el flujo y reflujo; **to be at a low ~** (*fig: person*) estar de capa caída.
ebb tide *n* marea menguante.
ebony ['ɛbənɪ] *n* ébano.
ebullient [ɪ'bʌlɪənt] *adj* entusiasta, animado.
EC *n abbr* (= *European Community*) CE *f*.
eccentric [ɪk'sɛntrɪk] *adj, n* excéntrico/a.
ecclesiastical [ɪkliːzɪ'æstɪkəl] *adj* eclesiástico.
ECG *n abbr* (= *electrocardiogram*) E.C. *m*.
ECGD *n abbr* (= *Export Credits Guarantee Department*) *servicio de garantía financiera a la exportación*.
echo, **~es** ['ɛkəʊ] *n* eco *m* ♦ *vt* (*sound*) repetir ♦ *vi* resonar, hacer eco.
ECLA *n abbr* (= *Economic Commission for Latin America*) CEPAL *f*.
éclair ['eɪkleə*] *n* petisú *m*.
eclipse [ɪ'klɪps] *n* eclipse *m* ♦ *vt* eclipsar.
ECM *n abbr* (*US*: = *European Common Market*) MCE *m*.
eco- ['iːkəʊ] *pref* eco-.
eco-friendly ['iːkəʊfrɛndlɪ] *adj* ecológico.
ecological [iːkə'lɒdʒɪkl] *adj* ecológico.
ecologist [ɪ'kɒlədʒɪst] *n* ecologista *m/f*; (*scientist*) ecólogo/a *m/f*.
ecology [ɪ'kɒlədʒɪ] *n* ecología.
economic [iːkə'nɒmɪk] *adj* (*profitable: price*) económico; (: *business etc*) rentable.
economical [iːkə'nɒmɪkl] *adj* económico.
economically [iːkə'nɒmɪklɪ] *adv* económicamente.
economics [iːkə'nɒmɪks] *n* economía ♦ *npl* (*financial aspects*) finanzas *fpl*.
economic warfare *n* guerra económica.
economist [ɪ'kɒnəmɪst] *n* economista *m/f*.
economize [ɪ'kɒnəmaɪz] *vi* economizar,

ahorrar.
economy [ɪ'kɒnəmɪ] *n* economía; **economies of scale** economías *fpl* de escala.
economy class *n* (*AVIAT etc*) clase *f* turista.
economy size *n* tamaño familiar.
ecosystem ['iːkəʊsɪstəm] *n* ecosistema *m*.
eco-tourism [iːkəʊ'tʊərɪzm] *n* turismo verde *or* ecológico.
ECSC *n abbr* (= *European Coal and Steel Community*) CECA *f*.
ecstasy ['ɛkstəsɪ] *n* éxtasis *m inv*.
ecstatic [ɛks'tætɪk] *adj* extático, extasiado.
ECT *n abbr see* **electroconvulsive therapy.**
ECU, ecu *n abbr* (= *European Currency Unit*) ECU, ecu *m*.
Ecuador ['ɛkwədɔː*] *n* Ecuador *m*.
Ecuador(i)an [ɛkwə'dɔːr(ɪ)ən] *adj, n* ecuatoriano/a *m/f*.
ecumenical [iːkju'mɛnɪkl] *adj* ecuménico.
eczema ['ɛksɪmə] *n* eczema *m*.
eddy ['ɛdɪ] *n* remolino *m*.
Eden ['iːdn] *n* Edén *m*.
edge [ɛdʒ] *n* (*of knife etc*) filo; (*of object*) borde *m*; (*of lake etc*) orilla ♦ *vt* (*SEWING*) ribetear ♦ *vi*: **to ~ past** pasar con dificultad; **on ~** (*fig*) = **edgy; to ~ away from** alejarse poco a poco de; **to ~ forward** avanzar poco a poco; **to ~ up** subir lentamente.
edgeways ['ɛdʒweɪz] *adv*: **he couldn't get a word in ~** no pudo meter baza.
edging ['ɛdʒɪŋ] *n* (*SEWING*) ribete *m*; (*of path*) borde *m*.
edgy ['ɛdʒɪ] *adj* nervioso, inquieto.
edible ['ɛdɪbl] *adj* comestible.
edict ['iːdɪkt] *n* edicto.
edifice ['ɛdɪfɪs] *n* edificio.
edifying ['ɛdɪfaɪɪŋ] *adj* edificante.
Edinburgh ['ɛdɪnbərə] *n* Edimburgo.
edit ['ɛdɪt] *vt* (*be editor of*) dirigir; (*re-write*) redactar; (*cut*) cortar; (*COMPUT*) editar.
edition [ɪ'dɪʃən] *n* (*gen*) edición *f*; (*number printed*) tirada.
editor ['ɛdɪtə*] *n* (*of newspaper*) director(a) *m/f*; (*of book*) redactor(a) *m/f*; (*film ~*) montador(a) *m/f*.
editorial [ɛdɪ'tɔːrɪəl] *adj* editorial ♦ *n* editorial *m*; **~ staff** redacción *f*.
EDP *n abbr* (= *electronic data processing*) PED *m*.
EDT *n abbr* (*US*: = *Eastern Daylight Time*) *hora de verano de Nueva York*.
educate ['ɛdjukeɪt] *vt* (*gen*) educar; (*instruct*) instruir.
educated guess ['ɛdjukeɪtɪd-] *n* hipótesis *f* sólida.
education [ɛdju'keɪʃən] *n* educación *f*;

(*schooling*) enseñanza; (*SCOL: subject etc*) pedagogía; **primary/secondary** ~ enseñanza primaria/secundaria.
educational [ɛdjuˈkeɪʃənl] *adj* (*policy etc*) de educación, educativo; (*teaching*) docente; (*instructive*) educativo; ~ **technology** tecnología educacional.
Edwardian [ɛdˈwɔːdɪən] *adj* eduardiano.
E.E. *abbr* = **electrical engineer.**
EEC *n abbr* (= *European Economic Community*) CEE *f.*
EEG *n abbr see* **electroencephalogram.**
eel [iːl] *n* anguila.
EENT *n abbr* (*US MED*) = *eye, ear, nose and throat.*
EEOC *n abbr* (*US*: = *Equal Employment Opportunities Commission*) *comisión que investiga discriminación racial o sexual en el empleo.*
eerie [ˈɪərɪ] *adj* (*sound, experience*) espeluznante.
EET *n abbr* (= *Eastern European Time*) *hora de Europa oriental.*
efface [ɪˈfeɪs] *vt* borrar.
effect [ɪˈfɛkt] *n* efecto ♦ *vt* efectuar, llevar a cabo; ~**s** *npl* (*property*) efectos *mpl*; **to take** ~ (*law*) entrar en vigor *or* vigencia; (*drug*) surtir efecto; **in** ~ en realidad; **to have an** ~ **on sb/sth** hacerle efecto a algn/afectar algo; **to put into** ~ (*plan*) llevar a la práctica; **his letter is to the** ~ **that...** su carta viene a decir que....
effective [ɪˈfɛktɪv] *adj* (*gen*) eficaz; (*striking: display, outfit*) impresionante; (*real*) efectivo; **to become** ~ (*LAW*) entrar en vigor; ~ **date** fecha de vigencia.
effectively [ɪˈfɛktɪvlɪ] *adv* (*efficiently*) eficazmente; (*strikingly*) de manera impresionante; (*in reality*) en efecto.
effectiveness [ɪˈfɛktɪvnɪs] *n* eficacia.
effeminate [ɪˈfɛmɪnɪt] *adj* afeminado.
effervescent [ɛfəˈvɛsnt] *adj* efervescente.
efficacy [ˈɛfɪkəsɪ] *n* eficacia.
efficiency [ɪˈfɪʃənsɪ] *n* (*gen*) eficiencia; (*of machine*) rendimiento.
efficient [ɪˈfɪʃənt] *adj* eficiente; (*remedy, product, system*) eficaz; (*machine, car*) de buen rendimiento.
effigy [ˈɛfɪdʒɪ] *n* efigie *f.*
effluent [ˈɛfluənt] *n* vertidos *mpl.*
effort [ˈɛfət] *n* esfuerzo; **to make an** ~ **to do sth** estar deseoso de hacer algo.
effortless [ˈɛfətlɪs] *adj* sin ningún esfuerzo.
effrontery [ɪˈfrʌntərɪ] *n* descaro.
effusive [ɪˈfjuːsɪv] *adj* efusivo.
EFL *n abbr* (*SCOL*) = *English as a foreign language.*
EFTA [ˈɛftə] *n abbr* (= *European Free Trade*

Association) EFTA *f.*
e.g. *adv abbr* (= *exempli gratia*) p.ej.
egg [ɛg] *n* huevo; **hard-boiled/soft-boiled/ poached** ~ huevo duro *or* a la copa (*LAM*) *or* tibio (*LAM*)/pasado por agua/escalfado; **scrambled** ~**s** huevos revueltos.
▶**egg on** *vt* incitar.
eggcup [ˈɛgkʌp] *n* huevera.
eggnog [ˈɛgˈnɔg] *n* ponche *m* de huevo.
eggplant [ˈɛgplɑːnt] *n* (*esp US*) berenjena.
eggshell [ˈɛgʃɛl] *n* cáscara de huevo.
egg-timer [ˈɛgtaɪmə*] *n* reloj *m* de arena (*para cocer huevos*).
egg white *n* clara de huevo.
egg yolk *n* yema de huevo.
ego [ˈiːgəu] *n* ego.
egotism [ˈɛgəutɪzəm] *n* egoísmo.
egotist [ˈɛgəutɪst] *n* egoísta *m/f.*
ego trip *n*: **to be on an** ~ creerse el centro del mundo.
Egypt [ˈiːdʒɪpt] *n* Egipto.
Egyptian [ɪˈdʒɪpʃən] *adj, n* egipcio/a *m/f.*
eiderdown [ˈaɪdədaun] *n* edredón *m.*
eight [eɪt] *num* ocho.
eighteen [eɪˈtiːn] *num* dieciocho.
eighth [eɪtθ] *num* octavo.
eighty [ˈeɪtɪ] *num* ochenta.
Eire [ˈɛərə] *n* Eire *m.*
EIS *n abbr* (= *Educational Institute of Scotland*) *sindicato de profesores escoceses.*
either [ˈaɪðə*] *adj* cualquiera de los dos ...; (*both, each*) cada ♦ *pron*: ~ (**of them**) cualquiera (de los dos) ♦ *adv* tampoco ♦ *conj*: ~ **yes or no** o sí o no; **on** ~ **side** en ambos lados; **I don't like** ~ no me gusta ninguno de los dos; **no, I don't** ~ no, yo tampoco.
eject [ɪˈdʒɛkt] *vt* echar; (*tenant*) desahuciar ♦ *vi* eyectarse.
ejector seat [ɪˈdʒɛktə-] *n* asiento proyectable.
eke out [iːk-] *vt fus* (*money*) hacer que llegue.
EKG *n abbr* (*US*) *see* **electrocardiogram.**
el [ɛl] *n abbr* (*US col*) = **elevated railroad.**
elaborate *adj* [ɪˈlæbərɪt] (*design, pattern*) complicado ♦ *vb* [ɪˈlæbəreɪt] *vt* elaborar ♦ *vi* explicarse con muchos detalles.
elaborately [ɪˈlæbərɪtlɪ] *adv* de manera complicada; (*decorated*) profusamente.
elaboration [ɪlæbəˈreɪʃən] *n* elaboración *f.*
elapse [ɪˈlæps] *vi* transcurrir.
elastic [ɪˈlæstɪk] *adj, n* elástico.
elastic band *n* (*BRIT*) gomita.
elated [ɪˈleɪtɪd] *adj*: **to be** ~ estar eufórico.
elation [ɪˈleɪʃən] *n* euforia.
elbow [ˈɛlbəu] *n* codo ♦ *vt*: **to** ~ **one's way through the crowd** abrirse paso a

codazos por la muchedumbre.

elbow grease n (col): **to use some** or **a bit of** ~ menearse.

elder ['ɛldə*] adj mayor ♦ n (tree) saúco; (person) mayor; (of tribe) anciano.

elderly ['ɛldəlɪ] adj de edad, mayor ♦ npl: **the** ~ la gente mayor, los ancianos.

elder statesman n estadista m veterano; (fig) figura respetada.

eldest ['ɛldɪst] adj, n el/la mayor.

elect [ɪ'lɛkt] vt elegir; (choose): **to** ~ **to do** optar por hacer ♦ adj: **the president** ~ el presidente electo.

election [ɪ'lɛkʃən] n elección f; **to hold an** ~ convocar elecciones.

election campaign n campaña electoral.

electioneering [ɪlɛkʃə'nɪərɪŋ] n campaña electoral.

elector [ɪ'lɛktə*] n elector(a) m/f.

electoral [ɪ'lɛktərəl] adj electoral.

electoral college n colegio electoral.

electoral roll n censo electoral.

electorate [ɪ'lɛktərɪt] n electorado.

electric [ɪ'lɛktrɪk] adj eléctrico.

electrical [ɪ'lɛktrɪkl] adj eléctrico.

electrical engineer n ingeniero/a electricista.

electrical failure n fallo eléctrico.

electric blanket n manta eléctrica.

electric chair n silla eléctrica.

electric cooker n cocina eléctrica.

electric current n corriente f eléctrica.

electric fire n estufa eléctrica.

electrician [ɪlɛk'trɪʃən] n electricista m/f.

electricity [ɪlɛk'trɪsɪtɪ] n electricidad f; **to switch on/off the** ~ conectar/desconectar la electricidad.

electricity board n (BRIT) compañía eléctrica (estatal).

electric light n luz f eléctrica.

electric shock n electrochoque m.

electrification [ɪlɛktrɪfɪ'keɪʃən] n electrificación f.

electrify [ɪ'lɛktrɪfaɪ] vt (RAIL) electrificar; (fig: audience) electrizar.

electro... [ɪ'lɛktrəu] pref electro....

electrocardiogram (ECG, (US) EKG) [ɪ'lɛktrə'kɑːdɪəgræm] n electro-cardiograma m.

electrocardiograph [ɪ'lɛktrəu'kɑːdɪəgræf] n electrocardiógrafo.

electro-convulsive therapy (ECT) [ɪ'lɛktrəkən'vʌlsɪv-] n electroterapia.

electrocute [ɪ'lɛktrəukjuːt] vt electrocutar.

electrode [ɪ'lɛktrəud] n electrodo.

electroencephalogram (EEG) [ɪ'lɛktrəuɛn'sɛfələgræm] n electroencefalograma m.

electrolysis [ɪlɛk'trɒlɪsɪs] n electrólisis f inv.

electromagnetic [ɪ'lɛktrəmæg'nɛtɪk] adj electromagnético.

electron [ɪ'lɛktrɒn] n electrón m.

electronic [ɪlɛk'trɒnɪk] adj electrónico.

electronic data processing (EDP) n tratamiento or proceso electrónico de datos.

electronic mail n correo electrónico.

electronics [ɪlɛk'trɒnɪks] n electrónica.

electron microscope n microscopio electrónico.

electroplated [ɪ'lɛktrə'pleɪtɪd] adj galvanizado.

electrotherapy [ɪ'lɛktrə'θɛrəpɪ] n electroterapia.

elegance ['ɛlɪgəns] n elegancia.

elegant ['ɛlɪgənt] adj elegante.

elegy ['ɛlɪdʒɪ] n elegía.

element ['ɛlɪmənt] n (gen) elemento; (of heater, kettle etc) resistencia.

elementary [ɛlɪ'mɛntərɪ] adj elemental; (primitive) rudimentario; (school, education) primario.

En Estados Unidos y Canadá se llama **elementary school** al centro estatal en el que los niños reciben los primeros seis u ocho años de su educación, también llamado **grade school** o **grammar school**.

elephant ['ɛlɪfənt] n elefante m.

elevate ['ɛlɪveɪt] vt (gen) elevar; (in rank) ascender.

elevated railroad n (US) ferrocarril m urbano elevado.

elevation [ɛlɪ'veɪʃən] n elevación f; (rank) ascenso; (height) altitud f.

elevator ['ɛlɪveɪtə*] n (US) ascensor m, elevador m (LAM).

eleven [ɪ'lɛvn] num once.

elevenses [ɪ'lɛvnzɪz] npl (BRIT) ≈ café m de media mañana.

eleventh [ɪ'lɛvnθ] adj undécimo; **at the** ~ **hour** (fig) a última hora.

elf, pl **elves** [ɛlf, ɛlvz] n duende m.

elicit [ɪ'lɪsɪt] vt: **to** ~ **sth (from sb)** obtener algo (de algn).

eligible ['ɛlɪdʒəbl] adj cotizado; **to be** ~ **for a pension** tener derecho a una pensión.

eliminate [ɪ'lɪmɪneɪt] vt eliminar; (score out) suprimir; (a suspect, possibility) descartar.

elimination [ɪlɪmɪ'neɪʃən] n eliminación f; supresión f; **by process of** ~ por eliminación.

elite [eɪ'liːt] n élite f.

elitist [eɪ'liːtɪst] adj (pej) elitista.

elixir [ɪˈlɪksɪə*] n elixir m.
Elizabethan [ɪlɪzəˈbiːθən] adj isabelino.
elm [ɛlm] n olmo.
elocution [ɛləˈkjuːʃən] n elocución f.
elongated [ˈiːlɒŋgeɪtɪd] adj alargado.
elope [ɪˈləup] vi fugarse.
elopement [ɪˈləupmənt] n fuga.
eloquence [ˈɛləkwəns] n elocuencia.
eloquent [ˈɛləkwənt] adj elocuente.
else [ɛls] adv: **or ~** si no; **something ~** otra cosa or algo más; **somewhere ~** en otra parte; **everywhere ~** en los demás sitios; **everyone ~** todos los demás; **nothing ~** nada más; **is there anything ~ I can do?** ¿puedo hacer algo más?; **where ~?** ¿dónde más?, ¿en qué otra parte?; **there was little ~ to do** apenas quedaba otra cosa que hacer; **nobody ~ spoke** no habló nadie más.
elsewhere [ɛlsˈwɛə*] adv (be) en otra parte; (go) a otra parte.
ELT n abbr (SCOL) = English Language Teaching.
elucidate [ɪˈluːsɪdeɪt] vt esclarecer, elucidar.
elude [ɪˈluːd] vt eludir; (blow, pursuer) esquivar.
elusive [ɪˈluːsɪv] adj escurridizo; (answer) difícil de encontrar; **he is very ~** no es fácil encontrarlo.
elves [ɛlvz] npl of elf.
emaciated [ɪˈmeɪsɪeɪtɪd] adj escuálido.
E-Mail, e-mail [ˈiːmeɪl] n abbr (= electronic mail) correo electrónico ♦ vt: **to ~ sb** mandar un mensaje por correo electrónico a algn.
emanate [ˈɛməneɪt] vi emanar, provenir.
emancipate [ɪˈmænsɪpeɪt] vt emancipar.
emancipated [ɪˈmænsɪpeɪtɪd] adj liberado.
emancipation [ɪmænsɪˈpeɪʃən] n emancipación f, liberación f.
emasculate [ɪˈmæskjuleɪt] vt castrar; (fig) debilitar.
embalm [ɪmˈbɑːm] vt embalsamar.
embankment [ɪmˈbæŋkmənt] n (of railway) terraplén m; (riverside) dique m.
embargo, pl **~es** [ɪmˈbɑːgəu] n prohibición f; (COMM, NAUT) embargo; **to put an ~ on sth** poner un embargo en algo.
embark [ɪmˈbɑːk] vi embarcarse ♦ vt embarcar; **to ~ on** (journey) comenzar, iniciar; (fig) emprender.
embarkation [ɛmbɑːˈkeɪʃən] n (people) embarco; (goods) embarque m.
embarkation card n tarjeta de embarque.
embarrass [ɪmˈbærəs] vt avergonzar, dar vergüenza a; (financially etc) poner en un aprieto.

embarrassed [ɪmˈbærəst] adj azorado, violento; **to be ~** sentirse azorado or violento.
embarrassing [ɪmˈbærəsɪŋ] adj (situation) violento; (question) embarazoso.
embarrassment [ɪmˈbærəsmənt] n vergüenza, azoramiento; (financial) apuros mpl.
embassy [ˈɛmbəsɪ] n embajada; **the Spanish E~** la embajada española.
embed [ɪmˈbɛd] vt (jewel) empotrar; (teeth etc) clavar.
embellish [ɪmˈbɛlɪʃ] vt embellecer; (fig: story, truth) adornar.
embers [ˈɛmbəz] npl rescoldo sg, ascuas.
embezzle [ɪmˈbɛzl] vt desfalcar, malversar.
embezzlement [ɪmˈbɛzlmənt] n desfalco, malversación f.
embezzler [ɪmˈbɛzlə*] n malversador(a) m/f.
embitter [ɪmˈbɪtə*] vt (person) amargar; (relationship) envenenar.
embittered [ɪmˈbɪtəd] adj resentido, amargado.
emblem [ˈɛmbləm] n emblema m.
embody [ɪmˈbɒdɪ] vt (spirit) encarnar; (ideas) expresar.
embolden [ɪmˈbəuldən] vt envalentonar; (TYP) poner en negrita.
embolism [ˈɛmbəlɪzəm] n embolia.
emboss [ɪmˈbɒs] vt estampar en relieve; (metal, leather) repujar.
embossed [ɪmˈbɒst] adj realzado; **~ with ...** con ... en relieve.
embrace [ɪmˈbreɪs] vt abrazar, dar un abrazo a; (include) abarcar; (adopt: idea) adherirse a ♦ vi abrazarse ♦ n abrazo.
embroider [ɪmˈbrɔɪdə*] vt bordar; (fig: story) adornar, embellecer.
embroidery [ɪmˈbrɔɪdərɪ] n bordado.
embroil [ɪmˈbrɔɪl] vt: **to become ~ed (in sth)** enredarse (en algo).
embryo [ˈɛmbrɪəu] n (also fig) embrión m.
emcee [ɛmˈsiː] n (US) presentador(a) m/f.
emend [ɪˈmɛnd] vt (text) enmendar.
emerald [ˈɛmərəld] n esmeralda.
emerge [ɪˈmɜːdʒ] vi (gen) salir; (arise) surgir; **it ~s that** resulta que.
emergence [ɪˈmɜːdʒəns] n (of nation) surgimiento.
emergency [ɪˈmɜːdʒənsɪ] n (event) emergencia; (crisis) crisis f inv; **in an ~** en caso de urgencia; **(to declare a) state of ~** (declarar) estado de emergencia or de excepción.
emergency cord n (US) timbre m de alarma.

emergency exit *n* salida de emergencia.
emergency landing *n* aterrizaje *m* forzoso.
emergency lane *n* (*US*) arcén *m*.
emergency meeting *n* reunión *f* extraordinaria.
emergency service *n* servicio de urgencia.
emergency stop *n* (*AUT*) parada en seco.
emergent [ɪ'məːdʒənt] *adj* (*nation*) recientemente independizado.
emery board ['ɛmərɪ-] *n* lima de uñas.
emetic [ɪ'mɛtɪk] *n* vomitivo, emético.
emigrant ['ɛmɪgrənt] *n* emigrante *m/f*.
emigrate ['ɛmɪgreɪt] *vi* emigrar.
emigration [ɛmɪ'greɪʃən] *n* emigración *f*.
émigré ['ɛmɪgreɪ] *n* emigrado/a.
eminence ['ɛmɪnəns] *n* eminencia; **to gain** *or* **win** ~ ganarse fama.
eminent ['ɛmɪnənt] *adj* eminente.
eminently ['ɛmɪnəntlɪ] *adv* eminentemente.
emirate ['ɛmɪrɪt] *n* emirato.
emission [ɪ'mɪʃən] *n* emisión *f*.
emit [ɪ'mɪt] *vt* emitir; (*smell, smoke*) despedir.
emolument [ɪ'mɔljumənt] *n* (*often pl: formal*) honorario, emolumento.
emotion [ɪ'məuʃən] *n* emoción *f*.
emotional [ɪ'məuʃənl] *adj* (*person*) sentimental; (*scene*) conmovedor(a), emocionante.
emotionally [ɪ'məuʃnəlɪ] *adv* (*behave, speak*) con emoción; (*be involved*) sentimentalmente.
emotive [ɪ'məutɪv] *adj* emotivo.
empathy ['ɛmpəθɪ] *n* empatía; **to feel** ~ **with sb** sentirse identificado con algn.
emperor ['ɛmpərə*] *n* emperador *m*.
emphasis, *pl* **emphases** ['ɛmfəsɪs, -siːz] *n* énfasis *m inv*; **to lay** *or* **place** ~ **on sth** (*fig*) hacer hincapié en algo; **the** ~ **is on sport** se da mayor importancia al deporte.
emphasize ['ɛmfəsaɪz] *vt* (*word, point*) subrayar, recalcar; (*feature*) hacer resaltar.
emphatic [ɛm'fætɪk] *adj* (*condemnation*) enérgico; (*denial*) rotundo.
emphatically [ɛm'fætɪklɪ] *adv* con énfasis.
emphysema [ɛmfɪ'siːmə] *n* (*MED*) enfisema *m*.
empire ['ɛmpaɪə*] *n* imperio.
empirical [ɛm'pɪrɪkl] *adj* empírico.
employ [ɪm'plɔɪ] *vt* (*give job to*) emplear; (*make use of: thing, method*) emplear, usar; **he's ~ed in a bank** está empleado en un banco.
employee [ɪmplɔɪ'iː] *n* empleado/a.
employer [ɪm'plɔɪə*] *n* patrón/ona *m/f*;

(*businessman*) empresario/a.
employment [ɪm'plɔɪmənt] *n* empleo; **full** ~ pleno empleo; **without** ~ sin empleo; **to find** ~ encontrar trabajo; **place of** ~ lugar *m* de trabajo.
employment agency *n* agencia de colocaciones *or* empleo.
employment exchange *n* bolsa de trabajo.
empower [ɪm'pauə*] *vt*: **to** ~ **sb to do sth** autorizar a algn para hacer algo.
empress ['ɛmprɪs] *n* emperatriz *f*.
emptiness ['ɛmptɪnɪs] *n* vacío.
empty ['ɛmptɪ] *adj* vacío; (*street, area*) desierto; (*threat*) vano ♦ *n* (*bottle*) envase *m* ♦ *vt* vaciar; (*place*) dejar vacío ♦ *vi* vaciarse; (*house*) quedar(se) vacío *or* desocupado; (*place*) quedar(se) desierto; **to** ~ **into** (*river*) desembocar en.
empty-handed ['ɛmptɪ'hændɪd] *adj* con las manos vacías.
empty-headed ['ɛmptɪ'hɛdɪd] *adj* casquivano.
EMS *n abbr* (= *European Monetary System*) SME *m*.
EMT *n abbr* = *emergency medical technician*.
EMU *n abbr* (= *European Monetary Union*) UME *f*.
emulate ['ɛmjuleɪt] *vt* emular.
emulsion [ɪ'mʌlʃən] *n* emulsión *f*.
enable [ɪ'neɪbl] *vt*: **to** ~ **sb to do sth** (*allow*) permitir a algn hacer algo; (*prepare*) capacitar a algn para hacer algo.
enact [ɪn'ækt] *vt* (*law*) promulgar; (*play, scene, role*) representar.
enamel [ɪ'næməl] *n* esmalte *m*.
enamel paint *n* esmalte *m*.
enamoured [ɪ'næməd] *adj*: **to be** ~ **of** (*person*) estar enamorado de; (*activity etc*) tener gran afición a; (*idea*) aferrarse a.
encampment [ɪn'kæmpmənt] *n* campamento.
encase [ɪn'keɪs] *vt*: **to** ~ **in** (*contain*) encajar; (*cover*) cubrir.
encased [ɪn'keɪst] *adj*: ~ **in** (*covered*) revestido de.
enchant [ɪn'tʃɑːnt] *vt* encantar.
enchanting [ɪn'tʃɑːntɪŋ] *adj* encantador(a).
encircle [ɪn'səːkl] *vt* (*gen*) rodear; (*waist*) ceñir.
encl. *abbr* (= *enclosed*) adj.
enclave ['ɛnkleɪv] *n* enclave *m*.
enclose [ɪn'kləuz] *vt* (*land*) cercar; (*with letter etc*) adjuntar; (*in receptacle*) **to** ~ **(with)** encerrar (con); **please find ~d** le mandamos adjunto.
enclosure [ɪn'kləuʒə*] *n* cercado, recinto; (*COMM*) carta adjunta.

encoder [ɪn'kəudə*] n (*COMPUT*) codificador m.

encompass [ɪn'kʌmpəs] vt abarcar.

encore [ɔŋ'kɔː*] excl ¡otra!, ¡bis! ♦ n bis m.

encounter [ɪn'kauntə*] n encuentro ♦ vt encontrar, encontrarse con; (*difficulty*) tropezar con.

encourage [ɪn'kʌrɪdʒ] vt alentar, animar; (*growth*) estimular; **to ~ sb (to do sth)** animar a algn (a hacer algo).

encouragement [ɪn'kʌrɪdʒmənt] n estímulo; (*of industry*) fomento.

encouraging [ɪn'kʌrɪdʒɪŋ] adj alentador(a).

encroach [ɪn'krəutʃ] vi: **to ~ (up)on** (*gen*) invadir; (*time*) adueñarse de.

encrust [ɪn'krʌst] vt incrustar.

encrusted [ɪn'krʌstəd] adj: **~ with** recubierto de.

encumber [ɪn'kʌmbə*] vt: **to be ~ed with** (*carry*) estar cargado de; (*debts*) estar gravado de.

encyclop(a)edia [ɛnsaɪkləu'piːdɪə] n enciclopedia.

end [ɛnd] n (*gen, also aim*) fin m; (*of table*) extremo; (*of line, rope etc*) cabo; (*of pointed object*) punta; (*of town*) barrio; (*of street*) final m; (*SPORT*) lado ♦ vt terminar, acabar; (*also*: **bring to an ~, put an ~ to**) acabar con ♦ vi terminar, acabar; **to ~ (with)** terminar (con); **in the ~** al final; **to be at an ~** llegar a su fin; **at the ~ of the day** (*fig*) al fin y al cabo, a fin de cuentas; **to this ~, with this ~ in view** con este propósito; **from ~ to ~** de punta a punta; **on ~** (*object*) de punta, de cabeza; **to stand on ~** (*hair*) erizarse, ponerse de punta; **for hours on ~** hora tras hora.

▸**end up** vi: **to ~ up in** terminar en; (*place*) ir a parar a.

endanger [ɪn'deɪndʒə*] vt poner en peligro; **an ~ed species** (*of animal*) una especie en peligro de extinción.

endear [ɪn'dɪə*] vt: **to ~ o.s. to sb** ganarse la simpatía de algn.

endearing [ɪn'dɪərɪŋ] adj entrañable.

endearment [ɪn'dɪərmənt] n cariño, palabra cariñosa; **to whisper ~s** decir unas palabras cariñosas al oído; **term of ~** nombre m cariñoso.

endeavour, (*US*) **endeavor** [ɪn'dɛvə*] n esfuerzo; (*attempt*) tentativa ♦ vi: **to ~ to do** esforzarse por hacer; (*try*) procurar hacer.

endemic [ɛn'dɛmɪk] adj (*poverty, disease*) endémico.

ending ['ɛndɪŋ] n fin m, final m; (*of book*) desenlace m; (*LING*) terminación f.

endive ['ɛndaɪv] n (*curly*) escarola; (*smooth, flat*) endibia.

endless ['ɛndlɪs] adj interminable, inacabable; (*possibilities*) infinito.

endorse [ɪn'dɔːs] vt (*cheque*) endosar; (*approve*) aprobar.

endorsee [ɪndɔː'siː] n endorsatario/a.

endorsement [ɪn'dɔːsmənt] n (*approval*) aprobación f; (*signature*) endoso; (*BRIT: on driving licence*) nota de sanción.

endorser [ɪn'dɔːsə*] n avalista m/f.

endow [ɪn'dau] vt (*provide with money*) dotar; (*found*) fundar; **to be ~ed with** (*fig*) estar dotado de.

endowment [ɪn'daumənt] adj (*amount*) donación f.

endowment mortgage n hipoteca dotal.

endowment policy n póliza dotal.

end product n (*INDUSTRY*) producto final; (*fig*) resultado.

end result n resultado.

endurable [ɪn'djuərəbl] adj soportable, tolerable.

endurance [ɪn'djuərəns] n resistencia.

endurance test n prueba de resistencia.

endure [ɪn'djuə*] vt (*bear*) aguantar, soportar; (*resist*) resistir ♦ vi (*last*) perdurar; (*resist*) resistir.

enduring [ɪn'djuərɪŋ] adj duradero.

end user n (*COMPUT*) usuario final.

enema ['ɛnɪmə] n (*MED*) enema m.

enemy ['ɛnəmɪ] adj, n enemigo/a m/f; **to make an ~ of sb** enemistarse con algn.

energetic [ɛnə'dʒɛtɪk] adj enérgico.

energy ['ɛnədʒɪ] n energía.

energy crisis n crisis f energética.

energy-saving ['ɛnədʒɪseɪvɪŋ] adj (*policy*) para ahorrar energía; (*device*) que ahorra energía ♦ n ahorro de energía.

enervating ['ɛnəveɪtɪŋ] adj deprimente.

enforce [ɪn'fɔːs] vt (*LAW*) hacer cumplir.

enforced [ɪn'fɔːst] adj forzoso, forzado.

enfranchise [ɪn'fræntʃaɪz] vt (*give vote to*) conceder el derecho de voto a; (*set free*) emancipar.

engage [ɪn'geɪdʒ] vt (*attention*) captar; (*in conversation*) abordar; (*worker, lawyer*) contratar ♦ vi (*TECH*) engranar; **to ~ in** dedicarse a, ocuparse en; **to ~ sb in conversation** entablar conversación con algn; **to ~ the clutch** embragar.

engaged [ɪn'geɪdʒd] adj (*BRIT: busy, in use*) ocupado; (*betrothed*) prometido; **to get ~** prometerse; **he is ~ in research** se dedica a la investigación.

engaged tone n (*BRIT TEL*) señal f de comunicado.

engagement [ɪn'geɪdʒmənt] n

(*appointment*) compromiso, cita; (*battle*) combate *m*; (*to marry*) compromiso; (*period*) noviazgo; **I have a previous** ~ ya tengo un compromiso.

engagement ring *n* anillo de pedida.

engaging [ɪn'geɪdʒɪŋ] *adj* atractivo, simpático.

engender [ɪn'dʒɛndə*] *vt* engendrar.

engine ['ɛndʒɪn] *n* (*AUT*) motor *m*; (*RAIL*) locomotora.

engine driver *n* (*BRIT: of train*) maquinista *m/f*.

engineer [ɛndʒɪ'nɪə*] *n* ingeniero/a; (*BRIT: for repairs*) técnico/a; (*US RAIL*) maquinista *m/f*; **civil/mechanical** ~ ingeniero/a de caminos, canales y puertos/industrial.

engineering [ɛndʒɪ'nɪərɪŋ] *n* ingeniería ♦ *cpd* (*works, factory*) de componentes mecánicos.

engine failure, engine trouble *n* avería del motor.

England ['ɪŋglənd] *n* Inglaterra.

English ['ɪŋglɪʃ] *adj* inglés/esa ♦ *n* (*LING*) el inglés; **the** ~ *npl* los ingleses.

English Channel *n*: **the** ~ el Canal de la Mancha.

Englishman ['ɪŋglɪʃmən], **Englishwoman** ['ɪŋglɪʃwumən] *n* inglés/esa *m/f*.

English-speaker ['ɪŋglɪʃspi:kə*] *n* persona de habla inglesa.

English-speaking ['ɪŋglɪʃspi:kɪŋ] *adj* de habla inglesa.

engraving [ɪn'greɪvɪŋ] *n* grabado.

engrossed [ɪn'grəust] *adj*: ~ **in** absorto en.

engulf [ɪn'gʌlf] *vt* sumergir, hundir; (*subj: fire*) devorar.

enhance [ɪn'hɑ:ns] *vt* (*gen*) aumentar; (*beauty*) realzar; (*position, reputation*) mejorar.

enigma [ɪ'nɪgmə] *n* enigma *m*.

enigmatic [ɛnɪg'mætɪk] *adj* enigmático.

enjoy [ɪn'dʒɔɪ] *vt* (*have: health, fortune*) disfrutar de, gozar de; (*food*) comer con gusto; **I** ~ **doing...** me gusta hacer...; **to** ~ **o.s.** divertirse, pasarlo bien.

enjoyable [ɪn'dʒɔɪəbl] *adj* (*pleasant*) agradable; (*amusing*) divertido.

enjoyment [ɪn'dʒɔɪmənt] *n* (*use*) disfrute *m*; (*joy*) placer *m*.

enlarge [ɪn'lɑ:dʒ] *vt* aumentar; (*broaden*) extender; (*PHOT*) ampliar ♦ *vi*: **to** ~ **on** (*subject*) tratar con más detalles.

enlarged [ɪn'lɑ:dʒd] *adj* (*edition*) aumentado, (*MED: organ, gland*) dilatado.

enlargement [ɪn'lɑ:dʒmənt] *n* (*PHOT*) ampliación *f*.

enlighten [ɪn'laɪtn] *vt* informar, instruir.

enlightened [ɪn'laɪtnd] *adj* iluminado;

(*tolerant*) comprensivo.

enlightening [ɪn'laɪtnɪŋ] *adj* informativo, instructivo.

Enlightenment [ɪn'laɪtnmənt] *n* (*HISTORY*): **the** ~ la Ilustración, el Siglo de las Luces.

enlist [ɪn'lɪst] *vt* alistar; (*support*) conseguir ♦ *vi* alistarse; ~**ed man** (*US: MIL*) soldado raso.

enliven [ɪn'laɪvn] *vt* (*people*) animar; (*events*) avivar, animar.

enmity ['ɛnmɪtɪ] *n* enemistad *f*.

ennoble [ɪ'nəubl] *vt* ennoblecer.

enormity [ɪ'nɔ:mɪtɪ] *n* enormidad *f*.

enormous [ɪ'nɔ:məs] *adj* enorme.

enough [ɪ'nʌf] *adj*: ~ **time/books** bastante tiempo/bastantes libros ♦ *n*: **have you got** ~? ¿tiene usted bastante? ♦ *adv*: **big** ~ bastante grande; **he has not worked** ~ no ha trabajado bastante; (*that's*) ~! ¡basta ya!, ¡ya está bien!; **that's** ~, **thanks** con eso basta, gracias; **will 5 be** ~? ¿bastará con 5?; **I've had** ~ estoy harto; **he was kind** ~ **to lend me the money** tuvo la bondad *or* amabilidad de prestarme el dinero; ... **which, funnily** ~ ... ... lo que, por extraño que parezca ... .

enquire [ɪn'kwaɪə*] *vt, vi* = **inquire**.

enrage [ɪn'reɪdʒ] *vt* enfurecer.

enrich [ɪn'rɪtʃ] *vt* enriquecer.

enrol, (*US*) **enroll** [ɪn'rəul] *vt* (*members*) inscribir; (*SCOL*) matricular ♦ *vi* inscribirse; (*SCOL*) matricularse.

enrol(l)ment [ɪn'rəulmənt] *n* inscripción *f*; matriculación *f*.

en route [ɔn'ru:t] *adv* durante el viaje; ~ **for/from/to** camino de/de/a.

ensconce [ɪn'skɔns] *vt*: **to** ~ **o.s.** instalarse cómodamente, acomodarse.

ensemble [ɔn'sɔmbl] *n* (*MUS*) conjunto.

enshrine [ɪn'ʃraɪn] *vt* recoger.

ensign ['ɛnsaɪn] *n* (*flag*) bandera; (*NAUT*) alférez *m*.

enslave [ɪn'sleɪv] *vt* esclavizar.

ensue [ɪn'sju:] *vi* seguirse; (*result*) resultar.

ensuing [ɪn'sju:ɪŋ] *adj* subsiguiente.

ensure [ɪn'ʃuə*] *vt* asegurar.

ENT *n abbr* (= *Ear, Nose and Throat*) otorrinolaringología.

entail [ɪn'teɪl] *vt* (*imply*) suponer; (*result in*) acarrear.

entangle [ɪn'tæŋgl] *vt* (*thread etc*) enredar, enmarañar; **to become** ~**d in sth** (*fig*) enredarse en algo.

entanglement [ɪn'tæŋglmənt] *n* enredo.

enter ['ɛntə*] *vt* (*room, profession*) entrar en; (*club*) hacerse socio de; (*army*) alistarse en; (*sb for a competition*) inscribir; (*write down*) anotar, apuntar; (*COMPUT*) introducir ♦ *vi* entrar; **to ~ for** *vt fus* presentarse a; **to ~ into** *vt fus* (*relations*) establecer; (*plans*) formar parte de; (*debate*) tomar parte en; (*negotiations*) entablar; (*agreement*) llegar a, firmar; **to ~ (up)on** *vt fus* (*career*) emprender.

enteritis [ɛntəˈraɪtɪs] *n* enteritis *f.*

enterprise [ˈɛntəpraɪz] *n* empresa; (*spirit*) iniciativa; **free ~** la libre empresa; **private ~** la iniciativa privada.

enterprising [ˈɛntəpraɪzɪŋ] *adj* emprendedor(a).

entertain [ɛntəˈteɪn] *vt* (*amuse*) divertir; (*receive: guest*) recibir (en casa); (*idea*) abrigar.

entertainer [ɛntəˈteɪnə*] *n* artista *m/f.*

entertaining [ɛntəˈteɪnɪŋ] *adj* divertido, entretenido ♦ *n*: **to do a lot of ~** dar muchas fiestas, tener muchos invitados.

entertainment [ɛntəˈteɪnmənt] *n* (*amusement*) diversión *f*; (*show*) espectáculo; (*party*) fiesta.

entertainment allowance *n* (*COMM*) gastos *mpl* de representación.

enthral [ɪnˈθrɔːl] *vt* embelesar, cautivar.

enthralled [ɪnˈθrɔːld] *adj* cautivado.

enthralling [ɪnˈθrɔːlɪŋ] *adj* cautivador(a).

enthuse [ɪnˈθuːz] *vi*: **to ~ about** *or* **over** entusiasmarse por.

enthusiasm [ɪnˈθuːzɪæzəm] *n* entusiasmo.

enthusiast [ɪnˈθuːzɪæst] *n* entusiasta *m/f.*

enthusiastic [ɪnθuːzɪˈæstɪk] *adj* entusiasta; **to be ~ about sb/sth** estar entusiasmado con algn/algo.

entice [ɪnˈtaɪs] *vt* tentar; (*seduce*) seducir.

entire [ɪnˈtaɪə*] *adj* entero, todo.

entirely [ɪnˈtaɪəlɪ] *adv* totalmente.

entirety [ɪnˈtaɪərətɪ] *n*: **in its ~** en su totalidad.

entitle [ɪnˈtaɪtl] *vt*: **to ~ sb to sth** dar a algn derecho a algo.

entitled [ɪnˈtaɪtld] *adj* (*book*) titulado; **to be ~ to sth/to do sth** tener derecho a algo/a hacer algo.

entity [ˈɛntɪtɪ] *n* entidad *f.*

entourage [ɔntuˈrɑːʒ] *n* séquito.

entrails [ˈɛntreɪlz] *npl* entrañas *fpl*; (*US*) asadura *sg*, menudos *mpl.*

entrance [ˈɛntrəns] *n* entrada ♦ *vt* [ɪnˈtraːns] encantar, hechizar; **to gain ~ to** (*university etc*) ingresar en.

entrance examination *n* (*to school*) examen *m* de ingreso.

entrance fee *n* entrada.

entrance ramp *n* (*US AUT*) rampa de acceso.

entrancing [ɪnˈtraːnsɪŋ] *adj* encantador(a).

entrant [ˈɛntrənt] *n* (*in race, competition*) participante *m/f*; (*in exam*) candidato/a.

entreat [ɛnˈtriːt] *vt* rogar, suplicar.

entrenched [ɛnˈtrɛntʃd] *adj*: **~ interests** intereses *mpl* creados.

entrepreneur [ɔntrəprəˈnəː*] *n* empresario/a, capitalista *m/f.*

entrepreneurial [ɔntrəprəˈnəːrɪəl] *adj* empresarial.

entrust [ɪnˈtrʌst] *vt*: **to ~ sth to sb** confiar algo a algn.

entry [ˈɛntrɪ] *n* entrada; (*permission to enter*) acceso; (*in register, diary, ship's log*) apunte *m*; (*in account book, ledger, list*) partida; **no ~** prohibido el paso; (*AUT*) dirección prohibida; **single/double ~ book-keeping** contabilidad *f* simple/por partida doble.

entry form *n* boletín *m* de inscripción.

entry phone *n* (*BRIT*) portero automático.

E-number [ˈiːnʌmbə*] *n* número E.

enumerate [ɪˈnjuːməreɪt] *vt* enumerar.

enunciate [ɪˈnʌnsɪeɪt] *vt* pronunciar; (*principle etc*) enunciar.

envelop [ɪnˈvɛləp] *vt* envolver.

envelope [ˈɛnvələup] *n* sobre *m.*

enviable [ˈɛnvɪəbl] *adj* envidiable.

envious [ˈɛnvɪəs] *adj* envidioso; (*look*) de envidia.

environment [ɪnˈvaɪərnmənt] *n* medio ambiente; (*surroundings*) entorno; **Department of the E~** ministerio del medio ambiente.

environmental [ɪnvaɪərnˈmɛntl] *adj* (*medio*) ambiental; **~ studies** (*in school etc*) ecología *sg.*

environmentalist [ɪnvaɪərnˈmɛntlɪst] *n* ecologista *m/f.*

environmentally [ɪnvaɪərnˈmɛntlɪ] *adv*: **~ sound/friendly** ecológico.

envisage [ɪnˈvɪzɪdʒ] *vt* (*foresee*) prever; (*imagine*) concebir.

envision [ɪnˈvɪʒən] *vt* imaginar.

envoy [ˈɛnvɔɪ] *n* enviado/a.

envy [ˈɛnvɪ] *n* envidia ♦ *vt* tener envidia a; **to ~ sb sth** envidiar algo a algn.

enzyme [ˈɛnzaɪm] *n* enzima *m or f.*

EPA *n abbr* (*US*: = *Environmental Protection Agency*) Agencia del Medio Ambiente.

ephemeral [ɪˈfɛmərl] *adj* efímero.

epic [ˈɛpɪk] *n* epopeya ♦ *adj* épico.

epicentre, (US**) epicenter** [ˈɛpɪsɛntə*] *n* epicentro.

epidemic [ɛpɪˈdɛmɪk] *n* epidemia.

epigram [ˈɛpɪgræm] *n* epigrama *m.*

epilepsy [ˈɛpɪlɛpsɪ] *n* epilepsia.

epileptic [ɛpɪˈlɛptɪk] *adj, n* epiléptico/a *m/f.*

epilogue [ˈɛpɪlɔg] *n* epílogo.

episcopal [ɪ'pɪskəpl] *adj* episcopal.
episode ['epɪsəud] *n* episodio.
epistle [ɪ'pɪsl] *n* epístola.
epitaph ['epɪtɑːf] *n* epitafio.
epithet ['epɪθet] *n* epíteto.
epitome [ɪ'pɪtəmɪ] *n* arquetipo.
epitomize [ɪ'pɪtəmaɪz] *vt* representar.
epoch ['iːpɔk] *n* época.
eponymous [ɪ'pɔnɪməs] *adj* epónimo.
equable ['ekwəbl] *adj* (*climate*) estable; (*character*) ecuánime.
equal ['iːkwl] *adj* (*gen*) igual; (*treatment*) equitativo ♦ *n* igual *m/f* ♦ *vt* ser igual a; (*fig*) igualar; **to be ~ to** (*task*) estar a la altura de; **the E~ Opportunities Commission** (*BRIT*) comisión para la igualdad de la mujer en el trabajo.
equality [iː'kwɔlɪtɪ] *n* igualdad *f*.
equalize ['iːkwəlaɪz] *vt, vi* igualar; (*SPORT*) empatar.
equalizer ['iːkwəlaɪzə*] *n* igualada.
equally ['iːkwəlɪ] *adv* igualmente; (*share etc*) a partes iguales; **they are ~ clever** son tan listos uno como otro.
equals sign *n* signo igual.
equanimity [ekwə'nɪmɪtɪ] *n* ecuanimidad *f*.
equate [ɪ'kweɪt] *vt*: **to ~ sth with** equiparar algo con.
equation [ɪ'kweɪʒən] *n* (*MATH*) ecuación *f*.
equator [ɪ'kweɪtə*] *n* ecuador *m*.
equatorial [ekwə'tɔːrɪəl] *adj* ecuatorial.
Equatorial Guinea *n* Guinea Ecuatorial.
equestrian [ɪ'kwestrɪən] *adj* ecuestre ♦ *n* jinete *m/f*.
equilibrium [iːkwɪ'lɪbrɪəm] *n* equilibrio.
equinox ['iːkwɪnɔks] *n* equinoccio.
equip [ɪ'kwɪp] *vt* (*gen*) equipar; (*person*) proveer; **~ped with** (*machinery etc*) provisto de; **to be well ~ped** estar bien equipado; **he is well ~ped for the job** está bien preparado para este puesto.
equipment [ɪ'kwɪpmənt] *n* equipo.
equitable ['ekwɪtəbl] *adj* equitativo.
equities ['ekwɪtɪz] *npl* (*BRIT COMM*) acciones *fpl* ordinarias.
equity ['ekwɪtɪ] *n* (*fairness*) equidad *f*; (*ECON: of debtor*) valor *m* líquido.
equity capital *n* capital *m* propio, patrimonio neto.
equivalent [ɪ'kwɪvəlnt] *adj, n* equivalente *m*; **to be ~ to** equivaler a.
equivocal [ɪ'kwɪvəkl] *adj* equívoco.
equivocate [ɪ'kwɪvəkeɪt] *vi* andarse con ambigüedades.
equivocation [ɪkwɪvə'keɪʃən] *n* ambigüedad *f*.
ER *abbr* (*BRIT*: = *Elizabeth Regina*) la reina Isabel.

er [əː] *interj* (*col: in hesitation*) esto, este (*LAM*).
ERA *n abbr* (*US POL*: = *Equal Rights Amendment*) enmienda sobre la igualdad de derechos de la mujer.
era ['ɪərə] *n* era, época.
eradicate [ɪ'rædɪkeɪt] *vt* erradicar, extirpar.
erase [ɪ'reɪz] *vt* (*also COMPUT*) borrar.
eraser [ɪ'reɪzə*] *n* goma de borrar.
erect [ɪ'rekt] *adj* erguido ♦ *vt* erigir, levantar; (*assemble*) montar.
erection [ɪ'rekʃən] *n* (*of building*) construcción *f*; (*of machinery*) montaje *m*; (*structure*) edificio; (*MED*) erección *f*.
ergonomics [əːgə'nɔmɪks] *n* ergonomía.
ERISA *n abbr* (*US*: = *Employee Retirement Income Security Act*) ley que regula las pensiones de jubilados.
Eritrea [erɪ'treɪə] *n* Eritrea.
ERM *n abbr* (= *Exchange Rate Mechanism*) (mecanismo de cambios del) SME *m*.
ermine ['əːmɪn] *n* armiño.
ERNIE ['əːnɪ] *n abbr* (*BRIT*: = *Electronic Random Number Indicating Equipment*) ordenador que elige al azar los números ganadores de los bonos del Estado.
erode [ɪ'rəud] *vt* (*GEO*) erosionar; (*metal*) corroer, desgastar.
erogenous zone [ɪ'rɔdʒənəs-] *n* zona erógena.
erosion [ɪ'rəuʒən] *n* erosión *f*; desgaste *m*.
erotic [ɪ'rɔtɪk] *adj* erótico.
eroticism [ɪ'rɔtɪsɪzm] *n* erotismo.
err [əː*] *vi* errar; (*REL*) pecar.
errand ['ernd] *n* recado, mandado; **to run ~s** hacer recados; **~ of mercy** misión *f* de caridad.
errand boy *n* recadero.
erratic [ɪ'rætɪk] *adj* variable; (*results etc*) desigual, poco uniforme.
erroneous [ɪ'rəunɪəs] *adj* erróneo.
error ['erə*] *n* error *m*, equivocación *f*; **typing/spelling ~** error *m* de mecanografía/ortografía; **in ~** por equivocación; **~s and omissions excepted** salvo error u omisión.
error message *n* (*COMPUT*) mensaje *m* de error.
erstwhile ['əːstwaɪl] *adj* antiguo, previo.
erudite ['erudaɪt] *adj* erudito.
erudition [eru'dɪʃən] *n* erudición *f*.
erupt [ɪ'rʌpt] *vi* entrar en erupción; (*MED*) hacer erupción; (*fig*) estallar.
eruption [ɪ'rʌpʃən] *n* erupción *f*; (*fig: of anger, violence*) explosión *f*, estallido.
ESA *n abbr* (= *European Space Agency*) Agencia Espacial Europea.

escalate ['ɛskəleɪt] *vi* extenderse, intensificarse; (*costs*) aumentar vertiginosamente.

escalation clause [ɛskə'leɪʃən-] *n* cláusula de reajuste de los precios.

escalator ['ɛskəleɪtə*] *n* escalera mecánica.

escapade [ɛskə'peɪd] *n* aventura.

escape [ɪ'skeɪp] *n* (*gen*) fuga; (*TECH*) escape *m*; (*from duties*) escapatoria; (*from chase*) evasión *f* ♦ *vi* (*gen*) escaparse; (*flee*) huir, evadirse ♦ *vt* evitar, eludir; (*consequences*) escapar a; **to ~ from** (*place*) escaparse de; (*person*) huir de; (*clutches*) librarse de; **to ~ to** (*another place, freedom, safety*) huir a; **to ~ notice** pasar desapercibido.

escape artist *n* artista *m/f* de la evasión.

escape clause *n* (*fig: in agreement*) cláusula de excepción.

escapee [ɪskeɪ'piː] *n* fugado/a.

escape hatch *n* (*in submarine, space rocket*) escotilla de salvamento.

escape key *n* (*COMPUT*) tecla de escape.

escape route *n* (*from fire*) vía de escape.

escapism [ɪ'skeɪpɪzəm] *n* escapismo, evasión *f*.

escapist [ɪ'skeɪpɪst] *adj* escapista, de evasión ♦ *n* escapista *m/f*.

escapologist [ɛskə'pɒlədʒɪst] *n* (*BRIT*) = **escape artist**.

escarpment [ɪ'skɑːpmənt] *n* escarpa.

eschew [ɪs'tʃuː] *vt* evitar, abstenerse de.

escort ['ɛskɔːt] *n* acompañante *m/f*; (*MIL*) escolta; (*NAUT*) convoy *m* ♦ *vt* [ɪ'skɔːt] acompañar; (*MIL, NAUT*) escoltar.

escort agency *n* agencia de acompañantes.

Eskimo ['ɛskɪməʊ] *adj* esquimal ♦ *n* esquimal *m/f*; (*LING*) esquimal *m*.

ESL *n abbr* (*SCOL*) = *English as a Second Language*.

esophagus [iː'sɒfəɡəs] *n* (*US*) = **oesophagus**.

esoteric [ɛsəʊ'tɛrɪk] *adj* esotérico.

ESP *n abbr* = **extrasensory perception**; (*SCOL: English for Special Purposes*) *inglés especializado*.

esp. *abbr* = **especially**.

especially [ɪ'spɛʃlɪ] *adv* (*gen*) especialmente; (*above all*) sobre todo; (*particularly*) en especial.

espionage ['ɛspɪɒnɑːʒ] *n* espionaje *m*.

esplanade [ɛsplə'neɪd] *n* (*by sea*) paseo marítimo.

espouse [ɪ'spaʊz] *vt* adherirse a.

Esq. *abbr* (= *Esquire*) D.

Esquire [ɪ'skwaɪə*] *n*: **J. Brown, ~**
Sr. D. J. Brown.

essay ['ɛseɪ] *n* (*SCOL*) redacción *f*; (: *longer*) trabajo.

essayist ['ɛseɪɪst] *n* ensayista *m/f*.

essence ['ɛsns] *n* esencia; **in ~** esencialmente; **speed is of the ~** es esencial hacerlo con la mayor prontitud.

essential [ɪ'sɛnʃl] *adj* (*necessary*) imprescindible; (*basic*) esencial ♦ *n* (*often pl*) lo esencial; **it is ~ that** es imprescindible que.

essentially [ɪ'sɛnʃlɪ] *adv* esencialmente.

EST *n abbr* (*US:* = *Eastern Standard Time*) hora de invierno de Nueva York.

est. *abbr* (= *established*) fundado; (= *estimated*) aprox.

establish [ɪ'stæblɪʃ] *vt* establecer; (*prove: fact, identity*) comprobar, verificar; (*prove*) demostrar; (*relations*) entablar.

established [ɪ'stæblɪʃt] *adj* (*business*) de buena reputación; (*staff*) de plantilla.

establishment [ɪ'stæblɪʃmənt] *n* (*also business*) establecimiento; **the E~** la clase dirigente; **a teaching ~** un centro de enseñanza.

estate [ɪ'steɪt] *n* (*land*) finca, hacienda; (*property*) propiedad *f*; (*inheritance*) herencia; (*POL*) estado; **housing ~** (*BRIT*) urbanización *f*; **industrial ~** polígono industrial.

estate agency *n* (*BRIT*) agencia inmobiliaria.

estate agent *n* (*BRIT*) agente *m/f* inmobiliario/a.

estate car *n* (*BRIT*) ranchera.

esteem [ɪ'stiːm] *n*: **to hold sb in high ~** estimar en mucho a algn ♦ *vt* estimar.

esthetic [iːs'θɛtɪk] *adj* (*US*) = **aesthetic**.

estimate ['ɛstɪmət] *n* estimación *f*; (*assessment*) tasa, cálculo; (*COMM*) presupuesto ♦ *vt* ['ɛstɪmeɪt] estimar; tasar, calcular; **to give sb an ~ of** presentar a algn un presupuesto de; **at a rough ~** haciendo un cálculo aproximado; **to ~ for** (*COMM*) hacer un presupuesto de, presupuestar.

estimation [ɛstɪ'meɪʃən] *n* opinión *f*, juicio; (*esteem*) aprecio; **in my ~** a mi juicio.

Estonia [ɛ'stəʊnɪə] *n* Estonia.

Estonian [ɛ'stəʊnɪən] *adj* estonio ♦ *n* estonio/a; (*LING*) estonio.

estranged [ɪ'streɪndʒd] *adj* separado.

estrangement [ɪ'streɪndʒmənt] *n* alejamiento, distanciamiento.

estrogen ['iːstrəʊdʒən] *n* (*US*) = **oestrogen**.

estuary ['ɛstjʊərɪ] *n* estuario, ría.

ET *n abbr* (*BRIT:* = *Employment Training*) *plan estatal de formación para los*

desempleados ♦ *abbr* (*US*) = *Eastern Time*.
et al. *abbr* (= *et alii: and others*) et al.
etc *abbr* (= *et cetera*) etc.
etch [etʃ] *vt* grabar al aguafuerte.
etching ['etʃɪŋ] *n* aguafuerte *m or f*.
ETD *n abbr* = *estimated time of departure*.
eternal [ɪ'tə:nl] *adj* eterno.
eternity [ɪ'tə:nɪtɪ] *n* eternidad *f*.
ether ['i:θə*] *n* éter *m*.
ethereal [ɪ'θɪərɪəl] *adj* etéreo.
ethical ['eθɪkl] *adj* ético; (*honest*) honrado.
ethics ['eθɪks] *n* ética ♦ *npl* moralidad *f*.
Ethiopia [i:θɪ'əʊpɪə] *n* Etiopía.
Ethiopian [i:θɪ'əʊpɪən] *adj*, *n* etíope *m/f*.
ethnic ['eθnɪk] *adj* étnico.
ethnic cleansing [-klenzɪŋ] *n* limpieza étnica.
ethos ['i:θɔs] *n* (*of culture, group*) sistema *m* de valores.
etiquette ['etɪket] *n* etiqueta.
ETV *n abbr* (*US*: = *Educational Television*) televisión *f* escolar.
etymology [etɪ'mɔlədʒɪ] *n* etimología.
EU *n abbr* (= *European Union*) UE *f*.
eucalyptus [ju:kə'lɪptəs] *n* eucalipto.
Eucharist ['ju:kərɪst] *n* Eucaristía.
eulogy ['ju:lədʒɪ] *n* elogio, encomio.
eunuch ['ju:nək] *n* eunuco.
euphemism ['ju:fəmɪzm] *n* eufemismo.
euphemistic [ju:fə'mɪstɪk] *adj* eufemístico.
euphoria [ju:'fɔ:rɪə] *n* euforia.
Eurasia [juə'reɪʃə] *n* Eurasia.
Eurasian [juə'reɪʃən] *adj*, *n* eurasiático/a *m/f*.
Euratom [juə'rætəm] *n abbr* (= *European Atomic Energy Commission*) Euratom *m*.
Euro- *pref* euro-.
Eurocheque ['juərəutʃek] *n* Eurocheque *m*.
Eurocrat ['juərəukræt] *n* eurócrata *m/f*.
Eurodollar ['juərəudɔlə*] *n* eurodólar *m*.
Europe ['juərəp] *n* Europa.
European [juərə'pi:ən] *adj*, *n* europeo/a *m/f*.
European Court of Justice *n* Tribunal *m* de Justicia de las Comunidades Europeas.
European Economic Community *n* Comunidad *f* Económica Europea.
Euro-sceptic [juərəu'skeptɪk] *n* euroescéptico/a.
euthanasia [ju:θə'neɪzɪə] *n* eutanasia.
evacuate [ɪ'vækjueɪt] *vt* evacuar; (*place*) desocupar.
evacuation [ɪvækju'eɪʃən] *n* evacuación *f*.
evacuee [ɪvækju'i:] *n* evacuado/a.
evade [ɪ'veɪd] *vt* evadir, eludir.
evaluate [ɪ'væljueɪt] *vt* evaluar; (*value*) tasar; (*evidence*) interpretar.
evangelical [i:væn'dʒelɪkəl] *adj* evangélico.
evangelist [ɪ'vændʒəlɪst] *n* evangelista *m*;

(*preacher*) evangelizador(a) *m/f*.
evaporate [ɪ'væpəreɪt] *vi* evaporarse; (*fig*) desvanecerse ♦ *vt* evaporar.
evaporated milk [ɪ'væpəreɪtɪd-] *n* leche *f* evaporada.
evaporation [ɪvæpə'reɪʃən] *n* evaporación *f*.
evasion [ɪ'veɪʒən] *n* evasión *f*.
evasive [ɪ'veɪsɪv] *adj* evasivo.
eve [i:v] *n*: **on the ~ of** en vísperas de.
even ['i:vn] *adj* (*level*) llano; (*smooth*) liso; (*speed, temperature*) uniforme; (*number*) par; (*SPORT*) igual(es) ♦ *adv* hasta, incluso; **~ if**, **~ though** aunque + *subjun*, así + *subjun* (*LAM*); **~ more** aun más; **~ so** aun así; **not ~** ni siquiera; **~ he was there** hasta él estaba allí; **~ on Sundays** incluso los domingos; **~ faster** aún más rápido; **to break ~** cubrir los gastos; **to get ~ with sb** ajustar cuentas con algn; **to ~ out** *vi* nivelarse.
even-handed [i:vn'hændɪd] *adj* imparcial.
evening ['i:vnɪŋ] *n* tarde *f*; (*dusk*) atardecer *m*; (*night*) noche *f*; **in the ~** por la tarde; **this ~** esta tarde *or* noche; **tomorrow/yesterday ~** mañana/ayer por la tarde *or* noche.
evening class *n* clase *f* nocturna.
evening dress *n* (*man's*) traje *m* de etiqueta; (*woman's*) traje *m* de noche.
evenly ['i:vnlɪ] *adv* (*distribute, space, spread*) de modo uniforme; (*divide*) equitativamente.
evensong ['i:vnsɔŋ] *n* vísperas *fpl*.
event [ɪ'vent] *n* suceso, acontecimiento; (*SPORT*) prueba; **in the ~ of** en caso de; **in the ~** en realidad; **in the course of ~s** en el curso de los acontecimientos; **at all ~s**, **in any ~** en cualquier caso.
eventful [ɪ'ventful] *adj* azaroso; (*game etc*) lleno de emoción.
eventing [ɪ'ventɪŋ] *n* (*HORSERIDING*) competición *f*.
eventual [ɪ'ventʃuəl] *adj* final.
eventuality [ɪventʃu'ælɪtɪ] *n* eventualidad *f*.
eventually [ɪ'ventʃuəlɪ] *adv* (*finally*) por fin; (*in time*) con el tiempo.
ever ['evə*] *adv* nunca, jamás; (*at all times*) siempre; **for ~** (para) siempre; **the best ~** lo nunca visto; **did you ~ meet him?** ¿llegaste a conocerle?; **have you ~ been there?** ¿has estado allí alguna vez?; **have you ~ seen it?** ¿lo has visto alguna vez?; **better than ~** mejor que nunca; **thank you ~ so much** muchísimas gracias; **yours ~** (*in letters*) un abrazo de; **~ since** *adv* desde entonces ♦ *conj* después de que.
Everest ['evərɪst] *n* (*also*: **Mount ~**) el Everest *m*.

evergreen ['ɛvəgriːn] n árbol m de hoja perenne.
everlasting [ɛvə'lɑːstɪŋ] adj eterno, perpetuo.

================= KEYWORD

every ['ɛvrɪ] adj **1** (*each*) cada; ~ **one of them** (*persons*) todos ellos/as; (*objects*) cada uno de ellos/as; ~ **shop in the town was closed** todas las tiendas de la ciudad estaban cerradas
2 (*all possible*) todo/a; **I gave you ~ assistance** te di toda la ayuda posible; **I have ~ confidence in him** tiene toda mi confianza; **we wish you ~ success** te deseamos toda suerte de éxitos
3 (*showing recurrence*) todo/a; ~ **day/week** todos los días/todas las semanas; ~ **other car had been broken into** habían forzado uno de cada dos coches; **she visits me ~ other/third day** me visita cada dos/tres días; ~ **now and then** de vez en cuando.

everybody ['ɛvrɪbɔdɪ] pron todos pl, todo el mundo; ~ **knows about it** todo el mundo lo sabe; ~ **else** todos los demás.
everyday ['ɛvrɪdeɪ] adj (*daily: use, occurrence, experience*) diario, cotidiano; (*usual: expression*) corriente; (*common*) vulgar; (*routine*) rutinario.
everyone ['ɛvrɪwʌn] = **everybody**.
everything ['ɛvrɪθɪŋ] pron todo; ~ **is ready** todo está dispuesto; **he did ~ possible** hizo todo lo posible.
everywhere ['ɛvrɪwɛə*] adv (*be*) en todas partes; (*go*) a or por todas partes; ~ **you go you meet...** en todas partes encontrarás....
evict [ɪ'vɪkt] vt desahuciar.
eviction [ɪ'vɪkʃən] n desahucio.
eviction notice n orden f de desahucio or desalojo (*LAM*).
evidence ['ɛvɪdəns] n (*proof*) prueba; (*of witness*) testimonio; (*facts*) datos mpl, hechos mpl; **to give ~** prestar declaración, dar testimonio.
evident ['ɛvɪdənt] adj evidente, manifiesto.
evidently ['ɛvɪdəntlɪ] adv (*obviously*) obviamente, evidentemente; (*apparently*) por lo visto.
evil ['iːvl] adj malo; (*influence*) funesto; (*smell*) horrible ♦ n mal m.
evildoer ['iːvlduːə*] n malhechor(a) m/f.
evince [ɪ'vɪns] vt mostrar, dar señales de.
evocative [ɪ'vɔkətɪv] adj sugestivo, evocador(a).
evoke [ɪ'vəuk] vt evocar; (*admiration*)

provocar.
evolution [iːvə'luːʃən] n evolución f, desarrollo.
evolve [ɪ'vɔlv] vt desarrollar ♦ vi evolucionar, desarrollarse.
ewe [juː] n oveja.
ex- [ɛks] pref (*former: husband, president etc*) ex-; (*out of*): **the price ~ works** precio de fábrica.
exacerbate [ɛk'sæsəbeɪt] vt exacerbar.
exact [ɪg'zækt] adj exacto ♦ vt: **to ~ sth (from)** exigir algo (de).
exacting [ɪg'zæktɪŋ] adj exigente; (*conditions*) arduo.
exactitude [ɪg'zæktɪtjuːd] n exactitud f.
exactly [ɪg'zæktlɪ] adv exactamente; (*time*) en punto; ~! ¡exacto!
exactness [ɪg'zæktnɪs] n exactitud f.
exaggerate [ɪg'zædʒəreɪt] vt, vi exagerar.
exaggerated [ɪg'zædʒəreɪtɪd] adj exagerado.
exaggeration [ɪgzædʒə'reɪʃən] n exageración f.
exalt [ɪg'zɔːlt] vt (*praise*) ensalzar; (*elevate*) elevar.
exalted [ɪg'zɔːltɪd] adj (*position*) elevado; (*elated*) enardecido.
exam [ɪg'zæm] n abbr (*SCOL*) = **examination**.
examination [ɪgzæmɪ'neɪʃən] n (*gen*) examen m; (*LAW*) interrogación f; (*inquiry*) investigación f; **to take** or **sit an ~** hacer un examen; **the matter is under ~** se está examinando el asunto.
examine [ɪg'zæmɪn] vt (*gen*) examinar; (*inspect: machine, premises*) inspeccionar; (*SCOL, LAW: person*) interrogar; (*at customs: luggage, passport*) registrar; (*MED*) hacer un reconocimiento médico de, examinar.
examiner [ɪg'zæmɪnə*] n examinador(a) m/f.
example [ɪg'zɑːmpl] n ejemplo; **for ~** por ejemplo; **to set a good/bad ~** dar buen/mal ejemplo.
exasperate [ɪg'zɑːspəreɪt] vt exasperar, irritar; ~**d by** or **at** or **with** exasperado por or con.
exasperating [ɪg'zɑːspəreɪtɪŋ] adj irritante.
exasperation [ɪgzɑːspə'reɪʃən] n exasperación f, irritación f.
excavate ['ɛkskəveɪt] vt excavar.
excavation [ɛkskə'veɪʃən] n excavación f.
excavator ['ɛkskəveɪtə*] n excavadora.
exceed [ɪk'siːd] vt exceder; (*number*) pasar de; (*speed limit*) sobrepasar; (*limits*) rebasar; (*powers*) excederse en; (*hopes*) superar.
exceedingly [ɪk'siːdɪŋlɪ] adv sumamente,

sobremanera.
excel [ɪk'sɛl] *vi* sobresalir; **to ~ o.s.** lucirse.
excellence ['ɛksələns] *n* excelencia.
Excellency ['ɛksələnsɪ] *n*: **His ~** Su
Excelencia.
excellent ['ɛksələnt] *adj* excelente.
except [ɪk'sɛpt] *prep* (*also:* **~ for, ~ing**)
excepto, salvo ♦ *vt* exceptuar, excluir; **~
if/when** excepto si/cuando; **~ that** salvo
que.
exception [ɪk'sɛpʃən] *n* excepción *f*; **to take
~ to** ofenderse por; **with the ~ of** a
excepción de; **to make an ~** hacer una
excepción.
exceptional [ɪk'sɛpʃənl] *adj* excepcional.
excerpt ['ɛksə:pt] *n* extracto.
excess [ɪk'sɛs] *n* exceso; **in ~ of** superior a;
see also **excesses.**
excess baggage *n* exceso de equipaje.
excesses *npl* excesos *mpl.*
excess fare *n* suplemento.
excessive [ɪk'sɛsɪv] *adj* excesivo.
excess supply *n* exceso de oferta.
excess weight *n* exceso de peso.
exchange [ɪks'tʃeɪndʒ] *n* cambio; (*of
prisoners*) canje *m*; (*of ideas*) intercambio;
(*also:* **telephone ~**) central *f* (telefónica)
♦ *vt* intercambiar; **to ~ (for)** cambiar
(por); **in ~ for** a cambio de; **foreign ~**
(*COMM*) divisas *fpl.*
exchange control *n* control *m* de divisas.
exchange rate *n* tipo de cambio.
exchequer [ɪks'tʃɛkə*] *n*: **the ~** (*BRIT*)
Hacienda.
excisable [ɛk'saɪzəbl] *adj* sujeto al pago de
impuestos sobre el consumo.
excise ['ɛksaɪz] *n* impuestos *mpl* sobre el
consumo interior.
excitable [ɪk'saɪtəbl] *adj* excitable.
excite [ɪk'saɪt] *vt* (*stimulate*) entusiasmar;
(*anger*) suscitar, provocar; (*move*)
emocionar; **to get ~d** emocionarse.
excitement [ɪk'saɪtmənt] *n* emoción *f.*
exciting [ɪk'saɪtɪŋ] *adj* emocionante.
excl. *abbr* = **excluding; exclusive (of).**
exclaim [ɪk'skleɪm] *vi* exclamar.
exclamation [ɛksklə'meɪʃən] *n*
exclamación *f.*
exclamation mark *n* signo de admiración.
exclude [ɪk'sklu:d] *vt* excluir; (*except*)
exceptuar.
excluding [ɪks'klu:dɪŋ] *prep*: **~ VAT** IVA no
incluido.
exclusion [ɪk'sklu:ʒən] *n* exclusión *f*; **to the
~ of** con exclusión de.
exclusion clause *n* cláusula de exclusión.
exclusion zone *n* zona de exclusión.
exclusive [ɪk'sklu:sɪv] *adj* exclusivo; (*club,*

district) selecto; **~ of tax** excluyendo
impuestos; **~ of postage/service**
franqueo/servicio no incluido; **from 1st
to 13th March ~** del 1 al 13 de marzo
exclusive.
exclusively [ɪk'sklu:sɪvlɪ] *adv* únicamente.
excommunicate [ɛkskə'mju:nɪkeɪt] *vt*
excomulgar.
excrement ['ɛkskrəmənt] *n* excremento.
excrete [ɪk'skri:t] *vi* excretar.
excruciating [ɪk'skru:ʃɪeɪtɪŋ] *adj* (*pain*)
agudísimo, atroz.
excursion [ɪk'skə:ʃən] *n* excursión *f.*
excursion ticket *n* billete *m* (especial) de
excursión.
excusable [ɪk'skju:səbl] *adj* perdonable.
excuse *n* [ɪk'skju:s] disculpa, excusa;
(*evasion*) pretexto ♦ *vt* [ɪk'skju:z]
disculpar, perdonar; (*justify*) justificar; **to
make ~s for sb** presentar disculpas por
algn; **to ~ sb from doing sth** dispensar a
algn de hacer algo; **to ~ o.s. (for (doing)
sth)** pedir disculpas a algn (por (hacer)
algo); **~ me!** ¡perdone!; (*attracting
attention*) ¡oiga(, por favor)!; **if you will ~
me** con su permiso.
ex-directory ['ɛksdɪ'rɛktərɪ] *adj* (*BRIT*): **~
(phone) number** número que no figura en
la guía (telefónica).
execrable ['ɛksɪkrəbl] *adj* execrable,
abominable; (*manners*) detestable.
execute ['ɛksɪkju:t] *vt* (*plan*) realizar;
(*order*) cumplir; (*person*) ajusticiar,
ejecutar.
execution [ɛksɪ'kju:ʃən] *n* realización *f*;
cumplimiento; ejecución *f.*
executioner [ɛksɪ'kju:ʃənə*] *n* verdugo.
executive [ɪg'zɛkjutɪv] *n* (*COMM*)
ejecutivo/a; (*POL*) poder *m* ejecutivo ♦ *adj*
ejecutivo; (*car, plane, position*) de
ejecutivo; (*offices, suite*) de la dirección;
(*secretary*) de dirección.
executive director *n* director(a) *m/f*
ejecutivo/a.
executor [ɪg'zɛkjutə*] *n* albacea *m*,
testamentario.
exemplary [ɪg'zɛmplərɪ] *adj* ejemplar.
exemplify [ɪg'zɛmplɪfaɪ] *vt* ejemplificar.
exempt [ɪg'zɛmpt] *adj*: **~ from** exento de
♦ *vt*: **to ~ sb from** eximir a algn de.
exemption [ɪg'zɛmpʃən] *n* exención *f*;
(*immunity*) inmunidad *f.*
exercise ['ɛksəsaɪz] *n* ejercicio ♦ *vt* ejercer;
(*patience etc*) proceder con; (*dog*) sacar
de paseo ♦ *vi* hacer ejercicio.
exercise bike *n* bicicleta estática.
exercise book *n* cuaderno de ejercicios.
exert [ɪg'zə:t] *vt* ejercer; (*strength, force*)

emplear; **to ~ o.s.** esforzarse.
exertion [ɪgˈzɜːʃən] *n* esfuerzo.
exfoliant [ɛksˈfəʊliənt] *n* exfoliante *m*.
ex gratia [ˈɛksˈgreɪʃə] *adj*: **~ payment** pago
a título voluntario.
exhale [ɛksˈheɪl] *vt* despedir, exhalar ♦ *vi*
espirar.
exhaust [ɪgˈzɔːst] *n* (*pipe*) (tubo de) escape
m; (*fumes*) gases *mpl* de escape ♦ *vt* agotar;
to ~ o.s. agotarse.
exhausted [ɪgˈzɔːstɪd] *adj* agotado.
exhausting [ɪgˈzɔːstɪŋ] *adj*: **an ~ journey/
day** un viaje/día agotador.
exhaustion [ɪgˈzɔːstʃən] *n* agotamiento;
nervous ~ agotamiento nervioso.
exhaustive [ɪgˈzɔːstɪv] *adj* exhaustivo.
exhibit [ɪgˈzɪbɪt] *n* (*ART*) obra expuesta;
(*LAW*) objeto expuesto ♦ *vt* (*show:
emotions*) manifestar; (: *courage, skill*)
demostrar; (*paintings*) exponer.
exhibition [ɛksɪˈbɪʃən] *n* exposición *f*.
exhibitionist [ɛksɪˈbɪʃənɪst] *n*
exhibicionista *m/f*.
exhibitor [ɪgˈzɪbɪtə*] *n* expositor(a) *m/f*.
exhilarating [ɪgˈzɪləreɪtɪŋ] *adj* estimulante,
tónico.
exhilaration [ɪgzɪləˈreɪʃən] *n* júbilo.
exhort [ɪgˈzɔːt] *vt* exhortar.
exile [ˈɛksaɪl] *n* exilio; (*person*) exiliado/a
♦ *vt* desterrar, exiliar.
exist [ɪgˈzɪst] *vi* existir.
existence [ɪgˈzɪstəns] *n* existencia.
existentialism [ɛgzɪsˈtɛnʃəlɪzəm] *n*
existencialismo.
existing [ɪgˈzɪstɪŋ] *adj* existente, actual.
exit [ˈɛksɪt] *n* salida ♦ *vi* (*THEAT*) hacer
mutis; (*COMPUT*) salir (del sistema).
exit poll *n* encuesta a la salida de los
colegios electorales.
exit ramp *n* (*US AUT*) vía de acceso.
exit visa *n* visado de salida.
exodus [ˈɛksədəs] *n* éxodo.
ex officio [ˈɛksəˈfɪʃɪəʊ] *adj* de pleno
derecho ♦ *adv* ex oficio.
exonerate [ɪgˈzɒnəreɪt] *vt*: **to ~ from**
exculpar de.
exorbitant [ɪgˈzɔːbɪtənt] *adj* (*price,
demands*) exorbitante, excesivo.
exorcize [ˈɛksɔːsaɪz] *vt* exorcizar.
exotic [ɪgˈzɒtɪk] *adj* exótico.
expand [ɪkˈspænd] *vt* ampliar, extender;
(*number*) aumentar ♦ *vi* (*trade etc*)
ampliarse, expandirse; (*gas, metal*)
dilatarse; **to ~ on** (*notes, story etc*)
ampliar.
expanse [ɪkˈspæns] *n* extensión *f*.
expansion [ɪkˈspænʃən] *n* ampliación *f*;
aumento; (*of trade*) expansión *f*.

expansionism [ɪkˈspænʃənɪzəm] *n*
expansionismo.
expansionist [ɪkˈspænʃənɪst] *adj*
expansionista.
expatriate [ɛksˈpætrɪət] *n* expatriado/a.
expect [ɪkˈspɛkt] *vt* (*gen*) esperar; (*count
on*) contar con; (*suppose*) suponer ♦ *vi*: **to
be ~ing** estar encinta; **to ~ to do sth**
esperar hacer algo; **as ~ed** como era de
esperar; **I ~ so** supongo que sí.
expectancy [ɪkˈspɛktənsɪ] *n* (*anticipation*)
expectación *f*; **life ~** esperanza de vida.
expectantly [ɪkˈspɛktəntlɪ] *adv* (*look, listen*)
con expectación.
expectant mother [ɪkˈspɛktənt-] *n* futura
madre *f*.
expectation [ɛkspɛkˈteɪʃən] *n* esperanza,
expectativa; **in ~ of** esperando; **against**
or **contrary to all ~(s)** en contra de todas
las previsiones; **to come** *or* **live up to sb's
~s** resultar tan bueno como se esperaba;
to fall short of sb's ~s no cumplir las
esperanzas de algn, decepcionar a algn.
expedience [ɪkˈspiːdɪəns], **expediency**
[ɪkˈspiːdɪənsɪ] *n* conveniencia.
expedient [ɪkˈspiːdɪənt] *adj* conveniente,
oportuno ♦ *n* recurso, expediente *m*.
expedite [ˈɛkspɪdaɪt] *vt* (*speed up*) acelerar;
(: *progress*) facilitar.
expedition [ɛkspəˈdɪʃən] *n* expedición *f*.
expeditionary force [ɛkspəˈdɪʃnrɪ-] *n*
cuerpo expedicionario.
expel [ɪkˈspɛl] *vt* expulsar.
expend [ɪkˈspɛnd] *vt* gastar; (*use up*)
consumir.
expendable [ɪkˈspɛndəbl] *adj* prescindible.
expenditure [ɪkˈspɛndɪtʃə*] *n* gastos *mpl*,
desembolso; (*of time, effort*) gasto.
expense [ɪkˈspɛns] *n* gasto, gastos *mpl*;
(*high cost*) coste *m*; **~s** *npl* (*COMM*) gastos
mpl; **at the ~ of** a costa de; **to meet the ~**
of hacer frente a los gastos de.
expense account *n* cuenta de gastos (de
representación).
expensive [ɪkˈspɛnsɪv] *adj* caro, costoso.
experience [ɪkˈspɪərɪəns] *n* experiencia ♦ *vt*
experimentar; (*suffer*) sufrir; **to learn by
~** aprender con la experiencia.
experienced [ɪkˈspɪərɪənst] *adj*
experimentado.
experiment [ɪkˈspɛrɪmənt] *n* experimento
♦ *vi* hacer experimentos, experimentar;
to perform *or* **carry out an ~** realizar un
experimento; **as an ~** como experimento;
to ~ with a new vaccine experimentar
con una vacuna nueva.
experimental [ɪkspɛrɪˈmɛntl] *adj*
experimental; **the process is still at the ~**

stage el proceso está todavía en prueba.
expert ['ɛkspəːt] *adj* experto, perito ♦ *n*
experto/a, perito/a; (*specialist*)
especialista *m/f*; ~ **witness** (*LAW*) testigo
pericial; ~ **in** *or* **at doing sth** experto *or*
perito en hacer algo; **an** ~ **on sth** un
experto en algo.
expertise [ɛkspəːˈtiːz] *n* pericia.
expiration [ɛkspɪˈreɪʃən] *n* (*gen*) expiración
f, vencimiento.
expire [ɪkˈspaɪə*] *vi* (*gen*) caducar,
vencerse.
expiry [ɪkˈspaɪərɪ] *n* caducidad *f*,
vencimiento.
explain [ɪkˈspleɪn] *vt* explicar; (*mystery*)
aclarar.
► **explain away** *vt* justificar.
explanation [ɛkspləˈneɪʃən] *n* explicación *f*;
aclaración *f*; **to find an** ~ **for sth**
encontrarle una explicación a algo.
explanatory [ɪkˈsplænətrɪ] *adj* explicativo;
aclaratorio.
expletive [ɪkˈspliːtɪv] *n* imprecación *f*.
explicable [ɪkˈsplɪkəbl] *adj* explicable.
explicit [ɪkˈsplɪsɪt] *adj* explícito.
explicitly [ɪkˈsplɪsɪtlɪ] *adv* explícitamente.
explode [ɪkˈspləud] *vi* estallar, explotar;
(*with anger*) reventar ♦ *vt* hacer explotar;
(*fig: theory, myth*) demoler.
exploit ['ɛksplɔɪt] *n* hazaña ♦ *vt* [ɪkˈsplɔɪt]
explotar.
exploitation [ɛksplɔɪˈteɪʃən] *n* explotación
f.
exploration [ɛkspləˈreɪʃən] *n* exploración *f*.
exploratory [ɪkˈsplɔrətrɪ] *adj* (*fig: talks*)
exploratorio, preliminar.
explore [ɪkˈsplɔː*] *vt* explorar; (*fig*)
examinar, sondear.
explorer [ɪkˈsplɔːrə*] *n* explorador(a) *m/f*.
explosion [ɪkˈspləuʒən] *n* explosión *f*.
explosive [ɪkˈspləusɪv] *adj*, *n* explosivo.
exponent [ɪkˈspəunənt] *n* partidario/a; (*of
skill, activity*) exponente *m/f*.
export *vt* [ɛkˈspɔːt] exportar ♦ *n* ['ɛkspɔːt]
exportación *f* ♦ *cpd* de exportación.
exportation [ɛkspɔːˈteɪʃən] *n* exportación *f*.
export drive *n* campaña de exportación.
exporter [ɛkˈspɔːtə*] *n* exportador(a) *m/f*.
export licence *n* licencia de exportación.
export manager *n* gerente *m/f* de
exportación.
export trade *n* comercio exterior.
expose [ɪkˈspəuz] *vt* exponer; (*unmask*)
desenmascarar.
exposé [ɪkˈspəuzeɪ] *n* relevación *f*.
exposed [ɪkˈspəuzd] *adj* expuesto; (*land,
house*) desprotegido; (*ELEC: wire*) al aire;
(*pipe, beam*) al descubierto.

exposition [ɛkspəˈzɪʃən] *n* exposición *f*.
exposure [ɪkˈspəuʒə*] *n* exposición *f*;
(*PHOT: speed*) (tiempo *m* de) exposición *f*;
(: *shot*) fotografía; **to die from** ~ (*MED*)
morir de frío.
exposure meter *n* fotómetro.
expound [ɪkˈspaund] *vt* exponer; (*theory,
text*) comentar; (*one's views*) explicar.
express [ɪkˈsprɛs] *adj* (*definite*) expreso,
explícito; (*BRIT: letter etc*) urgente ♦ *n*
(*train*) rápido ♦ *adv* (*send*) por correo
extraordinario ♦ *vt* expresar; (*squeeze*)
exprimir; **to send sth** ~ enviar algo por
correo urgente; **to** ~ **o.s.** expresarse.
expression [ɪkˈsprɛʃən] *n* expresión *f*.
expressionism [ɪkˈsprɛʃənɪzm] *n*
expresionismo.
expressive [ɪkˈsprɛsɪv] *adj* expresivo.
expressly [ɪkˈsprɛslɪ] *adv* expresamente.
expressway [ɪkˈsprɛsweɪ] *n* (*US: urban
motorway*) autopista.
expropriate [ɛksˈprəuprɪeɪt] *vt* expropiar.
expulsion [ɪkˈspʌlʃən] *n* expulsión *f*.
expurgate ['ɛkspəgeɪt] *vt* expurgar.
exquisite [ɛkˈskwɪzɪt] *adj* exquisito.
exquisitely [ɛkˈskwɪzɪtlɪ] *adv*
exquisitamente.
ex-serviceman ['ɛksˈsəːvɪsmən] *n*
ex-combatiente *m*.
ext. *abbr* (*TEL*) = **extension**.
extemporize [ɪkˈstɛmpəraɪz] *vi* improvisar.
extend [ɪkˈstɛnd] *vt* (*visit, street*) prolongar;
(*building*) ampliar; (*thanks, friendship etc*)
extender; (*COMM: credit*) conceder;
(*deadline*) prorrogar ♦ *vi* (*land*)
extenderse; **the contract** ~**s to/for** ... el
contrato se prolonga hasta/por ....
extension [ɪkˈstɛnʃən] *n* extensión *f*;
(*building*) ampliación *f*; (*TEL: line*)
extensión *f*; (: *telephone*) supletorio *m*; (*of
deadline*) prórroga; ~ **3718** extensión
3718.
extension cable *n* (*ELEC*) alargador *m*.
extensive [ɪkˈstɛnsɪv] *adj* (*gen*) extenso;
(*damage*) importante; (*knowledge*) amplio.
extensively [ɪkˈstɛnsɪvlɪ] *adv* (*altered,
damaged etc*) extensamente; **he's travelled**
~ ha viajado por muchos países.
extent [ɪkˈstɛnt] *n* (*breadth*) extensión *f*;
(*scope: of knowledge, activities*) alcance *m*;
(*degree: of damage, loss*) grado; **to some** ~
hasta cierto punto; **to a certain** ~ hasta
cierto punto; **to a large** ~ en gran parte;
to the ~ **of...** hasta el punto de...; **to such
an** ~ **that...** hasta tal punto que...; **to what**
~? ¿hasta qué punto?; **debts to the** ~ **of**
£5000 deudas por la cantidad de £5000.
extenuating [ɪkˈstɛnjueɪtɪŋ] *adj*: ~

circumstances circunstancias *fpl* atenuantes.

exterior [ɛk'stɪərɪə*] *adj* exterior, externo ♦ *n* exterior *m*.

exterminate [ɪk'stə:mɪneɪt] *vt* exterminar.

extermination [ɪkstə:mɪ'neɪʃən] *n* exterminio.

external [ɛk'stə:nl] *adj* externo, exterior ♦ *n*: **the ~s** la apariencia exterior; **~ affairs** asuntos *mpl* exteriores; **for ~ use only** (*MED*) para uso tópico.

externally [ɛk'stə:nəlɪ] *adv* por fuera.

extinct [ɪk'stɪŋkt] *adj* (*volcano*) extinguido, apagado; (*race*) extinguido.

extinction [ɪk'stɪŋkʃən] *n* extinción *f*.

extinguish [ɪk'stɪŋgwɪʃ] *vt* extinguir, apagar.

extinguisher [ɪk'stɪŋgwɪʃə*] *n* extintor *m*.

extol, (*US*) **extoll** [ɪk'stəul] *vt* (*merits, virtues*) ensalzar, alabar; (*person*) alabar, elogiar.

extort [ɪk'stɔ:t] *vt* sacar a la fuerza; (*confession*) arrancar.

extortion [ɪk'stɔ:ʃən] *n* extorsión *f*.

extortionate [ɪk'stɔ:ʃnət] *adj* excesivo, exorbitante.

extra ['ɛkstrə] *adj* adicional ♦ *adv* (*in addition*) más ♦ *n* (*addition*) extra *m*, suplemento; (*THEAT*) extra *m/f*, comparsa *m/f*; (*newspaper*) edición *f* extraordinaria; **wine will cost ~** el vino se paga aparte; **~ large sizes** tallas extragrandes; *see also* **extras**.

extra... ['ɛkstrə] *pref* extra... .

extract *vt* [ɪk'strækt] sacar; (*tooth*) extraer; (*confession*) arrancar ♦ *n* ['ɛkstrækt] fragmento; (*CULIN*) extracto.

extraction [ɪk'strækʃən] *n* extracción *f*; (*origin*) origen *m*.

extractor fan [ɪk'stræktə-] *n* extractor *m* de humos.

extracurricular [ɛkstrəkə'rɪkjulə*] *adj* (*SCOL*) extraescolar.

extradite ['ɛkstrədaɪt] *vt* extraditar.

extradition [ɛkstrə'dɪʃən] *n* extradición *f*.

extramarital [ɛkstrə'mærɪtl] *adj* extramatrimonial.

extramural [ɛkstrə'mjuərl] *adj* extra-académico.

extraneous [ɪk'streɪnɪəs] *adj* extraño, ajeno.

extraordinary [ɪk'strɔ:dnrɪ] *adj* extraordinario; (*odd*) raro; **the ~ thing is that ...** lo más extraordinario es que ....

extraordinary general meeting *n* junta general extraordinaria.

extrapolation [ɪkstræpə'leɪʃən] *n* extrapolación *f*.

extras *npl* (*additional expense*) extras *mpl*.

extrasensory perception (ESP) ['ɛkstrə'sɛnsərɪ-] *n* percepción *f* extrasensorial.

extra time *n* (*FOOTBALL*) prórroga.

extravagance [ɪk'strævəgəns] *n* (*excessive spending*) derroche *m*; (*thing bought*) extravagancia.

extravagant [ɪk'strævəgənt] *adj* (*wasteful*) derrochador(a); (*taste, gift*) excesivamente caro; (*price*) exorbitante; (*praise*) excesivo.

extreme [ɪk'stri:m] *adj* extremo; (*poverty etc*) extremado; (*case*) excepcional ♦ *n* extremo; **the ~ left/right** (*POL*) la extrema izquierda/derecha; **~s of temperature** temperaturas extremas.

extremely [ɪk'stri:mlɪ] *adv* sumamente, extremadamente.

extremist [ɪk'stri:mɪst] *adj*, *n* extremista *m/f*.

extremity [ɪk'stremətɪ] *n* extremidad *f*, punta; (*need*) apuro, necesidad *f*; **extremities** *npl* (*hands and feet*) extremidades *fpl*.

extricate ['ɛkstrɪkeɪt] *vt*: **to ~ o.s. from** librarse de.

extrovert ['ɛkstrəvə:t] *n* extrovertido/a.

exuberance [ɪg'zju:bərns] *n* exuberancia.

exuberant [ɪg'zju:bərnt] *adj* (*person*) eufórico; (*style*) exuberante.

exude [ɪg'zju:d] *vt* rezumar.

exult [ɪg'zʌlt] *vi* regocijarse.

exultant [ɪg'zʌltənt] *adj* (*person*) regocijado, jubiloso; (*shout, expression, smile*) de júbilo.

exultation [ɛgzʌl'teɪʃən] *n* regocijo, júbilo.

eye [aɪ] *n* ojo ♦ *vt* mirar; **to keep an ~ on** vigilar; **as far as the ~ can see** hasta donde alcanza la vista; **with an ~ to doing sth** con vistas *or* miras a hacer algo; **to have an ~ for sth** tener mucha vista *or* buen ojo para algo; **there's more to this than meets the ~** esto tiene su miga.

eyeball ['aɪbɔ:l] *n* globo ocular.

eyebath ['aɪba:θ] *n* baño ocular, lavaojos *m inv*.

eyebrow ['aɪbrau] *n* ceja.

eyebrow pencil *n* lápiz *m* de cejas.

eye-catching ['aɪkætʃɪŋ] *adj* llamativo.

eye cup *n* (*US*) = **eyebath**.

eyedrops ['aɪdrɒps] *npl* gotas *fpl* para los ojos.

eyeful ['aɪful] *n* (*col*): **to get an ~ of sth** ver bien algo.

eyelash ['aɪlæʃ] *n* pestaña.

eyelet ['aɪlɪt] *n* ojete *m*.

eye-level ['aɪlɛvl] *adj* a la altura de los ojos.

eyelid ['aɪlɪd] *n* párpado.
eyeliner ['aɪlaɪnə*] *n* lápiz *m* de ojos.
eye-opener ['aɪəupnə*] *n* revelación *f*, gran sorpresa.
eyeshadow ['aɪʃædəu] *n* sombra de ojos.
eyesight ['aɪsaɪt] *n* vista.
eyesore ['aɪsɔ:*] *n* monstruosidad *f*.
eyestrain ['aɪstreɪn] *n*: **to get ~** cansar la vista *or* los ojos.
eyetooth, *pl* **eyeteeth** ['aɪtu:θ, -ti:θ] *n* colmillo; **to give one's eyeteeth for sth/to do sth** (*col, fig*) dar un ojo de la cara por algo/por hacer algo.
eyewash ['aɪwɔʃ] *n* (*fig*) disparates *mpl*, tonterías *fpl*.
eye witness *n* testigo *m/f* ocular.
eyrie ['ɪərɪ] *n* aguilera.

Ff

F, f [ɛf] *n* (*letter*) F, f *f*; (*MUS*) fa *m*; **F for Frederick,** (*US*) **F for Fox** F de Francia.
F. *abbr* = **Fahrenheit.**
FA *n abbr* (*BRIT*: = Football Association) ≈ AFE *f* (*SP*).
FAA *n abbr* (*US*) = Federal Aviation Administration.
fable ['feɪbl] *n* fábula.
fabric ['fæbrɪk] *n* tejido, tela.
fabricate ['fæbrɪkeɪt] *vt* fabricar; (*fig*) inventar.
fabrication [fæbrɪ'keɪʃən] *n* fabricación *f*; (*fig*) invención *f*.
fabric ribbon *n* (*for typewriter*) cinta de tela.
fabulous ['fæbjuləs] *adj* fabuloso.
façade [fə'sɑ:d] *n* fachada.
face [feɪs] *n* (*ANAT*) cara, rostro; (*of clock*) esfera, cara; (*side*) cara; (*surface*) superficie *f* ♦ *vt* mirar a; (*fig*) enfrentarse a; **~ down** (*person, card*) boca abajo; **to lose ~** desprestigiarse; **to save ~** salvar las apariencias; **to make** *or* **pull a ~** hacer muecas; **in the ~ of** (*difficulties etc*) en vista de, ante; **on the ~ of it** a primera vista; **~ to ~** cara a cara; **to ~ the fact that ...** reconocer que ....
▶**face up to** *vt fus* hacer frente a, enfrentarse a.
face cloth *n* (*BRIT*) toallita.
face cream *n* crema (de belleza).

faceless ['feɪslɪs] *adj* (*fig*) anónimo.
face lift *n* lifting *m*, estirado facial.
face powder *n* polvos *mpl* para la cara.
face-saving ['feɪsseɪvɪŋ] *adj* para salvar las apariencias.
facet ['fæsɪt] *n* faceta.
facetious [fə'si:ʃəs] *adj* chistoso.
facetiously [fə'si:ʃəslɪ] *adv* chistosamente.
face value *n* (*of stamp*) valor *m* nominal; **to take sth at ~** (*fig*) tomar algo en sentido literal, aceptar las apariencias de algo.
facial ['feɪʃəl] *adj* de la cara ♦ *n* (*also*: **beauty ~**) tratamiento facial, limpieza.
facile ['fæsaɪl] *adj* superficial.
facilitate [fə'sɪlɪteɪt] *vt* facilitar.
facility [fə'sɪlɪtɪ] *n* facilidad *f*; **facilities** *npl* instalaciones *fpl*; **credit ~** facilidades de crédito.
facing ['feɪsɪŋ] *prep* frente a ♦ *adj* de enfrente.
facsimile [fæk'sɪmɪlɪ] *n* facsímil(e) *m*.
fact [fækt] *n* hecho; **in ~** en realidad; **to know for a ~ that ...** saber a ciencia cierta que ....
fact-finding ['fæktfaɪndɪŋ] *adj*: **a ~ tour/ mission** un viaje/una misión de reconocimiento.
faction ['fækʃən] *n* facción *f*.
factional ['fækʃənl] *adj* (*fighting*) entre distintas facciones.
factor ['fæktə*] *n* factor *m*; (*COMM*: *person*) agente *m/f* comisionado/a ♦ *vi* (*COMM*) comprar deudas; **safety ~** factor de seguridad.
factory ['fæktərɪ] *n* fábrica.
factory farming *n* cría industrial.
factory floor *n* (*workers*) trabajadores *mpl*, mano *f* de obra directa; (*area*) talleres *mpl*.
factory ship *n* buque *m* factoría.
factual ['fæktjuəl] *adj* basado en los hechos.
faculty ['fækəltɪ] *n* facultad *f*; (*US*: *teaching staff*) personal *m* docente.
fad [fæd] *n* novedad *f*, moda.
fade [feɪd] *vi* descolorarse, desteñirse; (*sound, hope*) desvanecerse; (*light*) apagarse; (*flower*) marchitarse.
▶**fade away** *vi* (*sound*) apagarse.
▶**fade in** *vt* (*TV, CINE*) fundir; (*RADIO*: *sound*) mezclar ♦ *vi* (*TV, CINE*) fundirse; (*RADIO*) oírse por encima.
▶**fade out** *vt* (*TV, CINE*) fundir; (*RADIO*) apagar, disminuir el volumen de ♦ *vi* (*TV, CINE*) desvanecerse; (*RADIO*) apagarse, dejarse de oír.
faded ['feɪdɪd] *adj* (*clothes, colour*) descolorido; (*flower*) marchito.
faeces, (*US*) **feces** ['fi:si:z] *npl* excremento

sg, heces *fpl*.

fag [fæg] *n* (*BRIT col: cigarette*) pitillo (*SP*), cigarro; (*US col: homosexual*) maricón *m*.

fag end *n* (*BRIT col*) colilla.

fagged [fægd] *adj* (*BRIT col: exhausted*) rendido, agotado.

Fahrenheit ['fɑːrənhaɪt] *n* Fahrenheit *m*.

fail [feɪl] *vt* suspender; (*subj: memory etc*) fallar a ♦ *vi* suspender; (*be unsuccessful*) fracasar; (*strength, brakes, engine*) fallar; **to ~ to do sth** (*neglect*) dejar de hacer algo; (*be unable*) no poder hacer algo; **without ~** sin falta; **words ~ me!** ¡no sé qué decir!

failing ['feɪlɪŋ] *n* falta, defecto ♦ *prep* a falta de; **~ that** de no ser posible eso.

failsafe ['feɪlseɪf] *adj* (*device etc*) de seguridad.

failure ['feɪljə*] *n* fracaso; (*person*) fracasado/a; (*mechanical etc*) fallo; (*in exam*) suspenso; (*of crops*) pérdida, destrucción *f*; **it was a complete ~** fue un fracaso total.

faint [feɪnt] *adj* débil; (*smell, breeze, trace*) leve; (*recollection*) vago; (*mark*) apenas visible ♦ *n* desmayo ♦ *vi* desmayarse; **to feel ~** estar mareado, marearse.

faintest ['feɪntɪst] *adj*: **I haven't the ~ idea** no tengo la más remota idea.

faint-hearted ['feɪnt'hɑːtɪd] *adj* apocado.

faintly ['feɪntlɪ] *adv* débilmente; (*vaguely*) vagamente.

faintness ['feɪntnɪs] *n* debilidad *f*; vaguedad *f*.

fair [fɛə*] *adj* justo; (*hair, person*) rubio; (*weather*) bueno; (*good enough*) suficiente; (*sizeable*) considerable ♦ *adv*: **to play ~** jugar limpio ♦ *n* feria; (*BRIT: funfair*) parque *m* de atracciones; **it's not ~!** ¡no es justo!, ¡no hay derecho!; **~ copy** copia en limpio; **~ play** juego limpio; **a ~ amount of** bastante; **~ wear and tear** desgaste *m* natural; **trade ~** feria de muestras.

fair game *n*: **to be ~** ser presa fácil.

fairground ['fɛəgraund] *n* recinto ferial.

fair-haired [fɛə'hɛəd] *adj* (*person*) rubio.

fairly ['fɛəlɪ] *adv* (*justly*) con justicia; (*equally*) equitativamente; (*quite*) bastante; **I'm ~ sure** estoy bastante seguro.

fairness ['fɛənɪs] *n* justicia; (*impartiality*) imparcialidad *f*; **in all ~** a decir verdad.

fairy ['fɛərɪ] *n* hada.

fairy godmother *n* hada madrina.

fairyland ['fɛərɪlænd] *n* el país de ensueño.

fairy lights *npl* bombillas *fpl* de colores.

fairy tale *n* cuento de hadas.

faith [feɪθ] *n* fe *f*; (*trust*) confianza; (*sect*) religión *f*; **to have ~ in sb/sth** confiar en algn/algo.

faithful ['feɪθful] *adj* fiel.

faithfully ['feɪθfulɪ] *adv* fielmente; **yours ~** (*BRIT: in letters*) le saluda atentamente.

faith healer *n* curador(a) *m/f* por fe.

fake [feɪk] *n* (*painting etc*) falsificación *f*; (*person*) impostor(a) *m/f* ♦ *adj* falso ♦ *vt* fingir; (*painting etc*) falsificar.

falcon ['fɔːlkən] *n* halcón *m*.

Falkland Islands ['fɔːlklənd-] *npl* Islas *fpl* Malvinas.

fall [fɔːl] *n* caída; (*US*) otoño; (*decrease*) disminución *f* ♦ *vi*, *pt* **fell**, *pp* **fallen** ['fɔːlən] caer; (*accidentally*) caerse; (*price*) bajar; **~s** *npl* (*waterfall*) cataratas *fpl*, salto *sg* de agua; **a ~ of earth** un desprendimiento de tierra; **a ~ of snow** una nevada; **to ~ flat** *vi* (*on one's face*) caerse de bruces; (*joke, story*) no hacer gracia; **to ~ short of sb's expectations** decepcionar a algn; **to ~ in love (with sb/sth)** enamorarse (de algn/algo).

▶**fall apart** *vi* deshacerse.

▶**fall back** *vi* retroceder.

▶**fall back on** *vt fus* (*remedy etc*) recurrir a; **to have sth to ~ back on** tener algo a que recurrir.

▶**fall behind** *vi* quedarse atrás; (*fig: with payments*) retrasarse.

▶**fall down** *vi* (*person*) caerse; (*building, hopes*) derrumbarse.

▶**fall for** *vt fus* (*trick*) tragar; (*person*) enamorarse de.

▶**fall in** *vi* (*roof*) hundirse; (*MIL*) alinearse.

▶**fall in with** *vt fus*: **to ~ in with sb's plans** acomodarse con los planes de algn.

▶**fall off** *vi* caerse; (*diminish*) disminuir.

▶**fall out** *vi* (*friends etc*) reñir; (*MIL*) romper filas.

▶**fall over** *vi* caer(se).

▶**fall through** *vi* (*plan, project*) fracasar.

fallacy ['fæləsɪ] *n* error *m*.

fallback position ['fɔːlbæk-] *n* posición *f* de repliegue.

fallen ['fɔːlən] *pp of* **fall**.

fallible ['fæləbl] *adj* falible.

falling ['fɔːlɪŋ] *adj*: **~ market** mercado en baja.

falling-off ['fɔːlɪŋ'ɔf] *n* (*reduction*) disminución *f*.

Fallopian tube [fə'ləupɪən-] *n* (*ANAT*) trompa de Falopio.

fallout ['fɔːlaut] *n* lluvia radioactiva.

fallout shelter *n* refugio antinuclear.

fallow ['fæləu] *adj* (*land, field*) en barbecho.

false [fɔːls] *adj* (*gen*) falso; (*teeth etc*)

postizo; (*disloyal*) desleal, traidor(a);
under ~ **pretences** con engaños.
false alarm *n* falsa alarma.
falsehood ['fɔːlshud] *n* falsedad *f*.
falsely ['fɔːlslɪ] *adv* falsamente.
false teeth *npl* (*BRIT*) dentadura *sg* postiza.
falsify ['fɔːlsɪfaɪ] *vt* falsificar.
falter ['fɔːltə*] *vi* vacilar.
fame [feɪm] *n* fama.
familiar [fə'mɪlɪə*] *adj* familiar; (*well-known*) conocido; (*tone*) de confianza; **to be ~ with** (*subject*) estar enterado de; **to make o.s. ~ with** familiarizarse con; **to be on ~ terms with sb** tener confianza con algn.
familiarity [fəmɪlɪ'ærɪtɪ] *n* familiaridad *f*.
familiarize [fə'mɪlɪəraɪz] *vt*: **to ~ o.s. with** familiarizarse con.
family ['fæmɪlɪ] *n* familia.
family allowance *n* subsidio que se recibe *por cada hijo.*
family business *n* negocio familiar.
family credit *n* (*BRIT*) ≃ ayuda familiar.
family doctor *n* médico/a de cabecera.
family life *n* vida doméstica *or* familiar.
family man *n* (*home-loving*) hombre *m* casero; (*having family*) padre *m* de familia.
family planning *n* planificación *f* familiar.
family planning clinic *n* clínica de planificación familiar.
family tree *n* árbol *m* genealógico.
famine ['fæmɪn] *n* hambre *f*, hambruna.
famished ['fæmɪʃt] *adj* hambriento; **I'm ~!** (*col*) ¡estoy muerto de hambre!, ¡tengo un hambre canina!
famous ['feɪməs] *adj* famoso, célebre.
famously ['feɪməslɪ] *adv* (*get on*) estupendamente.
fan [fæn] *n* abanico *m*; (*ELEC*) ventilador *m*; (*person*) aficionado/a; (*SPORT*) hincha *m/f*; (*of pop star*) fan *m/f* ♦ *vt* abanicar; (*fire, quarrel*) atizar.
▶**fan out** *vi* desplegarse.
fanatic [fə'nætɪk] *n* fanático/a.
fanatical [fə'nætɪkəl] *adj* fanático.
fan belt *n* correa de ventilador.
fancied ['fænsɪd] *adj* imaginario.
fanciful ['fænsɪful] *adj* (*gen*) fantástico; (*imaginary*) fantasioso; (*design*) rebuscado.
fan club *n* club *m* de fans.
fancy ['fænsɪ] *n* (*whim*) capricho, antojo; (*imagination*) imaginación *f* ♦ *adj* (*luxury*) de lujo; (*price*) exorbitado ♦ *vt* (*feel like, want*) tener ganas de; (*imagine*) imaginarse, figurarse; **to take a ~ to sb** tomar cariño a algn; **when the ~ takes him** cuando se le antoja; **it took** *or* **caught**

my ~ me cayó en gracia; **to ~ that ...** imaginarse que ...; **he fancies her** le gusta (ella) mucho.
fancy dress *n* disfraz *m*.
fancy-dress ball ['fænsɪdrɛs-] *n* baile *m* de disfraces.
fancy goods *n* artículos *mpl* de fantasía.
fanfare ['fænfɛə*] *n* fanfarria (de trompeta).
fanfold paper ['fænfəuld-] *n* papel *m* plegado en abanico *or* en acordeón.
fang [fæŋ] *n* colmillo.
fan heater *n* calefactor *m* de aire.
fanlight ['fænlaɪt] *n* (montante *m* en) abanico.
fanny ['fænɪ] *n* (*BRIT col!*) chocho (*!*); (*US col*) pompis *m*, culo.
fantasize ['fæntəsaɪz] *vi* fantasear, hacerse ilusiones.
fantastic [fæn'tæstɪk] *adj* fantástico.
fantasy ['fæntəzɪ] *n* fantasía.
fanzine ['fænziːn] *n* fanzine *m*.
FAO *n abbr* (= *Food and Agriculture Organization*) FAO *f*, OAA *f*.
FAQ *abbr* (= *free alongside quay*) franco sobre muelle.
far [fɑː*] *adj* (*distant*) lejano ♦ *adv* lejos; **the ~ left/right** (*POL*) la extrema izquierda/derecha; **~ away, ~ off** (a lo) lejos; **~ better** mucho mejor; **~ from** lejos de; **by ~** con mucho; **it's by ~ the best** es con mucho el mejor; **go as ~ as the farm** vaya hasta la granja; **is it ~ to London?** ¿a cuánto está Londres?; **it's not ~ (from here)** no está lejos (de aquí); **as ~ as I know** que yo sepa; **how ~ have you got with your work?** ¿hasta dónde has llegado en tu trabajo?
faraway ['fɑːrəweɪ] *adj* remoto; (*look*) ausente, perdido.
farce [fɑːs] *n* farsa.
farcical ['fɑːsɪkəl] *adj* absurdo.
fare [fɛə*] *n* (*on trains, buses*) precio (del billete); (*in taxi: cost*) tarifa; (: *passenger*) pasajero; (*food*) comida; **half/full ~** medio billete *m*/billete *m* completo.
Far East *n*: **the ~** el Extremo *or* Lejano Oriente.
farewell [fɛə'wɛl] *excl, n* adiós *m*.
far-fetched [fɑː'fɛtʃt] *adj* inverosímil.
farm [fɑːm] *n* granja, finca, estancia (*LAM*), chacra (*LAM*), rancho (*LAM*) ♦ *vt* cultivar.
▶**farm out** *vt* (*work*): **to ~ out (to sb)** mandar hacer fuera (a algn).
farmer ['fɑːmə*] *n* granjero/a, estanciero/a (*LAM*).
farmhand ['fɑːmhænd] *n* peón *m*.
farmhouse ['fɑːmhaus] *n* granja, casa de

hacienda (*LAM*).

farming ['fɑːmɪŋ] n (*gen*) agricultura; (*tilling*) cultivo; **sheep ~** cría de ovejas.

farm labourer n = **farmhand**.

farmland ['fɑːmlænd] n tierra de cultivo.

farm produce n productos *mpl* agrícolas.

farm worker n = **farmhand**.

farmyard ['fɑːmjɑːd] n corral m.

Faroe Islands ['fɛərəu-], **Faroes** ['fɛərəuz] *npl:* **the ~** las Islas Feroe.

far-reaching [fɑːˈriːtʃɪŋ] adj (*reform, effect*) de gran alcance.

far-sighted [fɑːˈsaɪtɪd] adj previsor(a).

fart [fɑːt] (*col!*) n pedo (*!*) ♦ vi tirarse un pedo (*!*).

farther ['fɑːðə*] adv más lejos, más allá ♦ adj más lejano.

farthest ['fɑːðɪst] *superlative of* **far**.

FAS *abbr* (= *free alongside ship*) franco al costado del buque.

fascinate ['fæsɪneɪt] vt fascinar.

fascinating ['fæsɪneɪtɪŋ] adj fascinante.

fascination [fæsɪˈneɪʃən] n fascinación f.

fascism ['fæʃɪzəm] n fascismo.

fascist ['fæʃɪst] adj, n fascista *m/f*.

fashion ['fæʃən] n moda; (*manner*) manera ♦ vt formar; **in ~** a la moda; **out of ~** pasado de moda; **in the Greek ~** a la griega, al estilo griego; **after a ~** (*finish, manage etc*) en cierto modo.

fashionable ['fæʃnəbl] adj de moda; (*writer*) de moda, popular; **it is ~ to do ...** está de moda hacer ....

fashion designer n diseñador(a) *m/f* de modas, modisto/a.

fashion show n desfile m de modelos.

fast [fɑːst] adj (*also PHOT: film*) rápido; (*dye, colour*) sólido; (*clock*): **to be ~** estar adelantado ♦ adv rápidamente, de prisa; (*stuck, held*) firmemente ♦ n ayuno ♦ vi ayunar; **~ asleep** profundamente dormido; **in the ~ lane** (*AUT*) en el carril de adelantamiento; **my watch is 5 minutes ~** mi reloj está adelantado 5 minutos; **as ~ as I** *etc* **can** lo más rápido posible; **to make a boat ~** amarrar una barca.

fasten ['fɑːsn] vt asegurar, sujetar; (*coat, belt*) abrochar ♦ vi cerrarse.

▶**fasten (up)on** vt fus (*idea*) aferrarse a.

fastener ['fɑːsnə*] n cierre m; (*of door etc*) cerrojo; (*BRIT: zip ~*) cremallera.

fastening ['fɑːsnɪŋ] n = **fastener**.

fast food n comida rápida, platos *mpl* preparados.

fastidious [fæsˈtɪdɪəs] adj (*fussy*) delicado; (*demanding*) exigente.

fat [fæt] adj gordo; (*meat*) con mucha grasa;

(*greasy*) grasiento ♦ n grasa; (*on person*) carnes *fpl*; (*lard*) manteca; **to live off the ~ of the land** vivir a cuerpo de rey.

fatal ['feɪtl] adj (*mistake*) fatal; (*injury*) mortal; (*consequence*) funesto.

fatalism ['feɪtəlɪzəm] n fatalismo.

fatality [fəˈtælɪtɪ] n (*road death etc*) víctima f mortal.

fatally ['feɪtəlɪ] adv: **~ injured** herido de muerte.

fate [feɪt] n destino, sino.

fated ['feɪtɪd] adj predestinado.

fateful ['feɪtful] adj fatídico.

fat-free ['fætfriː] adj sin grasa.

father ['fɑːðə*] n padre m.

Father Christmas n Papá m Noel.

fatherhood ['fɑːðəhud] n paternidad f.

father-in-law ['fɑːðərɪnlɔː] n suegro.

fatherland ['fɑːðəlænd] n patria.

fatherly ['fɑːðəlɪ] adj paternal.

fathom ['fæðəm] n braza ♦ vt (*unravel*) desentrañar; (*understand*) explicarse.

fatigue [fəˈtiːg] n fatiga, cansancio; **metal ~** fatiga del metal.

fatness ['fætnɪs] n gordura.

fatten ['fætn] vt, vi engordar; **chocolate is ~ing** el chocolate engorda.

fatty ['fætɪ] adj (*food*) graso ♦ n (*fam*) gordito/a, gordinflón/ona *m/f*.

fatuous ['fætjuəs] adj fatuo, necio.

faucet ['fɔːsɪt] n (*US*) grifo, llave f, canilla (*LAM*).

fault [fɔːlt] n (*blame*) culpa; (*defect: in character*) defecto; (*in manufacture*) desperfecto; (*GEO*) falla ♦ vt criticar; **it's my ~** es culpa mía; **to find ~ with** criticar, poner peros a; **at ~** culpable.

faultless ['fɔːltlɪs] adj (*action*) intachable; (*person*) sin defectos.

faulty ['fɔːltɪ] adj defectuoso.

fauna ['fɔːnə] n fauna.

faux pas ['fəuˈpɑː] n desacierto.

favour, (*US*) **favor** ['feɪvə*] n favor m; (*approval*) aprobación f ♦ vt (*proposition*) estar a favor de, aprobar; (*person etc*) preferir; (*assist*) favorecer; **to ask a ~ of** pedir un favor a; **to do sb a ~** hacer un favor a algn; **to find ~ with sb** (*subj: person*) caerle bien a algn; (: *suggestion*) tener buena acogida por parte de algn; **in ~ of** a favor de; **to be in ~ of sth/of doing sth** ser partidario *or* estar a favor de algo/de hacer algo.

favo(u)rable ['feɪvərəbl] adj favorable.

favo(u)rably ['feɪvərəblɪ] adv favorablemente.

favo(u)rite ['feɪvərɪt] adj, n favorito/a *m/f*, preferido/a *m/f*.

favo(u)ritism ['feɪvərɪtɪzəm] *n* favoritismo.
fawn [fɔːn] *n* cervato ♦ *adj* (*also*: ~-coloured) de color cervato, leonado ♦ *vi*: to ~ (up)on adular.
fax [fæks] *n* fax *m* ♦ *vt* mandar *or* enviar por fax.
FBI *n abbr* (*US*: =*Federal Bureau of Investigation*) FBI *m*.
FCC *n abbr* (*US*) = *Federal Communications Commission*.
FCO *n abbr* (*BRIT*: = *Foreign and Commonwealth Office*) ≈ Min. de AA. EE.
FD *n abbr* (*US*) = **fire department**.
FDA *n abbr* (*US*: = *Food and Drug Administration*) oficina que se ocupa del control de los productos alimentarios y farmacéuticos.
FE *n abbr* = **further education**.
fear [fɪə*] *n* miedo, temor *m* ♦ *vt* temer; for ~ of por temor a; ~ of heights vértigo; to ~ for/that temer por/que.
fearful ['fɪəful] *adj* temeroso; (*awful*) espantoso; to be ~ of (*frightened*) tener miedo de.
fearfully ['fɪəfulɪ] *adv* (*timidly*) con miedo; (*col: very*) terriblemente.
fearless ['fɪəlɪs] *adj* (*gen*) sin miedo *or* temor; (*bold*) audaz.
fearlessly ['fɪəlɪslɪ] *adv* temerariamente.
fearsome ['fɪəsəm] *adj* (*opponent*) temible; (*sight*) espantoso.
feasibility [fiːzə'bɪlɪtɪ] *n* factibilidad *f*, viabilidad *f*.
feasibility study *n* estudio de viabilidad.
feasible ['fiːzəbl] *adj* factible, viable.
feast [fiːst] *n* banquete *m*; (*REL: also:* ~ day) fiesta ♦ *vi* banquetear.
feat [fiːt] *n* hazaña.
feather ['fɛðə*] *n* pluma ♦ *vt*: to ~ one's nest (*fig*) hacer su agosto, sacar tajada ♦ *cpd* (*mattress, bed, pillow*) de plumas.
feather-weight ['fɛðəweɪt] *n* (*BOXING*) peso pluma.
feature ['fiːtʃə*] *n* (*gen*) característica; (*ANAT*) rasgo; (*article*) reportaje *m* ♦ *vt* (*subj: film*) presentar ♦ *vi* figurar; ~s *npl* (*of face*) facciones *fpl*; a (special) ~ on sth/sb un reportaje (especial) sobre algo/algn; it ~d prominently in ... tuvo un papel destacado en ....
feature film *n* largometraje *m*.
Feb. *abbr* (= *February*) feb.
February ['fɛbruərɪ] *n* febrero.
feces ['fiːsiːz] *npl* (*US*) = **faeces**.
feckless ['fɛklɪs] *adj* irresponsable, irreflexivo.
Fed *abbr* (*US*) = **federal, federation**.

fed [fɛd] *pt, pp of* **feed**.
Fed. [fɛd] *n abbr* (*US col*) = *Federal Reserve Board*.
federal ['fɛdərəl] *adj* federal.
Federal Republic of Germany *n* República Federal de Alemania.
federation [fɛdə'reɪʃən] *n* federación *f*.
fed-up [fɛd'ʌp] *adj*: to be ~ (with) estar harto (de).
fee [fiː] *n* (*professional*) honorarios *mpl*; (*for examination*) derechos *mpl*; (*of school*) matrícula; (*membership* ~) cuota; (*entrance* ~) entrada; for a small ~ por poco dinero.
feeble ['fiːbl] *adj* débil.
feeble-minded [fiːbl'maɪndɪd] *adj* imbécil.
feed [fiːd] *n* (*gen, of baby*) comida; (*of animal*) pienso; (*on printer*) dispositivo de alimentación ♦ *vt* (*pt, pp* **fed**) (*gen*) alimentar; (*BRIT: breastfeed*) dar el pecho a; (*animal, baby*) dar de comer a ♦ *vi* (*baby, animal*) comer.
▶**feed back** *vt* (*results*) pasar.
▶**feed in** *vt* (*COMPUT*) introducir.
▶**feed into** *vt* (*data, information*) suministrar a; to ~ sth into a machine introducir algo en una máquina.
▶**feed on** *vt fus* alimentarse de.
feedback ['fiːdbæk] *n* (*from person*) reacción *f*; (*TECH*) realimentación *f*, feedback *m*.
feeder ['fiːdə*] *n* (*bib*) babero.
feeding bottle ['fiːdɪŋ-] *n* (*BRIT*) biberón *m*.
feel [fiːl] *n* (*sensation*) sensación *f*; (*sense of touch*) tacto ♦ *vt* (*pt, pp* **felt**) tocar; (*cold, pain etc*) sentir; (*think, believe*) creer; to get the ~ of sth (*fig*) acostumbrarse a algo; to ~ hungry/cold tener hambre/frío; to ~ lonely/better sentirse solo/mejor; I don't ~ well no me siento bien; it ~s soft es suave al tacto; it ~s colder out here se siente más frío aquí fuera; to ~ like (*want*) tener ganas de; I'm still ~ing my way (*fig*) todavía me estoy orientando; I ~ that you ought to do it creo que debes hacerlo; to ~ about *or* around *vi* tantear.
feeler ['fiːlə*] *n* (*of insect*) antena; to put out ~s (*fig*) tantear el terreno.
feeling ['fiːlɪŋ] *n* (*physical*) sensación *f*; (*foreboding*) presentimiento; (*impression*) impresión *f*; (*emotion*) sentimiento; what are your ~s about the matter? ¿qué opinas tú del asunto?; to hurt sb's ~s herir los sentimientos de algn; ~s ran high about it causó mucha controversia; I got the ~ that ... me dio la impresión de que ...; there was a general ~ that ... la

opinión general fue que ....
fee-paying school ['fi:peiɪŋ-] *n* colegio de pago.
feet [fi:t] *npl of* **foot**.
feign [feɪn] *vt* fingir.
feigned [feɪnd] *adj* fingido.
feline ['fi:laɪn] *adj* felino.
fell [fɛl] *pt of* **fall** ♦ *vt* (*tree*) talar ♦ *adj*: **with one ~ blow** con un golpe feroz; **at one ~ swoop** de un solo golpe ♦ *n* (*BRIT: mountain*) montaña; (: *moorland*): **the ~s** los páramos.
fellow ['fɛləu] *n* tipo, tío (*SP*); (*of learned society*) socio/a; (*UNIV*) *miembro de la junta de gobierno de un colegio* ♦ *cpd*: **~ students** compañeros/as *m/fpl* de curso, condiscípulos/as *m/fpl*.
fellow citizen *n* conciudadano/a.
fellow countryman *n* compatriota *m*.
fellow feeling *n* compañerismo.
fellow men *npl* semejantes *mpl*.
fellowship ['fɛləuʃɪp] *n* compañerismo; (*grant*) beca.
fellow traveller *n* compañero/a de viaje; (*POL: with communists*) simpatizante *m/f*.
fellow worker *n* colega *m/f*.
felon ['fɛlən] *n* criminal *m/f*.
felony ['fɛlənɪ] *n* crimen *m*, delito mayor.
felt [fɛlt] *pt, pp of* **feel** ♦ *n* fieltro.
felt-tip pen ['fɛlttɪp-] *n* rotulador *m*.
female ['fi:meɪl] *n* (*woman*) mujer *f*; (*ZOOL*) hembra ♦ *adj* femenino.
feminine ['fɛmɪnɪn] *adj* femenino.
femininity [fɛmɪ'nɪnɪtɪ] *n* feminidad *f*.
feminism ['fɛmɪnɪzəm] *n* feminismo.
feminist ['fɛmɪnɪst] *n* feminista *m/f*.
fence [fɛns] *n* valla, cerca; (*RACING*) valla ♦ *vt* (*also*: **~ in**) cercar ♦ *vi* hacer esgrima; **to sit on the ~** (*fig*) nadar entre dos aguas.
▶**fence in** *vt* cercar.
▶**fence off** *vt* separar con cerca.
fencing ['fɛnsɪŋ] *n* esgrima.
fend [fɛnd] *vi*: **to ~ for o.s.** valerse por sí mismo.
▶**fend off** *vt* (*attack, attacker*) rechazar, repeler; (*blow*) desviar; (*awkward question*) esquivar.
fender ['fɛndə*] *n* pantalla; (*US: AUT*) parachoques *m inv*; (: *RAIL*) trompa.
fennel ['fɛnl] *n* hinojo.
Fens [fɛnz] *npl* (*BRIT*): **the ~** *las tierras bajas de Norfolk (antiguamente zona de marismas)*.
ferment *vi* [fə'mɛnt] fermentar ♦ *n* ['fə:mɛnt] (*fig*) agitación *f*.
fermentation [fə:mɛn'teɪʃən] *n* fermentación *f*.

fern [fə:n] *n* helecho.
ferocious [fə'rəuʃəs] *adj* feroz.
ferociously [fə'rəuʃəslɪ] *adv* ferozmente, con ferocidad.
ferocity [fə'rɔsɪtɪ] *n* ferocidad *f*.
ferret ['fɛrɪt] *n* hurón *m*.
▶**ferret about, ferret around** *vi* rebuscar.
▶**ferret out** *vt* (*secret, truth*) desentrañar.
ferry ['fɛrɪ] *n* (*small*) barca (de pasaje), balsa; (*large: also*: **~boat**) transbordador *m*, ferry *m* ♦ *vt* transportar; **to ~ sth/sb across** *or* **over** transportar algo/a algn a la otra orilla; **to ~ sb to and fro** llevar a algn de un lado para otro.
ferryman ['fɛrɪmən] *n* barquero.
fertile ['fə:taɪl] *adj* fértil; (*BIOL*) fecundo.
fertility [fə'tɪlɪtɪ] *n* fertilidad *f*; fecundidad *f*.
fertility drug *n* medicamento contra la infertilidad.
fertilization [fə:tɪlaɪ'zeɪʃən] *n* fertilización *f*; (*BIOL*) fecundación *f*.
fertilize ['fə:tɪlaɪz] *vt* fertilizar; (*BIOL*) fecundar; (*AGR*) abonar.
fertilizer ['fə:tɪlaɪzə*] *n* abono, fertilizante *m*.
fervent ['fə:vənt] *adj* ferviente.
fervour, (*US*) **fervor** ['fə:və*] *n* fervor *m*, ardor *m*.
fester ['fɛstə*] *vi* supurar.
festival ['fɛstɪvəl] *n* (*REL*) fiesta; (*ART, MUS*) festival *m*.
festive ['fɛstɪv] *adj* festivo; **the ~ season** (*BRIT: Christmas*) las Navidades.
festivities [fɛs'tɪvɪtɪz] *npl* festejos *mpl*.
festoon [fɛs'tu:n] *vt*: **to ~ with** festonear *or* engalanar de.
fetch [fɛtʃ] *vt* ir a buscar; (*BRIT: sell for*) venderse por; **how much did it ~?** ¿por cuánto se vendió?
▶**fetch up** *vi* ir a parar.
fetching ['fɛtʃɪŋ] *adj* atractivo.
fête [feɪt] *n* fiesta.
fetid ['fɛtɪd] *adj* fétido.
fetish ['fɛtɪʃ] *n* fetiche *m*.
fetter ['fɛtə*] *vt* (*person*) encadenar, poner grillos a; (*horse*) trabar; (*fig*) poner trabas a.
fetters ['fɛtəz] *npl* grillos *mpl*.
fettle ['fɛtl] *n*: **in fine ~** en buenas condiciones.
fetus ['fi:təs] *n* (*US*) = **foetus**.
feud [fju:d] *n* (*hostility*) enemistad *f*; (*quarrel*) disputa; **a family ~** una pelea familiar.
feudal ['fju:dl] *adj* feudal.
feudalism ['fju:dəlɪzəm] *n* feudalismo.
fever ['fi:və*] *n* fiebre *f*; **he has a ~** tiene

fiebre.

feverish ['fiːvərɪʃ] adj febril.

feverishly ['fiːvərɪʃlɪ] adv febrilmente.

few [fjuː] adj (not many) pocos; (some) algunos, unos ♦ pron algunos; **a ~** adj unos pocos; **~ people** poca gente; **a good ~, quite a ~** bastantes; **in** or **over the next ~ days** en los próximos días; **every ~ weeks** cada 2 o 3 semanas; **a ~ more days** unos días más.

fewer ['fjuːə*] adj menos.

fewest ['fjuːɪst] adj los/las menos.

FFA n abbr = Future Farmers of America.

FH abbr (BRIT) = fire hydrant.

FHA n abbr (US: = Federal Housing Association) oficina federal de la vivienda.

fiancé [fɪ'ãːŋseɪ] n novio, prometido.

fiancée [fɪ'ãːŋseɪ] n novia, prometida.

fiasco [fɪ'æskəʊ] n fiasco.

fib [fɪb] n mentirijilla ♦ vi decir mentirijillas.

fibre, (US) fiber ['faɪbə*] n fibra.

fibreboard, (US) fiberboard ['faɪbəbɔːd] n fibra vulcanizada.

fibreglass, (US) fiberglass ['faɪbəglɑːs] n fibra de vidrio.

fibrositis [faɪbrə'saɪtɪs] n fibrositis f inv.

FICA n abbr (US) = Federal Insurance Contributions Act.

fickle ['fɪkl] adj inconstante.

fiction ['fɪkʃən] n (gen) ficción f.

fictional ['fɪkʃənl] adj novelesco.

fictionalize ['fɪkʃənəlaɪz] vt novelar.

fictitious [fɪk'tɪʃəs] adj ficticio.

fiddle ['fɪdl] n (MUS) violín m; (cheating) trampa ♦ vt (BRIT: accounts) falsificar; **tax ~** evasión f fiscal; **to work a ~** hacer trampa.

▶**fiddle with** vt fus juguetear con.

fiddler ['fɪdlə*] n violinista m/f.

fiddly ['fɪdlɪ] adj (task) delicado, mañoso; (object) enrevesado.

fidelity [fɪ'delɪtɪ] n fidelidad f.

fidget ['fɪdʒɪt] vi moverse (nerviosamente).

fidgety ['fɪdʒɪtɪ] adj nervioso.

fiduciary [fɪ'duːʃɪərɪ] n fiduciario/a.

field [fiːld] n (gen, COMPUT) campo; (fig) campo, esfera; (SPORT) campo, cancha (LAM); (competitors) competidores mpl ♦ cpd: **to have a ~ day** (fig) ponerse las botas; **to lead the ~** (SPORT, COMM) llevar la delantera; **to give sth a year's trial in the ~** (fig) sacar algo al mercado a prueba por un año; **my particular ~** mi especialidad.

field glasses npl gemelos mpl.

field hospital n hospital m de campaña.

field marshal n mariscal m.

fieldwork ['fiːldwɜːk] n (ARCHAEOLOGY, GEO) trabajo de campo.

fiend [fiːnd] n demonio.

fiendish ['fiːndɪʃ] adj diabólico.

fierce [fɪəs] adj feroz; (wind, attack) violento; (heat) intenso; (fighting, enemy) encarnizado.

fiercely ['fɪəslɪ] adv con ferocidad; violentamente; intensamente; encarnizadamente.

fierceness ['fɪəsnɪs] n ferocidad f; violencia; intensidad f; encarnizamiento.

fiery ['faɪərɪ] adj (burning) ardiente; (temperament) apasionado.

FIFA ['fiːfə] n abbr (= Fédération Internationale de Football Association) FIFA f.

fifteen [fɪf'tiːn] num quince.

fifth [fɪfθ] num quinto.

fiftieth ['fɪftɪɪθ] num quincuagésimo.

fifty ['fɪftɪ] num cincuenta; **the fifties** los años cincuenta; **to be in one's fifties** andar por los cincuenta.

fifty-fifty ['fɪftɪ'fɪftɪ] adv: **to go ~ with sb** ir a medias con algn ♦ adj: **we have a ~ chance of success** tenemos un cincuenta por ciento de posibilidades de tener éxito.

fig [fɪg] n higo.

fight [faɪt] n (gen) pelea; (MIL) combate m; (struggle) lucha ♦ vb (pt, pp fought) vt luchar contra; (cancer, alcoholism) combatir; (LAW): **to ~ a case** defenderse; (quarrel): **to ~ (with sb)** pelear (con algn) ♦ vi pelear, luchar; (fig): **to ~ (for/against)** luchar por/contra.

▶**fight back** vi defenderse; (after illness) recuperarse ♦ vt (tears) contener.

▶**fight down** vt (anger, anxiety, urge) reprimir.

▶**fight off** vt (attack, attacker) rechazar; (disease, sleep, urge) luchar contra.

▶**fight out** vt: **to ~ it out** decidirlo en una pelea.

fighter ['faɪtə*] n combatiente m/f; (fig) luchador(a) m/f; (plane) caza m.

fighter-bomber ['faɪtəbɒmə*] n cazabombardero.

fighter pilot n piloto de caza.

fighting ['faɪtɪŋ] n (gen) el luchar; (battle) combate m; (in streets) disturbios mpl.

figment ['fɪgmənt] n: **a ~ of the imagination** un producto de la imaginación.

figurative ['fɪgjʊrətɪv] adj (meaning) figurado; (ART) figurativo.

figure ['fɪgə*] n (DRAWING, GEOM) figura,

dibujo; (*number, cipher*) cifra; (*person, outline*) figura; (*body shape*) línea; (: *attractive*) tipo ♦ *vt* (*esp US: think, calculate*) calcular, imaginarse ♦ *vi* (*appear*) figurar; (*esp US: make sense*) ser lógico; ~ **of speech** (*LING*) figura retórica; **public** ~ personaje *m*.
▶**figure on** *vt fus* (*US*) contar con.
▶**figure out** *vt* (*understand*) comprender.
figurehead ['fɪɡəhɛd] *n* (*fig*) figura decorativa.
figure skating *n* patinaje *m* artístico.
Fiji (Islands) ['fiːdʒiː-] *n*(*pl*) (Islas *fpl*) Fiji *fpl*.
filament ['fɪləmənt] *n* (*ELEC*) filamento.
filch [fɪltʃ] *vt* (*col: steal*) birlar.
file [faɪl] *n* (*tool*) lima; (*for nails*) lima de uñas; (*dossier*) expediente *m*; (*folder*) carpeta; (*in cabinet*) archivo; (*COMPUT*) fichero; (*row*) fila ♦ *vt* limar; (*papers*) clasificar; (*LAW: claim*) presentar; (*store*) archivar; **to open/close a** ~ (*COMPUT*) abrir/cerrar un fichero; **to** ~ **in/out** *vi* entrar/salir en fila; **to** ~ **a suit against sb** entablar pleito contra algn; **to** ~ **past** desfilar ante.
file name *n* (*COMPUT*) nombre *m* de fichero.
filibuster ['fɪlɪbʌstə*] (*esp US: POL*) *n* obstruccionista *m/f*, filibustero/a ♦ *vi* usar maniobras obstruccionistas.
filing ['faɪlɪŋ] *n*: **to do the** ~ llevar los archivos.
filing cabinet *n* fichero, archivo.
filing clerk *n* oficinista *m/f*.
fill [fɪl] *vt* llenar; (*tooth*) empastar; (*vacancy*) cubrir ♦ *n*: **to eat one's** ~ comer hasta hartarse; **we've already** ~**ed that vacancy** ya hemos cubierto esa vacante; ~**ed with admiration (for)** lleno de admiración (por).
▶**fill in** *vt* rellenar; (*details, report*) completar; **to** ~ **sb in on sth** (*col*) poner a algn al corriente *or* al día sobre algo.
▶**fill out** *vt* (*form, receipt*) rellenar.
▶**fill up** *vt* llenar (hasta el borde) ♦ *vi* (*AUT*) echar gasolina.
fillet ['fɪlɪt] *n* filete *m*.
fillet steak *n* filete *m* de ternera.
filling ['fɪlɪŋ] *n* (*CULIN*) relleno; (*for tooth*) empaste *m*.
filling station *n* estación *f* de servicio.
fillip ['fɪlɪp] *n* estímulo.
filly ['fɪlɪ] *n* potra.
film [fɪlm] *n* película ♦ *vt* (*scene*) filmar ♦ *vi* rodar.
film script *n* guión *m*.
film star *n* estrella de cine.
filmstrip ['fɪlmstrɪp] *n* tira de diapositivas.

film studio *n* estudio de cine.
Filofax ® ['faɪləufæks] *n* agenda (profesional).
filter ['fɪltə*] *n* filtro ♦ *vt* filtrar.
▶**filter in, filter through** *vi* filtrarse.
filter coffee *n* café *m* (molido) para filtrar.
filter lane *n* (*BRIT*) carril *m* de selección.
filter-tipped ['fɪltətɪpt] *adj* con filtro.
filth [fɪlθ] *n* suciedad *f*.
filthy ['fɪlθɪ] *adj* sucio; (*language*) obsceno.
fin [fɪn] *n* (*gen*) aleta.
final ['faɪnl] *adj* (*last*) final, último; (*definitive*) definitivo ♦ *n* (*SPORT*) final *f*; ~**s** *npl* (*SCOL*) exámenes *mpl* finales; ~ **demand** (*on invoice etc*) último aviso; ~ **dividend** dividendo final.
finale [fɪ'nɑːlɪ] *n* final *m*.
finalist ['faɪnəlɪst] *n* (*SPORT*) finalista *m/f*.
finality [faɪ'nælɪtɪ] *n* finalidad *f*; **with an air of** ~ en tono resuelto, de modo terminante.
finalize ['faɪnəlaɪz] *vt* ultimar.
finally ['faɪnəlɪ] *adv* (*lastly*) por último, finalmente; (*eventually*) por fin; (*irrevocably*) de modo definitivo; (*once and for all*) definitivamente.
finance [faɪ'næns] *n* (*money, funds*) fondos *mpl*; ~**s** *npl* finanzas *fpl* ♦ *cpd* (*page, section, company*) financiero ♦ *vt* financiar.
financial [faɪ'nænʃəl] *adj* financiero.
financially [faɪ'nænʃəlɪ] *adv* económicamente.
financial management *n* gestión *f* financiera.
financial statement *n* estado financiero.
financial year *n* ejercicio (financiero).
financier [faɪ'nænsɪə*] *n* financiero/a.
find [faɪnd] *vt* (*pt, pp* **found** [faund]) (*gen*) encontrar, hallar; (*come upon*) descubrir ♦ *n* hallazgo; descubrimiento; **to** ~ **sb guilty** (*LAW*) declarar culpable a algn; **I** ~ **it easy** me resulta fácil.
▶**find out** *vt* averiguar; (*truth, secret*) descubrir ♦ *vi*: **to** ~ **out about** enterarse de.
findings ['faɪndɪŋz] *npl* (*LAW*) veredicto *sg*, fallo *sg*; (*of report*) recomendaciones *fpl*.
fine [faɪn] *adj* (*delicate*) fino; (*beautiful*) hermoso ♦ *adv* (*well*) bien ♦ *n* (*LAW*) multa ♦ *vt* (*LAW*) multar; **the weather is** ~ hace buen tiempo; **he's** ~ está muy bien; **you're doing** ~ lo estás haciendo muy bien; **to cut it** ~ (*of time, money*) calcular muy justo; **to get a** ~ **for (doing) sth** recibir una multa por (hacer) algo.
fine arts *npl* bellas artes *fpl*.
finely ['faɪnlɪ] *adv* (*splendidly*) con elegancia; (*chop*) en trozos pequeños,

fino; (*adjust*) con precisión.
fineness ['faɪnnɪs] *n* (*of cloth*) finura; (*of idea*) sutilidad *f*.
fine print *n*: **the ~** la letra pequeña *or* menuda.
finery ['faɪnərɪ] *n* galas *fpl*.
finesse [fɪ'nɛs] *n* sutileza.
fine-tooth comb ['faɪntuːθ-] *n*: **to go through sth with a ~** revisar algo a fondo.
finger ['fɪŋgə*] *n* dedo ♦ *vt* (*touch*) manosear; (*MUS*) puntear; **little/index ~** (dedo) meñique *m*/índice *m*.
fingernail ['fɪŋgəneɪl] *n* uña.
fingerprint ['fɪŋgəprɪnt] *n* huella dactilar ♦ *vt* tomar las huellas dactilares de.
fingertip ['fɪŋgətɪp] *n* yema del dedo; **to have sth at one's ~s** saberse algo al dedillo.
finicky ['fɪnɪkɪ] *adj* (*fussy*) delicado.
finish ['fɪnɪʃ] *n* (*end*) fin *m*; (*SPORT*) meta; (*polish etc*) acabado ♦ *vt*, *vi* acabar, terminar; **to ~ doing sth** acabar de hacer algo; **to ~ first/second/third** (*SPORT*) llegar el primero/segundo/tercero; **I've ~ed with the paper** he terminado con el periódico; **she's ~ed with him** ha roto *or* acabado con él.
►**finish off** *vt* acabar, terminar; (*kill*) rematar.
►**finish up** *vt* acabar, terminar ♦ *vi* ir a parar, terminar.
finished ['fɪnɪʃt] *adj* (*product*) acabado; (*performance*) pulido; (*col: tired*) rendido, hecho polvo.
finishing ['fɪnɪʃɪŋ] *adj*: **~ touches** toque *m* final.
finishing line *n* línea de llegada *or* meta.
finishing school *n* colegio para la educación social de señoritas.
finite ['faɪnaɪt] *adj* finito.
Finland ['fɪnlənd] *n* Finlandia.
Finn [fɪn] *n* finlandés/esa *m/f*.
Finnish ['fɪnɪʃ] *adj* finlandés/esa ♦ *n* (*LING*) finlandés *m*.
fiord [fjɔːd] *n* fiordo.
fir [fəː*] *n* abeto.
fire ['faɪə*] *n* fuego; (*accidental, damaging*) incendio ♦ *vt* (*gun*) disparar; (*set fire to*) incendiar; (*excite*) exaltar; (*interest*) despertar; (*dismiss*) despedir ♦ *vi* encenderse; (*AUT: subj: engine*) encender; **electric/gas ~** estufa eléctrica/de gas; **on ~** ardiendo, en llamas; **to be on ~** estar ardiendo; **to catch ~** prenderse fuego; **to set ~ to sth, set sth on ~** prender fuego a algo; **insured against ~** asegurado contra incendios; **to be/come under ~** estar/caer

bajo el fuego enemigo.
fire alarm *n* alarma de incendios.
firearm ['faɪərɑːm] *n* arma de fuego.
fire brigade, (*US*) **fire department** *n* (cuerpo de) bomberos *mpl*.
fire door *n* puerta contra incendios.
fire drill *n* (ejercicio de) simulacro de incendio.
fire engine *n* coche *m* de bomberos.
fire escape *n* escalera de incendios.
fire extinguisher *n* extintor *m*.
fireguard ['faɪəgɑːd] *n* pantalla (guardallama).
fire hazard *n* = **fire risk**.
fire hydrant *n* boca de incendios.
fire insurance *n* seguro contra incendios.
fireman ['faɪəmən] *n* bombero.
fireplace ['faɪəpleɪs] *n* chimenea.
fireplug ['faɪəplʌg] *n* (*US*) boca de incendios.
fire practice *n* = **fire drill**.
fireproof ['faɪəpruːf] *adj* a prueba de fuego; (*material*) incombustible.
fire regulations *npl* reglamentos *mpl* contra incendios.
fire risk *n* peligro de incendio.
firescreen ['faɪəskriːn] *n* pantalla refractaria.
fireside ['faɪəsaɪd] *n*: **by the ~** al lado de la chimenea.
fire station *n* parque *m* de bomberos.
firewood ['faɪəwud] *n* leña.
fireworks ['faɪəwəːks] *npl* fuegos *mpl* artificiales.
firing ['faɪərɪŋ] *n* (*MIL*) disparos *mpl*, tiroteo.
firing line *n* línea de fuego; **to be in the ~** (*fig: liable to be criticised*) estar en la línea de fuego.
firing squad *n* pelotón *m* de ejecución.
firm [fəːm] *adj* firme; (*offer, decision*) en firme ♦ *n* empresa; **to be a ~ believer in sth** ser un partidario convencido de algo; **to stand ~** *or* **take a ~ stand on sth** (*fig*) mantenerse firme ante algo.
firmly ['fəːmlɪ] *adv* firmemente.
firmness ['fəːmnɪs] *n* firmeza.
first [fəːst] *adj* primero ♦ *adv* (*before others*) primero; (*when listing reasons etc*) en primer lugar, primeramente ♦ *n* (*person: in race*) primero/a; (*AUT: also*: **~ gear**) primera; **at ~** al principio; **~ of all** ante todo; **the ~ of January** el uno *or* primero de enero; **in the ~ instance** en primer lugar; **I'll do it ~ thing tomorrow** lo haré mañana a primera hora; **for the ~ time** por primera vez; **head ~** de cabeza; **from the (very) ~** desde el principio.
first aid *n* primeros auxilios *mpl*.

first aid kit *n* botiquín *m*.
first aid post, (*US*) **first aid station** *n* puesto de auxilio.
first-class [ˈfəːstklɑːs] *adj* de primera clase; ~ **ticket** (*RAIL etc*) billete *m or* boleto (*LAM*) de primera clase; ~ **mail** correo de primera clase.
first-hand [fəːstˈhænd] *adj* de primera mano.
first lady *n* (*esp US*) primera dama.
firstly [ˈfəːstlɪ] *adv* en primer lugar.
first name *n* nombre *m* de pila.
first night *n* estreno.
first-rate [fəːstˈreɪt] *adj* de primera (clase).
first-time buyer [fəːsttaɪm-] *n persona que compra su primera vivienda.*
fir tree *n* abeto.
FIS *n abbr* (*BRIT*: = *Family Income Supplement*) *ayuda estatal familiar.*
fiscal [ˈfɪskəl] *adj* fiscal; ~ **year** año fiscal, ejercicio.
fish [fɪʃ] *n, pl inv* pez *m*; (*food*) pescado ♦ *vt* pescar en ♦ *vi* pescar; **to go ~ing** ir de pesca.
►**fish out** *vt* (*from water, box etc*) sacar.
fish-and-chip shop *n* = **chip shop**.
fishbone [ˈfɪʃbəun] *n* espina.
fisherman [ˈfɪʃəmən] *n* pescador *m*.
fishery [ˈfɪʃərɪ] *n* pesquería.
fish factory *n* fábrica de elaboración de pescado.
fish farm *n* piscifactoría.
fish fingers *npl* (*BRIT*) palitos *mpl* de pescado (empanado).
fishing boat [ˈfɪʃɪŋ-] *n* barca de pesca.
fishing industry *n* industria pesquera.
fishing line *n* sedal *m*.
fishing net *n* red *f* de pesca.
fishing rod *n* caña (de pescar).
fishing tackle *n* aparejo (de pescar).
fish market *n* mercado de pescado.
fishmonger [ˈfɪʃmʌŋgə*] *n* (*BRIT*) pescadero/a.
fishmonger's (shop) *n* (*BRIT*) pescadería.
fishseller [ˈfɪʃselə*] *n* (*US*) = **fishmonger**.
fish slice *n* paleta para pescado.
fish sticks *npl* (*US*) = **fish fingers**.
fishstore [ˈfɪʃstɔː*] *n* (*US*) = **fishmonger's (shop)**.
fishy [ˈfɪʃɪ] *adj* (*fig*) sospechoso.
fission [ˈfɪʃən] *n* fisión *f*; **atomic/nuclear ~** fisión *f* atómica/nuclear.
fissure [ˈfɪʃə*] *n* fisura.
fist [fɪst] *n* puño.
fistfight [ˈfɪstfaɪt] *n* lucha a puñetazos.
fit [fɪt] *adj* (*MED, SPORT*) en (buena) forma; (*proper*) adecuado, apropiado ♦ *vt* (*subj: clothes*) quedar bien a; (*try on: clothes*)

probar; (*match: facts*) cuadrar *or* corresponder *or* coincidir con; (*description*) estar de acuerdo con; (*accommodate*) ajustar, adaptar ♦ *vi* (*clothes*) quedar bien; (*in space, gap*) caber; (*facts*) coincidir ♦ *n* (*MED*) ataque *m*; (*outburst*) arranque *m*; ~ **to** apto para; ~ **for** apropiado para; **do as you think** *or* **see** ~ haz lo que te parezca mejor; **to keep** ~ mantenerse en forma; **to be ~ for work** (*after illness*) estar en condiciones para trabajar; ~ **of coughing** acceso de tos; ~ **of anger/enthusiasm** arranque de cólera/entusiasmo; **to have** *or* **suffer a** ~ tener un ataque *or* acceso; **this dress is a good** ~ este vestido me queda bien; **by ~s and starts** a rachas.
►**fit in** *vi* encajar ♦ *vt* (*object*) acomodar; (*fig: appointment, visitor*) encontrar un hueco para; **to ~ in with sb's plans** acomodarse a los planes de algn.
►**fit out** *vt* (*BRIT: also:* **fit up**) equipar.
fitful [ˈfɪtful] *adj* espasmódico, intermitente.
fitfully [ˈfɪtfəlɪ] *adv* irregularmente; **to sleep** ~ dormir a rachas.
fitment [ˈfɪtmənt] *n* mueble *m*.
fitness [ˈfɪtnɪs] *n* (*MED*) forma física; (*of remark*) conveniencia.
fitted carpet [ˈfɪtɪd-] *n* moqueta.
fitted cupboards [ˈfɪtɪd-] *npl* armarios *mpl* empotrados.
fitted kitchen [ˈfɪtɪd-] *n* cocina amueblada.
fitter [ˈfɪtə*] *n* ajustador(a) *m/f*.
fitting [ˈfɪtɪŋ] *adj* apropiado ♦ *n* (*of dress*) prueba; *see also* **fittings**.
fitting room *n* (*in shop*) probador *m*.
fittings [ˈfɪtɪŋz] *npl* instalaciones *fpl*.
five [faɪv] *num* cinco; **she is** ~ **(years old)** tiene cinco años (de edad); **it costs** ~ **pounds** cuesta cinco libras; **it's** ~ **(o'clock)** son las cinco.
five-day week [ˈfaɪvdeɪ] *n* semana inglesa.
fiver [ˈfaɪvə*] *n* (*col: BRIT*) billete *m* de cinco libras; (*: US*) billete *m* de cinco dólares.
fix [fɪks] *vt* (*secure*) fijar, asegurar; (*mend*) arreglar; (*make ready: meal, drink*) preparar ♦ *n*: **to be in a** ~ estar en un aprieto; **to ~ sth in one's mind** fijar algo en la memoria; **the fight was a** ~ (*col*) la pelea estaba amañada.
►**fix on** *vt* (*decide on*) fijar.
►**fix up** *vt* (*arrange: date, meeting*) arreglar; **to ~ sb up with sth** conseguirle algo a algn.
fixation [fɪkˈseɪʃən] *n* (*PSYCH, fig*) fijación *f*.
fixative [ˈfiksətɪv] *n* fijador *m*.
fixed [fɪkst] *adj* (*prices etc*) fijo; **how are you**

~ **for money?** (*col*) ¿qué tal andas de dinero?

fixed assets *npl* activo *sg* fijo.

fixed charge *n* gasto fijo.

fixed-price contract ['fɪkstpraɪs-] *n* contrato a precio fijo.

fixture ['fɪkstʃə*] *n* (*SPORT*) encuentro; ~**s** *npl* instalaciones *fpl* fijas.

fizz [fɪz] *vi* burbujear.

fizzle out ['fɪzl-] *vi* apagarse; (*enthusiasm, interest*) decaer; (*plan*) quedar en agua de borrajas.

fizzy ['fɪzɪ] *adj* (*drink*) gaseoso.

fjord [fjɔːd] *n* = **fiord.**

FL *abbr* (*US*) = Florida.

Fla. *abbr* (*US*) = Florida.

flabbergasted ['flæbəgɑːstɪd] *adj* pasmado.

flabby ['flæbɪ] *adj* flojo (de carnes); (*skin*) fofo.

flag [flæg] *n* bandera; (*stone*) losa ♦ *vi* decaer; ~ **of convenience** pabellón *m* de conveniencia.

▶**flag down** *vt:* **to ~ sb down** hacer señas a algn para que se pare.

flagpole ['flægpəul] *n* asta de bandera.

flagrant ['fleɪgrənt] *adj* flagrante.

flagship ['flægʃɪp] *n* buque *m* insignia *or* almirante.

flagstone ['flægstəun] *n* losa.

flag stop *n* (*US*) parada discrecional.

flair [fleə*] *n* aptitud *f* especial.

flak [flæk] *n* (*MIL*) fuego antiaéreo; (*col: criticism*) lluvia de críticas.

flake [fleɪk] *n* (*of rust, paint*) desconchón *m*; (*of snow*) copo; (*of soap powder*) escama ♦ *vi* (*also:* ~ **off**) (*paint*) desconcharse; (*skin*) descamarse.

flaky ['fleɪkɪ] *adj* (*paintwork*) desconchado; (*skin*) escamoso.

flaky pastry *n* (*CULIN*) hojaldre *m*.

flamboyant [flæm'bɔɪənt] *adj* (*dress*) vistoso; (*person*) extravagante.

flame [fleɪm] *n* llama; **to burst into** ~**s** incendiarse; **old** ~ (*col*) antiguo amor *m/f*.

flamingo [flə'mɪŋgəu] *n* flamenco.

flammable ['flæməbl] *adj* inflamable.

flan [flæn] *n* (*BRIT*) tarta.

flank [flæŋk] *n* flanco; (*of person*) costado ♦ *vt* flanquear.

flannel ['flænl] *n* (*BRIT: also:* **face** ~) toallita; (*fabric*) franela; ~**s** *npl* pantalones *mpl* de franela.

flannelette [flænə'lɛt] *n* franela de algodón.

flap [flæp] *n* (*of pocket, envelope*) solapa; (*of table*) hoja (plegadiza); (*wing movement*) aletazo; (*AVIAT*) flap *m* ♦ *vt* (*wings*) batir ♦ *vi* (*sail, flag*) ondear.

flapjack ['flæpdʒæk] *n* (*US: pancake*) torta, panqueque *m* (*LAM*).

flare [fleə*] *n* llamarada; (*MIL*) bengala; (*in skirt etc*) vuelo.

▶**flare up** *vi* encenderse; (*fig: person*) encolerizarse; (: *revolt*) estallar.

flash [flæʃ] *n* relámpago; (*also: news* ~) noticias *fpl* de última hora; (*PHOT*) flash *m*; (*US: torch*) linterna ♦ *vt* (*light, headlights*) lanzar destellos con; (*torch*) encender ♦ *vi* destellar; **in a** ~ en un santiamén; ~ **of inspiration** ráfaga de inspiración; **to** ~ **sth about** (*fig, col: flaunt*) ostentar algo, presumir con algo; **he** ~**ed by** *or* **past** pasó como un rayo.

flashback ['flæʃbæk] *n* flashback *m*, escena retrospectiva.

flashbulb ['flæʃbʌlb] *n* bombilla de flash.

flash card *n* (*SCOL*) tarjeta.

flash cube *n* cubo *m* de flash.

flasher ['flæʃə*] *n* exhibicionista *m*.

flashlight ['flæʃlaɪt] *n* (*US: torch*) linterna.

flashpoint ['flæʃpɔɪnt] *n* punto de inflamación; (*fig*) punto de explosión.

flashy ['flæʃɪ] *adj* (*pej*) ostentoso.

flask [flɑːsk] *n* petaca; (*also: vacuum* ~) termo.

flat [flæt] *adj* llano; (*smooth*) liso; (*tyre*) desinflado; (*battery*) descargado; (*beer*) sin gas; (*MUS: instrument*) desafinado ♦ *n* (*BRIT: apartment*) piso (*SP*), departamento (*LAM*), apartamento; (*AUT*) pinchazo; (*MUS*) bemol *m*; (**to work**) ~ **out** (trabajar) a tope; ~ **rate of pay** sueldo fijo.

flatfooted [flæt'futɪd] *adj* de pies planos.

flatly ['flætlɪ] *adv* rotundamente, de plano.

flatmate ['flætmeɪt] *n* compañero/a de piso.

flatness ['flætnɪs] *n* (*of land*) llanura, lo llano.

flat-screen ['flætskriːn] *adj* de pantalla plana.

flatten ['flætn] *vt* (*also:* ~ **out**) allanar; (*smooth out*) alisar; (*house, city*) arrasar.

flatter ['flætə*] *vt* adular, halagar; (*show to advantage*) favorecer.

flatterer ['flætərə*] *n* adulador(a) *m/f*.

flattering ['flætərɪŋ] *adj* halagador(a); (*clothes etc*) que favorece, favorecedor(a).

flattery ['flætərɪ] *n* adulación *f*.

flatulence ['flætjuləns] *n* flatulencia.

flaunt [flɔːnt] *vt* ostentar, lucir.

flavour, (*US*) **flavor** ['fleɪvə*] *n* sabor *m*, gusto ♦ *vt* sazonar, condimentar; **strawberry** ~**ed** con sabor a fresa.

flavo(u)ring ['fleɪvərɪŋ] *n* (*in product*) aromatizante *m*.

flaw [flɔː] *n* defecto.
flawless ['flɔːlɪs] *adj* intachable.
flax [flæks] *n* lino.
flaxen ['flæksən] *adj* muy rubio.
flea [fliː] *n* pulga.
flea market *n* rastro, mercadillo.
fleck [flɛk] *n* mota ♦ *vt* (*with blood, mud etc*) salpicar; **brown ~ed with white** marrón con motas blancas.
fledg(e)ling ['flɛdʒlɪŋ] *n* (*fig*) novato/a, principiante *m/f*.
flee [fliː], *pt, pp* **fled** [flɛd] *vt* huir de, abandonar ♦ *vi* huir.
fleece [fliːs] *n* vellón *m*; (*wool*) lana ♦ *vt* (*col*) desplumar.
fleecy ['fliːsɪ] *adj* (*blanket*) lanoso, lanudo; (*cloud*) aborregado.
fleet [fliːt] *n* flota; (*of cars, lorries etc*) parque *m*.
fleeting ['fliːtɪŋ] *adj* fugaz.
Flemish ['flɛmɪʃ] *adj* flamenco ♦ *n* (*LING*) flamenco; **the ~** los flamencos.
flesh [flɛʃ] *n* carne *f*; (*of fruit*) pulpa; **of ~ and blood** de carne y hueso.
flesh wound *n* herida superficial.
flew [fluː] *pt of* **fly**.
flex [flɛks] *n* cable *m* ♦ *vt* (*muscles*) tensar.
flexibility [flɛksɪ'bɪlɪtɪ] *n* flexibilidad *f*.
flexible ['flɛksəbl] *adj* (*gen, disk*) flexible; **~ working hours** horario *sg* flexible.
flexitime ['flɛksɪtaɪm] *n* horario flexible.
flick [flɪk] *n* golpecito; (*with finger*) capirotazo; (*BRIT: col: film*) película ♦ *vt* dar un golpecito a.
▶**flick off** *vt* quitar con el dedo.
▶**flick through** *vt fus* hojear.
flicker ['flɪkə*] *vi* (*light*) parpadear; (*flame*) vacilar ♦ *n* parpadeo.
flick knife *n* navaja de muelle.
flier ['flaɪə*] *n* aviador(a) *m/f*.
flies [flaɪz] *npl of* **fly**.
flight [flaɪt] *n* vuelo; (*escape*) huida, fuga; (*also: ~ of steps*) tramo (de escaleras); **to take ~** huir, darse a la fuga; **to put to ~** ahuyentar; **how long does the ~ take?** ¿cuánto dura el vuelo?
flight attendant *n* (*US*) auxiliar *m/f* de vuelo.
flight deck *n* (*AVIAT*) cabina de mandos.
flight path *n* trayectoria de vuelo.
flight recorder *n* registrador *m* de vuelo.
flighty ['flaɪtɪ] *adj* caprichoso.
flimsy ['flɪmzɪ] *adj* (*thin*) muy ligero; (*excuse*) flojo.
flinch [flɪntʃ] *vi* encogerse.
fling [flɪŋ] *vt* (*pt, pp* **flung** [flʌŋ]) arrojar ♦ *n* (*love affair*) aventura amorosa.
flint [flɪnt] *n* pedernal *m*; (*in lighter*) piedra.

flip [flɪp] *vt*: **to ~ a coin** echar a cara o cruz.
▶**flip over** *vt* dar la vuelta a.
▶**flip through** *vt fus* (*book*) hojear; (*records*) ver de pasada.
flippancy ['flɪpənsɪ] *n* ligereza.
flippant ['flɪpənt] *adj* poco serio.
flipper ['flɪpə*] *n* (*of seal etc, for swimming*) aleta.
flip side *n* (*of record*) cara B.
flirt [fləːt] *vi* coquetear, flirtear ♦ *n* coqueta *f*.
flirtation [fləː'teɪʃən] *n* coqueteo, flirteo.
flit [flɪt] *vi* revolotear.
float [fləut] *n* flotador *m*; (*in procession*) carroza; (*sum of money*) (dinero suelto para) cambio ♦ *vi* (*also COMM: currency*) flotar ♦ *vt* (*gen*) hacer flotar; (*company*) lanzar; **to ~ an idea** plantear una idea.
floating ['fləutɪŋ] *adj*: **~ vote** voto indeciso; **~ voter** votante *m/f* indeciso/a.
flock [flɔk] *n* (*of sheep*) rebaño; (*of birds*) bandada; (*of people*) multitud *f*.
floe [fləu] *n*: **ice ~** témpano de hielo.
flog [flɔg] *vt* azotar; (*col*) vender.
flood [flʌd] *n* inundación *f*; (*of words, tears etc*) torrente *m* ♦ *vt* (*also AUT: carburettor*) inundar; **to ~ the market** (*COMM*) inundar el mercado.
flooding ['flʌdɪŋ] *n* inundación *f*.
floodlight ['flʌdlaɪt] *n* foco ♦ *vt* (*irreg: like* **light**) iluminar con focos.
floodlit ['flʌdlɪt] *pt, pp of* **floodlight** ♦ *adj* iluminado.
flood tide *n* pleamar *f*.
floodwater ['flʌdwɔːtə*] *n* aguas *fpl* (de la inundación).
floor [flɔː*] *n* suelo, piso (*LAM*); (*storey*) piso; (*of sea, valley*) fondo; (*dance ~*) pista ♦ *vt* (*fig: baffle*) dejar anonadado; **ground ~, (US) first ~** planta baja; **first ~, (US) second ~** primer piso; **top ~** último piso; **to have the ~** (*speaker*) tener la palabra.
floorboard ['flɔːbɔːd] *n* tabla.
flooring ['flɔːrɪŋ] *n* suelo; (*material*) solería.
floor lamp *n* (*US*) lámpara de pie.
floor show *n* cabaret *m*.
floorwalker ['flɔːwɔːkə*] *n* (*US COMM*) supervisor(a) *m/f*.
flop [flɔp] *n* fracaso ♦ *vi* (*fail*) fracasar.
floppy ['flɔpɪ] *adj* flojo ♦ *n* = **floppy disk**.
floppy disk *n* (*COMPUT*) floppy *m*, floppy-disk *m*, disco flexible.
flora ['flɔːrə] *n* flora.
floral ['flɔːrl] *adj* floral; (*dress, wallpaper*) de flores.
Florence ['flɔrəns] *n* Florencia.
Florentine ['flɔrəntaɪn] *adj, n* florentino/a *m/f*.

florid ['florɪd] *adj* (*style*) florido.
florist ['florɪst] *n* florista *m/f*; ~'s (**shop**) *n* floristería.
flotation [fləu'teɪʃən] *n* (*of shares*) emisión *f*; (*of company*) lanzamiento.
flounce [flauns] *n* volante *m*.
▶**flounce in** *vi* entrar con gesto exagerado.
▶**flounce out** *vi* salir con gesto airado.
flounder ['flaundə*] *vi* tropezar ♦ *n* (*ZOOL*) platija.
flour ['flauə*] *n* harina.
flourish ['flʌrɪʃ] *vi* florecer ♦ *n* ademán *m*, movimiento (ostentoso).
flourishing ['flʌrɪʃɪŋ] *adj* floreciente.
flout [flaut] *vt* burlarse de; (*order*) no hacer caso de, hacer caso omiso de.
flow [fləu] *n* (*movement*) flujo; (*direction*) curso; (*of river, also ELEC*) corriente *f* ♦ *vi* correr, fluir.
flow chart *n* organigrama *m*.
flow diagram *n* organigrama *m*.
flower ['flauə*] *n* flor *f* ♦ *vi* florecer; **in** ~ en flor.
flower bed *n* macizo.
flowerpot ['flauəpot] *n* tiesto.
flowery ['flauərɪ] *adj* florido; (*perfume, pattern*) de flores.
flowing ['fləuɪŋ] *adj* (*hair, clothes*) suelto; (*style*) fluido.
flown [fləun] *pp of* **fly**.
flu [fluː] *n* gripe *f*.
fluctuate ['flʌktjueɪt] *vi* fluctuar.
fluctuation [flʌktju'eɪʃən] *n* fluctuación *f*.
flue [fluː] *n* cañón *m*.
fluency ['fluːənsɪ] *n* fluidez *f*, soltura.
fluent ['fluːənt] *adj* (*speech*) elocuente; **he speaks** ~ **French, he's** ~ **in French** domina el francés.
fluently ['fluːəntlɪ] *adv* con soltura.
fluff [flʌf] *n* pelusa.
fluffy ['flʌfɪ] *adj* lanoso.
fluid ['fluːɪd] *adj, n* fluido, líquido; (*in diet*) líquido.
fluke [fluːk] *n* (*col*) chiripa.
flummox ['flʌməks] *vt* desconcertar.
flung [flʌŋ] *pt, pp of* **fling**.
flunky ['flʌŋkɪ] *n* lacayo.
fluorescent [fluə'rɛsnt] *adj* fluorescente.
fluoride ['fluəraɪd] *n* fluoruro.
fluoride toothpaste *n* pasta de dientes con flúor.
flurry ['flʌrɪ] *n* (*of snow*) ventisca; (*haste*) agitación *f*; ~ **of activity** frenesí *m* de actividad.
flush [flʌʃ] *n* (*on face*) rubor *m*; (*fig: of youth, beauty*) resplandor *m* ♦ *vt* limpiar con agua; (*also*: ~ **out**) (*game, birds*) levantar;

(*fig: criminal*) poner al descubierto ♦ *vi* ruborizarse ♦ *adj*: ~ **with** a ras de; **to** ~ **the toilet** tirar de la cadena (del wáter); **hot** ~**es** (*MED*) sofocos *mpl*.
flushed [flʌʃt] *adj* ruborizado.
fluster ['flʌstə*] *n* aturdimiento ♦ *vt* aturdir.
flustered ['flʌstəd] *adj* aturdido.
flute [fluːt] *n* flauta travesera.
flutter ['flʌtə*] *n* (*of wings*) revoloteo, aleteo; (*fam: bet*) apuesta ♦ *vi* revolotear; **to be in a** ~ estar nervioso.
flux [flʌks] *n* flujo; **in a state of** ~ cambiando continuamente.
fly [flaɪ] *n* (*insect*) mosca; (*on trousers: also*: **flies**) bragueta ♦ *vb* (*pt* **flew**, *pp* **flown**) *vt* (*plane*) pilotar; (*cargo*) transportar (en avión); (*distances*) recorrer (en avión) ♦ *vi* volar; (*passengers*) ir en avión; (*escape*) evadirse; (*flag*) ondear.
▶**fly away** *vi* (*bird, insect*) irse volando.
▶**fly in** *vi* (*person*) llegar en avión; (*plane*) aterrizar; **he flew in from Bilbao** llegó en avión desde Bilbao.
▶**fly off** *vi* irse volando.
▶**fly out** *vi* irse en avión.
fly-fishing ['flaɪfɪʃɪŋ] *n* pesca con mosca.
flying ['flaɪɪŋ] *n* (*activity*) (el) volar ♦ *adj*: ~ **visit** visita relámpago; **with** ~ **colours** con lucimiento.
flying buttress *n* arbotante *m*.
flying picket *n* piquete *m* volante.
flying saucer *n* platillo volante.
flying squad *n* (*POLICE*) brigada móvil.
flying start *n*: **to get off to a** ~ empezar con buen pie.
flyleaf, *pl* **flyleaves** ['flaɪliːf, -liːvz] *n* (hoja de) guarda.
flyover ['flaɪəuvə*] *n* (*BRIT: bridge*) paso elevado or a desnivel (*LAM*).
flypast ['flaɪpɑːst] *n* desfile *m* aéreo.
flysheet ['flaɪʃiːt] *n* (*for tent*) doble techo.
flyswatter ['flaɪswɔtə*] *n* matamoscas *m inv*.
flyweight ['flaɪweɪt] *adj* de peso mosca ♦ *n* peso mosca.
flywheel ['flaɪwiːl] *n* volante *m* (de motor).
FM *abbr* (*BRIT MIL*) = **field marshal**; (*RADIO*: = *frequency modulation*) FM.
FMB *n abbr* (*US*) = *Federal Maritime Board*.
FMCS *n abbr* (*US*: = *Federal Mediation and Conciliation Services*) *organismo de conciliación en conflictos laborales*.
FO *n abbr* (*BRIT*: = *Foreign Office*) ≈ Min. de AA. EE.
foal [fəul] *n* potro.
foam [fəum] *n* espuma ♦ *vi* hacer espuma.
foam rubber *n* goma espuma.

FOB *abbr* (= *free on board*) f.a.b.
fob [fɔb] *n* (*also:* watch ~) leontina ♦ *vt*: to
~ **sb off with sth** deshacerse de algn con
algo.
foc *abbr* (*BRIT*: = *free of charge*) gratis.
focal ['fəukəl] *adj* focal; ~ **point** punto
focal; (*fig*) centro de atención.
focus ['fəukəs] (*pl:* ~es) *n* foco ♦ *vt* (*field
glasses etc*) enfocar ♦ *vi*: to ~ (on) enfocar
(a); (*issue etc*) centrarse en; in/out of ~
enfocado/desenfocado.
fodder ['fɔdə*] *n* pienso.
FOE *n abbr* (= *Friends of the Earth*) Amigos
mpl de la Tierra; (*US*: = *Fraternal Order of
Eagles*) organización benéfica.
foe [fəu] *n* enemigo.
foetus, (*US*) **fetus** ['fiːtəs] *n* feto.
fog [fɔg] *n* niebla.
fogbound ['fɔgbaund] *adj* inmovilizado por
la niebla.
foggy ['fɔgɪ] *adj*: it's ~ hay niebla.
fog lamp, (*US*) **fog light** *n* (*AUT*) faro
antiniebla.
foible ['fɔɪbl] *n* manía.
foil [fɔɪl] *vt* frustrar ♦ *n* hoja; (*kitchen* ~)
papel *m* (de) aluminio; (*FENCING*) florete
m.
foist [fɔɪst] *vt*: to ~ **sth on sb** endilgarle
algo a algn.
fold [fəuld] *n* (*bend, crease*) pliegue *m*; (*AGR*)
redil *m* ♦ *vt* doblar; (*map etc*) plegar; to ~
one's arms cruzarse de brazos.
▶**fold up** *vi* plegarse, doblarse; (*business*)
quebrar.
folder ['fəuldə*] *n* (*for papers*) carpeta;
(*binder*) carpeta de anillas; (*brochure*)
folleto.
folding ['fəuldɪŋ] *adj* (*chair, bed*) plegable.
foliage ['fəulɪɪdʒ] *n* follaje *m*.
folio ['fəulɪəu] *n* folio.
folk [fəuk] *npl* gente *f* ♦ *adj* popular,
folklórico; ~s *npl* familia, parientes *mpl*.
folklore ['fəuklɔː*] *n* folklore *m*.
folk music *n* música folk.
folk singer *n* cantante *m/f* de música folk.
folk song *n* canción *f* popular *or* folk.
follow ['fɔləu] *vt* seguir ♦ *vi* seguir; (*result*)
resultar; he ~ed suit hizo lo mismo; to ~
sb's advice seguir el consejo de algn; I
don't quite ~ you no te comprendo muy
bien; to ~ in sb's footsteps seguir los
pasos de algn; it doesn't ~ that ... no se
deduce que ....
▶**follow on** *vi* seguir; (*continue*): to ~ on
from ser la consecuencia lógica de.
▶**follow out** *vt* (*implement: idea, plan*)
realizar, llevar a cabo.
▶**follow through** *vt* llevar hasta el fin ♦ *vi*

(*SPORT*) dar el remate.
▶**follow up** *vt* (*letter, offer*) responder a;
(*case*) investigar.
follower ['fɔləuə*] *n* seguidor(a) *m/f*; (*POL*)
partidario/a.
following ['fɔləuɪŋ] *adj* siguiente ♦ *n*
seguidores *mpl*.
follow-up ['fɔləuʌp] *n* continuación *f*.
follow-up letter *n* carta recordatoria.
folly ['fɔlɪ] *n* locura.
fond [fɔnd] *adj* (*loving*) cariñoso; to be ~ of
sb tener cariño a algn; she's ~ of
swimming tiene afición a la natación, le
gusta nadar.
fondle ['fɔndl] *vt* acariciar.
fondly ['fɔndlɪ] *adv* (*lovingly*) con cariño; he
~ believed that ... creía ingenuamente
que ....
fondness ['fɔndnɪs] *n* (*for things*) afición *f*;
(*for people*) cariño.
font [fɔnt] *n* pila bautismal.
food [fuːd] *n* comida.
food chain *n* cadena alimenticia.
food mixer *n* batidora.
food poisoning *n* intoxicación *f*
alimentaria.
food processor *n* robot *m* de cocina.
food stamp *n* (*US*) vale *m* para comida.
foodstuffs ['fuːdstʌfs] *npl* comestibles *mpl*.
fool [fuːl] *n* tonto/a; (*CULIN*) mousse *m* de
frutas ♦ *vt* engañar; to make a ~ of o.s.
ponerse en ridículo; you can't ~ me a mí
no me engañas; *see also* April Fool's Day.
▶**fool about, fool around** *vi* hacer el
tonto.
foolhardy ['fuːlhɑːdɪ] *adj* temerario.
foolish ['fuːlɪʃ] *adj* tonto; (*careless*)
imprudente.
foolishly ['fuːlɪʃlɪ] *adv* tontamente,
neciamente.
foolproof ['fuːlpruːf] *adj* (*plan etc*) infalible.
foolscap ['fuːlskæp] *n* ~ papel *m* tamaño
folio.
foot [fut], *pl* feet *n* (*gen, also: of page, stairs
etc*) pie *m*; (*measure*) pie (= 304 mm); (*of
animal, table*) pata ♦ *vt* (*bill*) pagar; on ~ a
pie; to find one's feet acostumbrarse; to
put one's ~ down (*say no*) plantarse; (*AUT*) pisar el acelerador.
footage ['futɪdʒ] *n* (*CINE*) imágenes *fpl*.
foot-and-mouth (disease) [futənd'mauθ-]
n fiebre *f* aftosa.
football ['futbɔːl] *n* balón *m*; (*game: BRIT*)
fútbol *m*; (: *US*) fútbol *m* americano.
footballer ['futbɔːlə*] *n* (*BRIT*) = football
player.
football match *n* partido de fútbol.
football player *n* futbolista *m/f*, jugador(a)

m/f de fútbol.

footbrake ['futbreɪk] *n* freno de pie.

footbridge ['futbrɪdʒ] *n* pasarela, puente *m* para peatones.

foothills ['futhɪlz] *npl* estribaciones *fpl*.

foothold ['futhəuld] *n* pie *m* firme.

footing ['futɪŋ] *n* (*fig*) nivel *m*; **to lose one's ~** perder el equilibrio; **on an equal ~** en pie de igualdad.

footlights ['futlaɪts] *npl* candilejas *fpl*.

footman ['futmən] *n* lacayo.

footnote ['futnəut] *n* nota (de pie de página).

footpath ['futpɑːθ] *n* sendero.

footprint ['futprɪnt] *n* huella, pisada.

footrest ['futrɛst] *n* apoyapiés *m inv*.

footsie ['futsɪ] *n*: **to play ~ with sb** (*col*) juguetear con los pies de algn.

footsore ['futsɔː*] *adj* con los pies doloridos.

footstep ['futstɛp] *n* paso.

footwear ['futwɛə*] *n* calzado.

FOR *abbr* (= *free on rail*) franco (puesto sobre) vagón.

=========== *KEYWORD* ===========

for [fɔː] *prep* **1** (*indicating destination, intention*) para; **the train ~ London** el tren para Londres; (*in announcements*) el tren con destino a Londres; **he left ~ Rome** marchó para Roma; **he went ~ the paper** fue por el periódico; **is this ~ me?** ¿es esto para mí?; **it's time ~ lunch** es la hora de comer

2 (*indicating purpose*) para; **what('s it) ~?** ¿para qué (es)?; **what's this button ~?** ¿para qué sirve este botón?; **to pray ~ peace** rezar por la paz

3 (*on behalf of, representing*): **the MP ~ Hove** el diputado por Hove; **he works ~ the government/a local firm** trabaja para el gobierno/en una empresa local; **I'll ask him ~ you** se lo pediré por ti; **G ~ George** G de Gerona

4 (*because of*) por esta razón; **~ fear of being criticized** por temor a ser criticado

5 (*with regard to*) para; **it's cold ~ July** hace frío para julio; **he has a gift ~ languages** tiene don de lenguas

6 (*in exchange for*) por; **I sold it ~ £5** lo vendí por £5; **to pay 50 pence ~ a ticket** pagar 50 peniques por un billete

7 (*in favour of*): **are you ~ or against us?** ¿estás con nosotros o contra nosotros?; **I'm all ~ it** estoy totalmente a favor; **vote ~ X** vote (a) X

8 (*referring to distance*): **there are roadworks ~ 5 km** hay obras en 5 km; **we walked ~ miles** caminamos kilómetros y kilómetros

9 (*referring to time*): **he was away ~ 2 years** estuvo fuera (durante) dos años; **it hasn't rained ~ 3 weeks** no ha llovido durante or en 3 semanas; **I have known her ~ years** la conozco desde hace años; **can you do it ~ tomorrow?** ¿lo podrás hacer para mañana?

10 (*with infinitive clauses*): **it is not ~ me to decide** la decisión no es cosa mía; **it would be best ~ you to leave** sería mejor que te fueras; **there is still time ~ you to do it** todavía te queda tiempo para hacerlo; **~ this to be possible** ... para que esto sea posible ...

11 (*in spite of*) a pesar de; **~ all his complaints** a pesar de sus quejas

♦ *conj* (*since, as: rather formal*) puesto que.

forage ['fɒrɪdʒ] *n* forraje *m*.

foray ['fɒreɪ] *n* incursión *f*.

forbid *pt* **forbad(e)**, *pp* **forbidden** [fə'bɪd, -'bæd, -'bɪdn] *vt* prohibir; **to ~ sb to do sth** prohibir a algn hacer algo.

forbidding [fə'bɪdɪŋ] *adj* (*landscape*) inhóspito; (*severe*) severo.

force [fɔːs] *n* fuerza ♦ *vt* obligar, forzar; **to ~ o.s. to do** hacer un esfuerzo por hacer; **the F~s** *npl* (*BRIT*) las Fuerzas Armadas; **sales ~** (*COMM*) personal *m* de ventas; **a ~ 5 wind** un viento fuerza 5; **to join ~s** unir fuerzas; **in ~** (*law etc*) en vigor; **to ~ sb to do sth** obligar a algn a hacer algo.

►**force back** *vt* (*crowd, enemy*) hacer retroceder; (*tears*) reprimir.

►**force down** *vt* (*food*) tragar con esfuerzo.

forced [fɔːst] *adj* (*smile*) forzado; (*landing*) forzoso.

force-feed ['fɔːsfiːd] *vt* (*animal, prisoner*) alimentar a la fuerza.

forceful ['fɔːsful] *adj* enérgico.

forcemeat ['fɔːsmiːt] *n* (*CULIN*) relleno.

forceps ['fɔːsɛps] *npl* fórceps *m inv*.

forcible ['fɔːsəbl] *adj* (*violent*) a la fuerza; (*telling*) convincente.

forcibly ['fɔːsəblɪ] *adv* a la fuerza.

ford [fɔːd] *n* vado ♦ *vt* vadear.

fore [fɔː*] *n*: **to bring to the ~** sacar a la luz pública; **to come to the ~** empezar a destacar.

forearm ['fɔːrɑːm] *n* antebrazo.

forebear ['fɔːbɛə*] *n* antepasado.

foreboding [fɔː'bəudɪŋ] *n* presentimiento.

forecast ['fɔːkɑːst] *n* pronóstico ♦ *vt* (*irreg: like* **cast**) pronosticar; **weather ~** previsión *f* meteorológica.

foreclose [fɔː'kləuz] *vt* (*LAW: also:* ~ **on**) extinguir el derecho de redimir.

foreclosure [fɔː'kləuʒə*] *n* apertura de un juicio hipotecario.

forecourt ['fɔːkɔːt] *n* (*of garage*) área de entrada.

forefathers ['fɔːfɑːðəz] *npl* antepasados *mpl*.

forefinger ['fɔːfɪŋɡə*] *n* (dedo) índice *m*.

forefront ['fɔːfrʌnt] *n*: **in the** ~ **of** en la vanguardia de.

forego, *pt* **forewent**, *pp* **foregone** [fɔː'ɡəu, -'wɛnt, -'ɡɔn] *vt* = **forgo**.

foregoing ['fɔːɡəuɪŋ] *adj* anterior, precedente.

foregone ['fɔːɡɔn] *pp of* **forego** ♦ *adj*: **it's a** ~ **conclusion** es una conclusión inevitable.

foreground ['fɔːɡraund] *n* primer plano.

forehand ['fɔːhænd] *n* (*TENNIS*) derechazo directo.

forehead ['fɔrɪd] *n* frente *f*.

foreign ['fɔrɪn] *adj* extranjero; (*trade*) exterior.

foreign currency *n* divisas *fpl*.

foreigner ['fɔrɪnə*] *n* extranjero/a.

foreign exchange *n* (*system*) cambio de divisas; (*money*) divisas *fpl*, moneda extranjera.

foreign investment *n* inversión *f* en el extranjero; (*money, stock*) inversiones *fpl* extranjeras.

Foreign Minister *n* Ministro/a de Asuntos Exteriores, Canciller *m* (*LAM*).

Foreign Office *n* Ministerio de Asuntos Exteriores.

Foreign Secretary *n* (*BRIT*) Ministro/a de Asuntos Exteriores, Canciller *m* (*LAM*).

foreleg ['fɔːlɛɡ] *n* pata delantera.

foreman ['fɔːmən] *n* capataz *m*; (*LAW: of jury*) presidente *m/f*.

foremost ['fɔːməust] *adj* principal ♦ *adv*: **first and** ~ ante todo, antes que nada.

forename ['fɔːneɪm] *n* nombre *m* (de pila).

forensic [fə'rɛnsɪk] *adj* forense; ~ **scientist** forense *m/f*.

foreplay ['fɔːpleɪ] *n* preámbulos *mpl* (*de estimulación sexual*).

forerunner ['fɔːrʌnə*] *n* precursor(a) *m/f*.

foresee, *pt* **foresaw**, *pp* **foreseen** [fɔː'siː, -'sɔː, -'siːn] *vt* prever.

foreseeable [fɔː'siːəbl] *adj* previsible.

foreshadow [fɔː'ʃædəu] *vt* prefigurar, anunciar.

foreshore ['fɔːʃɔː*] *n* playa.

foreshorten [fɔː'ʃɔːtn] *vt* (*figure, scene*) escorzar.

foresight ['fɔːsaɪt] *n* previsión *f*.

foreskin ['fɔːskɪn] *n* (*ANAT*) prepucio.

forest ['fɔrɪst] *n* bosque *m*.

forestall [fɔː'stɔːl] *vt* anticiparse a.

forestry ['fɔrɪstrɪ] *n* silvicultura.

foretaste ['fɔːteɪst] *n* anticipo.

foretell, *pt*, *pp* **foretold** [fɔː'tɛl, -'təuld] *vt* predecir, pronosticar.

forethought ['fɔːθɔːt] *n* previsión *f*.

forever [fə'rɛvə*] *adv* siempre; (*for good*) para siempre.

forewarn [fɔː'wɔːn] *vt* avisar, advertir.

forewent [fɔː'wɛnt] *pt of* **forego**.

foreword ['fɔːwəːd] *n* prefacio.

forfeit ['fɔːfɪt] *n* (*in game*) prenda ♦ *vt* perder (derecho a).

forgave [fə'ɡeɪv] *pt of* **forgive**.

forge [fɔːdʒ] *n* fragua; (*smithy*) herrería ♦ *vt* (*signature: BRIT: money*) falsificar; (*metal*) forjar.

►**forge ahead** *vi* avanzar mucho.

forger ['fɔːdʒə*] *n* falsificador(a) *m/f*.

forgery ['fɔːdʒərɪ] *n* falsificación *f*.

forget, *pt* **forgot**, *pp* **forgotten** [fə'ɡɛt, -'ɡɔt, -'ɡɔtn] *vt* olvidar, olvidarse de ♦ *vi* olvidarse.

forgetful [fə'ɡɛtful] *adj* olvidadizo.

forget-me-not [fə'ɡɛtmɪnɔt] *n* nomeolvides *f inv*.

forgive, *pt* **forgave**, *pp* **forgiven** [fə'ɡɪv, -'ɡeɪv, -'ɡɪvn] *vt* perdonar; **to** ~ **sb for sth/ for doing sth** perdonar algo a algn/a algn por haber hecho algo.

forgiveness [fə'ɡɪvnɪs] *n* perdón *m*.

forgiving [fə'ɡɪvɪŋ] *adj* compasivo.

forgo, *pt* **forwent**, *pp* **forgone** [fɔː'ɡəu, -'wɛnt, -'ɡɔn] *vt* (*give up*) renunciar a; (*go without*) privarse de.

forgot [fə'ɡɔt] *pt of* **forget**.

forgotten [fə'ɡɔtn] *pp of* **forget**.

fork [fɔːk] *n* (*for eating*) tenedor *m*; (*for gardening*) horca; (*of roads*) bifurcación *f*; (*in tree*) horcadura ♦ *vi* (*road*) bifurcarse.

►**fork out** *vt* (*col: pay*) soltar.

forked [fɔːkt] *adj* (*lightning*) en zigzag.

fork-lift truck ['fɔːklɪft-] *n* máquina elevadora.

forlorn [fə'lɔːn] *adj* (*person*) triste, melancólico; (*deserted: cottage*) abandonado; (*desperate: attempt*) desesperado.

form [fɔːm] *n* forma; (*BRIT SCOL*) curso; (*document*) formulario, planilla (*LAM*) ♦ *vt* formar; **in the** ~ **of** en forma de; **in top** ~ en plena forma; **to be in good** ~ (*SPORT, fig*) estar en plena forma; **to** ~ **part of sth** formar parte de algo; **to** ~ **a circle/a queue** hacer una curva/una cola.

formal ['fɔːməl] *adj* (*offer, receipt*) por escrito; (*person etc*) correcto; (*occasion, dinner*) ceremonioso; ~ **dress** traje *m* de

vestir; (*evening dress*) traje *m* de etiqueta.
formalities [fɔː'mælɪtɪz] *npl* formalidades
fpl.
formality [fɔː'mælɪtɪ] *n* ceremonia.
formalize ['fɔːməlaɪz] *vt* formalizar.
formally ['fɔːməlɪ] *adv* oficialmente.
format ['fɔːmæt] *n* formato ♦ *vt* (*COMPUT*)
formatear.
formation [fɔː'meɪʃən] *n* formación *f.*
formative ['fɔːmətɪv] *adj* (*years*) de
formación.
format line *n* (*COMPUT*) línea de formato.
former ['fɔːmə*] *adj* anterior; (*earlier*)
antiguo; (*ex*) ex; **the** ~ ... **the latter** ...
aquél ... éste ...; **the** ~ **president** el
antiguo *or* ex presidente; **the** ~
Yugoslavia/Soviet Union la antigua *or* ex
Yugoslavia/Unión Soviética.
formerly ['fɔːməlɪ] *adv* antiguamente.
form feed *n* (*on printer*) salto de página.
Formica ® [fɔː'maɪkə] *n* formica ®.
formidable ['fɔːmɪdəbl] *adj* formidable.
formula ['fɔːmjulə] *n* fórmula; **F~ One**
(*AUT*) Fórmula Uno.
formulate ['fɔːmjuleɪt] *vt* formular.
fornicate ['fɔːnɪkeɪt] *vi* fornicar.
forsake, *pt* **forsook**, *pp* **forsaken** [fə'seɪk,
-'suk, -'seɪkən] *vt* (*gen*) abandonar; (*plan*)
renunciar a.
fort [fɔːt] *n* fuerte *m;* **to hold the** ~ (*fig*)
quedarse a cargo.
forte ['fɔːtɪ] *n* fuerte *m.*
forth [fɔːθ] *adv:* **back and** ~ de acá para
allá; **and so** ~ y así sucesivamente.
forthcoming [fɔːθ'kʌmɪŋ] *adj* próximo,
venidero; (*character*) comunicativo.
forthright ['fɔːθraɪt] *adj* franco.
forthwith ['fɔːθ'wɪθ] *adv* en el acto, acto
seguido.
fortification [fɔːtɪfɪ'keɪʃən] *n* fortificación *f.*
fortified wine ['fɔːtɪfaɪd-] *n* vino
encabezado.
fortify ['fɔːtɪfaɪ] *vt* fortalecer.
fortitude ['fɔːtɪtjuːd] *n* fortaleza.
fortnight ['fɔːtnaɪt] *n* (*BRIT*) quincena; **it's a**
~ **since** ... hace quince días que ....
fortnightly ['fɔːtnaɪtlɪ] *adj* quincenal ♦ *adv*
quincenalmente.
FORTRAN ['fɔːtræn] *n* FORTRAN *m.*
fortress ['fɔːtrɪs] *n* fortaleza.
fortuitous [fɔː'tjuːɪtəs] *adj* fortuito.
fortunate ['fɔːtʃənɪt] *adj:* **it is** ~ **that** ... (es
una) suerte que ....
fortunately ['fɔːtʃənɪtlɪ] *adv*
afortunadamente.
fortune ['fɔːtʃən] *n* suerte *f;* (*wealth*)
fortuna; **to make a** ~ hacer un dineral.
fortuneteller ['fɔːtʃəntɛlə*] *n* adivino/a.

forty ['fɔːtɪ] *num* cuarenta.
forum ['fɔːrəm] *n* (*also fig*) foro.
forward ['fɔːwəd] *adj* (*position*) avanzado;
(*movement*) hacia delante; (*front*)
delantero; (*not shy*) atrevido ♦ *n* (*SPORT*)
delantero ♦ *vt* (*career*) remitir; (*career*)
promocionar; **to move** ~ avanzar;
"please ~**"** "remítase al destinatario".
forward contract *n* contrato a término.
forward exchange *n* cambio a término.
forward planning *n* planificación *f* por
anticipado.
forward rate *n* tipo a término.
forward(s) ['fɔːwəd(z)] *adv* (hacia)
adelante.
forward sales *npl* ventas *fpl* a término.
forwent [fɔː'wɛnt] *pt of* **forgo.**
fossil ['fɔsl] *n* fósil *m;* ~ **fuel** combustible *m*
fósil.
foster ['fɔstə*] *vt* (*child*) acoger en familia;
(*idea*) fomentar.
foster brother *n* hermano de leche.
foster child *n* hijo/a adoptivo/a.
foster mother *n* madre *f* adoptiva.
fought [fɔːt] *pt, pp of* **fight.**
foul [faul] *adj* (*gen*) sucio, puerco; (*weather,*
smell etc) asqueroso ♦ *n* (*FOOTBALL*) falta
♦ *vt* (*dirty*) ensuciar; (*block*) atascar;
(*entangle: anchor, propeller*) atascar,
enredarse en; (*football player*) cometer
una falta contra.
foul play *n* (*SPORT*) mala jugada; (*LAW*)
muerte *f* violenta.
found [faund] *pt, pp of* **find** ♦ *vt* (*establish*)
fundar.
foundation [faun'deɪʃən] *n* (*act*) fundación
f; (*basis*) base *f*; (*also:* ~ **cream**) base *f* de
maquillaje.
foundations [faun'deɪʃənz] *npl* (*of building*)
cimientos *mpl;* **to lay the** ~ poner los
cimientos.
foundation stone *n:* **to lay the** ~ poner la
primera piedra.
founder ['faundə*] *n* fundador(a) *m/f* ♦ *vi*
irse a pique.
founding ['faundɪŋ] *adj:* ~ **fathers** (*esp US*)
fundadores *mpl*, próceres *mpl;* ~ **member**
miembro fundador.
foundry ['faundrɪ] *n* fundición *f.*
fountain ['fauntɪn] *n* fuente *f.*
fountain pen *n* (pluma) estilográfica,
(*LAM*) plumafuente *f.*
four [fɔː*] *num* cuatro; **on all** ~**s** a gatas.
four-footed [fɔː'futɪd] *adj* cuadrúpedo.
four-letter word ['fɔːlɛtə-] *n* taco.
four-poster ['fɔː'pəustə*] *n* (*also:* ~ **bed**)
cama de columnas.
foursome ['fɔːsəm] *n* grupo de cuatro

personas.

fourteen ['fɔː'tiːn] *num* catorce.

fourteenth [fɔː'tiːnθ] *num* decimocuarto.

fourth [fɔːθ] *num* cuarto ♦ *n* (*AUT: also:* ~ **gear**) cuarta (velocidad).

four-wheel drive ['fɔːwiːl-] *n* tracción *f* a las cuatro ruedas.

fowl [faul] *n* ave *f* (de corral).

fox [fɔks] *n* zorro ♦ *vt* confundir.

fox fur *n* piel *f* de zorro.

foxglove ['fɔksglʌv] *n* (*BOT*) dedalera.

fox-hunting ['fɔkshʌntɪŋ] *n* caza de zorros.

foxtrot ['fɔkstrɔt] *n* fox(trot) *m*.

foyer ['fɔɪeɪ] *n* vestíbulo.

FP *n abbr* (*BRIT*) = *former pupil*; (*US*) = *fireplug*.

FPA *n abbr* (*BRIT*: = *Family Planning Association*) *asociación de planificación familiar.*

Fr. *abbr* (*REL*) (= *Father*) P.; (= *friar*) Fr.

fr. *abbr* (= *franc*) f.

fracas ['frækɑː] *n* gresca, refriega.

fraction ['frækʃən] *n* fracción *f*.

fractionally ['frækʃnəlɪ] *adv* ligeramente.

fractious ['frækʃəs] *adj* (*person, mood*) irascible.

fracture ['fræktʃə*] *n* fractura ♦ *vt* fracturar.

fragile ['frædʒaɪl] *adj* frágil.

fragment ['frægmənt] *n* fragmento.

fragmentary [fræg'mɛntərɪ] *adj* fragmentario.

fragrance ['freɪgrəns] *n* fragancia.

fragrant ['freɪgrənt] *adj* fragante, oloroso.

frail [freɪl] *adj* (*fragile*) frágil, quebradizo; (*weak*) delicado.

frame [freɪm] *n* (*TECH*) armazón *f*; (*of picture, door etc*) marco; (*of spectacles: also:* ~**s**) montura ♦ *vt* encuadrar; (*picture*) enmarcar; (*reply*) formular; **to** ~ **sb** (*col*) inculpar por engaños a algn.

frame of mind *n* estado de ánimo.

framework ['freɪmwɜːk] *n* marco.

France [frɑːns] *n* Francia.

franchise ['fræntʃaɪz] *n* (*POL*) derecho al voto, sufragio; (*COMM*) licencia, concesión *f*.

franchisee [fræntʃaɪ'ziː] *n* concesionario/a.

franchiser ['fræntʃaɪzə*] *n* compañía concesionaria.

frank [fræŋk] *adj* franco ♦ *vt* (*BRIT: letter*) franquear.

frankfurter ['fræŋkfɔːtə*] *n* salchicha de Frankfurt.

frankincense ['fræŋkɪnsɛns] *n* incienso.

franking machine ['fræŋkɪŋ-] *n* máquina de franqueo.

frankly ['fræŋklɪ] *adv* francamente.

frankness ['fræŋknɪs] *n* franqueza.

frantic ['fræntɪk] *adj* (*desperate: need, desire*) desesperado; (: *search*) frenético; (: *person*) desquiciado.

fraternal [frə'tɜːnl] *adj* fraterno.

fraternity [frə'tɜːnɪtɪ] *n* (*club*) fraternidad *f*; (*US*) club *m* de estudiantes; (*guild*) gremio.

fraternization [frætənaɪ'zeɪʃən] *n* fraternización *f*.

fraternize ['frætənaɪz] *vi* confraternizar.

fraud [frɔːd] *n* fraude *m*; (*person*) impostor(a) *m/f*.

fraudulent ['frɔːdjulənt] *adj* fraudulento.

fraught [frɔːt] *adj* (*tense*) tenso; ~ **with** cargado de.

fray [freɪ] *n* combate *m*, lucha, refriega ♦ *vi* deshilacharse; **tempers were** ~**ed** el ambiente se ponía tenso.

FRB *n abbr* (*US*) = *Federal Reserve Board*.

FRCM *n abbr* (*BRIT*) = *Fellow of the Royal College of Music*.

FRCO *n abbr* (*BRIT*) = *Fellow of the Royal College of Organists*.

FRCP *n abbr* (*BRIT*) = *Fellow of the Royal College of Physicians*.

FRCS *n abbr* (*BRIT*) = *Fellow of the Royal College of Surgeons*.

freak [friːk] *n* (*person*) fenómeno; (*event*) suceso anormal; (*col: enthusiast*) adicto/a ♦ *adj* (*storm, conditions*) anormal; **health** ~ (*col*) maniático/a en cuestión de salud.

▶**freak out** *vi* (*col: on drugs*) flipar.

freakish ['friːkɪʃ] *adj* (*result*) inesperado; (*appearance*) estrambótico; (*weather*) cambiadizo.

freckle ['frɛkl] *n* peca.

freckled ['frɛkld] *adj* pecoso, lleno de pecas.

free [friː] *adj* (*person: at liberty*) libre (*not fixed*) suelto; (*gratis*) gratuito; (*unoccupied*) desocupado; (*liberal*) generoso ♦ *vt* (*prisoner etc*) poner en libertad; (*jammed object*) soltar; **to give sb a** ~ **hand** dar carta blanca a algn; ~ **and easy** despreocupado; **is this seat** ~**?** ¿está libre este asiento?; ~ **of tax** libre de impuestos; **admission** ~ entrada libre; ~ (**of charge**), **for** ~ *adv* gratis.

freebie ['friːbɪ] *n* (*col*): **it's a** ~ es gratis.

freedom ['friːdəm] *n* libertad *f*; ~ **of association** libertad *f* de asociación.

freedom fighter *n* luchador(a) *m/f* por la libertad.

free enterprise *n* libre empresa.

Freefone ® ['friːfəun] *n* (*BRIT*) número gratuito.

free-for-all ['friːfərɔːl] *n* riña general.

free gift n regalo.
freehold ['fri:hǝuld] n propiedad f absoluta.
free kick n tiro libre.
freelance ['fri:lɑ:ns] adj, adv por cuenta
  propia; **to do ~ work** trabajar por su
  cuenta.
freely ['fri:lɪ] adv libremente; (liberally)
  generosamente.
free-market economy ['fri:'mɑ:kɪt-] n
  economía de libre mercado.
freemason ['fri:meɪsn] n francmasón m.
freemasonry ['fri:meɪsnrɪ] n
  (franc)masonería.
freepost ['fri:pǝust] n porte m pagado.
free-range ['fri:'reɪndʒ] adj (hen, eggs) de
  granja.
free sample n muestra gratuita.
freesia ['fri:ʒǝ] n fresia.
free speech n libertad f de expresión.
free trade n libre comercio.
freeway ['fri:weɪ] n (US) autopista.
freewheel [fri:'wi:l] vi ir en punto muerto.
freewheeling [fri:'wi:lɪŋ] adj libre,
  espontáneo; (careless) irresponsable.
free will n libre albedrío; **of one's own ~**
  por su propia voluntad.
freeze [fri:z] vb (pt **froze**, pp **frozen** [frǝuz,
  frǝuzn]) vi helarse, congelarse ♦ vt helar;
  (prices, food, salaries) congelar ♦ n helada;
  congelación f.
▶**freeze over** vi (lake, river) helarse,
  congelarse; (window, windscreen)
  cubrirse de escarcha.
▶**freeze up** vi helarse, congelarse.
freeze-dried ['fri:zdraɪd] adj liofilizado.
freezer ['fri:zǝ*] n congelador m,
  congeladora f.
freezing ['fri:zɪŋ] adj helado.
freezing point n punto de congelación; **3
  degrees below ~** tres grados bajo cero.
freight [freɪt] n (goods) carga; (money
  charged) flete m; **~ forward** contra
  reembolso del flete, flete por pagar; **~
  inward** flete sobre compras.
freight car n vagón m de mercancías.
freighter ['freɪtǝ*] n buque m de carga;
  (AVIAT) avión m de transporte de
  mercancías.
freight forwarder [-'fɔ:wǝdǝ*] n agente m
  expedidor.
freight train n (US) tren m de mercancías.
French [frentʃ] adj francés/esa ♦ n (LING)
  francés m; **the ~** npl los franceses.
French bean n judía verde.
French bread n pan m francés.
French Canadian adj, n francocanadiense
  m/f.
French dressing n (CULIN) vinagreta.

French fried potatoes, (US) **French fries**
  npl patatas fpl or papas fpl (LAM) fritas.
French Guiana [-gaɪ'ænǝ] n la Guayana
  Francesa.
French loaf n barra de pan.
Frenchman ['frentʃmǝn] n francés m.
French Riviera n: **the ~** la Riviera, la
  Costa Azul.
French stick n barra de pan.
French window n puertaventana.
Frenchwoman ['frentʃwumǝn] n francesa.
frenetic [frǝ'netɪk] adj frenético.
frenzy ['frenzɪ] n frenesí m.
frequency ['fri:kwǝnsɪ] n frecuencia.
frequency modulation (FM) n
  frecuencia modulada.
frequent adj ['fri:kwǝnt] frecuente ♦ vt
  [frɪ'kwent] frecuentar.
frequently ['fri:kwǝntlɪ] adv
  frecuentemente, a menudo.
fresco ['freskǝu] n fresco.
fresh [freʃ] adj (gen) fresco; (new) nuevo;
  (water) dulce; **to make a ~ start** empezar
  de nuevo.
freshen ['freʃǝn] vi (wind) arreciar; (air)
  refrescar.
▶**freshen up** vi (person) refrescarse.
freshener ['freʃnǝ*] n: **air ~** ambientador m;
  skin ~ tónico.
fresher ['freʃǝ*] n (BRIT SCOL: col)
  estudiante m/f de primer año.
freshly ['freʃlɪ] adv: **~ painted/arrived**
  recién pintado/llegado.
freshman ['freʃmǝn] n (US: SCOL) = **fresher**.
freshness ['freʃnɪs] n frescura.
freshwater ['freʃwɔ:tǝ*] adj (fish) de agua
  dulce.
fret [fret] vi inquietarse.
fretful ['fretful] adj (child) quejumbroso.
Freudian ['frɔɪdɪǝn] adj freudiano; **~ slip**
  lapsus m (freudiano).
FRG n abbr (= Federal Republic of Germany)
  RFA f.
Fri. abbr (= Friday) vier.
friar ['fraɪǝ*] n fraile m; (before name) fray.
friction ['frɪkʃǝn] n fricción f.
friction feed n (on printer) avance m por
  fricción.
Friday ['fraɪdɪ] n viernes m inv.
fridge [frɪdʒ] n (BRIT) nevera, frigo,
  refrigeradora (LAM), heladera (LAM).
fridge-freezer ['frɪdʒ'fri:zǝ*] n frigorífico-
  congelador m, combi m.
fried [fraɪd] pt, pp of **fry** ♦ adj: **~ egg** huevo
  frito, huevo estrellado.
friend [frend] n amigo/a.
friendliness ['frendlɪnɪs] n simpatía.
friendly ['frendlɪ] adj simpático.

friendly fire *n* fuego amigo, disparos *mpl* del propio bando.

friendly society *n* mutualidad *f*, montepío.

friendship ['frɛndʃɪp] *n* amistad *f*.

frieze [friːz] *n* friso.

frigate ['frɪgɪt] *n* fragata.

fright [fraɪt] *n* susto; **to take** ~ asustarse.

frighten ['fraɪtn] *vt* asustar.

▶**frighten away, frighten off** *vt* (*birds, children etc*) espantar, ahuyentar.

frightened ['fraɪtnd] *adj* asustado.

frightening ['fraɪtnɪŋ] *adj*: **it's** ~ da miedo.

frightful ['fraɪtful] *adj* espantoso, horrible.

frightfully ['fraɪtfulɪ] *adv* terriblemente; **I'm** ~ **sorry** lo siento muchísimo.

frigid ['frɪdʒɪd] *adj* (*MED*) frígido.

frigidity [frɪ'dʒɪdɪtɪ] *n* (*MED*) frigidez *f*.

frill [frɪl] *n* volante *m*; **without** ~**s** (*fig*) sin adornos.

frilly ['frɪlɪ] *adj* con volantes.

fringe [frɪndʒ] *n* (*BRIT: of hair*) flequillo; (*edge: of forest etc*) borde *m*, margen *m*.

fringe benefits *npl* ventajas *fpl* complementarias.

fringe theatre *n* teatro experimental.

Frisbee ® ['frɪzbɪ] *n* frisbee ® *m*.

frisk [frɪsk] *vt* cachear, registrar.

frisky ['frɪskɪ] *adj* juguetón/ona.

fritter ['frɪtə*] *n* buñuelo.

▶**fritter away** *vt* desperdiciar.

frivolity [frɪ'vɔlɪtɪ] *n* frivolidad *f*.

frivolous ['frɪvələs] *adj* frívolo.

frizzy ['frɪzɪ] *adj* crespo.

fro [frəu] *see* **to**.

frock [frɔk] *n* vestido.

frog [frɔg] *n* rana; **to have a** ~ **in one's throat** tener carraspera.

frogman ['frɔgmən] *n* hombre-rana *m*.

frogmarch ['frɔgmɑːtʃ] *vt*: **to** ~ **sb in/out** meter/sacar a algn a rastras.

frolic ['frɔlɪk] *vi* juguetear.

===================== *KEYWORD*

from [frɔm] *prep* **1** (*indicating starting place*) de, desde; **where do you come** ~**?, where are you** ~**?** ¿de dónde eres?; **where has he come** ~**?** ¿de dónde ha venido?; ~ **London to Glasgow** de Londres a Glasgow; **to escape** ~ **sth/sb** escaparse de algo/algn

2 (*indicating origin etc*) de; **a letter/ telephone call** ~ **my sister** una carta/ llamada de mi hermana; **tell him** ~ **me that ...** dígale de mi parte que ...

3 (*indicating time*): ~ **one o'clock to** *or* **until** *or* **till nine** de la una a las nueve, desde la una hasta las nueve; ~ **January (on)** a partir de enero; **(as)** ~ **Friday** a

partir del viernes

4 (*indicating distance*) de; **the hotel is 1 km from the beach** el hotel está a 1 km de la playa

5 (*indicating price, number etc*) de; **prices range** ~ **£10 to £50** los precios van desde £10 a *or* hasta £50; **the interest rate was increased** ~ **9% to 10%** el tipo de interés fue incrementado de un 9% a un 10%

6 (*indicating difference*) de; **he can't tell red** ~ **green** no sabe distinguir el rojo del verde; **to be different** ~ **sb/sth** ser diferente a algn/algo

7 (*because of, on the basis of*): ~ **what he says** por lo que dice; **weak** ~ **hunger** debilitado por el hambre.

frond [frɔnd] *n* fronda.

front [frʌnt] *n* (*foremost part*) parte *f* delantera; (*of house*) fachada; (*promenade: also:* **sea** ~) paseo marítimo; (*MIL, POL, METEOROLOGY*) frente *m*; (*fig: appearances*) apariencia ♦ *adj* (*wheel, leg*) delantero; (*row, line*) primero ♦ *vi*: **to** ~ **onto sth** dar a algo; **in** ~ (**of**) delante (de).

frontage ['frʌntɪdʒ] *n* (*of building*) fachada.

frontal ['frʌntl] *adj* frontal.

El término genérico **front bench** *se usa para referirse a los escaños situados en primera fila a ambos lados del Presidente (Speaker) de la Cámara de los Comunes (House of Commons) del Parlamento británico. Dichos escaños son ocupados por los miembros del gobierno a un lado y los del gobierno en la oposición (shadow cabinet) al otro. Por esta razón a todos ellos se les denomina* **frontbenchers**.

frontbencher ['frʌnt'bentʃə*] *n* (*BRIT*) *see* **front bench**.

front desk *n* (*US*) recepción *f*.

front door *n* puerta principal.

frontier ['frʌntɪə*] *n* frontera.

frontispiece ['frʌntɪspiːs] *n* frontispicio.

front page *n* primera plana.

front room *n* (*BRIT*) salón *m*, sala.

front runner *n* favorito/a.

front-wheel drive ['frʌntwiːl-] *n* tracción *f* delantera.

frost [frɔst] *n* (*gen*) helada; (*also:* **hoar**~) escarcha ♦ *vt* (*US CULIN*) escarchar.

frostbite ['frɔstbaɪt] *n* congelación *f*.

frosted ['frɔstɪd] *adj* (*glass*) esmerilado; (*esp US: cake*) glaseado.

frosting ['frɔstɪŋ] *n* (*esp US: icing*) glaseado.

frosty ['frɔstɪ] *adj* (*surface*) cubierto de

escarcha; (*welcome etc*) glacial.
froth [frɔθ] *n* espuma.
frothy ['frɔθɪ] *adj* espumoso.
frown [fraun] *vi* fruncir el ceño ♦ *n*: **with a**
~ frunciendo el entrecejo.
▶**frown on** *vt fus* desaprobar.
froze [frəuz] *pt of* **freeze**.
frozen ['frəuzn] *pp of* **freeze** ♦ *adj* (*food*)
congelado; (*COMM*): ~ **assets** activos *mpl*
congelados *or* bloqueados.
FRS *n* (*BRIT*: = Fellow of the Royal Society)
*miembro de la principal asociación de
investigación científica*; (*US*: = Federal
Reserve System) *banco central de
los EE. UU.*
frugal ['fru:gəl] *adj* (*person*) frugal.
fruit [fru:t] *n* (*pl inv*) fruta.
fruiterer ['fru:tərə*] *n* frutero/a; ~'**s (shop)**
frutería.
fruit fly *n* mosca de la fruta.
fruitful ['fru:tful] *adj* provechoso.
fruition [fru:'ɪʃən] *n*: **to come to** ~
realizarse.
fruit juice *n* jugo *or* zumo (*SP*) de fruta.
fruitless ['fru:tlɪs] *adj* (*fig*) infructuoso,
inútil.
fruit machine *n* (*BRIT*) máquina
tragaperras.
fruit salad *n* macedonia *or* ensalada (*LAM*)
de frutas.
frump [frʌmp] *n* espantajo, adefesio.
frustrate [frʌs'treɪt] *vt* frustrar.
frustrated [frʌs'treɪtɪd] *adj* frustrado.
frustrating [frʌs'treɪtɪŋ] *adj* (*job, day*)
frustrante.
frustration [frʌs'treɪʃən] *n* frustración *f*.
fry, *pt, pp* **fried** [fraɪ, -d] *vt* freír ♦ *n*: **small** ~
gente *f* menuda.
frying pan ['fraɪŋ-] *n* sartén *f or m* (*LAM*).
FT *n abbr* (*BRIT*: = Financial Times) *periódico
financiero*; **the** ~ **index** *el índice de
valores del Financial Times*.
ft. *abbr* = **foot, feet**.
FTC *n abbr* (*US*) = Federal Trade Commission.
FTSE 100 Index *n abbr* (= Financial Times
Stock Exchange 100 Index) *índice bursátil
del Financial Times*.
fuchsia ['fju:ʃə] *n* fucsia.
fuck [fʌk] (*col!*) *vt* joder (*SP!*), coger (*LAM!*)
♦ *vi* joder (*SP!*), coger (*LAM!*); ~ **off!** ¡vete
a tomar por culo! (*!*).
fuddled ['fʌdld] *adj* (*muddled*) confuso,
aturdido; (*col: tipsy*) borracho.
fuddy-duddy ['fʌdɪdʌdɪ] (*pej*) *n* carcamal
m, carroza *m/f* ♦ *adj* chapado a la antigua.
fudge [fʌdʒ] *n* (*CULIN*) caramelo blando ♦ *vt*
(*issue, problem*) rehuir, esquivar.
fuel [fjuəl] *n* (*for heating*) combustible *m*;

(*coal*) carbón *m*; (*wood*) leña; (*for engine*)
carburante *m* ♦ *vt* (*furnace etc*) alimentar;
(*aircraft, ship etc*) aprovisionar de
combustible.
fuel oil *n* fuel oil *m*.
fuel pump *n* (*AUT*) surtidor *m* de gasolina.
fuel tank *n* depósito de combustible.
fug [fʌg] *n* aire *m* viciado.
fugitive ['fju:dʒɪtɪv] *n* (*from prison*)
fugitivo/a.
fulfil, (*US*) **fulfill** [ful'fɪl] *vt* (*function*)
desempeñar; (*condition*) cumplir; (*wish,
desire*) realizar.
fulfilled [ful'fɪld] *adj* (*person*) realizado.
fulfil(l)ment [ful'fɪlmənt] *n* realización *f*; (*of
promise*) cumplimiento.
full [ful] *adj* lleno; (*fig*) pleno; (*complete*)
completo; (*information*) detallado; (*price*)
íntegro, sin descuento ♦ *adv*: ~ **well**
perfectamente; **we're** ~ **up for July**
estamos completos para julio; **I'm** ~ **(up)**
estoy lleno; ~ **employment** pleno empleo;
~ **name** nombre *m* completo; **a** ~ **two
hours** dos horas enteras; **at** ~ **speed** a
toda velocidad; **in** ~ (*reproduce, quote*)
íntegramente; **to write sth in** ~ escribir
algo por extenso; **to pay in** ~ pagar la
deuda entera.
fullback ['fulbæk] *n* (*FOOTBALL*) defensa *m*;
(*RUGBY*) zaguero.
full-blooded ['ful'blʌdɪd] *adj* (*vigorous:
attack*) vigoroso; (*pure*) puro.
full-cream ['ful'kri:m] *adj*: ~ **milk** leche *f*
entera.
full driving licence *n* (*BRIT AUT*) carnet *m*
de conducir (*definitivo*); *see also* **L-plates**.
full-fledged ['fulfledʒd] *adj* (*US*) = **fully-
fledged**.
full-grown ['ful'grəun] *adj* maduro.
full-length ['ful'leŋθ] *adj* (*portrait*) de
cuerpo entero; (*film*) de largometraje.
full moon *n* luna llena, plenilunio.
fullness ['fulnɪs] *n* plenitud *f*, amplitud *f*.
full-scale ['fulskeɪl] *adj* (*attack, war, search,
retreat*) en gran escala; (*plan, model*) de
tamaño natural.
full stop *n* punto.
full-time ['fultaɪm] *adj* (*work*) de tiempo
completo ♦ *adv*: **to work** ~ trabajar a
tiempo completo.
fully ['fulɪ] *adv* completamente; (*at least*) al
menos.
fully-fledged ['fulɪ'fledʒd], (*US*) **full-
fledged** *adj* (*teacher, barrister*) diplomado;
(*bird*) con todas sus plumas, capaz de
volar; (*fig*) de pleno derecho.
fully-paid ['fulɪpeɪd] *adj*: ~ **share** acción *f*
liberada.

fulsome ['fulsəm] *adj* (*pej: praise, gratitude*) excesivo, exagerado; (*: manner*) obsequioso.

fumble with ['fʌmbl-] *vt fus* manosear.

fume [fju:m] *vi* humear, echar humo.

fumes [fju:mz] *npl* humo *sg*, gases *mpl*.

fumigate ['fju:mɪɡeɪt] *vt* fumigar.

fun [fʌn] *n* (*amusement*) diversión *f*; (*joy*) alegría; **to have ~** divertirse; **for ~** por gusto; **to make ~ of** reírse de.

function ['fʌŋkʃən] *n* función *f* ♦ *vi* funcionar; **to ~ as** hacer (las veces) de, fungir de (*LAM*).

functional ['fʌŋkʃənl] *adj* funcional.

function key *n* (*COMPUT*) tecla de función.

fund [fʌnd] *n* fondo; (*reserve*) reserva; **~s** *npl* fondos *mpl*.

fundamental [fʌndə'mɛntl] *adj* fundamental ♦ *n*: **~s** fundamentos *mpl*.

fundamentalism [fʌndə'mɛntəlɪzəm] *n* fundamentalismo, integrismo.

fundamentalist [fʌndə'mɛntəlɪst] *n* fundamentalista *m/f*, integrista *m/f*.

fundamentally [fʌndə'mɛntəlɪ] *adv* fundamentalmente.

funding ['fʌndɪŋ] *n* financiación *f*.

fund-raising ['fʌndreɪzɪŋ] *n* recaudación *f* de fondos.

funeral ['fju:nərəl] *n* (*burial*) entierro; (*ceremony*) funerales *mpl*.

funeral director *n* director(a) *m/f* de pompas fúnebres.

funeral parlour *n* (*BRIT*) funeraria.

funeral service *n* misa de cuerpo presente.

funereal [fju:'nɪərɪəl] *adj* fúnebre.

funfair ['fʌnfɛə*] *n* (*BRIT*) parque *m* de atracciones; (*travelling*) feria.

fungus, *pl* **fungi** ['fʌŋɡəs, -ɡaɪ] *n* hongo.

funicular [fju:'nɪkjulə*] *n* (*also:* **~ railway**) funicular *m*.

funky ['fʌŋkɪ] *adj* (*music*) funky; (*col: good*) guay.

funnel ['fʌnl] *n* embudo; (*of ship*) chimenea.

funnily ['fʌnɪlɪ] *adv* de modo divertido, graciosamente; (*oddly*) de una manera rara; **~ enough** aunque parezca extraño.

funny ['fʌnɪ] *adj* gracioso, divertido; (*strange*) curioso, raro.

funny bone *n* hueso de la alegría.

fun run *n* maratón *m* popular.

fur [fə:*] *n* piel *f*; (*BRIT: on tongue etc*) sarro.

fur coat *n* abrigo de pieles.

furious ['fjuərɪəs] *adj* furioso; (*effort, argument*) violento; **to be ~ with sb** estar furioso con algn.

furiously ['fjuərɪəslɪ] *adv* con furia.

furl [fə:l] *vt* (*sail*) recoger.

furlong ['fə:lɔŋ] *n* octava parte de una milla.

furlough ['fə:ləu] *n* (*MIL, US*) permiso.

furnace ['fə:nɪs] *n* horno.

furnish ['fə:nɪʃ] *vt* amueblar; (*supply*) proporcionar; (*information*) facilitar.

furnished ['fə:nɪʃt] *adj*: **~ flat** *or* (*US*) **apartment** piso amueblado.

furnishings ['fə:nɪʃɪŋz] *npl* mobiliario *sg*.

furniture ['fə:nɪtʃə*] *n* muebles *mpl*; **piece of ~** mueble *m*.

furniture polish *n* cera para muebles.

furore [fjuə'rɔ:rɪ] *n* (*protests*) escándalo.

furrier ['fʌrɪə*] *n* peletero/a.

furrow ['fʌrəu] *n* surco ♦ *vt* (*forehead*) arrugar.

furry ['fə:rɪ] *adj* peludo; (*toy*) de peluche.

further ['fə:ðə*] *adj* (*new*) nuevo; (*place*) más lejano ♦ *adv* más lejos; (*more*) más; (*moreover*) además ♦ *vt* hacer avanzar; **how much ~ is it?** ¿a qué distancia queda?; **~ to your letter of ...** (*COMM*) con referencia a su carta de ...; **to ~ one's interests** fomentar sus intereses.

further education *n* educación *f* postescolar.

furthermore [fə:ðə'mɔ:*] *adv* además.

furthermost ['fə:ðəməust] *adj* más lejano.

furthest ['fə:ðɪst] *superlative of* **far**.

furtive ['fə:tɪv] *adj* furtivo.

furtively ['fə:tɪvlɪ] *adv* furtivamente, a escondidas.

fury ['fjuərɪ] *n* furia.

fuse, (*US*) **fuze** [fju:z] *n* fusible *m*; (*for bomb etc*) mecha ♦ *vt* (*metal*) fundir; (*fig*) fusionar ♦ *vi* fundirse; fusionarse; (*BRIT: ELEC*): **to ~ the lights** fundir los plomos; **a ~ has blown** se ha fundido un fusible.

fuse box *n* caja de fusibles.

fuselage ['fju:zəlɑ:ʒ] *n* fuselaje *m*.

fuse wire *n* hilo fusible.

fusillade [fju:zɪ'leɪd] *n* descarga cerrada; (*fig*) lluvia.

fusion ['fju:ʒən] *n* fusión *f*.

fuss [fʌs] *n* (*noise*) bulla; (*dispute*) lío, jaleo; (*complaining*) protesta ♦ *vi* preocuparse (por pequeñeces) ♦ *vt* (*person*) molestar; **to make a ~** armar jaleo.

▶**fuss over** *vt fus* (*person*) contemplar, mimar.

fusspot ['fʌspɔt] *n* (*col*) quisquilloso/a.

fussy ['fʌsɪ] *adj* (*person*) quisquilloso; **I'm not ~** (*col*) me da igual.

fusty ['fʌstɪ] *adj* (*pej*) rancio; **to smell ~** oler a cerrado.

futile ['fju:taɪl] *adj* vano.

futility [fju:'tɪlɪtɪ] *n* inutilidad *f*.

futon ['fu:tɔn] *n* futón ṁ.

future ['fjuːtʃə*] adj (gen) futuro; (coming) venidero ♦ n futuro, porvenir; **in** ~ **de** ahora en adelante.

futures ['fjuːtʃəz] npl (COMM) operaciones fpl a término, futuros mpl.

futuristic [fjuːtʃə'rıstık] adj futurista.

fuze [fjuːz] (US) = **fuse**.

fuzzy ['fʌzɪ] adj (PHOT) borroso; (hair) muy rizado.

fwd. abbr = **forward**.

fwy abbr (US) = **freeway**.

FY abbr = **fiscal year**.

FYI abbr = for your information.

Gg

G, g [dʒiː] n (letter) G, g f; **G** (MUS) sol m; **G for George** G de Gerona.

G n abbr (BRIT SCOL: = good) N; (US CINE: = general audience) todos los públicos.

g. abbr (= gram(s), gravity) g.

G7 n abbr (POL = Group of Seven) G7 m.

GA abbr (US) = Georgia.

gab [gæb] n: **to have the gift of the** ~ (col) tener mucha labia.

gabble ['gæbl] vi hablar atropelladamente; (gossip) cotorrear.

gaberdine [gæbə'diːn] n gabardina.

gable ['geɪbl] n aguilón m.

Gabon [gə'bɒn] n Gabón m.

gad about [gæd-] vi (col) moverse mucho.

gadget ['gædʒɪt] n aparato.

gadgetry ['gædʒɪtrɪ] n chismes mpl.

Gaelic ['geɪlɪk] adj, n (LING) gaélico.

gaffe [gæf] n plancha, patinazo, metedura de pata.

gaffer ['gæfə*] n (BRIT col) jefe m; ((old) man) vejete m.

gag [gæg] n (on mouth) mordaza; (joke) chiste m ♦ vt (prisoner etc) amordazar ♦ vi (choke) tener arcadas.

gaga ['gɑːgɑː] adj: **to go** ~ (senile) chochear; (ecstatic) caérsele a algn la baba.

gage [geɪdʒ] n, vt (US) = **gauge**.

gaiety ['geɪtɪ] n alegría.

gaily ['geɪlɪ] adv alegremente.

gain [geɪn] n ganancia ♦ vt ganar ♦ vi (watch) adelantarse; **to** ~ **by sth** ganar con algo; **to** ~ **ground** ganar terreno; **to** ~ **3 lbs (in weight)** engordar 3 libras.

►**gain (up)on** vt fus alcanzar.

gainful ['geɪnful] adj (employment) remunerado.

gainfully ['geɪnfulɪ] adv: **to be** ~ **employed** tener un trabajo remunerado.

gait [geɪt] n forma de andar, andares mpl.

gala ['gɑːlə] n gala; **swimming** ~ certamen m de natación.

Galapagos Islands [gə'læpəgəs-] npl: **the** ~ las Islas Galápagos.

galaxy ['gæləksɪ] n galaxia.

gale [geɪl] n (wind) vendaval m; ~ **force 10** vendaval de fuerza 10.

gall [gɔːl] n (ANAT) bilis f, hiel f; (fig: impudence) descaro, caradura ♦ vt molestar.

gal(l). abbr = **gallon(s)**.

gallant ['gælənt] adj valeroso; (towards ladies) galante.

gallantry ['gæləntrɪ] n valentía; (courtesy) galantería.

gall bladder n vesícula biliar.

galleon ['gælɪən] n galeón m.

gallery ['gælərɪ] n (also THEAT) galería; (for spectators) tribuna; (also: **art** ~: state-owned) pinacoteca or museo de arte; (: private) galería de arte.

galley ['gælɪ] n (ship's kitchen) cocina; (ship) galera.

galley proof n (TYP) prueba de galera, galerada.

Gallic ['gælɪk] adj galo.

gallon ['gælən] n galón m (= 8 pints; BRIT = 4,546 litros, US = 3,785 litros).

gallop ['gæləp] n galope m ♦ vi galopar; ~**ing inflation** inflación f galopante.

gallows ['gæləuz] n horca.

gallstone ['gɔːlstəun] n cálculo biliar.

Gallup poll ['gæləp-] n sondeo de opinión.

galore [gə'lɔː*] adv en cantidad, en abundancia.

galvanize ['gælvənaɪz] vt (metal) galvanizar; (fig): **to** ~ **sb into action** mover or impulsar a algn a actuar.

Gambia ['gæmbɪə] n Gambia.

gambit ['gæmbɪt] n (fig): **opening** ~ táctica inicial.

gamble ['gæmbl] n (risk) jugada arriesgada; (bet) apuesta ♦ vt: **to** ~ **on** apostar a; (fig) confiar en que ♦ vi jugar; (COMM) especular; **to** ~ **on the Stock Exchange** jugar a la bolsa.

gambler ['gæmblə*] n jugador(a) m/f.

gambling ['gæmblɪŋ] n juego.

gambol ['gæmbl] vi brincar, juguetear.

game [geɪm] n (gen) juego; (match) partido; (of cards) partida; (HUNTING) caza ♦ adj valiente; (ready): **to be** ~ **for anything**

estar dispuesto a todo; ~s (*SCOL*) deportes *mpl*; **big** ~ caza mayor.
game bird *n* ave *f* de caza.
gamekeeper ['geɪmkiːpə*] *n* guardabosque *m/f*.
gamely ['geɪmlɪ] *adv* con decisión.
game reserve *n* coto de caza.
games console [geɪmz-] *n* consola de juegos.
game show *n* programa *m* concurso *inv*, concurso.
gamesmanship ['geɪmzmənʃɪp] *n* (uso de) artimañas *fpl* para ganar.
gaming ['geɪmɪŋ] *n* juego.
gammon ['gæmən] *n* (*bacon*) tocino ahumado; (*ham*) jamón *m* ahumado.
gamut ['gæmət] *n* (*MUS*) gama; **to run the (whole)** ~ **of emotions** (*fig*) recorrer toda la gama de emociones.
gander ['gændə*] *n* ganso.
gang [gæŋ] *n* pandilla; (*of criminals etc*) banda; (*of kids*) pandilla; (*of colleagues*) peña; (*of workmen*) brigada ♦ *vi*: **to** ~ **up on sb** conchabarse contra algn.
Ganges ['gændʒiːz] *n*: **the** ~ el Ganges.
gangland ['gæŋglænd] *adj*: ~ **bosses** cabecillas mafiosos; ~ **killings** asesinatos entre bandas.
gangling ['gæŋglɪŋ] *adj* larguirucho.
gangly ['gæŋglɪ] *adj* desgarbado.
gangplank ['gæŋplæŋk] *n* pasarela, plancha.
gangrene ['gæŋgriːn] *n* gangrena.
gangster ['gæŋstə*] *n* gángster *m*.
gang warfare *n* guerra entre bandas.
gangway ['gæŋweɪ] *n* (*BRIT: in theatre, bus etc*) pasillo; (*on ship*) pasarela.
gantry ['gæntrɪ] *n* (*for crane, railway signal*) pórtico; (*for rocket*) torre *f* de lanzamiento.
GAO *n abbr* (*US*: = *General Accounting Office*) *tribunal de cuentas*.
gaol [dʒeɪl] *n*, *vt* (*BRIT*) = **jail**.
gap [gæp] *n* hueco; (*in trees, traffic*) claro; (*in market, records*) laguna; (*in time*) intervalo.
gape [geɪp] *vi* mirar boquiabierto.
gaping ['geɪpɪŋ] *adj* (*hole*) muy abierto.
garage ['gærɑːʒ] *n* garaje *m*.
garb [gɑːb] *n* atuendo.
garbage ['gɑːbɪdʒ] *n* (*US*) basura; (*nonsense*) bobadas *fpl*; (*fig: film, book etc*) basura.
garbage can *n* (*US*) cubo *or* balde *m* (*LAM*) *or* bote *m* (*LAM*) de la basura.
garbage collector *n* (*US*) basurero/a.
garbage disposal unit *n* triturador *m* (de basura).

garbage man *n* basurero.
garbage truck *n* (*US*) camión *m* de la basura.
garbled ['gɑːbld] *adj* (*account, explanation*) confuso.
garden ['gɑːdn] *n* jardín *m*; ~**s** *npl* (*public*) parque *m*, jardines *mpl*; (*private*) huertos *mpl*.
garden centre *n* centro de jardinería.
garden city *n* (*BRIT*) ciudad *f* jardín.
gardener ['gɑːdnə*] *n* jardinero/a.
gardening ['gɑːdnɪŋ] *n* jardinería.
garden party *n* recepción *f* al aire libre.
gargle ['gɑːgl] *vi* hacer gárgaras, gargarear (*LAM*).
gargoyle ['gɑːgɔɪl] *n* gárgola.
garish ['gɛərɪʃ] *adj* chillón/ona.
garland ['gɑːlənd] *n* guirnalda.
garlic ['gɑːlɪk] *n* ajo.
garment ['gɑːmənt] *n* prenda (de vestir).
garner ['gɑːnə*] *vt* hacer acopio de.
garnish ['gɑːnɪʃ] *vt* adornar; (*CULIN*) aderezar.
garret ['gærɪt] *n* desván *m*, buhardilla.
garrison ['gærɪsn] *n* guarnición *f* ♦ *vt* guarnecer.
garrulous ['gærjuləs] *adj* charlatán/ana.
garter ['gɑːtə*] *n* (*US*) liga.
garter belt *n* (*US*) liguero, portaligas *m inv*.
gas [gæs] *n* gas *m*; (*US: gasoline*) gasolina ♦ *vt* asfixiar con gas; **Calor** ~ ® (gas *m*) butano.
gas chamber *n* cámara de gas.
Gascony ['gæskənɪ] *n* Gascuña.
gas cooker *n* (*BRIT*) cocina de gas.
gas cylinder *n* bombona de gas.
gaseous ['gæsɪəs] *adj* gaseoso.
gas fire *n* estufa de gas.
gas-fired ['gæsfaɪəd] *adj* de gas.
gash [gæʃ] *n* brecha, raja; (*from knife*) cuchillada ♦ *vt* rajar; (*with knife*) acuchillar.
gasket ['gæskɪt] *n* (*AUT*) junta.
gas mask *n* careta antigás.
gas meter *n* contador *m* de gas.
gasoline ['gæsəliːn] *n* (*US*) gasolina.
gasp [gɑːsp] *n* grito sofocado ♦ *vi* (*pant*) jadear.
▶**gasp out** *vt* (*say*) decir jadeando.
gas pedal *n* (*esp US*) acelerador *m*.
gas ring *n* hornillo de gas.
gas station *n* (*US*) gasolinera.
gas stove *n* cocina de gas.
gassy ['gæsɪ] *adj* con mucho gas.
gas tank *n* (*US AUT*) depósito (de gasolina).
gas tap *n* llave *f* del gas.
gastric ['gæstrɪk] *adj* gástrico.
gastric ulcer *n* úlcera gástrica.

gastroenteritis ['gæstrɔuɛntə'raɪtɪs] *n* gastroenteritis *f*.

gasworks ['gæswɔːks] *nsg or npl* fábrica de gas.

gate [geɪt] *n* (*also at airport*) puerta; (*RAIL: at level crossing*) barrera; (*metal*) verja.

gâteau, *pl* ~**x** ['gætəu, z] *n* tarta.

gatecrash ['geɪtkræʃ] *vt* colarse en.

gatecrasher ['geɪtkræʃə*] *n* intruso/a.

gatehouse ['geɪthaus] *n* casa del guarda.

gateway ['geɪtweɪ] *n* puerta.

gather ['gæðə*] *vt* (*flowers, fruit*) coger (*SP*), recoger (*LAM*); (*assemble*) reunir; (*pick up*) recoger; (*SEWING*) fruncir; (*understand*) sacar en consecuencia ♦ *vi* (*assemble*) reunirse; (*dust*) acumularse; (*clouds*) cerrarse; **to ~ speed** ganar velocidad; **to ~ (from/that)** deducir (por/ que); **as far as I can ~** por lo que tengo entendido.

gathering ['gæðərɪŋ] *n* reunión *f*, asamblea.

GATT [gæt] *n abbr* (= *General Agreement on Tariffs and Trade*) GATT *m*.

gauche [gəuʃ] *adj* torpe.

gaudy ['gɔːdɪ] *adj* chillón/ona.

gauge, (*US*) **gage** [geɪdʒ] *n* calibre *m*; (*RAIL*) ancho de vía, entrevía; (*instrument*) indicador *m* ♦ *vt* medir; (*fig: sb's capabilities, character*) juzgar, calibrar; **petrol ~** indicador *m* (del nivel) de gasolina; **to ~ the right moment** elegir el momento (oportuno).

Gaul [gɔːl] *n* Galia.

gaunt [gɔːnt] *adj* descarnado; (*fig*) adusto.

gauntlet ['gɔːntlɪt] *n* (*fig*): **to run the ~ of sth** exponerse a algo; **to throw down the ~** arrojar el guante.

gauze [gɔːz] *n* gasa.

gave [geɪv] *pt of* **give**.

gawk [gɔːk] *vi* mirar pasmado.

gawky ['gɔːkɪ] *adj* desgarbado.

gay [geɪ] *adj* (*colour, person*) alegre; (*homosexual*) gay.

gaze [geɪz] *n* mirada fija ♦ *vi*: **to ~ at sth** mirar algo fijamente.

gazelle [gə'zɛl] *n* gacela.

gazette [gə'zɛt] *n* (*newspaper*) gaceta; (*official publication*) boletín *m* oficial.

gazetteer [gæzə'tɪə*] *n* índice geográfico.

gazump [gə'zʌmp] *vti* (*BRIT*) echarse atrás en la venta ya acordada de una casa por haber una oferta más alta.

GB *abbr* (= *Great Britain*) G.B.

GBH *n abbr* (*BRIT LAW: col*) = **grievous bodily harm**.

GC *n abbr* (*BRIT:* = *George Cross*) distinción honorífica.

GCE *n abbr* (*BRIT:* = *General Certificate of Education*) ≈ certificado de bachillerato.

GCHQ *n abbr* (*BRIT:* = *Government Communications Headquarters*) *centro de intercepción de las telecomunicaciones internacionales*.

GCSE *n abbr* (*BRIT:* = *General Certificate of Secondary Education*) ≈ certificado de bachillerato.

Gdns. *abbr* (= *gardens*) jdns.

GDP *n abbr* (= *gross domestic product*) PIB *m*.

GDR *n abbr* (= *German Democratic Republic*) RDA *f*.

gear [gɪə*] *n* equipo; (*TECH*) engranaje *m*; (*AUT*) velocidad *f*, marcha ♦ *vt* (*fig: adapt*): **to ~ sth to** adaptar *or* ajustar algo a; **top** *or* (*US*) **high/low ~** cuarta/primera; **in ~** con la marcha metida; **our service is ~ed to meet the needs of the disabled** nuestro servicio va enfocado a responder a las necesidades de los minusválidos.

▶**gear up** *vi* prepararse.

gear box *n* caja de cambios.

gear lever, (*US*) **gear shift** *n* palanca de cambio.

gear wheel *n* rueda dentada.

GED *n abbr* (*US SCOL*) = *general educational development*.

geese [giːs] *npl of* **goose**.

geezer ['giːzə*] *n* (*BRIT col*) tipo, maromo (*SP*).

Geiger counter ['gaɪgə-] *n* contador *m* Geiger.

gel [dʒɛl] *n* gel *m*.

gelatin(e) ['dʒɛlətiːn] *n* gelatina.

gelignite ['dʒɛlɪgnaɪt] *n* gelignita.

gem [dʒɛm] *n* gema, piedra preciosa; (*fig*) joya.

Gemini ['dʒɛmɪnaɪ] *n* Géminis *m*.

gen [dʒɛn] *n* (*BRIT col*): **to give sb the ~ on sth** poner a algn al tanto de algo.

Gen. *abbr* (*MIL:* = *General*) Gen., Gral.

gen. *abbr* (= *general*) grl.; = **generally**.

gender ['dʒɛndə*] *n* género.

gene [dʒiːn] *n* gen(e) *m*.

genealogy [dʒiːnɪ'ælədʒɪ] *n* genealogía.

general ['dʒɛnərl] *n* general *m* ♦ *adj* general; **in ~** en general; **~ audit** auditoría general; **the ~ public** el gran público.

general anaesthetic, (*US*) **general anesthetic** *n* anestesia general.

general delivery *n* (*US*) lista de correos.

general election *n* elecciones *fpl* generales.

generalization [dʒɛnrəlaɪ'zeɪʃən] *n* generalización *f*.

generalize ['dʒɛnrəlaɪz] *vi* generalizar.

generally ['dʒɛnrəlɪ] *adv* generalmente, en

general.
general manager n director(a) m/f general.
general practitioner (GP) n médico/a de medicina general.
general strike n huelga general.
generate ['dʒenəreɪt] vt generar.
generation [dʒenə'reɪʃən] n (of electricity etc) generación f; **first/second/third/fourth** ~ (of computer) primera/segunda/tercera/cuarta generación.
generator ['dʒenəreɪtə*] n generador m.
generic [dʒɪ'nerɪk] adj genérico.
generosity [dʒenə'rɒsɪtɪ] n generosidad f.
generous ['dʒenərəs] adj generoso; (copious) abundante.
generously ['dʒenərəslɪ] adv generosamente; abundantemente.
genesis ['dʒenɪsɪs] n génesis f.
genetic [dʒɪ'netɪk] adj genético.
genetic engineering n ingeniería genética.
genetic fingerprinting [-'fɪŋgəprɪntɪŋ] n identificación f genética.
genetics [dʒɪ'netɪks] n genética.
Geneva [dʒɪ'niːvə] n Ginebra.
genial ['dʒiːnɪəl] adj afable.
genitals ['dʒenɪtlz] npl (órganos mpl) genitales mpl.
genitive ['dʒenɪtɪv] n genitivo.
genius ['dʒiːnɪəs] n genio.
Genoa ['dʒenəuə] n Génova.
genocide ['dʒenəusaɪd] n genocidio.
gent [dʒent] n abbr (BRIT col) = **gentleman**.
genteel [dʒen'tiːl] adj fino, distinguido.
Gentile ['dʒentaɪl] n gentil m/f.
gentle ['dʒentl] adj (sweet) dulce; (touch etc) ligero, suave.
gentleman ['dʒentlmən] n señor m; (well-bred man) caballero; ~'s **agreement** acuerdo entre caballeros.
gentlemanly ['dʒentlmənlɪ] adj caballeroso.
gentleness ['dʒentlnɪs] n dulzura; (of touch) suavidad f.
gently ['dʒentlɪ] adv suavemente.
gentrification [dʒentrɪfɪ'keɪʃən] n aburguesamiento.
gentry ['dʒentrɪ] npl pequeña nobleza sg.
gents [dʒents] n servicios mpl (de caballeros).
genuine ['dʒenjuɪn] adj auténtico; (person) sincero.
genuinely ['dʒenjuɪnlɪ] adv sinceramente.
geographer [dʒɪ'ɒgrəfə*] n geógrafo/a.
geographic(al) [dʒɪə'græfɪk(l)] adj geográfico.
geography [dʒɪ'ɒgrəfɪ] n geografía.
geological [dʒɪə'lɒdʒɪkl] adj geológico.

geologist [dʒɪ'ɒlədʒɪst] n geólogo/a.
geology [dʒɪ'ɒlədʒɪ] n geología.
geometric(al) [dʒɪə'metrɪk(l)] adj geométrico.
geometry [dʒɪ'ɒmətrɪ] n geometría.
Geordie ['dʒɔːdɪ] n habitante m/f de Tyneside.
Georgia ['dʒɔːdʒə] n Georgia.
Georgian ['dʒɔːdʒən] adj georgiano ♦ n georgiano/a; (LING) georgiano.
geranium [dʒɪ'reɪnjəm] n geranio.
geriatric [dʒerɪ'ætrɪk] adj, n geriátrico/a m/f.
germ [dʒɜːm] n (microbe) microbio, bacteria; (seed, fig) germen m.
German ['dʒɜːmən] adj alemán/ana ♦ n alemán/ana m/f; (LING) alemán m.
German Democratic Republic n República Democrática Alemana.
germane [dʒə'meɪn] adj: ~ **(to)** pertinente (a).
German measles n rubeola, rubéola.
German Shepherd n (dog) pastor m alemán.
Germany ['dʒɜːmənɪ] n Alemania; **East/West** ~ Alemania Oriental or Democrática/Occidental or Federal.
germination [dʒɜːmɪ'neɪʃən] n germinación f.
germ warfare n guerra bacteriológica.
gesticulate [dʒes'tɪkjuleɪt] vi gesticular.
gesticulation [dʒestɪkju'leɪʃən] n gesticulación f.
gesture ['dʒestjə*] n gesto; **as a** ~ **of friendship** en señal de amistad.

===================================== *KEYWORD*

get [get] (pt, pp **got**, pp **gotten** (US)) vi **1** (become, be) ponerse, volverse; **to** ~ **old/tired** envejecer/cansarse; **to** ~ **drunk** emborracharse; **to** ~ **dirty** ensuciarse; **to** ~ **ready/washed** prepararse/lavarse; **to** ~ **married** casarse; **when do I** ~ **paid?** ¿cuándo me pagan or se me paga?; **it's** ~**ting late** se está haciendo tarde
2 (go): **to** ~ **to/from** llegar a/de; **to** ~ **home** llegar a casa; **he got under the fence** pasó por debajo de la barrera
3 (begin) empezar a; **to** ~ **to know sb** (llegar a) conocer a algn; **I'm** ~**ting to like him** me está empezando a gustar; **let's** ~ **going** or **started** ¡vamos (a empezar)!
4 (modal aux vb): **you've got to do it** tienes que hacerlo
♦ vt **1**: **to** ~ **sth done** (finish) hacer algo; (have done) mandar hacer algo; **to** ~ **one's hair cut** cortarse el pelo; **to** ~ **the car going** or **to go** arrancar el coche; **to** ~

sb to do sth conseguir *or* hacer que algn haga algo; **to ~ sth/sb ready** preparar algo/a algn
2 (*obtain: money, permission, results*) conseguir; (*find: job, flat*) encontrar; (*fetch: person, doctor*) buscar; (*object*) ir a buscar, traer; **to ~ sth for sb** conseguir algo para algn; **~ me Mr Jones, please** (*TEL*) póngame *or* comuníqueme (*LAM*) con el Sr. Jones, por favor; **can I ~ you a drink?** ¿quieres algo de beber?
3 (*receive: present, letter*) recibir; (*acquire: reputation*) alcanzar; (: *prize*) ganar; **what did you ~ for your birthday?** ¿qué te regalaron por tu cumpleaños?; **how much did you ~ for the painting?** ¿cuánto sacaste por el cuadro?
4 (*catch*) coger (*SP*), agarrar (*LAM*); (*hit: target etc*) dar en; **to ~ sb by the arm/throat** coger *or* agarrar a algn por el brazo/cuello; **~ him!** ¡cógelo! (*SP*), ¡atrápalo! (*LAM*); **the bullet got him in the leg** la bala le dio en la pierna
5 (*take, move*) llevar; **to ~ sth to sb** hacer llegar algo a algn; **do you think we'll ~ it through the door?** ¿crees que lo podremos meter en la puerta?
6 (*catch, take: plane, bus etc*) coger (*SP*), tomar (*LAM*); **where do I ~ the train for Birmingham?** ¿dónde se coge *or* se toma el tren para Birmingham?
7 (*understand*) entender; (*hear*) oír; **I've got it!** ¡ya lo tengo!, ¡eureka!; **I don't ~ your meaning** no te entiendo; **I'm sorry, I didn't ~ your name** lo siento, no me he enterado de tu nombre
8 (*have, possess*): **to have got** tener
9 (*col: annoy*) molestar; (: *thrill*) chiflar
▶**get about** *vi* salir mucho; (*news*) divulgarse
▶**get across** *vt* (*message, meaning*) lograr comunicar ♦ *vi*: **to ~ across to sb** hacer que algn comprenda
▶**get along** *vi* (*agree*) llevarse bien; (*depart*) marcharse; (*manage*) = **get by**
▶**get at** *vt fus* (*attack*) meterse con; (*reach*) alcanzar; (*the truth*) descubrir; **what are you ~ting at?** ¿qué insinúas?
▶**get away** *vi* marcharse; (*escape*) escaparse
▶**get away with** *vt fus* hacer impunemente
▶**get back** *vi* (*return*) volver ♦ *vt* recobrar
▶**get back at** *vt fus* (*col*): **to ~ back at sb (for sth)** vengarse de algn (por algo)
▶**get by** *vi* (*pass*) (lograr) pasar; (*manage*) arreglárselas; **I can ~ by in Dutch** me defiendo en holandés
▶**get down** *vi* bajar(se) ♦ *vt fus* bajar ♦ *vt*

bajar; (*depress*) deprimir
▶**get down to** *vt fus* (*work*) ponerse a
▶**get in** *vi* entrar; (*train*) llegar; (*arrive home*) volver a casa, regresar; (*political party*) salir ♦ *vt* (*bring in: harvest*) recoger; (: *coal, shopping, supplies*) comprar, traer; (*insert*) meter
▶**get into** *vt fus* entrar en; (*vehicle*) subir a; **to ~ into a rage** enfadarse
▶**get off** *vi* (*from train etc*) bajar(se); (*depart: person, car*) marcharse ♦ *vt* (*remove*) quitar; (*send off*) mandar; (*have as leave: day, time*) tener libre ♦ *vt fus* (*train, bus*) bajar(se) de; **to ~ off to a good start** (*fig*) empezar muy bien *or* con buen pie
▶**get on** *vi* (*at exam etc*): **how are you ~ting on?** ¿cómo te va?; (*agree*): **to ~ on (with)** llevarse bien (con) ♦ *vt fus* subir(se) a
▶**get on to** *vt fus* (*deal with*) ocuparse de; (*col: contact: on phone etc*) hablar con
▶**get out** *vi* salir; (*of vehicle*) bajar(se); (*news*) saberse ♦ *vt* sacar
▶**get out of** *vt fus* salir de; (*duty etc*) escaparse de; (*gain from: pleasure, benefit*) sacar de
▶**get over** *vt fus* (*illness*) recobrarse de
▶**get round** *vt fus* rodear; (*fig: person*) engatusar a ♦ *vi*: **to ~ round to doing sth** encontrar tiempo para hacer algo
▶**get through** *vt fus* (*finish*) acabar ♦ *vi* (*TEL*) (lograr) comunicar
▶**get through to** *vt fus* (*TEL*) comunicar con
▶**get together** *vi* reunirse ♦ *vt* reunir, juntar
▶**get up** *vi* (*rise*) levantarse ♦ *vt fus* subir; **to ~ up enthusiasm for sth** cobrar entusiasmo por algo
▶**get up to** *vt fus* (*reach*) llegar a; (*prank*) hacer.

getaway ['gɛtəweɪ] *n* fuga.
getaway car *n*: **the thieves' ~** el coche en que huyeron los ladrones.
get-together ['gɛttəgɛðə*] *n* reunión *f*; (*party*) fiesta.
get-up ['gɛtʌp] *n* (*BRIT col: outfit*) atavío, atuendo.
get-well card [gɛt'wɛl-] *n tarjeta en la que se desea a un enfermo que se mejore.*
geyser ['giːzə*] *n* (*water heater*) calentador *m* de agua; (*GEO*) géiser *m*.
Ghana ['gɑːnə] *n* Ghana.
Ghanaian [gɑː'neɪən] *adj, n* ganés/esa *m/f*.
ghastly ['gɑːstlɪ] *adj* horrible; (*pale*) pálido.
gherkin ['gəːkɪn] *n* pepinillo.
ghetto ['gɛtəu] *n* gueto.

ghetto blaster [-'blɑːstə*] *n*
radiocas(s)et(t)e *m* portátil (*de gran tamaño*).
ghost [gəust] *n* fantasma *m* ♦ *vt* (*book*)
escribir por otro.
ghostly ['gəustlɪ] *adj* fantasmal.
ghost story *n* cuento de fantasmas.
ghostwriter ['gəustraɪtə*] *n* negro/a.
ghoul [guːl] *n* espíritu *m* necrófago.
GHQ *n abbr* (*MIL*: = *general headquarters*)
E.M.
GI *n abbr* (*US col*: = *government issue*)
soldado del ejército norteamericano.
giant ['dʒaɪənt] *n* gigante *m/f* ♦ *adj*
gigantesco, gigante; ~ (*size*) **packet**
paquete *m* (de tamaño) gigante *or*
familiar.
giant killer *n* (*SPORT*) matagigantes *m inv*.
gibber ['dʒɪbə*] *vi* farfullar.
gibberish ['dʒɪbərɪʃ] *n* galimatías *m*.
gibe [dʒaɪb] *n* pulla.
giblets ['dʒɪblɪts] *npl* menudillos *mpl*.
Gibraltar [dʒɪ'brɔːltə*] *n* Gibraltar *m*.
giddiness ['gɪdɪnɪs] *n* mareo.
giddy ['gɪdɪ] *adj* (*dizzy*) mareado; (*height,
speed*) vertiginoso; **it makes me** ~ me
marea; **I feel** ~ me siento mareado.
gift [gɪft] *n* (*gen*) regalo; (*COMM: also*: **free**
~) obsequio; (*ability*) don *m*; **to have a** ~
for sth tener dotes para algo.
gifted ['gɪftɪd] *adj* dotado.
gift token, gift voucher *n* vale-regalo *m*.
gig [gɪg] *n* (*col: concert*) actuación *f*.
gigabyte ['dʒɪgəbaɪt] *n* gigabyte *m*.
gigantic [dʒaɪ'gæntɪk] *adj* gigantesco.
giggle ['gɪgl] *vi* reírse tontamente ♦ *n*
risilla.
GIGO ['gaɪgəu] *abbr* (*COMPUT: col*) = *garbage
in, garbage out.*
gill [dʒɪl] *n* (*measure*) = 0.25 *pints* (*BRIT*
= 0.148 *l*, *US* = 0.118 *l*).
gills [gɪlz] *npl* (*of fish*) branquias *fpl*, agallas
fpl.
gilt [gɪlt] *adj, n* dorado.
gilt-edged ['gɪltedʒd] *adj* (*COMM: stocks,
securities*) de máxima garantía.
gimlet ['gɪmlɪt] *n* barrena de mano.
gimmick ['gɪmɪk] *n* reclamo; **sales** ~
reclamo promocional.
gimmicky ['gɪmɪkɪ] *adj* de reclamo.
gin [dʒɪn] *n* (*liquor*) ginebra.
ginger ['dʒɪndʒə*] *n* jengibre *m*.
ginger ale *n* ginger ale *m*.
ginger beer *n* refresco *m* de jengibre.
gingerbread ['dʒɪndʒəbred] *n* pan *m* de
jengibre.
ginger-haired [dʒɪndʒə'heəd] *adj* pelirrojo.
gingerly ['dʒɪndʒəlɪ] *adv* con pies de plomo.

ginseng ['dʒɪnsɛŋ] *n* ginseng *m*.
gipsy ['dʒɪpsɪ] *n* gitano/a.
giraffe [dʒɪ'rɑːf] *n* jirafa.
girder ['gɜːdə*] *n* viga.
girdle ['gɜːdl] *n* (*corset*) faja ♦ *vt* ceñir.
girl [gɜːl] *n* (*small*) niña; (*young woman*)
chica, joven *f*, muchacha; **an English** ~
una (chica) inglesa.
girlfriend ['gɜːlfrend] *n* (*of girl*) amiga; (*of
boy*) novia.
Girl Guide *n* exploradora.
girlish ['gɜːlɪʃ] *adj* de niña.
Girl Scout *n* (*US*) = **Girl Guide**.
giro ['dʒaɪrəu] *n* (*BRIT: bank* ~) giro
bancario; (*post office* ~) giro postal.
girth [gɜːθ] *n* circunferencia; (*of saddle*)
cincha.
gist [dʒɪst] *n* lo esencial.
give [gɪv] *vb* (*pt* **gave**, *pp* **given** [geɪv, 'gɪvn])
vt dar; (*deliver*) entregar; (*as gift*) regalar
♦ *vi* (*break*) romperse; (*stretch: fabric*) dar
de sí; **to** ~ **sb sth**, ~ **sth to sb** dar algo a
algn; **how much did you** ~ **for it?** ¿cuánto
pagaste por él?; **12 o'clock**, ~ **or take a
few minutes** más o menos las doce; ~
them my regards dales recuerdos de mi
parte; **I can** ~ **you 10 minutes** le puedo
conceder 10 minutos; **to** ~ **way** (*BRIT AUT*)
ceder el paso; **to** ~ **way to despair** ceder
a la desesperación.
▶**give away** *vt* (*give free*) regalar; (*betray*)
traicionar; (*disclose*) revelar.
▶**give back** *vt* devolver.
▶**give in** *vi* ceder ♦ *vt* entregar.
▶**give off** *vt* despedir.
▶**give out** *vt* distribuir ♦ *vi* (*be exhausted:
supplies*) agotarse; (*fail: engine*) averiarse;
(*strength*) fallar.
▶**give up** *vi* rendirse, darse por vencido
♦ *vt* renunciar a; **to** ~ **up smoking** dejar
de fumar; **to** ~ **o.s. up** entregarse.
give-and-take ['gɪvənd'teɪk] *n* (*col*) toma y
daca *m*.
giveaway ['gɪvəweɪ] *n* (*col*): **her expression
was a** ~ su expresión la delataba; **the
exam was a** ~! ¡el examen estaba tirado!
♦ *cpd*: ~ **prices** precios *mpl* de regalo.
given ['gɪvn] *pp of* **give** ♦ *adj* (*fixed: time,
amount*) determinado ♦ *conj*: ~ (**that**) ...
dado (que) ...; ~ **the circumstances** ...
dadas las circunstancias ....
glacial ['gleɪsɪəl] *adj* glacial.
glacier ['glæsɪə*] *n* glaciar *m*.
glad [glæd] *adj* contento; **to be** ~ **about
sth/that** alegrarse de algo/de que; **I was**
~ **of his help** agradecí su ayuda.
gladden ['glædn] *vt* alegrar.
glade [gleɪd] *n* claro.

gladiator ['glædɪeɪtə*] n gladiador m.
gladioli [glædɪ'əʊlaɪ] npl gladiolos mpl.
gladly ['glædlɪ] adv con mucho gusto.
glamorous ['glæmərəs] adj con encanto,
atractivo.
glamour ['glæmə*] n encanto, atractivo.
glance [glɑːns] n ojeada, mirada ♦ vi: **to ~
at** echar una ojeada a.
▶**glance off** vt fus (bullet) rebotar en.
glancing ['glɑːnsɪŋ] adj (blow) oblicuo.
gland [glænd] n glándula.
glandular ['glændjʊlə*] adj: **~ fever**
mononucleosis f infecciosa.
glare [glɛə*] n deslumbramiento, brillo ♦ vi
deslumbrar; **to ~ at** mirar con odio.
glaring ['glɛərɪŋ] adj (mistake) manifiesto.
glasnost ['glæznɔst] n glasnost f.
glass [glɑːs] n vidrio, cristal m; (for
drinking) vaso; (: with stem) copa; (also:
looking ~) espejo.
glass-blowing ['glɑːsbləʊɪŋ] n soplado de
vidrio.
glass ceiling n (fig) techo or barrera
invisible (que impide ascender
profesionalmente a las mujeres o miembros
de minorías étnicas).
glasses ['glɑːsəs] npl gafas fpl, anteojos mpl
(LAM).
glass fibre, (US) **glass fiber** n fibra de
vidrio.
glasshouse ['glɑːshaus] n invernadero.
glassware ['glɑːswɛə*] n cristalería.
glassy ['glɑːsɪ] adj (eyes) vidrioso.
Glaswegian [glæs'wiːdʒən] adj de Glasgow
♦ n nativo/a (or habitante m/f) de Glasgow.
glaze [gleɪz] vt (window) acristalar;
(pottery) vidriar; (CULIN) glasear ♦ n
barniz m; (CULIN) vidriado.
glazed [gleɪzd] adj (eye) vidrioso; (pottery)
vidriado.
glazier ['gleɪzɪə*] n vidriero/a.
gleam [gliːm] n destello ♦ vi relucir; **a ~ of
hope** un rayo de esperanza.
gleaming ['gliːmɪŋ] adj reluciente.
glean [gliːn] vt (gather: information) recoger.
glee [gliː] n alegría, regocijo.
gleeful ['gliːful] adj alegre.
glen [glɛn] n cañada.
glib [glɪb] adj (person) de mucha labia;
(comment) fácil.
glibly ['glɪblɪ] adv (explain) con mucha labia.
glide [glaɪd] vi deslizarse; (AVIAT, birds)
planear.
glider ['glaɪdə*] n (AVIAT) planeador m.
gliding ['glaɪdɪŋ] n (AVIAT) vuelo sin motor.
glimmer ['glɪmə*] n luz f tenue.
glimpse [glɪmps] n vislumbre m ♦ vt
vislumbrar, entrever; **to catch a ~ of**

vislumbrar.
glint [glɪnt] n destello; (in the eye) chispa
♦ vi centellear.
glisten ['glɪsn] vi relucir, brillar.
glitter ['glɪtə*] vi relucir, brillar ♦ n brillo.
glittering ['glɪtərɪŋ] adj reluciente,
brillante.
glitz [glɪts] n (col) vistosidad f.
gloat [gləʊt] vi: **to ~ over** regodearse con.
global ['gləʊbl] adj (world-wide) mundial;
(comprehensive) global.
global warming [-'wɔːmɪŋ] n
(re)calentamiento global or de la tierra.
globe [gləʊb] n globo, esfera; (model) bola
del mundo; globo terráqueo.
globetrotter ['gləʊbtrɔtə*] n trotamundos
m inv.
globule ['glɔbjuːl] n glóbulo.
gloom [gluːm] n penumbra; (sadness)
desaliento, melancolía.
gloomily ['gluːmɪlɪ] adv tristemente; de
modo pesimista.
gloomy ['gluːmɪ] adj (dark) oscuro; (sad)
triste; (pessimistic) pesimista; **to feel ~**
sentirse pesimista.
glorification [glɔːrɪfɪ'keɪʃən] n glorificación f.
glorify ['glɔːrɪfaɪ] vt glorificar.
glorious ['glɔːrɪəs] adj glorioso; (weather,
sunshine) espléndido.
glory ['glɔːrɪ] n gloria.
glory hole n (col) trastero.
Glos abbr (BRIT) = Gloucestershire.
gloss [glɔs] n (shine) brillo; (also: **~ paint**)
(pintura) esmalte m.
▶**gloss over** vt fus restar importancia a;
(omit) pasar por alto.
glossary ['glɔsərɪ] n glosario.
glossy ['glɔsɪ] adj (hair) brillante;
(photograph) con brillo; (magazine) de
papel satinado or cuché.
glove [glʌv] n guante m.
glove compartment n (AUT) guantera.
glow [gləʊ] vi (shine) brillar ♦ n brillo.
glower ['glaʊə*] vi: **to ~ at** mirar con
ceño.
glowing ['gləʊɪŋ] adj (fire) vivo;
(complexion) encendido; (fig: report,
description) entusiasta.
glow-worm ['gləʊwɜːm] n luciérnaga.
glucose ['gluːkəʊs] n glucosa.
glue [gluː] n pegamento, cemento (LAM) ♦ vt
pegar.
glue-sniffing ['gluːsnɪfɪŋ] n inhalación f de
pegamento or cemento (LAM).
glum [glʌm] adj (mood) abatido; (person,
tone) melancólico.
glut [glʌt] n superabundancia.
glutinous ['gluːtɪnəs] adj glutinoso,

pegajoso.

glutton ['glʌtn] *n* glotón/ona *m/f*; **~ for punishment** masoquista *m/f*.

gluttony ['glʌtənɪ] *n* gula, glotonería.

glycerin(e) ['glɪsəriːn] *n* glicerina.

gm *abbr* (= *gram*) g.

GMAT *n abbr* (*US*: = *Graduate Management Admissions Test*) *examen de admisión al segundo ciclo de la enseñanza superior*.

GMB *n abbr* (*BRIT*: = *General Municipal and Boilermakers (Union)*) *sindicato obrero*.

GMT *abbr* (= *Greenwich Mean Time*) GMT.

gnarled [nɑːld] *adj* nudoso.

gnash [næʃ] *vt*: **to ~ one's teeth** hacer rechinar los dientes.

gnat [næt] *n* mosquito.

gnaw [nɔː] *vt* roer.

gnome [nəum] *n* gnomo.

GNP *n abbr* (= *gross national product*) PNB *m*.

go [gəu] *vb* (*pt* **went**, *pp* **gone** [wɛnt, gɔn]) *vi* ir; (*travel*) viajar; (*depart*) irse, marcharse; (*work*) funcionar, marchar; (*be sold*) venderse; (*time*) pasar; (*become*) ponerse; (*break etc*) estropearse, romperse; (*fit, suit*): **to ~ with** hacer juego con ♦ *n* (*pl* **~es**): **to have a ~ (at)** probar suerte (con); **to be on the ~** no parar; **whose ~ is it?** ¿a quién le toca?; **to ~ by car/on foot** ir en coche/a pie; **he's ~ing to do it** va a hacerlo; **to ~ for a walk** ir a dar un paseo; **to ~ dancing** ir a bailar; **to ~ looking for sth/sb** ir a buscar algo/a algn; **to make sth ~, get sth ~ing** poner algo en marcha; **my voice has gone** he perdido la voz; **the cake is all gone** se acabó la tarta; **the money will ~ towards our holiday** el dinero es para (ayuda de) nuestras vacaciones; **how did it ~?** ¿qué tal salió *or* resultó?, ¿cómo ha ido?; **the meeting went well** la reunión salió bien; **to ~ and see sb, ~ to see sb** ir a ver a algn; **to ~ to sleep** dormirse; **I'll take whatever is ~ing** acepto lo que haya; ... **to ~** (*US*: *food*) ... para llevar; **to ~ round the back** pasar por detrás.

▶**go about** *vi* (*rumour*) propagarse; (*also*: **~ round**: *wander about*) andar (de un sitio para otro) ♦ *vt fus*: **how do I ~ about this?** ¿cómo me las arreglo para hacer esto?; **to ~ about one's business** ocuparse de sus asuntos.

▶**go after** *vt fus* (*pursue*) perseguir; (*job, record etc*) andar tras.

▶**go against** *vt fus* (*be unfavourable to*: *results*) ir en contra de; (*be contrary to*: *principles*) ser contrario a.

▶**go ahead** *vi* seguir adelante.

▶**go along** *vi* ir; **as you ~ along** sobre la marcha ♦ *vt fus* bordear.

▶**go along with** *vt fus* (*accompany*) acompañar; (*agree with*: *idea*) estar de acuerdo con.

▶**go around** *vi* = **go round**.

▶**go away** *vi* irse, marcharse.

▶**go back** *vi* volver.

▶**go back on** *vt fus* (*promise*) faltar a.

▶**go by** *vi* (*years, time*) pasar ♦ *vt fus* guiarse por.

▶**go down** *vi* bajar; (*ship*) hundirse; (*sun*) ponerse ♦ *vt fus* bajar por; **that should ~ down well with him** eso le va a gustar; **she's gone down with the flu** ha cogido la gripe.

▶**go for** *vt fus* (*fetch*) ir por; (*like*) gustar; (*attack*) atacar.

▶**go in** *vi* entrar.

▶**go in for** *vt fus* (*competition*) presentarse a.

▶**go into** *vt fus* entrar en; (*investigate*) investigar; (*embark on*) dedicarse a.

▶**go off** *vi* irse, marcharse; (*food*) pasarse; (*lights etc*) apagarse; (*explode*) estallar; (*event*) realizarse ♦ *vt fus* perder el interés por; **the party went off well** la fiesta salió bien.

▶**go on** *vi* (*continue*) seguir, continuar; (*lights*) encenderse; (*happen*) pasar, ocurrir; (*be guided by*: *evidence etc*) partir de; **to ~ on doing sth** seguir haciendo algo; **what's ~ing on here?** ¿qué pasa aquí?

▶**go on at** *vt fus* (*nag*) soltarle el rollo a.

▶**go out** *vi* salir; (*fire, light*) apagarse; (*ebb*: *tide*) bajar, menguar; **to ~ out with sb** salir con algn.

▶**go over** *vi* (*ship*) zozobrar ♦ *vt fus* (*check*) revisar; **to ~ over sth in one's mind** repasar algo mentalmente.

▶**go round** *vi* (*circulate*: *news, rumour*) correr; (*suffice*) alcanzar, bastar; (*revolve*) girar, dar vueltas; (*visit*): **to ~ round (to sb's)** pasar a ver (a algn); **to ~ round (by)** (*make a detour*) dar la vuelta (por).

▶**go through** *vt fus* (*town etc*) atravesar; (*search through*) revisar; (*perform*: *ceremony*) realizar; (*examine*: *list, book*) repasar.

▶**go through with** *vt fus* (*plan, crime*) llevar a cabo; **I couldn't ~ through with it** no pude llevarlo a cabo.

▶**go together** *vi* (*harmonize*: *people etc*) entenderse.

▶**go under** *vi* (*sink*: *ship, person*) hundirse; (*fig*: *business, firm*) quebrar.

▶**go up** *vi* subir; **to ~ up in flames** estallar

en llamas.

▶**go without** vt fus pasarse sin.

goad [gəud] vt aguijonear.

go-ahead ['gəuəhɛd] adj emprendedor(a) ♦ n luz f verde; **to give sth/sb the ~** dar luz verde a algo/algn.

goal [gəul] n meta, arco (LAM); (score) gol m.

goal difference n diferencia por goles.

goalie ['gəulɪ] n (col) portero, guardameta m/f, arquero (LAM).

goalkeeper ['gəulkiːpə*] n portero, guardameta m/f, arquero (LAM).

goal post n poste m (de la portería).

goat [gəut] n cabra f.

gobble ['gɔbl] vt (also: ~ **down**, ~ **up**) engullir.

go-between ['gəubɪtwiːn] n intermediario/a.

Gobi Desert ['gəubɪ-] n Desierto de Gobi.

goblet ['gɔblɪt] n copa.

goblin ['gɔblɪn] n duende m.

go-cart ['gəukaːt] n = **go-kart**.

god [gɔd] n dios m; **G~** Dios m.

god-awful [gɔd'ɔːfəl] adj (col) de puta pena.

godchild ['gɔdtʃaɪld] n ahijado/a.

goddamn ['gɔddæm] adj (col: also: **goddamned**) maldito, puñetero ♦ excl: ~! ¡cagüen diez!

goddess ['gɔdɪs] n diosa.

godfather ['gɔdfɑːðə*] n padrino.

god-fearing ['gɔdfɪərɪŋ] adj temeroso de Dios.

god-forsaken ['gɔdfəseɪkən] adj dejado de la mano de Dios.

godmother ['gɔdmʌðə*] n madrina.

godparents ['gɔdpɛərənts] npl: **the ~** los padrinos.

godsend ['gɔdsɛnd] n: **to be a ~** venir como llovido del cielo.

godson ['gɔdsʌn] n ahijado.

goes [gəuz] vb see **go**.

gofer ['gəufə*] n (col) chico/a para todo.

go-getter ['gəugɛtə*] n ambicioso/a.

goggle ['gɔgl] vi: **to ~ (at)** mirar con ojos desorbitados.

goggles ['gɔglz] npl (AUT) gafas fpl, anteojos mpl (LAM); (diver's) gafas fpl submarinas.

going ['gəuɪŋ] n (conditions) cosas fpl ♦ adj: **the ~ rate** la tarifa corriente or en vigor; **it was slow ~** las cosas iban lentas.

going-over [gəuɪŋ'əuvə*] n revisión f; (col: beating) paliza.

goings-on ['gəuɪŋz'ɔn] npl (col) tejemanejes mpl.

go-kart ['gəukaːt] n kart m.

gold [gəuld] n oro ♦ adj (reserves) de oro.

golden ['gəuldn] adj (made of gold) de oro; (~ in colour) dorado.

Golden Age n Siglo de Oro.

golden handshake n cuantiosa gratificación por los servicios prestados.

golden rule n regla de oro.

goldfish ['gəuldfɪʃ] n pez m de colores.

gold leaf n pan m de oro.

gold medal n (SPORT) medalla de oro.

goldmine ['gəuldmaɪn] n mina de oro.

gold-plated ['gəuld'pleɪtɪd] adj chapado en oro.

goldsmith ['gəuldsmɪθ] n orfebre m/f.

gold standard n patrón m oro.

golf [gɔlf] n golf m.

golf ball n (for game) pelota de golf; (on typewriter) esfera impresora.

golf club n club m de golf; (stick) palo (de golf).

golf course n campo de golf.

golfer ['gɔlfə*] n jugador(a) m/f de golf, golfista m/f.

golfing ['gɔlfɪŋ] n: **to go ~** jugar al golf.

gondola ['gɔndələ] n góndola.

gondolier [gɔndə'lɪə*] n gondolero.

gone [gɔn] pp of **go**.

goner ['gɔnə*] n (col): **to be a ~** estar en las últimas.

gong [gɔŋ] n gong m.

gonorrhea [gɔnə'rɪə] n gonorrea.

good [gud] adj bueno, (before m sing n buen); (well-behaved) educado ♦ n bien m; ~! ¡qué bien!; **he's ~ at** se le da bien; **to be ~ for** servir para; **it's ~ for you** te hace bien; **would you be ~ enough to...?** ¿podría hacerme el favor de...?, ¿sería tan amable de...?; **that's very ~ of you** es usted muy amable; **to feel ~** sentirse bien; **it's ~ to see you** me alegro de verte; **a ~ deal (of)** mucho; **a ~ many** muchos; **to make ~** reparar; **it's no ~ complaining** no sirve de nada quejarse; **is this any ~?** (will it do?) ¿sirve esto?; (what's it like?) ¿qué tal es esto?; **it's a ~ thing you were there** menos mal que estabas allí; **for ~** (for ever) para siempre, definitivamente; ~ **morning/afternoon** ¡buenos días/buenas tardes!; ~ **evening!** ¡buenas noches!; ~ **night!** ¡buenas noches!; **he's up to no ~** está tramando algo; **for the common ~** para el bien común; see also **goods**.

goodbye [gud'baɪ] excl ¡adiós!; **to say ~ (to)** (person) despedirse (de).

good faith n buena fe f.

good-for-nothing ['gudfənʌθɪŋ] n inútil m/f.

Good Friday n Viernes m Santo.

good-humoured ['gud'hju:məd] *adj* (*person*) afable, de buen humor; (*remark, joke*) bien intencionado.

good-looking ['gud'lukɪŋ] *adj* guapo.

good-natured ['gud'neɪtʃəd] *adj* (*person*) de buen carácter; (*discussion*) cordial.

goodness ['gudnɪs] *n* (*of person*) bondad *f*; **for ~ sake!** ¡por Dios!; **~ gracious!** ¡madre mía!

goods [gudz] *npl* bienes *mpl*; (*COMM etc*) géneros *mpl*, mercancías *fpl*, artículos *mpl*; **all his ~ and chattels** todos sus bienes.

goods train *n* (*BRIT*) tren *m* de mercancías.

goodwill [gud'wɪl] *n* buena voluntad *f*; (*COMM*) fondo de comercio; (*customer connections*) clientela.

goody-goody ['gudɪgudɪ] *n* (*pej*) santurrón/ona *m/f*.

gooey ['gu:ɪ] *adj* (*BRIT col*) pegajoso; (*cake, behaviour*) empalagoso.

goose, *pl* **geese** [gu:s, gi:s] *n* ganso, oca.

gooseberry ['guzbərɪ] *n* grosella espinosa *or* silvestre.

gooseflesh ['gu:sfleʃ] *n*, **goosepimples** ['gu:spɪmplz] *npl* carne *f* de gallina.

goose step *n* (*MIL*) paso de la oca.

GOP *n abbr* (*US POL: col = Grand Old Party*) *Partido Republicano.*

gopher ['gəufə*] *n* = **gofer.**

gore [gɔ:*] *vt* dar una cornada a, cornear ♦ *n* sangre *f*.

gorge [gɔ:dʒ] *n* garganta ♦ *vr*: **to ~ o.s. (on)** atracarse (de).

gorgeous ['gɔ:dʒəs] *adj* precioso; (*weather*) estupendo; (*person*) guapísimo.

gorilla [gə'rɪlə] *n* gorila *m*.

gormless ['gɔ:mlɪs] *adj* (*col*) ceporro, zoquete.

gorse [gɔ:s] *n* tojo.

gory ['gɔ:rɪ] *adj* sangriento.

go-slow ['gəu'sləu] *n* (*BRIT*) huelga de celo.

gospel ['gɔspl] *n* evangelio.

gossamer ['gɔsəmə*] *n* gasa.

gossip ['gɔsɪp] *n* cotilleo; (*person*) cotilla *m/f* ♦ *vi* cotillear, comadrear (*LAM*); **a piece of ~** un cotilleo.

gossip column *n* ecos *mpl* de sociedad.

got [gɔt] *pt, pp of* **get.**

Gothic ['gɔθɪk] *adj* gótico.

gotten ['gɔtn] (*US*) *pp of* **get.**

gouge [gaudʒ] *vt* (*also: ~ out: hole etc*) excavar; (*: initials*) grabar; **to ~ sb's eyes out** sacar los ojos a algn.

goulash ['gu:læʃ] *n* g(o)ulash *m*.

gourd [guəd] *n* calabaza.

gourmet ['guəmeɪ] *n* gastrónomo/a *m/f*.

gout [gaut] *n* gota.

govern ['gʌvən] *vt* (*gen*) gobernar; (*event,*

conduct) regir.

governess ['gʌvənɪs] *n* institutriz *f*.

governing ['gʌvənɪŋ] *adj* (*POL*) de gobierno, gubernamental; **~ body** organismo de gobierno.

government ['gʌvnmənt] *n* gobierno; **local ~** administración *f* municipal.

governmental [gʌvn'mɛntl] *adj* gubernamental.

government stock *n* papel *m* del Estado.

governor ['gʌvənə*] *n* gobernador(a) *m/f*; (*of jail*) director(a) *m/f*.

Govt. *abbr* (= *Government*) gobno.

gown [gaun] *n* vestido; (*of teacher, BRIT: of judge*) toga.

GP *n abbr see* **general practitioner.**

GPMU *n abbr* (*BRIT: = Graphical, Paper and Media Union*) *sindicato de trabajadores del sector editorial.*

GPO *n abbr* (*BRIT: old*) = *General Post Office*; (*US*) = *Government Printing Office.*

gr. *abbr* (*COMM: = gross*) bto.

grab [græb] *vt* coger (*SP*) *or* agarrar; **to ~ at** intentar agarrar.

grace [greɪs] *n* (*REL*) gracia; (*gracefulness*) elegancia, gracia; (*graciousness*) cortesía, gracia ♦ *vt* (*favour*) honrar; (*adorn*) adornar; **5 days' ~** un plazo de 5 días; **to say ~** bendecir la mesa; **his sense of humour is his saving ~** lo que le salva es su sentido del humor.

graceful ['greɪsful] *adj* elegante.

gracious ['greɪʃəs] *adj* amable ♦ *excl*: **good ~!** ¡Dios mío!

grade [greɪd] *n* (*quality*) clase *f*, calidad *f*; (*in hierarchy*) grado; (*US: SCOL*) curso (*: gradient*) pendiente *f*, cuesta ♦ *vt* clasificar; **to make the ~** (*fig*) dar el nivel; *see also* **high school.**

grade crossing *n* (*US*) paso a nivel.

grade school *n* (*US*) escuela primaria; *see also* **elementary school.**

gradient ['greɪdɪənt] *n* pendiente *f*.

gradual ['grædjuəl] *adj* gradual.

gradually ['grædjuəlɪ] *adv* gradualmente.

graduate *n* ['grædjuɪt] licenciado/a, graduado/a, egresado/a (*LAM*); (*US: SCOL*) bachiller *m/f* ♦ *vi* ['grædjueɪt] licenciarse, graduarse, recibirse (*LAM*); (*US*) obtener el título de bachillerato.

graduated pension ['grædjueɪtɪd-] *n* pensión *f* escalonada.

graduation [grædju'eɪʃən] *n* graduación *f*; (*US SCOL*) entrega de los títulos de bachillerato.

graffiti [grə'fi:tɪ] *npl* pintadas *fpl*.

graft [grɑ:ft] *n* (*AGR, MED*) injerto; (*bribery*) corrupción *f* ♦ *vt* injertar; **hard ~** (*col*) trabajo duro.

grain [greɪn] n (*single particle*) grano; (*no pl*: *cereals*) cereales mpl; (*US*: *corn*) trigo; (*in wood*) veta.

gram [græm] n (*US*) gramo.

grammar ['græmə*] n gramática.

grammar school n (*BRIT*) ≈ instituto (de segunda enseñanza); (*US*) escuela primaria; *see also* **comprehensive school**.

grammatical [grə'mætɪkl] adj gramatical.

gramme [græm] n = **gram**.

gramophone ['græməfəun] n (*BRIT*) gramófono.

granary ['grænərɪ] n granero.

grand [grænd] adj grandioso ♦ n (*US*: *col*) mil dólares mpl.

grandchildren ['græntʃɪldrən] npl nietos mpl.

granddad ['grændæd] n yayo, abuelito.

granddaughter ['grændɔːtə*] n nieta.

grandeur ['grændjə*] n grandiosidad f.

grandfather ['grænfɑːðə*] n abuelo.

grandiose ['grændɪəuz] adj grandioso; (*pej*) pomposo.

grand jury n (*US*) jurado de acusación.

grandma ['grænmɑː] n yaya, abuelita.

grandmother ['grænmʌðə*] n abuela.

grandpa ['grænpɑː] n = **granddad**.

grandparents ['grændpɛərənts] npl abuelos mpl.

grand piano n piano de cola.

Grand Prix ['grɑ̃ː'priː] n (*AUT*) gran premio, Grand Prix m.

grandson ['grænsʌn] n nieto.

grandstand ['grændstænd] n (*SPORT*) tribuna.

grand total n suma total, total m.

granite ['grænɪt] n granito.

granny ['grænɪ] n abuelita, yaya.

grant [grɑːnt] vt (*concede*) conceder; (*admit*): **to ~ (that)** reconocer (que) ♦ n (*SCOL*) beca; **to take sth for ~ed** dar algo por sentado.

granulated sugar ['grænjuleɪtɪd-] n (*BRIT*) azúcar m granulado.

granule ['grænjuːl] n gránulo.

grape [greɪp] n uva; **sour ~s** (*fig*) envidia sg; **a bunch of ~s** un racimo de uvas.

grapefruit ['greɪpfruːt] n pomelo, toronja.

grape juice n jugo *or* zumo (*SP*) de uva.

grapevine ['greɪpvaɪn] n vid f, parra; **I heard it on the ~** (*fig*) me enteré, me lo contaron.

graph [grɑːf] n gráfica.

graphic ['græfɪk] adj gráfico.

graphic designer n diseñador(a) m/f gráfico/a.

graphic equalizer n ecualizador m gráfico.

graphics ['græfɪks] n (*art, process*) artes fpl gráficas ♦ npl (*drawings*: *also COMPUT*) gráficos mpl.

graphite ['græfaɪt] n grafito.

graph paper n papel m cuadriculado.

grapple ['græpl] vi: **to ~ with a problem** enfrentarse a un problema.

grappling iron ['græplɪŋ-] n (*NAUT*) rezón m.

grasp [grɑːsp] vt agarrar, asir; (*understand*) comprender ♦ n (*grip*) asimiento; (*reach*) alcance m; (*understanding*) comprensión f; **to have a good ~ of** (*subject*) dominar.

▶**grasp at** vt fus (*rope etc*) tratar de agarrar; (*fig*: *opportunity*) aprovechar.

grasping ['grɑːspɪŋ] adj avaro.

grass [grɑːs] n hierba, grama (*LAM*); (*lawn*) césped m; (*pasture*) pasto; (*col*: *informer*) soplón/ona m/f.

grasshopper ['grɑːshɔpə*] n saltamontes m inv.

grassland ['grɑːslænd] n pradera, pampa (*LAM*).

grass roots adj de base ♦ npl (*POL*) bases fpl.

grass snake n culebra.

grassy ['grɑːsɪ] adj cubierto de hierba.

grate [greɪt] n parrilla ♦ vi chirriar, rechinar ♦ vt (*CULIN*) rallar.

grateful ['greɪtful] adj agradecido.

gratefully ['greɪtfəlɪ] adv con agradecimiento.

grater ['greɪtə*] n rallador m.

gratification [grætɪfɪ'keɪʃən] n satisfacción f.

gratify ['grætɪfaɪ] vt complacer; (*whim*) satisfacer.

gratifying ['grætɪfaɪɪŋ] adj gratificante.

grating ['greɪtɪŋ] n (*iron bars*) rejilla ♦ adj (*noise*) chirriante.

gratitude ['grætɪtjuːd] n agradecimiento.

gratuitous [grə'tjuːɪtəs] adj gratuito.

gratuity [grə'tjuːɪtɪ] n gratificación f.

grave [greɪv] n tumba ♦ adj serio, grave.

gravedigger ['greɪvdɪgə*] n sepulturero/a.

gravel ['grævl] n grava.

gravely ['greɪvlɪ] adv seriamente; **~ ill** muy grave.

gravestone ['greɪvstəun] n lápida.

graveyard ['greɪvjɑːd] n cementerio, camposanto.

gravitate ['grævɪteɪt] vi gravitar.

gravitation [grævɪ'teɪʃən] n gravitación f.

gravity ['grævɪtɪ] n gravedad f; (*seriousness*) seriedad f.

gravy ['greɪvɪ] n salsa de carne.

gravy boat n salsera.

gravy train n (*esp US*: *col*): **to get on the ~** coger un chollo.

gray [greɪ] *adj* (*US*) = **grey**.
graze [greɪz] *vi* pacer ♦ *vt* (*touch lightly, scrape*) rozar ♦ *n* (*MED*) rozadura.
grazing ['greɪzɪŋ] *n* (*for livestock*) pastoreo.
grease [griːs] *n* (*fat*) grasa; (*lubricant*) lubricante *m* ♦ *vt* engrasar; **to ~ the skids** (*US: fig*) engrasar el mecanismo.
grease gun *n* pistola engrasadora.
greasepaint ['griːspeɪnt] *n* maquillaje *m*.
greaseproof ['griːspruːf] *adj* a prueba de grasa; (*BRIT: paper*) de grasa.
greasy ['griːsɪ] *adj* (*hands, clothes*) grasiento; (*road, surface*) resbaladizo.
great [greɪt] *adj* grande, (*before n sing*) gran; (*col*) estupendo, macanudo (*LAM*), regio (*LAM*), chévere (*LAM*); (*pain, heat*) intenso; **we had a ~ time** nos lo pasamos muy bien; **they're ~ friends** son íntimos *or* muy amigos; **it was ~!** ¡fue estupendo!
Great Barrier Reef *n* Gran Barrera de Coral.
Great Britain *n* Gran Bretaña.
greater ['greɪtə*] *adj* mayor; **G~ London** el área metropolitana de Londres.
greatest ['greɪtɪst] *adj* (el/la) mayor.
great-grandchild, *pl* **-children** [greɪt'grændtʃaɪld, 'tʃɪldrən] *n* bisnieto/a.
great-grandfather [greɪt'grændfɑːðə*] *n* bisabuelo.
great-grandmother [greɪt'grændmʌðə*] *n* bisabuela.
Great Lakes *npl*: **the ~** los Grandes Lagos.
greatly ['greɪtlɪ] *adv* sumamente, muy.
greatness ['greɪtnɪs] *n* grandeza.
Greece [griːs] *n* Grecia.
greed [griːd] *n* (*also:* ~**iness**) codicia; (*for food*) gula.
greedily ['griːdɪlɪ] *adv* con avidez.
greedy ['griːdɪ] *adj* codicioso; (*for food*) glotón/ona.
Greek [griːk] *adj* griego ♦ *n* griego/a; (*LING*) griego; **ancient/modern ~** griego antiguo/moderno.
green [griːn] *adj* verde; (*inexperienced*) novato ♦ *n* verde *m*; (*stretch of grass*) césped *m*; (*of golf course*) campo, "green" *m*; **the G~ party** (*POL*) el partido verde; **~s** *npl* verduras *fpl*; **to have ~ fingers** (*fig*) tener buena mano para las plantas.
green belt *n* cinturón *m* verde.
green card *n* (*AUT*) carta verde.
greenery ['griːnərɪ] *n* vegetación *f*.
greenfly ['griːnflaɪ] *n* pulgón *m*.
greengage ['griːngeɪdʒ] *n* (*ciruela*) claudia.
greengrocer ['griːngrəusə*] *n* (*BRIT*) frutero/a, verdulero/a.
greenhouse ['griːnhaus] *n* invernadero.
greenhouse effect *n*: **the ~** el efecto invernadero.
greenhouse gas *n* gas *m* que produce el efecto invernadero.
greenish ['griːnɪʃ] *adj* verdoso.
Greenland ['griːnlənd] *n* Groenlandia.
Greenlander ['griːnləndə*] *n* groenlandés/esa *m/f*.
green light *n* luz *f* verde.
green pepper *n* pimiento verde.
greet [griːt] *vt* saludar; (*news*) recibir.
greeting ['griːtɪŋ] *n* (*gen*) saludo; (*welcome*) bienvenida; **~s** saludos *mpl*; **season's ~s** Felices Pascuas.
greeting(s) card *n* tarjeta de felicitación.
gregarious [grə'gɛərɪəs] *adj* gregario.
grenade [grə'neɪd] *n* (*also:* **hand ~**) granada.
grew [gruː] *pt of* **grow**.
grey [greɪ] *adj* gris; **to go ~** salirle canas.
grey-haired [greɪ'hɛəd] *adj* canoso.
greyhound ['greɪhaund] *n* galgo.
grid [grɪd] *n* rejilla; (*ELEC*) red *f*.
griddle ['grɪdl] *n* (*esp US*) plancha.
gridiron ['grɪdaɪən] *n* (*CULIN*) parrilla.
gridlock ['grɪdlɔk] *n* (*esp US*) retención *f*.
grief [griːf] *n* dolor *m*, pena; **to come to ~** (*plan*) fracasar, ir al traste; (*person*) acabar mal, desgraciarse.
grievance ['griːvəns] *n* (*cause for complaint*) motivo de queja, agravio.
grieve [griːv] *vi* afligirse, acongojarse ♦ *vt* afligir, apenar; **to ~ for** llorar por; **to ~ for sb** (*dead person*) llorar la pérdida de algn.
grievous ['griːvəs] *adj* grave; (*loss*) cruel; **~ bodily harm** (*LAW*) daños *mpl* corporales graves.
grill [grɪl] *n* (*on cooker*) parrilla ♦ *vt* (*BRIT*) asar a la parrilla; (*question*) interrogar; **~ed meat** carne *f* (asada) a la parrilla *or* plancha.
grille [grɪl] *n* rejilla.
grim [grɪm] *adj* (*place*) lúgubre; (*person*) adusto.
grimace [grɪ'meɪs] *n* mueca ♦ *vi* hacer muecas.
grime [graɪm] *n* mugre *f*.
grimly ['grɪmlɪ] *adv* (*say*) sombríamente.
grimy ['graɪmɪ] *adj* mugriento.
grin [grɪn] *n* sonrisa abierta ♦ *vi*: **to ~ (at)** sonreír abiertamente (a).
grind [graɪnd] *vb* (*pt, pp* **ground** [graund]) *vt* (*coffee, pepper etc*) moler; (*US: meat*) picar; (*make sharp*) afilar; (*polish: gem, lens*) esmerilar ♦ *vi* (*car gears*) rechinar

♦ *n*: **the daily ~** (*col*) la rutina diaria; **to ~ one's teeth** hacer rechinar los dientes; **to ~ to a halt** (*vehicle*) pararse con gran estruendo de frenos; (*fig: talks, scheme*) interrumpirse; (*work, production*) paralizarse.

grinder ['graɪndə*] *n* (*machine*: *for coffee*) molinillo.

grindstone ['graɪndstəun] *n*: **to keep one's nose to the ~** trabajar sin descanso.

grip [grɪp] *n* (*hold*) asimiento; (*of hands*) apretón *m*; (*handle*) asidero; (*of racquet etc*) mango; (*understanding*) comprensión *f* ♦ *vt* agarrar; **to get to ~s** with enfrentarse con; **to lose one's ~** (*fig*) perder el control; **he lost his ~ of the situation** la situación se le fue de las manos.

gripe [graɪp] *n* (*col: complaint*) queja ♦ *vi* (*col: complain*): **to ~ (about)** quejarse (de); **~s** *npl* retortijones *mpl*.

gripping ['grɪpɪŋ] *adj* absorbente.

grisly ['grɪzlɪ] *adj* horripilante, horrible.

gristle ['grɪsl] *n* cartílago.

grit [grɪt] *n* gravilla; (*courage*) valor *m* ♦ *vt* (*road*) poner gravilla en; **I've got a piece of ~ in my eye** tengo una arenilla en el ojo; **to ~ one's teeth** apretar los dientes.

grits [grɪts] *npl* (*US*) maíz *msg* a medio moler.

grizzle ['grɪzl] *vi* (*cry*) lloriquear.

grizzly ['grɪzlɪ] *n* (*also*: **~ bear**) oso pardo.

groan [grəun] *n* gemido, quejido ♦ *vi* gemir, quejarse.

grocer ['grəusə*] *n* tendero (de ultramarinos); **~'s (shop)** *n* tienda de ultramarinos *or* de abarrotes (*LAM*).

groceries ['grəusərɪz] *npl* comestibles *mpl*.

grocery ['grəusərɪ] *n* (*shop*) tienda de ultramarinos.

grog [grɔg] *n* (*BRIT*) grog *m*.

groggy ['grɔgɪ] *adj* atontado.

groin [grɔɪn] *n* ingle *f*.

groom [gruːm] *n* mozo/a de cuadra; (*also*: **bride~**) novio ♦ *vt* (*horse*) almohazar; **well-~ed** acicalado.

groove [gruːv] *n* ranura; (*of record*) surco.

grope [grəup] *vi* ir a tientas; **to ~ for** buscar a tientas.

gross [grəus] *adj* grueso; (*COMM*) bruto ♦ *vt* (*COMM*) recaudar en bruto.

gross domestic product (GDP) *n* producto interior bruto (PIB).

gross income *n* ingresos *mpl* brutos.

grossly ['grəuslɪ] *adv* (*greatly*) enormemente.

gross national product (GNP) *n* producto nacional bruto (PNB).

gross profit *n* beneficios *mpl* brutos.

gross sales *npl* ventas *fpl* brutas.

grotesque [grə'tɛsk] *adj* grotesco.

grotto ['grɔtəu] *n* gruta.

grotty ['grɔtɪ] *adj* asqueroso.

grouch [grautʃ] *vi* (*col*) refunfuñar ♦ *n* (*col: person*) refunfuñón/ona *m/f*.

ground [graund] *pt, pp of* **grind** ♦ *n* suelo, tierra; (*SPORT*) campo, terreno; (*reason: gen pl*) motivo, razón *f*; (*US: also*: **~ wire**) tierra ♦ *vt* (*plane*) mantener en tierra; (*US: ELEC*) conectar con tierra ♦ *vi* (*ship*) varar, encallar ♦ *adj* (*coffee etc*) molido; **~s** *npl* (*of coffee etc*) poso *sg*; (*gardens etc*) jardines *mpl*, parque *m*; **on the ~** en el suelo; **common ~** terreno común; **to gain/lose ~** ganar/perder terreno; **to the ~** al suelo; **below ~** bajo tierra; **he covered a lot of ~ in his lecture** abarcó mucho en la clase.

ground cloth *n* (*US*) = **groundsheet**.

ground control *n* (*AVIAT, SPACE*) control *m* desde tierra.

ground floor *n* (*BRIT*) planta baja.

grounding ['graundɪŋ] *n* (*in education*) conocimientos *mpl* básicos.

groundkeeper ['graundkiːpə*] *n* = **groundsman**.

groundless ['graundlɪs] *adj* infundado, sin fundamento.

groundnut ['graundnʌt] *n* cacahuete *m*.

ground rent *n* alquiler *m* del terreno.

ground rules *npl* normas básicas.

groundsheet ['graundʃiːt] (*BRIT*) *n* tela impermeable.

groundsman ['graundzmən], (*US*) **groundskeeper** ['graundzkiːpə*] *n* (*SPORT*) encargado de pista de deportes.

ground staff *n* personal *m* de tierra.

ground swell *n* mar *m or f* de fondo; (*fig*) ola.

ground-to-air ['grauntə'εə] *adj* tierra-aire.

ground-to-ground ['grauntə'graund] *adj* tierra-tierra.

groundwork ['graundwəːk] *n* trabajo preliminar.

group [gruːp] *n* grupo; (*MUS: pop* **~**) conjunto, grupo ♦ (*vb: also*: **~ together**) *vt* agrupar ♦ *vi* agruparse.

groupie ['gruːpɪ] *n* groupie *f*.

group therapy *n* terapia de grupo.

grouse [graus] *n* (*pl inv*) (*bird*) urogallo ♦ *vi* (*complain*) quejarse.

grove [grəuv] *n* arboleda.

grovel ['grɔvl] *vi* (*fig*) arrastrarse.

grow, *pt* **grew**, *pp* **grown** [grəu, gruː, grəun] *vi* crecer; (*increase*) aumentar; (*expand*) desarrollarse; (*become*) volverse ♦ *vt*

cultivar; (*hair, beard*) dejar crecer; **to ~ rich/weak** enriquecerse/debilitarse; **to ~ tired of waiting** cansarse de esperar.
▶**grow apart** *vi* (*fig*) alejarse uno del otro.
▶**grow away from** *vt fus* (*fig*) alejarse de.
▶**grow on** *vt fus*: **that painting is ~ing on me** ese cuadro me gusta cada vez más.
▶**grow out of** *vt fus* (*clothes*): **I've grown out of this shirt** esta camisa se me ha quedado pequeña; (*habit*) perder.
▶**grow up** *vi* crecer, hacerse hombre/mujer.
grower ['grəuə*] *n* (*AGR*) cultivador(a) *m/f*, productor(a) *m/f*.
growing ['grəuɪŋ] *adj* creciente; **~ pains** (*also fig*) problemas *mpl* de crecimiento.
growl [graul] *vi* gruñir.
grown [grəun] *pp of* **grow**.
grown-up [grəun'ʌp] *n* adulto/a, mayor *m/f*.
growth [grəuθ] *n* crecimiento, desarrollo; (*what has grown*) brote *m*; (*MED*) tumor *m*.
growth rate *n* tasa de crecimiento.
GRSM *n abbr* (*BRIT*) = *Graduate of the Royal Schools of Music.*
grub [grʌb] *n* gusano; (*col: food*) comida.
grubby ['grʌbɪ] *adj* sucio, mugriento, mugroso (*LAM*).
grudge [grʌdʒ] *n* rencor ♦ *vt*: **to ~ sb sth** dar algo a algn de mala gana; **to bear sb a ~** guardar rencor a algn; **he ~s (giving) the money** da el dinero de mala gana.
grudgingly ['grʌdʒɪŋlɪ] *adv* de mala gana.
gruelling, (*US*) **grueling** ['gruəlɪŋ] *adj* agotador.
gruesome ['gru:səm] *adj* horrible.
gruff [grʌf] *adj* (*voice*) ronco; (*manner*) brusco.
grumble ['grʌmbl] *vi* refunfuñar, quejarse.
grumpy ['grʌmpɪ] *adj* gruñón/ona.
grunge [grʌndʒ] *n* (*MUS, fashion*) grunge *m*.
grunt [grʌnt] *vi* gruñir ♦ *n* gruñido.
G-string ['dʒi:strɪŋ] *n* tanga *m*.
GSUSA *n abbr* = *Girl Scouts of the United States of America.*
GT *abbr* (*AUT*: = *gran turismo*) GT.
GU *abbr* (*US*) = *Guam.*
guarantee [gærən'ti:] *n* garantía ♦ *vt* garantizar; **he can't ~ (that) he'll come** no está seguro de poder venir.
guarantor [gærən'tɔ:*] *n* garante *m/f*, fiador(a) *m/f*.
guard [ga:d] *n* guardia; (*person*) guarda *m/f*; (*BRIT RAIL*) jefe *m* de tren; (*safety device: on machine*) cubierta de protección; (*protection*) protección *f*; (*fire~*) pantalla; (*mud~*) guardabarros *m inv* ♦ *vt* guardar; **to ~ (against or from)** proteger (de); **to be on one's ~** (*fig*) estar en guardia.

▶**guard against** *vi*: **to ~ against doing sth** guardarse de hacer algo.
guard dog *n* perro guardián.
guarded ['ga:dɪd] *adj* (*fig*) cauteloso.
guardian ['ga:dɪən] *n* guardián/ana *m/f*; (*of minor*) tutor(a) *m/f*.
guardrail ['ga:dreɪl] *n* pretil *m*.
guard's van *n* (*BRIT RAIL*) furgón *m* del jefe de tren.
Guatemala [gwa:tə'ma:lə] *n* Guatemala.
Guatemalan [gwa:tə'ma:lən] *adj, n* guatemalteco/a *m/f*.
Guernsey ['gə:nzɪ] *n* Guernsey *m*.
guerrilla [gə'rɪlə] *n* guerrillero/a.
guerrilla warfare *n* guerra de guerrillas.
guess [gɛs] *vi, vt* (*gen*) adivinar; (*suppose*) suponer ♦ *n* suposición *f*, conjetura; **I ~ you're right** (*esp US*) supongo que tienes razón; **to keep sb ~ing** mantener a algn a la expectativa; **to take** *or* **have a ~** tratar de adivinar; **my ~ is that ...** yo creo que ....
guesstimate ['gɛstɪmɪt] *n* cálculo aproximado.
guesswork ['gɛswə:k] *n* conjeturas *fpl*; **I got the answer by ~** acerté a ojo de buen cubero.
guest [gɛst] *n* invitado/a; (*in hotel*) huésped(a) *m/f*; **be my ~** (*col*) estás en tu casa.
guest-house ['gɛsthaus] *n* casa de huéspedes, pensión *f*.
guest room *n* cuarto de huéspedes.
guff [gʌf] *n* (*col*) bobadas *fpl*.
guffaw [gʌ'fɔ:] *n* carcajada ♦ *vi* reírse a carcajadas.
guidance ['gaɪdəns] *n* (*gen*) dirección *f*; (*advice*) consejos *mpl*; **marriage/vocational ~** orientación *f* matrimonial/profesional.
guide [gaɪd] *n* (*person*) guía *m/f*; (*book, fig*) guía *f*; (*also*: **girl ~**) exploradora ♦ *vt* guiar; **to be ~d by sb/sth** dejarse guiar por algn/algo.
guidebook ['gaɪdbuk] *n* guía.
guided missile ['gaɪdɪd-] *n* misil *m* teledirigido.
guide dog *n* perro guía.
guidelines ['gaɪdlaɪnz] *npl* (*fig*) directrices *fpl*.
guild [gɪld] *n* gremio.
guildhall ['gɪldhɔ:l] *n* (*BRIT: town hall*) ayuntamiento.
guile [gaɪl] *n* astucia.
guileless ['gaɪllɪs] *adj* cándido.
guillotine ['gɪləti:n] *n* guillotina.
guilt [gɪlt] *n* culpabilidad *f*.
guilty ['gɪltɪ] *adj* culpable; **to feel ~ (about)** sentirse culpable (de); **to plead ~/not ~**

declararse culpable/inocente.

Guinea ['gɪnɪ] *n*: **Republic of** ~ República de Guinea.

guinea ['gɪnɪ] *n* (*BRIT*: *old*) guinea (= *21 chelines: en la actualidad ya no se usa esta moneda*).

guinea pig *n* cobaya; (*fig*) conejillo de Indias.

guise [gaɪz] *n*: **in** *or* **under the** ~ **of** bajo la apariencia de.

guitar [gɪ'tɑː*] *n* guitarra.

guitarist [gɪ'tɑːrɪst] *n* guitarrista *m/f*.

gulch [gʌltʃ] *n* (*US*) barranco.

gulf [gʌlf] *n* golfo; (*abyss*) abismo; **the G~** el Golfo (Pérsico).

Gulf States *npl*: **the** ~ los países del Golfo.

Gulf Stream *n*: **the** ~ la Corriente del Golfo.

gull [gʌl] *n* gaviota.

gullet ['gʌlɪt] *n* esófago.

gullibility [gʌlɪ'bɪlɪtɪ] *n* credulidad *f*.

gullible ['gʌlɪbl] *adj* crédulo.

gully ['gʌlɪ] *n* barranco.

gulp [gʌlp] *vi* tragar saliva ♦ *vt* (*also*: ~ **down**) tragarse ♦ *n* (*of liquid*) trago; (*of food*) bocado; **in** *or* **at one** ~ de un trago.

gum [gʌm] *n* (*ANAT*) encía; (*glue*) goma, cemento (*LAM*); (*sweet*) gominola; (*also*: **chewing-**~) chicle *m* ♦ *vt* pegar con goma.

▶**gum up** *vt*: **to** ~ **up the works** (*col*) entorpecerlo todo.

gumboots ['gʌmbuːts] *npl* (*BRIT*) botas *fpl* de goma.

gumption ['gʌmpʃən] *n* (*col*) iniciativa.

gum tree *n* árbol *m* gomero.

gun [gʌn] *n* (*small*) pistola; (*shotgun*) escopeta; (*rifle*) fusil *m*; (*cannon*) cañón *m* ♦ *vt* (*also*: ~ **down**) abatir a tiros; **to stick to one's** ~**s** (*fig*) mantenerse firme *or* en sus trece.

gunboat ['gʌnbəut] *n* cañonero.

gun dog *n* perro de caza.

gunfire ['gʌnfaɪə*] *n* disparos *mpl*.

gung-ho [gʌŋ'həu] *adj* (*col*) patriotero.

gunk [gʌŋk] *n* (*col*) masa viscosa.

gunman ['gʌnmən] *n* pistolero.

gunner ['gʌnə*] *n* artillero.

gunpoint ['gʌnpɔɪnt] *n*: **at** ~ a mano armada.

gunpowder ['gʌnpaudə*] *n* pólvora.

gunrunner ['gʌnrʌnə*] *n* traficante *m/f* de armas.

gunrunning ['gʌnrʌnɪŋ] *n* tráfico de armas.

gunshot ['gʌnʃɒt] *n* disparo.

gunsmith ['gʌnsmɪθ] *n* armero.

gurgle ['gəːgl] *vi* gorgotear.

guru ['guːruː] *n* guru *m*.

gush [gʌʃ] *vi* chorrear; (*fig*) deshacerse en efusiones.

gushing ['gʌʃɪŋ] *adj* efusivo.

gusset ['gʌsɪt] *n* (*in tights, pants*) escudete *m*.

gust [gʌst] *n* (*of wind*) ráfaga.

gusto ['gʌstəu] *n* entusiasmo.

gusty ['gʌstɪ] *adj* racheado.

gut [gʌt] *n* intestino; (*MUS etc*) cuerda de tripa ♦ *vt* (*poultry, fish*) destripar; (*building*): **the blaze** ~**ted the entire building** el fuego destruyó el edificio entero.

gut reaction *n* reacción *f* instintiva.

guts [gʌts] *npl* (*courage*) agallas *fpl*, valor *m*; (*col*: *innards*: *of people, animals*) tripas *fpl*; **to hate sb's** ~ odiar a algn (a muerte).

gutsy ['gʌtsɪ] *adj*: **to be** ~ (*col*) tener agallas.

gutted ['gʌtɪd] *adj* (*col*: *disappointed*): **I was** ~ me quedé hecho polvo.

gutter ['gʌtə*] *n* (*of roof*) canalón *m*; (*in street*) cuneta; **the** ~ (*fig*) el arroyo.

gutter press *n* (*col*): **the** ~ la prensa sensacionalista *or* amarilla; *see also* **tabloid press**.

guttural ['gʌtərl] *adj* gutural.

guy [gaɪ] *n* (*also*: ~**rope**) viento, cuerda; (*col*: *man*) tío (*SP*), tipo.

Guyana [gaɪ'ænə] *n* Guayana.

La noche del cinco de noviembre, **Guy Fawkes' Night,** *se celebra el fracaso de la conspiración de la pólvora (***Gunpowder Plot**), *el intento fallido de volar el parlamento de Jaime 1 en 1605. Esa noche se lanzan fuegos artificiales y se queman en muchas hogueras muñecos de trapo que representan a* **Guy Fawkes,** *uno de los cabecillas. Días antes los niños tienen por costumbre pedir a los viandantes* "**a penny for the guy**", *dinero para comprar los cohetes.*

---

guzzle ['gʌzl] *vi* tragar ♦ *vt* engullir.

gym [dʒɪm] *n* (*also*: **gymnasium**) gimnasio; (*also*: **gymnastics**) gimnasia.

gymkhana [dʒɪm'kɑːnə] *n* gincana.

gymnast ['dʒɪmnæst] *n* gimnasta *m/f*.

gymnastics [dʒɪm'næstɪks] *n* gimnasia.

gym shoes *npl* zapatillas *fpl* de gimnasia.

gym slip *n* (*BRIT*) pichi *m*.

gynaecologist, (*US*) **gynecologist** [gaɪnɪ'kɒlədʒɪst] *n* ginecólogo/a.

gynaecology, (*US*) **gynecology** [gaɪnə'kɒlədʒɪ] *n* ginecología.

gypsy ['dʒɪpsɪ] *n* = **gipsy**.

gyrate [dʒaɪ'reɪt] *vi* girar.

gyroscope ['dʒaɪrəskəup] *n* giroscopio.

H h

H, h [eɪtʃ] *n (letter)* H, h *f*; **H for Harry,** (*US*) **H for How** H de Historia.
habeas corpus [ˈheɪbɪəsˈkɔːpəs] *n* (*LAW*) hábeas corpus *m*.
haberdashery [ˈhæbəˈdæʃərɪ] *n* (*BRIT*) mercería; (*US: men's clothing*) prendas *fpl* de caballero.
habit [ˈhæbɪt] *n* hábito, costumbre *f*; **to get out of/into the ~ of doing sth** perder la costumbre de/acostumbrarse a hacer algo.
habitable [ˈhæbɪtəbl] *adj* habitable.
habitat [ˈhæbɪtæt] *n* hábitat *m*.
habitation [hæbɪˈteɪʃən] *n* habitación *f*.
habitual [həˈbɪtjuəl] *adj* acostumbrado, habitual; (*drinker, liar*) empedernido.
habitually [həˈbɪtjuəlɪ] *adv* por costumbre.
hack [hæk] *vt (cut)* cortar; (*slice*) tajar ♦ *n* corte *m*; (*axe blow*) hachazo; (*pej: writer*) escritor(a) *m/f* a sueldo; (*old horse*) jamelgo.
hacker [ˈhækə*] *n* (*COMPUT*) pirata *m* informático.
hackles [ˈhæklz] *npl:* **to make sb's ~ rise** (*fig*) poner furioso a algn.
hackney cab [ˈhæknɪ-] *n* coche *m* de alquiler.
hackneyed [ˈhæknɪd] *adj* trillado, gastado.
hacksaw [ˈhæksɔː] *n* sierra para metales.
had [hæd] *pt, pp of* **have**.
haddock, *pl* ~ *or* ~**s** [ˈhædək] *n especie de merluza*.
hadn't [ˈhædnt] = **had not**.
haematology, (*US*) **hematology** [ˈhiːməˈtɔlədʒɪ] *n* hematología.
haemoglobin, (*US*) **hemoglobin** [ˈhiːməˈgləubɪn] *n* hemoglobina.
haemophilia, (*US*) **hemophilia** [ˈhiːməˈfɪlɪə] *n* hemofilia.
haemorrhage, (*US*) **hemorrhage** [ˈhɛmərɪdʒ] *n* hemorragia.
haemorrhoids, (*US*) **hemorrhoids** [ˈhɛmərɔɪdz] *npl* hemorroides *fpl*, almorranas *fpl*.
hag [hæg] *n (ugly)* vieja fea, tarasca; (*nasty*) bruja; (*witch*) hechicera.
haggard [ˈhægəd] *adj* ojeroso.

haggis [ˈhægɪs] *n (Scottish) asadura de cordero cocida; see also* **Burns' Night**.
haggle [ˈhægl] *vi (argue)* discutir; (*bargain*) regatear.
haggling [ˈhæglɪŋ] *n* regateo.
Hague [heɪg] *n:* **The ~** La Haya.
hail [heɪl] *n (weather)* granizo ♦ *vt* saludar; (*call*) llamar a ♦ *vi* granizar; **to ~ (as)** aclamar (como), celebrar (como); **he ~s from Scotland** es natural de Escocia.
hailstone [ˈheɪlstəun] *n* (piedra de) granizo.
hailstorm [ˈheɪlstɔːm] *n* granizada.
hair [hɛə*] *n (gen)* pelo, cabellos *mpl*; (*one* ~) pelo, cabello; (*head of* ~) pelo, cabellera; (*on legs etc*) vello; **to do one's ~** arreglarse el pelo; **grey ~** canas *fpl*.
hairbrush [ˈhɛəbrʌʃ] *n* cepillo (para el pelo).
haircut [ˈhɛəkʌt] *n* corte *m* de pelo.
hairdo [ˈhɛəduː] *n* peinado.
hairdresser [ˈhɛədrɛsə*] *n* peluquero/a; **~'s** peluquería.
hair-dryer [ˈhɛədraɪə*] *n* secador *m* (de pelo).
-haired [hɛəd] *adj suff:* **fair/long~** (de pelo) rubio *or* güero (*LAM*)/de pelo largo.
hairgrip [ˈhɛəgrɪp] *n* horquilla.
hairline [ˈhɛəlaɪn] *n* nacimiento del pelo.
hairline fracture *n* fractura muy fina.
hairnet [ˈhɛənɛt] *n* redecilla.
hair oil *n* brillantina.
hairpiece [ˈhɛəpiːs] *n* trenza postiza.
hairpin [ˈhɛəpɪn] *n* horquilla.
hairpin bend, (*US*) **hairpin curve** *n* curva muy cerrada.
hair-raising [ˈhɛəreɪzɪŋ] *adj* espeluznante.
hair remover *n* depilatorio.
hair's breadth *n:* **by a ~** por un pelo.
hair spray *n* laca.
hairstyle [ˈhɛəstaɪl] *n* peinado.
hairy [ˈhɛərɪ] *adj* peludo, velludo.
Haiti [ˈheɪtɪ] *n* Haití *m*.
hake [heɪk] *n* merluza.
halcyon [ˈhælsɪən] *adj* feliz.
hale [heɪl] *adj:* **~ and hearty** sano y fuerte.
half [hɑːf] *n (pl* **halves** [hɑːvz]) mitad *f*; (*SPORT: of match*) tiempo, parte *f*; (: *of ground*) campo ♦ *adj* medio ♦ *adv* medio, a medias; **~-an-hour** media hora; **two and a ~** dos y media; **~ a dozen** media docena; **~ a pound** media libra, ≈ 250 gr.; **to cut sth in ~** cortar algo por la mitad; **to go halves (with sb)** ir a medias (con algn); **~empty/closed** medio vacío/entreabierto; **~ asleep** medio dormido; **~ past 3** las 3 y media.
half-back [ˈhɑːfbæk] *n* (*SPORT*) medio.
half-baked [ˈhɑːfˈbeɪkt] *adj* (*col: idea,*

scheme) mal concebido *or* pensado.
half-breed ['hɑːfbriːd] *n* = **half-caste.**
half-brother ['hɑːfbrʌðə*] *n* hermanastro.
half-caste ['hɑːfkɑːst] *n* mestizo/a.
half-hearted ['hɑːf'hɑːtɪd] *adj* indiferente, poco entusiasta.
half-hour [hɑːf'auə*] *n* media hora.
half-mast ['hɑːf'mɑːst] *n*: **at ~** (*flag*) a media asta.
halfpenny ['heɪpnɪ] *n* medio penique *m.*
half-price ['hɑːf'praɪs] *adj* a mitad de precio.
half term *n* (*BRIT SCOL*) vacaciones de mediados del trimestre.
half-time [hɑːf'taɪm] *n* descanso.
halfway ['hɑːf'weɪ] *adv* a medio camino; **to meet sb ~** (*fig*) llegar a un acuerdo con algn.
halfway house *n centro de readaptación de antiguos presos;* (*fig*) solución *f* intermedia.
half-wit ['hɑːfwɪt] *n* (*col*) zoquete *m.*
half-yearly [hɑːf'jɪəlɪ] *adv* semestralmente ♦ *adj* semestral.
halibut ['hælɪbət] *n, pl inv* halibut *m.*
halitosis [hælɪ'təusɪs] *n* halitosis *f.*
hall [hɔːl] *n* (*for concerts*) sala; (*entrance way*) entrada, vestíbulo.
hallmark ['hɔːlmɑːk] *n* (*mark*) rasgo distintivo; (*seal*) sello.
hallo [hə'ləu] *excl* = **hello.**
hall of residence *n* (*BRIT*) colegio mayor, residencia universitaria.
Hallowe'en [hæləu'iːn] *n* víspera de Todos los Santos.

La tradición anglosajona dice que en la noche del 31 de octubre, **Hallowe'en,** *víspera de Todos los Santos, es fácil ver a brujas y fantasmas. Es una ocasión festiva en la que los niños se disfrazan y van de puerta en puerta llevando un farol hecho con una calabaza en forma de cabeza humana. Cuando se les abre la puerta gritan* **"trick or treat"** *para indicar que gastarán una broma a quien no les dé un pequeño regalo (como golosinas o dinero).*

hallucination [həluːsɪ'neɪʃən] *n* alucinación *f.*
hallucinogenic [həluːsɪnəu'dʒɛnɪk] *adj* alucinógeno.
hallway ['hɔːlweɪ] *n* vestíbulo.
halo ['heɪləu] *n* (*of saint*) aureola.
halt [hɔːlt] *n* (*stop*) alto, parada; (*RAIL*) apeadero ♦ *vt* parar ♦ *vi* pararse; (*process*) interrumpirse; **to call a ~** (**to sth**) (*fig*) poner fin (a algo).

halter ['hɔːltə*] *n* (*for horse*) cabestro.
halterneck ['hɔːltənɛk] *adj* de espalda escotada.
halve [hɑːv] *vt* partir por la mitad.
halves [hɑːvz] *pl of* **half.**
ham [hæm] *n* jamón *m* (cocido); (*col: also:* **radio ~**) radioaficionado/a *m/f*; (: *also:* **~ actor**) comicastro.
hamburger ['hæmbɜːgə*] *n* hamburguesa.
ham-fisted ['hæm'fɪstɪd] *adj* torpe, desmañado.
hamlet ['hæmlɪt] *n* aldea.
hammer ['hæmə*] *n* martillo ♦ *vt* (*nail*) clavar; **to ~ a point home to sb** remacharle un punto a algn.
▶**hammer out** *vt* (*metal*) forjar a martillo; (*fig: solution, agreement*) elaborar (trabajosamente).
hammock ['hæmək] *n* hamaca.
hamper ['hæmpə*] *vt* estorbar ♦ *n* cesto.
hamster ['hæmstə*] *n* hámster *m.*
hand [hænd] *n* mano *f*; (*of clock*) aguja, manecilla; (*writing*) letra; (*worker*) obrero; (*measurement: of horse*) palmo ♦ *vt* (*give*) dar, pasar; (*deliver*) entregar; **to give sb a ~** echar una mano a algn, ayudar a algn; **to force sb's ~** forzarle la mano a algn; **at ~** a mano; **in ~** entre manos; **we have the matter in ~** tenemos el asunto entre manos; **to have in one's ~** (*knife, victory*) tener en la mano; **to have a free ~** tener carta blanca; **on ~** (*person, services*) a mano, al alcance; **to ~** (*information etc*) a mano; **on the one ~ ..., on the other ~ ...** por una parte ... por otra (parte) ....
▶**hand down** *vt* pasar, bajar; (*tradition*) transmitir; (*heirloom*) dejar en herencia; (*US: sentence, verdict*) imponer.
▶**hand in** *vt* entregar.
▶**hand out** *vt* (*leaflets, advice*) repartir, distribuir.
▶**hand over** *vt* (*deliver*) entregar; (*surrender*) ceder.
▶**hand round** *vt* (*BRIT: information, papers*) pasar (de mano en mano); (: *chocolates etc*) ofrecer.
handbag ['hændbæg] *n* bolso, cartera (*LAM*).
hand baggage *n* = **hand luggage.**
handball ['hændbɔːl] *n* balonmano.
handbasin ['hændbeɪsn] *n* lavabo.
handbook ['hændbuk] *n* manual *m.*
handbrake ['hændbreɪk] *n* freno de mano.
hand cream *n* crema para las manos.
handcuffs ['hændkʌfs] *npl* esposas *fpl.*
handful ['hændful] *n* puñado.
hand-held ['hænd'hɛld] *adj* de mano.
handicap ['hændɪkæp] *n* desventaja;

(*SPORT*) hándicap *m* ♦ *vt* estorbar.
handicapped ['hændɪkæpt] *adj*: **to be mentally** ~ ser deficiente *m/f* mental; **to be physically** ~ ser minusválido/a.
handicraft ['hændɪkrɑ:ft] *n* artesanía.
handiwork ['hændɪwɔ:k] *n* manualidad(es) *f(pl)*; (*fig*) obra; **this looks like his** ~ (*pej*) es obra de él, parece.
handkerchief ['hæŋkətʃɪf] *n* pañuelo.
handle ['hændl] *n* (*of door etc*) pomo; (*of cup etc*) asa; (*of knife etc*) mango; (*for winding*) manivela ♦ *vt* (*touch*) tocar; (*deal with*) encargarse de; (*treat: people*) manejar; "~ **with care**" "(manéjese) con cuidado"; **to fly off the** ~ perder los estribos.
handlebar(s) ['hændlbɑ:(z)] *n(pl)* manillar *msg*.
handling ['hændlɪŋ] *n* (*AUT*) conducción *f*; **his** ~ **of the matter** su forma de llevar el asunto.
handling charges *npl* gastos *mpl* de tramitación.
hand luggage *n* equipaje *m* de mano.
handmade ['hændmeɪd] *adj* hecho a mano.
handout ['hændaut] *n* (*distribution*) repartición *f*; (*charity*) limosna; (*leaflet*) folleto, octavilla; (*press* ~) nota.
hand-picked ['hænd'pɪkt] *adj* (*produce*) escogido a mano; (*staff etc*) seleccionado cuidadosamente.
handrail ['hændreɪl] *n* (*on staircase etc*) pasamanos *m inv*, barandilla.
handset ['hændset] *n* (*TEL*) auricular *m*.
handshake ['hændʃeɪk] *n* apretón *m* de manos; (*COMPUT*) coloquio.
handsome ['hænsəm] *adj* guapo.
hands-on ['hændz'ɔn] *adj* práctico; **she has a very** ~ **approach** le gusta tomar parte activa; ~ **experience** (*COMPUT*) experiencia práctica.
handstand ['hændstænd] *n* voltereta, salto mortal.
hand-to-mouth ['hændtə'mauθ] *adj* (*existence*) precario.
handwriting ['hændraɪtɪŋ] *n* letra.
handwritten ['hændrɪtn] *adj* escrito a mano, manuscrito.
handy ['hændɪ] *adj* (*close at hand*) a mano; (*useful: machine, tool etc*) práctico; (*skilful*) hábil, diestro; **to come in** ~ venir bien.
handyman ['hændɪmæn] *n* manitas *m inv*.
hang, *pt, pp* **hung** [hæŋ, hʌŋ] *vt* colgar; (*head*) bajar; (*criminal: pt, pp* **hanged**) ahorcar; **to get the** ~ **of sth** (*col*) coger el tranquillo a algo.
▶**hang about** *vi* haraganear.
▶**hang back** *vi* (*hesitate*): **to** ~ **back (from doing)** vacilar (en hacer).

▶**hang on** *vi* (*wait*) esperar ♦ *vt fus* (*depend on: decision etc*) depender de; **to** ~ **on to** (*keep hold of*) agarrarse or aferrarse a; (*keep*) guardar, quedarse con.
▶**hang out** *vt* (*washing*) tender, colgar ♦ *vi* (*col: live*) vivir; (*: often be found*) moverse; **to** ~ **out of sth** colgar fuera de algo.
▶**hang together** *vi* (*cohere: argument etc*) sostenerse.
▶**hang up** *vt* (*coat*) colgar ♦ *vi* (*TEL*) colgar; **to** ~ **up on sb** colgarle a algn.
hangar ['hæŋə*] *n* hangar *m*.
hangdog ['hæŋdɔg] *adj* (*guilty: look, expression*) avergonzado.
hanger ['hæŋə*] *n* percha.
hanger-on [hæŋər'ɔn] *n* parásito.
hang-glider ['hæŋglaɪdə*] *n* ala delta.
hang-gliding ['hæŋglaɪdɪŋ] *n* vuelo con ala delta.
hanging ['hæŋɪŋ] *n* (*execution*) ejecución *f* (en la horca).
hangman ['hæŋmən] *n* verdugo.
hangover ['hæŋəuvə*] *n* (*after drinking*) resaca.
hang-up ['hæŋʌp] *n* complejo.
hanker ['hæŋkə*] *vi*: **to** ~ **after** (*miss*) echar de menos; (*long for*) añorar.
hankie, hanky ['hæŋkɪ] *n abbr* = **handkerchief**.
Hansard ['hænsɑ:d] *n actas oficiales de las sesiones del parlamento británico.*
Hants *abbr* (*BRIT*) = *Hampshire.*
haphazard [hæp'hæzəd] *adj* fortuito.
hapless ['hæplɪs] *adj* desventurado.
happen ['hæpən] *vi* suceder, ocurrir; (*take place*) tener lugar, realizarse; **as it** ~**s** da la casualidad de que; **what's** ~**ing?** ¿qué pasa?
▶**happen (up)on** *vt fus* tropezar *or* dar con.
happening ['hæpnɪŋ] *n* suceso, acontecimiento.
happily ['hæpɪlɪ] *adv* (*luckily*) afortunadamente; (*cheerfully*) alegremente.
happiness ['hæpɪnɪs] *n* (*contentment*) felicidad *f*; (*joy*) alegría.
happy ['hæpɪ] *adj* feliz; (*cheerful*) alegre; **to be** ~ (**with**) estar contento (con); **yes, I'd be** ~ **to** sí, con mucho gusto; **H**~ **Christmas/New Year!** ¡Feliz Navidad!/ ¡Feliz Año Nuevo!; ~ **birthday!** ¡felicidades!, ¡feliz cumpleaños!
happy-go-lucky ['hæpɪgəu'lʌkɪ] *adj* despreocupado.
happy hour *n horas en las que la bebida es más barata en un bar.*
harangue [hə'ræŋ] *vt* arengar.

harass ['hærəs] *vt* acosar, hostigar.

harassed ['hærəst] *adj* agobiado, presionado.

harassment ['hærəsmənt] *n* persecución *f*, acoso; (*worry*) preocupación *f*.

harbour, (*US*) **harbor** ['hɑːbə*] *n* puerto ♦ *vt* (*hope etc*) abrigar; (*hide*) dar abrigo a; (*retain*: *grudge etc*) guardar.

harbo(u)r dues *npl* derechos *mpl* portuarios.

hard [hɑːd] *adj* duro; (*difficult*) difícil; (*person*) severo ♦ *adv* (*work*) mucho, duro; (*think*) profundamente; **to look ~ at sb/ sth** clavar los ojos en algn/algo; **to try ~** esforzarse; **no ~ feelings!** ¡sin rencor(es)!; **to be ~ of hearing** ser duro de oído; **to be ~ done by** ser tratado injustamente; **to be ~ on sb** ser muy duro con algn; **I find it ~ to believe that ...** me cuesta trabajo creer que ....

hard-and-fast ['hɑːdən'fɑːst] *adj* rígido, definitivo.

hardback ['hɑːdbæk] *n* libro de tapas duras.

hard cash *n* dinero en efectivo.

hard copy *n* (*COMPUT*) copia impresa.

hard-core ['hɑːd'kɔː*] *adj* (*pornography*) duro; (*supporters*) incondicional.

hard court *n* (*TENNIS*) pista *or* cancha (de tenis) de cemento.

hard disk *n* (*COMPUT*) disco duro.

harden ['hɑːdn] *vt* endurecer; (*steel*) templar; (*fig*) curtir; (: *determination*) fortalecer ♦ *vi* (*substance*) endurecerse.

hardened ['hɑːdnd] *adj* (*criminal*) habitual; **to be ~ to sth** estar acostumbrado a algo.

hard-headed ['hɑːd'hɛdɪd] *adj* poco sentimental, realista.

hard-hearted ['hɑːd'hɑːtɪd] *adj* insensible.

hard-hitting ['hɑːd'hɪtɪŋ] *adj* (*speech, article*) contundente.

hard labour *n* trabajos *mpl* forzados.

hardliner [hɑːd'laɪnə*] *n* partidario/a de la línea dura.

hard-luck story ['hɑːdlʌk-] *n* dramón *m*.

hardly ['hɑːdlɪ] *adv* (*scarcely*) apenas; **that can ~ be true** eso difícilmente puede ser cierto; **~ ever** casi nunca; **I can ~ believe it** apenas me lo puedo creer.

hardness ['hɑːdnɪs] *n* dureza.

hard-nosed ['hɑːd'nəuzd] *adj* duro, sin contemplaciones.

hard-pressed ['hɑːd'prɛst] *adj* en apuros.

hard sell *n* publicidad *f* agresiva; **~ techniques** técnicas *fpl* agresivas de venta.

hardship ['hɑːdʃɪp] *n* (*troubles*) penas *fpl*; (*financial*) apuro.

hard shoulder *n* (*AUT*) arcén *m*.

hard-up [hɑːd'ʌp] *adj* (*col*) sin un duro (*SP*) *or* plata (*LAM*).

hardware ['hɑːdwɛə*] *n* ferretería; (*COMPUT*) hardware *m*.

hardware shop *n* ferretería.

hard-wearing [hɑːd'wɛərɪŋ] *adj* resistente, duradero; (*shoes*) resistente.

hard-won ['hɑːd'wʌn] *adj* ganado con esfuerzo.

hard-working [hɑːd'wəːkɪŋ] *adj* trabajador(a).

hardy ['hɑːdɪ] *adj* fuerte; (*plant*) resistente.

hare [hɛə*] *n* liebre *f*.

hare-brained ['hɛəbreɪnd] *adj* atolondrado.

harelip ['hɛəlɪp] *n* labio leporino.

harem [hɑː'riːm] *n* harén *m*.

haricot (bean) ['hærɪkəu-] *n* alubia.

hark back [hɑːk-] *vi*: **to ~ back to** (*former days, earlier occasion*) recordar.

harm [hɑːm] *n* daño, mal *m* ♦ *vt* (*person*) hacer daño a; (*health, interests*) perjudicar; (*thing*) dañar; **out of ~'s way** a salvo; **there's no ~ in trying** no se pierde nada con intentar.

harmful ['hɑːmful] *adj* (*gen*) dañino; (*reputation*) perjudicial.

harmless ['hɑːmlɪs] *adj* (*person*) inofensivo; (*drugs*) inocuo.

harmonica [hɑː'mɔnɪkə] *n* armónica.

harmonious [hɑː'məunɪəs] *adj* armonioso.

harmonize ['hɑːmənaɪz] *vt, vi* armonizar.

harmony ['hɑːmənɪ] *n* armonía.

harness ['hɑːnɪs] *n* arreos *mpl* ♦ *vt* (*horse*) enjaezar; (*resources*) aprovechar.

harp [hɑːp] *n* arpa ♦ *vi*: **to ~ on (about)** machacar (con).

harpoon [hɑː'puːn] *n* arpón *m*.

harrow ['hærəu] *n* grada ♦ *vt* gradar.

harrowing ['hærəuɪŋ] *adj* angustioso.

harry ['hærɪ] *vt* (*MIL*) acosar; (*person*) hostigar.

harsh [hɑːʃ] *adj* (*cruel*) duro, cruel; (*severe*) severo; (*words*) hosco; (*colour*) chillón/ ona; (*contrast*) violento.

harshly ['hɑːʃlɪ] *adv* (*say*) con aspereza; (*treat*) con mucha dureza.

harshness ['hɑːʃnɪs] *n* dureza.

harvest ['hɑːvɪst] *n* cosecha; (*of grapes*) vendimia ♦ *vt, vi* cosechar.

harvester ['hɑːvɪstə*] *n* (*machine*) cosechadora; (*person*) segador(a) *m/f*; **combine ~** segadora trilladora.

has [hæz] *vb see* **have**.

has-been ['hæzbiːn] *n* (*col*: *person*) persona acabada; (: *thing*) vieja gloria.

hash [hæʃ] *n* (*CULIN*) picadillo; (*fig*: *mess*) lío.

hashish ['hæʃɪʃ] n hachís m.
hasn't ['hæznt] = **has not**.
hassle ['hæsl] n (col) lío, rollo ♦ vt incordiar.
haste [heɪst] n prisa.
hasten ['heɪsn] vt acelerar ♦ vi darse prisa; **I ~ to add that...** me apresuro a añadir que ....
hastily ['heɪstɪlɪ] adv de prisa.
hasty ['heɪstɪ] adj apresurado.
hat [hæt] n sombrero.
hatbox ['hætbɔks] n sombrerera.
hatch [hætʃ] n (NAUT: also: ~**way**) escotilla ♦ vi salir del cascarón ♦ vt incubar; (fig: scheme, plot) idear, tramar.
hatchback ['hætʃbæk] n (AUT) tres or cinco puertas m.
hatchet ['hætʃɪt] n hacha.
hatchet job n (col) varapalo.
hatchet man n (col) ejecutor m de faenas desagradables por cuenta de otro.
hate [heɪt] vt odiar, aborrecer ♦ n odio; **I ~ to trouble you, but ...** siento or lamento molestarle, pero ....
hateful ['heɪtful] adj odioso.
hatred ['heɪtrɪd] n odio.
hat trick n: **to score a ~** (BRIT SPORT) marcar tres tantos (or triunfos) seguidos.
haughtily ['hɔːtɪlɪ] adv con arrogancia.
haughty ['hɔːtɪ] adj altanero, arrogante.
haul [hɔːl] vt tirar, jalar (LAM); (by lorry) transportar ♦ n (of fish) redada; (of stolen goods etc) botín m.
haulage ['hɔːlɪdʒ] n (BRIT) transporte m; (costs) gastos mpl de transporte.
haulage contractor n (firm) empresa de transportes; (person) transportista m/f.
haulier ['hɔːlɪə*], (US) **hauler** ['hɔːlə*] n transportista m/f.
haunch [hɔːntʃ] n anca; (of meat) pierna.
haunt [hɔːnt] vt (subj: ghost) aparecer en; (frequent) frecuentar; (obsess) obsesionar ♦ n guarida.
haunted ['hɔːntɪd] adj (castle etc) embrujado; (look) de angustia.
haunting ['hɔːntɪŋ] adj (sight, music) evocativo.
Havana [hə'vɑːnə] n La Havana.

═══════ KEYWORD

have [hæv] (pt, pp **had**) aux vb 1 (gen) haber; **to ~ arrived/eaten** haber llegado/comido; **having finished** or **when he had finished, he left** cuando hubo acabado, se fue

2 (in tag questions): **you've done it, ~n't you?** lo has hecho, ¿verdad? or ¿no?
3 (in short answers and questions): **I ~n't** no; **so I ~** pues, es verdad; **we ~n't paid — yes we ~!** no hemos pagado — ¡sí que hemos pagado!; **I've been there before, ~ you?** he estado allí antes, ¿y tú?

♦ modal aux vb (be obliged): **to ~ (got) to do sth** tener que hacer algo; **you ~n't to tell her** no hay que or no debes decírselo

♦ vt 1 (possess) tener; **he has (got) blue eyes/dark hair** tiene los ojos azules/el pelo negro
2 (referring to meals etc): **to ~ breakfast/lunch/dinner** desayunar/comer/cenar; **to ~ a drink/a cigarette** tomar algo/fumar un cigarrillo
3 (receive) recibir; (obtain) obtener; **may I ~ your address?** ¿puedes darme tu dirección?; **you can ~ it for £5** te lo puedes quedar por £5; **I must ~ it by tomorrow** lo necesito para mañana; **to ~ a baby** tener un niño or bebé
4 (maintain, allow): **I won't ~ it/this nonsense!** ¡no lo permitiré!/¡no permitiré estas tonterías!; **we can't ~ that** no podemos permitir eso
5: **to ~ sth done** hacer or mandar hacer algo; **to ~ one's hair cut** cortarse el pelo; **to ~ sb do sth** hacer que algn haga algo
6 (experience, suffer): **to ~ a cold/flu** tener un resfriado/la gripe; **she had her bag stolen/her arm broken** le robaron el bolso/se rompió un brazo; **to ~ an operation** operarse
7 (+ noun): **to ~ a swim/walk/bath/rest** nadar/dar un paseo/darse un baño/descansar; **let's ~ a look** vamos a ver; **to ~ a meeting/party** celebrar una reunión/una fiesta; **let me ~ a try** déjame intentarlo

▶**have in** vt: **to ~ it in for sb** (col) tenerla tomada con algn
▶**have on** vt: **~ you anything on tomorrow?** ¿vas a hacer algo mañana?; **I don't ~ any money on me** no llevo dinero (encima); **to ~ sb on** (BRIT col) tomarle el pelo a algn
▶**have out** vt: **to ~ it out with sb** (settle a problem etc) dejar las cosas en claro con algn.

haven ['heɪvn] n puerto; (fig) refugio.
haven't ['hævnt] = **have not**.
haversack ['hævəsæk] n macuto.
haves [hævz] npl: **the ~ and the have-nots** los ricos y los pobres.
havoc ['hævək] n estragos mpl; **to play ~**

with sth hacer estragos en algo.
Hawaii [hə'waɪi:] n (Islas fpl) Hawai m.
Hawaiian [hə'waɪjən] adj, n hawaiano/a m/f.
hawk [hɔ:k] n halcón m ♦ vt (goods for sale) pregonar.
hawkish ['hɔ:kɪʃ] adj beligerante.
hawthorn ['hɔ:θɔ:n] n espino.
hay [heɪ] n heno.
hay fever n fiebre f del heno.
haystack ['heɪstæk] n almiar m.
haywire ['heɪwaɪə*] adj (col): **to go ~** (person) volverse loco; (plan) irse al garete.
hazard ['hæzəd] n riesgo; (danger) peligro ♦ vt (remark) aventurar; (one's life) arriesgar; **to be a health ~** ser un peligro para la salud; **to ~ a guess** aventurar una respuesta or hipótesis.
hazardous ['hæzədəs] adj (dangerous) peligroso; (risky) arriesgado.
hazard warning lights npl (AUT) señales fpl de emergencia.
haze [heɪz] n neblina.
hazel ['heɪzl] n (tree) avellano ♦ adj (eyes) color m de avellano.
hazelnut ['heɪzlnʌt] n avellana.
hazy ['heɪzɪ] adj brumoso; (idea) vago.
H-bomb ['eɪtʃbɔm] n bomba H.
h & c abbr (BRIT) = hot and cold (water).
HE abbr = high explosive; (REL, DIPLOMACY: = His (or Her) Excellency) S. Exc^a.
he [hi:] pron él; **~ who...** aquél que..., quien....
head [hɛd] n cabeza; (leader) jefe/a m/f; (COMPUT) cabeza (grabadora) ♦ vt (list) encabezar; (group) capitanear; **~s (or tails)** cara (o cruz); **~ first** de cabeza; **~ over heels** patas arriba; **~ over heels in love** perdidamente enamorado; **on your ~ be it!** ¡allá tú!; **they went over my ~ to the manager** fueron directamente al gerente sin hacerme caso; **it was above or over their ~s** no alcanzaron a entenderlo; **to come to a ~** (fig: situation etc) llegar a un punto crítico; **to have a ~ for business** tener talento para los negocios; **to have no ~ for heights** no resistir las alturas; **to lose/keep one's ~** perder la cabeza/mantener la calma; **to sit at the ~ of the table** sentarse a la cabecera de la mesa; **to ~ the ball** cabecear (el balón).
▶**head for** vt fus dirigirse a.
▶**head off** vt (threat, danger) evitar.
headache ['hɛdeɪk] n dolor m de cabeza; **to have a ~** tener dolor de cabeza.
headband ['hɛdbænd] n cinta (para la cabeza), vincha (LAM).

headboard ['hɛdbɔ:d] n cabecera.
headdress ['hɛddrɛs] n (of bride, Indian) tocado.
headed notepaper ['hɛdɪd-] n papel m con membrete.
header ['hɛdə*] n (BRIT col: FOOTBALL) cabezazo; (: fall) caída de cabeza.
headfirst [hɛd'fɜ:st] adv de cabeza.
headhunt ['hɛdhʌnt] vt: **to be ~ed** ser seleccionado por un cazatalentos.
headhunter ['hɛdhʌntə*] n (fig) cazaejecutivos m inv.
heading ['hɛdɪŋ] n título.
headlamp ['hɛdlæmp] n (BRIT) = **headlight**.
headland ['hɛdlənd] n promontorio.
headlight ['hɛdlaɪt] n faro.
headline ['hɛdlaɪn] n titular m.
headlong ['hɛdlɔŋ] adv (fall) de cabeza; (rush) precipitadamente.
headmaster/mistress [hɛd'mɑ:stə*/mɪstrɪs] n director(a) m/f (de escuela).
head office n oficina central, central f.
head-on [hɛd'ɔn] adj (collision) de frente.
headphones ['hɛdfəʊnz] npl auriculares mpl.
headquarters (HQ) ['hɛdkwɔ:təz] npl sede f central; (MIL) cuartel m general.
head-rest ['hɛdrɛst] n reposa-cabezas m inv.
headroom ['hɛdrʊm] n (in car) altura interior; (under bridge) (límite m de) altura.
headscarf ['hɛdskɑ:f] n pañuelo.
headset ['hɛdsɛt] n cascos mpl.
headstone ['hɛdstəʊn] n lápida.
headstrong ['hɛdstrɔŋ] adj testarudo.
head waiter n maître m.
headway ['hɛdweɪ] n: **to make ~** (fig) hacer progresos.
headwind ['hɛdwɪnd] n viento contrario.
heady ['hɛdɪ] adj (experience, period) apasionante; (wine) fuerte.
heal [hi:l] vt curar ♦ vi cicatrizar.
health [hɛlθ] n salud f.
health care n asistencia sanitaria.
health centre n ambulatorio, centro médico.
health food(s) n(pl) alimentos mpl orgánicos.
health hazard n riesgo para la salud.
Health Service n (BRIT) servicio de salud pública, ≈ Insalud m (SP).
healthy ['hɛlθɪ] adj (gen) sano; (economy, bank balance) saludable.
heap [hi:p] n montón m ♦ vt amontonar; (plate) colmar; **~s (of)** (col: lots) montones (de); **to ~ favours/praise/gifts etc on sb** colmar a algn de favores/elogios/regalos etc.

hear, *pt, pp* **heard** [hɪə*, hɜːd] *vt* oír; (*perceive*) sentir; (*listen to*) escuchar; (*lecture*) asistir a; (*LAW: case*) ver ♦ *vi* oír; **to ~ about** oír hablar de; **to ~ from sb** tener noticias de alguien; **I've never heard of that book** nunca he oído hablar de ese libro.

▶**hear out** *vt*: **to ~ sb out** dejar que algn termine de hablar.

hearing ['hɪərɪŋ] *n* (*sense*) oído; (*LAW*) vista; **to give sb a ~** dar a algn la oportunidad de hablar, escuchar a algn.

hearing aid *n* audífono.

hearsay ['hɪəseɪ] *n* rumores *mpl*, habladurías *fpl*.

hearse [hɜːs] *n* coche *m* fúnebre.

heart [hɑːt] *n* corazón *m*; **~s** *npl* (*CARDS*) corazones *mpl*; **at ~** en el fondo; **by ~** (*learn, know*) de memoria; **to have a weak ~** tener el corazón débil; **to set one's ~ on sth/on doing sth** anhelar algo/hacer algo; **I did not have the ~ to tell her** no tuve valor para decírselo; **to take ~** cobrar ánimos; **the ~ of the matter** esencial *or* el meollo del asunto.

heartache ['hɑːteɪk] *n* angustia.

heart attack *n* infarto (de miocardio).

heartbeat ['hɑːtbiːt] *n* latido (del corazón).

heartbreak ['hɑːtbreɪk] *n* angustia, congoja.

heartbreaking ['hɑːtbreɪkɪŋ] *adj* desgarrador(a).

heartbroken ['hɑːtbrəukən] *adj*: **she was ~ about it** le partió el corazón.

heartburn ['hɑːtbɜːn] *n* acedía.

-hearted ['hɑːtɪd] *adj suff*: **a kind~ person** una persona bondadosa.

heartening ['hɑːtnɪŋ] *adj* alentador(a).

heart failure *n* (*MED*) paro cardíaco.

heartfelt ['hɑːtfɛlt] *adj* (*cordial*) cordial; (*deeply felt*) sincero.

hearth [hɑːθ] *n* (*gen*) hogar *m*; (*fireplace*) chimenea.

heartily ['hɑːtɪlɪ] *adv* sinceramente, cordialmente; (*laugh*) a carcajadas; (*eat*) con buen apetito; **to be ~ sick of** estar completamente harto de.

heartland ['hɑːtlænd] *n* zona interior *or* central; (*fig*) corazón *m*.

heartless ['hɑːtlɪs] *adj* despiadado.

heartstrings ['hɑːtstrɪŋz] *npl*: **to tug (at) sb's ~** tocar la fibra sensible de algn.

heart-throb ['hɑːtθrɔb] *n* ídolo.

heart-to-heart ['hɑːttə'hɑːt] *n* (*also*: **~ talk**) conversación *f* íntima.

heart transplant *n* transplante *m* de corazón.

hearty ['hɑːtɪ] *adj* cordial.

heat [hiːt] *n* (*gen*) calor *m*; (*SPORT: also*: **qualifying ~**) prueba eliminatoria; (*ZOOL*): **in** *or* **on ~** en celo ♦ *vt* calentar.

▶**heat up** *vi* (*gen*) calentarse.

heated ['hiːtɪd] *adj* caliente; (*fig*) acalorado.

heater ['hiːtə*] *n* calentador *m*.

heath [hiːθ] *n* (*BRIT*) brezal *m*.

heathen ['hiːðn] *adj, n* pagano/a *m/f*.

heather ['hɛðə*] *n* brezo.

heating ['hiːtɪŋ] *n* calefacción *f*.

heat-resistant ['hiːtrɪzɪstənt] *adj* refractario.

heart-seeking ['hiːtsiːkɪŋ-] *adj* guiado por infrarrojos, termoguiado.

heatstroke ['hiːtstrəuk] *n* insolación *f*.

heatwave ['hiːtweɪv] *n* ola de calor.

heave [hiːv] *vt* (*pull*) tirar; (*push*) empujar con esfuerzo; (*lift*) levantar (con esfuerzo) ♦ *vi* (*water*) subir y bajar ♦ *n* tirón *m*; empujón *m*; (*effort*) esfuerzo; (*throw*) echada; **to ~ a sigh** dar *or* echar un suspiro, suspirar.

▶**heave to** *vi* (*NAUT*) ponerse al pairo.

heaven ['hɛvn] *n* cielo; (*REL*) paraíso; **thank ~!** ¡gracias a Dios!; **for ~'s sake!** (*pleading*) ¡por el amor de Dios!, ¡por lo que más quiera!; (*protesting*) ¡por Dios!

heavenly ['hɛvnlɪ] *adj* celestial; (*REL*) divino.

heavenly body *n* cuerpo celeste.

heavily ['hɛvɪlɪ] *adv* pesadamente; (*drink, smoke*) en exceso; (*sleep, sigh*) profundamente.

heavy ['hɛvɪ] *adj* pesado; (*work*) duro; (*sea, rain, meal*) fuerte; (*drinker, smoker*) empedernido; (*eater*) comilón/ona.

heavy-duty ['hɛvɪ'djuːtɪ] *adj* resistente.

heavy goods vehicle (HGV) *n* (*BRIT*) vehículo pesado.

heavy-handed ['hɛvɪ'hændɪd] *adj* (*clumsy, tactless*) torpe.

heavy industry *n* industria pesada.

heavy metal *n* (*MUS*) heavy *m* (metal).

heavy-set [hɛvɪ'sɛt] *adj* (*esp US*) corpulento, fornido.

heavy user *n* consumidor *m* intensivo.

heavyweight ['hɛvɪweɪt] *n* (*SPORT*) peso pesado.

Hebrew ['hiːbruː] *adj, n* (*LING*) hebreo.

Hebrides ['hɛbrɪdiːz] *npl*: **the ~** las Hébridas.

heck [hɛk] *n* (*col*): **why the ~ ...?** ¿por qué porras ...?; **a ~ of a lot of** cantidad de.

heckle ['hɛkl] *vt* interrumpir.

heckler ['hɛklə*] *n* el/la que interrumpe a un orador.

hectare ['hɛktɑː*] *n* (*BRIT*) hectárea.

hectic ['hɛktɪk] *adj* agitado; (*busy*) ocupado.

hector ['hɛktə*] vt intimidar con bravatas.
he'd [hiːd] = he would; he had.
hedge [hɛdʒ] n seto ♦ vt cercar (con un seto) ♦ vi contestar con evasivas; **as a ~ against inflation** como protección contra la inflación; **to ~ one's bets** (fig) cubrirse.
hedgehog ['hɛdʒhɔg] n erizo.
hedgerow ['hɛdʒrəu] n seto vivo.
hedonism ['hiːdənɪzəm] n hedonismo.
heed [hiːd] vt (also: **take ~ of**) (pay attention) hacer caso de; (bear in mind) tener en cuenta; **to pay (no) ~ to, take (no) ~ of** (no) hacer caso a, (no) tener en cuenta.
heedless ['hiːdlɪs] adj desatento.
heel [hiːl] n talón m ♦ vt (shoe) poner tacón a; **to take to one's ~s** (col) poner pies en polvorosa; **to bring to ~** meter en cintura.
hefty ['hɛftɪ] adj (person) fornido; (piece) grande; (price) alto.
heifer ['hɛfə*] n novilla, ternera.
height [haɪt] n (of person) talla f; (of building) altura; (high ground) cerro; (altitude) altitud f; **what ~ are you?** ¿cuánto mides?; **of average ~** de estatura mediana; **to be afraid of ~s** tener miedo a las alturas; **it's the ~ of fashion** es el último grito en moda.
heighten ['haɪtn] vt elevar; (fig) aumentar.
heinous ['heɪnəs] adj atroz, nefasto.
heir [ɛə*] n heredero.
heir apparent n presunto heredero.
heiress ['ɛərɛs] n heredera.
heirloom ['ɛəluːm] n reliquia de familia.
heist [haɪst] n (col: hold-up) atraco a mano armada.
held [hɛld] pt, pp of **hold**.
helicopter ['hɛlɪkɔptə*] n helicóptero.
heliport ['hɛlɪpɔːt] n (AVIAT) helipuerto.
helium ['hiːlɪəm] n helio.
hell [hɛl] n infierno; **oh ~!** (col) ¡demonios!, ¡caramba!
he'll [hiːl] = he will, he shall.
hellbent [hɛl'bɛnt] adj (col): **he was ~ on going** se le metió entre ceja y ceja ir.
hellish ['hɛlɪʃ] adj infernal; (col) horrible.
hello [hə'ləu] excl ¡hola!; (surprise) ¡caramba!; (TEL) ¡dígame! (esp SP), ¡aló! (LAM).
helm [hɛlm] n (NAUT) timón m.
helmet ['hɛlmɪt] n casco.
helmsman ['hɛlmzmən] n timonel m.
help [hɛlp] n ayuda; (charwoman) criada, asistenta ♦ vt ayudar; **~!** ¡socorro!; **with the ~ of** con la ayuda de; **can I ~ you?** (in shop) ¿qué desea?; **to be of ~ to sb** servir a algn; **to ~ sb (to) do sth** echarle una mano or ayudar a algn a hacer algo; **~**

yourself sírvete; **he can't ~ it** no lo puede evitar.
helper ['hɛlpə*] n ayudante m/f.
helpful ['hɛlpful] adj útil; (person) servicial.
helping ['hɛlpɪŋ] n ración f.
helping hand n: **to give sb a ~** echar una mano a algn.
helpless ['hɛlplɪs] adj (incapable) incapaz; (defenceless) indefenso.
helpline ['hɛlplaɪn] n teléfono de asistencia al público.
Helsinki ['hɛlsɪŋkɪ] n Helsinki m.
helter-skelter ['hɛltə'skɛltə*] n (in funfair) tobogán m.
hem [hɛm] n dobladillo ♦ vt poner or coser el dobladillo a.
▶**hem in** vt cercar; **to feel ~med in** (fig) sentirse acosado.
he-man ['hiːmæn] n macho.
hematology [hiːmə'tɔlədʒɪ] n (US) = **haematology**.
hemisphere ['hɛmɪsfɪə*] n hemisferio.
hemline ['hɛmlaɪn] n bajo (del vestido).
hemlock ['hɛmlɔk] n cicuta.
hemoglobin [hiːmə'gləubɪn] n (US) = **haemoglobin**.
hemophilia [hiːmə'fɪlɪə] n (US) = **haemophilia**.
hemorrhage ['hɛmərɪdʒ] n (US) = **haemorrhage**.
hemorrhoids ['hɛmərɔɪdz] npl (US) = **haemorrhoids**.
hemp [hɛmp] n cáñamo.
hen [hɛn] n gallina; (female bird) hembra.
hence [hɛns] adv (therefore) por lo tanto; **2 years ~** de aquí a 2 años.
henceforth [hɛns'fɔːθ] adv de hoy en adelante.
henchman ['hɛntʃmən] n (pej) secuaz m.
henna ['hɛnə] n alheña.
hen night n (col) despedida de soltera.
hen party n (col) reunión f de mujeres.
henpecked ['hɛnpɛkt] adj: **to be ~** ser un calzonazos.
hepatitis [hɛpə'taɪtɪs] n hepatitis f inv.
her [həː*] pron (direct) la; (indirect) le; (stressed, after prep) ella ♦ adj su; see also **me; my**.
herald ['hɛrəld] n (forerunner) precursor(a) m/f ♦ vt anunciar.
heraldic [hɛ'rældɪk] adj heráldico.
heraldry ['hɛrəldrɪ] n heráldica.
herb [həːb] n hierba.
herbaceous [həː'beɪʃəs] adj herbáceo.
herbal ['həːbl] adj de hierbas.
herbicide ['həːbɪsaɪd] n herbicida m.
herd [həːd] n rebaño; (of wild animals, swine) piara ♦ vt (drive, gather: animals) llevar en

manada; (: *people*) reunir.
►**herd together** *vt* agrupar, reunir ♦ *vi* apiñarse, agruparse.
here [hɪə*] *adv* aquí; ~! (*present*) ¡presente!; ~ **is/are** aquí está/están; ~ **she is** aquí está; **come** ~! ¡ven aquí *or* acá!; ~ **and there** aquí y allá.
hereabouts ['hɪərə'bauts] *adv* por aquí (cerca).
hereafter [hɪər'ɑːftə*] *adv* en el futuro ♦ *n*: **the** ~ el más allá.
hereby [hɪə'baɪ] *adv* (*in letter*) por la presente.
hereditary [hɪ'redɪtrɪ] *adj* hereditario.
heredity [hɪ'redɪtɪ] *n* herencia.
heresy ['herəsɪ] *n* herejía.
heretic ['herətɪk] *n* hereje *m/f*.
heretical [hɪ'retɪkəl] *adj* herético.
herewith [hɪə'wɪð] *adv*: **I send you** ~ ... le mando adjunto ....
heritage ['herɪtɪdʒ] *n* (*gen*) herencia; (*fig*) patrimonio; **our national** ~ nuestro patrimonio nacional.
hermetically [həː'metɪkəlɪ] *adv*: ~ **sealed** herméticamente cerrado.
hermit ['həːmɪt] *n* ermitaño/a.
hernia ['həːnɪə] *n* hernia.
hero, *pl* ~**es** ['hɪərəu] *n* héroe *m*; (*in book, film*) protagonista *m*.
heroic [hɪ'rəuɪk] *adj* heroico.
heroin ['herəuɪn] *n* heroína.
heroin addict *n* heroinómano/a, adicto/a a la heroína.
heroine ['herəuɪn] *n* heroína; (*in book, film*) protagonista.
heroism ['herəuɪzm] *n* heroísmo.
heron ['herən] *n* garza.
hero worship *n* veneración *f*.
herring ['herɪŋ] *n* arenque *m*.
hers [həːz] *pron* (el) suyo/(la) suya *etc*; **a friend of** ~ un amigo suyo; **this is** ~ esto es suyo *or* de ella; *see also* **mine**.
herself [həː'self] *pron* (*reflexive*) se; (*emphatic*) ella misma; (*after prep*) sí (misma); *see also* **oneself**.
Herts *abbr* (*BRIT*) = *Hertfordshire*.
he's [hiːz] = **he is**; **he has**.
hesitant ['hezɪtənt] *adj* indeciso; **to be** ~ **about doing sth** no decidirse a hacer algo.
hesitate ['hezɪteɪt] *vi* dudar, vacilar; **don't** ~ **to ask (me)** no dudes en pedírmelo.
hesitation [hezɪ'teɪʃən] *n* indecisión *f*; **I have no** ~ **in saying (that)** ... no tengo el menor reparo en afirmar que ....
hessian ['hesɪən] *n* arpillera.
heterogeneous ['hetərə'dʒiːnɪəs] *adj* heterogéneo.

heterosexual [hetərəu'seksjuəl] *adj, n* heterosexual *m/f*.
het up [het'ʌp] *adj* (*col*) agitado, nervioso.
HEW *n abbr* (*US*: = *Department of Health, Education and Welfare*) ministerio de sanidad, educación y bienestar público.
hew [hjuː] *vt* cortar.
hex [heks] (*US*) *n* maleficio, mal *m* de ojo ♦ *vt* embrujar.
hexagon ['heksəgən] *n* hexágono.
hexagonal [hek'sægənl] *adj* hexagonal.
hey [heɪ] *excl* ¡oye!, ¡oiga!
heyday ['heɪdeɪ] *n*: **the** ~ **of** el apogeo de.
HF *n abbr* = *high frequency*.
HGV *n abbr see* **heavy goods vehicle**.
HI *abbr* (*US*) = *Hawaii*.
hi [haɪ] *excl* ¡hola!
hiatus [haɪ'eɪtəs] *n* vacío, interrupción *f*; (*LING*) hiato.
hibernate ['haɪbəneɪt] *vi* invernar.
hibernation [haɪbə'neɪʃən] *n* hibernación *f*.
hiccough, hiccup ['hɪkʌp] *vi* hipar; ~**s** *npl* hipo *sg*.
hid [hɪd] *pt of* **hide**.
hick [hɪk] *n* (*US col*) paleto/a.
hidden ['hɪdn] *pp of* **hide** ♦ *adj*: **there are no** ~ **extras** no hay suplementos ocultos; ~ **agenda** plan *m* encubierto.
hide [haɪd] *n* (*skin*) piel *f* ♦ *vb* (*pt* **hid**, *pp* **hidden** [hɪd, 'hɪdn]) *vt* esconder, ocultar; (*feelings, truth*) encubrir, ocultar ♦ *vi*: **to** ~ (**from sb**) esconderse *or* ocultarse (de algn).
hide-and-seek ['haɪdən'siːk] *n* escondite *m*.
hideaway ['haɪdəweɪ] *n* escondite *m*.
hideous ['hɪdɪəs] *adj* horrible.
hideously ['hɪdɪəslɪ] *adv* horriblemente.
hide-out ['haɪdaut] *n* escondite *m*, refugio.
hiding ['haɪdɪŋ] *n* (*beating*) paliza; **to be in** ~ (*concealed*) estar escondido.
hiding place *n* escondrijo.
hierarchy ['haɪərɑːkɪ] *n* jerarquía.
hieroglyphic [haɪərə'glɪfɪk] *adj* jeroglífico ♦ *n*: ~**s** jeroglíficos *mpl*.
hi-fi ['haɪfaɪ] *abbr* (= *high fidelity*) *n* estéreo, hifi *m* ♦ *adj* de alta fidelidad.
higgledy-piggledy ['hɪgldɪ'pɪgldɪ] *adv* en desorden, de cualquier modo.
high [haɪ] *adj* alto; (*speed, number*) grande, alto; (*price*) elevado; (*wind*) fuerte; (*voice*) agudo; (*col: on drugs*) colocado; (: *on drink*) borracho; (*CULIN: meat, game*) pasado; (: *spoilt*) estropeado ♦ *adv* alto, a gran altura ♦ *n*: **exports have reached a new** ~ las exportaciones han alcanzado niveles inusitados; **it is 20 m** ~ tiene 20 m de altura; ~ **in the air** en las alturas; **to pay a** ~ **price for sth** pagar algo muy caro.

highball ['haɪbɔːl] n (US: drink) whisky m soda, highball m (LAM), jaibol m (LAM).
highboy ['haɪbɔɪ] n (US) cómoda alta.
highbrow ['haɪbrau] adj culto.
highchair ['haɪtʃɛə*] n silla alta (para niños).
high-class ['haɪ'klɑːs] adj (neighbourhood) de alta sociedad; (hotel) de lujo; (person) distinguido, de categoría; (food) de alta categoría.
High Court n (LAW) tribunal m supremo.

En el sistema legal de Inglaterra y Gales **High Court** es la forma abreviada de **High Court of Justice**, tribunal superior que junto con el de apelación (**Court of Appeal**) forma el Tribunal Supremo (**Supreme Court of Judicature**).
En el sistema legal escocés es la forma abreviada de **High Court of Justiciary**, tribunal con jurado que juzga los delitos más serios, que pueden dar lugar a una pena de gran severidad.

higher ['haɪə*] adj (form of life, study etc) superior ♦ adv más alto.
higher education n educación f or enseñanza superior.
high explosive n explosivo de gran potencia.
highfalutin [haɪfə'luːtɪn] adj (col) de altos vuelos, encopetado.
high finance n altas finanzas fpl.
high-flier, high-flyer [haɪ'flaɪə*] n ambicioso/a.
high-handed [haɪ'hændɪd] adj despótico.
high-heeled [haɪ'hiːld] adj de tacón alto.
highjack ['haɪdʒæk] = hijack.
high jump n (SPORT) salto de altura.
highlands ['haɪləndz] npl tierras fpl altas; **the H~** (in Scotland) las Tierras Altas de Escocia.
high-level ['haɪlɛvl] adj (talks etc) de alto nivel; ~ **language** (COMPUT) lenguaje m de alto nivel.
highlight ['haɪlaɪt] n (fig: of event) punto culminante ♦ vt subrayar.
highly ['haɪlɪ] adv sumamente; ~ **paid** muy bien pagado; **to speak** ~ **of** hablar muy bien de.
highly-strung ['haɪlɪ'strʌŋ] adj muy excitable.
High Mass n misa mayor.
highness ['haɪnɪs] n altura; **Her** or **His H~** Su Alteza.
high-pitched [haɪ'pɪtʃt] adj agudo.
high point n: **the** ~ el punto culminante.
high-powered ['haɪ'pauəd] adj (engine) de

gran potencia; (fig: person) importante.
high-pressure ['haɪprɛʃə*] adj de alta presión; (fig: salesman etc) enérgico.
high-rise ['haɪraɪz] n (also: ~ **block**, ~ **building**) torre f de pisos.
high school n centro de enseñanza secundaria, ≈ Instituto Nacional de Bachillerato (SP), liceo (LAM).

El término **high school** se aplica en Estados Unidos a dos tipos de centros de educación secundaria: **Junior High Schools**, en los que se imparten normalmente del 7º al 9º curso (llamado **grade**) y **Senior High Schools**, que abarcan los cursos 10º, 11º y 12º y en ocasiones el 9º. Aquí pueden estudiarse asignaturas tanto de contenido académico como profesional. En Gran Bretaña también se llaman **high school** algunos centros de enseñanza secundaria.

high season n (BRIT) temporada alta.
high-speed ['haɪspiːd] adj de alta velocidad.
high-spirited [haɪ'spɪrɪtɪd] adj animado.
high spirits npl ánimos mpl.
high street n (BRIT) calle f mayor.
high tide n marea alta.
highway ['haɪweɪ] n carretera; (US) autopista; **the information** ~ la autopista de la información.
Highway Code n (BRIT) código de la circulación.
highwayman ['haɪweɪmən] n salteador m de caminos.
hijack ['haɪdʒæk] vt secuestrar ♦ n (also: ~**ing**) secuestro.
hijacker ['haɪdʒækə*] n secuestrador(a) m/f.
hike [haɪk] vi (go walking) ir de excursión (a pie); (tramp) caminar ♦ n caminata; (col: in prices etc) aumento.
►**hike up** vt (raise) aumentar.
hiker ['haɪkə*] n excursionista m/f.
hilarious [hɪ'lɛərɪəs] adj divertidísimo.
hilarity [hɪ'lærɪtɪ] n (laughter) risas fpl, carcajadas fpl.
hill [hɪl] n colina; (high) montaña; (slope) cuesta.
hillbilly ['hɪlbɪlɪ] n (US) rústico/a montañés/esa; (pej) palurdo/a.
hillock ['hɪlək] n montecillo, altozano.
hillside ['hɪlsaɪd] n ladera.
hilltop ['hɪltɔp] n cumbre f.
hilly ['hɪlɪ] adj montañoso; (uneven) accidentado.
hilt [hɪlt] n (of sword) empuñadura; **to the** ~ (fig: support) incondicionalmente; **to be in debt up to the** ~ estar hasta el cuello de

deudas.

him [hɪm] *pron* (*direct*) le, lo; (*indirect*) le; (*stressed, after prep*) él; *see also* **me**.

Himalayas [hɪmə'leɪəz] *npl*: **the** ~ el Himalaya.

himself [hɪm'sɛlf] *pron* (*reflexive*) se; (*emphatic*) él mismo; (*after prep*) sí (mismo); *see also* **oneself**.

hind [haɪnd] *adj* posterior ♦ *n* cierva.

hinder ['hɪndə*] *vt* estorbar, impedir.

hindquarters ['haɪndkwɔːtəz] *npl* (*ZOOL*) cuartos *mpl* traseros.

hindrance ['hɪndrəns] *n* estorbo, obstáculo.

hindsight ['haɪndsaɪt] *n* percepción *f* tardía *or* retrospectiva; **with the benefit of** ~ con la perspectiva del tiempo transcurrido.

Hindu ['hɪnduː] *n* hindú *m/f*.

hinge [hɪndʒ] *n* bisagra, gozne *m* ♦ *vi* (*fig*): **to** ~ **on** depender de.

hint [hɪnt] *n* indirecta; (*advice*) consejo ♦ *vt*: **to** ~ **that** insinuar que ♦ *vi*: **to** ~ **at** aludir a; **to drop a** ~ soltar *or* tirar una indirecta; **give me a** ~ dame una pista.

hip [hɪp] *n* cadera; (*BOT*) escaramujo.

hip flask *n* petaca.

hip-hop ['hɪphɔp] *n* hip hop *m*.

hippie ['hɪpɪ] *n* hippie *m/f*, jipi *m/f*.

hip pocket *n* bolsillo de atrás.

hippopotamus, *pl* ~**es** *or* **hippopotami** [hɪpə'pɔtəməs, -'pɔtəmaɪ] hipopótamo.

hippy ['hɪpɪ] *n* = **hippie**.

hire ['haɪə*] *vt* (*BRIT: car, equipment*) alquilar; (*worker*) contratar ♦ *n* alquiler *m*; **for** ~ se alquila; (*taxi*) libre; **on** ~ de alquiler.

▶**hire out** *vt* alquilar, arrendar.

hire(d) car *n* (*BRIT*) coche *m* de alquiler.

hire purchase (H.P.) *n* (*BRIT*) compra a plazos; **to buy sth on** ~ comprar algo a plazos.

his [hɪz] *pron* (el) suyo/(la) suya *etc* ♦ *adj* su; **this is** ~ esto es suyo *or* de él; *see also* **my**, **mine**.

Hispanic [hɪs'pænɪk] *adj* hispánico.

hiss [hɪs] *vi* sisear; (*in protest*) silbar ♦ *n* siseo; silbido.

histogram ['hɪstəgræm] *n* histograma *m*.

historian [hɪ'stɔːrɪən] *n* historiador(a) *m/f*.

historic(al) [hɪ'stɔrɪk(l)] *adj* histórico.

history ['hɪstərɪ] *n* historia; **there's a long** ~ **of that illness in his family** esa enfermedad corre en su familia.

histrionics [hɪstrɪ'ɔnɪks] *npl* histrionismo.

hit [hɪt] *vt* (*pt, pp* **hit**) (*strike*) golpear, pegar; (*reach: target*) alcanzar; (*collide with: car*) chocar contra; (*fig: affect*) afectar ♦ *n* golpe *m*; (*success*) éxito; **to** ~ **the**

headlines salir en primera plana; **to** ~ **the road** (*col*) largarse; **to** ~ **it off with sb** llevarse bien con algn.

▶**hit back** *vi* defenderse; (*fig*) devolver golpe por golpe.

▶**hit out at** *vt fus* asestar un golpe a; (*fig*) atacar.

▶**hit (up)on** *vt fus* (*answer*) dar con; (*solution*) hallar, encontrar.

hit and miss *adj*: **it's very** ~, **it's a** ~ **affair** es cuestión de suerte.

hit-and-run driver ['hɪtən'rʌn-] *n* conductor(a) que tras atropellar a algn se da a la fuga.

hitch [hɪtʃ] *vt* (*fasten*) atar, amarrar; (*also*: ~ **up**) arremangarse ♦ *n* (*difficulty*) problema, pega; **to** ~ **a lift** hacer autostop; **technical** ~ problema *m* técnico.

▶**hitch up** *vt* (*horse, cart*) enganchar, uncir.

hitch-hike ['hɪtʃhaɪk] *vi* hacer autostop.

hitch-hiker ['hɪtʃhaɪkə*] *n* autostopista *m/f*.

hi-tech [haɪ'tɛk] *adj* de alta tecnología.

hitherto ['hɪðə'tuː] *adv* hasta ahora, hasta aquí.

hit list *n* lista negra.

hitman ['hɪtmæn] *n* asesino a sueldo.

hit or miss ['hɪtə'mɪs] *adj* = **hit and miss**.

hit parade *n*: **the** ~ los cuarenta principales.

HIV *n abbr* (= *human immunodeficiency virus*) VIH *m*; ~**-negative** no portador(a) del virus del sida, no seropositivo; ~**-positive** portador(a) del virus del sida, seropositivo.

hive [haɪv] *n* colmena; **the shop was a** ~ **of activity** (*fig*) la tienda era una colmena humana.

▶**hive off** *vt* (*col: separate*) separar; (: *privatize*) privatizar.

hl *abbr* (= *hectolitre*) hl.

HM *abbr* (= *His (or Her) Majesty*) S.M.

HMG *abbr* = *His (or Her) Majesty's Government*.

HMI *n abbr* (*BRIT SCOL*) = *His (or Her) Majesty's Inspector*.

HMO *n abbr* (*US*: = *health maintenance organization*) seguro médico global.

HMS *abbr* = *His (or Her) Majesty's Ship*.

HMSO *n abbr* (*BRIT* = *His (or Her) Majesty's Stationery Office*) distribuidor oficial de las publicaciones del gobierno del Reino Unido.

HNC *n abbr* (*BRIT*: = *Higher National Certificate*) título académico.

HND *n abbr* (*BRIT*: = *Higher National Diploma*) título académico.

hoard [hɔːd] *n* (*treasure*) tesoro; (*stockpile*) provisión *f* ♦ *vt* acumular.

hoarding ['hɔ:dɪŋ] n (for posters) valla
publicitaria.
hoarfrost ['hɔ:frɔst] n escarcha.
hoarse [hɔ:s] adj ronco.
hoax [həuks] n engaño.
hob [hɔb] n quemador m.
hobble ['hɔbl] vi cojear.
hobby ['hɔbɪ] n pasatiempo, afición f.
hobby-horse ['hɔbɪhɔ:s] n (fig) tema
preferido.
hobnob ['hɔbnɔb] vi: **to ~ (with)** alternar
(con).
hobo ['həubəu] n (US) vagabundo.
hock [hɔk] n (of animal, CULIN) corvejón m;
(col): **to be in ~** (person) estar empeñado
or endeudado; (object) estar empeñado.
hockey ['hɔkɪ] n hockey m.
hocus-pocus [həukəs'pəukəs] n (trickery)
engañifa; (words: of magician)
abracadabra m.
hod [hɔd] n capacho.
hodge-podge ['hɔdʒpɔdʒ] n (US)
= **hotchpotch.**
hoe [həu] n azadón m ♦ vt azadonar.
hog [hɔg] n cerdo, puerco ♦ vt (fig)
acaparar; **to go the whole ~** echar el
todo por el todo.
Hogmanay [hɔgmə'neɪ] n (Scottish)
Nochevieja.
hoist [hɔɪst] n (crane) grúa ♦ vt levantar,
alzar.
hoity-toity [hɔɪtɪ'tɔɪtɪ] adj (col): **to be ~**
darse humos.
hold [həuld] vb (pt, pp **held** [hɛld]) vt tener;
(contain) contener; (keep back) retener;
(believe) sostener; (take ~ of) coger (SP),
agarrar (LAM); (take weight) soportar;
(meeting) celebrar ♦ vi (withstand pressure)
resistir; (be valid) ser válido; (stick)
pegarse ♦ n (grasp) asimiento; (fig)
dominio; (WRESTLING) presa; (NAUT)
bodega; **~ the line!** (TEL) ¡no cuelgue!; **to
~ one's own** (fig) defenderse; **to ~ office**
(POL) ocupar un cargo; **to ~ firm** or **fast**
mantenerse firme; **he ~s the view that ...**
opina or es su opinión que ...; **to ~ sb
responsible for sth** culpar or echarle la
culpa a algn de algo; **where can I get ~ of
...?** ¿dónde puedo encontrar (a) ...?; **to
catch** or **get (a) ~ of** agarrarse or asirse
de.
▶**hold back** vt retener; (secret) ocultar; **to
~ sb back from doing sth** impedir a algn
hacer algo, impedir que algn haga algo.
▶**hold down** vt (person) sujetar; (job)
mantener.
▶**hold forth** vi perorar.
▶**hold off** vt (enemy) rechazar ♦ vi: **if the**

rain **~s off** si no llueve.
▶**hold on** vi agarrarse bien; (wait) esperar.
▶**hold on to** vt fus agarrarse a; (keep)
guardar.
▶**hold out** vt ofrecer ♦ vi (resist) resistir; **to
~ out (against)** resistir (a), sobrevivir.
▶**hold over** vt (meeting etc) aplazar.
▶**hold up** vt (raise) levantar; (support)
apoyar; (delay) retrasar; (: traffic)
demorar; (rob: bank) asaltar, atracar.
holdall ['həuldɔ:l] n (BRIT) bolsa.
holder ['həuldə*] n (of ticket, record)
poseedor(a) m/f; (of passport, post, office,
title etc) titular m/f.
holding ['həuldɪŋ] n (share) participación f.
holding company n holding m.
holdup ['həuldʌp] n (robbery) atraco; (delay)
retraso; (BRIT: in traffic) embotellamiento.
hole [həul] n agujero ♦ vt agujerear; **~ in
the heart** (MED) boquete m en el corazón;
to pick ~s in (fig) encontrar defectos en;
the ship was ~d se abrió una vía de agua
en el barco.
▶**hole up** vi esconderse.
holiday ['hɔlədɪ] n vacaciones fpl; (day off)
(día m de) fiesta, día m festivo or feriado
(LAM); **on ~** de vacaciones; **to be on ~**
estar de vacaciones.
holiday camp n colonia or centro
vacacional; (for children) colonia
veraniega infantil.
holidaymaker ['hɔlədɪmeɪkə*] n (BRIT)
turista m/f.
holiday pay n paga de las vacaciones.
holiday resort n centro turístico.
holiday season n temporada de
vacaciones.
holiness ['həulɪnɪs] n santidad f.
holistic [həu'lɪstɪk] adj holístico.
Holland ['hɔlənd] n Holanda.
holler ['hɔlə*] vi (col) gritar, vocear.
hollow ['hɔləu] adj hueco; (fig) vacío; (eyes)
hundido; (sound) sordo ♦ n (gen) hueco;
(in ground) hoyo ♦ vt: **to ~ out** ahuecar.
holly ['hɔlɪ] n acebo.
hollyhock ['hɔlɪhɔk] n malva loca.
holocaust ['hɔləkɔ:st] n holocausto.
hologram ['hɔləgræm] n holograma m.
hols [hɔlz] npl (col): **the ~** las vacaciones.
holster ['həulstə*] n pistolera.
holy ['həulɪ] adj (gen) santo, sagrado;
(water) bendito; **the H~ Father** el Santo
Padre.
Holy Communion n Sagrada Comunión f.
Holy Ghost, Holy Spirit n Espíritu m
Santo.
homage ['hɔmɪdʒ] n homenaje m; **to pay ~**
to rendir homenaje a.

home [həum] *n* casa; (*country*) patria;
(*institution*) asilo; (*COMPUT*) punto inicial
or de partida ♦ *adj* (*domestic*) casero, de
casa; (*ECON, POL*) nacional; (*SPORT: team*)
de casa; (: *match, win*) en casa ♦ *adv*
(*direction*) a casa; **to go/
come** ~ ir/volver a casa; **make yourself at**
~ ¡estás en tu casa!; **it's near my** ~ está
cerca de mi casa.
►**home in on** *vt fus* (*missiles*) dirigirse
hacia.
home address *n* domicilio.
home-brew [həum'bru:] *n* cerveza *etc*
casera.
homecoming ['həumkʌmɪŋ] *n* regreso (al
hogar).
home computer *n* ordenador *m*
doméstico.
Home Counties *npl* condados que rodean
Londres.
home economics *n* economía doméstica.
home ground *n*: **to be on** ~ estar en su
etc terreno.
home-grown ['həumgrəun] *adj* de cosecha
propia.
home help *n* (*BRIT*) trabajador(a) *m/f* del
servicio de atención domiciliaria.
home key *n* (*COMPUT*) tecla home.
homeland ['həumlænd] *n* tierra natal.
homeless ['həumlɪs] *adj* sin hogar, sin casa
♦ *npl*: **the** ~ las personas sin hogar.
home loan *n* préstamo para la vivienda.
homely ['həumlɪ] *adj* (*domestic*) casero;
(*simple*) sencillo.
home-made [həum'meɪd] *adj* hecho en
casa.
Home Office *n* (*BRIT*) Ministerio del
Interior.
homeopathy [həumɪ'ɔpəθɪ] *etc* (*US*)
= **homoeopathy** *etc*.
home rule *n* autonomía.
Home Secretary *n* (*BRIT*) Ministro del
Interior.
homesick ['həumsɪk] *adj*: **to be** ~ tener
morriña *or* nostalgia.
homestead ['həumstɛd] *n* hacienda.
home town *n* ciudad *f* natal.
home truth *n*: **to tell sb a few** ~**s** decir
cuatro verdades a algn.
homeward ['həumwəd] *adj* (*journey*) de
vuelta.
homeward(s) ['həumwəd(z)] *adv* hacia
casa.
homework ['həumwə:k] *n* deberes *mpl*.
homicidal [hɔmɪ'saɪdl] *adj* homicida.
homicide ['hɔmɪsaɪd] *n* (*US*) homicidio.
homily ['hɔmɪlɪ] *n* homilía.
homing ['həumɪŋ] *adj* (*device, missile*)

buscador(a); ~ **pigeon** paloma
mensajera.
homoeopath, (*US*) **homeopath**
['həumɪəupæθ] *n* homeópata *m/f*.
homoeopathic, (*US*) **homeopathic**
[həumɪəu'pæθɪk] *adj* homeopático.
homoeopathy, (*US*) **homeopathy**
[həumɪ'ɔpəθɪ] *n* homeopatía.
homogeneous [hɔmə'dʒi:nɪəs] *adj*
homogéneo.
homogenize [hə'mɔdʒənaɪz] *vt*
homogeneizar.
homosexual [hɔməu'sɛksjuəl] *adj, n*
homosexual *m/f*.
Hon. *abbr* (= *honourable, honorary*) en
títulos.
Honduras [hɔn'djuərəs] *n* Honduras *fpl*.
hone [həun] *vt* (*sharpen*) afilar; (*fig*)
perfeccionar.
honest ['ɔnɪst] *adj* honrado; (*sincere*)
franco, sincero; **to be quite** ~ **with you** ...
para serte franco ....
honestly ['ɔnɪstlɪ] *adv* honradamente;
francamente, de verdad.
honesty ['ɔnɪstɪ] *n* honradez *f*.
honey ['hʌnɪ] *n* miel *f*; (*US col*) cariño; (: *to
strangers*) guapo, linda.
honeycomb ['hʌnɪkəum] *n* panal *m*; (*fig*)
laberinto.
honeymoon ['hʌnɪmu:n] *n* luna de miel.
honeysuckle ['hʌnɪsʌkl] *n* madreselva.
Hong Kong ['hɔŋ'kɔŋ] *n* Hong-Kong *m*.
honk [hɔŋk] *vi* (*AUT*) tocar la bocina.
Honolulu [hɔnə'lu:lu:] *n* Honolulú *m*.
honorary ['ɔnərərɪ] *adj* no remunerado;
(*duty, title*) honorario.
honour, (*US*) **honor** ['ɔnə*] *vt* honrar ♦ *n*
honor *m*, honra; **in** ~ **of** en honor de; **it's a
great** ~ es un gran honor.
hono(u)rable ['ɔnərəbl] *adj* honrado,
honorable.
hono(u)r-bound ['ɔnə'baund] *adj*
moralmente obligado.
hono(u)rs degree *n* (*UNIV*) licenciatura
superior.

---

*Tras un período de estudios de tres años
normalmente (cuatro en Escocia), los
universitarios obtienen una licenciatura
llamada* **honours degree**. *La calificación
global que se recibe, en una escala de
mayor a menor es la siguiente:* **first class** (I),
upper-second class (II:1), **lower-second class**
(II:2) *y* **third class** (III). *El licenciado puede
añadir las letras* **Hons** *al título obtenido tras
su nombre y apellidos, por ejemplo* **BA Hons**;
ver también **ordinary degree**.

honours list n (BRIT) lista de distinciones honoríficas que entrega la reina.

A la lista con los títulos honoríficos y condecoraciones que el monarca británico otorga en Año Nuevo y en el día de su cumpleaños se la conoce con el nombre de **honours list**. Las personas que reciben dichas distinciones suelen ser miembros destacados de la vida pública (ámbito empresarial, ejército, deportes, espectáculos), aunque últimamente también se reconoce con ellas el trabajo abnegado y anónimo de la gente de la calle.

Hons. abbr (UNIV) = **hono(u)rs degree.**
hood [hud] n capucha; (BRIT AUT) capota; (US AUT) capó m; (US col) matón m.
hooded ['hudɪd] adj (robber) encapuchado.
hoodlum ['huːdləm] n matón m.
hoodwink ['hudwɪŋk] vt (BRIT) timar, engañar.
hoof, pl ~s or **hooves** [huːf, huːvz] n pezuña.
hook [huk] n gancho; (on dress) corchete m, broche m; (for fishing) anzuelo ♦ vt enganchar; ~s and eyes corchetes mpl, macho y hembra m; **by ~ or by crook** por las buenas o por las malas, cueste lo que cueste; **to be ~ed on** (col) estar enganchado a.
►**hook up** vt (RADIO, TV) transmitir en cadena.
hooligan ['huːlɪgən] n gamberro.
hooliganism ['huːlɪgənɪzəm] n gamberrismo.
hoop [huːp] n aro.
hoot [huːt] vi (BRIT AUT) tocar la bocina; (siren) sonar la sirena; (owl) ulular ♦ n bocinazo, toque m de sirena; **to ~ with laughter** morirse de risa.
hooter ['huːtə*] n (BRIT AUT) bocina; (of ship, factory) sirena.
hoover ® ['huːvə*] (BRIT) n aspiradora ♦ vt pasar la aspiradora por.
hooves [huːvz] pl of **hoof.**
hop [hɔp] vi saltar, brincar; (on one foot) saltar con un pie ♦ n salto, brinco; see also **hops.**
hope [həup] vt, vi esperar ♦ n esperanza; **I ~ so/not** espero que sí/no.
hopeful ['həupful] adj (person) optimista; (situation) prometedor(a); **I'm ~ that she'll manage to come** confío en que podrá venir.
hopefully ['həupfulɪ] adv con optimismo, con esperanza.
hopeless ['həuplɪs] adj desesperado.
hopelessly ['həuplɪslɪ] adv (live etc) sin

esperanzas; **I'm ~ confused/lost** estoy totalmente despistado/perdido.
hopper ['hɔpə*] n (chute) tolva.
hops [hɔps] npl lúpulo sg.
horde [hɔːd] n horda.
horizon [hə'raɪzn] n horizonte m.
horizontal [hɔrɪ'zɔntl] adj horizontal.
hormone ['hɔːməun] n hormona.
hormone replacement therapy n terapia hormonal sustitutiva.
horn [hɔːn] n cuerno, cacho (LAM); (MUS: also: **French ~**) trompa; (AUT) bocina, claxon m.
horned [hɔːnd] adj con cuernos.
hornet ['hɔːnɪt] n avispón m.
horny ['hɔːnɪ] adj (material) córneo; (hands) calloso; (US col) cachondo.
horoscope ['hɔrəskəup] n horóscopo.
horrendous [hə'rendəs] adj horrendo.
horrible ['hɔrɪbl] adj horrible.
horribly ['hɔrɪblɪ] adv horriblemente.
horrid ['hɔrɪd] adj horrible, horroroso.
horridly ['hɔrɪdlɪ] adv (behave) tremendamente mal.
horrific [hə'rɪfɪk] adj (accident) horroroso; (film) horripilante.
horrify ['hɔrɪfaɪ] vt horrorizar.
horrifying ['hɔrɪfaɪɪŋ] adj horroroso.
horror ['hɔrə*] n horror m.
horror film n película de terror or miedo.
horror-struck ['hɔrəstrʌk], **horror-stricken** ['hɔrəstrɪkn] adj horrorizado.
hors d'œuvre [ɔː'dəːvrə] n entremeses mpl.
horse [hɔːs] n caballo.
horseback ['hɔːsbæk] n: **on ~** a caballo.
horsebox ['hɔːsbɔks] n remolque m para transportar caballos.
horse chestnut n (tree) castaño de Indias.
horsedrawn ['hɔːsdrɔːn] adj de tracción animal.
horsefly ['hɔːsflaɪ] n tábano.
horseman ['hɔːsmən] n jinete m.
horsemanship ['hɔːsmənʃɪp] n equitación f, manejo del caballo.
horseplay ['hɔːspleɪ] n pelea amistosa.
horsepower (hp) ['hɔːspauə*] n caballo (de fuerza), potencia en caballos.
horse-racing ['hɔːsreɪsɪŋ] n carreras fpl de caballos.
horseradish ['hɔːsrædɪʃ] n rábano picante.
horseshoe ['hɔːsʃuː] n herradura.
horse show n concurso hípico.
horse-trader ['hɔːstreɪdə*] n chalán/ana m/f.
horse trials npl = **horse show.**
horsewhip ['hɔːswɪp] vt azotar.
horsewoman ['hɔːswumən] n amazona.
horsey ['hɔːsɪ] adj (col: person) aficionado a los caballos.

horticulture ['hɔːtɪkʌltʃə*] *n* horticultura.
hose [həuz] *n* (*also:* ~**pipe**) manguera.
▶**hose down** *vt* limpiar con manguera.
hosiery ['həuzɪərɪ] *n* calcetería.
hospice ['hɔspɪs] *n* hospicio.
hospitable ['hɔspɪtəbl] *adj* hospitalario.
hospital ['hɔspɪtl] *n* hospital *m*.
hospitality [hɔspɪ'tælɪtɪ] *n* hospitalidad *f*.
hospitalize ['hɔspɪtəlaɪz] *vt* hospitalizar.
host [həust] *n* anfitrión *m*; (*TV, RADIO*) presentador(a) *m/f*; (*of inn etc*) mesonero; (*REL*) hostia; (*large number*): **a** ~ **of** multitud de.
hostage ['hɔstɪdʒ] *n* rehén *m*.
hostel ['hɔstl] *n* hostal *m*; (*for students, nurses etc*) residencia; (*also:* **youth** ~) albergue *m* juvenil; (*for homeless people*) hospicio.
hostelling ['hɔstlɪŋ] *n*: **to go (youth)** ~ hospedarse en albergues.
hostess ['həustɪs] *n* anfitriona; (*BRIT: air* ~) azafata; (*in night-club*) señorita de compañía.
hostile ['hɔstaɪl] *adj* hostil.
hostility [hɔ'stɪlɪtɪ] *n* hostilidad *f*.
hot [hɔt] *adj* caliente; (*weather*) caluroso, de calor; (*as opposed to only warm*) muy caliente; (*spicy*) picante; (*fig*) ardiente, acalorado; **to be** ~ (*person*) tener calor; (*object*) estar caliente; (*weather*) hacer calor.
▶**hot up** *vi* (*col: situation*) ponerse difícil *or* apurado; (: *party*) animarse ♦ *vt* (*col: pace*) apretar; (: *engine*) aumentar la potencia de.
hot air *n* (*col*) palabras *fpl* huecas.
hot-air balloon [hɔt'ɛə-] *n* (*AVIAT*) globo aerostático *or* de aire caliente.
hotbed ['hɔtbɛd] *n* (*fig*) semillero.
hot-blooded [hɔt'blʌdɪd] *adj* impetuoso.
hotchpotch ['hɔtʃpɔtʃ] *n* mezcolanza, baturrillo.
hot dog *n* perrito caliente.
hotel [həu'tɛl] *n* hotel *m*.
hotelier [həu'tɛlɪə*] *n* hotelero.
hotel industry *n* industria hotelera.
hotel room *n* habitación *f* de hotel.
hot flush *n* (*BRIT*) sofoco.
hotfoot ['hɔtfut] *adv* a toda prisa.
hothead ['hɔthɛd] *n* (*fig*) exaltado/a.
hotheaded [hɔt'hɛdɪd] *adj* exaltado.
hothouse ['hɔthaus] *n* invernadero.
hot line *n* (*POL*) teléfono rojo, línea directa.
hotly ['hɔtlɪ] *adv* con pasión, apasionadamente.
hotplate ['hɔtpleɪt] *n* (*on cooker*) hornillo.
hotpot ['hɔtpɔt] *n* (*BRIT CULIN*) estofado.

hot potato *n* (*BRIT col*) asunto espinoso; **to drop sth/sb like a** ~ no querer saber ya nada de algo/algn.
hot seat *n* primera fila.
hot spot *n* (*trouble spot*) punto caliente; (*night club etc*) lugar *m* popular.
hot spring *n* terma, fuente *f* de aguas termales.
hot-tempered ['hɔt'tɛmpəd] *adj* de mal genio *or* carácter.
hot-water bottle [hɔt'wɔːtə-] *n* bolsa de agua caliente.
hot-wire ['hɔtwaɪə*] *vt* (*col: car*) hacer el puente en.
hound [haund] *vt* acosar ♦ *n* perro de caza.
hour ['auə*] *n* hora; **at 30 miles an** ~ a 30 millas por hora; **lunch** ~ la hora del almuerzo *or* de comer; **to pay sb by the** ~ pagar a algn por horas.
hourly ['auəlɪ] *adj* (de) cada hora; (*rate*) por hora ♦ *adv* cada hora.
house *n* [haus] (*pl* ~**s** ['hauzɪz]) (*also firm*) casa; (*POL*) cámara; (*THEAT*) sala ♦ *vt* [hauz] (*person*) alojar; **at/to my** ~ en/a mi casa; **the H**~ **(of Commons/Lords)** (*BRIT*) la Cámara de los Comunes/Lores; **the H**~ **(of Representatives)** (*US*) la Cámara de Representantes; **on the** ~ (*fig*) la casa invita.
house arrest *n* arresto domiciliario.
houseboat ['hausbəut] *n* casa flotante.
housebound ['hausbaund] *adj* confinado en casa.
housebreaking ['hausbreɪkɪŋ] *n* allanamiento de morada.
house-broken ['hausbrəukən] *adj* (*US*) = **house-trained**.
housecoat ['hauskəut] *n* bata.
household ['haushəuld] *n* familia.
householder ['haushəuldə*] *n* propietario/a; (*head of house*) cabeza de familia.
househunting ['haushʌntɪŋ] *n*: **to go** ~ ir en busca de vivienda.
housekeeper ['hauskiːpə*] *n* ama de llaves.
housekeeping ['hauskiːpɪŋ] *n* (*work*) trabajos *mpl* domésticos; (*COMPUT*) gestión *f* interna; (*also:* ~ **money**) dinero para gastos domésticos.
houseman ['hausmən] *n* (*BRIT MED*) médico residente.
house-owner ['hausəunə*] *n* propietario/a de una vivienda.
house plant *n* planta de interior.
house-proud ['hauspraud] *adj* preocupado por el embellecimiento de la casa.
house-to-house ['haustə'haus] *adj* (*collection*) de casa en casa; (*search*) casa por casa.

house-train ['haustreɪn] *vt* (*pet*) enseñar (*a hacer sus necesidades en el sitio apropiado*).
house-trained ['haustreɪnd] *adj* (*BRIT*: *animal*) enseñado.
house-warming ['hauswɔːmɪŋ] *n* (*also*: ~ *party*) fiesta de estreno de una casa.
housewife ['hauswaɪf] *n* ama de casa.
housework ['hauswəːk] *n* faenas *fpl* (de la casa).
housing ['hauzɪŋ] *n* (*act*) alojamiento; (*houses*) viviendas *fpl* ♦ *cpd* (*problem, shortage*) de (la) vivienda.
housing association *n* asociación *f* de la vivienda.
housing benefit *n* (*BRIT*) subsidio por alojamiento.
housing conditions *npl* condiciones *fpl* de habitabilidad.
housing development, (*BRIT*) **housing estate** *n* urbanización *f*.
hovel ['hɔvl] *n* casucha.
hover ['hɔvə*] *vi* flotar (en el aire); (*helicopter*) cernerse; **to ~ on the brink of disaster** estar al borde mismo del desastre.
hovercraft ['hɔvəkrɑːft] *n* aerodeslizador *m*, hovercraft *m*.
hoverport ['hɔvəpɔːt] *n* puerto de aerodeslizadores.
how [hau] *adv* cómo; ~ **are you?** ¿cómo está usted?, ¿cómo estás?; ~ **do you do?** encantado, mucho gusto; ~ **far is it to ...?** ¿qué distancia hay de aquí a ...?; ~ **long have you been here?** ¿cuánto (tiempo) hace que estás aquí?, ¿cuánto tiempo llevas aquí?; ~ **lovely!** ¡qué bonito!; ~ **many/much?** ¿cuántos/cuánto?; ~ **old are you?** ¿cuántos años tienes?; ~ **is school?** ¿qué tal la escuela?; ~ **about a drink?** ¿te gustaría algo de beber?, ¿qué te parece una copa?
however [hau'ɛvə*] *adv* de cualquier manera; (+ *adjective*) por muy ... que; (*in questions*) cómo ♦ *conj* sin embargo, no obstante.
howitzer ['hauɪtsə*] *n* (*MIL*) obús *m*.
howl [haul] *n* aullido ♦ *vi* aullar.
howler ['haulə*] *n* plancha, falta garrafal.
howling ['haulɪŋ] *adj* (*wind*) huracanado.
HP *n abbr see* **hire purchase.**
hp *abbr see* **horsepower.**
HQ *n abbr see* **headquarters.**
HR *n abbr* (*US*) = **House of Representatives.**
HRH *abbr* (= *His (or Her) Royal Highness*) S.A.R.
hr(s) *abbr* (= *hour(s)*) h.
HRT *n abbr see* **hormone replacement therapy.**

HS *abbr* (*US*) = **high school.**
HST *abbr* (*US*: = *Hawaiian Standard Time*) hora de Hawai.
hub [hʌb] *n* (*of wheel*) cubo; (*fig*) centro.
hubbub ['hʌbʌb] *n* barahúnda, barullo.
hubcap ['hʌbkæp] *n* tapacubos *m inv.*
HUD *n abbr* (*US*: = *Department of Housing and Urban Development*) ministerio de la vivienda y urbanismo.
huddle ['hʌdl] *vi*: **to ~ together** amontonarse.
hue [hjuː] *n* color *m*, matiz *m*; ~ **and cry** *n* protesta.
huff [hʌf] *n*: **in a ~** enojado.
huffy ['hʌfɪ] *adj* (*col*) mosqueado.
hug [hʌg] *vt* abrazar ♦ *n* abrazo.
huge [hjuːdʒ] *adj* enorme.
hulk [hʌlk] *n* (*ship*) barco viejo; (*person, building etc*) mole *f*.
hulking ['hʌlkɪŋ] *adj* pesado.
hull [hʌl] *n* (*of ship*) casco.
hullabaloo ['hʌləbə'luː] *n* (*col: noise*) algarabía, jaleo.
hullo [hə'ləu] *excl* = **hello.**
hum [hʌm] *vt* tararear, canturrear ♦ *vi* tararear, canturrear; (*insect*) zumbar ♦ *n* (*also ELEC*) zumbido; (*of traffic, machines*) zumbido, ronroneo; (*of voices etc*) murmullo.
human ['hjuːmən] *adj* humano ♦ *n* (*also*: ~ *being*) ser *m* humano.
humane [hjuː'meɪn] *adj* humano, humanitario.
humanism ['hjuːmənɪzəm] *n* humanismo.
humanitarian [hjuːmænɪ'tɛərɪən] *adj* humanitario.
humanity [hjuː'mænɪtɪ] *n* humanidad *f*.
humanly ['hjuːmənlɪ] *adv* humanamente.
humanoid ['hjuːmənɔɪd] *adj, n* humanoide *m/f*.
human relations *npl* relaciones *fpl* humanas.
human rights *npl* derechos *mpl* humanos.
humble ['hʌmbl] *adj* humilde ♦ *vt* humillar.
humbly ['hʌmblɪ] *adv* humildemente.
humbug ['hʌmbʌg] *n* patrañas *fpl*; (*BRIT*: *sweet*) caramelo de menta.
humdrum ['hʌmdrʌm] *adj* (*boring*) monótono, aburrido; (*routine*) rutinario.
humid ['hjuːmɪd] *adj* húmedo.
humidifier [hjuː'mɪdɪfaɪə*] *n* humectador *m*.
humidity [hjuː'mɪdɪtɪ] *n* humedad *f*.
humiliate [hjuː'mɪlɪeɪt] *vt* humillar.
humiliation [hjuːmɪlɪ'eɪʃən] *n* humillación *f*.
humility [hjuː'mɪlɪtɪ] *n* humildad *f*.
humorist ['hjuːmərɪst] *n* humorista *m/f*.
humorous ['hjuːmərəs] *adj* gracioso,

divertido.
humour, (US) **humor** ['hju:mə*] n
humorismo, sentido del humor; (mood)
humor m ♦ vt (person) complacer; **sense of**
~ sentido del humor; **to be in a good/bad**
~ estar de buen/mal humor.
humo(u)rless ['hju:məlɪs] adj serio.
hump [hʌmp] n (in ground) montículo;
(camel's) giba.
humus ['hju:məs] n (BIO) humus m.
hunch [hʌntʃ] n (premonition)
presentimiento; **I have a** ~ **that** tengo la
corazonada or el presentimiento de que.
hunchback ['hʌntʃbæk] n jorobado/a.
hunched [hʌntʃt] adj jorobado.
hundred ['hʌndrəd] num ciento; (before n)
cien; **about a** ~ **people** unas cien
personas, alrededor de cien personas; ~**s**
of centenares de; ~**s of people**
centenares de personas; **I'm a** ~ **per cent**
sure estoy completamente seguro.
hundredweight ['hʌndrədweɪt] n (BRIT)
= 50.8 kg; 112 lb; (US) = 45.3 kg; 100 lb.
hung [hʌŋ] pt, pp of **hang**.
Hungarian [hʌŋ'gɛərɪən] adj húngaro ♦ n
húngaro/a m/f; (LING) húngaro.
Hungary ['hʌŋgərɪ] n Hungría.
hunger ['hʌŋgə*] n hambre f ♦ vi: **to** ~ **for**
(fig) tener hambre de, anhelar.
hunger strike n huelga de hambre.
hungover [hʌŋ'əuvə*] adj (col): **to be** ~
tener resaca.
hungrily ['hʌŋgrəlɪ] adv ávidamente, con
ganas.
hungry ['hʌŋgrɪ] adj hambriento; **to be** ~
tener hambre; ~ **for** (fig) sediento de.
hunk [hʌŋk] n (of bread etc) trozo, pedazo.
hunt [hʌnt] vt (seek) buscar; (SPORT) cazar
♦ vi cazar ♦ n caza, cacería.
►**hunt down** vt acorralar, seguir la pista
a.
hunter ['hʌntə*] n cazador(a) m/f; (horse)
caballo de caza.
hunting ['hʌntɪŋ] n caza.
hurdle ['hə:dl] n (SPORT) valla; (fig)
obstáculo.
hurl [hə:l] vt lanzar, arrojar.
hurling ['hə:lɪŋ] n (SPORT) juego irlandés
semejante al hockey.
hurly-burly ['hə:lɪ'bə:lɪ] n jaleo, follón m.
hurrah [hu'rɑ:], **hurray** [hu'reɪ] n ¡viva!,
¡hurra!
hurricane ['hʌrɪkən] n huracán m.
hurried ['hʌrɪd] adj (fast) apresurado;
(rushed) hecho de prisa.
hurriedly ['hʌrɪdlɪ] adv con prisa,
apresuradamente.
hurry ['hʌrɪ] n prisa ♦ vb (also: ~ **up**) vi

apresurarse, darse prisa, apurarse (LAM)
♦ vt (person) dar prisa a; (work)
apresurar, hacer de prisa; **to be in a** ~
tener prisa, tener apuro (LAM), estar
apurado (LAM); **to** ~ **back/home** darse
prisa en volver/volver a casa.
►**hurry along** vi pasar de prisa.
►**hurry away, hurry off** vi irse corriendo.
►**hurry on** vi: **to** ~ **on to say** apresurarse a
decir.
►**hurry up** vi darse prisa, apurarse (esp
LAM).
hurt [hə:t] vb (pt, pp hurt) vt hacer daño a;
(business, interests etc) perjudicar ♦ vi
doler ♦ adj lastimado; **I** ~ **my arm** me
lastimé el brazo; **where does it** ~**?**
¿dónde te duele?
hurtful ['hə:tful] adj (remark etc) hiriente,
dañino.
hurtle ['hə:tl] vi: **to** ~ **past** pasar como un
rayo.
husband ['hʌzbənd] n marido.
hush [hʌʃ] n silencio ♦ vt hacer callar;
(cover up) encubrir; ~**!** ¡chitón!, ¡cállate!
►**hush up** vt (fact) encubrir, callar.
hushed [hʌʃt] adj (voice) bajo.
hush-hush [hʌʃ'hʌʃ] adj (col) muy secreto.
husk [hʌsk] n (of wheat) cáscara.
husky ['hʌskɪ] adj ronco; (burly) fornido ♦ n
perro esquimal.
hustings ['hʌstɪŋz] npl (POL) mítin msg
preelectoral.
hustle ['hʌsl] vt (push) empujar; (hurry) dar
prisa a ♦ n bullicio, actividad f febril; ~
and bustle ajetreo.
hut [hʌt] n cabaña; (shed) cobertizo.
hutch [hʌtʃ] n conejera.
hyacinth ['haɪəsɪnθ] n jacinto.
hybrid ['haɪbrɪd] adj, n híbrido.
hydrant ['haɪdrənt] n (also: fire ~) boca de
incendios.
hydraulic [haɪ'drɔ:lɪk] adj hidráulico.
hydraulics [haɪ'drɔ:lɪks] n hidráulica.
hydrochloric [haɪdrəu'klɔrɪk] adj: ~ **acid**
ácido clorhídrico.
hydroelectric [haɪdrəuɪ'lɛktrɪk] adj
hidroeléctrico.
hydrofoil ['haɪdrəfɔɪl] n aerodeslizador m.
hydrogen ['haɪdrədʒən] n hidrógeno.
hydrogen bomb n bomba de hidrógeno.
hydrophobia [haɪdrə'fəubɪə] n hidrofobia.
hydroplane ['haɪdrəpleɪn] n hidroavión m,
hidroavioneta.
hyena [haɪ'i:nə] n hiena.
hygiene ['haɪdʒi:n] n higiene f.
hygienic [haɪ'dʒi:nɪk] adj higiénico.
hymn [hɪm] n himno.
hype [haɪp] n (col) bombo.

hyperactive [haɪpər'æktɪv] *adj* hiperactivo.
hypermarket ['haɪpəmɑːkɪt] *n* hipermercado.
hypertension ['haɪpə'tɛnʃən] *n* hipertensión *f*.
hyphen ['haɪfn] *n* guión *m*.
hypnosis [hɪp'nəusɪs] *n* hipnosis *f*.
hypnotic [hɪp'nɔtɪk] *adj* hipnótico.
hypnotism ['hɪpnətɪzəm] *n* hipnotismo.
hypnotist ['hɪpnətɪst] hipnotista *m/f*.
hypnotize ['hɪpnətaɪz] *vt* hipnotizar.
hypoallergenic ['haɪpəuælə'dʒɛnɪk] *adj* hipoalérgeno.
hypochondriac [haɪpəu'kɔndrɪæk] *n* hipocondríaco/a.
hypocrisy [hɪ'pɔkrɪsɪ] *n* hipocresía.
hypocrite ['hɪpəkrɪt] *n* hipócrita *m/f*.
hypocritical [hɪpə'krɪtɪkl] *adj* hipócrita.
hypodermic [haɪpə'dəːmɪk] *adj* hipodérmico ♦ *n* (*syringe*) aguja hipodérmica.
hypotenuse [haɪ'pɔtɪnjuːz] *n* hipotenusa.
hypothermia [haɪpəu'θəːmɪə] *n* hipotermia.
hypothesis, *pl* **hypotheses** [haɪ'pɔθɪsɪs, -siːz] *n* hipótesis *f inv*.
hypothetical [haɪpə'θɛtɪkl] *adj* hipotético.
hysterectomy [hɪstə'rɛktəmɪ] *n* histerectomía.
hysteria [hɪ'stɪərɪə] *n* histeria.
hysterical [hɪ'stɛrɪkl] *adj* histérico.
hysterics [hɪ'stɛrɪks] *npl* histeria *sg*, histerismo *sg*; **to have ~** ponerse histérico.
Hz *abbr* (= *Hertz*) Hz.

I i

I, i [aɪ] *n* (*letter*) I, i *f*; **I for Isaac**, (*US*) **I for Item** I de Inés, I de Israel.
I [aɪ] *pron* yo ♦ *abbr* = **island; isle.**
IA, Ia. *abbr* (*US*) = **Iowa.**
IAEA *n abbr see* **International Atomic Energy Agency.**
IBA *n abbr* (*BRIT*) = **Independent Broadcasting Authority;** *see* **ITV.**
Iberian [aɪ'bɪərɪən] *adj* ibero, ibérico.
Iberian Peninsula *n*: **the ~** la Península Ibérica.
IBEW *n abbr* (*US*: = *International Brotherhood of Electrical Workers*) sindicato internacional de electricistas.

ib(id). *abbr* (= *ibidem: from the same source*) ibídem.
i/c *abbr* (*BRIT*) = **in charge.**
ICBM *n abbr* (= *intercontinental ballistic missile*) misil *m* balístico intercontinental.
ICC *n abbr* (= *International Chamber of Commerce*) CCI *f*; (*US*) = *Interstate Commerce Commission.*
ice [aɪs] *n* hielo ♦ *vt* (*cake*) alcorzar ♦ *vi* (*also:* ~ **over,** ~ **up**) helarse; **to keep sth on** ~ (*fig: plan, project*) tener algo en reserva.
ice age *n* período glaciar.
ice axe *n* piqueta (de alpinista).
iceberg ['aɪsbəːg] *n* iceberg *m*; **the tip of the** ~ la punta del iceberg.
icebox ['aɪsbɔks] *n* (*BRIT*) congelador *m*; (*US*) nevera, refrigeradora (*LAM*).
icebreaker ['aɪsbreɪkə*] *n* rompehielos *m inv*.
ice bucket *n* cubo para el hielo.
icecap ['aɪskæp] *n* casquete *m* polar.
ice-cold [aɪs'kəuld] *adj* helado.
ice cream *n* helado.
ice-cream soda *n* soda mezclada con helado.
ice cube *n* cubito de hielo.
iced [aɪst] *adj* (*drink*) con hielo; (*cake*) escarchado.
ice hockey *n* hockey *m* sobre hielo.
Iceland ['aɪslənd] *n* Islandia.
Icelander ['aɪsləndə*] *n* islandés/esa *m/f*.
Icelandic [aɪs'lændɪk] *adj* islandés/esa ♦ *n* (*LING*) islandés *m*.
ice lolly *n* (*BRIT*) polo.
ice pick *n* piolet *m*.
ice rink *n* pista de hielo.
ice-skate ['aɪsskeɪt] *n* patín *m* de hielo ♦ *vi* patinar sobre hielo.
ice-skating ['aɪsskeɪtɪŋ] *n* patinaje *m* sobre hielo.
icicle ['aɪsɪkl] *n* carámbano.
icing ['aɪsɪŋ] *n* (*CULIN*) alcorza; (*AVIAT etc*) formación *f* de hielo.
icing sugar *n* (*BRIT*) azúcar *m* glas(eado).
ICJ *n abbr see* **International Court of Justice.**
icon ['aɪkɔn] *n* (*gen, COMPUT*) icono.
ICR *n abbr* (*US*) = *Institute for Cancer Research.*
ICRC *n abbr* (= *International Committee of the Red Cross*) CICR.
ICU *n abbr* (= *intensive care unit*) UVI *f*.
icy ['aɪsɪ] *adj* (*road*) helado; (*fig*) glacial.
ID *abbr* (*US*) = *Idaho.*
I'd [aɪd] = **I would; I had.**
Ida. *abbr* (*US*) = *Idaho.*
ID card *n* (= *identity card*) DNI *m*.
IDD *n abbr* (*BRIT TEL*: = *international direct dialling*) servicio automático

internacional.

idea [aɪ'dɪə] *n* idea; **good ~!** ¡buena idea!; **to have an ~ that ...** tener la impresión de que ...; **I haven't the least ~** no tengo ni (la más remota) idea.

ideal [aɪ'dɪəl] *n* ideal *m* ♦ *adj* ideal.

idealism [aɪ'dɪəlɪzəm] *n* idealismo.

idealist [aɪ'dɪəlɪst] *n* idealista *m/f.*

ideally [aɪ'dɪəlɪ] *adv* perfectamente; **~, the book should have ...** idealmente, el libro debería tener ....

identical [aɪ'dɛntɪkl] *adj* idéntico.

identification [aɪdɛntɪfɪ'keɪʃən] *n* identificación *f;* **means of ~** documentos *mpl* personales.

identify [aɪ'dɛntɪfaɪ] *vt* identificar ♦ *vi:* **to ~ with** identificarse con.

Identikit ® [aɪ'dɛntɪkɪt] *n:* **~ (picture)** retrato-robot *m.*

identity [aɪ'dɛntɪtɪ] *n* identidad *f.*

identity card *n* carnet *m* de identidad, cédula (de identidad) (*LAM*).

identity papers *npl* documentos *mpl* (de identidad), documentación *fsg.*

identity parade *n* identificación *f* de acusados.

ideological [aɪdɪə'lɔdʒɪkəl] *adj* ideológico.

ideology [aɪdɪ'ɔlədʒɪ] *n* ideología.

idiocy ['ɪdɪəsɪ] *n* idiotez *f;* (*stupid act*) estupidez *f.*

idiom ['ɪdɪəm] *n* modismo; (*style of speaking*) lenguaje *m.*

idiomatic [ɪdɪə'mætɪk] *adj* idiomático.

idiosyncrasy [ɪdɪəu'sɪŋkrəsɪ] *n* idiosincrasia.

idiot ['ɪdɪət] *n* (*gen*) idiota *m/f;* (*fool*) tonto/a.

idiotic [ɪdɪ'ɔtɪk] *adj* idiota; tonto.

idle ['aɪdl] *adj* (*lazy*) holgazán/ana; (*unemployed*) parado, desocupado; (*talk*) frívolo ♦ *vi* (*machine*) funcionar *or* marchar en vacío; **~ capacity** (*COMM*) capacidad *f* sin utilizar; **~ money** (*COMM*) capital *m* improductivo; **~ time** (*COMM*) tiempo de paro.

▶**idle away** *vt:* **to ~ away one's time** malgastar *or* desperdiciar el tiempo.

idleness ['aɪdlnɪs] *n* holgazanería; paro, desocupación *f.*

idler ['aɪdlə*] *n* holgazán/ana *m/f,* vago/a.

idol ['aɪdl] *n* ídolo.

idolize ['aɪdəlaɪz] *vt* idolatrar.

idyllic [ɪ'dɪlɪk] *adj* idílico.

i.e. *abbr* (= *id est: that is*) es decir.

if [ɪf] *conj* si ♦ *n:* **there are a lot of ~s and buts** hay muchas dudas sin resolver; **(even) ~** aunque, si bien; **I'd be pleased ~ you could do it** yo estaría contento si pudieras hacerlo; **~ necessary** si

resultase necesario; **~ only** si solamente; **as ~** como si.

iffy ['ɪfɪ] *adj* (*col*) dudoso.

igloo ['ɪgluː] *n* iglú *m.*

ignite [ɪg'naɪt] *vt* (*set fire to*) encender ♦ *vi* encenderse.

ignition [ɪg'nɪʃən] *n* (*AUT*) encendido; **to switch on/off the ~** arrancar/apagar el motor.

ignition key *n* (*AUT*) llave *f* de contacto.

ignoble [ɪg'nəubl] *adj* innoble, vil.

ignominious [ɪgnə'mɪnɪəs] *adj* ignominioso, vergonzoso.

ignoramus [ɪgnə'reɪməs] *n* ignorante *m/f,* inculto/a.

ignorance ['ɪgnərəns] *n* ignorancia; **to keep sb in ~ of sth** ocultarle algo a algn.

ignorant ['ɪgnərənt] *adj* ignorante; **to be ~ of** (*subject*) desconocer; (*events*) ignorar.

ignore [ɪg'nɔː*] *vt* (*person*) no hacer caso de; (*fact*) pasar por alto.

ikon ['aɪkɔn] *n* = **icon.**

IL *abbr* (*US*) = *Illinois.*

ILA *n abbr* (*US:* = *International Longshoremen's Association*) *sindicato internacional de trabajadores portuarios.*

ill [ɪl] *adj* enfermo, malo ♦ *n* mal *m;* (*fig*) infortunio ♦ *adv* mal; **to take** *or* **be taken ~** caer *or* ponerse enfermo; **to feel ~ (with)** encontrarse mal (de); **to speak/ think ~ of sb** hablar/pensar mal de algn; *see also* **ills.**

Ill. *abbr* (*US*) = *Illinois.*

I'll [aɪl] = **I will, I shall.**

ill-advised [ɪləd'vaɪzd] *adj* poco recomendable; **he was ~ to go** se equivocaba al ir.

ill-at-ease [ɪlət'iːz] *adj* incómodo.

ill-considered [ɪlkən'sɪdəd] *adj* (*plan*) poco pensado.

ill-disposed [ɪldɪs'pəuzd] *adj:* **to be ~ towards sb/sth** estar maldispuesto hacia algn/algo.

illegal [ɪ'liːgl] *adj* ilegal.

illegible [ɪ'lɛdʒɪbl] *adj* ilegible.

illegitimate [ɪlɪ'dʒɪtɪmət] *adj* ilegítimo.

ill-fated [ɪl'feɪtɪd] *adj* malogrado.

ill-favoured, (*US*) **ill-favored** [ɪl'feɪvəd] *adj* poco agraciado.

ill feeling *n* rencor *m.*

ill-gotten ['ɪlgɔtn] *adj* (*gains etc*) mal adquirido.

ill health *n* mala salud *f;* **to be in ~** estar mal de salud.

illicit [ɪ'lɪsɪt] *adj* ilícito.

ill-informed [ɪlɪn'fɔːmd] *adj* (*judgement*) erróneo; (*person*) mal informado.

illiterate [ɪ'lɪtərət] adj analfabeto.
ill-mannered [ɪl'mænəd] adj mal educado.
illness ['ɪlnɪs] n enfermedad f.
illogical [ɪ'lɔdʒɪkl] adj ilógico.
ills [ɪlz] npl males mpl.
ill-suited [ɪl'su:tɪd] adj (couple)
incompatible; **he is ~ to the job** no es la
persona indicada para el trabajo.
ill-timed [ɪl'taɪmd] adj inoportuno.
ill-treat [ɪl'tri:t] vt maltratar.
ill-treatment [ɪl'tri:tmənt] n malos tratos
mpl.
illuminate [ɪ'lu:mɪneɪt] vt (room, street)
iluminar, alumbrar; (subject) aclarar; ~d
sign letrero luminoso.
illuminating [ɪ'lu:mɪneɪtɪŋ] adj
revelador(a).
illumination [ɪlu:mɪ'neɪʃən] n alumbrado;
~s npl luminarias fpl, luces fpl.
illusion [ɪ'lu:ʒən] n ilusión f; **to be under the
~ that**... estar convencido de que ....
illusive [ɪ'lu:sɪv], **illusory** [ɪ'lu:sərɪ] adj
ilusorio.
illustrate ['ɪləstreɪt] vt ilustrar.
illustration [ɪlə'streɪʃən] n (example)
ejemplo, ilustración f; (in book) lámina,
ilustración f.
illustrator ['ɪləstreɪtə*] n ilustrador(a) m/f.
illustrious [ɪ'lʌstrɪəs] adj ilustre.
ill will n rencor m.
ILO n abbr (= International Labour
Organization) OIT f.
ILWU n abbr (US: = International
Longshoremen's and Warehousemen's
Union) sindicato internacional de
trabajadores portuarios y almacenistas.
I'm [aɪm] = **I am**.
image ['ɪmɪdʒ] n imagen f.
imagery ['ɪmɪdʒərɪ] n imágenes fpl.
imaginable [ɪ'mædʒɪnəbl] adj imaginable.
imaginary [ɪ'mædʒɪnərɪ] adj imaginario.
imagination [ɪmædʒɪ'neɪʃən] n imaginación
f; (inventiveness) inventiva; (illusion)
fantasía.
imaginative [ɪ'mædʒɪnətɪv] adj
imaginativo.
imagine [ɪ'mædʒɪn] vt imaginarse;
(suppose) suponer.
imbalance [ɪm'bæləns] n desequilibrio.
imbecile ['ɪmbəsi:l] n imbécil m/f.
imbue [ɪm'bju:] vt: **to ~ sth with** imbuir
algo de.
IMF n abbr see **International Monetary Fund**.
imitate ['ɪmɪteɪt] vt imitar.
imitation [ɪmɪ'teɪʃən] n imitación f; (copy)
copia; (pej) remedo.
imitator ['ɪmɪteɪtə*] n imitador(a) m/f.
immaculate [ɪ'mækjulət] adj limpísimo,

inmaculado; (REL) inmaculado.
immaterial [ɪmə'tɪərɪəl] adj incorpóreo; **it is
~ whether**... no importa si... .
immature [ɪmə'tjuə*] adj (person)
inmaduro; (of one's youth) joven.
immaturity [ɪmə'tjuərɪtɪ] n inmadurez f.
immeasurable [ɪ'mɛʒrəbl] adj
inconmensurable.
immediacy [ɪ'mi:dɪəsɪ] n urgencia,
proximidad f.
immediate [ɪ'mi:dɪət] adj inmediato;
(pressing) urgente, apremiante; **in the ~
future** en un futuro próximo.
immediately [ɪ'mi:dɪətlɪ] adv (at once) en
seguida; **~ next to** justo al lado de.
immense [ɪ'mɛns] adj inmenso, enorme.
immensely [ɪ'mɛnslɪ] adv enormemente.
immensity [ɪ'mɛnsɪtɪ] n (of size, difference)
inmensidad f; (of problem) enormidad f.
immerse [ɪ'mə:s] vt (submerge) sumergir;
to be ~d in (fig) estar absorto en.
immersion heater [ɪ'mə:ʃən-] n (BRIT)
calentador m de inmersión.
immigrant ['ɪmɪgrənt] n inmigrante m/f.
immigrate ['ɪmɪgreɪt] vi inmigrar.
immigration [ɪmɪ'greɪʃən] n inmigración f.
immigration authorities npl servicio sg
de inmigración.
immigration laws npl leyes fpl de
inmigración.
imminent ['ɪmɪnənt] adj inminente.
immobile [ɪ'məubaɪl] adj inmóvil.
immobilize [ɪ'məubɪlaɪz] vt inmovilizar.
immoderate [ɪ'mɔdərɪt] adj (person)
desmesurado; (opinion, reaction, demand)
excesivo.
immodest [ɪ'mɔdɪst] adj (indecent)
desvergonzado, impúdico; (boasting)
jactancioso.
immoral [ɪ'mɔrl] adj inmoral.
immorality [ɪmə'rælɪtɪ] n inmoralidad f.
immortal [ɪ'mɔ:tl] adj inmortal.
immortality [ɪmɔ:'tælɪtɪ] n inmortalidad f.
immortalize [ɪ'mɔ:tlaɪz] vt inmortalizar.
immovable [ɪ'mu:vəbl] adj (object)
imposible de mover; (person)
inconmovible.
immune [ɪ'mju:n] adj: **~ (to)** inmune (a).
immune system n sistema m inmunitario.
immunity [ɪ'mju:nɪtɪ] n (MED, of diplomat)
inmunidad f; (COMM) exención f.
immunization [ɪmjunaɪ'zeɪʃən] n
inmunización f.
immunize ['ɪmjunaɪz] vt inmunizar.
imp [ɪmp] n (small devil, also fig: child)
diablillo.
impact ['ɪmpækt] n (gen) impacto.
impair [ɪm'pɛə*] vt perjudicar.

-impaired [ɪmˈpɛəd] *suff*: **visually~** con defectos de visión.
impale [ɪmˈpeɪl] *vt* (*with sword*) atravesar.
impart [ɪmˈpɑːt] *vt* comunicar; (*make known*) participar; (*bestow*) otorgar.
impartial [ɪmˈpɑːʃl] *adj* imparcial.
impartiality [ɪmpɑːʃɪˈælɪtɪ] *n* imparcialidad *f*.
impassable [ɪmˈpɑːsəbl] *adj* (*barrier*) infranqueable; (*road*) intransitable.
impasse [ɪmˈpɑːs] *n* callejón *m* sin salida; **to reach an ~** llegar a un punto muerto.
impassioned [ɪmˈpæʃənd] *adj* apasionado, exaltado.
impassive [ɪmˈpæsɪv] *adj* impasible.
impatience [ɪmˈpeɪʃəns] *n* impaciencia.
impatient [ɪmˈpeɪʃənt] *adj* impaciente; **to get** *or* **grow ~** impacientarse.
impatiently [ɪmˈpeɪʃəntlɪ] *adv* con impaciencia.
impeachment [ɪmˈpiːtʃmənt] *n* denuncia, acusación *f*.
impeccable [ɪmˈpɛkəbl] *adj* impecable.
impecunious [ɪmpɪˈkjuːnɪəs] *adj* sin dinero.
impede [ɪmˈpiːd] *vt* estorbar, dificultar.
impediment [ɪmˈpɛdɪmənt] *n* obstáculo, estorbo; (*also*: **speech ~**) defecto (del habla).
impel [ɪmˈpɛl] *vt* (*force*): **to ~ sb (to do sth)** obligar a algn (a hacer algo).
impending [ɪmˈpɛndɪŋ] *adj* inminente.
impenetrable [ɪmˈpɛnɪtrəbl] *adj* (*jungle, fortress*) impenetrable; (*unfathomable*) insondable.
imperative [ɪmˈpɛrətɪv] *adj* (*tone*) imperioso; (*necessary*) imprescindible ♦ *n* (*LING*) imperativo.
imperceptible [ɪmpəˈsɛptɪbl] *adj* imperceptible.
imperfect [ɪmˈpəːfɪkt] *adj* imperfecto; (*goods etc*) defectuoso.
imperfection [ɪmpəˈfɛkʃən] *n* (*blemish*) desperfecto; (*fault, flaw*) defecto.
imperial [ɪmˈpɪərɪəl] *adj* imperial.
imperialism [ɪmˈpɪərɪəlɪzəm] *n* imperialismo.
imperil [ɪmˈpɛrɪl] *vt* poner en peligro.
imperious [ɪmˈpɪərɪəs] *adj* señorial, apremiante.
impersonal [ɪmˈpəːsənl] *adj* impersonal.
impersonate [ɪmˈpəːsəneɪt] *vt* hacerse pasar por.
impersonation [ɪmpəːsəˈneɪʃən] *n* imitación *f*.
impersonator [ɪmˈpəːsəneɪtə*] *n* (*THEAT etc*) imitador(a) *m/f*.
impertinence [ɪmˈpəːtɪnəns] *n* impertinencia, insolencia.

impertinent [ɪmˈpəːtɪnənt] *adj* impertinente, insolente.
imperturbable [ɪmpəˈtəːbəbl] *adj* imperturbable, impasible.
impervious [ɪmˈpəːvɪəs] *adj* impermeable; (*fig*): **~ to** insensible a.
impetuous [ɪmˈpɛtjuəs] *adj* impetuoso.
impetus [ˈɪmpətəs] *n* ímpetu *m*; (*fig*) impulso.
impinge [ɪmˈpɪndʒ]: **to ~ on** *vt fus* (*affect*) afectar a.
impish [ˈɪmpɪʃ] *adj* travieso.
implacable [ɪmˈplækəbl] *adj* implacable.
implant [ɪmˈplɑːnt] *vt* (*MED*) injertar, implantar; (*fig: idea, principle*) inculcar.
implausible [ɪmˈplɔːzɪbl] *adj* implausible.
implement *n* [ˈɪmplɪmənt] instrumento, herramienta ♦ *vt* [ˈɪmplɪmɛnt] hacer efectivo; (*carry out*) realizar.
implicate [ˈɪmplɪkeɪt] *vt* (*compromise*) comprometer; (*involve*) enredar; **to ~ sb in sth** comprometer a algn en algo.
implication [ɪmplɪˈkeɪʃən] *n* consecuencia; **by ~** indirectamente.
implicit [ɪmˈplɪsɪt] *adj* (*gen*) implícito; (*complete*) absoluto.
implicitly [ɪmˈplɪsɪtlɪ] *adv* implícitamente.
implore [ɪmˈplɔː*] *vt* (*person*) suplicar.
imploring [ɪmˈplɔːrɪŋ] *adj* de súplica.
imply [ɪmˈplaɪ] *vt* (*involve*) implicar, suponer; (*hint*) insinuar.
impolite [ɪmpəˈlaɪt] *adj* mal educado.
impolitic [ɪmˈpɒlɪtɪk] *adj* poco diplomático.
imponderable [ɪmˈpɒndərəbl] *adj* imponderable.
import *vt* [ɪmˈpɔːt] importar ♦ *n* [ˈɪmpɔːt] (*COMM*) importación *f*; (*meaning*) significado, sentido ♦ *cpd* (*duty, licence etc*) de importación.
importance [ɪmˈpɔːtəns] *n* importancia; **to be of great/little ~** tener mucha/poca importancia.
important [ɪmˈpɔːtənt] *adj* importante; **it's not ~** no importa, no tiene importancia; **it is ~ that** es importante que.
importantly [ɪmˈpɔːtəntlɪ] *adv* (*pej*) dándose importancia; **but, more ~** ... pero, lo que es aún más importante ....
import duty *n* derechos *mpl* de importación.
imported [ɪmˈpɔːtɪd] *adj* importado.
importer [ɪmˈpɔːtə*] *n* importador(a) *m/f*.
import licence, (*US*) **import license** *n* licencia de importación.
impose [ɪmˈpəuz] *vt* imponer ♦ *vi*: **to ~ on sb** abusar de algn.
imposing [ɪmˈpəuzɪŋ] *adj* imponente, impresionante.

imposition [ɪmpə'zɪʃn] n (of tax etc)
imposición f; **to be an ~** (on person)
molestar.
impossibility [ɪmpɒsə'bɪlɪtɪ] n
imposibilidad f.
impossible [ɪm'pɒsɪbl] adj imposible;
(person) insoportable; **it is ~ for me to
leave now** me es imposible salir ahora.
impossibly [ɪm'pɒsɪblɪ] adv
imposiblemente.
impostor [ɪm'pɒstə*] n impostor(a) m/f.
impotence ['ɪmpətəns] n impotencia.
impotent ['ɪmpətənt] adj impotente.
impound [ɪm'paund] vt embargar.
impoverished [ɪm'pɒvərɪʃt] adj necesitado;
(land) agotado.
impracticable [ɪm'præktɪkəbl] adj no
factible, irrealizable.
impractical [ɪm'præktɪkl] adj (person) poco
práctico.
imprecise [ɪmprɪ'saɪs] adj impreciso.
impregnable [ɪm'prɛgnəbl] adj
invulnerable; (castle) inexpugnable.
impregnate ['ɪmprɛgneɪt] vt (gen)
impregnar; (soak) empapar; (fertilize)
fecundar.
impresario [ɪmprɪ'sɑːrɪəu] n empresario/a.
impress [ɪm'prɛs] vt impresionar; (mark)
estampar ♦ vi causar buena impresión; **to
~ sth on sb** convencer a algn de la
importancia de algo.
impression [ɪm'prɛʃən] n impresión f;
(footprint etc) huella; (print run) edición f;
to be under the ~ that tener la idea de
que; **to make a good/bad ~ on sb** causar
buena/mala impresión a algn.
impressionable [ɪm'prɛʃnəbl] adj
impresionable.
impressionist [ɪm'prɛʃənɪst] n
impresionista m/f.
impressive [ɪm'prɛsɪv] adj impresionante.
imprint ['ɪmprɪnt] n (PUBLISHING) pie m de
imprenta; (fig) sello.
imprison [ɪm'prɪzn] vt encarcelar.
imprisonment [ɪm'prɪznmənt] n
encarcelamiento; (term of ~) cárcel f; **life
~** cadena perpetua.
improbable [ɪm'prɒbəbl] adj improbable,
inverosímil.
impromptu [ɪm'prɒmptjuː] adj improvisado
♦ adv de improviso.
improper [ɪm'prɒpə*] adj (incorrect)
impropio; (unseemly) indecoroso;
(indecent) indecente.
impropriety [ɪmprə'praɪətɪ] n falta de
decoro; (indecency) indecencia; (of
language) impropiedad f.
improve [ɪm'pruːv] vt mejorar; (foreign

language) perfeccionar ♦ vi mejorar.
►**improve (up)on** vt fus (offer) mejorar.
improvement [ɪm'pruːvmənt] n mejora;
perfeccionamiento; **to make ~s to**
mejorar.
improvise ['ɪmprəvaɪz] vt, vi improvisar.
imprudence [ɪm'pruːdns] n imprudencia.
imprudent [ɪm'pruːdnt] adj imprudente.
impudent ['ɪmpjudnt] adj descarado,
insolente.
impugn [ɪm'pjuːn] vt impugnar.
impulse ['ɪmpʌls] n impulso; **to act on ~**
sin reflexión dejarse llevar por el
impulso.
impulse buying n compra impulsiva.
impulsive [ɪm'pʌlsɪv] adj irreflexivo,
impulsivo.
impunity [ɪm'pjuːnɪtɪ] n: **with ~**
impunemente.
impure [ɪm'pjuə*] adj (adulterated)
adulterado; (morally) impuro.
impurity [ɪm'pjuərɪtɪ] n impureza.
IN abbr (US) = Indiana.

═══════════════════ KEYWORD

in [ɪn] prep **1** (indicating place, position, with
place names) en; **~ the house/garden** en
(la) casa/el jardín; **~ here/there** aquí/ahí
or allí dentro; **~ London/England** en
Londres/Inglaterra; **~ town** en el centro
(de la ciudad)
2 (indicating time) en; **~ spring** en (la)
primavera; **in 1888/May** en 1888/mayo; **~
the afternoon** por la tarde; **at 4 o'clock ~
the afternoon** a las 4 de la tarde; **I did it ~
3 hours/days** lo hice en 3 horas/días; **I'll
see you ~ 2 weeks** or **~ 2 weeks' time** te
veré dentro de 2 semanas; **once ~ a
hundred years** una vez cada cien años
3 (indicating manner etc) en; **~ a loud/soft
voice** en voz alta/baja; **~ pencil/ink** a
lápiz/bolígrafo; **the boy ~ the blue shirt**
el chico de la camisa azul; **~ writing** por
escrito; **to pay ~ dollars** pagar en dólares
4 (indicating circumstances): **~ the sun/
shade** al sol/a la sombra; **~ the rain** bajo
la lluvia; **a change ~ policy** un cambio de
política; **a rise ~ prices** un aumento de
precios
5 (indicating mood, state): **~ tears**
llorando; **~ anger/despair** enfadado/
desesperado; **to live ~ luxury** vivir
lujosamente
6 (with ratios, numbers): **1 ~ 10
households, 1 household ~ 10** una de
cada 10 familias; **20 pence ~ the pound**
20 peniques por libra; **they lined up ~
twos** se alinearon de dos en dos; **~**

hundreds a *or* por centenares
7 (*referring to people, works*) en; entre; **the disease is common ~ children** la enfermedad es común entre los niños; **~ (the works of) Dickens** en (las obras de) Dickens
8 (*indicating profession etc*): **to be ~ teaching** dedicarse a la enseñanza
9 (*after superlative*) de; **the best pupil ~ the class** el/la mejor alumno/a de la clase
10 (*with present participle*): **~ saying this** al decir esto
◆ *adv*: **to be ~** (*person: at home*) estar en casa; (: *work*) estar; (*train, ship, plane*) haber llegado; (*in fashion*) estar de moda; **she'll be ~ later today** llegará más tarde hoy; **to ask sb ~** hacer pasar a algn; **to run/limp** *etc* **~** entrar corriendo/cojeando *etc*
◆ **~ that** *conj* ya que
◆ *npl*: **the ~s and outs** (*of proposal, situation etc*) los detalles.

in., ins *abbr* = **inch(es)**.
inability [ɪnəˈbɪlɪtɪ] *n* incapacidad *f*; **~ to pay** insolvencia en el pago.
inaccessible [ɪnəkˈsɛsɪbl] *adj* inaccesible.
inaccuracy [ɪnˈækjurəsɪ] *n* inexactitud *f*.
inaccurate [ɪnˈækjurət] *adj* inexacto, incorrecto.
inaction [ɪnˈækʃən] *n* inacción *f*.
inactive [ɪnˈæktɪv] *adj* inactivo.
inactivity [ɪnækˈtɪvɪtɪ] *n* inactividad *f*.
inadequacy [ɪnˈædɪkwəsɪ] *n* insuficiencia; incapacidad *f*.
inadequate [ɪnˈædɪkwət] *adj* (*insufficient*) insuficiente; (*unsuitable*) inadecuado; (*person*) incapaz.
inadmissible [ɪnədˈmɪsəbl] *adj* improcedente, inadmisible.
inadvertent [ɪnədˈvəːtənt] *adj* descuidado, involuntario.
inadvertently [ɪnədˈvəːtntlɪ] *adv* por descuido.
inadvisable [ɪnədˈvaɪzəbl] *adj* poco aconsejable.
inane [ɪˈneɪn] *adj* necio, fatuo.
inanimate [ɪnˈænɪmət] *adj* inanimado.
inapplicable [ɪnˈæplɪkəbl] *adj* inaplicable.
inappropriate [ɪnəˈprəuprɪət] *adj* inadecuado.
inapt [ɪnˈæpt] *adj* impropio.
inaptitude [ɪnˈæptɪtjuːd] *n* incapacidad *f*.
inarticulate [ɪnɑːˈtɪkjulət] *adj* (*person*) incapaz de expresarse; (*speech*) mal pronunciado.
inartistic [ɪnɑːˈtɪstɪk] *adj* antiestético.
inasmuch as [ɪnəzˈmʌtʃ-] *adv* en la medida en que.

inattention [ɪnəˈtɛnʃən] *n* desatención *f*.
inattentive [ɪnəˈtɛntɪv] *adj* distraído.
inaudible [ɪnˈɔːdɪbl] *adj* inaudible.
inaugural [ɪˈnɔːgjurəl] *adj* inaugural; (*speech*) de apertura.
inaugurate [ɪˈnɔːgjureɪt] *vt* inaugurar; (*president, official*) investir.
inauguration [ɪnɔːgjuˈreɪʃən] *n* inauguración *f*; (*of official*) investidura; (*of event*) ceremonia de apertura.
inauspicious [ɪnɔːsˈpɪʃəs] *adj* poco propicio, inoportuno.
in-between [ɪnbɪˈtwiːn] *adj* intermedio.
inborn [ɪnˈbɔːn] *adj* (*feeling*) innato.
inbred [ɪnˈbrɛd] *adj* innato; (*family*) consanguíneo.
inbreeding [ɪnˈbriːdɪŋ] *n* endogamia.
Inc. *abbr* = **incorporated**.
Inca [ˈɪŋkə] *adj* (*also*: **~n**) inca, de los incas
◆ *n* inca *m/f*.
incalculable [ɪnˈkælkjuləbl] *adj* incalculable.
incapability [ɪnkeɪpəˈbɪlɪtɪ] *n* incapacidad *f*.
incapable [ɪnˈkeɪpəbl] *adj*: **~ (of doing sth)** incapaz (de hacer algo).
incapacitate [ɪnkəˈpæsɪteɪt] *vt*: **to ~ sb** incapacitar a algn.
incapacitated [ɪnkəˈpæsɪteɪtɪd] *adj* incapacitado.
incapacity [ɪnkəˈpæsɪtɪ] *n* (*inability*) incapacidad *f*.
incarcerate [ɪnˈkɑːsəreɪt] *vt* encarcelar.
incarnate *adj* [ɪnˈkɑːnɪt] en persona ◆ *vt* [ˈɪnkɑːneɪt] encarnar.
incarnation [ɪnkɑːˈneɪʃən] *n* encarnación *f*.
incendiary [ɪnˈsɛndɪərɪ] *adj* incendiario ◆ *n* (*bomb*) bomba incendiaria.
incense *n* [ˈɪnsɛns] incienso ◆ *vt* [ɪnˈsɛns] (*anger*) indignar, encolerizar.
incentive [ɪnˈsɛntɪv] *n* incentivo, estímulo.
incentive bonus *n* prima.
incentive scheme *n* plan *m* de incentivos.
inception [ɪnˈsɛpʃən] *n* comienzo, principio.
incessant [ɪnˈsɛsnt] *adj* incesante, continuo.
incessantly [ɪnˈsɛsəntlɪ] *adv* constantemente.
incest [ˈɪnsɛst] *n* incesto.
inch [ɪntʃ] *n* pulgada; **to be within an ~ of** estar a dos dedos de; **he didn't give an ~** no hizo la más mínima concesión; **a few ~es** unas pulgadas.
▶**inch forward** *vi* avanzar palmo a palmo.
incidence [ˈɪnsɪdns] *n* (*of crime, disease*) incidencia.
incident [ˈɪnsɪdnt] *n* incidente *m*; (*in book*)

episodio.

incidental [ɪnsɪ'dɛntl] *adj* circunstancial, accesorio; (*unplanned*) fortuito; ~ **to** relacionado con; ~ **expenses** (gastos *mpl*) imprevistos *mpl*.

incidentally [ɪnsɪ'dɛntəlɪ] *adv* (*by the way*) por cierto.

incidental music *n* música de fondo.

incident room *n* (*POLICE*) centro de coordinación.

incinerate [ɪn'sɪnəreɪt] *vt* incinerar, quemar.

incinerator [ɪn'sɪnəreɪtə*] *n* incinerador *m*, incineradora.

incipient [ɪn'sɪpɪənt] *adj* incipiente.

incision [ɪn'sɪʒən] *n* incisión *f*.

incisive [ɪn'saɪsɪv] *adj* (*mind*) penetrante; (*remark etc*) incisivo.

incisor [ɪn'saɪzə*] *n* incisivo.

incite [ɪn'saɪt] *vt* provocar, incitar.

incl. *abbr* = **including; inclusive (of)**.

inclement [ɪn'klɛmənt] *adj* inclemente.

inclination [ɪnklɪ'neɪʃən] *n* (*tendency*) tendencia, inclinación *f*.

incline *n* ['ɪnklaɪn] pendiente *f*, cuesta ♦ *vb* [ɪn'klaɪn] *vt* (*slope*) inclinar; (*head*) poner de lado ♦ *vi* inclinarse; **to be** ~**d to** (*tend*) ser propenso a; (*be willing*) estar dispuesto a.

include [ɪn'kluːd] *vt* incluir, comprender; (*in letter*) adjuntar; **the tip is/is not** ~**d** la propina está/no está incluida.

including [ɪn'kluːdɪŋ] *prep* incluso, inclusive; ~ **tip** propina incluida.

inclusion [ɪn'kluːʒən] *n* inclusión *f*.

inclusive [ɪn'kluːsɪv] *adj* inclusivo ♦ *adv* inclusive; ~ **of tax** incluidos los impuestos; **$50,** ~ **of all surcharges** 50 dólares, incluidos todos los recargos.

incognito [ɪnkɔg'niːtəu] *adv* de incógnito.

incoherent [ɪnkəu'hɪərənt] *adj* incoherente.

income ['ɪnkʌm] *n* (*personal*) ingresos *mpl*; (*from property etc*) renta; (*profit*) rédito; **gross/net** ~ ingresos *mpl* brutos/netos; ~ **and expenditure account** cuenta de gastos e ingresos.

income bracket *n* categoría económica.

income support *n* (*BRIT*) ≈ ayuda familiar.

income tax *n* impuesto sobre la renta.

income tax inspector *n* inspector(a) *m/f* de Hacienda.

income tax return *n* declaración *f* de ingresos.

incoming ['ɪnkʌmɪŋ] *adj* (*passengers, flight*) de llegada; (*government*) entrante; (*tenant*) nuevo.

incommunicado ['ɪnkəmjunɪ'kɑːdəu] *adj*: **to**

hold sb ~ mantener incomunicado a algn.

incomparable [ɪn'kɔmpərəbl] *adj* incomparable, sin par.

incompatible [ɪnkəm'pætɪbl] *adj* incompatible.

incompetence [ɪn'kɔmpɪtəns] *n* incompetencia.

incompetent [ɪn'kɔmpɪtənt] *adj* incompetente.

incomplete [ɪnkəm'pliːt] *adj* incompleto; (*unfinished*) sin terminar.

incomprehensible [ɪnkɔmprɪ'hɛnsɪbl] *adj* incomprensible.

inconceivable [ɪnkən'siːvəbl] *adj* inconcebible.

inconclusive [ɪnkən'kluːsɪv] *adj* sin resultado (definitivo); (*argument*) poco convincente.

incongruity [ɪnkɔŋ'gruːɪtɪ] *n* incongruencia.

incongruous [ɪn'kɔŋgruəs] *adj* discordante.

inconsequential [ɪnkɔnsɪ'kwɛnʃl] *adj* intrascendente.

inconsiderable [ɪnkən'sɪdərəbl] *adj* insignificante.

inconsiderate [ɪnkən'sɪdərət] *adj* desconsiderado; **how** ~ **of him!** ¡qué falta de consideración (de su parte)!

inconsistency [ɪnkən'sɪstənsɪ] *n* inconsecuencia; (*of actions etc*) falta de lógica; (*of work*) carácter *m* desigual, inconsistencia; (*of statement etc*) contradicción *f*.

inconsistent [ɪnkən'sɪstnt] *adj* inconsecuente; ~ **with** que no concuerda con.

inconsolable [ɪnkən'səuləbl] *adj* inconsolable.

inconspicuous [ɪnkən'spɪkjuəs] *adj* (*discreet*) discreto; (*person*) que llama poco la atención.

inconstancy [ɪn'kɔnstənsɪ] *n* inconstancia.

inconstant [ɪn'kɔnstənt] *adj* inconstante.

incontinence [ɪn'kɔntɪnəns] *n* incontinencia.

incontinent [ɪn'kɔntɪnənt] *adj* incontinente.

incontrovertible [ɪnkɔntrə'vəːtəbl] *adj* incontrovertible.

inconvenience [ɪnkən'viːnjəns] *n* (*gen*) inconvenientes *mpl*; (*trouble*) molestia ♦ *vt* incomodar; **to put sb to great** ~ causar mucha molestia a algn; **don't** ~ **yourself** no se moleste.

inconvenient [ɪnkən'viːnjənt] *adj* incómodo, poco práctico; (*time, place*) inoportuno; **that time is very** ~ **for me** esa hora me es muy inconveniente.

incorporate [ɪn'kɔːpəreɪt] *vt* incorporar; (*contain*) comprender; (*add*) agregar.
incorporated [ɪn'kɔːpəreɪtɪd] *adj*: ~ **company** (*US: abbr* **Inc.**) ≈ Sociedad *f* Anónima (S.A.).
incorrect [ɪnkə'rɛkt] *adj* incorrecto.
incorrigible [ɪn'kɔrɪdʒəbl] *adj* incorregible.
incorruptible [ɪnkə'rʌptɪbl] *adj* incorruptible.
increase *n* ['ɪnkriːs] aumento ♦ *vb* [ɪn'kriːs] *vi* aumentar; (*grow*) crecer; (*price*) subir ♦ *vt* aumentar; **an ~ of 5%** un aumento de 5%; **to be on the ~** ir en aumento.
increasing [ɪn'kriːsɪŋ] *adj* (*number*) creciente, que va en aumento.
increasingly [ɪn'kriːsɪŋlɪ] *adv* cada vez más.
incredible [ɪn'krɛdɪbl] *adj* increíble.
incredibly [ɪn'krɛdɪblɪ] *adv* increíblemente.
incredulity [ɪnkrɪ'djuːlɪtɪ] *n* incredulidad *f*.
incredulous [ɪn'krɛdjuləs] *adj* incrédulo.
increment ['ɪnkrɪmənt] *n* aumento, incremento.
incriminate [ɪn'krɪmɪneɪt] *vt* incriminar.
incriminating [ɪn'krɪmɪneɪtɪŋ] *adj* incriminatorio.
incrust [ɪn'krʌst] *vt* = **encrust**.
incubate ['ɪnkjubeɪt] *vt* (*eggs*) incubar, empollar ♦ *vi* (*egg, disease*) incubar.
incubation [ɪnkju'beɪʃən] *n* incubación *f*.
incubation period *n* período de incubación.
incubator ['ɪnkjubeɪtə*] *n* incubadora.
inculcate ['ɪnkʌlkeɪt] *vt*: **to ~ sth in sb** inculcar algo en algn.
incumbent [ɪn'kʌmbənt] *n* ocupante *m/f* ♦ *adj*: **it is ~ on him to...** le incumbe....
incur [ɪn'kɜː*] *vt* (*expenses*) incurrir en; (*loss*) sufrir.
incurable [ɪn'kjuərəbl] *adj* incurable.
incursion [ɪn'kɜːʃən] *n* incursión *f*.
Ind. *abbr* (*US*) = *Indiana*.
indebted [ɪn'dɛtɪd] *adj*: **to be ~ to sb** estar agradecido a algn.
indecency [ɪn'diːsnsɪ] *n* indecencia.
indecent [ɪn'diːsnt] *adj* indecente.
indecent assault *n* (*BRIT*) atentado contra el pudor.
indecent exposure *n* exhibicionismo.
indecipherable [ɪndɪ'saɪfərəbl] *adj* indescifrable.
indecision [ɪndɪ'sɪʒən] *n* indecisión *f*.
indecisive [ɪndɪ'saɪsɪv] *adj* indeciso; (*discussion*) no resuelto, inconcluyente.
indeed [ɪn'diːd] *adv* efectivamente, en realidad; **yes ~!** ¡claro que sí!
indefatigable [ɪndɪ'fætɪgəbl] *adj* incansable, infatigable.
indefensible [ɪndɪ'fɛnsəbl] *adj* (*conduct*) injustificable.
indefinable [ɪndɪ'faɪnəbl] *adj* indefinible.
indefinite [ɪn'dɛfɪnɪt] *adj* indefinido; (*uncertain*) incierto.
indefinitely [ɪn'dɛfɪnɪtlɪ] *adv* (*wait*) indefinidamente.
indelible [ɪn'dɛlɪbl] *adj* imborrable.
indelicate [ɪn'dɛlɪkɪt] *adj* (*tactless*) indiscreto, inoportuno; (*not polite*) poco delicado.
indemnify [ɪn'dɛmnɪfaɪ] *vt* indemnizar, resarcir.
indemnity [ɪn'dɛmnɪtɪ] *n* (*insurance*) indemnidad *f*; (*compensation*) indemnización *f*.
indent [ɪn'dɛnt] *vt* (*text*) sangrar.
indentation [ɪndɛn'teɪʃən] *n* mella; (*TYP*) sangría.
indenture [ɪn'dɛntʃə*] *n* escritura, instrumento.
independence [ɪndɪ'pɛndns] *n* independencia.

El cuatro de julio es la fiesta nacional de los Estados Unidos, **Independence Day,** *en conmemoración de la Declaración de Independencia escrita por Thomas Jefferson y adoptada en 1776. En ella se proclamaba la ruptura total con Gran Bretaña de las trece colonias americanas que fueron el origen de los Estados Unidos de América.*

---

independent [ɪndɪ'pɛndənt] *adj* independiente; **to become ~** independizarse.
in-depth ['ɪndɛpθ] *adj* en profundidad, a fondo.
indescribable [ɪndɪ'skraɪbəbl] *adj* indescriptible.
indestructible [ɪndɪs'trʌktəbl] *adj* indestructible.
indeterminate [ɪndɪ'təːmɪnɪt] *adj* indeterminado.
index ['ɪndɛks] *n* (*pl:* ~**es:** *in book*) índice *m*; (: *in library etc*) catálogo; (*pl:* **indices** ['ɪndɪsiːz]: *ratio, sign*) exponente *m*.
index card *n* ficha.
index finger *n* índice *m*.
index-linked ['ɪndɛks'lɪŋkt], (*US*) **indexed** ['ɪndɛkst] *adj* indexado.
India ['ɪndɪə] *n* la India.
Indian ['ɪndɪən] *adj, n* indio/a *m/f*; (*American* ~) indio/a *m/f* de América, amerindio/a *m/f*; **Red ~** piel roja *m/f*.
Indian Ocean *n*: **the ~** el Océano Índico, el Mar de las Indias.
Indian summer *n* (*fig*) veranillo de San

Martín.
india rubber *n* caucho.
indicate ['ɪndɪkeɪt] *vt* indicar ♦ *vi* (*BRIT AUT*):
to ~ left/right indicar a la izquierda/a la
derecha.
indication [ɪndɪ'keɪʃən] *n* indicio, señal *f*.
indicative [ɪn'dɪkətɪv] *adj*: **to be ~ of sth**
indicar algo ♦ *n* (*LING*) indicativo.
indicator ['ɪndɪkeɪtə*] *n* (*gen*) indicador *m*;
(*AUT*) intermitente *m*, direccional *m*
(*LAM*).
indices ['ɪndɪsiːz] *npl of* **index**.
indict [ɪn'daɪt] *vt* acusar.
indictable [ɪn'daɪtəbl] *adj*: **~ offence** delito
procesable.
indictment [ɪn'daɪtmənt] *n* acusación *f*.
indifference [ɪn'dɪfrəns] *n* indiferencia.
indifferent [ɪn'dɪfrənt] *adj* indiferente;
(*poor*) regular.
indigenous [ɪn'dɪdʒɪnəs] *adj* indígena.
indigestible [ɪndɪ'dʒɛstɪbl] *adj* indigesto.
indigestion [ɪndɪ'dʒɛstʃən] *n* indigestión *f*.
indignant [ɪn'dɪgnənt] *adj*: **to be ~ about**
sth indignarse por algo.
indignation [ɪndɪg'neɪʃən] *n* indignación *f*.
indignity [ɪn'dɪgnɪtɪ] *n* indignidad *f*.
indigo ['ɪndɪgəu] *adj* (*colour*) (de color) añil
♦ *n* añil *m*.
indirect [ɪndɪ'rɛkt] *adj* indirecto.
indirectly [ɪndɪ'rɛktlɪ] *adv* indirectamente.
indiscernible [ɪndɪ'səːnəbl] *adj*
imperceptible.
indiscreet [ɪndɪ'skriːt] *adj* indiscreto,
imprudente.
indiscretion [ɪndɪ'skrɛʃən] *n* indiscreción *f*,
imprudencia.
indiscriminate [ɪndɪ'skrɪmɪnət] *adj*
indiscriminado.
indispensable [ɪndɪ'spɛnsəbl] *adj*
indispensable, imprescindible.
indisposed [ɪndɪ'spəuzd] *adj* (*unwell*)
indispuesto.
indisposition [ɪndɪspə'zɪʃən] *n*
indisposición *f*.
indisputable [ɪndɪ'spjuːtəbl] *adj*
incontestable.
indistinct [ɪndɪ'stɪŋkt] *adj* indistinto.
indistinguishable [ɪndɪ'stɪŋgwɪʃəbl] *adj*
indistinguible.
individual [ɪndɪ'vɪdjuəl] *n* individuo ♦ *adj*
individual; (*personal*) personal; (*for/of one*
only) particular.
individualist [ɪndɪ'vɪdjuəlɪst] *n*
individualista *m/f*.
individuality [ɪndɪvɪdju'ælɪtɪ] *n*
individualidad *f*.
individually [ɪndɪ'vɪdjuəlɪ] *adv*
individualmente; particularmente.

indivisible [ɪndɪ'vɪzəbl] *adj* indivisible.
Indo-China ['ɪndəu'tʃaɪnə] *n* Indochina.
indoctrinate [ɪn'dɔktrɪneɪt] *vt* adoctrinar.
indoctrination [ɪndɔktrɪ'neɪʃən] *n*
adoctrinamiento.
indolence ['ɪndələns] *n* indolencia.
indolent ['ɪndələnt] *adj* indolente, perezoso.
Indonesia [ɪndə'niːzɪə] *n* Indonesia.
Indonesian [ɪndə'niːzɪən] *adj* indonesio ♦ *n*
indonesio/a; (*LING*) indonesio.
indoor ['ɪndɔː*] *adj* (*swimming pool*)
cubierto; (*plant*) de interior; (*sport*) bajo
cubierta.
indoors [ɪn'dɔːz] *adv* dentro; (*at home*) en
casa.
indubitable [ɪn'djuːbɪtəbl] *adj* indudable.
indubitably [ɪn'djuːbɪtəblɪ] *adv*
indudablemente.
induce [ɪn'djuːs] *vt* inducir, persuadir;
(*bring about*) producir; **to ~ sb to do sth**
persuadir a algn a que haga algo.
inducement [ɪn'djuːsmənt] *n* (*incentive*)
incentivo, aliciente *m*.
induct [ɪn'dʌkt] *vt* iniciar; (*in job, rank,*
position) instalar.
induction [ɪn'dʌkʃən] *n* (*MED: of birth*)
inducción *f*.
induction course *n* (*BRIT*) cursillo
introductorio *or* de iniciación.
indulge [ɪn'dʌldʒ] *vt* (*whim*) satisfacer;
(*person*) complacer; (*child*) mimar ♦ *vi*:
~ in darse el gusto de.
indulgence [ɪn'dʌldʒəns] *n* vicio.
indulgent [ɪn'dʌldʒənt] *adj* indulgente.
industrial [ɪn'dʌstrɪəl] *adj* industrial.
industrial action *n* huelga.
industrial estate *n* (*BRIT*) polígono *or* zona
(*LAM*) industrial.
industrial goods *npl* bienes *mpl* de
producción.
industrialist [ɪn'dʌstrɪəlɪst] *n* industrial *m/f*.
industrialize [ɪn'dʌstrɪəlaɪz] *vt*
industrializar.
industrial park *n* (*US*) = **industrial estate**.
industrial relations *npl* relaciones *fpl*
empresariales.
industrial tribunal *n* magistratura de
trabajo, tribunal *m* laboral.
industrial unrest *n* (*BRIT*) agitación *f*
obrera.
industrious [ɪn'dʌstrɪəs] *adj* (*gen*)
trabajador(a); (*student*) aplicado.
industry ['ɪndəstrɪ] *n* industria; (*diligence*)
aplicación *f*.
inebriated [ɪ'niːbrɪeɪtɪd] *adj* borracho.
inedible [ɪn'ɛdɪbl] *adj* incomible; (*plant etc*)
no comestible.
ineffective [ɪnɪ'fɛktɪv], **ineffectual**

[ɪnɪˈfɛktʃʊəl] *adj* ineficaz, inútil.

inefficiency [ɪnɪˈfɪʃənsɪ] *n* ineficacia.

inefficient [ɪnɪˈfɪʃənt] *adj* ineficaz, ineficiente.

inelegant [ɪnˈɛlɪgənt] *adj* poco elegante.

ineligible [ɪnˈɛlɪdʒɪbl] *adj* inelegible.

inept [ɪˈnɛpt] *adj* incompetente, incapaz.

ineptitude [ɪˈnɛptɪtjuːd] *n* incapacidad *f*, ineptitud *f*.

inequality [ɪnɪˈkwɔlɪtɪ] *n* desigualdad *f*.

inequitable [ɪnˈɛkwɪtəbl] *adj* injusto.

ineradicable [ɪnɪˈrædɪkəbl] *adj* inextirpable.

inert [ɪˈnɜːt] *adj* inerte, inactivo; (*immobile*) inmóvil.

inertia [ɪˈnɜːʃə] *n* inercia; (*laziness*) pereza.

inertia-reel seat-belt [ɪˈnɜːʃəˈriːl-] *n* cinturón *m* de seguridad retráctil.

inescapable [ɪnɪˈskeɪpəbl] *adj* ineludible, inevitable.

inessential [ɪnɪˈsɛnʃl] *adj* no esencial.

inestimable [ɪnˈɛstɪməbl] *adj* inestimable.

inevitability [ɪnɛvɪtəˈbɪlɪtɪ] *n* inevitabilidad *f*.

inevitable [ɪnˈɛvɪtəbl] *adj* inevitable; (*necessary*) forzoso.

inevitably [ɪnˈɛvɪtəblɪ] *adv* inevitablemente; **as ~ happens** ... como siempre pasa ....

inexact [ɪnɪgˈzaekt] *adj* inexacto.

inexcusable [ɪnɪksˈkjuːzəbl] *adj* imperdonable.

inexhaustible [ɪnɪgˈzɔːstɪbl] *adj* inagotable.

inexorable [ɪnˈɛksərəbl] *adj* inexorable, implacable.

inexpensive [ɪnɪkˈspɛnsɪv] *adj* económico.

inexperience [ɪnɪkˈspɪərɪəns] *n* falta de experiencia.

inexperienced [ɪnɪkˈspɪərɪənst] *adj* inexperto; **to be ~ in sth** no tener experiencia en algo.

inexplicable [ɪnɪkˈsplɪkəbl] *adj* inexplicable.

inexpressible [ɪnɪkˈsprɛsəbl] *adj* inexpresable.

inextricable [ɪnɪksˈtrɪkəbl] *adj* inseparable.

inextricably [ɪnɪksˈtrɪkəblɪ] *adv* indisolublemente.

infallibility [ɪnfælɪˈbɪlɪtɪ] *n* infalibilidad *f*.

infallible [ɪnˈfælɪbl] *adj* infalible.

infamous [ˈɪnfəməs] *adj* infame.

infamy [ˈɪnfəmɪ] *n* infamia.

infancy [ˈɪnfənsɪ] *n* infancia.

infant [ˈɪnfənt] *n* niño/a.

infantile [ˈɪnfəntaɪl] *adj* infantil; (*pej*) aniñado.

infant mortality *n* mortalidad *f* infantil.

infantry [ˈɪnfəntrɪ] *n* infantería.

infantryman [ˈɪnfəntrɪmən] *n* soldado de

infantería.

infant school *n* (*BRIT*) escuela de párvulos; *see also* **primary school**.

infatuated [ɪnˈfætjʊeɪtɪd] *adj*: ~ **with** (*in love*) loco por; **to become ~ (with sb)** enamoriscarse (de algn), encapricharse (con algn).

infatuation [ɪnfætjʊˈeɪʃən] *n* enamoramiento.

infect [ɪnˈfɛkt] *vt* (*wound*) infectar; (*person*) contagiar; (*fig*: *pej*) corromper; **~ed with** (*illness*) contagiado de; **to become ~ed** (*wound*) infectarse.

infection [ɪnˈfɛkʃən] *n* infección *f*; (*fig*) contagio.

infectious [ɪnˈfɛkʃəs] *adj* contagioso; (*also fig*) infeccioso.

infer [ɪnˈfɜː*] *vt* deducir, inferir; **to ~ (from)** inferir (de), deducir (de).

inference [ˈɪnfərəns] *n* deducción *f*, inferencia.

inferior [ɪnˈfɪərɪə*] *adj*, *n* inferior *m/f*; **to feel ~** sentirse inferior.

inferiority [ɪnfɪərɪˈɔrətɪ] *n* inferioridad *f*.

inferiority complex *n* complejo de inferioridad.

infernal [ɪnˈfɜːnl] *adj* infernal.

inferno [ɪnˈfɜːnəʊ] *n* infierno; (*fig*) hoguera.

infertile [ɪnˈfɜːtaɪl] *adj* estéril; (*person*) infecundo.

infertility [ɪnfəˈtɪlɪtɪ] *n* esterilidad *f*; infecundidad *f*.

infest [ɪnˈfɛst] *vt* infestar.

infested [ɪnˈfɛstɪd] *adj*: ~ **(with)** plagado (de).

infidel [ˈɪnfɪdəl] *n* infiel *m/f*.

infidelity [ɪnfɪˈdɛlɪtɪ] *n* infidelidad *f*.

in-fighting [ˈɪnfaɪtɪŋ] *n* (*fig*) lucha(s) *f(pl)* interna(s).

infiltrate [ˈɪnfɪltreɪt] *vt* (*troops etc*) infiltrarse en ♦ *vi* infiltrarse.

infinite [ˈɪnfɪnɪt] *adj* infinito; **an ~ amount of money/time** un sinfín de dinero/tiempo.

infinitely [ˈɪnfɪnɪtlɪ] *adv* infinitamente.

infinitesimal [ɪnfɪnɪˈtɛsɪməl] *adj* infinitésimo.

infinitive [ɪnˈfɪnɪtɪv] *n* infinitivo.

infinity [ɪnˈfɪnɪtɪ] *n* (*also MATH*) infinito; (*an ~*) infinidad *f*.

infirm [ɪnˈfɜːm] *adj* enfermizo, débil.

infirmary [ɪnˈfɜːmərɪ] *n* hospital *m*.

infirmity [ɪnˈfɜːmɪtɪ] *n* debilidad *f*; (*illness*) enfermedad *f*, achaque *m*.

inflame [ɪnˈfleɪm] *vt* inflamar.

inflamed [ɪnˈfleɪmd] *adj*: **to become ~** inflamarse.

inflammable [ɪnˈflæməbl] *adj* (*BRIT*)

inflamable; (*situation etc*) explosivo.

inflammation [ɪnfləˈmeɪʃən] *n* inflamación *f*.

inflammatory [ɪnˈflæmətərɪ] *adj* (*speech*) incendiario.

inflatable [ɪnˈfleɪtəbl] *adj* inflable.

inflate [ɪnˈfleɪt] *vt* (*tyre, balloon*) inflar; (*fig*) hinchar.

inflated [ɪnˈfleɪtɪd] *adj* (*tyre etc*) inflado; (*price, self-esteem etc*) exagerado.

inflation [ɪnˈfleɪʃən] *n* (*ECON*) inflación *f*.

inflationary [ɪnˈfleɪʃnərɪ] *adj* inflacionario.

inflationary spiral *n* espiral *f* inflacionista.

inflexible [ɪnˈflɛksɪbl] *adj* inflexible.

inflict [ɪnˈflɪkt] *vt*: **to ~ on** infligir en; (*tax etc*) imponer a.

infliction [ɪnˈflɪkʃən] *n* imposición *f*.

in-flight [ˈɪnflaɪt] *adj* durante el vuelo.

inflow [ˈɪnfləu] *n* afluencia.

influence [ˈɪnfluəns] *n* influencia ♦ *vt* influir en, influenciar; **under the ~ of alcohol** en estado de embriaguez.

influential [ɪnfluˈɛnʃl] *adj* influyente.

influenza [ɪnfluˈɛnzə] *n* gripe *f*.

influx [ˈɪnflʌks] *n* afluencia.

inform [ɪnˈfɔːm] *vt*: **to ~ sb of sth** informar a algn sobre *or* de algo; (*warn*) avisar a algn de algo; (*communicate*) comunicar algo a algn ♦ *vi*: **to ~ on sb** delatar a algn.

informal [ɪnˈfɔːml] *adj* (*manner, tone*) desenfadado; (*dress, interview, occasion*) informal.

informality [ɪnfɔːˈmælɪtɪ] *n* falta de ceremonia; (*intimacy*) intimidad *f*; (*familiarity*) familiaridad *f*; (*ease*) afabilidad *f*.

informally [ɪnˈfɔːməlɪ] *adv* sin ceremonia; (*invite*) informalmente.

informant [ɪnˈfɔːmənt] *n* informante *m/f*.

informatics [ɪnfɔːˈmætɪks] *n* informática.

information [ɪnfəˈmeɪʃən] *n* información *f*; (*news*) noticias *fpl*; (*knowledge*) conocimientos *mpl*; (*LAW*) delación *f*; **a piece of ~** un dato; **for your ~** para su información.

information bureau *n* oficina de información.

information processing *n* procesamiento de datos.

information retrieval *n* recuperación *f* de información.

information science *n* gestión *f* de la información.

information technology (IT) *n* informática.

informative [ɪnˈfɔːmətɪv] *adj* informativo.

informed [ɪnˈfɔːmd] *adj* (*observer*) informado, al corriente; **an ~ guess** una

opinión bien fundamentada.

informer [ɪnˈfɔːmə*] *n* delator(a) *m/f*; (*also*: **police ~**) soplón/ona *m/f*.

infra dig [ˈɪnfrəˈdɪg] *adj abbr* (*col*: = *infra dignitatem*) denigrante.

infra-red [ɪnfrəˈrɛd] *adj* infrarrojo.

infrastructure [ˈɪnfrəstrʌktʃə*] *n* (*of system etc, ECON*) infraestructura.

infrequent [ɪnˈfriːkwənt] *adj* infrecuente.

infringe [ɪnˈfrɪndʒ] *vt* infringir, violar ♦ *vi*: **to ~ on** invadir.

infringement [ɪnˈfrɪndʒmənt] *n* infracción *f*; (*of rights*) usurpación *f*; (*SPORT*) falta.

infuriate [ɪnˈfjuərɪeɪt] *vt*: **to become ~d** ponerse furioso.

infuriating [ɪnˈfjuərɪeɪtɪŋ] *adj*: **I find it ~** me saca de quicio.

infuse [ɪnˈfjuːz] *vt* (*with courage, enthusiasm*): **to ~ sb with sth** infundir algo a algn.

infusion [ɪnˈfjuːʒən] *n* (*tea etc*) infusión *f*.

ingenious [ɪnˈdʒiːnjəs] *adj* ingenioso.

ingenuity [ɪndʒɪˈnjuːɪtɪ] *n* ingeniosidad *f*.

ingenuous [ɪnˈdʒɛnjuəs] *adj* ingenuo.

ingot [ˈɪŋgət] *n* lingote *m*, barra.

ingrained [ɪnˈgreɪnd] *adj* arraigado.

ingratiate [ɪnˈgreɪʃɪeɪt] *vt*: **to ~ o.s. with** congraciarse con.

ingratiating [ɪnˈgreɪʃɪeɪtɪŋ] *adj* (*smile, speech*) insinuante; (*person*) zalamero, congraciador(a).

ingratitude [ɪnˈgrætɪtjuːd] *n* ingratitud *f*.

ingredient [ɪnˈgriːdɪənt] *n* ingrediente *m*.

ingrowing [ˈɪngrəuɪŋ] *adj*: **~ (toe)nail** uña encarnada.

inhabit [ɪnˈhæbɪt] *vt* vivir en; (*occupy*) ocupar.

inhabitable [ɪnˈhæbɪtəbl] *adj* habitable.

inhabitant [ɪnˈhæbɪtənt] *n* habitante *m/f*.

inhale [ɪnˈheɪl] *vt* inhalar ♦ *vi* (*in smoking*) tragar.

inhaler [ɪnˈheɪlə*] *n* inhalador *m*.

inherent [ɪnˈhɪərənt] *adj*: **~ in** or **to** inherente a.

inherently [ɪnˈhɪərəntlɪ] *adv* intrínsecamente.

inherit [ɪnˈhɛrɪt] *vt* heredar.

inheritance [ɪnˈhɛrɪtəns] *n* herencia; (*fig*) patrimonio.

inhibit [ɪnˈhɪbɪt] *vt* inhibir, impedir; **to ~ sb from doing sth** impedir a algn hacer algo.

inhibited [ɪnˈhɪbɪtɪd] *adj* (*person*) cohibido.

inhibition [ɪnhɪˈbɪʃən] *n* cohibición *f*.

inhospitable [ɪnhɔsˈpɪtəbl] *adj* (*person*) inhospitalario; (*place*) inhóspito.

in-house [ˈɪnhaus] *adj* dentro de la empresa.

inhuman [ɪnˈhjuːmən] *adj* inhumano.

inhumane [ɪnhjuː'meɪn] adj inhumano.
inimitable [ɪ'nɪmɪtəbl] adj inimitable.
iniquity [ɪ'nɪkwɪtɪ] n iniquidad f; (injustice) injusticia.
initial [ɪ'nɪʃl] adj inicial; (first) primero ♦ n inicial f ♦ vt firmar con las iniciales; ~s npl iniciales fpl; (abbreviation) siglas fpl.
initialize [ɪ'nɪʃəlaɪz] vt (COMPUT) inicializar.
initially [ɪ'nɪʃəlɪ] adv en un principio.
initiate [ɪ'nɪʃɪeɪt] vt (start) iniciar; **to ~ sb into a secret** iniciar a algn en un secreto; **to ~ proceedings against sb** (LAW) poner una demanda contra algn.
initiation [ɪnɪʃɪ'eɪʃən] n (into secret etc) iniciación f; (beginning) comienzo.
initiative [ɪ'nɪʃətɪv] n iniciativa; **to take the ~** tomar la iniciativa.
inject [ɪn'dʒɛkt] vt inyectar; (money, enthusiasm) aportar.
injection [ɪn'dʒɛkʃən] n inyección f; **to have an ~** ponerse una inyección.
injudicious [ɪndʒu'dɪʃəs] adj imprudente, indiscreto.
injunction [ɪn'dʒʌŋkʃən] n entredicho, interdicto.
injure ['ɪndʒə*] vt herir; (hurt) lastimar; (fig: reputation etc) perjudicar; (feelings) herir; **to ~ o.s** hacerse daño, lastimarse.
injured ['ɪndʒəd] adj (also fig) herido; ~ **party** (LAW) parte f perjudicada.
injurious [ɪn'dʒuərɪəs] adj: ~ **(to)** perjudicial (para).
injury ['ɪndʒərɪ] n herida, lesión f; (wrong) perjuicio, daño; **to escape without ~** salir ileso.
injury time n (SPORT) descuento.
injustice [ɪn'dʒʌstɪs] n injusticia; **you do me an ~** usted es injusto conmigo.
ink [ɪŋk] n tinta.
ink-jet printer ['ɪŋkdʒɛt-] n impresora de chorro de tinta.
inkling ['ɪŋklɪŋ] n sospecha; (idea) idea.
inkpad ['ɪŋkpæd] n almohadilla.
inlaid ['ɪnleɪd] adj (wood) taraceado; (tiles) entarimado.
inland adj ['ɪnlənd] interior; (town) del interior ♦ adv [ɪn'lænd] tierra adentro.
Inland Revenue n (BRIT) Hacienda.
in-laws ['ɪnlɔːz] npl suegros mpl.
inlet ['ɪnlɛt] n (GEO) ensenada, cala; (TECH) admisión f, entrada.
inmate ['ɪnmeɪt] n (in prison) preso/a, presidiario/a; (in asylum) internado/a.
inmost ['ɪnməust] adj más íntimo, más secreto.
inn [ɪn] n posada, mesón m; **the I~s of Court** see **barrister**.
innards ['ɪnədz] npl (col) tripas fpl.

innate [ɪ'neɪt] adj innato.
inner ['ɪnə*] adj interior, interno.
inner city n barrios deprimidos del centro de una ciudad.
innermost ['ɪnəməust] adj más íntimo, más secreto.
inner tube n (of tyre) cámara, llanta (LAM).
innings ['ɪnɪŋz] n (CRICKET) entrada, turno.
innocence ['ɪnəsns] n inocencia.
innocent ['ɪnəsnt] adj inocente.
innocuous [ɪ'nɔkjuəs] adj inocuo.
innovation [ɪnəu'veɪʃən] n novedad f.
innuendo, ~es [ɪnju'ɛndəu] n indirecta.
innumerable [ɪ'njuːmrəbl] adj innumerable.
inoculate [ɪ'nɔkjuleɪt] vt: **to ~ sb with sth/ against sth** inocular or vacunar a algn con algo/contra algo.
inoculation [ɪnɔkju'leɪʃən] n inoculación f.
inoffensive [ɪnə'fɛnsɪv] adj inofensivo.
inopportune [ɪn'ɔpətjuːn] adj inoportuno.
inordinate [ɪ'nɔːdɪnət] adj excesivo, desmesurado.
inordinately [ɪ'nɔːdɪnətlɪ] adv excesivamente, desmesuradamente.
inorganic [ɪnɔː'gænɪk] adj inorgánico.
in-patient ['ɪnpeɪʃənt] n (paciente m/f) interno/a.
input ['ɪnput] n (ELEC) entrada; (COMPUT) entrada de datos ♦ vt (COMPUT) introducir, entrar.
inquest ['ɪnkwɛst] n (coroner's) investigación f post-mortem.
inquire [ɪn'kwaɪə*] vi preguntar ♦ vt: **to ~ when/where/whether** preguntar cuándo/dónde/si; **to ~ about** (person) preguntar por; (fact) informarse de.
▶**inquire into** vt fus: **to ~ into sth** investigar or indagar algo.
inquiring [ɪn'kwaɪərɪŋ] adj (mind) inquieto; (look) interrogante.
inquiry [ɪn'kwaɪərɪ] n pregunta; (LAW) investigación f, pesquisa; (commission) comisión f investigadora; **to hold an ~ into sth** emprender una investigación sobre algo.
inquiry desk n mesa de información.
inquiry office n (BRIT) oficina de información.
inquisition [ɪnkwɪ'zɪʃən] n inquisición f.
inquisitive [ɪn'kwɪzɪtɪv] adj (mind) inquisitivo; (person) fisgón/ona.
inroad ['ɪnrəud] n incursión f; (fig) invasión f; **to make ~s into** (time) ocupar parte de; (savings, supplies) agotar parte de.
insane [ɪn'seɪn] adj loco; (MED) demente.
insanitary [ɪn'sænɪtərɪ] adj insalubre.
insanity [ɪn'sænɪtɪ] n demencia, locura.

insatiable [ɪnˈseɪʃəbl] *adj* insaciable.
inscribe [ɪnˈskraɪb] *vt* inscribir; (*book etc*): **to ~ (to sb)** dedicar (a algn).
inscription [ɪnˈskrɪpʃən] *n* (*gen*) inscripción *f*; (*in book*) dedicatoria.
inscrutable [ɪnˈskruːtəbl] *adj* inescrutable, insondable.
inseam measurement [ˈɪnsiːm-] *n* (*US*) = **inside leg measurement**.
insect [ˈɪnsɛkt] *n* insecto.
insect bite *n* picadura.
insecticide [ɪnˈsɛktɪsaɪd] *n* insecticida *m*.
insect repellent *n* loción *f* contra los insectos.
insecure [ɪnsɪˈkjuə*] *adj* inseguro.
insecurity [ɪnsɪˈkjuərɪtɪ] *n* inseguridad *f*.
insemination [ɪnsɛmɪˈneɪʃn] *n*: **artificial ~** inseminación *f* artificial.
insensible [ɪnˈsɛnsɪbl] *adj* inconsciente; (*unconscious*) sin conocimiento.
insensitive [ɪnˈsɛnsɪtɪv] *adj* insensible.
insensitivity [ɪnsɛnsɪˈtɪvɪtɪ] *n* insensibilidad *f*.
inseparable [ɪnˈsɛprəbl] *adj* inseparable; **they were ~ friends** los unía una estrecha amistad.
insert *vt* [ɪnˈsəːt] (*into sth*) introducir; (*COMPUT*) insertar ♦ *n* [ˈɪnsəːt] encarte *m*.
insertion [ɪnˈsəːʃən] *n* inserción *f*.
in-service [ɪnˈsəːvɪs] *adj* (*training, course*) en el trabajo, a cargo de la empresa.
inshore [ɪnˈʃɔː*] *adj*: **~ fishing** pesca *f* costera ♦ *adv* (*fish*) a lo largo de la costa; (*move*) hacia la orilla.
inside [ˈɪnˈsaɪd] *n* interior *m*; (*lining*) forro; (*of road*: *BRIT*) izquierdo; (: *US, Europe etc*) derecho ♦ *adj* interior, interno; (*information*) confidencial ♦ *adv* (*within*) (por) dentro, adentro (*esp LAM*); (*with movement*) hacia dentro; (*fam*: *in prison*) en chirona ♦ *prep* dentro de; (*of time*): **~ 10 minutes** en menos de 10 minutos; **~s** *npl* (*col*) tripas *fpl*; **~ out** *adv* (*turn*) al revés; (*know*) a fondo.
inside forward *n* (*SPORT*) interior *m*.
inside information *n* información *f* confidencial.
inside lane *n* (*AUT*: *in Britain*) carril *m* izquierdo; (: *in US, Europe*) carril *m* derecho.
inside leg measurement *n* medida de pernera.
insider [ɪnˈsaɪdə*] *n* enterado/a.
insider dealing, insider trading *n* (*STOCK EXCHANGE*) abuso de información privilegiada.
inside story *n* historia íntima.
insidious [ɪnˈsɪdɪəs] *adj* insidioso.

insight [ˈɪnsaɪt] *n* perspicacia, percepción *f*; **to gain** *or* **get an ~ into sth** comprender algo mejor.
insignia [ɪnˈsɪgnɪə] *npl* insignias *fpl*.
insignificant [ɪnsɪgˈnɪfɪknt] *adj* insignificante.
insincere [ɪnsɪnˈsɪə*] *adj* poco sincero.
insincerity [ɪnsɪnˈsɛrɪtɪ] *n* falta de sinceridad, doblez *f*.
insinuate [ɪnˈsɪnjueɪt] *vt* insinuar.
insinuation [ɪnsɪnjuˈeɪʃən] *n* insinuación *f*.
insipid [ɪnˈsɪpɪd] *adj* soso, insulso.
insist [ɪnˈsɪst] *vi* insistir; **to ~ on doing** empeñarse en hacer; **to ~ that** insistir en que; (*claim*) exigir que.
insistence [ɪnˈsɪstəns] *n* insistencia; (*stubbornness*) empeño.
insistent [ɪnˈsɪstənt] *adj* insistente; empeñado.
insofar as [ɪnsəʊˈfɑː-] *conj* en la medida en que, en tanto que.
insole [ˈɪnsəʊl] *n* plantilla.
insolence [ˈɪnsələns] *n* insolencia, descaro.
insolent [ˈɪnsələnt] *adj* insolente, descarado.
insoluble [ɪnˈsɔljubl] *adj* insoluble.
insolvency [ɪnˈsɔlvənsɪ] *n* insolvencia.
insolvent [ɪnˈsɔlvənt] *adj* insolvente.
insomnia [ɪnˈsɔmnɪə] *n* insomnio.
insomniac [ɪnˈsɔmnɪæk] *n* insomne *m/f*.
inspect [ɪnˈspɛkt] *vt* inspeccionar, examinar; (*troops*) pasar revista a.
inspection [ɪnˈspɛkʃən] *n* inspección *f*, examen *m*.
inspector [ɪnˈspɛktə*] *n* inspector(a) *m/f*; (*BRIT*: *on buses, trains*) revisor(a) *m/f*.
inspiration [ɪnspəˈreɪʃən] *n* inspiración *f*.
inspire [ɪnˈspaɪə*] *vt* inspirar; **to ~ sb (to do sth)** alentar a algn (a hacer algo).
inspired [ɪnˈspaɪəd] *adj* (*writer, book etc*) inspirado, genial, iluminado; **in an ~ moment** en un momento de inspiración.
inspiring [ɪnˈspaɪərɪŋ] *adj* inspirador(a).
inst. *abbr* (*BRIT COMM*: = *instant, of the present month*) cte.
instability [ɪnstəˈbɪlɪtɪ] *n* inestabilidad *f*.
install [ɪnˈstɔːl] *vt* instalar.
installation [ɪnstəˈleɪʃən] *n* instalación *f*.
installment plan *n* (*US*) compra a plazos.
instalment, (*US*) **installment** [ɪnˈstɔːlmənt] *n* plazo; (*of story*) entrega; (*of TV serial etc*) capítulo; **in ~s** (*pay, receive*) a plazos; **to pay in ~s** pagar a plazos *or* por abonos.
instance [ˈɪnstəns] *n* ejemplo, caso; **for ~** por ejemplo; **in the first ~** en primer lugar; **in that ~** en ese caso.
instant [ˈɪnstənt] *n* instante *m*, momento

♦ *adj* inmediato; (*coffee*) instantáneo.
instantaneous [ɪnstən'teɪnɪəs] *adj* instantáneo.
instantly ['ɪnstəntlɪ] *adv* en seguida, al instante.
instant replay *n* (*US TV*) repetición *f* de la jugada.
instead [ɪn'stɛd] *adv* en cambio; ~ **of** en lugar de, en vez de.
instep ['ɪnstɛp] *n* empeine *m*.
instigate ['ɪnstɪgeɪt] *vt* (*rebellion, strike, crime*) instigar; (*new ideas etc*) fomentar.
instigation [ɪnstɪ'geɪʃən] *n* instigación *f*; **at sb's** ~ a instigación de algn.
instil [ɪn'stɪl] *vt*: **to** ~ **into** inculcar a.
instinct ['ɪnstɪŋkt] *n* instinto.
instinctive [ɪn'stɪŋktɪv] *adj* instintivo.
instinctively [ɪn'stɪŋktɪvlɪ] *adv* por instinto.
institute ['ɪnstɪtjuːt] *n* instituto; (*professional body*) colegio ♦ *vt* (*begin*) iniciar, empezar; (*proceedings*) entablar.
institution [ɪnstɪ'tjuːʃən] *n* institución *f*; (*beginning*) iniciación *f*; (*MED: home*) asilo; (*asylum*) manicomio; (*custom*) costumbre *f* arraigada.
institutional [ɪnstɪ'tjuːʃənl] *adj* institucional.
instruct [ɪn'strʌkt] *vt*: **to** ~ **sb in sth** instruir a algn en *or* sobre algo; **to** ~ **sb to do sth** dar instrucciones a algn de *or* mandar a algn hacer algo.
instruction [ɪn'strʌkʃən] *n* (*teaching*) instrucción *f*; ~**s** *npl* órdenes *fpl*; ~**s (for use)** modo *sg* de empleo.
instruction book *n* manual *m*.
instructive [ɪn'strʌktɪv] *adj* instructivo.
instructor [ɪn'strʌktə*] *n* instructor(a) *m/f*.
instrument ['ɪnstrəmənt] *n* instrumento.
instrumental [ɪnstrə'mɛntl] *adj* (*MUS*) instrumental; **to be** ~ **in** ser el artífice de; **to be** ~ **in sth/in doing sth** ser responsable de algo/de hacer algo.
instrumentalist [ɪnstrə'mɛntəlɪst] *n* instrumentista *m/f*.
instrument panel *n* tablero (de instrumentos).
insubordinate [ɪnsə'bɔːdənɪt] *adj* insubordinado.
insubordination [ɪnsəbɔːdə'neɪʃən] *n* insubordinación *f*.
insufferable [ɪn'sʌfrəbl] *adj* insoportable.
insufficient [ɪnsə'fɪʃənt] *adj* insuficiente.
insufficiently [ɪnsə'fɪʃəntlɪ] *adv* insuficientemente.
insular ['ɪnsjulə*] *adj* insular; (*outlook*) estrecho de miras.
insularity [ɪnsju'lærɪtɪ] *n* insularidad *f*.
insulate ['ɪnsjuleɪt] *vt* aislar.

insulating tape ['ɪnsjuleɪtɪŋ-] *n* cinta aislante.
insulation [ɪnsju'leɪʃən] *n* aislamiento.
insulator ['ɪnsjuleɪtə*] *n* aislante *m*.
insulin ['ɪnsjulɪn] *n* insulina.
insult *n* ['ɪnsʌlt] insulto; (*offence*) ofensa ♦ *vt* [ɪn'sʌlt] insultar; ofender.
insulting [ɪn'sʌltɪŋ] *adj* insultante; ofensivo.
insuperable [ɪn'sjuːprəbl] *adj* insuperable.
insurance [ɪn'ʃuərəns] *n* seguro; **fire/life** ~ seguro de incendios/vida; **to take out** ~ (**against**) hacerse un seguro (contra).
insurance agent *n* agente *m/f* de seguros.
insurance broker *n* corredor(a) *m/f* *or* agente *m/f* de seguros.
insurance policy *n* póliza (de seguros).
insurance premium *n* prima de seguros.
insure [ɪn'ʃuə*] *vt* asegurar; **to** ~ **sb** *or* **sb's life** hacer un seguro de vida a algn; **to** ~ (**against**) asegurar (contra); **to be** ~**d for £5000** tener un seguro de 5000 libras.
insured [ɪn'ʃuəd] *n*: **the** ~ el/la asegurado/a.
insurer [ɪn'ʃuərə*] *n* asegurador(a).
insurgent [ɪn'sɜːdʒənt] *adj, n* insurgente *m/f*, insurrecto/a *m/f*.
insurmountable [ɪnsə'mauntəbl] *adj* insuperable.
insurrection [ɪnsə'rɛkʃən] *n* insurrección *f*.
intact [ɪn'tækt] *adj* íntegro; (*untouched*) intacto.
intake ['ɪnteɪk] *n* (*TECH*) entrada, toma; (: *pipe*) tubo de admisión; (*of food*) ingestión *f*; (*BRIT SCOL*): **an** ~ **of 200 a year** 200 matriculados al año.
intangible [ɪn'tændʒɪbl] *adj* intangible.
integer ['ɪntɪdʒə*] *n* (número) entero.
integral ['ɪntɪgrəl] *adj* (*whole*) íntegro; (*part*) integrante.
integrate ['ɪntɪgreɪt] *vt* integrar ♦ *vi* integrarse.
integrated circuit ['ɪntɪgreɪtɪd-] *n* (*COMPUT*) circuito integrado.
integration [ɪntɪ'greɪʃən] *n* integración *f*; **racial** ~ integración de razas.
integrity [ɪn'tɛgrɪtɪ] *n* honradez *f*, rectitud *f*; (*COMPUT*) integridad *f*.
intellect ['ɪntəlɛkt] *n* intelecto.
intellectual [ɪntə'lɛktjuəl] *adj, n* intelectual *m/f*.
intelligence [ɪn'tɛlɪdʒəns] *n* inteligencia.
intelligence quotient (IQ) *n* coeficiente *m* intelectual.
Intelligence Service *n* Servicio de Inteligencia.
intelligence test *n* prueba de inteligencia.
intelligent [ɪn'tɛlɪdʒənt] *adj* inteligente.
intelligently [ɪn'tɛlɪdʒəntlɪ] *adv*

inteligentemente.
intelligentsia [ɪntɛlɪ'dʒɛntsɪə] *n*
intelectualidad *f*.
intelligible [ɪn'tɛlɪdʒɪbl] *adj* inteligible,
comprensible.
intemperate [ɪn'tɛmpərət] *adj* inmoderado.
intend [ɪn'tɛnd] *vt* (*gift etc*): **to ~ sth for**
destinar algo a; **to ~ to do sth** tener
intención de *or* pensar hacer algo.
intended [ɪn'tɛndɪd] *adj* (*effect*) deseado.
intense [ɪn'tɛns] *adj* intenso; **to be ~**
(*person*) tomárselo todo muy en serio.
intensely [ɪn'tɛnslɪ] *adv* intensamente;
(*very*) sumamente.
intensify [ɪn'tɛnsɪfaɪ] *vt* intensificar;
(*increase*) aumentar.
intensity [ɪn'tɛnsɪtɪ] *n* (*gen*) intensidad *f*.
intensive [ɪn'tɛnsɪv] *adj* intensivo.
intensive care *n*: **to be in ~** estar bajo
cuidados intensivos; **~ unit** *n* unidad *f* de
vigilancia intensiva.
intensively [ɪn'tɛnsɪvlɪ] *adv*
intensamente.
intent [ɪn'tɛnt] *n* propósito ♦ *adj* (*absorbed*)
absorto; (*attentive*) atento; **to all ~s and
purposes** a efectos prácticos; **to be ~ on
doing sth** estar resuelto *or* decidido a
hacer algo.
intention [ɪn'tɛnʃən] *n* intención *f*,
propósito.
intentional [ɪn'tɛnʃənl] *adj* deliberado.
intentionally [ɪn'tɛnʃnəlɪ] *adv* a propósito.
intently [ɪn'tɛntlɪ] *adv* atentamente,
fijamente.
inter [ɪn'təː*] *vt* enterrar, sepultar.
inter- ['ɪntə*] *pref* inter-.
interact [ɪntər'ækt] *vi* (*substances*) influirse
mutuamente; (*people*) relacionarse.
interaction [ɪntər'ækʃən] *n* interacción *f*,
acción *f* recíproca.
interactive [ɪntər'æktɪv] *adj* (*also COMPUT*)
interactivo.
intercede [ɪntə'siːd] *vi*: **to ~ (with)**
interceder (con); **to ~ with sb/on behalf
of sb** interceder con algn/en nombre de
algn.
intercept [ɪntə'sɛpt] *vt* interceptar; (*stop*)
detener.
interception [ɪntə'sɛpʃən] *n* interceptación
f, detención *f*.
interchange *n* ['ɪntətʃeɪndʒ] intercambio;
(*on motorway*) intersección *f* ♦ *vt*
[ɪntə'tʃeɪndʒ] intercambiar.
interchangeable [ɪntə'tʃeɪndʒəbl] *adj*
intercambiable.
intercity [ɪntə'sɪtɪ] *adj*: **~ (train)** (tren *m*)
intercity *m*.
intercom ['ɪntəkɔm] *n* interfono.

interconnect [ɪntəkə'nɛkt] *vi* (*rooms*)
comunicar(se).
intercontinental ['ɪntəkɔntɪ'nɛntl] *adj*
intercontinental.
intercourse ['ɪntəkɔːs] *n* (*sexual ~*)
relaciones *fpl* sexuales, contacto sexual;
(*social*) trato.
interdependence [ɪntədɪ'pɛndəns] *n*
interdependencia.
interdependent [ɪntədɪ'pɛndənt] *adj*
interdependiente.
interest ['ɪntrɪst] *n* (*also COMM*) interés *m*
♦ *vt* interesar; **compound/simple ~** interés
compuesto/simple; **business ~s** negocios
mpl; **British ~s in the Middle East** los
intereses británicos en el Medio Oriente.
interested ['ɪntrɪstɪd] *adj* interesado; **to be
~ in** interesarse por.
interest-free ['ɪntrɪst'friː] *adj* libre de
interés.
interesting ['ɪntrɪstɪŋ] *adj* interesante.
interest rate *n* tipo de interés.
interface ['ɪntəfeɪs] *n* (*COMPUT*) junción *f*,
interface *m*.
interfere [ɪntə'fɪə*] *vi*: **to ~ in** (*quarrel, other
people's business*) entrometerse en; **to ~
with** (*hinder*) estorbar; (*damage*)
estropear; (*radio*) interferir con.
interference [ɪntə'fɪərəns] *n* (*gen*)
intromisión *f*; (*RADIO, TV*) interferencia.
interfering [ɪntə'fɪərɪŋ] *adj* entrometido.
interim ['ɪntərɪm] *adj*: **~ dividend** dividendo
parcial ♦ *n*: **in the ~** en el ínterin.
interior [ɪn'tɪərɪə*] *n* interior *m* ♦ *adj*
interior.
interior decorator, interior designer *n*
interiorista *m/f*, diseñador(a) *m/f* de
interiores.
interjection [ɪntə'dʒɛkʃən] *n* interrupción *f*.
interlock [ɪntə'lɔk] *vi* entrelazarse; (*wheels
etc*) endentarse.
interloper ['ɪntələupə*] *n* intruso/a.
interlude ['ɪntəluːd] *n* intervalo; (*rest*)
descanso; (*THEAT*) intermedio.
intermarriage [ɪntə'mærɪdʒ] *n* endogamia.
intermarry [ɪntə'mærɪ] *vi* casarse (entre
parientes).
intermediary [ɪntə'miːdɪərɪ] *n*
intermediario/a.
intermediate [ɪntə'miːdɪət] *adj* intermedio.
interminable [ɪn'təːmɪnəbl] *adj* inacabable.
intermission [ɪntə'mɪʃən] *n* (*THEAT*)
descanso.
intermittent [ɪntə'mɪtnt] *adj* intermitente.
intermittently [ɪntə'mɪtntlɪ] *adv*
intermitentemente.
intern *vt* [ɪn'təːn] internar; (*enclose*)
encerrar ♦ *n* ['ɪntəːn] (*US*) médico/a *m/f*

interno/a.

internal [ɪn'tɜːnl] *adj* interno, interior; ~ **injuries** heridas *fpl or* lesiones *fpl* internas.

internally [ɪn'tɜːnəlɪ] *adv* interiormente; "**not to be taken ~**" "uso externo".

Internal Revenue Service (IRS) *n* (*US*) Hacienda.

international [ɪntə'næʃənl] *adj* internacional; ~ (**game**) partido internacional; ~ (**player**) jugador(a) *m/f* internacional.

International Atomic Energy Agency (IAEA) *n* Organismo Internacional de Energía Atómica.

International Chamber of Commerce (ICC) *n* Cámara de Comercio Internacional (CCI *f*).

International Court of Justice (ICJ) *n* Corte *f* Internacional de Justicia (CIJ *f*).

international date line *n* línea de cambio de fecha.

internationally [ɪntə'næʃnəlɪ] *adv* internacionalmente.

International Monetary Fund (IMF) *n* Fondo Monetario Internacional (FMI *m*).

internecine [ɪntə'niːsaɪn] *adj* de aniquilación mutua.

internee [ɪntɜː'niː] *n* interno/a, recluso/a.

internment [ɪn'tɜːnmənt] *n* internamiento.

interplanetary [ɪntə'plænɪtərɪ] *adj* interplanetario.

interplay ['ɪntəpleɪ] *n* interacción *f*.

Interpol ['ɪntəpɔl] *n* Interpol *f*.

interpret [ɪn'tɜːprɪt] *vt* interpretar; (*translate*) traducir; (*understand*) entender ♦ *vi* hacer de intérprete.

interpretation [ɪntɜːprɪ'teɪʃən] *n* interpretación *f*; traducción *f*.

interpreter [ɪn'tɜːprɪtə*] *n* intérprete *m/f*.

interrelated [ɪntərɪ'leɪtɪd] *adj* interrelacionado.

interrogate [ɪn'tɛrəugeɪt] *vt* interrogar.

interrogation [ɪntɛrəu'geɪʃən] *n* interrogatorio.

interrogative [ɪntə'rɔgətɪv] *adj* interrogativo.

interrupt [ɪntə'rʌpt] *vt, vi* interrumpir.

interruption [ɪntə'rʌpʃən] *n* interrupción *f*.

intersect [ɪntə'sɛkt] *vt* cruzar ♦ *vi* (*roads*) cruzarse.

intersection [ɪntə'sɛkʃən] *n* intersección *f*; (*of roads*) cruce *m*.

intersperse [ɪntə'spɜːs] *vt*: **to ~ with** salpicar de.

intertwine [ɪntə'twaɪn] *vt* entrelazar ♦ *vi* entrelazarse.

interval ['ɪntəvl] *n* intervalo; (*BRIT: THEAT, SPORT*) descanso; **at ~s** a ratos, de vez en

cuando; **sunny ~s** (*METEOROLOGY*) claros *mpl*.

intervene [ɪntə'viːn] *vi* intervenir; (*take part*) participar; (*occur*) sobrevenir.

intervening [ɪntə'viːnɪŋ] *adj* intermedio.

intervention [ɪntə'vɛnʃən] *n* intervención *f*.

interview ['ɪntəvjuː] *n* (*RADIO, TV etc*) entrevista ♦ *vt* entrevistar a.

interviewee [ɪntəvjuː'iː] *n* entrevistado/a.

interviewer ['ɪntəvjuːə*] *n* entrevistador(a) *m/f*.

intestate [ɪn'tɛsteɪt] *adj* intestado.

intestinal [ɪn'tɛstɪnl] *adj* intestinal.

intestine [ɪn'tɛstɪn] *n*: **large/small ~** intestino grueso/delgado.

intimacy ['ɪntɪməsɪ] *n* intimidad *f*; (*relations*) relaciones *fpl* íntimas.

intimate *adj* ['ɪntɪmət] íntimo; (*friendship*) estrecho; (*knowledge*) profundo ♦ *vt* ['ɪntɪmeɪt] (*announce*) dar a entender.

intimately ['ɪntɪmətlɪ] *adv* íntimamente.

intimidate [ɪn'tɪmɪdeɪt] *vt* intimidar, amedrentar.

intimidation [ɪntɪmɪ'deɪʃən] *n* intimidación *f*.

into ['ɪntuː] *prep* (*gen*) en; (*towards*) a; (*inside*) hacia el interior de; ~ **3 pieces/ French** en 3 pedazos/al francés; **to change pounds ~ dollars** cambiar libras por dólares.

intolerable [ɪn'tɔlərəbl] *adj* intolerable, insoportable.

intolerance [ɪn'tɔlərəns] *n* intolerancia.

intolerant [ɪn'tɔlərənt] *adj*: ~ (**of**) intolerante (con).

intonation [ɪntəu'neɪʃən] *n* entonación *f*.

intoxicate [ɪn'tɔksɪkeɪt] *vt* embriagar.

intoxicated [ɪn'tɔksɪkeɪtɪd] *adj* embriagado.

intoxication [ɪntɔksɪ'keɪʃən] *n* embriaguez *f*.

intractable [ɪn'træktəbl] *adj* (*person*) intratable; (*problem*) irresoluble; (*illness*) incurable.

intransigence [ɪn'trænsɪdʒəns] *n* intransigencia.

intransigent [ɪn'trænsɪdʒənt] *adj* intransigente.

intransitive [ɪn'trænsɪtɪv] *adj* intransitivo.

intravenous [ɪntrə'viːnəs] *adj* intravenoso.

in-tray ['ɪntreɪ] *n* bandeja de entrada.

intrepid [ɪn'trɛpɪd] *adj* intrépido.

intricacy ['ɪntrɪkəsɪ] *n* complejidad *f*.

intricate ['ɪntrɪkət] *adj* intrincado; (*plot, problem*) complejo.

intrigue [ɪn'triːg] *n* intriga ♦ *vt* fascinar ♦ *vi* andar en intrigas.

intriguing [ɪn'triːgɪŋ] *adj* fascinante.

intrinsic [ɪn'trɪnsɪk] *adj* intrínseco.

introduce [ɪntrə'djuːs] *vt* introducir, meter; **to ~ sb (to sb)** presentar algn (a otro); **to ~ sb to** (*pastime, technique*) introducir a algn a; **may I ~ ...?** permítame presentarle a ....

introduction [ɪntrə'dʌkʃən] *n* introducción *f*; (*of person*) presentación *f*; **a letter of ~** una carta de recomendación.

introductory [ɪntrə'dʌktərɪ] *adj* introductorio; **an ~ offer** una oferta introductoria; **~ remarks** comentarios *mpl* preliminares.

introspection [ɪntrəu'spɛkʃən] *n* introspección *f*.

introspective [ɪntrəu'spɛktɪv] *adj* introspectivo.

introvert ['ɪntrəuvəːt] *adj, n* introvertido/a *m/f*.

intrude [ɪn'truːd] *vi* (*person*) entrometerse; **to ~ on** estorbar.

intruder [ɪn'truːdə*] *n* intruso/a.

intrusion [ɪn'truːʒən] *n* invasión *f*.

intrusive [ɪn'truːsɪv] *adj* intruso.

intuition [ɪntju:'ɪʃən] *n* intuición *f*.

intuitive [ɪn'tjuːɪtɪv] *adj* intuitivo.

intuitively [ɪn'tjuːɪtɪvlɪ] *adv* por intuición, intuitivamente.

inundate ['ɪnʌndeɪt] *vt*: **to ~ with** inundar de.

inure [ɪn'juə*] *vt*: **to ~ (to)** acostumbrar *or* habituar (a).

invade [ɪn'veɪd] *vt* invadir.

invader [ɪn'veɪdə*] *n* invasor(a) *m/f*.

invalid *n* ['ɪnvəlɪd] minusválido/a ♦ *adj* [ɪn'vælɪd] (*not valid*) inválido, nulo.

invalidate [ɪn'vælɪdeɪt] *vt* invalidar, anular.

invalid chair *n* silla de ruedas.

invaluable [ɪn'væljuəbl] *adj* inestimable.

invariable [ɪn'vɛərɪəbl] *adj* invariable.

invariably [ɪn'vɛərɪəblɪ] *adv* sin excepción, siempre; **she is ~ late** siempre llega tarde.

invasion [ɪn'veɪʒən] *n* invasión *f*.

invective [ɪn'vɛktɪv] *n* invectiva.

inveigle [ɪn'viːgl] *vt*: **to ~ sb into (doing) sth** embaucar *or* engatusar a algn para (que haga) algo.

invent [ɪn'vɛnt] *vt* inventar.

invention [ɪn'vɛnʃən] *n* invento; (*inventiveness*) inventiva; (*lie*) invención *f*.

inventive [ɪn'vɛntɪv] *adj* inventivo.

inventiveness [ɪn'vɛntɪvnɪs] *n* ingenio, inventiva.

inventor [ɪn'vɛntə*] *n* inventor(a) *m/f*.

inventory ['ɪnvəntrɪ] *n* inventario.

inventory control *n* control *m* de existencias.

inverse [ɪn'vəːs] *adj, n* inverso; **in ~**

proportion (to) en proporción inversa (a).

inversely [ɪn'vəːslɪ] *adv* a la inversa.

invert [ɪn'vəːt] *vt* invertir.

invertebrate [ɪn'vəːtɪbrət] *n* invertebrado.

inverted commas [ɪn'vəːtɪd] *npl* (*BRIT*) comillas *fpl*.

invest [ɪn'vɛst] *vt* invertir; (*fig: time, effort*) dedicar ♦ *vi* invertir; **to ~ sb with sth** conferir algo a algn.

investigate [ɪn'vɛstɪgeɪt] *vt* investigar; (*study*) estudiar, examinar.

investigation [ɪnvɛstɪ'geɪʃən] *n* investigación *f*, pesquisa; examen *m*.

investigative journalism [ɪn'vɛstɪgətɪv-] *n* periodismo de investigación.

investigator [ɪn'vɛstɪgeɪtə*] *n* investigador(a) *m/f*; **private ~** investigador(a) *m/f* privado/a.

investiture [ɪn'vɛstɪtʃə*] *n* investidura.

investment [ɪn'vɛstmənt] *n* inversión *f*.

investment grant *n* subvención *f* para la inversión.

investment income *n* ingresos *mpl* procedentes de inversiones.

investment portfolio *n* cartera de inversiones.

investment trust *n* compañía inversionista, sociedad *f* de cartera.

investor [ɪn'vɛstə*] *n* inversor(a) *m/f*.

inveterate [ɪn'vɛtərət] *adj* empedernido.

invidious [ɪn'vɪdɪəs] *adj* odioso.

invigilate [ɪn'vɪdʒɪleɪt] *vt, vi* (*in exam*) vigilar.

invigilator [ɪn'vɪdʒɪleɪtə*] *n* celador(a) *m/f*.

invigorating [ɪn'vɪgəreɪtɪŋ] *adj* vigorizante.

invincible [ɪn'vɪnsɪbl] *adj* invencible.

inviolate [ɪn'vaɪələt] *adj* inviolado.

invisible [ɪn'vɪzɪbl] *adj* invisible.

invisible assets *npl* activo invisible.

invisible ink *n* tinta simpática.

invisible mending *n* puntada invisible.

invitation [ɪnvɪ'teɪʃən] *n* invitación *f*; **at sb's ~** a invitación de algn; **by ~ only** solamente por invitación.

invite [ɪn'vaɪt] *vt* invitar; (*opinions etc*) solicitar, pedir; (*trouble*) buscarse; **to ~ sb (to do)** invitar a algn (a hacer); **to ~ sb to dinner** invitar a algn a cenar.

▶**invite out** *vt* invitar a salir.

▶**invite over** *vt* invitar a casa.

inviting [ɪn'vaɪtɪŋ] *adj* atractivo; (*look*) provocativo; (*food*) apetitoso.

invoice ['ɪnvɔɪs] *n* factura ♦ *vt* facturar; **to ~ sb for goods** facturar a algn las mercancías.

invoicing ['ɪnvɔɪsɪŋ] *n* facturación *f*.

invoke [ɪn'vəuk] *vt* invocar; (*aid*) pedir; (*law*) recurrir a.

involuntary [ɪn'vɔləntrɪ] *adj* involuntario.
involve [ɪn'vɔlv] *vt* (*entail*) suponer, implicar; **to ~ sb (in)** involucrar a algn (en).
involved [ɪn'vɔlvd] *adj* complicado; **to be/ become ~ in sth** estar involucrado/ involucrarse en algo.
involvement [ɪn'vɔlvmənt] *n* (*gen*) enredo; (*obligation*) compromiso; (*difficulty*) apuro.
invulnerable [ɪn'vʌlnərəbl] *adj* invulnerable.
inward ['ɪnwəd] *adj* (*movement*) interior, interno; (*thought, feeling*) íntimo.
inwardly ['ɪnwədlɪ] *adv* (*feel, think etc*) para sí, para dentro.
inward(s) ['ɪnwəd(z)] *adv* hacia dentro.
I/O *abbr* (*COMPUT = input/output*) E/S; ~ **error** error *m* de E/S.
IOC *n abbr* (= *International Olympic Committee*) COI *m*.
iodine ['aɪəudiːn] *n* yodo.
ion ['aɪən] *n* ion *m*.
Ionian Sea [aɪ'əunɪən-] *n*: **the ~** el Mar Jónico.
ioniser ['aɪənaɪzə*] *n* ionizador *m*.
iota [aɪ'əutə] *n* (*fig*) jota, ápice *m*.
IOU *n abbr* (= *I owe you*) pagaré *m*.
IOW *abbr* (*BRIT*) = Isle of Wight.
IPA *n abbr* (= *International Phonetic Alphabet*) AFI *m*.
IQ *n abbr* (= *intelligence quotient*) C.I. *m*.
IRA *n abbr* (= *Irish Republican Army*) IRA *m*; (*US*) = *individual retirement account.*
Iran [ɪ'rɑːn] *n* Irán *m*.
Iranian [ɪ'reɪnɪən] *adj* iraní ♦ *n* iraní *m/f*; (*LING*) iraní *m*.
Iraq [ɪ'rɑːk] *n* Irak *m*.
Iraqi [ɪ'rɑːkɪ] *adj, n* irakí *m/f*.
irascible [ɪ'ræsɪbl] *adj* irascible.
irate [aɪ'reɪt] *adj* enojado, airado.
Ireland ['aɪələnd] *n* Irlanda; **Republic of ~** República de Irlanda.
iris, ~es ['aɪrɪs, -ɪz] *n* (*ANAT*) iris *m*; (*BOT*) lirio.
Irish ['aɪrɪʃ] *adj* irlandés/esa ♦ *n* (*LING*) irlandés *m*; **the ~** *npl* los irlandeses.
Irishman ['aɪrɪʃmən] *n* irlandés *m*.
Irish Sea *n*: **the ~** el Mar de Irlanda.
Irishwoman ['aɪrɪʃwumən] *n* irlandesa.
irk [əːk] *vt* fastidiar.
irksome ['əːksəm] *adj* fastidioso.
IRN *n abbr* (= *Independent Radio News*) *servicio de noticias en las cadenas de radio privadas.*
IRO *n abbr* (*US*) = *International Refugee Organization.*
iron ['aɪən] *n* hierro; (*for clothes*) plancha ♦ *adj* de hierro ♦ *vt* (*clothes*) planchar; **~s**

npl (*chains*) grilletes *mpl*.
►**iron out** *vt* (*crease*) quitar; (*fig*) allanar, resolver.
Iron Curtain *n*: **the ~** el Telón de Acero.
iron foundry *n* fundición *f*, fundidora.
ironic(al) [aɪ'rɔnɪk(l)] *adj* irónico.
ironically [aɪ'rɔnɪklɪ] *adv* irónicamente.
ironing ['aɪənɪŋ] *n* (*act*) planchado; (*ironed clothes*) ropa planchada; (*to be ironed*) ropa por planchar.
ironing board *n* tabla de planchar.
iron lung *n* (*MED*) pulmón *m* de acero.
ironmonger ['aɪənmʌŋgə*] *n* (*BRIT*) ferretero/a; ~**'s (shop)** ferretería.
iron ore *n* mineral *m* de hierro.
ironworks ['aɪənwəːks] *n* fundición *f*.
irony ['aɪrənɪ] *n* ironía; **the ~ of it is that ...** lo irónico del caso es que ....
irrational [ɪ'ræʃənl] *adj* irracional.
irreconcilable [ɪrɛkən'saɪləbl] *adj* inconciliable; (*enemies*) irreconciliable.
irredeemable [ɪrɪ'diːməbl] *adj* irredimible.
irrefutable [ɪrɪ'fjuːtəbl] *adj* irrefutable.
irregular [ɪ'rɛgjulə*] *adj* irregular; (*surface*) desigual.
irregularity [ɪrɛgju'lærɪtɪ] *n* irregularidad *f*; desigualdad *f*.
irrelevance [ɪ'rɛləvəns] *n* irrelevancia.
irrelevant [ɪ'rɛləvənt] *adj* irrelevante; **to be ~** estar fuera de lugar, no venir al caso.
irreligious [ɪrɪ'lɪdʒəs] *adj* irreligioso.
irreparable [ɪ'rɛprəbl] *adj* irreparable.
irreplaceable [ɪrɪ'pleɪsəbl] *adj* irremplazable.
irrepressible [ɪrɪ'prɛsəbl] *adj* incontenible.
irreproachable [ɪrɪ'prəutʃəbl] *adj* irreprochable.
irresistible [ɪrɪ'zɪstɪbl] *adj* irresistible.
irresolute [ɪ'rɛzəluːt] *adj* indeciso.
irrespective [ɪrɪ'spɛktɪv]: ~ **of** *prep* sin tener en cuenta, no importa.
irresponsibility [ɪrɪspɔnsɪ'bɪlɪtɪ] *n* irresponsabilidad *f*.
irresponsible [ɪrɪ'spɔnsɪbl] *adj* (*act*) irresponsable; (*person*) poco serio.
irretrievable [ɪrɪ'triːvəbl] *adj* (*object*) irrecuperable; (*loss, damage*) irremediable, irreparable.
irretrievably [ɪrɪ'triːvəblɪ] *adv* irremisiblemente.
irreverence [ɪ'rɛvərns] *n* irreverencia.
irreverent [ɪ'rɛvərnt] *adj* irreverente, irrespetuoso.
irrevocable [ɪ'rɛvəkəbl] *adj* irrevocable.
irrigate ['ɪrɪgeɪt] *vt* regar.
irrigation [ɪrɪ'geɪʃən] *n* riego.
irritability [ɪrɪtə'bɪlɪtɪ] *n* irritabilidad *f*.
irritable ['ɪrɪtəbl] *adj* (*person: temperament*)

irritable; (: *mood*) de mal humor.
irritant ['ɪrɪtənt] *n* agente *m* irritante.
irritate ['ɪrɪteɪt] *vt* fastidiar; (*MED*) picar.
irritating ['ɪrɪteɪtɪŋ] *adj* fastidioso.
irritation [ɪrɪ'teɪʃən] *n* fastidio; picazón *f*, picor *m*.
IRS *n abbr* (*US*) *see* **Internal Revenue Service**.
is [ɪz] *vb see* **be**.
ISBN *n abbr* (= *International Standard Book Number*) ISBN *m*.
Islam ['ɪzlɑːm] *n* Islam *m*.
island ['aɪlənd] *n* isla; (*also*: **traffic** ~) isleta.
islander ['aɪləndə*] *n* isleño/a.
isle [aɪl] *n* isla.
isn't ['ɪznt] = **is not**.
isobar ['aɪsəubɑː*] *n* isobara.
isolate ['aɪsəleɪt] *vt* aislar.
isolated ['aɪsəleɪtɪd] *adj* aislado.
isolation [aɪsə'leɪʃən] *n* aislamiento.
isolationism [aɪsə'leɪʃənɪzəm] *n* aislacionismo.
isolation ward *n* pabellón *m* de aislamiento.
isotope ['aɪsəutəup] *n* isótopo.
Israel ['ɪzreɪl] *n* Israel *m*.
Israeli [ɪz'reɪlɪ] *adj, n* israelí *m/f*.
issue ['ɪsjuː] *n* cuestión *f*, asunto; (*outcome*) resultado; (*of banknotes etc*) emisión *f*; (*of newspaper etc*) número; (*offspring*) sucesión *f*, descendencia ♦ *vt* (*rations, equipment*) distribuir, repartir; (*orders*) dar; (*certificate, passport*) expedir; (*decree*) promulgar; (*magazine*) publicar; (*cheques*) extender; (*banknotes, stamps*) emitir ♦ *vi*: **to ~ (from)** derivar (de), brotar (de); **at ~** en cuestión; **to take ~ with sb (over)** disentir con algn (en); **to avoid the ~** andarse con rodeos; **to confuse** *or* **obscure the ~** confundir las cosas; **to make an ~ of sth** dar a algo más importancia de lo necesario; **to ~ sth to sb, ~ sb with sth** entregar algo a algn.
Istanbul [ɪstæn'buːl] *n* Estambul *m*.
isthmus ['ɪsməs] *n* istmo.
IT *n abbr* = **information technology**.

========================= *KEYWORD*

it [ɪt] *pron* **1** (*specific*: *subject*: *not generally translated*) él/ella; (: *direct object*) lo, la; (: *indirect object*) le; (*after prep*) él/ella; (*abstract concept*) ello; ~**'s on the table** está en la mesa; **I can't find** ~ no lo (*or* la) encuentro; **give** ~ **to me** dámelo (*or* dámela); **I spoke to him about** ~ le hablé del asunto; **what did you learn from** ~? ¿qué aprendiste de él (*or* ella)?; **did you go to** ~? (*party, concert etc*) ¿fuiste?

2 (*impersonal*): ~**'s raining** llueve, está lloviendo; ~**'s 6 o'clock/the 10th of August** son las 6/es el 10 de agosto; **how far is** ~? — ~**'s 10 miles/2 hours on the train** ¿a qué distancia está? — a 10 millas/2 horas en tren; **who is** ~? — ~**'s me** ¿quién es? — soy yo.

ITA *n abbr* (*BRIT*: = *initial teaching alphabet*) alfabeto parcialmente fonético, ayuda para enseñar a leer.
Italian [ɪ'tæljən] *adj* italiano ♦ *n* italiano/a; (*LING*) italiano.
italic [ɪ'tælɪk] *adj* cursivo; ~**s** *npl* cursiva *sg*.
Italy ['ɪtəlɪ] *n* Italia.
itch [ɪtʃ] *n* picazón *f*; (*fig*) prurito ♦ *vi* (*person*) sentir *or* tener comezón; (*part of body*) picar; **to be ~ing to do sth** rabiar por *or* morirse de ganas de hacer algo.
itching ['ɪtʃɪŋ] *n* picazón *f*, comezón *f*.
itchy ['ɪtʃɪ] *adj*: **to be ~** picar.
it'd ['ɪtd] = **it would**; **it had**.
item ['aɪtəm] *n* artículo; (*on agenda*) asunto (a tratar); (*in programme*) número; (*also*: **news ~**) noticia; ~**s of clothing** prendas *fpl* de vestir.
itemize ['aɪtəmaɪz] *vt* detallar.
itemized bill ['aɪtəmaɪzd-] *n* recibo detallado.
itinerant [ɪ'tɪnərənt] *adj* ambulante.
itinerary [aɪ'tɪnərərɪ] *n* itinerario.
it'll ['ɪtl] = **it will**; **it shall**.
ITN *n abbr see* **ITV**.
its [ɪts] *adj* su.
it's [ɪts] = **it is**; **it has**.
itself [ɪt'sɛlf] *pron* (*reflexive*) sí mismo/a; (*emphatic*) él mismo/ella misma.

En el Reino Unido la **ITV (Independent Television)** *es una cadena de emisoras comerciales regionales con licencia exclusiva para emitir en su región. Suelen producir sus propios programas, se financian con publicidad y están bajo el control del organismo oficial independiente* **Independent Broadcasting Authority (IBA)**. *El servicio de noticias nacionales e internacionales,* **ITN (Independent Television News)**, *funciona como una compañía productora para toda la cadena.*

IUD *n abbr* (= *intra-uterine device*) DIU *m*.
I've [aɪv] = **I have**.
ivory ['aɪvərɪ] *n* marfil *m*.
Ivory Coast *n*: **the ~** la Costa de Marfil.
ivory tower *n* (*fig*) torre *f* de marfil.
ivy ['aɪvɪ] *n* hiedra.

Las ocho universidades más prestigiosas del nordeste de los Estados Unidos reciben el nombre colectivo de **Ivy League,** *por sus muros cubiertos de hiedra. Son: Brown, Columbia, Cornell, Dartmouth College, Harvard, Princeton, la universidad de Pennsylvania y Yale. También se llaman así las competiciones deportivas que celebran entre ellas.*

J j

J, j [dʒeɪ] n (*letter*) J, j *f*; **J for Jack,** (*US*) **J for Jig** J de José.
JA n abbr = **judge advocate.**
J/A abbr = **joint account.**
jab [dʒæb] vt (*elbow*) dar un codazo a; (*punch*) dar un golpe rápido a ♦ vi: **to ~ at** intentar golpear a; **to ~ sth into sth** clavar algo en algo ♦ n codazo; golpe m (rápido); (*MED col*) pinchazo.
jabber ['dʒæbə*] vt, vi farfullar.
jack [dʒæk] n (*AUT*) gato; (*BOWLS*) boliche m; (*CARDS*) sota.
▶**jack in** vt (*col*) dejar.
▶**jack up** vt (*AUT*) levantar con el gato.
jackal ['dʒækl] n (*ZOOL*) chacal m.
jackass ['dʒækæs] n (*also fig*) asno, burro.
jackdaw ['dʒækdɔ:] n grajo/a, chova.
jacket ['dʒækɪt] n chaqueta, americana, saco (*LAM*); (*of boiler etc*) camisa; (*of book*) sobrecubierta.
jacket potato n patata asada (con piel).
jack-in-the-box ['dʒækɪnðəbɔks] n caja sorpresa, caja de resorte.
jack-knife ['dʒæknaɪf] vi colear.
jack-of-all-trades ['dʒækəv'ɔ:ltreɪdz] n aprendiz m de todo.
jack plug n (*ELEC*) enchufe m de clavija.
jackpot ['dʒækpɔt] n premio gordo.
Jacuzzi ® [dʒə'ku:zɪ] n jacuzzi ® m.
jade [dʒeɪd] n (*stone*) jade m.
jaded ['dʒeɪdɪd] adj (*tired*) cansado; (*fed up*) hastiado.
jagged ['dʒægɪd] adj dentado.
jaguar ['dʒægjuə*] n jaguar m.
jail [dʒeɪl] n cárcel f ♦ vt encarcelar.
jailbird ['dʒeɪlbɜ:d] n preso/a reincidente.
jailbreak ['dʒeɪlbreɪk] n fuga or evasión f

(de la cárcel).
jailer ['dʒeɪlə*] n carcelero/a.
jalopy [dʒə'lɔpɪ] n (*col*) cacharro, armatoste m.
jam [dʒæm] n mermelada; (*also:* **traffic ~**) atasco, embotellamiento; (*difficulty*) apuro ♦ vt (*passage etc*) obstruir; (*mechanism, drawer etc*) atascar; (*RADIO*) interferir ♦ vi atascarse, trabarse; **to get sb out of a ~** sacar a algn del paso or de un apuro; **to ~ sth into sth** meter algo a la fuerza en algo; **the telephone lines are ~med** las líneas están saturadas.
Jamaica [dʒə'meɪkə] n Jamaica.
Jamaican [dʒə'meɪkən] adj, n jamaicano/a m/f.
jamb [dʒæm] n jamba.
jamboree [dʒæmbə'ri:] n congreso de niños exploradores.
jam-packed [dʒæm'pækt] adj: ~ **(with)** atestado (de).
jam session n concierto improvisado de jazz/rock etc.
Jan. abbr (= *January*) ene.
jangle ['dʒæŋgl] vi sonar (de manera) discordante.
janitor ['dʒænɪtə*] n (*caretaker*) portero, conserje m.
January ['dʒænjuərɪ] n enero.
Japan [dʒə'pæn] n (el) Japón.
Japanese [dʒæpə'ni:z] adj japonés/esa ♦ n (pl inv) japonés/esa m/f; (*LING*) japonés m.
jar [dʒɑ:*] n (*glass: large*) jarra; (: *small*) tarro ♦ vi (*sound*) chirriar; (*colours*) desentonar.
jargon ['dʒɑ:gən] n jerga.
jarring ['dʒɑ:rɪŋ] adj (*sound*) discordante, desafinado; (*colour*) chocante.
Jas. abbr = *James.*
jasmin(e) ['dʒæzmɪn] n jazmín m.
jaundice ['dʒɔ:ndɪs] n ictericia.
jaundiced ['dʒɔ:ndɪst] adj (*fig: embittered*) amargado; (: *disillusioned*) desilusionado.
jaunt [dʒɔ:nt] n excursión f.
jaunty ['dʒɔ:ntɪ] adj alegre; (*relaxed*) desenvuelto.
Java ['dʒɑ:və] n Java.
javelin ['dʒævlɪn] n jabalina.
jaw [dʒɔ:] n mandíbula; ~**s** npl (*TECH: of vice etc*) mordaza sg.
jawbone ['dʒɔ:bəun] n mandíbula, quijada.
jay [dʒeɪ] n (*ZOOL*) arrendajo.
jaywalker ['dʒeɪwɔ:kə*] n peatón/ona m/f imprudente.
jazz [dʒæz] n jazz m.
▶**jazz up** vt (*liven up*) animar.
jazz band n orquesta de jazz.
jazzy ['dʒæzɪ] adj de colores llamativos.

JCB ® *n abbr* excavadora.
JCS *n abbr* (*US*) = *Joint Chiefs of Staff.*
JD *n abbr* (*US:* = *Doctor of Laws*) título universitario; (: = *Justice Department*) Ministerio de Justicia.
jealous ['dʒɛləs] *adj* (*gen*) celoso; (*envious*) envidioso; **to be** ~ tener celos.
jealously ['dʒɛləslɪ] *adv* (*enviously*) envidiosamente; (*watchfully*) celosamente.
jealousy ['dʒɛləsɪ] *n* celos *mpl*; envidia.
jeans [dʒiːnz] *npl* (pantalones *mpl*) vaqueros *mpl or* tejanos *mpl*, bluejean *m inv* (*LAM*).
Jeep ® [dʒiːp] *n* jeep *m*.
jeer [dʒɪə*] *vi:* **to** ~ **(at)** (*boo*) abuchear; (*mock*) mofarse (de).
jeering ['dʒɪərɪŋ] *adj* (*crowd*) insolente, ofensivo ♦ *n* protestas *fpl*; (*mockery*) burlas *fpl*.
jelly ['dʒɛlɪ] *n* gelatina, jalea.
jellyfish ['dʒɛlɪfɪʃ] *n* medusa.
jemmy ['dʒɛmɪ] *n* palanqueta.
jeopardize ['dʒɛpədaɪz] *vt* arriesgar, poner en peligro.
jeopardy ['dʒɛpədɪ] *n:* **to be in** ~ estar en peligro.
jerk [dʒəːk] *n* (*jolt*) sacudida; (*wrench*) tirón *m*; (*US col*) imbécil *m/f*, pendejo/a (*LAM*) ♦ *vt* dar una sacudida a; tirar bruscamente de ♦ *vi* (*vehicle*) dar una sacudida.
jerkin ['dʒəːkɪn] *n* chaleco.
jerky ['dʒəːkɪ] *adj* espasmódico.
jerry-built ['dʒɛrɪbɪlt] *adj* mal construido.
jerry can ['dʒɛrɪ-] *n* bidón *m*.
Jersey ['dʒəːzɪ] *n* Jersey *m*.
jersey ['dʒəːzɪ] *n* jersey *m*; (*fabric*) tejido de punto.
Jerusalem [dʒəˈruːsləm] *n* Jerusalén *m*.
jest [dʒɛst] *n* broma.
jester ['dʒɛstə*] *n* bufón *m*.
Jesus ['dʒiːzəs] *n* Jesús *m*; ~ **Christ** Jesucristo.
jet [dʒɛt] *n* (*of gas, liquid*) chorro; (*AVIAT*) avión *m* a reacción.
jet-black ['dʒɛt'blæk] *adj* negro como el azabache.
jet engine *n* motor *m* a reacción.
jet lag *n* desorientación *f* por desfase horario.
jetsam ['dʒɛtsəm] *n* echazón *f*.
jet-setter ['dʒɛtsɛtə*] *n* personaje *m* de la jet.
jettison ['dʒɛtɪsn] *vt* desechar.
jetty ['dʒɛtɪ] *n* muelle *m*, embarcadero.
Jew [dʒuː] *n* judío.
jewel ['dʒuːəl] *n* joya; (*in watch*) rubí *m*.
jeweller, (*US*) **jeweler** ['dʒuːələ*] *n* joyero/a; ~**'s (shop)** joyería.

jewellery, (*US*) **jewelry** ['dʒuːəlrɪ] *n* joyas *fpl*, alhajas *fpl*.
Jewess ['dʒuːɪs] *n* judía.
Jewish ['dʒuːɪʃ] *adj* judío.
JFK *n abbr* (*US*) = *John Fitzgerald Kennedy International Airport.*
jib [dʒɪb] *vi* (*horse*) plantarse; **to** ~ **at doing sth** resistirse a hacer algo.
jibe [dʒaɪb] *n* mofa.
jiffy ['dʒɪfɪ] *n* (*col*): **in a** ~ en un santiamén.
jig [dʒɪg] *n* (*dance, tune*) giga.
jigsaw ['dʒɪgsɔː] *n* (*also:* ~ **puzzle**) rompecabezas *m inv*; (*tool*) sierra de vaivén.
jilt [dʒɪlt] *vt* dejar plantado a.
jingle ['dʒɪŋgl] *n* (*advert*) musiquilla ♦ *vi* tintinear.
jingoism ['dʒɪŋgəuɪzəm] *n* patriotería, jingoísmo.
jinx [dʒɪŋks] *n:* **there's a** ~ **on it** está gafado.
jitters ['dʒɪtəz] *npl* (*col*): **to get the** ~ ponerse nervioso.
jittery ['dʒɪtərɪ] *adj* (*col*) agitado.
jiujitsu [dʒuːˈdʒɪtsuː] *n* ju-jitsu *m*.
job [dʒɔb] *n* trabajo; (*task*) tarea; (*duty*) deber *m*; (*post*) empleo; (*fam: difficulty*) dificultad *f*; **it's a good** ~ **that...** menos mal que...; **just the** ~! ¡justo lo que necesito!; **a part-time/full-time** ~ un trabajo a tiempo parcial/tiempo completo; **that's not my** ~ eso no me incumbe *or* toca a mí; **he's only doing his** ~ está cumpliendo nada más.
job centre *n* (*BRIT*) oficina de empleo.
job creation scheme *n* plan *m* de creación de puestos de trabajo.
job description *n* descripción *f* del puesto de trabajo.
jobless ['dʒɔblɪs] *adj* sin trabajo ♦ *n:* **the** ~ los parados.
job lot *n* lote *m* de mercancías, saldo.
job satisfaction *n* satisfacción *f* en el trabajo.
job security *n* garantía de trabajo.
job specification *n* especificación *f* del trabajo, profesiograma *m*.
Jock *n* (*col: Scotsman*) escocés *m*.
jockey ['dʒɔkɪ] *n* jockey *m/f* ♦ *vi:* **to** ~ **for position** maniobrar para sacar delantera.
jockey box *n* (*US AUT*) guantera.
jockstrap ['dʒɔkstræp] *n* suspensorio.
jocular ['dʒɔkjulə*] *adj* (*humorous*) gracioso; (*merry*) alegre.
jodhpurs ['dʒɔdpəːz] *npl* pantalón *msg* de montar.
jog [dʒɔg] *vt* empujar (ligeramente) ♦ *vi* (*run*) hacer footing; **to** ~ **along** (*fig*) ir tirando; **to** ~ **sb's memory** refrescar la

memoria a algn.
jogger ['dʒɔgə*] n corredor(a) m/f.
jogging ['dʒɔgɪŋ] n footing m.
john [dʒɔn] n (US col) wáter m.
join [dʒɔɪn] vt (things) unir, juntar; (become member of: club) hacerse socio de; (POL: party) afiliarse a; (meet: people) reunirse con; (fig) unirse a ♦ vi (roads) empalmar; (rivers) confluir ♦ n juntura; **will you ~ us for dinner?** ¿quieres cenar con nosotros?; **I'll ~ you later** me reuniré contigo luego; **to ~ forces (with)** aliarse (con).
▶**join in** vi tomar parte, participar ♦ vt fus tomar parte or participar en.
▶**join up** vi unirse; (MIL) alistarse.
joiner ['dʒɔɪnə*] n carpintero/a.
joinery ['dʒɔɪnərɪ] n carpintería.
joint [dʒɔɪnt] n (TECH) juntura, unión f; (ANAT) articulación f; (BRIT CULIN) pieza de carne (para asar); (col: place) garito ♦ adj (common) común; (combined) conjunto; (responsibility) compartido; (committee) mixto.
joint account (J/A) n (with bank etc) cuenta común.
jointly ['dʒɔɪntlɪ] adv (gen) en común; (together) conjuntamente.
joint owners npl copropietarios mpl.
joint ownership n copropiedad f, propiedad f común.
joint-stock bank ['dʒɔɪntstɔk-] n banco por acciones.
joint-stock company ['dʒɔɪntstɔk-] n sociedad f anónima.
joint venture n empresa conjunta.
joist [dʒɔɪst] n viga.
joke [dʒəuk] n chiste m; (also: **practical ~**) broma ♦ vi bromear; **to play a ~ on** gastar una broma a.
joker ['dʒəukə*] n chistoso/a, bromista m/f; (CARDS) comodín m.
joking ['dʒəukɪŋ] n bromas fpl.
jokingly ['dʒəukɪŋlɪ] adv en broma.
jollity ['dʒɔlɪtɪ] n alegría.
jolly ['dʒɔlɪ] adj (merry) alegre; (enjoyable) divertido ♦ adv (col) muy, la mar de ♦ vt: **to ~ sb along** animar or darle ánimos a algn; **~ good!** ¡estupendo!
jolt [dʒəult] n (shake) sacudida f; (blow) golpe m; (shock) susto ♦ vt sacudir.
Jordan ['dʒɔ:dən] n (country) Jordania; (river) Jordán m.
joss stick [dʒɔs-] n barrita de incienso, pebete m.
jostle ['dʒɔsl] vt dar empujones or empellones a.
jot [dʒɔt] n: **not one ~** ni pizca, ni un ápice.
▶**jot down** vt apuntar.

jotter ['dʒɔtə*] n (BRIT) bloc m.
journal ['dʒə:nl] n (paper) periódico; (magazine) revista; (diary) diario.
journalese [dʒə:nə'li:z] n (pej) lenguaje m periodístico.
journalism ['dʒə:nəlɪzəm] n periodismo.
journalist ['dʒə:nəlɪst] n periodista m/f.
journey ['dʒə:nɪ] n viaje m; (distance covered) trayecto ♦ vi viajar; **return ~** viaje de regreso; **a 5-hour ~** un viaje de 5 horas.
jovial ['dʒəuvɪəl] adj risueño, alegre.
jowl [dʒaul] n quijada.
joy [dʒɔɪ] n alegría.
joyful ['dʒɔɪful] adj alegre.
joyfully ['dʒɔɪfulɪ] adv alegremente.
joyous ['dʒɔɪəs] adj alegre.
joyride ['dʒɔɪraɪd] n: **to go for a ~** darse una vuelta en un coche robado.
joyrider ['dʒɔɪraɪdə*] n persona que se da una vuelta en un coche robado.
joystick ['dʒɔɪstɪk] n (AVIAT) palanca de mando; (COMPUT) palanca de control.
JP n abbr see **Justice of the Peace**.
Jr. abbr = **junior**.
JTPA n abbr (US: = Job Training Partnership Act) programa gubernamental de formación profesional.
jubilant ['dʒu:bɪlnt] adj jubiloso.
jubilation [dʒu:bɪ'leɪʃən] n júbilo.
jubilee ['dʒu:bɪli:] n aniversario; **silver ~** vigésimo quinto aniversario.
judge [dʒʌdʒ] n juez m/f ♦ vt juzgar; (competition) actuar de or ser juez en; (estimate) considerar; (: weight, size etc) calcular ♦ vi: **judging or to ~ by his expression** a juzgar por su expresión; **as far as I can ~** por lo que puedo entender, a mi entender; **I ~d it necessary to inform him** consideré necesario informarle.
judge advocate n (MIL) auditor m de guerra.
judg(e)ment ['dʒʌdʒmənt] n juicio; (punishment) sentencia, fallo; **to pass ~ (on)** (LAW) pronunciar or dictar sentencia (sobre); (fig) emitir un juicio crítico or dictaminar (sobre); **in my ~** a mi juicio.
judicial [dʒu:'dɪʃl] adj judicial.
judiciary [dʒu:'dɪʃɪərɪ] n poder m judicial, magistratura.
judicious [dʒu:'dɪʃəs] adj juicioso.
judo ['dʒu:dəu] n judo.
jug [dʒʌg] n jarro.
jugged hare [dʒʌgd-] n (BRIT) estofado de liebre.
juggernaut ['dʒʌgənɔ:t] n (BRIT: huge truck) camión m de carga pesada.
juggle ['dʒʌgl] vi hacer juegos malabares.

juggler ['dʒʌglə*] *n* malabarista *m/f*.
Jugoslav ['juːgəuslɑːv] *etc* = **Yugoslav** *etc*.
jugular ['dʒʌgjulə*] *adj*: ~ **vein** (vena) yugular *f*.
juice [dʒuːs] *n* jugo, zumo (*SP*); (*of meat*) jugo; (*col: petrol*): **we've run out of** ~ se nos acabó la gasolina.
juiciness ['dʒuːsɪnɪs] *n* jugosidad *f*.
juicy ['dʒuːsɪ] *adj* jugoso.
jujitsu [dʒuː'dʒɪtsuː] *n* = **juijitsu**.
jukebox ['dʒuːkbɔks] *n* máquina de discos.
Jul. *abbr* (= *July*) jul.
July [dʒuː'laɪ] *n* julio; **the first of** ~ el uno *or* primero de julio; **during** ~ en el mes de julio; **in** ~ **of next year** en julio del año que viene.
jumble ['dʒʌmbl] *n* revoltijo ♦ *vt* (*also*: ~ **together,** ~ **up**: *mix up*) revolver; (: *disarrange*) mezclar.
jumble sale *n* (*BRIT*) mercadillo.

En cada **jumble sale** *pueden comprarse todo tipo de objetos baratos de segunda mano, especialmente ropa, juguetes, libros, vajillas y muebles. Suelen organizarse en los locales de un colegio, iglesia, ayuntamiento o similar, con fines benéficos, bien en ayuda de una organización benéfica conocida o para solucionar problemas más concretos de la comunidad.*

jumbo (jet) ['dʒʌmbəu-] *n* jumbo.
jump [dʒʌmp] *vi* saltar, dar saltos; (*start*) sobresaltarse; (*increase*) aumentar ♦ *vt* saltar ♦ *n* salto; (*fence*) obstáculo; (*increase*) aumento; **to** ~ **the queue** (*BRIT*) colarse.
►**jump about** *vi* dar saltos, brincar.
►**jump at** *vt fus* (*fig*) apresurarse a aprovechar; **he** ~**ed at the offer** se apresuró a aceptar la oferta.
►**jump down** *vi* bajar de un salto, saltar a tierra.
►**jump up** *vi* levantarse de un salto.
jumped-up ['dʒʌmptʌp] *adj* (*pej*) engreído.
jumper ['dʒʌmpə*] *n* (*BRIT: pullover*) jersey *m*, suéter *m*; (*US: pinafore dress*) pichi *m*; (*SPORT*) saltador(a) *m/f*.
jump leads, (*US*) **jumper cables** *npl* cables *mpl* puente de batería.
jump-start ['dʒʌmpstɑːt] *vt* (*car*) arrancar con ayuda de otra batería *or* empujando; (*fig: economy*) reactivar.
jump suit *n* mono.
jumpy ['dʒʌmpɪ] *adj* nervioso.
Jun. *abbr* = **junior; (**= *June*) jun.
junction ['dʒʌŋkʃən] *n* (*BRIT: of roads*) cruce *m*; (*RAIL*) empalme *m*.

juncture ['dʒʌŋktʃə*] *n*: **at this** ~ en este momento, en esta coyuntura.
June [dʒuːn] *n* junio.
jungle ['dʒʌŋgl] *n* selva, jungla.
junior ['dʒuːnɪə*] *adj* (*in age*) menor, más joven; (*competition*) juvenil; (*position*) subalterno ♦ *n* menor *m/f*, joven *m/f*; **he's** ~ **to me** es menor que yo.
junior executive *n* ejecutivo/a subalterno/a.
junior high school *n* (*US*) centro de educación secundaria; *see also* **high school**.
junior school *n* (*BRIT*) escuela primaria; *see also* **primary school**.
junk [dʒʌŋk] *n* (*cheap goods*) baratijas *fpl*; (*lumber*) trastos *mpl* viejos; (*rubbish*) basura; (*ship*) junco ♦ *vt* (*esp US*) deshacerse de.
junk bond *n* (*COMM*) obligación *f* basura *inv*.
junk dealer *n* vendedor(a) *m/f* de objetos usados.
junket ['dʒʌŋkɪt] *n* (*CULIN*) dulce de leche cuajada; (*BRIT col*): **to go on a** ~, **go** ~**ing** viajar a costa ajena *or* del erario público.
junk food *n* comida basura *or* de plástico.
junkie ['dʒʌŋkɪ] *n* (*col*) yonqui *m/f*, heroinómano/a.
junk mail *n* propaganda (buzoneada).
junk room *n* trastero.
junk shop *n* tienda de objetos usados.
junta ['dʒʌntə] *n* junta militar.
Jupiter ['dʒuːpɪtə*] *n* (*MYTHOLOGY, ASTRO*) Júpiter *m*.
jurisdiction [dʒuərɪs'dɪkʃən] *n* jurisdicción *f*; **it falls** *or* **comes within/outside our** ~ es/no es de nuestra competencia.
jurisprudence [dʒuərɪs'pruːdəns] *n* jurisprudencia.
juror ['dʒuərə*] *n* jurado.
jury ['dʒuərɪ] *n* jurado.
jury box *n* tribuna del jurado.
juryman ['dʒuərɪmən] *n* miembro del jurado.
just [dʒʌst] *adj* justo ♦ *adv* (*exactly*) exactamente; (*only*) sólo, solamente, no más (*LAM*); **he's** ~ **done it/left** acaba de hacerlo/irse; **I've** ~ **seen him** acabo de verle; ~ **right** perfecto; ~ **two o'clock** las dos en punto; **she's** ~ **as clever as you** es tan lista como tú; ~ **as well that...** menos mal que...; **it's** ~ **as well you didn't go** menos mal que no fuiste; **it's** ~ **as good (as)** es igual (que), es tan bueno (como); ~ **as he was leaving** en el momento en que se marchaba; **we were** ~ **going** ya nos íbamos; **I was** ~ **about to phone**

estaba a punto de llamar; ~ **before/ enough** justo antes/lo suficiente; ~ **here** aquí mismo; **he** ~ **missed** falló por poco; ~ **listen to this** escucha esto un momento; ~ **ask someone the way** simplemente pregúntale a algn por dónde se va; **not** ~ **now** ahora no.

justice ['dʒʌstɪs] n justicia; **this photo doesn't do you** ~ esta foto no te favorece.

Justice of the Peace (JP) n juez m/f de paz; see also **Crown Court.**

justifiable [dʒʌstɪ'faɪəbl] adj justificable, justificado.

justifiably [dʒʌstɪ'faɪəblɪ] adv justificadamente, con razón.

justification [dʒʌstɪfɪ'keɪʃən] n justificación f.

justify ['dʒʌstɪfaɪ] vt justificar; (text) alinear, justificar; **to be justified in doing sth** tener motivo para or razón al hacer algo.

justly ['dʒʌstlɪ] adv (gen) justamente; (with reason) con razón.

justness ['dʒʌstnɪs] n justicia.

jut [dʒʌt] vi (also: ~ **out**) sobresalir.

jute [dʒuːt] n yute m.

juvenile ['dʒuːvənaɪl] adj juvenil; (court) de menores ♦ n joven m/f, menor m/f de edad.

juvenile delinquency n delincuencia juvenil.

juvenile delinquent n delincuente m/f juvenil.

juxtapose ['dʒʌkstəpəuz] vt yuxtaponer.

juxtaposition ['dʒʌkstəpə'zɪʃən] n yuxtaposición f.

Kk

K, k [keɪ] n (letter) K, k f; **K for King** K de Kilo.

K abbr (= one thousand) K; = **kilobyte**; (BRIT: = Knight) caballero de una orden.

kaftan ['kæftæn] n caftán m.

Kalahari Desert [kælə'hɑːrɪ-] n desierto de Kalahari.

kale [keɪl] n col f rizada.

kaleidoscope [kə'laɪdəskəup] n calidoscopio.

kamikaze [kæmɪ'kɑːzɪ] adj kamikaze.

Kampala [kæm'pɑːlə] n Kampala.

Kampuchea [kæmpu'tʃɪə] n Kampuchea.

kangaroo [kæŋgə'ruː] n canguro.

Kans. abbr (US) = Kansas.

kaput [kə'put] adj (col) roto, estropeado.

karaoke [kɑːrə'əukɪ] n karaoke.

karate [kə'rɑːtɪ] n karate m.

Kashmir [kæʃ'mɪə*] n Cachemira.

kayak ['kaɪæk] n kayak m.

Kazakhstan [kɑːzɑːk'stæn] n Kazajstán m.

KC n abbr (BRIT LAW: = King's Counsel) título concedido a determinados abogados.

kd abbr (US: = knocked down) desmontado.

kebab [kə'bæb] n pincho moruno, brocheta.

keel [kiːl] n quilla; **on an even** ~ (fig) en equilibrio.

►**keel over** vi (NAUT) zozobrar, volcarse; (person) desplomarse.

keen [kiːn] adj (interest, desire) grande, vivo; (eye, intelligence) agudo; (competition) intenso; (edge) afilado; (BRIT: eager) entusiasta; **to be** ~ **to do** or **on doing sth** tener muchas ganas de hacer algo; **to be** ~ **on sth/sb** interesarse por algo/uno; **I'm not** ~ **on going** no tengo ganas de ir.

keenly ['kiːnlɪ] adv (enthusiastically) con entusiasmo; (acutely) vivamente; (intensely) intensamente.

keenness ['kiːnnɪs] n (eagerness) entusiasmo, interés m.

keep [kiːp] vb (pt, pp **kept** [kɛpt]) vt (retain, preserve) guardar; (hold back) quedarse con; (shop) ser propietario de; (feed: family etc) mantener; (promise) cumplir; (chickens, bees etc) criar ♦ vi (food) conservarse; (remain) seguir, continuar ♦ n (of castle) torreón m; (food etc) comida, sustento; **to** ~ **doing sth** seguir haciendo algo; **to** ~ **sb from doing sth** impedir a algn hacer algo; **to** ~ **sth from happening** impedir que algo ocurra; **to** ~ **sb happy** tener a algn contento; **to** ~ **sb waiting** hacer esperar a algn; **to** ~ **a place tidy** mantener un lugar limpio; **to** ~ **sth to o.s.** no decirle algo a nadie; **to** ~ **time** (clock) mantener la hora exacta; ~ **the change** quédese con la vuelta; **to** ~ **an appointment** acudir a una cita; **to** ~ **a record** or **note of sth** tomar nota de or apuntar algo; see also **keeps.**

►**keep away** vt: **to** ~ **sth/sb away from sb** mantener algo/a algn apartado de algn ♦ vi: **to** ~ **away (from)** mantenerse apartado (de).

►**keep back** vt (crowd, tears) contener; (money) quedarse con; (conceal: information): **to** ~ **sth back from sb** ocultar algo a algn ♦ vi hacerse a un lado.

►**keep down** vt (control: prices, spending)

controlar; (*retain: food*) retener ♦ *vi* seguir agachado, no levantar la cabeza.

►**keep in** *vt* (*invalid, child*) impedir que salga, no dejar salir; (*SCOL*) castigar (a quedarse en el colegio) ♦ *vi* (*col*): **to ~ in with sb** mantener la relación con algn.

►**keep off** *vt* (*dog, person*) mantener a distancia ♦ *vi* evitar; **~ your hands off!** ¡no toques!; **"~ off the grass"** "prohibido pisar el césped".

►**keep on** *vi* seguir, continuar.

►**keep out** *vi* (*stay out*) permanecer fuera; **"~ out"** "prohibida la entrada".

►**keep up** *vt* mantener, conservar ♦ *vi* no rezagarse; (*fig: in comprehension*) seguir (el hilo); **to ~ up with** (*pace*) ir al paso de; (*level*) mantenerse a la altura de; **to ~ up with sb** seguir el ritmo a algn; (*fig*) seguir a algn.

keeper ['ki:pə*] *n* guarda *m/f*.

keep-fit [ki:p'fɪt] *n* gimnasia (de mantenimiento).

keeping ['ki:pɪŋ] *n* (*care*) cuidado; **in ~ with** de acuerdo con.

keeps [ki:ps] *n*: **for ~** (*col*) para siempre.

keepsake ['ki:pseɪk] *n* recuerdo.

keg [kɛg] *n* barrilete *m*, barril *m*.

Ken. *abbr* (*US*) = *Kentucky.*

kennel ['kɛnl] *n* perrera; **~s** *npl* perrera.

Kenya ['ki:njə] *n* Kenia.

Kenyan ['ki:njən] *adj, n* keniata *m/f*, keniano/a *m/f*.

kept [kɛpt] *pt, pp of* **keep.**

kerb [kə:b] *n* (*BRIT*) bordillo.

kerb crawler [-krɔ:lə*] *n conductor en busca de prostitutas desde su coche.*

kernel ['kə:nl] *n* (*nut*) fruta; (*fig*) meollo.

kerosene ['kɛrəsi:n] *n* keroseno.

kestrel ['kɛstrəl] *n* cernícalo.

ketchup ['kɛtʃəp] *n* salsa de tomate, ketchup *m*.

kettle ['kɛtl] *n* hervidor *m*.

kettle drum *n* (*MUS*) timbal *m*.

key [ki:] *n* (*gen*) llave *f*; (*MUS*) tono; (*of piano, typewriter*) tecla; (*on map*) clave *f* ♦ *cpd* (*vital: position, industry etc*) clave ♦ *vt* (*also:* **~ in**) teclear.

keyboard ['ki:bɔ:d] *n* teclado ♦ *vt* (*text*) teclear.

keyboarder ['ki:bɔ:də*] *n* teclista *m/f*.

keyed up [ki:d-] *adj* (*person*) nervioso; **to be (all) ~** estar nervioso *or* emocionado.

keyhole ['ki:həʊl] *n* ojo (de la cerradura).

keyhole surgery *n* cirugía cerrada *or* no invasiva.

key man *n* hombre *m* clave.

keynote ['ki:nəʊt] *n* (*MUS*) tónica; (*fig*) idea fundamental.

keynote speech *n* discurso de apertura.

keypad ['ki:pæd] *n* teclado numérico.

keyring ['ki:rɪŋ] *n* llavero.

keystone ['ki:stəʊn] *n* piedra clave.

keystroke ['ki:strəʊk] *n* pulsación *f* (de una tecla).

kg *abbr* (= *kilogram*) kg.

KGB *n abbr* KGB *m*.

khaki ['kɑ:kɪ] *n* caqui.

kibbutz, ~im [kɪ'bʊts, -ɪm] *n* kibutz *m*.

kick [kɪk] *vt* (*person*) dar una patada a; (*ball*) dar un puntapié a ♦ *vi* (*horse*) dar coces ♦ *n* patada; puntapié *m*, tiro; (*of rifle*) culetazo; (*col: thrill*): **he does it for ~s** lo hace por pura diversión.

►**kick around** *vt* (*idea*) dar vueltas a; (*person*) tratar a patadas a.

►**kick off** *vi* (*SPORT*) hacer el saque inicial.

kick-start ['kɪkstɑ:t] *n* (*also:* **~er**) (pedal *m* de) arranque *m*.

kid [kɪd] *n* (*col: child*) niño/a, chiquillo/a; (*animal*) cabrito; (*leather*) cabritilla ♦ *vi* (*col*) bromear.

kid gloves *npl*: **to treat sb with ~** andarse con pies de plomo con algn.

kidnap ['kɪdnæp] *vt* secuestrar.

kidnapper ['kɪdnæpə*] *n* secuestrador(a) *m/f*.

kidnapping ['kɪdnæpɪŋ] *n* secuestro.

kidney ['kɪdnɪ] *n* riñón *m*.

kidney bean *n* judía, alubia.

kidney machine *n* riñón *m* artificial.

Kilimanjaro [kɪlɪmæn'dʒɑ:rəʊ] *n* Kilimanjaro.

kill [kɪl] *vt* matar; (*murder*) asesinar; (*fig: rumour, conversation*) acabar con ♦ *n* matanza; **to ~ time** matar el tiempo.

►**kill off** *vt* exterminar, terminar con; (*fig*) echar por tierra.

killer ['kɪlə*] *n* asesino/a.

killer instinct *n*: **to have the ~** ir a por todas.

killing ['kɪlɪŋ] *n* (*one*) asesinato; (*several*) matanza; (*COMM*): **to make a ~** tener un gran éxito financiero.

killjoy ['kɪldʒɔɪ] *n* (*BRIT*) aguafiestas *m/f inv*.

kiln [kɪln] *n* horno.

kilo ['ki:ləʊ] *n* (*abbr. = kilogram(me)*) kilo.

kilobyte ['kɪləʊbaɪt] *n* (*COMPUT*) kilobyte *m*, kilooteto.

kilogram(me) ['kɪləʊɡræm] *n* kilogramo.

kilometre, (*US*) **kilometer** ['kɪləmi:tə*] *n* kilómetro.

kilowatt ['kɪləʊwɒt] *n* kilovatio.

kilt [kɪlt] *n* falda escocesa.

kilter ['kɪltə*] *n*: **out of ~** desbaratado.

kimono [kɪ'məʊnəʊ] *n* quimono.

kin [kɪn] *n* parientes *mpl*.

kind [kaɪnd] *adj* (*treatment*) bueno, cariñoso; (*person, act, word*) amable, atento ♦ *n* clase *f*, especie *f*; (*species*) género; in ~ (*COMM*) en especie; a ~ of una especie de; to be two of a ~ ser tal para cual; would you be ~ enough to ...?, would you be so ~ as to ...? ¿me hace el favor de ...?; it's very ~ of you (to do) le agradezco mucho (el que haya hecho).

kindergarten ['kɪndəgɑːtn] *n* jardín *m* de infancia.

kind-hearted [kaɪnd'hɑːtɪd] *adj* bondadoso, de buen corazón.

kindle ['kɪndl] *vt* encender.

kindliness ['kaɪndlɪnəs] *n* bondad *f*, amabilidad *f*.

kindling ['kɪndlɪŋ] *n* leña (menuda).

kindly ['kaɪndlɪ] *adj* bondadoso; (*gentle*) cariñoso ♦ *adv* bondadosamente, amablemente; will you ~ ... sería usted tan amable de ....

kindness ['kaɪndnɪs] *n* bondad *f*, amabilidad *f*.

kindred ['kɪndrɪd] *n* familia, parientes *mpl* ♦ *adj*: ~ spirits almas *fpl* gemelas.

kinetic [kɪ'nɛtɪk] *adj* cinético.

king [kɪŋ] *n* rey *m*.

kingdom ['kɪŋdəm] *n* reino.

kingfisher ['kɪŋfɪʃə*] *n* martín *m* pescador.

kingpin ['kɪŋpɪn] *n* (*TECH*) perno real *or* pinzote; (*fig*) persona clave.

king-size(d) ['kɪŋsaɪz(d)] *adj* de tamaño gigante; (*cigarette*) extra largo.

kink [kɪŋk] *n* (*in rope etc*) enroscadura; (*in hair*) rizo; (*fig: emotional, psychological*) manía.

kinky ['kɪŋkɪ] *adj* (*pej*) perverso.

kinship ['kɪnʃɪp] *n* parentesco; (*fig*) afinidad *f*.

kinsman ['kɪnzmən] *n* pariente *m*.

kinswoman ['kɪnzwumən] *n* parienta.

kiosk ['kiːɔsk] *n* quiosco; (*BRIT TEL*) cabina; newspaper ~ quiosco, kiosco.

kipper ['kɪpə*] *n* arenque *m* ahumado.

Kirghizia [kəː'gɪzɪə] *n* Kirguizistán *m*.

kiss [kɪs] *n* beso ♦ *vt* besar; ~ of life (*artificial respiration*) respiración *f* artificial; to ~ sb goodbye dar un beso de despedida a algn; to ~ (each other) besarse.

kissogram ['kɪsəgræm] *n servicio de felicitaciones mediante el que se envía a una persona vestida de manera sugerente para besar a algn.*

kit [kɪt] *n* equipo; (*set of tools etc*) (caja de) herramientas *fpl*; (*assembly ~*) juego de armar; tool ~ juego *or* estuche *m* de herramientas.

►**kit out** *vt* equipar.

kitbag ['kɪtbæg] *n* (*MIL*) macuto.

kitchen ['kɪtʃɪn] *n* cocina.

kitchen garden *n* huerto.

kitchen sink *n* fregadero.

kitchen unit *n* módulo de cocina.

kitchenware ['kɪtʃɪnwɛə*] *n* batería de cocina.

kite [kaɪt] *n* (*toy*) cometa.

kith [kɪθ] *n*: ~ and kin parientes *mpl* y allegados.

kitten ['kɪtn] *n* gatito/a.

kitty ['kɪtɪ] *n* (*pool of money*) fondo común; (*CARDS*) bote *m*.

kiwi ['kiːwiː] *n* (*col: New Zealander*) neozelandés/esa *m/f*; (*also*: ~ fruit) kiwi *m*.

KKK *n abbr* (*US*) = Ku Klux Klan.

kleptomaniac [klɛptəu'meɪnɪæk] *n* cleptómano/a.

km *abbr* (= *kilometre*) km.

km/h *abbr* (= *kilometres per hour*) km/h.

knack [næk] *n*: to have the ~ of doing sth tener facilidad para hacer algo.

knackered ['nækəd] *adj* (*col*) hecho polvo.

knapsack ['næpsæk] *n* mochila.

knead [niːd] *vt* amasar.

knee [niː] *n* rodilla.

kneecap ['niːkæp] *vt* destrozar a tiros la rótula de ♦ *n* rótula.

knee-deep ['niː'diːp] *adj*: the water was ~ el agua llegaba hasta la rodilla.

kneel [niːl], *pt, pp* knelt [niːl, nɛlt] *vi* (*also*: ~ down) arrodillarse.

kneepad ['niːpæd] *n* rodillera.

knell [nɛl] *n* toque *m* de difuntos.

knelt [nɛlt] *pt, pp of* kneel.

knew [njuː] *pt of* know.

knickers ['nɪkəz] *npl* (*BRIT*) bragas *fpl*, calzones *mpl* (*LAM*).

knick-knack ['nɪknæk] *n* chuchería, baratija.

knife [naɪf] (*pl* knives) *n* cuchillo ♦ *vt* acuchillar; ~, fork and spoon cubiertos *mpl*.

knife edge *n*: to be on a ~ estar en la cuerda floja.

knight [naɪt] *n* caballero; (*CHESS*) caballo.

knighthood ['naɪthud] *n* (*title*): to get a ~ recibir el título de *Sir*.

knit [nɪt] *vt* tejer, tricotar; (*brows*) fruncir; (*fig*): to ~ together unir, juntar ♦ *vi* hacer punto, tejer, tricotar; (*bones*) soldarse.

knitted ['nɪtɪd] *adj* de punto.

knitting ['nɪtɪŋ] *n* labor *f* de punto.

knitting machine *n* máquina de tricotar.

knitting needle, (*US*) **knit pin** *n* aguja de hacer punto *or* tejer.

knitting pattern *n* patrón *m* para tricotar.

knitwear ['nɪtwɛə*] *n* prendas *fpl* de punto.

knives [naɪvz] *pl of* **knife**.
knob [nɒb] *n* (*of door*) pomo; (*of stick*) puño; (*lump*) bulto; (*fig*): **a ~ of butter** (*BRIT*) un pedazo de mantequilla.
knobbly ['nɒblɪ], (*US*) **knobby** ['nɒbɪ] *adj* (*wood, surface*) nudoso; (*knee*) huesudo.
knock [nɒk] *vt* (*strike*) golpear; (*bump into*) chocar contra; (*fig: col*) criticar ♦ *vi* (*at door etc*): **to ~ at/on** llamar a ♦ *n* golpe *m*; (*on door*) llamada; **he ~ed at the door** llamó a la puerta.
►**knock down** *vt* (*pedestrian*) atropellar; (*price*) rebajar.
►**knock off** *vi* (*col: finish*) salir del trabajo ♦ *vt* (*col: steal*) birlar; (*strike off*) quitar; (*fig: from price, record*): **to ~ off £10** rebajar en £10.
►**knock out** *vt* dejar sin sentido; (*BOXING*) poner fuera de combate, dejar K.O.; (*stop*) estropear, dejar fuera de servicio.
►**knock over** *vt* (*object*) derribar, tirar; (*pedestrian*) atropellar.
knockdown ['nɒkdaun] *adj* (*price*) de saldo.
knocker ['nɒkə*] *n* (*on door*) aldaba.
knocking ['nɒkɪŋ] *n* golpes *mpl*, golpeteo.
knock-kneed [nɒk'niːd] *adj* patizambo.
knockout ['nɒkaut] *n* (*BOXING*) K.O. *m*, knockout *m*.
knock-up ['nɒkʌp] *n* (*TENNIS*) peloteo.
knot [nɒt] *n* (*gen*) nudo ♦ *vt* anudar; **to tie a ~** hacer un nudo.
knotted ['nɒtɪd] *adj* anudado.
knotty ['nɒtɪ] *adj* (*fig*) complicado.
know [nəu] *vb* (*pt* **knew**, *pp* **known** [njuː, nəun]) *vt* (*gen*) saber; (*person, author, place*) conocer ♦ *vi*: **as far as I ~** ... que yo sepa ...; **yes, I ~** sí, ya lo sé; **I don't ~** no lo sé; **to ~ how to do** saber hacer; **to ~ how to swim** saber nadar; **to ~ about** *or* **of sb/sth** saber de algn/algo; **to get to ~ sth** enterarse de algo; **I ~ nothing about it** no sé nada de eso; **I don't ~ him** no lo *or* le conozco; **to ~ right from wrong** saber distinguir el bien del mal.
know-all ['nəuɔːl] *n* (*BRIT pej*) sabelotodo *m/f inv*, sabihondo/a.
know-how ['nəuhau] *n* conocimientos *mpl*.
knowing ['nəuɪŋ] *adj* (*look etc*) de complicidad.
knowingly ['nəuɪŋlɪ] *adv* (*purposely*) a sabiendas; (*smile, look*) con complicidad.
know-it-all ['nəuɪtɔːl] *n* (*US*) = **know-all**.
knowledge ['nɒlɪdʒ] *n* (*gen*) conocimiento; (*learning*) saber *m*, conocimientos *mpl*; **to have no ~ of** no saber nada de; **with my ~** con mis conocimientos, sabiéndolo; **to (the best of) my ~** a mi entender, que yo sepa; **not to my ~** que yo sepa, no; **it is**

common ~ that ... es del dominio público que ...; **it has come to my ~ that ...** me he enterado de que ...; **to have a working ~ of Spanish** defenderse con el español.
knowledgeable ['nɒlɪdʒəbl] *adj* entendido, erudito.
known [nəun] *pp of* **know** ♦ *adj* (*thief, facts*) conocido; (*expert*) reconocido.
knuckle ['nʌkl] *n* nudillo.
►**knuckle down** *vi* (*col*) ponerse a trabajar en serio.
►**knuckle under** *vi* someterse.
knuckleduster ['nʌkldʌstə*] *n* puño de hierro.
KO *abbr n* (= *knockout*) K.O. *m* ♦ *vt* (= *knock out*) dejar K.O.
koala [kəu'ɑːlə] *n* (*also*: **~ bear**) koala *m*.
kook [kuːk] *n* (*US col*) chiflado/a *m/f*, majareta *m/f*.
Koran [kɔ'rɑːn] *n* Corán *m*.
Korea [kə'rɪə] *n* Corea; **North/South ~** Corea del Norte/Sur.
Korean [kə'rɪən] *adj*, *n* coreano/a *m/f*.
kosher ['kəuʃə*] *adj* autorizado por la ley judía.
kowtow ['kau'tau] *vi*: **to ~ to sb** humillarse ante algn.
KS *abbr* (*US*) = *Kansas*.
Kt *abbr* (*BRIT*: = *Knight*) *caballero de una orden*.
Kuala Lumpur ['kwɑːlə'lumpuə*] *n* Kuala Lumpur *m*.
kudos ['kjuːdɒs] *n* gloria, prestigio.
Kurd [kɜːd] *n* kurdo/a.
Kuwait [ku'weɪt] *n* Kuwait *m*.
Kuwaiti [ku'weɪtɪ] *adj*, *n* Kuwaití *m/f*.
kW *abbr* (= *kilowatt*) Kv.
KY, Ky. *abbr* (*US*) = *Kentucky*.

L l

L, l [ɛl] *n* (*letter*) L, l *f*; **L for Lucy**, (*US*) **L for Love** L de Lorenzo.
L *abbr* (*on maps etc*) = **lake**; **large**; (= *left*) izq.; (*BRIT AUT*: = *learner*) L.
l. *abbr* = **litre**.
LA *n abbr* (*US*) = *Los Angeles* ♦ *abbr* (*US*) = *Louisiana*.
La. *abbr* (*US*) = *Louisiana*.
lab [læb] *n abbr* = **laboratory**.
Lab. *abbr* (*Canada*) = *Labrador*.

label ['leɪbl] *n* etiqueta; (*brand: of record*) sello (discográfico) ♦ *vt* poner una etiqueta a, etiquetar.

labor *etc* ['leɪbə*] (*US*) = **labour**.

laboratory [lə'bɔrətərɪ] *n* laboratorio.

Labor Day *n* (*US*) día *m* de los trabajadores (*primer lunes de septiembre*).

laborious [lə'bɔːrɪəs] *adj* penoso.

laboriously [lə'bɔːrɪəslɪ] *adv* penosamente.

labor union *n* (*US*) sindicato.

labor unrest *n* (*US*) conflictividad *f* laboral.

Labour ['leɪbə*] *n* (*BRIT POL: also*: **the** ~ **Party**) el partido laborista, los laboristas.

labour, (*US*) **labor** ['leɪbə*] *n* (*task*) trabajo; (~ *force*) mano *f* de obra; (*workers*) trabajadores *mpl*; (*MED*) (dolores *mpl* de) parto ♦ *vi*: **to** ~ (**at**) trabajar (en) ♦ *vt* insistir en; **hard** ~ trabajos *mpl* forzados; **to be in** ~ estar de parto.

labo(u)r cost *n* costo de la mano de obra.

labo(u)r dispute *n* conflicto laboral.

labo(u)red ['leɪbəd] *adj* (*breathing*) fatigoso; (*style*) forzado, pesado.

labo(u)rer ['leɪbərə*] *n* peón *m*; (*on farm*) peón *m*, obrero; (*day* ~) jornalero.

labo(u)r force *n* mano *f* de obra.

labo(u)r-intensive [leɪbərɪn'tɛnsɪv] *adj* que necesita mucha mano de obra.

labo(u)r relations *npl* relaciones *fpl* laborales.

labo(u)r-saving ['leɪbəseɪvɪŋ] *adj* que ahorra trabajo.

laburnum [lə'bɜːnəm] *n* codeso.

labyrinth ['læbɪrɪnθ] *n* laberinto.

lace [leɪs] *n* encaje *m*; (*of shoe etc*) cordón *m* ♦ *vt* (*shoes: also*: ~ **up**) atarse; (*drink: fortify with spirits*) echar licor a.

lacemaking ['leɪsmeɪkɪŋ] *n* obra de encaje.

lacerate ['læsəreɪt] *vt* lacerar.

laceration [læsə'reɪʃən] *n* laceración *f*.

lace-up ['leɪsʌp] *adj* (*shoes etc*) con cordones.

lack [læk] *n* (*absence*) falta, carencia; (*scarcity*) escasez *f* ♦ *vt* faltarle a algn, carecer de; **through** *or* **for** ~ **of** por falta de; **to be** ~**ing** faltar, no haber.

lackadaisical [lækə'deɪzɪkl] *adj* (*careless*) descuidado; (*indifferent*) indiferente.

lackey ['lækɪ] *n* (*also fig*) lacayo.

lacklustre, (*US*) **lackluster** ['læklʌstə*] *adj* (*surface*) deslustrado, deslucido; (*style*) inexpresivo; (*eyes*) apagado.

laconic [lə'kɔnɪk] *adj* lacónico.

lacquer ['lækə*] *n* laca; **hair** ~ laca para el pelo.

lacrosse [lə'krɔs] *n* lacrosse *f*.

lacy ['leɪsɪ] *adj* (*like lace*) parecido al encaje.

lad [læd] *n* muchacho, chico; (*in stable etc*) mozo.

ladder ['lædə*] *n* escalera (de mano); (*BRIT: in tights*) carrera ♦ *vt* (*BRIT: tights*) hacer una carrera en.

laden ['leɪdn] *adj*: ~ (**with**) cargado (de); **fully** ~ (*truck, ship*) cargado hasta el tope.

ladle ['leɪdl] *n* cucharón *m*.

lady ['leɪdɪ] *n* señora; (*distinguished, noble*) dama; **young** ~ señorita; **the ladies'** (**room**) los servicios de señoras.

ladybird ['leɪdɪbəːd], (*US*) **ladybug** ['leɪdɪbʌg] *n* mariquita.

lady doctor *n* médica, doctora.

lady-in-waiting ['leɪdɪɪn'weɪtɪŋ] *n* dama de honor.

ladykiller ['leɪdɪkɪlə*] *n* robacorazones *m inv*.

ladylike ['leɪdɪlaɪk] *adj* fino.

Ladyship ['leɪdɪʃɪp] *n*: **your** ~ su Señoría.

LAFTA *n abbr* (= *Latin American Free Trade Association*) ALALC *f*.

lag [læg] *vi* (*also*: ~ **behind**) retrasarse, quedarse atrás ♦ *vt* (*pipes*) revestir.

lager ['lɑːgə*] *n* cerveza (rubia).

lager lout *n* (*BRIT col*) gamberro borracho.

lagging ['lægɪŋ] *n* revestimiento.

lagoon [lə'guːn] *n* laguna.

Lagos ['leɪgɔs] *n* Lagos *m*.

laid [leɪd] *pt, pp of* **lay**.

laid-back [leɪd'bæk] *adj* (*col*) tranquilo, relajado.

laid up *adj*: **to be** ~ (*person*) tener que guardar cama.

lain [leɪn] *pp of* **lie**.

lair [lɛə*] *n* guarida.

laissez-faire [lɛseɪ'fɛə*] *n* laissez-faire *m*.

laity ['leɪtɪ] *n* laicado.

lake [leɪk] *n* lago.

Lake District *n* (*BRIT*): **the** ~ la Región de los Lagos.

lamb [læm] *n* cordero; (*meat*) carne *f* de cordero.

lamb chop *n* chuleta de cordero.

lambswool ['læmzwul] *n* lana de cordero.

lame [leɪm] *adj* cojo, rengo (*LAM*); (*weak*) débil, poco convincente; ~ **duck** (*fig: person*) inútil *m/f*; (: *firm*) empresa en quiebra.

lamely ['leɪmlɪ] *adv* (*fig*) sin convicción.

lament [lə'mɛnt] *n* lamento ♦ *vt* lamentarse de.

lamentable ['læməntəbl] *adj* lamentable.

lamentation [læmən'teɪʃən] *n* lamento.

laminated ['læmɪneɪtɪd] *adj* laminado.

lamp [læmp] *n* lámpara.

lamplight ['læmplaɪt] *n*: **by** ~ a la luz de la lámpara.

lampoon [læm'pu:n] *vt* satirizar.
lamppost ['læmppəust] *n* (*BRIT*) farola.
lampshade ['læmpʃeɪd] *n* pantalla.
lance [lɑ:ns] *n* lanza ♦ *vt* (*MED*) abrir con lanceta.
lance corporal *n* (*BRIT*) soldado de primera clase.
lancet ['lɑ:nsɪt] *n* (*MED*) lanceta.
Lancs [læŋks] *abbr* (*BRIT*) = *Lancashire*.
land [lænd] *n* tierra; (*country*) país *m*; (*piece of ~*) terreno; (*estate*) tierras *fpl*, finca; (*AGR*) campo ♦ *vi* (*from ship*) desembarcar; (*AVIAT*) aterrizar; (*fig: fall*) caer ♦ *vt* (*obtain*) conseguir; (*passengers, goods*) desembarcar; **to go/travel by ~** ir/viajar por tierra; **to own ~** ser dueño de tierras; **to ~ on one's feet** caer de pie; (*fig: to be lucky*) salir bien parado.
▶**land up** *vi*: **to ~ up in/at** ir a parar a/en.
landed ['lændɪd] *adj*: **~ gentry** terratenientes *mpl*.
landfill site ['lændfɪl-] *n* vertedero.
landing ['lændɪŋ] *n* desembarco; aterrizaje *m*; (*of staircase*) rellano.
landing card *n* tarjeta de desembarque.
landing craft *n* lancha de desembarco.
landing gear *n* (*AVIAT*) tren *m* de aterrizaje.
landing stage *n* (*BRIT*) desembarcadero.
landing strip *n* pista de aterrizaje.
landlady ['lændleɪdɪ] *n* (*of boarding house*) patrona; (*owner*) dueña.
landlocked ['lændlɔkt] *adj* cercado de tierra.
landlord ['lændlɔ:d] *n* propietario; (*of pub etc*) patrón *m*.
landlubber ['lændlʌbə*] *n* marinero de agua dulce.
landmark ['lændmɑ:k] *n* lugar *m* conocido; **to be a ~** (*fig*) hacer época.
landowner ['lændəunə*] *n* terrateniente *m/f*.
landscape ['lænskeɪp] *n* paisaje *m*.
landscape architecture *n* arquitectura paisajista.
landscaped ['lænskeɪpt] *adj* reformado artísticamente.
landscape gardener *n* diseñador(a) *m/f* de paisajes.
landscape gardening *n* jardinería paisajista.
landscape painting *n* (*ART*) paisaje *m*.
landslide ['lændslaɪd] *n* (*GEO*) corrimiento de tierras; (*fig: POL*) victoria arrolladora.
lane [leɪn] *n* (*in country*) camino; (*in town*) callejón *m*; (*AUT*) carril *m*; (*in race*) calle *f*; (*for air or sea traffic*) ruta; **shipping ~** ruta marina.

language ['læŋgwɪdʒ] *n* lenguaje *m*; (*national tongue*) idioma *m*, lengua; **bad ~** palabrotas *fpl*.
language laboratory *n* laboratorio de idiomas.
language studies *npl* estudios *mpl* filológicos.
languid ['læŋgwɪd] *adj* lánguido.
languish ['læŋgwɪʃ] *vi* languidecer.
languor ['læŋgə*] *n* languidez *f*.
languorous ['læŋgərəs] *adj* lánguido.
lank [læŋk] *adj* (*hair*) lacio.
lanky ['læŋkɪ] *adj* larguirucho.
lanolin(e) ['lænəlɪn] *n* lanolina.
lantern ['læntn] *n* linterna, farol *m*.
lanyard ['lænjed] *n* acollador *m*.
Laos [laus] *n* Laos *m*.
lap [læp] *n* (*of track*) vuelta; (*of body*): **to sit on sb's ~** sentarse en las rodillas de algn ♦ *vt* (*also: ~ up*) beber a lengüetadas *or* con la lengua ♦ *vi* (*waves*) chapotear.
▶**lap up** *vt* beber a lengüetadas *or* con la lengua; (*fig: compliments, attention*) disfrutar; (*lies etc*) tragarse.
La Paz [læ'pæz] *n* La Paz.
lapdog ['læpdɔg] *n* perro faldero.
lapel [lə'pɛl] *n* solapa.
Lapland ['læplænd] *n* Laponia.
Laplander ['læplændə*] *n* lapón/ona *m/f*.
lapse [læps] *n* (*fault*) error *m*, fallo; (*moral*) desliz *m* ♦ *vi* (*expire*) caducar; (*morally*) cometer un desliz; (*time*) pasar, transcurrir; **to ~ into bad habits** volver a las andadas; **~ of time** lapso, período; **a ~ of memory** un lapsus de memoria.
laptop ['læptɔp] *n* (*also: ~ computer*) (ordenador *m*) portátil *m*.
larceny ['lɑ:sənɪ] *n* latrocinio.
lard [lɑ:d] *n* manteca (de cerdo).
larder ['lɑ:də*] *n* despensa.
large [lɑ:dʒ] *adj* grande ♦ *adv*: **by and ~** en general, en términos generales; **at ~** (*free*) en libertad; (*generally*) en general; **to make ~(r)** hacer mayor *or* más extenso; **a ~ number of people** una gran cantidad de personas; **on a ~ scale** a gran escala.
largely ['lɑ:dʒlɪ] *adv* en gran parte.
large-scale ['lɑ:dʒ'skeɪl] *adj* (*map, drawing*) a gran escala; (*reforms, business activities*) importante.
largesse [lɑ:'ʒɛs] *n* generosidad *f*.
lark [lɑ:k] *n* (*bird*) alondra; (*joke*) broma.
▶**lark about** *vi* bromear, hacer el tonto.
larva, *pl* **larvae** ['lɑ:və, -i:] *n* larva.
laryngitis [lærɪn'dʒaɪtɪs] *n* laringitis *f*.
larynx ['lærɪŋks] *n* laringe *f*.
lasagne [lə'zænjə] *n* lasaña.

lascivious [ləˈsɪvɪəs] *adj* lascivo.
laser [ˈleɪzə*] *n* láser *m*.
laser beam *n* rayo láser.
laser printer *n* impresora láser.
lash [læʃ] *n* latigazo; (*punishment*) azote *m*; (*also*: **eye~**) pestaña ♦ *vt* azotar; (*tie*) atar.
▶**lash down** *vt* sujetar con cuerdas ♦ *vi* (*rain*) caer a trombas.
▶**lash out** *vi* (*col: spend*) gastar a la loca; **to ~ out at** *or* **against sb** lanzar invectivas contra algn.
lashing [ˈlæʃɪŋ] *n* (*beating*) azotaina, flagelación *f*; **~s of** (*col*) montones *mpl* de.
lass [læs] *n* chica.
lassitude [ˈlæsɪtjuːd] *n* lasitud *f*.
lasso [læˈsuː] *n* lazo ♦ *vt* coger con lazo.
last [lɑːst] *adj* (*gen*) último; (*final*) último, final ♦ *adv* por último ♦ *vi* (*endure*) durar; (*continue*) continuar, seguir; **~ night** anoche; **~ week** la semana pasada; **at ~** por fin; **~ but one** penúltimo; **~ time** la última vez; **it ~s (for) 2 hours** dura dos horas.
last-ditch [ˈlɑːstˈdɪtʃ] *adj* (*attempt*) de último recurso, último, desesperado.
lasting [ˈlɑːstɪŋ] *adj* duradero.
lastly [ˈlɑːstlɪ] *adv* por último, finalmente.
last-minute [ˈlɑːstmɪnɪt] *adj* de última hora.
latch [lætʃ] *n* picaporte *m*, pestillo.
▶**latch on to** *vt fus* (*cling to: person*) pegarse a; (: *idea*) agarrarse de.
latchkey [ˈlætʃkiː] *n* llavín *m*.
latchkey child *n* niño cuyos padres trabajan.
late [leɪt] *adj* (*not on time*) tarde, atrasado; (*towards end of period, life*) tardío; (*hour*) avanzado; (*dead*) fallecido ♦ *adv* tarde; (*behind time, schedule*) con retraso; **to be (10 minutes) ~** llegar con (diez minutos de) retraso; **to be ~ with** estar atrasado con; **~ delivery** entrega tardía; **~ in life** a una edad avanzada; **of ~** últimamente; **in ~ May** hacia fines de mayo; **the ~ Mr X** el difunto Sr X; **to work ~** trabajar hasta tarde.
latecomer [ˈleɪtkʌmə*] *n* recién llegado/a.
lately [ˈleɪtlɪ] *adv* últimamente.
lateness [ˈleɪtnɪs] *n* (*of person*) demora; (*of event*) tardanza.
latent [ˈleɪtnt] *adj* latente; **~ defect** defecto latente.
later [ˈleɪtə*] *adj* (*date etc*) posterior; (*version etc*) más reciente ♦ *adv* más tarde, después; **~ on today** hoy más tarde.
lateral [ˈlætərl] *adj* lateral.
latest [ˈleɪtɪst] *adj* último; **at the ~** a más tardar.

latex [ˈleɪtɛks] *n* látex *m*.
lathe [leɪð] *n* torno.
lather [ˈlɑːðə*] *n* espuma (de jabón) ♦ *vt* enjabonar.
Latin [ˈlætɪn] *n* latín *m* ♦ *adj* latino.
Latin America *n* América Latina, Latinoamérica.
Latin American *adj*, *n* latinoamericano/a *m/f*.
Latino [læˈtiːnəu] *adj*, *n* latino/a *m/f*.
latitude [ˈlætɪtjuːd] *n* latitud *f*; (*fig: freedom*) libertad *f*.
latrine [ləˈtriːn] *n* letrina.
latter [ˈlætə*] *adj* último; (*of two*) segundo ♦ *n*: **the ~** el último, éste.
latter-day [ˈlætədeɪ] *adj* moderno.
latterly [ˈlætəlɪ] *adv* últimamente.
lattice [ˈlætɪs] *n* enrejado.
lattice window *n* ventana enrejada *or* de celosía.
lattice work *n* enrejado.
Latvia [ˈlætvɪə] *n* Letonia.
Latvian [ˈlætvɪən] *adj* letón/ona ♦ *n* letón/ona *m/f*; (*LING*) letón *m*.
laudable [ˈlɔːdəbl] *adj* loable.
laugh [lɑːf] *n* risa; (*loud*) carcajada ♦ *vi* reírse, reír; reírse a carcajadas.
▶**laugh at** *vt fus* reírse de.
▶**laugh off** *vt* tomar a risa.
laughable [ˈlɑːfəbl] *adj* ridículo.
laughing [ˈlɑːfɪŋ] *adj* risueño ♦ *n*: **it's no ~ matter** no es cosa de risa.
laughing gas *n* gas *m* hilarante.
laughing stock *n*: **to be the ~ of the town** ser el hazmerreír de la ciudad.
laughter [ˈlɑːftə*] *n* risa.
launch [lɔːntʃ] *n* (*boat*) lancha; *see also* **launching** ♦ *vt* (*ship*) botar; (*rocket, plan*) lanzar.
▶**launch forth** *vi*: **to ~ forth (into)** lanzarse a *or* en, emprender.
▶**launch out** *vi* = **launch forth**.
launching [ˈlɔːntʃɪŋ] *n* (*of rocket etc*) lanzamiento; (*inauguration*) estreno.
launch(ing) pad *n* plataforma de lanzamiento.
launder [ˈlɔːndə*] *vt* lavar.
Launderette ® [lɔːnˈdrɛt], (*US*) **Laundromat** ® [ˈlɔːndrəmæt] *n* lavandería (automática).
laundry [ˈlɔːndrɪ] *n* lavandería; (*clothes*) ropa sucia; **to do the ~** hacer la colada.
laureate [ˈlɔːrɪət] *adj see* **poet**.
laurel [ˈlɔrl] *n* laurel *m*; **to rest on one's ~s** dormirse en *or* sobre los laureles.
lava [ˈlɑːvə] *n* lava.
lavatory [ˈlævətərɪ] *n* wáter *m*; **lavatories** *npl* servicios *mpl*, aseos *mpl*, sanitarios *mpl*

(*LAM*).
lavatory paper *n* papel *m* higiénico.
lavender ['lævəndə*] *n* lavanda.
lavish ['lævɪʃ] *adj* abundante; (*giving freely*):
~ **with** pródigo en ♦ *vt*: **to ~ sth on sb**
colmar a algn de algo.
lavishly ['lævɪʃlɪ] *adv* (*give, spend*)
generosamente; (*furnished*) lujosamente.
law [lɔ:] *n* ley *f*; (*study*) derecho; (*of game*)
regla; **against the ~** contra la ley; **to**
study ~ estudiar derecho; **to go to ~**
recurrir a la justicia.
law-abiding ['lɔ:əbaɪdɪŋ] *adj* respetuoso
con la ley.
law and order *n* orden *m* público.
lawbreaker ['lɔ:breɪkə*] *n* infractor(a) *m/f*
de la ley.
law court *n* tribunal *m* (de justicia).
lawful ['lɔ:ful] *adj* legítimo, lícito.
lawfully ['lɔ:fulɪ] *adv* legalmente.
lawless ['lɔ:lɪs] *adj* (*act*) ilegal; (*person*)
rebelde; (*country*) ingobernable.
Law Lord *n* (*BRIT*) *miembro de la Cámara*
de los Lores y del más alto tribunal de
apelación.
lawmaker ['lɔ:meɪkə*] *n* legislador(a) *m/f*.
lawn [lɔ:n] *n* césped *m*.
lawnmower ['lɔ:nməuə*] *n* cortacésped *m*.
lawn tennis *n* tenis *m* sobre hierba.
law school *n* (*US*) facultad *f* de derecho.
law student *n* estudiante *m/f* de derecho.
lawsuit ['lɔ:su:t] *n* pleito; **to bring a ~**
against entablar un pleito contra.
lawyer ['lɔ:jə*] *n* abogado/a; (*for sales, wills*
etc) notario/a.
lax [læks] *adj* (*discipline*) relajado; (*person*)
negligente.
laxative ['læksətɪv] *n* laxante *m*.
laxity ['læksɪtɪ] *n* flojedad *f*; (*moral*)
relajamiento; (*negligence*) negligencia.
lay [leɪ] *pt of* lie ♦ *adj* laico; (*not expert*) lego
♦ *vt* (*pt, pp* laid [leɪd]) (*place*) colocar; (*eggs,*
table) poner; (*trap*) tender; **to ~ the facts/**
one's proposals before sb presentar los
hechos/sus propuestas a algn.
►**lay aside, lay by** *vt* dejar a un lado.
►**lay down** *vt* (*pen etc*) dejar; (*arms*)
rendir; (*policy*) trazar; **to ~ down the law**
imponer las normas.
►**lay in** *vt* abastecerse de.
►**lay into** *vt fus* (*col: attack, scold*) arremeter
contra.
►**lay off** *vt* (*workers*) despedir.
►**lay on** *vt* (*water, gas*) instalar; (*meal,*
facilities) proveer.
►**lay out** *vt* (*plan*) trazar; (*display*) exponer;
(*spend*) gastar.
►**lay up** *vt* (*store*) guardar; (*ship*)

desarmar; (*subj: illness*) obligar a guardar
cama.
layabout ['leɪəbaut] *n* vago/a.
lay-by ['leɪbaɪ] *n* (*BRIT AUT*) apartadero.
lay days *npl* días *mpl* de inactividad.
layer ['leɪə*] *n* capa.
layette [leɪˈɛt] *n* ajuar *m* (de niño).
layman ['leɪmən] *n* lego.
lay-off ['leɪɔf] *n* despido, paro forzoso.
layout ['leɪaut] *n* (*design*) plan *m*, trazado;
(*disposition*) disposición *f*; (*PRESS*)
composición *f*.
laze [leɪz] *vi* no hacer nada; (*pej*)
holgazanear.
lazily ['leɪzɪlɪ] *adv* perezosamente.
laziness ['leɪzɪnɪs] *n* pereza.
lazy ['leɪzɪ] *adj* perezoso, vago, flojo (*LAM*).
LB *abbr* (*Canada*) = *Labrador*.
lb. *abbr* = **pound** (*weight*).
lbw *abr* (*CRICKET*) = *leg before wicket*.
LC *n abbr* (*US*) = *Library of Congress*.
lc *abbr* (*TYP*: = *lower case*) min.
L/C *abbr* = **letter of credit.**
LCD *n abbr see* **liquid crystal display.**
Ld *abbr* (= *Lord*) título de nobleza.
LDS *n abbr* (= *Licentiate in Dental Surgery*)
diploma universitario; (= *Latter-day*
Saints) Iglesia de Jesucristo de los Santos
del último día.
LEA *n abbr* (*BRIT*: = *local education authority*)
organismos locales encargados de la
enseñanza.
lead [li:d] *n* (*front position*) delantera;
(*distance, time ahead*) ventaja; (*clue*) pista;
(*ELEC*) cable *m*; (*for dog*) correa; (*THEAT*)
papel *m* principal; [lɛd] (*metal*) plomo; (*in*
pencil) mina ♦ *vb* (*pt, pp* led [lɛd]) *vt*
conducir; (*life*) llevar; (*be leader of*)
dirigir; (*SPORT*) ir en cabeza de;
(*orchestra: BRIT*) ser el primer violín en;
(: *US*) dirigir ♦ *vi* ir primero; **to be in the**
~ (*SPORT*) llevar la delantera; (*fig*) ir a la
cabeza; **to take the ~** (*SPORT*) tomar la
delantera; (*fig*) tomar la iniciativa; **to ~**
sb to believe that ... hacer creer a algn
que ...; **to ~ sb to do sth** llevar a algn a
hacer algo.
►**lead astray** *vt* llevar por mal camino.
►**lead away** *vt* llevar.
►**lead back** *vt* hacer volver.
►**lead off** *vt* llevar ♦ *vi* (*in game*) abrir.
►**lead on** *vt* (*tease*) engañar; **to ~ sb on to**
(*induce*) incitar a algn a.
►**lead to** *vt fus* producir, provocar.
►**lead up to** *vt fus* conducir a.
leaded ['lɛdɪd] *adj*: ~ **windows** ventanas *fpl*
emplomadas.
leaden ['lɛdn] *adj* (*sky, sea*) plomizo; (*heavy:*

footsteps) pesado.

leader ['li:də*] n jefe/a m/f, líder m; (*of union etc*) dirigente m/f; (*guide*) guía m/f; (*of newspaper*) editorial m; **they are ~s in their field** (*fig*) llevan la delantera en su especialidad.

leadership ['li:dəʃɪp] n dirección f; **qualities of ~** iniciativa sg; **under the ~ of ...** bajo la dirección de ..., al mando de ....

lead-free ['lɛdfriː] adj sin plomo.

leading ['li:dɪŋ] adj (*main*) principal; (*outstanding*) destacado; (*first*) primero; (*front*) delantero; **a ~ question** una pregunta tendenciosa.

leading lady n (THEAT) primera actriz f.

leading light n (*fig: person*) figura principal.

leading man n (THEAT) primer actor m.

leading role n papel m principal.

lead pencil n lápiz m.

lead poisoning n envenenamiento plúmbico.

lead time n (COMM) plazo de entrega.

lead-up ['li:dʌp] n: **in the ~ to the election** cuando falta *etc* poco para las elecciones.

lead weight n peso de plomo.

leaf, pl **leaves** [li:f, li:vz] n hoja; **to turn over a new ~** (*fig*) volver la hoja, hacer borrón y cuenta nueva; **to take a ~ out of sb's book** (*fig*) seguir el ejemplo de algn.

►**leaf through** vt fus (*book*) hojear.

leaflet ['li:flɪt] n folleto.

leafy ['li:fɪ] adj frondoso.

league [li:g] n sociedad f; (FOOTBALL) liga; **to be in ~ with** estar confabulado con.

league table n clasificación f.

leak [li:k] n (*of liquid, gas*) escape m, fuga; (*in pipe*) agujero; (*in roof*) gotera; (*fig: of information, in security*) filtración f ♦ vi (*ship*) hacer agua; (*shoes*) tener un agujero; (*pipe*) tener un escape; (*roof*) tener goteras; (*also: ~ out: liquid, gas*) escaparse, salirse; (*fig: news*) trascender, divulgarse ♦ vt (*gen*) dejar escapar; (*fig: information*) filtrar.

leakage ['li:kɪdʒ] n (*of water, gas etc*) escape m, fuga.

leaky ['li:kɪ] adj (*roof*) con goteras; (*bucket, shoe*) con agujeros; (*pipe*) con un escape; (*boat*) que hace agua.

lean [li:n] adj (*thin*) flaco; (*meat*) magro ♦ vb (pt, pp **leaned** or **leant** [lɛnt]) vt: **to ~ sth on sth** apoyar algo en algo ♦ vi (*slope*) inclinarse; (*rest*): **to ~ against** apoyarse contra; **to ~ on** apoyarse en.

►**lean back** vi inclinarse hacia atrás.

►**lean forward** vi inclinarse hacia

adelante.

►**lean out** vi: **to ~ out (of)** asomarse (a).

►**lean over** vi inclinarse.

leaning ['li:nɪŋ] adj inclinado ♦ n: **~ (towards)** inclinación f (hacia); **the L~ Tower of Pisa** la Torre Inclinada de Pisa.

leant [lɛnt] pt, pp of **lean**.

lean-to ['li:ntu:] n (*roof*) tejado de una sola agua; (*building*) cobertizo.

leap [li:p] n salto ♦ vi (pt, pp **leaped** or **leapt** [lɛpt]) saltar; **to ~ at an offer** apresurarse a aceptar una oferta.

►**leap up** vi (*person*) saltar.

leapfrog ['li:pfrɔg] n pídola ♦ vi: **to ~ over sb/sth** saltar por encima de algn/algo.

leapt [lɛpt] pt, pp of **leap**.

leap year n año bisiesto.

learn, pt, pp **learned** or **learnt** [lə:n, -t] vt (*gen*) aprender; (*come to know of*) enterarse de ♦ vi aprender; **to ~ how to do sth** aprender a hacer algo; **to ~ that ...** enterarse or informarse de que ...; **to ~ about sth** (SCOL) aprender algo; (*hear*) enterarse or informarse de algo; **we were sorry to ~ that ...** nos dio tristeza saber que ....

learned ['lə:nɪd] adj erudito.

learner ['lə:nə*] n principiante m/f; (BRIT: also: ~ driver) conductor(a) m/f en prácticas; see also **L-plates**.

learning ['lə:nɪŋ] n saber m, conocimientos mpl.

learnt [lə:nt] pp of **learn**.

lease [li:s] n arriendo ♦ vt arrendar; **on ~** en arriendo.

►**lease back** vt subarrendar.

leaseback ['li:sbæk] n subarriendo.

leasehold ['li:shəuld] n (*contract*) derechos mpl de arrendamiento ♦ adj arrendado.

leash [li:ʃ] n correa.

least [li:st] adj (*slightest*) menor, más pequeño; (*smallest amount of*) mínimo ♦ adv menos ♦ n: **the ~** lo menos; **the ~ expensive car** el coche menos caro; **at ~** por lo menos, al menos; **not in the ~** en absoluto.

leather ['lɛðə*] n cuero ♦ cpd: **~ goods** artículos mpl de cuero or piel.

leathery ['lɛðərɪ] adj (*skin*) curtido.

leave [li:v] vb (pt, pp **left** [lɛft]) vt dejar; (*go away from*) abandonar ♦ vi irse; (*train*) salir ♦ n permiso; **to ~ school** dejar la escuela or el colegio; **~ it to me!** ¡yo me encargo!; **he's already left for the airport** ya se ha marchado al aeropuerto; **to be left** quedar, sobrar; **there's some milk left over** sobra or queda algo de leche; **on ~**

de permiso; **to take one's ~ of** despedirse de.

▶**leave behind** vt (on purpose) dejar (atrás); (accidentally) olvidar.

▶**leave off** vt (lid) no poner; (switch) no encender; (col: stop): **to ~ off doing sth** dejar de hacer algo.

▶**leave on** vt (lid) dejar puesto; (light, fire, cooker) dejar encendido.

▶**leave out** vt omitir.

▶**leave over** vt (postpone) dejar, aplazar.

leave of absence n excedencia.

leaves [li:vz] pl of **leaf**.

leavetaking ['li:vteɪkɪŋ] n despedida.

Lebanon ['lɛbənən] n: **the ~** el Líbano.

lecherous ['lɛtʃərəs] adj lascivo.

lectern ['lɛktəːn] n atril m.

lecture ['lɛktʃə*] n conferencia; (SCOL) clase f ♦ vi dar clase(s) ♦ vt (scold) sermonear; (reprove) echar una reprimenda a; **to give a ~ on** dar una conferencia sobre.

lecture hall n sala de conferencias; (UNIV) aula.

lecturer ['lɛktʃərə*] n conferenciante m/f; (BRIT: at university) profesor(a) m/f.

lecture theatre n = **lecture hall**.

LED n abbr (= light-emitting diode) LED m.

led [lɛd] pt, pp of **lead**.

ledge [lɛdʒ] n (of window, on wall) repisa, reborde m; (of mountain) saliente m.

ledger ['lɛdʒə*] n libro mayor.

lee [li:] n sotavento; **in the ~ of** al abrigo de.

leech [li:tʃ] n sanguijuela.

leek [li:k] n puerro.

leer [lɪə*] vi: **to ~ at sb** mirar de manera lasciva a algn.

leeward ['li:wəd] adj (NAUT) de sotavento ♦ n (NAUT) sotavento; **to ~** a sotavento.

leeway ['li:weɪ] n (fig): **to have some ~** tener cierta libertad de acción.

left [lɛft] pt, pp of **leave** ♦ adj izquierdo ♦ n izquierda ♦ adv a la izquierda; **on** or **to the ~** a la izquierda; **the L~** (POL) la izquierda.

left-hand drive ['lɛfthænd-] n conducción f por la izquierda.

left-handed [lɛft'hændɪd] adj zurdo; **~ scissors** tijeras fpl zurdas or para zurdos.

left-hand side ['lɛfthænd-] n izquierda.

leftie ['lɛftɪ] n = **lefty**.

leftist ['lɛftɪst] adj (POL) izquierdista.

left-luggage (office) [lɛft'lʌgɪdʒ(-)] n (BRIT) consigna.

left-overs ['lɛftəuvəz] npl sobras fpl.

left-wing [lɛft'wɪŋ] adj (POL) de izquierda(s), izquierdista.

left-winger ['lɛft'wɪŋə*] n (POL) izquierdista m/f.

lefty ['lɛftɪ] n (col: POL) rojillo/a.

leg [lɛg] n pierna; (of animal, chair) pata; (CULIN: of meat) pierna; (of journey) etapa; **1st/2nd ~** (SPORT) partido de ida/de vuelta; **to pull sb's ~** tomar el pelo a algn; **to stretch one's ~s** dar una vuelta.

legacy ['lɛgəsɪ] n herencia; (fig) herencia, legado.

legal ['li:gl] adj (permitted by law) lícito; (of law) legal; (inquiry etc) jurídico; **to take ~ action** or **proceedings against sb** entablar or levantar un pleito contra algn.

legal adviser n asesor(a) m/f jurídico/a.

legal holiday n (US) fiesta oficial.

legality [lɪ'gælɪtɪ] n legalidad f.

legalize ['li:gəlaɪz] vt legalizar.

legally ['li:gəlɪ] adv legalmente; **~ binding** con fuerza legal.

legal tender n moneda de curso legal.

legatee [lɛgə'ti:] n legatario/a.

legation [lɪ'geɪʃən] n legación f.

legend ['lɛdʒənd] n leyenda.

legendary ['lɛdʒəndərɪ] adj legendario.

-legged ['lɛgɪd] suff: **two-~** (table etc) de dos patas.

leggings ['lɛgɪŋz] npl mallas fpl, leggins mpl.

leggy ['lɛgɪ] adj de piernas largas.

legibility [lɛdʒɪ'bɪlɪtɪ] n legibilidad f.

legible ['lɛdʒəbl] adj legible.

legibly ['lɛdʒəblɪ] adv legiblemente.

legion ['li:dʒən] n legión f.

legionnaire [li:dʒə'nɛə*] n legionario.

legionnaire's disease n enfermedad f del legionario.

legislation [lɛdʒɪs'leɪʃən] n legislación f; **a piece of ~** (bill) un proyecto de ley; (act) una ley.

legislative ['lɛdʒɪslətɪv] adj legislativo.

legislator ['lɛdʒɪsleɪtə*] n legislador(a) m/f.

legislature ['lɛdʒɪslətʃə*] n cuerpo legislativo.

legitimacy [lɪ'dʒɪtɪməsɪ] n legitimidad f.

legitimate [lɪ'dʒɪtɪmət] adj legítimo.

legitimize [lɪ'dʒɪtɪmaɪz] vt legitimar.

legless ['lɛglɪs] adj (BRIT col) mamado.

leg-room ['lɛgru:m] n espacio para las piernas.

Leics abbr (BRIT) = **Leicestershire**.

leisure ['lɛʒə*] n ocio, tiempo libre; **at ~** con tranquilidad.

leisure centre n centro recreativo.

leisurely ['lɛʒəlɪ] adj sin prisa; lento.

leisure suit n conjunto tipo chandal.

lemon ['lɛmən] n limón m.

lemonade [lɛmə'neɪd] n (fruit juice) limonada; (fizzy) gaseosa.

lemon cheese, lemon curd *n* queso de limón.
lemon juice *n* zumo de limón.
lemon tea *n té m* con limón.
lend, *pt, pp* **lent** [lɛnd, lɛnt] *vt:* **to ~ sth to sb** prestar algo a algn.
lender ['lɛndə*] *n* prestamista *m/f.*
lending library ['lɛndɪŋ-] *n* biblioteca de préstamo.
length [lɛŋθ] *n (size)* largo, longitud *f; (section: of road, pipe)* tramo; (*: of rope etc*) largo; **at ~** (*at last*) por fin, finalmente; (*lengthily*) largamente; **it is 2 metres in ~** tiene dos metros de largo; **what ~ is it?** ¿cuánto tiene de largo?; **to fall full ~** caer de bruces; **to go to any ~(s) to do sth** ser capaz de hacer cualquier cosa para hacer algo.
lengthen ['lɛŋθn] *vt* alargar ♦ *vi* alargarse.
lengthways ['lɛŋθweɪz] *adv* a lo largo.
lengthy ['lɛŋθɪ] *adj* largo, extenso; (*meeting*) prolongado.
lenient ['liːnɪənt] *adj* indulgente.
lens [lɛnz] *n (of spectacles)* lente *f; (of camera)* objetivo.
Lent [lɛnt] *n* Cuaresma.
lent [lɛnt] *pt, pp of* **lend.**
lentil ['lɛntl] *n* lenteja.
Leo ['liːəu] *n* Leo.
leopard ['lɛpəd] *n* leopardo.
leotard ['liːətɑːd] *n* leotardo.
leper ['lɛpə*] *n* leproso/a.
leper colony *n* colonia de leprosos.
leprosy ['lɛprəsɪ] *n* lepra.
lesbian ['lɛzbɪən] *adj* lesbiano ♦ *n* lesbiana.
lesion ['liːʒən] *n (MED)* lesión *f.*
Lesotho [lɪ'suːtuː] *n* Lesotho.
less [lɛs] *adj (in size, degree etc)* menor; (*in quantity*) menos ♦ *pron, adv* menos; **~ than** half menos de la mitad; **~ than £1/a kilo/ 3 metres** menos de una libra/un kilo/tres metros; **~ than ever** menos que nunca; **~ 5%** menos el cinco por ciento; **~ and ~** cada vez menos; **the ~ he works...** cuanto menos trabaja ....
lessee [lɛ'siː] *n* inquilino/a, arrendatario/a.
lessen ['lɛsn] *vi* disminuir, reducirse ♦ *vt* disminuir, reducir.
lesser ['lɛsə*] *adj* menor; **to a ~ extent** *or* **degree** en menor grado.
lesson ['lɛsn] *n* clase *f;* **a maths ~** una clase de matemáticas; **to give ~s in** dar clases de; **it taught him a ~** (*fig*) le sirvió de lección.
lessor ['lɛsɔː* *or* lɛ'sɔː*] *n* arrendador(a) *m/f.*
lest [lɛst] *conj:* **~ it happen** para que no pase.
let, *pt, pp* **let** [lɛt] *vt (allow)* dejar, permitir;

(*BRIT: lease*) alquilar; **to ~ sb do sth** dejar que algn haga algo; **to ~ sb have sth** dar algo a algn; **to ~ sb know sth** comunicar algo a algn; **~'s go** ¡vamos!; **~ him come** que venga; **"to ~"** "se alquila".
►**let down** *vt (lower)* bajar; (*dress*) alargar; (*tyre*) desinflar; (*hair*) soltar; (*disappoint*) defraudar.
►**let go** *vi* soltar; (*fig*) dejarse ir ♦ *vt* soltar.
►**let in** *vt* dejar entrar; (*visitor etc*) hacer pasar; **what have you ~ yourself in for?** ¿en qué te has metido?
►**let off** *vt* dejar escapar; (*firework etc*) disparar; (*bomb*) accionar; (*passenger*) dejar, bajar; **to ~ off steam** (*fig, col*) desahogarse, desfogarse.
►**let on** *vi:* **to ~ on that ...** revelar que ...
►**let out** *vt* dejar salir; (*dress*) ensanchar; (*rent out*) alquilar.
►**let up** *vi* disminuir; (*rain etc*) amainar.
let-down ['lɛtdaun] *n (disappointment)* decepción *f.*
lethal ['liːθl] *adj (weapon)* mortífero; (*poison, wound*) mortal.
lethargic [lɛ'θɑːdʒɪk] *adj* aletargado.
lethargy ['lɛθədʒɪ] *n* letargo.
letter ['lɛtə*] *n (of alphabet)* letra; (*correspondence*) carta; **~s** *npl (literature, learning)* letras *fpl;* **small/capital ~** minúscula/mayúscula; **covering ~** carta adjunta.
letter bomb *n* carta-bomba.
letterbox ['lɛtəbɔks] *n (BRIT)* buzón *m.*
letterhead ['lɛtəhɛd] *n* membrete *m,* encabezamiento.
lettering ['lɛtərɪŋ] *n* letras *fpl.*
letter of credit *n* carta de crédito; **documentary ~** carta de crédito documentaria; **irrevocable ~** carta de crédito irrevocable.
letter-opener ['lɛtərəupnə*] *n* abrecartas *m inv.*
letterpress ['lɛtəprɛs] *n (method)* prensa de copiar; (*printed page*) impresión *f* tipográfica.
letter quality *n* calidad *f* de correspondencia.
letters patent *npl* letra *sg* de patente.
lettuce ['lɛtɪs] *n* lechuga.
let-up ['lɛtʌp] *n* descanso, tregua.
leukaemia, (*US*) **leukemia** [luː'kiːmɪə] *n* leucemia.
level ['lɛvl] *adj (flat)* llano; (*flattened*) nivelado; (*uniform*) igual ♦ *adv* a nivel ♦ *n* nivel *m* ♦ *vt* nivelar, allanar; (*gun*) apuntar; (*accusation*): **to ~ (against)** levantar (contra) ♦ *vi (col):* **to ~ with sb** ser franco con algn; **to be ~ with** estar a

nivel de; **a ~ spoonful** (*CULIN*) una
cucharada rasa; **to draw ~ with** (*team*)
igualar; (*runner, car*) alcanzar a; **"A" ~s**
npl (*BRIT*) ≈ Bachillerato Superior *sg*,
B.U.P. *msg*; **"O" ~s** *npl* (*BRIT*) ≈
bachillerato *sg* elemental, octavo *sg* de
Básica; **on the ~** (*fig: honest*) en serio;
talks at ministerial ~ charlas *fpl* a nivel
ministerial.
▶**level off** *or* **out** *vi* (*prices etc*)
estabilizarse; (*ground*) nivelarse; (*aircraft*)
ponerse en una trayectoria horizontal.
level crossing *n* (*BRIT*) paso a nivel.
level-headed [lɛvl'hɛdɪd] *adj* sensato.
levelling, (*US*) **leveling** ['lɛvlɪŋ] *adj*
(*process, effect*) de nivelación ♦ *n*
igualación *f*, allanamiento.
level playing field *n* situación *f* de
igualdad; **to compete on a ~** competir en
igualdad de condiciones.
lever ['liːvə*] *n* palanca ♦ *vt*: **to ~ up**
levantar con palanca.
leverage ['liːvərɪdʒ] *n* (*fig: influence*)
influencia.
levity ['lɛvɪtɪ] *n* frivolidad *f*, informalidad *f*.
levy ['lɛvɪ] *n* impuesto ♦ *vt* exigir, recaudar.
lewd [luːd] *adj* lascivo; obsceno, colorado
(*LAM*).
lexicographer [lɛksɪ'kɔɡrəfə*] *n*
lexicógrafo/a *m/f*.
lexicography [lɛksɪ'kɔɡrəfɪ] *n* lexicografía.
LGV *n abbr* (= *Large Goods Vehicle*) vehículo
pesado.
LI *abbr* (*US*) = *Long Island*.
liabilities [laɪə'bɪlɪtɪz] *npl* obligaciones *fpl*;
pasivo *sg*.
liability [laɪə'bɪlɪtɪ] *n* responsabilidad *f*;
(*handicap*) desventaja.
liable ['laɪəbl] *adj* (*subject*): **~ to** sujeto a;
(*responsible*): **~ for** responsable de;
(*likely*): **~ to do** propenso a hacer; **to be ~
to a fine** exponerse a una multa.
liaise [liː'eɪz] *vi*: **to ~ (with)** colaborar
(con); **to ~ with sb** mantener informado
a algn.
liaison [liː'eɪzɔn] *n* (*coordination*) enlace *m*;
(*affair*) relación *f*.
liar ['laɪə*] *n* mentiroso/a.
libel ['laɪbl] *n* calumnia ♦ *vt* calumniar.
libellous ['laɪbləs] *adj* difamatorio,
calumnioso.
liberal ['lɪbərl] *adj* (*gen*) liberal; (*generous*):
~ with generoso con ♦ *n*: **L~** (*POL*) liberal
m/f.
Liberal Democrat *n* (*BRIT*) demócrata *m/f*
liberal.
liberality [lɪbə'rælɪtɪ] *n* (*generosity*)
liberalidad *f*, generosidad *f*.

liberalize ['lɪbərəlaɪz] *vt* liberalizar.
liberally ['lɪbərəlɪ] *adv* liberalmente.
liberal-minded ['lɪbərl'maɪndɪd] *adj* de
miras anchas, liberal.
liberate ['lɪbəreɪt] *vt* liberar.
liberation [lɪbə'reɪʃən] *n* liberación *f*.
liberation theology *n* teología de la
liberación.
Liberia [laɪ'bɪərɪə] *n* Liberia.
Liberian [laɪ'bɪərɪən] *adj, n* liberiano/a *m/f*.
liberty ['lɪbətɪ] *n* libertad *f*; **to be at ~ to do**
estar libre para hacer; **to take the ~ of
doing sth** tomarse la libertad de hacer
algo.
libido [lɪ'biːdəu] *n* libido.
Libra ['liːbrə] *n* Libra.
librarian [laɪ'brɛərɪən] *n* bibliotecario/a.
library ['laɪbrərɪ] *n* biblioteca.
library book *n* libro de la biblioteca.
libretto [lɪ'brɛtəu] *n* libreto.
Libya ['lɪbɪə] *n* Libia.
Libyan ['lɪbɪən] *adj, n* libio/a *m/f*.
lice [laɪs] *pl of* **louse**.
licence, (*US*) **license** ['laɪsns] *n* licencia;
(*permit*) permiso; (*also*: **driving licence**,
(*US*) **driver's license**) carnet *m* de
conducir; (*excessive freedom*) libertad *f*;
import ~ licencia *or* permiso de
importación; **produced under ~**
elaborado bajo licencia.
licence number *n* (número de) matrícula.
licence plate *n* (placa de) matrícula.
license ['laɪsns] (*US*) = **licence** ♦ *vt*
autorizar, dar permiso a; (*car*) sacar la
matrícula de *or* la patente (*LAM*) de.
licensed ['laɪsnst] *adj* (*for alcohol*)
autorizado para vender bebidas
alcohólicas.
licensed trade *n* comercio *or* negocio
autorizado.
licensee [laɪsən'siː] *n* (*in a pub*)
concesionario/a, dueño/a de un bar.
licentious [laɪ'sɛnʃəs] *adj* licencioso.
lichen ['laɪkən] *n* liquen *m*.
lick [lɪk] *vt* lamer; (*col: defeat*) dar una
paliza a ♦ *n* lamedura; **a ~ of paint** una
mano de pintura.
licorice ['lɪkərɪs] *n* = **liquorice**.
lid [lɪd] *n* (*of box, case*) tapa; (*of pan*)
cobertera; **to take the ~ off sth** (*fig*)
exponer algo a la luz pública.
lido ['laɪdəu] *n* (*BRIT*) piscina, alberca (*LAM*).
lie [laɪ] *n* mentira ♦ *vi* mentir; (*pt* **lay**, *pp* **lain**
[leɪ, leɪn]) (*rest*) estar echado, estar
acostado; (*of object: be situated*) estar,
encontrarse; **to tell ~s** mentir; **to ~ low**
(*fig*) mantenerse a escondidas.
▶**lie about**, **lie around** *vi* (*things*) estar

tirado; (*BRIT: people*) estar acostado *or* tumbado.
▶**lie back** *vi* recostarse.
▶**lie down** *vi* echarse, tumbarse.
▶**lie up** *vi* (*hide*) esconderse.
Liechtenstein ['lıktənstaın] *n* Liechtenstein *m*.
lie detector *n* detector *m* de mentiras.
lie-down ['laıdaun] *n* (*BRIT*): **to have a ~** echarse (una siesta).
lie-in ['laıın] *n* (*BRIT*): **to have a ~** quedarse en la cama.
lieu [luː]: **in ~ of** *prep* en lugar de.
Lieut *abbr* = **lieutenant**.
lieutenant [lɛf'tɛnənt, (*US*) luː'tɛnənt] *n* (*MIL*) teniente *m*.
lieutenant colonel *n* teniente *m* coronel.
life, *pl* **lives** [laɪf, laɪvz] *n* vida; (*of licence etc*) vigencia; **to be sent to prison for ~** ser condenado a cadena perpetua; **country/city ~** la vida en el campo/en la ciudad; **true to ~** fiel a la realidad; **to paint from ~** pintar del natural; **to put** *or* **breathe new ~ into** (*person*) reanimar; (*project, area etc*) infundir nueva vida a.
life annuity *n* pensión *f* anual vitalicia.
life assurance *n* (*BRIT*) seguro de vida.
lifebelt ['laıfbɛlt] *n* (*BRIT*) cinturón *m* salvavidas.
lifeblood ['laıfblʌd] *n* (*fig*) alma, nervio.
lifeboat ['laıfbəut] *n* lancha de socorro.
life-buoy ['laıfbɔı] *n* boya *or* guindola salvavidas.
life expectancy *n* esperanza de vida.
lifeguard ['laıfgɑːd] *n* vigilante *m/f*.
life imprisonment *n* cadena perpetua.
life insurance *n* = **life assurance**.
life jacket *n* chaleco salvavidas.
lifeless ['laıflıs] *adj* sin vida; (*dull*) soso.
lifelike ['laıflaık] *adj* natural.
lifeline ['laıflaın] *n* (*fig*) cordón *m* umbilical.
lifelong ['laıflɔŋ] *adj* de toda la vida.
life preserver *n* (*US*) = **lifebelt**.
lifer ['laıfə*] *n* (*col*) condenado/a *m/f* a cadena perpetua.
life-saver ['laıfseıvə*] *n* socorrista *m/f*.
life sentence *n* cadena perpetua.
life-sized ['laıfsaızd] *adj* de tamaño natural.
life span *n* vida.
lifestyle ['laıfstaıl] *n* estilo de vida.
life support system *n* (*MED*) sistema *m* de respiración asistida.
lifetime ['laıftaım] *n*: **in his ~** durante su vida; **once in a ~** una vez en la vida; **the chance of a ~** una oportunidad única.
lift [lıft] *vt* levantar; (*copy*) plagiar ♦ *vi* (*fog*) disiparse ♦ *n* (*BRIT: elevator*) ascensor *m*, elevador *m* (*LAM*); **to give sb a ~** (*BRIT*)

llevar a algn en coche.
▶**lift off** *vt* levantar, quitar ♦ *vi* (*rocket, helicopter*) despegar.
▶**lift out** *vt* sacar; (*troops, evacuees etc*) evacuar.
▶**lift up** *vt* levantar.
lift-off ['lıftɔf] *n* despegue *m*.
ligament ['lıgəmənt] *n* ligamento.
light [laıt] *n* luz *f*; (*flame*) lumbre *f*; (*lamp*) luz *f*, lámpara; (*daylight*) luz *f* del día; (*headlight*) faro; (*rear ~*) luz *f* trasera; (*for cigarette etc*): **have you got a ~?** ¿tienes fuego? ♦ *vt* (*pt, pp* **lighted** *or* **lit** [lıt]) (*candle, cigarette, fire*) encender; (*room*) alumbrar ♦ *adj* (*colour*) claro; (*not heavy, also fig*) ligero, liviano (*esp LAM*); (*room*) alumbrado ♦ *adv* (*travel*) con poco equipaje; **to turn the ~ on/off** encender/apagar la luz; **in the ~ of** a la luz de; **to come to ~** salir a la luz; **to cast** *or* **shed** *or* **throw ~ on** arrojar luz sobre; **to make ~ of sth** (*fig*) no dar importancia a algo.
▶**light up** *vi* (*smoke*) encender un cigarrillo; (*face*) iluminarse ♦ *vt* (*illuminate*) iluminar, alumbrar.
light bulb *n* bombilla, bombillo (*LAM*), foco (*LAM*).
lighten ['laıtn] *vi* (*grow light*) clarear ♦ *vt* (*give light to*) iluminar; (*make lighter*) aclarar; (*make less heavy*) aligerar.
lighter ['laıtə*] *n* (*also*: **cigarette ~**) encendedor *m* (*esp LAM*), mechero.
light-fingered [laıt'fıŋgəd] *adj* de manos largas.
light-headed [laıt'hɛdıd] *adj* (*dizzy*) mareado; (*excited*) exaltado; (*by nature*) atolondrado.
light-hearted [laıt'hɑːtıd] *adj* alegre.
lighthouse ['laıthaus] *n* faro.
lighting ['laıtıŋ] *n* (*act*) iluminación *f*; (*system*) alumbrado.
lighting-up time [laıtıŋ'ʌp-] *n* (*BRIT*) hora de encendido del alumbrado.
lightly ['laıtlı] *adv* ligeramente; (*not seriously*) con poca seriedad; **to get off ~** ser castigado con poca severidad.
light meter *n* (*PHOT*) fotómetro.
lightness ['laıtnıs] *n* claridad *f*; (*in weight*) ligereza.
lightning ['laıtnıŋ] *n* relámpago, rayo.
lightning conductor, (*US***) lightning rod** *n* pararrayos *m inv*.
lightning strike *n* huelga relámpago.
light pen *n* lápiz *m* óptico.
lightweight ['laıtweıt] *adj* (*suit*) ligero ♦ *n* (*BOXING*) peso ligero.
light year *n* año luz.
like [laık] *vt* (*person*) querer a; (*thing*): **I ~**

swimming/apples me gusta nadar/me gustan las manzanas ♦ *prep* como ♦ *adj* parecido, semejante ♦ *n*: **did you ever see the ~ (of it)?** ¿has visto cosa igual?; **his ~s and dislikes** sus gustos y aversiones; **the ~s of him** personas como él; **I would ~, I'd ~** me gustaría; (*for purchase*) quisiera; **would you ~ a coffee?** ¿te apetece un café?; **to be** *or* **look ~ sb/sth** parecerse a algn/algo; **that's just ~ him** es muy de él, es típico de él; **do it ~ this** hazlo así; **it is nothing ~...** no tiene parecido alguno con...; **what's he ~?** ¿cómo es (él)?; **what's the weather ~?** ¿qué tiempo hace?; **something ~ that** algo así *or* por el estilo; **I feel ~ a drink** me apetece algo de beber; **if you ~** si quieres.

likeable ['laɪkəbl] *adj* simpático, agradable.

likelihood ['laɪklɪhud] *n* probabilidad *f*; **in all ~** según todas las probabilidades.

likely ['laɪklɪ] *adj* probable, capaz (*LAM*); **he's ~ to leave** es probable *or* capaz (*LAM*) que se vaya; **not ~!** ¡ni hablar!

like-minded [laɪk'maɪndɪd] *adj* de la misma opinión.

liken ['laɪkən] *vt*: **to ~** comparar con.

likeness ['laɪknɪs] *n* (*similarity*) semejanza, parecido.

likewise ['laɪkwaɪz] *adv* igualmente.

liking ['laɪkɪŋ] *n*: **~ (for)** (*person*) cariño (a); (*thing*) afición (a); **to take a ~ to sb** tomar cariño a algn; **to be to sb's ~** ser del gusto de algn.

lilac ['laɪlək] *n* lila ♦ *adj* (*colour*) de color lila.

Lilo ® ['laɪləʊ] *n* colchoneta inflable.

lilt [lɪlt] *n* deje *m*.

lilting ['lɪltɪŋ] *adj* melodioso.

lily ['lɪlɪ] *n* lirio, azucena.

lily of the valley *n* lirio de los valles.

Lima ['liːmə] *n* Lima.

limb [lɪm] *n* miembro; (*of tree*) rama; **to be out on a ~** (*fig*) estar aislado.

limber up ['lɪmbə*-] *vi* (*fig*) entrenarse; (*SPORT*) hacer (ejercicios de) precalentamiento.

limbo ['lɪmbəʊ] *n*: **to be in ~** (*fig*) quedar a la expectativa.

lime [laɪm] *n* (*tree*) limero; (*fruit*) lima; (*GEO*) cal *f*.

lime juice *n* zumo (*SP*) *or* jugo de lima.

limelight ['laɪmlaɪt] *n*: **to be in the ~** (*fig*) ser el centro de atención.

limerick ['lɪmərɪk] *n* quintilla humorística.

limestone ['laɪmstəʊn] *n* piedra caliza.

limit ['lɪmɪt] *n* límite *m* ♦ *vt* limitar; **weight/speed ~** peso máximo/velocidad *f* máxima; **within ~s** entre límites.

limitation [lɪmɪ'teɪʃən] *n* limitación *f*.

limited ['lɪmɪtɪd] *adj* limitado; **to be ~ to** limitarse a; **~ edition** edición limitada.

limited (liability) company (Ltd) *n* (*BRIT*) sociedad *f* anónima (SA).

limitless ['lɪmɪtlɪs] *adj* sin límites.

limousine ['lɪməziːn] *n* limusina.

limp [lɪmp] *n*: **to have a ~** tener cojera ♦ *vi* cojear, renguear (*LAM*) ♦ *adj* flojo.

limpet ['lɪmpɪt] *n* lapa.

limpid ['lɪmpɪd] *adj* (*poetic*) límpido, cristalino.

limply ['lɪmplɪ] *adv* desmayadamente; **to say ~** decir débilmente.

linchpin ['lɪntʃpɪn] *n* pezonera; (*fig*) eje *m*.

Lincs [lɪŋks] *abbr* (*BRIT*) = Lincolnshire.

line [laɪn] *n* (*also COMM*) línea; (*straight ~*) raya; (*rope*) cuerda; (*for fishing*) sedal *m*; (*wire*) hilo; (*row, series*) fila, hilera; (*of writing*) renglón *m*; (*on face*) arruga; (*speciality*) rama ♦ *vt* (*SEWING*): **to ~ (with)** forrar (de); **to ~ the streets** ocupar las aceras; **in ~ with** de acuerdo con; **she's in ~ for promotion** (*fig*) tiene muchas posibilidades de que la asciendan; **to bring sth into ~ with** sth poner algo de acuerdo con algo; **~ of research/business** campo de investigación/comercio; **to take the ~ that ...** ser de la opinión que ...; **hold the ~ please** (*TEL*) no cuelgue usted, por favor; **to draw the ~ at doing sth** negarse a hacer algo; no permitir que se haga algo; **on the right ~s** por buen camino; **a new ~ in cosmetics** una nueva línea en cosméticos; *see also* **lines**.

► **line up** *vi* hacer cola ♦ *vt* alinear, poner en fila; **to have sth ~d up** tener algo arreglado.

linear ['lɪnɪə*] *adj* lineal.

lined [laɪnd] *adj* (*face*) arrugado; (*paper*) rayado; (*clothes*) forrado.

line editing *n* (*COMPUT*) corrección *f* por líneas.

line feed *n* (*COMPUT*) avance *m* de línea.

lineman ['laɪnmən] *n* (*US*) técnico de las líneas; (*FOOTBALL*) delantero.

linen ['lɪnɪn] *n* ropa blanca; (*cloth*) lino.

line printer *n* impresora de línea.

liner ['laɪnə*] *n* vapor *m* de línea, transatlántico; **dustbin ~** bolsa de la basura.

lines [laɪnz] *npl* (*RAIL*) vía *sg*, raíles *mpl*.

linesman ['laɪnzmən] *n* (*SPORT*) juez *m* de línea.

line-up ['laɪnʌp] *n* alineación *f*.

linger ['lɪŋgə*] *vi* retrasarse, tardar en marcharse; (*smell, tradition*) persistir.

lingerie ['lænʒəriː] *n* ropa interior *or* íntima

(de mujer).

lingering ['lɪŋgərɪŋ] *adj* persistente; (*death*) lento.

lingo, ~**es** ['lɪŋgəu] *n* (*pej*) jerga.

linguist ['lɪŋgwɪst] *n* lingüista *m/f*.

linguistic [lɪŋ'gwɪstɪk] *adj* lingüístico.

linguistics [lɪŋ'gwɪstɪks] *n* lingüística.

liniment ['lɪnɪmənt] *n* linimento.

lining ['laɪnɪŋ] *n* forro; (*TECH*) revestimiento; (*of brake*) guarnición *f*.

link [lɪŋk] *n* (*of a chain*) eslabón *m*; (*connection*) conexión *f*; (*bond*) vínculo, lazo ♦ *vt* vincular, unir; **rail** ~ línea de ferrocarril, servicio de trenes.

▶**link up** *vt* acoplar ♦ *vi* unirse.

links [lɪŋks] *npl* (*GOLF*) campo *sg* de golf.

link-up ['lɪŋkʌp] *n* (*gen*) unión *f*; (*meeting*) encuentro, reunión *f*; (*of roads*) empalme *m*; (*of spaceships*) acoplamiento; (*RADIO*, *TV*) enlace *m*.

lino ['laɪnəu] (*BRIT*), **linoleum** [lɪ'nəulɪəm] *n* linóleo.

linseed oil ['lɪnsiːd-] *n* aceite *m* de linaza.

lint [lɪnt] *n* gasa.

lintel ['lɪntl] *n* dintel *m*.

lion ['laɪən] *n* león *m*.

lioness ['laɪənɪs] *n* leona.

lip [lɪp] *n* labio; (*of jug*) pico; (*of cup etc*) borde *m*.

liposuction ['lɪpəusʌkʃən] *n* liposucción *f*.

lipread ['lɪpriːd] *vi* leer los labios.

lip salve *n* crema protectora para labios.

lip service *n*: **to pay** ~ **to sth** alabar algo pero sin hacer nada.

lipstick ['lɪpstɪk] *n* lápiz *m or* barra de labios, carmín *m*.

liquefy ['lɪkwɪfaɪ] *vt* licuar ♦ *vi* licuarse.

liqueur [lɪ'kjuə*] *n* licor *m*.

liquid ['lɪkwɪd] *adj*, *n* líquido.

liquidate ['lɪkwɪdeɪt] *vt* liquidar.

liquidation [lɪkwɪ'deɪʃən] *n* liquidación *f*; **to go into** ~ entrar en liquidación.

liquid crystal display (LCD) *n* pantalla de cristal líquido.

liquidity [lɪ'kwɪdɪtɪ] *n* (*COMM*) liquidez *f*.

liquidize ['lɪkwɪdaɪz] *vt* (*CULIN*) licuar.

liquidizer ['lɪkwɪdaɪzə*] *n* (*CULIN*) licuadora.

liquor ['lɪkə*] *n* licor *m*, bebidas *fpl* alcohólicas.

liquorice ['lɪkərɪs] *n* regaliz *m*.

liquor store *n* (*US*) bodega, *tienda de vinos y bebidas alcohólicas*.

Lisbon ['lɪzbən] *n* Lisboa.

lisp [lɪsp] *n* ceceo.

lissom ['lɪsəm] *adj* ágil.

list [lɪst] *n* lista; (*of ship*) inclinación *f* ♦ *vt* (*write down*) hacer una lista de; (*enumerate*) catalogar; (*COMPUT*) hacer un

listado de ♦ *vi* (*ship*) inclinarse; **shopping** ~ lista de las compras; *see also* **lists**.

listed building ['lɪstɪd-] *n* (*ARCHIT*) edificio de interés histórico-artístico.

listed company ['lɪstɪd-] *n* compañía cotizable.

listen ['lɪsn] *vi* escuchar, oír; (*pay attention*) atender.

listener ['lɪsnə*] *n* oyente *m/f*.

listeria [lɪs'tɪərɪə] *n* listeria.

listing ['lɪstɪŋ] *n* (*COMPUT*) listado.

listless ['lɪstlɪs] *adj* apático, indiferente.

listlessly ['lɪstlɪslɪ] *adv* con indiferencia.

listlessness ['lɪstlɪsnɪs] *n* indiferencia, apatía.

list price *n* precio de catálogo.

lists [lɪsts] *npl* (*HISTORY*) liza *sg*; **to enter the** ~ **(against sb/sth)** salir a la palestra (contra algn/algo).

lit [lɪt] *pt*, *pp of* **light**.

litany ['lɪtənɪ] *n* letanía.

liter ['liːtə*] *n* (*US*) = **litre**.

literacy ['lɪtərəsɪ] *n* capacidad *f* de leer y escribir; ~ **campaign** campaña de alfabetización.

literal ['lɪtərl] *adj* literal.

literally ['lɪtrəlɪ] *adv* literalmente.

literary ['lɪtərərɪ] *adj* literario.

literate ['lɪtərət] *adj* que sabe leer y escribir; (*fig*) culto.

literature ['lɪtərɪtʃə*] *n* literatura; (*brochures etc*) folletos *mpl*.

lithe [laɪð] *adj* ágil.

litho(graph) ['lɪθəu(grɑːf)] *n* litografía.

lithography [lɪ'θɔgrəfɪ] *n* litografía.

Lithuania [lɪθju'eɪnɪə] *n* Lituania.

Lithuanian [lɪθju'eɪnɪən] *adj* lituano ♦ *n* lituano/a; (*LING*) lituano.

litigate ['lɪtɪgeɪt] *vi* litigar.

litigation [lɪtɪ'geɪʃən] *n* litigio.

litmus paper ['lɪtməs-] *n* papel *m* de tornasol.

litre, (*US*) **liter** ['liːtə*] *n* litro.

litter ['lɪtə*] *n* (*rubbish*) basura; (*paper*) papeles *mpl* (tirados); (*young animals*) camada, cría.

litter bin *n* (*BRIT*) papelera.

littered ['lɪtəd] *adj*: ~ **with** lleno de.

litter lout, (*US*) **litterbug** ['lɪtəbʌg] *n persona que tira papeles usados en la vía pública*.

little ['lɪtl] *adj* (*small*) pequeño, chico (*esp LAM*); (*not much*) poco; (*often translated by suffix, eg*): ~ **house** casita ♦ *adv* poco; **a** ~ un poco (de); ~ **by** ~ poco a poco; ~ **finger** (dedo) meñique *m*; **for a** ~ **while** (durante) un rato; **with** ~ **difficulty** sin problema *or* dificultad; **as** ~ **as possible**

lo menos posible.
little-known ['lɪtl'nəun] *adj* poco conocido.
liturgy ['lɪtədʒɪ] *n* liturgia.
live *vb* [lɪv] *vi* vivir ♦ *vt* (*a life*) llevar;
(*experience*) vivir ♦ *adj* [laɪv] (*animal*) vivo;
(*wire*) conectado; (*broadcast*) en directo;
(*issue*) de actualidad; (*unexploded*) sin
explotar; **to ~ in London** vivir en
Londres; **to ~ together** vivir juntos.
►**live down** *vt* hacer olvidar.
►**live off** *vt fus* (*land, fish etc*) vivir de; (*pej*:
parents etc) vivir a costa de.
►**live on** *vt fus* (*food*) vivir de, alimentarse
de; **to ~ on £50 a week** vivir con 50 libras
semanales *or* a la semana.
►**live out** *vi* (*students*) ser externo ♦ *vt*: **to**
~ out one's days *or* **life** pasar el resto de
la vida.
►**live up** *vt*: **to ~ it up** (*col*) tirarse la gran
vida.
►**live up to** *vt fus* (*fulfil*) cumplir con;
(*justify*) justificar.
live-in ['lɪvɪn] *adj*: **~ partner** pareja,
compañero/a sentimental; **~ maid**
asistenta interna.
livelihood ['laɪvlɪhud] *n* sustento.
liveliness ['laɪvlɪnɪs] *n* viveza.
lively ['laɪvlɪ] *adj* (*gen*) vivo; (*talk*) animado;
(*pace*) rápido; (*party, tune*) alegre.
liven up ['laɪvn-] *vt* (*discussion, evening*)
animar.
liver ['lɪvə*] *n* hígado.
liverish ['lɪvərɪʃ] *adj*: **to feel ~** sentirse *or*
encontrarse mal, no estar muy católico.
Liverpudlian [lɪvə'pʌdlɪən] *adj* de Liverpool
♦ *n* nativo/a (*or* habitante *m/f*) de
Liverpool.
livery ['lɪvərɪ] *n* librea.
lives [laɪvz] *npl of* **life**.
livestock ['laɪvstɔk] *n* ganado.
live wire [laɪv-] *n* (*fig, col*): **he's a real ~!**
¡tiene una marcha!
livid ['lɪvɪd] *adj* lívido; (*furious*) furioso.
living ['lɪvɪŋ] *adj* (*alive*) vivo ♦ *n*: **to earn** *or*
make a ~ ganarse la vida; **cost of ~** coste
m de la vida; **in ~ memory** que se
recuerde *or* recuerda.
living conditions *npl* condiciones *fpl* de
vida.
living expenses *npl* gastos *mpl* de
mantenimiento.
living room *n* sala (de estar), living *m*
(*LAM*).
living standards *npl* nivel *msg* de vida.
living wage *n* sueldo suficiente para vivir.
lizard ['lɪzəd] *n* lagartija.
llama ['lɑːmə] *n* llama.
LLB *n abbr* (= *Bachelor of Laws*) Ldo./a. en

Dcho; *see also* **Bachelor's Degree**.
LLD *n abbr* (= *Doctor of Laws*) Dr(a). en
Dcho.
LMT *n abbr* (*US*: = *Local Mean Time*) hora
local.
load [ləud] *n* (*gen*) carga; (*weight*) peso ♦ *vt*
(*COMPUT*) cargar; (*also*: ~ **up**): **to ~** (**with**)
cargar (con *or* de); **a ~ of**, **~s of** (*fig*)
(gran) cantidad de, montones de.
loaded ['ləudɪd] *adj* (*dice*) cargado;
(*question*) intencionado; (*col*: *rich*) forrado
(de dinero).
loading ['ləudɪŋ] *n* (*COMM*) sobreprima.
loading bay *n* área de carga y descarga.
loaf, *pl* **loaves** [ləuf, ləuvz] *n* (barra de) pan
m ♦ *vi* (*also*: ~ **about**, ~ **around**)
holgazanear.
loam [ləum] *n* marga.
loan [ləun] *n* préstamo; (*COMM*) empréstito
♦ *vt* prestar; **on ~** (*book, painting*)
prestado; **to raise a ~** (*money*) procurar
un empréstito.
loan account *n* cuenta de crédito.
loan capital *n* empréstito.
loan shark *n* (*col*: *pej*) prestamista *m/f* sin
escrúpulos.
loath [ləuθ] *adj*: **to be ~ to do sth** ser reacio
a hacer algo.
loathe [ləuð] *vt* aborrecer; (*person*) odiar.
loathing ['ləuðɪŋ] *n* aversión *f*; odio.
loathsome ['ləuðsəm] *adj* asqueroso,
repugnante; (*person*) odioso.
loaves [ləuvz] *pl of* **loaf**.
lob [lɔb] *vt* (*ball*) volear por alto.
lobby ['lɔbɪ] *n* vestíbulo, sala de espera;
(*POL*: *pressure group*) grupo de presión ♦ *vt*
presionar.
lobbyist ['lɔbɪɪst] *n* cabildero/a.
lobe [ləub] *n* lóbulo.
lobster ['lɔbstə*] *n* langosta.
lobster pot *n* nasa, langostera.
local ['ləukl] *adj* local ♦ *n* (*pub*) bar *m*; **the**
~s *npl* los vecinos, los del lugar.
local anaesthetic *n* (*MED*) anestesia local.
local authority *n* municipio,
ayuntamiento (*SP*).
local call *n* (*TEL*) llamada local.
local government *n* gobierno municipal.
locality [ləu'kælɪtɪ] *n* localidad *f*.
localize ['ləukəlaɪz] *vt* localizar.
locally ['ləukəlɪ] *adv* en la vecindad.
locate [ləu'keɪt] *vt* (*find*) localizar; (*situate*)
situar, ubicar (*LAM*).
location [ləu'keɪʃən] *n* situación *f*; **on ~**
(*CINE*) en exteriores, fuera del estudio.
loch [lɔx] *n* lago.
lock [lɔk] *n* (*of door, box*) cerradura, chapa
(*LAM*); (*of canal*) esclusa; (*of hair*) mechón

m ♦ *vt* (*with key*) cerrar con llave; (*immobilize*) inmovilizar ♦ *vi* (*door etc*) cerrarse con llave; (*wheels*) trabarse; ~ **stock and barrel** (*fig*) por completo *or* entero; **on full** ~ (*AUT*) con el volante girado al máximo.

►**lock away** *vt* (*valuables*) guardar bajo llave; (*criminal*) encerrar.

►**lock out** *vt*: **the workers were** ~**ed out** los trabajadores tuvieron que enfrentarse con un cierre patronal.

►**lock up** *vi* echar la llave.

locker ['lɔkə*] *n* casillero.

locker-room ['lɔkərum] *n* (*US SPORT*) vestuario.

locket ['lɔkɪt] *n* medallón *m*.

lockout ['lɔkaut] *n* (*INDUSTRY*) paro *or* cierre *m* patronal, lockout *m*.

locksmith ['lɔksmɪθ] *n* cerrajero/a.

lock-up ['lɔkʌp] *n* (*prison*) cárcel *f*; (*cell*) jaula; (~ *garage*) jaula, cochera.

locomotive [ləukə'məutɪv] *n* locomotora.

locum ['ləukəm] *n* (*MED*) (médico/a) suplente *m/f*.

locust ['ləukəst] *n* langosta.

lodge [lɔdʒ] *n* casa del guarda; (*porter's*) portería; (*FREEMASONRY*) logia ♦ *vi* (*person*): **to** ~ (**with**) alojarse (en casa de) ♦ *vt* (*complaint*) presentar.

lodger ['lɔdʒə*] *n* huésped(a) *m/f*.

lodging house ['lɔdʒɪŋ-] *n* pensión *f*, casa de huéspedes.

lodgings ['lɔdʒɪŋz] *npl* alojamiento *sg*; (*house*) casa *sg* de huéspedes.

loft [lɔft] *n* desván *m*.

lofty ['lɔftɪ] *adj* alto; (*haughty*) altivo, arrogante; (*sentiments, aims*) elevado, noble.

log [lɔg] *n* (*of wood*) leño, tronco; (*book*) = **logbook** ♦ *n abbr* (= *logarithm*) log. ♦ *vt* anotar, registrar.

►**log in, log on** *vi* (*COMPUT*) iniciar la (*or* una) sesión.

►**log off, log out** *vi* (*COMPUT*) finalizar la sesión.

logarithm ['lɔgərɪðəm] *n* logaritmo.

logbook ['lɔgbuk] *n* (*NAUT*) diario de a bordo; (*AVIAT*) libro de vuelo; (*of car*) documentación *f* (del coche).

log cabin *n* cabaña de troncos.

log fire *n* fuego de leña.

logger ['lɔgə*] *n* leñador(a) *m/f*.

loggerheads ['lɔgəhɛdz] *npl*: **at** ~ (**with**) de pique (con).

logic ['lɔdʒɪk] *n* lógica.

logical ['lɔdʒɪkl] *adj* lógico.

logically ['lɔdʒɪkəlɪ] *adv* lógicamente.

logistics [lɔ'dʒɪstɪks] *n* logística.

log jam *n*: **to break the** ~ poner fin al estancamiento.

logo ['ləugəu] *n* logotipo.

loin [lɔɪn] *n* (*CULIN*) lomo, solomillo; ~**s** *npl* lomos *mpl*.

loin cloth *n* taparrabos *m inv*.

loiter ['lɔɪtə*] *vi* vagar; (*pej*) merodear.

loll [lɔl] *vi* (*also*: ~ **about**) repantigarse.

lollipop ['lɔlɪpɔp] *n* pirulí *m*, chupachup(s) ® *m inv*; (*iced*) polo.

Se llama **lollipop man** *o* **lollipop lady** *a la persona encargada de parar el tráfico en las carreteras cercanas a los colegios británicos para que los niños los crucen sin peligro. Suelen ser personas ya jubiladas, vestidas con un abrigo de color luminoso y llevando una señal de stop en un poste portátil, la cual recuerda por su forma a un chupachups, de ahí su nombre.*

---

lollop ['lɔləp] *vi* (*BRIT*) moverse desgarbadamente.

lolly ['lɔlɪ] *n* (*col: ice cream*) polo; (: *lollipop*) piruleta; (: *money*) guita.

Lombardy ['lɔmbədɪ] *n* Lombardía.

London ['lʌndən] *n* Londres *m*.

Londoner ['lʌndənə*] *n* londinense *m/f*.

lone [ləun] *adj* solitario.

loneliness ['ləunlɪnɪs] *n* soledad *f*, aislamiento.

lonely ['ləunlɪ] *adj* solitario, solo.

lonely hearts *adj*: ~ **ad** anuncio de la sección de contactos; ~ **column** sección *f* de contactos.

lone parent family *n* familia monoparental.

loner ['ləunə*] *n* solitario/a.

lonesome ['ləunsəm] *adj* (*esp US*) = **lonely**.

long [lɔŋ] *adj* largo ♦ *adv* mucho tiempo, largamente ♦ *vi*: **to** ~ **for sth** anhelar algo ♦ *n*: **the** ~ **and the short of it is that ...** (*fig*) en resumidas cuentas ...; **in the** ~ **run** a la larga; **so** *or* **as** ~ **as** mientras, con tal de que; **don't be** ~! ¡no tardes!, ¡vuelve pronto!; **how** ~ **is the street?** ¿cuánto tiene la calle de largo?; **how** ~ **is the lesson?** ¿cuánto dura la clase?; **6 metres** ~ que mide 6 metros, de 6 metros de largo; **6 months** ~ que dura 6 meses, de 6 meses de duración; **all night** ~ toda la noche; **he came mucho (tiempo)**; **he no** ~**er comes** ya no viene; ~ **before** mucho antes; **before** ~ (+ *future*) dentro de poco; (+ *past*) poco tiempo después; **at** ~ **last** al fin, por fin; **I shan't be** ~ termino pronto.

long-distance [lɔŋ'dɪstəns] *adj* (*race*) de

larga distancia; (*call*) interurbano.
longevity [lɔn'dʒɛvɪtɪ] *n* longevidad *f*.
long-haired ['lɔŋ'hɛəd] *adj* de pelo largo.
longhand ['lɔŋhænd] *n* escritura
(corriente).
longing ['lɔŋɪŋ] *n* anhelo, ansia; (*nostalgia*)
nostalgia ♦ *adj* anhelante.
longingly ['lɔŋɪŋlɪ] *adv* con ansia.
longitude ['lɔŋgɪtjuːd] *n* longitud *f*.
long jump *n* salto de longitud.
long-lost ['lɔŋlɔst] *adj* desaparecido hace
mucho tiempo.
long-playing record (LP) ['lɔŋpleɪŋ-] *n*
elepé *m*, disco de larga duración.
long-range ['lɔŋ'reɪndʒ] *adj* de gran
alcance; (*weather forecast*) a largo plazo.
longshoreman ['lɔŋʃɔːmən] *n* (*US*)
estibador *m*.
long-sighted ['lɔŋ'saɪtɪd] *adj* (*BRIT*)
présbita.
long-standing ['lɔŋ'stændɪŋ] *adj* de mucho
tiempo.
long-suffering [lɔŋ'sʌfərɪŋ] *adj* sufrido.
long-term ['lɔŋtəːm] *adj* a largo plazo.
long wave *n* onda larga.
long-winded [lɔŋ'wɪndɪd] *adj* prolijo.
loo [luː] *n* (*BRIT*: *col*) wáter *m*.
loofah ['luːfə] *n* esponja de lufa.
look [luk] *vi* mirar; (*seem*) parecer;
(*building etc*): **to ~ south/on to the sea**
dar al sur/al mar ♦ *n* mirada; (*glance*)
vistazo; (*appearance*) aire *m*, aspecto; ~s
npl físico *sg*, belleza *sg*; **to ~ ahead** mirar
hacia delante; **it ~s about 4 metres long**
yo calculo que tiene unos 4 metros de
largo; **it ~s all right to me** a mí me
parece que está bien; **to have a ~ at sth**
echar un vistazo a algo; **to have a ~ for**
sth buscar algo.
► **look after** *vt fus* cuidar.
► **look around** *vi* echar una mirada
alrededor.
► **look at** *vt fus* mirar; (*consider*) considerar.
► **look back** *vi* mirar hacia atrás; **to ~ back**
at sb/sth mirar hacia atrás algo/a algn;
to ~ back on (*event, period*) recordar.
► **look down on** *vt fus* (*fig*) despreciar,
mirar con desprecio.
► **look for** *vt fus* buscar.
► **look forward to** *vt fus* esperar con
ilusión; (*in letters*): **we ~ forward to**
hearing from you quedamos a la espera
de su respuesta *or* contestación; **I'm not**
~ing forward to it no tengo ganas de eso,
no me hace ilusión.
► **look in** *vi*: **to ~ in on sb** (*visit*) pasar por
casa de algn.
► **look into** *vt fus* investigar.

► **look on** *vi* mirar (como espectador).
► **look out** *vi* (*beware*): **to ~ out (for)** tener
cuidado (de).
► **look out for** *vt fus* (*seek*) buscar; (*await*)
esperar.
► **look over** *vt* (*essay*) revisar; (*town,*
building) inspeccionar, registrar; (*person*)
examinar.
► **look round** *vi* (*turn*) volver la cabeza; **to**
~ round for sth buscar algo.
► **look through** *vt fus* (*papers, book*) hojear;
(*briefly*) echar un vistazo a; (*telescope*)
mirar por.
► **look to** *vt fus* ocuparse de; (*rely on*) contar
con.
► **look up** *vi* mirar hacia arriba; (*improve*)
mejorar ♦ *vt* (*word*) buscar; (*friend*)
visitar.
► **look up to** *vt fus* admirar.
look-out ['lukaut] *n* (*tower etc*) puesto de
observación; (*person*) vigía *m/f*; **to be on**
the ~ for sth estar al acecho de algo.
look-up table ['lukʌp-] *n* (*COMPUT*) tabla de
consulta.
LOOM *n abbr* (*US*: = *Loyal Order of Moose*)
asociación benéfica.
loom [luːm] *n* telar *m* ♦ *vi* (*threaten*)
amenazar.
loony ['luːnɪ] *adj*, *n* (*col*) loco/a *m/f*.
loop [luːp] *n* lazo; (*bend*) vuelta, recodo;
(*COMPUT*) bucle *m*.
loophole ['luːphəul] *n* laguna.
loose [luːs] *adj* (*gen*) suelto; (*not tight*) flojo;
(*wobbly etc*) movedizo; (*clothes*) ancho;
(*morals, discipline*) relajado ♦ *vt* (*free*)
soltar; (*slacken*) aflojar; (*also*: ~ **off**: *arrow*)
disparar, soltar; ~ **connection** (*ELEC*) hilo
desempalmado; **to be at a ~ end** *or* (*US*)
at ~ ends no saber qué hacer; **to tie up ~**
ends (*fig*) no dejar ningún cabo suelto,
atar cabos.
loose change *n* cambio.
loose chippings [-'tʃɪpɪŋz] *npl* (*on road*)
gravilla *sg* suelta.
loose-fitting ['luːsfɪtɪŋ] *adj* suelto.
loose-leaf ['luːsliːf] *adj*: ~ **binder** *or* **folder**
carpeta de anillas.
loose-limbed ['luːslɪmd] *adj* ágil, suelto.
loosely ['luːslɪ] *adv* libremente,
aproximadamente.
loosely-knit [-nɪt] *adj* de estructura
abierta.
loosen ['luːsn] *vt* (*free*) soltar; (*untie*)
desatar; (*slacken*) aflojar.
► **loosen up** *vi* (*before game*) hacer
(ejercicios de) precalentamiento; (*col*:
relax) soltarse, relajarse.
looseness ['luːsnɪs] *n* soltura; flojedad *f*.

loot [luːt] *n* botín *m* ♦ *vt* saquear.
looter ['luːtə*] *n* saqueador(a) *m/f*.
looting ['luːtɪŋ] *n* pillaje *m*.
lop [lɔp]: **to ~ off** *vt* cortar; (*branches*) podar.
lop-sided ['lɔp'saɪdɪd] *adj* desequilibrado.
lord [lɔːd] *n* señor *m*; **L~ Smith** Lord Smith; **the L~** el Señor; **the (House of) L~s** (*BRIT*) la Cámara de los Lores.
lordly ['lɔːdlɪ] *adj* señorial.
Lordship ['lɔːdʃɪp] *n*: **your ~** su Señoría.
lore [lɔː*] *n* saber *m* popular, tradiciones *fpl*.
lorry ['lɔrɪ] *n* (*BRIT*) camión *m*.
lorry driver *n* camionero/a.
lorry load *n* carga.
lose, *pt, pp* **lost** [luːz, lɔst] *vt* perder ♦ *vi* perder, ser vencido; **to ~ (time)** (*clock*) atrasarse; **to ~ no time (in doing sth)** no tardar (en hacer algo); **to get lost** (*object*) extraviarse; (*person*) perderse.
▶**lose out** *vi* salir perdiendo.
loser ['luːzə*] *n* perdedor(a) *m/f*; **to be a bad ~** no saber perder.
losing ['luːzɪŋ] *adj* (*team etc*) vencido, perdedor(a).
loss [lɔs] *n* pérdida; **heavy ~es** (*MIL*) grandes pérdidas *fpl*; **to be at a ~** no saber qué hacer; **to be a dead ~** ser completamente inútil; **to cut one's ~es** reducir las pérdidas; **to sell sth at a ~** vender algo perdiendo dinero.
loss adjuster *n* (*INSURANCE*) perito/a *m/f or* tasador(a) *m/f* de pérdidas.
loss leader *n* (*COMM*) artículo de promoción.
lost [lɔst] *pt, pp of* **lose** ♦ *adj* perdido; **~ in thought** absorto, ensimismado.
lost and found *n* (*US*) = **lost property, lost property office** *or* **department.**
lost cause *n* causa perdida.
lost property *n* (*BRIT*) objetos *mpl* perdidos.
lost property office *or* **department** *n* (*BRIT*) departamento de objetos perdidos.
lot [lɔt] *n* (*at auctions*) lote *m*; (*destiny*) suerte *f*; **the ~** el todo, todos *mpl*, todas *fpl*; **a ~** mucho, bastante; **a ~ of, ~s of** mucho(s)/a(s) (*pl*); **I read a ~** leo bastante; **to draw ~s (for sth)** echar suertes (para decidir algo).
lotion ['ləuʃən] *n* loción *f*.
lottery ['lɔtərɪ] *n* lotería.
loud [laud] *adj* (*voice, sound*) fuerte; (*laugh, shout*) estrepitoso; (*gaudy*) chillón/ona ♦ *adv* (*speak etc*) fuerte; **out ~** en voz alta.
loudhailer [laud'heɪlə*] *n* (*BRIT*) megáfono.
loudly ['laudlɪ] *adv* (*noisily*) fuerte; (*aloud*) en alta voz.

loudness ['laudnɪs] *n* (*of sound etc*) fuerza.
loudspeaker [laud'spiːkə*] *n* altavoz *m*.
lounge [laundʒ] *n* salón *m*, sala de estar; (*of hotel*) salón *m*; (*of airport*) sala de embarque ♦ *vi* (*also:* **~ about, ~ around**) holgazanear, no hacer nada; *see also* **pub.**
lounge bar *n* salón *m*.
lounge suit *n* (*BRIT*) traje *m* de calle.
louse, *pl* **lice** [laus, laɪs] *n* piojo.
▶**louse up** *vt* (*col*) echar a perder.
lousy ['lauzɪ] *adj* (*fig*) vil, asqueroso.
lout [laut] *n* gamberro/a.
louvre, (*US*) **louver** ['luːvə*] *adj*: **~ door** puerta de rejilla; **~ window** ventana de libro.
lovable ['lʌvəbl] *adj* amable, simpático.
love [lʌv] *n* amor *m* ♦ *vt* amar, querer; **to send one's ~ to sb** dar sus recuerdos a algn; **~ from Anne** (*in letter*) con cariño de Anne; **I ~ to read** me encanta leer; **to be in ~ with** estar enamorado de; **to make ~** hacer el amor; **for the ~ of** por amor a; **"15 ~"** (*TENNIS*) "15 a cero"; **I ~ paella** me encanta la paella; **I'd ~ to come** me gustaría muchísimo venir.
love affair *n* aventura sentimental *or* amorosa.
love child *n* hijo/a natural.
loved ones ['lʌvdwʌnz] *npl* seres *mpl* queridos.
love-hate relationship ['lʌvheɪt-] *n* relación *f* de amor y odio.
love letter *n* carta de amor.
love life *n* vida sentimental.
lovely ['lʌvlɪ] *adj* (*delightful*) precioso, encantador(a), lindo (*esp LAM*); (*beautiful*) hermoso, lindo (*esp LAM*); **we had a ~ time** lo pasamos estupendo.
lovemaking ['lʌvmeɪkɪŋ] *n* relaciones *fpl* sexuales.
lover ['lʌvə*] *n* amante *m/f*; (*amateur*): **a ~ of** un(a) aficionado/a *or* un(a) amante de.
lovesick ['lʌvsɪk] *adj* enfermo de amor, amartelado.
lovesong ['lʌvsɔŋ] *n* canción *f* de amor.
loving ['lʌvɪŋ] *adj* amoroso, cariñoso.
lovingly ['lʌvɪŋlɪ] *adv* amorosamente, cariñosamente.
low [ləu] *adj, adv* bajo ♦ *n* (*METEOROLOGY*) área de baja presión ♦ *vi* (*cow*) mugir; **to feel ~** sentirse deprimido; **to turn (down) ~** llegar a su punto más bajo; **to reach a new ~ or an all-time ~** llegar a su punto más bajo.
low-alcohol [ləu'ælkəhɔl] *adj* bajo en alcohol.
lowbrow ['ləubrau] *adj* (*person*) de poca cultura.
low-calorie ['ləu'kælərɪ] *adj* bajo en

calorías.
low-cut ['ləʊkʌt] *adj* (*dress*) escotado.
low-down ['ləʊdaʊn] *n* (*col*): **he gave me the ~ on it** me puso al corriente ♦ *adj* (*mean*) vil, bajo.
lower ['ləʊə*] *vt* bajar; (*reduce*: *price*) reducir, rebajar; (: *resistance*) debilitar: **to ~ o.s. to** (*fig*) rebajarse a ♦ *vi* ['ləʊə*]: **to ~ (at sb)** fulminar (a algn) con la mirada.
lower case *n* (*TYP*) minúscula.
Lower House *n* (*POL*): **the ~** la Cámara baja.
lowering ['laʊərɪŋ] *adj* (*sky*) amenazador(a).
low-fat ['ləʊ'fæt] *adj* (*milk, yoghurt*) desnatado; (*diet*) bajo en calorías.
low-key ['ləʊ'ki:] *adj* de mínima intensidad; (*operation*) de poco perfil.
lowland ['ləʊlənd] *n* tierra baja.
low-level ['ləʊlɛvl] *adj* de bajo nivel; (*flying*) a poca altura.
low-loader ['ləʊləʊdə*] *n* camión *m* de caja a bajo nivel.
lowly ['ləʊlɪ] *adj* humilde.
low-lying [ləʊ'laɪɪŋ] *adj* bajo.
low-rise ['ləʊraɪz] *adj* bajo.
low-tech ['ləʊtɛk] *adj* de baja tecnología, tradicional.
loyal ['lɔɪəl] *adj* leal.
loyalist ['lɔɪəlɪst] *n* legitimista *m/f*.
loyally ['lɔɪəlɪ] *adv* lealmente.
loyalty ['lɔɪəltɪ] *n* lealtad *f*.
lozenge ['lɔzɪndʒ] *n* (*MED*) pastilla.
LP *n abbr see* **long-playing record**.
L-plates ['ɛlpleɪts] *npl* (*BRIT*) (placas *fpl* de) la L.

En el Reino Unido las personas que están aprendiendo a conducir han de llevar indicativos blancos con una L en rojo llamados normalmente **L-plates** *(de* **learner***) en la parte delantera y trasera de los automóviles que conducen. No tienen que ir a clases teóricas, sino que desde el principio se les entrega un carnet de conducir provisional (***provisional driving licence***) para que realicen sus prácticas, que han de estar supervisadas por un conductor con carnet definitivo (***full driving licence***). Tampoco se les permite hacer prácticas en autopistas aunque vayan acompañados.*

LPN *n abbr* (*US*: = *Licensed Practical Nurse*) enfermero/a practicante.
LRAM *n abbr* (*BRIT*) = *Licentiate of the Royal Academy of Music.*
LSAT *n abbr* (*US*) = *Law School Admissions Test.*

LSD *n abbr* (= *lysergic acid diethylamide*) LSD *m*; (*BRIT*: = *pounds, shillings and pence*) *sistema monetario usado en Gran Bretaña hasta 1971.*
LSE *n abbr* = *London School of Economics.*
Ltd *abbr* (= *limited company*) S.A.
lubricant ['lu:brɪkənt] *n* lubricante *m*.
lubricate ['lu:brɪkeɪt] *vt* lubricar, engrasar.
lubrication [lu:brɪ'keɪʃən] *n* lubricación *f*.
lucid ['lu:sɪd] *adj* lúcido.
lucidity [lu:'sɪdɪtɪ] *n* lucidez *f*.
lucidly ['lu:sɪdlɪ] *adv* lúcidamente.
luck [lʌk] *n* suerte *f*; **good/bad ~** buena/ mala suerte; **good ~!** ¡(que tengas) suerte!; **to be in ~** estar de suerte; **to be out of ~** tener mala suerte.
luckily ['lʌkɪlɪ] *adv* afortunadamente.
luckless ['lʌklɪs] *adj* desafortunado.
lucky ['lʌkɪ] *adj* afortunado.
lucrative ['lu:krətɪv] *adj* lucrativo.
ludicrous ['lu:dɪkrəs] *adj* absurdo.
ludo ['lu:dəʊ] *n* parchís *m*.
lug [lʌg] *vt* (*drag*) arrastrar.
luggage ['lʌgɪdʒ] *n* equipaje *m*.
luggage rack *n* (*in train*) rejilla, redecilla; (*on car*) baca, portaequipajes *m inv*.
luggage van *n* furgón *m or* vagón *m* de equipaje.
lugubrious [lu'gu:brɪəs] *adj* lúgubre.
lukewarm [lu:kwɔ:m] *adj* tibio, templado.
lull [lʌl] *n* tregua ♦ *vt* (*child*) acunar; (*person, fear*) calmar.
lullaby ['lʌləbaɪ] *n* nana.
lumbago [lʌm'beɪgəʊ] *n* lumbago.
lumber ['lʌmbə*] *n* (*junk*) trastos *mpl* viejos; (*wood*) maderos *mpl* ♦ *vt* (*BRIT col*): **to ~ sb with sth/sb** hacer que algn cargue con algo/algn ♦ *vi* (*also*: ~ **about**, ~ **along**) moverse pesadamente.
lumberjack ['lʌmbədʒæk] *n* maderero.
lumber room *n* (*BRIT*) cuarto trastero.
lumber yard *n* (*US*) almacén *m* de madera.
luminous ['lu:mɪnəs] *adj* luminoso.
lump [lʌmp] *n* terrón *m*; (*fragment*) trozo; (*in sauce*) grumo; (*in throat*) nudo; (*swelling*) bulto ♦ *vt* (*also*: ~ **together**) juntar; (*persons*) poner juntos.
lump sum *n* suma global.
lumpy ['lʌmpɪ] *adj* (*sauce*) lleno de grumos.
lunacy ['lu:nəsɪ] *n* locura.
lunar ['lu:nə*] *adj* lunar.
lunatic ['lu:nətɪk] *adj* *n* loco/a *m/f*.
lunatic asylum *n* manicomio.
lunch [lʌntʃ] *n* almuerzo, comida ♦ *vi* almorzar; **to invite sb to** *or* **for ~** invitar a algn a almorzar.
lunch break, lunch hour *n* hora del almuerzo.

luncheon ['lʌntʃən] n almuerzo.
luncheon meat n tipo de fiambre.
luncheon voucher n vale m de comida.
lunchtime ['lʌntʃtaɪm] n hora del almuerzo or de comer.
lung [lʌŋ] n pulmón m.
lung cancer n cáncer m del pulmón.
lunge [lʌndʒ] vi (also: ~ forward) abalanzarse; **to ~ at** arremeter contra.
lupin ['luːpɪn] n altramuz m.
lurch [ləːtʃ] vi dar sacudidas ♦ n sacudida; **to leave sb in the ~** dejar a algn plantado.
lure [luə*] n (bait) cebo; (decoy) señuelo ♦ vt convencer con engaños.
lurid ['luərɪd] adj (colour) chillón/ona; (account) sensacional; (detail) horripilante.
lurk [ləːk] vi (hide) esconderse; (wait) estar al acecho.
luscious ['lʌʃəs] adj delicioso.
lush [lʌʃ] adj exuberante.
lust [lʌst] n lujuria; (greed) codicia.
▶**lust after** vt fus codiciar.
lustful ['lʌstful] adj lascivo, lujurioso.
lustre, (US) **luster** ['lʌstə*] n lustre m, brillo.
lustrous ['lʌstrəs] adj brillante.
lusty ['lʌstɪ] adj robusto, fuerte.
lute [luːt] n laúd m.
Luxembourg ['lʌksəmbəːg] n Luxemburgo.
luxuriant [lʌg'zjuərɪənt] adj exuberante.
luxurious [lʌg'zjuərɪəs] adj lujoso.
luxury ['lʌkʃərɪ] n lujo ♦ cpd de lujo.
luxury tax n impuesto de lujo.
LV n abbr (BRIT) = **luncheon voucher.**
LW abbr (RADIO) = **long wave.**
Lycra ® ['laɪkrə] n licra ®.
lying ['laɪɪŋ] n mentiras fpl ♦ adj (statement, story) falso; (person) mentiroso.
lynch [lɪntʃ] vt linchar.
lynx [lɪŋks] n lince m.
Lyons ['laɪənz] n Lyón m.
lyre ['laɪə*] n lira.
lyric ['lɪrɪk] adj lírico; **~s** npl (of song) letra sg.
lyrical ['lɪrɪkl] adj lírico.

M m

M, m [ɛm] n (letter) M, m f; **M for Mary**, (US) **M for Mike** M de Madrid.
M n abbr = **million(s)**; (= medium) M; (BRIT: = motorway): **the M8** ≈ la A8.
m abbr (= metre) m.; = **mile(s).**
MA n abbr (US) = Military Academy; see **Master of Arts** ♦ abbr (US) = Massachusetts.
mac [mæk] n (BRIT) impermeable m.
macabre [mə'kɑːbrə] adj macabro.
macaroni [mækə'rəʊnɪ] n macarrones mpl.
macaroon [mækə'ruːn] n macarron m, mostachón m.
mace [meɪs] n (weapon, ceremonial) maza; (spice) macis f.
Macedonia [mæsɪ'dəʊnɪə] n Macedonia.
Macedonian [mæsɪ'dəʊnɪən] adj macedonio ♦ n macedonio/a; (LING) macedonio.
machinations [mæʃɪ'neɪʃənz] npl intrigas fpl, maquinaciones fpl.
machine [mə'ʃiːn] n máquina ♦ vt (dress etc) coser a máquina; (TECH) trabajar a máquina.
machine code n (COMPUT) código máquina.
machine gun n ametralladora.
machine language n (COMPUT) lenguaje m máquina.
machine readable adj (COMPUT) legible por máquina.
machinery [mə'ʃiːnərɪ] n maquinaria; (fig) mecanismo.
machine shop n taller m de máquinas.
machine tool n máquina herramienta.
machine translation n traducción f automática.
machine washable adj lavable a máquina.
machinist [mə'ʃiːnɪst] n operario/a m/f (de máquina).
macho ['mætʃəʊ] adj macho.
mackerel ['mækrl] n, pl inv caballa.
mackintosh ['mækɪntɔʃ] n (BRIT) impermeable m.
macro ... ['mækrəʊ] pref macro....
macro-economics ['mækrəʊiːkə'nɔmɪks] n macroeconomía.
mad [mæd] adj loco; (idea) disparatado;

(*angry*) furioso, enojado (*LAM*); ~ (**at** *or* **with sb**) furioso con algn; **to be** ~ (**keen**) **about** *or* **on sth** estar loco por algo; **to go** ~ volverse loco, enloquecer(se).

madam ['mædəm] *n* señora; **can I help you** ~**?** ¿le puedo ayudar, señora?; **M**~ **Chairman** señora presidenta.

madcap ['mædkæp] *adj* (*col*) alocado, disparatado.

mad cow disease *n* encefalopatía espongiforme bovina.

madden ['mædn] *vt* volver loco.

maddening ['mædnɪŋ] *adj* enloquecedor(a).

made [meɪd] *pt, pp of* **make**.

Madeira [mə'dɪərə] *n* (*GEO*) Madeira; (*wine*) madeira *m*.

made-to-measure ['meɪdtəmɛʒə*] *adj* (*BRIT*) hecho a la medida.

made-up ['meɪdʌp] *adj* (*story*) ficticio.

madhouse ['mædhaus] *n* (*also fig*) manicomio.

madly ['mædlɪ] *adv* locamente.

madman ['mædmən] *n* loco.

madness ['mædnɪs] *n* locura.

Madonna [mə'dɒnə] *n* Virgen *f*.

Madrid [mə'drɪd] *n* Madrid *m*.

madrigal ['mædrɪgəl] *n* madrigal *m*.

Mafia ['mæfɪə] *n* Mafia.

mag [mæg] *n abbr* (*BRIT col*) = **magazine**.

magazine [mægə'ziːn] *n* revista; (*MIL: store*) almacén *m*; (*of firearm*) recámara.

maggot ['mægət] *n* gusano.

magic ['mædʒɪk] *n* magia ♦ *adj* mágico.

magical ['mædʒɪkəl] *adj* mágico.

magician [mə'dʒɪʃən] *n* mago/a.

magistrate ['mædʒɪstreɪt] *n* juez *m/f* (municipal); **M**~**s' Courts** *see* **crown court**.

magnanimity [mægnə'nɪmɪtɪ] *n* magnanimidad *f*.

magnanimous [mæg'nænɪməs] *adj* magnánimo.

magnate ['mægneɪt] *n* magnate *m/f*.

magnesium [mæg'niːzɪəm] *n* magnesio.

magnet ['mægnɪt] *n* imán *m*.

magnetic [mæg'nɛtɪk] *adj* magnético.

magnetic disk *n* (*COMPUT*) disco magnético.

magnetic tape *n* cinta magnética.

magnetism ['mægnɪtɪzəm] *n* magnetismo.

magnification [mægnɪfɪ'keɪʃən] *n* aumento.

magnificence [mæg'nɪfɪsns] *n* magnificencia.

magnificent [mæg'nɪfɪsnt] *adj* magnífico.

magnificently [mæg'nɪfɪsntlɪ] *adv* magníficamente.

magnify ['mægnɪfaɪ] *vt* aumentar; (*fig*) exagerar.

magnifying glass ['mægnɪfaɪɪŋ-] *n* lupa.

magnitude ['mægnɪtjuːd] *n* magnitud *f*.

magnolia [mæg'nəʊlɪə] *n* magnolia.

magpie ['mægpaɪ] *n* urraca.

maharajah [mɑːhə'rɑːdʒə] *n* maharajá *m*.

mahogany [mə'hɒgənɪ] *n* caoba ♦ *cpd* de caoba.

maid [meɪd] *n* criada; **old** ~ (*pej*) solterona.

maiden ['meɪdn] *n* doncella ♦ *adj* (*aunt etc*) solterona; (*speech, voyage*) inaugural.

maiden name *n* apellido de soltera.

mail [meɪl] *n* correo; (*letters*) cartas *fpl* ♦ *vt* (*post*) echar al correo; (*send*) mandar por correo; **by** ~ por correo.

mailbox ['meɪlbɒks] *n* (*US: for letters etc; COMPUT*) buzón *m*.

mailing list ['meɪlɪŋ-] *n* lista de direcciones.

mailman ['meɪlmæn] *n* (*US*) cartero.

mail-order ['meɪlɔːdə*] *n* pedido postal; (*business*) venta por correo ♦ *adj*: ~ **firm** *or* **house** casa de venta por correo.

mailshot ['meɪlʃɒt] *n* mailing *m inv*.

mailtrain ['meɪltreɪn] *n* tren *m* correo.

mail van, (*US*) **mail truck** *n* (*AUT*) camioneta de correos *or* de reparto.

maim [meɪm] *vt* mutilar, lisiar.

main [meɪn] *adj* principal, mayor ♦ *n* (*pipe*) cañería principal *or* maestra; (*US*) red *f* eléctrica; **the** ~**s** (*BRIT ELEC*) la red eléctrica; **in the** ~ en general.

main course *n* (*CULIN*) plato principal.

mainframe ['meɪnfreɪm] *n* (*also:* ~ **computer**) ordenador *m or* computadora central.

mainland ['meɪnlənd] *n* continente *m*.

main line *n* línea principal.

mainly ['meɪnlɪ] *adv* principalmente, en su mayoría.

main road *n* carretera principal.

mainstay ['meɪnsteɪ] *n* (*fig*) pilar *m*.

mainstream ['meɪnstriːm] *n* (*fig*) corriente *f* principal.

main street *n* calle *f* mayor.

maintain [meɪn'teɪn] *vt* mantener; (*affirm*) sostener; **to** ~ **that** ... mantener *or* sostener que ... .

maintenance ['meɪntənəns] *n* mantenimiento; (*alimony*) pensión *f* alimenticia.

maintenance contract *n* contrato de mantenimiento.

maintenance order *n* (*LAW*) obligación *f* de pagar una pensión alimenticia al cónyuge.

maisonette [meɪzə'nɛt] *n* dúplex *m*.

maize [meɪz] *n* (*BRIT*) maíz *m*, choclo (*LAM*).

Maj. *abbr* (*MIL*) = **major**.

majestic [mə'dʒɛstɪk] *adj* majestuoso.

majesty ['mædʒɪstɪ] n majestad f.
major ['meɪdʒə*] n (MIL) comandante m
♦ adj principal; (MUS) mayor ♦ vi (US
UNIV): **to ~ (in)** especializarse en; **a ~
operation** una operación or intervención
de gran importancia.
Majorca [mə'jɔːkə] n Mallorca.
major general n (MIL) general m de
división.
majority [mə'dʒɔrɪtɪ] n mayoría ♦ cpd
(verdict) mayoritario.
majority holding n (COMM): **to have a ~**
tener un interés mayoritario.
make [meɪk] vt (pt, pp **made** [meɪd]) hacer;
(manufacture) hacer, fabricar; (cause to
be): **to ~ sb sad** poner triste or
entristecer a algn; (force): **to ~ sb do sth**
obligar a algn a hacer algo; (equal): **2 and
2 ~ 4** 2 y 2 son 4 ♦ n marca; **to ~ a fool of
sb** poner a algn en ridículo; **to ~ a
profit/loss** obtener ganancias/sufrir
pérdidas; **to ~ a profit of £500** sacar una
ganancia de 500 libras; **to ~ it** (arrive)
llegar; (achieve sth) tener éxito; **what
time do you ~ it?** ¿qué hora tienes?; **to ~
do with** contentarse con.
►**make for** vt fus (place) dirigirse a.
►**make off** vi largarse.
►**make out** vt (decipher) descifrar;
(understand) entender; (see) distinguir;
(write: cheque) extender; **to ~ out (that)**
(claim, imply) dar a entender (que); **to ~
out a case for sth** dar buenas razones en
favor de algo.
►**make over** vt (assign): **to ~ over (to)**
ceder or traspasar (a).
►**make up** vt (invent) inventar; (parcel)
hacer ♦ vi reconciliarse; (with cosmetics)
maquillarse; **to be made up of** estar
compuesto de.
►**make up for** vt fus compensar.
make-believe ['meɪkbɪliːv] n ficción f,
fantasía.
maker ['meɪkə*] n fabricante m/f.
makeshift ['meɪkʃɪft] adj improvisado.
make-up ['meɪkʌp] n maquillaje m.
make-up bag n bolsita del maquillaje or
de los cosméticos.
make-up remover n desmaquillador m.
making ['meɪkɪŋ] n (fig): **in the ~** en vías de
formación; **to have the ~s of** (person)
tener madera de.
maladjusted [mælə'dʒʌstɪd] adj
inadaptado.
maladroit [mælə'drɔɪt] adj torpe.
malaise [mæ'leɪz] n malestar m.
malaria [mə'lɛərɪə] n malaria.
Malawi [mə'lɑːwɪ] n Malawi m.

Malay [mə'leɪ] adj malayo ♦ n
malayo/a; (LING) malayo. .
Malaya [mə'leɪə] n Malaya, Malaca.
Malayan [mə'leɪən] adj, n = **Malay**.
Malaysia [mə'leɪzɪə] n Malaisia, Malaysia.
Malaysian [mə'leɪzɪən] adj, n malaisio/a m/f,
malaysio/a m/f.
Maldive Islands ['mɔːldaɪv-], **Maldives**
['mɔːldaɪvz] npl: **the ~** las Maldivas.
male [meɪl] n (BIOL, ELEC) macho ♦ adj (sex,
attitude) masculino; (child etc) varón.
male chauvinist (pig) n machista m.
male nurse n enfermero.
malevolence [mə'lɛvələns] n malevolencia.
malevolent [mə'lɛvələnt] adj malévolo.
malfunction [mæl'fʌŋkʃən] n mal
funcionamiento.
malice ['mælɪs] n (ill will) malicia; (rancour)
rencor m.
malicious [mə'lɪʃəs] adj malicioso;
rencoroso.
maliciously [mə'lɪʃəslɪ] adv con
malevolencia, con malicia;
rencorosamente.
malign [mə'laɪn] vt difamar, calumniar
♦ adj maligno.
malignant [mə'lɪgnənt] adj (MED) maligno.
malinger [mə'lɪŋgə*] vi fingirse enfermo.
malingerer [mə'lɪŋgərə*] n enfermo/a
fingido/a.
mall [mɔːl] n (US: also: **shopping ~**) centro
comercial.
malleable ['mælɪəbl] adj maleable.
mallet ['mælɪt] n mazo.
malnutrition [mælnjuː'trɪʃən] n
desnutrición f.
malpractice [mæl'præktɪs] n negligencia
profesional.
malt [mɔːlt] n malta.
Malta ['mɔːltə] n Malta.
Maltese [mɔːl'tiːz] adj maltés/esa ♦ n, pl inv
maltés/esa m/f; (LING) maltés m.
maltreat [mæl'triːt] vt maltratar.
mammal ['mæml] n mamífero.
mammoth ['mæməθ] n mamut m ♦ adj
gigantesco.
man, pl men [mæn, mɛn] n hombre m;
(CHESS) pieza ♦ vt (NAUT) tripular; (MIL)
defender; **an old ~** un viejo; **~ and wife**
marido y mujer.
Man. abbr (Canada) = Manitoba.
manacle ['mænəkl] n esposa, manilla; **~s**
npl grillos mpl.
manage ['mænɪdʒ] vi arreglárselas ♦ vt (be
in charge of) dirigir; (person etc) manejar;
to ~ to do sth conseguir hacer algo; **to ~
without sth/sb** poder prescindir de algo/
algn.

manageable ['mænɪdʒəbl] *adj* manejable.
management ['mænɪdʒmənt] *n* dirección *f*, administración *f*; **"under new ~"** "bajo nueva dirección".
management accounting *n* contabilidad *f* de gestión.
management consultant *n* consultor(a) *m/f* en dirección de empresas.
manager ['mænɪdʒə*] *n* director *m*; (SPORT) entrenador *m*; **sales ~** jefe/a *m/f* de ventas.
manageress ['mænɪdʒərɛs] *n* directora; (SPORT) entrenadora.
managerial [mænə'dʒɪərɪəl] *adj* directivo.
managing director (MD) ['mænɪdʒɪŋ-] *n* director(a) *m/f* general.
Mancunian [mæŋ'kjuːnɪən] *adj* de Manchester ♦ *n* nativo/a (*or* habitante *m/f*) de Manchester.
mandarin ['mændərɪn] *n* (*also*: **~ orange**) mandarina; (*person*) mandarín *m*.
mandate ['mændeɪt] *n* mandato.
mandatory ['mændətərɪ] *adj* obligatorio.
mandolin(e) ['mændəlɪn] *n* mandolina.
mane [meɪn] *n* (*of horse*) crin *f*; (*of lion*) melena.
maneuver [mə'nuːvə*] (US) = **manoeuvre**.
manful ['mænful] *adj* resuelto.
manfully ['mænfəlɪ] *adv* resueltamente.
mangetout [mɒnʒ'tuː] *n* tirabeque *m*.
mangle ['mæŋgl] *vt* mutilar, destrozar ♦ *n* escurridor *m*.
mango, ~es ['mæŋgəu] *n* mango.
mangrove ['mæŋgrəuv] *n* mangle *m*.
mangy ['meɪndʒɪ] *adj* roñoso; (MED) sarnoso.
manhandle ['mænhændl] *vt* maltratar; (*move by hand*: *goods*) manipular.
manhole ['mænhəul] *n* boca de acceso.
manhood ['mænhud] *n* edad *f* viril; (*manliness*) virilidad *f*.
man-hour ['mæn'auə*] *n* hora-hombre *f*.
manhunt ['mænhʌnt] *n* caza de hombre.
mania ['meɪnɪə] *n* manía.
maniac ['meɪnɪæk] *n* maníaco/a; (*fig*) maniático.
manic ['mænɪk] *adj* (*behaviour*, *activity*) frenético.
manic-depressive ['mænɪkdɪ'presɪv] *adj*, *n* maniacodepresivo/a *m/f*.
manicure ['mænɪkjuə*] *n* manicura.
manicure set *n* estuche *m* de manicura.
manifest ['mænɪfɛst] *vt* manifestar, mostrar ♦ *adj* manifiesto ♦ *n* manifiesto.
manifestation [mænɪfɛs'teɪʃən] *n* manifestación *f*.
manifestly ['mænɪfɛstlɪ] *adv* evidentemente.

manifesto [mænɪ'fɛstəu] *n* manifiesto.
manifold ['mænɪfəuld] *adj* múltiples ♦ *n* (AUT *etc*): **exhaust ~** colector *m* de escape.
Manila [mə'nɪlə] *n* Manila.
manil(l)a [mə'nɪlə] *n* (*paper*, *envelope*) manila.
manipulate [mə'nɪpjuleɪt] *vt* manipular.
manipulation [mənɪpju'leɪʃən] *n* manipulación *f*, manejo.
mankind [mæn'kaɪnd] *n* humanidad *f*, género humano.
manliness ['mænlɪnɪs] *n* virilidad *f*, hombría.
manly ['mænlɪ] *adj* varonil.
man-made ['mæn'meɪd] *adj* artificial.
manna ['mænə] *n* maná *m*.
mannequin ['mænɪkɪn] *n* (*dummy*) maniquí *m*; (*fashion model*) maniquí *m/f*.
manner ['mænə*] *n* manera, modo; (*behaviour*) conducta, manera de ser; (*type*) clase *f*; **~s** *npl* modales *mpl*, educación *f sg*; (**good**) **~s** (buena) educación *f sg*, (buenos) modales *mpl*; **bad ~s** falta *sg* de educación, pocos modales *mpl*; **all ~ of** toda clase *or* suerte de.
mannerism ['mænərɪzəm] *n* gesto típico.
mannerly ['mænəlɪ] *adj* bien educado, formal.
man(o)euvrable [mə'nuːvrəbl] *adj* (*car etc*) manejable.
manoeuvre, (US) **maneuver** [mə'nuːvə*] *vt*, *vi* maniobrar ♦ *n* maniobra; **to ~ sb into doing sth** manipular a algn para que haga algo.
manor ['mænə*] *n* (*also*: **~ house**) casa solariega.
manpower ['mænpauə*] *n* mano *f* de obra.
Manpower Services Commission (MSC) *n* (BRIT) comisión para el aprovechamiento de los recursos humanos.
manservant ['mænsəːvənt] *n* criado.
mansion ['mænʃən] *n* mansión *f*.
manslaughter ['mænslɔːtə*] *n* homicidio involuntario.
mantelpiece ['mæntlpiːs] *n* repisa de la chimenea.
mantle ['mæntl] *n* manto.
man-to-man ['mæntə'mæn] *adj* de hombre a hombre.
manual ['mænjuəl] *adj* manual ♦ *n* manual *m*; **~ worker** obrero, trabajador *m* manual.
manufacture [mænju'fæktʃə*] *vt* fabricar ♦ *n* fabricación *f*.
manufactured goods [mænju'fæktʃəd-] *npl* manufacturas *fpl*, bienes *mpl* manufacturados.

manufacturer [mænjuˈfæktʃərə*] n
fabricante m/f.
manufacturing industries [mænjuˈfæk
tʃərɪŋ-] npl industrias fpl manufactureras.
manure [məˈnjuə*] n estiércol m, abono.
manuscript [ˈmænjuskrɪpt] n manuscrito.
Manx [mæŋks] adj de la Isla de Man.
many [ˈmɛnɪ] adj muchos/as ♦ pron muchos/
as; **a great** ~ muchísimos, un buen
número de; ~ **a time** muchas veces; **too**
~ **difficulties** demasiadas dificultades;
twice as ~ el doble; **how** ~? ¿cuántos?
Maori [ˈmaurɪ] adj, n maorí m/f.
map [mæp] n mapa m ♦ vt trazar el mapa
de.
►**map out** vt (fig: career, holiday, essay)
proyectar, planear.
maple [ˈmeɪpl] n arce m, maple m (LAM).
mar [maː*] vt estropear.
Mar. abbr (= March) mar.
marathon [ˈmærəθən] n maratón m ♦ adj: **a**
~ **session** una sesión maratoniana.
marathon runner n corredor(a) m/f de
maratones.
marauder [məˈrɔːdə*] n merodeador(a) m/f.
marble [ˈmaːbl] n mármol m; (toy) canica.
March [maːtʃ] n marzo.
march [maːtʃ] vi (MIL) marchar; (fig)
caminar con resolución ♦ n marcha;
(demonstration) manifestación f.
marcher [ˈmaːtʃə*] n manifestante m/f.
marching [ˈmaːtʃɪŋ] n: **to give sb his** ~
orders (fig) mandar a paseo a algn;
(employee) poner de patitas en la calle a
algn.
march-past [ˈmaːtʃpaːst] n desfile m.
mare [mɛə*] n yegua f.
margarine [maːdʒəˈriːn] n margarina.
marg(e) [maːdʒ] n abbr = **margarine**.
margin [ˈmaːdʒɪn] n margen m.
marginal [ˈmaːdʒɪnl] adj marginal.
marginally [ˈmaːdʒɪnəlɪ] adv ligeramente.
marginal seat n (POL) circunscripción f
políticamente no definida.
marigold [ˈmærɪɡəuld] n caléndula.
marijuana [mærɪˈwaːnə] n marihuana.
marina [məˈriːnə] n marina.
marinade [mærɪˈneɪd] n adobo.
marinate [ˈmærɪneɪt] vt adobar.
marine [məˈriːn] adj marino ♦ n soldado de
infantería de marina.
marine insurance n seguro marítimo.
mariner [ˈmærɪnə*] n marinero, marino.
marionette [mærɪəˈnɛt] n marioneta, títere
m.
marital [ˈmærɪtl] adj matrimonial; ~ **status**
estado civil.
maritime [ˈmærɪtaɪm] adj marítimo.

marjoram [ˈmaːdʒərəm] n mejorana.
mark [maːk] n marca, señal f; (imprint)
huella; (stain) mancha; (BRIT SCOL) nota;
(currency) marco ♦ vt (also SPORT: player)
marcar; (stain) manchar; (BRIT SCOL)
calificar, corregir; **punctuation** ~**s** signos
mpl de puntuación; **to be quick off the** ~
(fig) ser listo; **up to the** ~ (in efficiency) a
la altura de las circunstancias; **to** ~ **time**
marcar el paso.
►**mark down** vt (reduce: prices, goods)
rebajar.
►**mark off** vt (tick) indicar, señalar.
►**mark out** vt trazar.
►**mark up** vt (price) aumentar.
marked [maːkt] adj marcado, acusado.
markedly [ˈmaːkɪdlɪ] adv marcadamente,
apreciablemente.
marker [ˈmaːkə*] n (sign) marcador m;
(bookmark) registro.
market [ˈmaːkɪt] n mercado ♦ vt (COMM)
comercializar; (promote) publicitar; **open**
~ mercado libre; **to be on the** ~ estar en
venta; **to play the** ~ jugar a la bolsa.
marketable [ˈmaːkɪtəbl] adj comerciable.
market analysis n análisis m del mercado.
market day n día m de mercado.
market demand n demanda de mercado.
market economy n economía de
mercado.
market forces npl tendencias fpl del
mercado.
market garden n (BRIT) huerto.
marketing [ˈmaːkɪtɪŋ] n marketing m,
mercadotecnia.
marketing manager n director m de
marketing.
market leader n líder m de ventas.
marketplace [ˈmaːkɪtpleɪs] n mercado.
market price n precio de mercado.
market research n (COMM) estudios mpl de
mercado.
market value n valor m en el mercado.
marking [ˈmaːkɪŋ] n (on animal) pinta; (on
road) señal f.
marksman [ˈmaːksmən] n tirador m.
marksmanship [ˈmaːksmənʃɪp] n puntería.
mark-up [ˈmaːkʌp] n (COMM: margin)
margen m de beneficio; (: increase)
aumento.
marmalade [ˈmaːməleɪd] n mermelada de
naranja.
maroon [məˈruːn] vt: **to be** ~**ed**
(shipwrecked) naufragar; (fig) quedar
abandonado ♦ adj granate inv.
marquee [maːˈkiː] n carpa, entoldado.

marquess, marquis ['mɑːkwɪs] n marqués m.

Marrakech, Marrakesh [mærə'keʃ] n Marrakech m.

marriage ['mærɪdʒ] n (state) matrimonio; (wedding) boda; (act) casamiento.

marriage bureau n agencia matrimonial.

marriage certificate n partida de casamiento.

marriage guidance, (US) **marriage counseling** n orientación f matrimonial.

marriage of convenience n matrimonio de conveniencia.

married ['mærɪd] adj casado; (life, love) conyugal.

marrow ['mærəu] n médula; (vegetable) calabacín m.

marry ['mærɪ] vt casarse con; (subj: father, priest etc) casar ♦ vi (also: get married) casarse.

Mars [mɑːz] n Marte m.

Marseilles [mɑː'seɪ] n Marsella.

marsh [mɑːʃ] n pantano; (salt ~) marisma.

marshal ['mɑːʃl] n (MIL) mariscal m; (at sports meeting, demonstration etc) oficial m; (US: of police, fire department) jefe/a m/f ♦ vt (facts) ordenar; (soldiers) formar.

marshalling yard ['mɑːʃəlɪŋ-] n (RAIL) estación f clasificadora.

marshmallow ['mɑːʃmæləu] n (BOT) malvavisco; (sweet) esponja, dulce m de merengue blando.

marshy ['mɑːʃɪ] adj pantanoso.

marsupial [mɑː'suːpɪəl] adj, n marsupial m.

martial ['mɑːʃl] adj marcial.

martial arts npl artes fpl marciales.

martial law n ley f marcial.

martin ['mɑːtɪn] n (also: house ~) avión m.

martyr ['mɑːtə*] n mártir m/f ♦ vt martirizar.

martyrdom ['mɑːtədəm] n martirio.

marvel ['mɑːvl] n maravilla, prodigio ♦ vi: to ~ (at) maravillarse (de).

marvellous, (US) **marvelous** ['mɑːvləs] adj maravilloso.

marvel(l)ously ['mɑːvləslɪ] adv maravillosamente.

Marxism ['mɑːksɪzəm] n marxismo.

Marxist ['mɑːksɪst] adj, n marxista m/f.

marzipan ['mɑːzɪpæn] n mazapán m.

mascara [mæs'kɑːrə] n rimel m.

mascot ['mæskət] n mascota.

masculine ['mæskjulɪn] adj masculino.

masculinity [mæskju'lɪnɪtɪ] n masculinidad f.

MASH [mæʃ] n abbr (US) = mobile army surgical hospital.

mash [mæʃ] n (mix) mezcla; (CULIN) puré m; (pulp) amasijo.

mashed potatoes [mæʃt-] npl puré m de patatas or papas (LAM).

mask [mɑːsk] n (also ELEC) máscara ♦ vt enmascarar.

masochism ['mæsəkɪzəm] n masoquismo.

masochist ['mæsəukɪst] n masoquista m/f.

mason ['meɪsn] n (also: stone~) albañil m; (also: free~) masón m.

masonic [mə'sɒnɪk] adj masónico.

masonry ['meɪsnrɪ] n masonería; (building) mampostería.

masquerade [mæskə'reɪd] n baile m de máscaras; (fig) mascarada ♦ vi: to ~ as disfrazarse de, hacerse pasar por.

mass [mæs] n (people) muchedumbre f; (PHYSICS) masa; (REL) misa; (great quantity) montón m ♦ vi reunirse; (MIL) concentrarse; **the ~es** las masas; **to go to ~** ir a or oír misa.

Mass. abbr (US) = Massachusetts.

massacre ['mæsəkə*] n masacre f ♦ vt masacrar.

massage ['mæsɑːʒ] n masaje m ♦ vt dar masajes or un masaje a.

masseur [mæ'səː*] n masajista m.

masseuse [mæ'səːz] n masajista f.

massive ['mæsɪv] adj enorme; (support, intervention) masivo.

mass media npl medios mpl de comunicación de masas.

mass meeting n (of everyone concerned) reunión f en masa; (huge) mitin m.

mass-produce ['mæsprə'djuːs] vt fabricar en serie.

mass-production ['mæsprə'dʌkʃən] n fabricación f or producción f en serie.

mast [mɑːst] n (NAUT) mástil m; (RADIO etc) torre f, antena.

mastectomy [mæs'tektəmɪ] n mastectomía.

master ['mɑːstə*] n (of servant, animal) amo; (fig: of situation) dueño; (ART, MUS) maestro; (in secondary school) profesor m; (title for boys): **M~ X** Señorito X ♦ vt dominar.

master disk n (COMPUT) disco maestro.

masterful ['mɑːstəful] adj magistral, dominante.

master key n llave f maestra.

masterly ['mɑːstəlɪ] adj magistral.

mastermind ['mɑːstəmaɪnd] n inteligencia superior ♦ vt dirigir, planear.

Master of Arts (MA) n licenciatura superior en Letras; see also **master's degree.**

Master of Ceremonies n encargado de protocolo.

Master of Science (MSc) *n* licenciatura superior en Ciencias; *see also* **master's degree.**
masterpiece ['mɑːstəpiːs] *n* obra maestra.
master plan *n* plan *m* rector.

Los estudios de postgrado británicos que llevan a la obtención de un **master's degree** *consisten generalmente en una combinación de curso(s) académico(s) y tesina (***dissertation***) sobre un tema original, o bien únicamente la redacción de una tesina. El primer caso es el más frecuente para los títulos de* **MA (Master of Arts)** *y* **MSc (Master of Science)**, *mientras que los de* **MLitt (Master of Letters)** *o* **MPhil (Master of Philosophy)** *se obtienen normalmente mediante tesina. En algunas universidades, como las escocesas, el título de* **master's degree** *no es de postgrado, sino que corresponde a la licenciatura.*

---

master stroke *n* golpe *m* maestro.
mastery ['mɑːstərɪ] *n* maestría.
mastiff ['mæstɪf] *n* mastín *m*.
masturbate ['mæstəbeɪt] *vi* masturbarse.
masturbation [mæstə'beɪʃən] *n* masturbación *f*.
mat [mæt] *n* alfombrilla; (*also:* door~) felpudo ♦ *adj* = **matt.**
MAT *n abbr* (= *machine-assisted translation*) TAO.
match [mætʃ] *n* cerilla, fósforo; (*game*) partido; (*fig*) igual *m/f* ♦ *vt* emparejar; (*go well with*) hacer juego con; (*equal*) igualar ♦ *vi* hacer juego; **to be a good** ~ hacer buena pareja.
matchbox ['mætʃbɔks] *n* caja de cerillas.
matching ['mætʃɪŋ] *adj* que hace juego.
matchless ['mætʃlɪs] *adj* sin par, incomparable.
matchmaker ['mætʃmeɪkə*] *n* casamentero.
mate [meɪt] *n* (work~) compañero/a, colega *m/f*; (*col: friend*) amigo/a, compadre *m/f* (*LAM*); (*animal*) macho/hembra; (*in merchant navy*) primer oficial *m* ♦ *vi* acoplarse, parearse ♦ *vt* acoplar, parear.
maté ['mɑːteɪ] *n* mate *m* (cocido), yerba mate.
material [mə'tɪərɪəl] *n* (*substance*) materia; (*equipment*) material *m*; (*cloth*) tela, tejido ♦ *adj* material; (*important*) esencial; ~**s** *npl* materiales *mpl*; (*equipment etc*) artículos *mpl*.
materialistic [mətɪərɪə'lɪstɪk] *adj* materialista.
materialize [mə'tɪərɪəlaɪz] *vi*

materializarse.
materially [mə'tɪərɪəlɪ] *adv* materialmente.
maternal [mə'təːnl] *adj* maternal; ~ **grandmother** abuela materna.
maternity [mə'təːnɪtɪ] *n* maternidad *f*.
maternity benefit *n* subsidio por maternidad.
maternity dress *n* vestido premamá.
maternity hospital *n* hospital *m* de maternidad.
maternity leave *n* baja por maternidad.
math [mæθ] *n abbr* (*US:* = *mathematics*) matemáticas *fpl*.
mathematical [mæθə'mætɪkl] *adj* matemático.
mathematically [mæθɪ'mætɪklɪ] *adv* matemáticamente.
mathematician [mæθəmə'tɪʃən] *n* matemático.
mathematics [mæθə'mætɪks] *n* matemáticas *fpl*.
maths [mæθs] *n abbr* (*BRIT:* = *mathematics*) matemáticas *fpl*.
matinée ['mætɪneɪ] *n* función *f* de la tarde, vermú(t) *m* (*LAM*).
mating ['meɪtɪŋ] *n* apareajmiento.
mating call *n* llamada del macho.
mating season *n* época de celo.
matins ['mætɪnz] *n* maitines *mpl*.
matriarchal [meɪtrɪ'ɑːkl] *adj* matriarcal.
matrices ['meɪtrɪsiːz] *pl of* **matrix.**
matriculation [mətrɪkju'leɪʃən] *n* matriculación *f*, matrícula.
matrimonial [mætrɪ'məunɪəl] *adj* matrimonial.
matrimony ['mætrɪmənɪ] *n* matrimonio.
matrix, *pl* **matrices** ['meɪtrɪks, 'meɪtrɪsiːz] *n* matriz *f*.
matron ['meɪtrən] *n* (*in hospital*) enfermera jefe; (*in school*) ama de llaves.
matronly ['meɪtrənlɪ] *adj* de matrona; (*fig: figure*) corpulento.
matt [mæt] *adj* mate.
matted ['mætɪd] *adj* enmarañado.
matter ['mætə*] *n* cuestión *f*, asunto; (*PHYSICS*) sustancia, materia; (*content*) contenido; (*MED: pus*) pus *m* ♦ *vi* importar; **it doesn't** ~ no importa; **what's the** ~? ¿qué pasa?; **no** ~ **what** pase lo que pase; **as a** ~ **of course** por rutina; **as a** ~ **of fact** en realidad; **printed** ~ impresos *mpl*; **reading** ~ material *m* de lectura, lecturas *fpl*.
matter-of-fact ['mætərəv'fækt] *adj* (*style*) prosaico; (*person*) práctico; (*voice*) neutro.
mattress ['mætrɪs] *n* colchón *m*.

mature [mə'tjuə*] adj maduro ♦ vi madurar.
mature student n estudiante de más de 21 años.
maturity [mə'tjuərɪtɪ] n madurez f.
maudlin ['mɔːdlɪn] adj llorón/ona.
maul [mɔːl] vt magullar.
Mauritania [mɔːrɪ'teɪnɪə] n Mauritania.
Mauritius [mə'rɪʃəs] n Mauricio.
mausoleum [mɔːsə'lɪəm] n mausoleo.
mauve [məuv] adj de color malva.
maverick ['mævrɪk] n (fig) inconformista m/f, persona independiente.
mawkish ['mɔːkɪʃ] adj sensiblero, empalagoso.
max. abbr = **maximum**.
maxim ['mæksɪm] n máxima.
maxima ['mæksɪmə] pl of **maximum**.
maximize ['mæksɪmaɪz] vt (profits etc) llevar al máximo; (chances) maximizar.
maximum ['mæksɪməm] adj máximo ♦ n (pl **maxima** ['mæksɪmə]) máximo.
May [meɪ] n mayo.
may [meɪ] vi (conditional: **might**) (indicating possibility): **he ~ come** puede que venga; (be allowed to): ~ **I smoke?** ¿puedo fumar?; (wishes): ~ **God bless you!** ¡que Dios le bendiga!; ~ **I sit here?** ¿me puedo sentar aquí?
maybe ['meɪbiː] adv quizá(s); ~ **not** quizá(s) no.
May Day n el primero de Mayo.
mayday ['meɪdeɪ] n señal f de socorro.
mayhem ['meɪhɛm] n caos m total.
mayonnaise [meɪə'neɪz] n mayonesa.
mayor [mɛə*] n alcalde m.
mayoress ['mɛərɛs] n alcaldesa.
maypole ['meɪpəul] n mayo.
maze [meɪz] n laberinto.
MB abbr (COMPUT) = **megabyte**; (Canada) = Manitoba.
MBA n abbr (= Master of Business Administration) título universitario.
MBBS, MBChB n abbr (BRIT: = Bachelor of Medicine and Surgery) título universitario.
MBE n abbr (BRIT: = Member of the Order of the British Empire) título ceremonial.
MC n abbr (= master of ceremonies) e.p.; (US: = Member of Congress) diputado del Congreso de los Estados Unidos.
MCAT n abbr (US) = Medical College Admissions Test.
MCP n abbr (BRIT col) = **male chauvinist pig**.
MD n abbr (= Doctor of Medicine) título universitario; (COMM) = **managing director** ♦ abbr (US) = Maryland.
Md. abbr (US) = Maryland.
MDT n abbr (US: = mountain daylight time) hora de verano de las Montañas Rocosas.
ME abbr (US POST) = Maine ♦ n abbr (US MED) = medical examiner; (MED) = myalgic encephalomyelitis) encefalomielitis f miálgica.
me [miː] pron (direct) me; (stressed, after pronoun) mí; **can you hear** ~? ¿me oyes?; **he heard ME!** me oyó a mí; **it's** ~ soy yo; **give them to** ~ dámelos; **with/without** ~ conmigo/sin mí; **it's for** ~ es para mí.
meadow ['mɛdəu] n prado, pradera.
meagre, (US) meager ['miːgə*] adj escaso, pobre.
meal [miːl] n comida; (flour) harina; **to go out for a** ~ salir a comer.
meals on wheels nsg (BRIT) servicio de alimentación a domicilio para necesitados y tercera edad.
mealtime ['miːltaɪm] n hora de comer.
mealy-mouthed ['miːlɪmauðd] adj: **to be** ~ no decir nunca las cosas claras.
mean [miːn] adj (with money) tacaño; (unkind) mezquino, malo; (average) medio; (US: vicious: animal) resabiado; (: person) malicioso ♦ vt (pt, pp **meant** [mɛnt]) (signify) querer decir, significar; (intend): **to** ~ **to do sth** tener la intención de or pensar hacer algo ♦ n medio, término medio; **do you** ~ **it?** ¿lo dices en serio?; **what do you** ~? ¿qué quiere decir?; **to be meant for sb/sth** ser para algn/algo; see also **means**.
meander [mɪ'ændə*] vi (river) serpentear; (person) vagar.
meaning ['miːnɪŋ] n significado, sentido.
meaningful ['miːnɪŋful] adj significativo.
meaningless ['miːnɪŋlɪs] adj sin sentido.
meanness ['miːnnɪs] n (with money) tacañería; (unkindness) maldad f, mezquindad f.
means [miːnz] npl medio sg, manera sg; (resource) recursos mpl, medios mpl; **by** ~ **of** mediante, por medio de; **by all** ~! ¡naturalmente!, ¡claro que sí!
means test n control m de los recursos económicos.
meant [mɛnt] pt, pp of **mean**.
meantime ['miːntaɪm], **meanwhile** ['miːnwaɪl] adv (also: **in the meantime**) mientras tanto.
measles ['miːzlz] n sarampión m.
measly ['miːzlɪ] adj (col) miserable.
measurable ['mɛʒərəbl] adj mensurable, que se puede medir.
measure ['mɛʒə*] vt medir; (for clothes etc) tomar las medidas a ♦ vi medir ♦ n medida; (ruler) cinta métrica, metro; **a litre** ~ una medida de un litro; **some** ~ **of**

success cierto éxito; **to take ~s to do sth** tomar medidas para hacer algo.

▶**measure up** *vi*: **to ~ up (to)** estar a la altura (de).

measured ['mɛʒəd] *adj* moderado; *(tone)* mesurado.

measurement ['mɛʒəmənt] *n (measure)* medida; *(act)* medición *f*; **to take sb's ~s** tomar las medidas a algn.

meat [mi:t] *n* carne *f*; **cold ~s** fiambres *mpl*; **crab ~** carne *f* de cangrejo.

meatball ['mi:tbɔ:l] *n* albóndiga.

meat pie *n* pastel *m* de carne.

meaty ['mi:tɪ] *adj (person)* fuerte, corpulento; *(role)* sustancioso; **a ~ meal** una comida con bastante carne.

Mecca ['mɛkə] *n (city)* la Meca; *(fig)* meca.

mechanic [mɪ'kænɪk] *n* mecánico/a.

mechanical [mɪ'kænɪkl] *adj* mecánico.

mechanical engineering *n (science)* ingeniería mecánica; *(industry)* construcción *f* mecánica.

mechanics [mə'kænɪks] *n* mecánica ♦ *npl* mecanismo *sg*.

mechanism ['mɛkənɪzəm] *n* mecanismo.

mechanization [mɛkənaɪ'zeɪʃən] *n* mecanización *f*.

mechanize ['mɛkənaɪz] *vt* mecanizar; *(factory etc)* automatizar.

MEd *n abbr (= Master of Education)* título universitario.

medal ['mɛdl] *n* medalla.

medallion [mɪ'dælɪən] *n* medallón *m*.

medallist, *(US)* **medalist** ['mɛdlɪst] *n (SPORT)* medallista *m/f*.

meddle ['mɛdl] *vi*: **to ~ in** entrometerse en; **to ~ with sth** manosear algo.

meddlesome ['mɛdlsəm], **meddling** ['mɛdlɪŋ] *adj (interfering)* entrometido; *(touching things)* curioso.

media ['mi:dɪə] *npl* medios *mpl* de comunicación.

media circus *n* excesivo despliegue informativo.

mediaeval [mɛdɪ'i:vl] *adj* = **medieval**.

median ['mi:dɪən] *n (US: also: ~ strip)* mediana.

media research *n* estudio de los medios de publicidad.

mediate ['mi:dɪeɪt] *vi* mediar.

mediation [mi:dɪ'eɪʃən] *n* mediación *f*.

mediator ['mi:dɪeɪtə*] *n* mediador(a) *m/f*.

Medicaid ['mɛdɪkeɪd] *n (US)* programa de ayuda médica.

medical ['mɛdɪkl] *adj* médico ♦ *n (also: ~ examination)* reconocimiento médico.

medical certificate *n* certificado *m* médico.

Medicare ['mɛdɪkɛə*] *n (US)* seguro médico del Estado.

medicated ['mɛdɪkeɪtɪd] *adj* medicinal.

medication [mɛdɪ'keɪʃən] *n (drugs etc)* medicación *f*.

medicinal [mɛ'dɪsɪnl] *adj* medicinal.

medicine ['mɛdsɪn] *n* medicina; *(drug)* medicamento.

medicine chest *n* botiquín *m*.

medicine man *n* hechicero.

medieval, mediaeval [mɛdɪ'i:vl] *adj* medieval.

mediocre [mi:dɪ'əukə*] *adj* mediocre.

mediocrity [mi:dɪ'ɔkrɪtɪ] *n* mediocridad *f*.

meditate ['mɛdɪteɪt] *vi* meditar.

meditation [mɛdɪ'teɪʃən] *n* meditación *f*.

Mediterranean [mɛdɪtə'reɪnɪən] *adj* mediterráneo; **the ~ (Sea)** el (Mar *m*) Mediterráneo.

medium ['mi:dɪəm] *adj* mediano; *(level, height)* medio ♦ *n (pl media: means)* medio; *(pl* **mediums**: *person)* médium *m/f*; **happy ~** punto justo.

medium-dry ['mi:dɪəm'draɪ] *adj* semiseco.

medium-sized ['mi:dɪəm'saɪzd] *adj* de tamaño mediano; *(clothes)* de (la) talla mediana.

medium wave *n* onda media.

medley ['mɛdlɪ] *n* mezcla; *(MUS)* popurrí *m*.

meek [mi:k] *adj* manso, sumiso.

meekly ['mi:klɪ] *adv* mansamente, dócilmente.

meet [mi:t] *vb (pt, pp* met [mɛt]*) vt* encontrar; *(accidentally)* encontrarse con; *(by arrangement)* reunirse con; *(for the first time)* conocer; *(go and fetch)* ir a buscar; *(opponent)* enfrentarse con; *(obligations)* cumplir; *(bill, expenses)* pagar, costear ♦ *vi* encontrarse; *(in session)* reunirse; *(join: objects)* unirse; *(get to know)* conocerse ♦ *n (BRIT: HUNTING)* cacería; *(US: SPORT)* encuentro; **pleased to ~ you!** ¡encantado (de conocerle)!, ¡mucho gusto!

▶**meet up** *vi*: **to ~ up with sb** reunirse con algn.

▶**meet with** *vt fus* reunirse con; *(difficulty)* tropezar con.

meeting ['mi:tɪŋ] *n (also SPORT: rally)* encuentro; *(arranged)* cita, compromiso *(LAM)*; *(formal session, business meet)* reunión *f*; *(POL)* mitin *m*; **to call a ~** convocar una reunión.

meeting place *n* lugar *m* de reunión *or* encuentro.

megabyte ['mɛgə'baɪt] *n (COMPUT)* megabyte *m*, megaocteto.

megalomaniac [mɛgələu'meɪnɪæk] *adj, n* megalómano/a *m/f*.

megaphone ['mɛgəfəun] *n* megáfono.
megawatt ['mɛgəwɔt] *n* megavatio.
melancholy ['mɛlənkəlɪ] *n* melancolía ♦ *adj* melancólico.
melee ['mɛleɪ] *n* refriega.
mellow ['mɛləu] *adj* (*wine*) añejo; (*sound, colour*) suave; (*fruit*) maduro ♦ *vi* (*person*) madurar.
melodious [mɪ'ləudɪəs] *adj* melodioso.
melodrama ['mɛləudrɑːmə] *n* melodrama *m*.
melodramatic [mɛləudrə'mætɪk] *adj* melodramático.
melody ['mɛlədɪ] *n* melodía.
melon ['mɛlən] *n* melón *m*.
melt [mɛlt] *vi* (*metal*) fundirse; (*snow*) derretirse; (*fig*) ablandarse ♦ *vt* (*also*: ~ **down**) fundir; ~**ed butter** mantequilla derretida.
▶**melt away** *vi* desvanecerse.
meltdown ['mɛltdaun] *n* (*in nuclear reactor*) fusión *f* (de un reactor nuclear).
melting point ['mɛltɪŋ-] *n* punto de fusión.
melting pot ['mɛltɪŋ-] *n* (*fig*) crisol *m*; **to be in the** ~ estar sobre el tapete.
member ['mɛmbə*] *n* (*of political party*) miembro; (*of club*) socio/a; **M~ of Parliament (MP)** (*BRIT*) diputado/a; **M~ of the European Parliament (MEP)** (*BRIT*) eurodiputado/a; **M~ of the House of Representatives (MHR)** (*US*) diputado/a del Congreso de los Estados Unidos.
membership ['mɛmbəʃɪp] *n* (*members*) miembros *mpl*; socios *mpl*; (*numbers*) número de miembros *or* socios; **to seek** ~ **of** pedir el ingreso a.
membership card *n* carnet *m* de socio.
membrane ['mɛmbreɪn] *n* membrana.
memento [mə'mɛntəu] *n* recuerdo.
memo ['mɛməu] *n abbr* (= *memorandum*) nota (de servicio).
memoirs ['mɛmwɑːz] *npl* memorias *fpl*.
memo pad *n* bloc *m* de notas.
memorable ['mɛmərəbl] *adj* memorable.
memorandum, *pl* **memoranda** [mɛmə'rændəm, -də] *n* nota (de servicio); (*POL*) memorándum *m*.
memorial [mɪ'mɔːrɪəl] *n* monumento conmemorativo ♦ *adj* conmemorativo.
Memorial Day *n* (*US*) día de conmemoración de los caídos en la guerra.
memorize ['mɛməraɪz] *vt* aprender de memoria.
memory ['mɛmərɪ] *n* memoria; (*recollection*) recuerdo; (*COMPUT*) memoria; **to have a good/bad** ~ tener buena/mala memoria; **loss of** ~ pérdida

de memoria.
men [mɛn] *pl of* **man**.
menace ['mɛnəs] *n* amenaza; (*col: nuisance*) lata ♦ *vt* amenazar; **a public** ~ un peligro público.
menacing ['mɛnɪsɪŋ] *adj* amenazador(a).
menacingly ['mɛnɪsɪŋlɪ] *adv* amenazadoramente.
menagerie [mɪ'nædʒərɪ] *n* casa de fieras.
mend [mɛnd] *vt* reparar, arreglar; (*darn*) zurcir ♦ *vi* reponerse ♦ *n* (*gen*) remiendo; (*darn*) zurcido; **to be on the** ~ ir mejorando.
mending ['mɛndɪŋ] *n* arreglo, reparación *f*; (*clothes*) ropa por remendar.
menial ['miːnɪəl] *adj* (*pej*) bajo, servil.
meningitis [mɛnɪn'dʒaɪtɪs] *n* meningitis *f*.
menopause ['mɛnəupɔːz] *n* menopausia.
men's room *n* (*US*): **the** ~ el servicio de caballeros.
menstrual ['mɛnstruəl] *adj* menstrual.
menstruate ['mɛnstrueɪt] *vi* menstruar.
menstruation [mɛnstru'eɪʃən] *n* menstruación *f*.
menswear ['mɛnzwɛə*] *n* confección *f* de caballero.
mental ['mɛntl] *adj* mental; ~ **illness** enfermedad *f* mental.
mental hospital *n* (hospital *m*) psiquiátrico.
mentality [mɛn'tælɪtɪ] *n* mentalidad *f*.
mentally ['mɛntlɪ] *adv*: **to be** ~ **handicapped** ser un disminuido mental.
menthol ['mɛnθɔl] *n* mentol *m*.
mention ['mɛnʃən] *n* mención *f* ♦ *vt* mencionar; (*speak of*) hablar de; **don't** ~ **it!** ¡de nada!; **I need hardly** ~ **that** ... huelga decir que ...; **not to** ~, **without** ~**ing** sin contar.
mentor ['mɛntɔː*] *n* mentor *m*.
menu ['mɛnjuː] *n* (*set* ~) menú *m*; (*printed*) carta; (*COMPUT*) menú *m*.
menu-driven ['mɛnjuːdrɪvn] *adj* (*COMPUT*) guiado por menú.
MEP *n abbr see* **Member of the European Parliament**.
mercantile ['mɜːkəntaɪl] *adj* mercantil.
mercenary ['mɜːsɪnərɪ] *adj*, *n* mercenario.
merchandise ['mɜːtʃəndaɪz] *n* mercancías *fpl*.
merchandiser ['mɜːtʃəndaɪzə*] *n* comerciante *m/f*, tratante *m*.
merchant ['mɜːtʃənt] *n* comerciante *m/f*.
merchant bank *n* (*BRIT*) banco comercial.
merchantman ['mɜːtʃəntmən] *n* buque *m* mercante.
merchant navy, (*US*) **merchant marine** *n* marina mercante.

merciful ['mə:sɪful] adj compasivo.
mercifully ['mə:sɪfulɪ] adv con compasión; (fortunately) afortunadamente.
merciless ['mə:sɪlɪs] adj despiadado.
mercilessly ['mə:sɪlɪslɪ] adv despiadadamente, sin piedad.
mercurial [mə:'kjuərɪəl] adj veleidoso, voluble.
mercury ['mə:kjurɪ] n mercurio.
mercy ['mə:sɪ] n compasión f; (REL) misericordia; **at the ~ of** a la merced de.
mercy killing n eutanasia.
mere [mɪə*] adj simple, mero.
merely ['mɪəlɪ] adv simplemente, sólo.
merge [mə:dʒ] vt (join) unir; (mix) mezclar; (fuse) fundir; (COMPUT: files, text) intercalar ♦ vi unirse; (COMM) fusionarse.
merger ['mə:dʒə*] n (COMM) fusión f.
meridian [mə'rɪdɪən] n meridiano.
meringue [mə'ræŋ] n merengue m.
merit ['mɛrɪt] n mérito ♦ vt merecer.
meritocracy [mɛrɪ'tɔkrəsɪ] n meritocracia.
mermaid ['mə:meɪd] n sirena.
merrily ['mɛrɪlɪ] adv alegremente.
merriment ['mɛrɪmənt] n alegría.
merry ['mɛrɪ] adj alegre; **M~ Christmas!** ¡Felices Pascuas!
merry-go-round ['mɛrɪɡəuraund] n tiovivo.
mesh [mɛʃ] n malla; (TECH) engranaje m ♦ vi (gears) engranar; **wire ~** tela metálica.
mesmerize ['mɛzmərɑɪz] vt hipnotizar.
mess [mɛs] n confusión f; (of objects) revoltijo; (tangle) lío; (MIL) comedor m; **to be (in) a ~** (room) estar revuelto; **to be/ get o.s. in a ~** estar/meterse en un lío.
▶**mess about, mess around** vi (col) perder el tiempo; (pass the time) pasar el rato.
▶**mess about** or **around with** vt fus (col: play with) divertirse con; (: handle) manosear.
▶**mess up** vt (disarrange) desordenar; (spoil) estropear; (dirty) ensuciar.
message ['mɛsɪdʒ] n recado, mensaje m; **to get the ~** (fig, col) enterarse.
message switching n (COMPUT) conmutación f de mensajes.
messenger ['mɛsɪndʒə*] n mensajero/a.
Messiah [mɪ'saɪə] n Mesías m.
Messrs abbr (on letters: = Messieurs) Sres.
messy ['mɛsɪ] adj (dirty) sucio; (untidy) desordenado; (confused: situation etc) confuso.
Met [mɛt] n abbr (US) = Metropolitan Opera.
met [mɛt] pt, pp of **meet** ♦ adj abbr = meteorological.
metabolism [mɛ'tæbəlɪzəm] n metabolismo.

metal ['mɛtl] n metal m.
metallic [mɛ'tælɪk] adj metálico.
metallurgy [mɛ'tælədʒɪ] n metalurgia.
metalwork ['mɛtlwə:k] n (craft) metalistería.
metamorphosis, pl **metamorphoses** [mɛtə'mɔ:fəsɪs, -siːz] n metamorfosis f inv.
metaphor ['mɛtəfə*] n metáfora.
metaphorical [mɛtə'fɔrɪkl] adj metafórico.
metaphysics [mɛtə'fɪzɪks] n metafísica.
mete [miːt]: **to ~ out** vt fus (punishment) imponer.
meteor ['miːtɪə*] n meteoro.
meteoric [miːtɪ'ɔrɪk] adj (fig) meteórico.
meteorite ['miːtɪərɑɪt] n meteorito.
meteorological [miːtɪərə'lɔdʒɪkl] adj meteorológico.
meteorology [miːtɪə'rɔlədʒɪ] n meteorología.
meter ['miːtə*] n (instrument) contador m; (US: unit) = **metre** ♦ vt (US POST) franquear; **parking ~** parquímetro.
methane ['miːθeɪn] n metano.
method ['mɛθəd] n método; **~ of payment** método de pago.
methodical [mɪ'θɔdɪkl] adj metódico.
Methodist ['mɛθədɪst] adj, n metodista m/f.
methodology [mɛθə'dɔlədʒɪ] n metodología.
meths [mɛθs], **methylated spirit(s)** ['mɛθɪleɪtɪd-] n (BRIT) alcohol m metilado or desnaturalizado.
meticulous [mɛ'tɪkjuləs] adj meticuloso.
metre, (US) **meter** ['miːtə*] n metro.
metric ['mɛtrɪk] adj métrico; **to go ~** pasar al sistema métrico.
metrication [mɛtrɪ'keɪʃən] n conversión f al sistema métrico.
metric system n sistema m métrico.
metric ton n tonelada métrica.
metronome ['mɛtrənəum] n metrónomo.
metropolis [mɪ'trɔpəlɪs] n metrópoli(s) f.
metropolitan [mɛtrə'pɔlɪtən] adj metropolitano.
Metropolitan Police n (BRIT): **the ~** la policía londinense.
mettle ['mɛtl] n valor m, ánimo.
mew [mjuː] vi (cat) maullar.
mews [mjuːz] n (BRIT): **~ cottage** casa acondicionada en antiguos establos o cocheras; **~ flat** piso en antiguos establos o cocheras.
Mexican ['mɛksɪkən] adj, n mejicano/a m/f, mexicano/a m/f (LAM).
Mexico ['mɛksɪkəu] n Méjico, México (LAM).
Mexico City n Ciudad f de Méjico or México (LAM).

mezzanine ['mɛtsəniːn] *n* entresuelo.
MFA *n abbr* (*US*: = *Master of Fine Arts*) *título universitario.*
mfr *abbr* (= *manufacturer*) fab.
mg *abbr* (= *milligram*) mg.
Mgr *abbr* (= *Monseigneur, Monsignor*) Mons.
mgr *abbr* = **manager.**
MHR *n abbr* (*US*) *see* **Member of the House of Representatives.**
MHz *abbr* (= *megahertz*) MHz.
MI *abbr* (*US*) = *Michigan.*
MI5 *n abbr* (*BRIT*: = *Military Intelligence 5*) *servicio de contraespionaje del gobierno británico.*
MI6 *n abbr* (*BRIT*: = *Military Intelligence 6*) *servicio de inteligencia del gobierno británico.*
MIA *abbr* (= *missing in action*) desaparecido.
miaow [miːˈau] *vi* maullar.
mice [maɪs] *pl of* **mouse.**
Mich. *abbr* (*US*) = *Michigan.*
mickey ['mɪkɪ] *n*: **to take the ~ out of sb** tomar el pelo a algn.
micro... [maɪkrəu] *pref* micro....
microbe ['maɪkrəub] *n* microbio.
microbiology [maɪkrəubaɪˈɔlədʒɪ] *n* microbiología.
microchip ['maɪkrəutʃɪp] *n* microchip *m*, microplaqueta.
micro(computer) ['maɪkrəu(kəmˈpjuːtə*)] *n* microordenador *m*, microcomputador *m*.
microcosm ['maɪkrəukɔzəm] *n* microcosmo.
microeconomics ['maɪkrəuiːkəˈnɔmɪks] *n* microeconomía.
microfiche ['maɪkrəufiːʃ] *n* microficha.
microfilm ['maɪkrəufɪlm] *n* microfilm *m*.
microlight ['maɪkrəulaɪt] *n* ultraligero.
micrometer [maɪˈkrɔmɪtə*] *n* micrómetro.
microphone ['maɪkrəfəun] *n* micrófono.
microprocessor ['maɪkrəuˈprəusesə*] *n* microprocesador *m*.
microscope ['maɪkrəskəup] *n* microscopio; **under the ~** al microscopio.
microscopic [maɪkrəˈskɔpɪk] *adj* microscópico.
microwave ['maɪkrəuweɪv] *n* (*also*: **~ oven**) horno microondas.
mid [mɪd] *adj*: **in ~ May** a mediados de mayo; **in ~ afternoon** a media tarde; **in ~ air** en el aire; **he's in his ~ thirties** tiene unos treinta y cinco años.
midday [mɪd'deɪ] *n* mediodía *m*.
middle ['mɪdl] *n* medio, centro; (*waist*) cintura ♦ *adj* de en medio; **in the ~ of the night** en plena noche; **I'm in the ~ of reading it** lo estoy leyendo ahora mismo.
middle-aged [mɪdl'eɪdʒd] *adj* de mediana

edad.
Middle Ages *npl*: **the ~** la Edad *sg* Media.
middle class *n*: **the ~(es)** la clase media ♦ *adj* (*also*: **middle-class**) de clase media.
Middle East *n* Oriente *m* Medio.
middleman ['mɪdlmæn] *n* intermediario.
middle management *n* dirección *f* de nivel medio.
middle name *n* segundo nombre *m*.
middle-of-the-road ['mɪdləvðə'rəud] *adj* moderado.
middleweight ['mɪdlweɪt] *n* (*BOXING*) peso medio.
middling ['mɪdlɪŋ] *adj* mediano.
Middx *abbr* (*BRIT*) = *Middlesex.*
midge [mɪdʒ] *n* mosquito.
midget ['mɪdʒɪt] *n* enano/a.
midi system *n* cadena midi.
Midlands ['mɪdləndz] *npl* región central de Inglaterra.
midnight ['mɪdnaɪt] *n* medianoche *f*; **at ~** a medianoche.
midriff ['mɪdrɪf] *n* diafragma *m*.
midst [mɪdst] *n*: **in the ~ of** entre, en medio de.
midsummer [mɪd'sʌmə*] *n*: **a ~ day** un día de pleno verano.
Midsummer's Day *n* Día *m* de San Juan.
midway [mɪd'weɪ] *adj, adv*: **~ (between)** a mitad de camino *or* a medio camino (entre).
midweek [mɪd'wiːk] *adv* entre semana.
midwife, *pl* **midwives** ['mɪdwaɪf, -waɪvz] *n* comadrona.
midwifery ['mɪdwɪfərɪ] *n* tocología.
midwinter [mɪd'wɪntə*] *n*: **in ~** en pleno invierno.
miffed [mɪft] *adj* (*col*) mosqueado.
might [maɪt] *vb see* **may** ♦ *n* fuerza, poder *m*; **he ~ be there** puede que esté allí, a lo mejor está allí; **I ~ as well go** más vale que vaya; **you ~ like to try** podría intentar.
mightily ['maɪtɪlɪ] *adv* fuertemente, poderosamente; **I was ~ surprised** me sorprendí enormemente.
mightn't ['maɪtnt] = **might not.**
mighty ['maɪtɪ] *adj* fuerte, poderoso.
migraine ['miːgreɪn] *n* jaqueca.
migrant ['maɪgrənt] *adj* migratorio ♦ *n* (*bird*) ave *f* migratoria; (*worker*) emigrante *m/f*.
migrate [maɪ'greɪt] *vi* emigrar.
migration [maɪ'greɪʃən] *n* emigración *f*.
mike [maɪk] *n abbr* (= *microphone*) micro.
Milan [mɪ'læn] *n* Milán *m*.
mild [maɪld] *adj* (*person*) apacible; (*climate*) templado; (*slight*) ligero; (*taste*) suave;

(*illness*) leve.
mildew ['mɪldjuː] *n* moho.
mildly ['maɪldlɪ] *adv* ligeramente; suavemente; **to put it ~** por no decir algo peor.
mildness ['maɪldnɪs] *n* suavidad *f*; (*of illness*) levedad *f*.
mile [maɪl] *n* milla; **to do 20 ~s per gallon** hacer 20 millas por galón.
mileage ['maɪlɪdʒ] *n* número de millas; (*AUT*) kilometraje *m*.
mileage allowance *n* ≈ asignación *f* por kilometraje.
mileometer [maɪ'lɔmɪtə*] *n* (*BRIT*) = **milometer**.
milestone ['maɪlstəun] *n* mojón *m*; (*fig*) hito.
milieu ['miːljəː] *n* (medio) ambiente *m*, entorno.
militant ['mɪlɪtnt] *adj, n* militante *m/f*.
militarism ['mɪlɪtərɪzəm] *n* militarismo.
militaristic [mɪlɪtə'rɪstɪk] *adj* militarista.
military ['mɪlɪtərɪ] *adj* militar.
military service *n* servicio militar.
militate ['mɪlɪteɪt] *vi*: **to ~ against** militar en contra de.
militia [mɪ'lɪʃə] *n* milicia.
milk [mɪlk] *n* leche *f* ♦ *vt* (*cow*) ordeñar; (*fig*) chupar.
milk chocolate *n* chocolate *m* con leche.
milk float *n* (*BRIT*) furgoneta de la leche.
milking ['mɪlkɪŋ] *n* ordeño.
milkman ['mɪlkmən] *n* lechero, repartidor *m* de la leche.
milk shake *n* batido, malteada (*LAM*).
milk tooth *n* diente *m* de leche.
milk truck *n* (*US*) = **milk float**.
milky ['mɪlkɪ] *adj* lechoso.
Milky Way *n* Vía Láctea.
mill [mɪl] *n* (*windmill etc*) molino; (*coffee ~*) molinillo; (*factory*) fábrica; (*spinning ~*) hilandería ♦ *vt* moler ♦ *vi* (*also: ~ about*) arremolinarse.
milled [mɪld] (*grain*) molido; (*coin, edge*) acordonado.
millennium, *pl* **~s** *or* **millennia** [mɪ'lenɪəm, 'lenɪə] *n* milenio, milenario.
miller ['mɪlə*] *n* molinero.
millet ['mɪlɪt] *n* mijo.
milli... ['mɪlɪ] *pref* mili....
milligram(me) ['mɪlɪgraem] *n* miligramo.
millilitre, (*US*) **milliliter** ['mɪlɪliːtə*] *n* mililitro.
millimetre, (*US*) **millimeter** ['mɪlɪmiːtə*] *n* milímetro.
milliner ['mɪlɪnə*] *n* sombrerero/a.
millinery ['mɪlɪnərɪ] *n* sombrerería.
million ['mɪljən] *n* millón *m*; **a ~ times** un

millón de veces.
millionaire [mɪljə'nɛə*] *n* millonario/a.
millipede ['mɪlɪpiːd] *n* milpiés *m inv*.
millstone ['mɪlstəun] *n* piedra de molino.
millwheel ['mɪlwiːl] *n* rueda de molino.
milometer [maɪ'lɔmɪtə*] *n* (*BRIT*) cuentakilómetros *m inv*.
mime [maɪm] *n* mímica; (*actor*) mimo/a ♦ *vt* remedar ♦ *vi* actuar de mimo.
mimic ['mɪmɪk] *n* imitador(a) *m/f* ♦ *adj* mímico ♦ *vt* remedar, imitar.
mimicry ['mɪmɪkrɪ] *n* imitación *f*.
Min. *abbr* (*BRIT POL: = Ministry*) Min.
min. *abbr* (= *minute(s)*) m.; = **minimum**.
minaret [mɪnə'rɛt] *n* alminar *m*, minarete *m*.
mince [mɪns] *vt* picar ♦ *vi* (*in walking*) andar con pasos menudos ♦ *n* (*BRIT CULIN*) carne *f* picada, picadillo.
mincemeat ['mɪnsmiːt] *n* conserva de fruta picada.
mince pie *n* pastelillo relleno de fruta picada.
mincer ['mɪnsə*] *n* picadora de carne.
mincing ['mɪnsɪŋ] *adj* afectado.
mind [maɪnd] *n* (*gen*) mente *f*; (*contrasted with matter*) espíritu *m* ♦ *vt* (*attend to, look after*) ocuparse de, cuidar; (*be careful of*) tener cuidado con; (*object to*): **I don't ~ the noise** no me molesta el ruido; **it is on my ~** me preocupa; **to my ~** a mi parecer *or* juicio; **to change one's ~** cambiar de idea *or* de parecer; **to bring** *or* **call sth to ~** recordar algo; **to have sth/sb in ~** tener algo/a algn en mente; **to be out of one's ~** haber perdido el juicio; **to bear sth in ~** tomar *or* tener algo en cuenta; **to make up one's ~** decidirse; **it went right out of my ~** se me fue por completo (de la cabeza); **to be in two ~s about sth** estar indeciso *or* dudar ante algo; **I don't ~** me es igual; **~ you, ...** te advierto que ...; **never ~!** ¡es igual!, ¡no importa!; (*don't worry*) ¡no te preocupes!; '~ **the step**' 'cuidado con el escalón'.
mind-boggling ['maɪndbɔglɪŋ] *adj* (*col*) alucinante, increíble.
-minded [-maɪndɪd] *adj*: **fair~** imparcial; **an industrially~ nation** una nación orientada a la industria.
minder ['maɪndə*] *n* guardaespaldas *m inv*.
mindful ['maɪndful] *adj*: **~ of** consciente de.
mindless ['maɪndlɪs] *adj* (*violence, crime*) sin sentido; (*work*) de autómata.
mine [maɪn] *pron* (el) mío/(la) mía *etc*; **a friend of ~** un(a) amigo/a mío/mía ♦ *adj*: **this book is ~** este libro es mío ♦ *n* mina ♦ *vt* (*coal*) extraer; (*ship, beach*) minar.

mine detector *n* detector *m* de minas.
minefield ['maɪnfiːld] *n* campo de minas.
miner ['maɪnə*] *n* minero/a.
mineral ['mɪnərəl] *adj* mineral ♦ *n* mineral *m*; ~**s** *npl* (*BRIT: soft drinks*) refrescos *mpl* con gas.
mineral water *n* agua mineral.
minesweeper ['maɪnswiːpə*] *n* dragaminas *m inv*.
mingle ['mɪŋgl] *vi*: **to ~ with** mezclarse con.
mingy ['mɪndʒɪ] *adj* (*col*) tacaño.
mini ... [mɪnɪ] *pref* mini..., micro....
miniature ['mɪnətʃə*] *adj* (en) miniatura ♦ *n* miniatura.
minibus ['mɪnɪbʌs] *n* microbús *m*.
minicab ['mɪnɪkæb] *n* taxi *m* (*que sólo puede pedirse por teléfono*).
minicomputer ['mɪnɪkəm'pjuːtə*] *n* miniordenador *m*.
minim ['mɪnɪm] *n* (*BRIT MUS*) blanca.
minimal ['mɪnɪml] *adj* mínimo.
minimalist ['mɪnɪməlɪst] *adj, n* minimalista *m/f*.
minimize ['mɪnɪmaɪz] *vt* minimizar.
minimum ['mɪnɪməm] *n* (*pl* **minima** ['mɪnɪmə]) mínimo ♦ *adj* mínimo; **to reduce to a ~** reducir algo al mínimo; **~ wage** salario mínimo.
minimum lending rate (MLR) *n* tipo de interés mínimo.
mining ['maɪnɪŋ] *n* minería ♦ *adj* minero.
minion ['mɪnjən] *n* secuaz *m*.
mini-series ['mɪnɪsɪərɪːz] *n* serie *f* de pocos capítulos, miniserie *f*.
miniskirt ['mɪnɪskəːt] *n* minifalda.
minister ['mɪnɪstə*] *n* (*BRIT POL*) ministro/a; (*REL*) pastor *m* ♦ *vi*: **to ~ to** atender a.
ministerial [mɪnɪs'tɪərɪəl] *adj* (*BRIT POL*) ministerial.
ministry ['mɪnɪstrɪ] *n* (*BRIT POL*) ministerio; (*REL*) sacerdocio; **M~ of Defence** Ministerio de Defensa.
mink [mɪŋk] *n* visón *m*.
mink coat *n* abrigo de visón.
Minn. *abbr* (*US*) = Minnesota.
minnow ['mɪnəu] *n* pececillo (de agua dulce).
minor ['maɪnə*] *adj* (*unimportant*) secundario; (*MUS*) menor ♦ *n* (*LAW*) menor *m/f* de edad.
Minorca [mɪ'nɔːkə] *n* Menorca.
minority [maɪ'nɔrɪtɪ] *n* minoría; **to be in a ~** estar en *or* ser minoría.
minority interest *n* participación *f* minoritaria.
minster ['mɪnstə*] *n* catedral *f*.
minstrel ['mɪnstrəl] *n* juglar *m*.

mint [mɪnt] *n* (*plant*) menta, hierbabuena; (*sweet*) caramelo de menta ♦ *vt* (*coins*) acuñar; **the (Royal) M~**, (*US*) **the (US) M~** la Casa de la Moneda; **in ~ condition** en perfecto estado.
mint sauce *n* salsa de menta.
minuet [mɪnju'ɛt] *n* minué *m*.
minus ['maɪnəs] *n* (*also:* **~ sign**) signo menos ♦ *prep* menos.
minuscule ['mɪnəskjuːl] *adj* minúsculo.
minute *n* ['mɪnɪt] minuto; (*fig*) momento; ~**s** *npl* actas *fpl* ♦ *adj* [maɪ'njuːt] diminuto; (*search*) minucioso; **it is 5 ~s past 3** son las 3 y 5 (minutos); **at the last ~** a última hora; **wait a ~!** ¡espera un momento!; **up to the ~** de última hora; **in ~ detail** con todo detalle.
minute book *n* libro de actas.
minute hand *n* minutero.
minutely [maɪ'njuːtlɪ] *adv* (*by a small amount*) por muy poco; (*in detail*) detalladamente, minuciosamente.
minutiae [mɪ'njuːʃiː] *npl* minucias *fpl*.
miracle ['mɪrəkl] *n* milagro.
miracle play *n* auto, milagro.
miraculous [mɪ'rækjuləs] *adj* milagroso.
miraculously [mɪ'rækjuləslɪ] *adv* milagrosamente.
mirage ['mɪrɑːʒ] *n* espejismo.
mire [maɪə*] *n* fango, lodo.
mirror ['mɪrə*] *n* espejo; (*in car*) retrovisor *m* ♦ *vt* reflejar.
mirror image *n* reflejo inverso.
mirth [məːθ] *n* alegría; (*laughter*) risa, risas *fpl*.
misadventure [mɪsəd'vɛntʃə*] *n* desventura; **death by ~** muerte *f* accidental.
misanthropist [mɪ'zænθrəpɪst] *n* misántropo/a.
misapply [mɪsə'plaɪ] *vt* emplear mal.
misapprehension ['mɪsæprɪ'hɛnʃən] *n* equivocación *f*.
misappropriate [mɪsə'prəuprɪeɪt] *vt* (*funds*) malversar.
misappropriation ['mɪsəprəuprɪ'eɪʃən] *n* malversación *f*, desfalco.
misbehave [mɪsbɪ'heɪv] *vi* portarse mal.
misbehaviour, (*US*) **misbehavior** [mɪsbɪ'heɪvjə*] *n* mala conducta.
misc. *abbr* = miscellaneous.
miscalculate [mɪs'kælkjuleɪt] *vt* calcular mal.
miscalculation [mɪskælkju'leɪʃən] *n* error *m* (de cálculo).
miscarriage ['mɪskærɪdʒ] *n* (*MED*) aborto (no provocado); ~ **of justice** error *m* judicial.

miscarry [mɪsˈkærɪ] *vi* (*MED*) abortar (de forma natural); (*fail: plans*) fracasar, malograrse.

miscellaneous [mɪsɪˈleɪnɪəs] *adj* varios/as, diversos/as; ~ **expenses** gastos diversos.

miscellany [mɪˈselənɪ] *n* miscelánea.

mischance [mɪsˈtʃɑːns] *n* desgracia, mala suerte *f*; **by (some)** ~ por (alguna) desgracia.

mischief [ˈmɪstʃɪf] *n* (*naughtiness*) travesura; (*harm*) mal *m*, daño; (*maliciousness*) malicia.

mischievous [ˈmɪstʃɪvəs] *adj* travieso; dañino; (*playful*) malicioso.

mischievously [ˈmɪstʃɪvəslɪ] *adv* por travesura; maliciosamente.

misconception [ˈmɪskənˈsepʃən] *n* concepto erróneo; equivocación *f*.

misconduct [mɪsˈkɔndʌkt] *n* mala conducta; **professional** ~ falta profesional.

miscount [mɪsˈkaunt] *vt, vi* contar mal.

misconstrue [mɪskənˈstruː] *vt* interpretar mal.

misdeed [mɪsˈdiːd] *n* (*old*) fechoría, delito.

misdemeanour, (*US*) **misdemeanor** [mɪsdɪˈmiːnə*] *n* delito, ofensa.

misdirect [mɪsdɪˈrekt] *vt* (*person*) informar mal; (*letter*) poner señas incorrectas en.

miser [ˈmaɪzə*] *n* avaro/a.

miserable [ˈmɪzərəbl] *adj* (*unhappy*) triste, desgraciado; (*wretched*) miserable; **to feel** ~ sentirse triste.

miserably [ˈmɪzərəblɪ] *adv* (*smile, answer*) tristemente; (*fail*) rotundamente; **to pay** ~ pagar una miseria.

miserly [ˈmaɪzəlɪ] *adj* avariento, tacaño.

misery [ˈmɪzərɪ] *n* (*unhappiness*) tristeza; (*wretchedness*) miseria, desdicha.

misfire [mɪsˈfaɪə*] *vi* fallar.

misfit [ˈmɪsfɪt] *n* (*person*) inadaptado/a.

misfortune [mɪsˈfɔːtʃən] *n* desgracia.

misgiving(s) [mɪsˈɡɪvɪŋ(z)] *n(pl)* (*mistrust*) recelo; (*apprehension*) presentimiento; **to have** ~**s about sth** tener dudas sobre algo.

misguided [mɪsˈɡaɪdɪd] *adj* equivocado.

mishandle [mɪsˈhændl] *vt* (*treat roughly*) maltratar; (*mismanage*) manejar mal.

mishap [ˈmɪshæp] *n* desgracia, contratiempo.

mishear [mɪsˈhɪə*] *vt, vi* (*irreg: like* **hear**) oír mal.

mishmash [ˈmɪʃmæʃ] *n* (*col*) revoltijo.

misinform [mɪsɪnˈfɔːm] *vt* informar mal.

misinterpret [mɪsɪnˈtəːprɪt] *vt* interpretar mal.

misinterpretation [ˈmɪsɪntəːprɪˈteɪʃən] *n* mala interpretación *f*.

misjudge [mɪsˈdʒʌdʒ] *vt* juzgar mal.

mislay [mɪsˈleɪ] *vt* (*irreg: like* **lay**) extraviar, perder.

mislead [mɪsˈliːd] *vt* (*irreg: like* **lead**) llevar a conclusiones erróneas; (*deliberately*) engañar.

misleading [mɪsˈliːdɪŋ] *adj* engañoso.

misled [mɪsˈled] *pt, pp of* **mislead**.

mismanage [mɪsˈmænɪdʒ] *vt* administrar mal.

mismanagement [mɪsˈmænɪdʒmənt] *n* mala administración *f*.

misnomer [mɪsˈnəumə*] *n* término inapropiado *or* equivocado.

misogynist [mɪˈsɔdʒɪnɪst] *n* misógino.

misplace [mɪsˈpleɪs] *vt* (*lose*) extraviar; ~**d** (*trust etc*) inmerecido.

misprint [ˈmɪsprɪnt] *n* errata, error *m* de imprenta.

mispronounce [mɪsprəˈnauns] *vt* pronunciar mal.

misquote [ˈmɪsˈkwəut] *vt* citar incorrectamente.

misread [mɪsˈriːd] *vt* (*irreg: like* **read**) leer mal.

misrepresent [mɪsreprɪˈzent] *vt* falsificar.

misrepresentation [mɪsreprɪzenˈteɪʃən] *n* (*LAW*) falsa declaración *f*.

Miss [mɪs] *n* Señorita; **Dear** ~ **Smith** Estimada Señorita Smith.

miss [mɪs] *vt* (*train etc*) perder; (*shot*) errar, fallar; (*appointment, class*) faltar a; (*escape, avoid*) evitar; (*notice loss of: money etc*) notar la falta de, echar en falta; (*regret the absence of*): **I** ~ **him** le echo de menos ♦ *vi* fallar ♦ *n* (*shot*) tiro fallido; **the bus just** ~**ed the wall** faltó poco para que el autobús se estrella contra el muro; **you're** ~**ing the point** no has entendido la idea.

▶**miss out** *vt* (*BRIT*) omitir.

▶**miss out on** *vt fus* (*fun, party, opportunity*) perderse.

Miss. *abbr* (*US*) = *Mississippi*.

missal [ˈmɪsl] *n* misal *m*.

misshapen [mɪsˈʃeɪpən] *adj* deforme.

missile [ˈmɪsaɪl] *n* (*AVIAT*) misil *m*; (*object thrown*) proyectil *m*.

missile base *n* base *f* de misiles.

missile launcher *n* lanzamisiles *m inv*.

missing [ˈmɪsɪŋ] *adj* (*pupil*) ausente, que falta; (*thing*) perdido; (*MIL*) desaparecido; **to be** ~ faltar; ~ **person** desaparecido/a.

mission [ˈmɪʃən] *n* misión *f*; **on a** ~ **for sb** en una misión para algn.

missionary [ˈmɪʃənrɪ] *n* misionero/a.

misspell [mɪsˈspel] *vt* (*irreg: like* **spell**)

escribir mal.

misspent ['mɪs'spɛnt] *adj*: **his ~ youth** su juventud disipada.

mist [mɪst] *n* (*light*) neblina; (*heavy*) niebla; (*at sea*) bruma ♦ *vi* (*also*: **~ over**, **~ up**: *weather*) nublarse; (: *BRIT*: *windows*) empañarse.

mistake [mɪs'teɪk] *n* error *m* ♦ *vt* (*irreg*: *like* **take**) entender mal; **by ~** por equivocación; **to make a ~** (*about sb/sth*) equivocarse; (*in writing, calculating etc*) cometer un error; **to ~ A for B** confundir A con B.

mistaken [mɪs'teɪkən] *pp of* **mistake** ♦ *adj* (*idea etc*) equivocado; **to be ~** equivocarse, engañarse; **~ identity** identificación *f* errónea.

mistakenly [mɪs'teɪkənlɪ] *adv* erróneamente.

mister ['mɪstə*] *n* (*col*) señor *m*; *see* **Mr.**

mistletoe ['mɪsltəu] *n* muérdago.

mistook [mɪs'tuk] *pt of* **mistake**.

mistranslation [mɪstræns'leɪʃən] *n* mala traducción *f.*

mistreat [mɪs'triːt] *vt* maltratar, tratar mal.

mistress ['mɪstrɪs] *n* (*lover*) amante *f*; (*of house*) señora (de la casa); (*BRIT*: *in primary school*) maestra; (*in secondary school*) profesora; *see* **Mrs.**

mistrust [mɪs'trʌst] *vt* desconfiar de ♦ *n*: **~ (of)** desconfianza (de).

mistrustful [mɪs'trʌstful] *adj*: **~ (of)** desconfiado (de), receloso (de).

misty ['mɪstɪ] *adj* nebuloso, brumoso; (*day*) de niebla; (*glasses*) empañado.

misty-eyed ['mɪstɪ'aɪd] *adj* sentimental.

misunderstand [mɪsʌndə'stænd] *vt, vi* (*irreg*: *like* **understand**) entender mal.

misunderstanding [mɪsʌndə'stændɪŋ] *n* malentendido.

misunderstood [mɪsʌndə'stud] *pt, pp of* **misunderstand** ♦ *adj* (*person*) incomprendido.

misuse *n* [mɪs'juːs] mal uso; (*of power*) abuso ♦ *vt* [mɪs'juːz] abusar de; (*funds*) malversar.

MIT *n abbr* (*US*) = *Massachusetts Institute of Technology.*

mite [maɪt] *n* (*small quantity*) pizca; **poor ~!** ¡pobrecito!

mitigate ['mɪtɪgeɪt] *vt* mitigar; **mitigating circumstances** circunstancias *fpl* atenuantes.

mitigation [mɪtɪ'geɪʃən] *n* mitigación *f*, alivio.

mitre, (*US*) **miter** ['maɪtə*] *n* mitra.

mitt(en) ['mɪt(n)] *n* manopla.

mix [mɪks] *vt* (*gen*) mezclar; (*combine*) unir ♦ *vi* mezclarse; (*people*) llevarse bien ♦ *n* mezcla; **to ~ sth with sth** mezclar algo con algo; **to ~ business with pleasure** combinar los negocios con el placer; **cake ~** preparado para pastel.

▶**mix in** *vt* (*eggs etc*) añadir.

▶**mix up** *vt* mezclar; (*confuse*) confundir; **to be ~ed up in sth** estar metido en algo.

mixed [mɪkst] *adj* (*assorted*) variado, surtido; (*school, marriage etc*) mixto.

mixed-ability ['mɪkstə'bɪlɪtɪ] *adj* (*class etc*) de alumnos de distintas capacidades.

mixed bag *n*: **these results are a bit of a ~** en estos resultados hay un poco de todo.

mixed blessing *n*: **it's a ~** tiene su lado bueno y su lado malo.

mixed doubles *n* (*SPORT*) mixtos *mpl*.

mixed economy *n* economía mixta.

mixed grill *n* (*BRIT*) parrillada mixta.

mixed-up [mɪkst'ʌp] *adj* (*confused*) confuso, revuelto.

mixer ['mɪksə*] *n* (*for food*) batidora; (*person*): **he's a good ~** tiene don de gentes.

mixer tap *n* (grifo) monomando.

mixture ['mɪkstʃə*] *n* mezcla.

mix-up ['mɪksʌp] *n* confusión *f.*

Mk *abbr* (*BRIT TECH*: = *mark*) Mk.

mk *abbr* = **mark** (*currency*).

mkt *abbr* = **market**.

MLitt *n abbr* (= *Master of Literature, Master of Letters*) título universitario de postgrado; *see also* **master's degree.**

MLR *n abbr* (*BRIT*) = **minimum lending rate.**

mm *abbr* (= *millimetre*) mm.

MN *abbr* (*BRIT*) = **Merchant Navy**; (*US*) = *Minnesota.*

MO *n abbr* (*MED*) = **medical officer**; (*US col*) = *modus operandi* ♦ *abbr* (*US*) = *Missouri.*

Mo. *abbr* (*US*) = *Missouri.*

m.o. *abbr* (= *money order*) g/.

moan [məun] *n* gemido ♦ *vi* gemir; (*col*: *complain*): **to ~ (about)** quejarse (de).

moaning ['məunɪŋ] *n* gemidos *mpl*; quejas *fpl.*

moat [məut] *n* foso.

mob [mɔb] *n* multitud *f*; (*pej*): **the ~** el populacho ♦ *vt* acosar.

mobile ['məubaɪl] *adj* móvil ♦ *n* móvil *m.*

mobile home *n* caravana.

mobile phone *n* teléfono móvil.

mobility [məu'bɪlɪtɪ] *n* movilidad *f*; **~ of labour** *or* (*US*) **labor** movilidad *f* de la mano de obra.

mobilize ['məubɪlaɪz] *vt* movilizar.

moccasin ['mɔkəsɪn] *n* mocasín *m.*

mock [mɔk] *vt* (*make ridiculous*) ridiculizar;

(*laugh at*) burlarse de ♦ *adj* fingido.
mockery ['mɔkərɪ] *n* burla; **to make a ~ of** desprestigiar.
mocking ['mɔkɪŋ] *adj* (*tone*) burlón/ona.
mockingbird ['mɔkɪŋbəːd] *n* sinsonte *m* (*LAM*), zenzontle (*LAM*).
mock-up ['mɔkʌp] *n* maqueta.
mod cons ['mɔd'kɔnz] *npl abbr* (= *modern conveniences*) *see* **convenience**.
mode [məud] *n* modo; (*of transport*) medio; (*COMPUT*) modo, modalidad *f*.
model ['mɔdl] *n* (*gen*) modelo; (*ARCH*) maqueta; (*person: for fashion, ART*) modelo *m/f* ♦ *adj* modelo *inv* ♦ *vt* modelar ♦ *vi* ser modelo; **~ railway** ferrocarril *m* de juguete; **to ~ clothes** pasar modelos, ser modelo; **to ~ on** crear a imitación de.
modelling, (*US*) **modeling** ['mɔdlɪŋ] *n* (*modelmaking*) modelado.
modem ['məudəm] *n* módem *m*.
moderate *adj, n* ['mɔdərət] moderado/a *m/f* ♦ (*vb*: ['mɔdəreɪt]) *vi* moderarse, calmarse ♦ *vt* moderar.
moderately ['mɔdərətlɪ] *adv* (*act*) con moderación; (*expensive, difficult*) medianamente; (*pleased, happy*) bastante.
moderation [mɔdə'reɪʃən] *n* moderación *f*; **in ~** con moderación.
moderator ['mɔdəreɪtə*] *n* (*mediator*) moderador(a) *m/f*.
modern ['mɔdən] *adj* moderno; **~ languages** lenguas *fpl* modernas.
modernity [mɔ'dɜːnɪtɪ] *n* modernidad *f*.
modernization [mɔdənaɪ'zeɪʃən] *n* modernización *f*.
modernize ['mɔdənaɪz] *vt* modernizar.
modest ['mɔdɪst] *adj* modesto.
modestly ['mɔdɪstlɪ] *adv* modestamente.
modesty ['mɔdɪstɪ] *n* modestia.
modicum ['mɔdɪkəm] *n*: **a ~ of** un mínimo de.
modification [mɔdɪfɪ'keɪʃən] *n* modificación *f*; **to make ~s** hacer cambios *or* modificaciones.
modify ['mɔdɪfaɪ] *vt* modificar.
modish ['məudɪʃ] *adj* de moda.
Mods [mɔdz] *n abbr* (*BRIT*: = (*Honour*) *Moderations*) *examen de licenciatura de la universidad de Oxford*.
modular ['mɔdjulə*] *adj* (*filing, unit*) modular.
modulate ['mɔdjuleɪt] *vt* modular.
modulation [mɔdju'leɪʃən] *n* modulación *f*.
module ['mɔdjuːl] *n* (*unit, component, SPACE*) módulo.
modus operandi ['məudəsɔpə'rændiː] *n* manera de actuar.
Mogadishu [mɔgə'dɪʃuː] *n* Mogadiscio.

mogul ['məugəl] *n* (*fig*) magnate *m*.
MOH *n abbr* (*BRIT*) = *Medical Officer of Health*.
mohair ['məuhɛə*] *n* mohair *m*.
Mohammed [mə'hæmed] *n* Mahoma *m*.
moist [mɔɪst] *adj* húmedo.
moisten ['mɔɪsn] *vt* humedecer.
moisture ['mɔɪstʃə*] *n* humedad *f*.
moisturize ['mɔɪstʃəraɪz] *vt* (*skin*) hidratar.
moisturizer ['mɔɪstʃəraɪzə*] *n* crema hidratante.
molar ['məulə*] *n* muela.
molasses [məu'læsɪz] *n* melaza.
mold [məuld] *n, vt* (*US*) = **mould**.
Moldavia [mɔl'deɪvɪə], **Moldova** [mɔl'dəuvə] *n* Moldavia, Moldova.
Moldavian [mɔl'deɪvɪən], **Moldovan** [mɔl'dəuvən] *adj, n* moldavo/a *m/f*.
mole [məul] *n* (*animal*) topo; (*spot*) lunar *m*.
molecular [məu'lɛkjulə*] *adj* molecular.
molecule ['mɔlɪkjuːl] *n* molécula.
molest [məu'lɛst] *vt* importunar; (*sexually*) abordar con propósitos deshonestos.
moll [mɔl] *n* (*slang*) amiga.
mollusc, (*US*) **mollusk** ['mɔləsk] *n* molusco.
mollycoddle ['mɔlɪkɔdl] *vt* mimar.
Molotov cocktail ['mɔlətɔf-] *n* cóctel *m* Molotov.
molt [məult] *vi* (*US*) = **moult**.
molten ['məultən] *adj* fundido; (*lava*) líquido.
mom [mɔm] *n* (*US*) = **mum**.
moment ['məumənt] *n* momento; **at** *or* **for the ~** de momento, por el momento, por ahora; **in a ~** dentro de un momento.
momentarily ['məuməntrɪlɪ] *adv* momentáneamente; (*US: very soon*) de un momento a otro.
momentary ['məuməntərɪ] *adj* momentáneo.
momentous [məu'mɛntəs] *adj* trascendental, importante.
momentum [məu'mɛntəm] *n* momento; (*fig*) ímpetu *m*; **to gather ~** cobrar velocidad; (*fig*) cobrar fuerza.
mommy ['mɔmɪ] *n* (*US*) = **mummy**.
Mon. *abbr* (= *Monday*) lun.
Monaco ['mɔnəkəu] *n* Mónaco.
monarch ['mɔnək] *n* monarca *m/f*.
monarchist ['mɔnəkɪst] *n* monárquico/a.
monarchy ['mɔnəkɪ] *n* monarquía.
monastery ['mɔnəstərɪ] *n* monasterio.
monastic [mə'næstɪk] *adj* monástico.
Monday ['mʌndɪ] *n* lunes *m inv*.
Monegasque [mɔnɪ'gæsk] *adj, n* monegasco/a *m/f*.
monetarist ['mʌnɪtərɪst] *n* monetarista *m*.

monetary ['mʌnɪtərɪ] adj monetario.
monetary policy n política monetaria.
money ['mʌnɪ] n dinero, plata (LAM); **to make ~** ganar dinero; **I've got no ~ left** no me queda dinero.
moneyed ['mʌnɪd] adj adinerado.
moneylender ['mʌnɪlɛndə*] n prestamista m/f.
moneymaker ['mʌnɪmeɪkə*] n (BRIT col: business) filón m.
moneymaking ['mʌnɪmeɪkɪŋ] adj rentable.
money market n mercado monetario.
money order n giro.
money-spinner ['mʌnɪspɪnə*] n (col: person, idea, business) filón m.
money supply n oferta monetaria, medio circulante, volumen m monetario.
Mongol ['mɔŋgəl] n mongol(a) m/f; (LING) mongol m.
mongol ['mɔŋgəl] adj, n (MED) mongólico.
Mongolia [mɔŋ'gəulɪə] n Mongolia.
Mongolian [mɔŋ'gəulɪən] adj mongol(a) ♦ n mongol(a) m/f; (LING) mongol m.
mongoose ['mɔŋguːs] n mangosta.
mongrel ['mʌŋgrəl] n (dog) perro cruzado.
monitor ['mɔnɪtə*] n monitor m ♦ vt controlar; (foreign station) escuchar.
monk [mʌŋk] n monje m.
monkey ['mʌŋkɪ] n mono.
monkey business n, **monkey tricks** npl tejemanejes mpl.
monkey nut n (BRIT) cacahuete m, maní (LAM).
monkey wrench n llave f inglesa.
mono ['mɔnəu] adj (broadcast etc) mono inv.
mono... [mɔnəu] pref mono ... .
monochrome ['mɔnəukrəum] adj monocromo.
monocle ['mɔnəkl] n monóculo.
monogamous [mə'nɔgəməs] adj monógamo.
monogram ['mɔnəgræm] n monograma m.
monolith ['mɔnəlɪθ] n monolito.
monolithic [mɔnə'lɪθɪk] adj monolítico.
monologue ['mɔnəlɔg] n monólogo.
monoplane ['mɔnəpleɪn] n monoplano.
monopolist [mə'nɔpəlɪst] n monopolista m/f.
monopolize [mə'nɔpəlaɪz] vt monopolizar.
monopoly [mə'nɔpəlɪ] n monopolio; **Monopolies and Mergers Commission** (BRIT) comisión reguladora de monopolios y fusiones.
monorail ['mɔnəureɪl] n monocarril m, monorraíl m.
monosodium glutamate [mɔnə'səudɪəm 'gluːtəmeɪt] n glutamato monosódico.
monosyllabic [mɔnəsɪ'læbɪk] adj monosílabo.

monosyllable ['mɔnəsɪləbl] n monosílabo.
monotone ['mɔnətəun] n voz f (or tono) monocorde.
monotonous [mə'nɔtənəs] adj monótono.
monotony [mə'nɔtənɪ] n monotonía.
monoxide [mə'nɔksaɪd] n: **carbon ~** monóxido de carbono.
monseigneur [mɔnsɛn'jə:*], **monsignor** [mɔn'siːnjə*] n monseñor m.
monsoon [mɔn'suːn] n monzón m.
monster ['mɔnstə*] n monstruo.
monstrosity [mɔns'trɔsɪtɪ] n monstruosidad f.
monstrous ['mɔnstrəs] adj (huge) enorme; (atrocious) monstruoso.
Mont. abbr (US) = Montana.
montage [mɔn'tɑːʒ] n montaje m.
Mont Blanc [mɔ̃'blɑ̃] n Mont Blanc m.
month [mʌnθ] n mes m; **300 dollars a ~** 300 dólares al mes; **every ~** cada mes.
monthly ['mʌnθlɪ] adj mensual ♦ adv mensualmente ♦ n (magazine) revista mensual; **twice ~** dos veces al mes; **~ instalment** mensualidad f.
monument ['mɔnjumənt] n monumento.
monumental [mɔnju'mɛntl] adj monumental.
moo [muː] vi mugir.
mood [muːd] n humor m; **to be in a good/bad ~** estar de buen/mal humor.
moodily ['muːdɪlɪ] adv malhumoradamente.
moodiness ['muːdɪnɪs] n humor m cambiante; (bad mood) mal humor m.
moody ['muːdɪ] adj (variable) de humor variable; (sullen) malhumorado.
moon [muːn] n luna.
moonbeam ['muːnbiːm] n rayo de luna.
moon landing n alunizaje m.
moonless ['muːnlɪs] adj sin luna.
moonlight ['muːnlaɪt] n luz f de la luna ♦ vi hacer pluriempleo.
moonlighting ['muːnlaɪtɪŋ] n pluriempleo.
moonlit ['muːnlɪt] adj: **a ~ night** una noche de luna.
moonshot ['muːnʃɔt] n lanzamiento de una astronave a la luna.
moonstruck ['muːnstrʌk] adj chiflado.
moony ['muːnɪ] adj: **to have ~ eyes** estar soñando despierto, estar pensando en las musarañas.
Moor [muə*] n moro/a.
moor [muə*] n páramo ♦ vt (ship) amarrar ♦ vi echar las amarras.
moorings ['muərɪŋz] npl (chains) amarras fpl; (place) amarradero sg.
Moorish ['muərɪʃ] adj moro; (architecture) árabe.
moorland ['muələnd] n páramo, brezal m.

moose [muːs] *n, pl inv* alce *m*.

moot [muːt] *vt* proponer para la discusión, sugerir ♦ *adj*: ~ **point** punto discutible.

mop [mɔp] *n* fregona; (*of hair*) greñas *fpl* ♦ *vt* fregar.

►**mop up** *vt* limpiar.

mope [məup] *vi* estar deprimido.

►**mope about, mope around** *vi* andar abatido.

moped ['məupɛd] *n* ciclomotor *m*.

moquette [mɔ'kɛt] *n* moqueta.

MOR *adj abbr* (*MUS*: = *middle-of-the-road*) para el gran público.

moral ['mɔrl] *adj* moral ♦ *n* moraleja; ~**s** *npl* moralidad *f*, moral *f*.

morale [mɔ'rɑːl] *n* moral *f*.

morality [mə'rælɪtɪ] *n* moralidad *f*.

moralize ['mɔrəlaɪz] *vi*: **to** ~ **(about)** moralizar (sobre).

morally ['mɔrəlɪ] *adv* moralmente.

moral victory *n* victoria moral.

morass [mə'ræs] *n* pantano.

moratorium [mɔrə'tɔːrɪəm] *n* moratoria.

morbid ['mɔːbɪd] *adj* (*interest*) morboso; (*MED*) mórbido.

======================== *KEYWORD*

more [mɔː*] *adj* **1** (*greater in number etc*) más; ~ **people/work than before** más gente/trabajo que antes

2 (*additional*) más; **do you want (some)** ~ **tea?** ¿quieres más té?; **is there any** ~ **wine?** ¿queda vino?; **it'll take a few** ~ **weeks** tardará unas semanas más; **it's 2 kms** ~ **to the house** faltan 2 kms para la casa; ~ **time/letters than we expected** más tiempo del que/más cartas de las que esperábamos; **I have no** ~ **money, I don't have any** ~ **money** (ya) no tengo más dinero

♦ *pron* (*greater amount, additional amount*) más; ~ **than 10** más de 10; **it cost** ~ **than the other one/than we expected** costó más que el otro/más de lo que esperábamos; **is there any** ~**?** ¿hay más?; **I want** ~ quiero más; **and what's** ~ ... y además ...; **many/much** ~ muchos(as)/mucho(a) más

♦ *adv* más; ~ **dangerous/easily (than)** más peligroso/fácilmente (que); ~ **and** ~ **expensive** cada vez más caro; ~ **or less** más o menos; ~ **than ever** más que nunca; **she doesn't live here any** ~ ya no vive aquí.

moreover [mɔː'rəuvə*] *adv* además, por otra parte.

morgue [mɔːg] *n* depósito de cadáveres.

MORI ['mɔːrɪ] *n abbr* (*BRIT*) = *Market and Opinion Research Institute*.

moribund ['mɔrɪbʌnd] *adj* moribundo.

Mormon ['mɔːmən] *n* mormón/ona *m/f*.

morning ['mɔːnɪŋ] *n* (*gen*) mañana; (*early* ~) madrugada; **in the** ~ por la mañana; **7 o'clock in the** ~ las 7 de la mañana; **this** ~ esta mañana.

morning-after pill ['mɔːnɪŋ'ɑːftə-] *n* píldora del día después.

morning sickness *n* (*MED*) náuseas *fpl* del embarazo.

Moroccan [mə'rɔkən] *adj, n* marroquí *m/f*.

Morocco [mə'rɔkəu] *n* Marruecos *m*.

moron ['mɔːrɔn] *n* imbécil *m/f*.

morose [mə'rəus] *adj* hosco, malhumorado.

morphine ['mɔːfiːn] *n* morfina.

morris dancing ['mɔrɪs] *n* (*BRIT*) *baile tradicional inglés en el que se llevan cascabeles en la ropa*.

Morse [mɔːs] *n* (*also*: ~ **code**) (alfabeto) morse *m*.

morsel ['mɔːsl] *n* (*of food*) bocado.

mortal ['mɔːtl] *adj, n* mortal *m*.

mortality [mɔː'tælɪtɪ] *n* mortalidad *f*.

mortality rate *n* tasa de mortalidad.

mortally ['mɔːtəlɪ] *adv* mortalmente.

mortar ['mɔːtə*] *n* argamasa; (*implement*) mortero.

mortgage ['mɔːgɪdʒ] *n* hipoteca ♦ *vt* hipotecar; **to take out a** ~ sacar una hipoteca.

mortgage company *n* (*US*) ≈ banco hipotecario.

mortgagee [mɔːgə'dʒiː] *n* acreedor(a) *m/f* hipotecario/a.

mortgager ['mɔːgədʒə*] *n* deudor(a) *m/f* hipotecario/a.

mortice ['mɔːtɪs] *n* = **mortise**.

mortician [mɔː'tɪʃən] *n* (*US*) director(a) *m/f* de pompas fúnebres.

mortification ['mɔːtɪfɪ'keɪʃən] *n* mortificación *f*, humillación *f*.

mortified ['mɔːtɪfaɪd] *adj*: **I was** ~ me dio muchísima vergüenza.

mortise (lock) ['mɔːtɪs-] *n* cerradura de muesca.

mortuary ['mɔːtjuərɪ] *n* depósito de cadáveres.

mosaic [məu'zeɪɪk] *n* mosaico.

Moscow ['mɔskəu] *n* Moscú *m*.

Moslem ['mɔzləm] *adj, n* = **Muslim**.

mosque [mɔsk] *n* mezquita.

mosquito, ~es [mɔs'kiːtəu] *n* mosquito.

moss [mɔs] *n* musgo.

mossy ['mɔsɪ] *adj* musgoso, cubierto de musgo.

most [məust] *adj* la mayor parte de, la

mayoría de ♦ *pron* la mayor parte, la
mayoría ♦ *adv* el más; (*very*) muy; **the ~**
(*also:* + *adjective*) el más; **~ of them** la
mayor parte de ellos; **I saw the ~** yo fui
el que más vi; **at the (very) ~** a lo sumo,
todo lo más; **to make the ~ of** aprovechar
(al máximo); **a ~ interesting book** un
libro interesantísimo.

mostly ['məustlɪ] *adv* en su mayor parte,
principalmente.

MOT *n abbr* (*BRIT* = *Ministry of Transport*):
the ~ (test) ≈ la ITV.

motel [məu'tɛl] *n* motel *m*.

moth [mɔθ] *n* mariposa nocturna; (*clothes*
~) polilla.

mothball ['mɔθbɔːl] *n* bola de naftalina.

moth-eaten ['mɔθiːtn] *adj* apolillado.

mother ['mʌðə*] *n* madre *f* ♦ *adj* materno
♦ *vt* (*care for*) cuidar (como una madre).

mother board *n* (*COMPUT*) placa madre.

motherhood ['mʌðəhud] *n* maternidad *f*.

mother-in-law ['mʌðərɪnlɔː] *n* suegra.

motherly ['mʌðəlɪ] *adj* maternal.

mother-of-pearl ['mʌðərəv'pəːl] *n* nácar *m*.

mother's help *n* niñera.

mother-to-be ['mʌðətə'biː] *n* futura
madre.

mother tongue *n* lengua materna.

mothproof ['mɔθpruːf] *adj* a prueba de
polillas.

motif [məu'tiːf] *n* motivo; (*theme*) tema *m*.

motion ['məuʃən] *n* movimiento; (*gesture*)
ademán *m*, señal *f*; (*at meeting*) moción *f*;
(*BRIT: also:* **bowel ~**) evacuación *f*
intestinal ♦ *vt, vi:* **to ~ (to) sb to do sth**
hacer señas a algn para que haga algo; **to
be in ~** (*vehicle*) estar en movimiento; **to
set in ~** poner en marcha; **to go through
the ~s of doing sth** (*fig*) hacer algo
mecánicamente *or* sin convicción.

motionless ['məuʃənlɪs] *adj* inmóvil.

motion picture *n* película.

motivate ['məutɪveɪt] *vt* motivar.

motivated ['məutɪveɪtɪd] *adj* motivado.

motivation [məutɪ'veɪʃən] *n* motivación *f*.

motivational research [məutɪ'veɪʃənl-] *n*
estudios *mpl* de motivación.

motive ['məutɪv] *n* motivo; **from the best
~s** con las mejores intenciones.

motley ['mɔtlɪ] *adj* variopinto.

motor ['məutə*] *n* motor *m*; (*BRIT: col:
vehicle*) coche *m*, carro (*LAM*), automóvil
m, auto *m* (*esp LAM*) ♦ *adj* motor (*f:* motora,
motriz).

motorbike ['məutəbaɪk] *n* moto *f*.

motorboat ['məutəbəut] *n* lancha motora.

motorcade ['məutəkeɪd] *n* desfile *m* de
automóviles.

motorcar ['məutəkɑː*] *n* (*BRIT*) coche *m*,
carro (*LAM*), automóvil *m*, auto *m* (*esp
LAM*).

motorcoach ['məutəkəutʃ] *n* autocar *m*,
autobús *m*, camión *m* (*LAM*).

motorcycle ['məutəsaɪkl] *n* motocicleta.

motorcycle racing *n* motociclismo.

motorcyclist ['məutəsaɪklɪst] *n*
motociclista *m/f*.

motoring ['məutərɪŋ] *n* (*BRIT*)
automovilismo ♦ *adj* (*accident, offence*) de
tráfico *or* tránsito.

motorist ['məutərɪst] *n* conductor(a) *m/f*,
automovilista *m/f*.

motorize ['məutəraɪz] *vt* motorizar.

motor oil *n* aceite *m* para motores.

motor racing *n* (*BRIT*) carreras *fpl* de
coches, automovilismo.

motor scooter *n* vespa ®.

motor vehicle *n* automóvil *m*.

motorway ['məutəweɪ] *n* (*BRIT*) autopista.

mottled ['mɔtld] *adj* moteado.

motto, ~es ['mɔtəu] *n* lema *m*; (*watchword*)
consigna.

mould, (*US*) **mold** [məuld] *n* molde *m*;
(*mildew*) moho ♦ *vt* moldear; (*fig*) formar.

mo(u)lder ['məuldə*] *vi* (*decay*) decaer.

mo(u)lding ['məuldɪŋ] *n* (*ARCH*) moldura.

mo(u)ldy ['məuldɪ] *adj* enmohecido.

moult, (*US*) **molt** [məult] *vi* mudar la piel;
(*bird*) mudar las plumas.

mound [maund] *n* montón *m*, montículo.

mount [maunt] *n* monte *m*; (*horse*)
montura; (*for jewel etc*) engarce *m*; (*for
picture*) marco ♦ *vt* montar en, subir a;
(*stairs*) subir; (*exhibition*) montar; (*attack*)
lanzar; (*stamp*) pegar, fijar; (*picture*)
enmarcar ♦ *vi* (*also:* **~ up**) subirse,
montarse.

mountain ['mauntɪn] *n* montaña ♦ *cpd* de
montaña; **to make a ~ out of a molehill**
hacer una montaña de un grano de
arena.

mountain bike *n* bicicleta de montaña.

mountaineer [mauntɪ'nɪə*] *n* montañero/a,
alpinista *m/f*, andinista *m/f* (*LAM*).

mountaineering [mauntɪ'nɪərɪŋ] *n*
montañismo, alpinismo, andinismo
(*LAM*).

mountainous ['mauntɪnəs] *adj* montañoso.

mountain range *n* sierra.

mountain rescue team *n* equipo de
rescate de montaña.

mountainside ['mauntɪnsaɪd] *n* ladera de la
montaña.

mounted ['mauntɪd] *adj* montado.

Mount Everest *n* Monte *m* Everest.

mourn [mɔːn] *vt* llorar, lamentar ♦ *vi:* **to ~**

for llorar la muerte de, lamentarse por.

mourner ['mɔːnə*] n doliente m/f.

mournful ['mɔːnful] adj triste, lúgubre.

mourning ['mɔːnɪŋ] n luto ♦ cpd (dress) de luto; **in** ~ de luto.

mouse, pl **mice** [maus, maɪs] n (also COMPUT) ratón m.

mousetrap ['maustræp] n ratonera.

moussaka [muˈsɑːkə] n moussaka.

mousse [muːs] n (CULIN) mousse f, (for hair) espuma (moldeadora).

moustache [məsˈtɑːʃ], (US) **mustache** ['mʌstæʃ] n bigote m.

mousy ['mausɪ] adj (person) tímido; (hair) pardusco.

mouth, pl **mouths** [mauθ, -ðz] n boca; (of river) desembocadura.

mouthful ['mauθful] n bocado.

mouth organ n armónica.

mouthpiece ['mauθpiːs] n (of musical instrument) boquilla; (TEL) micrófono; (spokesman) portavoz m/f.

mouth-to-mouth ['mauθtəˈmauθ] adj: ~ **resuscitation** boca a boca m.

mouthwash ['mauθwɔʃ] n enjuague m bucal.

mouth-watering ['mauθwɔːtərɪŋ] adj apetitoso.

movable ['muːvəbl] adj movible.

move [muːv] n (movement) movimiento; (in game) jugada; (: turn to play) turno; (change of house) mudanza ♦ vt mover; (emotionally) conmover; (POL: resolution etc) proponer ♦ vi (gen) moverse; (traffic) circular; (also: BRIT: ~ **house**) trasladarse, mudarse; **to** ~ **sb to do sth** mover a algn a hacer algo; **to be** ~**d** estar conmovido; **to get a** ~ **on** darse prisa.

▶**move about** or **around** vi moverse; (travel) viajar.

▶**move along** vi (stop loitering) circular; (along seat etc) correrse.

▶**move away** vi (leave) marcharse.

▶**move back** vi (return) volver.

▶**move down** vt (demote) degradar.

▶**move forward** vi avanzar ♦ vt adelantar.

▶**move in** vi (to a house) instalarse.

▶**move off** vi ponerse en camino.

▶**move on** vi seguir viaje ♦ vt (onlookers) hacer circular.

▶**move out** vi (of house) mudarse.

▶**move over** vi hacerse a un lado, correrse.

▶**move up** vi subir; (employee) ascender.

movement ['muːvmənt] n movimiento; (TECH) mecanismo; ~ **(of the bowels)** (MED) evacuación f.

mover ['muːvə*] n proponente m/f.

movie ['muːvɪ] n película; **to go to the** ~**s** ir al cine.

movie camera n cámara cinematográfica.

moviegoer ['muːvɪɡəuə*] n (US) aficionado/a al cine.

moving ['muːvɪŋ] adj (emotional) conmovedor(a); (that moves) móvil; (instigating) motor(a).

mow, pt **mowed**, pp **mowed** or **mown** [məu, -n] vt (grass) cortar; (corn: also: ~ **down**) segar; (shoot) acribillar.

mower ['məuə*] n (also: **lawn**~) cortacésped m.

Mozambique [məuzæmˈbiːk] n Mozambique m.

MP n abbr (= Military Police) PM; BRIT: = **Member of Parliament**; (Canada) = Mounted Police.

mpg n abbr (= miles per gallon) millas por galón.

mph abbr = miles per hour (60 mph = 96 km/h.).

MPhil n abbr (= Master of Philosophy) título universitario de postgrado; see also **master's degree**.

MPS n abbr (BRIT) = Member of the Pharmaceutical Society.

Mr, Mr. ['mɪstə*] n: ~ **Smith** (el) Sr. Smith.

MRC n abbr (BRIT: = Medical Research Council) departamento estatal que controla la investigación médica.

MRCP n abbr (BRIT) = Member of the Royal College of Physicians.

MRCS n abbr (BRIT) = Member of the Royal College of Surgeons.

MRCVS n abbr (BRIT) = Member of the Royal College of Veterinary Surgeons.

Mrs, Mrs. ['mɪsɪz] n: ~ **Smith** (la) Sra. de Smith.

MS n abbr (= manuscript) MS; = **multiple sclerosis**; (US: = Master of Science) título universitario ♦ abbr (US) = Mississippi.

Ms, Ms. [mɪz] n (= Miss or Mrs) abreviatura con la que se evita hacer expreso el estado civil de una mujer.

MSA n abbr (US: = Master of Science in Agriculture) título universitario.

MSc abbr see **Master of Science**.

MSG n abbr = monosodium glutamate.

MSS n abbr (= manuscripts) MSS.

MST abbr (US: = Mountain Standard Time) hora de invierno de las Montañas Rocosas.

MSW n abbr (US: = Master of Social Work) título universitario.

MT abbr (US) = Montana.

Mt abbr (GEO: = mount) m.

MTV n abbr = music television.

mth *abbr* (= *month*) m.

much [mʌtʃ] *adj* mucho ♦ *adv, n, pron* mucho; (*before pp*) muy; **how ~ is it?** ¿cuánto es?, ¿cuánto cuesta?; **too ~** demasiado; **so ~** tanto; **it's not ~** no es mucho; **as ~ as** tanto como; **however ~ he tries** por mucho que se esfuerce; **I like it very/so ~** me gusta mucho/tanto; **thank you very ~** muchas gracias, muy agradecido.

muck [mʌk] *n* (*dirt*) suciedad *f*; (*fig*) porquería.

▶**muck about** *or* **around** *vi* (*col*) perder el tiempo; (*enjoy o.s.*) entretenerse; (*tinker*) manosear.

▶**muck in** *vi* (*col*) arrimar el hombro.

▶**muck out** *vt* (*stable*) limpiar.

▶**muck up** *vt* (*col: dirty*) ensuciar; (: *spoil*) echar a perder; (: *ruin*) estropear.

muckraking ['mʌkreɪkɪŋ] (*fig col*) *n* amarillismo ♦ *adj* especializado en escándalos.

mucky ['mʌkɪ] *adj* (*dirty*) sucio.

mucus ['mjuːkəs] *n* mucosidad *f*, moco.

mud [mʌd] *n* barro, lodo.

muddle ['mʌdl] *n* desorden *m*, confusión *f*; (*mix-up*) embrollo, lío ♦ *vt* (*also:* **~ up**) embrollar, confundir.

▶**muddle along, muddle on** *vi* arreglárselas de alguna manera.

▶**muddle through** *vi* salir del paso.

muddle-headed [mʌdl'hedɪd] *adj* (*person*) despistado, confuso.

muddy ['mʌdɪ] *adj* fangoso, cubierto de lodo.

mudguard ['mʌdgɑːd] *n* guardabarros *m inv*.

mudpack ['mʌdpæk] *n* mascarilla.

mud-slinging ['mʌdslɪŋɪŋ] *n* injurias *fpl*, difamación *f*.

muesli ['mjuːzlɪ] *n* muesli *m*.

muff [mʌf] *n* manguito ♦ *vt* (*chance*) desperdiciar; (*lines*) estropear; (*shot, catch etc*) fallar; **to ~ it** fracasar.

muffin ['mʌfɪn] *n* bollo.

muffle ['mʌfl] *vt* (*sound*) amortiguar; (*against cold*) abrigar.

muffled ['mʌfld] *adj* sordo, apagado.

muffler ['mʌflə*] *n* (*scarf*) bufanda; (*US AUT*) silenciador *m*; (*on motorbike*) silenciador *m*, mofle *m*.

mufti ['mʌftɪ] *n*: **in ~** (vestido) de paisano.

mug [mʌg] *n* (*cup*) taza alta; (*for beer*) jarra; (*col: face*) jeta; (: *fool*) bobo ♦ *vt* (*assault*) atracar; **it's a ~'s game** es cosa de bobos.

▶**mug up** *vt* (*col: also:* **~ up on**) empollar.

mugger ['mʌgə*] *n* atracador(a) *m/f*.

mugging ['mʌgɪŋ] *n* atraco callejero.

muggins ['mʌgɪnz] *nsg* (*col*) tonto/a el bote.

muggy ['mʌgɪ] *adj* bochornoso.

mug shot *n* (*col*) foto *f* (para la ficha policial).

mulatto, ~es [mjuːˈlætəu] *n* mulato/a.

mulberry ['mʌlbrɪ] *n* (*fruit*) mora; (*tree*) morera, moral *m*.

mule [mjuːl] *n* mula.

mull [mʌl]: **to ~ over** *vt* meditar sobre.

mulled [mʌld] *adj*: **~ wine** vino caliente (*con especias*).

mullioned ['mʌlɪənd] *adj* (*windows*) dividido por parteluces.

multi... [mʌltɪ] *pref* multi....

multi-access ['mʌltɪˈækses] *adj* (*COMPUT*) multiacceso, de acceso múltiple.

multicoloured, (*US*) **multicolored** ['mʌltɪkʌləd] *adj* multicolor.

multifarious [mʌltɪˈfɛərɪəs] *adj* múltiple, vario.

multilateral [mʌltɪˈlætərl] *adj* (*POL*) multilateral.

multi-level [mʌltɪˈlevl] *adj* (*US*) = **multistorey**.

multimillionaire [mʌltɪmɪljəˈnɛə*] *n* multimillonario/a.

multinational [mʌltɪˈnæʃənl] *n* multinacional *f* ♦ *adj* multinacional.

multiple ['mʌltɪpl] *adj* múltiple ♦ *n* múltiplo; (*BRIT: also:* **~ store**) (cadena de) grandes almacenes *mpl*.

multiple choice *n* examen *m* de tipo test.

multiple crash *n* colisión *f* en cadena.

multiple sclerosis [-sklɪˈrəusɪs] *n* esclerosis *f* múltiple.

multiplex ['mʌltɪpleks] *n* (*also:* **~ cinema**) multicines *m inv*.

multiplication [mʌltɪplɪˈkeɪʃən] *n* multiplicación *f*.

multiplication table *n* tabla de multiplicar.

multiplicity [mʌltɪˈplɪsɪtɪ] *n* multiplicidad *f*.

multiply ['mʌltɪplaɪ] *vt* multiplicar ♦ *vi* multiplicarse.

multiracial [mʌltɪˈreɪʃl] *adj* multirracial.

multistorey [mʌltɪˈstɔːrɪ] *adj* (*BRIT: building, car park*) de muchos pisos.

multistrike ribbon ['mʌltɪstraɪk-] *n* (*COMPUT: on printer*) cinta de múltiples impactos.

multi-tasking ['mʌltɪtɑːskɪŋ] *n* (*COMPUT*) ejecución *f* de tareas múltiples, multitarea.

multitude ['mʌltɪtjuːd] *n* multitud *f*.

mum [mʌm] *n* (*BRIT*) mamá ♦ *adj*: **to keep ~ (about sth)** no decir ni mu (de algo).

mumble ['mʌmbl] *vt* decir entre dientes ♦ *vi* hablar entre dientes, musitar.

mumbo jumbo ['mʌmbəu-] *n* (*col*)

galimatías *m inv.*

mummify ['mʌmɪfaɪ] *vt* momificar.

mummy ['mʌmɪ] *n* (*BRIT: mother*) mamá; (*embalmed*) momia.

mumps [mʌmps] *n* paperas *fpl.*

munch [mʌntʃ] *vt, vi* mascar.

mundane [mʌn'deɪn] *adj* mundano.

municipal [mju:'nɪsɪpl] *adj* municipal.

municipality [mju:nɪsɪ'pælɪtɪ] *n* municipio.

munificence [mu:'nɪfɪsns] *n* munificencia.

munitions [mju:'nɪʃənz] *npl* municiones *fpl.*

mural ['mjuərl] *n* (*pintura*) mural *m.*

murder ['məːdə*] *n* asesinato; (*in law*) homicidio ♦ *vt* asesinar, matar; **to commit** ~ cometer un asesinato *or* homicidio.

murderer ['məːdərə*] *n* asesino.

murderess ['məːdərɪs] *n* asesina.

murderous ['məːdərəs] *adj* homicida.

murk [məːk] *n* oscuridad *f*, tinieblas *fpl.*

murky ['məːkɪ] *adj* (*water, past*) turbio; (*room*) sombrío.

murmur ['məːmə*] *n* murmullo ♦ *vt, vi* murmurar; **heart** ~ soplo cardíaco.

MusB(ac) *n abbr* (= *Bachelor of Music*) título universitario.

muscle ['mʌsl] *n* músculo.

▶**muscle in** *vi* entrometerse.

muscular ['mʌskjulə*] *adj* muscular; (*person*) musculoso.

muscular dystrophy *n* distrofia muscular.

MusD(oc) *n abbr* (= *Doctor of Music*) título universitario.

muse [mju:z] *vi* meditar ♦ *n* musa.

museum [mju:'zɪəm] *n* museo.

mush [mʌʃ] *n* gachas *fpl.*

mushroom ['mʌʃrum] *n* (*gen*) seta, hongo; (*small*) champiñón *m* ♦ *vi* (*fig*) crecer de la noche a la mañana.

mushy ['mʌʃɪ] *adj* (*vegetables*) casi hecho puré; (*story*) sentimentaloide.

music ['mju:zɪk] *n* música.

musical ['mju:zɪkl] *adj* melodioso; (*person*) musical ♦ *n* (*show*) (comedia) musical *m.*

music(al) box *n* caja de música.

musical chairs *n* juego de las sillas; (*fig*) **to play** ~ cambiar de puesto continuamente.

musical instrument *n* instrumento musical.

musically ['mju:zɪklɪ] *adv* melodiosamente, armoniosamente.

music centre *n* equipo de música.

music hall *n* teatro de variedades.

musician [mju:'zɪʃən] *n* músico/a.

music stand *n* atril *m.*

musk [mʌsk] *n* (*perfume m de*) almizcle *m.*

musket ['mʌskɪt] *n* mosquete *m.*

musk rat *n* ratón *m* almizclero.

musk rose *n* (*BOT*) rosa almizcleña.

Muslim ['mʌzlɪm] *adj, n* musulmán/ana *m/f.*

muslin ['mʌzlɪn] *n* muselina.

musquash ['mʌskwɔʃ] *n* (*fur*) piel *f* del ratón almizclero.

muss [mʌs] *vt* (*col: hair*) despeinar; (*: dress*) arrugar.

mussel ['mʌsl] *n* mejillón *m.*

must [mʌst] *aux vb* (*obligation*): **I** ~ **do it** debo hacerlo, tengo que hacerlo; (*probability*): **he** ~ **be there by now** ya debe (de) estar allí ♦ *n*: **it's a** ~ es imprescindible.

mustache ['mʌstæʃ] *n* (*US*) = **moustache.**

mustard ['mʌstəd] *n* mostaza.

mustard gas *n* gas *m* mostaza.

muster ['mʌstə*] *vt* juntar, reunir; (*also:* ~ **up**) reunir; (*: courage*) armarse de.

mustiness ['mʌstɪnɪs] *n* olor *m* a cerrado.

mustn't ['mʌsnt] = **must not.**

musty ['mʌstɪ] *adj* mohoso, que huele a humedad.

mutant ['mju:tənt] *adj, n* mutante *m.*

mutate [mju:'teɪt] *vi* sufrir mutación, transformarse.

mutation [mju:'teɪʃən] *n* mutación *f.*

mute [mju:t] *adj, n* mudo/a *m/f.*

muted ['mju:tɪd] *adj* (*noise*) sordo; (*criticism*) callado.

mutilate ['mju:tɪleɪt] *vt* mutilar.

mutilation [mju:tɪ'leɪʃən] *n* mutilación *f.*

mutinous ['mju:tɪnəs] *adj* (*troops*) amotinado; (*attitude*) rebelde.

mutiny ['mju:tɪnɪ] *n* motín *m* ♦ *vi* amotinarse.

mutter ['mʌtə*] *vt, vi* murmurar.

mutton ['mʌtn] *n* (*carne f de*) cordero.

mutual ['mju:tʃuəl] *adj* mutuo; (*friend*) común.

mutually ['mju:tʃuəlɪ] *adv* mutuamente.

Muzak ® ['mju:zæk] *n* hilo musical.

muzzle ['mʌzl] *n* hocico; (*protective device*) bozal *m*; (*of gun*) boca ♦ *vt* amordazar; (*dog*) poner un bozal a.

MVP *n abbr* (*US SPORT*) = *most valuable player.*

MW *abbr* (= *medium wave*) onda media.

my [maɪ] *adj* mi(s); ~ **house/brother/sisters** mi casa/hermano/mis hermanas; **I've washed** ~ **hair/cut** ~ **finger** me he lavado el pelo/cortado un dedo; **is this** ~ **pen or yours?** ¿este bolígrafo es mío o tuyo?

Myanmar ['maɪænmɑ:*] *n* Myanmar.

myopic [maɪ'ɔpɪk] *adj* miope.

myriad ['mɪrɪəd] *n* (*of people, things*) miríada.

myrrh [məː*] *n* mirra.

myself [maɪ'sɛlf] *pron (reflexive)* me; *(emphatic)* yo mismo; *(after prep)* mí *(mismo); see also* **oneself.**
mysterious [mɪs'tɪərɪəs] *adj* misterioso.
mysteriously [mɪs'tɪərɪəslɪ] *adv* misteriosamente.
mystery ['mɪstərɪ] *n* misterio.
mystery play *n* auto, misterio.
mystic ['mɪstɪk] *adj, n* místico/a *m/f.*
mystical ['mɪstɪkl] *adj* místico.
mysticism ['mɪstɪsɪzəm] *n* misticismo.
mystification [mɪstɪfɪ'keɪʃən] *n* perplejidad *f;* desconcierto.
mystify ['mɪstɪfaɪ] *vt (perplex)* dejar perplejo; *(disconcert)* desconcertar.
mystique [mɪs'tiːk] *n* misterio.
myth [mɪθ] *n* mito.
mythical ['mɪθɪkl] *adj* mítico.
mythological [mɪθə'lɔdʒɪkl] *adj* mitológico.
mythology [mɪ'θɔlədʒɪ] *n* mitología.

N n

N, n [ɛn] *n (letter)* N, n *f;* **N for Nellie,** *(US)* **N for Nan** N de Navarra.
N *abbr (= North)* N.
NA *n abbr (US: = Narcotics Anonymous) organización de ayuda a los drogadictos; (US) = National Academy.*
n/a *abbr (= not applicable)* no interesa; *(COMM etc) = no account.*
NAACP *n abbr (US) = National Association for the Advancement of Colored People.*
NAAFI ['næfɪ] *n abbr (BRIT: = Navy, Army & Air Force Institute) servicio de cantinas etc para las fuerzas armadas.*
nab [næb] *vt (col: grab)* coger *(SP),* agarrar *(LAM);* (: *catch out)* pillar.
NACU *n abbr (US) = National Association of Colleges and Universities.*
nadir ['neɪdɪə*] *n (ASTRO)* nadir *m; (fig)* punto más bajo.
NAFTA ['næftə] *n abbr (= North Atlantic Free Trade Agreement)* TLC *m.*
nag [næg] *n (pej: horse)* rocín *m* ♦ *vt (scold)* regañar; *(annoy)* fastidiar.
nagging ['nægɪŋ] *adj (doubt)* persistente; *(pain)* continuo ♦ *n* quejas *fpl.*
nail [neɪl] *n (human)* uña; *(metal)* clavo ♦ *vt* clavar; *(fig: catch)* coger *(SP),* pillar; **to pay cash on the ~** pagar a tocateja; **to ~**

sb down to a date/price hacer que algn se comprometa a una fecha/un precio.
nailbrush ['neɪlbrʌʃ] *n* cepillo para las uñas.
nailfile ['neɪlfaɪl] *n* lima para las uñas.
nail polish *n* esmalte *m or* laca para las uñas.
nail polish remover *n* quitaesmalte *m.*
nail scissors *npl* tijeras *fpl* para las uñas.
nail varnish *n (BRIT)* = **nail polish.**
Nairobi [naɪ'rəubɪ] *n* Nairobi *m.*
naïve [naɪ'iːv] *adj* ingenuo.
naïvely [naɪ'iːvlɪ] *adv* ingenuamente.
naïveté [nɑː'iːvteɪ], **naivety** [naɪ'iːvɪtɪ] *n* ingenuidad *f,* candidez *f.*
naked ['neɪkɪd] *adj (nude)* desnudo; *(flame)* expuesto al aire; **with the ~ eye** a simple vista.
NAM *n abbr (US) = National Association of Manufacturers.*
name [neɪm] *n (gen)* nombre *m; (surname)* apellido; *(reputation)* fama, renombre *m* ♦ *vt (child)* poner nombre a; *(appoint)* nombrar; **by ~** de nombre; **in the ~ of** en nombre de; **what's your ~?** ¿cómo se llama usted?; **my ~ is Peter** me llamo Pedro; **to give one's ~ and address** dar sus señas; **to take sb's ~ and address** apuntar las señas de algn; **to make a ~ for o.s.** hacerse famoso; **to get (o.s.) a bad ~** forjarse una mala reputación.
name-drop ['neɪmdrɔp] *vi:* **he's always ~ping** siempre está presumiendo de la gente que conoce.
nameless ['neɪmlɪs] *adj* anónimo, sin nombre.
namely ['neɪmlɪ] *adv* a saber.
nameplate ['neɪmpleɪt] *n (on door etc)* placa.
namesake ['neɪmseɪk] *n* tocayo/a.
nan bread [nɑːn-] *n pan indio sin apenas levadura.*
nanny ['nænɪ] *n* niñera.
nap [næp] *n (sleep)* sueñecito, siesta; **they were caught ~ping** les pilló desprevenidos.
NAPA *n abbr (US: = National Association of Performing Artists) sindicato de trabajadores del espectáculo.*
napalm ['neɪpɑːm] *n* napalm *m.*
nape [neɪp] *n:* **~ of the neck** nuca, cogote *m.*
napkin ['næpkɪn] *n (also:* **table ~**) servilleta.
Naples ['neɪplz] *n* Nápoles.
nappy ['næpɪ] *n (BRIT)* pañal *m.*
nappy liner *n* gasa.
nappy rash *n* prurito.
narcissism [nɑː'sɪsɪzəm] *n* narcisismo.

narcissus, *pl* **narcissi** [nɑː'sɪsəs, -saɪ] *n* narciso.
narcotic [nɑː'kɔtɪk] *adj, n* narcótico.
narrate [nə'reɪt] *vt* narrar, contar.
narration [nə'reɪʃən] *n* narración *f*, relato.
narrative ['nærətɪv] *n* narrativa ♦ *adj* narrativo.
narrator [nə'reɪtə*] *n* narrador(a) *m/f*.
narrow ['nærəu] *adj* estrecho; (*resources, means*) escaso ♦ *vi* estrecharse; (*diminish*) reducirse; **to have a ~ escape** escaparse por los pelos; **to ~ sth down** reducir algo.
narrow gauge *adj* (*RAIL*) de vía estrecha.
narrowly ['nærəlɪ] *adv* (*miss*) por poco.
narrow-minded [nærəu'maɪndɪd] *adj* de miras estrechas.
narrow-mindedness ['nærəu'maɪndɪdnɪs] *n* estrechez *f* de miras.
NAS *n abbr* (*US*) = *National Academy of Sciences.*
NASA *n abbr* (*US:* = *National Aeronautics and Space Administration*) NASA *f.*
nasal ['neɪzl] *adj* nasal.
Nassau ['næsɔː] *n* (*in Bahamas*) Nassau *m.*
nastily ['nɑːstɪlɪ] *adv* (*unpleasantly*) de mala manera; (*spitefully*) con rencor.
nastiness ['nɑːstɪnɪs] *n* (*malice*) malevolencia; (*rudeness*) grosería; (*of person, remark*) maldad *f*; (*spitefulness*) rencor *m.*
nasturtium [nəs'təːʃəm] *n* capuchina.
nasty ['nɑːstɪ] *adj* (*remark*) feo; (*person*) antipático; (*revolting: taste, smell*) asqueroso; (*wound, disease etc*) peligroso, grave; **to turn ~** (*situation*) ponerse feo; (*weather*) empeorar; (*person*) ponerse negro.
NAS/UWT *n abbr* (*BRIT:* = *National Association of Schoolmasters/Union of Women Teachers*) sindicato de profesores.
nation ['neɪʃən] *n* nación *f.*
national ['næʃənl] *adj* nacional ♦ *n* súbdito/a.
national anthem *n* himno nacional.
National Curriculum *n* (*BRIT*) plan *m* general de estudios (*en Inglaterra y Gales*).
national debt *n* deuda pública.
national dress *n* traje *m* típico del país.
National Guard *n* (*US*) Guardia Nacional.
National Health Service (NHS) *n* (*BRIT*) servicio nacional de sanidad, ≈ INSALUD *m* (*SP*).
National Insurance *n* (*BRIT*) seguro social nacional, ≈ Seguridad *f* Social.
nationalism ['næʃnəlɪzəm] *n* nacionalismo.
nationalist ['næʃnəlɪst] *adj, n* nacionalista *m/f.*

nationality [næʃə'nælɪtɪ] *n* nacionalidad *f.*
nationalization [næʃnəlaɪ'zeɪʃən] *n* nacionalización *f.*
nationalize ['næʃnəlaɪz] *vt* nacionalizar; **~d industry** industria nacionalizada.
nationally ['næʃnəlɪ] *adv* (*nationwide*) a escala nacional; (*as a nation*) como nación.
national press *n* prensa nacional.
national service *n* (*MIL*) servicio militar.
National Trust *n* (*BRIT*) organización encargada de preservar el patrimonio histórico británico.
nationwide ['neɪʃənwaɪd] *adj* a escala nacional.
native ['neɪtɪv] *n* (*local inhabitant*) natural *m/f*, (*in colonies*) indígena *m/f*, nativo/a ♦ *adj* (*indigenous*) indígena; (*country*) natal; (*innate*) natural, innato; **a ~ of Russia** un(a) natural de Rusia; **~ language** lengua materna; **a ~ speaker of French** un hablante nativo de francés.
Native American *adj*, *n* americano/a indígena *m/f*, amerindio/a *m/f.*
Nativity [nə'tɪvɪtɪ] *n*: **the ~** Navidad *f.*
nativity play *n* auto del nacimiento.
NATO ['neɪtəu] *n abbr* (= *North Atlantic Treaty Organization*) OTAN *f.*
natter ['nætə*] *vi* (*BRIT*) charlar ♦ *n*: **to have a ~** charlar.
natural ['nætʃrəl] *adj* natural; **death from ~ causes** (*LAW*) muerte *f* por causas naturales.
natural childbirth *n* parto natural.
natural gas *n* gas *m* natural.
natural history *n* historia natural.
naturalist ['nætʃrəlɪst] *n* naturalista *m/f.*
naturalization [nætʃrəlaɪ'zeɪʃən] *n* naturalización *f.*
naturalize ['nætʃrəlaɪz] *vt*: **to become ~d** (*person*) naturalizarse; (*plant*) aclimatarse.
naturally ['nætʃrəlɪ] *adv* (*speak etc*) naturalmente; (*of course*) desde luego, por supuesto, ¡cómo no! (*esp LAM*); (*instinctively*) por naturaleza.
naturalness ['nætʃrəlnɪs] *n* naturalidad *f.*
natural resources *npl* recursos *mpl* naturales.
natural selection *n* selección *f* natural.
natural wastage *n* (*INDUSTRY*) desgaste *m* natural.
nature ['neɪtʃə*] *n* naturaleza; (*group, sort*) género, clase *f*; (*character*) modo de ser, carácter *m*; **by ~** por naturaleza; **documents of a confidential ~** documentos *mpl* de tipo confidencial.
-natured ['neɪtʃəd] *suff*: **ill~** malhumorado.

nature reserve n reserva natural.
nature trail n camino forestal educativo.
naturist ['neɪtʃərɪst] n naturista m/f.
naught [nɔːt] = **nought**.
naughtily ['nɔːtɪlɪ] adv (behave) mal; (say) con malicia.
naughtiness ['nɔːtɪnɪs] n travesuras fpl.
naughty ['nɔːtɪ] adj (child) travieso; (story, film) picante, escabroso, colorado (LAM).
nausea ['nɔːsɪə] n náusea.
nauseate ['nɔːsɪeɪt] vt dar náuseas a; (fig) dar asco a.
nauseating ['nɔːsɪeɪtɪŋ] adj nauseabundo; (fig) asqueroso, repugnante.
nauseous ['nɔːsɪəs] adj nauseabundo; **to feel** ~ sentir náuseas.
nautical ['nɔːtɪkl] adj náutico, marítimo; ~ **mile** milla marina.
naval ['neɪvl] adj naval, de marina.
naval officer n oficial m/f de marina.
nave [neɪv] n nave f.
navel ['neɪvl] n ombligo.
navigable ['nævɪɡəbl] adj navegable.
navigate ['nævɪɡeɪt] vt (ship) gobernar; (river etc) navegar por ♦ vi navegar; (AUT) hacer de copiloto.
navigation [nævɪ'ɡeɪʃən] n (action) navegación f; (science) náutica.
navigator ['nævɪɡeɪtə*] n navegante m/f.
navvy ['nævɪ] n (BRIT) peón m caminero.
navy ['neɪvɪ] n marina de guerra; (ships) armada, flota.
navy(-blue) ['neɪvɪ('bluː)] adj azul marino.
Nazareth ['næzərɪθ] n Nazaret m.
Nazi ['nɑːtsɪ] adj, n nazi m/f.
NB abbr (= nota bene) nótese; (Canada) = New Brunswick.
NBA n abbr (US) = National Basketball Association, National Boxing Association.
NBC n abbr (US: = National Broadcasting Company) cadena de televisión.
NBS n abbr (US: = National Bureau of Standards) ≈ Oficina Nacional de Normalización.
NC abbr (COMM etc) = no charge; (US) = North Carolina.
NCC n abbr (BRIT: = Nature Conservancy Council) ≈ ICONA m; (US) = National Council of Churches.
NCCL n abbr (BRIT: = National Council for Civil Liberties) asociación para la defensa de las libertades públicas.
NCO n abbr = non-commissioned officer.
ND abbr (US) = North Dakota.
N. Dak. abbr (US) = North Dakota.
NE abbr (US) = Nebraska, New England.
NEA n abbr (US) = National Education Association.

Neapolitan [nɪə'pɔlɪtən] adj, n napolitano/a m/f.
neap tide [niːp-] n marea muerta.
near [nɪə*] adj (place, relation) cercano; (time) próximo ♦ adv cerca ♦ prep (also: ~ to: space) cerca de, junto a; (: time) cerca de ♦ vt acercarse a, aproximarse a; ~ **here/there** cerca de aquí/de allí; **£25,000 or** ~**est offer** 25,000 libras o precio a discutir; **in the** ~ **future** en fecha próxima; **the building is** ~**ing completion** el edificio está casi terminado.
nearby [nɪə'baɪ] adj cercano, próximo ♦ adv cerca.
nearly ['nɪəlɪ] adv casi, por poco; **I** ~ **fell** por poco me caigo; **not** ~ ni mucho menos, ni con mucho.
near miss n (shot) tiro casi en el blanco; (AVIAT) accidente evitado por muy poco.
nearness ['nɪənɪs] n cercanía, proximidad f.
nearside ['nɪəsaɪd] n (AUT: right-hand drive) lado izquierdo (: left-hand drive) lado derecho.
near-sighted [nɪə'saɪtɪd] adj miope, corto de vista.
neat [niːt] adj (place) ordenado, bien cuidado; (person) pulcro; (plan) ingenioso; (spirits) solo.
neatly ['niːtlɪ] adv (tidily) con esmero; (skilfully) ingeniosamente.
neatness ['niːtnɪs] n (tidiness) orden m; (skilfulness) destreza, habilidad f.
Nebr. abbr (US) = Nebraska.
nebulous ['nɛbjuləs] adj (fig) vago, confuso.
necessarily ['nɛsɪsrɪlɪ] adv necesariamente; **not** ~ no necesariamente.
necessary ['nɛsɪsrɪ] adj necesario, preciso; **he did all that was** ~ hizo todo lo necesario; **if** ~ si es necesario.
necessitate [nɪ'sɛsɪteɪt] vt necesitar, precisar.
necessity [nɪ'sɛsɪtɪ] n necesidad f; **necessities** npl artículos mpl de primera necesidad; **in case of** ~ en caso de urgencia.
neck [nɛk] n (ANAT) cuello; (of animal) pescuezo ♦ vi besuquearse; ~ **and** ~ parejos; **to stick one's** ~ **out** (col) arriesgarse.
necklace ['nɛklɪs] n collar m.
neckline ['nɛklaɪn] n escote m.
necktie ['nɛktaɪ] n (US) corbata.
nectar ['nɛktə*] n néctar m.
nectarine ['nɛktərɪn] n nectarina.
NEDC n abbr (BRIT: = National Economic Development Council) ≈ Consejo Económico y Social.

Neddy ['nɛdɪ] *n abbr* (*BRIT col*) = **NEDC**.

née [neɪ] *adj*: ~ **Scott** de soltera Scott.

need [niːd] *n* (*lack*) escasez *f*, falta; (*necessity*) necesidad *f* ♦ *vt* (*require*) necesitar; **in case of** ~ en caso de necesidad; **there's no** ~ **for** ... no hace(n) falta ...; **to be in** ~ **of, have** ~ **of** necesitar; **10 will meet my immediate** ~**s** 10 satisfacerán mis necesidades más apremiantes; **the** ~**s of industry** las necesidades de la industria; **I** ~ **it** lo necesito; **a signature is** ~**ed** se requiere una firma; **I** ~ **to do it** tengo que hacerlo; **you don't** ~ **to go** no hace falta que vayas.

needle ['niːdl] *n* aguja ♦ *vt* (*fig: col*) picar, fastidiar.

needless ['niːdlɪs] *adj* innecesario, inútil; ~ **to say** huelga decir que.

needlessly ['niːdlɪslɪ] *adv* innecesariamente, inútilmente.

needlework ['niːdlwəːk] *n* (*activity*) costura, labor *f* de aguja.

needn't ['niːdnt] = **need not**.

needy ['niːdɪ] *adj* necesitado.

negation [nɪ'geɪʃən] *n* negación *f*.

negative ['nɛgətɪv] *n* (*PHOT*) negativo; (*answer*) negativa; (*LING*) negación *f* ♦ *adj* negativo.

negative cash flow *n* flujo negativo de efectivo.

negative equity *n* situación en la que el valor de la vivienda es menor que el de la hipoteca que pesa sobre ella.

neglect [nɪ'glɛkt] *vt* (*one's duty*) faltar a, no cumplir con; (*child*) descuidar, desatender ♦ *n* (*state*) abandono; (*personal*) dejadez *f*; (*of duty*) incumplimiento; **to** ~ **to do sth** olvidarse de hacer algo.

neglected [nɪ'glɛktɪd] *adj* abandonado.

neglectful [nɪ'glɛktful] *adj* negligente; **to be** ~ **of sth/sb** desatender algo/a algn.

negligee ['nɛglɪʒeɪ] *n* (*nightdress*) salto de cama.

negligence ['nɛglɪdʒəns] *n* negligencia.

negligent ['nɛglɪdʒənt] *adj* negligente; (*casual*) descuidado.

negligently ['nɛglɪdʒəntlɪ] *adv* negligentemente; (*casually*) con descuido.

negligible ['nɛglɪdʒɪbl] *adj* insignificante, despreciable.

negotiable [nɪ'gəuʃɪəbl] *adj* (*cheque*) negociable; **not** ~ (*cheque*) no trasferible.

negotiate [nɪ'gəuʃɪeɪt] *vt* (*treaty, loan*) negociar; (*obstacle*) franquear; (*bend in road*) tomar ♦ *vi*: **to** ~ (**with**) negociar (con); **to** ~ **with sb for sth** tratar *or*

negociar con algn por algo.

negotiating table [nɪ'gəuʃɪeɪtɪŋ-] *n* mesa de negociaciones.

negotiation [nɪgəuʃɪ'eɪʃən] *n* negociación *f*, gestión *f*; **to enter into** ~**s with sb** entrar en negociaciones con algn.

negotiator [nɪ'gəuʃɪeɪtə*] *n* negociador(a) *m/f*.

Negress ['niːgrɪs] *n* negra.

Negro ['niːgrəu] *adj, n* negro.

neigh [neɪ] *n* relincho ♦ *vi* relinchar.

neighbour, (*US*) **neighbor** ['neɪbə*] *n* vecino/a.

neighbo(u)rhood ['neɪbəhud] *n* (*place*) vecindad *f*, barrio; (*people*) vecindario.

neighbourhood watch *n* (*BRIT: also:* ~ **scheme**) vigilancia del barrio por los propios vecinos.

neighbo(u)ring ['neɪbərɪŋ] *adj* vecino.

neighbo(u)rly ['neɪbəlɪ] *adj* amigable, sociable.

neither ['naɪðə*] *adj* ni ♦ *conj*: **I didn't move and** ~ **did John** no me he movido, ni Juan tampoco ♦ *pron* ninguno; ~ **is true** ninguno/a de los/las dos es cierto/a ♦ *adv*: ~ **good nor bad** ni bueno ni malo.

neo ... [niːəu] *pref* neo....

neolithic [niːəu'lɪθɪk] *adj* neolítico.

neologism [nɪ'ɔlədʒɪzəm] *n* neologismo.

neon ['niːɔn] *n* neón *m*.

neon light *n* lámpara de neón.

Nepal [nɪ'pɔːl] *n* Nepal *m*.

nephew ['nɛvjuː] *n* sobrino.

nepotism ['nɛpətɪzəm] *n* nepotismo.

nerd [nɔːd] *n* (*col*) primo/a.

nerve [nɔːv] *n* (*ANAT*) nervio; (*courage*) valor *m*; (*impudence*) descaro, frescura; **a fit of** ~**s** un ataque de nervios; **to lose one's** ~ (*self-confidence*) perder el valor.

nerve centre *n* (*ANAT*) centro nervioso; (*fig*) punto neurálgico.

nerve gas *n* gas *m* nervioso.

nerve-racking ['nɔːvrækɪŋ] *adj* angustioso.

nervous ['nɔːvəs] *adj* (*anxious, ANAT*) nervioso; (*timid*) tímido, miedoso.

nervous breakdown *n* crisis *f* nerviosa.

nervously ['nɔːvəslɪ] *adv* nerviosamente; tímidamente.

nervousness ['nɔːvəsnɪs] *n* nerviosismo; timidez *f*.

nervous wreck *n* (*col*): **to be a** ~ estar de los nervios.

nervy ['nɔːvɪ] *adj*: **to be** ~ estar nervioso.

nest [nɛst] *n* (*of bird*) nido ♦ *vi* anidar.

nest egg *n* (*fig*) ahorros *mpl*.

nestle ['nɛsl] *vi*: **to** ~ **down** acurrucarse.

nestling ['nɛstlɪŋ] *n* pajarito.

net [nɛt] *n* (*gen*) red *f*; (*fabric*) tul *m* ♦ *adj*

(*COMM*) neto, líquido; (*weight, price, salary*) neto ♦ *vt* coger (*SP*) or agarrar (*LAM*) con red; (*money: subj: person*) cobrar; (: *deal, sale*) conseguir; (*SPORT*) marcar; ~ **of tax** neto; **he earns £10,000 ~ per year** gana 10,000 libras netas por año.

netball ['nɛtbɔːl] *n* básquet *m*.

net curtain *n* visillo.

Netherlands ['nɛðələndz] *npl*: **the ~** los Países Bajos.

net income *n* renta neta.

net loss *n* pérdida neta.

net profit *n* beneficio neto.

nett [nɛt] *adj* = **net**.

netting ['nɛtɪŋ] *n* red *f*, redes *fpl*.

nettle ['nɛtl] *n* ortiga.

network ['nɛtwəːk] *n* red *f* ♦ *vt* (*RADIO, TV*) difundir por la red de emisores; **local area ~** red local.

neuralgia [njuə'rældʒə] *n* neuralgia.

neurological [njuərə'lɔdʒɪkl] *adj* neurológico.

neurosis, *pl* -ses [njuə'rəusɪs, -siːz] *n* neurosis *f inv*.

neurotic [njuə'rɔtɪk] *adj, n* neurótico/a *m/f*.

neuter ['njuːtə*] *adj* (*LING*) neutro ♦ *vt* castrar, capar.

neutral ['njuːtrəl] *adj* (*person*) neutral; (*colour etc, ELEC*) neutro ♦ *n* (*AUT*) punto muerto.

neutrality [njuː'trælɪtɪ] *n* neutralidad *f*.

neutralize ['njuːtrəlaɪz] *vt* neutralizar.

neutron ['njuːtrɔn] *n* neutrón *m*.

neutron bomb *n* bomba de neutrones.

Nev. *abbr* (*US*) = *Nevada*.

never ['nɛvə*] *adv* nunca, jamás; **I ~ went** no fui nunca; **~ in my life** jamás en la vida; *see also* **mind**.

never-ending [nɛvər'ɛndɪŋ] *adj* interminable, sin fin.

nevertheless [nɛvəðə'lɛs] *adv* sin embargo, no obstante.

new [njuː] *adj* nuevo; (*recent*) reciente; **as good as ~** como nuevo.

New Age *n* Nueva era.

newborn ['njuːbɔːn] *adj* recién nacido.

newcomer ['njuːkʌmə*] *n* recién venido or llegado.

new-fangled ['njuːfæŋgld] *adj* (*pej*) modernísimo.

new-found ['njuːfaund] *adj* (*friend*) nuevo; (*enthusiasm*) recién adquirido.

New Guinea *n* Nueva Guinea.

newly ['njuːlɪ] *adv* recién.

newly-weds ['njuːlɪwɛdz] *npl* recién casados.

new moon *n* luna nueva.

newness ['njuːnɪs] *n* novedad *f*; (*fig*)

inexperiencia.

news [njuːz] *n* noticias *fpl*; **a piece of ~** una noticia; **the ~** (*RADIO, TV*) las noticias *fpl*, el telediario; **good/bad ~** buenas/malas noticias *fpl*; **financial ~** noticias *fpl* financieras.

news agency *n* agencia de noticias.

newsagent ['njuːzeɪdʒənt] *n* (*BRIT*) vendedor(a) *m/f* de periódicos.

news bulletin *n* (*RADIO, TV*) noticiario.

newscaster ['njuːzkɑːstə*] *n* presentador(a) *m/f*, locutor(a) *m/f*.

news dealer *n* (*US*) = **newsagent**.

news flash *n* noticia de última hora.

newsletter ['njuːzlɛtə*] *n* hoja informativa, boletín *m*.

newspaper ['njuːzpeɪpə*] *n* periódico, diario; **daily ~** diario; **weekly ~** periódico semanal.

newsprint ['njuːzprɪnt] *n* papel *m* de periódico.

newsreader ['njuːzriːdə*] *n* = **newscaster**.

newsreel ['njuːzriːl] *n* noticiario.

newsroom ['njuːzruːm] *n* (*PRESS, RADIO, TV*) sala de redacción.

news stand *n* quiosco or puesto de periódicos.

newsworthy ['njuːzwəːðɪ] *adj*: **to be ~** ser de interés periodístico.

newt [njuːt] *n* tritón *m*.

new town *n* (*BRIT*) ciudad *f* nueva (*construida con subsidios estatales*).

New Year *n* Año Nuevo; **Happy ~!** ¡Feliz Año Nuevo!; **to wish sb a happy ~** desear a algn un feliz año nuevo.

New Year's Day *n* Día *m* de Año Nuevo.

New Year's Eve *n* Nochevieja.

New York [-'jɔːk] *n* Nueva York.

New Zealand [-'ziːlənd] *n* Nueva Zelanda (*SP*), Nueva Zelandia (*LAM*) ♦ *adj* neozelandés/esa.

New Zealander [-'ziːləndə*] *n* neozelandés/esa *m/f*.

next [nɛkst] *adj* (*house, room*) vecino, de al lado; (*meeting*) próximo; (*page*) siguiente ♦ *adv* después; **the ~ day** el día siguiente; **~ time** la próxima vez; **~ year** el año próximo or que viene; **~ month** el mes que viene or entrante; **the week after ~** no la semana que viene sino la otra; **"turn to the ~ page"** "vuelva a la página siguiente"; **you're ~** le toca; **~ to** *prep* junto a, al lado de; **~ to nothing** casi nada.

next door *adv* en la casa de al lado ♦ *adj* vecino, de al lado.

next-of-kin ['nɛkstəv'kɪn] *n* pariente(s) *m(pl)* más cercano(s).

NF *n abbr* (*BRIT POL*: = *National Front*) partido político de la extrema derecha ♦ *abbr* (*Canada*) = *Newfoundland*.
NFL *n abbr* (*US*) = *National Football League*.
Nfld. *abbr* (*Canada*) = *Newfoundland*.
NG *abbr* (*US*) = **National Guard.**
NGO *n abbr* (= *non-governmental organization*) ONG *f*.
NH *abbr* (*US*) = *New Hampshire*.
NHL *n abbr* (*US*) = *National Hockey League*.
NHS *n abbr see* **National Health Service.**
NI *abbr* = **Northern Ireland;** (*BRIT*) = **National Insurance.**
nib [nɪb] *n* plumilla.
nibble ['nɪbl] *vt* mordisquear.
Nicaragua [nɪkəˈrægjuə] *n* Nicaragua.
Nicaraguan [nɪkəˈrægjuən] *adj, n* nicaragüense *m/f*, nicaragüeño/a *m/f*.
Nice [niːs] *n* Niza.
nice [naɪs] *adj* (*likeable*) simpático, majo; (*kind*) amable; (*pleasant*) agradable; (*attractive*) bonito, mono; (*distinction*) fino; (*taste, smell, meal*) rico.
nice-looking ['naɪslukɪŋ] *adj* guapo.
nicely ['naɪslɪ] *adv* amablemente; (*of health etc*) bien; **that will do ~** perfecto.
niceties ['naɪsɪtɪz] *npl* detalles *mpl*.
niche [niːʃ] *n* (*ARCH*) nicho, hornacina.
nick [nɪk] *n* (*wound*) rasguño; (*cut, indentation*) mella, muesca ♦ *vt* (*cut*) cortar; (*col*) birlar, mangar; (: *arrest*) pillar; **in the ~ of time** justo a tiempo; **in good ~** en buen estado; **to ~ o.s.** cortarse.
nickel ['nɪkl] *n* níquel *m*; (*US*) moneda de 5 centavos.
nickname ['nɪkneɪm] *n* apodo, mote *m* ♦ *vt* apodar.
Nicosia [nɪkəˈsiːə] *n* Nicosía.
nicotine ['nɪkətiːn] *n* nicotina.
nicotine patch *n* parche *m* de nicotina.
niece [niːs] *n* sobrina.
nifty ['nɪftɪ] *adj* (*col*: *car, jacket*) elegante, chulo; (: *gadget, tool*) ingenioso.
Niger ['naɪdʒə*] *n* (*country, river*) Níger *m*.
Nigeria [naɪˈdʒɪərɪə] *n* Nigeria.
Nigerian [naɪˈdʒɪərɪən] *adj, n* nigeriano/a *m/f*.
niggardly ['nɪgədlɪ] *adj* (*person*) avaro, tacaño, avariento; (*allowance, amount*) miserable.
nigger ['nɪgə*] *n* (*coll: highly offensive*) negro/a.
niggle ['nɪgl] *vt* preocupar ♦ *vi* (*complain*) quejarse; (*fuss*) preocuparse por minucias.
niggling ['nɪglɪŋ] *adj* (*detail: trifling*) nimio, insignificante; (*annoying*) molesto; (*doubt, pain*) constante.

night [naɪt] *n* (*gen*) noche *f*; (*evening*) tarde *f*; **last ~** anoche; **the ~ before last** anteanoche, antes de ayer por la noche; **at ~, by ~** de noche, por la noche; **in the ~, during the ~** durante la noche, por la noche.
night-bird ['naɪtbɜːd] *n* pájaro nocturno; (*fig*) trasnochador(a) *m/f*, madrugador(a) *m/f* (*LAM*).
nightcap ['naɪtkæp] *n* (*drink*) bebida que se toma antes de acostarse.
night club *n* club nocturno, discoteca.
nightdress ['naɪtdres] *n* (*BRIT*) camisón *m*.
nightfall ['naɪtfɔːl] *n* anochecer *m*.
nightgown ['naɪtgaun], **nightie** ['naɪtɪ] (*BRIT*) *n* = **nightdress**.
nightingale ['naɪtɪŋgeɪl] *n* ruiseñor *m*.
night life *n* vida nocturna.
nightly ['naɪtlɪ] *adj* de todas las noches ♦ *adv* todas las noches, cada noche.
nightmare ['naɪtmɛə*] *n* pesadilla.
night porter *n* guardián *m* nocturno.
night safe *n* caja fuerte.
night school *n* clase(s) *f(pl)* nocturna(s).
nightshade ['naɪtʃeɪd] *n*: **deadly ~** (*BOT*) belladona.
night shift *n* turno nocturno *or* de noche.
night-time ['naɪttaɪm] *n* noche *f*.
night watchman *n* vigilante *m* nocturno, sereno.
nihilism ['naɪɪlɪzəm] *n* nihilismo.
nil [nɪl] *n* (*BRIT SPORT*) cero, nada.
Nile [naɪl] *n*: **the ~** el Nilo.
nimble ['nɪmbl] *adj* (*agile*) ágil, ligero; (*skilful*) diestro.
nimbly ['nɪmblɪ] *adv* ágilmente; con destreza.
nine [naɪn] *num* nueve.
nineteen ['naɪn'tiːn] *num* diecinueve.
nineteenth [naɪn'tiːnθ] *num* decimonoveno, decimonono.
ninety ['naɪntɪ] *num* noventa.
ninth [naɪnθ] *num* noveno.
nip [nɪp] *vt* (*pinch*) pellizcar; (*bite*) morder ♦ *vi* (*BRIT col*): **to ~ out/down/up** salir/bajar/subir un momento ♦ *n* (*drink*) trago.
nipple ['nɪpl] *n* (*ANAT*) pezón *m*; (*of bottle*) tetilla; (*TECH*) boquilla, manguito.
nippy ['nɪpɪ] *adj* (*BRIT*: *person*) rápido; (*taste*) picante; **it's a very ~ car** es un coche muy potente para el tamaño que tiene.
nit [nɪt] *n* (*of louse*) liendre *f*; (*col*: *idiot*) imbécil *m/f*.
nit-pick ['nɪtpɪk] *vi* (*col*) sacar punta a todo.
nitrogen ['naɪtrədʒən] *n* nitrógeno.
nitroglycerin(e) ['naɪtrəu'glɪsəriːn] *n* nitroglicerina.
nitty-gritty ['nɪtɪ'grɪtɪ] *n* (*col*): **to get down**

to the ~ ir al grano.

nitwit ['nɪtwɪt] *n* cretino/a.

NJ *abbr* (*US*) = New Jersey.

NLF *n abbr* (= *National Liberation Front*) FLN *m*.

NLQ *abbr* (= *near letter quality*) calidad *f* casi de correspondencia.

NLRB *n abbr* (*US*: = *National Labor Relations Board*) organismo de protección al trabajador.

NM, N. Mex. *abbr* (*US*) = New Mexico.

========================= *KEYWORD*

no [nəʊ] (*pl* ~**es**) *adv* (*opposite of "yes"*) no; **are you coming? — ~ (I'm not)** ¿vienes? — no; **would you like some more? — ~ thank you** ¿quieres más? — no gracias ♦ *adj* (*not any*): **I have ~ money/time/ books** no tengo dinero/tiempo/libros; ~ **other man would have done it** ningún otro lo hubiera hecho; "~ **entry**" "prohibido el paso"; "~ **smoking**" "prohibido fumar"
♦ *n* no *m*.

no. *abbr* (= *number*) nº., núm.

nobble ['nɔbl] *vt* (*BRIT col*: *bribe*) sobornar; (: *catch*) pescar; (: *RACING*) drogar.

Nobel prize [nəʊ'bɛl-] *n* premio Nobel.

nobility [nəʊ'bɪlɪtɪ] *n* nobleza.

noble ['nəʊbl] *adj* (*person*) noble; (*title*) de nobleza.

nobleman ['nəʊblmən] *n* noble *m*.

nobly ['nəʊblɪ] *adv* (*selflessly*) noblemente.

nobody ['nəʊbədɪ] *pron* nadie.

no-claims bonus ['nəʊkleɪmz-] *n* bonificación *f* por carencia de reclamaciones.

nocturnal [nɔk'tə:nl] *adj* nocturno.

nod [nɔd] *vi* saludar con la cabeza; (*in agreement*) asentir con la cabeza ♦ *vt*: **to ~ one's head** inclinar la cabeza ♦ *n* inclinación *f* de cabeza; **they ~ded their agreement** asintieron con la cabeza.

▶**nod off** *vi* cabecear.

no-fly zone [nəʊ'flaɪ-] *n* zona de exclusión aérea.

noise [nɔɪz] *n* ruido; (*din*) escándalo, estrépito.

noisily ['nɔɪzɪlɪ] *adv* ruidosamente, estrepitosamente.

noisy ['nɔɪzɪ] *adj* (*gen*) ruidoso; (*child*) escandaloso.

nomad ['nəʊmæd] *n* nómada *m/f*.

nomadic [nəʊ'mædɪk] *adj* nómada.

no man's land *n* tierra de nadie.

nominal ['nɔmɪnl] *adj* nominal.

nominate ['nɔmɪneɪt] *vt* (*propose*)

proponer; (*appoint*) nombrar.

nomination [nɔmɪ'neɪʃən] *n* propuesta; nombramiento.

nominee [nɔmɪ'ni:] *n* candidato/a.

non... [nɔn] *pref* no, des..., in....

nonalcoholic [nɔnælkə'hɔlɪk] *adj* sin alcohol.

nonaligned [nɔnə'laɪnd] *adj* no alineado.

nonarrival [nɔnə'raɪvl] *n* falta de llegada.

nonce word [nɔns-] *n* hápax *m*.

nonchalant ['nɔnʃələnt] *adj* indiferente.

noncommissioned [nɔnkə'mɪʃənd] *adj*: ~ **officer** suboficial *m/f*.

noncommittal ['nɔnkə'mɪtl] *adj* (*reserved*) reservado; (*uncommitted*) evasivo.

nonconformist [nɔnkən'fɔ:mɪst] *adj* inconformista ♦ *n* inconformista *m/f*; (*BRIT REL*) no conformista *m/f*.

noncontributory [nɔnkən'trɪbjutərɪ] *adj*: ~ **pension scheme** *or* (*US*) **plan** fondo de pensiones no contributivo.

noncooperation ['nɔnkəʊɔpə'reɪʃən] *n* no cooperación *f*.

nondescript ['nɔndɪskrɪpt] *adj* anodino, soso.

none [nʌn] *pron* ninguno/a ♦ *adv* de ninguna manera; ~ **of you** ninguno de vosotros; **I've ~ left** no me queda ninguno/a; **he's ~ the worse for it** no le ha perjudicado; **I have ~** no tengo ninguno; ~ **at all** (*not one*) ni uno.

nonentity [nɔ'nentɪtɪ] *n* cero a la izquierda, nulidad *f*.

nonessential [nɔnɪ'senʃl] *adj* no esencial ♦ *n*: ~**s** cosas *fpl* secundarias *or* sin importancia.

nonetheless [nʌnðə'les] *adv* sin embargo, no obstante, aún así.

non-event [nɔnɪ'vent] *n* acontecimiento sin importancia; **it was a ~** no pasó absolutamente nada.

nonexecutive [nɔnɪg'zekjutɪv] *adj*: ~ **director** director *m* no ejecutivo.

nonexistent [nɔnɪg'zɪstənt] *adj* inexistente.

nonfiction [nɔn'fɪkʃən] *n* no ficción *f*.

nonintervention [nɔnɪntə'venʃən] *n* no intervención *f*.

no-no ['nəʊnəʊ] *n* (*col*): **it's a ~** de eso ni hablar.

non obst. *abbr* (= *non obstante*: *notwithstanding*) no obstante.

no-nonsense [nəʊ'nɔnsəns] *adj* sensato.

nonpayment [nɔn'peɪmənt] *n* falta de pago.

nonplussed [nɔn'plʌst] *adj* perplejo.

non-profit-making [nɔn'prɔfɪtmeɪkɪŋ] *adj* no lucrativo.

nonsense ['nɔnsəns] *n* tonterías *fpl*,

disparates *fpl*; ~! ¡qué tonterías!; **it is ~ to say that** ... es absurdo decir que ....
nonsensical [nɔn'sɛnsɪkl] *adj* disparatado, absurdo.
nonshrink [nɔn'ʃrɪŋk] *adj* que no encoge.
nonskid [nɔn'skɪd] *adj* antideslizante.
nonsmoker ['nɔn'sməukə*] *n* no fumador(a) *m/f*.
nonstarter [nɔn'stɑːtə*] *n*: **it's a ~** no tiene futuro.
nonstick ['nɔn'stɪk] *adj* (*pan*, *surface*) antiadherente.
nonstop ['nɔn'stɔp] *adj* continuo; (*RAIL*) directo ♦ *adv* sin parar.
nontaxable [nɔn'tæksəbl] *adj*: **~ income** renta no imponible.
non-U ['nɔnjuː] *adj abbr* (*BRIT col*: = *non-upper class*) que no pertenece a la clase alta.
nonvolatile [nɔn'vɔlətaɪl] *adj*: **~ memory** (*COMPUT*) memoria permanente.
nonvoting [nɔn'vəutɪŋ] *adj*: **~ shares** acciones *fpl* sin derecho a voto.
nonwhite ['nɔn'waɪt] *adj* de color ♦ *n* (*person*) persona de color.
noodles ['nuːdlz] *npl* tallarines *mpl*.
nook [nuk] *n* rincón *m*; **~s and crannies** escondrijos *mpl*.
noon [nuːn] *n* mediodía *m*.
no-one ['nəuwʌn] *pron* = **nobody**.
noose [nuːs] *n* lazo corredizo.
nor [nɔː*] *conj* = **neither** ♦ *adv see* **neither**.
Norf *abbr* (*BRIT*) = **Norfolk**.
norm [nɔːm] *n* norma.
normal ['nɔːml] *adj* normal; **to return to ~** volver a la normalidad.
normality [nɔː'mælɪtɪ] *n* normalidad *f*.
normally ['nɔːməlɪ] *adv* normalmente.
Normandy ['nɔːməndɪ] *n* Normandía.
north [nɔːθ] *n* norte *m* ♦ *adj* del norte ♦ *adv* al *or* hacia el norte.
North Africa *n* África del Norte.
North African *adj*, *n* norteafricano/a *m/f*.
North America *n* América del Norte.
North American *adj*, *n* norteamericano/a *m/f*.
Northants *abbr* (*BRIT*) = **Northamptonshire**.
northbound ['nɔːθbaund] *adj* (*traffic*) que se dirige al norte; (*carriageway*) de dirección norte.
Northd *abbr* (*BRIT*) = **Northumberland**.
north-east [nɔːθ'iːst] *n* nor(d)este *m*.
northerly ['nɔːðəlɪ] *adj* (*point*, *direction*) hacia el norte, septentrional; (*wind*) del norte.
northern ['nɔːðən] *adj* norteño, del norte.
Northern Ireland *n* Irlanda del Norte.
North Korea *n* Corea del Norte.

North Pole *n*: **the ~** el Polo Norte.
North Sea *n*: **the ~** el Mar del Norte.
North Sea oil *n* petróleo del Mar del Norte.
northward(s) ['nɔːθwəd(z)] *adv* hacia el norte.
north-west [nɔːθ'wɛst] *n* noroeste *m*.
Norway ['nɔːweɪ] *n* Noruega.
Norwegian [nɔː'wiːdʒən] *adj* noruego ♦ *n* noruego/a; (*LING*) noruego.
nos. *abbr* (= *numbers*) núms.
nose [nəuz] *n* (*ANAT*) nariz *f*; (*ZOOL*) hocico; (*sense of smell*) olfato ♦ *vi* (*also*: **~ one's way**) avanzar con cautela; **to pay through the ~ (for sth)** (*col*) pagar un dineral (por algo).
►**nose about, nose around** *vi* curiosear.
nosebleed ['nəuzbliːd] *n* hemorragia nasal.
nose-dive ['nəuzdaɪv] *n* picado vertical.
nose drops *npl* gotas *fpl* para la nariz.
nosey ['nəuzɪ] *adj* curioso, fisgón(ona).
nostalgia [nɔs'tældʒɪə] *n* nostalgia.
nostalgic [nɔs'tældʒɪk] *adj* nostálgico.
nostril ['nɔstrɪl] *n* ventana *or* orificio de la nariz.
nosy ['nəuzɪ] *adj* = **nosey**.
not [nɔt] *adv* no; **~ at all** no ... en absoluto; **~ that...** no es que...; **it's too late, isn't it?** es demasiado tarde, ¿verdad?; **~ yet** todavía no; **~ now** ahora no; **why ~?** ¿por qué no?; **I hope ~** espero que no; **~ at all** no ... nada; (*after thanks*) de nada.
notable ['nəutəbl] *adj* notable.
notably ['nəutəblɪ] *adv* especialmente; (*in particular*) sobre todo.
notary ['nəutərɪ] *n* (*also*: **~ public**) notario/a.
notation [nəu'teɪʃən] *n* notación *f*.
notch [nɔtʃ] *n* muesca, corte *m*.
►**notch up** *vt* (*score, victory*) apuntarse.
note [nəut] *n* (*MUS*, *record*, *letter*) nota; (*banknote*) billete *m*; (*tone*) tono ♦ *vt* (*observe*) notar, observar; (*write down*) apuntar, anotar; **delivery ~** nota de entrega; **to compare ~s** (*fig*) cambiar impresiones; **of ~** conocido, destacado; **to take ~** prestar atención a; **just a quick ~ to let you know that** ... sólo unas líneas para informarte que ....
notebook ['nəutbuk] *n* libreta, cuaderno; (*for shorthand*) libreta.
notecase ['nəutkeɪs] *n* (*BRIT*) cartera, billetero.
noted ['nəutɪd] *adj* célebre, conocido.
notepad ['nəutpæd] *n* bloc *m*.
notepaper ['nəutpeɪpə*] *n* papel *m* para cartas.

noteworthy ['nəutwə:ðɪ] *adj* notable, digno de atención.

nothing ['nʌθɪŋ] *n* nada; (*zero*) cero; **he does** ~ no hace nada; ~ **new** nada nuevo; **for** ~ (*free*) gratis; (*in vain*) en balde; ~ **at all** nada en absoluto.

notice ['nəutɪs] *n* (*announcement*) anuncio; (*dismissal*) despido; (*resignation*) dimisión *f*; (*review: of play etc*) reseña ♦ *vt* (*observe*) notar, observar; **to take** ~ **of** hacer caso de, prestar atención a; **at short** ~ con poca antelación; **without** ~ sin previo aviso; **advance** ~ previo aviso; **until further** ~ hasta nuevo aviso; **to give sb** ~ **of sth** avisar a algn de algo; **to give** ~, **hand in one's** ~ dimitir, renunciar; **it has come to my** ~ **that ...** he llegado a saber que ...; **to escape** *or* **avoid** ~ pasar inadvertido.

noticeable ['nəutɪsəbl] *adj* evidente, obvio.

notice board *n* (*BRIT*) tablón *m* de anuncios.

notification [nəutɪfɪ'keɪʃən] *n* aviso, (*announcement*) anuncio.

notify ['nəutɪfaɪ] *vt*: **to** ~ **sb** (**of sth**) comunicar (algo) a algn.

notion ['nəuʃən] *n* noción *f*, concepto; (*opinion*) opinión *f*.

notions ['nəuʃənz] *npl* (*US*) mercería.

notoriety [nəutə'raɪətɪ] *n* notoriedad *f*, mala fama.

notorious [nəu'tɔ:rɪəs] *adj* notorio, tristemente célebre.

notoriously [nəu'tɔ:rɪəslɪ] *adv* notoriamente.

Notts *abbr* (*BRIT*) = *Nottinghamshire*.

notwithstanding [nɔtwɪθ'stændɪŋ] *adv* no obstante, sin embargo; ~ **this** a pesar de esto.

nougat ['nu:gɑ:] *n* turrón *m*.

nought [nɔ:t] *n* cero.

noun [naun] *n* nombre *m*, sustantivo.

nourish ['nʌrɪʃ] *vt* nutrir, alimentar; (*fig*) fomentar, nutrir.

nourishing ['nʌrɪʃɪŋ] *adj* nutritivo, rico.

nourishment ['nʌrɪʃmənt] *n* alimento, sustento.

Nov. *abbr* (= *November*) nov.

novel ['nɔvl] *n* novela ♦ *adj* (*new*) nuevo, original; (*unexpected*) insólito.

novelist ['nɔvəlɪst] *n* novelista *m/f*.

novelty ['nɔvəltɪ] *n* novedad *f*.

November [nəu'vɛmbə*] *n* noviembre *m*.

novice ['nɔvɪs] *n* principiante *m/f*, novato/a; (*REL*) novicio/a.

NOW [nau] *n abbr* (*US*) = *National Organization for Women*.

now [nau] *adv* (*at the present time*) ahora; (*these days*) actualmente, hoy día ♦ *conj*: ~ (*that*) ya que, ahora que; **right** ~ ahora mismo; **by** ~ ya; **just** ~: **I'll do it just** ~ ahora mismo lo hago; ~ **and then,** ~ **and again** de vez en cuando; **from** ~ **on** de ahora en adelante; **between** ~ **and Monday** entre hoy y el lunes; **in 3 days from** ~ de hoy en 3 días; **that's all for** ~ eso es todo por ahora.

nowadays ['nauədeɪz] *adv* hoy (en) día, actualmente.

nowhere ['nəuwɛə*] *adv* (*direction*) a ninguna parte; (*location*) en ninguna parte; ~ **else** en *or* a ninguna otra parte.

no-win situation [nəu'wɪn-] *n*: **I'm in a** ~ haga lo que haga, llevo las de perder.

noxious ['nɔkʃəs] *adj* nocivo.

nozzle ['nɔzl] *n* boquilla.

NP *n abbr* = **notary public.**

NS *abbr* (*Canada*) = *Nova Scotia.*

NSC *n abbr* (*US*) = *National Security Council.*

NSF *n abbr* (*US*) = *National Science Foundation.*

NSPCC *n abbr* (*BRIT*) = *National Society for the Prevention of Cruelty to Children.*

NSW *abbr* (*Australia*) = *New South Wales.*

NT *n abbr* = *New Testament* ♦ *abbr* (*Canada*) = *Northwest Territories.*

nth [ɛnθ] *adj*: **for the** ~ **time** (*col*) por enésima vez.

nuance ['nju:ɑ:ns] *n* matiz *m*.

nubile ['nju:baɪl] *adj* núbil.

nuclear ['nju:klɪə*] *adj* nuclear.

nuclear disarmament *n* desarme *m* nuclear.

nuclear family *n* familia nuclear.

nuclear-free zone ['nju:klɪə'fri:-] *n* zona desnuclearizada.

nucleus, *pl* **nuclei** ['nju:klɪəs, 'nju:klɪaɪ] *n* núcleo.

NUCPS *n abbr* (*BRIT* = *National Union of Civil and Public Servants*) sindicato de funcionarios.

nude [nju:d] *adj, n* desnudo/a *m/f*; **in the** ~ desnudo.

nudge [nʌdʒ] *vt* dar un codazo a.

nudist ['nju:dɪst] *n* nudista *m/f*.

nudist colony *n* colonia de desnudistas.

nudity ['nju:dɪtɪ] *n* desnudez *f*.

nugget ['nʌgɪt] *n* pepita.

nuisance ['nju:sns] *n* molestia, fastidio; (*person*) pesado, latoso; **what a** ~! ¡qué lata!

NUJ *n abbr* (*BRIT*: = *National Union of Journalists*) sindicato de periodistas.

nuke [nju:k] (*col*) *n* bomba atómica ♦ *vt* atacar con arma nuclear.

null [nʌl] *adj*: ~ **and void** nulo y sin efecto.

nullify ['nʌlɪfaɪ] *vt* anular, invalidar.
NUM *n abbr* (*BRIT:* = National Union of Mineworkers) sindicato de mineros.
numb [nʌm] *adj* entumecido; (*fig*) insensible ♦ *vt* quitar la sensación a, entumecer, entorpecer; **to be ~ with cold** estar entumecido de frío; **~ with fear** paralizado de miedo; **~ with grief** paralizado de dolor.
number ['nʌmbə*] *n* número; (*numeral*) número, cifra ♦ *vt* (*pages etc*) numerar, poner número a; (*amount to*) sumar, ascender a; **reference ~** número de referencia; **telephone ~** número de teléfono; **wrong ~** (*TEL*) número equivocado; **opposite ~** (*person*) homólogo/a; **to be ~ed among** figurar entre; **a ~ of** varios, algunos; **they were ten in ~** eran diez.
numbered account *n* (*in bank*) cuenta numerada.
number plate *n* (*BRIT*) matrícula, placa.
Number Ten *n* (*BRIT:* 10 Downing Street) residencia del primer ministro.
numbness ['nʌmnɪs] *n* insensibilidad *f*, parálisis *f inv*; (*due to cold*) entumecimiento.
numbskull ['nʌmskʌl] *n* (*col*) papanatas *m/f inv*.
numeral ['nju:mərəl] *n* número, cifra.
numerate ['nju:mərɪt] *adj* competente en aritmética.
numerical [nju:'mɛrɪkl] *adj* numérico.
numerous ['nju:mərəs] *adj* numeroso, muchos.
nun [nʌn] *n* monja, religiosa.
nunnery ['nʌnərɪ] *n* convento de monjas.
nuptial ['nʌpʃəl] *adj* nupcial.
nurse [nə:s] *n* enfermero/a; (*nanny*) niñera ♦ *vt* (*patient*) cuidar, atender; (*baby: Brit*) mecer; (: *US*) criar, amamantar; **male ~** enfermero.
nursery ['nə:sərɪ] *n* (*institution*) guardería infantil; (*room*) cuarto de los niños; (*for plants*) criadero, semillero.
nursery rhyme *n* canción *f* infantil.
nursery school *n* escuela de preescolar.
nursery slope *n* (*BRIT SKI*) cuesta para principiantes.
nursing ['nə:sɪŋ] *n* (*profession*) profesión *f* de enfermera; (*care*) asistencia, cuidado ♦ *adj* (*mother*) lactante.
nursing home *n* clínica de reposo.
nurture ['nə:tʃə*] *vt* (*child, plant*) alimentar, nutrir.
NUS *n abbr* (*BRIT:* = National Union of Students) sindicato de estudiantes.
NUT *n abbr* (*BRIT:* = National Union of

Teachers) sindicato de profesores.
nut [nʌt] *n* (*TECH*) tuerca; (*BOT*) nuez *f* ♦ *adj* (*chocolate etc*) con nueces; **~s** (*CULIN*) frutos secos.
nutcrackers ['nʌtkrækəz] *npl* cascanueces *m inv*.
nutmeg ['nʌtmɛg] *n* nuez *f* moscada.
nutrient ['nju:trɪənt] *adj* nutritivo ♦ *n* elemento nutritivo.
nutrition [nju:'trɪʃən] *n* nutrición *f*, alimentación *f*.
nutritionist [nju:'trɪʃənɪst] *n* dietista *m/f*.
nutritious [nju:'trɪʃəs] *adj* nutritivo.
nuts [nʌts] *adj* (*col*) chiflado.
nutshell ['nʌtʃɛl] *n* cáscara de nuez; **in a ~** en resumidas cuentas.
nutty ['nʌtɪ] *adj* (*flavour*) a frutos secos; (*col: foolish*) chalado.
nuzzle ['nʌzl] *vi:* **to ~ up to** arrimarse a.
NV *abbr* (*US*) = Nevada.
NWT *abbr* (*Canada*) = Northwest Territories.
NY *abbr* (*US*) = New York.
NYC *abbr* (*US*) = New York City.
nylon ['naɪlɔn] *n* nylon *m*, nilón *m* ♦ *adj* de nylon *or* nilón.
nymph [nɪmf] *n* ninfa.
nymphomaniac ['nɪmfəu'meɪnɪæk] *adj*, *n* ninfómana.
NYSE *n abbr* (*US*) = New York Stock Exchange.

O o

O, o [əu] (*letter*) O, o *f*; **O for Oliver**, (*US*) **O for Oboe** O de Oviedo.
oaf [əuf] *n* zoquete *m/f*.
oak [əuk] *n* roble *m* ♦ *adj* de roble.
OAP *abbr see* old-age pensioner.
oar [ɔː*] *n* remo; **to put** *or* **shove one's ~ in** (*fig: col*) entrometerse.
oarsman ['ɔːzmən] *n* remero.
OAS *n abbr* (= Organization of American States) OEA *f*.
oasis, *pl* **oases** [əu'eɪsɪs, əu'eɪsi:z] *n* oasis *m inv*.
oath [əuθ] *n* juramento; (*swear word*) palabrota; **on** (*BRIT*) *or* **under ~** bajo juramento.
oatmeal ['əutmi:l] *n* harina de avena.
oats [əuts] *n* avena.
OAU *n abbr* (= Organization of African Unity)

OUA *f.*

obdurate ['ɔbdjurɪt] *adj* (*stubborn*) terco, obstinado; (*sinner*) empedernido; (*unyielding*) inflexible, firme.

OBE *n abbr* (*BRIT*: = *Order of the British Empire*) título *ceremonial.*

obedience [ə'biːdɪəns] *n* obediencia; **in ~ to** de acuerdo con.

obedient [ə'biːdɪənt] *adj* obediente.

obelisk ['ɔbɪlɪsk] *n* obelisco.

obese [əu'biːs] *adj* obeso.

obesity [əu'biːsɪtɪ] *n* obesidad *f.*

obey [ə'beɪ] *vt* obedecer; (*instructions, regulations*) cumplir.

obituary [ə'bɪtjuərɪ] *n* necrología.

object ['ɔbdʒɪkt] *n* (*gen*) objeto; (*purpose*) objeto, propósito; (*LING*) objeto, complemento ♦ *vi* [ɔb'dʒɛkt]: **to ~ to** (*attitude*) protestar contra; (*proposal*) oponerse a; **expense is no ~** no importan los gastos; **I ~!** ¡protesto!; **to ~ that** objetar que.

objection [əb'dʒɛkʃən] *n* objeción *f*; **I have no ~ to** ... no tengo inconveniente en que ....

objectionable [əb'dʒɛkʃənəbl] *adj* (*gen*) desagradable; (*conduct*) censurable.

objective [əb'dʒɛktɪv] *adj, n* objetivo.

objectively [əb'dʒɛktɪvlɪ] *adv* objetivamente.

objectivity [ɔbdʒɪk'tɪvɪtɪ] *n* objetividad *f.*

object lesson *n* (*fig*) (buen) ejemplo.

objector [əb'dʒɛktə*] *n* objetor(a) *m/f.*

obligation [ɔblɪ'geɪʃən] *n* obligación *f*; (*debt*) deber *m*; "**without ~**" "sin compromiso"; **to be under an ~ to sb/to do sth** estar comprometido con algn/a hacer algo.

obligatory [ə'blɪgətərɪ] *adj* obligatorio.

oblige [ə'blaɪdʒ] *vt* (*do a favour for*) complacer, hacer un favor a; **to ~ sb to do sth** obligar a algn a hacer algo; **to be ~d to sb for sth** estarle agradecido a algn por algo; **anything to ~!** (*col*) todo sea por complacerte.

obliging [ə'blaɪdʒɪŋ] *adj* servicial, atento.

oblique [ə'bliːk] *adj* oblicuo; (*allusion*) indirecto ♦ *n* (*TYP*) barra.

obliterate [ə'blɪtəreɪt] *vt* arrasar; (*memory*) borrar.

oblivion [ə'blɪvɪən] *n* olvido.

oblivious [ə'blɪvɪəs] *adj*: **~ of** inconsciente de.

oblong ['ɔblɔŋ] *adj* rectangular ♦ *n* rectángulo.

obnoxious [əb'nɔkʃəs] *adj* odioso, detestable; (*smell*) nauseabundo.

o.b.o. *abbr* (*US*: = *or best offer: in classified ads*) abierto ofertas.

oboe ['əubəu] *n* oboe *m.*

obscene [əb'siːn] *adj* obsceno.

obscenity [əb'sɛnɪtɪ] *n* obscenidad *f.*

obscure [əb'skjuə*] *adj* oscuro ♦ *vt* oscurecer; (*hide: sun*) ocultar.

obscurity [əb'skjuərɪtɪ] *n* oscuridad *f*; (*obscure point*) punto oscuro; **to rise from ~** salir de la nada.

obsequious [əb'siːkwɪəs] *adj* servil.

observable [əb'zəːvəbl] *adj* observable, perceptible.

observance [əb'zəːvns] *n* observancia, cumplimiento; (*ritual*) práctica; **religious ~s** prácticas *fpl* religiosas.

observant [əb'zəːvnt] *adj* observador(a).

observation [ɔbzə'veɪʃən] *n* (*also MED*) observación *f*; (*by police etc*) vigilancia.

observation post *n* (*MIL*) puesto de observación.

observatory [əb'zəːvətrɪ] *n* observatorio.

observe [əb'zəːv] *vt* (*gen*) observar; (*rule*) cumplir.

observer [əb'zəːvə*] *n* observador(a) *m/f.*

obsess [əb'sɛs] *vt* obsesionar; **to be ~ed by** *or* **with sb/sth** estar obsesionado con algn/algo.

obsession [əb'sɛʃən] *n* obsesión *f.*

obsessive [əb'sɛsɪv] *adj* obsesivo.

obsolescence [ɔbsə'lɛsns] *n* obsolescencia.

obsolescent [ɔbsə'lɛsnt] *adj* que está cayendo en desuso.

obsolete ['ɔbsəliːt] *adj* obsoleto.

obstacle ['ɔbstəkl] *n* obstáculo; (*nuisance*) estorbo.

obstacle race *n* carrera de obstáculos.

obstetrician [ɔbstə'trɪʃən] *n* obstetra *m/f.*

obstetrics [ɔb'stɛtrɪks] *n* obstetricia.

obstinacy ['ɔbstɪnəsɪ] *n* terquedad *f*, obstinación *f*; tenacidad *f.*

obstinate ['ɔbstɪnɪt] *adj* terco, obstinado; (*determined*) tenaz.

obstinately ['ɔbstɪnɪtlɪ] *adv* tercamente, obstinadamente.

obstreperous [əb'strɛpərəs] *adj* ruidoso; (*unruly*) revoltoso.

obstruct [əb'strʌkt] *vt* (*block*) obstruir; (*hinder*) estorbar, obstaculizar.

obstruction [əb'strʌkʃən] *n* obstrucción *f*; estorbo, obstáculo.

obstructive [əb'strʌktɪv] *adj* obstruccionista; **stop being ~!** ¡deja de poner peros!

obtain [əb'teɪn] *vt* (*get*) obtener; (*achieve*) conseguir; **to ~ sth (for o.s.)** conseguir *or* adquirir algo.

obtainable [əb'teɪnəbl] *adj* asequible.

obtrusive [əb'truːsɪv] *adj* (*person*)

importuno; (: *interfering*) entrometido;
(*building etc*) demasiado visible.
obtuse [əb'tjuːs] *adj* obtuso.
obverse ['ɔbvəːs] *n* (*of medal*) anverso; (*fig*)
complemento.
obviate ['ɔbvieit] *vt* obviar, evitar.
obvious ['ɔbviəs] *adj* (*clear*) obvio,
evidente; (*unsubtle*) poco sutil; **it's ~ that**
... está claro que ..., es evidente que ....
obviously ['ɔbviəsli] *adv* obviamente,
evidentemente; **~ not!** ¡por supuesto que
no!; **he was ~ not drunk** era evidente que
no estaba borracho; **he was not ~ drunk**
no se le notaba que estaba borracho.
OCAS *n abbr* (= *Organization of Central
American States*) ODECA *f*.
occasion [ə'keɪʒən] *n* oportunidad *f*,
ocasión *f*; (*event*) acontecimiento ♦ *vt*
ocasionar, causar; **on that ~** esa vez, en
aquella ocasión; **to rise to the ~** ponerse
a la altura de las circunstancias.
occasional [ə'keɪʒənl] *adj* poco frecuente,
ocasional.
occasionally [ə'keɪʒənli] *adv* de vez en
cuando; **very ~** muy de tarde en tarde, en
muy contadas ocasiones.
occasional table *n* mesita.
occult [ɔ'kʌlt] *adj* (*gen*) oculto.
occupancy ['ɔkjupənsi] *n* ocupación *f*.
occupant ['ɔkjupənt] *n* (*of house*)
inquilino/a; (*of boat, car*) ocupante *m/f*.
occupation [ɔkju'peɪʃən] *n* (*of house*)
tenencia; (*job*) trabajo; (: *calling*) oficio.
occupational accident [ɔkju'peɪʃənl] *n*
accidente *m* laboral.
occupational guidance *n* orientación *f*
profesional.
occupational hazard *n* gajes *mpl* del
oficio.
occupational pension scheme *n* plan *m*
profesional de jubilación.
occupational therapy *n* terapia
ocupacional.
occupier ['ɔkjupaɪə*] *n* inquilino/a.
occupy ['ɔkjupaɪ] *vt* (*seat, post, time*)
ocupar; (*house*) habitar; **to ~ o.s. with** *or*
by doing (*as job*) dedicarse a hacer; (*to
pass time*) entretenerse haciendo; **to be
occupied with sth/in doing sth** estar
ocupado con algo/haciendo algo.
occur [ə'kəː*] *vi* ocurrir, suceder; **to ~ to
sb** ocurrírsele a algn.
occurrence [ə'kʌrəns] *n* suceso.
ocean ['əuʃən] *n* océano; **~s of** (*col*) la mar
de.
ocean bed *n* fondo del océano.
ocean-going ['əuʃəngəuɪŋ] *adj* de alta mar.
Oceania [əuʃɪ'eɪnɪə] *n* Oceanía.

ocean liner *n* buque *m* transoceánico.
ochre, (*US*) **ocher** ['əukə*] *n* ocre *m*.
o'clock [ə'klɔk] *adv*: **it is 5 ~** son las 5.
OCR *n abbr see* **optical character
recognition/reader**.
Oct. *abbr* (= *October*) oct.
octagonal [ɔk'tægənl] *adj* octagonal.
octane ['ɔkteɪn] *n* octano; **high ~ petrol** *or*
(*US*) **gas** gasolina de alto octanaje.
octave ['ɔktɪv] *n* octava.
October [ɔk'təubə*] *n* octubre *m*.
octogenarian ['ɔktəudʒɪ'nɛərɪən] *n*
octogenario/a.
octopus ['ɔktəpəs] *n* pulpo.
oculist ['ɔkjulɪst] *n* oculista *m/f*.
odd [ɔd] *adj* (*strange*) extraño, raro;
(*number*) impar; (*left over*) sobrante,
suelto; **60–~** 60 y pico; **at ~ times** de vez
en cuando; **to be the ~ one out** estar de
más; **if you have the ~ minute** si tienes
unos minutos libres; *see also* **odds**.
oddball ['ɔdbɔːl] *n* (*col*) bicho raro.
oddity ['ɔdɪtɪ] *n* rareza; (*person*)
excéntrico/a.
odd-job man [ɔd'dʒɔb-] *n* hombre *m* que
hace chapuzas.
odd jobs *npl* chapuzas *fpl*.
oddly ['ɔdlɪ] *adv* extrañamente.
oddments ['ɔdmənts] *npl* (*BRIT COMM*)
restos *mpl*.
odds [ɔdz] *npl* (*in betting*) puntos *mpl* de
ventaja; **it makes no ~** da lo mismo; **at ~**
reñidos/as; **to succeed against all the ~**
tener éxito contra todo pronóstico; **~ and
ends** cachivaches *mpl*.
odds-on [ɔdz'ɔn] *adj* (*col*): **the ~ favourite**
el máximo favorito; **it's ~ he'll come**
seguro que viene.
ode [əud] *n* oda.
odious ['əudɪəs] *adj* odioso.
odometer [ɔ'dɔmɪtə*] *n* (*US*)
cuentakilómetros *m inv*.
odour, (*US*) **odor** ['əudə*] *n* olor *m*;
(*perfume*) perfume *m*.
odo(u)rless ['əudəlɪs] *adj* sin olor.
OECD *n abbr* (= *Organization for
Economic Co-operation and Development*)
OCDE *f*.
oesophagus, (*US*) **esophagus** [iː'sɔfəgəs]
n esófago.
oestrogen, (*US*) **estrogen** ['iːstrədʒən] *n*
estrógeno.

═══════════ *KEYWORD*

of [ɔv, əv] *prep* **1** (*gen*) de; **a friend ~ ours** un
amigo nuestro; **a boy ~ 10** un chico de 10
años; **that was kind ~ you** eso fue muy
amable de tu parte

2 (*expressing quantity, amount, dates etc*) de; **a kilo ~ flour** un kilo de harina; **there were 3 ~ them** había tres; **3 ~ us went** tres de nosotros fuimos; **the 5th ~ July** el 5 de julio; **a quarter ~ 4** (*US*) las 4 menos cuarto
3 (*from, out of*) de; **made ~ wood** (hecho) de madera.

off [ɔf] *adj, adv* (*engine, light*) apagado; (*tap*) cerrado; (*BRIT: food: bad*) pasado, malo; (*: milk*) cortado; (*cancelled*) suspendido; (*removed*): **the lid was ~** no estaba puesta la tapadera ♦ *prep* de; **to be ~** (*to leave*) irse, marcharse; **to be ~ sick** estar enfermo *or* de baja; **a day ~** un día libre; **to have an ~ day** tener un mal día; **he had his coat ~** se había quitado el abrigo; **10% ~** (*COMM*) (con el) 10% de descuento; **it's a long way ~** está muy lejos; **5 km ~ (the road)** a 5 km (de la carretera); **~ the coast** frente a la costa; **I'm ~ meat** (*no longer eat/like it*) paso de la carne; **on the ~ chance** por si acaso; **~ and on, on and ~** de vez en cuando; **I must be ~** tengo que irme; **to be well/ badly ~** andar bien/mal de dinero; **I'm afraid the chicken is ~** desgraciadamente ya no queda pollo; **that's a bit ~, isn't it!** (*fig, col*) ¡eso no se hace!

offal ['ɔfl] *n* (*BRIT CULIN*) menudillos *mpl*, asaduras *fpl*.

off-centre, (*US*) **off-center** [ɔf'sɛntə*] *adj* descentrado, ladeado.

off-colour ['ɔf'kʌlə*] *adj* (*BRIT: ill*) indispuesto; **to feel ~** sentirse *or* estar mal.

offence, (*US*) **offense** [ə'fɛns] *n* (*crime*) delito; (*insult*) ofensa; **to take ~ at** ofenderse por; **to commit an ~** cometer un delito.

offend [ə'fɛnd] *vt* (*person*) ofender ♦ *vi*: **to ~ against** (*law, rule*) infringir.

offender [ə'fɛndə*] *n* delincuente *m/f*; (*against regulations*) infractor(a) *m/f*.

offending [ə'fɛndɪŋ] *adj* culpable; (*object*) molesto; (*word*) problemático.

offense [ə'fɛns] *n* (*US*) = **offence**.

offensive [ə'fɛnsɪv] *adj* ofensivo; (*smell etc*) repugnante ♦ *n* (*MIL*) ofensiva.

offer ['ɔfə*] *n* (*gen*) oferta, ofrecimiento; (*proposal*) propuesta ♦ *vt* ofrecer; "**on ~**" (*COMM*) "en oferta"; **to make an ~ for sth** hacer una oferta por algo; **to ~ sth to sb, ~ sb sth** ofrecer algo a algn; **to ~ to do sth** ofrecerse a hacer algo.

offering ['ɔfərɪŋ] *n* (*REL*) ofrenda.

offer price *n* precio de oferta.

offertory ['ɔfətrɪ] *n* (*REL*) ofertorio.

offhand [ɔf'hænd] *adj* informal; (*brusque*) desconsiderado ♦ *adv* de improviso, sin pensarlo; **I can't tell you ~** no te lo puedo decir así de improviso *or* así nomás (*LAM*).

office ['ɔfɪs] *n* (*place*) oficina; (*room*) despacho; (*position*) cargo, oficio; **doctor's ~** (*US*) consultorio; **to take ~** entrar en funciones; **through his good ~s** gracias a sus buenos oficios; **O~ of Fair Trading** (*BRIT*) *oficina que regula normas comerciales*.

office automation *n* ofimática, buromática.

office bearer *n* (*of club etc*) titular *m/f* (de una cartera).

office block, (*US*) **office building** *n* bloque *m* de oficinas.

office boy *n* ordenanza *m*.

office hours *npl* horas *fpl* de oficina; (*US MED*) horas *fpl* de consulta.

office manager *n* jefe/a *m/f* de oficina.

officer ['ɔfɪsə*] *n* (*MIL etc*) oficial *m/f*; (*of organization*) director(a) *m/f*; (*also*: **police ~**) agente *m/f* de policía.

office work *n* trabajo de oficina.

office worker *n* oficinista *m/f*.

official [ə'fɪʃl] *adj* (*authorized*) oficial, autorizado; (*strike*) oficial ♦ *n* funcionario/a.

officialdom [ə'fɪʃldəm] *n* burocracia.

officially [ə'fɪʃəlɪ] *adv* oficialmente.

official receiver *n* síndico.

officiate [ə'fɪʃɪeɪt] *vi* (*also REL*) oficiar; **to ~ as Mayor** ejercer las funciones de alcalde; **to ~ at a marriage** celebrar una boda.

officious [ə'fɪʃəs] *adj* oficioso.

offing ['ɔfɪŋ] *n*: **in the ~** (*fig*) en perspectiva.

off-key [ɔf'kiː] *adj* desafinado ♦ *adv* desafinadamente.

off-licence ['ɔflaɪsns] *n* (*BRIT: shop*) tienda de bebidas alcohólicas.

En el Reino Unido una **off-licence** es una tienda especializada en la venta de bebidas alcohólicas para el consumo fuera del establecimiento. De ahí su nombre, pues se necesita un permiso especial para tal venta, que está estrictamente regulada. Suelen vender además bebidas sin alcohol, tabaco, chocolate, patatas fritas etc y a menudo son parte de grandes cadenas nacionales.

off-limits [ɔf'lɪmɪts] *adj* (*US MIL*) prohibido al personal militar.

off line adj, adv (COMPUT) fuera de línea; (switched off) desconectado.

off-load ['ɔfləud] vt descargar, desembarcar.

off-peak ['ɔf'piːk] adj (holiday) de temporada baja; (electricity) de banda económica.

off-putting ['ɔfputɪŋ] adj (BRIT: person) poco amable, difícil; (behaviour) chocante.

off-season ['ɔf'siːzn] adj, adv fuera de temporada.

offset ['ɔfsɛt] vt (irreg: like set) (counteract) contrarrestar, compensar ♦ n (also: ~ printing) offset m.

offshoot ['ɔfʃuːt] n (BOT) vástago; (fig) ramificación f.

offshore [ɔf'ʃɔː*] adj (breeze, island) costero/a; (fishing) de bajura; ~ oilfield campo petrolífero submarino.

offside ['ɔf'saɪd] n (AUT: with right-hand drive) lado derecho; (: with left-hand drive) lado izquierdo ♦ adj (SPORT) fuera de juego; (AUT) del lado derecho; del lado izquierdo.

offspring ['ɔfsprɪŋ] n descendencia.

offstage [ɔf'steɪdʒ] adv entre bastidores.

off-the-cuff [ɔfðə'kʌf] adj espontáneo.

off-the-job [ɔfðə'dʒɔb] adj: ~ training formación f fuera del trabajo.

off-the-peg [ɔfðə'pɛg], (US) **off-the-rack** [ɔfðə'ræk] adv confeccionado.

off-the-record ['ɔfðə'rɛkɔːd] adj extraoficial, confidencial ♦ adv extraoficialmente, confidencialmente.

off-white ['ɔfwaɪt] adj blanco grisáceo.

Ofgas ['ɔfgæs] n (BRIT: = Office of Gas Supply) organismo que controla a las empresas del gas en Gran Bretaña.

Oftel ['ɔftɛl] n (BRIT: = Office of Telecommunications) organismo que controla las telecomunicaciones británicas.

often ['ɔfn] adv a menudo, con frecuencia, seguido (LAM); **how ~ do you go?** ¿cada cuánto vas?

Ofwat ['ɔfwɔt] n (BRIT: = Office of Water Services) organismo que controla a las empresas suministradoras del agua en Inglaterra y Gales.

ogle ['əugl] vt comerse con los ojos a.

ogre ['əugə*] n ogro.

OH abbr (US) = Ohio.

oh [əu] excl ¡ah!

OHMS abbr (BRIT) On His (or Her) Majesty's Service.

oil [ɔɪl] n aceite m; (petroleum) petróleo ♦ vt (machine) engrasar; **fried in ~** frito en aceite.

oilcan ['ɔɪlkæn] n lata de aceite.

oilfield ['ɔɪlfiːld] n campo petrolífero.

oil filter n (AUT) filtro de aceite.

oil-fired ['ɔɪlfaɪəd] adj de fuel-oil.

oil gauge n indicador m del aceite.

oil industry n industria petrolífera.

oil level n nivel m del aceite.

oil painting n pintura al óleo.

oil refinery n refinería de petróleo.

oil rig n torre f de perforación.

oilskins ['ɔɪlskɪnz] npl impermeable msg, chubasquero sg.

oil tanker n petrolero.

oil well n pozo (de petróleo).

oily ['ɔɪlɪ] adj aceitoso; (food) grasiento.

ointment ['ɔɪntmənt] n ungüento.

OK abbr (US) = Oklahoma.

O.K., okay ['əu'keɪ] excl O.K., ¡está bien!, ¡vale! ♦ adj bien ♦ n: **to give sth one's ~** dar el visto bueno a or aprobar algo ♦ vt dar el visto bueno a; **it's ~ with** or **by me** estoy de acuerdo, me parece bien; **are you ~ for money?** ¿andas or vas bien de dinero?

Okla. abbr (US) = Oklahoma.

old [əuld] adj viejo; (former) antiguo; **how ~ are you?** ¿cuántos años tienes?, ¿qué edad tienes?; **he's 10 years ~** tiene 10 años; **~er brother** hermano mayor; **any thing will do** sirve cualquier cosa.

old age n vejez f.

old-age pension ['əuldeɪdʒ-] n (BRIT) jubilación f, pensión f.

old-age pensioner (OAP) ['əuldeɪdʒ-] n (BRIT) jubilado/a.

olden ['əuldən] adj antiguo.

old-fashioned ['əuld'fæʃənd] adj anticuado, pasado de moda.

old maid n solterona.

old-style ['əuldstaɪl] adj tradicional, chapado a la antigua.

old-time ['əuld'taɪm] adj antiguo, de antaño.

old-timer [əuld'taɪmə*] n veterano/a; (old person) anciano/a.

old wives' tale n cuento de viejas, patraña.

olive ['ɔlɪv] n (fruit) aceituna; (tree) olivo ♦ adj (also: ~-green) verde oliva inv.

olive branch n (fig): **to offer an ~ to sb** ofrecer hacer las paces con algn.

olive oil n aceite m de oliva.

Olympic [əu'lɪmpɪk] adj olímpico; **the ~ Games, the ~s** npl las Olimpíadas.

OM n abbr (BRIT: = Order of Merit) título ceremonial.

O & M n abbr = organization and method.

Oman [əu'maːn] n Omán m.

OMB n abbr (US: = Office of Management and

Budget) servicio que asesora al presidente en materia presupuestaria.
omelet(te) ['ɔmlɪt] *n* tortilla, tortilla de huevo (*LAM*).
omen ['əumən] *n* presagio.
ominous ['ɔmɪnəs] *adj* de mal agüero, amenazador(a).
omission [əu'mɪʃən] *n* omisión *f*; (*error*) descuido.
omit [əu'mɪt] *vt* omitir; (*by mistake*) olvidar, descuidar; **to ~ to do sth** olvidarse *or* dejar de hacer algo.
omnivorous [ɔm'nɪvərəs] *adj* omnívoro.
ON *abbr* (*Canada*) = Ontario.

================ *KEYWORD*

on [ɔn] *prep* **1** (*indicating position*) en; sobre; **~ the wall** en la pared; **it's ~ the table** está sobre *or* en la mesa; **~ the left** a la izquierda; **I haven't got any money ~ me** no llevo dinero encima
2 (*indicating means, method, condition etc*): **~ foot** a pie; **~ the train/plane** (*go*) en tren/avión; (*be*) en el tren/el avión; **~ the radio/television** por *or* en la radio/televisión; **~ the telephone** al teléfono; **to be ~ drugs** drogarse; (*MED*) estar a tratamiento; **to be ~ holiday/business** estar de vacaciones/en viaje de negocios; **we're ~ irregular verbs** estamos con los verbos irregulares
3 (*referring to time*): **~ Friday** el viernes; **~ Fridays** los viernes; **~ June 20th** el 20 de junio; **a week ~ Friday** del viernes en una semana; **~ arrival** al llegar; **~ seeing this** al ver esto
4 (*about, concerning*) sobre, acerca de; **a book ~ physics** un libro de *or* sobre física
5 (*at the expense of*): **this round's ~ me** esta ronda la pago yo, invito yo (a esta ronda); (*earning*): **he's ~ £16,000 a year** gana dieciséis mil libras al año
♦ *adv* **1** (*referring to dress*): **to have one's coat ~** tener *or* llevar el abrigo puesto; **she put her gloves ~** se puso los guantes
2 (*referring to covering*): **"screw the lid ~ tightly"** "cerrar bien la tapa"
3 (*further, continuously*): **to walk/run** *etc* **~** seguir caminando/corriendo *etc*; **from that day ~** desde aquel día; **it was well ~ in the evening** estaba ya entrada la tarde
4 (*in phrases*): **I'm ~ to sth** creo haber encontrado algo; **my father's always ~ at me to get a job** (*col*) mi padre siempre me está dando la lata para que me ponga a trabajar
♦ *adj* **1** (*functioning, in operation: machine,*

radio, TV, light) encendido/a (*SP*), prendido/a (*LAM*); (: *tap*) abierto/a; (: *brakes*) echado/a, puesto/a; **is the meeting still ~?** (*in progress*) ¿todavía continúa la reunión?; (*not cancelled*) ¿va a haber reunión al fin?; **there's a good film ~ at the cinema** ponen una buena película en el cine
2: that's not ~! (*inf: not possible*) ¡eso ni hablar!; (: *not acceptable*) ¡eso no se hace!

ONC *n abbr* (*BRIT*: = Ordinary National Certificate*) título escolar.
once [wʌns] *adv* una vez; (*formerly*) antiguamente ♦ *conj* una vez que; **~ he had left/it was done** una vez que se había marchado/se hizo; **at ~** en seguida, inmediatamente; (*simultaneously*) a la vez; **~ a week** una vez a la semana; **~ more** otra vez; **~ and for all** de una vez por todas; **~ upon a time** érase una vez; **I knew him ~** le conocía hace tiempo.
oncoming ['ɔnkʌmɪŋ] *adj* (*traffic*) que viene de frente.
OND *n abbr* (*BRIT*: = Ordinary National Diploma*) título escolar.

================ *KEYWORD*

one [wʌn] *num* un(o)/una; **~ hundred and fifty** ciento cincuenta; **~ by ~** uno a uno; **it's ~** (*o'clock*) es la una
♦ *adj* **1** (*sole*) único; **the ~ book which** el único libro que; **the ~ man who** el único que
2 (*same*) mismo/a; **they came in the ~ car** vinieron en un solo coche
♦ *pron* **1: this ~** éste/ésta; **that ~** ése/ésa; (*more remote*) aquél/aquélla; **I've already got (a red) ~** ya tengo uno/a (rojo/a); **~ by ~** uno/a por uno/a; **to be ~ up on sb** llevar ventaja a algn; **to be at ~ (with sb)** estar completamente de acuerdo (con algn)
2: ~ another (*US*) nos; (*you*) os (*SP*); (*you: polite, them*) se; **do you two ever see ~ another?** ¿os veis alguna vez? (*SP*), ¿se ven alguna vez?; **the two boys didn't dare look at ~ another** los dos chicos no se atrevieron a mirarse (el uno al otro); **they all kissed ~ another** se besaron unos a otros
3 (*impers*): **~ never knows** nunca se sabe; **to cut ~'s finger** cortarse el dedo; **~ needs to eat** hay que comer.

one-armed bandit ['wʌnɑːmd-] *n* máquina tragaperras.
one-day excursion ['wʌndeɪ-] *n* (*US*)

billete *m* de ida y vuelta en un día.
One-hundred share index ['wʌnhʌndrəd-] *n* índice *m* bursátil (*del Financial Times*).
one-man ['wʌn'mæn] *adj* (*business*) individual.
one-man band *n* hombre-orquesta *m*.
one-off [wʌn'ɔf] *n* (*BRIT col: object*) artículo único; (: *event*) caso especial.
one-parent family ['wʌnpɛərənt-] *n* familia monoparental.
one-piece ['wʌnpiːs] *adj* (*bathing suit*) de una pieza.
onerous ['ɔnərəs] *adj* (*task, duty*) pesado; (*responsibility*) oneroso.
oneself [wʌn'sɛlf] *pron* uno mismo; (*after prep, also emphatic*) sí (mismo/a); **to do sth by** ~ hacer algo solo *or* por sí solo.
one-shot [wʌn'ʃɔt] *n* (*US*) = **one-off.**
one-sided [wʌn'saɪdɪd] *adj* (*argument*) parcial; (*decision, view*) unilateral; (*game, contest*) desigual.
one-time ['wʌntaɪm] *adj* antiguo, ex-.
one-to-one ['wʌntəwʌn] *adj* (*relationship*) individualizado.
one-upmanship [wʌn'ʌpmənʃɪp] *n*: **the art of** ~ el arte de quedar siempre por encima.
one-way ['wʌnweɪ] *adj* (*street, traffic*) de dirección única; (*ticket*) sencillo.
ongoing ['ɔngəʊɪŋ] *adj* continuo.
onion ['ʌnjən] *n* cebolla.
on line *adj, adv* (*COMPUT*) en línea; (*switched on*) conectado.
onlooker ['ɔnlukə*] *n* espectador(a) *m/f*.
only ['əunlɪ] *adv* solamente, sólo, nomás (*LAM*) ♦ *adj* único, solo ♦ *conj* solamente que, pero; **an** ~ **child** un hijo único; **not** ~ ... **but also**... no sólo ... sino también...; **I'd be** ~ **too pleased to help** encantado de ayudarles; **I saw her** ~ **yesterday** le vi ayer mismo; **I would come,** ~ **I'm very busy** iría, sólo que estoy muy atareado.
ono *abbr* (= *or nearest offer: in classified ads*) abierto ofertas.
onset ['ɔnsɛt] *n* comienzo.
onshore ['ɔnʃɔː*] *adj* (*wind*) que sopla del mar hacia la tierra.
onslaught ['ɔnslɔːt] *n* ataque *m*, embestida.
Ont. *abbr* (*Canada*) = Ontario.
on-the-job ['ɔnðə'dʒɔb] *adj*: ~ **training** formación *f* en el trabajo *or* sobre la práctica.
onto ['ɔntu] *prep* = **on to.**
onus ['əunəs] *n* responsabilidad *f*; **the** ~ **is upon him to prove it** le incumbe a él demostrarlo.
onward(s) ['ɔnwəd(z)] *adv* (*move*) (hacia) adelante.

onyx ['ɔnɪks] *n* ónice *m*, onyx *m*.
oops [ups] *excl* (*also:* ~-**a-daisy**!) ¡huy!
ooze [uːz] *vi* rezumar.
opal ['əupl] *n* ópalo.
opaque [əu'peɪk] *adj* opaco.
OPEC ['əupɛk] *n abbr* (= *Organization of Petroleum-Exporting Countries*) OPEP *f*.
open ['əupn] *adj* abierto; (*car*) descubierto; (*road, view*) despejado; (*meeting*) público; (*admiration*) manifiesto ♦ *vt* abrir ♦ *vi* (*flower, eyes, door, debate*) abrirse; (*book etc: commence*) comenzar; **in the** ~ **(air)** al aire libre; ~ **verdict** veredicto inconcluso; ~ **ticket** billete *m* sin fecha; ~ **ground** (*among trees*) claro; (*waste ground*) solar *m*; **to have an** ~ **mind (on sth)** estar sin decidirse aún (sobre algo); **to** ~ **a bank account** abrir una cuenta en el banco.
▶**open on to** *vt fus* (*subj: room, door*) dar a.
▶**open out** *vt* abrir ♦ *vi* (*person*) abrirse.
▶**open up** *vt* abrir; (*blocked road*) despejar ♦ *vi* abrirse.
open-and-shut ['əupənən'ʃʌt] *adj*: ~ **case** caso claro *or* evidente.
open day *n* (*BRIT*) jornada de puertas abiertas *or* acceso público.
open-ended [əupn'ɛndɪd] *adj* (*fig*) indefinido, sin definir.
opener ['əupnə*] *n* (*also:* **can** ~, **tin** ~) abrelatas *m inv*.
open-heart surgery [əupn'hɑːt-] *n* cirugía a corazón abierto.
opening ['əupnɪŋ] *n* abertura; (*beginning*) comienzo; (*opportunity*) oportunidad *f*; (*job*) puesto vacante, vacante *f*.
opening night *n* estreno.
open learning *n* enseñanza flexible a tiempo parcial.
openly ['əupnlɪ] *adv* abiertamente.
open-minded [əupn'maɪndɪd] *adj* de amplias miras, sin prejuicios.
open-necked ['əupnnɛkt] *adj* sin corbata.
openness ['əupnnɪs] *n* (*frankness*) franqueza.
open-plan ['əupn'plæn] *adj* sin tabiques, de plan abierto.
open prison *n* centro penitenciario de régimen abierto.
open return *n* vuelta con fecha abierta.
open shop *n empresa que contrata a mano de obra no afiliada a ningún sindicato.*
Open University *n* (*BRIT*) ≈ Universidad *f* Nacional de Enseñanza a Distancia, UNED *f*.

La **Open University**, *fundada en 1969, está especializada en impartir cursos a distancia y a tiempo parcial con sus propios materiales de apoyo diseñados para tal fin, entre ellos programas de radio y televisión emitidos por la* **BBC**. *Los trabajos se envían por correo y se complementan con la asistencia obligatoria a cursos de verano. Para obtener la licenciatura es necesario estudiar un mínimo de módulos y alcanzar un determinado número de créditos.*

opera ['ɔpərə] n ópera.
opera glasses npl gemelos mpl.
opera house n teatro de la ópera.
opera singer n cantante m/f de ópera.
operate ['ɔpəreɪt] vt (machine) hacer funcionar; (company) dirigir ♦ vi funcionar; (drug) hacer efecto; **to ~ on sb** (MED) operar a algn.
operatic [ɔpə'rætɪk] adj de ópera.
operating costs ['ɔpəreɪtɪŋ-] npl gastos mpl operacionales.
operating profit n beneficio de explotación.
operating room n (US) quirófano, sala de operaciones.
operating table n mesa de operaciones.
operating theatre n quirófano, sala de operaciones.
operation [ɔpə'reɪʃən] n (gen) operación f; (of machine) funcionamiento; **to be in ~** estar funcionando or en funcionamiento; **to have an ~** (MED) ser operado; **to have an ~ for** operarse de; **the company's ~s during the year** las actividades de la compañía durante el año.
operational [ɔpə'reɪʃənl] adj operacional, en buen estado; (COMM) en condiciones de servicio; (ready for use or action) en condiciones de funcionar; **when the service is fully ~** cuando el servicio esté en pleno funcionamiento.
operative ['ɔpərətɪv] adj (measure) en vigor; **the ~ word** la palabra clave.
operator ['ɔpəreɪtə*] n (of machine) operario/a; (TEL) operador(a) m/f, telefonista m/f.
operetta [ɔpə'rɛtə] n opereta.
ophthalmic [ɔf'θælmɪk] adj oftálmico.
ophthalmologist [ɔfθæl'mɔlədʒɪst] n oftalmólogo/a.
opinion [ə'pɪnjən] n (gen) opinión f; **in my ~** en mi opinión, a mi juicio; **to seek a second ~** pedir una segunda opinión.
opinionated [ə'pɪnjəneɪtɪd] adj testarudo.
opinion poll n encuesta, sondeo.

opium ['əupɪəm] n opio.
opponent [ə'pəunənt] n adversario/a, contrincante m/f.
opportune ['ɔpətjuːn] adj oportuno.
opportunism [ɔpə'tjuːnɪzm] n oportunismo.
opportunist [ɔpə'tjuːnɪst] n oportunista m/f.
opportunity [ɔpə'tjuːnɪtɪ] n oportunidad f, chance m or f (LAM); **to take the ~ to do** or **of doing** aprovechar la ocasión para hacer.
oppose [ə'pəuz] vt oponerse a; **to be ~d to sth** oponerse a algo; **as ~d to** en vez de; (unlike) a diferencia de.
opposing [ə'pəuzɪŋ] adj (side) opuesto, contrario.
opposite ['ɔpəzɪt] adj opuesto, contrario; (house etc) de enfrente ♦ adv en frente ♦ prep en frente de, frente a ♦ n lo contrario; **the ~ sex** el otro sexo, el sexo opuesto.
opposite number n (BRIT) homólogo/a.
opposition [ɔpə'zɪʃən] n oposición f.
oppress [ə'prɛs] vt oprimir.
oppression [ə'prɛʃən] n opresión f.
oppressive [ə'prɛsɪv] adj opresivo.
opprobrium [ə'prəubrɪəm] n (formal) oprobio.
opt [ɔpt] vi: **to ~ for** optar por; **to ~ to do** optar por hacer; **to ~ out** (of NHS etc) salirse.
optical ['ɔptɪkl] adj óptico.
optical character recognition/reader (OCR) n reconocimiento/lector m óptico de caracteres.
optical fibre n fibra óptica.
optician [ɔp'tɪʃən] n óptico m/f.
optics ['ɔptɪks] n óptica.
optimism ['ɔptɪmɪzəm] n optimismo.
optimist ['ɔptɪmɪst] n optimista m/f.
optimistic [ɔptɪ'mɪstɪk] adj optimista.
optimum ['ɔptɪməm] adj óptimo.
option ['ɔpʃən] n opción f; **to keep one's ~s open** (fig) mantener las opciones abiertas; **I have no ~** no tengo más or otro remedio.
optional ['ɔpʃənl] adj opcional; (course) optativo; **~ extras** opciones fpl extras.
opulence ['ɔpjuləns] n opulencia.
opulent ['ɔpjulənt] adj opulento.
OR abbr (US) = Oregon.
or [ɔː*] conj o; (before o, ho) u; (with negative): **he hasn't seen ~ heard anything** no ha visto ni oído nada; **~ else** si no; **let me go ~ I'll scream!** ¡suélteme, o me pongo a gritar!
oracle ['ɔrəkl] n oráculo.
oral ['ɔːrəl] adj oral ♦ n examen m oral.

orange ['ɔrɪndʒ] *n* (*fruit*) naranja ♦ *adj* (de color) naranja.

orangeade [ɔrɪndʒ'eɪd] *n* naranjada, refresco de naranja.

orange squash *n* zumo (*SP*) *or* jugo de naranja.

orang-outang, orang-utan [ɔ'ræŋuː'tæn] *n* orangután *m*.

oration [ɔː'reɪʃən] *n* discurso solemne; **funeral** ~ oración *f* fúnebre.

orator ['ɔrətə*] *n* orador(a) *m/f*.

oratorio [ɔrə'tɔːrɪəu] *n* oratorio.

orbit ['ɔːbɪt] *n* órbita ♦ *vt, vi* orbitar; **to be in/go into** ~ **(round)** estar en/entrar en órbita (alrededor de).

orbital ['ɔːbɪtl] *n* (*also*: ~ **motorway**) autopista de circunvalación.

orchard ['ɔːtʃəd] *n* huerto; **apple** ~ manzanar *m*, manzanal *m*.

orchestra ['ɔːkɪstrə] *n* orquesta; (*US*: *seating*) platea.

orchestral [ɔː'kɛstrəl] *adj* de orquesta.

orchestrate ['ɔːkɪstreɪt] *vt* (*MUS, fig*) orquestar.

orchid ['ɔːkɪd] *n* orquídea.

ordain [ɔː'deɪn] *vt* (*also REL*) ordenar.

ordeal [ɔː'diːl] *n* experiencia terrible.

order ['ɔːdə*] *n* orden *m*; (*command*) orden *f*; (*type, kind*) clase *f*; (*state*) estado; (*COMM*) pedido, encargo ♦ *vt* (*also*: **put in** ~) ordenar, poner en orden; (*COMM*) encargar, pedir; (*command*) mandar, ordenar; **in** ~ (*gen*) en orden; (*of document*) en regla; **in (working)** ~ en funcionamiento; **a machine in working** ~ una máquina en funcionamiento; **to be out of** ~ (*machine, toilets*) estar estropeado *or* descompuesto (*LAM*); **in** ~ **to do** para hacer; **in** ~ **that** para que + *subj*; **on** ~ (*COMM*) pedido; **to be on** ~ estar pedido; **we are under ~s to do it** tenemos orden de hacerlo; **a point of** ~ una cuestión de procedimiento; **to place an** ~ **for sth with sb** hacer un pedido de algo a algn; **made to** ~ hecho a la medida; **his income is of the** ~ **of £24,000 per year** sus ingresos son del orden de 24 mil libras al año; **to the** ~ **of** (*BANKING*) a la orden de; **to** ~ **sb to do sth** mandar a algn hacer algo.

order book *n* cartera de pedidos.

order form *n* hoja de pedido.

orderly ['ɔːdəlɪ] *n* (*MIL*) ordenanza *m*; (*MED*) auxiliar *m/f* (de hospital) ♦ *adj* ordenado.

orderly officer *n* (*MIL*) oficial *m* del día.

order number *n* número de pedido.

ordinal ['ɔːdɪnl] *adj* ordinal.

ordinarily ['ɔːdnrɪlɪ] *adv* por lo común.

ordinary ['ɔːdnrɪ] *adj* corriente, normal; (*pej*) común y corriente; **out of the** ~ fuera de lo común, extraordinario.

Después de tres años de estudios, algunos universitarios obtienen la titulación de **ordinary degree**. *Esto ocurre en el caso poco frecuente de que no aprueben los exámenes que conducen al título de* **honours degree** *pero sus examinadores consideren que a lo largo de la carrera han logrado unos resultados mínimos satisfactorios. También es una opción que tienen los estudiantes de las universidades escocesas no interesados en estudiar en la universidad más de tres años.*

ordinary seaman *n* (*BRIT*) marinero.

ordinary shares *npl* acciones *fpl* ordinarias.

ordination [ɔːdɪ'neɪʃən] *n* ordenación *f*.

ordnance ['ɔːdnəns] *n* (*MIL*: *unit*) artillería.

ordnance factory *n* fábrica de artillería.

Ordnance Survey *n* (*BRIT*) servicio oficial de topografía y cartografía.

ore [ɔː*] *n* mineral *m*.

Ore(g). *abbr* (*US*) = *Oregon*.

organ ['ɔːgən] *n* órgano.

organic [ɔː'gænɪk] *adj* orgánico.

organism ['ɔːgənɪzəm] *n* organismo.

organist ['ɔːgənɪst] *n* organista *m/f*.

organization [ɔːgənaɪ'zeɪʃən] *n* organización *f*.

organization chart *n* organigrama *m*.

organize ['ɔːgənaɪz] *vt* organizar; **to get ~d** organizarse.

organized crime *n* crimen organizado.

organizer ['ɔːgənaɪzə*] *n* organizador(a) *m/f*.

orgasm ['ɔːgæzəm] *n* orgasmo.

orgy ['ɔːdʒɪ] *n* orgía.

Orient ['ɔːrɪənt] *n* Oriente *m*.

oriental [ɔːrɪ'ɛntl] *adj* oriental.

orientate ['ɔːrɪənteɪt] *vt* orientar.

origin ['ɔrɪdʒɪn] *n* origen *m*; (*point of departure*) procedencia.

original [ə'rɪdʒɪnl] *adj* original; (*first*) primero; (*earlier*) primitivo ♦ *n* original *m*.

originality [ərɪdʒɪ'nælɪtɪ] *n* originalidad *f*.

originally [ə'rɪdʒɪnəlɪ] *adv* (*at first*) al principio; (*with originality*) con originalidad.

originate [ə'rɪdʒɪneɪt] *vi*: **to** ~ **from, to** ~ **in** surgir de, tener su origen en.

originator [ə'rɪdʒɪneɪtə*] *n* inventor(a) *m/f*, autor(a) *m/f*.

Orkneys ['ɔːknɪz] *npl*: **the** ~ (*also*: **the Orkney Islands**) las Orcadas.

ornament ['ɔːnəmənt] *n* adorno.
ornamental [ɔːnə'mentl] *adj* decorativo, de adorno.
ornamentation [ɔːnəmen'teɪʃən] *n* ornamentación *f*.
ornate [ɔː'neɪt] *adj* recargado.
ornithologist [ɔːnɪ'θɔlədʒɪst] *n* ornitólogo/a.
ornithology [ɔːnɪ'θɔlədʒɪ] *n* ornitología.
orphan ['ɔːfn] *n* huérfano/a ♦ *vt*: **to be ~ed** quedar huérfano/a.
orphanage ['ɔːfənɪdʒ] *n* orfanato.
orthodox ['ɔːθədɔks] *adj* ortodoxo.
orthodoxy ['ɔːθədɔksɪ] *n* ortodoxia.
orthopaedic, (*US*) **orthopedic** [ɔːθə'piːdɪk] *adj* ortopédico.
orthop(a)edics [ɔːθə'piːdɪks] *n* ortopedia.
OS *abbr* (*BRIT*: = *Ordnance Survey*) *servicio oficial de topografía y cartografía*; (: *NAUT*) = **ordinary seaman**; (: *DRESS*) = **outsize**.
O/S *abbr* = **out of stock**.
Oscar ['ɔskə*] *n* óscar *m*.
oscillate ['ɔsɪleɪt] *vi* oscilar; (*person*) vacilar.
oscillation [ɔsɪ'leɪʃən] *n* oscilación *f*; (*of prices*) fluctuación *f*.
OSHA *n abbr* (*US*: = *Occupational Safety and Health Administration*) *oficina de la higiene y la seguridad en el trabajo*.
Oslo ['ɔzləu] *n* Oslo.
ostensible [ɔs'tensɪbl] *adj* aparente.
ostensibly [ɔs'tensɪblɪ] *adv* aparentemente.
ostentatious [ɔsten'teɪʃəs] *adj* pretencioso, aparatoso; (*person*) ostentativo.
osteopath ['ɔstɪəpæθ] *n* osteópata *m/f*.
ostracize ['ɔstrəsaɪz] *vt* hacer el vacío a.
ostrich ['ɔstrɪtʃ] *n* avestruz *m*.
OT *n abbr* (= *Old Testament*) A.T. *m*.
OTB *n abbr* (*US*: = *off-track betting*) *apuestas hechas fuera del hipódromo*.
O.T.E. *abbr* (= *on-target earnings*) *beneficios según objetivos*.
other ['ʌðə*] *adj* otro ♦ *pron*: **the ~** (*one*) el/la otro/a; **~s** (*~ people*) otros; **~ than** (*apart from*) aparte de; **the ~ day** el otro día; **some ~ people have still to arrive** quedan por llegar otros; **some actor or ~** un actor cualquiera; **somebody or ~** alguien, alguno; **it was no ~ than the bishop** no era otro que el obispo.
otherwise ['ʌðəwaɪz] *adv, conj* de otra manera; (*if not*) si no; **an ~ good piece of work** un trabajo que, quitando eso, es bueno.
OTT *abbr* (*col*) = **over the top;** *see* **top**.
otter ['ɔtə*] *n* nutria.
OU *n abbr* (*BRIT*) = **Open University**.

ouch [autʃ] *excl* ¡ay!
ought, *pt* **ought** [ɔːt] *aux vb*: **I ~ to do it** debería hacerlo; **this ~ to have been corrected** esto debiera de haberse corregido; **he ~ to win** (*probability*) debiera ganar; **you ~ to go and see it** vale la pena ir a verlo.
ounce [auns] *n* onza (*28.35g; 16 in a pound*).
our ['auə*] *adj* nuestro; *see also* **my.**
ours ['auəz] *pron* (el) nuestro/(la) nuestra *etc*; *see also* **mine.**
ourselves [auə'selvz] *pron pl* (*reflexive, after prep*) nosotros; (*emphatic*) nosotros mismos; **we did it (all) by ~** lo hicimos nosotros solos; *see also* **oneself.**
oust [aust] *vt* desalojar.
out [aut] *adv* fuera, afuera; (*not at home*) fuera (de casa); (*light, fire*) apagado; (*on strike*) en huelga ♦ *vt*: **to ~ sb** revelar públicamente la homosexualidad de algn; **~ there** allí (fuera); **he's ~** (*absent*) no está, ha salido; **to be ~ in one's calculations** equivocarse (en sus cálculos); **to run ~** salir corriendo; **~ loud** en alta voz; **~ of** *prep* (*outside*) fuera de; (*because of: anger etc*) por; **to look ~ of the window** mirar por la ventana; **to drink ~ of a cup** beber de una taza; **made ~ of wood** de madera; **~ of petrol** sin gasolina; **"~ of order"** "no funciona"; **it's ~ of stock** (*COMM*) está agotado; **to be ~ and about again** estar repuesto y levantado; **the journey ~** el viaje de ida; **the boat was 10 km ~** el barco estaba a diez kilómetros de la costa; **before the week was ~** antes del fin de la semana; **he's ~ for all he can get** busca sus propios fines, anda detrás de lo suyo.
out-and-out ['autəndaut] *adj* (*liar, thief etc*) redomado, empedernido.
outback ['autbæk] *n* interior *m*.
outbid [aut'bɪd] *vt* pujar más alto que, sobrepujar.
outboard ['autbɔːd] *adj*: **~ motor** (motor *m*) fuera borda *m*.
outbound ['autbaund] *adj*: **~ from/for** con salida de/hacia.
outbreak ['autbreɪk] *n* (*of war*) comienzo; (*of disease*) epidemia; (*of violence etc*) ola.
outbuilding ['autbɪldɪŋ] *n* dependencia; (*shed*) cobertizo.
outburst ['autbəːst] *n* explosión *f*, arranque *m*.
outcast ['autkɑːst] *n* paria *m/f*.
outclass [aut'klɑːs] *vt* aventajar, superar.
outcome ['autkʌm] *n* resultado.
outcrop ['autkrɔp] *n* (*of rock*) afloramiento.
outcry ['autkraɪ] *n* protestas *fpl*.

outdated [aut'deɪtɪd] *adj* anticuado.
outdistance [aut'dɪstəns] *vt* dejar atrás.
outdo [aut'duː] *vt* (*irreg: like* **do**) superar.
outdoor [aut'dɔː*] *adj* al aire libre.
outdoors [aut'dɔːz] *adv* al aire libre.
outer ['autə*] *adj* exterior, externo.
outer space *n* espacio exterior.
outfit ['autfɪt] *n* equipo; (*clothes*) traje *m*; (*col: organization*) grupo, organización *f.*
outfitter's ['autfɪtəz] *n* (*BRIT*) sastrería.
outgoing ['autgəuɪŋ] *adj* (*president, tenant*) saliente; (*means of transport*) que sale; (*character*) extrovertido.
outgoings ['autgəuɪŋz] *npl* (*BRIT*) gastos *mpl.*
outgrow [aut'grəu] *vt*: (*irreg: like* **grow**) **he has ~n his clothes** su ropa le queda pequeña ya.
outhouse ['authaus] *n* dependencia.
outing ['autɪŋ] *n* excursión *f*, paseo.
outlandish [aut'lændɪʃ] *adj* estrafalario.
outlast [aut'lɑːst] *vt* durar más tiempo que, sobrevivir a.
outlaw ['autlɔː] *n* proscrito/a ♦ *vt* (*person*) declarar fuera de la ley; (*practice*) declarar ilegal.
outlay ['autleɪ] *n* inversión *f.*
outlet ['autlɛt] *n* salida; (*of pipe*) desagüe *m*; (*US ELEC*) toma de corriente; (*for emotion*) desahogo; (*also:* **retail ~**) punto de venta.
outline ['autlaɪn] *n* (*shape*) contorno, perfil *m*; **in ~** (*fig*) a grandes rasgos.
outlive [aut'lɪv] *vt* sobrevivir a.
outlook ['autluk] *n* perspectiva; (*opinion*) punto de vista.
outlying ['autlaɪɪŋ] *adj* remoto, aislado.
outmanoeuvre, (*US*) **outmaneuver** [autmə'nuːvə*] *vt* (*MIL, fig*) superar en la estrategia.
outmoded [aut'məudɪd] *adj* anticuado, pasado de moda.
outnumber [aut'nʌmbə*] *vt* exceder *or* superar en número.
out of bounds [autəv'baundz] *adj*: **it's ~** está prohibido el paso.
out-of-court [autəv'kɔːt] *adj, adv* sin ir a juicio.
out-of-date [autəv'deɪt] *adj* (*passport*) caducado, vencido; (*theory, idea*) anticuado; (*clothes, customs*) pasado de moda.
out-of-doors [autəv'dɔːz] *adv* al aire libre.
out-of-the-way [autəvðə'weɪ] *adj* (*remote*) apartado; (*unusual*) poco común *or* corriente.
out-of-touch [autəv'tʌtʃ] *adj*: **to be ~** estar desconectado.
outpatient ['autpeɪʃənt] *n* paciente *m/f* externo/a.

outpost ['autpəust] *n* puesto avanzado.
outpouring ['autpɔːrɪŋ] *n* (*fig*) efusión *f.*
output ['autput] *n* (volumen *m* de) producción *f*, rendimiento; (*COMPUT*) salida ♦ *vt* (*COMPUT: to power*) imprimir.
outrage ['autreɪdʒ] *n* (*scandal*) escándalo; (*atrocity*) atrocidad *f* ♦ *vt* ultrajar.
outrageous [aut'reɪdʒəs] *adj* (*clothes*) extravagante; (*behaviour*) escandaloso.
outright [aut'raɪt] *adv* (*win*) de manera absoluta; (*be killed*) en el acto; (*ask*) abiertamente; (*completely*) completamente ♦ *adj* ['autraɪt] completo; (*winner*) absoluto; (*refusal*) rotundo.
outrun [aut'rʌn] *vt* (*irreg: like* **run**) correr más que, dejar atrás.
outset ['autsɛt] *n* principio.
outshine [aut'ʃaɪn] *vt* (irreg: *like* **shine**) (*fig*) eclipsar, brillar más que.
outside [aut'saɪd] *n* exterior *m* ♦ *adj* exterior, externo ♦ *adv* fuera, afuera (*esp LAM*) ♦ *prep* fuera de; (*beyond*) más allá de; **at the ~** (*fig*) a lo sumo; **an ~ chance** una posibilidad remota; **~ left/right** (*FOOTBALL*) extremo izquierdo/derecho.
outside broadcast *n* (*RADIO, TV*) emisión *f* exterior.
outside contractor *n* contratista *m/f* independiente.
outside lane *n* (*AUT*) carril *m* de adelantamiento.
outside line *n* (*TEL*) línea (exterior).
outsider [aut'saɪdə*] *n* (*stranger*) forastero.
outsize ['autsaɪz] *adj* (*clothes*) de talla grande.
outskirts ['autskəːts] *npl* alrededores *mpl*, afueras *fpl.*
outsmart [aut'smɑːt] *vt* ser más listo que.
outspoken [aut'spəukən] *adj* muy franco.
outspread [aut'sprɛd] *adj* extendido; (*wings*) desplegado.
outstanding [aut'stændɪŋ] *adj* excepcional, destacado; (*unfinished*) pendiente.
outstay [aut'steɪ] *vt*: **to ~ one's welcome** quedarse más de la cuenta.
outstretched [aut'strɛtʃt] *adj* (*arm*) extendido.
outstrip [aut'strɪp] *vt* (*competitors, demand, also fig*) dejar atrás, aventajar.
out-tray ['auttreɪ] *n* bandeja de salida.
outvote [aut'vəut] *vt*: **it was ~d (by ...)** fue rechazado en el voto (por ...).
outward ['autwəd] *adj* (*sign, appearances*) externo; (*journey*) de ida.
outwardly ['autwədlɪ] *adv* por fuera.
outweigh [aut'weɪ] *vt* pesar más que.
outwit [aut'wɪt] *vt* ser más listo que.

outworn [aut'wɔːn] adj (expression) cansado.

oval ['əuvl] adj ovalado ♦ n óvalo.

ovarian [əu'vɛərɪən] adj ovárico; (cancer) de ovario.

ovary ['əuvərɪ] n ovario.

ovation [əu'veɪʃən] n ovación f.

oven ['ʌvn] n horno.

ovenproof ['ʌvnpruːf] adj refractario, resistente al horno.

oven-ready ['ʌvnrɛdɪ] adj listo para el horno.

ovenware ['ʌvnwɛə*] n artículos mpl para el horno.

over ['əuvə*] adv encima, por encima ♦ adj (or adv) (finished) terminado; (surplus) de sobra; (excessively) demasiado ♦ prep (por) encima de; (above) sobre; (on the other side of) al otro lado de; (more than) más de; (during) durante; (about, concerning): **they fell out ~ money** riñeron por una cuestión de dinero; **~ here** (por) aquí; **~ there** (por) allí or allá; **all ~** (everywhere) por todas partes; **~ and ~ (again)** una y otra vez; **~ and above** además de; **to ask sb ~** invitar a algn a casa; **to bend ~** inclinarse; **now ~ to our Paris correspondent** damos la palabra a nuestro corresponsal de París; **the world ~** en todo el mundo, en el mundo entero; **she's not ~ intelligent** no es muy lista que digamos.

over ... [əuvə*] pref sobre..., super....

overact [əuvər'ækt] vi (THEAT) exagerar el papel.

overall ['əuvərɔːl] adj (length) total; (study) de conjunto ♦ adv [əuvər'ɔːl] en conjunto ♦ n (BRIT) guardapolvo; **~s** npl mono sg, overol msg (LAM).

overall majority n mayoría absoluta.

overanxious [əuvər'æŋkʃəs] adj demasiado preocupado or ansioso.

overawe [əuvər'ɔː] vt intimidar.

overbalance [əuvə'bæləns] vi perder el equilibrio.

overbearing [əuvə'bɛərɪŋ] adj autoritario, imperioso.

overboard ['əuvəbɔːd] adv (NAUT) por la borda; **to go ~ for sth** (fig) enloquecer por algo.

overbook [əuvə'buk] vt sobrereservar, reservar con exceso.

overcapitalize [əuvə'kæpɪtəlaɪz] vi sobrecapitalizar.

overcast ['əuvəkɑːst] adj encapotado.

overcharge [əuvə'tʃɑːdʒ] vt: **to ~ sb** cobrar un precio excesivo a algn.

overcoat ['əuvəkəut] n abrigo.

overcome [əuvə'kʌm] vt (irreg: like **come**) (gen) vencer; (difficulty) superar; **she was quite ~ by the occasion** la ocasión le conmovió mucho.

overconfident [əuvə'kɔnfɪdənt] adj demasiado confiado.

overcrowded [əuvə'kraudɪd] adj atestado de gente; (city, country) superpoblado.

overcrowding [əuvə'kraudɪŋ] n (in town, country) superpoblación f; (in bus etc) hacinamiento, apiñamiento.

overdo [əuvə'duː] vt (irreg: like **do**) exagerar; (overcook) cocer demasiado; **to ~ it, to ~ things** (work too hard) trabajar demasiado.

overdose ['əuvədəus] n sobredosis f inv.

overdraft ['əuvədrɑːft] n saldo deudor.

overdrawn [əuvə'drɔːn] adj (account) en descubierto.

overdrive ['əuvədraɪv] n (AUT) sobremarcha, superdirecta.

overdue [əuvə'djuː] adj retrasado; (recognition) tardío; (bill) vencido y no pagado; **that change was long ~** ese cambio tenía que haberse hecho hace tiempo.

overemphasis [əuvər'ɛmfəsɪs] n: **to put an ~ on** poner énfasis excesivo en.

overenthusiastic ['əuvərənθuːzɪ'æstɪk] adj demasiado entusiasta.

overestimate [əuvər'ɛstɪmeɪt] vt sobreestimar.

overexcited [əuvərɪk'saɪtɪd] adj sobreexcitado.

overexertion [əuvərɪg'zəːʃən] n agotamiento, fatiga.

overexpose [əuvərɪk'spəuz] vt (PHOT) sobreexponer.

overflow [əuvə'fləu] vi desbordarse ♦ n ['əuvəfləu] (excess) exceso; (of river) desbordamiento; (also: ~ pipe) (cañería de) desagüe m.

overfly [əuvə'flaɪ] vt (irreg: like **fly**) sobrevolar.

overgenerous [əuvə'dʒɛnərəs] adj demasiado generoso.

overgrown [əuvə'grəun] adj (garden) cubierto de hierba; **he's just an ~ schoolboy** es un niño en grande.

overhang [əuvə'hæŋ] (irreg: like **hang**) vt sobresalir por encima de ♦ vi sobresalir.

overhaul vt [əuvə'hɔːl] revisar, repasar ♦ n ['əuvəhɔːl] revisión f.

overhead adv [əuvə'hɛd] por arriba or encima ♦ adj ['əuvəhɛd] (cable) aéreo; (railway) elevado, aéreo ♦ n ['əuvəhɛd] (US) = **overheads**.

overheads ['əuvəhɛdz] *npl* (*BRIT*) gastos *mpl* generales.

overhear [əuvə'hɪə*] *vt* (*irreg: like* **hear**) oír por casualidad.

overheat [əuvə'hiːt] *vi* (*engine*) recalentarse.

overjoyed [əuvə'dʒɔɪd] *adj* encantado, lleno de alegría.

overkill ['əuvəkɪl] *n* (*MIL*) capacidad *f* excesiva de destrucción; (*fig*) exceso.

overland ['əuvəlænd] *adj, adv* por tierra.

overlap *vi* [əuvə'læp] superponerse ♦ *n* ['əuvəlæp] superposición *f*.

overleaf [əuvə'liːf] *adv* al dorso.

overload [əuvə'ləud] *vt* sobrecargar.

overlook [əuvə'luk] *vt* (*have view of*) dar a, tener vistas a; (*miss*) pasar por alto; (*forgive*) hacer la vista gorda a.

overlord ['əuvəlɔːd] *n* señor *m*.

overmanning [əuvə'mænɪŋ] *n* exceso de mano de obra; (*in organization*) exceso de personal.

overnight [əuvə'naɪt] *adv* durante la noche; (*fig*) de la noche a la mañana ♦ *adj* de noche; **to stay ~** pasar la noche.

overnight bag *n* fin *m* de semana, neceser *m* de viaje.

overnight stay *n* estancia de una noche.

overpass ['əuvəpɑːs] *n* (*US*) paso elevado *or* a desnivel.

overpay [əuvə'peɪ] *vt*: **to ~ sb by £50** pagar 50 libras de más a algn.

overplay [əuvə'pleɪ] *vt* exagerar; **to ~ one's hand** desmedirse.

overpower [əuvə'pauə*] *vt* dominar; (*fig*) embargar.

overpowering [əuvə'pauərɪŋ] *adj* (*heat*) agobiante; (*smell*) penetrante.

overproduction [əuvəprə'dʌkʃən] *n* superproducción *f*.

overrate [əuvə'reɪt] *vt* sobrevalorar.

overreach [əuvə'riːtʃ] *vt*: **to ~ o.s.** ir demasiado lejos, pasarse.

override [əuvə'raɪd] *vt* (*irreg: like* **ride**) (*order, objection*) no hacer caso de.

overriding [əuvə'raɪdɪŋ] *adj* predominante.

overrule [əuvə'ruːl] *vt* (*decision*) anular; (*claim*) denegar.

overrun [əuvə'rʌn] *vt* (*irreg: like* **run**) (*MIL: country*) invadir; (*time limit*) rebasar, exceder ♦ *vi* rebasar el límite previsto; **the town is ~ with tourists** el pueblo está inundado de turistas.

overseas [əuvə'siːz] *adv* en ultramar; (*abroad*) en el extranjero ♦ *adj* (*trade*) exterior; (*visitor*) extranjero.

oversee [əuvə'siː] *vt* supervisar.

overseer ['əuvəsɪə*] *n* (*in factory*)

supervisor(a) *m/f*; (*foreman*) capataz *m*.

overshadow [əuvə'ʃædəu] *vt* (*fig*) eclipsar.

overshoot [əuvə'ʃuːt] *vt* (*irreg: like* **shoot**) excederse.

oversight ['əuvəsaɪt] *n* descuido; **due to an ~** a causa de un descuido *or* una equivocación.

oversimplify [əuvə'sɪmplɪfaɪ] *vt* simplificar demasiado.

oversleep [əuvə'sliːp] *vi* (*irreg: like* **sleep**) dormir más de la cuenta, no despertarse a tiempo.

overspend [əuvə'spɛnd] *vi* gastar más de la cuenta; **we have overspent by 5 dollars** hemos excedido el presupuesto en 5 dólares.

overspill ['əuvəspɪl] *n* exceso de población.

overstaffed [əuvə'stɑːft] *adj*: **to be ~** tener exceso de plantilla.

overstate [əuvə'steɪt] *vt* exagerar.

overstatement ['əuvəsteɪtmənt] *n* exageración *f*.

overstay [əuvə'steɪ] *vt*: **to ~ one's time** *or* **welcome** quedarse más de lo conveniente.

overstep [əuvə'stɛp] *vt*: **to ~ the mark** *or* **the limits** pasarse de la raya.

overstock [əuvə'stɔk] *vt* abarrotar.

overstretched [əuvə'strɛtʃt] *adj* utilizado por encima de su capacidad.

overstrike *n* ['əuvəstraɪk] (*on printer*) superposición *f* ♦ *vt* (*irreg: like* **strike**) [əuvə'straɪk] superponer.

oversubscribed [əuvəsəb'skraɪbd] *adj* suscrito en exceso.

overt [əu'vəːt] *adj* abierto.

overtake [əuvə'teɪk] *vt* (*irreg: like* **take**) sobrepasar; (*BRIT AUT*) adelantar.

overtax [əuvə'tæks] *vt* (*ECON*) exigir contribuciones *fpl* excesivas *or* impuestos *mpl* excesivos a; (*fig: strength, patience*) agotar, abusar de; **to ~ o.s.** fatigarse demasiado.

overthrow [əuvə'θrəu] *vt* (*irreg: like* **throw**) (*government*) derrocar.

overtime ['əuvətaɪm] *n* horas *fpl* extraordinarias; **to do** *or* **work ~** hacer *or* trabajar horas extraordinarias *or* extras.

overtime ban *n* prohibición *f* de (hacer) horas extraordinarias.

overtone ['əuvətəun] *n* (*fig*) tono.

overture ['əuvətʃuə*] *n* (*MUS*) obertura; (*fig*) propuesta.

overturn [əuvə'təːn] *vt, vi* volcar.

overview ['əuvəvjuː] *n* visión *f* de conjunto.

overweight [əuvə'weɪt] *adj* demasiado

gordo or pesado.

overwhelm [əuvə'wɛlm] vt aplastar.

overwhelming [əuvə'wɛlmɪŋ] adj (victory, defeat) arrollador(a); (desire) irresistible; **one's ~ impression is of heat** lo que más impresiona es el calor.

overwhelmingly [əuvə'wɛlmɪŋlɪ] adv abrumadoramente.

overwork [əuvə'wɜːk] n trabajo excesivo ♦ vt hacer trabajar demasiado ♦ vi trabajar demasiado.

overwrite [əuvə'raɪt] vt (irreg: like **write**) (COMPUT) sobreescribir.

overwrought [əuvə'rɔːt] adj sobreexcitado.

ovulation [ɔvju'leɪʃən] n ovulación f.

owe [əu] vt deber; **to ~ sb sth, to ~ sth to sb** deber algo a algn.

owing to ['əuɪŋtuː] prep debido a, por causa de.

owl [aul] n (long-eared ~) búho; (barn ~) lechuza.

own [əun] vt tener, poseer ♦ vi: **to ~ to sth/ to having done sth** confesar or reconocer algo/haber hecho algo ♦ adj propio; **a room of my ~** mi propia habitación; **to get one's ~ back** tomarse la revancha; **on one's ~** solo, a solas; **can I have it for my (very) ~?** ¿puedo quedarme con él?; **to come into one's ~** llegar a realizarse.

▶**own up** vi confesar.

own brand n (COMM) marca propia.

owner ['əunə*] n dueño/a.

owner-occupier ['əunər'ɔkjupaɪə*] n ocupante propietario/a m/f.

ownership ['əunəʃɪp] n posesión f; **it's under new ~** está bajo nueva dirección.

own goal n (SPORT) autogol m; **to score an ~** marcar un gol en propia puerta, marcar un autogol.

ox, pl **oxen** [ɔks, 'ɔksn] n buey m.

> El término **Oxbridge** es una fusión de Ox(ford) y (Cam)bridge, las dos universidades británicas más antiguas y con mayor prestigio académico y social. Muchos miembros destacados de la clase dirigente del país son antiguos alumnos de una de las dos. El mismo término suele aplicarse a todo lo que ambas representan en cuestión de prestigio y privilegios sociales.

Oxfam ['ɔksfæm] n abbr (BRIT: = Oxford Committee for Famine Relief) OXFAM.

oxide ['ɔksaɪd] n óxido.

Oxon. ['ɔksn] abbr (BRIT: = Oxoniensis) = of Oxford.

oxtail ['ɔksteɪl] n: **~ soup** sopa de rabo de buey.

oxyacetylene ['ɔksɪə'sɛtɪliːn] adj oxiacetilénico; **~ burner, ~ torch** soplete m oxiacetilénico.

oxygen ['ɔksɪdʒən] n oxígeno.

oxygen mask n máscara de oxígeno.

oxygen tent n tienda de oxígeno.

oyster ['ɔɪstə*] n ostra.

oz. abbr = **ounce(s)**.

ozone ['əuzəun] n ozono; **~ layer** capa de ozono.

P p

P, p [piː] n (letter) P, p f; **P for Peter** P de París.

P abbr = **president, prince**.

p abbr (= page) pág.; (BRIT) = **penny, pence**.

PA n abbr see **personal assistant, public address system** ♦ abbr (US) = Pennsylvania.

pa [paː] n (col) papá m.

p.a. abbr = **per annum**.

PAC n abbr (US) = political action committee.

pace [peɪs] n paso; (rhythm) ritmo ♦ vi: **to ~ up and down** pasearse de un lado a otro; **to keep ~ with** llevar el mismo paso que; (events) mantenerse a la altura de or al corriente de; **to set the ~** (running) marcar el paso; (fig) marcar la pauta; **to put sb through his ~s** (fig) poner a algn a prueba.

pacemaker ['peɪsmeɪkə*] n (MED) marcapasos m inv.

pacific [pə'sɪfɪk] adj pacífico ♦ n: **the P~ (Ocean)** el (Océano) Pacífico.

pacification [pæsɪfɪ'keɪʃən] n pacificación f.

pacifier ['pæsɪfaɪə*] n (US: dummy) chupete m.

pacifism ['pæsɪfɪzəm] n pacifismo.

pacifist ['pæsɪfɪst] n pacifista m/f.

pacify ['pæsɪfaɪ] vt (soothe) apaciguar; (country) pacificar.

pack [pæk] n (packet) paquete m; (COMM) embalaje m; (of hounds) jauría; (of wolves) manada; (of thieves etc) banda; (of cards) baraja; (bundle) fardo; (US: of cigarettes) paquete m, cajetilla ♦ vt (wrap) empaquetar; (fill) llenar; (in suitcase etc) meter, poner; (cram) llenar, atestar; (fig: meeting etc) llenar de partidarios; (COMPUT) comprimir; **to ~ (one's bags)**

hacer las maletas; **to ~ sb off** despachar a algn; **the place was ~ed** el local estaba (lleno) hasta los topes; **to send sb ~ing** (*col*) echar a algn con cajas destempladas.

▶**pack in** *vi* (*break down: watch, car*) estropearse ♦ *vt* (*col*) dejar; **~ it in!** ¡para!, ¡basta ya!

▶**pack up** *vi* (*col: machine*) estropearse; (*person*) irse ♦ *vt* (*belongings, clothes*) recoger; (*goods, presents*) empaquetar, envolver.

package ['pækɪdʒ] *n* paquete *m*; (*bulky*) bulto; (*also: ~ **deal**) acuerdo global ♦ *vt* (*COMM: goods*) envasar, embalar.

package holiday *n* viaje *m* organizado (con todo incluido).

package tour *n* viaje *m* organizado.

packaging ['pækɪdʒɪŋ] *n* envase *m*.

packed lunch [pækt-] *n* almuerzo frío.

packer ['pækə*] *n* (*person*) empacador(a) *m/f*.

packet ['pækɪt] *n* paquete *m*.

packet switching [-'swɪtʃɪŋ] *n* (*COMPUT*) conmutación *f* por paquetes.

packhorse ['pækhɔːs] *n* caballo de carga.

pack ice *n* banco de hielo.

packing ['pækɪŋ] *n* embalaje *m*.

packing case *n* cajón *m* de embalaje.

pact [pækt] *n* pacto.

pad [pæd] *n* (*of paper*) bloc *m*; (*cushion*) cojinete *m*; (*launching ~*) plataforma (de lanzamiento); (*col: flat*) casa ♦ *vt* rellenar.

padded cell ['pædɪd-] *n* celda acolchada.

padding ['pædɪŋ] *n* relleno; (*fig*) paja.

paddle ['pædl] *n* (*oar*) canalete *m*, pala; (*US: for table tennis*) pala ♦ *vt* remar ♦ *vi* (*with feet*) chapotear.

paddle steamer *n* vapor *m* de ruedas.

paddling pool ['pædlɪŋ-] *n* (*BRIT*) piscina para niños.

paddock ['pædək] *n* (*field*) potrero.

paddy field ['pædɪ-] *n* arrozal *m*.

padlock ['pædlɔk] *n* candado ♦ *vt* cerrar con candado.

padre ['pɑːdrɪ] *n* capellán *m*.

paediatrician, (*US*) **pediatrician** [piːdɪə'trɪʃən] *n* pediatra *m/f*.

paediatrics, (*US*) **pediatrics** [piːdɪ'ætrɪks] *n* pediatría.

paedophile, (*US*) **pedophile** ['piːdəufaɪl] *adj* de pedófilos ♦ *n* pedófilo/a.

pagan ['peɪgən] *adj, n* pagano/a *m/f*.

page [peɪdʒ] *n* página; (*also: ~ **boy**) paje *m* ♦ *vt* (*in hotel etc*) llamar por altavoz a.

pageant ['pædʒənt] *n* (*procession*) desfile *m*; (*show*) espectáculo.

pageantry ['pædʒəntrɪ] *n* pompa.

page break *n* límite *m* de la página.

pager ['peɪdʒə*] *n* busca *m*.

paginate ['pædʒɪneɪt] *vt* paginar.

pagination [pædʒɪ'neɪʃən] *n* paginación *f*.

pagoda [pə'gəudə] *n* pagoda.

paid [peɪd] *pt, pp of* **pay** ♦ *adj* (*work*) remunerado; (*official*) asalariado; **to put ~ to** (*BRIT*) acabar con.

paid-up ['peɪdʌp], (*US*) **paid-in** ['peɪdɪn] *adj* (*member*) con sus cuotas pagadas *or* al día; (*share*) liberado; **~ capital** capital *m* desembolsado.

pail [peɪl] *n* cubo, balde *m*.

pain [peɪn] *n* dolor *m*; **to be in ~** sufrir; **on ~ of death** so *or* bajo pena de muerte; *see also* **pains**.

pained [peɪnd] *adj* (*expression*) afligido.

painful ['peɪnful] *adj* (*doloroso*; (*difficult*) penoso; (*disagreeable*) desagradable.

painfully ['peɪnfəlɪ] *adv* (*fig: very*) terriblemente.

painkiller ['peɪnkɪlə*] *n* analgésico.

painless ['peɪnlɪs] *adj* sin dolor; (*method*) fácil.

pains [peɪnz] *npl* (*efforts*) esfuerzos *mpl*; **to take ~ to do sth** tomarse trabajo en hacer algo.

painstaking ['peɪnzteɪkɪŋ] *adj* (*person*) concienzudo, esmerado.

paint [peɪnt] *n* pintura ♦ *vt* pintar; **a tin of ~** un bote de pintura; **to ~ the door blue** pintar la puerta de azul.

paintbox ['peɪntbɔks] *n* caja de pinturas.

paintbrush ['peɪntbrʌʃ] *n* (*artist's*) pincel *m*; (*decorator's*) brocha.

painter ['peɪntə*] *n* pintor(a) *m/f*.

painting ['peɪntɪŋ] *n* pintura.

paintwork ['peɪntwɔːk] *n* pintura.

pair [pɛə*] *n* (*of shoes, gloves etc*) par *m*; (*of people*) pareja; **a ~ of scissors** unas tijeras; **a ~ of trousers** unos pantalones, un pantalón.

▶**pair off** *vi*: **to ~ off (with sb)** hacer pareja (con algn).

pajamas [pɪ'dʒɑːməz] *npl* (*US*) pijama *msg*, piyama *msg* (*LAM*).

Pakistan [pɑːkɪ'stɑːn] *n* Paquistán *m*.

Pakistani [pɑːkɪ'stɑːnɪ] *adj, n* paquistaní *m/f*.

PAL [pæl] *n abbr* (*TV*) = *phase alternation line*.

pal [pæl] *n* (*col*) amiguete/a *m/f*, colega *m/f*.

palace ['pæləs] *n* palacio.

palatable ['pælɪtəbl] *adj* sabroso; (*acceptable*) aceptable.

palate ['pælɪt] *n* paladar *m*.

palatial [pə'leɪʃəl] *adj* (*surroundings, residence*) suntuoso, espléndido.

palaver [pə'lɑːvə*] *n* (*fuss*) lío.

pale [peɪl] *adj* (*gen*) pálido; (*colour*) claro

paleness – pants

♦ n: **to be beyond the** ~ pasarse de la raya ♦ vi palidecer; **to grow** or **turn** ~ palidecer; **to** ~ **into insignificance (beside)** no poderse comparar (con).
paleness ['peɪlnɪs] n palidez f.
Palestine ['pælɪstaɪn] n Palestina.
Palestinian [pælɪs'tɪnɪən] adj, n palestino/a m/f.
palette ['pælɪt] n paleta.
paling ['peɪlɪŋ] n (stake) estaca; (fence) valla.
palisade [pælɪ'seɪd] n palizada.
pall [pɔːl] n (of smoke) cortina ♦ vi cansar.
pallbearer ['pɔːlbɛərə*] n portador m del féretro.
pallet ['pælɪt] n (for goods) pallet m.
palletization [pælɪtaɪ'zeɪʃən] n paletización f.
palliative ['pælɪətɪv] n paliativo.
pallid ['pælɪd] adj pálido.
pallor ['pælə*] n palidez f.
pally ['pælɪ] adj (col): **to be very** ~ **with sb** ser muy amiguete de algn.
palm [pɑːm] n (ANAT) palma; (also: ~ **tree**) palmera, palma ♦ vt: **to** ~ **sth off on sb** (BRIT col) endosarle algo a algn.
palmist ['pɑːmɪst] n quiromántico/a, palmista m/f.
Palm Sunday n Domingo de Ramos.
palpable ['pælpəbl] adj palpable.
palpably ['pælpəblɪ] adv obviamente.
palpitation [pælpɪ'teɪʃən] n palpitación f; **to have** ~s tener palpitaciones.
paltry ['pɔːltrɪ] adj (amount etc) miserable; (insignificant: person) insignificante.
pamper ['pæmpə*] vt mimar.
pamphlet ['pæmflət] n folleto; (political: handed out in street) panfleto.
pan [pæn] n (also: **sauce**~) cacerola, cazuela, olla; (also: **frying** ~) sartén m; (of lavatory) taza ♦ vi (CINE) tomar panorámicas; **to** ~ **for gold** cribar oro.
pan- [pæn] pref pan-.
panacea [pænə'sɪə] n panacea.
panache [pə'næʃ] n gracia, garbo.
Panama ['pænəmɑː] n Panamá m.
Panama Canal n el Canal de Panamá.
pancake ['pænkeɪk] n crepe f, panqueque m (LAM).
Pancake Day n martes m de carnaval.
pancake roll n rollito de primavera.
pancreas ['pæŋkrɪəs] n páncreas m.
panda ['pændə] n panda m.
panda car n (BRIT) coche m de la policía.
pandemonium [pændɪ'məʊnɪəm] n (noise): **there was** ~ se armó un tremendo jaleo; (mess) caos m.
pander ['pændə*] vi: **to** ~ **to** complacer a.

p&h abbr (US: = postage and handling) gastos de envío.
P&L abbr = profit and loss.
p & p abbr (BRIT: = postage and packing) gastos de envío.
pane [peɪn] n cristal m.
panel ['pænl] n (of wood) panel m; (of cloth) paño; (RADIO, TV) panel m de invitados.
panel game n (TV) programa m concurso para equipos.
panelling, (US) paneling ['pænəlɪŋ] n paneles mpl.
panellist, (US) panelist ['pænəlɪst] n miembro del jurado.
pang [pæŋ] n: ~s **of conscience** remordimientos mpl; ~s **of hunger** dolores mpl del hambre.
panhandler ['pænhændlə*] n (US col) mendigo/a.
panic ['pænɪk] n pánico ♦ vi dejarse llevar por el pánico.
panic buying [-baɪɪŋ] n compras masivas por miedo a futura escasez.
panicky ['pænɪkɪ] adj (person) asustadizo.
panic-stricken ['pænɪkstrɪkən] adj preso del pánico.
pannier ['pænɪə*] n (on bicycle) cartera; (on mule etc) alforja.
panorama [pænə'rɑːmə] n panorama m.
panoramic [pænə'ræmɪk] adj panorámico.
pansy ['pænzɪ] n (BOT) pensamiento; (col: pej) maricón m.
pant [pænt] vi jadear.
panther ['pænθə*] n pantera.
panties ['pæntɪz] npl bragas fpl.
pantihose ['pæntɪhəʊz] n (US) medias fpl, panties mpl.
panto ['pæntəʊ] n (BRIT col) = **pantomime**.
pantomime ['pæntəmaɪm] n (BRIT) representación f musical navideña.

En época navideña los teatros británicos ponen en escena representaciones llamadas **pantomimes**, versiones libres de cuentos tradicionales como Aladino o El gato con botas. En ella nunca faltan personajes como la dama (**dame**), papel que siempre interpreta un actor; el protagonista joven (**principal boy**), normalmente interpretado por una actriz, y el malvado (**villain**). Es un espectáculo familiar dirigido a los niños pero con grandes dosis de humor para adultos en el que se alienta la participación del público.

pantry ['pæntrɪ] n despensa.
pants [pænts] n (BRIT: underwear: woman's) bragas fpl; (: man's) calzoncillos mpl; (US:

trousers) pantalones *mpl*.
pantsuit ['pæntsjuːt] *n* (*US*) traje *m* de chaqueta y pantalón.
papal ['peɪpəl] *adj* papal.
paparazzi [pæpə'rætsɪ] *npl* paparazzi *mpl*.
paper ['peɪpə*] *n* papel *m*; (*also*: **news~**) periódico, diario; (*study, article*) artículo; (*exam*) examen *m* ♦ *adj* de papel ♦ *vt* empapelar; (**identity**) **~s** *npl* papeles *mpl*, documentos *mpl*; **a piece of ~** un papel; **to put sth down on ~** poner algo por escrito.
paper advance *n* (*on printer*) avance *m* de papel.
paperback ['peɪpəbæk] *n* libro de bolsillo.
paper bag *n* bolsa de papel.
paperboy ['peɪpəbɔɪ] *n* (*selling*) vendedor *m* de periódicos; (*delivering*) repartidor *m* de periódicos.
paper clip *n* clip *m*.
paper hankie *n* pañuelo de papel.
paper money *n* papel *m* moneda.
paper profit *n* beneficio no realizado.
paper shop *n* (*BRIT*) tienda de periódicos.
paperweight ['peɪpəweɪt] *n* pisapapeles *m inv*.
paperwork ['peɪpəwɜːk] *n* trabajo administrativo; (*pej*) papeleo.
papier-mâché ['pæpɪeɪ'mæʃeɪ] *n* cartón *m* piedra.
paprika ['pæprɪkə] *n* pimentón *m*.
Pap test ['pæp-] *n* (*MED*) frotis *m* (cervical).
papyrus [pə'paɪərəs] *n* papiro.
par [pɑː*] *n* par *f*; (*GOLF*) par *m* ♦ *adj* a la par; **to be on a ~ with** estar a la par con; **at ~** a la par; **to be above/below ~** estar sobre/bajo par; **to feel under ~** sentirse en baja forma.
parable ['pærəbl] *n* parábola.
parachute ['pærəʃuːt] *n* paracaídas *m inv* ♦ *vi* lanzarse en paracaídas.
parachutist ['pærəʃuːtɪst] *n* paracaidista *m/ f*.
parade [pə'reɪd] *n* desfile *m* ♦ *vt* (*gen*) recorrer, desfilar por; (*show off*) hacer alarde de ♦ *vi* desfilar; (*MIL*) pasar revista; **a fashion ~** un desfile de modelos.
parade ground *n* plaza de armas.
paradise ['pærədaɪs] *n* paraíso.
paradox ['pærədɔks] *n* paradoja.
paradoxical [pærə'dɔksɪkl] *adj* paradójico.
paradoxically [pærə'dɔksɪklɪ] *adv* paradójicamente.
paraffin ['pærəfɪn] *n* (*BRIT*): **~ (oil)** parafina.
paraffin heater *n* estufa de parafina.
paraffin lamp *n* quinqué *m*.
paragon ['pærəgən] *n* modelo.

paragraph ['pærəgrɑːf] *n* párrafo, acápite *m* (*LAM*); **new ~** punto y aparte, punto acápite (*LAM*).
Paraguay ['pærəgwaɪ] *n* Paraguay *m*.
Paraguayan [pærə'gwaɪən] *adj, n* paraguayo/a *m/f*, paraguayano/a *m/f*.
parallel ['pærəlɛl] *adj*: **~ (with/to)** en paralelo (con/a); (*fig*) semejante (a) ♦ *n* (*line*) paralela; (*fig, GEO*) paralelo.
paralysis [pə'rælɪsɪs] *n* parálisis *f inv*.
paralytic [pærə'lɪtɪk] *adj* paralítico.
paralyze ['pærəlaɪz] *vt* paralizar.
paramedic [pærə'mɛdɪk] *n* auxiliar *m/f* sanitario/a.
parameter [pə'ræmɪtə*] *n* parámetro.
paramilitary [pærə'mɪlɪtərɪ] *adj* (*organization, operations*) paramilitar.
paramount ['pærəmaunt] *adj*: **of ~ importance** de suma importancia.
paranoia [pærə'nɔɪə] *n* paranoia.
paranoid ['pærənɔɪd] *adj* (*person, feeling*) paranoico.
paranormal [pærə'nɔːml] *adj* paranormal.
parapet ['pærəpɪt] *n* parapeto.
paraphernalia [pærəfə'neɪlɪə] *n* parafernalia.
paraphrase ['pærəfreɪz] *vt* parafrasear.
paraplegic [pærə'pliːdʒɪk] *n* parapléjico/a.
parapsychology [pærəsaɪ'kɔlədʒɪ] *n* parasicología.
parasite ['pærəsaɪt] *n* parásito/a.
parasol ['pærəsɔl] *n* sombrilla, quitasol *m*.
paratrooper ['pærətruːpə*] *n* paracaidista *m/f*.
parcel ['pɑːsl] *n* paquete *m* ♦ *vt* (*also*: **~ up**) empaquetar, embalar; **to be part and ~ of** ser parte integrante de.
► **parcel out** *vt* parcelar, repartir.
parcel bomb *n* paquete *m* bomba.
parcel post *n* servicio de paquetes postales.
parch [pɑːtʃ] *vt* secar, resecar.
parched [pɑːtʃt] *adj* (*person*) muerto de sed.
parchment ['pɑːtʃmənt] *n* pergamino.
pardon ['pɑːdn] *n* perdón *m*; (*LAW*) indulto ♦ *vt* perdonar; indultar; **~ me!, I beg your ~!** ¡perdone usted!; (**I beg your**) **~?**, (*US*) **~ me?** ¿cómo (dice)?
pare [pɛə*] *vt* (*nails*) cortar; (*fruit etc*) pelar.
parent ['pɛərənt] *n*: **~s** *npl* padres *mpl*.
parentage ['pɛərəntɪdʒ] *n* familia, linaje *m*; **of unknown ~** de padres desconocidos.
parental [pə'rɛntl] *adj* paternal/maternal.
parent company *n* casa matriz.
parenthesis, *pl* **parentheses** [pə'rɛnθɪsɪs, -θɪsiːz] *n* paréntesis *m inv*; **in parentheses** entre paréntesis.

parenthood ['pɛərənthud] n el ser padres.
parent ship n buque m nodriza.
Paris ['pærɪs] n París m.
parish ['pærɪʃ] n parroquia.
parish council n consejo parroquial.
parishioner [pə'rɪʃənə*] n feligrés/esa m/f.
Parisian [pə'rɪzɪən] adj, n parisino/a m/f,
parisiense m/f.
parity ['pærɪtɪ] n paridad f, igualdad f.
park [pɑːk] n parque m, jardín m público
♦ vt aparcar, estacionar ♦ vi aparcar,
estacionar.
parka ['pɑːkə] n parka.
parking ['pɑːkɪŋ] n aparcamiento,
estacionamiento; "no ~" "prohibido
aparcar or estacionarse".
parking lights npl luces fpl de
estacionamiento.
parking lot n (US) parking m,
aparcamiento, playa f de estacionamiento
(LAM).
parking meter n parquímetro.
parking offence, (US) **parking violation**
n ofensa por aparcamiento indebido.
parking place n sitio para aparcar,
aparcamiento.
parking ticket n multa de aparcamiento.
Parkinson's n (also: ~ **disease**)
(enfermedad f de) Parkinson m.
parkway ['pɑːkweɪ] n (US) alameda.
parlance ['pɑːləns] n lenguaje m; in
common/modern ~ en lenguaje
corriente/moderno.
parliament ['pɑːləmənt] n parlamento;
(Spanish) las Cortes fpl.

---

*El Parlamento británico (Parliament) tiene
como sede el palacio de Westminster,
también llamado* **Houses of Parliament**.
*Consta de dos cámaras: la Cámara de los
Comunes* (**House of Commons**) *está formada
por 650 diputados* (**Members of Parliament**)
*que acceden a ella tras ser elegidos por
sufragio universal en su respectiva área o
circunscripción electoral* (**constituency**). *Se
reúne 175 días al año y sus sesiones son
presididas y moderadas por el Presidente
de la Cámara* (**Speaker**). *La cámara alta es
la Cámara de los Lores* (**House of Lords**) *y
sus miembros son nombrados por el
monarca o bien han heredado su escaño. Su
poder es limitado, aunque actúa como
tribunal supremo de apelación, excepto en
Escocia.*

---

parliamentary [pɑːlə'mɛntərɪ] adj
parlamentario.
parlour, (US) **parlor** ['pɑːlə*] n salón m,

living m (LAM).
parlous ['pɑːləs] adj peligroso, alarmante.
Parmesan [pɑːmɪ'zæn] n (also: ~ **cheese**)
queso parmesano.
parochial [pə'rəʊkɪəl] adj parroquial; (pej)
de miras estrechas.
parody ['pærədɪ] n parodia ♦ vt parodiar.
parole [pə'rəʊl] n: on ~ en libertad
condicional.
paroxysm ['pærəksɪzəm] n (MED)
paroxismo, ataque m; (of anger, laughter,
coughing) ataque m; (of grief) crisis f.
parquet ['pɑːkeɪ] n: ~ **floor(ing)** parquet m.
parrot ['pærət] n loro, papagayo.
parrot fashion adv como un loro.
parry ['pærɪ] vt parar.
parsimonious [pɑːsɪ'məʊnɪəs] adj tacaño.
parsley ['pɑːslɪ] n perejil m.
parsnip ['pɑːsnɪp] n chirivía.
parson ['pɑːsn] n cura m.
part [pɑːt] n (gen, MUS) parte f; (bit) trozo;
(of machine) pieza; (THEAT etc) papel m; (of
serial) entrega; (US: in hair) raya ♦ adv
= **partly** ♦ vt separar; (break) partir ♦ vi
(people) separarse; (roads) bifurcarse;
(crowd) apartarse; (break) romperse; **to
take** ~ **in** participar or tomar parte en; **to
take sb's** ~ tomar partido por algn; **for
my** ~ por mi parte; **for the most** ~ en su
mayor parte; (people) en su mayoría; **for
the better** ~ **of the day** durante la mayor
parte del día; ~ **of speech** (LING)
categoría gramatical, parte f de la
oración; **to take sth in good/bad** ~
aceptar algo bien/tomarse algo a mal.
▶**part with** vt fus ceder, entregar; (money)
pagar; (get rid of) deshacerse de.
partake [pɑː'teɪk] vi (irreg: like **take**)
(formal): **to** ~ **of sth** (food) comer algo;
(drink) tomar or beber algo.
part exchange n (BRIT): **in** ~ como parte
del pago.
partial ['pɑːʃl] adj parcial; **to be** ~ **to** (like)
ser aficionado a.
partially ['pɑːʃəlɪ] adv en parte,
parcialmente.
participant [pɑː'tɪsɪpənt] n (in competition)
concursante m/f.
participate [pɑː'tɪsɪpeɪt] vi: **to** ~ **in**
participar en.
participation [pɑːtɪsɪ'peɪʃən] n
participación f.
participle ['pɑːtɪsɪpl] n participio.
particle ['pɑːtɪkl] n partícula; (of dust)
mota; (fig) pizca.
particular [pə'tɪkjulə*] adj (special)
particular; (concrete) concreto; (given)
determinado; (detailed) detallado,

minucioso; (*fussy*) quisquilloso, exigente; ~s *npl* (*information*) datos *mpl*, detalles *mpl*; (*details*) pormenores *mpl*; **in** ~ en particular; **to be very** ~ **about** ser muy exigente en cuanto a; **I'm not** ~ me es *or* da igual.

particularly [pə'tɪkjulǝlɪ] *adv* especialmente, en particular.

parting ['pɑːtɪŋ] *n* (*act of*) separación *f*; (*farewell*) despedida; (*BRIT: in hair*) raya ♦ *adj* de despedida; ~ **shot** (*fig*) golpe *m* final.

partisan [pɑːtɪ'zæn] *adj* partidista ♦ *n* partidario/a; (*fighter*) partisano/a.

partition [pɑː'tɪʃən] *n* (*POL*) división *f*; (*wall*) tabique *m* ♦ *vt* dividir; dividir con tabique.

partly ['pɑːtlɪ] *adv* en parte.

partner ['pɑːtnə*] *n* (*COMM*) socio/a; (*SPORT, at dance*) pareja; (*spouse*) cónyuge *m/f*; (*friend etc*) compañero/a ♦ *vt* acompañar.

partnership ['pɑːtnəʃɪp] *n* (*gen*) asociación *f*; (*COMM*) sociedad *f*; **to go into** ~ (**with**), **form a** ~ (**with**) asociarse (con).

part payment *n* pago parcial.

partridge ['pɑːtrɪdʒ] *n* perdiz *f*.

part-time ['pɑːt'taɪm] *adj, adv* a tiempo parcial.

part-timer [pɑːt'taɪmə*] *n* trabajador(a) *m/f* a tiempo parcial.

party ['pɑːtɪ] *n* (*POL*) partido; (*celebration*) fiesta; (*group*) grupo; (*LAW*) parte *f*, interesado ♦ *adj* (*POL*) de partido; (*dress etc*) de fiesta, de gala; **to have** *or* **give** *or* **throw a** ~ organizar una fiesta; **dinner** ~ cena; **to be a** ~ **to a crime** ser cómplice *m/f* de un crimen.

party line *n* (*POL*) línea política del partido; (*TEL*) línea compartida.

party piece *n*: **to do one's** ~ hacer su numerito (de fiesta).

party political broadcast *n* ≈ espacio electoral.

pass [pɑːs] *vt* (*time, object*) pasar; (*place*) pasar por; (*exam, law*) aprobar; (*overtake, surpass*) rebasar; (*approve*) aprobar ♦ *vi* pasar; (*SCOL*) aprobar ♦ *n* (*permit*) permiso, pase *m*; (*membership card*) carnet *m*; (*in mountains*) puerto; (*SPORT*) pase *m*; (*SCOL: also:* ~ **mark**) aprobado; **to** ~ **sth through sth** pasar algo por algo; **to** ~ **the time of day with sb** pasar el rato con algn; **things have come to a pretty** ~! ¡hasta dónde hemos llegado!; **to make a** ~ **at sb** (*col*) insinuársele a algn.

▶**pass away** *vi* fallecer.

▶**pass by** *vi* pasar ♦ *vt* (*ignore*) pasar por alto.

▶**pass down** *vt* (*customs, inheritance*) pasar, transmitir.

▶**pass for** *vt fus* pasar por; **she could** ~ **for twenty-five** se podría creer que sólo tiene 25 años.

▶**pass on** *vi* (*die*) fallecer, morir ♦ *vt* (*hand on*): **to** ~ **on** (**to**) transmitir (a); (*cold, illness*) pegar (a); (*benefits*) dar (a); (*price rises*) pasar (a).

▶**pass out** *vi* desmayarse; (*MIL*) graduarse.

▶**pass over** *vi* (*die*) fallecer ♦ *vt* omitir, pasar por alto.

▶**pass up** *vt* (*opportunity*) dejar pasar, no aprovechar.

passable ['pɑːsəbl] *adj* (*road*) transitable; (*tolerable*) pasable.

passably ['pɑːsəblɪ] *adv* pasablemente.

passage ['pæsɪdʒ] *n* pasillo; (*act of passing*) tránsito; (*fare, in book*) pasaje *m*; (*by boat*) travesía.

passageway ['pæsɪdʒweɪ] *n* (*in house*) pasillo, corredor *m*; (*between buildings etc*) pasaje *m*, pasadizo.

passenger ['pæsɪndʒə*] *n* pasajero/a, viajero/a.

passer-by [pɑːsə'baɪ] *n* transeúnte *m/f*.

passing ['pɑːsɪŋ] *adj* (*fleeting*) pasajero; **in** ~ de paso.

passing place *n* (*AUT*) apartadero.

passion ['pæʃən] *n* pasión *f*.

passionate ['pæʃənɪt] *adj* apasionado.

passionately ['pæʃənɪtlɪ] *adv* apasionadamente, con pasión.

passion fruit *n* fruta de la pasión, granadilla.

passion play *n* drama *m* de la Pasión.

passive ['pæsɪv] *adj* (*also LING*) pasivo.

passive smoking *n efectos del tabaco en fumadores pasivos*.

passkey ['pɑːskiː] *n* llave *f* maestra.

Passover ['pɑːsəuvə*] *n* Pascua (de los judíos).

passport ['pɑːspɔːt] *n* pasaporte *m*.

passport control *n* control *m* de pasaporte.

password ['pɑːswəːd] *n* (*also COMPUT*) contraseña.

past [pɑːst] *prep* (*further than*) más allá de; (*later than*) después de ♦ *adj* pasado; (*president etc*) antiguo ♦ *n* (*time*) pasado; (*of person*) antecedentes *mpl*; **quarter/half** ~ **four** las cuatro y cuarto/media; **he's** ~ **forty** tiene más de cuarenta años; **I'm** ~ **caring** ya no me importa; **to be** ~ **it** (*col: person*) estar acabado; **for the** ~ **few/3 days** durante los últimos días/últimos 3 días; **to run** ~ pasar corriendo por; **in the** ~ en el pasado, antes.

pasta ['pæstə] *n* pasta.
paste [peɪst] *n* (*gen*) pasta; (*glue*) engrudo ♦ *vt* (*stick*) pegar; (*glue*) engomar; **tomato** ~ tomate concentrado.
pastel ['pæstl] *adj* pastel; (*painting*) al pastel.
pasteurized ['pæstəraɪzd] *adj* pasteurizado.
pastille ['pæstl] *n* pastilla.
pastime ['pɑːstaɪm] *n* pasatiempo.
past master *n*: **to be a** ~ **at** ser un maestro en.
pastor ['pɑːstə*] *n* pastor *m*.
pastoral ['pɑːstərl] *adj* pastoral.
pastry ['peɪstrɪ] *n* (*dough*) pasta; (*cake*) pastel *m*.
pasture ['pɑːstʃə*] *n* (*grass*) pasto.
pasty *n* ['pæstɪ] empanada ♦ *adj* ['peɪstɪ] pastoso; (*complexion*) pálido.
pat [pæt] *vt* dar una palmadita a; (*dog etc*) acariciar ♦ *n* (*of butter*) porción *f* ♦ *adj*: **he knows it (off)** ~ se lo sabe de memoria *or* al dedillo; **to give sb/o.s. a** ~ **on the back** (*fig*) felicitar a algn/felicitarse.
patch [pætʃ] *n* (*of material*) parche *m*; (*mended part*) remiendo; (*of land*) terreno; (*COMPUT*) ajuste *m* ♦ *vt* (*clothes*) remendar; **(to go through) a bad** ~ (pasar por) una mala racha.
▶**patch up** *vt* (*mend temporarily*) reparar; **to** ~ **up a quarrel** hacer las paces.
patchwork ['pætʃwɜːk] *n* labor *f* de retales.
patchy ['pætʃɪ] *adj* desigual.
pate [peɪt] *n*: **bald** ~ calva.
pâté ['pæteɪ] *n* paté *m*.
patent ['peɪtnt] *n* patente *f* ♦ *vt* patentar ♦ *adj* patente, evidente.
patent leather *n* charol *m*.
patently ['peɪtntlɪ] *adv* evidentemente.
patent medicine *n* específico.
patent office *n* oficina de patentes y marcas.
patent rights *npl* derechos *mpl* de patente.
paternal [pə'tɜːnl] *adj* paternal; (*relation*) paterno.
paternalistic [pətə:nə'lɪstɪk] *adj* paternalista.
paternity [pə'tɜːnɪtɪ] *n* paternidad *f*.
paternity suit *n* (*LAW*) caso de paternidad.
path [pɑːθ] *n* camino, sendero; (*trail, track*) pista; (*of missile*) trayectoria.
pathetic [pə'θetɪk] *adj* (*pitiful*) penoso, patético; (*very bad*) malísimo; (*moving*) conmovedor(a).
pathetically [pə'θetɪklɪ] *adv* penosamente, patéticamente; (*very badly*) malísimamente mal, de pena.
pathological [pæθə'lɔdʒɪkəl] *adj* patológico.
pathologist [pə'θɔlədʒɪst] *n* patólogo/a.

pathology [pə'θɔlədʒɪ] *n* patología.
pathos ['peɪθɔs] *n* patetismo.
pathway ['pɑːθweɪ] *n* sendero, vereda.
patience ['peɪʃns] *n* paciencia; (*BRIT CARDS*) solitario; **to lose one's** ~ perder la paciencia.
patient ['peɪʃnt] *n* paciente *m/f* ♦ *adj* paciente, sufrido; **to be** ~ **with sb** tener paciencia con algn.
patiently ['peɪʃəntlɪ] *adv* pacientemente, con paciencia.
patio ['pætɪəu] *n* patio.
patriot ['peɪtrɪət] *n* patriota *m/f*.
patriotic [pætrɪ'ɔtɪk] *adj* patriótico.
patriotism ['pætrɪətɪzəm] *n* patriotismo.
patrol [pə'trəul] *n* patrulla ♦ *vt* patrullar por; **to be on** ~ patrullar, estar de patrulla.
patrol boat *n* patrullero, patrullera.
patrol car *n* coche *m* patrulla.
patrolman [pə'trəulmən] *n* (*US*) policía *m*.
patron ['peɪtrən] *n* (*in shop*) cliente *m/f*; (*of charity*) patrocinador(a) *m/f*; ~ **of the arts** mecenas.
patronage ['pætrənɪdʒ] *n* patrocinio, protección *f*.
patronize ['pætrənaɪz] *vt* (*shop*) ser cliente de; (*look down on*) tratar con condescendencia a.
patronizing ['pætrənaɪzɪŋ] *adj* condescendiente.
patron saint *n* santo/a patrón/ona.
patter ['pætə*] *n* golpeteo; (*sales talk*) labia ♦ *vi* (*rain*) tamborilear.
pattern ['pætən] *n* (*SEWING*) patrón *m*; (*design*) dibujo; (*behaviour, events*) esquema *m*; ~ **of events** curso de los hechos; **behaviour** ~**s** modelos *mpl* de comportamiento.
patterned ['pætənd] *adj* (*material*) estampado.
paucity ['pɔːsɪtɪ] *n* escasez *f*.
paunch [pɔːntʃ] *n* panza, barriga.
pauper ['pɔːpə*] *n* pobre *m/f*.
pause [pɔːz] *n* pausa; (*interval*) intervalo ♦ *vi* hacer una pausa; **to** ~ **for breath** detenerse para tomar aliento.
pave [peɪv] *vt* pavimentar; **to** ~ **the way for** preparar el terreno para.
pavement ['peɪvmənt] *n* (*BRIT*) acera, vereda (*LAM*), andén *m* (*LAM*), banqueta (*LAM*); (*US*) calzada, pavimento.
pavilion [pə'vɪlɪən] *n* pabellón *m*; (*SPORT*) vestuarios *mpl*.
paving ['peɪvɪŋ] *n* pavimento.
paving stone *n* losa.
paw [pɔː] *n* pata; (*claw*) garra ♦ *vt* (*animal*) tocar con la pata; (*pej: touch*) tocar,

manosear.
pawn [pɔːn] *n* (*CHESS*) peón *m*; (*fig*)
instrumento ♦ *vt* empeñar.
pawnbroker ['pɔːnbrəukə*] *n* prestamista
m/f.
pawnshop ['pɔːnʃɔp] *n* casa de empeños.
pay [peɪ] *n* paga; (*wage etc*) sueldo, salario
♦ (*vb: pt, pp* **paid**) *vt* pagar; (*visit*) hacer;
(*respect*) ofrecer ♦ *vi* pagar; (*be profitable*)
rendir, compensar, ser rentable; **to be in
sb's** ~ estar al servicio de algn; **to** ~
attention (to) prestar atención (a); **I paid
£5 for that record** pagué 5 libras por ese
disco; **how much did you** ~ **for it?**
¿cuánto pagaste por él?; **to** ~ **one's way**
(*contribute one's share*) pagar su parte;
(*remain solvent: company*) ser solvente; **to**
~ **dividends** (*COMM*) pagar dividendos;
(*fig*) compensar; **it won't** ~ **you to do that**
no te merece la pena hacer eso; **to put
paid to** (*plan, person*) acabar con.
▶**pay back** *vt* (*money*) devolver,
reembolsar; (*person*) pagar.
▶**pay for** *vt fus* pagar.
▶**pay in** *vt* ingresar.
▶**pay off** *vt* liquidar; (*person*) pagar; (*debts*)
liquidar, saldar; (*creditor*) cancelar,
redimir; (*workers*) despedir; (*mortgage*)
cancelar, redimir ♦ *vi* (*scheme, decision*)
dar resultado; **to** ~ **sth off in instalments**
pagar algo a plazos.
▶**pay out** *vt* (*rope*) ir dando; (*money*)
gastar, desembolsar.
▶**pay up** *vt* pagar.
payable ['peɪəbl] *adj* pagadero; **to make a
cheque** ~ **to sb** extender un cheque a
favor de algn.
pay award *n* aumento de sueldo.
pay day *n* día *m* de paga.
PAYE *n abbr* (*BRIT*: = *pay as you earn*)
*sistema de retención fiscal en la fuente
de ingresos.*
payee [peɪ'iː] *n* portador(a) *m/f.*
pay envelope *n* (*US*) = **pay packet**.
paying ['peɪɪŋ] *adj*: ~ **guest** huésped(a) *m/f*
que la paga.
payload ['peɪləud] *n* carga útil.
payment ['peɪmənt] *n* pago; **advance** ~
(*part sum*) anticipo, adelanto; (*total sum*)
saldo; **monthly** ~ mensualidad *f*; **deferred**
~, ~ **by instalments** pago a plazos *or*
diferido; **on** ~ **of £5** mediante pago de *or*
pagando £5; **in** ~ **for** (*goods, sum owed*) en
pago de.
pay packet *n* (*BRIT*) sobre *m* (de la paga).
pay-phone ['peɪfəun] *n* teléfono público.
payroll ['peɪrəul] *n* nómina; **to be on a
firm's** ~ estar en la nómina de una

compañía.
pay slip *n* hoja del sueldo.
pay station *n* (*US*) teléfono público.
PBS *n abbr* (*US*: = *Public Broadcasting
Service*) *agrupación de ayuda a la
realización de emisiones para la TV
pública.*
PC *n abbr see* **personal computer**; (*BRIT*) =
police constable ♦ *abbr* (*BRIT*) = *Privy
Councillor* ♦ *adj abbr* = **politically correct**.
pc *abbr* = **per cent, postcard**.
p/c *abbr* = **petty cash**.
PCB *n abbr see* **printed circuit board**.
PD *n abbr* (*US*) = **police department**.
pd *abbr* = **paid**.
PDSA *n abbr* (*BRIT*) = *People's Dispensary for
Sick Animals.*
PDT *n abbr* (*US*: = *Pacific Daylight Time*) *hora
de verano del Pacífico.*
PE *n abbr* (= *physical education*) ed. física
♦ *abbr* (*Canada*) = *Prince Edward Island.*
pea [piː] *n* guisante *m*, chícharo (*LAM*),
arveja (*LAM*).
peace [piːs] *n* paz *f*; (*calm*) paz *f*,
tranquilidad *f*; **to be at** ~ **with sb/sth**
estar en paz con algn/algo; **to keep the** ~
(*policeman*) mantener el orden; (*citizen*)
guardar el orden.
peaceable ['piːsəbl] *adj* pacífico.
peaceably ['piːsəblɪ] *adv* pacíficamente.
peaceful ['piːsful] *adj* (*gentle*) pacífico;
(*calm*) tranquilo, sosegado.
peacekeeping ['piːskiːpɪŋ] *adj* de
pacificación ♦ *n* pacificación *f*.
peacekeeping force *n* fuerza de
pacificación.
peace offering *n* (*fig*) prenda de paz.
peacetime ['piːstaɪm] *n*: **in** ~ en tiempo de
paz.
peach [piːtʃ] *n* melocotón *m*, durazno (*LAM*).
peacock ['piːkɔk] *n* pavo real.
peak [piːk] *n* (*of mountain: top*) cumbre *f*,
cima; (: *point*) pico; (*of cap*) visera; (*fig*)
cumbre *f*.
peak-hour ['piːkauə*] *adj* (*traffic etc*) de
horas punta.
peak hours *npl*, **peak period** *n* horas *fpl*
punta.
peak rate *n* tarifa máxima.
peaky ['piːkɪ] *adj* (*BRIT col*) pálido,
paliducho; **I'm feeling a bit** ~ estoy
malucho, no me encuentro bien.
peal [piːl] *n* (*of bells*) repique *m*; ~ **of
laughter** carcajada.
peanut ['piːnʌt] *n* cacahuete *m*, maní *m*
(*LAM*).
peanut butter *n* mantequilla de
cacahuete.

pear [pɛə*] n pera.
pearl [pəːl] n perla.
peasant ['pɛznt] n campesino/a.
peat [piːt] n turba.
pebble ['pɛbl] n guijarro.
peck [pɛk] vt (also: ~ at) picotear; (food)
comer sin ganas ♦ n picotazo; (kiss)
besito.
pecking order ['pɛkɪŋ-] n orden m de
jerarquía.
peckish ['pɛkɪʃ] adj (BRIT col): **I feel** ~ tengo
ganas de picar algo.
peculiar [pɪ'kjuːlɪə*] adj (odd) extraño,
raro; (typical) propio, característico;
(particular: importance, qualities)
particular; ~ **to** propio de.
peculiarity [pɪkjuːlɪ'ærɪtɪ] n peculiaridad f,
característica.
peculiarly [pɪ'kjuːlɪəlɪ] adv extrañamente;
particularmente.
pedal ['pɛdl] n pedal m ♦ vi pedalear.
pedal bin n cubo de la basura con pedal.
pedant ['pɛdənt] n pedante m/f.
pedantic [pɪ'dæntɪk] adj pedante.
pedantry ['pɛdəntrɪ] n pedantería.
peddle ['pɛdl] vt (goods) ir vendiendo or
vender de puerta en puerta; (drugs)
traficar con; (gossip) divulgar.
peddler ['pɛdlə*] n vendedor(a) m/f
ambulante.
pedestal ['pɛdəstl] n pedestal m.
pedestrian [pɪ'dɛstrɪən] n peatón m ♦ adj
pedestre.
pedestrian crossing n (BRIT) paso de
peatones.
pedestrian precinct n zona reservada
para peatones.
pediatrics [piːdɪ'ætrɪks] n (US)
= **paediatrics**.
pedigree ['pɛdɪgriː] n genealogía; (of
animal) pedigrí m ♦ cpd (animal) de raza,
de casta.
pedlar ['pɛdlə*] n (BRIT) = **peddler**.
pee [piː] vi (col) mear.
peek [piːk] vi mirar a hurtadillas; (COMPUT)
inspeccionar.
peel [piːl] n piel f; (of orange, lemon)
cáscara; (: removed) peladuras fpl ♦ vt
pelar ♦ vi (paint etc) desconcharse;
(wallpaper) despegarse, desprenderse.
▶**peel back** vt pelar.
peeler ['piːlə*] n: **potato** ~ mondador m or
pelador m de patatas, pelapatatas m inv.
peep [piːp] n (BRIT: look) mirada furtiva;
(sound) pío ♦ vi (BRIT) piar.
▶**peep out** vi asomar la cabeza.
peephole ['piːphəul] n mirilla.
peer [pɪə*] vi: **to** ~ **at** escudriñar ♦ n (noble)

par m; (equal) igual m.
peerage ['pɪərɪdʒ] n nobleza.
peerless ['pɪəlɪs] adj sin par, incomparable,
sin igual.
peeved [piːvd] adj enojado.
peevish ['piːvɪʃ] adj malhumorado.
peevishness ['piːvɪʃnɪs] n mal humor m.
peg [pɛg] n clavija; (for coat etc) gancho,
colgador m; (BRIT: also: **clothes** ~) pinza;
(tent ~) estaca ♦ vt (clothes) tender;
(groundsheet) fijar con estacas; (fig:
wages, prices) fijar.
pejorative [pɪ'dʒɔrətɪv] adj peyorativo.
Pekin [piː'kɪn], **Peking** [piː'kɪŋ] n Pekín m.
pekinese [piːkɪ'niːz] n pequinés/esa m/f.
pelican ['pɛlɪkən] n pelícano.
pelican crossing n (BRIT AUT) paso de
peatones señalizado.
pellet ['pɛlɪt] n bolita; (bullet) perdigón m.
pell-mell ['pɛl'mɛl] adv en tropel.
pelmet ['pɛlmɪt] n galería.
pelt [pɛlt] vt: **to** ~ **sb with sth** arrojarle
algo a algn ♦ vi (rain: also: ~ **down**) llover
a cántaros ♦ n pellejo.
pelvis ['pɛlvɪs] n pelvis f.
pen [pɛn] n (ballpoint ~) bolígrafo; (fountain
~) pluma; (for sheep) redil m; (US col:
prison) cárcel f, chirona; **to put** ~ **to paper**
tomar la pluma.
penal ['piːnl] adj penal; ~ **servitude**
trabajos mpl forzados.
penalize ['piːnəlaɪz] vt (punish) castigar;
(SPORT) sancionar, penalizar.
penalty ['pɛnltɪ] n (gen) pena; (fine) multa;
(SPORT) sanción f; ~ **(kick)** (FOOTBALL)
penalty m.
penalty area n (BRIT SPORT) área de
castigo.
penalty clause n cláusula de penalización.
penalty shoot-out [-'ʃuːtaut] n (FOOTBALL)
tanda de penaltis.
penance ['pɛnəns] n penitencia.
pence [pɛns] pl of **penny**.
penchant ['pãːʃãːŋ] n predilección f,
inclinación f.
pencil ['pɛnsl] n lápiz m, lapicero (esp LAM)
♦ vt (also: ~ **in**) escribir con lápiz.
pencil case n estuche m.
pencil sharpener n sacapuntas m inv.
pendant ['pɛndnt] n pendiente m.
pending ['pɛndɪŋ] prep antes de ♦ adj
pendiente; ~ **the arrival of** ... hasta que
llegue ..., hasta llegar ... .
pendulum ['pɛndjuləm] n péndulo.
penetrate ['pɛnɪtreɪt] vt penetrar.
penetrating ['pɛnɪtreɪtɪŋ] adj penetrante.
penetration [pɛnɪ'treɪʃən] n penetración f.
penfriend ['pɛnfrɛnd] n (BRIT) amigo/a por

correspondencia.
penguin ['pɛŋgwɪn] n pingüino.
penicillin [pɛnɪ'sɪlɪn] n penicilina.
peninsula [pə'nɪnsjulə] n península.
penis ['piːnɪs] n pene m.
penitence ['pɛnɪtns] n penitencia.
penitent ['pɛnɪtnt] adj arrepentido; (REL) penitente.
penitentiary [pɛnɪ'tɛnʃərɪ] n (US) cárcel f, presidio.
penknife ['pɛnnaɪf] n navaja.
Penn(a). abbr (US) = Pennsylvania.
pen name n seudónimo.
pennant ['pɛnənt] n banderola; banderín m.
penniless ['pɛnɪlɪs] adj sin dinero.
Pennines ['pɛnaɪnz] npl (Montes mpl) Peninos mpl.
penny, pl **pennies** or (BRIT) **pence** ['pɛnɪ, 'pɛnɪz, pɛns] n penique m; (US) centavo.
penpal ['pɛnpæl] n amigo/a por correspondencia.
penpusher ['pɛnpuʃə*] n (pej) chupatintas m/f inv.
pension ['pɛnʃən] n (allowance, state payment) pensión f; (old-age) jubilación f.
▶**pension off** vt jubilar.
pensioner ['pɛnʃənə*] n (BRIT) jubilado/a.
pension fund n fondo de pensiones.
pensive ['pɛnsɪv] adj pensativo; (withdrawn) preocupado.
pentagon ['pɛntəgən] n pentágono; **the P~** (US POL) el Pentágono.

---
*Se conoce como el Pentágono (**the Pentagon**) al edificio de planta pentagonal que acoge las dependencias del Ministerio de Defensa estadounidense (**Department of Defense**) en Arlington, Virginia. En lenguaje periodístico se aplica también a la dirección militar del país.*

Pentecost ['pɛntɪkɔst] n Pentecostés m.
penthouse ['pɛnthaus] n ático (de lujo).
pent-up ['pɛntʌp] adj (feelings) reprimido.
penultimate [pɛ'nʌltɪmət] adj penúltimo.
penury ['pɛnjurɪ] n miseria, pobreza.
people ['piːpl] npl gente f; (citizens) pueblo sg, ciudadanos mpl ♦ n (nation, race) pueblo, nación f ♦ vt poblar; **several ~ came** vinieron varias personas; **~ say that ...** dice la gente que ...; **old/young ~** los ancianos/jóvenes; **~ at large** la gente en general; **a man of the ~** un hombre del pueblo.
PEP n abbr (= Personal Equity Plan) plan personal de inversión con desgravación fiscal.
pep [pɛp] n (col) energía.

▶**pep up** vt animar.
pepper ['pɛpə*] n (spice) pimienta; (vegetable) pimiento, ají m (LAM), chile m (LAM) ♦ vt (fig) salpicar.
peppermint ['pɛpəmɪnt] n menta; (sweet) pastilla de menta.
pepperoni [pɛpə'rəunɪ] n ≈ salchichón m picante.
pepperpot ['pɛpəpɔt] n pimentero.
peptalk ['pɛptɔːk] n (col): **to give sb a ~** darle a algn una inyección de ánimo.
per [pə:*] prep por; **~ day/person** por día/persona; **as ~ your instructions** de acuerdo con sus instrucciones.
per annum adv al año.
per capita adj, adv per cápita.
perceive [pə'siːv] vt percibir; (realize) darse cuenta de.
per cent, (US) **percent** [pə'sɛnt] n por ciento; **a 20 ~ discount** un descuento del 20 por ciento.
percentage [pə'sɛntɪdʒ] n porcentaje m; **to get a ~ on all sales** percibir un tanto por ciento sobre todas las ventas; **on a ~ basis** a porcentaje.
percentage point n punto (porcentual).
perceptible [pə'sɛptəbl] adj perceptible; (notable) sensible.
perception [pə'sɛpʃən] n percepción f; (insight) perspicacia.
perceptive [pə'sɛptɪv] adj perspicaz.
perch [pə:tʃ] n (fish) perca; (for bird) percha ♦ vi posarse.
percolate ['pə:kəleɪt] vt (coffee) filtrar ♦ vi (coffee, fig) filtrarse.
percolator ['pə:kəleɪtə*] n cafetera de filtro.
percussion [pə'kʌʃən] n percusión f.
percussionist [pə'kʌʃənɪst] n percusionista m/f.
peremptory [pə'rɛmptərɪ] adj perentorio.
perennial [pə'rɛnɪəl] adj perenne.
perfect adj ['pə:fɪkt] perfecto ♦ n (also: ~ tense) perfecto ♦ vt [pə'fɛkt] perfeccionar; **he's a ~ stranger to me** no le conozco de nada, me es completamente desconocido.
perfection [pə'fɛkʃən] n perfección f.
perfectionist [pə'fɛkʃənɪst] n perfeccionista m/f.
perfectly ['pə:fɪktlɪ] adv perfectamente; **I'm ~ happy with the situation** estoy muy contento con la situación; **you know ~ well** lo sabes muy bien or perfectamente.
perforate ['pə:fəreɪt] vt perforar.
perforated ulcer n úlcera perforada.
perforation [pə:fə'reɪʃən] n perforación f.
perform [pə'fɔ:m] vt (carry out) realizar,

llevar a cabo; (*THEAT*) representar; (*piece of music*) interpretar ♦ *vi* (*THEAT*) actuar; (*TECH*) funcionar.

performance [pə'fɔːməns] *n* (*of task*) realización *f*; (*of a play*) representación *f*; (*of player etc*) actuación *f*; (*of engine*) rendimiento; (*of car*) prestaciones *fpl*; (*of function*) desempeño; **the team put up a good** ~ el equipo se defendió bien.

performer [pə'fɔːmə*] *n* (*actor*) actor *m*, actriz *f*; (*MUS*) intérprete *m/f*.

performing [pə'fɔːmɪŋ] *adj* (*animal*) amaestrado.

performing arts *npl*: **the** ~ las artes teatrales.

perfume ['pəːfjuːm] *n* perfume *m*.

perfunctory [pə'fʌŋktərɪ] *adj* superficial.

perhaps [pə'hæps] *adv* quizá(s), tal vez; ~ **so/not** puede que sí/no.

peril ['pɛrɪl] *n* peligro, riesgo.

perilous ['pɛrɪləs] *adj* peligroso.

perilously ['pɛrɪləslɪ] *adv*: **they came** ~ **close to being caught** por poco les cogen *or* agarran.

perimeter [pə'rɪmɪtə*] *n* perímetro.

period ['pɪərɪəd] *n* período, periodo; (*HISTORY*) época; (*SCOL*) clase *f*; (*full stop*) punto; (*MED*) regla, periodo; (*US SPORT*) tiempo ♦ *adj* (*costume, furniture*) de época; **for a** ~ **of three weeks** durante (un período de) tres semanas; **the holiday** ~ el período de vacaciones.

periodic [pɪərɪ'ɔdɪk] *adj* periódico.

periodical [pɪərɪ'ɔdɪkl] *adj* periódico ♦ *n* revista, publicación *f* periódica.

periodically [pɪərɪ'ɔdɪklɪ] *adv* de vez en cuando, cada cierto tiempo.

period pains *npl* dolores *mpl* de la regla *or* de la menstruación.

peripatetic [pɛrɪpə'tɛtɪk] *adj* (*salesman*) ambulante; (*teacher*) con trabajo en varios colegios.

peripheral [pə'rɪfərəl] *adj* periférico ♦ *n* (*COMPUT*) periférico, unidad *f* periférica.

periphery [pə'rɪfərɪ] *n* periferia.

periscope ['pɛrɪskəup] *n* periscopio.

perish ['pɛrɪʃ] *vi* perecer; (*decay*) echarse a perder.

perishable ['pɛrɪʃəbl] *adj* perecedero.

perishables ['pɛrɪʃəblz] *npl* productos *mpl* perecederos.

peritonitis [pɛrɪtə'naɪtɪs] *n* peritonitis *f*.

perjure ['pəːdʒə*] *vt*: **to** ~ **o.s.** perjurar.

perjury ['pəːdʒərɪ] *n* (*LAW*) perjurio.

perk [pəːk] *n* beneficio, extra *m*.

►**perk up** *vi* (*cheer up*) animarse.

perky ['pəːkɪ] *adj* alegre, animado.

perm [pəːm] *n* permanente *f* ♦ *vt*: **to have**

one's hair ~**ed** hacerse una permanente.

permanence ['pəːmənəns] *n* permanencia.

permanent ['pəːmənənt] *adj* permanente; (*job, position*) fijo; (*dye, ink*) indeleble; ~ **address** domicilio permanente; **I'm not** ~ **here** no estoy fijo aquí.

permanently ['pəːmənəntlɪ] *adv* (*lastingly*) para siempre, de modo definitivo; (*all the time*) permanentemente.

permeate ['pəːmɪeɪt] *vi* penetrar, trascender ♦ *vt* penetrar, trascender a.

permissible [pə'mɪsɪbl] *adj* permisible, lícito.

permission [pə'mɪʃən] *n* permiso; **to give sb** ~ **to do sth** autorizar a algn para que haga algo; **with your** ~ con su permiso.

permissive [pə'mɪsɪv] *adj* permisivo.

permit *n* ['pəːmɪt] permiso, licencia; (*entrance pass*) pase *m* ♦ *vt* [pə'mɪt] permitir; (*accept*) tolerar ♦ *vi* [pə'mɪt]: **weather** ~**ting** si el tiempo lo permite; **fishing** ~ permiso de pesca; **building/ export** ~ licencia *or* permiso de construcción/exportación.

permutation [pəːmju'teɪʃən] *n* permutación *f*.

pernicious [pəː'nɪʃəs] *adj* nocivo; (*MED*) pernicioso.

pernickety [pə'nɪkɪtɪ] *adj* (*col: person*) quisquilloso; (: *task*) delicado.

perpendicular [pəːpən'dɪkjulə*] *adj* perpendicular.

perpetrate ['pəːpɪtreɪt] *vt* cometer.

perpetual [pə'pɛtjuəl] *adj* perpetuo.

perpetually [pə'pɛtjuəlɪ] *adv* (*eternally*) perpetuamente; (*continuously*) constantemente, continuamente.

perpetuate [pə'pɛtjueɪt] *vt* perpetuar.

perpetuity [pəːpɪ'tjuɪtɪ] *n*: **in** ~ a perpetuidad.

perplex [pə'plɛks] *vt* dejar perplejo.

perplexed [pə'plɛkst] *adj* perplejo, confuso.

perplexing [pə'plɛksɪŋ] *adj* que causa perplejidad.

perplexity [pə'plɛksɪtɪ] *n* perplejidad *f*, confusión *f*.

perquisites ['pəːkwɪzɪts] *npl* (*also*: **perks**) beneficios *mpl*.

persecute ['pəːsɪkjuːt] *vt* (*pursue*) perseguir; (*harass*) acosar.

persecution [pəːsɪ'kjuːʃən] *n* persecución *f*.

perseverance [pəːsɪ'vɪərəns] *n* perseverancia.

persevere [pəːsɪ'vɪə*] *vi* perseverar.

Persia ['pəːʃə] *n* Persia.

Persian ['pəːʃən] *adj, n* persa *m/f* ♦ *n* (*LING*) persa *m*; **the** ~ **Gulf** el Golfo Pérsico.

Persian cat *n* gato persa.

persist [pə'sɪst] *vi* persistir; **to ~ in doing sth** empeñarse en hacer algo.

persistence [pə'sɪstəns] *n* empeño.

persistent [pə'sɪstənt] *adj* (*lateness, rain*) persistente; (*determined*) porfiado; (*continuing*) constante; ~ **offender** (*LAW*) multirreincidente *m/f*.

persistently [pə'sɪstəntlɪ] *adv* persistentemente; (*continually*) constantemente.

persnickety [pə'snɪkətɪ] *adj* (*US col*) = **pernickety.**

person ['pəːsn] *n* persona; **in ~** en persona; **on** *or* **about one's ~** (*weapon, money*) encima; **a ~ to ~ call** (*TEL*) una llamada (de) persona a persona.

personable ['pəːsnəbl] *adj* atractivo.

personal ['pəːsnl] *adj* personal, individual; (*visit*) en persona; (*BRIT TEL*) persona a persona.

personal allowance *n* desgravación *f* personal.

personal assistant (PA) *n* ayudante *m/f* personal.

personal belongings *npl* efectos *mpl* personales.

personal column *n* anuncios *mpl* personales.

personal computer (PC) *n* ordenador *m* personal.

personal effects *npl* efectos *mpl* personales.

personal identification number (PIN) *n* (*COMPUT, BANKING*) número personal de identificación.

personality [pəːsə'nælɪtɪ] *n* personalidad *f*.

personal loan *n* préstamo personal.

personally ['pəːsnlɪ] *adv* personalmente.

personal organizer *n* agenda (*profesional*); (*electronic*) organizador *m* personal.

personal property *n* bienes *mpl* muebles.

personal stereo *n* walkman ® *m*.

personification [pəːsɔnɪfɪ'keɪʃən] *n* personificación *f*.

personify [pəː'sɔnɪfaɪ] *vt* encarnar, personificar.

personnel [pəːsə'nɛl] *n* personal *m*.

personnel department *n* departamento de personal.

personnel management *n* gestión *f* de personal.

personnel manager *n* jefe *m* de personal.

perspective [pə'spɛktɪv] *n* perspectiva; **to get sth into ~** ver algo en perspectiva *or* como es.

Perspex ® ['pəːspɛks] *n* (*BRIT*) vidrio acrílico, plexiglás *m* ®.

perspiration [pəːspɪ'reɪʃən] *n* transpiración *f*, sudor *m*.

perspire [pə'spaɪə*] *vi* transpirar, sudar.

persuade [pə'sweɪd] *vt*: **to ~ sb to do sth** persuadir a algn para que haga algo; **to ~ sb of sth/that** persuadir *or* convencer a algn de algo/de que; **I am ~d that ...** estoy convencido de que ....

persuasion [pə'sweɪʒən] *n* persuasión *f*; (*persuasiveness*) persuasiva; (*creed*) creencia.

persuasive [pə'sweɪsɪv] *adj* persuasivo.

persuasively [pə'sweɪsɪvlɪ] *adv* de modo persuasivo.

pert [pəːt] *adj* impertinente, fresco, atrevido.

pertaining [pəː'teɪnɪŋ]: ~ **to** *prep* relacionado con.

pertinent ['pəːtɪnənt] *adj* pertinente, a propósito.

perturb [pə'təːb] *vt* perturbar.

perturbing [pə'təːbɪŋ] *adj* inquietante, perturbador(a).

Peru [pə'ruː] *n* el Perú.

perusal [pə'ruːzəl] *n* (*quick*) lectura somera; (*careful*) examen *m*.

peruse [pə'ruːz] *vt* (*examine*) leer con detención, examinar; (*glance at*) mirar por encima.

Peruvian [pə'ruːvɪən] *adj, n* peruano/a *m/f*.

pervade [pə'veɪd] *vt* impregnar; (*influence, ideas*) extenderse por.

pervasive [pə'veɪsɪv] *adj* (*smell*) penetrante; (*influence*) muy extendido; (*gloom, feelings, ideas*) reinante.

perverse [pə'vəːs] *adj* perverso; (*stubborn*) terco; (*wayward*) travieso.

perversely [pə'vəːslɪ] *adv* perversamente; tercamente; traviesamente.

perverseness [pə'vəːsnɪs] *n* perversidad *f*; terquedad *f*; travesura.

perversion [pə'vəːʃən] *n* perversión *f*.

pervert *n* ['pəːvəːt] pervertido/a ♦ *vt* [pə'vəːt] pervertir.

pessary ['pɛsərɪ] *n* pesario.

pessimism ['pɛsɪmɪzəm] *n* pesimismo.

pessimist ['pɛsɪmɪst] *n* pesimista *m/f*.

pessimistic [pɛsɪ'mɪstɪk] *adj* pesimista.

pest [pɛst] *n* (*insect*) insecto nocivo; (*fig*) lata, molestia; ~**s** *npl* plaga.

pest control *n* control *m* de plagas.

pester ['pɛstə*] *vt* molestar, acosar.

pesticide ['pɛstɪsaɪd] *n* pesticida *m*.

pestilence ['pɛstɪləns] *n* pestilencia.

pestle ['pɛsl] *n* mano *f* de mortero *or* de almirez.

pet [pɛt] *n* animal *m* doméstico; (*favourite*) favorito/a ♦ *vt* acariciar ♦ *vi* (*col*)

besuquearse ◊ *cpd*: my ~ aversion mi manía.
petal ['pɛtl] *n* pétalo.
peter ['piːtə*]: **to ~ out** *vi* agotarse, acabarse.
petite [pə'tiːt] *adj* menuda, chiquita.
petition [pə'tɪʃən] *n* petición *f* ◊ *vt* presentar una petición a ◊ *vi*: **to ~ for divorce** pedir el divorcio.
pet name *n* nombre *m* cariñoso, apodo.
petrified ['pɛtrɪfaɪd] *adj* (*fig*) pasmado, horrorizado.
petrochemical [pɛtrə'kɛmɪkl] *adj* petroquímico.
petrodollars ['pɛtrəudɔləz] *npl* petrodólares *mpl*.
petrol ['pɛtrəl] (*BRIT*) *n* gasolina; (*for lighter*) bencina; **two/four-star ~** gasolina normal/súper.
petrol bomb *n* cóctel *m* Molotov.
petrol can *n* bidón *m* de gasolina.
petrol engine *n* (*BRIT*) motor *m* de gasolina.
petroleum [pə'trəulɪəm] *n* petróleo.
petroleum jelly *n* vaselina.
petrol pump *n* (*BRIT*) (*in car*) bomba de gasolina; (*in garage*) surtidor *m* de gasolina.
petrol station *n* (*BRIT*) gasolinera.
petrol tank *n* (*BRIT*) depósito (de gasolina).
petticoat ['pɛtɪkaut] *n* combinación *f*, enagua(s) *f(pl)* (*LAM*).
pettifogging ['pɛtɪfɔɡɪŋ] *adj* quisquilloso.
pettiness ['pɛtɪnɪs] *n* mezquindad *f*.
petty ['pɛtɪ] *adj* (*mean*) mezquino; (*unimportant*) insignificante.
petty cash *n* dinero para gastos menores.
petty cash book *n* libro de caja auxiliar.
petty officer *n* contramaestre *m*.
petulant ['pɛtjulənt] *adj* malhumorado.
pew [pjuː] *n* banco.
pewter ['pjuːtə*] *n* peltre *m*.
Pfc *abbr* (*US MIL*) = *private first class*.
PG *n abbr* (*CINE*) = *parental guidance*.
PGA *n abbr* = *Professional Golfers' Association*.
PH *n abbr* (*US MIL*: = *Purple Heart*) decoración *f* otorgada a los heridos de guerra.
pH *n abbr* (= *pH value*) pH.
PHA *n abbr* (*US*) = *Public Housing Administration*.
phallic ['fælɪk] *adj* fálico.
phantom ['fæntəm] *n* fantasma *m*.
Pharaoh ['fɛərəu] *n* faraón *m*.
pharmaceutical [faːmə'sjuːtɪkl] *adj* farmacéutico.
pharmacist ['faːməsɪst] *n* farmacéutico/a.

pharmacy ['faːməsɪ] *n* (*US*) farmacia.
phase [feɪz] *n* fase *f* ◊ *vt*: **to ~ sth in/out** introducir/retirar algo por etapas; **~d withdrawal** retirada progresiva.
PhD *abbr* = *Doctor of Philosophy*.
pheasant ['fɛznt] *n* faisán *m*.
phenomenal [fɪ'nɔmɪnl] *adj* fenomenal, extraordinario.
phenomenally [fɪ'nɔmɪnlɪ] *adv* extraordinariamente.
phenomenon, *pl* **phenomena** [fə'nɔmɪnən, -nə] *n* fenómeno.
phial ['faɪəl] *n* ampolla.
philanderer [fɪ'lændərə*] *n* donjuán *m*, don Juan *m*.
philanthropic [fɪlən'θrɔpɪk] *adj* filantrópico.
philanthropist [fɪ'lænθrəpɪst] *n* filántropo/a.
philatelist [fɪ'lætəlɪst] *n* filatelista *m/f*.
philately [fɪ'lætəlɪ] *n* filatelia.
Philippines ['fɪlɪpiːnz] *npl*: **the ~** (las Islas) Filipinas.
philosopher [fɪ'lɔsəfə*] *n* filósofo/a.
philosophical [fɪlə'sɔfɪkl] *adj* filosófico.
philosophy [fɪ'lɔsəfɪ] *n* filosofía.
phlegm [flɛm] *n* flema.
phlegmatic [flɛɡ'mætɪk] *adj* flemático.
phobia ['fəubjə] *n* fobia.
phone [fəun] *n* teléfono ◊ *vt* telefonear, llamar por teléfono; **to be on the ~** tener teléfono; (*be calling*) estar hablando por teléfono.
▶**phone back** *vt*, *vi* volver a llamar.
▶**phone up** *vt*, *vi* llamar por teléfono.
phone book *n* guía telefónica.
phone box, **phone booth** *n* cabina telefónica.
phone call *n* llamada (telefónica).
phonecard ['fəunkaːd] *n* tarjeta telefónica.
phone-in ['fəunɪn] *n* (*BRIT RADIO*, *TV*) programa de radio *or* televisión con las líneas abiertas al público.
phone tapping [-tæpɪŋ] *n* escuchas telefónicas.
phonetics [fə'nɛtɪks] *n* fonética.
phon(e)y ['fəunɪ] *adj* falso ◊ *n* (*person*) farsante *m/f*.
phonograph ['fəunəɡræf] *n* (*US*) fonógrafo, tocadiscos *m inv*.
phonology [fəu'nɔlədʒɪ] *n* fonología.
phosphate ['fɔsfeɪt] *n* fosfato.
phosphorus ['fɔsfərəs] *n* fósforo.
photo ['fəutəu] *n* foto *f*.
photo... ['fəutəu] *pref* foto....
photocall ['fəutəukɔːl] *n* sesión *f* fotográfica para la prensa.
photocopier ['fəutəukɔpɪə*] *n* fotocopiadora.
photocopy ['fəutəukɔpɪ] *n* fotocopia ◊ *vt*

fotocopiar.

photoelectric [fəutəuɪˈlɛktrɪk] *adj:* ~ **cell** célula fotoeléctrica.

photo finish *n* resultado comprobado por fotocontrol.

Photofit ® [ˈfəutəufɪt] *n* (*also:* ~ **picture**) retrato robot.

photogenic [fəutəuˈdʒɛnɪk] *adj* fotogénico.

photograph [ˈfəutəgræf] *n* fotografía ♦ *vt* fotografiar; **to take a** ~ **of sb** sacar una foto de algn.

photographer [fəˈtɔgrəfə*] *n* fotógrafo.

photographic [fəutəˈgræfɪk] *adj* fotográfico.

photography [fəˈtɔgrəfɪ] *n* fotografía.

photo opportunity *n* oportunidad de salir en la foto.

Photostat ® [ˈfəutəustæt] *n* fotóstato.

photosynthesis [fəutəuˈsɪnθəsɪs] *n* fotosíntesis *f*.

phrase [freɪz] *n* frase *f* ♦ *vt* (*letter*) expresar, redactar.

phrase book *n* libro de frases.

physical [ˈfɪzɪkl] *adj* físico; ~ **examination** reconocimiento médico; ~ **exercises** ejercicios *mpl* físicos.

physical education *n* educación *f* física.

physically [ˈfɪsɪklɪ] *adv* físicamente.

physical training *n* gimnasia.

physician [fɪˈzɪʃən] *n* médico/a.

physicist [ˈfɪzɪsɪst] *n* físico/a.

physics [ˈfɪzɪks] *n* física.

physiological [fɪzɪəˈlɔdʒɪkl] *adj* fisiológico.

physiology [fɪzɪˈɔlədʒɪ] *n* fisiología.

physiotherapy [fɪzɪəuˈθerəpɪ] *n* fisioterapia.

physique [fɪˈziːk] *n* físico.

pianist [ˈpɪənɪst] *n* pianista *m/f*.

piano [pɪˈænəu] *n* piano.

piano accordion *n* (*BRIT*) acordeón-piano *m*.

piccolo [ˈpɪkələu] *n* (*MUS*) flautín *m*.

pick [pɪk] *n* (*tool: also:* ~**-axe**) pico, piqueta ♦ *vt* (*select*) elegir, escoger; (*gather*) coger (*SP*), recoger (*LAM*); (*lock*) abrir con ganzúa; (*scab, spot*) rascar ♦ *vi:* **to** ~ **and choose** ser muy exigente; **take your** ~ escoja lo que quiera; **the** ~ **of** lo mejor de; **to** ~ **one's nose/teeth** hurgarse las narices/escarbarse los dientes; **to** ~ **pockets** ratear, ser carterista; **to** ~ **one's way through** andar a tientas, abrirse camino; **to** ~ **a fight/quarrel with sb** buscar pelea/camorra con algn; **to** ~ **sb's brains** aprovecharse de los conocimientos de algn.

▶**pick at** *vt fus:* **to** ~ **at one's food** comer con poco apetito.

▶**pick off** *vt* (*kill*) matar de un tiro.

▶**pick on** *vt fus* (*person*) meterse con.

▶**pick out** *vt* escoger; (*distinguish*) identificar.

▶**pick up** *vi* (*improve: sales*) ir mejor; (: *patient*) reponerse; (: *FINANCE*) recobrarse ♦ *vt* (*from floor*) recoger; (*buy*) comprar; (*find*) encontrar; (*learn*) aprender; (*RADIO, TV, TEL*) captar; **to** ~ **up speed** acelerarse; **to** ~ **o.s. up** levantarse; **to** ~ **up where one left off** reempezar algo donde lo había dejado.

pickaxe, (*US*) **pickax** [ˈpɪkæks] *n* pico, zapapico.

picket [ˈpɪkɪt] *n* (*in strike*) piquete *m* ♦ *vt* hacer un piquete en, piquetear; **to be on** ~ **duty** estar de piquete.

picketing [ˈpɪkɪtɪŋ] *n* organización *f* de piquetes.

picket line *n* piquete *m*.

pickings [ˈpɪkɪŋz] *npl* (*pilferings*): **there are good** ~ **to be had here** se pueden sacar buenas ganancias de aquí.

pickle [ˈpɪkl] *n* (*also:* ~**s:** *as condiment*) escabeche *m*; (*fig: mess*) apuro ♦ *vt* conservar en escabeche; (*in vinegar*) conservar en vinagre; **in a** ~ en un lío, en apuros.

pick-me-up [ˈpɪkmɪʌp] *n* reconstituyente *m*.

pickpocket [ˈpɪkpɔkɪt] *n* carterista *m/f*.

pickup [ˈpɪkʌp] *n* (*BRIT: on record player*) brazo; (*small truck: also:* ~ **truck,** ~ **van**) furgoneta.

picnic [ˈpɪknɪk] *n* picnic *m*, merienda ♦ *vi* merendar en el campo.

pictorial [pɪkˈtɔːrɪəl] *adj* pictórico; (*magazine etc*) ilustrado.

picture [ˈpɪktʃə*] *n* cuadro; (*painting*) pintura; (*photograph*) fotografía; (*film*) película; (*TV*) imagen *f* ♦ *vt* pintar; **the ~s** (*BRIT*) el cine; **we get a good** ~ **here** captamos bien la imagen aquí; **to take a** ~ **of sb/sth** hacer *or* sacar una foto a algn/de algo; **the garden is a** ~ **in June** el jardín es una preciosidad en junio; **the overall** ~ la impresión general; **to put sb in the** ~ poner a algn al corriente *or* al tanto.

picture book *n* libro de dibujos.

picturesque [pɪktʃəˈrɛsk] *adj* pintoresco.

piddling [ˈpɪdlɪŋ] *adj* insignificante.

pidgin [ˈpɪdʒɪn] *adj:* ~ **English** lengua franca basada en el inglés.

pie [paɪ] *n* (*of meat etc: large*) pastel *m*; (: *small*) empanada; (*sweet*) tarta.

piebald [ˈpaɪbɔːld] *adj* pío.

piece [piːs] *n* pedazo, trozo; (*of cake*) trozo;

(*DRAUGHTS etc*) ficha; (*CHESS, part of a set*) pieza; (*item*): **a ~ of furniture/advice** un mueble/un consejo ♦ *vt*: **to ~ together** juntar; (*TECH*) armar; **to take to ~s** desmontar; **a ~ of news** una noticia; **a 10p ~** una moneda de 10 peniques; **a six-~ band** un conjunto de seis (músicos); **in one ~** (*object*) de una sola pieza; **~ by ~** pieza por *or* a pieza; **to say one's ~** decir su parecer.

piecemeal ['piːsmiːl] *adv* poco a poco.

piece rate *n* tarifa a destajo.

piecework ['piːswəːk] *n* trabajo a destajo.

pie chart *n* gráfico de sectores *or* de tarta.

pier [pɪə*] *n* muelle *m*, embarcadero.

pierce [pɪəs] *vt* penetrar en, perforar; **to have one's ears ~d** hacerse los agujeros de las orejas.

piercing ['pɪəsɪŋ] *adj* (*cry*) penetrante.

piety ['paɪətɪ] *n* piedad *f*.

pig [pɪg] *n* cerdo, puerco, chancho (*LAM*); (*person: greedy*) tragón/ona *m/f*, comilón/ona *m/f*; (: *nasty*) cerdo/a.

pigeon ['pɪdʒən] *n* paloma; (*as food*) pichón *m*.

pigeonhole ['pɪdʒənhəul] *n* casilla.

piggy bank ['pɪgɪbæŋk] *n* hucha (*en forma de cerdito*).

pigheaded ['pɪg'hɛdɪd] *adj* terco, testarudo.

piglet ['pɪglɪt] *n* cerdito, cochinillo.

pigment ['pɪgmənt] *n* pigmento.

pigmentation [pɪgmən'teɪʃən] *n* pigmentación *f*.

pigmy ['pɪgmɪ] *n* = **pygmy**.

pigskin ['pɪgskɪn] *n* piel *f* de cerdo.

pigsty ['pɪgstaɪ] *n* pocilga.

pigtail ['pɪgteɪl] *n* (*girl's*) trenza; (*Chinese, TAUR*) coleta.

pike [paɪk] *n* (*spear*) pica; (*fish*) lucio.

pilchard ['pɪltʃəd] *n* sardina.

pile [paɪl] *n* (*heap*) montón *m*; (*of carpet*) pelo ♦ (*vb: also: ~ up*) *vt* amontonar; (*fig*) acumular ♦ *vi* amontonarse; **in a ~** en un montón; **to ~ into** (*car*) meterse en.

►**pile on** *vt*: **to ~ it on** (*col*) exagerar.

piles [paɪlz] *npl* (*MED*) almorranas *fpl*, hemorroides *mpl*.

pile-up ['paɪlʌp] *n* (*AUT*) accidente *m* múltiple.

pilfer ['pɪlfə*] *vt*, *vi* ratear, robar, sisar.

pilfering ['pɪlfərɪŋ] *n* ratería.

pilgrim ['pɪlgrɪm] *n* peregrino/a; **the Pilgrim Fathers** *or* **Pilgrims** *los primeros colonos norteamericanos*; *see also* **Thanksgiving (Day)**.

pilgrimage ['pɪlgrɪmɪdʒ] *n* peregrinación *f*, romería.

pill [pɪl] *n* píldora; **the ~** la píldora; **to be on**

the ~ tomar la píldora (anticonceptiva).

pillage ['pɪlɪdʒ] *vt* pillar, saquear.

pillar ['pɪlə*] *n* pilar *m*, columna.

pillar box *n* (*BRIT*) buzón *m*.

pillion ['pɪljən] *n* (*of motorcycle*) asiento trasero; **to ride ~** ir en el asiento trasero.

pillion passenger *n* pasajero que va detrás.

pillory ['pɪlərɪ] *vt* poner en ridículo.

pillow ['pɪləu] *n* almohada.

pillowcase ['pɪləukeɪs], **pillowslip** ['pɪləuslɪp] *n* funda (de almohada).

pilot ['paɪlət] *n* piloto *inv* ♦ *adj* (*scheme etc*) piloto ♦ *vt* pilotar; (*fig*) guiar, conducir.

pilot light *n* piloto.

pimento [pɪ'mɛntəu] *n* pimiento morrón.

pimp [pɪmp] *n* chulo, cafiche *m* (*LAM*).

pimple ['pɪmpl] *n* grano.

pimply ['pɪmplɪ] *adj* lleno de granos.

PIN *n abbr see* **personal identification number**.

pin [pɪn] *n* alfiler *m*; (*ELEC: of plug*) clavija; (*TECH*) perno; (: *wooden*) clavija; (*drawing ~*) chincheta; (*in grenade*) percutor *m* ♦ *vt* prender (con alfiler); sujetar con perno; **~s and needles** hormigueo *sg*; **to ~ sth on sb** (*fig*) cargar a algn con la culpa de algo.

►**pin down** *vt* (*fig*): **there's something strange here, but I can't quite ~ it down** aquí hay algo raro pero no puedo precisar qué es; **to ~ sb down** hacer que algn concrete.

pinafore ['pɪnəfɔː*] *n* delantal *m*.

pinafore dress *n* (*BRIT*) pichi *m*.

pinball ['pɪnbɔːl] *n* (*also: ~ machine*) millón *m*, flíper *m*.

pincers ['pɪnsəz] *npl* pinzas *fpl*, tenazas *fpl*.

pinch [pɪntʃ] *n* pellizco; (*of salt etc*) pizca ♦ *vt* pellizcar; (*col: steal*) birlar ♦ *vi* (*shoe*) apretar; **at a ~** en caso de apuro; **to feel the ~** (*fig*) pasar apuros *or* estrecheces.

pinched [pɪntʃt] *adj* (*drawn*) cansado; **~ with cold** transido de frío; **~ for money/space** mal *or* falto de dinero/espacio *or* sitio.

pincushion ['pɪnkuʃən] *n* acerico.

pine [paɪn] *n* (*also: ~ tree*) pino ♦ *vi*: **to ~ for** suspirar por.

►**pine away** *vi* morirse de pena.

pineapple ['paɪnæpl] *n* piña, ananá(s) (*LAM*) *m*.

pine cone *n* piña.

pine needle *n* aguja de pino.

ping [pɪŋ] *n* (*noise*) sonido agudo.

Ping-Pong ® ['pɪŋpɔŋ] *n* pingpong *m*.

pink [pɪŋk] *adj* (de color) rosa ♦ *n* (*colour*) rosa; (*BOT*) clavel *m*.

pinking shears ['pɪŋkɪŋ-] *npl* tijeras *fpl* dentadas.
pin money *n* dinero para gastos extra.
pinnacle ['pɪnəkl] *n* cumbre *f*.
pinpoint ['pɪnpɔɪnt] *vt* precisar.
pinstripe ['pɪnstraɪp] *adj*: ~ **suit** traje *m* a rayas.
pint [paɪnt] *n* pinta (*BRIT* = *0.57 l*; *US* = *0.47 l*); (*BRIT col: of beer*) pinta de cerveza, ≈ jarra (*SP*).
pin-up ['pɪnʌp] *n* (*picture*) fotografía de *mujer u hombre medio desnudos*; ~ (**girl**) ≈ chica de calendario.
pioneer [paɪə'nɪə*] *n* pionero/a ♦ *vt* promover.
pious ['paɪəs] *adj* piadoso, devoto.
pip [pɪp] *n* (*seed*) pepita; **the** ~**s** (*BRIT TEL*) la señal.
pipe [paɪp] *n* tubería, cañería; (*for smoking*) pipa, cachimba (*LAM*), cachimbo (*LAM*) ♦ *vt* conducir en cañerías; (**bag**)~**s** *npl* gaita *sg*.
►**pipe down** *vi* (*col*) callarse.
pipe cleaner *n* limpiapipas *m inv*.
piped music [paɪpt-] *n* música ambiental.
pipe dream *n* sueño imposible.
pipeline ['paɪplaɪn] *n* tubería, cañería; (*for oil*) oleoducto; (*for natural gas*) gaseoducto; **it is in the** ~ (*fig*) está en trámite.
piper ['paɪpə*] *n* (*gen*) flautista *m/f*; (*with bagpipes*) gaitero/a.
pipe tobacco *n* tabaco de pipa.
piping ['paɪpɪŋ] *adv*: **to be** ~ **hot** estar calentito.
piquant ['piːkənt] *adj* picante.
pique [piːk] *n* pique *m*, resentimiento.
pirate ['paɪərət] *n* pirata *m/f* ♦ *vt* (*record, video, book*) hacer una copia pirata de.
pirated ['paɪərətɪd] *adj* (*book, record etc*) pirata *inv*.
pirate radio *n* (*BRIT*) emisora pirata.
pirouette [pɪru'εt] *n* pirueta ♦ *vi* piruetear.
Pisces ['paɪsiːz] *n* Piscis *m*.
piss [pɪs] *vi* (*col*) mear.
pissed [pɪst] *adj* (*col: drunk*) mamado.
pistol ['pɪstl] *n* pistola.
piston ['pɪstən] *n* pistón *m*, émbolo.
pit [pɪt] *n* hoyo; (*also*: **coal** ~) mina; (*in garage*) foso de inspección; (*also*: **orchestra** ~) foso de la orquesta; (*quarry*) cantera ♦ *vt* (*subj: chickenpox*) picar; (: *rust*) comer; **to** ~ **A against B** oponer A a B; ~**s** *npl* (*AUT*) box *msg*; ~**ted with** (*chickenpox*) picado de.
pitapat ['pɪtə'pæt] *adv*: **to go** ~ (*heart*) latir rápidamente; (*rain*) golpetear.
pitch [pɪtʃ] *n* (*throw*) lanzamiento; (*MUS*)

tono; (*BRIT SPORT*) campo, terreno; (*tar*) brea; (*in market etc*) puesto; (*fig: degree*) nivel *m*, grado ♦ *vt* (*throw*) arrojar, lanzar ♦ *vi* (*fall*) caer(se); (*NAUT*) cabecear; **I can't keep working at this** ~ no puedo seguir trabajando a este ritmo; **at its** (**highest**) ~ en su punto máximo; **his anger reached such a** ~ **that** ... su ira *or* cólera llegó a tal extremo que ...; **to** ~ **a tent** montar una tienda (de campaña); **to** ~ **one's aspirations too high** tener ambiciones desmesuradas.
pitch-black ['pɪtʃ'blæk] *adj* negro como boca de lobo.
pitched battle [pɪtʃt-] *n* batalla campal.
pitcher ['pɪtʃə*] *n* cántaro, jarro.
pitchfork ['pɪtʃfɔːk] *n* horca.
piteous ['pɪtɪəs] *adj* lastimoso.
pitfall ['pɪtfɔːl] *n* riesgo.
pith [pɪθ] *n* (*of orange*) piel *f* blanca; (*fig*) meollo.
pithead ['pɪthɛd] *n* (*BRIT*) bocamina.
pithy ['pɪθɪ] *adj* jugoso.
pitiful ['pɪtɪful] *adj* (*touching*) lastimoso, conmovedor(a); (*contemptible*) lamentable.
pitifully ['pɪtɪfəlɪ] *adv*: **it's** ~ **obvious** es tan evidente que da pena.
pitiless ['pɪtɪlɪs] *adj* despiadado, implacable.
pitilessly ['pɪtɪlɪslɪ] *adv* despiadadamente, implacablemente.
pittance ['pɪtns] *n* miseria.
pity ['pɪtɪ] *n* (*compassion*) compasión *f*, piedad *f*; (*shame*) lástima ♦ *vt* compadecer(se de); **to have** *or* **take** ~ **on sb** compadecerse de algn; **what a** ~! ¡qué pena!; **it is a** ~ **that you can't come** ¡qué pena que no puedas venir!
pitying ['pɪtɪɪŋ] *adj* compasivo, de lástima.
pivot ['pɪvət] *n* eje *m* ♦ *vi*: **to** ~ **on** girar sobre; (*fig*) depender de.
pixel ['pɪksl] *n* (*COMPUT*) pixel *m*, punto.
pixie ['pɪksɪ] *n* duendecillo.
pizza ['piːtsə] *n* pizza.
placard ['plækaːd] *n* (*in march etc*) pancarta.
placate [plə'keɪt] *vt* apaciguar.
place [pleɪs] *n* lugar *m*, sitio; (*rank*) rango; (*seat*) plaza, asiento; (*post*) puesto; (*in street names*) plaza; (*home*): **at/to his** ~ en/a su casa ♦ *vt* (*object*) poner, colocar; (*identify*) reconocer; (*find a post for*) dar un puesto a, colocar; (*goods*) vender; **to take** ~ tener lugar; **to be** ~**d** (*in race, exam*) colocarse; **out of** ~ (*not suitable*) fuera de lugar; **in the first** ~ (*first of all*) en primer lugar; **to change** ~**s with sb** cambiarse de sitio con algn; **from** ~ **to** ~

de un sitio a or para otro; **all over the ~** por todas partes; **he's going ~s** (*fig, col*) llegará lejos; **I feel rather out of ~ here** me encuentro algo desplazado; **to put sb in his ~** (*fig*) poner a algn en su lugar; **it is not my ~ to do it** no me incumbe a mí hacerlo; **to ~ an order with sb (for)** hacer un pedido a algn (de); **we are better ~d than a month ago** estamos en mejor posición que hace un mes.

placebo [plə'si:bəu] *n* placebo.

place mat *n* (*wooden etc*) salvamanteles *m inv*; (*in linen etc*) mantel *m* individual.

placement ['pleismənt] *n* colocación *f*.

place name *n* topónimo.

placenta [plə'sɛntə] *n* placenta.

placid ['plæsɪd] *adj* apacible, plácido.

placidity [plæ'sɪdɪtɪ] *n* placidez *f*.

plagiarism ['pleɪdʒjərɪzm] *n* plagio.

plagiarist ['pleɪdʒjərɪst] *n* plagiario/a.

plagiarize ['pleɪdʒjəraɪz] *vt* plagiar.

plague [pleɪg] *n* plaga; (*MED*) peste *f* ♦ *vt* (*fig*) acosar, atormentar; **to ~ sb with questions** acribillar a algn a preguntas.

plaice [pleɪs] *n*, *pl inv* platija.

plaid [plæd] *n* (*material*) tela de cuadros.

plain [pleɪn] *adj* (*clear*) claro, evidente; (*simple*) sencillo; (*frank*) franco, abierto; (*not handsome*) poco atractivo; (*pure*) natural, puro ♦ *adv* claramente ♦ *n* llano, llanura; **in ~ clothes** (*police*) vestido de paisano; **to make sth ~ to sb** dejar algo en claro a algn.

plain chocolate *n* chocolate *m* oscuro or amargo.

plainly ['pleɪnlɪ] *adv* claramente, evidentemente; (*frankly*) francamente.

plainness ['pleɪnnɪs] *n* (*clarity*) claridad *f*; (*simplicity*) sencillez *f*; (*of face*) falta de atractivo.

plain speaking *n*: **there has been some ~** se ha hablado claro.

plaintiff ['pleɪntɪf] *n* demandante *m/f*.

plaintive ['pleɪntɪv] *adj* (*cry, voice*) lastimero, quejumbroso; (*look*) que da lástima.

plait [plæt] *n* trenza ♦ *vt* trenzar.

plan [plæn] *n* (*drawing*) plano; (*scheme*) plan *m*, proyecto ♦ *vt* (*think*) pensar; (*prepare*) proyectar, planear; (*intend*) pensar, tener la intención de ♦ *vi* hacer proyectos; **have you any ~s for today?** ¿piensas hacer algo hoy?; **to ~ to do** pensar hacer; **how long do you ~ to stay?** ¿cuánto tiempo piensas quedarte?; **to ~ (for)** planear, proyectar.

▶**plan out** *vt* planear detalladamente.

plane [pleɪn] *n* (*AVIAT*) avión *m*; (*tree*)

plátano; (*tool*) cepillo; (*MATH*) plano.

planet ['plænɪt] *n* planeta *m*.

planetarium [plænɪ'tɛərɪəm] *n* planetario.

planetary ['plænɪtərɪ] *adj* planetario.

plank [plæŋk] *n* tabla.

plankton ['plæŋktən] *n* plancton *m*.

planned economy [plænd-] *n* economía planificada.

planner ['plænə*] *n* planificador(a) *m/f*; (*chart*) diagrama *m* de planificación; **town ~** urbanista *m/f*.

planning ['plænɪŋ] *n* (*POL, ECON*) planificación *f*; **family ~** planificación familiar.

planning committee *n* (*in local government*) comité *m* de planificación.

planning permission *n* licencia de obras.

plant [plɑːnt] *n* planta; (*machinery*) maquinaria; (*factory*) fábrica ♦ *vt* plantar; (*field*) sembrar; (*bomb*) colocar.

plantain ['plæntein] *n* llantén *m*.

plantation [plæn'teɪʃən] *n* plantación *f*; (*estate*) hacienda.

planter ['plɑːntə*] *n* hacendado.

plant pot *n* maceta, tiesto.

plaque [plæk] *n* placa.

plasma ['plæzmə] *n* plasma *m*.

plaster ['plɑːstə*] *n* (*for walls*) yeso; (*also: ~ of Paris*) yeso mate; (*MED: for broken leg etc*) escayola; (*BRIT: also: sticking ~*) tirita, esparadrapo ♦ *vt* enyesar; (*cover*): **to ~ with** llenar or cubrir de; **to be ~ed with mud** estar cubierto de barro.

plasterboard ['plɑːstəbɔːd] *n* cartón *m* yeso.

plaster cast *n* (*MED*) escayola; (*model, statue*) vaciado de yeso.

plastered ['plɑːstəd] *adj* (*col*) borracho.

plasterer ['plɑːstərə*] *n* yesero.

plastic ['plæstɪk] *n* plástico ♦ *adj* de plástico.

plastic bag *n* bolsa de plástico.

plastic bullet *n* bala de goma.

plastic explosive *n* goma 2 ®.

plasticine ® ['plæstɪsiːn] *n* (*BRIT*) plastilina ®.

plastic surgery *n* cirujía plástica.

plate [pleɪt] *n* (*dish*) plato; (*metal, in book*) lámina; (*PHOT, on door*) placa; (*AUT: number ~*) matrícula.

plateau, **~s** or **~x** ['plætəu, -z] *n* meseta, altiplanicie *f*.

plateful ['pleɪtful] *n* plato.

plate glass *n* vidrio or cristal *m* cilindrado.

platen ['plætən] *n* (*on typewriter, printer*) rodillo.

plate rack *n* escurreplatos *m inv*.

platform ['plætfɔːm] n (*RAIL*) andén m; (*stage*) plataforma; (*at meeting*) tribuna; (*POL*) programa m (electoral); **the train leaves from ~ 7** el tren sale del andén número 7.

platform ticket n (*BRIT*) billete m de andén.

platinum ['plætɪnəm] n platino.

platitude ['plætɪtjuːd] n tópico, lugar m común.

platonic [plə'tɒnɪk] adj platónico.

platoon [plə'tuːn] n pelotón m.

platter ['plætə*] n fuente f.

plaudits ['plɔːdɪts] npl aplausos mpl.

plausibility [plɔːzɪ'bɪlɪtɪ] n verosimilitud f, credibilidad f.

plausible ['plɔːzɪbl] adj verosímil; (*person*) convincente.

play [pleɪ] n (*gen*) juego; (*THEAT*) obra ♦ vt (*game*) jugar; (*instrument*) tocar; (*THEAT*) representar; (: *part*) hacer el papel de; (*fig*) desempeñar ♦ vi jugar; (*frolic*) juguetear; **to ~ safe** ir a lo seguro; **to bring** or **call into ~** poner en juego; **to ~ a trick on sb** gastar una broma a algn; **they're ~ing at soldiers** están jugando a (los) soldados; **to ~ for time** (*fig*) tratar de ganar tiempo; **to ~ into sb's hands** (*fig*) hacerle el juego a algn; **a smile ~ed on his lips** una sonrisa le bailaba en los labios.

►**play about, play around** vi (*person*) hacer el tonto; **to ~ about** or **around with** (*fiddle with*) juguetear con; (*idea*) darle vueltas a.

►**play along** vi: **to ~ along with** seguirle el juego a ♦ vt: **to ~ sb along** (*fig*) jugar con algn.

►**play back** vt poner.

►**play down** vt quitar importancia a.

►**play on** vt fus (*sb's feelings, credulity*) aprovecharse de; **to ~ on sb's nerves** atacarle los nervios a algn.

►**play up** vi (*cause trouble*) dar guerra.

playact ['pleɪækt] vi (*fig*) hacer comedia or teatro.

play-acting ['pleɪæktɪŋ] n teatro.

playboy ['pleɪbɔɪ] n playboy m.

player ['pleɪə*] n jugador(a) m/f; (*THEAT*) actor m, actriz f; (*MUS*) músico/a.

playful ['pleɪful] adj juguetón/ona.

playground ['pleɪgraund] n (*in school*) patio de recreo.

playgroup ['pleɪgruːp] n jardín m de infancia.

playing card ['pleɪɪŋ-] n naipe m, carta.

playing field n campo de deportes.

playmaker ['pleɪmeɪkə*] n (*SPORT*) jugador encargado de facilitar buenas jugadas a sus compañeros.

playmate ['pleɪmeɪt] n compañero/a de juego.

play-off ['pleɪɔf] n (*SPORT*) (partido de) desempate m.

playpen ['pleɪpɛn] n corral m.

playroom ['pleɪruːm] n cuarto de juego.

playschool ['pleɪskuːl] n = **playgroup**.

plaything ['pleɪθɪŋ] n juguete m.

playtime ['pleɪtaɪm] n (*SCOL*) (hora de) recreo.

playwright ['pleɪraɪt] n dramaturgo/a.

plc abbr (= *public limited company*) S.A.

plea [pliː] n (*request*) súplica, petición f; (*excuse*) pretexto, disculpa; (*LAW*) alegato, defensa.

plea bargaining n (*LAW*) acuerdo entre fiscal y defensor para agilizar los trámites judiciales.

plead [pliːd] vt (*LAW*): **to ~ sb's case** defender a alguien; (*give as excuse*) poner como pretexto ♦ vi (*LAW*) declararse; (*beg*): **to ~ with sb** suplicar or rogar a algn; **to ~ guilty/not guilty** (*defendant*) declararse culpable/inocente; **to ~ for sth** (*beg for*) suplicar algo.

pleasant ['plɛznt] adj agradable.

pleasantly ['plɛzntlɪ] adv agradablemente.

pleasantries ['plɛzntrɪz] npl (*polite remarks*) cortesías fpl; **to exchange ~** conversar amablemente.

please [pliːz] vt (*give pleasure to*) dar gusto a, agradar ♦ vi (*think fit*): **do as you ~** haz lo que quieras or lo que te dé la gana; **to ~ o.s.** hacer lo que le parezca; **~!** ¡por favor!; **~ yourself!** ¡haz lo que quieras!, ¡como quieras!; **~ don't cry!** ¡no llores! te lo ruego.

pleased [pliːzd] adj (*happy*) alegre, contento; (*satisfied*): **~ (with)** satisfecho (de); **~ to meet you** (*col*) ¡encantado!, ¡tanto or mucho gusto!; **to be ~ (about sth)** alegrarse (de algo); **we are ~ to inform you that ...** tenemos el gusto de comunicarle que ....

pleasing ['pliːzɪŋ] adj agradable, grato.

pleasurable ['plɛʒərəbl] adj agradable, grato.

pleasurably ['plɛʒərəblɪ] adv agradablemente, gratamente.

pleasure ['plɛʒə*] n placer m, gusto; (*will*) voluntad f ♦ cpd de recreo; "**it's a ~**" "el gusto es mío"; **it's a ~ to see him** da gusto verle; **I have much ~ in informing you that ...** tengo el gran placer de comunicarles que ...; **with ~** con mucho or todo gusto; **is this trip for business or**

~? ¿este viaje es de negocios o de placer?

pleasure cruise n crucero de placer.

pleasure ground n parque m de atracciones.

pleasure-seeking ['plɛʒəsiːkɪŋ] adj hedonista.

pleat [pliːt] n pliegue m.

pleb [plɛb] n: **the ~s** la gente baja, la plebe.

plebeian [plɪ'biːən] n plebeyo/a ♦ adj plebeyo; (pej) ordinario.

plebiscite ['plɛbɪsɪt] n plebiscito.

plectrum ['plɛktrəm] n plectro.

pledge [plɛdʒ] n (object) prenda; (promise) promesa, voto ♦ vt (pawn) empeñar; (promise) prometer; **to ~ support for sb** prometer su apoyo a algn; **to ~ sb to secrecy** hacer jurar a algn que guardará el secreto.

plenary ['pliːnərɪ] adj: **in ~ session** en sesión plenaria.

plentiful ['plɛntɪful] adj copioso, abundante.

plenty ['plɛntɪ] n abundancia; **~ of** mucho(s)/a(s); **we've got ~ of time to get there** tenemos tiempo de sobra para llegar.

plethora ['plɛθərə] n plétora.

pleurisy ['pluərɪsɪ] n pleuresía.

pliability [plaɪə'bɪlɪtɪ] n flexibilidad f.

pliable ['plaɪəbl] adj flexible.

pliers ['plaɪəz] npl alicates mpl, tenazas fpl.

plight [plaɪt] n condición f or situación f difícil.

plimsolls ['plɪmsəlz] npl (BRIT) zapatillas fpl de tenis.

plinth [plɪnθ] n plinto.

PLO n abbr (= Palestine Liberation Organization) OLP f.

plod [plɔd] vi caminar con paso pesado; (fig) trabajar laboriosamente.

plodder ['plɔdə*] n trabajador(a) diligente pero lento/a.

plodding ['plɔdɪŋ] adj (student) empollón(ona); (worker) más aplicado que brillante.

plonk [plɔŋk] (col) n (BRIT: wine) vino peleón ♦ vt: **to ~ sth down** dejar caer algo.

plot [plɔt] n (scheme) complot m, conjura; (of story, play) argumento m; (of land) terreno, parcela ♦ vt (mark out) trazar; (conspire) tramar, urdir ♦ vi conspirar; **a vegetable ~** un cuadro de hortalizas.

plotter ['plɔtə*] n (instrument) trazador m (de gráficos); (COMPUT) trazador m.

plotting ['plɔtɪŋ] n conspiración f, intrigas fpl.

plough, (US) **plow** [plau] n arado ♦ vt (earth) arar.

▶**plough back** vt (COMM) reinvertir.

▶**plough through** vt fus (crowd) abrirse paso a la fuerza por.

ploughing ['plauɪŋ] n labranza.

ploughman ['plaumən] n: **~'s lunch** pan m con queso y cebolla.

plow [plau] (US) = **plough.**

ploy [plɔɪ] n truco, estratagema.

pluck [plʌk] vt (fruit) coger (SP), recoger (LAM); (musical instrument) puntear; (bird) desplumar ♦ n valor m, ánimo; **to ~ up courage** hacer de tripas corazón; **to ~ one's eyebrows** depilarse las cejas.

plucky ['plʌkɪ] adj valiente.

plug [plʌg] n tapón m; (ELEC) enchufe m, clavija; (AUT: also: **spark(ing) ~**) bujía ♦ vt (hole) tapar; (col: advertise) dar publicidad a; **to give sb/sth a ~** dar publicidad a algn/algo; **to ~ a lead into a socket** enchufar un hilo en una toma.

▶**plug in** vt, vi (ELEC) enchufar.

plughole ['plʌɡhəul] n desagüe m.

plum [plʌm] n (fruit) ciruela; (also ~ **job**) chollo.

plumage ['pluːmɪdʒ] n plumaje m.

plumb [plʌm] adj vertical ♦ n plomo ♦ adv (exactly) exactamente, en punto ♦ vt sondar; (fig) sondear.

▶**plumb in** vt (washing machine) conectar.

plumber ['plʌmə*] n fontanero/a, plomero/a (LAM).

plumbing ['plʌmɪŋ] n (trade) fontanería, plomería (LAM); (piping) cañerías.

plume [pluːm] n (gen) pluma; (on helmet) penacho.

plummet ['plʌmɪt] vi: **to ~ (down)** caer a plomo.

plump [plʌmp] adj rechoncho, rollizo ♦ vt: **to ~ sth (down) on** dejar caer algo en.

▶**plump for** vt fus (col: choose) optar por.

▶**plump up** vt ahuecar.

plumpness ['plʌmpnɪs] n gordura.

plunder ['plʌndə*] n pillaje m; (loot) botín m ♦ vt saquear, pillar.

plunge [plʌndʒ] n zambullida ♦ vt sumergir, hundir ♦ vi (fall) caer; (dive) saltar; (person) arrojarse; (sink) hundirse; **to take the ~** lanzarse; **to ~ a room into darkness** sumir una habitación en la oscuridad.

plunger ['plʌndʒə*] n émbolo; (for drain) desatascador m.

plunging ['plʌndʒɪŋ] adj (neckline) escotado.

pluperfect [pluː'pəːfɪkt] n pluscuamperfecto.

plural ['pluərl] n plural m.

plus [plʌs] n (also: ~ **sign**) signo más; (fig) punto a favor ♦ adj: **a ~ factor** (fig) un

factor *m* a favor ♦ *prep* más, y, además de;
ten/twenty ~ más de diez/veinte.
plush [plʌʃ] *adj* de felpa.
plutonium [pluː'təʊnɪəm] *n* plutonio.
ply [plaɪ] *vt* (*a trade*) ejercer ♦ *vi* (*ship*) ir y
venir; (*for hire*) ofrecerse (para alquilar);
three ~ (*wool*) de tres cabos; **to** ~ **sb with
drink** no dejar de ofrecer copas a algn.
plywood ['plaɪwʊd] *n* madera
contrachapada.
PM *abbr* (*BRIT*) *see* **Prime Minister**.
p.m. *adv abbr* (= *post meridiem*) de la tarde
or noche.
PMS *n abbr* (= *premenstrual syndrome*) SPM
m.
PMT *n abbr* (= *premenstrual tension*) SPM *m*.
pneumatic [njuː'mætɪk] *adj* neumático.
pneumatic drill *n* taladradora neumática.
pneumonia [njuː'məʊnɪə] *n* pulmonía,
neumonía.
PO *n abbr* (= *Post Office*) Correos *mpl*; (*NAUT*)
= **petty officer**.
po *abbr* = **postal order**.
POA *n abbr* (*BRIT*) = *Prison Officers'
Association*.
poach [pəʊtʃ] *vt* (*cook*) escalfar; (*steal*)
cazar/pescar en vedado ♦ *vi* cazar/pescar
en vedado.
poached [pəʊtʃt] *adj* (*egg*) escalfado.
poacher ['pəʊtʃə*] *n* cazador(a) *m/f* furtivo/
a.
poaching ['pəʊtʃɪŋ] *n* caza/pesca furtiva.
PO Box *n abbr see* **Post Office Box**.
pocket ['pɒkɪt] *n* bolsillo; (*of air, GEO, fig*)
bolsa; (*BILLIARDS*) tronera ♦ *vt* meter en el
bolsillo; (*steal*) embolsarse; (*BILLIARDS*)
entronerar; **breast** ~ bolsillo de pecho; ~
of resistance foco de resistencia; ~ **of
warm air** bolsa de aire caliente; **to be out
of** ~ salir perdiendo; **to be £5 in/out of** ~
salir ganando/perdiendo 5 libras.
pocketbook ['pɒkɪtbʊk] *n* (*US: wallet*)
cartera; (: *handbag*) bolso.
pocketful ['pɒkɪtfʊl] *n* bolsillo lleno.
pocket knife *n* navaja.
pocket money *n* asignación *f*.
pockmarked ['pɒkmɑːkt] *adj* (*face*) picado
de viruelas.
pod [pɒd] *n* vaina.
podgy ['pɒdʒɪ] *adj* gordinflón/ona.
podiatrist [pɒ'diːətrɪst] *n* (*US*) podólogo/a.
podiatry [pɒ'diːətrɪ] *n* (*US*) podología.
podium ['pəʊdɪəm] *n* podio.
POE *n abbr* = *port of embarkation, port of
entry*.
poem ['pəʊɪm] *n* poema *m*.
poet ['pəʊɪt] *n* poeta *m/f*.
poetic [pəʊ'etɪk] *adj* poético.

poet laureate [-'lɔːrɪɪt] *n* poeta *m* laureado.

El poeta de la corte, denominado **Poet
Laureate**, *ocupa como tal un puesto vitalicio
al servicio de la Casa Real británica. Era
tradición que escribiera poemas
conmemorativos para ocasiones oficiales,
aunque hoy día esto es poco frecuente. El
primer poeta así distinguido fue Ben
Jonson, en 1616.*

poetry ['pəʊɪtrɪ] *n* poesía.
poignant ['pɔɪnjənt] *adj* conmovedor(a).
poignantly ['pɔɪnjəntlɪ] *adv* de modo
conmovedor.
point [pɔɪnt] *n* punto; (*tip*) punta; (*purpose*)
fin *m*, propósito; (*BRIT ELEC: also:* **power** ~)
toma de corriente, enchufe *m*; (*use*)
utilidad *f*; (*significant part*) lo esencial;
(*place*) punto, lugar *m*; (*also:* **decimal** ~): **2**
~ **3 (2.3)** dos coma tres (2,3) ♦ *vt* (*gun etc*):
to ~ **sth at sb** apuntar con algo a algn ♦ *vi*
señalar con el dedo; ~**s** *npl* (*AUT*)
contactos *mpl*; (*RAIL*) agujas *fpl*; **to be on
the** ~ **of doing sth** estar a punto de hacer
algo; **to make a** ~ **of doing sth** poner
empeño en hacer algo; **to get the** ~
comprender; **to come to the** ~ ir al
meollo; **there's no** ~ **(in doing)** no tiene
sentido (hacer); ~ **of departure** (*also fig*)
punto de partida; ~ **of order** cuestión *f* de
procedimiento; ~ **of sale** (*COMM*) punto
de venta; ~**-of-sale advertising** publicidad
f en el punto de venta; **the train stops at
Carlisle and all** ~**s south** el tren para en
Carlisle, y en todas las estaciones al sur;
when it comes to the ~ a la hora de la
verdad; **in** ~ **of fact** en realidad; **that's
the whole** ~! ¡de eso se trata!; **to be
beside the** ~ no venir al caso; **you've got
a** ~ **there!** ¡tienes razón!
▶**point out** *vt* señalar.
▶**point to** *vt fus* indicar con el dedo; (*fig*)
indicar, señalar.
point-blank ['pɔɪnt'blæŋk] *adv* (*also:* **at** ~
range) a quemarropa.
point duty *n* (*BRIT*) control *m* de
circulación.
pointed ['pɔɪntɪd] *adj* (*shape*) puntiagudo,
afilado; (*remark*) intencionado.
pointedly ['pɔɪntɪdlɪ] *adv*
intencionadamente.
pointer ['pɔɪntə*] *n* (*stick*) puntero; (*needle*)
aguja, indicador *m*; (*clue*) indicación *f*,
pista; (*advice*) consejo.
pointless ['pɔɪntlɪs] *adj* sin sentido.
pointlessly ['pɔɪntlɪslɪ] *adv* inútilmente, sin
motivo.

point of view *n* punto de vista.
poise [pɔɪz] *n* (*of head, body*) porte *m*; (*calmness*) aplomo.
poised [pɔɪzd] *adj* (*in temperament*) sereno.
poison ['pɔɪzn] *n* veneno ♦ *vt* envenenar.
poisoning ['pɔɪznɪŋ] *n* envenenamiento.
poisonous ['pɔɪznəs] *adj* venenoso; (*fumes etc*) tóxico; (*fig: ideas, literature*) pernicioso; (: *rumours, individual*) nefasto.
poke [pəuk] *vt* (*fire*) hurgar, atizar; (*jab with finger, stick etc*) dar; (*COMPUT*) almacenar; (*put*): **to ~ sth in(to)** introducir algo en ♦ *n* (*jab*) empujoncito; (*with elbow*) codazo; **to ~ one's head out of the window** asomar la cabeza por la ventana; **to ~ fun at sb** ridiculizar a algn; **to give the fire a ~** atizar el fuego.
▶**poke about** *vi* fisgonear.
poker ['pəukə*] *n* atizador *m*; (*CARDS*) póker *m*.
poker-faced ['pəukə'feɪst] *adj* de cara impasible.
poky ['pəukɪ] *adj* estrecho.
Poland ['pəulənd] *n* Polonia.
polar ['pəulə*] *adj* polar.
polar bear *n* oso polar.
polarization [pəuləraɪ'zeɪʃən] *n* polarización *f*.
polarize ['pəuləraɪz] *vt* polarizar.
Pole [pəul] *n* polaco/a.
pole [pəul] *n* palo; (*GEO*) polo; (*TEL*) poste *m*; (*flag* ~) asta; (*tent* ~) mástil *m*.
poleaxe ['pəulæks] *vt* (*fig*) desnucar.
pole bean *n* (*US*) judía trepadora.
polecat ['pəulkæt] *n* (*BRIT*) turón *m*; (*US*) mofeta.
Pol. Econ. ['pɔlɪkɔn] *n abbr* = *political economy*.
polemic [pɔ'lɛmɪk] *n* polémica.
polemicist [pɔ'lɛmɪsɪst] *n* polemista *m/f*.
pole star *n* estrella polar.
pole vault *n* salto con pértiga.
police [pə'liːs] *n* policía ♦ *vt* (*streets, city, frontier*) vigilar.
police car *n* coche-patrulla *m*.
police constable *n* (*BRIT*) guardia *m*, policía *m*.
police department *n* (*US*) policía.
police force *n* cuerpo de policía.
policeman [pə'liːsmən] *n* guardia *m*, policía *m*, agente *m* (*LAM*).
police officer *n* guardia *m*, policía *m*.
police record *n*: **to have a ~** tener antecedentes penales.
police state *n* estado policial.
police station *n* comisaría.
policewoman [pə'liːswumən] *n* mujer *f* policía.

policy ['pɔlɪsɪ] *n* política; (*also:* **insurance ~**) póliza; (*of newspaper, company*) política; **it is our ~ to do that** tenemos por norma hacer eso; **to take out a ~** sacar una póliza, hacerse un seguro.
policy holder *n* asegurado/a.
policy-making ['pɔlɪsɪmeɪkɪŋ] *n* elaboración *f* de directrices generales; **~ body** organismo encargado de elaborar las directrices generales.
polio ['pəulɪəu] *n* polio *f*.
Polish ['pəulɪʃ] *adj* polaco ♦ *n* (*LING*) polaco.
polish ['pɔlɪʃ] *n* (*for shoes*) betún *m*; (*for floor*) cera (de lustrar); (*for nails*) esmalte *m*; (*shine*) brillo, lustre *m*; (*fig: refinement*) refinamiento ♦ *vt* (*shoes*) limpiar; (*make shiny*) pulir, sacar brillo a; (*fig: improve*) perfeccionar, refinar.
▶**polish off** *vt* (*work*) terminar; (*food*) despachar.
▶**polish up** *vt* (*shoes, furniture etc*) limpiar, sacar brillo a; (*fig: language*) perfeccionar.
polished ['pɔlɪʃt] *adj* (*fig: person*) refinado.
polite [pə'laɪt] *adj* cortés, atento; (*formal*) correcto; **it's not ~ to do that** es de mala educación hacer eso.
politely [pə'laɪtlɪ] *adv* cortésmente.
politeness [pə'laɪtnɪs] *n* cortesía.
politic ['pɔlɪtɪk] *adj* prudente.
political [pə'lɪtɪkl] *adj* político.
political asylum *n* asilo político.
politically [pə'lɪtɪkəlɪ] *adv* políticamente.
politically correct *adj* políticamente correcto.
politician [pɔlɪ'tɪʃən] *n* político/a.
politics ['pɔlɪtɪks] *n* política.
polka ['pɔlkə] *n* polca.
polka dot *n* lunar *m*.
poll [pəul] *n* (*votes*) votación *f*, votos *mpl*; (*also:* **opinion ~**) sondeo, encuesta ♦ *vt* (*votes*) obtener; (*in opinion ~*) encuestar; **to go to the ~s** (*voters*) votar; (*government*) acudir a las urnas.
pollen ['pɔlən] *n* polen *m*.
pollen count *n* índice *m* de polen.
pollination [pɔlɪ'neɪʃən] *n* polinización *f*.
polling ['pəulɪŋ] *n* (*BRIT POL*) votación *f*; (*TEL*) interrogación *f*.
polling booth *n* cabina de votar.
polling day *n* día *m* de elecciones.
polling station *n* centro electoral.
pollster ['pəulstə*] *n* (*person*) encuestador(a) *m/f*; (*organization*) empresa de encuestas *or* sondeos.
poll tax *n* (*BRIT, formerly*) contribución *f* municipal (*no progresiva*).
pollutant [pə'luːtənt] *n* (agente *m*)

contaminante *m*.
pollute [pə'luːt] *vt* contaminar.
pollution [pə'luːʃən] *n* contaminación *f*,
polución *f*.
polo ['pəuləu] *n* (*sport*) polo.
polo-neck ['pəuləunɛk] *adj* de cuello vuelto
♦ *n* (*sweater*) suéter *m* de cuello vuelto.
poly ['pɒlɪ] *n abbr* (*BRIT*) = **polytechnic**.
poly... [pɒlɪ] *pref* poli....
poly bag *n* (*BRIT col*) bolsa de polietileno.
polyester [pɒlɪ'ɛstə*] *n* poliéster *m*.
polyethylene [pɒlɪ'ɛθɪliːn] *n* (*US*)
polietileno.
polygamy [pə'lɪɡəmɪ] *n* poligamia.
polygraph ['pɒlɪɡrɑːf] *n* polígrafo.
polymath ['pɒlɪmæθ] *n* erudito/a.
Polynesia [pɒlɪ'niːzɪə] *n* Polinesia.
Polynesian [pɒlɪ'niːzɪən] *adj*, *n* polinesio/a
m/f.
polyp ['pɒlɪp] *n* (*MED*) pólipo.
polystyrene [pɒlɪ'staɪriːn] *n* poliestireno.
polytechnic [pɒlɪ'tɛknɪk] *n* escuela
politécnica.
polythene ['pɒlɪθiːn] *n* (*BRIT*) polietileno.
polythene bag *n* bolsa de plástico.
polyurethane [pɒlɪ'juərɪθeɪn] *n*
poliuretano.
pomegranate ['pɒmɪɡrænɪt] *n* granada.
pommel ['pɒml] *n* pomo ♦ *vt* = **pummel**.
pomp [pɒmp] *n* pompa.
pompom ['pɒmpɒm] *n* borla.
pompous ['pɒmpəs] *adj* pomposo; (*person*)
presumido.
pond [pɒnd] *n* (*natural*) charca; (*artificial*)
estanque *m*.
ponder ['pɒndə*] *vt* meditar.
ponderous ['pɒndərəs] *adj* pesado.
pong [pɒŋ] *n* (*BRIT col*) peste *f* ♦ *vi* (*BRIT col*)
apestar.
pontiff ['pɒntɪf] *n* pontífice *m*.
pontificate [pɒn'tɪfɪkeɪt] *vi* (*fig*): **to ~
(about)** pontificar (sobre).
pontoon [pɒn'tuːn] *n* pontón *m*; (*BRIT: card
game*) veintiuna.
pony ['pəunɪ] *n* poney *m*, potro.
ponytail ['pəunɪteɪl] *n* coleta, cola de
caballo.
pony trekking *n* (*BRIT*) excursión *f* a
caballo.
poodle ['puːdl] *n* caniche *m*.
pooh-pooh [puː'puː] *vt* desdeñar.
pool [puːl] *n* (*natural*) charca; (*pond*)
estanque *m*; (*also:* **swimming** ~) piscina,
alberca (*LAM*); (*billiards*) billar *m*
americano; (*COMM: consortium*)
consorcio; (: *US: monopoly trust*) trust *m*
♦ *vt* juntar; **typing ~** servicio de
mecanografía; **(football) ~s** *npl*

quinielas *fpl*.
poor [puə*] *adj* pobre; (*bad*) malo ♦ *npl*: **the
~** los pobres.
poorly ['puəlɪ] *adj* mal, enfermo.
pop [pɒp] *n* ¡pum!; (*sound*) ruido seco;
(*MUS*) (música) pop *m*; (*US col: father*)
papá *m*; (*col: drink*) gaseosa ♦ *vt* (*burst*)
hacer reventar ♦ *vi* reventar; (*cork*)
saltar; **she ~ped her head out (of the
window)** sacó de repente la cabeza (por
la ventana).
▶**pop in** *vi* entrar un momento.
▶**pop out** *vi* salir un momento.
▶**pop up** *vi* aparecer inesperadamente.
pop concert *n* concierto pop.
popcorn ['pɒpkɔːn] *n* palomitas *fpl* (de
maíz).
pope [pəup] *n* papa *m*.
poplar ['pɒplə*] *n* álamo.
poplin ['pɒplɪn] *n* popelina.
popper ['pɒpə*] *n* corchete *m*, botón *m*
automático.
poppy ['pɒpɪ] *n* amapola; *see also*
Remembrance Sunday.
poppycock ['pɒpɪkɒk] *n* (*col*) tonterías *fpl*.
Popsicle ® ['pɒpsɪkl] *n* (*US*) polo.
populace ['pɒpjuləs] *n* pueblo.
popular ['pɒpjulə*] *adj* popular; **a ~ song**
una canción popular; **to be ~ (with)**
(*person*) caer bien (a); (*decision*) ser
popular (entre).
popularity [pɒpju'lærɪtɪ] *n* popularidad *f*.
popularize ['pɒpjuləraɪz] *vt* popularizar;
(*disseminate*) vulgarizar.
populate ['pɒpjuleɪt] *vt* poblar.
population [pɒpju'leɪʃən] *n* población *f*.
population explosion *n* explosión *f*
demográfica.
populous ['pɒpjuləs] *adj* populoso.
porcelain ['pɔːslɪn] *n* porcelana.
porch [pɔːtʃ] *n* pórtico, entrada.
porcupine ['pɔːkjupaɪn] *n* puerco *m* espín.
pore [pɔː*] *n* poro ♦ *vi*: **to ~ over**
enfrascarse en.
pork [pɔːk] *n* (carne *f* de) cerdo *or* chancho
(*LAM*).
pork chop *n* chuleta de cerdo.
porn [pɔːn] *adj* (*col*) porno *inv* ♦ *n* porno.
pornographic [pɔːnə'ɡræfɪk] *adj*
pornográfico.
pornography [pɔː'nɒɡrəfɪ] *n* pornografía.
porous ['pɔːrəs] *adj* poroso.
porpoise ['pɔːpəs] *n* marsopa.
porridge ['pɒrɪdʒ] *n* gachas *fpl* de avena.
port [pɔːt] *n* (*harbour*) puerto; (*NAUT: left
side*) babor *m*; (*wine*) oporto; (*COMPUT*)
puerta, puerto, port *m*; **~ of call** puerto de
escala.

portable ['pɔːtəbl] *adj* portátil.

portal ['pɔːtl] *n* puerta (grande), portalón *m*.

port authorities *npl* autoridades *fpl* portuarias.

portcullis [pɔːt'kʌlɪs] *n* rastrillo.

portend [pɔː'tend] *vt* presagiar, anunciar.

portent ['pɔːtent] *n* presagio, augurio.

porter ['pɔːtə*] *n* (*for luggage*) maletero; (*doorkeeper*) portero/a, conserje *m/f*; (*US RAIL*) mozo de los coches-cama.

portfolio [pɔːt'fəuliəu] *n* (*case, of artist*) cartera, carpeta; (*POL, FINANCE*) cartera.

porthole ['pɔːthəul] *n* portilla.

portico ['pɔːtɪkəu] *n* pórtico.

portion ['pɔːʃən] *n* porción *f*; (*helping*) ración *f*.

portly ['pɔːtlɪ] *adj* corpulento.

portrait ['pɔːtreɪt] *n* retrato.

portray [pɔː'treɪ] *vt* retratar; (*in writing*) representar.

portrayal [pɔː'treɪəl] *n* representación *f*.

Portugal ['pɔːtjugl] *n* Portugal *m*.

Portuguese [pɔːtju'giːz] *adj* portugués/esa ♦ *n, pl inv* portugués/esa *m/f*; (*LING*) portugués *m*.

Portuguese man-of-war [-mænəu'wɔː*] *n* (*jellyfish*) especie de medusa.

pose [pəuz] *n* postura, actitud *f*; (*pej*) afectación *f*, pose *f* ♦ *vi* posar; (*pretend*): **to ~ as** hacerse pasar por ♦ *vt* (*question*) plantear; **to strike a ~** tomar *or* adoptar una pose *or* actitud.

poser ['pəuzə*] *n* problema *m*/pregunta difícil; (*person*) = **poseur**.

poseur [pəu'zəː*] *n* presumido/a, persona afectada.

posh [pɔʃ] *adj* (*col*) elegante, de lujo ♦ *adv* (*col*): **to talk ~** hablar con acento afectado.

position [pə'zɪʃən] *n* posición *f*; (*job*) puesto ♦ *vt* colocar; **to be in a ~ to do sth** estar en condiciones de hacer algo.

positive ['pɔzɪtɪv] *adj* positivo; (*certain*) seguro; (*definite*) definitivo; **we look forward to a ~ reply** (*COMM*) esperamos que pueda darnos una respuesta en firme; **he's a ~ nuisance** es un auténtico pelmazo; **~ cash flow** (*COMM*) flujo positivo de efectivo.

positively ['pɔzɪtɪvlɪ] *adv* (*affirmatively, enthusiastically*) de forma positiva; (*col: really*) absolutamente.

posse ['pɔsɪ] *n* (*US*) pelotón *m*.

possess [pə'zes] *vt* poseer; **like one ~ed** como un poseído; **whatever can have ~ed you?** ¿cómo se te ocurrió?

possessed [pə'zest] *adj* poseso, poseído.

possession [pə'zeʃən] *n* posesión *f*; **to take ~ of sth** tomar posesión de algo.

possessive [pə'zesɪv] *adj* posesivo.

possessiveness [pə'zesɪvnɪs] *n* posesividad *f*.

possessor [pə'zesə*] *n* poseedor(a) *m/f*, dueño/a.

possibility [pɔsɪ'bɪlɪtɪ] *n* posibilidad *f*; **he's a ~ for the part** es uno de los posibles para el papel.

possible ['pɔsɪbl] *adj* posible; **as big as ~** lo más grande posible; **it is ~ to do it** es posible hacerlo; **as far as ~** en la medida de lo posible; **a ~ candidate** un(a) posible candidato/a.

possibly ['pɔsɪblɪ] *adv* (*perhaps*) posiblemente, tal vez; **I cannot ~ come** me es imposible venir; **could you ~ ...?** ¿podrías ...?

post [pəust] *n* (*BRIT: letters, delivery*) correo; (*job, situation*) puesto; (*trading ~*) factoría; (*pole*) poste *m* ♦ *vt* (*BRIT: send by ~*) mandar por correo; (*: put in mailbox*) echar al correo; (*MIL*) apostar; (*bills*) fijar, pegar; (*BRIT: appoint*): **to ~ to** destinar a; **by ~** por correo; **by return of ~** a vuelta de correo; **to keep sb ~ed** tener a algn al corriente.

post ... [pəust] *pref* post..., pos...; **~ 1950** pos(t) 1950.

postage ['pəustɪdʒ] *n* porte *m*, franqueo.

postage stamp *n* sello (de correo).

postal ['pəustl] *adj* postal, de correos.

postal order *n* giro postal.

postbag ['pəustbæg] *n* (*BRIT*) correspondencia, cartas *fpl*.

postbox ['pəustbɔks] *n* (*BRIT*) buzón *m*.

postcard ['pəustkɑːd] *nf* (tarjeta) postal *f*.

postcode ['pəustkəud] *n* (*BRIT*) código postal.

postdate [pəust'deɪt] *vt* (*cheque*) poner fecha adelantada a.

poster ['pəustə*] *n* cartel *m*, afiche *m* (*LAM*).

poste restante [pəust'restɔnt] *n* (*BRIT*) lista de correos.

posterior [pɔs'tɪərɪə*] *n* (*col*) trasero.

posterity [pɔs'terɪtɪ] *n* posteridad *f*.

poster paint *n* pintura al agua.

post-free [pəust'friː] *adj* (con) porte pagado.

postgraduate ['pəust'grædjuɪt] *n* posgraduado/a.

posthumous ['pɔstjuməs] *adj* póstumo.

posthumously ['pɔstjuməslɪ] *adv* póstumamente, con carácter póstumo.

posting ['pəustɪŋ] *n* destino.

postman ['pəustmən] *n* cartero.

postmark ['pəustmɑːk] *n* matasellos

m inv.

postmaster ['pəustmɑːstə*] *n* administrador *m* de correos.

Postmaster General *n* director *m* general de correos.

postmistress ['pəustmɪstrɪs] *n* administradora de correos.

post-mortem [pəust'mɔːtəm] *n* autopsia.

postnatal ['pəust'neɪtl] *adj* postnatal, postparto.

post office *n* (*building*) (oficina de) correos *m*; (*organization*): **the P~ O~** Administración *f* General de Correos.

Post Office Box (PO Box) *n* apartado postal, casilla de correos (*LAM*).

post-paid ['pəust'peɪd] *adj* porte pagado.

postpone [pəs'pəun] *vt* aplazar, postergar (*LAM*).

postponement [pəs'pəunmənt] *n* aplazamiento.

postscript ['pəustskrɪpt] *n* posdata.

postulate ['pɔstjuleɪt] *vt* postular.

posture ['pɔstʃə*] *n* postura, actitud *f*.

postwar [pəust'wɔː*] *adj* de la posguerra.

posy ['pəuzɪ] *n* ramillete *m* (de flores).

pot [pɔt] *n* (*for cooking*) olla; (*for flowers*) maceta; (*for jam*) tarro, pote *m* (*LAM*); (*piece of pottery*) cacharro; (*col: marijuana*) costo ♦ *vt* (*plant*) poner en tiesto; (*conserve*) conservar (en tarros); **~s of** (*col*) montones de; **to go to ~** (*col: work, performance*) irse al traste.

potash ['pɔtæʃ] *n* potasa.

potassium [pə'tæsɪəm] *n* potasio.

potato, ~es [pə'teɪtəu] *n* patata, papa (*LAM*).

potato crisps, (US) potato chips *npl* patatas *fpl or* papas *fpl* (*LAM*) fritas.

potato peeler *n* pelapatatas *m inv*.

potbellied ['pɔtbelɪd] *adj* (*from overeating*) barrigón/ona; (*from malnutrition*) con el vientre hinchado.

potency ['pəutnsɪ] *n* potencia.

potent ['pəutnt] *adj* potente, poderoso; (*drink*) fuerte.

potentate ['pəutnteɪt] potentado.

potential [pə'tenʃl] *adj* potencial, posible ♦ *n* potencial *m*; **to have ~** prometer.

potentially [pə'tenʃəlɪ] *adv* en potencia.

pothole ['pɔthəul] *n* (*in road*) bache *m*; (*BRIT: underground*) gruta.

potholer ['pɔthəulə*] *n* (*BRIT*) espeleólogo/a.

potholing ['pɔthəulɪŋ] *n* (*BRIT*): **to go ~** dedicarse a la espeleología.

potion ['pəuʃən] *n* poción *f*, pócima.

potluck [pɔt'lʌk] *n*: **to take ~** conformarse con lo que haya.

pot roast *n* carne *f* asada.

potshot ['pɔtʃɔt] *n*: **to take a ~ at sth** tirar a algo sin apuntar.

potted ['pɔtɪd] *adj* (*food*) en conserva; (*plant*) en tiesto *or* maceta; (*fig: shortened*) resumido.

potter ['pɔtə*] *n* alfarero/a ♦ *vi*: **to ~ around, ~ about** entretenerse haciendo cosillas; **to ~ round the house** estar en casa haciendo cosillas; **~'s wheel** torno de alfarero.

pottery ['pɔtərɪ] *n* cerámica, alfarería; **a piece of ~** un objeto de cerámica.

potty ['pɔtɪ] *adj* (*col: mad*) chiflado ♦ *n* orinal *m* de niño.

potty-trained ['pɔtɪtreɪnd] *adj* que ya no necesita pañales.

pouch [pautʃ] *n* (*ZOOL*) bolsa; (*for tobacco*) petaca.

pouf(fe) [puːf] *n* (*stool*) pouf *m*.

poultry ['pəultrɪ] *n* aves *fpl* de corral; (*dead*) pollos *mpl*.

poultry farm *n* granja avícola.

poultry farmer *n* avicultor(a) *m/f*.

pounce [pauns] *vi*: **to ~ on** precipitarse sobre ♦ *n* salto, ataque *m*.

pound [paund] *n* libra; (*for dogs*) perrera; (*for cars*) depósito ♦ *vt* (*beat*) golpear; (*crush*) machacar ♦ *vi* (*beat*) dar golpes; **half a ~** media libra; **a one ~ note** un billete de una libra.

pounding ['paundɪŋ] *n*: **to take a ~** (*team*) recibir una paliza.

pound sterling *n* libra esterlina.

pour [pɔː*] *vt* echar; (*tea*) servir ♦ *vi* correr, fluir; (*rain*) llover a cántaros.

▶**pour away, pour off** *vt* vaciar, verter.

▶**pour in** *vi* (*people*) entrar en tropel; **to come ~ing in** (*water*) entrar a raudales; (*letters*) llegar a montones; (*cars, people*) llegar en tropel.

▶**pour out** *vi* (*people*) salir en tropel ♦ *vt* (*drink*) echar, servir.

pouring ['pɔːrɪŋ] *adj*: **~ rain** lluvia torrencial.

pout [paut] *vi* hacer pucheros.

poverty ['pɔvətɪ] *n* pobreza, miseria; (*fig*) falta, escasez *f*.

poverty line *n*: **below the ~** por debajo del umbral de pobreza.

poverty-stricken ['pɔvətɪstrɪkn] *adj* necesitado.

poverty trap *n* trampa de la pobreza.

POW *n abbr* = prisoner of war.

powder ['paudə*] *n* polvo; (*face ~*) polvos *mpl*; (*gun~*) pólvora ♦ *vt* empolvar; **to ~ one's face** ponerse polvos; **to ~ one's nose** empolvarse la nariz, ponerse polvos; (*euphemism*) ir al baño.

powder compact n polvera.
powdered milk ['paudǝd-] n leche f en polvo.
powder keg n (fig) polvorín m.
powder puff n borla (para empolvarse).
powder room n aseos mpl.
powdery ['paudǝrɪ] adj polvoriento.
power ['pauǝ*] n poder m; (strength) fuerza; (nation) potencia; (drive) empuje m; (TECH) potencia; (ELEC) energía ♦ vt impulsar; **to be in** ~ (POL) estar en el poder; **to do all in one's** ~ **to help sb** hacer todo lo posible por ayudar a algn; **the world** ~**s** las potencias mundiales.
powerboat ['pauǝbǝut] n lancha a motor.
power cut n (BRIT) apagón m.
powered ['pauǝd] adj: ~ **by** impulsado por; **nuclear-**~ **submarine** submarino nuclear.
power failure n = **power cut.**
powerful ['pauǝful] adj poderoso; (engine) potente; (strong) fuerte; (play, speech) conmovedor(a).
powerhouse ['pauǝhaus] n (fig: person) fuerza motriz; **a** ~ **of ideas** una cantera de ideas.
powerless ['pauǝlɪs] adj impotente, ineficaz.
power line n línea de conducción eléctrica.
power of attorney n poder m, procuración f.
power point n (BRIT) enchufe m.
power station n central f eléctrica.
power steering n (AUT) dirección f asistida.
powwow ['pauwau] n conferencia ♦ vi conferenciar.
pp abbr (= per procurationem: by proxy) p.p.
PPE n abbr (BRIT SCOL) = philosophy, politics and economics.
PPS abbr (= post postscriptum) posdata adicional; (BRIT: = Parliamentary Private Secretary) ayudante de un ministro.
PQ abbr (Canada) = Province of Quebec.
PR n abbr see **proportional representation**; (= public relations) relaciones fpl públicas ♦ abbr (US) = **Puerto Rico.**
Pr. abbr (= prince) P.
practicability [præktɪkǝ'bɪlɪtɪ] n factibilidad f.
practicable ['præktɪkǝbl] adj (scheme) factible.
practical ['præktɪkl] adj práctico.
practicality [præktɪ'kælɪtɪ] n (of situation etc) aspecto práctico.
practical joke n broma pesada.
practically ['præktɪklɪ] adv (almost) casi, prácticamente.

practice ['præktɪs] n (habit) costumbre f; (exercise) práctica; (training) adiestramiento; (MED) clientela ♦ vt, vi (US) = **practise; in** ~ (in reality) en la práctica; **out of** ~ desentrenado; **to put sth into** ~ poner algo en práctica; **it's common** ~ es bastante corriente; **target** ~ práctica de tiro; **he has a small** ~ (doctor) tiene pocos pacientes; **to set up in** ~ **as** establecerse como.
practise, (US) **practice** ['præktɪs] vt (carry out) practicar; (profession) ejercer; (train at) practicar ♦ vi ejercer; (train) practicar.
practised, (US) **practiced** ['præktɪst] adj (person) experto; (performance) bien ensayado; (liar) consumado; **with a** ~ **eye** con ojo experto.
practising, (US) **practicing** ['præktɪsɪŋ] adj (Christian etc) practicante; (lawyer) que ejerce; (homosexual) activo.
practitioner [præk'tɪʃǝnǝ*] n practicante m/f; (MED) médico/a.
pragmatic [præg'mætɪk] adj pragmático.
pragmatism ['prægmǝtɪzǝm] n pragmatismo.
pragmatist ['prægmǝtɪst] n pragmatista m/f.
Prague [prɑːg] n Praga.
prairie ['prɛǝrɪ] n (US) pampa.
praise [preɪz] n alabanza(s) f(pl), elogio(s) m(pl).
praiseworthy ['preɪzwǝ:ðɪ] adj loable.
pram [præm] n (BRIT) cochecito de niño.
prance [prɑːns] vi (horse) hacer cabriolas.
prank [præŋk] n travesura.
prat [præt] n (BRIT col) imbécil m/f.
prattle ['prætl] vi parlotear; (child) balbucear.
prawn [prɔːn] n gamba.
pray [preɪ] vi rezar; **to** ~ **for forgiveness** pedir perdón.
prayer [prɛǝ*] n oración f, rezo; (entreaty) ruego, súplica.
prayer book n devocionario, misal m.
pre- ['priː] pref pre..., ante-; ~**1970** pre 1970.
preach [priːtʃ] vi predicar.
preacher ['priːtʃǝ*] n predicador(a) m/f; (US: minister) pastor(a) m/f.
preamble [prɪ'æmbl] n preámbulo.
prearrange [priːǝ'reɪndʒ] vt organizar or acordar de antemano.
prearrangement [priːǝ'reɪndʒmǝnt] n: **by** ~ por previo acuerdo.
precarious [prɪ'kɛǝrɪǝs] adj precario.
precariously [prɪ'kɛǝrɪǝslɪ] adv precariamente.
precaution [prɪ'kɔːʃǝn] n precaución f.
precautionary [prɪ'kɔːʃǝnrɪ] adj (measure)

de precaución.
precede [prɪˈsiːd] vt, vi preceder.
precedence [ˈprɛsɪdəns] n precedencia;
(priority) preferencia.
precedent [ˈprɛsɪdənt] n precedente m; **to
establish** or **set a** ~ sentar un
precedente.
preceding [prɪˈsiːdɪŋ] adj precedente.
precept [ˈpriːsɛpt] n precepto.
precinct [ˈpriːsɪŋkt] n recinto; (US: district)
distrito, barrio; ~**s** npl recinto; **pedestrian**
~ (BRIT) zona peatonal; **shopping** ~ (BRIT)
centro comercial.
precious [ˈprɛʃəs] adj precioso; (treasured)
querido; (stylized) afectado ♦ adv (col): ~
little/few muy poco/pocos; **your** ~ **dog**
(ironic) tu querido perro.
precipice [ˈprɛsɪpɪs] n precipicio.
precipitate adj [prɪˈsɪpɪtɪt] (hasty)
precipitado ♦ vt [prɪˈsɪpɪteɪt] precipitar.
precipitation [prɪsɪpɪˈteɪʃən] n
precipitación f.
precipitous [prɪˈsɪpɪtəs] adj (steep)
escarpado; (hasty) precipitado.
précis [ˈpreɪsiː] n resumen m.
precise [prɪˈsaɪs] adj preciso, exacto;
(person) escrupuloso.
precisely [prɪˈsaɪslɪ] adv exactamente,
precisamente.
precision [prɪˈsɪʒən] n precisión f.
preclude [prɪˈkluːd] vt excluir.
precocious [prɪˈkəʊʃəs] adj precoz.
preconceived [priːkənˈsiːvd] adj (idea)
preconcebido.
preconception [priːkənˈsɛpʃən] n (idea)
idea preconcebida.
precondition [priːkənˈdɪʃən] n condición f
previa.
precursor [priːˈkɜːsə*] n precursor(a) m/f.
predate [ˈpriːˈdeɪt] vt (precede) preceder.
predator [ˈprɛdətə*] n depredador m.
predatory [ˈprɛdətərɪ] adj depredador(a).
predecessor [ˈpriːdɪsɛsə*] n antecesor(a)
m/f.
predestination [priːdɛstɪˈneɪʃən] n
predestinación f.
predestine [priːˈdɛstɪn] vt predestinar.
predetermine [priːdɪˈtɜːmɪn] vt
predeterminar.
predicament [prɪˈdɪkəmənt] n apuro.
predicate [ˈprɛdɪkɪt] n predicado.
predict [prɪˈdɪkt] vt predecir, pronosticar.
predictable [prɪˈdɪktəbl] adj previsible.
predictably [prɪˈdɪktəblɪ] adv (behave, react)
de forma previsible; ~ **she didn't arrive**
como era de prever, no llegó.
prediction [prɪˈdɪkʃən] n pronóstico,
predicción f.

predispose [ˈpriːdɪsˈpəʊz] vt predisponer.
predominance [prɪˈdɒmɪnəns] n
predominio.
predominant [prɪˈdɒmɪnənt] adj
predominante.
predominantly [prɪˈdɒmɪnəntlɪ] adv en su
mayoría.
predominate [prɪˈdɒmɪneɪt] vi predominar.
pre-eminent [priːˈɛmɪnənt] adj
preeminente.
pre-empt [priːˈɛmt] vt (BRIT) adelantarse a.
pre-emptive [priːˈɛmtɪv] adj: ~ **strike**
ataque m preventivo.
preen [priːn] vt: **to** ~ **itself** (bird) limpiarse
las plumas; **to** ~ **o.s.** pavonearse.
prefab [ˈpriːfæb] n casa prefabricada.
prefabricated [priːˈfæbrɪkeɪtɪd] adj
prefabricado.
preface [ˈprɛfəs] n prefacio.
prefect [ˈpriːfɛkt] n (BRIT: in school)
monitor(a) m/f.
prefer [prɪˈfɜː*] vt preferir; (LAW: charges,
complaint) presentar; (: action) entablar;
to ~ **coffee to tea** preferir el café al té.
preferable [ˈprɛfrəbl] adj preferible.
preferably [ˈprɛfrəblɪ] adv
preferentemente, más bien.
preference [ˈprɛfrəns] n preferencia; **in** ~
to sth antes que algo.
preference shares npl acciones fpl
privilegiadas.
preferential [prɛfəˈrɛnʃəl] adj preferente.
prefix [ˈpriːfɪks] n prefijo.
pregnancy [ˈprɛgnənsɪ] n embarazo.
pregnancy test n prueba del embarazo.
pregnant [ˈprɛgnənt] adj embarazada; **3
months** ~ embarazada de tres meses; ~
with meaning cargado de significado.
prehistoric [ˈpriːhɪsˈtɒrɪk] adj prehistórico.
prehistory [priːˈhɪstərɪ] n prehistoria.
prejudge [priːˈdʒʌdʒ] vt prejuzgar.
prejudice [ˈprɛdʒʊdɪs] n (bias) prejuicio;
(harm) perjuicio ♦ vt (bias) predisponer;
(harm) perjudicar; **to** ~ **sb in favour of/
against** (bias) predisponer a algn a favor
de/en contra de.
prejudiced [ˈprɛdʒʊdɪst] adj (person)
predispuesto; (view) parcial, interesado;
to be ~ **against sb/sth** estar predispuesto
en contra de algn/algo.
prelate [ˈprɛlət] n prelado.
preliminaries [prɪˈlɪmɪnərɪz] npl
preliminares mpl, preparativos mpl.
preliminary [prɪˈlɪmɪnərɪ] adj preliminar.
prelude [ˈprɛljuːd] n preludio.
premarital [ˈpriːˈmærɪtl] adj
prematrimonial, premarital.
premature [ˈprɛmətʃʊə*] adj (arrival etc)

prematuro; **you are being a little** ~ te has adelantado.

prematurely [prɛməˈtʃuəlɪ] *adv* prematuramente, antes de tiempo.

premeditate [priːˈmɛdɪteɪt] *vt* premeditar.

premeditated [priːˈmɛdɪteɪtɪd] *adj* premeditado.

premeditation [priːmɛdɪˈteɪʃən] *n* premeditación *f.*

premenstrual [priːˈmɛnstruəl] *adj* premenstrual.

premenstrual tension *n* (*MED*) tensión *f* premenstrual.

premier [ˈprɛmɪə*] *adj* primero, principal ♦ *n* (*POL*) primer(a) ministro/a.

première [ˈprɛmɪə*] *n* estreno.

premise [ˈprɛmɪs] *n* premisa.

premises [ˈprɛmɪsɪs] *npl* local *msg*; **on the** ~ en el lugar mismo; **business** ~ locales *mpl* comerciales.

premium [ˈpriːmɪəm] *n* prima; **to be at a** ~ estar muy solicitado; **to sell at a** ~ (*shares*) vender caro.

premium bond *n* (*BRIT*) bono del estado que participa en una lotería nacional.

Se conoce como **Premium Bonds** o **Premium Savings Bonds** a los bonos emitidos por el Ministerio de Economía británico (**Treasury**) en los que se pueden invertir los ahorros. No producen intereses, pero dan acceso a un sorteo mensual de premios en metálico.

premium deal *n* (*COMM*) oferta extraordinaria.

premium gasoline *n* (*US*) (gasolina) súper *m.*

premonition [prɛməˈnɪʃən] *n* presentimiento.

preoccupation [priːɔkjuˈpeɪʃən] *n* preocupación *f.*

preoccupied [priːˈɔkjupaɪd] *adj* (*worried*) preocupado; (*absorbed*) ensimismado.

prep [prɛp] *adj abbr*: ~ **school** = **preparatory school** ♦ *n abbr* (*SCOL*: = *preparation*) deberes *mpl.*

prepaid [priːˈpeɪd] *adj* porte pagado; ~ **envelope** sobre *m* de porte pagado.

preparation [prɛpəˈreɪʃən] *n* preparación *f*; ~**s** *npl* preparativos *mpl*; **in** ~ **for sth** en preparación para algo.

preparatory [prɪˈpærətərɪ] *adj* preparatorio, preliminar; ~ **to sth/to doing sth** como preparación para algo/para hacer algo.

preparatory school *n* (*BRIT*) colegio privado de enseñanza primaria; (*US*) colegio privado de enseñanza

secundaria; *see also* **public school.**

prepare [prɪˈpɛə*] *vt* preparar, disponer ♦ *vi*: **to** ~ **for** prepararse *or* disponerse para; (*make preparations*) hacer preparativos para.

prepared [prɪˈpɛəd] *adj* (*willing*): **to be** ~ **to help sb** estar dispuesto a ayudar a algn.

preponderance [prɪˈpɔndərns] *n* preponderancia, predominio.

preposition [prɛpəˈzɪʃən] *n* preposición *f.*

prepossessing [priːpəˈzɛsɪŋ] *adj* agradable, atractivo.

preposterous [prɪˈpɔstərəs] *adj* absurdo, ridículo.

prerecorded [ˈpriːrɪˈkɔːdɪd] *adj*: ~ **broadcast** programa *m* grabado de antemano; ~ **cassette** cassette *f* pregrabada.

prerequisite [priːˈrɛkwɪzɪt] *n* requisito previo.

prerogative [prɪˈrɔgətɪv] *n* prerrogativa.

Presbyterian [prɛzbɪˈtɪərɪən] *adj, n* presbiteriano/a *m/f.*

presbytery [ˈprɛzbɪtərɪ] *n* casa parroquial.

preschool [ˈpriːˈskuːl] *adj* (*child, age*) preescolar.

prescribe [prɪˈskraɪb] *vt* prescribir; (*MED*) recetar; ~**d books** (*BRIT SCOL*) libros *mpl* del curso.

prescription [prɪˈskrɪpʃən] *n* (*MED*) receta; **to make up** *or* (*US*) **fill a** ~ preparar una receta; **only available on** ~ se vende solamente con receta (médica).

prescription charges *npl* (*BRIT*) precio *sg* de las recetas.

prescriptive [prɪˈskrɪptɪv] *adj* normativo.

presence [ˈprɛzns] *n* presencia; (*attendance*) asistencia.

presence of mind *n* aplomo.

present *adj* [ˈprɛznt] (*in attendance*) presente; (*current*) actual ♦ *n* (*gift*) regalo; (*actuality*) actualidad *f*, presente *m* ♦ *vt* [prɪˈzɛnt] (*introduce*) presentar; (*expound*) exponer; (*give*) presentar, dar, ofrecer; (*THEAT*) representar; **to be** ~ **at** asistir a, estar presente en; **those** ~ los presentes; **to give sb a** ~, **make sb a** ~ **of sth** regalar algo a algn; **at** ~ actualmente; **to** ~ **o.s. for an interview** presentarse a una entrevista; **may I** ~ **Miss Clark** permítame presentarle *or* le presento a la Srta Clark.

presentable [prɪˈzɛntəbl] *adj*: **to make o.s.** ~ arreglarse.

presentation [prɛznˈteɪʃən] *n* presentación *f*; (*gift*) obsequio; (*of case*) exposición *f*; (*THEAT*) representación *f*; **on** ~ **of the voucher** al presentar el vale.

present-day ['prɛzntdeɪ] *adj* actual.
presenter [prɪ'zɛntə*] *n* (*RADIO, TV*) locutor(a) *m/f*.
presently ['prɛzntlɪ] *adv* (*soon*) dentro de poco; (*US: now*) ahora.
present participle *n* participio (de) presente.
present tense *n* (tiempo) presente *m*.
preservation [prɛzə'veɪʃən] *n* conservación *f*.
preservative [prɪ'zə:vətɪv] *n* conservante *m*.
preserve [prɪ'zə:v] *vt* (*keep safe*) preservar, proteger; (*maintain*) mantener; (*food*) conservar; (*in salt*) salar ♦ *n* (*for game*) coto, vedado; (*often pl: jam*) confitura.
preshrunk [priː'ʃrʌŋk] *adj* inencogible.
preside [prɪ'zaɪd] *vi* presidir.
presidency ['prɛzɪdənsɪ] *n* presidencia.
president ['prɛzɪdənt] *n* presidente *m/f*; (*US: of company*) director(a) *m/f*.
presidential [prɛzɪ'dɛnʃl] *adj* presidencial.
press [prɛs] *n* (*tool, machine, newspapers*) prensa; (*printer's*) imprenta; (*of hand*) apretón *m* ♦ *vt* (*push*) empujar; (*squeeze*) apretar; (*grapes*) pisar; (*clothes: iron*) planchar; (*pressure*) presionar; (*doorbell*) apretar, pulsar, tocar; (*insist*): **to ~ sth on sb** insistir en que algn acepte algo ♦ *vi* (*squeeze*) apretar; (*pressurize*) ejercer presión; **to go to ~** (*newspaper*) entrar en prensa; **to be in the ~** (*being printed*) estar en prensa; (*in the newspapers*) aparecer en la prensa; **we are ~ed for time** tenemos poco tiempo; **to ~ sb to do** *or* **into doing sth** (*urge, entreat*) presionar a algn para que haga algo; **to ~ sb for an answer** insistir a algn para que conteste; **to ~ charges against sb** (*LAW*) demandar a algn.
▶**press ahead** *vi* seguir adelante.
▶**press on** *vi* avanzar; (*hurry*) apretar el paso.
press agency *n* agencia de prensa.
press clipping *n* = **press cutting**.
press conference *n* rueda de prensa.
press cutting *n* recorte *m* (de periódico).
pressing ['prɛsɪŋ] *adj* apremiante.
pressman ['prɛsmæn] *n* periodista *m*.
press officer *n* jefe/a *m/f* de prensa.
press release *n* comunicado de prensa.
press stud *n* (*BRIT*) botón *m* de presión.
press-up ['prɛsʌp] *n* (*BRIT*) flexión *f*.
pressure ['prɛʃə*] *n* presión *f*; (*urgency*) apremio, urgencia; (*influence*) influencia; **high/low ~** alta/baja presión; **to put ~ on sb** presionar a algn, hacer presión sobre algn.

pressure cooker *n* olla a presión.
pressure gauge *n* manómetro.
pressure group *n* grupo de presión.
pressurize ['prɛʃəraɪz] *vt* presurizar; **to ~ sb (into doing sth)** presionar a algn (para que haga algo).
pressurized ['prɛʃəraɪzd] *adj* (*container*) a presión.
Prestel ® ['prɛstɛl] *n* videotex *m*.
prestige [prɛs'tiːʒ] *n* prestigio.
prestigious [prɛs'tɪdʒəs] *adj* prestigioso.
presumably [prɪ'zjuːməblɪ] *adv* es de suponer que, cabe presumir que; **~ he did it** es de suponer que lo hizo él.
presume [prɪ'zjuːm] *vt* suponer, presumir; **to ~ to do** (*dare*) atreverse a hacer.
presumption [prɪ'zʌmpʃən] *n* suposición *f*; (*pretension*) presunción *f*.
presumptuous [prɪ'zʌmptjuəs] *adj* presumido.
presuppose [priːsə'pəuz] *vt* presuponer.
presupposition [priːsʌpə'zɪʃən] *n* presuposición *f*.
pre-tax [priː'tæks] *adj* anterior al impuesto.
pretence, (*US*) **pretense** [prɪ'tɛns] *n* (*claim*) pretensión *f*; (*pretext*) pretexto; (*make-believe*) fingimiento; **on** *or* **under the ~ of doing sth** bajo *or* con el pretexto de hacer algo; **she is devoid of all ~** no es pretenciosa.
pretend [prɪ'tɛnd] *vt* (*feign*) fingir ♦ *vi* (*feign*) fingir; (*claim*): **to ~ to sth** pretender a algo.
pretense [prɪ'tɛns] *n* (*US*) = **pretence**.
pretension [prɪ'tɛnʃən] *n* (*claim*) pretensión *f*; **to have no ~s to sth/to being sth** no engañarse en cuanto a algo/a ser algo.
pretentious [prɪ'tɛnʃəs] *adj* pretencioso.
pretext ['priːtɛkst] *n* pretexto; **on** *or* **under the ~ of doing sth** con el pretexto de hacer algo.
prettily ['prɪtɪlɪ] *adv* encantadoramente, con gracia.
pretty ['prɪtɪ] *adj* (*gen*) bonito, lindo (*LAM*) ♦ *adv* bastante.
prevail [prɪ'veɪl] *vi* (*gain mastery*) prevalecer; (*be current*) predominar; (*persuade*): **to ~ (up)on sb to do sth** persuadir a algn para que haga algo.
prevailing [prɪ'veɪlɪŋ] *adj* (*dominant*) predominante.
prevalent ['prɛvələnt] *adj* (*dominant*) dominante; (*widespread*) extendido; (*fashionable*) de moda.
prevarication [prɪværɪ'keɪʃən] *n* evasivas *fpl*.
prevent [prɪ'vɛnt] *vt*: **to ~ (sb) from doing sth** impedir (a algn) hacer algo.

preventable [prɪ'vɛntəbl] *adj* evitable.
preventative [prɪ'vɛntətɪv] *adj* preventivo.
prevention [prɪ'vɛnʃən] *n* prevención *f*.
preventive [prɪ'vɛntɪv] *adj* preventivo.
preview ['priːvjuː] *n* (*of film*) preestreno.
previous ['priːvɪəs] *adj* previo, anterior; **he has no ~ experience in that field** no tiene experiencia previa en ese campo; **I have a ~ engagement** tengo un compromiso anterior.
previously ['priːvɪəslɪ] *adv* antes.
prewar [priː'wɔː*] *adj* antes de la guerra.
prey [preɪ] *n* presa ♦ *vi*: **to ~ on** vivir a costa de; (*feed on*) alimentarse de; **it was ~ing on his mind** le obsesionaba.
price [praɪs] *n* precio; (*BETTING: odds*) puntos *mpl* de ventaja ♦ *vt* (*goods*) fijar el precio de; **to go up** *or* **rise in ~** subir de precio; **what is the ~ of ...?** ¿qué precio tiene ...?; **to put a ~ on sth** poner precio a algo; **what ~ his promises now?** ¿para qué sirven ahora sus promesas?; **he regained his freedom, but at a ~** recobró su libertad, pero le había costado caro; **to be ~d out of the market** (*article*) no encontrar comprador por ese precio; (*nation*) no ser competitivo.
price control *n* control *m* de precios.
price-cutting ['praɪskʌtɪŋ] *n* reducción *f* de precios.
priceless ['praɪslɪs] *adj* que no tiene precio; (*col: amusing*) divertidísimo.
price list *n* tarifa.
price range *n* gama de precios; **it's within my ~** está al alcance de mi bolsillo.
price tag *n* etiqueta.
price war *n* guerra de precios.
pricey ['praɪsɪ] *adj* (*BRIT col*) caro.
prick [prɪk] *n* pinchazo; (*with pin*) alfilerazo; (*sting*) picadura ♦ *vt* pinchar; picar; **to ~ up one's ears** aguzar el oído.
prickle ['prɪkl] *n* (*sensation*) picor *m*; (*BOT*) espina; (*ZOOL*) púa.
prickly ['prɪklɪ] *adj* espinoso; (*fig: person*) enojadizo.
prickly heat *n* sarpullido causado por exceso de calor.
prickly pear *n* higo chumbo.
pride [praɪd] *n* orgullo; (*pej*) soberbia ♦ *vt*: **to ~ o.s. on** enorgullecerse de; **to take (a) ~ in** enorgullecerse de; **her ~ and joy** su orgullo; **to have ~ of place** tener prioridad.
priest [priːst] *n* sacerdote *m*.
priestess ['priːstɪs] *n* sacerdotisa.
priesthood ['priːsthud] *n* (*practice*) sacerdocio; (*priests*) clero.
prig [prɪg] *n* gazmoño/a.

prim [prɪm] *adj* (*demure*) remilgado; (*prudish*) gazmoño.
primacy ['praɪməsɪ] *n* primacía.
prima donna ['priːmə'dɒnə] *n* primadonna, diva.
prima facie ['praɪmə'feɪʃɪ] *adj*: **to have a ~ case** (*LAW*) tener razón a primera vista.
primal ['praɪml] *adj* original; (*important*) principal.
primarily ['praɪmərɪlɪ] *adv* (*above all*) ante todo, primordialmente.
primary ['praɪmərɪ] *adj* primario; (*first in importance*) principal ♦ *n* (*US: also: ~ election*) (elección *f*) primaria.

*Las elecciones primarias (**primaries**) sirven para preseleccionar a los candidatos de los partidos Demócrata (**Democratic**) y Republicano (**Republican**) durante la campaña que precede a las elecciones a presidente de los Estados Unidos. Se inician en New Hampshire y tienen lugar en 35 estados de febrero a junio. El número de votos obtenidos por cada candidato determina el número de delegados que votarán en el congreso general (**National Convention**) de julio y agosto, cuando se decide el candidato definitivo de cada partido.*

primary colour, (*US*) **primary color** *n* color *m* primario.
primary education *n* enseñanza primaria.
primary school *n* (*BRIT*) escuela primaria.

*En el Reino Unido la escuela a la que van los niños entre cinco y once años se llama **primary school**, a menudo dividida en **infant school** (entre cinco y siete años de edad) y **junior school** (entre siete y once).*

primate *n* ['praɪmɪt] (*REL*) primado ♦ *n* ['praɪmeɪt] (*ZOOL*) primate *m*.
prime [praɪm] *adj* primero, principal; (*basic*) fundamental; (*excellent*) selecto, de primera clase ♦ *n*: **in the ~ of life** en la flor de la vida ♦ *vt* (*gun, pump*) cebar; (*fig*) preparar.
Prime Minister (PM) *n* primer(a) ministro/a; *see also* **Downing Street**.
primer ['praɪmə*] *n* (*book*) texto elemental; (*paint*) capa preparatoria.
prime time *n* (*RADIO, TV*) horas *fpl* de mayor audiencia.
primeval [praɪ'miːvl] *adj* primitivo.
primitive ['prɪmɪtɪv] *adj* primitivo; (*crude*) rudimentario; (*uncivilized*) inculto.
primly ['prɪmlɪ] *adv* remilgadamente; con

gazmoñería.

primrose ['prɪmrəuz] *n* primavera, prímula.

primus (stove) ® ['praɪməs-] *n* (*BRIT*) hornillo de camping.

prince [prɪns] *n* príncipe *m*.

prince charming *n* príncipe *m* azul.

princess [prɪn'sɛs] *n* princesa.

principal ['prɪnsɪpl] *adj* principal ♦ *n* director(a) *m/f*; (*in play*) protagonista principal *m/f*; (*COMM*) capital *m*, principal *m*; *see also* **pantomime**.

principality [prɪnsɪ'pælɪtɪ] *n* principado.

principle ['prɪnsɪpl] *n* principio; **in** ~ en principio; **on** ~ por principio.

print [prɪnt] *n* (*impression*) marca, impresión *f*; huella; (*letters*) letra de molde; (*fabric*) estampado; (*ART*) grabado; (*PHOT*) impresión *f* ♦ *vt* (*gen*) imprimir; (*on mind*) grabar; (*write in capitals*) escribir en letras de molde; **out of** ~agotado.

▶**print out** *vt* (*COMPUT*) imprimir.

printed circuit ['prɪntɪd-] *n* circuito impreso.

printed circuit board (PCB) *n* tarjeta de circuito impreso (TCI).

printed matter *n* impresos *mpl*.

printer ['prɪntə*] *n* (*person*) impresor(a) *m/f*; (*machine*) impresora.

printhead ['prɪnthɛd] *n* cabeza impresora.

printing ['prɪntɪŋ] *n* (*art*) imprenta; (*act*) impresión *f*; (*quantity*) tirada.

printing press *n* prensa.

printout ['prɪntaut] *n* (*COMPUT*) printout *m*.

print wheel *n* rueda impresora.

prior ['praɪə*] *adj* anterior, previo ♦ *n* prior *m*; ~ **to doing** antes de *or* hasta hacer; **without** ~ **notice** sin previo aviso; **to have a** ~ **claim to sth** tener prioridad en algo.

prioress [praɪə'rɛs] *n* priora.

priority [praɪ'ɒrɪtɪ] *n* prioridad *f*; **to have** *or* **take** ~ **over sth** tener prioridad sobre algo.

priory ['praɪərɪ] *n* priorato.

prise, (*US*) **prize** [praɪz] *vt*: **to** ~ **open** abrir con palanca.

prism ['prɪzəm] *n* prisma *m*.

prison ['prɪzn] *n* cárcel *f*, prisión *f* ♦ *cpd* carcelario.

prison camp *n* campamento para prisioneros.

prisoner ['prɪznə*] *n* (*in prison*) preso/a; (*under arrest*) detenido/a; (*in dock*) acusado/a; **the** ~ **at the bar** el/la acusado/a; **to take sb** ~ hacer *or* tomar prisionero a algn.

prisoner of war *n* prisionero/a *or* preso/a de guerra.

prissy ['prɪsɪ] *adj* remilgado.

pristine ['prɪstiːn] *adj* pristino.

privacy ['prɪvəsɪ] *n* (*seclusion*) soledad *f*; (*intimacy*) intimidad *f*; **in the strictest** ~ con el mayor secreto.

private ['praɪvɪt] *adj* (*personal*) particular; (*confidential*) secreto, confidencial; (*intimate*) privado, íntimo; (*sitting etc*) a puerta cerrada ♦ *n* soldado raso; "~" (*on envelope*) "confidencial"; (*on door*) "privado"; **in** ~ en privado; **in (his)** ~ **life** en su vida privada; **to be in** ~ **practice** tener consulta particular.

private enterprise *n* la empresa privada.

private eye *n* detective *m/f* privado/a.

private hearing *n* (*LAW*) vista a puerta cerrada.

private limited company *n* (*BRIT*) sociedad *f* de responsabilidad limitada.

privately ['praɪvɪtlɪ] *adv* en privado; (*in o.s.*) en secreto.

private parts *npl* partes *fpl* pudendas.

private property *n* propiedad *f* privada.

private school *n* colegio privado.

privation [praɪ'veɪʃən] *n* (*state*) privación *f*; (*hardship*) privaciones *fpl*, estrecheces *fpl*.

privatize ['praɪvɪtaɪz] *vt* privatizar.

privet ['prɪvɪt] *n* alheña.

privilege ['prɪvɪlɪdʒ] *n* privilegio; (*prerogative*) prerrogativa.

privileged ['prɪvɪlɪdʒd] *adj* privilegiado; **to be** ~ **to do sth** gozar del privilegio de hacer algo.

privy ['prɪvɪ] *adj*: **to be** ~ **to** estar enterado de.

Privy Council *n* consejo privado (de la Corona).

El consejo de asesores de la Corona conocido como **Privy Council** *tuvo su origen en la época de los normandos, y fue adquiriendo mayor importancia hasta ser substituido en 1688 por el actual Consejo de Ministros (***Cabinet***). Hoy día sigue existiendo con un carácter fundamentalmente honorífico y los ministros del gobierno y otras personalidades políticas, eclesiásticas y jurídicas adquieren el rango de* **privy councillors** *de manera automática.*

---

prize [praɪz] *n* premio ♦ *adj* (*first class*) de primera clase ♦ *vt* apreciar, estimar; (*US*) = **prise**.

prize fighter *n* boxeador *m* profesional.

prize fighting *n* boxeo *m* profesional.

prize-giving ['praɪzgɪvɪŋ] n distribución f de premios.
prize money n (SPORT) bolsa.
prizewinner ['praɪzwɪnə*] n premiado/a.
prizewinning ['praɪzwɪnɪŋ] adj (novel, essay) premiado.
PRO n abbr = **public relations officer**.
pro [prəu] n (SPORT) profesional m/f; **the ~s and cons** los pros y los contras.
pro- [prəu] pref (in favour of) pro, en pro de; **~Soviet** pro-soviético.
proactive [prəu'æktɪv] adj: **to be ~** impulsar la actividad.
probability [prɔbə'bɪlɪtɪ] n probabilidad f; **in all ~** lo más probable.
probable ['prɔbəbl] adj probable; **it is ~/ hardly ~ that** es probable/poco probable que.
probably ['prɔbəblɪ] adv probablemente.
probate ['prəubeɪt] n (LAW) legalización f de un testamento.
probation [prə'beɪʃən] n: **on ~** (employee) a prueba; (LAW) en libertad condicional.
probationary [prə'beɪʃənrɪ] adj: **~ period** período de prueba.
probationer [prə'beɪʃənə*] n (LAW) persona en libertad condicional; (nurse) ≈ ATS m/f (SP) or enfermero/a en prácticas.
probation officer n persona a cargo de los presos en libertad condicional.
probe [prəub] n (MED, SPACE) sonda; (enquiry) investigación f ♦ vt sondar; (investigate) investigar.
probity ['prəubɪtɪ] n probidad f.
problem ['prɔbləm] n problema m; **what's the ~?** ¿cuál es el problema?, ¿qué pasa?; **no ~!** ¡por supuesto!; **to have ~s with the car** tener problemas con el coche.
problematic(al) [prɔblə'mætɪk(l)] adj problemático.
problem-solving [prɔbləm'sɔlvɪŋ] n resolución f de problemas; **~ skills** técnicas de resolución de problemas.
procedural [prəu'siːdʒərəl] adj de procedimiento; (LAW) procesal.
procedure [prə'siːdʒə*] n procedimiento; (bureaucratic) trámites mpl; **cashing a cheque is a simple ~** cobrar un cheque es un trámite sencillo.
proceed [prə'siːd] vi proceder; (continue): **to ~ (with)** continuar (con); **to ~ against sb** (LAW) proceder contra algn; **I am not sure how to ~** no sé cómo proceder; see also **proceeds**.
proceedings [prə'siːdɪŋz] npl acto sg, actos mpl; (LAW) proceso sg; (meeting) función fsg; (records) actas fpl.
proceeds ['prəusiːdz] npl ganancias fpl,

ingresos mpl.
process ['prəusɛs] n proceso; (method) método, sistema m; (proceeding) procedimiento ♦ vt tratar, elaborar ♦ vi [prə'sɛs] (BRIT formal: go in procession) desfilar; **in ~** en curso; **we are in the ~ of moving to ...** estamos en vías de mudarnos a ....
processed cheese ['prəusɛst-], (US) **process cheese** n queso fundido.
processing ['prəusɛsɪŋ] n elaboración f.
procession [prə'sɛʃən] n desfile m; **funeral ~** cortejo fúnebre.
pro-choice [prəu'tʃɔɪs] adj en favor del derecho de elegir de la madre.
proclaim [prə'kleɪm] vt proclamar; (announce) anunciar.
proclamation [prɔklə'meɪʃən] n proclamación f; (written) proclama.
proclivity [prə'klɪvɪtɪ] n propensión f, inclinación f.
procrastinate [prəu'kræstɪneɪt] vi demorarse.
procrastination [prəukræstɪ'neɪʃən] n dilación f.
procreation [prəukrɪ'eɪʃən] n procreación f.
Procurator Fiscal ['prɔkjureɪtə-] n (Scottish) fiscal m/f.
procure [prə'kjuə*] vt conseguir, obtener.
procurement [prə'kjuəmənt] n obtención f.
prod [prɔd] vt (push) empujar; (with elbow) dar un codazo a ♦ n empujoncito; codazo.
prodigal ['prɔdɪgl] adj pródigo.
prodigious [prə'dɪdʒəs] adj prodigioso.
prodigy ['prɔdɪdʒɪ] n prodigio.
produce n ['prɔdjuːs] (AGR) productos mpl agrícolas ♦ vt [prə'djuːs] producir; (yield) rendir; (bring) sacar; (show) presentar, mostrar; (proof of identity) enseñar, presentar; (THEAT) presentar, poner en escena; (offspring) dar a luz.
produce dealer n (US) verdulero/a.
producer [prə'djuːsə*] n (THEAT) director(a) m/f; (AGR, CINE) productor(a) m/f.
product ['prɔdʌkt] n producto.
production [prə'dʌkʃən] n (act) producción f; (THEAT) representación f, montaje m; **to put into ~** lanzar a la producción.
production agreement n (US) acuerdo de productividad.
production line n línea de producción.
production manager n jefe/jefa m/f de producción.
productive [prə'dʌktɪv] adj productivo.
productivity [prɔdʌk'tɪvɪtɪ] n productividad f.
productivity agreement n (BRIT) acuerdo

de productividad.

productivity bonus *n* bono de productividad.

Prof. [prɔf] *abbr* (= *professor*) Prof.

profane [prəˈfeɪn] *adj* profano.

profess [prəˈfɛs] *vt* profesar; **I do not ~ to be an expert** no pretendo ser experto.

professed [prəˈfɛst] *adj* (*self-declared*) declarado.

profession [prəˈfɛʃən] *n* profesión *f*.

professional [prəˈfɛʃnl] *n* profesional *m/f* ♦ *adj* profesional; (*by profession*) de profesión; **to take ~ advice** buscar un consejo profesional.

professionalism [prəˈfɛʃnəlɪzm] *n* profesionalismo.

professionally [prəˈfɛʃnəlɪ] *adv*: **I only know him ~** sólo le conozco por nuestra relación de trabajo.

professor [prəˈfɛsə*] *n* (*BRIT*) catedrático/a; (*US*: *teacher*) profesor(a) *m/f*.

professorship [prəˈfɛsəʃɪp] *n* cátedra.

proffer [ˈprɔfə*] *vt* ofrecer.

proficiency [prəˈfɪʃənsɪ] *n* capacidad *f*, habilidad *f*.

proficiency test *n* prueba de capacitación.

proficient [prəˈfɪʃənt] *adj* experto, hábil.

profile [ˈprəufaɪl] *n* perfil *m*; **to keep a high/low ~** tratar de llamar la atención/pasar inadvertido.

profit [ˈprɔfɪt] *n* (*COMM*) ganancia; (*fig*) provecho ♦ *vi*: **to ~ by** *or* **from** aprovechar *or* sacar provecho de; **~ and loss account** cuenta de ganancias y pérdidas; **with ~s endowment assurance** seguro dotal con beneficios; **to sell sth at a ~** vender algo con ganancia.

profitability [prɔfɪtəˈbɪlɪtɪ] *n* rentabilidad *f*.

profitable [ˈprɔfɪtəbl] *adj* (*ECON*) rentable; (*beneficial*) provechoso, útil.

profitably [ˈprɔfɪtəblɪ] *adv* rentablemente; provechosamente.

profit centre, (*US*) **profit center** *n* centro de beneficios.

profiteering [prɔfɪˈtɪərɪŋ] *n* (*pej*) explotación *f*.

profit-making [ˈprɔfɪtmeɪkɪŋ] *adj* rentable.

profit margin *n* margen *m* de ganancia.

profit-sharing [ˈprɔfɪtʃɛərɪŋ] *n* participación *f* de empleados en los beneficios.

profits tax *n* impuesto sobre los beneficios.

profligate [ˈprɔflɪgɪt] *adj* (*dissolute*: *behaviour, act*) disoluto; (: *person*) libertino; (*extravagant*): **he's very ~ with his money** es muy derrochador.

pro forma [ˈprəuˈfɔːmə] *adj*: **~ invoice** factura pro-forma.

profound [prəˈfaund] *adj* profundo.

profoundly [prəˈfaundlɪ] *adv* profundamente.

profusely [prəˈfjuːslɪ] *adv* profusamente.

profusion [prəˈfjuːʒən] *n* profusión *f*, abundancia.

progeny [ˈprɔdʒɪnɪ] *n* progenie *f*.

programme, (*US*) **program** [ˈprəugræm] *n* programa *m* ♦ *vt* programar.

program(m)er [ˈprəugræmə*] *n* programador(a) *m/f*.

program(m)ing [ˈprəugræmɪŋ] *n* programación *f*.

program(m)ing language *n* lenguaje *m* de programación.

progress *n* [ˈprəugrɛs] progreso; (*development*) desarrollo ♦ *vi* [prəˈgrɛs] progresar, avanzar; desarrollarse; **in ~** (*meeting, work etc*) en curso; **as the match ~ed** a medida que avanzaba el partido.

progression [prəˈgrɛʃən] *n* progresión *f*.

progressive [prəˈgrɛsɪv] *adj* progresivo; (*person*) progresista.

progressively [prəˈgrɛsɪvlɪ] *adv* progresivamente, poco a poco.

progress report *n* (*MED*) informe *m* sobre el estado del paciente; (*ADMIN*) informe *m* sobre la marcha del trabajo.

prohibit [prəˈhɪbɪt] *vt* prohibir; **to ~ sb from doing sth** prohibir a algn hacer algo; **"smoking ~ed"** "prohibido fumar".

prohibition [prəuɪˈbɪʃən] *n* (*US*) prohibicionismo.

prohibitive [prəˈhɪbɪtɪv] *adj* (*price etc*) prohibitivo.

project *n* [ˈprɔdʒɛkt] proyecto; (*SCOL, UNIV*: *research*) trabajo, proyecto ♦ (*vb*: [prəˈdʒɛkt]) *vt* proyectar ♦ *vi* (*stick out*) salir, sobresalir.

projectile [prəˈdʒɛktaɪl] *n* proyectil *m*.

projection [prəˈdʒɛkʃən] *n* proyección *f*; (*overhang*) saliente *m*.

projectionist [prəˈdʒɛkʃənɪst] *n* (*CINE*) operador(a) *m/f* de cine.

projection room *n* (*CINE*) cabina de proyección.

projector [prəˈdʒɛktə*] *n* proyector *m*.

proletarian [prəulɪˈtɛərɪən] *adj* proletario.

proletariat [prəulɪˈtɛərɪət] *n* proletariado.

pro-life [prəuˈlaɪf] *adj* pro-vida.

proliferate [prəˈlɪfəreɪt] *vi* proliferar, multiplicarse.

proliferation [prəlɪfəˈreɪʃən] *n* proliferación *f*.

prolific [prəˈlɪfɪk] *adj* prolífico.

prologue, (*US*) **prolog** [ˈprəulɔg] *n* prólogo.

prolong [prə'lɔŋ] vt prolongar, extender.
prom [prɔm] n abbr (BRIT) = **promenade**, **promenade concert** ♦ n (US: ball) baile m de gala.

Los conciertos de música clásica más conocidos en Inglaterra son los llamados **Proms** (= **promenade concerts**), que tienen lugar en el **Royal Albert Hall** de Londres, aunque también se llama así a cualquier concierto de esas características. Su nombre se debe al hecho de que en un principio el público paseaba durante las actuaciones; en la actualidad parte de la gente que acude a ellos permanece de pie. En Estados Unidos se llama **prom** a un baile de gala en un colegio o universidad.

---

promenade [prɔmə'nɑːd] n (by sea) paseo marítimo ♦ vi (stroll) pasearse.
promenade concert n concierto (en que parte del público permanece de pie).
promenade deck n cubierta de paseo.
prominence ['prɔmɪnəns] n (fig) importancia.
prominent ['prɔmɪnənt] adj (standing out) saliente; (important) eminente, importante; **he is ~ in the field of** ... destaca en el campo de ....
prominently ['prɔmɪnəntlɪ] adv (display, set) muy a la vista; **he figured ~ in the case** desempeñó un papel destacado en el juicio.
promiscuity [prɔmɪs'kjuːɪtɪ] n promiscuidad f.
promiscuous [prə'mɪskjuəs] adj (sexually) promiscuo.
promise ['prɔmɪs] n promesa ♦ vt, vi prometer; **to make sb a ~** prometer algo a algn; **a young man of ~** un joven con futuro; **to ~ (sb) to do sth** prometer (a algn) hacer algo; **to ~ well** ser muy prometedor.
promising ['prɔmɪsɪŋ] adj prometedor(a).
promissory note ['prɔmɪsərɪ-] n pagaré m.
promontory ['prɔməntrɪ] n promontorio.
promote [prə'məut] vt promover; (new product) dar publicidad a, lanzar; (MIL) ascender; **the team was ~d to the second division** (BRIT FOOTBALL) el equipo ascendió a la segunda división.
promoter [prə'məutə*] n (of sporting event) promotor(a) m/f; (of company, business) patrocinador(a) m/f.
promotion [prə'məuʃən] n (gen) promoción f; (MIL) ascenso.
prompt [prɔmpt] adj pronto ♦ adv: **at 6 o'clock ~** a las seis en punto ♦ n (COMPUT) aviso, guía ♦ vt (urge) mover, incitar; (THEAT) apuntar; **to ~ sb to do sth** instar a algn a hacer algo; **to be ~ to do sth** no tardar en hacer algo; **they're very ~** (punctual) son muy puntuales.
prompter ['prɔmptə*] n (THEAT) apuntador(a) m/f.
promptly ['prɔmptlɪ] adv (punctually) puntualmente; (rapidly) rápidamente.
promptness ['prɔmptnɪs] n puntualidad f; rapidez f.
promulgate ['prɔməlgeɪt] vt promulgar.
prone [prəun] adj (lying) postrado; **~ to** propenso a.
prong [prɔŋ] n diente m, punta.
pronoun ['prəunaun] n pronombre m.
pronounce [prə'nauns] vt pronunciar; (declare) declarar ♦ vi: **to ~ (up)on** pronunciarse sobre; **they ~d him unfit to plead** le declararon incapaz de defenderse.
pronounced [prə'naunst] adj (marked) marcado.
pronouncement [prə'naunsmənt] n declaración f.
pronunciation [prənʌnsɪ'eɪʃən] n pronunciación f.
proof [pruːf] n prueba; **70° ~** graduación f del 70 por 100 ♦ adj: **~ against** a prueba de ♦ vt (tent, anorak) impermeabilizar.
proofreader ['pruːfriːdə*] n corrector(a) m/f de pruebas.
prop [prɔp] n apoyo; (fig) sostén m ♦ vt (also: **~ up**) apoyar; (lean) **to ~ sth against** apoyar algo contra.
Prop. abbr (COMM) = **proprietor**.
propaganda [prɔpə'gændə] n propaganda.
propagate ['prɔpəgeɪt] vt propagar.
propagation [prɔpə'geɪʃən] n propagación f.
propel [prə'pɛl] vt impulsar, propulsar.
propeller [prə'pɛlə*] n hélice f.
propelling pencil [prə'pɛlɪŋ-] n (BRIT) lapicero.
propensity [prə'pɛnsɪtɪ] n propensión f.
proper ['prɔpə*] adj (suited, right) propio; (exact) justo; (apt) apropiado, conveniente; (timely) oportuno; (seemly) correcto, decente; (authentic) verdadero; (col: real) auténtico; **to go through the ~ channels** (ADMIN) ir por la vía oficial.
properly ['prɔpəlɪ] adv (adequately) correctamente; (decently) decentemente.
proper noun n nombre m propio.
properties ['prɔpətɪz] npl (THEAT) accesorios mpl, atrezzo msg.
property ['prɔpətɪ] n propiedad f; (estate) finca; **lost ~** objetos mpl perdidos;

personal ~ bienes *mpl* muebles.
property developer *n* promotor(a) *m/f* de construcciones.
property owner *n* dueño/a de propiedades.
property tax *n* impuesto sobre la propiedad.
prophecy ['prɒfɪsɪ] *n* profecía.
prophesy ['prɒfɪsaɪ] *vt* profetizar; (*fig*) predecir.
prophet ['prɒfɪt] *n* profeta *m/f*.
prophetic [prə'fɛtɪk] *adj* profético.
proportion [prə'pɔːʃən] *n* proporción *f*; (*share*) parte *f*; **to be in/out of ~ to** *or* **with sth** estar en/no guardar proporción con algo; **to see sth in ~** (*fig*) ver algo en su justa medida.
proportional [prə'pɔːʃənl] *adj* proporcional.
proportionally [prəpɔːʃnəlɪ] *adv* proporcionalmente, en proporción.
proportional representation (PR) *n* (*POL*) representación *f* proporcional.
proportional spacing *n* (*on printer*) espaciado proporcional.
proportionate [prə'pɔːʃənɪt] *adj* proporcionado.
proportionately [prə'pɔːʃnɪtlɪ] *adv* proporcionadamente, en proporción.
proportioned [prə'pɔːʃənd] *adj* proporcionado.
proposal [prə'pəuzl] *n* propuesta; (*offer of marriage*) oferta de matrimonio; (*plan*) proyecto; (*suggestion*) sugerencia.
propose [prə'pəuz] *vt* proponer; (*have in mind*): **to ~ sth/to do** *or* **doing sth** proponer algo/proponerse hacer algo ♦ *vi* declararse.
proposer [prə'pəuzə*] *n* (*of motion*) proponente *m/f*.
proposition [prɒpə'zɪʃən] *n* propuesta, proposición *f*; **to make sb a ~** proponer algo a algn.
propound [prə'paund] *vt* (*theory*) exponer.
proprietary [prə'praɪətərɪ] *adj* (*COMM*): **~ article** artículo de marca; **~ brand** marca comercial.
proprietor [prə'praɪətə*] *n* propietario/a, dueño/a.
propriety [prə'praɪətɪ] *n* decoro.
propulsion [prə'pʌlʃən] *n* propulsión *f*.
pro rata [prəu'rɑːtə] *adv* a prorrata.
prosaic [prəu'zeɪɪk] *adj* prosaico.
Pros. Atty. *abbr* (*US*) = *prosecuting attorney*.
proscribe [prə'skraɪb] *vt* proscribir.
prose [prəuz] *n* prosa; (*SCOL*) traducción *f* inversa.
prosecute ['prɒsɪkjuːt] *vt* (*LAW*) procesar; "trespassers will be ~d" (*LAW*) "se

procesará a los intrusos".
prosecution [prɒsɪ'kjuːʃən] *n* proceso, causa; (*accusing side*) acusación *f*.
prosecutor ['prɒsɪkjuːtə*] *n* acusador(a) *m/f*; (*also*: **public ~**) fiscal *m/f*.
prospect *n* ['prɒspɛkt] (*chance*) posibilidad *f*; (*outlook*) perspectiva; (*hope*) esperanza ♦ (*vb*: [prə'spɛkt]) *vt* explorar ♦ *vi* buscar; **~s** *npl* (*for work etc*) perspectivas *fpl*; **to be faced with the ~ of** tener que enfrentarse a la posibilidad de que ...; **we were faced with the ~ of leaving early** se nos planteó la posibilidad de marcharnos pronto; **there is every ~ of an early victory** hay buenas perspectivas de una pronta victoria.
prospecting [prə'spɛktɪŋ] *n* prospección *f*.
prospective [prə'spɛktɪv] *adj* (*possible*) probable, eventual; (*certain*) futuro; (*buyer*) presunto; (*legislation, son-in-law*) futuro.
prospector [prə'spɛktə*] *n* explorador(a) *m/f*; **gold ~** buscador *m* de oro.
prospectus [prə'spɛktəs] *n* prospecto.
prosper ['prɒspə*] *vi* prosperar.
prosperity [prɒ'spɛrɪtɪ] *n* prosperidad *f*.
prosperous ['prɒspərəs] *adj* próspero.
prostate ['prɒsteɪt] *n* (*also*: ~ **gland**) próstata.
prostitute ['prɒstɪtjuːt] *n* prostituta; **male ~** prostituto.
prostitution [prɒstɪ'tjuːʃən] *n* prostitución *f*.
prostrate ['prɒstreɪt] *adj* postrado; (*fig*) abatido ♦ *vt*: **to ~ o.s.** postrarse.
protagonist [prə'tægənɪst] *n* protagonista *m/f*.
protect [prə'tɛkt] *vt* proteger.
protection [prə'tɛkʃən] *n* protección *f*; **to be under sb's ~** estar amparado por algn.
protectionism [prə'tɛkʃənɪzəm] *n* proteccionismo.
protection racket *n* chantaje *m*.
protective [prə'tɛktɪv] *adj* protector(a); **~ custody** (*LAW*) detención *f* preventiva.
protector [prə'tɛktə*] *n* protector(a) *m/f*.
protégé ['prəutɛʒeɪ] *n* protegido/a.
protein ['prəutiːn] *n* proteína.
pro tem [prəu'tɛm] *adv abbr* (= *pro tempore*: *for the time being*) provisionalmente.
protest *n* ['prəutɛst] protesta ♦ (*vb*: [prə'tɛst]) *vi* protestar ♦ *vt* (*affirm*) afirmar, declarar; **to do sth under ~** hacer algo bajo protesta; **to ~ against/about** protestar en contra de/por.
Protestant ['prɒtɪstənt] *adj, n* protestante *m/f*.
protester, protestor [prə'tɛstə*] *n* (*in

demonstration) manifestante *m/f*.

protest march *n* manifestación *f or* marcha (de protesta).

protocol ['prəʊtəkɔl] *n* protocolo.

prototype ['prəʊtətaɪp] *n* prototipo.

protracted [prə'træktɪd] *adj* prolongado.

protractor [prə'træktə*] *n* (*GEOM*) transportador *m*.

protrude [prə'truːd] *vi* salir, sobresalir.

protuberance [prə'tjuːbərəns] *n* protuberancia.

proud [praʊd] *adj* orgulloso; (*pej*) soberbio, altanero ♦ *adv*: **to do sb ~** tratar a algn a cuerpo de rey; **to do o.s. ~** no privarse de nada; **to be ~ to do sth** estar orgulloso de hacer algo.

proudly ['praʊdlɪ] *adv* orgullosamente, con orgullo; (*pej*) con soberbia, con altanería.

prove [pruːv] *vt* probar; (*verify*) comprobar; (*show*) demostrar ♦ *vi*: **to ~ correct** resultar correcto; **to ~ o.s.** ponerse a prueba; **he was ~d right in the end** al final se vio que tenía razón.

proverb ['prɔvəːb] *n* refrán *m*.

proverbial [prə'vəːbɪəl] *adj* proverbial.

proverbially [prə'vəːbɪəlɪ] *adv* proverbialmente.

provide [prə'vaɪd] *vt* proporcionar, dar; **to ~ sb with sth** proveer a algn de algo; **to be ~d with** ser provisto de.

►provide for *vt fus* (*person*) mantener a; (*problem etc*) tener en cuenta.

provided [prə'vaɪdɪd] *conj*: **~ (that)** con tal de que, a condición de que.

Providence ['prɔvɪdəns] *n* Divina Providencia.

providing [prə'vaɪdɪŋ] *conj* a condición de que, con tal de que.

province ['prɔvɪns] *n* provincia; (*fig*) esfera.

provincial [prə'vɪnʃəl] *adj* provincial; (*pej*) provinciano.

provision [prə'vɪʒən] *n* provisión *f*; (*supply*) suministro, abastecimiento; **~s** *npl* provisiones *fpl*, víveres *mpl*; **to make ~ for** (*one's family, future*) atender las necesidades de.

provisional [prə'vɪʒənl] *adj* provisional, provisorio (*LAM*); (*temporary*) interino ♦ *n*: **P~** (*Irish POL*) Provisional *m* (*miembro de la tendencia activista del IRA*).

provisional driving licence *n* (*BRIT AUT*) carnet *m* de conducir provisional; *see also* **L-plates**.

proviso [prə'vaɪzəʊ] *n* condición *f*, estipulación *f*; **with the ~ that** a condición de que.

Provo ['prɔvəʊ] *n abbr* (*col*) = **Provisional**.

provocation [prɔvə'keɪʃən] *n* provocación *f*.

provocative [prə'vɔkətɪv] *adj* provocativo.

provoke [prə'vəʊk] *vt* (*arouse*) provocar, incitar; (*cause*) causar, producir; (*anger*) enojar; **to ~ sb to sth/to do** *or* **into doing sth** provocar a algn a algo/a hacer algo.

provoking [prə'vəʊkɪŋ] *adj* provocador(a).

provost ['prɔvəst] *n* (*BRIT: of university*) rector(a) *m/f*; (*Scottish*) alcalde(sa) *m/f*.

prow [praʊ] *n* proa.

prowess ['praʊɪs] *n* (*skill*) destreza, habilidad *f*; (*courage*) valor *m*; **his ~ as a footballer** (*skill*) su habilidad como futbolista.

prowl [praʊl] *vi* (*also*: **~ about, ~ around**) merodear ♦ *n*: **on the ~** de merodeo, merodeando.

prowler ['praʊlə*] *n* merodeador(a) *m/f*.

proximity [prɔk'sɪmɪtɪ] *n* proximidad *f*.

proxy ['prɔksɪ] *n* poder *m*; (*person*) apoderado/a; **by ~** por poderes.

PRP *n abbr* (= *performance related pay*) *retribución en función del rendimiento en el trabajo*.

prude [pruːd] *n* gazmoño/a, mojigato/a.

prudence ['pruːdns] *n* prudencia.

prudent ['pruːdnt] *adj* prudente.

prudently ['pruːdntlɪ] *adv* prudentemente, con prudencia.

prudish ['pruːdɪʃ] *adj* gazmoño.

prudishness [pruːdɪʃnɪs] *n* gazmoñería, ñoñería.

prune [pruːn] *n* ciruela pasa ♦ *vt* podar.

pry [praɪ] *vi*: **to ~ into** entrometerse en.

PS *abbr* (= *postscript*) P.D.

psalm [sɑːm] *n* salmo.

PSAT *n abbr* (*US*) = *Preliminary Scholastic Aptitude Test*.

PSBR *n abbr* (*BRIT*: = *public sector borrowing requirement*) endeudamiento público.

pseud [sjuːd] *n* (*BRIT col: intellectually*) farsante *m/f*; (: *socially*) pretencioso/a.

pseudo ... [sjuːdəʊ] *pref* seudo....

pseudonym ['sjuːdənɪm] *n* seudónimo.

PST *n abbr* (*US*: = *Pacific Standard Time*) *hora de invierno del Pacífico*.

PSV *n abbr* (*BRIT*) *see* **public service vehicle**.

psyche ['saɪkɪ] *n* psique *f*.

psychiatric [saɪkɪ'ætrɪk] *adj* psiquiátrico.

psychiatrist [saɪ'kaɪətrɪst] *n* psiquiatra *m/f*.

psychiatry [saɪ'kaɪətrɪ] *n* psiquiatría.

psychic ['saɪkɪk] *adj* (*also*: **~al**) psíquico.

psycho ['saɪkəʊ] *n* (*col*) psicópata *m/f*, pirado/a.

psychoanalyse, psychoanalyze [saɪkəʊ-'ænəlaɪz] *vt* psicoanalizar.

psychoanalysis, *pl* **psychoanalyses**

[saɪkəuə'nælɪsɪs, -siːz] *n* psicoanálisis *m inv.*
psychoanalyst [saɪkəu'ænəlɪst] *n* psicoanalista *m/f.*
psychological [saɪkə'lɒdʒɪkl] *adj* psicológico.
psychologically [saɪkə'lɒdʒɪklɪ] *adv* psicológicamente.
psychologist [saɪ'kɒlədʒɪst] *n* psicólogo/a.
psychology [saɪ'kɒlədʒɪ] *n* psicología.
psychopath ['saɪkəupæθ] *n* psicópata *m/f.*
psychosis, *pl* **psychoses** [saɪ'kəusɪs, -siːz] *n* psicosis *f inv.*
psychosomatic ['saɪkəusə'mætɪk] *adj* psicosomático.
psychotherapy [saɪkəu'θerəpɪ] *n* psicoterapia.
psychotic [saɪ'kɒtɪk] *adj*, *n* psicótico/a.
PT *n abbr* (*BRIT:* = *Physical Training*) Ed. Fís.
pt *abbr* = **pint(s), point(s).**
Pt. *abbr* (*GEO:* = *Point*) Pta.
PTA *n abbr* (*BRIT:* = *Parent-Teacher Association*) ≈ Asociación *f* de Padres de Alumnos.
Pte. *abbr* (*BRIT MIL*) = **private.**
PTO *abbr* (= *please turn over*) sigue.
PTV *n abbr* (*US*) = *pay television, public television.*
pub [pʌb] *n abbr* (= *public house*) pub *m*, bar *m.*

En un **pub** (**public house**) *se pueden consumir fundamentalmente bebidas alcohólicas, aunque en la actualidad también se sirven platos ligeros durante el almuerzo. Es, además, un lugar de encuentro donde se juega a los dardos o al billar, entre otras actividades. La estricta regulación sobre la venta de alcohol controla las horas de apertura, aunque éstas son más flexibles desde hace unos años. No se puede servir alcohol a los menores de 18 años.*

pub crawl *n* (*col*): **to go on a** ~ ir a recorrer bares.
puberty ['pjuːbətɪ] *n* pubertad *f.*
pubic ['pjuːbɪk] *adj* púbico.
public ['pʌblɪk] *adj*, *n* público; **in** ~ en público; **to make sth** ~ revelar or hacer público algo; **to be** ~ **knowledge** ser del dominio público; **to go** ~ (*COMM*) proceder a la venta pública de acciones.
public address system (PA) *n* megafonía, sistema *m* de altavoces.
publican ['pʌblɪkən] *n* dueño/a or encargado/a de un bar.
publication [pʌblɪ'keɪʃən] *n* publicación *f.*
public company *n* sociedad *f* anónima.
public convenience *n* (*BRIT*) aseos *mpl*

públicos, sanitarios *mpl* (*LAM*).
public holiday *n* día *m* de fiesta, (día) feriado (*LAM*).
public house *n* (*BRIT*) bar *m*, pub *m.*
publicity [pʌb'lɪsɪtɪ] *n* publicidad *f.*
publicize ['pʌblɪsaɪz] *vt* publicitar; (*advertise*) hacer propaganda para.
public limited company (plc) *n* sociedad *f* anónima (S.A.).
publicly ['pʌblɪklɪ] *adv* públicamente, en público.
public opinion *n* opinión *f* pública.
public ownership *n* propiedad *f* pública; **to be taken into** ~ ser nacionalizado.
Public Prosecutor *n* Fiscal *m/f* del Estado.
public relations (PR) *n* relaciones *fpl* públicas.
public relations officer *n* encargado/a de relaciones públicas.
public school *n* (*BRIT*) colegio privado; (*US*) instituto.

En Inglaterra el término **public school** *se usa para referirse a un colegio privado de pago, generalmente de alto prestigio social y en régimen de internado. Algunos de los más conocidos son Eton o Harrow. Muchos de sus alumnos estudian previamente hasta los 13 años en un centro privado de pago llamado* **prep**(**aratory**) **school** *y al terminar el bachiller pasan a estudiar en las universidades de Oxford y Cambridge. En otros lugares como Estados Unidos el mismo término se refiere a una escuela pública de enseñanza gratuita administrada por el Estado.*

public sector *n* sector *m* público.
public service vehicle (PSV) *n* vehículo de servicio público.
public-spirited [pʌblɪk'spɪrɪtɪd] *adj* cívico.
public transport, (*US*) **public transportation** *n* transporte *m* público.
public utility *n* servicio público.
public works *npl* obras *fpl* públicas.
publish ['pʌblɪʃ] *vt* publicar.
publisher ['pʌblɪʃə*] *n* (*person*) editor(a) *m/f*; (*firm*) editorial *f.*
publishing ['pʌblɪʃɪŋ] *n* (*industry*) industria del libro.
publishing company *n* (casa) editorial *f.*
puce [pjuːs] *adj* de color pardo rojizo.
puck [pʌk] *n* (*ICE HOCKEY*) puck *m.*
pucker ['pʌkə*] *vt* (*pleat*) arrugar; (*brow etc*) fruncir.
pudding ['pudɪŋ] *n* pudín *m*; (*BRIT: sweet*) postre *m*; **black** ~ morcilla; **rice** ~ arroz *m* con leche.

puddle ['pʌdl] n charco.
puerile ['pjuərail] adj pueril.
Puerto Rican ['pwɔːtəu'riːkən] adj, n puertorriqueño/a m/f.
Puerto Rico [-'riːkəu] n Puerto Rico.
puff [pʌf] n soplo; (of smoke) bocanada; (of breathing, engine) resoplido; (powder ~) borla ♦ vt: **to ~ one's pipe** dar chupadas a la pipa; (also: ~ **out**: sails, cheeks) hinchar, inflar ♦ vi (gen) soplar; (pant) jadear; **to ~ out smoke** echar humo.
puffed [pʌft] adj (col: out of breath) sin aliento.
puffin ['pʌfɪn] n frailecillo.
puff pastry, (US) **puff paste** n hojaldre m.
puffy ['pʌfɪ] adj hinchado.
pull [pul] n (tug): **to give sth a ~** dar un tirón a algo; (fig: advantage) influencia ♦ vt tirar de, jalar (LAM); (haul) tirar, jalar (LAM), arrastrar; (strain): **to ~ a muscle** sufrir un tirón ♦ vi tirar, jalar (LAM); **to ~ to pieces** hacer pedazos; **to ~ one's punches** andarse con bromas; **to ~ one's weight** hacer su parte; **to ~ o.s. together** tranquilizarse; **to ~ sb's leg** tomar el pelo a algn; **to ~ strings (for sb)** enchufar (a algn).
▶**pull about** vt (handle roughly: object) manosear; (: person) maltratar.
▶**pull apart** vt (take apart) desmontar.
▶**pull down** vt (house) derribar.
▶**pull in** vi (AUT: at the kerb) parar (junto a la acera); (RAIL) llegar.
▶**pull off** vt (deal etc) cerrar.
▶**pull out** vi irse, marcharse; (AUT: from kerb) salir ♦ vt sacar, arrancar.
▶**pull over** vi (AUT) hacerse a un lado.
▶**pull round, pull through** vi salvarse; (MED) recobrar la salud.
▶**pull up** vi (stop) parar ♦ vt (uproot) arrancar, desarraigar; (stop) parar.
pulley ['pulɪ] n polea.
pull-out ['pulaut] n suplemento ♦ cpd (pages, magazine) separable.
pullover ['puləuvə*] n jersey m, suéter m.
pulp [pʌlp] n (of fruit) pulpa; (for paper) pasta; (pej: also: ~ **magazines** etc) prensa amarilla; **to reduce sth to ~** hacer algo papilla.
pulpit ['pulpɪt] n púlpito.
pulsate [pʌl'seɪt] vi pulsar, latir.
pulse [pʌls] n (ANAT) pulso; (of music, engine) pulsación f; (BOT) legumbre f; **to feel** or **take sb's ~** tomar el pulso a algn.
pulverize ['pʌlvəraɪz] vt pulverizar; (fig) hacer polvo.
puma ['pjuːmə] n puma m.
pumice (stone) ['pʌmɪs-] n piedra pómez.

pummel ['pʌml] vt aporrear.
pump [pʌmp] n bomba; (shoe) zapatilla de tenis ♦ vt sacar con una bomba; (fig: col) (son)sacar; **to ~ sb for information** (son)sacarle información a algn.
▶**pump up** vt inflar.
pumpkin ['pʌmpkɪn] n calabaza.
pun [pʌn] n juego de palabras.
punch [pʌntʃ] n (blow) golpe m, puñetazo; (tool) punzón m; (for paper) perforadora; (for tickets) taladro; (drink) ponche m ♦ vt (hit): **to ~ sb/sth** dar un puñetazo or golpear a algn/algo; (make a hole in) punzar; perforar.
punch-drunk ['pʌntʃdrʌŋk] adj (BRIT) grogui, sonado.
punch(ed) card [pʌntʃ(t)-] n tarjeta perforada.
punch line n (of joke) remate m.
punch-up ['pʌntʃʌp] n (BRIT col) riña.
punctual ['pʌŋktjuəl] adj puntual.
punctuality [pʌŋktju'ælɪtɪ] n puntualidad f.
punctually ['pʌŋktjuəlɪ] adv: **it will start ~ at 6** empezará a las 6 en punto.
punctuate ['pʌŋktjueɪt] vt puntuar; (fig) interrumpir.
punctuation [pʌŋktju'eɪʃən] n puntuación f.
punctuation mark n signo de puntuación.
puncture ['pʌŋktʃə*] (BRIT) n pinchazo ♦ vt pinchar; **to have a ~** tener un pinchazo.
pundit ['pʌndɪt] n experto/a.
pungent ['pʌndʒənt] adj acre.
punish ['pʌnɪʃ] vt castigar; **to ~ sb for sth/ for doing sth** castigar a algn por algo/por haber hecho algo.
punishable ['pʌnɪʃəbl] adj punible, castigable.
punishing ['pʌnɪʃɪŋ] adj (fig: exhausting) agotador(a).
punishment ['pʌnɪʃmənt] n castigo; (fig, col): **to take a lot of ~** (boxer) recibir una paliza; (car) ser maltratado.
punitive ['pjuːnɪtɪv] adj punitivo.
punk [pʌŋk] n (also: ~ **rocker**) punki m/f; (also: ~ **rock**) música punk; (US col: hoodlum) matón m.
punt [pʌnt] n (boat) batea; (IRELAND) libra irlandesa ♦ vi (bet) apostar.
punter ['pʌntə*] n (gambler) jugador(a) m/f.
puny ['pjuːnɪ] adj enclenque.
pup [pʌp] n cachorro.
pupil ['pjuːpl] n alumno/a; (of eye) pupila.
puppet ['pʌpɪt] n títere m.
puppet government n gobierno títere.
puppy ['pʌpɪ] n cachorro, perrito.
purchase ['pɜːtʃɪs] n compra; (grip) agarre m, asidero ♦ vt comprar.
purchase order n orden f de compra.

purchase price *n* precio de compra.
purchaser ['pɜːtʃɪsə*] *n* comprador(a) *m/f.*
purchase tax *n* (*BRIT*) impuesto sobre la venta.
purchasing power ['pɜːtʃɪsɪŋ-] *n* poder *m* adquisitivo.
pure [pjuə*] *adj* puro; **a ~ wool jumper** un jersey de pura lana; **it's laziness, ~ and simple** es pura vagancia.
purebred ['pjuəbred] *adj* de pura sangre.
purée ['pjuəreɪ] *n* puré *m.*
purely ['pjuəlɪ] *adv* puramente.
purgatory ['pɜːgətərɪ] *n* purgatorio.
purge [pɜːdʒ] *n* (*MED, POL*) purga ♦ *vt* purgar.
purification [pjuərɪfɪ'keɪʃən] *n* purificación *f*, depuración *f.*
purify ['pjuərɪfaɪ] *vt* purificar, depurar.
purist ['pjuərɪst] *n* purista *m/f.*
puritan ['pjuərɪtən] *n* puritano/a.
puritanical [pjuərɪ'tænɪkl] *adj* puritano.
purity ['pjuərɪtɪ] *n* pureza.
purl [pɜːl] *n* punto del revés.
purloin [pɜː'lɔɪn] *vt* hurtar, robar.
purple ['pɜːpl] *adj* morado.
purport [pɜː'pɔːt] *vi*: **to ~ to be/do** dar a entender que es/hace.
purpose ['pɜːpəs] *n* propósito; **on ~** a propósito, adrede; **to no ~** para nada, en vano; **for teaching ~s** con fines pedagógicos; **for the ~s of this meeting** para los fines de esta reunión.
purpose-built ['pɜːpəs'bɪlt] *adj* (*BRIT*) construido especialmente.
purposeful ['pɜːpəsful] *adj* resuelto, determinado.
purposely ['pɜːpəslɪ] *adv* a propósito, adrede.
purr [pɜː*] ♦ *vi* ronronear.
purse [pɜːs] *n* monedero; (*US: handbag*) bolso ♦ *vt* fruncir.
purser ['pɜːsə*] *n* (*NAUT*) comisario/a.
purse snatcher [-snætʃə*] *n* (*US*) persona que roba por el procedimiento del tirón.
pursue [pə'sjuː] *vt* seguir; (*harass*) perseguir; (*profession*) ejercer; (*pleasures*) buscar; (*inquiry, matter*) seguir.
pursuer [pə'sjuːə*] *n* perseguidor(a) *m/f.*
pursuit [pə'sjuːt] *n* (*chase*) caza; (*of pleasure etc*) busca; (*occupation*) actividad *f*; **in (the) ~ of sth** en busca de algo.
purveyor [pə'veɪə*] *n* proveedor(a) *m/f.*
pus [pʌs] *n* pus *m.*
push [puʃ] *n* empujón *m*; (*MIL*) ataque *m*; (*drive*) empuje *m* ♦ *vt* empujar; (*button*) apretar; (*promote*) promover; (*fig: press, advance: views*) fomentar; (*thrust*): **to ~ sth (into)** meter algo a la fuerza (en) ♦ *vi*

empujar; (*fig*) hacer esfuerzos; **at a ~** (*col*) a duras penas; **she is ~ing 50** (*col*) raya en los 50; **to be ~ed for time/money** andar justo de tiempo/escaso de dinero; **to ~ a door open/shut** abrir/cerrar una puerta empujándola; **to ~ for** (*better pay, conditions*) reivindicar; *"~"* (*on door*) "empujar"; (*on bell*) "pulse".
▶**push aside** *vt* apartar con la mano.
▶**push in** *vi* colarse.
▶**push off** *vi* (*col*) largarse.
▶**push on** *vi* (*continue*) seguir adelante.
▶**push through** *vt* (*measure*) despachar.
▶**push up** *vt* (*total, prices*) hacer subir.
push-bike ['puʃbaɪk] *n* (*BRIT*) bicicleta.
push-button ['puʃbʌtn] *adj* con botón de mando.
pushchair ['puʃtʃeə*] *n* (*BRIT*) silla de niño.
pusher ['puʃə*] *n* (*drug ~*) traficante *m/f* de drogas.
pushover ['puʃəuvə*] *n* (*col*): **it's a ~** está tirado.
push-up ['puʃʌp] *n* (*US*) flexión *f.*
pushy ['puʃɪ] *adj* (*pej*) agresivo.
puss [pus], **pussy(-cat)** ['pusɪ(kæt)] *n* minino.
put [put], *pt, pp* **put** *vt* (*place*) poner, colocar; (*~ into*) meter; (*express, say*) expresar; (*a question*) hacer; (*estimate*) calcular; (*cause to be*): **to ~ sb in a good/bad mood** poner a algn de buen/mal humor; **to ~ a lot of time into sth** dedicar mucho tiempo a algo; **to ~ money on a horse** apostar dinero en un caballo; **to ~ money into a company** invertir dinero en una compañía; **to ~ sb to a lot of trouble** causar mucha molestia a algn; **we ~ the children to bed** acostamos a los niños; **how shall I ~ it?** ¿cómo puedo explicarlo or decirlo?; **I ~ it to you that ...** le sugiero que ...; **to stay ~** no moverse.
▶**put about** *vi* (*NAUT*) virar ♦ *vt* (*rumour*) hacer correr.
▶**put across** *vt* (*ideas etc*) comunicar.
▶**put aside** *vt* (*lay down: book etc*) dejar *or* poner a un lado; (*save*) ahorrar; (*in shop*) guardar.
▶**put away** *vt* (*store*) guardar.
▶**put back** *vt* (*replace*) devolver a su lugar; (*postpone*) posponer; (*set back: watch, clock*) retrasar; **this will ~ us back 10 years** esto nos retrasará 10 años.
▶**put by** *vt* (*money*) guardar.
▶**put down** *vt* (*on ground*) poner en el suelo; (*animal*) sacrificar; (*in writing*) apuntar; (*suppress: revolt etc*) sofocar; (*attribute*) atribuir; **~ me down for £15** apúntame por 15 libras; **~ it down on my**

account (*COMM*) póngalo en mi cuenta.
▶**put forward** *vt* (*ideas*) presentar, proponer; (*date*) adelantar.
▶**put in** *vt* (*application, complaint*) presentar.
▶**put in for** *vt fus* (*job*) solicitar; (*promotion*) pedir.
▶**put off** *vt* (*postpone*) aplazar; (*discourage*) desanimar, quitar las ganas a.
▶**put on** *vt* (*clothes, lipstick etc*) ponerse; (*light etc*) encender; (*play etc*) presentar; (*brake*) echar; (*assume: accent, manner*) afectar, fingir; (*airs*) adoptar, darse; (*concert, exhibition etc*) montar; (*extra bus, train etc*) poner; (*col: kid, have on: esp US*) tomar el pelo a; (*inform, indicate*): **to ~ sb on to sb/sth** informar a algn de algn/algo; **to ~ on weight** engordar.
▶**put out** *vt* (*fire, light*) apagar; (*one's hand*) alargar; (*news, rumour*) hacer circular; (*tongue etc*) sacar; (*person: inconvenience*) molestar, fastidiar; (*dislocate: shoulder, vertebra, knee*) dislocar(se) ♦ *vi* (*NAUT*): **to ~ out to sea** hacerse a la mar; **to ~ out from Plymouth** salir de Plymouth.
▶**put through** *vt* (*call*) poner; **~ me through to Miss Blair** póngame *or* comuníqueme (*LAM*) con la Señorita Blair.
▶**put together** *vt* unir, reunir; (*assemble: furniture*) armar, montar; (*meal*) preparar.
▶**put up** *vt* (*raise*) levantar, alzar; (*hang*) colgar; (*build*) construir; (*increase*) aumentar; (*accommodate*) alojar; (*incite*): **to ~ sb up to doing sth** instar *or* incitar a algn a hacer algo; **to ~ sth up for sale** poner algo a la venta.
▶**put upon** *vt fus*: **to be ~ upon** (*imposed upon*) dejarse explotar.
▶**put up with** *vt fus* aguantar.
putrid ['pjuːtrɪd] *adj* podrido.
putsch [putʃ] *n* golpe *m* de estado.
putt [pʌt] *vt* hacer un putt ♦ *n* putt *m*, golpe *m* corto.
putter ['pʌtə*] *n* putter *m*.
putting green ['pʌtɪŋ-] *n* green *m*, minigolf *m*.
putty ['pʌtɪ] *n* masilla.
put-up ['putʌp] *adj*: **~ job** (*BRIT*) estafa.
puzzle ['pʌzl] *n* (*riddle*) acertijo; (*jigsaw*) rompecabezas *m inv*; (*also*: **crossword ~**) crucigrama *m*; (*mystery*) misterio ♦ *vt* dejar perplejo, confundir ♦ *vi*: **to ~ about** quebrar la cabeza por; **to ~ over** (*sb's actions*) quebrarse la cabeza por; (*mystery, problem*) devanarse los sesos sobre; **to be ~d about sth** no llegar a entender algo.

puzzling ['pʌzlɪŋ] *adj* (*question*) misterioso, extraño; (*attitude, set of instructions*) extraño.
PVC *n abbr* (= *polyvinyl chloride*) P.V.C. *m*.
Pvt. *abbr* (*US MIL*) = **private**.
PW *n abbr* (*US*) = **prisoner of war**.
pw *abbr* (= *per week*) por semana.
PX *n abbr* (*US*: = *post exchange*) *economato militar*.
pygmy ['pɪgmɪ] *n* pigmeo/a.
pyjamas, (*US*) **pajamas** [pɪ'dʒɑːməz] *npl* (*BRIT*) pijama *m*, piyama *m* (*LAM*); **a pair of ~** un pijama.
pylon ['paɪlən] *n* torre *f* de conducción eléctrica.
pyramid ['pɪrəmɪd] *n* pirámide *f*.
Pyrenean [pɪrə'niːən] *adj* pirenaico.
Pyrenees [pɪrə'niːz] *npl*: **the ~** los Pirineos.
Pyrex ® ['paɪreks] *n* pírex *m* ♦ *cpd*: **~ casserole** cazuela de pírex.
python ['paɪθən] *n* pitón *m*.

Q q

Q, q [kjuː] *n* (*letter*) Q, q *f*; **Q for Queen** Q de Quebec.
Qatar [kæ'tɑː] *n* Qatar *m*.
QC *n abbr* (*BRIT*: = *Queen's Council*) *título concedido a determinados abogados*.
QED *abbr* (= *quod erat demonstrandum*) Q.E.D.
QM *n abbr* = **quartermaster**.
q.t. *n abbr* (*col*: = *quiet*): **on the ~** a hurtadillas.
qty *abbr* (= *quantity*) ctdad.
quack [kwæk] *n* (*of duck*) graznido; (*pej: doctor*) curandero/a, matasanos *m inv* ♦ *vi* graznar.
quad [kwɔd] *abbr* = **quadrangle, quadruple, quadruplet**.
quadrangle ['kwɔdræŋgl] *n* (*BRIT: courtyard: abbr*: **quad**) patio.
quadruple [kwɔ'druːpl] *vt, vi* cuadruplicar.
quadruplet [kwɔ'druːplɪt] *n* cuatrillizo.
quagmire ['kwægmaɪə*] *n* lodazal *m*, cenegal *m*.
quail [kweɪl] *n* (*bird*) codorniz *f* ♦ *vi* amedrentarse.
quaint [kweɪnt] *adj* extraño; (*picturesque*) pintoresco.
quaintly ['kweɪntlɪ] *adv* extrañamente;

pintorescamente.

quaintness ['kweɪntnɪs] *n* lo pintoresco, tipismo.

quake [kweɪk] *vi* temblar ♦ *n abbr* = **earthquake**.

Quaker ['kweɪkə*] *n* cuáquero/a.

qualification [kwɔlɪfɪ'keɪʃən] *n* (*reservation*) reserva; (*modification*) modificación *f*; (*act*) calificación *f*; (*paper ~*) título; **what are your ~s?** ¿qué títulos tienes?

qualified ['kwɔlɪfaɪd] *adj* (*trained*) cualificado; (*fit*) capacitado; (*limited*) limitado; (*professionally*) titulado; **~ for/to do sth** capacitado para/para hacer algo; **he's not ~ for the job** no está capacitado para ese trabajo; **it was a ~ success** fue un éxito relativo.

qualify ['kwɔlɪfaɪ] *vt* (*LING*) calificar a; (*capacitate*) capacitar; (*modify*) matizar; (*limit*) moderar ♦ *vi* (*SPORT*) clasificarse; **to ~ (as)** calificarse (de), graduarse (en), recibirse (de) (*LAM*); **to ~ (for)** reunir los requisitos (para); **to ~ as an engineer** sacar el título de ingeniero.

qualifying ['kwɔlɪfaɪɪŋ] *adj* (*exam, round*) eliminatorio.

qualitative ['kwɔlɪtətɪv] *adj* cualitativo.

quality ['kwɔlɪtɪ] *n* calidad *f*; (*moral*) cualidad *f*; **of good/poor ~** de buena *or* alta/poca calidad.

quality control *n* control *m* de calidad.

quality of life *n* calidad *f* de vida.

> *La expresión* **quality press** *se refiere los periódicos que dan un tratamiento serio de las noticias, ofreciendo información detallada sobre un amplio espectro de temas y análisis en profundidad de la actualidad. Por su tamaño, considerablemente mayor que el de los periódicos sensacionalistas, se les llama también* **broadsheets**.

qualm [kwɑːm] *n* escrúpulo; **to have ~s about sth** sentir escrúpulos por algo.

quandary ['kwɔndrɪ] *n*: **to be in a ~** verse en un dilema.

quango ['kwæŋɡəʊ] *n abbr* (*BRIT*: = *quasi-autonomous non-governmental organization*) *organismo semi-autónomo de subvención estatal*.

quantifiable [kwɔntɪ'faɪəbl] *adj* cuantificable.

quantitative ['kwɔntɪtətɪv] *adj* cuantitativo.

quantity ['kwɔntɪtɪ] *n* cantidad *f*; **in ~** en grandes cantidades.

quantity surveyor *n* aparejador(a)

m/f.

quantum leap ['kwɔntəm-] *n* (*fig*) avance *m* espectacular.

quarantine ['kwɔrntiːn] *n* cuarentena.

quark [kwɑːk] *n* cuark *m*.

quarrel ['kwɔrl] *n* riña, pelea ♦ *vi* reñir, pelearse; **to have a ~ with sb** reñir *or* pelearse con algn; **I can't ~ with that** no le veo pegas.

quarrelsome ['kwɔrəlsəm] *adj* pendenciero.

quarry ['kwɔrɪ] *n* (*for stone*) cantera; (*animal*) presa.

quart [kwɔːt] *n cuarto de galón* = *1.136 l.*

quarter ['kwɔːtə*] *n* cuarto, cuarta parte *f*; (*of year*) trimestre *m*; (*district*) barrio; (*US, Canada*: 25 *cents*) cuarto de dólar ♦ *vt* dividir en cuartos; (*MIL: lodge*) alojar; **~s** *npl* (*barracks*) cuartel *m*; (*living ~s*) alojamiento *sg*; **a ~ of an hour** un cuarto de hora; **to pay by the ~** pagar trimestralmente *or* cada 3 meses; **it's a ~ to** *or* (*US*) **of 3** son las 3 menos cuarto; **it's a ~ past** *or* (*US*) **after 3** son las 3 y cuarto; **from all ~s** de todas partes; **at close ~s** de cerca.

quarterback ['kwɔːtəbæk] *n* (*US: football*) mariscal *m* de campo.

quarter-deck ['kwɔːtədɛk] *n* (*NAUT*) alcázar *m*.

quarter final *n* cuarto de final.

quarterly ['kwɔːtəlɪ] *adj* trimestral ♦ *adv* cada 3 meses, trimestralmente.

quartermaster ['kwɔːtəmɑːstə*] *n* (*MIL*) comisario, intendente *m* militar.

quartet(te) [kwɔː'tɛt] *n* cuarteto.

quarto ['kwɔːtəʊ] *n* tamaño holandés ♦ *adj* de tamaño holandés.

quartz [kwɔːts] *n* cuarzo.

quash [kwɔʃ] *vt* (*verdict*) anular, invalidar.

quasi- ['kweɪzaɪ] *pref* cuasi.

quaver ['kweɪvə*] *n* (*BRIT MUS*) corchea ♦ *vi* temblar.

quay [kiː] *n* (*also: ~side*) muelle *m*.

Que. *abbr* (*Canada*) = *Quebec*.

queasiness ['kwiːzɪnɪs] *n* malestar *m*, náuseas *fpl*.

queasy ['kwiːzɪ] *adj*: **to feel ~** tener náuseas.

Quebec [kwɪ'bɛk] *n* Quebec *m*.

queen [kwiːn] *n* reina; (*CARDS etc*) dama.

queen mother *n* reina madre.

> *Se llama* **Queen's Speech** (*o* **King's Speech**) *al discurso que pronuncia el monarca durante la sesión de apertura del Parlamento británico, en el que se expresan*

las líneas generales de la política del gobierno para la nueva legislatura. El Primer Ministro se encarga de redactarlo con la ayuda del Consejo de Ministros y es leído en la Cámara de los Lores (House of Lords) ante los miembros de ambas cámaras.

queer [kwɪə*] *adj* (*odd*) raro, extraño ♦ *n* (*pej: col*) marica *m*.

quell [kwɛl] *vt* calmar; (*put down*) sofocar.

quench [kwɛntʃ] *vt* (*flames*) apagar; **to ~ one's thirst** apagar la sed.

querulous [ˈkwɛrʊləs] *adj* (*person, voice*) quejumbroso.

query [ˈkwɪərɪ] *n* (*question*) pregunta; (*doubt*) duda ♦ *vt* preguntar; (*disagree with, dispute*) no estar conforme con, dudar de.

quest [kwɛst] *n* busca, búsqueda.

question [ˈkwɛstʃən] *n* pregunta; (*matter*) asunto, cuestión *f* ♦ *vt* (*doubt*) dudar de; (*interrogate*) interrogar, hacer preguntas a; **to ask sb a ~, put a ~ to sb** hacerle una pregunta a algn; **the ~ is ...** el asunto es ...; **to bring** *or* **call sth into ~** poner algo en (tela de) duda; **beyond ~** fuera de toda duda; **it's out of the ~** imposible, ni hablar.

questionable [ˈkwɛstʃənəbl] *adj* discutible; (*doubtful*) dudoso.

questioner [ˈkwɛstʃənə*] *n* interrogador(a) *m/f*.

questioning [ˈkwɛstʃənɪŋ] *adj* inquisitivo ♦ *n* preguntas *fpl*; (*by police etc*) interrogatorio.

question mark *n* punto de interrogación.

questionnaire [kwɛstʃəˈnɛə*] *n* cuestionario.

queue [kjuː] (*BRIT*) *n* cola ♦ *vi* hacer cola; **to jump the ~** colarse.

quibble [ˈkwɪbl] *vi* andarse con sutilezas.

quick [kwɪk] *adj* rápido; (*temper*) vivo; (*agile*) ágil; (*mind*) listo; (*eye*) agudo; (*ear*) fino ♦ *n*: **cut to the ~** (*fig*) herido en lo más vivo; **be ~!** ¡date prisa!; **to be ~ to act** obrar con prontitud; **she was ~ to see that** se dio cuenta de eso en seguida.

quicken [ˈkwɪkən] *vt* apresurar ♦ *vi* apresurarse, darse prisa.

quick-fire [ˈkwɪkfaɪə*] *adj* (*questions etc*) rápido, (hecho) a quemarropa.

quick fix *n* (*pej*) parche *m*.

quickly [ˈkwɪklɪ] *adv* rápidamente, de prisa; **we must act ~** tenemos que actuar cuanto antes.

quickness [ˈkwɪknɪs] *n* rapidez *f*; (*of temper*) viveza; (*agility*) agilidad *f*; (*of mind, eye etc*) agudeza.

quicksand [ˈkwɪksænd] *n* arenas *fpl* movedizas.

quickstep [ˈkwɪkstɛp] *n* baile de ritmo rápido.

quick-tempered [kwɪkˈtɛmpəd] *adj* de genio vivo.

quick-witted [kwɪkˈwɪtɪd] *adj* listo, despabilado.

quid [kwɪd] *n, pl inv* (*BRIT col*) libra.

quid pro quo [ˈkwɪdprəʊˈkwəʊ] *n* quid pro quo *m*, compensación *f*.

quiet [ˈkwaɪət] *adj* (*not busy: day*) tranquilo; (*silent*) callado; (*reserved*) reservado; (*discreet*) discreto; (*not noisy: engine*) silencioso ♦ *n* tranquilidad *f* ♦ *vt, vi* (*US*) = **quieten; keep ~!** ¡cállate!, ¡silencio!; **business is ~ at this time of year** hay poco movimiento en esta época.

quieten [ˈkwaɪətn] (*also: ~ down*) *vi* (*grow calm*) calmarse; (*grow silent*) callarse ♦ *vt* calmar; hacer callar.

quietly [ˈkwaɪətlɪ] *adv* tranquilamente; (*silently*) silenciosamente.

quietness [ˈkwaɪətnɪs] *n* (*silence*) silencio; (*calm*) tranquilidad *f*.

quill [kwɪl] *n* (*of porcupine*) púa; (*pen*) pluma.

quilt [kwɪlt] *n* (*BRIT*) edredón *m*.

quin [kwɪn] *n abbr* = **quintuplet**.

quince [kwɪns] *n* membrillo.

quinine [kwɪˈniːn] *n* quinina.

quintet(te) [kwɪnˈtɛt] *n* quinteto.

quintuplet [kwɪnˈtjuːplɪt] *n* quintillizo.

quip [kwɪp] *n* ocurrencia ♦ *vi* decir con ironía.

quire [ˈkwaɪə*] *n* mano *f* de papel.

quirk [kwəːk] *n* peculiaridad *f*; **by some ~ of fate** por algún capricho del destino.

quit *pt, pp* **quit** *or* **quitted** [kwɪt] *vt* dejar, abandonar; (*premises*) desocupar; (*COMPUT*) abandonar ♦ *vi* (*give up*) renunciar; (*go away*) irse; (*resign*) dimitir; **~ stalling!** (*US col*) ¡déjate de evasivas!

quite [kwaɪt] *adv* (*rather*) bastante; (*entirely*) completamente; **~ a few of them** un buen número de ellos; **~ (so)!** ¡así es!, ¡exactamente!; **~ new** bastante nuevo; **that's not ~ right** eso no está del todo bien; **not ~ as many as last time** no tantos como la última vez; **she's ~ pretty** es bastante guapa.

Quito [ˈkiːtəʊ] *n* Quito.

quits [kwɪts] *adj*: **~ (with)** en paz (con); **let's call it ~** quedamos en paz.

quiver [ˈkwɪvə*] *vi* estremecerse ♦ *n* (*for arrows*) carcaj *m*.

quiz [kwɪz] *n* (*game*) concurso; (: *TV, RADIO*)

programa-concurso; (*questioning*)
interrogatorio ♦ *vt* interrogar.
quizzical ['kwɪzɪkl] *adj* burlón(ona).
quoits [kwɔɪts] *npl* juego de aros.
quorum ['kwɔːrəm] *n* quórum *m*.
quota ['kwəutə] *n* cuota.
quotation [kwəu'teɪʃən] *n* cita; (*estimate*)
presupuesto.
quotation marks *npl* comillas *fpl*.
quote [kwəut] *n* cita ♦ *vt* (*sentence*) citar;
(*COMM: sum, figure*) cotizar ♦ *vi*: **to ~ from**
citar de; **~s** *npl* (*inverted commas*)
comillas *fpl*; **in ~s** entre comillas; **the
figure ~d for the repairs** el presupuesto
dado para las reparaciones; **~ ... unquote**
(*in dictation*) comillas iniciales ... finales.
quotient ['kwəuʃənt] *n* cociente *m*.
qv *n abbr* (= *quod vide: which see*) q.v.
qwerty keyboard ['kwəːtɪ-] *n* teclado
QWERTY.

R r

R, r [ɑː*] *n* (*letter*) R, r *f*; **R for Robert**, (*US*) **R
for Roger** R de Ramón.
R *abbr* (= *right*) dcha.; (= *river*) R.;
(= *Réaumur (scale)*) R; (*US CINE*: =
restricted) sólo mayores; (*US POL*) =
republican; (*BRIT*: = *Rex, Regina*) R.
RA *abbr* = *rear admiral* ♦ *n abbr* (*BRIT*) = **Royal
Academy, Royal Academician**.
RAAF *n abbr* = *Royal Australian Air Force*.
Rabat [rə'bɑːt] *n* Rabat *m*.
rabbi ['ræbaɪ] *n* rabino.
rabbit ['ræbɪt] *n* conejo ♦ *vi*: **to ~ (on)** (*BRIT
col*) hablar sin ton ni son.
rabbit hutch *n* conejera.
rabble ['ræbl] *n* (*pej*) chusma, populacho.
rabies ['reɪbiːz] *n* rabia.
RAC *n abbr* (*BRIT*: = *Royal Automobile Club*)
≈ RACE *m* (*SP*).
raccoon [rə'kuːn] *n* mapache *m*.
race [reɪs] *n* carrera; (*species*) raza ♦ *vt*
(*horse*) hacer correr; (*person*) competir
contra; (*engine*) acelerar ♦ *vi* (*compete*)
competir; (*run*) correr; (*pulse*) latir a
ritmo acelerado; **the arms ~** la carrera
armamentista; **the human ~** el género
humano; **he ~d across the road** cruzó
corriendo la carretera; **to ~ in/out**
entrar/salir corriendo.

race car *n* (*US*) = **racing car**.
race car driver *n* (*US*) = **racing driver**.
racecourse ['reɪskɔːs] *n* hipódromo.
racehorse ['reɪshɔːs] *n* caballo de carreras.
race meeting *n* concurso hípico.
race relations *npl* relaciones *fpl* raciales.
racetrack ['reɪstræk] *n* hipódromo; (*for cars*)
circuito de carreras.
racial ['reɪʃl] *adj* racial.
racial discrimination *n* discriminación *f*
racial.
racial integration *n* integración *f* racial.
racialism ['reɪʃəlɪzəm] *n* racismo.
racialist ['reɪʃəlɪst] *adj, n* racista *m/f*.
racing ['reɪsɪŋ] *n* carreras *fpl*.
racing car *n* (*BRIT*) coche *m* de carreras.
racing driver *n* (*BRIT*) corredor(a) *m/f* de
coches.
racism ['reɪsɪzəm] *n* racismo.
racist ['reɪsɪst] *adj, n* racista *m/f*.
rack [ræk] *n* (*also*: **luggage ~**) rejilla
(portaequipajes); (*shelf*) estante *m*; (*also*:
roof ~) baca; (*clothes ~*) perchero ♦ *vt*
(*cause pain to*) atormentar; **to go to ~ and
ruin** venirse abajo; **to ~ one's brains**
devanarse los sesos.
▶**rack up** *vt* conseguir, ganar.
racket ['rækɪt] *n* (*for tennis*) raqueta; (*noise*)
ruido, estrépito; (*swindle*) estafa, timo.
racketeer [rækɪ'tɪə*] *n* (*esp US*)
estafador(a) *m/f*.
racoon [rə'kuːn] *n* = **raccoon**.
racquet ['rækɪt] *n* raqueta.
racy ['reɪsɪ] *adj* picante, subido.
RADA ['rɑːdə] *n abbr* (*BRIT*) = *Royal Academy
of Dramatic Art*.
radar ['reɪdɑː*] *n* radar *m*.
radar trap *n* trampa radar.
radial ['reɪdɪəl] *adj* (*tyre: also*: **~-ply**) radial.
radiance ['reɪdɪəns] *n* brillantez *f*,
resplandor *m*.
radiant ['reɪdɪənt] *adj* brillante,
resplandeciente.
radiate ['reɪdɪeɪt] *vt* (*heat*) radiar, irradiar
♦ *vi* (*lines*) extenderse.
radiation [reɪdɪ'eɪʃən] *n* radiación *f*.
radiation sickness *n* enfermedad *f* de
radiación.
radiator ['reɪdɪeɪtə*] *n* (*AUT*) radiador *m*.
radiator cap *n* tapón *m* de radiador.
radiator grill *n* (*AUT*) rejilla del radiador.
radical ['rædɪkl] *adj* radical.
radically ['rædɪkəlɪ] *adv* radicalmente.
radii ['reɪdɪaɪ] *npl of* **radius**.
radio ['reɪdɪəu] *n* radio *f* or *m* (*LAM*) ♦ *vi*: **to ~
to sb** mandar un mensaje por radio a
algn ♦ *vt* (*information*) radiar, transmitir
por radio; (*one's position*) indicar por

radio; (*person*) llamar por radio; **on the ~** en *or* por la radio.

radioactive [reɪdɪəu'æktɪv] *adj* radi(o)activo.

radioactivity [reɪdɪəuæk'tɪvɪtɪ] *n* radi(o)actividad *f*.

radio announcer *n* locutor(a) *m/f* de radio.

radio-controlled [reɪdɪəukən'trəuld] *adj* teledirigido.

radiographer [reɪdɪ'ɔgrəfə*] *n* radiógrafo/a.

radiography [reɪdɪ'ɔgrəfɪ] *n* radiografía.

radiology [reɪdɪ'ɔlədʒɪ] *n* radiología.

radio station *n* emisora.

radio taxi *n* radio taxi *m*.

radiotelephone [reɪdɪəu'tɛlɪfəun] *n* radioteléfono.

radiotelescope [reɪdɪəu'tɛlɪskəup] *n* radiotelescopio.

radiotherapist [reɪdɪəu'θɛrəpɪst] *n* radioterapeuta *m/f*.

radiotherapy ['reɪdɪəuθɛrəpɪ] *n* radioterapia.

radish ['rædɪʃ] *n* rábano.

radium ['reɪdɪəm] *n* radio.

radius, *pl* **radii** ['reɪdɪəs, -ɪaɪ] *n* radio; **within a ~ of 50 miles** en un radio de 50 millas.

RAF *n abbr see* **Royal Air Force.**

raffia ['ræfɪə] *n* rafia.

raffle ['ræfl] *n* rifa, sorteo ♦ *vt* (*object*) rifar.

raft [rɑːft] *n* (*craft*) balsa; (*also*: **life ~**) balsa salvavidas.

rafter ['rɑːftə*] *n* viga.

rag [ræg] *n* (*piece of cloth*) trapo; (*torn cloth*) harapo; (*pej: newspaper*) periodicucho; (*for charity*) actividades estudiantiles benéficas ♦ *vt* (*BRIT*) tomar el pelo a; **~s** *npl* harapos *mpl*; **in ~s** en harapos, hecho jirones.

> *En la universidad los estudiantes suelen organizar cada año lo que llaman* **rag day** *o, con más frecuencia,* **rag week**, *según sea un sólo día o una semana. Consiste en una serie de actos festivos y de participación general como teatro en la calle, marchas patrocinadas etc, para hacer colectas con fines benéficos. En ocasiones hacen también una revista (***rag mag***), que consiste básicamente en chistes más bien picantes para vender a los transeúntes, e incluso un baile de gala (***rag ball***).*

rag-and-bone man [ræɡən'bəunmæn] *n* (*BRIT*) trapero.

rag doll *n* muñeca de trapo.

rage [reɪdʒ] *n* (*fury*) rabia, furor *m* ♦ *vi* (*person*) rabiar, estar furioso; (*storm*)

bramar; **to fly into a ~** montar en cólera; **it's all the ~** es lo último.

ragged ['ræɡɪd] *adj* (*edge*) desigual, mellado; (*cuff*) roto; (*appearance*) andrajoso, harapiento; **~ left/right** (*text*) margen *m* izquierdo/derecho irregular.

raging ['reɪdʒɪŋ] *adj* furioso; **in a ~ temper** de un humor de mil demonios.

rag trade *n*: **the ~** (*col*) el ramo de la confección.

rag week *n see* **rag.**

raid [reɪd] *n* (*MIL*) incursión *f*; (*criminal*) asalto; (*by police*) redada, allanamiento (*LAM*) ♦ *vt* invadir, atacar; asaltar.

raider ['reɪdə*] *n* invasor(a) *m/f*.

rail [reɪl] *n* (*on stair*) barandilla, pasamanos *m inv*; (*on bridge*) pretil *m*; (*of balcony, ship*) barandilla; (*for train*) riel *m*, carril *m*; **~s** *npl* vía *sg*; **by ~** por ferrocarril, en tren.

railcard ['reɪlkɑːd] *n* (*BRIT*) *tarjeta para obtener descuentos en el tren*; **Young Person's ~** ≈ Tarjeta joven (*ESP*).

railing(s) ['reɪlɪŋz] *n(pl)* verja *sg*.

railway ['reɪlweɪ], (*US*) **railroad** ['reɪlrəud] *n* ferrocarril *m*, vía férrea.

railway engine *n* (máquina) locomotora.

railway line *n* (*BRIT*) línea (de ferrocarril).

railwayman ['reɪlweɪmən] *n* (*BRIT*) ferroviario.

railway station *n* (*BRIT*) estación *f* de ferrocarril.

rain [reɪn] *n* lluvia ♦ *vi* llover; **in the ~** bajo la lluvia; **it's ~ing** llueve, está lloviendo; **it's ~ing cats and dogs** está lloviendo a cántaros *or* a mares.

rainbow ['reɪnbəu] *n* arco iris.

raincoat ['reɪnkəut] *n* impermeable *m*.

raindrop ['reɪndrɔp] *n* gota de lluvia.

rainfall ['reɪnfɔːl] *n* lluvia.

rainforest ['reɪnfɔrɪst] *n* selva tropical.

rainproof ['reɪnpruːf] *adj* impermeable, a prueba de lluvia.

rainstorm ['reɪnstɔːm] *n* temporal *m* (de lluvia).

rainwater ['reɪnwɔːtə*] *n* agua de lluvia.

rainy ['reɪnɪ] *adj* lluvioso.

raise [reɪz] *n* aumento ♦ *vt* (*lift*) levantar; (*build*) erigir, edificar; (*increase*) aumentar; (*doubts*) suscitar; (*a question*) plantear; (*cattle, family*) criar; (*crop*) cultivar; (*army*) reclutar; (*funds*) reunir; (*loan*) obtener; (*end: embargo*) levantar; **to ~ one's voice** alzar la voz; **to ~ one's glass to sb/sth** brindar por algn/algo; **to ~ a laugh/a smile** provocar risa/una sonrisa; **to ~ sb's hopes** dar esperanzas a algn.

raisin ['reɪzn] *n* pasa de Corinto.

rake [reɪk] n (*tool*) rastrillo; (*person*) libertino ♦ vt (*garden*) rastrillar; (*fire*) hurgar; (*with machine gun*) barrer.
▶**rake in, rake together** vt sacar.
rake-off ['reɪkɔf] n (*col*) comisión f, tajada.
rakish ['reɪkɪʃ] adj (*dissolute*) libertino; **at a ~ angle** (*hat*) echado a un lado, de lado.
rally ['rælɪ] n reunión f; (*POL*) mitin m; (*AUT*) rallye m; (*TENNIS*) peloteo ♦ vt reunir ♦ vi reunirse; (*sick person, STOCK EXCHANGE*) recuperarse.
▶**rally round** vt fus (*fig*) dar apoyo a.
rallying point ['rælɪɪŋ-] n (*POL, MIL*) punto de reunión.
RAM [ræm] n abbr (= *random access memory*) RAM f.
ram [ræm] n carnero; (*TECH*) pisón m ♦ vt (*crash into*) dar contra, chocar con; (*tread down*) apisonar.
ramble ['ræmbl] n caminata, excursión f en el campo ♦ vi (*pej: also:* ~ **on**) divagar.
rambler ['ræmblə*] n excursionista m/f; (*BOT*) trepadora f.
rambling ['ræmblɪŋ] adj (*speech*) inconexo; (*BOT*) trepador(a); (*house*) laberíntico.
rambunctious [ræm'bʌŋkʃəs] adj (*US*) = **rumbustious**.
RAMC n abbr (*BRIT*) = *Royal Army Medical Corps.*
ramification [ræmɪfɪ'keɪʃən] n ramificación f.
ramp [ræmp] n rampa; **on/off** ~ n (*US AUT*) vía de acceso/salida; "~" (*AUT*) "rampa".
rampage [ræm'peɪdʒ] n: **to be on the ~** desmandarse.
rampant ['ræmpənt] adj (*disease etc*): **to be ~** estar muy extendido.
rampart ['ræmpɑːt] n terraplén m; (*wall*) muralla.
ram raid vt atracar (*rompiendo el escaparate con un coche*).
ramshackle ['ræmʃækl] adj destartalado.
RAN n abbr = *Royal Australian Navy.*
ran [ræn] pt of **run**.
ranch [rɑːntʃ] n (*US*) hacienda, estancia.
rancher ['rɑːntʃə*] n ganadero.
rancid ['rænsɪd] adj rancio.
rancour, (*US*) **rancor** ['ræŋkə*] n rencor m.
random ['rændəm] adj fortuito, sin orden; (*COMPUT, MATH*) aleatorio ♦ n: **at** ~ al azar.
random access n (*COMPUT*) acceso aleatorio.
randy ['rændɪ] adj (*BRIT col*) cachondo, caliente.
rang [ræŋ] pt of **ring**.
range [reɪndʒ] n (*of mountains*) cadena de montañas, cordillera; (*of missile*) alcance

m; (*of voice*) registro; (*series*) serie f; (*of products*) surtido; (*MIL: also:* **shooting** ~) campo de tiro; (*also:* **kitchen** ~) fogón m ♦ vt (*place*) colocar; (*arrange*) arreglar ♦ vi: **to** ~ **over** (*wander*) recorrer; (*extend*) extenderse por; **within** (*firing*) ~ a tiro; **do you have anything else in this price** ~? ¿tiene algo más de esta gama de precios?; **intermediate-/short-**~ **missile** proyectil m de medio/corto alcance; **to** ~ **from ... to...** oscilar entre ... y...; ~**d left/ right** (*text*) alineado a la izquierda/ derecha.
ranger [reɪndʒə*] n guardabosques m inv.
Rangoon [ræŋ'guːn] n Rangún m.
rangy ['reɪndʒɪ] adj alto y delgado.
rank [ræŋk] n (*row*) fila; (*MIL*) rango; (*status*) categoría; (*BRIT: also:* **taxi** ~) parada ♦ vi: **to** ~ **among** figurar entre ♦ adj (*stinking*) fétido, rancio; (*hypocrisy, injustice etc*) manifiesto; **the** ~ **and file** (*fig*) las bases; **to close** ~**s** (*MIL*) cerrar filas; (*fig*) hacer un frente común; ~ **outsider** participante m/f sin probabilidades de vencer; **I** ~ **him 6th** yo le pongo en sexto lugar.
rankle ['ræŋkl] vi (*insult*) doler.
ransack ['rænsæk] vt (*search*) registrar; (*plunder*) saquear.
ransom ['rænsəm] n rescate m; **to hold sb to** ~ (*fig*) poner a algn entre la espada y la pared.
rant [rænt] vi despotricar.
ranting ['ræntɪŋ] n desvaríos mpl.
rap [ræp] vt golpear, dar un golpecito en.
rape [reɪp] n violación f; (*BOT*) colza ♦ vt violar.
rape(seed) oil ['reɪp(siːd)-] n aceite m de colza.
rapid ['ræpɪd] adj rápido.
rapidity [rə'pɪdɪtɪ] n rapidez f.
rapidly ['ræpɪdlɪ] adv rápidamente.
rapids ['ræpɪdz] npl (*GEO*) rápidos mpl.
rapier ['reɪpɪə*] n estoque m.
rapist ['reɪpɪst] n violador m.
rapport [ræ'pɔː*] n entendimiento.
rapprochement [ræ'prɔʃmɑːŋ] n acercamiento.
rapt [ræpt] adj (*attention*) profundo; **to be ~ in contemplation** estar ensimismado.
rapture ['ræptʃə*] n éxtasis m.
rapturous ['ræptʃərəs] adj extático; (*applause*) entusiasta; **a** ~ (*party*) macrofiesta con música máquina; ~ **music** música máquina.
rare [rɛə*] adj raro, poco común; (*CULIN: steak*) poco hecho; **it is** ~ **to find that ...** es raro descubrir que ....
rarefied ['rɛərɪfaɪd] adj (*air, atmosphere*)

enrarecido.

rarely ['rɛəlɪ] *adv* rara vez, pocas veces.

raring ['rɛərɪŋ] *adj*: **to be ~ to go** (*col*) tener muchas ganas de empezar.

rarity ['rɛərɪtɪ] *n* rareza.

rascal ['rɑːskl] *n* pillo/a, pícaro/a.

rash [ræʃ] *adj* imprudente, precipitado ♦ *n* (*MED*) salpullido, erupción *f* (cutánea); **to come out in a ~** salir salpullidos.

rasher ['ræʃə*] *n* loncha.

rashly ['ræʃlɪ] *adv* imprudentemente, precipitadamente.

rashness ['ræʃnɪs] *n* imprudencia, precipitación *f*.

rasp [rɑːsp] *n* (*tool*) escofina ♦ *vt* (*speak: also*: **~ out**) decir con voz áspera.

raspberry ['rɑːzbərɪ] *n* frambuesa.

rasping ['rɑːspɪŋ] *adj*: **a ~ noise** un ruido áspero.

Rastafarian [ræstə'fɛərɪən] *adj, n* rastafari *m/f*.

rat [ræt] *n* rata.

ratchet ['rætʃɪt] *n* (*TECH*) trinquete *m*.

rate [reɪt] *n* (*ratio*) razón *f*; (*percentage*) tanto por ciento; (*price*) precio; (: *of hotel*) tarifa; (*of interest*) tipo; (*speed*) velocidad *f* ♦ *vt* (*value*) tasar; (*estimate*) estimar; **to ~ as** ser considerado como; **~s** *npl* (*BRIT*) impuesto *sg* municipal; (*fees*) tarifa *sg*; **failure ~** porcentaje *m* de fallos; **pulse ~** pulsaciones *fpl* por minuto; **~ of pay** tipos *mpl* de sueldo; **at a ~ of 60 kph** a una velocidad de 60 kph; **~ of growth** ritmo de crecimiento; **~ of return** (*COMM*) tasa de rendimiento; **bank ~** tipo *or* tasa de interés bancario; **at any ~** en todo caso; **to ~ sb/sth highly** tener a algn/algo en alta estima; **the house is ~d at £84 per annum** (*BRIT*) la casa está tasada en 84 libras al año.

rateable value ['reɪtəbl-] *n* (*BRIT*) valor *m* impuesto.

rate-capping ['reɪtkæpɪŋ] *n* (*BRIT*) fijación *f* de las contribuciones.

ratepayer ['reɪtpeɪə*] *n* (*BRIT*) contribuyente *m/f*.

rather ['rɑːðə*] *adv* antes, más bien; (*somewhat*) algo, un poco; (*quite*) bastante; **it's ~ expensive** es algo caro; (*too much*) es demasiado caro; **there's ~ a lot** hay bastante; **I would** *or* **I'd ~ go** preferiría ir; **I'd ~ not** prefiero que no; **I ~ think he won't come** me inclino a creer que no vendrá; **or ~** (*more accurately*) o mejor dicho.

ratification [rætɪfɪ'keɪʃən] *n* ratificación *f*.

ratify ['rætɪfaɪ] *vt* ratificar.

rating ['reɪtɪŋ] *n* (*valuation*) tasación *f*;

(*standing*) posición *f*; (*BRIT NAUT*: *sailor*) marinero; **~s** *npl* (*RADIO*, *TV*) clasificación *f*.

ratio ['reɪʃɪəu] *n* razón *f*; **in the ~ of 100 to 1** a razón de *or* en la proporción de 100 a 1.

ration ['ræʃən] *n* ración *f*; **~s** *npl* víveres *mpl* ♦ *vt* racionar.

rational ['ræʃənl] *adj* racional; (*solution, reasoning*) lógico, razonable; (*person*) cuerdo, sensato.

rationale [ræʃə'nɑːl] *n* razón *f* fundamental.

rationalism ['ræʃnəlɪzəm] *n* racionalismo.

rationalization [ræʃnəlaɪ'zeɪʃən] *n* racionalización *f*.

rationalize ['ræʃnəlaɪz] *vt* (*reorganize*: *industry*) racionalizar.

rationally ['ræʃnəlɪ] *adv* racionalmente; (*logically*) lógicamente.

rationing ['ræʃnɪŋ] *n* racionamiento.

ratpack ['rætpæk] *n* (*BRIT col*) *periodistas que persiguen a los famosos*.

rat race *n* lucha incesante por la supervivencia.

rattan [ræ'tæn] *n* rota, caña de Indias.

rattle ['rætl] *n* golpeteo; (*of train etc*) traqueteo; (*object*: *of baby*) sonaja, sonajero; (: *of sports fan*) matraca ♦ *vi* sonar, golpear; traquetear; (*small objects*) castañetear ♦ *vt* hacer sonar agitando; (*col*: *disconcert*) poner nervioso a.

rattlesnake ['rætlsneɪk] *n* serpiente *f* de cascabel.

ratty ['rætɪ] *adj* (*col*) furioso; **to get ~** mosquearse.

raucous ['rɔːkəs] *adj* estridente, ronco.

raucously ['rɔːkəslɪ] *adv* de modo estridente, roncamente.

raunchy ['rɔːntʃɪ] *adj* (*col*) lascivo.

ravage ['rævɪdʒ] *vt* hacer estragos en, destrozar; **~s** *npl* estragos *mpl*.

rave [reɪv] *vi* (*in anger*) encolerizarse; (*with enthusiasm*) entusiasmarse; (*MED*) delirar, desvariar ♦ *cpd*: **~ review** reseña entusiasta; **a ~** (*party*) *macrofiesta con música máquina*; **~ music** música máquina.

raven ['reɪvən] *n* cuervo.

ravenous ['rævənəs] *adj*: **to be ~** tener un hambre canina.

ravine [rə'viːn] *n* barranco.

raving ['reɪvɪŋ] *adj*: **~ lunatic** loco de atar.

ravings ['reɪvɪŋz] *npl* desvaríos *mpl*.

ravioli [rævɪ'əulɪ] *n* ravioles *mpl*, ravioli *mpl*.

ravish ['rævɪʃ] *vt* (*charm*) encantar, embelesar; (*rape*) violar.

ravishing ['rævɪʃɪŋ] *adj* encantador(a).

raw [rɔː] *adj* (*uncooked*) crudo; (*not processed*) bruto; (*sore*) vivo;

(*inexperienced*) novato, inexperto.

Rawalpindi [rɔːlˈpɪndɪ] *n* Rawalpindi *m*.

raw data *n* (*COMPUT*) datos *mpl* en bruto.

raw deal *n* (*col: bad deal*) mala pasada *or* jugada; (: *harsh treatment*) injusticia.

raw material *n* materia prima.

ray [reɪ] *n* rayo; ~ **of hope** (rayo de) esperanza.

rayon [ˈreɪɔn] *n* rayón *m*.

raze [reɪz] *vt* (*also*: ~ **to the ground**) arrasar, asolar.

razor [ˈreɪzə*] *n* (*open*) navaja; (*safety* ~) máquina de afeitar.

razor blade *n* hoja de afeitar.

razzle(-dazzle) [ˈræzl(ˈdæzl)] *n* (*BRIT col*): **to be/go on the** ~ estar/irse de juerga.

razzmatazz [ˈræzməˈtæz] *n* (*col*) animación *f*, bullicio.

R & B *n abbr* = *rhythm and blues*.

RC *abbr* = **Roman Catholic**.

RCAF *n abbr* = *Royal Canadian Air Force*.

RCMP *n abbr* = *Royal Canadian Mounted Police*.

RCN *n abbr* = *Royal Canadian Navy*.

RD *abbr* (*US POST*) = *rural delivery*.

Rd *abbr* = **road**.

R & D *n abbr* (= *research and development*) I + D.

RDC *n abbr* (*BRIT*) = *rural district council*.

RE *n abbr* (*BRIT*) = *religious education*; (*BRIT MIL*) = *Royal Engineers*.

re [riː] *prep* con referencia a.

re ... [riː] *pref* re....

reach [riːtʃ] *n* alcance *m*; (*BOXING*) envergadura; (*of river etc*) extensión *f* entre dos recodos ♦ *vt* alcanzar, llegar a; (*achieve*) lograr ♦ *vi* extenderse; (*stretch out hand: also*: ~ **down**, ~ **over**, ~ **across** *etc*) tender la mano; **within** ~ al alcance (de la mano); **out of** ~ fuera del alcance; **to** ~ **out for sth** alargar *or* tender la mano para tomar algo; **can I** ~ **you at your hotel?** ¿puedo localizarte en tu hotel?; **to** ~ **sb by phone** comunicarse con algn por teléfono.

react [riːˈækt] *vi* reaccionar.

reaction [riːˈækʃən] *n* reacción *f*.

reactionary [riːˈækʃənrɪ] *adj, n* reaccionario/a *m/f*.

reactor [riːˈæktə*] *n* reactor *m*.

read, *pt, pp* **read** [riːd, rɛd] *vi* leer ♦ *vt* leer; (*understand*) entender; (*study*) estudiar; **to take sth as read** (*fig*) dar algo por sentado; **do you** ~ **me?** (*TEL*) ¿me escucha?; **to** ~ **between the lines** leer entre líneas.

▶**read out** *vt* leer en alta voz.

▶**read over** *vt* repasar.

▶**read through** *vt* (*quickly*) leer rápidamente, echar un vistazo a; (*thoroughly*) leer con cuidado *or* detenidamente.

▶**read up** *vt*, **read up on** *vt fus* documentarse sobre.

readable [ˈriːdəbl] *adj* (*writing*) legible; (*book*) que merece la pena leer.

reader [ˈriːdə*] *n* lector(a) *m/f*; (*book*) libro de lecturas; (*BRIT: at university*) profesor(a) *m/f*.

readership [ˈriːdəʃɪp] *n* (*of paper etc*) número de lectores.

readily [ˈrɛdɪlɪ] *adv* (*willingly*) de buena gana; (*easily*) fácilmente; (*quickly*) en seguida.

readiness [ˈrɛdɪnɪs] *n* buena voluntad; (*preparedness*) preparación *f*; **in** ~ (*prepared*) listo, preparado.

reading [ˈriːdɪŋ] *n* lectura; (*understanding*) comprensión *f*; (*on instrument*) indicación *f*.

reading lamp *n* lámpara portátil.

reading matter *n* lectura.

reading room *n* sala de lectura.

readjust [riːəˈdʒʌst] *vt* reajustar ♦ *vi* (*person*): **to** ~ **to** reajustarse a.

readjustment [riːəˈdʒʌstmənt] *n* reajuste *m*.

ready [ˈrɛdɪ] *adj* listo, preparado; (*willing*) dispuesto; (*available*) disponible ♦ *n*: **at the** ~ (*MIL*) listo para tirar; ~ **for use** listo para usar; **to be** ~ **to do sth** estar listo para hacer algo; **to get** ~ *vi* prepararse ♦ *vt* preparar.

ready cash *n* efectivo.

ready-made [ˈrɛdɪˈmeɪd] *adj* confeccionado.

ready money *n* dinero contante.

ready reckoner *n* tabla de cálculos hechos.

ready-to-wear [ˈrɛdɪtəˈwɛə*] *adj* confeccionado.

reaffirm [riːəˈfəːm] *vt* reafirmar.

reagent [riːˈeɪdʒənt] *n* reactivo.

real [rɪəl] *adj* verdadero, auténtico; **in** ~ **terms** en términos reales; **in** ~ **life** en la vida real, en la realidad.

real ale *n* cerveza elaborada tradicionalmente.

real estate *n* bienes *mpl* raíces.

real estate agency *n* = **estate agency**.

realism [ˈrɪəlɪzəm] *n* (*also ART*) realismo.

realist [ˈrɪəlɪst] *n* realista *m/f*.

realistic [rɪəˈlɪstɪk] *adj* realista.

realistically [rɪəˈlɪstɪklɪ] *adv* de modo realista.

reality [riːˈælɪtɪ] *n* realidad *f*; **in** ~ en

realidad.

realization [rɪəlaɪ'zeɪʃən] *n* comprensión *f*; (*of a project*; COMM: *of assets*) realización *f*.

realize ['rɪəlaɪz] *vt* (*understand*) darse cuenta de; (*a project*; COMM: *asset*) realizar; **I ~ that ...** comprendo *or* entiendo que ....

really ['rɪəlɪ] *adv* realmente; **~?** ¿de veras?

realm [rɛlm] *n* reino; (*fig*) esfera.

real time *n* (COMPUT) tiempo real.

Realtor ® ['rɪəltɔ:*] *n* (*US*) corredor(a) *m/f* de bienes raíces.

ream [ri:m] *n* resma; **~s** (*fig, col*) montones *mpl*.

reap [ri:p] *vt* segar; (*fig*) cosechar, recoger.

reaper ['ri:pə*] *n* segador(a) *m/f*.

reappear [ri:ə'pɪə*] *vi* reaparecer.

reappearance [ri:ə'pɪərəns] *n* reaparición *f*.

reapply [ri:ə'plaɪ] *vi* volver a presentarse, hacer *or* presentar una nueva solicitud.

reappoint [ri:ə'pɔɪnt] *vt* volver a nombrar.

reappraisal [ri:ə'preɪzl] *n* revaluación *f*.

rear [rɪə*] *adj* trasero ♦ *n* parte *f* trasera ♦ *vt* (*cattle, family*) criar ♦ *vi* (*also:* **~ up**) (*animal*) encabritarse.

rear-engined ['rɪər'ɛndʒɪnd] *adj* (AUT) con motor trasero.

rearguard ['rɪəgɑ:d] *n* retaguardia.

rearm [ri:'ɑ:m] *vt* rearmar ♦ *vi* rearmarse.

rearmament [ri:'ɑ:məmənt] *n* rearme *m*.

rearrange [ri:ə'reɪndʒ] *vt* ordenar *or* arreglar de nuevo.

rear-view ['rɪəvju:]: **~ mirror** *n* (AUT) espejo retrovisor.

reason ['ri:zn] *n* razón *f* ♦ *vi*: **to ~ with sb** tratar de que algn entre en razón; **it stands to ~ that** es lógico que; **the ~ for/ why** la causa de/la razón por la cual; **she claims with good ~ that she's underpaid** dice con razón que está mal pagada; **all the more ~ why you should not sell it** razón de más para que no lo vendas.

reasonable ['ri:znəbl] *adj* razonable; (*sensible*) sensato.

reasonably ['ri:znəblɪ] *adv* razonablemente; **a ~ accurate report** un informe bastante exacto.

reasoned ['ri:znd] *adj* (*argument*) razonado.

reasoning ['ri:znɪŋ] *n* razonamiento, argumentos *mpl*.

reassemble [ri:ə'sɛmbl] *vt* volver a reunir; (*machine*) montar de nuevo ♦ *vi* volver a reunirse.

reassert [ri:ə'sə:t] *vt* reafirmar, reiterar.

reassurance [ri:ə'ʃuərəns] *n* consuelo.

reassure [ri:ə'ʃuə*] *vt* tranquilizar; **to ~ sb that** tranquilizar a algn asegurándole que.

reassuring [ri:ə'ʃuərɪŋ] *adj* tranquilizador(a).

reawakening [ri:ə'weɪknɪŋ] *n* despertar *m*.

rebate ['ri:beɪt] *n* (*on product*) rebaja; (*on tax etc*) desgravación *f*; (*repayment*) reembolso.

rebel ['rɛbl] *n* rebelde *m/f* ♦ *vi* [rɪ'bɛl] rebelarse, sublevarse.

rebellion [rɪ'bɛljən] *n* rebelión *f*, sublevación *f*.

rebellious [rɪ'bɛljəs] *adj* rebelde; (*child*) revoltoso.

rebirth [ri:'bə:θ] *n* renacimiento.

rebound [rɪ'baund] *vi* (*ball*) rebotar ♦ *n* ['ri:baund] rebote *m*.

rebuff [rɪ'bʌf] *n* desaire *m*, rechazo ♦ *vt* rechazar.

rebuild [ri:'bɪld] *vt* (*irreg: like* **build**) reconstruir.

rebuilding [ri:'bɪldɪŋ] *n* reconstrucción *f*.

rebuke [rɪ'bju:k] *n* reprimenda ♦ *vt* reprender.

rebut [rɪ'bʌt] *vt* rebatir.

recalcitrant [rɪ'kælsɪtrənt] *adj* reacio.

recall [rɪ'kɔ:l] *vt* (*remember*) recordar; (*ambassador etc*) retirar; (COMPUT) volver a llamar ♦ *n* recuerdo.

recant [rɪ'kænt] *vi* retractarse.

recap ['ri:kæp] *vt, vi* recapitular.

recapitulate [ri:kə'pɪtjuleɪt] *vt, vi* = **recap**.

recapture [ri:'kæptʃə*] *vt* (*town*) reconquistar; (*atmosphere*) hacer revivir.

recd., rec'd *abbr* (= *received*) rbdo.

recede [rɪ'si:d] *vi* retroceder.

receding [rɪ'si:dɪŋ] *adj* (*forehead, chin*) hundido; **~ hairline** entradas *fpl*.

receipt [rɪ'si:t] *n* (*document*) recibo; (*act of receiving*) recepción *f*; **~s** *npl* (COMM) ingresos *mpl*; **to acknowledge ~ of** acusar recibo de; **we are in ~ of ...** obra en nuestro poder ....

receivable [rɪ'si:vəbl] *adj* (COMM) a cobrar.

receive [rɪ'si:v] *vt* recibir; (*guest*) acoger; (*wound*) sufrir; **"~ed with thanks"** (COMM) "recibí".

Received Pronunciation [rɪ'si:vd-] *n see* **RP**.

receiver [rɪ'si:və*] *n* (TEL) auricular *m*; (RADIO) receptor *m*; (*of stolen goods*) perista *m/f*; (LAW) administrador *m* jurídico.

receivership [rɪ'si:vəʃɪp] *n*: **to go into ~** entrar en liquidación.

recent ['ri:snt] *adj* reciente; **in ~ years** en los últimos años.

recently ['ri:sntlɪ] *adv* recientemente, recién (LAM); **~ arrived** recién llegado; **until ~** hasta hace poco.

receptacle [rɪ'sɛptɪkl] *n* receptáculo.
reception [rɪ'sɛpʃən] *n* (*in building, office etc*) recepción *f*; (*welcome*) acogida.
reception centre *n* (*BRIT*) centro de recepción.
reception desk *n* recepción *f*.
receptionist [rɪ'sɛpʃənɪst] *n* recepcionista *m/f*.
receptive [rɪ'sɛptɪv] *adj* receptivo.
recess [rɪ'sɛs] *n* (*in room*) hueco; (*for bed*) nicho; (*secret place*) escondrijo; (*POL etc*: *holiday*) período vacacional; (*US LAW*: *short break*) descanso; (*SCOL: esp US*) recreo.
recession [rɪ'sɛʃən] *n* recesión *f*, depresión *f*.
recharge [riː'tʃɑːdʒ] *vt* (*battery*) recargar.
rechargeable [riː'tʃɑːdʒəbl] *adj* recargable.
recipe ['rɛsɪpɪ] *n* receta.
recipient [rɪ'sɪpɪənt] *n* recibidor(a) *m/f*; (*of letter*) destinatario/a.
reciprocal [rɪ'sɪprəkl] *adj* recíproco.
reciprocate [rɪ'sɪprəkeɪt] *vt* devolver, corresponder a ♦ *vi* corresponder.
recital [rɪ'saɪtl] *n* (*MUS*) recital *m*.
recitation [rɛsɪ'teɪʃən] *n* (*of poetry*) recitado; (*of complaints etc*) enumeración *f*, relación *f*.
recite [rɪ'saɪt] *vt* (*poem*) recitar; (*complaints etc*) enumerar.
reckless ['rɛkləs] *adj* temerario, imprudente; (*speed*) peligroso.
recklessly ['rɛkləslɪ] *adv* imprudentemente; de modo peligroso.
recklessness ['rɛkləsnɪs] *n* temeridad *f*, imprudencia.
reckon ['rɛkən] *vt* (*count*) contar; (*consider*) considerar ♦ *vi*: **to ~ without sb/sth** dejar de contar con algn/algo; **he is somebody to be ~ed with** no se le puede descartar; **I ~ that ...** me parece que ..., creo que ....
▶**reckon on** *vt fus* contar con.
reckoning ['rɛkənɪŋ] *n* (*calculation*) cálculo.
reclaim [rɪ'kleɪm] *vt* (*land*) recuperar; (: *from sea*) rescatar; (*demand back*) reclamar.
reclamation [rɛklə'meɪʃən] *n* recuperación *f*; rescate *m*.
recline [rɪ'klaɪn] *vi* reclinarse.
reclining [rɪ'klaɪnɪŋ] *adj* (*seat*) reclinable.
recluse [rɪ'kluːs] *n* recluso/a.
recognition [rɛkəg'nɪʃən] *n* reconocimiento; **transformed beyond ~** irreconocible; **in ~ of** en reconocimiento de.
recognizable ['rɛkəgnaɪzəbl] *adj*: **~ (by)** reconocible (por).
recognize ['rɛkəgnaɪz] *vt* reconocer,

conocer; **to ~ (by/as)** reconocer (por/como).
recoil [rɪ'kɔɪl] *vi* (*person*): **to ~ from doing sth** retraerse de hacer algo ♦ *n* (*of gun*) retroceso.
recollect [rɛkə'lɛkt] *vt* recordar, acordarse de.
recollection [rɛkə'lɛkʃən] *n* recuerdo; **to the best of my ~** que yo recuerde.
recommend [rɛkə'mɛnd] *vt* recomendar; **she has a lot to ~ her** tiene mucho a su favor.
recommendation [rɛkəmɛn'deɪʃən] *n* recomendación *f*.
recommended retail price (RRP) *n* (*BRIT*) precio (recomendado) de venta al público.
recompense ['rɛkəmpɛns] *vt* recompensar ♦ *n* recompensa.
reconcilable ['rɛkənsaɪləbl] *adj* (re)conciliable.
reconcile ['rɛkənsaɪl] *vt* (*two people*) reconciliar; (*two facts*) conciliar; **to ~ o.s. to sth** resignarse *or* conformarse a algo.
reconciliation [rɛkənsɪlɪ'eɪʃən] *n* reconciliación *f*.
recondite [rɪ'kɔndaɪt] *adj* recóndito.
recondition [riːkən'dɪʃən] *vt* (*machine*) reparar, reponer.
reconditioned [riːkən'dɪʃənd] *adj* renovado, reparado.
reconnaissance [rɪ'kɔnɪsns] *n* (*MIL*) reconocimiento.
reconnoitre, (US**) reconnoiter** [rɛkə'nɔɪtə*] *vt, vi* (*MIL*) reconocer.
reconsider [riːkən'sɪdə*] *vt* repensar.
reconstitute [riː'kɔnstɪtjuːt] *vt* reconstituir.
reconstruct [riːkən'strʌkt] *vt* reconstruir.
reconstruction [riːkən'strʌkʃən] *n* reconstrucción *f*.
reconvene [riːkən'viːn] *vt* volver a convocar ♦ *vi* volver a reunirse.
record *n* ['rɛkɔːd] (*MUS*) disco; (*of meeting etc*) relación *f*; (*register*) registro, partida; (*file*) archivo; (*also*: **police** *or* **criminal ~**) antecedentes *mpl* penales; (*written*) expediente *m*; (*SPORT*) récord *m*; (*COMPUT*) registro ♦ *vt* [rɪ'kɔːd] (*set down, also COMPUT*) registrar; (*relate*) hacer constar; (*MUS: song etc*) grabar; **in ~ time** en un tiempo récord; **public ~s** archivos *mpl* nacionales; **he is on ~ as saying that ...** hay pruebas de que ha dicho públicamente que ...; **Spain's excellent ~** el excelente historial de España; **off the ~** *adj* no oficial ♦ *adv* confidencialmente.
record card *n* (*in file*) ficha.

recorded delivery letter [rɪˈkɔːdɪd-] n (*BRIT POST*) carta de entrega con acuse de recibo.

recorded music n música grabada.

recorder [rɪˈkɔːdə*] n (*MUS*) flauta de pico; (*TECH*) contador m.

record holder n (*SPORT*) actual poseedor(a) m/f del récord.

recording [rɪˈkɔːdɪŋ] n (*MUS*) grabación f.

recording studio n estudio de grabación.

record library n discoteca.

record player n tocadiscos m inv.

recount vt [rɪˈkaunt] contar.

re-count [ˈriːkaunt] n (*POL: of votes*) segundo escrutinio, recuento ♦ vt [riːˈkaunt] volver a contar.

recoup [rɪˈkuːp] vt: to ~ one's losses recuperar las pérdidas.

recourse [rɪˈkɔːs] n recurso; to have ~ to recurrir a.

recover [rɪˈkʌvə*] vt recuperar; (*rescue*) rescatar ♦ vi recuperarse.

recovery [rɪˈkʌvərɪ] n recuperación f; rescate m; (*MED*): to make a ~ restablecerse.

recreate [riːkrɪˈeɪt] vt recrear.

recreation [rɛkrɪˈeɪʃən] n recreación f; (*amusement*) recreo.

recreational [rɛkrɪˈeɪʃənl] adj de recreo.

recreational drug n droga recreativa.

recreational vehicle n (*US*) caravana or roulotte f pequeña.

recrimination [rɪkrɪmɪˈneɪʃən] n recriminación f.

recruit [rɪˈkruːt] n recluta m/f ♦ vt reclutar; (*staff*) contratar.

recruiting office [rɪˈkruːtɪŋ-] n caja de reclutas.

recruitment [rɪˈkruːtmənt] n reclutamiento.

rectangle [ˈrɛktæŋgl] n rectángulo.

rectangular [rɛkˈtæŋgjulə*] adj rectangular.

rectify [ˈrɛktɪfaɪ] vt rectificar.

rector [ˈrɛktə*] n (*REL*) párroco; (*SCOL*) rector(a) m/f.

rectory [ˈrɛktərɪ] n casa del párroco.

rectum [ˈrɛktəm] n (*ANAT*) recto.

recuperate [rɪˈkuːpəreɪt] vi reponerse, restablecerse.

recur [rɪˈkəː*] vi repetirse; (*pain, illness*) producirse de nuevo.

recurrence [rɪˈkəːrns] n repetición f.

recurrent [rɪˈkəːrnt] adj repetido.

recycle [riːˈsaɪkl] vt reciclar.

red [rɛd] n rojo ♦ adj rojo; to be in the ~ (*account*) estar en números rojos;

(*business*) tener un saldo negativo; to give sb the ~ carpet treatment recibir a algn con todos los honores.

El término **redbrick university** se aplica a las universidades construidas en los grandes centros urbanos industriales como Birmingham, Liverpool o Manchester a finales del siglo XIX o principios del XX. Deben su nombre a que sus edificios son normalmente de ladrillo, a diferencia de las universidades tradicionales de Oxford y Cambridge, cuyos edificios suelen ser de piedra.

red alert n alerta roja.

red-blooded [ˈrɛdˈblʌdɪd] adj (*col*) viril.

Red Cross n Cruz f Roja.

redcurrant [ˈrɛdkʌrənt] n grosella.

redden [ˈrɛdn] vt enrojecer ♦ vi enrojecerse.

reddish [ˈrɛdɪʃ] adj (*hair*) rojizo.

redecorate [riːˈdɛkəreɪt] pintar de nuevo; volver a decorar.

redecoration [riːdɛkəˈreɪʃən] n renovación f.

redeem [rɪˈdiːm] vt (*sth in pawn*) desempeñar; (*fig, also REL*) rescatar.

redeemable [rɪˈdiːməbl] adj canjeable.

redeeming [rɪˈdiːmɪŋ] adj: ~ feature punto bueno or favorable.

redefine [riːdɪˈfaɪn] vt redefinir.

redemption [rɪˈdɛmpʃən] n (*REL*) redención f; to be past or beyond ~ no tener remedio.

redeploy [riːdɪˈplɔɪ] vt (*resources*) disponer de nuevo.

redeployment [riːdɪˈplɔɪmənt] n redistribución f.

redevelop [riːdɪˈvɛləp] vt reorganizar.

redevelopment [riːdɪˈvɛləpmənt] n reorganización f.

red-handed [rɛdˈhændɪd] adj: he was caught ~ le pillaron con las manos en la masa.

redhead [ˈrɛdhɛd] n pelirrojo/a.

red herring n (*fig*) pista falsa.

red-hot [rɛdˈhɔt] adj candente.

redirect [riːdaɪˈrɛkt] vt (*mail*) reexpedir.

rediscover [riːdɪsˈkʌvə*] vt redescubrir.

rediscovery [riːdɪsˈkʌvərɪ] n redescubrimiento.

redistribute [riːdɪsˈtrɪbjuːt] vt redistribuir, hacer una nueva distribución de.

red-letter day [rɛdˈlɛtə-] n día m señalado, día m especial.

red light n: to go through or jump a ~ (*AUT*) saltarse un semáforo.

red-light district n barrio chino, zona de

tolerancia.
red meat *n* carne *f* roja.
redness ['rɛdnɪs] *n* rojez *f*.
redo [riː'duː] *vt* (*irreg: like* **do**) rehacer.
redolent ['rɛdələnt] *adj*: ~ **of** (*smell*) con
fragancia a; **to be** ~ **of** (*fig*) evocar.
redouble [riː'dʌbl] *vt*: **to** ~ **one's efforts**
redoblar los esfuerzos.
redraft [riː'drɑːft] *vt* volver a redactar.
redress [rɪ'drɛs] *n* reparación *f* ♦ *vt* reparar,
corregir; **to** ~ **the balance** restablecer el
equilibrio.
Red Sea *n*: **the** ~ el mar Rojo.
redskin ['rɛdskɪn] *n* piel roja *m/f*.
red tape *n* (*fig*) trámites *mpl*, papeleo (*col*).
reduce [rɪ'djuːs] *vt* reducir; (*lower*) rebajar;
to ~ **sth by/to** reducir algo en/a; **to** ~ **sb**
to silence/despair/tears hacer callar/
desesperarse/llorar a algn; "~ **speed**
now" (*AUT*) "reduzca la velocidad".
reduced [rɪ'djuːst] *adj* (*decreased*) reducido,
rebajado; **at a** ~ **price** con rebaja *or*
descuento; "**greatly** ~ **prices**" "grandes
rebajas".
reduction [rɪ'dʌkʃən] *n* reducción *f*; (*of*
price) rebaja; (*discount*) descuento.
redundancy [rɪ'dʌndənsɪ] *n* despido;
(*unemployment*) desempleo; **voluntary** ~
baja voluntaria.
redundancy payment *n* indemnización *f*
por desempleo.
redundant [rɪ'dʌndənt] *adj* (*BRIT: worker*)
parado, sin trabajo; (*detail, object*)
superfluo; **to be made** ~ quedar(se) sin
trabajo, perder el empleo.
reed [riːd] *n* (*BOT*) junco, caña; (*MUS: of*
clarinet etc) lengüeta.
re-educate [riː'ɛdjukeɪt] *vt* reeducar.
reedy ['riːdɪ] *adj* (*voice, instrument*)
aflautado.
reef [riːf] *n* (*at sea*) arrecife *m*.
reek [riːk] *vi*: **to** ~ (**of**) oler *or* apestar (a).
reel [riːl] *n* carrete *m*, bobina; (*of film*) rollo
♦ *vt* (*TECH*) devanar; (*also*: ~ **in**) sacar ♦ *vi*
(*sway*) tambalear(se); **my head is** ~**ing**
me da vueltas la cabeza.
▶**reel off** *vt* recitar de memoria.
re-election [riː'ɪlɛkʃən] *n* reelección *f*.
re-engage [riːɪn'geɪdʒ] *vt* contratar de
nuevo.
re-enter [riː'ɛntə*] *vt* reingresar en, volver
a entrar en.
re-entry [riː'ɛntrɪ] *n* reingreso, reentrada.
re-examine [riːɪg'zæmɪn] *vt* reexaminar.
re-export *vt* ['riːɪks'pɔːt] reexportar ♦ *n*
[riː'ɛkspɔːt] reexportación *f*.
ref [rɛf] *n abbr* (*col*) = **referee**.
ref. *abbr* (*COMM*: = *with reference to*) Ref.

refectory [rɪ'fɛktərɪ] *n* comedor *m*.
refer [rɪ'fɜː*] *vt* (*send*) remitir; (*ascribe*)
referir a, relacionar con ♦ *vi*: **to** ~ **to**
(*allude to*) referirse a, aludir a; (*apply to*)
relacionarse con; (*consult*) remitirse a; **he**
~**red me to the manager** me envió al
gerente.
referee [rɛfə'riː] *n* árbitro; (*BRIT: for job*
application) persona que da referencias
de otro ♦ *vt* (*match*) arbitrar en.
reference ['rɛfrəns] *n* (*mention, in book*)
referencia; (*sending*) remisión *f*;
(*relevance*) relación *f*; (*for job application:*
letter) carta de recomendación; **with** ~ **to**
con referencia a; (*COMM: in letter*) me
remito a.
reference book *n* libro de consulta.
reference library *n* biblioteca de consulta.
reference number *n* número de
referencia.
referendum, *pl* **referenda** [rɛfə'rɛndəm,
-də] *n* referéndum *m*.
referral [rɪ'fɜːrəl] *n* remisión *f*.
refill *vt* [riː'fɪl] rellenar ♦ *n* ['riːfɪl] repuesto,
recambio.
refine [rɪ'faɪn] *vt* (*sugar, oil*) refinar.
refined [rɪ'faɪnd] *adj* (*person, taste*) refinado,
culto.
refinement [rɪ'faɪnmənt] *n* (*of person*)
cultura, educación *f*.
refinery [rɪ'faɪnərɪ] *n* refinería.
refit (*NAUT*) *n* ['riːfɪt] reparación *f* ♦ *vt*
[riː'fɪt] reparar.
reflate [riː'fleɪt] *vt* (*economy*) reflacionar.
reflation [riː'fleɪʃən] *n* reflación *f*.
reflationary [riː'fleɪʃənrɪ] *adj* reflacionario.
reflect [rɪ'flɛkt] *vt* (*light, image*) reflejar ♦ *vi*
(*think*) reflexionar, pensar; **it** ~**s badly/**
well on him le perjudica/le hace honor.
reflection [rɪ'flɛkʃən] *n* (*act*) reflexión *f*;
(*image*) reflejo; (*discredit*) crítica; **on** ~
pensándolo bien.
reflector [rɪ'flɛktə*] *n* (*AUT*) catafaros *m inv*;
(*telescope*) reflector *m*.
reflex ['riːflɛks] *adj, n* reflejo.
reflexive [rɪ'flɛksɪv] *adj* (*LING*) reflexivo.
reform [rɪ'fɔːm] *n* reforma ♦ *vt* reformar.
reformat [riː'fɔːmæt] *vt* (*COMPUT*)
recomponer.
Reformation [rɛfə'meɪʃən] *n*: **the** ~ la
Reforma.
reformatory [rɪ'fɔːmətərɪ] *n* (*US*)
reformatorio.
reformer [rɪ'fɔːmə*] *n* reformador(a) *m/f*.
refrain [rɪ'freɪn] *vi*: **to** ~ **from doing**
abstenerse de hacer ♦ *n* (*MUS etc*)
estribillo.
refresh [rɪ'frɛʃ] *vt* refrescar.

refresher course [rɪ'frɛʃə-] n (BRIT) curso de repaso.

refreshing [rɪ'frɛʃɪŋ] adj (drink) refrescante; (sleep) reparador; (change etc) estimulante; (idea, point of view) estimulante, interesante.

refreshments [rɪ'frɛʃmənts] npl (drinks) refrescos mpl.

refrigeration [rɪfrɪdʒə'reɪʃən] n refrigeración f.

refrigerator [rɪ'frɪdʒəreɪtə*] n frigorífico, refrigeradora (LAM), heladera (LAM).

refuel [riː'fjuəl] vi repostar (combustible).

refuelling, (US) **refueling** [riː'fjuəlɪŋ] n reabastecimiento de combustible.

refuge ['rɛfjuːdʒ] n refugio, asilo; **to take ~ in** refugiarse en.

refugee [rɛfju'dʒiː] n refugiado/a.

refugee camp n campamento para refugiados.

refund n ['riːfʌnd] reembolso ♦ vt [rɪ'fʌnd] devolver, reembolsar.

refurbish [riː'fəːbɪʃ] vt restaurar, renovar.

refurnish [riː'fəːnɪʃ] vt amueblar de nuevo.

refusal [rɪ'fjuːzəl] n negativa; **first ~** primera opción; **to have first ~ on sth** tener la primera opción a algo.

refuse n ['rɛfjuːs] basura ♦ (vb: [rɪ'fjuːz]) vt (reject) rehusar; (say no to) negarse a ♦ vi negarse; (horse) rehusar; **to ~ to do sth** negarse a or rehusar hacer algo.

refuse bin n cubo or bote m (LAM) or balde m (LAM) de la basura.

refuse collection n recogida de basuras.

refuse disposal n eliminación f de basuras.

refusenik [rɪ'fjuːznɪk] n judío/a que tenía prohibido emigrar de la ex-URSS.

refuse tip n vertedero.

refute [rɪ'fjuːt] vt refutar, rebatir.

regain [rɪ'geɪn] vt recobrar, recuperar.

regal ['riːgl] adj regio, real.

regale [rɪ'geɪl] vt agasajar, entretener.

regalia [rɪ'geɪlɪə] n galas fpl.

regard [rɪ'gɑːd] n (gaze) mirada; (aspect) respecto; (esteem) respeto, consideración f ♦ vt (consider) considerar; (look at) mirar; **to give one's ~s to** saludar de su parte a; **"(kind) ~s"** "muy atentamente"; **"with kindest ~s"** "con muchos recuerdos"; **~s to María, please give my ~s to María** recuerdos a María, dele recuerdos a María de mi parte; **as ~s, with ~ to** con respecto a, en cuanto a.

regarding [rɪ'gɑːdɪŋ] prep con respecto a, en cuanto a.

regardless [rɪ'gɑːdlɪs] adv a pesar de todo; **~ of** sin reparar en.

regatta [rɪ'gætə] n regata.

regency ['riːdʒənsɪ] n regencia.

regenerate [rɪ'dʒɛnəreɪt] vt regenerar.

regent ['riːdʒənt] n regente m/f.

reggae ['rɛgeɪ] n reggae m.

régime [reɪ'ʒiːm] n régimen m.

regiment n ['rɛdʒɪmənt] regimiento ♦ vt ['rɛdʒɪment] reglamentar.

regimental [rɛdʒɪ'mɛntl] adj militar.

regimentation [rɛdʒɪmɛn'teɪʃən] n regimentación f.

region ['riːdʒən] n región f; **in the ~ of** (fig) alrededor de.

regional ['riːdʒənl] adj regional.

regional development n desarrollo regional.

register ['rɛdʒɪstə*] n registro ♦ vt registrar; (birth) declarar; (letter) certificar; (subj: instrument) marcar, indicar ♦ vi (at hotel) registrarse; (sign on) inscribirse; (make impression) producir impresión; **to ~ a protest** presentar una queja; **to ~ for a course** matricularse or inscribirse en un curso.

registered ['rɛdʒɪstəd] adj (design) registrado; (BRIT: letter) certificado; (student) matriculado; (voter) registrado.

registered company n sociedad f legalmente constituida.

registered nurse n (US) enfermero/a titulado/a.

registered office n domicilio social.

registered trademark n marca registrada.

registrar ['rɛdʒɪstrɑː*] n secretario/a (del registro civil).

registration [rɛdʒɪs'treɪʃən] n (act) declaración f; (AUT: also: ~ number) matrícula.

registry ['rɛdʒɪstrɪ] n registro.

registry office n (BRIT) registro civil; **to get married in a ~** casarse por lo civil.

regret [rɪ'grɛt] n sentimiento, pesar m; (remorse) remordimiento ♦ vt sentir, lamentar; (repent of) arrepentirse de; **we ~ to inform you that ...** sentimos informarle que ....

regretful [rɪ'grɛtful] adj pesaroso, arrepentido.

regretfully [rɪ'grɛtfəlɪ] adv con pesar, sentidamente.

regrettable [rɪ'grɛtəbl] adj lamentable; (loss) sensible.

regrettably [rɪ'grɛtəblɪ] adv desgraciadamente.

regroup [riː'gruːp] vt reagrupar ♦ vi reagruparse.

regt abbr = **regiment**.

regular ['rɛgjulə*] *adj* regular; (*soldier*) profesional; (*col: intensive*) verdadero; (*listener, reader*) asiduo, habitual ♦ *n* (*client etc*) cliente/a *m/f* habitual.

regularity [rɛgju'lærɪtɪ] *n* regularidad *f*.

regularly ['rɛgjulǝlɪ] *adv* con regularidad.

regulate ['rɛgjuleɪt] *vt* (*gen*) controlar; (*TECH*) regular, ajustar.

regulation [rɛgju'leɪʃǝn] *n* (*rule*) regla, reglamento; (*adjustment*) regulación *f*.

rehabilitate [ri:ǝ'bɪlɪteɪt] *vt* rehabilitar.

rehabilitation ['ri:ǝbɪlɪ'teɪʃǝn] *n* rehabilitación *f*.

rehash [ri:'hæʃ] *vt* (*col*) hacer un refrito de.

rehearsal [rɪ'hǝːsǝl] *n* ensayo; **dress ~** ensayo general *or* final.

rehearse [rɪ'hǝːs] *vt* ensayar.

rehouse [ri:'hauz] *vt* dar nueva vivienda a.

reign [reɪn] *n* reinado; (*fig*) predominio ♦ *vi* reinar; (*fig*) imperar.

reigning ['reɪnɪŋ] *adj* (*monarch*) reinante, actual; (*predominant*) imperante.

reimburse [ri:ɪm'bǝːs] *vt* reembolsar.

rein [reɪn] *n* (*for horse*) rienda; **to give sb free ~** dar rienda suelta a algn.

reincarnation [ri:ɪnkɑː'neɪʃǝn] *n* reencarnación *f*.

reindeer ['reɪndɪǝ*] *n* (*pl inv*) reno.

reinforce [ri:ɪn'fɔːs] *vt* reforzar.

reinforced concrete [ri:ɪn'fɔːst-] *n* hormigón armado.

reinforcement [ri:ɪn'fɔːsmǝnt] *n* (*action*) refuerzo; **~s** *npl* (*MIL*) refuerzos *mpl*.

reinstate [ri:ɪn'steɪt] *vt* (*worker*) reintegrar (a su puesto).

reinstatement [ri:ɪn'steɪtmǝnt] *n* reintegración *f*.

reissue [ri:'ɪʃuː] *vt* (*record, book*) reeditar.

reiterate [ri:'ɪtǝreɪt] *vt* reiterar, repetir.

reject *n* ['ri:dʒɛkt] (*thing*) desecho ♦ *vt* [rɪ'dʒɛkt] rechazar; (*proposition, offer etc*) descartar.

rejection [rɪ'dʒɛkʃǝn] *n* rechazo.

rejoice [rɪ'dʒɔɪs] *vi*: **to ~ at** *or* **over** regocijarse *or* alegrarse de.

rejoinder [rɪ'dʒɔɪndǝ*] *n* (*retort*) réplica.

rejuvenate [rɪ'dʒuːvǝneɪt] *vt* rejuvenecer.

rekindle [ri:'kɪndl] *vt* volver a encender; (*fig*) despertar.

relapse [rɪ'læps] *n* (*MED*) recaída; (*into crime*) reincidencia.

relate [rɪ'leɪt] *vt* (*tell*) contar, relatar; (*connect*) relacionar ♦ *vi* relacionarse; **to ~ to** (*connect*) relacionarse *or* tener que ver con.

related [rɪ'leɪtɪd] *adj* afín; (*person*) emparentado; **~ to** con referencia a, relacionado con.

relating [rɪ'leɪtɪŋ]: **~ to** *prep* referente a.

relation [rɪ'leɪʃǝn] *n* (*person*) pariente *m/f*; (*link*) relación *f*; **in ~ to** en relación con, en lo que se refiere a; **to bear a ~ to** guardar relación con; **diplomatic/ international ~s** relaciones *fpl* diplomáticas/internacionales.

relationship [rɪ'leɪʃǝnʃɪp] *n* relación *f*; (*personal*) relaciones *fpl*; (*also:* **family ~**) parentesco.

relative ['rɛlǝtɪv] *n* pariente *m/f*, familiar *m/f* ♦ *adj* relativo.

relatively ['rɛlǝtɪvlɪ] *adv* (*fairly, rather*) relativamente.

relative pronoun *n* pronombre *m* relativo.

relax [rɪ'læks] *vi* descansar; (*quieten down*) relajarse ♦ *vt* relajar; (*grip*) aflojar; **~!** (*calm down*) ¡tranquilo!

relaxation [ri:læk'seɪʃǝn] *n* (*rest*) descanso; (*easing*) relajación *f*, relajamiento *m*; (*amusement*) recreo; (*entertainment*) diversión *f*.

relaxed [rɪ'lækst] *adj* relajado; (*tranquil*) tranquilo.

relaxing [rɪ'læksɪŋ] *adj* relajante.

relay *n* ['ri:leɪ] (*race*) carrera de relevos ♦ *vt* [rɪ'leɪ] (*RADIO, TV, pass on*) retransmitir.

release [rɪ'li:s] *n* (*liberation*) liberación *f*; (*discharge*) puesta en libertad *f*; (*of gas etc*) escape *m*; (*of film etc*) estreno ♦ *vt* (*prisoner*) poner en libertad; (*film*) estrenar; (*book*) publicar; (*piece of news*) difundir; (*gas etc*) despedir, arrojar; (*free: from wreckage etc*) liberar; (*TECH: catch, spring etc*) desenganchar; (*let go*) soltar, aflojar.

relegate ['rɛlǝgeɪt] *vt* relegar; (*SPORT*): **to be ~d to** bajar a.

relent [rɪ'lɛnt] *vi* ceder, ablandarse; (*let up*) descansar.

relentless [rɪ'lɛntlɪs] *adj* implacable.

relentlessly [rɪ'lɛntlɪslɪ] *adv* implacablemente.

relevance ['rɛlǝvǝns] *n* relación *f*.

relevant ['rɛlǝvǝnt] *adj* (*fact*) pertinente; **~ to** relacionado con.

reliability [rɪlaɪǝ'bɪlɪtɪ] *n* fiabilidad *f*; seguridad *f*; veracidad *f*.

reliable [rɪ'laɪǝbl] *adj* (*person, firm*) de confianza, de fiar; (*method, machine*) seguro; (*source*) fidedigno.

reliably [rɪ'laɪǝblɪ] *adv*: **to be ~ informed that ...** saber de fuente fidedigna que ....

reliance [rɪ'laɪǝns] *n*: **~ (on)** dependencia (de).

reliant [rɪ'laɪǝnt] *adj*: **to be ~ on sth/sb**

depender de algo/algn.
relic ['rɛlɪk] *n* (*REL*) reliquia; (*of the past*)
vestigio.
relief [rɪ'liːf] *n* (*from pain, anxiety*) alivio,
desahogo; (*help, supplies*) socorro, ayuda;
(*ART, GEO*) relieve *m*; **by way of light** ~ a
modo de diversión.
relief road *n* carretera de
descongestionamiento.
relieve [rɪ'liːv] *vt* (*pain, patient*) aliviar;
(*bring help to*) ayudar, socorrer; (*burden*)
aligerar; (*take over from: gen*) sustituir a;
(*: guard*) relevar; **to** ~ **sb of sth** quitar
algo a algn; **to** ~ **sb of his command** (*MIL*)
relevar a algn de su mando; **to** ~ **o.s.**
hacer sus necesidades; **I am** ~**d to hear
you are better** me alivia saber que estás
or te encuentras mejor.
religion [rɪ'lɪdʒən] *n* religión *f*.
religious [rɪ'lɪdʒəs] *adj* religioso.
religious education *n* educación *f*
religiosa.
religiously [rɪ'lɪdʒəslɪ] *adv* religiosamente.
relinquish [rɪ'lɪŋkwɪʃ] *vt* abandonar; (*plan,
habit*) renunciar a.
relish ['rɛlɪʃ] *n* (*CULIN*) salsa; (*enjoyment*)
entusiasmo; (*flavour*) sabor *m*, gusto ♦ *vt*
(*food, challenge etc*) saborear; **to** ~ **doing**
gozar haciendo.
relive [riː'lɪv] *vt* vivir de nuevo, volver a
vivir.
relocate [riːləʊ'keɪt] *vt* trasladar ♦ *vi*
trasladarse.
reluctance [rɪ'lʌktəns] *n* desgana,
renuencia.
reluctant [rɪ'lʌktənt] *adj* reacio; **to be** ~ **to
do sth** resistirse a hacer algo.
reluctantly [rɪ'lʌktəntlɪ] *adv* de mala
gana.
rely [rɪ'laɪ]: **to** ~ **on** *vt fus* confiar en, fiarse
de; (*be dependent on*) depender de; **you
can** ~ **on my discretion** puedes contar
con mi discreción.
remain [rɪ'meɪn] *vi* (*survive*) quedar; (*be left*)
sobrar; (*continue*) quedar(se),
permanecer; **to** ~ **silent** permanecer
callado; **I** ~, **yours faithfully** (*in letters*) le
saluda atentamente.
remainder [rɪ'meɪndə*] *n* resto.
remaining [rɪ'meɪnɪŋ] *adj* sobrante.
remains [rɪ'meɪnz] *npl* restos *mpl*.
remand [rɪ'mɑːnd] *n*: **on** ~ detenido (bajo
custodia) ♦ *vt*: **to** ~ **in custody** mantener
bajo custodia.
remand home *n* (*BRIT*) reformatorio.
remark [rɪ'mɑːk] *n* comentario ♦ *vt*
comentar; **to** ~ **on sth** hacer
observaciones sobre algo.

remarkable [rɪ'mɑːkəbl] *adj* notable;
(*outstanding*) extraordinario.
remarkably [rɪ'mɑːkəblɪ] *adv*
extraordinariamente.
remarry [riː'mærɪ] *vi* casarse por segunda
vez, volver a casarse.
remedial [rɪ'miːdɪəl] *adj*: ~ **education**
educación *f* de los niños atrasados.
remedy ['rɛmədɪ] *n* remedio ♦ *vt* remediar,
curar.
remember [rɪ'mɛmbə*] *vt* recordar,
acordarse de; (*bear in mind*) tener
presente; **I** ~ **seeing it, I** ~ **having seen it**
recuerdo haberlo visto; **she** ~**ed doing it**
se acordó de hacerlo; ~ **me to your wife
and children!** ¡déle recuerdos a su
familia!
remembrance [rɪ'mɛmbrəns] *n* (*memory,
souvenir*) recuerdo; **in** ~ **of** en
conmemoración de.

En el Reino Unido el domingo más cercano
al 11 de noviembre es **Remembrance Sunday**
o **Remembrance Day**, aniversario de la firma
del armisticio de 1918 que puso fin a la
Primera Guerra Mundial. Tal día se
recuerda a todos aquellos que murieron en
las dos guerras mundiales con dos minutos
de silencio a las once de la mañana hora en
que se firmó el armisticio durante los actos
de conmemoración celebrados en los
monumentos a los caídos. Allí se colocan
coronas de amapolas, flor que también se
suele llevar prendida en el pecho tras pagar
un donativo para los inválidos de guerra.

remind [rɪ'maɪnd] *vt*: **to** ~ **sb to do sth**
recordar a algn que haga algo; **to** ~ **sb of
sth** recordar algo a algn; **she** ~**s me of
her mother** me recuerda a su madre; **that**
~**s me!** ¡a propósito!
reminder [rɪ'maɪndə*] *n* notificación *f*;
(*memento*) recuerdo.
reminisce [rɛmɪ'nɪs] *vi* recordar (viejas
historias).
reminiscences [rɛmɪ'nɪsnsɪz] *npl*
reminiscencias *fpl*, recuerdos *mpl*.
reminiscent [rɛmɪ'nɪsnt] *adj*: **to be** ~ **of sth**
recordar algo.
remiss [rɪ'mɪs] *adj* descuidado; **it was** ~ **of
me** fue un descuido de mi parte.
remission [rɪ'mɪʃən] *n* remisión *f*; (*of
sentence*) reducción *f* de la pena.
remit [rɪ'mɪt] *vt* (*send: money*) remitir,
enviar.
remittance [rɪ'mɪtns] *n* remesa, envío.
remnant ['rɛmnənt] *n* resto; (*of cloth*) retal
m, retazo; ~**s** *npl* (*COMM*) restos de serie.

remonstrate ['rɛmənstreɪt] *vi* protestar.
remorse [rɪ'mɔːs] *n* remordimientos *mpl*.
remorseful [rɪ'mɔːsful] *adj* arrepentido.
remorseless [rɪ'mɔːslɪs] *adj* (*fig*)
  implacable, inexorable.
remorselessly [rɪ'mɔːslɪslɪ] *adv*
  implacablemente, inexorablemente.
remote [rɪ'məʊt] *adj* remoto; (*distant*)
  lejano; (*person*) distante; **there is a ~**
  possibility that ... hay una posibilidad
  remota de que ....
remote control *n* mando a distancia.
remote-controlled [rɪ'məʊtkən'trəʊld] *adj*
  teledirigido, con mando a distancia.
remotely [rɪ'məʊtlɪ] *adv* remotamente;
  (*slightly*) levemente.
remoteness [rɪ'məʊtnɪs] *n* alejamiento;
  distancia.
remould ['riːməʊld] *n* (*BRIT: tyre*) neumático
  or llanta (*LAM*) recauchutado/a.
removable [rɪ'muːvəbl] *adj* (*detachable*)
  separable.
removal [rɪ'muːvəl] *n* (*taking away*) (el)
  quitar; (*BRIT: from house*) mudanza; (*from*
  office: dismissal) destitución *f*; (*MED*)
  extirpación *f*.
removal van *n* (*BRIT*) camión *m* de
  mudanzas.
remove [rɪ'muːv] *vt* quitar; (*employee*)
  destituir; (*name: from list*) tachar, borrar;
  (*doubt*) disipar; (*TECH*) retirar, separar;
  (*MED*) extirpar; **first cousin once ~d**
  (*parent's cousin*) tío/a segundo/a; (*cousin's*
  child) sobrino/a segundo/a.
remover [rɪ'muːvə*] *n*: **make-up ~**
  desmaquilladora.
remunerate [rɪ'mjuːnəreɪt] *vt* remunerar.
remuneration [rɪmjuːnə'reɪʃən] *n*
  remuneración *f*.
Renaissance [rɪ'neɪsõns] *n*: **the ~** el
  Renacimiento.
rename [riː'neɪm] *vt* poner nuevo nombre
  a.
render ['rɛndə*] *vt* (*thanks*) dar; (*aid*)
  proporcionar; (*honour*) dar, conceder;
  (*assistance*) dar, prestar; **to ~ sth +** *adj*
  volver algo + *adj*.
rendering ['rɛndərɪŋ] *n* (*MUS etc*)
  interpretación *f*.
rendez-vous ['rɒndɪvuː] *n* cita ♦ *vi*
  reunirse, encontrarse; (*spaceship*)
  efectuar una reunión espacial.
rendition [rɛn'dɪʃən] *n* (*MUS*)
  interpretación *f*.
renegade ['rɛnɪgeɪd] *n* renegado/a.
renew [rɪ'njuː] *vt* renovar; (*resume*)
  reanudar; (*extend date*) prorrogar;
  (*negotiations*) volver a.

renewable [rɪ'njuːəbl] *adj* renovable; ~
  energy, ~**s** energías renovables.
renewal [rɪ'njuːəl] *n* renovación *f*;
  reanudación *f*; prórroga.
renounce [rɪ'naʊns] *vt* renunciar a; (*right*,
  inheritance) renunciar.
renovate ['rɛnəveɪt] *vt* renovar.
renovation [rɛnə'veɪʃən] *n* renovación *f*.
renown [rɪ'naʊn] *n* renombre *m*.
renowned [rɪ'naʊnd] *adj* renombrado.
rent [rɛnt] *n* alquiler *m*; (*for house*)
  arriendo, renta ♦ *vt* (*also:* ~ **out**) alquilar.
rental ['rɛntl] *n* (*for television, car*) alquiler
  m.
rent boy *n* (*BRIT col*) chapero.
renunciation [rɪnʌnsɪ'eɪʃən] *n* renuncia.
reopen [riː'əʊpən] *vt* volver a abrir,
  reabrir.
reorder [riː'ɔːdə*] *vt* volver a pedir, repetir
  el pedido de; (*rearrange*) volver a ordenar
  or arreglar.
reorganization [riːɔːgənaɪ'zeɪʃən] *n*
  reorganización *f*.
reorganize [riː'ɔːgənaɪz] *vt* reorganizar.
rep [rɛp] *n abbr* (*COMM*) = **representative**;
  (*THEAT*) = **repertory**.
Rep. *abbr* (*US POL*) = **representative,**
  republican.
repair [rɪ'pɛə*] *n* reparación *f*, arreglo;
  (*patch*) remiendo ♦ *vt* reparar, arreglar;
  in good/bad ~ en buen/mal estado; **under**
  ~ en obras.
repair kit *n* caja de herramientas.
repair man *n* mecánico.
repair shop *n* taller *m* de reparaciones.
repartee [rɛpɑː'tiː] *n* réplicas *fpl* agudas.
repast [rɪ'pɑːst] *n* (*formal*) comida.
repatriate [riː'pætrɪeɪt] *vt* repatriar.
repay [riː'peɪ] *vt* (*irreg: like pay*) (*money*)
  devolver, reembolsar; (*person*) pagar;
  (*debt*) liquidar; (*sb's efforts*) devolver,
  corresponder a.
repayment [riː'peɪmənt] *n* reembolso,
  devolución *f*; (*sum of money*) recompensa.
repeal [rɪ'piːl] *n* revocación *f* ♦ *vt* revocar.
repeat [rɪ'piːt] *n* (*RADIO, TV*) reposición *f* ♦ *vt*
  repetir ♦ *vi* repetirse.
repeatedly [rɪ'piːtɪdlɪ] *adv* repetidas veces.
repeat order *n* (*COMM*): **to place a ~ for**
  renovar un pedido de.
repel [rɪ'pɛl] *vt* repugnar.
repellent [rɪ'pɛlənt] *adj* repugnante ♦ *n*:
  insect ~ crema/loción *f* anti-insectos.
repent [rɪ'pɛnt] *vi*: **to ~ (of)** arrepentirse
  (de).
repentance [rɪ'pɛntəns] *n* arrepentimiento.
repercussion [riːpə'kʌʃən] *n* (*consequence*)
  repercusión *f*; **to have ~s** repercutir.

repertoire ['rɛpətwɑː*] n repertorio.
repertory ['rɛpətərɪ] n (also: ~ **theatre**) teatro de repertorio.
repertory company n compañía de repertorio.
repetition [rɛpɪ'tɪʃən] n repetición f.
repetitious [rɛpɪ'tɪʃəs] adj repetidor(a), que se repite.
repetitive [rɪ'pɛtɪtɪv] adj (movement, work) repetitivo, reiterativo; (speech) lleno de repeticiones.
rephrase [riː'freɪz] vt decir or formular de otro modo.
replace [rɪ'pleɪs] vt (put back) devolver a su sitio; (take the place of) reemplazar, sustituir.
replacement [rɪ'pleɪsmənt] n reemplazo; (act) reposición f; (thing) recambio; (person) suplente m/f.
replacement cost n costo de sustitución.
replacement part n repuesto.
replacement value n valor m de sustitución.
replay ['riːpleɪ] n (SPORT) partido de desempate; (TV: playback) repetición f.
replenish [rɪ'plɛnɪʃ] vt (tank etc) rellenar; (stock etc) reponer; (with fuel) repostar.
replete [rɪ'pliːt] adj repleto, lleno.
replica ['rɛplɪkə] n réplica, reproducción f.
reply [rɪ'plaɪ] n respuesta, contestación f ♦ vi contestar, responder; **in ~** en respuesta; **there's no ~** (TEL) no contestan.
reply coupon n cupón-respuesta m.
reply-paid [rɪ'plaɪ'peɪd] adj: ~ **postcard** tarjeta postal con respuesta pagada.
report [rɪ'pɔːt] n informe m; (PRESS etc) reportaje m; (BRIT: also: **school** ~) informe m escolar; (of gun) detonación f ♦ vt informar sobre; (PRESS etc) hacer un reportaje sobre; (notify: accident, culprit) denunciar ♦ vi (make a ~) presentar un informe; (present o.s.): **to ~ (to sb)** presentarse (ante algn); **annual ~** (COMM) informe m anual; **to ~ (on)** hacer un informe (sobre); **it is ~ed from Berlin that ...** se informa desde Berlín que ....
report card n (US, Scottish) cartilla escolar.
reportedly [rɪ'pɔːtɪdlɪ] adv según se dice, según se informa.
reporter [rɪ'pɔːtə*] n (PRESS) periodista m/f, reportero/a; (RADIO, TV) locutor(a) m/f.
repose [rɪ'pəʊz] n: **in ~** (face, mouth) en reposo.
repossess [riːpə'zɛs] vt recuperar.
repossession order [riːpə'zɛʃən-] n orden de devolución de la vivienda por el

impago de la hipoteca.
reprehensible [rɛprɪ'hɛnsɪbl] adj reprensible, censurable.
represent [rɛprɪ'zɛnt] vt representar; (COMM) ser agente de.
representation [rɛprɪzɛn'teɪʃən] n representación f; (petition) petición f; ~**s** npl (protest) quejas fpl.
representative [rɛprɪ'zɛntətɪv] n (US POL) representante m/f, diputado/a; (COMM) representante m/f ♦ adj: ~ **(of)** representativo (de).
repress [rɪ'prɛs] vt reprimir.
repression [rɪ'prɛʃən] n represión f.
repressive [rɪ'prɛsɪv] adj represivo.
reprieve [rɪ'priːv] n (LAW) indulto; (fig) alivio ♦ vt indultar; (fig) salvar.
reprimand ['rɛprɪmɑːnd] n reprimenda ♦ vt reprender.
reprint ['riːprɪnt] n reimpresión f ♦ vt [riː'prɪnt] reimprimir.
reprisal [rɪ'praɪzl] n represalia; **to take ~s** tomar represalias.
reproach [rɪ'prəʊtʃ] n reproche m ♦ vt: **to ~ sb with sth** reprochar algo a algn; **beyond ~** intachable.
reproachful [rɪ'prəʊtʃful] adj de reproche, de acusación.
reproduce [riːprə'djuːs] vt reproducir ♦ vi reproducirse.
reproduction [riːprə'dʌkʃən] n reproducción f.
reproductive [riːprə'dʌktɪv] adj reproductor(a).
reproof [rɪ'pruːf] n reproche m.
reprove [rɪ'pruːv] vt: **to ~ sb for sth** reprochar algo a algn.
reptile ['rɛptaɪl] n reptil m.
republic [rɪ'pʌblɪk] n república.
republican [rɪ'pʌblɪkən] adj, n republicano/a m/f.
repudiate [rɪ'pjuːdɪeɪt] vt (accusation) rechazar; (obligation) negarse a reconocer.
repudiation [rɪpjuːdɪ'eɪʃən] n incumplimiento.
repugnance [rɪ'pʌgnəns] n repugnancia.
repugnant [rɪ'pʌgnənt] adj repugnante.
repulse [rɪ'pʌls] vt rechazar.
repulsion [rɪ'pʌlʃən] n repulsión f, repugnancia.
repulsive [rɪ'pʌlsɪv] adj repulsivo.
repurchase [riː'pɔːtʃəs] vt volver a comprar, readquirir.
reputable ['rɛpjutəbl] adj (make etc) de renombre.
reputation [rɛpju'teɪʃən] n reputación f; **he has a ~ for being awkward** tiene fama de

difícil.

repute [rɪ'pjuːt] *n* reputación *f*, fama.

reputed [rɪ'pjuːtɪd] *adj* supuesto; **to be ~ to be rich/intelligent** *etc* tener fama de rico/inteligente *etc*.

reputedly [rɪ'pjuːtɪdlɪ] *adv* según dicen *or* se dice.

request [rɪ'kwest] *n* solicitud *f*, petición *f* ♦ *vt*: **to ~ sth of** *or* **from sb** solicitar algo a algn; **at the ~ of** a petición de; **"you are ~ed not to smoke"** "se ruega no fumar".

request stop *n* (*BRIT*) parada discrecional.

requiem ['rekwɪəm] *n* réquiem *m*.

require [rɪ'kwaɪə*] *vt* (*need*: *subj*: *person*) necesitar, tener necesidad de; (: *thing*, *situation*) exigir, requerir; (*want*) pedir; (*demand*) insistir en que; **to ~ sb to do sth/sth of sb** exigir que algn haga algo; **what qualifications are ~d?** ¿qué títulos se requieren?; **~d by law** requerido por la ley.

requirement [rɪ'kwaɪəmənt] *n* requisito; (*need*) necesidad *f*.

requisite ['rekwɪzɪt] *n* requisito ♦ *adj* necesario, requerido.

requisition [rekwɪ'zɪʃən] *n* solicitud *f*; (*MIL*) requisa ♦ *vt* (*MIL*) requisar.

reroute [riː'ruːt] *vt* desviar.

resale ['riːseɪl] *n* reventa.

resale price maintenance *n* mantenimiento del precio de venta.

rescind [rɪ'sɪnd] *vt* (*LAW*) abrogar; (*contract*) rescindir; (*order etc*) anular.

rescue ['reskjuː] *n* rescate *m* ♦ *vt* rescatar; **to come/go to sb's ~** ir en auxilio de uno, socorrer a algn; **to ~ from** librar de.

rescue party *n* equipo de salvamento.

rescuer ['reskjuə*] *n* salvador(a) *m/f*.

research [rɪ'səːtʃ] *n* investigaciones *fpl* ♦ *vt* investigar; **a piece of ~** un trabajo de investigación; **to ~ (into sth)** investigar (algo).

research and development (R & D) *n* investigación *f* y desarrollo.

researcher [rɪ'səːtʃə*] *n* investigador(a) *m/f*.

research work *n* investigación *f*.

resell [riː'sel] *vt* revender.

resemblance [rɪ'zembləns] *n* parecido; **to bear a strong ~ to** parecerse mucho a.

resemble [rɪ'zembl] *vt* parecerse a.

resent [rɪ'zent] *vt* resentirse por, ofenderse por; **he ~s my being here** le molesta que esté aquí.

resentful [rɪ'zentful] *adj* resentido.

resentment [rɪ'zentmənt] *n* resentimiento.

reservation [rezə'veɪʃən] *n* reserva; (*BRIT*: *also*: **central ~**) mediana; **with ~s** con reservas.

reservation desk *n* (*US*: *in hotel*) recepción *f*.

reserve [rɪ'zəːv] *n* reserva; (*SPORT*) suplente *m/f* ♦ *vt* (*seats etc*) reservar; **~s** *npl* (*MIL*) reserva *sg*; **in ~** en reserva.

reserve currency *n* divisa de reserva.

reserved [rɪ'zəːvd] *adj* reservado.

reserve price *n* (*BRIT*) precio mínimo.

reserve team *n* (*SPORT*) equipo de reserva.

reservist [rɪ'zəːvɪst] *n* (*MIL*) reservista *m*.

reservoir ['rezəvwaː*] *n* (*artificial lake*) embalse *m*, represa; (*small*) depósito.

reset [riː'set] *vt* (*COMPUT*) reinicializar.

reshape [riː'ʃeɪp] *vt* (*policy*) reformar, rehacer.

reshuffle [riː'ʃʌfl] *n*: **Cabinet ~** (*POL*) remodelación *f* del gabinete.

reside [rɪ'zaɪd] *vi* residir.

residence ['rezɪdəns] *n* residencia; (*formal*: *home*) domicilio; (*length of stay*) permanencia; **in ~** (*doctor*) residente; **to take up ~** instalarse.

residence permit *n* (*BRIT*) permiso de residencia.

resident ['rezɪdənt] *n* vecino/a; (*in hotel*) huésped/a *m/f* ♦ *adj* residente; (*population*) permanente.

residential [rezɪ'denʃəl] *adj* residencial.

residue ['rezɪdjuː] *n* resto, residuo.

resign [rɪ'zaɪn] *vt* (*gen*) renunciar a ♦ *vi*: **to ~ (from)** dimitir (de), renunciar (a); **to ~ o.s. to** (*endure*) resignarse a.

resignation [rezɪg'neɪʃən] *n* dimisión *f*; (*state of mind*) resignación *f*; **to tender one's ~** presentar la dimisión.

resigned [rɪ'zaɪnd] *adj* resignado.

resilience [rɪ'zɪlɪəns] *n* (*of material*) elasticidad *f*; (*of person*) resistencia.

resilient [rɪ'zɪlɪənt] *adj* (*person*) resistente.

resin ['rezɪn] *n* resina.

resist [rɪ'zɪst] *vt* resistirse a; (*temptation*, *damage*) resistir.

resistance [rɪ'zɪstəns] *n* resistencia.

resistant [rɪ'zɪstənt] *adj*: **~ (to)** resistente (a).

resolute ['rezəluːt] *adj* resuelto.

resolutely ['rezəlutlɪ] *adv* resueltamente.

resolution [rezə'luːʃən] *n* (*gen*) resolución *f*; (*purpose*) propósito; (*COMPUT*) definición *f*; **to make a ~** tomar una resolución.

resolve [rɪ'zɔlv] *n* (*determination*) resolución *f*; (*purpose*) propósito ♦ *vt* resolver ♦ *vi* resolverse; **to ~ to do** resolver hacer.

resolved [rɪ'zɔlvd] *adj* resuelto.

resonance ['rezənəns] *n* resonancia.

resonant ['rɛzənənt] *adj* resonante.
resort [rɪ'zɔːt] *n* (*town*) centro turístico;
(*recourse*) recurso ♦ *vi*: **to ~ to** recurrir a;
in the last ~ como último recurso;
seaside/winter sports ~ playa, estación *f*
balnearia/centro de deportes de
invierno.
resound [rɪ'zaund] *vi*: **to ~ (with)** resonar
(con).
resounding [rɪ'zaundɪŋ] *adj* sonoro; (*fig*)
clamoroso.
resource [rɪ'sɔːs] *n* recurso; **~s** *npl*
recursos *mpl*; **natural ~s** recursos *mpl*
naturales; **to leave sb to his/her own ~s**
(*fig*) abandonar a algn/a a sus propios
recursos.
resourceful [rɪ'sɔːsful] *adj* ingenioso.
resourcefulness [rɪ'sɔːsfulnɪs] *n* inventiva,
iniciativa.
respect [rɪs'pɛkt] *n* (*consideration*) respeto;
(*relation*) respecto; **~s** *npl* recuerdos *mpl*,
saludos *mpl* ♦ *vt* respetar; **with ~ to** con
respecto a; **in this ~** en cuanto a eso; **to
have** *or* **show ~ for** tener *or* mostrar
respeto a; **out of ~ for** por respeto a; **in
some ~s** en algunos aspectos; **with due ~
I still think you're wrong** con el respeto
debido, sigo creyendo que está
equivocado.
respectability [rɪspɛktə'bɪlɪtɪ] *n*
respetabilidad *f*.
respectable [rɪs'pɛktəbl] *adj* respetable;
(*quite big: amount etc*) apreciable;
(*passable*) tolerable; (*quite good: player,
result etc*) bastante bueno.
respected [rɪs'pɛktɪd] *adj* respetado,
estimado.
respectful [rɪs'pɛktful] *adj* respetuoso.
respectfully [rɪs'pɛktfulɪ] *adv*
respetuosamente; **Yours ~** Le saluda
atentamente.
respecting [rɪs'pɛktɪŋ] *prep* (con) respecto
a, en cuanto a.
respective [rɪs'pɛktɪv] *adj* respectivo.
respectively [rɪs'pɛktɪvlɪ] *adv*
respectivamente.
respiration [rɛspɪ'reɪʃən] *n* respiración *f*.
respiratory [rɛs'pɪrətərɪ] *adj* respiratorio.
respite ['rɛspaɪt] *n* respiro; (*LAW*) prórroga.
resplendent [rɪs'plɛndənt] *adj*
resplandeciente.
respond [rɪs'pɔnd] *vi* responder; (*react*)
reaccionar.
respondent [rɪs'pɔndənt] *n* (*LAW*)
demandado/a.
response [rɪs'pɔns] *n* respuesta; (*reaction*)
reacción *f*; **in ~ to** como respuesta a.
responsibility [rɪspɔnsɪ'bɪlɪtɪ] *n*
responsabilidad *f*; **to take ~ for sth/sb**
admitir responsabilidad por algo/uno.
responsible [rɪs'pɔnsɪbl] *adj* (*liable*): **~ (for)**
responsable (de); (*character*) serio,
formal; (*job*) de responsabilidad; **to be ~
to sb (for sth)** ser responsable ante algn
(de algo).
responsibly [rɪs'pɔnsɪblɪ] *adv* con seriedad.
responsive [rɪs'pɔnsɪv] *adj* sensible.
rest [rɛst] *n* descanso, reposo; (*MUS*) pausa,
silencio; (*support*) apoyo; (*remainder*)
resto ♦ *vi* descansar; (*be supported*): **to ~
on** apoyarse en ♦ *vt* (*lean*): **to ~ sth on/
against** apoyar algo en *or* sobre/contra;
the ~ of them (*people, objects*) los demás;
to set sb's mind at ~ tranquilizar a algn;
to ~ one's eyes *or* **gaze on** fijar la mirada
en; **it ~s with him** depende de él; **~
assured that ...** tenga por seguro que ....
restaurant ['rɛstərɔŋ] *n* restaurante *m*.
restaurant car *n* (*BRIT*) coche-comedor *m*.
restaurant owner *n* dueño/a *or*
propietario/a de un restaurante.
rest cure *n* cura de reposo.
restful ['rɛstful] *adj* descansado, tranquilo.
rest home *n* residencia de ancianos.
restitution [rɛstɪ'tjuːʃən] *n*: **to make ~ to
sb for sth** restituir algo a algn; (*paying*)
indemnizar a algn por algo.
restive ['rɛstɪv] *adj* inquieto; (*horse*)
rebelón/ona.
restless ['rɛstlɪs] *adj* inquieto; **to get ~**
impacientarse.
restlessly ['rɛstlɪslɪ] *adv* inquietamente,
con inquietud *f*.
restlessness ['rɛstlɪsnɪs] *n* inquietud *f*.
restock [riː'stɔk] *vt* reaprovisionar.
restoration [rɛstə'reɪʃən] *n* restauración *f*;
(*giving back*) devolución *f*, restitución *f*.
restorative [rɪ'stɔːrətɪv] *adj*
reconstituyente, fortalecedor(a) ♦ *n*
reconstituyente *m*.
restore [rɪ'stɔː*] *vt* (*building*) restaurar; (*sth
stolen*) devolver, restituir; (*health*)
restablecer.
restorer [rɪ'stɔːrə*] *n* (*ART etc*)
restaurador(a) *m/f*.
restrain [rɪs'treɪn] *vt* (*feeling*) contener,
refrenar; (*person*): **to ~ (from doing)**
disuadir (de hacer).
restrained [rɪs'treɪnd] *adj* (*style*) reservado.
restraint [rɪs'treɪnt] *n* (*restriction*) freno,
control *m*; (*of style*) reserva; **wage ~**
control *m* de los salarios.
restrict [rɪs'trɪkt] *vt* restringir, limitar.
restricted [rɪs'trɪktɪd] *adj* restringido,
limitado.
restriction [rɪs'trɪkʃən] *n* restricción *f*,

limitación *f*.
restrictive [rɪs'trɪktɪv] *adj* restrictivo.
restrictive practices *npl* (*INDUSTRY*)
prácticas *fpl* restrictivas.
rest room *n* (*US*) aseos *mpl*.
restructure [riː'strʌktʃə*] *vt* reestructurar.
result [rɪ'zʌlt] *n* resultado ♦ *vi*: **to ~ in**
terminar en, tener por resultado; **as a ~
of** a *or* como consecuencia de; **to ~ (from)**
resultar (de).
resultant [rɪ'zʌltənt] *adj* resultante.
resume [rɪ'zjuːm] *vt* (*work, journey*)
reanudar; (*sum up*) resumir ♦ *vi* (*meeting*)
continuar.
résumé ['reɪzjuːmeɪ] *n* resumen *m*.
resumption [rɪ'zʌmpʃən] *n* reanudación *f*.
resurgence [rɪ'səːdʒəns] *n* resurgimiento.
resurrection [rɛzə'rekʃən] *n* resurrección *f*.
resuscitate [rɪ'sʌsɪteɪt] *vt* (*MED*) resucitar.
resuscitation [rɪsʌsɪ'teɪʃn] *n* resucitación *f*.
retail ['riːteɪl] *n* venta al por menor ♦ *cpd* al
por menor ♦ *vt* vender al por menor *or* al
detalle ♦ *vi*: **to ~ at** (*COMM*) tener precio
de venta al público de.
retailer ['riːteɪlə*] *n* minorista *m/f*, detallista
m/f.
retail outlet *n* punto de venta.
retail price *n* precio de venta al público,
precio al detalle *or* al por menor.
retail price index *n* índice *m* de precios al
por menor.
retain [rɪ'teɪn] *vt* (*keep*) retener, conservar;
(*employ*) contratar.
retainer [rɪ'teɪnə*] *n* (*servant*) criado; (*fee*)
anticipo.
retaliate [rɪ'tælɪeɪt] *vi*: **to ~ (against)** tomar
represalias (contra).
retaliation [rɪtælɪ'eɪʃən] *n* represalias *fpl*; **in
~ for** como represalia por.
retaliatory [rɪ'tælɪətərɪ] *adj* de represalia.
retarded [rɪ'tɑːdɪd] *adj* retrasado.
retch [retʃ] *vi* darle a algn arcadas.
retentive [rɪ'tentɪv] *adj* (*memory*) retentivo.
rethink [riː'θɪŋk] *vt* repensar.
reticence ['retɪsns] *n* reticencia, reserva.
reticent ['retɪsnt] *adj* reticente, reservado.
retina ['retɪnə] *n* retina.
retinue ['retɪnjuː] *n* séquito, comitiva.
retire [rɪ'taɪə*] *vi* (*give up work*) jubilarse;
(*withdraw*) retirarse; (*go to bed*)
acostarse.
retired [rɪ'taɪəd] *adj* (*person*) jubilado.
retirement [rɪ'taɪəmənt] *n* jubilación *f*;
early ~ jubilación *f* anticipada.
retiring [rɪ'taɪərɪŋ] *adj* (*departing: chairman*)
saliente; (*shy*) retraído.
retort [rɪ'tɔːt] *n* (*reply*) réplica ♦ *vi* replicar.
retrace [riː'treɪs] *vt*: **to ~ one's steps** volver

sobre sus pasos, desandar lo andado.
retract [rɪ'trækt] *vt* (*statement*) retirar;
(*claws*) retraer; (*undercarriage, aerial*)
replegar ♦ *vi* retractarse.
retractable [rɪ'træktəbl] *adj* replegable.
retrain [riː'treɪn] *vt* reciclar.
retraining [riː'treɪnɪŋ] *n* reciclaje *m*,
readaptación *f* profesional.
retread ['riːtred] *n* neumático *or* llanta
(*LAM*) recauchutado/a.
retreat [rɪ'triːt] *n* (*place*) retiro; (*MIL*)
retirada ♦ *vi* retirarse; (*flood*) bajar; **to
beat a hasty ~** (*fig*) retirarse en
desbandada.
retrial [riː'traɪəl] *n* nuevo proceso.
retribution [retrɪ'bjuːʃən] *n* desquite *m*.
retrieval [rɪ'triːvəl] *n* recuperación *f*;
information ~ recuperación *f* de datos.
retrieve [rɪ'triːv] *vt* recobrar; (*situation,
honour*) salvar; (*COMPUT*) recuperar;
(*error*) reparar.
retriever [rɪ'triːvə*] *n* perro cobrador.
retroactive [retrəu'æktɪv] *adj* retroactivo.
retrograde ['retrəgreɪd] *adj* retrógrado.
retrospect ['retrəspekt] *n*: **in ~**
retrospectivamente.
retrospective [retrə'spektɪv] *adj*
retrospectivo; (*law*) retroactivo ♦ *n*
exposición *f* retrospectiva.
return [rɪ'təːn] *n* (*going or coming back*)
vuelta, regreso; (*of sth stolen etc*)
devolución *f*; (*recompense*) recompensa;
(*FINANCE: from land, shares*) ganancia,
ingresos *mpl*; (*COMM: of merchandise*)
devolución *f* ♦ *cpd* (*journey*) de regreso;
(*BRIT: ticket*) de ida y vuelta; (*match*) de
vuelta ♦ *vi* (*person etc: come or go back*)
volver, regresar; (*symptoms etc*)
reaparecer ♦ *vt* devolver; (*favour, love etc*)
corresponder a; (*verdict*) pronunciar;
(*POL: candidate*) elegir; **~s** *npl* (*COMM*)
ingresos *mpl*; **tax ~** declaración *f* de la
renta; **in ~ (for)** a cambio (de); **by ~ of
post** a vuelta de correo; **many happy ~s
(of the day)!** ¡feliz cumpleaños!
returnable [rɪ'təːnəbl] *adj*: **~ bottle** envase
m retornable.
returner [rɪ'təːnə*] *n* mujer que vuelve a
trabajar tras un tiempo dedicada a la
familia.
returning officer [rɪ'təːnɪŋ-] *n* (*BRIT POL*)
escrutador(a) *m/f*.
return key *n* (*COMPUT*) tecla de retorno.
reunion [riː'juːnɪən] *n* reencuentro.
reunite [riːjuː'naɪt] *vt* reunir; (*reconcile*)
reconciliar.
rev [rev] *n abbr* (*AUT*: = *revolution*)
revolución *f* ♦ (*vb*: *also*: **~ up**) *vt* acelerar.

revaluation [riːvæljuːˈeɪʃən] n revalorización f.

revamp [riːˈvæmp] vt renovar.

Rev(d). abbr (= reverend) R., Rvdo.

reveal [rɪˈviːl] vt (make known) revelar.

revealing [rɪˈviːlɪŋ] adj revelador(a).

reveille [rɪˈvælɪ] n (MIL) diana.

revel [ˈrɛvl] vi: **to ~ in sth/in doing sth** gozar de algo/haciendo algo.

revelation [rɛvəˈleɪʃən] n revelación f.

reveller, (US) **reveler** [ˈrɛvlə*] n jaranero, juerguista m/f.

revelry [ˈrɛvlrɪ] n jarana, juerga.

revenge [rɪˈvɛndʒ] n venganza; (in sport) revancha; **to take ~ on** vengarse de; **to get one's ~ (for sth)** vengarse (de algo).

revengeful [rɪˈvɛndʒful] adj vengativo.

revenue [ˈrɛvənjuː] n ingresos mpl, rentas fpl.

revenue account n cuenta de ingresos presupuestarios.

revenue expenditure n gasto corriente.

reverberate [rɪˈvəːbəreɪt] vi (sound) resonar, retumbar.

reverberation [rɪvəːbəˈreɪʃən] n resonancia.

revere [rɪˈvɪə*] vt reverenciar, venerar.

reverence [ˈrɛvərəns] n reverencia.

Reverend [ˈrɛvərənd] adj (in titles): **the ~ John Smith** (Anglican) el Reverendo John Smith; (Catholic) el Padre John Smith; (Protestant) el Pastor John Smith.

reverent [ˈrɛvərənt] adj reverente.

reverie [ˈrɛvərɪ] n ensueño.

reversal [rɪˈvəːsl] n (of order) inversión f; (of policy) cambio de rumbo; (of decision) revocación f.

reverse [rɪˈvəːs] n (opposite) contrario; (back: of cloth) revés m; (: of coin) reverso; (: of paper) dorso; (AUT: also: ~ **gear**) marcha atrás ♦ adj (order) inverso; (direction) contrario ♦ vt (decision, AUT) dar marcha atrás a; (position, function) invertir ♦ vi (BRIT AUT) poner en marcha atrás; **in ~ order** en orden inverso; **the ~** lo contrario; **to go into ~** dar marcha atrás.

reverse-charge call [rɪˈvəːstʃɑːdʒ-] n (BRIT) llamada a cobro revertido.

reverse video n vídeo inverso.

reversible [rɪˈvəːsəbl] adj (garment, procedure) reversible.

reversing lights [rɪˈvəːsɪŋ-] npl (BRIT AUT) luces fpl de marcha atrás.

revert [rɪˈvəːt] vi: **to ~ to** volver or revertir a.

review [rɪˈvjuː] n (magazine, MIL) revista; (of book, film) reseña; (US: examination)

repaso, examen m ♦ vt repasar, examinar; (MIL) pasar revista a; (book, film) reseñar; **to come under ~** ser examinado.

reviewer [rɪˈvjuːə*] n crítico/a.

revile [rɪˈvaɪl] vt injuriar, vilipendiar.

revise [rɪˈvaɪz] vt (manuscript) corregir; (opinion) modificar; (BRIT: study: subject) repasar; (look over) revisar; **~d edition** edición f corregida.

revision [rɪˈvɪʒən] n corrección f; modificación f; (of subject) repaso; (revised version) revisión f.

revisit [riːˈvɪzɪt] vt volver a visitar.

revitalize [riːˈvaɪtəlaɪz] vt revivificar.

revival [rɪˈvaɪvəl] n (recovery) reanimación f; (POL) resurgimiento; (of interest) renacimiento; (THEAT) reestreno; (of faith) despertar m.

revive [rɪˈvaɪv] vt resucitar; (custom) restablecer; (hope, courage) reanimar; (play) reestrenar ♦ vi (person) volver en sí; (from tiredness) reponerse; (business) reactivarse.

revoke [rɪˈvəuk] vt revocar.

revolt [rɪˈvəult] n rebelión f ♦ vi rebelarse, sublevarse ♦ vt dar asco a, repugnar; **to ~ (against sb/sth)** rebelarse (contra algn/algo).

revolting [rɪˈvəultɪŋ] adj asqueroso, repugnante.

revolution [rɛvəˈluːʃən] n revolución f.

revolutionary [rɛvəˈluːʃənrɪ] adj, n revolucionario/a m/f.

revolutionize [rɛvəˈluːʃənaɪz] vt revolucionar.

revolve [rɪˈvɒlv] vi dar vueltas, girar.

revolver [rɪˈvɒlvə*] n revólver m.

revolving [rɪˈvɒlvɪŋ] adj (chair, door etc) giratorio.

revue [rɪˈvjuː] n (THEAT) revista.

revulsion [rɪˈvʌlʃən] n asco, repugnancia.

reward [rɪˈwɔːd] n premio, recompensa ♦ vt: **to ~ (for)** recompensar or premiar (por).

rewarding [rɪˈwɔːdɪŋ] adj (fig) gratificante; **financially ~** económicamente provechoso.

rewind [riːˈwaɪnd] vt (watch) dar cuerda a; (wool etc) devanar.

rewire [riːˈwaɪə*] vt (house) renovar la instalación eléctrica de.

reword [riːˈwəːd] vt expresar en otras palabras.

rewrite [riːˈraɪt] vt (irreg: like **write**) reescribir.

Reykjavik [ˈreɪkjəviːk] n Reykjavik m.

RFD abbr (US POST)= rural free delivery.

Rh abbr (= rhesus) Rh m.

rhapsody ['ræpsədɪ] n (MUS) rapsodia; (fig): **to go into rhapsodies over** extasiarse por.

rhesus negative ['riːsəs-] adj (MED) Rh negativo.

rhesus positive adj (MED) Rh positivo.

rhetoric ['rɛtərɪk] n retórica.

rhetorical [rɪ'tɔrɪkl] adj retórico.

rheumatic [ruː'mætɪk] adj reumático.

rheumatism ['ruːmətɪzəm] n reumatismo, reúma.

rheumatoid arthritis ['ruːmətɔɪd-] n reúma m articular.

Rhine [raɪn] n: **the ~** el (río) Rin.

rhinestone ['raɪnstəun] n diamante m de imitación.

rhinoceros [raɪ'nɔsərəs] n rinoceronte m.

Rhodes [rəudz] n Rodas f.

rhododendron [rəudə'dɛndrn] n rododendro.

Rhone [rəun] n: **the ~** el (río) Ródano.

rhubarb ['ruːbɑːb] n ruibarbo.

rhyme [raɪm] n rima; (verse) poesía ♦ vi: **to ~ (with)** rimar (con); **without ~ or reason** sin ton ni son.

rhythm ['rɪðm] n ritmo.

rhythmic(al) ['rɪðmɪk(l)] adj rítmico.

rhythmically ['rɪðmɪklɪ] adv rítmicamente.

rhythm method n método (de) Ogino.

RI n abbr (BRIT: = religious instruction) ed. religiosa ♦ abbr (US) = Rhode Island.

rib [rɪb] n (ANAT) costilla ♦ vt (mock) tomar el pelo a.

ribald ['rɪbəld] adj escabroso.

ribbon ['rɪbən] n cinta; **in ~s** (torn) hecho trizas.

rice [raɪs] n arroz m.

ricefield ['raɪsfiːld] n arrozal m.

rice pudding n arroz m con leche.

rich [rɪtʃ] adj rico; (soil) fértil; (food) pesado; (: sweet) empalagoso; **the ~** npl los ricos; **~es** npl riqueza sg; **to be ~ in sth** abundar en algo.

richly ['rɪtʃlɪ] adv ricamente.

richness ['rɪtʃnɪs] n riqueza; (of soil) fertilidad f.

rickets ['rɪkɪts] n raquitismo.

rickety ['rɪkɪtɪ] adj (old) desvencijado; (shaky) tambaleante.

rickshaw ['rɪkʃɔː] n carro de culí.

ricochet ['rɪkəʃeɪ] n rebote m ♦ vi rebotar.

rid, pt, pp rid [rɪd] vt: **to ~ sb of sth** librar a algn de algo; **to get ~ of** deshacerse or desembarazarse de.

riddance ['rɪdns] n: **good ~!** ¡y adiós muy buenas!

ridden ['rɪdn] pp of ride.

-ridden ['rɪdn] suff: **disease~** plagado de enfermedades; **inflation~** minado por la inflación.

riddle ['rɪdl] n (conundrum) acertijo; (mystery) enigma m, misterio ♦ vt: **to be ~d with** ser lleno or plagado de.

ride [raɪd] n paseo; (distance covered) viaje m, recorrido ♦ vb (pt **rode**, pp **ridden**) vi (horse: as sport) montar; (go somewhere: on horse, bicycle) dar un paseo, pasearse; (journey: on bicycle, motor cycle, bus) viajar ♦ vt (a horse) montar a; (distance) viajar; **to ~ a bicycle** andar en bicicleta; **to ~ at anchor** (NAUT) estar fondeado; **can you ~ a bike?** ¿sabes montar en bici(cleta)?; **to go for a ~** dar un paseo; **to take sb for a ~** (fig) tomar el pelo a algn.

▶**ride out** vt: **to ~ out the storm** (fig) capear el temporal.

rider ['raɪdə*] n (on horse) jinete m; (on bicycle) ciclista m/f; (on motorcycle) motociclista m/f.

ridge [rɪdʒ] n (of hill) cresta; (of roof) caballete m; (wrinkle) arruga.

ridicule ['rɪdɪkjuːl] n irrisión f, burla ♦ vt poner en ridículo a, burlarse de; **to hold sth/sb up to ~** poner algo/a algn en ridículo.

ridiculous [rɪ'dɪkjuləs] adj ridículo.

ridiculously [rɪ'dɪkjuləslɪ] adv ridículamente, de modo ridículo.

riding ['raɪdɪŋ] n equitación f; **I like ~** me gusta montar a caballo.

riding habit n traje m de montar.

riding school n escuela de equitación.

rife [raɪf] adj: **to be ~** ser muy común; **to be ~ with** abundar en.

riffraff ['rɪfræf] n chusma, gentuza.

rifle ['raɪfl] n rifle m, fusil m ♦ vt saquear.

▶**rifle through** vt fus saquear.

rifle range n campo de tiro; (at fair) tiro al blanco.

rift [rɪft] n (fig: between friends) desavenencia; (: in party) escisión f.

rig [rɪg] n (also: oil ~: on land) torre f de perforación; (: at sea) plataforma petrolera ♦ vt (election etc) amañar los resultados de.

▶**rig out** vt (BRIT) ataviar.

▶**rig up** vt improvisar.

rigging ['rɪgɪŋ] n (NAUT) aparejo.

right [raɪt] adj (true, correct) correcto, exacto; (suitable) indicado, debido; (proper) apropiado, propio; (just) justo; (morally good) bueno; (not left) derecho ♦ n (title, claim) derecho; (not left) derecha ♦ adv (correctly) bien, correctamente; (straight) derecho, directamente; (not on the left) a la derecha; (to the ~) hacia la derecha ♦ vt (put straight) enderezar ♦ excl ¡bueno!, ¡está bien!; **to be** ~ (person) tener razón; **to get sth** ~ acertar en algo; **you did the** ~ **thing** hiciste bien; **let's get it** ~ **this time!** ¡a ver si esta vez nos sale bien!; **to put a mistake** ~ corregir un error; **the** ~ **time** la hora exacta; (fig) el momento oportuno; **by** ~s en justicia; ~ **and wrong** el bien y el mal; **film** ~s derechos mpl de la película; **on the** ~ a la derecha; **to be in the** ~ tener razón; ~ **now** ahora mismo; ~ **before/after** inmediatamente antes/después; ~ **in the middle** exactamente en el centro; ~ **away** en seguida; **to go** ~ **to the end of sth** llegar hasta el final de algo; ~, **who's next?** bueno, ¿quién sigue?; **all** ~! ¡vale!; **I'm/I feel all** ~ **now** ya estoy bien.

right angle n ángulo recto.

righteous ['raɪtʃəs] adj justo, honrado; (anger) justificado.

righteousness ['raɪtʃəsnɪs] n justicia.

rightful ['raɪtful] adj (heir) legítimo.

right-hand ['raɪthænd] adj (drive, turn) por la derecha.

right-handed [raɪt'hændɪd] adj (person) que usa la mano derecha.

right-hand man n brazo derecho.

right-hand side n derecha.

rightly ['raɪtlɪ] adv correctamente, debidamente; (with reason) con razón; **if I remember** ~ si recuerdo bien.

right-minded ['raɪt'maɪndɪd] adj (sensible) sensato; (decent) honrado.

right of way n (on path etc) derecho de paso; (AUT) prioridad f de paso.

rights issue n (STOCK EXCHANGE) emisión f gratuita de acciones.

right-wing [raɪt'wɪŋ] adj (POL) de derechas, derechista.

right-winger [raɪt'wɪŋə*] n (POL) persona de derechas, derechista m/f; (SPORT) extremo derecha.

rigid ['rɪdʒɪd] adj rígido; (person, ideas) inflexible.

rigidity [rɪ'dʒɪdɪtɪ] n rigidez f; inflexibilidad f.

rigidly ['rɪdʒɪdlɪ] adv rígidamente; (inflexibly) inflexiblemente.

rigmarole ['rɪgmərəul] n galimatías m inv.

rigor mortis ['rɪgə'mɔːtɪs] n rigidez f cadavérica.

rigorous ['rɪgərəs] adj riguroso.

rigorously ['rɪgərəslɪ] adv rigurosamente.

rigour, (US) **rigor** ['rɪgə*] n rigor m, severidad f.

rig-out ['rɪgaut] n (BRIT col) atuendo.

rile [raɪl] vt irritar.

rim [rɪm] n borde m; (of spectacles) montura, aro; (of wheel) llanta.

rimless ['rɪmlɪs] adj (spectacles) sin aros.

rimmed [rɪmd] adj: ~ **with** con un borde de, bordeado de.

rind [raɪnd] n (of bacon, cheese) corteza; (of lemon etc) cáscara.

ring [rɪŋ] n (of metal) aro; (on finger) anillo; (of people) corro; (of objects) círculo; (gang) banda; (for boxing) cuadrilátero; (of circus) pista; (bull ~) ruedo, plaza; (sound of bell) toque m; (telephone call) llamada ♦ vb (pt **rang**, pp **rung** [ræŋ, rʌŋ]) vi (on telephone) llamar por teléfono; (large bell) repicar; (also: ~ **out**: voice, words) sonar; (ears) zumbar ♦ vt (BRIT TEL: also: ~ **up**) llamar; (bell etc) hacer sonar; (doorbell) tocar; **that has the** ~ **of truth about it** eso suena a verdad; **to give sb a** ~ (BRIT TEL) llamar por teléfono a algn, dar un telefonazo a algn; **the name doesn't** ~ **a bell (with me)** el nombre no me suena; **to** ~ **sb (up)** llamar a algn.

▶**ring back** vt, vi (TEL) devolver la llamada.

▶**ring off** vi (BRIT TEL) colgar, cortar la comunicación.

ring binder n carpeta de anillas.

ring finger n (dedo) anular m.

ringing ['rɪŋɪŋ] n (of bell) toque m, tañido; (louder. of large bell) repique m; (in ears) zumbido.

ringing tone n (TEL) tono de llamada.

ringleader ['rɪŋliːdə*] n (of gang) cabecilla m/f.

ringlets ['rɪŋlɪts] npl tirabuzones mpl, bucles mpl.

ring road n (BRIT) carretera periférica or de circunvalación.

rink [rɪŋk] n (also: **ice** ~) pista de hielo; (for roller-skating) pista de patinaje.

rinse [rɪns] n (of dishes) enjuague m; (of clothes) aclarado; (of hair) reflejo ♦ vt enjuagar; aclarar; dar reflejos a.

Rio (de Janeiro) ['riːəu(dədʒə'nɪərəu)] n Río de Janeiro.

riot ['raɪət] n motín m, disturbio ♦ vi amotinarse; **to run** ~ desmandarse.

rioter ['raɪətə*] n amotinado/a.

riot gear n uniforme m antidisturbios inv.

riotous ['raɪətəs] adj alborotado; (party) bullicioso; (uncontrolled) desenfrenado.

riotously ['raɪətəslɪ] adv bulliciosamente.

riot police n policía antidisturbios.

RIP abbr (= rest in peace) q.e.p.d.

rip [rɪp] n rasgón m, desgarrón m ♦ vt rasgar, desgarrar ♦ vi rasgarse.

▶**rip up** vt hacer pedazos.

ripcord ['rɪpkɔːd] n cabo de desgarre.

ripe [raɪp] *adj (fruit)* maduro.
ripen ['raɪpən] *vt, vi* madurar.
ripeness ['raɪpnɪs] *n* madurez *f*.
rip-off ['rɪpɔf] *n (col)*: **it's a ~!** ¡es una estafa!, ¡es un timo!
riposte [rɪ'pɔst] *n* respuesta aguda, réplica.
ripple ['rɪpl] *n* onda, rizo; *(sound)* murmullo
♦ *vi* rizarse ♦ *vt* rizar.
rise [raɪz] *n (slope)* cuesta, pendiente *f*; *(hill)* altura; *(increase: in wages: Brit)* aumento; *(: in prices, temperature)* subida, alza; *(fig: to power etc)* ascenso; *(: ascendancy)* auge *m* ♦ *vi (pt* **rose**, *pp* **risen** [rəuz, 'rɪzn]) *(gen)* elevarse; *(prices)* subir; *(waters)* crecer; *(river)* nacer; *(sun)* salir; *(person: from bed etc)* levantarse; *(also: ~ up: rebel)* sublevarse; *(in rank)* ascender; **~ to power** ascenso al poder; **to give ~ to** dar lugar *or* origen a; **to ~ to the occasion** ponerse a la altura de las circunstancias.
rising ['raɪzɪŋ] *adj (increasing: number)* creciente; *(: prices)* en aumento *or* alza; *(tide)* creciente; *(sun, moon)* naciente ♦ *n (uprising)* sublevación *f*.
rising damp *n* humedad *f* de paredes.
rising star *n (fig)* figura en alza.
risk [rɪsk] *n* riesgo, peligro ♦ *vt (gen)* arriesgar; *(dare)* atreverse a; **to take** *or* **run the ~ of doing** correr el riesgo de hacer; **at ~** en peligro; **at one's own ~** bajo su propia responsabilidad; **fire/ health/security ~** peligro de incendio/ para la salud/para la seguridad.
risk capital *n* capital *m* de riesgo.
risky ['rɪskɪ] *adj* arriesgado, peligroso.
risqué ['riːskeɪ] *adj (joke)* subido de color.
rissole ['rɪsəul] *n* croqueta.
rite [raɪt] *n* rito; **last ~s** últimos sacramentos *mpl*.
ritual ['rɪtjuəl] *adj* ritual ♦ *n* ritual *m*, rito.
rival ['raɪvl] *n* rival *m/f*; *(in business)* competidor(a) *m/f* ♦ *adj* rival, opuesto ♦ *vt* competir con.
rivalry ['raɪvlrɪ] *n* rivalidad *f*, competencia.
river ['rɪvə*] *n* río ♦ *cpd (port, traffic)* de río, del río; **up/down ~** río arriba/abajo.
riverbank ['rɪvəbæŋk] *n* orilla (del río).
riverbed ['rɪvəbɛd] *n* lecho, cauce *m*.
rivet ['rɪvɪt] *n* roblón *m*, remache *m* ♦ *vt* remachar; *(fig)* fascinar.
riveting ['rɪvɪtɪŋ] *adj (fig)* fascinante.
Riviera [rɪvɪ'ɛərə] *n*: **the (French) ~** la Costa Azul, la Riviera (francesa); **the Italian ~** la Riviera italiana.
Riyadh [rɪ'jɑːd] *n* Riyadh *m*.
RMT *n abbr (=Rail, Maritime and Transport)* sindicato de transportes.
RN *n abbr (BRIT) see* **Royal Navy**; *(US)*

= **registered nurse.**
RNA *n abbr (= ribonucleic acid)* ARN *m*, RNA *m*.
RNLI *n abbr (BRIT: = Royal National Lifeboat Institution)* organización benéfica que proporciona un servicio de lanchas de socorro.
RNZAF *n abbr = Royal New Zealand Air Force.*
RNZN *n abbr = Royal New Zealand Navy.*
road [rəud] *n (gen)* camino; *(motorway etc)* carretera; *(in town)* calle *f*; **major/minor ~** carretera general/secundaria; **main ~** carretera; **it takes 4 hours by ~** se tarda 4 horas por carretera; **on the ~ to success** camino del éxito.
roadblock ['rəudblɔk] *n* barricada, control *m*, retén *m (LAM)*.
road haulage *n* transporte *m* por carretera.
roadhog ['rəudhɔg] *n* loco/a del volante.
road map *n* mapa *m* de carreteras.
road safety *n* seguridad *f* vial.
roadside ['rəudsaɪd] *n* borde *m* (del camino) ♦ *cpd* al lado de la carretera; **by the ~** al borde del camino.
roadsign ['rəudsaɪn] *n* señal *f* de tráfico.
roadsweeper ['rəudswiːpə*] *n (BRIT: person)* barrendero/a.
road user *n* usuario/a de la vía pública.
roadway ['rəudweɪ] *n* calzada.
roadworks ['rəudwəːks] *npl* obras *fpl*.
roadworthy ['rəudwəːðɪ] *adj (car)* en buen estado para circular.
roam [rəum] *vi* vagar ♦ *vt* vagar por.
roar [rɔː*] *n (of animal)* rugido, bramido; *(of crowd)* clamor *m*, rugido; *(of vehicle, storm)* estruendo; *(of laughter)* carcajada ♦ *vi* rugir, bramar; hacer estruendo; **to ~ with laughter** reírse a carcajadas.
roaring ['rɔːrɪŋ] *adj*: **a ~ success** un tremendo éxito; **to do a ~ trade** hacer buen negocio.
roast [rəust] *n* carne *f* asada, asado ♦ *vt (meat)* asar; *(coffee)* tostar.
roast beef *n* rosbif *m*.
roasting ['rəustɪŋ] *n*: **to give sb a ~** *(col)* echar una buena bronca a algn.
rob [rɔb] *vt* robar; **to ~ sb of sth** robar algo a algn; *(fig: deprive)* quitar algo a algn.
robber ['rɔbə*] *n* ladrón/ona *m/f*.
robbery ['rɔbərɪ] *n* robo.
robe [rəub] *n (for ceremony etc)* toga; *(also: bath ~)* bata.
robin ['rɔbɪn] *n* petirrojo.
robot ['rəubɔt] *n* robot *m*.
robotics [rəu'bɔtɪks] *n* robótica.
robust [rəu'bʌst] *adj* robusto, fuerte.
rock [rɔk] *n (gen)* roca; *(boulder)* peña,

peñasco; (*BRIT: sweet*) ≈ pirulí *m* ♦ *vt* (*swing gently*) mecer; (*shake*) sacudir ♦ *vi* mecerse, balancearse; sacudirse; **on the ~s** (*drink*) con hielo; **their marriage is on the ~s** su matrimonio se está yendo a pique; **to ~ the boat** (*fig*) crear problemas.

rock and roll *n* rock and roll *m*, rocanrol *m*.

rock-bottom ['rɔk'bɒtəm] *adj* (*fig*) por los suelos; **to reach** *or* **touch ~** (*price*) estar por los suelos; (*person*) tocar fondo.

rock cake *n* (*BRIT*) *bollito de pasas con superficie rugosa.*

rock climber *n* escalador(a) *m/f*.

rock climbing *n* (*SPORT*) escalada.

rockery ['rɔkərɪ] *n* cuadro alpino.

rocket ['rɔkɪt] *n* cohete *m* ♦ *vi* (*prices*) dispararse, ponerse por las nubes.

rocket launcher *n* lanzacohetes *m inv*.

rock face *n* pared *f* de roca.

rocking chair ['rɔkɪŋ-] *n* mecedora.

rocking horse *n* caballo de balancín.

rocky ['rɔkɪ] *adj* (*gen*) rocoso; (*unsteady: table*) inestable.

Rocky Mountains *npl*: **the ~** las Montañas Rocosas.

rococo [rə'kəukəu] *adj* rococó *inv* ♦ *n* rococó.

rod [rɔd] *n* vara, varilla; (*TECH*) barra; (*also: fishing ~*) caña.

rode [rəud] *pt of* ride.

rodent ['rəudnt] *n* roedor *m*.

rodeo ['rəudɪəu] *n* rodeo.

roe [rəu] *n* (*species: also: ~ deer*) corzo; (*of fish*): **hard/soft ~** hueva/lecha.

rogue [rəug] *n* pícaro, pillo.

roguish ['rəugɪʃ] *adj* (*child*) travieso; (*smile etc*) pícaro.

role [rəul] *n* papel *m*, rol *m*.

role-model ['rəulmɔdl] *n* modelo a imitar.

role play *n* (*also: ~ing*) juego de papeles *or* roles.

roll [rəul] *n* rollo; (*of bank notes*) fajo; (*also: bread ~*) panecillo; (*register*) lista, nómina; (*sound: of drums etc*) redoble *m*; (*movement: of ship*) balanceo ♦ *vt* hacer rodar; (*also: ~ up: string*) enrollar; (: *sleeves*) arremangar; (*cigarettes*) liar; (*also: ~ out: pastry*) aplanar ♦ *vi* (*gen*) rodar; (*drum*) redoblar; (*in walking*) bambolearse; (*ship*) balancearse; **cheese ~** panecillo de queso.

►**roll about, roll around** *vi* (*person*) revolcarse.

►**roll by** *vi* (*time*) pasar.

►**roll in** *vi* (*mail, cash*) entrar a raudales.

►**roll over** *vi* dar una vuelta.

►**roll up** *vi* (*col: arrive*) presentarse,

aparecer ♦ *vt* (*carpet, cloth, map*) arrollar; (*sleeves*) arremangar; **to ~ o.s. up into a ball** acurrucarse, hacerse un ovillo.

roll call *n*: **to take a ~** pasar lista.

rolled [rəuld] *adj* (*umbrella*) plegado.

roller ['rəulə*] *n* rodillo; (*wheel*) rueda.

roller blind *n* (*BRIT*) persiana (enrollable).

roller coaster *n* montaña rusa.

roller skates *npl* patines *mpl* de rueda.

rollicking ['rɔlɪkɪŋ] *adj*: **we had a ~ time** nos divertimos una barbaridad.

rolling ['rəulɪŋ] *adj* (*landscape*) ondulado.

rolling mill *n* taller *m* de laminación.

rolling pin *n* rodillo (de cocina).

rolling stock *n* (*RAIL*) material *m* rodante.

ROM [rɔm] *n abbr* (= *read only memory*) (memoria) ROM *f*.

Roman ['rəumən] *adj*, *n* romano/a *m/f*.

Roman Catholic *adj*, *n* católico/a *m/f* (romano/a).

romance [rə'mæns] *n* (*love affair*) amor *m*, idilio; (*charm*) lo romántico; (*novel*) novela de amor.

romanesque [rəumə'nɛsk] *adj* románico.

Romania [ru:'meɪnɪə] *n* = **Rumania.**

Romanian [ru:'meɪnɪən] *adj*, *n* = **Rumanian.**

Roman numeral *n* número romano.

romantic [rə'mæntɪk] *adj* romántico.

romanticism [rə'mæntɪsɪzəm] *n* romanticismo.

Romany ['rəumənɪ] *adj* gitano ♦ *n* (*person*) gitano/a; (*LING*) lengua gitana, caló (*SP*).

Rome [rəum] *n* Roma.

romp [rɔmp] *n* retozo, jugueteo ♦ *vi* (*also: ~ about*) juguetear; **to ~ home** (*horse*) ganar fácilmente.

rompers ['rɔmpəz] *npl* pelele *m*.

roof [ru:f] *n* (*gen*) techo; (*of house*) tejado ♦ *vt* techar, poner techo a; **~ of the mouth** paladar *m*.

roofing ['ru:fɪŋ] *n* techumbre *f*.

roof rack *n* (*AUT*) baca.

rook [ruk] *n* (*bird*) graja; (*CHESS*) torre *f*.

rookie ['rukɪ] *n* (*col*) novato/a; (*MIL*) chivo.

room [ru:m] *n* (*in house*) cuarto, habitación *f*, pieza (*esp LAm*); (*also: bed~*) dormitorio; (*in school etc*) sala; (*space*) sitio; **~s** *npl* (*lodging*) alojamiento *sg*; "**~s to let**", (*US*) "**~s for rent**" "se alquilan pisos *or* cuartos"; **single/double ~** habitación individual/doble *or* para dos personas; **is there ~ for this?** ¿cabe esto?; **to make ~ for sb** hacer sitio para algn; **there is ~ for improvement** podría mejorarse.

roominess ['ru:mɪnɪs] *n* amplitud *f*, espaciosidad *f*.

rooming house ['ru:mɪŋ-] *n* (*US*) pensión *f*.

roommate ['ruːmmeɪt] n compañero/a de cuarto.

room service n servicio de habitaciones.

room temperature n temperatura ambiente.

roomy ['ruːmɪ] adj espacioso.

roost [ruːst] n percha ♦ vi pasar la noche.

rooster ['ruːstə*] n gallo.

root [ruːt] n (BOT, MATH) raíz f ♦ vi (plant, belief) arraigar(se); **to take ~** (plant) echar raíces; (idea) arraigar(se); **the ~ of the problem is that ...** la raíz del problema es que ....
  ►**root about** vi (fig) rebuscar.
  ►**root for** vt fus apoyar a.
  ►**root out** vt desarraigar.

root beer n (US) refresco sin alcohol de extractos de hierbas.

rooted ['ruːtɪd] adj enraizado; (opinions etc) arraigado.

rope [rəup] n cuerda; (NAUT) cable m ♦ vt (box) atar or amarrar con (una) cuerda; (climbers: also: ~ **together**) encordarse; **to ~ sb in** (fig) persuadir a algn a tomar parte; **to know the ~s** (fig) conocer los trucos (del oficio).

rope ladder n escala de cuerda.

ropey ['rəupɪ] adj (col) chungo.

rosary ['rəuzərɪ] n rosario.

rose [rəuz] pt of **rise** ♦ n rosa; (also: ~**bush**) rosal m; (on watering can) roseta ♦ adj color de rosa.

rosé ['rəuzeɪ] n vino rosado, clarete m.

rosebed ['rəuzbɛd] n rosaleda.

rosebud ['rəuzbʌd] n capullo de rosa.

rosebush ['rəuzbʊʃ] n rosal m.

rosemary ['rəuzmərɪ] n romero.

rosette [rəu'zɛt] n rosetón m.

ROSPA ['rɔspə] n abbr (BRIT) = Royal Society for the Prevention of Accidents.

roster ['rɔstə*] n: **duty ~** lista de tareas.

rostrum ['rɔstrəm] n tribuna.

rosy ['rəuzɪ] adj rosado, sonrosado; **the future looks ~** el futuro parece prometedor.

rot [rɔt] n (decay) putrefacción f, podredumbre f; (fig: pej) tonterías fpl ♦ vt pudrir, corromper ♦ vi pudrirse, corromperse; **it has ~ted** está podrido; **to stop the ~** (fig) poner fin a las pérdidas.

rota ['rəutə] n lista (de tareas).

rotary ['rəutərɪ] adj rotativo.

rotate [rəu'teɪt] vt (revolve) hacer girar, dar vueltas a; (change round: crops) cultivar en rotación; (: jobs) alternar ♦ vi (revolve) girar, dar vueltas.

rotating [rəu'teɪtɪŋ] adj (movement) rotativo.

rotation [rəu'teɪʃən] n rotación f; **in ~** por turno.

rote [rəut] n: **by ~** de memoria.

rotor ['rəutə*] n rotor m.

rotten ['rɔtn] adj (decayed) podrido; (: wood) carcomido; (fig) corrompido; (col: bad) pésimo; **to feel ~** (ill) sentirse fatal; **~ to the core** completamente podrido.

rotund [rəu'tʌnd] adj rotundo.

rouble, (US) **ruble** ['ruːbl] n rublo.

rouge [ruːʒ] n colorete m.

rough [rʌf] adj (skin, surface) áspero; (terrain) accidentado; (road) desigual; (voice) bronco; (person, manner: coarse) tosco, grosero; (weather) borrascoso; (treatment) brutal; (sea) embravecido; (cloth) basto; (plan) preliminar; (guess) aproximado; (violent) violento ♦ n (GOLF): **in the ~** en las hierbas altas; **to ~ it** vivir sin comodidades; **to sleep ~** (BRIT) pasar la noche al raso; **the sea is ~ today** el mar está agitado hoy; **to have a ~ time (of it)** pasar una mala racha; **~ estimate** cálculo aproximado.

roughage ['rʌfɪdʒ] n fibra(s) f(pl), forraje m.

rough-and-ready ['rʌfən'rɛdɪ] adj improvisado, tosco.

rough-and-tumble ['rʌfən'tʌmbl] n pelea.

roughcast ['rʌfkɑːst] n mezcla gruesa.

rough copy, rough draft n borrador m.

roughen ['rʌfn] vt (a surface) poner áspero.

roughly ['rʌflɪ] adv (handle) torpemente; (make) toscamente; (approximately) aproximadamente; **~ speaking** más o menos.

roughness ['rʌfnɪs] n aspereza; tosquedad f; brutalidad f.

roughshod ['rʌfʃɔd] adv: **to ride ~ over** (person) pisotear a; (objections) hacer caso omiso de.

rough work n (SCOL etc) borrador m.

roulette [ruː'lɛt] n ruleta.

Roumania [ruː'meɪnɪə] n = **Rumania**.

round [raund] adj redondo ♦ n círculo; (of policeman) ronda; (of milkman) recorrido; (of doctor) visitas fpl; (game: of cards, in competition) partida; (of ammunition) cartucho; (BOXING) asalto; (of talks) ronda ♦ vt (corner) doblar ♦ prep alrededor de ♦ adv: **all ~** por todos lados; **the long way ~** por el camino menos directo; **all the year ~** durante todo el año; **it's just ~ the corner** (fig) está a la vuelta de la esquina; **to ask sb ~** invitar a algn a casa; **I'll be ~ at 6 o'clock** llegaré a eso de las 6; **she arrived ~ (about) noon** llegó alrededor del mediodía; **~ the clock** adv las 24 horas; **to go ~ to sb's (house)** ir a casa de algn; **to go ~ the back** pasar por atrás; **to go ~ a house** visitar una casa; **enough to go ~** bastante (para todos); **in ~ figures** en números redondos; **to go the ~s** (story) divulgarse; **a ~ of applause** una salva de aplausos; **a ~ of drinks/ sandwiches** una ronda de bebidas/ bocadillos; **a ~ of toast** (BRIT) una tostada; **the daily ~** la rutina cotidiana.

▶**round off** vt (speech etc) acabar, poner término a.

▶**round up** vt (cattle) acorralar; (people) reunir; (prices) redondear.

roundabout ['raundəbaut] n (BRIT: AUT) glorieta, rotonda; (: at fair) tiovivo ♦ adj (route, means) indirecto.

rounded ['raundɪd] adj redondeado, redondo.

rounders ['raundəz] n (BRIT: game) juego similar al béisbol.

roundly ['raundlɪ] adv (fig) rotundamente.

round-robin ['raundrɔbɪn] n (SPORT: also: ~ tournament) liguilla.

round-shouldered ['raund'ʃəuldəd] adj cargado de espaldas.

round trip n viaje m de ida y vuelta.

roundup ['raundʌp] n rodeo; (of criminals) redada; **a ~ of the latest news** un resumen de las últimas noticias.

rouse [rauz] vt (wake up) despertar; (stir up) suscitar.

rousing ['rauzɪŋ] adj (applause) caluroso; (speech) conmovedor(a).

rout [raut] n (MIL) derrota; (flight) desbandada ♦ vt derrotar.

route [ruːt] n ruta, camino; (of bus) recorrido; (of shipping) rumbo, derrota; **the best ~ to London** el mejor camino or la mejor ruta para ir a Londres; **en ~ from ... to** en el viaje de ... a; **en ~ for** rumbo a, con destino en.

route map n (BRIT: for journey) mapa m de carreteras.

routine [ruːˈtiːn] adj (work) rutinario ♦ n rutina; (THEAT) número; (COMPUT) rutina; **~ procedure** trámite m rutinario.

rover ['rəuvə*] n vagabundo/a.

roving ['rəuvɪŋ] adj (wandering) errante; (salesman) ambulante; (reporter) volante.

row [rəu] n (line) fila, hilera; (KNITTING) vuelta; [rau] (noise) escándalo; (dispute) bronca, pelea; (fuss) jaleo; (scolding) reprimenda ♦ vi (in boat) remar; [rau] reñir(se) ♦ vt (boat) conducir remando; **4 days in a ~** 4 días seguidos; **to make a ~** armar un lío; **to have a ~** pelearse, reñir.

rowboat ['rəubəut] n (US) bote m de remos.

rowdy ['raudɪ] adj (person: noisy) ruidoso; (: quarrelsome) pendenciero; (occasion) alborotado ♦ n pendenciero.

rowdyism ['raudɪzəm] n gamberrismo.

row houses npl (US) casas fpl adosadas.

rowing ['rəuɪŋ] n remo.

rowing boat n (BRIT) bote m or barco de remos.

rowlock ['rɔlək] n (BRIT) chumacera.

royal ['rɔɪəl] adj real.

La **Royal Academy** o **Royal Academy of Arts**, fundada en 1768 durante el reinado de Jorge III, es una institución dedicada al fomento de la pintura, escultura y arquitectura en el Reino Unido. Además de dar cursos de arte, presenta una exposición anual de artistas contemporáneos en su sede de Burlington House, en el centro de Londres. No existe una institución equivalente a la Real Academia de la Lengua.

Royal Air Force (RAF) n Fuerzas Aéreas Británicas fpl.

royal blue n azul m marino.

royalist ['rɔɪəlɪst] adj, n monárquico/a m/f.

Royal Navy (RN) n (BRIT) Marina Británica.

royalty ['rɔɪəltɪ] n (royal persons) (miembros mpl de la) familia real; (payment to author) derechos mpl de autor.

El acento con el que suelen hablar las clases medias y altas de Inglaterra se denomina **RP (Received Pronunciation)**. Es el acento estándar, sin variaciones regionales, que aún usan los locutores en los informativos nacionales de la **BBC**. También suele tomarse como norma en la enseñanza del inglés británico como lengua extranjera. Todavía conserva un gran prestigio, aunque la gran mayoría de la población habla con el acento de su región, que puede ser más o menos fuerte según su educación o clase social.

---

rpm abbr (= revs per minute) r.p.m.

RR abbr (US) = **railroad**.

R & R n abbr (US MIL) = rest and recreation.

RSA n abbr (BRIT) = Royal Society of Arts, Royal Scottish Academy.

RSI n abbr (MED: = repetitive strain injury) traumatismo producido por un esfuerzo continuado (como el de las mecanógrafas).

RSPB n abbr (BRIT) = Royal Society for the Protection of Birds.

RSPCA n abbr (BRIT) = Royal Society for the

Prevention of Cruelty to Animals.

R.S.V.P. *abbr* (= *répondez s'il vous plaît*) SRC.

RTA *n abbr* (= *road traffic accident*) accidente *m* de carretera.

Rt. Hon. *abbr* (*BRIT:* = *Right Honourable*) *tratamiento honorífico de diputado.*

Rt. Rev. *abbr* (= *Right Reverend*) Rvdo.

rub [rʌb] *vt* (*gen*) frotar; (*hard*) restregar ♦ *n* (*gen*) frotamiento; (*touch*) roce *m;* **to ~ sb up** *or* (*US*) **~ sb the wrong way** sacar de quicio a algn.

►**rub down** *vt* (*body*) secar frotando; (*horse*) almohazar.

►**rub in** *vt* (*ointment*) frotar.

►**rub off** *vt* borrarse ♦ *vi* quitarse (frotando); **to ~ off on sb** influir en algn, pegársele a algn.

►**rub out** *vt* borrar ♦ *vi* borrarse.

rubber ['rʌbə*] *n* caucho, goma; (*BRIT: eraser*) goma de borrar.

rubber band *n* goma, gomita.

rubber bullet *n* bala de goma.

rubber plant *n* ficus *m*.

rubber ring *n* (*for swimming*) flotador *m*.

rubber stamp *n* sello (de caucho) ♦ *vt:* **rubber-stamp** (*fig*) aprobar maquinalmente.

rubbery ['rʌbəri] *adj* (como) de goma.

rubbish ['rʌbɪʃ] (*BRIT*) *n* (*from household*) basura; (*waste*) desperdicios *mpl;* (*fig: pej*) tonterías *fpl;* (*trash*) basura, porquería ♦ *vt* (*col*) poner por los suelos; **what you've just said is ~** lo que acabas de decir es una tontería.

rubbish bin *n* cubo *or* bote *m* (*LAM*) de la basura.

rubbish dump *n* (*in town*) vertedero, basurero.

rubbishy ['rʌbɪʃɪ] *adj* de mala calidad, de pacotilla.

rubble ['rʌbl] *n* escombros *mpl*.

ruby ['ruːbɪ] *n* rubí *m*.

RUC *n abbr* (= *Royal Ulster Constabulary*) *fuerza de policía en Irlanda del Norte.*

rucksack ['rʌksæk] *n* mochila.

ructions ['rʌkʃənz] *npl:* **there will be ~** se va a armar la gorda.

ruddy ['rʌdɪ] *adj* (*face*) rubicundo; (*col: damned*) condenado.

rude [ruːd] *adj* (*impolite: person*) grosero, maleducado; (: *word, manners*) rudo, grosero; (*indecent*) indecente; **to be ~ to sb** ser grosero con algn.

rudeness ['ruːdnɪs] *n* grosería, tosquedad *f*.

rudiment ['ruːdɪmənt] *n* rudimento.

rudimentary [ruːdɪ'mɛntərɪ] *adj*

rudimentario.

rue [ruː] *vt* arrepentirse de.

rueful ['ruːful] *adj* arrepentido.

ruffian ['rʌfɪən] *n* matón *m*, criminal *m*.

ruffle ['rʌfl] *vt* (*hair*) despeinar; (*clothes*) arrugar; (*fig: person*) agitar.

rug [rʌg] *n* alfombra; (*BRIT: for knees*) manta.

rugby ['rʌgbɪ] *n* (*also:* ~ **football**) rugby *m*.

rugged ['rʌgɪd] *adj* (*landscape*) accidentado; (*features*) robusto.

rugger ['rʌgə*] *n* (*BRIT col*) rugby *m*.

ruin ['ruːɪn] *n* ruina ♦ *vt* arruinar; (*spoil*) estropear; **~s** *npl* ruinas *fpl*, restos *mpl;* **in ~s** en ruinas.

ruinous ['ruːɪnəs] *adj* ruinoso.

rule [ruːl] *n* (*norm*) norma, costumbre *f;* (*regulation, ruler*) regla; (*government*) dominio; (*dominion etc*): **under British ~** bajo el dominio británico ♦ *vt* (*country, person*) gobernar; (*decide*) disponer; (*draw lines*) trazar ♦ *vi* gobernar; (*LAW*) fallar; **to ~ against/in favour of/on** fallar en contra de/a favor de/sobre; **to ~ that ...** (*umpire, judge*) fallar que ...; **it's against the ~s** está prohibido; **as a ~** por regla general, generalmente; **by ~ of thumb** por experiencia; **majority ~** (*POL*) gobierno mayoritario.

►**rule out** *vt* excluir.

ruled [ruːld] *adj* (*paper*) rayado.

ruler ['ruːlə*] *n* (*sovereign*) soberano; (*for measuring*) regla.

ruling ['ruːlɪŋ] *adj* (*party*) gobernante; (*class*) dirigente ♦ *n* (*LAW*) fallo, decisión *f*.

rum [rʌm] *n* ron *m*.

Rumania [ruː'meɪnɪə] *n* Rumanía.

Rumanian [ruː'meɪnɪən] *adj, n* rumano/a *m/f*.

rumble ['rʌmbl] *n* ruido sordo; (*of thunder*) redoble *m* ♦ *vi* retumbar, hacer un ruido sordo; (*stomach, pipe*) sonar.

rumbustious [rʌm'bʌstʃəs] *adj* (*person*) bullicioso.

rummage ['rʌmɪdʒ] *vi* revolverlo todo.

rumour, (*US*) **rumor** ['ruːmə*] *n* rumor *m* ♦ *vt:* **it is ~ed that ...** se rumorea que ...; **~ has it that ...** corre la voz de que ...

rump [rʌmp] *n* (*of animal*) ancas *fpl*, grupa.

rumple ['rʌmpl] *vt* (*clothes*) arrugar; (*hair*) despeinar.

rump steak *n* filete *m* de lomo.

rumpus ['rʌmpəs] *n* (*col*) lío, jaleo; (*quarrel*) pelea, riña; **to kick up a ~** armar un follón *or* armar bronca.

run [rʌn] *n* (*SPORT*) carrera; (*outing*) paseo, excursión *f;* (*distance travelled*) trayecto; (*series*) serie *f;* (*THEAT*) temporada; (*SKI*) pista; (*in tights, stockings*) carrera; ♦ *vb* (*pt*

ran, *pp* **run** [ræn, rʌn]) *vt* (*operate: business*) dirigir; (: *competition, course*) organizar; (: *hotel, house*) administrar, llevar; (*COMPUT: program*) ejecutar; (*to pass: hand*) pasar; (*bath*): **to ~ a bath** llenar la bañera ♦ *vi* (*gen*) correr; (*work: machine*) funcionar, marchar; (*bus, train: operate*) circular, ir; (: *travel*) ir; (*continue: play*) seguir en cartel; (: *contract*) ser válido; (*flow: river, bath*) fluir; (*colours, washing*) desteñirse; (*in election*) ser candidato; **to go for a ~** ir a correr; **to make a ~ for it** echar(se) a correr, escapar(se), huir; **to have the ~ of sb's house** tener el libre uso de la casa de algn; **a ~ of luck** una racha de suerte; **there was a ~ on** (*meat, tickets*) hubo mucha demanda de; **in the long ~** a la larga; **on the ~** en fuga; **I'll ~ you to the station** te llevaré a la estación en coche; **to ~ a risk** correr un riesgo; **to ~ errands** hacer recados; **it's very cheap to ~** es muy económico; **to be ~ off one's feet** estar ocupadísimo; **to ~ for the bus** correr tras el autobús; **we shall have to ~ for it** tendremos que escapar; **the train ~s between Gatwick and Victoria** el tren circula entre Gatwick y Victoria; **the bus ~s every 20 minutes** el autobús pasa cada 20 minutos; **to ~ on petrol/on diesel/off batteries** funcionar con gasolina/gasoil/baterías; **my salary won't ~ to a car** mi sueldo no me da para comprarme un coche; **the car ran into the lamppost** el coche chocó contra el farol.
▶**run about, run around** *vi* (*children*) correr por todos lados.
▶**run across** *vt fus* (*find*) dar *or* topar con.
▶**run away** *vi* huir.
▶**run down** *vi* (*clock*) pararse ♦ *vt* (*reduce: production*) ir reduciendo; (*factory*) restringir la producción de; (*AUT*) atropellar; (*criticize*) criticar; **to be ~ down** (*person: tired*) encontrarse agotado.
▶**run in** *vt* (*BRIT: car*) rodar.
▶**run into** *vt fus* (*meet: person, trouble*) tropezar con; (*collide with*) chocar con; **to ~ into debt** contraer deudas, endeudarse.
▶**run off** *vt* (*water*) dejar correr ♦ *vi* huir corriendo.
▶**run out** *vi* (*person*) salir corriendo; (*liquid*) irse; (*lease*) caducar, vencer; (*money*) acabarse.
▶**run out of** *vt fus* quedar sin; **I've ~ out of petrol** se me acabó la gasolina.
▶**run over** *vt* (*AUT*) atropellar ♦ *vt fus* (*revise*) repasar.
▶**run through** *vt fus* (*instructions*) repasar.

▶**run up** *vt* (*debt*) incurrir en; **to ~ up against** (*difficulties*) tropezar con.
run-around ['rʌnəraund] *n*: **to give sb the ~** traer a algn al retortero.
runaway ['rʌnəweɪ] *adj* (*horse*) desbocado; (*truck*) sin frenos; (*person*) fugitivo.
rundown ['rʌndaun] *n* (*BRIT: of industry etc*) cierre *m* gradual.
rung [rʌŋ] *pp of* **ring** ♦ *n* (*of ladder*) escalón *m*, peldaño.
run-in ['rʌnɪn] *n* (*col*) altercado.
runner ['rʌnə*] *n* (*in race: person*) corredor(a) *m/f*; (: *horse*) caballo; (*on sledge*) patín *m*; (*wheel*) ruedecilla.
runner bean *n* (*BRIT*) judía escarlata.
runner-up [rʌnər'ʌp] *n* subcampeón/ona *m/f*.
running ['rʌnɪŋ] *n* (*sport*) atletismo; (*race*) carrera ♦ *adj* (*costs, water*) corriente; (*commentary*) en directo; **to be in/out of the ~ for sth** tener/no tener posibilidades de ganar algo; **6 days ~** 6 días seguidos.
running costs *npl* (*of business*) gastos *mpl* corrientes; (*of car*) gastos *mpl* de mantenimiento.
running head *n* (*TYP, WORD PROCESSING*) encabezamiento normal.
running mate *n* (*US POL*) candidato/a a la vice-presidencia.
runny ['rʌnɪ] *adj* derretido.
run-off ['rʌnɔf] *n* (*in contest, election*) desempate *m*; (*extra race*) carrera de desempate.
run-of-the-mill ['rʌnəvðə'mɪl] *adj* común y corriente.
runt [rʌnt] *n* (*also pej*) enano.
run-up ['rʌnʌp] *n*: **~ to** (*election etc*) período previo a.
runway ['rʌnweɪ] *n* (*AVIAT*) pista (de aterrizaje).
rupee [ruː'piː] *n* rupia.
rupture ['rʌptʃə*] *n* (*MED*) hernia ♦ *vt*: **to ~ o.s.** causarse una hernia.
rural ['ruərl] *adj* rural.
ruse [ruːz] *n* ardid *m*.
rush [rʌʃ] *n* ímpetu *m*; (*hurry*) prisa, apuro (*LAM*); (*COMM*) demanda repentina; (*BOT*) junco; (*current*) corriente *f* fuerte, ráfaga ♦ *vt* apresurar; (*work*) hacer de prisa; (*attack: town etc*) asaltar ♦ *vi* correr, precipitarse; **gold ~** fiebre *f* del oro; **we've had a ~ of orders** ha habido una gran demanda; **I'm in a ~ (to do)** tengo prisa *or* apuro (*LAM*) (por hacer); **is there any ~ for this?** ¿te corre prisa esto?; **to ~ sth off** hacer algo de prisa y corriendo.
▶**rush through** *vt fus* (*meal*) comer de prisa; (*book*) leer de prisa; (*work*) hacer de prisa; (*town*) atravesar a toda

velocidad; (*COMM*: *order*) despachar rápidamente.
rush hour *n* horas *fpl* punta.
rush job *n* (*urgent*) trabajo urgente.
rusk [rʌsk] *n* bizcocho tostado.
Russia ['rʌʃə] *n* Rusia.
Russian ['rʌʃən] *adj* ruso ♦ *n* ruso/a; (*LING*) ruso.
rust [rʌst] *n* herrumbre *f*, moho ♦ *vi* oxidarse.
rustic ['rʌstɪk] *adj* rústico.
rustle ['rʌsl] *vi* susurrar ♦ *vt* (*paper*) hacer crujir; (*US*: *cattle*) hurtar, robar.
rustproof ['rʌstpruːf] *adj* inoxidable.
rusty ['rʌstɪ] *adj* oxidado.
rut [rʌt] *n* surco; (*ZOOL*) celo; **to be in a** ~ ser esclavo de la rutina.
ruthless ['ruːθlɪs] *adj* despiadado.
RV *abbr* (= *revised version*) traducción inglesa de la Biblia de 1855 ♦ *n abbr* (*US*) = **recreational vehicle**.
rye [raɪ] *n* centeno.
rye bread *n* pan de centeno.

S s

S, s [ɛs] *n* (*letter*) S, s *f*; **S for Sugar** S de sábado.
S *abbr* (= *Saint*) Sto./a.; (*US SCOL*: *mark*: = *satisfactory*) suficiente; (= *south*) S; = **small**.
SA *n abbr* = **South Africa, South America**.
sabbath ['sæbəθ] *n* domingo; (*Jewish*) sábado.
sabbatical [sə'bætɪkl] *adj*: ~ **year** año sabático.
sabotage ['sæbətɑːʒ] *n* sabotaje *m* ♦ *vt* sabotear.
sabre, (*US*) **saber** ['seɪbə*] *n* sable *m*.
saccharin(e) ['sækərɪn] *n* sacarina.
sachet ['sæʃeɪ] *n* sobrecito.
sack [sæk] *n* (*bag*) saco, costal *m* ♦ *vt* (*dismiss*) despedir, echar; (*plunder*) saquear; **to get the** ~ ser despedido; **to give sb the** ~ despedir *or* echar a algn.
sackful ['sækful] *n* saco.
sacking ['sækɪŋ] *n* (*material*) arpillera.
sacrament ['sækrəmənt] *n* sacramento.
sacred ['seɪkrɪd] *adj* sagrado, santo.
sacred cow *n* (*fig*) vaca sagrada.
sacrifice ['sækrɪfaɪs] *n* sacrificio ♦ *vt*

sacrificar; **to make** ~**s (for sb)** sacrificarse (por algn).
sacrilege ['sækrɪlɪdʒ] *n* sacrilegio.
sacrosanct ['sækrəusæŋkt] *adj* sacrosanto.
sad [sæd] *adj* (*unhappy*) triste; (*deplorable*) lamentable.
sadden ['sædn] *vt* entristecer.
saddle ['sædl] *n* silla (de montar); (*of cycle*) sillín *m* ♦ *vt* (*horse*) ensillar; **to** ~ **sb with sth** (*col*: *task, bill, name*) cargar a algn con algo; (: *responsibility*) gravar a algn con algo; **to be** ~**d with sth** (*col*) quedar cargado con algo.
saddlebag ['sædlbæg] *n* alforja.
sadism ['seɪdɪzm] *n* sadismo.
sadist ['seɪdɪst] *n* sádico/a.
sadistic [sə'dɪstɪk] *adj* sádico.
sadly ['sædlɪ] *adv* tristemente; (*regrettably*) desgraciadamente; ~ **lacking (in)** muy deficiente (en).
sadness ['sædnɪs] *n* tristeza.
sado-masochism [seɪdəu'mæsəkɪzɪm] *n* sadomasoquismo.
sae *abbr* (*BRIT*: = *stamped addressed envelope*) *sobre con las propias señas de uno y con sello.*
safari [sə'fɑːrɪ] *n* safari *m*.
safari park *n* safari *m*.
safe [seɪf] *adj* (*out of danger*) fuera de peligro; (*not dangerous, sure*) seguro; (*unharmed*) ileso; (*trustworthy*) digno de confianza ♦ *n* caja de caudales, caja fuerte; ~ **and sound** sano y salvo; **(just) to be on the** ~ **side** para mayor seguridad; ~ **journey!** ¡buen viaje!; **it is** ~ **to say that ...** se puede decir con confianza que ...
safe bet *n* apuesta segura; **it's a** ~ **she'll turn up** seguro que viene.
safe-breaker ['seɪfbreɪkə*] *n* (*BRIT*) ladrón/ona *m/f* de cajas fuertes.
safe-conduct [seɪf'kɔndʌkt] *n* salvoconducto.
safe-cracker ['seɪfkrækə*] *n* (*US*) = **safe-breaker**.
safe-deposit ['seɪfdɪpɔzɪt] *n* (*vault*) cámara acorazada; (*box*) caja de seguridad *or* de caudales.
safeguard ['seɪfgɑːd] *n* protección *f*, garantía ♦ *vt* proteger, defender.
safe haven *n* refugio.
safekeeping ['seɪf'kiːpɪŋ] *n* custodia.
safely ['seɪflɪ] *adv* seguramente, con seguridad; (*without mishap*) sin peligro; **I can** ~ **say** puedo decir *or* afirmar con toda seguridad.
safeness ['seɪfnɪs] *n* seguridad *f*.
safe passage *n* garantías *fpl* para

marcharse en libertad.

safe sex *n* sexo seguro *or* sin riesgo.

safety ['seɪftɪ] *n* seguridad *f* ♦ *cpd* de seguridad; **road** ~ seguridad *f* en carretera; ~ **first!** ¡precaución!

safety belt *n* cinturón *m* (de seguridad).

safety catch *n* seguro.

safety net *n* red *f* (de seguridad).

safety pin *n* imperdible *m*, seguro (*LAM*).

safety valve *n* válvula de seguridad *or* de escape.

saffron ['sæfrən] *n* azafrán *m*.

sag [sæg] *vi* aflojarse.

saga ['sɑːgə] *n* (*HISTORY*) saga; (*fig*) epopeya.

sage [seɪdʒ] *n* (*herb*) salvia; (*man*) sabio.

Sagittarius [sædʒɪ'tɛərɪəs] *n* Sagitario.

sago ['seɪgəu] *n* sagú *m*.

Sahara [sə'hɑːrə] *n*: **the** ~ **(Desert)** el Sáhara.

Sahel [sæ'hɛl] *n* Sahel *m*.

said [sɛd] *pt, pp of* **say**.

Saigon [saɪ'gɔn] *n* Saigón *m*.

sail [seɪl] *n* (*on boat*) vela ♦ *vt* (*boat*) gobernar ♦ *vi* (*travel: ship*) navegar; (: *passenger*) pasear en barco; (*set off: also*: **to set** ~) zarpar; **to go for a** ~ dar un paseo en barco; **they** ~**ed into Copenhagen** arribaron a Copenhague.

▶**sail through** *vt fus* (*exam*) aprobar fácilmente.

sailboat ['seɪlbəut] *n* (*US*) velero, barco de vela.

sailing ['seɪlɪŋ] *n* (*SPORT*) balandrismo; **to go** ~ salir en balandro.

sailing ship *n* barco de vela.

sailor ['seɪlə*] *n* marinero, marino.

saint [seɪnt] *n* santo; **S~ John** San Juan.

saintliness ['seɪntlɪnɪs] *n* santidad *f*.

saintly ['seɪntlɪ] *adj* santo.

sake [seɪk] *n*: **for the** ~ **of** por; **for the** ~ **of argument** digamos, es un decir; **art for art's** ~ el arte por el arte.

salad ['sæləd] *n* ensalada; **tomato** ~ ensalada de tomate.

salad bowl *n* ensaladera.

salad cream *n* (*BRIT*) mayonesa.

salad dressing *n* aliño.

salad oil *n* aceite *m* para ensalada.

salami [sə'lɑːmɪ] *n* salami *m*, salchichón *m*.

salaried ['sælərɪd] *adj* asalariado.

salary ['sælərɪ] *n* sueldo.

salary earner *n* asalariado/a.

salary scale *n* escala salarial.

sale [seɪl] *n* venta; (*at reduced prices*) liquidación *f*, saldo; "**for** ~" "se vende"; **on** ~ en venta; **on** ~ **or return** (*goods*) venta por reposición; **closing-down** *or*

(*US*) **liquidation** ~ liquidación *f*; ~ **and lease back** venta y arrendamiento al vendedor.

saleroom ['seɪlruːm] *n* sala de subastas.

sales assistant *n* (*BRIT*) dependiente/a *m/f*.

sales campaign *n* campaña de venta.

sales clerk *n* (*US*) dependiente/a *m/f*.

sales conference *n* conferencia de ventas.

sales drive *n* promoción *f* de ventas.

sales figures *npl* cifras *fpl* de ventas.

sales force *n* personal *m* de ventas.

salesman ['seɪlzmən] *n* vendedor *m*; (*in shop*) dependiente *m*; (*representative*) viajante *m*.

sales manager *n* gerente *m/f* de ventas.

salesmanship ['seɪlzmənʃɪp] *n* arte *m* de vender.

sales meeting *n* reunión *f* de ventas.

sales tax *n* (*US*) = **purchase tax**.

saleswoman ['seɪlzwumən] *n* vendedora; (*in shop*) dependienta; (*representative*) viajante *f*.

salient ['seɪlɪənt] *adj* (*features, points*) sobresaliente.

saline ['seɪlaɪn] *adj* salino.

saliva [sə'laɪvə] *n* saliva.

sallow ['sæləu] *adj* cetrino.

sally forth, sally out *vi* salir, ponerse en marcha.

salmon ['sæmən] *n* (*pl inv*) salmón *m*.

salon ['sælɔn] *n* (*hairdressing* ~, *beauty* ~) salón *m*.

saloon [sə'luːn] *n* (*US*) bar *m*, taberna; (*BRIT AUT*) (coche *m* de) turismo; (*ship's lounge*) cámara, salón *m*.

SALT [sɔːlt] *n abbr* (= *Strategic Arms Limitation Treaty*) tratado SALT.

salt [sɔːlt] *n* sal *f* ♦ *vt* salar; (*put* ~ *on*) poner sal en; **an old** ~ un lobo de mar.

▶**salt away** *vt* (*col: money*) ahorrar.

salt cellar *n* salero.

salt mine *n* mina de sal.

saltwater ['sɔːlt'wɔːtə*] *adj* (*fish etc*) de agua salada, de mar.

salty ['sɔːltɪ] *adj* salado.

salubrious [sə'luːbrɪəs] *adj* sano; (*fig: district etc*) atractivo.

salutary ['sæljutərɪ] *adj* saludable.

salute [sə'luːt] *n* saludo; (*of guns*) salva ♦ *vt* saludar.

salvage ['sælvɪdʒ] *n* (*saving*) salvamento, recuperación *f*; (*things saved*) objetos *mpl* salvados ♦ *vt* salvar.

salvage vessel *n* buque *m* de salvamento.

salvation [sæl'veɪʃən] *n* salvación *f*.

Salvation Army *n* Ejército de Salvación.

salve [sælv] *n* (*cream etc*) ungüento,

bálsamo.
salver ['sælvə*] n bandeja.
salvo ['sælvəu] n (MIL) salva.
Samaritan [sə'mærɪtən] n: **to call the ~s**
llamar al teléfono de la esperanza.
same [seɪm] adj mismo ♦ pron: **the ~ el**
mismo/la misma; **the ~ book as** el mismo
libro que; **on the ~ day** el mismo día; **at
the ~ time** (at the ~ moment) al mismo
tiempo; (yet) sin embargo; **all or just the
~** sin embargo, aun así; **they're one and
the ~** (person) son la misma persona;
(thing) son iguales; **to do the ~ (as sb)**
hacer lo mismo (que otro); **and the ~ to
you!** ¡igualmente!; ~ **here!** ¡yo también!;
the ~ again (in bar etc) otro igual.
sampan ['sæmpæn] n sampán m.
sample ['sɑːmpl] n muestra ♦ vt (food, wine)
probar; **to take a ~** tomar una muestra;
free ~ muestra gratuita.
sanatorium, pl -ria [sænə'tɔːrɪəm, -rɪə] n
(BRIT) sanatorio.
sanctify ['sæŋktɪfaɪ] vt santificar.
sanctimonious [sæŋktɪ'məunɪəs] adj
santurrón/ona.
sanction ['sæŋkʃən] n sanción f ♦ vt
sancionar; **to impose economic ~s on** or
against imponer sanciones económicas a
or contra.
sanctity ['sæŋktɪtɪ] n (gen) santidad f;
(inviolability) inviolabilidad f.
sanctuary ['sæŋktjuərɪ] n (gen) santuario;
(refuge) asilo, refugio.
sand [sænd] n arena; (beach) playa ♦ vt
(also: ~ **down**: wood etc) lijar.
sandal ['sændl] n sandalia.
sandalwood ['sændlwud] n sándalo.
sandbag ['sændbæg] n saco de arena.
sandblast ['sændblɑːst] vt limpiar con
chorro de arena.
sandbox ['sændbɔks] n (US) = sandpit.
sandcastle ['sændkɑːsl] n castillo de arena.
sand dune n duna.
sander ['sændə*] n pulidora.
S & M n abbr (= sadomasochism)
sadomasoquismo.
sandpaper ['sændpeɪpə*] n papel m de lija.
sandpit ['sændpɪt] n (for children) cajón m
de arena.
sands [sændz] npl playa sg de arena.
sandstone ['sændstəun] n piedra arenisca.
sandstorm ['sændstɔːm] n tormenta de
arena.
sandwich ['sændwɪtʃ] n bocadillo (SP),
sandwich m (LAM) ♦ vt (also: ~ **in**)
intercalar; **to be ~ed between** estar
apretujado entre; **cheese/ham ~**
sandwich de queso/jamón.

sandwich board n cartelón m.
sandwich course n (BRIT) programa que
intercala períodos de estudio con
prácticas profesionales.
sandy ['sændɪ] adj arenoso; (colour) rojizo.
sane [seɪn] adj cuerdo, sensato.
sang [sæŋ] pt of **sing**.
sanitarium [sænɪ'tɛərɪəm] n (US)
= **sanatorium**.
sanitary ['sænɪtərɪ] adj (system,
arrangements) sanitario; (clean) higiénico.
sanitary towel, (US) **sanitary napkin** n
paño higiénico, compresa.
sanitation [sænɪ'teɪʃən] n (in house)
servicios mpl higiénicos; (in town)
servicio de desinfección.
sanitation department n (US)
departamento de limpieza y recogida de
basuras.
sanity ['sænɪtɪ] n cordura; (of judgment)
sensatez f.
sank [sæŋk] pt of **sink**.
San Marino ['sænmə'riːnəu] n San Marino.
Santa Claus [sæntə'klɔːz] n San Nicolás m,
Papá Noel m.
Santiago [sæntɪ'ɑːgəu] n (also: ~ **de Chile**)
Santiago (de Chile).
sap [sæp] n (of plants) savia ♦ vt (strength)
minar, agotar.
sapling ['sæplɪŋ] n árbol nuevo or joven.
sapphire ['sæfaɪə*] n zafiro.
Saragossa [særə'gɔsə] n Zaragoza.
sarcasm ['sɑːkæzm] n sarcasmo.
sarcastic [sɑː'kæstɪk] adj sarcástico; **to be
~** ser sarcástico.
sarcophagus, pl sarcophagi [sɑː'kɔfəgəs,
-gaɪ] n sarcófago.
sardine [sɑː'diːn] n sardina.
Sardinia [sɑː'dɪnɪə] n Cerdeña.
Sardinian [sɑː'dɪnɪən] adj, n sardo/a m/f.
sardonic [sɑː'dɔnɪk] adj sardónico.
sari ['sɑːrɪ] n sari m.
SAS n abbr (BRIT MIL: = Special Air Service)
cuerpo del ejército británico encargado
de misiones clandestinas.
SASE n abbr (US: = self-addressed stamped
envelope) sobre con las propias señas de
uno y con sello.
sash [sæʃ] n faja.
Sask. abbr (Canada) = Saskatchewan.
SAT n abbr (US) = Scholastic Aptitude Test.
sat [sæt] pt, pp of **sit**.
Sat. abbr (= Saturday) sáb.
Satan ['seɪtn] n Satanás m.
satanic [sə'tænɪk] adj satánico.
satchel ['sætʃl] n bolsa; (child's) cartera,
mochila (LAM).
sated ['seɪtɪd] adj (appetite, person) saciado.

satellite ['sætəlaɪt] *n* satélite *m*.
satellite television *n* televisión *f* por satélite.
satiate ['seɪʃɪeɪt] *vt* saciar, hartar.
satin ['sætɪn] *n* raso ♦ *adj* de raso; **with a ~ finish** satinado.
satire ['sætaɪə*] *n* sátira.
satirical [sə'tɪrɪkl] *adj* satírico.
satirist ['sætɪrɪst] *n* (*writer etc*) escritor(a) *m/f* satírico/a; (*cartoonist*) caricaturista *m/f*.
satirize ['sætɪraɪz] *vt* satirizar.
satisfaction [sætɪs'fækʃən] *n* satisfacción *f*; **it gives me great ~** es para mí una gran satisfacción; **has it been done to your ~?** ¿se ha hecho a su satisfacción?
satisfactorily [sætɪs'fæktərɪlɪ] *adv* satisfactoriamente, de modo satisfactorio.
satisfactory [sætɪs'fæktərɪ] *adj* satisfactorio.
satisfied ['sætɪsfaɪd] *adj* satisfecho; **to be ~ (with sth)** estar satisfecho (de algo).
satisfy ['sætɪsfaɪ] *vt* satisfacer; (*pay*) liquidar; (*convince*) convencer; **to ~ the requirements** llenar los requisitos; **to ~ sb that** convencer a algn de que; **to ~ o.s. of sth** convencerse de algo.
satisfying ['sætɪsfaɪɪŋ] *adj* satisfactorio.
satsuma [sæt'suːmə] *n* satsuma.
saturate ['sætʃəreɪt] *vt*: **to ~ (with)** empapar *or* saturar (de).
saturated fat [sætʃəreɪtɪd-] *n* grasa saturada.
saturation [sætʃə'reɪʃən] *n* saturación *f*.
Saturday ['sætədɪ] *n* sábado.
sauce [sɔːs] *n* salsa; (*sweet*) crema; (*fig: cheek*) frescura.
saucepan ['sɔːspən] *n* cacerola, olla.
saucer ['sɔːsə*] *n* platillo.
saucily ['sɔːsɪlɪ] *adv* con frescura, descaradamente.
sauciness ['sɔːsɪnɪs] *n* frescura, descaro.
saucy ['sɔːsɪ] *adj* fresco, descarado.
Saudi Arabia ['saʊdɪ-] *n* Arabia Saudí *or* Saudita.
Saudi (Arabian) ['saʊdɪ-] *adj, n* saudí *m/f*, saudita *m/f*.
sauna ['sɔːnə] *n* sauna.
saunter ['sɔːntə*] *vi* deambular.
sausage ['sɔsɪdʒ] *n* salchicha; (*salami etc*) salchichón *m*.
sausage roll *n* empanadilla.
sauté ['səʊteɪ] *adj* (*CULIN: potatoes*) salteado; (: *onions*) dorado, rehogado ♦ *vt* saltear; dorar.
savage ['sævɪdʒ] *adj* (*cruel, fierce*) feroz, furioso; (*primitive*) salvaje ♦ *n* salvaje *m/f* ♦ *vt* (*attack*) embestir.

savagely ['sævɪdʒlɪ] *adv* con ferocidad, furiosamente; de modo salvaje.
savagery ['sævɪdʒrɪ] *n* ferocidad *f*; salvajismo.
save [seɪv] *vt* (*rescue*) salvar, rescatar; (*money, time*) ahorrar; (*put by*) guardar; (*COMPUT*) salvar (y guardar); (*avoid: trouble*) evitar ♦ *vi* (*also: ~ up*) ahorrar ♦ *n* (*SPORT*) parada ♦ *prep* salvo, excepto; **to ~ face** salvar las apariencias; **God ~ the Queen!** ¡Dios guarde a la Reina!, ¡Viva la Reina!; **I ~d you a piece of cake** te he guardado un trozo de tarta; **it will ~ me an hour** con ello ganaré una hora.
saving ['seɪvɪŋ] *n* (*on price etc*) economía ♦ *adj*: **the ~ grace of** el único mérito de; **~s** *npl* ahorros *mpl*; **to make ~s** economizar.
savings account *n* cuenta de ahorros.
savings bank *n* caja de ahorros.
saviour, (US) savior ['seɪvjə*] *n* salvador(a) *m/f*.
savoir-faire ['sævwɑː'fɛə*] *n* don *m* de gentes.
savour, (US) savor ['seɪvə*] *n* sabor *m*, gusto ♦ *vt* saborear.
savo(u)ry ['seɪvərɪ] *adj* sabroso; (*dish: not sweet*) salado.
savvy ['sævɪ] *n* (*col*) conocimiento, experiencia.
saw [sɔː] *pt of* **see** ♦ *n* (*tool*) sierra ♦ *vt* (*pt* **sawed**, *pp* **sawed** *or* **sawn** [sɔːn]) serrar; **to ~ sth up** (a)serrar algo.
sawdust ['sɔːdʌst] *n* (a)serrín *m*.
sawmill ['sɔːmɪl] *n* aserradero.
sawn [sɔːn] *pp of* **saw**.
sawn-off ['sɔːnɔf], (*US*) **sawed-off** ['sɔːdɔf] *adj*: **~ shotgun** escopeta de cañones recortados.
saxophone ['sæksəfəʊn] *n* saxófono.
say [seɪ] *n*: **to have one's ~** expresar su opinión; **to have a ~ or some ~ in sth** tener voz y voto en algo ♦ *vt, vi* (*pt, pp* **said** [sɛd]) decir; **to ~ yes/no** decir que sí/no; **my watch ~s 3 o'clock** mi reloj marca las tres; **that is to ~** es decir; **that goes without ~ing** ni que decir tiene; **she said (that) I was to give you this** me pidió que te diera esto; **I should ~ it's worth about £100** yo diría que vale unas 100 libras; **~ after me** repite lo que yo diga; **shall we ~ Tuesday?** ¿quedamos, por ejemplo, el martes?; **that doesn't ~ much for him** eso no dice nada a su favor; **when all is said and done** al fin y al cabo, a fin de cuentas; **there is something** *or* **a lot to be said for it** hay algo *or* mucho que decir a su favor.
saying ['seɪɪŋ] *n* dicho, refrán *m*.
say-so ['seɪsəʊ] *n* (*col*) autorización *f*.

SBA n abbr (US) = Small Business Administration.
SC n abbr (US) = **Supreme Court** ♦ abbr (US) = South Carolina.
s/c abbr = self-contained.
scab [skæb] n costra; (pej) esquirol(a) m/f.
scaffold ['skæfəld] n (for execution) cadalso.
scaffolding ['skæfəldɪŋ] n andamio, andamiaje m.
scald [skɔːld] n escaldadura ♦ vt escaldar.
scalding ['skɔːldɪŋ] adj (also: ~ **hot**) hirviendo, que arde.
scale [skeɪl] n (gen, MUS) escala; (of fish) escama; (of salaries, fees etc) escalafón m ♦ vt (mountain) escalar; (tree) trepar; ~**s** npl (small) balanza sg; (large) báscula sg; **on a large** ~ a gran escala; ~ **of charges** tarifa, lista de precios; **pay** ~ escala salarial; **to draw sth to** ~ dibujar algo a escala.
▶**scale down** vt reducir.
scaled-down [skeɪld'daun] adj reducido proporcionalmente.
scale model n modelo a escala.
scallop ['skɔləp] n (ZOOL) venera; (SEWING) festón m.
scalp [skælp] n cabellera ♦ vt escalpar.
scalpel ['skælpl] n bisturí m.
scam [skæm] n (col) estafa, timo.
scamper ['skæmpə*] vi: **to** ~ **away**, ~ **off** escabullirse.
scampi ['skæmpɪ] npl gambas fpl.
scan [skæn] vt (examine) escudriñar; (glance at quickly) dar un vistazo a; (TV, RADAR) explorar, registrar ♦ n (MED) examen m ultrasónico.
scandal ['skændl] n escándalo; (gossip) chismes mpl.
scandalize ['skændəlaɪz] vt escandalizar.
scandalous ['skændələs] adj escandaloso.
Scandinavia [skændɪ'neɪvɪə] n Escandinavia.
Scandinavian [skændɪ'neɪvɪən] adj, n escandinavo/a m/f.
scanner ['skænə*] n (RADAR, MED) escáner m.
scant [skænt] adj escaso.
scantily ['skæntɪlɪ] adv: ~ **clad** or **dressed** ligero de ropa.
scantiness ['skæntɪnɪs] n escasez f, insuficiencia.
scanty ['skæntɪ] adj (meal) insuficiente; (clothes) ligero.
scapegoat ['skeɪpgəut] n cabeza de turco, chivo expiatorio.
scar [skɑː] n cicatriz f ♦ vt marcar con una cicatriz ♦ vi cicatrizarse.
scarce [skɛəs] adj escaso.

scarcely ['skɛəslɪ] adv apenas; ~ **anybody** casi nadie; **I can** ~ **believe it** casi no puedo creerlo.
scarceness ['skɛəsnɪs], **scarcity** ['skɛəsɪtɪ] n escasez f.
scarcity value n valor m de escasez.
scare [skɛə*] n susto, sobresalto; (panic) pánico ♦ vt asustar, espantar; **to** ~ **sb stiff** dar a algn un susto de muerte; **bomb** ~ amenaza de bomba.
▶**scare away, scare off** vt espantar, ahuyentar.
scarecrow ['skɛəkrəu] n espantapájaros m inv.
scared [skɛəd] adj: **to be** ~ asustarse, estar asustado.
scaremonger ['skɛəmʌŋgə*] n alarmista m/f.
scarf, pl **scarves** [skɑːf, skɑːvz] n (long) bufanda; (square) pañuelo.
scarlet ['skɑːlɪt] adj escarlata.
scarlet fever n escarlatina.
scarper ['skɑːpə*] vi (BRIT col) largarse.
scarred [skɑːd] adj lleno de cicatrices.
scarves [skɑːvz] npl of **scarf**.
scary ['skɛərɪ] adj (col) de miedo; **it's** ~ **da** miedo.
scathing ['skeɪðɪŋ] adj mordaz; **to be** ~ **about sth** criticar algo duramente.
scatter ['skætə*] vt (spread) esparcir, desparramar; (put to flight) dispersar ♦ vi desparramarse; dispersarse.
scatterbrained ['skætəbreɪnd] adj ligero de cascos.
scavenge ['skævɪndʒ] vi: **to** ~ **(for)** (person) revolver entre la basura (para encontrar); **to** ~ **for food** (hyenas etc) nutrirse de carroña.
scavenger ['skævɪndʒə*] n (person) mendigo/a que rebusca en la basura; (ZOOL: animal) animal m de carroña; (: bird) ave f de carroña.
SCE n abbr = Scottish Certificate of Education.
scenario [sɪ'nɑːrɪəu] n (THEAT) argumento; (CINE) guión m; (fig) escenario.
scene [siːn] n (THEAT, fig etc) escena; (of crime, accident) escenario; (sight, view) vista, perspectiva; (fuss) escándalo; **the political** ~ **in Spain** el panorama político español; **behind the** ~**s** (also fig) entre bastidores; **to appear** or **come on the** ~ (also fig) aparecer, presentarse; **to make a** ~ (col: fuss) armar un escándalo.
scenery ['siːnərɪ] n (THEAT) decorado; (landscape) paisaje m.
scenic ['siːnɪk] adj (picturesque) pintoresco.
scent [sɛnt] n perfume m, olor m; (fig: track) rastro, pista; (sense of smell) olfato ♦ vt

perfumar; (*suspect*) presentir; **to put** *or*
throw sb off the ~ (*fig*) despistar a algn.
sceptic, (*US*) **skeptic** ['skɛptɪk] *n*
escéptico/a.
sceptical, (*US*) **skeptical** ['skɛptɪkl] *adj*
escéptico.
scepticism, (*US*) **skepticism** ['skɛptɪsɪzm]
n escepticismo.
sceptre, (*US*) **scepter** ['sɛptə*] *n* cetro.
schedule ['ʃɛdjuːl, (*US*) 'skɛdjuːl] *n* (*of
trains*) horario; (*of events*) programa *m*;
(*list*) lista ♦ *vt* (*timetable*) establecer el
horario de; (*list*) catalogar; (*visit*) fijar la
hora de; **on** ~ a la hora, sin retraso; **to be
ahead of/behind** ~ estar adelantado/
retrasado; **we are working to a very tight**
~ tenemos un programa de trabajo muy
apretado; **everything went according to** ~
todo salió según lo previsto; **the meeting
is** ~**d for 7** *or* **to begin at 7** la reunión está
fijada para las 7.
scheduled ['ʃɛdjuːld, (*US*) 'skɛdjuːld] *adj*
(*date, time*) fijado; (*visit, event, bus, train*)
programado; (*stop*) previsto; ~ **flight**
vuelo regular.
schematic [skɪ'mætɪk] *adj* (*diagram etc*)
esquemático.
scheme [skiːm] *n* (*plan*) plan *m*, proyecto;
(*method*) esquema *m*; (*plot*) intriga; (*trick*)
ardid *m*; (*arrangement*) disposición *f*;
(*pension* ~ *etc*) sistema *m* ♦ *vt* proyectar
♦ *vi* (*plan*) hacer proyectos; (*intrigue*)
intrigar; **colour** ~ combinación *f* de
colores.
scheming ['skiːmɪŋ] *adj* intrigante.
schism ['skɪzəm] *n* cisma *m*.
schizophrenia [skɪtsə'friːnɪə] *n*
esquizofrenia.
schizophrenic [skɪtsə'frɛnɪk] *adj*
esquizofrénico.
scholar ['skɔlə*] *n* (*pupil*) alumno/a,
estudiante *m/f*; (*learned person*) sabio/a,
erudito/a.
scholarly ['skɔləlɪ] *adj* erudito.
scholarship ['skɔləʃɪp] *n* erudición *f*; (*grant*)
beca.
school [skuːl] *n* (*gen*) escuela, colegio; (*in
university*) facultad *f*; (*of fish*) banco ♦ *vt*
(*animal*) amaestrar; **to be at** *or* **go to** ~ ir
al colegio *or* a la escuela.
school age *n* edad *f* escolar.
schoolbook ['skuːlbuk] *n* libro de texto.
schoolboy ['skuːlbɔɪ] *n* alumno.
schoolchild, *pl* **-children** ['skuːltʃaɪld,
-tʃɪldrən] *n* alumno/a.
schooldays ['skuːldeɪz] *npl* años *mpl* del
colegio.
schoolgirl ['skuːlgəːl] *n* alumna.

schooling ['skuːlɪŋ] *n* enseñanza.
school-leaver ['skuːlliːvə*] *n* (*BRIT*) joven
*que ha terminado la educación
secundaria.*
schoolmaster ['skuːlmɑːstə*] *n* (*primary*)
maestro; (*secondary*) profesor *m*.
schoolmistress ['skuːlmɪstrɪs] *n* (*primary*)
maestra; (*secondary*) profesora.
schoolroom ['skuːlrum] *n* clase *f*.
schoolteacher ['skuːltiːtʃə*] *n* (*primary*)
maestro/a; (*secondary*) profesor(a) *m/f*.
schoolyard ['skuːljɑːd] *n* (*US*) patio del
colegio.
schooner ['skuːnə*] *n* (*ship*) goleta.
sciatica [saɪ'ætɪkə] *n* ciática.
science ['saɪəns] *n* ciencia; **the** ~**s** las
ciencias.
science fiction *n* ciencia-ficción *f*.
scientific [saɪən'tɪfɪk] *adj* científico.
scientist ['saɪəntɪst] *n* científico/a.
sci-fi ['saɪfaɪ] *n abbr* (*col*) = **science fiction**.
Scilly Isles ['sɪlɪ-], **Scillies** ['sɪlɪz] *npl*: **the** ~
las Islas Sorlingas.
scintillating ['sɪntɪleɪtɪŋ] *adj* (*wit,
conversation, company*) brillante,
chispeante, ingenioso.
scissors ['sɪzəz] *npl* tijeras *fpl*; **a pair of** ~
unas tijeras.
scoff [skɔf] *vt* (*BRIT col: eat*) engullir ♦ *vi*: **to**
~ **(at)** (*mock*) mofarse (de).
scold [skəuld] *vt* regañar.
scolding ['skəuldɪŋ] *n* riña, reprimenda.
scone [skɔn] *n pastel de pan.*
scoop [skuːp] *n* cucharón *m*; (*for flour etc*)
pala; (*PRESS*) exclusiva ♦ *vt* (*COMM:
market*) adelantarse a; (: *profit*) sacar;
(*COMM, PRESS: competitors*) adelantarse a.
▶**scoop out** *vt* excavar.
▶**scoop up** *vt* recoger.
scooter ['skuːtə*] *n* (*motor cycle*) Vespa ®;
(*toy*) patinete *m*.
scope [skəup] *n* (*of plan, undertaking*)
ámbito; (*reach*) alcance *m*; (*of person*)
competencia; (*opportunity*) libertad *f* (de
acción); **there is plenty of** ~ **for
improvement** hay bastante campo para
efectuar mejoras.
scorch [skɔːtʃ] *vt* (*clothes*) chamuscar;
(*earth, grass*) quemar, secar.
scorcher ['skɔːtʃə*] *n* (*col: hot day*) día *m*
abrasador.
scorching ['skɔːtʃɪŋ] *adj* abrasador(a).
score [skɔː*] *n* (*points etc*) puntuación *f*;
(*MUS*) partitura; (*reckoning*) cuenta;
(*twenty*) veintena ♦ *vt* (*goal, point*) ganar;
(*mark, cut*) rayar ♦ *vi* marcar un tanto;
(*FOOTBALL*) marcar un gol; (*keep score*)
llevar el tanteo; **to keep (the)** ~ llevar la

cuenta; **to have an old ~ to settle with sb** (*fig*) tener cuentas pendientes con algn; **on that ~** en lo que se refiere a eso; **~s of people** (*fig*) muchísima gente, cantidad de gente; **to ~ 6 out of 10** obtener una puntuación de 6 sobre 10.
▶**score out** *vt* tachar.
scoreboard ['skɔːbɔːd] *n* marcador *m*.
scoreline ['skɔːlaɪn] *n* (*SPORT*) resultado final.
scorer ['skɔːrə*] *n* marcador *m*; (*keeping score*) encargado/a del marcador.
scorn [skɔːn] *n* desprecio ♦ *vt* despreciar.
scornful ['skɔːnful] *adj* desdeñoso, despreciativo.
scornfully ['skɔːnfulɪ] *adv* desdeñosamente, con desprecio.
Scorpio ['skɔːpɪəu] *n* Escorpión *m*.
scorpion ['skɔːpɪən] *n* alacrán *m*, escorpión *m*.
Scot [skɔt] *n* escocés/esa *m/f*.
Scotch [skɔtʃ] *n* whisky *m* escocés.
scotch [skɔtʃ] *vt* (*rumour*) desmentir; (*plan*) frustrar.
Scotch tape ® *n* (*US*) cinta adhesiva, celo, scotch ® *m*.
scot-free [skɔt'friː] *adv*: **to get off ~** (*unpunished*) salir impune; (*unhurt*) salir ileso.
Scotland ['skɔtlənd] *n* Escocia.
Scots [skɔts] *adj* escocés/esa.
Scotsman ['skɔtsmən] *n* escocés *m*.
Scotswoman ['skɔtswumən] *n* escocesa.
Scottish ['skɔtɪʃ] *adj* escocés/esa; **the ~ National Party** *partido político independista escocés*.
scoundrel ['skaundrəl] *n* canalla *m/f*, sinvergüenza *m/f*.
scour ['skauə*] *vt* (*clean*) fregar, estregar; (*search*) recorrer, registrar.
scourer ['skauərə*] *n* (*pad*) estropajo; (*powder*) limpiador *m*.
scourge [skɜːdʒ] *n* azote *m*.
scout [skaut] *n* (*MIL, also*: **boy ~**) explorador *m*.
▶**scout around** *vi* reconocer el terreno.
scowl [skaul] *vi* fruncir el ceño; **to ~ at sb** mirar con ceño a algn.
scrabble ['skræbl] *vi* (*claw*): **to ~ (at)** arañar ♦ *n*: **S~** ® Intelect *m* ®; **to ~ about** *or* **around for sth** revolver todo buscando algo.
scraggy ['skrægɪ] *adj* flaco, delgaducho.
scram [skræm] *vi* (*col*) largarse.
scramble ['skræmbl] *n* (*climb*) subida (difícil); (*struggle*) pelea ♦ *vi*: **to ~ out/ through** salir/abrirse paso con dificultad; **to ~ for** pelear por; **to go scrambling**

(*SPORT*) hacer motocrós.
scrambled eggs ['skræmbld-] *npl* huevos *mpl* revueltos.
scrap [skræp] *n* (*bit*) pedacito; (*fig*) pizca; (*fight*) riña, bronca; (*also*: **~ iron**) chatarra, hierro viejo ♦ *vt* (*discard*) desechar, descartar ♦ *vi* reñir, armar (una) bronca; **~s** *npl* (*waste*) sobras *fpl*, desperdicios *mpl*; **to sell sth for ~** vender algo como chatarra.
scrapbook ['skræpbuk] *n* álbum *m* de recortes.
scrap dealer *n* chatarrero/a.
scrape [skreɪp] *n* (*fig*) lío, apuro ♦ *vt* raspar; (*skin etc*) rasguñar; (**~ against**) rozar.
▶**scrape through** *vi* (*succeed*) salvarse por los pelos; (*exam*) aprobar por los pelos.
scraper ['skreɪpə*] *n* raspador *m*.
scrap heap *n* (*fig*): **on the ~** desperdiciado; **to throw sth on the ~** desechar *or* descartar algo.
scrap iron *n* chatarra.
scrap merchant *n* (*BRIT*) chatarrero/a.
scrap metal *n* chatarra, desecho de metal.
scrap paper *n* pedazos *mpl* de papel.
scrappy ['skræpɪ] *adj* (*essay etc*) deshilvanado; (*education*) incompleto.
scrap yard *n* depósito de chatarra; (*for cars*) cementerio de coches.
scratch [skrætʃ] *n* rasguño; (*from claw*) arañazo ♦ *adj*: **~ team** equipo improvisado ♦ *vt* (*record*) rayar; (*with claw, nail*) rasguñar, arañar; (*COMPUT*) borrar ♦ *vi* rascarse; **to start from ~** partir de cero; **to be up to ~** cumplir con los requisitos.
scratchpad ['skrætʃpæd] *n* (*US*) bloc *m* de notas.
scrawl [skrɔːl] *n* garabatos *mpl* ♦ *vi* hacer garabatos.
scrawny ['skrɔːnɪ] *adj* (*person, neck*) flaco.
scream [skriːm] *n* chillido ♦ *vi* chillar; **it was a ~** (*fig, col*) fue para morirse de risa *or* muy divertido; **he's a ~** (*fig, col*) es muy divertido *or* de lo más gracioso; **to ~ at sb (to do sth)** gritarle a algn (para que haga algo).
scree [skriː] *n* cono de desmoronamiento.
screech [skriːtʃ] *vi* chirriar.
screen [skriːn] *n* (*CINE, TV*) pantalla; (*movable*) biombo; (*wall*) tabique *m*; (*also*: **wind~**) parabrisas *m inv* ♦ *vt* (*conceal*) tapar; (*from the wind etc*) proteger; (*film*) proyectar; (*fig: person: for security*) investigar; (: *for illness*) hacer una exploración a.
screen editing *n* (*COMPUT*) corrección *f* en pantalla.

screening ['skri:nɪŋ] n (of film) proyección f; (for security) investigación f; (MED) exploración f.

screen memory n (COMPUT) memoria de la pantalla.

screenplay ['skri:npleɪ] n guión m.

screen test n prueba de pantalla.

screw [skru:] n tornillo; (propeller) hélice f ♦ vt atornillar; **to ~ sth to the wall** fijar algo a la pared con tornillos.

▶**screw up** vt (paper, material etc) arrugar; (col: ruin) fastidiar; **to ~ up one's eyes** arrugar el entrecejo; **to ~ up one's face** torcer or arrugar la cara.

screwdriver ['skru:draɪvə*] n destornillador m.

screwed-up ['skru:d'ʌp] adj (col): **she's totally ~** está trastornada.

screwy ['skru:ɪ] adj (col) chiflado.

scribble ['skrɪbl] n garabatos mpl ♦ vt escribir con prisa; **to ~ sth down** garabatear algo.

script [skrɪpt] n (CINE etc) guión m; (writing) escritura, letra.

scripted ['skrɪptɪd] adj (RADIO, TV) escrito.

Scripture ['skrɪptʃə*] n Sagrada Escritura.

scriptwriter ['skrɪptraɪtə*] n guionista m/f.

scroll [skrəul] n rollo ♦ vt (COMPUT) desplazar.

scrotum ['skrəutəm] n escroto.

scrounge [skraundʒ] (col) vt: **to ~ sth off or from sb** gorronear algo a algn ♦ vi: **to ~ on sb** vivir a costa de algn.

scrounger ['skraundʒə*] n gorrón/ona m/f.

scrub [skrʌb] n (clean) fregado; (land) maleza ♦ vt fregar, restregar; (reject) cancelar, anular.

scrubbing brush ['skrʌbɪŋ-] n cepillo de fregar.

scruff [skrʌf] n: **by the ~ of the neck** por el pescuezo.

scruffy ['skrʌfɪ] adj desaliñado, desaseado.

scrum(mage) ['skrʌm(mɪdʒ)] n (RUGBY) melée f.

scruple ['skru:pl] n escrúpulo; **to have no ~s about doing sth** no tener reparos en or escrúpulos para hacer algo.

scrupulous ['skru:pjuləs] adj escrupuloso.

scrupulously ['skru:pjuləslɪ] adv escrupulosamente; **to be ~ fair/honest** ser sumamente justo/honesto.

scrutinize ['skru:tɪnaɪz] vt escudriñar; (votes) escrutar.

scrutiny ['skru:tɪnɪ] n escrutinio, examen m; **under the ~ of sb** bajo la mirada or el escrutinio de algn.

scuba ['sku:bə] n escafandra autónoma.

scuba diving n buceo con escafandra autónoma.

scuff [skʌf] vt (shoes, floor) rayar.

scuffle ['skʌfl] n refriega.

scullery ['skʌlərɪ] n trascocina.

sculptor ['skʌlptə*] n escultor(a) m/f.

sculpture ['skʌlptʃə*] n escultura.

scum [skʌm] n (on liquid) espuma; (pej: people) escoria.

scupper ['skʌpə*] vt (BRIT: boat) hundir; (: fig: plans etc) acabar con.

scurrilous ['skʌrɪləs] adj difamatorio, calumnioso.

scurry ['skʌrɪ] vi: **to ~ off** escabullirse.

scurvy ['skə:vɪ] n escorbuto.

scuttle ['skʌtl] n (also: **coal ~**) cubo, carbonera ♦ vt (ship) barrenar ♦ vi (scamper): **to ~ away, ~ off** escabullirse.

scythe [saɪð] n guadaña.

SD, S. Dak. abbr (US) = **South Dakota.**

SDI n abbr (= Strategic Defense Initiative) IDE f.

SDLP n abbr (BRIT POL) = **Social Democratic and Labour Party.**

SDP n abbr (BRIT POL) = **Social Democratic Party.**

sea [si:] n mar m/f; **by ~** (travel) en barco; **on the ~** (boat) en el mar; (town) junto al mar; **to be all at ~** (fig) estar despistado; **out to or at ~** en alta mar; **to go by ~** ir en barco; **heavy or rough ~s** marejada; **by or beside the ~** (holiday) en la playa; (village) a orillas del mar; **a ~ of faces** una multitud de caras.

sea bed n fondo del mar.

sea bird n ave f marina.

seaboard ['si:bɔ:d] n litoral m.

sea breeze n brisa de mar.

seadog ['si:dɔg] n lobo de mar.

seafarer ['si:fɛərə*] n marinero.

seafaring ['si:fɛərɪŋ] adj (community) marinero; (life) de marinero.

seafood ['si:fu:d] n mariscos mpl.

sea front n (beach) playa; (prom) paseo marítimo.

seagoing ['si:gəuɪŋ] adj (ship) de alta mar.

seagull ['si:gʌl] n gaviota.

seal [si:l] n (animal) foca; (stamp) sello ♦ vt (close) cerrar; (: with ~) sellar; (decide: sb's fate) decidir; (: bargain) cerrar; **~ of approval** sello de aprobación.

▶**seal off** vt obturar.

seal cull n matanza de crías de foca.

sea level n nivel m del mar.

sealing wax ['si:lɪŋ-] n lacre m.

sea lion n león m marino.

sealskin ['si:lskɪn] n piel f de foca.

seam [si:m] n costura; (of metal) juntura; (of coal) veta, filón m; **the hall was**

bursting at the ~**s** la sala rebosaba de gente.
seaman ['siːmən] *n* marinero.
seamanship ['siːmənʃɪp] *n* náutica.
seamless ['siːmlɪs] *adj* sin costura(s).
seamy ['siːmɪ] *adj* sórdido.
seance ['seɪɔns] *n* sesión *f* de espiritismo.
seaplane ['siːpleɪn] *n* hidroavión *m*.
seaport ['siːpɔːt] *n* puerto de mar.
search [sɔːtʃ] *n* (*for person, thing*) busca, búsqueda; (*of drawer, pockets*) registro; (*inspection*) reconocimiento ♦ *vt* (*look in*) buscar en; (*examine*) examinar; (*person, place*) registrar; (*COMPUT*) buscar ♦ *vi*: **to ~ for** buscar; **in ~ of** en busca de; "**~ and replace**" (*COMPUT*) "buscar y reemplazar".
►**search through** *vt fus* registrar.
searcher ['sɔːtʃə*] *n* buscador(a) *m/f*.
searching ['sɔːtʃɪŋ] *adj* (*question*) penetrante.
searchlight ['sɔːtʃlaɪt] *n* reflector *m*.
search party *n* equipo de salvamento.
search warrant *n* mandamiento judicial.
searing ['sɪərɪŋ] *adj* (*heat*) abrasador(a); (*pain*) agudo.
seashore ['siːʃɔː*] *n* playa, orilla del mar; **on the ~** a la orilla del mar.
seasick ['siːsɪk] *adj* mareado; **to be ~** marearse.
seaside ['siːsaɪd] *n* playa, orilla del mar; **to go to the ~** ir a la playa.
seaside resort *n* playa.
season ['siːzn] *n* (*of year*) estación *f*; (*sporting etc*) temporada; (*gen*) época, período ♦ *vt* (*food*) sazonar; **to be in/out of ~** estar en sazón/fuera de temporada; **the busy ~** (*for shops, hotels etc*) la temporada alta; **the open ~** (*HUNTING*) la temporada de caza *or* de pesca.
seasonal ['siːznl] *adj* estacional.
seasoned ['siːznd] *adj* (*wood*) curado; (*fig: worker, actor*) experimentado; (*troops*) curtido; **~ campaigner** veterano/a.
seasoning ['siːznɪŋ] *n* condimento.
season ticket *n* abono.
seat [siːt] *n* (*in bus, train: place*) asiento; (*chair*) silla; (*PARLIAMENT*) escaño; (*buttocks*) trasero; (*centre: of government etc*) sede *f* ♦ *vt* sentar; (*have room for*) tener cabida para; **are there any ~s left?** ¿quedan plazas?; **to take one's ~** sentarse, tomar asiento; **to be ~ed** estar sentado, sentarse.
seat belt *n* cinturón *m* de seguridad.
seating ['siːtɪŋ] *n* asientos *mpl*.
seating arrangements *npl* distribución *fsg* de los asientos.

seating capacity *n* número de asientos, aforo.
SEATO ['siːtəu] *n abbr* (= *Southeast Asia Treaty Organization*) OTASE *f*.
sea water *n* agua *m* del mar.
seaweed ['siːwiːd] *n* alga marina.
seaworthy ['siːwɔːðɪ] *adj* en condiciones de navegar.
SEC *n abbr* (*US*: = *Securities and Exchange Commission*) comisión de operaciones bursátiles.
sec. *abbr* = **second(s)**.
secateurs [sɛkə'tɔːz] *npl* podadera *sg*.
secede [sɪ'siːd] *vi*: **to ~ (from)** separarse (de).
secluded [sɪ'kluːdɪd] *adj* retirado.
seclusion [sɪ'kluːʒən] *n* retiro.
second ['sɛkənd] *adj* segundo ♦ *adv* (*in race etc*) en segundo lugar ♦ *n* (*gen*) segundo; (*AUT: also*: ~ **gear**) segunda; (*COMM*) artículo con algún desperfecto; (*BRIT SCOL: degree*) título universitario de segunda clase ♦ *vt* (*motion*) apoyar; [sɪ'kɔnd] (*employee*) trasladar temporalmente; **~ floor** (*BRIT*) segundo piso; (*US*) primer piso; **Charles the S~** Carlos Segundo; **to ask for a ~ opinion** (*MED*) pedir una segunda opinión; **just a ~!** ¡un momento!; **to have ~ thoughts** cambiar de opinión; **on ~ thoughts** *or* (*US*) **thought** pensándolo bien; **~ mortgage** segunda hipoteca.
secondary ['sɛkəndərɪ] *adj* secundario.
secondary education *n* enseñanza secundaria.
secondary school *n* escuela secundaria.

*En el Reino Unido se llama **secondary school** a un centro educativo para alumnos de 11 a 18 años, si bien muchos estudiantes acaban a los 16, edad mínima de escolarización obligatoria. La mayor parte de estos centros funcionan como **comprehensive schools**, aunque aún existen algunos de tipo selectivo.*

second-best [sɛkənd'bɛst] *n* segundo.
second-class ['sɛkənd'klɑːs] *adj* de segunda clase ♦ *adv*: **to send sth ~** enviar algo por correo de segunda clase; **to travel ~** viajar en segunda; **~ citizen** ciudadano/a de segunda (clase).
second cousin *n* primo/a segundo/a.
seconder ['sɛkəndə*] *n* el/la que apoya una moción.
second-guess ['sɛkənd'gɛs] *vt* (*evaluate*) juzgar (a posteriori); (*anticipate*): **to ~ sth/sb** (intentar) adivinar algo/lo que va

a hacer algn.

secondhand ['sɛkənd'hænd] adj de segunda mano, usado ♦ adv: **to buy sth** ~ comprar algo de segunda mano; **to hear sth** ~ oír algo indirectamente.

second hand n (on clock) segundero.

second-in-command ['sɛkəndɪnkə'mɑːnd] n (MIL) segundo en el mando; (ADMIN) segundo/a, ayudante m/f.

secondly ['sɛkəndlɪ] adv en segundo lugar.

secondment [sɪ'kɔndmənt] n (BRIT) traslado temporal.

second-rate ['sɛkənd'reɪt] adj de segunda categoría.

secrecy ['siːkrəsɪ] n secreto.

secret ['siːkrɪt] adj, n secreto; **in** ~ adv en secreto; **to keep sth** ~ **(from sb)** ocultarle algo (a algn); **to make no** ~ **of sth** no ocultar algo.

secret agent n agente m/f secreto/a, espía m/f.

secretarial [sɛkrɪ'tɛərɪəl] adj (course) de secretariado; (staff) de secretaría; (work, duties) de secretaria.

secretariat [sɛkrɪ'tɛərɪət] n secretaría.

secretary ['sɛkrətərɪ] n secretario/a; **S~ of State** (BRIT POL) Ministro (con cartera).

secretary-general ['sɛkrətərɪ'dʒɛnərl] n secretario/a general.

secretary pool n (US) = **typing pool**.

secrete [sɪ'kriːt] vt (MED, ANAT, BIO) secretar; (hide) ocultar, esconder.

secretion [sɪ'kriːʃən] n secreción f.

secretive ['siːkrətɪv] adj reservado, sigiloso.

secretly ['siːkrɪtlɪ] adv en secreto.

secret police n policía secreta.

secret service n servicio secreto.

sect [sɛkt] n secta.

sectarian [sɛk'tɛərɪən] adj sectario.

section ['sɛkʃən] n sección f; (part) parte f; (of document) artículo; (of opinion) sector m; **business** ~ (PRESS) sección f de economía.

sectional ['sɛkʃənl] adj (regional) regional, local.

sector ['sɛktə*] n (gen, COMPUT) sector m.

secular ['sɛkjulə*] adj secular, seglar.

secure [sɪ'kjuə*] adj (free from anxiety) seguro; (firmly fixed) firme, fijo ♦ vt (fix) asegurar, afianzar; (get) conseguir; (COMM: loan) garantizar; **to make sth** ~ afianzar algo; **to** ~ **sth for sb** conseguir algo para algn.

secured creditor [sɪ'kjuəd-] n acreedor(a) m/f con garantía.

securely [sɪ'kjuəlɪ] adv firmemente; **it is** ~ **fastened** está bien sujeto.

security [sɪ'kjuərɪtɪ] n seguridad f; (for loan) fianza; (: object) prenda; **securities** npl (COMM) valores mpl, títulos mpl; ~ **of tenure** tenencia asegurada; **to increase/ tighten** ~ aumentar/estrechar las medidas de seguridad; **job** ~ seguridad f en el empleo.

Security Council n: **the** ~ el Consejo de Seguridad.

security forces npl fuerzas fpl de seguridad.

security guard n guardia m/f de seguridad.

security risk n riesgo para la seguridad.

secy. abbr (= secretary) Srio/a.

sedan [sɪ'dæn] n (US AUT) sedán m.

sedate [sɪ'deɪt] adj tranquilo ♦ vt administrar sedantes a, sedar.

sedation [sɪ'deɪʃən] n (MED) sedación f; **to be under** ~ estar bajo sedación.

sedative ['sɛdɪtɪv] n sedante m, calmante m.

sedentary ['sɛdntrɪ] adj sedentario.

sediment ['sɛdɪmənt] n sedimento.

sedimentary [sɛdɪ'mɛntərɪ] adj (GEO) sedimentario.

sedition [sɪ'dɪʃən] n sedición f.

seduce [sɪ'djuːs] vt (gen) seducir.

seduction [sɪ'dʌkʃən] n seducción f.

seductive [sɪ'dʌktɪv] adj seductor(a).

see [siː] vb (pt **saw**, pp **seen** [sɔː, siːn]) vt (gen) ver; (understand) ver, comprender; (look at) mirar ♦ vi ver ♦ n sede f; **to** ~ **sb to the door** acompañar a algn a la puerta; **to** ~ **that** (ensure) asegurarse de que; ~ **you soon/later/tomorrow!** ¡hasta pronto/ luego/mañana!; **as far as I can** ~ por lo visto or por lo que veo; **there was nobody to be** ~**n** no se veía a nadie; **let me** ~ (show me) a ver; (let me think) vamos a ver; **to go and** ~ **sb** ir a ver a algn; ~ **for yourself** compruébalo tú mismo; **I don't know what she** ~**s in him** no sé qué le encuentra.

▶**see about** vt fus atender a, encargarse de.

▶**see off** vt despedir.

▶**see through** vt fus calar ♦ vt llevar a cabo.

▶**see to** vt fus atender a, encargarse de.

seed [siːd] n semilla; (in fruit) pepita; (fig) germen m; (TENNIS) preseleccionado/a; **to go to** ~ (plant) granar; (fig) descuidarse.

seedless ['siːdlɪs] adj sin semillas or pepitas.

seedling ['siːdlɪŋ] n planta de semillero.

seedy ['siːdɪ] adj (person) desaseado; (place) sórdido.

seeing ['siːɪŋ] conj: ~ **(that)** visto que, en vista de que.

seek, *pt, pp* **sought** [siːk, sɔːt] *vt (gen)*
buscar; *(post)* solicitar; **to ~ advice/help
from sb** pedir consejos/solicitar ayuda a
algn.
▶**seek out** *vt (person)* buscar.
seem [siːm] *vi* parecer; **there ~s to be...**
parece que hay ...; **it ~s (that)** ... parece
que ...; **what ~s to be the trouble?** ¿qué
pasa?; **I did what ~ed best** hice lo que
parecía mejor.
seemingly ['siːmɪŋlɪ] *adv* aparentemente,
según parece.
seen [siːn] *pp of* **see.**
seep [siːp] *vi* filtrarse.
seer [sɪə*] *n* vidente *m/f*, profeta *m/f*.
seersucker [sɪə'sʌkə*] *n* sirsaca.
seesaw ['siːsɔː] *n* balancín *m*, subibaja *m*.
seethe [siːð] *vi* hervir; **to ~ with anger**
enfurecerse.
see-through ['siːθruː] *adj* transparente.
segment ['sɛgmənt] *n* segmento.
segregate ['sɛgrɪgeɪt] *vt* segregar.
segregation [sɛgrɪ'geɪʃən] *n* segregación *f*.
Seine [seɪn] *n* Sena *m*.
seismic ['saɪzmɪk] *adj* sísmico.
seize [siːz] *vt (grasp)* agarrar, asir; *(take
possession of)* secuestrar; *(: territory)*
apoderarse de; *(opportunity)*
aprovecharse de.
▶**seize up** *vi (TECH)* agarrotarse.
▶**seize (up)on** *vt fus* valerse de.
seizure ['siːʒə*] *n (MED)* ataque *m*; *(LAW)*
incautación *f*.
seldom ['sɛldəm] *adv* rara vez.
select [sɪ'lɛkt] *adj* selecto, escogido; *(hotel,
restaurant, clubs)* exclusivo ♦ *vt* escoger,
elegir; *(SPORT)* seleccionar; **a ~ few** una
minoría selecta.
selection [sɪ'lɛkʃən] *n* selección *f*, elección
f; *(COMM)* surtido.
selection committee *n* comisión *f* de
nombramiento.
selective [sɪ'lɛktɪv] *adj* selectivo.
self [sɛlf] *n (pl* **selves** [sɛlvz]) uno mismo
♦ *pref* auto ...; **the ~** el yo.
self-addressed ['sɛlfə'drɛst] *adj*: **~
envelope** sobre *m* con la dirección propia.
self-adhesive [sɛlfəd'hiːzɪv] *adj*
autoadhesivo, autoadherente.
self-appointed [sɛlfə'pɔɪntɪd] *adj*
autonombrado.
self-assurance [sɛlfə'ʃuərəns] *n* confianza
en sí mismo.
self-assured [sɛlfə'ʃuəd] *adj* seguro de sí
mismo.
self-catering [sɛlf'keɪtərɪŋ] *adj (BRIT)* sin
pensión *or* servicio de comida; **~
apartment** apartamento con cocina

propia.
self-centred, *(US)* **self-centered**
[sɛlf'sɛntəd] *adj* egocéntrico.
self-cleaning [sɛlf'kliːnɪŋ] *adj*
autolimpiador.
self-confessed [sɛlfkən'fɛst] *adj (alcoholic
etc)* confeso.
self-confidence [sɛlf'kɔnfɪdns] *n* confianza
en sí mismo.
self-confident [sɛlf'kɔnfɪdnt] *adj* seguro de
sí (mismo), lleno de confianza en sí
mismo.
self-conscious [sɛlf'kɔnʃəs] *adj* cohibido.
self-contained [sɛlfkən'teɪnd] *adj (gen)*
independiente; *(BRIT: flat)* con entrada
particular.
self-control [sɛlfkən'trəul] *n* autodominio.
self-defeating [sɛlfdɪ'fiːtɪŋ] *adj*
contraproducente.
self-defence, *(US)* **self-defense**
[sɛlfdɪ'fɛns] *n* defensa propia.
self-discipline [sɛlf'dɪsɪplɪn] *n*
autodisciplina.
self-employed [sɛlfɪm'plɔɪd] *adj* que
trabaja por cuenta propia, autónomo.
self-esteem [sɛlfɪ'stiːm] *n* amor *m* propio.
self-evident [sɛlf'ɛvɪdnt] *adj* patente.
self-explanatory [sɛlfɪks'plænətərɪ] *adj* que
no necesita explicación.
self-financing [sɛlffaɪ'nænsɪŋ] *adj*
autofinanziado.
self-governing [sɛlf'gʌvənɪŋ] *adj*
autónomo.
self-help ['sɛlf'hɛlp] *n* autosuficiencia,
ayuda propia.
self-importance [sɛlfɪm'pɔːtns] *n*
presunción *f*, vanidad *f*.
self-important [sɛlfɪm'pɔːtnt] *adj* vanidoso.
self-indulgent [sɛlfɪn'dʌldʒənt] *adj*
indulgente consigo mismo.
self-inflicted [sɛlfɪn'flɪktɪd] *adj* infligido a sí
mismo.
self-interest [sɛlf'ɪntrɪst] *n* egoísmo.
selfish ['sɛlfɪʃ] *adj* egoísta.
selfishly ['sɛlfɪʃlɪ] *adv* con egoísmo, de
modo egoísta.
selfishness ['sɛlfɪʃnɪs] *n* egoísmo.
selflessly ['sɛlflɪslɪ] *adv*
desinteresadamente.
selfless ['sɛlflɪs] *adj* desinteresado.
self-made man ['sɛlfmeɪd-] *n* hombre que
ha triunfado por su propio esfuerzo.
self-pity [sɛlf'pɪtɪ] *n* lástima de sí mismo.
self-portrait [sɛlf'pɔːtreɪt] *n* autorretrato.
self-possessed [sɛlfpə'zɛst] *adj* sereno,
dueño de sí mismo.
self-preservation ['sɛlfprɛzə'veɪʃən] *n*
propia conservación *f*.

self-propelled [sɛlfprə'pɛld] *adj* autopropulsado, automotor/triz.

self-raising [sɛlf'reɪzɪŋ], (*US*) **self-rising** [sɛlf'raɪzɪŋ] *adj*: ~ **flour** harina con levadura.

self-reliant [sɛlfrɪ'laɪənt] *adj* independiente, autosuficiente.

self-respect [sɛlfrɪ'spɛkt] *n* amor *m* propio.

self-respecting [sɛlfrɪ'spɛktɪŋ] *adj* que tiene amor propio.

self-righteous [sɛlf'raɪtʃəs] *adj* santurrón/ona.

self-rising [sɛlf'raɪzɪŋ] *adj* (*US*) = **self-raising.**

self-sacrifice [sɛlf'sækrɪfaɪs] *n* abnegación *f*.

self-same [sɛlfseɪm] *adj* mismo, mismísimo.

self-satisfied [sɛlf'sætɪsfaɪd] *adj* satisfecho de sí mismo.

self-service [sɛlf'səːvɪs] *adj* de autoservicio.

self-styled ['sɛlfstaɪld] *adj* supuesto, sedicente.

self-sufficient [sɛlfsə'fɪʃənt] *adj* autosuficiente.

self-supporting [sɛlfsə'pɔːtɪŋ] *adj* económicamente independiente.

self-taught [sɛlf'tɔːt] *adj* autodidacta.

self-test ['sɛlftɛst] *n* (*COMPUT*) autocomprobación *f*.

sell, *pt, pp* **sold** [sɛl, səʊld] *vt* vender ♦ *vi* venderse; **to ~ at** *or* **for £10** venderse a 10 libras; **to ~ sb an idea** (*fig*) convencer a algn de una idea.

▶**sell off** *vt* liquidar.

▶**sell out** *vi* transigir, transar (*LAM*); **to ~ out (to sb/sth)** (*COMM*) vender su negocio (a algn/algo) ♦ *vt* agotar las existencias de, venderlo todo; **the tickets are all sold out** las entradas están agotadas.

▶**sell up** *vi* (*COMM*) liquidarse.

sell-by date ['sɛlbaɪ-] *n* fecha de caducidad.

seller ['sɛlə*] *n* vendedor(a) *m/f*; ~**'s market** mercado de demanda.

selling price ['sɛlɪŋ-] *n* precio de venta.

Sellotape ® ['sɛləʊteɪp] *n* (*BRIT*) cinta adhesiva, celo, scotch ® *m*.

sellout ['sɛlaʊt] *n* traición *f*; **it was a ~** (*THEAT etc*) fue un éxito de taquilla.

selves [sɛlvz] *npl of* **self.**

semantic [sɪ'mæntɪk] *adj* semántico.

semaphore ['sɛməfɔː*] *n* semáforo.

semblance ['sɛmbləns] *n* apariencia.

semen ['siːmən] *n* semen *m*.

semester [sɪ'mɛstə*] *n* (*US*) semestre *m*.

semi ['sɛmɪ] *n* = **semidetached house.**

semi... [sɛmɪ] *pref* semi..., medio....

semicircle ['sɛmɪsəːkl] *n* semicírculo.

semicircular ['sɛmɪ'səːkjulə*] *adj* semicircular.

semicolon [sɛmɪ'kəʊlən] *n* punto y coma.

semiconductor [sɛmɪkən'dʌktə*] *n* semiconductor *m*.

semiconscious [sɛmɪ'kɔnʃəs] *adj* semiconsciente.

semidetached (house) [sɛmɪdɪ'tætʃt-] *n* casa adosada.

semi-final [sɛmɪ'faɪnl] *n* semi-final *f*.

seminar ['sɛmɪnɑː*] *n* seminario.

seminary ['sɛmɪnərɪ] *n* (*REL*) seminario.

semiprecious stone [sɛmɪ'prɛʃəs-] *n* piedra semipreciosa.

semiquaver ['sɛmɪkweɪvə*] *n* (*BRIT*) semicorchea.

semiskilled ['sɛmɪskɪld] *adj* (*work, worker*) semicualificado.

semi-skimmed *adj* semidesnatado.

semitone ['sɛmɪtəʊn] *n* semitono.

semolina [sɛmə'liːnə] *n* sémola.

SEN *n abbr* (*BRIT*) = **State Enrolled Nurse.**

Sen., sen. *abbr* = **senator, senior.**

senate ['sɛnɪt] *n* senado; *see also* **Congress.**

senator ['sɛnɪtə*] *n* senador(a) *m/f*.

send, *pt, pp* **sent** [sɛnd, sɛnt] *vt* mandar, enviar; **to ~ by post** mandar por correo; **to ~ sb for sth** mandar a algn a buscar algo; **to ~ word that ...** avisar *or* mandar aviso de que ...; **she ~s (you) her love** te manda *or* envía cariñosos recuerdos; **to ~ sb to sleep/into fits of laughter** dormir/hacer reír a algn; **to ~ sb flying** echar a algn; **to ~ sth flying** tirar algo.

▶**send away** *vt* (*letter, goods*) despachar.

▶**send away for** *vt fus* pedir.

▶**send back** *vt* devolver.

▶**send for** *vt fus* mandar traer; (*by post*) escribir pidiendo algo.

▶**send in** *vt* (*report, application, resignation*) mandar.

▶**send off** *vt* (*goods*) despachar; (*BRIT SPORT: player*) expulsar.

▶**send on** *vt* (*letter*) mandar, expedir; (*luggage etc: in advance*) facturar.

▶**send out** *vt* (*invitation*) mandar; (*emit: light, heat*) emitir, difundir; (: *signal*) emitir.

▶**send round** *vt* (*letter, document etc*) hacer circular.

▶**send up** *vt* (*person, price*) hacer subir; (*BRIT: parody*) parodiar.

sender ['sɛndə*] *n* remitente *m/f*.

send-off ['sɛndɔf] *n*: **a good ~** una buena despedida.

send-up ['sɛndʌp] *n* (*col*) parodia, sátira.

Senegal [sɛnɪˈgɔːl] n Senegal m.
Senegalese [sɛnɪɡəˈliːz] adj, n senegalés/esa m/f.
senile [ˈsiːnaɪl] adj senil.
senility [sɪˈnɪlɪtɪ] n senilidad f.
senior [ˈsiːnɪə*] adj (older) mayor, más viejo; (: on staff) más antiguo; (of higher rank) superior ♦ n mayor m; **P. Jones ~ P.** Jones padre.
senior citizen n persona de la tercera edad.
senior high school n (US) ≈ instituto de enseñanza media; see also **high school**.
seniority [siːnɪˈɔrɪtɪ] n antigüedad f; (in rank) rango superior.
sensation [sɛnˈseɪʃən] n (physical feeling, impression) sensación f.
sensational [sɛnˈseɪʃənl] adj sensacional.
sense [sɛns] n (faculty, meaning) sentido; (feeling) sensación f; (good ~) sentido común, juicio ♦ vt sentir, percibir; ~ **of** **humour** sentido del humor; **it makes ~** tiene sentido; **there is no ~ in (doing) that** no tiene sentido (hacer) eso; **to come to** **one's ~s** (regain consciousness) volver en sí, recobrar el sentido; **to take leave of** **one's ~s** perder el juicio.
senseless [ˈsɛnslɪs] adj estúpido, insensato; (unconscious) sin conocimiento.
senselessly [ˈsɛnslɪslɪ] adv estúpidamente, insensatamente.
sensibility [sɛnsɪˈbɪlɪtɪ] n sensibilidad f; **sensibilities** npl delicadeza sg.
sensible [ˈsɛnsɪbl] adj sensato; (reasonable) razonable, lógico.
sensibly [ˈsɛnsɪblɪ] adv sensatamente, razonablemente, de modo lógico.
sensitive [ˈsɛnsɪtɪv] adj sensible; (touchy) susceptible; **he is very ~ about it** es muy susceptible acerca de eso.
sensitivity [sɛnsɪˈtɪvɪtɪ] n sensibilidad f; susceptibilidad f.
sensual [ˈsɛnsjuəl] adj sensual.
sensuous [ˈsɛnsjuəs] adj sensual.
sent [sɛnt] pt, pp of **send**.
sentence [ˈsɛntəns] n (LING) frase f, oración f; (LAW) sentencia, fallo ♦ vt: **to ~ sb to** **death/to 5 years** condenar a algn a muerte/a 5 años de cárcel; **to pass ~ on** **sb** (also fig) sentenciar or condenar a algn.
sentiment [ˈsɛntɪmənt] n sentimiento; (opinion) opinión f.
sentimental [sɛntɪˈmɛntl] adj sentimental.
sentimentality [sɛntɪmɛnˈtælɪtɪ] n sentimentalismo, sensiblería.
sentinel [ˈsɛntɪnl] n centinela m.
sentry [ˈsɛntrɪ] n centinela m.

sentry duty n: **to be on ~** estar de guardia, hacer guardia.
Seoul [səul] n Seúl m.
separable [ˈsɛpərəbl] adj separable.
separate adj [ˈsɛprɪt] separado; (distinct) distinto ♦ (vb: [ˈsɛpəreɪt]) vt separar; (part) dividir ♦ vi separarse; ~ **from** separado or distinto de; **under ~ cover** (COMM) por separado; **to ~ into** dividir or separar en; **he is ~d from his wife, but not divorced** está separado de su mujer, pero no (está) divorciado.
separately [ˈsɛprɪtlɪ] adv por separado.
separates [ˈsɛprɪts] npl (clothes) coordinados mpl.
separation [sɛpəˈreɪʃən] n separación f.
sepia [ˈsiːpɪə] adj color sepia inv.
Sept. abbr (= September) sep.
September [sɛpˈtɛmbə*] n se(p)tiembre m.
septic [ˈsɛptɪk] adj séptico; **to go ~** ponerse séptico.
septicaemia, (US) **septicemia** [sɛptɪˈsiːmɪə] n septicemia.
septic tank n fosa séptica.
sequel [ˈsiːkwl] n consecuencia, resultado; (of story) continuación f.
sequence [ˈsiːkwəns] n sucesión f, serie f; (CINE) secuencia; **in ~** en orden or serie.
sequential [sɪˈkwɛnʃəl] adj: ~ **access** (COMPUT) acceso en serie.
sequin [ˈsiːkwɪn] n lentejuela.
Serb [səːb] adj, n = **Serbian**.
Serbia [ˈsəːbɪə] n Serbia.
Serbian [ˈsəːbɪən] adj serbio ♦ n serbio/a; (LING) serbio.
Serbo-Croat [ˈsəːbəuˈkrəuæt] n (LING) serbocroata m.
serenade [sɛrəˈneɪd] n serenata ♦ vt dar serenata a.
serene [sɪˈriːn] adj sereno, tranquilo.
serenely [sɪˈriːnlɪ] adv serenamente, tranquilamente.
serenity [səˈrɛnɪtɪ] n serenidad f, tranquilidad f.
sergeant [ˈsɑːdʒənt] n sargento.
sergeant major n sargento mayor.
serial [ˈsɪərɪəl] n novela por entregas; (TV) telenovela.
serial access n (COMPUT) acceso en serie.
serial interface n (COMPUT) interface m en serie.
serialize [ˈsɪərɪəlaɪz] vt publicar/televisar por entregas.
serial killer n asesino/a múltiple.
serial number n número de serie.
serial printer n (COMPUT) impresora en serie.
series [ˈsɪəriːz] n, pl inv serie f.

serious ['sɪərɪəs] adj serio; (grave) grave;
are you ~ (about it)? ¿lo dices en serio?
seriously ['sɪərɪəslɪ] adv en serio; (ill,
wounded etc) gravemente; (col: extremely)
de verdad; **to take sth/sb ~** tomar algo/a
algn en serio; **he's ~ rich** es una pasada
de rico.
seriousness ['sɪərɪəsnɪs] n seriedad f;
gravedad f.
sermon ['sɜːmən] n sermón m.
serpent ['sɜːpənt] n serpiente f.
serrated [sɪ'reɪtɪd] adj serrado, dentellado.
serum ['sɪərəm] n suero.
servant ['sɜːvənt] n (gen) servidor(a) m/f;
(house ~) criado/a.
serve [sɜːv] vt servir; (customer) atender;
(subj: train) tener parada en;
(apprenticeship) hacer; (prison term)
cumplir ♦ vi (servant, soldier etc) servir;
(TENNIS) sacar ♦ n (TENNIS) saque m; **it ~s
him right** se lo merece, se lo tiene
merecido; **to ~ a summons on sb**
entregar una citación a algn; **it ~s my
purpose** me sirve para lo que quiero; **are
you being ~d?** ¿le atienden?; **the power
station ~s the entire region** la central
eléctrica abastece a toda la región; **to ~
as/for/to do** servir de/para/para hacer; **to
~ on a committee/a jury** ser miembro de
una comisión/un jurado.
▶**serve out, serve up** vt (food) servir.
service ['sɜːvɪs] n (gen) servicio; (REL:
Catholic) misa; (: other) oficio (religioso);
(AUT) mantenimiento; (of dishes) juego
♦ vt (car, washing machine) mantener;
(: repair) reparar; **the S~s** las fuerzas
armadas; **funeral ~** exequias fpl; **to hold a
~** celebrar un oficio religioso; **the
essential ~s** los servicios esenciales;
medical/social ~s servicios mpl médicos/
sociales; **the train ~ to London** los trenes
a Londres; **to be of ~ to sb** ser útil a algn.
serviceable ['sɜːvɪsəbl] adj servible,
utilizable.
service area n (on motorway) área de
servicios.
service charge n (BRIT) servicio.
service industries npl industrias fpl del
servicio.
serviceman ['sɜːvɪsmən] n militar m.
service station n estación f de servicio.
servicing ['sɜːvɪsɪŋ] n (of car) revisión f; (of
washing machine etc) servicio de
reparaciones.
serviette [sɜːvɪ'ɛt] n (BRIT) servilleta.
servile ['sɜːvaɪl] adj servil.
session ['sɛʃən] n (sitting) sesión f; **to be in
~** estar en sesión.

session musician n músico m/f de estudio.
set [sɛt] n juego; (RADIO) aparato; (TV)
televisor m; (of utensils) batería; (of
cutlery) cubierto; (of books) colección f;
(TENNIS) set m; (group of people) grupo;
(CINE) plató m; (THEAT) decorado;
(HAIRDRESSING) marcado ♦ adj (fixed) fijo;
(ready) listo; (resolved) resuelto, decidido
♦ (vb: pt, pp set) vt (place) poner, colocar;
(fix) fijar; (adjust) ajustar, arreglar;
(decide: rules etc) establecer, decidir;
(assign: task) asignar; (: homework) poner
♦ vi (sun) ponerse; (jam, jelly) cuajarse;
(concrete) fraguar; **a ~ of false teeth** una
dentadura postiza; **a ~ of dining-room
furniture** muebles mpl de comedor; **~ in
one's ways** con costumbres arraigadas; **a
~ phrase** una frase hecha; **to be all ~ to
do sth** estar listo para hacer algo; **to be
~ on doing sth** estar empeñado en hacer
algo; **a novel ~ in Valencia** una novela
ambientada en Valencia; **to ~ to music**
poner música a; **to ~ on fire** incendiar,
prender fuego a; **to ~ free** poner en
libertad; **to ~ sth going** poner algo en
marcha; **to ~ sail** zarpar, hacerse a la
mar.
▶**set about** vt fus: **to ~ about doing sth**
ponerse a hacer algo.
▶**set aside** vt poner aparte, dejar de lado.
▶**set back** vt (progress): **to ~ back (by)**
retrasar (por); **a house ~ back from the
road** una casa apartada de la carretera.
▶**set down** vt (subj: bus, train) dejar;
(record) poner por escrito.
▶**set in** vi (infection) declararse;
(complications) comenzar; **the rain has ~
in for the day** parece que va a llover todo
el día.
▶**set off** vi partir ♦ vt (bomb) hacer
estallar; (cause to start) poner en marcha;
(show up well) hacer resaltar.
▶**set out** vi: **to ~ out to do sth** proponerse
hacer algo ♦ vt (arrange) disponer; (state)
exponer; **to ~ out (from)** salir (de).
▶**set up** vt (organization) establecer.
setback ['sɛtbæk] n (hitch) revés m,
contratiempo; (in health) recaída.
set menu n menú m.
set phrase n frase f hecha.
set square n cartabón m.
settee [sɛ'tiː] n sofá m.
setting ['sɛtɪŋ] n (scenery) marco; (of jewel)
engaste m, montadura.
setting lotion n fijador m (para el pelo).
settle ['sɛtl] vt (argument, matter) resolver;
(pay: bill, accounts) pagar, liquidar;
(colonize: land) colonizar; (MED: calm)

calmar, sosegar ♦ *vi* (*dust etc*)
depositarse; (*weather*) estabilizarse; (*also*:
~ **down**) instalarse; (*calm down*)
tranquilizarse; **to ~ for sth** convenir en
aceptar algo; **to ~ on sth** decidirse por
algo; **that's ~d then** bueno, está
arreglado; **to ~ one's stomach** asentar el
estómago.
►**settle in** *vi* instalarse.
►**settle up** *vi*: **to ~ up with sb** ajustar
cuentas con algn.
settlement ['sɛtlmənt] *n* (*payment*)
liquidación *f*; (*agreement*) acuerdo,
convenio; (*village etc*) poblado; **in ~ of our
account** (*COMM*) en pago *or* liquidación
de nuestra cuenta.
settler ['sɛtlə*] *n* colono/a, colonizador(a)
m/f.
setup ['sɛtʌp] *n* sistema *m*.
seven ['sɛvn] *num* siete.
seventeen [sɛvn'tiːn] *num* diez y siete,
diecisiete.
seventh ['sɛvnθ] *adj* séptimo.
seventy ['sɛvntɪ] *num* setenta.
sever ['sɛvə*] *vt* cortar; (*relations*) romper.
several ['sɛvərl] *adj, pron* varios/as *m/fpl*,
algunos/as *m/fpl*; ~ **of us** varios de
nosotros; ~ **times** varias veces.
severance ['sɛvərəns] *n* (*of relations*)
ruptura.
severance pay *n* indemnización *f* por
despido.
severe [sɪ'vɪə*] *adj* severo; (*serious*) grave;
(*hard*) duro; (*pain*) intenso.
severely [sɪ'vɪəlɪ] *adv* severamente;
(*wounded, ill*) de gravedad, gravemente.
severity [sɪ'vɛrɪtɪ] *n* severidad *f*; gravedad
f; intensidad *f*.
Seville [sə'vɪl] *n* Sevilla.
sew, *pt* **sewed**, *pp* **sewn** [səu, səud, səun] *vt,
vi* coser.
►**sew up** *vt* coser.
sewage ['suːɪdʒ] *n* (*effluence*) aguas *fpl*
residuales; (*system*) alcantarillado.
sewage works *n* estación *f* depuradora
(de aguas residuales).
sewer ['suːə*] *n* alcantarilla, cloaca.
sewing ['səuɪŋ] *n* costura.
sewing machine *n* máquina de coser.
sewn [səun] *pp of* **sew**.
sex [sɛks] *n* sexo; **the opposite ~** el sexo
opuesto; **to have ~ with sb** tener
relaciones (sexuales) con algn.
sex act *n* acto sexual, coito.
sex appeal *n* sex-appeal *m*, gancho.
sex education *n* educación *f* sexual.
sexism ['sɛksɪzəm] *n* sexismo.
sexist ['sɛksɪst] *adj, n* sexista *m/f*.

sex life *n* vida sexual.
sex object *n* objeto sexual.
sextant ['sɛkstənt] *n* sextante *m*.
sextet [sɛks'tɛt] *n* sexteto.
sexual ['sɛksjuəl] *adj* sexual; ~ **assault**
atentado contra el pudor; ~ **harassment**
acoso sexual; ~ **intercourse** relaciones *fpl*
sexuales.
sexually ['sɛksjuəlɪ] *adv* sexualmente.
sexy ['sɛksɪ] *adj* sexy.
Seychelles [seɪ'ʃɛlz] *npl*: **the ~** las
Seychelles.
SF *n abbr* = **science fiction**.
SG *n abbr* (*US*: = *Surgeon General*) jefe del
servicio federal de sanidad.
Sgt *abbr* (= *sergeant*) sgto.
shabbily ['ʃæbɪlɪ] *adv* (*treat*) injustamente;
(*dressed*) pobremente.
shabbiness ['ʃæbɪnɪs] *n* (*of dress, person*)
aspecto desharrapado; (*of building*) mal
estado.
shabby ['ʃæbɪ] *adj* (*person*) desharrapado;
(*clothes*) raído, gastado.
shack [ʃæk] *n* choza, chabola.
shackle ['ʃækl] *vt* encadenar; (*fig*): **to be ~d
by sth** verse obstaculizado por algo.
shackles ['ʃæklz] *npl* grillos *mpl*, grilletes
mpl.
shade [ʃeɪd] *n* sombra; (*for lamp*) pantalla;
(*for eyes*) visera; (*of colour*) tono *m*,
tonalidad *f*; (*US: window ~*) persiana ♦ *vt*
dar sombra a; ~**s** *npl* (*US: sunglasses*)
gafas *fpl* de sol; **in the ~** a la sombra;
(*small quantity*): **a ~ of** un poquito de; **a ~
smaller** un poquito más pequeño.
shadow ['ʃædəu] *n* sombra ♦ *vt* (*follow*)
seguir y vigilar; **without** *or* **beyond a ~
of doubt** sin lugar a dudas.
shadow cabinet *n* (*BRIT POL*) gobierno en
la oposición.
shadowy ['ʃædəuɪ] *adj* oscuro; (*dim*)
indistinto.
shady ['ʃeɪdɪ] *adj* sombreado; (*fig:
dishonest*) sospechoso; (*: deal*) turbio.
shaft [ʃɑːft] *n* (*of arrow, spear*) astil *m*; (*AUT,
TECH*) eje *m*, árbol *m*; (*of mine*) pozo; (*of
lift*) hueco, caja; (*of light*) rayo; **ventilator
~** chimenea de ventilación.
shaggy ['ʃægɪ] *adj* peludo.
shake [ʃeɪk] *vb* (*pt* **shook**, *pp* **shaken** [ʃuk,
'ʃeɪkn]) *vt* sacudir; (*building*) hacer
temblar; (*perturb*) inquietar, perturbar;
(*weaken*) debilitar; (*alarm*) trastornar ♦ *vi*
estremecerse; (*tremble*) temblar ♦ *n*
(*movement*) sacudida; **to ~ one's head** (*in
refusal*) negar con la cabeza; (*in dismay*)
mover *or* menear la cabeza, incrédulo; **to
~ hands with sb** estrechar la mano a

algn; **to ~ in one's shoes** (*fig*) temblar de miedo.

►**shake off** *vt* sacudirse; (*fig*) deshacerse de.

►**shake up** *vt* agitar.

shake-up ['ʃeɪkʌp] *n* reorganización *f*.

shakily ['ʃeɪkɪlɪ] *adv* (*reply*) con voz temblorosa *or* trémula; (*walk*) con paso vacilante; (*write*) con mano temblorosa.

shaky ['ʃeɪkɪ] *adj* (*unstable*) inestable, poco firme; (*trembling*) tembloroso; (*health*) delicado; (*memory*) defectuoso; (*person: from illness*) temblando; (*premise etc*) incierto.

shale [ʃeɪl] *n* esquisto.

shall [ʃæl] *aux vb*: **I ~ go** iré.

shallot [ʃə'lɔt] *n* (*BRIT*) cebollita, chalote *m*.

shallow ['ʃæləu] *adj* poco profundo; (*fig*) superficial.

shallows ['ʃæləuz] *npl* bajío *sg*, bajos *mpl*.

sham [ʃæm] *n* fraude *m*, engaño ♦ *adj* falso, fingido ♦ *vt* fingir, simular.

shambles ['ʃæmblz] *n* desorden *m*, confusión *f*; **the economy is (in) a complete ~** la economía está en un estado desastroso.

shambolic [ʃæm'bɔlɪk] *adj* (*col*) caótico.

shame [ʃeɪm] *n* vergüenza; (*pity*) lástima, pena ♦ *vt* avergonzar; **it is a ~ that/to do** es una lástima *or* pena que/hacer; **what a ~!** ¡qué lástima *or* pena!; **to put sth/sb to ~** (*fig*) ridiculizar algo/a algn.

shamefaced ['ʃeɪmfeɪst] *adj* avergonzado.

shameful ['ʃeɪmful] *adj* vergonzoso.

shamefully ['ʃeɪmfulɪ] *adv* vergonzosamente.

shameless ['ʃeɪmlɪs] *adj* descarado.

shampoo [ʃæm'pu:] *n* champú *m* ♦ *vt* lavar con champú.

shampoo and set *n* lavado y marcado.

shamrock ['ʃæmrɔk] *n* trébol *m*.

shandy ['ʃændɪ], (*US*) **shandygaff** ['ʃændɪgæf] *n* clara, cerveza con gaseosa.

shan't [ʃɑ:nt] = **shall not**.

shanty town ['ʃæntɪ-] *n* barrio de chabolas.

SHAPE [ʃeɪp] *n abbr* (= *Supreme Headquarters Allied Powers, Europe*) *cuartel general de las fuerzas aliadas en Europa*.

shape [ʃeɪp] *n* forma ♦ *vt* formar, dar forma a; (*clay*) modelar; (*stone*) labrar; (*sb's ideas*) determinar; (*sb's life*) determinar ♦ *vi* (*also*: **~ up**) (*events*) desarrollarse; (*person*) formarse; **to take ~** tomar forma; **to get o.s. into ~** ponerse en forma *or* en condiciones; **in the ~ of a heart** en forma de corazón; **I can't bear gardening in any ~ or form** no aguanto la jardinería de ningún modo.

-shaped *suff*: **heart~** en forma de corazón.

shapeless ['ʃeɪplɪs] *adj* informe, sin forma definida.

shapely ['ʃeɪplɪ] *adj* bien formado *or* proporcionado.

share [ʃɛə*] *n* (*part*) parte *f*, porción *f*; (*contribution*) cuota; (*COMM*) acción *f* ♦ *vt* dividir; (*fig: have in common*) compartir; **to have a ~ in the profits** tener una proporción de las ganancias; **he has a 50% ~ in a new business venture** tiene una participación del 50% en un nuevo negocio; **to ~ in** participar en; **to ~ out (among or between)** repartir (entre).

share capital *n* (*COMM*) capital *m* social en acciones.

share certificate *n* certificado *or* título de una acción.

shareholder ['ʃɛəhəuldə*] *n* (*BRIT*) accionista *m/f*.

share index *n* (*COMM*) índice *m* de la bolsa.

share issue *n* emisión *f* de acciones.

share price *n* (*COMM*) cotización *f*.

shark [ʃɑ:k] *n* tiburón *m*.

sharp [ʃɑ:p] *adj* (*razor, knife*) afilado; (*point*) puntiagudo; (*outline*) definido; (*pain*) intenso; (*MUS*) desafinado; (*contrast*) marcado; (*voice*) agudo; (*curve, bend*) cerrado; (*person: quick-witted*) avispado; (: *dishonest*) poco escrupuloso ♦ *n* (*MUS*) sostenido ♦ *adv*: **at 2 o'clock ~** a las 2 en punto; **to be ~ with sb** hablar a algn de forma brusca y tajante; **turn ~ left** tuerce del todo a la izquierda.

sharpen ['ʃɑ:pn] *vt* afilar; (*pencil*) sacar punta a; (*fig*) agudizar.

sharpener ['ʃɑ:pnə*] *n* (*gen*) afilador *m*; (*pencil ~*) sacapuntas *m inv*.

sharp-eyed [ʃɑ:p'aɪd] *adj* de vista aguda.

sharpish ['ʃɑ:pɪʃ] *adv* (*BRIT col: quickly*) prontito, bien pronto.

sharply ['ʃɑ:plɪ] *adv* (*abruptly*) bruscamente; (*clearly*) claramente; (*harshly*) severamente.

sharp-tempered [ʃɑ:p'tɛmpəd] *adj* de genio arisco.

sharp-witted [ʃɑ:p'wɪtɪd] *adj* listo, despabilado.

shatter ['ʃætə*] *vt* hacer añicos *or* pedazos; (*fig: ruin*) destruir, acabar con ♦ *vi* hacerse añicos.

shattered ['ʃætəd] *adj* (*grief-stricken*) destrozado, deshecho; (*exhausted*) agotado, hecho polvo.

shattering ['ʃætərɪŋ] *adj* (*experience*) devastador(a), anonadante.

shatterproof ['ʃætəpru:f] *adj* inastillable.

shave [ʃeɪv] *vt* afeitar, rasurar ♦ *vi* afeitarse ♦ *n*: **to have a** ~ afeitarse.

shaven ['ʃeɪvn] *adj (head)* rapado.

shaver ['ʃeɪvə*] *n (also*: **electric** ~*)* máquina de afeitar (eléctrica).

shaving ['ʃeɪvɪŋ] *n (action)* afeitado, ~s *npl (of wood etc)* virutas *fpl*.

shaving brush *n* brocha (de afeitar).

shaving cream *n* crema (de afeitar).

shaving point *n* enchufe *m* para máquinas de afeitar.

shaving soap *n* jabón *m* de afeitar.

shawl [ʃɔ:l] *n* chal *m*.

she [ʃi:] *pron* ella; **there** ~ **is** allí está; ~**-cat** gata; *NB: for ships, countries follow the gender of your translation.*

sheaf, *pl* **sheaves** [ʃi:f, ʃi:vz] *n (of corn)* gavilla; *(of arrows)* haz *m*; *(of papers)* fajo.

shear [ʃɪə*] *vt (pt* ~**ed**, *pp* ~**ed** *or* **shorn** [ʃɔ:n]) *(sheep)* esquilar, trasquilar.

►**shear off** *vi* romperse.

shears ['ʃɪəz] *npl (for hedge)* tijeras *fpl* de jardín.

sheath [ʃi:θ] *n* vaina; *(contraceptive)* preservativo.

sheath knife *n* cuchillo de monte.

sheaves [ʃi:vz] *npl of* **sheaf**.

shed [ʃɛd] *n* cobertizo; *(INDUSTRY, RAIL)* nave *f* ♦ *vt (pt, pp* **shed**) *(skin)* mudar; *(tears)* derramar; **to** ~ **light on** *(problem, mystery)* aclarar, arrojar luz sobre.

she'd [ʃi:d] = **she had, she would.**

sheen [ʃi:n] *n* brillo, lustre *m*.

sheep [ʃi:p] *n (pl inv)* oveja.

sheepdog ['ʃi:pdɔg] *n* perro pastor.

sheep farmer *n* ganadero (de ovejas).

sheepish ['ʃi:pɪʃ] *adj* tímido, vergonzoso.

sheepskin ['ʃi:pskɪn] *n* piel *f* de carnero.

sheepskin jacket *n* zamarra.

sheer [ʃɪə*] *adj (utter)* puro, completo; *(steep)* escarpado; *(material)* diáfano ♦ *adv* verticalmente; **by** ~ **chance** de pura casualidad.

sheet [ʃi:t] *n (on bed)* sábana; *(of paper)* hoja; *(of glass, metal)* lámina.

sheet feed *n (on printer)* alimentador *m* de papel.

sheet lightning *n* relámpago (difuso).

sheet metal *n* metal *m* en lámina.

sheet music *n* hojas *fpl* de partitura.

sheik(h) [ʃeɪk] *n* jeque *m*.

shelf, *pl* **shelves** [ʃɛlf, ʃɛlvz] *n* estante *m*.

shelf life *n (COMM)* periodo de conservación antes de la venta.

shell [ʃɛl] *n (on beach)* concha, caracol *(LAM)*; *(of egg, nut etc)* cáscara; *(explosive)* proyectil *m*, obús *m*; *(of building)* armazón *m* ♦ *vt (peas)* desenvainar; *(MIL)* bombardear.

►**shell out** *vi (col)*: **to** ~ **out (for)** soltar el dinero (para), desembolsar (para).

she'll [ʃi:l] = **she will, she shall.**

shellfish ['ʃɛlfɪʃ] *n (pl inv)* crustáceo; *(pl: as food)* mariscos *mpl.*

shellsuit ['ʃɛlsu:t] *n* chándal *m* (de tactel ®).

shelter ['ʃɛltə*] *n* abrigo, refugio ♦ *vt (aid)* amparar, proteger; *(give lodging to)* abrigar; *(hide)* esconder ♦ *vi* abrigarse, refugiarse; **to take** ~ **(from)** refugiarse *or* asilarse (de); **bus** ~ parada de autobús cubierta.

sheltered ['ʃɛltəd] *adj (life)* protegido; *(spot)* abrigado.

shelve [ʃɛlv] *vt (fig)* dar carpetazo a.

shelves [ʃɛlvz] *npl of* **shelf**.

shelving ['ʃɛlvɪŋ] *n* estantería.

shepherd ['ʃɛpəd] *n* pastor *m* ♦ *vt (guide)* guiar, conducir.

shepherdess ['ʃɛpədɪs] *n* pastora.

shepherd's pie *n* pastel de carne y puré de patatas.

sherbert ['ʃə:bət] *n (BRIT: powder)* polvos *mpl* azucarados; *(US: water ice)* sorbete *m*.

sheriff ['ʃɛrɪf] *n (US)* sheriff *m*.

sherry ['ʃɛrɪ] *n* jerez *m*.

she's [ʃi:z] = **she is, she has.**

Shetland ['ʃɛtlənd] *n (also*: **the** ~**s, the** ~ **Isles)** las Islas *fpl* Shetland.

Shetland pony *n* pony *m* de Shetland.

shield [ʃi:ld] *n* escudo; *(TECH)* blindaje *m* ♦ *vt*: **to** ~ **(from)** proteger (de).

shift [ʃɪft] *n (change)* cambio; *(at work)* turno ♦ *vt* trasladar; *(remove)* quitar ♦ *vi* moverse; *(change place)* cambiar de sitio; **the wind has** ~**ed to the south** el viento ha virado al sur; **a** ~ **in demand** *(COMM)* un desplazamiento de la demanda.

shift key *n (on typewriter)* tecla de mayúsculas.

shiftless ['ʃɪftlɪs] *adj (person)* vago.

shift work *n (BRIT)* trabajo por turnos; **to do** ~ trabajar por turnos.

shifty ['ʃɪftɪ] *adj* tramposo; *(eyes)* furtivo.

Shiite ['ʃi:aɪt] *adj, n* shiíta *m/f*.

shilling ['ʃɪlɪŋ] *n (BRIT)* chelín *m* (= *12 old pence; 20 in a pound*).

shilly-shally ['ʃɪlɪʃælɪ] *vi* titubear, vacilar.

shimmer ['ʃɪmə*] *n* reflejo trémulo ♦ *vi* relucir.

shimmering ['ʃɪmərɪŋ] *adj* reluciente; *(haze)* trémulo; *(satin etc)* lustroso.

shin [ʃɪn] *n* espinilla ♦ *vi*: **to** ~ **down/up a tree** bajar de/trepar un árbol.

shindig ['ʃɪndɪg] *n (col)* fiesta, juerga.

shine [ʃaɪn] *n* brillo, lustre *m* ♦ *(vb: pt, pp*

shone [ʃɔn]) *vi* brillar, relucir ♦ *vt* (*shoes*) lustrar, sacar brillo a; **to ~ a torch on sth** dirigir una linterna hacia algo.

shingle ['ʃɪŋgl] *n* (*on beach*) guijarras *fpl.*

shingles ['ʃɪŋglz] *n* (*MED*) herpes *msg.*

shining ['ʃaɪnɪŋ] *adj* (*surface, hair*) lustroso; (*light*) brillante.

shiny ['ʃaɪnɪ] *adj* brillante, lustroso.

ship [ʃɪp] *n* buque *m*, barco ♦ *vt* (*goods*) embarcar; (*oars*) desarmar; (*send*) transportar *or* enviar por vía marítima; **~'s manifest** manifiesto del buque; **on board ~** a bordo.

shipbuilder ['ʃɪpbɪldə*] *n* constructor(a) *m/f* naval.

shipbuilding ['ʃɪpbɪldɪŋ] *n* construcción *f* naval.

ship canal *n* canal *m* de navegación.

ship chandler [-'tʃɑ:ndlə*] *n* proveedor *m* de efectos navales.

shipment ['ʃɪpmənt] *n* (*act*) embarque *m*; (*goods*) envío.

shipowner ['ʃɪpəʊnə*] *n* naviero, armador *m*.

shipper ['ʃɪpə*] *n* compañía naviera.

shipping ['ʃɪpɪŋ] *n* (*act*) embarque *m*; (*traffic*) buques *mpl.*

shipping agent *n* agente *m/f* marítimo/a.

shipping company *n* compañía naviera.

shipping lane *n* ruta de navegación.

shipping line *n* = **shipping company**.

shipshape ['ʃɪpʃeɪp] *adj* en buen orden.

shipwreck ['ʃɪprek] *n* naufragio ♦ *vt*: **to be ~ed** naufragar.

shipyard ['ʃɪpjɑ:d] *n* astillero.

shire ['ʃaɪə*] *n* (*BRIT*) condado.

shirk [ʃə:k] *vt* eludir, esquivar; (*obligations*) faltar a.

shirt [ʃə:t] *n* camisa; **in ~ sleeves** en mangas de camisa.

shirty ['ʃə:tɪ] *adj* (*BRIT col*): **to be ~** estar de malas pulgas.

shit [ʃɪt] (*col!*) *n* mierda; (*nonsense*) chorradas *fpl*; **to be a ~** ser un cabrón ♦ *excl* ¡mierda!; **tough ~!** ¡te jodes!

shiver ['ʃɪvə*] *vi* temblar, estremecerse; (*with cold*) tiritar.

shoal [ʃəʊl] *n* (*of fish*) banco.

shock [ʃɔk] *n* (*impact*) choque *m*; (*ELEC*) descarga (eléctrica); (*emotional*) conmoción *f*; (*start*) sobresalto, susto; (*MED*) postración *f* nerviosa ♦ *vt* dar un susto a; (*offend*) escandalizar; **to get a ~** (*ELEC*) sentir una sacudida eléctrica; **to give sb a ~** dar un susto a algn; **to be suffering from ~** padecer una postración nerviosa; **it came as a ~ to hear that ...**

me (*etc*) asombró descubrir que ....

shock absorber [-əbsɔːbə*] *n* amortiguador *m*.

shocker ['ʃɔkə*] *n* (*col*): **it was a real ~** fue muy fuerte.

shocking ['ʃɔkɪŋ] *adj* (*awful: weather, handwriting*) espantoso, horrible; (*improper*) escandaloso; (*result*) inesperado.

shock therapy, shock treatment *n* (*MED*) terapia de choque.

shock wave *n* onda expansiva *or* de choque.

shod [ʃɔd] *pt, pp of* **shoe** ♦ *adj* calzado.

shoddiness ['ʃɔdɪnɪs] *n* baja calidad *f.*

shoddy ['ʃɔdɪ] *adj* de pacotilla.

shoe [ʃuː] *n* zapato; (*for horse*) herradura; (*brake ~*) zapata ♦ *vt* (*pt, pp* **shod** [ʃɔd]) (*horse*) herrar.

shoebrush ['ʃuːbrʌʃ] *n* cepillo para zapatos.

shoehorn ['ʃuːhɔːn] *n* calzador *m*.

shoelace ['ʃuːleɪs] *n* cordón *m*.

shoemaker ['ʃuːmeɪkə*] *n* zapatero/a.

shoe polish *n* betún *m*.

shoeshop ['ʃuːʃɔp] *n* zapatería.

shoestring ['ʃuːstrɪŋ] *n* (*shoelace*) cordón *m*; (*fig*): **on a ~** con muy poco dinero, a lo barato.

shone [ʃɔn] *pt, pp of* **shine**.

shoo [ʃuː] *excl* ¡fuera!; (*to animals*) ¡zape! ♦ *vt* (*also: ~ away, ~ off*) ahuyentar.

shook [ʃʊk] *pt of* **shake**.

shoot [ʃuːt] *n* (*on branch, seedling*) retoño, vástago; (*shooting party*) cacería; (*competition*) concurso de tiro; (*preserve*) coto de caza ♦ (*vb: pt, pp* **shot** [ʃɔt]) *vt* disparar; (*kill*) matar a tiros; (*execute*) fusilar; (*CINE: film, scene*) rodar, filmar ♦ *vi* (*FOOTBALL*) chutar; **to ~ (at)** tirar (a); **to ~ past** pasar como un rayo; **to ~ in/out** *vi* entrar corriendo/salir disparado.

▶**shoot down** *vt* (*plane*) derribar.

▶**shoot up** *vi* (*prices*) dispararse.

shooting ['ʃuːtɪŋ] *n* (*shots*) tiros *mpl*, tiroteo; (*HUNTING*) caza con escopeta; (*act: murder*) asesinato (a tiros); (*CINE*) rodaje *m*.

shooting star *n* estrella fugaz.

shop [ʃɔp] *n* tienda; (*workshop*) taller *m* ♦ *vi* (*also: go ~ping*) ir de compras; **to talk ~** (*fig*) hablar del trabajo; **repair ~** taller *m* de reparaciones.

▶**shop around** *vi* comparar precios.

shopaholic ['ʃɔpəhɔlɪk] *n* (*col*) adicto/a a las compras.

shop assistant *n* (*BRIT*) dependiente/a *m/f.*

shop floor *n* (*BRIT fig*) taller *m*, fábrica.

shopkeeper ['ʃɒpkiːpə*] n (BRIT) tendero/a.
shoplift ['ʃɒplɪft] vi robar en las tiendas.
shoplifter ['ʃɒplɪftə*] n ratero/a.
shoplifting ['ʃɒplɪftɪŋ] n ratería, robo (en las tiendas).
shopper ['ʃɒpə*] n comprador(a) m/f.
shopping ['ʃɒpɪŋ] n (goods) compras fpl.
shopping bag n bolsa (de compras).
shopping centre, (US) **shopping center** n centro comercial.
shopping mall n centro comercial.
shop-soiled ['ʃɒpsɔɪld] adj (BRIT) usado.
shop steward n (BRIT INDUSTRY) enlace m/f sindical.
shop window n escaparate m, vidriera (LAM).
shopworn ['ʃɒpwɔːn] adj (US) usado.
shore [ʃɔː*] n (of sea, lake) orilla ♦ vt: **to ~ (up)** reforzar; **on ~** en tierra.
shore leave n (NAUT) permiso para bajar a tierra.
shorn [ʃɔːn] pp of **shear**.
short [ʃɔːt] adj (not long) corto; (in time) breve, de corta duración; (person) bajo; (curt) brusco, seco ♦ vi (ELEC) ponerse en cortocircuito ♦ n (also: ~ **film**) cortometraje m; **(a pair of)** ~s (unos) pantalones mpl cortos; **to be ~ of sth** estar falto de algo; **in ~** en pocas palabras; **a ~ time ago** hace poco (tiempo); **in the ~ term** a corto plazo; **to be in ~ supply** escasear, haber escasez de; **I'm ~ of time** me falta tiempo; **~ of doing...** a menos que hagamos etc...; **everything ~ of...** todo menos...; **it is ~ for** es la forma abreviada de; **to cut ~** (speech, visit) interrumpir, terminar inesperadamente; **to fall ~ of** no alcanzar; **to run ~ of sth** acabársele algo; **to stop ~** parar en seco; **to stop ~ of** detenerse antes de.
shortage ['ʃɔːtɪdʒ] n escasez f, falta.
shortbread ['ʃɔːtbred] n pasta de mantequilla.
short-change [ʃɔːt'tʃeɪndʒ] vt: **to ~ sb** no dar el cambio completo a algn.
short-circuit [ʃɔːt'səːkɪt] n cortocircuito ♦ vt poner en cortocircuito ♦ vi ponerse en cortocircuito.
shortcoming ['ʃɔːtkʌmɪŋ] n defecto, deficiencia.
short(crust) pastry ['ʃɔːt(krʌst)-] n (BRIT) pasta quebradiza.
shortcut ['ʃɔːtkʌt] n atajo.
shorten ['ʃɔːtn] vt acortar; (visit) interrumpir.
shortfall ['ʃɔːtfɔːl] n déficit m, deficiencia.
shorthand ['ʃɔːthænd] n (BRIT) taquigrafía;

to take sth down in ~ taquigrafiar algo.
shorthand notebook n cuaderno de taquigrafía.
shorthand typist n (BRIT) taquimecanógrafo/a.
short list n (BRIT: for job) lista de candidatos pre-seleccionados.
short-lived ['ʃɔːt'lɪvd] adj efímero.
shortly ['ʃɔːtlɪ] adv en breve, dentro de poco.
shortness ['ʃɔːtnɪs] n (of distance) cortedad f; (of time) brevedad f; (manner) brusquedad f.
short-sighted [ʃɔːt'saɪtɪd] adj (BRIT) miope, corto de vista; (fig) imprudente.
short-sightedness [ʃɔːt'saɪtɪdnɪs] n miopía; (fig) falta de previsión, imprudencia.
short-staffed [ʃɔːt'stɑːft] adj falto de personal.
short story n cuento.
short-tempered [ʃɔːt'tempəd] adj enojadizo.
short-term ['ʃɔːttəːm] adj (effect) a corto plazo.
short time n: **to work ~, be on ~** (INDUSTRY) trabajar con sistema de horario reducido.
short-time working ['ʃɔːttaɪm-] n trabajo de horario reducido.
short wave n (RADIO) onda corta.
shot [ʃɒt] pt, pp of **shoot** ♦ n (sound) tiro, disparo; (person) tirador(a) m/f; (try) tentativa; (injection) inyección f; (PHOT) toma, fotografía; (shotgun pellets) perdigones mpl; **to fire a ~ at sb/sth** tirar or disparar contra algn/algo; **to have a ~ at (doing) sth** probar suerte con algo; **like a ~** (without any delay) como un rayo; **a big ~** (col) un pez gordo; **to get ~ of sth/sb** (col) deshacerse de algo/algn, quitarse algo/a algn de encima.
shotgun ['ʃɒtgʌn] n escopeta.
should [ʃud] aux vb: **I ~ go now** debo irme ahora; **he ~ be there now** debe de haber llegado (ya); **I ~ go if I were you** yo en tu lugar me iría; **I ~ like to** me gustaría; **~ he phone ...** si llamara ..., en caso de que llamase ....
shoulder ['ʃəuldə*] n hombro; (BRIT: of road): **hard ~** arcén m ♦ vt (fig) cargar con; **to look over one's ~** mirar hacia atrás; **to rub ~s with sb** (fig) codearse con algn; **to give sb the cold ~** (fig) dar de lado a algn.
shoulder blade n omóplato.
shoulder bag n bolso de bandolera.
shoulder strap n tirante m.
shouldn't ['ʃudnt] = **should not**.

shout [ʃaut] *n* grito ♦ *vt* gritar ♦ *vi* gritar, dar voces.
▶**shout down** *vt* hundir a gritos.
shouting [ˈʃautɪŋ] *n* griterío.
shouting match *n* (*col*) discusión *f* a voz en grito.
shove [ʃʌv] *n* empujón *m* ♦ *vt* empujar; (*col*: *put*): **to ~ sth in** meter algo a empellones; **he ~d me out of the way** me quitó de en medio de un empujón.
▶**shove off** *vi* (*NAUT*) alejarse del muelle; (*fig*: *col*) largarse.
shovel [ˈʃʌvl] *n* pala; (*mechanical*) excavadora ♦ *vt* mover con pala.
show [ʃəu] *n* (*of emotion*) demostración *f*; (*semblance*) apariencia; (*COMM, TECH*: *exhibition*) exhibición *f*, exposición *f*; (*THEAT*) función *f*, espectáculo; (*organization*) negocio, empresa ♦ *vb* (*pt* **showed**, *pp* **shown** [ʃəun]) *vt* mostrar, enseñar; (*courage etc*) mostrar, manifestar; (*exhibit*) exponer; (*film*) proyectar ♦ *vi* mostrarse; (*appear*) aparecer; **on ~** (*exhibits etc*) expuesto; **to be on ~** estar expuesto; **it's just for ~** es sólo para impresionar; **to ask for a ~ of hands** pedir una votación a mano alzada; **who's running the ~ here?** ¿quién manda aquí?; **to ~ a profit/loss** (*COMM*) arrojar un saldo positivo/negativo; **I have nothing to ~ for it** no saqué ningún provecho (de ello); **to ~ sb to his seat/to the door** acompañar a algn a su asiento/a la puerta; **as ~n in the illustration** como se ve en el grabado; **it just goes to ~ that ...** queda demostrado que ...; **it doesn't ~** no se ve *or* nota.
▶**show in** *vt* (*person*) hacer pasar.
▶**show off** *vi* (*pej*) presumir ♦ *vt* (*display*) lucir; (*pej*) hacer alarde de.
▶**show out** *vt*: **to ~ sb out** acompañar a algn a la puerta.
▶**show up** *vi* (*stand out*) destacar; (*col*: *turn up*) presentarse ♦ *vt* descubrir; (*unmask*) desenmascarar.
showbiz [ˈʃəubɪz] *n* (*col*) = **show business**.
show business *n* el mundo del espectáculo.
showcase [ˈʃəukeɪs] *n* vitrina; (*fig*) escaparate *m*.
showdown [ˈʃəudaun] *n* crisis *f*, momento decisivo.
shower [ˈʃauə*] *n* (*rain*) chaparrón *m*, chubasco; (*of stones etc*) lluvia; (*also*: ~ **bath**) ducha ♦ *vi* llover ♦ *vt*: **to ~ sb with sth** colmar a algn de algo; **to have** *or* **take a ~** ducharse.
shower cap *n* gorro de baño.

showerproof [ˈʃauəpruːf] *adj* impermeable.
showery [ˈʃauərɪ] *adj* (*weather*) lluvioso.
showground [ˈʃəugraund] *n* ferial *m*, real *m* (de la feria).
showing [ˈʃəuɪŋ] *n* (*of film*) proyección *f*.
show jumping *n* hípica.
showman [ˈʃəumən] *n* (*at fair, circus*) empresario (de espectáculos); (*fig*) actor *m* consumado.
showmanship [ˈʃəumənʃɪp] *n* dotes *fpl* teatrales.
shown [ʃəun] *pp of* **show**.
show-off [ˈʃəuɔf] *n* (*col*: *person*) fantasmón/ona *m/f*.
showpiece [ˈʃəupiːs] *n* (*of exhibition etc*) objeto más valioso, joya; **that hospital is a ~** ese hospital es un modelo del género.
showroom [ˈʃəuruːm] *n* sala de muestras.
show trial *n* juicio propagandístico.
showy [ˈʃəuɪ] *adj* ostentoso.
shrank [ʃræŋk] *pt of* **shrink**.
shrapnel [ˈʃræpnl] *n* metralla.
shred [ʃrɛd] *n* (*gen pl*) triza, jirón *m*; (*fig*: *of truth, evidence*) pizca, chispa ♦ *vt* hacer trizas; (*documents*) triturar; (*CULIN*) desmenuzar.
shredder [ˈʃrɛdə*] *n* (*vegetable* ~) picadora; (*document* ~) trituradora (de papel).
shrewd [ʃruːd] *adj* astuto.
shrewdly [ˈʃruːdlɪ] *adv* astutamente.
shrewdness [ˈʃruːdnɪs] *n* astucia.
shriek [ʃriːk] *n* chillido ♦ *vt, vi* chillar.
shrill [ʃrɪl] *adj* agudo, estridente.
shrimp [ʃrɪmp] *n* camarón *m*.
shrine [ʃraɪn] *n* santuario, sepulcro.
shrink, *pt* **shrank,** *pp* **shrunk** [ʃrɪŋk, ʃræŋk, ʃrʌŋk] *vi* encogerse; (*be reduced*) reducirse ♦ *vt* encoger; **to ~ from (doing) sth** no atreverse a hacer algo.
▶**shrink away** *vi* retroceder, retirarse.
shrinkage [ˈʃrɪŋkɪdʒ] *n* encogimiento; reducción *f*; (*COMM*: *in shops*) pérdidas *fpl*.
shrink-wrap [ˈʃrɪŋkræp] *vt* empaquetar en envase termoretráctil.
shrivel [ˈʃrɪvl] (*also*: ~ **up**) *vt* (*dry*) secar; (*crease*) arrugar ♦ *vi* secarse; arrugarse.
shroud [ʃraud] *n* sudario ♦ *vt*: **~ed in mystery** envuelto en el misterio.
Shrove Tuesday [ˈʃrəuv-] *n* martes *m* de carnaval.
shrub [ʃrʌb] *n* arbusto.
shrubbery [ˈʃrʌbərɪ] *n* arbustos *mpl*.
shrug [ʃrʌg] *n* encogimiento de hombros ♦ *vt, vi*: **to ~ (one's shoulders)** encogerse de hombros.
▶**shrug off** *vt* negar importancia a; (*cold, illness*) deshacerse de.

shrunk [ʃrʌŋk] *pp of* **shrink**.
shrunken ['ʃrʌŋkn] *adj* encogido.
shudder ['ʃʌdə*] *n* estremecimiento, escalofrío ♦ *vi* estremecerse.
shuffle ['ʃʌfl] *vt* (*cards*) barajar; **to ~ (one's feet)** arrastrar los pies.
shun [ʃʌn] *vt* rehuir, esquivar.
shunt [ʃʌnt] *vt* (*RAIL*) maniobrar.
shunting yard ['ʃʌntɪŋ-] *n* estación *f* de maniobras.
shut, *pt, pp* **shut** [ʃʌt] *vt* cerrar ♦ *vi* cerrarse.
▶**shut down** *vt, vi* cerrar; (*machine*) parar.
▶**shut off** *vt* (*stop: power, water supply etc*) interrumpir, cortar; (: *engine*) parar.
▶**shut out** *vt* (*person*) excluir, dejar fuera; (*noise, cold*) no dejar entrar; (*block: view*) tapar; (: *memory*) tratar de olvidar.
▶**shut up** *vi* (*col: keep quiet*) callarse ♦ *vt* (*close*) cerrar; (*silence*) callar.
shutdown ['ʃʌtdaun] *n* cierre *m*.
shutter ['ʃʌtə*] *n* contraventana; (*PHOT*) obturador *m*.
shuttle ['ʃʌtl] *n* lanzadera; (*also:* **~ service**: *AVIAT*) puente *m* aéreo ♦ *vi* (*subj: vehicle, person*) ir y venir ♦ *vt* (*passengers*) transportar, trasladar.
shuttlecock ['ʃʌtlkɔk] *n* volante *m*.
shuttle diplomacy *n* viajes *mpl* diplomáticos.
shy [ʃaɪ] *adj* tímido ♦ *vi*: **to ~ away from doing sth** (*fig*) rehusar hacer algo; **to be ~ of doing sth** esquivar hacer algo.
shyly ['ʃaɪlɪ] *adv* tímidamente.
shyness ['ʃaɪnɪs] *n* timidez *f*.
Siam [saɪ'æm] *n* Siam *m*.
Siamese [saɪə'miːz] *adj* siamés/esa ♦ *n* (*person*) siamés/esa *m/f*; (*LING*) siamés *m*; **~ cat** gato siamés; **~ twins** gemelos/as *m/fpl* siameses/as.
Siberia [saɪ'bɪərɪə] *n* Siberia.
sibling ['sɪblɪŋ] *n* (*formal*) hermano/a.
Sicilian [sɪ'sɪlɪən] *adj, n* siciliano/a *m/f*.
Sicily ['sɪsɪlɪ] *n* Sicilia.
sick [sɪk] *adj* (*ill*) enfermo; (*nauseated*) mareado; (*humour*) morboso; **to be ~** (*BRIT*) vomitar; **to feel ~** estar mareado; **to be ~ of** (*fig*) estar harto de; **a ~ person** un(a) enfermo/a; **to be (off) ~** estar ausente por enfermedad; **to fall** *or* **take ~** ponerse enfermo.
sickbag ['sɪkbæg] *n* bolsa para el mareo.
sick bay *n* enfermería.
sickbed ['sɪkbɛd] *n* lecho de enfermo.
sick building syndrome *n enfermedad causada por falta de ventilación y luz natural en un edificio.*
sicken ['sɪkn] *vt* dar asco a ♦ *vi* enfermar; **to be ~ing for** (*cold, flu etc*) mostrar

síntomas de.
sickening ['sɪknɪŋ] *adj* (*fig*) asqueroso.
sickle ['sɪkl] *n* hoz *f*.
sick leave *n* baja por enfermedad.
sickle-cell anaemia ['sɪklsɛl-] *n* anemia de células falciformes, drepanocitosis *f*.
sick list *n*: **to be on the ~** estar de baja.
sickly ['sɪklɪ] *adj* enfermizo; (*taste*) empalagoso.
sickness ['sɪknɪs] *n* enfermedad *f*, mal *m*; (*vomiting*) náuseas *fpl*.
sickness benefit *n* subsidio de enfermedad.
sick pay *n prestación por enfermedad pagada por la empresa.*
sickroom ['sɪkruːm] *n* cuarto del enfermo.
side [saɪd] *n* (*gen*) lado; (*face, surface*) cara; (*of paper*) cara; (*slice of bread*) rebanada; (*of body*) costado; (*of animal*) ijar *m*, ijada; (*of lake*) orilla; (*part*) lado; (*aspect*) aspecto; (*team: SPORT*) equipo; (: *POL etc*) partido; (*of hill*) ladera ♦ *adj* (*door, entrance*) lateral ♦ *vi*: **to ~ with sb** ponerse de parte de algn; **by the ~ of** al lado de; **~ by ~** juntos/as; **from all ~s** de todos lados; **to take ~s (with)** tomar partido (por); **~ of beef** flanco de vaca; **the right/wrong ~** el derecho/revés; **from ~ to ~** de un lado a otro.
sideboard ['saɪdbɔːd] *n* aparador *m*.
sideboards ['saɪdbɔːdz] (*BRIT*), **sideburns** ['saɪdbɔːnz] *npl* patillas *fpl*.
sidecar ['saɪdkɑː*] *n* sidecar *m*.
side dish *n* entremés *m*.
side drum *n* (*MUS*) tamboril *m*.
side effect *n* efecto secundario.
sidekick ['saɪdkɪk] *n* compinche *m*.
sidelight ['saɪdlaɪt] *n* (*AUT*) luz *f* lateral.
sideline ['saɪdlaɪn] *n* (*SPORT*) línea lateral; (*fig*) empleo suplementario.
sidelong ['saɪdlɔŋ] *adj* de soslayo; **to give a ~ glance at sth** mirar algo de reojo.
side plate *n* platito.
side road *n* (*BRIT*) calle *f* lateral.
sidesaddle ['saɪdsædl] *adv* a la amazona.
side show *n* (*stall*) caseta; (*fig*) atracción *f* secundaria.
sidestep ['saɪdstɛp] *vt* (*question*) eludir; (*problem*) esquivar ♦ *vi* (*BOXING etc*) dar un quiebro.
side street *n* calle *f* lateral.
sidetrack ['saɪdtræk] *vt* (*fig*) desviar (de su propósito).
sidewalk ['saɪdwɔːk] *n* (*US*) acera, vereda (*LAM*), andén *n* (*LAM*), banqueta (*LAM*).
sideways ['saɪdweɪz] *adv* de lado.
siding ['saɪdɪŋ] *n* (*RAIL*) apartadero, vía muerta.

sidle ['saɪdl] *vi*: **to ~ up (to)** acercarse furtivamente (a).

SIDS [sɪdz] *n abbr* (= *sudden infant death syndrome*) (síndrome *m* de la) muerte *f* súbita.

siege [siːdʒ] *n* cerco, sitio; **to lay ~ to** cercar, sitiar.

siege economy *n* economía de sitio *or* de asedio.

Sierra Leone [sɪˈerəlɪˈəun] *n* Sierra Leona.

siesta [sɪˈestə] *n* siesta.

sieve [sɪv] *n* colador *m* ♦ *vt* cribar.

sift [sɪft] *vt* cribar ♦ *vi*: **to ~ through** pasar por una criba; (*information*) analizar cuidadosamente.

sigh [saɪ] *n* suspiro ♦ *vi* suspirar.

sight [saɪt] *n* (*faculty*) vista; (*spectacle*) espectáculo; (*on gun*) mira, alza ♦ *vt* ver, divisar; **in ~** a la vista; **out of ~** fuera de (la) vista; **at ~** a la vista; **at first ~** a primera vista; **to lose ~ of sth/sb** perder algo/a algn de vista; **to catch ~ of sth/sb** divisar algo/a algn; **I know her by ~** la conozco de vista; **to set one's ~s on (doing) sth** aspirar a *or* ambicionar (hacer) algo.

sighted ['saɪtɪd] *adj* vidente, de vista normal; **partially ~** de vista limitada.

sightseer ['saɪtsiːə*] *n* excursionista *m/f*, turista *m/f*.

sightseeing ['saɪtsiːɪŋ] *n* excursionismo, turismo; **to go ~** visitar monumentos.

sign [saɪn] *n* (*with hand*) señal *f*, seña; (*trace*) huella, rastro; (*notice*) letrero; (*written*) signo; (*road ~*) indicador *m*; (: *with instructions*) señal *f* de tráfico ♦ *vt* firmar; **as a ~ of** en señal de; **it's a good/bad ~** es buena/mala señal; **plus/minus ~** signo de más/de menos; **to ~ one's name** firmar.

▶**sign away** *vt* (*rights etc*) ceder.

▶**sign off** *vi* (*RADIO, TV*) cerrar el programa.

▶**sign on** *vi* (*MIL*) alistarse; (*as unemployed*) apuntarse al paro; (*employee*) firmar un contrato ♦ *vt* (*MIL*) alistar; (*employee*) contratar; **to ~ on for a course** matricularse en un curso.

▶**sign out** *vi* firmar el registro (al salir).

▶**sign over** *vt*: **to ~ sth over to sb** traspasar algo a algn.

▶**sign up** *vi* (*MIL*) alistarse ♦ *vt* (*contract*) contratar.

signal ['sɪgnl] *n* señal *f* ♦ *vi* (*AUT*) señalizar ♦ *vt* (*person*) hacer señas a; (*message*) transmitir; **the engaged ~** (*TEL*) la señal de comunicando; **the ~ is very weak** (*TV*) no captamos bien el canal; **to ~ a left/**
right turn (*AUT*) indicar que se va a doblar a la izquierda/derecha; **to ~ to sb (to do sth)** hacer señas a algn (para que haga algo).

signal box *n* (*RAIL*) garita de señales.

signalman ['sɪgnlmən] *n* (*RAIL*) guardavía *m*.

signatory ['sɪgnətərɪ] *n* firmante *m/f*.

signature ['sɪgnətʃə*] *n* firma.

signature tune *n* sintonía.

signet ring ['sɪgnət-] *n* (anillo de) sello.

significance [sɪgˈnɪfɪkəns] *n* significado; (*importance*) trascendencia; **that is of no ~** eso no tiene importancia.

significant [sɪgˈnɪfɪkənt] *adj* significativo; trascendente; **it is ~ that ...** es significativo que ....

significantly [sɪgˈnɪfɪkəntlɪ] *adv* (*smile*) expresivamente; (*improve, increase*) sensiblemente; **and, ~ ...** y debe notarse que ....

signify ['sɪgnɪfaɪ] *vt* significar.

sign language *n* mímica, lenguaje *m* por *or* de señas.

signpost ['saɪnpəust] *n* indicador *m*.

silage ['saɪlɪdʒ] *n* ensilaje *m*.

silence ['saɪlns] *n* silencio ♦ *vt* hacer callar; (*guns*) reducir al silencio.

silencer ['saɪlnsə*] *n* (*on gun, BRIT AUT*) silenciador *m*.

silent ['saɪlnt] *adj* (*gen*) silencioso; (*not speaking*) callado; (*film*) mudo; **to keep** *or* **remain ~** guardar silencio.

silently ['saɪlntlɪ] *adv* silenciosamente, en silencio.

silent partner *n* (*COMM*) socio/a comanditario/a.

silhouette [sɪluːˈet] *n* silueta; **~d against** destacado sobre *or* contra.

silicon ['sɪlɪkən] *n* silicio.

silicon chip *n* chip *m*, plaqueta de silicio.

silicone ['sɪlɪkəun] *n* silicona.

silk [sɪlk] *n* seda ♦ *cpd* de seda.

silky ['sɪlkɪ] *adj* sedoso.

sill [sɪl] *n* (*also*: **window~**) alféizar *m*; (*AUT*) umbral *m*.

silliness ['sɪlɪnɪs] *n* (*of person*) necedad *f*; (*of idea*) lo absurdo.

silly ['sɪlɪ] *adj* (*person*) tonto; (*idea*) absurdo; **to do sth ~** hacer una tontería.

silo ['saɪləu] *n* silo.

silt [sɪlt] *n* sedimento.

silver ['sɪlvə*] *n* plata; (*money*) moneda suelta ♦ *adj* de plata.

silver paper (*BRIT*), **silver foil** *n* papel *m* de plata.

silver plate *n* vajilla de plata.

silver-plated [sɪlvəˈpleɪtɪd] *adj* plateado.

silversmith ['sɪlvəsmɪθ] n platero/a.
silverware ['sɪlvəwɛə*] n plata.
silver wedding (anniversary) n (BRIT)
bodas fpl de plata.
silvery ['sɪlvrɪ] adj plateado.
similar ['sɪmɪlə*] adj: ~ **to** parecido or
semejante a.
similarity [sɪmɪ'lærɪtɪ] n parecido,
semejanza.
similarly ['sɪmɪləlɪ] adv del mismo modo; (in
a similar way) de manera parecida;
(equally) igualmente.
simile ['sɪmɪlɪ] n símil m.
simmer ['sɪmə*] vi hervir a fuego lento.
▶**simmer down** vi (fig, col) calmarse,
tranquilizarse.
simpering ['sɪmpərɪŋ] adj afectado; (foolish)
bobo.
simple ['sɪmpl] adj (easy) sencillo; (foolish,
COMM) simple; **the** ~ **truth** la pura
verdad.
simple interest n (COMM) interés m
simple.
simple-minded [sɪmpl'maɪndɪd] adj simple,
ingenuo.
simpleton ['sɪmpltən] n inocentón/ona m/f.
simplicity [sɪm'plɪsɪtɪ] n sencillez f;
(foolishness) ingenuidad f.
simplification [sɪmplɪfɪ'keɪʃən] n
simplificación f.
simplify ['sɪmplɪfaɪ] vt simplificar.
simply ['sɪmplɪ] adv (in a simple way: live,
talk) sencillamente; (just, merely) sólo.
simulate ['sɪmjuleɪt] vt simular.
simulation [sɪmju'leɪʃən] n simulación f.
simultaneous [sɪməl'teɪnɪəs] adj
simultáneo.
simultaneously [sɪməl'teɪnɪəslɪ] adv
simultáneamente, a la vez.
sin [sɪn] n pecado ♦ vi pecar.
since [sɪns] adv desde entonces ♦ prep desde
♦ conj (time) desde que; (because) ya que,
puesto que; ~ **then** desde entonces; ~
Monday desde el lunes; (ever) ~ **I arrived**
desde que llegué.
sincere [sɪn'sɪə*] adj sincero.
sincerely [sɪn'sɪəlɪ] adv sinceramente;
yours ~ (in letters) le saluda
(afectuosamente); ~ **yours** (US: in letters)
le saluda atentamente.
sincerity [sɪn'sɛrɪtɪ] n sinceridad f.
sinecure ['saɪnɪkjuə*] n chollo.
sinew ['sɪnjuː] n tendón m.
sinful ['sɪnful] adj (thought) pecaminoso;
(person) pecador(a).
sing, pt **sang,** pp **sung** [sɪŋ, sæŋ, sʌŋ] vt
cantar ♦ vi (gen) cantar; (bird) trinar;
(ears) zumbar.

Singapore [sɪŋə'pɔː*] n Singapur m.
singe [sɪndʒ] vt chamuscar.
singer ['sɪŋə*] n cantante m/f.
Singhalese [sɪŋə'liːz] adj = **Sinhalese.**
singing ['sɪŋɪŋ] n (of person, bird) canto;
(songs) canciones fpl; (in the ears)
zumbido; (of kettle) silbido.
single ['sɪŋgl] adj único, solo; (unmarried)
soltero; (not double) individual, sencillo
♦ n (BRIT: also: ~ **ticket**) billete m sencillo;
(record) sencillo, single m; ~**s** npl (TENNIS)
individual msg; **not a** ~ **one was left** no
quedaba ni uno; **every** ~ **day** todos los
días (sin excepción).
▶**single** vt (choose) escoger; (point out)
singularizar.
single bed n cama individual.
single-breasted [sɪŋgl'brɛstɪd] adj (jacket,
suit) recto, sin cruzar.
single-density ['sɪŋgldɛnsɪtɪ] adj (COMPUT:
disk) de densidad sencilla.
single-entry book-keeping ['sɪŋglɛntrɪ-] n
contabilidad f por partida simple.
Single European Market n: **the** ~ el
Mercado Único Europeo.
single file n: **in** ~ en fila de uno.
single-handed [sɪŋgl'hændɪd] adv sin
ayuda.
single-minded [sɪŋgl'maɪndɪd] adj resuelto,
firme.
single parent n (mother) madre f soltera;
(father) padre m soltero.
single-parent family ['sɪŋglpɛərənt-] n
familia monoparental.
single room n habitación f individual.
singles bar n (esp US) bar m para solteros.
single-sex school ['sɪŋglsɛks-] n escuela
no mixta.
single-sided [sɪŋgl'saɪdɪd] adj (COMPUT:
disk) de una cara.
single spacing n (TYP): **in** ~ a un espacio.
singlet ['sɪŋglɪt] n camiseta.
singly ['sɪŋglɪ] adv uno por uno.
singsong ['sɪŋsɔŋ] adj (tone) cantarín/ina
♦ n (songs): **to have a** ~ tener un
concierto improvisado.
singular ['sɪŋgjulə*] adj singular,
extraordinario; (odd) extraño; (LING)
singular ♦ n (LING) singular m; **in the
feminine** ~ en femenino singular.
singularly ['sɪŋgjuləlɪ] adv singularmente,
extraordinariamente.
Sinhalese [sɪnhə'liːz] adj singhalese.
sinister ['sɪnɪstə*] adj siniestro.
sink [sɪŋk] n fregadero ♦ vb (pt **sank,** pp **sunk**
[sæŋk, sʌŋk]) vt (ship) hundir, echar a
pique; (foundations) excavar; (piles etc): **to**
~ **sth into** hundir algo en ♦ vi (gen)

hundirse; **he sank into a chair/the mud** se dejó caer en una silla/se hundió en el barro; **the shares** or **share prices have sunk to 3 dollars** las acciones han bajado a 3 dólares.

▶**sink in** vi (fig) penetrar, calar; **the news took a long time to ~ in** la noticia tardó mucho en hacer mella en él (or mí etc).

sinking ['sɪŋkɪŋ] adj: **that ~ feeling** la sensación esa de desmoralización.

sinking fund n fondo de amortización.

sink unit n fregadero.

sinner ['sɪnə*] n pecador(a) m/f.

Sinn Féin [ʃɪn'feɪn] n partido político republicano de Irlanda del Norte.

sinuous ['sɪnjuəs] adj sinuoso.

sinus ['saɪnəs] n (ANAT) seno.

sip [sɪp] n sorbo ♦ vt sorber, beber a sorbitos.

siphon ['saɪfən] n sifón m ♦ vt (also: ~ **off**) (funds) desviar.

sir [sə:*] n señor m; **S~ John Smith** el Señor John Smith; **yes ~** sí, señor; **Dear S~** (in letter) Muy señor mío, Estimado Señor; **Dear S~s** Muy señores nuestros, Estimados Señores.

siren ['saɪərn] n sirena.

sirloin ['sə:lɔɪn] n solomillo; **~ steak** filete m de solomillo.

sisal ['saɪsəl] n pita, henequén m (LAM).

sissy ['sɪsɪ] n (col) marica m.

sister ['sɪstə*] n hermana; (BRIT: nurse) enfermera jefe.

sister-in-law ['sɪstərɪnlɔ:] n cuñada.

sister organization n organización f hermana.

sister ship n barco gemelo.

sit, pt, pp **sat** [sɪt, sæt] vi sentarse; (be sitting) estar sentado; (assembly) reunirse; (dress etc) caer, sentar ♦ vt (exam) presentarse a; **that jacket ~s well** esa chaqueta sienta bien; **to ~ on a committee** ser miembro de una comisión or un comité.

▶**sit about, sit around** vi holgazanear.

▶**sit back** vi (in seat) recostarse.

▶**sit down** vi sentarse; **to be ~ting down** estar sentado.

▶**sit in on** vt fus: **to ~ in on a discussion** asistir a una discusión.

▶**sit up** vi incorporarse; (not go to bed) no acostarse.

sitcom ['sɪtkɔm] n abbr (= situation comedy) telecomedia.

sit-down ['sɪtdaun] adj: **~ strike** huelga de brazos caídos; **a ~ meal** una comida sentada.

site [saɪt] n sitio; (also: **building ~**) solar m ♦ vt situar.

sit-in ['sɪtɪn] n (demonstration) sentada f.

siting ['saɪtɪŋ] n (location) situación f, emplazamiento.

sitter ['sɪtə*] n (ART) modelo m/f; (baby~) canguro m/f.

sitting ['sɪtɪŋ] n (of assembly etc) sesión f; (in canteen) turno.

sitting member n (POL) titular m/f de un escaño.

sitting room n sala de estar.

sitting tenant n inquilino con derechos de estancia en una vivienda.

situate ['sɪtjueɪt] vt situar, ubicar (LAM).

situated ['sɪtjueɪtɪd] adj situado, ubicado (LAM).

situation [sɪtju'eɪʃən] n situación f; "**~s vacant**" (BRIT) "ofertas de trabajo".

situation comedy n (TV, RADIO) serie f cómica, comedia de situación.

six [sɪks] num seis.

six-pack ['sɪkspæk] n (esp US) paquete m de seis cervezas.

sixteen [sɪks'ti:n] num dieciséis.

sixth [sɪksθ] adj sexto; **the upper/lower ~** (SCOL) el séptimo/sexto año.

sixty ['sɪkstɪ] num sesenta.

size [saɪz] n (gen) tamaño; (extent) extensión f; (of clothing) talla; (of shoes) número; **I take ~ 5 shoes** calzo el número cinco; **I take ~ 14** mi talla es la 42; **I'd like the small/large ~** (of soap powder etc) quisiera el tamaño pequeño/grande.

▶**size up** vt formarse una idea de.

sizeable ['saɪzəbl] adj importante, considerable.

sizzle ['sɪzl] vi crepitar.

SK abbr (Canada) = Saskatchewan.

skate [skeɪt] n patín m; (fish: pl inv) raya ♦ vi patinar.

▶**skate over, skate round** vt fus (problem, issue) pasar por alto.

skateboard ['skeɪtbɔ:d] n monopatín m.

skater ['skeɪtə*] n patinador(a) m/f.

skating ['skeɪtɪŋ] n patinaje m; **figure ~** patinaje m artístico.

skating rink n pista de patinaje.

skeleton ['skelɪtn] n esqueleto; (TECH) armazón m; (outline) esquema m.

skeleton key n llave f maestra.

skeleton staff n personal m reducido.

skeptic ['skeptɪk] etc (US) = **sceptic**.

sketch [sketʃ] n (drawing) dibujo; (outline) esbozo, bosquejo; (THEAT) pieza corta ♦ vt dibujar; esbozar.

sketch book n bloc m de dibujo.

sketching ['sketʃɪŋ] n dibujo.

sketch pad n bloc m de dibujo.

sketchy ['sketʃɪ] adj incompleto.

skewer ['skjuːə*] n broqueta.

ski [skiː] n esquí m ♦ vi esquiar.

ski boot n bota de esquí.

skid [skɪd] n patinazo ♦ vi patinar; **to go into a** ~ comenzar a patinar.

skid mark n señal f de patinazo.

skier ['skiːə*] n esquiador(a) m/f.

skiing ['skiːɪŋ] n esquí m; **to go** ~ practicar el esquí, (ir a) esquiar.

ski instructor n instructor(a) m/f de esquí.

ski jump n pista para salto de esquí.

skilful, (US) **skillful** ['skɪlful] adj diestro, experto.

ski lift n telesilla m, telesquí m.

skill [skɪl] n destreza, pericia; (technique) arte m, técnica; **there's a certain** ~ **to doing it** se necesita cierta habilidad para hacerlo.

skilled [skɪld] adj hábil, diestro; (worker) cualificado.

skillet ['skɪlɪt] n sartén f pequeña.

skillful ['skɪlful] etc (US) = **skilful** etc.

skil(l)fully ['skɪlfulɪ] adv hábilmente, con destreza.

skim [skɪm] vt (milk) desnatar; (glide over) rozar, rasar ♦ vi: **to** ~ **through** (book) hojear.

skimmed milk [skɪmd-] n leche f desnatada or descremada.

skimp [skɪmp] vt (work) chapucear; (cloth etc) escatimar; **to** ~ **on** (material etc) economizar; (work) escatimar.

skimpy ['skɪmpɪ] adj (meagre) escaso; (skirt) muy corto.

skin [skɪn] n (gen) piel f; (complexion) cutis m; (of fruit, vegetable) piel f, cáscara; (crust: on pudding, paint) nata ♦ vt (fruit etc) pelar; (animal) despellejar; **wet** or **soaked to the** ~ calado hasta los huesos.

skin cancer n cáncer m de piel.

skin-deep ['skɪn'diːp] adj superficial.

skin diver n buceador(a) m/f.

skin diving n buceo.

skinflint ['skɪnflɪnt] n tacaño/a, roñoso/a.

skinhead ['skɪnhɛd] n cabeza m/f rapada, skin(head) m/f.

skinny ['skɪnɪ] adj flaco, magro.

skintight ['skɪntaɪt] adj (dress etc) muy ajustado.

skip [skɪp] n brinco, salto; (container) contenedor m ♦ vi brincar; (with rope) saltar a la comba ♦ vt (pass over) omitir, saltar.

ski pants npl pantalones mpl de esquí.

ski pole n bastón m de esquiar.

skipper ['skɪpə*] n (NAUT, SPORT) capitán m.

skipping rope ['skɪpɪŋ-] n (BRIT) comba, cuerda (de saltar).

ski resort n estación f de esquí.

skirmish ['skəːmɪʃ] n escaramuza.

skirt [skəːt] n falda, pollera (LAM) ♦ vt (surround) ceñir, rodear; (go round) ladear.

skirting board ['skəːtɪŋ-] n (BRIT) rodapié m.

ski run n pista de esquí.

ski suit n traje m de esquiar.

skit [skɪt] n sátira, parodia.

ski tow n arrastre m (de esquí).

skittle ['skɪtl] n bolo; ~**s** (game) boliche m.

skive [skaɪv] vi (BRIT col) gandulear.

skulk [skʌlk] vi esconderse.

skull [skʌl] n calavera; (ANAT) cráneo.

skullcap ['skʌlkæp] n (worn by Jews) casquete m; (worn by Pope) solideo.

skunk [skʌŋk] n mofeta.

sky [skaɪ] n cielo; **to praise sb to the skies** poner a algn por las nubes.

sky-blue [skaɪ'bluː] adj (azul) celeste.

skydiving ['skaɪdaɪvɪŋ] n paracaidismo acrobático.

sky-high ['skaɪ'haɪ] adj (col) por las nubes ♦ adv (throw) muy alto; **prices have gone** ~ (col) los precios están por las nubes.

skylark ['skaɪlɑːk] n (bird) alondra.

skylight ['skaɪlaɪt] n tragaluz m, claraboya.

skyline ['skaɪlaɪn] n (horizon) horizonte m; (of city) perfil m.

skyscraper ['skaɪskreɪpə*] n rascacielos m inv.

slab [slæb] n (stone) bloque m; (of wood) tabla, plancha; (flat) losa; (of cake) trozo; (of meat, cheese) tajada, trozo.

slack [slæk] adj (loose) flojo; (slow) de poca actividad; (careless) descuidado; (COMM: market) poco activo; (: demand) débil; (period) bajo; **business is** ~ hay poco movimiento en el negocio.

slacken ['slækn] (also: ~ **off**) vi aflojarse ♦ vt aflojar; (speed) disminuir.

slackness ['slæknɪs] n flojedad f; negligencia.

slacks [slæks] npl pantalones mpl.

slag [slæg] n escoria, escombros mpl.

slag heap n escorial m, escombrera.

slain [sleɪn] pp of **slay**.

slake [sleɪk] vt (one's thirst) apagar.

slalom ['slɑːləm] n eslálom m.

slam [slæm] vt (door) cerrar de golpe; (throw) arrojar (violentamente); (criticize) vapulear, vituperar ♦ vi cerrarse de golpe.

slammer [slæmə*] n (col): **the** ~ la trena, el talego.

slander ['slɑːndə*] n calumnia, difamación f ♦ vt calumniar, difamar.

slanderous ['slɑːndərəs] *adj* calumnioso, difamatorio.

slang [slæŋ] *n* argot *m*; (*jargon*) jerga.

slanging match ['slæŋɪŋ-] *n* (*BRIT col*) bronca gorda.

slant [slɑːnt] *n* sesgo, inclinación *f*; (*fig*) punto de vista; **to get a new ~ on sth** obtener un nuevo punto de vista sobre algo.

slanted ['slɑːntɪd], **slanting** ['slɑːntɪŋ] *adj* inclinado.

slap [slæp] *n* palmada; (*in face*) bofetada ♦ *vt* dar una palmada/bofetada a ♦ *adv* (*directly*) de lleno.

slapdash ['slæpdæʃ] *adj* chapucero.

slaphead ['slæphɛd] *n* (*BRIT col*) colgado/a.

slapstick ['slæpstɪk] *n*: **~ comedy** comedia de payasadas.

slap-up ['slæpʌp] *adj*: **a ~ meal** (*BRIT*) un banquetazo, una comilona.

slash [slæʃ] *vt* acuchillar; (*fig: prices*) quemar.

slat [slæt] *n* (*of wood, plastic*) tablilla, listón *m*.

slate [sleɪt] *n* pizarra ♦ *vt* (*BRIT: fig: criticize*) vapulear.

slaughter ['slɔːtə*] *n* (*of animals*) matanza; (*of people*) carnicería ♦ *vt* matar.

slaughterhouse ['slɔːtəhaus] *n* matadero.

Slav [slɑːv] *adj* eslavo.

slave [sleɪv] *n* esclavo/a ♦ *vi* (*also*: **~ away**) trabajar como un negro; **to ~ (away) at sth** trabajar como un negro en algo.

slave driver *n* (*col, pej*) tirano/a.

slave labour, (*US*) **slave labor** *n* trabajo de esclavos.

slaver ['slævə*] *vi* (*dribble*) babear.

slavery ['sleɪvərɪ] *n* esclavitud *f*.

slavish ['sleɪvɪʃ] *adj* (*devotion*) de esclavo; (*imitation*) servil.

slay, *pt* **slew**, *pp* **slain** [sleɪ, sluː, sleɪn] *vt* (*literary*) matar.

SLD *n abbr* (*BRIT POL*) = Social and Liberal Democrats.

sleazy ['sliːzɪ] *adj* (*fig: place*) sórdido.

sledge [slɛdʒ], (*US*) **sled** [slɛd] *n* trineo.

sledgehammer ['slɛdʒhæmə*] *n* mazo.

sleek [sliːk] *adj* (*shiny*) lustroso.

sleep [sliːp] *n* sueño ♦ *vb* (*pt, pp* **slept** [slɛpt]) *vi* dormir ♦ *vt*: **we can ~ 4** podemos alojar a 4, tenemos cabida para 4; **to go to ~** dormirse; **to have a good night's ~** dormir toda la noche; **to put to ~** (*patient*) dormir; (*animal: euphemism: kill*) sacrificar; **to ~ lightly** tener el sueño ligero; **to ~ with sb** (*euphemism*) acostarse con algn.

▶**sleep in** *vi* (*oversleep*) quedarse dormido.

sleeper ['sliːpə*] *n* (*person*) durmiente *m/f*; (*BRIT RAIL: on track*) traviesa; (: *train*) coche-cama *m*.

sleepiness ['sliːpɪnɪs] *n* somnolencia.

sleeping bag ['sliːpɪŋ-] *n* saco de dormir.

sleeping car *n* coche-cama *m*.

sleeping partner *n* (*COMM*) socio/a comanditario/a.

sleeping pill *n* somnífero.

sleeping sickness *n* enfermedad *f* del sueño.

sleepless ['sliːplɪs] *adj*: **a ~ night** una noche en blanco.

sleeplessness ['sliːplɪsnɪs] *n* insomnio.

sleepwalk ['sliːpwɔːk] *vi* caminar dormido; (*habitually*) ser sonámbulo.

sleepwalker ['sliːpwɔːkə*] *n* sonámbulo/a.

sleepy ['sliːpɪ] *adj* soñoliento; **to be** *or* **feel ~** tener sueño.

sleet [sliːt] *n* aguanieve *f*.

sleeve [sliːv] *n* manga; (*TECH*) manguito; (*of record*) funda.

sleeveless ['sliːvlɪs] *adj* (*garment*) sin mangas.

sleigh [sleɪ] *n* trineo.

sleight [slaɪt] *n*: **~ of hand** prestidigitación *f*.

slender ['slɛndə*] *adj* delgado; (*means*) escaso.

slept [slɛpt] *pt, pp of* **sleep**.

sleuth [sluːθ] *n* (*col*) detective *m/f*.

slew [sluː] *vi* (*veer*) torcerse ♦ *pt of* **slay**.

slice [slaɪs] *n* (*of meat*) tajada; (*of bread*) rebanada; (*of lemon*) rodaja; (*utensil*) paleta ♦ *vt* cortar, tajar; rebanar; **~d bread** pan *m* de molde.

slick [slɪk] *adj* (*skilful*) hábil, diestro ♦ *n* (*also*: **oil ~**) capa de aceite.

slid [slɪd] *pt, pp of* **slide**.

slide [slaɪd] *n* (*in playground*) tobogán *m*; (*PHOT*) diapositiva; (*microscope ~*) portaobjetos *m inv*, plaquilla de vidrio; (*BRIT: also*: **hair ~**) pasador *m* ♦ *vb* (*pt, pp* **slid** [slɪd]) *vt* correr, deslizar ♦ *vi* (*slip*) resbalarse; (*glide*) deslizarse; **to let things ~** (*fig*) dejar que ruede la bola.

slide projector *n* (*PHOT*) proyector *m* de diapositivas.

slide rule *n* regla de cálculo.

sliding ['slaɪdɪŋ] *adj* (*door*) corredizo; **~ roof** (*AUT*) techo de corredera.

sliding scale *n* escala móvil.

slight [slaɪt] *adj* (*slim*) delgado; (*frail*) delicado; (*pain etc*) leve; (*trifling*) insignificante; (*small*) pequeño ♦ *n* desaire *m* ♦ *vt* (*offend*) ofender, desairar; **a ~ improvement** una ligera mejora; **not in the ~est** en absoluto; **there's not the**

~**est possibility** no hay la menor *or* más mínima posibilidad.

slightly ['slaɪtlɪ] *adv* ligeramente, un poco; ~ **built** delgado.

slim [slɪm] *adj* delgado, esbelto ♦ *vi* adelgazar.

slime [slaɪm] *n* limo, cieno.

slimming ['slɪmɪŋ] *n* adelgazamiento ♦ *adj* (*diet, pills*) adelgazante.

slimness ['slɪmnɪs] *n* delgadez *f.*

slimy ['slaɪmɪ] *adj* limoso; (*covered with mud*) fangoso; (*also fig: person*) adulón, zalamero.

sling [slɪŋ] *n* (*MED*) cabestrillo; (*weapon*) honda ♦ *vt* (*pt, pp* **slung** [slʌŋ]) tirar, arrojar; **to have one's arm in a** ~ llevar el brazo en cabestrillo.

slink, *pt, pp* **slunk** [slɪŋk, slʌŋk] *vi:* **to** ~ **away,** ~ **off** escabullirse.

slinky ['slɪŋkɪ] *adj* (*clothing*) pegado al cuerpo, superajustado.

slip [slɪp] *n* (*slide*) resbalón *m*; (*mistake*) descuido; (*underskirt*) combinación *f*; (*of paper*) papelito ♦ *vt* (*slide*) deslizar ♦ *vi* (*slide*) deslizarse; (*stumble*) resbalar(se); (*decline*) decaer; (*move smoothly*): **to** ~ **into/out of** (*room etc*) colarse en/salirse de; **to let a chance** ~ **by** dejar escapar la oportunidad; **to** ~ **sth on/off** ponerse/ quitarse algo; **to** ~ **on a jumper** ponerse un jersey *or* un suéter; **it** ~**ped from her hand** se la cayó de la mano; **to give sb the** ~ dar esquinazo a algn; **wages** ~ (*BRIT*) hoja del sueldo; **a** ~ **of the tongue** un lapsus.

►**slip away** *vi* escabullirse.

►**slip in** *vt* meter ♦ *vi* meterse, colarse.

►**slip out** *vi* (*go out*) salir (un momento).

slip-on ['slɪpɔn] *adj* de quita y pon; (*shoes*) sin cordones.

slipped disc [slɪpt-] *n* vértebra dislocada.

slipper ['slɪpə*] *n* zapatilla, pantufla.

slippery ['slɪpərɪ] *adj* resbaladizo.

slip road *n* (*BRIT*) carretera de acceso.

slipshod ['slɪpʃɔd] *adj* descuidado, chapucero.

slipstream ['slɪpstriːm] *n* viento de la hélice.

slip-up ['slɪpʌp] *n* (*error*) desliz *m.*

slipway ['slɪpweɪ] *n* grada, gradas *fpl.*

slit [slɪt] *n* raja; (*cut*) corte *m* ♦ *vt* (*pt, pp* **slit**) rajar, cortar; **to** ~ **sb's throat** cortarle el pescuezo a algn.

slither ['slɪðə*] *vi* deslizarse.

sliver ['slɪvə*] *n* (*of glass, wood*) astilla; (*of cheese, sausage*) lonja, loncha.

slob [slɔb] *n* (*col*) patán/ana *m/f*, palurdo/a.

slog [slɔg] (*BRIT*) *vi* sudar tinta ♦ *n:* **it was a** ~ **costó trabajo (hacerlo).**

slogan ['sləugən] *n* eslogan *m*, lema *m.*

slop [slɔp] *vi* (*also:* ~ **over**) derramarse, desbordarse ♦ *vt* derramar, verter.

slope [sləup] *n* (*up*) cuesta, pendiente *f*; (*down*) declive *m*; (*side of mountain*) falda, vertiente *f* ♦ *vi:* **to** ~ **down** estar en declive; **to** ~ **up** subir (en pendiente).

sloping ['sləupɪŋ] *adj* en pendiente; en declive.

sloppily ['slɔpɪlɪ] *adv* descuidadamente; con descuido *or* desaliño.

sloppiness ['slɔpɪnɪs] *n* descuido; desaliño.

sloppy ['slɔpɪ] *adj* (*work*) descuidado; (*appearance*) desaliñado.

slosh [slɔʃ] *vi:* **to** ~ **about** *or* **around** chapotear.

sloshed [slɔʃt] *adj* (*col: drunk*): **to get** ~ agarrar una trompa.

slot [slɔt] *n* ranura; (*fig: in timetable*) hueco; (*RADIO, TV*) espacio ♦ *vt:* **to** ~ **into** encajar en.

sloth [sləuθ] *n* (*vice*) pereza; (*ZOOL*) oso perezoso.

slot machine *n* (*BRIT: vending machine*) máquina expendedora, (*for gambling*) máquina tragaperras.

slot meter *n* contador *m.*

slouch [slautʃ] *vi:* **to** ~ **about,** ~ **around** (*laze*) gandulear.

Slovak ['sləuvæk] *adj* eslovaco ♦ *n* eslovaco/a; (*LING*) eslovaco; **the** ~ **Republic** Eslovaquia.

Slovakia [sləu'vækɪə] *n* Eslovaquia.

Slovakian [sləu'vækɪən] *adj, n* = **Slovak.**

Slovene [sləu'viːn] *adj* esloveno ♦ *n* esloveno/a; (*LING*) esloveno.

Slovenia [sləu'viːnɪə] *n* Eslovenia.

Slovenian [sləu'viːnɪən] *adj, n* = **Slovene.**

slovenly ['slʌvənlɪ] *adj* (*dirty*) desaliñado, desaseado; (*careless*) descuidado.

slow [sləu] *adj* lento; (*watch*): **to be** ~ estar atrasado ♦ *adv* lentamente, despacio ♦ *vt* (*also:* ~ **down,** ~ **up**) retardar; (*engine, machine*) reducir la marcha de ♦ *vi* (*also:* ~ **down,** ~ **up**) ir más despacio; "~" (*road sign*) "disminuir la velocidad"; **at a** ~ **speed** a una velocidad lenta; **the** ~ **lane** el carril derecho; **business is** ~ (*COMM*) hay poca actividad; **my watch is 20 minutes** ~ mi reloj lleva 20 minutos de retraso; **bake for two hours in a** ~ **oven** cocer *or* asar 2 horas en el horno a fuego lento; **to be** ~ **to act/decide** tardar en obrar/decidir; **to go** ~ (*driver*) conducir despacio; (*in industrial dispute*) trabajar a ritmo lento.

slow-acting [sləu'æktɪŋ] *adj* de efecto

retardado.

slowcoach ['sləukəutʃ] *n* (*BRIT col*) tortuga.

slowdown ['sləudaun] *n* (*US*) huelga de celo.

slowly ['sləulı] *adv* lentamente, despacio; **to drive ~** conducir despacio; **~ but surely** lento pero seguro.

slow motion *n*: **in ~** a cámara lenta.

slow-moving ['sləu'muːvıŋ] *adj* lento.

slowpoke ['sləupəuk] *n* (*US col*) = **slowcoach**.

sludge [slʌdʒ] *n* lodo, fango.

slug [slʌg] *n* babosa; (*bullet*) posta.

sluggish ['slʌgıʃ] *adj* (*slow*) lento; (*lazy*) perezoso; (*business, market, sales*) inactivo.

sluggishly ['slʌgıʃlı] *adv* lentamente.

sluggishness ['slʌgıʃnıs] *n* lentitud *f*.

sluice [sluːs] *n* (*gate*) esclusa; (*channel*) canal *m* ♦ *vt*: **to ~ down** *or* **out** regar.

slum [slʌm] *n* (*area*) barrios *mpl* bajos; (*house*) casucha.

slumber ['slʌmbə*] *n* sueño.

slum clearance (programme) *n* (programa *m* de) deschabolización *f*.

slump [slʌmp] *n* (*economic*) depresión *f* ♦ *vi* hundirse; **the ~ in the price of copper** la baja repentina del precio del cobre; **he was ~ed over the wheel** se había desplomado encima del volante.

slung [slʌŋ] *pt, pp of* **sling**.

slunk [slʌŋk] *pt, pp of* **slink**.

slur [slɔː*] *n* calumnia ♦ *vt* calumniar, difamar; (*word*) pronunciar mal; **to cast a ~ on sb** manchar la reputación de algn, difamar a algn.

slurp [slɔːp] *vt, vi* sorber ruidosamente.

slurred [slɔːd] *adj* (*pronunciation*) poco claro.

slush [slʌʃ] *n* nieve *f* a medio derretir.

slush fund *n* fondos *mpl* para sobornar.

slushy ['slʌʃı] *adj* (*col: poetry etc*) sentimentaloide.

slut [slʌt] *n* marrana.

sly [slaı] *adj* (*clever*) astuto; (*nasty*) malicioso.

slyly ['slaılı] *adv* astutamente; taimadamente.

slyness ['slaınıs] *n* astucia.

smack [smæk] *n* (*slap*) manotada; (*blow*) golpe *m* ♦ *vt* dar una manotada a; golpear con la mano ♦ *vi*: **to ~ of** saber a, oler a ♦ *adv*: **it fell ~ in the middle** (*col*) cayó justo en medio.

smacker ['smækə*] *n* (*col: kiss*) besazo; (: *BRIT: pound note*) billete *m* de una libra; (: *US: dollar bill*) billete *m* de un dólar.

small [smɔːl] *adj* pequeño, chico (*esp LAM*);

(*in height*) bajo, chaparro (*LAM*); (*letter*) en minúscula ♦ *n*: **~ of the back** región *f* lumbar; **~ shopkeeper** pequeño/a comerciante *m/f*; **to get** *or* **grow ~er** (*stain, town*) empequeñecer; (*debt, organization, numbers*) reducir, disminuir; **to make ~er** (*amount, income*) reducir; (*garden, object, garment*) achicar.

small ads *npl* (*BRIT*) anuncios *mpl* por palabras.

small arms *npl* armas *fpl* cortas.

small business *n* pequeño negocio; **~es** la pequeña empresa.

small change *n* suelto, cambio.

smallholder ['smɔːlhəuldə*] *n* (*BRIT*) granjero/a, parcelero/a.

smallholding ['smɔːlhəuldıŋ] *n* parcela, minifundio.

small hours *npl*: **in the ~** a altas horas de la noche.

smallish ['smɔːlıʃ] *adj* más bien pequeño.

small-minded [smɔːl'maındıd] *adj* mezquino, de miras estrechas.

smallness ['smɔːlnıs] *n* pequeñez *f*.

smallpox ['smɔːlpɒks] *n* viruela.

small print *n* letra pequeña *or* menuda.

small-scale ['smɔːlskeıl] *adj* (*map, model*) a escala reducida; (*business, farming*) en pequeña escala.

small talk *n* cháchara.

small-time ['smɔːltaım] *adj* (*col*) de poca categoría *or* monta; **a ~ thief** un(a) ratero/a.

small-town ['smɔːltəun] *adj* de provincias.

smarmy ['smɑːmı] *adj* (*BRIT pej*) pelotillero (*fam*).

smart [smɑːt] *adj* elegante; (*clever*) listo, inteligente; (*quick*) rápido, vivo; (*weapon*) inteligente ♦ *vi* escocer, picar; **the ~ set** la gente de buen tono; **to look ~** estar elegante; **my eyes are ~ing** me pican los ojos.

smartcard ['smɑːtkɑːd] *n* tarjeta inteligente.

smarten up ['smɑːtn-] *vi* arreglarse ♦ *vt* arreglar.

smartness ['smɑːtnıs] *n* elegancia; (*cleverness*) inteligencia.

smash [smæʃ] *n* (*also*: **~-up**) choque *m*; (*sound*) estrépito ♦ *vt* (*break*) hacer pedazos; (*car etc*) estrellar; (*SPORT: record*) batir ♦ *vi* hacerse pedazos; (*against wall etc*) estrellarse.

▶**smash up** *vt* (*car*) hacer pedazos; (*room*) destrozar.

smash hit *n* exitazo.

smashing ['smæʃıŋ] *adj* (*col*) cojonudo.

smattering ['smætərıŋ] *n*: **a ~ of Spanish**

algo de español.

smear [smɪə*] n mancha; (*MED*) frotis m inv (cervical); (*insult*) calumnia ♦ vt untar; (*fig*) calumniar, difamar; **his hands were ~ed with oil/ink** tenía las manos manchadas de aceite/tinta.

smear campaign n campaña de calumnias.

smear test n (*MED*) citología, frotis m inv (cervical).

smell [smɛl] n olor m; (*sense*) olfato ♦ (vb: pt, pp **smelt** or **~ed** [smɛlt, smɛld]) vt, vi oler; **it ~s good/of garlic** huele bien/a ajo.

smelly ['smɛlɪ] adj maloliente.

smelt [smɛlt] vt (*ore*) fundir ♦ pt, pp of **smell**.

smile [smaɪl] n sonrisa ♦ vi sonreír.

smiling ['smaɪlɪŋ] adj sonriente, risueño.

smirk [smə:k] n sonrisa falsa or afectada.

smith [smɪθ] n herrero.

smithy ['smɪðɪ] n herrería.

smitten ['smɪtn] adj: **he's really ~ with her** está totalmente loco por ella.

smock [smɔk] n blusón; (*children's*) babi m; (*US: overall*) guardapolvo, bata.

smog [smɔg] n smog m.

smoke [sməuk] n humo ♦ vi fumar; (*chimney*) echar humo ♦ vt (*cigarettes*) fumar; **to go up in ~** (*house etc*) quemarse; (*fig*) quedar en agua de borrajas; **do you ~?** ¿fumas?

smoked [sməukt] adj (*bacon, glass*) ahumado.

smokeless fuel ['sməuklɪs-] n combustible m sin humo.

smokeless zone ['sməuklɪs-] n zona libre de humo.

smoker ['sməukə*] n (*person*) fumador(a) m/f; (*RAIL*) coche m de fumadores.

smoke screen n cortina de humo.

smoke shop n (*US*) estanco, tabaquería.

smoking ['sməukɪŋ] n: **"no ~"** "prohibido fumar"; **he's given up ~** ha dejado de fumar.

smoking compartment, (*US*) **smoking car** n departamento de fumadores.

smoky ['sməukɪ] adj (*room*) lleno de humo.

smolder ['sməuldə*] vi (*US*) = **smoulder**.

smoochy ['smu:tʃɪ] adj (*col*) blandengue.

smooth [smu:ð] adj liso; (*sea*) tranquilo; (*flavour, movement*) suave; (*person: pej*) meloso ♦ vt alisar; (*also: ~ out*) (*creases*) alisar; (*difficulties*) allanar.

▶**smooth over** vt: **to ~ things over** (*fig*) limar las asperezas.

smoothly ['smu:ðlɪ] adv (*easily*) fácilmente; **everything went ~** todo fue sobre ruedas.

smoothness ['smu:ðnɪs] n (*of skin, cloth*) tersura; (*of surface, flavour, movement*)

suavidad f.

smother ['smʌðə*] vt sofocar; (*repress*) contener.

smoulder, (*US*) **smolder** ['sməuldə*] vi arder sin llama.

smudge [smʌdʒ] n mancha ♦ vt manchar.

smug [smʌg] adj engreído.

smuggle ['smʌgl] vt pasar de contrabando; **to ~ in/out** (*goods etc*) meter/sacar de contrabando.

smuggler ['smʌglə*] n contrabandista m/f.

smuggling ['smʌglɪŋ] n contrabando.

smugly ['smʌglɪ] adv con suficiencia.

smugness ['smʌgnɪs] n suficiencia.

smut [smʌt] n (*grain of soot*) carbonilla, hollín m; (*mark*) tizne m; (*in conversation etc*) obscenidades fpl.

smutty ['smʌtɪ] adj (*fig*) verde, obsceno.

snack [snæk] n bocado, tentempié m; **to have a ~** tomar un bocado.

snack bar n cafetería.

snag [snæg] n problema m; **to run into** or **hit a ~** encontrar inconvenientes, dar con un obstáculo.

snail [sneɪl] n caracol m.

snake [sneɪk] n (*gen*) serpiente f; (*harmless*) culebra; (*poisonous*) víbora.

snap [snæp] n (*sound*) chasquido; golpe m seco; (*photograph*) foto f ♦ adj (*decision*) instantáneo ♦ vt (*fingers etc*) castañetear; (*break*) partir, quebrar; (*photograph*) tomar una foto de ♦ vi (*break*) partirse, quebrarse; (*fig: person*) contestar bruscamente; **to ~ (at sb)** (*subj: person*) hablar con brusquedad (a algn); (: *dog*) intentar morder (a algn); **to ~ shut** cerrarse de golpe; **to ~ one's fingers at sth/sb** (*fig*) burlarse de algo/uno; **a cold ~** (*of weather*) una ola de frío.

▶**snap off** vi (*break*) partirse.

▶**snap up** vt agarrar.

snap fastener n (*US*) botón m de presión.

snappy ['snæpɪ] adj (*col: answer*) instantáneo; (*slogan*) conciso; **make it ~!** (*hurry up*) ¡date prisa!

snapshot ['snæpʃɔt] n foto f (instantánea).

snare [snɛə*] n trampa ♦ vt cazar con trampa; (*fig*) engañar.

snarl [snɑ:l] n gruñido ♦ vi gruñir; **to get ~ed up** (*wool, plans*) enmarañarse, enredarse; (*traffic*) quedar atascado.

snatch [snætʃ] n (*fig*) robo; **~es of trocitos** mpl de ♦ vt (~ *away*) arrebatar; (*grasp*) coger (*SP*), agarrar; **~es of conversation** fragmentos mpl de conversación; **to ~ a sandwich** comer un bocadillo a prisa; **to ~ some sleep** buscar tiempo para dormir; **don't ~!** ¡no me lo quites!

▶**snatch up** *vt* agarrar.

snazzy ['snæzɪ] *adj* (*col*) guapo.

sneak [sniːk] *vi*: to ~ **in/out** entrar/salir a hurtadillas ♦ *vt*: to ~ **a look at sth** mirar algo de reojo ♦ *n* (*fam*) soplón/ona *m/f*.

sneakers ['sniːkəz] *npl* (*US*) zapatos *mpl* de lona, zapatillas *fpl*.

sneaking ['sniːkɪŋ] *adj*: **to have a ~ feeling/ suspicion that ...** tener la sensación/ sospecha de que ....

sneaky ['sniːkɪ] *adj* furtivo.

sneer [snɪə*] *n* sonrisa de desprecio ♦ *vi* sonreír con desprecio; **to ~ at sth/sb** burlarse *or* mofarse de algo/uno.

sneeze [sniːz] *n* estornudo ♦ *vi* estornudar.

snide [snaɪd] *adj* (*col*: *sarcastic*) sarcástico.

sniff [snɪf] *vi* sorber (por la nariz) ♦ *vt* husmear, oler; (*glue, drug*) esnifar.

▶**sniff at** *vt fus*: **it's not to be ~ed at** no es de despreciar.

sniffer dog ['snɪfə-] *n* (*for drugs*) perro antidroga; (*for explosives*) perro antiexplosivos.

snigger ['snɪgə*] *n* risa disimulada ♦ *vi* reírse con disimulo.

snip [snɪp] *n* (*piece*) recorte *m*; (*bargain*) ganga ♦ *vt* tijeretear.

sniper ['snaɪpə*] *n* francotirador(a) *m/f*.

snippet ['snɪpɪt] *n* retazo.

snivelling, (*US*) **sniveling** ['snɪvlɪŋ] *adj* llorón/ona.

snob [snɔb] *n* (e)snob *m/f*.

snobbery ['snɔbərɪ] *n* (e)snobismo.

snobbish ['snɔbɪʃ] *adj* (e)snob.

snobbishness ['snɔbɪʃnɪs] *n* (e)snobismo.

snog [snɔg] *vi* (*BRIT col*) besuquearse, morrear; **to ~ sb** besuquear a algn.

snooker ['snuːkə*] *n* snooker *m*.

snoop [snuːp] *vi*: **to ~ about** fisgonear.

snooper ['snuːpə*] *n* fisgón/ona *m/f*.

snooty ['snuːtɪ] *adj* (e)snob.

snooze [snuːz] *n* siesta ♦ *vi* echar una siesta.

snore [snɔː*] *vi* roncar ♦ *n* ronquido.

snoring ['snɔːrɪŋ] *n* ronquidos *mpl*.

snorkel ['snɔːkl] *n* tubo de respiración.

snort [snɔːt] *n* bufido ♦ *vi* bufar ♦ *vt* (*col*: *drugs*) esnifar.

snotty ['snɔtɪ] *adj* (*col*) creído.

snout [snaut] *n* hocico, morro.

snow [snəu] *n* nieve *f* ♦ *vi* nevar ♦ *vt*: **to be ~ed under with work** estar agobiado de trabajo.

snowball ['snəubɔːl] *n* bola de nieve ♦ *vi* ir aumentándose.

snow-blind ['snəublaɪnd] *adj* cegado por la nieve.

snowbound ['snəubaund] *adj* bloqueado por la nieve.

snow-capped ['snəukæpt] *adj* (*peak*) cubierto de nieve, nevado.

snowdrift ['snəudrɪft] *n* ventisquero.

snowdrop ['snəudrɔp] *n* campanilla.

snowfall ['snəufɔːl] *n* nevada.

snowflake ['snəufleɪk] *n* copo de nieve.

snowline ['snəulaɪn] *n* límite *m* de las nieves perpetuas.

snowman ['snəumæn] *n* figura de nieve.

snowplough, (*US*) **snowplow** ['snəuplau] *n* quitanieves *m inv*.

snowshoe ['snəuʃuː] *n* raqueta (de nieve).

snowstorm ['snəustɔːm] *n* tormenta de nieve, nevasca.

Snow White *n* Blancanieves *f*.

snowy ['snəuɪ] *adj* de (mucha) nieve.

SNP *n abbr* (*BRIT POL*) = *Scottish National Party.*

snub [snʌb] *vt*: **to ~ sb** desairar a algn ♦ *n* desaire *m*, repulsa.

snub-nosed [snʌb'nəuzd] *adj* chato.

snuff [snʌf] *n* rapé *m* ♦ *vt* (*also*: ~ **out**: *candle*) apagar.

snuffbox ['snʌfbɔks] *n* caja de rapé.

snuff movie *n* (*col*) película porno (*que acaba con un asesinato real*).

snug [snʌg] *adj* (*cosy*) cómodo; (*fitted*) ajustado.

snuggle ['snʌgl] *vi*: **to ~ down in bed** hacerse un ovillo *or* acurrucarse en la cama; **to ~ up to sb** acurrucarse junto a algn.

snugly ['snʌglɪ] *adv* cómodamente; **it fits ~** (*object in pocket etc*) cabe perfectamente; (*garment*) ajusta perfectamente.

SO *abbr* (*BANKING*) = **standing order.**

═══════════════════════ *KEYWORD*

so [səu] *adv* **1** (*thus, likewise*) así, de este modo; **if ~** de ser así; **I like swimming — ~ do I** a mí me gusta nadar — a mí también; **I've got work to do — ~ has Paul** tengo trabajo que hacer — Paul también; **it's 5 o'clock — ~ it is!** son las cinco — ¡pues es verdad!; **I hope/think ~** espero/creo que sí; **~ far** hasta ahora; (*in past*) hasta este momento; **~ to speak** por decirlo así

2 (*in comparisons etc: to such a degree*) tan; **~ quickly (that)** tan rápido (que); **~ big (that)** tan grande (que); **she's not ~ clever as her brother** no es tan lista como su hermano; **we were ~ worried** estábamos preocupadísimos

3: **~ much** *adj* tanto/a ♦ *adv* tanto; **~ many** tantos/as

4 (*phrases*): **10 or ~** unos 10, 10 o así; **~**

long! (*inf: goodbye*) ¡hasta luego!; **she didn't ~ much as send me a birthday card** no me mandó ni una tarjeta siquiera por mi cumpleaños; **~ (what)?** (*col*) ¿y (qué)? ♦ *conj* **1** (*expressing purpose*): **~ as to do** para hacer; **~ (that)** para que +*sub*; **we hurried ~ (that) we wouldn't be late** nos dimos prisa por no llegar tarde **2** (*expressing result*) así que; **~ you see, I could have gone** así que ya ves, (yo) podría haber ido; **~ that's the reason!** ¡así que es por eso *or* por eso es!

soak [səuk] *vt* (*drench*) empapar; (*put in water*) remojar ♦ *vi* remojarse, estar a remojo.
▶**soak in** *vi* penetrar.
▶**soak up** *vt* absorber.
soaking ['səukɪŋ] *adj* (*also*: **~ wet**) calado *or* empapado (hasta los huesos *or* el tuétano).
so-and-so ['səuənsəu] *n* (*somebody*) fulano/a de tal.
soap [səup] *n* jabón *m*.
soapbox ['səupbɒks] *n* tribuna improvisada.
soapflakes ['səupfleɪks] *npl* jabón *msg* en escamas.
soap opera *n* (*TV*) telenovela; (*RADIO*) radionovela.
soap powder *n* jabón *m* en polvo.
soapsuds ['səupsʌdz] *npl* espuma *sg*.
soapy ['səupɪ] *adj* jabonoso.
soar [sɔ:*] *vi* (*on wings*) remontarse; (*building etc*) elevarse; (*price*) subir vertiginosamente; (*morale*) elevarse.
soaring ['sɔ:rɪŋ] *adj* (*flight*) por lo alto; (*prices*) en alza *or* aumento; **~ inflation** inflación *f* altísima *or* en aumento.
sob [sɒb] *n* sollozo ♦ *vi* sollozar.
s.o.b. *n abbr* (*US col!* = *son of a bitch*) hijo de puta (*!*).
sober ['səubə*] *adj* (*moderate*) moderado; (*serious*) serio; (*not drunk*) sobrio; (*colour, style*) discreto.
▶**sober up** *vi* pasársele a algn la borrachera.
soberly ['səubəlɪ] *adv* sobriamente.
sobriety [sə'braɪətɪ] *n* (*not being drunk*) sobriedad *f*; (*seriousness, sedateness*) seriedad *f*, sensatez *f*.
sob story *n* (*col, pej*) dramón *m*.
Soc. *abbr* (= *society*) S.
so-called ['səu'kɔ:ld] *adj* presunto, supuesto.
soccer ['sɒkə*] *n* fútbol *m*.
soccer pitch *n* campo *or* cancha (*LAM*) de fútbol.

soccer player *n* jugador(a) *m/f* de fútbol.
sociability [səuʃə'bɪlɪtɪ] *n* sociabilidad *f*.
sociable ['səuʃəbl] *adj* sociable.
social ['səuʃl] *adj* social ♦ *n* velada, fiesta.
social class *n* clase *f* social.
social climber *n* arribista *m/f*.
social club *n* club *m*.
Social Democrat *n* socialdemócrata *m/f*.
social insurance *n* (*US*) seguro social.
socialism ['səuʃəlɪzəm] *n* socialismo.
socialist ['səuʃəlɪst] *adj, n* socialista *m/f*.
socialite ['səuʃəlaɪt] *n persona que alterna con la buena sociedad*.
socialize ['səuʃəlaɪz] *vi* hacer vida social; **to ~ with** (*colleagues*) salir con.
social life *n* vida social
socially ['səuʃəlɪ] *adv* socialmente.
social science(s) *n(pl)* ciencias *fpl* sociales.
social security *n* seguridad *f* social.
social services *npl* servicios *mpl* sociales.
social welfare *n* asistencia social.
social work *n* asistencia social.
social worker *n* asistente/a *m/f* social.
society [sə'saɪətɪ] *n* sociedad *f*; (*club*) asociación *f*; (*also*: **high ~**) buena sociedad ♦ *cpd* (*party, column*) social, de sociedad.
socio-economic ['səusɪəui:kə'nɔmɪk] *adj* socioeconómico.
sociological [səusɪə'lɒdʒɪkəl] *adj* sociológico.
sociologist [səusɪ'ɔlədʒɪst] *n* sociólogo/a.
sociology [səusɪ'ɔlədʒɪ] *n* sociología.
sock [sɒk] *n* calcetín *m*, media (*LAM*); **to pull one's ~s up** (*fig*) hacer esfuerzos, despabilarse.
socket ['sɒkɪt] *n* (*ELEC*) enchufe *m*.
sod [sɒd] *n* (*of earth*) césped *m*; (*col!*) cabrón/ona *m/f* (*!*) ♦ *excl*: **~ off!** (*col!*) ¡vete a la porra!
soda ['səudə] *n* (*CHEM*) sosa; (*also*: **~ water**) soda; (*US: also*: **~ pop**) gaseosa.
sodden ['sɒdn] *adj* empapado.
sodium ['səudɪəm] *n* sodio.
sodium chloride *n* cloruro sódico *or* de sodio.
sofa ['səufə] *n* sofá *m*.
Sofia ['səufɪə] *n* Sofía.
soft [sɒft] *adj* (*teacher, parent*) blando; (*gentle, not loud*) suave; (*stupid*) bobo; **~ currency** divisa blanda *or* débil.
soft-boiled ['sɒftbɔɪld] *adj* (*egg*) pasado por agua.
soft copy *n* (*COMPUT*) copia transitoria.
soft drink *n* bebida no alcohólica.
soft drugs *npl* drogas *fpl* blandas.
soften ['sɒfn] *vt* ablandar; suavizar ♦ *vi*

ablandarse; suavizarse.
softener ['sɔfnə*] n suavizante m.
soft fruit n bayas fpl.
soft furnishings npl tejidos mpl para el hogar.
soft-hearted [sɔft'hɑːtɪd] adj bondadoso.
softly ['sɔftlɪ] adv suavemente; (gently) delicadamente, con delicadeza.
softness ['sɔftnɪs] n blandura; suavidad f.
soft option n alternativa fácil.
soft sell n venta persuasiva.
soft target n blanco or objetivo fácil.
soft toy n juguete m de peluche.
software ['sɔftwɛə*] n (COMPUT) software m.
soft water n agua blanda.
soggy ['sɔgɪ] adj empapado.
soil [sɔɪl] n (earth) tierra, suelo ♦ vt ensuciar.
soiled [sɔɪld] adj sucio, manchado.
sojourn ['sɔdʒəːn] n (formal) estancia.
solace ['sɔlɪs] n consuelo.
solar ['səʊlə*] adj solar.
solarium, pl **solaria** [sə'lɛərɪəm, -rɪə] n solario.
solar panel n panel m solar.
solar plexus [-'plɛksəs] n (ANAT) plexo solar.
solar power n energía solar.
solar system n sistema m solar.
sold [səʊld] pt, pp of **sell**.
solder ['səʊldə*] vt soldar ♦ n soldadura.
soldier ['səʊldʒə*] n (gen) soldado; (army man) militar m ♦ vi: **to ~ on** seguir adelante; **toy ~** soldadito de plomo.
sold out adj (COMM) agotado.
sole [səʊl] n (of foot) planta; (of shoe) suela; (fish: pl inv) lenguado ♦ adj único; **the ~ reason** la única razón.
solely ['səʊllɪ] adv únicamente, sólo, solamente; **I will hold you ~ responsible** le consideraré el único responsable.
solemn ['sɔləm] adj solemne.
sole trader n (COMM) comerciante m/f exclusivo/a.
solicit [sə'lɪsɪt] vt (request) solicitar ♦ vi (prostitute) abordar clientes.
solicitor [sə'lɪsɪtə*] n abogado/a; see also **barrister**.
solid ['sɔlɪd] adj sólido; (gold etc) macizo; (line) continuo; (vote) unánime ♦ n sólido; **we waited 2 ~ hours** esperamos 2 horas enteras; **to be on ~ ground** estar en tierra firme; (fig) estar seguro.
solidarity [sɔlɪ'dærɪtɪ] n solidaridad f.
solid fuel n combustible m sólido.
solidify [sə'lɪdɪfaɪ] vi solidificarse.
solidity [sə'lɪdɪtɪ] n solidez f.

solidly ['sɔlɪdlɪ] adv sólidamente; (fig) unánimemente.
solid-state ['sɔlɪdsteɪt] adj (ELEC) estado sólido.
soliloquy [sə'lɪləkwɪ] n soliloquio.
solitaire [sɔlɪ'tɛə*] n (game, gem) solitario.
solitary ['sɔlɪtərɪ] adj solitario, solo; (isolated) apartado, aislado; (only) único.
solitary confinement n incomunicación f; **to be in ~** estar incomunicado.
solitude ['sɔlɪtjuːd] n soledad f.
solo ['səʊləʊ] n solo.
soloist ['səʊləʊɪst] n solista m/f.
Solomon Islands ['sɔləmən-] npl: **the ~** las Islas Salomón.
solstice ['sɔlstɪs] n solsticio.
soluble ['sɔljubl] adj soluble.
solution [sə'luːʃən] n solución f.
solve [sɔlv] vt resolver, solucionar.
solvency ['sɔlvənsɪ] n (COMM) solvencia.
solvent ['sɔlvənt] adj (COMM) solvente ♦ n (CHEM) solvente m.
solvent abuse n uso indebido de disolventes.
Som. abbr (BRIT) = **Somerset**.
Somali [sə'mɑːlɪ] adj, n somalí m/f.
Somalia [sə'mɑːlɪə] n Somalia.
Somaliland [sə'mɑːlɪlænd] n Somaliland f.
sombre, (US) **somber** ['sɔmbə*] adj sombrío.

=========================== KEYWORD

some [sʌm] adj **1** (a certain amount or number of): **~ tea/water/biscuits** té/agua/(unas) galletas; **have ~ tea** tómese un té; **there's ~ milk in the fridge** hay leche en el frigo; **there were ~ people outside** había algunas personas fuera; **I've got ~ money, but not much** tengo algo de dinero, pero no mucho
2 (certain: in contrasts) algunos/as; **~ people say that ...** hay quien dice que ...; **~ films were excellent, but most were mediocre** hubo películas excelentes, pero la mayoría fueron mediocres
3 (unspecified): **~ woman was asking for you** una mujer estuvo preguntando por ti; **~ day** algún día; **~ day next week** un día de la semana que viene; **he was asking for ~ book (or other)** pedía no se qué libro; **in ~ way or other** de alguna que otra manera
4 (considerable amount of) bastante; **~ days ago** hace unos cuantos días; **after ~ time** pasado algún tiempo; **at ~ length** con mucho detalle
5 (col: intensive): **that was ~ party!** ¡menuda fiesta!

♦ *pron* **1** (*a certain number*): **I've got** ~ (*books etc*) tengo algunos/as **2** (*a certain amount*) algo; **I've got** ~ (*money, milk*) tengo algo; **would you like** ~**?** (*coffee etc*) ¿quiere un poco?; (*books etc*) ¿quiere alguno?; **could I have** ~ **of that cheese?** ¿me puede dar un poco de ese queso?; **I've read** ~ **of the book** he leído parte del libro ♦ *adv:* ~ **10 people** unas 10 personas, una decena de personas.

somebody ['sʌmbədɪ] *pron* alguien; ~ **or other** alguien.
someday ['sʌmdeɪ] *adv* algún día.
somehow ['sʌmhau] *adv* de alguna manera; (*for some reason*) por una u otra razón.
someone ['sʌmwʌn] *pron* = **somebody**.
someplace ['sʌmpleɪs] *adv* (*US*) = **somewhere**.
somersault ['sʌməsɔːlt] *n* (*deliberate*) salto mortal; (*accidental*) vuelco ♦ *vi* dar un salto mortal; dar vuelcos.
something ['sʌmθɪŋ] *pron* algo ♦ *adv:* **he's** ~ **like me** es un poco como yo; ~ **to do** algo que hacer; **it's** ~ **of a problem** es bastante problemático.
sometime ['sʌmtaɪm] *adv* (*in future*) algún día, en algún momento; ~ **last month** durante el mes pasado; **I'll finish it** ~ lo terminaré un día de éstos.
sometimes ['sʌmtaɪmz] *adv* a veces.
somewhat ['sʌmwɔt] *adv* algo.
somewhere ['sʌmwɛə*] *adv* (*be*) en alguna parte; (*go*) a alguna parte; ~ **else** (*be*) en otra parte; (*go*) a otra parte.
son [sʌn] *n* hijo.
sonar ['səunɑ:*] *n* sonar *m*.
sonata [sə'nɑ:tə] *n* sonata.
song [sɔŋ] *n* canción *f*.
songwriter ['sɔŋraɪtə*] *n* compositor(a) *m/f* de canciones.
sonic ['sɔnɪk] *adj* (*boom*) sónico.
son-in-law ['sʌnɪnlɔ:] *n* yerno.
sonnet ['sɔnɪt] *n* soneto.
sonny ['sʌnɪ] *n* (*col*) hijo.
soon [su:n] *adv* pronto, dentro de poco; ~ **afterwards** poco después; **very/quite** ~ muy/bastante pronto; **how** ~ **can you be ready?** ¿cuánto tardas en prepararte?; **it's too** ~ **to tell** es demasiado pronto para saber; **see you** ~**!** ¡hasta pronto!; *see also* **as**.
sooner ['su:nə*] *adv* (*time*) antes, más temprano; **I would** ~ **do that** preferiría hacer eso; ~ **or later** tarde o temprano; **no** ~ **said than done** dicho y hecho; **the** ~ **the better** cuanto antes mejor; **no** ~ **had**

we left than ... apenas nos habíamos marchado cuando ....
soot [sut] *n* hollín *m*.
soothe [su:ð] *vt* tranquilizar; (*pain*) aliviar.
soothing ['su:ðɪŋ] *adj* (*ointment etc*) sedante; (*tone, words etc*) calmante, tranquilizante.
SOP *n abbr* = *standard operating procedure.*
sophisticated [sə'fɪstɪkeɪtɪd] *adj* sofisticado.
sophistication [səfɪstɪ'keɪʃən] *n* sofisticación *f*.
sophomore ['sɔfəmɔ:*] *n* (*US*) estudiante *m/f* de segundo año.
soporific [sɔpə'rɪfɪk] *adj* soporífero.
sopping ['sɔpɪŋ] *adj:* ~ (**wet**) empapado.
soppy ['sɔpɪ] *adj* (*pej*) bobo, tonto.
soprano [sə'prɑ:nəu] *n* soprano *f*.
sorbet ['sɔ:beɪ] *n* sorbete *m*.
sorcerer ['sɔ:sərə*] *n* hechicero.
sordid ['sɔ:dɪd] *adj* (*place etc*) sórdido; (*motive etc*) mezquino.
sore [sɔ:*] *adj* (*painful*) doloroso, que duele; (*offended*) resentido ♦ *n* llaga; ~ **throat** dolor *m* de garganta; **my eyes are** ~**, I have** ~ **eyes** me duelen los ojos; **it's a** ~ **point** es un asunto delicado or espinoso.
sorely *adv:* **I am** ~ **tempted to** (**do it**) estoy muy tentado a (hacerlo).
soreness ['sɔ:nɪs] *n* dolor *m*.
sorrel ['sɔrəl] *n* (*BOT*) acedera.
sorrow ['sɔrəu] *n* pena, dolor *m*.
sorrowful ['sɔrəuful] *adj* afligido, triste.
sorrowfully ['sɔrəfulɪ] *adv* tristemente.
sorry ['sɔrɪ] *adj* (*regretful*) arrepentido; (*condition, excuse*) lastimoso; (*sight, failure*) triste; ~**!** ¡perdón!, ¡perdone!; **I am** ~ lo siento; **I feel** ~ **for him** me da lástima *or* pena; **I'm** ~ **to hear that** ... siento saber que ...; **to be** ~ **about sth** lamentar algo.
sort [sɔ:t] *n* clase *f*, género, tipo; (*make: of coffee, car etc*) marca ♦ *vt* (*also:* ~ **out:** *papers*) clasificar; (: *problems*) arreglar, solucionar; (*COMPUT*) clasificar; **what** ~ **do you want?** (*make*) ¿qué marca quieres?; **what** ~ **of car?** ¿qué tipo de coche?; **I shall do nothing of the** ~ no pienso hacer nada parecido; **it's** ~ **of awkward** (*col*) es bastante difícil.
sortie ['sɔ:tɪ] *n* salida.
sorting office ['sɔ:tɪŋ-] *n* oficina de clasificación del correo.
SOS *n* SOS *m*.
so-so ['səusəu] *adv* regular, así así.
soufflé ['su:fleɪ] *n* suflé *m*.
sought [sɔ:t] *pt, pp of* **seek.**
sought-after ['sɔ:tɑ:ftə*] *adj* solicitado,

codiciado.

soul [səul] n alma f; **God rest his ~** Dios le reciba en su seno or en su gloria; **I didn't see a ~** no vi a nadie; **the poor ~ had nowhere to sleep** el pobre no tenía dónde dormir.

soul-destroying ['səuldɪstrɔɪɪŋ] adj (work) deprimente.

soulful ['səulful] adj lleno de sentimiento.

soulmate ['səulmeɪt] n compañero/a del alma.

soul-searching ['səulsə:tʃɪŋ] n: **after much ~** después de pensarlo mucho, después de darle muchas vueltas.

sound [saund] adj (healthy) sano; (safe, not damaged) en buen estado; (valid: argument, policy, claim) válido; (: move) acertado; (dependable: person) de fiar; (sensible) sensato, razonable ♦ adv: **~ asleep** profundamente dormido ♦ n (noise) sonido, ruido; (GEO) estrecho ♦ vt (alarm) sonar; (also: **~ out:** opinions) consultar, sondear ♦ vi sonar, resonar; (fig: seem) parecer; **to ~ like** sonar a; **to be of ~ mind** estar en su sano juicio; **I don't like the ~ of it** no me gusta nada; **it ~s as if ...** parece que ....

▶**sound off** vi (col): **to ~ off (about)** (give one's opinions) despotricar (contra).

sound barrier n barrera del sonido.

sound bite n cita jugosa.

sound effects npl efectos mpl sonoros.

sound engineer n ingeniero/a del sonido.

sounding ['saundɪŋ] n (NAUT etc) sondeo.

sounding board n caja de resonancia.

soundly ['saundlɪ] adv (sleep) profundamente; (beat) completamente.

soundproof ['saundpru:f] adj insonorizado.

sound system n equipo de sonido.

soundtrack ['saundtræk] n (of film) banda sonora.

sound wave n (PHYSICS) onda sonora.

soup [su:p] n (thick) sopa; (thin) caldo; **in the ~** (fig) en apuros.

soup kitchen n comedor m de beneficencia.

soup plate n plato sopero.

soupspoon ['su:pspu:n] n cuchara sopera.

sour ['sauə*] adj agrio; (milk) cortado; **it's just ~ grapes!** (fig) ¡pura envidia!, ¡están verdes!; **to go** or **turn ~** (milk) cortarse; (wine) agriarse; (fig: relationship) agriarse; (: plans) irse a pique.

source [sɔ:s] n fuente f; **I have it from a reliable ~ that ...** sé de fuente fidedigna que ....

source language n (COMPUT) lenguaje m

fuente or de origen.

south [sauθ] n sur m ♦ adj del sur ♦ adv al sur, hacia el sur; **(to the) ~ of** al sur de; **the S~ of France** el Sur de Francia; **to travel ~** viajar hacia el sur.

South Africa n Sudáfrica.

South African adj, n sudafricano/a m/f.

South America n América del Sur, Sudamérica.

South American adj, n sudamericano/a m/f.

southbound ['sauθbaund] adj (con) rumbo al sur.

south-east [sauθ'i:st] n sudeste m ♦ adj (counties etc) (del) sudeste.

Southeast Asia n Sudeste m asiático.

southerly ['sʌðəlɪ] adj sur; (from the south) del sur.

southern ['sʌðən] adj del sur, meridional; **the ~ hemisphere** el hemisferio sur.

South Korea n Corea del Sur.

South Pole n Polo Sur.

South Sea Islands npl: **the ~** Oceanía.

South Seas npl: **the ~** los Mares del Sur.

South Vietnam n Vietnam m del Sur.

southward(s) ['sauθwəd(z)] adv hacia el sur.

south-west [sauθ'wɛst] n suroeste m.

souvenir [su:və'nɪə*] n recuerdo.

sovereign ['sɔvrɪn] adj, n soberano/a m/f.

sovereignty ['sɔvrɪntɪ] n soberanía.

soviet ['səuvɪət] adj soviético.

Soviet Union n: **the ~** la Unión Soviética.

sow [sau] n cerda, puerca ♦ vt [səu] (pt **~ed**, pp **~n** [səun]) (gen) sembrar; (spread) esparcir.

soya ['sɔɪə], (US) **soy** [sɔɪ] n soja.

soy(a) bean n semilla de soja.

soy(a) sauce n salsa de soja.

sozzled ['sɔzld] adj (BRIT col) mamado.

spa [spa:] n balneario.

space [speɪs] n espacio; (room) sitio ♦ vt (also: **~ out**) espaciar; **to clear a ~ for sth** hacer sitio para algo; **in a confined ~** en un espacio restringido; **in a short ~ of time** en poco or un corto espacio de tiempo; **(with)in the ~ of an hour/three generations** en el espacio de una hora/ tres generaciones.

space bar n (on typewriter) barra espaciadora.

spacecraft ['speɪskra:ft] n nave f espacial, astronave f.

spaceman ['speɪsmæn] n astronauta m, cosmonauta m.

spaceship ['speɪsʃɪp] n = **spacecraft.**

space shuttle n transportador m espacial.

spacesuit ['speɪssu:t] n traje m espacial.

spacewoman ['speɪswumən] *n* astronauta, cosmonauta.
spacing ['speɪsɪŋ] *n* espacio.
spacious ['speɪʃəs] *adj* amplio.
spade [speɪd] *n (tool)* pala; ~s *npl (CARDS: British)* picas *fpl*; (: *Spanish)* espadas *fpl*.
spadework ['speɪdwəːk] *n (fig)* trabajo preliminar.
spaghetti [spə'gɛtɪ] *n* espaguetis *mpl*.
Spain [speɪn] *n* España.
span [spæn] *n (of bird, plane)* envergadura; *(of hand)* palmo; *(of arch)* luz *f*; *(in time)* lapso ♦ *vt* extenderse sobre, cruzar; *(fig)* abarcar.
Spaniard ['spænjəd] *n* español(a) *m/f*.
spaniel ['spænjəl] *n* perro de aguas.
Spanish ['spænɪʃ] *adj* español(a) ♦ *n (LING)* español *m*, castellano; **the** ~ *npl (people)* los españoles; ~ **omelette** tortilla española *or* de patata.
spank [spæŋk] *vt* zurrar, dar unos azotes a.
spanner ['spænə*] *n (BRIT)* llave *f* inglesa.
spar [spɑː*] *n* palo, verga ♦ *vi (BOXING)* entrenarse (en el boxeo).
spare [spɛə*] *adj* de reserva; *(surplus)* sobrante, de más ♦ *n (part)* pieza de repuesto ♦ *vt (do without)* pasarse sin; *(afford to give)* tener de sobra; *(refrain from hurting)* perdonar; *(details etc)* ahorrar; **to** ~ *(surplus)* sobrante, de sobra; **there are 2 going** ~ sobran *or* quedan 2; **to** ~ **no expense** no escatimar gastos; **can you** ~ **(me) £10?** ¿puedes prestarme *or* darme 10 libras?; **can you** ~ **the time?** ¿tienes tiempo?; **I've a few minutes to** ~ tengo unos minutos libres; **there is no time to** ~ no hay tiempo que perder.
spare part *n* pieza de repuesto.
spare room *n* cuarto de los invitados.
spare time *n* ratos *mpl* de ocio, tiempo libre.
spare tyre, (US) spare tire *n (AUT)* neumático *or* llanta *(LAM)* de recambio.
spare wheel *n (AUT)* rueda de recambio.
sparing ['spɛərɪŋ] *adj*: **to be** ~ **with** ser parco en.
sparingly ['spɛərɪŋlɪ] *adv* escasamente.
spark [spɑːk] *n* chispa; *(fig)* chispazo.
spark(ing) plug ['spɑːk(ɪŋ)-] *n* bujía.
sparkle ['spɑːkl] *n* centelleo, destello ♦ *vi* centellear; *(shine)* relucir, brillar.
sparkler ['spɑːklə*] *n* bengala.
sparkling ['spɑːklɪŋ] *adj* centelleante; *(wine)* espumoso.
sparring partner ['spɑːrɪŋ-] *n* sparring *m*; *(fig)* contrincante *m/f*.
sparrow ['spærəu] *n* gorrión *m*.

sparse [spɑːs] *adj* esparcido, escaso.
sparsely ['spɑːslɪ] *adv* escasamente; **a** ~ **furnished room** un cuarto con pocos muebles.
spartan ['spɑːtən] *adj (fig)* espartano.
spasm ['spæzəm] *n (MED)* espasmo; *(fig)* arranque *m*, ataque *m*.
spasmodic [spæz'mɔdɪk] *adj* espasmódico.
spastic ['spæstɪk] *n* espástico/a.
spat [spæt] *pt, pp of* **spit** ♦ *n (US)* riña.
spate [speɪt] *n (fig)*: ~ **of** torrente *m* de; **in** ~ *(river)* crecido.
spatial ['speɪʃl] *adj* espacial.
spatter ['spætə*] *vt*: **to** ~ **with** salpicar de.
spatula ['spætjulə] *n* espátula.
spawn [spɔːn] *vt (pej)* engendrar ♦ *vi* desovar, frezar ♦ *n* huevas *fpl*.
SPCA *n abbr (US)* = *Society for the Prevention of Cruelty to Animals.*
SPCC *n abbr (US)* = *Society for the Prevention of Cruelty to Children.*
speak, *pt* **spoke,** *pp* **spoken** [spiːk, spəuk, 'spəukn] *vt (language)* hablar; *(truth)* decir ♦ *vi* hablar; *(make a speech)* intervenir; **to** ~ **one's mind** hablar claro *or* con franqueza; **to** ~ **to sb/of** *or* **about sth** hablar con algn/de *or* sobre algo; **to** ~ **at a conference/in a debate** hablar en un congreso/un debate; **he has no money to** ~ **of** no tiene mucho dinero que digamos; ~**ing!** ¡al habla!; ~ **up!** ¡habla más alto!
▶**speak for** *vt fus*: **to** ~ **for sb** hablar por *or* en nombre de algn; **that picture is already spoken for** *(in shop)* ese cuadro está reservado.
speaker ['spiːkə*] *n (in public)* orador(a) *m/f*; *(also: loud~)* altavoz *m*; *(for stereo etc)* bafle *m*; *(POL)*: **the S~** *(BRIT)* el *Presidente de la Cámara de los Comunes; (US)* el *Presidente del Congreso*; **are you a Welsh** ~**?** ¿habla Ud galés?
speaking ['spiːkɪŋ] *adj* hablante.
-speaking ['spiːkɪŋ] *suff* -hablante; **Spanish~ people** los hispanohablantes.
spear [spɪə*] *n* lanza; *(for fishing)* arpón *m* ♦ *vt* alancear; arponear.
spearhead ['spɪəhɛd] *vt (attack etc)* encabezar ♦ *n* punta de lanza, vanguardia.
spearmint ['spɪəmɪnt] *n (BOT etc)* menta verde.
spec [spɛk] *n (col)*: **on** ~ por si acaso; **to buy on** ~ arriesgarse a comprar.
special ['spɛʃl] *adj* especial; *(edition etc)* extraordinario; *(delivery)* urgente ♦ *n (train)* tren *m* especial; **nothing** ~ nada de particular, nada extraordinario.
special agent *n* agente *m/f* especial.

special correspondent *n* corresponsal *m/f* especial.
special delivery *n* (*POST*): **by ~** por entrega urgente.
special effects *npl* (*CINE*) efectos *mpl* especiales.
specialist ['spɛʃəlɪst] *n* especialista *m/f*; **a heart ~** (*MED*) un(a) especialista del corazón.
speciality [spɛʃɪ'ælɪtɪ], (*US*) **specialty** ['spɛʃəltɪ] *n* especialidad *f*.
specialize ['spɛʃəlaɪz] *vi*: **to ~ (in)** especializarse (en).
specially ['spɛʃlɪ] *adv* especialmente.
special offer *n* (*COMM*) oferta especial.
special train *n* tren *m* especial.
specialty ['spɛʃəltɪ] *n* (*US*) = **speciality**.
species ['spiːʃiːz] *n* especie *f*.
specific [spə'sɪfɪk] *adj* específico.
specifically [spə'sɪfɪklɪ] *adv* (*explicitly*: *state, warn*) específicamente, expresamente; (*especially*: *design, intend*) especialmente.
specification [spɛsɪfɪ'keɪʃən] *n* especificación *f*; **~s** *npl* (*plan*) presupuesto *sg*; (*of car, machine*) descripción *f* técnica; (*for building*) plan *msg* detallado.
specify ['spɛsɪfaɪ] *vt, vi* especificar, precisar; **unless otherwise specified** salvo indicaciones contrarias.
specimen ['spɛsɪmən] *n* ejemplar *m*; (*MED*: *of urine*) espécimen *m*; (: *of blood*) muestra.
specimen copy *n* ejemplar *m* de muestra.
specimen signature *n* muestra de firma.
speck [spɛk] *n* grano, mota.
speckled ['spɛkld] *adj* moteado.
specs [spɛks] *npl* (*col*) gafas *fpl* (*SP*), anteojos *mpl*.
spectacle ['spɛktəkl] *n* espectáculo.
spectacle case *n* estuche *m* or funda (de gafas).
spectacles ['spɛktəklz] *npl* (*BRIT*) gafas *fpl* (*SP*), anteojos *mpl*.
spectacular [spɛk'tækjulə*] *adj* espectacular; (*success*) impresionante.
spectator [spɛk'teɪtə*] *n* espectador(a) *m/f*.
spectator sport *n* deporte *m* espectáculo.
spectra ['spɛktrə] *npl of* **spectrum**.
spectre, (*US*) **specter** ['spɛktə*] *n* espectro, fantasma *m*.
spectrum, *pl* **spectra** ['spɛktrəm, -trə] *n* espectro.
speculate ['spɛkjuleɪt] *vi* especular; (*try to guess*): **to ~ about** especular sobre.
speculation [spɛkju'leɪʃən] *n* especulación *f*.
speculative ['spɛkjulətɪv] *adj* especulativo.
speculator ['spɛkjuleɪtə*] *n* especulador(a)

m/f.
sped [spɛd] *pt, pp of* **speed**.
speech [spiːtʃ] *n* (*faculty*) habla; (*formal talk*) discurso; (*words*) palabras *fpl*; (*manner of speaking*) forma de hablar; (*language*) idioma *m*, lenguaje *m*.
speech day *n* (*BRIT SCOL*) ≈ día de reparto de premios.
speech impediment *n* defecto del habla.
speechless ['spiːtʃlɪs] *adj* mudo, estupefacto.
speech therapy *n* logopedia.
speed [spiːd] *n* (*also*: *AUT, TECH*: *gear*) velocidad *f*; (*haste*) prisa; (*promptness*) rapidez *f* ♦ *vi* (*pt, pp* **sped** [spɛd]) (*AUT*: *exceed ~ limit*) conducir con exceso de velocidad; **at full** *or* **top ~** a máxima velocidad; **at a ~ of 70 km/h** a una velocidad de 70 km por hora; **at ~** a gran velocidad; **a five-~ gearbox** una caja de cambios de 5 velocidades; **shorthand/ typing ~** rapidez *f* en taquigrafía/ mecanografía; **the years sped by** los años pasaron volando.
▶**speed up** *vi* acelerarse ♦ *vt* acelerar.
speedboat ['spiːdbəut] *n* lancha motora.
speedily ['spiːdɪlɪ] *adv* rápido, rápidamente.
speeding ['spiːdɪŋ] *n* (*AUT*) exceso de velocidad.
speed limit *n* límite *m* de velocidad, velocidad *f* máxima.
speedometer [spɪ'dɔmɪtə*] *n* velocímetro.
speed trap *n* (*AUT*) control *m* de velocidades.
speedway ['spiːdweɪ] *n* (*SPORT*) pista de carrera.
speedy ['spiːdɪ] *adj* (*fast*) veloz, rápido; (*prompt*) pronto.
spell [spɛl] *n* (*also*: **magic ~**) encanto, hechizo; (*period of time*) rato, período; (*turn*) turno ♦ *vt* (*pt, pp* **spelt** *or* **~ed** [spɛlt, spɛld]) (*also*: **~ out**) deletrear; (*fig*) anunciar, presagiar; **to cast a ~ on sb** hechizar a algn; **he can't ~** no sabe escribir bien, comete faltas de ortografía; **can you ~ it for me?** ¿cómo se deletrea *or* se escribe?; **how do you ~ your name?** ¿cómo se escribe tu nombre?
spellbound ['spɛlbaund] *adj* embelesado, hechizado.
spelling ['spɛlɪŋ] *n* ortografía.
spelling mistake *n* falta de ortografía.
spelt [spɛlt] *pt, pp of* **spell**.
spend, *pt, pp* **spent** [spɛnd, spɛnt] *vt* (*money*) gastar; (*time*) pasar; (*life*) dedicar; **to ~ time/money/effort on sth** gastar tiempo/ dinero/energías en algo.

spending ['spɛndɪŋ] *n*: **government** ~
gastos *mpl* del gobierno.
spending money *n* dinero para gastos.
spending power *n* poder *m* adquisitivo.
spendthrift ['spɛndθrɪft] *n* derrochador(a)
m/f, manirroto/a.
spent [spɛnt] *pt, pp of* **spend** ♦ *adj* (*cartridge,
bullets, match*) usado.
sperm [spə:m] *n* esperma.
sperm bank *n* banco de esperma.
sperm whale *n* cachalote *m*.
spew [spju:] *vt* vomitar, arrojar.
sphere [sfɪə*] *n* esfera.
spherical ['sfɛrɪkl] *adj* esférico.
sphinx [sfɪŋks] *n* esfinge *f*.
spice [spaɪs] *n* especia ♦ *vt* especiar.
spiciness ['spaɪsɪnɪs] *n* lo picante.
spicy ['spaɪsɪ] *adj* picante.
spick-and-span ['spɪkən'spæn] *adj*
impecable.
spider ['spaɪdə*] *n* araña.
spider's web *n* telaraña.
spiel [ʃpi:l] *n* (*col*) rollo.
spike [spaɪk] *n* (*point*) punta; (*ZOOL*) pincho,
púa; (*BOT*) espiga; (*ELEC*) pico parásito
♦ *vt*: **to** ~ **a quote** cancelar una cita; ~**s**
npl (*SPORT*) zapatillas *fpl* con clavos.
spiky ['spaɪkɪ] *adj* (*bush, branch*) cubierto de
púas; (*animal*) erizado.
spill, *pt, pp* **spilt** *or* ~**ed** [spɪl, spɪlt, spɪld] *vt*
derramar, verter; (*blood*) derramar ♦ *vi*
derramarse; **to** ~ **the beans** (*col*)
descubrir el pastel.
▶**spill out** *vi* derramarse, desparramarse.
▶**spill over** *vi* desbordarse.
spillage ['spɪlɪdʒ] *n* (*event*) derrame *m*;
(*substance*) vertidos.
spin [spɪn] *n* (*revolution of wheel*) vuelta,
revolución *f*; (*AVIAT*) barrena; (*trip in car*)
paseo (en coche) ♦ *vb* (*pt, pp* **spun** [spʌn])
vt (*wool etc*) hilar; (*wheel*) girar ♦ *vi* girar,
dar vueltas; **the car spun out of control** el
coche se descontroló y empezó a dar
vueltas.
▶**spin out** *vt* alargar, prolongar.
spina bifida ['spaɪnə'bɪfɪdə] *n* espina *f*
bífida.
spinach ['spɪnɪtʃ] *n* espinacas *fpl*.
spinal ['spaɪnl] *adj* espinal.
spinal column *n* columna vertebral.
spinal cord *n* médula espinal.
spindly ['spɪndlɪ] *adj* (*leg*) zanquivano.
spin doctor *n* (*col*) *informador(a) parcial
al servicio de un partido político*.
spin-dry ['spɪn'draɪ] *vt* centrifugar.
spin-dryer [spɪn'draɪə*] *n* (*BRIT*) secadora
centrífuga.
spine [spaɪn] *n* espinazo, columna

vertebral; (*thorn*) espina.
spine-chilling ['spaɪntʃɪlɪŋ] *adj* terrorífico.
spineless ['spaɪnlɪs] *adj* (*fig*) débil, flojo.
spinet [spɪ'nɛt] *n* espineta.
spinning ['spɪnɪŋ] *n* (*of thread*) hilado; (*art*)
hilandería.
spinning top *n* peonza.
spinning wheel *n* rueca, torno de hilar.
spin-off ['spɪnɔf] *n* derivado, producto
secundario.
spinster ['spɪnstə*] *n* soltera; (*pej*)
solterona.
spiral ['spaɪərl] *n* espiral *f* ♦ *adj* en espiral
♦ *vi* (*prices*) dispararse; **the inflationary**
~ la espiral inflacionista.
spiral staircase *n* escalera de caracol.
spire ['spaɪə*] *n* aguja, chapitel *m*.
spirit ['spɪrɪt] *n* (*soul*) alma *f*; (*ghost*)
fantasma *m*; (*attitude*) espíritu *m*;
(*courage*) valor *m*, ánimo; ~**s** *npl* (*drink*)
alcohol *msg*, bebidas *fpl* alcohólicas; **in
good** ~**s** alegre, de buen ánimo; **Holy S**~
Espíritu *m* Santo; **community** ~, **public** ~
civismo.
spirit duplicator *n* copiadora al alcohol.
spirited ['spɪrɪtɪd] *adj* enérgico, vigoroso.
spirit level *n* nivel *m* de aire.
spiritual ['spɪrɪtjuəl] *adj* espiritual ♦ *n* (*also*:
Negro ~) canción *f* religiosa, espiritual *m*.
spiritualism ['spɪrɪtjuəlɪzəm] *n*
espiritualismo.
spit [spɪt] *n* (*for roasting*) asador *m*, espetón
m; (*spittle*) esputo, escupitajo; (*saliva*)
saliva ♦ *vi* (*pt, pp* **spat** [spæt]) escupir;
(*sound*) chisporrotear.
spite [spaɪt] *n* rencor *m*, ojeriza ♦ *vt*
fastidiar; **in** ~ **of** a pesar de, pese a.
spiteful ['spaɪtful] *adj* rencoroso, malévolo.
spitting ['spɪtɪŋ] *n*: "~ **prohibited**" "se
prohíbe escupir" ♦ *adj*: **to be the** ~ **image
of sb** ser la viva imagen de algn.
spittle ['spɪtl] *n* saliva, baba.
splash [splæʃ] *n* (*sound*) chapoteo; (*of
colour*) mancha ♦ *vt* salpicar de ♦ *vi* (*also*:
~ **about**) chapotear; **to** ~ **paint on the
floor** manchar el suelo de pintura.
splashdown ['splæʃdaun] *n* amaraje *m*,
amerizaje *m*.
spleen [spli:n] *n* (*ANAT*) bazo.
splendid ['splɛndɪd] *adj* espléndido.
splendidly ['splɛndɪdlɪ] *adv*
espléndidamente; **everything went** ~
todo fue a las mil maravillas.
splendour, (*US*) **splendor** ['splɛndə*] *n*
esplendor *m*; (*of achievement*) brillo,
gloria.
splice [splaɪs] *vt* empalmar.
splint [splɪnt] *n* tablilla.

splinter ['splɪntə*] n astilla ♦ vi astillarse, hacer astillas.
splinter group n grupo disidente, facción f.
split [splɪt] n hendedura, raja; (fig) división f; (POL) escisión f ♦ (vb: pt, pp **split**) vt partir, rajar; (party) dividir; (work, profits) repartir ♦ vi (divide) dividirse, escindirse; **to ~ the difference** partir la diferencia; **to do the ~s** hacer el spagat; **to ~ sth down the middle** (also fig) dividir algo en dos.
▶**split up** vi (couple) separarse, romper; (meeting) acabarse.
split-level ['splɪtlɛvl] adj (house) dúplex.
split peas npl guisantes mpl secos.
split personality n doble personalidad f.
split second n fracción f de segundo.
splitting ['splɪtɪŋ] adj (headache) horrible.
splutter ['splʌtə*] vi chisporrotear; (person) balbucear.
spoil, pt, pp **spoilt** or ~ed [spɔɪl, spɔɪlt, spɔɪld] vt (damage) dañar; (ruin) estropear, echar a perder; (child) mimar, consentir; (ballot paper) invalidar ♦ vi: **to be ~ing for a fight** estar con ganas de lucha, andar con ganas de pelea.
spoiled [spɔɪld] adj (US: food: bad) pasado, malo; (: milk) cortado.
spoils [spɔɪlz] npl despojo sg, botín msg.
spoilsport ['spɔɪlspɔːt] n aguafiestas m inv.
spoilt [spɔɪlt] pt, pp of **spoil** ♦ adj (child) mimado, consentido; (ballot paper) invalidado.
spoke [spəuk] pt of **speak** ♦ n rayo, radio.
spoken ['spəukn] pp of **speak.**
spokesman ['spəuksmən] n portavoz m, vocero (LAM).
spokesperson ['spəukspə:sn] n portavoz m/f, vocero/a (LAM).
spokeswoman ['spəukswumən] n portavoz f, vocera (LAM).
sponge [spʌndʒ] n esponja; (CULIN: also: ~ cake) bizcocho ♦ vt (wash) lavar con esponja ♦ vi: **to ~ on** or (US) **off sb** vivir a costa de algn.
sponge bag n (BRIT) neceser m.
sponge cake n bizcocho, pastel m.
sponger ['spʌndʒə*] n gorrón/ona m/f.
spongy ['spʌndʒɪ] adj esponjoso.
sponsor ['spɔnsə*] n (RADIO, TV) patrocinador(a) m/f; (for membership) padrino/madrina; (COMM) fiador(a) m/f, avalador(a) m/f ♦ vt patrocinar; apadrinar; (parliamentary bill) apoyar, respaldar; (idea etc) presentar, promover; **I ~ed him at 3p a mile** (in fund-raising race) me apunté para darle 3 peniques la milla.

sponsorship ['spɔnsəʃɪp] n patrocinio.
spontaneity [spɔntə'neɪtɪ] n espontaneidad f.
spontaneous [spɔn'teɪnɪəs] adj espontáneo.
spontaneously [spɔn'teɪnɪəslɪ] adv espontáneamente.
spooky ['spuːkɪ] adj (col: place, atmosphere) espeluznante, horripilante.
spool [spuːl] n carrete m; (of sewing machine) canilla.
spoon [spuːn] n cuchara.
spoon-feed ['spuːnfiːd] vt dar de comer con cuchara a; (fig) dárselo todo mascado a.
spoonful ['spuːnful] n cucharada.
sporadic [spə'rædɪk] adj esporádico.
sport [spɔːt] n deporte m; (person) buen(a) perdedor(a) m/f; (amusement) juego, diversión f; **indoor/outdoor ~s** deportes mpl en sala cubierta/al aire libre; **to say sth in ~** decir algo en broma.
sport coat n (US) = **sports jacket.**
sporting ['spɔːtɪŋ] adj deportivo; **to give sb a ~ chance** darle a algn su oportunidad.
sports car n coche m sport.
sports coat n (US) = **sports jacket.**
sports ground n campo de deportes, centro deportivo.
sports jacket, (US) **sport jacket** n chaqueta deportiva.
sportsman ['spɔːtsmən] n deportista m.
sportsmanship ['spɔːtsmənʃɪp] n deportividad f.
sports pages npl páginas fpl deportivas.
sportswear ['spɔːtswɛə*] n ropa de deporte.
sportswoman ['spɔːtswumən] n deportista f.
sporty ['spɔːtɪ] adj deportivo.
spot [spɔt] n sitio, lugar m; (dot: on pattern) punto, mancha; (pimple) grano; (also: advertising ~) spot m; (small amount): **a ~ of** un poquito de ♦ vt (notice) notar, observar ♦ adj (COMM) inmediatamente efectivo; **on the ~** en el acto, acto seguido; (in difficulty) en un aprieto; **to do sth on the ~** hacer algo en el acto; **to put sb on the ~** poner a algn en un apuro.
spot check n reconocimiento rápido.
spotless ['spɔtlɪs] adj (clean) inmaculado; (reputation) intachable.
spotlessly ['spɔtlɪslɪ] adv: **~ clean** limpísimo.
spotlight ['spɔtlaɪt] n foco, reflector m; (AUT) faro auxiliar.
spot-on [spɔt'ɔn] adj (BRIT col) exacto.
spot price n precio de entrega inmediata.
spotted ['spɔtɪd] adj (pattern) de puntos.
spotty ['spɔtɪ] adj (face) con granos.

spouse [spauz] n cónyuge m/f.
spout [spaut] n (of jug) pico; (pipe) caño ♦ vi chorrear.
sprain [spreɪn] n torcedura, esguince m ♦ vt: **to ~ one's ankle** torcerse el tobillo.
sprang [spræŋ] pt of **spring**.
sprawl [sprɔːl] vi tumbarse ♦ n: **urban ~** crecimiento urbano descontrolado; **to send sb ~ing** tirar a algn al suelo.
sprawling ['sprɔːlɪŋ] adj (town) desparramado.
spray [spreɪ] n rociada; (of sea) espuma; (container) atomizador m; (of paint) pistola rociadora; (of flowers) ramita ♦ vt rociar; (crops) regar ♦ cpd (deodorant) en atomizador.
spread [sprɛd] n extensión f; (of idea) diseminación f; (col: food) comilona; (PRESS, TYP: two pages) plana ♦ vb (pt, pp **spread**) vt extender; diseminar; (butter) untar; (wings, sails) desplegar; (scatter) esparcir ♦ vi extenderse; diseminarse; untarse; desplegarse; esparcirse; **middle-age ~** gordura de la mediana edad; **repayments will be ~ over 18 months** los pagos se harán a lo largo de 18 meses.
spread-eagled ['sprɛdiːgld] adj: **to be ~** estar despatarrado.
spreadsheet ['sprɛdʃiːt] n (COMPUT) hoja de cálculo.
spree [spriː] n: **to go on a ~** ir de juerga or farra (LAM).
sprightly ['spraɪtlɪ] adj vivo, enérgico.
spring [sprɪŋ] n (season) primavera; (leap) salto, brinco; (coiled metal) resorte m; (of water) fuente f, manantial m; (bounciness) elasticidad f ♦ vb (pt **sprang**, pp **sprung** [spræŋ, sprʌŋ]) vi (arise) brotar, nacer; (leap) saltar, brincar ♦ vt: **to ~ a leak** (pipe etc) empezar a hacer agua; **he sprang the news on me** de repente me soltó la noticia; **in (the) ~** en (la) primavera; **to walk with a ~ in one's step** andar dando saltos or brincos; **to ~ into action** lanzarse a la acción.
▶**spring up** vi (problem) surgir.
springboard ['sprɪŋbɔːd] n trampolín m.
spring-clean [sprɪŋ'kliːn] n (also: **~ing**) limpieza general.
spring onion n cebolleta.
spring roll n rollito de primavera.
springtime ['sprɪŋtaɪm] n primavera.
springy ['sprɪŋɪ] adj elástico; (grass) mullido.
sprinkle ['sprɪŋkl] vt (pour) rociar; **to ~ water on, ~ with water** rociar or salpicar de agua.

sprinkler ['sprɪŋklə*] n (for lawn) aspersor m; (to put out fire) aparato de rociadura automática.
sprinkling ['sprɪŋklɪŋ] n (of water) rociada; (of salt, sugar) un poco de.
sprint [sprɪnt] n (e)sprint m ♦ vi (gen) correr a toda velocidad; (SPORT) esprintar; **the 200 metres ~** el (e)sprint de 200 metros.
sprinter ['sprɪntə*] n velocista m/f.
spritzer ['sprɪtsə*] n vino blanco con soda.
sprocket ['sprɔkɪt] n (on printer etc) rueda dentada.
sprocket feed n avance m por rueda dentada.
sprout [spraut] vi brotar, retoñar ♦ n: **(Brussels) ~s** npl coles fpl de Bruselas.
spruce [spruːs] n (BOT) pícea ♦ adj aseado, pulcro.
▶**spruce up** vt (tidy) arreglar, acicalar; (smarten up: room etc) ordenar; **to ~ o.s. up** arreglarse.
sprung [sprʌŋ] pp of **spring**.
spry [spraɪ] adj ágil, activo.
SPUC n abbr (= Society for the Protection of Unborn Children) ≈ Federación f Española de Asociaciones Pro-vida.
spun [spʌn] pt, pp of **spin**.
spur [spəː*] n espuela; (fig) estímulo, aguijón m ♦ vt (also: **~ on**) estimular, incitar; **on the ~ of the moment** de improviso.
spurious ['spjʊərɪəs] adj falso.
spurn [spəːn] vt desdeñar, rechazar.
spurt [spəːt] n chorro; (of energy) arrebato ♦ vi chorrear; **to put in** or **on a ~** (runner) acelerar; (fig: in work etc) hacer un gran esfuerzo.
sputter ['spʌtə*] vi = **splutter**.
spy [spaɪ] n espía m/f ♦ vi: **to ~ on** espiar a ♦ vt (see) divisar, lograr ver ♦ cpd (film, story) de espionaje.
spying ['spaɪɪŋ] n espionaje m.
Sq. abbr (in address: = Square) Plza.
sq. abbr (MATH etc) = **square**.
squabble ['skwɔbl] n riña, pelea ♦ vi reñir, pelear.
squad [skwɔd] n (MIL) pelotón m; (POLICE) brigada; (SPORT) equipo; **flying ~** (POLICE) brigada móvil.
squad car n (POLICE) coche-patrulla m.
squaddie ['skwɔdɪ] n (MIL: col) chivo.
squadron ['skwɔdrn] n (MIL) escuadrón m; (AVIAT, NAUT) escuadra.
squalid ['skwɔlɪd] adj miserable.
squall [skwɔːl] n (storm) chubasco; (wind) ráfaga.
squalor ['skwɔlə*] n miseria.
squander ['skwɔndə*] vt (money)

derrochar, despilfarrar; (*chances*) desperdiciar.

square [skwεə*] *n* cuadro; (*in town*) plaza; (*US: block of houses*) manzana, cuadra (*LAM*) ♦ *adj* cuadrado ♦ *vt* (*arrange*) arreglar; (*MATH*) cuadrar; (*reconcile*): **can you ~ it with your conscience?** ¿cómo se justifica ante sí mismo? ♦ *vi* cuadrar, conformarse; **all ~ igual(es); a ~ meal** una comida decente; **2 metres ~ 2** metros por 2; **1 ~ metre** un metro cuadrado; **to get one's accounts ~** dejar las cuentas claras; **I'll ~ it with him** (*col*) yo lo arreglo con él; **we're back to ~ one** (*fig*) hemos vuelto al punto de partida.

▶**square up** *vi* (*settle*): **to ~ up (with sb)** ajustar cuentas (con algn).

square bracket *n* (*TYP*) corchete *m*.

squarely ['skwεəlɪ] *adv* (*fully*) de lleno; (*honestly, fairly*) honradamente, justamente.

square root *n* raíz *f* cuadrada.

squash [skwɔʃ] *n* (*vegetable*) calabaza; (*SPORT*) squash *m*; (*BRIT: drink*): **lemon/ orange ~** zumo (*SP*) *or* jugo (*LAM*) de limón/naranja ♦ *vt* aplastar.

squat [skwɔt] *adj* achaparrado ♦ *vi* agacharse, sentarse en cuclillas; (*on property*) ocupar ilegalmente.

squatter ['skwɔtə*] *n* ocupante *m/f* ilegal, okupa *m/f*.

squawk [skwɔ:k] *vi* graznar.

squeak [skwi:k] *vi* (*hinge, wheel*) chirriar, rechinar; (*shoe, wood*) crujir ♦ *n* (*of hinge, wheel etc*) chirrido, rechinamiento; (*of shoes*) crujir *m*; (*of mouse etc*) chillido.

squeaky ['skwi:kɪ] *adj* que cruje; **to be ~ clean** (*fig*) ser superhonrado.

squeal [skwi:l] *vi* chillar, dar gritos agudos.

squeamish ['skwi:mɪʃ] *adj* delicado, remilgado.

squeeze [skwi:z] *n* presión *f*; (*of hand*) apretón *m*; (*COMM: credit ~*) restricción *f* ♦ *vt* (*lemon etc*) exprimir; (*hand, arm*) apretar; **a ~ of lemon** unas gotas de limón; **to ~ past/under sth** colarse al lado de/por debajo de algo.

▶**squeeze out** *vt* exprimir; (*fig*) excluir.

▶**squeeze through** *vi* abrirse paso con esfuerzos.

squelch [skwεltʃ] *vi* chapotear.

squid [skwɪd] *n* calamar *m*.

squiggle ['skwɪgl] *n* garabato.

squint [skwɪnt] *vi* entrecerrar los ojos ♦ *n* (*MED*) estrabismo; **to ~ at sth** mirar algo entornando los ojos.

squire ['skwaɪə*] *n* (*BRIT*) terrateniente *m*.

squirm [skwə:m] *vi* retorcerse, revolverse.

squirrel ['skwɪrəl] *n* ardilla.

squirt [skwə:t] *vi* salir a chorros.

Sr *abbr* = **senior, sister** (*REL*).

SRC *n abbr* (*BRIT*: = *Students' Representative Council*) consejo de estudiantes.

Sri Lanka [srɪ'læŋkə] *n* Sri Lanka *m*.

SRN *n abbr* (*BRIT*) = *State Registered Nurse*.

SRO *abbr* (*US*) = *standing room only*.

SS *abbr* (= *steamship*) M.V.

SSA *n abbr* (*US*: = *Social Security Administration*) ≈ Seguro Social.

SST *n abbr* (*US*) = *supersonic transport*.

ST *abbr* (*US*: = *Standard Time*) hora oficial.

St *abbr* (= *saint*) Sto./a.; (= *street*) c/.

stab [stæb] *n* (*with knife etc*) puñalada; (*of pain*) pinchazo; **to have a ~ at (doing) sth** (*col*) probar (a hacer) algo ♦ *vt* apuñalar; **to ~ sb to death** matar a algn a puñaladas.

stabbing ['stæbɪŋ] *n*: **there's been a ~** han apuñalado a alguien ♦ *adj* (*pain*) punzante.

stability [stə'bɪlɪtɪ] *n* estabilidad *f*.

stabilization [steɪbəlaɪ'zeɪʃən] *n* estabilización *f*.

stabilize ['steɪbəlaɪz] *vt* estabilizar ♦ *vi* estabilizarse.

stabilizer ['steɪbəlaɪzə*] *n* (*AVIAT, NAUT*) estabilizador *m*.

stable ['steɪbl] *adj* estable ♦ *n* cuadra, caballeriza; **riding ~s** escuela hípica.

staccato [stə'kɑ:təu] *adj, adv* staccato.

stack [stæk] *n* montón *m*, pila; (*col*) mar *f* ♦ *vt* amontonar, apilar; **there's ~s of time to finish it** hay cantidad de tiempo para acabarlo.

stacker ['stækə*] *n* (*for printer*) apiladora.

stadium ['steɪdɪəm] *n* estadio.

staff [stɑ:f] *n* (*work force*) personal *m*, plantilla; (*BRIT SCOL: also:* **teaching ~**) cuerpo docente; (*stick*) bastón *m* ♦ *vt* proveer de personal; **to be ~ed by Asians/women** tener una plantilla asiática/femenina.

staffroom ['stɑ:fru:m] *n* sala de profesores.

Staffs *abbr* (*BRIT*) = *Staffordshire*.

stag [stæg] *n* ciervo, venado; (*BRIT STOCK EXCHANGE*) especulador *m* con nuevas emisiones.

stage [steɪdʒ] *n* escena; (*point*) etapa; (*platform*) plataforma; **the ~** el escenario, el teatro ♦ *vt* (*play*) poner en escena, representar; (*organize*) montar, organizar; (*fig: perform: recovery etc*) efectuar; **in ~s** por etapas; **in the early/ final ~s** en las primeras/últimas etapas; **to go through a difficult ~** pasar una fase

or etapa mala.
stagecoach ['steɪdʒkəʊtʃ] *n* diligencia.
stage door *n* entrada de artistas.
stagehand ['steɪdʒhænd] *n* tramoyista *m/f.*
stage-manage ['steɪdʒmænɪdʒ] *vt* (*fig*) manipular.
stage manager *n* director(a) *m/f* de escena.
stagger ['stægə*] *vi* tambalear ♦ *vt* (*amaze*) asombrar; (*hours, holidays*) escalonar.
staggering ['stægərɪŋ] *adj* (*amazing*) asombroso, pasmoso.
staging post ['steɪdʒɪŋ-] *n* escala.
stagnant ['stægnənt] *adj* estancado.
stagnate [stæg'neɪt] *vi* estancarse; (*fig: economy, mind*) quedarse estancado.
stagnation [stæg'neɪʃən] *n* estancamiento.
stag night, stag party *n* despedida de soltero.
staid [steɪd] *adj* (*clothes*) serio, formal.
stain [steɪn] *n* mancha; (*colouring*) tintura ♦ *vt* manchar; (*wood*) teñir.
stained glass window [steɪnd-] *n* vidriera de colores.
stainless ['steɪnlɪs] *adj* (*steel*) inoxidable.
stain remover *n* quitamanchas *m inv.*
stair [stɛə*] *n* (*step*) peldaño, escalón *m*; ~**s** *npl* escaleras *fpl.*
staircase ['stɛəkeɪs], **stairway** ['stɛəweɪ] *n* escalera.
stairwell ['stɛəwɛl] *n* hueco *or* caja de la escalera.
stake [steɪk] *n* estaca, poste *m*; (*BETTING*) apuesta ♦ *vt* (*bet*) apostar; (*also*: ~ **out**: *area*) cercar con estacas; **to be at** ~ estar en juego; **to have a** ~ **in sth** tener interés en algo; **to** ~ **a claim to** (**sth**) presentar reclamación por *or* reclamar (algo).
stake-out ['steɪkaʊt] *n* vigilancia; **to be on a** ~ estar de vigilancia.
stalactite ['stæləktaɪt] *n* estalactita.
stalagmite ['stæləgmaɪt] *n* estalagmita.
stale [steɪl] *adj* (*bread*) duro; (*food*) pasado.
stalemate ['steɪlmeɪt] *n* tablas *fpl*; **to reach** ~ (*fig*) estancarse, alcanzar un punto muerto.
stalk [stɔːk] *n* tallo, caña ♦ *vt* acechar, cazar al acecho; **to** ~ **off** irse airado.
stall [stɔːl] *n* (*in market*) puesto; (*in stable*) casilla (de establo) ♦ *vt* (*AUT*) parar, calar ♦ *vi* (*AUT*) pararse, calarse; (*fig*) buscar evasivas; ~**s** *npl* (*BRIT: in cinema, theatre*) butacas *fpl*; **a newspaper** ~ un quiosco (de periódicos); **a flower** ~ un puesto de flores.
stallholder ['stɔːlhəʊldə*] *n* dueño/a de un puesto.
stallion ['stælɪən] *n* semental *m*, garañón *m.*

stalwart ['stɔːlwət] *n* partidario/a incondicional.
stamen ['steɪmən] *n* estambre *m.*
stamina ['stæmɪnə] *n* resistencia.
stammer ['stæmə*] *n* tartamudeo, balbuceo ♦ *vi* tartamudear, balbucir.
stamp [stæmp] *n* sello, estampilla (*LAM*); (*mark, also fig*) marca, huella; (*on document*) timbre *m* ♦ *vi* (*also*: ~ **one's foot**) patear ♦ *vt* patear, golpear con el pie; (*letter*) poner sellos en; (*with rubber* ~) marcar con sello; ~**ed addressed envelope (sae)** sobre *m* sellado con las señas propias.
▶**stamp out** *vt* (*fire*) apagar con el pie; (*crime, opposition*) acabar con.
stamp album *n* álbum *m* para sellos.
stamp collecting *n* filatelia.
stamp duty *n* (*BRIT*) derecho de timbre.
stampede [stæm'piːd] *n* (*of cattle*) estampida.
stamp machine *n* máquina (expendedora) de sellos.
stance [stæns] *n* postura.
stand [stænd] *n* (*attitude*) posición *f*, postura; (*for taxis*) parada; (*music* ~) atril *m*; (*SPORT*) tribuna; (*at exhibition*) stand *m* ♦ *vb* (*pt, pp* **stood** [stud]) *vi* (*be*) estar, encontrarse; (*be on foot*) estar de pie; (*rise*) levantarse; (*remain*) quedar en pie ♦ *vt* (*place*) poner, colocar; (*tolerate, withstand*) aguantar, soportar; **to make a** ~ resistir; (*fig*) mantener una postura firme; **to take a** ~ **on an issue** adoptar una actitud hacia una cuestión; **to** ~ **for parliament** (*BRIT*) presentarse (como candidato) a las elecciones; **nothing** ~**s in our way** nada nos lo impide; **to** ~ **still** quedarse inmóvil; **to let sth** ~ **as it is** dejar algo como está; **as things** ~ tal como están las cosas; **to** ~ **sb a drink/ meal** invitar a algn a una copa/a comer; **the company will have to** ~ **the loss** la empresa tendrá que hacer frente a las pérdidas; **I can't** ~ **him** no le aguanto, no le puedo ver; **to** ~ **guard** *or* **watch** (*MIL*) hacer guardia.
▶**stand aside** *vi* apartarse, mantenerse aparte.
▶**stand by** *vi* (*be ready*) estar listo ♦ *vt fus* (*opinion*) mantener.
▶**stand down** *vi* (*withdraw*) ceder el puesto; (*MIL, LAW*) retirarse.
▶**stand for** *vt fus* (*signify*) significar; (*tolerate*) aguantar, permitir.
▶**stand in for** *vt fus* suplir a.
▶**stand out** *vi* (*be prominent*) destacarse.
▶**stand up** *vi* (*rise*) levantarse, ponerse de

pie.

▶**stand up for** *vt fus* defender.

▶**stand up to** *vt fus* hacer frente a.

stand-alone ['stændələun] *adj* (*COMPUT*) autónomo.

standard ['stændəd] *n* patrón *m*, norma; (*flag*) estandarte *m* ♦ *adj* (*size etc*) normal, corriente, estándar; ~**s** *npl* (*morals*) valores *mpl* morales; **the gold** ~ (*COMM*) el patrón oro; **high/low** ~ de alto/bajo nivel; **below** *or* **not up to** ~ (*work*) de calidad inferior; **to be** *or* **come up to** ~ satisfacer los requisitos; **to apply a double** ~ aplicar un doble criterio.

standardization [stændədaɪ'zeɪʃən] *n* normalización *f*.

standardize ['stændədaɪz] *vt* estandarizar.

standard lamp *n* (*BRIT*) lámpara de pie.

standard model *n* modelo stándard.

standard of living *n* nivel *m* de vida.

standard practice *n* norma, práctica común.

standard rate *n* tasa de imposición.

stand-by ['stændbaɪ] *n* (*alert*) alerta, aviso; (*also:* ~ **ticket**: *THEAT*) *entrada reducida de última hora*; (: *AVIAT*) billete *m* standby; **to be on** ~ estar preparado; (*doctor*) estar listo para acudir; (*AVIAT*) estar en la lista de espera.

stand-by generator *n* generador *m* de reserva.

stand-by passenger *n* (*AVIAT*) pasajero/a en lista de espera.

stand-by ticket *n* (*AVIAT*) (billete *m*) standby *m*.

stand-in ['stændɪn] *n* suplente *m/f*; (*CINE*) doble *m/f*.

standing ['stændɪŋ] *adj* (*upright*) derecho; (*on foot*) de pie, en pie; (*permanent*: *committee*) permanente; (: *rule*) fijo; (: *army*) permanente, regular; (*grievance*) constante, viejo ♦ *n* reputación *f*; (*duration*): **of 6 months'** ~ que lleva 6 meses; **of many years'** ~ que lleva muchos años; **he was given a** ~ **ovation** le dieron una calurosa ovación de pie; ~ **joke** motivo constante de broma; **a man of some** ~ un hombre de cierta posición *or* categoría.

standing order *n* (*BRIT*: *at bank*) giro bancario; **standing orders** *npl* (*MIL*) reglamento *sg* general.

standing room *n* sitio para estar de pie.

stand-off ['stændɔf] *n* (*esp US*: *stalemate*) punto muerto.

stand-offish [stænd'ɔfɪʃ] *adj* distante.

standpat ['stændpæt] *adj* (*US*) inmovilista.

standpipe ['stændpaɪp] *n* tubo vertical.

standpoint ['stændpɔɪnt] *n* punto de vista.

standstill ['stændstɪl] *n*: **at a** ~ paralizado, en un punto muerto; **to come to a** ~ pararse, quedar paralizado.

stank [stæŋk] *pt of* **stink**.

staple ['steɪpl] *n* (*for papers*) grapa; (*product*) producto *or* artículo de primeva necesidad ♦ *adj* (*crop, industry, food etc*) básico ♦ *vt* grapar.

stapler ['steɪplə*] *n* grapadora.

star [stɑ:*] *n* estrella; (*celebrity*) estrella, astro ♦ *vi*: **to** ~ **in** ser la estrella de; **four-** ~ **hotel** hotel *m* de cuatro estrellas; **4-**~ **petrol** gasolina extra.

star attraction *n* atracción *f* principal.

starboard ['stɑ:bəd] *n* estribor *m*.

starch [stɑ:tʃ] *n* almidón *m*.

starchy ['stɑ:tʃɪ] *adj* (*food*) feculento.

stardom ['stɑ:dəm] *n* estrellato.

stare [stɛə*] *n* mirada fija ♦ *vi*: **to** ~ **at** mirar fijo.

starfish ['stɑ:fɪʃ] *n* estrella de mar.

stark [stɑ:k] *adj* (*bleak*) severo, escueto; (*simplicity, colour*) austero; (*reality, truth*) puro; (*poverty*) absoluto ♦ *adv*: ~ **naked** en cueros.

starkers ['stɑ:kəz] *adj* (*BRIT col*): **to be** ~ estar en cueros.

starlet ['stɑ:lɪt] *n* (*CINE*) actriz *f* principiante.

starling ['stɑ:lɪŋ] *n* estornino.

starry ['stɑ:rɪ] *adj* estrellado.

starry-eyed [stɑ:rɪ'aɪd] *adj* (*gullible, innocent*) inocentón/ona; (*idealistic*) idealista; (*from wonder*) asombrado; (*from love*) enamoradísimo.

Stars and Stripes *npl*: **the** ~ las barras y las estrellas, la bandera de EEUU.

star sign *n* signo del zodíaco.

star-studded ['stɑ:stʌdɪd] *adj*: **a** ~ **cast** un elenco estelar.

start [stɑ:t] *n* (*beginning*) principio, comienzo; (*departure*) salida; (*sudden movement*) sobresalto; (*advantage*) ventaja ♦ *vt* empezar, comenzar; (*cause*) causar; (*found*: *business, newspaper*) establecer, fundar; (*engine*) poner en marcha ♦ *vi* (*begin*) comenzar, empezar; (*with fright*) asustarse, sobresaltarse; (*train etc*) salir; **to give sb a** ~ dar un susto a algn; **at the** ~ al principio; **for a** ~ en primer lugar; **to make an early** ~ ponerse en camino temprano; **the thieves had 3 hours'** ~ los ladrones llevaban 3 horas de ventaja; **to** ~ **a fire** provocar un incendio; **to** ~ **doing** *or* **to do sth** empezar a hacer algo; **to** ~ **(off) with ...**

(*firstly*) para empezar; (*at the beginning*) al principio.

▶**start off** *vi* empezar, comenzar; (*leave*) salir, ponerse en camino.

▶**start over** *vi* (*US*) volver a empezar.

▶**start up** *vi* comenzar; (*car*) ponerse en marcha ♦ *vt* comenzar; (*car*) poner en marcha.

starter ['stɑːtə*] *n* (*AUT*) botón *m* de arranque; (*SPORT: official*) juez *m/f* de salida; (: *runner*) corredor(a) *m/f*; (*BRIT CULIN*) entrada.

starting point ['stɑːtɪŋ-] *n* punto de partida.

starting price *n* (*COMM*) precio inicial.

startle ['stɑːtl] *vt* asustar, sobresaltar.

startling ['stɑːtlɪŋ] *adj* alarmante.

star turn *n* (*BRIT*) atracción *f* principal.

starvation [stɑːˈveɪʃən] *n* hambre *f*, hambruna (*LAM*); (*MED*) inanición *f*.

starvation wages *npl* sueldo *sg* de hambre.

starve [stɑːv] *vi* pasar hambre; (*to death*) morir de hambre ♦ *vt* hacer pasar hambre; (*fig*) privar; **I'm starving** estoy muerto de hambre.

stash [stæʃ] *vt*: **to ~ sth away** (*col*) poner algo a buen recaudo.

state [steɪt] *n* estado; (*pomp*): **in ~** con mucha ceremonia ♦ *vt* (*say, declare*) afirmar; (*a case*) presentar, exponer; **~ of emergency** estado de excepción *or* emergencia; **~ of mind** estado de ánimo; **to lie in ~** (*corpse*) estar de cuerpo presente; **to be in a ~** estar agitado.

State Department *n* (*US*) Ministerio de Asuntos Exteriores.

state education *n* (*BRIT*) enseñanza pública.

stateless ['steɪtlɪs] *adj* desnacionalizado.

stately ['steɪtlɪ] *adj* majestuoso, imponente.

statement ['steɪtmənt] *n* afirmación *f*; (*LAW*) declaración *f*; (*COMM*) estado; **official ~** informe *m* oficial; **~ of account, bank ~** estado de cuenta.

state-of-the-art ['steɪtəvðɪˈɑːt] *adj* (*technology etc*) puntero.

state-owned ['steɪtəʊnd] *adj* estatal, del estado.

States [steɪts] *npl*: **the ~** los Estados Unidos.

state school *n* escuela *or* colegio estatal.

statesman ['steɪtsmən] *n* estadista *m*.

statesmanship ['steɪtsmənʃɪp] *n* habilidad *f* política, arte *m* de gobernar.

static ['stætɪk] *n* (*RADIO*) parásitos *mpl* ♦ *adj* estático.

static electricity *n* electricidad *f* estática.

station ['steɪʃən] *n* (*gen*) estación *f*; (*place*) puesto, sitio; (*RADIO*) emisora; (*rank*) posición *f* social ♦ *vt* colocar, situar; (*MIL*) apostar; **action ~s!** ¡a los puestos de combate!; **to be ~ed in** (*MIL*) estar estacionado en.

stationary ['steɪʃnərɪ] *adj* estacionario, fijo.

stationer ['steɪʃənə*] *n* papelero/a.

stationer's (shop) *n* (*BRIT*) papelería.

stationery ['steɪʃənərɪ] *n* (*writing paper*) papel *m* de escribir; (*writing materials*) artículos *mpl* de escritorio.

station master *n* (*RAIL*) jefe *m* de estación.

station wagon *n* (*US*) coche *m* familiar con ranchera.

statistic [stəˈtɪstɪk] *n* estadística.

statistical [stəˈtɪstɪkl] *adj* estadístico.

statistics [stəˈtɪstɪks] *n* (*science*) estadística.

statue ['stætjuː] *n* estatua.

statuette [stætjuˈɛt] *n* figurilla.

stature ['stætʃə*] *n* estatura; (*fig*) talla.

status ['steɪtəs] *n* condición *f*, estado; (*reputation*) reputación *f*, estatus *m*; **the ~ quo** el statu quo.

status line *n* (*COMPUT*) línea de situación *or* de estado.

status symbol *n* símbolo de prestigio.

statute ['stætjuːt] *n* estatuto, ley *f*.

statute book *n* código de leyes.

statutory ['stætjutrɪ] *adj* estatutario; **~ meeting** junta ordinaria.

staunch [stɔːntʃ] *adj* leal, incondicional ♦ *vt* (*flow, blood*) restañar.

stave [steɪv] *vt*: **to ~ off** (*attack*) rechazar; (*threat*) evitar.

stay [steɪ] *n* (*period of time*) estancia; (*LAW*): **~ of execution** aplazamiento de una sentencia ♦ *vi* (*remain*) quedar(se); (*as guest*) hospedarse; **to ~ put** seguir en el mismo sitio; **to ~ the night/5 days** pasar la noche/estar *or* quedarse 5 días.

▶**stay behind** *vi* quedar atrás.

▶**stay in** *vi* (*at home*) quedarse en casa.

▶**stay on** *vi* quedarse.

▶**stay out** *vi* (*of house*) no volver a casa; (*strikers*) no volver al trabajo.

▶**stay up** *vi* (*at night*) velar, no acostarse.

staying power ['steɪɪŋ-] *n* resistencia, aguante *m*.

STD *n abbr* (*BRIT*: = *subscriber trunk dialling*) *servicio de conferencias automáticas*; (= *sexually transmitted disease*) ETS *f*.

stead [stɛd] *n*: **in sb's ~** en lugar de algn; **stand sb in good ~** ser muy útil a algn.

steadfast ['stɛdfɑːst] *adj* firme, resuelto.

steadily ['stɛdɪlɪ] *adv* (*firmly*) firmemente; (*unceasingly*) sin parar; (*fixedly*) fijamente; (*walk*) normalmente; (*drive*) a velocidad constante.

steady ['stɛdɪ] *adj* (*fixed*) firme, fijo; (*regular*) regular; (*boyfriend etc*) formal, fijo; (*person, character*) sensato, juicioso ♦ *vt* (*hold*) mantener firme; (*stabilize*) estabilizar; (*nerves*) calmar; **to** ~ **o.s. on** *or* **against sth** afirmarse en algo.

steak [steɪk] *n* (*gen*) filete *m*; (*beef*) bistec *m*.

steal, *pt* **stole,** *pp* **stolen** [stiːl, stəul, 'stəuln] *vt*, *vi* robar.

▶**steal away, steal off** *vi* marcharse furtivamente, escabullirse.

stealth [stɛlθ] *n*: **by** ~ a escondidas, sigilosamente.

stealthy ['stɛlθɪ] *adj* cauteloso, sigiloso.

steam [stiːm] *n* vapor *m*; (*mist*) vaho, humo ♦ *vt* (*CULIN*) cocer al vapor ♦ *vi* echar vapor; (*ship*): **to** ~ **along** avanzar, ir avanzando; **under one's own** ~ (*fig*) por sus propios medios *or* propias fuerzas; **to run out of** ~ (*fig: person*) quedar(se) agotado, quemarse; **to let off** ~ (*fig*) desahogarse.

▶**steam up** *vi* (*window*) empañarse; **to get** ~**ed up about sth** (*fig*) ponerse negro por algo.

steam engine *n* máquina de vapor.

steamer ['stiːmə*] *n* (buque *m* de) vapor *m*; (*CULIN*) *recipiente para cocinar al vapor*.

steam iron *n* plancha de vapor.

steamroller ['stiːmrəulə*] *n* apisonadora.

steamship ['stiːmʃɪp] *n* = **steamer**.

steamy ['stiːmɪ] *adj* (*room*) lleno de vapor; (*window*) empañado.

steel [stiːl] *n* acero ♦ *adj* de acero.

steel band *n* banda de percusión del Caribe.

steel industry *n* industria siderúrgica.

steel mill *n* fábrica de acero.

steelworks ['stiːlwɜːks] *n* acería, fundición *f* de acero.

steely ['stiːlɪ] *adj* (*determination*) inflexible; (*gaze*) duro; (*eyes*) penetrante; ~ **grey** gris *m* metálico.

steelyard ['stiːljɑːd] *n* romana.

steep [stiːp] *adj* escarpado, abrupto; (*stair*) empinado; (*price*) exorbitante, excesivo ♦ *vt* empapar, remojar.

steeple ['stiːpl] *n* aguja, campanario.

steeplechase ['stiːpltʃeɪs] *n* carrera de obstáculos.

steeplejack ['stiːpldʒæk] *n* reparador(a) *m/f* de chimeneas *or* de campanarios.

steer [stɪə*] *vt* (*car*) conducir (*SP*), manejar (*LAM*); (*person*) dirigir, guiar ♦ *vi* conducir; **to** ~ **clear of sb/sth** (*fig*) esquivar a algn/evadir algo.

steering ['stɪərɪŋ] *n* (*AUT*) dirección *f*.

steering committee *n* comisión *f* directiva.

steering wheel *n* volante *m*.

stellar ['stɛlə*] *adj* estelar.

stem [stɛm] *n* (*of plant*) tallo; (*of glass*) pie *m*; (*of pipe*) cañón *m* ♦ *vt* detener; (*blood*) restañar.

▶**stem from** *vt fus* ser consecuencia de.

stench [stɛntʃ] *n* hedor *m*.

stencil ['stɛnsl] *n* (*typed*) cliché *m*, clisé *m*; (*lettering*) plantilla ♦ *vt* hacer un cliché de.

stenographer [stɛ'nɔgrəfə*] *n* (*US*) taquígrafo/a.

step [stɛp] *n* paso; (*sound*) paso, pisada; (*stair*) peldaño, escalón *m* ♦ *vi*: **to** ~ **forward** dar un paso adelante; ~**s** *npl* (*BRIT*) = ~**ladder**; ~ **by** ~ paso a paso; (*fig*) poco a poco; **to keep in** ~ (**with**) llevar el paso de; (*fig*) llevar el paso de, estar de acuerdo con; **to be in/out of** ~ **with** estar acorde con/estar en disonancia con; **to take** ~**s to solve a problem** tomar medidas para resolver un problema.

▶**step down** *vi* (*fig*) retirarse.

▶**step in** *vi* entrar; (*fig*) intervenir.

▶**step off** *vt fus* bajar de.

▶**step on** *vt fus* pisar.

▶**step over** *vt fus* pasar por encima de.

▶**step up** *vt* (*increase*) aumentar.

step aerobics *npl* step *m*.

stepbrother ['stɛpbrʌðə*] *n* hermanastro.

stepdaughter ['stɛpdɔːtə*] *n* hijastra.

stepfather ['stɛpfɑːðə*] *n* padrastro.

stepladder ['stɛplædə*] *n* escalera doble *or* de tijera.

stepmother ['stɛpmʌðə*] *n* madrastra.

stepping stone ['stɛpɪŋ-] *n* pasadera.

step Reebok ® [-'riːbɔk] *n* step *m*.

stepsister ['stɛpsɪstə*] *n* hermanastra.

stepson ['stɛpsʌn] *n* hijastro.

stereo ['stɛrɪəu] *n* estéreo ♦ *adj* (*also:* ~**phonic**) estéreo, estereofónico; **in** ~ en estéreo.

stereotype ['stɪərɪətaɪp] *n* estereotipo ♦ *vt* estereotipar.

sterile ['stɛraɪl] *adj* estéril.

sterilization [stɛrɪlaɪ'zeɪʃən] *n* esterilización *f*.

sterilize ['stɛrɪlaɪz] *vt* esterilizar.

sterling ['stɜːlɪŋ] *adj* (*silver*) de ley ♦ *n* (*ECON*) libras *fpl* esterlinas; **a pound** ~ una libra esterlina; **he is of** ~ **character** tiene un carácter excelente.

stern [stɜːn] *adj* severo, austero ♦ *n* (*NAUT*) popa.

sternum ['stɜːnəm] *n* esternón *m*.

steroid ['stɪərɔɪd] n esteroide m.
stethoscope ['stɛθəskəup] n estetoscopio.
stevedore ['sti:vədɔ:*] n estibador m.
stew [stju:] n cocido, estofado, guisado (LAM) ♦ vt, vi estofar, guisar; (fruit) cocer; ~ed fruit compota de fruta.
steward ['stju:əd] n (BRIT: gen) camarero; (shop ~) enlace m/f sindical.
stewardess ['stju:ədəs] n azafata.
stewardship ['stju:ədʃɪp] n tutela.
stewing steak ['stju:ɪŋ-], (US) **stew meat** n carne f de vaca.
St. Ex. abbr = **stock exchange**.
stg abbr (= sterling) ester.
stick [stɪk] n palo; (as weapon) porra; (walking ~) bastón m ♦ vb (pt, pp **stuck** [stʌk]) vt (glue) pegar; (col: put) meter; (: tolerate) aguantar, soportar ♦ vi pegarse; (come to a stop) quedarse parado; (get jammed: door, lift) atascarse; **to get hold of the wrong end of the ~** entender al revés; **to ~ to** (word, principles) atenerse a, ser fiel a; (promise) cumplir; **it stuck in my mind** se me quedó grabado; **to ~ sth into** clavar or hincar algo en.
▶**stick around** vi (col) quedarse.
▶**stick out** vi sobresalir ♦ vt: **to ~ it out** (col) aguantar.
▶**stick up** vi sobresalir.
▶**stick up for** vt fus defender.
sticker ['stɪkə*] n (label) etiqueta adhesiva; (with slogan) pegatina.
sticking plaster ['stɪkɪŋ-] n (BRIT) esparadrapo.
sticking point n (fig) punto de fricción.
stickler ['stɪklə*] n: **to be a ~ for** insistir mucho en.
stick shift n (US AUT) palanca de cambios.
stick-up ['stɪkʌp] n asalto, atraco.
sticky ['stɪki] adj pegajoso; (label) adhesivo; (fig) difícil.
stiff [stɪf] adj rígido, tieso; (hard) duro; (difficult) difícil; (person) inflexible; (price) exorbitante; **to have a ~ neck/back** tener tortícolis/dolor de espalda; **the door's ~** la puerta está atrancada.
stiffen ['stɪfn] vt hacer más rígido; (limb) entumecer ♦ vi endurecerse; (grow stronger) fortalecerse.
stiffness ['stɪfnɪs] n rigidez f.
stifle ['staɪfl] vt ahogar, sofocar.
stifling ['staɪflɪŋ] adj (heat) sofocante, bochornoso.
stigma, pl (BOT, MED, REL) ~**ta**, (fig) ~**s** ['stɪgmə, stɪg'mɑːtə] n estigma m.
stile [staɪl] n escalera (para pasar una cerca).
stiletto [stɪ'lɛtəu] n (BRIT: also: ~ **heel**) tacón m de aguja.

still [stɪl] adj inmóvil, quieto; (orange juice etc) sin gas ♦ adv (up to this time) todavía; (even) aún; (nonetheless) sin embargo, aun así ♦ n (CINE) foto f fija; **keep ~!** ¡estate quieto!, ¡no te muevas!; **he ~ hasn't arrived** todavía no ha llegado.
stillborn ['stɪlbɔ:n] adj nacido muerto.
still life n naturaleza muerta.
stilt [stɪlt] n zanco; (pile) pilar m, soporte m.
stilted ['stɪltɪd] adj afectado, artificial.
stimulant ['stɪmjulənt] n estimulante m.
stimulate ['stɪmjuleɪt] vt estimular.
stimulating ['stɪmjuleɪtɪŋ] adj estimulante.
stimulation [stɪmju'leɪʃən] n estímulo.
stimulus, pl **-li** ['stɪmjuləs, -laɪ] n estímulo, incentivo.
sting [stɪŋ] n (wound) picadura; (pain) escozor m, picazón m; (organ) aguijón m; (col: confidence trick) timo ♦ vb (pt, pp **stung** [stʌŋ]) vt picar ♦ vi picar, escocer; **my eyes are ~ing** me pican or escuecen los ojos.
stingy ['stɪndʒɪ] adj tacaño.
stink [stɪŋk] n hedor m, tufo ♦ vi (pt **stank**, pp **stunk** [stæŋk, stʌŋk]) heder, apestar.
stinking ['stɪŋkɪŋ] adj hediondo, fétido; (fig: col) horrible.
stint [stɪnt] n tarea, destajo; **to do one's ~ at sth** hacer su parte (de algo), hacer lo que corresponde (de algo) ♦ vi: **to ~ on** escatimar.
stipend ['staɪpɛnd] n salario, remuneración f.
stipendiary [staɪ'pɛndɪərɪ] adj: ~ **magistrate** magistrado/a estipendiario/a.
stipulate ['stɪpjuleɪt] vt estipular.
stipulation [stɪpju'leɪʃən] n estipulación f.
stir [stə:*] n (fig: agitation) conmoción f ♦ vt (tea etc) remover; (fire) atizar; (move) agitar; (fig: emotions) conmover ♦ vi moverse; **to give sth a ~** remover algo; **to cause a ~** causar conmoción or sensación.
▶**stir up** vt excitar; (trouble) fomentar.
stir-fry ['stə:fraɪ] vt sofreír removiendo ♦ n plato preparado sofriendo y removiendo los ingredientes.
stirrup ['stɪrəp] n estribo.
stitch [stɪtʃ] n (SEWING) puntada; (KNITTING) punto; (MED) punto (de sutura); (pain) punzada ♦ vt coser; (MED) suturar.
stoat [stəut] n armiño.
stock [stɔk] n (COMM: reserves) existencias fpl, stock m; (: selection) surtido; (AGR) ganado, ganadería; (CULIN) caldo; (fig: lineage) estirpe f, cepa; (FINANCE) capital m; (: shares) acciones fpl; (RAIL: rolling ~) material m rodante ♦ adj (COMM: goods,

size) normal, de serie; (*fig: reply etc*) clásico, trillado; (: *greeting*) acostumbrado ♦ *vt* (*have in* ~) tener existencias de; (*supply*) proveer, abastecer; **in** ~ en existencia *or* almacén; **to have sth in** ~ tener existencias de algo; **out of** ~ agotado; **to take** ~ **of** (*fig*) considerar, examinar; ~**s** *npl* (*HISTORY: punishment*) cepo *sg*; ~**s and shares** acciones y valores; **government** ~ papel *m* del Estado.

►**stock up with** *vt fus* abastecerse de.

stockbroker ['stɔkbrəukə*] *n* agente *m/f or* corredor(a) *m/f* de bolsa.

stock control *n* (*COMM*) control *m* de existencias.

stock cube *n* pastilla *or* cubito de caldo.

stock exchange *n* bolsa.

stockholder ['stɔkhəuldə*] *n* (*US*) accionista *m/f*.

Stockholm ['stɔkhəum] *n* Estocolmo.

stocking ['stɔkɪŋ] *n* media.

stock-in-trade ['stɔkɪn'treɪd] *n* (*tools etc*) herramientas *fpl*; (*stock*) existencia de mercancías; (*fig*): **it's his** ~ es su especialidad.

stockist ['stɔkɪst] *n* (*BRIT*) distribuidor(a) *m/f*.

stock market *n* bolsa (de valores).

stock phrase *n* vieja frase *f*.

stockpile ['stɔkpaɪl] *n* reserva ♦ *vt* acumular, almacenar.

stockroom ['stɔkru:m] *n* almacén *m*, depósito.

stocktaking ['stɔkteɪkɪŋ] *n* (*BRIT COMM*) inventario, balance *m*.

stocky ['stɔkɪ] *adj* (*strong*) robusto; (*short*) achaparrado.

stodgy ['stɔdʒɪ] *adj* indigesto, pesado.

stoical ['stəuɪkəl] *adj* estoico.

stoke [stəuk] *vt* atizar.

stole [stəul] *pt of* **steal** ♦ *n* estola.

stolen ['stəuln] *pp of* **steal**.

stolid ['stɔlɪd] *adj* (*person*) imperturbable, impasible.

stomach ['stʌmək] *n* (*ANAT*) estómago; (*belly*) vientre *m* ♦ *vt* tragar, aguantar.

stomach ache *n* dolor *m* de estómago.

stomach pump *n* bomba gástrica.

stomach ulcer *n* úlcera de estómago.

stomp [stɔmp] *vi*: **to** ~ **in/out** entrar/salir con pasos ruidosos.

stone [stəun] *n* piedra; (*in fruit*) hueso; (*BRIT: weight*) = 6.348 kg; 14 pounds ♦ *adj* de piedra ♦ *vt* apedrear; **within a** ~**'s throw of the station** a tiro de piedra *or* a dos pasos de la estación.

Stone Age *n*: **the** ~ la Edad de Piedra.

stone-cold ['stəun'kəuld] *adj* helado.

stoned [stəund] *adj* (*col: drunk*) trompa, borracho, colocado.

stone-deaf ['stəun'dɛf] *adj* sordo como una tapia.

stonemason ['stəunmeɪsən] *n* albañil *m*.

stonewall [stəun'wɔ:l] *vi* alargar la cosa innecesariamente ♦ *vt* dar largas a.

stonework ['stəunwɜ:k] *n* (*art*) cantería.

stony ['stəunɪ] *adj* pedregoso; (*glance*) glacial.

stood [stud] *pt, pp of* **stand**.

stooge [stu:dʒ] *n* (*col*) hombre *m* de paja.

stool [stu:l] *n* taburete *m*.

stoop [stu:p] *vi* (*also*: **have a** ~) ser cargado de espaldas; (*bend*) inclinarse, encorvarse; **to** ~ **to (doing) sth** rebajarse a (hacer) algo.

stop [stɔp] *n* parada, alto; (*in punctuation*) punto ♦ *vt* parar, detener; (*break off*) suspender; (*block*) tapar, cerrar; (*prevent*) impedir; (*also*: **put a** ~ **to**) poner término a ♦ *vi* pararse, detenerse; (*end*) acabarse; **to** ~ **doing sth** dejar de hacer algo; **to** ~ **sb (from) doing sth** impedir a algn hacer algo; **to** ~ **dead** pararse en seco; ~ **it!** ¡basta ya!, ¡párate!

►**stop by** *vi* pasar por.

►**stop off** *vi* interrumpir el viaje.

►**stop up** *vt* (*hole*) tapar.

stopcock ['stɔpkɔk] *n* llave *f* de paso.

stopgap ['stɔpgæp] *n* interino; (*person*) sustituto/a; (*measure*) medida provisional ♦ *cpd* (*situation*) provisional.

stoplights ['stɔplaɪts] *npl* (*AUT*) luces *fpl* de detención.

stopover ['stɔpəuvə*] *n* parada intermedia; (*AVIAT*) escala.

stoppage ['stɔpɪdʒ] *n* (*strike*) paro; (*temporary stop*) interrupción *f*; (*of pay*) suspensión *f*; (*blockage*) obstrucción *f*.

stopper ['stɔpə*] *n* tapón *m*.

stop press *n* noticias *fpl* de última hora.

stopwatch ['stɔpwɔtʃ] *n* cronómetro.

storage ['stɔːrɪdʒ] *n* almacenaje *m*; (*COMPUT*) almacenamiento.

storage capacity *n* espacio de almacenaje.

storage heater *n* acumulador *m* de calor.

store [stɔː*] *n* (*stock*) provisión *f*; (*depot*; *BRIT: large shop*) almacén *m*; (*US*) tienda; (*reserve*) reserva, repuesto ♦ *vt* (*gen*, *COMPUT*) almacenar; (*keep*) guardar; (*in filing system*) archivar; ~**s** *npl* víveres *mpl*; **who knows what is in** ~ **for us** quién sabe lo que nos espera; **to set great/little** ~ **by sth** dar mucha/poca importancia a algo, valorar mucho/poco algo.

▶**store up** *vt* acumular.

storehouse ['stɔːhaus] *n* almacén *m*, depósito.

storekeeper ['stɔːkiːpə*] *n* (*US*) tendero/a.

storeroom ['stɔːruːm] *n* despensa.

storey, (*US*) **story** ['stɔːrɪ] *n* piso.

stork [stɔːk] *n* cigüeña.

storm [stɔːm] *n* tormenta; (*wind*) vendaval *m*; (*fig*) tempestad *f* ♦ *vi* (*fig*) rabiar ♦ *vt* tomar por asalto, asaltar; **to take a town by** ~ (*MIL*) tomar una ciudad por asalto.

storm cloud *n* nubarrón *m*.

storm door *n* contrapuerta.

stormy ['stɔːmɪ] *adj* tempestuoso.

story ['stɔːrɪ] *n* historia; (*PRESS*) artículo; (*joke*) cuento, chiste *m*; (*plot*) argumento; (*lie*) cuento; (*US*) = **storey**.

storybook ['stɔːrɪbuk] *n* libro de cuentos.

storyteller ['stɔːrɪtɛlə*] *n* cuentista *m/f*.

stout [staut] *adj* (*strong*) sólido; (*fat*) gordo, corpulento ♦ *n* cerveza negra.

stove [stəuv] *n* (*for cooking*) cocina; (*for heating*) estufa; **gas/electric** ~ cocina de gas/eléctrica.

stow [stəu] *vt* meter, poner; (*NAUT*) estibar.

stowaway ['stəuəweɪ] *n* polizón/ona *m/f*.

straddle ['strædl] *vt* montar a horcajadas.

straggle ['strægl] *vi* (*wander*) vagar en desorden; (*lag behind*) rezagarse.

straggler ['stræglə*] *n* rezagado/a.

straggling ['stræglɪŋ], **straggly** ['stræglɪ] *adj* (*hair*) desordenado.

straight [streɪt] *adj* (*direct*) recto, derecho; (*plain, uncomplicated*) sencillo; (*frank*) franco, directo; (*in order*) en orden; (*continuous*) continuo; (*THEAT: part, play*) serio; (*person: conventional*) recto, convencional; (: *heterosexual*) heterosexual ♦ *adv* derecho, directamente; (*drink*) solo; **to put** *or* **get sth** ~ dejar algo en claro; **10** ~ **wins** 10 victorias seguidas; **to be (all)** ~ (*tidy*) estar en orden; (*clarified*) estar claro; **I went** ~ **home** (me) fui directamente a casa; ~ **away**, ~ **off** (*at once*) en seguida.

straighten ['streɪtn] *vt* (*also*: ~ **out**) enderezar, poner derecho; **to** ~ **things out** poner las cosas en orden.

straight-faced [streɪt'feɪst] *adj* serio ♦ *adv* sin mostrar emoción, impávido.

straightforward [streɪt'fɔːwəd] *adj* (*simple*) sencillo; (*honest*) sincero.

strain [streɪn] *n* (*gen*) tensión *f*; (*TECH*) esfuerzo; (*MED*) distensión *f*, torcedura; (*breed*) raza; (*lineage*) linaje *m*; (*of virus*) variedad *f* ♦ *vt* (*back etc*) distender, torcerse; (*tire*) cansar; (*stretch*) estirar; (*filter*) filtrar; (*meaning*) tergiversar ♦ *vi*

esforzarse; ~**s** *npl* (*MUS*) son *m*; **she's under a lot of** ~ está bajo mucha tensión.

strained [streɪnd] *adj* (*muscle*) torcido; (*laugh*) forzado; (*relations*) tenso.

strainer ['streɪnə*] *n* colador *m*.

strait [streɪt] *n* (*GEO*) estrecho; **to be in dire** ~**s** (*fig*) estar en un gran aprieto.

straitjacket ['streɪtdʒækɪt] *n* camisa de fuerza.

strait-laced [streɪt'leɪst] *adj* mojigato, gazmoño.

strand [strænd] *n* (*of thread*) hebra; (*of rope*) ramal *m*; **a** ~ **of hair** un pelo.

stranded ['strændɪd] *adj* (*person*) colgado.

strange [streɪndʒ] *adj* (*not known*) desconocido; (*odd*) extraño, raro.

stranger ['streɪndʒə*] *n* desconocido/a; (*from another area*) forastero/a; **I'm a** ~ **here** no soy de aquí.

strangle ['stræŋgl] *vt* estrangular.

stranglehold ['stræŋglhəuld] *n* (*fig*) dominio completo.

strangulation [stræŋgjuˈleɪʃən] *n* estrangulación *f*.

strap [stræp] *n* correa; (*of slip, dress*) tirante *m* ♦ *vt* atar con correa.

straphanging ['stræphæŋɪŋ] *n* viajar *m* de pie *or* parado (*LAM*).

strapless ['stræplɪs] *adj* (*bra, dress*) sin tirantes.

strapped [stræpt] *adj*: **to be** ~ **for cash** (*col*) andar mal de dinero.

strapping ['stræpɪŋ] *adj* robusto, fornido.

Strasbourg ['stræzbɔːg] *n* Estrasburgo.

strata ['strɑːtə] *npl of* **stratum**.

stratagem ['strætɪdʒəm] *n* estratagema.

strategic [strəˈtiːdʒɪk] *adj* estratégico.

strategy ['strætɪdʒɪ] *n* estrategia.

stratum, pl strata ['strɑːtəm, 'strɑːtə] *n* estrato.

straw [strɔː] *n* paja; (*drinking* ~) caña, pajita; **that's the last** ~! ¡eso es el colmo!

strawberry ['strɔːbərɪ] *n* fresa, frutilla (*LAM*).

stray [streɪ] *adj* (*animal*) extraviado; (*bullet*) perdido; (*scattered*) disperso ♦ *vi* extraviarse, perderse; (*wander: walker*) vagar, ir sin rumbo fijo; (: *speaker*) desvariar.

streak [striːk] *n* raya; (*fig: of madness etc*) vena ♦ *vt* rayar ♦ *vi*: **to** ~ **past** pasar como un rayo; **to have** ~**s in one's hair** tener vetas en el pelo; **a winning/losing** ~ una racha de buena/mala suerte.

streaker ['striːkə*] *n* corredor(a) *m/f* desnudo/a.

streaky ['striːkɪ] *adj* rayado.

stream [striːm] *n* riachuelo, arroyo; (*jet*)

chorro; (*flow*) corriente *f*; (*of people*) oleada ♦ *vt* (*SCOL*) dividir en grupos por habilidad ♦ *vi* correr, fluir; **to ~ in/out** (*people*) entrar/salir en tropel; **against the ~** a contracorriente; **on ~** (*new power plant etc*) en funcionamiento.

streamer ['stri:mə*] *n* serpentina.

stream feed *n* (*on photocopier etc*) alimentación *f* continua.

streamline ['stri:mlaɪn] *vt* aerodinamizar; (*fig*) racionalizar.

streamlined ['stri:mlaɪnd] *adj* aerodinámico.

street [stri:t] *n* calle *f* ♦ *adj* callejero; **the back ~s** las callejuelas; **to be on the ~s** (*homeless*) estar sin vivienda; (*as prostitute*) hacer la calle.

streetcar ['stri:tkɑ:] *n* (*US*) tranvía *m*.

street cred [-krɛd] *n* (*col*) *imagen de estar en la onda.*

street lamp *n* farol *m*.

street lighting *n* alumbrado público.

street market *n* mercado callejero.

street plan *n* plano callejero.

streetwise ['stri:twaɪz] *adj* (*col*) pícaro.

strength [strɛŋθ] *n* fuerza; (*of girder, knot etc*) resistencia; (*of chemical solution*) potencia; (*of wine*) graduación *f* de alcohol; **on the ~ of** a base de, en base a; **to be at full/below ~** tener/no tener completo el cupo.

strengthen ['strɛŋθn] *vt* fortalecer, reforzar.

strenuous ['strɛnjuəs] *adj* (*tough*) arduo; (*energetic*) enérgico; (*opposition*) firme, tenaz; (*efforts*) intensivo.

stress [strɛs] *n* (*force, pressure*) presión *f*; (*mental strain*) estrés *m*, tensión *f*; (*accent, emphasis*) énfasis *m*, acento; (*LING, POETRY*) tensión *f*, carga ♦ *vt* subrayar, recalcar; **to be under ~** estar estresado; **to lay great ~ on sth** hacer hincapié en algo.

stressful ['strɛsful] *adj* (*job*) estresante.

stretch [strɛtʃ] *n* (*of sand etc*) trecho; (*of road*) tramo; (*of time*) período, tiempo ♦ *vi* estirarse; (*extend*): **to ~ to** *or* **as far as** extenderse hasta; (*be enough: money, food*): **to ~ to** alcanzar para, dar de sí para ♦ *vt* extender, estirar; (*make demands of*) exigir el máximo esfuerzo a; **to ~ one's legs** estirar las piernas.

► **stretch out** *vi* tenderse ♦ *vt* (*arm etc*) extender; (*spread*) estirar.

stretcher ['strɛtʃə*] *n* camilla.

stretcher-bearer ['strɛtʃəbɛərə*] *n* camillero/a.

stretch marks *npl* estrías *fpl*.

strewn [stru:n] *adj*: **~ with** cubierto *or* sembrado de.

stricken ['strɪkən] *adj* (*person*) herido; (*city, industry etc*) condenado; **~ with** (*arthritis, disease*) afligido por; **grief-~** destrozado por el dolor.

strict [strɪkt] *adj* (*order, rule etc*) estricto; (*discipline, ban*) severo; **in ~ confidence** en la más absoluta confianza.

strictly ['strɪktlɪ] *adv* estrictamente; (*totally*) terminantemente; **~ confidential** estrictamente confidencial; **~ speaking** en (el) sentido estricto (de la palabra); **~ between ourselves** ... entre nosotros ....

stridden ['strɪdn] *pp of* **stride**.

stride [straɪd] *n* zancada, tranco ♦ *vi* (*pt* **strode**, *pp* **stridden** [strəud, 'strɪdn]) dar zancadas, andar a trancos; **to take in one's ~** (*fig: changes etc*) tomar con calma.

strident ['straɪdnt] *adj* estridente; (*colour*) chillón/ona.

strife [straɪf] *n* lucha.

strike [straɪk] *n* huelga; (*of oil etc*) descubrimiento; (*attack*) ataque *m*; (*SPORT*) golpe *m* ♦ *vb* (*pt, pp* **struck** [strʌk]) *vt* golpear, pegar; (*oil etc*) descubrir; (*obstacle*) topar con; (*produce: coin, medal*) acuñar; (: *agreement, deal*) concertar ♦ *vi* declarar la huelga; (*attack: MIL etc*) atacar; (*clock*) dar la hora; **on ~** (*workers*) en huelga; **to call a ~** declarar una huelga; **to go on** *or* **come out on ~** ponerse *or* declararse en huelga; **to ~ a match** encender una cerilla; **to ~ a balance** (*fig*) encontrar un equilibrio; **to ~ a bargain** cerrar un trato; **the clock struck 9 o'clock** el reloj dio las nueve.

► **strike back** *vi* (*MIL*) contraatacar; (*fig*) devolver el golpe.

► **strike down** *vt* derribar.

► **strike off** *vt* (*from list*) tachar; (*doctor etc*) suspender.

► **strike out** *vt* borrar, tachar.

► **strike up** *vt* (*MUS*) empezar a tocar; (*conversation*) entablar; (*friendship*) trabar.

strikebreaker ['straɪkbreɪkə*] *n* rompehuelgas *m/f inv*.

striker ['straɪkə*] *n* huelguista *m/f*; (*SPORT*) delantero.

striking ['straɪkɪŋ] *adj* (*colour*) llamativo; (*obvious*) notorio.

Strimmer ® ['strɪmə*] *n* cortacéspedes *m inv* (*especial para los bordes*).

string [strɪŋ] *n* (*gen*) cuerda; (*row*) hilera; (*COMPUT*) cadena ♦ *vt* (*pt, pp* **strung** [strʌŋ]): **to ~ together** ensartar; **to ~ out**

extenderse; **the ~s** *npl* (*MUS*) los instrumentos de cuerda; **to pull ~s** (*fig*) mover palancas; **to get a job by pulling ~s** conseguir un trabajo por enchufe; **with no ~s attached** (*fig*) sin compromiso.

string bean *n* judía verde, habichuela.

string(ed) instrument [strɪŋ(d)-] *n* (*MUS*) instrumento de cuerda.

stringent ['strɪndʒənt] *adj* riguroso, severo.

string quartet *n* cuarteto de cuerdas.

strip [strɪp] *n* tira; (*of land*) franja; (*of metal*) cinta, lámina ♦ *vt* desnudar; (*also: ~ down: machine*) desmontar ♦ *vi* desnudarse.

strip cartoon *n* tira cómica, historieta (*LAM*).

stripe [straɪp] *n* raya; (*MIL*) galón *m*; **white with green ~s** blanco con rayas verdes.

striped [straɪpt] *adj* a rayas, rayado.

strip lighting *n* alumbrado fluorescente.

stripper ['strɪpə*] *n* artista *m/f* de striptease.

strip-search ['strɪpsə:tʃ] *vt*: **to ~ sb** desnudar y registrar a algn.

striptease ['strɪptiːz] *n* striptease *m*.

strive, *pt* **strove**, *pp* **striven** [straɪv, strəʊv, 'strɪvn] *vi*: **to ~ to do sth** esforzarse *or* luchar por hacer algo.

strobe [strəʊb] *n* (*also: ~ light*) luz *f* estroboscópica.

strode [strəʊd] *pt of* **stride**.

stroke [strəʊk] *n* (*blow*) golpe *m*; (*MED*) apoplejía; (*caress*) caricia; (*of pen*) trazo; (*SWIMMING: style*) estilo; (*of piston*) carrera ♦ *vt* acariciar; **at a ~** de golpe; **a ~ of luck** un golpe de suerte; **two-~ engine** motor *m* de dos tiempos.

stroll [strəʊl] *n* paseo, vuelta ♦ *vi* dar un paseo *or* una vuelta; **to go for a ~, have** *or* **take a ~** dar un paseo.

stroller ['strəʊlə*] *n* (*US: pushchair*) cochecito.

strong [strɒŋ] *adj* fuerte; (*bleach, acid*) concentrado ♦ *adv*: **to be going ~** (*company*) marchar bien; (*person*) conservarse bien; **they are 50 ~** son 50.

strong-arm ['strɒŋɑːm] *adj* (*tactics, methods*) represivo.

strongbox ['strɒŋbɒks] *n* caja fuerte.

strong drink *n* bebida cargada *or* fuerte.

stronghold ['strɒŋhəʊld] *n* fortaleza; (*fig*) baluarte *m*.

strong language *n* lenguaje *m* fuerte.

strongly ['strɒŋlɪ] *adv* fuertemente, con fuerza; (*believe*) firmemente; **to feel ~ about sth** tener una opinión firme sobre algo.

strongman ['strɒŋmæn] *n* forzudo; (*fig*) hombre *m* robusto.

strongroom ['strɒŋruːm] *n* cámara acorazada.

stroppy ['strɒpɪ] *adj* (*BRIT col*) borde; **to get ~** ponerse borde.

strove [strəʊv] *pt of* **strive**.

struck [strʌk] *pt, pp of* **strike**.

structural ['strʌktʃərəl] *adj* estructural.

structure ['strʌktʃə*] *n* estructura; (*building*) construcción *f*.

struggle ['strʌgl] *n* lucha ♦ *vi* luchar; **to have a ~ to do sth** esforzarse por hacer algo.

strum [strʌm] *vt* (*guitar*) rasguear.

strung [strʌŋ] *pt, pp of* **string**.

strut [strʌt] *n* puntal *m* ♦ *vi* pavonearse.

strychnine ['strɪkniːn] *n* estricnina.

stub [stʌb] *n* (*of ticket etc*) matriz *f*; (*of cigarette*) colilla ♦ *vt*: **to ~ one's toe on sth** dar con el dedo del pie contra algo.

▶**stub out** *vt* (*cigarette*) apagar.

stubble ['stʌbl] *n* rastrojo; (*on chin*) barba (incipiente).

stubborn ['stʌbən] *adj* terco, testarudo.

stucco ['stʌkəʊ] *n* estuco.

stuck [stʌk] *pt, pp of* **stick** ♦ *adj* (*jammed*) atascado.

stuck-up [stʌk'ʌp] *adj* engreído, presumido.

stud [stʌd] *n* (*shirt ~*) corchete *m*; (*of boot*) taco; (*of horses*) caballeriza; (*also: ~ horse*) caballo semental ♦ *vt* (*fig*): **~ded with** salpicado de.

student ['stjuːdənt] *n* estudiante *m/f* ♦ *adj* estudiantil; **a law/medical ~** un(a) estudiante de derecho/medicina.

student driver *n* (*US AUT*) aprendiz(a) *m/f* de conductor.

students' union *n* (*BRIT: association*) sindicato de estudiantes; (*: building*) centro de estudiantes.

studio ['stjuːdɪəʊ] *n* estudio; (*artist's*) taller *m*.

studio flat, (*US*) **studio apartment** *n* estudio.

studious ['stjuːdɪəs] *adj* estudioso; (*studied*) calculado.

studiously ['stjuːdɪəslɪ] *adv* (*carefully*) con esmero.

study ['stʌdɪ] *n* estudio ♦ *vt* estudiar; (*examine*) examinar, investigar ♦ *vi* estudiar; **to make a ~ of sth** realizar una investigación de algo; **to ~ for an exam** preparar un examen.

stuff [stʌf] *n* materia; (*cloth*) tela; (*substance*) material *m*, sustancia; (*things, belongings*) cosas *fpl* ♦ *vt* llenar; (*CULIN*)

rellenar; (*animal: for exhibition*) disecar;
my nose is ~**ed up** tengo la nariz tapada;
~**ed toy** juguete *m* or muñeco de trapo.
stuffing ['stʌfɪŋ] *n* relleno.
stuffy ['stʌfɪ] *adj* (*room*) mal ventilado;
(*person*) de miras estrechas.
stumble ['stʌmbl] *vi* tropezar, dar un
traspié.
▶**stumble across** *vt fus* (*fig*) tropezar con.
stumbling block ['stʌmblɪŋ-] *n* tropiezo,
obstáculo.
stump [stʌmp] *n* (*of tree*) tocón *m*; (*of limb*)
muñón *m* ♦ *vt*: **to be** ~**ed** quedarse
perplejo; **to be** ~**ed for an answer**
quedarse sin saber qué contestar.
stun [stʌn] *vt* aturdir.
stung [stʌŋ] *pt, pp of* **sting**.
stunk [stʌŋk] *pp of* **stink**.
stunning ['stʌnɪŋ] *adj* (*fig*) pasmoso.
stunt [stʌnt] *n* (*AVIAT*) vuelo acrobático;
(*publicity* ~) truco publicitario.
stunted ['stʌntɪd] *adj* enano, achaparrado.
stuntman ['stʌntmæn] *n* especialista *m*.
stupefaction [stjuːpɪ'fækʃən] *n*
estupefacción *f*.
stupefy ['stjuːpɪfaɪ] *vt* dejar estupefacto.
stupendous [stjuː'pɛndəs] *adj* estupendo,
asombroso.
stupid ['stjuːpɪd] *adj* estúpido, tonto.
stupidity [stjuː'pɪdɪtɪ] *n* estupidez *f*.
stupor ['stjuːpə*] *n* estupor *m*.
sturdy ['stɜːdɪ] *adj* robusto, fuerte.
stutter ['stʌtə*] *n* tartamudeo ♦ *vi*
tartamudear.
sty [staɪ] *n* (*for pigs*) pocilga.
stye [staɪ] *n* (*MED*) orzuelo.
style [staɪl] *n* estilo; (*fashion*) moda; (*of
dress etc*) hechura; (*hair* ~) corte *m*; **in the
latest** ~ en el último modelo.
stylish ['staɪlɪʃ] *adj* elegante, a la moda.
stylist ['staɪlɪst] *n* (*hair* ~) peluquero/a
stylus, *pl* **styli** or **styluses** ['staɪləs, -laɪ] *n*
(*of record player*) aguja.
Styrofoam ® ['staɪrəfəum] *n* (*US*)
poliestireno ♦ *adj* (*cup*) de poliestireno.
suave [swaːv] *adj* cortés, fino.
sub [sʌb] *n abbr* = **submarine, subscription**.
sub... [sʌb] *pref* sub....
subcommittee ['sʌbkəmɪtɪ] *n* subcomisión
f.
subconscious [sʌb'kɔnʃəs] *adj*
subconsciente ♦ *n* subconsciente *m*.
subcontinent [sʌb'kɔntɪnənt] *n*: **the Indian**
~ el subcontinente (de la India).
subcontract *n* ['sʌb'kɔntrækt] subcontrato
♦ *vt* ['sʌbkən'trækt] subcontratar.
subcontractor ['sʌbkən'træktə*] *n*
subcontratista *m/f*.

subdivide [sʌbdɪ'vaɪd] *vt* subdividir.
subdue [səb'djuː] *vt* sojuzgar; (*passions*)
dominar.
subdued [səb'djuːd] *adj* (*light*) tenue;
(*person*) sumiso, manso.
sub-editor ['sʌb'ɛdɪtə*] *n* (*BRIT*) redactor(a)
m/f.
subject *n* ['sʌbdʒɪkt] súbdito; (*SCOL*) tema
m, materia ♦ *vt* [səb'dʒɛkt]: **to** ~ **sb to sth**
someter a algn a algo ♦ *adj* ['sʌbdʒɪkt]: **to
be** ~ **to** (*law*) estar sujeto a; ~ **to
confirmation in writing** sujeto a
confirmación por escrito; **to change the**
~ cambiar de tema.
subjective [səb'dʒɛktɪv] *adj* subjetivo.
subject matter *n* materia; (*content*)
contenido.
sub judice [sʌb'djuːdɪsɪ] *adj* (*LAW*)
pendiente de resolución.
subjugate ['sʌbdʒugeɪt] *vt* subyugar,
sojuzgar.
subjunctive [səb'dʒʌŋktɪv] *adj, n*
subjuntivo.
sublet [sʌb'lɛt] *vt, vi* subarrendar,
realquilar.
sublime [sə'blaɪm] *adj* sublime.
subliminal [sʌb'lɪmɪnl] *adj* subliminal.
submachine gun ['sʌbmə'ʃiːn-] *n*
metralleta.
submarine [sʌbmə'riːn] *n* submarino.
submerge [səb'mɜːdʒ] *vt* sumergir; (*flood*)
inundar ♦ *vi* sumergirse.
submersion [səb'mɜːʃən] *n* submersión *f*.
submission [səb'mɪʃən] *n* sumisión *f*; (*to
committee etc*) ponencia.
submissive [səb'mɪsɪv] *adj* sumiso.
submit [səb'mɪt] *vt* someter; (*proposal,
claim*) presentar ♦ *vi* someterse; **I** ~ **that
... me permito sugerir que ...**
subnormal [sʌb'nɔːməl] *adj* subnormal.
subordinate [sə'bɔːdɪnət] *adj, n*
subordinado/a *m/f*.
subpoena [səb'piːnə] (*LAW*) *n* citación *f* ♦ *vt*
citar.
subroutine [sʌbruː'tiːn] *n* (*COMPUT*)
subrutina.
subscribe [səb'skraɪb] *vi* suscribir; **to**
~ **to** (*fund*) suscribir, aprobar; (*opinion*)
estar de acuerdo con; (*newspaper*)
suscribirse a.
subscribed capital [səb'skraɪbd-] *n* capital
m suscrito.
subscriber [səb'skraɪbə*] *n* (*to periodical*)
suscriptor(a) *m/f*; (*to telephone*)
abonado/a.
subscript ['sʌbskrɪpt] *n* (*TYP*) subíndice *m*.
subscription [səb'skrɪpʃən] *n* (*to club*)
abono; (*to magazine*) suscripción *f*; **to take**

out a ~ **to** suscribirse a.
subsequent ['sʌbsɪkwənt] *adj* subsiguiente, posterior; ~ **to** posterior a.
subsequently ['sʌbsɪkwəntlɪ] *adv* posteriormente, más tarde.
subservient [səb'sə:vɪənt] *adj*: ~ **(to)** servil (a).
subside [səb'saɪd] *vi* hundirse; (*flood*) bajar; (*wind*) amainar.
subsidence [səb'saɪdns] *n* hundimiento; (*in road*) socavón *m*.
subsidiarity [səbsɪdɪ'ærɪtɪ] *n* (*POL*) subsidiariedad *f*.
subsidiary [səb'sɪdɪərɪ] *n* sucursal *f*, filial *f* ♦ *adj* (*UNIV: subject*) secundario.
subsidize ['sʌbsɪdaɪz] *vt* subvencionar.
subsidy ['sʌbsɪdɪ] *n* subvención *f*.
subsist [səb'sɪst] *vi*: **to** ~ **on sth** subsistir a base de algo, sustentarse con algo.
subsistence [səb'sɪstəns] *n* subsistencia.
subsistence allowance *n* dietas *fpl*.
subsistence level *n* nivel *m* de subsistencia.
subsistence wage *n* sueldo de subsistencia.
substance ['sʌbstəns] *n* sustancia; (*fig*) esencia; **to lack** ~ (*argument*) ser poco convincente; (*accusation*) no tener fundamento; (*film, book*) tener poca profundidad.
substance abuse *n* uso indebido de sustancias tóxicas.
substandard [sʌb'stændəd] *adj* (*goods*) inferior; (*housing*) deficiente.
substantial [səb'stænʃl] *adj* sustancial, sustancioso; (*fig*) importante.
substantially [səb'stænʃəlɪ] *adv* sustancialmente; ~ **bigger** bastante más grande.
substantiate [səb'stænʃɪeɪt] *vt* comprobar.
substitute ['sʌbstɪtju:t] *n* (*person*) suplente *m/f*; (*thing*) sustituto ♦ *vt*: **to** ~ **A for B** sustituir B por A, reemplazar A por B.
substitution [sʌbstɪ'tju:ʃən] *n* sustitución *f*.
subterfuge ['sʌbtəfju:dʒ] *n* subterfugio.
subterranean [sʌbtə'reɪnɪən] *adj* subterráneo.
subtitle ['sʌbtaɪtl] *n* subtítulo.
subtle ['sʌtl] *adj* sutil.
subtlety ['sʌtltɪ] *n* sutileza.
subtly ['sʌtlɪ] *adv* sutilmente.
subtotal [sʌb'təʊtl] *n* subtotal *m*.
subtract [səb'trækt] *vt* restar; sustraer.
subtraction [səb'trækʃən] *n* resta; sustracción *f*.
suburb ['sʌbə:b] *n* barrio residencial; **the** ~**s** las afueras (de la ciudad).
suburban [sə'bə:bən] *adj* suburbano; (*train*

etc) de cercanías.
suburbia [sə'bə:bɪə] *n* barrios *mpl* residenciales.
subversion [səb'və:ʃən] *n* subversión *f*.
subversive [səb'və:sɪv] *adj* subversivo.
subway ['sʌbweɪ] *n* (*BRIT*) paso subterráneo *or* inferior; (*US*) metro.
sub-zero [sʌb'zɪərəʊ] *adj*: ~ **temperatures** temperaturas *fpl* por debajo del cero.
succeed [sək'si:d] *vi* (*person*) tener éxito; (*plan*) salir bien ♦ *vt* suceder a; **to** ~ **in doing** lograr hacer.
succeeding [sək'si:dɪŋ] *adj* (*following*) sucesivo; ~ **generations** generaciones *fpl* futuras.
success [sək'sɛs] *n* éxito; (*gain*) triunfo.
successful [sək'sɛsful] *adj* (*venture*) de éxito, exitoso (*esp LAM*); **to be** ~ **(in doing)** lograr (hacer).
successfully [sək'sɛsfulɪ] *adv* con éxito.
succession [sək'sɛʃən] *n* (*series*) sucesión *f*, serie *f*; (*descendants*) descendencia; **in** ~ sucesivamente.
successive [sək'sɛsɪv] *adj* sucesivo, consecutivo; **on 3** ~ **days** tres días seguidos.
successor [sək'sɛsə*] *n* sucesor(a) *m/f*.
succinct [sək'sɪŋkt] *adj* sucinto.
succulent ['sʌkjulənt] *adj* suculento ♦ *n* (*BOT*): ~**s** plantas *fpl* carnosas.
succumb [sə'kʌm] *vi* sucumbir.
such [sʌtʃ] *adj* tal, semejante; (*of that kind*): ~ **a book** tal libro; ~ **books** tales libros; (*so much*): ~ **courage** tanto valor ♦ *adv* tan; ~ **a long trip** un viaje tan largo; ~ **a lot of** tanto; ~ **as** (*like*) tal como; **a noise** ~ **as to** un ruido tal que; ~ **books as I have** cuantos libros tengo; **I said no** ~ **thing** no dije tal cosa; **it's** ~ **a long time since we saw each other** hace tanto tiempo que no nos vemos; ~ **a long time ago** hace tantísimo tiempo; **as** ~ *adv* como tal.
such-and-such ['sʌtʃənsʌtʃ] *adj* tal o cual.
suchlike ['sʌtʃlaɪk] *pron* (*col*): **and** ~ y cosas por el estilo.
suck [sʌk] *vt* chupar; (*bottle*) sorber; (*breast*) mamar; (*subj: pump, machine*) aspirar.
sucker ['sʌkə*] *n* (*BOT*) serpollo; (*ZOOL*) ventosa; (*col*) bobo, primo.
sucrose ['su:krəʊz] *n* sacarosa.
suction ['sʌkʃən] *n* succión *f*.
suction pump *n* bomba aspirante *or* de succión.
Sudan [su'dæn] *n* Sudán *m*.
Sudanese [su:də'ni:z] *adj, n* sudanés/esa *m/f*.
sudden ['sʌdn] *adj* (*rapid*) repentino, súbito; (*unexpected*) imprevisto; **all of a** ~ de

repente.

sudden-death [sʌdn'dɛθ] n (also: ~ **play off**) desempate m instantáneo, muerte f súbita.

suddenly ['sʌdnlɪ] adv de repente.

suds [sʌdz] npl espuma sg de jabón.

sue [su:] vt demandar; **to** ~ **(for)** demandar (por); **to** ~ **for divorce** solicitar or pedir el divorcio; **to** ~ **for damages** demandar por daños y perjuicios.

suede [sweɪd] n ante m, gamuza (LAM).

suet ['suɪt] n sebo.

Suez Canal ['su:ɪz-] n Canal m de Suez.

Suff. abbr (BRIT) = Suffolk.

suffer ['sʌfə*] vt sufrir, padecer; (tolerate) aguantar, soportar; (undergo: loss, setback) experimentar ♦ vi sufrir, padecer; **to** ~ **from** sufrir, tener; **to** ~ **from the effects of alcohol/a fall** sufrir los efectos del alcohol/resentirse de una caída.

sufferance ['sʌfərns] n: **he was only there on** ~ estuvo allí sólo porque se lo toleraron.

sufferer ['sʌfərə*] n víctima f; (MED) ~ **from** enfermo/a de.

suffering ['sʌfərɪŋ] n (hardship, deprivation) sufrimiento m; (pain) dolor m.

suffice [sə'faɪs] vi bastar, ser suficiente.

sufficient [sə'fɪʃənt] adj suficiente, bastante.

sufficiently [sə'fɪʃəntlɪ] adv suficientemente, bastante.

suffix ['sʌfɪks] n sufijo.

suffocate ['sʌfəkeɪt] vi ahogarse, asfixiarse.

suffocation [sʌfə'keɪʃən] n sofocación f, asfixia.

suffrage ['sʌfrɪdʒ] n sufragio.

suffuse [sə'fju:z] vt: **to** ~ **(with)** (colour) bañar (de); **her face was** ~d **with joy** su cara estaba llena de alegría.

sugar ['ʃugə*] n azúcar m ♦ vt echar azúcar a, azucarar.

sugar basin n (BRIT) = sugar bowl.

sugar beet n remolacha.

sugar bowl n azucarero.

sugar cane n caña de azúcar.

sugar-coated [ʃugə'kəutɪd] adj azucarado.

sugar lump n terrón m de azúcar.

sugar refinery n refinería de azúcar.

sugary ['ʃugərɪ] adj azucarado.

suggest [sə'dʒɛst] vt sugerir; (recommend) aconsejar; **what do you** ~ **I do?** ¿qué sugieres que haga?; **this** ~s **that ...** esto hace pensar que ....

suggestion [sə'dʒɛstʃən] n sugerencia; **there's no** ~ **of ...** no hay indicación or evidencia de ....

suggestive [sə'dʒɛstɪv] adj sugestivo; (pej: indecent) indecente.

suicidal ['suɪsaɪdl] adj suicida; (fig) suicida, peligroso.

suicide ['suɪsaɪd] n suicidio; (person) suicida m/f; **to commit** ~ suicidarse.

suicide attempt, suicide bid n intento de suicidio.

suit [su:t] n (man's) traje m; (woman's) traje de chaqueta; (LAW) pleito; (CARDS) palo ♦ vt convenir; (clothes) sentar bien a, ir bien a; (adapt): **to** ~ **sth to** adaptar or ajustar algo a; **to be** ~**ed to sth** (suitable for) ser apto para algo; **well** ~**ed** (couple) hechos el uno para el otro; **to bring a** ~ **against sb** entablar demanda contra algn; **to follow** ~ (CARDS) seguir el palo; (fig) seguir el ejemplo (de algn); **that** ~s **me** me va bien.

suitable ['su:təbl] adj conveniente; (apt) indicado.

suitably ['su:təblɪ] adv convenientemente; (appropriately) en forma debida.

suitcase ['su:tkeɪs] n maleta, valija (LAM).

suite [swi:t] n (of rooms, MUS) suite f; (furniture): **bedroom/dining room** ~ (juego de) dormitorio/comedor m; **a three-piece** ~ un tresillo.

suitor ['su:tə*] n pretendiente m.

sulfate ['sʌlfeɪt] n (US) = sulphate.

sulfur ['sʌlfə*] n (US) = sulphur.

sulk [sʌlk] vi estar de mal humor.

sulky ['sʌlkɪ] adj malhumorado.

sullen ['sʌlən] adj hosco, malhumorado.

sulphate, (US) **sulfate** ['sʌlfeɪt] n sulfato; **copper** ~ sulfato de cobre.

sulphur, (US) **sulfur** ['sʌlfə*] n azufre m.

sulphur dioxide n dióxido de azufre.

sultan ['sʌltən] n sultán m.

sultana [sʌl'tɑːnə] n (fruit) pasa de Esmirna.

sultry ['sʌltrɪ] adj (weather) bochornoso; (seductive) seductor(a).

sum [sʌm] n suma; (total) total m.

▶**sum up** vt resumir; (evaluate rapidly) evaluar ♦ vi hacer un resumen.

Sumatra [su'mɑːtrə] n Sumatra.

summarize ['sʌməraɪz] vt resumir.

summary ['sʌmərɪ] n resumen m ♦ adj (justice) sumario.

summer ['sʌmə*] n verano ♦ adj de verano; **in (the)** ~ en (el) verano.

summerhouse ['sʌməhaus] n (in garden) cenador m, glorieta.

summertime ['sʌmətaɪm] n (season) verano.

summer time n (by clock) hora de verano.

summery ['sʌmərɪ] *adj* veraniego.
summing-up [sʌmɪŋ'ʌp] *n* (*LAW*) resumen *m*.
summit ['sʌmɪt] *n* cima, cumbre *f*.
summit (conference) *n* (conferencia) cumbre *f*.
summon ['sʌmən] *vt* (*person*) llamar; (*meeting*) convocar; **to ~ a witness** citar a un testigo.
▶**summon up** *vt* (*courage*) armarse de.
summons ['sʌmənz] *n* llamamiento, llamada ♦ *vt* citar, emplazar; **to serve a ~ on sb** citar a algn ante el juicio.
sumo ['su:məu] *n* (*also:* ~ **wrestling**) sumo.
sump [sʌmp] *n* (*BRIT AUT*) cárter *m*.
sumptuous ['sʌmptjuəs] *adj* suntuoso.
sun [sʌn] *n* sol *m*; **they have everything under the ~** no les falta nada, tienen de todo.
Sun. *abbr* (= *Sunday*) dom.
sunbathe ['sʌnbeɪð] *vi* tomar el sol.
sunbeam ['sʌnbi:m] *n* rayo de sol.
sunbed ['sʌnbed] *n* cama solar.
sunburn ['sʌnbə:n] *n* (*painful*) quemadura del sol; (*tan*) bronceado.
sunburnt ['sʌnbə:nt], **sunburned** ['sʌnbə:nd] *adj* (*tanned*) bronceado; (*painfully*) quemado por el sol.
sundae ['sʌndeɪ] *n* helado con frutas y nueces.
Sunday ['sʌndɪ] *n* domingo.
Sunday paper *n* (periódico) dominical *m*.
Sunday school *n* catequesis *f*.
sundial ['sʌndaɪəl] *n* reloj *m* de sol.
sundown ['sʌndaun] *n* anochecer *m*, puesta de sol.
sundries ['sʌndrɪz] *npl* géneros *mpl* diversos.
sundry ['sʌndrɪ] *adj* varios, diversos; **all and ~** todos sin excepción.
sunflower ['sʌnflauə*] *n* girasol *m*.
sung [sʌŋ] *pp of* **sing**.
sunglasses ['sʌngla:sɪz] *npl* gafas *fpl* de sol.
sunk [sʌŋk] *pp of* **sink**.
sunken ['sʌŋkn] *adj* (*bath*) hundido.
sunlamp ['sʌnlæmp] *n* lámpara solar ultravioleta.
sunlight ['sʌnlaɪt] *n* luz *f* del sol.
sunlit ['sʌnlɪt] *adj* iluminado por el sol.
sunny ['sʌnɪ] *adj* soleado; (*day*) de sol; (*fig*) alegre; **it is ~** hace sol.
sunrise ['sʌnraɪz] *n* salida del sol.
sun roof *n* (*AUT*) techo corredizo *or* solar; (*on building*) azotea, terraza.
sunscreen ['sʌnskri:n] *n* protector *m* solar.
sunset ['sʌnset] *n* puesta del sol.
sunshade ['sʌnʃeɪd] *n* (*over table*) sombrilla.

sunshine ['sʌnʃaɪn] *n* sol *m*.
sunstroke ['sʌnstrəuk] *n* insolación *f*.
suntan ['sʌntæn] *n* bronceado.
suntanned ['sʌntænd] *adj* bronceado.
suntan oil *n* aceite *m* bronceador.
super ['su:pə*] *adj* (*col*) bárbaro.
superannuation [su:pərænju'eɪʃən] *n* jubilación *f*, pensión *f*.
superb [su:'pə:b] *adj* magnífico, espléndido.
Super Bowl *n* (*US SPORT*) super copa de fútbol americano.
supercilious [su:pə'sɪlɪəs] *adj* (*disdainful*) desdeñoso; (*haughty*) altanero.
superconductor [su:pəkən'dʌktə*] *n* superconductor *m*.
superficial [su:pə'fɪʃəl] *adj* superficial.
superfluous [su'pə:fluəs] *adj* superfluo, de sobra.
superglue ['su:pəglu:] *n* cola de contacto, supercola.
superhighway ['su:pəhaɪweɪ] *n* (*US*) superautopista; **the information ~** la superautopista de la información.
superhuman [su:pə'hju:mən] *adj* sobrehumano.
superimpose ['su:pərɪm'pəuz] *vt* sobreponer.
superintend [su:pərɪn'tend] *vt* supervisar.
superintendent [su:pərɪn'tendənt] *n* director(a) *m/f*; (*police ~*) subjefe/a *m/f*.
superior [su'pɪərɪə*] *adj* superior; (*smug: person*) altivo, desdeñoso; (*: smile, air*) de suficiencia; (*: remark*) desdeñoso ♦ *n* superior *m*; **Mother S~** (*REL*) madre *f* superiora.
superiority [supɪərɪ'ɔrɪtɪ] *n* superioridad *f*; desdén *m*.
superlative [su'pə:lətɪv] *adj, n* superlativo.
superman ['su:pəmæn] *n* superhombre *m*.
supermarket ['su:pəma:kɪt] *n* supermercado.
supermodel ['su:pəmɔdl] *n* top model *f*, supermodelo *f*.
supernatural [su:pə'nætʃərəl] *adj* sobrenatural.
supernova [su:pə'nəuvə] *n* supernova.
superpower ['su:pəpauə*] *n* (*POL*) superpotencia.
supersede [su:pə'si:d] *vt* suplantar.
supersonic ['su:pə'sɔnɪk] *adj* supersónico.
superstar ['su:pəsta:*] *n* superestrella ♦ *adj* de superestrella.
superstition [su:pə'stɪʃən] *n* superstición *f*.
superstitious [su:pə'stɪʃəs] *adj* supersticioso.
superstore ['su:pəstɔ:*] *n* (*BRIT*) hipermercado.
supertanker ['su:pətæŋkə*] *n*

superpetrolero.

supertax ['suːpətæks] n sobretasa, sobreimpuesto.

supervise ['suːpəvaɪz] vt supervisar.

supervision [suːpə'vɪʒən] n supervisión f.

supervisor ['suːpəvaɪzə*] n (gen, UNIV) supervisor(a) m/f.

supervisory ['suːpəvaɪzərɪ] adj de supervisión.

supine ['suːpaɪn] adj supino.

supper ['sʌpə*] n cena; **to have** ~ cenar.

supplant [sə'plɑːnt] vt suplantar, reemplazar.

supple ['sʌpl] adj flexible.

supplement n ['sʌplɪmənt] suplemento ♦ vt [sʌplɪ'mɛnt] suplir.

supplementary [sʌplɪ'mɛntərɪ] adj suplementario.

supplementary benefit n (BRIT) subsidio adicional de la seguridad social.

supplier [sə'plaɪə*] n suministrador(a) m/f; (COMM) distribuidor(a) m/f.

supply [sə'plaɪ] vt (provide) suministrar; (information) facilitar; (fill: need, want) suplir, satisfacer; (equip): **to** ~ **(with)** proveer (de) ♦ n provisión f; (of gas, water etc) suministro ♦ adj (BRIT: teacher etc) suplente; **supplies** npl (food) víveres mpl; (MIL) pertrechos mpl; **office supplies** materiales mpl para oficina; **to be in short** ~ escasear, haber escasez de; **the electricity/water/gas** ~ el suministro de electricidad/agua/gas; ~ **and demand** la oferta y la demanda.

support [sə'pɔːt] n (moral, financial etc) apoyo; (TECH) soporte m ♦ vt apoyar; (financially) mantener; (uphold) sostener; (SPORT: team) seguir, ser hincha de; **they stopped work in** ~ **(of)** pararon de trabajar en apoyo (de); **to** ~ **o.s.** (financially) ganarse la vida.

support buying [-'baɪɪŋ] n compra proteccionista.

supporter [sə'pɔːtə*] n (POL etc) partidario/a; (SPORT) aficionado/a; (FOOTBALL) hincha m/f.

supporting [sə'pɔːtɪŋ] adj (wall) de apoyo; ~ **role** papel m secundario; ~ **actor/ actress** actor/actriz m/f secundario/a.

supportive [sə'pɔːtɪv] adj de apoyo; **I have a** ~ **family/wife** mi familia/mujer me apoya.

suppose [sə'pəuz] vt, vi suponer; (imagine) imaginarse; **to be** ~**d to do sth** deber hacer algo; **I don't** ~ **she'll come** no creo que venga; **he's** ~**d to be an expert** se le supone un experto.

supposedly [sə'pəuzɪdlɪ] adv según cabe

suponer.

supposing [sə'pəuzɪŋ] conj en caso de que; **always** ~ **(that) he comes** suponiendo que venga.

supposition [sʌpə'zɪʃən] n suposición f.

suppository [sə'pɔzɪtrɪ] n supositorio.

suppress [sə'prɛs] vt suprimir; (yawn) ahogar.

suppression [sə'prɛʃən] n represión f.

supremacy [su'prɛməsɪ] n supremacía f.

supreme [su'priːm] adj supremo.

Supreme Court n (US) Tribunal m Supremo, Corte f Suprema.

supremo [su'priːməu] n autoridad f máxima.

Supt. abbr (POLICE) = **superintendent**.

surcharge ['səːtʃɑːdʒ] n sobretasa, recargo.

sure [ʃuə*] adj seguro; (definite, convinced) cierto; (aim) certero ♦ adv: **that** ~ **is pretty, that's** ~ **pretty** (US) ¡qué bonito es!; **to be** ~ **of sth** estar seguro de algo; **to be** ~ **of o.s.** estar seguro de sí mismo; **to make** ~ **of sth/that** asegurarse de algo/asegurar que; **I'm not** ~ **how/why/ when** no estoy seguro de cómo/por qué/ cuándo; ~! (of course) ¡claro!, ¡por supuesto!; ~ **enough** efectivamente.

sure-fire ['ʃuəfaɪə*] adj (col) infalible.

sure-footed [ʃuə'futɪd] adj de pie firme.

surely ['ʃuəlɪ] adv (certainly) seguramente; ~ **you don't mean that!** ¡no lo dices en serio!

surety ['ʃuərətɪ] n fianza; (person) fiador(a) m/f; **to go** or **stand** ~ **for sb** ser fiador de algn, salir garante por algn.

surf [səːf] n olas fpl.

surface ['səːfɪs] n superficie f ♦ vt (road) revestir ♦ vi salir a la superficie ♦ cpd (MIL, NAUT) de (la) superficie; **on the** ~ **it seems that ...** (fig) a primera vista parece que ....

surface area n área de la superficie.

surface mail n vía terrestre.

surface-to-air ['səːfɪstə'ɛə*] adj (MIL) tierra-aire.

surface-to-surface ['səːfɪstə'səːfɪs] adj (MIL) tierra-tierra.

surfboard ['səːfbɔːd] n plancha (de surf).

surfeit ['səːfɪt] n: **a** ~ **of** un exceso de.

surfer ['səːfə*] n súrfer m/f.

surfing ['səːfɪŋ] n surf m.

surge [səːdʒ] n oleada, oleaje m; (ELEC) sobretensión f transitoria ♦ vi avanzar a tropel; **to** ~ **forward** avanzar rápidamente.

surgeon ['səːdʒən] n cirujano/a.

surgery ['səːdʒərɪ] n cirugía; (BRIT: room)

consultorio; (: *POL*) *horas en las que los electores pueden reunirse personalmente con su diputado*; **to undergo** ~ operarse; *see also* **constituency**.
surgery hours *npl* (*BRIT*) horas *fpl* de consulta.
surgical ['sɜːdʒɪkl] *adj* quirúrgico.
surgical spirit *n* (*BRIT*) alcohol *m*.
surly ['sɜːlɪ] *adj* hosco, malhumorado.
surmount [sɜː'maunt] *vt* superar, vencer.
surname ['sɜːneɪm] *n* apellido.
surpass [sɜː'pɑːs] *vt* superar, exceder.
surplus ['sɜːpləs] *n* excedente *m*; (*COMM*) superávit *m* ♦ *adj* (*COMM*) excedente, sobrante; **to have a** ~ **of sth** tener un excedente de algo; **it is** ~ **to our requirements** nos sobra; ~ **stock** saldos *mpl*.
surprise [sə'praɪz] *n* sorpresa ♦ *vt* sorprender; **to take by** ~ (*person*) coger a algn desprevenido *or* por sorpresa, sorprender a algn; (*MIL: town, fort*) atacar por sorpresa.
surprising [sə'praɪzɪŋ] *adj* sorprendente.
surprisingly [sə'praɪzɪŋlɪ] *adv* (*easy, helpful*) de modo sorprendente; **(somewhat)** ~, **he agreed** para sorpresa de todos, aceptó.
surrealism [sə'rɪəlɪzəm] *n* surrealismo.
surrealist [sə'rɪəlɪst] *adj*, *n* surrealista *m/f*.
surrender [sə'rɛndə*] *n* rendición *f*, entrega ♦ *vi* rendirse, entregarse ♦ *vt* (*claim, right*) renunciar.
surrender value *n* valor *m* de rescate.
surreptitious [sʌrəp'tɪʃəs] *adj* subrepticio.
surrogate ['sʌrəgɪt] *n* (*BRIT: substitute*) sustituto/a ♦ *adj*: ~ **coffee** sucedáneo de café.
surrogate mother *n* madre *f* de alquiler.
surround [sə'raund] *vt* rodear, circundar; (*MIL etc*) cercar.
surrounding [sə'raundɪŋ] *adj* circundante.
surroundings [sə'raundɪŋz] *npl* alrededores *mpl*, cercanías *fpl*.
surtax ['sɜːtæks] *n* sobretasa, sobreimpuesto.
surveillance [sɜː'veɪləns] *n* vigilancia.
survey *n* ['sɜːveɪ] inspección *f*, reconocimiento; (*inquiry*) encuesta; (*comprehensive view: of situation etc*) vista de conjunto ♦ *vt* [sɜː'veɪ] examinar, inspeccionar; (*SURVEYING: building*) inspeccionar; (: *land*) hacer un reconocimiento de, reconocer; (*look at*) mirar, contemplar; (*make inquiries about*) hacer una encuesta de; **to carry out a** ~ **of** inspeccionar, examinar.
surveyor [sɜː'veɪə*] *n* (*BRIT*) (*of building*) perito *m/f*; (*of land*) agrimensor(a) *m/f*.

survival [sə'vaɪvl] *n* supervivencia.
survival course *n* curso de supervivencia.
survival kit *n* equipo de emergencia.
survive [sə'vaɪv] *vi* sobrevivir; (*custom etc*) perdurar ♦ *vt* sobrevivir a.
survivor [sə'vaɪvə*] *n* superviviente *m/f*.
susceptibility [səseptə'bɪlɪtɪ] *n* (*to illness*) propensión *f*.
susceptible [sə'sɛptəbl] *adj* (*easily influenced*) influenciable; (*to disease, illness*): ~ **to** propenso a.
suspect *adj*, *n* ['sʌspɛkt] sospechoso/a *m/f* ♦ *vt* [səs'pɛkt] sospechar.
suspected [səs'pɛktɪd] *adj* presunto; **to have a** ~ **fracture** tener una posible fractura.
suspend [səs'pɛnd] *vt* suspender.
suspended animation [səs'pɛndəd-] *n*: **in a state of** ~ en (estado de) hibernación.
suspended sentence *n* (*LAW*) libertad *f* condicional.
suspender belt [səs'pɛndə*-] *n* (*BRIT*) liguero, portaligas *m inv* (*AM*).
suspenders [səs'pɛndəz] *npl* (*BRIT*) ligas *fpl*; (*US*) tirantes *mpl*.
suspense [səs'pɛns] *n* incertidumbre *f*, duda; (*in film etc*) suspense *m*.
suspension [səs'pɛnʃən] *n* (*gen, AUT*) suspensión *f*; (*of driving licence*) privación *f*.
suspension bridge *n* puente *m* colgante.
suspension file *n* archivador *m* colgante.
suspicion [səs'pɪʃən] *n* sospecha; (*distrust*) recelo; (*trace*) traza; **to be under** ~ estar bajo sospecha; **arrested on** ~ **of murder** detenido bajo sospecha de asesinato.
suspicious [səs'pɪʃəs] *adj* (*suspecting*) receloso; (*causing suspicion*) sospechoso; **to be** ~ **of** *or* **about sb/sth** tener sospechas de algn/algo.
suss out [sʌs-] *vt* (*BRIT col*) calar.
sustain [səs'teɪn] *vt* sostener, apoyar; (*suffer*) sufrir, padecer.
sustainable [səs'teɪnəbl] *adj* sostenible.
sustained [səs'teɪnd] *adj* (*effort*) sostenido.
sustenance ['sʌstɪnəns] *n* sustento.
suture ['suːtʃə*] *n* sutura.
SW *abbr* = **short wave**.
swab [swɔb] *n* (*MED*) algodón *m*, frotis *m inv* ♦ *vt* (*NAUT: also*: ~ **down**) limpiar, fregar.
swagger ['swægə*] *vi* pavonearse.
swallow ['swɔləu] *n* (*bird*) golondrina; (*of food*) bocado; (*of drink*) trago ♦ *vt* tragar.
►**swallow up** *vt* (*savings etc*) consumir.
swam [swæm] *pt of* **swim**.
swamp [swɔmp] *n* pantano, ciénaga ♦ *vt* abrumar, agobiar.
swampy ['swɔmpɪ] *adj* pantanoso.

swan [swɔn] *n* cisne *m*.

swank [swæŋk] (*col*) *n* (*vanity, boastfulness*) fanfarronada ♦ *vi* fanfarronear, presumir.

swan song *n* (*fig*) canto del cisne.

swap [swɔp] *n* canje *m*, trueque *m* ♦ *vt*: **to ~ (for)** canjear (por).

SWAPO ['swɑːpəu] *n abbr* (= *South-West Africa People's Organization*) SWAPO *f*.

swarm [swɔːm] *n* (*of bees*) enjambre *m*; (*fig*) multitud *f* ♦ *vi* (*fig*) hormiguear, pulular.

swarthy ['swɔːðɪ] *adj* moreno.

swashbuckling ['swɔʃbʌklɪŋ] *adj* (*person*) aventurero; (*film*) de capa y espada.

swastika ['swɔstɪkə] *n* esvástica, cruz *f* gamada.

swat [swɔt] *vt* aplastar ♦ *n* (*also:* **fly ~**) matamoscas *m inv*.

SWAT [swɔt] *n abbr* (*US*: = *Special Weapons and Tactics*) *unidad especial de la policía*.

swathe [sweɪð] *vt*: **to ~ in** (*blankets*) envolver en; (*bandages*) vendar en.

sway [sweɪ] *vi* mecerse, balancearse ♦ *vt* (*influence*) mover, influir en ♦ *n* (*rule, power*): **~ (over)** dominio (sobre); **to hold ~ over sb** dominar a algn, mantener el dominio sobre algn.

Swaziland ['swɑːzɪlænd] *n* Swazilandia.

swear, *pt* **swore,** *pp* **sworn** [swɛə*, swɔː*, swɔːn] *vi* jurar; (*with swearwords*) decir tacos ♦ *vt*: **to ~ an oath** prestar juramento, jurar; **to ~ to sth** declarar algo bajo juramento.

▶**swear in** *vt* tomar juramento (a).

swearword ['swɛəwɔːd] *n* taco, palabrota.

sweat [swɛt] *n* sudor *m* ♦ *vi* sudar.

sweatband ['swɛtbænd] *n* (*SPORT: on head*) banda; (: *on wrist*) muñequera.

sweater ['swɛtə*] *n* suéter *m*.

sweatshirt ['swɛtʃəːt] *n* sudadera.

sweatshop ['swɛtʃɔp] *n* fábrica donde se explota al obrero.

sweaty ['swɛtɪ] *adj* sudoroso.

Swede [swiːd] *n* sueco/a.

swede [swiːd] *n* (*BRIT*) nabo.

Sweden ['swiːdn] *n* Suecia.

Swedish ['swiːdɪʃ] *adj*, *n* (*LING*) sueco.

sweep [swiːp] *n* (*act*) barrida; (*of arm*) manotazo *m*; (*curve*) curva, alcance *m*; (*also:* **chimney ~**) deshollinador(a) *m/f* ♦ *vb* (*pt, pp* **swept** [swɛpt]) *vt* barrer; (*disease, fashion*) recorrer ♦ *vi* barrer.

▶**sweep away** *vt* barrer; (*rub out*) borrar.

▶**sweep past** *vi* pasar rápidamente; (*brush by*) rozar.

▶**sweep up** *vi* barrer.

sweeper ['swiːpə*] *n* (*person*) barrendero/ a; (*machine*) barredora; (*FOOTBALL*) líbero, libre *m*.

sweeping ['swiːpɪŋ] *adj* (*gesture*) dramático; (*generalized*) generalizado; (*changes, reforms*) radical.

sweepstake ['swiːpsteɪk] *n* lotería.

sweet [swiːt] *n* (*candy*) dulce *m*, caramelo; (*BRIT*: *pudding*) postre *m* ♦ *adj* dulce; (*sugary*) azucarado; (*charming*: *person*) encantador(a); (: *smile, character*) dulce, amable, agradable ♦ *adv*: **to smell/taste ~** oler/saber dulce.

sweet and sour *adj* agridulce.

sweetcorn ['swiːtkɔːn] *n* maíz *m* (dulce).

sweeten ['swiːtn] *vt* (*person*) endulzar; (*add sugar to*) poner azúcar a.

sweetener ['swiːtnə*] *n* (*CULIN*) edulcorante *m*.

sweetheart ['swiːthɑːt] *n* amor *m*, novio/a; (*in speech*) amor, cariño.

sweetness ['swiːtnɪs] *n* (*gen*) dulzura.

sweet pea *n* guisante *m* de olor.

sweet potato *n* batata, camote *m* (*LAM*).

sweetshop ['swiːtʃɔp] *n* (*BRIT*) confitería, bombonería.

swell [swɛl] *n* (*of sea*) marejada, oleaje *m* ♦ *adj* (*US*: *col*: excellent) estupendo, fenomenal ♦ *vb* (*pt* **~ed**, *pp* **swollen** *or* **~ed** ['swəulən]) *vt* hinchar, inflar ♦ *vi* hincharse, inflarse.

swelling ['swɛlɪŋ] *n* (*MED*) hinchazón *f*.

sweltering ['swɛltərɪŋ] *adj* sofocante, de mucho calor.

swept [swɛpt] *pt, pp of* **sweep**.

swerve [swəːv] *n* regate *m*; (*in car*) desvío brusco ♦ *vi* desviarse bruscamente.

swift [swɪft] *n* (*bird*) vencejo ♦ *adj* rápido, veloz.

swiftly ['swɪftlɪ] *adv* rápidamente.

swiftness ['swɪftnɪs] *n* rapidez *f*, velocidad *f*.

swig [swɪg] *n* (*col*: drink) trago.

swill [swɪl] *n* bazofia ♦ *vt* (*also:* **~ out, ~ down**) lavar, limpiar con agua.

swim [swɪm] *n*: **to go for a ~** ir a nadar *or* a bañarse ♦ *vb* (*pt* **swam**, *pp* **swum** [swæm, swʌm]) *vi* nadar; (*head, room*) dar vueltas ♦ *vt* pasar a nado; **to go ~ming** ir a nadar; **to ~ a length** nadar *or* hacer un largo.

swimmer ['swɪmə*] *n* nadador(a) *m/f*.

swimming ['swɪmɪŋ] *n* natación *f*.

swimming cap *n* gorro de baño.

swimming costume *n* bañador *m*, traje *m* de baño.

swimmingly ['swɪmɪŋlɪ] *adv*: **to go ~** (*wonderfully*) ir como una seda *or* sobre ruedas.

swimming pool *n* piscina, alberca (*LAM*).

swimming trunks *npl* bañador *msg.*
swimsuit ['swɪmsuːt] *n* = **swimming costume**.
swindle ['swɪndl] *n* estafa ♦ *vt* estafar.
swine [swaɪn] *n, pl inv* cerdo, puerco; (*col!*) canalla *m* (*!*).
swing [swɪŋ] *n* (*in playground*) columpio; (*movement*) balanceo, vaivén *m*; (*change of direction*) viraje *m*; (*rhythm*) ritmo; (*POL: in votes etc*): **there has been a ~ towards/away from Labour** ha habido un viraje en favor/en contra del Partido Laborista ♦ *vb* (*pt, pp* **swung** [swʌŋ]) *vt* balancear; (*on a ~*) columpiar; (*also:* **~ round**) voltear, girar ♦ *vi* balancearse, columpiarse; (*also:* **~ round**) dar media vuelta; **a ~ to the left** un movimiento hacia la izquierda; **to be in full ~** estar en plena marcha; **to get into the ~ of things** meterse en situación; **the road ~s south** la carretera gira hacia el sur.
swing bridge *n* puente *m* giratorio.
swing door, (*US*) **swinging door** ['swɪŋɪŋ-] *n* puerta giratoria.
swingeing ['swɪndʒɪŋ] *adj* (*BRIT*) abrumador(a).
swipe [swaɪp] *n* golpe *m* fuerte ♦ *vt* (*hit*) golpear fuerte; (*col: steal*) guindar; (*credit card etc*) pasar.
swirl [swəːl] *vi* arremolinarse.
swish [swɪʃ] *n* (*sound: of whip*) chasquido; (: *of skirts*) frufrú *m*; (: *of grass*) crujido ♦ *adj* (*col: smart*) elegante ♦ *vi* chasquear.
Swiss [swɪs] *adj, n* (*pl inv*) suizo/a *m/f.*
switch [swɪtʃ] *n* (*for light, radio etc*) interruptor *m*; (*change*) cambio ♦ *vt* (*change*) cambiar de; (*invert: also:* **~ round, ~ over**) intercambiar.
▶**switch off** *vt* apagar; (*engine*) parar.
▶**switch on** *vt* (*AUT: ignition*) encender, prender (*LAM*); (*engine, machine*) arrancar; (*water supply*) conectar.
switchboard ['swɪtʃbɔːd] *n* (*TEL*) centralita (de teléfonos), conmutador *m* (*LAM*).
Switzerland ['swɪtsələnd] *n* Suiza.
swivel ['swɪvl] *vi* (*also:* **~ round**) girar.
swollen ['swəʊlən] *pp of* **swell**.
swoon [swuːn] *vi* desmayarse.
swoop [swuːp] *n* (*by police etc*) redada; (*of bird etc*) descenso en picado, calada ♦ *vi* (*also:* **~ down**) caer en picado.
swop [swɔp] = **swap**.
sword [sɔːd] *n* espada.
swordfish ['sɔːdfɪʃ] *n* pez *m* espada.
swore [swɔː*] *pt of* **swear**.
sworn [swɔːn] *pp of* **swear**.
swot [swɔt] (*BRIT*) *vt, vi* empollar ♦ *n* empollón/ona *m/f.*

swum [swʌm] *pp of* **swim**.
swung [swʌŋ] *pt, pp of* **swing**.
sycamore ['sɪkəmɔː*] *n* sicomoro.
sycophant ['sɪkəfænt] *n* adulador(a) *m/f*, pelotillero/a.
Sydney ['sɪdnɪ] *n* Sidney *m.*
syllable ['sɪləbl] *n* sílaba.
syllabus ['sɪləbəs] *n* programa *m* de estudios; **on the ~** en el programa de estudios.
symbol ['sɪmbl] *n* símbolo.
symbolic(al) [sɪm'bɔlɪk(l)] *adj* simbólico; **to be ~ of sth** simbolizar algo.
symbolism ['sɪmbəlɪzəm] *n* simbolismo.
symbolize ['sɪmbəlaɪz] *vt* simbolizar.
symmetrical [sɪ'mɛtrɪkl] *adj* simétrico.
symmetry ['sɪmɪtrɪ] *n* simetría.
sympathetic [sɪmpə'θɛtɪk] *adj* compasivo; (*understanding*) comprensivo; **to be ~ to a cause** (*well-disposed*) apoyar una causa; **to be ~ towards** (*person*) ser comprensivo con.
sympathize ['sɪmpəθaɪz] *vi*: **to ~ with sb** compadecerse de algn; (*understand*) comprender a algn.
sympathizer ['sɪmpəθaɪzə*] *n* (*POL*) simpatizante *m/f.*
sympathy ['sɪmpəθɪ] *n* (*pity*) compasión *f*; (*understanding*) comprensión *f*; **a letter of ~** un pésame; **with our deepest ~** nuestro más sentido pésame.
symphony ['sɪmfənɪ] *n* sinfonía.
symposium [sɪm'pəʊzɪəm] *n* simposio.
symptom ['sɪmptəm] *n* síntoma *m*, indicio.
symptomatic [sɪmptə'mætɪk] *adj*: **~ (of)** sintomático (de).
synagogue ['sɪnəgɔg] *n* sinagoga.
sync [sɪŋk] *n* (*col*): **to be in/out of ~ (with)** ir/no ir al mismo ritmo (que); (*fig: people*) conectar/no conectar con.
synchromesh ['sɪŋkrəʊmɛʃ] *n* cambio sincronizado de velocidades.
synchronize ['sɪŋkrənaɪz] *vt* sincronizar ♦ *vi*: **to ~ with** sincronizarse con.
synchronized swimming ['sɪŋkrənaɪzd-] *n* natación *f* sincronizada.
syncopated ['sɪŋkəpeɪtɪd] *adj* sincopado.
syndicate ['sɪndɪkɪt] *n* (*gen*) sindicato; (*PRESS*) agencia (de noticias).
syndrome ['sɪndrəʊm] *n* síndrome *m.*
synonym ['sɪnənɪm] *n* sinónimo.
synonymous [sɪ'nɒnɪməs] *adj*: **~ (with)** sinónimo (con).
synopsis, *pl* **synopses** [sɪ'nɒpsɪs, -siːz] *n* sinopsis *f inv.*
syntax ['sɪntæks] *n* sintaxis *f.*
syntax error *n* (*COMPUT*) error *m* sintáctico.

synthesis, *pl* **syntheses** ['sɪnθəsɪs, -siːz] *n* síntesis *f inv.*
synthesizer ['sɪnθəsaɪzə*] *n* sintetizador *m.*
synthetic [sɪn'θεtɪk] *adj* sintético ♦ *n* sintético.
syphilis ['sɪfɪlɪs] *n* sífilis *f.*
syphon ['saɪfən] = **siphon.**
Syria ['sɪrɪə] *n* Siria.
Syrian ['sɪrɪən] *adj, n* sirio/a *m/f.*
syringe [sɪ'rɪndʒ] *n* jeringa.
syrup ['sɪrəp] *n* jarabe *m*, almíbar *m.*
system ['sɪstəm] *n* sistema *m*; (*ANAT*) organismo; **it was quite a shock to his ~** fue un golpe para él.
systematic [sɪstə'mætɪk] *adj* sistemático; metódico.
system disk *n* (*COMPUT*) disco del sistema.
systems analyst *n* analista *m/f* de sistemas.

T t

T, t [tiː] *n* (*letter*) T, t *f;* **T for Tommy** T de Tarragona.
TA *n abbr* (*BRIT*) = *Territorial Army.*
ta [tɑː] *excl* (*BRIT col*) ¡gracias!
tab [tæb] *n abbr* = **tabulator** ♦ *n* lengüeta; (*label*) etiqueta; **to keep ~s on** (*fig*) vigilar.
tabby ['tæbɪ] *n* (*also:* ~ **cat**) gato atigrado.
tabernacle ['tæbənækl] *n* tabernáculo.
table ['teɪbl] *n* mesa; (*chart: of statistics etc*) cuadro, tabla ♦ *vt* (*BRIT: motion etc*) presentar; **to lay** *or* **set the ~** poner la mesa; **to clear the ~** quitar *or* levantar la mesa; **league ~** (*FOOTBALL, RUGBY*) clasificación *f* del campeonato; **~ of contents** índice *m* de materias.
tablecloth ['teɪblklɔθ] *n* mantel *m.*
table d'hôte [tɑːbl'dəut] *n* menú *m.*
table lamp *n* lámpara de mesa.
tablemat ['teɪblmæt] *n* salvamanteles *m inv*, posaplatos *m inv.*
tablespoon ['teɪblspuːn] *n* cuchara grande; (*also:* ~**ful:** *as measurement*) cucharada.
tablet ['tæblɪt] *n* (*MED*) pastilla, comprimido; (*for writing*) bloc *m*; (*of stone*) lápida; ~ **of soap** pastilla de jabón.
table talk *n* conversación *f* de sobremesa.
table tennis *n* ping-pong *m*, tenis *m* de mesa.
table wine *n* vino de mesa.
tabloid ['tæblɔɪd] *n* (*newspaper*) periódico popular sensacionalista.

> *El término genérico* **tabloid press** *o* **tabloids** *se usa para referirse a los periódicos populares británicos, por su tamaño reducido. A diferencia de la llamada* **quality press**, *estos periódicos se caracterizan por su lenguaje sencillo, presentación llamativa y contenido a menudo sensacionalista, con gran énfasis en noticias sobre escándalos financieros y sexuales de los famosos, por lo que también reciben el nombre peyorativo de* **gutter press**.

taboo [tə'buː] *adj, n* tabú *m.*
tabulate ['tæbjuleɪt] *vt* disponer en tablas.
tabulator ['tæbjuleɪtə*] *n* tabulador *m.*
tachograph ['tækəgrɑːf] *n* tacógrafo.
tachometer [tæ'kɔmɪtə*] *n* taquímetro.
tacit ['tæsɪt] *adj* tácito.
tacitly ['tæsɪtlɪ] *adv* tácitamente.
taciturn ['tæsɪtəːn] *adj* taciturno.
tack [tæk] *n* (*nail*) tachuela; (*stitch*) hilván *m*; (*NAUT*) bordada ♦ *vt* (*nail*) clavar con tachuelas; (*stitch*) hilvanar ♦ *vi* virar; **to ~ sth on to (the end of) sth** (*of letter, book*) añadir algo a(l final de) algo.
tackle ['tækl] *n* (*gear*) equipo; (*fishing ~, for lifting*) aparejo; (*FOOTBALL*) entrada, tackle *m*; (*RUGBY*) placaje *m* ♦ *vt* (*difficulty*) enfrentarse a, abordar; (*grapple with*) agarrar; (*FOOTBALL*) entrar a; (*RUGBY*) placar.
tacky ['tækɪ] *adj* pegajoso; (*fam*) hortera *inv.*
tact [tækt] *n* tacto, discreción *f.*
tactful ['tæktful] *adj* discreto, diplomático; **to be ~** tener tacto, actuar discretamente.
tactfully ['tæktfulɪ] *adv* diplomáticamente, con tacto.
tactical ['tæktɪkl] *adj* táctico.
tactical voting *n* voto útil.
tactician [tæk'tɪʃən] *n* táctico/a.
tactics ['tæktɪks] *n, npl* táctica *sg.*
tactless ['tæktlɪs] *adj* indiscreto.
tactlessly ['tæktlɪslɪ] *adv* indiscretamente, sin tacto.
tadpole ['tædpəul] *n* renacuajo.
taffy ['tæfɪ] *n* (*US*) melcocha.
tag [tæg] *n* (*label*) etiqueta; **price/name ~** etiqueta del precio/con el nombre.
►**tag along** *vi:* **to ~ along with sb** engancharse a algn.
tag question *n* pregunta coletilla.
Tahiti [tɑː'hiːtɪ] *n* Tahití *m.*
tail [teɪl] *n* cola; (*ZOOL*) rabo; (*of shirt, coat*)

faldón *m* ♦ *vt* (*follow*) vigilar a; **heads or** ~**s** cara o cruz; **to turn** ~ volver la espalda.

►**tail away, tail off** *vi* (*in size, quality etc*) ir disminuyendo.

tailback ['teɪlbæk] *n* (*BRIT AUT*) cola.

tail coat *n* frac *m*.

tail end *n* cola, parte *f* final.

tailgate ['teɪlgeɪt] *n* (*AUT*) puerta trasera.

tail light *n* (*AUT*) luz *f* trasera.

tailor ['teɪlə*] *n* sastre *m* ♦ *vt*: **to** ~ **sth (to)** confeccionar algo a medida (para); ~**'s (shop)** sastrería.

tailoring ['teɪlərɪŋ] *n* (*cut*) corte *m*; (*craft*) sastrería.

tailor-made ['teɪlə'meɪd] *adj* (*also fig*) hecho a (la) medida.

tailwind ['teɪlwɪnd] *n* viento de cola.

taint [teɪnt] *vt* (*meat, food*) contaminar; (*fig: reputation*) manchar, tachar (*LAM*).

tainted ['teɪntɪd] *adj* (*water, air*) contaminado; (*fig*) manchado.

Taiwan [taɪ'wɑːn] *n* Taiwán *m*.

Tajikistan [tɑːdʒɪkɪ'stɑːn] *n* Tayikistán *m*.

take [teɪk] *vb* (*pt* **took**, *pp* **taken** [tuk, 'teɪkn]) *vt* tomar; (*grab*) coger (*SP*), agarrar (*LAM*); (*gain: prize*) ganar; (*require: effort, courage*) exigir; (*support weight of*) aguantar; (*hold: passengers etc*) tener cabida para; (*accompany, bring, carry*) llevar; (*exam*) presentarse a; (*conduct: meeting*) presidir ♦ *vi* (*fire*) prender; (*dye*) coger (*SP*), agarrar, tomar ♦ *n* (*CINE*) toma; **to** ~ **sth from** (*drawer etc*) sacar algo de; (*person*) coger (*SP*) algo a; **to** ~ **sb's hand** tomar de la mano a algn; **to** ~ **notes** tomar apuntes; **to be** ~**n ill** ponerse enfermo; ~ **the first on the left** toma la primera a la izquierda; **I only took Russian for one year** sólo estudié ruso un año; **I took him for a doctor** le tenía por médico; **it won't** ~ **long** durará poco; **it will** ~ **at least 5 litres** tiene cabida por lo menos para 5 litros; **to be** ~**n with sb/sth** (*attracted*) tomarle cariño a algn/tomarle gusto a algo; **I** ~ **it that** ... supongo que ....

►**take after** *vt fus* parecerse a.

►**take apart** *vt* desmontar.

►**take away** *vt* (*remove*) quitar; (*carry off*) llevar ♦ *vi*: **to** ~ **away from** quitar mérito a.

►**take back** *vt* (*return*) devolver; (*one's words*) retractar.

►**take down** *vt* (*building*) derribar; (*dismantle: scaffolding*) desmantelar; (*message etc*) apuntar, tomar nota de.

►**take in** *vt* (*BRIT: deceive*) engañar; (*understand*) entender; (*include*) abarcar;

(*lodger*) acoger, recibir; (*orphan, stray dog*) recoger; (*SEWING*) achicar.

►**take off** *vi* (*AVIAT*) despegar, decolar (*LAM*) ♦ *vt* (*remove*) quitar; (*imitate*) imitar, remedar.

►**take on** *vt* (*work*) emprender; (*employee*) contratar; (*opponent*) desafiar.

►**take out** *vt* sacar; (*remove*) quitar; **don't** ~ **it out on me!** ¡no te desquites conmigo!

►**take over** *vt* (*business*) tomar posesión de ♦ *vi*: **to** ~ **over from sb** reemplazar a algn.

►**take to** *vt fus* (*person*) coger cariño a (*SP*), encariñarse con (*LAM*); (*activity*) aficionarse a; **to** ~ **to doing sth** aficionarse a (hacer) algo.

►**take up** *vt* (*a dress*) acortar; (*occupy: time, space*) ocupar; (*engage in: hobby etc*) dedicarse a; (*absorb: liquids*) absorber; (*accept: offer, challenge*) aceptar ♦ *vi*: **to** ~ **up with sb** hacerse amigo de algn.

►**take upon** *vt*: **to** ~ **it upon o.s. to do sth** encargarse de hacer algo.

takeaway ['teɪkəweɪ] *adj* (*BRIT: food*) para llevar.

take-home pay ['teɪkhəum-] *n* salario neto.

taken ['teɪkən] *pp of* **take**.

takeoff ['teɪkɔf] *n* (*AVIAT*) despegue *m*, decolaje *m* (*LAM*).

takeover ['teɪkəuvə*] *n* (*COMM*) absorción *f*.

takeover bid *n* oferta pública de adquisición.

takings ['teɪkɪŋz] *npl* (*COMM*) ingresos *mpl*.

talc [tælk] *n* (*also*: ~**um powder**) talco.

tale [teɪl] *n* (*story*) cuento; (*account*) relación *f*; **to tell** ~**s** (*fig*) contar chismes.

talent ['tælnt] *n* talento.

talented ['tæləntɪd] *adj* talentoso, de talento.

talisman ['tælɪzmən] *n* talismán *m*.

talk [tɔːk] *n* charla; (*gossip*) habladurías *fpl*, chismes *mpl*; (*conversation*) conversación *f* ♦ *vi* (*speak*) hablar; (*chatter*) charlar; ~**s** *npl* (*POL etc*) conversaciones *fpl*; **to give a** ~ dar una charla *or* conferencia; **to** ~ **about** hablar de; **to** ~ **sb into doing sth** convencer a algn para que haga algo; **to** ~ **sb out of doing sth** disuadir a algn de que haga algo; ~**ing of films, have you seen** ...? hablando de películas, ¿has visto ...?

►**talk over** *vt* discutir.

talkative ['tɔːkətɪv] *adj* hablador(a).

talker ['tɔːkə*] *n* hablador(a) *m/f*.

talking point ['tɔːkɪŋ-] *n* tema *m* de conversación.

talking-to ['tɔːkɪŋtuː] *n*: **to give sb a good** ~ echar una buena bronca a algn.

talk show n programa m magazine.
tall [tɔːl] adj alto; (tree) grande; **to be 6 feet**
  ~ ≈ medir 1 metro 80, tener 1 metro 80
  de alto; **how ~ are you?** ¿cuánto mides?
tallboy ['tɔːlbɔɪ] n (BRIT) cómoda alta.
tallness ['tɔːlnɪs] n altura.
tall story n cuento chino.
tally ['tælɪ] n cuenta ♦ vi: **to ~ (with)**
  concordar (con), cuadrar (con); **to keep a**
  ~ **of sth** llevar la cuenta de algo.
talon ['tælən] n garra.
tambourine [tæmbə'riːn] n pandereta.
tame [teɪm] adj (mild) manso; (tamed)
  domesticado; (fig: story, style, person)
  soso, anodino.
tameness ['teɪmnɪs] n mansedumbre f.
Tamil ['tæmɪl] adj tamil ♦ n tamil m/f; (LING)
  tamil m.
tamper ['tæmpə*] vi: **to ~ with** (lock etc)
  intentar forzar; (papers) falsificar.
tampon ['tæmpən] n tampón m.
tan [tæn] n (also: **sun~**) bronceado ♦ vt
  broncear ♦ vi ponerse moreno ♦ adj
  (colour) marrón; **to get a ~** broncearse,
  ponerse moreno.
tandem ['tændəm] n tándem m.
tandoori [tæn'duərɪ] adj, n tandoori m (asado
  a la manera hindú, en horno de barro).
tang [tæŋ] n sabor m fuerte.
tangent ['tændʒənt] n (MATH) tangente f; **to**
  go off at a ~ (fig) salirse por la tangente.
tangerine [tændʒə'riːn] n mandarina.
tangible ['tændʒəbl] adj tangible; ~ **assets**
  bienes mpl tangibles.
Tangier [tæn'dʒɪə*] n Tánger m.
tangle ['tæŋgl] n enredo; **to get in(to) a** ~
  enredarse.
tango ['tæŋgəu] n tango.
tank [tæŋk] n (water ~) depósito, tanque m;
  (for fish) acuario; (MIL) tanque m.
tankard ['tæŋkəd] n bock m.
tanker ['tæŋkə*] n (ship) petrolero; (truck)
  camión m cisterna.
tankful ['tæŋkful] n: **to get a ~ of petrol**
  llenar el depósito de gasolina.
tanned [tænd] adj (skin) moreno,
  bronceado.
tannin ['tænɪn] n tanino.
tanning ['tænɪŋ] n (of leather) curtido.
tannoy ® ['tænɔɪ] n: **over the ~** por el
  altavoz.
tantalizing ['tæntəlaɪzɪŋ] adj tentador(a).
tantamount ['tæntəmaunt] adj: ~ **to**
  equivalente a.
tantrum ['tæntrəm] n rabieta; **to throw a** ~
  coger una rabieta.
Tanzania [tænzə'nɪə] n Tanzania.
Tanzanian [tænzə'nɪən] adj, n tanzano/a m/f.

tap [tæp] n (BRIT: on sink etc) grifo, canilla
  (LAM); (gentle blow) golpecito; (gas ~)
  llave f ♦ vt (table etc) tamborilear;
  (shoulder etc) dar palmaditas en;
  (resources) utilizar, explotar; (telephone
  conversation) intervenir, pinchar; **on** ~
  (fig: resources) a mano; **beer on** ~ cerveza
  de barril.
tap-dancing ['tæpdɑːnsɪŋ] n claqué m.
tape [teɪp] n cinta; (also: **magnetic** ~) cinta
  magnética; (sticky ~) cinta adhesiva ♦ vt
  (record) grabar (en cinta); **on** ~ (song etc)
  grabado (en cinta).
tape deck n pletina.
tape measure n cinta métrica, metro.
taper ['teɪpə*] n cirio ♦ vi afilarse.
tape-record ['teɪprɪkɔːd] vt grabar (en
  cinta).
tape recorder n grabadora.
tape recording n grabación f.
tapered ['teɪpəd], **tapering** ['teɪpərɪŋ] adj
  terminado en punta.
tapestry ['tæpɪstrɪ] n (object) tapiz m; (art)
  tapicería.
tape-worm ['teɪpwəːm] n solitaria, tenia.
tapioca [tæpɪ'əukə] n tapioca.
tappet ['tæpɪt] n excéntrica.
tar [tɑː*] n alquitrán m, brea; **low/middle** ~
  cigarettes cigarrillos con contenido
  bajo/medio de alquitrán.
tarantula [tə'ræntjulə] n tarántula.
tardy ['tɑːdɪ] adj (late) tardío; (slow) lento.
tare [tɛə*] n (COMM) tara.
target ['tɑːgɪt] n (gen) blanco; **to be on** ~
  (project) seguir el curso previsto.
target audience n público al que va
  destinado un programa etc.
target market n (COMM) mercado al que
  va destinado un producto etc.
target practice n tiro al blanco.
tariff ['tærɪf] n tarifa.
tariff barrier n (COMM) barrera
  arancelaria.
tarmac ['tɑːmæk] n (BRIT: on road)
  alquitranado; (AVIAT) pista (de
  aterrizaje).
tarn [tɑːn] n lago pequeño de montaña.
tarnish ['tɑːnɪʃ] vt deslustrar.
tarot ['tærəu] n tarot m.
tarpaulin [tɑː'pɔːlɪn] n alquitranado.
tarragon ['tærəgən] n estragón m.
tarry ['tærɪ] vi entretenerse, quedarse
  atrás.
tart [tɑːt] n (CULIN) tarta; (BRIT col: pej:
  woman) fulana ♦ adj (flavour) agrio, ácido.
▶**tart up** vt (room, building) dar tono a.
tartan ['tɑːtn] n tartán m ♦ adj de tartán.
tartar ['tɑːtə*] n (on teeth) sarro.

tartar sauce *n* salsa tártara.
tartly ['tɑːtlɪ] *adv* (*answer*) ásperamente.
task [tɑːsk] *n* tarea; **to take to** ~ reprender.
task force *n* (*MIL, POLICE*) grupo de operaciones.
taskmaster ['tɑːskmɑːstə*] *n*: **he's a hard** ~ es muy exigente.
Tasmania [tæz'meɪnɪə] *n* Tasmania.
tassel ['tæsl] *n* borla.
taste [teɪst] *n* sabor *m*, gusto; (*also*: **after~**) dejo; (*sip*) sorbo; (*fig*: *glimpse, idea*) muestra, idea ♦ *vt* probar ♦ *vi*: **to** ~ **of** *or* **like** (*fish etc*) saber a; **you can** ~ **the garlic (in it)** se nota el sabor a ajo; **can I have a** ~ **of this wine?** ¿puedo probar este vino?; **to have a** ~ **for sth** ser aficionado a algo; **in good/bad** ~ de buen/mal gusto; **to be in bad** *or* **poor** ~ ser de mal gusto.
taste bud *n* papila gustativa *or* del gusto.
tasteful ['teɪstful] *adj* de buen gusto.
tastefully ['teɪstfulɪ] *adv* elegantemente, con buen gusto.
tasteless ['teɪstlɪs] *adj* (*food*) soso; (*remark*) de mal gusto.
tastelessly ['teɪstlɪslɪ] *adv* con mal gusto.
tastily ['teɪstɪlɪ] *adv* sabrosamente.
tastiness ['teɪstɪnɪs] *n* (buen) sabor *m*, lo sabroso.
tasty ['teɪstɪ] *adj* sabroso, rico.
ta-ta ['tæ'tɑː] *interj* (*BRIT col*) hasta luego, adiós.
tatters ['tætəz] *npl*: **in** ~ (*also*: **tattered**) hecho jirones.
tattoo [tə'tuː] *n* tatuaje *m*; (*spectacle*) espectáculo militar ♦ *vt* tatuar.
tatty ['tætɪ] *adj* (*BRIT col*) cochambroso.
taught [tɔːt] *pt, pp* of **teach**.
taunt [tɔːnt] *n* pulla ♦ *vt* lanzar pullas a.
Taurus ['tɔːrəs] *n* Tauro.
taut [tɔːt] *adj* tirante, tenso.
tavern ['tævən] *n* (*old*) posada, fonda.
tawdry ['tɔːdrɪ] *adj* de mal gusto.
tawny ['tɔːnɪ] *adj* leonado.
tax [tæks] *n* impuesto ♦ *vt* gravar (con un impuesto); (*fig*: *test*) poner a prueba; (: *patience*) agotar; **before/after** ~ impuestos excluidos/incluidos; **free of** ~ libre de impuestos.
taxable ['tæksəbl] *adj* (*income*) imponible, sujeto a impuestos.
tax allowance *n* desgravación *f* fiscal.
taxation [tæk'seɪʃən] *n* impuestos *mpl*; **system of** ~ sistema *m* tributario.
tax avoidance *n* evasión *f* de impuestos.
tax collector *n* recaudador(a) *m/f*.
tax disc *n* (*BRIT AUT*) pegatina del impuesto de circulación.
tax evasion *n* evasión *f* fiscal.

tax exemption *n* exención *f* de impuestos.
tax-free ['tæksfriː] *adj* libre de impuestos.
tax haven *n* paraíso fiscal.
taxi ['tæksɪ] *n* taxi *m* ♦ *vi* (*AVIAT*) rodar por la pista.
taxidermist ['tæksɪdəːmɪst] *n* taxidermista *m/f*.
taxi driver *n* taxista *m/f*.
tax inspector *n* inspector(a) *m/f* de Hacienda.
taxi rank (*BRIT*), **taxi stand** *n* parada de taxis.
tax payer *n* contribuyente *m/f*.
tax rebate *n* devolución *f* de impuestos, reembolso fiscal.
tax relief *n* desgravación *f* fiscal.
tax return *n* declaración *f* de la renta.
tax shelter *n* protección *f* fiscal.
tax year *n* año fiscal.
TB *n abbr* = **tuberculosis**.
TD *n abbr* (*US*) = **Treasury Department**; (: *FOOTBALL*) = **touchdown**.
tea [tiː] *n* té *m*; (*BRIT*: *snack*) ≈ merienda; **high** ~ (*BRIT*) ≈ merienda-cena.
tea bag *n* bolsita de té.
tea break *n* (*BRIT*) descanso para el té.
teacake ['tiːkeɪk] *n* bollito, queque *m* (*LAM*).
teach, *pt, pp* **taught** [tiːtʃ, tɔːt] *vt*: **to** ~ **sb sth**, ~ **sth to sb** enseñar algo a algn ♦ *vi* enseñar; (*be a teacher*) ser profesor(a); **it taught him a lesson** (eso) le sirvió de escarmiento.
teacher ['tiːtʃə*] *n* (*in secondary school*) profesor(a) *m/f*; (*in primary school*) maestro/a; **Spanish** ~ profesor(a) *m/f* de español.
teacher training college *n* (*for primary schools*) escuela normal; (*for secondary schools*) centro de formación del profesorado.
teach-in ['tiːtʃɪn] *n* seminario.
teaching ['tiːtʃɪŋ] *n* enseñanza.
teaching aids *npl* materiales *mpl* pedagógicos.
teaching hospital *n* hospital universitario.
tea cosy *n* cubretetera *m*.
teacup ['tiːkʌp] *n* taza de té.
teak [tiːk] *n* (madera de) teca.
tea leaves *npl* hojas *fpl* de té.
team [tiːm] *n* equipo; (*of animals*) pareja.
▶**team up** *vi* asociarse.
team spirit *n* espíritu *m* de equipo.
teamwork ['tiːmwəːk] *n* trabajo en equipo.
tea party *n* té *m*.
teapot ['tiːpɔt] *n* tetera.
tear [tɛə*] *n* rasgón *m*, desgarrón *m*; [tɪə*] lágrima ♦ *vb* [tɛə*] (*pt* **tore**, *pp* **torn** [tɔː*,

tɔːn]) *vt* romper, rasgar ♦ *vi* rasgarse; **in ~s** llorando; **to burst into ~s** deshacerse en lágrimas; **to ~ to pieces** *or* **to bits** *or* **to shreds** (*also fig*) hacer pedazos, destrozar.

▶**tear along** *vi* (*rush*) precipitarse.

▶**tear apart** *vt* (*also fig*) hacer pedazos.

▶**tear away** *vt*: **to ~ o.s. away (from sth)** alejarse (de algo).

▶**tear out** *vt* (*sheet of paper, cheque*) arrancar.

▶**tear up** *vt* (*sheet of paper etc*) romper.

tearaway ['tɛərəweɪ] *n* (*col*) gamberro/a.

teardrop ['tɪədrɔp] *n* lágrima.

tearful ['tɪəful] *adj* lloroso.

tear gas *n* gas *m* lacrimógeno.

tearing ['tɛərɪŋ] *adj*: **to be in a ~ hurry** tener muchísima prisa.

tearoom ['tiːruːm] *n* salón *m* de té.

tease [tiːz] *n* bromista *m/f* ♦ *vt* tomar el pelo a.

tea set *n* servicio de té.

teashop ['tiːʃɔp] *n* café *m*, cafetería.

Teasmaid ® ['tiːzmeɪd] *n* tetera automática.

teaspoon ['tiːspuːn] *n* cucharita; (*also*: **~ful**: *as measurement*) cucharadita.

tea strainer *n* colador *m* de té.

teat [tiːt] *n* (*of bottle*) boquilla, tetilla.

teatime ['tiːtaɪm] *n* hora del té.

tea towel *n* (*BRIT*) paño de cocina.

tea urn *n* tetera grande.

tech [tɛk] *n abbr* (*col*) = **technology; technical college.**

technical ['tɛknɪkl] *adj* técnico.

technical college *n* centro de formación profesional.

technicality [tɛknɪ'kælɪtɪ] *n* detalle *m* técnico; **on a legal ~** por una cuestión formal.

technically ['tɛknɪklɪ] *adv* técnicamente.

technician [tɛk'nɪʃn] *n* técnico/a.

technique [tɛk'niːk] *n* técnica.

techno ['tɛknəʊ] *n* (*MUS*) (música) tecno.

technocrat ['tɛknəkræt] *n* tecnócrata *m/f*.

technological [tɛknə'lɔdʒɪkl] *adj* tecnológico.

technologist [tɛk'nɔlədʒɪst] *n* tecnólogo/a.

technology [tɛk'nɔlədʒɪ] *n* tecnología.

teddy (bear) ['tɛdɪ-] *n* osito de peluche.

tedious ['tiːdɪəs] *adj* pesado, aburrido.

tedium ['tiːdɪəm] *n* tedio.

tee [tiː] *n* (*GOLF*) tee *m*.

teem [tiːm] *vi*: **to ~ with** rebosar de; **it is ~ing (with rain)** llueve a mares.

teenage ['tiːneɪdʒ] *adj* (*fashions etc*) juvenil.

teenager ['tiːneɪdʒə*] *n* adolescente *m/f*, quinceañero/a.

teens [tiːnz] *npl*: **to be in one's ~** ser adolescente.

tee-shirt ['tiːʃəːt] *n* = **T-shirt.**

teeter ['tiːtə*] *vi* balancearse.

teeth [tiːθ] *npl of* **tooth.**

teethe [tiːð] *vi* echar los dientes.

teething ring ['tiːðɪŋ-] *n* mordedor *m*.

teething troubles ['tiːðɪŋ-] *npl* (*fig*) dificultades *fpl* iniciales.

teetotal ['tiː'təʊtl] *adj* (*person*) abstemio.

teetotaller, (*US*) **teetotaler** ['tiː'təʊtlə*] *n* (*person*) abstemio/a.

TEFL ['tɛfl] *n abbr* = *Teaching of English as a Foreign Language*; **~ qualification** *título para la enseñanza del inglés como lengua extranjera*.

Teflon ® ['tɛflɔn] *n* teflón *m* ®.

Teheran [tɛə'rɑːn] *n* Teherán *m*.

tel. *abbr* (= *telephone*) tel.

Tel Aviv ['tɛlə'viːv] *n* Tel Aviv *m*.

telecast ['tɛlɪkɑːst] *vt, vi* transmitir por televisión.

telecommunications ['tɛlɪkəmjuːnɪ'keɪʃənz] *n* telecomunicaciones *fpl*.

telefax ['tɛlɪfæks] *n* telefax *m*.

telegram ['tɛlɪgræm] *n* telegrama *m*.

telegraph ['tɛlɪgrɑːf] *n* telégrafo.

telegraphic [tɛlɪ'græfɪk] *adj* telegráfico.

telegraph pole *n* poste *m* telegráfico.

telegraph wire *n* hilo telegráfico.

telepathic [tɛlɪ'pæθɪk] *adj* telepático.

telepathy [tə'lɛpəθɪ] *n* telepatía.

telephone ['tɛlɪfəʊn] *n* teléfono ♦ *vt* llamar por teléfono, telefonear; **to be on the ~** (*subscriber*) tener teléfono; (*be speaking*) estar hablando por teléfono.

telephone booth, (*BRIT*) **telephone box** *n* cabina telefónica.

telephone call *n* llamada telefónica.

telephone directory *n* guía telefónica.

telephone exchange *n* central *f* telefónica.

telephone number *n* número de teléfono.

telephonist [tə'lɛfənɪst] *n* (*BRIT*) telefonista *m/f*.

telephoto ['tɛlɪ'fəʊtəʊ] *adj*: **~ lens** teleobjetivo.

teleprinter ['tɛlɪprɪntə*] *n* teletipo, teleimpresora.

teleprompter ® ['tɛlɪprɔmptə*] *n* teleapuntador *m*.

telesales ['tɛlɪseɪlz] *npl* televentas *fpl*.

telescope ['tɛlɪskəʊp] *n* telescopio.

telescopic [tɛlɪ'skɔpɪk] *adj* telescópico; (*umbrella*) plegable.

Teletext ® ['tɛlɪtɛkst] *n* telexexto *m*.

telethon ['tɛlɪθɔn] *n* telemaratón *m*,

maratón *m* televisivo (*con fines benéficos*).
televise ['tɛlɪvaɪz] *vt* televisar.
television ['tɛlɪvɪʒən] *n* televisión *f*; **to watch** ~ mirar *or* ver la televisión.
television licence *n* impuesto por uso de televisor.
television set *n* televisor *m*.
telex ['tɛlɛks] *n* télex *m* ♦ *vt* (*message*) enviar por télex; (*person*) enviar un télex a ♦ *vi* enviar un télex.
tell *pt, pp* **told** [tɛl, təuld] *vt* decir; (*relate: story*) contar; (*distinguish*): **to** ~ **sth from** distinguir algo de ♦ *vi* (*talk*): **to** ~ (**of**) contar; (*have effect*) tener efecto; **to** ~ **sb to do sth** decir a algn que haga algo; **to** ~ **sb about sth** contar algo a algn; **to** ~ **the time** dar *or* decir la hora; **can you** ~ **me the time?** ¿me puedes decir la hora?; (**I**) ~ **you what ...** fíjate ...; **I couldn't** ~ **them apart** no podía distinguirlos.
▶**tell off** *vt*: **to** ~ **sb off** regañar a algn.
▶**tell on** *vt fus*: **to** ~ **on sb** chivarse de algn.
teller ['tɛlə*] *n* (*in bank*) cajero/a.
telling ['tɛlɪŋ] *adj* (*remark, detail*) revelador(a).
telltale ['tɛlteɪl] *adj* (*sign*) indicador(a).
telly ['tɛlɪ] *n* (*BRIT col*) tele *f*.
temerity [tə'mɛrɪtɪ] *n* temeridad *f*.
temp [tɛmp] *n abbr* (*BRIT: = temporary office worker*) empleado/a eventual ♦ *vi* trabajar como empleado/a eventual.
temper ['tɛmpə*] *n* (*mood*) humor *m*; (*bad* ~) (mal) genio; (*fit of anger*) ira; (*of child*) rabieta ♦ *vt* (*moderate*) moderar; **to be in a** ~ estar furioso; **to lose one's** ~ enfadarse, enojarse (*LAM*); **to keep one's** ~ contenerse, no alterarse.
temperament ['tɛmprəmənt] *n* (*nature*) temperamento.
temperamental [tɛmprə'mɛntl] *adj* temperamental.
temperance ['tɛmpərns] *n* moderación *f*; (*in drinking*) sobriedad *f*.
temperate ['tɛmprət] *adj* moderado; (*climate*) templado.
temperature ['tɛmprətʃə*] *n* temperatura; **to have** *or* **run a** ~ tener fiebre.
tempered ['tɛmpəd] *adj* (*steel*) templado.
tempest ['tɛmpɪst] *n* tempestad *f*.
tempestuous [tɛm'pɛstjuəs] *adj* (*relationship, meeting*) tempestuoso.
tempi ['tɛmpiː] *npl of* **tempo**.
template ['tɛmplɪt] *n* plantilla.
temple ['tɛmpl] *n* (*building*) templo; (*ANAT*) sien *f*.
templet ['tɛmplɪt] *n* = **template**.
tempo, *pl* ~**s** *or* **tempi** ['tɛmpəu, 'tɛmpiː] *n* tempo; (*fig: of life etc*) ritmo.

temporal ['tɛmpərl] *adj* temporal.
temporarily ['tɛmpərərɪlɪ] *adv* temporalmente.
temporary ['tɛmpərərɪ] *adj* provisional, temporal; (*passing*) transitorio; (*worker*) eventual; ~ **teacher** maestro/a interino/a.
tempt [tɛmpt] *vt* tentar; **to** ~ **sb into doing sth** tentar *or* inducir a algn a hacer algo; **to be** ~**ed to do sth** (*person*) sentirse tentado de hacer algo.
temptation [tɛmp'teɪʃən] *n* tentación *f*.
tempting ['tɛmptɪŋ] *adj* tentador(a).
ten [tɛn] *num* diez; ~**s of thousands** decenas *fpl* de miles.
tenable ['tɛnəbl] *adj* sostenible.
tenacious [tə'neɪʃəs] *adj* tenaz.
tenaciously [tə'neɪʃəslɪ] *adv* tenazmente.
tenacity [tə'næsɪtɪ] *n* tenacidad *f*.
tenancy ['tɛnənsɪ] *n* alquiler *m*.
tenant ['tɛnənt] *n* (*rent-payer*) inquilino/a; (*occupant*) habitante *m/f*.
tend [tɛnd] *vt* (*sick etc*) cuidar, atender; (*cattle, machine*) vigilar, cuidar ♦ *vi*: **to** ~ **to do sth** tener tendencia a hacer algo.
tendency ['tɛndənsɪ] *n* tendencia.
tender ['tɛndə*] *adj* tierno, blando; (*delicate*) delicado; (*sore*) sensible; (*affectionate*) tierno, cariñoso ♦ *n* (*COMM: offer*) oferta; (*money*): **legal** ~ moneda de curso legal ♦ *vt* ofrecer; **to put in a** ~ (**for**) hacer una oferta (para); **to put work out to** ~ ofrecer un trabajo a contrata; **to** ~ **one's resignation** presentar la dimisión.
tenderize ['tɛndəraɪz] *vt* (*CULIN*) ablandar.
tenderly ['tɛndəlɪ] *adv* tiernamente.
tenderness ['tɛndənɪs] *n* ternura; (*of meat*) blandura.
tendon ['tɛndən] *n* tendón *m*.
tendril ['tɛndrɪl] *n* zarcillo.
tenement ['tɛnəmənt] *n* casa *or* bloque *m* de pisos *or* vecinos (*LAM*).
Tenerife [tɛnə'riːf] *n* Tenerife *m*.
tenet ['tɛnət] *n* principio.
Tenn. *abbr* (*US*) = **Tennessee**.
tenner ['tɛnə*] *n* (billete *m* de) diez libras *fpl*.
tennis ['tɛnɪs] *n* tenis *m*.
tennis ball *n* pelota de tenis.
tennis club *n* club *m* de tenis.
tennis court *n* cancha de tenis.
tennis elbow *n* (*MED*) sinovitis *f* del codo.
tennis match *n* partido de tenis.
tennis player *n* tenista *m/f*.
tennis racket *n* raqueta de tenis.
tennis shoes *npl* zapatillas *fpl* de tenis.
tenor ['tɛnə*] *n* (*MUS*) tenor *m*.
tenpin bowling *n* bolos *mpl*.
tense [tɛns] *adj* tenso; (*stretched*) tirante;

(*stiff*) rígido, tieso; (*person*) nervioso ♦ *n*
(*LING*) tiempo ♦ *vt* (*tighten: muscles*)
tensar.
tensely ['tɛnslɪ] *adv*: **they waited ~**
esperaban tensos.
tenseness ['tɛnsnɪs] *n* tirantez *f*, tensión *f*.
tension ['tɛnʃən] *n* tensión *f*.
tent [tɛnt] *n* tienda (de campaña), carpa
(*LAM*).
tentacle ['tɛntəkl] *n* tentáculo.
tentative ['tɛntətɪv] *adj* (*person*) indeciso;
(*provisional*) provisional.
tentatively ['tɛntətɪvlɪ] *adv* con indecisión;
(*provisionally*) provisionalmente.
tenterhooks ['tɛntəhuks] *npl*: **on ~** sobre
ascuas.
tenth [tɛnθ] *adj* décimo.
tent peg *n* clavija, estaca.
tent pole *n* mástil *m*.
tenuous ['tɛnjuəs] *adj* tenue.
tenure ['tɛnjuə*] *n* posesión *f*, tenencia; **to
have ~** tener posesión *or* título de
propiedad.
tepid ['tɛpɪd] *adj* tibio.
term [təːm] *n* (*limit*) límite *m*; (*COMM*) plazo;
(*word*) término; (*period*) período; (*SCOL*)
trimestre *m* ♦ *vt* llamar, calificar de; **~s**
npl (*conditions*) condiciones *fpl*; (*COMM*)
precio, tarifa; **in the short/long ~** a
corto/largo plazo; **during his ~ of office**
bajo su mandato; **to be on good ~s with
sb** llevarse bien con algn; **to come to ~s
with** (*problem*) aceptar; **in ~s of ...** en
cuanto a ..., en términos de ...
terminal ['təːmɪnl] *adj* terminal ♦ *n* (*ELEC*)
borne *m*; (*COMPUT*) terminal *m*; (*also:* **air
~**) terminal *f*; (*BRIT: also:* **coach ~**)
(estación *f*) terminal *f*.
terminate ['təːmɪneɪt] *vt* poner término a;
(*pregnancy*) interrumpir ♦ *vi*: **to ~ in**
acabar en.
termination [təːmɪ'neɪʃən] *n* fin *m*; (*of
contract*) terminación *f*; **~ of pregnancy**
interrupción *f* del embarazo.
termini ['təːmɪnaɪ] *npl of* **terminus**.
terminology [təːmɪ'nɔlədʒɪ] *n*
terminología.
terminus, *pl* **termini** ['təːmɪnəs, 'təːmɪnaɪ] *n*
término, (estación *f*) terminal *f*.
termite ['təːmaɪt] *n* termita, comején *m*.
term paper *n* (*US UNIV*) trabajo escrito
trimestral *or* semestral.
Ter(r). *abbr* = **terrace.**
terrace ['tɛrəs] *n* terraza; (*BRIT: row of
houses*) hilera de casas adosadas; **the ~s**
(*BRIT SPORT*) las gradas *fpl*.
terraced ['tɛrəst] *adj* (*garden*) escalonado;
(*house*) adosado.

terracotta ['tɛrə'kɔtə] *n* terracota.
terrain [tɛ'reɪn] *n* terreno.
terrible ['tɛrɪbl] *adj* terrible, horrible; (*fam*)
malísimo.
terribly ['tɛrɪblɪ] *adv* terriblemente; (*very
badly*) malísimamente.
terrier ['tɛrɪə*] *n* terrier *m*.
terrific [tə'rɪfɪk] *adj* fantástico, fenomenal,
macanudo (*LAM*); (*wonderful*) maravilloso.
terrify ['tɛrɪfaɪ] *vt* aterrorizar; **to be
terrified** estar aterrado *or* aterrorizado.
terrifying ['tɛrɪfaɪɪŋ] *adj* aterrador(a).
territorial [tɛrɪ'tɔːrɪəl] *adj* territorial.
territorial waters *npl* aguas *fpl*
jurisdiccionales.
territory ['tɛrɪtərɪ] *n* territorio.
terror ['tɛrə*] *n* terror *m*.
terrorism ['tɛrərɪzəm] *n* terrorismo.
terrorist ['tɛrərɪst] *n* terrorista *m/f*.
terrorize ['tɛrəraɪz] *vt* aterrorizar.
terse [təːs] *adj* (*style*) conciso; (*reply*)
brusco.
tertiary ['təːʃərɪ] *adj* terciario; **~ education**
enseñanza superior.
Terylene ® ['tɛrəliːn] *n* (*BRIT*) terylene *m* ®.
TESL [tɛsl] *n abbr* = *Teaching of English as a
Second Language.*
TESSA ['tɛsə] *n abbr* (*BRIT*: = *Tax Exempt
Special Savings Account*) plan de ahorro
por el que se invierte a largo plazo a
cambio de intereses libres de impuestos.
test [tɛst] *n* (*trial, check*) prueba, ensayo; (:
of goods in factory) control *m*; (*of courage
etc, CHEM, MED*) prueba; (*of blood, urine*)
análisis *m inv*; (*exam*) examen *m*, test *m*;
(*also:* **driving ~**) examen *m* de conducir
♦ *vt* probar, poner a prueba; (*MED*)
examinar; (: *blood*) analizar; **to put sth to
the ~** someter algo a prueba; **to ~ sth for
sth** analizar algo en busca de algo.
testament ['tɛstəmənt] *n* testamento; **the
Old/New T~** el Antiguo/Nuevo
Testamento.
test ban *n* (*also:* **nuclear ~**) suspensión *f* de
pruebas nucleares.
test card *n* (*TV*) carta de ajuste.
test case *n* (*JUR*) juicio que sienta
precedente.
testes ['tɛstiːz] *npl* testes *mpl*.
test flight *n* vuelo de ensayo.
testicle ['tɛstɪkl] *n* testículo.
testify ['tɛstɪfaɪ] *vi* (*LAW*) prestar
declaración; **to ~ to sth** atestiguar algo.
testimonial [tɛstɪ'məunɪəl] *n* (*of character*)
(carta de) recomendación *f*.
testimony ['tɛstɪmənɪ] *n* (*LAW*) testimonio,
declaración *f*.
testing ['tɛstɪŋ] *adj* (*difficult: time*) duro.

test match n (CRICKET, RUGBY) partido internacional.
testosterone [tɛsˈtɔstərəun] n testosterona.
test paper n examen m, test m.
test pilot n piloto m/f de pruebas.
test tube n probeta.
test-tube baby n bebé m probeta inv.
testy [ˈtɛstɪ] adj irritable.
tetanus [ˈtɛtənəs] n tétano.
tetchy [ˈtɛtʃɪ] adj irritable.
tether [ˈtɛðə*] vt atar (con una cuerda) ♦ n: **to be at the end of one's ~** no aguantar más.
Tex. abbr (US) = Texas.
text [tɛkst] n texto.
textbook [ˈtɛkstbuk] n libro de texto.
textiles [ˈtɛkstaɪlz] npl tejidos mpl.
textual [ˈtɛkstjuəl] adj del texto, textual.
texture [ˈtɛkstʃə*] n textura.
TGWU n abbr (BRIT: = Transport and General Workers' Union) sindicato de transportistas.
Thai [taɪ] adj, n tailandés/esa m/f.
Thailand [ˈtaɪlænd] n Tailandia.
thalidomide ® [θəˈlɪdəmaɪd] n talidomida ®.
Thames [tɛmz] n: **the ~** el (río) Támesis.
than [ðæn, ðən] conj que; (with numerals): **more ~ 10/once** más de 10/una vez; **I have more/less ~ you** tengo más/menos que tú; **it is better to phone ~ to write** es mejor llamar por teléfono que escribir; **no sooner did he leave ~ the phone rang** en cuanto se marchó, sonó el teléfono.
thank [θæŋk] vt dar las gracias a, agradecer; **~ you (very much)** muchas gracias; **~ heavens, ~ God!** ¡gracias a Dios!, ¡menos mal!
thankful [ˈθæŋkful] adj: **~ for** agradecido (por).
thankfully [ˈθæŋkfəlɪ] adv (gratefully) con agradecimiento; (with relief) por suerte; **~ there were few victims** afortunadamente hubo pocas víctimas.
thankless [ˈθæŋklɪs] adj ingrato.
thanks [θæŋks] npl gracias fpl ♦ excl ¡gracias!; **~ to** prep gracias a.
Thanksgiving (Day) [ˈθæŋksgɪvɪŋ-] n día m de Acción de Gracias.

En Estados Unidos el cuarto jueves de noviembre es **Thanksgiving Day**, fiesta oficial en la que se conmemora la celebración que tuvieron los primeros colonos norteamericanos (**Pilgrims** o **Pilgrim Fathers**) tras la estupenda cosecha de 1621, por la que se dan gracias a Dios. En Canadá se celebra una fiesta semejante el segundo lunes de octubre, aunque no está relacionada con dicha fecha histórica.

══════════════════════════ KEYWORD

that [ðæt](pl those) adj (demonstrative) ese/a, pl esos/as; (more remote) aquel/aquella, pl aquellos/as; **leave those books on the table** deja esos libros sobre la mesa; **~ one** ése/ésa; (more remote) aquél/aquélla, **~ one over there** ése/ésa de ahí; aquél/aquélla de allí
♦ pron 1 (demonstrative) ése/a, pl ésos/as; (neuter) eso; (more remote) aquél/aquélla, pl aquéllos/as; (neuter) aquello; **what's ~?** ¿qué es eso (or aquello)?; **who's ~?** ¿quién es?; (when pointing etc) ¿quién es ése/a?; **is ~ you?** ¿eres tú?; **will you eat all ~?** ¿vas a comer todo eso?; **~'s my house** ésa es mi casa; **~'s what he said** eso es lo que dijo; **~ is (to say)** es decir; **at or with ~ she ...** en eso, ella ...; **do it like ~** hazlo así
2 (relative: subject, object) que; (with preposition) (el/la) que, el/la cual; **the book (~) I read** el libro que leí; **the books ~ are in the library** los libros que están en la biblioteca; **all (~) I have** todo lo que tengo; **the box (~) I put it in** la caja en la que or donde lo puse; **the people (~) I spoke to** la gente con la que hablé; **not ~ I know of** que yo sepa, no
3 (relative: of time) que; **the day (~) he came** el día (en) que vino
♦ conj que; **he thought ~ I was ill** creyó que yo estaba enfermo
♦ adv (demonstrative): **I can't work ~ much** no puedo trabajar tanto; **I didn't realise it was ~ bad** no creí que fuera tan malo; **~ high** así de alto.

══════════════════════════

thatched [θætʃt] adj (roof) de paja; **~ cottage** casita con tejado de paja.
Thatcherism [ˈθætʃərɪzəm] n thatcherismo.
thaw [θɔː] n deshielo ♦ vi (ice) derretirse; (food) descongelarse ♦ vt (food) descongelar.

══════════════════════════ KEYWORD

the [ðiː, ðə] def art 1 (gen) el, f la, pl los, fpl las (NB = el immediately before feminine noun beginning with stressed (h)a; a+el = al; de+el = del); **~ boy/girl** el chico/la chica; **~ books/flowers** los libros/las flores; **to ~ postman/from ~ drawer** al cartero/del cajón; **I haven't ~ time/money** no tengo tiempo/dinero; **100 pesetas to ~ dollar**

100 pesetas por dólar; **paid by ~ hour** pagado por hora

2 (*+adj to form noun*) los; lo; **~ rich and ~ poor** los ricos y los pobres; **to attempt ~ impossible** intentar lo imposible

3 (*in titles, surnames*): **Elizabeth ~ First** Isabel Primera; **Peter ~ Great** Pedro el Grande; **do you know ~ Smiths?** ¿conoce a los Smith?

4 (*in comparisons*): **~ more he works ~ more he earns** cuanto más trabaja más gana.

theatre, (*US*) **theater** ['θɪətə*] *n* teatro.

theatre-goer, (*US*) **theater-goer** ['θɪətəgəuə*] *n* aficionado/a al teatro.

theatrical [θɪ'ætrɪkl] *adj* teatral.

theft [θɛft] *n* robo.

their [ðɛə*] *adj* su.

theirs [ðɛəz] *pron* (el) suyo/(la) suya *etc*; *see also* **my, mine.**

them [ðɛm, ðəm] *pron* (*direct*) los/las; (*indirect*) les; (*stressed, after prep*) ellos/ ellas; **I see ~** los veo; **both of ~** ambos/as, los/las dos; **give me a few of ~** dame algunos/as; *see also* **me.**

theme [θiːm] *n* tema *m*.

theme park *n* parque *m* temático.

theme song *n* tema *m* (musical).

themselves [ðəm'sɛlvz] *pl pron* (*subject*) ellos mismos/ellas mismas; (*complement*) se; (*after prep*) sí (mismos/as); *see also* **oneself.**

then [ðɛn] *adv* (*at that time*) entonces; (*next*) pues; (*later*) luego, después; (*and also*) además ♦ *conj* (*therefore*) en ese caso, entonces ♦ *adj*: **the ~ president** el entonces presidente; **from ~ on** desde entonces; **until ~** hasta entonces; **and ~ what?** y luego, ¿qué?; **what do you want me to do, ~?** ¿entonces, qué quiere que haga?

theologian [θɪə'ləudʒən] *n* teólogo/a.

theological [θɪə'lɔdʒɪkl] *adj* teológico.

theology [θɪ'ɔlədʒɪ] *n* teología.

theorem ['θɪərəm] *n* teorema *m*.

theoretical [θɪə'rɛtɪkl] *adj* teórico.

theoretically [θɪə'rɛtɪklɪ] *adv* teóricamente, en teoría.

theorize ['θɪəraɪz] *vi* teorizar.

theory ['θɪərɪ] *n* teoría.

therapeutic(al) [θɛrə'pjuːtɪk(l)] *adj* terapéutico.

therapist ['θɛrəpɪst] *n* terapeuta *m/f*.

therapy ['θɛrəpɪ] *n* terapia.

═══════════════ *KEYWORD*

there ['ðɛə*] *adv* **1:** **~ is, ~ are** hay; **~ is no-one here** no hay nadie aquí; **~ is no bread left** no queda pan; **~ has been an accident** ha habido un accidente

2 (*referring to place*) ahí; (*distant*) allí; **it's ~** está ahí; **put it in/on/up/down ~** ponlo ahí dentro/encima/arriba/abajo; **I want that book ~** quiero ese libro de ahí; **~ he is!** ¡ahí está!; **~'s the bus** ahí *or* ya viene el autobús; **back/down ~** allí atrás/abajo; **over ~, through ~** por allí

3: **~, ~** (*esp to child*) ¡venga, venga!

thereabouts ['ðɛərə'bauts] *adv* por ahí.

thereafter [ðɛər'ɑːftə*] *adv* después.

thereby ['ðɛəbaɪ] *adv* así, de ese modo.

therefore ['ðɛəfɔː*] *adv* por lo tanto.

there's [ðɛəz] = **there is; there has.**

thereupon [ðɛərə'pɔn] *adv* (*at that point*) en eso, en seguida.

thermal ['θəːml] *adj* termal.

thermal paper *n* papel *m* térmico.

thermal printer *n* termoimpresora.

thermodynamics ['θəːmədaɪnæmɪks] *n* termodinámica.

thermometer [θə'mɔmɪtə*] *n* termómetro.

thermonuclear [θəːməu'njuːklɪə*] *adj* termonuclear.

Thermos ® ['θəːməs] *n* (*also:* **~ flask**) termo.

thermostat ['θəːməustæt] *n* termostato.

thesaurus [θɪ'sɔːrəs] *n* tesoro, diccionario de sinónimos.

these [ðiːz] *pl adj* estos/as ♦ *pl pron* éstos/as.

thesis, *pl* **theses** ['θiːsɪs, -siːz] *n* tesis *f inv*; *see also* **doctorate.**

they [ðeɪ] *pl pron* ellos/ellas; **~ say that ... (***it is said that***)** se dice que ....

they'd [ðeɪd] = **they had; they would.**

they'll [ðeɪl] = **they shall, they will.**

they're [ðɛə*] = **they are.**

they've [ðeɪv] = **they have.**

thick [θɪk] *adj* (*wall, slice*) grueso; (*dense: liquid, smoke etc*) espeso; (*vegetation, beard*) tupido; (*stupid*) torpe ♦ *n*: **in the ~ of the battle** en lo más reñido de la batalla; **it's 20 cm ~** tiene 20 cm de espesor.

thicken ['θɪkn] *vi* espesarse ♦ *vt* (*sauce etc*) espesar.

thicket ['θɪkɪt] *n* espesura.

thickly ['θɪklɪ] *adv* (*spread*) en capa espesa; (*cut*) en rebanada gruesa; (*populated*) densamente.

thickness ['θɪknɪs] *n* espesor *m*, grueso.

thickset [θɪk'sɛt] *adj* fornido.

thickskinned [θɪk'skɪnd] *adj (fig)* insensible.

thief, *pl* **thieves** [θiːf, θiːvz] *n* ladrón/ona *m/f.*

thieving ['θiːvɪŋ] *n* tobo, hurto ♦ *adj* ladrón/ona.

thigh [θaɪ] *n* muslo.

thighbone ['θaɪbəun] *n* fémur *m.*

thimble ['θɪmbl] *n* dedal *m.*

thin [θɪn] *adj* delgado; *(wall, layer)* fino; *(watery)* aguado; *(light)* tenue; *(hair)* escaso; *(fog)* ligero; *(crowd)* disperso ♦ *vt:* **to ~ (down)** *(sauce, paint)* diluir ♦ *vi (fog)* aclararse; *(also:* **~ out:** *crowd)* dispersarse; **his hair is ~ning** se está quedando calvo.

thing [θɪŋ] *n* cosa; *(object)* objeto, artículo; *(contraption)* chisme *m; (mania)* manía; **~s** *npl (belongings)* cosas *fpl;* **the best ~ would be to...** lo mejor sería...; **the main ~ is ...** lo principal es ...; **first ~ (in the morning)** a primera hora (de la mañana); **last ~ (at night)** a última hora (de la noche); **the ~ is ...** lo que pasa es que ...; **how are ~s?** ¿qué tal van las cosas?; **she's got a ~ about mice** le dan no sé qué los ratones; **poor ~!** ¡pobre! *m/f,* ¡pobrecito/a!

think, *pt, pp* **thought** [θɪŋk, θɔːt] *vi* pensar ♦ *vt* pensar, creer; *(imagine)* imaginar; **what did you ~ of it?** ¿qué te parece?; **what did you ~ of them?** ¿qué te parecieron?; **to ~ about sth/sb** pensar en algo/uno; **I'll ~ about it** lo pensaré; **to ~ of doing sth** pensar en hacer algo; **I ~ so/not** creo que sí/no; **~ again!** ¡piénsalo bien!; **to ~ aloud** pensar en voz alta; **to ~ well of sb** tener buen concepto de algn.

▶**think out** *vt (plan)* elaborar, tramar; *(solution)* encontrar.

▶**think over** *vt* reflexionar sobre, meditar; **I'd like to ~ things over** me gustaría pensármelo.

▶**think through** *vt* pensar bien.

▶**think up** *vt* imaginar.

thinking ['θɪŋkɪŋ] *n:* **to my (way of) ~** a mi parecer.

think tank *n* grupo de expertos.

thinly ['θɪnlɪ] *adv (cut)* en lonchas finas; *(spread)* en una capa fina.

thinness ['θɪnnɪs] *n* delgadez *f.*

third [θɜːd] *adj (before nmsg:* **tercer)** tercero ♦ *n* tercero/a; *(fraction)* tercio; *(BRIT SCOL: degree)* título universitario de tercera clase.

third degree *adj (burns)* de tercer grado.

thirdly ['θɜːdlɪ] *adv* en tercer lugar.

third party insurance *n (BRIT)* seguro a terceros.

third-rate ['θɜːd'reɪt] *adj* de poca calidad.

Third World *n:* **the ~** el Tercer Mundo ♦ *cpd* tercermundista.

thirst [θɜːst] *n* sed *f.*

thirsty ['θɜːstɪ] *adj (person)* sediento; **to be ~** tener sed.

thirteen [θɜː'tiːn] *num* trece.

thirteenth [θɜː'tiːnθ] *adj* decimotercero ♦ *n (in series)* decimotercero/a; *(fraction)* decimotercio.

thirtieth ['θɜːtɪəθ] *adj* trigésimo ♦ *n (in series)* trigésimo/a; *(fraction)* treintavo.

thirty ['θɜːtɪ] *num* treinta.

═══════════════════════ *KEYWORD*

this [ðɪs] *(pl* **these)** *adj (demonstrative)* este/a; *pl* estos/as; *(neuter)* esto; **~ man/woman** este hombre/esta mujer; **these children/flowers** estos chicos/estas flores; **~ way** por aquí; **~ time last year** hoy hace un año; **~ one (here)** éste/a, esto (de aquí)
♦ *pron (demonstrative)* éste/a; *pl* éstos/as; *(neuter)* esto; **who is ~?** ¿quién es éste/ésta?; **what is ~?** ¿qué es esto?; **~ is where I live** aquí vivo; **~ is what he said** esto es lo que dijo; **~ is Mr Brown** *(in introductions)* le presento al Sr. Brown; *(photo)* éste es el Sr. Brown; *(on telephone)* habla el Sr. Brown; **they were talking of ~ and that** hablaban de esto y lo otro
♦ *adv (demonstrative):* **~ high/long** así de alto/largo; **~ far** hasta aquí.

thistle ['θɪsl] *n* cardo.

thong [θɔŋ] *n* correa.

thorn [θɔːn] *n* espina.

thorny ['θɔːnɪ] *adj* espinoso.

thorough ['θʌrə] *adj (search)* minucioso; *(knowledge)* profundo; *(research)* a fondo.

thoroughbred ['θʌrəbred] *adj (horse)* de pura sangre.

thoroughfare ['θʌrəfɛə*] *n* calle *f;* **"no ~"** "prohibido el paso".

thoroughgoing ['θʌrəgəuɪŋ] *adj* a fondo.

thoroughly ['θʌrəlɪ] *adv* minuciosamente; a fondo.

thoroughness ['θʌrənɪs] *n* minuciosidad *f.*

those [ðəuz] *pl pron* ésos/ésas; *(more remote)* aquéllos/as ♦ *pl adj* esos/esas; aquellos/as.

though [ðəu] *conj* aunque ♦ *adv* sin embargo, aún así; **even ~** aunque; **it's not so easy, ~** sin embargo no es tan fácil.

thought [θɔːt] *pt, pp of* **think** ♦ *n* pensamiento; *(opinion)* opinión *f;* *(intention)* intención *f;* **to give sth some ~**

pensar algo detenidamente; **after much ~** después de pensarlo bien; **I've just had a ~** se me acaba de ocurrir una idea.

thoughtful ['θɔːtful] *adj* pensativo; (*considerate*) atento.

thoughtfully ['θɔːtfəlɪ] *adv* pensativamente; atentamente.

thoughtless ['θɔːtlɪs] *adj* desconsiderado.

thoughtlessly ['θɔːtlɪslɪ] *adv* insensatamente.

thought-provoking ['θɔːtprəvəʊkɪŋ] *adj* estimulante.

thousand ['θauzənd] *num* mil; **two ~** dos mil; **~s of** miles de.

thousandth ['θauzəntθ] *num* milésimo.

thrash [θræʃ] *vt* dar una paliza a.

▶**thrash about** *vi* revolverse.

▶**thrash out** *vt* discutir a fondo.

thrashing ['θræʃɪŋ] *n*: **to give sb a ~** dar una paliza a algn.

thread [θrɛd] *n* hilo; (*of screw*) rosca ♦ *vt* (*needle*) enhebrar.

threadbare ['θrɛdbɛə*] *adj* raído.

threat [θrɛt] *n* amenaza; **to be under ~ of** estar amenazado de.

threaten ['θrɛtn] *vi* amenazar ♦ *vt*: **to ~ sb with sth/to do** amenazar a algn con algo/con hacer.

threatening ['θrɛtnɪŋ] *adj* amenazador(a), amenazante.

three [θriː] *num* tres.

three-dimensional [θriːdɪ'mɛnʃənl] *adj* tridimensional.

threefold ['θriːfəuld] *adv*: **to increase ~** triplicar.

three-piece ['θriːpiːs]: **~ suit** *n* traje *m* de tres piezas; **~ suite** *n* tresillo.

three-ply [θriː'plaɪ] *adj* (*wood*) de tres capas; (*wool*) triple.

three-quarter [θriː'kwɔːtə*] *adj*: **~ length sleeves** mangas *fpl* tres cuartos.

three-quarters [θriː'kwɔːtəz] *npl* tres cuartas partes; **~ full** tres cuartas partes lleno.

three-wheeler [θriː'wiːlə*] *n* (*car*) coche *m* cabina.

thresh [θrɛʃ] *vt* (*AGR*) trillar.

threshing machine ['θrɛʃɪŋ-] *n* trilladora.

threshold ['θrɛʃhəuld] *n* umbral *m*; **to be on the ~ of** (*fig*) estar al borde de.

threshold agreement *n* convenio de nivel crítico.

threw [θruː] *pt of* throw.

thrift [θrɪft] *n* economía.

thrifty ['θrɪftɪ] *adj* económico.

thrill [θrɪl] *n* (*excitement*) emoción *f* ♦ *vt* emocionar; **to be ~ed** (*with gift etc*) estar encantado.

thriller ['θrɪlə*] *n* película/novela de suspense.

thrilling ['θrɪlɪŋ] *adj* emocionante.

thrive, *pt* **thrived, throve,** *pp* **thrived, thriven** [θraɪv, θrəuv, 'θrɪvn] *vi* (*grow*) crecer; (*do well*) prosperar.

thriving ['θraɪvɪŋ] *adj* próspero.

throat [θrəut] *n* garganta; **I have a sore ~** me duele la garganta.

throb [θrɔb] *n* (*of heart*) latido; (*of engine*) vibración *f* ♦ *vi* latir; vibrar; (*with pain*) dar punzadas; **my head is ~bing** la cabeza me da punzadas.

throes [θrəuz] *npl*: **in the ~ of** en medio de.

thrombosis [θrɔm'bəusɪs] *n* trombosis *f*.

throne [θrəun] *n* trono.

throng [θrɔŋ] *n* multitud *f*, muchedumbre *f* ♦ *vt, vi* apiñarse, agolparse.

throttle ['θrɔtl] *n* (*AUT*) acelerador *m* ♦ *vt* estrangular.

through [θruː] *prep* por, a través de; (*time*) durante; (*by means of*) por medio de, mediante; (*owing to*) gracias a ♦ *adj* (*ticket, train*) directo ♦ *adv* completamente, de parte a parte; de principio a fin; **(from) Monday ~ Friday** (*US*) de lunes a viernes; **to go ~ sb's papers** mirar entre los papeles de algn; **I am halfway ~ the book** voy por la mitad del libro; **the soldiers didn't let us ~** los soldados no nos dejaron pasar; **to put sb ~ to sb** (*TEL*) poner *or* pasar a algn con algn; **to be ~** (*TEL*) tener comunicación; (*have finished*) haber terminado; **"no ~ road"** (*BRIT*) "calle sin salida".

throughout [θruː'aut] *prep* (*place*) por todas partes de, por todo; (*time*) durante todo ♦ *adv* por *or* en todas partes.

throughput ['θruːput] *n* (*of goods, materials*) producción *f*; (*COMPUT*) capacidad *f* de procesamiento.

throve [θrəuv] *pt of* thrive.

throw [θrəu] *n* tiro, (*SPORT*) lanzamiento ♦ *vt* (*pt* threw, *pp* thrown [θruː, θrəun]) tirar, echar, botar (*LAM*); (*SPORT*) lanzar; (*rider*) derribar; (*fig*) desconcertar; **to ~ a party** dar una fiesta.

▶**throw about, throw around** *vt* (*litter etc*) tirar, esparcir.

▶**throw away** *vt* tirar.

▶**throw off** *vt* deshacerse de.

▶**throw open** *vt* (*doors, windows*) abrir de par en par; (*house, gardens etc*) abrir al público; (*competition, race*) abrir a todos.

▶**throw out** *vt* tirar, botar (*LAM*).

▶**throw together** *vt* (*clothes*) amontonar; (*meal*) preparar a la carrera; (*essay*) hacer sin cuidado.

▶**throw up** *vi* vomitar, devolver.

throwaway ['θrəuəweɪ] *adj* para tirar, desechable.

throwback ['θrəubæk] *n*: **it's a ~ to** (*fig*) eso nos lleva de nuevo a.

throw-in ['θrəuɪn] *n* (*SPORT*) saque *m* de banda.

thrown [θrəun] *pp of* **throw**.

thru [θruː] (*US*) = **through**.

thrush [θrʌʃ] *n* zorzal *m*, tordo; (*MED*) candiasis *f*.

thrust [θrʌst] *n* (*TECH*) empuje *m* ♦ *vt* (*pt, pp* **thrust**) empujar; (*push in*) introducir.

thrusting ['θrʌstɪŋ] *adj* (*person*) dinámico, con empuje.

thud [θʌd] *n* golpe *m* sordo.

thug [θʌg] *n* gamberro/a.

thumb [θʌm] *n* (*ANAT*) pulgar *m* ♦ *vt*: **to ~ a lift** hacer dedo; **to give sth/sb the ~s up/ down** aprobar/desaprobar algo/a algn.

▶**thumb through** *vt fus* (*book*) hojear.

thumb index *n* uñero, índice *m* recortado.

thumbnail ['θʌmneɪl] *n* uña del pulgar.

thumbnail sketch *n* esbozo.

thumbtack ['θʌmtæk] *n* (*US*) chincheta, chinche *f*.

thump [θʌmp] *n* golpe *m*; (*sound*) ruido seco *or* sordo ♦ *vt, vi* golpear.

thumping ['θʌmpɪŋ] *adj* (*col: huge*) descomunal.

thunder ['θʌndə*] *n* trueno; (*of applause etc*) estruendo ♦ *vi* tronar; (*train etc*): **to ~ past** pasar como un trueno.

thunderbolt ['θʌndəbəult] *n* rayo.

thunderclap ['θʌndəklæp] *n* trueno.

thunderous ['θʌndərəs] *adj* ensordecedor(a), estruendoso.

thunderstorm ['θʌndəstɔːm] *n* tormenta.

thunderstruck ['θʌndəstrʌk] *adj* pasmado.

thundery ['θʌndərɪ] *adj* tormentoso.

Thur(s). *abbr* (= *Thursday*) juev.

Thursday ['θəːzdɪ] *n* jueves *m inv*.

thus [ðʌs] *adv* así, de este modo.

thwart [θwɔːt] *vt* frustrar.

thyme [taɪm] *n* tomillo.

thyroid ['θaɪrɔɪd] *n* tiroides *m inv*.

tiara [tɪ'ɑːrə] *n* tiara, diadema.

Tiber ['taɪbə*] *n* Tíber *m*.

Tibet [tɪ'bɛt] *n* el Tibet.

Tibetan [tɪ'bɛtən] *adj* tibetano ♦ *n* tibetano/ a; (*LING*) tibetano.

tibia ['tɪbɪə] *n* tibia.

tic [tɪk] *n* tic *m*.

tick [tɪk] *n* (*sound: of clock*) tictac *m*; (*mark*) señal *f* (de visto bueno), palomita (*LAM*); (*ZOOL*) garrapata; (*BRIT col*): **in a ~** en un instante; (*BRIT col: credit*): **to buy sth on ~** comprar algo a crédito ♦ *vi* hacer tictac

♦ *vt* marcar, señalar; **to put a ~ against** sth poner una señal en algo.

▶**tick off** *vt* marcar; (*person*) reñir.

▶**tick over** *vi* (*BRIT: engine*) girar en marcha lenta; (: *fig*) ir tirando.

ticker tape ['tɪkə-] *n* cinta perforada.

ticket ['tɪkɪt] *n* billete *m*, tíquet *m*, boleto (*LAM*); (*for cinema etc*) entrada, boleto (*LAM*); (*in shop: on goods*) etiqueta; (*for library*) tarjeta; (*US POL*) lista (de candidatos); **to get a parking ~** (*AUT*) ser multado por estacionamiento ilegal.

ticket agency *n* (*THEAT*) agencia de venta de entradas.

ticket collector *n* revisor(a) *m/f*.

ticket holder *n* poseedor(a) *m/f* de billete *or* entrada.

ticket inspector *n* revisor(a) *m/f*, inspector(a) *m/f* de boletos (*LAM*).

ticket office *n* (*THEAT*) taquilla, boletería (*LAM*); (*RAIL*) despacho de billetes *or* boletos (*LAM*).

ticking-off ['tɪkɪŋ'ɔf] *n* (*col*): **to give sb a ~** echarle una bronca a algn.

tickle ['tɪkl] *n*: **to give sb a ~** hacer cosquillas a algn ♦ *vt* hacer cosquillas a.

ticklish ['tɪklɪʃ] *adj* (*which tickles: blanket*) que pica; (: *cough*) irritante; **to be ~** tener cosquillas.

tidal ['taɪdl] *adj* de marea.

tidal wave *n* maremoto.

tidbit ['tɪdbɪt] (*US*) = **titbit**.

tiddlywinks ['tɪdlɪwɪŋks] *n* juego de la pulga.

tide [taɪd] *n* marea; (*fig: of events*) curso, marcha ♦ *vt*: **to ~ sb over** *or* **through (until)** sacar a algn del apuro (hasta); **high/low ~** marea alta/baja; **the ~ of public opinion** la tendencia de la opinión pública.

tidily ['taɪdɪlɪ] *adv* bien, ordenadamente; **to arrange ~** ordenar; **to dress ~** vestir bien.

tidiness ['taɪdɪnɪs] *n* (*order*) orden *m*; (*cleanliness*) aseo.

tidy ['taɪdɪ] *adj* (*room*) ordenado; (*drawing, work*) limpio; (*person*) (bien) arreglado; (: *in character*) metódico; (*mind*) claro, metódico ♦ *vt* (*also: ~ up*) ordenar, poner en orden.

tie [taɪ] *n* (*string etc*) atadura; (*BRIT: neck~*) corbata; (*fig: link*) vínculo, lazo; (*SPORT: draw*) empate *m* ♦ *vt* atar ♦ *vi* (*SPORT*) empatar; **family ~s** obligaciones *fpl* familiares; **cup ~** (*SPORT: match*) partido de copa; **to ~ in a bow** hacer un lazo; **to ~ a knot in sth** hacer un nudo en algo.

▶**tie down** *vt* atar; (*fig*): **to ~ sb down to**

obligar a algn a.

▶**tie in** *vi*: **to** ~ **in (with)** (*correspond*) concordar (con).

▶**tie on** *vt* (*BRIT: label etc*) atar.

▶**tie up** *vt* (*parcel*) envolver; (*dog*) atar; (*boat*) amarrar; (*arrangements*) concluir; **to be ~d up** (*busy*) estar ocupado.

tie-break(er) ['taɪbreɪk(ə*)] *n* (*TENNIS*) tiebreak *m*, muerte *f* súbita; (*in quiz*) punto decisivo.

tie-on ['taɪɒn] *adj* (*BRIT: label*) para atar.

tie-pin ['taɪpɪn] *n* (*BRIT*) alfiler *m* de corbata.

tier [tɪə*] *n* grada; (*of cake*) piso.

tie tack *n* (*US*) alfiler *m* de corbata.

tiff [tɪf] *n* (*col*) pelea, riña.

tiger ['taɪgə*] *n* tigre *m*.

tight [taɪt] *adj* (*rope*) tirante; (*money*) escaso; (*clothes, budget*) ajustado; (*programme*) apretado; (*col: drunk*) borracho ♦ *adv* (*squeeze*) muy fuerte; (*shut*) herméticamente; **to be packed** ~ (*suitcase*) estar completamente lleno; (*people*) estar apretados; **everybody hold** ~**!** ¡agárrense bien!

tighten ['taɪtn] *vt* (*rope*) tensar, estirar; (*screw*) apretar ♦ *vi* estirarse; apretarse.

tight-fisted [taɪt'fɪstɪd] *adj* tacaño.

tight-lipped ['taɪt'lɪpt] *adj*: **to be** ~ (*silent*) rehusar hablar; (*angry*) apretar los labios.

tightly ['taɪtlɪ] *adv* (*grasp*) muy fuerte.

tightness ['taɪtnɪs] *n* (*of rope*) tirantez *f*; (*of clothes*) estrechez *f*; (*of budget*) lo ajustado.

tightrope ['taɪtrəup] *n* cuerda floja.

tightrope walker *n* equilibrista *m/f*, funambulista *m/f*.

tights [taɪts] *npl* (*BRIT*) medias *fpl*, panties *mpl*.

tigress ['taɪgrɪs] *n* tigresa.

tilde ['tɪldə] *n* tilde *f*.

tile [taɪl] *n* (*on roof*) teja; (*on floor*) baldosa; (*on wall*) azulejo ♦ *vt* (*floor*) poner baldosas en; (*wall*) alicatar.

tiled [taɪld] *adj* (*floor*) embaldosado; (*wall, bathroom*) alicatado; (*roof*) con tejas.

till [tɪl] *n* caja (registradora) ♦ *vt* (*land*) cultivar ♦ *prep, conj* = **until.**

tiller ['tɪlə*] *n* (*NAUT*) caña del timón.

tilt [tɪlt] *vt* inclinar ♦ *vi* inclinarse ♦ *n* (*slope*) inclinación *f*; **to wear one's hat at a** ~ llevar el sombrero echado a un lado or terciado; **(at) full** ~ a toda velocidad or carrera.

timber ['tɪmbə*] *n* (*material*) madera; (*trees*) árboles *mpl*.

time [taɪm] *n* tiempo; (*epoch: often pl*) época; (*by clock*) hora; (*moment*) momento; (*occasion*) vez *f*; (*MUS*) compás *m* ♦ *vt* calcular or medir el tiempo de; (*race*) cronometrar; (*remark etc*) elegir el momento para; **a long** ~ mucho tiempo; **4 at a** ~ 4 a la vez; **for the** ~ **being** de momento, por ahora; **at** ~**s** a veces, a ratos; ~ **after** ~, ~ **and again** repetidas veces, una y otra vez; **from** ~ **to** ~ de vez en cuando; **in** ~ (*soon enough*) a tiempo; (*after some time*) con el tiempo; (*MUS*) al compás; **in a week's** ~ dentro de una semana; **in no** ~ en un abrir y cerrar de ojos; **any** ~ cuando sea; **on** ~ a la hora; **to be 30 minutes behind/ahead of** ~ llevar media hora de retraso/adelanto; **to take one's** ~ tomárselo con calma; **he'll do it in his own** ~ (*without being hurried*) lo hará sin prisa; (*out of working hours*) lo hará en su tiempo libre; **by the** ~ **he arrived** cuando llegó; **5 ~s 5** 5 por 5; **what** ~ **is it?** ¿qué hora es?; **what** ~ **do you make it?** ¿qué hora es or tiene?; **to be behind the** ~**s** estar atrasado; **to carry 3 boxes at a** ~ llevar 3 cajas a la vez; **to keep** ~ llevar el ritmo or el compás; **to have a good** ~ pasarlo bien, divertirse; **to** ~ **sth well/badly** elegir un buen/mal momento para algo; **the bomb was ~d to explode 5 minutes later** la bomba estaba programada para explotar 5 minutos más tarde.

time-and-motion expert ['taɪmənd'məuʃən-] *n* experto/a en la ciencia de la producción.

time-and-motion study ['taɪmənd'məuʃən-] *n* estudio de desplazamientos y tiempos.

time bomb *n* bomba de relojería.

time card *n* tarjeta de registro horario.

time clock *n* reloj *m* registrador.

time-consuming ['taɪmkənsjuːmɪŋ] *adj* que requiere mucho tiempo.

time frame *n* plazo.

time-honoured, (*US*) **time-honored** ['taɪmɒnəd] *adj* consagrado.

timekeeper ['taɪmkiːpə*] *n* (*SPORT*) cronómetro.

time lag *n* desfase *m*.

timeless ['taɪmlɪs] *adj* eterno.

time limit *n* (*gen*) límite *m* de tiempo; (*COMM*) plazo.

timely ['taɪmlɪ] *adj* oportuno.

time off *n* tiempo libre.

timer ['taɪmə*] *n* (~ *switch*) interruptor *m*; (*in kitchen, TECH*) temporizador *m*.

time-saving ['taɪmseɪvɪŋ] *adj* que ahorra tiempo.

time scale *n* escala de tiempo.

time sharing n (*COMPUT*) tiempo compartido.
time sheet n = **time card**.
time signal n señal f horaria.
time switch n (*BRIT*) interruptor m (horario).
timetable ['taɪmteɪbl] n horario; (*programme of events etc*) programa m.
time zone n huso horario.
timid ['tɪmɪd] adj tímido.
timidity [tɪ'mɪdɪtɪ] n timidez f.
timidly ['tɪmɪdlɪ] adv tímidamente.
timing ['taɪmɪŋ] n (*SPORT*) cronometraje m; **the ~ of his resignation** el momento que eligió para dimitir.
timpani ['tɪmpənɪ] npl tímpanos mpl.
tin [tɪn] n estaño; (*also*: ~ **plate**) hojalata; (*BRIT*: *can*) lata.
tinfoil ['tɪnfɔɪl] n papel m de estaño.
tinge [tɪndʒ] n matiz m ♦ vt: **~d with** teñido de.
tingle ['tɪŋgl] n hormigueo ♦ vi (*cheeks, skin*: *from cold*) sentir comezón; (: *from bad circulation*) sentir hormigueo.
tinker ['tɪŋkə*] n calderero/a; (*gipsy*) gitano/a.
▶**tinker with** vt fus jugar con, tocar.
tinkle ['tɪŋkl] vi tintinear.
tin mine n mina de estaño.
tinned [tɪnd] adj (*BRIT*: *food*) en lata, en conserva.
tinnitus ['tɪnɪtəs] n (*MED*) acufeno.
tinny ['tɪnɪ] adj (*sound, taste*) metálico; (*pej*: *car*) poco sólido, de pacotilla.
tin opener [-əupnə*] n (*BRIT*) abrelatas m inv.
tinsel ['tɪnsl] n oropel m.
tint [tɪnt] n matiz m; (*for hair*) tinte m ♦ vt (*hair*) teñir.
tinted ['tɪntɪd] adj (*hair*) teñido; (*glass, spectacles*) ahumado.
tiny ['taɪnɪ] adj minúsculo, pequeñito.
tip [tɪp] n (*end*) punta; (*gratuity*) propina; (*BRIT*: *for rubbish*) vertedero; (*advice*) consejo ♦ vt (*waiter*) dar una propina a; (*tilt*) inclinar; (*empty*: *also* ~ **out**) vaciar, echar; (*predict*: *winner*) pronosticar; (: *horse*) recomendar; **he ~ped out the contents of the box** volcó el contenido de la caja.
▶**tip off** vt avisar, poner sobreaviso a.
▶**tip over** vt volcar ♦ vi volcarse.
tip-off ['tɪpɔf] n (*hint*) advertencia.
tipped [tɪpt] adj (*BRIT*: *cigarette*) con filtro.
Tipp-Ex ® ['tɪpɛks] n Tipp-Ex ® m.
tipple ['tɪpl] n (*BRIT*): **his ~ is Cointreau** bebe Cointreau.
tipster ['tɪpstə*] n (*RACING*)

pronosticador(a) m/f.
tipsy ['tɪpsɪ] adj alegre, achispado.
tiptoe ['tɪptəu] n (*BRIT*): **on ~** de puntillas.
tiptop ['tɪptɔp] adj: **in ~ condition** en perfectas condiciones.
tirade [taɪ'reɪd] n diatriba.
tire ['taɪə*] n (*US*) = **tyre** ♦ vt cansar ♦ vi (*gen*) cansarse; (*become bored*) aburrirse.
▶**tire out** vt agotar, rendir.
tired ['taɪəd] adj cansado; **to be ~ of sth** estar harto de algo; **to be/feel/look ~** estar/sentirse/parecer cansado.
tiredness ['taɪədnɪs] n cansancio.
tireless ['taɪəlɪs] adj incansable.
tirelessly ['taɪəlɪslɪ] adv incansablemente.
tiresome ['taɪəsəm] adj aburrido.
tiring ['taɪərɪŋ] adj cansado.
tissue ['tɪʃuː] n tejido; (*paper handkerchief*) pañuelo de papel, kleenex m ®.
tissue paper n papel m de seda.
tit [tɪt] n (*bird*) herrerillo común; **to give ~ for tat** dar ojo por ojo.
titbit ['tɪtbɪt], (*US*) **tidbit** ['tɪdbɪt] n (*food*) golosina; (*news*) pedazo.
titillate ['tɪtɪleɪt] vt estimular, excitar.
titillation [tɪtɪ'leɪʃən] n estimulación f, excitación f.
titivate ['tɪtɪveɪt] vt emperejilar.
title ['taɪtl] n título; (*LAW*: *right*): ~ **(to)** derecho (a).
title deed n (*LAW*) título de propiedad.
title page n portada.
title role n papel m principal.
titter ['tɪtə*] vi reírse entre dientes.
tittle-tattle ['tɪtltætl] n chismes mpl.
titular ['tɪtjulə*] adj (*in name only*) nominal.
T-junction ['tiːdʒʌŋkʃən] n cruce m en T.
TM abbr (= *trademark*) marca de fábrica; = **transcendental meditation**.
TN abbr (*US*) = **Tennessee**.
TNT n abbr (= *trinitrotoluene*) TNT m.

═══════════════════════ *KEYWORD*

to [tuː, tə] prep **1** (*direction*) a; **to go ~ France/London/school/the station** ir a Francia/Londres/al colegio/a la estación; **to go ~ Claude's/the doctor's** ir a casa de Claude/al médico; **the road ~ Edinburgh** la carretera de Edimburgo; ~ **the left/right** a la izquierda/derecha
2 (*as far as*) hasta, a; **from here ~ London** de aquí a or hasta Londres; **to count ~ 10** contar hasta 10; **from 40 ~ 50 people** entre 40 y 50 personas
3 (*with expressions of time*): **a quarter/ twenty ~ 5** las 5 menos cuarto/veinte
4 (*for, of*): **the key ~ the front door** la llave de la puerta principal; **she is**

secretary ~ the director es la secretaria del director; a letter ~ his wife una carta a or para su mujer

5 (expressing indirect object) a; to give sth ~ sb darle algo a algn; give it ~ me dámelo; to talk ~ sb hablar con algn; to be a danger ~ sb ser un peligro para algn; to carry out repairs ~ sth hacer reparaciones en algo

6 (in relation to): 3 goals ~ 2 3 goles a 2; 30 miles ~ the gallon ≈ 9,4 litros a los cien (kilómetros); 8 apples ~ the kilo 8 manzanas por kilo

7 (purpose, result): to come ~ sb's aid venir en auxilio or ayuda de algn; to sentence sb ~ death condenar a algn a muerte; ~ my great surprise con gran sorpresa mía

♦ with vb 1 (simple infin): ~ go/eat ir/comer

2 (following another vb): to want/try/start ~ do querer/intentar/empezar a hacer; see also relevant vb

3 (with vb omitted): I don't want ~ no quiero

4 (purpose, result) para; I did it ~ help you lo hice para ayudarte; he came ~ see you vino a verte

5 (equivalent to relative clause): I have things ~ do tengo cosas que hacer; the main thing is ~ try lo principal es intentarlo

6 (after adj etc): ready ~ go listo para irse; too old ~ ... demasiado viejo (como) para ...

♦ adv: pull/push the door ~ tirar de/ empujar la puerta; to go ~ and fro ir y venir.

---

toad [təud] n sapo.

toadstool ['təudstuːl] n seta venenosa.

toady ['təudɪ] n pelota m/f ♦ vi: to ~ to sb hacer la pelota or dar coba a algn.

toast [təust] n (CULIN: also: piece of ~) tostada; (drink, speech) brindis m inv ♦ vt (CULIN) tostar; (drink to) brindar.

toaster ['təustə*] n tostador m.

toastmaster ['təustmɑːstə*] n persona que propone brindis y anuncia a los oradores en un banquete.

toast rack n rejilla para tostadas.

tobacco [tə'bækəu] n tabaco; **pipe ~** tabaco de pipa.

tobacconist [tə'bækənɪst] n estanquero/a, tabaquero/a (LAM); **~'s (shop)** (BRIT) estanco, tabaquería (LAM).

tobacco plantation n plantación f de tabaco, tabacal m.

Tobago [tə'beɪgəu] n see **Trinidad and Tobago.**

toboggan [tə'bɔgən] n tobogán m.

today [tə'deɪ] adv, n (also fig) hoy m; **what day is it ~?** ¿qué día es hoy?; **what date is it ~?** ¿a qué fecha estamos hoy?; **~ is the 4th of March** hoy es el 4 de marzo; **~'s paper** el periódico de hoy; **a fortnight ~** de hoy en 15 días, dentro de 15 días.

toddle ['tɔdl] vi empezar a andar, dar los primeros pasos.

toddler ['tɔdlə*] n niño/a (que empieza a andar).

toddy ['tɔdɪ] n ponche m.

to-do [tə'duː] n (fuss) lío.

toe [təu] n dedo (del pie); (of shoe) punta ♦ vt: to ~ the line (fig) acatar las normas; **big/little ~** dedo gordo/pequeño del pie.

TOEFL n abbr = Test(ing) of English as a Foreign Language.

toehold ['təuhəuld] n punto de apoyo (para el pie).

toenail ['təuneɪl] n uña del pie.

toffee ['tɔfɪ] n caramelo.

toffee apple n (BRIT) manzana de caramelo.

tofu ['təufuː] n tofu m.

toga ['təugə] n toga.

together [tə'gɛðə*] adv juntos; (at same time) al mismo tiempo, a la vez; **~ with** prep junto con.

togetherness [tə'gɛðənɪs] n compañerismo.

toggle switch ['tɔgl-] n (COMPUT) conmutador m de palanca.

Togo ['təugəu] n Togo m.

togs [tɔgz] npl (col: clothes) atuendo, ropa.

toil [tɔɪl] n trabajo duro, labor f ♦ vi esforzarse.

toilet ['tɔɪlət] n (BRIT: lavatory) servicios mpl, wáter m ♦ cpd (bag, soap etc) de aseo; to go to the ~ ir al baño; see also **toilets.**

toilet bag n neceser m, bolsa de aseo.

toilet bowl n taza (de retrete).

toilet paper n papel m higiénico.

toiletries ['tɔɪlətrɪz] npl artículos mpl de aseo; (make-up etc) artículos mpl de tocador.

toilet roll n rollo de papel higiénico.

toilets ['tɔɪləts] npl (BRIT) servicios mpl.

toilet soap n jabón m de tocador.

toilet water n (agua de) colonia.

to-ing and fro-ing ['tuɪŋən'frəuɪŋ] n vaivén m.

token ['təukən] n (sign) señal f, muestra; (souvenir) recuerdo; (voucher) vale m; (disc) ficha ♦ cpd (fee, strike) nominal, simbólico; **book/record ~** (BRIT) vale m para comprar libros/discos; **by the same**

~ (*fig*) por la misma razón.

tokenism ['təukənɪzəm] *n* (*POL*) política
simbólica *or* de fachada.

Tokyo ['təukjəu] *n* Tokio, Tokío.

told [təuld] *pt, pp of* **tell**.

tolerable ['tɔlərəbl] *adj* (*bearable*)
soportable; (*fairly good*) pasable.

tolerably ['tɔlərəblɪ] *adv* (*good, comfortable*)
medianamente.

tolerance ['tɔlərns] *n* (*also: TECH*)
tolerancia.

tolerant ['tɔlərnt] *adj*: ~ **of** tolerante con.

tolerantly ['tɔlərntlɪ] *adv* con tolerancia.

tolerate ['tɔləreɪt] *vt* tolerar.

toleration [tɔlə'reɪʃən] *n* tolerancia.

toll [təul] *n* (*of casualties*) número de
víctimas; (*tax, charge*) peaje *m* ♦ *vi* (*bell*)
doblar.

toll bridge *n* puente *m* de peaje.

toll call *n* (*US TELEC*) conferencia, llamada
interurbana.

toll-free *adj, adv* (*US*) gratis.

toll road *n* carretera de peaje.

tomato, ~**es** [tə'mɑːtəu] *n* tomate *m*.

tomato puree *n* puré *m* de tomate.

tomb [tuːm] *n* tumba.

tombola [tɔm'bəulə] *n* tómbola.

tomboy ['tɔmbɔɪ] *n* marimacho.

tombstone ['tuːmstəun] *n* lápida.

tomcat ['tɔmkæt] *n* gato.

tomorrow [tə'mɔrəu] *adv, n* (*also fig*)
mañana; **the day after** ~ pasado mañana;
~ **morning** mañana por la mañana; **a
week** ~ de mañana en ocho (días).

ton [tʌn] *n* (*BRIT* = 1016 kg; *US*: *also* **short** ~
= 907,18 kg) tonelada; ~**s of** (*col*)
montones de.

tonal ['təunl] *adj* tonal.

tone [təun] *n* tono ♦ *vi* armonizar; **dialling** ~
(*TEL*) señal *f* para marcar.

▶**tone down** *vt* (*criticism*) suavizar;
(*colour*) atenuar.

▶**tone up** *vt* (*muscles*) tonificar.

tone-deaf [təun'dɛf] *adj* sin oído musical.

toner ['təunə*] *n* (*for photocopier*) virador *m*.

Tonga ['tɔŋə] *n* Islas *fpl* Tonga.

tongs [tɔŋz] *npl* (*for coal*) tenazas *fpl*; (*for
hair*) tenacillas *fpl*.

tongue [tʌŋ] *n* lengua; ~ **in cheek** *adv* en
plan de broma.

tongue-tied ['tʌŋtaɪd] *adj* (*fig*) mudo.

tongue-twister ['tʌŋtwɪstə*] *n*
trabalenguas *m inv*.

tonic ['tɔnɪk] *n* (*MED*) tónico; (*MUS*) tónica;
(*also*: ~ **water**) (agua) tónica.

tonight [tə'naɪt] *adv, n* esta noche; **I'll see
you** ~ nos vemos esta noche.

tonnage ['tʌnɪdʒ] *n* (*NAUT*) tonelaje *m*.

tonsil ['tɔnsl] *n* amígdala; **to have one's** ~**s
out** sacarse las amígdalas *or* anginas.

tonsillitis [tɔnsɪ'laɪtɪs] *n* amigdalitis *f*; **to
have** ~ tener amigdalitis.

too [tuː] *adv* (*excessively*) demasiado; (*very*)
muy; (*also*) también; **it's** ~ **sweet** está
demasiado dulce; **I'm not** ~ **sure about
that** no estoy muy seguro de eso; **I went**
~ yo también fui; ~ **much** *adv, adj*
demasiado; ~ **many** *adj* demasiados/as; ~
bad! ¡mala suerte!

took [tuk] *pt of* **take**.

tool [tuːl] *n* herramienta; (*fig*: *person*)
instrumento.

tool box *n* caja de herramientas.

tool kit *n* juego de herramientas.

tool shed *n* cobertizo (para
herramientas).

toot [tuːt] *n* (*of horn*) bocinazo; (*of whistle*)
silbido ♦ *vi* (*with car horn*) tocar la bocina.

tooth, *pl* **teeth** [tuːθ, tiːθ] *n* (*ANAT, TECH*)
diente *m*; (*molar*) muela; **to clean one's
teeth** lavarse los dientes; **to have a** ~ **out**
sacarse una muela; **by the skin of one's
teeth** por un pelo.

toothache ['tuːθeɪk] *n* dolor *m* de muelas.

toothbrush ['tuːθbrʌʃ] *n* cepillo de dientes.

toothpaste ['tuːθpeɪst] *n* pasta de dientes.

toothpick ['tuːθpɪk]. *n* palillo.

tooth powder *n* polvos *mpl* dentífricos.

top [tɔp] *n* (*of mountain*) cumbre *f*, cima; (*of
head*) coronilla; (*of ladder*) (lo) alto; (*of
cupboard, table*) superficie *f*; (*lid: of box,
jar*) tapa; (: *of bottle*) tapón *m*; (*of list, table,
queue, page*) cabeza; (*toy*) peonza; (*DRESS:
blouse*) blusa; (: *T-shirt*) camiseta; (: *of
pyjamas*) chaqueta ♦ *adj* de arriba; (*in
rank*) principal, primero; (*best*) mejor ♦ *vt*
(*exceed*) exceder; (*be first in*) encabezar;
on ~ **of** sobre, encima de; **from** ~ **to
bottom** de pies a cabeza; **the** ~ **of the
milk** la nata; **at the** ~ **of the stairs** en lo
alto de la escalera; **at the** ~ **of the street**
al final de la calle; **at the** ~ **of one's voice**
(*fig*) a voz en grito; **at** ~ **speed** a máxima
velocidad; **a** ~ **surgeon** un cirujano
eminente; **over the** ~ (*col*) excesivo,
desmesurado; **to go over the** ~ pasarse.

▶**top up**, (*US*) **top off** *vt* volver a llenar.

topaz ['təupæz] *n* topacio.

top-class ['tɔp'klɑːs] *adj* de primera clase.

topcoat ['tɔpkəut] *n* sobretodo, abrigo.

topflight ['tɔpflaɪt] *adj* de primera
(categoría *or* clase).

top floor *n* último piso.

top hat *n* sombrero de copa.

top-heavy [tɔp'hɛvɪ] *adj* (*object*) con más
peso en la parte superior.

topic ['tɔpɪk] n tema m.
topical ['tɔpɪkl] adj actual.
topless ['tɔplɪs] adj (bather etc) topless.
top-level ['tɔplɛvl] adj (talks) al más alto nivel.
topmost ['tɔpməust] adj más alto.
top-notch ['tɔp'nɔtʃ] adj (col) de primerísima categoría.
topography [tə'pɔgrəfɪ] n topografía.
topping ['tɔpɪŋ] n (CULIN): **with a ~ of cream** con nata por encima.
topple ['tɔpl] vt volcar, derribar ♦ vi caerse.
top-ranking ['tɔprænkɪŋ] adj de alto rango.
top-secret [tɔp'siːkrɪt] adj de alto secreto.
top-security ['tɔpsɪ'kjuərɪtɪ] adj (BRIT) de máxima seguridad.
topsy-turvy ['tɔpsɪ'təːvɪ] adj, adv patas arriba.
top-up ['tɔpʌp] n: **would you like a ~?** ¿quiere que se lo vuelva a llenar?
top-up loan n (BRIT) préstamo complementario.
torch [tɔːtʃ] n antorcha; (BRIT: electric) linterna.
tore [tɔː*] pt of **tear**.
torment n ['tɔːmɛnt] tormento ♦ vt [tɔː'mɛnt] atormentar; (fig: annoy) fastidiar.
torn [tɔːn] pp of **tear**.
tornado, ~es [tɔː'neɪdəu] n tornado.
torpedo, ~es [tɔː'piːdəu] n torpedo.
torpedo boat n torpedero, lancha torpedera.
torpor ['tɔːpə*] n letargo.
torrent ['tɔrnt] n torrente m.
torrential [tɔ'rɛnʃl] adj torrencial.
torrid ['tɔrɪd] adj tórrido; (fig) apasionado.
torso ['tɔːsəu] n torso.
tortoise ['tɔːtəs] n tortuga.
tortoiseshell ['tɔːtəʃɛl] adj de carey.
tortuous ['tɔːtjuəs] adj tortuoso.
torture ['tɔːtʃə*] n tortura ♦ vt torturar; (fig) atormentar.
torturer ['tɔːtʃərə*] n torturador(a) m/f.
Tory ['tɔːrɪ] adj, n (BRIT POL) conservador(a) m/f.
toss [tɔs] vt tirar, echar; (head) sacudir ♦ n (movement: of head etc) sacudida; (of coin) tirada, echada (LAM); **to ~ a coin** echar a cara o cruz; **to ~ up for sth** jugar algo a cara o cruz; **to ~ and turn** (in bed) dar vueltas (en la cama); **to win/lose the ~** (also SPORT) ganar/perder (a cara o cruz).
tot [tɔt] n (BRIT: drink) copita; (child) nene/a m/f.
▶**tot up** vt sumar.
total ['təutl] adj total, entero ♦ n total m,

suma ♦ vt (add up) sumar; (amount to) ascender a; **grand ~** cantidad f total; (cost) importe m total; **in ~** en total, en suma.
totalitarian [təutælɪ'tɛərɪən] adj totalitario.
totality [təu'tælɪtɪ] n totalidad f.
total loss n siniestra total.
totally ['təutəlɪ] adv totalmente.
tote [təut] vt (col) acarrear, cargar con.
tote bag n bolsa.
totem pole ['təutəm-] n poste m totémico.
totter ['tɔtə*] vi tambalearse.
touch [tʌtʃ] n (sense) tacto; (contact) contacto; (FOOTBALL) fuera de juego ♦ vt tocar; (emotionally) conmover; **a ~ of** (fig) una pizca or un poquito de; **to get in ~ with sb** ponerse en contacto con algn; **I'll be in ~** le llamaré/escribiré; **to lose ~** (friends) perder contacto; **to be out of ~ with events** no estar al corriente (de los acontecimientos); **the personal ~** el toque personal; **to put the finishing ~es to sth** dar el último toque a algo; **no artist in the country can ~ him** no hay artista en todo el país que le iguale.
▶**touch on** vt fus (topic) aludir (brevemente) a.
▶**touch up** vt (paint) retocar.
touch-and-go ['tʌtʃən'gəu] adj arriesgado.
touchdown ['tʌtʃdaun] n aterrizaje m; (US FOOTBALL) ensayo.
touched [tʌtʃt] adj conmovido; (col) chiflado.
touchiness ['tʌtʃɪnɪs] n susceptibilidad f.
touching ['tʌtʃɪŋ] adj conmovedor(a).
touchline ['tʌtʃlaɪn] n (SPORT) línea de banda.
touch-sensitive ['tʌtʃ'sɛnsɪtɪv] adj sensible al tacto.
touch-type ['tʌtʃtaɪp] vi mecanografiar al tacto.
touchy ['tʌtʃɪ] adj (person) quisquilloso.
tough [tʌf] adj (meat) duro; (journey) penoso; (task, problem, situation) difícil; (resistant) resistente; (person) fuerte; (: pej) bruto ♦ n (gangster etc) gorila m; **they got ~ with the workers** se pusieron muy duros con los trabajadores.
toughen ['tʌfn] vt endurecer.
toughness ['tʌfnɪs] n dureza; (resistance) resistencia; (strictness) inflexibilidad f.
toupée ['tuːpeɪ] n peluquín m.
tour ['tuə*] n viaje m; (also: package ~) viaje m con todo incluido; (of town, museum) visita ♦ vt viajar por; **to go on a ~ of** (region, country) ir de viaje por; (museum, castle) visitar; **to go on ~** partir or ir de gira.

touring ['tuərɪŋ] *n* viajes *mpl* turísticos, turismo.

tourism ['tuərɪzm] *n* turismo.

tourist ['tuərɪst] *n* turista *m/f* ♦ *cpd* turístico; **the ~ trade** el turismo.

tourist class *n* (*AVIAT*) clase *f* turista.

tourist office *n* oficina de turismo.

tournament ['tuənəmənt] *n* torneo.

tourniquet ['tuənɪkeɪ] *n* (*MED*) torniquete *m*.

tour operator *n* touroperador(a) *m/f*, operador(a) *m/f* turístico/a.

tousled ['tauzld] *adj* (*hair*) despeinado.

tout [taut] *vi*: **to ~ for business** solicitar clientes ♦ *n*: **ticket ~** revendedor(a) *m/f*.

tow [təu] *n*: **to give sb a ~** (*AUT*) remolcar a algn ♦ *vt* remolcar; **"on** or (*US*) **in ~"** (*AUT*) **"a remolque"**.

toward(s) [tə'wɔːd(z)] *prep* hacia; (*of attitude*) respecto a, con; (*of purpose*) para; **~ noon** alrededor de mediodía; **~ the end of the year** hacia finales de año; **to feel friendly ~ sb** sentir amistad hacia algn.

towel ['tauəl] *n* toalla; **to throw in the ~** (*fig*) darse por vencido, renunciar.

towelling ['tauəlɪŋ] *n* (*fabric*) felpa.

towel rail, (*US*) **towel rack** *n* toallero.

tower ['tauə*] *n* torre *f* ♦ *vi* (*building, mountain*) elevarse; **to ~ above** or **over sth/sb** dominar algo/destacarse sobre algn.

tower block *n* (*BRIT*) bloque *m* de pisos.

towering ['tauərɪŋ] *adj* muy alto, imponente.

town [taun] *n* ciudad *f*; **to go to ~** ir a la ciudad; (*fig*) tirar la casa por la ventana; **in the ~** en la ciudad; **to be out of ~** estar fuera de la ciudad.

town centre *n* centro de la ciudad.

town clerk *n* secretario/a del Ayuntamiento.

town council *n* Ayuntamiento, consejo municipal.

town crier [-kraɪə*] *n* (*BRIT*) pregonero.

town hall *n* ayuntamiento.

townie ['taunɪ] *n* (*BRIT col*) persona de la ciudad.

town plan *n* plano de la ciudad.

town planner *n* urbanista *m/f*.

town planning *n* urbanismo.

township ['taunʃɪp] *n* municipio habitado sólo por negros en Sudáfrica.

townspeople ['taunzpiːpl] *npl* gente *f* de ciudad.

towpath ['təupɑːθ] *n* camino de sirga.

towrope ['təurəup] *n* cable *m* de remolque.

tow truck *n* (*US*) camión *m* grúa.

toxic ['tɔksɪk] *adj* tóxico.

toxin ['tɔksɪn] *n* toxina.

toy [tɔɪ] *n* juguete *m*.

▶**toy with** *vt fus* jugar con; (*idea*) acariciar.

toyshop ['tɔɪʃɔp] *n* juguetería.

toy train *n* tren *m* de juguete.

trace [treɪs] *n* rastro ♦ *vt* (*draw*) trazar, delinear; (*locate*) encontrar; **there was no ~ of it** no había ningún indicio de ello.

trace element *n* oligoelemento.

trachea [trə'kɪə] *n* (*ANAT*) tráquea.

tracing paper ['treɪsɪŋ-] *n* papel *m* de calco.

track [træk] *n* (*mark*) huella, pista; (*path: gen*) camino, senda; (: *of bullet etc*) trayectoria; (: *of suspect, animal*) pista, rastro; (*RAIL*) vía; (*COMPUT, SPORT*) pista; (*on record*) canción *f* ♦ *vt* seguir la pista de; **to keep ~ of** mantenerse al tanto de, seguir; **a 4-~ tape** una cinta de 4 pistas; **the first ~ on the record/tape** la primera canción en el disco/la cinta; **to be on the right ~** (*fig*) ir por buen camino.

▶**track down** *vt* (*person*) localizar; (*sth lost*) encontrar.

tracker dog ['trækə*-] *n* (*BRIT*) perro rastreador.

track events *npl* (*SPORT*) pruebas *fpl* en pista.

tracking station ['trækɪŋ-] *n* (*SPACE*) estación *f* de seguimiento.

track meet *n* (*US*) concurso de carreras y saltos.

track record *n*: **to have a good ~** (*fig*) tener un buen historial.

tracksuit ['træksuːt] *n* chandal *m*.

tract [trækt] *n* (*GEO*) región *f*; (*pamphlet*) folleto.

traction ['trækʃən] *n* (*AUT, power*) tracción *f*; **in ~** (*MED*) en tracción.

traction engine *n* locomotora de tracción.

tractor ['træktə*] *n* tractor *m*.

trade [treɪd] *n* comercio, negocio; (*skill, job*) oficio, empleo; (*industry*) industria ♦ *vi* negociar, comerciar; **foreign ~** comercio exterior.

▶**trade in** *vt* (*old car etc*) ofrecer como parte del pago.

trade barrier *n* barrera comercial.

trade deficit *n* déficit *m* comercial.

Trade Descriptions Act *n* (*BRIT*) *ley sobre descripciones comerciales.*

trade discount *n* descuento comercial.

trade fair *n* feria de muestras.

trade-in ['treɪdɪn] *adj*: **~ price/value** *precio/valor de un artículo usado que se descuenta del precio de otro nuevo.*

trademark ['treɪdmɑːk] *n* marca de fábrica.

trade mission *n* misión *f* comercial.

trade name *n* marca registrada.
trade-off *n*: **a ~ (between)** un equilibrio (entre).
trade price *n* precio al detallista.
trader ['treɪdə*] *n* comerciante *m/f*.
trade reference *n* referencia comercial.
trade secret *n* secreto profesional.
tradesman ['treɪdzmən] *n* (*shopkeeper*) comerciante *m/f*.
trade union *n* sindicato.
trade unionist [-'juːnjənɪst] *n* sindicalista *m/f*.
trade wind *n* viento alisio.
trading ['treɪdɪŋ] *n* comercio.
trading account *n* cuenta de compraventa.
trading estate *n* (*BRIT*) polígono industrial.
trading stamp *n* cupón *m*, sello de prima.
tradition [trə'dɪʃən] *n* tradición *f*.
traditional [trə'dɪʃənl] *adj* tradicional.
traditionally [trə'dɪʃənlɪ] *adv* tradicionalmente.
traffic ['træfɪk] *n* (*gen, AUT*) tráfico, circulación *f*, tránsito ♦ *vi*: **to ~ in** (*pej: liquor, drugs*) traficar en; **air ~** tráfico aéreo.
traffic calming [-'kɑːmɪŋ] *n* reducción *f* de la velocidad de la circulación.
traffic circle *n* (*US*) glorieta de tráfico.
traffic island *n* refugio, isleta.
traffic jam *n* embotellamiento, atasco.
trafficker ['træfɪkə*] *n* traficante *m/f*.
traffic lights *npl* semáforo *sg*.
traffic offence, (*US*) **traffic violation** *n* infracción *f* de tráfico.
traffic warden *n* guardia *m/f* de tráfico.
tragedy ['trædʒədɪ] *n* tragedia.
tragic ['trædʒɪk] *adj* trágico.
tragically ['trædʒɪkəlɪ] *adv* trágicamente.
trail [treɪl] *n* (*tracks*) rastro, pista; (*path*) camino, sendero; (*dust, smoke*) estela ♦ *vt* (*drag*) arrastrar; (*follow*) seguir la pista de; (*follow closely*) vigilar ♦ *vi* arrastrarse; **to be on sb's ~** seguir la pista de algn.
► **trail away, trail off** *vi* (*sound*) desvanecerse; (*interest, voice*) desaparecer.
► **trail behind** *vi* quedar a la zaga.
trailer ['treɪlə*] *n* (*AUT*) remolque *m*; (*caravan*) caravana; (*CINE*) trailer *m*, avance *m*.
trail truck *n* (*US*) trailer *m*.
train [treɪn] *n* tren *m*; (*of dress*) cola; (*series*): **~ of events** cadena de los acontecimientos ♦ *vt* (*educate*) formar; (*teach skills to*) adiestrar; (*sportsman*) entrenar; (*dog*) amaestrar; (*point: gun*

etc): **to ~ on** apuntar a ♦ *vi* (*SPORT*) entrenarse; (*be educated, learn a skill*) formarse; **to go by ~** ir en tren; **one's ~ of thought** el razonamiento de algn; **to ~ sb to do sth** enseñar a algn a hacer algo.
train attendant *n* (*US RAIL*) empleado/a de coches-cama.
trained [treɪnd] *adj* (*worker*) cualificado; (*animal*) amaestrado.
trainee [treɪ'niː] *n* trabajador(a) *m/f* en prácticas ♦ *cpd*: **he's a ~ teacher** (*primary*) es estudiante de magisterio; (*secondary*) está haciendo las prácticas del I.C.E.
trainer ['treɪnə*] *n* (*SPORT*) entrenador(a) *m/f*; (*of animals*) domador(a) *m/f*; **~s** *npl* (*shoes*) zapatillas *fpl* (de deporte).
training ['treɪnɪŋ] *n* formación *f*; entrenamiento; **to be in ~** (*SPORT*) estar entrenando; (: *fit*) estar en forma.
training college *n* (*gen*) colegio de formación profesional; (*for teachers*) escuela normal.
training course *n* curso de formación.
traipse [treɪps] *vi* andar penosamente.
trait [treɪt] *n* rasgo.
traitor ['treɪtə*] *n* traidor(a) *m/f*.
trajectory [trə'dʒektərɪ] *n* trayectoria, curso.
tram [træm] *n* (*BRIT: also:* **~car**) tranvía *m*.
tramline ['træmlaɪn] *n* carril *m* de tranvía.
tramp [træmp] *n* (*person*) vagabundo/a; (*col: offensive: woman*) puta ♦ *vi* andar con pasos pesados.
trample ['træmpl] *vt*: **to ~ (underfoot)** pisotear.
trampoline ['træmpəliːn] *n* trampolín *m*.
trance [trɑːns] *n* trance *m*; **to go into a ~** entrar en trance.
tranquil ['træŋkwɪl] *adj* tranquilo.
tranquillity, (*US*) **tranquility** [træŋ'kwɪlɪtɪ] *n* tranquilidad *f*.
tranquillizer, (*US*) **tranquilizer** ['træŋkwɪlaɪzə*] *n* (*MED*) tranquilizante *m*.
trans- [trænz] *pref* trans-, tras-.
transact [træn'zækt] *vt* (*business*) tramitar.
transaction [træn'zækʃən] *n* transacción *f*, operación *f*; **cash ~s** transacciones al contado.
transatlantic ['trænzət'læntɪk] *adj* transatlántico.
transcend [træn'send] *vt* rebasar.
transcendent [træn'sendənt] *adj* trascendente.
transcendental [trænsen'dentl] *adj*: **~ meditation** meditación *f* transcendental.
transcribe [træn'skraɪb] *vt* transcribir, copiar.
transcript ['trænskrɪpt] *n* copia.

transcription [træn'skrɪpʃən] n transcripción f.

transept ['trænsɛpt] n crucero.

transfer n ['trænsfə*] transferencia; (*SPORT*) traspaso; (*picture, design*) calcomanía ♦ vt [træns'fɔ:*] trasladar, pasar; **to ~ the charges** (*BRIT TEL*) llamar a cobro revertido; **by bank ~** por transferencia bancaria *or* giro bancario; **to ~ money from one account to another** transferir dinero de una cuenta a otra; **to ~ sth to sb's name** transferir algo al nombre de algn.

transferable [træns'fə:rəbl] adj: **not ~** intransferible.

transfix [træns'fɪks] vt traspasar; (*fig*): **~ed with fear** paralizado por el miedo.

transform [træns'fɔ:m] vt transformar.

transformation [trænsfə'meɪʃən] n transformación f.

transformer [træns'fɔ:mə*] n (*ELEC*) transformador m.

transfusion [træns'fju:ʒən] n transfusión f.

transgress [træns'grɛs] vt (*go beyond*) traspasar; (*violate*) violar, infringir.

tranship [træn'ʃɪp] vt trasbordar.

transient ['trænzɪənt] adj transitorio.

transistor [træn'zɪstə*] n (*ELEC*) transistor m.

transistorized [træn'zɪstəraɪzd] adj (*circuit*) transistorizado.

transistor radio n transistor m.

transit ['trænzɪt] n: **in ~** en tránsito.

transit camp n campamento de tránsito.

transition [træn'zɪʃən] n transición f.

transitional [træn'zɪʃənl] adj transitorio.

transition period n período de transición.

transitive ['trænzɪtɪv] adj (*LING*) transitivo.

transitively ['trænzɪtɪvlɪ] adv transitivamente.

transitory ['trænzɪtərɪ] adj transitorio.

transit visa n visado de tránsito.

translate [trænz'leɪt] vt: **to ~ (from/into)** traducir (de/a).

translation [trænz'leɪʃən] n traducción f.

translator [trænz'leɪtə*] n traductor(a) m/f.

translucent [trænz'lu:snt] adj traslúcido.

transmission [trænz'mɪʃən] n transmisión f.

transmit [trænz'mɪt] vt transmitir.

transmitter [trænz'mɪtə*] n transmisor m; (*station*) emisora.

transparency [træns'pɛərnsɪ] n (*BRIT PHOT*) diapositiva.

transparent [træns'pærnt] adj transparente.

transpire [træns'paɪə*] vi (*turn out*) resultar (ser); (*happen*) ocurrir, suceder; (*become known*): **it finally ~d that ...** por fin se supo que ....

transplant vt [træns'plɑ:nt] transplantar ♦ n ['trænsplɑ:nt] (*MED*) transplante m; **to have a heart ~** hacerse un transplante de corazón.

transport n ['trænspɔ:t] transporte m ♦ vt [træns'pɔ:t] transportar; **public ~** transporte m público.

transportable [træns'pɔ:təbl] adj transportable.

transportation [trænspɔ:'teɪʃən] n transporte m; (*of prisoners*) deportación f.

transport café n (*BRIT*) bar-restaurante m de carretera.

transpose [træns'pəuz] vt transponer.

transsexual [trænz'sɛksjuəl] adj, n transexual m/f.

transverse ['trænzvə:s] adj transverso, transversal.

transvestite [trænz'vɛstaɪt] n travesti m/f.

trap [træp] n (*snare, trick*) trampa; (*carriage*) cabriolé m ♦ vt coger (*SP*) *or* agarrar (*LAM*) en una trampa; (*immobilize*) bloquear; (*jam*) atascar; **to set** *or* **lay a ~ (for sb)** poner(le) una trampa (a algn); **to ~ one's finger in the door** pillarse el dedo en la puerta.

trap door n escotilla.

trapeze [trə'pi:z] n trapecio.

trapper ['træpə*] n trampero, cazador m.

trappings ['træpɪŋz] npl adornos mpl.

trash [træʃ] n basura; (*nonsense*) tonterías fpl.

trash can n (*US*) cubo, balde m (*LAM*) *or* bote m (*LAM*) de la basura.

trash can liner n (*US*) bolsa de basura.

trashy ['træʃɪ] adj (*col*) chungo.

trauma ['trɔ:mə] n trauma m.

traumatic [trɔ:'mætɪk] adj (*PSYCH, fig*) traumático.

travel ['trævl] n viaje m ♦ vi viajar ♦ vt (*distance*) recorrer; **this wine doesn't ~ well** este vino pierde con los viajes.

travel agency n agencia de viajes.

travel agent n agente m/f de viajes.

travel brochure n folleto turístico.

traveller, (*US*) **traveler** ['trævlə*] n viajero/a; (*COMM*) viajante m/f.

traveller's cheque, (*US*) **traveler's check** n cheque m de viaje.

travelling, (*US*) **traveling** ['trævlɪŋ] n los viajes, el viajar ♦ adj (*circus, exhibition*) ambulante ♦ cpd (*bag, clock*) de viaje.

travel(l)ing expenses npl dietas fpl.

travel(l)ing salesman n viajante m.

travelogue ['trævələg] n (*book*) relación f de viajes; (*film*) documental m de viajes;

(*talk*) recuento de viajes.

travel sickness *n* mareo.

traverse ['trævəs] *vt* atravesar.

travesty ['trævəstɪ] *n* parodia.

trawler ['trɔːlə*] *n* pesquero de arrastre.

tray [treɪ] *n* (*for carrying*) bandeja; (*on desk*) cajón *m*.

treacherous ['tretʃərəs] *adj* traidor(a); **road conditions are** ~ el estado de las carreteras es peligroso.

treachery ['tretʃərɪ] *n* traición *f*.

treacle ['triːkl] *n* (*BRIT*) melaza.

tread [tred] *n* paso, pisada; (*of tyre*) banda de rodadura ♦ *vi* (*pt* **trod**, *pp* **trodden** [trɔd, 'trɔdn]) pisar.

▶**tread on** *vt fus* pisar.

treas. *abbr* = **treasurer**.

treason ['triːzn] *n* traición *f*.

treasure ['treʒə*] *n* tesoro ♦ *vt* (*value*) apreciar, valorar.

treasure hunt *n* caza del tesoro.

treasurer ['treʒərə*] *n* tesorero/a.

treasury ['treʒərɪ] *n*: **the T~**, (*US*) **the T~ Department** ≈ el Ministerio de Economía y de Hacienda.

treasury bill *n* bono del Tesoro.

treat [triːt] *n* (*present*) regalo; (*pleasure*) placer *m* ♦ *vt* tratar; (*consider*) considerar; **to give sb a** ~ hacer un regalo a algn; **to** ~ **sb to sth** invitar a algn a algo; **to** ~ **sth as a joke** tomar algo a broma.

treatise ['triːtɪz] *n* tratado.

treatment ['triːtmənt] *n* tratamiento; **to have** ~ **for sth** recibir tratamiento por algo.

treaty ['triːtɪ] *n* tratado.

treble ['trebl] *adj* triple ♦ *vt* triplicar ♦ *vi* triplicarse.

treble clef *n* (*MUS*) clave *f* de sol.

tree [triː] *n* árbol *m*.

tree-lined ['triːlaɪnd] *adj* bordeado de árboles.

tree trunk *n* tronco de árbol.

trek [trek] *n* (*long journey*) expedición *f*; (*tiring walk*) caminata.

trellis ['trelɪs] *n* enrejado.

tremble ['trembl] *vi* temblar.

trembling ['tremblɪŋ] *n* temblor *m* ♦ *adj* tembloroso.

tremendous [trɪ'mendəs] *adj* tremendo; (*enormous*) enorme; (*excellent*) estupendo.

tremendously [trɪ'mendəslɪ] *adv* enormemente, sobremanera; **he enjoyed it** ~ lo disfrutó de lo lindo.

tremor ['tremə*] *n* temblor *m*; (*also*: **earth** ~) temblor *m* de tierra.

trench [trentʃ] *n* zanja; (*MIL*) trinchera.

trench coat *n* trinchera.

trench warfare *n* guerra de trincheras.

trend [trend] *n* (*tendency*) tendencia; (*of events*) curso; (*fashion*) moda; ~ **towards/away from sth** tendencia hacia/ en contra de algo; **to set the** ~ marcar la pauta.

trendy ['trendɪ] *adj* de moda.

trepidation [trepɪ'deɪʃən] *n* inquietud *f*.

trespass ['trespəs] *vi*: **to** ~ **on** entrar sin permiso en; **"no ~ing"** "prohibido el paso".

trespasser ['trespəsə*] *n* intruso/a *m/f*; **"~s will be prosecuted"** "se procesará a los intrusos".

tress [tres] *n* guedeja.

trestle ['tresl] *n* caballete *m*.

trestle table *n* mesa de caballete.

tri- [traɪ] *pref* tri-.

trial ['traɪəl] *n* (*LAW*) juicio, proceso; (*test: of machine etc*) prueba; (*hardship*) desgracia; ~**s** *npl* (*ATHLETICS, of horses*) pruebas *fpl*; **to bring sb to** ~ (**for a crime**) llevar a algn a juicio (por un delito); ~ **by jury** juicio ante jurado; **to be sent for** ~ ser remitido al tribunal; **by** ~ **and error** a fuerza de probar.

trial balance *n* balance *m* de comprobación.

trial basis *n*: **on a** ~ a modo de prueba.

trial offer *n* oferta de prueba.

trial run *n* prueba.

triangle ['traɪæŋgl] *n* (*MATH, MUS*) triángulo.

triangular [traɪ'æŋgjulə*] *adj* triangular.

triathlon [traɪ'æθlən] *n* triatlón *m*.

tribal ['traɪbəl] *adj* tribal.

tribe [traɪb] *n* tribu *f*.

tribesman ['traɪbzmən] *n* miembro de una tribu.

tribulation [trɪbju'leɪʃən] *n* tribulación *f*.

tribunal [traɪ'bjuːnl] *n* tribunal *m*.

tributary ['trɪbjuːtərɪ] *n* (*river*) afluente *m*.

tribute ['trɪbjuːt] *n* homenaje *m*, tributo; **to pay** ~ **to** rendir homenaje a.

trice [traɪs] *n*: **in a** ~ en un santiamén.

trick [trɪk] *n* trampa; (*conjuring* ~, *deceit*) truco; (*joke*) broma; (*CARDS*) baza ♦ *vt* engañar; **it's a** ~ **of the light** es una ilusión óptica; **to play a** ~ **on sb** gastar una broma a algn; **that should do the** ~ eso servirá; **to** ~ **sb out of sth** quitarle algo a algn con engaños; **to** ~ **sb into doing sth** hacer que algn haga algo con engaños.

trickery ['trɪkərɪ] *n* engaño.

trickle ['trɪkl] *n* (*of water etc*) hilo ♦ *vi* gotear.

trick question *n* pregunta capciosa.

trickster ['trɪkstə*] *n* estafador(a) *m/f*.
tricky ['trɪkɪ] *adj* difícil; (*problem*) delicado.
tricycle ['traɪsɪkl] *n* triciclo.
tried [traɪd] *adj* probado.
trifle ['traɪfl] *n* bagatela; (*CULIN*) dulce de bizcocho, gelatina, fruta y natillas ♦ *adv*: **a ~ long** un pelín largo ♦ *vi*: **to ~ with** jugar con.
trifling ['traɪflɪŋ] *adj* insignificante.
trigger ['trɪgə*] *n* (*of gun*) gatillo.
▶**trigger off** *vt* desencadenar.
trigonometry [trɪgə'nɔmətrɪ] *n* trigonometría.
trilby ['trɪlbɪ] *n* (*also*: ~ **hat**) sombrero flexible *or* tirolés.
trill [trɪl] *n* (*of bird*) gorjeo; (*MUS*) trino.
trilogy ['trɪlədʒɪ] *n* trilogía.
trim [trɪm] *adj* (*elegant*) aseado; (*house, garden*) en buen estado; (*figure*): **to be ~** tener buen talle ♦ *n* (*haircut etc*) recorte *m* ♦ *vt* (*neaten*) arreglar; (*cut*) recortar; (*decorate*) adornar; (*NAUT: a sail*) orientar; **to keep in (good) ~** mantener en buen estado.
trimmings ['trɪmɪŋz] *npl* (*extras*) accesorios *mpl*; (*cuttings*) recortes *mpl*.
Trinidad and Tobago ['trɪnɪdæd-] *n* Trinidad *f* y Tobago.
Trinity ['trɪnɪtɪ] *n*: **the ~** la Trinidad.
trinket ['trɪŋkɪt] *n* chuchería, baratija.
trio ['triːəu] *n* trío.
trip [trɪp] *n* viaje *m*; (*excursion*) excursión *f*; (*stumble*) traspié *m* ♦ *vi* (*stumble*) tropezar; (*go lightly*) andar a paso ligero; **on a ~** de viaje.
▶**trip over** *vt fus* tropezar con.
▶**trip up** *vi* tropezar, caerse ♦ *vt* hacer tropezar *or* caer.
tripartite [traɪ'pɑːtaɪt] *adj* (*agreement, talks*) tripartito.
tripe [traɪp] *n* (*CULIN*) callos *mpl*; (*pej: rubbish*) bobadas *fpl*.
triple ['trɪpl] *adj* triple ♦ *adv*: **~ the distance/the speed** 3 veces la distancia/la velocidad.
triple jump *n* triple salto.
triplets ['trɪplɪts] *npl* trillizos/as *m/fpl*.
triplicate ['trɪplɪkət] *n*: **in ~** por triplicado.
tripod ['traɪpɔd] *n* trípode *m*.
Tripoli ['trɪpəlɪ] *n* Trípoli *m*.
tripper ['trɪpə*] *n* turista *m/f*, excursionista *m/f*.
tripwire ['trɪpwaɪə*] *n* cable *m* de trampa.
trite [traɪt] *adj* trillado.
triumph ['traɪʌmf] *n* triunfo ♦ *vi*: **to ~ (over)** vencer.
triumphal [traɪ'ʌmfl] *adj* triunfal.
triumphant [traɪ'ʌmfənt] *adj* triunfante.

triumphantly [traɪ'ʌmfəntlɪ] *adv* triunfalmente, en tono triunfal.
trivia ['trɪvɪə] *npl* trivialidades *fpl*.
trivial ['trɪvɪəl] *adj* insignificante, trivial.
triviality [trɪvɪ'ælɪtɪ] *n* insignificancia, trivialidad *f*.
trivialize ['trɪvɪəlaɪz] *vt* trivializar.
trod [trɔd] *pt of* **tread**.
trodden ['trɔdn] *pp of* **tread**.
trolley ['trɔlɪ] *n* carrito; (*in hospital*) camilla.
trolley bus *n* trolebús *m*.
trombone [trɔm'bəun] *n* trombón *m*.
troop [truːp] *n* grupo, banda; *see also* **troops**.
▶**troop in** *vi* entrar en tropel.
▶**troop out** *vi* salir en tropel.
troop carrier *n* (*plane*) transporte *m* (militar); (*NAUT: also*: **troopship**) (buque *m* de) transporte *m*.
trooper ['truːpə*] *n* (*MIL*) soldado (de caballería); (*US: policeman*) policía *m/f* montado/a.
trooping the colour ['truːpɪŋ-] *n* (*ceremony*) presentación *f* de la bandera.
troopship ['truːpʃɪp] *n* (buque *m* de) transporte *m*.
trophy ['trəufɪ] *n* trofeo.
tropic ['trɔpɪk] *n* trópico; **the ~s** los trópicos, la zona tropical; **T~ of Cancer/Capricorn** trópico de Cáncer/Capricornio.
tropical ['trɔpɪkl] *adj* tropical.
trot [trɔt] *n* trote *m* ♦ *vi* trotar; **on the ~** (*BRIT fig*) seguidos/as.
▶**trot out** *vt* (*excuse, reason*) volver a usar; (*names, facts*) sacar a relucir.
trouble ['trʌbl] *n* problema *m*, dificultad *f*; (*worry*) preocupación *f*; (*bother, effort*) molestia, esfuerzo; (*unrest*) inquietud *f*; (*with machine etc*) fallo, avería; (*MED*): **stomach ~** problemas *mpl* gástricos ♦ *vt* molestar; (*worry*) preocupar, inquietar ♦ *vi*: **to ~ to do sth** molestarse en hacer algo; **~s** *npl* (*POL etc*) conflictos *mpl*; **to be in ~** estar en un apuro; (*for doing wrong*) tener problemas; **to have ~ doing sth** tener dificultad en *or* para hacer algo; **to go to the ~ of doing sth** tomarse la molestia de hacer algo; **what's the ~?** ¿qué pasa?; **the ~ is ...** el problema es ..., lo que pasa es ...; **please don't ~ yourself** por favor no se moleste.
troubled ['trʌbld] *adj* (*person*) preocupado; (*epoch, life*) agitado.
trouble-free ['trʌblfriː] *adj* sin problemas *or* dificultades.
troublemaker ['trʌblmeɪkə*] *n* agitador(a) *m/f*.
troubleshooter ['trʌblʃuːtə*] *n* (*in conflict*)

mediador(a) *m/f*.
troublesome ['trʌblsəm] *adj* molesto, inoportuno.
trouble spot *n* centro de fricción, punto caliente.
troubling ['trʌblɪŋ] *adj* (*thought*) preocupante; **these are ~ times** son malos tiempos.
trough [trɔf] *n* (*also*: **drinking ~**) abrevadero; (*also*: **feeding ~**) comedero; (*channel*) canal *m*.
trounce [trauns] *vt* dar una paliza a.
troupe [truːp] *n* grupo.
trouser press *n* prensa para pantalones.
trousers ['trauzəz] *npl* pantalones *mpl*; **short ~** pantalones *mpl* cortos.
trouser suit *n* traje *m* de chaqueta y pantalón.
trousseau, *pl* ~**x** *or* ~**s** ['truːsəu, -z] *n* ajuar *m*.
trout [traut] *n* (*pl inv*) trucha.
trowel ['trauəl] *n* paleta.
truant ['truənt] *n*: **to play ~** (*BRIT*) hacer novillos.
truce [truːs] *n* tregua.
truck [trʌk] *n* (*US*) camión *m*; (*RAIL*) vagón *m*.
truck driver *n* camionero/a.
trucker ['trʌkə*] *n* (*esp US*) camionero/a.
truck farm *n* (*US*) huerto de hortalizas.
trucking ['trʌkɪŋ] *n* (*esp US*) transporte *m* en camión.
trucking company *n* (*US*) compañía de transporte por carretera.
truckload ['trʌkləud] *n* camión *m* lleno.
truculent ['trʌkjulənt] *adj* agresivo.
trudge [trʌdʒ] *vi* caminar penosamente.
true [truː] *adj* verdadero; (*accurate*) exacto; (*genuine*) auténtico; (*faithful*) fiel; (*wheel*) centrado; a plomo; (*beam*) alineado; ~ **to life** verídico; **to come ~** realizarse, cumplirse.
truffle ['trʌfl] *n* trufa.
truly ['truːlɪ] *adv* realmente; (*faithfully*) fielmente; **yours ~** (*in letter-writing*) atentamente.
trump [trʌmp] *n* (*CARDS*) triunfo; **to turn up ~s** (*fig*) salir *or* resultar bien.
trump card *n* triunfo; (*fig*) baza.
trumped-up ['trʌmptʌp] *adj* inventado.
trumpet ['trʌmpɪt] *n* trompeta.
truncated [trʌŋ'keɪtɪd] *adj* truncado.
truncheon ['trʌntʃən] *n* (*BRIT*) porra.
trundle ['trʌndl] *vt, vi*: **to ~ along** rodar haciendo ruido.
trunk [trʌŋk] *n* (*of tree, person*) tronco; (*of elephant*) trompa; (*case*) baúl *m*; (*US AUT*) maletero, baúl *m* (*LAM*); *see also* **trunks**.

trunk call *n* (*BRIT TEL*) llamada interurbana.
trunk road *n* carretera principal.
trunks [trʌŋks] *npl* (*also*: **swimming ~**) bañador *m*.
truss [trʌs] *n* (*MED*) braguero ♦ *vt*: **to ~ (up)** atar.
trust [trʌst] *n* confianza; (*COMM*) trust *m*; (*LAW*) fideicomiso ♦ *vt* (*rely on*) tener confianza en; (*entrust*): **to ~ sth to sb** confiar algo a algn; (*hope*): **to ~ (that)** esperar (que); **in ~** en fideicomiso; **you'll have to take it on ~** tienes que aceptarlo a ojos cerrados.
trust company *n* banco fideicomisario.
trusted ['trʌstɪd] *adj* de confianza, fiable, de fiar.
trustee [trʌs'tiː] *n* (*LAW*) fideicomisario.
trustful ['trʌstful] *adj* confiado.
trust fund *n* fondo fiduciario *or* de fideicomiso.
trusting ['trʌstɪŋ] *adj* confiado.
trustworthy ['trʌstwəːðɪ] *adj* digno de confianza, fiable, de fiar.
trusty ['trʌstɪ] *adj* fiel.
truth, ~**s** [truːθ, truːðz] *n* verdad *f*.
truthful ['truːθful] *adj* (*person*) sincero; (*account*) fidedigno.
truthfully ['truːθfulɪ] *adv* (*answer*) con sinceridad.
truthfulness ['truːθfulnɪs] *n* (*of account*) verdad *f*; (*of person*) sinceridad *f*.
try [traɪ] *n* tentativa, intento; (*RUGBY*) ensayo ♦ *vt* (*LAW*) juzgar, procesar; (*test: sth new*) probar, someter a prueba; (*attempt*) intentar; (*strain: patience*) hacer perder ♦ *vi* probar; **to give sth a ~** intentar hacer algo; **to ~ one's (very) best** *or* **hardest** poner todo su empeño, esmerarse; **to ~ to do sth** intentar hacer algo.
▶**try on** *vt* (*clothes*) probarse.
▶**try out** *vt* probar, poner a prueba.
trying ['traɪɪŋ] *adj* cansado; (*person*) pesado.
tsar [zɑː*] *n* zar *m*.
T-shirt ['tiːʃəːt] *n* camiseta.
T-square ['tiːskwɛə*] *n* regla en T.
TT *adj abbr* (*BRIT col*) = **teetotal** ♦ *abbr* (*US*) = Trust Territory.
tub [tʌb] *n* cubo (*SP*), balde *m* (*LAM*); (*bath*) bañera, tina (*esp LAM*).
tuba ['tjuːbə] *n* tuba.
tubby ['tʌbɪ] *adj* regordete.
tube [tjuːb] *n* tubo; (*BRIT: underground*) metro; (*US col: television*) tele *f*.
tubeless ['tjuːblɪs] *adj* (*tyre*) sin cámara.
tuber ['tjuːbə*] *n* (*BOT*) tubérculo.
tuberculosis [tjubəːkju'ləusɪs] *n*

tuberculosis *f inv.*

tube station *n* (*BRIT*) estación *f* de metro.

tubing ['tjuːbɪŋ] *n* tubería (*SP*), cañería; **a piece of** ~ un trozo de tubo.

tubular ['tjuːbjulə*] *adj* tubular.

TUC *n abbr* (*BRIT*: = Trades Union Congress) *federación nacional de sindicatos.*

tuck [tʌk] *n* (*SEWING*) pliegue *m* ♦ *vt* (*put*) poner.

▶**tuck away** *vt* esconder.

▶**tuck in** *vt* meter; (*child*) arropar ♦ *vi* (*eat*) comer con apetito.

▶**tuck up** *vt* (*child*) arropar.

tuck shop *n* (*SCOL*) tienda de golosinas.

Tue(s). *abbr* (= *Tuesday*) mart.

Tuesday ['tjuːzdɪ] *n* martes *m inv*; **on** ~ el martes; **on** ~**s** los martes; **every** ~ todos los martes; **every other** ~ cada dos martes, un martes sí y otro no; **last/next** ~ el martes pasado/próximo; **a week/ fortnight on** ~, ~ **week/fortnight** del martes en 8/15 días, del martes en una semana/dos semanas.

tuft [tʌft] *n* mechón *m*; (*of grass etc*) manojo.

tug [tʌg] *n* (*ship*) remolcador *m* ♦ *vt* remolcar.

tug-of-love [tʌgəv'lʌv] *n*: ~ **children** hijos envueltos en el litigio de los padres por su custodia.

tug-of-war [tʌgəv'wɔː*] *n* juego de la cuerda.

tuition [tjuː'ɪʃən] *n* (*BRIT*) enseñanza; (: *private* ~) clases *fpl* particulares; (*US: school fees*) matrícula.

tulip ['tjuːlɪp] *n* tulipán *m.*

tumble ['tʌmbl] *n* (*fall*) caída ♦ *vi* caerse, tropezar; **to** ~ **to sth** (*col*) caer en la cuenta de algo.

tumbledown ['tʌmbldaun] *adj* ruinoso.

tumble dryer *n* (*BRIT*) secadora *f.*

tumbler ['tʌmblə*] *n* vaso.

tummy ['tʌmɪ] *n* (*col*) barriga, vientre *m.*

tumour, (*US*) **tumor** ['tjuːmə*] *n* tumor *m.*

tumult ['tjuːmʌlt] *n* tumulto.

tumultuous [tjuː'mʌltjuəs] *adj* tumultuoso.

tuna ['tjuːnə] *n* (*pl inv*) (*also*: ~ **fish**) atún *m.*

tundra ['tʌndrə] *n* tundra.

tune [tjuːn] *n* (*melody*) melodía ♦ *vt* (*MUS*) afinar; (*RADIO, TV, AUT*) sintonizar; **to be in/out of** ~ (*instrument*) estar afinado/ desafinado; (*singer*) afinar/desafinar; **to be in/out of** ~ **with** (*fig*) armonizar/ desentonar con; **to the** ~ **of** (*fig: amount*) por (la) cantidad de.

▶**tune in** *vi* (*RADIO, TV*): **to** ~ **in (to)** sintonizar (con).

▶**tune up** *vi* (*musician*) afinar (su instrumento).

tuneful ['tjuːnful] *adj* melodioso.

tuner ['tjuːnə*] *n* (*radio set*) sintonizador *m*; **piano** ~ afinador(a) *m/f* de pianos.

tungsten ['tʌŋstn] *n* tungsteno.

tunic ['tjuːnɪk] *n* túnica.

tuning ['tjuːnɪŋ] *n* sintonización *f*; (*MUS*) afinación *f.*

tuning fork *n* diapasón *m.*

Tunis ['tjuːnɪs] *n* Túnez *m.*

Tunisia [tjuː'nɪzɪə] *n* Túnez *m.*

Tunisian [tjuː'nɪzɪən] *adj, n* tunecino/a *m/f.*

tunnel ['tʌnl] *n* túnel *m*; (*in mine*) galería ♦ *vi* construir un túnel/una galería.

tunnel vision *n* (*MED*) visión *f* periférica restringida; (*fig*) estrechez *f* de miras.

tunny ['tʌnɪ] *n* atún *m.*

turban ['təːbən] *n* turbante *m.*

turbid ['təːbɪd] *adj* turbio.

turbine ['təːbaɪn] *n* turbina.

turbo ['təːbəu] *n* turbo.

turboprop ['təːbəuprɔp] *n* turbohélice *m.*

turbot ['təːbət] *n* (*pl inv*) rodaballo.

turbulence ['təːbjuləns] *n* (*AVIAT*) turbulencia.

turbulent ['təːbjulənt] *adj* turbulento.

tureen [tə'riːn] *n* sopera.

turf [təːf] *n* césped *m*; (*clod*) tepe *m* ♦ *vt* cubrir con césped.

▶**turf out** *vt* (*col*) echar a la calle.

turf accountant *n* corredor(a) *m/f* de apuestas.

turgid ['təːdʒɪd] *adj* (*prose*) pesado.

Turin [tjuə'rɪn] *n* Turín *m.*

Turk [təːk] *n* turco/a.

Turkey ['təːkɪ] *n* Turquía.

turkey ['təːkɪ] *n* pavo.

Turkish ['təːkɪʃ] *adj* turco ♦ *n* (*LING*) turco.

Turkish bath *n* baño turco.

turmeric ['təːmərɪk] *n* cúrcuma.

turmoil ['təːmɔɪl] *n* desorden *m*, alboroto.

turn [təːn] *n* turno; (*in road*) curva; (*THEAT*) número; (*MED*) ataque *m* ♦ *vt* girar, volver, voltear (*LAM*); (*collar, steak*) dar la vuelta a; (*shape: wood, metal*) tornear; (*change*): **to** ~ **sth into** convertir algo en ♦ *vi* volver, voltearse (*LAM*); (*person: look back*) volverse; (*reverse direction*) dar la vuelta, voltear (*LAM*); (*milk*) cortarse; (*change*) cambiar; (*become*): **to** ~ **into sth** convertirse *or* transformarse en algo; **a good** ~ un favor; **it gave me quite a** ~ me dio un susto; **"no left** ~**"** (*AUT*) "prohibido girar a la izquierda"; **it's your** ~ te toca a ti; **in** ~ por turnos; **to take** ~**s** turnarse; **at the** ~ **of the year/century** a fin de año/a finales de siglo; **to take a** ~ **for the worse** (*situation, patient*) empeorar; **they** ~**ed him against us** le pusieron en contra nuestra; **the car ~ed the corner** el coche dobló la esquina; **to ~ left** (*AUT*) torcer *or* girar a la izquierda; **she has no-one to ~** to no tiene a quién recurrir.

▶**turn away** *vi* apartar la vista ♦ *vt* (*reject*: *person, business*) rechazar.

▶**turn back** *vi* volverse atrás.

▶**turn down** *vt* (*refuse*) rechazar; (*reduce*) bajar; (*fold*) doblar.

▶**turn in** *vi* (*col: go to bed*) acostarse ♦ *vt* (*fold*) doblar hacia dentro.

▶**turn off** *vi* (*from road*) desviarse ♦ *vt* (*light, radio etc*) apagar; (*engine*) parar.

▶**turn on** *vt* (*light, radio etc*) encender, prender (*LAM*); (*engine*) poner en marcha.

▶**turn out** *vt* (*light, gas*) apagar; (*produce*: *goods, novel etc*) producir ♦ *vi* (*attend*: *troops*) presentarse; (: *doctor*) atender; **to ~ out to be ...** resultar ser ....

▶**turn over** *vi* (*person*) volverse ♦ *vt* (*mattress, card*) dar la vuelta a; (*page*) volver.

▶**turn round** *vi* volverse; (*rotate*) girar.

▶**turn to** *vt fus*: **to ~ to sb** acudir a algn.

▶**turn up** *vi* (*person*) llegar, presentarse; (*lost object*) aparecer ♦ *vt* (*radio*) subir, poner más alto; (*heat, gas*) poner más fuerte.

turnabout ['tə:nəbaut], **turnaround** ['tə:nəraund] *n* (*fig*) giro total.

turncoat ['tə:nkəut] *n* renegado/a.

turned-up ['tə:ndʌp] *adj* (*nose*) respingón/ ona.

turning ['tə:nıŋ] *n* (*side road*) bocacalle *f*; (*bend*) curva; **the first ~ on the right** la primera bocacalle a la derecha.

turning point *n* (*fig*) momento decisivo.

turnip ['tə:nıp] *n* nabo.

turnkey system ['tə:nki:-] *n* (*COMPUT*) sistema *m* de seguridad.

turnout ['tə:naut] *n* asistencia, número de asistentes, público.

turnover ['tə:nəuvə*] *n* (*COMM*: *amount of money*) facturación *f*; (: *of goods*) movimiento; **there is a rapid ~ in staff** hay mucho movimiento de personal.

turnpike ['tə:npaık] *n* (*US*) autopista de peaje.

turnstile ['tə:nstail] *n* torniquete *m*.

turntable ['tə:nteibl] *n* plato.

turn-up ['tə:nʌp] *n* (*BRIT*: *on trousers*) vuelta.

turpentine ['tə:pəntain] *n* (*also*: **turps**) trementina.

turquoise ['tə:kwɔiz] *n* (*stone*) turquesa ♦ *adj* color turquesa.

turret ['tʌrit] *n* torreón *m*.

turtle ['tə:tl] *n* tortuga (marina).

turtleneck (sweater) ['tə:tlnɛk-] *n* (jersey *m* de) cuello cisne.

Tuscany ['tʌskəni] *n* Toscana.

tusk [tʌsk] *n* colmillo.

tussle ['tʌsl] *n* lucha, pelea.

tutor ['tju:tə*] *n* profesor(a) *m/f*.

tutorial [tju:'tɔ:riəl] *n* (*SCOL*) seminario.

tuxedo [tʌk'si:dəu] *n* (*US*) smóking *m*, esmoquin *m*.

TV [ti:'vi:] *n abbr* (= *television*) televisión *f*.

TV dinner *n* cena precocinada.

TV licence *n* licencia que se paga por el uso del televisor, destinada a financiar la BBC.

twaddle ['twɔdl] *n* (*col*) tonterías *fpl*.

twang [twæŋ] *n* (*of instrument*) tañido; (*of voice*) timbre *m* nasal.

tweak [twi:k] *vt* (*nose, ear*) pellizcar; (*hair*) tirar.

tweed [twi:d] *n* tweed *m*.

tweezers ['twi:zəz] *npl* pinzas *fpl* (de depilar).

twelfth [twɛlfθ] *num* duodécimo.

Twelfth Night *n* (Día *m* de) Reyes *mpl*.

twelve [twɛlv] *num* doce; **at ~ o'clock** (*midday*) a mediodía; (*midnight*) a medianoche.

twentieth ['twɛntııθ] *num* vigésimo.

twenty ['twɛntı] *num* veinte.

twerp [twə:p] *n* (*col*) idiota *m/f*.

twice [twais] *adv* dos veces; **~ as much** dos veces más, el doble; **she is ~ your age** ella te dobla edad; **~ a week** dos veces a la *or* por semana.

twiddle ['twidl] *vt*, *vi*: **to ~ (with) sth** dar vueltas a algo; **to ~ one's thumbs** (*fig*) estar de brazos cruzados.

twig [twig] *n* ramita ♦ *vi* (*col*) caer en la cuenta.

twilight ['twailait] *n* crepúsculo; (*morning*) madrugada; **in the ~** en la media luz.

twill [twil] *n* sarga, estameña.

twin [twin] *adj*, *n* gemelo/a *m/f* ♦ *vt* hermanar.

twin(-bedded) room ['twin('bɛdid)-] *n* habitación *f* con dos camas.

twin beds *npl* camas *fpl* gemelas.

twin-carburettor ['twinkɑ:bju'rɛtə*] *adj* de dos carburadores.

twine [twain] *n* bramante *m* ♦ *vi* (*plant*) enroscarse.

twin-engined [twin'ɛndʒind] *adj* bimotor; **~ aircraft** avión *m* bimotor.

twinge [twindʒ] *n* (*of pain*) punzada; (*of conscience*) remordimiento.

twinkle ['twiŋkl] *n* centelleo ♦ *vi* centellear; (*eyes*) parpadear.

twin town *n* ciudad *f* hermanada *or*

gemela.

twirl [twɜːl] *n* giro ♦ *vt* dar vueltas a ♦ *vi* piruetear.

twist [twɪst] *n* (*action*) torsión *f*; (*in road, coil*) vuelta; (*in wire, flex*) doblez *f*; (*in story*) giro ♦ *vt* torcer, retorcer; (*roll around*) enrollar; (*fig*) deformar ♦ *vi* serpentear; **to ~ one's ankle/wrist** (*MED*) torcerse el tobillo/la muñeca.

twisted ['twɪstɪd] *adj* (*wire, rope*) trenzado, enroscado; (*ankle, wrist*) torcido; (*fig: logic, mind*) retorcido.

twit [twɪt] *n* (*col*) tonto.

twitch [twɪtʃ] *n* sacudida; (*nervous*) tic *m* nervioso ♦ *vi* moverse nerviosamente.

two [tuː] *num* dos; **~ by ~**, **in ~s** de dos en dos; **to put ~ and ~ together** (*fig*) atar cabos.

two-bit [tuːˈbɪt] *adj* (*esp US col, pej*) de poca monta, de tres al cuarto.

two-door [tuːˈdɔː*] *adj* (*AUT*) de dos puertas.

two-faced [tuːˈfeɪst] *adj* (*pej: person*) falso, hipócrita.

twofold ['tuːfəuld] *adv*: **to increase ~** duplicarse ♦ *adj* (*increase*) doble; (*reply*) en dos partes.

two-piece [tuːˈpiːs] *n* (*also*: **~ suit**) traje *m* de dos piezas; (*also*: **~ swimsuit**) dos piezas *m inv*, bikini *m*.

two-seater [tuːˈsiːtə*] *n* (*plane, car*) avión *m*/coche *m* de dos plazas, biplaza *m*.

twosome ['tuːsəm] *n* (*people*) pareja.

two-stroke ['tuːstrəuk] *n* (*also*: **~ engine**) motor *m* de dos tiempos ♦ *adj* de dos tiempos.

two-tone ['tuːtəun] *adj* (*colour*) bicolor, de dos tonos.

two-way [tuːˈweɪ] *adj*: **~ traffic** circulación *f* de dos sentidos; **~ radio** radio *f* emisora y receptora.

TX *abbr* (*US*) = **Texas**.

tycoon [taɪˈkuːn] *n*: **(business) ~** magnate *m/f*.

type [taɪp] *n* (*category*) tipo, género; (*model*) modelo; (*TYP*) tipo, letra ♦ *vt* (*letter etc*) escribir a máquina; **what ~ do you want?** ¿qué tipo quieres?; **in bold/italic ~** en negrita/cursiva.

type-cast ['taɪpkɑːst] *adj* (*actor*) encasillado.

typeface ['taɪpfeɪs] *n* tipo de letra.

typescript ['taɪpskrɪpt] *n* texto mecanografiado.

typeset ['taɪpsɛt] *vt* (*irreg: like* **set**) componer.

typesetter ['taɪpsɛtə*] *n* cajista *m/f*.

typewriter ['taɪpraɪtə*] *n* máquina de escribir.

typewritten ['taɪprɪtn] *adj* mecanografiado.

typhoid ['taɪfɔɪd] *n* (fiebre *f*) tifoidea.

typhoon [taɪˈfuːn] *n* tifón *m*.

typhus ['taɪfəs] *n* tifus *m*.

typical ['tɪpɪkl] *adj* típico.

typically ['tɪpɪklɪ] *adv* típicamente.

typify ['tɪpɪfaɪ] *vt* tipificar.

typing ['taɪpɪŋ] *n* mecanografía.

typing pool *n* (*BRIT*) servicio de mecanógrafos.

typist ['taɪpɪst] *n* mecanógrafo/a.

typography [taɪˈpɔgrəfɪ] *n* tipografía.

tyranny ['tɪrənɪ] *n* tiranía.

tyrant ['taɪərənt] *n* tirano/a.

tyre, (*US*) **tire** ['taɪə*] *n* neumático, llanta (*LAM*).

tyre pressure *n* presión *f* de los neumáticos.

Tyrol [tɪˈrəul] *n* Tirol *m*.

Tyrolean [tɪrəˈlɪən], **Tyrolese** [tɪrəˈliːz] *adj* tirolés/esa.

Tyrrhenian Sea [tɪˈriːnɪən-] *n* Mar *m* Tirreno.

tzar [zɑː*] *n* = **tsar**.

U u

U, u [juː] *n* (*letter*) U, u *f*; **U for Uncle** U de Uruguay.

U *n abbr* (*BRIT CINE*: = *universal*) todos los públicos.

UB40 *n abbr* (*BRIT*: = *unemployment benefit form 40*) número de referencia en la solicitud de inscripción en la lista de parados; por extensión, la tarjeta del paro o su beneficiario.

U-bend ['juːbɛnd] *n* (*AUT, in pipe*) recodo.

ubiquitous [juːˈbɪkwɪtəs] *adj* omnipresente, ubicuo.

UCAS ['juːkæs] *n abbr BRIT*: = *Universities and Colleges Admissions Service*.

UDA *n abbr* (*BRIT*: = *Ulster Defence Association*) organización paramilitar protestante de Irlanda del Norte.

UDC *n abbr* (*BRIT*) = *Urban District Council*.

udder ['ʌdə*] *n* ubre *f*.

UDI *n abbr* (*BRIT POL*) = *unilateral declaration of independence*.

UDR *n abbr* (*BRIT*: = *Ulster Defence Regiment*) fuerza de seguridad de Irlanda del Norte.

UEFA [juːˈeɪfə] *n abbr* (= *Union of European Football Associations*) U.E.F.A. *f.*

UFO [ˈjuːfəu] *n abbr* = (*unidentified flying object*) OVNI *m.*

Uganda [juːˈɡændə] *n* Uganda.

Ugandan [juːˈɡændən] *adj* de Uganda.

UGC *n abbr* (*BRIT*: = *University Grants Committee*) entidad gubernamental que controla las finanzas de las universidades.

ugh [əːh] *excl* ¡uf!

ugliness [ˈʌɡlɪnɪs] *n* fealdad *f.*

ugly [ˈʌɡlɪ] *adj* feo; (*dangerous*) peligroso.

UHF *abbr* (= *ultra-high frequency*) UHF *f.*

UHT *adj abbr* (= *ultra heat treated*): ~ **milk** leche *f* uperizada.

UK *n abbr* (= *United Kingdom*) Reino Unido, R.U.

Ukraine [juːˈkreɪn] *n* Ucrania.

Ukrainian [juːˈkreɪnɪən] *adj* ucraniano ♦ *n* ucraniano/a; (*LING*) ucraniano.

ulcer [ˈʌlsə*] *n* úlcera; **mouth** ~ úlcera bucal.

Ulster [ˈʌlstə*] *n* Ulster *m.*

ulterior [ʌlˈtɪərɪə*] *adj* ulterior; ~ **motive** segundas intenciones *fpl.*

ultimate [ˈʌltɪmət] *adj* último, final; (*greatest*) mayor ♦ *n*: **the** ~ **in luxury** el colmo del lujo.

ultimately [ˈʌltɪmətlɪ] *adv* (*in the end*) por último, al final; (*fundamentally*) a fin de cuentas.

ultimatum, *pl* ~**s** *or* **ultimata** [ʌltɪˈmeɪtəm, -tə] *n* ultimátum *m.*

ultra- [ˈʌltrə] *pref* ultra-.

ultrasonic [ʌltrəˈsɔnɪk] *adj* ultrasónico.

ultrasound [ˈʌltrəsaund] *n* (*MED*) ultrasonido.

ultraviolet [ˈʌltrəˈvaɪəlɪt] *adj* ultravioleta.

um [ʌm] *interj*; (*col*: *in hesitation*) esto, este (*LAM*).

umbilical cord [ʌmbɪˈlaɪkl-] *n* cordón *m* umbilical.

umbrage [ˈʌmbrɪdʒ] *n*: **to take** ~ (**at**) ofenderse (por).

umbrella [ʌmˈbrelə] *n* paraguas *m inv*; **under the** ~ **of** (*fig*) bajo la protección de.

umlaut [ˈumlaut] *n* diéresis *f inv.*

umpire [ˈʌmpaɪə*] *n* árbitro ♦ *vt* arbitrar.

umpteen [ʌmpˈtiːn] *num* enésimos/as; **for the** ~**th time** por enésima vez.

UMW *n abbr* (= *United Mineworkers of America*) sindicato de mineros.

UN *n abbr* (= *United Nations*) ONU *f.*

un- [ʌn] *pref* in-; des-; no ...; poco ...; nada ....

unabashed [ʌnəˈbæʃt] *adj* nada avergonzado.

unabated [ʌnəˈbeɪtɪd] *adj*: **to continue** ~ seguir con la misma intensidad.

unable [ʌnˈeɪbl] *adj*: **to be** ~ **to do sth** no poder hacer algo; (*not know how to*) ser incapaz de hacer algo, no saber hacer algo.

unabridged [ʌnəˈbrɪdʒd] *adj* íntegro.

unacceptable [ʌnəkˈsɛptəbl] *adj* (*proposal, behaviour, price*) inaceptable; **it's** ~ **that** no se puede aceptar que.

unaccompanied [ʌnəˈkʌmpənɪd] *adj* no acompañado; (*singing, song*) sin acompañamiento.

unaccountably [ʌnəˈkauntəblɪ] *adv* inexplicablemente.

unaccounted [ʌnəˈkauntɪd] *adj*: **two passengers are** ~ **for** faltan dos pasajeros.

unaccustomed [ʌnəˈkʌstəmd] *adj*: **to be** ~ **to** no estar acostumbrado a.

unacquainted [ʌnəˈkweɪntɪd] *adj*: **to be** ~ **with** (*facts*) desconocer, ignorar.

unadulterated [ʌnəˈdʌltəreɪtɪd] *adj* (*gen*) puro; (*wine*) sin mezcla.

unaffected [ʌnəˈfɛktɪd] *adj* (*person, behaviour*) sin afectación, sencillo; (*emotionally*): **to be** ~ **by** no estar afectado por.

unafraid [ʌnəˈfreɪd] *adj*: **to be** ~ no tener miedo.

unaided [ʌnˈeɪdɪd] *adj* sin ayuda, por sí solo.

unanimity [juːnəˈnɪmɪtɪ] *n* unanimidad *f.*

unanimous [juːˈnænɪməs] *adj* unánime.

unanimously [juːˈnænɪməslɪ] *adv* unánimemente.

unanswered [ʌnˈɑːnsəd] *adj* (*question, letter*) sin contestar; (*criticism*) incontestado.

unappetizing [ʌnˈæpɪtaɪzɪŋ] *adj* poco apetitoso.

unappreciative [ʌnəˈpriːʃɪətɪv] *adj* desagradecido.

unarmed [ʌnˈɑːmd] *adj* (*person*) desarmado; (*combat*) sin armas.

unashamed [ʌnəˈʃeɪmd] *adj* desvergonzado.

unassisted [ʌnəˈsɪstɪd] *adj, adv* sin ayuda.

unassuming [ʌnəˈsjuːmɪŋ] *adj* modesto, sin pretensiones.

unattached [ʌnəˈtætʃt] *adj* (*person*) soltero; (*part etc*) suelto.

unattended [ʌnəˈtɛndɪd] *adj* (*car, luggage*) sin atender.

unattractive [ʌnəˈtræktɪv] *adj* poco atractivo.

unauthorized [ʌnˈɔːθəraɪzd] *adj* no autorizado.

unavailable [ʌnəˈveɪləbl] *adj* (*article, room*,

book) no disponible; (*person*) ocupado.

unavoidable [ʌnə'vɔɪdəbl] *adj* inevitable.

unavoidably [ʌnə'vɔɪdəblɪ] *adv* (*detained*) por causas ajenas a su voluntad.

unaware [ʌnə'wɛə*] *adj*: **to be ~ of** ignorar.

unawares [ʌnə'wɛəz] *adv* de improviso.

unbalanced [ʌn'bælənst] *adj* desequilibrado; (*mentally*) trastornado.

unbearable [ʌn'bɛərəbl] *adj* insoportable.

unbeatable [ʌn'biːtəbl] *adj* (*gen*) invencible; (*price*) inmejorable.

unbeaten [ʌn'biːtn] *adj* (*team*) imbatido; (*army*) invicto; (*record*) no batido.

unbecoming [ʌnbɪ'kʌmɪŋ] *adj* (*unseemly: language, behaviour*) indecoroso, impropio; (*unflattering: garment*) poco favorecedor(a).

unbeknown(st) [ʌnbɪ'nəun(st)] *adv*: **~ to me** sin saberlo yo.

unbelief [ʌnbɪ'liːf] *n* incredulidad *f*.

unbelievable [ʌnbɪ'liːvəbl] *adj* increíble.

unbelievingly [ʌnbɪ'liːvɪŋlɪ] *adv* sin creer.

unbend [ʌn'bend] (*irreg: like* **bend**) *vi* (*fig: person*) relajarse ♦ *vt* (*wire*) enderezar.

unbending [ʌn'bendɪŋ] *adj* (*fig*) inflexible.

unbias(s)ed [ʌn'baɪəst] *adj* imparcial.

unblemished [ʌn'blemɪʃt] *adj* sin mancha.

unblock [ʌn'blɔk] *vt* (*pipe*) desatascar; (*road*) despejar.

unborn [ʌn'bɔːn] *adj* que va a nacer.

unbounded [ʌn'baundɪd] *adj* ilimitado, sin límite.

unbreakable [ʌn'breɪkəbl] *adj* irrompible.

unbridled [ʌn'braɪdld] *adj* (*fig*) desenfrenado.

unbroken [ʌn'brəukən] *adj* (*seal*) intacto; (*series*) continuo, ininterrumpido; (*record*) no batido; (*spirit*) indómito.

unbuckle [ʌn'bʌkl] *vt* desabrochar.

unburden [ʌn'bɜːdn] *vt*: **to ~ o.s.** desahogarse.

unbusinesslike [ʌn'bɪznɪslaɪk] *adj* (*trader*) poco profesional; (*transaction*) incorrecto; (*fig: person*) poco práctico; (*: without method*) desorganizado.

unbutton [ʌn'bʌtn] *vt* desabrochar.

uncalled-for [ʌn'kɔːldfɔː*] *adj* gratuito, inmerecido.

uncanny [ʌn'kænɪ] *adj* extraño, extraordinario.

unceasing [ʌn'siːsɪŋ] *adj* incesante.

unceremonious ['ʌnsɛrɪ'məunɪəs] *adj* (*abrupt, rude*) brusco, hosco.

uncertain [ʌn'sɜːtn] *adj* incierto; (*indecisive*) indeciso; **it's ~ whether** no se sabe si; **in no ~ terms** sin dejar lugar a dudas.

uncertainty [ʌn'sɜːtntɪ] *n* incertidumbre *f*.

unchallenged [ʌn'tʃælɪndʒd] *adj* (*LAW etc*)

incontestado; **to go ~** no encontrar respuesta.

unchanged [ʌn'tʃeɪndʒd] *adj* sin cambiar *or* alterar.

uncharitable [ʌn'tʃærɪtəbl] *adj* (*remark, behaviour*) demasiado duro.

uncharted [ʌn'tʃɑːtɪd] *adj* inexplorado.

unchecked [ʌn'tʃɛkt] *adj* desenfrenado.

uncivil [ʌn'sɪvɪl] *adj* descortés, grosero.

uncivilized [ʌn'sɪvɪlaɪzd] *adj* (*gen*) inculto, poco civilizado; (*fig: behaviour etc*) bárbaro.

uncle ['ʌŋkl] *n* tío.

unclear [ʌn'klɪə*] *adj* poco claro; **I'm still ~ about what I'm supposed to do** todavía no tengo muy claro lo que tengo que hacer.

uncoil [ʌn'kɔɪl] *vt* desenrollar ♦ *vi* desenrollarse.

uncomfortable [ʌn'kʌmfətəbl] *adj* incómodo; (*uneasy*) inquieto.

uncomfortably [ʌn'kʌmfətəblɪ] *adv* (*uneasily: say*) con inquietud; (*: think*) con remordimiento *or* nerviosismo.

uncommitted [ʌnkə'mɪtɪd] *adj* (*attitude, country*) no comprometido; **to remain ~ to** (*policy, party*) no comprometerse a.

uncommon [ʌn'kɔmən] *adj* poco común, raro.

uncommunicative [ʌnkə'mjuːnɪkətɪv] *adj* poco comunicativo, reservado.

uncomplicated [ʌn'kɔmplɪkeɪtɪd] *adj* sin complicaciones.

uncompromising [ʌn'kɔmprəmaɪzɪŋ] *adj* intransigente.

unconcerned [ʌnkən'sɜːnd] *adj* indiferente; **to be ~ about** ser indiferente a, no preocuparse de.

unconditional [ʌnkən'dɪʃənl] *adj* incondicional.

uncongenial [ʌnkən'dʒiːnɪəl] *adj* desagradable.

unconnected [ʌnkə'nɛktɪd] *adj* (*unrelated*): **to be ~ with** no estar relacionado con.

unconscious [ʌn'kɔnʃəs] *adj* sin sentido; (*unaware*) inconsciente ♦ *n*: **the ~** el inconsciente; **to knock sb ~** dejar a algn sin sentido.

unconsciously [ʌn'kɔnʃəslɪ] *adv* inconscientemente.

unconsciousness [ʌn'kɔnʃəsnɪs] *n* inconsciencia.

unconstitutional [ʌnkɔnstɪ'tjuːʃənl] *adj* anti-constitucional.

uncontested [ʌnkən'tɛstɪd] *adj* (*champion*) incontestado; (*PARLIAMENT: seat*) ganado sin oposición.

uncontrollable [ʌnkən'trəuləbl] *adj* (*temper*)

indomable; (*laughter*) incontenible.

uncontrolled [ʌnkən'trəʊld] *adj* (*child, dog, emotion*) incontrolado; (*inflation, price rises*) desenfrenado.

unconventional [ʌnkən'vɛnʃənl] *adj* poco convencional.

unconvinced [ʌnkən'vɪnst] *adj*: **to be** *or* **remain** ~ seguir sin convencerse.

unconvincing [ʌnkən'vɪnsɪŋ] *adj* poco convincente.

uncork [ʌn'kɔːk] *vt* descorchar.

uncorroborated [ʌnkə'rɔbəreɪtɪd] *adj* no confirmado.

uncouth [ʌn'kuːθ] *adj* grosero, inculto.

uncover [ʌn'kʌvə*] *vt* (*gen*) descubrir; (*take lid off*) destapar.

undamaged [ʌn'dæmɪdʒd] *adj* (*goods*) en buen estado; (*fig: reputation*) intacto.

undaunted [ʌn'dɔːntɪd] *adj*: ~ **by** sin dejarse desanimar por.

undecided [ʌndɪ'saɪdɪd] *adj* (*character*) indeciso; (*question*) no resuelto, pendiente.

undelivered [ʌndɪ'lɪvəd] *adj* no entregado al destinatario; **if** ~ **return to sender** en caso de no llegar a su destino devolver al remitente.

undeniable [ʌndɪ'naɪəbl] *adj* innegable.

undeniably [ʌndɪ'naɪəblɪ] *adv* innegablemente.

under ['ʌndə*] *prep* debajo de; (*less than*) menos de; (*according to*) según, de acuerdo con ♦ *adv* debajo, abajo; ~ **there** ahí debajo; ~ **construction** en construcción; en obras; ~ **the circumstances** dadas las circunstancias; **in** ~ **2 hours** en menos de dos horas; ~ **anaesthetic** bajo los efectos de la anestesia; ~ **discussion** en discusión, sobre el tapete.

under... [ʌndə*] *pref* sub....

under-age [ʌndər'eɪdʒ] *adj* menor de edad.

underarm ['ʌndərɑːm] *n* axila, sobaco ♦ *cpd*: ~ **deodorant** desodorante *m* corporal.

undercapitalised [ʌndə'kæpɪtəlaɪzd] *adj* descapitalizado.

undercarriage ['ʌndəkærɪdʒ] *n* (*BRIT AVIAT*) tren *m* de aterrizaje.

undercharge [ʌndə'tʃɑːdʒ] *vt* cobrar de menos.

underclass ['ʌndəklɑːs] *n* clase *f* marginada.

underclothes ['ʌndəkləʊðz] *npl* ropa *sg* interior *or* íntima (*LAM*).

undercoat ['ʌndəkəʊt] *n* (*paint*) primera mano.

undercover [ʌndə'kʌvə*] *adj* clandestino.

undercurrent ['ʌndəkʌrnt] *n* corriente *f*

submarina; (*fig*) tendencia oculta.

undercut ['ʌndəkʌt] *vt* (*irreg: like* **cut**) vender más barato que; fijar un precio más barato que.

underdeveloped [ʌndədɪ'vɛləpt] *adj* subdesarrollado.

underdog ['ʌndədɒg] *n* desvalido/a.

underdone [ʌndə'dʌn] *adj* (*CULIN*) poco hecho.

underemployment [ʌndərɪm'plɔɪmənt] *n* subempleo.

underestimate [ʌndər'ɛstɪmeɪt] *vt* subestimar.

underexposed [ʌndərɪks'pəʊzd] *adj* (*PHOT*) subexpuesto.

underfed [ʌndə'fɛd] *adj* subalimentado.

underfoot [ʌndə'fʊt] *adv*: **it's wet** ~ el suelo está mojado.

underfunded [ʌndə'fʌndɪd] *adj* infradotado (económicamente).

undergo [ʌndə'gəʊ] *vt* (*irreg: like* **go**) sufrir; (*treatment*) recibir, someterse a; **the car is** ~**ing repairs** están reparando el coche.

undergraduate ['ʌndə'grædjuət] *n* estudiante *m/f* ♦ *cpd*: ~ **courses** cursos *mpl* de licenciatura.

underground ['ʌndəgraund] *n* (*BRIT: railway*) metro; (*POL*) movimiento clandestino ♦ *adj* subterráneo.

undergrowth ['ʌndəgrəʊθ] *n* maleza.

underhand(ed) [ʌndə'hænd(ɪd)] *adj* (*fig*) poco limpio.

underinsured [ʌndərɪn'ʃʊəd] *adj* insuficientemente asegurado.

underlie [ʌndə'laɪ] *vt* (*irreg: like* **lie**) (*fig*) ser la razón fundamental de; **the underlying cause** la causa fundamental.

underline [ʌndə'laɪn] *vt* subrayar.

underling ['ʌndəlɪŋ] *n* (*pej*) subalterno/a.

undermanning [ʌndə'mænɪŋ] *n* falta de personal.

undermentioned [ʌndə'mɛnʃənd] *adj* abajo citado.

undermine [ʌndə'maɪn] *vt* socavar, minar.

underneath [ʌndə'niːθ] *adv* debajo ♦ *prep* debajo de, bajo.

undernourished [ʌndə'nʌrɪʃt] *adj* desnutrido.

underpaid [ʌndə'peɪd] *adj* mal pagado.

underpants ['ʌndəpænts] *npl* calzoncillos *mpl*.

underpass ['ʌndəpɑːs] *n* (*BRIT*) paso subterráneo.

underpin [ʌndə'pɪn] *vt* (*argument, case*) secundar, sostener.

underplay [ʌndə'pleɪ] *vt* (*BRIT*) minimizar.

underpopulated [ʌndə'pɒpjuleɪtɪd] *adj* poco poblado.

underprice [ˌʌndəˈpraɪs] *vt* vender demasiado barato.

underpriced [ˌʌndəˈpraɪst] *adj* con precio demasiado bajo.

underprivileged [ˌʌndəˈprɪvɪlɪdʒd] *adj* desvalido.

underrate [ˌʌndəˈreɪt] *vt* infravalorar, subestimar.

underscore [ˈʌndəskɔː*] *vt* subrayar, sostener.

underseal [ˌʌndəˈsiːl] *vt* (*AUT*) proteger contra la corrosión.

undersecretary [ˌʌndəˈsɛkrətrɪ] *n* subsecretario/a.

undersell [ˌʌndəˈsɛl] *vt* (*competitors*) vender más barato que.

undershirt [ˈʌndəʃəːt] *n* (*US*) camiseta.

undershorts [ˈʌndəʃɔːts] *npl* (*US*) calzoncillos *mpl*.

underside [ˈʌndəsaɪd] *n* parte *f* inferior, revés *m*.

undersigned [ˈʌndəsaɪnd] *adj, n*: **the ~** el/la *etc* abajo firmante.

underskirt [ˈʌndəskəːt] *n* (*BRIT*) enaguas *fpl*.

understaffed [ˌʌndəˈstɑːft] *adj* falto de personal.

understand [ˌʌndəˈstænd] (*irreg: like* **stand**) *vt, vi* entender, comprender; (*assume*) tener entendido; **to make o.s. understood** hacerse entender; **I ~ you have been absent** tengo entendido que (usted) ha estado ausente.

understandable [ˌʌndəˈstændəbl] *adj* comprensible.

understanding [ˌʌndəˈstændɪŋ] *adj* comprensivo ♦ *n* comprensión *f*, entendimiento; (*agreement*) acuerdo; **to come to an ~ with sb** llegar a un acuerdo con algn; **on the ~ that** a condición de que (+ *subjun*).

understate [ˌʌndəˈsteɪt] *vt* minimizar.

understatement [ˌʌndəˈsteɪtmənt] *n* subestimación *f*; (*modesty*) modestia (excesiva); **to say it was good is quite an ~** decir que estuvo bien es quedarse corto.

understood [ˌʌndəˈstʊd] *pt, pp of* **understand** ♦ *adj* entendido; (*implied*): **it is ~ that** se sobreentiende que.

understudy [ˈʌndəstʌdɪ] *n* suplente *m/f*.

undertake [ˌʌndəˈteɪk] (*irreg: like* **take**) *vt* emprender; **to ~ to do sth** comprometerse a hacer algo.

undertaker [ˈʌndəteɪkə*] *n* director(a) *m/f* de pompas fúnebres.

undertaking [ˈʌndəteɪkɪŋ] *n* empresa; (*promise*) promesa.

undertone [ˈʌndətəun] *n* (*of criticism*) connotación *f*; (*low voice*): **in an ~** en voz baja.

undervalue [ˌʌndəˈvæljuː] *vt* (*fig*) subestimar, infravalorar; (*COMM etc*) valorizar por debajo de su precio.

underwater [ˌʌndəˈwɔːtə*] *adv* bajo el agua ♦ *adj* submarino.

underwear [ˈʌndəwɛə*] *n* ropa interior *or* íntima (*LAM*).

underweight [ˌʌndəˈweɪt] *adj* de peso insuficiente; (*person*) demasiado delgado.

underworld [ˈʌndəwəːld] *n* (*of crime*) hampa, inframundo.

underwrite [ˌʌndəˈraɪt] (*irreg: like* **write**) *vt* (*COMM*) suscribir; (*INSURANCE*) asegurar (*contra riesgos*).

underwriter [ˈʌndəraɪtə*] *n* (*INSURANCE*) asegurador/a *m/f*.

undeserving [ˌʌndɪˈzəːvɪŋ] *adj*: **to be ~ of** no ser digno de.

undesirable [ˌʌndɪˈzaɪərəbl] *adj* indeseable.

undeveloped [ˌʌndɪˈvɛləpt] *adj* (*land, resources*) sin explotar.

undies [ˈʌndɪz] *npl* (*col*) paños *mpl* menores.

undiluted [ˌʌndaɪˈluːtɪd] *adj* (*concentrate*) concentrado.

undiplomatic [ˌʌndɪpləˈmætɪk] *adj* poco diplomático.

undischarged [ˌʌndɪsˈtʃɑːdʒd] *adj*: **~ bankrupt** quebrado/a no rehabilitado/a.

undisciplined [ʌnˈdɪsɪplɪnd] *adj* indisciplinado.

undiscovered [ˌʌndɪsˈkʌvəd] *adj* no descubierto; (*unknown*) desconocido.

undisguised [ˌʌndɪsˈgaɪzd] *adj* franco, abierto.

undisputed [ˌʌndɪsˈpjuːtɪd] *adj* incontestable.

undistinguished [ˌʌndɪsˈtɪŋgwɪʃt] *adj* mediocre.

undisturbed [ˌʌndɪsˈtəːbd] *adj* (*sleep*) ininterrumpido; **to leave sth ~** dejar algo tranquilo *or* como está.

undivided [ˌʌndɪˈvaɪdɪd] *adj*: **I want your ~ attention** quiero su completa atención.

undo [ʌnˈduː] *vt* (*irreg: like* **do**) deshacer.

undoing [ʌnˈduːɪŋ] *n* ruina, perdición *f*.

undone [ʌnˈdʌn] *pp of* **undo** ♦ *adj*: **to come ~** (*clothes*) desabrocharse; (*parcel*) desatarse.

undoubted [ʌnˈdautɪd] *adj* indudable.

undoubtedly [ʌnˈdautɪdlɪ] *adv* indudablemente, sin duda.

undress [ʌnˈdrɛs] *vi* desnudarse, desvestirse (*esp LAM*).

undrinkable [ʌnˈdrɪŋkəbl] *adj* (*unpalatable*) imbebible; (*poisonous*) no potable.

undue [ʌnˈdjuː] *adj* indebido, excesivo.

undulating [ˈʌndjuleɪtɪŋ] *adj* ondulante.
unduly [ʌnˈdjuːlɪ] *adv* excesivamente, demasiado.
undying [ʌnˈdaɪɪŋ] *adj* eterno.
unearned [ʌnˈɜːnd] *adj* (*praise, respect*) inmerecido; ~ **income** ingresos *mpl* no ganados, renta no ganada *or* salarial.
unearth [ʌnˈɜːθ] *vt* desenterrar.
unearthly [ʌnˈɜːθlɪ] *adj*: ~ **hour** (*col*) hora intempestiva.
unease [ʌnˈiːz] *n* malestar *m*.
uneasy [ʌnˈiːzɪ] *adj* intranquilo; (*worried*) preocupado; **to feel** ~ **about doing sth** sentirse incómodo con la idea de hacer algo.
uneconomic(al) [ˈʌniːkəˈnɒmɪk(l)] *adj* no económico.
uneducated [ʌnˈɛdjukeɪtɪd] *adj* ignorante, inculto.
unemployed [ʌnɪmˈplɔɪd] *adj* parado, sin trabajo ♦ *n*: **the** ~ los parados.
unemployment [ʌnɪmˈplɔɪmənt] *n* paro, desempleo, cesantía (*LAM*).
unemployment benefit *n* (*BRIT*) subsidio de desempleo *or* paro.
unending [ʌnˈɛndɪŋ] *adj* interminable.
unenviable [ʌnˈɛnvɪəbl] *adj* poco envidiable.
unequal [ʌnˈiːkwəl] *adj* (*length, objects etc*) desigual; (*amounts*) distinto; (*division of labour*) poco justo.
unequalled, (*US*) **unequaled** [ʌnˈiːkwəld] *adj* inigualado, sin par.
unequivocal [ʌnɪˈkwɪvəkəl] *adj* (*answer*) inequívoco, claro; (*person*) claro.
unerring [ʌnˈɜːrɪŋ] *adj* infalible.
UNESCO [juːˈnɛskəu] *n abbr* (= United Nations Educational, Scientific and Cultural Organization) UNESCO *f*.
unethical [ʌnˈɛθɪkəl] *adj* (*methods*) inmoral; (*doctor's behaviour*) que infringe la ética profesional.
uneven [ʌnˈiːvn] *adj* desigual; (*road etc*) con baches.
uneventful [ʌnɪˈvɛntful] *adj* sin incidentes.
unexceptional [ʌnɪkˈsɛpʃənl] *adj* sin nada de extraordinario, corriente.
unexciting [ʌnɪkˈsaɪtɪŋ] *adj* (*news*) sin interés; (*film, evening*) aburrido.
unexpected [ʌnɪkˈspɛktɪd] *adj* inesperado.
unexpectedly [ʌnɪkˈspɛktɪdlɪ] *adv* inesperadamente.
unexplained [ʌnɪksˈpleɪnd] *adj* inexplicado.
unexploded [ʌnɪksˈpləudɪd] *adj* sin explotar.
unfailing [ʌnˈfeɪlɪŋ] *adj* (*support*) indefectible; (*energy*) inagotable.
unfair [ʌnˈfɛə*] *adj*: ~ (**to sb**) injusto (con

algn); **it's** ~ **that** ... es injusto que ..., no es justo que ....
unfair dismissal *n* despido improcedente.
unfairly [ʌnˈfɛəlɪ] *adv* injustamente.
unfaithful [ʌnˈfeɪθful] *adj* infiel.
unfamiliar [ʌnfəˈmɪlɪə*] *adj* extraño, desconocido; **to be** ~ **with sth** desconocer *or* ignorar algo.
unfashionable [ʌnˈfæʃnəbl] *adj* (*clothes*) pasado *or* fuera de moda; (*district*) poco elegante.
unfasten [ʌnˈfɑːsn] *vt* desatar.
unfathomable [ʌnˈfæðəməbl] *adj* insondable.
unfavourable, (*US*) **unfavorable** [ʌnˈfeɪvərəbl] *adj* desfavorable.
unfavo(u)rably [ʌnˈfeɪvrəblɪ] *adv*: **to look** ~ **upon** ser adverso a.
unfeeling [ʌnˈfiːlɪŋ] *adj* insensible.
unfinished [ʌnˈfɪnɪʃt] *adj* inacabado, sin terminar.
unfit [ʌnˈfɪt] *adj* en baja forma; (*incompetent*) incapaz; ~ **for work** no apto para trabajar.
unflagging [ʌnˈflægɪŋ] *adj* incansable.
unflappable [ʌnˈflæpəbl] *adj* imperturbable.
unflattering [ʌnˈflætərɪŋ] *adj* (*dress, hairstyle*) poco favorecedor.
unflinching [ʌnˈflɪntʃɪŋ] *adj* impávido.
unfold [ʌnˈfəuld] *vt* desdoblar; (*fig*) revelar ♦ *vi* abrirse; revelarse.
unforeseeable [ʌnfɔːˈsiːəbl] *adj* imprevisible.
unforeseen [ˈʌnfɔːˈsiːn] *adj* imprevisto.
unforgettable [ʌnfəˈgɛtəbl] *adj* inolvidable.
unforgivable [ʌnfəˈgɪvəbl] *adj* imperdonable.
unformatted [ʌnˈfɔːmætɪd] *adj* (*disk, text*) sin formatear.
unfortunate [ʌnˈfɔːtʃnət] *adj* desgraciado; (*event, remark*) inoportuno.
unfortunately [ʌnˈfɔːtʃnətlɪ] *adv* desgraciadamente, por desgracia.
unfounded [ʌnˈfaundɪd] *adj* infundado.
unfriendly [ʌnˈfrɛndlɪ] *adj* antipático.
unfulfilled [ʌnfulˈfɪld] *adj* (*ambition*) sin realizar; (*prophecy, promise, terms of contract*) incumplido; (*desire, person*) insatisfecho.
unfurl [ʌnˈfɜːl] *vt* desplegar.
unfurnished [ʌnˈfɜːnɪʃt] *adj* sin amueblar.
ungainly [ʌnˈgeɪnlɪ] *adj* (*walk*) desgarbado.
ungodly [ʌnˈgɒdlɪ] *adj*: **at an** ~ **hour** a una hora intempestiva.
ungrateful [ʌnˈgreɪtful] *adj* ingrato.
unguarded [ʌnˈgɑːdɪd] *adj* (*moment*) de descuido.

unhappily [ʌn'hæpɪlɪ] *adv* (*unfortunately*) desgraciadamente.

unhappiness [ʌn'hæpɪnɪs] *n* tristeza.

unhappy [ʌn'haepɪ] *adj* (*sad*) triste; (*unfortunate*) desgraciado; (*childhood*) infeliz; ~ **with** (*arrangements etc*) poco contento con, descontento de.

unharmed [ʌn'hɑːmd] *adj* (*person*) ileso.

UNHCR *n abbr* (= *United Nations High Commission for Refugees*) ACNUR *m*.

unhealthy [ʌn'hɛlθɪ] *adj* (*gen*) malsano, insalubre; (*person*) enfermizo; (*interest*) morboso.

unheard-of [ʌn'hɜːdɔv] *adj* inaudito, sin precedente.

unhelpful [ʌn'hɛlpful] *adj* (*person*) poco servicial; (*advice*) inútil.

unhesitating [ʌn'hɛzɪteɪtɪŋ] *adj* (*loyalty*) automático; (*reply, offer*) inmediato; (*person*) resuelto.

unholy [ʌn'həulɪ] *adj*: **an ~ alliance** una alianza nefasta; **he returned at an ~ hour** volvió a una hora intempestiva.

unhook [ʌn'huk] *vt* desenganchar; (*from wall*) descolgar; (*undo*) desabrochar.

unhurt [ʌn'hɜːt] *adj* ileso.

unhygienic [ʌnhaɪ'dʒiːnɪk] *adj* antihigiénico.

UNICEF ['juːnɪsɛf] *n abbr* (= *United Nations International Children's Emergency Fund*) UNICEF *f*.

unidentified [ʌnaɪ'dɛntɪfaɪd] *adj* no identificado; ~ **flying object (UFO)** objeto volante no identificado.

unification [juːnɪfɪ'keɪʃən] *n* unificación *f*.

uniform ['juːnɪfɔːm] *n* uniforme *m* ♦ *adj* uniforme.

uniformity [juːnɪ'fɔːmɪtɪ] *n* uniformidad *f*.

unify ['juːnɪfaɪ] *vt* unificar, unir.

unilateral [juːnɪ'lætərəl] *adj* unilateral.

unimaginable [ʌnɪ'mædʒɪnəbl] *adj* inconcebible, inimaginable.

unimaginative [ʌnɪ'mædʒɪnətɪv] *adj* falto de imaginación.

unimpaired [ʌnɪm'pɛəd] *adj* (*unharmed*) intacto; (*not lessened*) no disminuido; (*unaltered*) inalterado.

unimportant [ʌnɪm'pɔːtənt] *adj* sin importancia.

unimpressed [ʌnɪm'prɛst] *adj* poco impresionado.

uninhabited [ʌnɪn'hæbɪtɪd] *adj* desierto; (*country*) despoblado; (*house*) deshabitado, desocupado.

uninhibited [ʌnɪn'hɪbɪtɪd] *adj* nada cohibido, desinhibido.

uninjured [ʌn'ɪndʒəd] *adj* (*person*) ileso.

uninspiring [ʌnɪn'spaɪərɪŋ] *adj* anodino.

unintelligent [ʌnɪn'tɛlɪdʒənt] *adj* poco inteligente.

unintentional [ʌnɪn'tɛnʃənəl] *adj* involuntario.

unintentionally [ʌnɪn'tɛnʃnəlɪ] *adv* sin querer.

uninvited [ʌnɪn'vaɪtɪd] *adj* (*guest*) sin invitación.

uninviting [ʌnɪn'vaɪtɪŋ] *adj* (*place, offer*) poco atractivo; (*food*) poco apetecible.

union ['juːnjən] *n* unión *f*; (*also:* **trade ~**) sindicato ♦ *cpd* sindical; **the U~** (*US*) la Unión.

union card *n* carnet *m* de sindicato.

unionize ['juːnjənaɪz] *vt* sindicalizar.

Union Jack *n* bandera del Reino Unido.

Union of Soviet Socialist Republics (USSR) *n* Unión *f* de Repúblicas Socialistas Soviéticas.

union shop *n* (*US*) empresa de afiliación sindical obligatoria.

unique [juː'niːk] *adj* único.

unisex ['juːnɪsɛks] *adj* unisex.

Unison ['juːnɪsn] *n* (*trade union*) gran sindicato de funcionarios.

unison ['juːnɪsn] *n*: **in ~** en armonía.

unissued capital [ʌn'ɪʃuːd-] *n* capital *m* no emitido.

unit ['juːnɪt] *n* unidad *f*; (*team, squad*) grupo; **kitchen ~** módulo de cocina; **production ~** taller *m* de fabricación; **sink ~** fregadero.

unit cost *n* costo unitario.

unite [juː'naɪt] *vt* unir ♦ *vi* unirse.

united [juː'naɪtɪd] *adj* unido.

United Arab Emirates *npl* Emiratos *mpl* Árabes Unidos.

United Kingdom (UK) *n* Reino Unido.

United Nations (Organization) (UN, UNO) *n* Naciones Unidas *fpl* (ONU *f*).

United States (of America) (US, USA) *n* Estados Unidos *mpl* (de América) (EE.UU. *mpl*).

unit price *n* precio unitario.

unit trust *n* (*BRIT*) bono fiduciario.

unity ['juːnɪtɪ] *n* unidad *f*.

Univ. *abbr* = **university**.

universal [juːnɪ'vɜːsl] *adj* universal.

universally [juːnɪ'vɜːsəlɪ] *adv* universalmente.

universe ['juːnɪvɜːs] *n* universo.

university [juːnɪ'vɜːsɪtɪ] *n* universidad *f* ♦ *cpd* (*student, professor, education, degree*) universitario; (*year*) académico; **to be at/ go to ~** estudiar en/ir a la universidad.

unjust [ʌn'dʒʌst] *adj* injusto.

unjustifiable [ʌndʒʌstɪ'faɪəbl] *adj* injustificable.

unjustified [ʌn'dʒʌstɪfaɪd] *adj* (*text*) no alineado *or* justificado.

unkempt [ʌn'kɛmpt] *adj* descuidado; (*hair*) despeinado.

unkind [ʌn'kaɪnd] *adj* poco amable; (*comment etc*) cruel.

unkindly [ʌn'kaɪndlɪ] *adv* (*speak*) severamente; (*treat*) cruelmente, mal.

unknown [ʌn'nəun] *adj* desconocido ♦ *adv*: ~ **to me** sin saberlo yo; ~ **quantity** (*MATH, fig*) incógnita.

unladen [ʌn'leɪdən] *adj* (*weight*) vacío, sin cargamento.

unlawful [ʌn'lɔːful] *adj* ilegal, ilícito.

unleaded [ʌn'lɛdɪd] *n* (*also*: ~ **petrol**) gasolina sin plomo.

unleash [ʌn'liːʃ] *vt* desatar.

unleavened [ʌn'lɛvənd] *adj* ácimo, sin levadura.

unless [ʌn'lɛs] *conj* a menos que; ~ **he comes** a menos que venga; ~ **otherwise stated** salvo indicación contraria; ~ **I am mistaken** si no mi equivoco.

unlicensed [ʌn'laɪsənst] *adj* (*BRIT: to sell alcohol*) no autorizado.

unlike [ʌn'laɪk] *adj* distinto ♦ *prep* a diferencia de.

unlikelihood [ʌn'laɪklɪhud] *n* improbabilidad *f*.

unlikely [ʌn'laɪklɪ] *adj* improbable.

unlimited [ʌn'lɪmɪtɪd] *adj* ilimitado; ~ **liability** responsabilidad *f* ilimitada.

unlisted [ʌn'lɪstɪd] *adj* (*US TEL*) que no figura en la guía; ~ **company** empresa sin cotización en bolsa.

unlit [ʌn'lɪt] *adj* (*room*) oscuro, sin luz.

unload [ʌn'ləud] *vt* descargar.

unlock [ʌn'lɔk] *vt* abrir (con llave).

unlucky [ʌn'lʌkɪ] *adj* desgraciado; (*object, number*) que da mala suerte; **to be** ~ (*person*) tener mala suerte.

unmanageable [ʌn'mænɪdʒəbl] *adj* (*unwieldy: tool, vehicle*) difícil de manejar; (*: situation*) incontrolable.

unmanned [ʌn'mænd] *adj* (*spacecraft*) sin tripulación.

unmannerly [ʌn'mænəlɪ] *adj* mal educado, descortés.

unmarked [ʌn'mɑːkt] *adj* (*unstained*) sin mancha; ~ **police car** vehículo policial camuflado.

unmarried [ʌn'mærɪd] *adj* soltero.

unmask [ʌn'mɑːsk] *vt* desenmascarar.

unmatched [ʌn'mætʃt] *adj* incomparable.

unmentionable [ʌn'mɛnʃnəbl] *adj* (*topic, vice*) indecible; (*word*) que no se debe decir.

unmerciful [ʌn'məːsɪful] *adj* despiadado.

unmistakable [ʌnmɪs'teɪkəbl] *adj* inconfundible.

unmistakably [ʌnmɪs'teɪkəblɪ] *adv* de modo inconfundible.

unmitigated [ʌn'mɪtɪgeɪtɪd] *adj* rematado, absoluto.

unnamed [ʌn'neɪmd] *adj* (*nameless*) sin nombre; (*anonymous*) anónimo.

unnatural [ʌn'nætʃrəl] *adj* (*gen*) antinatural; (*manner*) afectado; (*habit*) perverso.

unnecessary [ʌn'nɛsəsərɪ] *adj* innecesario, inútil.

unnerve [ʌn'nəːv] *vt* (*subj: accident*) poner nervioso; (*: hostile attitude*) acobardar; (*: long wait, interview*) intimidar.

unnoticed [ʌn'nəutɪst] *adj*: **to go** *or* **pass** ~ pasar desapercibido.

UNO ['juːnəu] *n abbr* = (*United Nations Organization*) ONU *f*.

unobservant [ʌnəb'zəːvnt] *adj*: **to be** ~ ser poco observador, ser distraído.

unobtainable [ʌnəb'teɪnəbl] *adj* inasequible; (*TEL*) inexistente.

unobtrusive [ʌnəb'truːsɪv] *adj* discreto.

unoccupied [ʌn'ɔkjupaɪd] *adj* (*house etc*) libre, desocupado.

unofficial [ʌnə'fɪʃl] *adj* no oficial; ~ **strike** huelga no oficial.

unopened [ʌn'əupənd] *adj* (*letter, present*) sin abrir.

unopposed [ʌnə'pəuzd] *adj* (*enter, be elected*) sin oposición.

unorthodox [ʌn'ɔːθədɔks] *adj* poco ortodoxo.

unpack [ʌn'pæk] *vi* deshacer las maletas, desempacar (*LAM*).

unpaid [ʌn'peɪd] *adj* (*bill, debt*) sin pagar, impagado; (*COMM*) pendiente; (*holiday*) sin sueldo; (*work*) sin pago, voluntario.

unpalatable [ʌn'pælətəbl] *adj* (*truth*) desagradable.

unparalleled [ʌn'pærəlɛld] *adj* (*unequalled*) sin par; (*unique*) sin precedentes.

unpatriotic [ʌnpætrɪ'ɔtɪk] *adj* (*person*) poco patriota; (*speech, attitude*) antipatriótico.

unplanned [ʌn'plænd] *adj* (*visit*) imprevisto; (*baby*) no planeado.

unpleasant [ʌn'plɛznt] *adj* (*disagreeable*) desagradable; (*person, manner*) antipático.

unplug [ʌn'plʌg] *vt* desenchufar, desconectar.

unpolluted [ʌnpə'luːtɪd] *adj* impoluto, no contaminado.

unpopular [ʌn'pɔpjulə*] *adj* poco popular; **to be** ~ **with sb** (*person, law*) no ser popular con algn; **to make o.s.** ~ **(with)**

hacerse impopular (con).

unprecedented [ʌn'prɛsɪdəntɪd] *adj* sin precedentes.

unpredictable [ʌnprɪ'dɪktəbl] *adj* imprevisible.

unprejudiced [ʌn'prɛdʒudɪst] *adj* (*not biased*) imparcial; (*having no prejudices*) sin prejuicio.

unprepared [ʌnprɪ'pɛəd] *adj* (*person*) desprevenido; (*speech*) improvisado.

unprepossessing [ʌnpriːpə'zɛsɪŋ] *adj* poco atractivo.

unprincipled [ʌn'prɪnsɪpld] *adj* sin escrúpulos.

unproductive [ʌnprə'dʌktɪv] *adj* improductivo; (*discussion*) infructuoso.

unprofessional [ʌnprə'fɛʃənl] *adj* poco profesional; ~ **conduct** negligencia.

unprofitable [ʌn'prɔfɪtəbl] *adj* poco provechoso, no rentable.

UNPROFOR *n abbr* (= *United Nations Protection Force*) FORPRONU *f*, Unprofor *f*.

unprotected ['ʌnprə'tɛktɪd] *adj* (*sex*) sin protección.

unprovoked [ʌnprə'vəukt] *adj* no provocado.

unpunished [ʌn'pʌnɪʃt] *adj*: **to go** ~ quedar sin castigo, salir impune.

unqualified [ʌn'kwɔlɪfaɪd] *adj* sin título, no cualificado; (*success*) total, incondicional.

unquestionably [ʌn'kwɛstʃənəblɪ] *adv* indiscutiblemente.

unquestioning [ʌn'kwɛstʃənɪŋ] *adj* (*obedience, acceptance*) incondicional.

unravel [ʌn'rævl] *vt* desenmarañar.

unreal [ʌn'rɪəl] *adj* irreal.

unrealistic [ʌnrɪə'lɪstɪk] *adj* poco realista.

unreasonable [ʌn'riːznəbl] *adj* irrazonable; **to make** ~ **demands on sb** hacer demandas excesivas a algn.

unrecognizable [ʌn'rɛkəgnaɪzəbl] *adj* irreconocible.

unrecognized [ʌn'rɛkəgnaɪzd] *adj* (*talent, genius*) ignorado; (*POL: regime*) no reconocido.

unrecorded [ʌnrɪ'kɔːdɪd] *adj* no registrado.

unrefined [ʌnrɪ'faɪnd] *adj* (*sugar, petroleum*) sin refinar.

unrehearsed [ʌnrɪ'həːst] *adj* (*THEAT etc*) improvisado; (*spontaneous*) espontáneo.

unrelated [ʌnrɪ'leɪtɪd] *adj* sin relación; (*family*) no emparentado.

unrelenting [ʌnrɪ'lɛntɪŋ] *adj* implacable.

unreliable [ʌnrɪ'laɪəbl] *adj* (*person*) informal; (*machine*) poco fiable.

unrelieved [ʌnrɪ'liːvd] *adj* (*monotony*) constante.

unremitting [ʌnrɪ'mɪtɪŋ] *adj* incesante.

unrepeatable [ʌnrɪ'piːtəbl] *adj* irrepetible.

unrepentant [ʌnrɪ'pɛntənt] *adj* (*smoker, sinner*) impenitente; **to be** ~ **about sth** no arrepentirse de algo.

unrepresentative [ʌnrɛprɪ'zɛntətɪv] *adj* (*untypical*) poco representativo.

unreserved [ʌnrɪ'zɔːvd] *adj* (*seat*) no reservado; (*approval, admiration*) total.

unreservedly [ʌnrɪ'zɔːvɪdlɪ] *adv* sin reserva.

unresponsive [ʌnrɪ'spɔnsɪv] *adj* insensible.

unrest [ʌn'rɛst] *n* inquietud *f*, malestar *m*; (*POL*) disturbios *mpl*.

unrestricted [ʌnrɪ'strɪktɪd] *adj* (*power, time*) sin restricción; (*access*) libre.

unrewarded [ʌnrɪ'wɔːdɪd] *adj* sin recompensa.

unripe [ʌn'raɪp] *adj* verde, inmaduro.

unrivalled, (*US*) **unrivaled** [ʌn'raɪvəld] *adj* incomparable, sin par.

unroll [ʌn'rəul] *vt* desenrollar.

unruffled [ʌn'rʌfld] *adj* (*person*) imperturbable; (*hair*) liso.

unruly [ʌn'ruːlɪ] *adj* indisciplinado.

unsafe [ʌn'seɪf] *adj* (*journey*) peligroso; (*car etc*) inseguro; (*method*) arriesgado; ~ **to drink/eat** no apto para el consumo humano.

unsaid [ʌn'sɛd] *adj*: **to leave sth** ~ dejar algo sin decir.

unsaleable, (*US*) **unsalable** [ʌn'seɪləbl] *adj* invendible.

unsatisfactory ['ʌnsætɪs'fæktərɪ] *adj* poco satisfactorio.

unsatisfied [ʌn'sætɪsfaɪd] *adj* (*desire, need etc*) insatisfecho.

unsavoury, (*US*) **unsavory** [ʌn'seɪvərɪ] *adj* (*fig*) repugnante.

unscathed [ʌn'skeɪðd] *adj* ileso.

unscientific [ʌnsaɪən'tɪfɪk] *adj* poco científico.

unscrew [ʌn'skruː] *vt* destornillar.

unscrupulous [ʌn'skruːpjuləs] *adj* sin escrúpulos.

unseat [ʌn'siːt] *vt* (*rider*) hacer caerse de la silla a; (*fig: official*) hacer perder su escaño a.

unsecured [ʌnsɪ'kjuəd] *adj*: ~ **creditor** acreedor(a) *m/f* común.

unseeded [ʌn'siːdɪd] *adj* (*SPORT*) no preseleccionado.

unseen [ʌn'siːn] *adj* (*person, danger*) oculto.

unselfish [ʌn'sɛlfɪʃ] *adj* generoso, poco egoísta; (*act*) desinteresado.

unsettled [ʌn'sɛtld] *adj* inquieto; (*situation*) inestable; (*weather*) variable.

unsettling [ʌn'sɛtlɪŋ] *adj* perturbador(a),

inquietante.

unshak(e)able [ʌn'ʃeɪkəbl] *adj* inquebrantable.

unshaven [ʌn'ʃeɪvn] *adj* sin afeitar.

unsightly [ʌn'saɪtlɪ] *adj* desagradable.

unskilled [ʌn'skɪld] *adj*: ~ **workers** mano *f* de obra no cualificada.

unsociable [ʌn'səʊʃəbl] *adj* insociable.

unsocial [ʌn'səʊʃl] *adj*: ~ **hours** horario nocturno.

unsold [ʌn'səʊld] *adj* sin vender.

unsolicited [ʌnsə'lɪsɪtɪd] *adj* no solicitado.

unsophisticated [ʌnsə'fɪstɪkeɪtɪd] *adj* (*person*) sencillo, ingenuo; (*method*) poco sofisticado.

unsound [ʌn'saʊnd] *adj* (*health*) malo; (*in construction: floor, foundations*) defectuoso; (*policy, advice, judgment*) erróneo; (*investment*) poco seguro.

unspeakable [ʌn'spiːkəbl] *adj* indecible; (*awful*) incalificable.

unspoken [ʌn'spəʊkn] *adj* (*words*) sobreentendido; (*agreement, approval*) tácito.

unstable [ʌn'steɪbl] *adj* inestable.

unsteady [ʌn'stedɪ] *adj* inestable.

unstinting [ʌn'stɪntɪŋ] *adj* (*support etc*) pródigo.

unstuck [ʌn'stʌk] *adj*: **to come** ~ despegarse; (*fig*) fracasar.

unsubstantiated [ʌnsəb'stænʃɪeɪtɪd] *adj* (*rumour, accusation*) no comprobado.

unsuccessful [ʌnsək'sɛsful] *adj* (*attempt*) infructuoso; (*writer, proposal*) sin éxito; **to be** ~ (*in attempting sth*) no tener éxito, fracasar.

unsuccessfully [ʌnsək'sɛsfulɪ] *adv* en vano, sin éxito.

unsuitable [ʌn'suːtəbl] *adj* inconveniente, inapropiado; (*time*) inoportuno.

unsuited [ʌn'suːtɪd] *adj*: **to be** ~ **for** *or* **to** no ser apropiado para.

unsung ['ʌnsʌŋ] *adj*: **an** ~ **hero** un héroe desconocido.

unsupported [ʌnsə'pɔːtɪd] *adj* (*claim*) sin fundamento; (*theory*) sin base firme.

unsure [ʌn'ʃʊə*] *adj* inseguro, poco seguro; **to be** ~ **of o.s.** estar poco seguro de sí mismo.

unsuspecting [ʌnsə'spɛktɪŋ] *adj* confiado.

unsweetened [ʌn'swiːtnd] *adj* sin azúcar.

unsympathetic [ʌnsɪmpə'θɛtɪk] *adj* (*attitude*) poco comprensivo; (*person*) sin compasión; ~ **(to)** indiferente (a).

untangle [ʌn'tæŋgl] *vt* desenredar.

untapped [ʌn'tæpt] *adj* (*resources*) sin explotar.

untaxed [ʌn'tækst] *adj* (*goods*) libre de

impuestos; (*income*) antes de impuestos.

unthinkable [ʌn'θɪŋkəbl] *adj* inconcebible, impensable.

unthinkingly [ʌn'θɪŋkɪŋlɪ] *adv* irreflexivamente.

untidy [ʌn'taɪdɪ] *adj* (*room*) desordenado, en desorden; (*appearance*) desaliñado.

untie [ʌn'taɪ] *vt* desatar.

until [ən'tɪl] *prep* hasta ♦ *conj* hasta que; ~ **he comes** hasta que venga; ~ **now** hasta ahora; ~ **then** hasta entonces; **from morning** ~ **night** de la mañana a la noche.

untimely [ʌn'taɪmlɪ] *adj* inoportuno; (*death*) prematuro.

untold [ʌn'təʊld] *adj* (*story*) nunca contado; (*suffering*) indecible; (*wealth*) incalculable.

untouched [ʌn'tʌtʃt] *adj* (*not used etc*) intacto, sin tocar; (*safe: person*) indemne, ileso; (*unaffected*): ~ **by** insensible a.

untoward [ʌntə'wɔːd] *adj* (*behaviour*) impropio; (*event*) adverso.

untrained [ʌn'treɪnd] *adj* (*worker*) sin formación; (*troops*) no entrenado; **to the** ~ **eye** para los no entendidos.

untrammelled, (*US*) **untrammeled** [ʌn'træməld] *adj* ilimitado.

untranslatable [ʌntrænz'leɪtəbl] *adj* intraducible.

untried [ʌn'traɪd] *adj* (*plan*) no probado.

untrue [ʌn'truː] *adj* (*statement*) falso.

untrustworthy [ʌn'trʌstwəːðɪ] *adj* (*person*) poco fiable.

unusable [ʌn'juːzəbl] *adj* inservible.

unused [ʌn'juːzd] *adj* sin usar, nuevo; **to be** ~ **to (doing) sth** no estar acostumbrado a (hacer) algo.

unusual [ʌn'juːʒʊəl] *adj* insólito, poco común.

unusually [ʌn'juːʒʊəlɪ] *adv*: **he arrived** ~ **early** llegó más temprano que de costumbre.

unveil [ʌn'veɪl] *vt* (*statue*) descubrir.

unwanted [ʌn'wɒntɪd] *adj* (*person, effect*) no deseado.

unwarranted [ʌn'wɒrəntɪd] *adj* injustificado.

unwary [ʌn'wɛərɪ] *adj* imprudente, incauto.

unwavering [ʌn'weɪvərɪŋ] *adj* inquebrantable.

unwelcome [ʌn'wɛlkəm] *adj* (*at a bad time*) inoportuno, molesto; **to feel** ~ sentirse incómodo.

unwell [ʌn'wɛl] *adj*: **to feel** ~ estar indispuesto, sentirse mal.

unwieldy [ʌn'wiːldɪ] *adj* difícil de manejar.

unwilling [ʌn'wɪlɪŋ] *adj*: **to be** ~ **to do sth** estar poco dispuesto a hacer algo.

unwillingly [ʌn'wɪlɪŋlɪ] *adv* de mala gana.

unwind [ʌn'waɪnd] (*irreg: like* **wind**) *vt* desenvolver ♦ *vi* (*relax*) relajarse.

unwise [ʌn'waɪz] *adj* imprudente.

unwitting [ʌn'wɪtɪŋ] *adj* inconsciente.

unworkable [ʌn'wɜːkəbl] *adj* (*plan*) impracticable.

unworthy [ʌn'wɜːðɪ] *adj* indigno; **to be ~ of sth/to do sth** ser indigno de algo/de hacer algo.

unwrap [ʌn'ræp] *vt* deshacer.

unwritten [ʌn'rɪtn] *adj* (*agreement*) tácito; (*rules, law*) no escrito.

unzip [ʌn'zɪp] *vt* abrir la cremallera de.

========================= *KEYWORD*

up [ʌp] *prep*: **to go/be ~ sth** subir/estar subido en algo; **he went ~ the stairs/the hill** subió las escaleras/la colina; **we walked/climbed ~ the hill** subimos la colina; **they live further ~ the street** viven más arriba en la calle; **go ~ that road and turn left** sigue por esa calle y gira a la izquierda

♦ *adv* **1** (*upwards, higher*) más arriba; **~ in the mountains** en lo alto (de la montaña); **put it a bit higher ~** ponlo un poco más arriba *or* alto; **to stop halfway ~** pararse a la mitad del camino *or* de la subida; **~ there** ahí *or* allí arriba; **~ above** en lo alto, por encima, arriba; **"this side ~"** "este lado hacia arriba"; **to live/go ~ North** vivir en el norte/ir al norte

2: **to be ~** (*out of bed*) estar levantado; (*prices, level*) haber subido; (*building*) estar construido; (*tent*) estar montado; (*curtains, paper etc*) estar puesto; **time's ~** se acabó el tiempo; **when the year was ~** al terminarse el año; **he's well ~ in *or* on politics** (*BRIT: knowledgeable*) está muy al día en política; **what's up?** (*wrong*) ¿qué pasa?; **what's ~ with him?** ¿qué le pasa?; **prices are ~ on last year** los precios han subido desde el año pasado

3: **~ to** (*as far as*) hasta; **~ to now** hasta ahora *or* la fecha

4: **to be ~ to** (*depending on*): **it's ~ to you** depende de ti; **he's not ~ to it** (*job, task etc*) no es capaz de hacerlo; **I don't feel ~ to it** no me encuentro con ánimos para ello; **his work is not ~ to the required standard** su trabajo no da la talla; (*inf: be doing*): **what is he ~ to?** ¿qué estará tramando?

♦ *vi* (*col*): **she ~ped and left** se levantó y se marchó

♦ *vt* (*col: price*) subir

♦ *n*: **~s and downs** altibajos *mpl*.

up-and-coming [ʌpənd'kʌmɪŋ] *adj* prometedor(a).

upbeat ['ʌpbiːt] *n* (*MUS*) tiempo no acentuado; (*in economy, prosperity*) aumento ♦ *adj* (*col*) optimista, animado.

upbraid [ʌp'breɪd] *vt* censurar, reprender.

upbringing ['ʌpbrɪŋɪŋ] *n* educación *f*.

upcoming ['ʌpkʌmɪŋ] *adj* próximo.

update [ʌp'deɪt] *vt* poner al día.

upend [ʌp'ɛnd] *vt* poner vertical.

upfront [ʌp'frʌnt] *adj* claro, directo ♦ *adv* a las claras; (*pay*) por adelantado; **to be ~ about sth** admitir algo claramente.

upgrade [ʌp'greɪd] *vt* ascender; (*COMPUT*) modernizar.

upheaval [ʌp'hiːvl] *n* trastornos *mpl*; (*POL*) agitación *f*.

uphill [ʌp'hɪl] *adj* cuesta arriba; (*fig: task*) penoso, difícil ♦ *adv*: **to go ~** ir cuesta arriba.

uphold [ʌp'həuld] (*irreg: like* **hold**) *vt* sostener.

upholstery [ʌp'həulstərɪ] *n* tapicería.

upkeep ['ʌpkiːp] *n* mantenimiento.

upmarket [ʌp'mɑːkɪt] *adj* (*product*) de categoría.

upon [ə'pɔn] *prep* sobre.

upper ['ʌpə*] *adj* superior, de arriba ♦ *n* (*of shoe: also:* **~s**) pala.

upper case *n* (*TYP*) mayúsculas *fpl*.

upper-class [ʌpə'klɑːs] *adj* (*district, people, accent*) de clase alta; (*attitude*) altivo.

uppercut ['ʌpəkʌt] *n* uppercut *m*, gancho a la cara.

upper hand *n*: **to have the ~** tener la sartén por el mango.

Upper House *n* (*POL*): **the ~** la Cámara alta.

uppermost ['ʌpəməust] *adj* el más alto; **what was ~ in my mind** lo que me preocupaba más.

Upper Volta [-'vəultə] *n* Alto Volta *m*.

upright ['ʌpraɪt] *adj* vertical; (*fig*) honrado.

uprising ['ʌpraɪzɪŋ] *n* sublevación *f*.

uproar ['ʌprɔː*] *n* tumulto, escándalo.

uproarious [ʌp'rɔːrɪəs] *adj* escandaloso; (*hilarious*) graciosísimo; (*exceptional*) espectacular.

uproot [ʌp'ruːt] *vt* desarraigar.

upset *n* ['ʌpsɛt] (*to plan etc*) revés *m*, contratiempo; (*MED*) trastorno ♦ *vt* [ʌp'sɛt] (*irreg: like* **set**) (*glass etc*) volcar; (*spill*) derramar; (*plan*) alterar; (*person*) molestar, perturbar ♦ *adj* [ʌp'sɛt] preocupado, perturbado; (*stomach*) revuelto; **to have a stomach ~** (*BRIT*) tener el estómago revuelto; **to get ~**

molestarse, llevarse un disgusto.
upset price *n* (*US, Scottish*) precio mínimo
or de reserva.
upsetting [ʌp'sɛtɪŋ] *adj* (*worrying*)
inquietante; (*offending*) ofensivo;
(*annoying*) molesto.
upshot ['ʌpʃɔt] *n* resultado.
upside-down ['ʌpsaɪd'daun] *adv* al revés.
upstage ['ʌp'steɪdʒ] *vt* robar protagonismo
a.
upstairs [ʌp'stɛəz] *adv* arriba ♦ *adj* (*room*)
de arriba ♦ *n* el piso superior.
upstart ['ʌpstɑːt] *n* advenedizo.
upstream [ʌp'striːm] *adv* río arriba.
upsurge ['ʌpsəːdʒ] *n* (*of enthusiasm etc*)
arrebato.
uptake ['ʌpteɪk] *n*: **he is quick/slow on the**
~ es muy listo/torpe.
uptight [ʌp'taɪt] *adj* tenso, nervioso.
up-to-date ['ʌptə'deɪt] *adj* moderno, actual;
to bring sb ~ **(on sth)** poner a algn al
corriente/tanto (de algo).
upturn ['ʌptəːn] *n* (*in luck*) mejora; (*COMM*:
in market) resurgimiento económico; (: *in
value of currency*) aumento.
upturned ['ʌptəːnd] *adj*: ~ **nose** nariz *f*
respingona.
upward ['ʌpwəd] *adj* ascendente.
upwardly-mobile ['ʌpwədlɪ'məubaɪl] *adj*: **to
be** ~ mejorar socialmente.
upward(s) ['ʌpwəd(z)] *adv* hacia arriba.
URA *n abbr* (*US*) = *Urban Renewal
Administration.*
Ural Mountains ['juərəl-] *npl*: **the** ~ (*also*:
the Urals) los Montes Urales.
uranium [juə'reɪnɪəm] *n* uranio.
Uranus [juə'reɪnəs] *n* (*ASTRO*) Urano.
urban ['əːbən] *adj* urbano.
urbane [əː'beɪn] *adj* cortés, urbano.
urbanization ['əːbənaɪ'zeɪʃən] *n*
urbanización *f.*
urchin ['əːtʃɪn] *n* pilluelo, golfillo.
Urdu ['uəduː] *n* urdu *m.*
urge [əːdʒ] *n* (*force*) impulso; (*desire*) deseo
♦ *vt*: **to** ~ **sb to do sth** animar a algn a
hacer algo.
▶**urge on** *vt* animar.
urgency ['əːdʒənsɪ] *n* urgencia.
urgent ['əːdʒənt] *adj* (*earnest, persistent*:
plea) insistente; (: *tone*) urgente.
urgently ['əːdʒəntlɪ] *adv* con urgencia,
urgentemente.
urinal ['juərɪnl] *n* (*building*) urinario;
(*vessel*) orinal *m.*
urinate ['juərɪneɪt] *vi* orinar.
urine ['juərɪn] *n* orina.
urn [əːn] *n* urna; (*also*: **tea** ~) tetera
(grande).

Uruguay ['juərəgwaɪ] *n* el Uruguay.
Uruguayan [juərə'gwaɪən] *adj, n*
uruguayo/a *m/f.*
US *n abbr* (= *United States*) EE.UU.
us [ʌs] *pron* nos; (*after prep*) nosotros/as;
(*col*: *me*): **give** ~ **a kiss** dame un beso; *see
also* **me.**
USA *n abbr see* **United States of America**;
(*MIL*) = *United States Army.*
usable ['juːzəbl] *adj* utilizable.
USAF *n abbr* = *United States Air Force.*
usage ['juːzɪdʒ] *n* (*LING*) uso; (*utilization*)
utilización *f.*
USCG *n abbr* = *United States Coast
Guard.*
USDA *n abbr* = *United States Department of
Agriculture.*
USDAW ['ʌzdɔː] *n abbr* (*BRIT*: = *Union
of Shop, Distributive and Allied Workers*)
sindicato de empleados de
comercio.
USDI *n abbr* = *United States Department of
the Interior.*
use *n* [juːs] uso, empleo; (*usefulness*)
utilidad *f* ♦ *vt* [juːz] usar, emplear; **in** ~ en
uso; **out of** ~ en desuso; **to be of** ~ servir;
ready for ~ listo (para usar); **to make** ~
of sth aprovecharse *or* servirse de algo;
it's no ~ (*pointless*) es inútil; (*not useful*)
no sirve; **what's this** ~**d for?** ¿para qué
sirve esto?; **to be** ~**d to** estar
acostumbrado a (*SP*), acostumbrar; **to
get** ~**d to** acostumbrarse a; **she** ~**d to do
it** (ella) solía *or* acostumbraba hacerlo.
▶**use up** *vt* agotar.
used [juːzd] *adj* (*car*) usado.
useful ['juːsful] *adj* útil; **to come in** ~ ser
útil.
usefulness ['juːsfəlnɪs] *n* utilidad.
useless ['juːslɪs] *adj* inútil; (*unusable*: *object*)
inservible.
uselessly ['juːslɪslɪ] *adv* inútilmente, en
vano.
uselessness ['juːslɪsnɪs] *n* inutilidad *f.*
user ['juːzə*] *n* usuario/a; (*of petrol, gas etc*)
consumidor(a) *m/f.*
user-friendly ['juːzə'frɛndlɪ] *adj* (*COMPUT*)
fácil de utilizar.
USES *n abbr* = *United States Employment
Service.*
usher ['ʌʃə*] *n* (*at wedding*) ujier *m*; (*in
cinema etc*) acomodador *m* ♦ *vt*: **to** ~ **sb in**
(*into room*) hacer pasar a algn; **it** ~**ed in a
new era** (*fig*) inició una nueva era.
usherette [ʌʃə'rɛt] *n* (*in cinema*)
acomodadora.
USIA *n abbr* = *United States Information
Agency.*

USM *n abbr* = United States Mail; United States Mint.
USN *n abbr* = United States Navy.
USPHS *n abbr* = United States Public Health Service.
USPO *n abbr* = United States Post Office.
USS *abbr* = United States Ship (*or* Steamer).
USSR *n abbr*: **the** ~ la U.R.S.S.
usu. *abbr* = **usually.**
usual ['juːʒuəl] *adj* normal, corriente; **as** ~ como de costumbre, como siempre.
usually ['juːʒuəli] *adv* normalmente.
usurer ['juːʒərə*] *n* usurero.
usurp [juː'zəːp] *vt* usurpar.
usury ['juːʒəri] *n* usura.
UT *abbr* (*US*) = Utah.
utensil [juː'tɛnsl] *n* utensilio; **kitchen ~s** batería de cocina.
uterus ['juːtərəs] *n* útero.
utilitarian [juːtɪlɪ'tɛərɪən] *adj* utilitario.
utility [juː'tɪlɪtɪ] *n* utilidad *f*.
utility room *n* trascocina.
utilization [juːtɪlaɪ'zeɪʃən] *n* utilización *f*.
utilize ['juːtɪlaɪz] *vt* utilizar.
utmost ['ʌtməust] *adj* mayor ♦ *n*: **to do one's** ~ hacer todo lo posible; **it is of the** ~ **importance that** ... es de la mayor importancia que ....
utter ['ʌtə*] *adj* total, completo ♦ *vt* pronunciar, proferir.
utterance ['ʌtrns] *n* palabras *fpl*, declaración *f*.
utterly ['ʌtəli] *adv* completamente, totalmente.
U-turn ['juː'təːn] *n* cambio de sentido; (*fig*) giro de 180 grados.
Uzbekistan [ʌzbɛkɪ'staːn] *n* Uzbekistán *m*.

V v

V, v [viː] (*letter*) V, v *f*; **V for Victor** V de Valencia.
v. *abbr* (= *verse*) vers.º (= *vide*: *see*) V, vid., vide; (= *versus*) vs.; = **volt.**
VA, Va. *abbr* (*US*) = Virginia.
vac [væk] *n abbr* (*BRIT col*) = **vacation.**
vacancy ['veɪkənsɪ] *n* (*BRIT*: *job*) vacante *f*; (*room*) cuarto libro; **have you any vacancies?** ¿tiene *or* hay alguna habitación *or* algún cuarto libre?

vacant ['veɪkənt] *adj* desocupado, libre; (*expression*) distraído.
vacant lot *n* (*US*) solar *m*.
vacate [və'keɪt] *vt* (*house*) desocupar; (*job*) dejar (vacante).
vacation [və'keɪʃən] *n* vacaciones *fpl*; **on** ~ de vacaciones; **to take a** ~ (*esp US*) tomarse unas vacaciones.
vacation course *n* curso de vacaciones.
vacationer [və'keɪʃənə*], **vacationist** [və'keɪʃənɪst] *n* (*US*) turista *m/f*.
vaccinate ['væksɪneɪt] *vt* vacunar.
vaccination [væksɪ'neɪʃən] *n* vacunación *f*.
vaccine ['væksiːn] *n* vacuna.
vacuum ['vækjum] *n* vacío.
vacuum bottle *n* (*US*) = **vacuum flask.**
vacuum cleaner *n* aspiradora.
vacuum flask *n* (*BRIT*) termo.
vacuum-packed ['vækjum'pækt] *adj* envasado al vacío.
vagabond ['vægəbɔnd] *n* vagabundo/a.
vagary ['veɪgərɪ] *n* capricho.
vagina [və'dʒaɪnə] *n* vagina.
vagrancy ['veɪgrənsɪ] *n* vagabundeo.
vagrant ['veɪgrənt] *n* vagabundo/a.
vague [veɪg] *adj* vago; (*blurred*: *memory*) borroso; (*uncertain*) incierto, impreciso; (*person*) distraído; **I haven't the ~st idea** no tengo la más remota idea.
vaguely ['veɪglɪ] *adv* vagamente.
vagueness ['veɪgnɪs] *n* vaguedad *f*; imprecisión *f*; (*absent-mindedness*) despiste *m*.
vain [veɪn] *adj* (*conceited*) presumido; (*useless*) vano, inútil; **in** ~ en vano.
vainly ['veɪnlɪ] *adv* (*to no effect*) en vano; (*conceitedly*) vanidosamente.
valance ['væləns] *n* (*for bed*) volante alrededor de la colcha o sábana que cuelga hasta el suelo.
valedictory [vælɪ'dɪktərɪ] *adj* de despedida.
valentine ['væləntaɪn] *n* (*also*: ~ **card**) tarjeta del Día de los Enamorados.
valet ['væleɪ] *n* ayuda *m* de cámara.
valet service *n* (*for clothes*) planchado.
valiant ['væljənt] *adj* valiente.
valiantly ['væljəntlɪ] *adv* valientemente, con valor.
valid ['vælɪd] *adj* válido; (*ticket*) valedero; (*law*) vigente.
validate ['vælɪdeɪt] *vt* (*contract, document*) convalidar; (*argument, claim*) dar validez a.
validity [və'lɪdɪtɪ] *n* validez *f*; vigencia.
valise [və'liːz] *n* maletín *m*.
valley ['vælɪ] *n* valle *m*.
valour, (*US*) **valor** ['vælə*] *n* valor *m*, valentía.

valuable ['væljuəbl] *adj* (*jewel*) de valor; (*time*) valioso; ~s *npl* objetos *mpl* de valor.

valuation [vælju'eɪʃən] *n* tasación *f*, valuación *f*.

value ['vælju:] *n* valor *m*; (*importance*) importancia ♦ *vt* (*fix price of*) tasar, valorar; (*esteem*) apreciar; ~s *npl* (*moral*) valores *mpl* morales; **to lose (in)** ~ (*currency*) bajar; (*property*) desvalorizarse; **to gain (in)** ~ (*currency*) subir; (*property*) valorizarse; **you get good** ~ **(for money) in that shop** la relación calidad-precio es muy buena en esa tienda; **to be of great** ~ **to sb** ser de gran valor para algn; **it is** ~**d at £8** está valorado en ocho libras.

value added tax (VAT) *n* (*BRIT*) impuesto sobre el valor añadido *or* agregado (*LAM*) (IVA *m*).

valued ['vælju:d] *adj* (*appreciated*) apreciado.

valueless ['vælju:lɪs] *adj* sin valor.

valuer ['vælju:ə*] *n* tasador(a) *m/f*.

valve [vælv] *n* (*ANAT, TECH*) válvula.

vampire ['væmpaɪə*] *n* vampiro.

van [væn] *n* (*AUT*) furgoneta, camioneta (*LAM*); (*BRIT RAIL*) furgón *m* (de equipajes).

V and A *n abbr* (*BRIT*) = *Victoria and Albert Museum*.

vandal ['vændl] *n* vándalo/a.

vandalism ['vændəlɪzəm] *n* vandalismo.

vandalize ['vændəlaɪz] *vt* dañar, destruir, destrozar.

vanguard ['vængɑ:d] *n* vanguardia.

vanilla [və'nɪlə] *n* vainilla.

vanish ['vænɪʃ] *vi* desaparecer, esfumarse.

vanity ['vænɪtɪ] *n* vanidad *f*.

vanity case *n* neceser *m*.

vantage point ['vɑ:ntɪdʒ-] *n* posición *f* ventajosa.

vaporize ['veɪpəraɪz] *vt* vaporizar ♦ *vi* vaporizarse.

vapour, (*US*) **vapor** ['veɪpə*] *n* vapor *m*; (*on breath, window*) vaho.

vapo(u)r trail *n* (*AVIAT*) estela.

variable ['veərɪəbl] *adj* variable ♦ *n* variable *f*.

variance ['veərɪəns] *n*: **to be at** ~ **(with)** estar en desacuerdo (con), no cuadrar (con).

variant ['veərɪənt] *n* variante *f*.

variation [veərɪ'eɪʃən] *n* variación *f*.

varicose ['værɪkəus] *adj*: ~ **veins** varices *fpl*.

varied ['veərɪd] *adj* variado.

variety [və'raɪətɪ] *n* variedad *f*, diversidad *f*; (*quantity*) surtido; **for a** ~ **of reasons** por varias *or* diversas razones.

variety show *n* espectáculo de

variedades.

various ['veərɪəs] *adj* varios/as, diversos/as; **at** ~ **times** (*different*) en distintos momentos; (*several*) varias veces.

varnish ['vɑ:nɪʃ] *n* (*gen*) barniz *m*; (*nail* ~) esmalte *m* ♦ *vt* (*gen*) barnizar; (*nails*) pintar (con esmalte).

vary ['veərɪ] *vt* variar; (*change*) cambiar ♦ *vi* variar; (*disagree*) discrepar; **to** ~ **with** *or* **according to** variar según *or* de acuerdo con.

varying ['veərɪɪŋ] *adj* diversos/as.

vase [vɑ:z] *n* florero.

vasectomy [və'sɛktəmɪ] *n* vasectomía.

Vaseline ® ['væsɪli:n] *n* vaselina ®.

vast [vɑ:st] *adj* enorme; (*success*) abrumador(a), arrollador(a).

vastly ['vɑ:stlɪ] *adv* enormemente.

vastness ['vɑ:stnɪs] *n* inmensidad *f*.

VAT [væt] *n abbr* (*BRIT*: = *value added tax*) IVA *m*.

vat [væt] *n* tina, tinaja.

Vatican ['vætɪkən] *n*: **the** ~ el Vaticano.

vatman ['vætmæn] *n* (*BRIT col*) inspector *m* *or* recaudador *m* del IVA; **"how to avoid the** ~**"** "cómo evitar pagar el IVA".

vaudeville ['vəudəvɪl] *n* (*US*) vodevil *m*.

vault [vɔ:lt] *n* (*of roof*) bóveda; (*tomb*) tumba; (*in bank*) cámara acorazada ♦ *vt* (*also*: ~ **over**) saltar (por encima de).

vaunted ['vɔ:ntɪd] *adj*: **much** ~ cacareado.

VC *n abbr* = **vice-chairman, vice-chancellor**; (*BRIT*: = *Victoria Cross*) *condecoración militar*.

VCR *n abbr* = **video cassette recorder**.

VD *n abbr see* **venereal disease**.

VDU *n abbr see* **visual display unit**.

veal [vi:l] *n* ternera.

veer [vɪə*] *vi* (*ship*) virar.

veg. [vɛdʒ] *n abbr* (*BRIT col*) = **vegetable(s)**.

vegan ['vi:gən] *n* vegetariano/a estricto/a.

vegeburger, veggieburger ['vɛdʒɪbə:gə*] *n* hamburguesa vegetal.

vegetable ['vɛdʒtəbl] *n* (*BOT*) vegetal *m*; (*edible plant*) legumbre *f*, hortaliza ♦ *adj* vegetal; ~s *npl* (*cooked*) verduras *fpl*.

vegetable garden *n* huerta, huerto.

vegetarian [vɛdʒɪ'teərɪən] *adj, n* vegetariano/a *m/f*.

vegetate ['vɛdʒɪteɪt] *vi* vegetar.

vegetation [vɛdʒɪ'teɪʃən] *n* vegetación *f*.

vegetative ['vɛdʒɪtətɪv] *adj* vegetativo; (*BOT*) vegetal.

vehemence ['vi:ɪməns] *n* vehemencia; violencia.

vehement ['vi:ɪmənt] *adj* vehemente, apasionado; (*dislike, hatred*) violento.

vehicle ['vi:ɪkl] *n* vehículo; (*fig*) vehículo,

medio.
vehicular [vɪ'hɪkjulə*] adj: ~ **traffic**
circulación f rodada.
veil [veɪl] n velo ♦ vt velar; **under a** ~ **of**
secrecy (fig) en el mayor secreto.
veiled [veɪld] adj (also fig) disimulado,
velado.
vein [veɪn] n vena; (of ore etc) veta.
Velcro ® ['vɛlkrəu] n velcro m ®.
vellum ['vɛləm] n (writing paper) papel m
vitela.
velocity [vɪ'lɒsɪtɪ] n velocidad f.
velour [və'luə*] n terciopelo.
velvet ['vɛlvɪt] n terciopelo ♦ adj
aterciopelado.
vendetta [vɛn'dɛtə] n vendetta.
vending machine ['vɛndɪŋ-] n máquina
expendedora, expendedor m.
vendor ['vɛndə*] n vendedor(a) m/f; **street**
~ vendedor(a) m/f callejero/a.
veneer [və'nɪə*] n chapa, enchapado; (fig)
barniz m.
venereal [vɪ'nɪərɪəl] adj: ~ **disease (VD)**
enfermedad f venérea.
Venetian blind [vɪ'niːʃən-] n persiana.
Venezuela [vɛnɛ'zweɪlə] n Venezuela.
Venezuelan [vɛnɛ'zweɪlən] adj, n
venezolano/a m/f.
vengeance ['vɛndʒəns] n venganza; **with a**
~ (fig) con creces.
vengeful ['vɛndʒful] adj vengativo.
Venice ['vɛnɪs] n Venecia.
venison ['vɛnɪsn] n carne f de venado.
venom ['vɛnəm] n veneno.
venomous ['vɛnəməs] adj venenoso.
venomously ['vɛnəməslɪ] adv con odio.
vent [vɛnt] n (opening) abertura; (air-hole)
respiradero; (in wall) rejilla (de
ventilación) ♦ vt (fig: feelings) desahogar.
ventilate ['vɛntɪleɪt] vt ventilar.
ventilation [vɛntɪ'leɪʃən] n ventilación f.
ventilation shaft n pozo de ventilación.
ventilator ['vɛntɪleɪtə*] n ventilador m.
ventriloquist [vɛn'trɪləkwɪst] n
ventrílocuo/a.
venture ['vɛntʃə*] n empresa ♦ vt
arriesgar; (opinion) ofrecer ♦ vi
arriesgarse, lanzarse; **a business** ~ una
empresa comercial; **to** ~ **to do sth**
aventurarse a hacer algo.
venture capital n capital m arriesgado.
venue ['vɛnjuː] n (meeting place) lugar m de
reunión; (for concert) local m.
Venus ['viːnəs] n (ASTRO) Venus m.
veracity [və'ræsɪtɪ] n veracidad f.
veranda(h) [və'rændə] n terraza; (with
glass) galería.
verb [vəːb] n verbo.

verbal ['vəːbl] adj verbal.
verbally ['vəːbəlɪ] adv verbalmente, de
palabra.
verbatim [vəː'beɪtɪm] adj, adv al pie de la
letra, palabra por palabra.
verbose [vəː'bəus] adj prolijo.
verdict ['vəːdɪkt] n veredicto, fallo; (fig:
opinion) opinión f, juicio; ~ **of guilty/not**
guilty veredicto de culpabilidad/
inocencia.
verge [vəːdʒ] n (BRIT) borde m; **to be on the**
~ **of doing sth** estar a punto de hacer
algo.
▶**verge on** vt fus rayar en.
verger ['vəːdʒə*] n sacristán m.
verification [vɛrɪfɪ'keɪʃən] n comprobación
f, verificación f.
verify ['vɛrɪfaɪ] vt comprobar, verificar;
(COMPUT) verificar; (prove the truth of)
confirmar.
veritable ['vɛrɪtəbl] adj verdadero,
auténtico.
vermin ['vəːmɪn] npl (animals) bichos mpl;
(insects, fig) sabandijas fpl.
vermouth ['vəːmǝθ] n vermut m.
vernacular [və'nækjulə*] n lengua
vernácula.
versatile ['vəːsətaɪl] adj (person)
polifacético; (machine, tool etc) versátil.
versatility [vəːsə'tɪlɪtɪ] n versatilidad f.
verse [vəːs] n versos mpl, poesía; (stanza)
estrofa; (in bible) versículo; **in** ~ en
verso.
versed [vəːst] adj: **(well-)**~ **in** versado en.
version ['vəːʃən] n versión f.
versus ['vəːsəs] prep contra.
vertebra, pl ~**e** ['vəːtɪbrə, briː] n vértebra.
vertebrate ['vəːtɪbrɪt] n vertebrado.
vertical ['vəːtɪkl] adj vertical.
vertically ['vəːtɪkəlɪ] adv verticalmente.
vertigo ['vəːtɪgəu] n vértigo; **to suffer from**
~ tener vértigo.
verve [vəːv] n brío.
very ['vɛrɪ] adv muy ♦ adj: **the** ~ **book which**
el mismo libro que; **the** ~ **last** el último
(de todos); **at the** ~ **least** al menos; ~
much muchísimo; ~ **well/little** muy bien/
poco; ~ **high frequency** (RADIO)
frecuencia muy alta; **it's** ~ **cold** hace
mucho frío; **the** ~ **thought (of it) alarms**
me con sólo pensarlo me entra miedo.
vespers ['vɛspəz] npl vísperas fpl.
vessel ['vɛsl] n (ANAT) vaso; (ship) barco;
(container) vasija.
vest [vɛst] n (BRIT) camiseta; (US: waistcoat)
chaleco.
vested interests ['vɛstɪd-] npl (COMM)
intereses mpl creados.

vestibule ['vɛstɪbjuːl] *n* vestíbulo.
vestige ['vɛstɪdʒ] *n* vestigio, rastro.
vestry ['vɛstrɪ] *n* sacristía.
Vesuvius [vɪ'suːvɪəs] *n* Vesubio.
vet [vɛt] *n abbr* = **veterinary surgeon** ♦ *vt* revisar; **to ~ sb for a job** someter a investigación a algn para un trabajo.
veteran ['vɛtərn] *n* veterano/a ♦ *adj*: **she is a ~ campaigner for ...** es una veterana de la campaña de ... .
veteran car *n* coche *m* antiguo.
veterinarian [vɛtrɪ'nɛərɪən] *n* (*US*) = **veterinary surgeon**.
veterinary ['vɛtrɪnərɪ] *adj* veterinario.
veterinary surgeon *n* (*BRIT*) veterinario/a.
veto ['viːtəu] *n* (*pl* ~**es**) veto ♦ *vt* prohibir, vedar; **to put a ~ on** vetar.
vetting ['vɛtɪŋ] *n*: **positive ~** *investigación gubernamental de los futuros altos cargos de la Administración*.
vex [vɛks] *vt* (*irritate*) fastidiar; (*make impatient*) impacientar.
vexed [vɛkst] *adj* (*question*) controvertido.
vexing ['vɛksɪŋ] *adj* molesto, engorroso.
VFD *n abbr* (*US*) = **voluntary fire department**.
VG *n abbr* (*BRIT SCOL etc*: = **very good**) S (= **sobresaliente**).
VHF *abbr* (= **very high frequency**) VHF *f*.
VI *abbr* (*US*) = **Virgin Islands**.
via ['vaɪə] *prep* por, por vía de.
viability [vaɪə'bɪlɪtɪ] *n* viabilidad *f*.
viable ['vaɪəbl] *adj* viable.
viaduct ['vaɪədʌkt] *n* viaducto.
vial ['vaɪəl] *n* frasco pequeño.
vibes [vaɪbz] *npl* (*col*): **I got good/bad ~ me** dio buen/mal rollo.
vibrant ['vaɪbrənt] *adj* (*lively, bright*) vivo; (*full of emotion: voice*) vibrante; (*colour*) fuerte.
vibraphone ['vaɪbrəfəun] *n* vibráfono.
vibrate [vaɪ'breɪt] *vi* vibrar.
vibration [vaɪ'breɪʃən] *n* vibración *f*.
vibrator [vaɪ'breɪtə*] *n* vibrador *m*.
vicar ['vɪkə*] *n* párroco.
vicarage ['vɪkərɪdʒ] *n* parroquia.
vicarious [vɪ'kɛərɪəs] *adj* indirecto; (*responsibility*) delegado.
vice [vaɪs] *n* (*evil*) vicio; (*TECH*) torno de banco.
vice- [vaɪs] *pref* vice....
vice-chairman ['vaɪs'tʃɛəmən] *n* vicepresidente *m*.
vice-chancellor [vaɪs'tʃɑːnsələ*] *n* (*BRIT UNIV*) rector(a) *m/f*.
vice-president [vaɪs'prɛzɪdənt] *n* vice-presidente/a *m/f*.
viceroy ['vaɪsrɔɪ] *n* virrey *m*.
vice versa ['vaɪsɪ'vɜːsə] *adv* viceversa.

vicinity [vɪ'sɪnɪtɪ] *n* (*area*) vecindad *f*; (*nearness*) proximidad *f*; **in the ~ (of)** cercano (a).
vicious ['vɪʃəs] *adj* (*remark*) malicioso; (*blow*) brutal; **a ~ circle** un círculo vicioso.
viciousness ['vɪʃəsnɪs] *n* brutalidad *f*.
vicissitudes [vɪ'sɪsɪtjuːdz] *npl* vicisitudes *fpl*, peripecias *fpl*.
victim ['vɪktɪm] *n* víctima *f*; **to be the ~ of** ser víctima de.
victimization [vɪktɪmaɪ'zeɪʃən] *n* persecución *f*; (*of striker etc*) represalias *fpl*.
victimize ['vɪktɪmaɪz] *vt* (*strikers etc*) tomar represalias contra.
victor ['vɪktə*] *n* vencedor(a) *m/f*.
Victorian [vɪk'tɔːrɪən] *adj* victoriano.
victorious [vɪk'tɔːrɪəs] *adj* vencedor(a).
victory ['vɪktərɪ] *n* victoria; **to win a ~ over sb** obtener una victoria sobre algn.
video ['vɪdɪəu] *cpd* de vídeo ♦ *n* vídeo.
video camera *n* videocámara, cámara de vídeo.
video cassette *n* videocassette *f*.
video (cassette) recorder *n* vídeo, videocassette *f*.
videodisk ['vɪdɪəudɪsk] *n* videodisco.
video game *n* videojuego.
video nasty *n* vídeo de violencia y/o porno duro.
videophone ['vɪdɪəufəun] *n* videoteléfono, videófono.
video recording *n* videograbación *f*.
video tape *n* cinta de vídeo.
vie [vaɪ] *vi*: **to ~ with** competir con.
Vienna [vɪ'ɛnə] *n* Viena.
Viennese [vɪə'niːz] *adj*, *n* vienés/esa *m/f*.
Vietnam, Viet Nam [vjɛt'næm] *n* Vietnam *m*.
Vietnamese [vjɛtnə'miːz] *adj* vietnamita ♦ *n* (*pl inv*) vietnamita *m/f*; (*LING*) vietnamita *m*.
view [vjuː] *n* vista; (*landscape*) paisaje *m*; (*opinion*) opinión *f*, criterio ♦ *vt* (*look at*) mirar; (*examine*) examinar; **on ~** (*in museum etc*) expuesto; **in full ~ of sb** a la vista de algn; **to be within ~ (of sth)** estar a la vista (de algo); **an overall ~ of the situation** una visión de conjunto de la situación; **in ~ of the fact that** en vista de que; **to take** *or* **hold the ~ that ...** opinar *or* pensar que ...; **with a ~ to doing sth** con miras *or* vistas a hacer algo.
viewdata ['vjuːdeɪtə] *n* (*BRIT*) videodatos *mpl*.
viewer ['vjuːə*] *n* (*small projector*) visionadora; (*TV*) televidente *m/f*,

telespectador(a) *m/f.*
viewfinder ['vjuːfaɪndə*] *n* visor *m* de imagen.
viewpoint ['vjuːpɔɪnt] *n* punto de vista.
vigil ['vɪdʒɪl] *n* vigilia; **to keep** ~ velar.
vigilance ['vɪdʒɪləns] *n* vigilancia.
vigilance committee *n* (*US*) comité *m* de autodefensa.
vigilant ['vɪdʒɪlənt] *adj* vigilante.
vigilante [vɪdʒɪ'læntɪ] *n* vecino/a que se toma la justicia por su mano.
vigorous ['vɪgərəs] *adj* enérgico, vigoroso.
vigorously ['vɪgərəslɪ] *adv* enérgicamente, vigorosamente.
vigour, (*US*) **vigor** ['vɪgə*] *n* energía, vigor *m.*
vile [vaɪl] *adj* (*action*) vil, infame; (*smell*) repugnante.
vilify ['vɪlɪfaɪ] *vt* denigrar, vilipendiar.
villa ['vɪlə] *n* (*country house*) casa de campo; (*suburban house*) chalet *m.*
village ['vɪlɪdʒ] *n* aldea.
villager ['vɪlɪdʒə*] *n* aldeano/a.
villain ['vɪlən] *n* (*scoundrel*) malvado/a; (*criminal*) maleante *m/f; see also* **pantomime.**
VIN *n abbr* (*US*) = *vehicle identification number.*
vinaigrette [vɪneɪ'grɛt] *n* vinagreta.
vindicate ['vɪndɪkeɪt] *vt* vindicar, justificar.
vindication [vɪndɪ'keɪʃən] *n*: **in** ~ **of** en justificación de.
vindictive [vɪn'dɪktɪv] *adj* vengativo.
vine [vaɪn] *n* vid *f.*
vinegar ['vɪnɪgə*] *n* vinagre *m.*
vine-growing ['vaɪngrəʊɪŋ] *adj* (*region*) viticultor(a).
vineyard ['vɪnjɑːd] *n* viña, viñedo.
vintage ['vɪntɪdʒ] *n* (*year*) vendimia, cosecha; **the 1970** ~ la cosecha de 1970.
vintage car *n* coche *m* antiguo *or* de época.
vintage wine *n* vino añejo.
vintage year *n*: **it's been a** ~ **for plays** ha sido un año destacado en lo que a teatro se refiere.
vinyl ['vaɪnl] *n* vinilo.
viola [vɪ'əʊlə] *n* (*MUS*) viola.
violate ['vaɪəleɪt] *vt* violar.
violation [vaɪə'leɪʃən] *n* violación *f*; **in** ~ **of** sth en violación de algo.
violence ['vaɪələns] *n* violencia; **acts of** ~ actos *mpl* de violencia.
violent ['vaɪələnt] *adj* (*gen*) violento; (*pain*) intenso; **a** ~ **dislike of sb/sth** una profunda antipatía *or* manía a algn/algo.
violently ['vaɪələntlɪ] *adv* (*severely: ill, angry*) muy.
violet ['vaɪələt] *adj* violado, violeta ♦ *n*

(*plant*) violeta.
violin [vaɪə'lɪn] *n* violín *m.*
violinist [vaɪə'lɪnɪst] *n* violinista *m/f.*
VIP *n abbr* (= *very important person*) VIP *m.*
viper ['vaɪpə*] *n* víbora.
viral ['vaɪərəl] *adj* vírico.
virgin ['vɜːdʒɪn] *n* virgen *m/f* ♦ *adj* virgen; **the Blessed V**~ la Santísima Virgen.
virginity [vɜː'dʒɪnɪtɪ] *n* virginidad *f.*
Virgo ['vɜːgəʊ] *n* Virgo.
virile ['vɪraɪl] *adj* viril.
virility [vɪ'rɪlɪtɪ] *n* virilidad *f.*
virtual ['vɜːtjuəl] *adj* virtual.
virtually ['vɜːtjuəlɪ] *adv* (*almost*) prácticamente, virtualmente; **it is** ~ **impossible** es prácticamente imposible.
virtual reality *n* realidad *f* virtual.
virtue ['vɜːtjuː] *n* virtud *f*; **by** ~ **of** en virtud de.
virtuosity [vɜːtju'ɔsɪtɪ] *n* virtuosismo.
virtuoso [vɜːtju'əʊsəʊ] *n* virtuoso.
virtuous ['vɜːtjuəs] *adj* virtuoso.
virulence ['vɪruləns] *n* virulencia.
virulent ['vɪrulənt] *adj* virulento, violento.
virus ['vaɪərəs] *n* virus *m.*
visa ['viːzə] *n* visado, visa (*LAM*).
vis-à-vis [viːzə'viː] *prep* con respecto a.
viscount ['vaɪkaunt] *n* vizconde *m.*
viscous ['vɪskəs] *adj* viscoso.
vise [vaɪs] *n* (*US TECH*) = **vice.**
visibility [vɪzɪ'bɪlɪtɪ] *n* visibilidad *f.*
visible ['vɪzəbl] *adj* visible; ~ **exports/imports** exportaciones *fpl*/importaciones *fpl* visibles.
visibly ['vɪzɪblɪ] *adv* visiblemente.
vision ['vɪʒən] *n* (*sight*) vista; (*foresight, in dream*) visión *f.*
visionary ['vɪʒənrɪ] *n* visionario/a.
visit ['vɪzɪt] *n* visita ♦ *vt* (*person*) visitar, hacer una visita a; (*place*) ir a, (ir a) conocer; **to pay a** ~ **to** (*person*) visitar a; **on a private/official** ~ en visita privada/oficial.
visiting ['vɪzɪtɪŋ] *adj* (*speaker, professor*) invitado; (*team*) visitante.
visiting card *n* tarjeta de visita.
visiting hours *npl* (*in hospital etc*) horas *fpl* de visita.
visitor *n* (*gen*) visitante *m/f*; (*to one's house*) visita; (*tourist*) turista *m/f*; (*tripper*) excursionista *m/f*; **to have** ~**s** (*at home*) tener visita.
visitors' book *n* libro de visitas.
visor ['vaɪzə*] *n* visera.
VISTA ['vɪstə] *n abbr* (= *Volunteers In Service to America*) programa de ayuda voluntaria a los necesitados.
vista ['vɪstə] *n* vista, panorama.

visual ['vɪzjuəl] *adj* visual.
visual aid *n* medio visual.
visual arts *npl* artes *fpl* plásticas.
visual display unit (VDU) *n* unidad *f* de despliegue visual, monitor *m*.
visualize ['vɪzjuəlaɪz] *vt* imaginarse; (*foresee*) prever.
visually ['vɪzjuəlɪ] *adv*: ~ **handicapped** con visión deficiente.
vital ['vaɪtl] *adj* (*essential*) esencial, imprescindible; (*crucial*) crítico; (*person*) enérgico, vivo; (*of life*) vital; **of ~ importance (to sb/sth)** de suma importancia (para algn/algo).
vitality [vaɪ'tælɪtɪ] *n* energía, vitalidad *f*.
vitally ['vaɪtəlɪ] *adv*: ~ **important** de suma importancia.
vital statistics *npl* (*of population*) estadísticas *fpl* demográficas; (*col*: *woman's*) medidas *fpl* (corporales).
vitamin ['vɪtəmɪn] *n* vitamina.
vitamin pill *n* pastilla de vitaminas.
vitreous ['vɪtrɪəs] *adj* (*china, enamel*) vítreo.
vitriolic [vɪtrɪ'ɒlɪk] *adj* mordaz.
viva ['vaɪvə] *n* (*also*: ~ **voce**) examen *m* oral.
vivacious [vɪ'veɪʃəs] *adj* vivaz, alegre.
vivacity [vɪ'væsɪtɪ] *n* vivacidad *f*.
vivid ['vɪvɪd] *adj* (*account*) gráfico; (*light*) intenso; (*imagination*) vivo.
vividly ['vɪvɪdlɪ] *adv* (*describe*) gráficamente; (*remember*) como si fuera hoy.
vivisection [vɪvɪ'sɛkʃən] *n* vivisección *f*.
vixen ['vɪksn] *n* (*ZOOL*) zorra, raposa; (*pej*: *woman*) arpía, bruja.
viz *abbr* (= *videlicet*: *namely*) v.gr.
VLF *abbr* = *very low frequency*.
V-neck ['viːnɛk] *n* cuello de pico.
VOA *n abbr* (= *Voice of America*) Voz *f* de América.
vocabulary [vəu'kæbjulərɪ] *n* vocabulario.
vocal ['vəukl] *adj* vocal; (*articulate*) elocuente.
vocal cords *npl* cuerdas *fpl* vocales.
vocalist ['vəukəlɪst] *n* cantante *m/f*.
vocation [vəu'keɪʃən] *n* vocación *f*.
vocational [vəu'keɪʃənl] *adj* vocacional; ~ **guidance** orientación *f* profesional; ~ **training** formación *f* profesional.
vociferous [və'sɪfərəs] *adj* vociferante.
vociferously [və'sɪfərəslɪ] *adv* a gritos.
vodka ['vɒdkə] *n* vodka *m*.
vogue [vəug] *n* boga, moda; **to be in ~, be the ~** estar de moda *or* en boga.
voice [vɔɪs] *n* voz *f* ♦ *vt* (*opinion*) expresar; **in a loud/soft ~** en voz alta/baja; **to give ~ to** expresar.
voice-over ['vɔɪsəuvə*] *n* voz *f* en off.

void [vɔɪd] *n* vacío; (*hole*) hueco ♦ *adj* (*invalid*) nulo, inválido; (*empty*): ~ **of** carente *or* desprovisto de.
voile [vɔɪl] *n* gasa.
vol. *abbr* (= *volume*) t.
volatile ['vɒlətaɪl] *adj* volátil; (*COMPUT*: *memory*) no permanente.
volcanic [vɒl'kænɪk] *adj* volcánico.
volcano, ~es [vɒl'keɪnəu] *n* volcán *m*.
volition [və'lɪʃən] *n*: **of one's own ~** por su propia voluntad.
volley ['vɒlɪ] *n* (*of gunfire*) descarga; (*of stones etc*) lluvia; (*TENNIS etc*) volea.
volleyball *n* voleibol *m*, balonvolea *m*.
volt [vəult] *n* voltio.
voltage ['vəultɪdʒ] *n* voltaje *m*; **high/low ~** alto/bajo voltaje, alta/baja tensión.
volte-face ['vɒlt'fɑːs] *n* viraje *m*.
voluble ['vɒljubl] *adj* locuaz, hablador(a).
volume ['vɒljuːm] *n* (*of tank*) volumen *m*; (*book*) tomo; ~ **one/two** (*of book*) tomo primero/segundo; ~**s** *npl* (*great quantities*) cantidad *fsg*; **his expression spoke ~s** su expresión (lo) decía todo.
volume control *n* (*RADIO*, *TV*) (botón *m* del) volumen *m*.
volume discount *n* (*COMM*) descuento por volumen de compras.
voluminous [və'luːmɪnəs] *adj* (*large*) voluminoso; (*prolific*) prolífico.
voluntarily ['vɒləntrɪlɪ] *adv* libremente, voluntariamente.
voluntary ['vɒləntərɪ] *adj* voluntario, espontáneo.
voluntary liquidation *n* (*COMM*) liquidación *f* voluntaria.
voluntary redundancy *n* (*BRIT*) despido voluntario.
volunteer [vɒlən'tɪə*] *n* voluntario/a ♦ *vi* ofrecerse (de voluntario); **to ~ to do** ofrecerse a hacer.
voluptuous [və'lʌptjuəs] *adj* voluptuoso.
vomit ['vɒmɪt] *n* vómito ♦ *vt*, *vi* vomitar.
voracious [və'reɪʃəs] *adj* voraz; (*reader*) ávido.
vote [vəut] *n* voto; (*votes cast*) votación *f*; (*right to* ~) derecho a votar; (*franchise*) sufragio ♦ *vt* (*chairman*) elegir ♦ *vi* votar, ir a votar; ~ **of thanks** voto de gracias; **to put sth to the ~, to take a ~ on sth** someter algo a votación; ~ **for** *or* **in favour of/against** voto a favor de/en contra de; **to ~ to do sth** votar por hacer algo; **he was ~d secretary** fue elegido secretario por votación; **to pass a ~ of confidence/no confidence** aprobar un voto de confianza/de censura.
voter ['vəutə*] *n* votante *m/f*.

voting ['vəutɪŋ] *n* votación *f*.
voting paper *n* (*BRIT*) papeleta de votación.
voting right *n* derecho a voto.
vouch [vautʃ]: **to ~ for** *vt fus* garantizar, responder de.
voucher ['vautʃə*] *n* (*for meal, petrol*) vale *m*; **luncheon/travel ~** vale *m* de comida/de viaje.
vow [vau] *n* voto ♦ *vi* hacer voto; **to take or make a ~ to do sth** jurar hacer algo, comprometerse a hacer algo.
vowel ['vauəl] *n* vocal *f*.
voyage ['vɔɪɪdʒ] *n* (*journey*) viaje *m*; (*crossing*) travesía.
voyeur [vwɑː'jəː*] *n* voyeur *m/f*, mirón/ona *m/f*.
VP *n abbr* (= *vice-president*) V.P.
vs *abbr* (= *versus*) vs.
VSO *n abbr* (*BRIT*: = *Voluntary Service Overseas*) *organización que envía jóvenes voluntarios a trabajar y enseñar en los países del Tercer Mundo.*
VT, Vt. *abbr* (*US*) = *Vermont*.
vulgar ['vʌlgə*] *adj* (*rude*) ordinario, grosero; (*in bad taste*) de mal gusto.
vulgarity [vʌl'gærɪtɪ] *n* grosería; mal gusto.
vulnerability [vʌlnərə'bɪlɪtɪ] *n* vulnerabilidad *f*.
vulnerable ['vʌlnərəbl] *adj* vulnerable.
vulture ['vʌltʃə*] *n* buitre *m*, gallinazo (*LAM*).

W w

W, w ['dʌblju:] *n* (*letter*) W, w *f*; **W for William** W de Washington.
W *abbr* (= *west*) O; (*ELEC*: = *watt*) v.
WA *abbr* (*US*) = *Washington*.
wad [wɔd] *n* (*of cotton wool, paper*) bolita; (*of banknotes etc*) fajo.
wadding ['wɔdɪŋ] *n* relleno.
waddle ['wɔdl] *vi* andar como un pato.
wade [weɪd] *vi*: **to ~ through** caminar por el agua; (*fig: a book*) leer con dificultad.
wading pool ['weɪdɪŋ-] *n* (*US*) piscina para niños.
wafer ['weɪfə*] *n* (*biscuit*) barquillo; (*REL*) oblea; (: *consecrated*) hostia; (*COMPUT*) oblea, microplaqueta.
wafer-thin ['weɪfə'θɪn] *adj* finísimo.

waffle ['wɔfl] *n* (*CULIN*) gofre *m* ♦ *vi* meter el rollo.
waffle iron *n* molde *m* para hacer gofres.
waft [wɔft] *vt* llevar por el aire ♦ *vi* flotar.
wag [wæg] *vt* menear, agitar ♦ *vi* moverse, menearse; **the dog ~ged its tail** el perro meneó la cola.
wage [weɪdʒ] *n* (*also*: **~s**) sueldo, salario ♦ *vt*: **to ~ war** hacer la guerra; **a day's ~** el sueldo de un día.
wage claim *n* reivindicación *f* salarial.
wage differential *n* diferencia salarial.
wage earner *n* asalariado/a.
wage freeze *n* congelación *f* de salarios.
wage packet *n* sobre *m* de la paga.
wager ['weɪdʒə*] *n* apuesta ♦ *vt* apostar.
waggle ['wægl] *vt* menear, mover.
wag(g)on ['wægən] *n* (*horse-drawn*) carro; (*BRIT RAIL*) vagón *m*.
wail [weɪl] *n* gemido ♦ *vi* gemir.
waist [weɪst] *n* cintura, talle *m*.
waistcoat ['weɪstkəut] *n* (*BRIT*) chaleco.
waistline ['weɪstlaɪn] *n* talle *m*.
wait [weɪt] *n* espera; (*interval*) pausa ♦ *vi* esperar; **to lie in ~ for** acechar a; **I can't ~ to** (*fig*) estoy deseando; **to ~ for** esperar (a); **to keep sb ~ing** hacer esperar a algn; **~ a moment!** ¡un momento!, ¡un momentito!; **"repairs while you ~"** "reparaciones en el acto".
▶**wait behind** *vi* quedarse.
▶**wait on** *vt fus* servir a.
▶**wait up** *vi* esperar levantado.
waiter ['weɪtə*] *n* camarero.
waiting ['weɪtɪŋ] *n*: **"no ~"** (*BRIT AUT*) "prohibido estacionarse".
waiting list *n* lista de espera.
waiting room *n* sala de espera.
waitress ['weɪtrɪs] *n* camarera.
waive [weɪv] *vt* suspender.
waiver ['weɪvə*] *n* renuncia.
wake [weɪk] *vb* (*pt* **woke** *or* **waked**, *pp* **woken** *or* **waked** [wəuk, 'wəukn]) *vt* (*also*: **~ up**) despertar ♦ *vi* (*also*: **~ up**) despertarse ♦ *n* (*for dead person*) velatorio; (*NAUT*) estela; **to ~ up to sth** (*fig*) darse cuenta de algo; **in the ~ of** tras, después de; **to follow in sb's ~** (*fig*) seguir las huellas de algn.
waken ['weɪkn] *vt, vi* = **wake**.
Wales [weɪlz] *n* País *m* de Gales.
walk [wɔːk] *n* (*stroll*) paseo; (*hike*) excursión *f* a pie, caminata; (*gait*) paso, andar *m*; (*in park etc*) paseo ♦ *vi* andar, caminar; (*for pleasure, exercise*) pasearse ♦ *vt* (*distance*) recorrer a pie, andar; (*dog*) (sacar a) pasear; **to go for a ~** ir a dar un paseo; **10 minutes' ~ from here** a 10

minutos de aquí andando; **people from all ~s of life** gente de todas las esferas; **to ~ in one's sleep** ser sonámbulo/a; **I'll ~ you home** te acompañaré a casa.

►**walk out** *vi* (*go out*) salir; (*as protest*) marcharse, salirse; (*strike*) declararse en huelga; **to ~ out on sb** abandonar a algn.

walkabout ['wɔ:kəbaut] *n*: **to go (on a) ~** darse un baño de multitudes.

walker ['wɔ:kə*] *n* (*person*) paseante *m/f*, caminante *m/f*.

walkie-talkie ['wɔ:kɪ'tɔ:kɪ] *n* walkie-talkie *m*.

walking ['wɔ:kɪŋ] *n* (el) andar; **it's within ~ distance** se puede ir andando *or* a pie.

walking shoes *npl* zapatos *mpl* para andar.

walking stick *n* bastón *m*.

Walkman ® *n* walkman *m* ®.

walk-on ['wɔ:kɔn] *adj* (*THEAT: part*) de comparsa.

walkout ['wɔ:kaut] *n* (*of workers*) huelga.

walkover ['wɔ:kəuvə*] *n* (*col*) pan *m* comido.

walkway ['wɔ:kweɪ] *n* paseo.

wall [wɔ:l] *n* pared *f*; (*exterior*) muro; (*city ~ etc*) muralla; **to go to the ~** (*fig: firm etc*) quebrar, ir a la bancarrota.

►**wall in** *vt* (*garden etc*) cercar con una tapia.

walled [wɔ:ld] *adj* (*city*) amurallado; (*garden*) con tapia.

wallet ['wɔlɪt] *n* cartera, billetera (*esp LAM*).

wallflower ['wɔ:lflauə*] *n* alhelí *m*; **to be a ~** (*fig*) comer pavo.

wall hanging *n* tapiz *m*.

wallop ['wɔləp] *vt* (*col*) zurrar.

wallow ['wɔləu] *vi* revolcarse; **to ~ in one's grief** sumirse en su pena.

wallpaper ['wɔ:lpeɪpə*] *n* papel *m* pintado.

wall-to-wall ['wɔ:ltə'wɔ:l] *adj*: **~ carpeting** moqueta.

wally ['wɔlɪ] *n* (*col*) majadero/a.

walnut ['wɔ:lnʌt] *n* nuez *f*; (*tree*) nogal *m*.

walrus, *pl* **~** *or* **~es** ['wɔ:lrəs] *n* morsa.

waltz [wɔ:lts] *n* vals *m* ♦ *vi* bailar el vals.

wan [wɔn] *adj* pálido.

wand [wɔnd] *n* (*also*: **magic ~**) varita (mágica).

wander ['wɔndə*] *vi* (*person*) vagar; deambular; (*thoughts*) divagar; (*get lost*) extraviarse ♦ *vt* recorrer, vagar por.

wanderer ['wɔndərə*] *n* vagabundo/a.

wandering ['wɔndərɪŋ] *adj* (*tribe*) nómada; (*minstrel, actor*) ambulante; (*path, river*) sinuoso; (*glance, mind*) distraído.

wane [weɪn] *vi* menguar.

wangle ['wæŋgl] (*BRIT col*) *vt*: **to ~ sth**

agenciarse *or* conseguir algo ♦ *n* chanchullo.

wanker ['wæŋkə*] *n* (*col!*) pajero/a (*!*); (*as insult*) mamón/ona (*!*) *m/f*.

want [wɔnt] *vt* (*wish for*) querer, desear; (*need*) necesitar; (*lack*) carecer de ♦ *n* (*poverty*) pobreza; **for ~ of** por falta de; **~s** *npl* (*needs*) necesidades *fpl*; **to ~ to do** querer hacer; **to ~ sb to do sth** querer que algn haga algo; **you're ~ed on the phone** te llaman al teléfono; **to be in ~** estar necesitado; **"cook ~ed"** "se necesita cocinero/a".

want ads *npl* (*US*) anuncios *mpl* por palabras.

wanting ['wɔntɪŋ] *adj*: **to be ~ (in)** estar falto (de); **to be found ~** no estar a la altura de las circunstancias.

wanton ['wɔntn] *adj* (*playful*) juguetón/ona; (*licentious*) lascivo.

war [wɔ:*] *n* guerra; **to make ~** hacer la guerra; **the First/Second World W~** la primera/segunda guerra mundial.

warble ['wɔ:bl] *n* (*of bird*) trino, gorjeo ♦ *vi* (*bird*) trinar.

war cry *n* grito de guerra.

ward [wɔ:d] *n* (*in hospital*) sala; (*POL*) distrito electoral; (*LAW: child*) pupilo/a.

►**ward off** *vt* desviar, parar; (*attack*) rechazar.

warden ['wɔ:dn] *n* (*BRIT: of institution*) director(a) *m/f*; (*of park, game reserve*) guardián/ana *m/f*; (*BRIT: also*: **traffic ~**) guardia *m/f*.

warder ['wɔ:də*] *n* (*BRIT*) guardián/ana *m/f*, carcelero/a.

wardrobe ['wɔ:drəub] *n* armario, guardarropa, ropero, clóset/closet *m* (*LAM*).

warehouse ['weəhaus] *n* almacén *m*, depósito.

wares [weəz] *npl* mercancías *fpl*.

warfare ['wɔ:feə*] *n* guerra.

war game *n* juego de estrategia militar.

warhead ['wɔ:hed] *n* cabeza armada; **nuclear ~s** cabezas *fpl* nucleares.

warily ['weərɪlɪ] *adv* con cautela, cautelosamente.

warlike ['wɔ:laɪk] *adj* guerrero.

warm [wɔ:m] *adj* caliente; (*person, greeting, heart*) afectuoso, cariñoso; (*supporter*) entusiasta; (*thanks, congratulations, apologies*) efusivo; (*clothes etc*) que abriga; (*welcome, day*) caluroso; **it's ~** hace calor; **I'm ~** tengo calor; **to keep sth ~** mantener algo caliente.

►**warm up** *vi* (*room*) calentarse; (*person*) entrar en calor; (*athlete*) hacer ejercicios

de calentamiento; (*discussion*) acalorarse
♦ *vt* calentar.
warm-blooded ['wɔːm'blʌdɪd] *adj* de
sangre caliente.
war memorial *n* monumento a los caídos.
warm-hearted [wɔːm'hɑːtɪd] *adj* afectuoso.
warmly ['wɔːmlɪ] *adv* afectuosamente.
warmonger ['wɔːmʌŋgə*] *n* belicista *m/f*.
warmongering ['wɔːmʌŋgrɪŋ] *n* belicismo.
warmth [wɔːmθ] *n* calor *m*.
warm-up ['wɔːmʌp] *n* (*SPORT*) ejercicios
mpl de calentamiento.
warn [wɔːn] *vt* avisar, advertir; **to ~ sb not
to do sth** *or* **against doing sth** aconsejar a
algn que no haga algo.
warning ['wɔːnɪŋ] *n* aviso, advertencia;
gale ~ (*METEOROLOGY*) aviso de vendaval;
without (any) ~ sin aviso *or* avisar.
warning light *n* luz *f* de advertencia.
warning triangle *n* (*AUT*) triángulo
señalizador.
warp [wɔːp] *vi* (*wood*) combarse.
warpath ['wɔːpɑːθ] *n*: **to be on the ~** (*fig*)
estar en pie de guerra.
warped [wɔːpt] *adj* (*wood*) alabeado; (*fig:
character, sense of humour etc*) pervertido.
warrant ['wɔrnt] *n* (*LAW: to arrest*) orden *f*
de detención; (: *to search*) mandamiento
de registro ♦ *vt* (*justify, merit*) merecer.
warrant officer *n* (*MIL*) brigada *m*; (*NAUT*)
contramaestre *m*.
warranty ['wɔrəntɪ] *n* garantía; **under ~**
(*COMM*) bajo garantía.
warren ['wɔrən] *n* (*of rabbits*) madriguera;
(*fig*) laberinto.
warring ['wɔːrɪŋ] *adj* (*interests etc*) opuesto;
(*nations*) en guerra.
warrior ['wɔrɪə*] *n* guerrero/a.
Warsaw ['wɔːsɔː] *n* Varsovia.
warship ['wɔːʃɪp] *n* buque *m or* barco de
guerra.
wart [wɔːt] *n* verruga.
wartime ['wɔːtaɪm] *n*: **in ~** en tiempos de
guerra, en la guerra.
wary ['wɛərɪ] *adj* cauteloso; **to be ~ about**
or **of doing sth** tener cuidado con hacer
algo.
was [wɔz] *pt of* **be**.
wash [wɔʃ] *vt* lavar; (*sweep, carry: sea etc*)
llevar ♦ *vi* lavarse ♦ *n* (*clothes etc*) lavado;
(*bath*) baño; (*of ship*) estela; **he was ~ed
overboard** fue arrastrado del barco por
las olas; **to have a ~** lavarse.
▶**wash away** *vt* (*stain*) quitar lavando;
(*subj: river etc*) llevarse; (*fig*) limpiar.
▶**wash down** *vt* lavar.
▶**wash off** *vt* quitar lavando.
▶**wash up** *vi* (*BRIT*) fregar los platos; (*US:*

have a wash) lavarse.
Wash. *abbr* (*US*) = Washington.
washable ['wɔʃəbl] *adj* lavable.
washbasin ['wɔʃbeɪsn], (*US*) **washbowl**
['wɔʃbəul] *n* lavabo.
washcloth ['wɔʃklɔθ] *n* (*US*) manopla.
washer ['wɔʃə*] *n* (*TECH*) arandela.
washing ['wɔʃɪŋ] *n* (*dirty*) ropa sucia;
(*clean*) colada.
washing line *n* cuerda de (colgar) la ropa.
washing machine *n* lavadora.
washing powder *n* (*BRIT*) detergente *m*
(en polvo).
Washington ['wɔʃɪŋtən] *n* (*city, state*)
Washington *m*.
washing-up [wɔʃɪŋ'ʌp] *n* fregado; (*dishes*)
platos *mpl* (para fregar); **to do the ~**
fregar los platos.
washing-up liquid *n* lavavajillas *m inv.*
wash leather *n* gamuza.
wash-out ['wɔʃaut] *n* (*col*) fracaso.
washroom ['wɔʃrum] *n* servicios *mpl.*
wasn't ['wɔznt] = **was not.**
Wasp, WASP [wɔsp] *n abbr* (*US col*: = *White
Anglo-Saxon Protestant*) sobrenombre, en
general peyorativo, que se da a los
americanos de origen anglosajón,
acomodada y de tendencia
conservadora.
wasp [wɔsp] *n* avispa.
waspish ['wɔspɪʃ] *adj* (*character*) irascible;
(*comment*) mordaz, punzante.
wastage ['weɪstɪdʒ] *n* desgaste *m*; (*loss*)
pérdida; **natural ~** desgaste natural.
waste [weɪst] *n* derroche *m*, despilfarro;
(*misuse*) desgaste *m*; (*of time*) pérdida;
(*food*) sobras *fpl*; (*rubbish*) basura,
desperdicios *mpl* ♦ *adj* (*material*) de
desecho; (*left over*) sobrante; (*energy,
heat*) desperdiciado; (*land, ground*: in city)
sin construir; (: *in country*) baldío ♦ *vt*
(*squander*) malgastar, derrochar; (*time*)
perder; (*opportunity*) desperdiciar; **~s** *npl*
(*area of land*) tierras *fpl* baldías; **to lay ~**
devastar, arrasar; **it's a ~ of money** es
tirar el dinero; **to go to ~**
desperdiciarse.
▶**waste away** *vi* consumirse.
wastebasket ['weɪstbɑːskɪt] *n* (*esp US*)
= **wastepaper basket**.
waste disposal (unit) *n* (*BRIT*) triturador
m de basura.
wasteful ['weɪstful] *adj* derrochador(a);
(*process*) antieconómico.
wastefully ['weɪstfulɪ] *adv*: **to spend money
~** derrochar dinero.
waste ground *n* (*BRIT*) terreno baldío.
wasteland ['weɪstlənd] *n* (*urban*)

descampados *mpl.*

wastepaper basket ['weɪstpeɪpə-] *n* papelera.

waste pipe *n* tubo de desagüe.

waste products *npl* (*INDUSTRY*) residuos *mpl.*

waster ['weɪstə*] *n* (*col*) gandul *m/f.*

watch [wɔtʃ] *n* reloj *m*; (*vigil*) vigilia; (*vigilance*) vigilancia; (*MIL: guard*) centinela *m*; (*NAUT: spell of duty*) guardia ♦ *vt* (*look at*) mirar, observar; (: *match, programme*) ver; (*spy on, guard*) vigilar; (*be careful of*) cuidar, tener cuidado de ♦ *vi* ver, mirar; (*keep guard*) montar guardia; **to keep a close ~ on sth/sb** vigilar algo/a algn de cerca; **~ how you drive/what you're doing** ten cuidado al conducir/con lo que haces.

▶**watch out** *vi* cuidarse, tener cuidado.

watch band *n* (*US*) pulsera (de reloj).

watchdog ['wɔtʃdɔg] *n* perro guardián; (*fig*) organismo de control.

watchful ['wɔtʃful] *adj* vigilante, sobre aviso.

watchfully ['wɔtʃfulɪ] *adv*: **to stand ~** permanecer vigilante.

watchmaker ['wɔtʃmeɪkə*] *n* relojero/a.

watchman *n* guardián *m*; (*also*: **night ~**) sereno, vigilante *m*; (*in factory*) vigilante *m* nocturno.

watch stem *n* (*US*) cuerda.

watch strap *n* pulsera (de reloj).

watchword ['wɔtʃwɔːd] *n* consigna, contraseña.

water ['wɔːtə*] *n* agua ♦ *vt* (*plant*) regar ♦ *vi* (*eyes*) llorar; **I'd like a drink of ~** quisiera un vaso de agua; **in British ~s** en aguas británicas; **to pass ~** orinar; **his mouth ~ed** se le hizo la boca agua.

▶**water down** *vt* (*milk etc*) aguar.

water closet *n* wáter *m.*

watercolour, (*US*) **watercolor** ['wɔːtəkʌlə*] *n* acuarela.

water-cooled ['wɔːtəkuːld] *adj* refrigerado (por agua).

watercress ['wɔːtəkrɛs] *n* berro.

waterfall ['wɔːtəfɔːl] *n* cascada, salto de agua.

waterfront ['wɔːtəfrʌnt] *n* (*seafront*) parte *f* que da al mar; (*at docks*) muelles *mpl.*

water heater *n* calentador *m* de agua.

water hole *n* abrevadero.

watering can ['wɔːtərɪŋ-] *n* regadera.

water level *n* nivel *m* del agua.

water lily *n* nenúfar *m.*

waterline ['wɔːtəlaɪn] *n* (*NAUT*) línea de flotación.

waterlogged ['wɔːtələgd] *adj* (*boat*)

anegado; (*ground*) inundado.

water main *n* cañería del agua.

watermark ['wɔːtəmɑːk] *n* (*on paper*) filigrana.

watermelon ['wɔːtəmɛlən] *n* sandía.

water polo *n* waterpolo, polo acuático.

waterproof ['wɔːtəpruːf] *adj* impermeable.

water-repellent ['wɔːtərɪ'pɛlənt] *adj* hidrófugo.

watershed ['wɔːtəʃɛd] *n* (*GEO*) cuenca; (*fig*) momento crítico.

water-skiing ['wɔːtəskiːɪŋ] *n* esquí *m* acuático.

water softener *n* ablandador *m* de agua.

water tank *n* depósito de agua.

watertight ['wɔːtətaɪt] *adj* hermético.

water vapour, (*US*) **water vapor** *n* vapor *m* de agua.

waterway ['wɔːtəweɪ] *n* vía fluvial *or* navegable.

waterworks ['wɔːtəwɔːks] *npl* central *fsg* depuradora.

watery ['wɔːtərɪ] *adj* (*colour*) desvaído; (*coffee*) aguado; (*eyes*) lloroso.

watt [wɔt] *n* vatio.

wattage ['wɔtɪdʒ] *n* potencia en vatios.

wattle ['wɔtl] *n* zarzo.

wave [weɪv] *n* ola; (*of hand*) señal *f* con la mano; (*RADIO, in hair*) onda; (*fig: of enthusiasm, strikes*) oleada ♦ *vi* agitar la mano; (*flag*) ondear ♦ *vt* (*handkerchief, gun*) agitar; **short/medium/long ~** (*RADIO*) onda corta/media/larga; **the new ~** (*CINE, MUS*) la nueva ola; **to ~ goodbye to sb** decir adiós a algn con la mano; **he ~d us over to his table** nos hizo señas (con la mano) para que nos acercásemos a su mesa.

▶**wave aside, wave away** *vt* (*person*): **to ~ sb aside** apartar a algn con la mano; (*fig: suggestion, objection*) rechazar; (*doubts*) desechar.

waveband ['weɪvbænd] *n* banda de ondas.

wavelength ['weɪvlɛŋθ] *n* longitud *f* de onda.

waver ['weɪvə*] *vi* oscilar; (*confidence*) disminuir; (*faith*) flaquear.

wavy ['weɪvɪ] *adj* ondulado.

wax [wæks] *n* cera ♦ *vt* encerar ♦ *vi* (*moon*) crecer.

waxen ['wæksn] *adj* (*fig: pale*) blanco como la cera.

waxworks ['wækswɔːks] *npl* museo *sg* de cera.

way [weɪ] *n* camino; (*distance*) trayecto, recorrido; (*direction*) dirección *f*, sentido; (*manner*) modo, manera; (*habit*) costumbre *f*; **which ~? — this ~** ¿por

dónde? *or* ¿en qué dirección? — por aquí;
on the ~ (*en route*) en (el) camino;
(*expected*) en camino; **to be on one's** ~
estar en camino; **you pass it on your** ~
home está de camino a tu casa; **to be in
the** ~ bloquear el camino; (*fig*) estorbar;
to keep out of sb's ~ esquivar a algn; **to
make** ~ **(for sb/sth)** dejar paso (a algn/
algo); (*fig*) abrir camino (a algn/algo); **to
go out of one's** ~ **to do sth** desvivirse
por hacer algo; **to lose one's** ~ perderse,
extraviarse; **to be the wrong** ~ **round**
estar del *or* al revés; **in a** ~ en cierto
modo *or* sentido; **by the** ~ a propósito; **by
** ~ **of** (*via*) pasando por; (*as a sort of*) como,
a modo de; *"*~ **in"** (*BRIT*) "entrada"; "~
out" (*BRIT*) "salida"; **the** ~ **back** el camino
de vuelta; **the village is rather out of the
** ~ el pueblo está un poco apartado *or*
retirado; **it's a long** ~ **away** está muy
lejos; **to get one's own** ~ salirse con la
suya; *"***give** ~*"* (*BRIT AUT*) "ceda el paso";
no ~! (*col*) ¡ni pensarlo!; **put it the right
** ~ **up** ponlo boca arriba; **he's in a bad**
~ está grave; **to be under** ~ (*work, project*)
estar en marcha.
waybill ['weɪbɪl] *n* (*COMM*) hoja de ruta,
carta de porte.
waylay [weɪ'leɪ] *vt* (*irreg: like* **lay**) atacar.
wayside ['weɪsaɪd] *n* borde *m* del camino;
to fall by the ~ (*fig*) fracasar.
way station *n* (*US RAIL*) apeadero; (*fig*)
paso intermedio.
wayward ['weɪwəd] *adj* díscolo,
caprichoso.
WC ['dʌblju:'si:] *n abbr* (*BRIT:* = *water closet*)
wáter *m*.
WCC *n abbr* = *World Council of Churches*.
we [wiː] *pl pron* nosotros/as; ~ **understand**
(nosotros) entendemos; **here** ~ **are** aquí
estamos.
weak [wiːk] *adj* débil, flojo; (*tea, coffee*)
flojo, aguado; **to grow** ~**(er)** debilitarse.
weaken ['wiːkən] *vi* debilitarse; (*give way*)
ceder ♦ *vt* debilitar.
weak-kneed [wiːk'niːd] *adj* (*fig*) sin
voluntad *or* carácter.
weakling ['wiːklɪŋ] *n* debilucho/a.
weakly ['wiːklɪ] *adj* enfermizo, débil ♦ *adv*
débilmente.
weakness ['wiːknɪs] *n* debilidad *f*; (*fault*)
punto débil.
wealth [wɛlθ] *n* (*money, resources*) riqueza;
(*of details*) abundancia.
wealth tax *n* impuesto sobre el
patrimonio.
wealthy ['wɛlθɪ] *adj* rico.
wean [wiːn] *vt* destetar.

weapon ['wɛpən] *n* arma.
wear [wɛə*] *n* (*use*) uso; (*deterioration
through use*) desgaste *m*; (*clothing*):
sports/baby~ ropa de deportes/de niños
♦ *vb* (*pt* **wore**, *pp* **worn** [wɔː*, wɔːn]) *vt*
(*clothes, beard*) llevar; (*shoes*) calzar;
(*look, smile*) tener; (*damage: through use*)
gastar, usar ♦ *vi* (*last*) durar; (*rub through
etc*) desgastarse; **evening** ~ (*man's*) traje
m de etiqueta; (*woman's*) traje *m* de
noche; **to** ~ **a hole in sth** hacer un
agujero en algo.
▶**wear away** *vt* gastar ♦ *vi* desgastarse.
▶**wear down** *vt* gastar; (*strength*) agotar.
▶**wear off** *vi* (*pain, excitement etc*) pasar,
desaparecer.
▶**wear out** *vt* desgastar; (*person, strength*)
agotar.
wearable ['wɛərəbl] *adj* que se puede
llevar, ponible.
wear and tear *n* desgaste *m*.
wearer ['wɛərə*] *n*: **the** ~ **of this jacket** el/la
que lleva puesta esta chaqueta.
wearily ['wɪərɪlɪ] *adv* con cansancio.
weariness ['wɪərɪnɪs] *n* cansancio;
abatimiento.
wearisome ['wɪərɪsəm] *adj* (*tiring*) cansado,
pesado; (*boring*) aburrido.
weary ['wɪərɪ] *adj* (*tired*) cansado;
(*dispirited*) abatido ♦ *vt* cansar ♦ *vi*: **to** ~ **of**
cansarse de, aburrirse de.
weasel ['wiːzl] *n* (*ZOOL*) comadreja.
weather ['wɛðə*] *n* tiempo ♦ *vt* (*storm,
crisis*) hacer frente a; **under the** ~ (*fig: ill*)
mal, pachucho; **what's the** ~ **like?** ¿qué
tiempo hace?, ¿cómo hace?
weather-beaten ['wɛðəbiːtn] *adj* curtido.
weathercock ['wɛðəkɔk] *n* veleta.
weather forecast *n* boletín *m*
meteorológico.
weatherman ['wɛðəmæn] *n* hombre *m* del
tiempo.
weatherproof ['wɛðəpruːf] *adj* (*garment*)
impermeable.
weather report *n* parte *m* meteorológico.
weather vane *n* = **weathercock**.
weave, *pt* **wove**, *pp* **woven** [wiːv, wəuv,
'wəuvn] *vt* (*cloth*) tejer; (*fig*) entretejer ♦ *vi*
(*fig:pt,pp* ~**d**: *move in and out*) zigzaguear.
weaver ['wiːvə*] *n* tejedor(a) *m/f*.
weaving ['wiːvɪŋ] *n* tejeduría.
web [wɛb] *n* (*of spider*) telaraña; (*on foot*)
membrana; (*network*) red *f*.
webbed [wɛbd] *adj* (*foot*) palmeado.
webbing ['wɛbɪŋ] *n* (*on chair*) cinchas *fpl*.
wed [wɛd] *vt* (*pt, pp* **wedded**) casar ♦ *n*: **the
newly-**~**s** los recién casados.
Wed. *abbr* (= *Wednesday*) miérc.

we'd [wiːd] = **we had; we would**.
wedded ['wɛdɪd] *pt, pp of* **wed**.
wedding ['wɛdɪŋ] *n* boda, casamiento.
wedding anniversary *adj* aniversario de boda; **silver/golden** ~ bodas *fpl* de plata/de oro.
wedding day *n* día *m* de la boda.
wedding dress *n* traje *m* de novia.
wedding present *n* regalo de boda.
wedding ring *n* alianza.
wedge [wɛdʒ] *n* (*of wood etc*) cuña; (*of cake*) trozo ♦ *vt* acuñar; (*push*) apretar.
wedge-heeled ['wɛdʒ'hiːld] *adj* con suela de cuña.
wedlock ['wɛdlɔk] *n* matrimonio.
Wednesday ['wɛdnzdɪ] *n* miércoles *m inv*.
wee [wiː] *adj* (*Scottish*) pequeñito.
weed [wiːd] *n* mala hierba, maleza ♦ *vt* escardar, desherbar.
►**weed out** *vt* eliminar.
weedkiller ['wiːdkɪlə*] *n* herbicida *m*.
weedy ['wiːdɪ] *adj* (*person*) debilucho.
week [wiːk] *n* semana; **a** ~ **today** de hoy en ocho días; **Tuesday** ~, **a** ~ **on Tuesday** del martes en una semana; **once/twice a** ~ una vez/dos veces a la semana; **this** ~ esta semana; **in 2** ~**s' time** dentro de 2 semanas; **every other** ~ cada 2 semanas.
weekday ['wiːkdeɪ] *n* día *m* laborable; **on** ~**s** entre semana, en días laborables.
weekend [wiːk'ɛnd] *n* fin *m* de semana.
weekend case *n* neceser *m*.
weekly ['wiːklɪ] *adv* semanalmente, cada semana ♦ *adj* semanal ♦ *n* semanario; ~ **newspaper** semanario.
weep, *pt, pp* **wept** [wiːp, wɛpt] *vi, vt* llorar; (*MED: wound etc*) supurar.
weeping willow ['wiːpɪŋ-] *n* sauce *m* llorón.
weepy ['wiːpɪ] *n* (*col: film*) película lacrimógena; (: *story*) historia lacrimógena.
weft [wɛft] *n* (*TEXTILES*) trama.
weigh [weɪ] *vt, vi* pesar; **to** ~ **anchor** levar anclas; **to** ~ **the pros and cons** pesar los pros y los contras.
►**weigh down** *vt* sobrecargar; (*fig: with worry*) agobiar.
►**weigh out** *vt* (*goods*) pesar.
►**weigh up** *vt* pesar.
weighbridge ['weɪbrɪdʒ] *n* báscula para camiones.
weighing machine ['weɪɪŋ-] *n* báscula, peso.
weight [weɪt] *n* peso; (*on scale*) pesa; **to lose/put on** ~ adelgazar/engordar; ~**s and measures** pesas y medidas.
weighting ['weɪtɪŋ] *n* (*allowance*): **(London)** ~ *dietas fpl* (*por residir en Londres*).
weightlessness ['weɪtlɪsnɪs] *n* ingravidez *f*.
weight lifter *n* levantador(a) *m/f* de pesas.
weight limit *n* límite *m* de peso.
weight training *n* musculación *f* (con pesas).
weighty ['weɪtɪ] *adj* pesado.
weir [wɪə*] *n* presa.
weird [wɪəd] *adj* raro, extraño.
weirdo ['wɪədəu] *n* (*col*) tío/a raro/a.
welcome ['wɛlkəm] *adj* bienvenido ♦ *n* bienvenida ♦ *vt* dar la bienvenida a; (*be glad of*) alegrarse de; **to make sb** ~ recibir *or* acoger bien a algn; **thank you** — **you're** ~ gracias — de nada; **you're** ~ **to try** puede intentar cuando quiera; **we** ~ **this step** celebramos esta medida.
weld [wɛld] *n* soldadura ♦ *vt* soldar.
welding ['wɛldɪŋ] *n* soldadura.
welfare ['wɛlfɛə*] *n* bienestar *m*; (*social aid*) asistencia social; **W**~ (*US*) subsidio de paro; **to look after sb's** ~ cuidar del bienestar de algn.
welfare state *n* estado del bienestar.
welfare work *n* asistencia social.
well [wɛl] *n* pozo ♦ *adv* bien ♦ *adj*: **to be** ~ estar bien (de salud) ♦ *excl* ¡vaya!, ¡bueno!; **as** ~ (*in addition*) además, también; **as** ~ **as** además de; **you might as** ~ **tell me** más vale que me lo digas; **it would be as** ~ **to ask** más valdría preguntar; ~ **done!** ¡bien hecho!; **get** ~ **soon!** ¡que te mejores pronto!; **to do** ~ (*business*) ir bien; **I did** ~ **in my exams** me han salido bien los exámenes; **they are doing** ~ **now** les va bien ahora; **to think** ~ **of sb** pensar bien de algn; **I don't feel** ~ no me encuentro *or* siento bien; ~, **as I was saying** ... bueno, como decía ....
►**well up** *vi* brotar.
we'll [wiːl] = **we will, we shall**.
well-behaved ['wɛlbɪ'heɪvd] *adj*: **to be** ~ portarse bien.
well-being ['wɛl'biːɪŋ] *n* bienestar *m*.
well-bred ['wɛl'brɛd] *adj* bien educado.
well-built ['wɛl'bɪlt] *adj* (*person*) fornido.
well-chosen ['wɛl'tʃəuzn] *adj* (*remarks, words*) acertado.
well-deserved ['wɛldɪ'zəːvd] *adj* merecido.
well-developed ['wɛldɪ'vɛləpt] *adj* (*arm, muscle etc*) bien desarrollado; (*sense*) agudo, fino.
well-disposed ['wɛldɪs'pəuzd] *adj*: ~ **to(wards)** bien dispuesto a.
well-dressed ['wɛl'drɛst] *adj* bien vestido.
well-earned ['wɛl'əːnd] *adj* (*rest*) merecido.
well-groomed ['wɛl'gruːmd] *adj* de apariencia cuidada.

well-heeled ['wɛl'hiːld] *adj (col: wealthy)* rico.

well-informed ['wɛlɪn'fɔːmd] *adj (having knowledge of sth)* enterado, al corriente.

Wellington ['wɛlɪŋtən] *n* Wellington *m*.

wellingtons ['wɛlɪŋtənz] *npl (also:* **Wellington boots)** botas *fpl* de goma.

well-kept ['wɛl'kɛpt] *adj (secret)* bien guardado; *(hair, hands, house, grounds)* bien cuidado.

well-known ['wɛl'nəun] *adj (person)* conocido.

well-mannered ['wɛl'mænəd] *adj* educado.

well-meaning ['wɛl'miːnɪŋ] *adj* bienintencionado.

well-nigh ['wɛl'naɪ] *adv:* ~ **impossible** casi imposible.

well-off ['wɛl'ɔf] *adj* acomodado.

well-read ['wɛl'rɛd] *adj* culto.

well-spoken ['wɛl'spəukən] *adj* bienhablado.

well-stocked ['wɛl'stɔkt] *adj (shop, larder)* bien surtido.

well-timed ['wɛl'taɪmd] *adj* oportuno.

well-to-do ['wɛltə'duː] *adj* acomodado.

well-wisher ['wɛlwɪʃə*] *n* admirador(a) *m/f*.

well-woman clinic ['wɛlwumən-] *n centro de prevención médica para mujeres.*

Welsh [wɛlʃ] *adj* galés/esa ♦ *n (LING)* galés *m;* **the** ~ *npl* los galeses.

Welshman ['wɛlʃmən] *n* galés *m*.

Welsh rarebit [-'rɛəbɪt] *n* pan *m* con queso tostado.

Welshwoman ['wɛlʃwumən] *n* galesa.

welter ['wɛltə*] *n* mescolanza, revoltijo.

went [wɛnt] *pt of* **go**.

wept [wɛpt] *pt, pp of* **weep**.

were [wəː*] *pt of* **be**.

we're [wɪə*] = **we are**.

weren't [wəːnt] = **were not**.

werewolf, *pl* **-wolves** ['wɪəwulf, -wulvz] *n* hombre *m* lobo.

west [wɛst] *n* oeste *m* ♦ *adj* occidental, del oeste ♦ *adv* al *or* hacia el oeste; **the W**~ Occidente *m*.

westbound ['wɛstbaund] *adj (traffic, carriageway)* con rumbo al oeste.

West Country *n:* **the** ~ el suroeste de Inglaterra.

westerly ['wɛstəlɪ] *adj (wind)* del oeste.

western ['wɛstən] *adj* occidental ♦ *n (CINE)* película del oeste.

westerner ['wɛstənə*] *n (POL)* occidental *m/f*.

westernized ['wɛstənaɪzd] *adj* occidentalizado.

West German *(formerly) adj* de Alemania Occidental ♦ *n* alemán/ana *m/f* (de Alemania Occidental.

West Germany *n (formerly)* Alemania Occidental.

West Indian *adj, n* antillano/a *m/f*.

West Indies [-'ɪndɪz] *npl:* **the** ~ las Antillas.

Westminster ['wɛstmɪnstə*] *n el parlamento británico,* Westminster *m*.

westward(s) ['wɛstwəd(z)] *adv* hacia el oeste.

wet [wɛt] *adj (damp)* húmedo; (~ **through)** mojado; *(rainy)* lluvioso ♦ *vt:* **to** ~ **one's pants** *or* **o.s.** mearse; **to get** ~ mojarse; "~ **paint"** 'recién pintado'.

wet blanket *n:* **to be a** ~ *(fig)* ser un/una aguafiestas.

wetness ['wɛtnɪs] *n* humedad *f*.

wet rot *n* putrefacción *f* por humedad.

wet suit *n* traje *m* de buzo.

we've [wiːv] = **we have**.

whack [wæk] *vt* dar un buen golpe a.

whale [weɪl] *n (ZOOL)* ballena.

whaler ['weɪlə*] *n (ship)* ballenero.

whaling ['weɪlɪŋ] *n* pesca de ballenas.

wharf, *pl* **wharves** [wɔːf, wɔːvz] *n* muelle *m*.

═══════════════════════════ *KEYWORD*

what [wɔt] *adj* **1** *(in direct/indirect questions)* qué; ~ **size is he?** ¿qué talla usa?; ~ **colour/shape is it?** ¿de qué color/forma es?; ~ **books do you need?** ¿qué libros necesitas?

2 *(in exclamations):* ~ **a mess!** ¡qué desastre!; ~ **a fool I am!** ¡qué tonto soy!

♦ *pron* **1** *(interrogative)* qué; ~ **are you doing?** ¿qué haces *or* estás haciendo?; ~ **is happening?** ¿qué pasa *or* está pasando?; ~ **is it called?** ¿cómo se llama?; ~ **about me?** ¿y yo qué?; ~ **about doing ...?** ¿qué tal si hacemos ...?; ~ **is his address?** ¿cuáles son sus señas?; ~ **will it cost?** ¿cuánto costará?

2 *(relative)* lo que; **I saw** ~ **you did/was on the table** vi lo que hiciste/había en la mesa; ~ **I want is a cup of tea** lo que quiero es una taza de té; **I don't know** ~ **to do** no sé qué hacer; **tell me** ~ **you're thinking about** dime en qué estás pensando

3 *(reported questions):* **she asked me** ~ **I wanted** me preguntó qué quería

♦ *excl (disbelieving)* ¡cómo!; ~, **no coffee!** ¡que no hay café!

whatever [wɔt'ɛvə*] *adj:* ~ **book you choose** cualquier libro que elijas ♦ *pron:* **do** ~ **is necessary** haga lo que sea necesario; **no reason** ~ ninguna razón en

absoluto; **nothing** ~ nada en absoluto; ~
it costs cueste lo que cueste.
wheat [wiːt] n trigo.
wheatgerm ['wiːtdʒɜːm] n germen m de
trigo.
wheatmeal ['wiːtmiːl] n harina de trigo.
wheedle ['wiːdl] vt: **to** ~ **sb into doing sth**
engatusar a algn para que haga algo; **to**
~ **sth out of sb** sonsacar algo a algn.
wheel [wiːl] n rueda; (AUT: also: **steering** ~)
volante m; (NAUT) timón m ♦ vt (pram etc)
empujar ♦ vi (also: ~ **round**) dar la vuelta,
girar; **four-**~ **drive** tracción f en las
cuatro ruedas; **front-/rear-**~ **drive**
tracción f delantera/trasera.
wheelbarrow ['wiːlbærəu] n carretilla.
wheelbase ['wiːlbeɪs] n batalla.
wheelchair ['wiːltʃɛəʳ] n silla de ruedas.
wheel clamp n (AUT) cepo.
wheeler-dealer ['wiːləˈdiːləʳ] n
chanchullero/a.
wheelie-bin ['wiːlɪbɪn] n (BRIT) contenedor
m de basura.
wheeling ['wiːlɪŋ] n: ~ **and dealing** (col)
chanchullos mpl.
wheeze [wiːz] vi resollar.
wheezy ['wiːzɪ] adj silbante.

when [wɛn] adv cuando; ~ **did it happen?**
¿cuándo ocurrió?; **I know** ~ **it happened**
sé cuándo ocurrió
♦ conj **1** (at, during, after the time that)
cuando; **be careful** ~ **you cross the road**
ten cuidado al cruzar la calle; **that was** ~
I needed you entonces era cuando te
necesitaba; **I'll buy you a car** ~ **you're 18**
te compraré un coche cuando cumplas
18 años
2 (on, at which): **on the day** ~ **I met him** el
día en qué le conocí
3 (whereas) cuando; **you said I was wrong**
~ **in fact I was right** dijiste que no tenía
razón, cuando en realidad sí la tenía.

whenever [wɛnˈɛvəʳ] conj cuando; (every
time) cada vez que; **I go** ~ **I can** voy
siempre or todas las veces que puedo.
where [wɛəʳ] adv dónde ♦ conj donde; **this is**
~ aquí es donde; ~ **possible** donde sea
posible; ~ **are you from?** ¿de dónde es
usted?
whereabouts ['wɛərəbauts] adv dónde ♦ n:
nobody knows his ~ nadie conoce su
paradero.
whereas [wɛərˈæz] conj mientras.
whereby [wɛəˈbaɪ] adv mediante el/la
cual etc.

whereupon [wɛərəˈpɔn] conj con lo cual,
después de lo cual.
wherever [wɛərˈɛvəʳ] adv dondequiera que;
(interrogative) dónde; **sit** ~ **you like**
siéntese donde quiera.
wherewithal ['wɛəwɪðɔːl] n recursos mpl;
the ~ **(to do sth)** los medios económicos
(para hacer algo).
whet [wɛt] vt estimular; (appetite) abrir.
whether ['wɛðəʳ] conj si; **I don't know** ~ **to**
accept or not no sé si aceptar o no; ~ **you**
go or not vayas o no vayas.
whey [weɪ] n suero.

which [wɪtʃ] adj **1** (interrogative: direct,
indirect) qué; ~ **picture(s) do you want?**
¿qué cuadro(s) quieres?; ~ **one?** ¿cuál?;
~ **one of you?** ¿cuál de vosotros?; **tell me**
~ **one you want** dime cuál (es el que)
quieres
2: **in** ~ **case** en cuyo caso; **we got there at**
8 pm, by ~ **time the cinema was full**
llegamos allí a las 8, cuando el cine
estaba lleno
♦ pron **1** (interrogative) cual; **I don't mind** ~
el/la que sea; ~ **do you want?** ¿cuál
quieres?
2 (relative: replacing noun) que; (: replacing
clause) lo que; (: after preposition) (el/la)
que, el/la cual; **the apple** ~ **you ate/**~ **is**
on the table la manzana que comiste/que
está en la mesa; **the chair on** ~ **you are**
sitting la silla en la que estás sentado; **he**
didn't believe it, ~ **upset me** no se lo
creyó, lo cual or lo que me disgustó; **after**
~ después de lo cual.

whichever [wɪtʃˈɛvəʳ] adj: **take** ~ **book**
you prefer coja el libro que prefiera;
~ **book you take** cualquier libro que
coja.
whiff [wɪf] n bocanada; **to catch a** ~ **of sth**
oler algo.
while [waɪl] n rato, momento ♦ conj
durante; (whereas) mientras; (although)
aunque ♦ vt: **to** ~ **away the time** pasar el
rato; **for a** ~ durante algún tiempo; **in a** ~
dentro de poco; **all the** ~ todo el tiempo;
we'll make it worth your ~ te
compensaremos generosamente.
whilst [waɪlst] conj = **while**.
whim [wɪm] n capricho.
whimper ['wɪmpəʳ] n (weeping) lloriqueo;
(moan) quejido ♦ vi lloriquear; quejarse.
whimsical ['wɪmzɪkl] adj (person)
caprichoso.
whine [waɪn] n (of pain) gemido; (of engine)

zumbido ♦ *vi* gemir; zumbar.
whip [wɪp] *n* látigo ♦ *vt* azotar; (*snatch*) arrebatar; (*US CULIN*) batir.
▶**whip up** *vt* (*cream etc*) batir (rápidamente); (*col: meal*) preparar rápidamente; (: *stir up: support, feeling*) avivar.

En el Parlamento británico la disciplina de partido (en concreto de voto y de asistencia a la Cámara de los Comunes) está a cargo de un grupo de parlamentarios llamados **whips**, *encabezados por el* **Chief Whip**. *Por lo general todos ellos tienen también altos cargos en la Administración del Estado si pertenecen al partido en el poder.*

---

whiplash ['wɪplæʃ] *n* (*MED: also:* ~ *injury*) latigazo.
whipped cream [wɪpt-] *n* nata montada.
whipping boy ['wɪpɪŋ-] *n* (*fig*) cabeza de turco.
whip-round ['wɪpraund] *n* (*BRIT*) colecta.
whirl [wəːl] *n* remolino ♦ *vt* hacer girar, dar vueltas a ♦ *vi* (*dancers*) girar, dar vueltas; (*leaves, dust, water etc*) arremolinarse.
whirlpool ['wəːlpuːl] *n* remolino.
whirlwind ['wəːlwɪnd] *n* torbellino.
whirr [wəː*] *vi* zumbar.
whisk [wɪsk] *n* (*BRIT CULIN*) batidor *m* ♦ *vt* (*BRIT CULIN*) batir; **to** ~ **sb away** *or* **off** llevarse volando a algn.
whiskers [wɪskəz] *npl* (*of animal*) bigotes *mpl*; (*of man*) patillas *fpl*.
whisky, (*US, Ireland*) **whiskey** ['wɪskɪ] *n* whisky *m*.
whisper ['wɪspə*] *n* cuchicheo; (*rumour*) rumor *m*; (*fig*) susurro, murmullo ♦ *vi* cuchichear, hablar bajo; (*fig*) susurrar ♦ *vt* decir en voz muy baja; **to** ~ **sth to sb** decirle algo al oído a algn.
whispering ['wɪspərɪŋ] *n* cuchicheo.
whist [wɪst] *n* (*BRIT*) whist *m*.
whistle ['wɪsl] *n* (*sound*) silbido; (*object*) silbato ♦ *vi* silbar; **to** ~ **a tune** silbar una melodía.
whistle-stop ['wɪslstɔp] *adj:* ~ **tour** (*US POL*) gira electoral rápida; (*fig*) recorrido rápido.
Whit [wɪt] *n* Pentecostés *m*.
white [waɪt] *adj* blanco; (*pale*) pálido ♦ *n* blanco; (*of egg*) clara; **to turn** *or* **go** ~ (*person*) palidecer, ponerse blanco; (*hair*) encanecer; **the** ~**s** (*washing*) la ropa blanca; **tennis** ~**s** ropa *f* de tenis.
whitebait ['waɪtbeɪt] *n* chanquetes *mpl*.
white coffee *n* (*BRIT*) café *m* con leche.
white-collar worker ['waɪtkɔlə-] *n*

oficinista *m/f*.
white elephant *n* (*fig*) maula.
white goods *npl* (*appliances*) electrodomésticos *mpl* de línea blanca; (*linen etc*) ropa blanca.
white-hot [waɪt'hɔt] *adj* (*metal*) candente, calentado al (rojo) blanco.
white lie *n* mentirijilla.
whiteness ['waɪtnɪs] *n* blancura.
white noise *n* sonido blanco.
whiteout ['waɪtaut] *n* resplandor *m* sin sombras; (*fig*) masa confusa.
white paper *n* (*POL*) libro blanco.
whitewash ['waɪtwɔʃ] *n* (*paint*) cal *f*, jalbegue *m* ♦ *vt* encalar, blanquear; (*fig*) encubrir.
whiting ['waɪtɪŋ] *n* (*pl inv*) (*fish*) pescadilla.
Whit Monday *n* lunes *m* de Pentecostés.
Whitsun ['wɪtsn] *n* (*BRIT*) Pentecostés *m*.
whittle ['wɪtl] *vt:* **to** ~ **away**, ~ **down** ir reduciendo.
whizz [wɪz] *vi:* **to** ~ **past** *or* **by** pasar a toda velocidad.
whizz kid *n* (*col*) prodigio/a.
WHO *n abbr* (= *World Health Organization*) OMS *f*.

========================= KEYWORD

who [huː] *pron* **1** (*interrogative*) quién; ~ **is it?**, ~'**s there?** ¿quién es?; ~ **are you looking for?** ¿a quién buscas?; **I told her** ~ **I was** le dije quién era yo
2 (*relative*) que; **the man/woman** ~ **spoke to me** el hombre/la mujer que habló conmigo; **those** ~ **can swim** los que saben *or* sepan nadar.

---

whodun(n)it [huː'dʌnɪt] *n* (*col*) novela policíaca.
whoever [huː'ɛvə*] *pron:* ~ **finds it** cualquiera *or* quienquiera que lo encuentre; **ask** ~ **you like** pregunta a quien quieras; ~ **he marries** se case con quien se case.
whole [həul] *adj* (*complete*) todo, entero; (*not broken*) intacto ♦ *n* (*total*) total *m*; (*sum*) conjunto; ~ **villages were destroyed** pueblos enteros fueron destruídos; **the** ~ **of the town** toda la ciudad, la ciudad entera; **on the** ~, **as a** ~ en general.
wholehearted [həul'haːtɪd] *adj* (*support, approval*) total; (*sympathy*) todo.
wholeheartedly [həul'haːtɪdlɪ] *adv* con entusiasmo.
wholemeal ['həulmiːl] *adj* (*BRIT: flour, bread*) integral.

wholesale ['həʊseɪl] *n* venta al por mayor
♦ *adj* al por mayor; (*destruction*)
sistemático.
wholesaler ['həʊseɪlə*] *n* mayorista
m/f.
wholesome ['həʊlsəm] *adj* sano.
wholewheat ['həʊlwiːt] *adj*
= **wholemeal.**
wholly ['həʊlɪ] *adv* totalmente,
enteramente.

═══════════════ *KEYWORD*

whom [huːm] *pron* **1** (*interrogative*): ~ **did
you see?** ¿a quién viste?; **to** ~ **did you
give it?** ¿a quién se lo diste?; **tell me from
~ you received it** dígame de quién lo
recibiste
2 (*relative*) que; **to** ~ a quien(es); **of** ~
de quien(es), del/de la que; **the man** ~ **I
saw** el hombre qui vi; **the man to** ~ **I
wrote** el hombre a quien escribí; **the lady
about** ~ **I was talking** la señora de (la)
que hablaba; **the lady with** ~ **I was
talking** la señora con quien *or* (la) que
hablaba.

whooping cough ['huːpɪŋ-] *n* tos *f*
ferina.
whoops [wuːps] *excl* (*also*: ~-**a-daisy!**)
¡huy!
whoosh [wuːʃ] *n*: **it came out with a** ~
(*sauce etc*) salió todo de repente; (*air*)
salió con mucho ruido.
whopper ['wɔpə*] *n* (*col: lie*) embuste *m*;
(: *large thing*): **a** ~ una/o enorme.
whopping ['wɔpɪŋ] *adj* (*col*) enorme.
whore [hɔː*] *n* (*col: pej*) puta.

═══════════════ *KEYWORD*

whose [huːz] *adj* **1** (*possessive: interrogative*)
de quién; ~ **book is this?**, ~ **is this book?**
¿de quién es este libro?; ~ **pencil have
you taken?** ¿de quién es el lápiz que has
cogido?; ~ **daughter are you?** ¿de quién
eres hija?
2 (*possessive: relative*) cuyo/a, *pl* cuyos/as;
the man ~ **son they rescued** el hombre
cuyo hijo rescataron; **the girl** ~ **sister he
was speaking to** la chica con cuya
hermana estaba hablando; **those** ~
passports I have aquellas personas cuyos
pasaportes tengo; **the woman** ~ **car was
stolen** la mujer a quien le robaron el
coche
♦ *pron* de quién; ~ **is this?** ¿de quién
es esto?; **I know** ~ **it is** sé de quién
es.

═══════════════ *KEYWORD*

why [waɪ] *adv* por qué; ~ **not?** ¿por qué
no?; ~ **not do it now?** ¿por qué no lo
haces (*or* hacemos) ahora?
♦ *conj*: **I wonder** ~ **he said that** me
pregunto por qué dijo eso; **that's not** ~
I'm here no es por eso (por lo) que estoy
aquí; **the reason** ~ la razón por la que
♦ *excl* (*expressing surprise, shock,
annoyance*) ¡hombre!, ¡vaya!; (*explaining*):
~, **it's you!** ¡hombre, eres tú!; ~, **that's
impossible!** ¡pero si eso es imposible!

whyever [waɪ'ɛvə*] *adv* por qué.
WI *n abbr* (*BRIT*: = *Women's Institute*)
asociación de amas de casa ♦ *abbr* (*GEO*)
= **West Indies**; (*US*) = **Wisconsin.**
wick [wɪk] *n* mecha.
wicked ['wɪkɪd] *adj* malvado, cruel.
wickedness ['wɪkɪdnɪs] *n* maldad *f*,
crueldad *f.*
wicker ['wɪkə*] *n* mimbre *m.*
wickerwork ['wɪkəwɜːk] *n* artículos *mpl* de
mimbre.
wicket ['wɪkɪt] *n* (*CRICKET*) palos *mpl.*
wicket keeper *n* guardameta *m.*
wide [waɪd] *adj* ancho; (*area, knowledge*)
vasto, grande; (*choice*) grande ♦ *adv*: **to
open** ~ abrir de par en par; **to shoot** ~
errar el tiro; **it is 3 metres** ~ tiene 3
metros de ancho.
wide-angle lens ['waɪdæŋgl-] *n* (objetivo)
gran angular *m.*
wide-awake [waɪdə'weɪk] *adj* bien
despierto.
wide-eyed [waɪd'aɪd] *adj* con los ojos muy
abiertos; (*fig*) ingenuo.
widely ['waɪdlɪ] *adv* (*differing*) muy; **it is** ~
believed that ... existe la creencia
generalizada de que ...; **to be** ~ **read**
(*author*) ser muy leído; (*reader*) haber
leído mucho.
widen ['waɪdn] *vt* ensanchar.
wideness ['waɪdnɪs] *n* anchura; amplitud *f.*
wide open *adj* abierto de par en par.
wide-ranging [waɪd'reɪndʒɪŋ] *adj* (*survey,
report*) de gran alcance; (*interests*) muy
diversos.
widespread ['waɪdspred] *adj* (*belief etc*)
extendido, general.
widow ['wɪdəʊ] *n* viuda.
widowed ['wɪdəʊd] *adj* viudo.
widower ['wɪdəʊə*] *n* viudo.
width [wɪdθ] *n* anchura; (*of cloth*) ancho;
it's 7 metres in ~ tiene 7 metros de
ancho.
widthways ['wɪdθweɪz] *adv* a lo ancho.

wield [wiːld] *vt* (*sword*) manejar; (*power*) ejercer.

wife, *pl* **wives** [waɪf, waɪvz] *n* mujer *f*, esposa.

wig [wɪg] *n* peluca.

wigging ['wɪgɪŋ] *n* (*BRIT col*) rapapolvo, bronca.

wiggle ['wɪgl] *vt* menear ♦ *vi* menearse.

wiggly ['wɪglɪ] *adj* (*line*) ondulado.

wigwam ['wɪgwæm] *n* tipi *m*, tienda india.

wild [waɪld] *adj* (*animal*) salvaje; (*plant*) silvestre; (*rough*) furioso, violento; (*idea*) descabellado; (*col: angry*) furioso ♦ *n*: **the ~** la naturaleza; **~s** *npl* regiones *fpl* salvajes, tierras *fpl* vírgenes; **to be ~ about** (*enthusiastic*) estar *or* andar loco por; **in its ~ state** en estado salvaje.

wild card *n* (*COMPUT*) comodín *m*.

wildcat ['waɪldkæt] *n* gato montés.

wildcat strike *n* huelga salvaje.

wilderness ['wɪldənɪs] *n* desierto; (*jungle*) jungla.

wildfire ['waɪldfaɪə*] *n*: **to spread like ~** correr como un reguero de pólvora.

wild-goose chase [waɪld'guːs-] *n* (*fig*) búsqueda inútil.

wildlife ['waɪldlaɪf] *n* fauna.

wildly ['waɪldlɪ] *adv* (*roughly*) violentamente; (*foolishly*) locamente; (*rashly*) descabelladamente.

wiles [waɪlz] *npl* artimañas *fpl*, ardides *mpl*.

wilful, (*US*) **willful** ['wɪlful] *adj* (*action*) deliberado; (*obstinate*) testarudo.

═══════════════════════ *KEYWORD*

will [wɪl] *aux vb* **1** (*forming future tense*): **I ~ finish it tomorrow** lo terminaré *or* voy a terminar mañana; **I ~ have finished it by tomorrow** lo habré terminado para mañana; **~ you do it? — yes I ~/no I won't** ¿lo harás? — sí/no; **you won't lose it, ~ you?** no lo vayas a perder *or* no lo perderás ¿verdad?

2 (*in conjectures, predictions*): **he ~** *or* **he'll be there by now** ya habrá llegado, ya debe (de) haber llegado; **that ~ be the postman** será el cartero, debe ser el cartero

3 (*in commands, requests, offers*): **~ you be quiet!** ¿quieres callarte?; **~ you help me?** ¿quieres ayudarme?; **~ you have a cup of tea?** ¿te apetece un té?; **I won't put up with it!** ¡no lo soporto!

4 (*habits, persistence*): **the car won't start** el coche no arranca; **accidents ~ happen** son cosas que pasan

♦ *vt* (*pt, pp* **willed**): **to ~ sb to do sth** desear que algn haga algo; **he ~ed himself to go**

on con gran fuerza de voluntad, continuó

♦ *n* **1** (*desire*) voluntad *f*; **against sb's ~** contra la voluntad de algn; **he did it of his own free ~** lo hizo por su propia voluntad

2 (*LAW*) testamento; **to make a** *or* **one's ~** hacer su testamento.

willful ['wɪlful] *adj* (*US*) = **wilful**.

willing ['wɪlɪŋ] *adj* (*with goodwill*) de buena voluntad; complaciente; **he's ~ to do it** está dispuesto a hacerlo; **to show ~** mostrarse dispuesto.

willingly ['wɪlɪŋlɪ] *adv* con mucho gusto.

willingness ['wɪlɪŋnɪs] *n* buena voluntad.

will-o'-the-wisp ['wɪləðə'wɪsp] *n* fuego fatuo; (*fig*) quimera.

willow ['wɪləu] *n* sauce *m*.

willpower ['wɪlpauə*] *n* fuerza de voluntad.

willy-nilly [wɪlɪ'nɪlɪ] *adv* quiérase o no.

wilt [wɪlt] *vi* marchitarse.

Wilts *abbr* (*BRIT*) = Wiltshire.

wily ['waɪlɪ] *adj* astuto.

wimp [wɪmp] *n* (*col*) enclenque *m/f*; (*character*) calzonazos *m inv*.

win [wɪn] *n* (*in sports etc*) victoria, triunfo ♦ *vb* (*pt, pp* **won** [wʌn]) *vt* ganar; (*obtain: contract etc*) conseguir, lograr ♦ *vi* ganar.

►**win over,** (*BRIT*) **win round** *vt* convencer a.

wince [wɪns] *vi* encogerse.

winch [wɪntʃ] *n* torno.

Winchester disk ® ['wɪntʃɪstə-] *n* (*COMPUT*) disco Winchester ®.

wind *n* [wɪnd] viento; (*MED*) gases *mpl*; (*breath*) aliento ♦ *vb* (*pt, pp* **wound** [waund]) *vt* enrollar; (*wrap*) envolver; (*clock, toy*) dar cuerda a; [wɪnd] (*take breath away from*) dejar sin aliento a ♦ *vi* (*road, river*) serpentear; **into** *or* **against the ~** contra el viento; **to get ~ of sth** enterarse de algo; **to break ~** ventosear.

►**wind down** *vt* (*car window*) bajar; (*fig: production, business*) disminuir.

►**wind up** *vt* (*clock*) dar cuerda a; (*debate*) concluir, terminar.

windbreak ['wɪndbreɪk] *n* barrera contra el viento.

windcheater ['wɪndtʃiːtə*], (*US*) **windbreaker** ['wɪndbreɪkə*] *n* cazadora.

winder ['waɪndə*] *n* (*on watch*) cuerda.

wind erosion *n* erosión *f* del viento.

windfall ['wɪndfɔːl] *n* golpe *m* de suerte.

winding ['waɪndɪŋ] *adj* (*road*) tortuoso.

wind instrument *n* (*MUS*) instrumento de viento.

windmill ['wɪndmɪl] *n* molino de viento.

window ['wɪndəu] *n* ventana; (*in car, train*)

ventana; (*in shop etc*) escaparate *m*, vitrina (*LAM*), vidriera (*LAM*); (*COMPUT*) ventana.
window box *n* jardinera (de ventana).
window cleaner *n* (*person*) limpiacristales *m inv*.
window dressing *n* decoración *f* de escaparates.
window envelope *n* sobre *m* de ventanilla.
window frame *n* marco de ventana.
window ledge *n* alféizar *m*, repisa.
window pane *n* cristal *m*.
window-shopping [ˈwɪndəuˈʃɔpɪŋ] *n*: **to go ~** ir a ver *or* mirar escaparates.
windowsill [ˈwɪndəusɪl] *n* alféizar *m*, repisa.
windpipe [ˈwɪndpaɪp] *n* tráquea.
wind power *n* energía eólica.
windscreen [ˈwɪndskriːn], (*US*) **windshield** [ˈwɪndʃiːld] *n* parabrisas *m inv*.
windscreen washer, (*US*) **windshield washer** *n* lavaparabrisas *m inv*.
windscreen wiper, (*US*) **windshield wiper** *n* limpiaparabrisas *m inv*.
windsurfing [ˈwɪndsəːfɪŋ] *n* windsurf *m*.
windswept [ˈwɪndswɛpt] *adj* azotado por el viento.
wind tunnel *n* túnel *m* aerodinámico.
windy [ˈwɪndɪ] *adj* de mucho viento; **it's ~** hace viento.
wine [waɪn] *n* vino ♦ *vt*: **to ~ and dine sb** agasajar *or* festejar a algn.
wine bar *n bar especializado en vinos*.
wine cellar *n* bodega.
wine glass *n* copa (de *or* para vino).
wine-growing [ˈwaɪngrəuɪŋ] *adj* viticultor(a).
wine list *n* lista de vinos.
wine merchant *n* vinatero.
wine tasting *n* degustación *f* de vinos.
wine waiter *n* escanciador *m*.
wing [wɪŋ] *n* ala; (*BRIT AUT*) aleta; **~s** *npl* (*THEAT*) bastidores *mpl*.
winger [ˈwɪŋə*] *n* (*SPORT*) extremo.
wing mirror *n* (espejo) retrovisor *m*.
wing nut *n* tuerca (de) mariposa.
wingspan [ˈwɪŋspaen], **wingspread** [ˈwɪŋsprɛd] *n* envergadura.
wink [wɪŋk] *n* guiño; (*blink*) pestañeo ♦ *vi* guiñar; (*blink*) pestañear; (*light etc*) parpadear.
winkle [ˈwɪŋkl] *n* bígaro, bigarro.
winner [ˈwɪnə*] *n* ganador(a) *m/f*.
winning [ˈwɪnɪŋ] *adj* (*team*) ganador(a); (*goal*) decisivo; (*charming*) encantador(a).
winning post *n* meta.

winnings [ˈwɪnɪŋz] *npl* ganancias *fpl*.
winsome [ˈwɪnsəm] *adj* atractivo.
winter [ˈwɪntə*] *n* invierno ♦ *vi* invernar.
winter sports *npl* deportes *mpl* de invierno.
wintry [ˈwɪntrɪ] *adj* invernal.
wipe [waɪp] *n*: **to give sth a ~** pasar un trapo sobre algo ♦ *vt* limpiar; **to ~ one's nose** limpiarse la nariz.
▶**wipe off** *vt* limpiar con un trapo.
▶**wipe out** *vt* (*debt*) liquidar; (*memory*) borrar; (*destroy*) destruir.
▶**wipe up** *vt* limpiar.
wire [waɪə*] *n* alambre *m*; (*ELEC*) cable *m* (eléctrico); (*TEL*) telegrama *m* ♦ *vt* (*house*) poner la instalación eléctrica en; (*also*: **~ up**) conectar.
wire cutters *npl* cortaalambres *msg inv*.
wireless [ˈwaɪəlɪs] *n* (*BRIT*) radio *f*.
wire mesh, **wire netting** *n* tela metálica.
wire service *n* (*US*) agencia de noticias.
wire-tapping [ˈwaɪəˈtæpɪŋ] *n* intervención *f* telefónica.
wiring [ˈwaɪərɪŋ] *n* instalación *f* eléctrica.
wiry [ˈwaɪərɪ] *adj* enjuto y fuerte.
Wis(c). *abbr* (*US*) = Wisconsin.
wisdom [ˈwɪzdəm] *n* sabiduría, saber *m*; (*good sense*) cordura.
wisdom tooth *n* muela del juicio.
wise [waɪz] *adj* sabio; (*sensible*) juicioso; **I'm none the ~r** sigo sin entender.
▶**wise up** *vi* (*col*): **to ~ up (to sth)** enterarse (de algo).
...wise [waɪz] *suff*: **time~** en cuanto a *or* respecto al tiempo.
wisecrack [ˈwaɪzkræk] *n* broma.
wish [wɪʃ] *n* (*desire*) deseo ♦ *vt* desear; (*want*) querer; **best ~es** (*on birthday etc*) felicidades *fpl*; **with best ~es** (*in letter*) saludos *mpl*, recuerdos *mpl*; **to ~ sb goodbye** despedirse de algn; **he ~ed me well** me deseó mucha suerte; **to ~ sth on sb** imponer algo a algn; **to ~ to do/sb to do sth** querer hacer/que algn haga algo; **to ~ for** desear.
wishbone [ˈwɪʃbəun] *n* espoleta (*de la que tiran dos personas; quien se quede con el hueso más largo pide un deseo*).
wishful [ˈwɪʃful] *n*: **it's ~ thinking** eso es hacerse ilusiones.
wishy-washy [ˈwɪʃɪwɔʃɪ] *adj* (*col: colour*) desvaído; (: *ideas, thinking*) flojo.
wisp [wɪsp] *n* mechón *m*; (*of smoke*) voluta.
wistful [ˈwɪstful] *adj* pensativo; (*nostalgic*) nostálgico.
wit [wɪt] *n* (*wittiness*) ingenio, gracia; (*intelligence*: *also*: **~s**) inteligencia; (*person*) chistoso/a; **to have** *or* **keep one's**

~s about one no perder la cabeza.
witch [wɪtʃ] *n* bruja.
witchcraft ['wɪtʃkrɑːft] *n* brujería.
witch doctor *n* hechicero.
witch-hunt ['wɪtʃhʌnt] *n* (*POL*) caza de
brujas.

================================ *KEYWORD*

with [wɪð, wɪθ] *prep* **1** (*accompanying, in the
company of*) con (*con+mí, ti, sí = conmigo,
contigo, consigo*); **I was ~ him** estaba con
él; **we stayed ~ friends** nos quedamos en
casa de unos amigos
2 (*descriptive, indicating manner etc*) con;
de; **a room ~ a view** una habitación con
vistas; **the man ~ the grey hat/blue eyes**
el hombre del sombrero gris/de los ojos
azules; **red ~ anger** rojo de ira; **to shake
~ fear** temblar de miedo; **to fill sth ~
water** llenar algo de agua
3: **I'm ~ you/I'm not ~ you** (*understand*)
ya te entiendo/no te entiendo; **I'm not
really ~ it today** no doy pie con bola hoy.

withdraw [wɪθ'drɔː] *vb* (*irreg: like* **draw**) *vt*
retirar ♦ *vi* retirarse; (*go back on promise*)
retractarse; **to ~ money** (*from the bank*)
retirar fondos (del banco); **to ~ into o.s.**
ensimismarse.
withdrawal [wɪθ'drɔːəl] *n* retirada.
withdrawal symptoms *npl* síndrome *m*
de abstinencia.
withdrawn [wɪθ'drɔːn] *adj* (*person*)
reservado, introvertido ♦ *pp of* **withdraw**.
wither ['wɪðə*] *vi* marchitarse.
withered ['wɪðəd] *adj* marchito, seco.
withhold [wɪθ'həuld] *vt* (*irreg: like* **hold**)
(*money*) retener; (*decision*) aplazar;
(*permission*) negar; (*information*) ocultar.
within [wɪð'ɪn] *prep* dentro de ♦ *adv* dentro;
~ **reach** al alcance de la mano; ~ **sight of**
a la vista de; ~ **the week** antes de que
acabe la semana; **to be ~ the law**
atenerse a la legalidad; ~ **an hour from
now** dentro de una hora.
without [wɪð'aut] *prep* sin; **to go** *or* **do ~
sth** prescindir de algo; ~ **anybody
knowing** sin saberlo nadie.
withstand [wɪθ'stænd] *vt* (*irreg: like* **stand**)
resistir a.
witness ['wɪtnɪs] *n* (*person*) testigo *m/f*;
(*evidence*) testimonio ♦ *vt* (*event*)
presenciar, ser testigo de; (*document*)
atestiguar la veracidad de; ~ **for the
prosecution/defence** testigo de cargo/
descargo; **to ~ to** (*having seen*) **sth** dar
testimonio de (haber visto) algo.
witness box, (*US*) **witness stand** *n*

tribuna de los testigos.
witticism ['wɪtɪsɪzm] *n* dicho ingenioso.
wittily ['wɪtɪlɪ] *adv* ingeniosamente.
witty ['wɪtɪ] *adj* ingenioso.
wives [waɪvz] *npl of* **wife**.
wizard ['wɪzəd] *n* hechicero.
wizened ['wɪznd] *adj* arrugado, marchito.
wk *abbr* = **week**.
Wm. *abbr* = *William*.
WO *n abbr* = **warrant officer**.
wobble ['wɔbl] *vi* tambalearse.
wobbly ['wɔblɪ] *adj* (*hand, voice*)
tembloroso; (*table, chair*) tambaleante,
cojo.
woe [wəu] *n* desgracia.
woeful ['wəuful] *adj* (*bad*) lamentable; (*sad*)
apesadumbrado.
wok [wɔk] *n* wok *m*.
woke [wəuk] *pt of* **wake**.
woken ['wəukn] *pp of* **wake**.
wolf, *pl* **wolves** [wulf, wulvz] *n* lobo.
woman, *pl* **women** ['wumən, 'wɪmɪn] *n*
mujer *f*; **young ~** (mujer *f*) joven *f*;
women's page (*PRESS*) sección *f* de la
mujer.
woman doctor *n* doctora.
woman friend *n* amiga.
womanize ['wumənaɪz] *vi* ser un
mujeriego.
womanly ['wumənlɪ] *adj* femenino.
womb [wuːm] *n* (*ANAT*) matriz *f*, útero.
women ['wɪmɪn] *npl of* **woman**.
Women's (Liberation) Movement *n*
(*also:* **women's lib**) Movimiento de
liberación de la mujer.
won [wʌn] *pt, pp of* **win**.
wonder ['wʌndə*] *n* maravilla, prodigio;
(*feeling*) asombro ♦ *vi*: **to ~ whether**
preguntarse si; **to ~ at** asombrarse de; **to
~ about** pensar sobre *or* en; **it's no ~ that**
no es de extrañar que.
wonderful ['wʌndəful] *adj* maravilloso.
wonderfully ['wʌndəfəlɪ] *adv*
maravillosamente, estupendamente.
wonky ['wɔŋkɪ] *adj* (*BRIT col: unsteady*) poco
seguro, cojo; (: *broken down*) estropeado.
wont [wɔnt] *n*: **as is his/her ~** como tiene
por costumbre.
won't [wəunt] = **will not**.
woo [wuː] *vt* (*woman*) cortejar.
wood [wud] *n* (*timber*) madera; (*forest*)
bosque *m* ♦ *cpd* de madera.
wood alcohol *n* (*US*) alcohol *m*
desnaturalizado.
wood carving *n* tallado en madera.
wooded ['wudɪd] *adj* arbolado.
wooden ['wudn] *adj* de madera; (*fig*)
inexpresivo.

woodland ['wudlənd] *n* bosque *m*.

woodpecker ['wudpɛkə*] *n* pájaro carpintero.

wood pigeon *n* paloma torcaz.

woodwind ['wudwɪnd] *n* (*MUS*) instrumentos *mpl* de viento de madera.

woodwork ['wudwə:k] *n* carpintería.

woodworm ['wudwə:m] *n* carcoma.

woof [wuf] *n* (*of dog*) ladrido ♦ *vi* ladrar; ~, ~! ¡guau, guau!

wool [wul] *n* lana; **knitting** ~ lana (de hacer punto); **to pull the** ~ **over sb's eyes** (*fig*) dar a algn gato por liebre.

woollen, (*US*) **woolen** ['wulən] *adj* de lana ♦ *n*: ~s géneros *mpl* de lana.

woolly, (*US*) **wooly** ['wulɪ] *adj* de lana; (*fig: ideas*) confuso.

woozy ['wu:zɪ] *adj* (*col*) mareado.

word [wə:d] *n* palabra; (*news*) noticia; (*promise*) palabra (de honor) ♦ *vt* redactar; ~ **for** ~ palabra por palabra; **what's the** ~ **for "pen" in Spanish?** ¿cómo se dice "pen" en español?; **to put sth into** ~s expresar algo en palabras; **to have a** ~ **with sb** hablar (dos palabras) con algn; **in other** ~s en otras palabras; **to break/ keep one's** ~ faltar a la palabra/cumplir la promesa; **to leave** ~ **(with/for sb) that** ... dejar recado (con/para algn) de que ...; **to have** ~s **with sb** (*quarrel with*) discutir *or* reñir con algn.

wording ['wə:dɪŋ] *n* redacción *f*.

word-of-mouth [wə:dəv'mauθ] *n*: **by** *or* **through** ~ de palabra, por el boca a boca.

word-perfect ['wə:d'pə:fɪkt] *adj* (*speech etc*) sin faltas de expresión.

word processing *n* procesamiento *or* tratamiento de textos.

word processor [-'prəusɛsə*] *n* procesador *m* de textos.

wordwrap ['wə:dræp] *n* (*COMPUT*) salto de línea automático.

wordy ['wə:dɪ] *adj* verboso, prolijo.

wore [wɔ:*] *pt of* **wear**.

work [wə:k] *n* trabajo; (*job*) empleo, trabajo; (*ART*, *LIT*) obra ♦ *vi* trabajar; (*mechanism*) funcionar, marchar; (*medicine*) ser eficaz, surtir efecto ♦ *vt* (*shape*) trabajar; (*stone etc*) tallar; (*mine etc*) explotar; (*machine*) manejar, hacer funcionar; (*cause*) producir; **to go to** ~ ir a trabajar *or* al trabajo; **to be at** ~ **(on sth)** estar trabajando (en algo); **to set to** ~, **start** ~ ponerse a trabajar; **to be out of** ~ estar parado, no tener trabajo; **his life's** ~ el trabajo de su vida; **to** ~ **hard** trabajar mucho *or* duro; **to** ~ **to rule** (*INDUSTRY*) hacer una huelga de celo; **to**

~ **loose** (*part*) desprenderse; (*knot*) aflojarse; *see also* **works**.

▶**work off** *vt*: **to** ~ **off one's feelings** desahogarse.

▶**work on** *vt fus* trabajar en, dedicarse a; (*principle*) basarse en; **he's** ~**ing on the car** está reparando el coche.

▶**work out** *vi* (*plans etc*) salir bien, funcionar; (*SPORT*) hacer ejercicios ♦ *vt* (*problem*) resolver; (*plan*) elaborar; **it** ~**s out at £100** asciende a 100 libras.

▶**work up** *vt*: **he** ~**ed his way up in the company** ascendió en la compañía mediante sus propios esfuerzos.

workable ['wə:kəbl] *adj* (*solution*) práctico, factible.

workaholic [wə:kə'hɔlɪk] *n* adicto/a al trabajo.

workbench ['wə:kbɛntʃ] *n* banco *or* mesa de trabajo.

worked up [wə:kt-] *adj*: **to get** ~ excitarse.

worker ['wə:kə*] *n* trabajador(a) *m/f*, obrero/a; **office** ~ oficinista *m/f*.

work force *n* mano *f* de obra.

work-in ['wə:kɪn] *n* (*BRIT*) ocupación *f* (de la empresa) sin interrupción del trabajo.

working ['wə:kɪŋ] *adj* (*day, week*) laborable; (*tools, conditions, clothes*) de trabajo; (*wife*) que trabaja; (*partner*) activo.

working capital *n* (*COMM*) capital *m* circulante.

working class *n* clase *f* obrera ♦ *adj*: **working-class** obrero.

working knowledge *n* conocimientos *mpl* básicos.

working man *n* obrero.

working order *n*: **in** ~ en funcionamiento.

working party *n* comisión *f* de investigación, grupo de trabajo.

working week *n* semana laboral.

work-in-progress ['wə:kɪn'prəugrɛs] *n* (*COMM*) trabajo en curso.

workload ['wə:kləud] *n* cantidad *f* de trabajo.

workman ['wə:kmən] *n* obrero.

workmanship ['wə:kmənʃɪp] *n* (*art*) hechura; (*skill*) habilidad *f*.

workmate ['wə:kmeɪt] *n* compañero/a de trabajo.

workout ['wə:kaut] *n* (*SPORT*) sesión *f* de ejercicios.

work permit *n* permiso de trabajo.

works [wə:ks] *nsg* (*BRIT*: *factory*) fábrica ♦ *npl* (*of clock, machine*) mecanismo; **road** ~ obras *fpl*.

works council *n* comité *m* de empresa.

worksheet ['wə:kʃi:t] *n* (*COMPUT*) hoja de trabajo.

workshop ['wəːkʃɔp] *n* taller *m*.
work station *n* estación *f* de trabajo.
work study *n* estudio del trabajo.
worktop ['wəːktɔp] *n* encimera.
work-to-rule ['wəːktə'ruːl] *n* (*BRIT*) huelga de celo.
world [wəːld] *n* mundo ♦ *cpd* (*champion*) del mundo; (*power, war*) mundial; **all over the** ~ por todo el mundo, en el mundo entero; **the business** ~ el mundo de los negocios; **what in the** ~ **is he doing?** ¿qué diablos está haciendo?; **to think the** ~ **of sb** (*fig*) tener un concepto muy alto de algn; **to do sb a** ~ **of good** sentar muy bien a algn; **W~ War One/Two** la primera/segunda Guerra Mundial.
World Cup *n* (*FOOTBALL*): **the** ~ el Mundial, los Mundiales.
world-famous [wəːld'feiməs] *adj* de fama mundial, mundialmente famoso.
worldly ['wəːldlɪ] *adj* mundano.
world music *n* música étnica.
World Series *n*: **the** ~ (*US BASEBALL*) el campeonato nacional de béisbol de EEUU.
World Service *n see* **BBC**.
world-wide ['wəːldwaid] *adj* mundial, universal.
worm [wəːm] *n* gusano; (*earth*~) lombriz *f*.
worn [wɔːn] *pp of* **wear** ♦ *adj* usado.
worn-out ['wɔːnaut] *adj* (*object*) gastado; (*person*) rendido, agotado.
worried ['wʌrid] *adj* preocupado; **to be** ~ **about sth** estar preocupado por algo.
worrisome ['wʌrisəm] *adj* preocupante, inquietante.
worry ['wʌrɪ] *n* preocupación *f* ♦ *vt* preocupar, inquietar ♦ *vi* preocuparse; **to** ~ **about** *or* **over sth/sb** preocuparse por algo/algn.
worrying ['wʌriɪŋ] *adj* inquietante.
worse [wəːs] *adj, adv* peor ♦ *n* el peor, lo peor; **a change for the** ~ un empeoramiento; **so much the** ~ **for you** tanto peor para ti; **he is none the** ~ **for it** se ha quedado tan fresco *or* tan tranquilo; **to get** ~, **to grow** ~ empeorar.
worsen ['wəːsn] *vt, vi* empeorar.
worse off *adj* (*fig*): **you'll be** ~ **this way** de esta forma estarás peor que antes.
worship ['wəːʃɪp] *n* (*organized* ~) culto; (*act*) adoración *f* ♦ *vt* adorar; **Your W~** (*BRIT: to mayor*) su Ilustrísima; (: *to judge*) su señoría.
worshipper, (*US*) **worshiper** ['wəːʃɪpə*] *n* devoto/a.
worst [wəːst] *adj* (el/la) peor ♦ *adv* peor ♦ *n* lo peor; **at** ~ en el peor de los casos; **to**

come off ~ llevar la peor parte; **if the** ~ **comes to the** ~ en el peor de los casos.
worst-case ['wəːstkeis] *adj*: **the** ~ **scenario** el peor de los casos.
worsted ['wustid] *n*: (**wool**) ~ estambre *m*.
worth [wəːθ] *n* valor *m* ♦ *adj*: **to be** ~ valer; **how much is it** ~? ¿cuánto vale?; **it's** ~ **it** vale *or* merece la pena; **to be** ~ **one's while (to do)** merecer la pena (hacer); **it's not** ~ **the trouble** no vale *or* merece la pena.
worthless ['wəːθlɪs] *adj* sin valor; (*useless*) inútil.
worthwhile ['wəːθwail] *adj* (*activity*) que merece la pena; (*cause*) loable.
worthy ['wəːðɪ] *adj* (*person*) respetable; (*motive*) honesto; ~ **of** digno de.

================================= *KEYWORD*

would [wud] *aux vb* **1** (*conditional tense*): **if you asked him he** ~ **do it** si se lo pidieras, lo haría; **if you had asked him he** ~ **have done it** si se lo hubieras pedido, lo habría *or* hubiera hecho
2 (*in offers, invitations, requests*): ~ **you like a biscuit?** ¿quieres una galleta?; (*formal*) ¿querría una galleta?; ~ **you ask him to come in?** ¿quiere hacerle pasar?; ~ **you open the window please?** ¿quiere *or* podría abrir la ventana, por favor?
3 (*in indirect speech*): **I said I** ~ **do it** dije que lo haría
4 (*emphatic*): **it WOULD have to snow today!** ¡tenía que nevar precisamente hoy!
5 (*insistence*): **she** ~**n't behave** no quiso comportarse bien
6 (*conjecture*): **it** ~ **have been midnight** sería medianoche; **it** ~ **seem so** parece ser que sí
7 (*indicating habit*): **he** ~ **go there on Mondays** iba allí los lunes.

would-be ['wudbiː] *adj* (*pej*) presunto.
wouldn't ['wudnt] = **would not**.
wound *vb* [waund] *pt, pp of* **wind** ♦ *n, vt* [wuːnd] *n* herida ♦ *vt* herir.
wove [wəuv] *pt of* **weave**.
woven ['wəuvən] *pp of* **weave**.
WP *n abbr* = **word processing; word processor** ♦ *abbr* (*BRIT col*: = *weather permitting*) si lo permite el tiempo.
WPC *n abbr* (*BRIT*) = **woman police constable**.
wpm *abbr* (= *words per minute*) p.p.m.
WRAC *n abbr* (*BRIT*: = *Women's Royal Army Corps*) cuerpo auxiliar femenino del ejército de tierra.
WRAF *n abbr* (*BRIT*: = *Women's Royal Air*

Force) cuerpo auxiliar femenino del ejército del aire.

wrangle ['ræŋgl] *n* riña ♦ *vi* reñir.

wrap [ræp] *n (stole)* chal *m* ♦ *vt (also:* ~ **up)** envolver; **under** ~**s** *(fig: plan, scheme)* oculto, tapado.

wrapper ['ræpə*] *n (BRIT: of book)* sobrecubierta; *(on chocolate etc)* envoltura.

wrapping paper ['ræpɪŋ-] *n* papel *m* de envolver.

wrath [rɔθ] *n* cólera.

wreak [riːk] *vt (destruction)* causar; **to** ~ **havoc (on)** hacer *or* causar estragos (en); **to** ~ **vengeance (on)** vengarse (en).

wreath, ~**s** [riːθ, riːðz] *n (funeral* ~) corona; *(of flowers)* guirnalda.

wreck [rɛk] *n (ship: destruction)* naufragio; *(: remains)* restos *mpl* del barco; *(pej: person)* ruina ♦ *vt* destrozar; **to be** ~**ed** *(NAUT)* naufragar.

wreckage ['rɛkɪdʒ] *n (remains)* restos *mpl*; *(of building)* escombros *mpl*.

wrecker ['rɛkə*] *n (US: breakdown van)* camión-grúa *m*.

WREN [rɛn] *n abbr (BRIT) miembro del WRNS.*

wren [rɛn] *n (ZOOL)* reyezuelo.

wrench [rɛntʃ] *n (TECH)* llave *f* inglesa; *(tug)* tirón *m* ♦ *vt* arrancar; **to** ~ **sth from sb** arrebatar algo violentamente a algn.

wrest [rɛst] *vt:* **to** ~ **sth from sb** arrebatar *or* arrancar algo a algn.

wrestle ['rɛsl] *vi:* **to** ~ **(with sb)** luchar (con *or* contra algn).

wrestler ['rɛslə*] *n* luchador(a) *m/f* (de lucha libre).

wrestling ['rɛslɪŋ] *n* lucha libre.

wrestling match *n* combate *m* de lucha libre.

wretch [rɛtʃ] *n* desgraciado/a, miserable *m/f*; **little** ~! *(often humorous)* ¡granuja!

wretched ['rɛtʃɪd] *adj* miserable.

wriggle ['rɪgl] *vi* serpentear.

wring *pt, pp* **wrung** [rɪŋ, rʌŋ] *vt* torcer, retorcer; *(wet clothes)* escurrir; *(fig):* **to** ~ **sth out of sb** sacar algo por la fuerza a algn.

wringer ['rɪŋə*] *n* escurridor *m*.

wringing ['rɪŋɪŋ] *adj (also:* ~ **wet)** empapado.

wrinkle ['rɪŋkl] *n* arruga ♦ *vt* arrugar ♦ *vi* arrugarse.

wrinkled ['rɪŋkld], **wrinkly** ['rɪŋklɪ] *adj (fabric, paper, etc)* arrugado.

wrist [rɪst] *n* muñeca.

wristband ['rɪstbænd] *n (BRIT: of shirt)* puño; *(: of watch)* correa.

wrist watch *n* reloj *m* de pulsera.

writ [rɪt] *n* mandato judicial; **to serve a** ~ **on sb** notificar un mandato judicial a algn.

write, *pt* **wrote,** *pp* **written** [raɪt, rəut, 'rɪtn] *vt, vi* escribir; **to** ~ **sb a letter** escribir una carta a algn.

▶**write away** *vi:* **to** ~ **away for** *(information, goods)* pedir por escrito *or* carta.

▶**write down** *vt* escribir; *(note)* apuntar.

▶**write off** *vt (debt)* borrar (como incobrable); *(fig)* desechar por inútil; *(smash up: car)* destrozar.

▶**write out** *vt* escribir.

▶**write up** *vt* redactar.

write-off ['raɪtɔf] *n* siniestro total; **the car is a** ~ el coche es pura chatarra.

write-protect ['raɪtprə'tɛkt] *vt (COMPUT)* proteger contra escritura.

writer ['raɪtə*] *n* escritor(a) *m/f*.

write-up ['raɪtʌp] *n (review)* crítica, reseña.

writhe [raɪð] *vi* retorcerse.

writing ['raɪtɪŋ] *n* escritura; *(hand*~) letra; *(of author)* obras; **in** ~ por escrito; **to put sth in** ~ poner algo por escrito; **in my own** ~ escrito por mí; *see also* **writings.**

writing case *n* estuche *m* de papel de escribir.

writing desk *n* escritorio.

writing paper *n* papel *m* de escribir.

writings *npl* obras *fpl*.

written ['rɪtn] *pp of* **write.**

WRNS *n abbr (BRIT: = Women's Royal Naval Service)* cuerpo auxiliar femenino de la armada.

wrong [rɔŋ] *adj (wicked)* malo; *(unfair)* injusto; *(incorrect)* equivocado, incorrecto; *(not suitable)* inoportuno, inconveniente ♦ *adv* mal ♦ *n* mal *m*; *(injustice)* injusticia ♦ *vt* ser injusto con; *(hurt)* agraviar; **to be** ~ *(answer)* estar equivocado; *(in doing, saying)* equivocarse; **it's** ~ **to steal, stealing is** ~ es mal robar; **you are** ~ **to do it** haces mal en hacerlo; **you are** ~ **about that, you've got it** ~ en eso estás equivocado; **to be in the** ~ no tener razón; *(guilty)* tener la culpa; **what's** ~? ¿qué pasa?; **what's** ~ **with the car?** ¿qué le pasa al coche?; **there's nothing** ~ no pasa nada; **you have the** ~ **number** *(TEL)* se ha equivocado de número; **to go** ~ *(person)* equivocarse; *(plan)* salir mal; *(machine)* estropearse.

wrongdoer ['rɔŋduə*] *n* malhechor(a) *m/f*.

wrong-foot [rɔŋ'fut] *vt (SPORT)* hacer perder el equilibrio a; *(fig)* poner en un aprieto a.

wrongful ['rɒŋful] *adj* injusto; ~ **dismissal** (*INDUSTRY*) despido improcedente.

wrongly ['rɒŋlɪ] *adv* (*answer, do, count*) incorrectamente; (*treat*) injustamente.

wrote [rəut] *pt of* **write.**

wrought [rɔːt] *adj*: ~ **iron** hierro forjado.

wrung [rʌŋ] *pt, pp of* **wring.**

WRVS *n abbr* (*BRIT*: = *Women's Royal Voluntary Service*) cuerpo de voluntarias al servicio de la comunidad.

wry [raɪ] *adj* irónico.

wt. *abbr* = **weight.**

WV, W. Va. *abbr* (*US*) = *West Virginia.*

WY, Wyo. *abbr* (*US*) = *Wyoming.*

WYSIWYG ['wɪzɪwɪg] *abbr* (*COMPUT*: = *what you see is what you get*) tipo de presentación en un procesador de textos.

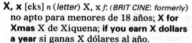

Xx

X, x [eks] *n* (*letter*) X, x *f*: (*BRIT CINE: formerly*) no apto para menores de 18 años; **X for Xmas** X de Xiquena; **if you earn X dollars a year** si ganas X dólares al año.

X-certificate ['ɛkssə'tɪfɪkɪt] *adj* (*BRIT: film: formerly*) no apto para menores de 18 años.

Xerox ® ['zɪərɒks] *n* (*also*: ~ **machine**) fotocopiadora; (*photocopy*) fotocopia ♦ *vt* fotocopiar.

XL *abbr* = *extra large.*

Xmas ['ɛksməs] *n abbr* = **Christmas.**

X-rated ['eks'reɪtɪd] *adj* (*US: film*) no apto para menores de 18 años.

X-ray [ɛks'reɪ] *n* radiografía; ~**s** *npl* rayos *mpl* X ♦ *vt* radiografiar.

xylophone ['zaɪləfəun] *n* xilófono.

Yy

Y, y [waɪ] *n* (*letter*) Y, y *f*; **Y for Yellow**, (*US*) **Y for Yoke** Y de Yegua.

yacht [jɒt] *n* yate *m*.

yachting ['jɒtɪŋ] *n* (*sport*) balandrismo.

yachtsman ['jɒtsmən] *n* balandrista *m*.

yachtswoman ['jɒtswumən] balandrista.

yam [jæm] *n* ñame *m*; (*sweet potato*) batata, camote *m* (*LAM*).

Yank [jæŋk], **Yankee** ['jæŋkɪ] *n* (*pej*) yanqui *m/f*.

yank [jæŋk] *vt* tirar de, jalar de (*LAM*) ♦ *n* tirón *m*.

yap [jæp] *vi* (*dog*) aullar.

yard [jɑːd] *n* patio *m*; (*US: garden*) jardín *m*; (*measure*) yarda; **builder's** ~ almacén *m*.

yardstick ['jɑːdstɪk] *n* (*fig*) criterio, norma.

yarn [jɑːn] *n* hilo; (*tale*) cuento (chino), historia.

yawn [jɔːn] *n* bostezo ♦ *vi* bostezar.

yawning ['jɔːnɪŋ] *adj* (*gap*) muy abierto.

yd. *abbr* (= *yard*) yda.

yeah [jɛə] *adv* (*col*) sí.

year [jɪə*] *n* año; (*SCOL, UNIV*) curso; **this** ~ este año; ~ **in**, ~ **out** año tras año; **a** *or* **per** ~ al año; **to be 8** ~**s old** tener 8 años; **she's three** ~**s old** tiene tres años; **an eight-**~**-old child** un niño de ocho años (de edad).

yearbook ['jɪəbuk] *n* anuario.

yearling ['jɪəlɪŋ] *n* (*racehorse*) potro de un año.

yearly ['jɪəlɪ] *adj* anual ♦ *adv* anualmente, cada año; **twice** ~ dos veces al año.

yearn [jɜːn] *vi*: **to** ~ **for sth** añorar algo, suspirar por algo.

yearning ['jɜːnɪŋ] *n* ansia; (*longing*) añoranza.

yeast [jiːst] *n* levadura.

yell [jɛl] *n* grito, alarido ♦ *vi* gritar.

yellow ['jɛləu] *adj*, *n* amarillo.

yellow fever *n* fiebre *f* amarilla.

yellowish ['jɛləuɪʃ] *adj* amarillento.

Yellow Pages ® *npl* páginas *fpl* amarillas.

Yellow Sea *n*: **the** ~ el Mar Amarillo.

yelp [jɛlp] *n* aullido ♦ *vi* aullar.

Yemen ['jɛmən] *n* Yemen *m*.

Yemeni ['jɛmənɪ] *adj*, *n* yemení *m/f*, yemenita *m/f*.

yen [jɛn] *n* (*currency*) yen *m*.

yeoman ['jəumən] *n*: **Y~ of the Guard** *alabardero de la Casa Real*.

yes [jɛs] *adv, n* sí *m*; **to say/answer ~** decir/ contestar que sí; **to say ~ (to)** decir que sí (a), conformarse (con).

yes man *n* pelotillero.

yesterday ['jɛstədɪ] *adv, n* ayer *m*; **~ morning/evening** ayer por la mañana/ tarde; **all day ~** todo el día de ayer; **the day before ~** antes de ayer, anteayer.

yet [jɛt] *adv* todavía ♦ *conj* sin embargo, a pesar de todo; **~ again** de nuevo; **it is not finished ~** todavía no está acabado; **the best ~** el/la mejor hasta ahora; **as ~** hasta ahora, todavía.

yew [juː] *n* tejo.

Y-fronts ® ['waɪfrʌnts] *npl* (*BRIT*) calzoncillos *mpl*, eslip *msg* tradicional.

YHA *n abbr* (*BRIT*: = Youth Hostel Association) ≈ Red *f* Española de Albergues Juveniles.

Yiddish ['jɪdɪʃ] *n* yiddish *m*.

yield [jiːld] *n* producción *f*; (*AGR*) cosecha; (*COMM*) rendimiento ♦ *vt* producir, dar; (*profit*) rendir ♦ *vi* rendirse, ceder; (*US AUT*) ceder el paso; **a ~ of 5%** un rédito del 5 por ciento.

YMCA *n abbr* (= Young Men's Christian Association) Asociación *f* de Jóvenes Cristianos.

yob(bo) ['jɔb(bəu)] *n* (*BRIT col*) gamberro.

yodel ['jəudl] *vi* cantar a la tirolesa.

yoga ['jəugə] *n* yoga *m*.

yog(h)ourt, yog(h)urt ['jəugət] *n* yogur *m*.

yoke [jəuk] *n* (*of oxen*) yunta; (*on shoulders*) balancín *m*; (*fig*) yugo ♦ *vt* (*also*: **~ together**: *oxen*) uncir.

yolk [jəuk] *n* yema (de huevo).

yonder ['jɔndə*] *adv* allá (a lo lejos).

yonks [jɔŋks] *npl* (*col*): **I haven't seen him for ~** hace siglos que no lo veo.

Yorks *abbr* (*BRIT*) = Yorkshire.

======================== *KEYWORD*

you [juː] *pron* **1** (*subject: familiar*) tú, *pl* vosotros/as (*SP*), ustedes (*LAM*); (*polite*) usted, *pl* ustedes; **~ are very kind** eres/es *etc* muy amable; **~ French enjoy your food** a vosotros (*or* ustedes) los franceses os (*or* les) gusta la comida; **~ and I will go** iremos tú y yo
2 (*object: direct: familiar*) te, *pl* os (*SP*), les (*LAM*); (*polite*) lo *or* le, *pl* los *or* les, *f* la, *pl* las; **I know ~** te/le *etc* conozco
3 (*object: indirect: familiar*) te, *pl* os (*SP*), les (*LAM*); (*polite*) le, *pl* les; **I gave the letter to ~ yesterday** te/os *etc* di la carta ayer
4 (*stressed*): **I told YOU to do it** te dije a ti que lo hicieras, es a ti a quien dije que lo hicieras; *see also* **3, 5**
5 (*after prep*: NB: con+ti = contigo: familiar) ti, *pl* vosotros/as (*SP*), ustedes (*LAM*); (*: polite*) usted, *pl* ustedes; **it's for ~** es para ti/vosotros *etc*
6 (*comparisons: familiar*) tú, *pl* vosotros/as (*SP*), ustedes (*LAM*); (*: polite*) usted, *pl* ustedes; **she's younger than ~** es más joven que tú/vosotros *etc*
7 (*impersonal: one*): **fresh air does ~ good** el aire puro (te) hace bien; **~ never know** nunca se sabe; **~ can't do that!** ¡eso no se hace!

you'd [juːd] = you had; you would.

you'll [juːl] = you will, you shall.

young [jʌŋ] *adj* joven ♦ *npl* (*of animal*) cría; (*people*): **the ~** los jóvenes, la juventud; **a ~ man/lady** un(a) joven; **my ~er brother** mi hermano menor *or* pequeño; **the ~er generation** la nueva generación.

youngster ['jʌŋstə*] *n* joven *m/f*.

your [jɔː*] *adj* tu; (*pl*) vuestro; (*formal*) su; **~ house** tu *etc* casa; *see also* **my**.

you're [juə*] = you are.

yours [jɔːz] *pron* tuyo; (*: pl*) vuestro; (*formal*) suyo; **a friend of ~** un amigo tuyo *etc*; *see also* **faithfully, mine, sincerely**.

yourself [jɔː'sɛlf] *pron* (*reflexive*) tú mismo; (*complement*) te; (*after prep*) tí (mismo); (*formal*) usted mismo; (*: complement*) se; (*: after prep*) sí (mismo); **you ~ told me** me lo dijiste tú mismo; **(all) by ~** sin ayuda de nadie, solo; *see also* **oneself**.

yourselves [jɔː'sɛlvz] *pl pron* vosotros mismos; (*after prep*) vosotros (mismos); (*formal*) ustedes (mismos); (*: complement*) se; (*: after prep*) sí mismos.

youth [juːθ] *n* juventud *f*; (*young man*) (*pl* **~s** [juːðz]) joven *m*; **in my ~** en mi juventud.

youth club *n* club *m* juvenil.

youthful ['juːθful] *adj* juvenil.

youthfulness ['juːθfəlnɪs] *n* juventud *f*.

youth hostel *n* albergue *m* juvenil.

youth movement *n* movimiento juvenil.

you've [juːv] = you have.

yowl [jaul] *n* (*of animal, person*) aullido ♦ *vi* aullar.

yr. *abbr* (= year) a.

YT *abbr* (*Canada*) = Yukon Territory.

Yugoslav ['juːgəuslɑːv] *adj, n* yugoslavo/a *m/f*.

Yugoslavia [juːgəu'slɑːvɪə] *n* Yugoslavia.

Yugoslavian [juːgəu'slɑːvɪən] *adj* yugoslavo/a.

yuppie ['jʌpɪ] (*col*) *adj, n* yuppie *m/f*.
YWCA *n abbr* (= *Young Women's Christian Association*) Asociación *f* de Jóvenes Cristianas.

Z, z [zɛd, (*US*) zi:] *n* (*letter*) Z, z *f*; **Z for Zebra** Z de Zaragoza.
Zaire [zɑːˈiːə*] *n* Zaire *m*.
Zambia [ˈzæmbɪə] *n* Zambia.
Zambian [ˈzæmbɪən] *adj, n* zambiano/a *m/f*.
zany [ˈzeɪnɪ] *adj* estrafalario.
zap [zæp] *vt* (*COMPUT*) borrar.
zeal [ziːl] *n* celo, entusiasmo.
zealot [ˈzɛlət] *n* fanático/a.
zealous [ˈzɛləs] *adj* celoso, entusiasta.
zebra [ˈziːbrə] *n* cebra.
zebra crossing *n* (*BRIT*) paso de peatones.
zenith [ˈzɛnɪθ] *n* (*ASTRO*) cénit *m*; (*fig*) apogeo.
zero [ˈzɪərəu] *n* cero; **5 degrees below ~ 5** grados bajo cero.
zero hour *n* hora cero.
zero option *n* (*POL*) opción *f* cero.

zero-rated [ˈzɪərəureɪtɪd] *adj* (*BRIT*) de tasa cero.
zest [zɛst] *n* entusiasmo; **~ for living** brío.
zigzag [ˈzɪgzæg] *n* zigzag *m* ♦ *vi* zigzaguear.
Zimbabwe [zɪmˈbɑːbwɪ] *n* Zimbabwe *m*.
Zimbabwean [zɪmˈbɑːbwɪən] *adj, n* zimbabuo/a *m/f*.
Zimmer ® [ˈzɪmə*] *n* (*also*: **~ frame**) andador *m*, andaderas *fpl*.
zinc [zɪŋk] *n* cinc *m*, zinc *m*.
Zionism [ˈzaɪənɪzm] *n* sionismo.
Zionist [ˈzaɪənɪst] *adj, n* sionista *m/f*.
zip [zɪp] *n* (*also*: **~ fastener**, (*US*) **~per**) cremallera, cierre *m* relámpago (*LAM*); (*energy*) energía, vigor *m* ♦ *vt* (*also*: **~ up**) cerrar la cremallera de ♦ *vi*: **to ~ along to the shops** ir de compras volando.
zip code *n* (*US*) código postal.
zither [ˈzɪðə*] *n* cítara.
zodiac [ˈzəudɪæk] *n* zodíaco.
zombie [ˈzɔmbɪ] *n* zombi *m*.
zone [zəun] *n* zona.
zonked [zɔŋkt] *adj* (*col*) hecho polvo.
zoo [zuː] *n* zoo, (parque *m*) zoológico.
zoological [zuːəˈlɔdʒɪkəl] *adj* zoológico.
zoologist [zuːˈɔlədʒɪst] *n* zoólogo/a.
zoology [zuːˈɔlədʒɪ] *n* zoología.
zoom [zuːm] *vi*: **to ~ past** pasar zumbando; **to ~ in (on sth/sb)** (*PHOT, CINE*) enfocar (algo/a algn) con el zoom.
zoom lens *n* zoom *m*.
zucchini [zuːˈkiːnɪ] *n(pl)* (*US*) calabacín(ines) *m(pl)*.

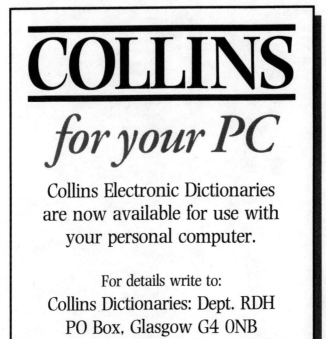